BIG LONDON

A-Z®

T0364382

9780008663506

Published by Geographers' A-Z Map Company Limited
An imprint of HarperCollins Publishers
Westerhill Road
Bishopbriggs
Glasgow G64 2QT

www.az.co.uk
a-z.maps@harpercollins.co.uk

HarperCollinsPublishers
Macken House, 39/40 Mayor Street Upper, Dublin 1, D01 C9W8, Ireland

15th edition 2024

A catalogue record for this book is available from the British Library.

ISBN 978-0-00-866350-6

10 9 8 7 6 5 4 3 2

Printed in Malaysia

Key to Map Pages	2-3
Large Scale Map Pages @ 8.5" to 1 mile	4-19
Map Pages @ 4.25" to 1 mile	20-174
Congestion Charging Overview Map and Information	175
Index to Streets, Places, Areas and selected Places of Interest	176-310
Index to Hospitals etc.	311-313
Index to Stations	314-315
Railway Connections Map	316-317
West End Cinema and Theatres Map	318
Underground Railway Map	Back Cover

REFERENCE

Motorway M1

A Road A2

B Road B408

Dual Carriageway

One-way Street
Traffic flow on A Roads is also indicated by a heavy line on the driver's left.

Road Under Construction
Opening dates are correct at the time of publication.

Proposed Road

Junction Name MARBLE ARCH

Restricted Access

Pedestrianized Road

Track / Footpath

Residential Walkway

Congestion Charging Zone — Zone edge. Within Zone.
See page 175 for more information.

Ultra Low and Low Emission Zones — Zone edge. Within Zone.
Visit www.tfl.gov.uk/modes/driving for more information on London's driving zones.

Railway — Level Crossing, Tunnel

Stations: (Large Scale Map Pages)

- National Rail Network
- Elizabeth Line
- Docklands Light Railway DLR
- Overground
- Underground

London Tramlink — Tunnel, Stop
The boarding of Tramlink trams at stops may be limited to a single direction, indicated by the arrow.

Built-up Area MILL STREET

Postcode Boundary

Map Continuation 82 — Large Scale Map Pages 10

Airport

Car Park (selected)

Church or Chapel

Fire Station

Hospital

House Numbers (A & B Roads only) 35 154

Information Centre

National Grid Reference 530

Police Station

Post Office

River Bus Stop

Toilet

Educational Establishment

Hospital or Healthcare Building

Industrial Building

Leisure or Recreational Facility

Place of Interest

Public Building

Shopping Centre or Market

Other Selected Buildings

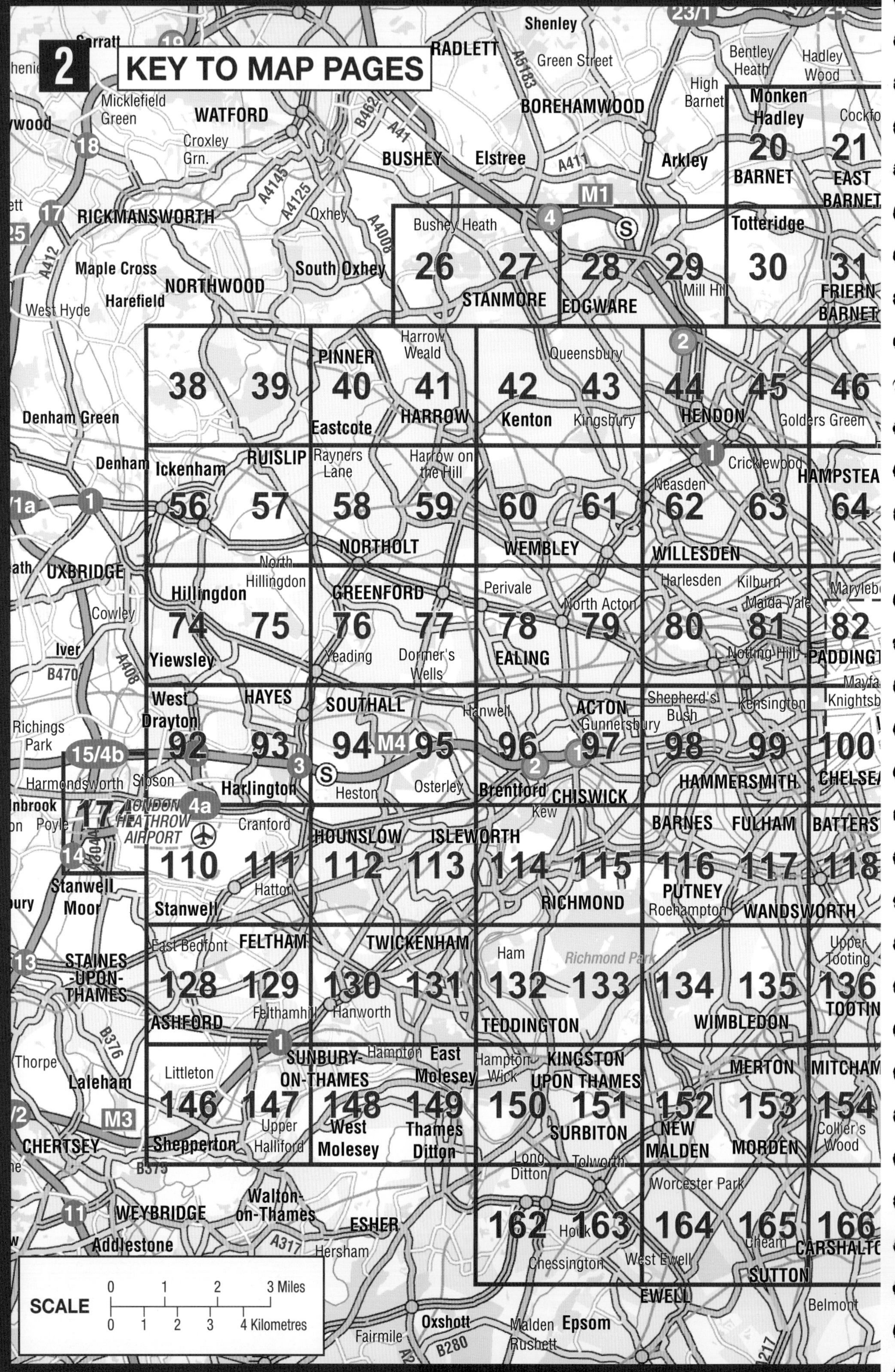

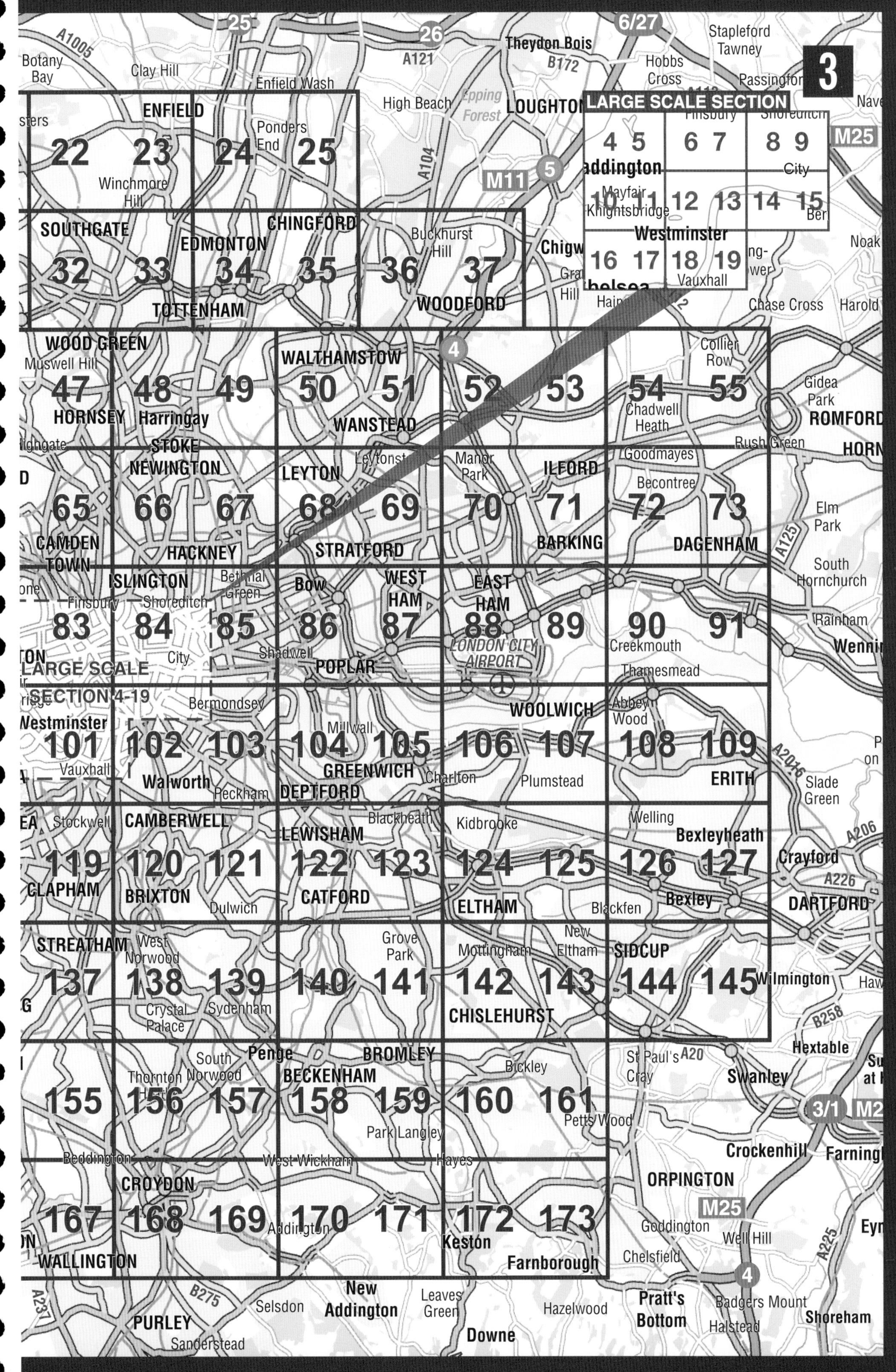
LARGE SCALE SECTION
4 5 Paddington
6 7 Finsbury
8 9 Shoreditch City
10 11 Mayfair Knightsbridge
12 13 14 15
Westminster
16 17 Chelsea
18 19 Vauxhall
Botany Bay
Clay Hill
Enfield Wash
Theydon Bois
Stapleford Tawney
Hobbs Cross
Passingford
High Beach
Epping Forest
LOUGHTON
ENFIELD
22 23 24 25
Ponders End
Winchmore Hill
SOUTHGATE
EDMONTON
CHINGFORD
Buckhurst Hill
32 33 34 35 36 37
TOTTENHAM
WOODFORD
Chigwell
Grange Hill
Hainault
Chase Cross
Harold
Noak
WOOD GREEN
Muswell Hill
WALTHAMSTOW
Collier Row
47 48 49 50 51 52 53 54 55
HORNSEY
Harringay
WANSTEAD
Chadwell Heath
Gidea Park
ROMFORD
Highgate
STOKE NEWINGTON
LEYTON
Leytonstone
Manor Park
ILFORD
Goodmayes
Becontree
Rush Green
HORN
65 66 67 68 69 70 71 72 73
CAMDEN TOWN
HACKNEY
STRATFORD
BARKING
DAGENHAM
Elm Park
South Hornchurch
ISLINGTON
Bethnal Green
Bow
WEST HAM
EAST HAM
Finsbury
Shoreditch
83 84 85 86 87 88 89 90 91
Rainham
LONDON CITY AIRPORT
Creekmouth
City
Shadwell
POPLAR
Thamesmead
LARGE SCALE SECTION 4-19
Westminster
Bermondsey
Millwall
WOOLWICH
Abbey Wood
101 102 103 104 105 106 107 108 109
Vauxhall
Walworth
Peckham
DEPTFORD
GREENWICH
Charlton
Plumstead
ERITH
Slade Green
Stockwell
CAMBERWELL
LEWISHAM
Blackheath
Kidbrooke
Welling
Bexleyheath
119 120 121 122 123 124 125 126 127
CLAPHAM
BRIXTON
Dulwich
CATFORD
ELTHAM
Blackfen
Bexley
Crayford
DARTFORD
STREATHAM
West Norwood
Grove Park
Mottingham
New Eltham
SIDCUP
137 138 139 140 141 142 143 144 145
Wilmington
Crystal Palace
Sydenham
CHISLEHURST
Hextable
South Norwood
Thornton Heath
Penge
BECKENHAM
BROMLEY
Bickley
St Paul's Cray
Swanley
155 156 157 158 159 160 161
Petts Wood
Park Langley
Beddington
West Wickham
Hayes
Crockenhill
Farningham
ORPINGTON
CROYDON
167 168 169 170 171 172 173
Addington
Keston
Goddington
Well Hill
WALLINGTON
Farnborough
Chelsfield
New Addington
Leaves Green
Pratt's Bottom
Badgers Mount
Shoreham
PURLEY
Selsdon
Hazelwood
Halstead
Sanderstead
Downe
A1005
A121
B172
A104
M11
M25
A125
A2016
A206
A226
B258
A20
A225
A237
B275
25 26 6/27 5 4 3/1 4

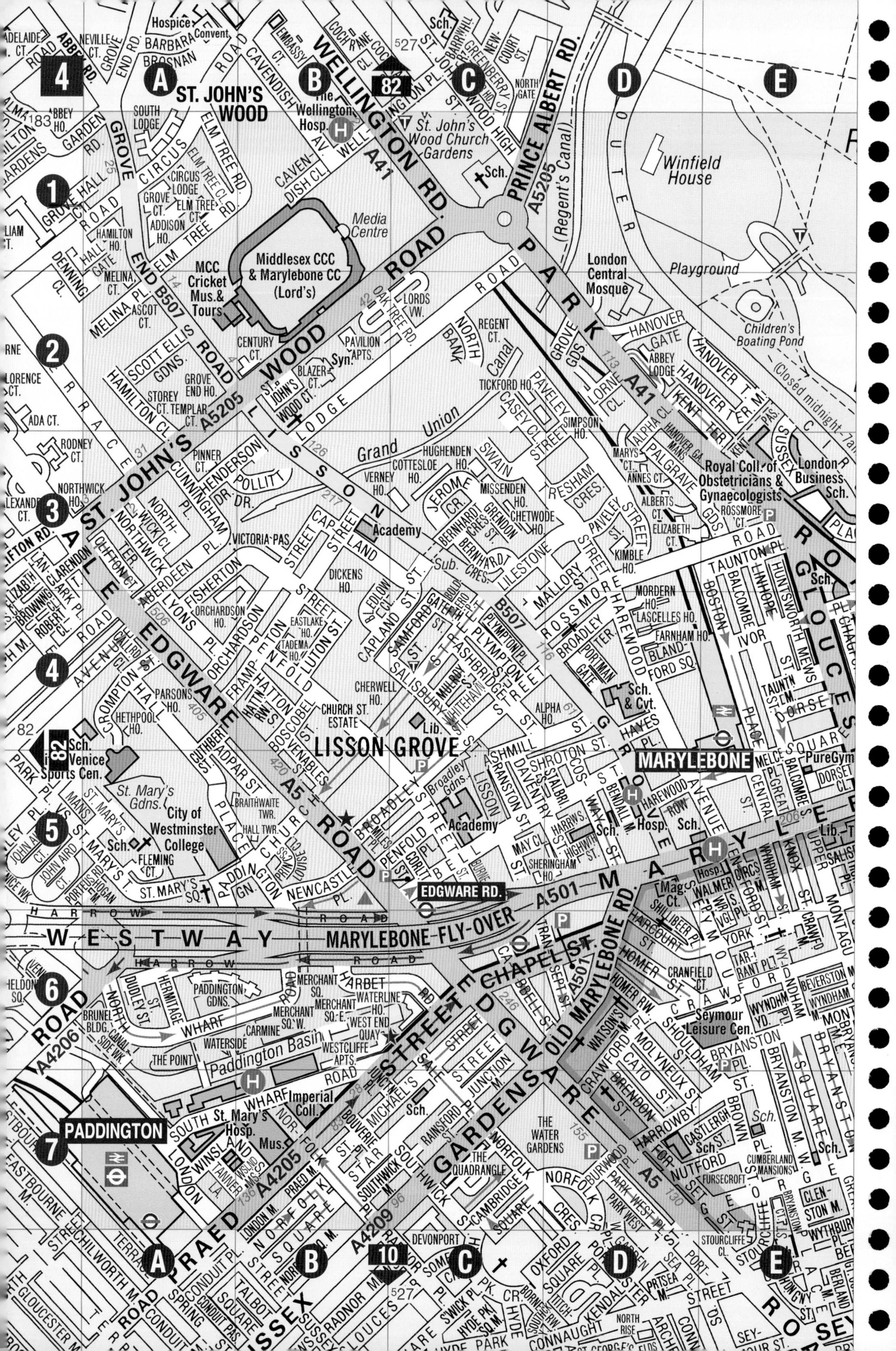
4
A
B
C
D
E
82
527
ST. JOHN'S WOOD
WELLINGTON RD.
PRINCE ALBERT RD.
A5205 (Regent's Canal)
OUTER
Winfield House
St. John's Wood Church Gardens
The Wellington Hosp.
Sch.
Middlesex CCC & Marylebone CC (Lord's)
MCC Cricket Mus.& Tours
Media Centre
ST. JOHN'S WOOD ROAD
A5205
A41
PARK ROAD
London Central Mosque
Playground
Children's Boating Pond
(Closed midnight-7am)
Grand Union Canal
LISSON GROVE
Royal Coll. of Obstetricians & Gynaecologists
London Business Sch.
GLOUCESTER PL.
Academy
CHURCH ST. ESTATE
Lib.
Lisson Grove
EDGWARE ROAD
A5
B507
MARYLEBONE
EDGWARE RD.
PureGym
Little Venice Sports Cen.
St. Mary's Gdns.
City of Westminster College
WESTWAY
HARROW ROAD
MARYLEBONE FLY-OVER
A501
MARYLEBONE RD.
CHAPEL ST.
OLD MARYLEBONE RD.
Seymour Leisure Cen.
Paddington Basin
PADDINGTON
Imperial Coll.
St. Mary's Hosp.
Mus.
A4206
A4205
A4209
PRAED
SUSSEX GARDENS
EDGWARE ROAD
THE WATER GARDENS
THE QUADRANGLE
10
1
2
3
4
5
6
7

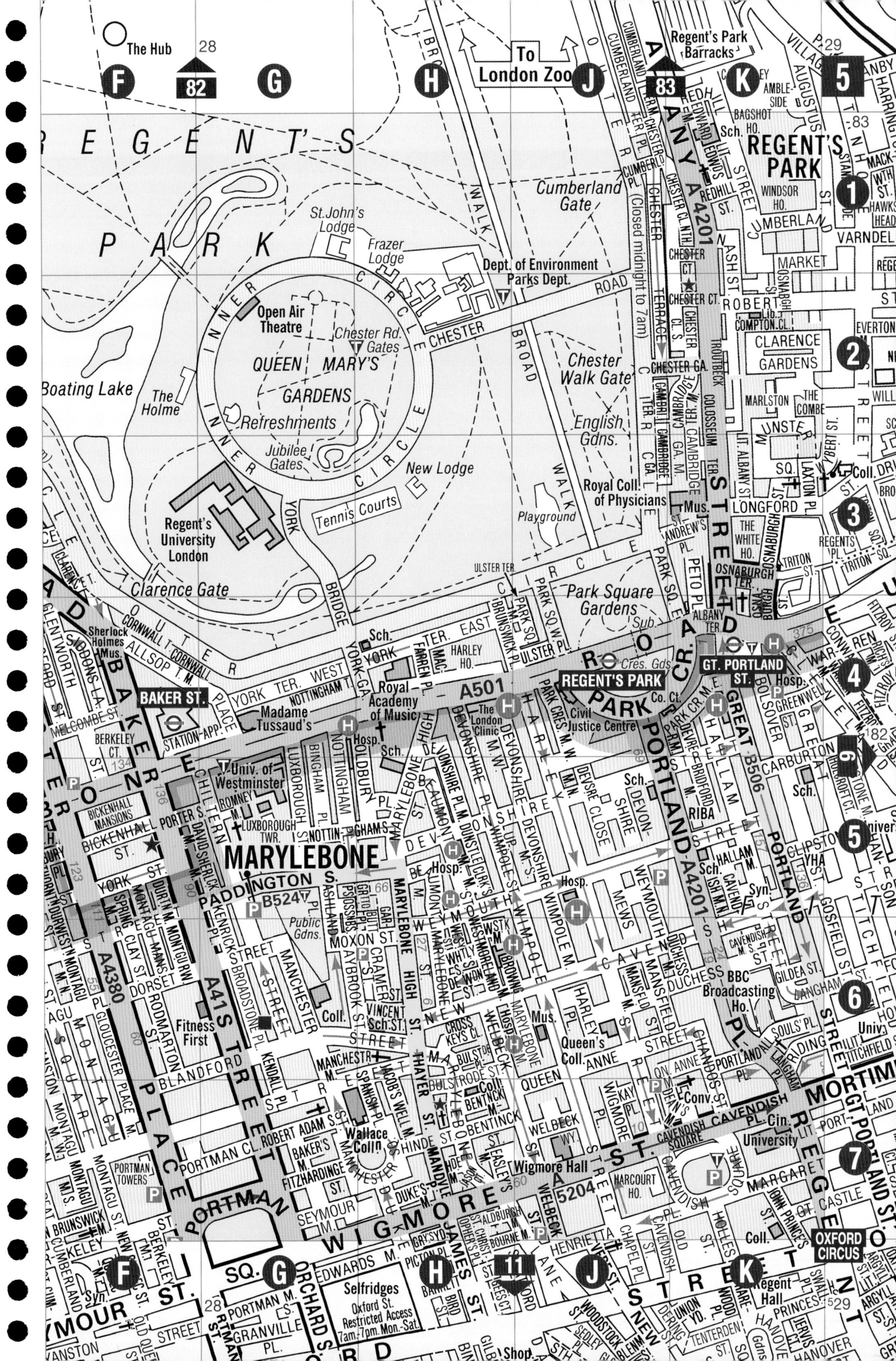

The Hub
F
82
G
H
To London Zoo
J
83
K
5
Regent's Park Barracks
REGENT'S PARK
REGENT'S PARK
Boating Lake
Cumberland Gate
St.John's Lodge
Frazer Lodge
Dept. of Environment Parks Dept.
INNER CIRCLE
Open Air Theatre
Chester Rd. Gates
QUEEN MARY'S GARDENS
Refreshments
Jubilee Gates
New Lodge
The Holme
Regent's University London
Tennis Courts
Chester Walk Gate
English Gdns.
Royal Coll. of Physicians
Playground
Clarence Gate
OUTER CIRCLE
Park Square Gardens
CHESTER ROAD
BROAD WALK
(Closed midnight to 7am)
CLARENCE GARDENS
MUNSTER SQ.
LONGFORD
OSNABURGH
ROBERT
CUMBERLAND MARKET
WINDSOR HO.
1
2
3
4
5
6
7
Sherlock Holmes Mus.
BAKER ST.
REGENT'S PARK
GT. PORTLAND ST.
Madame Tussaud's
Royal Academy of Music
The London Clinic
Civil Justice Centre
Univ. of Westminster
MARYLEBONE
A501
MARYLEBONE ROAD
PADDINGTON ST.
B524
Public Gdns.
Fitness First
BAKER STREET
GLOUCESTER PLACE
PORTMAN SQ.
Wallace Colln.
Wigmore Hall
WIGMORE STREET
CAVENDISH SQUARE
Queen's Coll.
BBC Broadcasting Ho.
University
OXFORD CIRCUS
Selfridges
Oxford St. Restricted Access 7am-7pm. Mon.-Sat.
Regent Hall
OXFORD STREET
REGENT STREET
GREAT PORTLAND STREET
PORTLAND PLACE
HARLEY STREET
WIMPOLE ST.
MARYLEBONE HIGH ST.
A4201
A41
A4380
A5204
B506
11

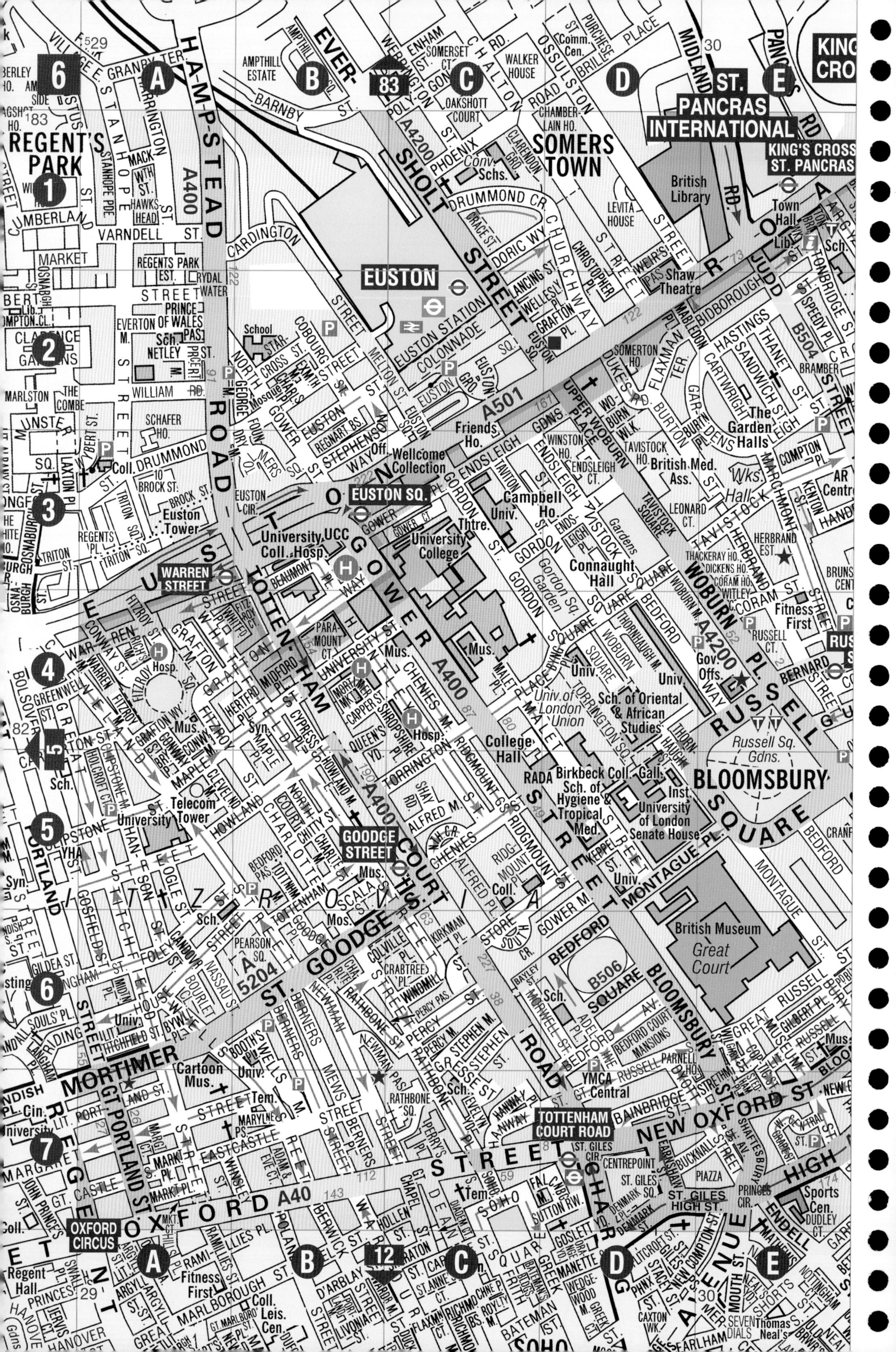

6
A
B
C
D
E
1
2
3
4
5
6
7
83
12
5
30
REGENT'S PARK
SOMERS TOWN
ST. PANCRAS INTERNATIONAL
KING'S CROSS ST. PANCRAS
EUSTON
EUSTON SQ.
WARREN STREET
GOODGE STREET
TOTTENHAM COURT ROAD
OXFORD CIRCUS
BLOOMSBURY
British Library
British Museum
Great Court
Euston Tower
Telecom Tower
University College
Wellcome Collection
Sch. of Oriental & African Studies
University of London Senate House
Birkbeck Coll.
Sch. of Hygiene & Tropical Med.
Russell Sq. Gdns.
Gordon Sq. Garden
Connaught Hall
College Hall
The Garden Halls
British Med. Ass.
Shaw Theatre
Campbell Ho.
YMCA Central
Cartoon Mus.
Fitness First
Sports Cen.
HAMPSTEAD ROAD
EUSTON ROAD
GOWER STREET
TOTTENHAM COURT ROAD
OXFORD STREET
NEW OXFORD ST.
GOODGE ST.
MORTIMER ST.
GT. PORTLAND ST.
REGENT ST.
EVERSHOLT STREET
RUSSELL SQUARE
BEDFORD SQUARE
BLOOMSBURY ST.
WOBURN PL.
MALET STREET
MONTAGUE PL.
GREAT RUSSELL ST.
CHARING CROSS RD.
SHAFTESBURY AV.
SOHO SQ.
ST. GILES HIGH ST.
A400
A4200
A501
A40
A5204
B506
B504

83
84
7
F
G
H
J
K
1
2
3
4
5
6
7
8
13
PENTONVILLE ROAD
KING'S CROSS
ST. PANCRAS
A5200
SWINTON ST.
ACTON ST.
GRAY'S INN ROAD
A201
FARRINGDON ROAD
ROSEBERY AV.
CLERKENWELL
CLERKENWELL ROAD
A401
THEOBALD'S ROAD
SOUTHAMPTON ROW
HOLBORN
HIGH HOLBORN
KINGSWAY
A4200
CHANCERY LA.
FETTER LA.
NEW FETTER LA.
A40
A4
B400
B402
B501
B502
B521
A5201
A210
St. John's Gardens
FARRINGDON
Sadler's Wells
Myddelton Square
New River Head
The Hydra Building
Spa Green Estate
Mount Pleasant Sorting Office
Postmark Development
The Postal Museum
London Metropolitan Archives
Westminster Kingsway Coll.
The Foundling Museum
The Wolfson Assessment Cen.
Coram's Fields
Mecklenburgh Sq. Gds.
St. George's Gdns.
St. Andrew's Gds.
The Charles Dickens Mus.
International Hall
Great Ormond Street Hosp. for Children
The National Hosp.
Gray's Inn Gdns.
Gray's Inn
Bourne Estate
Islamic Cen.
Lincoln's Inn Fields
Lincoln's Inn Liby.
Lincoln's Inn Hall
Royal Coll. of Surgeons
Law Ct's.
King's Coll. Maughan Library
Royal Courts of Justice
Grand Connaught Rooms
Freemasons' Hall
Temple Bar
FLEET ST.
LSE
Holford Gds.
ITN
Dania Sch.
Joseph Trotter Cl.
Finsbury Estate
Michael Cliffe Ho.
The Old Sessions Ho.
Hlth. Club
Budd. Cen.

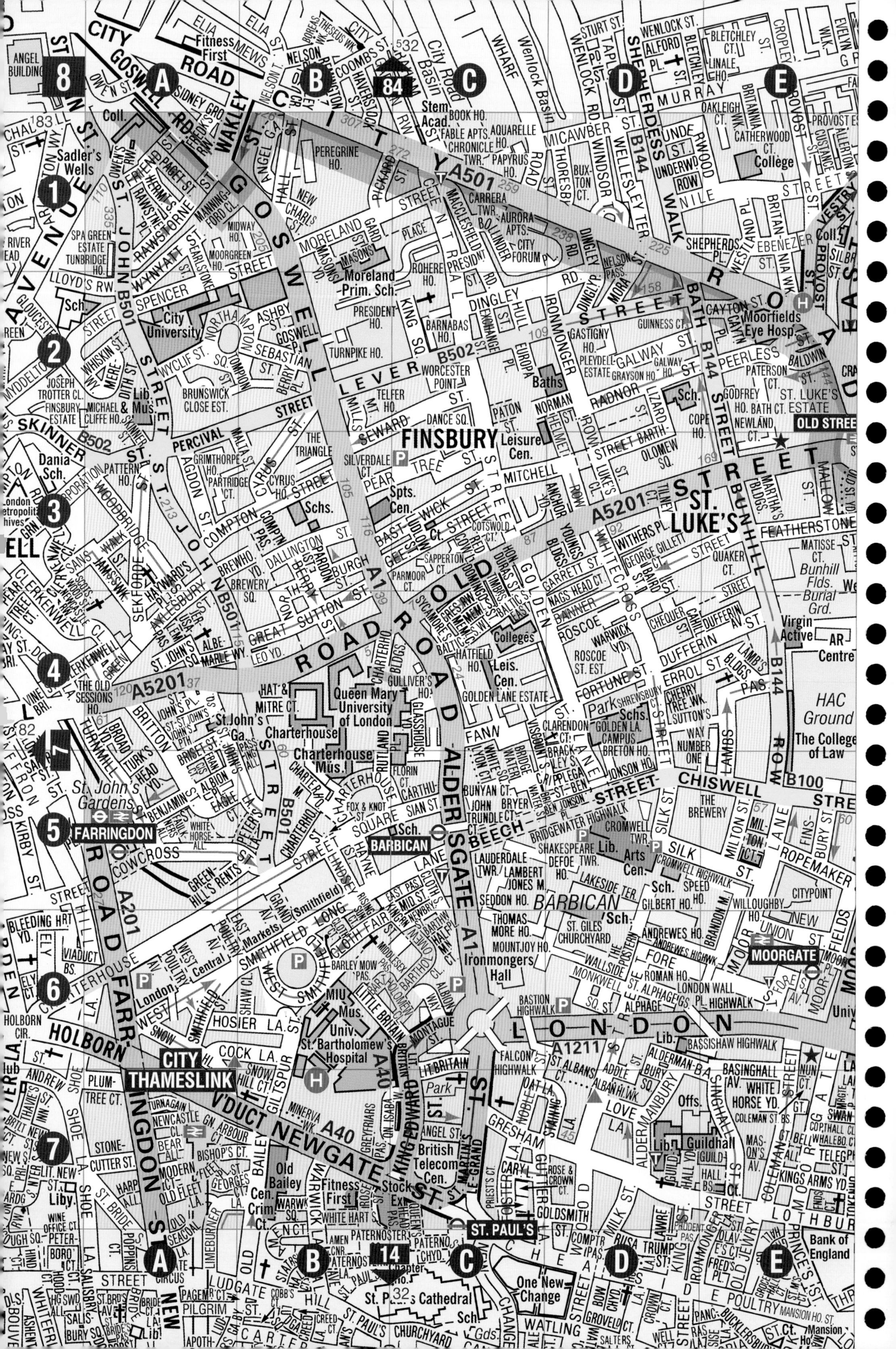

8
A
B
84
C
D
E
1
2
3
4
5
6
7
A
B
14
C
D
E
7
CITY ROAD
GOSWELL ROAD
A501
FINSBURY
ST. LUKE'S
OLD STREET
A5201
OLD ROAD
ROAD
ALDERSGATE
A1
BEECH STREET
CHISWELL STREET
LONDON WALL
A1211
NEWGATE ST.
KING EDWARD ST.
V'DUCT
HOLBORN
FARRINGDON ROAD
A201
A40
ST. JOHN STREET
B501
B502
B144
B100
BUNHILL ROW
ST. MARTIN'S LE GRAND
FARRINGDON
BARBICAN
MOORGATE
ST. PAUL'S
CITY THAMESLINK
OLD STREET
BARBICAN
Queen Mary University of London
Charterhouse
City University
St. Bartholomew's Hospital
Moorfields Eye Hosp.
Old Bailey
St. Paul's Cathedral
HAC Ground
The College of Law
Guildhall
Bank of England
One New Change
British Telecom Cen.
Ironmongers Hall
Sadler's Wells
Angel Building
Moreland Prim. Sch.
Leisure Cen.
Virgin Active
St. John's Gardens
Smithfield
Central Markets
Bunhill Flds. Burial Grd.
Fitness First

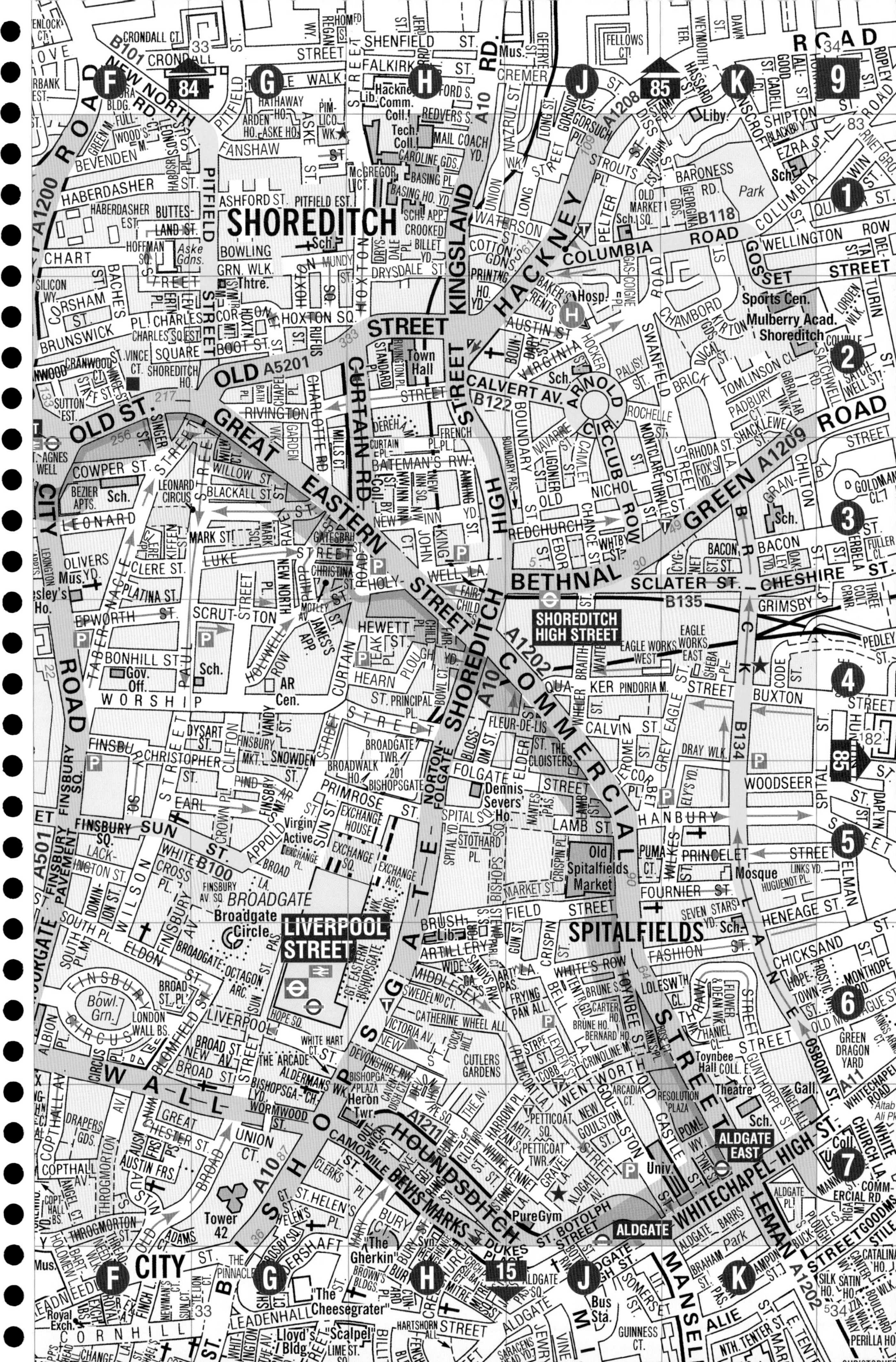

84
85
15
85
F
G
H
J
K
9
1
2
3
4
5
6
7
SHOREDITCH
SPITALFIELDS
CITY
LIVERPOOL STREET
SHOREDITCH HIGH STREET
ALDGATE
ALDGATE EAST
NEW NORTH RD.
CRONDALL ST.
SHENFIELD ST.
FALKIRK ST.
KINGSLAND RD.
A10
HACKNEY RD.
A1208
COLUMBIA ROAD
B118
HABERDASHER ST.
PITFIELD ST.
PITFIELD EST.
ASHFORD ST.
FANSHAW ST.
BOWLING GRN. WLK.
HOXTON ST.
HOXTON SQ.
OLD STREET
A5201
OLD ST.
CITY ROAD
A1200
CHARLES SQUARE
BRUNSWICK PL.
CORSHAM ST.
CHART ST.
SHOREDITCH HO.
GREAT EASTERN STREET
CURTAIN RD.
RIVINGTON ST.
CHARLOTTE RD.
Town Hall
CALVERT AV.
B122
ARNOLD CIR.
BOUNDARY
SWANFIELD ST.
CHAMBORD ST.
Sports Cen.
Mulberry Acad. Shoreditch
GOSSET STREET
WELLINGTON ROW
VIRGINIA RD.
BRICK LANE
GREEN A1209 ROAD
REDCHURCH ST.
CLUB ROW
BETHNAL GREEN
SCLATER ST.
CHESHIRE ST.
B135
COMMERCIAL
A1202
LEONARD ST.
CLERE ST.
LUKE ST.
EPWORTH ST.
SCRUTTON ST.
TABERNACLE ST.
PAUL ST.
BONHILL ST.
WORSHIP ST.
Gov. Off.
HOLYWELL ROW
HEWETT ST.
HEARN ST.
PRINCIPAL PL.
FINSBURY SQ.
CHRISTOPHER ST.
EARL ST.
SUN ST.
APPOLD ST.
PRIMROSE ST.
EXCHANGE HOUSE
EXCHANGE SQ.
BROADGATE
Broadgate Circle
FINSBURY PAVEMENT
A501
WILSON ST.
ELDON ST.
FINSBURY CIRCUS
LONDON WALL
MOORGATE
BISHOPSGATE
NORTON FOLGATE
FOLGATE ST.
Dennis Severs' Ho.
SPITAL SQ.
LAMB ST.
Old Spitalfields Market
HANBURY ST.
PRINCELET STREET
FOURNIER ST.
Mosque
HENEAGE ST.
FASHION ST.
WHITE'S ROW
TOYNBEE ST.
COMMERCIAL STREET
WENTWORTH ST.
Toynbee Hall
Theatre
Gall.
WHITECHAPEL HIGH ST.
A11
LEMAN STREET
OSBORN ST.
BRICK LANE
CHICKSAND ST.
WOODSEER ST.
BUXTON STREET
QUAKER ST.
CALVIN ST.
BRUSHFIELD ST.
ARTILLERY LA.
MIDDLESEX ST.
CUTLERS GARDENS
PETTICOAT LA.
HOUNDSDITCH
A1211
BEVIS MARKS
CAMOMILE ST.
WORMWOOD ST.
Heron Twr.
Tower 42
OLD BROAD ST.
THROGMORTON ST.
AUSTIN FRS.
COPTHALL AV.
"The Gherkin"
"The Cheesegrater"
Lloyd's Bldg.
"Scalpel"
LEADENHALL ST.
CORNHILL
Royal Exch.
ST. BOTOLPH STREET
PureGym
DUKES PLACE
ALDGATE
Bus Sta.
MANSELL ST.
ALIE ST.
GOODMAN'S STILE
CHURCH LA.
COMMERCIAL RD.
Univ.
Sch.
Hosp.
Liby.
Park

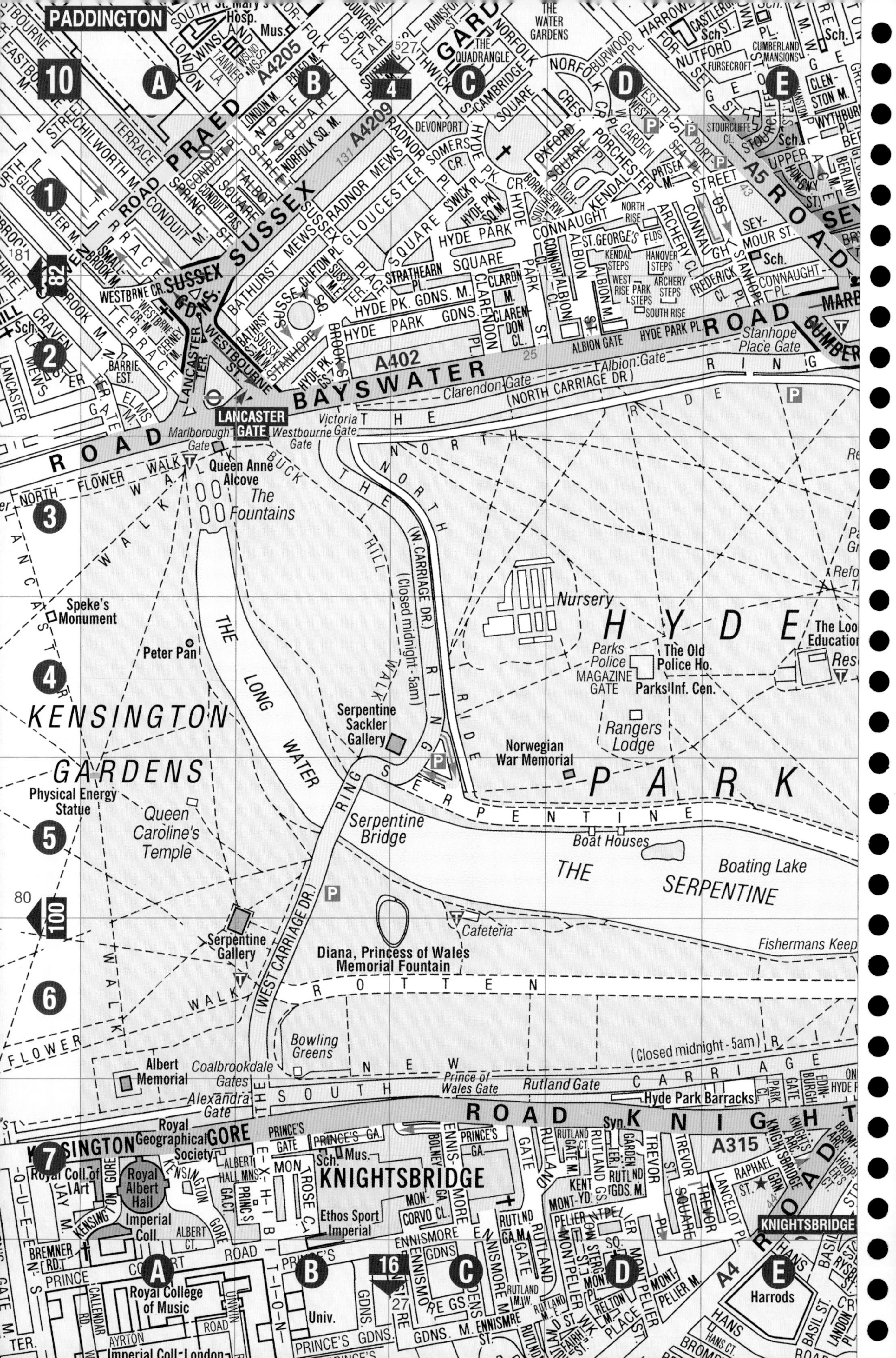

PADDINGTON
10
A
B
C
D
E
1
2
3
4
5
6
7
4
82
100
16
PRAED
SUSSEX
BAYSWATER
ROAD
A4205
A4209
A402
A5
A315
A4
LANCASTER GATE
KNIGHTSBRIDGE
Marlborough Gate
Westbourne Gate
Victoria Gate
Clarendon Gate
Albion Gate
Stanhope Place Gate
Queen Anne Alcove
The Fountains
Speke's Monument
Peter Pan
KENSINGTON GARDENS
Physical Energy Statue
Queen Caroline's Temple
Serpentine Gallery
THE LONG WATER
Serpentine Sackler Gallery
Nursery
HYDE PARK
Parks Police
MAGAZINE GATE
The Old Police Ho.
Parks Inf. Cen.
Rangers Lodge
Norwegian War Memorial
Serpentine Bridge
Boat Houses
THE SERPENTINE
Boating Lake
Cafeteria
Diana, Princess of Wales Memorial Fountain
Fishermans Keep
ROTTEN ROW
Bowling Greens
(Closed midnight - 5am)
(Closed midnight - 5am)
(W. CARRIAGE DR.)
(WEST CARRIAGE DR.)
(NORTH CARRIAGE DR.)
THE RING
NORTH RIDE
Albert Memorial
Coalbrookdale Gates
Alexandra Gate
Prince of Wales Gate
Rutland Gate
Hyde Park Barracks
SOUTH CARRIAGE DR.
Royal Geographical Society
KENSINGTON GORE
Royal Coll. of Art
Royal Albert Hall
Imperial Coll.
Royal College of Music
Imperial Coll. London
KNIGHTSBRIDGE
Ethos Sport Imperial
Univ.
Harrods
Mus.
Sch.
Syn.
St. Mary's Hosp.
THE WATER GARDENS
THE QUADRANGLE
CONNAUGHT SQUARE
HYDE PARK SQUARE
HYDE PARK GDNS.
SUSSEX GDNS.
WESTBOURNE TERRACE
GLOUCESTER SQUARE
NORFOLK SQUARE
OXFORD SQUARE
SEYMOUR ST.
CONNAUGHT ST.
HYDE PARK PL.
MONTPELIER SQ.
TREVOR SQUARE
ENNISMORE GDNS.
PRINCE'S GATE
EXHIBITION ROAD
PRINCE CONSORT ROAD
QUEEN'S GATE

Wallace Colln
University
Wigmore Hall
Portman Towers
Harcourt Ho.
Cavendish Square
Oxford Circus
11
5
Selfridges
Oxford St. Restricted Access 7am.-7pm. Mon.-Sat.
Bond St.
Regent Hall
Marble Arch
Virgin Active
Tyburn Tree (site of)
Speakers' Corner
Roosevelt Memorial
Three Kings Yd.
Mayfair
Fitness First
The Faraday Mus.
St. George's Gdns.
Lib.
Sch.
Grosvenor Square
Oxford Street
New Bond Street
Park Lane
Brook Street
Mount Street
South Audley St.
Berkeley Square
Piccadilly
Curzon St.
Green Park
12
Refreshment Kiosk
7/7 Memorial
Bandstand
Cavalry Memorial
Achilles Statue
Nannies Lawn
The Dell
The Holocaust Memorial Gdn.
Rose Garden
Queen Elizabeth Gate
Apsley House
Hyde Pk. Cnr.
Hyde Park Corner
Wellington Mon.
Wellington Arch
RAF Bomber Command Memorial
Commonwealth Memorial Gates
Constitution (Closed to traffic on Sundays) Hill
Green Park
Knightsbridge
Buckingham Palace Gardens
Buckingham Palace
The Quadrangle
Queen Victoria Memorial
Ambassadors' Ct.
Queen's Gallery
The Royal Mews
Belgrave Square
Grosvenor Place
Buckingham Palace Road
Lwr. Grosvenor Pl.
Sloane
17
A40
A4202
A4201
A4
A302
B406
B310
F
G
H
J
K
1
2
3
4
5
6
7
28
29

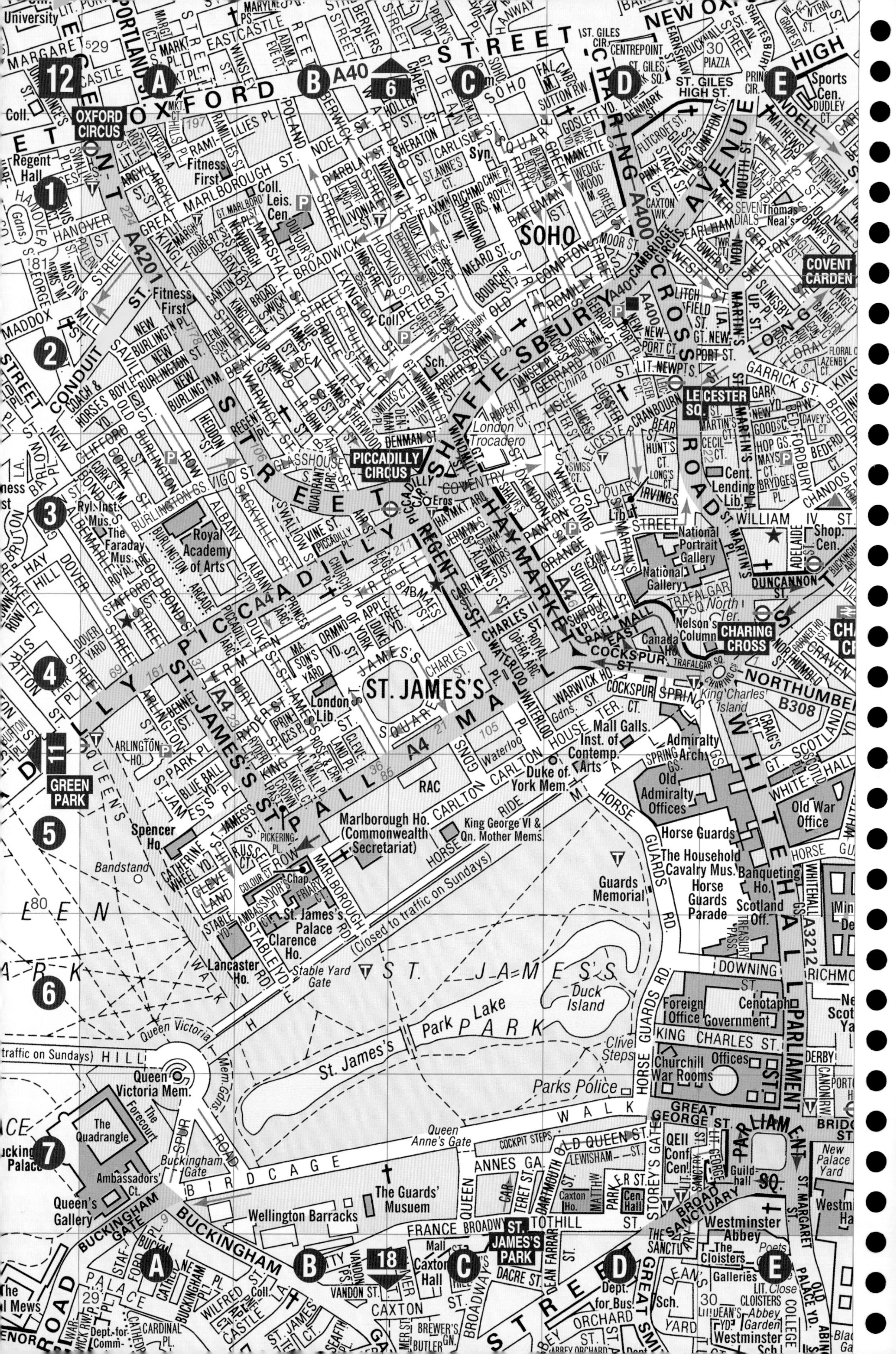

12
A
B
C
D
E
A40
6
1
2
3
4
5
6
7
11
18
OXFORD CIRCUS
OXFORD STREET
NEW OXFORD STREET
Regent Hall
Fitness First
Coll. Leis. Cen.
SOHO
SOHO SQUARE
CHARING CROSS ROAD
A400
A401
SHAFTESBURY AVENUE
CAMBRIDGE CIRCUS
SEVEN DIALS
Thomas Neal's
COVENT GARDEN
LONG ACRE
GARRICK ST.
LEICESTER SQ.
China Town
GERRARD ST.
London Trocadero
PICCADILLY CIRCUS
Eros
REGENT STREET
A4201
CONDUIT STREET
NEW BOND ST.
OLD BOND ST.
Ryl. Inst. Mus.
The Faraday Mus.
Royal Academy of Arts
BURLINGTON ARC.
PICCADILLY
A4
HAYMARKET
JERMYN ST.
ST. JAMES'S SQUARE
London Lib.
ST. JAMES'S ST.
PALL MALL
RAC
GREEN PARK
Spencer Ho.
Lancaster Ho.
St. James's Palace
Clarence Ho.
Marlborough Ho. (Commonwealth Secretariat)
King George VI & Qn. Mother Mems.
THE MALL
(Closed to traffic on Sundays)
Duke of York Mem.
Inst. of Contemp. Arts
Mall Galls.
Admiralty Arch
Old Admiralty Offices
National Portrait Gallery
National Gallery
TRAFALGAR SQ.
Nelson's Column
Canada Ho.
CHARING CROSS
Cent. Lending Lib.
Shop. Cen.
WILLIAM IV ST.
DUNCANNON ST.
NORTHUMBERLAND
B308
COCKSPUR ST.
King Charles Island
WHITEHALL
Old War Office
Horse Guards
The Household Cavalry Mus.
Horse Guards Parade
Banqueting Ho.
Scotland Off.
Guards Memorial
HORSE GUARDS RD.
DOWNING ST.
Foreign Office
Government Offices
Cenotaph
KING CHARLES ST.
Churchill War Rooms
PARLIAMENT ST.
A3212
PARLIAMENT SQ.
ST. JAMES'S PARK
Duck Island
Lake
Clive Steps
Parks Police
Stable Yard Gate
Bandstand
Queen Victoria Mem.
The Forecourt
The Quadrangle
Buckingham Palace
Ambassadors' Ct.
Queen's Gallery
Buckingham Gate
BIRDCAGE WALK
The Guards' Museum
Wellington Barracks
Queen Anne's Gate
QUEEN ANNE'S GATE
GREAT GEORGE ST.
QEII Conf. Cen.
Guild-hall
Westminster Abbey
The Cloisters
Westminster Sch.
BROADWAY
TOTHILL ST.
ST. JAMES'S PARK
Caxton Hall
CAXTON ST.
BUCKINGHAM GATE
Dept. for Bus.
VICTORIA ST.

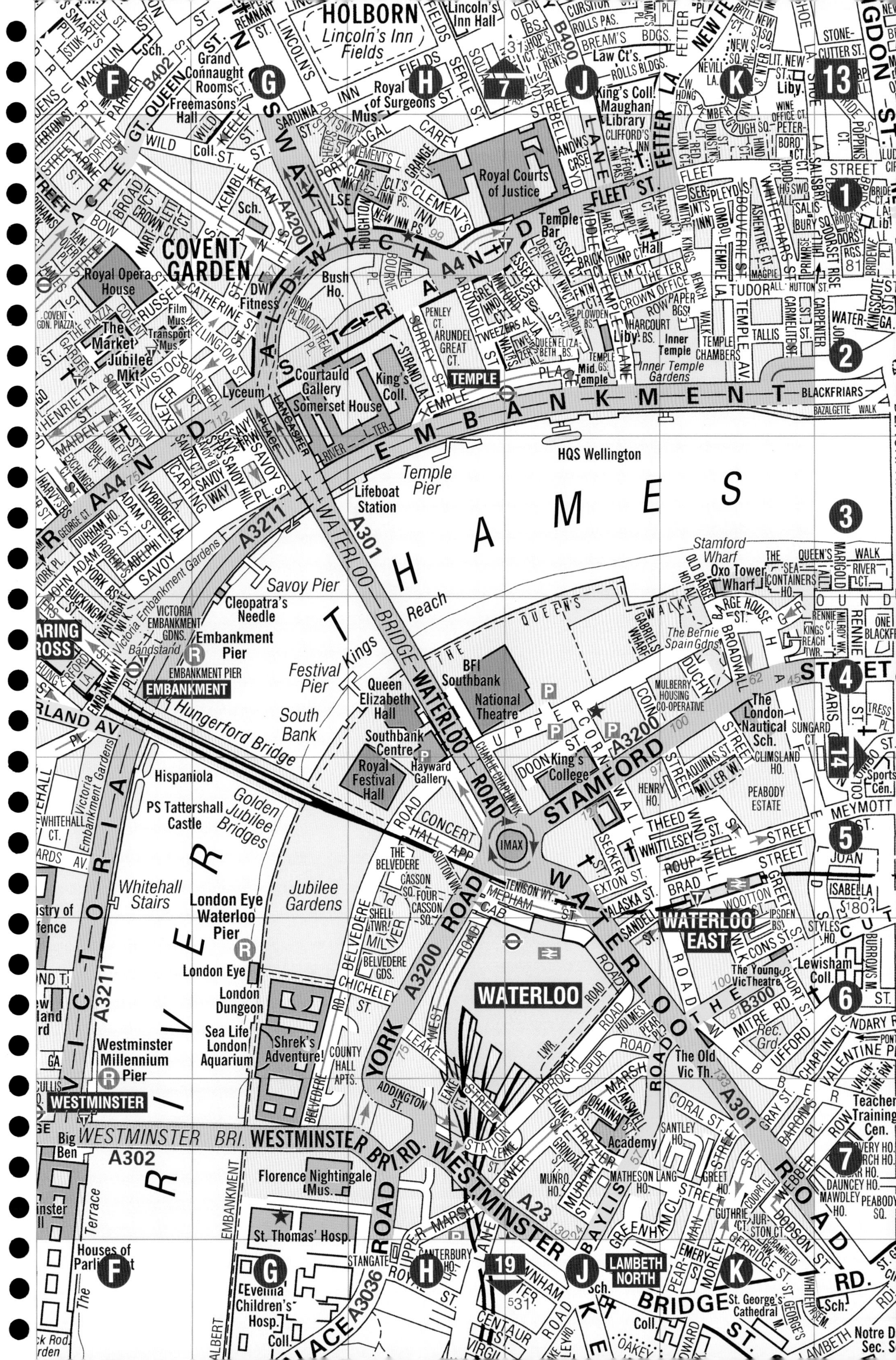

HOLBORN
Lincoln's Inn Fields
Lincoln's Inn Hall
Grand Connaught Rooms
Freemasons' Hall
Royal Coll. of Surgeons Mus.
Royal Courts of Justice
King's Coll. Maughan Library
LSE
Law Ct's.
Liby.
F
G
H
J
K
7
13
1
2
3
4
5
6
7
14
19
B400
B402
A4200
A4
A4
A3211
A301
A3200
A3200
A3036
A302
A23
B300
A301
ALDWYCH
STRAND
FLEET ST.
FETTER LA.
TEMPLE BAR
COVENT GARDEN
Royal Opera House
The Market
Jubilee Mkt
Film Mus.
Transport Mus.
DW Fitness
Lyceum
Bush Ho.
Courtauld Gallery
Somerset House
King's Coll.
TEMPLE
Inner Temple
Temple Chambers
Inner Temple Gardens
Mid. Temple
Hall
BLACKFRIARS
BAZALGETTE WALK
EMBANKMENT
HQS Wellington
Temple Pier
Lifeboat Station
THAMES
Savoy Pier
Cleopatra's Needle
Embankment Pier
EMBANKMENT PIER
EMBANKMENT
Bandstand
Victoria Embankment Gardens
CHARING CROSS
Hungerford Bridge
Hispaniola
PS Tattershall Castle
Golden Jubilee Bridges
Whitehall Stairs
Festival Pier
Kings Reach
South Bank
Queen Elizabeth Hall
Southbank Centre
Royal Festival Hall
Hayward Gallery
BFI Southbank
National Theatre
Stamford Wharf
Oxo Tower Wharf
Sea Containers Ho.
The Bernie Spain Gdns.
Mulberry Housing Co-operative
King's College
The London Nautical Sch.
Sports Cen.
Peabody Estate
IMAX
STAMFORD STREET
UPPER GROUND
WATERLOO BRIDGE
WATERLOO ROAD
Jubilee Gardens
London Eye Waterloo Pier
London Eye
London Dungeon
Sea Life London Aquarium
Shrek's Adventure!
County Hall Apts.
WATERLOO
WATERLOO EAST
The Young Vic Theatre
Lewisham Coll.
The Old Vic Th.
Teacher Training Cen.
Academy
Westminster Millennium Pier
WESTMINSTER
Big Ben
WESTMINSTER BRIDGE
WESTMINSTER BRI. RD.
YORK ROAD
RIVER
VICTORIA EMBANKMENT
Florence Nightingale Mus.
St. Thomas' Hosp.
Evelina Children's Hosp.
Houses of Parliament
LAMBETH NORTH
St. George's Cathedral
Notre Dame Sec. Sch.
BRIDGE ST.
LAMBETH PALACE RD.

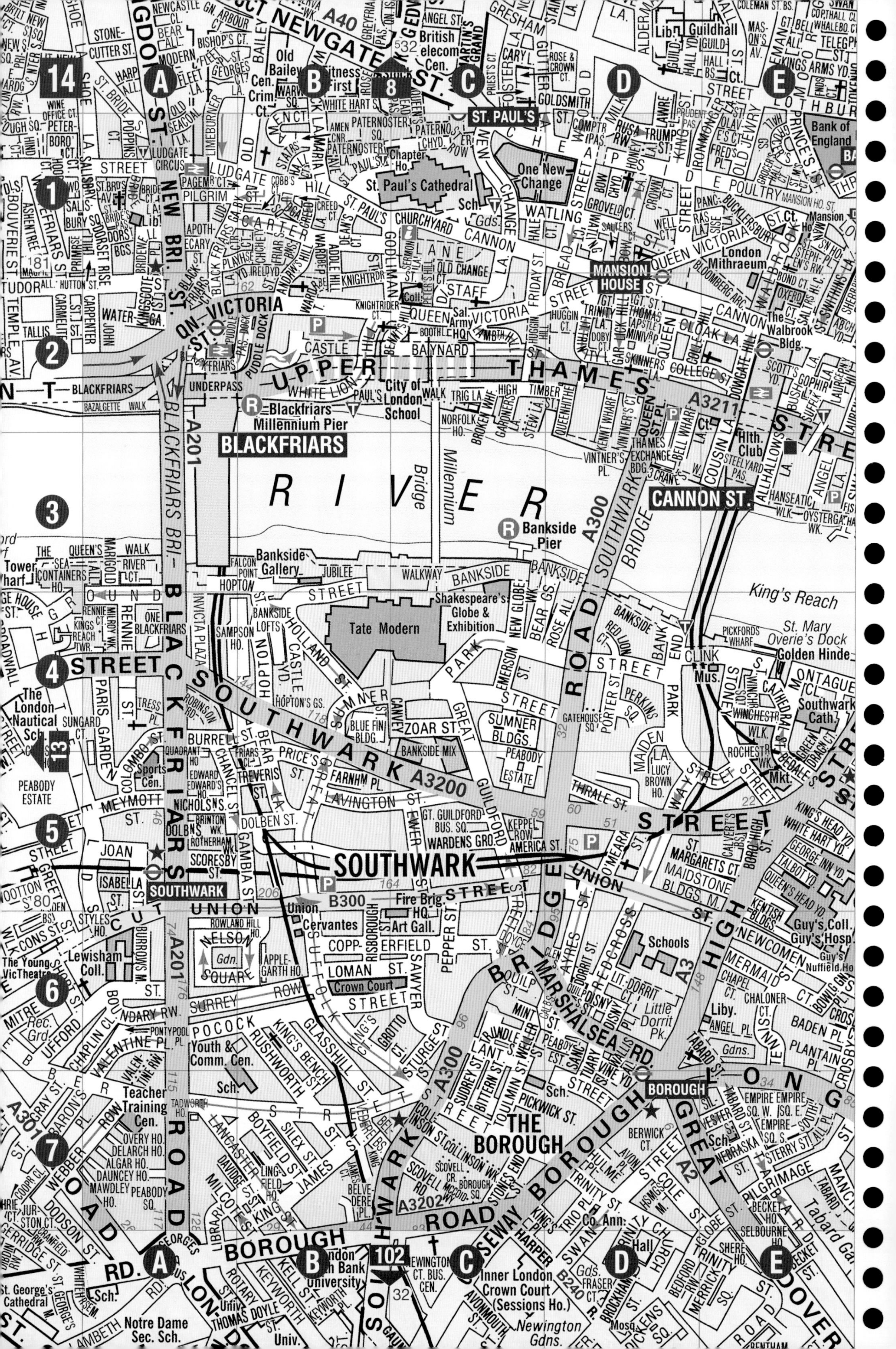
14
8
13
102
A
B
C
D
E
1
2
3
4
5
6
7
NEWGATE ST.
A40
Old Bailey
Cen. Crim. Ct.
British Telecom Cen.
Fitness First
ST. PAUL'S
St. Paul's Cathedral
Chapter Ho.
One New Change
Guildhall
Lib.
Bank of England
LUDGATE CIRCUS
LUDGATE HILL
FLEET ST.
NEW BRI. ST.
CHEAPSIDE
POULTRY
QUEEN VICTORIA ST.
CANNON ST.
MANSION HOUSE
London Mithraeum
The Walbrook Bldg.
WATLING ST.
FRIDAY ST.
BREAD ST.
OLD CHANGE CT.
KNIGHTRIDER ST.
BAYNARD
Sal. Army HQ
UPPER THAMES ST.
WHITE LION HILL
City of London School
BLACKFRIARS
UNDERPASS
Blackfriars Millennium Pier
BAZALGETTE WALK
A201
A3211
Hlth. Club
CANNON ST.
RIVER
Millennium Bridge
Bankside Pier
SOUTHWARK BRIDGE
A300
King's Reach
St. Mary Overie's Dock
Golden Hinde
Clink Mus.
Southwark Cath.
Bankside Gallery
JUBILEE WALKWAY
BANKSIDE
HOPTON ST.
Tate Modern
Shakespeare's Globe & Exhibition
NEW GLOBE WK.
BEAR GS.
ROSE ALL.
PARK ST.
STONEY ST.
SOUTHWARK ST.
A3200
SUMNER ST.
ZOAR ST.
BANKSIDE MIX
BLUE FIN BLDG.
GREAT GUILDFORD ST.
SUMNER BLDGS.
PEABODY ESTATE
THRALE ST.
LAVINGTON ST.
BLACKFRIARS BRI.
BLACKFRIARS RD.
The London Nautical Sch.
Sports Cen.
STAMFORD ST.
MEYMOTT ST.
SOUTHWARK
UNION ST.
B300
Fire Brig. HQ
Art Gall.
Cervantes
Union
NELSON SQUARE
Gdn.
COPPERFIELD ST.
LOMAN ST.
Crown Court
SURREY ROW
POCOCK ST.
Youth & Comm. Cen.
Sch.
SOUTHWARK BRIDGE RD.
MARSHALSEA RD.
BOROUGH HIGH ST.
A3
Schools
Little Dorrit Pk.
Liby.
BOROUGH
THE BOROUGH
BOROUGH RD.
A3202
LONG LANE
GREAT DOVER ST.
A2
Guy's Coll.
Guy's Hosp.
The Young Vic Theatre
Lewisham Coll.
THE CUT
Teacher Training Cen.
A301
WEBBER ST.
London South Bank University
Inner London Crown Court (Sessions Ho.)
Newington Gdns.
St. George's Cathedral
Notre Dame Sec. Sch.
LONDON RD.
ST. GEORGE'S RD.
Tabard Gdns.

F
G
H
J
K
15
9
1
2
3
4
5
6
7
CITY
Tower 42
"The Gherkin"
"The Cheesegrater"
"Scalpel"
Lloyd's Bldg
"Walkie-Talkie"
ALDGATE
ALDGATE EAST
FENCHURCH ST.
MONUMENT
TOWER HILL
TOWER GATEWAY
LONDON BRIDGE
HOUNDSDITCH
WHITECHAPEL HIGH ST.
LEMAN STREET
MANSELL
MINORIES
PRESCOT
ROYAL MINT ST.
CORNHILL
LEADENHALL
FENCHURCH
GRACECHURCH
EASTCHEAP
GREAT TOWER ST.
LWR. THAMES ST.
BYWARD ST.
TOWER HILL
EAST SMITHFIELD
TOWER BRI. APP.
A3211
A1203
A1202
THAMES
Old Billingsgate Market
Custom Ho.
The Tower of London
Chapel
Traitors Gate
Tower Beach
Tower Millennium Pier
London Bridge City Pier
HMS Belfast
St. Katharine Docks
St. Katharine's Pier
Tower Bri. Exhibition
Royal Mint Court
UPPER POOL
Hay's Galleria
Southwark Crown Court
The Scoop
City Hall
More London Riverside
London Bridge City Park
The Shard
Guy's Hospital
TOOLEY ST.
BERMONDSEY ST.
TOWER BRIDGE ROAD
A200
A100
A3
A2198
A2205
A2207
B202
CRUCIFIX LA.
DRUID ST.
JAMAICA ROAD
BERMONDSEY
Leathermarket Gdns.
Guy St. Park
Butlers Wharf Pier
ANCHOR BREWHOUSE
SHAD THAMES
102
103

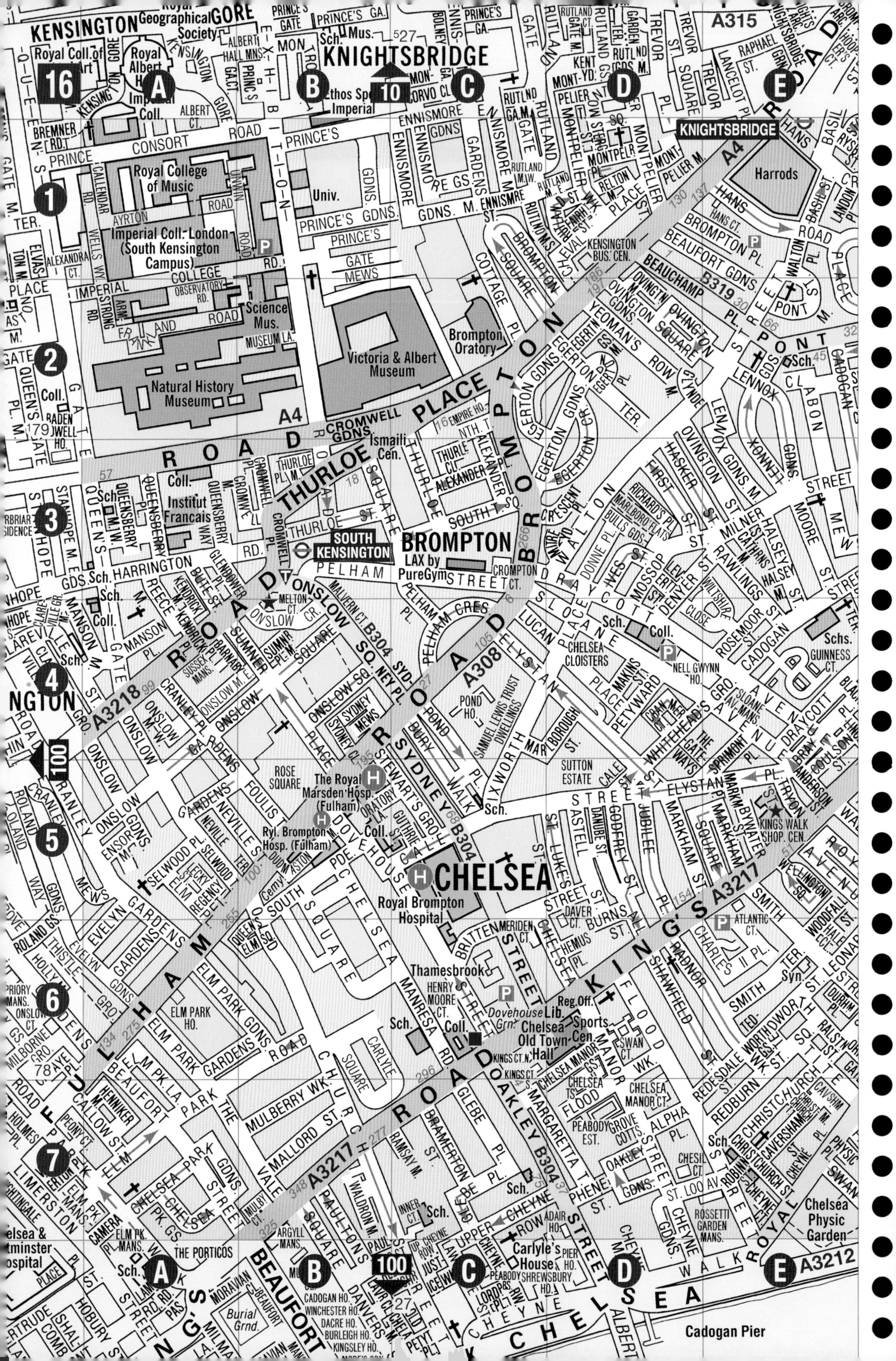
KENSINGTON GORE
Royal Geographical Society
Royal Coll. of Art
Royal Albert Hall
16
A
B
C
D
E
KNIGHTSBRIDGE
10
A315
Imperial Coll.
Ethos Sports Imperial
CONSORT ROAD
PRINCE CONSORT ROAD
Royal College of Music
Imperial Coll. London (South Kensington Campus)
IMPERIAL COLLEGE RD.
EXHIBITION ROAD
Science Mus.
Natural History Museum
Victoria & Albert Museum
Univ.
PRINCE'S GDNS.
PRINCE'S GATE MEWS
ENNISMORE GDNS.
ENNISMORE GARDENS M.
RUTLAND GATE
MONTPELIER SQ.
MONTPELIER PLACE
KNIGHTSBRIDGE
Harrods
HANS ROAD
BROMPTON PL.
BEAUFORT GDNS.
BEAUCHAMP PL.
B319
WALTON STREET
PONT STREET
LENNOX GDNS.
KENSINGTON BUS. CEN.
BROMPTON SQUARE
Brompton Oratory
COTTAGE PL.
A4
CROMWELL ROAD
CROMWELL GDNS.
Ismaili Cen.
THURLOE PLACE
THURLOE SQUARE
EGERTON GDNS.
EGERTON CRESCENT
YEOMAN'S ROW
OVINGTON SQUARE
HASKER ST.
MILNER ST.
RAWLINGS ST.
MOORE ST.
Institut Francais
QUEENSBERRY PL.
HARRINGTON RD.
SOUTH KENSINGTON
BROMPTON
LAX by PureGym
PELHAM STREET
PELHAM CRES.
ONSLOW SQUARE
ONSLOW GARDENS
SUMNER PL.
A3218
FULHAM ROAD
BROMPTON ROAD
A308
SYDNEY STREET
B304
DRAYCOTT AVENUE
WALTON ST.
SLOANE AVENUE
ELYSTAN STREET
ELYSTAN PL.
CADOGAN ST.
Schs.
CHELSEA CLOISTERS
NELL GWYNN HO.
SUTTON ESTATE
SAMUEL LEWIS TRUST DWELLINGS
IXWORTH PL.
JUBILEE PL.
MARKHAM SQUARE
KINGS WALK SHOP. CEN.
ROSE SQUARE
The Royal Marsden Hosp. (Fulham)
Ryl. Brompton Hosp. (Fulham)
CHELSEA
Royal Brompton Hospital
EVELYN GARDENS
ELM PARK GARDENS
ELM PARK HO.
CHELSEA SQUARE
DOVEHOUSE STREET
MANRESA RD.
Thamesbrook
HENRY MOORE CT.
Dovehouse Grn.
Reg.Off.
Lib.
Chelsea Old Town Hall
Sports Cen.
KING'S ROAD
A3217
FLOOD STREET
SHAWFIELD ST.
RADNOR WK.
SMITH ST.
CHRISTCHURCH ST.
MULBERRY WK.
MALLORD ST.
OAKLEY STREET
GLEBE PL.
CHEYNE WALK
CHELSEA EMBANKMENT
Carlyle's House
BEAUFORT ST.
THE PORTICOS
Burial Grnd.
PAULTONS SQUARE
100
Chelsea Physic Garden
ROSSETTI GARDEN MANS.
ROYAL HOSPITAL ROAD
A3212
Cadogan Pier
ALBERT BRIDGE
1
2
3
4
5
6
7

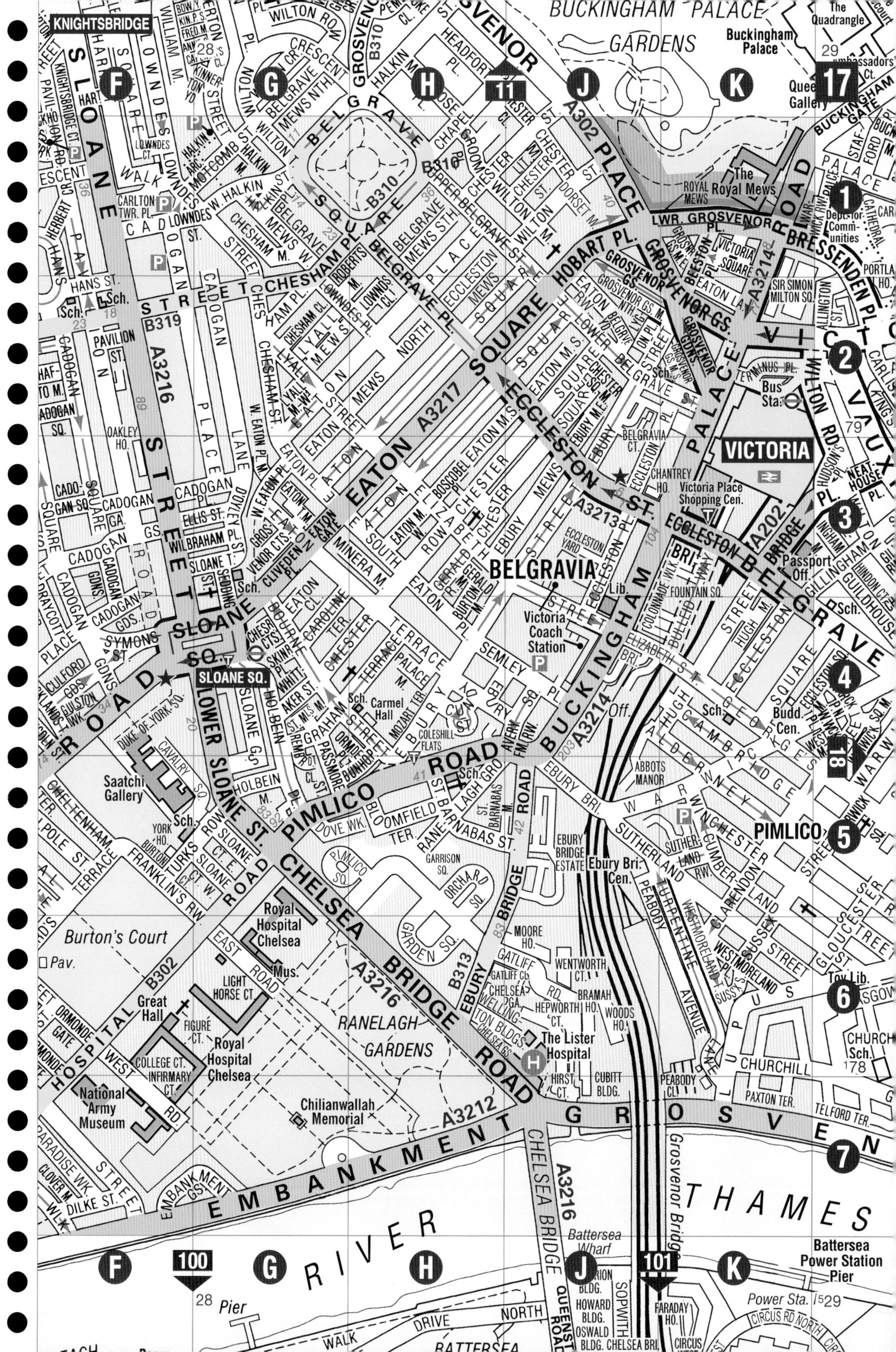

KNIGHTSBRIDGE
BUCKINGHAM PALACE GARDENS
Buckingham Palace
The Quadrangle
Queen's Gallery
17
11
18
100
101
F
G
H
J
K
1
2
3
4
5
6
7
SLOANE STREET
BELGRAVE SQUARE
EATON SQUARE
ECCLESTON ST.
GROSVENOR PLACE
BUCKINGHAM PALACE ROAD
BELGRAVE ROAD
VICTORIA
Victoria Place Shopping Cen.
Victoria Coach Station
BELGRAVIA
SLOANE SQ.
PIMLICO ROAD
PIMLICO
LOWER SLOANE ST.
CHELSEA BRIDGE ROAD
ROYAL HOSPITAL ROAD
Royal Hospital Chelsea
National Army Museum
Saatchi Gallery
Burton's Court
RANELAGH GARDENS
Chilianwallah Memorial
The Lister Hospital
GROSVENOR ROAD
EMBANKMENT
CHELSEA BRIDGE
RIVER THAMES
Grosvenor Bridge
Battersea Power Station Pier
The Royal Mews
Passport Off.
Ebury Bri. Cen.
EBURY BRIDGE ESTATE

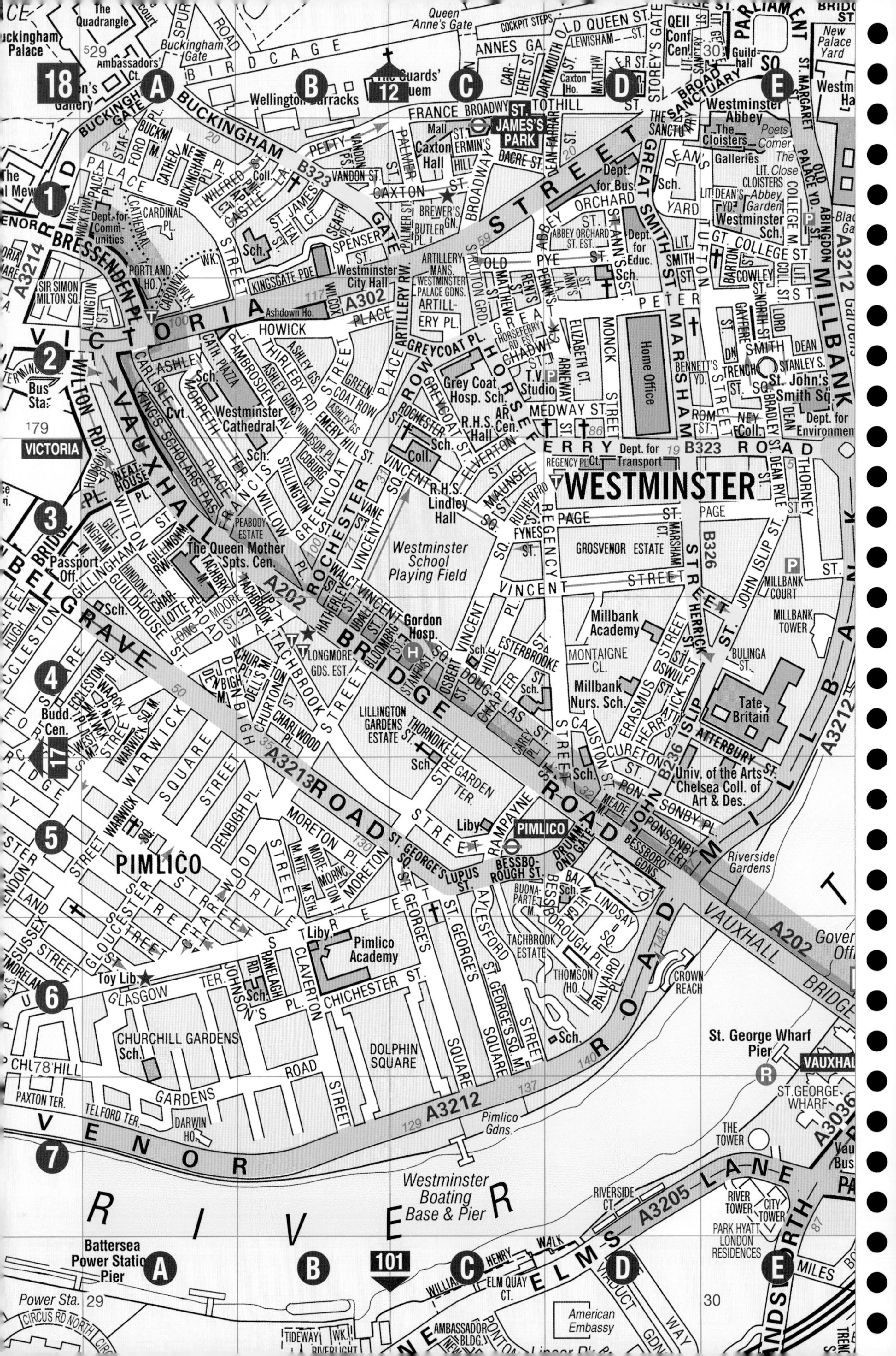

The Quadrangle
Buckingham Palace
Queen Anne's Gate
COCKPIT STEPS
OLD QUEEN ST.
PARLIAMENT SQ.
New Palace Yard
18
A
B
C
D
E
Ambassadors' Ct.
BIRDCAGE
ANNES GA.
LEWISHAM ST.
Caxton Ho.
Guildhall
Wellington Barracks
12
BUCKINGHAM GATE
BROADWAY
ST. JAMES'S PARK
TOTHILL ST.
THE SANCTUARY
BROAD SANCTUARY
Westminster Abbey
The Cloisters
Poets' Corner
Galleries
ST. MARGARET ST.
Caxton Hall
PETTY FRANCE
VANDON ST.
DACRE ST.
CAXTON ST.
PALMER ST.
DEAN FARRAR ST.
DEAN'S YARD
Dept. for Bus.
LIT. CLOSE
CLOISTERS
Abbey Garden
Westminster Sch.
1
PALACE ST.
CATHEDRAL PL.
BUCKINGHAM PL.
WILFRED ST.
CASTLE LA.
ST. JAMES CT.
BREWER'S GN.
BUTLER PL.
ABBEY ORCHARD ST.
ABBEY ORCHARD ST. EST.
Dept. for Educ.
GT. COLLEGE ST.
COWLEY ST.
ABINGDON ST.
MILLBANK
A3212
Dept. for Communities
Sch.
Westminster City Hall
SPENSER ST.
ARTILLERY MANS.
WESTMINSTER PALACE GDNS.
ARTILLERY PL.
OLD PYE ST.
GREAT SMITH ST.
TUFTON ST.
BARTON ST.
BRESSENDEN PL.
A3214
SIR SIMON MILTON SQ.
PORTLAND HO.
KINGSGATE PDE.
A302
PETER ST.
VICTORIA STREET
Ashdown Ho.
HOWICK PL.
ELIZABETH CT.
MONCK ST.
Home Office
MARSHAM ST.
SMITH SQ.
St. John's Smith Sq.
DEAN TRENCH ST.
STANLEY S.
2
Bus Sta.
ASHLEY PL.
CARLISLE PL.
AMBROSDEN AV.
THIRLEBY RD.
ASHLEY GDNS.
GREEN COAT ROW
GREYCOAT PL.
GREYCOAT ST.
HORSEFERRY RD.
CHADWICK ST.
ARNEWAY
T.V. Studio
BENNETT'S YD.
Westminster Cathedral
Grey Coat Hosp. Sch.
R.H.S. Hall
AR. Cen.
MEDWAY ST.
ROMNEY ST.
NEY Coll.
Dept. for Environment
179
VICTORIA
WILTON RD.
VAUXHALL BRIDGE ROAD
MORPETH TER.
EMERY HILL ST.
ROCHESTER ROW
ELVERTON ST.
HORSEFERRY ROAD
B323
Dept. for Transport
REGENCY PL.
WESTMINSTER
THORNEY ST.
DEAN RYLE ST.
HUDSON'S PL.
NEATHOUSE PL.
STILLINGTON ST.
WINDSOR PL.
COBURG CL.
VINCENT SQ.
R.H.S. Lindley Hall
MAUNSEL ST.
3
FRANCIS ST.
PEABODY ESTATE
VANE ST.
VINCENT ST.
FYNES ST.
REGENCY ST.
PAGE ST.
GROSVENOR ESTATE
MARSHAM CT.
B326
JOHN ISLIP ST.
Passport Off.
GILLINGHAM ST.
WILTON RD.
The Queen Mother Spts. Cen.
Westminster School Playing Field
VINCENT ST.
VINCENT ST.
MILLBANK COURT
A202
ROCHESTER ST.
GUILDHOUSE ST.
CHARLOTTE PL.
MOORE ST.
TACHBROOK ST.
HATHERLEY ST.
UDALL ST.
Gordon Hosp.
Millbank Academy
MILLBANK TOWER
BELGRAVE ROAD
LONGMORE GDS. EST.
BLOOMBURG ST.
ESTERBROOKE ST.
MONTAIGNE CL.
HERRICK ST.
BULINGA ST.
4
ECCLESTON SQ.
WARWICK WAY
DENBIGH ST.
CHURTON ST.
CHARLWOOD PL.
LILLINGTON GARDENS ESTATE
DOUGLAS ST.
CHAPTER ST.
Millbank Nurs. Sch.
ERASMUS ST.
OSWULF ST.
Tate Britain
Budd. Cen.
17
WARWICK SQ. M.
WARWICK SQUARE
THORNDIKE ST.
GARDEN TER.
CAREY PL.
CAUSTON ST.
CURETON ST.
B236
ATTERBURY ST.
Univ. of the Arts Chelsea Coll. of Art & Des.
A3213
ST. GEORGE'S DRIVE
DENBIGH PL.
MORETON PL.
MORETON ST.
ST. GEORGE'S SQ.
Liby.
RAMPAYNE ST.
PIMLICO
DRUMMOND GATE
PONSONBY PL.
PONSONBY TER.
JOHN ISLIP ST.
5
PIMLICO
LUPUS ST.
BESSBOROUGH ST.
BESSBOROUGH GDNS.
Riverside Gardens
VAUXHALL BRIDGE
A202
Govern. Offi.
GLOUCESTER STREET
CHARLWOOD STREET
SUSSEX STREET
MORETON TER.
Liby.
Pimlico Academy
ST. GEORGE'S SQUARE
AYLESFORD ST.
BUONAPARTE M.
LINDSAY SQ.
TACHBROOK ESTATE
6
Toy Lib.
GLASGOW TER.
JOHNSON'S PL.
RANELAGH RD.
CLAVERTON ST.
CHICHESTER ST.
ST. GEORGE'S SQ. M.
THOMSON HO.
BALVAIRD PL.
CROWN REACH
CHURCHILL GARDENS
DOLPHIN SQUARE
CHURCHILL GARDENS ROAD
ROAD
St. George Wharf Pier
VAUXHALL
78
PAXTON TER.
TELFORD TER.
DARWIN HO.
A3212
Pimlico Gdns.
ST. GEORGE WHARF
THE TOWER
A3036
GROSVENOR ROAD
7
RIVER THAMES
Westminster Boating Base & Pier
RIVERSIDE CT.
A3205
NINE ELMS LANE
RIVER TOWER
CITY TOWER
PARK HYATT LONDON RESIDENCES
WANDSWORTH RD.
Battersea Power Station Pier
101
HENRY WALK
ELM QUAY CT.
MILES ST.
Power Sta.
29
30
CIRCUS RD NORTH
TIDEWAY WK.
AMBASSADOR BLDG.
American Embassy

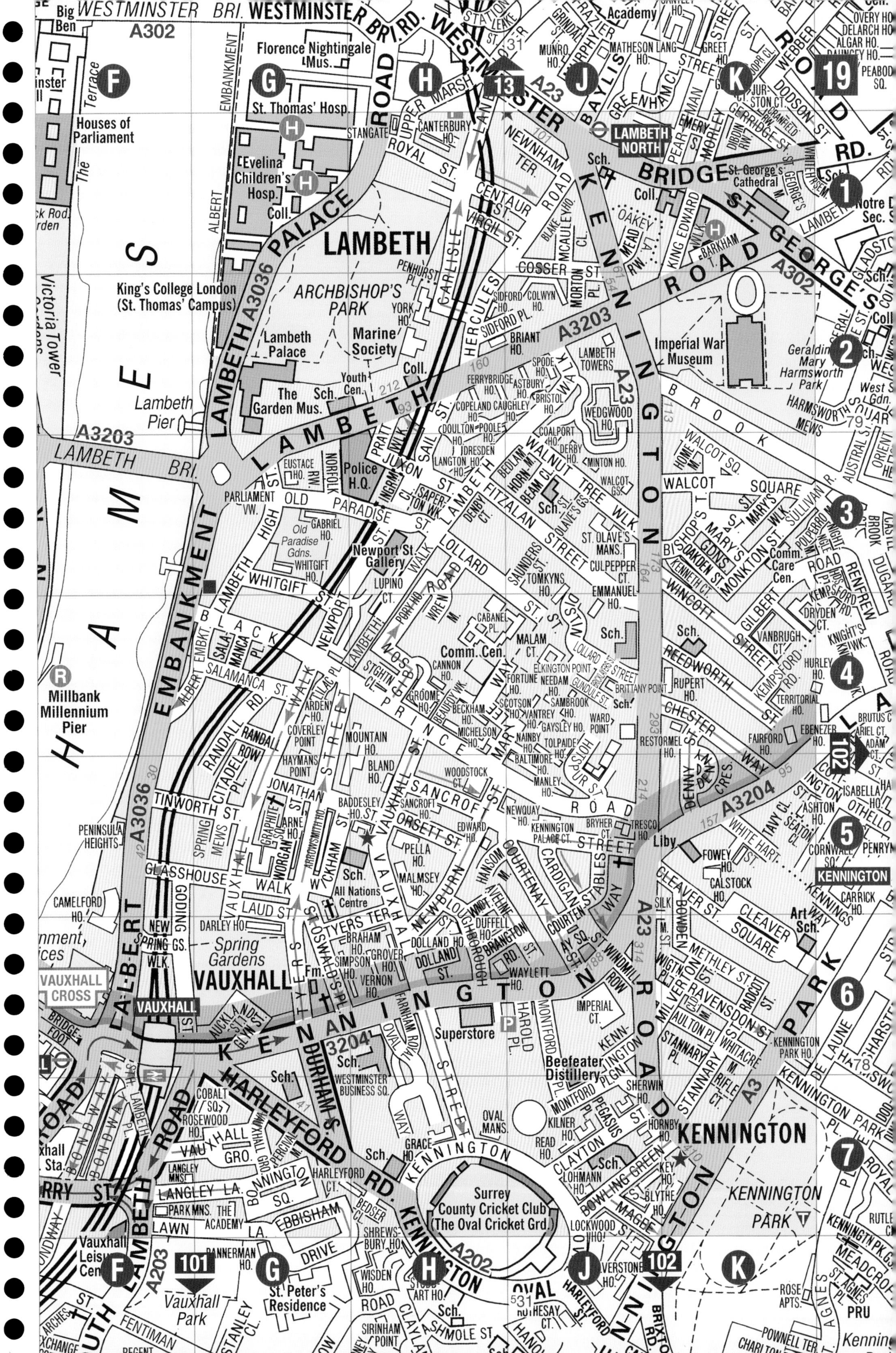

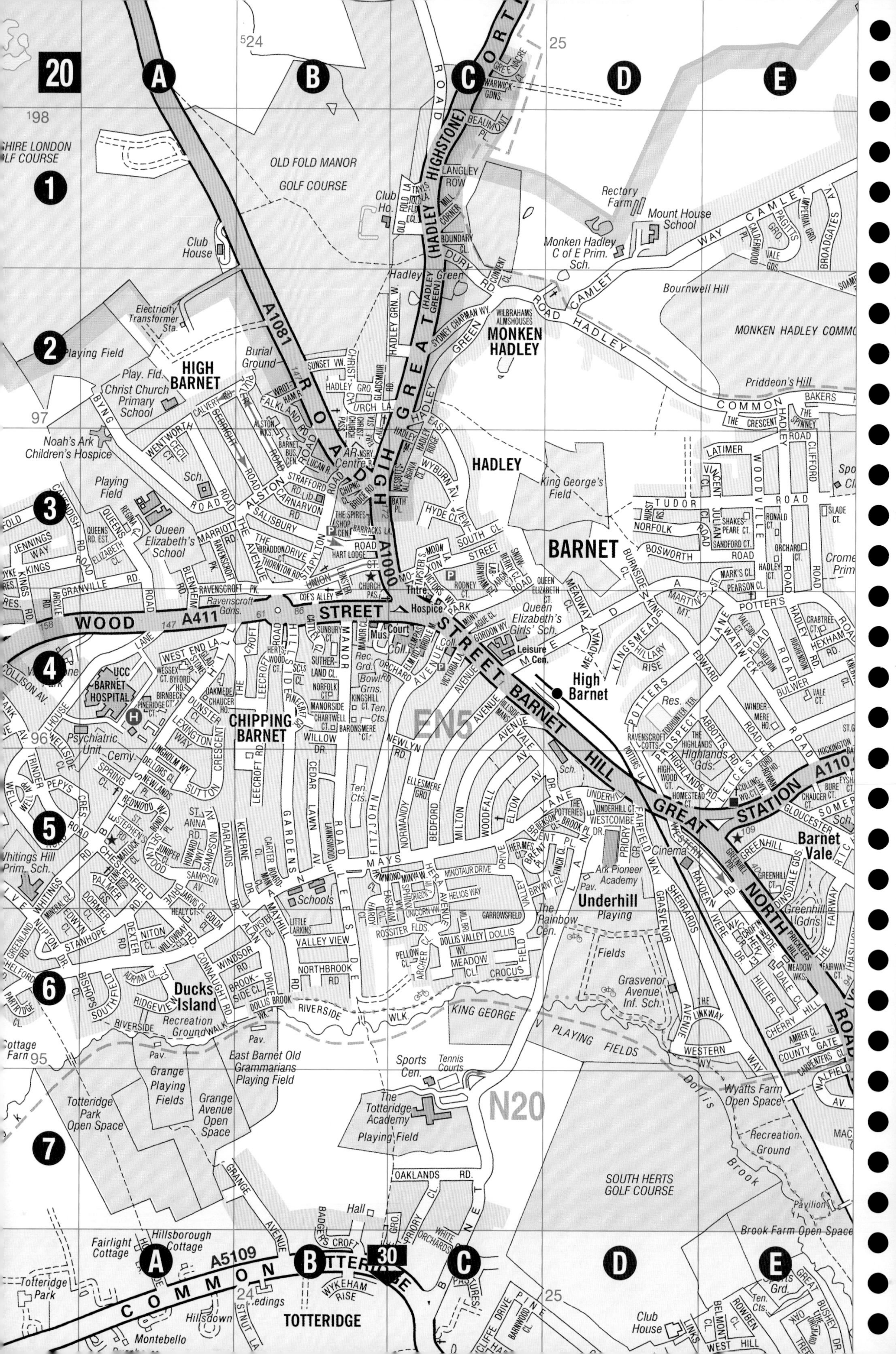
20
A
B
C
D
E
1
2
3
4
5
6
7
OLD FOLD MANOR GOLF COURSE
Club House
HIGH BARNET
Playing Field
Electricity Transformer Sta.
Burial Ground
Play. Fld.
Christ Church Primary School
Noah's Ark Children's Hospice
Queen Elizabeth's School
A1081
GREAT NORTH ROAD
HIGH STREET
A1000
HADLEY GREEN
Hadley Green
MONKEN HADLEY
Monken Hadley C of E Prim. Sch.
Mount House School
Rectory Farm
CAMLET WAY
HADLEY ROAD
Bournwell Hill
MONKEN HADLEY COMMON
Priddeon's Hill
COMMON
HADLEY
King George's Field
BARNET
WOOD STREET
A411
Hospice
Mus.
Court
Queen Elizabeth's Girls' Sch.
Leisure Cen.
High Barnet
BARNET HILL
GREAT NORTH ROAD
STATION ROAD
A110
Barnet Vale
UCC BARNET HOSPITAL
Psychiatric Unit
Cemy.
CHIPPING BARNET
EN5
Whitings Hill Prim. Sch.
Schools
Underhill
Ark Pioneer Academy
Underhill Playing Fields
Cinema
Ducks Island
Recreation Ground
RIVERSIDE WALK
KING GEORGE PLAYING FIELDS
Gravenor Avenue Inf. Sch.
Grange Playing Fields
East Barnet Old Grammarians Playing Field
Grange Avenue Open Space
Totteridge Park Open Space
Sports Cen.
Tennis Courts
The Totteridge Academy Playing Field
N20
Dollis Brook
Wyatts Farm Open Space
Recreation Ground
SOUTH HERTS GOLF COURSE
Pavilion
Brook Farm Open Space
Fairlight Cottage
Hillsborough Cottage
A5109
TOTTERIDGE COMMON
Totteridge Park
Hillsdown
Montebello
TOTTERIDGE
30
Club House
Sports Grd.
524
25
198
97
96
95
24

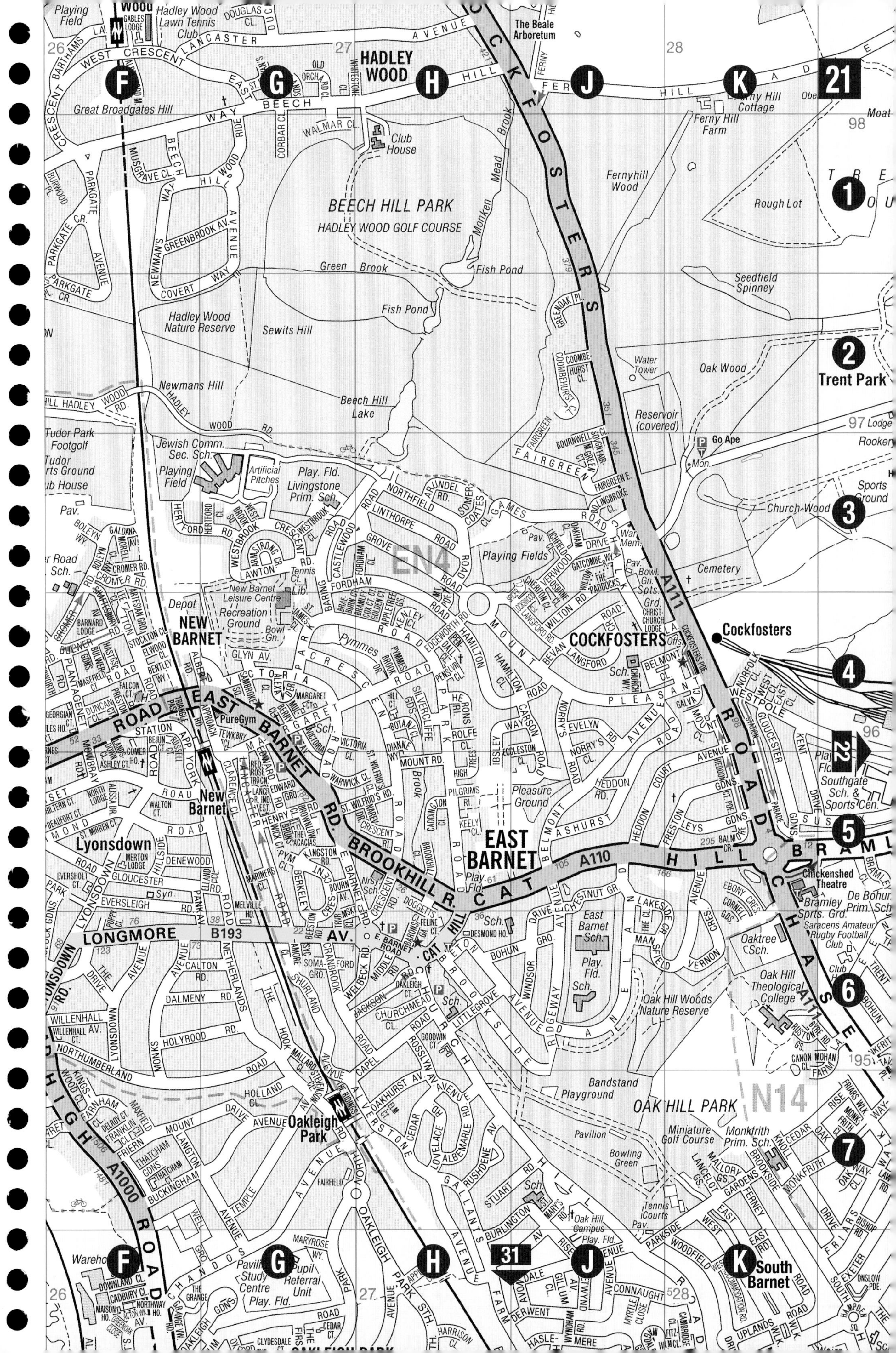

21
22
31
Hadley Wood
Playing Field
Hadley Wood Lawn Tennis Club
The Beale Arboretum
Great Broadgates Hill
Club House
Beech Hill Park
Hadley Wood Golf Course
Monken Mead Brook
Green Brook
Fish Pond
Hadley Wood Nature Reserve
Sewits Hill
Newmans Hill
Beech Hill Lake
Ferny Hill Cottage
Ferny Hill Farm
Fernyhill Wood
Rough Lot
Seedfield Spinney
Oak Wood
Water Tower
Reservoir (covered)
Trent Park
Go Ape
Church Wood
Sports Ground
Cemetery
Cockfosters
Jewish Comm. Sec. Sch.
Artificial Pitches
Play. Fld.
Livingstone Prim. Sch.
Tudor Park Footgolf
Playing Fields
EN4
New Barnet Leisure Centre
Recreation Ground
New Barnet
PureGym
Lyonsdown
Pleasure Ground
East Barnet
Chickenshed Theatre
Southgate Sch. & Sports Cen.
Bramley Sprts. Grd.
De Bohun Prim. Sch.
Saracens Amateur Rugby Football Club
Oaktree Sch.
Oak Hill Theological College
East Barnet Sch.
Oak Hill Woods Nature Reserve
Bandstand
Playground
Oak Hill Park
Miniature Golf Course
Pavilion
Bowling Green
Monkfrith Prim. Sch.
N14
Oak Hill Campus Play. Fld.
Oakleigh Park
South Barnet
Pupil Referral Unit
Pavilion Study Centre
COCKFOSTERS ROAD
A111
EAST BARNET RD.
BROOKHILL RD.
CAT HILL
A110
LONGMORE AV.
B193
HIGH ROAD
A1000
CHASE SIDE
HADLEY WOOD RD.
BEECH HILL
FERNY HILL
MOUNT PLEASANT
STATION ROAD
OAKLEIGH PARK NTH.
OAKLEIGH PARK STH.
CHURCH HILL ROAD
ALVERSTONE AVENUE
PARKSIDE

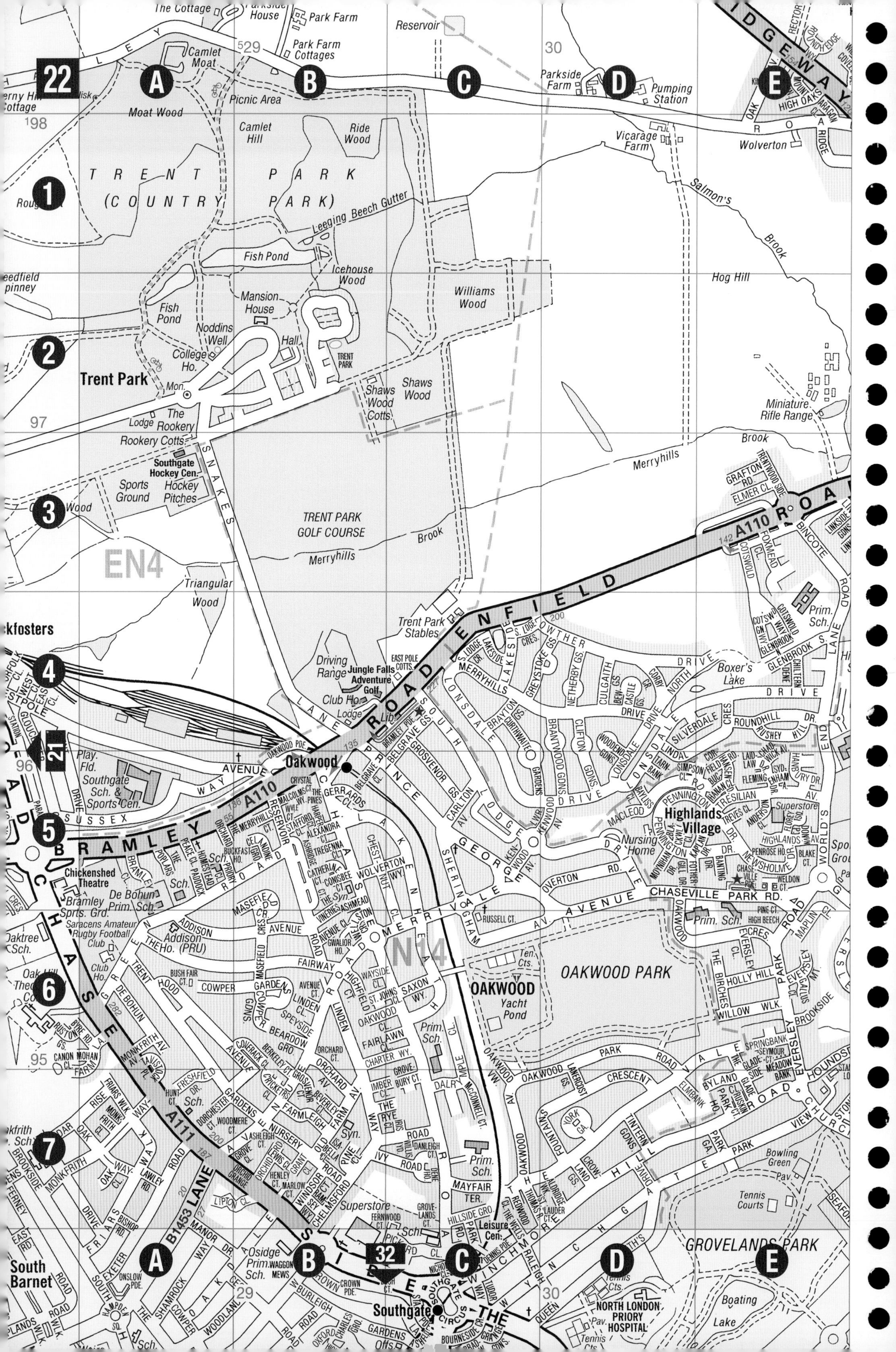

22
21
32
Trent Park
TRENT PARK (COUNTRY PARK)
Camlet Moat
Moat Wood
Picnic Area
Camlet Hill
Ride Wood
Park Farm
Park Farm Cottages
Reservoir
Parkside Farm
Pumping Station
Vicarage Farm
Wolverton
Leeging Beech Gutter
Fish Pond
Icehouse Wood
Mansion House
Williams Wood
Noddins Well
College Ho.
Hall
Shaws Wood Cotts.
Shaws Wood
The Rookery
Lodge
Rookery Cotts.
Southgate Hockey Cen.
Sports Ground
Hockey Pitches
TRENT PARK GOLF COURSE
Merryhills Brook
Salmon's Brook
Hog Hill
Miniature Rifle Range
EN4
Triangular Wood
Trent Park Stables
Driving Range
Jungle Falls Adventure Golf
Club Ho.
Oakwood
ENFIELD ROAD
A110
BRAMLEY ROAD
SNAKES LANE
PRINCE GEORGE AV.
Southgate Sch. & Sports Cen.
Chickenshed Theatre
Bramley Sprts. Grd.
De Bohun Prim. Sch.
Saracens Amateur Rugby Football Club
Addison Ho. (PRU)
Highlands Village
Nursing Home
Superstore
Boxer's Lake
N14
OAKWOOD PARK
Yacht Pond
Prim. Sch.
CHASEVILLE PARK RD.
MERRIVALE
AVENUE
A111
B1453 LANE
Superstore
Leisure Cen.
Southgate
Southgate Circus
Osidge Prim. Sch.
South Barnet
GROVELANDS PARK
Bowling Green
Tennis Courts
Boating Lake
NORTH LONDON PRIORY HOSPITAL
RIDGEWAY
1 2 3 4 5 6 7
A B C D E
29 30 529
198 97 96 95

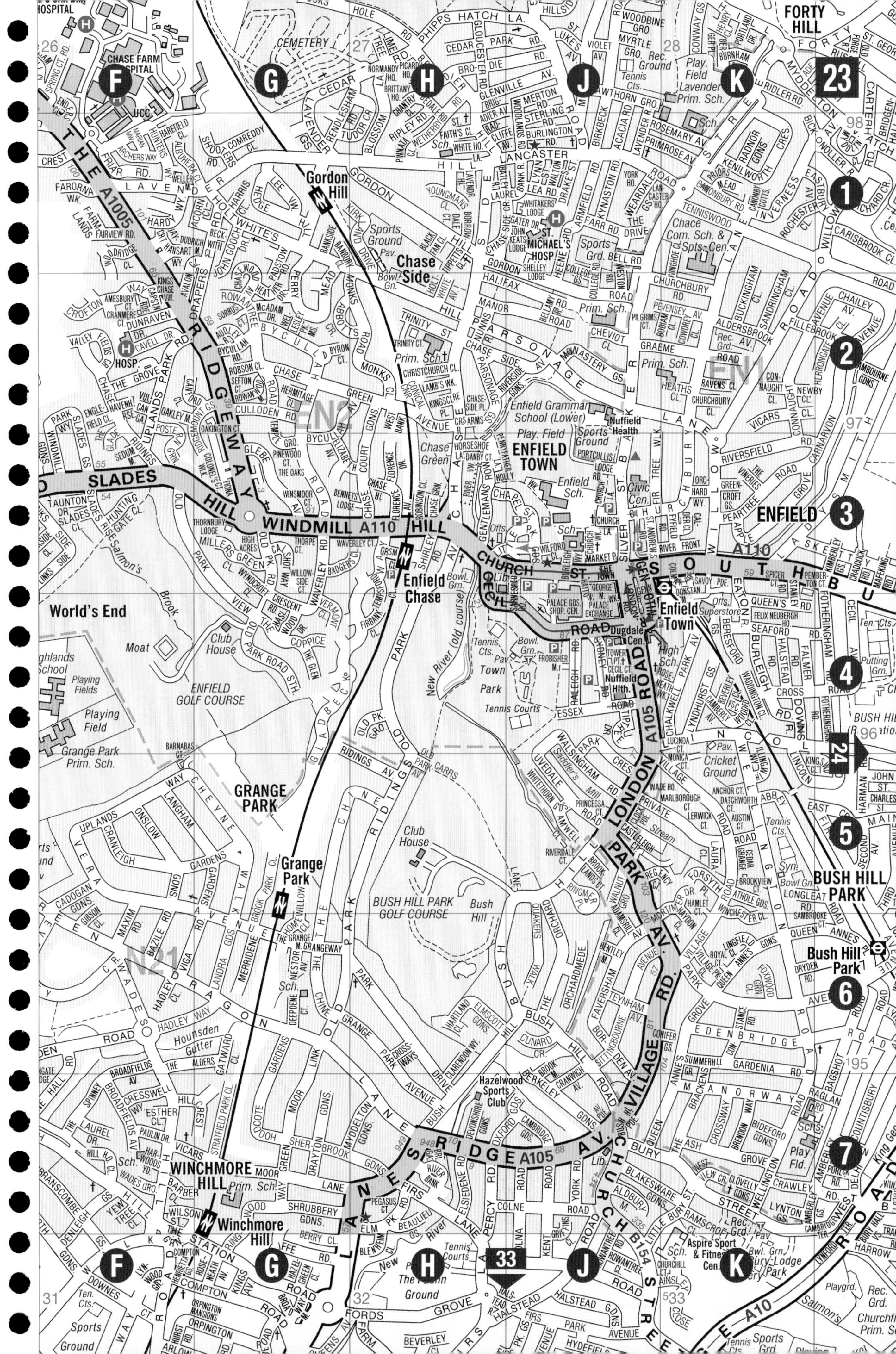
23
24
33
F
G
H
J
K
1
2
3
4
5
6
7
26
27
28
31
32
33
98
97
96
195
FORTY HILL
CHASE FARM HOSPITAL
CEMETERY
Gordon Hill
Chase Side
ST. MICHAEL'S HOSP.
Enfield Grammar School (Lower)
Nuffield Health
ENFIELD TOWN
Enfield Sch.
Civic Cen.
ENFIELD
EN1
EN2
N21
Enfield Chase
Enfield Town
Lib.
PALACE GDS. SHOP. CEN.
PALACE EXCHANGE
Dugdale Cen.
Town Park
World's End
Moat
Club House
ENFIELD GOLF COURSE
Playing Fields
Playing Field
Grange Park Prim. Sch.
GRANGE PARK
Grange Park
BUSH HILL PARK GOLF COURSE
Bush Hill
BUSH HILL PARK
Bush Hill Park
Hazelwood Sports Club
WINCHMORE HILL
Winchmore Hill
New River
Aspire Sport & Fitness Cen.
Bury Lodge Park
Salmon's Brook
THE RIDGEWAY
A1005
SLADES HILL
WINDMILL A110 HILL
CHURCH ST.
SOUTHBURY
A110
CECIL ROAD
LONDON ROAD
A105
PARK AV.
VILLAGE RD.
BUSH HILL
RIDGE AV.
GREEN LANES
CHURCH STREET
B154
A10
GORDON HILL
LAVENDER HILL
LANCASTER ROAD
BAKER STREET
SILVER STREET
CHASE SIDE
PARSONAGE LANE
WINDMILL HILL
BYCULLAH RD.
CHASE GREEN AVENUE
OLD PARK RIDINGS
BOURNE HILL
ORANGE GROVE
THE CHINE
ENFIELD ROAD
VICARS MOOR LANE
STATION ROAD
QUEEN ANNES GDS.
SHRUBBERY GDNS.
FORTY HILL
PHIPPS HATCH LA.
PRIMROSE AV.
CHURCHBURY LANE
RIVERSFIELD RD.
LINCOLN ROAD
DRAPERS RD.
PARK AVENUE
UPLANDS WAY
CHEYNE WALK
GRANGE PARK AVENUE
HALSTEAD ROAD
ALDERSBROOK AV.
BAGSHOT RD.
EDENBRIDGE RD.
GARDENIA RD.
MANORWAY
BURY STREET

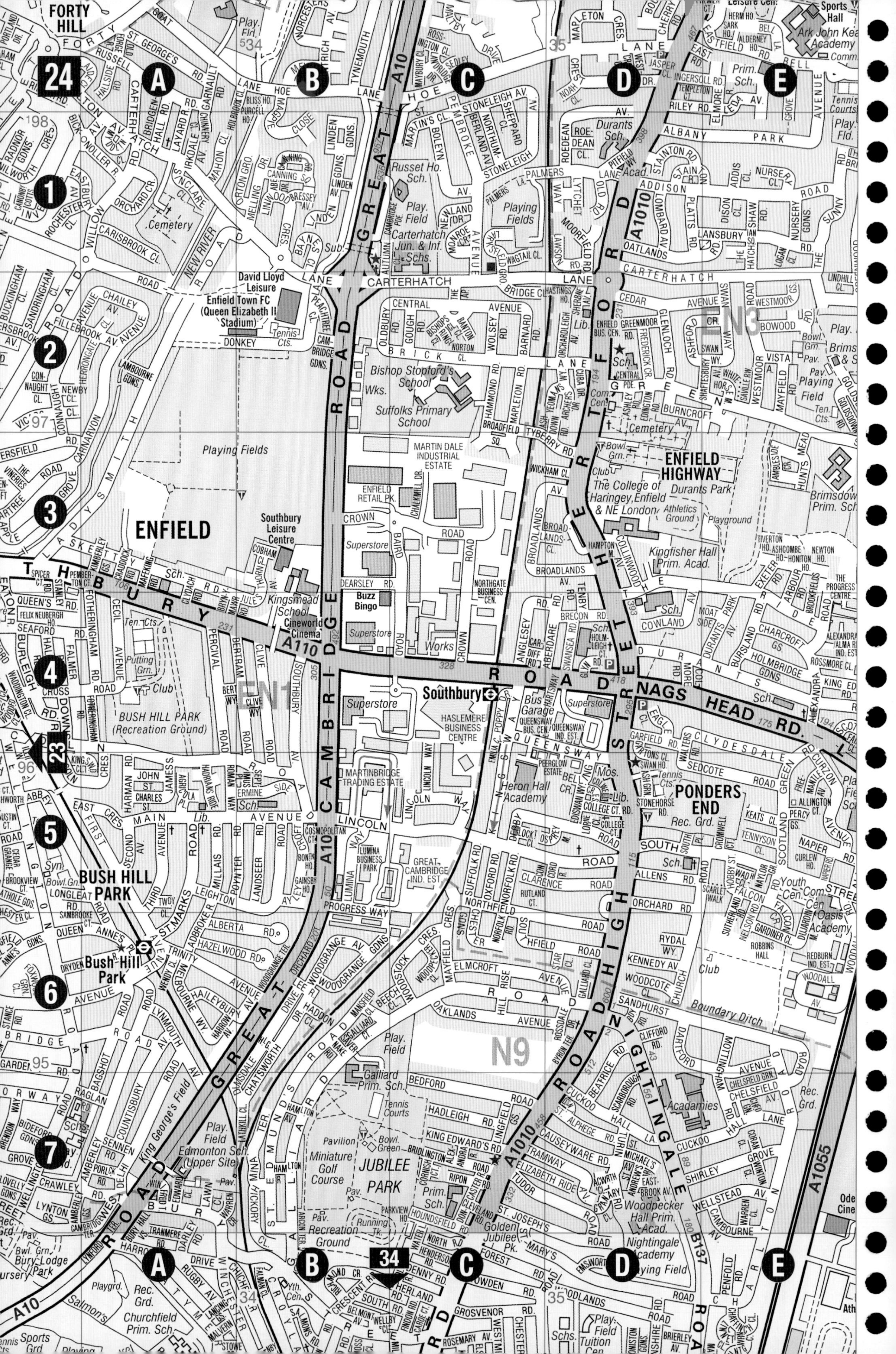
24
23
34
A
B
C
D
E
1
2
3
4
5
6
7
FORTY HILL
ENFIELD
EN1
EN3
N9
ENFIELD HIGHWAY
PONDERS END
BUSH HILL PARK
Bush Hill Park
Southbury
GREAT CAMBRIDGE ROAD
A10
A110
A1010
A1055
B137
SOUTHBURY ROAD
NAGS HEAD RD.
HERTFORD ROAD
HIGH STREET
NIGHTINGALE ROAD
CARTERHATCH LANE
HOE LANE
David Lloyd Leisure
Enfield Town FC (Queen Elizabeth II Stadium)
Southbury Leisure Centre
Kingsmead School
Cineworld Cinema
Buzz Bingo
Playing Fields
BUSH HILL PARK (Recreation Ground)
MARTIN DALE INDUSTRIAL ESTATE
ENFIELD RETAIL PK.
NORTHGATE BUSINESS CEN.
HASLEMERE BUSINESS CENTRE
MARTINBRIDGE TRADING ESTATE
GREAT CAMBRIDGE IND. EST.
Heron Hall Academy
The College of Haringey, Enfield & NE London
Durants Park
Kingfisher Hall Prim. Acad.
Bishop Stopford's School
Suffolks Primary School
Carterhatch Jun. & Inf. Schs.
Russet Ho. Sch.
Durants Sch.
Ark John Keats Academy
Galliard Prim. Sch.
JUBILEE PARK
Miniature Golf Course
Edmonton Sch. (Upper Site)
King George's Field
Woodpecker Hall Prim. Acad.
Nightingale Academy
Oasis Academy
Boundary Ditch
Churchfield Prim. Sch.
Bury Lodge Park
Salmon's Brook
Brimsdown Prim. Sch.

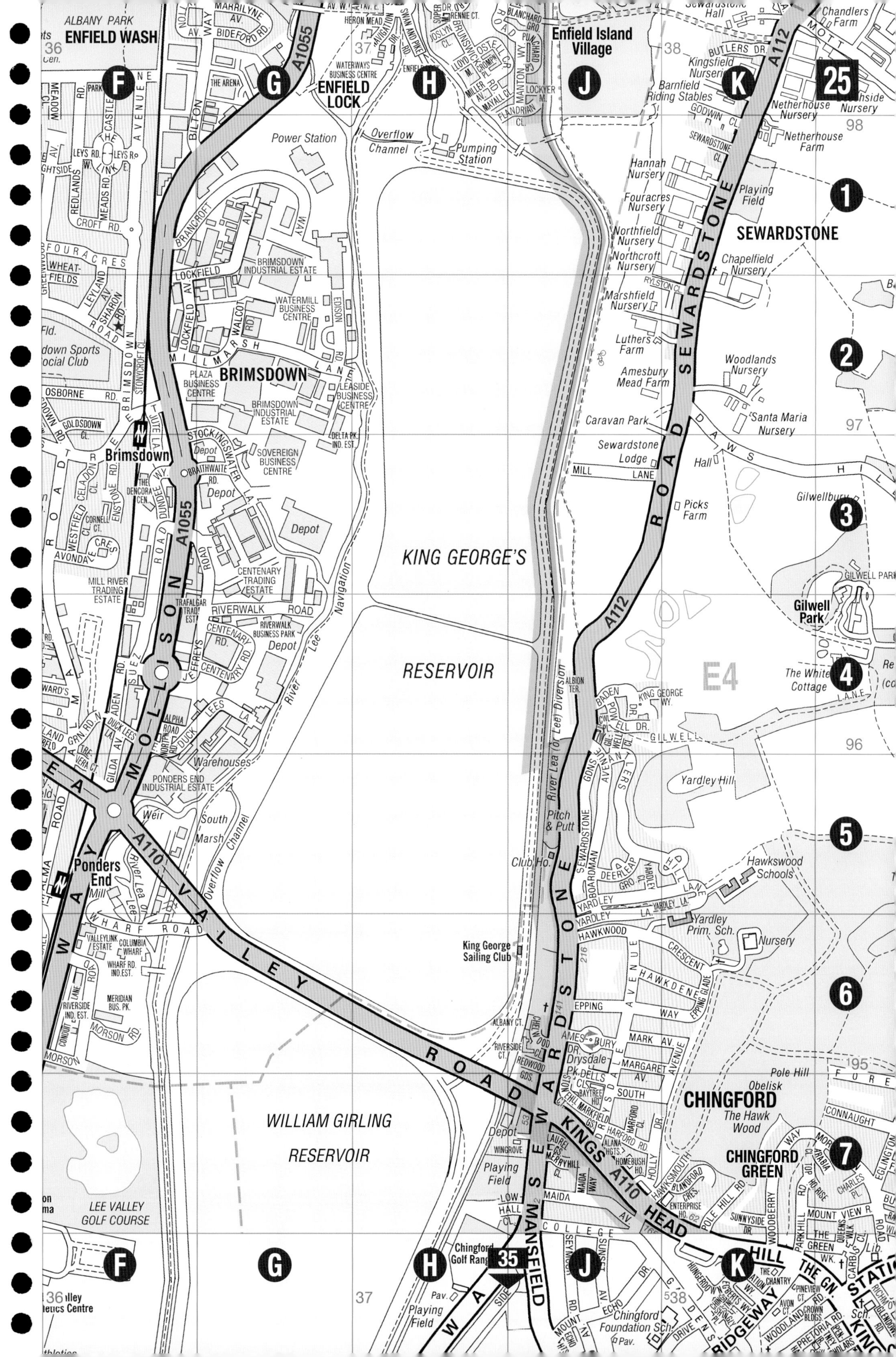
ALBANY PARK
ENFIELD WASH
ENFIELD LOCK
Enfield Island Village
SEWARDSTONE
BRIMSDOWN
Brimsdown
Ponders End
KING GEORGE'S
RESERVOIR
WILLIAM GIRLING
RESERVOIR
LEE VALLEY
GOLF COURSE
CHINGFORD
CHINGFORD GREEN
E4
A1055
A112
A110
MOLLISON AVENUE
LEA VALLEY ROAD
SEWARDSTONE ROAD
KINGS HEAD HILL
MANSFIELD
Power Station
Overflow Channel
Pumping Station
River Lee Navigation
River Lea (or Lee) Diversion
Overflow Channel
BRIMSDOWN INDUSTRIAL ESTATE
WATERMILL BUSINESS CENTRE
PLAZA BUSINESS CENTRE
LEASIDE BUSINESS CENTRE
SOVEREIGN BUSINESS CENTRE
CENTENARY TRADING ESTATE
MILL RIVER TRADING ESTATE
RIVERWALK BUSINESS PARK
PONDERS END INDUSTRIAL ESTATE
VALLEYLINK ESTATE
MERIDIAN BUS. PK.
Depot
Warehouses
Weir
South Marsh
Hannah Nursery
Fouracres Nursery
Northfield Nursery
Northcroft Nursery
Marshfield Nursery
Chapelfield Nursery
Luthers Farm
Amesbury Mead Farm
Woodlands Nursery
Santa Maria Nursery
Caravan Park
Sewardstone Lodge
Picks Farm
Gilwell Park
The White Cottage
Yardley Hill
Hawkswood Schools
Yardley Prim. Sch.
King George Sailing Club
Pitch & Putt
Club Ho.
Pole Hill
Obelisk
The Hawk Wood
Chingford Golf Range
Playing Field
Chingford Foundation Sch.
Kingsfield Nursery
Barnfield Riding Stables
Netherhouse Nursery
Netherhouse Farm
Chandlers Farm
Playing Field
F G H J K
1 2 3 4 5 6 7
36 37 38
98 97 96 195
25
35

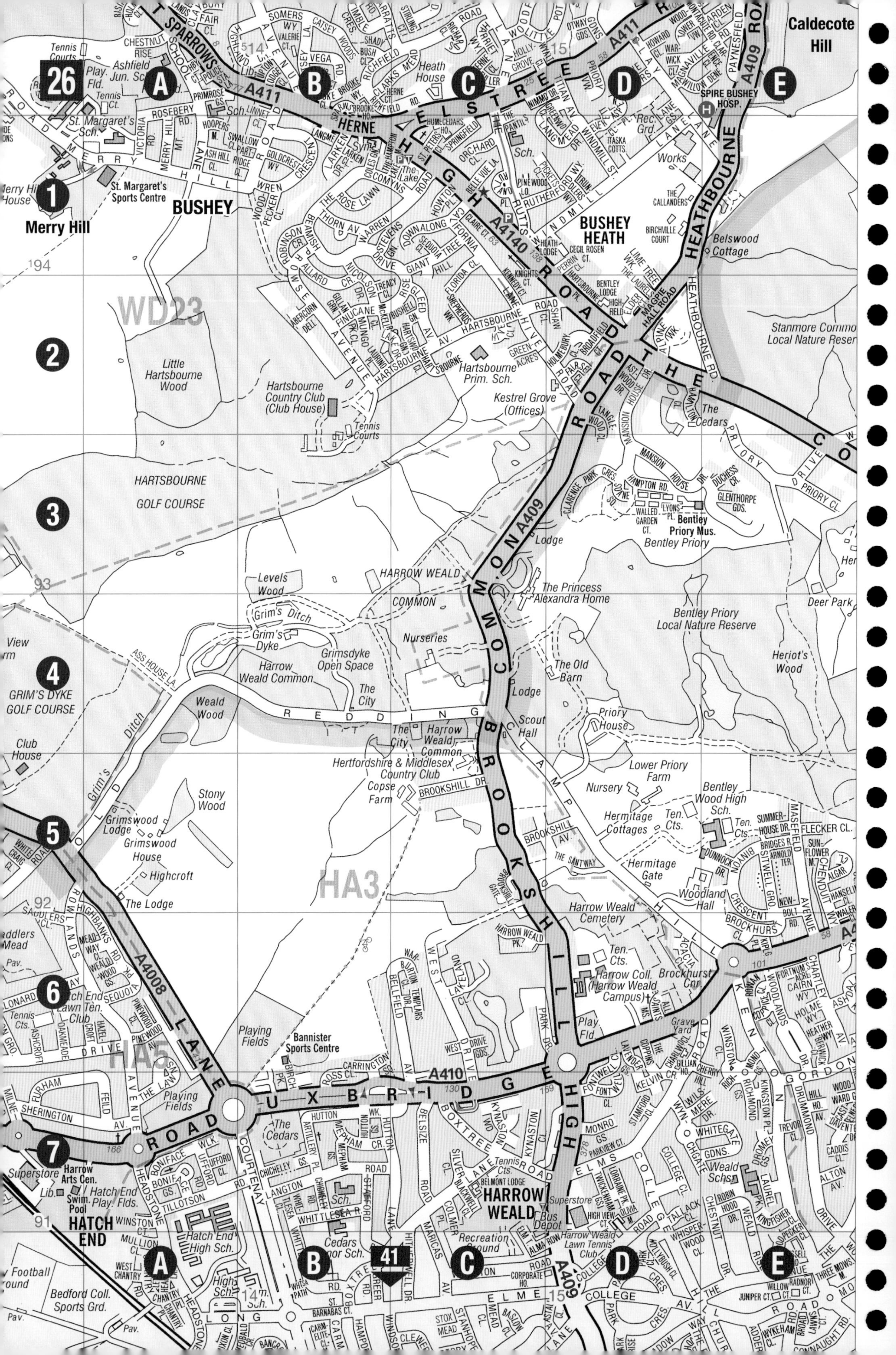

26
41
A
B
C
D
E
1
2
3
4
5
6
7
Caldecote Hill
Merry Hill
BUSHEY
BUSHEY HEATH
WD23
HA3
HA5
HATCH END
HARROW WEALD
ELSTREE
HIGH ROAD
THE COMMON
HEATHBOURNE ROAD
COMMON
BROOKSHILL
UXBRIDGE ROAD
LANE
HIGH
REDDING
CLAMP
HILL
A411
A4140
A409
A4008
A410
Spire Bushey Hosp.
St. Margaret's Sports Centre
St. Margaret's Sch.
Ashfield Jun. Sch.
Little Hartsbourne Wood
Hartsbourne Country Club (Club House)
Hartsbourne Prim. Sch.
Kestrel Grove (Offices)
HARTSBOURNE GOLF COURSE
Stanmore Common Local Nature Reserve
Belswood Cottage
The Cedars
Bentley Priory Mus.
Bentley Priory
Bentley Priory Local Nature Reserve
Deer Park
Heriot's Wood
Levels Wood
HARROW WEALD COMMON
Grim's Ditch
Grim's Dyke
Grimsdyke Open Space
Harrow Weald Common
The City
The Princess Alexandra Home
Nurseries
The Old Barn
Lodge
Scout Hall
Priory House
GRIM'S DYKE GOLF COURSE
Club House
Weald Wood
Hertfordshire & Middlesex Country Club
Copse Farm
Lower Priory Farm
Nursery
Hermitage Cottages
Hermitage Gate
Woodland Hall
Bentley Wood High Sch.
Stony Wood
Grimswood Lodge
Grimswood House
Highcroft
The Lodge
Harrow Weald Cemetery
Harrow Coll. (Harrow Weald Campus)
Brockhurst Cnr.
Playing Fields
Bannister Sports Centre
Harrow Arts Cen.
Hatch End Play. Flds.
Hatch End High Sch.
Cedars Manor Sch.
Recreation Ground
Harrow Weald Lawn Tennis Club
Bedford Coll. Sports Grd.
Weald Schs.
Superstore
Bus Depot

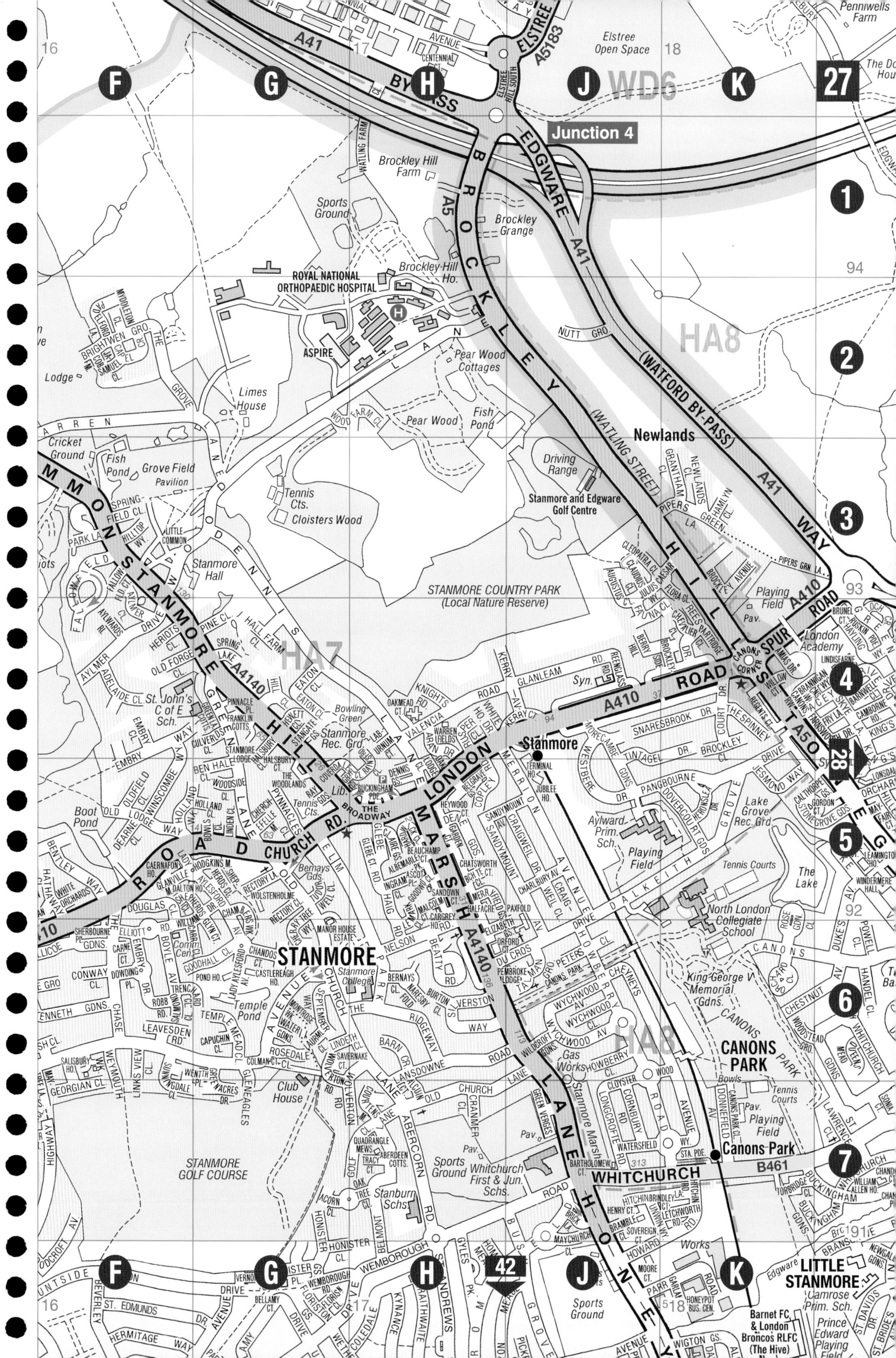

F
G
H
J
K
WD6
27
Junction 4
A41
BY PASS
ELSTREE
A5183
Elstree Open Space
Penniwells Farm
EDGWARE
BROCKLEY
A5
Brockley Hill Farm
Sports Ground
Brockley Grange
ROYAL NATIONAL ORTHOPAEDIC HOSPITAL
Brockley Hill Ho.
ASPIRE
Pear Wood Cottages
Limes House
Pear Wood
Fish Pond
HA8
(WATFORD BY-PASS)
(WATLING STREET)
Newlands
Driving Range
Stanmore and Edgware Golf Centre
Cricket Ground
Grove Field Pavilion
Tennis Cts.
Cloisters Wood
Stanmore Hall
STANMORE COUNTRY PARK
(Local Nature Reserve)
HA7
A4140
A410
ROAD
SPUR
Canons Corner
London Academy
Playing Field
A41 WAY
Stanmore
STANMORE HILL
LONDON RD.
CHURCH RD.
THE BROADWAY
MARSH
Bowling Green
Stanmore Rec. Grd.
St. John's C of E Sch.
Boot Pond
Aylward Prim. Sch.
Lake Grove Rec. Grd.
The Lake
Tennis Courts
North London Collegiate School
28
STANMORE
Stanmore College
Temple Pond
King George V Memorial Gdns.
CANONS PARK
Gas Works
Stanmore Marsh
Club House
STANMORE GOLF COURSE
Sports Ground
Whitchurch First & Jun. Schs.
Stanburn Schs.
WHITCHURCH
B461
Canons Park
HONEYPOT LANE
42
LITTLE STANMORE
Camrose Prim. Sch.
Prince Edward Playing Field
Barnet FC & London Broncos RLFC (The Hive)
Works
Sports Ground
1
2
3
4
5
6
7
94
93
92
91
16
17
18

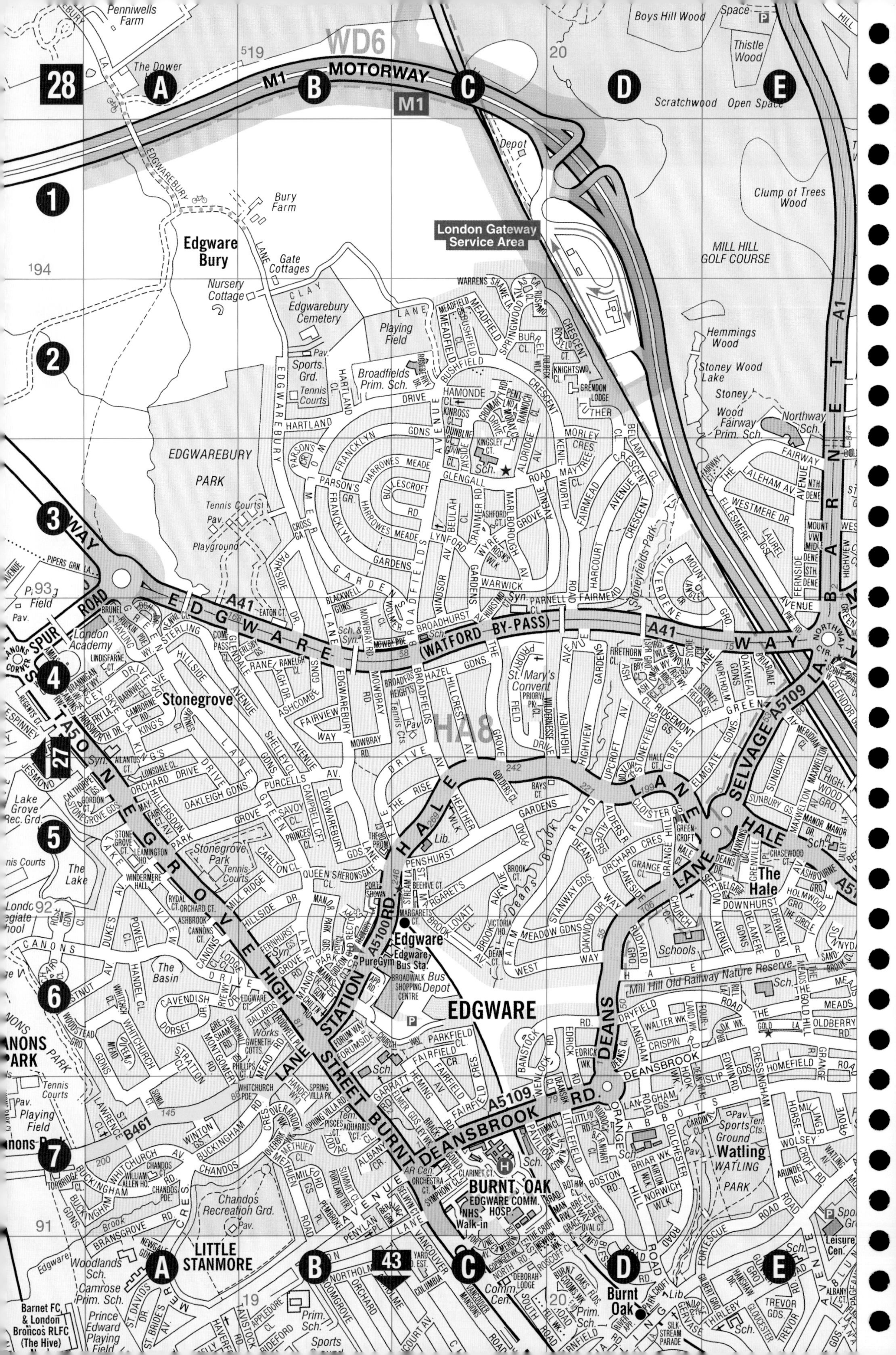

28
27
43
WD6
M1 MOTORWAY
M1
Penniwells Farm
The Dower
Boys Hill Wood
Thistle Wood
Scratchwood Open Space
Depot
Bury Farm
London Gateway Service Area
Clump of Trees Wood
MILL HILL GOLF COURSE
Edgware Bury
Gate Cottages
Nursery Cottage
Edgwarebury Cemetery
Playing Field
Sports Grd.
Tennis Courts
Broadfields Prim. Sch.
Hemmings Wood
Stoney Wood Lake
Stoney Wood
Fairway Prim. Sch.
Northway Sch.
EDGWAREBURY PARK
Tennis Courts
Pav.
Playground
EDGWARE WAY
A41
(WATFORD BY-PASS)
London Academy
Stonegrove
St. Mary's Convent
HA8
Stoneyfields Park
Stonegrove Park
Lake Grove Rec. Grd.
The Lake
The Basin
EDGWARE
Edgware
Edgware Bus Sta.
Bus Depot
BROADWALK SHOPPING CENTRE
PureGym
Lib.
Schools
The Hale
Mill Hill Old Railway Nature Reserve
Chandos Recreation Grd.
BURNT OAK
EDGWARE COMM. HOSP.
NHS Walk-in
Watling
WATLING PARK
Sports Ground
Leisure Cen.
LITTLE STANMORE
Woodlands Sch.
Camrose Prim. Sch.
Prince Edward Playing Field
Barnet FC & London Broncos RLFC (The Hive)
Burnt Oak
Comm. Cen.
Prim. Sch.
STONEGROVE
HIGH STREET
BURNT OAK
DEANSBROOK RD.
A5109
A5100
A510
B461
SELVAGE LA.
HALE LANE
DEANS LANE
BARNET WAY
A1
CANONS PARK

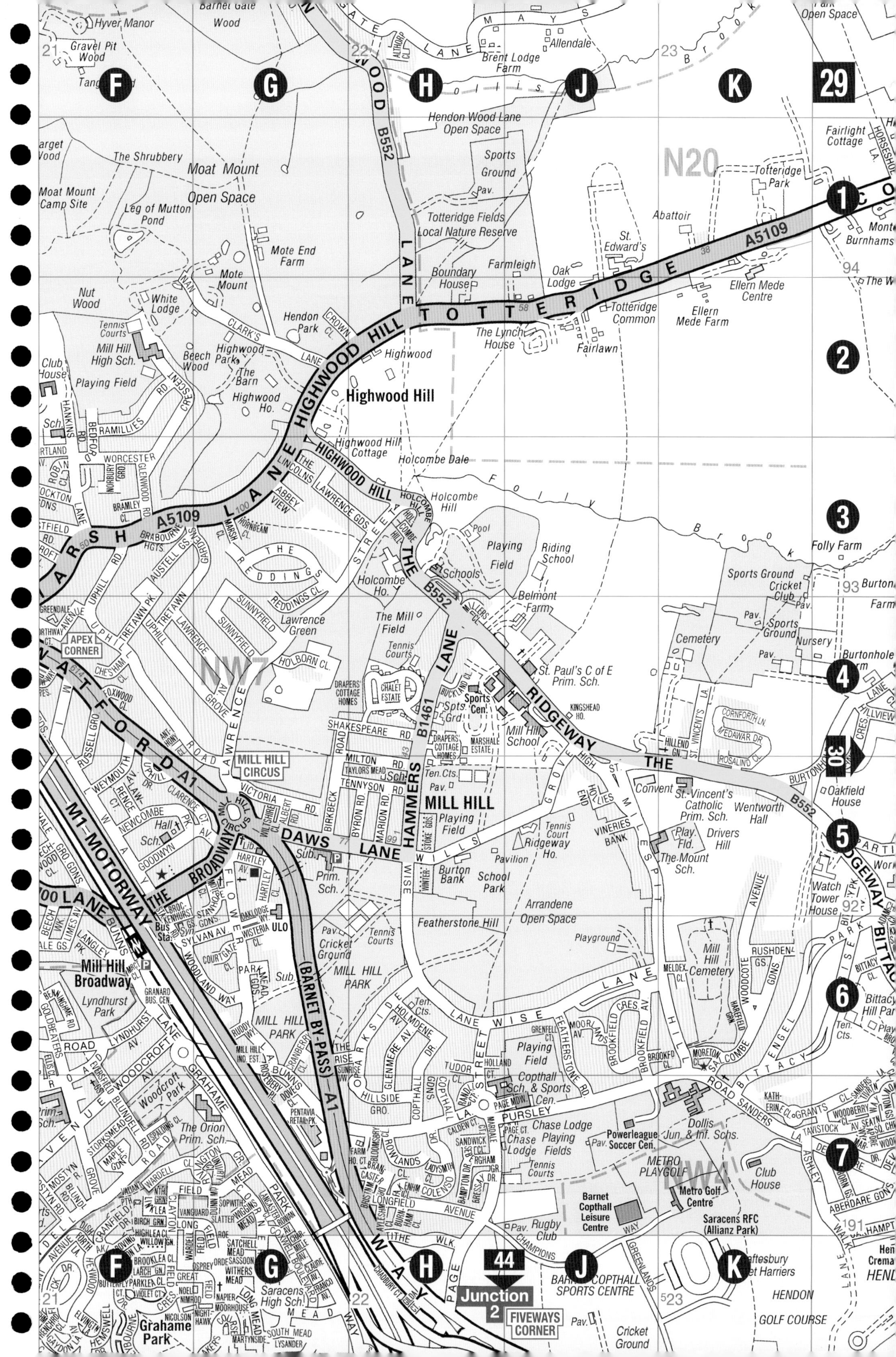29
30
44
Junction 2
FIVEWAYS CORNER
F
G
H
J
K
1
2
3
4
5
6
7
21
22
23
N20
NW7
Hyver Manor
Gravel Pit Wood
Barnet Gate Wood
Brent Lode Farm
Allendale
Hendon Wood Lane Open Space
Sports Ground
Pav.
Fairlight Cottage
Totteridge Park
Abattoir
The Shrubbery
Moat Mount Open Space
Moat Mount Camp Site
Leg of Mutton Pond
Totteridge Fields Local Nature Reserve
Mote End Farm
Mote Mount
St. Edward's
Oak Lodge
Boundary House
Farmleigh
Ellern Mede Centre
Ellern Mede Farm
Totteridge Common
The Lynch House
Fairlawn
Nut Wood
White Lodge
Tennis Courts
Mill Hill High Sch.
Club House
Playing Field
Hendon Park
Highwood Park
Beech Wood
The Barn
Highwood Ho.
Highwood
Highwood Hill
Highwood Hill Cottage
Holcombe Dale
Holcombe Hill
Pool
Playing Field
Riding School
Schools
Holcombe Ho.
Belmont Farm
Folly Farm
Sports Ground
Cricket Club
Sports Ground
Nursery
Cemetery
Burtonhole Farm
APEX CORNER
Lawrence Green
The Mill Field
Tennis Courts
St. Paul's C of E Prim. Sch.
Sports Cen.
Mill Hill School
MILL HILL CIRCUS
MILL HILL
Playing Field
Convent
St. Vincent's Catholic Prim. Sch.
Wentworth Hall
Oakfield House
Ridgeway Ho.
Tennis Court
Pavilion
Burton Bank
School Park
Arrandene Open Space
Drivers Hill
The Mount Sch.
Watch Tower House
Featherstone Hill
Playground
Mill Hill Cemetery
Cricket Ground
MILL HILL PARK
Mill Hill Broadway
Lyndhurst Park
Woodcroft Park
The Orion Prim. Sch.
Playing Field
Copthall Sch. & Sports Cen.
Chase Lodge Playing Fields
Powerleague Soccer Cen.
Dollis Jun. & Inf. Schs.
METRO PLAYGOLF
Club House
Metro Golf Centre
Barnet Copthall Leisure Centre
Saracens RFC (Allianz Park)
Rugby Club
BARNET COPTHALL SPORTS CENTRE
HENDON GOLF COURSE
Cricket Ground
Saracens High Sch.
Grahame Park
Bus Sta.
ULO
A5109
B552
B1461
A1
M1 MOTORWAY
TOTTERIDGE
HIGHWOOD HILL
HIGHWOOD LANE
MARSH LANE
THE RIDGEWAY
WATFORD WAY
THE BROADWAY
DAWS LANE
HAMMERS LANE
WISE LANE
(BARNET BY-PASS)
Folly Brook
Dollis Brook

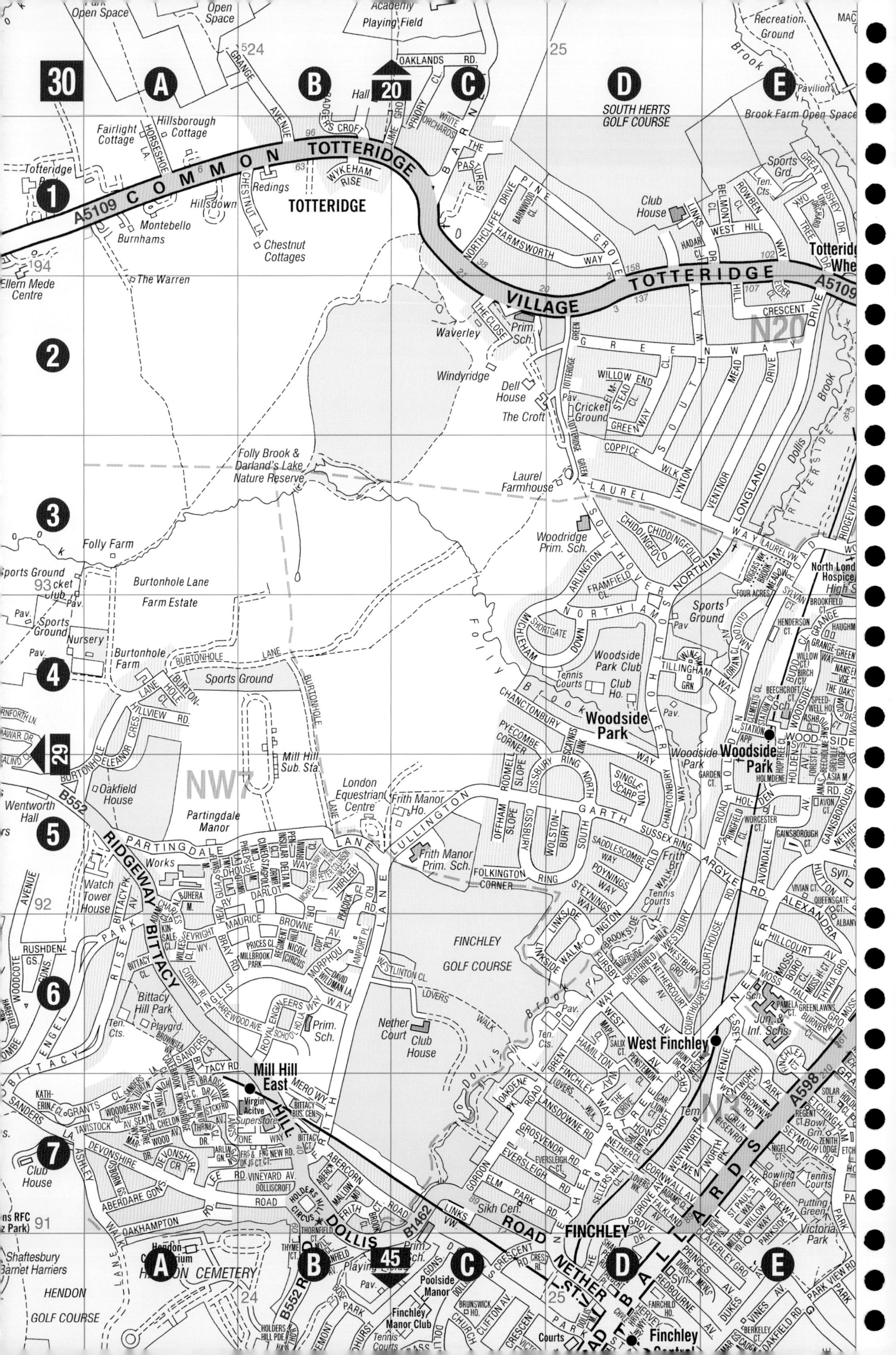
TOTTERIDGE
SOUTH HERTS GOLF COURSE
Woodside Park
NW7
N20
FINCHLEY GOLF COURSE
Mill Hill East
West Finchley
FINCHLEY
HENDON CEMETERY
HENDON GOLF COURSE

26
27
28
F
G
H
J
K
21
31
32
46
1
2
3
4
5
6
7
Oakleigh Park
Miniature Golf Course
Monkfrith Prim. Sch.
Pavilion
Bowling Green
Oak Hill Campus Play. Fld.
Tennis Courts Pav.
South Barnet
EN4
N14
N12
N11
N2
Warehouses
Pavilion Study Centre Play. Fld.
Pupil Referral Unit
OAKLEIGH PARK
OAKLEIGH
LANE
OSIDGE
B1453
Weirs Club
Brunswick Park Prim. Sch.
Lib.
Syn.
A109
Prim. Sch.
Tennis Club
Sch.
RUSSELL
ROAD
Barnet Tunnel
Sports Ground Pav.
North London Bus. Pk
St Andrew the Apostle Greek Orthodox School
NEW SOUTHGATE CEMETERY
War Mem.
New Southgate Crematorium
BRUNSWICK PARK
WHETSTONE
Swan Lane Open Space
HIGH ROAD
FRIERN
B550
BARNET
NORTH
NORTH MIDDLESEX GOLF COURSE
Club House
Bookbinders Cottage Homes
Bethune Park
Recreation Ground
Cricket Ground
Curtis Family Centre
Friary Park
Library
Superstore
A1000
FRIERN BARNET
NORTH FINCHLEY
Wren Academy
Woodhouse College
Spts. Grd. Pav.
Tally Ho Corner
Arts Depot
Bus Sta.
WOODHOUSE
RD.
A1003
COLNEY HATCH
Colney Hatch Works
Coppetts Wood & Glebelands Local Nature Reserve
Nuffield Health Fitness
FRIERN BRIDGE RETAIL PARK
NEW SOUTHGATE
Compton Leisure Cen.
Artificial Pitch
Recycling Centre
Superstore
Coppetts Centre
Powerleague Soccer Cen.
PINKHAM
ROAD
A406
NORTH CIRCULAR
David Lloyd Leisure
Wingate & Finchley FC
Rugby Football Ground
Cricket & Football Grounds
Finchley Lido Leisure Cen.
Great North Leisure Park
Glebe Land Open Space
FINCHLEY MEM. HOSP.
NHS Walk-in
Fallow Corner
Bowl. Alley
Cinema
Brook
Sports Ground
Playing Field
Islington Crematorium
Recreation Ground
Liby.

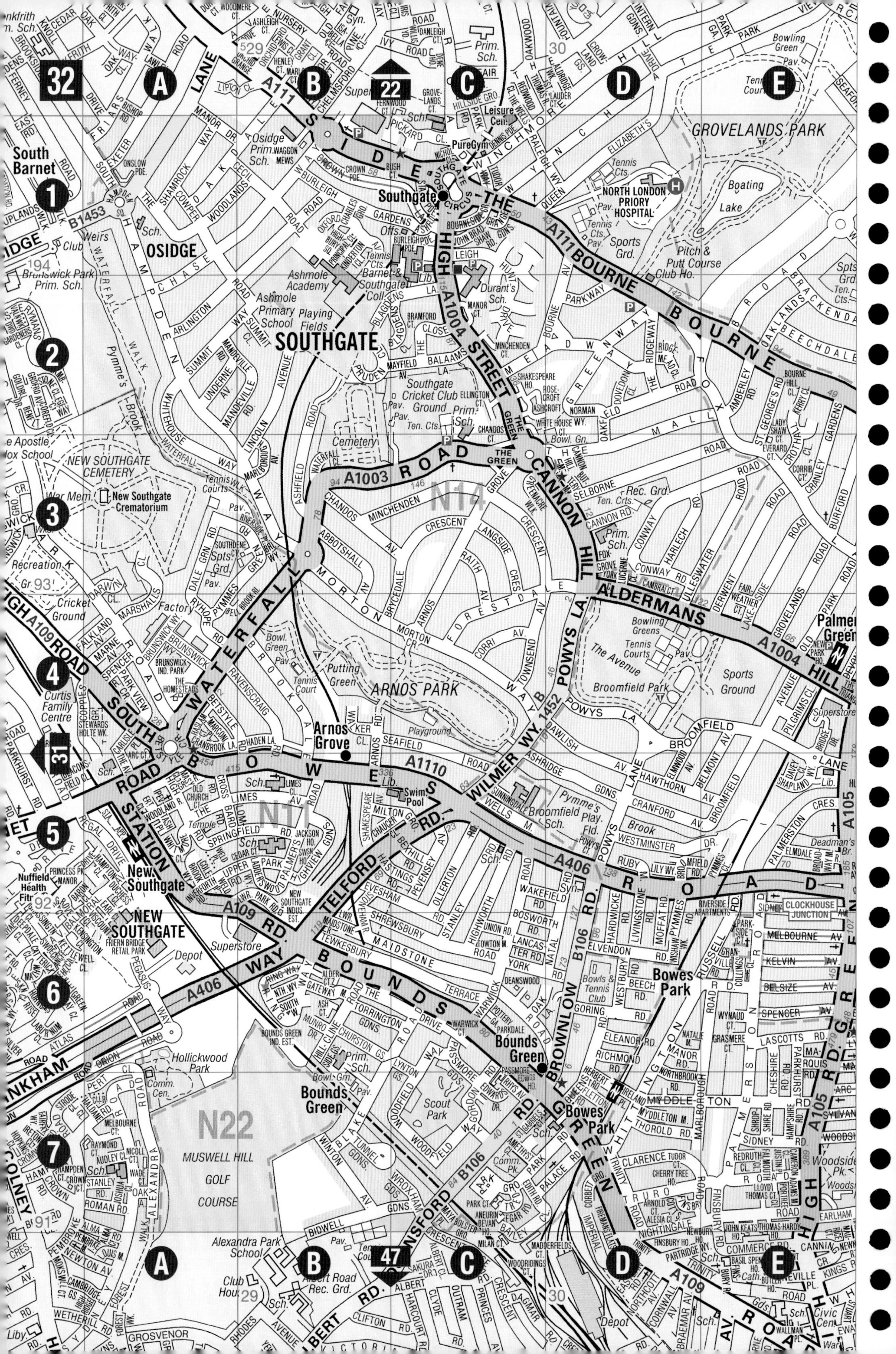

32
22
31
47
A
B
C
D
E
1
2
3
4
5
6
7
South Barnet
OSIDGE
SOUTHGATE
Southgate
GROVELANDS PARK
NORTH LONDON PRIORY HOSPITAL
Boating Lake
Pitch & Putt Course
Sports Grd.
NEW SOUTHGATE CEMETERY
New Southgate Crematorium
Ashmole Academy
Ashmole Primary School
Barnet & Southgate Coll.
Southgate Cricket Club Ground
Cemetery
ARNOS PARK
Arnos Grove
N14
N11
N22
Broomfield Park
Sports Ground
Palmers Green
New Southgate
NEW SOUTHGATE
Bounds Green
Bowes Park
MUSWELL HILL GOLF COURSE
Hollickwood Park
Alexandra Park School
Scout Park
Friern Bridge Retail Park
Superstore
Depot
Curtis Family Centre
Cricket Ground
Recreation Grd.
A111
A1004
A1003
A1110
A406
A109
A105
B1453
B1452
B106
HIGH STREET
BOURNE HILL
THE BOURNE
CANNON HILL
ALDERMANS HILL
WATERFALL ROAD
BOWES ROAD
BOUNDS GREEN ROAD
TELFORD RD.
NORTH CIRCULAR ROAD
GREEN LANES
HIGH ROAD
BROWNLOW RD.
POWYS LA.
BROOMFIELD LANE
WILMER WY.
STATION ROAD
FRIERN BARNET ROAD
HAMPDEN WAY
CHASE SIDE
CLOCKHOUSE JUNCTION

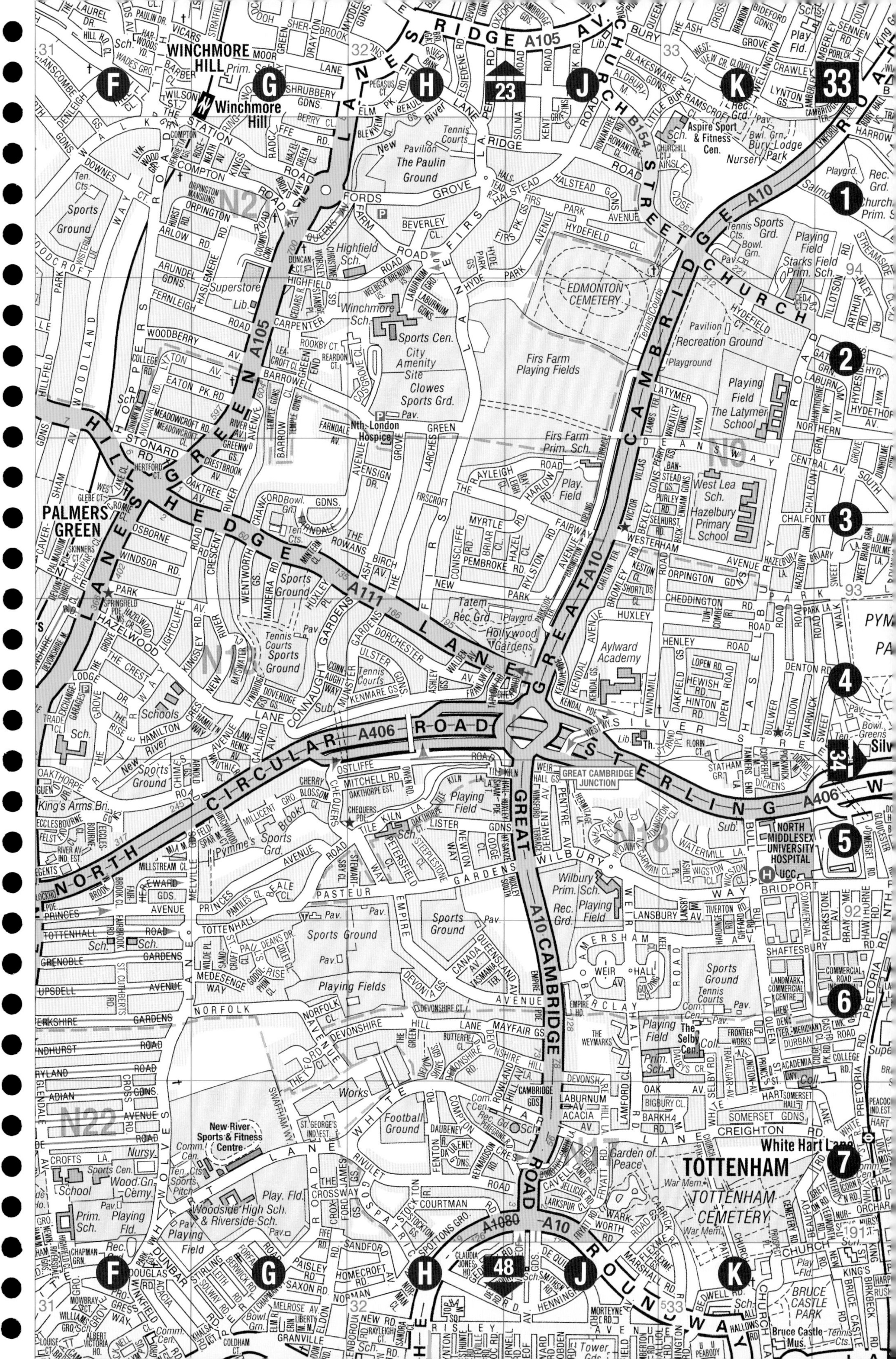

33
23
48
34
F
G
H
J
K
1
2
3
4
5
6
7
31
32
33
94
93
92
91
WINCHMORE HILL
Winchmore Hill
PALMERS GREEN
TOTTENHAM
N21
N13
N9
N18
N17
N22
RIDGE A105 AV.
GREEN LANES
A105
HEDGE LANE
A111
NORTH CIRCULAR ROAD A406
STERLING WAY A406
GREAT CAMBRIDGE ROAD
A10 CAMBRIDGE ROAD
GREAT CAMBRIDGE JUNCTION
CAMBRIDGE RD. A10
CHURCH STREET B154
CHURCH ROAD
SILVER STREET
WHITE HART LANE
LORDSHIP LANE
A1080
A10
The Paulin Ground
Pavilion
New River
Highfield Sch.
Winchmore Sch.
Sports Cen.
City Amenity Site
Clowes Sports Grd.
Nth. London Hospice
Firs Farm Playing Fields
Firs Farm Prim. Sch.
EDMONTON CEMETERY
Recreation Ground
Playing Field
The Latymer School
West Lea Sch.
Hazelbury Primary School
Aylward Academy
Tatem Rec. Grd.
Hollywood Gardens
Aspire Sport & Fitness Cen.
Bury Lodge Park
Starks Field Prim. Sch.
Sports Ground
Pymme's Sports Grd.
Playing Fields
Wilbury Prim. Sch.
NORTH MIDDLESEX UNIVERSITY HOSPITAL
UCC
The Selby Cen.
Football Ground
New River Sports & Fitness Centre
Woodside High Sch. & Riverside Sch.
Garden of Peace
TOTTENHAM CEMETERY
White Hart Lane
BRUCE CASTLE PARK
Bruce Castle Mus.
Superstore
Schools
King's Arms Bri.
Works
Wood Gn. Cemy.

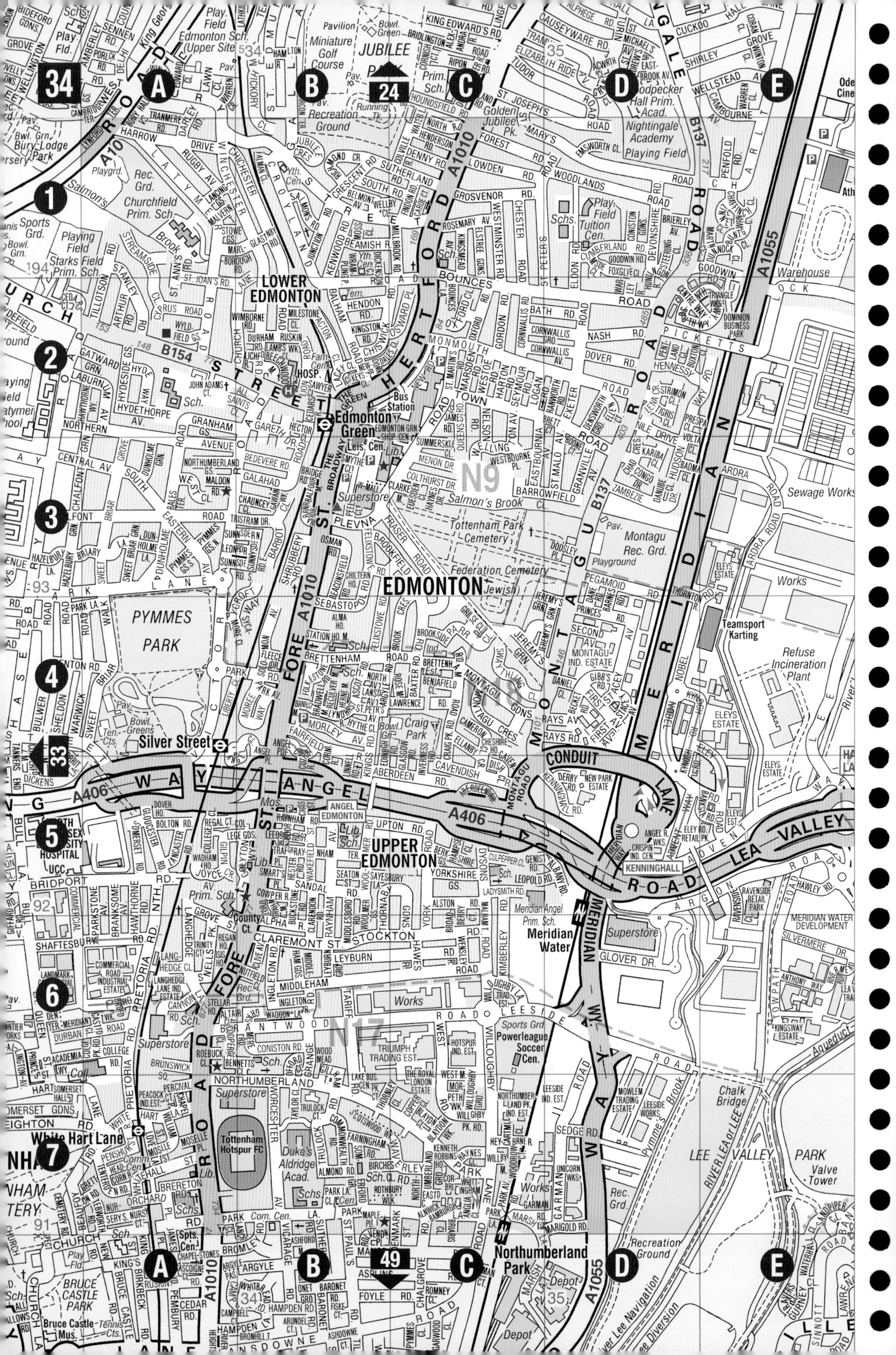

34
24
49
33
A
B
C
D
E
1
2
3
4
5
6
7
LOWER EDMONTON
EDMONTON
UPPER EDMONTON
N9
N17
JUBILEE PARK
Miniature Golf Course
Recreation Ground
Edmonton Sch. (Upper Site)
Churchfield Prim. Sch.
Starks Field Prim. Sch.
Sports Grd.
Playing Field
Salmon's Brook
Golden Jubilee Pk.
Nightingale Academy
Woodpecker Hall Prim. Acad.
Play Field
Tuition Cen.
Edmonton Green
Bus Station
Leis. Cen.
Superstore
Tottenham Park Cemetery
Federation Cemetery (Jewish)
Montagu Rec. Grd.
Playground
Sewage Works
Works
Teamsport Karting
Refuse Incineration Plant
ELEYS ESTATE
PYMMES PARK
Silver Street
Craig Park
ANGEL EDMONTON
KENNINGHALL
Meridian Water
Meridian Angel Prim. Sch.
MERIDIAN WATER DEVELOPMENT
RAVENSIDE RETAIL PARK
Sports Grd.
Powerleague Soccer Cen.
TRIUMPH TRADING EST.
Tottenham Hotspur FC
Duke's Aldridge Acad.
White Hart Lane
Northumberland Park
LEE VALLEY PARK
Valve Tower
Chalk Bridge
Recreation Ground
NORTH MIDDLESEX UNIVERSITY HOSPITAL
BRUCE CASTLE PARK
Bruce Castle Mus.
A10
A1010
A406
A1055
B137
B154
FORE STREET
HERTFORD ROAD
MONTAGU ROAD
MERIDIAN WAY
NORTH CIRCULAR ROAD
ANGEL ROAD
LEA VALLEY ROAD
CONDUIT LANE
LEESIDE ROAD
NORTHUMBERLAND PARK
TOTTENHAM HIGH ROAD

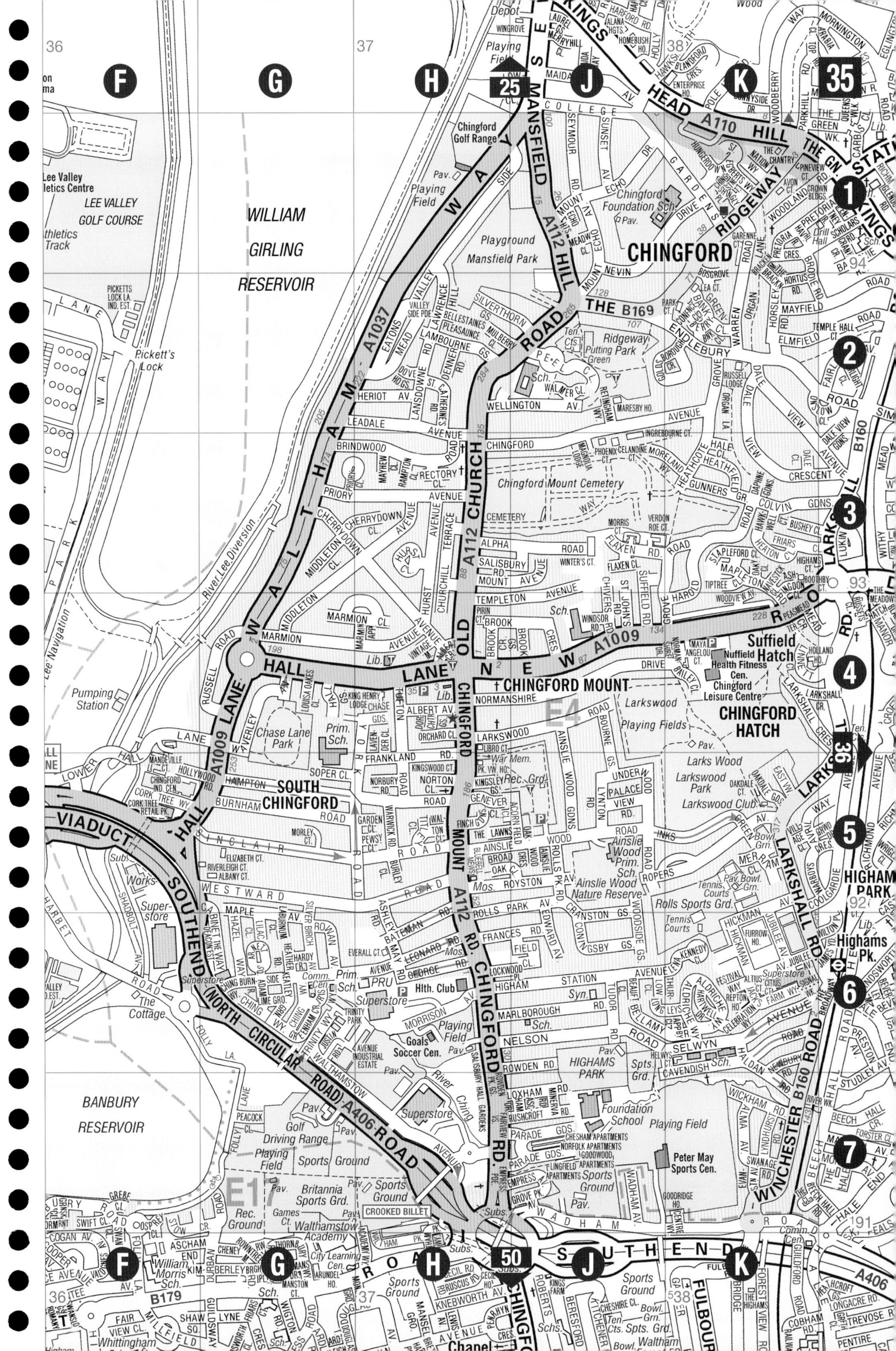

36
37
38
F
G
H
J
K
25
35
36
50
1
2
3
4
5
6
7
CHINGFORD
SOUTH CHINGFORD
CHINGFORD MOUNT
CHINGFORD HATCH
HIGHAM PARK
WILLIAM GIRLING RESERVOIR
BANBURY RESERVOIR
LEE VALLEY GOLF COURSE
Lee Valley Athletics Centre
Athletics Track
Pickett's Lock
PICKETTS LOCK LA. IND. EST.
River Lee Diversion
Lee Navigation
Pumping Station
Chingford Golf Range
Playing Field
Playground
Mansfield Park
Chingford Foundation Sch.
Ridgeway Putting Park Green
Chingford Mount Cemetery
Chase Lane Park
Prim. Sch.
Larkswood Playing Fields
Larks Wood
Larkswood Park
Larkswood Club
Suffield Hatch
Nuffield Health Fitness Cen.
Chingford Leisure Centre
Ainslie Wood Prim. Sch.
Ainslie Wood Nature Reserve
Rolls Sports Grd.
Tennis Courts
Highams Park
Highams Pk.
Foundation School
Playing Field
Peter May Sports Cen.
Sports Ground
Superstore
Hlth. Club
Goals Soccer Cen.
Walthamstow Avenue Industrial Estate
Golf Driving Range
Sports Ground
Britannia Sports Grd.
Rec. Ground
Walthamstow Academy
City Learning Cen.
William Morris Sch.
CROOKED BILLET
The Cottage
E4
E17
WALTHAM WAY A1037
MANSFIELD HILL A112
THE RIDGEWAY B169
OLD CHURCH ROAD A112
NEW ROAD A1009
HALL LANE A1009
CHINGFORD MOUNT RD. A112
KINGS HEAD HILL A110
LARKSHALL RD.
WINCHESTER ROAD B160
SOUTHEND ROAD (NORTH CIRCULAR ROAD) A406
VIADUCT
SOUTHEND ROAD A406
WADHAM ROAD
CHINGFORD AVENUE
HIGHAM STATION AVENUE
NELSON RD.
MARLBOROUGH RD.
LARKSWOOD RD.
PRIORY AVENUE
CHINGFORD AVENUE
WELLINGTON AV.
LEADALE AVENUE
HERIOT AV.
MARMION AVENUE
MIDDLETON AVENUE
CHERRYDOWN AVENUE
SALISBURY RD.
TEMPLETON AVENUE
ALPHA ROAD
HAROLD ROAD
NORMANSHIRE DRIVE
FRANKLAND RD.
BURNHAM ROAD
SINCLAIR ROAD
WESTWARD ROAD
ROLLS PARK AV.
ROYSTON AV.
FRANCES RD.
LOWER HALL LANE
COLLEGE GDNS.
ENDLEBURY RD.

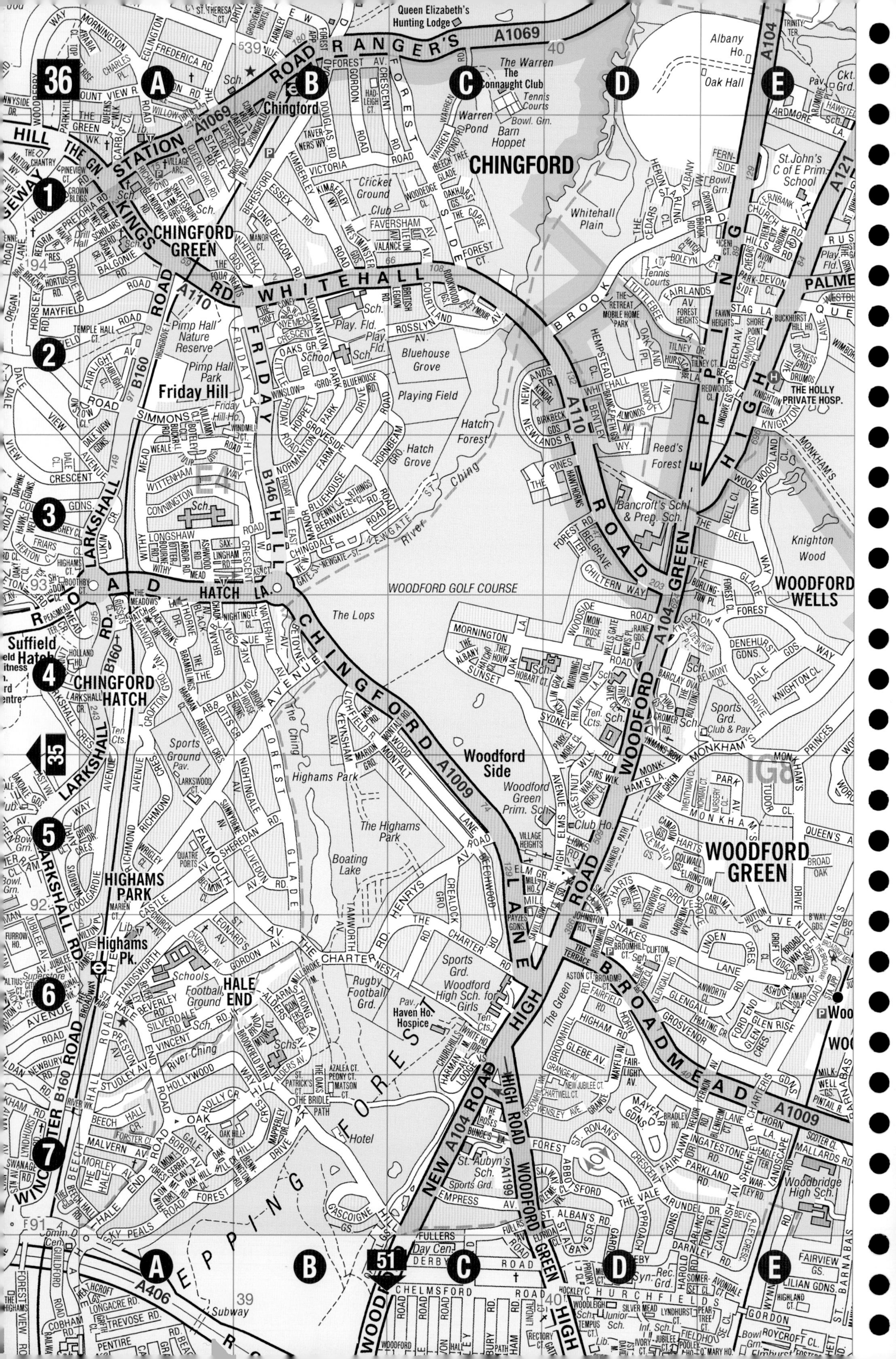

36
35
51
A
B
C
D
E
1
2
3
4
5
6
7
39
40
Queen Elizabeth's Hunting Lodge
RANGER'S ROAD
A1069
The Warren
The Connaught Club
Tennis Courts
Warren Pond
Bowl. Grn.
Barn Hoppet
CHINGFORD
Albany Ho.
Oak Hall
A104
Chingford
STATION ROAD
THE GN.
HILL
KINGS
CHINGFORD GREEN
Whitehall Plain
St. John's C of E Prim. School
Cricket Ground
Club
WHITEHALL RD.
A110
Pimp Hall Nature Reserve
Pimp Hall Park
Friday Hill
FRIDAY HILL
B146
B160
LARKSHALL
Bluehouse Grove
Playing Field
Hatch Forest
Hatch Grove
River Ching
THE HOLLY PRIVATE HOSP.
Reed's Forest
Bancroft's Schl & Prep. Sch.
Knighton Wood
WOODFORD WELLS
HATCH LA.
WOODFORD GOLF COURSE
The Lops
CHINGFORD ROAD
A1009
Suffield Hatch
CHINGFORD HATCH
E4
Sports Ground
Pav.
Highams Park
The Highams Park
Boating Lake
Woodford Side
Woodford Green Prim. Sch.
Club Ho.
IG8
WOODFORD GREEN
HIGHAMS PARK
Highams Pk.
HALE END
Schools
Football Ground
Rugby Football Grd.
Sports Grd.
Woodford High Sch. for Girls
Haven Ho. Hospice
HIGH ROAD
BROADMEAD ROAD
NEW A104 ROAD
A1199
St. Aubyn's Sch.
Sports Grd.
Hotel
EPPING FOREST
A406
Subway
Woodbridge High Sch.
WOODFORD GREEN
CHURCHFIELDS
CHELMSFORD ROAD
DERBY ROAD
Day Cen.
Syn.
Rec. Grd.
Junior Sch.
Inf. Sch.
Bowl Grn.

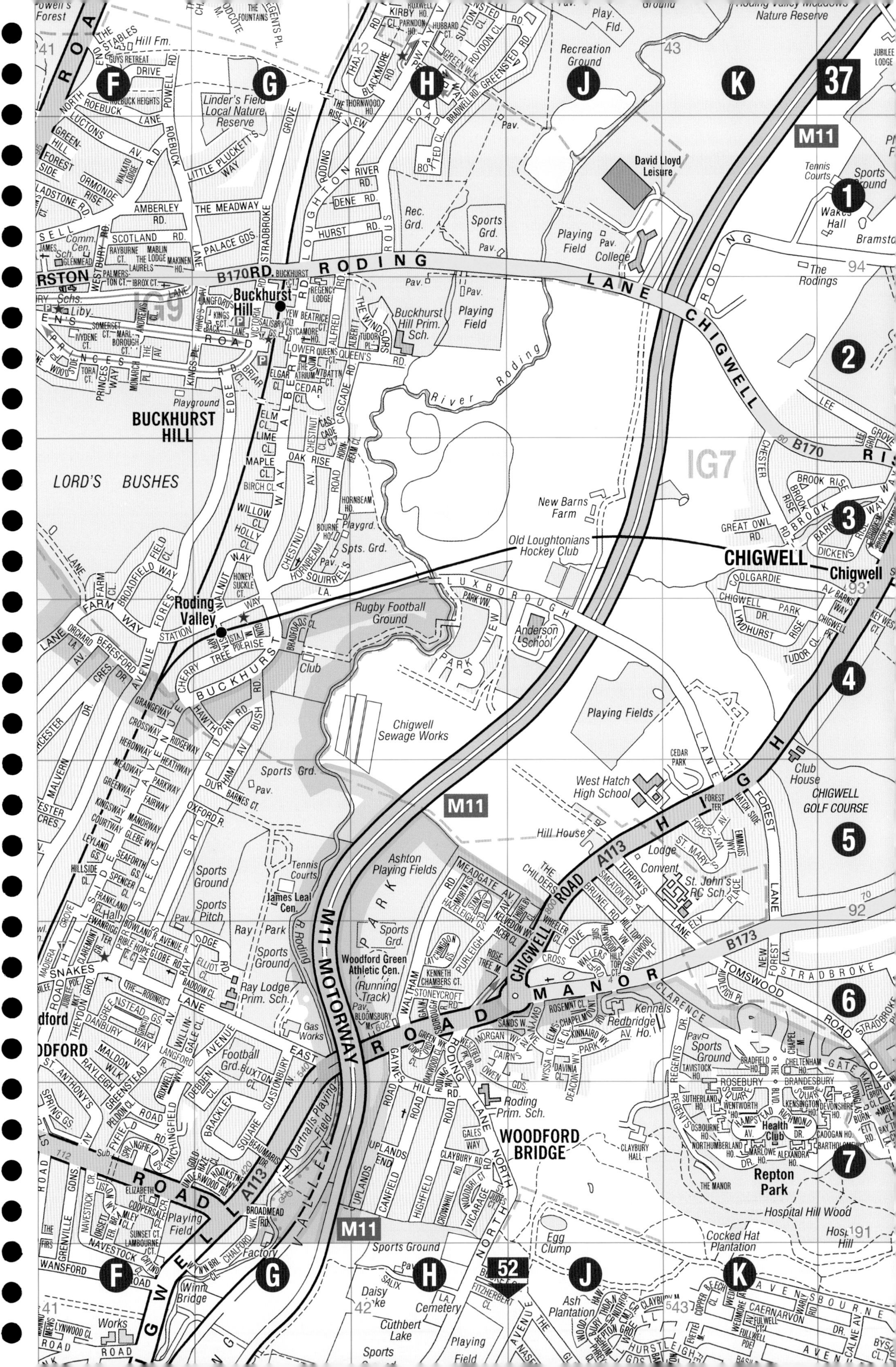
37
52
M11
M11 MOTORWAY
BUCKHURST HILL
Buckhurst Hill
Roding Valley
CHIGWELL
Chigwell
WOODFORD BRIDGE
LORD'S BUSHES
IG9
IG7
F
G
H
J
K
1
2
3
4
5
6
7
Linder's Field Local Nature Reserve
Hill Fm.
Recreation Ground
Play. Fld.
Nature Reserve
David Lloyd Leisure
Playing Field
College
Sports Grd.
Rec. Grd.
Tennis Courts
Sports Ground
Wakes Hall
The Rodings
Buckhurst Hill Prim. Sch.
River Roding
New Barns Farm
Old Loughtonians Hockey Club
Rugby Football Ground
Anderson School
Club
Chigwell Sewage Works
Playing Fields
West Hatch High School
Hill House
Club House
CHIGWELL GOLF COURSE
Ashton Playing Fields
James Leal Cen.
Ray Park
Woodford Green Athletic Cen. (Running Track)
Ray Lodge Prim. Sch.
Gas Works
Football Grd.
Dartnalls Playing Field
Convent
St. John's RC Sch.
Kennels
Redbridge Ho.
Roding Prim. Sch.
Health Club
Claybury Hall
The Manor
Repton Park
Hospital Hill Wood
Cocked Hat Plantation
Egg Clump
Ash Plantation
Sports Ground
Daisy Lake
Cemetery
Cuthbert Lake
Playing Field
Factory
Works
Playground
RODING RD.
RODING LANE
CHIGWELL LANE
B170
B173
A113
HIGH RD.
MANOR ROAD
CHIGWELL ROAD
BUCKHURST WAY
LUXBOROUGH LANE
QUEEN'S ROAD
PRINCES WAY
FOREST EDGE
FOREST AVENUE
TOMSWOOD ROAD
STRADBROKE GROVE
WOODFORD AVENUE
RODING LANE NORTH
SNAKES LANE
PROSPECT ROAD
ALBERT ROAD
CASCADE RD.

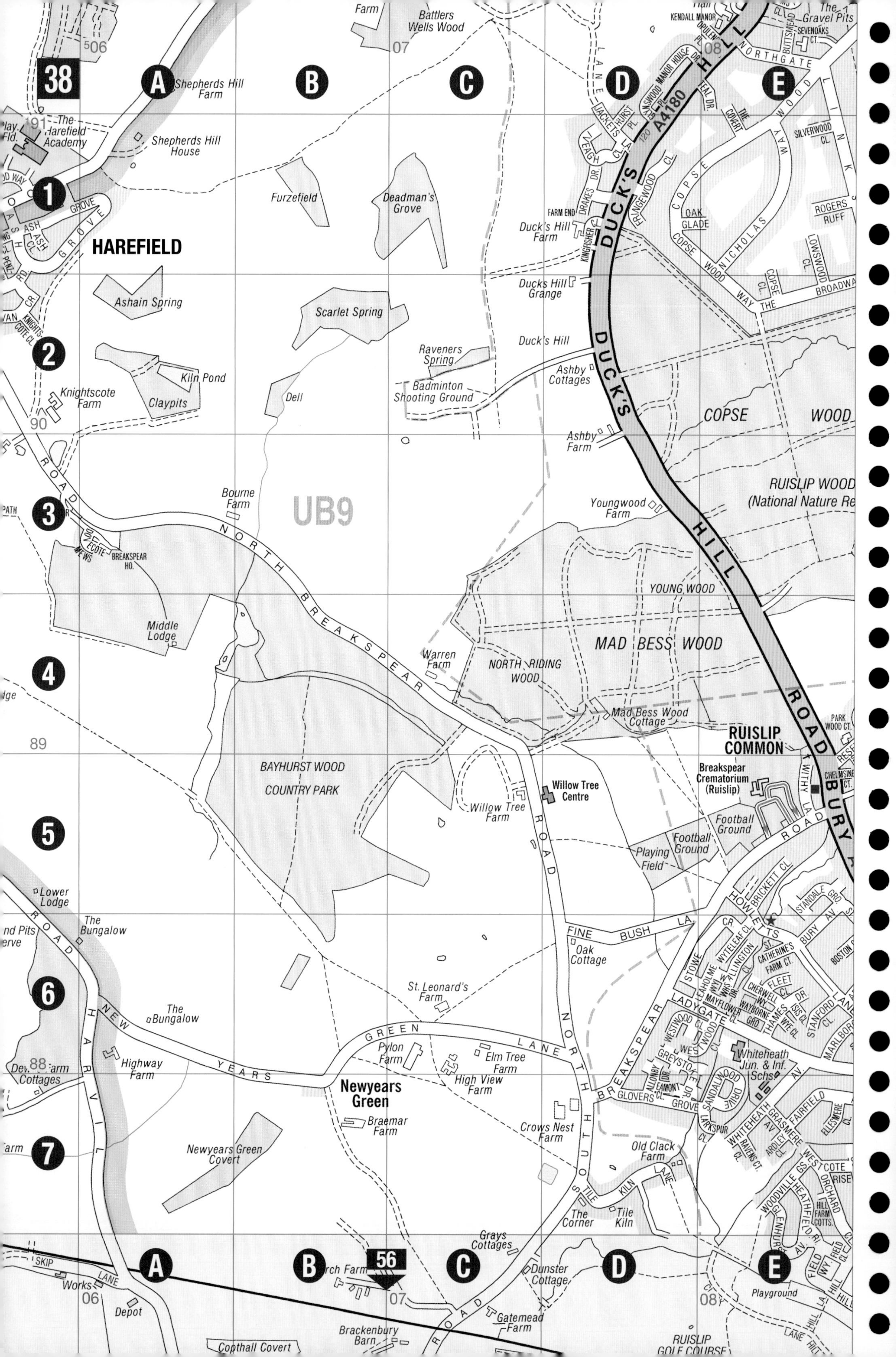

38
56
A
B
C
D
E
1
2
3
4
5
6
7
HAREFIELD
UB9
Shepherds Hill Farm
Shepherds Hill House
The Harefield Academy
Battlers Wells Wood
Furzefield
Deadman's Grove
Ashain Spring
Scarlet Spring
Kiln Pond
Claypits
Knightscote Farm
Dell
Raveners Spring
Badminton Shooting Ground
Duck's Hill Farm
Ducks Hill Grange
Duck's Hill
Ashby Cottages
Ashby Farm
Youngwood Farm
COPSE WOOD
RUISLIP WOOD (National Nature Re
YOUNG WOOD
MAD BESS WOOD
NORTH RIDING WOOD
Mad Bess Wood Cottage
Bourne Farm
NORTH BREAKSPEAR ROAD
Middle Lodge
Warren Farm
BAYHURST WOOD COUNTRY PARK
Willow Tree Centre
Willow Tree Farm
RUISLIP COMMON
Breakspear Crematorium (Ruislip)
Football Ground
Playing Field
FINE BUSH LA.
Oak Cottage
St. Leonard's Farm
Lower Lodge
The Bungalow
HARVIL ROAD
NEW YEARS GREEN LANE
Highway Farm
Pylon Farm
Elm Tree Farm
High View Farm
Newyears Green
Braemar Farm
Crows Nest Farm
Newyears Green Covert
Old Clack Farm
TILE KILN LANE
The Corner
Tile Kiln
Whiteheath Jun. & Inf. Schs.
DUCK'S HILL ROAD
A4180
BURY AV.
LADYGATE LA.
SOUTH ROAD
BREAKSPEAR ROAD
Grays Cottages
Dunster Cottage
Gatemead Farm
Brackenbury Barn
Copthall Covert
Works
Depot
SKIP LANE
Playground
RUISLIP GOLF COURSE

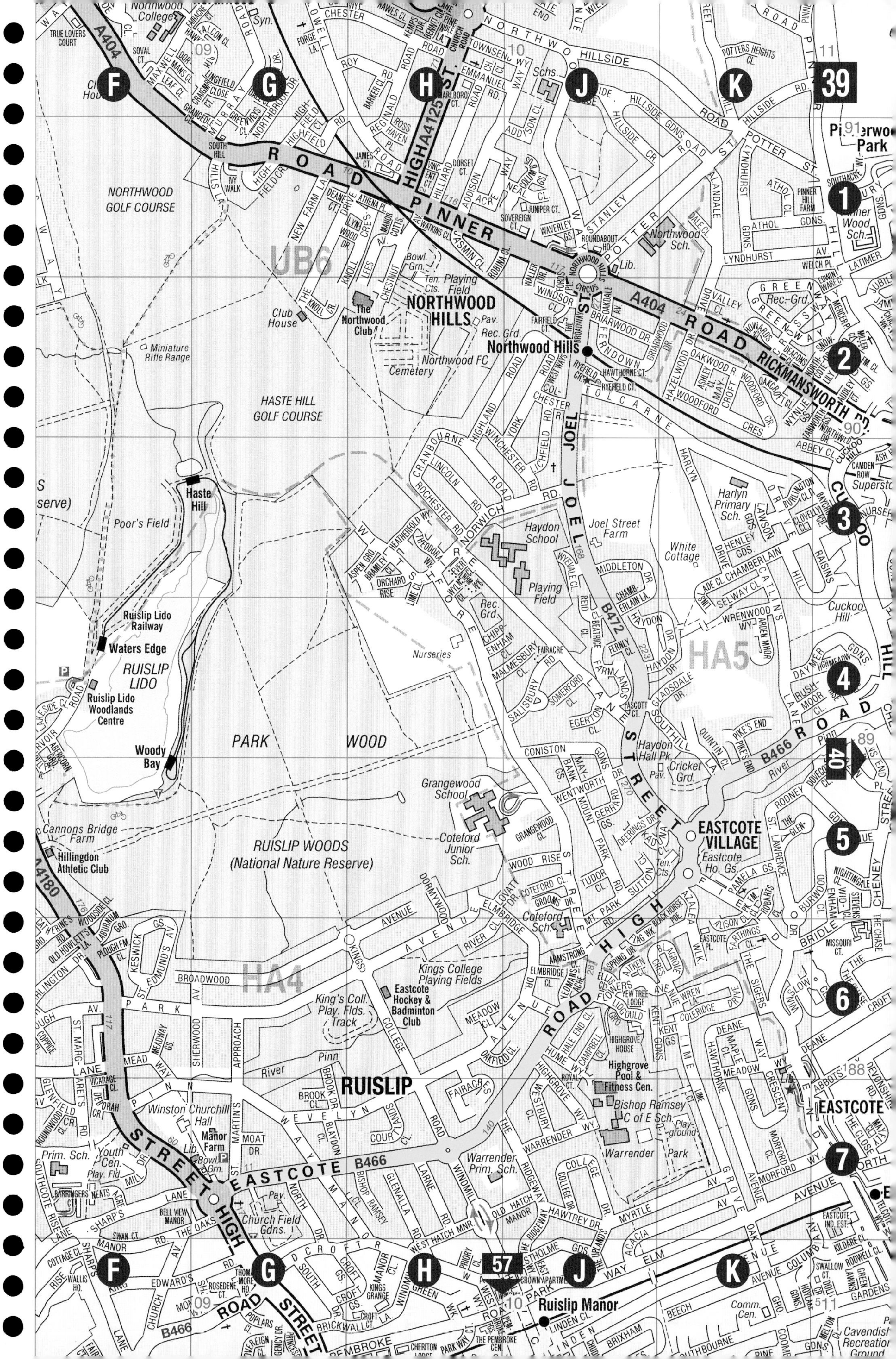

39
40
57
NORTHWOOD HILLS
Northwood Hills
EASTCOTE VILLAGE
RUISLIP
Ruislip Manor
EASTCOTE
NORTHWOOD GOLF COURSE
HASTE HILL GOLF COURSE
RUISLIP LIDO
PARK WOOD
RUISLIP WOODS
(National Nature Reserve)
PINNER ROAD
RICKMANSWORTH RD.
JOEL ST.
HIGH ST.
EASTCOTE ROAD
HIGH STREET
UB6
HA5
HA4

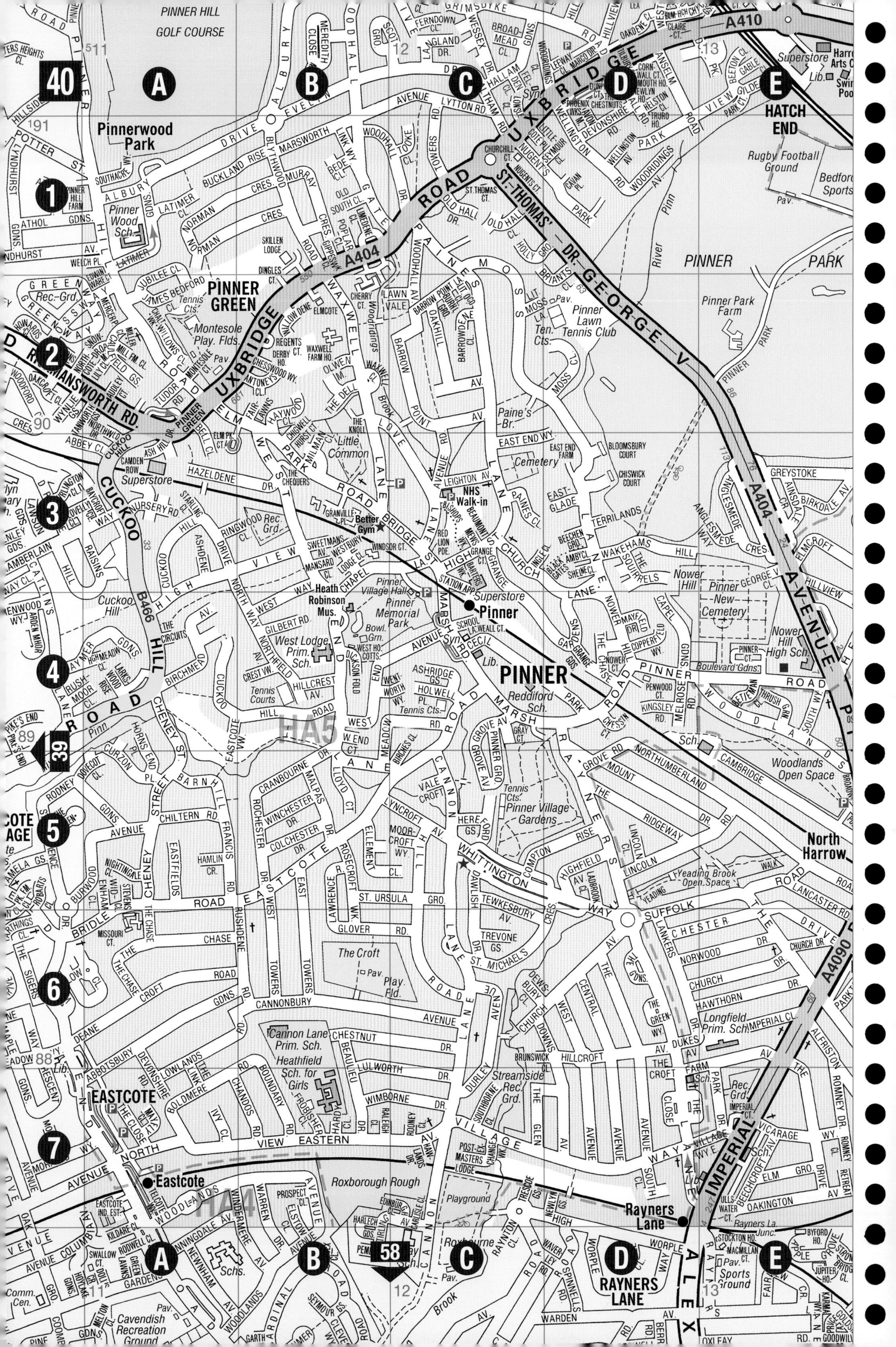

40
39
58
A
B
C
D
E
1
2
3
4
5
6
7
PINNER HILL
GOLF COURSE
Pinnerwood
Park
HATCH
END
Rugby Football
Ground
PINNER
PARK
Pinner Park
Farm
PINNER
GREEN
Montesole
Play. Flds.
Pinner Lawn
Tennis Club
Paine's
Br.
Cemetery
Little
Common
NHS
Walk-in
Better
Gym
Superstore
Pinner
Heath
Robinson
Mus.
Pinner
Village Hall
Pinner
Memorial
Park
West Lodge
Prim.
Sch.
Cuckoo
Hill
Nower
Hill
Pinner
New
Cemetery
Nower
Hill
High Sch.
PINNER
Reddiford
Sch.
HA5
Woodlands
Open Space
North
Harrow
Pinner Village
Gardens
Yeading Brook
Open Space
The Croft
Play.
Fld.
Cannon Lane
Prim. Sch.
Heathfield
Sch. for
Girls
Streamside
Rec.
Grd.
Longfield
Prim. Sch.
EASTCOTE
Eastcote
Roxborough Rough
Playground
HA4
Rayners
Lane
RAYNERS
LANE
Sports
Ground
Cavendish
Recreation
Ground
Rayners La
Junc.
A410
A404
A4090
B466
UXBRIDGE
ROAD
ST. THOMAS' DR.
GEORGE V
AVENUE
CUCKOO HILL
RICKMANSWORTH RD.
MARSH RD.
IMPERIAL
EASTERN AVENUE

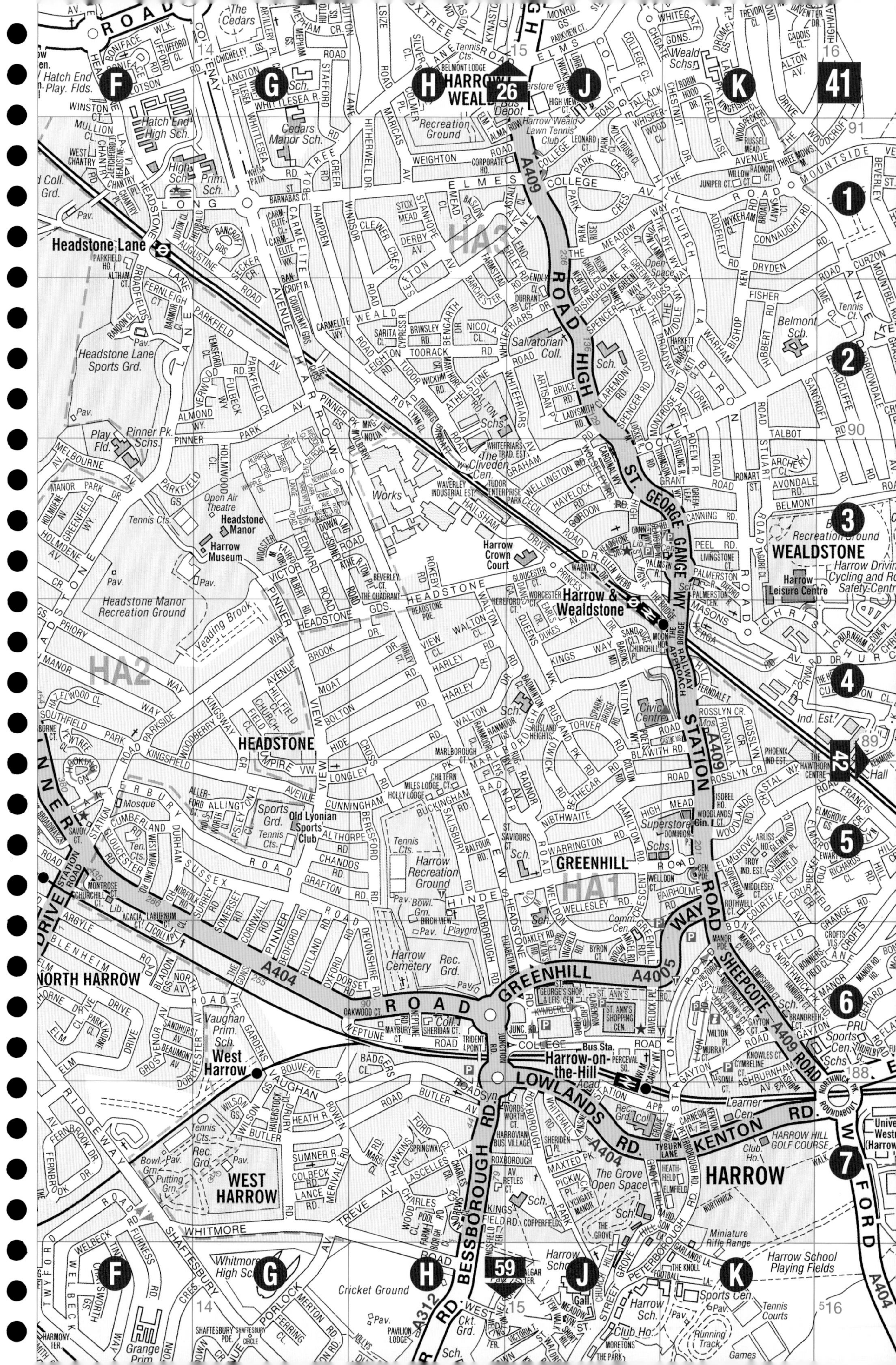

F
G
H
J
K
41
26
42
59
14
15
16
91
90
89
188
1
2
3
4
5
6
7
HARROW WEALD
Headstone Lane
Hatch End High Sch.
Cedars Manor Sch.
Recreation Ground
Harrow Weald Lawn Tennis Club
Bus Depot
HA3
Headstone Lane Sports Grd.
Pinner Pk. Schs.
Salvatorian Coll.
Belmont Sch.
WEALDSTONE
Recreation Ground
Harrow Leisure Centre
Harrow Driving Cycling and Road Safety Centre
Harrow & Wealdstone
Harrow Crown Court
Headstone Manor
Harrow Museum
Open Air Theatre
Headstone Manor Recreation Ground
Yeading Brook
HA2
HEADSTONE
Civic Centre
Works
The Clivedon Cen.
WAVERLEY INDUSTRIAL EST.
TUDOR ENTERPRISE PARK
WHITEFRIARS TRAD. EST.
Old Lyonian Sports Club
Harrow Recreation Ground
GREENHILL
HA1
Superstore
NORTH HARROW
Harrow Cemetery
Rec. Grd.
Vaughan Prim. Sch.
West Harrow
WEST HARROW
Harrow-on-the-Hill
Bus Sta.
ST. ANN'S SHOPPING CEN.
HARROW
HARROW HILL GOLF COURSE
The Grove Open Space
Miniature Rifle Range
Harrow School Playing Fields
Whitmore High Sch.
Cricket Ground
Harrow Sch.
Sports Cen.
Running Track
Tennis Courts
A409
A404
A4005
A312
STATION ROAD
HIGH ROAD
ST. GEORGE GANGE WAY
GREENHILL WAY
LOWLANDS RD.
KENTON RD.
PINNER ROAD
HEADSTONE DRIVE
HEADSTONE GDS.
HEADSTONE LANE
LONG ELMES
ELMES
WEALD LANE
BOXTREE RD.
HARROW VIEW
PINNER VIEW
PINNER PARK
VAUGHAN RD.
BESSBOROUGH RD.
SHEEPCOTE ROAD
WATFORD RD.
WHITMORE RD.
SHAFTESBURY AV.
RIDGEWAY
PINNER RD.

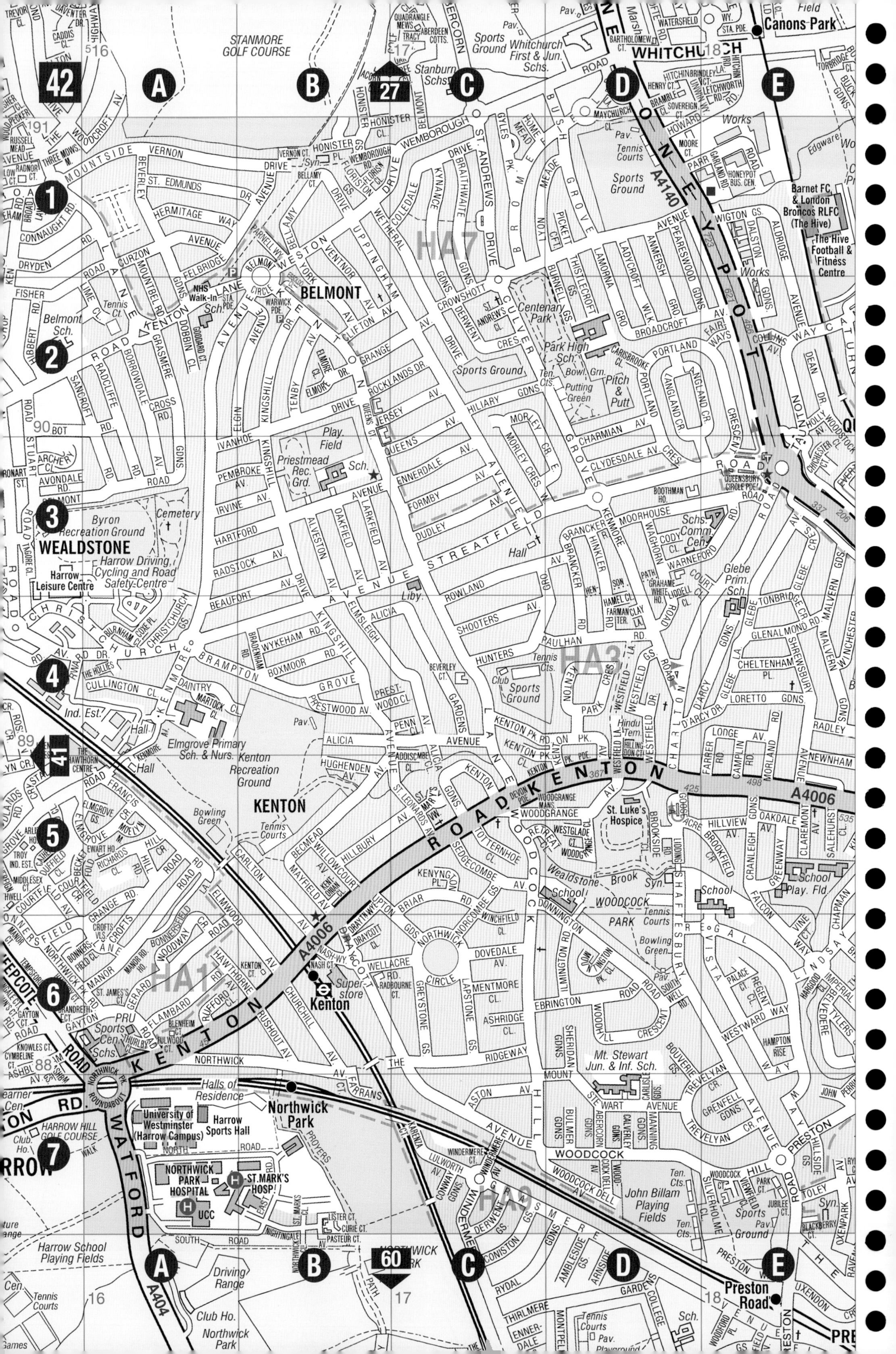

42
27
41
60
A
B
C
D
E
1
2
3
4
5
6
7
STANMORE GOLF COURSE
Stanburn Schs.
Sports Ground
Whitchurch First & Jun. Schs.
Canons Park
WHITCHURCH
Works
Barnet FC & London Broncos RLFC (The Hive)
The Hive Football & Fitness Centre
A4140
HA7
BELMONT
NHS Walk-In
Belmont Sch.
Centenary Park
Park High Sch.
Pitch & Putt
Putting Green
Sports Ground
Play. Field
Priestmead Rec. Grd.
Cemetery
Byron Recreation Ground
WEALDSTONE
Harrow Driving, Cycling and Road Safety Centre
Harrow Leisure Centre
Liby.
Hall
Schs. Comm. Cen.
Glebe Prim. Sch.
HA3
Hindu Tem.
Elmgrove Primary Sch. & Nurs.
Kenton Recreation Ground
Ind. Est.
Bowling Green
KENTON
Tennis Courts
Club Sports Ground
KENTON ROAD
A4006
St. Luke's Hospice
Wealdstone Brook
School
WOODCOCK PARK
Tennis Courts
Bowling Green
Play. Fld.
HA1
Super store
Kenton
Sports Cen.
Mt. Stewart Jun. & Inf. Sch.
Halls of Residence
Northwick Park
University of Westminster (Harrow Campus)
Harrow Sports Hall
NORTHWICK PARK HOSPITAL
ST. MARK'S HOSP.
UCC
HARROW HILL GOLF COURSE
HA9
John Billam Playing Fields
Sports Ground
Harrow School Playing Fields
Driving Range
Club Ho.
Northwick Park
Preston Road
WATFORD
A404
16
17
18

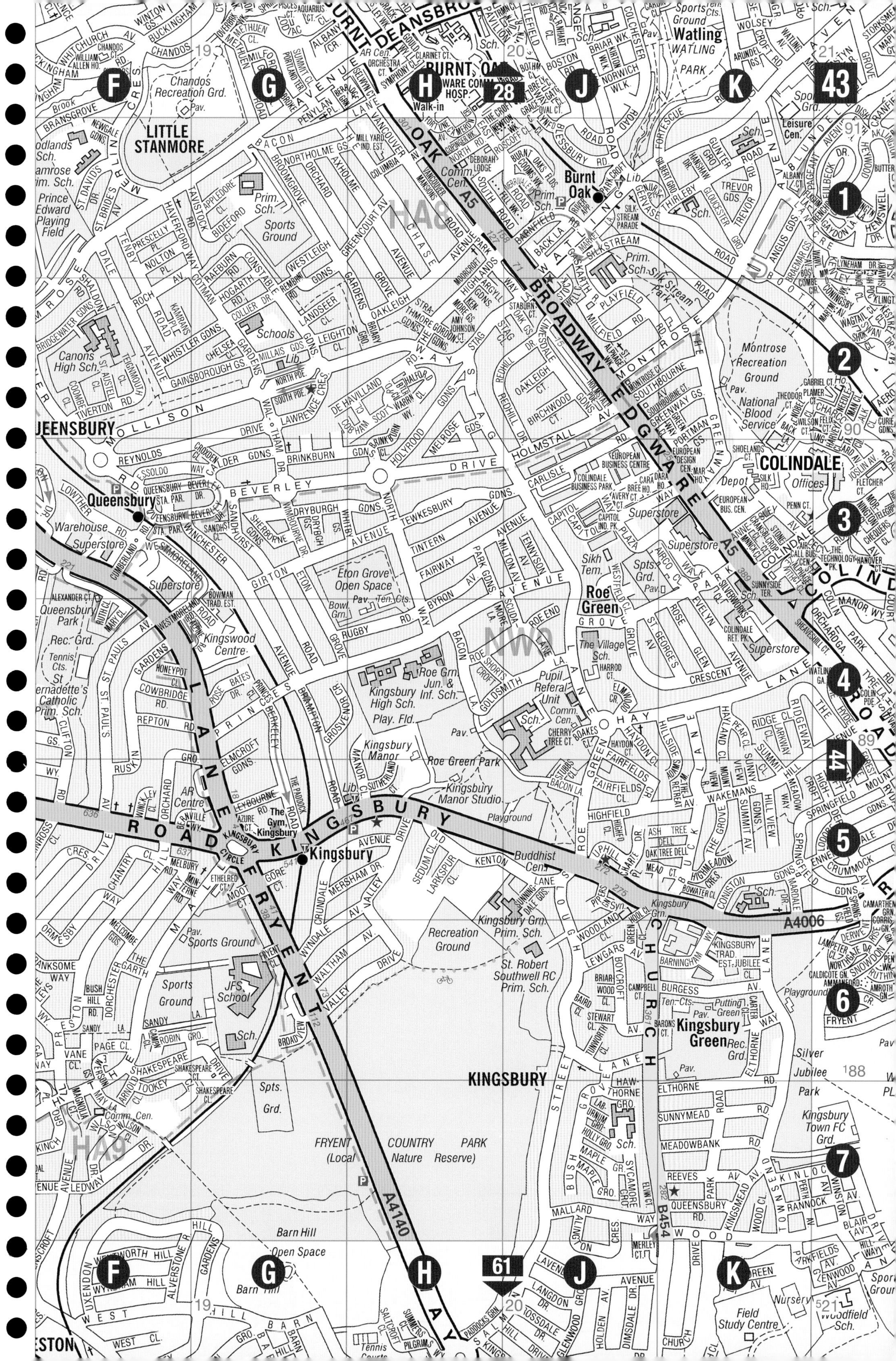

43
28
44
61
F
G
H
J
K
1
2
3
4
5
6
7
19
20
21
91
90
89
188
HA8
NW9
HA9
LITTLE STANMORE
Chandos Recreation Grd.
BURNT OAK
Burnt Oak
Watling Park
Montrose Recreation Ground
National Blood Service
COLINDALE
QUEENSBURY
Queensbury
Roe Green
Eton Grove Open Space
Roe Green Park
Kingsbury Manor Studio
Kingsbury High Sch.
Roe Grn. Jun. & Inf. Sch.
Kingsbury
KINGSBURY
Kingsbury Green
FRYENT COUNTRY PARK (Local Nature Reserve)
Barn Hill Open Space
Silver Jubilee Park
Kingsbury Town FC Grd.
Field Study Centre
Canons High Sch.
Prince Edward Playing Field
Queensbury Park Rec. Grd.
Kingswood Centre
JFS School
Recreation Ground
St. Robert Southwell RC Prim. Sch.
Kingsbury Grn. Prim. Sch.
The Village Sch.
Pupil Referal Unit
Buddhist Cen.
BROADWAY
EDGWARE
KINGSBURY ROAD
FRYENT WAY
A5
A4006
A4140
B454
MOLLISON WAY
BEVERLEY DRIVE
STAG LANE
MONTROSE AV.
COLINDALE AV.
CHURCH LANE
DEANSBROOK RD.
BURNT OAK
WATLING AV.
SILKSTREAM RD.
HONEYPOT LANE
BARN HILL

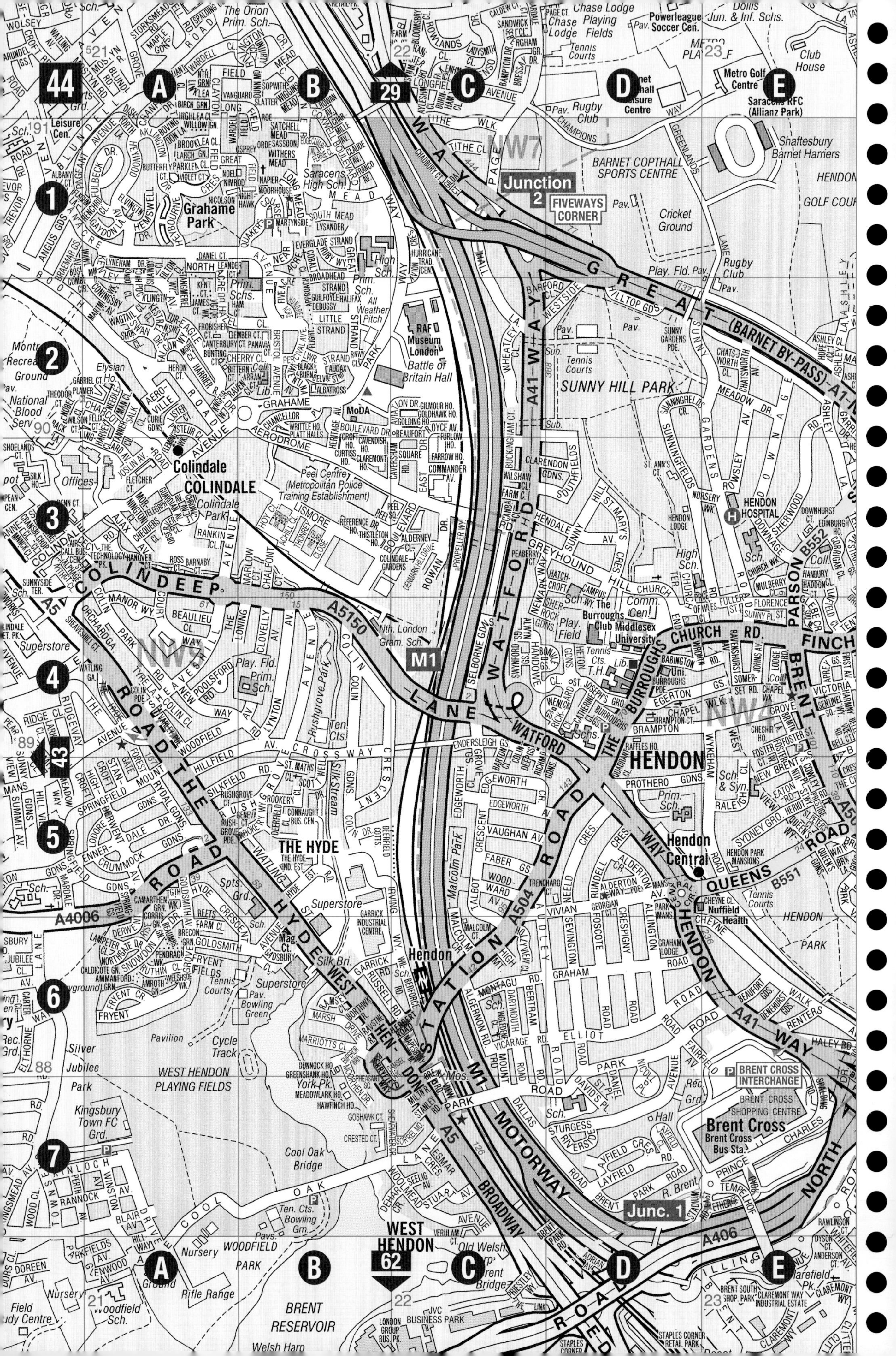

44
29
43
62
A
B
C
D
E
1
2
3
4
5
6
7
21
22
23
NW7
NW9
NW4
Junction 2
FIVEWAYS CORNER
Junc. 1
The Orion Prim. Sch.
Chase Lodge Playing Fields
Powerleague Soccer Cen.
Dollis Jun. & Inf. Schs.
Metro Golf Centre
Club House
Saracens RFC (Allianz Park)
Rugby Club
Copthall Leisure Centre
BARNET COPTHALL SPORTS CENTRE
Shaftesbury Barnet Harriers
HENDON GOLF COURSE
Cricket Ground
Grahame Park
Saracens High Sch.
Leisure Cen.
Montrose Recreation Ground
National Blood Service
Elysian Ho.
RAF Museum London
Battle of Britain Hall
MoDA
Colindale
COLINDALE
Colindale Park
Peel Centre (Metropolitan Police Training Establishment)
Offices
Superstore
SUNNY HILL PARK
HENDON HOSPITAL
Nth. London Gram. Sch.
The Burroughs
Middlesex University
HENDON
Hendon Central
Nuffield Health
HENDON PARK
THE HYDE
Silk Stream
Rushgrove Park
Malcolm Park
Hendon
WEST HENDON PLAYING FIELDS
Cycle Track
Silver Jubilee Park
Kingsbury Town FC Grd.
Cool Oak Bridge
York Pk.
BRENT CROSS INTERCHANGE
BRENT CROSS SHOPPING CENTRE
Brent Cross
Brent Cross Bus Sta.
WEST HENDON
WOODFIELD PARK
Rifle Range
BRENT RESERVOIR
Welsh Harp
Old Welsh Harp
Brent Bridge
JVC BUSINESS PARK
LONDON GROUP BUS. PK.
BRENT SOUTH SHOP. PARK
CLAREMONT WAY INDUSTRIAL ESTATE
STAPLES CORNER RETAIL PARK
STAPLES CORNER
WATFORD WAY
GREAT NORTH WAY (BARNET BY-PASS)
A1
A41
A5
A5150
A504
A4006
A406
B551
B552
M1
COLINDEEP LANE
WATFORD WAY
THE BURROUGHS
CHURCH RD.
QUEENS ROAD
HENDON WAY
STATION ROAD
WEST HENDON BROADWAY
THE HYDE
EDGWARE ROAD
MOTORWAY
NORTH CIRCULAR ROAD
COOL OAK LANE
PAGE STREET
AERODROME ROAD
GRAHAME PARK WAY
COLINDALE AVENUE

F
G
H
J
K
24
25
26
30
45
46
63
FINCHLEY
Victoria Park
Finchley Central
CHURCH END
Holders Hill
Hendon Crematorium
HENDON CEMETERY
NW7
N3
N2
NW11
NW2
DOLLIS ROAD
B1462
B552 ROAD
NETHER ST.
BALLARDS LANE
A598
REGENTS PARK ROAD
EAST END ROAD
A504
HENDON LANE
HOLDERS HILL
Poolside Manor
Finchley Manor Club
Playing Fields
Windsor Open Space
College Farm
Avenue House Grounds
Sports Ground
Courts
Lib.
Pentland Centre
The Sternberg Centre
PureGym
The Academy
St. Marylebone Crematorium
EAST FINCHLEY CEMETERY
Christ's College Finchley
HENLYS CORNER
A1
FALLODEN WAY
A1 WAY
A406
NORTH CIRCULAR ROAD
Mutton Brook
Little Wood
Big Wood
Willifred Green
Temple Fortune
Princes Park
FINCHLEY ROAD
Jewish Cemetery
Golders Green Crematorium
GOLDERS GREEN
A502
GOLDERS GREEN ROAD
Brent Cross
HIGHFIELD
Curtis & Staub
Golders Green
NORTH END
HAMPSTEAD
HEATH
Bunkers Hill
Works
Yth. Hostel
Leisure Cen.
Superstores
HENDON WAY
A41
Clitterhouse
1
2
3
4
5
6
7
89
90
91
188

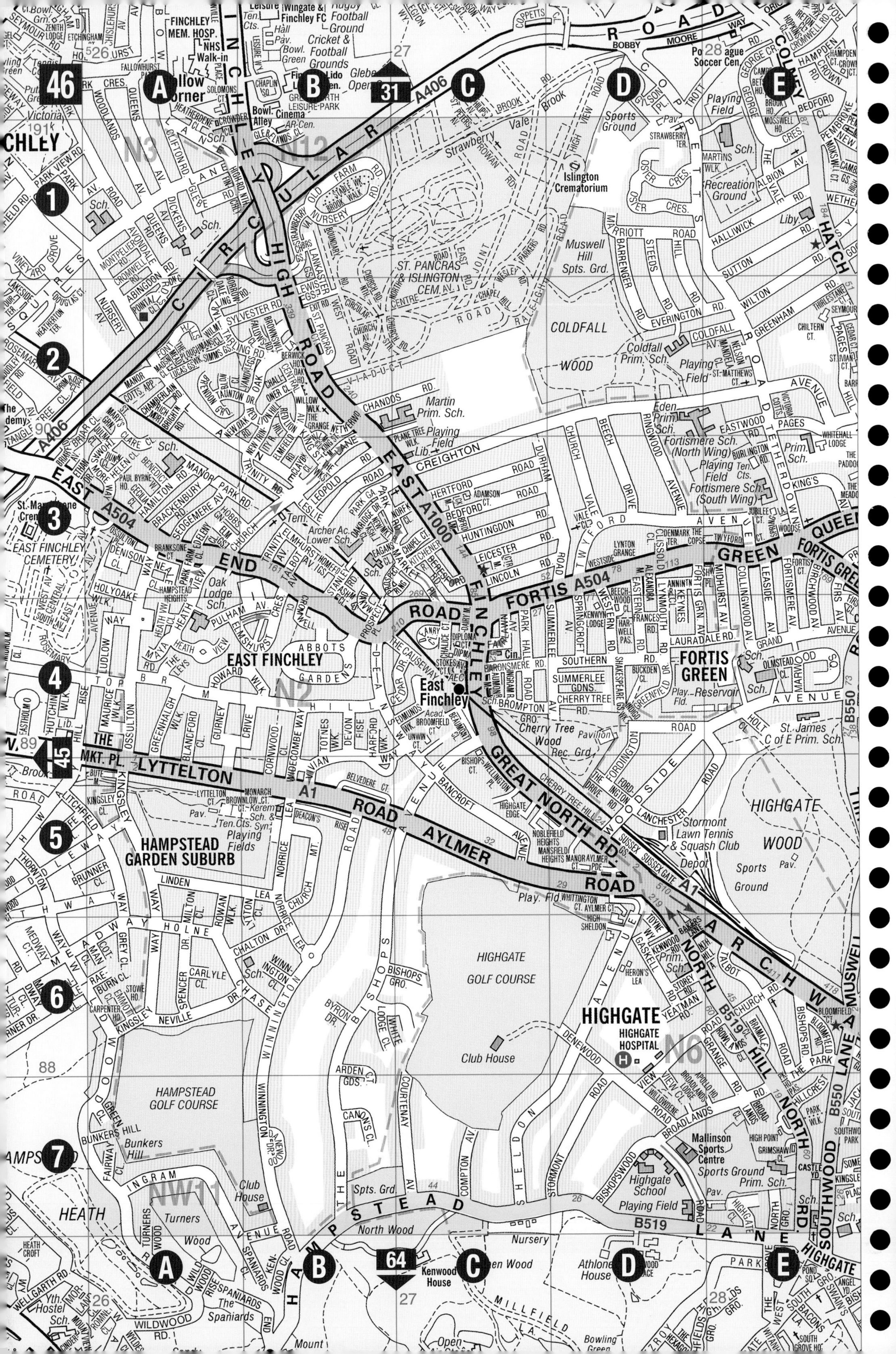

46
31
45
64
A
B
C
D
E
1
2
3
4
5
6
7
N3
N12
N2
N6
NW11
FINCHLEY MEM. HOSP.
NHS Walk-in
Wingate & Finchley FC
Rugby Football Ground
Cricket & Football Grounds
Finchley Lido Leisure Cen.
Bowl. Alley
Cinema
Great North Leisure Park
NORTH CIRCULAR ROAD
A406
BOBBY MOORE WAY
COPPETTS RD.
COLNEY HATCH LANE
Prague Soccer Cen.
Sports Ground
Strawberry Vale
Islington Crematorium
ST. PANCRAS & ISLINGTON CEM.
Muswell Hill Spts. Grd.
COLDFALL WOOD
Coldfall Prim. Sch.
Recreation Ground
Playing Field
HIGH ROAD
EAST END ROAD
A504
St. Marylebone Crem.
EAST FINCHLEY CEMETERY
EAST FINCHLEY
East Finchley
Archer Ac. Lower Sch.
Martin Prim. Sch.
Eden Prim. Sch.
Fortismere Sch. (North Wing)
Fortismere Sch. (South Wing)
EAST END ROAD
FORTIS GREEN
A504
A1000
FORTIS GREEN
Oak Lodge Sch.
Cherry Tree Wood
Rec. Grd.
Stormont Lawn Tennis & Squash Club
HIGHGATE WOOD
Sports Ground
St. James C of E Prim. Sch.
LYTTELTON ROAD
A1
AYLMER ROAD
GREAT NORTH RD.
ARCHWAY ROAD
HAMPSTEAD GARDEN SUBURB
Playing Fields
HIGHGATE GOLF COURSE
Club House
HIGHGATE
HIGHGATE HOSPITAL
NORTH HILL
B519
Mallinson Sports Centre
Sports Ground
Prim. Sch.
Highgate School Playing Field
HAMPSTEAD GOLF COURSE
Bunkers Hill
Turners Wood
HEATH
HAMPSTEAD LANE
B519
North Wood
Kenwood House
Ken Wood
Athlone House
MUSWELL HILL
SOUTHWOOD LANE
B550
HIGHGATE
Yth. Hostel
The Spaniards
WILDWOOD RD.
MILLFIELD LA.

F
G
H
J
K
F
G
H
J
K
1
2
3
4
5
6
7
47
32
48
65
29
30
31
MUSWELL HILL GOLF COURSE
Alexandra Park School
Club House
Albert Road Rec. Grd.
N11
N22
N10
N8
N4
N19
ALEXANDRA PARK RD.
ALBERT RD.
DURNSFORD RD.
VICTORIA RD.
ALEXANDRA PARK RD.
PALACE GATES RD.
Go Ape Alexandra Palace
The Lake
Skate Park
Theatre
Ice Rink
Alexandra Palace
Pitch & Putt Course
ALEXANDRA PARK
Cricket Ground
Playing Field
Health Club
Alexandra Palace
WOOD GREEN
Heartlands High Sch.
Wood Gn. Common
Reservoir
Filter Beds
New River
Nightingale Gdns.
Avenue Gds.
STATION RD.
MAYES RD.
PARK AV.
A109
B151
B106
B550
B138
A504
A1201
A103
B540
A1
Wood Green
SHOPPING CITY
Civic Cen.
War Mem.
TURNPIKE LA.
HORNSEY PARK RD.
HIGH RD.
Gas Works
OLYMPIA IND. EST.
HORNSEY
Hornsey
MUSWELL HILL
The Grove
Muswell Hill Prim. Sch.
MUSWELL HILL
Gym
Arts Cen.
Parkland Walk
Cranley Gardens
QUEEN'S WOOD
Shepherd's Hill Gds.
PRIORY RD.
HIGH STREET A504
PRIORY PARK
PARK ROAD
Park Road Pools & Fitness
Ckt. Grd. Hornsey Cricket Club
Play. Flds.
Sports Gd.
TOTTENHAM LA.
CHURCH LA.
Academy
HORNSEY VALE
Stationers Park
TOTTENHAM LA.
THE BROADWAY
CROUCH END HILL
CROUCH HILL
CROUCH END
St. Aloysius College Sports Ground
Coolhurst Club
Highgate
Lib.
HIGHGATE
HORNSEY LANE
Nature Res.
Reservoirs (covered)
STROUD GREEN
Crouch Hill
STROUD GREEN RD.
HORNSEY RISE
HORNSEY RD.
Lauderdale House
Tennis Courts
Parkland Walk
ARCHWAY RD.
HIGH ST.

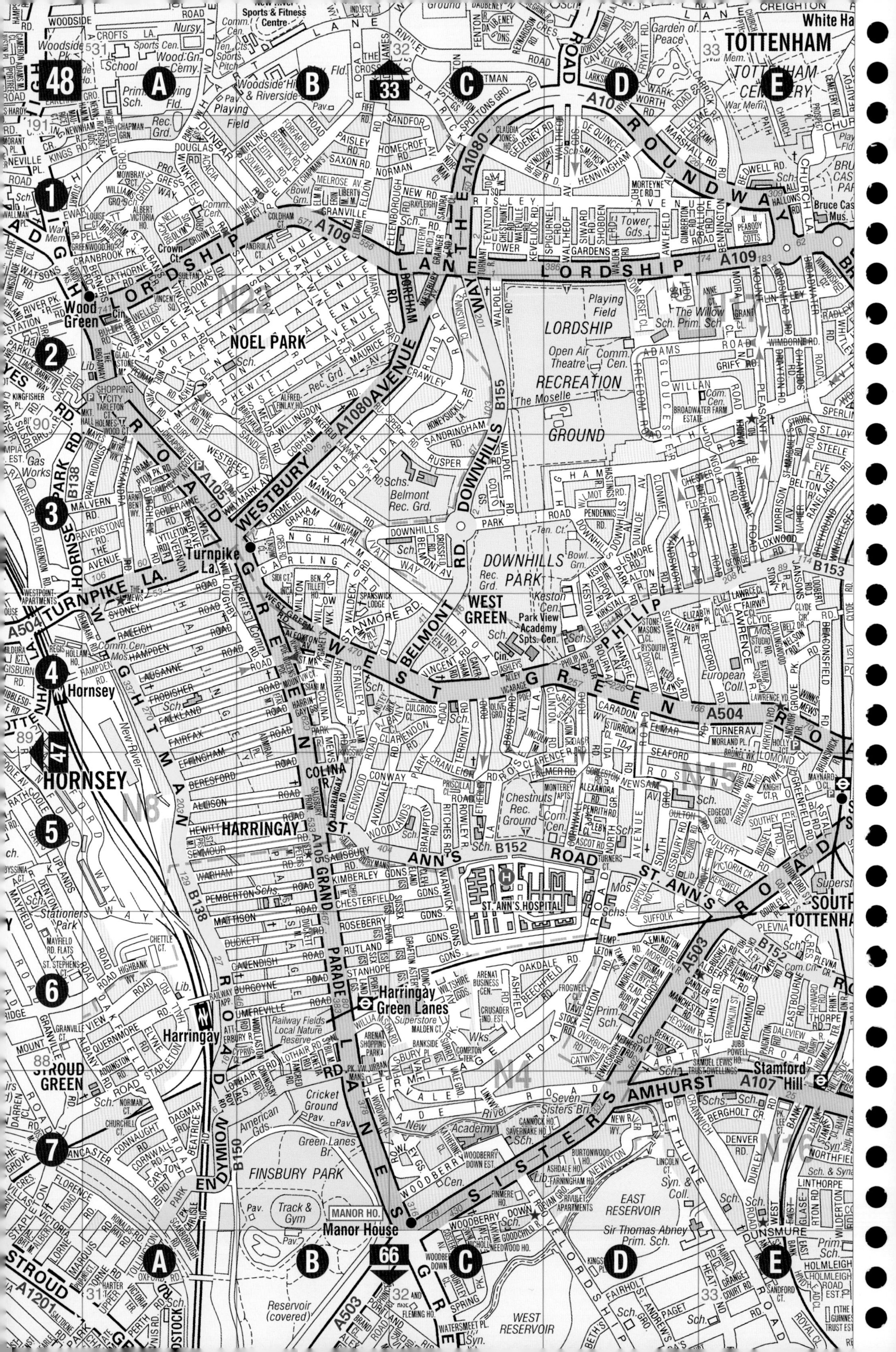

48
33
47
66
A
B
C
D
E
1
2
3
4
5
6
7
TOTTENHAM
NOEL PARK
LORDSHIP RECREATION GROUND
DOWNHILLS PARK
WEST GREEN
HARRINGAY
HORNSEY
STROUD GREEN
FINSBURY PARK
EAST RESERVOIR
WEST RESERVOIR
Wood Green
Turnpike La.
Harringay
Harringay Green Lanes
Manor House
Stamford Hill
St. Ann's Hospital
LORDSHIP LANE
WESTBURY AVENUE
GREEN LANES
WEST GREEN ROAD
ST. ANN'S ROAD
SEVEN SISTERS ROAD
AMHURST
THE ROUNDWAY
HIGH ROAD
PHILIP LA.
GRAND PARADE
WIGHTMAN ROAD
HORNSEY PARK RD.
TURNPIKE LA.
ENDYMION ROAD
DOWNHILLS WAY
N22
N8
N15
N4
N16
A109
A10
A1080
A105
A504
A503
A107
A1201
B138
B150
B152
B153
B155

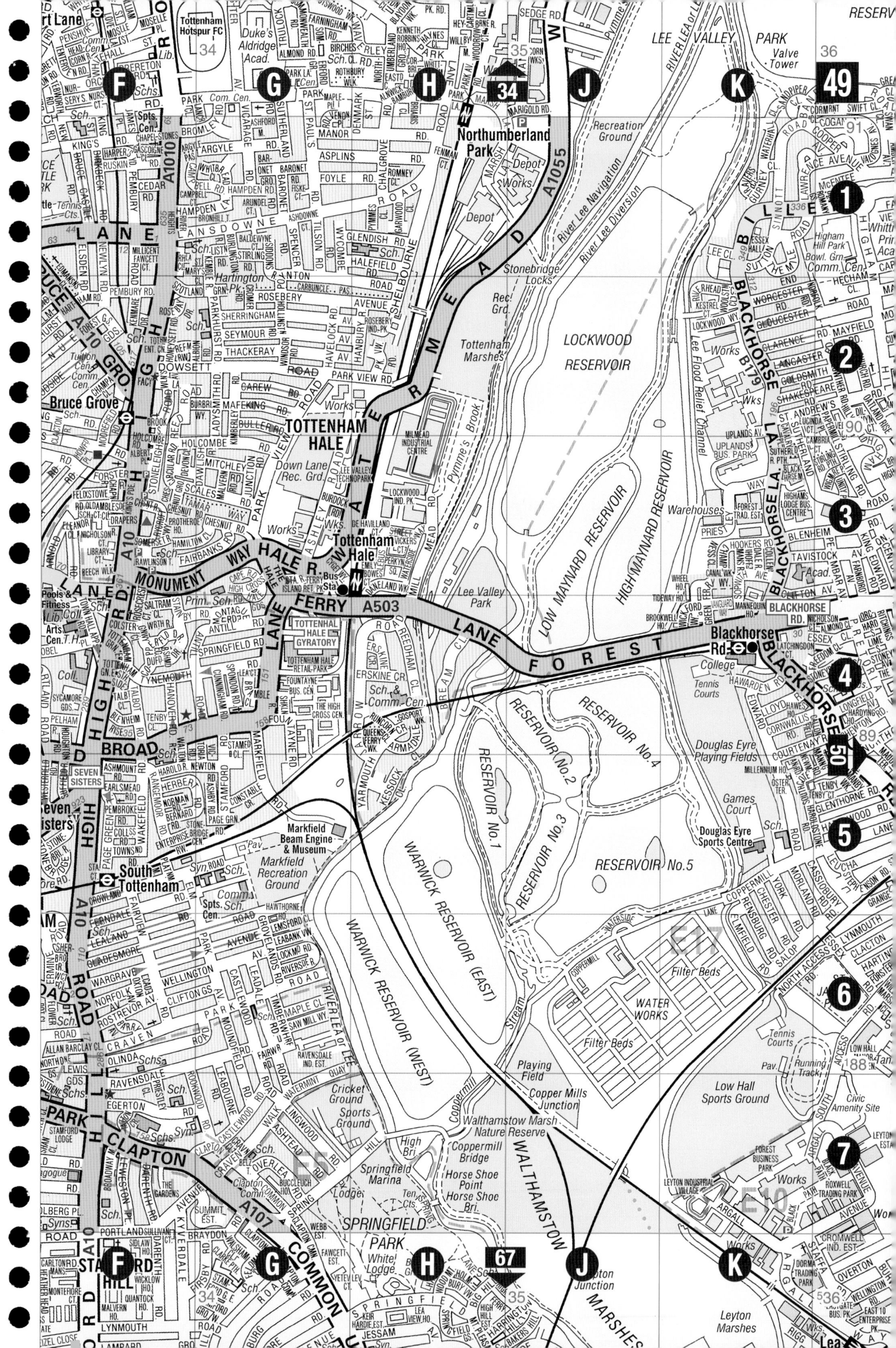

Tottenham Hotspur FC
34
35
36
49
50
67
F
G
H
J
K
1
2
3
4
5
6
7
LEE VALLEY PARK
Valve Tower
Northumberland Park
Recreation Ground
River Lee Navigation
River Lee Diversion
Stonebridge Locks
LOCKWOOD RESERVOIR
LOW MAYNARD RESERVOIR
HIGH MAYNARD RESERVOIR
Tottenham Marshes
Lee Valley Park
TOTTENHAM HALE
Tottenham Hale
MILLMEAD INDUSTRIAL CENTRE
LOCKWOOD IND. PK.
TOTTENHAM HALE GYRATORY
TOTTENHAM HALE RETAIL PARK
Down Lane Rec. Grd.
Bruce Grove
MONUMENT WAY
FERRY LANE
FOREST ROAD
A503
A1055
A10
A1010
A107
B179
BROAD LANE
BLACKHORSE LANE
BLACKHORSE RD.
Blackhorse Rd.
Higham Hill Park
Douglas Eyre Playing Fields
Douglas Eyre Sports Centre
Games Court
RESERVOIR No.1
RESERVOIR No.2
RESERVOIR No.3
RESERVOIR No.4
RESERVOIR No.5
WARWICK RESERVOIR (EAST)
WARWICK RESERVOIR (WEST)
Markfield Beam Engine & Museum
Markfield Recreation Ground
South Tottenham
Seven Sisters
SEVEN SISTERS
E17
E5
E10
Filter Beds
WATER WORKS
Playing Field
Copper Mills Junction
Walthamstow Marsh Nature Reserve
Coppermill Bridge
Horse Shoe Point
Horse Shoe Bri.
Springfield Marina
SPRINGFIELD PARK
White Lodge
WALTHAMSTOW MARSHES
Low Hall Sports Ground
Civic Amenity Site
FOREST BUSINESS PARK
LEYTON INDUSTRIAL VILLAGE
ROXWELL TRADING PARK
Leyton Marshes
CLAPTON COMMON
STAMFORD HILL
HIGH ROAD

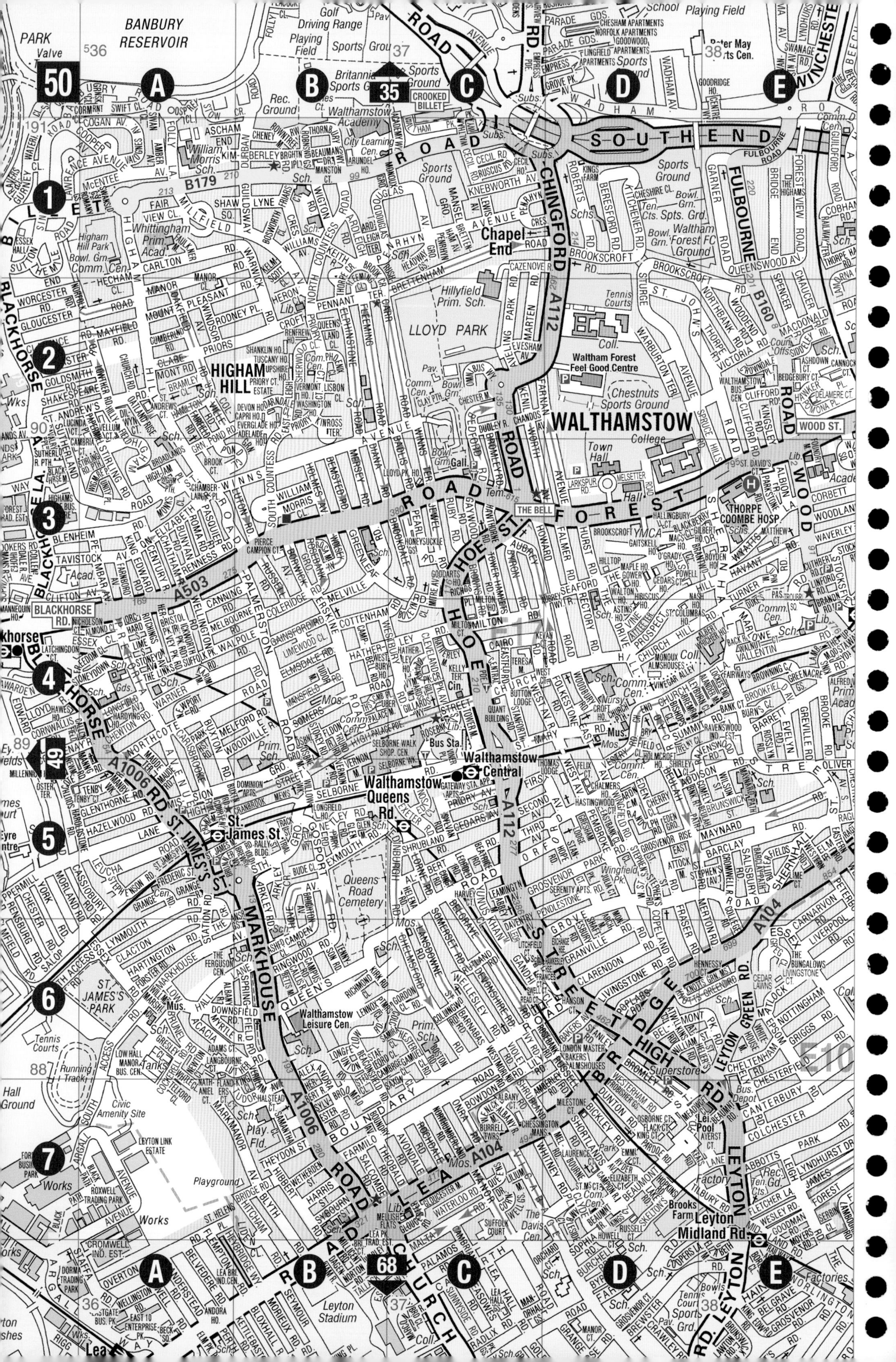

50
A
B
35
C
D
E
BANBURY RESERVOIR
Golf Driving Range
Playing Field
Sports Ground
CROOKED BILLET
Walthamstow Academy
SOUTHEND ROAD
CHINGFORD ROAD
A112
B179
Higham Hill Park
HIGHAM HILL
Chapel End
Hillyfield Prim. Sch.
LLOYD PARK
Waltham Forest Feel Good Centre
Chestnuts Sports Ground
WALTHAMSTOW
Town Hall
College
WOOD ST.
FOREST ROAD
THE BELL
THORPE COOMBE HOSP.
HOE ST.
A503
BLACKHORSE RD.
BLACKHORSE LA.
E17
Walthamstow Central
Walthamstow Queens Rd.
St. James St.
A1006
ST. JAMES'S ST.
MARKHOUSE ROAD
Queens Road Cemetery
Walthamstow Leisure Cen.
ST. JAMES'S PARK
Running Track
Civic Amenity Site
LEYTON LINK ESTATE
ROXWELL TRADING PARK
CROMWELL IND. EST.
A104
LEA BRIDGE ROAD
HIGH RD.
LEYTON
Leyton Midland Rd.
Brooks Farm
E10
Leyton Stadium
CHURCH ROAD
49
68
1
2
3
4
5
6
7
36
37
38
88
89
90
191

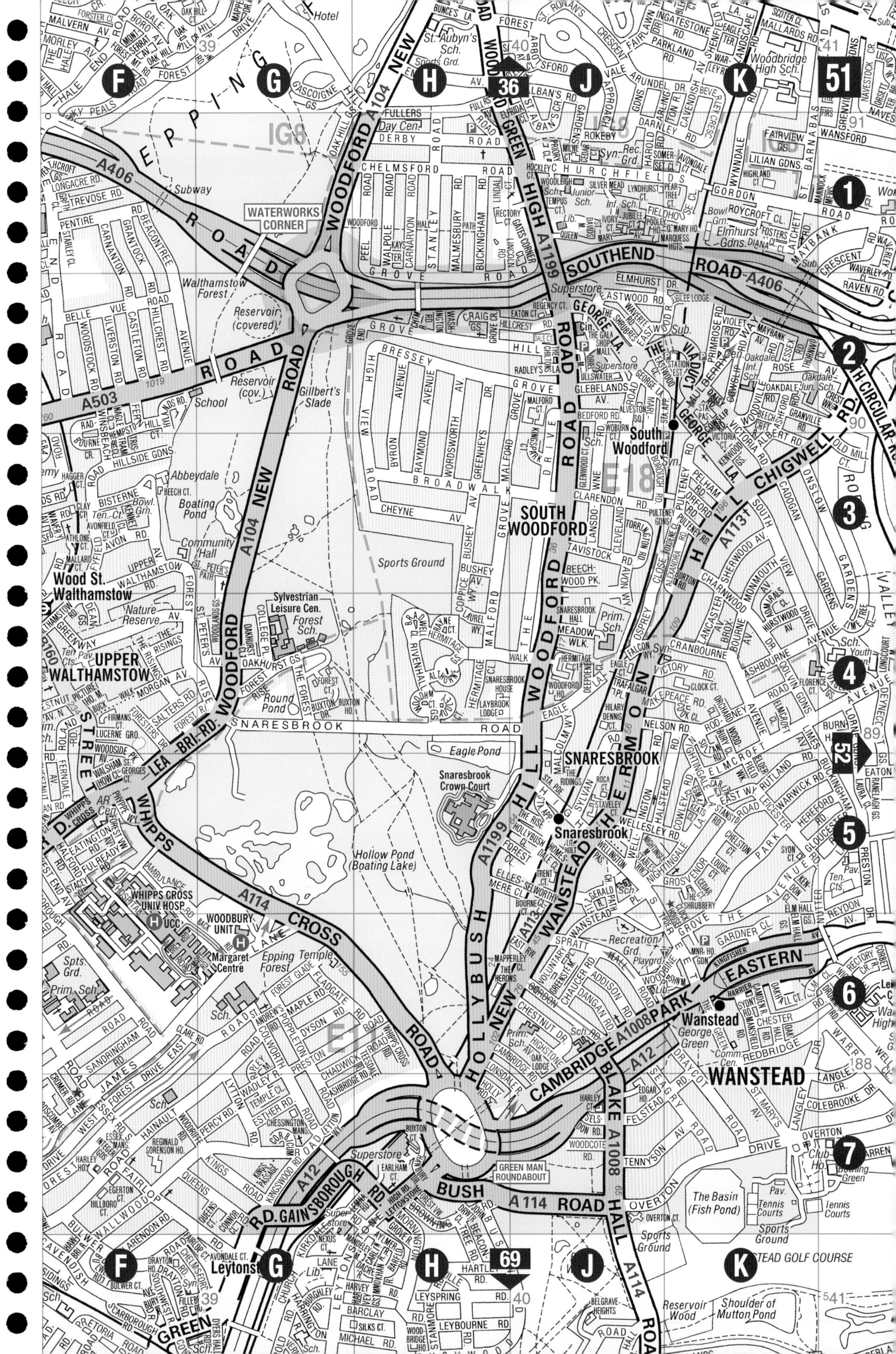

51
36
52
69
F
G
H
J
K
1
2
3
4
5
6
7
39
40
41
91
90
89
88
EPPING
IG8
E18
E11
A406
A503
A104
A1199
A113
A114
A1008
A12
A406 ROAD
SOUTHEND ROAD A406
WATERWORKS CORNER
Subway
Walthamstow Forest
Reservoir (covered)
Reservoir (cov.)
School
Gillbert's Slade
WOODFORD NEW ROAD
WOODFORD HIGH ROAD
WOODFORD NEW RD.
Abbeydale
Boating Pond
Community Hall
Wood St. Walthamstow
Nature Reserve
UPPER WALTHAMSTOW
Sylvestrian Leisure Cen.
Forest Sch.
Round Pond
SNARESBROOK ROAD
Eagle Pond
Snaresbrook Crown Court
Hollow Pond (Boating Lake)
WHIPPS CROSS ROAD
WHIPPS CROSS UNIV. HOSP
WOODBURY UNIT
Margaret Centre
Epping Forest
Sports Ground
SOUTH WOODFORD
South Woodford
GEORGE LA.
CHIGWELL RD.
HERMON HILL
SNARESBROOK
Snaresbrook
HOLLYBUSH HILL
NEW WANSTEAD
CAMBRIDGE PARK
EASTERN AV.
Wanstead
George Green
WANSTEAD
GREEN MAN ROUNDABOUT
BLAKE HALL ROAD
BUSH ROAD
GAINSBOROUGH RD.
Superstore
Leytonstone
The Basin (Fish Pond)
Sports Ground
Tennis Courts
WANSTEAD GOLF COURSE
Reservoir Wood
Shoulder of Mutton Pond
Woodbridge High Sch.
St. Aubyn's Sch.
Hotel
Recreation Grd.
NORTH CIRCULAR RD.

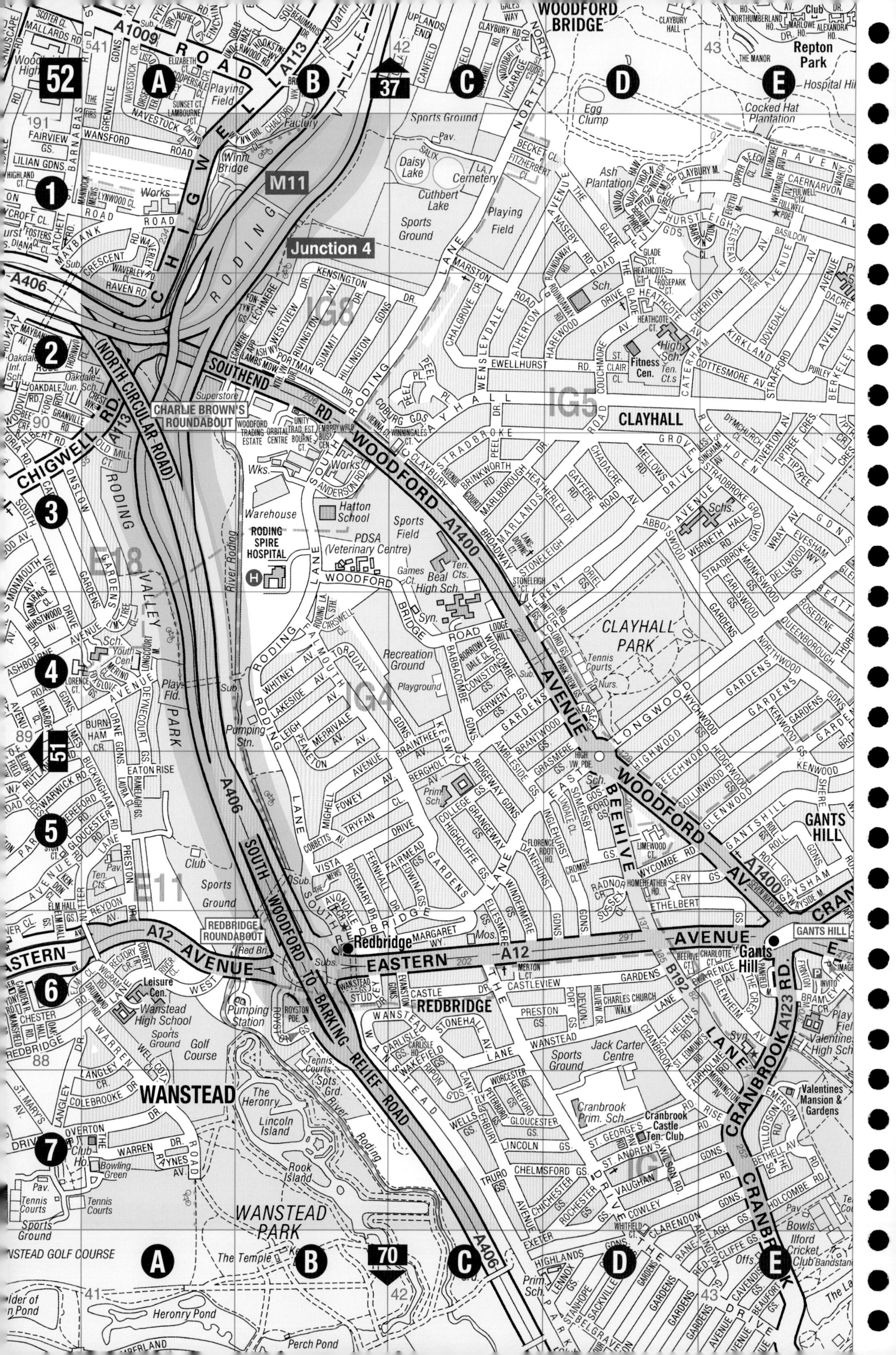
52
37
51
70
A
B
C
D
E
1
2
3
4
5
6
7
WOODFORD BRIDGE
Repton Park
Egg Clump
Cocked Hat Plantation
Ash Plantation
Sports Ground
Daisy Lake
Cuthbert Lake
Cemetery
Playing Field
M11
Junction 4
A406
A1009
A113
A1400
A12
A123
B192
IG8
IG5
IG4
E18
E11
CLAYHALL
CLAYHALL PARK
GANTS HILL
REDBRIDGE
WANSTEAD
WANSTEAD PARK
CHARLIE BROWN'S ROUNDABOUT
REDBRIDGE ROUNDABOUT
RODING SPIRE HOSPITAL
River Roding
Hatton School
PDSA (Veterinary Centre)
Beal High Sch.
Recreation Ground
Wanstead High School
Jack Carter Centre
Cranbrook Prim. Sch.
Valentines Mansion & Gardens
Heronry Pond
Perch Pond
Lincoln Island
Rook Island
The Heronry
The Temple
SOUTHEND RD.
WOODFORD AVENUE
EASTERN AVENUE
SOUTH WOODFORD TO BARKING RELIEF ROAD
NORTH CIRCULAR ROAD
CHIGWELL ROAD
CRANBROOK RD.
BEEHIVE LANE
VALLEY PARK
WANSTEAD GOLF COURSE
41
42
43

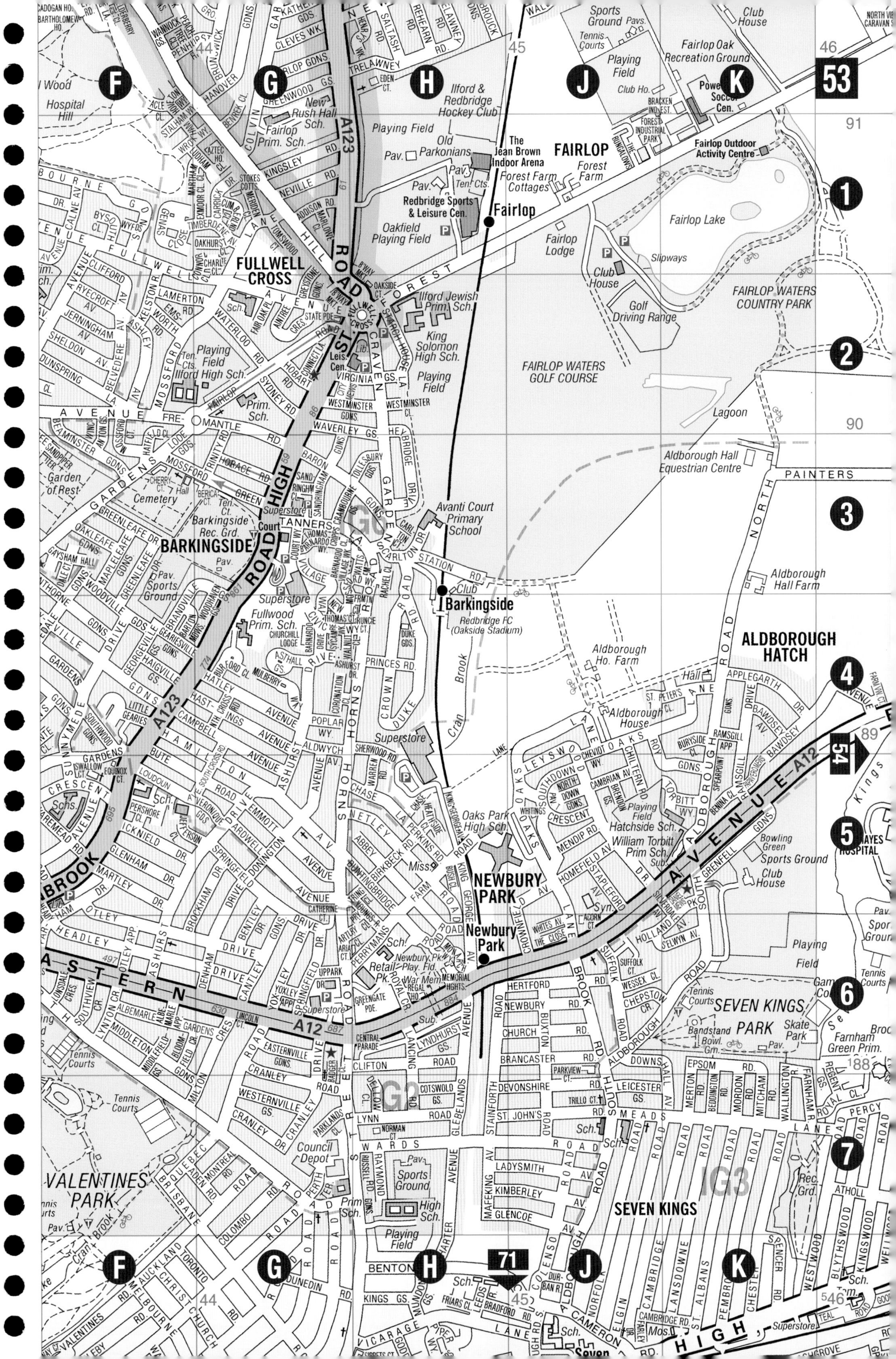
53
54
71
FULLWELL CROSS
BARKINGSIDE
FAIRLOP
ALDBOROUGH HATCH
NEWBURY PARK
SEVEN KINGS
Fairlop Lake
FAIRLOP WATERS COUNTRY PARK
FAIRLOP WATERS GOLF COURSE
Fairlop Oak Recreation Ground
Ilford & Redbridge Hockey Club
Redbridge Sports & Leisure Cen.
Oakfield Playing Field
The Jean Brown Indoor Arena
Fairlop Outdoor Activity Centre
King Solomon High Sch.
Ilford Jewish Prim. Sch.
Avanti Court Primary School
Aldborough Hall Equestrian Centre
Aldborough Hall Farm
Redbridge FC (Oakside Stadium)
Oaks Park High Sch.
Hatchside Sch.
William Torbitt Prim Sch.
SEVEN KINGS PARK
VALENTINES PARK
Fairlop
Barkingside
Newbury Park
HIGH ROAD
EASTERN AVENUE
A12
A123
IG2
IG3
IG6

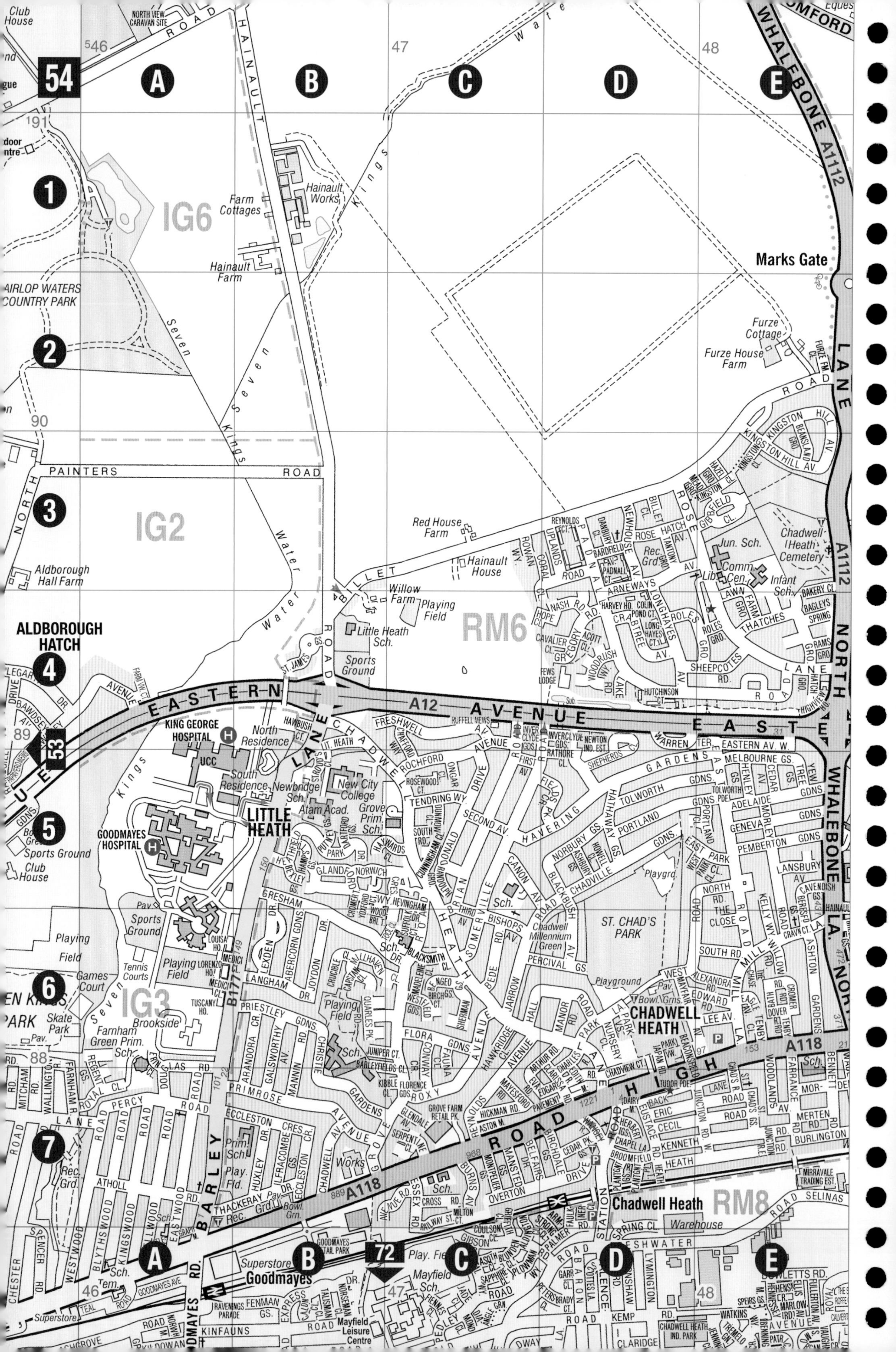

54
A
B
C
D
E
1
2
3
4
5
6
7
46
47
48
88
89
90
191
53
72
Club House
NORTH VIEW CARAVAN SITE
ROAD
HAINAULT
Wate
WHALEBONE
A1112
IG6
Farm Cottages
Hainault Works
Hainault Farm
Kings
Seven
FAIRLOP WATERS COUNTRY PARK
Marks Gate
Furze Cottage
Furze House Farm
FURZE FM. CL.
LANE
ROAD
KINGSTON HILL AV.
KINGSTON CL.
BEANSLAND GRO.
HAZEL GRO.
GIBBFIELD CL.
PAINTERS ROAD
NORTH
IG2
Water
Red House Farm
Hainault House
Aldborough Hall Farm
ALDBOROUGH HATCH
BILLET
Willow Farm
Playing Field
Little Heath Sch.
Sports Ground
RM6
ROSE HATCH AV.
Rec. Grd.
Jun. Sch.
Chadwell Heath Cemetery
Comm. Cen.
Lib.
Infant Sch.
BAKERY CL.
BAGLEYS SPRING
THATCHES GRO.
SHEEPCOTES RD.
ARNEWAYS AV.
HUTCHINSON CT.
EASTERN
A12
AVENUE
EAST
KING GEORGE HOSPITAL
North Residence
UCC
South Residence
Newbridge Sch.
New City College
Atam Acad.
Grove Prim. Sch.
LITTLE HEATH
GOODMAYES HOSPITAL
Sports Ground
Club House
CHADWELL
ROCHFORD
TENDRING WY.
SECOND AV.
HAVERING
PORTLAND
TOLWORTH GDNS.
EASTERN AV. W.
MELBOURNE GS.
ADELAIDE GDNS.
GENEVA GDNS.
PEMBERTON GDNS.
LANSBURY AV.
WHALEBONE LA. NORTH
St. Chad's Park
Playgrd.
Chadwell Millennium Green
Sch.
HEATH
Sports Ground
Playing Field
Games Court
Tennis Courts
Playing Field
IG3
Brookside
Skate Park
Farnham Green Prim. Sch.
B177
BARLEY
LANGHAM DR.
PRIESTLEY GDNS.
PRIMROSE
GRESHAM
Playing Field
Sch.
FLORA GDNS.
ROXY
GROVE FARM RETAIL PK.
CHADWELL HEATH
Playground
SOUTH RD.
WEST RD.
ALEXANDRA RD.
A118
HIGH
ROAD
WOODLANDS AV.
BURLINGTON
MIRRAVALE TRADING EST.
SELINAS
RM8
Warehouse
Chadwell Heath
STATION
Superstore
Goodmayes
GOODMAYES RETAIL PARK
Play. Fields
Mayfield Sch.
Mayfield Leisure Centre
KINFAUNS
GOODMAYES RD.
CHESTER RD.
SPENCER RD.
WESTWOOD
BLYTHSWOOD
KINGSWOOD
ATHOLL
PERCY ROAD
Prim. Sch.
Play. Fld.
THACKERAY
Rec. Grd.
Works
GLENDALE
LYMINGTON
CHADWELL HEATH IND. PARK
KEMP
CLARIDGE
Rec. Grd.

55
F
G
H
J
K
Cold Blow Farm
B174
ROAD
HOG HILL RD.
COLLIER ROW
B1459
Gobions Farm
COLLIER ROW
RISE PARK
RM5
RM1
RM7
Mawney
Rollerbowl Laserquest
The City Pavilion
Whites Farm
Football Grd.
Works
NORTHGATE INDUSTRIAL PARK
Crownfield Jun. & Inf. Schs.
King Georges Field
MAWNEY PARK
Warehouse
HUBBINET IND. EST.
EASTERN AV. RETAIL PK.
Bus Depot
Comm. Cen.
Moat
Warren Farm
MOBY DICK
Moby Golf
Driving Range
Golf Kingdom
Warren Sports Centre
Warren Jun. Sch.
Playing Field
Golf Course
Crown Farm
Crown Cottages
Sports Ground
ART Cen.
Cottons Park
Tennis Cts
Romford Greyhound Stadium
St. Edward's C of E Sch.
Westlands Playing Field
West Ham FC Training Grd.
Crowlands
Works
Jutsums Rec. Grd.
Gas Works
ROMFORD
Nuffield Health Fitness Cen.
Namco Funscape
Helipad
Oldchurch Park
Romford Cemetery
Crowlands Sports Ground
RUSH GREEN
CROWLANDS HEATH GOLF COURSE
Club House
Football Ground
Fords Sports Ground
BEACONTREE HEATH
Robert Clack Leisure Cen.
Robert Clack Sch. (Upper Site)
All Saints Cath. Sch.
Superstore
73
EASTERN AVENUE A12
NORTH STREET A125
ST. EDWARDS WAY
WATERLOO RD.
LONDON ROAD
A118
WHALEBONE LANE A1112
CROW LANE
RUSH GREEN ROAD A124
HAVERING ROAD
MAWNEY ROAD
HAINAULT ROAD
MARKS ROAD
B175
1
2
3
4
5
6
7

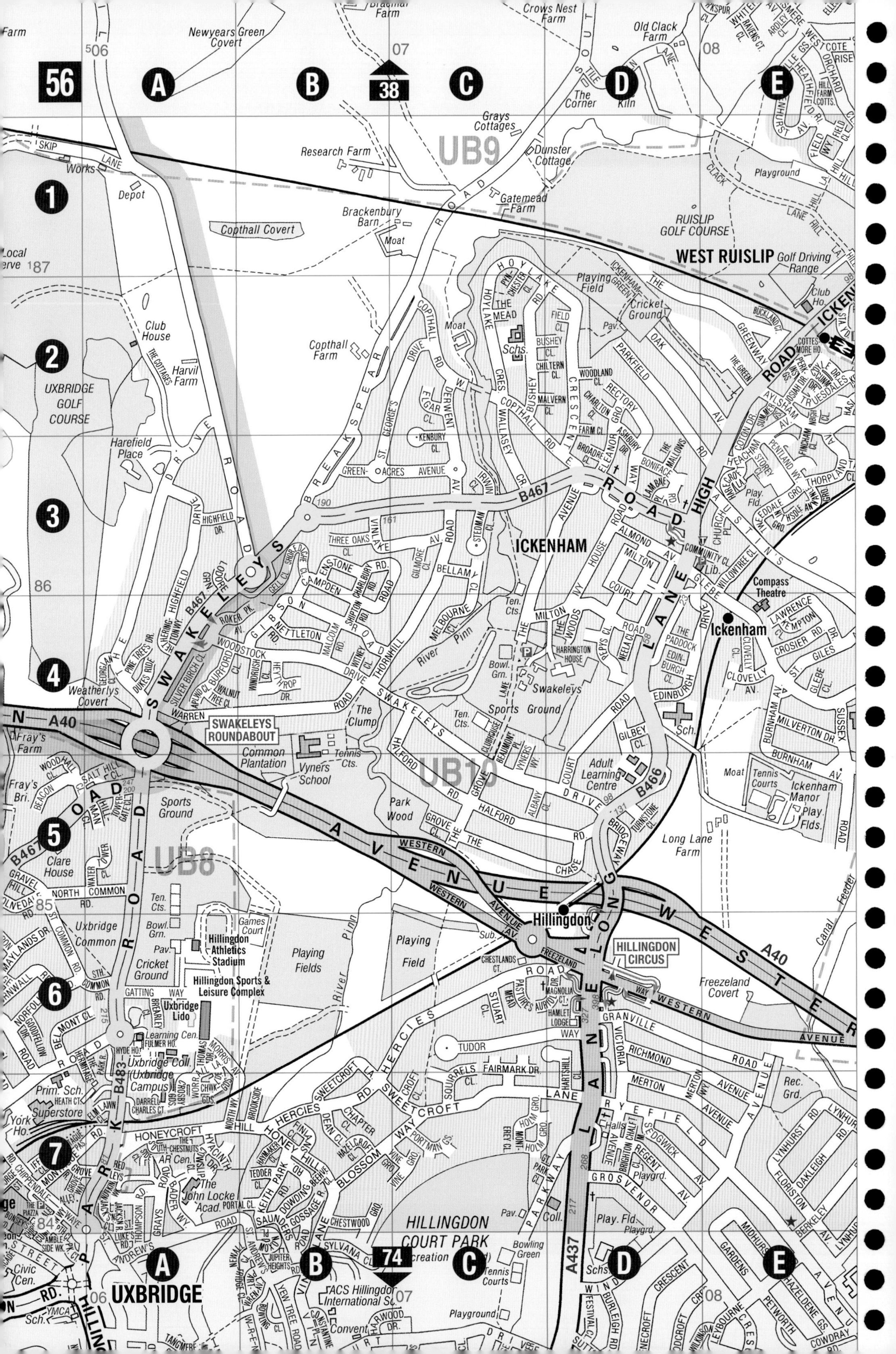

56
A
B
C
D
E
38
74
1
2
3
4
5
6
7
UB9
UB10
UB8
Newyears Green Covert
Crows Nest Farm
Old Clack Farm
The Corner
Kiln
Grays Cottages
Research Farm
Dunster Cottage
Gatemead Farm
Brackenbury Barn
Moat
Copthall Covert
Works
Depot
Club House
Harvil Farm
UXBRIDGE GOLF COURSE
Harefield Place
Copthall Farm
RUISLIP GOLF COURSE
WEST RUISLIP
Golf Driving Range
Playground
Playing Field
Cricket Ground
Pav.
Schs.
THE MEAD
HOYLAKE
BREAKSPEAR ROAD
COPTHALL RD. W.
DERWENT AV.
GREEN-ACRES AVENUE
KENBURY CL.
ELGAR CL.
WALLASEY CR.
CRESCENT
BUSHEY RD.
CHILTERN CL.
MALVERN CL.
WOODLAND CL.
RECTORY
CHARLTON
ASHBURY DR.
BROADRE CL.
ELEANOR GRO.
BONIFACE RD.
THE MALLOWS
PARKFIELD AV.
GREENWAY
THE GREEN
OAK AV.
ICKENHAM ROAD
HIGH ROAD
B467
ROAD
ICKENHAM
SWAKELEYS ROAD
HIGHFIELD DR.
DRIVE ROAD
THREE OAKS CL.
VINLAKE AV.
GILMORE RD.
BELLAMY CL.
STEDMAN CL.
MELBOURNE AV.
CAMPDEN RD.
ENSTONE RD.
CHARLBURY RD.
SHIPTON CL.
NETTLETON RD.
GIBSON RD.
MALCOLM RD.
THORNHILL
ROKER PK. AV.
WOODSTOCK DRIVE
BURFORD CL.
HEYTHROP DR.
WINDRUSH CL.
WITNEY CL.
SILVER BIRCH CL.
WALNUT TREE CL.
PINE TREES DR.
DUKE'S RIDE
GEORGIAN
Weatherlys Covert
WARREN ROAD
SWAKELEYS ROUNDABOUT
A40
Fray's Farm
Fray's Bri.
Common Plantation
Vyners School
Tennis Cts.
The Clump
River Pinn
Ten. Cts.
Bowl. Grn.
Swakeleys
HARRINGTON HOUSE
Sports Ground
THE MILTON WOODS
MILTON COURT
ALMOND AV.
PEPYS CL.
NEELA CL.
COMMUNITY CL.
Lib.
GLEBE AV.
WILLOWTREE CL.
Compass Theatre
Ickenham
LAWRENCE
KEMPTON
CROSIER RD.
ST. GILES
CLOVELLY AV.
EDINBURGH DR.
THE PADDOCK
Sch.
BURNHAM AV.
MILVERTON DR.
SUSSEX
Moat
Tennis Courts
Ickenham Manor
Play. Flds.
Long Lane Farm
GILBEY CL.
Adult Learning Centre
COURT DRIVE
ALBANY CL.
HALFORD RD.
GROVE
THE GROVE
CLUBHOUSE
VYNERS WY.
BEAUMONT PL.
Park Wood
B466
BRIDGEWAY
TURNSTONE CL.
THE CHASE
LONG LANE
AVENUE
WESTERN AVENUE
WESTERN AVENUE
Hillingdon
HILLINGDON CIRCUS
Sub.
FREEZELAND WAY
Freezeland Covert
Canal Feeder
Sports Ground
Clare House
B467
WATER TOWER CL.
TOWER GATE CL.
WOODHALL CL.
SALT HILL CL.
BEACON
GRAVEL HILL
NORTH COMMON RD.
Uxbridge Common
Hillingdon Athletics Stadium
Games Court
Cricket Ground
Hillingdon Sports & Leisure Complex
Uxbridge Lido
Playing Fields
Playing Field
MAYLANDS DR.
COMMON RD.
STH. COMMON RD.
GATTING WAY
BREARLEY
NORFOLK
GOODFELLOW
BELMONT CL.
Learning Cen.
FULMER HO.
HYDE HO.
THOMAS
MORRIS
Uxbridge Coll. (Uxbridge Campus)
CROSBY
DARRELL CHARLES CT.
Prim. Sch.
HEATH CT.
Superstore
York Ho.
B483
PARK ROAD
CHESTLANDS CT.
STUART CL.
MEAD
PASTURES
MAGNOLIA CT.
HAMLET LODGE
GRANVILLE
VICTORIA
RICHMOND ROAD
MERTON AVENUE
TUDOR WAY
FAIRMARK DR.
SQUIRRELS CL.
HERCIES ROAD
SWEETCROFT LA.
SWEETCROFT
CHAPTER CL.
HONEYCROFT HILL
BROOKSIDE
NORTH WY.
HYACINTH
BLOSSOM WAY
PORTMAN GS.
HARTSHILL CL.
LANE
HOLM GRO.
RYEFIELD AV.
SEDGWICK
BRIGHTON
REGENT AV.
GROSVENOR AV.
Playgrd.
Halls
The John Locke Acad.
AR Cen.
BADER WY.
THOMPSON RD.
GRAYS ROAD
ST. ANDREW'S
KEITH PARK RD.
DOWDING
GOSSAGE RD.
SAUNDERS
CHESTWOOD GRO.
SYLVANA CL.
HILLINGDON COURT PARK
Pav.
Coll.
Play. Fld.
Playgrd.
Bowling Green
Tennis Courts
Playground
Schs.
A437
PARKWAY
WINDSOR
CRESCENT
MIDHURST
GARDENS
BERKELEY AV.
AVENUE
HAZELDENE GS.
PETWORTH
COWDRAY
LYNHURST RD.
OAKLEIGH
FLORISTON
Rec. Grd.
ACS Hillingdon International Sc.
Convent
UXBRIDGE
Civic Cen.
YMCA
Sch.
RD.
06
07
08
187
86
85
84

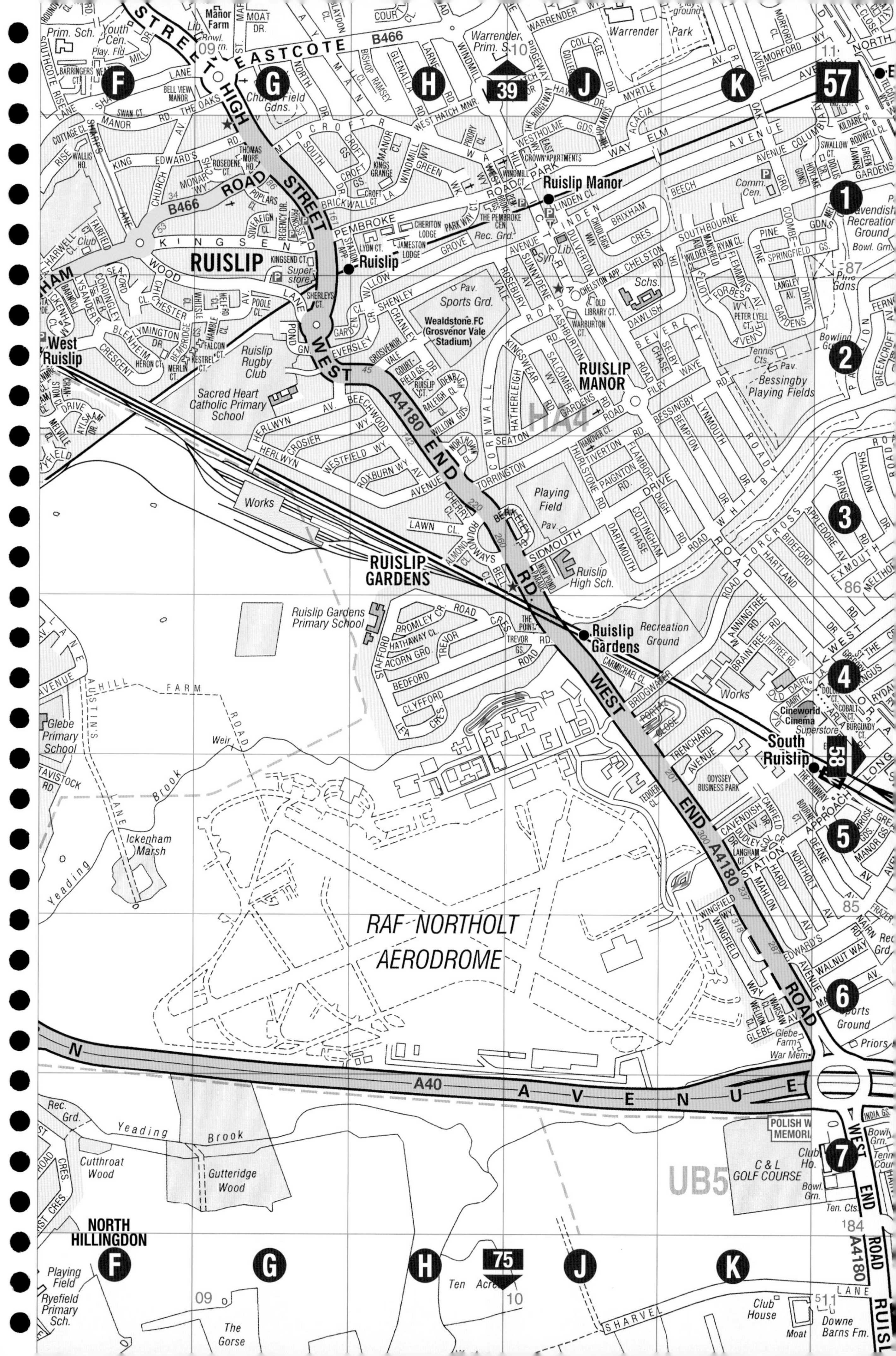

RUISLIP
Ruislip Manor
Ruislip
West Ruislip
RUISLIP MANOR
RUISLIP GARDENS
Ruislip Gardens
South Ruislip
RAF NORTHOLT AERODROME
NORTH HILLINGDON
HA4
UB5
EASTCOTE
HIGH STREET
WEST END ROAD
A4180
B466
A40
AVENUE
WHITBY ROAD
VICTORIA ROAD
KINGSEND
Wealdstone FC (Grosvenor Vale Stadium)
Sports Grd.
Ruislip Rugby Club
Sacred Heart Catholic Primary School
Ruislip Gardens Primary School
Ruislip High Sch.
Playing Field
Recreation Ground
Bessingby Playing Fields
Cavendish Recreation Ground
Works
Cineworld Cinema
Superstore
Odyssey Business Park
Glebe Primary School
Ickenham Marsh
Yeading Brook
Cutthroat Wood
Gutteridge Wood
C & L Golf Course
Polish War Memorial
Ryefield Primary Sch.
The Gorse
Ten Acre
Downe Barns Fm.
Warrender Park
Warrender Prim. S.
Manor Farm
39
57
58
75
F
G
H
J
K
1
2
3
4
5
6
7

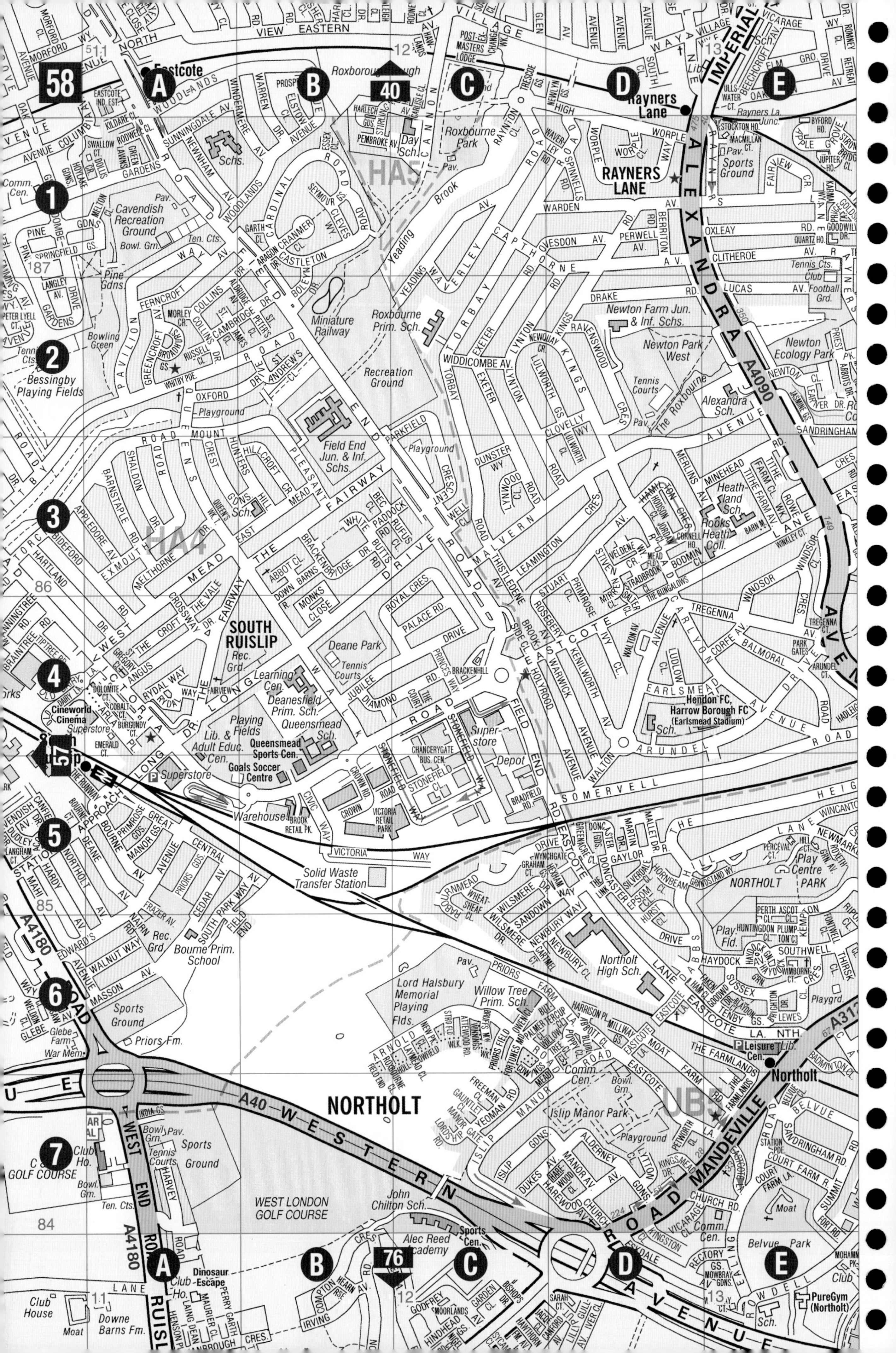

58
40
57
76
Eastcote
Rayners Lane
RAYNERS LANE
SOUTH RUISLIP
NORTHOLT
Northolt
HA5
HA4
UB5
Cavendish Recreation Ground
Roxbourne Park
Miniature Railway
Recreation Ground
Field End Jun. & Inf. Schs.
Roxbourne Prim. Sch.
Newton Farm Jun. & Inf. Schs.
Newton Park West
Newton Ecology Park
Alexandra Sch.
Heathland Sch.
Rooks Heath Coll.
Deane Park
Deanesfield Prim. Sch.
Queensmead Sch.
Queensmead Sports Cen.
Goals Soccer Centre
Cineworld Cinema
Hendon FC, Harrow Borough FC (Earlsmead Stadium)
Northolt High Sch.
Willow Tree Prim. Sch.
Lord Halsbury Memorial Playing Flds.
Islip Manor Park
Bourne Prim. School
Solid Waste Transfer Station
Victoria Retail Park
Brook Retail Pk.
Northolt Park
West London Golf Course
John Chilton Sch.
Alec Reed Academy
Belvue Park
PureGym (Northolt)
Dinosaur Escape
Bessingby Playing Fields
Pine Gdns.
Priors Fm.
Downe Barns Fm.
A4090
A4180
A40 WESTERN AVENUE
ALEXANDRA AVENUE
MANDEVILLE ROAD
VICTORIA ROAD
EASTCOTE ROAD
FIELD END ROAD
LONG DRIVE
WEST END ROAD

WEST HARROW
HARROW
59
41
F
G
H
J
K
14
15
16
Harrow Hill Golf Course
Harrow School Playing Fields
Whitmore High Sch.
Cricket Ground
Harrow School
The Grove Open Space
Miniature Rifle Range
Sports Cen.
Tennis Courts
Harrow Sch.
Running Track
Games Court
HARROW ON THE HILL
School Lake
Harrow Sch. Golf Course
Har. School Farm
HA1
HA2
HA0
UB6
ROXETH
Grange Prim. Sch.
Superstore
Cricket Ground
YMCA
HARROW CYGNET HOSPITAL
Kennet End
Burial Ground
THE CLEMENTINE CHURCHILL BMI HOSPITAL
BMI UCC
St. George's Prim. Sch.
South Harrow
Orley Farm Sch.
Playing Fld.
Toll Gate
Bowling Green
Roxeth Rec. Grd.
Tennis Courts
SOUTH HARROW
Welldon Park Inf. Sch.
Harrow Ckt. Club
Playing Fields
Sudbury Hill Harrow
Sudbury Hill Play. Flds.
Sudbury Hill
ALEXANDRA PARK
Northolt Pk.
Rec. Grd.
David Lloyd Leisure
Ealing Northern Sports Centre
KELLOGG TOWER
Wood End
Prim. Sch.
Academy
Inf. Sch.
Liby.
WHITTON
WEST WHITTON AVENUE A4090
A4090
A312
A4127
A4005
LOWER RD.
BESSBOROUGH RD.
SUDBURY HILL
SUDBURY COURT
NORTHOLT ROAD
HORSENDEN LANE NORTH
Greenford Green
Schools
Bowling Green
Pavilion
Factory
BERKELEY FIELDS
Horsenden Hill Rec. Grd.
Nature Reserve
Radio Station
Warehouses
Works
GRAND UNION CANAL
Lyon's Dock
Youth & Comm. Cen.
GREENFORD INDUSTRIAL ESTATE
Depot
Wks.
Mosque
Greenford
77
60
Sports Ground
Oldfield Rec. Grd.
Sorting Office
Perivale Wood Local Nature Reserve
Comm. Centre
1
2
3
4
5
6
7

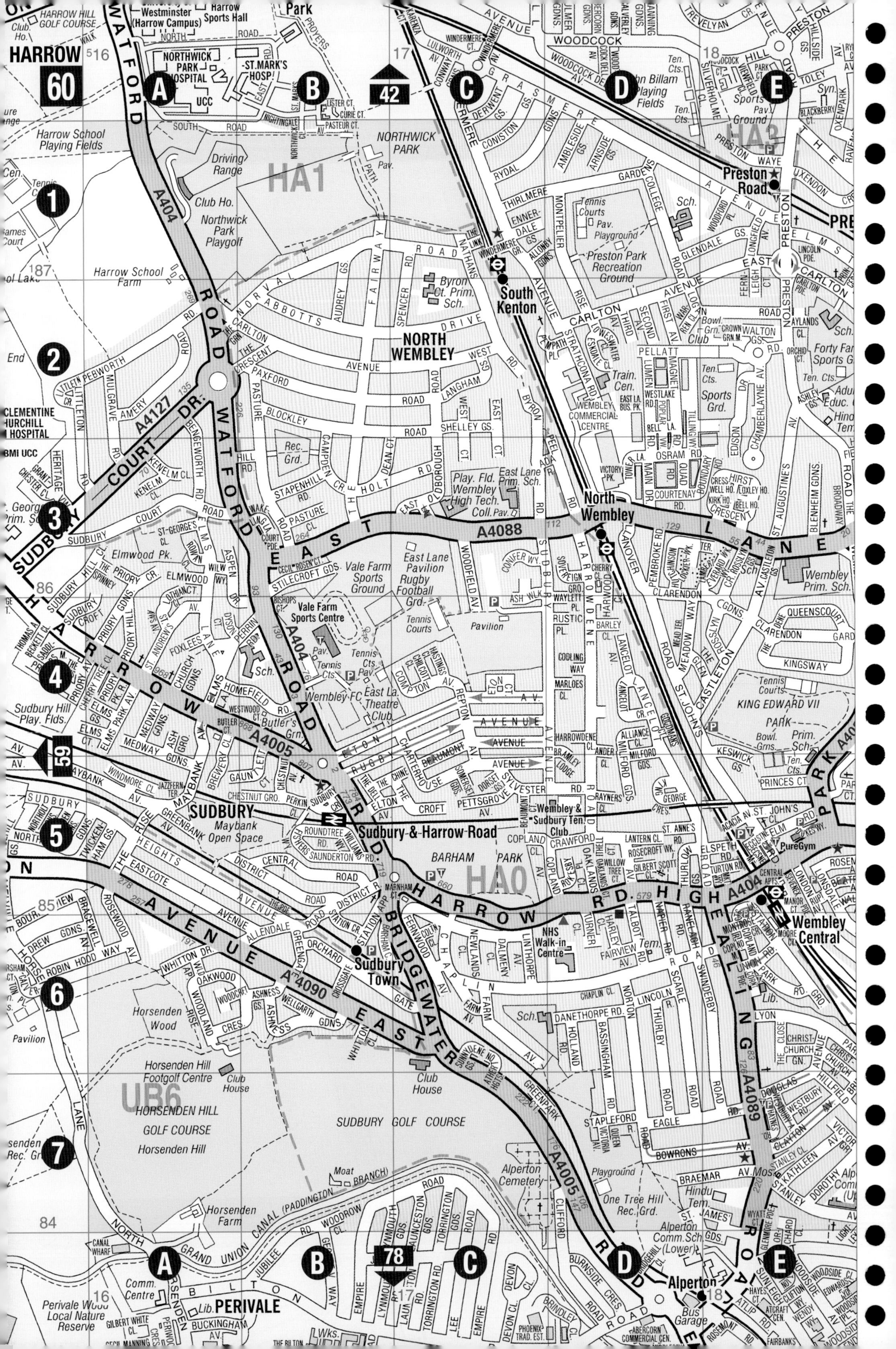

HARROW
60
42
59
78
A
B
C
D
E
1
2
3
4
5
6
7
16
17
18
187
86
85
84
HA1
HA3
HA0
UB6
Westminster (Harrow Campus)
Harrow Sports Hall
Northwick Park Hospital
St. Mark's Hosp.
UCC
Harrow Hill Golf Course
Harrow School Playing Fields
Northwick Park
Driving Range
Club Ho.
Northwick Park Playgolf
Harrow School Farm
Clementine Churchill Hospital
BMI UCC
Watford Road
A404
A4127
Court Dr.
Sudbury Court Road
Harrow Road
A4005
North Wembley
South Kenton
Preston Road
Woodcock Hill
John Billam Playing Fields
Preston Park Recreation Ground
Byron Ct. Prim. Sch.
East Lane
A4088
North Wembley
Vale Farm Sports Ground
Vale Farm Sports Centre
East Lane Pavilion Rugby Football Grd.
Wembley Commercial Centre
Sports Grd.
Forty Farm Sports Grd.
Wembley Prim. Sch.
King Edward VII Park
Sudbury
Maybank Open Space
Sudbury & Harrow Road
Barham Park
Wembley & Sudbury Ten. Club
Sudbury Hill Play. Flds.
Elmwood Pk.
Sudbury Town
Bridgewater Rd.
Harrow Rd.
High Road
Ealing Road
A4089
Wembley Central
PureGym
NHS Walk-in Centre
Whitton Avenue East
A4090
Horsenden Wood
Horsenden Hill Footgolf Centre
Horsenden Hill Golf Course
Horsenden Hill
Horsenden Farm
Sudbury Golf Course
Club House
Alperton Cemetery
One Tree Hill Rec. Grd.
Hindu Tem.
Alperton Comm. Sch. (Lower)
Alperton
Bus Garage
Grand Union Canal (Paddington Branch)
Perivale
Perivale Wood Local Nature Reserve
Comm. Centre
Canal Wharf
Abercorn Commercial Cen.
Phoenix Trad. Est.

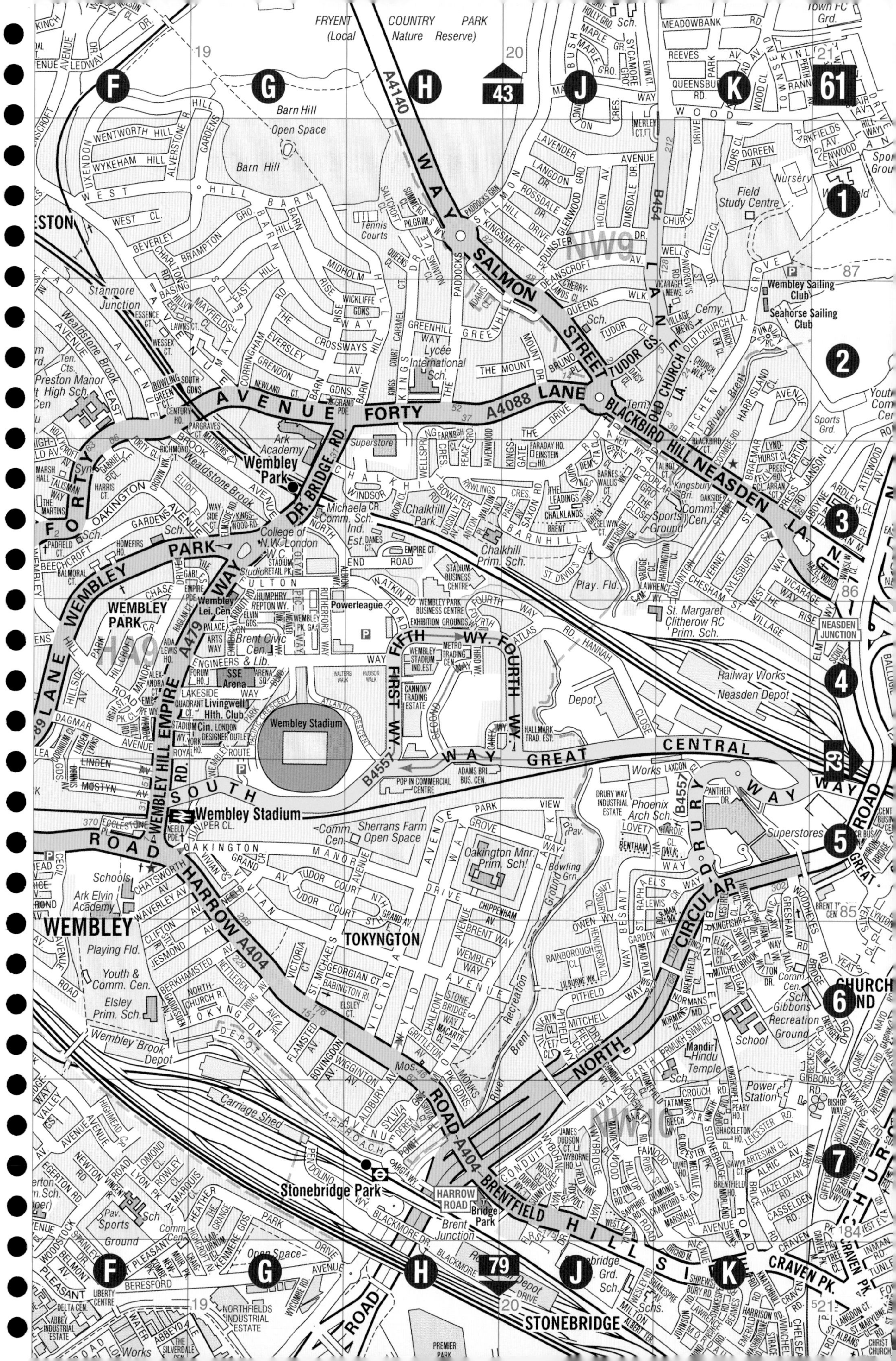

FRYENT COUNTRY PARK
(Local Nature Reserve)
43
61
62
79
F
G
H
J
K
1
2
3
4
5
6
7
19
20
21
84
85
86
87
Barn Hill
Open Space
Barn Hill
A4140
WAY
SALMON STREET
NW9
B454
LANE
Field Study Centre
Nursery
Wembley Sailing Club
Seahorse Sailing Club
Cemy.
Lycée International Sch.
THE MOUNT
A4088
FORTY AVENUE
LANE
BLACKBIRD HILL
NEASDEN LA.
OLD CHURCH LA.
Stanmore Junction
Preston Manor High Sch.
Wembley Park
Ark Academy
Superstore
Chalkhill Park
Michaela Comm. Sch.
Ind. Est.
College of N.W. London
Chalkhill Prim. Sch.
Kingsbury Comm. Cen.
Sports Ground
Play. Fld.
St. Margaret Clitherow RC Prim. Sch.
NEASDEN JUNCTION
Railway Works
Neasden Depot
WEMBLEY PARK
HA9
Wembley Lei. Cen.
Brent Civic Cen.
Engineers & Lib.
SSE Arena
Livingwell Hlth. Club
LONDON DESIGNER OUTLET
Powerleague
WEMBLEY PARK BUSINESS CENTRE
EXHIBITION GROUNDS
Wembley Stadium
WEMBLEY LANE
EMPIRE WAY
A479
B4557
GREAT CENTRAL WAY
SOUTH WAY
Depot
HALLMARK TRAD. EST.
Works
DRURY WAY INDUSTRIAL ESTATE
Phoenix Arch Sch.
Superstores
Wembley Stadium
HARROW ROAD
A404
Sherrans Farm Open Space
Oakington Mnr. Prim. Sch.
Bowling Grn
Recreation Ground
River Brent
TOKYNGTON
Schools
Ark Elvin Academy
WEMBLEY
Playing Fld.
Youth & Comm. Cen.
Elsley Prim. Sch.
Wembley Brook Depot
Carriage Shed
NORTH CIRCULAR ROAD
BRENTFIELD
NW10
Mandir Hindu Temple
School
Gibbons Recreation Ground
CHURCH END
Power Station
Stonebridge Park
Brent Junction
HARROW ROAD
Bridge Park
HILLSIDE
Stonebridge Grd. Sch.
Schs.
STONEBRIDGE
Sports Ground
Open Space
NORTHFIELDS INDUSTRIAL ESTATE
ABBEY INDUSTRIAL ESTATE
Works
PREMIER PARK
CRAVEN PK.

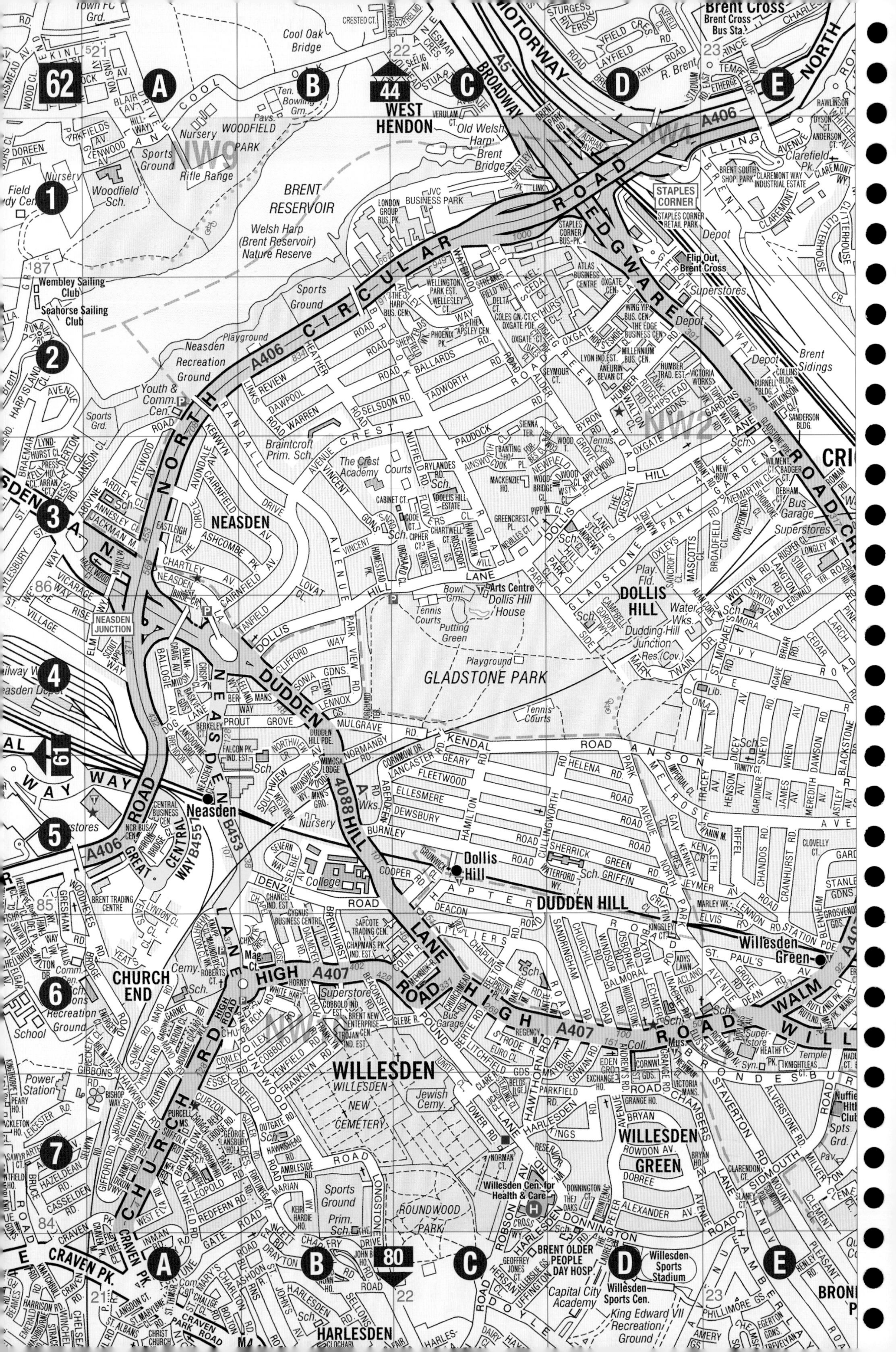
62
44
61
80
A
B
C
D
E
1
2
3
4
5
6
7
WEST HENDON
Cool Oak Bridge
WOODFIELD PARK
NW9
Sports Ground
Nursery
Rifle Range
Woodfield Sch.
BRENT RESERVOIR
Welsh Harp (Brent Reservoir) Nature Reserve
Wembley Sailing Club
Seahorse Sailing Club
Neasden Recreation Ground
Playground
Youth & Comm. Cen.
Sports Grd.
Old Welsh Harp
Brent Bridge
LONDON GROUP BUS. PK.
JVC BUSINESS PARK
NORTH CIRCULAR ROAD
A406
EDGWARE ROAD
MOTORWAY
A5
BROADWAY
Brent Cross
Brent Cross Bus Sta.
R. Brent
STAPLES CORNER
STAPLES CORNER RETAIL PARK
STAPLES CORNER BUS. PK.
BRENT SOUTH SHOP. PARK
CLAREMONT WAY INDUSTRIAL ESTATE
Clarefield Pk.
Depot
Flip Out, Brent Cross
Superstores
Brent Sidings
NW2
WELLINGTON PARK EST.
THE HARP BUS. CEN.
PHOENIX PK.
THE APSLEY CEN.
ATLAS BUSINESS CENTRE
OXGATE CEN.
WING YIP BUS. CEN.
THE EDGE BUSINESS CEN.
MILLENNIUM BUS. CEN.
LYON IND. EST.
HUMBER TRAD. EST.
VICTORIA WORKS
Braintcroft Prim. Sch.
The Crest Academy
Courts
DOLLIS HILL ESTATE
NEASDEN
NEASDEN JUNCTION
Neasden Depot
Neasden
DOLLIS HILL
Dudding Hill Junction
Water Wks.
Play. Fld.
Arts Centre
Dollis Hill House
Tennis Courts
Putting Green
Playground
GLADSTONE PARK
DUDDEN HILL
DUDDEN HILL LANE
B4088
B4557
B453
FALCON PK. IND. EST.
Nursery
College
Dollis Hill
CHANCEL IND. EST.
CYGNUS BUSINESS CENTRE
SAPCOTE TRADING CEN.
CHAPMANS PK. IND. EST.
BRENT TRADING CENTRE
CENTRAL BUSINESS CEN.
CHURCH END
Cemy.
Mag. Ct.
HIGH ROAD
A407
Superstore
COBBOLD IND. EST.
BRENT NEW ENTERPRISE CEN.
TROJAN IND. EST.
NW10
WILLESDEN
WILLESDEN NEW CEMETERY
Jewish Cemy.
Power Station
Recreation Ground
School
Sports Ground
Prim. Sch.
ROUNDWOOD PARK
Willesden Cen. for Health & Care
BRENT OLDER PEOPLE DAY HOSP.
Capital City Academy
Willesden Sports Stadium
Willesden Sports Cen.
King Edward VII Recreation Ground
WILLESDEN GREEN
Willesden Green
Coll.
Mus.
Syn.
Temple
HARLESDEN
CRAVEN PK.
CHURCH RD
NEASDEN LANE
HIGH ROAD
ANSON ROAD
KENDAL ROAD
MULGRAVE RD.
DOLLIS HILL LANE
GLADSTONE PARK
OXGATE LANE
BRONDESBURY

NW11
NW3
NW6
HAMPSTEAD
Golders Green
GOLDERS HILL PARK
CHILD'S HILL
Fortune Green
WEST HAMPSTEAD
SOUTH HAMPSTEAD
BRONDESBURY
CRICKLEWOOD
Cricklewood
Kilburn
Brondesbury
Brondesbury Park
West Hampstead
West Hampstead Thameslink
Finchley Rd. & Frognal
Clitterhouse Recreation Ground
Basing Hill Park
Leg of Mutton Pond
West Heath
Jack Straw's Castle
Hampstead Cemetery
Sports Ground
Kilburn Grange Park
Paddington Old Cemetery
(Willesden Lane Cemetery)
HENDON WAY
FINCHLEY ROAD
NORTH END ROAD
CRICKLEWOOD BROADWAY
SHOOT UP HILL
KILBURN HIGH RD.
WILLESDEN LANE
CHICHELE RD.
A41
A5
A407
A598
A502
A4003
B510
B520
B509
B507
F
G
H
J
K
1
2
3
4
5
6
7
24
25
26
45
63
64
81

64
46
63
82
A
B
C
D
E
1
2
3
4
5
6
7
HAMPSTEAD HEATH
HAMPSTEAD
PARLIAMENT HILL
NW11
NW3
NW6
N6
Kenwood House
Caen Wood
KEN WOOD
Open Air Stage
Mount Tyndal
North Wood
Club House
Turners Wood
Bunkers Hill
Sandy Heath
The Spaniards
North End
The Hill
West Heath
Jack Straw's Castle
VALE OF HEALTH
East Heath
Sports Ground
Ladies Bathing Pond
Highgate Ponds
Men's Bathing Pond
Bathing Pond
Hampstead Ponds
Bowling Green
Nursery
Athlone House
Highgate School
Mallinson Sports Centre
HIGHGATE CEMETERY
Parliament Hill Fields
Hampstead Heath Educ. Centre
William Ellis Sch.
Parliament Hill School
Parliament Hill Fields Athletics Track
Lido
Gospel Oak
Hampstead Heath
Hampstead
Burgh Ho.
Keats Ho.
2 Willow Rd.
ROYAL FREE HOSPITAL
UCC
University College School
Camden Arts Cen.
Finchley Rd. & Frognal
Finchley Rd.
Freud Mus.
Sigmund Freud Statue
Hospice
Belsize Pk.
Swiss Cottage
SWISS COTTAGE
South Hampstead
SOUTH HAMPSTEAD
UCL Academy
Chalk Farm
PRIMROSE HILL
Reservoir (covered)
SPANIARDS ROAD
HAMPSTEAD LANE
NORTH END ROAD
HEATH ST.
FITZJOHN'S AVENUE
ROSSLYN HILL
HAVERSTOCK HILL
POND ST.
FLEET ROAD
MANSFIELD ROAD
MALDEN ROAD
FINCHLEY ROAD
ADELAIDE ROAD
AVENUE ROAD
CHALK FARM ROAD
A502
A41
B519
B518
B511
B509
B525
B517

F
G
H
J
K
65
47
83
66
1
2
3
4
5
6
7
29
30
31
Crouch Hill
HIGHGATE
HORNSEY ROAD
HORNSEY RISE
STROUD GREEN
Lauderdale House
WATERLOW PARK
Waterlow Park Cen.
Highgate Mental Health Centre
WHITTINGTON HOSPITAL
HIGHGATE CEMETERY
Archway
HOLLOWAY
Upper Holloway
UPPER HOLLOWAY
DARTMOUTH PARK
Elthorne Park
Whittington Park
Foxham Gdns.
Sports Grd.
HOLLOWAY
TUFNELL PARK
Tufnell Pk.
JUNCTION RD
BRECKNOCK RD
FORTESS RD
HIGHGATE RD
KENTISH TOWN
Kentish Town
02 Forum Kentish Town
KENTISH TOWN RD
CAMDEN RD
SEVEN SISTERS
Odeon Cinema
NAG'S HEAD
Sobell Leisure Cen.
Holloway Rd.
LOWER HOLLOWAY
CALEDONIAN RD
Caledonian Rd.
Caledonian Park
Islington Ten. Cen.
HMP PENTONVILLE
YORK WAY
CAMDEN PARK RD.
ST. PANCRAS WAY
Camden Rd.
Camden Town
CAMDEN TOWN
BARNSBURY
Caledonian Rd & Barnsbury
City Farm
Cally Pool & Gym
COPENHAGEN ST.
Finsbury Pk.
Park Theatre
University
A1
A1201
A400
A503
A5200
A5203
A103
B540
B519

66
48
65
84
A
B
C
D
E
1
2
3
4
5
6
7
FINSBURY PARK
Manor House
Reservoir (covered)
WEST RESERVOIR
West Reservoir Centre
The Castle Climbing Cen.
Sir Thomas Abney Prim. Sch.
Finsbury Park
Park Theatre
Rowans Tenpin
Interchange
BROWNSWOOD PARK
LORDSHIP PARK MANOR
STOKE NEWINGTON
Abney Park Cemetery (Local Nature Reserve)
CLISSOLD PARK
Clissold Ho.
Council Offices
Tennis Courts
Bowl. Grn.
Paddling Pool
Clissold Leisure Cen.
STOKE NEWINGTON CHURCH
Isledon Village
Gillespie Park Local Nature Res.
Arsenal
Ecology Cen.
Fitness First
Sobell Leisure Cen.
Ashburton Grove
Arsenal FC (Emirates Stadium)
Drayton Pk.
HIGHBURY
University
Holloway Rd.
Highbury Leis. Cen.
Highbury & Islington
HIGHBURY CNR.
City Farm
Paradise Park
Canonbury
CANONBURY
Dalston Kingsland
BALLS POND ROAD
KINGSLAND
The Cube
Butterfield Grn.
Essex Rd.
BARNSBURY
ISLINGTON
DE BEAUVOIR TOWN
Kingsland Basin
Barnard Park
Nuffield
SEVEN SISTERS ROAD
GREEN LANES
BLACKSTOCK ROAD
HIGHBURY PARK
HIGHBURY GROVE
ST. PAUL'S ROAD
CANONBURY RD.
UPPER STREET
LIVERPOOL ROAD
HOLLOWAY ROAD
NEWINGTON GRN. RD.
ALBION ROAD
SOUTHGATE ROAD
ESSEX ROAD
NEW NORTH RD.
A1201
A503
A105
A1199
A104
A1
B150
B104
B105
B102
A103
B515

49
67
68
85
F
G
H
J
K
1
2
3
4
5
6
7
34
35
36
CLAPTON
STAMFORD HILL
UPPER CLAPTON
Stoke Newington
NORTHWOLD RD.
SPRINGFIELD PARK
Springfield Marina
Walthamstow Marsh Nature Reserve
Coppermill Bridge
Horse Shoe Point
WALTHAMSTOW
E17
Clapton Junction
MARSHES
Leyton Marshes
Lea Valley Riding Centre
Playing Field
E10
Lee Valley Ice Centre
LEA BRIDGE
Lea Bridge
LEA BRIDGE RD.
North Millfields Recreation Ground
Middlesex Filter Beds Nature Reserve
LEA BRIDGE SOUTH MILL FIELDS
South Millfields Rec. Grd.
Clapton
E5
UPPER CLAPTON RD.
LOWER CLAPTON RD.
Rectory Road
RECTORY RD.
STOKE NEWINGTON HIGH ST.
SHACKLEWELL
LOWER CLAPTON
HACKNEY DOWNS
Stormont House Sch.
Mossbourne Community Academy
PEMBURY R.
CRICKETFIELD R.
AMHURST RD.
DALSTON LA.
Hackney Downs
Hackney Cen.
HOMERTON UNIVERSITY HOSP.
CITY & HACKNEY
HOMERTON HIGH ST.
Homerton
URSWICK RD.
LWR. CLAPTON R.
MORNING LA.
MARE STREET
GRAHAM RD.
DALSTON
Dalston Junc.
QUEENSBRIDGE RD.
HACKNEY
London Fields Lido
London Fields
LONDON FIELDS
E8
WICK RD.
CASSLAND RD.
WELL STREET COMMON
SOUTH HACKNEY
VICTORIA PARK
Victoria Fountain
Royal Gate East
Haggerston
Regent's Canal
Anton's Lock
KINGSLAND HIGH ST.
WELL ST.

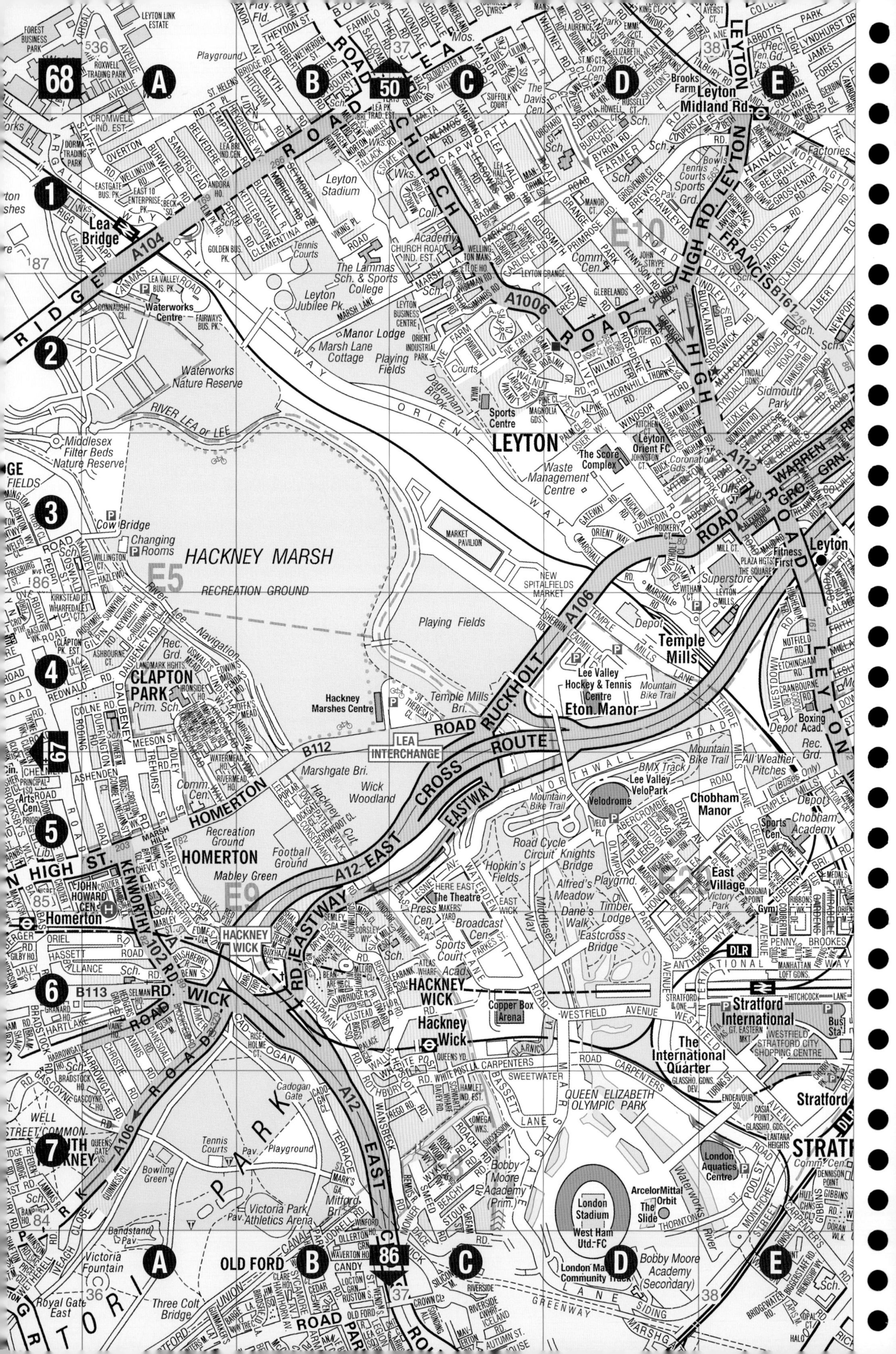

68
50
67
86
A
B
C
D
E
1
2
3
4
5
6
7
36
37
38
E10
E5
E9
LEYTON
HACKNEY MARSH
RECREATION GROUND
HOMERTON
HACKNEY WICK
CLAPTON PARK
OLD FORD
Lea Bridge
Leyton Midland Rd.
Leyton
Homerton
Hackney Wick
Stratford International
Stratford
LEA BRIDGE ROAD
A104
CHURCH ROAD
A1006
HIGH RD. LEYTON
A112
RUCKHOLT ROAD
A106
EAST CROSS ROUTE
A12
EASTWAY
HOMERTON HIGH ST.
B112
B113
B161
ORIENT WAY
LEA INTERCHANGE
Leyton Stadium
Leyton Jubilee Pk.
Leyton Orient FC
The Score Complex
Waterworks Nature Reserve
Waterworks Centre
Middlesex Filter Beds Nature Reserve
RIVER LEA or LEE
Hackney Marshes Centre
Lee Valley Hockey & Tennis Centre
Eton Manor
Temple Mills
NEW SPITALFIELDS MARKET
MARKET PAVILION
Velodrome
Lee Valley VeloPark
Chobham Manor
Chobham Academy
East Village
Copper Box Arena
The International Quarter
WESTFIELD STRATFORD CITY SHOPPING CENTRE
QUEEN ELIZABETH OLYMPIC PARK
London Stadium
West Ham Utd. FC
ArcelorMittal Orbit
The Slide
London Aquatics Centre
Bobby Moore Academy (Prim.)
Bobby Moore Academy (Secondary)
London Marathon Community Track
Victoria Park Athletics Arena
Victoria Fountain
VICTORIA PARK
Mabley Green
Wick Woodland
Hackney Cut
Marsh Lane Cottage
Manor Lodge
Playing Fields
Sports Centre
Waste Management Centre
Superstore
Fitness First
Mountain Bike Trail
BMX Track
Road Cycle Circuit
Knights Bridge
Alfred's Meadow
Dane's Walk
Timber Lodge
Eastcross Bridge
Hopkin's Fields
Here East
The Theatre
Press Cen.
Broadcast Cen.
Sports Court
Temple Mills Bri.
Marshgate Bri.
Cow Bridge
Changing Rooms
Mitford Bri.
Three Colt Bridge
Royal Gate East
Cadogan Gate
Bowling Green
Tennis Courts
Playground
JOHN HOWARD CEN.

69
70
87
51
F
G
H
J
K
1
2
3
4
5
6
7
39
40
41
84
85
86
87
Leytonstone
LEYTONSTONE
Leytonstone High Rd.
E11
E12
E15
E7
WANSTEAD GOLF COURSE
Bush Wood
Reservoir Wood
Shoulder of Mutton Pond
Sports Ground
The Basin (Fish Pond)
WANSTEAD FLATS
Playing Field
Horse Ride
St. Patrick's RC Cemetery
Langthorne Park
Cann Hall
West Ham Cemetery
Wanstead Pk.
Forest Gate
FOREST GATE
Maryland
Stratford New Town
Stratford High St.
WEST HAM PARK
WEST HAM
Football Ground
Netball Court
Playground
Football Pitch
Tennis Courts
Public Gardens
UPTON
Upton Park
GAINSBOROUGH RD.
CENTRE ROAD
WOODFORD ROAD
WOODGRANGE RD.
HALL ROAD
ALDERSBROOK RD.
DAMES ROAD
HARROW ROAD
CANN HALL ROAD
ROMFORD ROAD
UPTON LANE
GREEN STREET
PORTWAY
PLASHET ROAD
BROADWAY
WEST HAM LANE
GREAT EASTERN RD.
LEYTON RD.
CATHALL ROAD
GROVE GREEN ROAD
VICARAGE LANE
FOREST LANE
EARLHAM GROVE
CHOBHAM ROAD
WOODLANDS AVENUE
CAPEL ROAD
SEBERT ROAD
HAMPTON ROAD
OSBORNE ROAD
CLAREMONT ROAD
WINDSOR ROAD
BOLEYN ROAD
A114
A116
A118
A12
A112
A106
B161
B164
B165

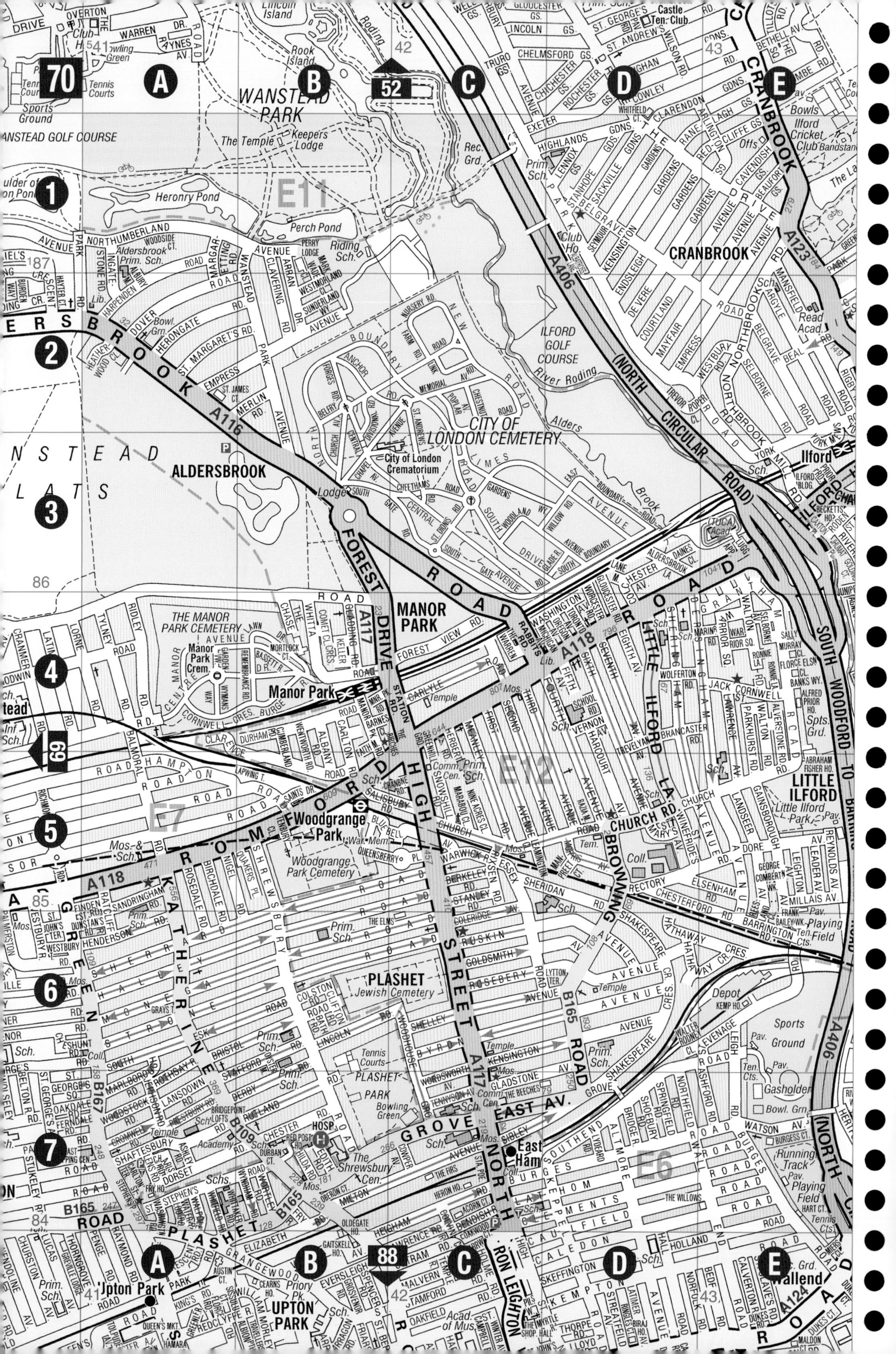
70
52
69
88
A
B
C
D
E
1
2
3
4
5
6
7
WANSTEAD PARK
WANSTEAD GOLF COURSE
The Temple
Keepers Lodge
Heronry Pond
Perch Pond
Rook Island
Lincoln Island
E11
ALDERSBROOK
WANSTEAD FLATS
ALDERSBROOK ROAD
A116
CITY OF LONDON CEMETERY
City of London Crematorium
ILFORD GOLF COURSE
River Roding
Alders Brook
CRANBROOK
CRANBROOK ROAD
A123
NORTH CIRCULAR ROAD
A406
Ilford
MANOR PARK
Manor Park
THE MANOR PARK CEMETERY
Manor Park Crem.
FOREST DRIVE
A117
ROMFORD ROAD
A118
E12
E7
Woodgrange Park
Woodgrange Park Cemetery
HIGH STREET NORTH
LITTLE ILFORD LA.
LITTLE ILFORD
Little Ilford Park
CHURCH RD.
BROWNING ROAD
B165
PLASHET
Jewish Cemetery
PLASHET PARK
KATHERINE ROAD
B109
GREEN STREET
B167
PLASHET ROAD
East Ham
E6
Sports Ground
Gasholder
Running Track
Playing Field
SOUTH WOODFORD TO BARKING RELIEF ROAD
Upton Park
UPTON PARK
Wallend
A124
RON LEIGHTON WAY
The Shrewsbury Cen.

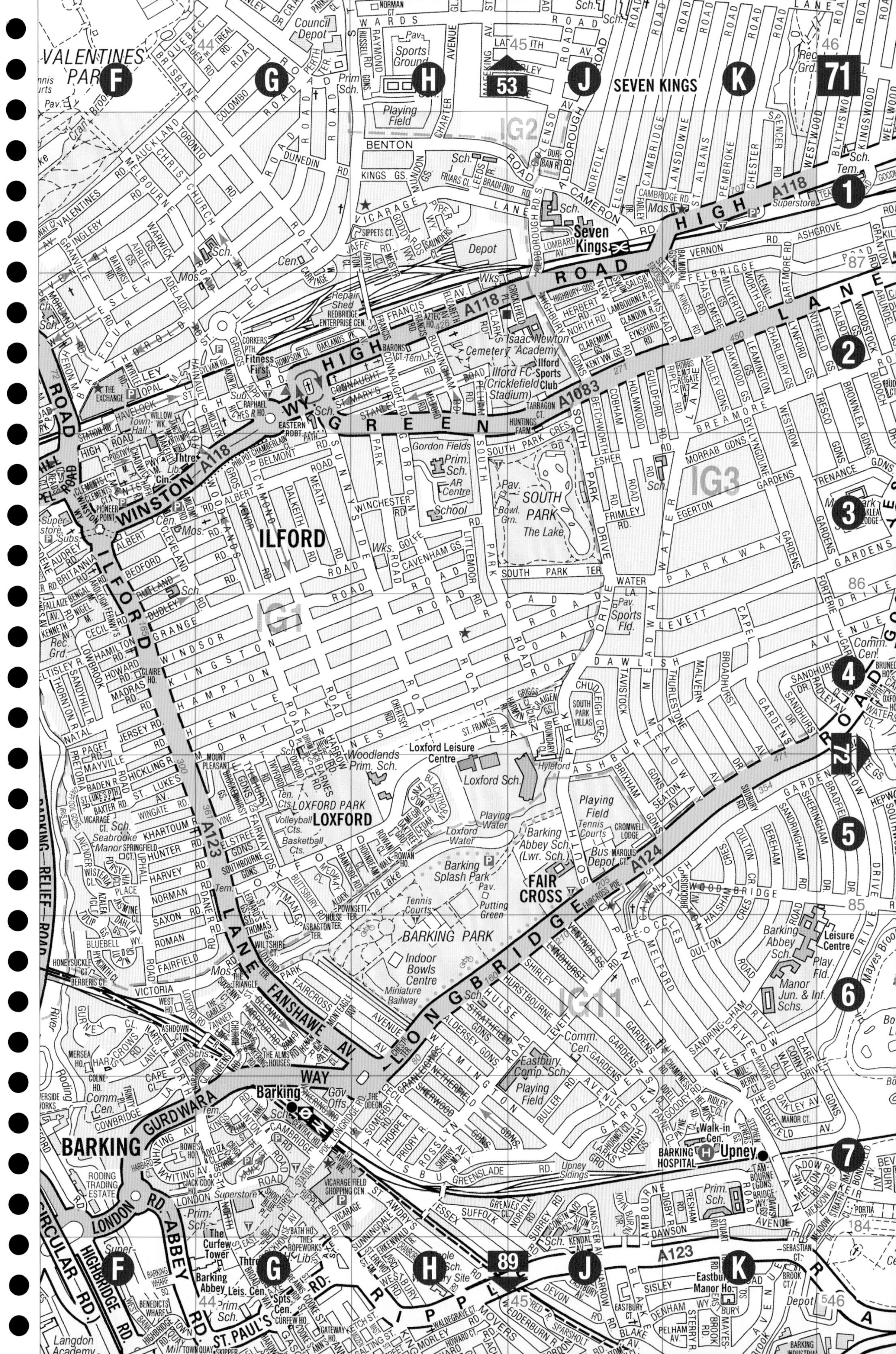

VALENTINES PARK
F
G
H
J
K
53
71
72
89
SEVEN KINGS
IG2
IG1
IG3
IG11
ILFORD
LOXFORD
FAIR CROSS
BARKING
Seven Kings
Barking
Upney
HIGH ROAD A118
GREEN LANE A1083
WINSTON WY. A118
ILFORD LANE A123
FANSHAWE AV.
LONGBRIDGE RD. A124
GURDWARA WAY
RIPPLE RD.
A123
HIGH WY.
SOUTH PARK
The Lake
SOUTH PARK DRIVE
LOXFORD PARK
BARKING PARK
Barking Splash Park
Indoor Bowls Centre
Miniature Railway
Loxford Leisure Centre
Loxford Sch.
Woodlands Prim. Sch.
Isaac Newton Academy
Ilford FC (Cricklefield Stadium)
Ilford Sports Club
Cemetery
Depot
Sports Ground
Playing Field
Council Depot
Barking Abbey Sch. (Lwr. Sch.)
Barking Abbey Sch.
Leisure Centre
Manor Jun. & Inf. Schs.
Eastbury Comp. Sch.
BARKING HOSPITAL
Walk-in Cen.
Eastbury Manor Ho.
RODING TRADING ESTATE
The Curfew Tower
Barking Abbey
VICARAGE FIELD SHOPPING CEN.
Fitness First
THE EXCHANGE
PIONEER POINT
Town Hall
BARKING RELIEF ROAD
HIGHBRIDGE RD.
CIRCULAR RD.
ABBEY RD.
LONDON RD.
River Roding
Langdon Academy
1
2
3
4
5
6
7
44
45
46
84
85
86
87
184

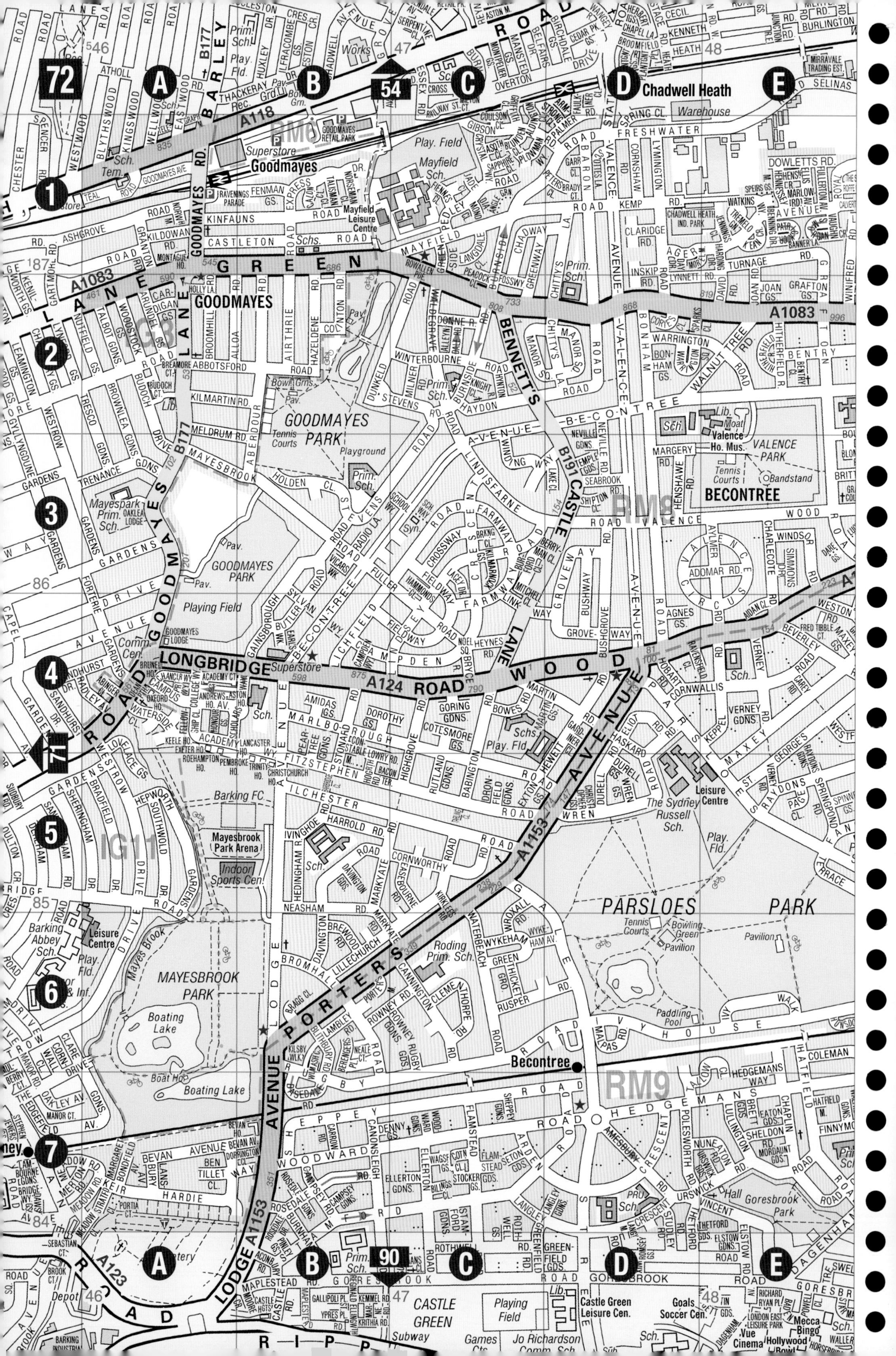
72
54
71
90
A
B
C
D
E
1
2
3
4
5
6
7
Chadwell Heath
Goodmayes
GOODMAYES
Superstore
GOODMAYES RETAIL PARK
RM6
IG3
IG11
RM8
RM9
A118
A1083
A124
A1153
A123
B177
B191
HIGH ROAD
BARLEY LANE
GOODMAYES RD.
GOODMAYES LANE
GREEN LANE
GOODMAYES ROAD
LONGBRIDGE ROAD
WOOD LANE
CASTLE LANE
BENNETT'S CASTLE LANE
BECONTREE AVENUE
PORTERS AVENUE
LODGE AVENUE
VALENCE AVENUE
VALENCE WOOD ROAD
PARSLOES AVENUE
FRESHWATER ROAD
KEMP RD.
TURNAGE RD.
MAYESBROOK ROAD
MARLBOROUGH RD.
FITZSTEPHEN RD.
ILCHESTER RD.
HEATHWAY
GORESBROOK ROAD
HEDGEMANS ROAD
IVYHOUSE ROAD
WOODWARD RD.
BEVAN AVENUE
CASTLETON ROAD
KINFAUNS
FENMAN GS.
Mayfield Sch.
Mayfield Leisure Centre
Play. Field
Warehouse
MIRRAVALE TRADING EST.
CHADWELL HEATH IND. PARK
Chitty's Prim. Sch.
GOODMAYES PARK
Tennis Courts
Playground
Prim. Sch.
Pav.
Playing Field
Mayespark Prim. Sch.
Oaklea Lodge
Barking FC.
Mayesbrook Park Arena
Indoor Sports Cen.
Barking Abbey Sch.
Leisure Centre
Play. Fld.
MAYESBROOK PARK
Mayes Brook
Boating Lake
Boat Ho.
Roding Prim. Sch.
PARSLOES PARK
Bowling Green
Pavilion
Paddling Pool
Becontree
VALENCE PARK
Valence Ho. Mus.
Moat
Lib.
Bandstand
BECONTREE
The Sydney Russell Sch.
Leisure Centre
Schs.
Sch.
Comm. Cen.
Syn.
Cemetery
CASTLE GREEN
Playing Field
Castle Green Leisure Cen.
Goals Soccer Cen.
Jo Richardson Comm. Sch.
Subway
Games Cts.
Goresbrook Park
Hall
Vue Cinema
Hollywood Bowl
Mecca Bingo
LONDON EAST LEISURE PARK
Depot
BARKING INDUSTRIAL
RIPPLE ROAD
46
47
48
84
85
86
187

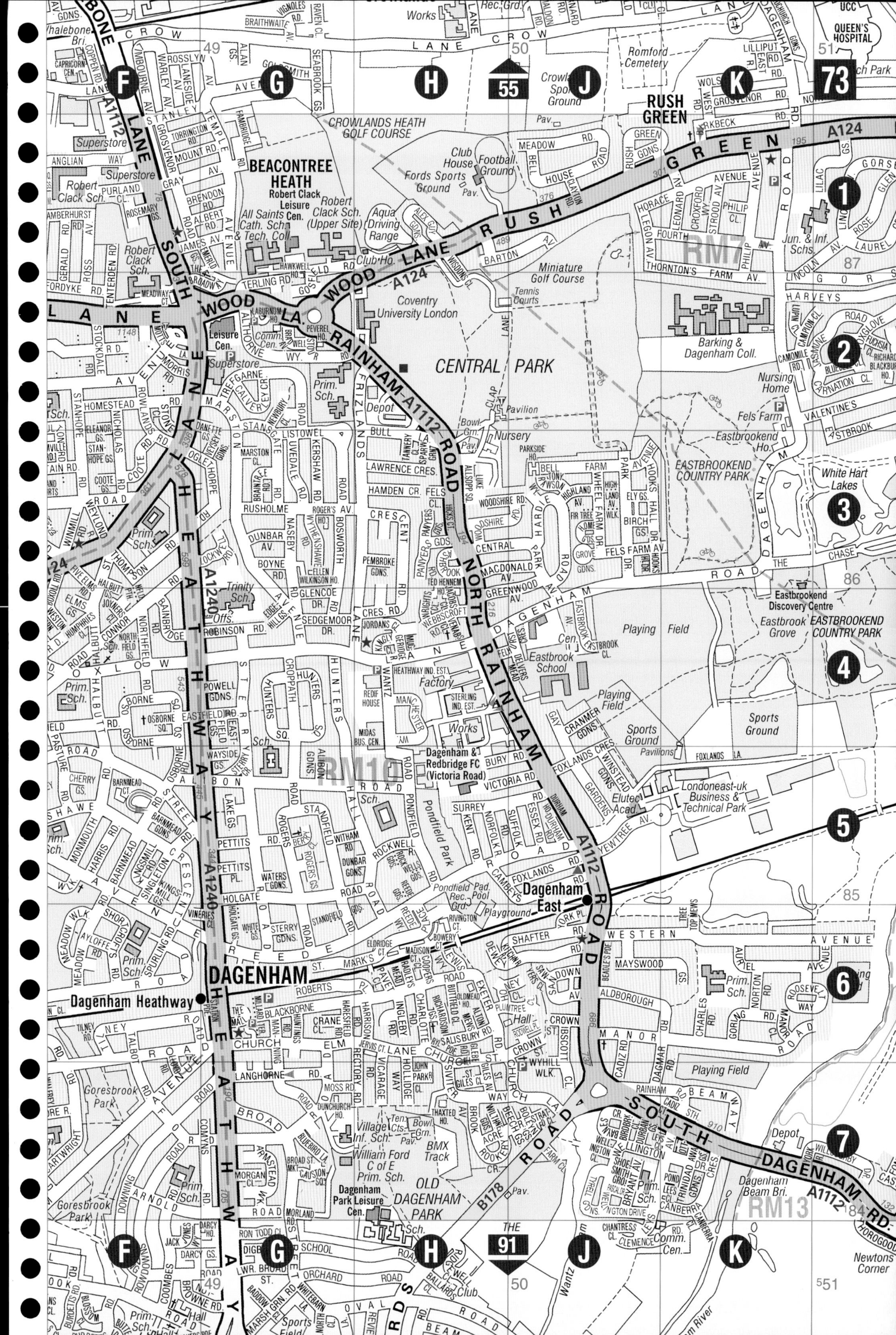

F
G
H
55
J
K
73
QUEEN'S HOSPITAL
UCC
Romford Cemetery
Crowlands Sports Ground
RUSH GREEN
CROWLANDS HEATH GOLF COURSE
BEACONTREE HEATH
Robert Clack Leisure Cen.
Robert Clack Sch. (Upper Site)
All Saints Cath. Sch. & Tech. Coll.
Fords Sports Ground
Club House
Football Ground
Aqua Driving Range
Miniature Golf Course
Tennis Courts
Coventry University London
CENTRAL PARK
Barking & Dagenham Coll.
Nursing Home
Fels Farm
Eastbrookend Ho.
EASTBROOKEND COUNTRY PARK
White Hart Lakes
Eastbrookend Discovery Centre
Eastbrook Grove
Playing Field
Eastbrook School
Sports Ground
Pavilions
Londoneast-uk Business & Technical Park
Eluteq Acad.
Dagenham & Redbridge FC (Victoria Road)
Pondfield Park
Pondfield Rec. Grd.
Playground
Dagenham East
DAGENHAM
Dagenham Heathway
Goresbrook Park
Village Inf. Sch.
William Ford C of E Prim. Sch.
BMX Track
OLD DAGENHAM PARK
Dagenham Park Leisure Cen.
Dagenham Beam Bri.
Newtons Corner
RM7
RM10
RM13
A124
A1112
A1240
B178
RUSH GREEN RD.
WOOD LANE
RAINHAM ROAD NORTH
SOUTH LANE
HEATHWAY
DAGENHAM RD.
CROW LANE
1
2
3
4
5
6
7
91
49
50
51
87
86
85
84

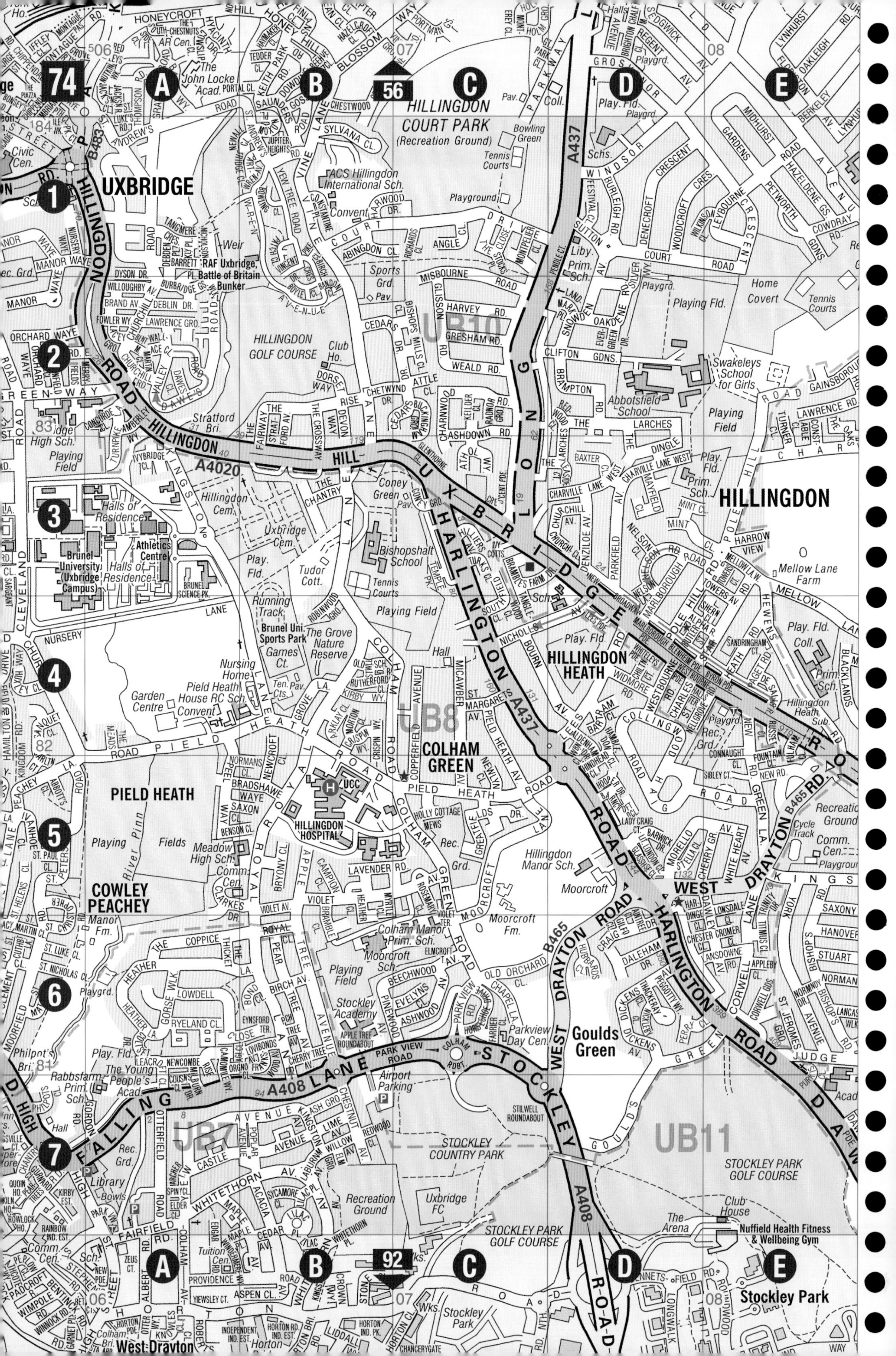

74
56
92
A
B
C
D
E
1
2
3
4
5
6
7
06
07
08
UXBRIDGE
HILLINGDON
HILLINGDON HEATH
COLHAM GREEN
PIELD HEATH
COWLEY PEACHEY
WEST DRAYTON
Goulds Green
Stockley Park
West Drayton
UB10
UB8
UB7
UB11
HILLINGDON COURT PARK (Recreation Ground)
HILLINGDON GOLF COURSE
STOCKLEY COUNTRY PARK
STOCKLEY PARK GOLF COURSE
Brunel University (Uxbridge Campus)
Athletics Centre
Halls of Residence
Hillingdon Cem.
Uxbridge Cem.
RAF Uxbridge, Battle of Britain Bunker
The John Locke Acad.
TACS Hillingdon International Sch.
Swakeleys School for Girls
Abbotsfield School
Bishopshalt School
HILLINGDON HOSPITAL
UCC
Meadow High Sch.
Pield Heath House RC Sch.
Hillingdon Manor Sch.
Colham Manor Prim. Sch.
Moorcroft Sch.
Stockley Academy
The Young People's Acad.
Rabbsfarm Prim. Sch.
Brunel Uni. Sports Park
The Grove Nature Reserve
Uxbridge FC
Nuffield Health Fitness & Wellbeing Gym
Airport Parking
Parkview Day Cen.
Home Covert
Mellow Lane Farm
A4020
A437
A408
B465
B483
HILLINGDON ROAD
HILLINGDON HILL
UXBRIDGE ROAD
HARLINGTON ROAD
LONG LANE
FALLING LANE
STOCKLEY ROAD
WEST DRAYTON ROAD
PIELD HEATH ROAD
ROYAL LANE
COLHAM GREEN ROAD
KINGSTON LANE
HIGH ROAD
HORTON ROAD

NORTH HILLINGDON
HAYES END
WOOD END GREEN
WOOD END
YEADING
HAYES
UB5
UB4
UB3
Yeading Brook
Cutthroat Wood
Gutteridge Wood
C & L GOLF COURSE
Ten Acres
The Gorse
Recreation Ground
Westways Fm.
Lane Covert
West London Shooting Grounds
Hedgewood School
Charville Prim. Sch.
Grosvenor Playing Field
Hayes Shrub
Hayes Park
Yeading Brook Meadows Nature Reserve
Belmore Playing Fields
Barnhill High Sch.
Belmore Prim. Sch.
Grange Park Jun. & Inf. Schs.
Rosedale College
Barra Hall
Town Hall Park
Uxbridge Coll. (Hayes Campus)
Lake Farm Country Park
Minet Jun. & Inf. Schs.
Hillingdon Cycle Circuit
Goals Soccer Centre (Hayes)
Lombardy Retail Park
Mecca Bingo
County Court
UXBRIDGE ROAD
A4020
A312
A437
OSSIE GARVIN ROUNDABOUT
WEST END ROAD
RUISLIP
SHARVEL LANE
KINGSHILL AVENUE
57
75
76
93

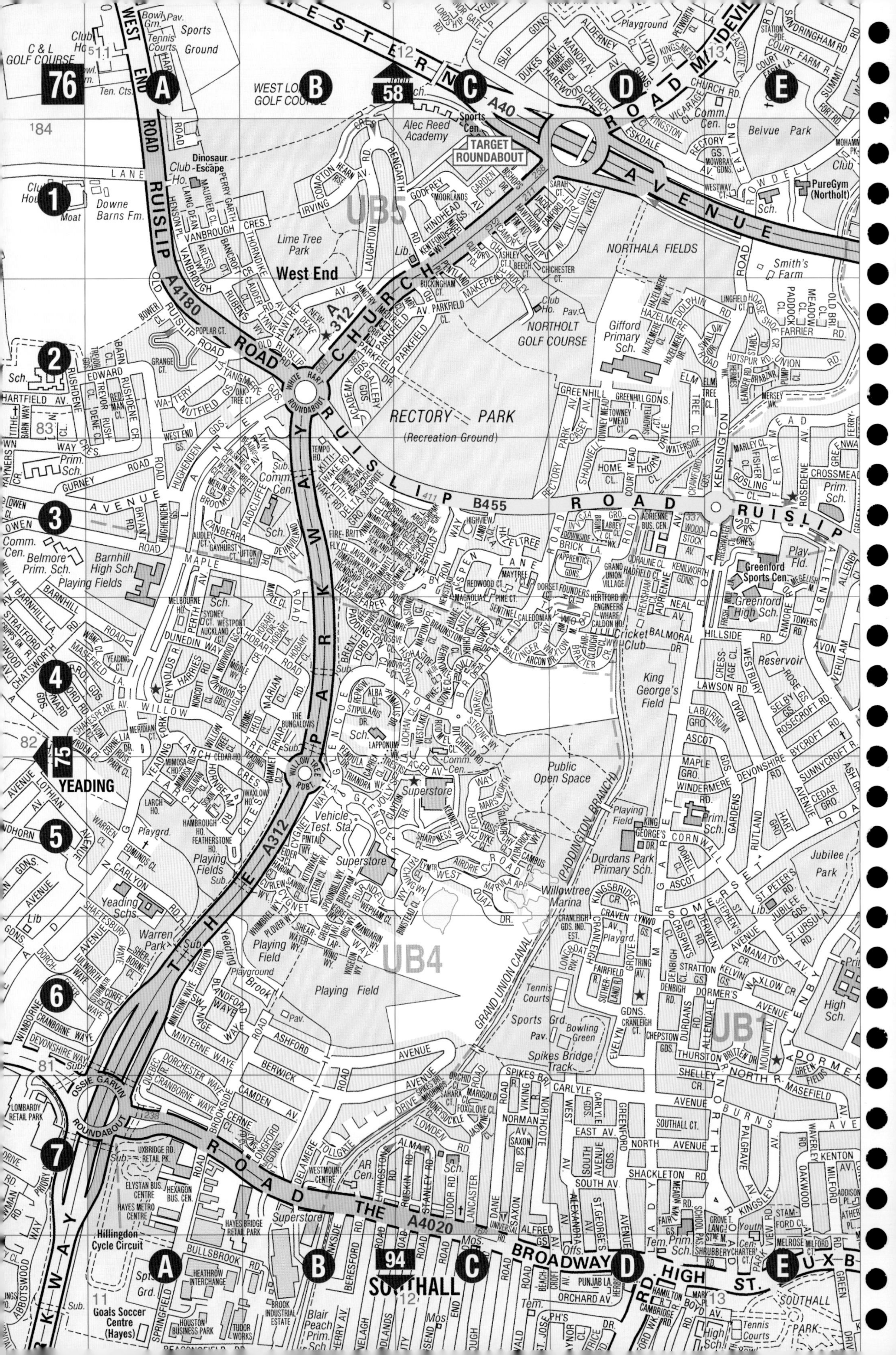

76
58
75
YEADING
94
SOUTHALL
A
B
C
D
E
1
2
3
4
5
6
7
C & L GOLF COURSE
WEST LONDON GOLF COURSE
WESTERN AVENUE
A40
TARGET ROUNDABOUT
Alec Reed Academy
Sports Cen.
Dinosaur Escape
Downe Barns Fm.
Moat
UB5
Lime Tree Park
West End
WEST END ROAD
RUISLIP ROAD
A4180
CHURCH ROAD
A312
WHITE HART ROUNDABOUT
RECTORY PARK
(Recreation Ground)
RUISLIP ROAD
B455
NORTHALA FIELDS
NORTHOLT GOLF COURSE
Gifford Primary Sch.
Belvue Park
PureGym (Northolt)
Smith's Farm
Greenford Sports Cen.
Greenford High Sch.
Barnhill High Sch.
Playing Fields
Belmore Prim. Sch.
Comm. Cen.
King George's Field
Public Open Space
Cricket Club
Reservoir
PARKWAY
WILLOW TREE RDBT.
Superstore
Vehicle Test. Sta.
Willowtree Marina
Durdans Park Primary Sch.
GRAND UNION CANAL (PADDINGTON BRANCH)
Yeading Schs.
Warren Park
Yeading Brook
Playing Field
UB4
UB1
Jubilee Park
High Sch.
Sports Grd.
Bowling Green
Tennis Courts
Spikes Bridge Track
OSSIE GARVIN ROUNDABOUT
LOMBARDY RETAIL PARK
UXBRIDGE RD. RETAIL PK.
ELYSTAN BUS. CENTRE
HEXAGON BUS. CEN.
HAYES METRO CENTRE
HAYES BRIDGE RETAIL PARK
Hillingdon Cycle Circuit
HEATHROW INTERCHANGE
Goals Soccer Centre (Hayes)
HOUSTON BUSINESS PARK
TUDOR WORKS
BROOK INDUSTRIAL ESTATE
Blair Peach Prim. Sch.
THE BROADWAY
A4020
UXBRIDGE ROAD
HIGH ST.
SOUTHALL PARK

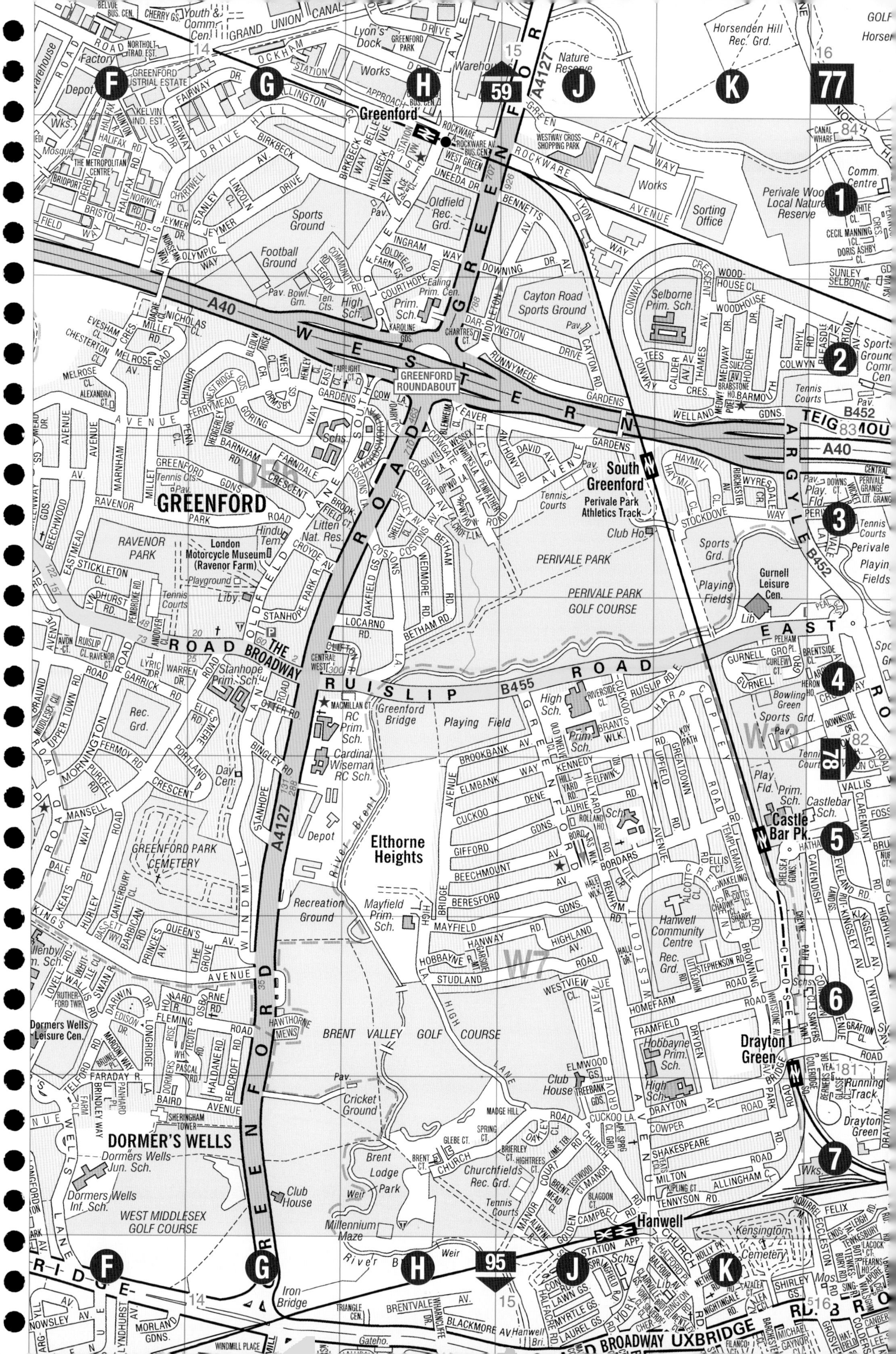

GRAND UNION CANAL
Youth & Comm. Cen.
Lyon's Dock
GREENFORD PARK
Horsenden Hill Rec. Grd.
GOLF
NORTHOLT TRAD. EST.
Factory
Warehouse
Depot
GREENFORD INDUSTRIAL ESTATE
KELVIN IND. EST.
OCKHAM DRIVE
STATION APPROACH
Works
Warehouse
Nature Reserve
F
G
H
J
K
14
15
16
59
77
A4127
Greenford
ROCKWARE AV. BUS. CEN.
WESTWAY CROSS SHOPPING PARK
ROCKWARE AVENUE
Works
Sorting Office
Comm. Centre
Perivale Wood Local Nature Reserve
1
Mosque
THE METROPOLITAN CENTRE
BIRKBECK AV.
Oldfield Rec. Grd.
Sports Ground
Football Ground
UNEEDA DR.
BENNETTS AV.
LYON WAY
CECIL MANNING CL.
DORIS ASHBY CL.
SUNLEY GDNS.
SELBORNE AV.
A40
WESTERN AVENUE
GREENFORD ROUNDABOUT
Ealing Prim. Cen.
Prim. Sch.
High Sch.
Cayton Road Sports Ground
Selborne Prim. Sch.
WOODHOUSE AV.
Sports Ground
2
Tennis Courts
B452
TEIGNMOUTH
ARGYLE
UB6
GREENFORD
RAVENOR PARK
London Motorcycle Museum (Ravenor Farm)
Playground
Liby.
Hindu Tem.
Litten Nat. Res.
South Greenford
Perivale Park Athletics Track
Tennis Courts
Club Ho.
PERIVALE PARK
PERIVALE PARK GOLF COURSE
Sports Grd.
Playing Fields
Gurnell Leisure Cen.
Lib.
Play. Fld.
3
Perivale Playing Fields
THE BROADWAY
RUISLIP ROAD
B455
RUISLIP ROAD EAST
Stanhope Prim. Sch.
Rec. Grd.
MACMILLAN CT.
RC Prim. Sch.
Cardinal Wiseman RC Sch.
Greenford Bridge
Playing Field
High Sch.
Prim. Sch.
Bowling Green
Sports Grd.
4
W13
78
82
Day Cen.
Depot
River Brent
Elthorne Heights
Castle Bar Pk.
Castlebar Sch.
Play Fld.
Prim. Sch.
5
GREENFORD PARK CEMETERY
Recreation Ground
Mayfield Prim. Sch.
Hanwell Community Centre
Rec. Grd.
W7
6
Dormers Wells Leisure Cen.
HAWTHORNE MEWS
BRENT VALLEY GOLF COURSE
Club House
Hobbayne Prim. Sch.
High Sch.
Drayton Green
Running Track
Drayton Green
181
Cricket Ground
Pav.
DORMER'S WELLS
Dormers Wells Jun. Sch.
Dormers Wells Inf. Sch.
WEST MIDDLESEX GOLF COURSE
Club House
Brent Lodge Park
Millennium Maze
Churchfields Rec. Grd.
Tennis Courts
Hanwell
Wks.
7
Kensington Cemetery
95
River Brent
Weir
Iron Bridge
BRENTVALE AV.
BLACKMORE AV.
UXBRIDGE ROAD
BROADWAY

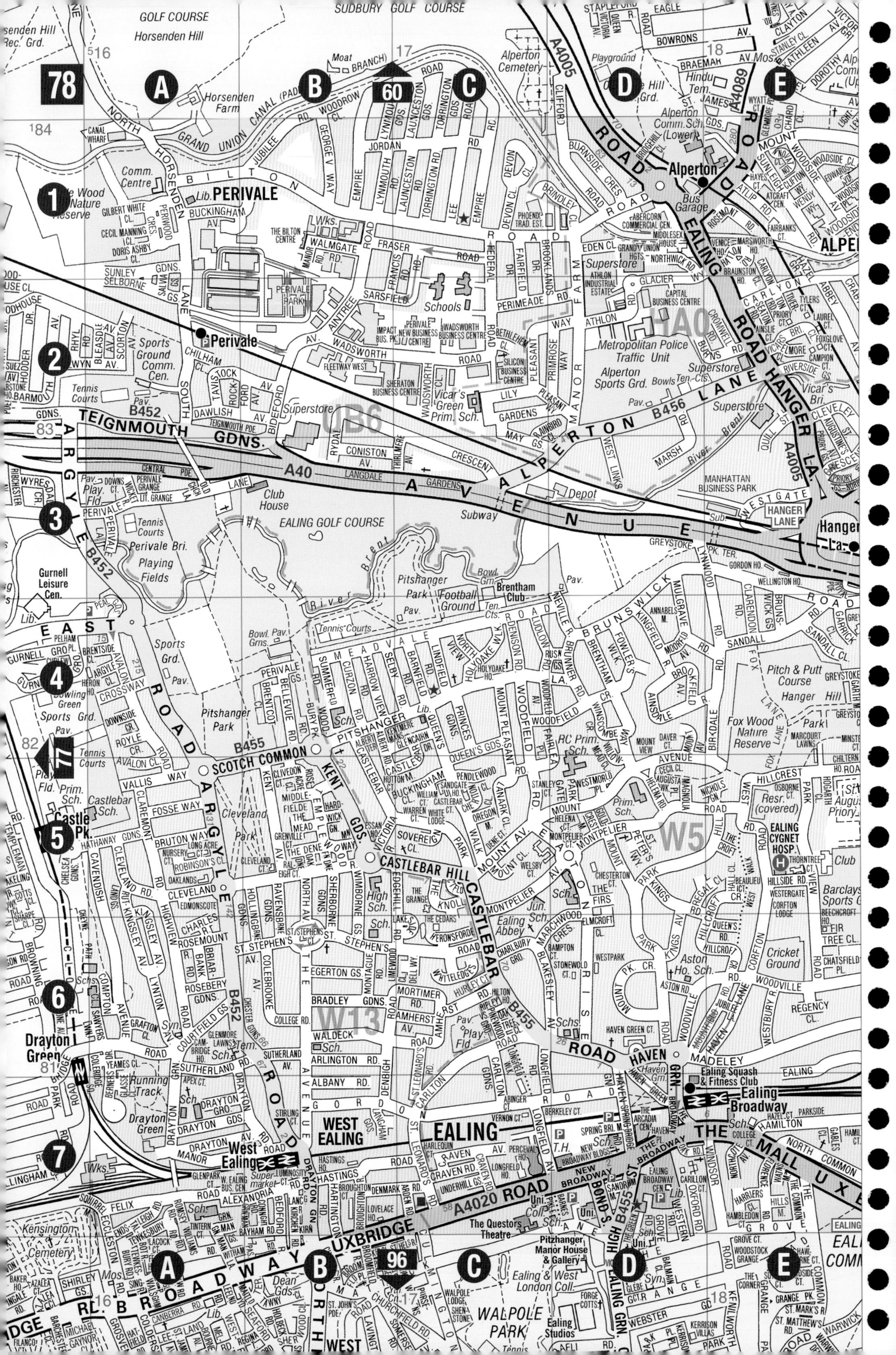

78
60
77
96
A
B
C
D
E
1
2
3
4
5
6
7
SUDBURY GOLF COURSE
GOLF COURSE
Horsenden Hill
Horsenden Farm
GRAND UNION CANAL (PADDINGTON BRANCH)
Moat
Alperton Cemetery
A4005
A4089
Alperton
Bus Garage
Hindu Tem.
Alperton Comm.Sch. (Lower)
PERIVALE
Perivale
Comm. Centre
BILTON
Lib.
Sports Ground Comm. Cen.
Tennis Courts
Schools
Superstore
Athlon Industrial Estate
Capital Business Centre
HA0
Metropolitan Police Traffic Unit
Alperton Sports Grd.
UB6
TEIGNMOUTH GDNS.
B452
B456
ALPERTON LANE
A40
WESTERN AVENUE
EALING ROAD
HANGER LANE
Hanger La.
Manhattan Business Park
Vicar's Green Prim. Sch.
Club House
EALING GOLF COURSE
Subway
Depot
Perivale Bri. Playing Fields
Gurnell Leisure Cen.
River Brent
Pitshanger Park
Football Ground
Brentham Club
Sports Grd.
Bowling Green
Pitshanger Park
SCOTCH COMMON
B455
ARGYLE ROAD
KENT GDNS.
PITSHANGER LA.
Cleveland Park
Castlebar Sch.
Castle Bar Pk.
CASTLEBAR HILL
CASTLEBAR ROAD
High Sch.
Ealing Abbey
Jun. Sch.
RC Prim. Sch.
Prim. Sch.
W5
Pitch & Putt Course
Hanger Hill Park
Fox Wood Nature Reserve
Resr. (covered)
Ealing Cygnet Hosp.
Cricket Ground
Aston Ho. Sch.
W13
Running Track
Drayton Green
West Ealing
WEST EALING
EALING
Ealing Broadway
Ealing Squash & Fitness Club
HAVEN GRN.
THE MALL
UXBRIDGE ROAD
A4020
BROADWAY
The Questors Theatre
Pitzhanger Manor House & Gallery
Ealing & West London Coll.
WALPOLE PARK
Ealing Studios
Kensington Cemetery
EALING GRN.

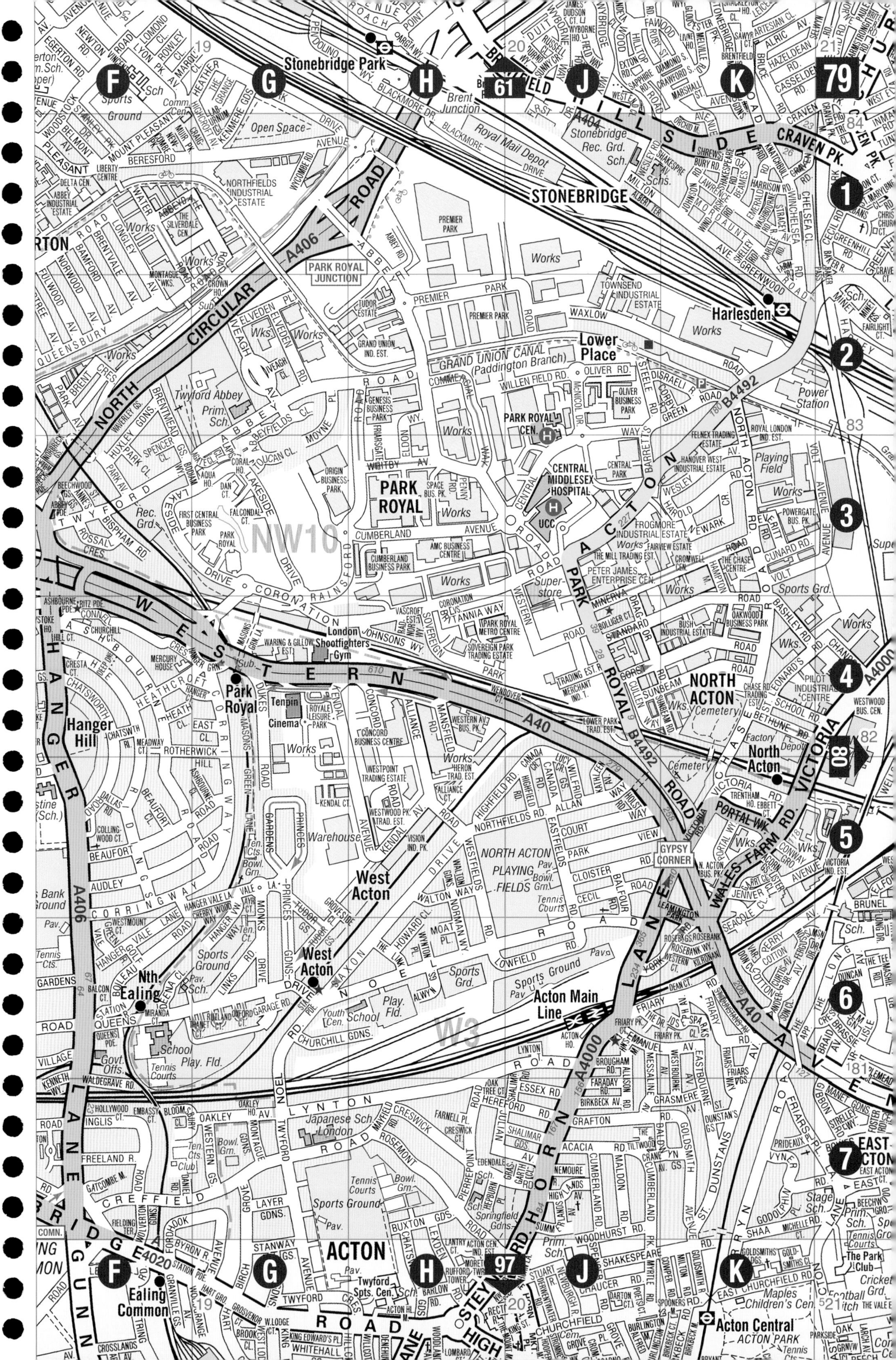

79
61
80
97
F
G
H
J
K
1
2
3
4
5
6
7
19
20
21
Stonebridge Park
Brent Junction
Open Space
Royal Mail Depot
STONEBRIDGE
Stonebridge Rec. Grd.
HILLSIDE
CRAVEN PK.
A404
NORTH CIRCULAR ROAD
A406
PARK ROYAL JUNCTION
NORTHFIELDS INDUSTRIAL ESTATE
PREMIER PARK
TOWNSEND INDUSTRIAL ESTATE
Harlesden
Lower Place
GRAND UNION CANAL (Paddington Branch)
Power Station
Twyford Abbey
PARK ROYAL CEN.
CENTRAL MIDDLESEX HOSPITAL
UCC
PARK ROYAL
NW10
Works
Playing Field
ACTON
B4492
PARK ROYAL ROAD
WESTERN AVENUE
A40
London Shootfighters Gym
Park Royal
Hanger Hill
Tenpin
Cinema
NORTH ACTON
Cemetery
North Acton
VICTORIA RD.
WALES FARM RD.
GYPSY CORNER
NORTH ACTON PLAYING FIELDS
West Acton
W3
Acton Main Line
HANGER LANE
Sports Ground
Nth. Ealing
HORN LANE
A4000
Japanese Sch. London
EAST ACTON
ACTON
Ealing Common
Acton Central
ACTON PARK
E4020
HIGH ST.
Maples Children's Cen.
The Park Club

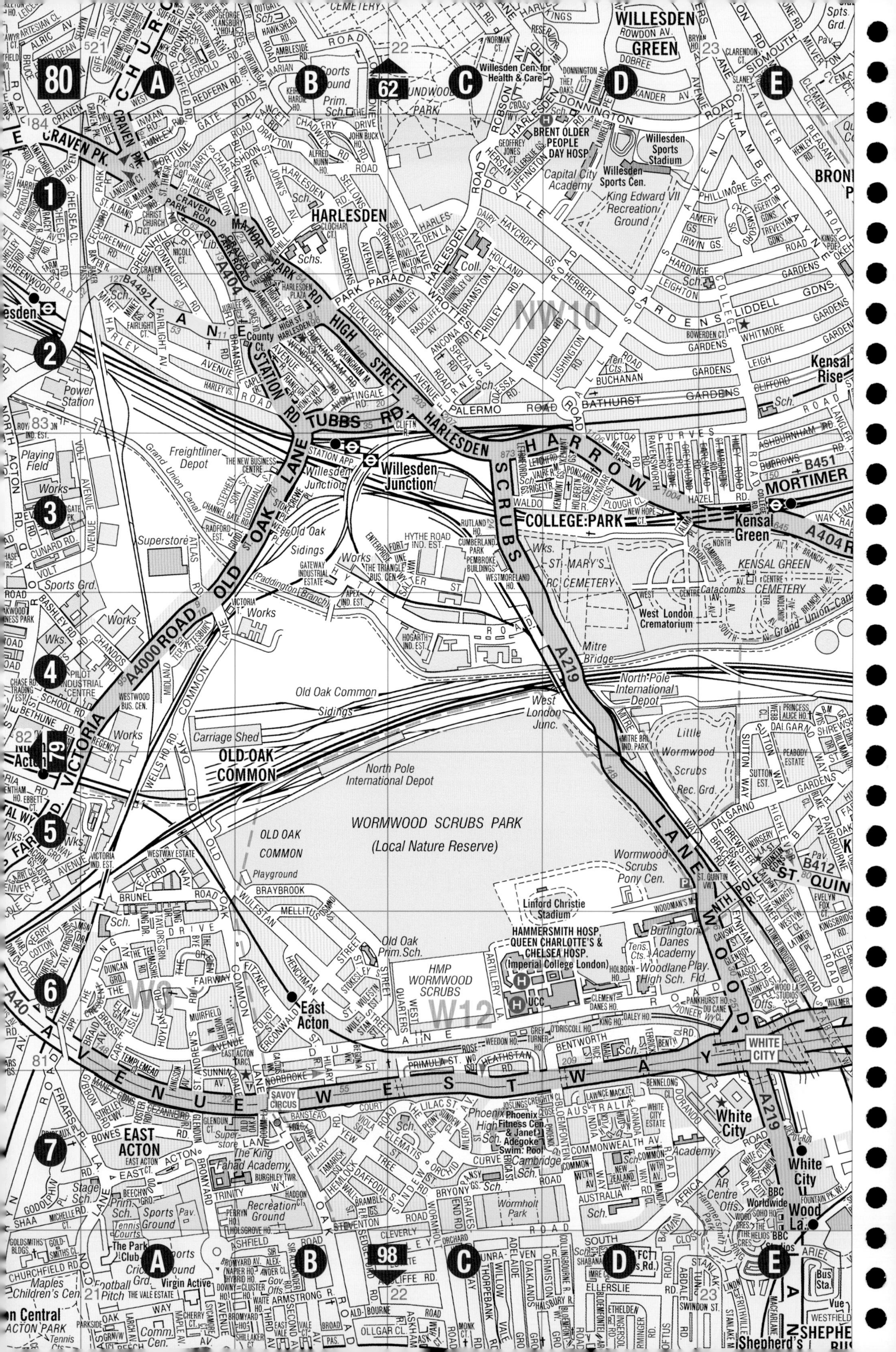
80
62
98
79
WILLESDEN GREEN
HARLESDEN
NW10
Kensal Rise
Kensal Green
KENSAL GREEN CEMETERY
ST. MARY'S RC CEMETERY
West London Crematorium
COLLEGE PARK
Willesden Junction
Willesden Sports Stadium
Willesden Sports Cen.
King Edward VII Recreation Ground
Capital City Academy
BRENT OLDER PEOPLE DAY HOSP.
Willesden Cen. for Health & Care
ROUNDWOOD PARK
HIGH STREET
HARLESDEN ROAD
CRAVEN PK.
CRAVEN PARK ROAD
MANOR PARK RD.
TUBBS RD.
STATION RD.
OLD OAK LANE
A4000 ROAD
VICTORIA
SCRUBS LANE
A219
HARROW ROAD
MORTIMER
B451
A404
A404R
B4492 LANE
Power Station
Freightliner Depot
Grand Union Canal
Superstore
Old Oak Sidings
Old Oak Common Sidings
Carriage Shed
OLD OAK COMMON
North Pole International Depot
West London Junc.
Mitre Bridge
WORMWOOD SCRUBS PARK
(Local Nature Reserve)
Little Wormwood Scrubs Rec. Grd.
Wormwood Scrubs Pony Cen.
Linford Christie Stadium
HAMMERSMITH HOSP. QUEEN CHARLOTTE'S & CHELSEA HOSP.
(Imperial College London)
UCC
HMP WORMWOOD SCRUBS
Burlington Danes Academy
Woodlane High Sch.
Old Oak Prim. Sch.
East Acton
W3
W12
WESTWAY
WOOD LANE
WHITE CITY
White City
DU CANE ROAD
ST. QUINTIN
B412
EAST ACTON
SAVOY CIRCUS
AVENUE
A40
The King Fahad Academy
Recreation Ground
Wormholt Park
Phoenix High Sch.
Phoenix Fitness Cen. & Janet Adegoke Swim. Pool
Cambridge Sch.
BBC Worldwide
Wood La.
Hammersmith Park
Academy
Sports Ground
Maples Children's Cen.
Virgin Active
Acton Central
ACTON PARK
North Acton
Sports Grd.
Playing Field
PILOT INDUSTRIAL CENTRE
Works
Old Oak Common
1
2
3
4
5
6
7
A
B
C
D
E
21
22
23

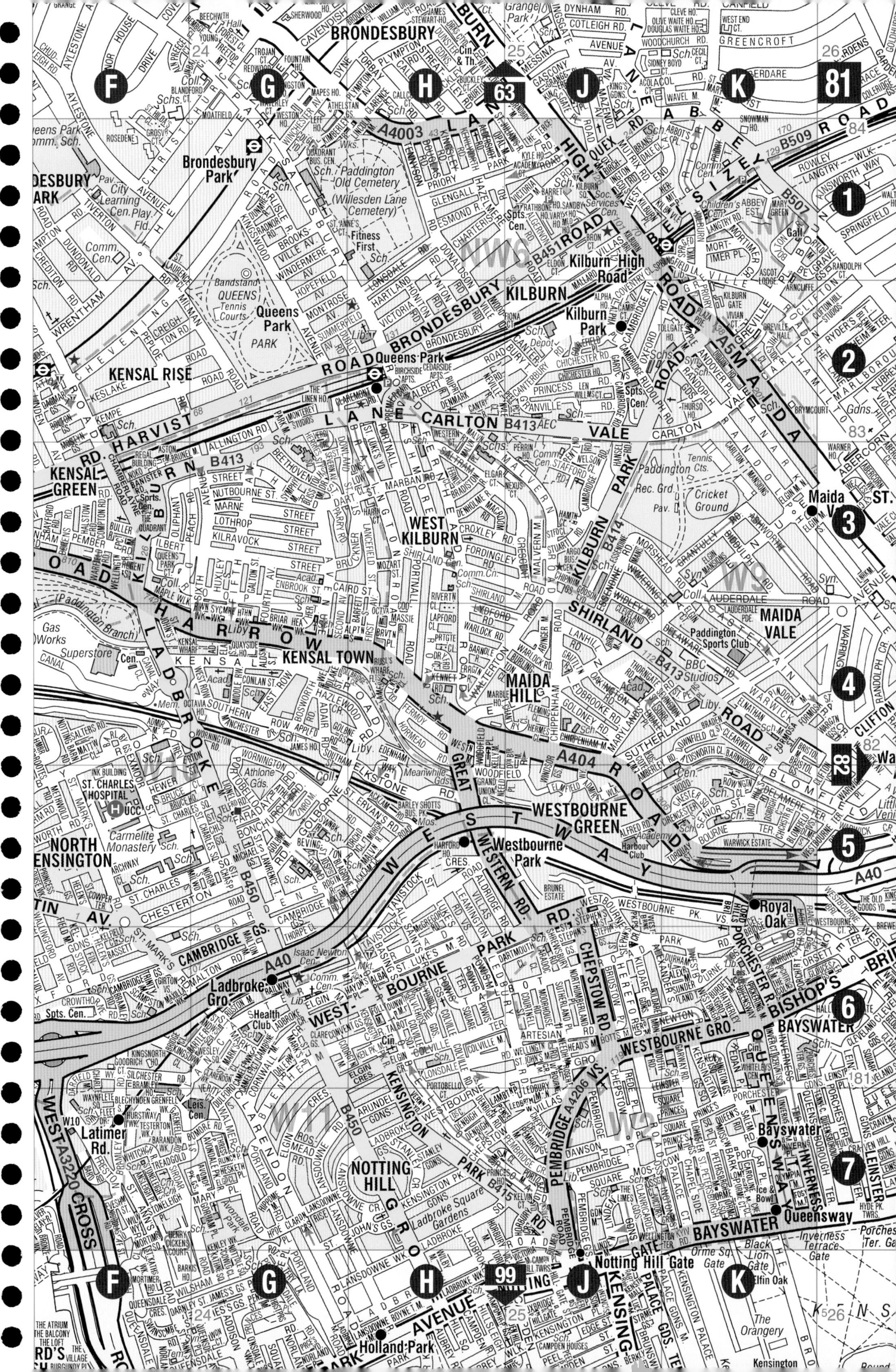

81
63
82
99
F
G
H
J
K
1
2
3
4
5
6
7
24
25
26
BRONDESBURY
Brondesbury Park
Paddington Old Cemetery
(Willesden Lane Cemetery)
Queens Park
QUEENS PARK
KENSAL RISE
KENSAL GREEN
HARVIST ROAD
BRONDESBURY ROAD
KILBURN
Kilburn High Road
Kilburn Park
NW6
CARLTON VALE
KILBURN LANE
WEST KILBURN
KILBURN PARK
HARROW ROAD
KENSAL TOWN
Gas Works
Superstore
Grand Union Canal (Paddington Branch)
MAIDA HILL
MAIDA VALE
Maida Vale
W9
Paddington Rec. Grd.
Cricket Ground
Paddington Sports Club
BBC Studios
SHIRLAND ROAD
ELGIN AV.
WARWICK AV.
ABBEY ROAD
BELSIZE ROAD
HIGH ROAD
A5 MAIDA VALE
ABERCORN PL.
ST. CHARLES HOSPITAL
Carmelite Monastery
NORTH KENSINGTON
W10
LADBROKE GROVE
Ladbroke Gro.
WESTWAY
A40
WESTBOURNE GREEN
Westbourne Park
GREAT WESTERN RD.
Royal Oak
WESTBOURNE PARK RD.
WESTBOURNE GRO.
BAYSWATER
Bayswater
Queensway
QUEENSWAY
CHEPSTOW RD.
PEMBRIDGE VS.
W11
W2
NOTTING HILL
KENSINGTON PARK RD.
Ladbroke Square Gardens
Notting Hill Gate
BAYSWATER ROAD
Latimer Rd.
WEST CROSS
A3220
Holland Park
HOLLAND PARK AVENUE
The Orangery
Kensington Gardens
Black Lion Gate
Elfin Oak
Orme Sq. Gate
Inverness Terrace Gate

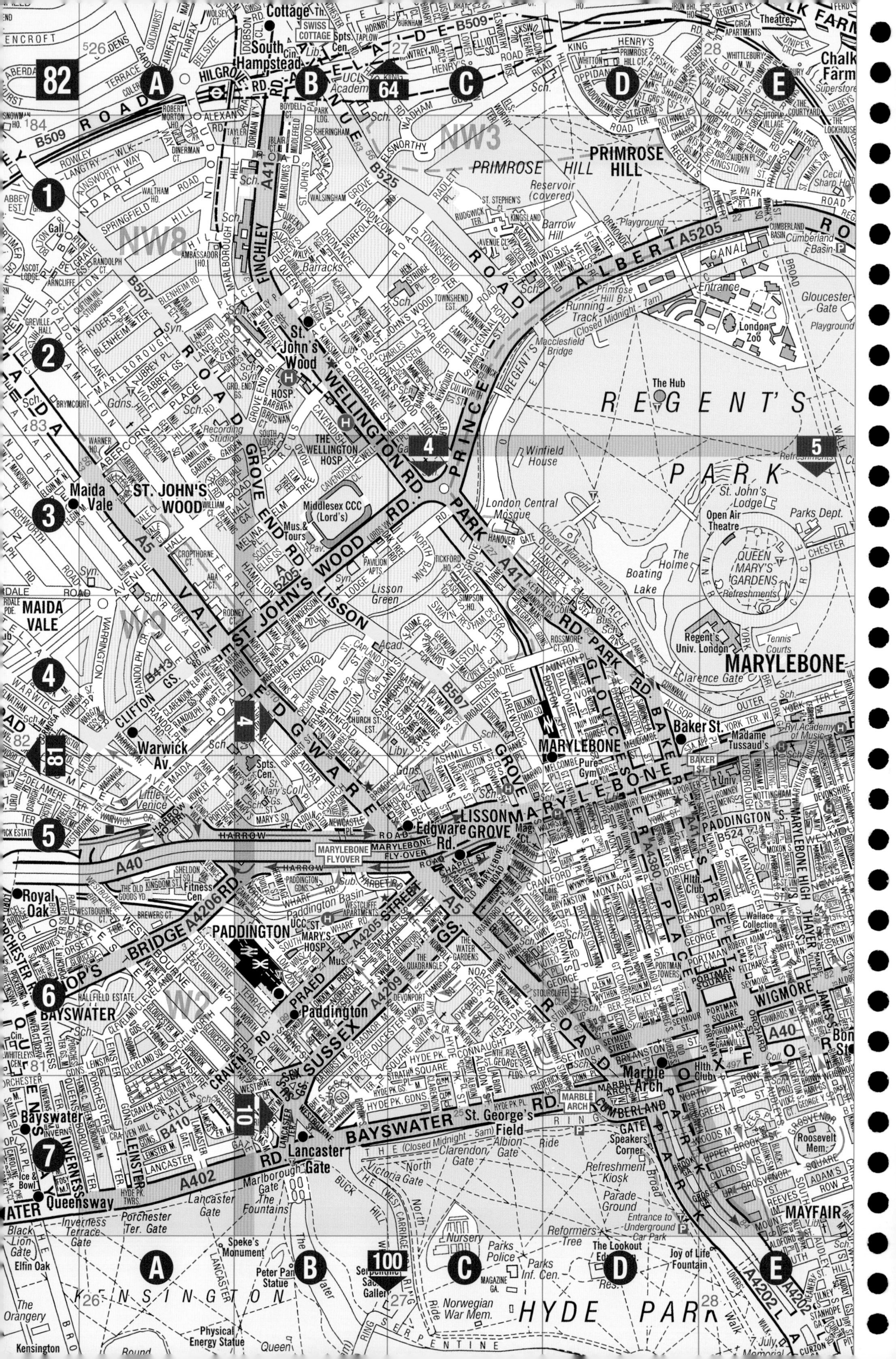

64
NW3
PRIMROSE HILL
Primrose Hill
NW8
ST. JOHN'S WOOD
St. John's Wood
Maida Vale
MAIDA VALE
REGENT'S PARK
London Zoo
The Hub
Winfield House
London Central Mosque
Middlesex CCC (Lord's)
THE WELLINGTON HOSP
Lisson Green
MARYLEBONE
Baker St.
Madame Tussaud's
Boating Lake
QUEEN MARY'S GARDENS
Open Air Theatre
Regent's Univ. London
Warwick Av.
Little Venice
PADDINGTON
Paddington
Paddington Basin
Edgware Rd.
LISSON GROVE
MARYLEBONE FLYOVER
Royal Oak
BAYSWATER
Bayswater
Queensway
W2
W9
Lancaster Gate
Marble Arch
MARBLE ARCH
Speakers' Corner
Wallace Collection
PORTMAN SQUARE
MAYFAIR
Roosevelt Mem.
KENSINGTON
HYDE PARK
Kensington
The Orangery
Elfin Oak
Peter Pan Statue
Speke's Monument
Physical Energy Statue
Serpentine Sackler Gallery
Norwegian War Mem.
The Lookout Edu. Cen.
Joy of Life Fountain
St. George's Field
Chalk Farm
81
100
10

F
G
H
J
K
83
65
CAMDEN TOWN
Camden Town
Camden Rd.
Caledonian Rd. & Barnsbury
Kentish Town Rd.
Camden High St.
Parkway
Albany St.
Regent's Park
Mornington Cres.
Hampstead Rd.
Eversholt St.
St. Pancras Way
Pancras Rd.
St. Pancras International
King's Cross
Caledonian Rd.
Copenhagen St.
Pentonville
Pentonville Rd.
Somers Town
British Library
Euston
Euston Rd.
Euston Sq.
Warren St.
Great Portland St.
Regent's Pk.
Gower St.
University College London
Woburn Pl.
Russell Sq.
Bloomsbury
Southampton Row
Theobalds Rd.
St. Pancras
Gray's Inn Rd.
King's Cross Rd.
Farringdon Rd.
Clerkenwell
Rosebery Av.
Goodge St.
Tottenham Ct. Rd.
Tottenham Court Rd.
British Museum
Bloomsbury St.
New Oxford St.
High Holborn
Holborn
Kingsway
Chancery La.
Royal Courts of Justice
Fleet St.
Oxford Circus
Regent St.
Portland Pl.
New Bond St.
Conduit St.
Soho
Charing Cross Rd.
Shaftesbury Av.
Leicester Sq.
Covent Gdn.
Piccadilly Circus
Haymarket
Strand
Aldwych
Temple
Victoria Embankment
Waterloo Bri.
National Gallery
Nelson's Col.
101
Charing Cross
Embankment
Cleopatra's Needle
Northumberland Av.
Admiralty Arch
Pall Mall
St. James's St.
Green Park
Royal Festival Hall
National Theatre
Southbank Cen.
1
2
3
4
5
6
7
6
7
84
29
30
31

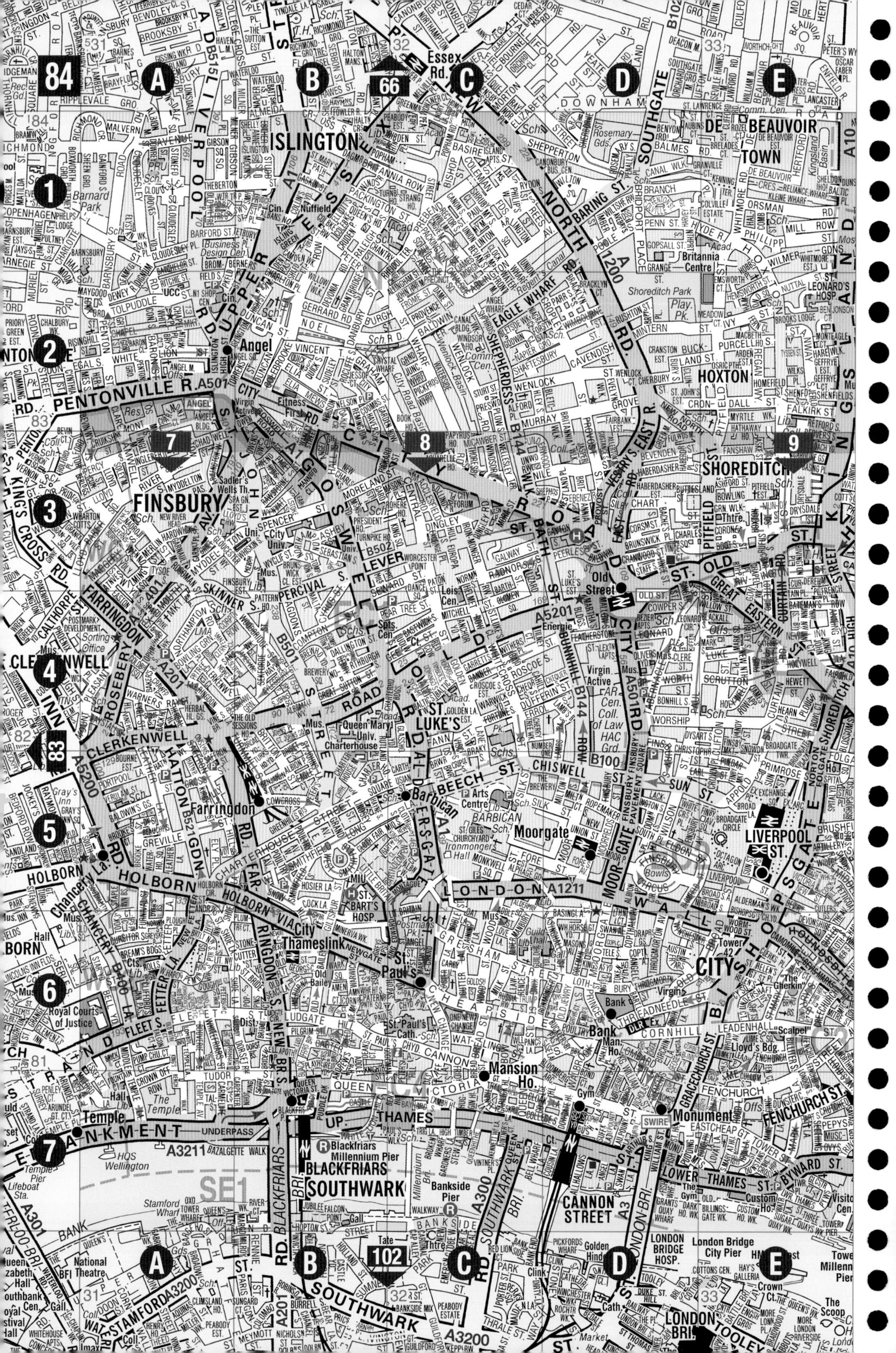

84
A
B
66
Essex Rd.
C
D
E
ISLINGTON
DE BEAUVOIR TOWN
DOWNHAM
SOUTHGATE
1
Barnard Park
LIVERPOOL
UPPER
NORTH
A1200
Britannia Centre
Shoreditch Park
BARING ST.
Nuffield
Acad.
Regent's Canal
EAGLE WHARF RD.
SHEPHERDESS
2
Angel
PENTONVILLE R.
A507
ANGEL
CITY
HOXTON
NEW NORTH RD.
Fitness First
Virgin Active
83
7
8
9
SHOREDITCH
FINSBURY
Sadler's Wells Th.
3
KING'S CROSS RD.
City Univ.
LEVER
B502
PITFIELD
Old Street
OLD ST.
OLD ST.
GREAT EASTERN
CURTAIN RD.
CITY RD.
FARRINGDON
CALTHORPE
4
CLERKENWELL
ROSEBERY
SKINNER S.
PERCIVAL S.
B501
GOSWELL RD.
ROAD
ST. LUKE'S
Queen Mary Univ.
Charterhouse
A5201
BUNHILL ROW
B144
A501
Virgin Active
CLERKENWELL
A5200
HATTON
CHISWELL
BEECH ST.
Barbican
Arts Centre
BARBICAN
Farringdon
Moorgate
MOORGATE
FINSBURY PAVEMENT
LIVERPOOL ST.
5
HOLBORN
Chancery La.
HOLBORN
CHARTERHOUSE
LONDON WALL
A1211
SMITHFIELD
St. Bart's Hosp.
City Thameslink
St. Paul's
GRESHAM ST.
Tower 42
CITY
BISHOPSGATE
HOUNDSDITCH
"The Gherkin"
6
Royal Courts of Justice
FLEET ST.
LUDGATE HILL
St. Paul's Cath.
CHEAPSIDE
Bank
Bank
CORNHILL
LEADENHALL
"Scalpel"
Lloyd's Bdg.
STRAND
Mansion Ho.
CANNON ST.
QUEEN VICTORIA ST.
FENCHURCH
FENCHURCH ST.
GRACECHURCH ST.
Temple
UP. THAMES ST.
Monument
EMBANKMENT
UNDERPASS
A3211
7
HQS Wellington
BLACKFRIARS
Blackfriars Millennium Pier
BLACKFRIARS
SOUTHWARK
SE1
Bankside Pier
CANNON STREET
LOWER THAMES ST.
Custom Ho.
A300
A3
SOUTHWARK BRI.
LONDON BRI.
National Theatre
A
B
102
C
D
E
LONDON BRIDGE HOSP.
London Bridge City Pier
Golden Hinde
Clink
STAMFORD
A3200
SOUTHWARK
A3200
Crown Ct.
The Scoop
LONDON BRI.
TOOLEY

DALSTON
London Fields
LONDON FIELDS
SOUTH HACKNEY
85
67
F
G
H
J
K
Haggerston
HAGGERSTON
Victoria Fountain
Royal Gate East
VICTORIA PARK ROAD
VICTORIA
GROVE ROAD
Regent's Canal
Anton's Lock
Bus Garage
St. Agnes Gate
Gore Gate
Bonner Hall Bri.
Crown Gate West
Crown Gate East
Skew Bridge
Hackney City Farm
Football Pitch
Haggerston Park
Cambridge Heath
BISHOP'S WAY
SEWARDSTONE RD.
ROMAN ROAD
Hoxton
HACKNEY RD.
A1208
York Hall
V&A Mus.
OLD FORD
GLOBE TOWN
Meath Gdns.
Bethnal Grn.
BETHNAL GREEN
BETHNAL GREEN RD.
A1209
COLUMBIA RD.
MILE END
Halls of Residence
TOWER HAMLETS CEN.
MILE END HOSPITAL
Queen Mary University of London
Shoreditch High St.
SPITALFIELDS
Old Spitalfields Mkt.
CAMBRIDGE HEATH RD.
A107
Bethnal Grn
THREE COLTS LA.
Stepney Green
MILE END RD.
Whitechapel
THE ROYAL LONDON HOSP.
Swanlea School
Burial Grnd.
Youth Cen.
WHITECHAPEL RD.
A11
STEPNEY
STEPNEY GREEN
Stepney Grn. Pk.
Nursing Home
E1
RATCLIFF
Aldgate East
Aldgate
WHITECHAPEL
COMMERCIAL RD.
A13
COMMERCIAL ST.
CANNON ST. RD.
NEW RD.
MINORIES
MANSELL ST.
Shadwell
CABLE ST.
THE HIGHWAY
A1203
B126
DLR
Tower Gateway
Tower Hill
TOWER HILL
The Fusilier Mus.
The Tower of London
St. Katharine Docks
St. Katharine's Pier
Tobacco Dock
SHADWELL
Shadwell Basin
King Edward Mem. Park
Shadwell Dock Stairs
Pelican Stairs
New Crane Stairs
Wapping
103
ROTHERHITHE TUNNEL
A101
John Orwell Sports Cen.
TOWER BRIDGE
A100
Butlers Wharf Pier
1
2
3
4
5
6
7
86
15
9
34
35
36

86
68
85
104
A
B
C
D
E
1
2
3
4
5
6
7
SOUTH HACKNEY
Victoria Park Athletics Arena
Victoria Fountain
Three Colt Bridge
Skew Bridge
Crown Gate East
Crown Gate West
E9
OLD FORD
VICTORIA PARK
Bobby Moore Academy (Prim.)
ArcelorMittal Orbit
The Slide
London Stadium
West Ham Utd. FC
Bobby Moore Academy (Secondary)
London Marathon Community Track
E20
GREENWAY
Pudding Mill Lane
STRATFORD
London Aquatics Centre
EAST CROSS ROUTE
A12 BLACKWALL
PARNELL RD.
ROMAN ROAD
FAIRFIELD RD.
OLD FORD ROAD
BOW ROAD
BOW INTERCHANGE
HIGH STREET
Bow Church
Bow Rd.
E3
MILE END
MILE END PARK
MILE END HOSPITAL
TOWER HAMLETS CEN.
Queen Mary University of London
Mile End
A11
A1205
BURDETT ROAD
TOWER HAMLETS CEMETERY PARK
BOW COMMON
DEVONS ROAD
Devons Rd.
BROMLEY
Bromley-by-Bow
NORTHERN APPROACH
BLACKWALL TUNNEL
Three Mills Green
The House Mill
THREE MILL LA.
Mile End Park Leisure Centre
Mile End Stadium
BEN JONSON RD.
ST. PAUL'S
RATCLIFF
LIMEHOUSE
Limehouse
Limehouse Basin
COMMERCIAL ROAD
LIMEHOUSE LINK
NARROW ST.
EAST INDIA DOCK ROAD
Langdon Pk.
All Saints
POPLAR
Poplar
Westferry
West India Quay
Canary Wharf
Billingsgate Market
WEST INDIA DOCKS
A12
A1261
RIVER THAMES
SE16
Canary Wharf Pier
Doubletree Docklands / Nelson Dock Pier
Blackwall Basin
E14

87
69
88
105
F
G
H
J
K
1
2
3
4
5
6
7
WEST HAM
WEST HAM PARK
PLAISTOW
CANNING TOWN
LEAMOUTH
Stratford High St.
Abbey Road
West Ham
Plaistow
Star La.
Canning Town
East India
Royal Victoria
Custom House for ExCeL
Prince Regent
Upton Park
Mill Meads
Prescott Channel
Pumping Station
Jubilee Line Depot
East London Crematorium
EAST LONDON CEMETERY
Memorial Recreation Ground
Star Park
Bow Creek Ecology Park
East India Dock Basin Nature Reserve
Virginia Quay
Blackwall Pier
ROYAL VICTORIA DOCK
ExCeL
Emirates Royal Docks
Millennium Mill
Pontoon Dock
Hollywood Bowl
North Greenwich
PORTWAY
NEW PLAISTOW RD.
PLAISTOW RD.
HIGH ST.
GREENGATE ST.
PRINCE REGENT LANE
BARKING ROAD
NEWHAM WAY
MANOR ROAD
A1011
A124
A13
A112
A114
A1020
B164
B165
B166
LOWER LEA CROSSING
SILVERTOWN VIADUCT
SILVERTOWN WY.
BALAAM ST.
STEPHENSON ST.
VICTORIA DOCK ROAD
BOW CREEK
BLACKWALL REACH
BLACKWALL TUNNEL
E13
E15
E16

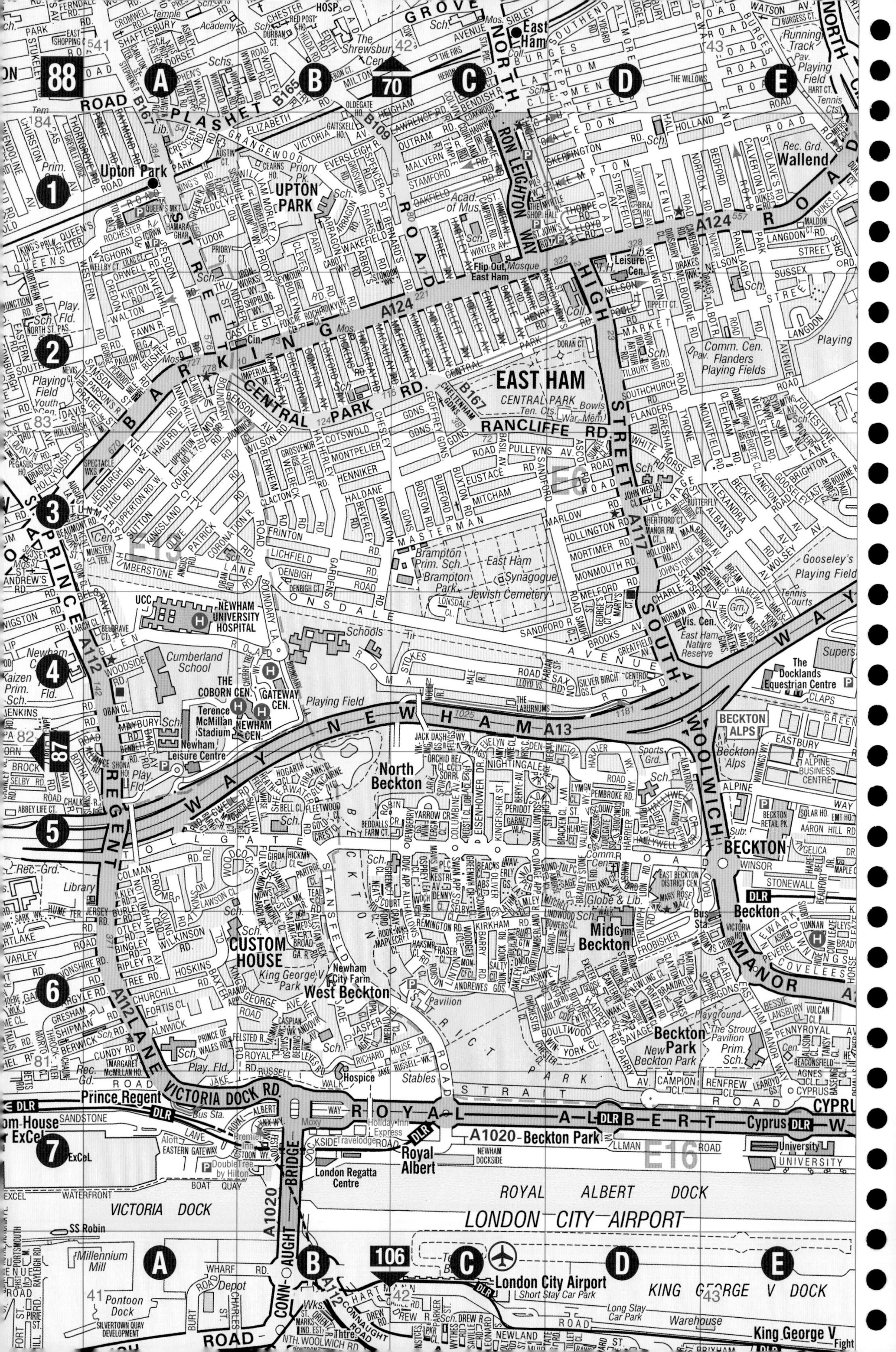

88
A
B
C
D
E
1
2
3
4
5
6
7
70
87
106
Upton Park
UPTON PARK
East Ham
EAST HAM
CENTRAL PARK
Wallend
PLASHET
GROVE
BARKING RD.
A124
B167
B165
B109
CENTRAL PARK RD.
RANCLIFFE RD.
HIGH STREET SOUTH
A117
HIGH ST. NORTH
RON LEIGHTON WAY
GREEN ST.
NEWHAM WAY
A13
PRINCE REGENT LANE
A112
WOOLWICH MANOR WAY
ROYAL ALBERT WAY
ROYAL DOCKS ROAD
A1020
VICTORIA DOCK RD.
CONNAUGHT BRIDGE
TOLLGATE RD.
PARK STRAIT
LONSDALE AVENUE
ROMAN ROAD
E6
E13
E16
NEWHAM UNIVERSITY HOSPITAL
Cumberland School
THE COBORN CEN.
GATEWAY CEN.
Terence McMillan Stadium
NEWHAM CEN.
Newham Leisure Centre
Playing Field
East Ham Jewish Cemetery
Synagogue
Brampton Prim. Sch.
Brampton Park
East Ham Nature Reserve
Vis. Cen.
Comm. Cen.
Flanders Playing Fields
Gooseley's Playing Field
Tennis Courts
The Docklands Equestrian Centre
BECKTON ALPS
Beckton Alps
ALPINE BUSINESS CENTRE
BECKTON RETAIL PK.
BECKTON
Beckton
DLR
North Beckton
Mid Beckton
West Beckton
Newham City Farm
King George V Park
CUSTOM HOUSE
Custom House for ExCeL
ExCeL
Prince Regent
Royal Albert
Beckton Park
New Beckton Park
Cyprus
CYPRUS
Globe & Lib.
EAST BECKTON DISTRICT CEN.
Hospice
Stables
Pavilion
Library
Rec. Grd.
Play. Fld.
Holiday Inn Express
Travelodge
Premier Inn
DoubleTree by Hilton
Aloft
London Regatta Centre
NEWHAM DOCKSIDE
University
UNIVERSITY
ROYAL ALBERT DOCK
LONDON CITY AIRPORT
London City Airport
Short Stay Car Park
Long Stay Car Park
Warehouse
KING GEORGE V DOCK
King George V
VICTORIA DOCK
SS Robin
Millennium Mill
Pontoon Dock
SILVERTOWN QUAY DEVELOPMENT
EXCEL WATERFRONT
BOAT QUAY
WHARF RD.
Depot
HARTMANN RD.
NEWLAND
NTH. WOOLWICH RD.
Running Track
Playing Field
Rec. Grd.
Leisure Cen.
Flip Out, East Ham
Mosque
Acad. of Mus.
Priory Pk.
The Shrewsbury Cen.
Newham Kaizen Prim. Sch.

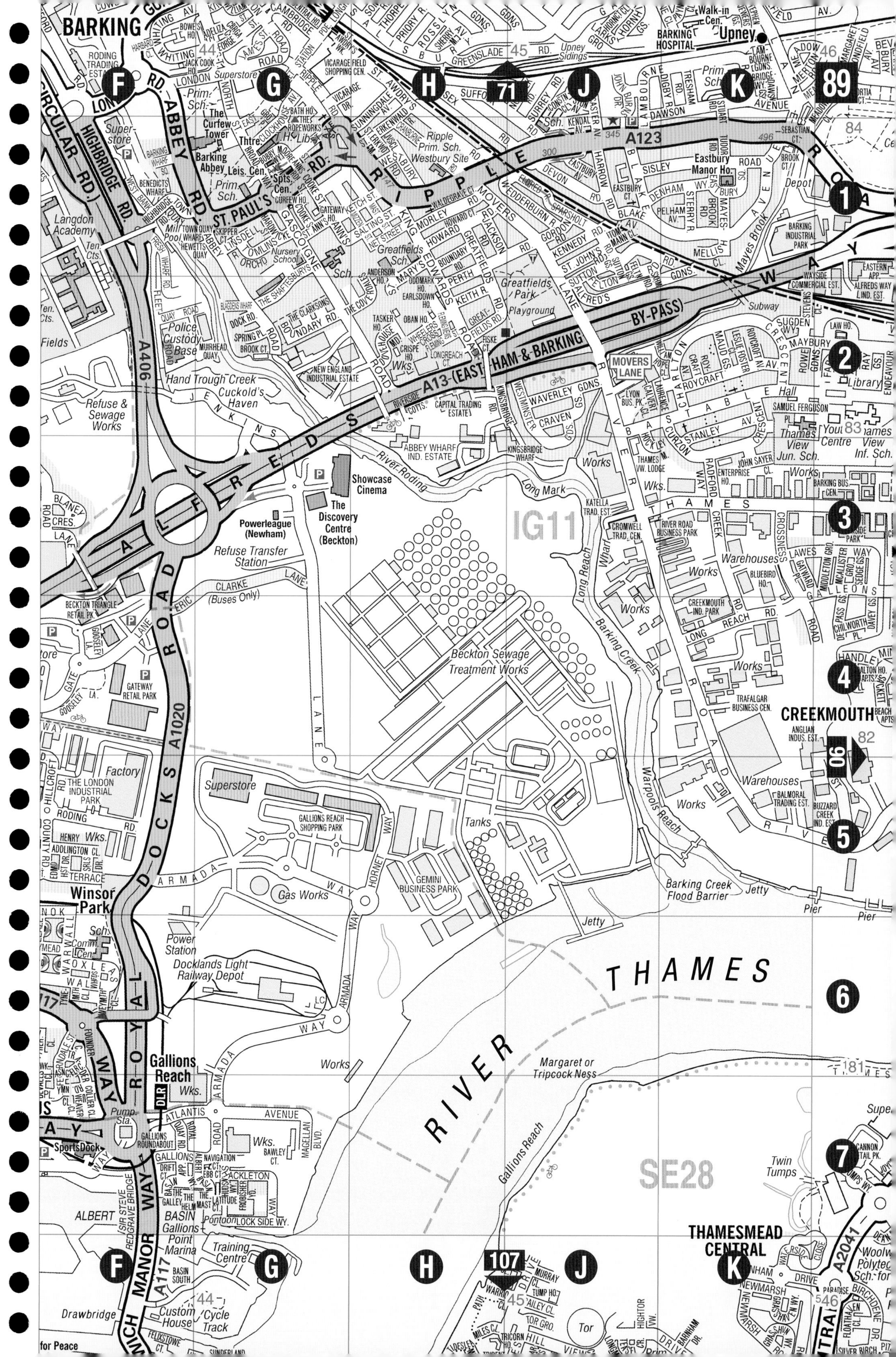

BARKING
Upney
BARKING HOSPITAL
Walk-in Cen.
89
71
Upney Sidings
GREENSLADE RD.
VICARAGE FIELD SHOPPING CEN.
Superstore
The Curfew Tower
Barking Abbey
Leis. Cen.
Prim. Sch.
ST. PAUL'S RD.
RIPPLE RD.
A123
Ripple Prim. Sch. Westbury Site
Eastbury Manor Ho.
RODING TRADING ESTATE
HIGHBRIDGE RD.
CIRCULAR RD.
ABBEY RD.
Langdon Academy
Police Custody Base
Greatfields Sch.
Greatfields Park
Playground
Nursery School
NEW ENGLAND INDUSTRIAL ESTATE
A13 (EAST HAM & BARKING BY-PASS)
ALFREDS WAY
MOVERS LANE
WAVERLEY GDNS.
CRAVEN GDNS.
BARKING INDUSTRIAL PARK
WAYSIDE COMMERCIAL EST.
EASTERN APP.
ALFREDS WAY IND. EST.
Subway
Library
Hall
Thames View Jun. Sch.
Youth Centre
Thames View Inf. Sch.
Hand Trough Creek
Cuckold's Haven
Refuse & Sewage Works
JENKINS LANE
CAPITAL TRADING ESTATE
ABBEY WHARF IND. ESTATE
KINGSBRIDGE WHARF
River Roding
Long Mark
Showcase Cinema
The Discovery Centre (Beckton)
Powerleague (Newham)
Refuse Transfer Station
CLARKE LANE (Buses Only)
IG11
KATELLA TRAD. EST.
CROMWELL TRAD. CEN.
RIVER ROAD BUSINESS PARK
THAMES RD.
Works
Warehouses
CREEKMOUTH IND. PARK
TRAFALGAR BUSINESS CEN.
CREEKMOUTH
ANGLIAN INDUS. EST.
90
BALMORAL TRADING EST.
BUZZARD CREEK IND. EST.
RIVER RD.
Long Reach
Barking Creek
Wharf
Beckton Sewage Treatment Works
BECKTON TRIANGLE RETAIL PK.
GATEWAY RETAIL PARK
A406
A1020
ROYAL DOCKS ROAD
Factory
THE LONDON INDUSTRIAL PARK
Superstore
GALLIONS REACH SHOPPING PARK
Tanks
GEMINI BUSINESS PARK
Gas Works
ARMADA WAY
HORNET WAY
Warpools Reach
Barking Creek Flood Barrier
Jetty
Pier
Winsor Park
Power Station
Docklands Light Railway Depot
RIVER THAMES
Margaret or Tripcock Ness
Gallions Reach
Works
Gallions Reach
DLR
Pump Sta.
GALLIONS ROUNDABOUT
SportsDock
ATLANTIS AVENUE
MAGELLAN BLVD.
BAWLEY CT.
Wks.
ALBERT BASIN
Gallions Point Marina
Training Centre
Custom House
Cycle Track
Drawbridge
A117
MANOR WAY
SIR STEVE REDGRAVE BRIDGE
107
SE28
Twin Tumps
THAMESMEAD CENTRAL
A2041
Woolwich Polytechnic Sch. for
Tor
for Peace
F G H J K
1 2 3 4 5 6 7

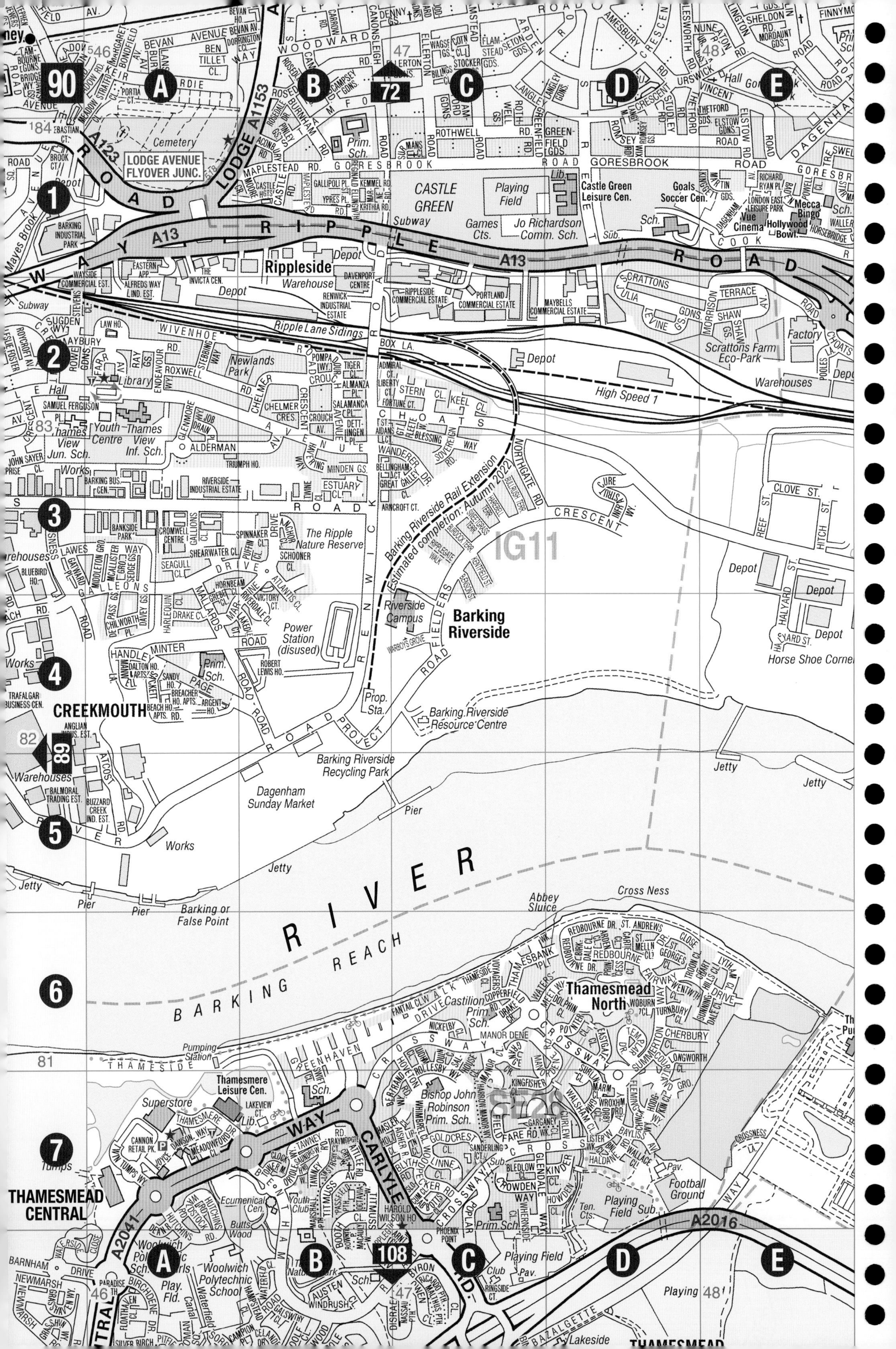

90
72
89
108
A
B
C
D
E
1
2
3
4
5
6
7
46
47
48
184
83
82
81
LODGE AVENUE
FLYOVER JUNC.
Cemetery
A123
A1153
LODGE AVENUE
A13
RIPPLE ROAD
ALFREDS WAY
Barking Industrial Park
Mayes Brook
Depot
BEVAN AVENUE
WOODWARD RD.
GORESBROOK ROAD
CASTLE GREEN
Playing Field
Castle Green Leisure Cen.
Goals Soccer Cen.
Jo Richardson Comm. Sch.
Games Cts.
Subway
Vue Cinema
Hollywood Bowl
Mecca Bingo
London East Leisure Park
Rippleside
Warehouse
Eastern App.
The Invicta Cen.
Alfreds Way Ind. Est.
Wayside Commercial Est.
Renwick Industrial Estate
Rippleside Commercial Estate
Portland Commercial Estate
Maybells Commercial Estate
Davenport Centre
Ripple Lane Sidings
Box La.
High Speed 1
Scrattons Farm Eco-Park
Factory
Warehouses
Newlands Park
Library
Hall
Youth Centre
Thames View Inf. Sch.
Thames View Jun. Sch.
Works
Riverside Industrial Estate
Alderman
Triumph Ho.
Choats
Renwick Road
Northgate Rd.
Crescent
IG11
Barking Riverside Rail Extension
Estimated completion: Autumn 2022
The Ripple Nature Reserve
Power Station (disused)
Riverside Campus
Barking Riverside
Fielders
Prop. Sta.
Barking Riverside Resource Centre
Barking Riverside Recycling Park
Dagenham Sunday Market
Creekmouth
Trafalgar Business Cen.
Anglian Indus. Est.
Balmoral Trading Est.
Buzzard Creek Ind. Est.
River Road
Works
Jetty
Pier
Clove St.
Reef St.
Hitch St.
Halyard St.
Depot
Horse Shoe Corner
Barking or False Point
RIVER
BARKING REACH
Abbey Sluice
Cross Ness
Thamesmead North
Pumping Station
Thameside
Thamesmere Leisure Cen.
Superstore
Cannon Retail Pk.
Lib.
Way
Carlyle
Bishop John Robinson Prim. Sch.
Crossway
Castilion Prim. Sch.
Manor Dene
SE28
Ecumenical Cen.
Youth Club
Butts Wood
Woolwich Polytechnic Sch.
Woolwich Polytechnic School
Play. Fld.
Canal
Football Ground
Playing Field
Ten. Cts.
Prim. Sch.
Playing Field
A2016
A2041
Thamesmead Central
Tumps
Barnham Drive
Lakeside
Bazalgette
Harold Wilson Ho.
Phoenix Point
Ringside Ct.
Thamesmead

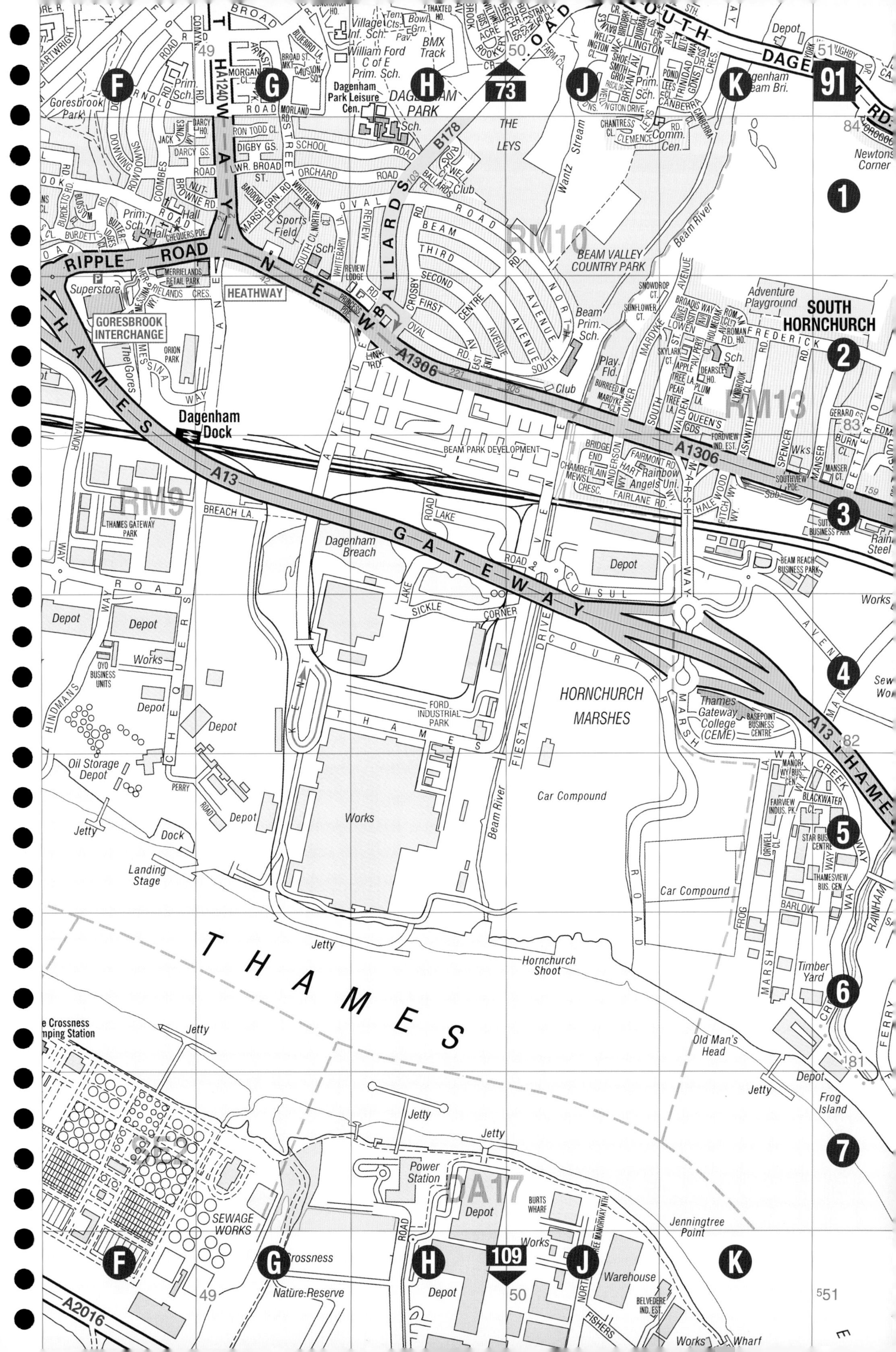73
91
109
F
G
H
J
K
1
2
3
4
5
6
7
49
50
51
84
83
82
181
551
Goresbrook Park
RIPPLE ROAD
NEW ROAD
HEATHWAY
GORESBROOK INTERCHANGE
Superstore
MERRIELANDS RETAIL PARK
ORION PARK
Dagenham Dock
Dagenham Leisure Park Leisure Cen.
DAGENHAM PARK
William Ford C of E Prim. Sch.
Village Inf. Sch.
BMX Track
Sports Field
BALLARDS
B178
THE LEYS
Wantz Stream
BEAM VALLEY COUNTRY PARK
Beam River
RM10
RM13
RM9
DA17
Beam Prim. Sch.
Play. Fld.
Club
A1306
A13
Adventure Playground
SOUTH HORNCHURCH
Dagenham Beam Bri.
Newtons Corner
BEAM PARK DEVELOPMENT
Rainbow Angels Uni.
THAMES GATEWAY PARK
BREACH LA.
Dagenham Breach
GATEWAY
Depot
Works
OYO BUSINESS UNITS
Oil Storage Depot
Jetty
Dock
Landing Stage
FORD INDUSTRIAL PARK
HORNCHURCH MARSHES
Car Compound
Thames Gateway College (CEME)
BASEPOINT BUSINESS CENTRE
BEAM REACH BUSINESS PARK
FAIRVIEW INDUS. PK.
STAR BUS. CENTRE
THAMESVIEW BUS. CEN.
Timber Yard
THAMES
Hornchurch Shoot
Old Man's Head
Frog Island
Crossness Pumping Station
SEWAGE WORKS
Crossness Nature Reserve
Power Station
BURTS WHARF
Warehouse
Jenningtree Point
BELVEDERE IND. EST.
Wharf
A2016

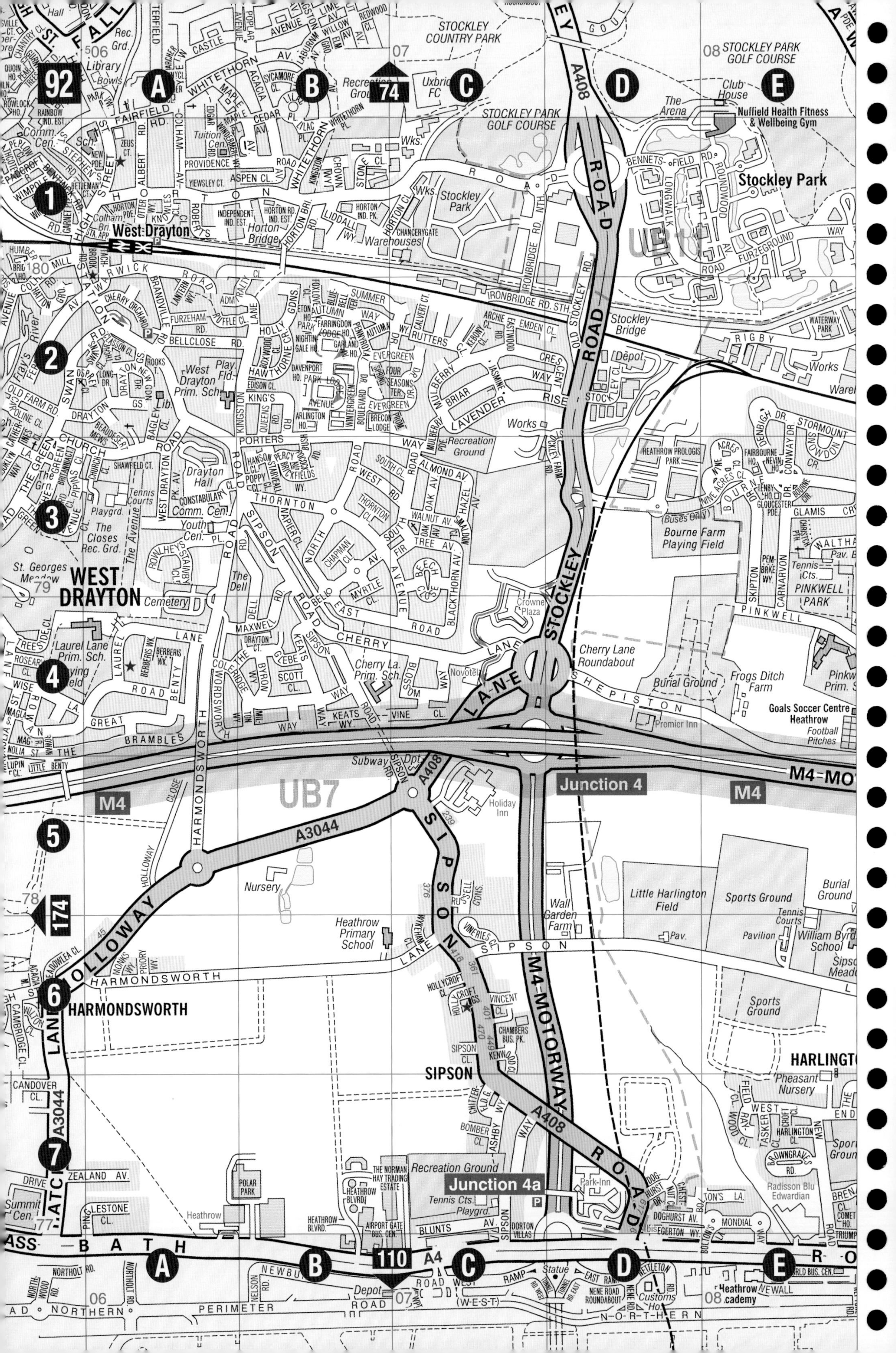

92
74
174
110
A
B
C
D
E
1
2
3
4
5
6
7
06
07
08
79
78
77
180
STOCKLEY COUNTRY PARK
STOCKLEY PARK GOLF COURSE
Club House
The Arena
Nuffield Health Fitness & Wellbeing Gym
Stockley Park
UB11
UB7
West Drayton
WEST DRAYTON
HARMONDSWORTH
SIPSON
HARLINGTON
Library
Bowls
Rec. Grd.
Recreation Ground
Uxbridge FC
Wks.
Tuition Cen.
Comm. Cen.
Sch.
Colham Bri.
Horton Bridge
Warehouses
INDEPENDENT IND. EST.
HORTON RD. IND. EST.
HORTON IND. PK.
CHANCERYGATE
Stockley Bridge
Depot
Works
Warehouses
HEATHROW PROLOGIS PARK
West Drayton Prim. Sch.
Play. Fld.
Lib.
Drayton Hall
Comm. Cen.
Tennis Courts
Playgrd.
Youth Cen.
The Closes Rec. Grd.
The Avenue
St. Georges Meadow
Cemetery
The Dell
Laurel Lane Prim. Sch.
Playing Field
Recreation Ground
Crowne Plaza
Novotel
Cherry La. Prim. Sch.
Cherry Lane Roundabout
Burial Ground
Frogs Ditch Farm
Promier Inn
Goals Soccer Centre Heathrow
Football Pitches
Bourne Farm Playing Field
(Buses Only)
PINKWELL PARK
Tennis Cts.
Pav.
Pinkwell Prim. Sch.
Subway
Dpts.
Holiday Inn
Junction 4
M4
M4-MOTORWAY
A408
A3044
A4
Nursery
Heathrow Primary School
Wall Garden Farm
Little Harlington Field
Sports Ground
Tennis Courts
Pavilion
William Byrd School
Burial Ground
Sipson Meadow
Sports Ground
CHAMBERS BUS. PK.
Pheasant Nursery
Recreation Ground
Junction 4a
Tennis Cts.
Playgrd.
Park Inn
Radisson Blu Edwardian
THE NORMAN HAY TRADING ESTATE
HEATHROW BLVRD.
AIRPORT GATE BUS. CEN.
POLAR PARK
Heathrow
Summit Cen.
DORTON VILLAS
Statue
NENE ROAD ROUNDABOUT
Customs Ho.
Depot
Heathrow Academy
WORLD BUS. CEN.
STOCKLEY ROAD
SIPSON ROAD
HOLLOWAY LANE
HARMONDSWORTH LANE
SIPSON LANE
CHERRY LANE
SHEPISTON LANE
BATH ROAD
NORTHERN PERIMETER ROAD
HORTON ROAD
STATION ROAD
HIGH STREET
PORTERS WAY
THORNTON AVENUE
PINKWELL LANE
RIGBY LANE
BENNETSFIELD RD.
FURZEGROUND WAY
IRONBRIDGE RD. STH.
WHITETHORN AV.
FAIRFIELD RD.

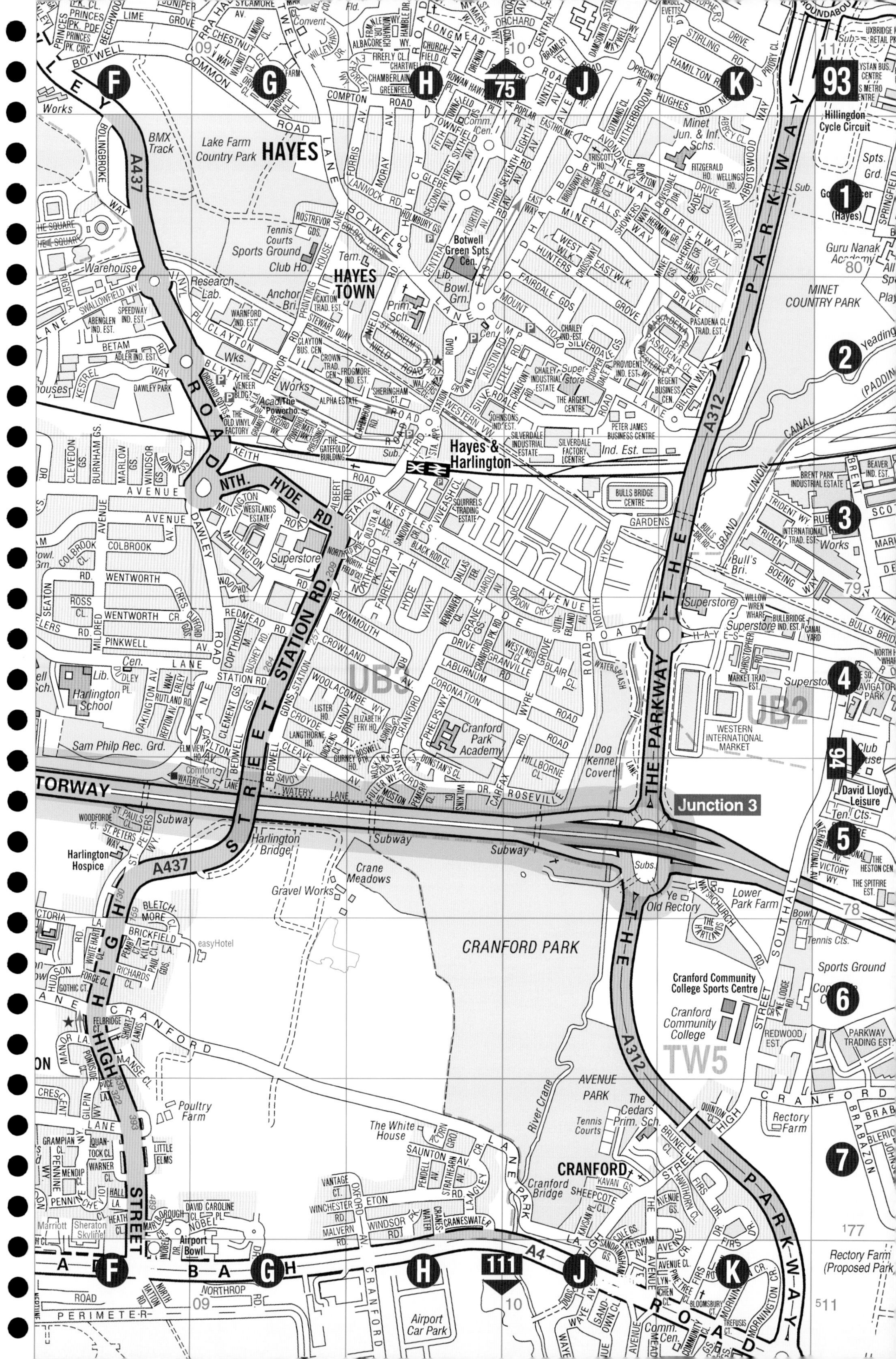

HAYES
HAYES TOWN
Lake Farm Country Park
BMX Track
Hayes & Harlington
Botwell Green Spts. Cen.
Sports Ground
Minet Jun. & Inf. Schs.
Hillingdon Cycle Circuit
MINET COUNTRY PARK
Guru Nanak Academy
Harlington School
Sam Philp Rec. Grd.
Harlington Hospice
Harlington Bridge
Crane Meadows
Gravel Works
CRANFORD PARK
Cranford Park Academy
Dog Kennel Covert
Junction 3
Ye Old Rectory
Lower Park Farm
Cranford Community College Sports Centre
Cranford Community College
AVENUE PARK
The Cedars Prim. Sch.
CRANFORD
Cranford Bridge
Poultry Farm
The White House
Airport Bowl
Airport Car Park
Rectory Farm
Rectory Farm (Proposed Park)
David Lloyd Leisure
WESTERN INTERNATIONAL MARKET
BULLS BRIDGE CENTRE
Superstore
UB3
UB2
TW5
A437
A312
A4
THE PARKWAY
STATION RD.
HIGH STREET
BATH ROAD
CRANFORD LANE
DAWLEY ROAD
NTH. HYDE RD.
NORTH HYDE ROAD
BOTWELL LANE
PUMP LANE
COLDHARBOUR LANE
UXBRIDGE ROAD
GRAND UNION CANAL
MOTORWAY
F
G
H
J
K
1
2
3
4
5
6
7
75
93
94
111

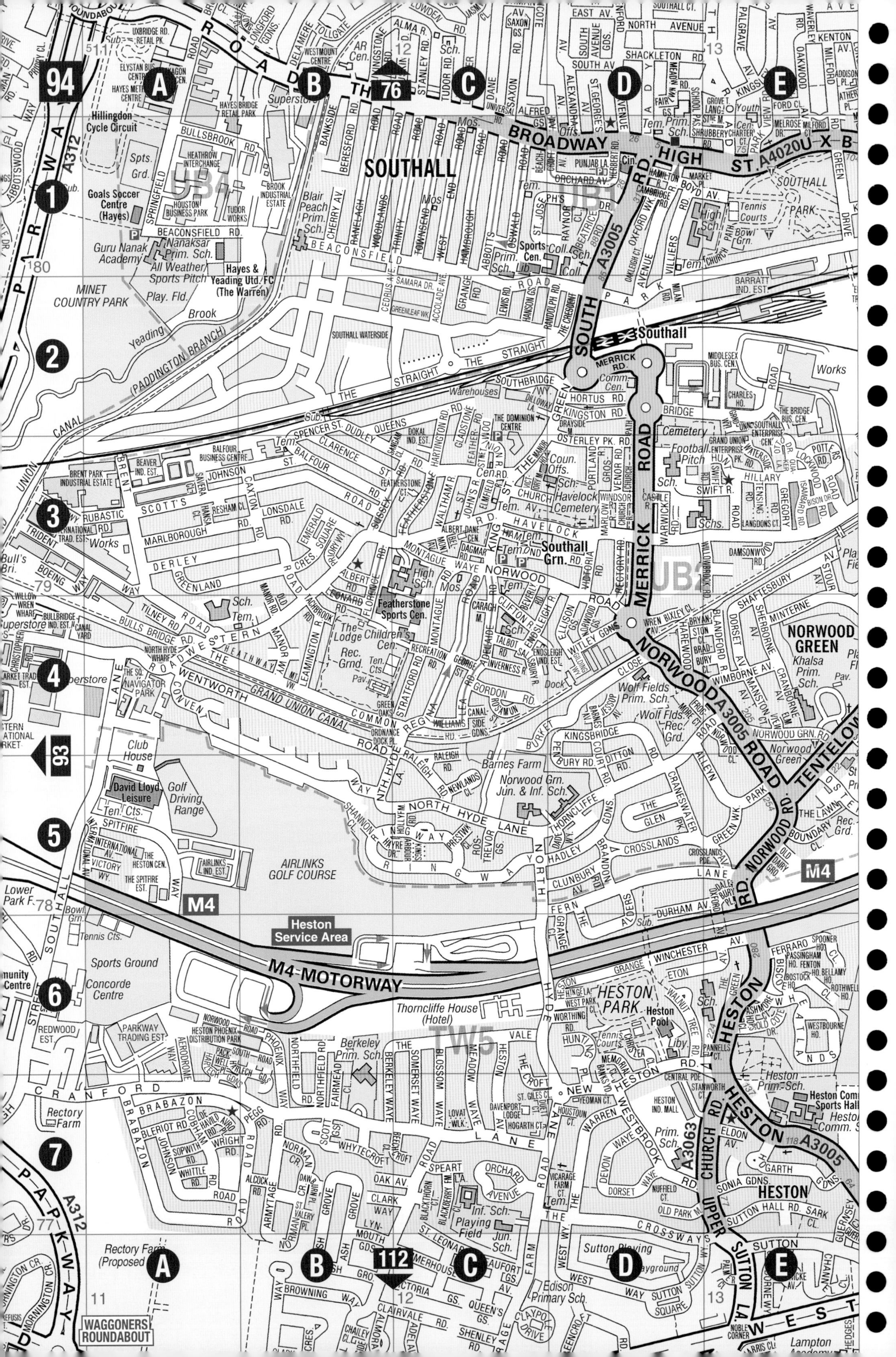

76
93
112
A
B
C
D
E
1
2
3
4
5
6
7
11
12
13
SOUTHALL
BROADWAY
HIGH ST. A4020 U X B
SOUTH RD. A3005
MERRICK ROAD
NORWOOD A3005 ROAD
NORWOOD GREEN
TENTELOW
HESTON A3005
HESTON RD.
HESTON PARK
HESTON
TW5
UB1
UB2
UB4
PARKWAY A312
M4
M4 MOTORWAY
Heston Service Area
AIRLINKS GOLF COURSE
MINET COUNTRY PARK
GRAND UNION CANAL
(PADDINGTON BRANCH)
Yeading Brook
Hillingdon Cycle Circuit
Goals Soccer Centre (Hayes)
Guru Nanak Academy
Nanaksar Prim. Sch.
All Weather Sports Pitch
Hayes & Yeading Utd. FC (The Warren)
BEACONSFIELD RD.
UXBRIDGE ROAD
THE STRAIGHT
SOUTHALL WATERSIDE
Southall
BRENT PARK INDUSTRIAL ESTATE
Blair Peach Prim. Sch.
Featherstone Sports Cen.
The Lodge Children's Cen.
Southall Grn.
Havelock Cemetery
Wolf Fields Prim. Sch.
Barnes Farm
Norwood Grn. Jun. & Inf. Sch.
Khalsa Prim. Sch.
David Lloyd Leisure
Golf Driving Range
NORTH HYDE LANE
RINGWAY
Sports Ground
Concorde Centre
Thorncliffe House (Hotel)
Berkeley Prim. Sch.
Heston Pool
Heston Prim. Sch.
Heston Comm. Sports Hall
Sutton Playing Fields
Edison Primary Sch.
Rectory Farm
Rectory Farm (Proposed)
WAGGONERS ROUNDABOUT
CRANFORD LANE
SUTTON LA.
WEST
SOUTHALL PARK
Tennis Courts
Lower Park F.

DORMER'S WELLS
WEST MIDDLESEX GOLF COURSE
Brent Lodge Park
Millennium Maze
River Brent
Hanwell
HANWELL
Kensington Cemetery
City of Westminster Cemetery
UXBRIDGE ROAD
BROADWAY
A4020
A3002
BOSTON RD.
ST. BERNARD'S HOSPITAL
EALING HOSP.
Meadow Ho. Hospice
Hanwell Locks
GREAT WESTERN INDUSTRIAL PARK
Glade Lane Canalside Park
Windmill Bridge
GRAND UNION CANAL
WINDMILL LANE
B454
QPR Training Academy & Community Sports Complex
Sports Ground
Osterley Sports Club
The Aviary Farm
The Aviary
Elthorne Park
Elthorne Park High Sch.
Elthorne Sports Cen.
Playing Field
Wincott Farm
Osterley Lock
OSTERLEY
M4
Long Wood
Trumpers Wood
OSTERLEY LANE
Osterley Park Farm
Bothy Cottage
Osterley Park & House
PARK
TW7
WYKE GREEN GOLF COURSE
Wyke Green
SYON LANE
Sky Studios
Goals Soccer Centre
Bolder Academy
Nishkam School
JERSEY ROAD
GREAT WEST ROAD
A4
Osterley
Osterley Sports & Athletics Centre
Isleworth Crown Court
SPRING GROVE
77
95
96
113
1
2
3
4
5
6
7
F
G
H
J
K

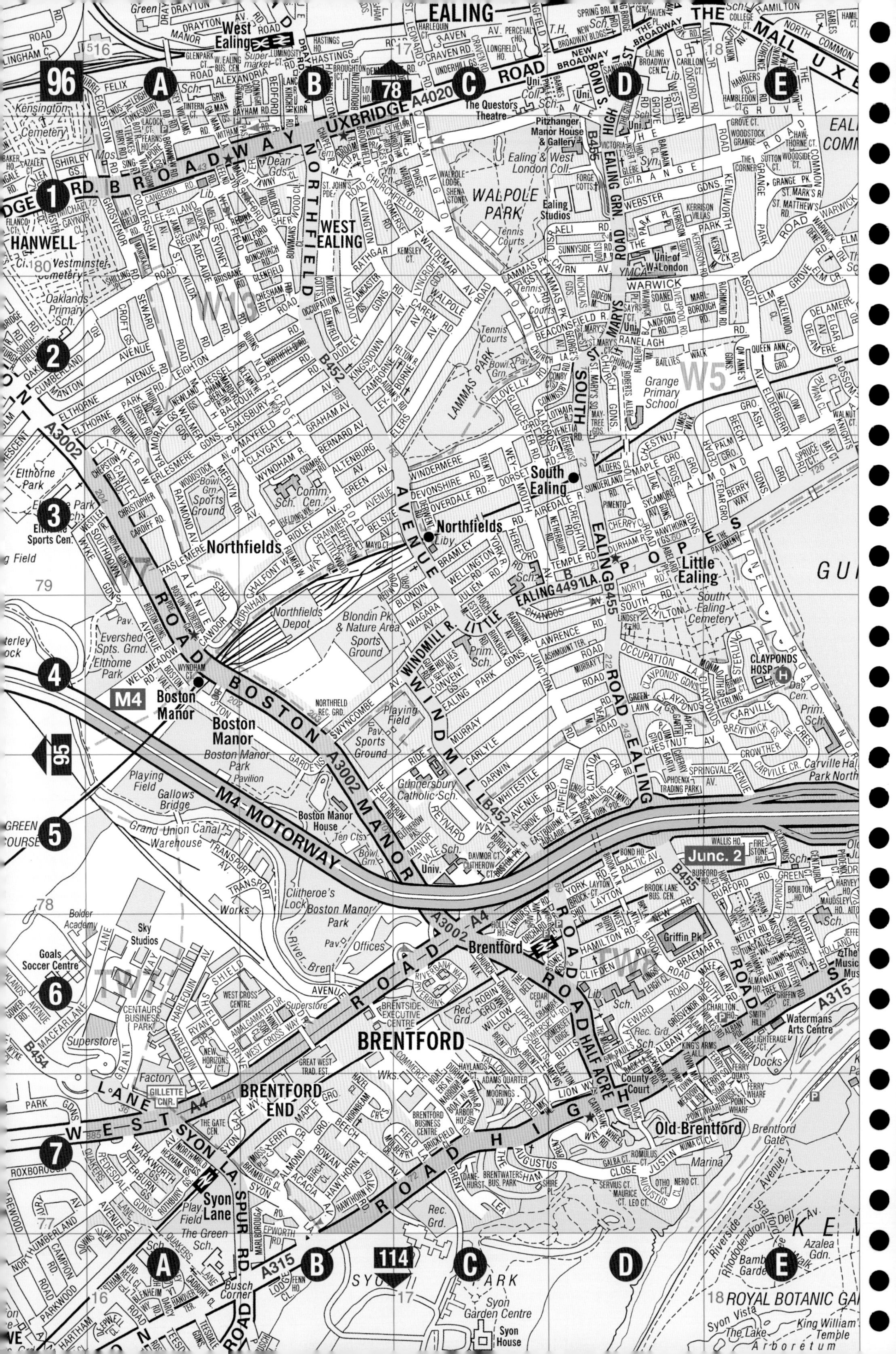

96
78
95
114
A
B
C
D
E
1
2
3
4
5
6
7
EALING
West Ealing
UXBRIDGE ROAD A4020
BROADWAY
THE MALL
NEW BROADWAY
The Questors Theatre
Pitzhanger Manor House & Gallery
Ealing & West London Coll.
WALPOLE PARK
Ealing Studios
Uni. of W. London
YMCA
HANWELL
Westminster Cemetery
Kensington Cemetery
Oaklands Primary Sch.
W13
WEST EALING
NORTHFIELD AVENUE
B452
LAMMAS PARK
South Ealing
SOUTH EALING ROAD
B455
W5
Grange Primary School
Little Ealing
POPES LA.
South Ealing Cemetery
CLAYPONDS HOSP.
Northfields
Elthorne Park
Elthorne Sports Cen.
Northfields Depot
Blondin Pk. & Nature Area Sports Ground
WINDMILL ROAD
LITTLE EALING LA. B4491
Evershed Spts. Grnd.
M4
Boston Manor
BOSTON MANOR ROAD A3002
A3002
Boston Manor Park
Boston Manor House
M4 MOTORWAY
Gunnersbury Catholic Sch.
Junc. 2
Grand Union Canal
Clitheroe's Lock
Gallows Bridge
Sky Studios
Goals Soccer Centre
Bolder Academy
TW7
Superstore
CENTAURS BUSINESS PARK
WEST CROSS CENTRE
BRENTSIDE EXECUTIVE CENTRE
River Brent
Brentford
BRENTFORD
TW8
Griffin Pk.
County Court
HIGH ROAD
HALF ACRE
KEW BRIDGE ROAD
A315
GREAT WEST ROAD A4
WEST CROSS WAY
GILLETTE CNR.
BRENTFORD END
LONDON ROAD
Syon Lane
SYON LA.
SPUR RD.
Busch Corner
SYON PARK
Syon Garden Centre
Syon House
Old Brentford
Watermans Arts Centre
Marina
Brentford Gate
ROYAL BOTANIC GARDENS
KEW
Azalea Gdn.
Rhododendron Dell
Syon Vista
The Lake
King William's Temple
Arboretum
Carville Hall Park North

F
G
H
J
K
79
97
98
115
1
2
3
4
5
6
7
ACTON
EAST ACTON
Ealing Common
Acton Central
ACTON PARK
Acton Town
SOUTH ACTON
South Acton
ACTON GREEN
SOUTHFIELD
BEDFORD PARK
Chiswick Pk.
GUNNERSBURY
Gunnersbury
TURNHAM GREEN
CHISWICK
Chiswick
GROVE PARK
KEW
Kew Bridge
Kew Gds.
W3
W4
TW9
A406
A4020
A4000
A315
A4
A3000
A307
A205
A316
B4491
B491
B409
B490
M4
M4 MOTORWAY
Junc. 1
GUNNERSBURY AVENUE
GUNNERSBURY LANE
UXBRIDGE RD.
TWYFORD AV.
HIGH ST.
THE VALE
CHISWICK HIGH RD.
HEATHFIELD TER.
CEDARS RD.
ELLESMERE RD.
HOGARTH
GT. WEST RD.
WELLESLEY RD.
SOUTH PARADE
ACTON LANE
BURLINGTON LANE
KEW RD.
MORTLAKE RD.
KEW GREEN
STRAND ON THE GREEN
Strand on the Green
London Transport Mus. Depot
Museum
Reynolds Sports Cen.
Twyford Spts. Cen.
West London Coll.
Acton Central
Southfields Rec. Grd.
Popefield Playing Flds.
Gunnersbury Park Mus.
Boating Lake
Miniature Golf Course
International Sch. of London
Kensington Cemetery
Kew East Junc.
Potomac (Fish Pond)
Virgin Active Health Club
Nature Res.
Gunnersby Junc.
Brentford FC Comm. Stadium
Brentford Fountain Leis. Cen.
Mus. of Water & Steam
Kew Pier
Oliver's Island
Botanical Library
Kew Gardens Gallery
Davies Alpine House
Princess of Wales Conservatory
Plants & People Exhibition
Palm House
Rose Garden
Temple of Bellona
The National Archives
Chiswick House & Gardens
Cricket Ground
Chiswick Cemetery
Sports Hall
Quintin Hogg Memorial Sports Ground
Acton Grn. Comm.
Chiswick Common
The Park Club
Maples Children's Cen.

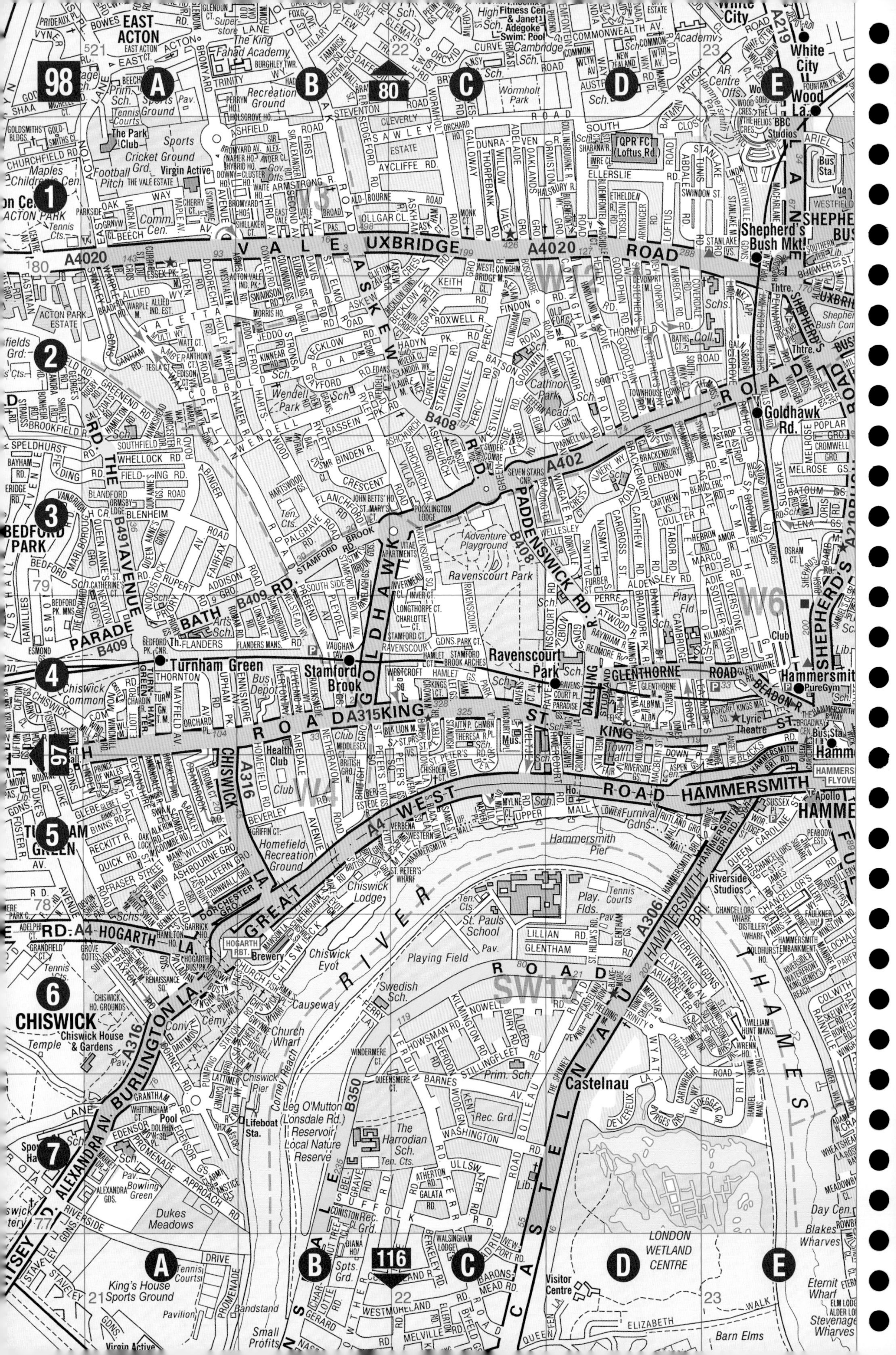

98
80
97
116
A
B
C
D
E
1
2
3
4
5
6
7
EAST ACTON
ACTON PARK
BEDFORD PARK
CHISWICK
Chiswick House & Gardens
White City
Wood La.
BBC Studios
Shepherd's Bush Mkt
Goldhawk Rd.
Hammersmith
Ravenscourt Park
Stamford Brook
Turnham Green
Castelnau
LONDON WETLAND CENTRE
Visitor Centre
Barn Elms
King's House Sports Ground
Dukes Meadows
Chiswick Pier
Lifeboat Sta.
Chiswick Eyot
Hammersmith Pier
St. Pauls School
Playing Field
The Harrodian Sch.
Leg O'Mutton (Lonsdale Rd.) Reservoir Local Nature Reserve
Swedish Sch.
Riverside Studios
Lyric Theatre
Town Hall
Apollo
Adventure Playground
Wormholt Park
QPR FC (Loftus Rd.)
The Park Club
Virgin Active
Cricket Ground
Football Pitch
Recreation Ground
Homefield Recreation Ground
Cathnor Park
Wendell Park
Chiswick Common
Hogarth Rbt.
Brewery
Corney Reach
Church Wharf
Causeway
Furnival Gdns.
Blakes Wharves
Eternit Wharf
Stevenage Wharves
RIVER THAMES
W3
W4
W6
W12
SW13
A4020
UXBRIDGE ROAD
VALE
ASKEW ROAD
GOLDHAWK ROAD
A402
B408
PADDENSWICK RD.
KING ST.
A315
CHISWICK HIGH ROAD
A316
GREAT WEST ROAD
A4
HOGARTH LA.
BURLINGTON LA.
ALEXANDRA AV.
HAMMERSMITH BRI. RD.
A306
CASTELNAU
LONSDALE ROAD
B350
HAMMERSMITH ROAD
SHEPHERD'S BUSH ROAD
GLENTHORNE ROAD
BATH RD.
B409
THE AVENUE
B491
STAMFORD BROOK
UPPER MALL

F
G
H
J
K
1
2
3
4
5
6
7
81
99
100
117
NOTTING HILL
Notting Hill Gate
KENSINGTON
Holland Park
HOLLAND PARK
Kensington Palace
Round Pond
The Orangery
High St. Kensington
Kensington Olympia
Olympia
Shepherd's Bush
Brook Green
WEST KENSINGTON
West Kensington
Barons Court
EARL'S COURT
Earl's Court
West Brompton
WEST BROMPTON
Brompton Cemetery
SOUTH KENSINGTON
Gloucester Rd.
Fulham Broadway
Chelsea FC (Stamford Bridge)
WALHAM GREEN
FULHAM
SANDS END
Imperial Wharf
HAMMERSMITH
TALGARTH RD.
CROMWELL ROAD
KENSINGTON HIGH STREET
HOLLAND PARK AVENUE
LILLIE ROAD
DAWES ROAD
FULHAM ROAD
OLD BROMPTON ROAD
NORTH END ROAD
WARWICK ROAD
EARLS COURT ROAD
FULHAM PALACE ROAD

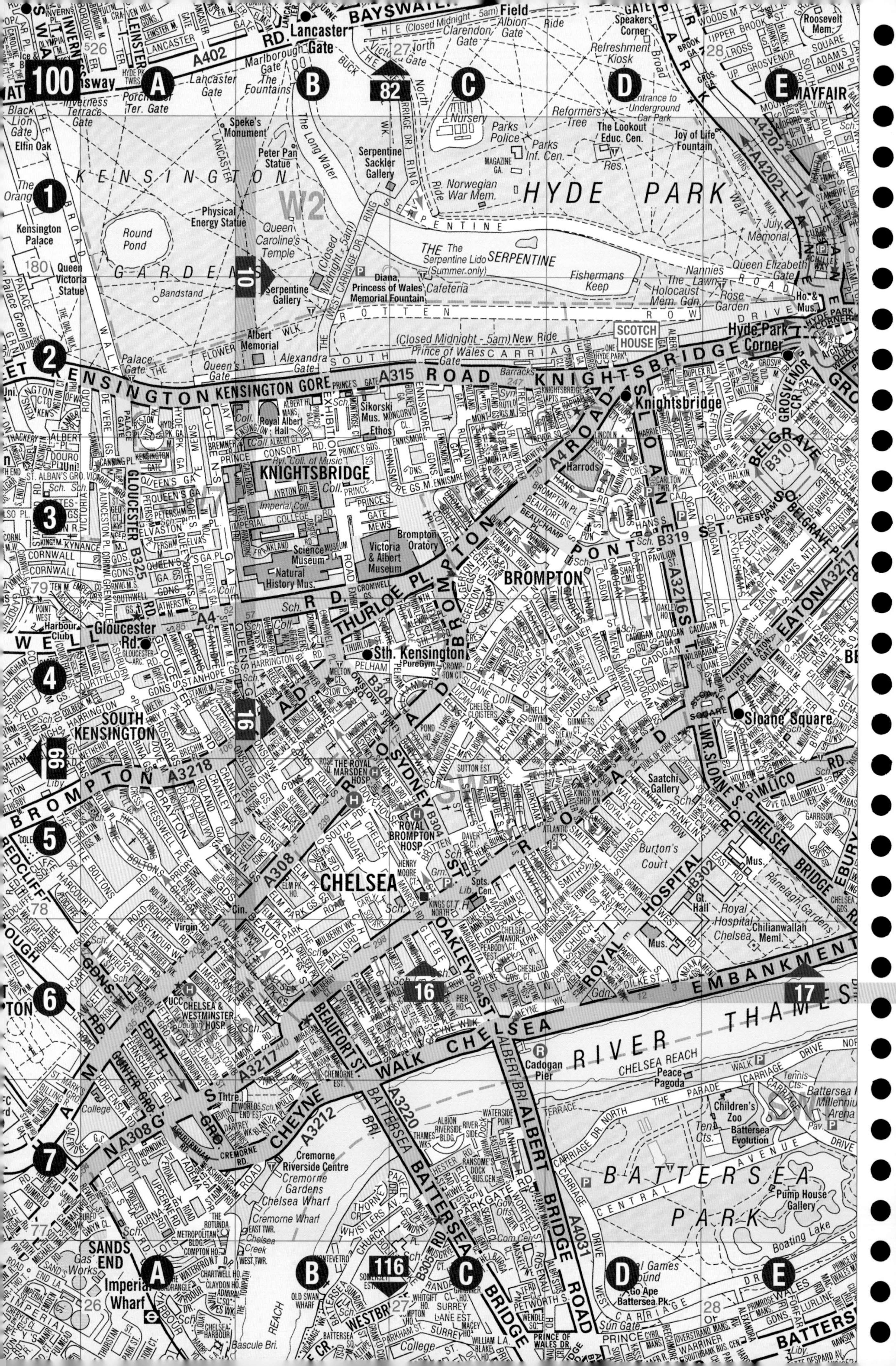
A
B
C
D
E
1
2
3
4
5
6
7
82
10
16
16
17
66
116
BAYSWATER
Lancaster Gate
Field
Speakers Corner
Roosevelt Mem.
MAYFAIR
Albion Gate
Clarendon Gate
Victoria Gate
Marlborough Gate
The Fountains
Lancaster Gate
Porchester Ter. Gate
Inverness Terrace Gate
Black Lion Gate
Elfin Oak
Refreshment Kiosk
Entrance to Underground Car Park
Reformers Tree
The Lookout Educ. Cen.
Joy of Life Fountain
Speke's Monument
Peter Pan Statue
The Long Water
Nursery
Parks Police
Parks Inf. Cen.
Serpentine Sackler Gallery
Norwegian War Mem.
KENSINGTON
HYDE PARK
W2
Kensington Palace
Physical Energy Statue
Round Pond
Queen Caroline's Temple
THE SERPENTINE
The Serpentine Lido (Summer only)
Queen Victoria Statue
GARDENS
Bandstand
Serpentine Gallery
Diana, Princess of Wales Memorial Fountain
Cafeteria
Fishermans Keep
The Holocaust Mem. Gdn.
Nannies Lawn
Rose Garden
Queen Elizabeth Gate
7 July Memorial
ROTTEN ROW
Albert Memorial
Alexandra Gate
Palace Gate
Queen's Gate
(Closed Midnight - 5am) New Ride
Prince of Wales Gate
SOUTH CARRIAGE
SCOTCH HOUSE
Hyde Park Corner
KENSINGTON GORE
KENSINGTON ROAD
A315
KNIGHTSBRIDGE
Knightsbridge
Royal Albert Hall
Sikorski Mus.
Ethos
Ryl. Coll. of Music
KNIGHTSBRIDGE
Imperial Coll.
IMPERIAL COLLEGE
Science Museum
Natural History Mus.
Victoria & Albert Museum
Brompton Oratory
Harrods
BELGRAVE SQ.
BROMPTON
BROMPTON ROAD
THURLOE PL.
CROMWELL ROAD
A4
Gloucester Rd.
GLOUCESTER ROAD
Sth. Kensington
PureGym
SOUTH KENSINGTON
Sloane Square
SLOANE SQUARE
SLOANE ST.
A3216
B319
PONT ST.
CADOGAN
EATON SQ.
A3217
PIMLICO RD
BROMPTON ROAD
A3218
THE ROYAL MARSDEN HOSP
ROYAL BROMPTON HOSP
SYDNEY ST.
FULHAM ROAD
A308
KING'S ROAD
CHELSEA
Saatchi Gallery
Burton's Court
ROYAL HOSPITAL RD.
Royal Hospital Chelsea
Chilianwallah Meml.
Ranelagh Gardens
CHELSEA BRIDGE
Gt. Hall
Mus.
UCC
CHELSEA & WESTMINSTER HOSP.
Virgin
Cin.
CHEYNE WALK
CHELSEA EMBANKMENT
RIVER THAMES
Cadogan Pier
CHELSEA REACH
Peace Pagoda
Children's Zoo
Battersea Evolution
Battersea Park Millennium Arena
BATTERSEA PARK
Pump House Gallery
Boating Lake
ALBERT BRIDGE
ALBERT BRIDGE ROAD
A4031
BATTERSEA BRIDGE
A3220
A3212
Cremorne Riverside Centre
Cremorne Gardens
Chelsea Wharf
Cremorne Wharf
Chelsea Creek
SANDS END
Gas Works
Imperial Wharf
College
Go Ape Battersea Pk.
Sun Gate
BATTERSEA
Bascule Bri.

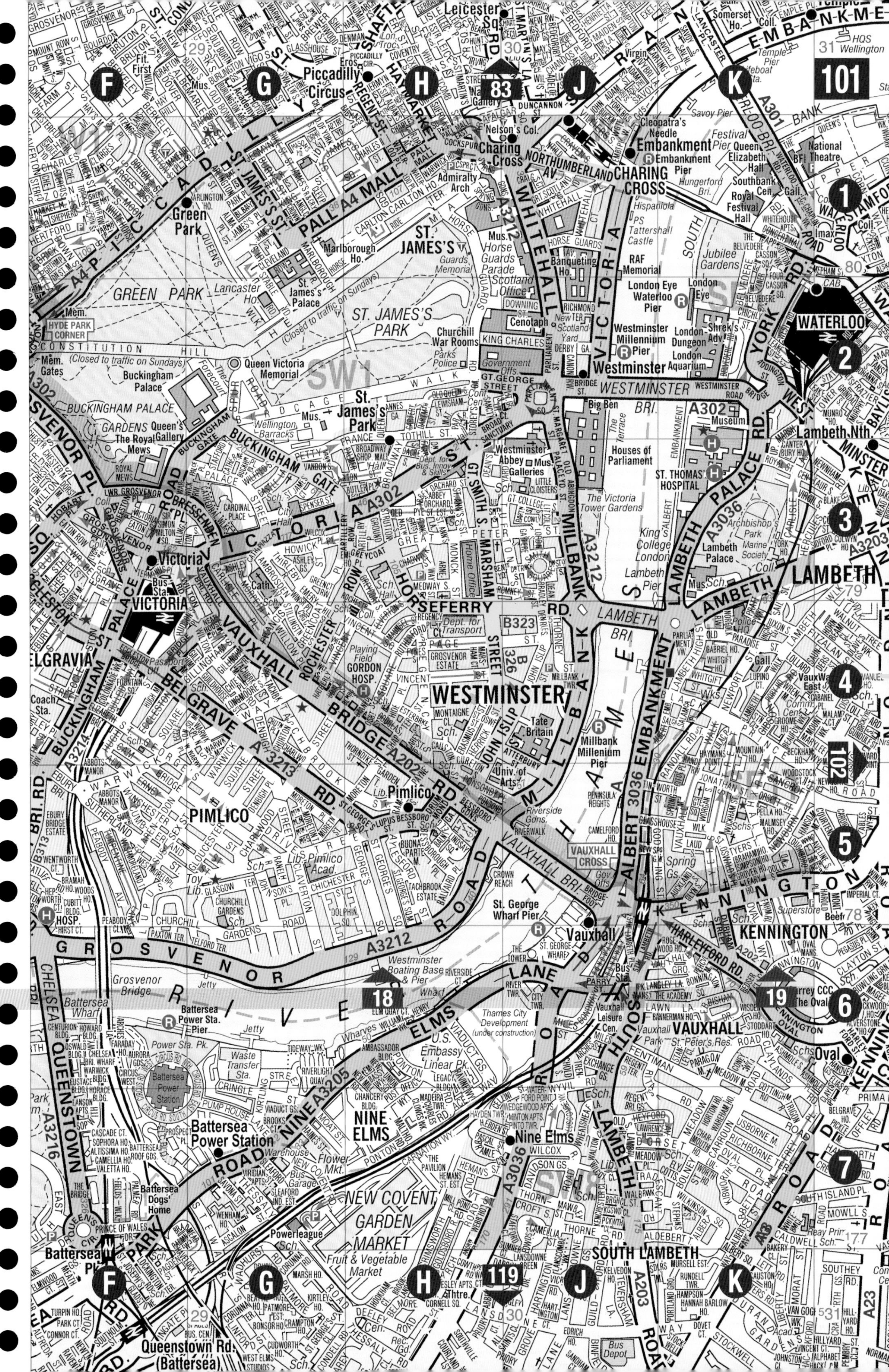

101
83
102
18
19
119
F
G
H
J
K
1
2
3
4
5
6
7
Piccadilly Circus
Leicester Sq.
Green Park
GREEN PARK
HYDE PARK CORNER
CONSTITUTION HILL
(Closed to traffic on Sundays)
Buckingham Palace
BUCKINGHAM PALACE GARDENS
Queen Victoria Memorial
The Royal Mews
Queen's Gallery
St. James's Palace
ST. JAMES'S PARK
ST. JAMES'S
Marlborough Ho.
PALL MALL
A4
PICCADILLY
THE MALL
Admiralty Arch
Nelson's Col.
Charing Cross
CHARING CROSS
Embankment
Cleopatra's Needle
Embankment Pier
Hungerford Bri.
Festival Pier
Queen Elizabeth Hall
Southbank Cen.
Royal Festival Hall
National Theatre
Imax
Horse Guards Parade
Banqueting Ho.
Scotland Office
Cenotaph
Churchill War Rooms
Government Offs.
Westminster
Westminster Millennium Pier
London Eye
London Eye Waterloo Pier
London Dungeon
London Aquarium
Jubilee Gardens
RAF Memorial
WATERLOO
Big Ben
Houses of Parliament
Westminster Abbey
ST. THOMAS'S HOSPITAL
Lambeth Palace
LAMBETH
Lambeth Nth.
King's College London
Lambeth Pier
The Victoria Tower Gardens
WHITEHALL
MILLBANK
VICTORIA
Victoria
VICTORIA
SW1
St. James's Park
HORSEFERRY RD.
Home Office
Dept. for Transport
WESTMINSTER
Tate Britain
Millbank Millennium Pier
Univ. of Arts
Pimlico
PIMLICO
BELGRAVIA
VAUXHALL BRIDGE RD.
BELGRAVE RD.
Riverside Gdns.
VAUXHALL CROSS
Vauxhall
VAUXHALL
ALBERT EMBANKMENT
St. George Wharf Pier
KENNINGTON
Oval
Surrey CCC The Oval
GROSVENOR ROAD
RIVER THAMES
Grosvenor Bridge
Battersea Power Sta. Pier
Battersea Power Station
Westminster Boating Base & Pier
Thames City Development (under construction)
U.S. Embassy
NINE ELMS
NINE ELMS LANE
Nine Elms
NEW COVENT GARDEN MARKET
Fruit & Vegetable Market
SOUTH LAMBETH
QUEENSTOWN RD.
Queenstown Rd. (Battersea)
Battersea Park
Battersea Dogs' Home
SW8

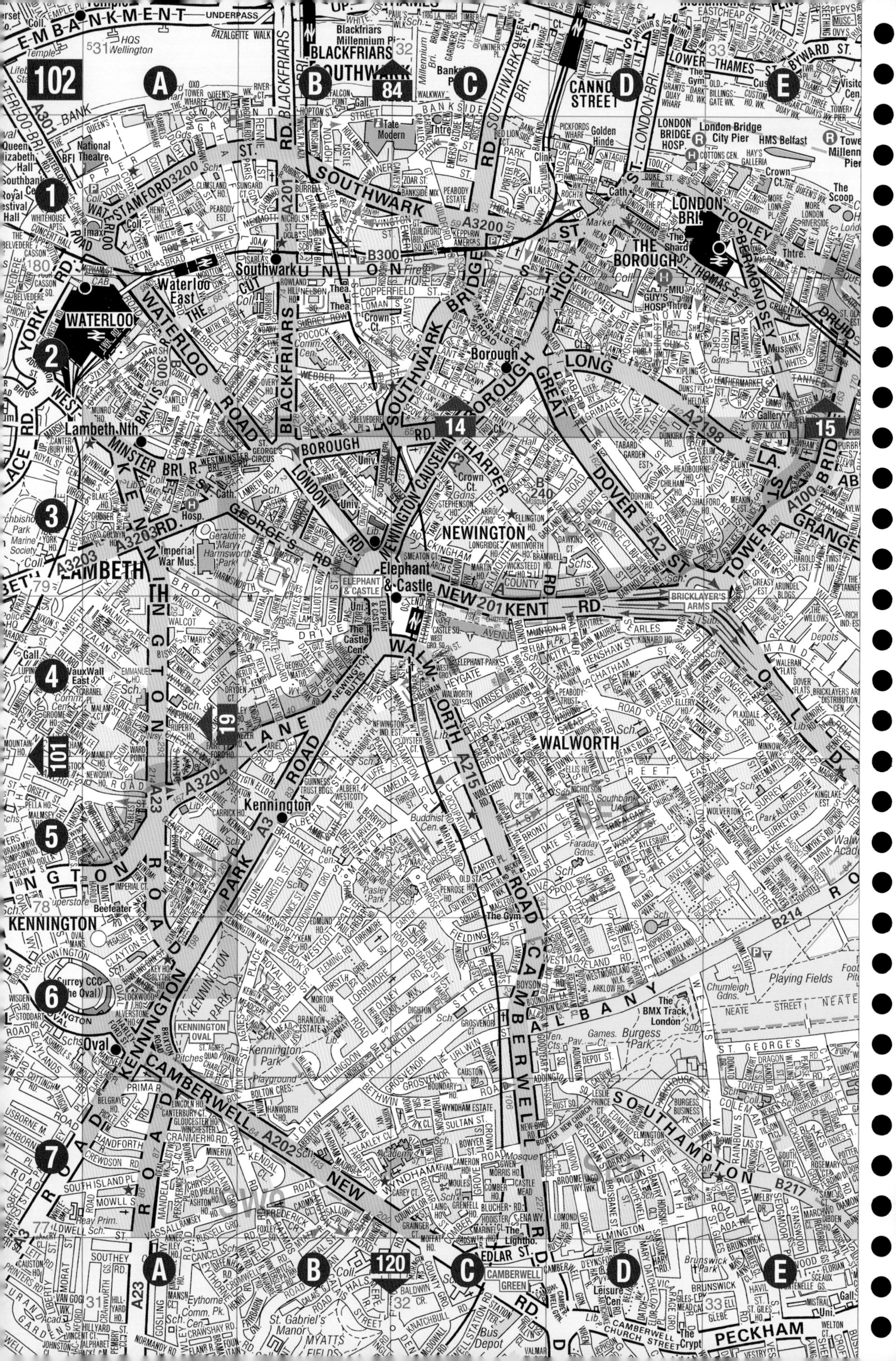
EMBANKMENT
UNDERPASS
BLACKFRIARS
SOUTHWARK
84
CANNON STREET
LOWER THAMES ST.
BYWARD ST.
National Theatre
Tate Modern
Golden Hinde
London Bridge City Pier
HMS Belfast
Tower Millennium Pier
LONDON BRIDGE HOSP.
STAMFORD ST.
A3200
SOUTHWARK ST.
LONDON BRI.
TOOLEY ST.
The Shard
THE BOROUGH
GUY'S HOSP.
B300
UNION ST.
Southwark
Waterloo East
WATERLOO
WATERLOO RD.
BLACKFRIARS RD.
SOUTHWARK BRIDGE RD.
BOROUGH HIGH ST.
Borough
LONG LANE
BERMONDSEY ST.
GREAT DOVER ST.
A2198
14
15
Lambeth Nth.
WESTMINSTER BRI. RD.
ST. GEORGE'S RD.
BOROUGH RD.
LONDON RD.
NEWINGTON CAUSEWAY
HARPER RD.
A2
TOWER BRIDGE RD.
A100
GRANGE RD.
Imperial War Mus.
Geraldine Mary Harmsworth Park
A3203
LAMBETH
NEWINGTON
Elephant & Castle
ELEPHANT & CASTLE
NEW KENT RD.
A201
BRICKLAYER'S ARMS
19
101
KENNINGTON LANE
A3204
WALWORTH RD.
A215
WALWORTH
OLD KENT RD.
Kennington
A3
KENNINGTON PARK RD.
A23
KENNINGTON
Surrey CCC (The Oval)
Oval
KENNINGTON OVAL
CAMBERWELL NEW RD.
A202
CAMBERWELL RD.
ALBANY RD.
Burgess Park
The BMX Track, London
Playing Fields
SOUTHAMPTON WAY
B217
B214
120
CAMBERWELL GREEN
Eythorne Comm. Pk.
St. Gabriel's Manor
MYATTS FIELDS
Brunswick Park
PECKHAM
CAMBERWELL CHURCH STREET
The Crypt
A
B
C
D
E
1
2
3
4
5
6
7

103
Tower Hill
Tower Gateway
The Tower of London
Tower Bridge
St. Katharine Docks
St. Katharine's Pier
EAST SMITHFIELD
THE HIGHWAY
WAPPING
Wapping
Shadwell Basin
Shadwell Dock Stairs
King Edward Mem. Park
ROTHERHITHE TUNNEL
SALTER RD.
Bellamy's Wharf
New Crane Stairs
Wapping Dock Stairs
Thames Police Mus.
Wapping Old Stairs
Wapping New Stairs
Cumberland Wharf
UPPER POOL
LOWER POOL
Cherry Garden Pier
King's Stairs
BERMONDSEY
Bermondsey
Rotherhithe
Canada Water
ROTHERHITHE
Surrey Quays
Stave Hill Ecological Park
JAMAICA ROAD
BRUNEL RD.
LOWER RD.
REDRIFF RD.
PLOUGH WAY
SOUTHWARK PARK RD.
Southwark Park
SE16
Printing Works
Bowl. Alley & Gala Bingo
Odeon Cinema
Leisure Cen.
Gallery By The Pool
Southwark Pk. Sports Cen. Track
Sports Complex
TeamSport Indoor Karting
Harris Academy
RAYMOUTH RD.
A2206
A2208
ROTHERHITHE NEW RD.
South Bermondsey
Lewisham Lions Cen.
Millwall FC (The Den)
New Bermondsey (Proposed)
Waste Transfer Station
Silwood Triangle
ROLLS RD.
DUNTON RD.
OLD KENT ROAD
TRAFALGAR AV.
South Eastern Gas Wks.
Waste Processing Facility
CANAL BRIDGE
Burgess Pk.
PECKHAM PARK RD.
PECKHAM HILL ST.
SE15
SE14
Brimmington Pk.
NEW CROSS RD.
New Cross Gate
NEW CROSS GATE
Bus Garage
QUEEN'S RD.
Queens Rd. (Peckham)
PECKHAM HIGH ST.
Bus Station
NEW POMEROY ST.
Hatcham Gs.
Eckington Gs.
85
15
104
121
34
35
36
F
G
H
J
K
1
2
3
4
5
6
7

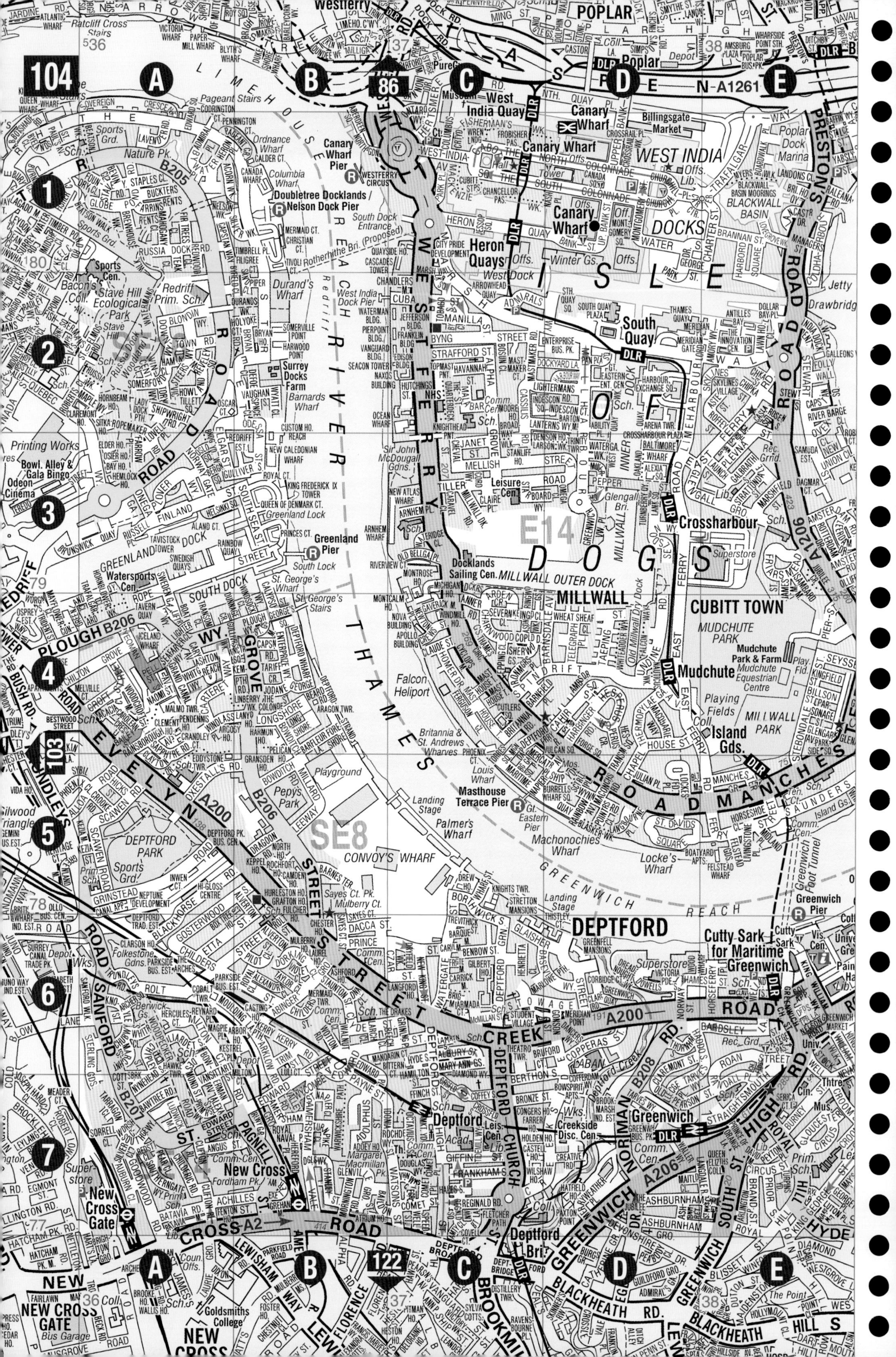

A
B
C
D
E
1
2
3
4
5
6
7
86
103
122
POPLAR
Poplar
West India Quay
Canary Wharf
Billingsgate Market
WEST INDIA
DOCKS
Heron Quays
South Quay
Crossharbour
Mudchute
Island Gds.
Cutty Sark for Maritime Greenwich
Greenwich
Deptford
Deptford Bri.
New Cross
New Cross Gate
NEW CROSS GATE
DEPTFORD
MILLWALL
CUBITT TOWN
ISLE OF DOGS
E14
SE8
RIVER THAMES
LIMEHOUSE REACH
GREENWICH REACH
Canary Wharf Pier
Doubletree Docklands / Nelson Dock Pier
Masthouse Terrace Pier
Greenland Pier
Greenwich Pier
Surrey Docks Farm
Stave Hill Ecological Park
Redriff Prim. Sch.
Printing Works
Bowl. Alley & Gala Bingo
Odeon Cinema
Watersports Cen.
Dockslands Sailing Cen.
MILLWALL OUTER DOCK
MUDCHUTE PARK
Mudchute Park & Farm
MILLWALL PARK
DEPTFORD PARK
Pepys Park
CONVOY'S WHARF
Falcon Heliport
Goldsmiths College
Creekside Disc. Cen.
EVELYN STREET
ROTHERHITHE
CREEK ROAD
MANCHESTER ROAD
WESTFERRY ROAD
PRESTONS ROAD
LOWER ROAD
PLOUGH WY
SALTER ROAD
NEW CROSS ROAD
GREENWICH HIGH ROAD
DEPTFORD CHURCH STREET
DEPTFORD HIGH STREET
GREENWICH SOUTH STREET
BLACKHEATH RD.
EAST INDIA DOCK ROAD
A200
A206
A1206
A1261
A2
B205
B206
B207
B208

105
87
106
123
F
G
H
J
K
1
2
3
4
5
6
7
East India
Blackwall
LEAMOUTH
East India Dock Basin Nature Reserve
Virginia Quay
Blackwall Pier
Wharves
Jetty
Works
DLR
Custom House for ExCeL
ExCeL
ROYAL VICTORIA
SS Robin
Millennium Mill
Emirates Royal Docks
Wakeup Docklands
SILVERTOWN WY.
NORTH WOOLWICH ROAD
A1020
West Silvertown
E16
Blackwall Point
BLACKWALL TUNNEL
A102
Hollywood Bowl
The O2
indigo at The O2
Up at The O2
North Greenwich
North Greenwich Pier
Emirates Air Line Cable Car
SILVERTOWN TUNNEL (PROPOSED)
Thames Wharf
Brewery
RIVER THAMES
Gallery
Emirates Greenwich Peninsula
Delta Wharf
Greenwich Peninsula Golf Driving Range
Victoria Deep Water Terminal
Central Park
Gas Works
Lorry Park
Manhattan Wharf
Lyle Park
Royal Wharf Pier
Thames Barrier Yacht Club Marina
Greenwich Yacht Club
Greenwich Peninsula Ecology Park
Swan Lake
Southern Park
Christie's Wharf
Depot
MERIDIAN TRADING ESTATE
SE7
Superstore
Cinema
Superstores
Nature Res.
Warehouse
BLACKWALL TUNNEL SOUTHERN APPROACH
A2203
Primrose Wharf
Morden Wharf
Pier
Jetty
Enderby's Wharf
Pipers Wharf
Cubitt Town Wharf
Newcastle Drawdock
Granite Wharf
Lovell's Wharf
WOOLWICH RD.
A206
TRAFALGAR RD.
Westcombe Park
Charlton
Trident Hall
Trinity Hospital
Maze Hill
E. Greenwich Pleasaunce
National Maritime Museum
GREENWICH
GREENWICH PARK
St. Mary's Gate
Prime Meridian Line
Peter Harrison Planetarium
Royal Observatory Greenwich
Bandstand
Reservoir (covered)
Playground
Tennis Courts
Parks Police
The Wilderness (Deer Park)
The Gardens
SE3
Woodland Dell
CHARLTON RD.
B210
Blackheath RUFC (Rectory Fld.)
Leigh Acad.
OLD DOVER ROAD
SHOOTERS HILL ROAD
A2
KIDBROOKE
Blackheath Nursy. & Prep. Sch.
SUN-IN-THE-SANDS
Bowls Ground
VANBRUGH PARK

106
88
105
124
A
B
C
D
E
1
2
3
4
5
6
7
ROYAL ALBERT DOCK
LONDON CITY AIRPORT
E16
Terminal Building
London City Airport
KING GEORGE V DOCK
Beckton Park
Cyprus
University
Royal Albert
London Regatta Centre
Millennium Mill
Pontoon Dock
SS Robin
WOOLWICH A1020 ROAD
CONNAUGHT BRIDGE
A1020
A112
ALBERT ROAD
FACTORY ROAD
Pontoon Dock
SILVERTOWN
Thames Barrier Park
THAMESIDE INDUSTRIAL ESTATE
Sugar Refinery
Works
STANDARD INDUSTRIAL ESTATE
King George V
NORTH WOOLWICH
PIER RD.
A117
North Woolwich Pier
North Terminal
WOOLWICH REACH
RIVER
THAMES BARRIER
WOOLWICH FREE FERRY
Subway
Barrier Gardens Pier
Thames Barrier Info. Cen.
South Terminal
Waterfront Leisure Cen.
WOOLWICH HIGH ST.
WOOLWICH CHURCH ST.
WOOLWICH ROAD
A206
New Charlton
Woolwich Dockyard
WOOLWICH
JOHN WILSON ST.
ARTILLERY PL.
WELLINGTON ST.
Maryon Park
MARYON WILSON PARK
Charlton
Charlton Athletic FC (The Valley)
SE7
LITTLE HEATH
HILL REACH
B210
Gun Park
Royal Artillery Barracks
Repository Woods
Rifle Range
Playground
Barrack Field
Blue Gate
GRAND DEPOT RD.
A205
CHARLTON PARK RD.
CHARLTON
Charlton Ho.
Library
THE VILLAGE
CHARLTON PARK
Cricket Ground
Charlton Park Academy
CHARLTON CEMETERY
QUEEN ELIZABETH HOSPITAL
UCC
WOOLWICH COMMON
WOOLWICH COMMON ROAD
Playing Field
Sports Ground
Hornfair Park
Charlton Lido Lifestyle Club
Blackheath RUFC (Rectory Fld.)
Leigh Acad.
SHOOTERS HILL ROAD
A207
Recreation Ground
Bowls Ground
Greenwich Free School
Reservoir (covered)
ACADEMY ROAD
Shooters Hill Post 16 Campus
41
42
43
77
78
79
180

F
G
H
J
K
89
107
108
125
THAMESMEAD CENTRAL
THAMESMEAD WEST
Thamesmead South West
THAMES
GALLIONS REACH
WOOLWICH REACH
Gallions Point
Gallions Point Marina
Training Centre
Custom House
Cycle Track
Drawbridge
Hoba Wharf
Royal Gardens
Woolwich Arsenal Pier
Royal Arsenal West
Royal Brass Fdy.
Woolwich
Woolwich Arsenal
PLUMSTEAD
Plumstead
PLUMSTEAD MARSHES
HMP ISIS
HMP BELMARSH
HMP THAMESIDE
SE28
SE18
Crown Ct. & Magistrates Ct.
WEST THAMESMEAD BUSINESS PK.
WHITE HART TRIANGLE
Gallions Park
Gallions Lake
Broadwater
Broadwater Green
Tor
Recreation Ground
Plumstead Gdns.
Plumstead Common
SHREWSBURY PARK
Clothworkers Wood
Woolwich Cemetery
East Wickham Open Space
SHOOTERS HILL GOLF COURSE
Winn's Common
WOOLWICH MANOR WAY
A117
A206
A2016
A2041
A209
WESTERN WAY
PLUMSTEAD RD.
PLUMSTEAD HIGH STREET
WICKHAM STREET
BERESFORD ST.
WALMER TERRACE
Bleak Hill
Twin Tumps
Woolwich Polytec Sch. for
1
2
3
4
5
6
7
44
45
46
177

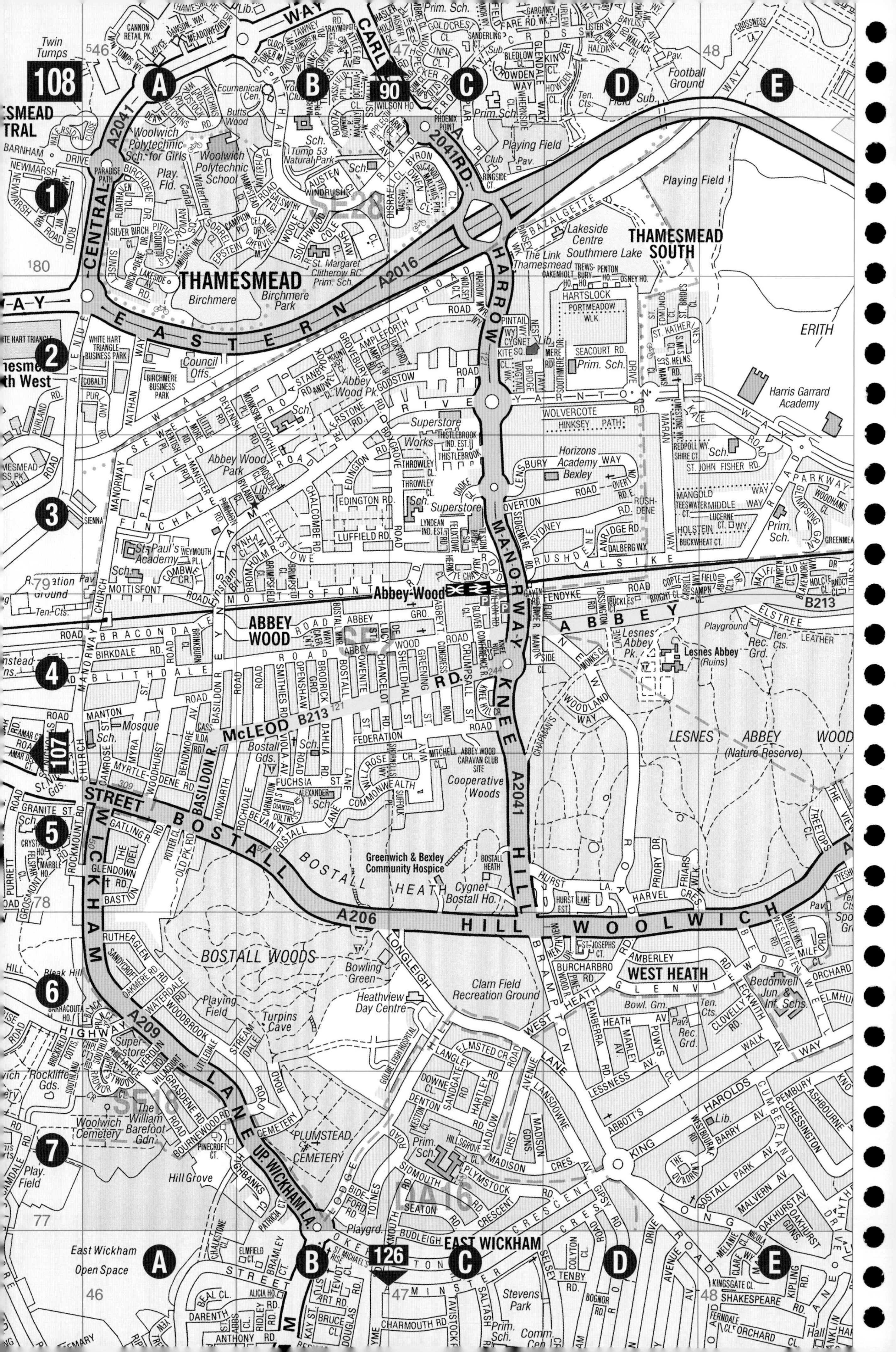
108
A
B
C
D
E
1
2
3
4
5
6
7
90
126
107
46
47
48
180
79
78
77
Twin Tumps
THAMESMEAD
THAMESMEAD SOUTH
SE28
SE2
SE18
DA16
ABBEY WOOD
WEST HEATH
EAST WICKHAM
ERITH
Woolwich Polytechnic Sch. for Girls
Woolwich Polytechnic School
Birchmere
Birchmere Park
Playing Field
Lakeside Centre
Southmere Lake
The Link Thamesmead
Harris Garrard Academy
Horizons Academy Bexley
Abbey Wood Park
Abbey Wood
Lesnes Abbey (Ruins)
LESNES ABBEY WOOD (Nature Reserve)
Cooperative Woods
Greenwich & Bexley Community Hospice
BOSTALL WOODS
Bostall Heath
Clam Field Recreation Ground
Heathview Day Centre
Turpins Cave
Bowling Green
PLUMSTEAD CEMETERY
Woolwich Cemetery
The William Barefoot Gdn.
Hill Grove
East Wickham Open Space
Stevens Park
Bedonwell Jun. & Inf. Schs.
St. Paul's Academy
Football Ground
A2041
A2016
A206
A209
B213
EASTERN WAY
HARROW MANORWAY
KNEE HILL
BOSTALL HILL
WOOLWICH ROAD
WICKHAM LANE
UP. WICKHAM LA.
McLEOD RD.
ABBEY ROAD
CENTRAL WAY
YARNTON WAY
SEWELL ROAD
MOTTISFONT ROAD
BOSTALL HEATH
KING HAROLDS WAY
LONG LANE

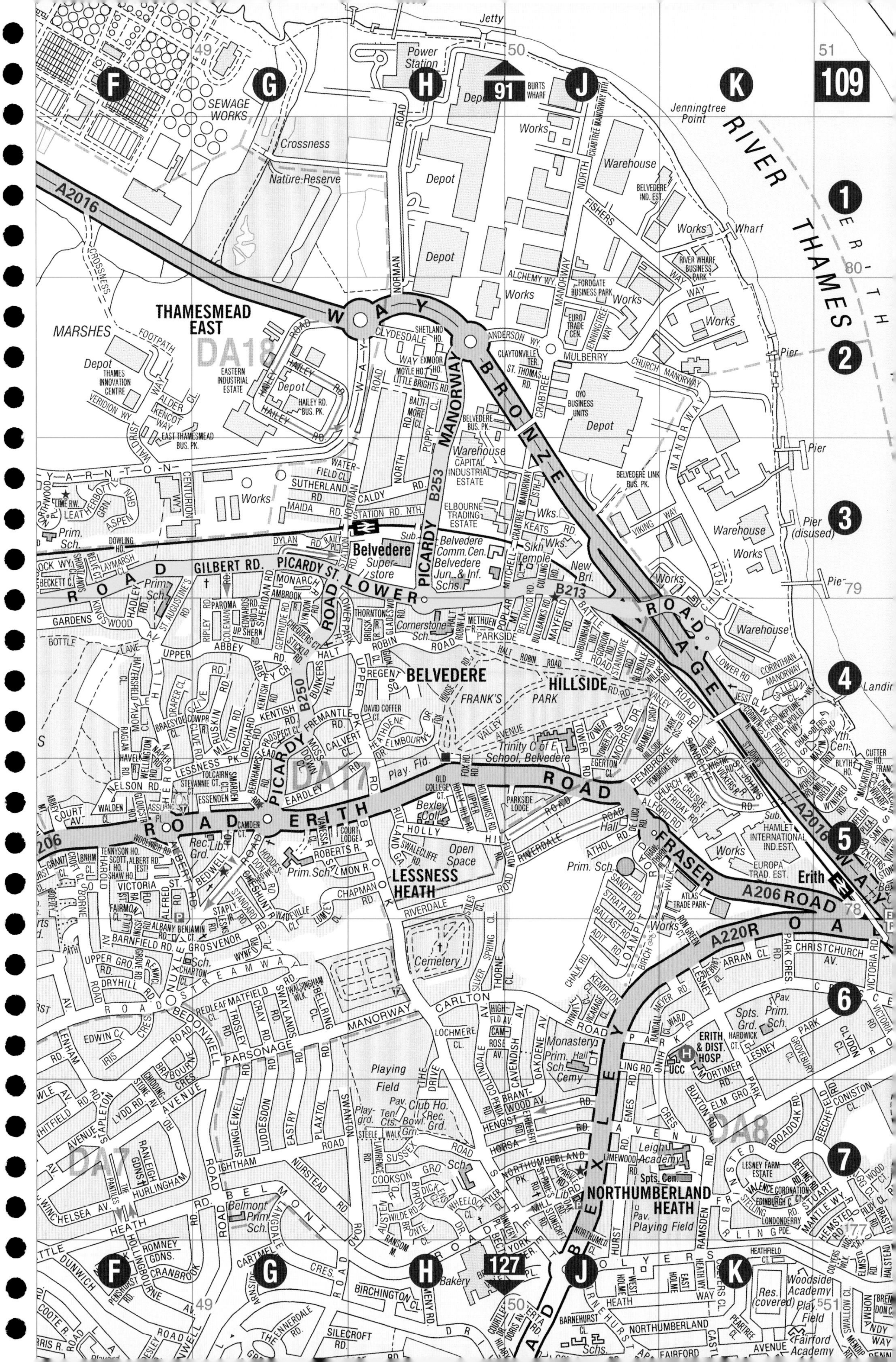

F
G
H
J
K
49
50
51
1
2
3
4
5
6
7
80
79
78
77
91
127
Jetty
Power Station
Depot
BURTS WHARF
Jenningtree Point
RIVER THAMES
ERITH
SEWAGE WORKS
Crossness
Nature Reserve
A2016
Warehouse
BELVEDERE IND. EST.
Works
Wharf
RIVER WHARF BUSINESS PARK
FORDGATE BUSINESS PARK
EURO TRADE CEN.
ALCHEMY WY.
Pier
THAMESMEAD EAST
MARSHES
FOOTPATH
DA18
EASTERN INDUSTRIAL ESTATE
THAMES INNOVATION CENTRE
VERIDION WY
HAILEY RD. BUS. PK.
EAST THAMESMEAD BUS. PK.
WAY
BRONZE
CLYDESDALE
SHETLAND HO.
EXMOOR HO.
MOYLE HO.
LITTLE BRIGHTS RD.
ANDERSON WY.
CLAYTONVILLE TER.
ST. THOMAS RD.
MULBERRY
CHURCH MANORWAY
OYO BUSINESS UNITS
BELVEDERE BUS. PK.
CAPITAL INDUSTRIAL ESTATE
ELBOURNE TRADING ESTATE
BELVEDERE LINK BUS. PK.
VIKING WAY
Pier (disused)
YARNTON
CENTURION WY.
SUTHERLAND RD.
MAIDA RD.
CALDY RD.
STATION RD. NTH.
NORMAN ROAD
B253
PICARDY MANORWAY
Prim. Sch.
DOWLING HO.
DYLAN RD.
Belvedere
Superstore
Belvedere Comm. Cen.
Belvedere Jun. & Inf. Schs.
Sikh Temple
New Bri.
B213
LOWER
PICARDY ST.
GILBERT RD.
ROAD
KEATS RD.
Cornerstone Sch.
PARKSIDE
HALT ROBIN ROAD
ASHBURNHAM
STANMORE
GLENDALE
LOWER RD
CORINTHIAN MANORWAY
Landing
Yth. Cen.
BELVEDERE
HILLSIDE
FRANK'S PARK
B250
BUNKERS HILL
UPPER ABBEY
REGENT SQ.
DAVID COFFER CT.
FREMANTLE
CALVERT
ELMBOURNE DR.
VALLEY AVENUE
Trinity C of E School, Belvedere
PEMBROKE
DA17
Play. Fld.
ERITH ROAD
OLD COLLEGE CT.
Bexley Coll.
PARKSIDE LODGE
HOLLY HILL
RIVERDALE
Open Space
LESSNESS HEATH
FRASER
A206 ROAD
A2016
HAMLET INTERNATIONAL IND. EST.
EUROPA TRAD. EST.
Erith
ATLAS TRADE PARK
Works
Prim. Sch.
Rec. Grd.
Lib.
NELSON RD.
WALDEN
ABBEY
COURT AV.
TENNYSON HO.
SCOTT, ALBERT RD.
SHAW HO.
VICTORIA ST.
Cemetery
A220
CHRISTCHURCH AV.
ARRAN CL.
PARK CRES
VICTORIA RD.
Spts. Grd.
Prim. Sch.
Pav.
LESNEY PARK
ERITH & DIST. HOSP.
UCC
MORTIMER RD.
Monastery Prim. Sch.
Hall
Cemy.
BEXLEY
CARLTON
MANORWAY
PARSONAGE
Playing Field
Club Ho.
Rec. Grd.
Bowl. Grn.
Ten. Cts.
Play-grd.
Sch.
HENGIST
HORSA
NORTHUMBERLAND
Leigh Academy
Spts. Cen.
NORTHUMBERLAND HEATH
Pav. Playing Field
DA8
LESNEY FARM ESTATE
CORONATION CT.
EDINBURGH C.
LONDONDERRY
MANTLE WY.
HEMSTED
DA7
STAPLETON
RANLEIGH GDNS.
HURLINGHAM
AVENUE
HEATH
CHELSEA AV.
BELMONT
Belmont Prim. Sch.
LANGDALE
DUNWICH
ROMNEY GDNS.
CRANBROOK
CARTMEL
BIRCHINGTON CL.
Bakery
YORK
A2
NORTHUMBERLAND
COLYERS
HEATHFIELD
Res. (covered)
Woodside Academy
Play. Field
Fairford Academy
Schs.
BARNEHURST

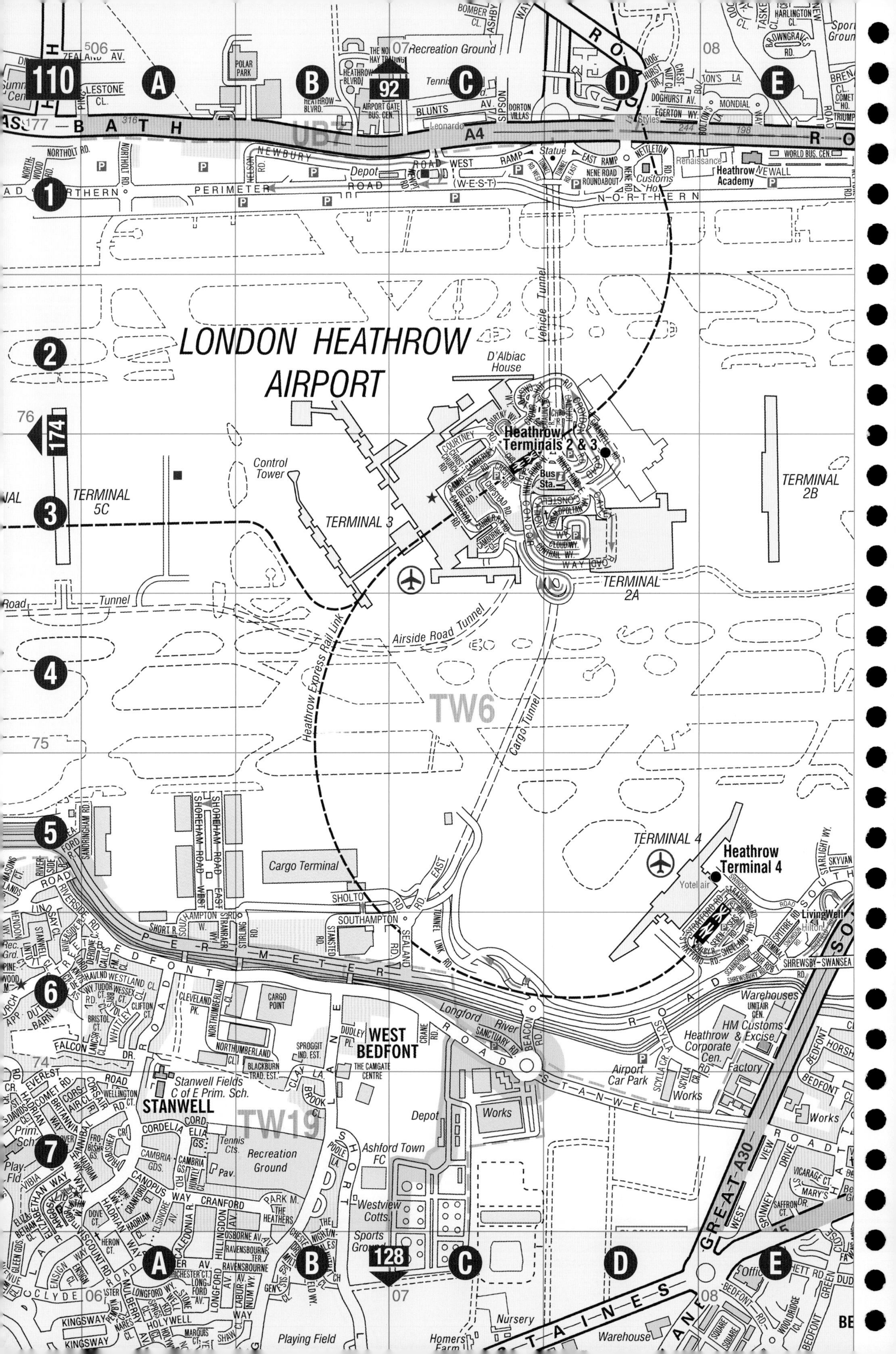

110
92
174
128
A
B
C
D
E
1
2
3
4
5
6
7
06
07
08
76
75
74
LONDON HEATHROW AIRPORT
Heathrow Terminals 2 & 3
Heathrow Terminal 4
TERMINAL 3
TERMINAL 2A
TERMINAL 2B
TERMINAL 5C
TERMINAL 4
Control Tower
D'Albiac House
Bus Sta.
Vehicle Tunnel
Airside Road Tunnel
Cargo Tunnel
Heathrow Express Rail Link
Cargo Terminal
TW6
UB7
TW19
BATH ROAD
A4
NORTHERN PERIMETER ROAD
NORTHERN
PERIMETER ROAD
BEDFONT ROAD
STANWELL
WEST BEDFONT
POLAR PARK
Recreation Ground
AIRPORT GATE BUS. CEN.
HEATHROW BLVRD.
BLUNTS AV.
DORTON VILLAS
Leonardo
Statue
Customs Ho.
NENE ROAD ROUNDABOUT
Heathrow Academy
WORLD BUS. CEN.
Renaissance
Styles
NEWALL
Depot
SOUTHAMPTON
SHOLTO
SEALAND RD.
TUNNEL LINK RD.
SHOREHAM ROAD WEST
SHOREHAM ROAD EAST
Longford River
SANCTUARY RD.
BEACON RD.
CARGO POINT
CLEVELAND PK.
NORTHUMBERLAND CL.
BLACKBURN TRAD. EST.
SPROGGIT IND. EST.
THE CAMGATE CENTRE
Stanwell Fields C of E Prim. Sch.
Recreation Ground
Tennis Cts.
Pav.
Ashford Town FC
Westview Cotts.
Sports Ground
Works
Airport Car Park
HM Customs & Excise
Heathrow Corporate Cen.
Factory
Warehouses
UNITAIR CEN.
Yotel air
LivingWell
Hilton
GREAT SOUTH WEST ROAD
A30
STAINES ROAD
CLYDE RD.
KINGSWAY
HOLYWELL WAY
LONGFORD WY.
MULBERRY AV.
VISCOUNT RD.
CANOPUS WAY
CRANFORD
HADRIAN WAY
CORDELIA
FALCON DR.
Playing Field
Nursery
Homers Farm
Warehouse
Office

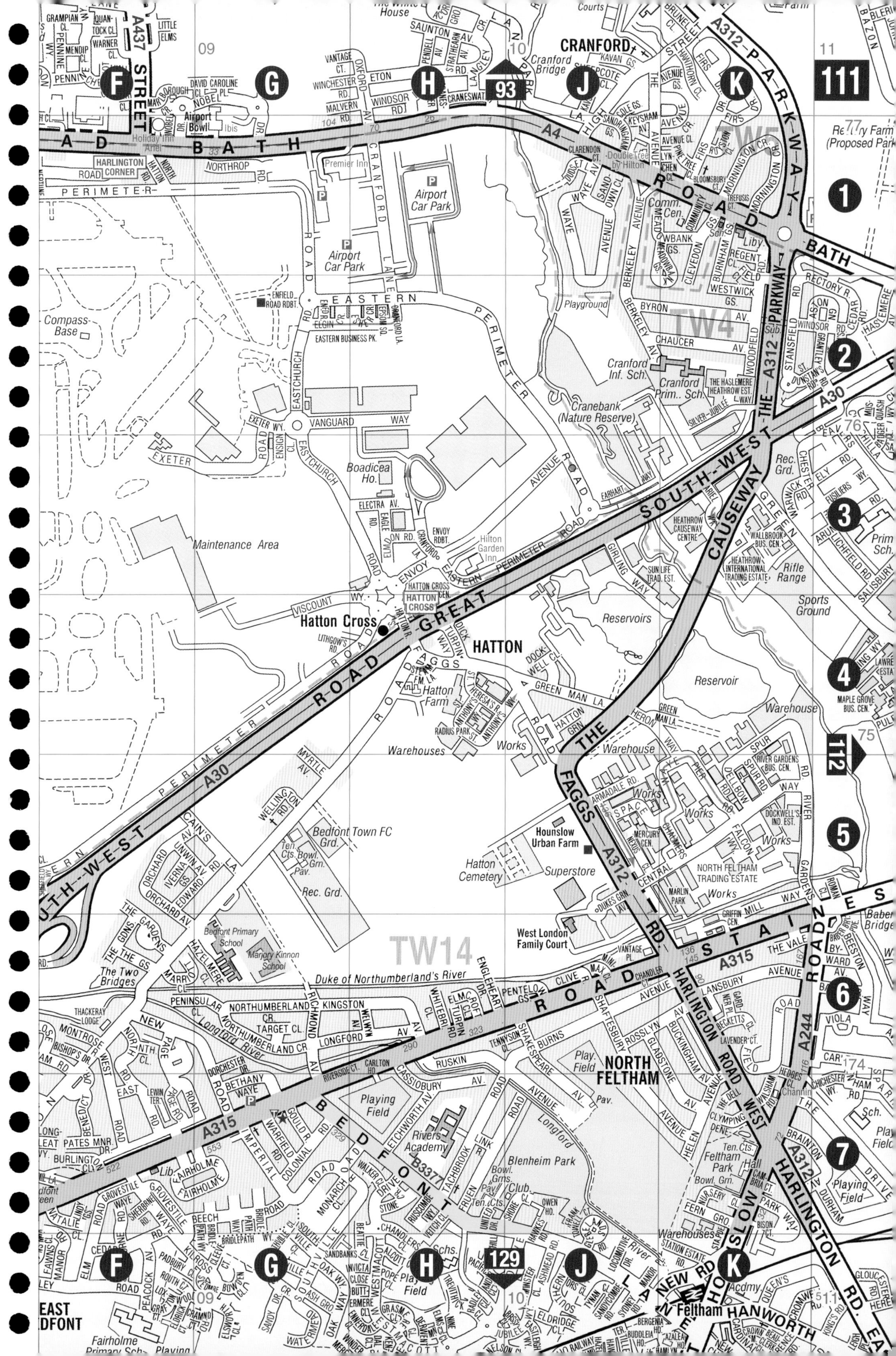

111
CRANFORD
Cranford Bridge
93
BATH ROAD
A4
A437
A312 PARKWAY
Airport Bowl
Ibis
Holiday Inn Ariel
HARLINGTON CORNER
PERIMETER ROAD
NORTHROP RD.
Premier Inn
Airport Car Park
EASTERN PERIMETER ROAD
ENFIELD ROAD RDBT.
EASTERN BUSINESS PK.
Compass Base
EASTCHURCH RD.
VANGUARD WAY
EXETER WY.
Boadicea Ho.
Maintenance Area
ELECTRA AV.
ENVOY RDBT.
Hilton Garden Inn
HATTON CROSS
Hatton Cross
VISCOUNT WY.
HATTON
Hatton Farm
Warehouses
Works
GREAT SOUTH-WEST ROAD
A30
THE CAUSEWAY
HEATHROW CAUSEWAY CENTRE
HEATHROW INTERNATIONAL TRADING ESTATE
SUN LIFE TRAD. EST.
Reservoirs
Reservoir
Rifle Range
Sports Ground
Rec. Grd.
DoubleTree by Hilton
Comm. Cen.
Playground
Cranford Inf. Sch.
Cranford Prim. Sch.
Cranebank (Nature Reserve)
TW4
TW5
TW14
Rectory Farm (Proposed Park)
MAPLE GROVE BUS. CEN.
112
THE FAGGS RD.
A312
Hounslow Urban Farm
Hatton Cemetery
Superstore
West London Family Court
NORTH FELTHAM TRADING ESTATE
DOCKWELL'S IND. EST.
RIVER GARDENS BUS. CEN.
Bedfont Town FC Grd.
Rec. Grd.
Bedfont Primary School
Marjory Kinnon School
The Two Bridges
Duke of Northumberland's River
Longford River
STAINES ROAD
A315
A244
NORTH FELTHAM
Playing Field
Rivers Academy
Blenheim Park
BEDFONT ROAD
B3377
HARLINGTON ROAD WEST
HOUNSLOW RD.
Feltham Park
Feltham
HANWORTH
EAST BEDFONT
Fairholme Primary Sch.
129
09
10
11
F
G
H
J
K
1
2
3
4
5
6
7

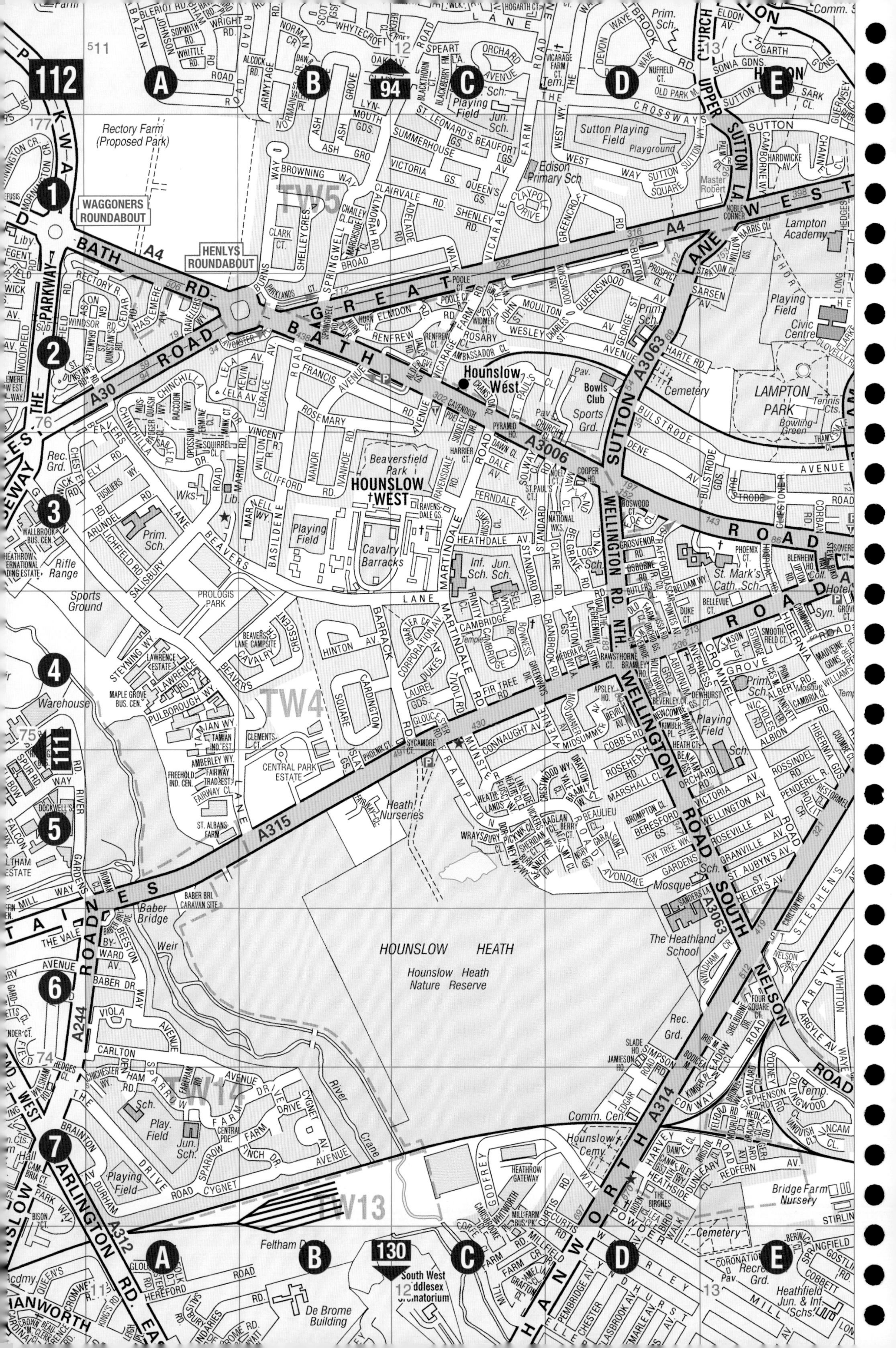
112
94
111
130
A
B
C
D
E
1
2
3
4
5
6
7
TW5
TW4
TW14
TW13
WAGGONERS ROUNDABOUT
HENLYS ROUNDABOUT
Rectory Farm (Proposed Park)
BATH RD.
BATH ROAD
GREAT WEST ROAD
A4
A30
A3006
A3063
A315
A244
A312
A314
Hounslow West
HOUNSLOW †WEST
Beaversfield Park
Playing Field
Cavalry Barracks
PROLOGIS PARK
CENTRAL PARK ESTATE
Sports Ground
Rifle Range
Warehouse
Heath Nurseries
HOUNSLOW HEATH
Hounslow Heath Nature Reserve
Baber Bridge
BABER BRI. CARAVAN SITE
Weir
River Crane
Feltham
De Brome Building
South West Middlesex Crematorium
Hounslow Cemy.
Comm. Cen.
HEATHROW GATEWAY
The Heathland School
Mosque
Rec. Grd.
Bridge Farm Nursery
Cemetery
Heathfield Jun. & Inf. Schs.
Sutton Playing Field
Playground
Edison Primary Sch.
Master Robert
NOBLE CORNER
Lampton Academy
Civic Centre
LAMPTON PARK
Tennis Cts.
Bowling Green
Bowls Club
Sports Grd.
St. Mark's Cath. Sch.
Syn.
Hotel
BEAVERS LANE
SALISBURY
BEAVERS LANE CAMPSITE
MARTINDALE
BARRACK RD.
WELLINGTON RD. NTH.
WELLINGTON ROAD SOUTH
SUTTON LANE
UPPER SUTTON LA.
HANWORTH ROAD
HANWORTH
STAINES ROAD
NELSON ROAD
ARLINGTON RD.
CROSSWAYS
BULSTRODE AVENUE
HIBERNIA GDS.
CROMWELL
VICTORIA AV.
WELLINGTON AV.
ROSEVILLE AV.
GRANVILLE AV.
ST. AUBYN'S AV.
AVONDALE GARDENS
CYGNET AVENUE
SPARROW FARM DRIVE
FELTHAM HILL ROAD

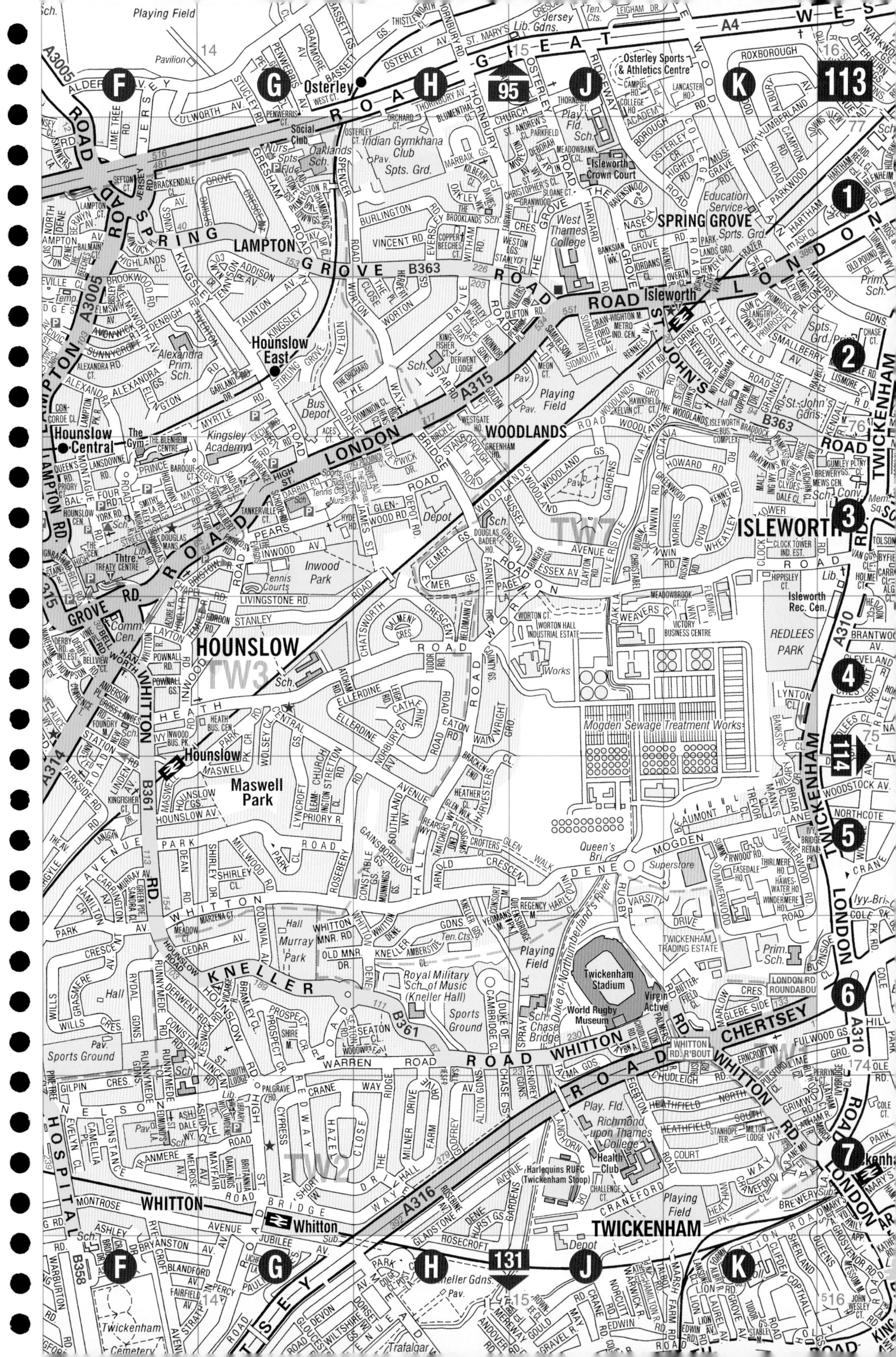113
F
G
H
J
K
95
114
131
1
2
3
4
5
6
7
14
15
16
77
76
75
174
516
Osterley
Osterley Sports & Athletics Centre
GREAT WEST ROAD
A4
Isleworth Crown Court
Indian Gymkhana Club
Oaklands Sch.
LAMPTON
SPRING GROVE
Hounslow East
Hounslow Central
Alexandra Prim. Sch.
West Thames College
Isleworth
LONDON ROAD
A315
B363
Bus Depot
Kingsley Academy
WOODLANDS
ISLEWORTH
Clock Tower Ind. Est.
TW7
TW3
HOUNSLOW
Inwood Park
Tennis Courts
Isleworth Rec. Cen.
REDLEES PARK
Mogden Sewage Treatment Works
Worton Hall Industrial Estate
Victory Business Centre
Hounslow
Maswell Park
Queen's Bri.
Superstore
Twickenham Trading Estate
Twickenham Stadium
World Rugby Museum
Virgin Active
Royal Military Sch. of Music (Kneller Hall)
Sports Ground
Murray Park
Playing Field
KNELLER ROAD
B361
WHITTON ROAD
CHERTSEY ROAD
WHITTON RD. R'BOUT
LONDON RD ROUNDABOUT
Richmond upon Thames College
Harlequins RUFC (Twickenham Stoop)
Health Club
TW2
WHITTON
Whitton
TWICKENHAM
A316
A310
A3005
A314
B358
HOSPITAL ROAD
Twickenham Cemetery
Kneller Gdns.
Play. Fld.
Duke of Northumberland's River
TWICKENHAM ROAD

114
96
113
132
A
B
C
D
E
1
2
3
4
5
6
7
Old Brentford
Brentford Gate
Syon Lane
Busch Corner
The Green Sch.
Hilton Syon Park
SYON PARK
Syon Garden Centre
Syon House
TW8
DUKE OF NORTHUMBERLAND ESTATE
Syon Reach
Isleworth Ferry Gate (Closed)
KEW
Azalea Gdn.
Bamboo Garden
ROYAL BOTANIC GA
Syon Vista
The Lake
King William's Temple
Arboretum
GARDEN
Evolution House
Waterlilly Pond
Temperate House
Conservation Area
Queen Charlotte's Cottage
Pavilion Restaura
Japanese Gateway & Landscape
Pagoda
OLD DEER PARK
ROYAL MID-SURREY GOLF COURSE
London Welsh RFC (Old Deer Park)
King's Observatory
Richmond Athletic Ground
Richmond and London Scottish RUFC
Club House
Richmond Olympus Gym & Squash Club
Tennis Courts
Pools on the Park
Obelisk
Old Deer Park Recreation Ground
Richmond Cricket Grnd.
Bowling Green
RICHMOND CIRCUS
Richmond
Richmond Lock
RICHMOND
Richmond Green
Asgill Ho.
Corporation Island
Visitor Cen.
Terrace Gardens
The Amer Int. Univ Londo
Terrace Fld.
Royal Star & Garter Home
Petersham Common
Buccleugh Gdns.
Glover's Island
Petersham Meadows
Petersham Farm
Petersham Gate
MARBLE HILL PARK
Marble Hill House
Tennis Courts
Sports Cen.
Playing Field
Orleans Ho. Gallery
Foot Ferry
Orleans Gns.
RIVER THAMES
Sports Grd.
The German Sch. London
WEST MIDDLESEX UNIVERSITY HOSP.
UCC
Old Isleworth
Isleworth Ait Nature Reserve
ISLEWORTH
CLOCK TOWER IND. EST.
Isleworth Rec. Cen.
REDLEES PARK
ST. MARGARETS
St. Margarets
ST. MARGARETS R'BOUT
Moor Mead Bridge
Cole Park
Moor Mead Gd.
Twickenham
Civic Cen.
Theatre
TW1
TWICKENHAM ROAD
LONDON ROAD
RICHMOND ROAD
ST. MARGARETS ROAD
PETERSHAM ROAD
A310
A315
A316
A3004
A305
A307
B454
B321

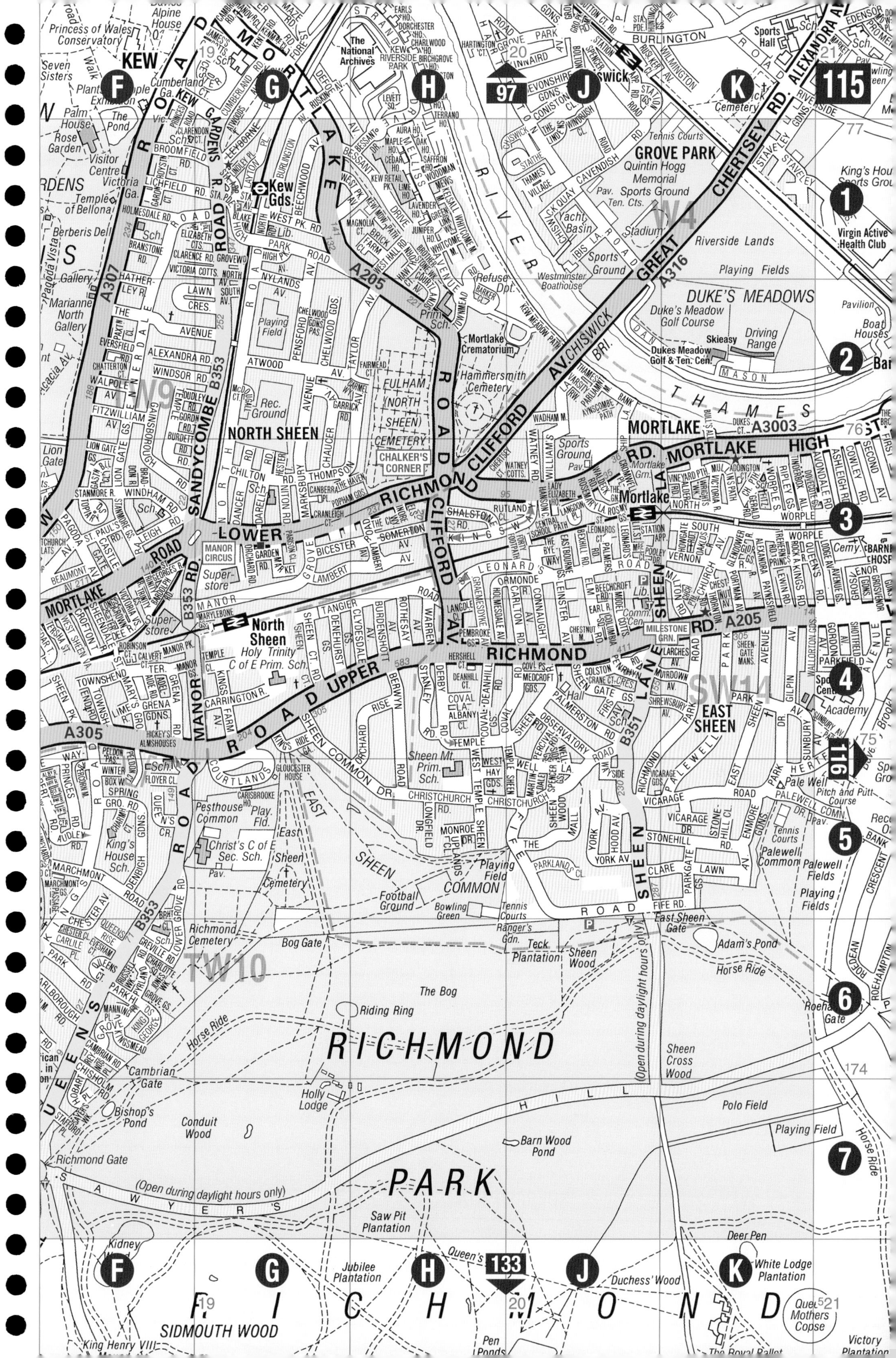
115
97
116
133
F
G
H
J
K
1
2
3
4
5
6
7
19
20
21
77
76
75
174
KEW
Princess of Wales Conservatory
Davies Alpine House
Seven Sisters
Plant Temple Exhibition
The Pond
Palm House
Rose Garden
Visitor Centre
Victoria Ga.
Temple of Bellona
Berberis Dell
Pagoda Vista
Gallery
Marianne North Gallery
Acacia Av.
Lion Gate
Cumberland Ga.
KEW GARDENS
Kew Gds.
The National Archives
KEW RETAIL PK.
A307
A205
B353
A316
A3003
A305
B351
TW9
TW10
W4
SW14
SANDYCOMBE ROAD
MORTLAKE ROAD
LOWER RICHMOND ROAD
UPPER RICHMOND ROAD
CLIFFORD AVENUE
CHISWICK BRI.
GREAT CHERTSEY RD.
MORTLAKE HIGH ST.
RIVER THAMES
NORTH SHEEN
Playing Field
Rec. Ground
FULHAM (NORTH SHEEN) CEMETERY
CHALKER'S CORNER
Mortlake Crematorium
Hammersmith Cemetery
Refuse Dpt.
Westminster Boathouse
GROVE PARK
Quintin Hogg Memorial Sports Ground
Yacht Basin
Stadium
Sports Ground
Riverside Lands
Playing Fields
DUKE'S MEADOWS
Duke's Meadow Golf Course
Skieasy
Driving Range
Dukes Meadow Golf & Ten. Cen.
Pavilion
Boat Houses
Virgin Active Health Club
King's House Sports Ground
Chiswick Cemetery
Sports Hall
MORTLAKE
Mortlake
MANOR CIRCUS
Superstore
North Sheen
Holy Trinity C of E Prim. Sch.
MILESTONE GRN.
EAST SHEEN
Academy
Hickey's Almshouses
King's House Sch.
Pesthouse Common
Christ's C of E Sec. Sch.
East Sheen Cemetery
Richmond Cemetery
Sheen Mt. Prim. Sch.
SHEEN COMMON
Playing Field
Football Ground
Bowling Green
Tennis Courts
Ranger's Gdn.
Teck Plantation
Sheen Wood
East Sheen Gate
Adam's Pond
Horse Ride
Pale Well
Pitch and Putt Course
Palewell Common
Palewell Fields
Playing Fields
Bog Gate
The Bog
Riding Ring
RICHMOND PARK
Cambrian Gate
Holly Lodge
Bishop's Pond
Conduit Wood
Barn Wood Pond
(Open during daylight hours only)
Sheen Cross Wood
Polo Field
Playing Field
Roehampton Gate
Richmond Gate
SAWYER'S HILL
Saw Pit Plantation
Kidney Wood
Queen's Ride
Jubilee Plantation
Duchess' Wood
Deer Pen
White Lodge Plantation
Queen Mothers Copse
SIDMOUTH WOOD
King Henry VIII's Mound
Pen Ponds
Victory Plantation

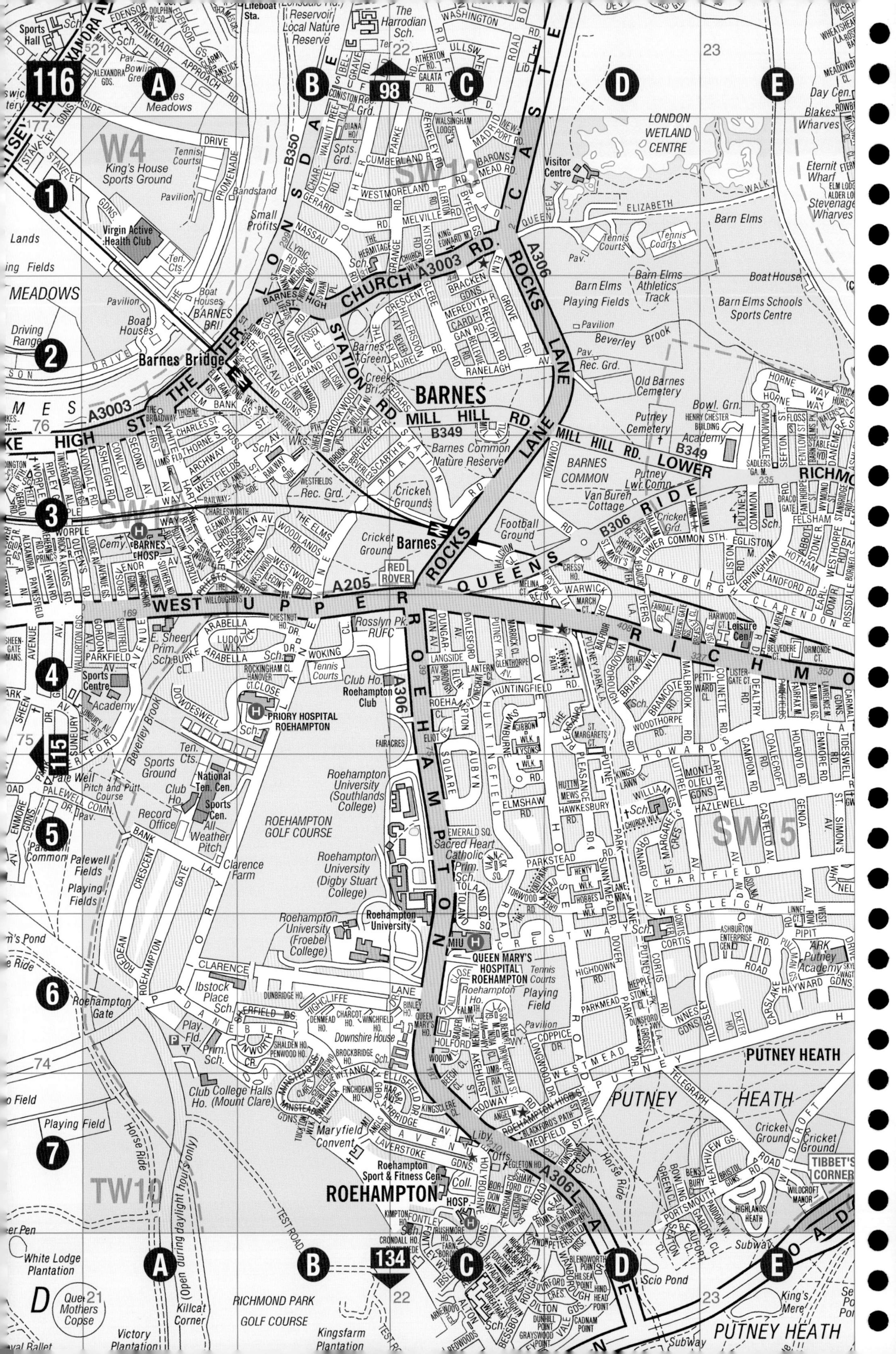

116
98
115
134
A
B
C
D
E
1
2
3
4
5
6
7
22
23
21
76
75
74
W4
SW13
SW15
TW10
BARNES
ROEHAMPTON
PUTNEY HEATH
PUTNEY
HEATH
LONDON WETLAND CENTRE
Visitor Centre
Barn Elms
Barn Elms Athletics Track
Barn Elms Playing Fields
Barn Elms Schools Sports Centre
Boat House
Blakes Wharves
Eternit Wharf
Stevenage Wharves
Day Cen.
King's House Sports Ground
Virgin Active Health Club
Small Profits
Bandstand
Pavilion
Boat Houses
BARNES BRI.
Barnes Bridge
Driving Range
MEADOWS
Lands
Beverley Brook
Old Barnes Cemetery
Putney Cemetery
Bowl. Grn.
HENRY CHESTER BUILDING
Academy
BARNES COMMON
Putney Lwr. Comn.
Van Buren Cottage
Barnes Common Nature Reserve
Cricket Grounds
Cricket Ground
Football Ground
Barnes
RED ROVER
Westfields Rec. Grd.
BARNES HOSP.
Cemy.
Rosslyn Pk. RUFC
Club Ho.
Roehampton Club
PRIORY HOSPITAL ROEHAMPTON
E. Sheen Prim. Sch.
Sports Centre
Sports Ground
National Ten. Cen.
Sports Cen.
All Weather Pitch
Record Office
Clarence Farm
Pitch and Putt Course
Pale Well
Palewell Common
Palewell Fields
Playing Fields
ROEHAMPTON GOLF COURSE
Roehampton University (Southlands College)
Roehampton University (Digby Stuart College)
Roehampton University (Froebel College)
Roehampton University
Sacred Heart Catholic Prim. Sch.
QUEEN MARY'S HOSPITAL ROEHAMPTON
Tennis Courts
Playing Field
Pavilion
Leisure Cen.
ARK Putney Academy
ASHBURTON ENTERPRISE CEN.
Roehampton Gate
Ibstock Place Sch.
Play. Fld.
Prim. Sch.
Downshire House
Club College Halls Ho. (Mount Clare)
Maryfield Convent
Roehampton Sport & Fitness Cen.
Coll.
HOSP.
Liby.
Horse Ride
(Open during daylight hours only)
Killcat Corner
RICHMOND PARK GOLF COURSE
Kingsfarm Plantation
Victory Plantation
White Lodge Plantation
Queen Mothers Copse
Deer Pen
Playing Field
Scio Pond
King's Mere
Cricket Ground
TIBBET'S CORNER
HIGHLANDS HEATH
WILDCROFT MANOR
Subway
A3003
A306
A205
B349
B350
B306
HIGH ST.
CHURCH RD.
STATION RD.
MILL HILL RD.
LOWER RICHMOND RD.
ROCKS LANE
CASTELNAU
LONSDALE RD.
UPPER RICHMOND RD. WEST
QUEENS RIDE
ROEHAMPTON LANE
DANEBURY AV.
CLARENCE LA.
PRIORY LA.
ROEHAMPTON GATE
WESTMEAD
PUTNEY PARK LA.
DOVER HOUSE RD.
CRESTWAY
CHARTFIELD AV.
WESTLEIGH AV.
HOWARDS LA.
TELEGRAPH RD.
PORTSMOUTH RD.
ROEHAMPTON HIGH ST.
MEDFIELD ST.
ALTON RD.
HOLYBOURNE AV.
HIGHCLIFFE DR.

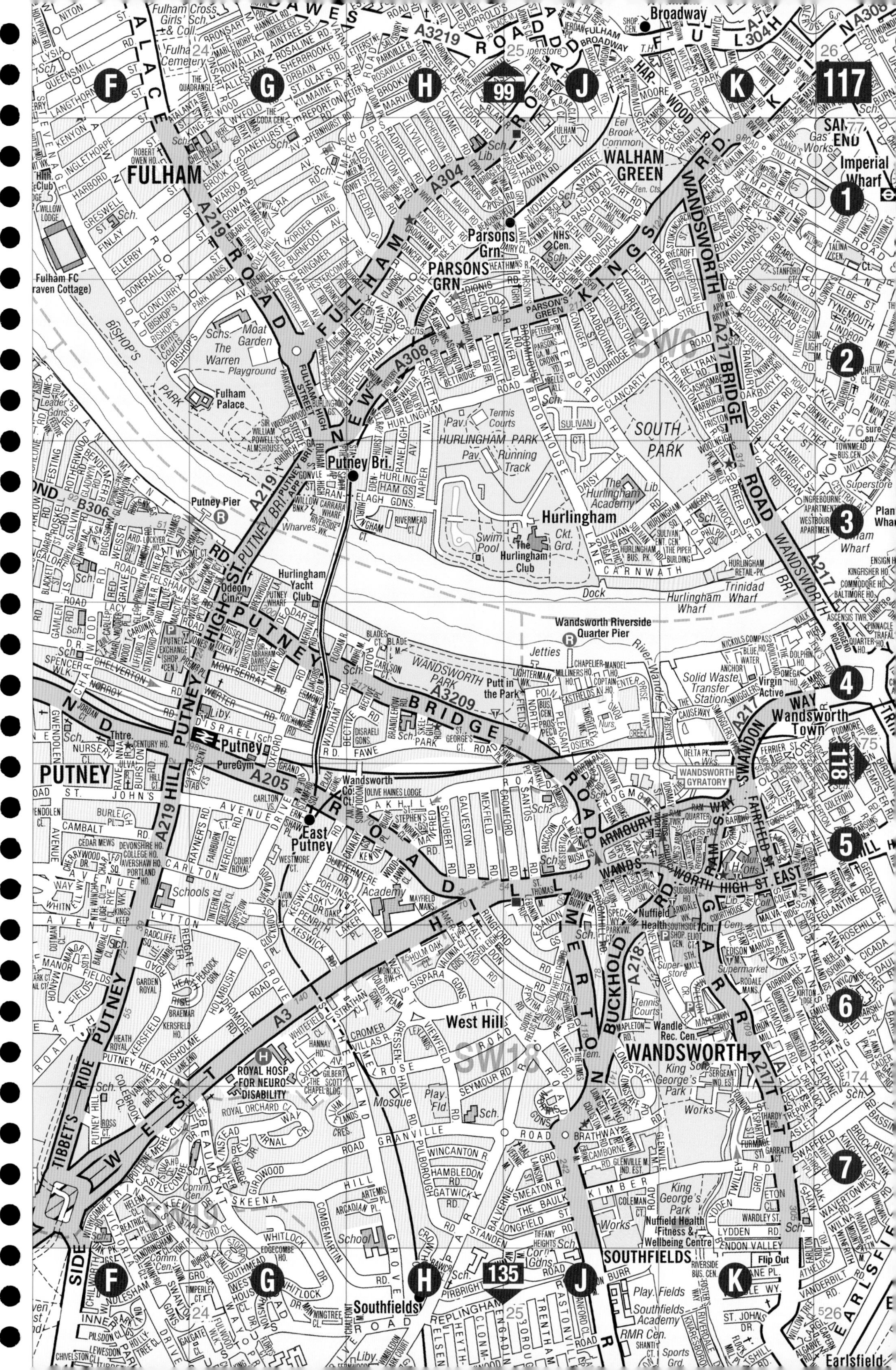

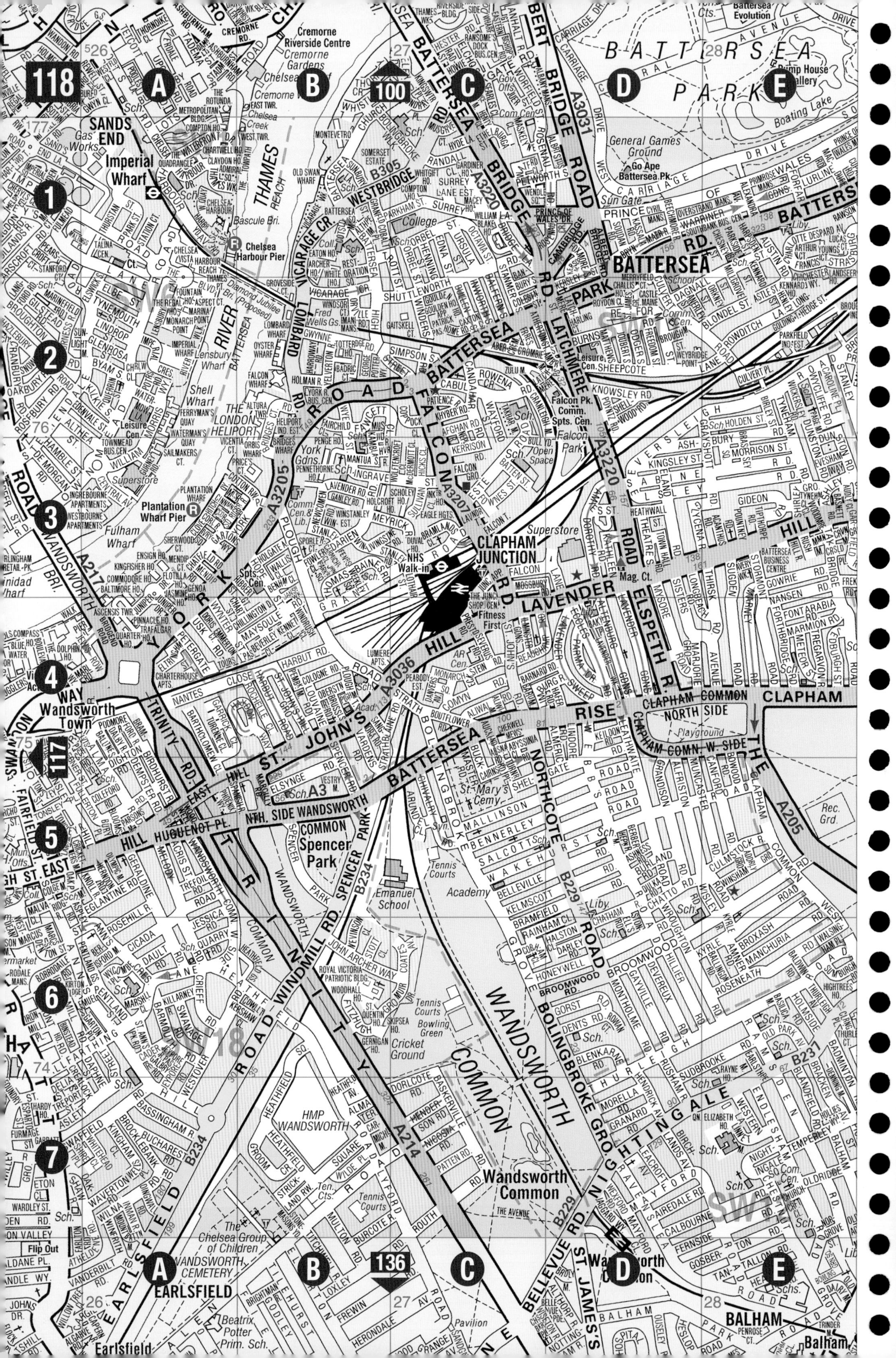

118
100
117
136
A
B
C
D
E
1
2
3
4
5
6
7
SANDS END
Imperial Wharf
Cremorne Riverside Centre
Cremorne Gardens
Chelsea Harbour Pier
Bascule Bri.
THAMES REACH
RIVER
Lensbury Wharf
Shell Wharf
THE LONDON HELIPORT
Plantation Wharf Pier
Fulham Wharf
Superstore
BATTERSEA PARK
Pump House Gallery
Boating Lake
General Games Ground
Go Ape Battersea Pk.
Sun Gate
CARRIAGE DRIVE
PRINCE OF WALES DR.
BATTERSEA
BATTERSEA BRIDGE ROAD
A3031
A3220
LATCHMERE RD.
BATTERSEA PARK RD.
Falcon Pk. Comm. Spts. Cen.
Falcon Park
Open Space
CLAPHAM JUNCTION
NHS Walk-in
Fitness First
LAVENDER HILL
FALCON RD.
A3207
YORK RD.
A3205
PLOUGH RD.
St. John's Hill
A3036
ST. JOHN'S HILL
BATTERSEA RISE
CLAPHAM COMMON NORTH SIDE
CLAPHAM COMMON
Playground
CLAPHAM COMN. W. SIDE
THE CLAPHAM COMMON
A205
Rec. Grd.
ELSPETH R.
NORTHCOTE ROAD
B229
St. Mary's Cemy.
WANDSWORTH COMMON
Tennis Courts
Academy
Emanuel School
Spencer Park
SPENCER PARK
B234
WINDMILL RD.
TRINITY RD.
A214
Wandsworth Town
A217
WANDSWORTH BRI.
NTH. SIDE WANDSWORTH COMMON
HUGUENOT PL.
EAST HILL
A3
SW18
SW11
SW17
HMP WANDSWORTH
Cricket Ground
Bowling Green
Wandsworth Common
BOLINGBROKE GRO.
NIGHTINGALE LA.
BELLEVUE RD.
THE AVENUE
B231
EARLSFIELD
EARLSFIELD RD.
WANDSWORTH CEMETERY
The Chelsea Group of Children
Beatrix Potter Prim. Sch.
Pavilion
Earlsfield
BALHAM
Balham
Wandsworth Common
ST. JAMES'S DR.

F
G
H
J
K
101
1
2
3
4
5
6
7
120
137
29
30
31
Power Station
Nine Elms
NEW COVENT GARDEN MARKET
Fruit & Vegetable Market
Battersea Pk.
Queenstown Rd. (Battersea)
SOUTH LAMBETH
Larkhall Park
Stockwell
Angell Town
Platanos College
Heathbrook Park
Wandsworth Rd.
STOCKWELL
CLAPHAM
Clapham High St.
Clapham North
LAMBETH HOSPITAL
Landor Space
Trinity Hospice
Clapham Comm.
CLAPHAM COMMON
COMMON NORTH SIDE
LONG A3 RD.
CLAPHAM COMMON SOUTH SIDE
CLAPHAM PARK RD.
ACRE LANE
A2217
BEDFORD RD.
B221
BRIXTON
Lambeth Coll.
Lambeth Academy
CLAPHAM PARK
Sudbourne Prim. Sch.
Windmill Gdns.
Sports Ground
HMP BRIXTON
Eagle Pond
Mount Pond
Bandstand
Long Pond
Basketball Courts
Clapham Sth.
CLAPHAM PARK RD.
CAVENDISH RD.
POYNDERS RD.
A205
ATKINS RD.
KING'S AVENUE
STREATHAM PL.
BRIXTON HILL
A23
CHRISTCHURCH RD.
A205
BALHAM HILL
A24
STOCKWELL RD.
CLAPHAM RD.
A3036
A203
A3216
QUEENSTOWN RD.
WANDSWORTH RD.
BRIXTON RD.
STREATHAM
SW8
SW4
SW9
SW2

A
B
C
D
E
1
2
3
4
5
6
7
102
119
136
CAMBERWELL
CAMBERWELL GREEN
STOCKWELL
Angell Town
Brixton
Loughborough Junc.
Herne Hill
North Dulwich
East Dulwich
Denmark Hill
DULWICH VILLAGE
HERNE HILL
PECKHAM
CAMBERWELL CHURCH STREET
COLDHARBOUR LANE
COLDHARBOUR
DENMARK HILL
CHAMPION PK.
DULWICH ROAD
HALF MOON LA.
VILLAGE WAY
EAST DULWICH
CROXTED ROAD
NORWOOD ROAD
MILKWOOD RD.
RAILTON RD.
EFFRA RD.
BRIXTON RD.
TULSE HILL
BROCKWELL PARK
Brockwell Park Lido
The Mansion
RUSKIN PARK
MYATTS FIELDS
KINGS COLLEGE HOSPITAL
THE MAUDSLEY HOSP.
William Booth Coll.
Dulwich Hamlet FC (Champion Hill Stadium)
DULWICH COMMUNITY HOSP.
The Charter School
James Allen's Girls' Sch.
Alleyn's Sch.
Herne Hill Velodrome
Dulwich Old College
Dulwich Picture Gallery
Belair Park
TURNEY ROAD
GROVE LA.
DOG KENNEL HILL
Dog Kennel Hill Open Space
Lettsom Gds.
Lucas Gds.
Sports Ground
Playing Fields
SE5
SE24
SE21
SW9
SW2
A23
A202
A2217
A2216
A215
A2214
A204
A2199
B217
B222
B223
31
32
33
76
75
74
177
TULSE HILL

121
103
122
139
F
G
H
J
K
1
2
3
4
5
6
7
34
35
36
PECKHAM
Peckham Rye
NEW CROSS GATE
NUNHEAD
BROCKLEY
EAST DULWICH
HONOR OAK
Honor Oak Park
Newlands
SE15
SE14
SE4
SE22
SE23
PECKHAM RYE COMMON
PECKHAM RYE PARK
NUNHEAD CEMETERY
Nunhead Cemetery Nature Reserve
AQUARIUS GOLF COURSE
DULWICH PARK
Camberwell Old Cemetery
One Tree Hill Local Nature Reserve
Honor Oak Crematorium
Telegraph Hill Park
Horniman Gardens
Horniman Museum
Warwick Gardens
Queens Rd. (Peckham)
Nunhead
Peckhamplex
PECKHAM HIGH ST.
QUEEN'S ROAD
NEW CROSS ROAD
PECKHAM RD.
EAST DULWICH ROAD
NUNHEAD LA.
EVELINA ROAD
PECKHAM RYE
FOREST HILL ROAD
HONOR OAK ROAD
LORDSHIP LANE
BARRY ROAD
DRAKEFELL RD.
LAUSANNE RD.
CONSORT RD.
CLAYTON RD.
COPELAND RD.
HEATON RD.
BRENCHLEY GARDENS
COMMON
A202
A2214
A2216
B215
B219
B238
B2142
Reservoirs (covered)
Harris Sports Cen.
Playing Field
Bus Station
Bus Garage
Court La. Gate
Lordship La.
Visitor Centre
Nature Reserves

122
104
121
140
A
B
C
D
E
1
2
3
4
5
6
7
36
37
38
NEW CROSS
New Cross Gate
New Cross
Goldsmiths College
Deptford Bri.
ST. JOHNS
St. Johns
Elverson Rd.
Lewisham
LEWISHAM
BROCKLEY
Brockley
Crofton Park
Crofton Pk.
HONOR OAK PARK
Honor Oak Park
Honor Oak Crematorium
Ladywell
LADYWELL
UNIVERSITY HOSPITAL LEWISHAM
Lewisham Park
Ladywell Arena (Running Track)
Blythe Hill
Blythe Hill Fields
Catford Bridge
Catford
CATFORD
Hilly Fields
Brockley Cemetery
Ladywell Cemetery
NEW CROSS ROAD A2
A20
LEWISHAM WAY
LOAMPIT HILL
LOAMPIT VALE
BROOKMILL ROAD A2210
BLACKHEATH RD.
BROCKLEY ROAD B218
ADELAIDE AV.
LADYWELL RD.
LEWISHAM HIGH STREET A21
RUSHEY GRN.
CATFORD RD.
STANSTEAD ROAD A205
B2142
B236
B238
SE14
SE4
SE13
SE23
SE6
SE10

Peter Harrison Planetarium
Royal Observatory Greenwich
PARK
Bandstand
The Wilderness (Deer Park)
The Gardens
Reservoir (covered)
Tennis Courts
Parks Police
Ranger's House
VANBRUGH PARK
OLD DOVER ROAD
105
123
F
G
H
J
K
1
2
3
4
5
6
7
39
40
41
A2
B209
B210
B212
B220
SHOOTERS HILL ROAD
HILL
BLACK HEATH
Blackheath Vale
PRINCE OF WALES RD.
KIDBROOKE PARK RD.
A2213
ROCHESTER WAY RELIEF ROAD
Blackheath Nursy. & Prep. Sch.
Morden College (Almshouses)
Thomas Tallis Sch.
Thomas Tallis Sports Cen.
Sports Grd.
Warehouse
Kidbrooke Nature Reserve
Superstore
BLACKHEATH
Blackheath
SE3
Concert Halls
College Academy
Hollyhedge Ho.
Heathfield House
BELMONT HILL
LEE TERRACE
BLACKHEATH PARK
The Priory
Kidbrooke
Sports Ground
Sports Grounds
David Lloyd Leis.
Quaggy River
Roan School Playing Fields
124
SUTCLIFFE PARK
Sutcliffe Athletic Track
A210
A20
LEE HIGH ROAD
Manor House Gdns.
Manor Park
Euro Cen.
LEE GRN.
ELTHAM ROAD
BURNT ASH RD.
A2212
Brindishe Lee Sch.
LEE
Horn Park
Colfes Senior Sch.
Colfes Prep. Sch.
Colfes Leisure Cen.
Lee
SE12
Hither Green
HITHER GREEN
Depot
CHILTONIAN IND. EST.
WESTHORNE AV.
A205
ST. MILDREDS ROAD
BURNT ASH HILL
BARING RD.
Horn Park Prim. Sch.
Horn Park
Rehab. Cen.
141
Northbrook Park
Green Sidings
Grove Park Nature Reserve
GA2212
Warehouse
MOTTINGHAM
Chapel

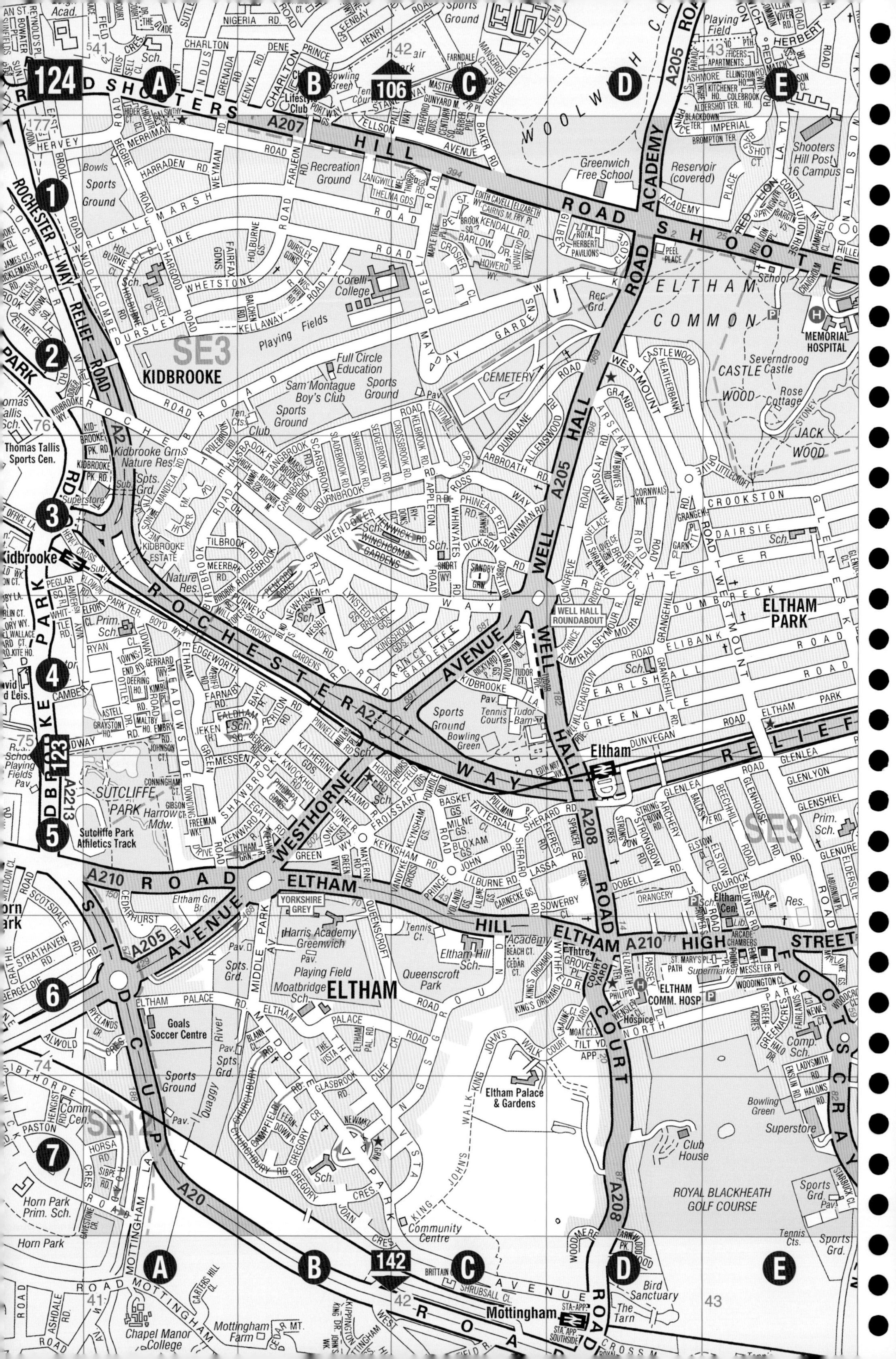
124
106
142
123
A
B
C
D
E
1
2
3
4
5
6
7
SHOOTERS HILL ROAD
A207
A205
A2
A20
A208
A210
A2213
ROCHESTER WAY RELIEF ROAD
ROCHESTER WAY
ACADEMY ROAD
WELL HALL ROAD
WELL HALL ROUNDABOUT
WESTHORNE AVENUE
ELTHAM ROAD
ELTHAM HILL
ELTHAM HIGH STREET
COURT ROAD
SIDCUP ROAD
FOOTSCRAY ROAD
MOTTINGHAM ROAD
KIDBROOKE
KIDBROOKE PARK ROAD
Kidbrooke
SE3
SE9
SE12
ELTHAM
ELTHAM PARK
ELTHAM COMMON
WOOLWICH COMMON
CASTLE WOOD
JACK WOOD
SUTCLIFFE PARK
Sutcliffe Park Athletics Track
Thomas Tallis Sports Cen.
Kidbrooke Grn. Nature Res.
Corelli College
Greenwich Free School
Reservoir (covered)
Shooters Hill Post 16 Campus
MEMORIAL HOSPITAL
Severndroog Castle
Rose Cottage
CEMETERY
Recreation Ground
Playing Fields
Full Circle Education
Sam Montague Boy's Club
Sports Ground
Bowls
Eltham
Harris Academy Greenwich
Playing Field
Eltham Hill Sch.
Queenscroft Park
Goals Soccer Centre
Eltham Palace & Gardens
ELTHAM COMM. HOSP
Hospice
ROYAL BLACKHEATH GOLF COURSE
Club House
Superstore
Community Centre
Mottingham
Chapel Manor College
Mottingham Farm
Horn Park
Horn Park Prim. Sch.
Bird Sanctuary
The Tarn
Eltham Cen.
YORKSHIRE GREY
Moatbridge Sch.
Quaggy River
41
42
43
74
75
76

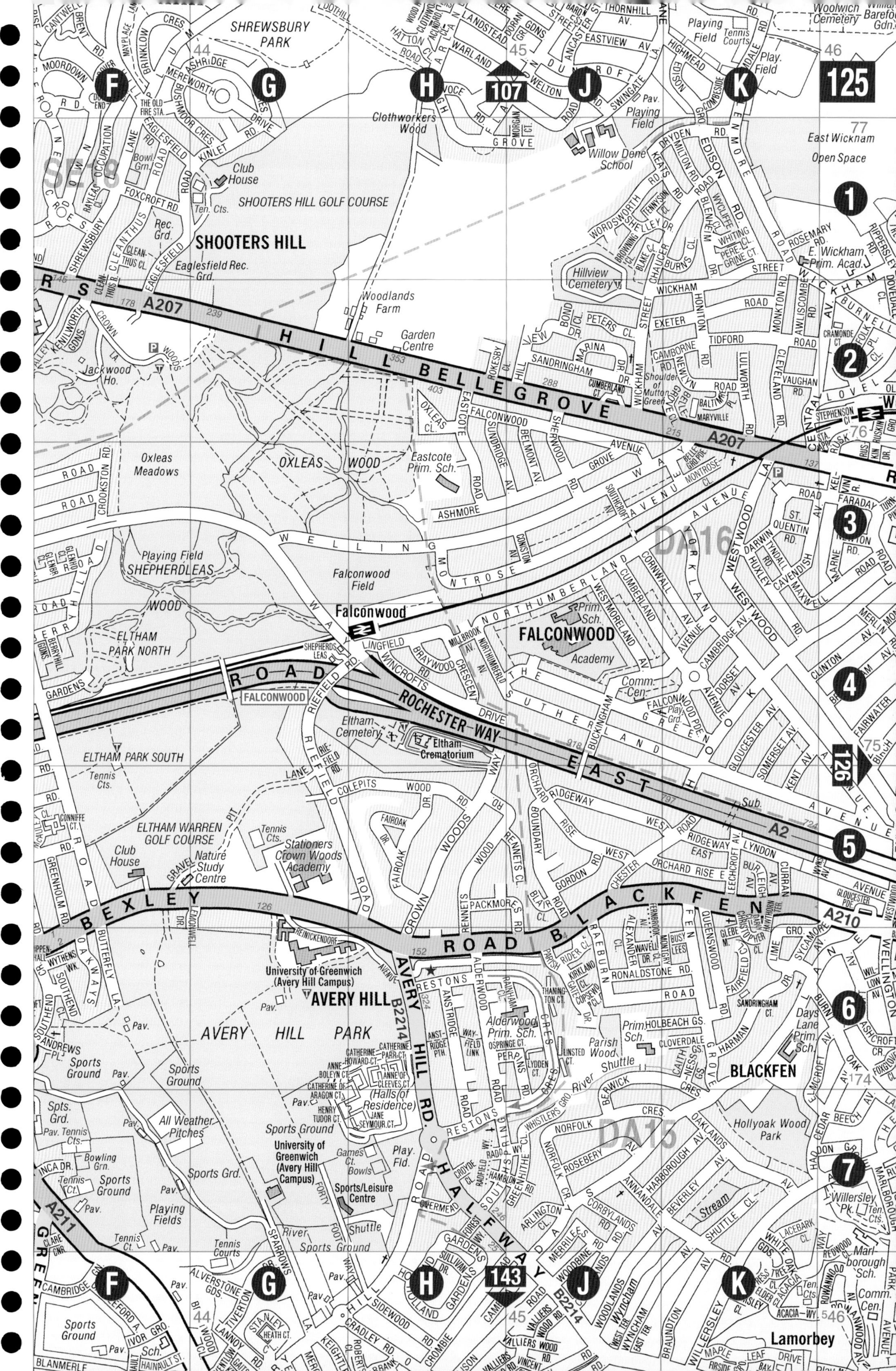

125
107
126
143
F
G
H
J
K
1
2
3
4
5
6
7
44
45
46
77
76
75
74
SE18
DA16
DA15
SHREWSBURY PARK
Woolwich Cemetery
Playing Field
Tennis Courts
Play. Field
Clothworkers Wood
Willow Dene School
East Wickham Open Space
Club House
SHOOTERS HILL GOLF COURSE
SHOOTERS HILL
Eaglesfield Rec. Grd.
Rec. Grd.
Hillview Cemetery
E. Wickham Prim. Acad.
A207
SHOOTERS HILL
BELLEGROVE ROAD
Woodlands Farm
Garden Centre
Jackwood Ho.
Oxleas Meadows
OXLEAS WOOD
Eastcote Prim. Sch.
WELLING WAY
Playing Field
SHEPHERDLEAS WOOD
ELTHAM PARK NORTH
Falconwood Field
Falconwood
FALCONWOOD
Falconwood Academy
Prim. Sch.
Comm. Cen.
ROCHESTER WAY
ROCHESTER WAY RELIEF ROAD
EAST ROCHESTER WAY
A2
Eltham Cemetery
Eltham Crematorium
ELTHAM PARK SOUTH
Tennis Cts.
ELTHAM WARREN GOLF COURSE
Club House
Nature Study Centre
Stationers Crown Woods Academy
BEXLEY ROAD
BLACKFEN ROAD
A210
University of Greenwich (Avery Hill Campus)
AVERY HILL
AVERY HILL PARK
B2214
AVERY HILL RD.
Alderwood Prim. Sch.
(Halls of Residence)
Parish Wood
Prim. Sch.
River Shuttle
BLACKFEN
Days Lane Prim. Sch.
Hollyoak Wood Park
Sports Ground
Sports Grd.
All Weather Pitches
Bowling Grn.
Tennis Ct.
Playing Fields
Sports/Leisure Centre
Play. Fld.
HALFWAY STREET
Stream
Willersley Pk.
Marlborough Sch.
Comm. Cen.
Lamorbey
A211

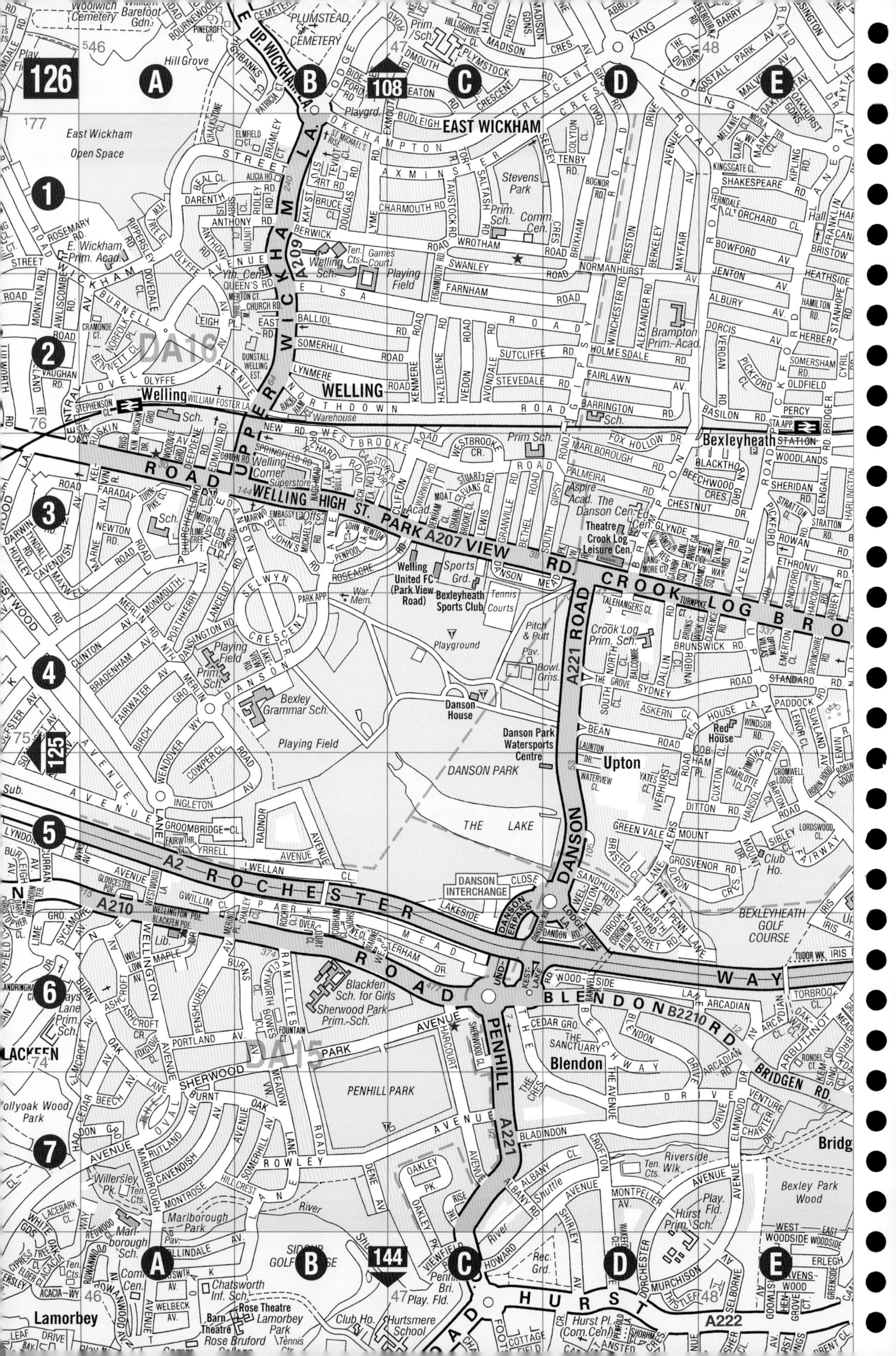

126
108
125
144
A
B
C
D
E
1
2
3
4
5
6
7
Woolwich Cemetery
Plumstead Cemetery
Hill Grove
East Wickham Open Space
EAST WICKHAM
Stevens Park
E. Wickham Prim. Acad.
Welling Sch.
Playing Field
Brampton Prim. Acad.
DA16
WELLING
Welling
Bexleyheath
BEXLEYHEATH STATION
Welling Corner
Superstore
Welling United FC (Park View Road)
Bexleyheath Sports Club
Aspire Acad.
The Danson Cen.
Theatre
Crook Log Leisure Cen.
Crook Log Prim. Sch.
Bexley Grammar Sch.
Danson House
Danson Park Watersports Centre
DANSON PARK
THE LAKE
Playground
Pitch & Putt
Upton
Red House
Club Ho.
BEXLEYHEATH GOLF COURSE
DANSON INTERCHANGE
A2 ROCHESTER WAY
A207
A209
A210
A221
A222
B2210
UPPER WICKHAM LA.
WELLING HIGH ST.
PARK VIEW RD.
CROOK LOG
DANSON ROAD
BLENDON RD.
PENHILL RD.
BRIDGEN RD.
Blackfen Sch. for Girls
Sherwood Park Prim. Sch.
DA15
Penhill Park
PENHILL PARK
Blendon
Lacey Lane Prim. Sch.
Hollyoak Wood Park
Willersley Pk.
Marlborough Park
Marlborough Sch.
Sidcup Golf Course
Chatsworth Inf. Sch.
Rose Theatre
Lamorbey Park
Barn Theatre
Rose Bruford
Hurtsmere School
Lamorbey
Hurst Prim. Sch.
Riverside Wlk.
Bexley Park Wood
Hurst Pl. (Com. Cen.)
Rec. Grd.
Bridg

127
109
145
F
G
H
J
K
1
2
3
4
5
6
7
49
50
51
77
76
75
74
NORTHUMBERLAND HEATH
BARNEHURST
BEXLEYHEATH
BEXLEY
OLD BEXLEY
CRAYFORD
DA8
DA7
DA6
DA5
DA1
Barnehurst
Bexley
BARNEHURST GOLF COURSE
Bursted Wood
Russell Park
Martens Grove Park
Hall Place Gardens
Churchfield Wood
BLACK PRINCE INTERCHANGE
Crayford Stadium (Greyhound)
Crayford Manor House
Bexleyheath Academy
Goals Soccer Cen.
BROADWAY SHOP. CEN.
Civic Offices
St. Catherine's Catholic School for Girls
St. Columba's Catholic Boys Sch.
Gravel Hill Prim. Sch.
Bursted Wood Prim. Sch.
Mayplace Prim. Sch.
VCD Athletic FC Ground
Hall Place & Gardens
Hall Place Sports Pav.
Bexley Lawn Tennis Club
Old Bexley C of E Prim. Sch.
Cricket Ground
Woodside Academy
Fairford Academy
A2
A207
A220
A221
A223
B2210
BROADWAY
WATLING ST.
LONDON ROAD
ROCHESTER WAY
EAST ROCHESTER WAY
BOURNE ROAD
GRAVEL HILL
PARKHILL ROAD
BEXLEY HIGH ST.
BELMONT ROAD
LONG LANE
MAYPLACE ROAD EAST
NORTHUMBERLAND AVENUE
EVERSLEY ROAD
PARKSIDE
COLYERS LANE
ALBION ROAD
ARNSBERG WAY
A2 DARTFORD HEATH

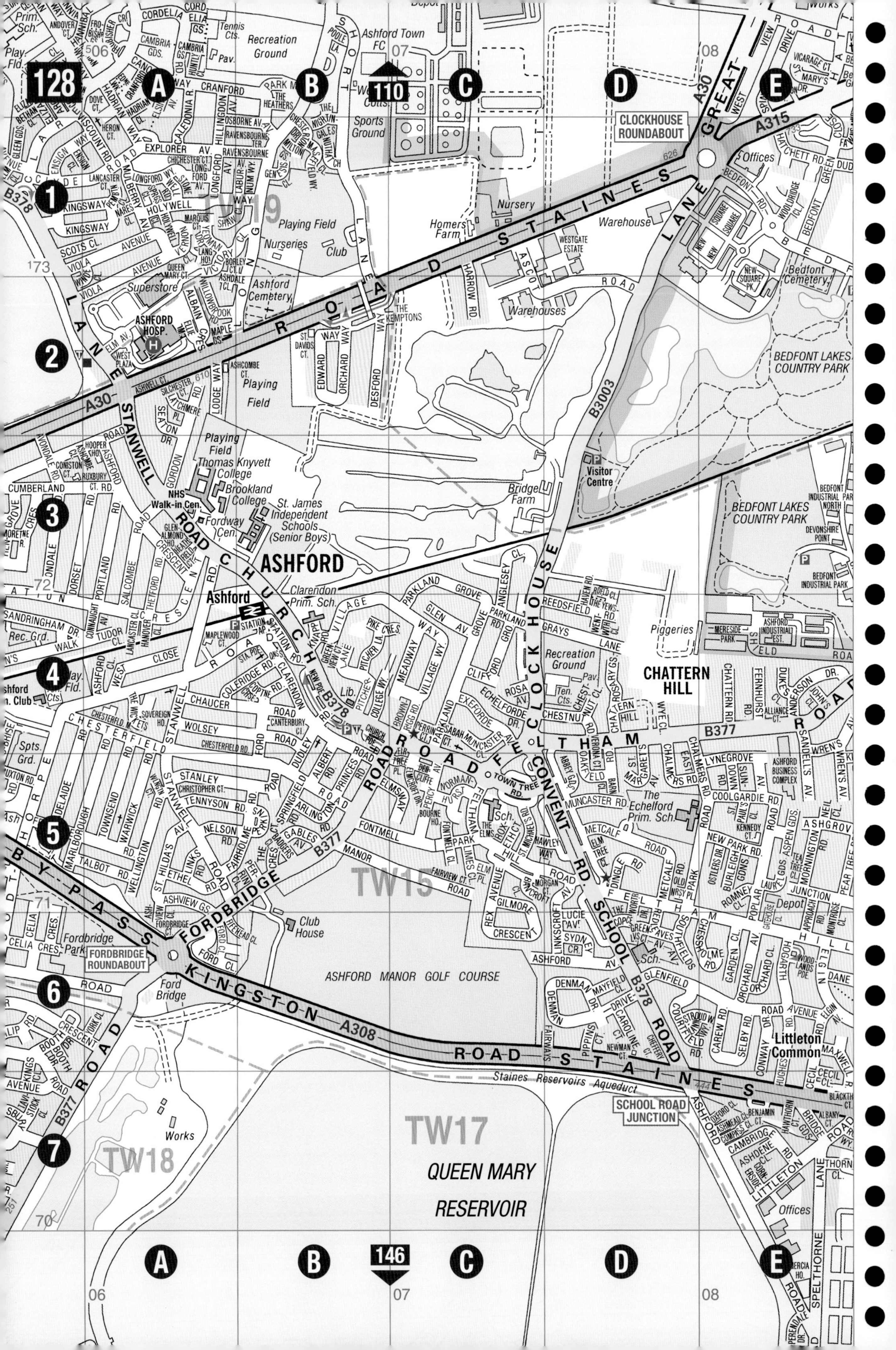

128
110
146
A
B
C
D
E
1
2
3
4
5
6
7
06
07
08
173
72
71
70
TW19
TW15
TW17
TW18
ASHFORD
CHATTERN HILL
Littleton Common
Ashford Town FC
Recreation Ground
Tennis Cts.
Pav.
Sports Ground
West Cotts.
CLOCKHOUSE ROUNDABOUT
GREAT WEST ROAD
A30
A315
STAINES ROAD
Nursery
Homers Farm
Warehouse
WESTGATE ESTATE
Playing Field
Nurseries
Club
Ashford Cemetery
Superstore
ASHFORD HOSP.
WEST PLAZA
THE KEMPTONS
Warehouses
Offices
Bedfont Cemetery
BEDFONT LAKES COUNTRY PARK
B3003
Visitor Centre
Bridge Farm
Thomas Knyvett College
Brookland College
NHS Walk-in Cen.
Fordway Cen.
St. James Independent Schools (Senior Boys)
Clarendon Prim. Sch.
Ashford
BEDFONT INDUSTRIAL PARK NORTH
DEVONSHIRE POINT
BEDFONT INDUSTRIAL PARK
MERESIDE PARK
ASHFORD INDUSTRIAL EST.
Piggeries
Recreation Ground
Ten. Cts.
Lib.
CHURCH ROAD
B378
FELTHAM ROAD
B377
CLOCKHOUSE LANE
CONVENT RD.
SCHOOL ROAD
The Echelford Prim. Sch.
ASHFORD BUSINESS COMPLEX
Depot
Sch.
TOWN TREE RD.
STANWELL ROAD
CHESTERFIELD ROAD
FORDBRIDGE ROAD
BY-PASS
Fordbridge Park
FORDBRIDGE ROUNDABOUT
Ford Bridge
KINGSTON ROAD
A308
Club House
ASHFORD MANOR GOLF COURSE
Staines Reservoirs Aqueduct
SCHOOL ROAD JUNCTION
QUEEN MARY RESERVOIR
Works
STANWELL LANE
B377 ROAD
SPELTHORNE LANE

129
111
130
147
EAST BEDFONT
Fairholme Primary Sch.
TW14
Bedfont Trading Estate
Edward Pauling Prim. Sch.
Vineyard Nurseries
HMYOI FELTHAM
LOWER FELTHAM
Feltham Hill Inf. Sch.
Oak Hill Academy
Cemetery
Grosvenor Park
Rivers Academy
Blenheim Park
FELTHAM
Feltham
Feltham Park
Superstore
Reach Acad. Feltham
Buzz Bingo
Tenpin
Cineworld
Leisure West
Feltham Business Complex
Ordnance Depot
Sports Ground
Feltham Corporate Centre
Five Ways Bus. Cen.
Felthambrook Ind. Est.
Croft Farm
TW13
Garden Centre
Rugby Football Ground
Club Ho.
FELTHAMHILL
Playing Field
Kenyngton Manor Prim. Sch.
King George's Fld.
Spelthorne School
Laboratories
Offices
ASHFORD COMMON
SUNBURY COMMON
Junc. 1
SUNBURY CROSS
Kempton Park
Kempton Steam Museum
Staines Reservo
Filter Beds
Grandstand
Sunbury
Sunbury Manor Sch.
Adult Ed. Cen.
Nuffield Health
St. Paul's
Kidabulous
M3
A244
A308
A316
B377
B3377
CHERTSEY ROAD
ASHFORD ROAD
HIGH ST.
HOUNSLOW
HANWORTH RD.
HARLINGTON RD. EAST
SNAKEY LANE
STAINES RD. WEST
STAINES RD.
COUNTY WAY
CADBURY ROAD
GROVELEY RD.
VICARAGE RD.
SUNBURY WAY
HAMILTON ROAD
CRANLEIGH ROAD
ELLINGTON ROAD

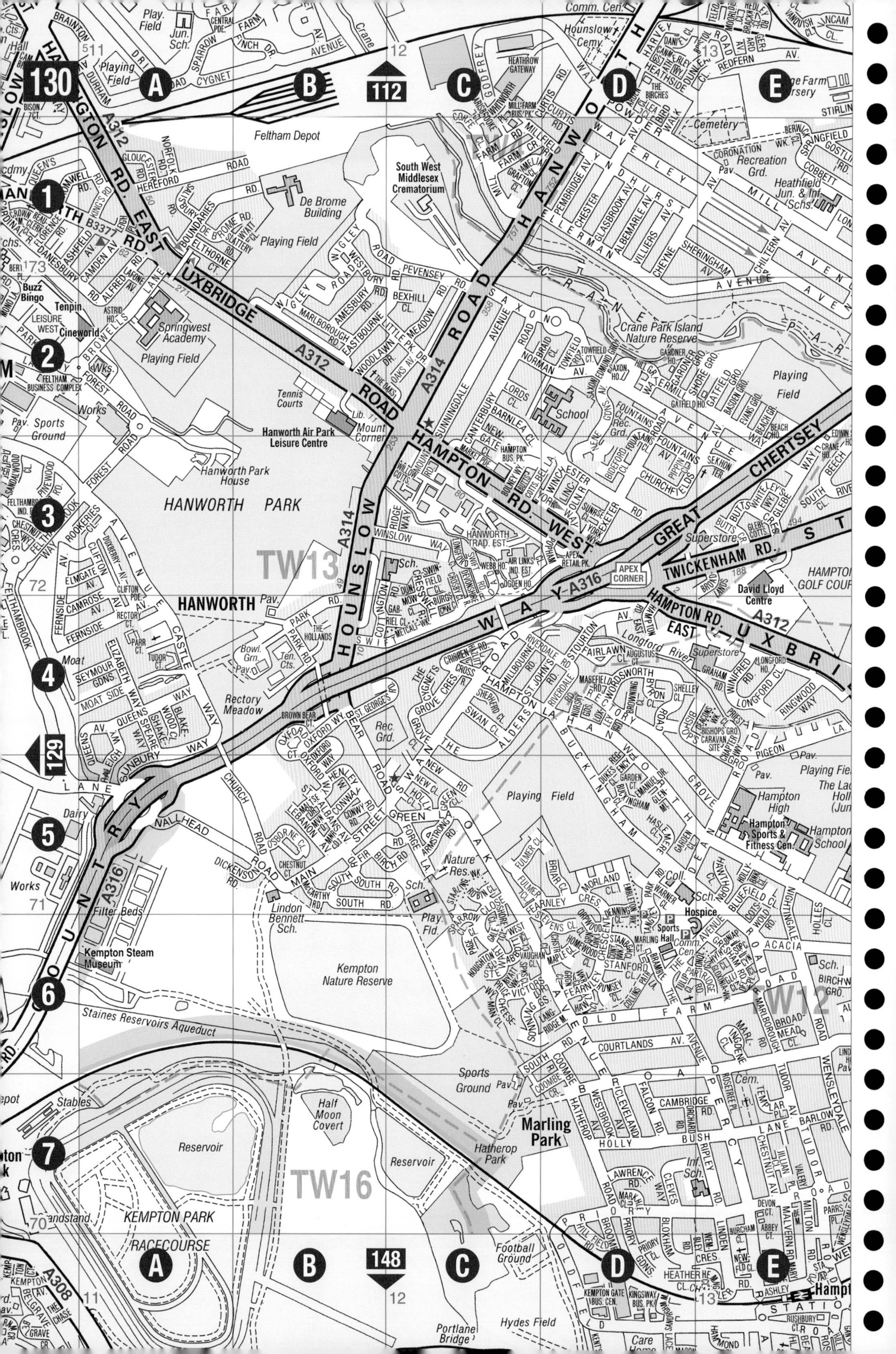

130
112
148
129
A
B
C
D
E
1
2
3
4
5
6
7
Feltham Depot
South West Middlesex Crematorium
De Brome Building
Playing Field
UXBRIDGE
A312
ROAD
HANWORTH ROAD
A314
HOUNSLOW ROAD
HAMPTON RD. WEST
GREAT CHERTSEY
TWICKENHAM RD.
HAMPTON RD. EAST
APEX CORNER
A316
Springwest Academy
Tenpin
Cineworld
Buzz Bingo
FELTHAM BUSINESS COMPLEX
Pav. Sports Ground
Hanworth Park House
HANWORTH PARK
TW13
HANWORTH
Hanworth Air Park Leisure Centre
Tennis Courts
Mount Corner
Crane Park Island Nature Reserve
School
Hounslow Cemy.
HEATHROW GATEWAY
Cemetery
Recreation Grd.
Heathfield Jun. & Inf. Schs.
Superstore
David Lloyd Centre
HAMPTON GOLF COURSE
Longford River
Rectory Meadow
Moat
Dairy
Works
Filter Beds
Kempton Steam Museum
Staines Reservoirs Aqueduct
Kempton Nature Reserve
Lindon Bennett Sch.
Nature Res.
Playing Field
Hampton High
Hampton Sports & Fitness Cen.
Hampton School
Hospice
Sports Hall
TW12
Sports Ground
Marling Park
Hatherop Park
Half Moon Covert
Reservoir
TW16
KEMPTON PARK
RACECOURSE
Stables
Stand
Football Ground
Hydes Field
Portlane Bridge
KEMPTON GATE BUS. CEN.
KINGSWAY BUS. PK.
A308

WHITTON
Whitton
113
TWICKENHAM
131
Harlequins RUFC (Twickenham Stoop)
Twickenham Cemetery
Kneller Gdns.
Trafalgar Inf. Sch.
TW2
TW1
CHERTSEY ROAD
A316
HEATH ROAD
A305
THE GREEN
HOSPITAL BRIDGE ROUNDABOUT
Hospital Bridge
Sports Ground
Twickenham Green
STAINES ROAD
SIXTH CROSS ROAD
B358
Fulwell Park
FULWELL GOLF COURSE
Fulwell
Club House
Bus Garage
Waldegrave Sch. for Girls
St. James's Catholic Primary School
STRAWBERRY HILL GOLF COURSE
Strawberry Hill
Stanley Prim. Sch.
Cemetery
St. Mary's University College
STRAWBERRY HILL
Sports Cen.
Radnor Gardens
WALDEGRAVE ROAD
A309
Newland Ho.Sch.
132
TEDDINGTON
TW11
HAMPTON HILL
HAMPTON ROAD
A313
A312
A311
WELLINGTON ROAD
HAMPTON RD.
PARK ROAD
Playing Field The Lady Eleanor Holles Sch. (Senior Dept.)
Cricket Grd.
National Phy. Lab.
HOSP. UCC
BROAD ST.
HIGH ST.
Canal Plantation
Upper Lodge
Pantile Bridge
The Brew House
Bartons Cottage
Cricket Ground
Bushy House
Tennis Courts
Bowling Green
Sports Ground
Teddington Lodge
Round Plantation
Longford River
Hampton Open Air Pool
Carlisle Park
Clarendon Sch.
BUSHY
149
HAMPTON
Hampton & Richmond Borough FC (Beveree Stadium)
The Pheasantry Welcome Centre
Broom Clumps
River Lodge
Willow Plantation
Deer Pen
170
F G H J K
1 2 3 4 5 6 7
14 15 16

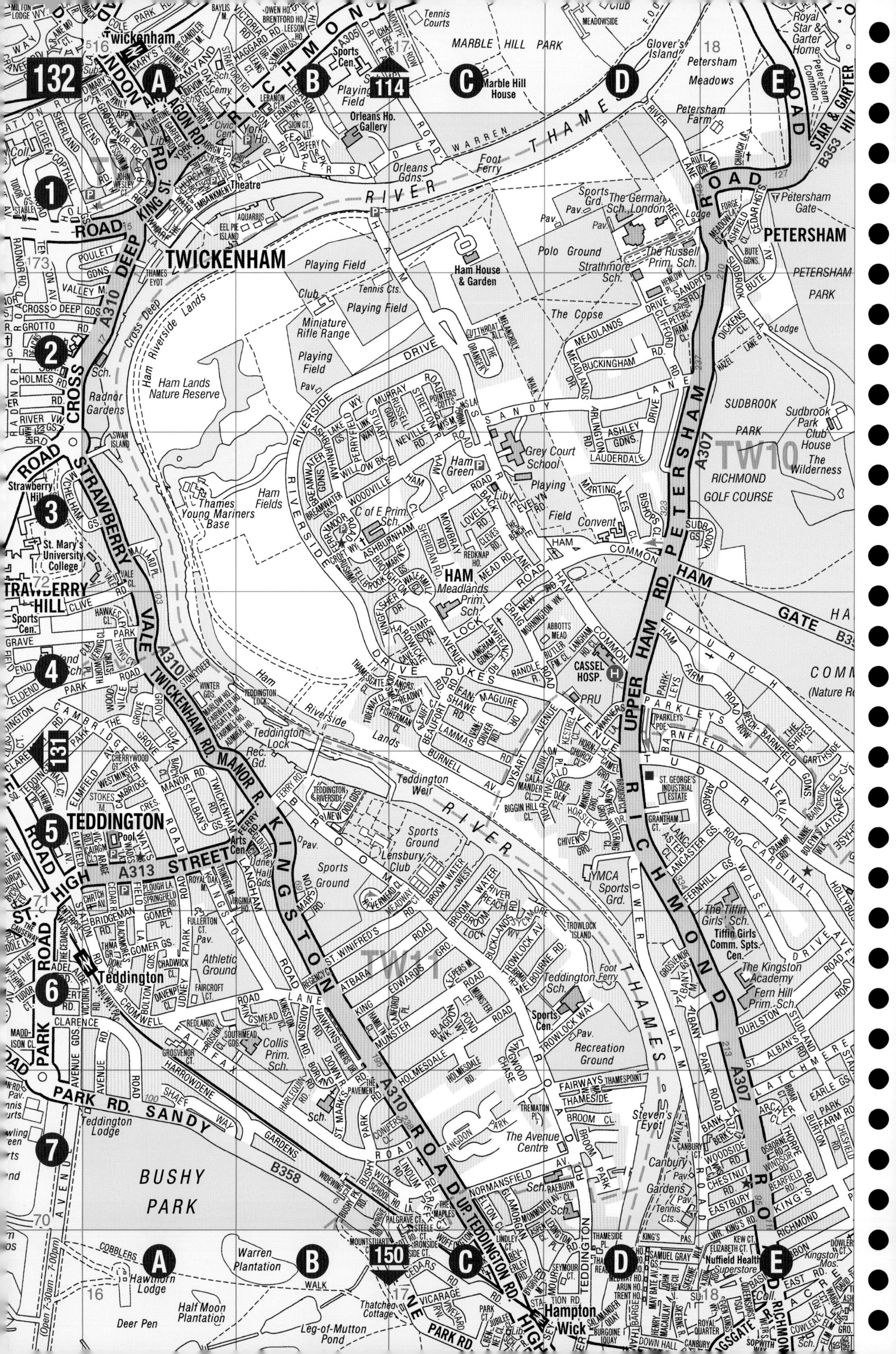

132
114
131
150
A
B
C
D
E
1
2
3
4
5
6
7
Twickenham
TWICKENHAM
MARBLE HILL PARK
Marble Hill House
Orleans Ho. Gallery
Orleans Gdns.
Glover's Island
Petersham Meadows
Petersham Farm
Royal Star & Garter Home
Petersham Common
Petersham Gate
PETERSHAM
PETERSHAM PARK
RIVER THAMES
WARREN
Foot Ferry
Theatre
EEL PIE ISLAND
THAMES EYOT
Playing Field
Tennis Cts.
Club
Miniature Rifle Range
Ham House & Garden
Polo Ground
The German Sch. London
The Russell Prim. Sch.
Strathmore Sch.
The Copse
Cross Deep
Ham Riverside Lands
Ham Lands Nature Reserve
Radnor Gardens
SWAN ISLAND
Strawberry Hill
St. Mary's University College
Thames Young Mariners Base
Ham Fields
Grey Court School
Ham Green
C of E Prim. Sch.
HAM
Meadlands Prim. Sch.
Convent
SUDBROOK PARK
Sudbrook Park Club House
The Wilderness
RICHMOND GOLF COURSE
TW10
HAM COMMON
HAM GATE
COMM (Nature R
CASSEL HOSP.
PRU
ST. GEORGE'S INDUSTRIAL ESTATE
Teddington Lock
Ham Riverside Lands
Rec. Gd.
Teddington Weir
TEDDINGTON RIVERSIDE
Sports Ground
Lensbury Club
Udney Hall Gds.
Arts Cen.
TEDDINGTON
Pool
Teddington
Athletic Ground
Collis Prim. Sch.
TW11
YMCA Sports Grd.
TROWLOCK ISLAND
Teddington Sch.
Sports Cen.
Recreation Ground
The Avenue Centre
Steven's Eyot
Canbury Gardens
The Tiffin Girls' Sch.
Tiffin Girls Comm. Spts. Cen.
The Kingston Academy
Fern Hill Prim. Sch.
Nuffield Health Superstore
Kingston Mos.
BUSHY PARK
Teddington Lodge
Hawthorn Lodge
Warren Plantation
Half Moon Plantation
Deer Pen
Thatched Cottage
Leg-of-Mutton Pond
Hampton Wick
(Open 7-30am - 7-00pm)
A310
A305
A307
A313
B358
B353
STRAWBERRY VALE
TWICKENHAM RD.
KINGSTON ROAD
UPPER HAM RD.
PETERSHAM ROAD
RICHMOND ROAD
HIGH STREET
SANDY LANE
RIVERSIDE DRIVE
LOWER HAM ROAD
BROOM ROAD
PARK RD.
SANDY LANE
UP. TEDDINGTON RD.
CROSS DEEP
STAR & GARTER HILL
16
17
18

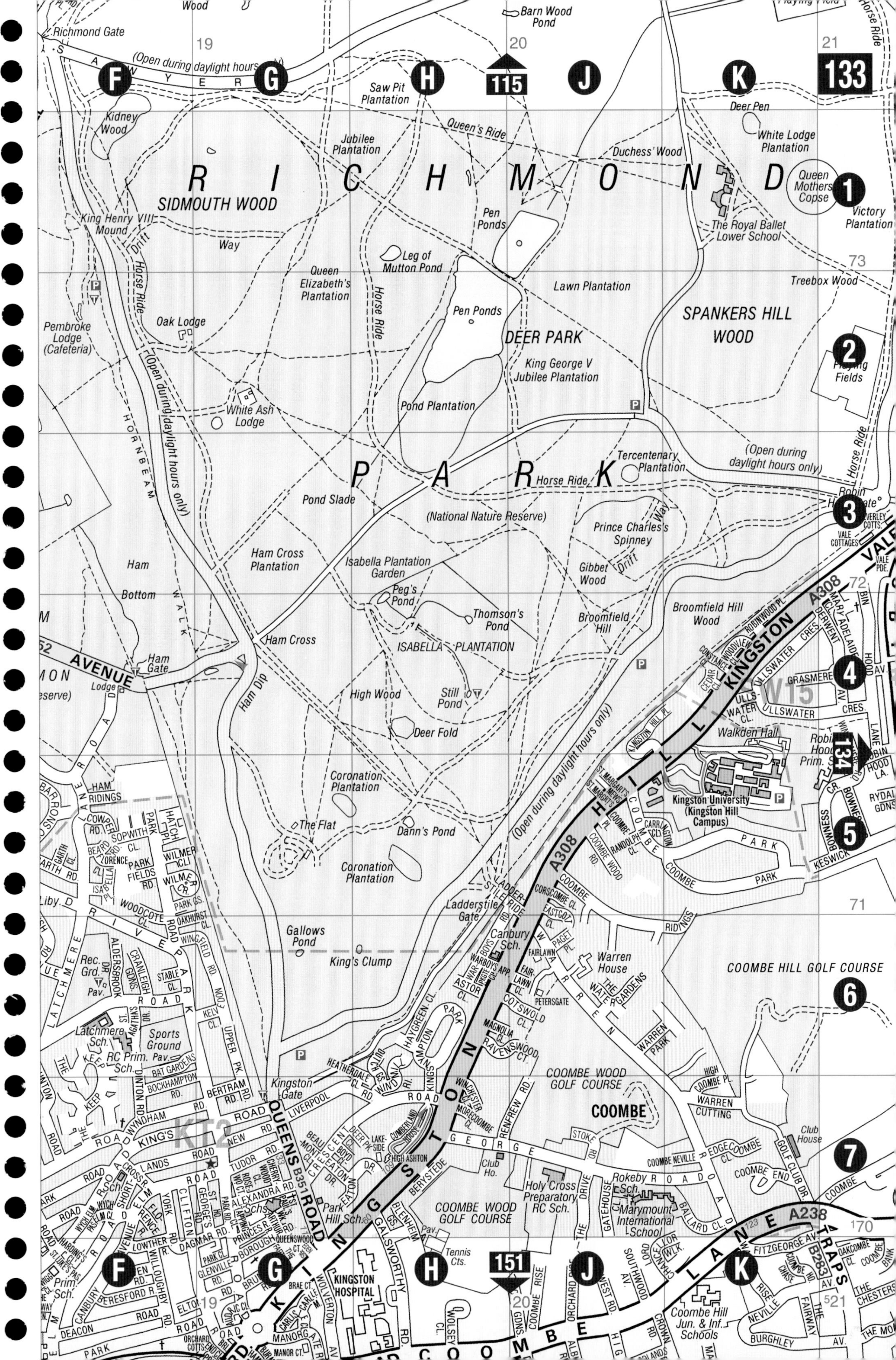

133
115
134
151
F
G
H
J
K
1
2
3
4
5
6
7
19
20
21
73
72
71
170
RICHMOND PARK
(National Nature Reserve)
Richmond Gate
Barn Wood Pond
(Open during daylight hours only)
Saw Pit Plantation
Kidney Wood
Jubilee Plantation
Queen's Ride
Duchess' Wood
Deer Pen
White Lodge Plantation
Queen Mothers Copse
Victory Plantation
The Royal Ballet Lower School
SIDMOUTH WOOD
King Henry VIII Mound
Pen Ponds
Leg of Mutton Pond
Queen Elizabeth's Plantation
Lawn Plantation
Treebox Wood
Pembroke Lodge (Cafeteria)
Oak Lodge
DEER PARK
SPANKERS HILL WOOD
King George V Jubilee Plantation
Playing Fields
Pond Plantation
White Ash Lodge
Tercentenary Plantation
Horse Ride
Robin Hood Gate
Pond Slade
Prince Charles's Spinney
Ham Cross Plantation
Isabella Plantation Garden
Gibbet Wood
Ham Bottom
Peg's Pond
Thomson's Pond
Broomfield Hill
Broomfield Hill Wood
Ham Cross
ISABELLA PLANTATION
Ham Gate
AVENUE
Ham Dip
High Wood
Still Pond
Deer Fold
Coronation Plantation
The Flat
Dann's Pond
Ladderstile Gate
Gallows Pond
King's Clump
Kingston Gate
Walkden Hall
Kingston University (Kingston Hill Campus)
KINGSTON HILL
A308
KT2
KT15
Canbury Sch.
Warren House
COOMBE HILL GOLF COURSE
COOMBE WOOD GOLF COURSE
COOMBE
Club House
Holy Cross Preparatory RC Sch.
Marymount International School
Rokeby Sch.
Coombe Hill Jun. & Inf. Schools
KINGSTON HOSPITAL
Park Hill Sch.
Tennis Cts.
Latchmere Sch.
RC Prim. Sch.
Sports Ground
Rec. Grd.
QUEENS ROAD B351
KING'S ROAD
GEORGE ROAD
COOMBE LANE A238
TRAPS LANE B283
COOMBE ROAD
COOMBE PARK
WARREN ROAD
LIVERPOOL ROAD
PARK ROAD
RICHMOND ROAD

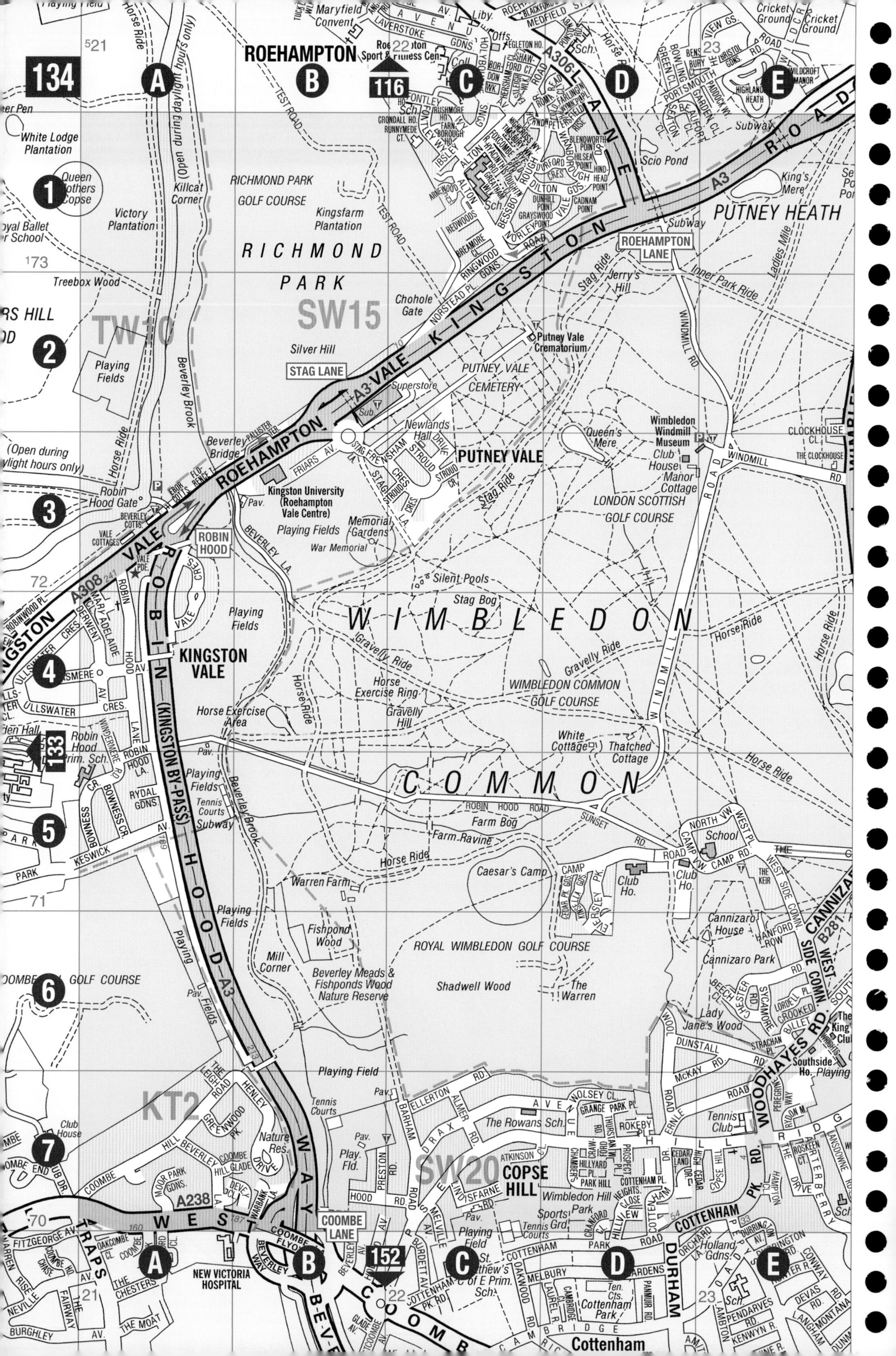

134
ROEHAMPTON
116
Roehampton Sport & Fitness Cen.
Maryfield Convent
White Lodge Plantation
Queen Mothers Copse
Royal Ballet School
Victory Plantation
Killcat Corner
Treebox Wood
TW10
Playing Fields
Beverley Brook
RICHMOND PARK GOLF COURSE
Kingsfarm Plantation
RICHMOND PARK
SW15
Chohole Gate
Silver Hill
STAG LANE
KINGSTON VALE
ROEHAMPTON VALE
A3
A306
ROEHAMPTON LANE
PUTNEY HEATH
King's Mere
Scio Pond
Jerry's Hill
Inner Park Ride
Ladies Mile
Putney Vale Crematorium
PUTNEY VALE CEMETERY
Superstore
PUTNEY VALE
Kingston University (Roehampton Vale Centre)
Playing Fields
Memorial Gardens
War Memorial
Robin Hood Gate
ROBIN HOOD
Queen's Mere
Wimbledon Windmill Museum
Club House
Manor Cottage
LONDON SCOTTISH GOLF COURSE
WINDMILL RD.
Silent Pools
Stag Bog
WIMBLEDON COMMON
Gravelly Ride
Horse Exercise Ring
Gravelly Hill
WIMBLEDON COMMON GOLF COURSE
KINGSTON VALE
Horse Exercise Area
White Cottage
Thatched Cottage
ROBIN HOOD ROAD
Farm Bog
Farm Ravine
Caesar's Camp
Warren Farm
Fishpond Wood
Mill Corner
ROYAL WIMBLEDON GOLF COURSE
Beverley Meads & Fishponds Wood Nature Reserve
Shadwell Wood
The Warren
Cannizaro House
Cannizaro Park
Lady Jane's Wood
ROBIN HOOD WAY (KINGSTON BY-PASS)
COOMBE HILL GOLF COURSE
KT2
A238
WEST
COOMBE LANE
152
NEW VICTORIA HOSPITAL
SW20
COPSE HILL
Wimbledon Hill Park
The Rowans Sch.
Cottenham Park
DURHAM RD.
COTTENHAM PARK RD.
WOODHAYES RD.
RIDGWAY
Holland Gdns.

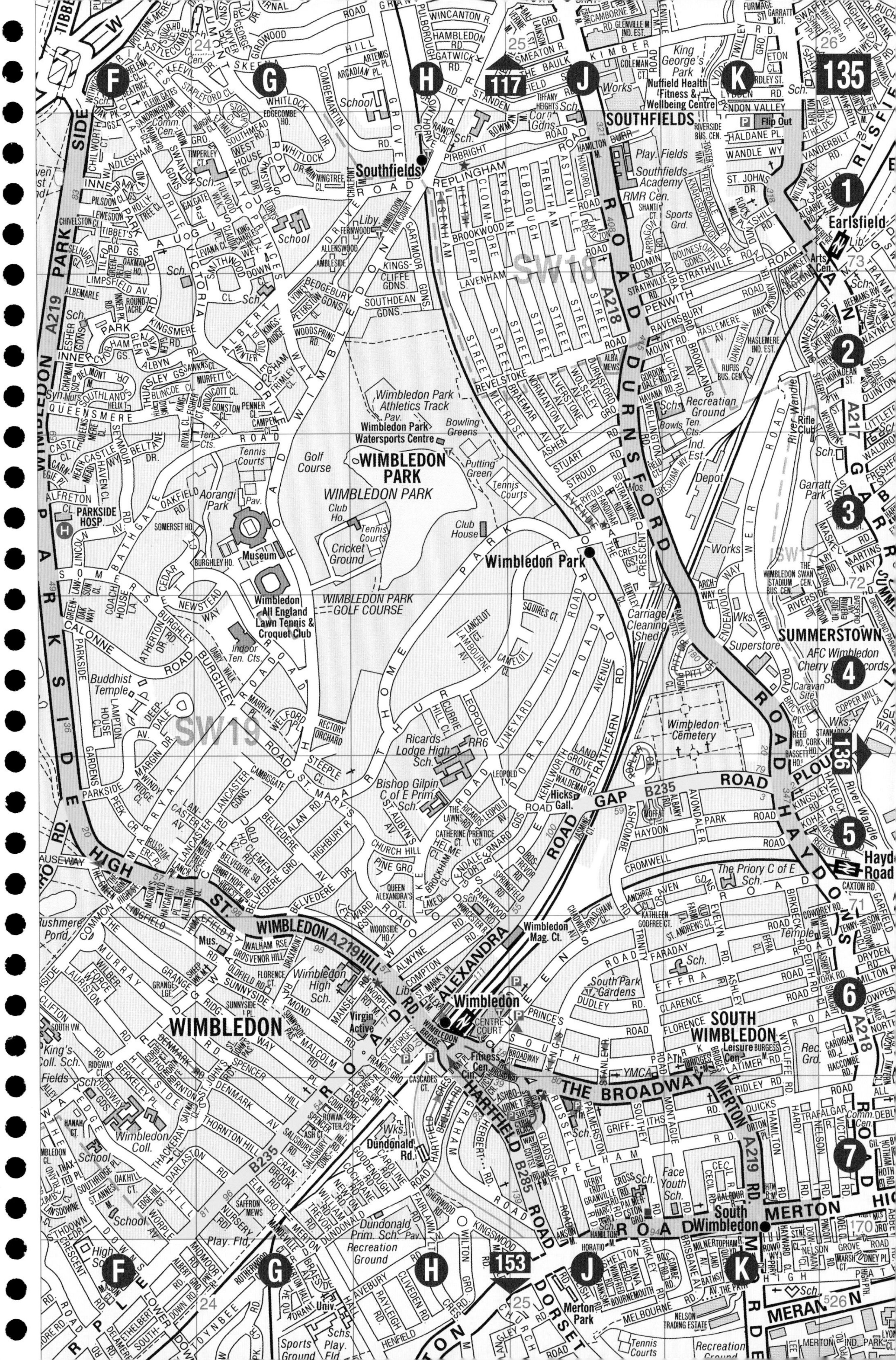

135
117
153
136
F
G
H
J
K
1
2
3
4
5
6
7
24
25
26
73
72
71
170
SW18
SW19
SW17
SOUTHFIELDS
Southfields
Earlsfield
SUMMERSTOWN
WIMBLEDON
SOUTH WIMBLEDON
MERTON
Merton Park
Wimbledon
Wimbledon Park
Haydons Road
South Wimbledon
Dundonald Rd.
WIMBLEDON PARK
Wimbledon Park Athletics Track
Wimbledon Park Watersports Centre
Golf Course
WIMBLEDON PARK GOLF COURSE
Cricket Ground
Bowling Greens
Putting Green
Tennis Courts
Club House
Museum
Wimbledon All England Lawn Tennis & Croquet Club
Indoor Ten. Cts.
Aorangi Park
Buddhist Temple
PARKSIDE HOSP.
Wimbledon Cemetery
Carriage Cleaning Shed
Superstore
AFC Wimbledon
Caravan Site
Ricards Lodge High Sch.
Bishop Gilpin C of E Prim. Sch.
Wimbledon High Sch.
Wimbledon Coll.
King's Coll. Sch.
Virgin Active
Wimbledon Mag. Ct.
Centre Court
Fitness Cen.
Dundonald Prim. Sch.
Recreation Ground
Rushmere Pond
The Priory C of E Sch.
South Park Gardens
Leisure Cen.
YMCA
Face Youth Sch.
King George's Park
Nuffield Health Fitness & Wellbeing Centre
Flip Out
Southfields Academy
RMR Cen.
Sports Grd.
Play. Fields
Rifle Club
Garratt Park
Works
Depot
Ind. Est.
Hicks Gall.
Nelson Trading Estate
Merton Ind. Park
WIMBLEDON PARK SIDE
PARKSIDE
A219
A218
A217
B235
B285
DURNSFORD ROAD
HAYDONS ROAD
PLOUGH LANE
GAP ROAD
HIGH ST.
WIMBLEDON HILL
THE BROADWAY
MERTON ROAD
HARTFIELD ROAD
ALEXANDRA RD.
HOME PARK ROAD
ARTHUR RD.
CHURCH ROAD
VICTORIA DRIVE
AUGUSTUS RD.
REPLINGHAM RD.
WIMBLEDON PARK RD.
BURGHLEY RD.
SOMERSET RD.
CALONNE RD.
QUEENSMERE RD.
KINGSMERE
WORPLE RD.
KINGSWOOD RD.
MERTON HIGH ST.

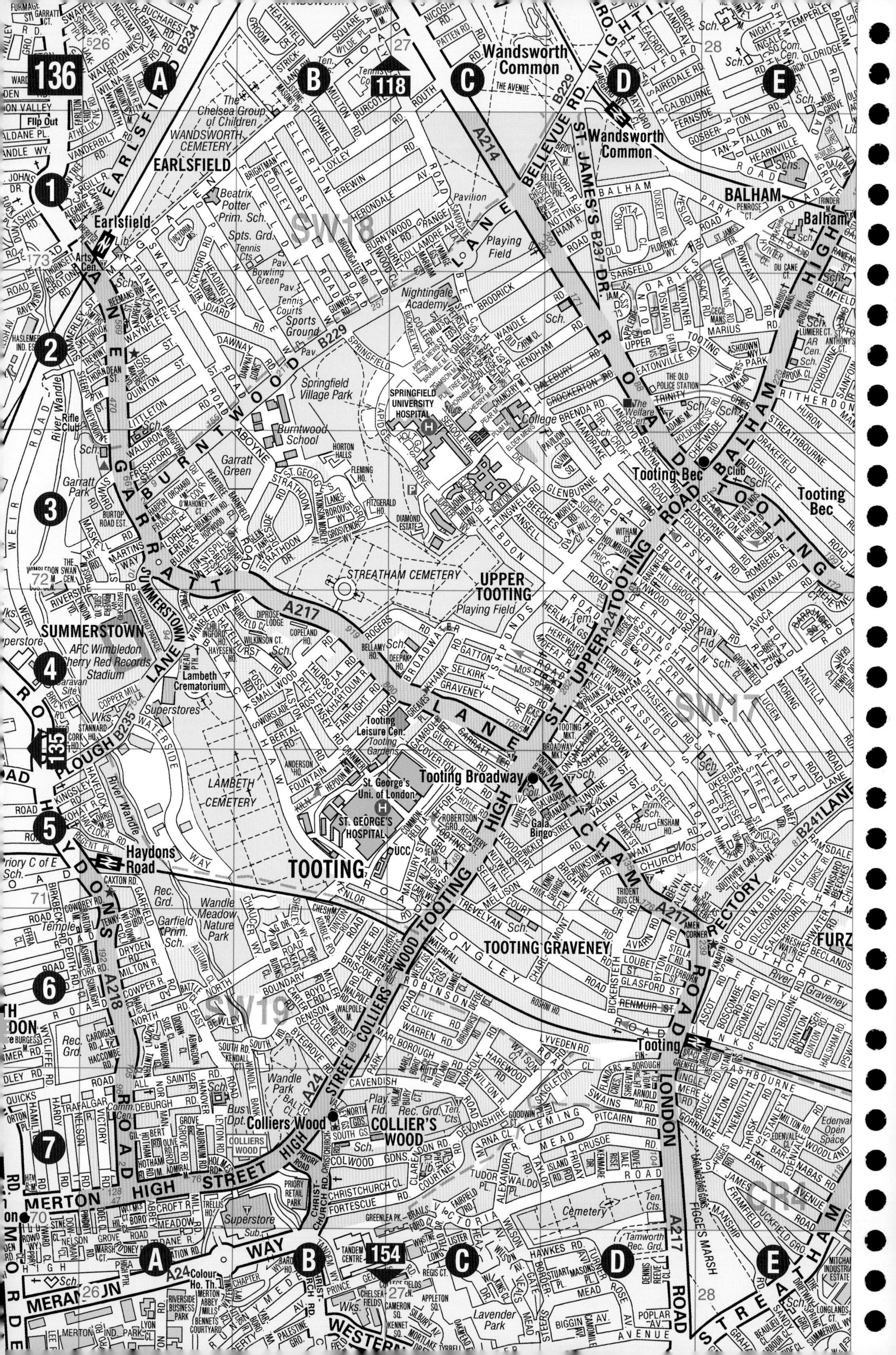

136
118
135
154
A
B
C
D
E
1
2
3
4
5
6
7
26
27
28
Wandsworth Common
EARLSFIELD
Earlsfield
The Chelsea Group of Children
WANDSWORTH CEMETERY
Beatrix Potter Prim. Sch.
SW18
BALHAM
Balham
BURNTWOOD LANE
B229
A214
B237
A217
A24
A218
B235
B241
Nightingale Academy
Springfield Village Park
SPRINGFIELD UNIVERSITY HOSPITAL
Burntwood School
Garratt Green
Garratt Park
Rifle Club
River Wandle
STREATHAM CEMETERY
UPPER TOOTING
Playing Field
Tooting Bec
SUMMERSTOWN
AFC Wimbledon Cherry Red Records Stadium
Lambeth Crematorium
LAMBETH CEMETERY
Tooting Leisure Cen.
Tooting Broadway
St. George's Uni. of London
ST. GEORGE'S HOSPITAL
TOOTING
Haydons Road
Wandle Meadow Nature Park
SW17
SW19
TOOTING GRAVENEY
Gala Bingo
Tooting
Colliers Wood
COLLIER'S WOOD
Wandle Park
Superstore
PRIORY RETAIL PARK
Cemetery
Lavender Park
Tamworth Rec. Grd.
Edenvale Open Space
CR4
MITCHAM INDUSTRIAL ESTATE
MERTON
HIGH STREET
COLLIERS WOOD HIGH STREET
UPPER TOOTING ROAD
TOOTING BEC ROAD
BALHAM HIGH ROAD
GARRATT LANE
MITCHAM ROAD
LONDON ROAD
STREATHAM ROAD
ROCTORY
FIGGE'S MARSH
WESTERN ROAD
MERANTUN WAY
PLOUGH LANE
HAYDONS ROAD

137
138
119
155
F
G
H
J
K
1
2
3
4
5
6
7
29
30
31
SW12
SW2
SW16
STREATHAM HILL
STREATHAM
STREATHAM PARK
STREATHAM VALE
NORBURY
TOOTING BEC COMMON
STREATHAM COMMON
Tooting Graveney Common
Tooting Bec Lido
Tooting Bec Athletic Track
Streatham Common
Streatham Hill
Streatham
Norbury
Streatham Ice & Leisure Cen.
Bishop Thomas Grant Sch.
Norwood Recreation Gd.
NORBURY PARK
Streatham Vale Park
School Playing Fields
Sports Ground
Football Pitch
Train Depot
Leisure Cen.
Lonesome
Beecholme Prim. Sch.
Hitherfield Prim. Sch.
Odeon Cin.
Virgin Active
Superstore
Bus Depot
The Rookery
CHRISTCHURCH HILL
STREATHAM HIGH ROAD
BEDFORD HILL
TOOTING BEC ROAD
BEC ROAD
STREATHAM COMMON NORTH
THORNTON AV.
STERNHOLD AV.
MITCHAM ROAD
GREYHOUND LA.
GARRAD'S RD.
STREATHAM VALE
GREEN LANE
EMMANUEL RD.
A23
A24
A205
A214
A216
B221
B242
B272
B273

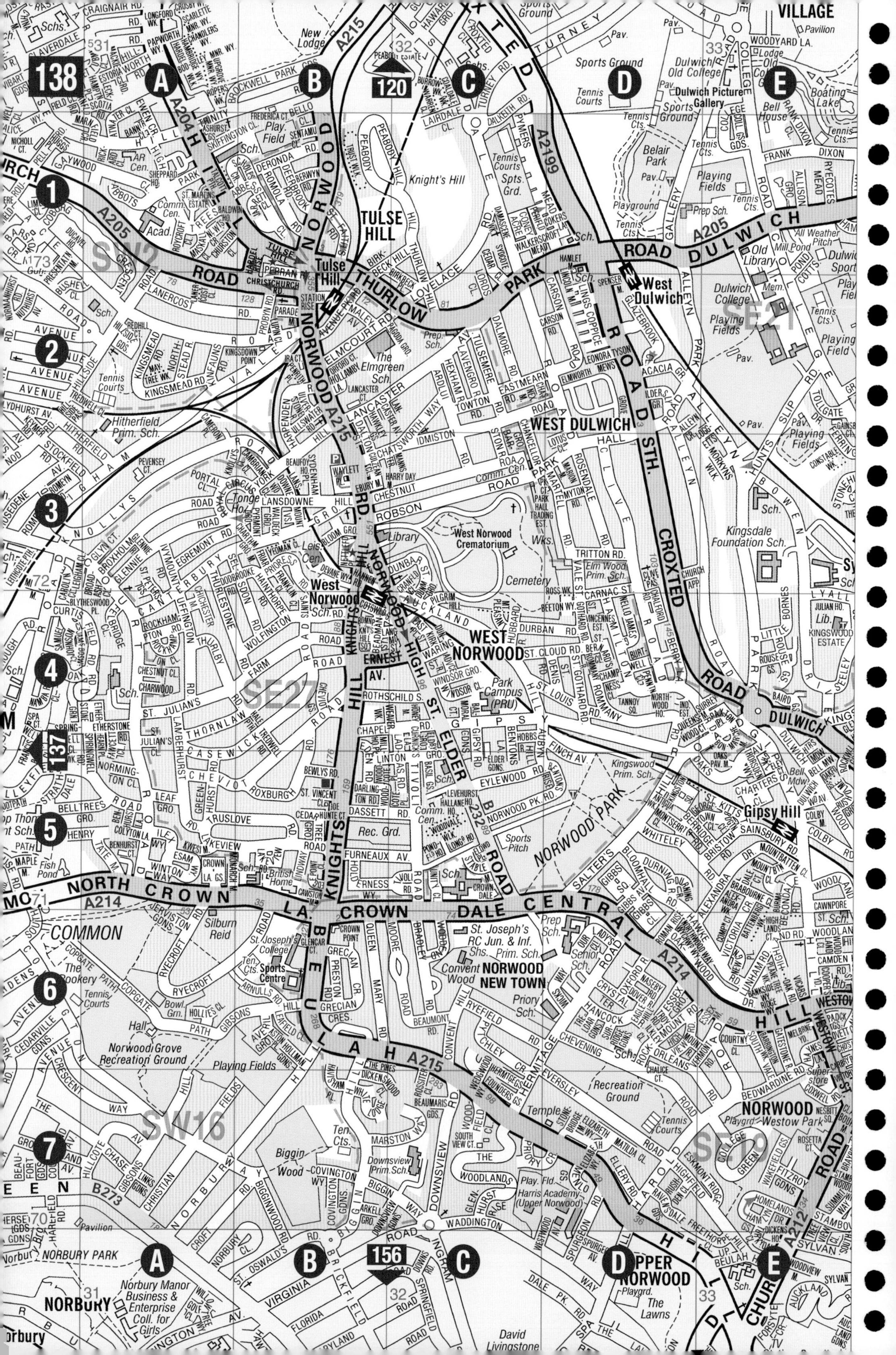

138
120
156
137
A
B
C
D
E
1
2
3
4
5
6
7
31
32
33
VILLAGE
Dulwich Old College
Dulwich Picture Gallery
Sports Ground
Tennis Courts
Belair Park
Playing Fields
Boating Lake
Bell House
Knight's Hill
TULSE HILL
Tulse Hill
THURLOW PARK ROAD
DULWICH ROAD
A205
A215
A2199
A204
NORWOOD ROAD
West Dulwich
WEST DULWICH
Dulwich College
SE21
SW2
The Elmgreen Sch.
Hitherfield Prim. Sch.
Tonge Ho.
West Norwood Crematorium
Cemetery
Library
West Norwood
WEST NORWOOD
SE27
CROXTED ROAD
Kingsdale Foundation Sch.
Park Campus (PRU)
Kingswood Prim. Sch.
NORWOOD PARK
Gipsy Hill
NORTH CROWN
CROWN DALE
CENTRAL HILL
A214
COMMON
St. Joseph's RC Jun. & Inf. Shs.
NORWOOD NEW TOWN
Norwood Grove Recreation Ground
Playing Fields
BEULAH HILL
Recreation Ground
SW16
SE19
Biggin Wood
Downsview Prim.Sch.
Harris Academy (Upper Norwood)
NORWOOD
Westow Park
UPPER NORWOOD
NORBURY PARK
Norbury Manor Business & Enterprise Coll. for Girls
NORBURY
Norbury
The Lawns
David Livingstone
B273
A212

139
121
140
157
F
G
H
J
K
1
2
3
4
5
6
7
DULWICH PARK
Aviary
COMMON
THE GROVE
DULWICH & SYDENHAM HILL GOLF COURSE
The Grange
Club House
DULWICH
Sydenham Hill Wood & Cox's Walk Nature Reserve
Dulwich Wood
PECKARMANS WOOD
UPPER SYDENHAM
Sydenham Wells Park
Horniman Gardens
Horniman Museum
LONDON ROAD
A205
SE22
SE23
SE26
SE20
Forest Hill
FOREST HILL
DARTMOUTH RD.
KIRKDALE
A2216
PERRY
DACRES
B227
LOWER SYDENHAM
Mayow Park
SYDENHAM
Sydenham
PureGym
WESTWOOD
CRYSTAL PALACE PARK
A234
A212
HILL
A213
NEWLANDS PARK
TV Transmitter
Camping Site
Intermediate Lake
The Maze
Crystal Palace National Sports Centre
Sydenham Entrance
Playing Field
Site of Crystal Palace
Hostel
Bus Terminal
CRYSTAL PALACE
Crystal Palace Museum
Crystal Palace Athletics Stadium
Crystal Palace
Crystal Palace Pk. Farm
Crystal Palace Dinosaurs
Anerley Entrance
Lower Lake
Penge Entrance
Penge West
Penge East
St. Christopher's Hospice
Alexandra Rec. Grd.
Alexandra Jun. Sch.
PARISH LANE
HIGH ST.
ANERLEY
A214
ANERLEY HILL
CHURCH RD.
PENGE
Anerley
Harris City Academy
Civic Halls
Superstore
The Kentwood Cen.
Kent House
BECKENHAM
James Dixon Prim. Sch.

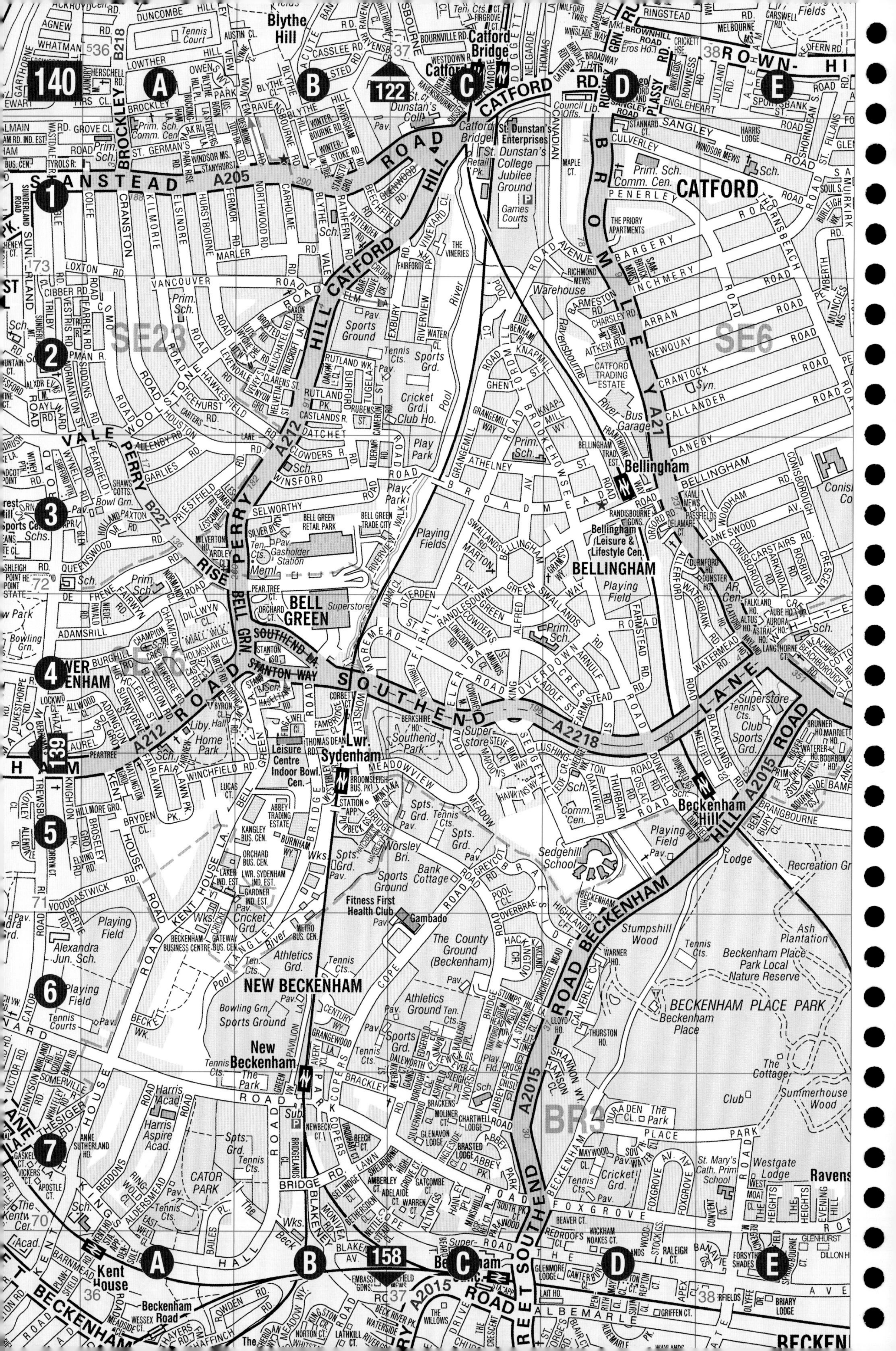

140
A
B
C
D
E
1
2
3
4
5
6
7
122
139
158
Blythe Hill
Catford Bridge
CATFORD
CATFORD RD.
STANSTEAD A205
CATFORD HILL
BROMLEY RD. A21
SE23
SE6
SE26
BR3
Bellingham
BELLINGHAM
BELL GREEN
PERRY RISE B227
PERRY HILL A212
VALE
BELL GRN
ROAD A212
SOUTHEND LA.
SOUTHEND LANE A2218
STANTON WAY
Lwr. Sydenham
NEW BECKENHAM
New Beckenham
BECKENHAM HILL ROAD A2015
Beckenham Hill
BECKENHAM ROAD
SOUTHEND ROAD A2015
BECKENHAM PLACE PARK
Beckenham Place
Beckenham Place Park Local Nature Reserve
Stumpshill Wood
Summerhouse Wood
Ash Plantation
Recreation Gr
CATOR PARK
Kent House
Beckenham Road
Sedgehill School
The County Ground (Beckenham)
Fitness First Health Club
Gambado
Sports Ground
Athletics Grd.
Playing Fields
Bellingham Leisure & Lifestyle Cen.
St. Dunstan's College Jubilee Ground
St. Dunstan's Enterprises
St. Dunstan's Coll.
Catford Bridge Retail Pk.
CATFORD TRADING ESTATE
BELL GREEN RETAIL PARK
BELL GREEN TRADE CITY
Gasholder Station
Leisure Centre Indoor Bowl. Cen.
Harris Acad.
Harris Aspire Acad.
Alexandra Jun. Sch.
River Pool
Ravensbourne
RAVENSBOURNE RD.
RIVERVIEW WALK
Bus Garage
Warehouse
THE PRIORY APARTMENTS
36
37
38
70
71
72
173

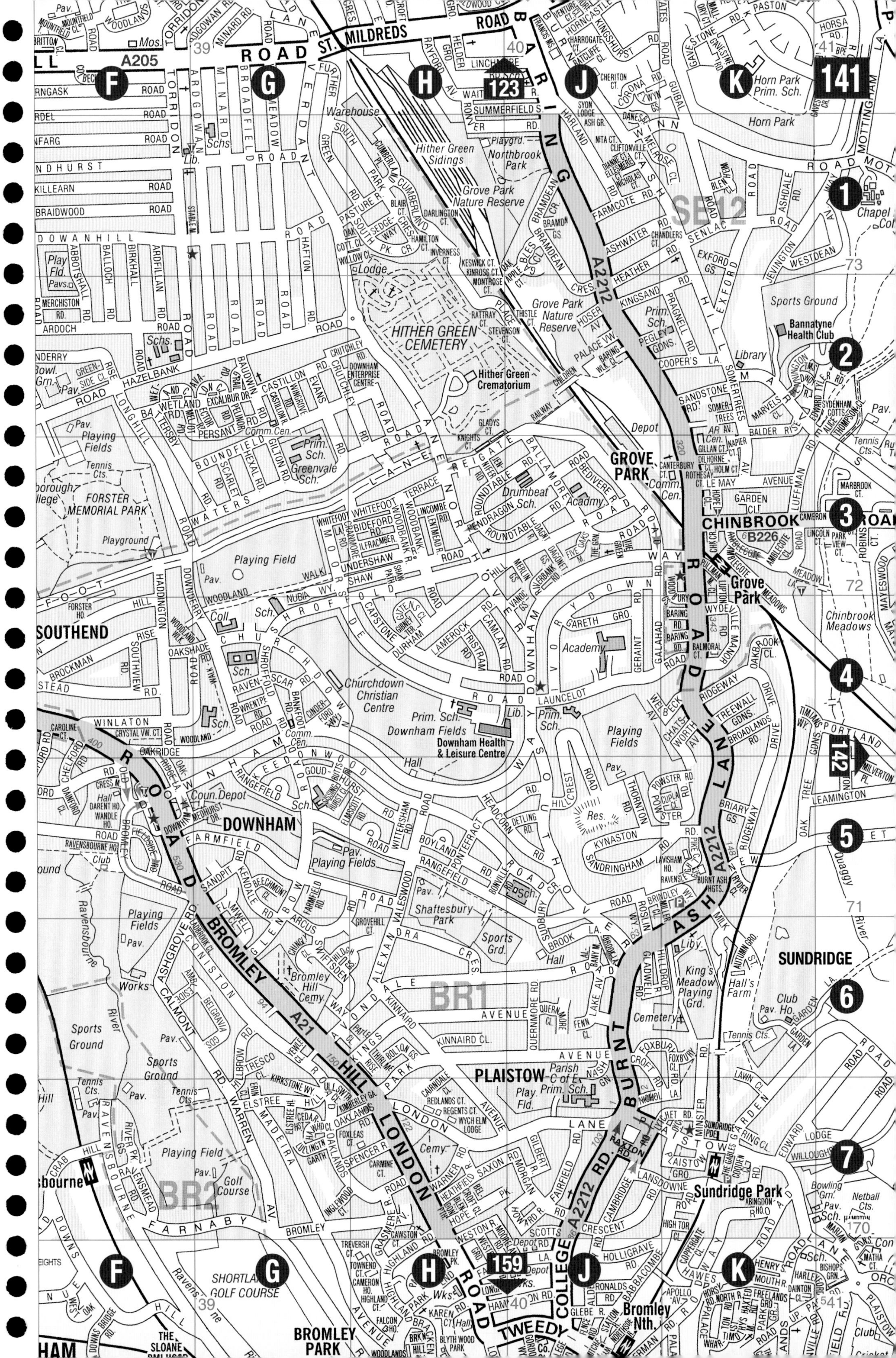

141
123
142
159
F
G
H
J
K
1
2
3
4
5
6
7
39
40
41
73
72
71
170
A205
ST. MILDREDS ROAD
BARING ROAD
A2212
SE12
Horn Park
Horn Park Prim. Sch.
MOTTINGHAM LA.
Hither Green Sidings
Northbrook Park
Grove Park Nature Reserve
HITHER GREEN CEMETERY
Hither Green Crematorium
Sports Ground
Bannatyne Health Club
Library
GROVE PARK
Depot
Comm. Cen.
CHINBROOK ROAD
B226
Grove Park
Chinbrook Meadows
FORSTER MEMORIAL PARK
Playing Fields
Playing Field
SOUTHEND
DOWNHAM
Drumbeat Sch.
Academy
Churchdown Christian Centre
Downham Fields
Downham Health & Leisure Centre
Coun. Depot
BROMLEY ROAD
A21
BROMLEY HILL
LONDON ROAD
Shaftesbury Park
Sports Grd.
Bromley Hill Cemy.
BR1
BR2
PLAISTOW
Parish C of E Prim. Sch.
BURNT ASH LANE
BURNT ASH HILL
King's Meadow Playing Grd.
Cemetery
SUNDRIDGE
Hall's Farm
Quaggy River
Sundridge Park
Ravensbourne
Ravensbourne River
SHORTLANDS GOLF COURSE
Golf Course
BROMLEY PARK
COLLEGE RD.
TWEEDY
Bromley Nth.
WARREN AV.
FARNABY

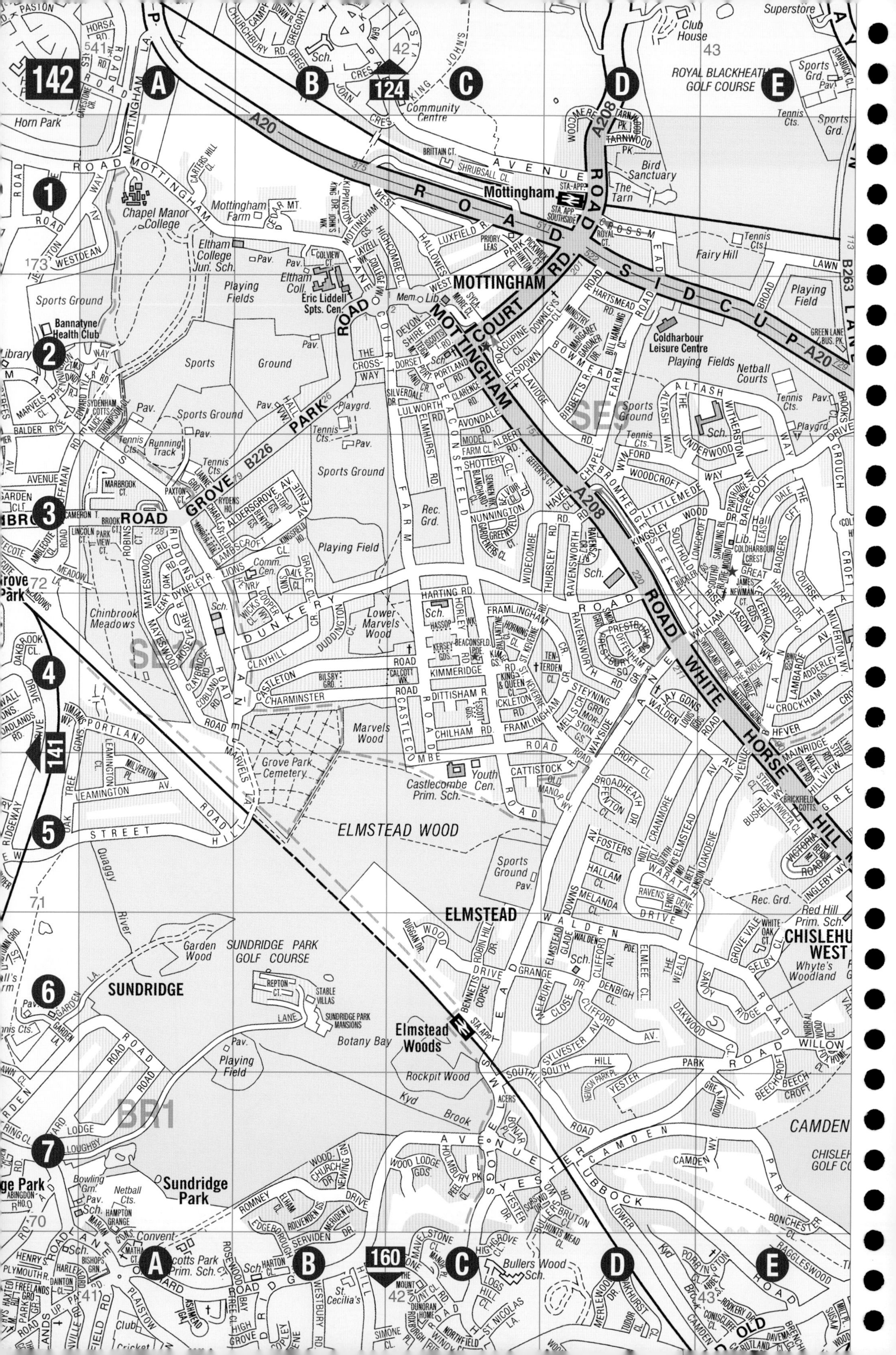

142
124
160
141
A
B
C
D
E
1
2
3
4
5
6
7
41
42
43
70
71
72
173
Horn Park
Chapel Manor College
Mottingham Farm
Eltham College Jun. Sch.
Eltham Coll.
Eric Liddell Spts. Cen.
Playing Fields
Sports Ground
Bannatyne Health Club
Library
Running Track
Community Centre
Club House
ROYAL BLACKHEATH GOLF COURSE
Superstore
Sports Grd.
Tennis Cts.
Bird Sanctuary
The Tarn
Mottingham
Fairy Hill
Coldharbour Leisure Centre
Playing Field
Netball Courts
MOTTINGHAM
Mem.
Lib.
Sch.
Rec. Grd.
Playing Field
Lower Marvels Wood
Marvels Wood
Chinbrook Meadows
SE12
SE9
Grove Park
Grove Park Cemetery
Castlecombe Prim. Sch.
Youth Cen.
ELMSTEAD WOOD
ELMSTEAD
Sports Ground
SUNDRIDGE PARK GOLF COURSE
Garden Wood
SUNDRIDGE
Quaggy River
Botany Bay
Elmstead Woods
Rockpit Wood
Kyd Brook
Playing Field
BR1
Sundridge Park
Bowling Grn.
Netball Cts.
Convent
Holy Trinity Prim. Sch.
St. Cecilia's
Bullers Wood Sch.
Red Hill Prim. Sch.
Whyte's Woodland
CHISLEHURST WEST
Rec. Grd.
CAMDEN
CHISLEHURST GOLF COURSE
Club
Cricket
A20
A208
B226
B263
MOTTINGHAM ROAD
COURT RD.
SIDCUP ROAD
GROVE PARK ROAD
WHITE HORSE HILL
MOTTINGHAM LANE
BEACONSFIELD ROAD
FARM
DUNKERY
MARVELS LANE
WESTDEAN
AVENUE
PORTLAND
LEAMINGTON AV.
STREET
WALDEN
ELMSTEAD
CAMDEN PARK ROAD
SOUTHILL
YESTER
LUBBOCK
WILLOW GROVE
LODGE
BAKER
OLD

143
125
144
161
F
G
H
J
K
1
2
3
4
5
6
7
University of Greenwich (Avery Hill Campus)
Sports/Leisure Centre
Sports Ground
Playing Fields
New Eltham
NEW ELTHAM
FIVEWAYS
A211
A20
B2214
A222
A208
B263
B264
DA15
DA14
BR7
Lamorbey
Old Farm Park
Playground
King George's Rec. Grd.
Dulverton Sch.
St. Olave's Prep. School
Marjorie McLure School
Edgebury Prim. Sch.
LONGLANDS
Sidcup Family Golf
Cray Wanderers FC (Est. Comp.-2024)
Flamingo Park
Pitch & Putt Course
Kemnal Park Cemetery
Ashen Grove
Partridge Shaw
Nuffield Health & Fitness Centre
Beaver's Wood
Chislehurst Cemetery
Hoblands Wood
SIDCUP
Sports Ground
Christ The King (St Mary's) Sixth Form College
FROGNAL CORNER
Foxbury
Old Elthamians Sports Club
Chislehurst Sch. for Girls
Darul Uloom London
Mead Rd. Inf. Sch.
Selwood
Farringtons School
Icehouse Wood
SCADBURY PARK (Nature Reserve)
Square Clump
Bushy Clump
Bank's Shaw
Spring Shaw
CHISLEHURST
CHISLEHURST COMMON
Camden Place Club House
War Mem.
Prim. Sch.
PARK WOOD
Hadresham
Fantails
Holbrook Wood
Lodge
Peasons
SIDCUP BY-PASS
MAIN ROAD
SIDCUP ROAD
PERRY STREET
BROMLEY RD.
BROMLEY LANE
ST. PAUL'S
CENTRE COMN. RD.
ROYAL PDE.
IMPERIAL WAY
CHISLEHURST RD.
FARM AV.
HALL WAY

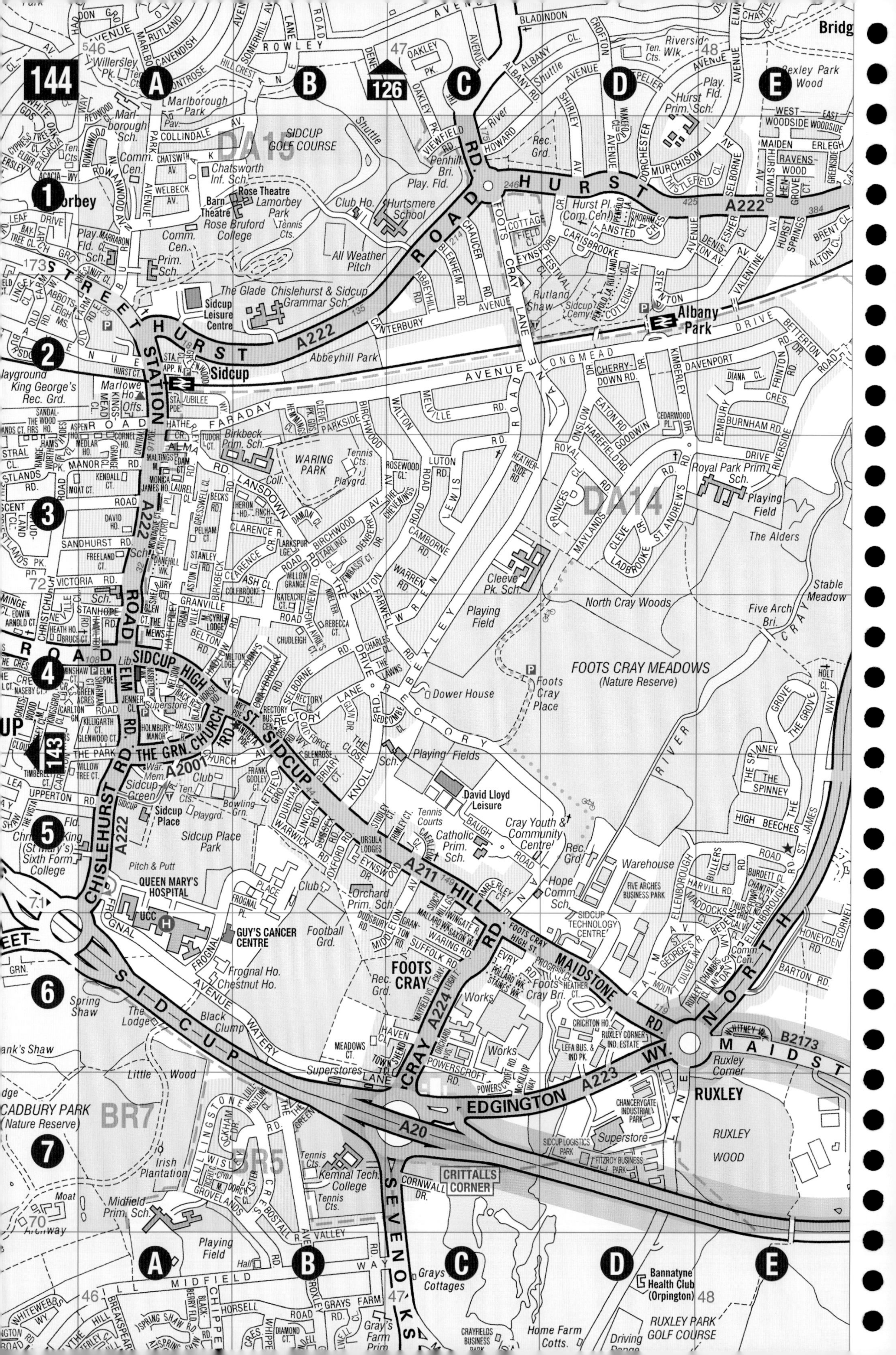
144
126
143
A
B
C
D
E
1
2
3
4
5
6
7
46
47
48
DA15
DA14
BR7
BR5
Willersley Pk.
Marlborough Park
Marlborough Sch.
SIDCUP GOLF COURSE
Chatsworth Inf. Sch.
Rose Theatre
Lamorbey Park
Barn Theatre
Rose Bruford College
Comm. Cen.
Prim. Sch.
Play. Fld.
Club Ho.
Hurtsmere School
All Weather Pitch
The Glade
Chislehurst & Sidcup Grammar Sch.
Sidcup Leisure Centre
Abbeyhill Park
Penhill Bri.
Play. Fld.
Rec. Grd.
Hurst Prim. Sch.
Bexley Park Wood
Hurst Pl. (Com.Cen.)
Rutland Shaw
Sidcup Cemy.
Albany Park
Sidcup
King George's Rec. Grd.
Marlowe Ho. Offs.
Birkbeck Prim. Sch.
WARING PARK
Royal Park Prim. Sch.
Playing Field
The Alders
Cleeve Pk. Sch.
North Cray Woods
Stable Meadow
Five Arch Bri.
Playing Field
FOOTS CRAY MEADOWS
(Nature Reserve)
Foots Cray Place
Dower House
Playing Fields
David Lloyd Leisure
Cray Youth & Community Centre
Catholic Prim. Sch.
Rec. Grd.
Warehouse
FIVE ARCHES BUSINESS PARK
Hope Comm. Sch.
SIDCUP TECHNOLOGY CENTRE
Sidcup Green
Sidcup Place
Sidcup Place Park
Pitch & Putt
QUEEN MARY'S HOSPITAL
UCC
GUY'S CANCER CENTRE
Frognal Ho.
Chestnut Ho.
Christ the King (St Mary's) Sixth Form College
Orchard Prim. Sch.
Football Grd.
FOOTS CRAY
Rec. Grd.
Works
Foots Cray Bri.
RUXLEY CORNER IND. ESTATE
LEFA BUS. & IND PK.
Ruxley Corner
RUXLEY
RUXLEY WOOD
CHANCERYGATE INDUSTRIAL PARK
Superstore
SIDCUP LOGISTICS PARK
FITZROY BUSINESS PARK
Spring Shaw
The Lodge
Black Clump
Little Wood
CADBURY PARK (Nature Reserve)
Irish Plantation
Moat
Midfield Prim. Sch.
Archway
Kemnal Tech. College
Tennis Cts.
CRITTALLS CORNER
Playing Field
Grays Cottages
Bannatyne Health Club (Orpington)
RUXLEY PARK GOLF COURSE
Home Farm Cotts.
Driving Range
CRAYFIELDS BUSINESS PARK
Gray's Farm Prim.
HURST ROAD A222
STATION ROAD
SIDCUP HIGH ST.
CHISLEHURST RD. A222
THE GRN.
CHURCH RD.
A2001
A211
SIDCUP HILL
MAIDSTONE RD.
NORTH CRAY ROAD
FOOTS CRAY LANE
BEXLEY LANE
RECTORY LANE
LONGMEAD DRIVE
AVENUE RD.
FARADAY AVENUE
SIDCUP BY-PASS
EDGINGTON WY. A223
A20
A224 CRAY RD.
MAIDSTONE RD. B2173
SEVENOAKS WAY
FROGNAL AVENUE
WATERY LANE
MIDFIELD WAY
VALLEY RD.
GRAYS FARM RD.
RUXLEY LANE
PALM AV.
HIGH BEECHES
ST. JAMES
THE SPINNEY
THE GROVE
ROWLEY AVENUE
BLADINDON
ALBANY RD.
HOWARD
CHAUCER RD.
BLENHEIM RD.
CANTERBURY AVENUE
CARISBROOKE
DAVENPORT
BETTERTON ROAD
PEMBURY
BURNHAM RD.
RIVERSIDE
ST. ANDREW'S RD.
MAYLANDS
ONSLOW
HAREFIELD RD.
GOODWIN
BIRCHWOOD
WALTON
MELVILLE RD.
LUTON RD.
CAMBORNE RD.
WARREN RD.
LANSDOWN RD.
GRANVILLE
BELTON RD.
VICTORIA RD.
SANDHURST RD.
MANOR RD.
ELM RD.
UPPERTON RD.
FROGNAL PL.
SUFFOLK RD.
WARING RD.
POWERSCROFT RD.
CORNWALL DR.
LULLINGSTONE
GROVELANDS
BOSTALL
HORSELL
BREAKSPEAR
HONEYDEN RD.
BARTON RD.
ELLENBOROUGH
ST. GEORGE'S RD.

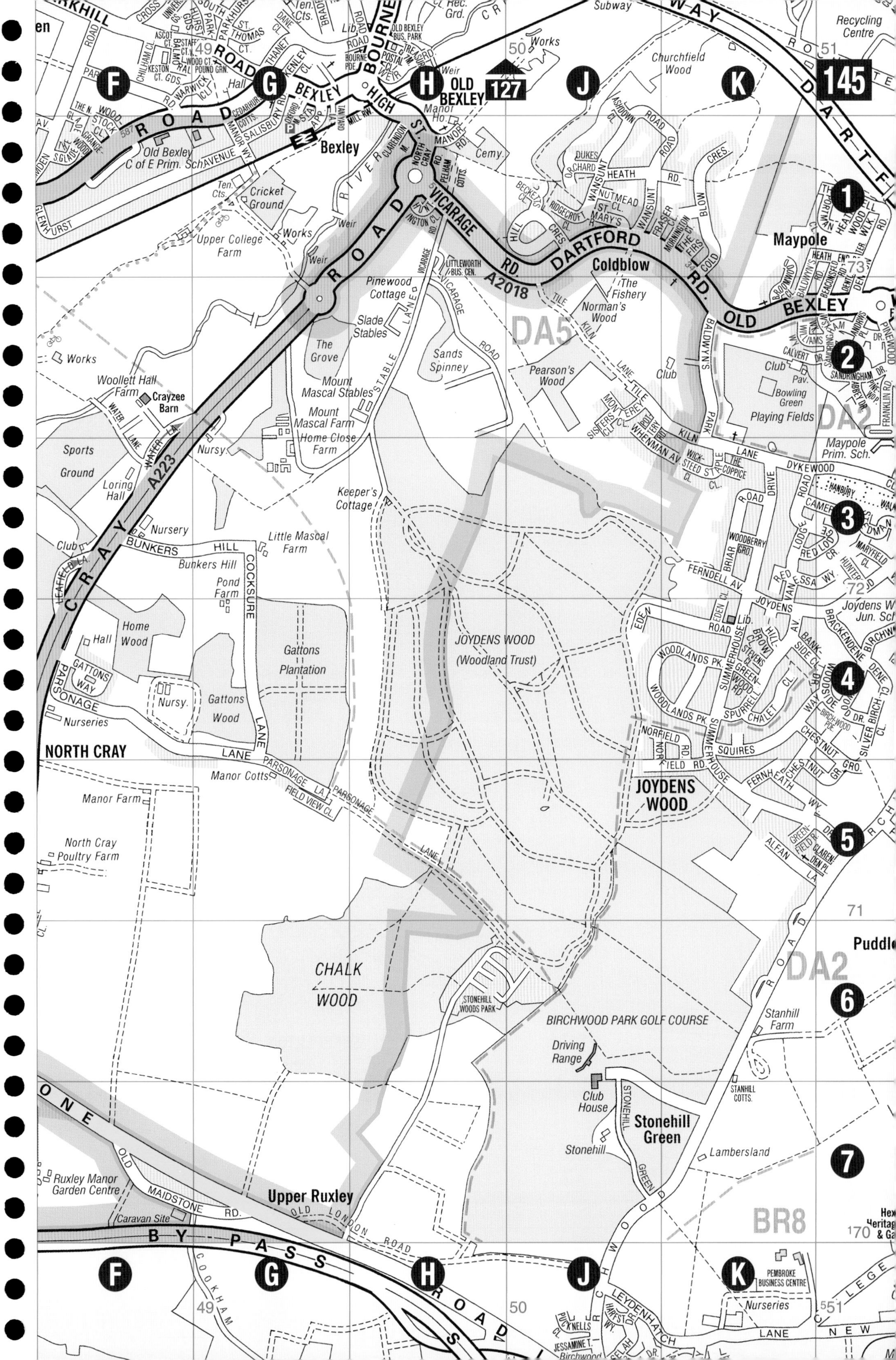

145
127
OLD BEXLEY
Bexley
Old Bexley C of E Prim. Sch.
Cricket Ground
Upper College Farm
Works
Weir
Cemy.
Churchfield Wood
Recycling Centre
Maypole
Coldblow
The Fishery
Norman's Wood
Pearson's Wood
DA5
DA2
BR8
Playing Fields
Bowling Green
Maypole Prim. Sch.
Pinewood Cottage
Slade Stables
The Grove
Sands Spinney
Mount Mascal Stables
Mount Mascal Farm
Home Close Farm
Keeper's Cottage
Woollett Hall Farm
Crayzee Barn
Sports Ground
Loring Hall
Nursery
Little Mascal Farm
Bunkers Hill
Pond Farm
Home Wood
Gattons Plantation
Gattons Wood
JOYDENS WOOD (Woodland Trust)
JOYDENS WOOD
Joydens Wood Jun. Sch.
NORTH CRAY
Nurseries
Manor Cotts
Manor Farm
North Cray Poultry Farm
CHALK WOOD
STONEHILL WOODS PARK
BIRCHWOOD PARK GOLF COURSE
Driving Range
Club House
Stonehill
Stonehill Green
Stanhill Farm
STANHILL COTTS.
Lambersland
Upper Ruxley
Ruxley Manor Garden Centre
Caravan Site
PEMBROKE BUSINESS CENTRE
Nurseries
Puddledock
CRAY ROAD
A223
VICARAGE RD.
DARTFORD RD.
A2018
OLD BEXLEY LANE
BUNKERS HILL
COCKSURE LANE
PARSONAGE LANE
MAIDSTONE RD.
OLD LONDON ROAD
BY-PASS
TILE KILN LANE
DYKEWOOD
FERNDELL AV.
EDEN ROAD
WOODLANDS PK.
SUMMERHOUSE DRIVE
SQUIRES
NORFIELD RD.
ALFAN LA.
LEYDENHATCH LANE
BIRCHWOOD ROAD
F
G
H
J
K
1
2
3
4
5
6
7
49
50
51
71
72
73
170

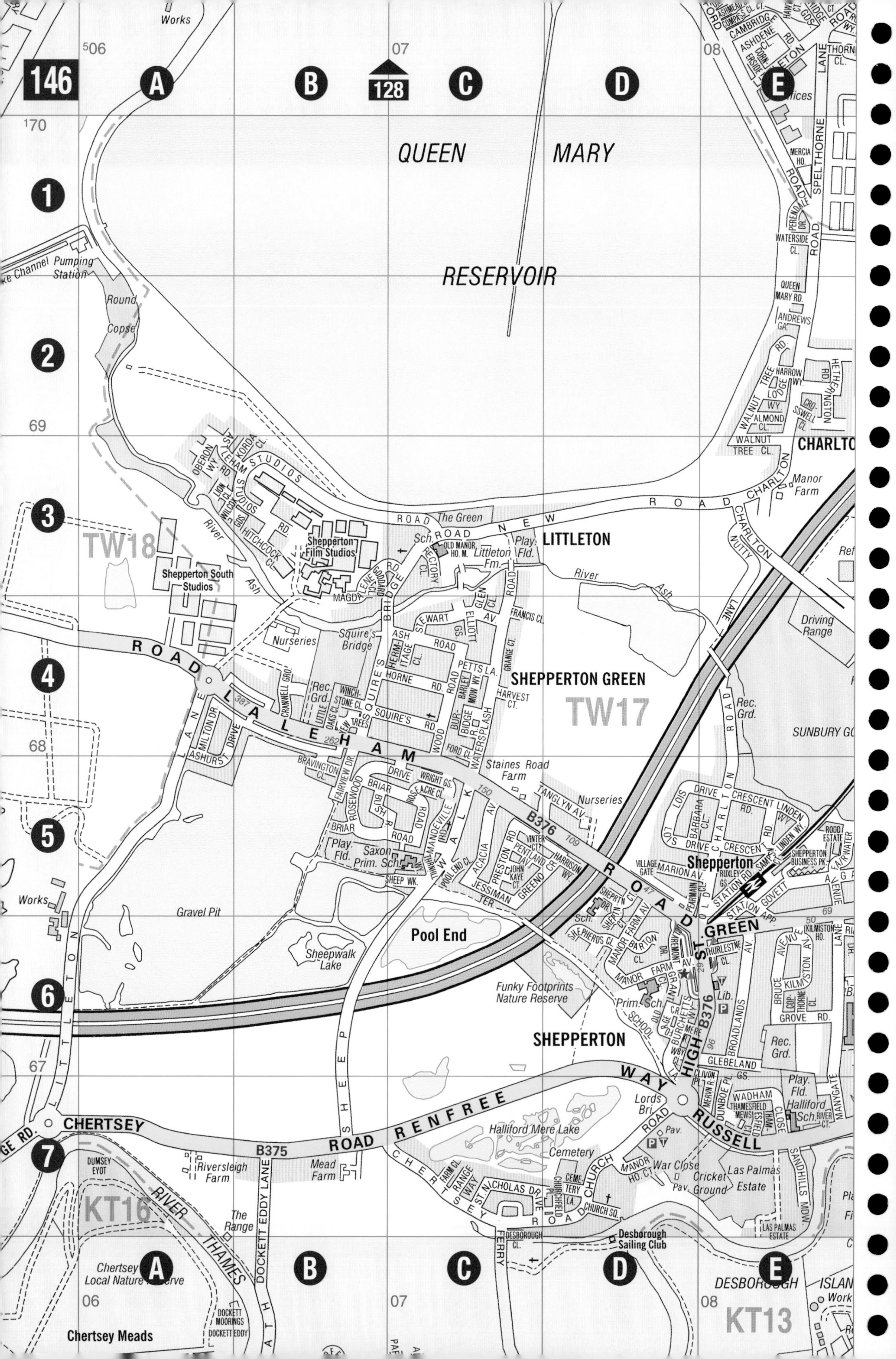
146
128
A
B
C
D
E
1
2
3
4
5
6
7
506
07
08
170
69
68
67
06
Works
QUEEN
MARY
RESERVOIR
Pumping Station
Round Copse
River Ash
TW18
TW17
KT16
KT13
Shepperton Film Studios
Shepperton South Studios
LITTLETON
SHEPPERTON GREEN
SHEPPERTON
Shepperton
NEW ROAD
CHARLTON ROAD
CHARLTON LANE
SPELTHORNE ROAD
LALEHAM ROAD
B376
B375
CHERTSEY ROAD
RENFREE WAY
RUSSELL ROAD
HIGH ST.
GREEN
LITTLETON LANE
SHEEP WALK
SQUIRE'S BRIDGE RD.
STUDIOS RD.
Squire's Bridge
Nurseries
Rec. Grd.
Staines Road Farm
Play. Fld.
Saxon Prim. Sch.
Pool End
Sheepwalk Lake
Gravel Pit
Funky Footprints Nature Reserve
Halliford Mere Lake
Cemetery
Lords Bri.
War Close
Cricket Ground
Las Palmas Estate
Desborough Sailing Club
Riversleigh Farm
Mead Farm
The Range
DOCKETT EDDY LANE
RIVER THAMES
DUMSEY EYOT
Chertsey Local Nature Reserve
Chertsey Meads
DESBOROUGH
Manor Farm
Driving Range
SUNBURY GOLF
Littleton Fm.
The Green
OLD MANOR HO. M.
CHARLTON
Halliford Sch.
CHURCH ROAD
MANOR FARM AV.
GLEBELAND GS.
BROADLANDS AV.
GROVE RD.
STATION RD.
STATION APP.
CRESCENT RD.
LOIS DRIVE
WAINUT TREE CL.
QUEEN MARY RD.
WATERSIDE CL.
MERCIA HO.
ST. NICHOLAS DRIVE
FERRY LA.
ACACIA AV.
PRESTON RD.
JESSIMAN TER.
TANGLYN AV.
HARRISON WY.
STEWART AV.
ASH RD.
HORNE RD.
PETTS LA.
WATERSPLASH RD.
BARLEY MOW WY.
FORD CL.
MILTON DR.
ASHURST DRIVE
CRANWELL GRO.
BRAVINGTON CL.
FAIRVIEW DR.
ROSEWOOD
BRIAR ROAD
MANDEVILLE RD.
POOL END CL.
SHEEP WK.
HITCHCOCK CL.
OBERON WY.
KORDA CL.
FRANCIS CL.
GRANGE CT.
HARVEST CT.
BRUCE AV.
KILMISTON AV.
SANDHILLS MDW.
CHURCH SQ.
DESBOROUGH CL.

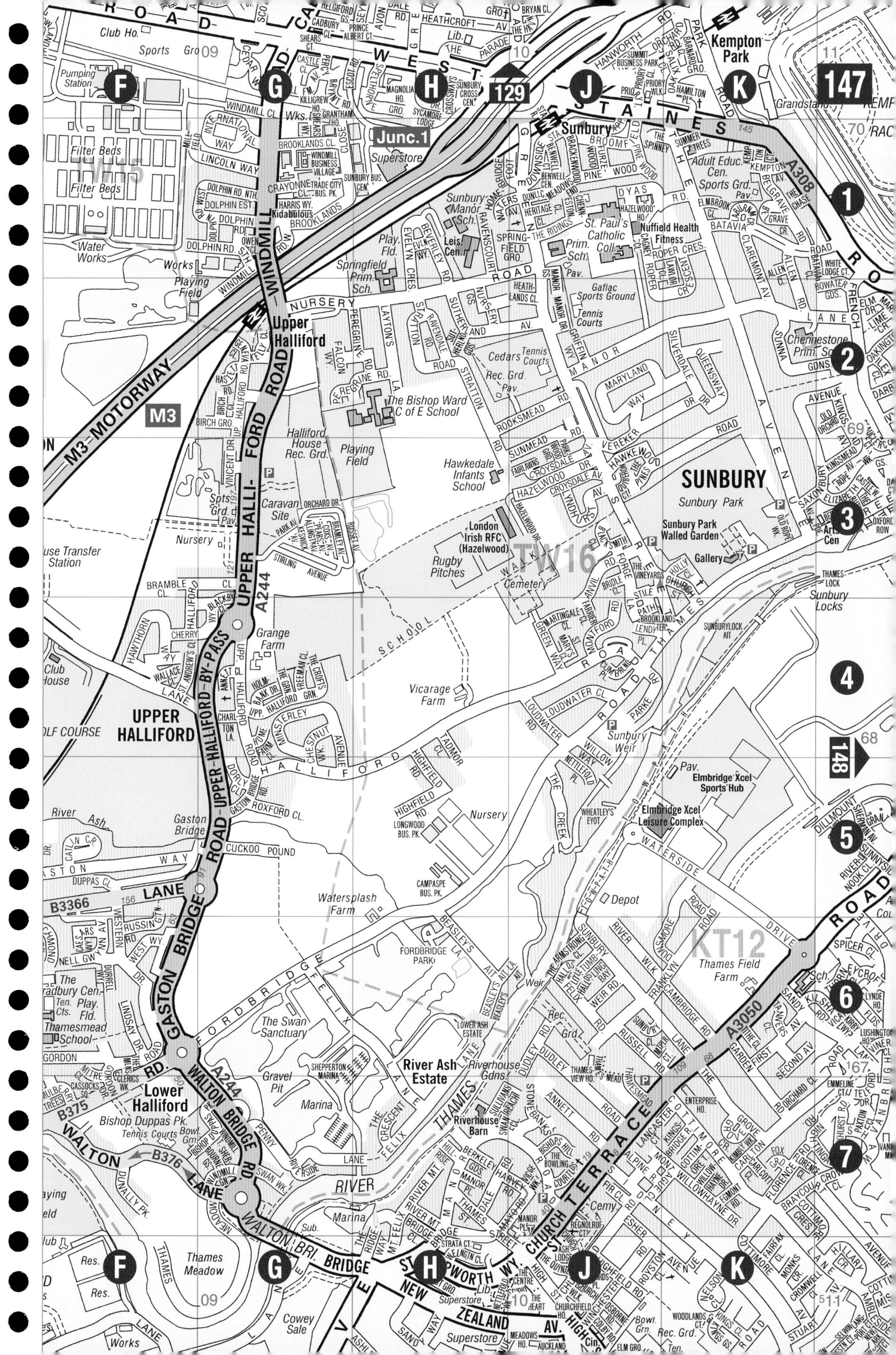147
148
129
Kempton Park
Grandstand
Junc.1
Superstore
M3
M3-MOTORWAY
SUNBURY
Sunbury Park
Sunbury Park Walled Garden
Gallery
Arts Cen
Sunbury Locks
Sunbury
Upper Halliford
UPPER HALLIFORD
Lower Halliford
TW16
TW15
KT12
A308
A244
A3050
B3366
B375
B376
STAINES ROAD WEST
STAINES ROAD
UPPER HALLIFORD ROAD
UPPER HALLIFORD BY-PASS
GASTON BRIDGE ROAD
WALTON BRIDGE RD.
WALTON LANE
CHURCH TERRACE
NEW ZEALAND AV.
THAMES STREET
HALLIFORD ROAD
NURSERY ROAD
FORDBRIDGE ROAD
MANOR LANE
FRENCH STREET
GREEN STREET
SCHOOL WALK
Filter Beds
Water Works
Pumping Station
Sports Grd.
Club Ho.
Playing Field
Sunbury Manor Sch.
Leis. Cen.
Springfield Prim. Sch.
St. Paul's Catholic Coll.
Nuffield Health Fitness
Adult Educ. Cen.
Sports Grd.
Chennestone Prim. Sch.
Gaflac Sports Ground
Tennis Courts
Cedars Rec. Grd.
The Bishop Ward C of E School
Halliford House Rec. Grd.
Hawkedale Infants School
London Irish RFC (Hazelwood)
Rugby Pitches
Cemetery
Caravan Site
Grange Farm
Vicarage Farm
Sunbury Weir
Elmbridge Xcel Sports Hub
Elmbridge Xcel Leisure Complex
Depot
Thames Field Farm
Nursery
Watersplash Farm
The Swan Sanctuary
Gravel Pit
Marina
River Ash Estate
Riverhouse Gdns.
Riverhouse Barn
Thames Meadow
Bishop Duppas Pk.
Thamesmead School
The Bradbury Cen.
Gaston Bridge
River Ash
RIVER THAMES
Cowey Sale
Superstore
Lib.
Cemy.
Rec. Grd.
Kidabulous
F
G
H
J
K
1
2
3
4
5
6
7
09
10
11
68
69
70

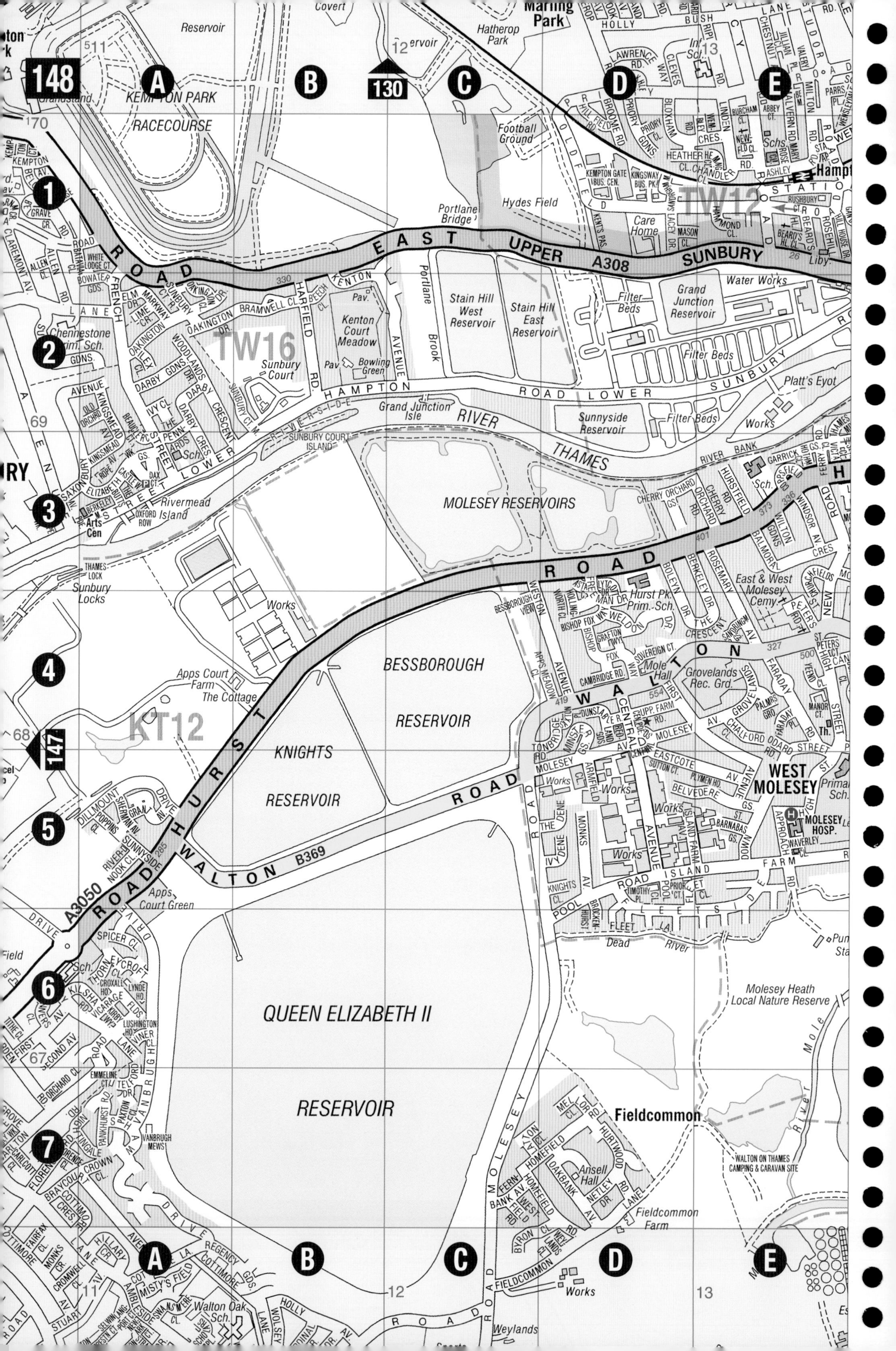

148
130
147
A
B
C
D
E
1
2
3
4
5
6
7
KEMPTON PARK RACECOURSE
Reservoir
Marling Park
Hatherop Park
Football Ground
Hydes Field
Portlane Bridge
UPPER SUNBURY ROAD EAST A308
TW12
TW16
KT12
Stain Hill West Reservoir
Stain Hill East Reservoir
Grand Junction Reservoir
Water Works
Filter Beds
Kenton Court Meadow
Sunbury Court
HAMPTON ROAD
LOWER SUNBURY ROAD
Platt's Eyot
Grand Junction Isle
RIVER THAMES
Sunnyside Reservoir
Works
SUNBURY COURT ISLAND
MOLESEY RESERVOIRS
Rivermead Island
Sunbury Locks
THAMES LOCK
Arts Cen
Hurst Pk. Prim. Sch.
East & West Molesey Cemy.
BESSBOROUGH RESERVOIR
KNIGHTS RESERVOIR
Apps Court Farm
The Cottage
HURST ROAD
WALTON ROAD B369
A3050
Apps Court Green
Grovelands Rec. Grd.
Mole Hall
WEST MOLESEY
MOLESEY HOSP.
Dead River
Molesey Heath Local Nature Reserve
River Mole
QUEEN ELIZABETH II RESERVOIR
Fieldcommon
Ansell Hall
Fieldcommon Farm
WALTON ON THAMES CAMPING & CARAVAN SITE
Walton Oak Sch.
Weylands
MOLESEY ROAD
11
12
13
67
68
69
170

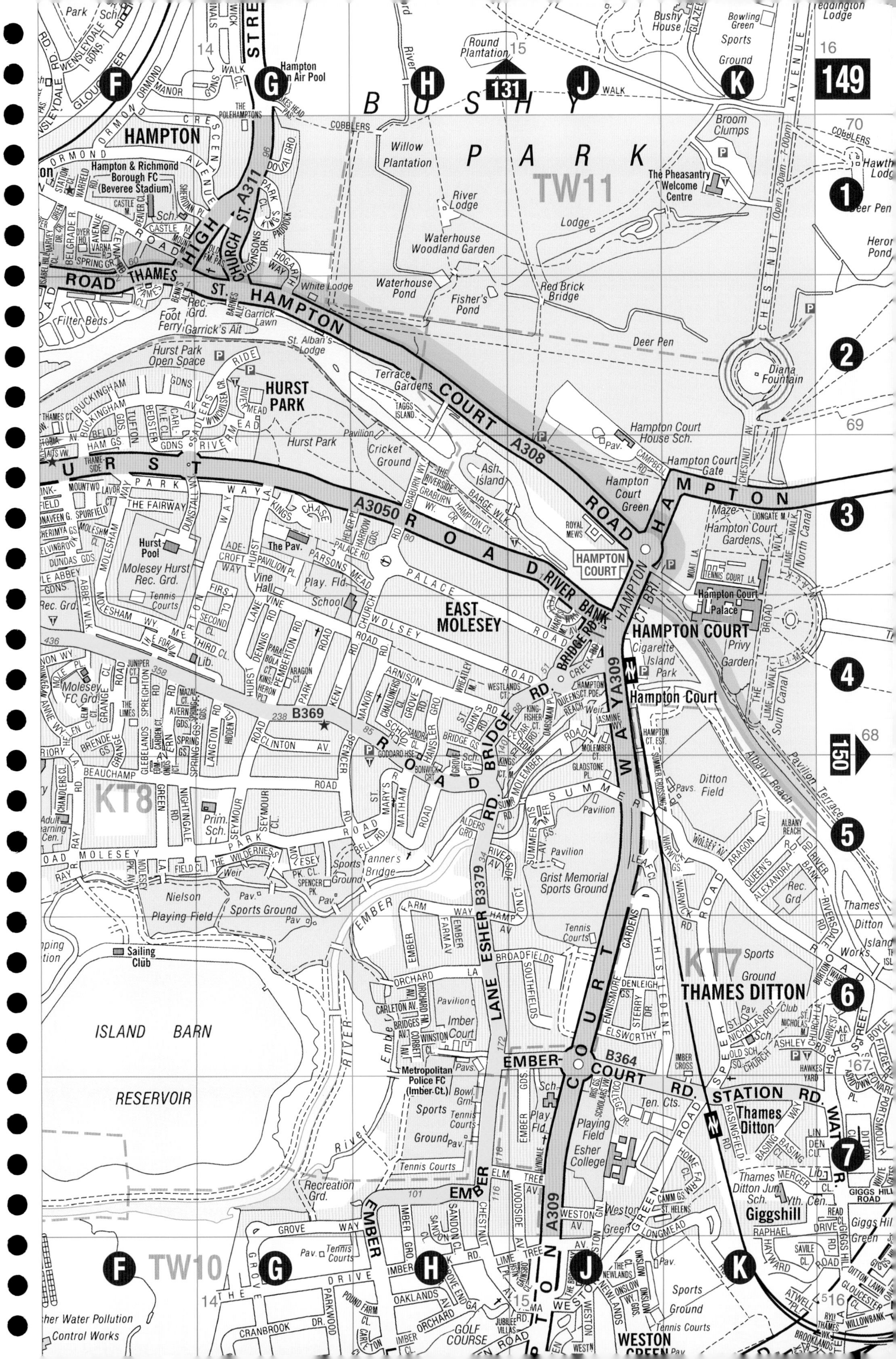

149
131
150
BUSHY PARK
TW11
TW10
KT8
KT7
HAMPTON
HAMPTON COURT
EAST MOLESEY
HURST PARK
THAMES DITTON
WESTON GREEN
Giggshill
ISLAND BARN RESERVOIR
Hampton & Richmond Borough FC (Beveree Stadium)
Hampton Open Air Pool
Bushy House
Round Plantation
Willow Plantation
Broom Clumps
The Pheasantry Welcome Centre
Waterhouse Woodland Garden
Waterhouse Pond
Fisher's Pond
Red Brick Bridge
Deer Pen
Heron Pond
Diana Fountain
Hampton Court House Sch.
Hampton Court Gate
Hampton Court Green
Royal Mews
Maze
Hampton Court Gardens
Hampton Court Palace
Privy Garden
Cigarette Island Park
Hampton Court
Ditton Field
Garrick's Ait
Garrick Lawn
Foot Ferry
Filter Beds
Hurst Park Open Space
Ash Island
Taggs Island
Cricket Ground
Terrace Gardens
Hurst Pool
Molesey Hurst Rec. Grd.
Molesey FC Grd.
Nielson Playing Field
Sailing Club
Grist Memorial Sports Ground
Metropolitan Police FC (Imber Ct.)
Esher College
Thames Ditton Jun. Sch.
Recreation Grd.
Golf Course
Thames Ditton Island
A308
A3050
A309
A311
B369
B364
B3379
THAMES ROAD
HAMPTON COURT ROAD
HAMPTON COURT WAY
HAMPTON COURT ROAD
HURST ROAD
BRIDGE ROAD
EMBER COURT RD.
STATION RD.
ESHER LANE
CHESTNUT AVENUE
HIGH STREET
CHURCH ST.
PALACE ROAD
WOLSEY ROAD
WALTON ROAD
SUMMER ROAD
EMBER LANE

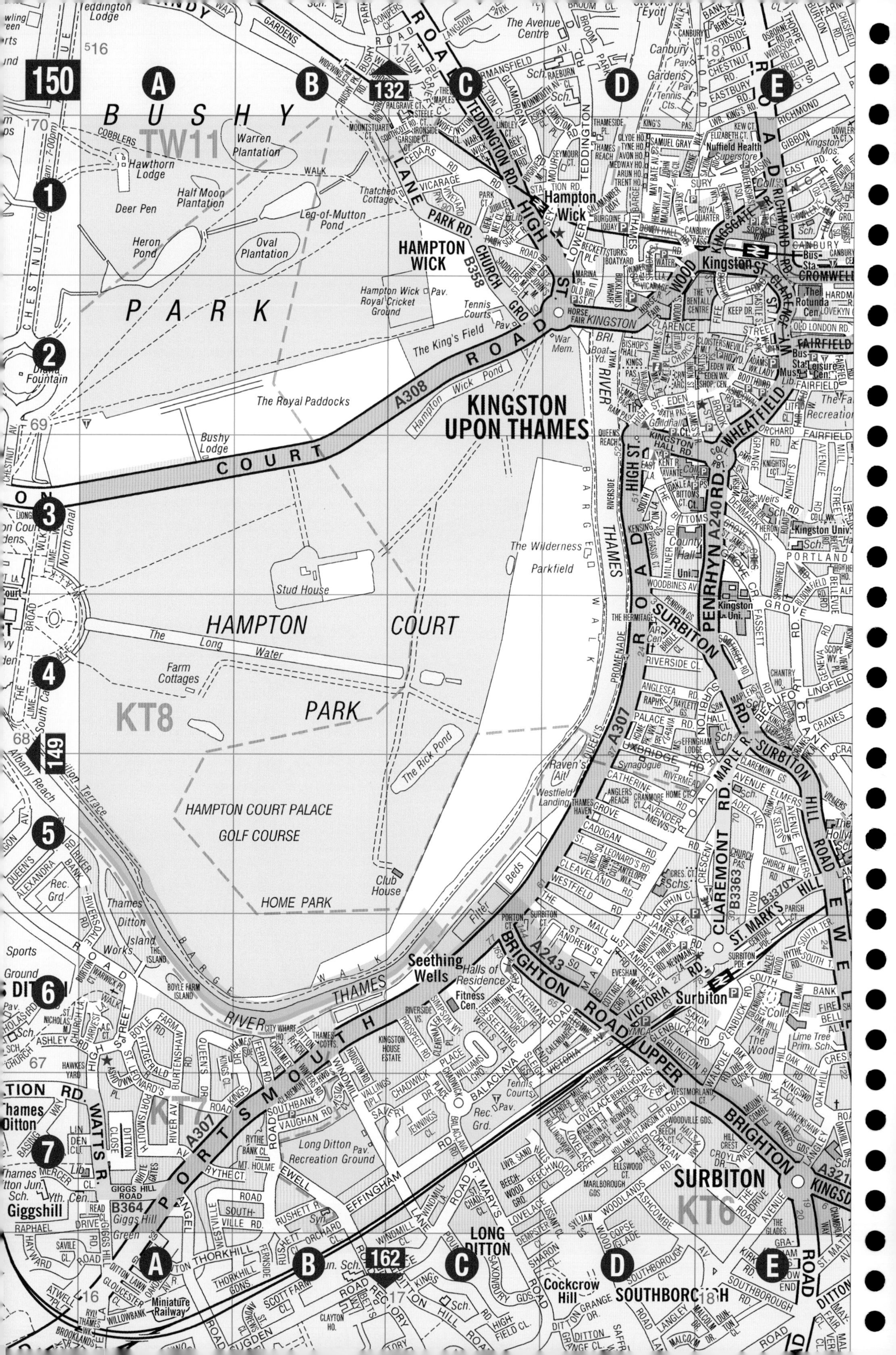

150
A
B
C
D
E
132
1
2
3
4
5
6
7
149
162
BUSHY
PARK
TW11
Warren Plantation
Hawthorn Lodge
Half Moon Plantation
Deer Pen
Heron Pond
Oval Plantation
Leg-of-Mutton Pond
Thatched Cottage
Diana Fountain
The Royal Paddocks
Bushy Lodge
HAMPTON WICK
Hampton Wick
Hampton Wick Royal Cricket Ground
The King's Field
Tennis Courts
COURT ROAD
A308
Hampton Wick Pond
KINGSTON UPON THAMES
Kingston
TEDDINGTON RD.
HIGH ST.
B358
CHURCH GRO.
PARK RD.
LANE
The Avenue Centre
Canbury Gardens
Nuffield Health Superstore
RICHMOND RD.
CROMWELL
The Rotunda Cen.
FAIRFIELD
The Bentall Centre
KINGSGATE RD.
CLARENCE ST.
WOOD ST.
EDEN ST.
WHEATFIELD WAY
Kingston Univ.
County Hall
PENRHYN RD. A240
SURBITON RD.
PORTLAND
GROVE
The Wilderness
Parkfield
RIVER THAMES
BARGE WALK
Stud House
HAMPTON COURT
The Long Water
Farm Cottages
KT8
PARK
The Rick Pond
HAMPTON COURT PALACE GOLF COURSE
Club House
HOME PARK
Raven's Ait
Westfield Landing
A307
PORTSMOUTH ROAD
Seething Wells
Halls of Residence
Fitness Cen.
BRIGHTON ROAD
A243
UPPER BRIGHTON ROAD
VICTORIA RD.
Surbiton
CLAREMONT RD.
B3363
ST. MARK'S HILL
SURBITON HILL ROAD
EWELL ROAD
SURBITON
KT6
A321
Lime Tree Prim. Sch.
The Wood
Thames Ditton Island
Works
Boyle Farm Island
Sports Ground
Thames Ditton
WATTS R.
KT7
B364
Giggs Hill Green
Giggshill
Long Ditton Recreation Ground
Rec. Grd.
LONG DITTON
Cockcrow Hill
SOUTHBOROUGH
Miniature Railway
EFFINGHAM
WINDMILL LANE

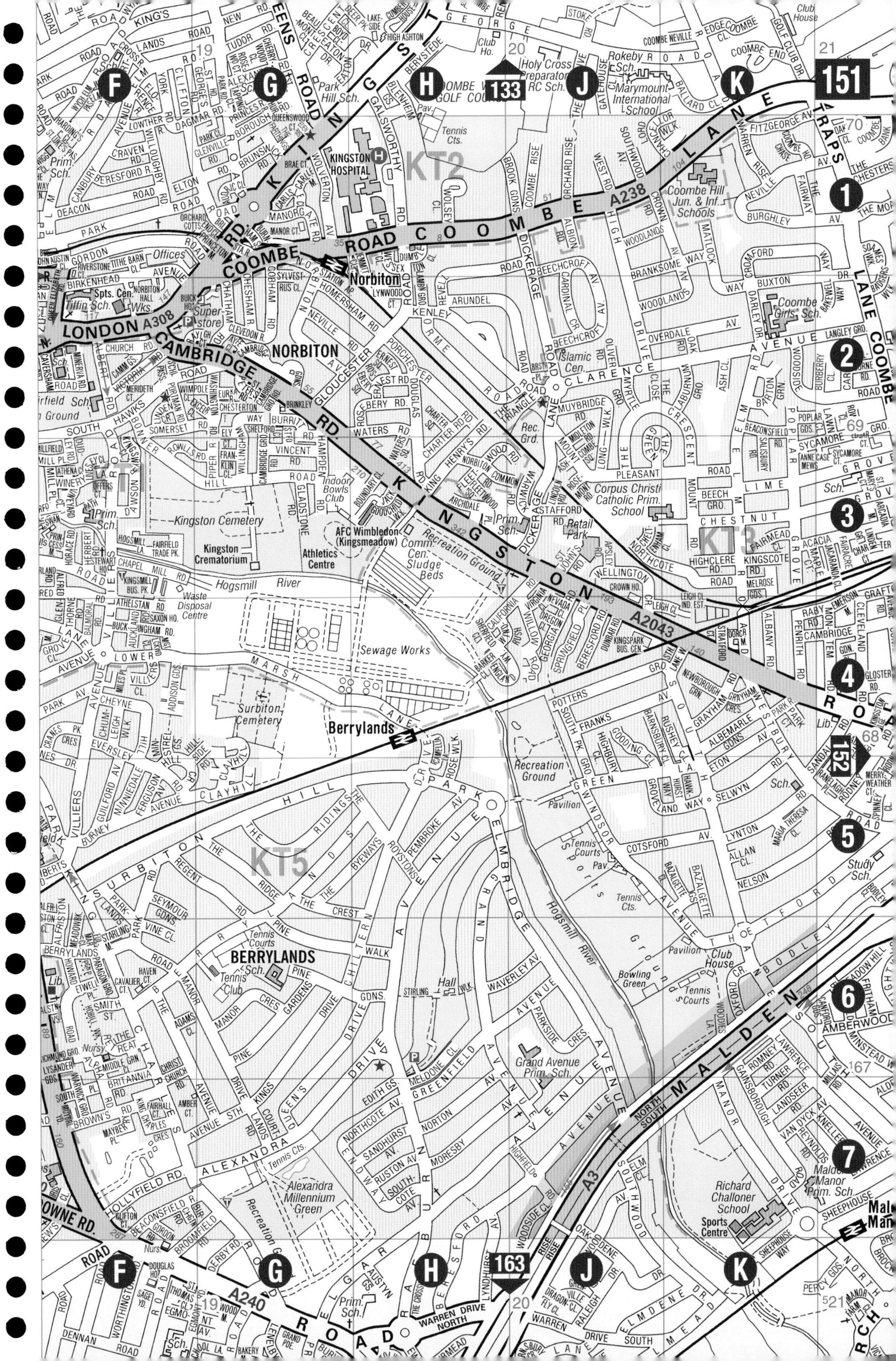

151
133
152
163
F
G
H
J
K
1
2
3
4
5
6
7
19
20
21
KT2
KT3
KT5
COOMBE LANE
A238
COOMBE ROAD
KINGSTON RD.
A2043
LONDON ROAD
A308
CAMBRIDGE RD.
NORBITON
Norbiton
KINGSTON HOSPITAL
Kingston Cemetery
Kingston Crematorium
Athletics Centre
AFC Wimbledon (Kingsmeadow)
Hogsmill River
Sewage Works
Waste Disposal Centre
Surbiton Cemetery
Berrylands
BERRYLANDS
Recreation Ground
Coombe Hill Jun. & Inf. Schools
Coombe Girls' Sch.
Holy Cross Preparatory RC Sch.
Marymount International School
Rokeby Sch.
Corpus Christi Catholic Prim. School
Retail Park
Islamic Cen.
Tiffin Sch.
Grand Avenue Prim. Sch.
Richard Challoner School
Sports Centre
Malden Manor Prim. Sch.
Alexandra Millennium Green
SURBITON HILL PARK
MALDEN RD.
A3
A240
ROAD
WARREN DRIVE NORTH
ELGAR AV.
THE AVENUE
ALEXANDRA
HOLLYFIELD RD.
BEACONSFIELD RD.
WOODSIDE CL.
CLARENCE AVENUE
GEORGE RD.
KING'S RD.
PARK RD.
DEACON RD.
BURGHLEY AV.
NEVILLE AV.
TRAPS LANE

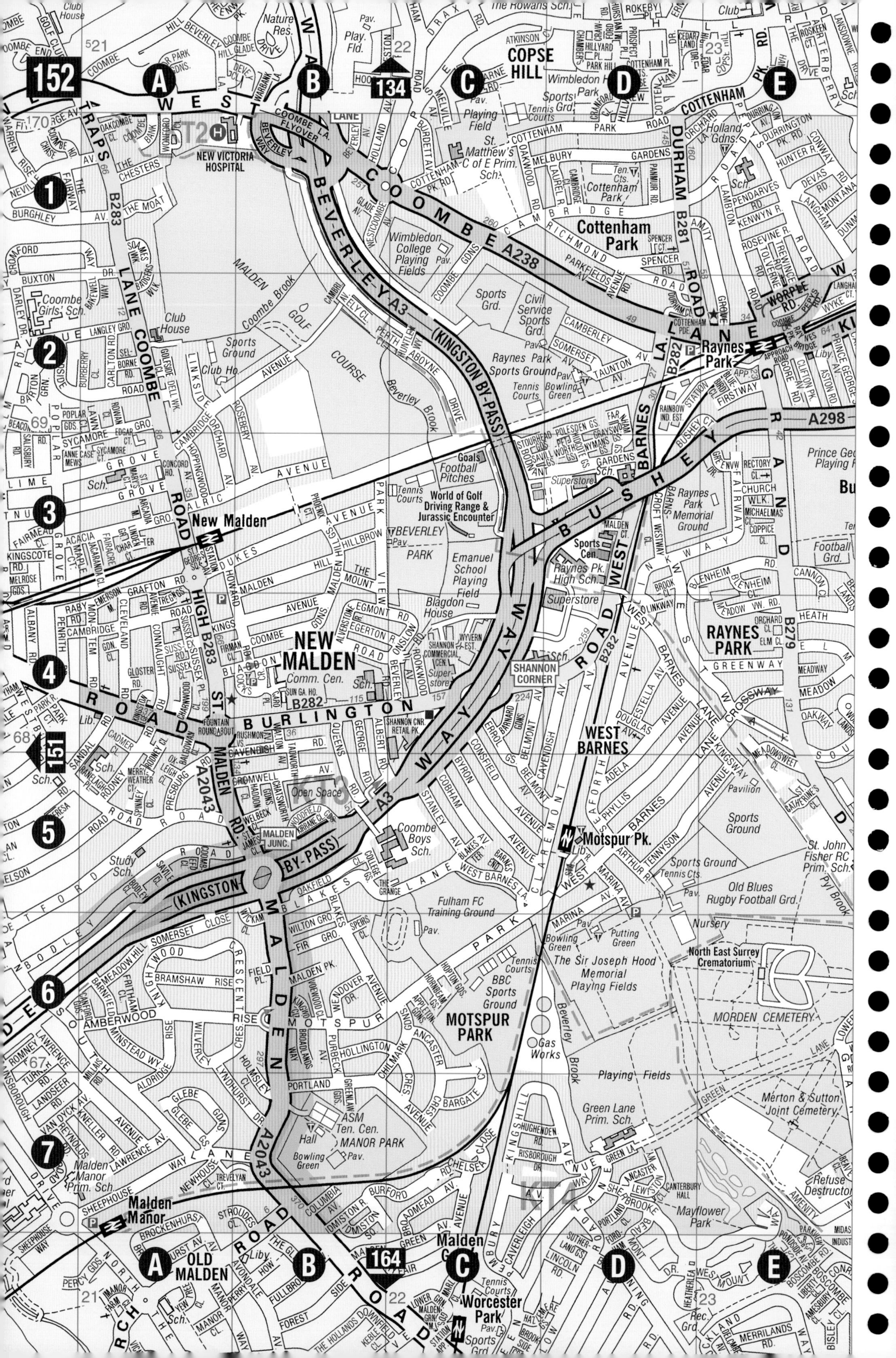

152
134
151
164
A
B
C
D
E
1
2
3
4
5
6
7
COPSE HILL
Wimbledon Park
COTTENHAM PARK ROAD
Cottenham Park
NEW VICTORIA HOSPITAL
KT2
COOMBE LANE
COOMBE A238
COOMBE FLYOVER
BEVERLEY WAY A3
KINGSTON BY-PASS
Wimbledon College Playing Fields
St. Matthew's C of E Prim. Sch.
Holland Gdns.
DURHAM ROAD B281
TRAPS LANE B283
COOMBE LANE
COOMBE ROAD
Coombe Girls' Sch.
Club House
Sports Ground
Club Ho.
MALDEN GOLF COURSE
Coombe Brook
Beverley Brook
Civil Service Sports Grd.
Raynes Park Sports Ground
Raynes Park
WORPLE RD
A298
BUSHEY ROAD
Prince George's Playing Field
Raynes Park Memorial Ground
Football Grd.
Goals Football Pitches
World of Golf Driving Range & Jurassic Encounter
BEVERLEY PARK
Emanuel School Playing Field
Blagdon House
Sports Cen.
Raynes Pk. High Sch.
Superstore
New Malden
NEW MALDEN
Comm. Cen.
HIGH ST. B283
BURLINGTON ROAD B282
SHANNON CORNER
WEST BARNES
WEST BARNES LANE
RAYNES PARK
KT3
MALDEN ROAD A2043
MALDEN JUNC.
Open Space
Coombe Boys Sch.
Motspur Pk.
Fulham FC Training Ground
Sports Ground
Old Blues Rugby Football Grd.
St. John Fisher RC Prim. Sch.
North East Surrey Crematorium
MORDEN CEMETERY
The Sir Joseph Hood Memorial Playing Fields
BBC Sports Ground
MOTSPUR PARK
Gas Works
Playing Fields
Merton & Sutton Joint Cemetery
Green Lane Prim. Sch.
ASM Ten. Cen.
MANOR PARK
Mayflower Park
Refuse Destructor
KT4
Malden Manor
Malden Manor Prim. Sch.
OLD MALDEN
Malden Green
Worcester Park
Sports Grd.
Rec. Grd.

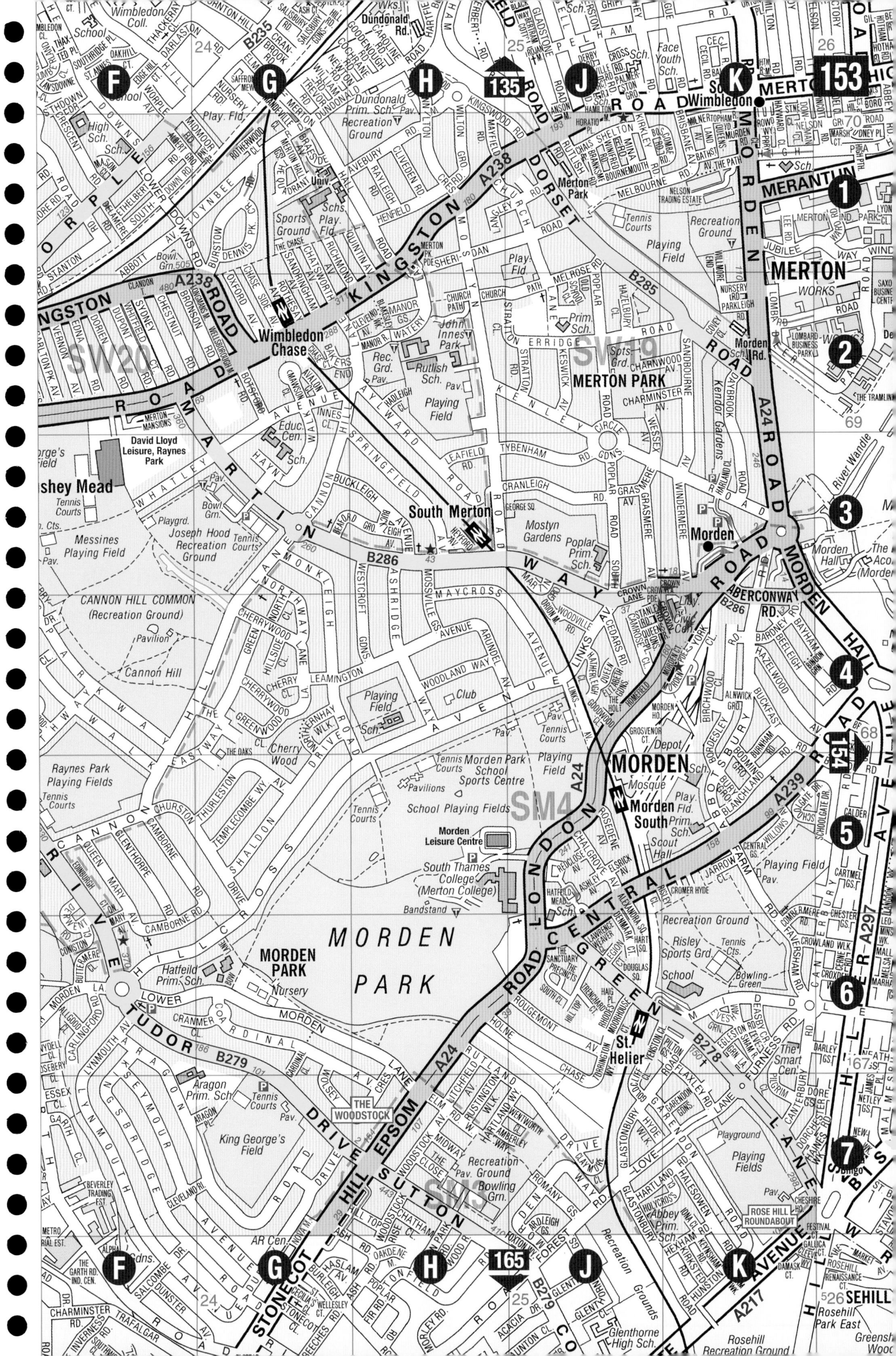

153
135
154
165
167
F
G
H
J
K
1
2
3
4
5
6
7
24
25
26
69
70
68
Wimbledon Coll.
Dundonald Rd.
Dundonald Prim. Sch.
Recreation Ground
Wimbledon
MERTON ROAD
KINGSTON ROAD
A238
A24
A239
A297
A217
B235
B285
B286
B279
B278
Merton Park
MERTON
WORKS
MERANTUN WAY
MERTON IND. PARK
LOMBARD BUSINESS PARK
Morden Rd.
Wimbledon Chase
SW20
SW19
SM4
SM3
MERTON PARK
Rutlish Sch.
John Innes Park
Playing Field
David Lloyd Leisure, Raynes Park
Tennis Courts
Messines Playing Field
Joseph Hood Recreation Ground
CANNON HILL COMMON (Recreation Ground)
Cannon Hill
Raynes Park Playing Fields
South Merton
Mostyn Gardens
Poplar Prim. Sch.
Morden
Morden Hall
River Wandle
MORDEN
Morden South
Depot
Mosque
Morden Park School Sports Centre
School Playing Fields
Morden Leisure Centre
South Thames College (Merton College)
Bandstand
MORDEN PARK
Nursery
Hatfeild Prim. Sch.
Aragon Prim. Sch.
King George's Field
THE WOODSTOCK
Recreation Ground
Risley Sports Grd.
St. Helier
Abbey Prim. Sch.
ROSE HILL ROUNDABOUT
Playing Fields
The Smart Cen.
Recreation Grounds
Rosehill Recreation Ground
Glenthorne High Sch.
Rosehill Park East
TUDOR DRIVE
EPSOM ROAD
LONDON ROAD
CENTRAL ROAD
MARTIN WAY
GREEN LANE
STONECOT HILL
SUTTON COMMON ROAD
AVENUE
MORDEN HALL ROAD

154
136
153
166
A
B
C
D
E
1
2
3
4
5
6
7
26
27
28
67
68
69
70
Colliers Wood
COLLIER'S WOOD
HIGH STREET
MERANTUN WAY
A24
MERTON
Merton Abbey Mills
Superstore
Tandem Centre
Colour Ho. Th.
Deen City Farm
Morden Rd.
MORDEN ROAD
MORDEN HALL ROAD
A297
MORDEN HALL PARK
Morden Hall
The London Acorn Sch. (Morden Cottage)
Morden Lodge
Phipps Bridge
Belgrave Wlk.
River Wandle
WESTERN ROAD
A236
Lavender Park
Cemetery
Tamworth Rec. Grd.
LONDON RD.
A217
STREATHAM ROAD
FIGGES MARSH
CR4
MITCHAM
COMMONSIDE
COMMONSIDE WEST
CRICKET GRN.
Cricket Green
Canons Leisure Centre
Canons House
Sports Ground
Running Track
MADEIRA RD.
A239
CRANMER RD.
Cranmer Bri.
The Wilson Hospital
Blue Houses Bridge
Beehive Bridge
CARSHALTON ROAD
A237
MORDEN ROAD
Ravensbury Park
Mitcham
TRAMWAY PATH
Watermeads
Tooting & Mitcham United FC (Imperial Fields)
Poulter Park
Bennett's Hole
Bishopsford House
Harris Academy Morden
SM4
SM5
ST. HELIER AVENUE
BISHOPSFORD ROAD
ST. HELIER
Open Space
Playing Fields
Willow Lane Business Park
Willow Lane Industrial Estate
Willow Lane Bri.
Mitcham Junction
Mill Green
Wandle Valley Comm. Hall
Nature Reserves
David Weir Leisure Centre
Mecca Bingo
St. Helier Open Space
ST. HELIER HOSPITAL
ROSEHILL
Rosehill Park East
Greenshaw Wood
Hackbridge Prim. Sch.
BEDDING CORN
Playing Field
Moreton Green

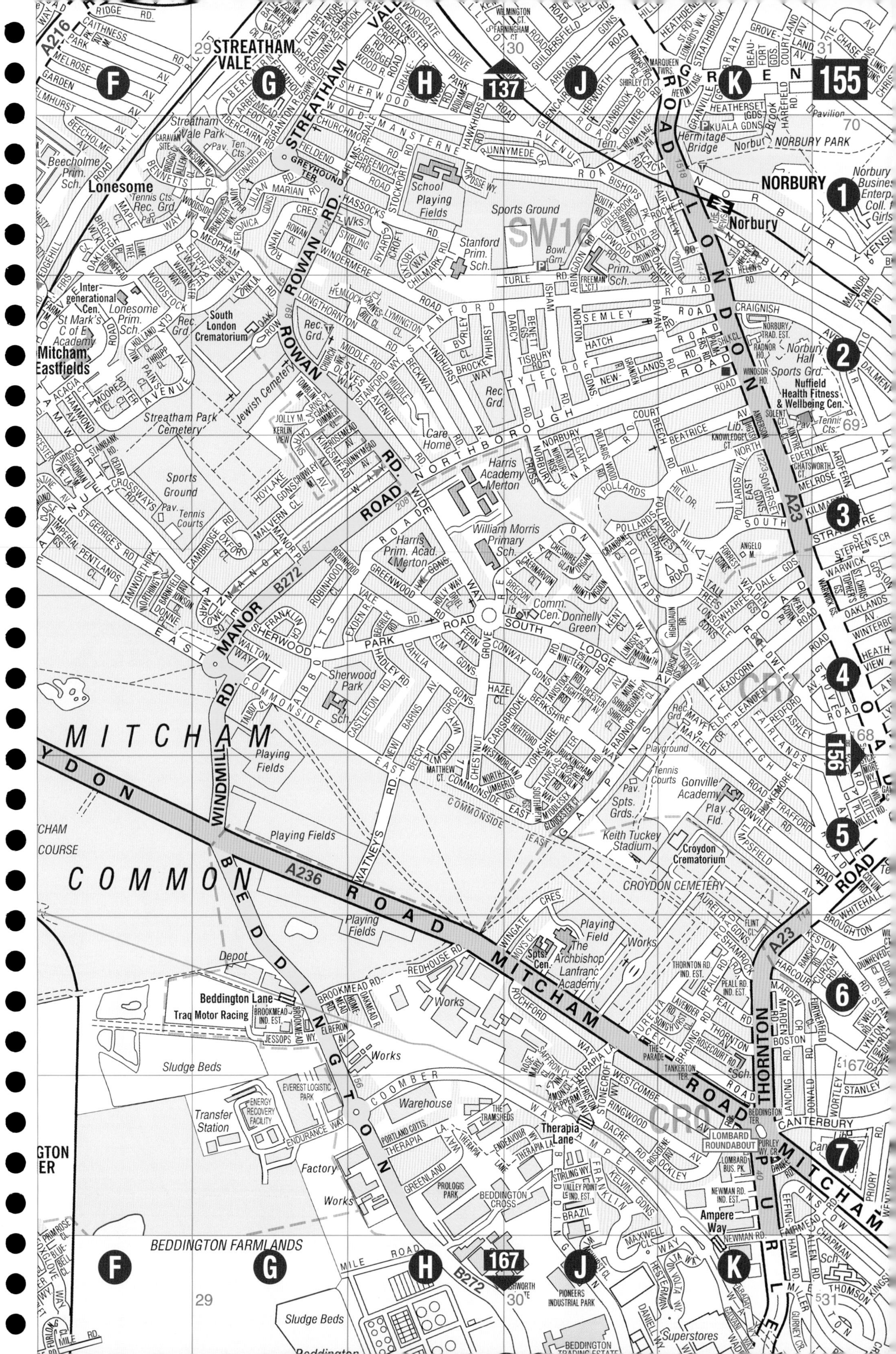

155
137
156
167
STREATHAM VALE
NORBURY
Norbury
Lonesome
Mitcham Eastfields
MITCHAM COMMON
SW16
CR7
CR0
A216
A23
A236
B272
Streatham Vale Park
Streatham Park Cemetery
South London Crematorium
Jewish Cemetery
Sports Ground
School Playing Fields
Stanford Prim. Sch.
Harris Academy Merton
William Morris Primary Sch.
Harris Prim. Acad. Merton
Sherwood Park Sch.
Lonesome Prim. Sch.
St Mark's C of E Academy
Inter-generational Cen.
Beecholme Prim. Sch.
Norbury Park
Norbury Hall
Nuffield Health Fitness & Wellbeing Cen.
Donnelly Green
Gonville Academy
Keith Tuckey Stadium
Croydon Crematorium
CROYDON CEMETERY
The Archbishop Lanfranc Academy
Beddington Lane
Traq Motor Racing
Sludge Beds
Transfer Station
Everest Logistic Park
Energy Recovery Facility
Therapia Lane
Ampere Way
Lombard Roundabout
Prologis Park
Beddington Cross
Pioneers Industrial Park
Superstores
BEDDINGTON FARMLANDS
Playing Fields
Hermitage Bridge
Kuala Gdns
Norbury Business Enterp. Coll. for Girls
STREATHAM RD.
ROWAN RD.
MANOR ROAD
WINDMILL RD.
MITCHAM ROAD
BEDDINGTON LANE
LONDON ROAD
THORNTON ROAD
PURLEY WAY
NORTHBOROUGH ROAD
COMMONSIDE EAST
GALPINS ROAD
NORBURY AVENUE
F
G
H
J
K
1
2
3
4
5
6
7
29
30
31

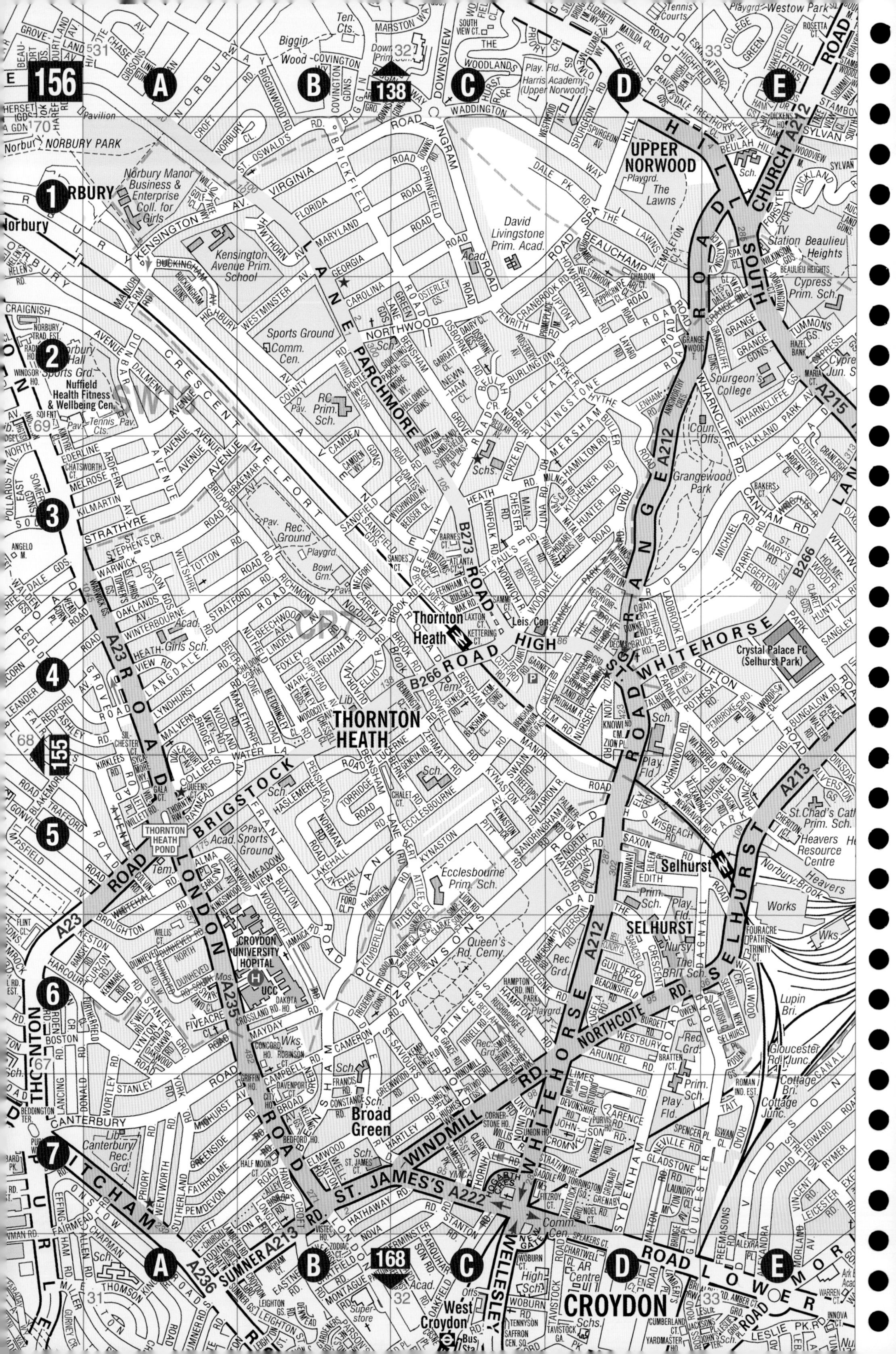

156
138
155
168
A
B
C
D
E
1
2
3
4
5
6
7
NORBURY
Norbury
NORBURY PARK
UPPER NORWOOD
THORNTON HEATH
Thornton Heath
SELHURST
Selhurst
Broad Green
CROYDON
West Croydon
SW16
CR7
Biggin Wood
Norbury Manor Business & Enterprise Coll. for Girls
Kensington Avenue Prim. School
Sports Ground
Comm. Cen.
RC Prim. Sch.
Nuffield Health Fitness & Wellbeing Cen.
Norbury Hall
David Livingstone Prim. Acad.
Harris Academy (Upper Norwood)
The Lawns
Spurgeon's College
Grangewood Park
Coun. Offs.
TV Station
Beaulieu Heights
Cypress Prim. Sch.
Crystal Palace FC (Selhurst Park)
Rec. Ground
Leis. Cen.
Ecclesbourne Prim. Sch.
Queen's Rd. Cemy.
CROYDON UNIVERSITY HOSPITAL
THORNTON HEATH POND
Canterbury Rec. Grd.
St. Chad's Cath. Prim. Sch.
Heavers Resource Centre
Norbury Brook
Gloucester Rd. Junc.
Cottage Bri.
Cottage Junc.
Lupin Bri.
Works
A23
A212
A215
A235
A222
A213
A236
B266
B273
LONDON ROAD
BRIGSTOCK ROAD
PARCHMORE ROAD
GRANGE ROAD
WHITEHORSE ROAD
WINDMILL ROAD
ST. JAMES'S ROAD
SELHURST ROAD
NORTHCOTE RD.
HIGH STREET
WELLESLEY ROAD
MITCHAM ROAD
LOWER ADDISCOMBE ROAD
CHURCH ROAD
SOUTH NORWOOD HILL
MELFORT ROAD
QUEENS ROAD
SUMNER ROAD

157
139
158
169
F
G
H
J
K
1
2
3
4
5
6
7
34
35
36
70
69
68
67
PENGE
Anerley
ANERLEY
SE20
SE19
SE25
BR3
SOUTH NORWOOD
WOODSIDE
CROYDON ROAD
ELMERS END ROAD
BECKENHAM ROAD
PORTLAND ROAD
SPRING LANE
LONG LANE
WOODSIDE GREEN
HIGH STREET
SOUTH NORWOOD HILL
ADDISCOMBE ROAD
SHIRLEY ROAD
A213
A214
A215
A222
B243
Kent House
Avenue Road
Birkbeck
Elmers End
Harrington Rd.
Norwood Junc.
Woodside
Blackhorse La.
Arena
Addiscombe
Bromley Junction
Beckenham Crematorium
SOUTH NORWOOD COUNTRY PARK
Pitch & Putt Course
Blind Corner
Visitor Centre
Playground
Croydon Sports Arena
Croydon FC Grd.
Oasis Academy Arena
World of Golf Centre
South Norwood Lake
Croydon Sailing Club
Harris City Academy
Phil Edwards PRU
James Dixon Prim. Sch.
Orchard School Sports Centre
Nursing Home
Playing Field
Bowling Green
Tennis Courts
Harris Academy
Recreation Ground
Brickfields Mdw.
Ashburton Park
Ashburton Playing Fields
Oasis Academy Shirley Park (Seniors)
SHIRLEY OAKS BMI HOSPITAL
Shirley Oaks
Monks Orchard Prim. Sch.
Glade Wood
Long Lane Wood
Bird Sanctuary
Chaffinch Brook Sch.
Davidson Prim. Sch.
Beavers Farm Prim. Sch.
Superstore
Recyling Cen.
Playing Field
Primary School
Kentwood Cen.
Betts Pk.
Bowls
Temple
Leis. Cen.

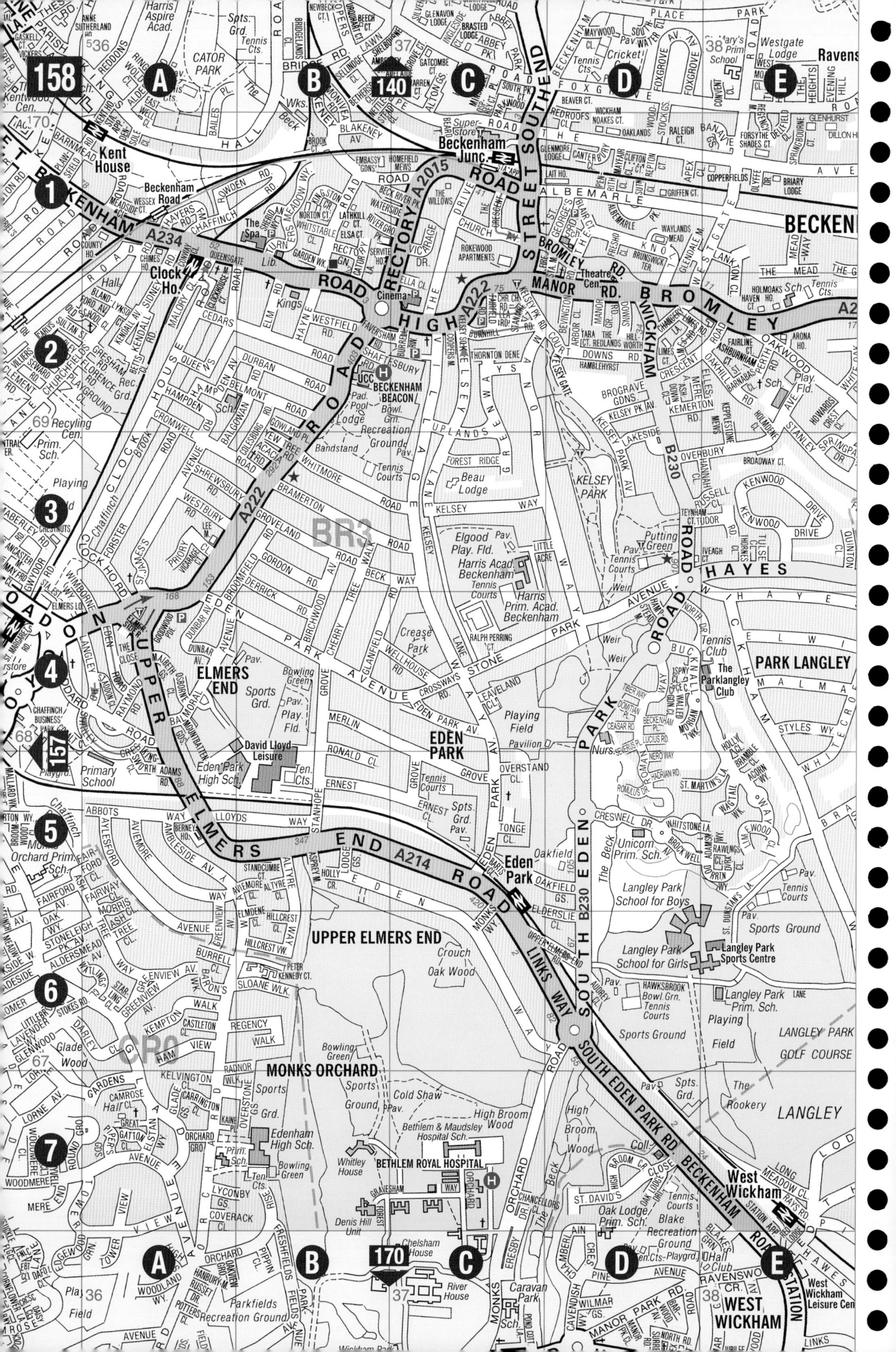

158
140
157
170
A
B
C
D
E
1
2
3
4
5
6
7
Kent House
Beckenham Road
Clock Ho.
Beckenham Junc.
BECKENHAM ROAD
A234
ROAD
RECTORY ROAD
A2015
HIGH STREET
SOUTHEND ROAD
MANOR RD.
BROMLEY RD.
A222
BR3
Harris Aspire Acad.
CATOR PARK
The Spa
Lib.
Cinema
BECKENHAM BEACON
Recreation Ground
Bandstand
Tennis Courts
Beau Lodge
KELSEY PARK
Putting Green
Elgood Play. Fld.
Harris Acad. Beckenham
Harris Prim. Acad. Beckenham
Crease Park
ELMERS END
Sports Grd.
Bowling Green
David Lloyd Leisure
Eden Park High Sch.
EDEN PARK
Playing Field
Pavilion
Eden Park
HAYES ROAD
PARK LANGLEY
The Parklangley Club
Tennis Club
Unicorn Prim. Sch.
Langley Park School for Boys
Langley Park School for Girls
Langley Park Sports Centre
Langley Park Prim. Sch.
Sports Ground
LANGLEY PARK GOLF COURSE
The Rookery
LANGLEY
ELMERS END ROAD
A214
UPPER ELMERS END
Crouch Oak Wood
LINKS WAY
SOUTH EDEN PARK RD
B230
MONKS ORCHARD
Sports Ground
Cold Shaw
High Broom Wood
Bethlem & Maudsley Hospital Sch.
BETHLEM ROYAL HOSPITAL
Whitley House
Denis Hill Unit
Chelsham House
River House
Edenham High Sch.
Monks Orchard Prim. Sch.
CR0
Glade Wood
Parkfields Recreation Ground
Oak Lodge Prim. Sch.
Blake Recreation Ground
West Wickham
WEST WICKHAM
West Wickham Leisure Cen
Caravan Park
Primary School
Recyling Cen.
Playing Field
BECKENHAM
Westgate Lodge
Ravens

159
141
160
171
F
G
H
J
K
1
2
3
4
5
6
7
Sundridge Park
Bromley Nth.
Shortlands
Bromley South
BROMLEY
BROMLEY PARK
SHORTLANDS
HAYES
Hayes
BR1
BR2
BR4
SHORTLANDS GOLF COURSE
Golf Course
Playing Field
THE SLOANE BMI HOSP.
Bishop Challoner Sch.
TWEEDY
COLLEGE
HIGH ST.
WIDMORE
KENTISH
WAY
BECKENHAM
LANE
ROAD
A21
B228
B251
B212
B265
WESTMORELAND
PICKHURST
LANE
HAYES
ROAD
MASONS HILL
Queens Gdn.
THE GLADES
Leisure Cen.
Churchill Theatre
Bromley Civic Centre
Moat
Church Ho. Gdns.
Martin's Hill
War Meml
Rec. Grd. Queen's Mead
Harris Prim. Acad.
Highfield Inf. Sch.
Highfield Jun. Sch.
South Hill Wood
Rec. Grd.
Cupola Wood
Recreation Ground
Pickhurst Jun. & Inf. Schs.
Pickhurst Green
Nuffield Health Fitness & Wellbeing Centre
Cricket Ground
Bromley FC & Cray Wanderers FC (Courage Stadium)
Fishers Wood
NORMAN PARK
Norman Park Community Sports Cen.
Norman Park Athletics Track
The Ravensbourne Sch.
Playing Field
Hayesford
Bowling Green
Club House
PARK
Sports Ground
Hayes Prim. Sch.
Brook Wood
Cricket Ground
Playground
Hall
Liby.
Rec. Grd

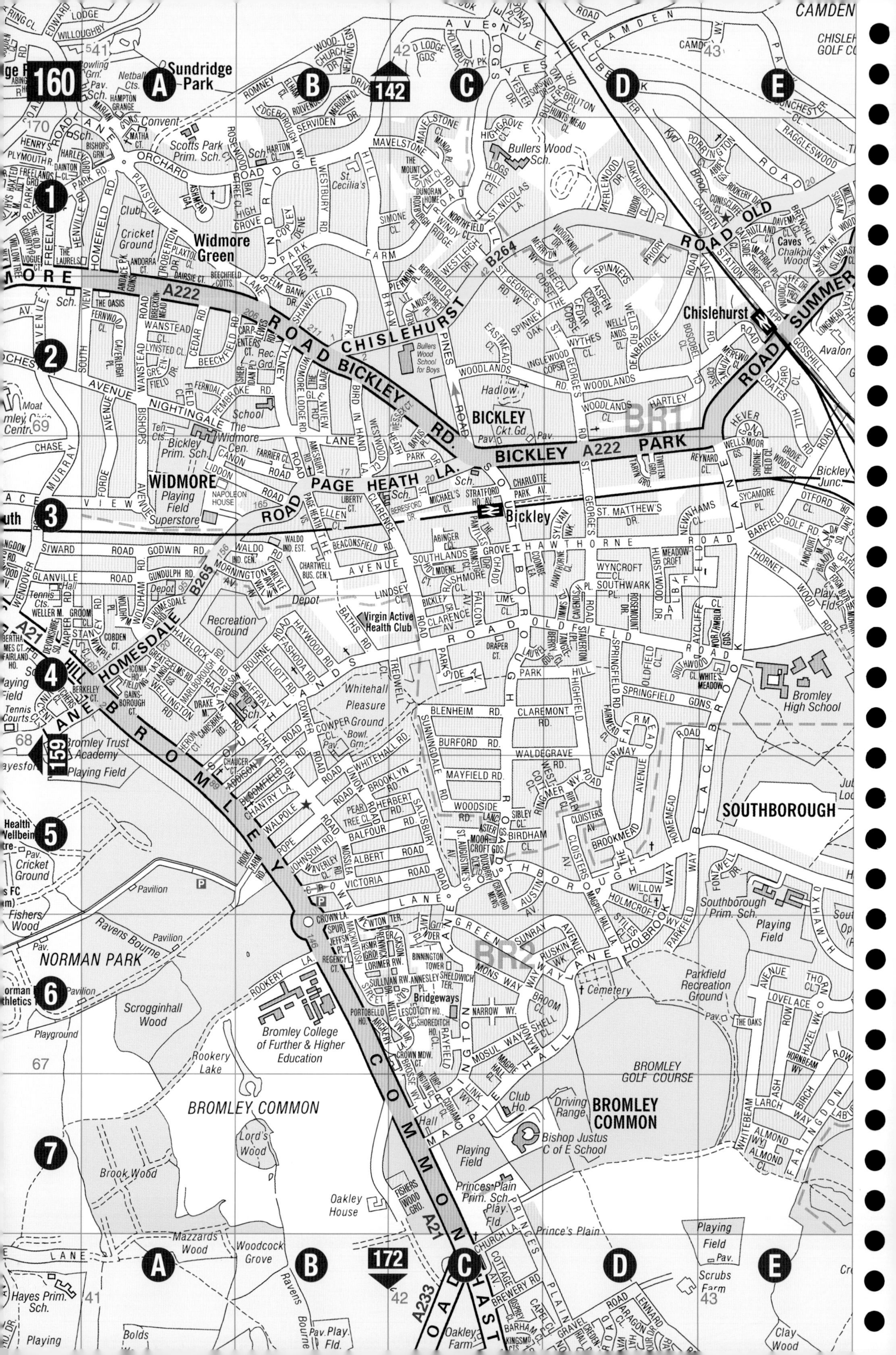

160
142
A
B
C
D
E
Sundridge Park
CAMDEN
Chislehurst Golf Course
Scotts Park Prim. Sch.
Convent
Bullers Wood Sch.
Widmore Green
Cricket Ground
A222
B264
CHISLEHURST ROAD
BICKLEY ROAD
BICKLEY RD.
BICKLEY PARK
OLD ROAD
SUMMER
Chislehurst
Caves
Chalkpit Wood
Avalon
Bullers Wood School for Boys
Hadlow
BICKLEY
Ckt. Gd.
BR1
Bickley Junc.
WIDMORE
Playing Field
Superstore
Napoleon House
The Widmore Cen.
Bickley Prim. Sch.
PAGE HEATH LA.
Bickley
ST. GEORGE'S
HAWTHORNE ROAD
Recreation Ground
Virgin Active Health Club
Depot
B265
HOMESDALE
A21
Whitehall Pleasure Ground
Bromley High School
SOUTHBOROUGH
Bromley Trust Academy Playing Field
159
BROMLEY
SOUTHBOROUGH LANE
Southborough Prim. Sch.
Playing Field
Health Wellbeing Ctre.
Cricket Ground
Pavilion
Fishers Wood
Ravens Bourne
NORMAN PARK
BR2
Cemetery
Parkfield Recreation Ground
Scrogginhall Wood
Bromley College of Further & Higher Education
Bridgeways
Rookery Lake
BROMLEY GOLF COURSE
BROMLEY COMMON
Driving Range
Club Ho.
Bishop Justus C of E School
Lord's Wood
Brook Wood
Playing Field
Princes Plain Prim. Sch.
Oakley House
Mazzards Wood
Woodcock Grove
Prince's Plain
172
A233
A21
Hayes Prim. Sch.
Scrubs Farm
Clay Wood
Oakley Farm
Bolds

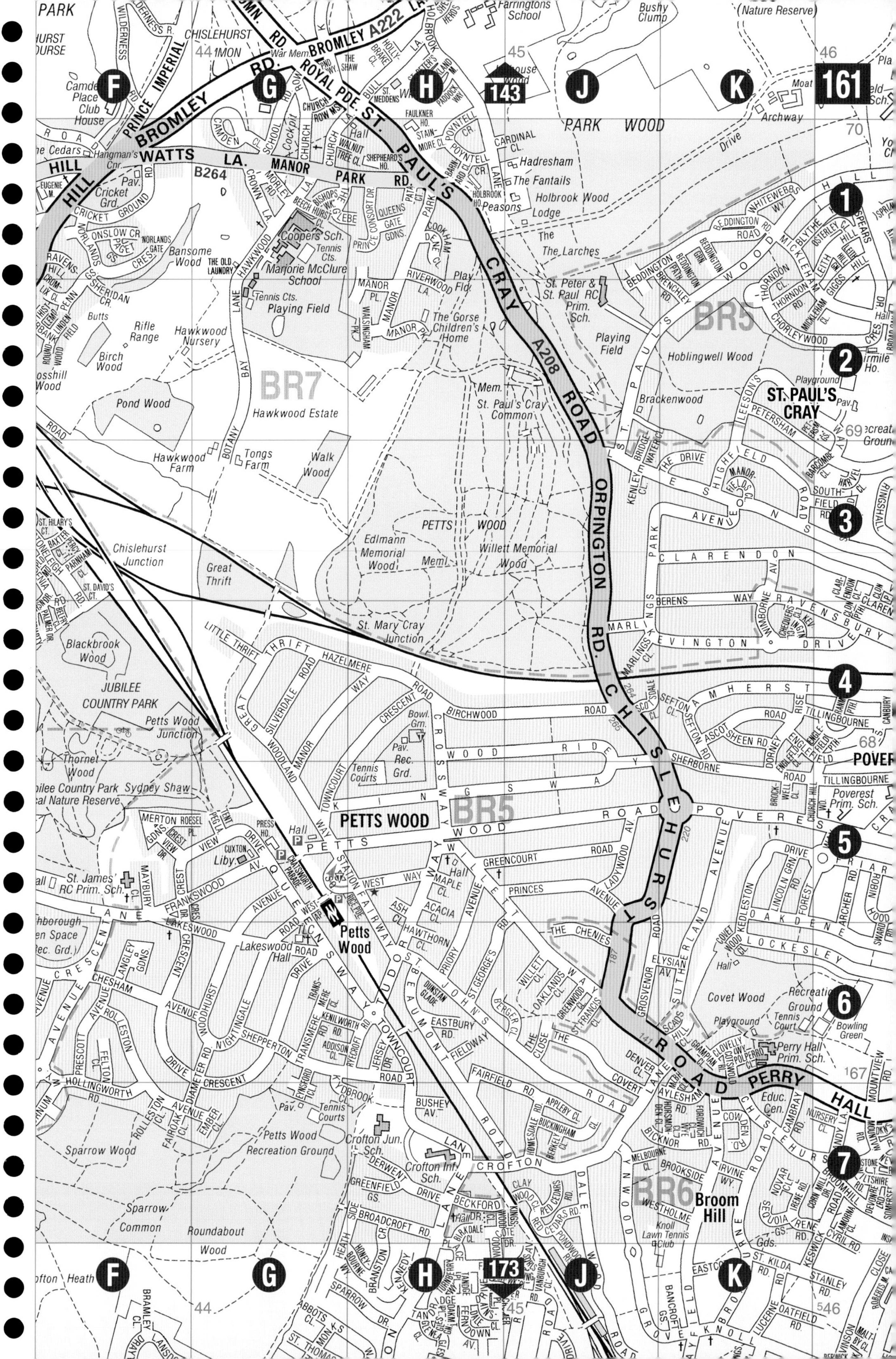

161
143
173
167
F
G
H
J
K
1
2
3
4
5
6
7
44
45
46
70
69
68
BR7
BR5
BR6
PETTS WOOD
ST. PAUL'S CRAY
Broom Hill
Petts Wood
ST. PAUL'S CRAY A208 ROAD
ORPINGTON RD.
CHISLEHURST ROAD
PERRY HALL
BROMLEY RD.
WATTS LA.
MANOR PARK RD.
B264
HILL
ROYAL PDE.
BROMLEY A222
PRINCE IMPERIAL
Farringtons School
Bushy Clump
(Nature Reserve)
PARK WOOD
Hadresham
The Fantails
Holbrook Wood Lodge
Peasons
The Larches
Coopers Sch.
Marjorie McClure School
Playing Field
Tennis Cts.
THE OLD LAUNDRY
Bansome Wood
Rifle Range
Hawkwood Nursery
Birch Wood
Butts
Pond Wood
Hawkwood Estate
Hawkwood Farm
Tongs Farm
Walk Wood
The Gorse Children's Home
Mem.
St. Paul's Cray Common
St. Peter & St. Paul RC Prim. Sch.
Hoblingwell Wood
Brackenwood
Playground
Chislehurst Junction
Great Thrift
Edlmann Memorial Wood
PETTS WOOD
Willett Memorial Wood
St. Mary Cray Junction
Blackbrook Wood
JUBILEE COUNTRY PARK
Petts Wood Junction
Thornet Wood
Jubilee Country Park Sydney Shaw Local Nature Reserve
St. James' RC Prim. Sch.
Liby.
Hall
Lakeswood Hall
Bowl. Grn.
Pav.
Rec. Grd.
Tennis Courts
Poverest Prim. Sch.
Covet Wood
Recreation Ground
Tennis Court
Bowling Green
Perry Hall Prim. Sch.
Educ. Cen.
Petts Wood Recreation Ground
Tennis Courts
Crofton Jun. Sch.
Crofton Inf. Sch.
Sparrow Wood
Sparrow Common
Roundabout Wood
Knoll Lawn Tennis Club
Cricket Grd.
Camden Place Club House
Hangman's Cnr.
CRICKET GROUND
ONSLOW CR.
SHERIDAN CR.
HAWKWOOD LANE
BOTANY BAY LANE
LITTLE THRIFT
HAZELMERE WAY
CRESCENT ROAD
BIRCHWOOD ROAD
WOOD RIDE
KINGSWAY
SILVERDALE ROAD
WOODLAND
MANOR
TOWNCOURT
GREAT THRIFT
CROSSWAY
PETTS WOOD ROAD
QUEENSWAY
FRANKSWOOD AV.
CHESHAM AVENUE
HOLLINGWORTH RD.
WOODHURST
NIGHTINGALE
SHEPPERTON
TUDOR WAY
ST. JOHN'S
BEAUMONT
FIELDWAY
FAIRFIELD RD.
EASTBURY RD.
CROFTON LANE
CROFTON
GREENFIELD GS.
BROADCROFT RD.
WILLETT WAY
GREENCOURT ROAD
PRINCES AVENUE
LADYWOOD AV.
THE CHENIES
GROSVENOR ROAD
SUTHERLAND AVENUE
POVEREST ROAD
OAKDENE
LOCKESLEY
MARLINGS PARK
CLARENDON WAY
BERENS WAY
KEVINGTON DRIVE
RAVENSBURY
AMHERST
SEFTON RD.
SHERBORNE ROAD
TILLINGBOURNE
CHORLEYWOOD
WOOD
BEDDINGTON ROAD
PETERSHAM
HIGHFIELD
AVENUE
THE DRIVE
SOUTHFIELD RD.
ELYSIAN AV.
AYLESHAM
BICKNOR RD.
BROOKSIDE
WESTHOLME
MELBOURNE CL.
IRVINE WY.
DENVER CL.
COVERT
SANDY LA.
MOUNTVIEW
KESWICK RD.
ST. KILDA RD.
STANLEY RD.
OATFIELD RD.
LUCERNE
EASTCOTE
BANCROFT GS.
MANOR WY.
LAKESWOOD
DALE WOOD
KINGS
BECKFORD DR.

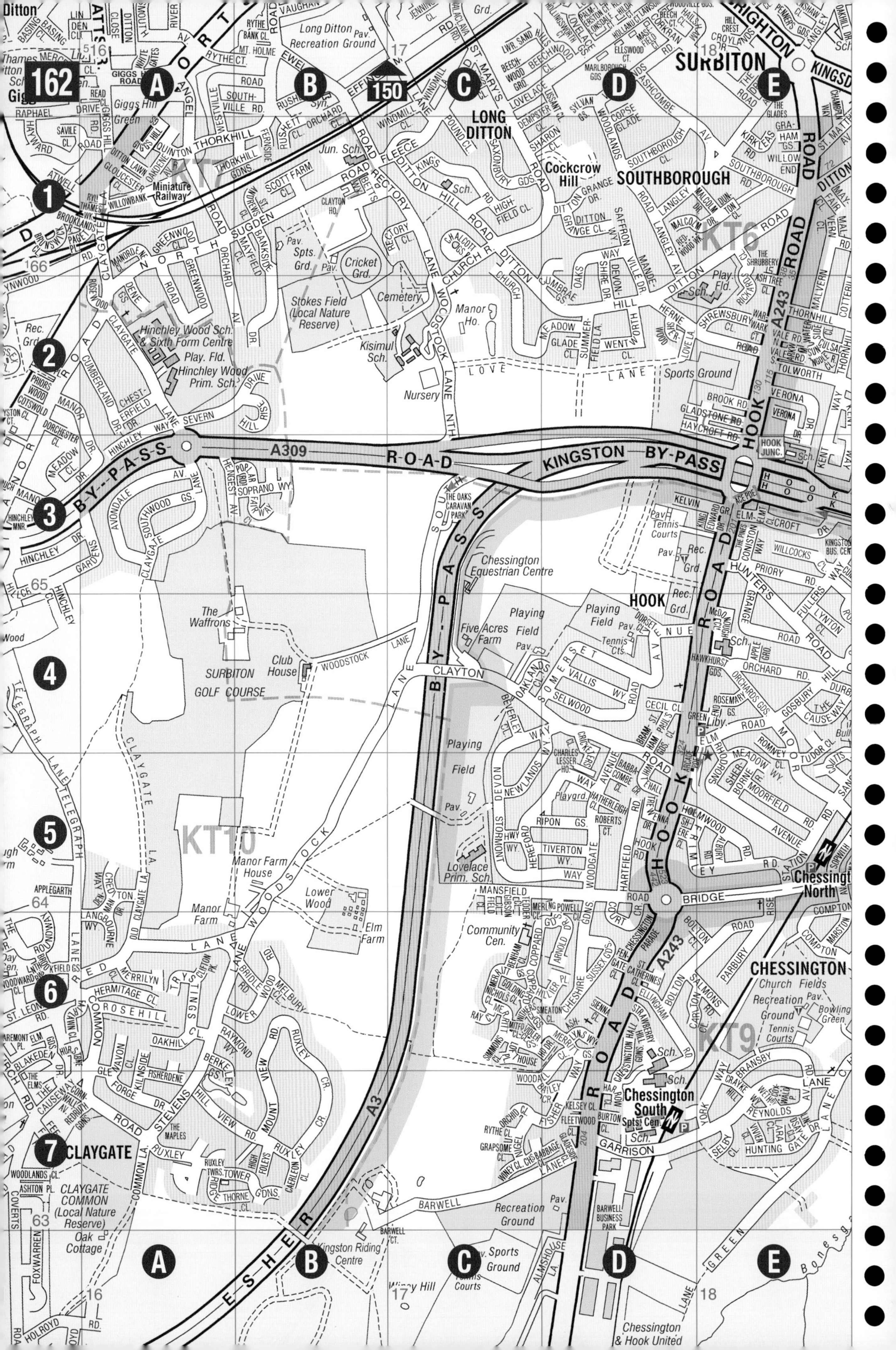

162
150
A
B
C
D
E
1
2
3
4
5
6
7
SURBITON
LONG DITTON
Cockcrow Hill
SOUTHBOROUGH
KT6
KT7
KT10
KT9
HOOK
CHESSINGTON
CLAYGATE
Long Ditton Pav. Recreation Ground
Giggs Hill Green
Miniature Railway
Stokes Field (Local Nature Reserve)
Cricket Grd.
Cemetery
Kisimul Sch.
Manor Ho.
Nursery
Hinchley Wood Sch. & Sixth Form Centre
Play. Fld.
Hinchley Wood Prim. Sch.
Sports Ground
KINGSTON BY-PASS
A309
ROAD
HOOK JUNC.
Chessington Equestrian Centre
Five Acres Farm
Playing Field
The Waffrons
Club House
SURBITON GOLF COURSE
Manor Farm House
Manor Farm
Lower Wood
Elm Farm
Lovelace Prim. Sch.
Community Cen.
Chessington North
Chessington South
Church Fields Recreation Ground
Bowling Green
Tennis Courts
CLAYGATE COMMON (Local Nature Reserve)
Oak Cottage
Kingston Riding Centre
Recreation Ground
Sports Ground
Winey Hill
BARWELL BUSINESS PARK
Chessington & Hook United
A3
A243
ESHER ROAD
BY-PASS
THE MAPLES
16
17
18
63
64
65
166
516

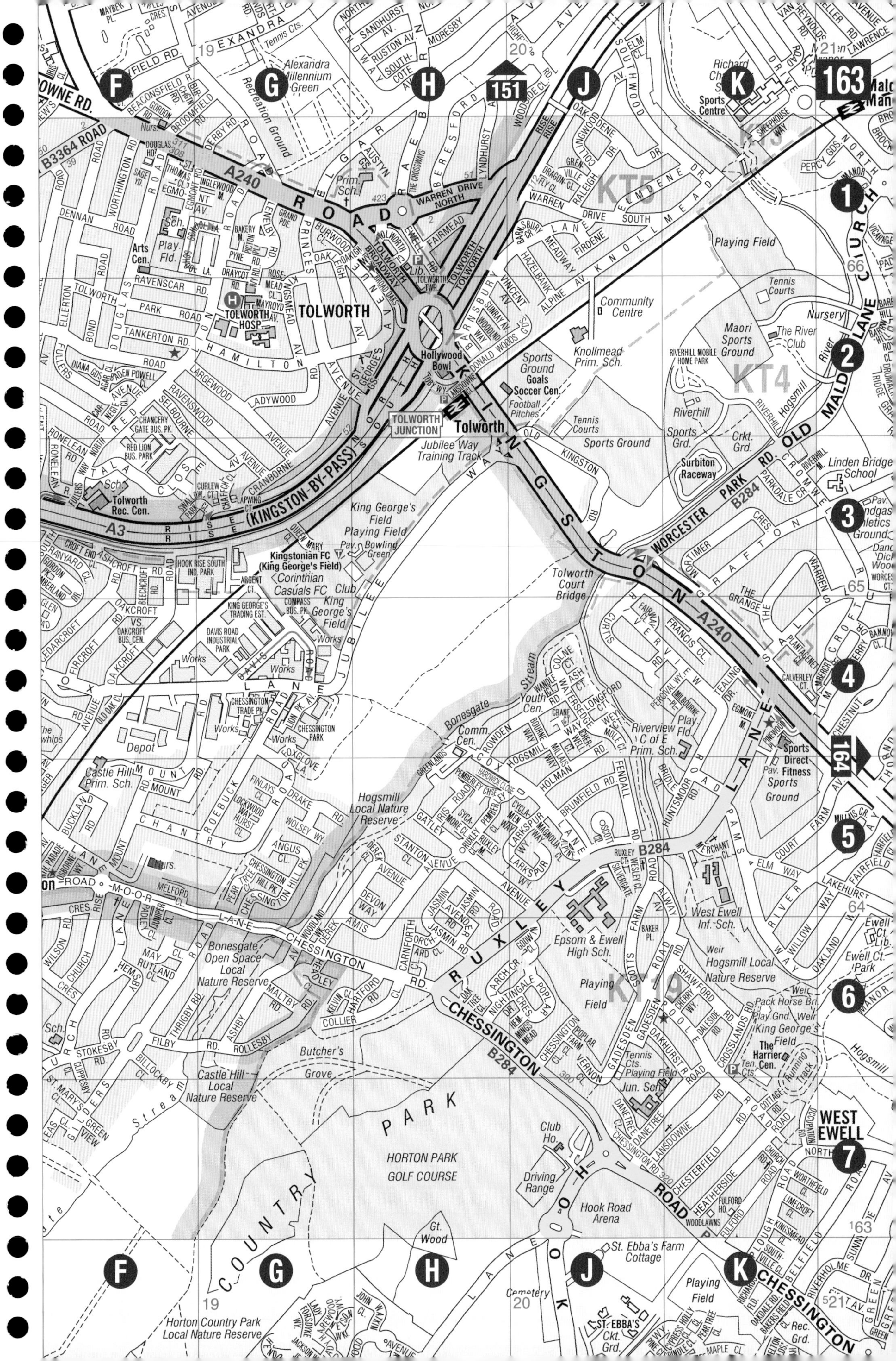

163
151
164
F
G
H
J
K
1
2
3
4
5
6
7
TOLWORTH
Tolworth
TOLWORTH JUNCTION
KT5
KT4
KT19
A240
A3
B284
B3364 ROAD
(KINGSTON-BY-PASS)
KINGSTON ROAD
Alexandra Millennium Green
Recreation Ground
Tennis Cts.
Richard Challoner Sch.
Sports Centre
Playing Field
Tennis Courts
Nursery
The River Club
Maori Sports Ground
Community Centre
Knollmead Prim. Sch.
Sports Ground
Goals Soccer Cen.
Football Pitches
Hollywood Bowl
TOLWORTH HOSP.
Arts Cen.
Play. Fld.
Sch.
Prim. Sch.
Lib.
TOLWORTH TWR.
RIVERHILL MOBILE HOME PARK
Riverhill Sports Grd.
Crkt. Grd.
Surbiton Raceway
Linden Bridge School
Jubilee Way Training Track
King George's Field Playing Field
Bowling Green
Kingstonian FC (King George's Field)
Corinthian Casuals FC
Club King George's Field
Tolworth Court Bridge
Tolworth Rec. Cen.
CHANCERY GATE BUS. PK.
RED LION BUS. PARK
HOOK RISE SOUTH IND. PARK
KING GEORGE'S TRADING EST.
COMPASS BUS. PK.
DAVIS ROAD INDUSTRIAL PARK
OAKCROFT VS. OAKCROFT BUS. CEN.
CHESSINGTON TRADE PK.
CHESSINGTON PARK
Works
Depot
Castle Hill Prim. Sch.
Comm. Cen.
Youth Cen.
Riverview C of E Prim. Sch.
Play. Fld.
Sports Direct Fitness
Pav. Sports Ground
Hogsmill Local Nature Reserve
Bonesgate Stream
Bonesgate Open Space Local Nature Reserve
Epsom & Ewell High Sch.
West Ewell Inf. Sch.
Playing Field
Hogsmill Local Nature Reserve
Pack Horse Bri.
Play. Gnd.
Weir
King George's Field
The Harrier Cen.
Running Track
Ten. Cts.
Tennis Cts.
Jun. Sch.
Castle Hill Local Nature Reserve
Butcher's Grove
HORTON COUNTRY PARK
HORTON PARK GOLF COURSE
Club Ho.
Driving Range
Hook Road Arena
Gt. Wood
St. Ebba's Farm Cottage
Cemetery
ST. EBBA'S Ckt. Grd.
Horton Country Park Local Nature Reserve
WEST EWELL
Ewell Ct. Lib.
Ewell Ct. Park
Hogsmill
Rec. Grd.
HOOK ROAD
CHESSINGTON ROAD
RUXLEY LANE
OLD MALDEN LANE
WORCESTER PARK RD.
CHURCH ROAD
MOOR LANE
CHESSINGTON RD.
WARREN DRIVE NORTH
WARREN DRIVE SOUTH
KNOLLMEAD
ELMDENE
ALPINE AV.
JUBILEE WAY
HOOK RISE SOUTH
DAVIS ROAD
CHANTRY ROAD
MOUNT RD.
COX LANE
GRAFTON ROAD
THE GRANGE
FRANCIS CL.
GATLEY AVENUE
STANTON AVENUE
DEVON WAY
COLLIER CL.
FILBY RD.
ROLLESBY RD.
THRIGBY RD.
HAMILTON AVENUE
TOLWORTH PARK ROAD
TANKERTON RD.
RAVENSCAR RD.
DENNAN ROAD
WORTHINGTON RD.
DOUGLAS RD.
ELLERTON RD.
FULLERS AV.
LARGEWOOD AV.
RAVENSWOOD AV.
SELBOURNE AV.
ADYWOOD
CRANBORNE AVENUE
TOLWORTH RISE SOUTH
PRINCES AVENUE
ELGAR AVENUE
BERESFORD AV.
LYNDHURST AV.
VINCENT AV.
HAZELBANK
MEADWAY
FIRDENE
RALEIGH DR.
COLLINGWOOD AV.
MORTIMER CRES.
WARREN RISE
PARKDALE CRES.
CURTIS RD.
TEALING DR.
EGMONT RD.
HUNTSMOOR RD.
FENDALL RD.
BRUMFIELD RD.
HOLMAN RD.
HOGSMILL WAY
ROWDEN RD.
LONGFORD CT.
LARKSPUR WY.
IRIS RD.
FINLAYS CL.
ROEBUCK RD.
DRAKE RD.
WOLSEY WY.
ANGUS CL.
MELFORD CL.
WOODLAND WAY
HARTFORD RD.
CARNFORTH RD.
JASMIN RD.
NIGHTINGALE RD.
POPLAR CRES.
GADESDEN RD.
OAKHURST RD.
DALESIDE RD.
CROSSLANDS RD.
SHAWFORD RD.
LANSDOWNE RD.
CHESTERFIELD RD.
HEATHERSIDE RD.
FULFORD RD.
WOODLAWNS
WORTHFIELD CL.
LIMECROFT CL.
OAKLAND WAY
WILLOW WAY
FAIRFIELD
ELM WAY
COURT FARM AV.
LAKEHURST
RIVERHOLME DR.
THORNDON GDNS.
LANE
COUNTRY PARK

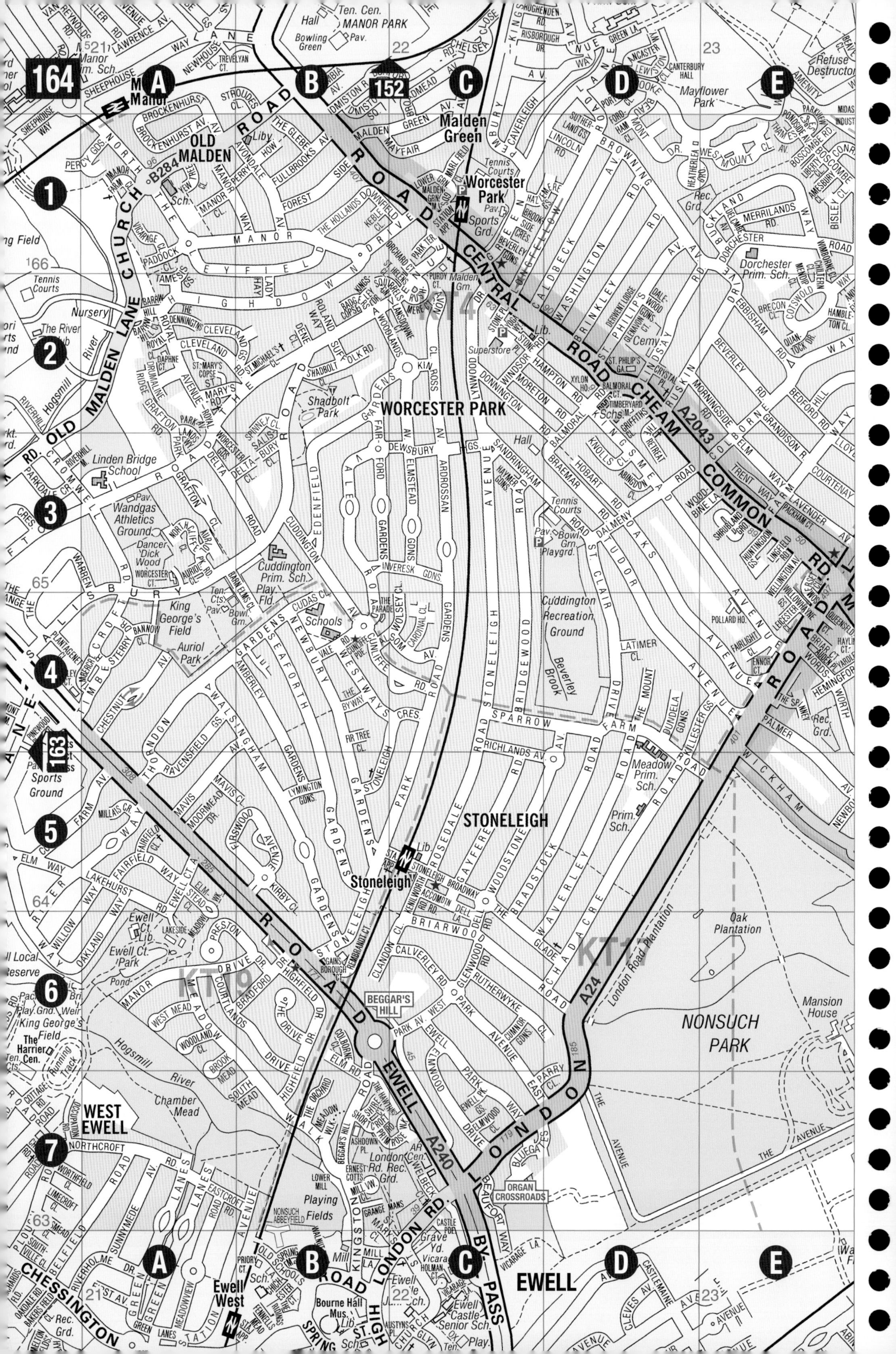

164
152
163
A
B
C
D
E
1
2
3
4
5
6
7
21
22
23
166
65
64
63
OLD MALDEN
Malden Green
Worcester Park
WORCESTER PARK
STONELEIGH
Stoneleigh
WEST EWELL
EWELL
Ewell West
NONSUCH PARK
KT4
KT19
KT17
Malden Manor
MALDEN ROAD
CENTRAL ROAD
CHEAM COMMON RD.
A2043
B284
A24
A240
OLD MALDEN LANE
CHURCH ROAD
EWELL ROAD
LONDON ROAD
EWELL BY PASS
KINGSTON ROAD
HIGH ST.
CHESSINGTON ROAD
SALISBURY ROAD
HIGHDOWN
MANOR DRIVE
STONELEIGH PARK ROAD
STONELEIGH AVENUE
SPARROW FARM ROAD
WICKHAM AV.
BEGGAR'S HILL
ORGAN CROSSROADS
Linden Bridge School
Wandgas Athletics Ground
Dancer Dick Wood
Cuddington Prim. Sch.
King George's Field
Auriol Park
Shadbolt Park
Cuddington Recreation Ground
Beverley Brook
Meadow Prim. Sch.
Dorchester Prim. Sch.
Mayflower Park
Refuse Destructor
Oak Plantation
Mansion House
London Road Plantation
Hogsmill River
Chamber Mead
Playing Fields
Bourne Hall Mus.
Ewell Castle Senior Sch.
The Harrier Cen.
Sports Ground
Ewell Ct. Park
Tennis Courts
Superstore
Sports Grd.
Schools
Cemy.

165
153
166
163
1
2
3
4
5
6
7
F
G
H
J
K
ROSEHILL
BENHILTON
NORTH CHEAM
CHEAM
SUTTON
BELMONT
SM1
SM2
SM3
SM4
King George's Field
Rosehill Recreation Ground
Sutton Sports Village
Sutton Tennis Academy
Sutton Cemetery
Glenthorne High Sch.
Recreation Grounds
Sutton Common
West Sutton
Westbourne Prim. Sch.
Collingwood Road Recreation Ground
Sutton United FC (The Knights Comm. Stadium)
Cheam High Sch.
Cheam Leisure Cen.
Goals Soccer Cen. (Sutton)
St. Anthony's Hosp.
St. Raphael's Hospice
Perrett's Field
Seears Park
Cheam Recreation Ground
Cheam Park
David Lloyd Leisure Cen.
Nonsuch High Sch.
Overton Grange Sch.
Overton Park
Sutton Ckt. Grd.
Fitness4Less (Sutton)
Superstore
Recycling Cen.
Mecca Bingo
A24
A217
A232
A2043
B279
B2230
B283
LONDON ROAD
STONECOT HILL
ST. DUNSTAN'S HILL
OLDFIELDS ROAD
REIGATE AVENUE
COMMON ROAD
ROSE HILL
ANGEL HILL
HIGH ST.
ST. NICHOLAS WAY
THROWLEY WAY
CHEAM ROAD
MALDEN ROAD
EWELL RD.
BELMONT RISE
BURDON LANE
MULGRAVE ROAD
GANDER GREEN LANE

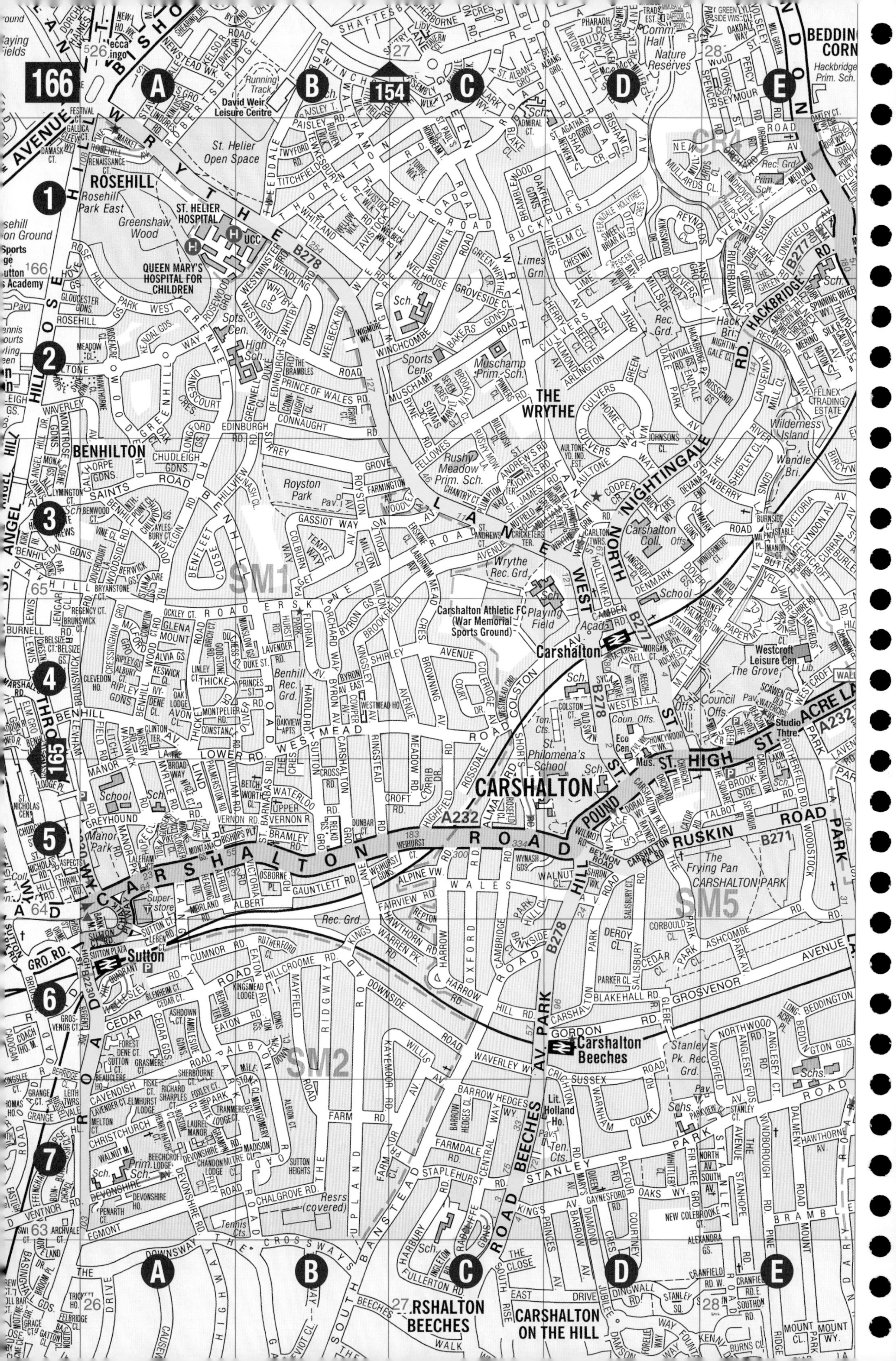

166
154
165
A
B
C
D
E
1
2
3
4
5
6
7
ROSEHILL
Rosehill Park East
Greenshaw Wood
ST. HELIER HOSPITAL
QUEEN MARY'S HOSPITAL FOR CHILDREN
St. Helier Open Space
David Weir Leisure Centre
Running Track
BENHILTON
THE WRYTHE
SM1
SM2
SM5
CR4
Royston Park
Rushy Meadow Prim. Sch.
Muschamp Prim. Sch.
Wrythe Rec. Grd.
Carshalton Athletic FC (War Memorial Sports Ground)
Playing Field
Carshalton
CARSHALTON
St. Philomena's School
Carshalton Coll.
Westcroft Leisure Cen.
The Grove
Council Offs.
Studio Thtre.
The Frying Pan
CARSHALTON PARK
Benhill Rec. Grd.
Manor Park
Sutton
Carshalton Beeches
Stanley Pk. Rec. Grd.
Lit. Holland Ho.
Resrs (covered)
CARSHALTON BEECHES
CARSHALTON ON THE HILL
Wilderness Island
Wandle Bri.
FELNEX TRADING ESTATE
Hackbridge Prim. Sch.
BEDDINGTON CORNER
Comm. Hall
Nature Reserves
Limes Grn.
CARSHALTON ROAD
A232
B278
B277
B271
B2230
WRYTHE LANE
WEST ST.
NORTH ST.
HIGH ST.
RUSKIN ROAD
POUND ST.
BEECHES AV.
HACKBRIDGE RD.
NIGHTINGALE RD.
ACRE LANE
PARK LANE
GROSVENOR AVENUE
ST. HELIER AVENUE
ERSKINE ROAD
WESTMEAD ROAD
MUSCHAMP ROAD
STANLEY PARK ROAD

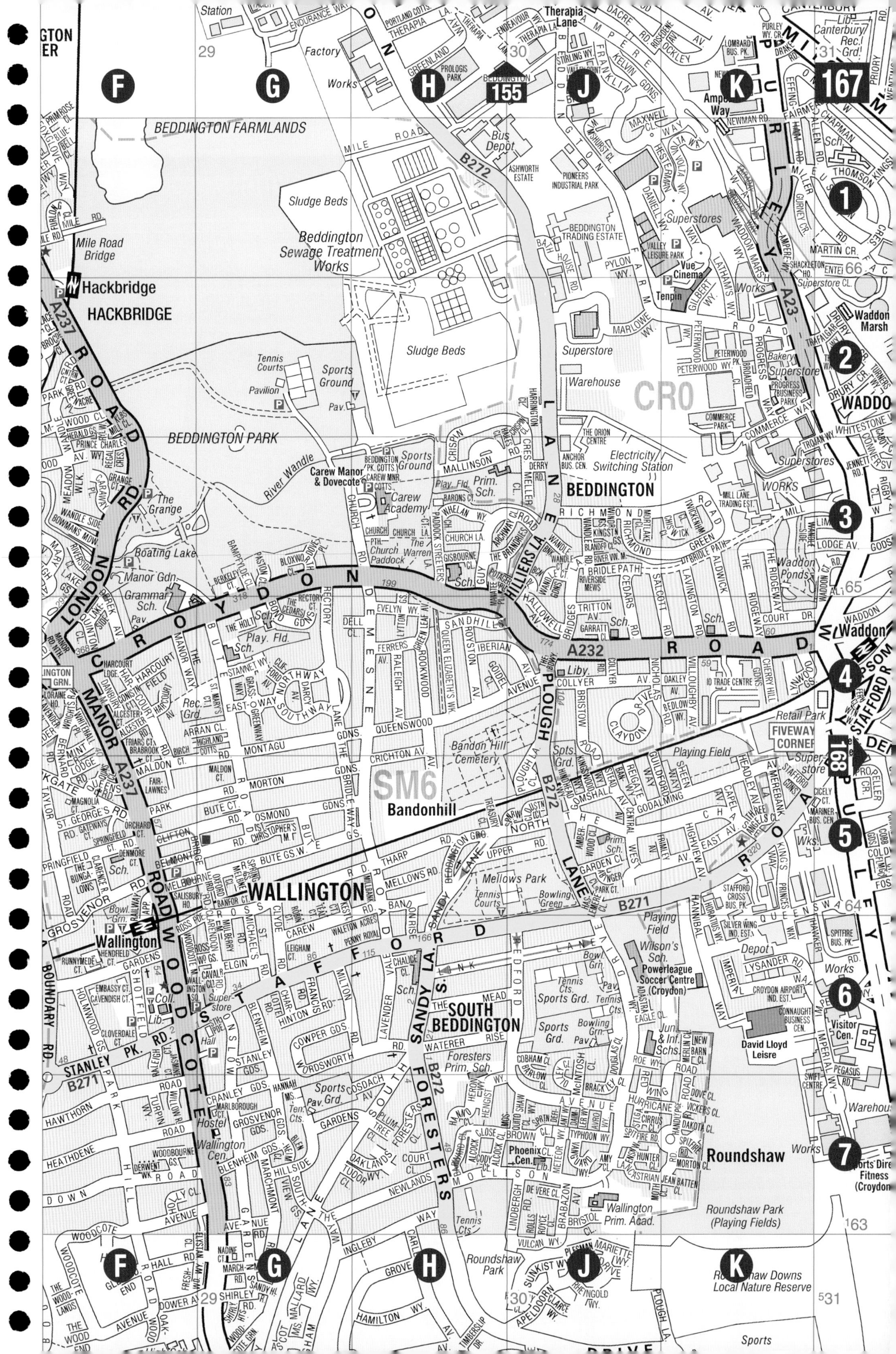

F
G
H
J
K
29
30
31
155
167
168
163
64
65
66
1
2
3
4
5
6
7
Station
Factory
Works
Therapia Lane
PROLOGIS PARK
Ampere Way
BEDDINGTON FARMLANDS
MILE ROAD
B272
Bus Depot
ASHWORTH ESTATE
PIONEERS INDUSTRIAL PARK
Sludge Beds
Beddington Sewage Treatment Works
BEDDINGTON TRADING ESTATE
VALLEY LEISURE PARK
Superstores
Vue Cinema
Tenpin
Mile Road Bridge
Hackbridge
HACKBRIDGE
A237
LONDON ROAD
Tennis Courts
Sports Ground
Pavilion
Pav.
Superstore
Warehouse
CR0
Waddon Marsh
A23
PURLEY WAY
BEDDINGTON PARK
River Wandle
Carew Manor & Dovecote
Carew Academy
Sports Ground
Prim. Sch.
THE ORION CENTRE
ANCHOR BUS. CEN.
Electricity Switching Station
BEDDINGTON
MILL LANE TRADING EST.
WORKS
The Grange
Boating Lake
Manor Gdn.
Grammar Sch.
The Warren Paddock
Church Paddock
CROYDON ROAD
A232
ROAD
Waddon Ponds
Waddon
THE RIDGEWAY
Play. Fld.
Sch.
Rec. Grd.
Liby.
PLOUGH LANE
Bandon Hill Cemetery
SM6
Bandonhill
CLAYDON DRIVE
Retail Park
FIVEWAYS CORNER
Playing Field
Super-store
MANOR ROAD
WALLINGTON
Mellows Park
Tennis Courts
Bowling Green
B271
Playing Field
Wilson's Sch.
Powerleague Soccer Centre (Croydon)
STAFFORD ROAD
Wallington
WOODCOTE ROAD
SANDY LA.
SOUTH BEDDINGTON
Foresters Prim. Sch.
FORESTERS DRIVE
Sports Grd.
Tennis Cts.
Jun. & Inf. Schs.
Phoenix Cen.
CROYDON AIRPORT IND. EST.
David Lloyd Leisure
Visitor Cen.
Roundshaw
Sports Direct Fitness (Croydon)
Warehouse
Wallington Cen.
Hostel
Coll.
Lib.
Hall
STANLEY PARK ROAD
B271
Wallington Prim. Acad.
Roundshaw Park (Playing Fields)
Roundshaw Park
Roundshaw Downs Local Nature Reserve
Sports
BOUNDARY RD.

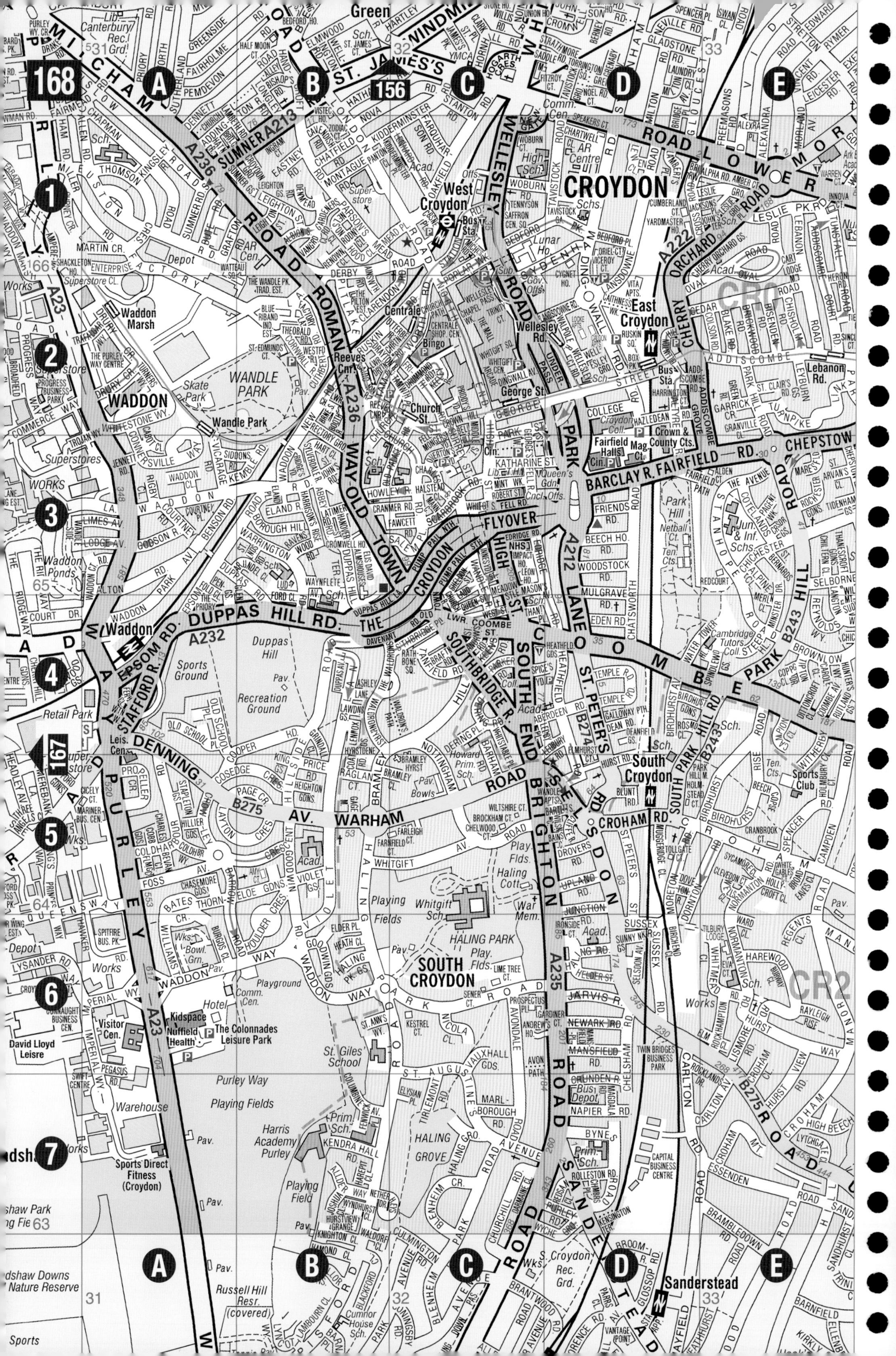
168
156
167
A
B
C
D
E
1
2
3
4
5
6
7
31
32
33
CROYDON
WADDON
SOUTH CROYDON
CR0
CR2
West Croydon
East Croydon
South Croydon
Sanderstead
Waddon
Waddon Marsh
Wandle Park
Reeves Cnr.
Centrale
Church St.
Wellesley Rd.
George St.
Lebanon Rd.
WANDLE PARK
Duppas Hill
Sports Ground
Recreation Ground
Purley Way Playing Fields
Haling Grove
HALING PARK Play. Flds.
Whitgift Sch.
St. Giles' School
Harris Academy Purley
Playing Field
Russell Hill Resr. (covered)
S. Croydon Rec. Grd.
Fairfield Halls
Croydon Coll.
Crown & County Cts.
Cambridge Tutors Coll.
Howard Prim. Sch.
The Colonnades Leisure Park
Kidspace
Nuffield Health
Visitor Cen.
David Lloyd Leisre
Sports Direct Fitness (Croydon)
Retail Park
Superstore
Superstores
Warehouse
Twin Bridges Business Park
Capital Business Centre
Sports Club
ROMAN WAY
PURLEY WAY
DUPPAS HILL RD.
DENNING AV.
WARHAM AV.
WADDON WAY
PARK LANE
SOUTH END
BRIGHTON ROAD
SANDERSTEAD ROAD
COOMBE ROAD
PARK HILL RD.
FAIRFIELD RD.
BARCLAY R.
CHEPSTOW ROAD
ADDISCOMBE RD.
LOWER ADDISCOMBE ROAD
CHERRY ORCHARD ROAD
WELLESLEY ROAD
SYDENHAM ROAD
MITCHAM ROAD
SUMNER ROAD
CROHAM ROAD
THE FLYOVER
A23
A232
A235
A236
A212
A213
A222
B243
B274
B275

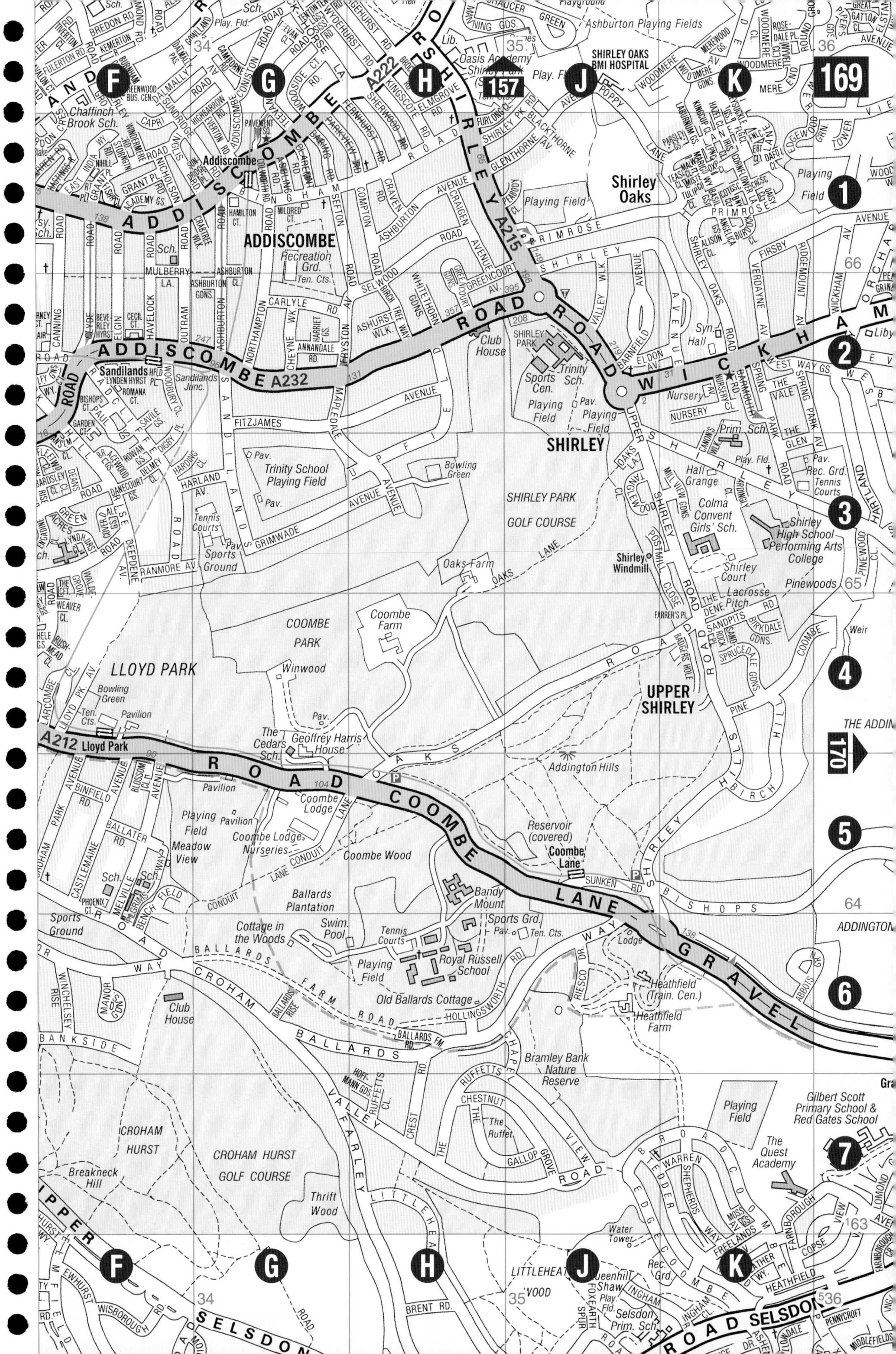
ADDISCOMBE
SHIRLEY
UPPER SHIRLEY
Shirley Oaks
LLOYD PARK
COOMBE PARK
SHIRLEY PARK GOLF COURSE
CROHAM HURST GOLF COURSE
Addington Hills
Coombe Wood
Ballards Plantation
Bramley Bank Nature Reserve
Royal Russell School
Trinity School Playing Field
Shirley High School Performing Arts College
Colma Convent Girls' Sch.
Shirley Windmill
SHIRLEY OAKS BMI HOSPITAL
Oasis Academy Shirley Park
Gilbert Scott Primary School & Red Gates School
The Quest Academy
Selsdon Prim. Sch.
ADDISCOMBE ROAD A232
SHIRLEY ROAD A215
WICKHAM ROAD
COOMBE ROAD A212
COOMBE LANE
GRAVEL HILL
UPPER SHIRLEY ROAD
SELSDON ROAD
157
170
163

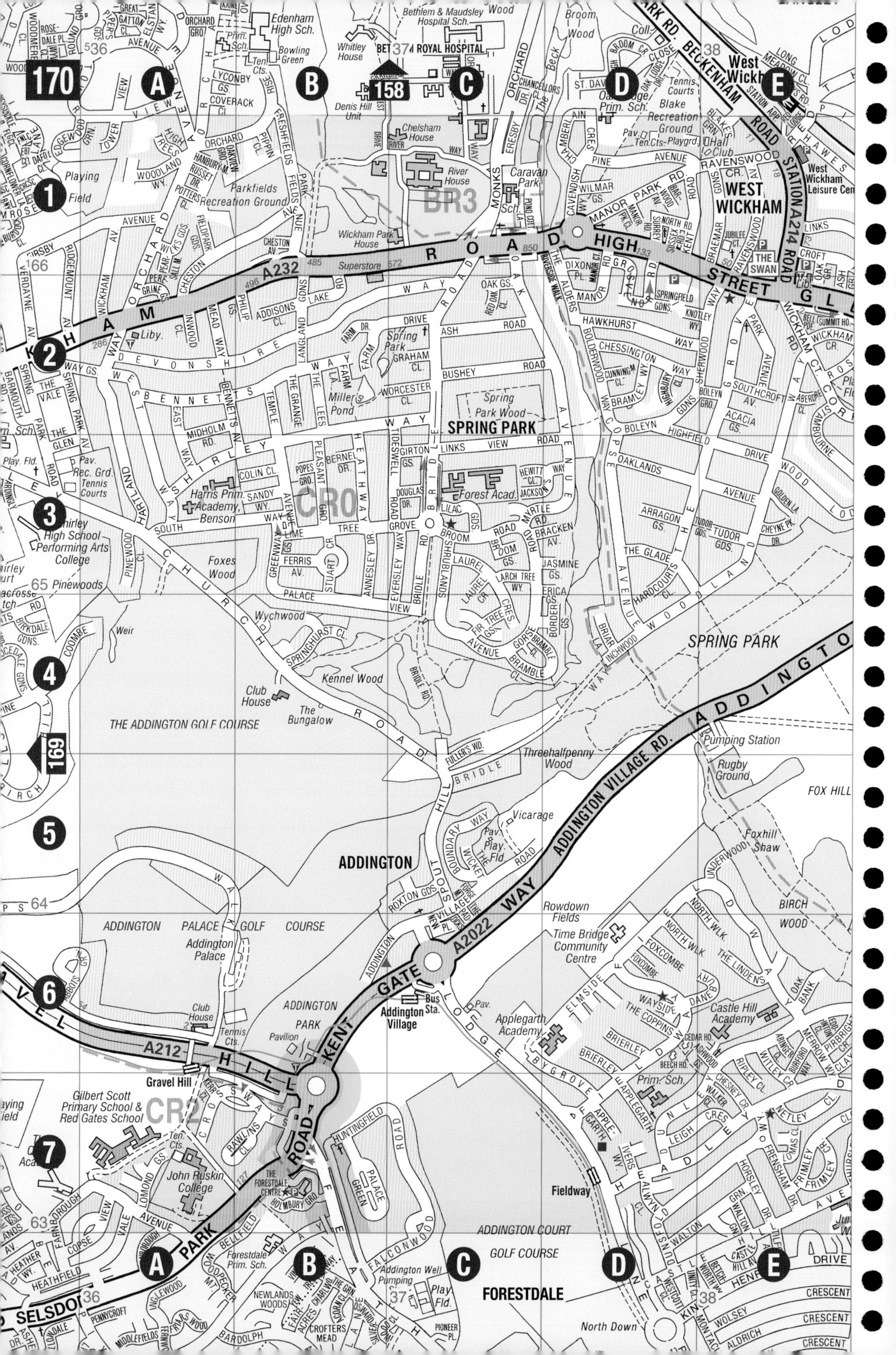

A
B
C
D
E
1
2
3
4
5
6
7
158
169
Edenham High Sch.
Bethlem & Maudsley Hospital Sch.
ROYAL HOSPITAL
Whitley House
Denis Hill Unit
Chelsham House
River House
BR3
Wickham Park House
Caravan Park
Broom Wood
Oak Lodge Prim. Sch.
Blake Recreation Ground
West Wickham
WEST WICKHAM
West Wickham Leisure Cen
THE SWAN
Playing Field
Parkfields Recreation Ground
Bowling Green
Superstore
A232
WICKHAM ROAD
HIGH STREET
A214
STATION ROAD
Liby.
Spring Park
Miller's Pond
Spring Park Wood
SPRING PARK
Forest Acad.
Harris Prim. Academy, Benson
CR0
Shirley High School Performing Arts College
Rec. Grd.
Tennis Courts
Foxes Wood
Pinewoods
Wychwood
Weir
Kennel Wood
Club House
The Bungalow
THE ADDINGTON GOLF COURSE
Threehalfpenny Wood
SPRING PARK
ADDINGTON VILLAGE RD.
A2022
ADDINGTON WAY
Pumping Station
Rugby Ground
FOX HILL
Foxhill Shaw
BIRCH WOOD
Vicarage
Pav. Play. Fld.
ADDINGTON
ADDINGTON PALACE GOLF COURSE
Addington Palace
Rowdown Fields
Time Bridge Community Centre
Addington Village
Bus Sta.
Applegarth Academy
Castle Hill Academy
Prim. Sch.
Club House
Tennis Cts.
Pavilion
A212
GRAVEL HILL
Gravel Hill
KENT GATE
Gilbert Scott Primary School & Red Gates School
CR2
John Ruskin College
THE FORESTDALE CENTRE
Fieldway
ADDINGTON COURT GOLF COURSE
Forestdale Prim. Sch.
Addington Well Pumping
Play. Fld.
FORESTDALE
North Down
PARK
SELSDON

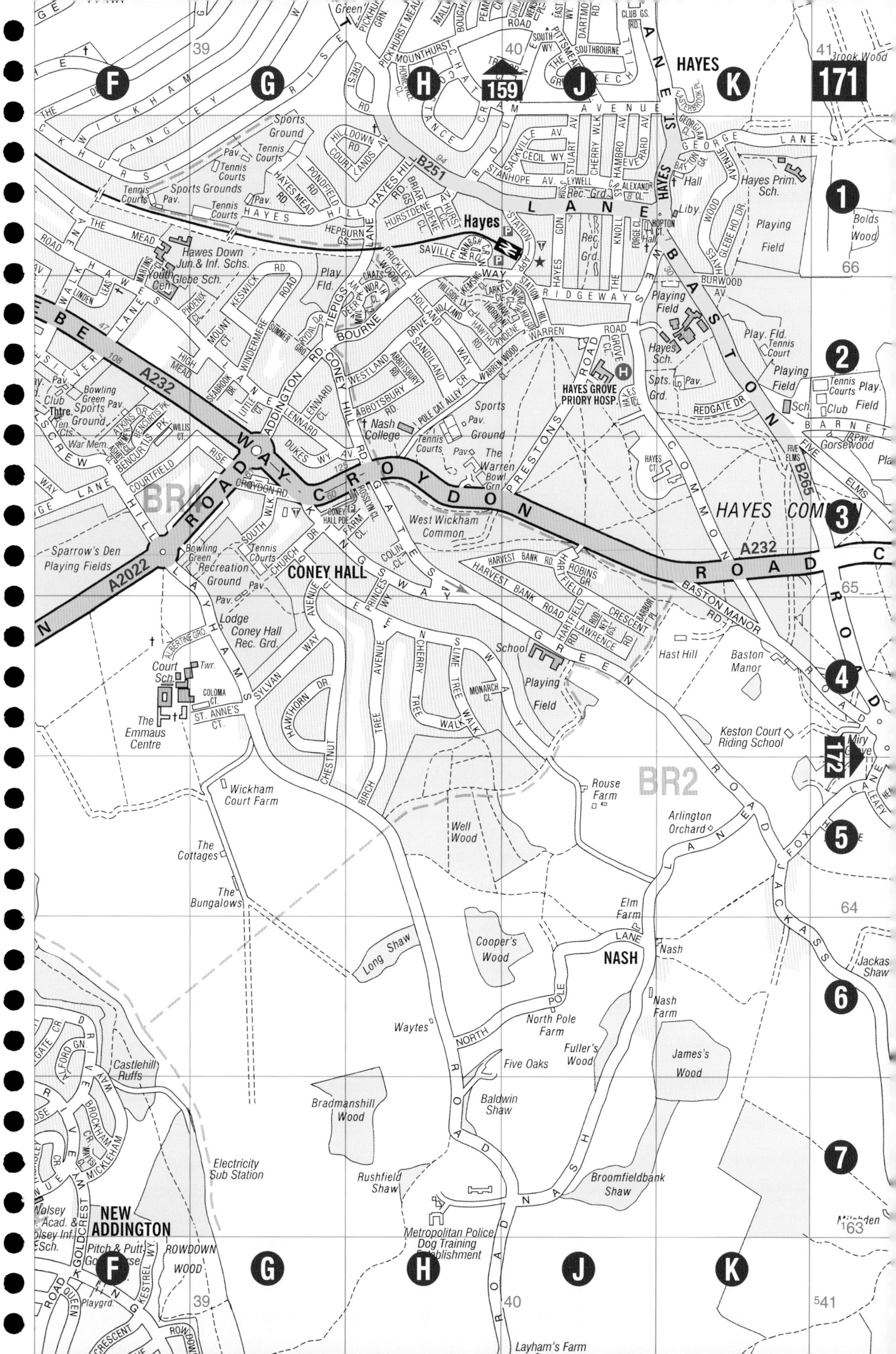

171
159
172
F
G
H
J
K
1
2
3
4
5
6
7
39
40
41
66
65
64
163
HAYES
Hayes
CONEY HALL
NASH
NEW ADDINGTON
BR4
BR2
A232
A2022
B251
B265
CROYDON ROAD
HAYES LANE
BASTON ROAD
WEST WICKHAM
LANGLEY RISE
WICKHAM
PICKHURST MEAD
MOUNTHURST
CHATHAM AVENUE
BOURNE WAY
RIDGEWAY
STANHOPE AV.
SACKVILLE AV.
CECIL WY.
STUART AV.
CHERRY WLK.
HAMBRO AV.
EVERARD AV.
ALEXANDER CL.
HAYES ST.
GEORGE LANE
BAFTON GA.
GEORGIAN CL.
EASTERBROOK PL.
GLEBE HO. DR.
BURWOOD AV.
REDGATE DR.
BARNET WOOD
FIVE ELMS
HAYES HILL
HAYES HILL RD.
HILLDOWN RD.
PONDFIELD RD.
HAYES MEAD RD.
BRIAR GS.
HURSTDENE AV.
HEPBURN GS.
SAVILLE ROW
STATION APP.
STATION HILL
TIEPIGS LANE
CONEY HILL RD.
ADDINGTON RD.
WESTLAND DR.
ABBOTSBURY RD.
SANDILAND CR.
HOLLAND WAY
HOLLAND DRIVE
HAWTHORNDENE RD.
WARREN ROAD
WARREN WOOD CL.
POLE CAT ALLEY
PRESTONS ROAD
HAYES COMMON
COMMON ROAD
BASTON MANOR RD.
HARVEST BANK RD.
HARTFIELD CRESCENT
HARTFIELD RD.
LAWRENCE RD.
BARBOR PL.
GREEN LANE
KINGSWAY
GATES GREEN RD.
COLIN CL.
ROSSLYN CL.
CONEY HALL PDE.
FARM CL.
CROYDON RD.
SOUTH WLK.
CHURCH DR.
PRINCES WY.
AVENUE
CHERRY TREE WALK
LIME TREE WALK
MONARCH CL.
SYLVAN WAY
HAWTHORN DR.
CHESTNUT AVENUE
BIRCH TREE AVENUE
LAYHAMS ROAD
ALBERTINE GRO.
COLOMA CT.
ST. ANNE'S CT.
WICKHAM WAY
GLEBE WAY
COURTFIELD RISE
SILVER LANE
KESWICK RD.
WINDERMERE RD.
MOUNT CT.
HIGH MEAD
LENNARD RD.
DUKES WY.
BENCURTIS PK.
WILLIS CT.
ATKINS DR.
LINDEN LEAS
MARTINS CL.
PHOENIX CL.
THE MEAD
NASH LANE
NORTH POLE LANE
FOX LANE
JACKASS LANE
ELM FARM LANE
LEAFY WAY
Sports Ground
Tennis Courts
Sports Grounds
Pav.
Hawes Down Jun.& Inf. Schs.
Glebe Sch.
Youth Cen.
Bowling Green
Club
Thtre.
War Mem.
Play. Fld.
Nash College
Tennis Courts
Sports Ground
The Warren
Bowl. Grn.
West Wickham Common
Rec. Grd.
Hall
Liby.
Hayes Prim. Sch.
Playing Field
Bolds Wood
Playing Field
Hayes Sch.
Spts. Grd.
Play. Fld.
Tennis Court
Club
Sch.
HAYES GROVE PRIORY HOSP.
Gorsewood
Sparrow's Den Playing Fields
Bowling Green
Recreation Ground
Lodge
Coney Hall Rec. Grd.
Court Sch.
Twr.
The Emmaus Centre
School
Playing Field
Hast Hill
Baston Manor
Keston Court Riding School
Miry Grove
Rouse Farm
Wickham Court Farm
Arlington Orchard
Well Wood
The Cottages
The Bungalows
Elm Farm
Nash
Long Shaw
Cooper's Wood
Nash Farm
North Pole Farm
Waytes
Fuller's Wood
Five Oaks
James's Wood
Jackass Shaw
Castlehill Ruffs
Bradmanshill Wood
Baldwin Shaw
Electricity Sub Station
Rushfield Shaw
Broomfieldbank Shaw
Metropolitan Police Dog Training Establishment
Wolsey Acad. & Wolsey Inf. Sch.
Pitch & Putt Golf Course
ROWDOWN WOOD
Playgrd.
KESTREL WY.
GOLDCREST WAY
BROCKHAM
MICKLEHAM
ALFORD GN.
QUEEN ELIZABETH
CRESCENT
ROWDOWN
Layham's Farm
Brook Wood

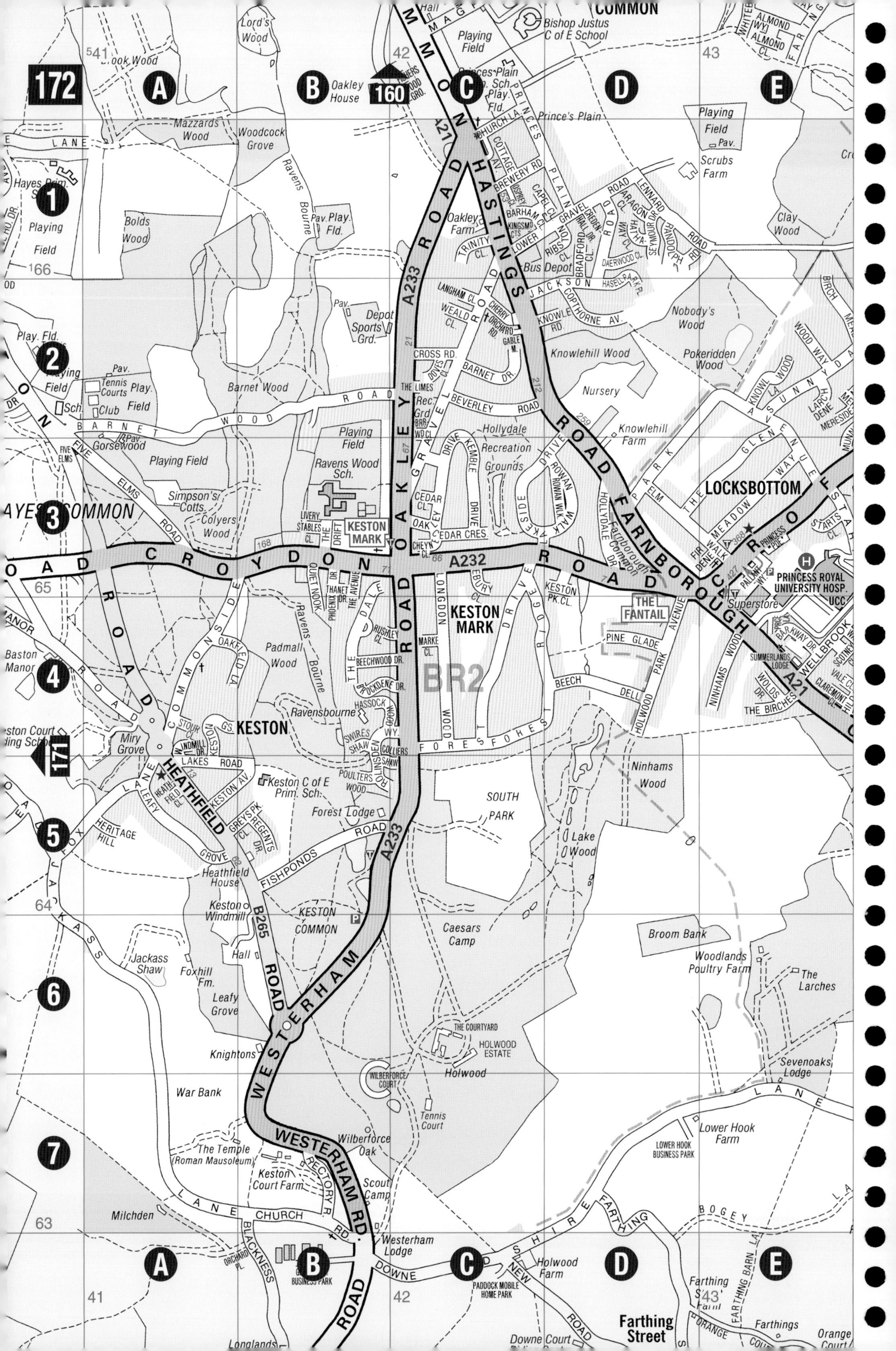
A
B
C
D
E
1
2
3
4
5
6
7
160
171
LOCKSBOTTOM
KESTON MARK
KESTON
HAYES COMMON
BR2
CROYDON ROAD
OAKLEY ROAD
HASTINGS ROAD
FARNBOROUGH COMMON
WESTERHAM ROAD
WESTERHAM RD.
HEATHFIELD
A233
A232
A21
B265
PRINCESS ROYAL UNIVERSITY HOSP.
Keston C of E Prim. Sch.
Ravens Wood Sch.
Bishop Justus C of E School
Caesars Camp
Holwood
Keston Windmill
Heathfield House
Wilberforce Oak
The Temple (Roman Mausoleum)
Keston Court Farm
Lower Hook Farm
LOWER HOOK BUSINESS PARK
Farthing Street
Nobody's Wood
Pokeridden Wood
Knowlehill Wood
Ninhams Wood
Padmall Wood
Barnet Wood
Bolds Wood
Clay Wood
Lord's Wood
Mazzards Wood
Woodcock Grove
Jackass Shaw
Leafy Grove
Foxhill Fm.
Knightons
War Bank
Milchden
Broom Bank
Woodlands Poultry Farm
The Larches
Sevenoaks Lodge
Scrubs Farm
Oakley Farm
Oakley House
SOUTH PARK
Lake Wood
Hollydale Recreation Grounds
Knowlehill Farm
Nursery
Baston Manor
Miry Grove
Ravensbourne
Forest Lodge
KESTON COMMON
THE COURTYARD
HOLWOOD ESTATE
WILBERFORCE COURT
Scout Camp
Westerham Lodge
Holwood Farm
PADDOCK MOBILE HOME PARK
Downe Court
Longlands
Farthings
Orange Court
THE FANTAIL
Superstore
41
42
43
63
64
65
166
168

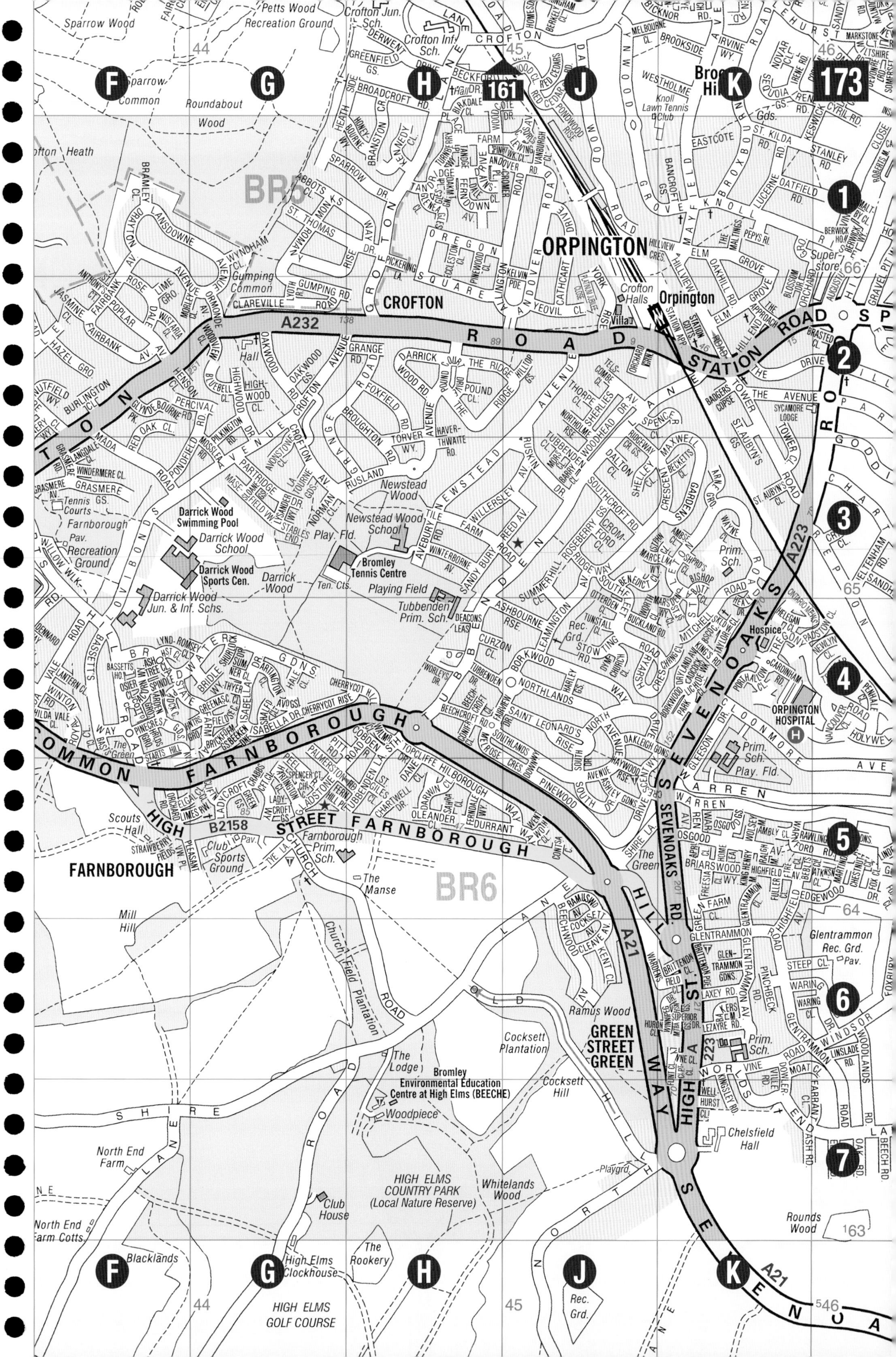

161
173
163
F
G
H
J
K
1
2
3
4
5
6
7
44
45
46
BR5
BR6
ORPINGTON
Orpington
CROFTON
FARNBOROUGH
GREEN STREET GREEN
A232
A223
A21
B2158
CROFTON ROAD
STATION ROAD
FARNBOROUGH COMMON
FARNBOROUGH HILL
HIGH STREET FARNBOROUGH
SEVENOAKS ROAD
SEVENOAKS WAY
SEVENOAKS RD.
HIGH ST.
SHIRE LANE
NORTH END LANE
NORTH HILL ROAD
CHURCH ROAD
LOVIBONDS AVENUE
CROFTON LANE
CROFTON AVENUE
Sparrow Wood
Petts Wood Recreation Ground
Crofton Jun. Sch.
Crofton Inf. Sch.
Sparrow Common
Roundabout Wood
Crofton Heath
Gumping Common
Broom Hill
Knoll Lawn Tennis Club
Crofton Halls
Villa
Super-store
Darrick Wood Swimming Pool
Darrick Wood School
Darrick Wood Sports Cen.
Darrick Wood
Darrick Wood Jun. & Inf. Schs.
Tennis Courts
Farnborough Pav.
Recreation Ground
Newstead Wood
Newstead Wood School
Play. Fld.
Bromley Tennis Centre
Ten. Cts.
Playing Field
Tubbenden Prim. Sch.
Prim. Sch.
Rec. Grd.
Hospice
ORPINGTON HOSPITAL
Sycamore Lodge
Scouts Hall
Club Sports Ground
Pav.
Farnborough Prim. Sch.
The Manse
The Green
Mill Hill
Church Field Plantation
Glentrammon Rec. Grd.
Ramus Wood
Cocksett Plantation
Cocksett Hill
The Lodge
Bromley Environmental Education Centre at High Elms (BEECHE)
Woodpiece
Chelsfield Hall
North End Farm
North End Farm Cotts.
HIGH ELMS COUNTRY PARK (Local Nature Reserve)
Whitelands Wood
Playgrd.
Club House
Blacklands
High Elms Clockhouse
The Rookery
HIGH ELMS GOLF COURSE
Rounds Wood
Rec. Grd.

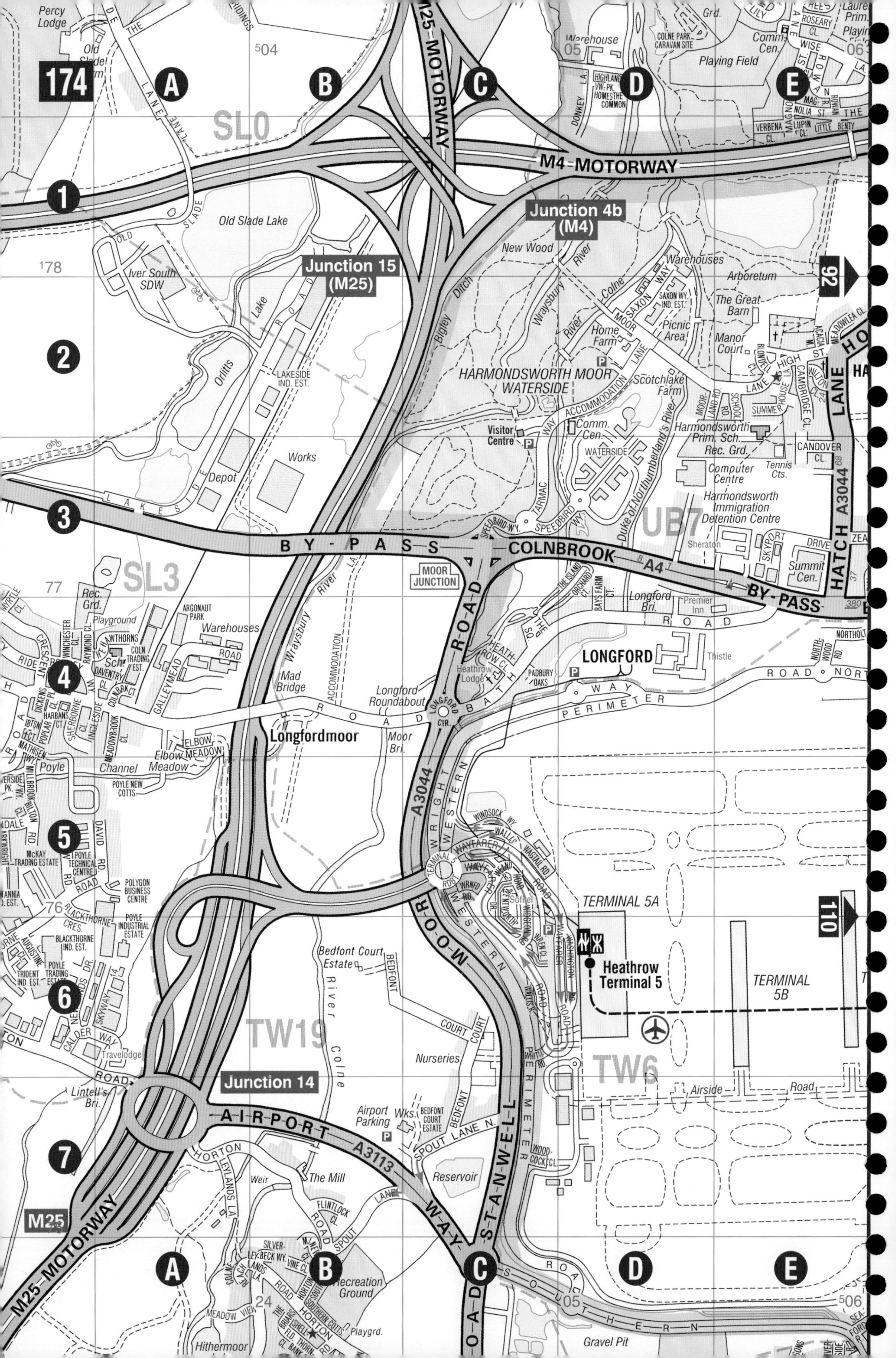
174
92
110
M4-MOTORWAY
M25-MOTORWAY
Junction 4b (M4)
Junction 15 (M25)
Junction 14
SL0
SL3
UB7
TW19
TW6
Old Slade Lake
Iver South SDW
Orlitts
LAKESIDE IND. EST.
Works
Depot
HARMONDSWORTH MOOR WATERSIDE
Visitor Centre
New Wood
Warehouses
Arboretum
The Great Barn
Manor Court
Picnic Area
Home Farm
Scotchlake Farm
Harmondsworth Prim. Sch.
Rec. Grd.
Computer Centre
Harmondsworth Immigration Detention Centre
Tennis Cts.
Summit Cen.
COLNBROOK BY-PASS
A4
MOOR JUNCTION
LONGFORD
Longford Bri.
Premier Inn
Thistle
Heathrow Lodge
Longford Roundabout
Longfordmoor
Mad Bridge
Moor Bri.
Poyle
Channel
Elbow Meadow
POYLE NEW COTTS.
McKAY TRADING ESTATE
POYLE TECHNICAL CENTRE
POLYGON BUSINESS CENTRE
POYLE INDUSTRIAL ESTATE
BLACKTHORNE IND. EST.
POYLE TRADING ESTATE
TRIDENT IND. EST.
Travelodge
Lintell's Bri.
ARGONAUT PARK
COLN TRADING EST.
Rec. Grd.
Playground
A3044
WRIGHT WAY
WESTERN PERIMETER ROAD
STANWELL MOOR ROAD
TERMINAL 5A
Heathrow Terminal 5
TERMINAL 5B
Sofitel
Sheraton
Bedfont Court Estate
Nurseries
Reservoir
Airport Parking
AIRPORT WAY
A3113
HORTON ROAD
The Mill
Weir
Recreation Ground
Playgrd.
Hithermoor
Gravel Pit
SOUTHERN PERIMETER ROAD
Airside Road
River Colne
Wraysbury River
Duke of Northumberland's River
Bigley Ditch
Colne Park Caravan Site
Playing Field
Comm. Cen.
Percy Lodge
A B C D E
1 2 3 4 5 6 7

Congestion Charging Zone

The daily charge applies Monday to Friday, 7.00am to 6.00pm, 12.00pm to 6.00pm Saturday and Sunday, and bank holidays. No charge between Christmas Day and New Year's Day bank holiday (inclusive).

Payment of the daily charge allows you to drive in, around, leave and re-enter the charging zone as many times as required on the same day.

Payment can be made in advance, or on the day of travel, or by midnight of the third day after travel. Payment after the day of travel will incur an increased cost.

You can pay using Auto Pay (registration required), online, or using the official TfL App.

Some vehicle types and classes are exempt, and some classes of road users can apply for a discount scheme.

Penalty charge for non-payment of the daily charge by midnight on the third day after the day of travel.

Ultra Low Emission Zone (ULEZ), and Low Emission Zone (LEZ)

The Ultra Low Emissions Zone (ULEZ) is a specified area covering all London boroughs, which also operates 24 hours a day, every day of the year, except Christmas Day (ULEZ only).

A daily charge applies to a range of vehicles which fail to meet specific emissions standards.
A small number of vehicles are exempt.

The Low Emission Zone (LEZ) covers lorries, vans or specialist heavy vehicles (all over 3.5 tonnes), and buses, minibuses and coaches (all over 5 tonnes).

You can pay using Auto Pay (registration required), online, or using the official TfL App.

This information is correct at the time of publication.

Visit www.tfl.gov.uk/modes/driving for more information on London's driving zones.

INDEX

Including Streets, Places & Areas, Industrial Estates, Selected Flats & Walkways, Junction Names & Service Areas, Stations and Selected Places of Interest.

HOW TO USE THIS INDEX

1. Each street name is followed by its Postcode District (or, if outside the London Postcodes, by its Locality Abbreviation(s)) and then by its map reference; e.g. **Abbey Av.** HA0: Wemb.....2E **78** is in the HA0 Postcode District and the Wembley locality and is to be found in square 2E on page **78**. The page number is shown in bold type.
2. A strict alphabetical order is followed in which Av., Rd., St., etc. (though abbreviated) are read in full and as part of the street name; e.g. **Alder M.** appears after **Aldermary Rd.** but before **Aldermoor Rd.**
3. Streets and a selection of flats and walkways that cannot be shown on the mapping, appear in the index with the thoroughfare to which they are connected shown in brackets; e.g. **Abady Ho.** SW1: .....3D **18** (4H **101**) *(off Page St.)*
4. Addresses that are in more than one part are referred to as not continuous.
5. Places and areas are shown in the index in BLUE TYPE and the map reference is to the actual map square in which the town centre or area is located and not to the place name shown on the map; e.g. ABBEY WOOD.....4C 108
6. An example of a selected place of interest is **Barnet Mus. 4B 20**
7. Junction names and Service Areas are shown in the index in **BOLD CAPITAL TYPE**; e.g. **ANGEL EDMONTON.....5B 34**
8. Map references for entries that appear on the large scale pages **4–19** are shown first, with small scale map references shown in brackets; e.g. **Abbey St.** SE1.....7H **15** (3E **102**)

GENERAL ABBREVIATIONS

All. : Alley
Apts. : Apartments
App. : Approach
Arc. : Arcade
Av. : Avenue
Bk. : Back
Blvd. : Boulevard
Bri. : Bridge
B'way. : Broadway
Bldg. : Building
Bldgs. : Buildings
Bus. : Business
C'way. : Causeway
Cen. : Centre
Chu. : Church
Chyd. : Churchyard
Circ. : Circle
Cir. : Circus
Cl. : Close
Coll. : College
Comn. : Common
Cnr. : Corner
Cott. : Cottage
Cotts. : Cottages
Ct. : Court
Ctyd. : Courtyard
Cres. : Crescent
Cft. : Croft
Dpt. : Depot
Dr. : Drive
E. : East
Emb. : Embankment
Ent. : Enterprise
Est. : Estate
Fld. : Field
Flds. : Fields
Gdn. : Garden
Gdns. : Gardens
Gth. : Garth
Ga. : Gate
Gt. : Great
Grn. : Green
Gro. : Grove
Hgts. : Heights
Ho. : House
Ho's. : Houses
Ind. : Industrial
Info. : Information
Intl. : International
Junc. : Junction
La. : Lane
Lit. : Little
Lwr. : Lower
Mnr. : Manor
Mans. : Mansions
Mkt. : Market
Mdw. : Meadow
Mdws. : Meadows
M. : Mews
Mt. : Mount
Mus. : Museum
Nth. : North
No. : Number
Pal. : Palace
Pde. : Parade
Pk. : Park
Pas. : Passage
Pav. : Pavilion
Pl. : Place
Pct. : Precinct
Prom. : Promenade
Quad. : Quadrant
Ri. : Rise
Rd. : Road
Rdbt. : Roundabout
Shop. : Shopping
Sth. : South
Sq. : Square
Sta. : Station
St. : Street
Ter. : Terrace
Twr. : Tower
Trad. : Trading
Up. : Upper
Va. : Vale
Vw. : View
Vs. : Villas
Vis. : Visitors
Wlk. : Walk
W. : West
Yd. : Yard

LOCALITY ABBREVIATIONS

Addington: BR4,CR0 ..... Addtn
Arkley: EN5 ..... Ark
Ashford: TW15 ..... Ashf
Barking: IG11,IG3,RM8-9 ..... Bark
Barnet: EH5,EN4-EN5 ..... Barn
Beckenham: BR3 ..... Beck
Beddington: CR0,SM6 ..... Bedd
Bedfont: TW14 ..... Bedf
Belvedere: DA7,DA17-18 ..... Belv
Bexley: DA1,DA5,DA15 ..... Bexl
Bexleyheath: DA5-7 ..... Bex
Brentford: TW7-8 ..... Bford
Brimsdown: EN3 ..... Brim
Dromley: DR1-2 ..... Broml
Buckhurst Hill: IG8-9 ..... Buck H
Bushey: WD23 ..... Bush
Bushy Heath: WD23 ..... B Hea
Carshalton: CR4,SM4-5 ..... Cars
Chadwell Heath: RM6-7 ..... Chad H
Cheam: SM2-3 ..... Cheam
Chelsfield: BR6 ..... Chels
Chertsey: KT16 ..... Chert
Chessington: KT9 ..... Chess
Chigwell: IG6-7 ..... Chig
Chislehurst: BR7 ..... Chst
Claygate: KT10 ..... Clay
Cockfosters: EN4-5 ..... Cockf
Collier Row: RM5-7 ..... Col R
Colnbrook: SL3 ..... Coln
Cowley: UB8 ..... Cowl
Cranford: TW4-6,UB3 ..... Cran
Crayford: DA1 ..... Cray
Croydon: CR0 ..... C'don
Dagenham: IG11,RM6,RM8-10 ..... Dag
Dartford: DA1,DA5 ..... Dart
Downe: BR6 ..... Downe
East Barnet: EN4 ..... E Barn
East Molesey: KT1,KT8,TW12 ..... E Mos
Eastcote: HA4-5,HA8 ..... Edg
Elstree: WD6 ..... E'tree
Enfield: EN1-2 ..... Enf
Enfield Highway: EN3 ..... Enf H
Enfield Lock: EN3 ..... Enf L
Enfield Wash: EN3 ..... Enf W
Epsom: KT19 ..... Eps
Erith: DA7-8,DA17-18 ..... Erith
Esher: KT10 ..... Esh
Ewell: KT17,KT19 ..... Ewe
Farnborough: BR5-6 ..... Farnb
Feltham: TW13-14 ..... Felt
Greenford: UB6 ..... G'frd
Hadley Wood: EN4 ..... Had W
Ham: TW10 ..... Ham
Hampton: TW12 ..... Hamp
Hampton Hill: TW12 ..... Hamp H
Hampton Wick: KT1,TW11 ..... Hamp W
Hanworth: TW13 ..... Hanw
Harefield: UB9 ..... Hare
Harlington: UB3,UB7 ..... Harl
Harmondsworth: UB7 ..... Harm
Harrow Weald: HA3 ..... Hrw W
Harrow: HA1-3 ..... Harr
Hatch End: HA5 ..... Hat E
Hayes: BR2,BR4,UB3-4 ..... Hayes
Heston: TW5 ..... Hest
Hextable: BR8 ..... Hext
Hillingdon: UB4,UB8,UB10 ..... Hil
Hinchley Wood: KT10 ..... Hin W
Hounslow: TW3-4,TW7,TW14 ..... Houn
Ickenham: UB10 ..... Ick
Ilford: IG1-6,IG8,IG10,RM6 ..... Ilf
Isleworth: TW1,TW3,TW5,TW7 ..... Isle
Kenley: CR8 ..... Kenley
Kenton: HA3,HA7,HA9, ... Kenton
Keston: BR2 ..... Kes
Kew: TW9 ..... Kew
Kingston upon Thames: KT1-2 ..... King T
London Heathrow Airport: TW6 ..... H'row A
Longford: TW6,UB7 ..... Lford
Loughton: IG9-10 ..... Lough
Mawney: RM7 ..... Mawney
Mitcham: CR0,CR4 ..... Mitc
Morden: SM4 ..... Mord
New Addington: CR0 ..... New Ad
New Barnet: EN5 ..... New Bar
New Malden: KT3 ..... N Mald
Northolt: UB4-5 ..... N'olt
Northwood: HA6 ..... Nwood
Orpington: BR5-6 ..... Orp
Petts Wood: BR5-6 ..... Pet W
Pinner: HA5-6 ..... Pinn
Ponders End: EN3 ..... Pond E
Poyle: SL3 ..... Poyle
Pratts Bottom: BR6 ..... Prat B
Purley: CR8 ..... Purl
Rainham: RM9,RM13 ..... Rain
Richings Park: SL0,SL3 ..... Rich P
Richmond: TW9,TW10 ..... Rich
Romford: RM1,RM5-7 ..... Rom
Ruislip: HA4 ..... Ruis
Rush Green: RM1,RM7,RM10 ..... Rush G
Sanderstead: CR2 ..... Sande
Selsdon: CR0,CR2 ..... Sels
Shepperton: TW17 ..... Shep
Sidcup: DA14-15,SE9,UB7 ..... Sip
South Croydon: CR2 ..... S Croy
Southall: UB1-2 ..... S'hall
St Mary Cray: BR5-6 ..... St M Cry
St Pauls Cray: BR5 ..... St P
Staines: TW18 ..... Staines
Stanmore: HA3,HA7 ..... Stan
Stanwell Moor: TW19 ..... Stanw M
Stanwell: TW6,TW19 ..... Stanw
Stockley Park: UB11 ..... Stock P
Sunbury: TW16 ..... Sun
Surbiton: KT1,KT5-6,KT10 ..... Surb
Sutton: SM1 ..... Sutt
Sutton: SM2 ..... Sutt
Sutton: SM3 ..... Sutt
Swanley: BR8 ..... Swan
Swanley: DA14 ..... Swan
Teddington: TW1,TW11 ..... Tedd
Thames Ditton: KT7 ..... T Ditt
Thornton Heath: CR7 ..... Thor H
Twickenham: TW1-2,TW7,TW13 ..... Twick
Uxbridge: UB8,UB10 ..... Uxb
Waddon: CR0 ..... Wadd
Wallington: SM5-6 ..... W'gton
Walton-on-Thames: KT12 ..... Walt T
Wealdstone: HA3 ..... W'stone
Welling: DA16 ..... Well
Wembley: HA0,HA9-10 ..... Wemb
Wennington: RM13 ..... Wenn
West Drayton: UB7 ..... W Dray
West Molesey: KT8 ..... W Mole
West Wickham: BR4 ..... W W'ck
Whitton: TW2 ..... Whitt
Wilmington: DA2 ..... Wilm
Woodford Green: IG4,IG8-9 ..... Wfd G
Worcester Park: KT4,SM3 ..... Wor Pk
Yeading: UB4 ..... Yead
Yiewsley: UB7 ..... Yiew

2 Temple Place ..... 2J 13 (7A 84) *(off Temple Pl.)*
2 Willow Rd. 4C 64
7 July Memorial 5H 11 (1E 100)
10 Brock St. NW1 ..... 3A **6** (4G **83**) *(off Triton Sq.)*
18 Stafford Terrace ..... 3J 99 *(off Stafford Ter.)*
60 St Martins La. WC2 ..... 2E **12** (7J **83**) *(off St Martin's La.)*
198 Contemporary Arts & Learning ..... 6B 120 *(off Railton Rd.)*
201 Bishopsgate EC2 ..... 5H **9** (5E **84**) *(off Bishopsgate)*

A

Aaron Hill Rd. E6 ..... 5E **88**
Abady Ho. SW1 ..... 3D **18** (4H **101**) *(off Page St.)*
Abberley M. SW4 ..... 3F **119**
Abbess Cl. E6 ..... 5C **88**
Abbess Cl. SW2 ..... 1B **138**
Abbeville M. SW4 ..... 4H **119**
Abbeville Rd. N8 ..... 5H **47**
Abbeville Rd. SW4 ..... 6G **119**
Abbey Av. HA0: Wemb 2E **78**
Abbey Cl. E5 ..... 4G **67**
Abbey Cl. HA5: Pinn 3K **39**
Abbey Cl. SW8 ..... 1H **119**
Abbey Cl. UB3: Hayes 1K **93**
Abbey Cl. UB5: N'olt 3D **76**
Abbey Ct. NW8 ..... 2A **82** *(off Abbey Rd.)*
Abbey Ct. SE17 ..... 5C **102** *(off Macleod St.)*
Abbey Ct. SE6 ..... 6C **122**
Abbey Ct. TW12: Hamp 7E **130**
Abbey Cres. DA17: Belv 4G **109**
Abbeydale Rd. HA0: Wemb 1F **79**
Abbey Dr. DA2: Wilm 2K **145**
Abbey Dr. SW17 ..... 5E **136**
Abbey Est. NW8 ..... 1K **81**
Abbeyfield Cl. CR4: Mitc 2C **154**
Abbeyfield Est. SE16 ..... 4J **103**
Abbeyfield Rd. SE16 ..... 4J **103** (not continuous)
Abbeyfields Cl. NW10 ..... 3G **79**
Abbey Gdns. BR7: Chst 1E **160**
Abbey Gdns. NW8 ..... 2A **82**
Abbey Gdns. SE16 ..... 4G **103**
Abbey Gdns. SW1 ..... 1E **18** (3J **101**) *(off Great College St.)*
Abbey Gdns. TW15: Ashf 5D **128**
Abbey Gdns. W6 ..... 6G **99**
Abbey Gro. SE2 ..... 4B **108**
Abbeyhill Rd. DA15: Sidc 2C **144**
Abbey Ho. E15 ..... 2G **87** *(off Baker's Row)*
Abbey Ho. NW8 ..... 1A **4** (3A **82**) *(off Garden Rd.)*
Abbey Ind. Est. CR4: Mitc 5D **154**
Abbey Ind. Est. HA0: Wemb 1F **79**
Abbey La. BR3: Beck 7C **140**
Abbey La. E15 ..... 2E **86** (not continuous)
Abbey La. Commercial Est. E15 ..... 2G **87**
Abbey Leisure Cen. Barking 1G 89
Abbey Life Ct. E16 ..... 5K **87**
Abbey Lodge NW8 ..... 2D **4** (3C **82**) *(off Park Rd.)*
Abbey Mansion M. SE24 ..... 5B **120**
Abbey M. E17 ..... 5C **50**
Abbey M. SW2 ..... 7J **119**
Abbey M. TW7: Isle 1B **114**
Abbey Mt. DA17: Belv 5F **109**
Abbey Orchard St. SW1 ..... 1C **18** (3H **101**)
Abbey Orchard St. Est. SW1 ..... 1D **18** (3H **101**) (not continuous)
Abbey Pde. SW19 ..... 7A **136** *(off Merton High St.)*
Abbey Pde. W5 ..... 3F **79**
Abbey Pk. BR3: Beck 7C **140**
Abbey Rd. CR0: C'don 3B **168**
Abbey Rd. DA17: Belv 4D **108**
Abbey Rd. DA7: Bex 4E **126**
Abbey Rd. E15 ..... 2F **87**
Abbey Rd. EN1: Enf 5K **23**
Abbey Rd. IG11: Bark 1F **89**
Abbey Rd. IG2: Ilf 5H **53**
Abbey Rd. NW10 ..... 1H **79**
Abbey Rd. NW6 ..... 7K **63**
Abbey Rd. NW8 ..... 1A **82**
Abbey Rd. SE2 ..... 4D **108**
Abbey Rd. SW19 ..... 7A **136**
Abbey Rd. Apts. NW8 ..... 1A **4** (2A **82**) *(off Abbey Rd.)*
Abbey Sports Cen. Barking 1G 89
Abbey St. E13 ..... 4J **87**
Abbey St. SE1 ..... 7H **15** (3E **102**)
Abbey St. SE16 ..... 7K **15** (3G **103**)
Abbey Ter. SE2 ..... 4C **108**
Abbey Trad. Est. SE26 ..... 5B **140**
Abbey Vw. NW7 ..... 3G **29**
Abbey Wlk. KT8: W Mole 3F **149**
Abbey Wharf Ind. Est. IG11: Bark 3H **89**
ABBEY WOOD 4C 108
Abbey Wood Cvn. Club Site SE2 ..... 4C **108**
Abbey Wood Rd. SE2 ..... 4B **108**
Abbot Cl. HA4: Ruis 3B **58**
Abbot Ct. SW8 ..... 7J **101** *(off Hartington Rd.)*
Abbot Ho. E14 ..... 7D **86** *(off Smythe St.)*
Abbotsbury NW1 ..... 7H **65** *(off Camley St.)*
Abbotsbury Cl. E15 ..... 2E **86**
Abbotsbury Cl. W14 ..... 2G **99**
Abbotsbury Gdns. HA5: Eastc 7A **40**
Abbotsbury Ho. W14 ..... 2G **99**
Abbotsbury M. SE15 ..... 3J **121**
Abbotsbury Rd. BR2: Hayes 2H **171**
Abbotsbury Rd. SM4: Mord 5K **153**
Abbotsbury Rd. W14 ..... 2G **99**
Abbots Cl. BR5: Farnb 1G **173**
Abbots Ct. W8 ..... 2K **99** *(off Thackeray St.)*
Abbots Dr. HA2: Harr 2E **58**
Abbotsford Av. N15 ..... 4C **48**
Abbotsford Gdns. IG8: Wfd G 7D **36**
Abbotsford Rd. IG3: Ilf 2A **72**
Abbots Gdns. N2 ..... 4B **46**
Abbots Grn. CR0: Addtn 6K **169**
Abbotshade Rd. SE16 ..... 1K **103**
Abbotshall Av. N14 ..... 3B **32**
Abbotshall Rd. SE6 ..... 1F **141**
Abbot's Ho. W14 ..... 3H **99** *(off St Mary Abbot's Ter.)*
Abbots La. SE1 ..... 5H **15** (1E **102**)
Abbotsleigh Cl. SM2: Sutt 7K **165**
Abbotsleigh Ms. DA15: Sidc 2K **143**
Abbotsleigh Rd. SW16 ..... 4G **137**
Abbots Mnr. SW1 ..... 4J **17** (4F **101**) (not continuous)
Abbots Pk. SW2 ..... 1A **138**
Abbot's Pl. NW6 ..... 1K **81**
Abbot's Rd. E6 ..... 1B **88**
Abbots Rd. HA8: Edg 7D **28**
Abbots Ter. N8 ..... 6J **47**
Abbotstone Rd. SW15 ..... 3E **116**
Abbot St. E8 ..... 6F **67**
Abbots Wlk. W8 ..... 3K **99**
Abbots Way BR3: Beck 5A **158**
Abbotswell Rd. SE4 ..... 5B **122**
Abbotswood Cl. DA17: Belv 3E **108**
Abbotswood Gdns. IG5: Ilf 3D **52**
Abbotswood Rd. SE22 ..... 4E **120**
Abbotswood Rd. SW16 ..... 3H **137**
Abbotswood Way UB3: Hayes 1K **93**
Abbott Av. SW20 ..... 1F **153**
Abbott Cl. TW12: Hamp 6C **130**
Abbott Cl. UB5: N'olt 6D **58**
Abbott Rd. E14 ..... 5E **86** (not continuous)
Abbott's Cl. UB8: Cowl 5A **74**
Abbotts Cl. N1 ..... 6C **66**
Abbotts Cl. RM7: Mawney 3H **55**
Abbotts Cl. SE28 ..... 7C **90**
Abbotts Cres. E4 ..... 4A **36**
Abbotts Cres. EN2: Enf 2G **23**
Abbotts Dr. HA0: Wemb 2B **60**
Abbotts Ho. SW1 ..... 6C **18** (5H **101**) *(off Aylesford St.)*
Abbotts Mead TW10: Ham 4D **132**
Abbottsmede Cl. TW1: Twick 2K **131**
Abbotts Pk. Rd. E10 ..... 7E **50**
Abbotts Rd. CR4: Mitc 4G **155**
Abbotts Rd. EN5: New Bar 4E **20**
Abbotts Rd. SM3: Cheam 4G **165**
Abbotts Rd. UB1: S'hall 1C **94**
Abbott's Wlk. DA7: Bex 7D **108**
Abbott's Wharf E14 ..... 6C **86** *(off Stainsby Pl.)*
Abbotts Wharf Moorings E14 ..... 6C **86** *(off Stainsby Rd.)*
Abchurch La. EC4 ..... 2F **15** (7D **84**) (not continuous)
Abchurch Yd. EC4 ..... 2E **14** (7D **84**)
Abdale Rd. W12 ..... 1D **98**
Abelard Pl. W5 ..... 3D **96**
Abel Ho. SE11 ..... 7K **19** (6A **102**) *(off Kennington Rd.)*
Abenglen Ind. Est. UB3: Hayes 2F **93**
Aberavon Rd. E3 ..... 3A **86**
Abercairn Rd. SW16 ..... 7G **137**
Aberconway Rd. SM4: Mord 4K **153**
Abercorn Cl. NW7 ..... 7B **30**
Abercorn Cl. NW8 ..... 3A **82**
Abercorn Commercial Cen. HA0: Wemb 1D **78**
Abercorn Cotts. NW8 ..... 3A **82** *(off Abercorn Pl.)*
Abercorn Cres. HA2: Harr 1F **59**
Abercorn Dell WD23: B Hea 2B **26**
Abercorn Gdns. HA3: Kenton 7D **42**
Abercorn Gdns. RM6: Chad H 6B **54**
Abercorn Gro. HA4: Ruis 4F **39**
Abercorn Mans. NW8 ..... 2A **82** *(off Abercorn Pl.)*
Abercorn M. TW10: Rich 5F **115**
Abercorn Pl. NW8 ..... 3A **82**
Abercorn Rd. HA7: Stan 7H **27**
Abercorn Rd. NW7 ..... 7B **30**
Abercorn Wlk. NW8 ..... 3A **82**
Abercorn Way SE1 ..... 5G **103**
Abercrombie Dr. EN1: Enf 1B **24**
Abercrombie Rd. E20 ..... 5D **68**

Abercrombie St. – Air Call Bus. Cen.

Abercrombie St. SW11 2C 118
Aberdale Ct. SE16 2K 103
(off Garter Way)
Aberdare Cl. BR4: W W'ck 2E 170
Aberdare Gdns. NW6 7K 63
Aberdare Gdns. NW7 7A 30
Aberdare Rd. EN3: Pond E 4D 24
Aberdeen Cotts. HA7: Stan 7H 27
Aberdeen Ct. W9 4A 4 (4B 82)
(off Maida Vale)
Aberdeen La. N5 5C 66
Aberdeen Mans. WC1 3E 6 (4J 83)
(off Kenton St.)
Aberdeen Pde. N18 5C 34
(off Aberdeen Rd.)
Aberdeen Pk. N5 5C 66
Aberdeen Pl. NW8 4A 4 (4B 82)
Aberdeen Rd. CR0: C'don 4C 168
Aberdeen Rd. HA3: W'stone 2K 41
Aberdeen Rd. N18 5B 34
(not continuous)
Aberdeen Rd. N5 4C 66
Aberdeen Rd. NW10 5B 62
Aberdeen Sq. E14 1B 104
Aberdeen Ter. SE3 2F 123
Aberdeen Wharf E1 1H 103
(off Wapping High St.)
Aberdour Rd. IG3: Ilf 3B 72
Aberdour St. SE1 4E 102
Aberfeldy Ho. SE5 7B 102
(not continuous)
Aberfeldy St. E14 5E 86
(not continuous)
Aberford Gdns. SE18 1C 124
Aberfoyle Rd. SW16 6H 137
(not continuous)
Abergeldie Rd. SE12 6K 123
Abernethy Ho. EC1 6C 8 (5C 84)
(off Bartholomew Cl.)
Abernethy Rd. SE13 4G 123
Abersham Rd. E8 5F 67
Abery St. SE18 4J 107
Abid M. SE15 2G 121
Ability Pl. E14 2D 104
Ability Plaza E8 7F 67
(off Arbutus St.)
Ability Towers EC1 1C 8 (3C 84)
(off Macclesfield Rd.)
Abingdon W14 4H 99
(off Kensington Village)
Abingdon Cl. KT4: Wor Pk 3D 164
Abingdon Cl. NW1 6H 65
Abingdon Cl. SE1 4F 103
(off Bushwood Dr.)
Abingdon Cl. SW19 6A 136
Abingdon Cl. UB10: Hil 1B 74
Abingdon Ct. W8 3J 99
(off Abingdon Vs.)
Abingdon Gdns. W8 3J 99
Abingdon Ho. BR1: Broml 7K 141
Abingdon Ho. E2 3J 9 (4F 85)
(off Boundary St.)
Abingdon Lodge BR2: Broml 2H 159
(off Beckenham La.)
Abingdon Lodge W8 3J 99
Abingdon Mans. W8 3J 99
(off Pater St.)
Abingdon Rd. N3 2A 46
Abingdon Rd. SW16 2J 155
Abingdon Rd. W8 3J 99
Abingdon St. SW1 1E 18 (3J 101)
Abingdon Vs. W8 3J 99
Abinger Cl. BR1: Broml 3C 160
Abinger Cl. CR0: New Ad 6E 170
Abinger Cl. IG11: Bark 4A 72
Abinger Cl. SM6: W'gton 5J 167
Abinger Ct. SM6: W'gton 5J 167
(off Abinger Cl.)
Abinger Ct. W5 7C 78
Abinger Gdns. TW7: Isle 3J 113
Abinger Gro. SE8 6B 104
Abinger Ho. SE1 7E 14 (2D 102)
(off Gt. Dover St.)
Abinger M. W9 4J 81
Abinger Rd. W4 3A 98
Ablett St. SE16 5J 103
Abney Gdns. N16 2F 67
Abney Pk. Cemetery Local Nature Reserve 2E 66
Abney Pk. Ter. N16 2F 67
(off Cazenove Rd.)
Aborfield NW5 5G 65
Aboyne Dr. SW20 2C 152
Aboyne Rd. NW10 3A 62
Aboyne Rd. SW17 3B 136
Abraham Fisher Ho. E12 5E 70
Abyssinia Cl. SW11 4C 118
Abyssinia Ct. N8 5K 47
Abyssinia Rd. SW11 4C 118
Acacia Av. HA4: Ruis 1J 57
Acacia Av. HA9: Wemb 5E 60
Acacia Av. N17 7J 33
Acacia Av. TW17: Shep 5C 146
Acacia Av. TW8: Bford 7B 96
Acacia Av. UB3: Hayes 6H 75
Acacia Av. UB7: Yiew 7B 74
Acacia Bus. Cen. E11 3G 69
Acacia Cl. BR5: Pet W 5H 161
Acacia Cl. HA7: Stan 6D 26
Acacia Cl. SE20 2G 157
Acacia Cl. SE8 4A 104
Acacia Ct. HA1: Harr 5F 41
Acacia Dr. SM3: Sutt 1H 165
Acacia Gdns. BR4: W W'ck 2E 170
Acacia Gdns. NW8 2B 82
Acacia Gro. KT3: N Mald 3K 151
Acacia Gro. SE21 2D 138
Acacia Ho. N22 1A 48
(off Douglas Rd.)
Acacia M. UB7: Harm 2E 174
Acacia Pl. NW8 2B 82
Acacia Rd. BR3: Beck 3B 158
Acacia Rd. CR4: Mitc 3E 154
Acacia Rd. E11 2G 69
Acacia Rd. E17 6A 50
Acacia Rd. EN2: Enf 1J 23
Acacia Rd. N22 1A 48
Acacia Rd. NW8 2B 82
Acacia Rd. SW16 1J 155
Acacia Rd. TW12: Hamp 6E 130
Acacia Rd. W3 7J 79
Acacias, The EN4: E Barn 5G 21
Acacia Wlk. SW10 7A 100
(off Tadema Rd.)
Acacia Way DA15: Sidc 1K 143
Academia Way N17 6K 33
Academy Middlesex County Cricket Club, The 2K 45
Academy, The SW8 7G 19 (6K 101)
Academy Apts. E8 5H 67
(off Dalston La.)
Academy Bldgs. N1 1G 9 (3E 84)
(off Fanshaw St.)
Academy Ct. DA5: Bexl 2K 145
(off Beaconsfield Rd.)
Academy Ct. E2 3J 85
(off Kirkwall Pl.)
Academy Ct. NW6 1J 81
Academy Ct. RM8: Dag 4A 72
Academy Gdns. CR0: C'don 1F 169
Academy Gdns. UB5: N'olt 2B 76
Academy Gdns. W8 2J 99
Academy Ho. E3 5D 86
(off Violet Rd.)
Academy Pl. SE18 1D 124
Academy Pl. TW7: Isle 1J 113
Academy Rd. SE18 1D 124
Academy Way E17 1C 50
Academy Way RM8: Dag 4A 72
Acanthus Dr. SE1 5G 103
Acanthus Rd. SW11 3E 118
Accolade Av. UB1: S'hall 2C 94
Accommodation La. UB7: Harm 2D 174
Accommodation La. UB7: Lford 4B 174
Accommodation Rd. E4 3A 36
(off Ashwood Rd.)
Accommodation Rd. EN4: E Barn 1K 31
Accommodation Rd. KT17: Ewe 5C 164
Accommodation Rd. NW11 1H 63
AC Ct. KT7: T Ditt 6A 150
Ace Pde. KT9: Chess 3E 162
Acer Av. UB4: Yead 5C 76
Acer Cl. IG8: Wfd G 6H 37
Acer Ct. EN3: Enf H 3F 25
(off Enstone Rd.)
Acer Rd. E8 7F 67
Acers BR7: Chst 7C 142
Aces Ct. TW3: Houn 2G 113
Ace Way SW11 7D 18 (6H 101)
Acfold Rd. SW6 1K 117
Achill Cl. NW9 3B 44
Achilles Cl. SE1 5G 103
Achilles Ho. E2 2H 85
(off Old Bethnal Grn. Rd.)
Achilles Rd. NW6 5J 63
Achilles Statue 5H 11 (1E 100)
Achilles St. SE14 7A 104
Achilles Way W1 5H 11 (1E 100)
Acklam Rd. W10 5G 81
(not continuous)
Acklington Dr. NW9 1A 44
Ackmar Rd. SW6 1J 117
Ackroyd Dr. E3 5B 86
Ackroyd Rd. SE23 7K 121
Acland Cl. SE18 7H 107
Acland Cres. SE5 3D 120
Acland Ho. SW9 1K 119
Acland Rd. NW2 6D 62
Acle Cl. IG6: Ilf 1F 53
Acme Studios E14 Gillender St. 5E 86
Acme Studios E14 Leven Rd. 5E 86
(off Leven Rd.)
Acock Gro. UB5: N'olt 4F 59
Acol Ct. NW6 7J 63
Acol Cres. HA4: Ruis 5K 57
Acol Rd. NW6 7J 63
Aconbury Rd. RM9: Dag 1B 90
Acorn Cl. BR7: Chst 5G 143
Acorn Cl. E4 5J 35
Acorn Cl. EN2: Enf 1G 23
Acorn Cl. HA7: Stan 7G 27
Acorn Cl. TW12: Hamp 6F 131
Acorn Ct. E3 2C 86
(off Morville St.)
Acorn Ct. E6 7C 70
Acorn Ct. IG2: Ilf 6J 53
Acorn Gdns. SE19 1F 157
Acorn Gdns. W3 5K 79
Acorn Gro. HA4: Ruis 4H 57
Acorn Gro. UB3: Harl 7H 93
Acorn Pde. SE15 7H 103
Acorn Production Cen. N7 7J 65
Acorn Wlk. SE16 1A 104
Acorn Way BR3: Beck 5E 158
Acorn Way BR6: Farnb 4F 173
Acorn Way SE23 3K 139
Acqua Ho. TW9: Kew 7H 97
Acre Dr. SE22 4G 121
Acrefield Ho. NW4 4F 45
(off Belle Vue Est.)
Acre La. SM5: Cars 4E 166
Acre La. SM6: W'gton 4F 167
Acre La. SW2 4J 119
Acre Path UB5: N'olt 6C 58
(off Arnold Rd.)
Acre Rd. KT2: King T 1E 150
Acre Rd. RM10: Dag 7H 73
Acre Rd. SW19 6B 136
Acre Way HA6: Nwood 1H 39
Acris St. SW18 5A 118
Acropolis Ho. KT1: King T 3F 151
(off Winery La.)
Actaeon M. SE18 6F 107
ACTON 1J 97
Acton Apts. N1 1D 84
(off Branch Pl.)
Acton Central Ind. Est. W3 1H 97
Acton Cl. N9 2B 34
ACTON GREEN 3J 97
Acton Hill M. W3 1H 97
Acton Ho. E8 1F 85
(off Lee St.)
Acton Ho. W3 6J 79
Acton La. NW10 3J 79
Acton La. W3 2J 97
Acton La. W4 4J 97
(not continuous)
Acton M. E8 1F 85
Acton Pk. Est. W3 2K 97
Acton St. WC1 2G 7 (3K 83)
Acton Swimming Baths 1J 97
(off Salisbury St.)
Acton Va. Ind. Pk. W3 2B 98
Acton Wlk. N20 1F 31
Acuba Rd. SW18 2K 135
Acworth Cl. N9 7D 24
Acworth Ho. SE18 6F 107
(off Barnfield Rd.)
Ada Cl. N11 3J 31
Ada Ct. N1 1C 84
(off Packington St.)
Ada Ct. W9 2A 4 (3A 82)
Ada Gdns. E14 6F 87
Ada Gdns. E15 1H 87
Adagio Point SE8 6D 104
(off Copperas St.)
Ada Ho. E2 1G 85
(off Ada Pl.)
Adair Cl. SE25 3H 157
Adair Ho. SW3 7D 16 (6C 100)
(off Oakley St.)
Adair Rd. W10 4G 81
Adair Twr. W10 4G 81
(off Appleford Rd.)
Ada Kennedy Ct. SE10 7E 104
(off Greenwich Sth. St.)
Ada Lewis Ho. HA9: Wemb 4F 61
Adam & Eve Ct. W1 7B 6 (6G 83)
(off Oxford St.)
Adam & Eve M. W8 3J 99
Ada Maria Ct. E1 6H 85
(off James Voller Way)
Adam Cl. NW7 6A 30
Adam Cl. SE6 4B 140
Adam Ct. SE11 4K 19 (4B 102)
(off Opal St.)
Adam Ct. SW7 4A 100
(off Gloucester Rd.)
Adamfields NW3 7B 64
(off Adamson Rd.)
Adam Rd. E4 6G 35
Adams Bri. Bus. Cen. HA9: Wemb 5H 61
Adams Cl. KT5: Surb 6F 151
Adams Cl. N3 7D 30
Adams Cl. NW9 2H 61
Adams Cl. RM5: Col R 1J 55
Adams Ct. E17 6A 50
Adams Ct. EC2 7G 9 (6E 84)
Adams Gdns. Est. SE16 2J 103
Adams Ho. E14 6F 87
(off Aberfeldy St.)
Adams M. N22 7E 32
Adams M. SW17 2D 136
Adamson Ct. N2 3C 46
Adamson Rd. E16 6J 87
Adamson Rd. NW3 7B 64
Adamson Way BR3: Beck 5E 158
Adams Pl. E14 1D 104
(off The Nth. Colonnade)
Adams Pl. N7 5K 65
Adams Quarter TW8: Bford 7C 96
Adamsrill Cl. EN1: Enf 6J 23
Adamsrill Rd. SE26 4K 139
Adams Rd. BR3: Beck 5A 158
Adams Rd. N17 2D 48
Adam's Row W1 3H 11 (7E 82)
Adams Sq. DA6: Bex 3E 126
Adams Ter. E3 3C 86
(off Rainhill Way)
Adam St. WC2 3F 13 (7J 83)
Adams Wlk. KT1: King T 2E 150
Adams Way CR0: C'don 6F 157
Adams Way SE25 5H 157
Adam Wlk. SW6 7E 98
Adana SE13 2E 122
Ada Pl. E2 1G 85
Adare Wlk. SW16 3K 137
Ada Rd. HA0: Wemb 3D 60
Ada Rd. SE5 7E 102
Adastral Ho. WC1 5G 7 (5K 83)
(off Harpur St.)
Adastra Way SM6: W'gton 6J 167
Ada St. E8 1H 85
Adcock Wlk. BR6: Orp 4K 173
Adderley Gdns. SE9 4E 142
Adderley Gro. SW11 5E 118
Adderley Rd. HA3: W'stone 1K 41
Adderley St. E14 6E 86
Addey Ho. SE8 7B 104
ADDINGTON 5C 170
Addington Cl. UB2: S'hall 1H 95
Addington Ct. SW14 3K 115
Addington Dr. N12 6G 31
Addington Golf Course, The 4B 170
Addington Gro. SE26 4A 140
Addington Hill Viewpoint 5J 169
Addington Ho. SW9 2K 119
(off Stockwell Rd.)
Addington Lofts SE5 7C 102
(off Bethwin Rd.)
Addington Palace Golf Course 6A 170
Addington Rd. BR4: W W'ck 4E 170
Addington Rd. CR0: C'don 1A 168
Addington Rd. E16 4G 87
Addington Rd. E3 3C 86
Addington Rd. N4 6A 48
Addington Sq. SE5 6D 102
(not continuous)
Addington St. SE1 7H 13 (2K 101)
Addington Village Rd. CR0: Addtn 6B 170
(not continuous)
Addis Cl. EN3: Enf H 1E 24
ADDISCOMBE 1G 169
Addiscombe Av. CR0: C'don 1G 169
Addiscombe Cl. HA3: Kenton 5C 42
Addiscombe Ct. Rd. CR0: C'don 1E 168
Addiscombe Gro. CR0: C'don 2E 168
Addiscombe Rd. CR0: C'don 2D 168
(not continuous)
Addis Ho. E1 5J 85
(off Lindley St.)
Addisland Ct. W14 2G 99
(off Holland Vs. Rd.)
Addison Av. N14 6A 22
Addison Av. TW3: Houn 1G 113
Addison Av. W11 1G 99
Addison Bri. Pl. W14 4H 99
Addison Cl. BR5: Pet W 6G 161
Addison Cl. HA6: Nwood 1J 39
Addison Ct. NW6 1J 81
(off Brondesbury Rd.)
Addison Cres. W14 3G 99
(not continuous)
Addison Dr. SE12 5K 123
Addison Gdns. KT5: Surb 4F 151
Addison Gdns. W14 3F 99
Addison Gro. W4 3A 98
Addison Ho. NW8 1A 4 (3B 82)
(off Grove End Rd.)
Addison Pk. Mans. W14 3F 99
(off Richmond Way)
Addison Pl. SE25 4G 157
Addison Pl. UB1: S'hall 7E 76
Addison Pl. W11 1G 99
Addison Rd. BR2: Broml 5A 160
Addison Rd. E11 6J 51
Addison Rd. E17 5D 50
Addison Rd. EN3: Enf H 1D 24
Addison Rd. IG6: Ilf 1G 53
Addison Rd. SE25 4G 157
Addison Rd. TW11: Tedd 6B 132
Addison Rd. W14 2G 99
Addisons Cl. CR0: C'don 2B 170
Addison Ter. W4 4J 97
(off Chiswick Rd.)
Addison Way HA6: Nwood 1H 39
Addison Way NW11 4H 45
Addison Way UB3: Hayes 6J 75
Addle Hill EC4 1B 14 (6B 84)
Addlestone Ho. W10 5E 80
(off Sutton Way)
Addle St. EC2 7D 8 (6C 84)
Addy Ho. SE16 4J 103
Adecroft Way KT8: W Mole 3G 149
Adela Av. KT3: N Mald 5D 152
Adela Ho. W6 5E 98
(off Queen Caroline St.)
Adelaide Av. SE4 4B 122
Adelaide Cl. EN1: Enf 1K 23
Adelaide Cl. HA7: Stan 4F 27
Adelaide Cl. SW9 4A 120
Adelaide Community Gdn. 7D 64
(off Adelaide Rd.)
Adelaide Ct. BR3: Beck 7C 140
Adelaide Ct. E9 5A 68
(off Kenworthy Rd.)
Adelaide Ct. NW8 1A 4 (2A 82)
(off Abbey Rd.)
Adelaide Ct. W7 2K 95
Adelaide Gdns. RM6: Chad H 5E 54
Adelaide Gro. W12 1C 98
Adelaide Ho. E15 2H 87
Adelaide Ho. E17 2B 50
Adelaide Ho. SE5 2E 120
Adelaide Ho. W11 6H 81
(off Portobello Rd.)
Adelaide Rd. BR7: Chst 5F 143
Adelaide Rd. E10 3D 68
Adelaide Rd. IG1: Ilf 2F 71
Adelaide Rd. KT6: Surb 5E 150
Adelaide Rd. NW3 7B 64
Adelaide Rd. SW18 5J 117
Adelaide Rd. TW11: Tedd 6K 131
Adelaide Rd. TW15: Ashf 5A 128
Adelaide Rd. TW5: Hest 1C 112
Adelaide Rd. TW9: Rich 4F 115
Adelaide Rd. UB2: S'hall 4C 94
Adelaide Rd. W13 1A 96
Adelaide St. WC2 3E 12 (7J 83)
(not continuous)
Adelaide Ter. TW8: Bford 5D 96
Adela St. W10 4G 81
Adelina Gro. E1 5J 85
Adelina M. SW12 1H 137
Adelina Yd. E1 5J 85
(off Adelina Gro.)
Adeline Pl. WC1 6D 6 (5H 83)
Adeliza Cl. IG11: Bark 7G 71
Adelphi Ct. E8 7F 67
(off Celandine Dr.)
Adelphi Ct. SE16 2K 103
(off Garter Way)
Adelphi Ct. W4 6K 97
Adelphi Cres. UB4: Hayes 3G 75
Adelphi Ter. WC2 3F 13 (7J 83)
Adelphi Theatre 3F 13 (7J 83)
(off Strand)
Adelphi Way UB4: Hayes 3H 75
Adeney Cl. W6 6F 99
Aden Gro. N16 4D 66
Adenmore Rd. SE6 7C 122
Aden Rd. EN3: Brim 4F 25
Aden Rd. IG1: Ilf 7G 53
Aden Ter. N16 4D 66
Adeyfield Ho. EC1 2F 9 (3D 84)
(off Cranwood St.)
Adie Rd. W6 3E 98
Adine Rd. E13 4K 87
Adit Rd. DA8: Erith 6J 109
Adler Ind. Est. UB3: Hayes 2F 93
Adler St. E1 6G 85
Adley St. E5 5A 68
Adlington Cl. N18 5J 33
Admaston Rd. SE18 7G 107
Admiral Ct. IG11: Bark 2B 90
Admiral Ct. SE5 1E 120
(off Havil St.)
Admiral Ct. SM5: Cars 1C 166
Admiral Ct. SW10 1A 118
(off Admiral Sq.)
Admiral Ct. W1 6G 5 (5E 82)
(off Blandford St.)
Admiral Ho. SW1 3B 18 (4G 101)
(off Willow Pl.)
Admiral Ho. TW11: Tedd 4A 132
Admiral Hyson Ind. Est. SE16 5H 103
Admiral M. SW19 7A 136
Admiral M. W10 4F 81
Admiral Pl. N8 4B 48
Admiral Pl. SE16 1A 104
Admirals Cl. E18 4K 51
Admirals Ct. E6 6F 89
(off Trader Rd.)
Admirals Ct. SE1 5J 15 (1F 103)
(off Horselydown La.)
Admiral Seymour Rd. SE9 4D 124
Admiral's Ga. SE10 1D 122
Admiral Sq. SW10 1A 118
Admiral's Twr. SE10 6D 104
(off Dowells St.)
Admiral St. SE8 2C 122
Admirals Wlk. NW3 3A 64
Admirals Way E14 2C 104
Admiralty & Commercial Court 7J 7 (6A 84)
Admiralty Arch London 4D 12 (1H 101)
Admiralty Av. E16 2K 105
Admiralty Bldg. KT2: King T 1D 150
(off Down Hall Rd.)
Admiralty Cl. SE8 7C 104
Admiralty Cl. UB7: W Dray 2A 92
Admiralty Ho. E1 7G 85
(off Vaughan Way)
Admiralty Rd. TW11: Tedd 6K 131
Admiralty Way TW11: Tedd 6K 131
Admiral Wlk. W9 5J 81
Adolf St. SE6 4D 140
Adolphus Rd. N4 2B 66
Adolphus St. SE8 7B 104
Adomar Rd. RM8: Dag 3E 72
Adpar St. W2 5A 4 (5B 82)
Adrian Av. NW2 1D 62
Adrian Boult Ho. E2 3H 85
(off Mansford St.)
Adrian Cl. EN5: Barn 6A 20
Adrian Ho. E15 7F 69
(off Jupp Rd.)
Adrian Ho. N1 1K 83
(off Barnsbury Est.)
Adrian Ho. SW8 7J 101
(off Wyvil Rd.)
Adrian M. SW10 6K 99
Adriatic Apts. E16 7J 87
(off Western Gateway)
Adriatic Bldg. E14 7A 86
(off Horseferry Rd.)
Adriatic Ho. E1 4K 85
(off Ernest St.)
Adrienne Av. UB1: S'hall 4D 76
Adrienne Bus. Cen. UB1: S'hall 3D 76
Adron Ho. SE16 4J 103
(off Millender Wlk.)
Adstock Ho. N1 7B 66
(off The Sutton Est.)
Advance Rd. SE27 4C 138
Adventure Kingdom 2K 159
(off Stockwell Cl.)
Adventurers Ct. E14 7F 87
(off Newport Av.)
Advent Way N18 5D 34
Adys Lawn NW2 6D 62
Ady's Rd. SE15 3F 121
Aegean Apts. E16 7J 87
(off Western Gateway)
Aegon Ho. E14 3D 104
(off Lanark Sq.)
Aerodrome Rd. NW9 2B 44
Aerodrome Way TW5: Hest 6A 94
Aeroville NW9 2A 44
AFC Wimbledon 3G 151
AFC Wimbledon Plough La. Stadium 4A 136
Affleck St. N1 1H 7 (2K 83)
Afghan Rd. SW11 2C 118
Afsil Ho. EC1 6K 7 (5A 84)
(off Viaduct Bldgs.)
Aftab Ter. E1 4H 85
(off Tent St.)
Agamemnon Rd. NW6 4H 63
Agar Cl. KT6: Surb 2F 163
Agar Gro. NW1 7G 65
Agar Gro. Est. NW1 7H 65
Agar Ho. KT1: King T 3E 150
(off Denmark Rd.)
Agar Pl. NW1 7G 65
Agar St. WC2 3E 12 (7J 83)
Agate Cl. E16 6B 88
Agate Cl. NW10 3G 79
Agate Rd. W6 3E 98
Agatha Cl. E1 1H 103
Agaton Path SE9 2G 143
Agaton Rd. SE9 2G 143
Agave Rd. NW2 4E 62
Agdon St. EC1 3A 8 (4B 84)
Ager Av. RM8: Dag 1D 72
Agincourt Rd. NW3 4D 64
Agnes Av. IG1: Ilf 4E 70
Agnes Cl. E6 7E 88
Agnesfield Cl. N12 6H 31
Agnes Gdns. RM8: Dag 4D 72
Agnes George Wlk. E16 1B 106
Agnes Ho. W11 7F 81
(off St Ann's Rd.)
Agnes Rd. W3 1B 98
Agnes St. E14 6B 86
Agnew Rd. SE23 7K 121
Agricola Ct. E3 1B 86
(off Parnell Rd.)
Agricola Pl. EN1: Enf 5A 24
Ahoy Cen, The 5C 104
(off Stretton Mans.)
Aidan Cl. RM8: Dag 4E 72
Aigburth Mans. SW9 7A 102
(off Mowll St.)
Ailantus Ct. HA8: Edg 5A 28
Aileen Wlk. E15 7H 69
Ailsa Av. TW1: Twick 5A 114
Ailsa Ho. E16 7E 88
(off University Way)
Ailsa Rd. TW1: Twick 5B 114
Ailsa St. E14 5E 86
Ainger M. NW3 7D 64
(off Ainger Rd.)
Ainger Rd. NW3 7D 64
Ainsdale NW1 1A 6 (2G 83)
(off Harrington St.)
Ainsdale Cl. BR6: Orp 1H 173
Ainsdale Cres. HA5: Pinn 3E 40
Ainsdale Dr. SE1 5G 103
Ainsdale Rd. W5 4D 78
Ainsley Av. RM7: Rom 6H 55
Ainsley Cl. N9 1K 33
Ainsley St. E2 3H 85
Ainslie Ct. HA0: Wemb 2E 78
Ainslie Wlk. SW12 7F 119
Ainslie Wood Cres. E4 5J 35
Ainslie Wood Gdns. E4 4J 35
Ainslie Wood Local Nature Reserve 5J 35
Ainslie Wood Rd. E4 5H 35
Ainsty Est. SE16 2K 103
Ainsty St. SE16 2J 103
Ainsworth Cl. N20 2G 31
Ainsworth Cl. NW2 3C 62
Ainsworth Cl. SE15 2E 120
Ainsworth Ct. NW10 3D 80
(off Plough Cl.)
Ainsworth Ho. NW8 1K 81
(off Ainsworth Way)
Ainsworth Ho. W10 3G 81
(off Kilburn La.)
Ainsworth Rd. CR0: C'don 1B 168
Ainsworth Rd. E9 7J 67
Ainsworth Way NW8 1A 82
Aintree Av. E6 1C 88
Aintree Cl. UB8: Hil 6D 74
Aintree Cres. IG6: Ilf 2G 53
Aintree Est. SW6 7G 99
Aintree Rd. UB6: G'frd 2B 78
Aintree St. SW6 7G 99
Airbourne Ho. SM6: W'gton 4G 167
(off Maldon Rd.)
Air Call Bus. Cen. NW9 3K 43

A–Z London 177

Airco Cl. NW9 3K 43
Aird Ho. SE1 3C 102
(off Rockingham St.)
Aird Point E16 7G 89
(off Lock Side Way)
Airdrie Cl. N1 7K 65
Airdrie Cl. UB4: Yead 5C 76
Airedale Av. W4 4B 98
Airedale Av. Sth. W4 5B 98
Airedale Rd. SW12 7D 118
Airedale Rd. W5 3C 96
Airlie Gdns. IG1: Ilf 1F 71
Airlie Gdns. W8 1J 99
Airlinks Golf Course 5A 94
Air Links Ind. Est. TW13: Hanw 3C 130
Airlinks Ind. Est. TW5: Cran 5A 94
Air Pk. Way TW13: Felt 2K 129
Airport Bowl 1G 111
Airport Ga. Bus. Cen. UB7: Sip 7B 92
Airport Way TW19: Stanw M 7A 174
Air Sea M. TW2: Twick 2H 131
Air St. W1 3B 12 (7G 83)
Airthrie Rd. IG3: Ilf 2B 72
Aisgill Av. W14 5H 99
(not continuous)
Aisher Rd. SE28 7C 90
Aislibie Rd. SE12 4G 123
Aiten Pl. W6 4C 98
Aithan Ho. E14 6B 86
(off Copenhagen Pl.)
Aitken Cl. CR4: Mitc 7D 154
Aitken Cl. E8 1G 85
Aitken Cl. HA4: Eastc 6J 39
Aitken Rd. SE6 2D 140
Aitman Dr. TW8: Bford 5G 97
Aitons Ho. TW8: Bford 5E 96
Aits Vw. KT8: W Mole 3F 149
Ajax Av. NW9 3A 44
Ajax Ho. E2 2H 85
(off Old Bethnal Grn. Rd.)
Ajax Rd. NW6 4H 63
Akabusi Cl. CR0: C'don 6G 157
Akbar Ho. E14 4D 104
(off Cahir St.)
Akehurst St. SW15 6C 116
Akenside Rd. NW3 5B 64
Akerman Rd. KT6: Surb 6C 150
Akerman Rd. SW9 2B 120
Akintaro Ho. SE8 6B 104
(off Alverton St.)
Alabama St. SE18 7H 107
Alacia Ct. W3 3J 97
(off Bassington Rd.)
Alacross Rd. W5 2C 96
Alamaro Lodge SE10 3H 105
(off Teal St.)
Alameda Pl. E3 2D 86
Alana Hgts. E4 7J 25
Alan Coren Cl. NW2 4E 62
Alandale Dr. HA5: Pinn 1K 39
Aland Ct. SE16 3A 104
Alander M. E17 4E 50
Alan Dr. EN5: Barn 6B 20
Alan Gdns. RM7: Rush G 7G 55
Alan Hocken Way E15 2G 87
Alan Preece Ct. NW6 7F 63
Alan Rd. SW19 5G 135
Alanthus Cl. SE12 6J 123
Alaska Apts. E16 7J 87
(off Western Gateway)
Alaska Bldg. SE13 1D 122
(off Deal's Gateway)
Alaska Bldgs. SE1 3F 103
Alaska St. SE1 5J 13 (1A 102)
Alastor Ho. E14 3E 104
(off Strattondale Ho.)
Alba Cl. UB4: Yead 4B 76
Albacore Cres. SE13 6D 122
Albacore Way UB3: Hayes 7H 75
Alba Gdns. NW11 6G 45
Albain Cres. TW15: Ashf 2A 128
Alba M. SW18 2J 135
Alban Highwalk EC2 6D 8 (5C 84)
(off Wood St.)
Albany N12 6E 30
Albany W1 3A 12 (7G 83)
Albany, The IG8: Wfd G 4C 36
Albany, The 7C 104
Albany Cl. DA5: Bexl 7C 126
Albany Cl. N15 4B 48
Albany Cl. SW14 4H 115
Albany Cl. UB10: Ick 5C 56
Albany Ct. E4 Chelwood Cl. 6H 25
Albany Ct. E4 Westward Rd. 5G 35
Albany Ct. E1 6G 85
(off Plumber's Row)
Albany Ct. E10 7C 50
Albany Ct. HA8: Edg 1K 43
Albany Ct. NW10 3D 80
(off Trenmar Gdns.)
Albany Ct. NW8 1A 4 (2B 82)
(off Abbey Rd.)
Albany Ct. TW15: Ashf 7E 128
Albany Ctyd. W1 3A 12 (7G 83)
Albany Cres. HA8: Edg 7B 28
Albany Mans. SW11 7C 100
Albany M. BR1: Broml 6J 141
Albany M. KT2: King T 6D 132
Albany M. N1 7A 66
Albany M. SE5 6C 102
Albany M. SM1: Sutt 5K 165
Albany Pde. TW8: Bford 6E 96
Albany Pk. Av. EN3: Enf W 1D 24
Albany Pk. Rd. KT2: King T 6D 132
Albany Pas. TW10: Rich 5E 114
Albany Pl. TW8: Bford 6D 96
Albany Reach KT7: T Ditt 5K 149
Albany Rd. BR7: Chst 5F 143
Albany Rd. DA17: Belv 6F 109
Albany Rd. DA5: Bexl 7C 126
Albany Rd. E10 7C 50
Albany Rd. E12 4B 70
Albany Rd. E17 6A 50
Albany Rd. KT3: N Mald 4K 151
Albany Rd. N18 5D 34
Albany Rd. N4 6A 48
Albany Rd. RM6: Chad H 6F 55
Albany Rd. SE5 6C 102
Albany Rd. SW19 5K 135
Albany Rd. TW10: Rich 5F 115
Albany Rd. TW8: Bford 6D 96
Albany Rd. W13 7B 78
Albany St. NW1 2F 83
Albany Ter. NW1 4K 5 (4F 83)
(off Marylebone Rd.)
Albany Ter. TW10: Rich 5F 115
(off Albany Pas.)
Albany Vw. IG9: Buck H 1D 36
Albany Works E3 1A 86
(off Gunmakers La.)
Alba Pl. W11 6H 81
Albatross NW9 2B 44
Albatross Cl. E6 5D 88
Albatross La. IG10: Ilf 1D 70
Albatross St. SE18 7J 107
Albatross Way SE16 2K 103
Albemarle SW19 2F 135
Albemarle App. IG2: Ilf 6F 53
Albemarle Av. TW2: Whitt 1D 130
Albemarle Ct. N17 3H 49
(off Perkyn Sq.)
Albemarle Gdns. IG2: Ilf 6F 53
Albemarle Gdns. KT3: N Mald 4K 151
Albemarle Ho. SE8 4B 104
(off Foreshore)
Albemarle Pk. BR3: Beck 1D 158
Albemarle Pk. HA7: Stan 5H 27
Albemarle Rd. BR3: Beck 1D 158
Albemarle Rd. EN4: E Barn 7H 21
Albemarle St. W1 3K 11 (7F 83)
Albemarle Wlk. SW9 3A 120
Albemarle Way EC1 4A 8 (4B 84)
Alberon Gdns. NW11 4H 45
Alberta Av. SM1: Sutt 4G 165
Alberta Est. SE17 5B 102
(off Alberta St.)
Alberta Ho. UB4: Yead 3K 75
(off Ayles Rd.)
Alberta Rd. DA8: Erith 1J 127
Alberta Rd. EN1: Enf 6A 24
Alberta St. SE17 5B 102
Albert Av. E4 4H 35
Albert Av. SW8 7K 101
Albert Barnes Ho. SE1 3C 102
(off New Kent Rd.)
Albert Basin 7F 89
Albert Basin Way E16 7G 89
Albert Bigg Point E15 2E 86
(off Godfrey St.)
ALBERT BRI. 6C 100
Albert Bri. Rd. SW11 7C 100
Albert Carr Gdns. SW16 5J 137
Albert Cl. E9 1H 85
Albert Cl. N22 1H 47
Albert Cotts. E1 5G 85
(off Deal St.)
Albert Ct. E7 4J 69
Albert Ct. SW7 1A 16 (3B 100)
Albert Ct. Ga. SW1 7E 10 (2D 100)
(off Knightsbridge)
Albert Cres. E4 4H 35
Albert Dane Cen. UB2: S'hall 3C 94
Albert Dr. SW19 2G 135
Albert Emb. SE1 Kennington La.
6F 19 (5J 101)
Albert Emb. SE1 Lambeth Pal. Rd.
2G 19 (3K 101)
Albert Gdns. E1 6K 85
Albert Ga. SW1 6F 11 (2D 100)
Albert Gray Ho. SW10 7B 100
(off Worlds End Est.)
Albert Gro. SW20 1F 153
Albert Hall Mans. SW7 7A 10 (2B 100)
Albert Ho. E18 3K 51
(off Albert Rd.)
Albert Ho. SE28 3G 107
Albertine Gr. BR4: W W'ck 4F 171
Albertine Gro. BR4: W W'ck 4F 171
Albert Mans. CR0: C'don 1D 168
(off Lansdowne Rd.)
Albert Mans. SW11 1D 118
(off Albert Bri. Rd.)
Albert Memorial London 7A 10 (2B 100)
Albert M. E14 7A 86
(off Northey St.)
Albert M. N4 1K 65
Albert M. SE4 4A 122
Albert M. W8 3A 100
Albert Pal. Mans. SW11 1F 119
(off Lurline Gdns.)
Albert Pl. N17 3F 49
Albert Pl. N3 1J 45
Albert Pl. W8 3K 99
Albert Rd. BR2: Broml 5B 160
Albert Rd. CR4: Mitc 3D 154
Albert Rd. DA17: Belv 5F 109
Albert Rd. DA5: Bexl 6G 127
Albert Rd. E10 2E 68
Albert Rd. E16 1C 106
Albert Rd. E17 5C 50
Albert Rd. E18 3K 51
Albert Rd. EN4: E Barn 4F 21
Albert Rd. HA2: Harr 3G 41
Albert Rd. IG1: Ilf 3F 71
Albert Rd. IG9: Buck H 2G 37
Albert Rd. KT1: King T 2F 151
Albert Rd. KT3: N Mald 4B 152
Albert Rd. N15 6E 48
Albert Rd. N22 1G 47
Albert Rd. N4 1K 65
Albert Rd. NW4 4F 45
Albert Rd. NW6 2H 81
Albert Rd. NW7 5G 29
Albert Rd. RM8: Dag 1G 73
Albert Rd. SE20 6K 139
Albert Rd. SE25 4G 157
Albert Rd. SE9 3C 142
Albert Rd. SM1: Sutt 5B 166
Albert Rd. TW1: Twick 1K 131
Albert Rd. TW10: Rich 5E 114
Albert Rd. TW11: Tedd 6K 131
Albert Rd. TW12: Hamp H 5G 131
Albert Rd. TW15: Ashf 5B 128
Albert Rd. TW3: Houn 4E 112
Albert Rd. UB2: S'hall 3B 94
Albert Rd. UB3: Hayes 3G 93
Albert Rd. UB7: Yiew 1A 92
Albert Rd. W5 4B 78
Albert Rd. Est. DA17: Belv 5F 109
Alberts Ct. NW1 3D 4 (4C 82)
(off Palgrave Gdns.)
Albert Sleet Ct. N9 3C 34
(off Colthurst Dr.)
Albert Sq. E15 5G 69
Albert Sq. SW8 7K 101
Albert Starr Ho. SE8 4K 103
(off Haddonfield)
Albert St. N12 5F 31
Albert St. NW1 1F 83
Albert Studios SW11 1D 118
Albert Ter. IG9: Buck H 2H 37
Albert Ter. NW1 1E 82
Albert Ter. NW10 1J 79
Albert Ter. W5 4B 78
Albert Ter. W6 5C 98
(off Beavor La.)
Albert Ter. M. NW1 1E 82
Albert Victoria Ho. N22 1A 48
Albert Wlk. E16 2E 106
Albert Way SE15 7H 103
Albert Westcott Ho. SE17 5B 102
Albert Whicher Ho. E17 4E 50
Albert Yd. SE19 6F 139
Albery Ct. E8 7F 67
(off Middleton Rd.)
Albion Av. N10 1E 46
Albion Av. SW8 2H 119
Albion Bldgs. N1 1F 7 (2J 83)
(off Albion Yd.)
Albion Cl. RM7: Rom 6K 55
Albion Cl. W2 2D 10 (7C 82)
Albion Ct. SE10 4G 105
(off Azof St.)
Albion Ct. SM2: Sutt 7B 166
Albion Ct. W6 4D 98
(off Albion Pl.)
Albion Dr. E8 7F 67
Albion Est. SE16 2K 103
Albion Gdns. W6 4D 98
Albion Ga. W2 2D 10 (7C 82)
(off Albion St.)
Albion Gro. N16 4E 66
Albion Ho. E16 1F 107
(off Church St.)
Albion Ho. SE8 7C 104
(off Watsons St.)
Albion M. N1 1A 84
Albion M. NW6 7H 63
Albion M. W2 2D 10 (7C 82)
Albion M. W6 4D 98
Albion Pde. N16 4D 66
Albion Pl. EC1 5A 8 (5B 84)
Albion Pl. EC2 6F 9 (5D 84)
Albion Pl. W6 4D 98
Albion Riverside Bldg. SW11 7C 100
Albion Rd. DA6: Bex 4F 127
Albion Rd. E17 3E 50
Albion Rd. KT2: King T 1J 151
Albion Rd. N16 4D 66
Albion Rd. N17 2G 49
Albion Rd. SM2: Sutt 6B 166
Albion Rd. TW2: Twick 1J 131
Albion Rd. TW3: Houn 4E 112
Albion Rd. UB3: Hayes 6G 75
Albion Sq. E8 7F 67
(not continuous)
Albion St. CR0: C'don 1B 168
Albion St. SE16 2J 103
Albion St. W2 1D 10 (6C 82)
Albion Ter. E4 4J 25
Albion Ter. E8 7F 67
Albion Vs. Rd. SE26 3J 139
Albion Wlk. N1 1F 7 (2J 83)
(off York Way)
Albion Way E6 1B 88
Albion Way EC1 6C 8 (5C 84)
Albion Way HA9: Wemb 3G 61
Albion Way SE13 4E 122
Albion Yd. E1 5H 85
Albion Yd. N1 2J 83
Albon Ho. SW18 6K 117
(off Neville Gill Cl.)
Albrighton Rd. SE22 3E 120
Albuhera Cl. EN2: Enf 1F 23
Albuhera M. NW7 5A 30
Albury Av. DA7: Bex 2E 126
Albury Av. TW7: Isle 7K 95
Albury Cl. TW12: Hamp 6F 131
Albury Ct. CR0: C'don 4C 168
(off Tanfield Rd.)
Albury Ct. CR4: Mitc 2B 154
Albury Ct. SE8 6C 104
(off Albury St.)
Albury Ct. SM1: Sutt 4A 166
Albury Ct. UB5: N'olt 3A 76
(off Canberra Dr.)
Albury Dr. HA5: Pinn 1C 40
Albury Ho. SE1 7B 14 (2B 102)
(off Boyfield St.)
Albury M. E12 2A 70
Albury Rd. KT9: Chess 5E 162
Albury St. SE8 6C 104
Albyfield BR1: Broml 4D 160
Albyn Rd. SE8 1C 122
Alcester Ct. SM6: W'gton 4F 167
Alcester Cres. E5 2H 67
Alcester Rd. SM6: W'gton 4F 167
Alchemy Wy. DA17: Belv 1J 109
Alcock Cl. SM6: W'gton 7H 167
Alcock Rd. TW5: Hest 7B 94
Alconbury DA6: Bex 5H 127
Alconbury Rd. E5 2G 67
Alcorn Cl. SM3: Sutt 2J 165
Alcott Cl. TW14: Felt 1H 129
Alcott Cl. W7 5K 77
Alcuin Ct. HA7: Stan 7H 27
Aldam Pl. N16 2F 67
Aldborough Ct. IG2: Ilf 5K 53
(off Aldborough Rd. Nth.)
Aldborough Hall Equestrian Cen. 3K 53
ALDBOROUGH HATCH 4K 53
Aldborough Rd. RM10: Dag 6J 73
Aldborough Rd. Nth. IG2: Ilf 5K 53
Aldborough Rd. Sth. IG3: Ilf 1J 71
Aldbourne Rd. W12 1B 98
Aldbridge St. SE17 5E 102
Aldburgh M. W1 7H 5 (6E 82)
Aldbury Av. HA9: Wemb 7H 61
Aldbury Ho. SW3 4C 16 (4C 100)
(off Cale St.)
Aldbury M. N9 7J 23
Aldebert Ter. SW8 7J 101
Aldeburgh Cl. E5 2H 67
Aldeburgh Pl. IG8: Wfd G 4D 36
Aldeburgh Pl. SE10 4J 105
(off Aldeburgh St.)
Aldeburgh St. SE10 5J 105
Alden Av. E15 3H 87
Alden Ct. CR0: C'don 3E 168
Aldenham Dr. UB8: Hil 4D 74
Aldenham Ho. NW1 1B 6 (2G 83)
(off Aldenham St.)
Aldenham St. NW1 1B 6 (2G 83)
Alden Ho. E8 1H 85
(off Duncan Rd.)
Aldensley Rd. W6 3D 98
Alderbrook Rd. SW12 6F 119
Alderbury Rd. SW13 6C 98
Alder Cl. DA18: Erith 2F 109
Alder Cl. SE15 6F 103
Alder Ct. E7 5J 69
Alder Ct. N11 6B 32
Alder Gro. NW2 2C 62
Aldergrove Gdns. TW3: Houn 2C 112
Alder Ho. E3 1B 86
(off Hornbeam Sq.)
Alder Ho. NW3 6D 64
Alder Ho. SE15 6F 103
(off Alder Cl.)
Alder Ho. SE4 3C 122
Alder Lodge SW6 1E 116
Alderman Av. IG11: Bark 3A 90
Aldermanbury EC2 7D 8 (6C 84)
Aldermanbury Sq. EC2 6D 8 (5C 84)
Alderman Judge Mall
KT1: King T 2E 150
(off Eden St.)
Aldermans Hill N13 4D 32
Aldermans Ho. E9 5A 68
(off Ward La.)
Aldermans Wlk. EC2 6G 9 (5E 84)
Aldermary Rd. BR1: Broml 1J 159
Alder M. N19 2G 65
Aldermoor Rd. SE6 3B 140
Alderney Av. TW5: Hest 7F 95
Alderney Av. TW5: Isle 7F 95
Alderney Cl. NW9 3C 44
Alderney Ct. SE10 6F 105
(off Trafalgar Rd.)
Alderney Gdns. UB5: N'olt 7D 58
Alderney Ho. EN3: Enf W 1E 24
Alderney Ho. N1 6C 66
(off Arran Wlk.)
Alderney M. SE1 3D 102
Alderney Rd. E1 4K 85
Alderney St. SW1 4K 17 (4F 101)
Alder Rd. DA14: Sidc 3K 143
Alder Rd. SW14 3K 115
Alders, The BR4: W W'ck 1D 170
Alders, The N21 6F 23
Alders, The SW16 4G 137
Alders, The TW13: Hanw 4C 130
Alders, The TW5: Hest 6D 94
Alders Av. IG8: Wfd G 6B 36
ALDERSBROOK 2K 69
Aldersbrook Av. EN1: Enf 2K 23
Aldersbrook Dr. KT2: King T 6F 133
Aldersbrook La. E12 3D 70
Aldersbrook Rd. E11 2K 69
Aldersbrook Rd. E12 2K 69
Alders Cl. E11 2K 69
Alders Cl. HA8: Edg 5D 28
Alders Cl. W5 3D 96
Aldersey Gdns. IG11: Bark 6H 71
Aldersford Cl. SE4 5K 121
Aldersgate Ct. EC1 6C 8 (5C 84)
(off Bartholomew Cl.)
Aldersgate St. EC1 5C 8 (5C 84)
Alders Gro. KT8: E Mos 5H 149
Aldersgrove Av. SE9 3B 142
Aldershot Rd. NW6 1H 81
Aldershot Ter. SE18 7E 106
Aldersmead Av. CR0: C'don 6K 157
Aldersmead Rd. BR3: Beck 7A 140
Alderson Pl. UB2: S'hall 1G 95
Alderson St. W10 4G 81
Alders Rd. HA8: Edg 5D 28
Alderton Cl. NW10 3K 61
Alderton Ct. KT8: W Mole 4D 148
(off Dunstable Rd.)
Alderton Cres. NW4 5D 44
Alderton Rd. CR0: C'don 7F 157
Alderton Rd. SE24 3C 120
Alderton Way NW4 5D 44
Alderville Rd. SW6 2H 117
Alder Wlk. IG1: Ilf 5G 71
Alderwick Ct. N7 6K 65
(off Cornelia St.)
Alderwick Dr. TW3: Houn 3H 113
Alderwood M. EN4: Had W 1F 21
Alderwood Rd. SE9 6H 125
Aldford Ho. W1 4G 11 (1E 100)
(off Park St.)
Aldford St. W1 4G 11 (1E 100)
Aldgate E1 7J 9 (6F 85)
(off Whitechapel High St.)
ALDGATE 1K 15 (6F 85)
(off Aldgate High St.)
Aldgate EC3 1J 15 (6F 85)
Aldgate Av. E1 7J 9 (6F 85)
Aldgate Barrs E1 7K 9 (6F 85)
(off Whitechapel High St.)
Aldgate High St. EC3 1J 15 (6F 85)
Aldgate Pl. E1 7K 9 (6F 85)
Aldgate Sq. EC3 1J 15 (6F 85)
Aldgate Twr. E1 7K 9 (6F 85)
Aldham Ho. SE4 2B 122
(off Malpas Rd.)
Aldine Ct. W12 2E 98
(off Aldine St.)
Aldine Pl. W12 2E 98
Aldine St. W12 2E 98
Aldington Cl. RM8: Dag 1C 72
Aldington Ct. E8 7G 67
(off London Flds. W. Side)
Aldington Rd. SE18 3B 106
Aldis M. SW17 5C 136
Aldis St. SW17 5C 136
Aldred Rd. NW6 5J 63
Aldren Rd. SW17 3A 136
Aldriche Way E4 6K 35
Aldrich Gdns. SM3: Cheam 3H 165
Aldrich Ter. SW18 2A 136
Aldrick Ho. N1 1K 83
(off Barnsbury Est.)
Aldridge Av. HA4: Ruis 2A 58
Aldridge Av. HA7: Stan 1E 42
Aldridge Av. HA8: Edg 3C 28
Aldridge Ct. W11 5H 81
(off Aldridge Rd. Vs.)
Aldridge Ri. KT3: N Mald 7A 152
Aldridge Rd. Vs. W11 5H 81
Aldridge Wlk. N14 7D 22
Aldrington Rd. SW16 5G 137
Aldsworth Cl. W9 4K 81
Aldwick Cl. SE9 3H 143
Aldwick Rd. CR0: Bedd 3K 167
Aldworth Gro. SE13 6E 122
Aldworth Rd. E15 7G 69
Aldwych WC2 1G 13 (6K 83)
Aldwych Av. IG6: Ilf 4G 53
Aldwych Bldgs. WC2 7F 7 (6J 83)
(off Parker M.)
Aldwych Ct. E8 7F 67
(off Middleton Rd.)
Aldwych Theatre 1G 13 (6K 83)
(off Aldwych)
Aldwyn Ho. SW8 7J 101
(off Davidson Gdns.)
Alers Rd. DA6: Bex 5D 126
Alesia Cl. N22 7D 32
Alestan Beck Rd. E16 6B 88
Alexa Ct. SM2: Sutt 6J 165
Alexa Ct. W8 4J 99
Alexander Av. NW10 7D 62
Alexander Cl. BR2: Hayes 1J 171
Alexander Cl. DA15: Sidc 6J 125
Alexander Cl. EN4: E Barn 4G 21
Alexander Cl. TW2: Twick 2J 131
Alexander Cl. UB2: S'hall 1G 95
Alexander Ct. BR3: Beck 1F 159
Alexander Ct. HA7: Stan 3F 43
Alexander Ct. TW16: Sun 6H 129
Alexander Evans M. SE23 2K 139
Alexander Fleming Laboratory Mus.
7B 4 (6B 82)
Aexander Ho. E14 3C 104
(off Tiller Rd.)
Alexander Ho. KT2: King T 1E 150
(off Seven Kings Way)
Alexander Ho. SE15 2H 121
(off Godman Rd.)
Alexander M. SW16 5G 137
Alexander M. W2 6K 81
Alexander Pl. SW7 3C 16 (4C 100)
Alexander Rd. BR7: Chst 6F 143
Alexander Rd. DA7: Bex 2D 126
Alexander Rd. N19 3J 65
Alexander Sq. SW3 3C 16 (4C 100)
Alexander St. W2 6J 81
Alexander Studios SW11 4B 118
(off Haydon Way)
Alexander Ter. SE2 5B 108
Alexandra Av. HA2: Harr 1D 58
Alexandra Av. N22 1H 47
Alexandra Av. SM1: Sutt 3J 165
Alexandra Av. SW11 1E 118
Alexandra Av. UB1: S'hall 7D 76
Alexandra Av. W4 7K 97
Alexandra Cl. HA2: Harr 3E 58
Alexandra Cl. SE8 6B 104
Alexandra Cl. TW15: Ashf 7F 129
Alexandra Cotts. SE14 1B 122
Alexandra Ct. HA9: Wemb 4F 61
Alexandra Ct. N14 5B 22
Alexandra Ct. SE5 6C 102
(off Urlwin St.)
Alexandra Ct. SW7 1A 16 (3A 100)
(off Queen's Ga.)
Alexandra Ct. TW15: Ashf 6F 129
Alexandra Ct. TW3: Houn 2F 113
Alexandra Ct. UB6: G'frd 2F 77
Alexandra Ct. W2 7K 81
(off Moscow Rd.)
Alexandra Ct. W9 4A 82
(off Maida Vale)
Alexandra Cres. BR1: Broml 6H 141
Alexandra Dr. KT5: Surb 7G 151
Alexandra Dr. SE19 5E 138
Alexandra Gdns. N10 4F 47
Alexandra Gdns. SM5: Cars 7E 166
Alexandra Gdns. TW3: Houn 2F 113
Alexandra Gdns. W4 7A 98
Alexandra Gro. N12 5E 30
Alexandra Gro. N4 1B 66
Alexandra Ho. E16 1K 105
(off Wesley Av.)
Alexandra Ho. IG8: Wfd G 7K 37
Alexandra Ho. W6 5E 98
(off Queen Caroline St.)
Alexandra Mans. SW3 7A 16 (6B 100)
(off King's Rd.)
Alexandra Mans. W12 1E 98
(off Stanlake Rd.)
Alexandra M. N2 3D 46
Alexandra M. N4 2B 66
Alexandra M. SW19 6H 135
Alexandra Palace Ice Rink 2H 47
Alexandra Palace Theatre 2H 47
Alexandra Pal. Way N22 4G 47
Alexandra Pal. Way N8 4G 47
Alexandra Pde. HA2: Harr 4F 59
Alexandra Pk. Rd. N10 2F 47
Alexandra Pk. Rd. N22 1G 47
Alexandra Pl. CR0: C'don 1E 168
Alexandra Pl. NW8 1A 82
Alexandra Pl. SE25 5D 156
Alexandra Rd. CR0: C'don 1E 168
Alexandra Rd. CR4: Mitc 7C 136
Alexandra Rd. E10 3E 68
Alexandra Rd. E17 6B 50
Alexandra Rd. E18 3K 51
Alexandra Rd. E6 3E 88
Alexandra Rd. EN3: Pond E 4E 24
Alexandra Rd. KT2: King T 7G 133
Alexandra Rd. KT7: T Ditt 5K 149
Alexandra Rd. N10 7A 32
Alexandra Rd. N15 5D 48
Alexandra Rd. N8 3A 48
Alexandra Rd. N9 7C 24
Alexandra Rd. NW4 4F 45
Alexandra Rd. NW8 1A 82
Alexandra Rd. RM6: Chad H 6E 54
Alexandra Rd. SE26 6K 139
Alexandra Rd. SW14 3K 115
Alexandra Rd. SW19 6H 135
Alexandra Rd. TW1: Twick 6C 114
Alexandra Rd. TW15: Ashf 7F 129
Alexandra Rd. TW3: Houn 2F 113
Alexandra Rd. TW8: Bford 6D 96
Alexandra Rd. TW9: Kew 2F 115
Alexandra Rd. W4 2K 97
Alexandra Rd. Ind. Est.
EN3: Pond E 4E 24
Alexandra Sq. SM4: Mord 5J 153
Alexandra St. E16 5J 87
Alexandra St. SE14 7A 104
Alexandra Ter. E14 5D 104
(off Westferry Rd.)
Alexandra Wlk. SE19 5E 138
Alexandra Wharf E2 1H 85
(off Darwen Pl.)
Alexandra Yd. E9 1K 85
Alexandria Apts. SE17 4E 102
(off Townsend St.)

Alexandria Rd. – Amyand La.

Alexandria Rd. W13 7A 78
Alex Guy Gdns. RM8: Dag 1H 73
Alexia Sq. E14 3D 104
Alexis St. SE16 4G 103
Alfan La. DA2: Wilm 5K 145
Alfearn Rd. E5 4J 67
Alford Ct. N1 1D 8 (2C 84)
(off Shepherdess Wlk.)
Alford Grn. CR0: New Ad 6F 171
Alford Ho. N6 6G 47
Alford Pl. N1 1D 8 (2C 84)
Alford Rd. DA8: Erith 5J 109
Alfoxton Av. N15 4B 48
Alfreda St. SW11 1F 119
Alfred Cl. W4 4K 97
Alfred Ct. SE16 4H 103
(off Bombay St.)
Alfred Dickens Ho. E16 6H 87
(off Hallsville Rd.)
Alfred Finlay Ho. N22 2B 48
Alfred Gdns. UB1: S'hall 7C 76
Alfred Ho. E12 7C 70
(off Tennyson Av.)
Alfred Ho. E9 5A 68
(off Homerton Rd.)
Alfred M. W1 5C 6 (5H 83)
Alfred Nunn Ho. NW10 1B 80
Alfred Pl. WC1 5C 6 (5H 83)
Alfred Prior Ho. E12 4E 70
Alfred Rd. DA17: Belv 5F 109
Alfred Rd. E15 5H 69
Alfred Rd. IG9: Buck H 2G 37
Alfred Rd. KT1: King T 3E 150
Alfred Rd. SE25 5G 157
Alfred Rd. SM1: Sutt 5A 166
Alfred Rd. TW13: Felt 2A 130
Alfred Rd. W2 5J 81
Alfred Rd. W3 1J 97
Alfred Salter Ho. SE1 4F 103
(off Fort Rd.)
Alfred's Gdns. IG11: Bark 2J 89
Alfred St. E3 3B 86
Alfreds Way IG11: Bark 3F 89
Alfreds Way Ind. Est. IG11: Bark 2A 90
Alfred Vs. E17 4E 50
Alfreton Cl. SW19 3F 135
Alfriston KT5: Surb 6F 151
Alfriston Av. CR0: C'don 7J 155
Alfriston Av. HA2: Harr 6E 40
Alfriston Cl. KT5: Surb 5F 151
Alfriston Rd. SW11 5D 118
Algar Cl. HA7: Stan 5E 26
Algar Cl. TW7: Isle 3A 114
Algar Ho. SE1 7A 14 (2B 102)
(off Webber Row)
Algar Rd. TW7: Isle 3A 114
Algarve Rd. SW18 1K 135
Algernon Rd. NW4 6C 44
Algernon Rd. NW6 1J 81
Algernon Rd. SE13 4D 122
Algiers Rd. SE13 4C 122
Alibon Gdns. RM10: Dag 5G 73
Alibon Rd. RM10: Dag 5G 73
Alibon Rd. RM9: Dag 5F 73
Alice Cl. EN5: New Bar 4F 21
(off Station App.)
Alice Gilliatt Ct. W14 6H 99
(off Star Rd.)
Alice La. E3 1B 86
Alice M. TW11: Tedd 5K 131
Alice Owen Technology Cen.
EC1 1A 8 (3B 84)
(off Goswell Rd.)
Alice Shepherd Ho. E14 2E 104
(off Manchester Rd.)
Alice St. SE1 3E 102
(not continuous)
Alice Thompson Cl. SE12 2A 142
Alice Walker Cl. SE24 4B 120
Alice Way TW3: Houn 4F 113
Alicia Av. HA3: Kenton 4B 42
Alicia Cl. HA3: Kenton 4C 42
Alicia Gdns. HA3: Kenton 4B 42
Alicia Ho. DA16: Well 1B 126
Alie St. E1 1K 15 (6F 85)
Alington Cres. NW9 7J 43
Alison Cl. CR0: C'don 1K 169
Alison Cl. E6 6E 88
Alison Cl. HA5: Eastc 6K 39
Alissa Dr. EN5: New Bar 5F 21
Aliwal M. SW11 4C 118
Aliwal Rd. SW11 4C 118
Alkerden Rd. W4 5A 98
Alkham Rd. N16 2F 67
Allan Barclay Cl. N15 6F 49
Allan Cl. KT3: N Mald 5K 151
Allandale Av. N3 3G 45
Allanson Ct. E10 2C 68
(off Leyton Grange Est.)
Allan Way W3 5J 79
Allard Cres. WD23: B Hea 1B 26
Allard Gdns. SW4 5H 119
Allard Ho. NW9 2B 44
(off Boulevard Dr.)
Allardyce St. SW4 4K 119
Allbrook Cl. TW11: Tedd 5J 131
Allcroft Rd. NW5 5E 64
Allder Way CR2: S Croy 7B 168
Allenby Cl. UB6: G'frd 3E 76
Allenby Rd. SE23 3A 140
Allenby Rd. SE28 3G 107
Allenby Rd. UB1: S'hall 3E 76
Allen Cl. CR4: Mitc 1F 155
Allen Cl. TW16: Sun 1K 147
Allen Ct. E17 6C 50
(off Yunus Khan Cl.)
Allendale Av. UB1: S'hall 6E 76
Allendale Cl. SE26 5K 139
Allendale Cl. SE5 2D 120
Allendale Rd. HA0: Wemb 6B 60
Allendale Rd. UB6: G'frd 6B 60
Allen Edwards Dr. SW8 1J 119
Allenford Ho. SW15 6B 116
(off Tunworth Cres.)
Allen Ho. W8 3J 99
(off Allen St.)
Allen Mans. W8 3J 99
(off Allen St.)
Allen Rd. BR3: Beck 2K 157
Allen Rd. CR0: C'don 1A 168
Allen Rd. E3 2B 86
Allen Rd. N16 4E 66
Allen Rd. TW16: Sun 1K 147
Allensbury Pl. NW1 7H 65
Allens Rd. EN3: Pond E 5D 24
Allen St. W8 3J 99
Allenswood SW19 1G 135
Allenswood Rd. SE9 3C 124
Allerford Ct. HA2: Harr 5G 41
Allerford Rd. SE6 3D 140
Allerton Ho. N1 1F 9 (3D 84)
(off Provost St.)
Allerton Rd. N16 2C 66
Allerton St. N1 1E 8 (3D 84)
Allerton Wlk. N7 2K 65
Allestree Rd. SW6 7G 99
Alleyn Cres. SE21 2D 138
Alleyndale Rd. RM8: Dag 2C 72
Alleyn Ho. SE1 3D 102
(off Burbage Cl.)
Alleyn Pk. SE21 2D 138
Alleyn Pk. UB2: S'hall 5E 94
Alleyn Rd. SE21 3D 138
Alley Way UB8: Uxb 7A 56
Allfarthing La. SW18 6K 117
Allgood Cl. SM4: Mord 6F 153
Allgood St. E2 1K 9 (2F 85)
Allhallows La. EC4 3E 14 (7D 84)
All Hallows Rd. N17 1E 48
Allhallows Rd. E6 5C 88
Alliance Cl. HA0: Wemb 4D 60
Alliance Cl. TW4: Houn 5D 112
Alliance Cl. TW15: Ashf 4E 128
Alliance Ct. W3 5H 79
Alliance Rd. E13 5A 88
Alliance Rd. SE18 6A 108
Alliance Rd. W3 4H 79
Allianz Pk. 7K 29
Allied Ct. N1 7E 66
(off Enfield Rd.)
Allied Ind. Est. W3 2A 98
Allied Way W3 2A 98
Allingham Cl. W7 7K 77
Allingham Ct. BR2: Broml 4H 159
Allingham M. N1 2C 84
(off Allingham St.)
Allingham Rd. SW4 6H 119
Allingham St. N1 2C 84
Allington Av. N17 6K 33
Allington Av. TW17: Shep 3G 147
Allington Cl. SW19 5F 135
Allington Cl. UB6: G'frd 7G 59
Allington Ct. CR0: C'don 6J 157
(off Chart Cl.)
Allington Ct. EN3: Pond E 5E 24
Allington Ct. SW8 2G 119
Allington Rd. BR6: Orp 2H 173
Allington Rd. HA2: Harr 5G 41
Allington Rd. NW4 5D 44
Allington Rd. W10 3G 81
Allington St. SW1 2K 17 (3F 101)
Allison Cl. SE10 1E 122
Allison Gro. SE21 1E 138
Allison Rd. N8 5A 48
Allison Rd. W3 6J 79
Alliston Ho. E2 2K 9 (3F 85)
(off Gibraltar Wlk.)
Allitsen Rd. NW8 2C 82
(not continuous)
All Nations Ho. E8 7H 67
(off Martello St.)
Allnutt Way SW4 5H 119
Alloa Rd. IG3: Ilf 2A 72
Alloa Rd. SE8 5K 103
Allom Ho. W11 7G 81
(off Clarendon Rd.)
Allonby Dr. HA4: Ruis 7D 38
Allonby Gdns. HA9: Wemb 1C 60
Allotment Way NW2 3F 63
Alloway Rd. E3 3A 86
Alloy Ho. SE14 6B 104
(off Moulding La.)
Allport Ho. SE5 3D 120
(off Champion Pk.)
Allport M. E1 4J 85
(off Hayfield Pas.)
All Saints Cl. N9 2B 34
All Saints Cl. SW8 1J 119
All Saint's Ct. TW5: Hest 1B 112
(off Springwell Rd.)
All Saints Ct. E1 7J 85
(off Johnson St.)
All Saints Ct. SW11 7F 101
(off Prince of Wales Dr.)
All Saints Dr. SE3 2G 123
(not continuous)
All Saints Ho. W11 5H 81
(off All Saints Rd.)
All Saints M. HA3: Hrw W 6D 26
All Saints Pas. SW18 5J 117
All Saints Rd. SM1: Sutt 3K 165
All Saints Rd. SW19 7A 136
(not continuous)
All Saints Rd. W11 5H 81
All Saints Rd. W3 3J 97
All Saints Russian Orthodox Cathedral
7C 10 (2C 100)
All Saints St. N1 2K 83
All Saints Wlk. SE15 7F 103
Allsop Pl. NW1 4F 5 (4D 82)
All Souls Av. NW10 2D 80
All Souls' Pl. W1 6K 5 (5F 83)
Allum Way N20 1F 31
Alluvium Ct. SE1 7G 15 (3E 102)
(off Long La.)
Allwood Cl. SE26 4K 139
Alma Av. E4 7K 35
Alma Birk Ho. NW6 7G 63
Almack Rd. E5 4J 67
Alma Cl. N10 1F 47
Alma Ct. HA2: Harr 2H 59
Alma Cres. SM1: Sutt 5G 165
Alma Gro. SE1 4F 103
Alma Ho. N9 4B 34
Alma Ho. TW8: Bford 6E 96
Almanza Pl. IG11: Bark 2B 90
Alma Pl. CR7: Thor H 5A 156
Alma Pl. NW10 3D 80
Alma Pl. SE19 7F 139
Alma Rd. DA14: Sidc 3A 144
Alma Rd. EN3: Enf H 5F 25
Alma Rd. EN3: Pond E 5F 25
Alma Rd. KT10: Esh 7J 149
Alma Rd. N10 7A 32
Alma Rd. SM5: Cars 5C 166
Alma Rd. SW18 4A 118
Alma Rd. UB1: S'hall 7C 76
Alma Rd. Ind. Est. EN3: Pond E 4E 24
Alma Row HA3: Hrw W 1H 41
Alma Sq. NW8 2A 82
Alma St. E15 6F 69
Alma St. NW5 6F 65
Alma Ter. E3 1B 86
(off Beale Rd.)
Alma Ter. SW18 7B 118
Alma Ter. W8 3J 99
Almeida St. N1 1B 84
Almeida Theatre 1B 84
(off Almeida St.)
Almeric Rd. SW11 4D 118
Almer Rd. SW20 7C 134
Almington St. N4 1K 65
Almond Av. SM5: Cars 2D 166
Almond Av. UB10: Ick 3D 56
Almond Av. UB7: W Dray 3C 92
Almond Av. W5 3D 96
Almond Cl. BR2: Broml 7E 160
Almond Cl. E17 4A 50
Almond Cl. HA4: Ruis 3H 57
Almond Cl. SE15 2G 121
Almond Cl. TW13: Felt 1J 129
Almond Cl. TW17: Shep 2E 146
Almond Cl. UB3: Hayes 7G 75
Almond Gro. TW8: Bford 7B 96
Almond Ho. E15 3G 87
(off Teasel Way)
Almond Rd. N17 7B 34
Almond Rd. SE16 4H 103
Almonds Av. IG9: Buck H 2D 36
Almond Way BR2: Broml 7E 160
Almond Way CR4: Mitc 5H 155
Almond Way HA2: Harr 2F 41
Almorah Rd. N1 7D 66
Almorah Rd. TW5: Hest 1B 112
Almshouse La. KT9: Chess 7C 162
Alms Ho's., The IG11: Bark 6G 71
Alnmouth Ct. UB1: S'hall 6G 77
(off Fleming Rd.)
Alnwick N17 7C 34
Alnwick Gro. SM4: Mord 4K 153
Alnwick Rd. E16 6A 88
Alnwick Rd. SE12 6K 123
ALPERTON 2E 78
Alperton La. HA0: Wemb 3D 78
Alperton La. UB6: G'frd 3C 78
Alperton St. W10 4H 81
Alphabet Gdns. SM5: Cars 6B 154
Alphabet M. SW9 1A 120
Alphabet Sq. E3 5C 86
Alpha Cl. NW1 3D 4 (4C 82)
Alpha Est. UB3: Hayes 2G 93
Alpha Gro. E14 2C 104
Alpha Ho. NW6 2J 81
Alpha Ho. NW8 4C 4 (4C 82)
(off Ashbridge St.)
Alpha Ho. SW4 4K 119
Alpha Pl. NW6 2J 81
Alpha Pl. SM4: Mord 1F 165
Alpha Pl. SW3 7D 16 (6C 100)
Alpha Rd. CR0: C'don 1E 168
Alpha Rd. E4 3H 35
Alpha Rd. EN3: Pond E 4F 25
Alpha Rd. KT5: Surb 6F 151
Alpha Rd. N18 6B 34
Alpha Rd. SE14 1B 122
Alpha Rd. TW11: Tedd 5H 131
Alpha Rd. UB10: Hil 4D 74
Alpha St. SE15 2G 121
Alphea Cl. SW19 7C 136
Alpine Av. KT5: Surb 2J 163
Alpine Bus. Cen. E6 5E 88
Alpine Cl. CR0: C'don 3E 168
Alpine Cl. KT19: Ewe 5J 163
Alpine Copse BR1: Broml 2E 160
Alpine Gro. E9 7J 67
Alpine Rd. E10 2D 68
Alpine Rd. KT12: Walt T 7J 147
Alpine Rd. NW9 4G 43
Alpine Rd. SE16 5K 103
Alpine Vw. SM5: Cars 5C 166
Alpine Wlk. HA7: Stan 2D 26
Alpine Way E6 5E 88
Alric Av. KT3: N Mald 3A 152
Alric Av. NW10 7K 61
Alroy Rd. N4 7A 48
Alsace Rd. SE17 5E 102
Alscot Rd. SE1 4F 103
Alscot Way SE1 4F 103
Alsike Rd. DA18: Erith 3D 108
Alsike Rd. SE2 3D 108
Alsom Av. KT4: Wor Pk 4C 164
Alston Cl. KT6: Surb 7B 150
Alston Rd. EN5: Barn 3B 20
Alston Rd. N18 5C 34
Alston Rd. SW17 4B 136
Alston Works EN5: Barn 2B 20
Altab Ali Pk. 6G 85
(off Adler St.)
Altair Cl. N17 6A 34
Altash Way SE9 2D 142
Altenburg Av. W13 3B 96
Altenburg Gdns. SW11 4D 118
Alt Gro. SW19 7H 135
Altham Ct. HA2: Harr 1F 41
Altham Rd. HA5: Pinn 1C 40
Althea St. SW6 2K 117
Althorne Gdns. E18 4H 51
Althorne Way RM10: Dag 2G 73
Althorp Cl. EN5: Ark 1H 29
Althorpe M. SW11 1B 118
Althorpe Rd. HA1: Harr 5G 41
Althorp Rd. SW17 1D 136
Altima Ct. SE22 4G 121
(off E. Dulwich Rd.)
Altior Ct. N6 6G 47
Altissima Ho. SW11 7F 101
Altitude Apts. CR0: C'don 3D 168
(off Altyre Rd.)
Altitude Point E1 7K 9 (6G 85)
(off Alie St.)
Altius Apts. E3 2C 86
(off Wick La.)
Altius Ct. E4 6K 35
Altius Wlk. E20 6E 68
Altmore Av. E6 7D 70
Alton Av. HA7: Stan 7E 26
Alton Cl. DA5: Bexl 1E 144
Alton Cl. TW7: Isle 2K 113
Alton Gdns. BR3: Beck 7C 140
Alton Gdns. TW2: Whitt 7H 113
Alton Ho. E3 3D 86
(off Bromley High St.)
Alton Rd. CR0: Wadd 3A 168
Alton Rd. N17 3D 48
Alton Rd. SW15 1C 134
Alton Rd. TW9: Rich 4E 114
Alton St. E14 5D 86
Altura Twr. SW11 2B 118
Altus Ho. SE6 4E 140
Altyre Cl. BR3: Beck 5B 158
Altyre Rd. CR0: C'don 2D 168
Altyre Way BR3: Beck 5B 158
Aluna Ct. SE15 3J 121
Alvanley Gdns. NW6 5K 63
Alverstone Av. EN4: E Barn 7H 21
Alverstone Av. SW19 2J 135
Alverstone Gdns. SE9 1G 143
Alverstone Ho. SE11 7J 19 (6A 102)
Alverstone Rd. E12 4E 70
Alverstone Rd. HA9: Wemb 1F 61
Alverstone Rd. KT3: N Mald 4B 152
Alverstone Rd. NW2 7E 62
Alverston Gdns. SE25 5E 156
Alverton St. SE8 5B 104
(not continuous)
Alveston Av. HA3: Kenton 3B 42
Alveston Sq. E18 2J 51
Alvey St. SE17 5E 102
Alvia Gdns. SM1: Sutt 4A 166
Alvington Cres. E8 5F 67
Alway Av. KT19: Ewe 5K 163
Alwold Cres. SE12 6K 123
Alwyn Av. W4 5K 97
Alwyn Cl. CR0: New Ad 7D 170
Alwyne La. N1 7B 66
Alwyne Pl. N1 6C 66
Alwyne Rd. N1 7C 66
Alwyne Rd. SW19 6H 135
Alwyne Rd. W7 7J 77
Alwyne Sq. N1 6C 66
Alwyne Vs. N1 7B 66
Alwyn Gdns. NW4 4C 44
Alwyn Gdns. W3 6H 79
Alyth Gdns. NW11 6J 45
Alzette Ho. E2 2K 85
(off Mace St.)
Amalgamated Dr. TW8: Bford 6B 96
Amanda Ct. TW15: Ashf 2B 128
(off Edward Way)
Amanda M. RM7: Rom 5J 55
Amar Ct. SE18 4K 107
Amar Deep Ct. SE18 5K 107
Amarelle Apts. CR0: C'don 1D 168
(off Cherry Orchard Rd.)
Amazon Bldg. N8 4K 47
Amazon St. E1 6G 85
Ambassador Bldg. SW11 7C 18 (6H 101)
Ambassador Cl. TW3: Houn 2C 112
Ambassador Gdns. E6 5D 88
Ambassador Ho. CR7: Thor H 4C 156
(off Brigstock Rd.)
Ambassador Ho. NW8 1A 82
Ambassador's Ct. SW1 5B 12 (1G 101)
(off St James's Pal.)
Ambassadors Ct. E8 7F 67
(off Holly St.)
Ambassador Sq. E14 4D 104
Ambassadors Theatre 2D 12 (7H 83)
(off West St.)
Amber Av. E17 1A 50
Amber Cl. EN5: New Bar 6E 20
Amber Ct. CR0: C'don 1E 168
Amber Ct. E15 1E 86
(off Warton Rd.)
Amber Ct. KT5: Surb 7F 151
Amber Ct. N7 6A 66
(off Bride St.)
Amber Ct. SW17 4E 136
(off Brudenell Rd.)
Amberden Av. N3 3J 45
Ambergate St. SE17 5B 102
Amber Gro. NW2 1F 63
Amber Ho. E1 6K 85
(off Aylward St.)
Amberley Cl. BR6: Chels 5K 173
Amberley Cl. HA5: Pinn 3D 40
Amberley Ct. BR3: Beck 7B 140
Amberley Ct. DA14: Sidc 5C 144
Amberley Gdns. EN1: Enf 7K 23
Amberley Gdns. KT19: Ewe 4B 164
Amberley Gro. CR0: C'don 7F 157
Amberley Gro. SE26 5H 139
Amberley Rd. E10 7C 50
Amberley Rd. EN1: Enf 7A 24
Amberley Rd. IG9: Buck H 1F 37
Amberley Rd. N13 2E 32
Amberley Rd. SE2 6D 108
Amberley Rd. W9 5J 81
Amberley Way RM7: Mawney 4H 55
Amberley Way SM4: Mord 7H 153
Amberley Way TW4: Houn 5A 112
Amberley Way UB10: Uxb 2A 74
Amberlith Ho. CR7: Thor H 5A 156
(off Thornton Rd.)
Amber M. N22 3A 48
(off High Rd.)
Amberside Cl. TW7: Isle 6H 113
Amber Way W3 2A 98
Amber Wharf E2 1F 85
(off Nursery La.)
Amberwood Cl. SM6: W'gton 5J 167
Amberwood Ri. KT3: N Mald 6A 152
Amblecote Cl. SE12 3K 141
Amblecote Mdws. SE12 3K 141
Amblecote Rd. SE12 3K 141
Ambler Rd. N4 3B 66
Ambleside BR1: Broml 6F 141
Ambleside NW1 1K 5 (2F 83)
(off Augustus St.)
Ambleside SW19 1G 135
Ambleside Av. BR3: Beck 5A 158
Ambleside Av. KT12: Walt T 7A 148
Ambleside Av. SW16 4H 137
Ambleside Cl. E10 7D 50
Ambleside Cl. E9 5J 67
Ambleside Cl. N17 3F 49
Ambleside Cres. EN3: Enf H 3E 24
Ambleside Dr. TW14: Felt 1H 129
Ambleside Gdns. HA9: Wemb 1D 60
Ambleside Gdns. IG4: Ilf 4C 52
Ambleside Gdns. SM2: Sutt 6A 166
Ambleside Gdns. SW16 5H 137
Ambleside Point SE15 7J 103
(off Tustin Est.)
Ambleside Rd. DA7: Bex 2G 127
Ambleside Rd. NW10 7B 62
Ambleside Wlk. UB8: Uxb 1A 74
Ambrook Rd. DA17: Belv 3G 109
Ambrosden Av. SW1 2A 18 (3G 101)
Ambrose Av. NW11 7G 45
Ambrose Cl. BR6: Orp 3K 173
Ambrose Cl. E6 5D 88
Ambrose Ct. N18 6A 34
(off Cannon Rd.)
Ambrose Ho. E14 5C 86
(off Selsey St.)
Ambrose M. SW11 2D 118
Ambrose St. SE16 4H 103
Ambrose Wlk. E3 2C 86
Ambulance Rd. E11 5F 51
AMC Bus. Cen. NW10 3H 79
Amelia Cl. TW4: Houn 1C 130
Amelia Cl. W3 1H 97
Amelia Ho. E14 6G 87
(off Lyell St.)
Amelia Ho. NW9 2B 44
(off Boulevard Dr.)
Amelia Ho. TW9: Kew 7H 97
Amelia Ho. W6 5E 98
(off Queen Caroline St.)
Amelia Mans. E20 6D 68
(off Olympic Pk. Av.)
Amelia St. SE17 5C 102
Amen Cnr. EC4 1B 14 (6B 84)
Amen Cnr. SW17 6D 136
Amen Ct. EC4 7B 8 (6B 84)
Amenity Way SM4: Mord 7E 152
American International University, The
in London Kensington Campus,
Ansdell Street 3K 99
(off Ansdell St.)
American International University, The
in London Kensington Campus,
St Albans Grove 3K 99
American International University, The
in London Kensington Campus,
Young Street 2K 99
American International University, The
in London Richmond Hill Campus
6E 114
American University of London, The
3K 65
America Sq. EC3 2J 15 (7F 85)
America St. SE1 5C 14 (1C 102)
Amerland Rd. SW18 5H 117
Amersham Av. N18 6J 33
Amersham Gro. SE14 7B 104
Amersham Rd. CR0: C'don 6C 156
Amersham Rd. SE14 1B 122
Amersham Va. SE14 7B 104
Amery Gdns. NW10 1E 80
Amery Ho. SE17 5E 102
(off Kinglake St.)
Amery Rd. HA1: Harr 2A 60
Amesbury Av. SW2 2J 137
Amesbury Cl. KT4: Wor Pk 1E 164
Amesbury Ct. EN2: Enf 2F 23
Amesbury Dr. E4 6J 25
Amesbury Rd. BR1: Broml 3B 160
Amesbury Rd. RM9: Dag 7D 72
Amesbury Rd. TW13: Felt 2B 130
Amesbury Twr. SW8 2G 119
Ames Cotts. E14 5A 86
(off Maroon St.)
Ames Ho. E2 2K 85
(off Mace St.)
Amethyst Cl. N11 7C 32
Amethyst Ct. BR6: Chels 5J 173
(off Farnborough Hill)
Amethyst Ct. EN3: Enf H 3F 25
(off Enstone Rd.)
Amethyst Rd. E15 4F 69
Amherst Av. W13 6C 78
Amherst Dr. BR5: St M Cry 4K 161
Amherst Gdns. W13 6C 78
(off Amherst Rd.)
Amherst Ho. SE16 2K 103
(off Wolfe Cres.)
Amherst Rd. W13 6C 78
Amhurst Gdns. TW7: Isle 2A 114
Amhurst Pde. N16 7F 49
(off Amhurst Pk.)
Amhurst Pk. N16 7D 48
Amhurst Pas. E8 4G 67
Amhurst Rd. E8 5H 67
Amhurst Rd. N16 4F 67
Amhurst Ter. E8 4G 67
Amhurst Wlk. SE28 1A 108
Amias Dr. HA8: Edg 4K 27
Amias Ho. EC1 3C 8 (4C 84)
(off Central St.)
Amidas Gdns. RM8: Dag 4B 72
Amiel St. E1 4J 85
Amies St. SW11 3D 118
Amigo Ho. SE1 1K 19 (3A 102)
(off Morley St.)
Amina Way SE16 3G 103
Amiot Ho. NW9 2B 44
(off Heritage Av.)
Amis Av. KT19: Ewe 6H 163
Amisha Ct. SE1 3F 103
(off Grange Rd.)
Amity Gro. SW20 1D 152
Amity Rd. E15 7H 69
Ammanford Grn. NW9 6A 44
Ammonite Ho. E15 7H 69
Amner Rd. SW11 6E 118
Amor Rd. W6 3E 98
Amory Ho. N1 1K 83
(off Barnsbury Est.)
Amott Rd. SE15 3G 121
Amoy Pl. E14 7C 86
(not continuous)
Ampere Way CR0: Wadd 7J 155
Ampleforth Rd. SE2 2B 108
Amport Pl. NW7 6B 30
Ampthill Est. NW1 1A 6 (2G 83)
Ampthill Sq. NW1 1B 6 (2G 83)
Ampton Pl. WC1 2G 7 (3K 83)
Ampton St. WC1 2G 7 (3K 83)
Amroth Cl. SE23 1H 139
Amroth Grn. NW9 6A 44
Amstel Ct. SE15 7F 103
Amsterdam Rd. E14 3E 104
Amundsen Ct. E14 5C 104
(off Napier Av.)
Amundsen Ho. NW10 7K 61
(off Stonebridge Pk.)
Amwell Cl. EN2: Enf 5J 23
Amwell Ct. Est. N4 2C 66
Amwell Ho. WC1 1J 7 (3A 84)
(off Cruikshank St.)
Amwell St. EC1 1J 7 (3A 84)
Amyand Cotts. TW1: Twick 6B 114
Amyand La. TW1: Twick 7B 114

A–Z London 179

Amyand Pk. Gdns. – Archer St.

Amyand Pk. Gdns. TW1: Twick 7B 114
Amyand Pk. Rd. TW1: Twick 7A 114
Amy Cl. SM6: W'gton 7J 167
Amy Ct. CR0: C'don 5B 168
Amy Johnson Ct. HA8: Edg 2H 43
Amyruth Rd. SE4 5C 122
Amy Warne Cl. E6 4C 88
Anastasia M. N12 5E 30
Anatola Rd. N19 2G 65
Anayah Apts. SE8 5K 103
(off Trundleys Rd.)
Ancaster Cres. KT3: N Mald 6C 152
Ancaster M. BR3: Beck 3K 157
Ancaster Rd. BR3: Beck 3K 157
Ancaster St. SE18 7J 107
Anchor SW18 4K 117
Anchorage Cl. SW19 5J 135
Anchorage Ho. E14 7F 87
(off Clove Cres.)
Anchorage Point E14 2B 104
(off Cuba St.)
Anchorage Point Ind. Est. SE7 3A 106
Anchor & Hope La. SE7 3K 105
Anchor Brewhouse SE1 5J 15 (1F 103)
Anchor Bus. Cen. CR0: Bedd 5J 167
Anchor Cl. IG11: Bark 3B 90
Anchor Ct. EN1: Enf 5K 23
Anchor Ct. SW1 4C 18 (4H 101)
(off Vauxhall Bri. Rd.)
Anchor Dr. N15 4E 48
Anchor Ho. E16 Barking Rd. 5H 87
(off Barking Rd.)
Anchor Ho. E16 Prince Regent La. 4A 88
(off Prince Regent La.)
Anchor Ho. EC1 3C 8 (4C 84)
(off Old St.)
Anchor Ho. SW10 6B 100
(off Cremorne Est.)
Anchor Iron Wharf SE10 5F 105
Anchor M. N1 6E 66
Anchor M. SW12 6F 119
Anchor Retail Pk. Stepney Green 4J 85
Anchor St. SE16 4H 103
Anchor Ter. E1 4J 85
Anchor Ter. SE1 4D 14 (1C 102)
(off Southwark Bri. Rd.)
Anchor Wharf E3 5D 86
(off Yeo St.)
Anchor Yd. EC1 3C 8 (4C 84)
Ancill Cl. W6 6G 99
Ancona Rd. NW10 2C 80
Ancona Rd. SE18 5H 107
Andace Pk. Gdns. BR1: Broml 2A 160
Andalus Rd. SW9 3J 119
Ander Cl. HA0: Wemb 4D 60
Anderson Cl. N21 5E 22
Anderson Cl. SM3: Sutt 1J 165
Anderson Cl. W3 6K 79
Anderson Ct. NW2 1E 62
Anderson Dr. TW15: Ashf 4E 128
Anderson Hgts. SW16 2K 155
Anderson Ho. E14 7E 86
(off Woolmore St.)
Anderson Ho. IG11: Bark 1H 89
Anderson Ho. SW17 5B 136
Anderson Pl. TW3: Houn 4F 113
Anderson Rd. E9 6K 67
Anderson Rd. IG8: Wfd G 3B 52
Anderson Rd. SE3 3K 123
Anderson Sq. N1 1B 84
(off Gaskin St.)
Anderson St. SW3 5E 16 (5D 100)
Anderson Way DA17: Belv 2H 109
Anderson Wy. RM13: Rain 3J 91
Anderton Cl. SE5 3D 120
Anderton Ct. N22 2H 47
Andora Ct. NW6 7G 63
(off Brondesbury Pk.)
Andora Ho. E10 1A 68
Andorra Ct. BR1: Broml 1A 160
Andover Av. E16 6B 88
Andover Cl. TW14: Felt 1H 129
Andover Cl. UB6: G'frd 4F 77
Andover Ct. E2 4H 85
(off Thee Colts La.)
Andover Ct. TW19: Stanw 7A 110
Andover Pl. NW6 2K 81
Andover Rd. BR6: Orp 1H 173
Andover Rd. N7 2K 65
Andover Rd. TW2: Twick 1H 131
Andoversford Ct. SE15 6E 102
(off Bibury Cl.)
Andover Ter. W6 4D 98
(off Raynham Rd.)
Andreck Ct. BR3: Beck 2E 158
(off Crescent Rd.)
Andre St. E8 5G 67
Andrew Cl. DA1: Cray 5K 127
Andrew Ct. SE23 2K 139
Andrewes Gdns. E6 6C 88
Andrewes Highwalk EC2 6D 8 (5C 84)
(off Fore St.)
Andrewes Ho. EC2 6D 8 (5C 84)
(off Fore St.)
Andrewes Ho. SM1: Sutt 4J 165
Andrew Gibb Memorial, The 1H 123
Andrew Pl. SW8 7H 101
Andrew Reed Ho. SW18 7G 117
(off Linstead Way)
Andrews Cl. HA1: Harr 7H 41
Andrews Cl. IG9: Buck H 2F 37
Andrews Cl. KT4: Wor Pk 2E 164
Andrews Crosse WC2 1J 13 (6A 84)
(off Chancery La.)
Andrews Ga. TW17: Shep 2E 146
Andrew's Ho. CR2: S Croy 6C 168
Andrews Ho. NW3 7D 64
(off Fellows Rd.)
Andrews Pl. DA2: Wilm 2K 145
Andrews Pl. SE9 6F 125
Andrew's Rd. E8 1H 85
Andrew St. E14 6E 86
Andrews Wlk. SE17 6B 102
Andringham Lodge BR1: Broml 1K 159
(off Palace Gro.)
Andrula Ct. N22 1B 48
Andwell Cl. SE2 2B 108
ANERLEY 1H 157
Anerley Gro. SE19 7F 139
Anerley Hill SE19 6F 139
Anerley Pk. SE20 7G 139
Anerley Pk. Rd. SE20 7H 139
Anerley Rd. SE19 7G 139
Anerley Rd. SE20 7G 139
Anerley Sta. Rd. SE20 1H 157
Anerley St. SW11 2D 118
Anerley Va. SE19 7F 139
Aneurin Bevan Ct. NW2 2D 62
Aneurin Bevan Ho. N11 7C 32
Anfield Cl. SW12 7G 119
ANGEL 1K 7 (2A 84)
Angela Carter Cl. SW9 3A 120
Angela Davies Ind. Est. SE24 4B 120
Angela Hooper Pl. SW1 1B 18 (3G 101)
(off Victoria St.)
Angel Bldg. N1 1K 7 (2A 84)
Angel Cl. N18 5A 34
Angel Cl. TW12: Hamp H 5G 131
Angel Cnr. Pde. N18 4B 34
Angel Ct. E15 6F 69
Angel Ct. EC2 7F 9 (6D 84)
Angel Ct. SW1 5B 12 (1G 101)
ANGEL EDMONTON 5B 34
Angelfield TW3: Houn 4F 113
Angel Ga. EC1 1B 8 (3B 84)
(not continuous)
Angel Hill SM1: Sutt 3K 165
Angel Hill Dr. SM1: Sutt 3K 165
Angel Ho. E3 3C 86
(off Campbell Rd.)
Angelica Cl. UB7: Yiew 6A 74
Angelica Dr. E6 5E 88
Angelica Gdns. CR0: C'don 1K 169
Angelica Ho. E3 1B 86
(off Sycamore Av.)
Angelina Ho. SE15 1G 121
(off Goldsmith Rd.)
Angelis Apts. N1 1B 8 (2B 84)
(off Graham St.)
Angel La. E15 6F 69
Angel La. EC4 3E 14 (7D 84)
Angel La. UB3: Hayes 5F 75
Angell Pk. Gdns. SW9 3A 120
Angell Rd. SW9 3A 120
ANGELL TOWN 1A 120
Angell Town Est. SW9 2A 120
Angel M. E1 7H 85
Angel M. N1 2A 84
Angel M. SW15 7C 116
Angelo M. SW16 3K 155
Angel Pl. N18 4B 34
Angel Pl. SE1 6E 14 (2D 102)
Angel Rd. HA1: Harr 6J 41
Angel Rd. KT7: T Ditt 7A 150
Angel Rd. N18 5B 34
Angel Rd. Works N18 5D 34
Angel Sq. EC1 2B 84
Angel St. EC1 7C 8 (6C 84)
Angel Wlk. W6 4E 98
Angel Way RM1: Rom 5K 55
Angel Wharf N1 2C 84
Angel Yd. N6 1E 64
Angerstein Bus. Pk. SE10 4J 105
Angerstein La. SE3 1H 123
Anglais M. NW9 4A 44
(off Colin Cl.)
Anglebury W2 6J 81
(off Talbot Rd.)
Angle Cl. UB10: Hil 1C 74
Angle Grn. RM8: Dag 1C 72
Anglers, The KT1: King T 3D 150
(off High St.)
Anglers Cl. TW10: Ham 4C 132
Angler's La. NW5 6F 65
Anglers Reach KT6: Surb 5D 150
Anglesea Av. SE18 4F 107
Anglesea Ho. KT1: King T 4D 150
(off Anglesea Rd.)
Anglesea M. SE18 4F 107
Anglesea Rd. KT1: King T 4D 150
Anglesea Rd. SE18 4F 107
Anglesea Ter. W6 3D 98
(off Wellesley Av.)
Anglesey Cl. TW15: Ashf 3C 128
Anglesey Ct. Rd. SM5: Cars 6E 166
Anglesey Gdns. SM5: Cars 6E 166
Anglesey Ho. E14 6C 86
(off Lindfield St.)
Anglesey Rd. EN3: Pond E 4C 24
Anglesmede Cres. HA5: Pinn 3E 40
Anglesmede Way HA5: Pinn 3E 40
Angles Rd. SW16 4J 137
Anglia Cl. N17 7C 34
Anglia Ct. RM8: Dag 1D 72
(off Spring Cl.)
Anglia Ho. E14 6A 86
(off Salmon La.)
Anglian Ind. Est. IG11: Bark 4K 89
Anglian Rd. E11 3F 69
Anglia Wlk. E6 1E 88
(off Napier Rd.)
Anglo Rd. E3 2B 86
Angora Cl. SM6: W'gton 3F 167
Angrave Ct. E8 1F 85
(off Scriven St.)
Angrave Pas. E8 1F 85
Angus Cl. KT9: Chess 5G 163
Angus Dr. HA4: Ruis 4A 58
Angus Gdns. NW9 1K 43
Angus Ho. SW2 7H 119
Angus Rd. E13 3A 88
Angus St. SE14 7A 104
Anhalt Rd. SW11 7C 100
Ankerdine Cres. SE18 7F 107
Anlaby Rd. TW11: Tedd 5J 131
Anley Rd. W14 2F 99
Anmersh Gro. HA7: Stan 1D 42
Annabel Cl. E14 6D 86
Annabels M. W5 4D 78
Anna Cl. E8 1F 85
Annandale Gro. UB10: Ick 3E 56
Annandale Rd. CR0: C'don 2G 169
Annandale Rd. DA15: Sidc 7J 125
Annandale Rd. SE10 6H 105
Annandale Rd. W4 5A 98
Anna Neagle Cl. E7 4J 69
Annan Way RM1: Rom 1K 55
Anne Boleyn Ct. SE9 6G 125
Anne Boleyn's Wlk. KT2: King T 5E 132
Anne Boleyn's Wlk. SM3: Cheam 7F 165
Anne Case M. KT3: N Mald 3K 151
Anne Compton M. SE12 7H 123
Anne Goodman Ho. E1 6J 85
(off Jubilee St.)
Anne Matthews Ct. E14 5C 86
(off Selsey St.)
Anne M. IG11: Bark 7G 71
Anne of Cleeves Ct. SE9 6H 125
Annes Ct. NW1 3D 4 (4C 82)
(off Palgrave Gdns.)
Annesley Apts. E3 5C 86
(off Gresham Pl.)
Annesley Av. NW9 3K 43
Annesley Cl. NW10 3A 62
Annesley Dr. CR0: C'don 3B 170
Annesley Ho. SW9 1A 120
Annesley Pl. BR2: Broml 6C 160
Annesley Rd. SE3 1K 123
Annesley Wlk. N19 2G 65
Annesmere Gdns. SE3 3B 124
Anne St. E13 4J 87
Anne Sutherland Ho. BR3: Beck 7A 140
Annett Cl. TW17: Shep 4G 147
Annette Cl. HA3: W'stone 2J 41
Annette Cres. N1 7C 66
Annette Rd. N7 3K 65
(not continuous)
Annett Rd. KT12: Walt T 7J 147
Anne Way KT8: W Mole 4F 149
Annexe Mkt. E1 5J 9 (5F 85)
(off Spital Sq.)
Annie Besant Cl. E3 1B 86
Annie Taylor Ho. E12 4E 70
(off Walton Rd.)
Anning St. EC2 3H 9 (4E 84)
Annington Rd. N2 3D 46
Annis Rd. E9 6A 68
Ann La. SW10 6B 100
Ann Moss Way SE16 3J 103
Ann's Cl. SW1 7F 11 (2D 100)
(off Kinnerton St.)
Ann's Pl. E1 6J 9 (5F 85)
(off Wentworth St.)
Ann St. N1 1C 84
Ann St. SE18 5G 107
(not continuous)
Ann Stroud Ct. SE12 5J 123
Annsworthy Av. CR7: Thor H 3D 156
Annsworthy Cres. SE25 2D 156
Ansar Gdns. E17 5B 50
Ansdell Rd. SE15 2J 121
Ansdell St. W8 3K 99
Ansdell Ter. W8 3K 99
Ansel Adams Way HA2: Harr 3G 41
Ansell Gro. SM5: Cars 1E 166
Ansell Ho. E1 5J 85
(off Mile End Rd.)
Ansell Rd. SW17 3C 136
Anselm Cl. CR0: C'don 3F 169
Anselm Rd. HA5: Hat E 1D 40
Anselm Rd. SW6 6J 99
Ansford Rd. BR1: Broml 5E 140
Ansleigh Pl. W11 7F 81
Anson Cl. RM7: Mawney 2H 55
Anson Ho. E1 4A 86
(off Shandy St.)
Anson Ho. SW1 7A 18 (6G 101)
(off Churchill Gdns.)
Anson M. SW19 7J 135
Anson Pl. SE28 2H 107
Anson Rd. N7 4G 65
Anson Rd. NW2 4D 62
Anson Ter. UB5: N'olt 6F 59
Anstey Ho. E9 1J 85
(off Templecombe Rd.)
Anstey Rd. SE15 3G 121
Anstey Wlk. N15 4B 48
Anstice Cl. W4 7A 98
Anstridge Path SE9 6H 125
Anstridge Rd. SE9 6H 125
Antelope Rd. SE18 3D 106
Antelope Wlk. KT6: Surb 5D 150
Antenor Ho. E2 2H 85
(off Old Bethnal Grn. Rd.)
Anthems Way E20 6D 68
Anthony Cl. NW7 4F 29
Anthony Cope Ct. N1 1F 9 (3D 84)
(off Chart St.)
Anthony Ct. W3 2A 98
Anthony Ho. NW8 4C 4 (4C 82)
(off Ashbridge St.)
Anthony Rd. DA16: Well 1A 126
Anthony Rd. SE25 6G 157
Anthony Rd. UB6: G'frd 3J 77
Anthony St. E1 6H 85
Anthony Way N18 6E 34
Antigua M. E13 3K 87
Antigua Wlk. SE19 5D 138
Antila Ct. E1 3K 9 (4F 85)
(off Sclater St.)
Antilles Bay E14 2E 104
Antill Rd. E3 3A 86
Antill Rd. N15 4G 49
Antill Ter. E1 6K 85
Antlers Hill E4 5J 25
Antoinette M. NW2 6C 62
Anton Cres. SM1: Sutt 3J 165
Antoneys Cl. HA5: Pinn 2B 40
Antonine Hgts. SE1 7G 15 (2E 102)
(off City Wlk.)
Anton Pl. HA9: Wemb 3H 61
Anton St. E8 5G 67
Antony Ho. SE16 4J 103
(off Raymouth Rd.)
Antrim Gro. NW3 6D 64
Antrim Rd. NW3 6D 64
Antrobus Cl. SM1: Sutt 5H 165
Antrobus Rd. W4 4J 97
Antwerp Way E16 2E 106
Anvil Cl. SW16 7G 137
Anvil Rd. TW16: Sun 3J 147
Anworth Cl. IG8: Wfd G 6E 36
Apeldoorn Dr. SM6: W'gton 7J 167
Apelles St. SE18 1C 124
(off Tellson Av.)
Apex Cl. BR3: Beck 1D 158
APEX CORNER Feltham 3D 130
APEX CORNER Mill Hill 4F 29
Apex Ct. W13 7A 78
Apex Ho. E1 3K 9 (4F 85)
(off Bacon St.)
Apex Ind. Est. NW10 4B 80
Apex Pde. NW7 4E 28
(off Selvage La.)
Apex Retail Pk. 3D 130
Aphrodite Ct. E14 4C 104
(off Homer Dr.)
Aphrodite Ct. E15 1E 86
(off Warton Rd.)
Aplin Way TW7: Isle 1J 113
Apollo Av. BR1: Broml 1K 159
Apollo Bldg. E14 4C 104
Apollo Bus. Cen. SE8 5K 103
Apollo Ct. E1 7G 85
(off Thomas More St.)
Apollo Ct. E15 1E 86
(off High St.)
Apollo Ct. SW9 1A 120
(off Southey Rd.)
Apollo Ho. E2 2H 85
(off St Jude's Rd.)
Apollo Ho. E3 2C 86
(off Garrison Rd.)
Apollo Ho. N6 7D 46
Apollo Ho. SW10 7B 100
(off Milman's St.)
Apollo Pl. E11 3G 69
Apollo Pl. SW10 7B 100
Apollo Theatre Piccadilly 2C 12 (7H 83)
(off Shaftesbury Av.)
Apollo Victoria Theatre 2A 18 (3G 101)
(off Wilton Rd.)
Apollo Way DA8: Erith 4K 109
Apollo Way SE28 3H 107
Apostle Ct. SE20 7K 139
Apostles, The SE23 2K 139
(off Church Ri.)
Apostle Way CR7: Thor H 2B 156
Apothecary St. EC4 1A 14 (6B 84)
Appach Rd. SW2 5A 120
Appian Ct. E3 2B 86
(off Parnell Rd.)
Apple Blossom Ct. SW8 7H 101
(off Pascal St.)
Appleby Cl. BR5: Pet W 7J 161
Appleby Cl. E4 6K 35
Appleby Cl. N15 5D 48
Appleby Cl. TW2: Twick 2H 131
Appleby Cl. UB8: Hil 6E 74
Appleby Ct. SE6 6C 122
Appleby Ct. W3 2J 97
(off Newport Rd.)
Appleby Gdns. TW14: Felt 1H 129
Appleby Rd. E16 6H 87
Appleby Rd. E8 7G 67
Appleby St. E2 2F 85
Appledore Av. DA7: Bex 1J 127
Appledore Av. HA4: Ruis 3K 57
Appledore Cl. BR2: Broml 5H 159
Appledore Cl. HA8: Edg 1G 43
Appledore Cl. SW17 2D 136
Appledore Cres. DA14: Sidc 3J 143
Appledore Way NW7 7A 30
Appleford Ho. W10 4G 81
(off Bosworth Rd.)
Appleford Rd. W10 4G 81
Apple Gth. TW8: Bford 4D 96
Applegarth CR0: New Ad 7D 170
(not continuous)
Applegarth KT10: Clay 5A 162
Applegarth Dr. IG2: Ilf 4K 53
Applegarth Ho. SE1 6B 14 (2B 102)
(off Nelson Sq.)
Applegarth Ho. SE15 7G 103
(off Bird in Bush Rd.)
Applegarth Rd. SE28 1B 108
Applegarth Rd. W14 3F 99
Applegate Ho. E20 5E 68
(off Victory Pde.)
Apple Gro. EN1: Enf 3K 23
Apple Gro. HA2: Harr 1E 58
Apple Gro. KT9: Chess 4E 162
Apple Gro. TW1: Twick 6A 114
Apple Mkt. KT1: King T 2D 150
(off Market Pl.)
Apple M. SW17 2C 136
Apple Rd. E11 3G 69
Appleshaw Ho. SE5 3E 120
Appleton Cl. DA7: Bex 2J 127
Appleton Gdns. KT3: N Mald 6C 152
Appleton Rd. SE9 3C 124
Appleton Sq. CR4: Mitc 1C 154
Apple Tree Av. UB7: Yiew 6B 74
Apple Tree Av. UB8: Hil 5B 74
Appletree Cl. SE20 1H 157
Appletree Gdns. EN4: E Barn 4H 21
Apple Tree La. RM13: Rain 2K 91
APPLE TREE RDBT. 6B 74
Apple Tree Yd. E1 3K 85
(off Longnor Rd.)
Apple Tree Yd. SW1 4B 12 (1G 101)
Applewood Cl. N20 1H 31
Applewood Cl. NW2 3D 62
Applewood Cl. UB10: Ick 4A 56
Applewood Dr. E13 4K 87
Apple Yd. SE20 1G 157
Appold St. EC2 5G 9 (5E 84)
Apprentice Gdns. UB5: N'olt 3D 76
Apprentice Way E5 4H 67
Approach, The BR6: Orp 2K 173
Approach, The EN1: Enf 2C 24
Approach, The NW4 5F 45
Approach, The W3 6K 79
Approach Cl. N16 4E 66
Approach Rd. E2 2J 85
Approach Rd. EN4: E Barn 4G 21
Approach Rd. HA8: Edg 6B 28
Approach Rd. KT8: W Mole 5E 148
Approach Rd. SW20 2E 152
Approach Rd. TW15: Ashf 6E 128
Apps Mdw. Cl. KT8: W Mole 4D 148
Aprey Gdns. NW4 4E 44
April Cl. BR6: Chels 5K 173
April Cl. TW13: Felt 3J 129
April Cl. W7 7J 77
April Ct. E2 2G 85
(off Teale St.)
April Glen SE23 3K 139
April St. E8 4F 67
Apsley Cen., The NW2 2C 62
Apsley Cl. HA2: Harr 5G 41
Apsley Ho. E1 5J 85
(off Stepney Way)
Apsley Ho. NW8 2B 82
(off Finchley Rd.)
Apsley Ho. SW15 6C 116
(off Holford Way)
Apsley Ho. TW4: Houn 4D 112
Apsley House 6H 11 (2E 100)
Apsley Rd. KT3: N Mald 3J 151
Apsley Rd. SE25 4H 157
Apsley Way NW2 2C 62
Apsley Way W1 6H 11 (2E 100)
(not continuous)
Aqua Ho. NW10 3G 79
Aquarelle Ho. EC1 1C 8 (3C 84)
Aquarius TW1: Twick 1B 132
Aquarius Bus. Pk. NW2 1C 62
(off Priestley Way)
Aquarius Ct. HA8: Edg 7B 28
Aquarius Golf Course 6J 121
Aqua Vista Sq. E3 5C 86
(off Bow Comn. La.)
Aquila St. NW8 2B 82
Aquinas St. SE1 5K 13 (1A 102)
Arabella Ct. NW8 2A 82
(off Marlborough Pl.)
Arabella Dr. SW15 4A 116
Arabella St. SE16 7K 15 (3G 103)
Arabia Cl. E4 1A 36
Arabian Ho. E1 4A 86
(off Ernest St.)
Arabin Rd. SE4 4A 122
Arado Ho. NW9 2B 44
(off Boulevard Dr.)
Aragon Av. KT7: T Ditt 5K 149
Aragon Cl. BR2: Broml 1D 172
Aragon Cl. EN2: Enf 1E 22
Aragon Cl. TW16: Sun 6H 129
Aragon Ct. KT8: E Mos 4G 149
Aragon Ct. SE11 5J 19 (5A 102)
(off Hotspur St.)
Aragon Dr. HA4: Ruis 1B 58
Aragon Ho. E16 1J 105
(off Capulet M.)
Aragon Pl. SM4: Mord 7G 153
Aragon Rd. KT2: King T 5E 132
Aragon Rd. SM4: Mord 6F 153
Aragon Twr. SE8 4B 104
Aral Ho. E1 4K 85
(off Ernest St.)
Arandora Cres. RM6: Chad H 7B 54
Aran Dr. HA7: Stan 4H 27
Aran Lodge NW6 7J 63
(off Woodchurch Rd.)
Aran M. N7 7A 66
(off St Clements St.)
Arapiles Ho. E14 6F 87
(off Blair St.)
Arbery Rd. E3 3A 86
Arbon Ct. N1 1C 84
(off Linton St.)
Arbor Cl. BR3: Beck 2D 158
Arbor Ct. N16 2D 66
Arboretum Ct. N1 6D 66
(off Dove Rd.)
Arboretum Pl. IG11: Bark 7G 71
(off Clockhouse Av.)
Arborfield Cl. SW2 1K 137
Arborfield Ho. E14 7C 86
(off E. India Dock Rd.)
Arbor Ho. BR6: Orp 2K 173
(off Orchard Gro.)
Arbor Ho. SE14 6B 104
Arbor Ho. TW8: Bford 7C 96
Arbor Rd. E4 3A 36
Arbot Ho. SE10 4G 105
(off Manilla Wlk.)
Arbour Ho. E1 6K 85
(off Arbour Sq.)
Arbour Rd. EN3: Pond E 3E 24
Arbour Sq. E1 6K 85
Arbroath Rd. SE9 3C 124
Arbury Ter. SE26 3G 139
Arbus Cres. HA2: Harr 3G 41
Arbuthnot La. DA5: Bexl 6E 126
Arbuthnot Rd. SE14 2K 121
Arbuthnot Rd. SM4: Mord 4A 154
Arbutus St. E8 1F 85
Arcade CR0: C'don 2C 168
Arcade, The CR0: C'don 3C 168
(off High St.)
Arcade, The E20 6E 68
(within Westfield Shop. Cen.)
Arcade, The EC2 6G 9 (5E 84)
(off Liverpool St.)
Arcade, The N7 4J 65
(off Macready Pl.)
Arcade, The SE9 6E 124
(off High St.)
Arcade Chambers SE9 6E 124
Arcade Pde. KT9: Chess 5D 162
Arcadia Av. N3 2J 45
Arcadia Cen., The 7D 78
Arcadia Cl. SM5: Cars 4E 166
Arcadia Ct. E1 7J 9 (6F 85)
(off Old Castle St.)
Arcadia M. KT3: N Mald 3A 152
Arcadian Av. DA5: Bexl 6E 126
Arcadian Cl. DA5: Bexl 6E 126
Arcadian Gdns. N22 7E 32
Arcadian Pl. SW18 7H 117
Arcadian Rd. DA5: Bexl 6E 126
Arcadia St. E14 6C 86
Arc Ct. N11 5A 32
Arc Ct. RM7: Rush G 6K 55
ArcelorMittal Orbit 7D 68
AR Cen. 3A 86
(off Rhondda Gro.)
AR Cen. 4G 9 (4E 84)
(off Worship St.)
Archangel St. SE16 2K 103
Archbishop Lanfranc School Sports Cen. 6J 155
Archbishop's Pl. SW2 7K 119
Archdale Bus. Cen. HA2: Harr 2G 59
Archdale Ct. W12 1D 98
Archdale Ho. SE1 7G 15 (3E 102)
(off Long La.)
Archdale Pl. KT3: N Mald 3H 151
Archdale Rd. SE22 5F 121
Archel Rd. W14 6H 99
Archer Apts. N1 2E 84
(off Fern Cl.)
Archer Cl. EN5: Barn 6C 20
Archer Cl. KT2: King T 7E 132
Archer Ho. N1 1E 84
(off Whitmore Est.)
Archer Ho. SE14 1A 122
Archer Ho. SW11 1B 118
Archer Ho. W11 7H 81
(off Westbourne Gro.)
Archer Ho. W13 1B 96
(off Sherwood Cl.)
Archer M. SW9 3J 119
Archer M. TW12: Hamp H 6G 131
Archer Rd. BR5: St M Cry 5K 161
Archer Rd. SE25 4H 157
Archers Ct. CR2: S Croy 5C 168
(off Nottingham Rd.)
Archers Dr. EN3: Enf H 2D 24
Archers Lodge SE16 5G 103
(off Culloden Cl.)
Archer Sq. SE14 6A 104
Archer St. W1 2C 12 (7H 83)

Archers Way – Ash Cl.

Archers Way EN2: Enf 1F 23
Archer Ter. UB7: Yiew 7A 74
Archery Cl. HA3: W'stone 3K 41
Archery Cl. W2 1D 10 (6C 82)
Archery Flds. Ho. WC1 1J 7 (3A 84)
(off Wharton St.)
Archery La. BR2: Broml 6B 160
Archery Rd. SE9 5D 124
Archery Steps W2 2D 10 (7C 82)
(off St George's Flds.)
Arches SW8 7E 18 (6J 101)
Arches, The E16 4G 87
Arches, The HA2: Harr 2F 59
Arches, The NW1 7F 65
Arches, The SE8 6A 104
Arches, The WC2 4F 13 (1J 101)
(off Villiers St.)
Arches Bus. Cen., The UB2: S'hall 2D 94
(off Merrick Rd.)
Arches La. SW11 7K 17 (6F 101)
Archgate Bus. Cen. N12 5F 31
Archibald M. W1 3J 11 (7F 83)
Archibald Rd. N7 4H 65
Archibald St. E3 3C 86
Archie Cl. UB7: W Dray 2C 92
Archie St. SE1 7H 15 (2E 102)
Arc Ho. SE1 7J 15 (2F 103)
(off Tanner St.)
Arch St. SE1 3C 102
ARCHWAY 2G 65
Archway Bus. Cen. N19 3H 65
Archway Cl. SM6: Bedd 3H 167
Archway Cl. SW19 3K 135
Archway Cl. W10 5F 81
Archway Leisure Cen. 2G 65
Archway Mall N19 2G 65
Archway M. SW15 4G 117
(off Putney Bri. Rd.)
Archway Rd. N19 1G 65
Archway Rd. N6 6E 46
Archway St. SW13 3A 116
Arcola St. E8 5F 67
Arcola Theatre 5F 67
Arcon Dr. UB5: N'olt 4C 76
Arcon Ter. N9 7B 24
Arctic Ho. NW9 2B 44
(off Heritage Av.)
Arctic St. NW5 5F 65
Arcus Rd. BR1: Broml 6G 141
Ardbeg Rd. SE24 5D 120
Arden Cl. HA1: Harr 3H 59
Arden Cl. SE28 6D 90
Arden Cl. TW2: Whitt 7D 112
Arden Cl. UB4: Yead 4K 75
Arden Cl. WD23: B Hea 1E 26
Arden Ct. Gdns. N2 6B 46
Arden Cres. E14 4C 104
Arden Cres. RM9: Dag 7C 72
Arden Est. N1 2E 84
Arden Grange N12 4F 31
Arden Gro. BR6: Farnb 4F 173
Arden Ho. N1 1G 9 (2E 84)
(off Arden Est.)
Arden Ho. SE11 4G 19 (4K 101)
(off Black Prince Rd.)
Arden Ho. SE13 3D 122
(off Thurston Rd.)
Arden Ho. SW9 2J 119
(off Grantham Rd.)
Arden M. E17 5D 50
Arden Mhor HA5: Eastc 4K 39
Arden Rd. N3 3H 45
Arden Rd. W13 7C 78
Ardent Cl. SE25 3E 156
Ardent Ho. E3 2A 86
(off Roman Rd.)
Ardfern Av. SW16 3A 156
Ardfillan Rd. SE6 1F 141
Ardgowan Rd. SE6 7G 123
Ardilaun Rd. N5 4C 66
Ardingly Cl. CR0: C'don 3K 169
Ardleigh Ct. BR1: Broml 7H 141
(off London Rd.)
Ardleigh Gdns. SM3: Sutt 7J 153
Ardleigh Ho. IG11: Bark 1G 89
(off Cooke St.)
Ardleigh M. IG1: Ilf 3F 71
Ardleigh Rd. E17 1B 50
Ardleigh Rd. N1 6E 66
Ardleigh Ter. E17 1B 50
Ardley Cl. HA4: Ruis 7E 38
Ardley Cl. NW10 3A 62
Ardley Cl. SE6 3A 140
Ardlui Rd. SE27 2C 138
Ardmay Gdns. KT6: Surb 5E 150
Ardmere Rd. SE13 6F 123
Ardmore La. IG9: Buck H 1E 36
Ardmore Pl. IG9: Buck H 1E 36
Ardoch Rd. SE6 2F 141
Ardra Rd. N9 3E 34
Ardrossan Gdns. KT4: Wor Pk 3C 164
Ardshiel Cl. SW15 3F 117
Ardwell Av. IG6: Ilf 5G 53
Ardwell Rd. SW2 2J 137
Ardwick Rd. NW2 4J 63
Arena, The EN3: Enf L 1G 25
Arena Bus. Cen. N4 6C 48
Arena Ho. E3 2C 86
(off Lefevre Wlk.)
Arena Shop. Pk. 6B 48
Arena Sq. HA9: Wemb 4G 61
Arena Twr. E14 2D 104
Ares Ct. E14 4C 104
(off Homer Dr.)
Arethusa Ho. E14 4C 104
(off Cahir St.)
Argali Ho. DA18: Erith 3E 108
(off Kale Rd.)
Argall Av. E10 7K 49
Argall Way E10 1K 67
Argan Cl. EN5: Barn 3C 20
Argenta Way NW10 7H 61
Argent Cen., The UB3: Hayes 2J 93
Argent Ct. E14 5C 86
(off Thomas Rd.)
Argent Ct. EN5: New Bar 4F 21
(off Leicester Rd.)
Argent Ct. KT6: Surb 3G 163
Argent Ho. IG11: Bark 4A 90
Argenton Twr. SW18 6K 117
(off Mapleton Cres.)
Argo Apts. E16 6H 87
(off Sylvia Pankhurst St.)
Argo Bus. Cen. NW6 3J 81
Argonaut Pk. SL3: Poyle 4A 174
Argon M. SW6 7J 99
Argon Rd. N18 5D 34
Argos Ct. SW9 1A 120
(off Caldwell St.)
Argos Ho. E2 2H 85
(off Old Bethnal Grn. Rd.)
Argosy Ho. SE8 4A 104
Argosy La. TW19: Stanw 7A 110
Argus Cl. RM7: Mawney 1H 55
Argus Way UB5: N'olt 3C 76
Argyle Av. TW3: Houn 6E 112
Argyle Cl. W13 4A 78
Argyle Ho. E14 3E 104
Argyle Pas. N17 1F 49
Argyle Pl. W6 4D 98
Argyle Rd. E1 4K 85
Argyle Rd. E15 4G 69
Argyle Rd. E16 6K 87
Argyle Rd. EN5: Barn 4A 20
Argyle Rd. HA2: Harr 6F 41
Argyle Rd. IG1: Ilf 2E 70
Argyle Rd. N12 5E 30
Argyle Rd. N17 1G 49
Argyle Rd. N18 4B 34
Argyle Rd. TW3: Houn 5F 113
Argyle Rd. UB6: G'frd 3K 77
Argyle Rd. W13 5A 78
Argyle Sq. WC1 1F 7 (3J 83)
(not continuous)
Argyle St. WC1 1E 6 (3J 83)
Argyle Wlk. WC1 2F 7 (3J 83)
Argyle Way SE16 5G 103
Argyll Av. UB1: S'hall 1F 95
Argyll Cl. SW9 3K 119
Argyll Ct. SW2 7J 119
(off New Pk. Rd.)
Argyll Gdns. HA8: Edg 2H 43
Argyll Mans. SW3 7B 16 (6B 100)
Argyll Mans. W14 4G 99
(off Hammersmith Rd.)
Argyll Rd. SE18 3G 107
Argyll Rd. W8 2J 99
Argyll St. W1 1A 12 (6G 83)
Aria Ct. IG2: Ilf 6G 53
Arica Ho. SE16 3H 103
(off Slippers Pl.)
Arica Rd. SE4 4A 122
Ariel Apts. E16 6J 87
Ariel Ct. SE11 4K 19 (4B 102)
Ariel Ho. E1 7G 85
(off Vaughan Way)
Ariel Rd. NW6 6J 63
Ariel Way TW4: Houn 3K 111
Ariel Way W12 1E 98
Aristotle Rd. SW4 3H 119
Arizona Bldg. SE13 1D 122
(off Deal's Gateway)
Ark, The W6 5F 99
(off Talgarth Rd.)
Arkell Gro. SE19 7B 138
Arkindale Rd. SE6 3E 140
Arklay Cl. UB8: Hil 4B 74
Arkley Cres. E17 5B 50
Arkley Rd. E17 5B 50
Arklow Ho. SE17 6D 102
Arklow M. KT6: Surb 2E 162
Arklow Rd. SE14 6B 104
Arkwright Rd. NW3 5A 64
Arla Pl. HA4: Ruis 4A 58
Arlesey Cl. SW15 5G 117
Arlesford Rd. SW9 3J 119
Arlidge Ho. EC1 5K 7 (5A 84)
(off Kirby St.)
Arlingford Rd. SW2 5A 120
Arlington N12 3D 30
Arlington Av. N1 2C 84
Arlington Bldg. E3 2C 86
Arlington Cl. DA15: Sidc 7J 125
Arlington Cl. SE13 5F 123
Arlington Cl. SM1: Sutt 2J 165
Arlington Cl. TW1: Twick 6C 114
Arlington Ct. W3 2H 97
(off Mill Hill Rd.)
Arlington Dr. HA4: Ruis 6F 39
Arlington Dr. SM5: Cars 2D 166
Arlington Gdns. IG1: Ilf 1E 70
Arlington Gdns. W4 5J 97
Arlington Grn. NW7 7A 30
Arlington Ho. EC1 1K 7 (3A 84)
(off Arlington Way)
Arlington Ho. SE8 6B 104
(off Evelyn St.)
Arlington Ho. SW1 4A 12 (1G 101)
Arlington Ho. TW9: Kew 7H 97
Arlington Ho. UB7: W Dray 2B 92
Arlington Ho. W12 1D 98
(off Tunis Rd.)
Arlington Lodge SW2 4K 119
Arlington M. SE13 5F 123
Arlington Pk. Mans. W4 5J 97
(off Sutton La. Nth.)
Arlington Pas. TW11: Tedd 4K 131
Arlington Pl. SE10 7E 104
Arlington Rd. IG8: Wfd G 1J 51
Arlington Rd. KT6: Surb 6D 150
Arlington Rd. N14 2A 32
Arlington Rd. NW1 1F 83
Arlington Rd. TW1: Twick 6C 114
Arlington Rd. TW10: Ham 2D 132
Arlington Rd. TW11: Tedd 4K 131
Arlington Rd. TW15: Ashf 5B 128
Arlington Rd. W13 6B 78
Arlington Sq. N1 1C 84
Arlington St. SW1 4A 12 (1G 101)
Arlington Way EC1 1K 7 (3A 84)
Arliss Ho. HA1: Harr 5K 41
Arliss Way UB5: N'olt 1A 76
Arlow Rd. N21 1F 33
Armada Ct. SE8 6C 104
Armadale Cl. N17 4H 49
Armadale Rd. SW6 7J 99
Armadale Rd. TW14: Felt 5J 111
Armada Way E6 5F 89
Armagh Rd. E3 1B 86
Arments Ct. SE5 6D 102
(off Albany Rd.)
Armfield Cl. KT8: W Mole 5D 148
Armfield Cres. CR4: Mitc 2D 154
Armfield Rd. EN2: Enf 1J 23
Arminger Rd. W12 1D 98
Armistice Gdns. SE25 3G 157
Armitage Ho. NW1 5D 4 (5C 82)
(off Lisson Gro.)
Armitage Rd. NW11 1G 63
Armitage Rd. SE10 5H 105
Armour Cl. N7 6K 65
Armoury, The 4C 64
(off Pond St.)
Armoury Ho. E3 1A 86
(off Gunmakers La.)
Armoury Rd. SE8 2D 122
Armoury Way SW18 5J 117
Armsby Ho. E1 5J 85
(off Stepney Way)
Armstead Wlk. RM10: Dag 7G 73
Armstrong Av. IG8: Wfd G 6B 36
Armstrong Cl. BR1: Broml 3C 160
Armstrong Cl. E6 6D 88
Armstrong Cl. HA5: Eastc 6J 39
Armstrong Cl. KT12: Walt T 6J 147
Armstrong Cl. RM8: Dag 7D 54
Armstrong Cl. SE3 4K 123
Armstrong Cres. EN4: Cockf 3G 21
Armstrong Ho. E14 6A 86
(off Commercial Rd.)
Armstrong Rd. NW10 7A 62
Armstrong Rd. SE18 3G 107
Armstrong Rd. SW7 2A 16 (3B 100)
Armstrong Rd. TW13: Hanw 5C 130
Armstrong Rd. W3 1B 98
Armstrong Way UB2: S'hall 2F 95
Armytage Rd. TW5: Hest 7B 94
Arnal Cres. SW18 7G 117
Arncliffe NW6 2K 81
Arncliffe Cl. N11 6K 31
Arncroft Ct. IG11: Bark 3B 90
Arndale Wlk. SW18 5K 117
Arne Gro. BR6: Orp 3K 173
Arne Ho. SE11 5G 19 (5K 101)
(off Tyers St.)
Arne St. WC2 1F 13 (6J 83)
Arnett Sq. E4 6G 35
Arne Wlk. SE3 4H 123
Arneways Av. RM6: Chad H 3D 54
Arneway St. SW1 2D 18 (3H 101)
Arnewood Cl. SW15 1C 134
Arneys La. CR4: Mitc 6E 154
Arngask Rd. SE6 7F 123
Arnhem Pl. E14 3C 104
Arnhem Way SE22 5E 120
Arnhem Wharf E14 3B 104
Arnison Rd. KT8: E Mos 4H 149
Arnold Bennett Way N8 3A 48
Arnold Cir. E2 2J 9 (3F 85)
Arnold Cl. HA3: Kenton 7F 43
Arnold Ct. N22 7D 32
Arnold Cres. TW7: Isle 5H 113
Arnold Dr. KT9: Chess 6D 162
Arnold Est. SE1 7K 15 (2F 103)
(not continuous)
Arnold Gdns. N13 5G 33
Arnold Ho. SE17 5B 102
(off Doddington Gro.)
Arnold Ho. SE3 7A 106
(off Shooters Hill Rd.)
Arnold Mans. W14 6H 99
(off Queen's Club Gdns.)
Arnold Rd. E3 3C 86
Arnold Rd. N15 3F 49
Arnold Rd. RM10: Dag 7G 73
Arnold Rd. RM9: Dag 7F 73
Arnold Rd. SW17 7D 136
Arnold Rd. UB5: N'olt 6B 58
Arnold Ter. HA7: Stan 5E 26
Arnos Gro. N14 4C 32
Arnos Gro. Ct. N11 5B 32
(off Palmer's Rd.)
Arnos Rd. N11 5B 32
Arnos Swimming Pool 5C 32
Arnot Ho. SE5 7C 102
(off Comber Gro.)
Arnott Cl. SE28 1C 108
Arnott Cl. W4 4K 97
Arnould Av. SE5 4D 120
Arnsberg Way DA6: Bex 4G 127
Arnsberg Way DA7: Bex 4G 127
Arnside Gdns. HA9: Wemb 1D 60
Arnside Ho. SE17 6D 102
(off Arnside St.)
Arnside Rd. DA7: Bex 1G 127
Arnside St. SE17 6D 102
Arnulf St. SE6 4D 140
Arnulls Rd. SW16 6B 138
Arodene Rd. SW2 6K 119
Arona Ho. BR3: Beck 2E 158
Arora Twr. SE10 1F 105
Arosa Rd. TW1: Twick 6D 114
Arpley Sq. SE20 7J 139
(off High St.)
Arragon Gdns. BR4: W W'ck 3D 170
Arragon Gdns. SW16 7J 137
Arragon Rd. E6 1B 88
Arragon Rd. SW18 1J 135
Arragon Rd. TW1: Twick 7A 114
Arran Cl. DA8: Erith 6K 109
Arran Cl. SM6: W'gton 4F 167
Arran Ct. NW10 3K 61
Arran Ct. NW9 2B 44
Arran Dr. E12 1B 70
Arran Ho. E14 1E 104
(off Raleana Rd.)
Arran M. W5 1F 97
Arran Rd. SE6 2D 140
Arran Wlk. N1 7C 66
Arras Av. SM4: Mord 5A 154
Arrival Sq. E1 7G 85
Arrol Ho. SE1 3C 102
Arrol Rd. BR3: Beck 3J 157
Arrow Ct. SW5 4J 99
(off W. Cromwell Rd.)
Arrowhead Quay E14 2C 104
Arrow Ho. N1 1E 84
(off Wilmer Gdns.)
Arrow Rd. E3 3D 86
Arrowscout Wlk. UB5: N'olt 3C 76
(off Argus Way)
Arrows Ho. SE15 7J 103
(off Clifton Way)
Arrowsmith Ho. SE11 5G 19 (5K 101)
(off Tyers St.)
Arsenal FC 4A 66
Arsenal Rd. SE9 2D 124
Arsenal Way SE18 3G 107
Arta Ho. E1 6J 85
(off Devonport St.)
Artbrand Ho. SE1 7G 15 (2E 102)
(off Leathermarket St.)
Artemis Ct. E14 4C 104
(off Homer Dr.)
Artemis Pl. SW18 7H 117
Arterberry Rd. SW20 7E 134
Artesian Cl. NW10 7K 61
Artesian Gro. EN5: New Bar 4F 21
Artesian Ho. SE1 3F 103
(off Grange Rd.)
Artesian Rd. W2 6J 81
Artesian Wlk. E11 3G 69
Arthaus Apts. E8 6H 67
(off Richmond Rd.)
Arthingworth St. E15 1G 87
Arthouse Crouch End 5J 47
Arthur Ct. CR0: C'don 3E 168
(off Fairfield Path)
Arthur Ct. SW11 1E 118
Arthur Ct. W10 6F 81
(off Silchester Rd.)
Arthur Ct. W2 6K 81
(off Queensway)
Arthur Deakin Ho. E1 5K 9 (5G 85)
(off Hunton St.)
Arthurdon Rd. SE4 5C 122
Arthur Gro. SE18 4G 107
Arthur Henderson Ho. SW6 2H 117
(off Fulham Rd.)
Arthur Horsley Wlk. E7 5H 69
(off Tower Hamlets Rd.)
Arthur Ho. N1 1E 84
(off Halcomb St.)
Arthur Lovell Ct. E14 6B 86
(off Lovat Cl.)
Arthur Newton Ho. SW11 3B 118
(off Winstanley Est.)
Arthur Rd. E6 2D 88
Arthur Rd. KT2: King T 7G 133
Arthur Rd. KT3: N Mald 5D 152
Arthur Rd. N7 4K 65
Arthur Rd. N9 2A 34
Arthur Rd. RM6: Chad H 6C 54
Arthur Rd. SW19 5H 135
Arthur St. EC4 2F 15 (7D 84)
Arthur Wade Ho. E2 1K 9 (3F 85)
(off Baroness Rd.)
Arthur Wallis Ho. E12 3E 70
(off Grantham Rd.)
Artichoke Hill E1 7H 85
Artichoke M. SE5 1D 120
(off Artichoke Pl.)
Artichoke Pl. SE5 1D 120
Artichoke Wlk. TW9: Rich 5D 114
(off Red Lion St.)
Artillery Bldg., The E1 6H 9 (5E 84)
(off Artillery La.)
Artillery Cl. IG2: Ilf 6G 53
Artillery Ho. E15 6G 69
Artillery Ho. E3 1A 86
(off Barge La.)
Artillery Ho. SE18 5E 106
(off Connaught M.)
Artillery La. E1 6H 9 (5E 84)
Artillery La. W12 6C 80
Artillery Mans. SW1 2C 18 (3H 101)
(off Victoria St.)
Artillery Pas. E1 6H 9 (5E 84)
(off Artillery La.)
Artillery Pl. HA3: Hrw W 7B 26
Artillery Pl. SE18 4D 106
Artillery Pl. SW1 2C 18 (3H 101)
Artillery Row SW1 2B 18 (3G 101)
Artillery Sq. SE18 3F 107
Artington Cl. BR6: Farnb 4G 173
Artisan Cl. E6 6F 89
Artisan Ct. E8 6G 67
Artisan M. NW10 3F 81
(off Warfield Rd.)
Artisan Pl. HA3: W'stone 2J 41
Artisan Quarter NW10 3F 81
(off Wellington Rd.)
Artizan St. E1 7J 9 (6F 85)
(off Harrow Pl.)
Arts Depot 5F 31
Arts La. SE16 3F 103
Arts Sq. E1 4A 86
Arts Theatre Covent Garden
2E 12 (7J 83)
(off Gt. Newport St.)
Arun Ct. SE25 5G 157
Arundale KT1: King T 4D 150
(off Anglesea Rd.)
Arundel Av. SM4: Mord 4H 153
Arundel Bldgs. SE1 3E 102
Arundel Cl. CR0: Wadd 3B 168
Arundel Cl. DA5: Bexl 6F 127
Arundel Cl. E15 4G 69
Arundel Cl. SW11 5C 118
Arundel Cl. TW12: Hamp H 5F 131
Arundel Ct. BR2: Broml 2G 159
Arundel Ct. HA2: Harr 4E 58
Arundel Ct. N12 6H 31
Arundel Ct. N17 1G 49
Arundel Ct. SE16 5H 103
(off Verney Rd.)
Arundel Ct. SW13 6D 98
(off Arundel Ter.)
Arundel Ct. SW3 5D 16 (5C 100)
(off Jubilee Pl.)
Arundel Ct. W11 7H 81
(off Arundel Gdns.)
Arundel Dr. HA2: Harr 4D 58
Arundel Dr. IG8: Wfd G 7D 36
Arundel Gdns. HA8: Edg 7E 28
Arundel Gdns. IG3: Ilf 2A 72
Arundel Gdns. N21 1F 33
Arundel Gdns. W11 7H 81
Arundel Gt. Ct. WC2 2H 13 (7K 83)
Arundel Gro. N16 5E 66
Arundel Ho. CR0: C'don 5D 168
(off Heathfield Rd.)
Arundel Ho. E17 1B 50
Arundel Ho. W3 2H 97
(off Park Rd. Nth.)
Arundel Mans. SW6 1H 117
(off Kelvedon Rd.)
Arundel Pl. N1 6A 66
Arundel Rd. CR0: C'don 6D 156
Arundel Rd. EN4: Cockf 3H 21
Arundel Rd. KT1: King T 2H 151
Arundel Rd. SM2: Cheam 7H 165
(not continuous)
Arundel Rd. SM2: Sutt 7H 165
(not continuous)
Arundel Rd. TW4: Houn 3A 112
Arundel Sq. N7 6A 66
Arundel St. WC2 2H 13 (7K 83)
Arundel Ter. SW13 6D 98
Arun Ho. KT2: King T 1D 150
Arvon Rd. N5 5A 66
(not continuous)
Asa Ct. UB3: Harl 3H 93
Asbaston Ter. IG1: Ilf 6G 71
Asbridge Ct. W6 3D 98
(off Dalling Rd.)
Asbury Ct. N21 5D 22
(off Pennington Dr.)
Ascalon Ho. SW8 7G 101
(off Thessaly Rd.)
Ascalon St. SW8 7G 101
Ascensis Twr. SW18 4A 118
Ascent Ho. NW9 2B 44
(off Boulevard Dr.)
Ascham Dr. E4 7J 35
Ascham End E17 1A 50
Ascham St. NW5 5G 65
Aschurch Rd. CR0: C'don 7F 157
Ascot Cl. UB5: N'olt 5E 58
Ascot Ct. DA5: Bexl 7F 127
Ascot Ct. NW8 2A 4 (3B 82)
(off Grove End Rd.)
Ascot Gdns. UB1: S'hall 4D 76
Ascot Ho. NW1 1K 5 (3F 83)
(off Redhill St.)
Ascot Ho. W9 4J 81
(off Harrow Rd.)
Ascot Lodge NW6 1K 81
Ascot Pl. HA7: Stan 5H 27
Ascot Rd. BR5: St M Cry 4K 161
Ascot Rd. E6 3D 88
Ascot Rd. N15 5D 48
Ascot Rd. N18 4B 34
Ascot Rd. SW17 6E 136
Ascot Rd. TW14: Bedf 1C 128
Ascott Av. W5 2E 96
Ascott Cl. HA5: Eastc 4J 39
Ashanti M. E8 5J 67
Ash Av. SE17 4C 102
Ashbee Ho. E2 3J 85
(off Portman Pl.)
Ashbourne Av. DA7: Bex 7E 108
Ashbourne Av. E18 4K 51
Ashbourne Av. HA2: Harr 2H 59
Ashbourne Av. N20 2J 31
Ashbourne Av. NW11 5H 45
Ashbourne Cl. N12 4E 30
Ashbourne Cl. W5 5G 79
Ashbourne Ct. E5 4A 68
Ashbourne Ct. N12 4E 30
(off Ashbourne Cl.)
Ashbourne Gro. NW7 5E 28
Ashbourne Gro. SE22 4F 121
Ashbourne Gro. W4 5A 98
Ashbourne Pde. NW11 4H 45
Ashbourne Pde. W5 4F 79
Ashbourne Ri. BR6: Orp 4J 173
Ashbourne Rd. CR4: Mitc 7E 136
Ashbourne Rd. W5 4F 79
Ashbourne Ter. SW19 7H 135
Ashbourne Way NW11 4H 45
Ashbridge Rd. E11 7G 51
Ashbridge St. NW8 4C 4 (4C 82)
Ashbrook HA8: Edg 6A 28
Ashbrook Rd. N19 1H 65
Ashbrook Rd. RM10: Dag 3H 73
Ashburn Gdns. SW7 4A 100
Ashburnham Av. HA1: Harr 6K 41
Ashburnham Cl. N2 3B 46
Ashburnham Ct. BR3: Beck 2E 158
Ashburnham Gdns. HA1: Harr 6K 41
Ashburnham Gro. SE10 7D 104
Ashburnham Mans. SW10 7A 100
(off Ashburnham Rd.)
Ashburnham M. SW1 3D 18 (4H 101)
(off Regency St.)
Ashburnham Pl. SE10 7D 104
Ashburnham Retreat SE10 7D 104
Ashburnham Rd. DA17: Belv 4J 109
Ashburnham Rd. NW10 3E 80
Ashburnham Rd. SW10 7A 100
Ashburnham Rd. TW10: Ham 3B 132
Ashburnham Twr. SW10 7B 100
(off Worlds End Est.)
Ashburn Pl. SW7 4A 100
Ashburton Av. CR0: C'don 1H 169
Ashburton Av. IG3: Ilf 5J 71
Ashburton Cl. CR0: C'don 1G 169
Ashburton Ent. Cen. SW15 6E 116
Ashburton Gdns. CR0: C'don 2G 169
ASHBURTON GROVE 4A 66
Ashburton Ho. W9 4H 81
(off Fernhead Rd.)
Ashburton Memorial Homes
CR0: C'don 7H 157
Ashburton Pl. W1 4K 11 (1F 101)
Ashburton Rd. CR0: C'don 2G 169
Ashburton Rd. E16 6J 87
Ashburton Rd. HA4: Ruis 2J 57
Ashburton Ter. E13 2J 87
Ashburton Triangle N5 4A 66
Ashbury Dr. UB10: Ick 3D 56
Ashbury Gdns. RM6: Chad H 5D 54
Ashbury Pl. SW19 6A 136
Ashbury Rd. SW11 3D 118
Ashby Av. KT9: Chess 6G 163
Ashby Cl. BR4: W W'ck 3F 171
Ashby Ct. NW8 3B 4 (4B 82)
(off Pollitt Dr.)
Ashby Gro. N1 7C 66
(not continuous)
Ashby Ho. N1 7C 66
(off Essex Rd.)
Ashby Ho. SW9 2B 120
Ashby Ho. UB5: N'olt 4D 76
(off Waxlow Way)
Ashby M. SE4 2B 122
Ashby M. SW2 5J 119
(off Prague Pl.)
Ashby Rd. N15 5G 49
Ashby Rd. SE4 2B 122
Ashbys Ct. E3 2B 86
(off Centurion La.)
Ashby St. EC1 2B 8 (3B 84)
Ashby Wlk. CR0: C'don 6C 156
Ashby Way UB7: Sip 7C 92
Ashchurch Gro. W12 3C 98
Ashchurch Pk. Vs. W12 3C 98
Ashchurch Ter. W12 3C 98
Ash Cl. BR5: Pet W 5H 161
Ash Cl. DA14: Sidc 3B 144
Ash Cl. HA7: Stan 6F 27
Ash Cl. HA8: Edg 4D 28
Ash Cl. KT3: N Mald 2K 151
Ash Cl. RM5: Col R 1H 55

A–Z London 181

Ash Cl. – Audleigh Pl.

Ash Cl. SE20 2J 157
Ash Cl. SM5: Cars 2D 166
Ash Cl. TW7: Isle 1K 113
Ash Cl. UB9: Hare 1A 38
Ashcombe Av. KT6: Surb 7D 150
Ashcombe Cl. TW15: Ashf 3A 128
Ashcombe Ct. TW15: Ashf 2B 128
Ashcombe Gdns. HA8: Edg 4B 28
Ashcombe Ho. E3 3D 86
(off Bruce Rd.)
Ashcombe Ho. EN3: Pond E 3E 24
Ashcombe Pk. NW2 3A 62
Ashcombe Rd. SM5: Cars 6E 166
Ashcombe Rd. SW19 5J 135
Ashcombe Sq. KT3: N Mald 3J 151
Ashcombe St. SW6 2K 117
Ash Ct. KT19: Ewe 4J 163
Ash Ct. N11 6B 32
Ash Ct. SW19 7G 135
Ashcroft HA5: Hat E 6A 26
Ashcroft N14 2C 32
Ashcroft Av. DA15: Sidc 6A 126
Ashcroft Ct. N20 2G 31
Ashcroft Cres. DA15: Sidc 6A 126
Ashcroft Ho. SW8 1G 119
(off Wadhurst Rd.)
Ashcroft Rd. KT9: Chess 3F 163
Ashcroft Sq. W6 4E 98
Ashcroft Theatre Croydon 3D 168
(within Fairfield Halls)
Ashdale Cl. TW19: Stanw 2A 128
Ashdale Cl. TW2: Whitt 7G 113
Ashdale Gro. HA7: Stan 6E 26
Ashdale Ho. N4 7D 48
Ashdale Rd. SE12 1K 141
Ashdale Way TW2: Whitt 7F 113
Ashdene HA5: Pinn 3A 40
Ashdene SE15 7H 103
Ashdene Cl. TW15: Ashf 7E 128
Ashdon Cl. IG8: Wfd G 6E 36
Ashdon Rd. NW10 1B 80
Ashdown W13 5B 78
(off Clivedon Ct.)
Ashdown Cl. BR3: Beck 2D 158
Ashdown Cl. DA5: Bexl 7J 127
Ashdown Ct. E17 2E 50
Ashdown Ct. IG11: Bark 6F 71
Ashdown Ct. SM2: Sutt 6A 166
Ashdown Cres. NW5 5E 64
Ashdowne Ct. N17 1G 49
Ashdown Pl. KT17: Ewe 7B 164
Ashdown Pl. KT7: T Ditt 7A 150
Ashdown Rd. EN3: Enf H 2D 24
Ashdown Rd. KT1: King T 2E 150
Ashdown Rd. UB10: Hil 2C 74
Ashdown Wlk. E14 4C 104
Ashdown Wlk. RM7: Mawney 1H 55
Ashdown Way SW17 2E 136
Ashe Ho. TW1: Twick 6D 114
Ashen E6 6E 88
Ashenden Rd. E5 5A 68
Ashen Gro. SW19 3J 135
Ashentree Ct. EC4 1K 13 (6A 84)
(off Whitefriars St.)
Asher Loftus Way N11 6J 31
Asher Way E1 7G 85
Ashfield Av. TW13: Felt 1K 129
Ashfield Cl. BR3: Beck 7C 140
Ashfield Cl. TW10: Ham 1E 132
Ashfield Ct. SW9 2J 119
(off Clapham Rd.)
Ashfield Ho. W14 5H 99
(off W. Cromwell Rd.)
Ashfield La. BR7: Chst 6F 143
(not continuous)
Ashfield Pde. N14 1C 32
Ashfield Rd. N14 3B 32
Ashfield Rd. N4 6C 48
Ashfield Rd. W3 1B 98
Ashfield St. E1 5H 85
(not continuous)
Ashfield Yd. E1 5J 85
ASHFORD 4B 128
Ashford Av. N8 4J 47
Ashford Av. TW15: Ashf 6D 128
Ashford Av. UB4: Yead 6B 76
Ashford Bus. Complex
TW15: Ashf 5E 128
Ashford Cl. TW15: Ashf West Cl. 4A 128
Ashford Cl. E17 6B 50
ASHFORD COMMON 7F 129
Ashford Ct. HA8: Edg 3C 28
Ashford Ct. NW2 4F 63
Ashford Cres. EN3: Enf H 2D 24
Ashford Cres. TW15: Ashf 3A 128
Ashford Ho. SE8 6B 104
Ashford Ind. Est. TW15: Ashf 4E 128
Ashford Manor Golf Course 6B 128
Ashford M. N17 1G 49
ASHFORD PARK 4A 128
Ashford Pas. NW2 4F 63
Ashford Rd. E18 2K 51
Ashford Rd. E6 7E 70
Ashford Rd. NW2 4F 63
Ashford Rd. TW13: Felt 4F 129
Ashford Rd. TW15: Ashf 7E 128
Ashford St. N1 1G 9 (3E 84)
Ashford Tennis Club 4A 128
Ash Gro. BR4: W W'ck 2E 170
Ash Gro. E8 1H 85
(not continuous)
Ash Gro. EN1: Enf 7K 23
Ash Gro. HA0: Wemb 4A 60
Ash Gro. N10 4F 47
Ash Gro. N13 3H 33
Ash Gro. NW2 4F 63
Ash Gro. SE12 1J 141
Ash Gro. SE20 2J 157
Ash Gro. TW14: Felt 1G 129
Ash Gro. TW5: Hest 1B 112
Ash Gro. UB1: S'hall 5E 76
Ash Gro. UB3: Hayes 7F 75
Ash Gro. UB7: Yiew 7B 74
Ash Gro. W5 2E 96
Ashgrove Ct. W9 5J 81
(off Elmfield Way)
Ashgrove Ho. SW1 5D 18 (5H 101)
(off Lindsay Sq.)
Ashgrove Rd. BR1: Broml 6F 141
Ashgrove Rd. IG3: Ilf 1K 71
Ashgrove Rd. TW15: Ashf 5E 128
Ash Hill Cl. WD23: Bush 1A 26
Ash Hill Dr. HA5: Pinn 3A 40
Ash Ho. E14 2E 104
(off E. Ferry Rd.)
Ash Ho. SE1 4F 103
(off Longfield Est.)
Ash Ho. W10 4G 81
(off Heather Wlk.)
Ashingdon Cl. E4 3K 35
Ashington Ho. E1 4H 85
(off Barnsley St.)
Ashington Rd. SW6 2H 117
Ash Island KT8: E Mos 3H 149
Ashlake Rd. SW16 4J 137
Ashland Pl. W1 5G 5 (5E 82)
Ashlar Pl. SE18 4F 107
Ashleigh Commercial Est. SE7 3A 106
Ashleigh Ct. N14 7B 22
Ashleigh Ct. W5 4D 96
(off Murray Rd.)
Ashleigh Gdns. SM1: Sutt 2K 165
Ashleigh M. SE15 3F 121
(off Oglander Rd.)
Ashleigh Point SE23 3K 139
Ashleigh Rd. SE20 3H 157
Ashleigh Rd. SW14 3A 116
Ashley Av. IG6: Ilf 2F 53
Ashley Av. SM4: Mord 5J 153
Ashley Cl. HA5: Pinn 2K 39
Ashley Cl. NW4 2E 44
Ashley Ct. E3 3E 86
(off Bolinder Way)
Ashley Ct. EN5: New Bar 5F 21
Ashley Ct. NW4 2E 44
Ashley Ct. SW1 2A 18 (3G 101)
(off Morpeth Ter.)
Ashley Ct. UB5: N'olt 1C 76
Ashley Cres. N22 2A 48
Ashley Cres. SW11 3E 118
Ashley Dr. TW2: Whitt 7F 113
Ashley Dr. TW7: Isle 6J 95
Ashley Gdns. BR6: Orp 5J 173
Ashley Gdns. HA9: Wemb 2E 60
Ashley Gdns. N13 4H 33
Ashley Gdns. SW1 2B 18 (3G 101)
(not continuous)
Ashley Gdns. TW10: Ham 2D 132
Ashley La. CR0: Wadd 4B 168
Ashley La. NW4 2E 44
Ashley Pl. SW1 2A 18 (3G 101)
(not continuous)
Ashley Rd. CR7: Thor H 4K 155
Ashley Rd. E4 6H 35
Ashley Rd. E7 7A 70
Ashley Rd. EN3: Enf H 2D 24
Ashley Rd. KT7: T Ditt 6K 149
Ashley Rd. N17 3G 49
Ashley Rd. N19 1J 65
Ashley Rd. SW19 6K 135
Ashley Rd. TW12: Hamp 1E 148
Ashley Rd. TW9: Rich 3E 114
Ashleys All. N15 4C 48
Ashley Wlk. NW7 7K 29
Ashling Rd. CR0: C'don 1G 169
Ashlin Rd. E15 4F 69
Ash Lodge KT12: Walt T 7J 147
Ash Lodge TW16: Sun 7H 129
(off Forest Dr.)
Ashlone Rd. SW15 3E 116
Ashlyns Way KT9: Chess 6D 162
Ashmead N14 5B 22
Ashmead Bus. Cen. E16 4F 87
Ashmead Cl. TW15: Ashf Oxford Cl.
7E 128
Ashmead Ga. BR1: Broml 1A 160
Ashmead Ho. E9 5A 68
(off Homerton Rd.)
Ashmead Ho. W13 1A 96
(off Tewkesbury Rd.)
Ashmead M. SE8 2C 122
Ashmead Rd. SE8 2C 122
Ashmead Rd. TW14: Felt 1J 129
Ashmere Av. BR3: Beck 2F 159
Ashmere Cl. SM3: Cheam 5F 165
Ashmere Gro. SW2 4J 119
Ash M. NW5 5G 65
Ashmill St. NW1 5C 4 (5C 82)
Ashmole Pl. SW8 6K 101
Ashmole St. SW8 7H 19 (6K 101)
Ashmore NW1 7H 65
(off Agar Gro.)
Ashmore Cl. SE15 7F 103
Ashmore Ct. N11 6J 31
Ashmore Ct. TW5: Hest 6E 94
Ashmore Gro. DA16: Well 3H 125
Ashmore Ho. W14 3G 99
(off Russell Rd.)
Ashmore Rd. SE18 7D 106
Ashmore Rd. W9 2H 81
Ashmount Est. N19 7H 47
Ashmount Rd. N15 5F 49
Ashmount Rd. N19 7G 47
Ashmount Ter. W5 4D 96
Ashmour Gdns. RM1: Rom 2K 55
Ashneal Gdns. HA1: Harr 3H 59
Ashness Gdns. UB6: G'frd 6B 60
Ashness Rd. SW11 5D 118
Ashpark Ho. E14 6B 86
(off Norbiton Rd.)
Ashridge Cl. HA3: Kenton 6C 42
Ashridge Ct. N3 3J 45
Ashridge Ct. N14 5B 22
Ashridge Ct. UB1: S'hall 6G 77
(off Redcroft Rd.)
Ashridge Cres. SE18 7G 107
Ashridge Gdns. HA5: Pinn 4C 40
Ashridge Gdns. N13 5C 32
Ashridge Way SM4: Mord 3H 153
Ashridge Way TW16: Sun 6J 129
Ash Rd. BR6: Chels 7K 173
Ash Rd. CR0: C'don 2C 170
Ash Rd. E15 5G 69
Ash Rd. SM3: Sutt 7G 153
Ash Rd. TW17: Shep 4C 146
Ash Row BR2: Broml 7E 160
Ashtead Rd. E5 7G 49
Ashton Cl. SM1: Sutt 4J 165
Ashton Ct. E4 3B 36
Ashton Ct. HA1: Harr 3K 59
Ashton Gdns. RM6: Chad H 6E 54
Ashton Gdns. TW4: Houn 4D 112
Ashton Hgts. SE23 1J 139
Ashton Ho. SE11 5K 19 (5B 102)
(off Cottington St.)
Ashton Ho. SW9 7A 102
Ashton Pl. KT10: Clay 7A 162
Ashton Reach SE16 4A 104
Ashton Rd. E15 5F 69
Ashton St. E14 7E 86
Ashtree Av. CR4: Mitc 2B 154
Ash Tree Cl. BR6: Farnb 4F 173
Ash Tree Cl. CR0: C'don 6A 158
Ash Tree Cl. KT6: Surb 2E 162
Ash Tree Ct. TW15: Ashf 5D 128
(off Feltham Hill Rd.)
Ash Tree Dell NW9 5J 43
Ash Tree Ho. SE5 7C 102
(off Pitman St.)
Ash Tree Way CR0: C'don 5K 157
Ashurst Cl. SE20 1H 157
Ashurst Dr. IG2: Ilf 6F 53
Ashurst Dr. IG6: Ilf 5G 53
Ashurst Dr. TW17: Shep 5A 146
Ashurst Gdns. SW2 1A 138
Ashurst Rd. EN4: Cockf 5J 21
Ashurst Rd. N12 5H 31
Ashurst Wlk. CR0: C'don 2H 169
Ashvale Ct. E3 2C 86
(off Matilda Gdns.)
Ashvale Rd. SW17 5D 136
Ashview Apts. N4 7C 48
(off Katherine Cl.)
Ashview Cl. TW15: Ashf 5A 128
Ashview Gdns. TW15: Ashf 5A 128
Ashville Rd. E11 2F 69
Ash Wlk. HA0: Wemb 4C 60
Ashwater Rd. SE12 1J 141
Ash Way IG8: Wfd G 2B 52
Ashway Cen., The KT2: King T 1E 150
Ashwell Cl. E6 6C 88
Ashwell Ct. TW15: Ashf 2A 128
Ashwin St. E8 6F 67
Ashwood Av. UB8: Hil 6C 74
Ashwood Gdns. CR0: New Ad 6E 170
Ashwood Gdns. UB3: Harl 4H 93
Ashwood Ho. NW4 4E 44
(off Belle Vue Est.)
Ashwood Rd. E4 3A 36
Ashworth Cl. SE5 2D 120
Ashworth Est. CR0: Bedd 1J 167
Ashworth Mans. W9 3K 81
(off Elgin Av.)
Ashworth Rd. W9 3K 81
Aske Ho. N1 1G 9 (3E 84)
(off Fanshaw St.)
Asker Ho. N7 4J 65
Askern Cl. DA6: Bex 4D 126
Aske St. N1 1G 9 (3E 84)
Askew Bldg., The EC1 6C 8 (5C 84)
(off Bartholomew Cl.)
Askew Cres. W12 2B 98
Askew Rd. W12 2B 98
Askham Ct. W12 1C 98
Askham Rd. W12 1C 98
Askill Dr. SW15 5G 117
Askwith Rd. RM13: Rain 3K 91
Asland Rd. E15 1G 87
Aslett St. SW18 7K 117
Asman Ho. N1 2B 84
(off Colebrooke Rd.)
Asmara Rd. NW2 5G 63
Asmuns Hill NW11 5J 45
Asmuns Pl. NW11 5H 45
Asolando Dr. SE17 4C 102
Aspect Ct. E14 2E 104
(off Manchester Rd.)
Aspect Ct. SW6 2A 118
Aspects SM1: Sutt 5K 165
Aspen Cl. KT1: Hamp W 1C 150
Aspen Cl. N19 2G 65
Aspen Cl. UB7: Yiew 1B 92
Aspen Cl. W5 2F 97
Aspen Copse BR1: Broml 2D 160
Aspen Ct. NW4 2G 45
Aspen Dr. HA0: Wemb 3A 60
Aspen Gdns. CR4: Mitc 5E 154
Aspen Gdns. TW15: Ashf 5E 128
Aspen Gdns. W6 5D 98
Aspen Grn. DA18: Erith 3F 109
Aspen Gro. HA5: Eastc 3H 39
Aspen Ho. DA15: Sidc 2A 144
Aspen Ho. E15 3G 87
(off Teasel Way)
Aspen Ho. SE15 6J 103
(off Sharratt St.)
Aspen La. UB5: N'olt 3C 76
Aspenlea Rd. W6 6F 99
Aspen Lodge W8 3K 99
(off Abbots Wlk.)
Aspen M. SE20 6J 139
Aspen Pl. WD23: B Hea 1D 26
Aspen Way E14 7D 86
Aspen Way TW13: Felt 3K 129
Aspern Gro. NW3 5C 64
Aspinall Rd. SE4 3K 121
(not continuous)
Aspinden Rd. SE16 4H 103
ASPIRE Nat. Training Cen. 2G 27
Aspire Sport & Fitness Cen. 1K 33
Aspland Gro. E8 6H 67
(off Amhurst Rd.)
Aspley Rd. SW18 5K 117
Asplins Rd. N17 1G 49
Asprey M. BR3: Beck 5B 158
Asprey Pl. BR1: Broml 2C 160
Asquith Cl. RM8: Dag 1C 72
Asquith Ho. SW1 2D 18 (3H 101)
(off Monck St.)
Assam St. E1 6G 85
(off White Church La.)
Assata M. N1 6B 66
Assembley Ho. SE14 6B 104
(off Arklow Rd.)
Assembly, The TW3: Houn 3H 113
Assembly Apts. SE15 1J 121
(off York Gro.)
Assembly Pas. E1 5J 85
Assembly Wlk. SM5: Cars 7C 154
Ass Ho. La. HA3: Hrw W 4A 26
Assurance Pl. DA17: Belv 5F 109
Astall Cl. HA3: Hrw W 1J 41
Astbury Bus. Pk. SE15 1J 121
Astbury Ho. SE11 2J 19 (3A 102)
(off Lambeth Wlk.)
Astbury Rd. SE15 1J 121
Astell Ho. E14 6G 87
(off Lyell St.)
Astell Ho. SW3 5D 16 (5C 100)
(off Astell St.)
Astell Rd. SE3 4A 124
Astell St. SW3 5D 16 (5C 100)
Asten Way RM7: Mawney 2H 55
Aster Ct. E5 2J 67
(off Woodmill Rd.)
Asterid Hgts. E20 5E 68
(off Liberty Bri. Rd.)
Aster Pl. E9 7J 67
(off Frampton Pk. Rd.)
Aste St. E14 2E 104
Astey's Row N1 7C 66
Asthall Gdns. IG6: Ilf 4G 53
Astins Ho. E17 4D 50
Astleham Rd. TW17: Shep 3A 146
Astle St. SW11 2E 118
Astley Av. NW2 5E 62
Astley Ho. SE1 5F 103
(off Rowcross St.)
Astley Ho. SW13 6D 98
(off Wyatt Dr.)
Astley Ho. W2 5J 81
(off Alfred Rd.)
Aston Av. HA3: Kenton 7C 42
Aston Cl. DA14: Sidc 3A 144
Aston Ct. IG8: Wfd G 6D 36
Aston Grn. TW4: Cran 2A 112
Aston Ho. EC4 6J 7 (5A 84)
(off Furnival St.)
Aston Ho. RM8: Dag 4A 72
Aston Ho. SW8 1H 119
Aston Ho. W11 7H 81
(off Westbourne Gro.)
Aston M. RM6: Chad H 7C 54
Aston M. W10 3F 81
Aston Pl. SW16 6B 138
Aston Rd. SW20 2E 152
Aston Rd. W5 6D 78
Aston St. E14 5A 86
Aston Ter. SW12 6F 119
Astonville St. SW18 1J 135
Aston Webb Ho. SE1 5G 15 (1E 102)
(off Tooley St.)
Astor Av. RM7: Rom 6J 55
Astor Cl. KT2: King T 6H 133
Astor Coll. W1 5B 6 (5G 83)
(off Charlotte St.)
Astor Ct. E16 6A 88
(off Ripley Rd.)
Astor Ct. SW6 7A 100
(off Maynard Cl.)
Astoria Ct. E8 7F 67
(off Queensbridge Rd.)
Astoria Ho. NW9 2B 44
(off Boulevard Dr.)
Astoria Mans. SW16 3J 137
Astoria Wlk. SW9 3A 120
Astra Ho. E3 3B 86
(off Alfred St.)
Astra Ho. SE14 6B 104
(off Arklow Rd.)
Astral Ho. E1 6H 9 (5E 84)
(off Middlesex Rd.)
Astral Ho. SE6 4E 140
Astrid Ho. TW13: Felt 2A 130
Astrop M. W6 3E 98
Astrop Ter. W6 2E 98
Astwood Dr. HA7: Stan 2D 26
Astwood M. SW7 4A 100
Asylum Rd. SE15 7H 103
Atalanta St. SW6 7F 99
Atbara Rd. TW11: Tedd 6B 132
Atcham Rd. TW3: Houn 4G 113
Atcost Rd. IG11: Bark 5A 90
Atcraft Cen. HA0: Wemb 1E 78
Atelier Ct. SE8 7C 104
(off Watson's St.)
Atelier Ct. Central E14 5E 86
(off Lovon Rd.)
Atelier Ct. Nth. E14 5E 86
(off Leven Rd.)
Atelier Ct. Sth. E14 5E 86
(off Leven Rd.)
Atheldene Rd. SW18 1K 135
Athelney St. SE6 3C 140
Athelstane Gro. E3 2B 86
Athelstane M. N4 1A 66
Athelstan Gdns. NW6 7G 63
Athelstan Ho. E9 5B 68
(off Homerton Rd.)
Athelstan Ho. KT1: King T 4F 151
(off Athelstan Rd.)
Athelstan Pl. TW2: Twick 1J 131
Athelstan Rd. KT1: King T 4F 151
Athelstone Rd. HA3: W'stone 2H 41
Athena Cl. HA2: Harr 2H 59
Athena Cl. KT1: King T 3F 151
Athena Ct. SE1 7G 15 (3E 102)
(off City Wlk.)
Athenaeum Ct. N5 4C 66
Athenaeum Lawn Tennis Club 6K 53
Athenaeum Pl. N10 3F 47
Athenaeum Rd. N20 1F 31
Athena Pl. HA6: Nwood 1H 39
Athene Pl. EC4 7K 7 (6A 84)
(off Thavie's Inn)
Athenia Ho. E14 6F 87
(off Blair St.)
Athenlay Rd. SE15 5K 121
Athens Gdns. W9 4J 81
(off Harrow Rd.)
Atherden Rd. E5 4J 67
Atherfold Rd. SW9 3J 119
Atherley Way TW4: Houn 7D 112
Atherstone Ct. W2 5K 81
(off Delamere Ter.)
Atherstone M. SW7 4A 100
Atherton Dr. SW19 4F 135
Atherton Hgts. HA0: Wemb 7C 60
Atherton Leisure Cen. 6H 69
Atherton M. E7 6H 69
Atherton Pl. HA2: Harr 3H 41
Atherton Pl. UB1: S'hall 7E 76
Atherton Rd. E7 6H 69
Atherton Rd. IG5: Ilf 2C 52
Atherton Rd. SW13 7C 98
Atherton St. SW11 2C 118
Athlone Cl. E5 5H 67
Athlone Ct. E17 3F 51
Athlone Ho. E1 6J 85
(off Sidney St.)
Athlone Pl. W10 5G 81
Athlone Rd. SW2 7K 119
Athlone St. NW5 6E 64
Athlon Ind. Est. HA0: Wemb 1D 78
Athlon Rd. HA0: Wemb 2D 78
Athol Cl. HA5: Pinn 1K 39
Athole Gdns. EN1: Enf 5K 23
Athol Gdns. HA5: Pinn 1K 39
Atholl Ho. W9 3A 82
(off Maida Vale)
Atholl Rd. IG3: Ilf 7A 54
Athol Rd. DA8: Erith 5J 109
Athol Sq. E14 6E 86
Athol Way UB10: Hil 3C 74
Atkin Bldg. WC1 5H 7 (5K 83)
(off Raymond Bldgs.)
Atkins Ct. E3 1B 86
(off Willow Tree Cl.)
Atkins Dr. BR4: W W'ck 2F 171
Atkins Lodge W8 2J 99
(off Thornwood Gdns.)
Atkinson Cl. BR6: Chels 5K 173
Atkinson Cl. SW20 7C 134
Atkinson Ct. E10 7D 50
(off Kings Cl.)
Atkinson Ho. E13 4H 87
(off Sutton Rd.)
Atkinson Ho. E2 2G 85
(off Pritchards Rd.)
Atkinson Ho. SE17 4D 102
(off Catesby St.)
Atkinson Ho. SW11 1E 118
(off Austin Rd.)
Atkinson Morley Av. SW17 3B 136
Atkinson Rd. E16 5A 88
Atkins Rd. E10 6D 50
Atkins Rd. SW12 7G 119
Atkins Sq. E8 5H 67
Atlanta Bldg. SE13 1D 122
(off Deal's Gateway)
Atlanta Ct. CR7: Thor H 3C 156
Atlanta Ho. SE16 3A 104
(off Brunswick Quay)
Atlantic Apts. E16 7J 87
(off Seagull La.)
Atlantic Bldg. E15 5F 69
(off Property Row)
Atlantic Ct. E14 7F 87
(off Jamestown Way)
Atlantic Ct. SW3 5E 16 (5D 100)
Atlantic Rd. SW9 4A 120
Atlantic Wharf E1 7K 85
Atlantis Av. E16 7F 89
Atlantis Cl. IG11: Bark 3B 90
Atlas Bus. Cen. NW2 1D 62
Atlas Cres. HA8: Edg 2C 28
Atlas Gdns. SE7 4A 106
Atlas M. E8 6F 67
Atlas M. N7 6K 65
Atlas M. SE13 4F 123
Atlas Rd. E13 2J 87
Atlas Rd. HA9: Wemb 4J 61
Atlas Rd. N11 7K 31
Atlas Rd. NW10 3A 80
Atlas Trade Pk. DA8: Erith 5K 109
Atlas Wharf E9 6C 68
Atlip Rd. HA0: Wemb 1E 78
Atney Rd. SW15 4G 117
Atrium, The IG9: Buck H 2G 37
Atrium, The W12 1F 99
Atrium Apts. N1 1D 84
(off Felton St.)
Atrium Hgts. SE8 6D 104
(off Creekside)
Atrium Ho. SE8 7B 104
Atterbury Rd. N4 6A 48
Atterbury St. SW1 4E 18 (4J 101)
Attewood Av. NW10 3A 62
Attewood Rd. UB5: N'olt 6C 58
Attfield Cl. N20 2G 31
Attfield Ct. KT1: King T 2F 151
(off Albert Rd.)
Attilburgh Ho. SE1 7J 15 (3F 103)
(off St Saviour's Est.)
Attleborough Ct. SE23 2G 139
Attle Cl. UB10: Hil 2C 74
Attlee Cl. CR7: Thor H 5C 156
Attlee Cl. UB4: Yead 3K 75
Attlee Cl. UB5: N'olt 3K 75
Attlee Ct. UB4: Yead 3K 75
Attlee Rd. SE28 7B 90
Attlee Rd. UB4: Yead 3J 75
Attlee Ter. E17 4D 50
Attneave St. WC1 2J 7 (3A 84)
Attock M. E17 5D 50
Attwood La. SE10 4G 105
Atunbi Ct. NW1 7G 65
(off Farrier St.)
Atwater Cl. SW2 1A 138
Atwell Cl. E10 6D 50
Atwell Pl. KT7: T Ditt 1A 162
Atwell Rd. SE15 2G 121
Atwood Av. TW9: Kew 2G 115
Atwood Ho. W14 4H 99
(off Beckford Cl.)
Atwood Rd. W6 4D 98
Atwoods All. TW9: Kew 1G 115
Aube Ho. SE6 4E 140
Aubers Ridge Ct. E3 2B 86
(off Festubert Pl.)
Aubert Ct. N5 4B 66
Aubert Pk. N5 4B 66
Aubert Rd. N5 4B 66
Aubrey Beardsley Ho.
SW1 4B 18 (4G 101)
(off Vauxhall Bri. Rd.)
Aubrey Mans. NW1 5C 4 (5C 82)
(off Lisson St.)
Aubrey Moore Point E15 2E 86
(off Abbey La.)
Aubrey Pl. NW8 2A 82
Aubrey Rd. E17 3C 50
Aubrey Rd. N8 5J 47
Aubrey Rd. W8 1H 99
Aubrey Wlk. W8 1H 99
Aubrey Way E17 4D 50
Auburn Cl. SE14 7A 104
Aubyn Hill SE27 4C 138
Aubyn Sq. SW15 5C 116
Auckland Cl. SE19 1F 157
Auckland Ct. UB4: Yead 4A 76
Auckland Gdns. SE19 1E 156
Auckland Hill SE27 4C 138
Auckland Ho. W12 7D 80
(off White City Est.)
Auckland Ri. SE19 1E 156
Auckland Rd. E10 3D 68
Auckland Rd. IG1: Ilf 1F 71
Auckland Rd. KT1: King T 4F 151
Auckland Rd. SE19 1F 157
Auckland Rd. SW11 4C 118
Auckland St. SE11 6G 19 (5K 101)
Audax NW9 2B 44
Auden Pl. NW1 1E 82
Auden Pl. SM3: Cheam 4E 164
Audleigh Pl. IG7: Chig 6K 37

Audley Cl. – Bakers Hill

Audley Cl. N10 7A 32
Audley Cl. SW11 3E 118
Audley Ct. E18 4H 51
Audley Ct. HA5: Pinn 2A 40
Audley Ct. TW2: Twick 3H 131
Audley Ct. UB5: N'olt 3A 76
Audley Dr. E16 1K 105
Audley Gdns. IG3: Ilf 2K 71
Audley Pl. SM2: Sutt 7K 165
Audley Rd. EN2: Enf 2G 23
Audley Rd. NW4 5C 44
Audley Rd. TW10: Rich 5F 115
Audley Rd. W5 5F 79
Audley Sq. W1 4H 11 (1E 100)
Audrey Cl. BR3: Beck 6D 158
Audrey Gdns. HA0: Wemb 2B 60
Audrey Rd. IG1: Ilf 3F 71
Audrey St. E2 2G 85
Audric Cl. KT2: King T 1G 151
Augurs La. E13 3K 87
Augusta Cl. KT8: W Mole 3D 148
Augusta Rd. TW2: Twick 2G 131
Augustas La. N1 7A 66
Augusta St. E14 6D 86
Augusta Wlk. W5 5D 78
Augustine Bell Twr. E3 2C 86
(off Pancras Way)
Augustine Rd. HA3: Hrw W 1F 41
Augustine Rd. W14 3F 99
Augustus Bldg. E1 6H 85
(off Tarling St.)
Augustus Cl. HA7: Stan 3J 27
Augustus Cl. TW8: Bford 7C 96
Augustus Cl. W12 2D 98
Augustus Ct. SE1 4E 102
(off Old Kent Rd.)
Augustus Ct. SW16 2H 137
Augustus Ct. TW13: Hanw 4D 130
Augustus Ho. NW1 1K 5 (2F 83)
(off Augustus St.)
Augustus La. BR6: Orp 2K 173
Augustus Rd. SW19 1F 135
Augustus St. NW1 1K 5 (2F 83)
Aulay Ho. SE16 3F 103
Aultone Way SM1: Sutt 2K 165
Aultone Way SM5: Cars 3D 166
Aultone Yd. Ind. Est. SM5: Cars 3D 166
Aulton Pl. SE11 6K 19 (5A 102)
Aumonier M. N2 4C 46
Aura Ct. SE15 4H 121
Aura Ho. TW9: Kew 1H 115
Aurelia Gdns. CR0: C'don 5K 155
Aurelia Ho. E20 5E 68
(off Sunrise Cl.)
Aurelia Rd. CR0: C'don 6J 155
Auriel Av. RM10: Dag 6K 73
Auriga M. N1 5D 66
Auriol Cl. KT4: Wor Pk 3A 164
Auriol Dr. UB10: Hil 6C 56
Auriol Dr. UB6: G'frd 7H 59
Auriol Ho. W12 1D 98
(off Ellerslie Rd.)
Auriol Mans. W14 4G 99
(off Edith Rd.)
Auriol Pk. Rd. KT4: Wor Pk 3A 164
Auriol Rd. W14 4G 99
Aurora Apts. EC1 1C 8 (3C 84)
(off Bollinder Pl.)
Aurora Apts. SW18 5J 117
(off Buckhold Rd.)
Aurora Bldg. E14 1E 104
(off Blackwall Way)
Aurora Bldg., The N1 1F 9 (3D 84)
(off East Rd.)
Aurora Gdns. 7K 17 (6F 101)
Aurora Ho. E14 6D 86
(off Kerbey St.)
Aurora Ho. SE6 4E 140
Aurora Point SE8 4B 104
(off Grove St.)
Austell Gdns. NW7 3F 29
Austell Hgts. NW7 3F 29
(off Austell Gdns.)
Austen Apts. SE20 2H 157
Austen Cl. SE28 1B 108
Austen Ho. NW6 3J 81
(off Cambridge Rd.)
Austen Ho. SW17 3B 136
(off St George's Gro.)
Austen Rd. DA8: Erith 7H 109
Austen Rd. HA2: Harr 2F 59
Austin Av. BR2: Broml 5C 160
Austin Cl. SE23 7A 122
Austin Cl. TW1: Twick 5C 114
Austin Ct. E6 1A 88
Austin Ct. EN1: Enf 5K 23
Austin Ct. SE15 3G 121
(off Peckham Rye)
Austin Friars EC2 7F 9 (6D 84)
Austin Friars Sq. EC2 7F 9 (6D 84)
(off Austin Friars)
Austin Ho. SE14 7B 104
(off Achilles St.)
Austin Rd. SW11 1E 118
Austin Rd. UB3: Hayes 2H 93
Austin's La. HA4: Ruis 5F 57
Austin's La. UB10: Ick 3E 56
Austin St. E2 2J 9 (3F 85)
Austin Ter. SE1 1K 19 (3A 102)
(off Morley St.)
Austral Cl. DA15: Sidc 3K 143
Australian War Memorial 6H 11 (2E 100)
Australia Rd. W12 7D 80
Austral St. SE11 3K 19 (4B 102)
Austyn Gdns. KT5: Surb 1H 163
Austyns Pl. KT17: Ewe 7C 164
Autumn Cl. EN1: Enf 1B 24
Autumn Cl. SW19 6A 136
Autumn Ct. RM7: Rom 6J 55
Autumn Gro. BR1: Broml 6K 141
Autumn Lodge CR2: S Croy 4E 168
(off South Pk. Hill Rd.)
Autumn St. E3 1C 86
Autumn Way UB7: W Dray 2B 92
Avalon Cl. EN2: Enf 2F 23
Avalon Cl. SE6 2G 141
Avalon Cl. SW20 2G 153
Avalon Cl. W13 5A 78
Avalon Ct. CR0: C'don 7F 157
Avalon Rd. SW6 1K 117
Avalon Rd. W13 4A 78
Avante KT1: King T 3D 150
Avantgarde Pl. E1 3K 9 (4F 85)
(off Sclater St.)
Avantgarde Twr. E1 3K 9 (4F 85)
(off Sclater St.)
Avard Gdns. BR6: Farnb 4G 173
Avarn Rd. SW17 6D 136
Avebury Ct. N1 1D 84
(off Imber St.)
Avebury Ct. SE16 4J 103
(off Debnams Rd.)
Avebury Pk. KT6: Surb 7D 150
Avebury Rd. BR6: Orp 3H 173
Avebury Rd. E11 1F 69
Avebury Rd. SW19 1H 153
Avebury St. N1 1D 84
Avedon Cl. HA2: Harr 2G 41
Aveley Mans. IG11: Bark 7F 71
(off Whiting Av.)
Aveley Rd. RM1: Rom 4K 55
Aveline St. SE11 6J 19 (5A 102)
Aveling Pk. Rd. E17 2C 50
Ave Maria La. EC4 1B 14 (6B 84)
Avenell Mans. N5 4B 66
Avenell Rd. N5 3B 66
Avenfield Ho. W1 2F 11 (7D 82)
(off Park La.)
Avening Rd. SW18 7J 117
Avening Ter. SW18 7J 117
Avenir Ho. E15 6F 69
(off Forrester Way)
Avenons Rd. E13 4J 87
Aventine Av. CR4: Mitc 3F 155
Avenue, The BR1: Broml 3B 160
Avenue, The BR2: Kes 4B 172
Avenue, The BR3: Beck 1D 158
Avenue, The BR4: W W'ck 7E 158
Avenue, The BR5: St P 7B 144
Avenue, The BR6: Orp 2K 173
Avenue, The CR0: C'don 3E 168
Avenue, The DA5: Bexl 7D 126
Avenue, The E11 6K 51
Avenue, The E3 4D 86
(off Devas St.)
Avenue, The E4 6A 36
Avenue, The EC2 7H 9 (6E 84)
Avenue, The EN5: Barn 3B 20
Avenue, The HA3: Hrw W 1K 41
Avenue, The HA5: Pinn 6D 40
Avenue, The HA9: Wemb 1E 60
Avenue, The IG9: Buck H 2F 37
Avenue, The KT17: Ewe 7D 164
Avenue, The KT4: Wor Pk 2B 164
Avenue, The KT5: Surb 6F 151
Avenue, The N10 2G 47
Avenue, The N11 5A 32
Avenue, The N17 3D 48
Avenue, The N3 2J 45
Avenue, The N8 3A 48
Avenue, The NW6 1F 81
Avenue, The RM1: Rom 4K 55
Avenue, The SE10 7F 105
Avenue, The SM2: Cheam 7H 165
Avenue, The SM5: Cars 7E 166
Avenue, The SW18 7C 118
Avenue, The SW4 4E 118
Avenue, The TW1: Twick 5B 114
Avenue, The TW12: Hamp 6D 130
Avenue, The TW16: Sun 1K 147
Avenue, The TW3: Houn 5F 113
Avenue, The TW5: Cran 7J 93
Avenue, The TW9: Kew 2F 115
Avenue, The UB10: Ick 4C 56
Avenue, The W13 6B 78
Avenue, The W4 3A 98
Avenue Cl. N14 6B 22
Avenue Cl. NW8 1C 82
(not continuous)
Avenue Cl. TW5: Cran 1K 111
Avenue Cl. UB7: W Dray 3A 92
Avenue Ct. IG5: Ilf 3C 52
Avenue Ct. N14 6B 22
Avenue Ct. NW2 3H 63
Avenue Ct. SW3 4E 16 (4D 100)
(off Draycott Av.)
Avenue Cres. TW5: Cran 1K 111
Avenue Cres. W3 2H 97
Avenue Elmers KT6: Surb 5E 150
Avenue Gdns. SE25 2G 157
Avenue Gdns. SW14 3A 116
Avenue Gdns. TW11: Tedd 7K 131
Avenue Gdns. TW5: Cran 7K 93
Avenue Gdns. W3 2H 97
Avenue Ho. NW10 2D 80
(off All Souls Av.)
Avenue Ho. NW6 7G 63
(off The Avenue)
Avenue Ho. NW8 2C 82
(off Allitsen Rd.)
Avenue Ind. Est. E4 6H 35
Avenue Lodge NW8 7B 64
(off Avenue Rd.)
Avenue Mans. NW3 5K 63
(off Finchley Rd.)
Avenue M. N10 3F 47
Avenue Pde. N21 7J 23
Avenue Pde. TW16: Sun 3K 147
Avenue Pk. Rd. SE27 2B 138
Avenue Rd. BR3: Beck 2K 157
Avenue Rd. DA17: Belv 4J 109
Avenue Rd. DA17: Erith 4J 109
Avenue Rd. DA7: Bex 3E 126
Avenue Rd. DA8: Erith 7J 109
Avenue Rd. E7 4K 69
Avenue Rd. HA5: Pinn 3C 40
Avenue Rd. IG8: Wfd G 6F 37
Avenue Rd. KT1: King T 3E 150
Avenue Rd. KT3: N Mald 4A 152
Avenue Rd. N12 4F 31
Avenue Rd. N14 7B 22
Avenue Rd. N15 5D 48
Avenue Rd. N6 7G 47
Avenue Rd. NW10 2B 80
Avenue Rd. NW3 7B 64
Avenue Rd. NW8 7B 64
Avenue Rd. RM6: Chad H 7B 54
Avenue Rd. SE20 1J 157
Avenue Rd. SE25 2F 157
Avenue Rd. SM6: W'gton 7G 167
Avenue Rd. SW16 2H 155
Avenue Rd. SW20 2D 152
Avenue Rd. TW11: Tedd 7A 132
Avenue Rd. TW12: Hamp 1F 149
Avenue Rd. TW13: Felt 3H 129
Avenue Rd. TW7: Isle 1K 113
Avenue Rd. TW8: Bford 5C 96
Avenue Rd. UB1: S'hall 1D 94
Avenue Rd. W3 2H 97
Avenue Sth. KT5: Surb 7G 151
Avenue Studios SW3 4B 16 (4D 100)
(off Sydney Cl.)
Averil Gro. SW16 6B 138
Averill St. W6 6F 99
Avern Gdns. KT8: W Mole 4F 149
Avern Rd. KT8: W Mole 4F 149
Avershaw Ho. SW15 5F 117
Avery Cl. BR3: Beck 6B 140
Avery Ct. NW9 3J 43
Avery Farm Row SW1 4H 17 (4E 100)
Avery Gdns. IG2: Ilf 5D 52
AVERY HILL 6H 125
Avery Hill Rd. SE9 6H 125
Avery Row W1 2J 11 (7F 83)
Avery Wlk. SW11 3E 118
Aviary Cl. E16 5H 87
Aviation Dr. NW9 2C 44
Aviemore Cl. BR3: Beck 5B 158
Aviemore Way BR3: Beck 5A 158
Avigdor M. N16 2D 66
Avignon Rd. SE4 3K 121
Avingdor Ct. W3 1J 97
(off Horn La.)
Avington Ct. SE1 4E 102
(off Old Kent Rd.)
Avington Gro. SE20 7J 139
Avion Cres. NW9 1C 44
Avis Sq. E1 6K 85
Avoca Rd. SW17 4E 136
Avocet Cl. SE1 5G 103
Avocet M. SE28 3H 107
Avon Cl. KT4: Wor Pk 2C 164
Avon Cl. SM1: Sutt 4A 166
Avon Cl. UB4: Yead 4A 76
Avon Ct. E4 1K 35
Avon Ct. IG9: Buck H 1E 36
Avon Ct. N12 5E 30
Avon Ct. SW15 5G 117
Avon Ct. UB6: G'frd 4F 77
Avon Ct. W9 5J 81
(off Elmfield Way)
Avondale Av. EN4: E Barn 1J 31
Avondale Av. KT10: Hin W 3A 162
Avondale Av. KT4: Wor Pk 1B 164
Avondale Av. N12 5E 30
Avondale Av. NW2 3A 62
Avondale Ct. E11 1G 69
Avondale Ct. E16 5G 87
Avondale Ct. E18 1K 51
Avondale Ct. SM2: Sutt 7A 166
(off Brighton Rd.)
Avondale Cres. EN3: Enf H 3F 25
Avondale Cres. IG4: Ilf 5B 52
Avondale Dr. UB3: Hayes 1J 93
Avondale Gdns. TW4: Houn 5D 112
Avondale Ho. SE1 5G 103
(off Avondale Sq.)
Avondale Mans. SW6 1H 117
(off Rostrevor Rd.)
Avondale Pk. Gdns. W11 7G 81
Avondale Pk. Rd. W11 7G 81
Avondale Pavement SE1 5G 103
Avondale Ri. SE15 3F 121
Avondale Rd. BR1: Broml 6G 141
Avondale Rd. CR2: S Croy 6C 168
Avondale Rd. DA16: Well 2C 126
Avondale Rd. E16 5G 87
Avondale Rd. E17 7C 50
Avondale Rd. HA3: W'stone 3K 41
Avondale Rd. N13 2F 33
Avondale Rd. N15 5B 48
Avondale Rd. N3 1A 46
Avondale Rd. SE9 2C 142
Avondale Rd. SW14 3A 116
Avondale Rd. SW19 5K 135
Avondale Rd. TW15: Ashf 3A 128
Avondale Sq. SE1 5G 103
Avonfield Ct. E17 3F 51
Avongrove Ct. EC1 1D 8 (3C 84)
(off Bollinder Pl.)
Avon Ho. KT2: King T 1D 150
Avon Ho. W14 4H 99
(off Kensington Village)
Avon Ho. W8 3J 99
(off Allen St.)
Avonhurst Ho. NW2 7G 63
Avonley Rd. SE14 7J 103
Avon M. HA5: Hat E 1D 40
Avonmore Gdns. W14 4H 99
Avonmore Mans. W14 4G 99
(off Avonmore Rd.)
Avonmore Pl. W14 4G 99
Avonmore Rd. W14 4G 99
Avonmouth Apts. SW11 4C 118
(off Monarch Sq.)
Avonmouth St. SE1 7C 14 (3C 102)
Avon Path CR2: S Croy 6C 168
Avon Pl. SE1 7D 14 (2C 102)
Avon Rd. E17 3F 51
Avon Rd. SE4 3C 122
Avon Rd. TW16: Sun 7H 129
Avon Rd. UB6: G'frd 4E 76
Avonstowe Cl. BR6: Farnb 3G 173
Avon Way E18 3J 51
Avonwick Rd. TW3: Houn 2F 113
Avril Way E4 5K 35
Avro Ct. E9 5A 68
(off Mabley St.)
Avro Ho. NW9 2B 44
(off Boulevard Dr.)
Avro Ho. SW8 7F 101
(off Havelock Ter.)
Avro Pl. TW5: Hest 7A 94
Avro Way SM6: W'gton 7J 167
Awlfield Av. N17 1D 48
Awliscombe Rd. DA16: Well 2K 125
Axe St. IG11: Bark 1G 89
(not continuous)
Axholme Av. HA8: Edg 1G 43
Axiom Apts. BR2: Broml 4K 159
(off Masons Hill)
Axio Way E3 5C 86
Axis Apts. E1 3K 9 (4F 85)
(off Sclater St.)
Axis Ct. SE10 6G 105
(off Woodland Cres.)
Axis Ct. SE16 2G 103
(off East La.)
Axis Ho. SE13 4E 122
(off Lewisham High St.)
Axminster Cres. DA16: Well 1C 126
Axminster Rd. N7 3J 65
Axon Pl. IG1: Ilf 2G 71
Aybrook St. W1 6G 5 (5E 82)
Aycliffe Cl. BR1: Broml 4D 160
Aycliffe Ho. SE17 6D 102
(off Portland St.)
Aycliffe Rd. W12 1C 98
Ayerst Ct. E10 7E 50
Aylands Cl. HA9: Wemb 2E 60
Aylesbury Cl. E7 6H 69
Aylesbury Ct. SM1: Sutt 3A 166
Aylesbury Ho. HA0: Wemb 1E 78
(off Hatton Rd.)
Aylesbury Ho. SE15 6G 103
(off Friary Est.)
Aylesbury Rd. BR2: Broml 3J 159
Aylesbury Rd. SE17 5D 102
Aylesbury St. EC1 4A 8 (4B 84)
Aylesbury St. NW10 3K 61
Aylesford Av. BR3: Beck 5A 158
Aylesford Ho. SE1 7F 15 (2D 102)
(off Long La.)
Aylesford St. SW1 5C 18 (5H 101)
Aylesham Cen. 1G 121
Aylesham Cl. NW7 7H 29
Aylesham Rd. BR6: Orp 7K 161
Ayles Rd. UB4: Yead 3K 75
Aylestone Av. NW6 7F 63
Aylett Rd. SE25 4H 157
Aylett Rd. TW7: Isle 2J 113
Ayley Cft. EN1: Enf 5B 24
Ayliffe Cl. KT1: King T 2G 151
Aylmer Cl. HA7: Stan 4F 27
Aylmer Ct. N2 5D 46
Aylmer Dr. HA7: Stan 4F 27
Aylmer Ho. SE10 5F 105
Aylmer Pde. N2 5D 46
Aylmer Rd. E11 1H 69
Aylmer Rd. N2 5C 46
Aylmer Rd. RM8: Dag 3E 72
Aylmer Rd. W12 2B 98
Ayloffe Rd. RM9: Dag 6F 73
Aylsham Dr. UB10: Ick 2E 56
Aylton Est. SE16 2J 103
Aylward Rd. SE23 2K 139
Aylward Rd. SW20 2H 153
Aylwards Ri. HA7: Stan 4F 27
Aylward St. E1 Jamaica St. 6J 85
Aylward St. E1 Jubilee St. 6J 85
Aylwin Est. SE1 3E 102
Aynhoe Mans. W14 4F 99
(off Aynhoe Rd.)
Aynhoe Rd. W14 4F 99
Aynscombe Path SW14 2J 115
Ayr Ct. W3 5G 79
Ayres Cl. E13 3J 87
Ayres St. SE1 6D 14 (2C 102)
Ayr Grn. RM1: Rom 1K 55
Ayrsome Rd. N16 3E 66
Ayrton Gould Ho. E2 3K 85
(off Roman Rd.)
Ayrton Rd. SW7 1A 16 (3B 100)
Ayr Way RM1: Rom 1K 55
Aysgarth Ct. SM1: Sutt 3K 165
Aysgarth Rd. SE21 7E 120
Ayston Ho. SE16 4K 103
(off Plough Way)
Aytoun Pl. SW9 2K 119
Aytoun Rd. SW9 2K 119
Azalea Cl. IG1: Ilf 5F 71
Azalea Cl. W7 1K 95
Azalea Ct. IG8: Wfd G 6B 36
Azalea Ct. W7 1K 95
Azalea Ho. SE14 7B 104
(off Achilles St.)
Azalea Ho. TW13: Felt 1K 129
Azalea Wlk. HA5: Eastc 5K 39
Azania M. NW5 6F 65
Azenby Rd. SE15 2F 121
Azof St. SE10 4G 105
Azov Ho. E1 4A 86
(off Commodore St.)
Aztec Ho. IG1: Ilf 2H 71
Aztec Ho. IG6: Ilf 1G 53
Azura Ct. E15 1E 86
(off Warton Rd.)
Azure Bldg. E15 7F 69
(off Gt. Eastern Rd.)
Azure Ct. NW9 5G 43
Azure Ho. E2 3G 85
(off Buckfast St.)
Azure Pl. TW3: Houn 4F 113

B

Baalbec Rd. N5 5B 66
Babbacombe Cl. KT9: Chess 5D 162
Babbacombe Gdns. IG4: Ilf 4C 52
Babbacombe Ho. BR1: Broml 1J 159
(off Babbacombe Rd.)
Babbacombe Rd. BR1: Broml 1J 159
Babbage Ct. SE17 6B 102
(off Cook's Rd.)
Babbage Point SE10 6D 104
(off Norman Rd.)
Babell Ho. N1 6B 66
(off Canonbury Rd.)
Baber Bri. Cvn. Site TW14: Felt 5A 112
Baber Bri. Pde. TW14: Felt 6A 112
Baber Dr. TW14: Felt 6A 112
Babington Ct. WC1 5F 7 (5J 83)
(off Orde Hall St.)
Babington Ho. SE1 6D 14 (2C 102)
(off Disney St.)
Babington Ri. HA9: Wemb 6G 61
Babington Rd. NW4 4D 44
Babington Rd. RM8: Dag 5C 72
Babington Rd. SW16 5H 137
Babmaes St. SW1 3C 12 (7H 83)
Bache's St. N1 1F 9 (3D 84)
Back All. EC3 1H 15 (6E 84)
(off Lloyd's Av.)
Back Church La. E1 6G 85
Back Hill EC1 4K 7 (4A 84)
Backhouse Pl. SE17 4E 102
Back La. DA5: Bexl 7G 127
Back La. HA8: Edg 1J 43
Back La. IG9: Buck H 2G 37
Back La. N8 5J 47
Back La. NW3 4A 64
Back La. NW9 2K 43
Back La. RM6: Chad H 7D 54
Back La. TW10: Ham 3C 132
Back La. TW8: Bford 6D 96
Backley Gdns. SE25 6G 157
Back Rd. DA14: Sidc 4A 144
Back Rd. E11 6G 51
Back Rd. E17 4E 50
Back Rd. TW11: Tedd 7J 131
Bacon Gro. SE1 3F 103
Bacon La. HA8: Edg 1G 43
Bacon La. NW9 4H 43
(not continuous)
Bacon's College Sports Cen. 1A 104
Bacons La. N6 1E 64
Bacon St. E1 3K 9 (4F 85)
Bacon St. E2 3K 9 (4F 85)
Bacon Ter. RM8: Dag 5B 72
Bacton NW5 5E 64
Bacton St. E2 3J 85
Baddeley Ho. KT8: W Mole 5E 148
(off Down St.)
Baddesley Ho. SE11 5H 19 (5K 101)
(off Jonathan St.)
Baddow Cl. IG8: Wfd G 6F 37
Baddow Cl. RM10: Dag 1G 91
Baden Dr. E4 4J 25
Baden Pl. SE1 6E 14 (2D 102)
Baden Powell Cl. KT6: Surb 2F 163
Baden Powell Cl. RM9: Dag 1E 90
Baden Powell Ho. DA17: Belv 3G 109
(off Ambrooke Rd.)
Baden Rd. IG1: Ilf 5F 71
Baden Rd. N8 4H 47
Bader Ct. NW9 2B 44
(off Runway Cl.)
Bader Way SW15 6C 116
Bader Way UB10: Uxb 7A 56
Badgemore Path SE18 5H 107
(off Tuscan Rd.)
Badger Cl. IG2: Ilf 6G 53
Badger Cl. TW13: Felt 3K 129
Badger Cl. TW4: Houn 3A 112
Badger Ct. NW2 3E 62
Badgers Cl. EN2: Enf 3G 23
Badgers Cl. HA1: Harr 6H 41
Badgers Cl. TW15: Ashf 5B 128
Badgers Cl. UB3: Hayes 7G 75
Badgers Copse BR6: Orp 2K 173
Badgers Copse KT4: Wor Pk 2B 164
Badgers Cft. N20 7B 20
Badgers Cft. SE9 3E 142
Badgers Hole CR0: C'don 4K 169
Badgers Wlk. KT3: N Mald 2A 152
Badlis Rd. E17 3C 50
Badma Cl. N9 3D 34
Badminton Cl. HA1: Harr 4J 41
Badminton Cl. UB5: N'olt 6E 58
Badminton M. E16 1J 105
Badminton Rd. SW12 6E 118
Badric Ct. SW11 2B 118
Badsworth Rd. SE5 1C 120
Baffin Way E14 1E 104
Bafton Ga. BR2: Hayes 1K 171
Bagley Cl. UB7: W Dray 2A 92
Bagley's La. SW6 1K 117
Bagleys Spring RM6: Chad H 4E 54
Bagley Wlk. N1 1H 83
Bagnigge Ho. WC1 2J 7 (3A 84)
(off Margery St.)
Bagshot Ct. SE18 1E 124
Bagshot Ho. NW1 1K 5 (3F 83)
(off Redhill St.)
Bagshot Rd. EN1: Enf 7A 24
Bagshot St. SE17 5E 102
Bahram Ct. E2 4H 85
(off Three Colts La.)
Baildon E2 2J 85
(off Cyprus St.)
Baildon St. SE8 7B 104
Bailes Pl. BR3: Beck 1A 158
Bailey Cl. E4 4K 35
Bailey Cl. N11 7C 32
Bailey Cl. SE28 1J 107
Bailey Cotts. E14 5A 86
(off Maroon St.)
Bailey Ct. NW9 3A 44
(off Lingard Av.)
Bailey Cres. KT9: Chess 7D 162
Bailey Ho. E3 3D 86
(off Talwin St.)
Bailey Ho. SW10 7K 99
(off Coleridge Gdns.)
Bailey M. SW2 5A 120
Bailey M. W4 6H 97
Bailey Pl. N16 5E 66
Bailey Pl. SE26 6K 139
Baileys Ho. SW11 7H 101
(off Charles Clowes Wlk.)
Bailey St. SE8 4A 104
Bailey Twr. E1 7H 85
Baillies Wlk. W5 2D 96
Bainbridge Cl. TW10: Ham 5E 132
Bainbridge Ct. SE10 3J 105
(off Rennie Street)
Bainbridge Rd. RM9: Dag 4F 73
Bainbridge St. WC1 7D 6 (6H 83)
Baines Cl. CR2: S Croy 5D 168
Baird Av. UB1: S'hall 7F 77
Baird Cl. E10 1C 68
Baird Cl. NW9 6J 43
Baird Gdns. SE19 4E 138
Baird Ho. W12 7D 80
(off White City Est.)
Baird Memorial Cotts. N14 2C 32
(off Balaams La.)
Baird Rd. EN1: Enf 3C 24
Baird St. EC1 3D 8 (4C 84)
Bairny Wood App. IG8: Wfd G 6E 36
Baizdon Rd. SE3 2G 123
Bakehouse M. TW12: Hamp 7E 130
Baker Beal Ct. DA7: Bex 3H 127
Baker Ho. E3 3D 86
(off Bromley High St.)
Baker Ho. W7 1K 95
Baker Ho. WC1 4F 7 (4J 83)
(off Colonnade)
Baker La. CR4: Mitc 2E 154
Baker Pas. NW10 1A 80
Baker Pl. KT19: Ewe 6J 163
Baker Rd. NW10 1A 80
Baker Rd. SE18 7C 106
Bakers Av. E17 6D 50
Bakers Ct. SE25 3E 156
Bakers End SW20 2G 153
Baker's Fld. N7 4H 65
Bakers Field Cl. KT19: Ewe 7K 163
Bakers Gdns. SM5: Cars 2C 166
Bakers Hall Ct. EC3 3H 15 (7E 84)
(off Harp La.)
Bakers Hill E5 1J 67
Bakers Hill EN5: New Bar 2E 20

Bakers Ho. W5 ....1D 96	Ballater Rd. CR2: S Croy 5F 169
Bakers La. N6 ....6D 46	Ballater Rd. SW2 ....4J 119
Baker's M. W1 ....7G 5 (6E 82)	Ball Ct. EC3 ....1F 15 (6D 84)
Bakers M. BR2: Chels 6K 173	*(off Birchin La.)*
Bakers Pas. NW3 ....4A 64	Balletica Apts. WC2 ......1F 13 (6J 83)
(off Heath St.)	*(off Long Acre)*
Baker's Rents E2 ....2J 9 (3F 85)	Ball Ho. NW9 ....3B 44
Baker's Row E15 ....2C 87	*(off Aerodrome Rd.)*
Baker's Row EC1 ....4J 7 (4A 84)	Ballie Apts. E16 ....1G 105
Baker St. EN1: Enf. 3J 23	*(off Lock Side Way)*
Baker St. NW1 ....4F 5 (4D 82)	Ballina St. SE23 ....7K 121
Baker St. W1 ....5F 5 (5D 82)	Ballin Ct. E14 ....2E 104
BAKER STREET 5F 5 (5D 82)	*(off Stewart St.)*
Baker's Yd. EC1 ....4J 7 (4A 84)	Ballingdon Rd. SW11 ....6E 118
(off Bakers Rd.)	Ballinger Point E3 ....3D 86
Bakery Cl. RM6: Chad H. 3E 54	*(off Bromley High St.)*
Bakery Cl. SW9 ....7K 101	Ballinger Way UB5: N'olt 4C 76
Bakery M. KT6: Surb. 1G 163	Balliol Av. E4 ....4B 36
Bakery Path HA8: Edg. 5C 28	Balliol Rd. DA16: Well 2B 126
(off St Margaret's Rd.)	Balliol Rd. N17 ....1E 48
Bakery Pl. SW11 ....4D 118	Balliol Rd. W10 ....6E 80
Bakery St. SE16 ....3F 103	Balloch Rd. SE6 ....1F 141
Bakewell Way KT3: N Mald ...2A 152	Ballogie Av. NW10 ....4A 62
Balaam Leisure Cen. 4J 87	Ballow Cl. SE5 ....7E 102
Balaam Ho. SM1: Sutt. 4J 165	Balmain Cl. W5 ....1D 96
Balaams La. N14 ....2C 32	Balmain Ct. TW3: Houn 1F 113
Balaam St. E13 ....4J 87	Balmain Lodge KT5: Surb 4E 150
Balaclava Rd. KT6: Surb 7C 150	*(off Cranes Pk. Av.)*
Balaclava Rd. SE1 ....4F 103	Balman Ho. SE16 ....4K 103
Bala Grn. NW9 ....6A 44	*(off Rotherhithe New Rd.)*
(off Ruthin Cl.)	Balmer Rd. E3 ....2B 86
Balboa Ct. E14 ....5A 86	Balmes Rd. N1 ....1D 84
(off Pechora Way)	Balmoral Apts. W2 ....6C 4 (5C 82)
Balcaskie Rd. SE9 ....5D 124	*(off Praed St.)*
Balchen Rd. SE3 ....2B 124	Balmoral Av. BR3: Beck 4A 158
Balchier Rd. SE22 ....6H 121	Balmoral Av. N11 ....6K 31
Balcombe Cl. DA6: Bex 4D 126	Balmoral Cl. SW15 ....6F 117
Balcombe Ho. NW1 ....3D 4 (4C 82)	*(off The Avenue)*
(off Taunton Pl.)	Balmoral Ct. HA9: Wemb 3F 61
Balcombe St. NW1 ....4E 4 (4D 82)	Balmoral Ct. KT4: Wor Pk.....2D 164
Balcon Ct. W5 ....6F 79	Balmoral Ct. NW8 ....2B 82
Balcony, The W12 ....1F 99	*(off Queen's Ter.)*
Balcorne St. E9 ....7J 67	Balmoral Ct. SE12 ....4K 141
Balder Ri. SE12 ....2K 141	Balmoral Ct. SE16 ....1K 103
Balderton Flats W1 ....1H 11 (6E 82)	*(off King & Queen Wharf)*
(off Balderton St.)	Balmoral Ct. SE17 ....5D 102
Balderton St. W1 ....1H 11 (6E 82)	*(off Merrow St.)*
Baldewyne Ct. N17 ....1G 49	Balmoral Ct. SE27 ....4C 138
Baldock St. E3 ....2D 86	Balmoral Ct. SM2: Sutt. 7J 165
Baldrey Ho. SE10 ....5H 105	Balmoral Cres. KT8: W Mole ...3E 148
(off Blackwall La.)	Balmoral Dr. UB1: S'hall 4D 76
Baldry Gdns. SW16 ....6J 137	Balmoral Dr. UB4: Hayes 4G 75
Baldwin Cres. SE5 ....1C 120	Balmoral Gdns. DA5: Bexl 7F 127
Baldwin Gdns. TW3: Houn 1G 113	Balmoral Gdns. IG3: Ilf 1K 71
Baldwin Ho. SW2 ....1A 138	Balmoral Gdns. W13 ....3A 96
Baldwin Rd. SW11 ....6E 118	Balmoral Ho. E14 ....3D 104
Baldwins EC1 ....5J 7 (5A 84)	*(off Lanark Sq.)*
Baldwin St. EC1 ....2E 8 (3D 84)	Balmoral Ho. E16 ....1K 105
Baldwin Ter. N1 ....2C 84	*(off Keats Av.)*
Baldwyn Gdns. W3 ....7K 79	Balmoral Ho. SE1 ....5J 15 (1F 103)
Baldwyn's Pk. DA5: Bexl 2K 145	*(off Duchess Wlk.)*
Baldwyn's Rd. DA5: Bexl 2K 145	Balmoral Ho. W14 ....4H 99
Balearic Apts. E16 ....7J 87	*(off Windsor Way)*
(off Western Gateway)	Balmoral M. W12 ....3B 98
Bale Rd. E1 ....5A 86	Balmoral Rd. E10 ....2D 68
Bales Ter. N9 ....3A 34	Balmoral Rd. E7 ....4A 70
Balfern Gro. W4 ....5A 98	Balmoral Rd. HA2: Harr 4E 58
Balfern St. SW11 ....2C 118	Balmoral Rd. KT1: King T 4F 151
Balfe St. N1 ....2J 83	Balmoral Rd. KT4: Wor Pk.....3D 164
Balfour Av. W7 ....1K 95	Balmoral Rd. NW2 ....6D 62
Balfour Bus. Cen. UB2: S'hall ..3A 94	Balmoral Trad. Est. IG11: Bark ..5K 89
Balfour Ho. N20 ....3J 31	Balmore Cl. E14 ....6E 86
Balfour Ho. SW11 ....1E 118	Balmore Cres. EN4: Cockf 5K 21
(off Forfar Rd.)	Balmore St. N19 ....2F 65
Balfour Ho. W10 ....5F 81	Balmuir Gdns. SW15 ....4E 116
(off St Charles Sq.)	Balnacraig Av. NW10 ....4J 62
Balfour M. N9 ....3B 34	Balniel Ga. SW1 ....5D 18 (5H 101)
Balfour M. W1 ....4H 11 (1E 100)	Balsam Ho. E14 ....7D 86
Balfour Pl. SW15 ....4D 116	*(off E. India Dock Rd.)*
Balfour Pl. W1 ....3H 11 (7E 82)	Baltic Apts. E16 ....7J 87
Balfour Rd. BR2: Broml 5B 160	*(off Western Gateway)*
Balfour Rd. HA1: Harr 5H 41	Baltic Av. TW8: Bford 5D 96
Balfour Rd. IG1: Ilf 2F 71	Baltic Cl. SW19 ....7B 136
Balfour Rd. N5 ....4C 66	Baltic Ct. E1 ....1J 103
Balfour Rd. SE25 ....5G 157	*(off Clave St.)*
Balfour Rd. SM5: Cars 7D 166	Baltic Ct. SE16 ....2K 103
Balfour Rd. SW19 ....7K 135	Baltic Ho. SE5 ....2C 120
Balfour Rd. TW3: Houn 3F 113	Baltic Pl. N1 ....1E 84
Balfour Rd. UB2: S'hall 3B 94	Baltic St. E. EC1 ....4C 8 (4C 84)
Balfour Rd. W13 ....2A 96	Baltic St. W. EC1 ....4C 8 (4C 84)
Balfour St. SE17 ....4D 102	Baltimore Cl. DA17: Belv 2H 109
Balfour Ter. N3 ....2K 45	Baltimore Ct. SW1 ....4C 18 (4H 101)
Balfron Twr. E14 ....1E 104	*(off Vauxhall Bri. Rd.)*
Balgonie Rd. E4 ....1A 36	Baltimore Ho. SE11 ......4J 19 (4A 102)
Balgove Ct. NW10 ....6A 62	*(off Hotspur St.)*
(off Eden Gro.)	Baltimore Ho. W12 ....1A 36
Balgowan Cl. KT3: N Mald 5A 152	Baltimore Pl. DA16: Well 2K 125
Balgowan Rd. BR3: Beck 3A 158	Baltimore Wharf E14 ....3D 104
Balgowan St. SE18 ....4K 107	Balvaird Pl. SW1 ....6D 18 (5H 101)
BALHAM 1E 136	Balvernie Gro. SW18 ....7H 117
Balham Gro. SW12 ....7E 118	Balvernie M. SW18 ....7J 117
Balham High Rd. SW12 ....1E 136	Bamber Rd. SE15 ....1F 121
Balham High Rd. SW17 ....3E 136	Bamboo Ct. E5 ....2J 67
Balham Hill SW12 ....7F 119	*(off Woodmill Rd.)*
Balham Leisure Cen. 2F 137	Bamborough Gdns. W12 ....2E 98
Balham New Rd. SW12 ....7F 119	Bamburgh N17 ....7C 34
Balham Pk. Rd. SW12 ....1D 136	Bamford Av. HA0: Wemb 1F 79
Balham Rd. N9 ....2B 34	Bamford Rd. BR1: Broml 5E 140
Balham Sta. Rd. SW12 ....1F 137	Bamford Rd. IG11: Bark 6G 71
Balin Ho. SE1 ....6E 14 (2D 102)	Bampfylde Cl. SM6: W'gton ...3G 167
(off Long La.)	Bampton Cl. W5 ....6D 78
Balladier Wlk. E14 ....5D 86	Bampton Dr. NW7 ....7H 29
Ballamore Rd. BR1: Broml 3J 141	Bampton Rd. SE23 ....3K 139
Ballance Rd. E9 ....6K 67	Banavie Gdns. BR3: Beck 1E 158
Ballantine St. SW18 ....4A 118	Banbury Cl. EN2: Enf 1G 23
Ballantrae Ho. NW2 ....4H 63	Banbury Ct. SM2: Sutt. 7J 165
Ballantyne Cl. SE9 ....4C 142	Banbury Ct. WC2 ....2E 12 (7J 83)
Ballard Cl. KT2: King T 7K 133	*(off Long Acre)*
Ballard Ho. SE10 ....6D 104	Banbury Ho. E9 ....7K 67
(off Thames St.)	Banbury Rd. E17 ....7F 34
Ballards Cl. RM10: Dag 1H 91	Banbury Rd. E9 ....7K 67
Ballards Farm Rd. CR0: C'don ..6K 169	Banbury St. SW11 ....2C 118
Ballards Farm Rd. CR2: S Croy ..6G 169	Banbury Wlk. UB5: N'olt 2E 76
Ballards La. N12 ....1J 45	*(off Brabazon Way)*
Ballards La. N3 ....1J 45	Banchory Rd. SE3 ....7K 105
Ballards M. HA8: Edg 6B 28	Bancroft Av. IG9: Buck H 2D 36
Ballards Ri. CR2: Sels 6G 169	Bancroft Av. N2 ....5C 46
Ballards Rd. NW2 ....2C 62	Bancroft Cl. TW15: Ashf 5C 128
Ballards Rd. RM10: Dag 2H 91	Bancroft Ct. SW8 ....7J 101
Ballards Way CR0: C'don 6H 169	*(off Allen Edwards Dr.)*
Ballards Way CR2: Sels 6G 169	Bancroft Ct. UB5: N'olt 1A 76
Ballast Quay SE10 ....5F 105	Bancroft Gdns. BR6: Orp 1K 173
Ballast Rd. DA8: Erith 5J 109	Bancroft Gdns. HA3: Hrw W ...1A 76

Bancroft Gdns. HA3: Hrw W ..1G 41	Barbers Rd. E15 ....2D 86
Bancroft Ho. E1 ....4J 85	Barbican EC2 ....5D 8 (5C 84)
(off Cephas St.)	*(off Silk St.)*
Bancroft Rd. E1 ....3J 85	Barbican Art Gallery 5D 8 (5C 84)
Bancroft Rd. HA3: Hrw W 2H 41	Barbican Arts Cen. 5D 8 (5C 84)
Bandon Cl. UB10: Uxb 2B 74	Barbican Cinema 1 Silk St. ...5D 8 (5C 84)
BANDONHILL 5H 167	Barbican Cinema 2 & 3 Whitecross St.
Bandon Ri. SM6: W'gton 5H 167	..............................5D 8 (5C 84)
Banfield Rd. SE15 ....3H 121	*(off Whitecross St.)*
Banfor Cl. SM6: W'gton 5G 167	Barbican Rd. UB6: G'frd 6F 77
Bangalore St. SW15 ....3E 116	Barbican Theatre London 5D 8 (5C 84)
Bangla Ho. E8 ....1F 85	*(within Arts Cen.)*
(off Clarissa St.)	Barb M. W6 ....3E 98
Bangor Cl. UB5: N'olt 5F 59	Barbon Cl. WC1 ....5G 7 (5K 83)
Banim St. W6 ....4D 98	Barbot Cl. N9 ....3B 34
Banister Ho. E9 ....5K 67	Barbridge Cl. HA8: Dag 5B 72
Banister Ho. SW8 ....1G 119	Barchard St. SW18 ....5K 117
(off Wadhurst St.)	Barchester Cl. W7 ....1K 95
Banister Ho. W10 ....7G 81	Barchester Rd. HA3: Hrw W ...2H 41
Banister M. NW6 ....7K 63	Barchester St. E14 ....5D 86
Banister Rd. W10 ....3F 81	Barclay Cl. SW6 ....7J 99
Bank, The N6 ....1F 65	Barclay Ho. E9 ....7J 67
Bank Av. CR4: Mitc 2B 154	*(off Well St.)*
Bank Bldgs. E4 ....6A 36	Barclay Oval IG8: Wfd G 4D 36
(off The Avenue)	Barclay Path E17 ....5E 50
Bank Ct. E17 ....4E 50	Barclay Rd. CR0: C'don 3D 168
Bank End SE1 ....4D 14 (1C 102)	Barclay Rd. E11 ....1H 69
Bankfoot Rd. BR1: Broml 4G 141	Barclay Rd. E13 ....4A 88
Bankhurst Rd. SE6 ....7B 122	Barclay Rd. E17 ....6E 50
Bank La. KT2: King T 7E 132	Barclay Rd. N18 ....6J 33
Bank La. SW15 ....5A 116	Barclay Rd. SW6 ....7J 99
Bank M. SM1: Sutt. 6A 166	Barcombe Av. SW2 ....2J 137
Bank of England 1E 14 (6D 84)	Barcombe Cl. BR5: St P 3K 161
Bank of England Mus. ...1F 15 (6D 84)	Bardell Ho. SE1 ....7K 15 (2G 103)
(off Bartholomew La.)	*(off Parkers Row)*
Bank of England Sports Cen. 5A 116	Barden St. SE18 ....7J 107
Banks Ho. SE1 ....3C 102	Bardfield Av. RM6: Chad H 3E 54
(off Rockingham St.)	Bardney Rd. SM4: Mord 4K 153
Banksian Wlk. TW7: Isle 1J 113	Bardolph Rd. N7 ....4J 65
Banksia Rd. N18 ....5E 34	Bardolph Rd. TW9: Rich 3F 115
Bankside CR2: S Croy 6F 169	Bard Rd. W10 ....7F 81
Bankside EN2: Enf 1G 23	Bardsey Pl. E1 ....4J 85
Bankside SE1 ....3C 14 (7C 84)	Bardsey Wlk. N1 ....6D 66
(not continuous)	*(off Douglas Rd. Nth.)*
Bankside UB1: S'hall 4D 94	Bardsley Cl. CR0: C'don 3F 169
Bankside Av. SE13 ....3E 122	Bardsley Ho. SE10 ....6E 104
Bankside Av. UB5: N'olt 2J 75	*(off Bardsley La.)*
Bankside Cl. DA5: Bexl 4K 145	Bardsley La. SE10 ....6E 104
Bankside Cl. SM5: Cars 6C 166	Barents Ho. E1 ....4K 85
Bankside Cl. TW7: Isle 4K 113	*(off White Horse La.)*
Bankside Dr. KT7: T Ditt 1B 162	Barfett St. W10 ....4H 81
Bankside Gallery 3B 14 (7B 84)	Barfield Av. N20 ....2J 31
Bankside Lofts SE1 ....4B 14 (1B 102)	Barfield Rd. BR1: Broml 3E 160
(off Hopton St.)	Barfield Rd. E11 ....1H 69
Bankside Mix 4C 14 (1C 102)	Barfleur La. SE8 ....4B 104
Bankside Pk. IG11: Bark 3A 90	Barford Cl. NW4 ....2C 44
Bankside Pl. N4 ....6C 48	Barford Ho. E3 ....2B 86
Bankside Rd. IG1: Ilf 5G 71	*(off Tredegar Rd.)*
Bankside SE19 ....6E 138	Barford St. N1 ....1A 84
Banks La. DA6: Bex 4F 127	Barforth Rd. SE15 ....3H 121
Bank St. E14 ....1D 104	Barfreston Way SE20 ....1H 157
Banks Way E12 ....4E 70	Bargate Cl. KT3: N Mald 7C 152
Banks Yd. TW5: Hest. 6D 94	Bargate Cl. SE18 ....5K 107
Bankton Rd. SW2 ....4A 120	Barge Dr. UB2: S'hall 3F 95
Bankwell Rd. SE13 ....4G 123	Barge Ho. Rd. E16 ....2F 107
Bannatyne Health Club Chingford	Barge Ho. St. SE1 ....4K 13 (1A 102)
....6H 35	Barge La. E3 ....1A 86
Bannatyne Health Club Grove Park	Bargery Rd. SE6 ....1D 140
....2K 141	Barge Wlk. KT8: E Mos Boyle Farm Island
Bannatyne Health Club Maida Vale	....3H 149
....2K 81	Barge Wlk. KT8: E Mos Hampton Ct. Cres.
(off Greville Rd.)	....3H 149
Bannatyne Health Club Orpington	Barge Wlk. KT1: Hamp W 3D 150
....7D 144	Barge Wlk. KT2: King T 1D 150
Bannatyne Health Club Russell Square	Barge Wlk. SE10 ....3H 105
........................3D 6 (4H 83)	Bargrove Cl. SE20 ....7G 139
(off Woburn Pl.)	Bargrove Cres. SE6 ....2B 140
Banner Ct. SE16 ....4J 103	Barham Cl. BR2: Broml 1C 172
(off Rotherhithe New Rd.)	Barham Cl. BR7: Chst. 5F 143
Banner Ho. EC1 ....4D 8 (4C 84)	Barham Cl. HA0: Wemb 6B 60
(off Roscoe St.)	Barham Cl. RM7: Mawney 2H 55
Banner La. RM8: Dag 1E 72	Barham Ct. CR2: S Croy 4C 168
Bannerman Ho. SW8 .....7G 19 (6K 101)	*(off Barham Rd.)*
Banner St. EC1 ....4D 8 (4C 84)	Barham Ho. SE17 ....5E 102
Banning Ho. SW19 ....5G 135	*(off Kinglake Est.)*
Bannister Cl. SW2 ....1A 138	Barham Rd. BR7: Chst. 5F 143
Bannister Cl. UB6: G'frd 5H 59	Barham Rd. CR2: S Croy 4C 168
Bannister Ho. HA3: W'stone ...3J 41	Barham Rd. SW20 ....7C 134
Bannister Ho. SE14 ....6B 104	Baring Cl. SE12 ....2J 141
(off John Williams Cl.)	Baring Ct. N1 ....1D 84
Bannister Ho. SE14 ....4K 103	*(off Baring St.)*
(off Headstone Dr.)	Baring Ho. E14 ....6C 86
Bannister Sports Cen. 6B 26	*(off Canton St.)*
Bannockburn Rd. SE18 ....4J 107	Baring Rd. CR0: C'don 1G 169
Bannon Ct. SW6 ....1K 117	Baring Rd. EN4: Cockf 4G 21
(off Michael Rd.)	Baring Rd. SE12 ....7J 123
Bannow Cl. KT19: Ewe 4A 164	Baring St. N1 ....1D 84
Banstead Ct. W12 ....7B 80	Baritone Ct. E15 ....1H 87
Banstead Gdns. N9 ....3K 33	Barker Cl. HA6: Nwood 1H 39
Banstead Rd. SM5: Cars 7B 166	Barker Cl. KT3: N Mald 4H 151
Banstead St. SE15 ....3J 121	Barker Cl. TW9: Kew 2H 115
Banstead Way SM6: W'gton ...5J 167	Barker Dr. NW1 ....7G 65
Banstock Rd. HA8: Edg 6C 28	Barker Ho. SE17 ....4E 102
Bantam Ho. NW9 ....2B 44	*(off Congreve St.)*
(off Heritage Av.)	Barker M. SW4 ....4F 119
Banting Dr. N21 ....5E 22	Barker's Arc. 4K 99
Banting Ho. NW2 ....3C 62	Barker St. SW10 ....6A 100
Bantock Ho. W10 ....3G 81	Barker Wlk. SW16 ....3H 137
(off Third Av.)	Barkham Rd. N17 ....7J 33
Banton Cl. EN1: Enf 2C 24	Barkham Ter. SE1 ....1K 19 (3A 102)
Bantry Ho. E1 ....4K 85	*(off Lambeth Rd.)*
(off Ernest St.)	BARKING 6G 71
Bantry St. SE5 ....7D 102	Barking Abbey School Leisure Cen.
Banwell Rd. DA5: Bexl 6D 126	....6A 72
Banyan Ct. E16 ....1K 105	Barking Bus. Cen. IG11: Bark ...3A 90
(off Regalia Close)	Barking Ind. Pk. IG11: Bark 1K 89
Banyard Rd. SE16 ....3H 103	Barking Pk. Miniature Railway ..6H 71
Baptist Gdns. NW5 ....6E 64	BARKING RIVERSIDE 3B 90
Baquba SE13 ....2D 122	Barking Rd. E13 ....4J 87
Barandon Rd. W11 ....7F 81	Barking Rd. E16 ....5G 87
(off Grenfell Rd.)	Barking Rd. E6 ....2B 88
Barandon Wlk. W11 ....7F 81	BARKINGSIDE 3G 53
Barbanel Ho. E1 ....4J 85	Barking Splash Pk. 5H 71
(off Cephas St.)	Barking Wharf Sq. IG11: Bark ..1F 89
Barbara Brosnan Ct. NW8 ...1A 4 (2B 82)	Barkis Ho. W11 ....1F 99
Barbara Castle Cl. SW6 ....6H 99	Bark Pl. W2 ....7K 81
Barbara Cl. TW17: Shep 5E 146	Barkston Gdns. SW5 ....4K 99
Barbara Hucklesby Cl. N22 ...2B 48	Barkway Ct. N4 ....3C 66
Barbauld Rd. N16 ....3E 66	Barkway Dr. BR6: Farnb 4E 172
Barber Beaumont Ho. E1 ....3K 85	Barkwith Ho. SE14 ....6K 103
(off Bancroft Rd.)	*(off Cold Blow La.)*
Barber Cl. N21 ....7F 23	Barkwood Cl. RM7: Rom 5J 55
Barberry Ct. E15 ....6G 69	Barkworth Rd. SE16 ....5H 103
Barbers All. E13 ....3K 87	

Barlborough St. SE14 ....7K 103	Barmouth Av. UB6: G'frd 2K 77
Barlby Gdns. W10 ....4F 81	Barmouth Rd. CR0: C'don 2K 169
Barlby Rd. W10 ....5E 80	Barmouth Rd. SW18 ....6A 118
Barley Cl. HA0: Wemb 4D 60	Barnabas Ct. EN2: Enf 4F 23
Barleycorn Way E14 ....7B 86	Barnabas Rd. EC1 ....2C 8 (3C 84)
Barley Ct. S 2J 67	*(off King Sq.)*
Barley Ct. RM13: Rain 2K 91	Barnabas Lodge SW8 ....1J 119
(off Lwr Mardyke Av.)	*(off Guildford Rd.)*
Barleyfields Cl. RM6: Chad H ...6B 54	Barnabas Rd. E9 ....5K 67
Barley La. IG3: Ilf 7A 54	Barnaby Cl. HA2: Harr 2G 59
Barley La. RM6: Chad H 4B 54	Barnaby Ct. SE16 ....2G 103
Barley Mow Pas. W4 ....5A 98	*(off Scott Lidgett Cres.)*
Barley Mow Way TW17: Shep ...4C 146	Barnaby Ho. SE15 ....6J 103
Barley Shotts Bus. Pk. W10 ...5H 81	Barnaby Pl. SW7 ....4A 16 (4B 100)
Barling NW1 ....6F 65	*(off Old Brompton Rd.)*
(off Castlehaven Rd.)	Barnaby Way IG7: Chig 3K 37
Barling Ct. SW4 ....1C 124	Barnard Cl. BR7: Chst 1H 161
Barlow Dr. SE18 ....1C 124	Barnard Cl. SE18 ....3E 106
Barlow Ho. N1 ....1E 8 (2D 84)	Barnard Cl. SM6: W'gton 7H 167
(off Provost St.)	Barnard Cl. TW16: Sun 7K 129
Barlow Ho. SE16 ....4H 103	Barnard Gdns. KT3: N Mald ...4C 152
(off Rennie Est.)	Barnard Gdns. UB4: Yead 4K 75
Barlow Ho. W11 ....7G 81	Barnard Gro. E15 ....7H 69
(off Walmer Rd.)	Barnard Hill N10 ....1F 47
Barlow Pl. W1 ....3K 11 (7F 83)	Barnard Ho. E2 ....3H 85
Barlow Rd. NW6 ....6H 63	*(off Ellsworth St.)*
Barlow Rd. TW12: Hamp 7E 130	Barnard Lodge EN5: New Bar ...4F 21
Barlow Rd. W3 ....1H 97	Barnard Lodge W9 ....5J 81
Barlow St. SE17 ....4D 102	*(off Admiral Wlk.)*
Barlow Way RM13: Rain 5K 91	Barnard M. SW11 ....4C 118
Barmeston Rd. SE6 ....2D 140	Barnardo Dr. IG6: Ilf 4G 53
Barmor Cl. HA2: Harr 2F 41	Barnardo Gdns. E1 ....7K 85
Barmouth Av. UB6: G'frd 2K 77	Barnardo St. E1 ....6K 85
Barmouth Rd. CR0: C'don 2K 169	Barnardo Village Wlk. IG6: Ilf ...3G 53
Barmouth Rd. SW18 ....6A 118	Barnard Rd. CR4: Mitc 3E 154
Barnabas Ct. EN2: Enf 4F 23	Barnard Rd. EN1: Enf 2C 24
Barnabas Rd. EC1 ....2C 8 (3C 84)	Barnard Rd. SW11 ....4C 118
(off King Sq.)	Barnards Ho. SE16 ....2B 104
Barnabas Lodge SW8 ....1J 119	*(off Wyatt Cl.)*
(off Guildford Rd.)	Barnard's Inn EC1 ....7K 7 (6A 84)
Barnabas Rd. E9 ....5K 67	*(off Fetter La.)*
Barnaby Cl. HA2: Harr 2G 59	Barnbrough NW1 ....1G 83
Barnaby Ct. SE16 ....2G 103	*(off Camden St.)*
(off Scott Lidgett Cres.)	Barnby Sq. E15 ....1G 87
Barnaby Ho. SE15 ....6J 103	Barnby St. E15 ....1G 87
Barnaby Pl. SW7 ....4A 16 (4B 100)	Barnby St. NW1 ....1B 6 (2G 83)
(off Old Brompton Rd.)	Barn Cl. NW5 ....5H 65
Barnaby Way IG7: Chig 3K 37	*(off Torriano Av.)*
Barnard Cl. BR7: Chst 1H 161	Barn Cl. TW15: Ashf 5D 128
Barnard Cl. SE18 ....3E 106	Barn Cl. UB5: N'olt 2A 76
Barnard Cl. SM6: W'gton 7H 167	Barn Cres. HA7: Stan 6H 27
Barnard Cl. TW16: Sun 7K 129	Barncroft Cl. UB8: Hil 5D 74
Barnard Gdns. KT3: N Mald ...4C 152	Barneby Cl. TW2: Twick 1J 131
Barnard Gdns. UB4: Yead 4K 75	BARNEHURST 3J 127
Barnard Gro. E15 ....7H 69	Barnehurst Av. DA7: Bex 1J 127
Barnard Hill N10 ....1F 47	Barnehurst Av. DA8: Erith 1J 127
Barnard Ho. E2 ....3H 85	Barnehurst Cl. DA8: Erith 1J 127
(off Ellsworth St.)	Barnehurst Golf Course. 3K 127
Barnard Lodge EN5: New Bar ...4F 21	Barnehurst Rd. DA7: Bex 2J 127
Barnard Lodge W9 ....5J 81	Barn Elms Athletics Track 2D 116
(off Admiral Wlk.)	Barn Elms Cl. KT4: Wor Pk. 3B 164
Barnard M. SW11 ....4C 118	Barn Elms Pk. SW15 ....3E 116
Barnardo Dr. IG6: Ilf 4G 53	BARNES 2B 116
Barnardo Gdns. E1 ....7K 85	Barnes All. TW12: Hamp 2G 149
Barnardo St. E1 ....6K 85	Barnes Av. SW13 ....7C 98
Barnardo Village Wlk. IG6: Ilf ...3G 53	Barnes Av. UB2: S'hall 4D 94
Barnard Rd. CR4: Mitc 3E 154	BARNES BRI. 2A 116
Barnard Rd. EN1: Enf 2C 24	Barnes Cl. E12 ....4B 70
Barnard Rd. SW11 ....4C 118	Barnes Cl. HA8: Edg 4A 28
Barnards Ho. SE16 ....2B 104	Barnes Common Nature Reserve
(off Wyatt Cl.)	....3C 116
Barnard's Inn EC1 ....7K 7 (6A 84)	Barnes Ct. CR7: Thor H 3C 156
(off Fetter La.)	Barnes Ct. E16 ....5A 88
Barnbrough NW1 ....1G 83	Barnes Ct. EN5: New Bar 4E 20
(off Camden St.)	Barnes Ct. IG8: Wfd G 5G 37
Barnby Sq. E15 ....1G 87	Barnes End KT3: N Mald 5C 152
Barnby St. E15 ....1G 87	Barnes High St. SW13 ....2B 116
Barnby St. NW1 ....1B 6 (2G 83)	Barnes Ho. E2 ....2J 85
Barn Cl. NW5 ....5H 65	*(off Wadeson St.)*
(off Torriano Av.)	Barnes Ho. NW1 ....7F 65
Barn Cl. TW15: Ashf 5D 128	*(off Camden St.)*
Barn Cl. UB5: N'olt 2A 76	Barnes Ho. SE14 ....6K 103
Barn Cres. HA7: Stan 6H 27	*(off John Williams Cl.)*
Barncroft Cl. UB8: Hil 5D 74	Barnes Pikle W5 ....7D 78
Barneby Cl. TW2: Twick 1J 131	Barnes Rd. IG1: Ilf 5G 71
BARNEHURST 3J 127	Barnes Rd. N18 ....4D 34
Barnehurst Av. DA7: Bex 1J 127	Barnes St. E14 ....6A 86
Barnehurst Av. DA8: Erith 1J 127	Barnes Ter. SE8 ....5B 104
Barnehurst Cl. DA8: Erith 1J 127	BARNET 3B 20
Barnehurst Golf Course. 3K 127	Barnet Burnt Oak Leisure Cen. ..1K 43
Barnehurst Rd. DA7: Bex 2J 127	Barnet Bus. Cen. EN5: Barn ...3B 20
Barn Elms Athletics Track 2D 116	Barnet By-Pass NW7 ....6G 29
Barn Elms Cl. KT4: Wor Pk. 3B 164	Barnet Copthall Leisure Cen. ...7J 29
Barn Elms Pk. SW15 ....3E 116	Barnet Copthall Sports Cen. ...1D 44
BARNES 2B 116	Barnet Dr. BR2: Broml 2C 172
Barnes All. TW12: Hamp 2G 149	Barnet FC 1E 42
Barnes Av. SW13 ....7C 98	Barnet Gro. E2 ....1K 9 (3G 85)
Barnes Av. UB2: S'hall 4D 94	Barnet Hill EN5: Barn 4C 20

Barnet Ho. – Beaconsfield Rd.

Barnet Ho. N20 2F 31
Barnet La. EN5: Barn 6C 20
Barnet La. N20 1C 30
Barnet Mus. 4B 20
Barnetts Ct. HA2: Harr 3F 59
Barnett St. E1 6H 85
BARNET VALE 5E 20
Barnet Way NW7 3E 28
Barnet Wood Rd. BR2: Broml 2A 172
Barney Cl. SE7 5A 106
Barn Fld. NW3 5D 64
Barnfield KT3: N Mald 6A 152
Barnfield Av. CR0: C'don 2J 169
Barnfield Av. CR4: Mitc 4F 155
Barnfield Av. KT2: King T 4D 132
Barnfield Cl. N4 7J 47
Barnfield Cl. SW17 3B 136
Barnfield Gdns. KT2: King T 4E 132
Barnfield Gdns. SE18 6F 107
Barnfield Pl. E14 4C 104
Barnfield Rd. CR2: Sande 7E 168
Barnfield Rd. DA17: Belv 6F 109
Barnfield Rd. HA8: Edg 1J 43
Barnfield Rd. SE18 6F 107
(not continuous)
Barnfield Rd. W5 4C 78
Barnfield Wood Cl. BR3: Beck 6F 159
Barnfield Wood Rd. BR3: Beck 6F 159
Barnham Dr. SE28 1K 107
(not continuous)
Barnham Rd. UB6: G'frd 3G 77
Barnham St. SE1 6H 15 (2E 102)
Barn Hill HA9: Wemb 1G 61
Barnhill HA5: Eastc 5A 40
Barnhill Av. BR2: Broml 5H 159
Barnhill La. UB4: Yead 3K 75
Barnhill Rd. HA9: Wemb 3J 61
Barnhill Rd. UB4: Yead 3K 75
Barningham Way NW9 6K 43
Barnlea Cl. TW13: Hanw 2C 130
Barnmead Ct. RM9: Dag 5F 73
Barnmead Gdns. RM9: Dag 5F 73
Barnmead Rd. BR3: Beck 1K 157
Barnmead Rd. RM9: Dag 5F 73
Barn M. HA2: Harr 3E 58
Barn Ri. HA9: Wemb 1G 61
BARNSBURY 7K 65
Barnsbury Cl. KT3: N Mald 4J 151
Barnsbury Cres. KT5: Surb 1J 163
Barnsbury Est. N1 1K 83
(not continuous)
Barnsbury Gro. N7 7K 65
Barnsbury Ho. SW4 6H 119
Barnsbury La. KT5: Surb 2H 163
Barnsbury Pk. N1 7A 66
Barnsbury Rd. N1 2A 84
Barnsbury Sq. N1 7A 66
Barnsbury St. N1 7A 66
Barnsbury Ter. N1 7K 65
Barnscroft SW20 3D 152
Barnsdale Av. E14 4D 104
Barnsdale Rd. W9 4H 81
Barnsley St. E1 4H 85
Barnstaple Ho. SE10 7D 104
(off Devonshire Dr.)
Barnstaple Ho. SE12 5H 123
(off Taunton Rd.)
Barnstaple La. SE13 4E 122
Barnstaple Rd. HA4: Ruis 3A 58
Barnston Wlk. N1 1C 84
(off Popham St.)
Barn St. N16 2E 66
Barn Theatre, The Sidcup 1A 144
Barn Theatre, The West Molesey 4E 148
Barn Way HA9: Wemb 1G 61
Barnwell Cl. HA8: Edg 4A 28
Barnwell Ho. SE5 1E 120
(off St Giles Rd.)
Barnwell Rd. SW2 5A 120
Barnwood Cl. HA4: Ruis 2F 57
Barnwood Cl. N20 1C 30
Barnwood Cl. W9 4K 81
Baron Cl. N1 2A 84
Baron Cl. N11 5K 31
Baroness Rd. E2 1K 9 (3F 85)
Baronet Gro. N17 1G 49
Baronet Rd. N17 1G 49
Baron Gdns. IG6: Ilf 3G 53
Baron Gro. CR4: Mitc 4C 154
Baron Ho. SW19 1B 154
Baron Rd. RM8: Dag 1D 72
Barons, The TW1: Twick 6B 114
Baronsclere Ct. N6 7G 47
BARONS COURT 5G 99
Barons Ct. IG1: Ilf 2H 71
Barons Ct. NW9 6K 43
Barons Ct. SM6: Bedd 3H 167
Baron's Ct. Rd. W14 5G 99
Barons Court Theatre 5G 99
(off Comeragh Rd.)
Baronsfield Rd. TW1: Twick 6B 114
Barons Ga. EN4: E Barn 6H 21
Barons Ga. W4 3J 97
Barons Keep W14 5G 99
Barons Lodge E14 4F 105
(off Manchester Rd.)
Barons Mead HA1: Harr 4J 41
Baronsmead Rd. SW13 1C 116
Baronsmede W5 2F 97
Baronsmere Ct. EN5: Barn 4B 20
Baronsmere Rd. N2 4C 46
Baron's Pl. SE1 7K 13 (2A 102)
Baron St. N1 2A 84
Baron's Wlk. CR0: C'don 6A 158
Baron Wlk. E16 Canning Town 5H 87
Baron Wlk. CR4: Mitc Mitcham 4C 154
Baroque Ct. TW3: Houn 3F 113
Baroque Gdns. SE8 4A 104
(off Grand Canal Av.)
Barque M. SE8 6C 104
Barquentine Hgts. SE10 3J 105
Barrack Rd. TW4: Houn 4B 112
Barracks La. EN5: Barn 3B 20
Barracouta Ho. SE18 6K 107
Barra Hall Cir. UB3: Hayes 7G 75
Barra Hall Rd. UB3: Hayes 7G 75
Barratt Av. N22 2K 47
Barratt Ho. N1 7B 66
(off Sable St.)
Barratt Ind. Est. UB1: S'hall 2E 94
Barratt Ind. Pk. E3 4E 86
Barratt Way HA3: W'stone 2H 41
Barra Wood Cl. UB3: Hayes 6G 75
Barrenger Rd. N10 1D 46
Barret Ho. NW6 1J 81
Barret Ho. SW9 3K 119
(off Benedict Rd.)
Barrett Ct. SE5 7D 102
(off Dobson Wlk.)
Barrett Ho. SE17 5C 102
(off Browning St.)
Barrett Pl. UB10: Uxb 1A 74
Barrett Rd. E17 4E 50
Barrett's Grn. Rd. NW10 3J 79
Barrett's Gro. N16 5E 66
Barrett St. W1 1H 11 (6E 82)
Barrhill Rd. SW2 2J 137
Barrie Ct. EN5: New Bar 5F 21
(off Lyonsdown Rd.)
Barriedale SE14 2A 122
Barrie Est. W2 2A 10 (7B 82)
Barrie Ho. NW8 1C 82
(off St Edmund's Ter.)
Barrie Ho. W2 7A 82
(off Lancaster Ga.)
Barrier App. SE7 3B 106
Barrier Point Rd. E16 1A 106
Barringers Ct. HA4: Ruis 7F 39
Barringer Sq. SW17 4E 136
Barrington Cl. IG5: Ilf 1D 52
Barrington Cl. NW5 5E 64
Barrington Ct. N10 2E 46
Barrington Ct. SW4 2J 119
Barrington Ct. W3 2H 97
(off Cheltenham Pl.)
Barrington Rd. DA7: Bex 2D 126
Barrington Rd. E12 6E 70
Barrington Rd. N8 5H 47
Barrington Rd. SM3: Sutt 2J 165
Barrington Rd. SW9 3B 120
Barrington Vs. SE18 1E 124
Barrington Wlk. SE19 6E 138
Barrons Chase TW10: Ham 5F 133
Barrow Av. SM5: Cars 7D 166
Barrow Cl. N21 3G 33
Barrow Ct. SE6 1H 141
(off Cumberland Pl.)
Barrowdene Cl. HA5: Pinn 2C 40
Barrowell Grn. N21 2G 33
Barrowfield Cl. N9 3C 34
Barrowgate Rd. W4 5J 97
Barrow Hedges Cl. SM5: Cars 7C 166
Barrow Hedges Way SM5: Cars 7C 166
Barrow Hill KT4: Wor Pk 2A 164
Barrow Hill Cl. KT4: Wor Pk 2A 164
Barrow Hill Est. NW8 2C 82
(off Barrow Hill Rd.)
Barrow Hill Rd. NW8 1C 4 (2C 82)
Barrow Point Av. HA5: Pinn 2C 40
Barrow Point La. HA5: Pinn 2C 40
Barrow Rd. CR0: Wadd 5A 168
Barrow Rd. SW16 6H 137
Barrow Store Ct. SE1 7G 15 (3E 102)
(off Decima St.)
Barrow Wlk. TW8: Bford 6C 96
Barrs Rd. NW10 7K 61
Barry Av. DA7: Bex 7E 108
Barry Av. N15 6F 49
Barry Blandford Way E3 4D 86
Barry Cl. BR6: Orp 3J 173
Barrydene N20 1G 31
Barry Ho. SE16 4H 103
(off Rennie Est.)
Barry Pde. SE22 5G 121
Barry Rd. E6 6C 88
Barry Rd. NW10 7J 61
Barry Rd. SE22 6G 121
Barry Ter. TW15: Ashf 2B 128
(off Orchard Way)
Barset Rd. SE15 3J 121
(not continuous)
Barson Cl. SE20 7J 139
Barston Rd. SE27 3C 138
Barstow Cres. SW2 1K 137
Barter St. WC1 6F 7 (5J 83)
Barters Wlk. HA5: Pinn 3C 40
Barth M. SE18 4J 107
Bartholomew Cl. EC1 6C 8 (5C 84)
(not continuous)
Bartholomew Cl. SW18 4A 118
Bartholomew Ct. E14 7F 87
(off Newport Av.)
Bartholomew Ct. EC1 3D 8 (4C 84)
(off Old St.)
Bartholomew Ct. HA8: Edg 7J 27
Bartholomew Ho. IG8: Wfd G 1F 53
Bartholomew Ho. W10 4G 81
(off Appleford Rd.)
Bartholomew La. EC2 1F 15 (6D 84)
Bartholomew Pl. EC1 6C 8 (5C 84)
(off Bartholomew Cl.)
Bartholomew Rd. NW5 6G 65
Bartholomew Sq. E1 4H 85
Bartholomew Sq. EC1 2D 8 (3C 84)
Bartholomew St. SE1 3D 102
Bartholomew Vs. NW5 6G 65
Barth Rd. SE18 4J 107
Bartle Av. E6 2C 88
Bartle Rd. W11 6G 81
Bartlett Cl. E14 6C 86
Bartlett Ct. EC4 7K 7 (6A 84)
Bartlett Ho. KT4: Wor Pk 2B 164
(off The Avenue)
Bartlett Ho's. RM10: Dag 7H 73
(off Vicarage Rd.)
Bartlett M. E14 5D 104
Bartletts Pas. EC4 7K 7 (6A 84)
(off Fetter La.)
Bartlett St. CR2: S Croy 5D 168
Bartlow Gdns. RM5: Col R 1K 55
Bartok Ho. W11 1H 99
(off Lansdowne Wlk.)
Barton Av. RM7: Rush G 1H 73
Barton Cl. DA6: Bex 5E 126
Barton Cl. E6 6D 88
Barton Cl. E9 5J 67
Barton Cl. NW4 5C 44
Barton Cl. SE15 3H 121
Barton Cl. TW17: Shep 6D 146
Barton Ct. W14 5G 99
(off Baron's Ct. Rd.)
Barton Grn. KT3: N Mald 2K 151
Barton Ho. E3 3D 86
(off Bow Rd.)
Barton Ho. N1 7B 66
(off Sable St.)
Barton Ho. SW6 3K 117
(off Wandsworth Bri. Rd.)
Barton Mdws. IG6: Ilf 4F 53
Barton M. E14 2D 104
Barton M. SW19 6A 136
Barton Rd. DA14: Sidc 6E 144
Barton Rd. W14 5G 99
Barton St. SW1 1E 18 (3J 101)
Bartonway NW8 1B 82
(off Queen's Ter.)
Bartram Cl. UB8: Hil 4D 74
Bartram Rd. SE4 5A 122
Bartrams La. EN4: Had W 1F 21
Bartrip St. E9 6B 68
Barts & The London School of Medicine & Dentistry Whitechapel Campus 5H 85
(off Turner St.)
Barts Cl. BR3: Beck 5C 158
Barville Cl. SE4 4A 122
Barwell Bus. Pk. KT9: Chess 7D 162
Barwell Ct. KT9: Chess 7B 162
Barwell Ho. E2 4G 85
(off Menotti St.)
Barwell La. KT9: Chess 7C 162
Barwick Dr. UB8: Hil 5D 74
Barwick Ho. W3 2J 97
(off Strafford Rd.)
Barwick Rd. E7 4K 69
Barwood Av. BR4: W W'ck 1D 170
Bascombe Gro. DA1: Bexl 7K 127
Bascombe Gro. DA1: Cray 7K 127
Bascombe St. SW2 6A 120
Basden Gro. TW13: Hanw 2E 130
Basden Ho. TW13: Hanw 2E 130
Basedale Rd. RM9: Dag 7B 72
Baseing Cl. E6 7E 88
Baseline Bus. Studios W11 7F 81
(off Barandon Wlk.)
Basepoint Bus. Cen. RM13: Rain 4K 91
Basevi Way SE8 6D 104
Bashley Rd. NW10 4K 79
Basil Av. E6 3C 88
Basildene Rd. TW4: Houn 3B 112
Basildon Av. IG5: Ilf 1E 52
Basildon Cl. SM2: Sutt 7K 165
Basildon Ct. W1 5H 5 (5E 82)
(off Devonshire Rd.)
Basildon Rd. SE2 5A 108
Basil Gdns. CR0: C'don 1K 169
Basil Gdns. SE27 5C 138
Basil Ho. E1 6G 85
(off Henriques St.)
Basil Ho. SW8 7J 101
(off Wyvil Rd.)
Basilica M. SW12 6E 118
Basilica Pl. E3 2B 86
Basil Mans. SW3 7F 11 (2D 100)
(off Basil St.)
Basilon Rd. DA7: Bex 2E 126
Basil Spence Ho. N22 1K 47
Basil St. SW3 1E 16 (3D 100)
Basin App. E14 6A 86
Basin App. E16 7F 89
Basing Cl. KT7: T Ditt 7K 149
Basing Ct. SE15 1F 121
Basingdon Way SE5 4D 120
Basing Dr. DA5: Bexl 6F 127
Basingfield Rd. KT7: T Ditt 7K 149
Basinghall Av. EC2 7E 8 (6D 84)
Basinghall Gdns. SM2: Sutt 7K 165
Basinghall St. EC2 7E 8 (6D 84)
Basing Hill HA9: Wemb 2F 61
Basing Hill NW11 1H 63
Basing Ho. Yd. E2 1H 9 (3E 84)
(off Kingsland Rd.)
Basing Pl. E2 1H 9 (3E 84)
Basing St. W11 6H 81
Basing Way KT7: T Ditt 7K 149
Basing Way N3 3J 45
Basin Mill Apts. E2 1F 85
(off Laburnum St.)
Basin Sth. E16 1F 107
Basire St. N1 1C 84
Baskerville Gdns. NW10 4A 62
Baskerville Rd. SW18 7C 118
Basket Gdns. SE9 5C 124
Baslow Cl. HA3: Hrw W 1H 41
Baslow Wlk. E5 4K 67
Basnett Rd. SW11 3E 118
Basque Ct. SE16 2K 103
(off Garter Way)
Bassano St. SE22 5F 121
Bassant Rd. SE18 6K 107
Bass Ct. E15 1H 87
(off Plaistow Rd.)
Bassein Pk. Rd. W12 2B 98
Bassett Gdns. TW7: Isle 7G 95
Bassett Ho. SW19 5K 135
Bassett La. E20 7C 68
Bassett Rd. W10 6F 81
Bassett's Cl. BR6: Farnb 4F 173
Bassetts Ho. BR6: Farnb 4F 173
Bassett St. NW5 6E 64
Bassett's Way BR6: Farnb 4F 173
Bassett Way UB6: G'frd 6F 77
Bassingbourn Ho. N1 7A 66
(off The Sutton Est.)
Bassingham Rd. HA0: Wemb 6D 60
Bassingham Rd. SW18 7A 118
Bassington Rd. W3 3J 97
Bassishaw Highwalk EC2 6E 8 (5D 84)
(off London Wall)
Bass M. SE22 4G 121
Basswood Cl. SE15 3H 121
Bastable Av. IG11: Bark 2J 89
Basterfield Ho. EC1 4C 8 (4C 84)
(off Golden La. Est.)
Bastion Highwalk EC2 6C 8 (5C 84)
(off London Wall)
Bastion Ho. EC2 6D 8 (5C 84)
(off London Wall)
Bastion Rd. SE2 5A 108
Baston Mnr. Rd. BR2: Hayes 3K 171
Baston Mnr. Rd. BR2: Kes 3K 171
Baston Rd. BR2: Hayes 2K 171
Bastwick St. EC1 3C 8 (4C 84)
Basuto Rd. SW6 1J 117
Batavia Cl. TW16: Sun 1K 147
Batavia Ho. SE14 7A 104
(off Batavia Rd.)
Batavia M. SE14 7A 104
Batavia Rd. SE14 7A 104
Batavia Rd. TW16: Sun 1K 147
Batchelor St. N1 1A 84
Bateman Cl. IG11: Bark 6G 71
Bateman Ho. SE17 6B 102
(off Otto St.)
Bateman M. SW4 6H 119
Bateman Rd. E4 6H 35
Bateman's Bldgs. W1 1C 12 (6H 83)
(off Bateman St.)
Bateman's Row EC2 3H 9 (4E 84)
Bateman St. W1 1C 12 (6H 83)
Bates Cres. CR0: Wadd 5A 168
Bates Cres. SW16 7G 137
Bateson St. SE18 4J 107
Bate St. E14 7B 86
Bat Gdns. KT2: King T 6F 133
Bath Cl. SE15 7H 103
Bath Ct. EC1 St Luke's Est. 2E 8 (3D 84)
(off St Luke's Est.)
Bath Ct. EC1 Warner St. 4J 7 (4A 84)
(off Warner St.)
Bath Ct. SE26 3G 139
(off Droitwich Cl.)
Bathgate Ho. SW9 1B 120
(off Lothian Rd.)
Bathgate Rd. SW19 3F 135
Bath Gro. E2 1K 9 (2G 85)
(off Horatio St.)
Bath Ho. E2 4G 85
(off Ramsey St.)
Bath Ho. IG11: Bark 7G 71
Bath Ho. SE1 3C 102
(off Bath Ter.)
Bath Ho. Rd. CR0: Bedd 1J 167
Bath Pas. KT1: King T 2D 150
Bath Pl. EC2 2G 9 (3E 84)
Bath Pl. EN5: Barn 3C 20
Bath Pl. W6 5E 98
(off Peabody Est.)
Bath Rd. E7 6B 70
Bath Rd. N9 2C 34
Bath Rd. RM6: Chad H 6E 54
Bath Rd. TW3: Houn 3F 113
Bath Rd. TW4: Houn 2B 112
Bath Rd. TW5: Cran 1A 112
Bath Rd. TW6: H'row A 1G 111
Bath Rd. UB3: Harl 1G 111
Bath Rd. UB7: Harm 4C 174
Bath Rd. UB7: Lford 4C 174
Bath Rd. UB7: Sip 4C 174
Bath Rd. W4 4A 98
Baths Ct. W12 2D 98
Baths Rd. BR2: Broml 4B 160
Bath St. EC1 2D 8 (3C 84)
Bath Ter. SE1 3C 102
Bathurst Av. SW19 1K 153
Bathurst Gdns. NW10 2D 80
Bathurst Ho. W12 7D 80
(off White City Est.)
Bathurst M. W2 1B 10 (6B 82)
Bathurst Rd. IG1: Ilf 1F 71
Bathurst Sq. N15 4E 48
Bathurst St. W2 2B 10 (7B 82)
Bathway SE18 4E 106
Batley Cl. CR4: Mitc 7D 154
Batley Pl. N16 3F 67
Batley Rd. EN2: Enf 1H 23
Batley Rd. N16 3F 67
Batman Cl. W12 1D 98
Batoum Gdns. W6 3E 98
Batsford Ho. SW19 4K 135
(off Durnsford Rd.)
Batson Ho. E1 6G 85
(off Fairclough St.)
Batson St. W12 2C 98
Batsworth Rd. CR4: Mitc 3B 154
Battalion Ho. NW9 2B 44
(off Heritage Av.)
Battenberg Wlk. SE19 6E 138
Batten Cl. E6 6D 88
Batten Cotts. E14 5A 86
(off Maroon St.)
Batten Ho. SW4 5G 119
Batten Ho. W10 3G 81
(off Third Av.)
Batten St. SW11 3C 118
Battersby Rd. SE6 2F 141
BATTERSEA 1E 118
Battersea Arts Cen. 3D 118
(off Lavender Hill)
BATTERSEA BRI. 7B 100
Battersea Bri. Rd. SW11 7C 100
Battersea Bus. Cen. SW11 3E 118
Battersea Bus. Pk. SW8 1G 119
Battersea Church Rd. SW11 1B 118
Battersea Dogs' Home 7F 101
Battersea Evolution 7E 100
Battersea High St. SW11 1B 118
(not continuous)
Battersea Pk. 7D 100
BATTERSEA PARK 7F 101
Battersea Pk. Children's Zoo 7E 100
Battersea Pk. Millennium Arena 7E 100
Battersea Pk. Rd. SW11 2C 118
Battersea Pk. Rd. SW8 1F 119
Battersea Power Sta. SW11 6F 101
Battersea Ri. SW11 5C 118
Battersea Roof Gdns. SW11 7F 101
Battersea Sports Cen. 3B 118
Battersea Sq. SW11 1B 118
Battery Rd. SE28 2J 107
Battishill St. N1 7B 66
Battlebridge Ct. N1 2J 83
(off Wharfdale Rd.)
Battle Bri. La. SE1 5G 15 (1E 102)
Battle Cl. SW19 6A 136
Battledean Rd. N5 5B 66
Battle Ho. SE15 6G 103
(off Haymerle Rd.)
Battle Rd. DA17: Belv 4J 109
Battle Rd. DA17: Erith 4J 109
Battle Rd. DA8: Erith 4J 109
Batty St. E1 6G 85
Batwa Ho. SE16 5H 103
Baudwin Rd. SE6 2G 141
Baugh Rd. DA14: Sidc 5C 144
Baulk, The SW18 7J 117
Bavant Rd. SW16 2J 155
Bavaria Rd. N19 2J 65
Bavdene M. NW4 4D 44
(off The Burroughs)
Bavent Rd. SE5 2C 120
Bawdale Rd. SE22 5F 121
Bawdsey Av. IG2: Ilf 4K 53
Bawley Ct. E16 7G 89
Bawley Ter. E15 1F 87
(off Rick Roberts Way)
Bawtree Rd. SE14 7A 104
Bawtry Rd. N20 3J 31
Baxendale N20 2F 31
Baxendale St. E2 3G 85
Baxter Cl. BR1: Broml 3F 161
Baxter Cl. UB10: Hil 3D 74
Baxter Cl. UB2: S'hall 3F 95
Baxter Ho. E3 3D 86
(off Bromley High St.)
Baxter Rd. E16 6A 88
Baxter Rd. IG1: Ilf 5F 71
Baxter Rd. N1 6D 66
Baxter Rd. N18 4C 34
Baxter Wlk. SW16 2H 137
Bayard Ct. DA6: Bex 4H 127
Bay Cl. RM7: Rush G 7J 55
Bay Ct. E1 4K 85
(off Frimley Way)
Bay Ct. W5 3E 96
Baycroft Cl. HA5: Eastc 3A 40
Baydon Ct. BR2: Broml 3H 159
Bayer Ho. EC1 4C 8 (4C 84)
(off Golden La. Est.)
Bayes Cl. SE26 5J 139
Bayes Ct. NW3 7D 64
(off Primrose Hill Rd.)
Bayes Ho. N1 7A 66
(off Augustas La.)
Bayfield Ho. SE4 4K 121
(off Coston Wlk.)
Bayfield Rd. SE9 4B 124
Bayford M. E8 7H 67
(off Bayford St.)
Bayford Rd. NW10 3F 81
Bayford St. E8 7H 67
Bayford St. Bus. Cen. E8 7H 67
(off Sidworth St.)
Baygrove M. KT1: Hamp W 1C 150
Bayham Pl. NW1 1G 83
Bayham Rd. SM4: Mord 4K 153
Bayham Rd. W13 7B 78
Bayham Rd. W4 3K 97
Bayham St. NW1 1G 83
Bay Ho. SE16 3A 104
Bayhurst Wood Country Pk. 5B 38
Bayleaf Cl. TW12: Hamp H 5H 131
Bayley St. WC1 6C 6 (5H 83)
Bayley Wlk. SE2 6E 108
Baylis Hgts. SE10 4J 105
(off Horn Link Way)
Baylis M. TW1: Twick 7A 114
Baylis Pl. BR1: Broml 3C 160
Baylis Rd. SE1 7J 13 (2A 102)
Bayliss Av. SE28 7D 90
Bayliss Cl. N21 5D 22
Bayliss Cl. UB1: S'hall 6F 77
(off Whitecote Rd.)
Baynard Ho. EC4 2B 14 (7B 84)
(off Queen Victoria St.)
Bayne Cl. E6 6D 88
Baynes Cl. EN1: Enf 1B 24
Baynes Cres. RM10: Dag 7J 73
Baynes M. NW3 6B 64
Baynes St. NW1 7G 65
Baynham Cl. DA5: Bexl 6F 127
Bayonne Rd. W6 6G 99
Bays Ct. HA8: Edg 5C 28
Bays Farm Ct. UB7: Lford 4D 174
Bayshill Ri. UB5: N'olt 6F 59
Baysixty6 Skate Pk. 5H 81
(off Acklam Rd.)
Bayston Rd. N16 3F 67
BAYSWATER 7A 82
Bayswater Cl. N13 4G 33
Bayswater Rd. W2 7K 81
Baythorne Ho. E16 6H 87
(off Turner St.)
Baythorne St. E3 5B 86
Bayton Ct. E8 7G 67
(off Lansdowne Dr.)
Bay Tree Cl. BR1: Broml 1B 160
Baytree Cl. DA15: Sidc 1K 143
Baytree Ct. SW2 4K 119
Bay Tree Ho. EC1 4J 7 (4A 84)
(off Baker's Row)
Baytree Ho. E4 7J 25
Baytree M. SE17 4D 102
Baytree Rd. SW2 4K 119
Baywillow Av. SM5: Cars 1D 166
Bazalgette Cl. KT3: N Mald 5K 151
Bazalgette Gdns. KT3: N Mald 5K 151
Bazalgette Ho. NW8 3B 4 (4B 82)
(off Orchardson St.)
Bazalgette Wlk. EC4 2K 13 (7A 84)
Bazalgette Way SE2 1C 108
Bazeley Ho. SE1 7A 14 (2B 102)
(off Library St.)
Bazely St. E14 7E 86
Bazile Rd. N21 6F 23
BBC Broadcasting House 6K 5 (5F 83)
BBC Maida Vale Studios 4K 81
(off Delaware Rd.)
BBC Studios 1E 98
BBC Worldwide 7E 80
BDA Dental Mus. 6J 5 (5F 83)
Beacham Cl. SE7 5B 106
Beachborough Rd. BR1: Broml 4E 140
Beach Ct. SE9 6C 124
Beachcroft Av. UB1: S'hall 1C 94
Beachcroft Rd. E11 3G 69
Beachcroft Way N19 1H 65
Beach Gro. TW13: Hanw 2E 130
Beach Ho. SW5 5J 99
(off Philbeach Gdns.)
Beach Ho. TW13: Hanw 2E 130
Beach Ho. Apts. IG11: Bark 4A 90
Beachy Rd. E3 7C 68
Beacon Bingo Cricklewood 4F 63
Beacon Cl. UB8: Uxb 5A 56
Beacon Ga. SE14 3K 121
Beacon Gro. SM5: Cars 4E 166
Beacon Hill N7 5J 65
Beacon Ho. E14 5D 104
(off Burrells Wharf Sq.)
Beacon Ho. SE5 7E 102
(off Southampton Way)
Beacon Pl. CR0: Bedd 3J 167
Beacon Point SE10 6D 104
(off Dowells St.)
Beacon Rd. SE13 6F 123
Beacon Rd. TW6: H'row A 6C 110
Beacons Cl. E6 5C 88
Beaconsfield WC1 6G 7 (5K 83)
(off Red Lion St.)
Beaconsfield Cl. N11 5K 31
Beaconsfield Cl. SE3 6J 105
Beaconsfield Cl. W4 5J 97
Beaconsfield Pde. SE9 4C 142
Beaconsfield Rd. BR1: Broml 3B 160

A–Z London 185

Beaconsfield Rd. – Beechwood Gdns.

Beaconsfield Rd. CR0: C'don........6D 156
Beaconsfield Rd. DA5: Bexl..........2K 145
Beaconsfield Rd. E10......................2E 68
Beaconsfield Rd. E16......................4H 87
Beaconsfield Rd. E17......................6B 50
Beaconsfield Rd. KT3: N Mald........2K 151
Beaconsfield Rd. KT5: Surb..........7F 151
Beaconsfield Rd. N11......................3K 31
Beaconsfield Rd. N15......................4E 48
Beaconsfield Rd. N9........................3B 34
Beaconsfield Rd. NW10....................6B 62
Beaconsfield Rd. SE17..................5D 102
Beaconsfield Rd. SE3....................7H 105
Beaconsfield Rd. SE9....................2C 142
Beaconsfield Rd. TW1: Twick........6B 114
Beaconsfield Rd. UB1: S'hall..........1B 94
Beaconsfield Rd. UB4: Yead............1A 94
Beaconsfield Rd. W4........................3K 97
Beaconsfield Rd. W5........................2C 96
Beaconsfield St. N1..........................1J 83
Beaconsfield Ter. RM6: Chad H........6D 54
Beaconsfield Ter. Rd. W14..............3G 99
Beaconsfield Wlk. E6 Beckton..........6E 88
Beaconsfield Wlk. SW6 Parsons Green
....1H 117
Beacontree Av. E17..........................1F 51
BEACONTREE HEATH........................1G 73
Beacontree Rd. E11..........................1H 69
Beadle's Pde. RM10: Dag..................6J 73
Beadlow Cl. SM5: Cars....................6B 154
Beadman Pl. SE27..........................4B 138
Beadman St. SE27..........................4B 138
Beadnell Ct. E1................................7G 85
(off Cable St.)
Beadnell Rd. SE23..........................1K 139
Beadon Rd. BR2: Broml..................4J 159
Beadon Rd. W6..................................4E 98
Beaford Gro. SW20..........................3G 153
Beagle Cl. TW13: Felt......................4K 129
Beak St. W1..........................2A 12 (7G 83)
Beal Cl. DA16: Well..........................1A 126
Beale Arboretum, The......................1J 21
Beale Cl. N13......................................5G 33
Beale Pl. E3..2B 86
Beale Rd. E3..1B 86
Beal Rd. IG1: Ilf..................................2E 70
Beam Av. RM10: Dag..........................1H 91
Beames Rd. NW10..............................1K 79
Beaminster Gdns. IG6: Ilf..................2F 53
Beaminster Ho. SW8........................7K 101
(off Dorset Rd.)
Beamish Dr. WD23: B Hea..................1B 26
Beamish Ho. SE16............................4H 103
(off Rennie Est.)
Beamish Rd. N9....................................1B 34
Beam Pk. Development RM9: Dag
....3H 91
Beam Reach Bus. Pk. RM13: Rain
....3K 91
Beam Valley Country Pk....................1J 91
Beamway RM10: Dag..........................7K 73
Beanacre Cl. E9....................................6B 68
Bean Rd. DA6: Bex............................4D 126
Beanshaw SE9....................................4E 142
Beansland Gro. RM6: Chad H..........3E 54
Bear All. EC4..........................7A 8 (6B 84)
Bear Cl. RM7: Rom..............................6H 55
Beardell St. SE19..............................6F 139
Beardow Gro. N14..............................6B 22
Beard Rd. KT2: King T......................5F 133
Beardsfield E13..................................2J 87
Beard's Hill TW12: Hamp..................1E 148
Beard's Hill Cl. TW12: Hamp............1E 148
Beardsley Ter. RM8: Dag..................5B 72
(off Stonard Rd.)
Beardsley Way W3..............................2K 97
Beard's Rd. TW15: Ashf....................6G 129
Bearfield Rd. KT2: King T................7E 132
Bear Gdns. SE1..............4C 14 (1C 102)
Bear La. SE1....................5B 14 (1B 102)
Bear Pit Apts. SE1............4C 14 (1C 102)
(off New Globe Wlk.)
Bear Rd. TW13: Hanw......................4B 130
Bearstead Ri. SE4............................5B 122
Bearsted Ter. BR3: Beck..................1C 158
Bear St. WC2..........................2D 12 (7H 83)
Beasley's Ait TW16: Sun..................6H 147
Beasley's Ait La. TW16: Sun............6H 147
Beaton Cl. SE15................................1F 121
Beatrice Av. HA9: Wemb......................5E 60
Beatrice Av. SW16............................3K 155
Beatrice Cl. E13....................................4J 87
Beatrice Cl. HA5: Eastc........................4J 39
Beatrice Ct. IG9: Buck H......................2G 37
Beatrice Ho. W6....................................5E 98
(off Queen Caroline St.)
Beatrice Pl. SW19............................7F 117
Beatrice Pl. W8....................................3K 99
Beatrice Rd. E17..................................5C 50
Beatrice Rd. N4....................................7A 48
Beatrice Rd. N9....................................7D 24
Beatrice Rd. SE1..............................4G 103
Beatrice Rd. TW10: Rich..................5F 115
Beatrice Rd. UB1: S'hall......................1D 94
Beatrice Webb Ho. E3..........................2A 86
(off Chisenhale Rd.)
Beatrix Apts. E3....................................4B 86
(off English St.)
Beatrix Ho. SW5....................................5K 99
(off Old Brompton Rd.)
Beatson Wlk. SE16............................1A 104
(not continuous)
Beattie Cl. TW14: Felt......................7H 111
Beattie Ho. SW8..............................1G 119
Beattock Ri. N10....................................4F 47
Beatty Ho. E14....................................2C 104
(off Admirals Way)
Beatty Ho. SW1..............6B 18 (5G 101)
(off Dolphin Sq.)
Beatty Rd. HA7: Stan..........................6H 27
Beatty Rd. N16..4E 66
Beatty St. NW1..2G 83
Beattyville Gdns. IG6: Ilf......................4E 52
Beauchamp Cl. W4..................................3J 97
Beauchamp Ct. EN5: Barn....................4C 20
(off Victors Way)
Beauchamp Ct. HA7: Stan....................5H 27
Beauchamp Pl. SW3........1D 16 (3C 100)
Beauchamp Rd. E7..................................7K 69
Beauchamp Rd. KT8: E Mos................5F 149
Beauchamp Rd. KT8: W Mole..............5F 149
Beauchamp Rd. SE19........................1D 156
Beauchamp Rd. SM1: Sutt..................4J 165
Beauchamp Rd. SW11........................4C 118
Beauchamp Rd. TW1: Twick................7A 114
Beauchamp St. EC1..............6J 7 (5A 84)
Beauchamp Ter. SW15........................3D 116
Beauclerc Ct. TW16: Sun....................2A 148
Beauclerc Rd. W6....................................3D 98
Beauclere Ho. SM2: Sutt....................6A 166
Beauclerk Cl. TW13: Felt....................1K 129
Beauclerk Ho. SW16..........................3J 137
Beau Ct. HA7: Stan................................7J 27
(off Hitchin La.)
Beaudesert M. UB7: W Dray..................2A 92
Beaufort E6..5E 88
Beaufort Av. HA3: Kenton......................4A 42
Beaufort Cl. E4..6J 35
Beaufort Cl. RM7: Mawney......................4J 55
Beaufort Cl. SW15..............................7D 116
Beaufort Cl. W5..5F 79
Beaufort Ct. E14....................................2C 104
(off Admirals Way)
Beaufort Ct. EN5: New Bar....................5F 21
Beaufort Ct. N11......................................5A 32
(off The Limes Av.)
Beaufort Ct. SW6......................................6J 99
Beaufort Ct. TW10: Ham......................4C 132
Beaufort Dr. NW11......................................4J 45
Beaufort Gdns. E1....................................5K 85
Beaufort Gdns. IG1: Ilf............................1E 70
Beaufort Gdns. NW4..................................6E 44
Beaufort Gdns. SW16..........................7K 137
Beaufort Gdns. SW3..............1D 16 (3C 100)
Beaufort Gdns. TW5: Hest....................1C 112
Beaufort Ho. E16....................................1K 105
(off Fairfax M.)
Beaufort Ho. SW1..............6C 18 (5H 101)
(off Aylesford St.)
Beaufort Ho. SW3..............7B 16 (6B 100)
(off Beaufort St.)
Beaufort Mans. SW3............7B 16 (6B 100)
Beaufort M. SW6..6H 99
Beaufort Pk. NW11....................................4J 45
Beaufort Rd. HA4: Ruis............................2F 57
Beaufort Rd. KT1: King T......................4E 150
Beaufort Rd. TW1: Twick......................7C 114
Beaufort Rd. TW10: Ham......................4C 132
Beaufort Rd. W5..5F 79
Beaufort Sq. NW9......................................2C 44
Beaufort St. SW3..............7A 16 (6B 100)
Beaufort Ter. E14....................................5E 104
(off Ferry St.)
Beaufort Way KT17: Ewe......................7C 164
Beaufoy Ho. SE27..................................3B 138
Beaufoy Ho. SW8....................................7K 101
(off Rita Rd.)
Beaufoy Rd. N17..7K 33
(not continuous)
Beaufoy Wlk. SE11..............4H 19 (4K 101)
Beaulieu Av. E16....................................1K 105
Beaulieu Av. SE26..................................4H 139
Beaulieu Cl. CR4: Mitc..........................1E 154
Beaulieu Cl. NW9......................................4A 44
Beaulieu Cl. SE5......................................3D 120
Beaulieu Cl. TW1: Twick........................6D 114
Beaulieu Cl. TW4: Houn........................5D 112
Beaulieu Ct. W5..5E 78
Beaulieu Dr. HA5: Pinn..............................6B 40
Beaulieu Gdns. N21....................................7H 23
Beaulieu Hgts. SE25................................1E 156
Beaulieu Lodge E14..................................3F 105
(off Schooner Cl.)
Beaulieu Pl. W4..3J 97
Beaumanor Gdns. SE9..........................4E 142
Beaumanor Mans. W2..............................7K 81
(off Queensway)
Beaumans Dr. E17......................................1B 50
Beaumaris Dr. IG8: Wfd G........................7G 37
Beaumaris Gdns. SE19..........................7C 138
Beaumaris Grn. NW9..................................6A 44
Beaumaris Twr. W3....................................2H 97
(off Park Rd. Nth.)
Beaumont W14..4H 99
(off Kensington Village)
Beaumont Av. HA0: Wemb........................5C 60
Beaumont Av. HA2: Harr............................6F 41
Beaumont Av. TW9: Rich..........................3F 115
Beaumont Av. W14......................................5H 99
Beaumont Bldgs. WC2..........1F 13 (6J 83)
(off Martlett Ct.)
Beaumont Cl. KT2: King T......................7G 133
Beaumont Cl. N2..4C 46
Beaumont Ct. E1..3K 85
Beaumont Ct. E5..3H 67
Beaumont Ct. HA0: Wemb........................5C 60
Beaumont Ct. NW1......................................1J 87
Beaumont Ct. NW9......................................2B 44
(off Cherry Cl.)
Beaumont Ct. W1....................5H 5 (5E 82)
(off Beaumont St.)
Beaumont Ct. W4..5J 97
Beaumont Cres. W14....................................5H 99
Beaumont Dr. KT4: Wor Pk......................7D 152
Beaumont Dr. TW15: Ashf........................5F 129
Beaumont Gdns. NW3..................................3J 63
Beaumont Gro. E1..4K 85
Beaumont Ho. E10..7D 50
(off Skelton's La.)
Beaumont Ho. W9..3H 81
(off Fernhead Rd.)
Beaumont Lodge E8..6G 67
(off Greenwood Rd.)
Beaumont M. HA5: Pinn..................................3C 40
Beaumont M. NW5..5H 65
(off Charlton King's Rd.)
Beaumont M. W1......................5H 5 (5E 82)
Beaumont Pl. EN5: Barn....................................1C 20
Beaumont Pl. TW7: Isle..................................5K 113
Beaumont Pl. UB10: Ick......................................5C 56
Beaumont Pl. W1......................3B 6 (4G 83)
Beaumont Ri. N19..1H 65
Beaumont Rd. BR5: Pet W..............................6H 161
Beaumont Rd. E10..7D 50
(not continuous)
Beaumont Rd. E13..3K 87
Beaumont Rd. SE19..6C 138
Beaumont Rd. SW19..7G 117
Beaumont Rd. W4..3J 97
Beaumont Sq. E1..5K 85
Beaumont St. W1......................5H 5 (5E 82)
Beaumont Ter. SE13..7G 123
(off Wellmeadow Rd.)
Beaumont Wlk. NW3..7D 64
Beauvais Ter. UB5: N'olt..3B 76
Beauvale NW1..7E 64
(off Ferdinand St.)
Beauval Rd. SE22..6F 121
Beaux Arts Bldg., The N7..3J 65
Beaverbank Rd. SE9..1H 143
Beaver Cl. SE20..7G 139
Beaver Cl. SM4: Mord..7E 152
Beaver Cl. TW12: Hamp..1F 149
Beaver Ct. BR3: Beck..7D 140
Beaver Gro. UB5: N'olt..3C 76
Beaver Ind. Est. UB2: S'hall......................................3A 94
Beavers Cres. TW4: Houn..4A 112
Beavers La. TW4: Houn..2A 112
Beavers La. Campsite TW4: Houn
....4B 112
Beavers Lodge DA14: Sidc......................................4K 143
Beaverwood Rd. BR7: Chst......................................6J 143
Beavor Gro. W6..5C 98
(off Beavor La.)
Beavor La. W6..5C 98
Bebbington Rd. SE18..4J 107
Beblets Cl. BR6: Chels..5K 173
Beccles Dr. IG11: Bark..6J 71
Beccles St. E14..6B 86
Bec Cl. HA4: Ruis..3B 58
Bechervaise Ct. E10..1D 68
(off Leyton Grange Est.)
Bechtel Ho. W6..4F 99
(off Hammersmith Rd.)
Beck Cl. SE13..1D 122
Beck Ct. BR3: Beck..3K 157
BECKENHAM..2C 158
Beckenham Bus. Cen. BR3: Beck
....6A 140
Beckenham Crematorium..3J 157
Beckenham Gdns. N9..3K 33
Beckenham Gro. BR2: Broml..2F 159
Beckenham Hill Est. BR3: Beck..5D 140
Beckenham Hill Rd. BR3: Beck..6D 140
Beckenham Hill Rd. SE6..5E 140
Beckenham La. BR2: Broml..2G 159
Beckenham Pl. BR3: Beck..4D 158
Beckenham Pl. Pk. BR3: Beck..7D 140
Beckenham Place Pk..6E 140
Beckenham Rd. BR3: Beck..1K 157
Beckenham Rd. BR4: W W'ck..7D 158
Beckenham Theatre Cen, The..2D 158
Beckers, The N16..4G 67
Becket Av. E6..3E 88
Becket Cl. IG8: Wfd G..1C 52
Becket Cl. SE25..6G 157
Becket Cl. SW19..1K 153
(off High Path)
Becket Fold HA1: Harr..5K 41
Becket Ho. E16..1K 105
(off Constable Av.)
Becket Ho. SE1..................................7E 14 (2D 102)
(off Tabard St.)
Becket Ho. WC1....................................2G 7 (3K 83)
(off Westking Pl.)
Becket Rd. N18..4D 34
Becket St. SE1....................................7E 14 (3D 102)
Beckett Cl. DA17: Belv..3F 109
Beckett Cl. NW10..6A 62
Beckett Cl. SW16..2H 137
Beckett Ho. E1..5J 85
(off Jubilee St.)
Beckett Ho. SW9..2J 119
Becketts Cl. BR6: Orp..3K 173
Becketts Cl. DA5: Bexl..1J 145
Becketts Cl. TW14: Felt..6K 111
Becketts Ho. IG1: Ilf..3E 70
Becketts Pl. KT1: Hamp W..1D 150
Becketts Wharf KT1: Hamp W..1D 150
(off Lwr. Teddington Rd.)
Beckett Wlk. BR3: Beck..6A 140
Beckfoot NW1....................................1B 6 (2G 83)
(off Ampthill Est.)
Beckford Cl. W14..4H 99
Beckford Dr. BR5: Orp..7H 161
Beckford Ho. N16..5E 66
Beckford Pl. SE17..5C 102
Beckford Rd. CR0: C'don..6F 157
Beckham Ho. SE11................................4H 19 (4K 101)
Beckhaven Ho. SE11................................4K 19 (4A 102)
(off Gilbert Rd.)
Beck Ho. N18..5C 34
(off Upton Rd.)
Beck La. BR3: Beck..3K 157
Beckley Ho. E3..4B 86
(off Hamlets Way)
Becklow Gdns. W12..2C 98
(off Becklow Rd.)
Becklow M. W12..2C 98
(off Becklow Rd.)
Becklow Rd. W12..2B 98
Beck River Pk. BR3: Beck..1B 158
Beck Rd. CR4: Mitc..6D 154
Beck Rd. E8..1H 85
Beck Sq. E10..1A 68
Becks Rd. DA14: Sidc..3A 144
Beck Theatre, The..6H 75
BECKTON..5E 88
BECKTON ALPS..4D 88
BECKTON PARK..6D 88
Beckton Retail Pk..5E 88
Beckton Rd. E16..5H 87
Beckton Triangle Retail Pk.................................4F 89
Beck Way BR3: Beck..3B 158
Beckway Rd. SW16..2H 155
Beckway St. SE17..4E 102
(not continuous)
Beckwith Cl. EN2: Enf..1G 23
Beckwith Ho. E2..2H 85
(off Wadeson St.)
Beckwith Rd. SE24..5D 120
Beclands Rd. SW17..6E 136
Becmead Av. HA3: Kenton..5B 42
Becmead Av. SW16..4H 137
Becondale Rd. SE19..5E 138
BECONTREE..4D 72
Becontree Av. RM8: Dag..4B 72
Becontree Heath Leisure Cen....................................2G 73
Becquerel Ct. SE10..3H 105
(off West Parkside)
Bective Pl. SW15..4H 117
Bective Rd. E7..4J 69
Bective Rd. SW15..4H 117
Becton Pl. DA8: Erith..1H 127
Bedale Rd. EN2: Enf..1H 23
Bedale St. SE1..........................5E 14 (1D 102)
Beddalls Farm Ct. E6..5B 88
BEDDINGTON..4J 167
BEDDINGTON CORNER..7E 154
Beddington Cross CR0: Bedd....................................7H 155
Beddington Farmlands SM6: Bedd
....1F 167
Beddington Farm Rd. CR0: Bedd..............................7J 155
Beddington Farm Rd. CR0: Wadd
....7J 155
Beddington Gdns. SM5: Cars..........................6E 166
Beddington Gdns. SM6: W'gton........................6F 167
Beddington Grn. BR5: St P..................................1K 161
Beddington Gro. SM6: W'gton..............................5H 167
Beddington La. CR0: Bedd......................................5G 155
Beddington La. CR0: C'don......................................5G 155
Beddington Pk..3F 167
Beddington Pk. Cotts. SM6: Bedd
....3H 167
Beddington Path BR5: St P......................................1K 161
Beddington Rd. BR5: St P..2J 161
Beddington Rd. IG3: Ilf..7K 53
Beddington Ter. CR0: C'don......................................7K 155
Beddington Trad. Est. CR0: Bedd..............................1J 167
Bede Cl. HA5: Pinn..1B 40
Bedefield WC1..................................2F 7 (3J 83)
Bede Ho. SE14..1B 122
(off Clare Rd.)
Bedens Rd. DA14: Sidc..6E 144
Bede Rd. RM6: Chad H..6C 54
Bede Sq. E3..4B 86
(off Joseph St.)
Bedevere Rd. N9..3B 34
Bedfont Cl. CR4: Mitc..2E 154
Bedfont Cl. TW14: Bedf..6E 110
Bedfont Ct. TW19: Stanw M..6B 174
Bedfont Ct. Est. TW19: Stanw M..7C 174
Bedfont Grn. Cl. TW14: Bedf..1E 128
Bedfont Ind. Pk. TW15: Ashf..3E 128
Bedfont Ind. Pk. Nth. TW15: Ashf..3E 128
Bedfont Lakes Country Pk..2E 128
Bedfont Lakes Country Pk. Vis. Cen.
....3D 128
Bedfont La. TW13: Felt..1K 129
Bedfont La. TW14: Felt..7G 111
Bedfont Rd. TW13: Felt..2G 129
Bedfont Rd. TW14: Bedf..1E 128
Bedfont Rd. TW19: Stanw..6A 110
Bedfont Trad. Est. TW14: Bedf..2F 129
Bedford Av. EN5: Barn..5C 20
Bedford Av. UB4: Yead..6K 75
Bedford Av. WC1..6D 6 (5H 83)
Bedfordbury WC2..2E 12 (7J 83)
(not continuous)
Bedford Cl. N10..7K 31
Bedford Cl. W4..6A 98
Bedford Cnr. W4..4A 98
(off South Pde.)
Bedford Ct. CR0: C'don..1D 168
(off Tavistock Rd.)
Bedford Ct. WC2..3E 12 (7J 83)
Bedford Ct. Mans. WC1....................................6D 6 (5H 83)
(off Bedford Av.)
Bedford Gdns. W8..1J 99
Bedford Gdns. Ho. W8..1J 99
(off Bedford Gdns.)
Bedford Hill SW12..1F 137
Bedford Hill SW16..3G 137
Bedford Ho. CR0: C'don..7B 156
Bedford Ho. SW4..4J 119
(off Solon New Rd. Est.)
Bedford M. N2..3C 46
Bedford M. SE6..2D 140
Bedford Pk. CR0: C'don..1C 168
BEDFORD PARK..3K 97
Bedford Pk. Cnr. W4..4A 98
Bedford Pk. Mans. W4..4K 97
Bedford Pas. SW6..7G 99
(off Dawes Rd.)
Bedford Pas. W1..5B 6 (5G 83)
Bedford Pl. CR0: C'don..1D 168
Bedford Pl. WC1..5E 6 (5J 83)
Bedford Rd. DA15: Sidc..3J 143
Bedford Rd. E17..2C 50
Bedford Rd. E18..2J 51
Bedford Rd. E6..1E 88
Bedford Rd. HA1: Harr..6G 41
Bedford Rd. HA4: Ruis..4H 57
Bedford Rd. IG1: Ilf..3F 71
Bedford Rd. KT4: Wor Pk..2E 164
Bedford Rd. N15..4E 48
Bedford Rd. N2..3C 46
Bedford Rd. N22..2J 47
Bedford Rd. N8..6H 47
Bedford Rd. N9..7C 24
Bedford Rd. NW7..2F 29
Bedford Rd. SW4..4J 119
Bedford Rd. TW2: Twick..3H 131
Bedford Rd. W13..7B 78
Bedford Rd. W4..3K 97
Bedford Row SE1..7D 14 (3C 102)
Bedford Row WC1..5H 7 (5K 83)
Bedford Sq. WC1..6D 6 (5H 83)
Bedford St. WC2..2E 12 (7J 83)
Bedford Ter. SM2: Sutt..6A 166
Bedford Ter. SW2..5J 119
Bedford Way WC1..4D 6 (4H 83)
Bedgebury Ct. E17..2E 50
Bedgebury Gdns. SW19..2G 135
Bedgebury Rd. SE9..4B 124
Bedivere Rd. BR1: Broml..3J 141
Bedlam M. SE11..3J 19 (4A 102)
(off Walnut Tree Wlk.)
Bedlow Way CR0: Bedd..4K 167
Bedmond Ho. SW3..5C 16 (5C 100)
(off Cale St.)
Bedonwell Rd. DA17: Belv..6E 108
Bedonwell Rd. DA7: Belv..6F 109
Bedonwell Rd. DA7: Bex..6F 109
Bedonwell Rd. DA7: Erith..6F 109
Bedonwell Rd. SE2..6E 108
Bedser Cl. CR7: Thor H..3C 156
Bedser Cl. SE11..7H 19 (6K 101)
Bedser Dr. UB6: G'frd..5H 59
Bedster Gdns. KT8: W Mole..2F 149
Bedwardine Rd. SE19..7E 138
Bedwell Cl. CR0: C'don..5D 156
Bedwell Ct. RM6: Chad H..7D 54
(off Chapel La.)
Bedwell Gdns. UB3: Harl..5G 93
(not continuous)
Bedwell Ho. SW9..2A 120
Bedwell Rd. DA17: Belv..5G 109
Bedwell Rd. N17..1E 48
Beeby Rd. E16..5K 87
Beech Av. DA15: Sidc..7A 126
Beech Av. HA4: Ruis..1K 57
Beech Av. IG9: Buck H..2E 36
Beech Av. N20..1H 31
Beech Av. TW8: Bford..7B 96
Beech Av. W3..1A 98
Beech Cl. N9..6B 24
Beech Cl. SE8..6C 104
Beech Cl. SM5: Cars..2D 166
Beech Cl. SW15..7C 116
Beech Cl. SW19..6E 134
Beech Cl. TW15: Ashf..5F 129
Beech Cl. TW16: Sun..2B 148
Beech Cl. UB7: W Dray..3C 92
Beech Copse BR1: Broml..1D 160
Beech Copse CR2: S Croy..5E 168
Beech Ct. BR1: Broml..1H 159
(off Blyth Rd.)
Beech Ct. BR3: Beck..7B 140
Beech Ct. E17..3F 51
Beech Ct. IG1: Ilf..3E 70
(off Riverdene Rd.)
Beech Ct. KT6: Surb..7D 150
Beech Ct. UB5: N'olt..1C 76
Beech Ct. W9..5J 81
(off Elmfield Way)
Beech Cres. Ct. N5..4B 66
Beechcroft BR7: Chst..7E 142
Beechcroft Av. DA7: Bex..1K 127
Beechcroft Av. HA2: Harr..7E 40
Beechcroft Av. KT3: N Mald..1J 151
Beechcroft Av. NW11..7H 45
Beechcroft Cl. BR6: Orp..4H 173
Beechcroft Cl. SW16..5K 137
Beechcroft Cl. TW5: Hest..7C 94
Beechcroft Ct. N12..4E 30
Beechcroft Ct. NW11..7H 45
(off Beechcroft Av.)
Beechcroft Gdns. HA9: Wemb..3F 61
Beechcroft Ho. W5..5E 78
Beechcroft Lodge SM2: Sutt..7A 166
Beechcroft Rd. BR6: Orp..4H 173
Beechcroft Rd. E18..2K 51
Beechcroft Rd. KT9: Chess..3F 163
Beechcroft Rd. SW14..3J 115
Beechcroft Rd. SW17..2C 136
Beechdale N21..2E 32
Beechdale Rd. SW2..6K 119
Beech Dell BR2: Kes..4D 172
Beechdene SE15..1H 121
(off Carlton Gro.)
Beech Dr. N2..2D 46
Beechen Cliff Way TW7: Isle..2K 113
Beechen Gro. HA5: Pinn..3D 40
Beechen Pl. SE23..2K 139
Beeches, The CR2: S Croy..5D 168
(off Blunt Rd.)
Beeches, The E12..7C 70
Beeches, The TW3: Houn..1F 113
Beeches Av. SM5: Cars..7C 166
Beeches Cl. SE20..1J 157
Beeches Rd. SM3: Sutt..1G 165
Beeches Rd. SW17..3C 136
Beeches Wlk. SM5: Cars..7B 166
Beechey Ho. E1..1H 103
(off Watts St.)
Beechfield Cotts. BR1: Broml..1A 160
Beechfield Ct. CR2: S Croy..4C 168
(off Bramley Hill)
Beechfield Gdns. RM7: Rush G..7J 55
Beechfield Rd. BR1: Broml..2A 160
Beechfield Rd. DA8: Erith..7K 109
Beechfield Rd. N4..6C 48
Beechfield Rd. SE6..1B 140
Beech Gdns. EC2....................................5C 8 (5C 84)
(off Beech St.)
Beech Gdns. RM10: Dag..7J 73
Beech Gdns. W5..2E 96
Beech Gro. CR4: Mitc..5H 155
Beech Gro. KT3: N Mald..3K 151
Beech Hall Cres. E4..7A 36
Beech Hall Rd. E4..7K 35
Beech Haven Ct. DA1: Cray..5K 127
(off London Rd.)
Beech Hill EN4: Had W..1G 21
Beech Hill Av. EN4: Had W..1F 21
Beechhill Rd. SE9..5E 124
Beech Ho. CR0: New Ad..6D 170
Beech Ho. SE16..2J 103
(off Ainsty Est.)
Beech Ho. Rd. CR0: C'don..3D 168
Beech Hurst Cl. BR7: Chst..1G 161
Beeching Ct. W3..3J 97
(off Bollo Bri. Rd.)
Beech La. IG9: Buck H..2E 36
Beech Lawns N12..5G 31
Beechmont Cl. BR1: Broml..5G 141
Beechmore Gdns. SM3: Cheam..2F 165
Beechmore Rd. SW11..1D 118
Beechmount Av. W7..5H 77
Beecholme N12..5E 30
Beecholme Av. CR4: Mitc..1F 155
Beecholme Est. E5..3H 67
Beech Rd. N11..6D 32
Beech Rd. SW16..2J 155
Beech Rd. TW14: Bedf..7G 111
Beechrow TW10: Ham..4E 132
Beech St. EC2..5C 8 (5C 84)
Beech St. RM7: Rom..4J 55
Beech Tree Cl. HA7: Stan..5H 27
Beech Tree Cl. N1..7A 66
Beech Tree Glade E4..1C 36
Beech Tree Pl. SM1: Sutt..5K 165
Beechvale Cl. N12..5H 31
Beech Wlk. N17..3F 49
Beech Wlk. NW7..6F 29
Beech Way NW10..7K 61
Beech Way TW2: Twick..3E 130
Beechway DA5: Bexl..6D 126
Beechwood Av. BR6: Chels..5J 173
Beechwood Av. CR7: Thor H..4B 156
Beechwood Av. HA2: Harr..3F 59
Beechwood Av. HA4: Ruis..2H 57
Beechwood Av. N3..3H 45
Beechwood Av. TW16: Sun..6J 129
Beechwood Av. TW9: Kew..1G 115
Beechwood Av. UB3: Hayes..7F 75
Beechwood Av. UB6: G'frd..3F 77
Beechwood Av. UB8: Hil..6C 74
Beechwood Cen., The BR2: Broml
....1D 172
(off Lwr. Gravel Rd.)
Beechwood Circ. HA2: Harr..3F 59
Beechwood Cl. KT6: Surb..7C 150
Beechwood Cl. N2..3D 46
Beechwood Cl. NW7..5F 29
Beechwood Ct. SM5: Cars..4D 166
Beechwood Ct. TW16: Sun..6J 129
Beechwood Ct. W4..6K 97
Beechwood Cres. DA7: Bex..3D 126
Beechwood Dr. BR2: Kes..4B 172
Beechwood Dr. IG8: Wfd G..5C 36
Beechwood Gdns. HA2: Harr..3F 59
Beechwood Gdns. IG5: Ilf..5D 52
Beechwood Gdns. NW10..3F 79

186 A–Z London

Beechwood Gro. – Bergen Ho.

Beechwood Gro. KT6: Surb 7C 150
Beechwood Gro. W3 7A 80
Beechwood Hall N3 3H 45
Beechwood Ho. E2 2G 85
(off Teale St.)
Beechwood M. N9 2B 34
Beechwood Pk. E18 3J 51
Beechwood Pl. SE10 1E 122
Beechwood Ri. BR7: Chst 4F 143
Beechwood Rd. E8 6F 67
Beechwood Rd. N8 4H 47
Beechwoods Ct. SE19 5F 139
Beechworth NW6 7G 63
Beechworth Cl. NW3 2J 63
Beecroft La. SE4 5A 122
Beecroft M. SE4 5A 122
Beecroft Rd. SE4 5A 122
Beefeater Distillery 6J 19 (5A 102)
Beehive Cl. E8 7F 67
Beehive Cl. UB10: Uxb 7B 56
Beehive Ct. HA8: Edg 5C 28
Beehive Ct. IG1: Ilf 6D 52
Beehive La. IG1: Ilf 6D 52
Beehive La. IG4: Ilf 5D 52
Beehive Pl. SW9 3A 120
Beeken Dene BR6: Farnb 4G 173
Beeleigh Rd. SM4: Mord 4K 153
Beemans Row SW18 2A 136
Beeston Cl. E8 5G 67
Beeston Ho. SE1 3D 102
(off Burbage Cl.)
Beeston Pl. SW1 1K 17 (3F 101)
Beeston Rd. EN4: E Barn 6G 21
Beeston Way TW14: Felt 6A 112
Beethoven St. W10 3G 81
Beeton Cl. HA5: Hat E 1E 40
Beeton Way SE27 4D 138
Begbie Rd. SE3 1A 124
Beggar's Hill KT17: Ewe 7B 164
BEGGAR'S HILL 6B 164
Beggars Roost La. SM1: Sutt 6J 165
Begonia Cl. E6 5D 88
Begonia Pl. TW12: Hamp 6E 130
Begonia Wlk. W12 6B 80
Beirach Moshe Sq. E5 2H 67
Beira St. SW12 7F 119
Bejun Ct. EN5: New Bar 4F 21
Bekesbourne St. E14 6A 86
Belcroft Cl. BR1: Broml 7H 141
Beldam Way TW3: Houn 3D 112
Beldanes Lodge NW10 7C 62
Beldham Gdns. KT8: W Mole 2F 149
Belfairs Dr. RM6: Chad H 7C 54
Belfast Rd. N16 2F 67
Belfast Rd. SE25 4H 157
Belfield Rd. KT19: Ewe 7K 163
Belfont Wlk. N7 4J 65
(not continuous)
Belford Gro. SE18 4E 106
Belford Ho. E8 1F 85
Belfort Rd. SE15 2J 121
Belfry Cl. BR1: Broml 4F 161
Belfry Cl. SE16 5H 103
Belgrade Rd. N16 4E 66
Belgrade Rd. TW12: Hamp 1F 149
Belgrave Cl. N14 5B 22
Belgrave Cl. NW7 5E 28
Belgrave Cl. W3 2H 97
Belgrave Ct. E13 4A 88
Belgrave Ct. E14 7B 86
(off Westferry Cir.)
Belgrave Ct. E2 2H 85
(off Temple St.)
Belgrave Ct. SW8 7G 101
(off Ascalon St.)
Belgrave Ct. W4 5J 97
Belgrave Cres. TW16: Sun 1K 147
Belgrave Gdns. HA7: Stan 5H 27
Belgrave Gdns. N14 5C 22
Belgrave Gdns. NW8 1K 81
Belgrave Hgts. E11 1J 69
Belgrave Ho. SW9 7A 102
Belgrave Mans. NW8 1K 81
(off Belgrave Gdns.)
Belgrave M. Nth. SW1 7G 11 (2E 100)
Belgrave M. Sth. SW1 1H 17 (3E 100)
Belgrave M. W. SW1 1G 17 (3E 100)
Belgrave Pl. SW1 1H 17 (3E 100)
Belgrave Rd. CR4: Mitc 3B 154
Belgrave Rd. E10 1E 68
Belgrave Rd. E11 2J 69
Belgrave Rd. E13 4A 88
Belgrave Rd. E17 5C 50
Belgrave Rd. IG1: Ilf 1D 70
Belgrave Rd. SE25 4F 157
Belgrave Rd. SW1 3K 17 (4F 101)
Belgrave Rd. SW13 7B 98
Belgrave Rd. TW16: Sun 1K 147
Belgrave Rd. TW4: Houn 3D 112
Belgrave Sq. SW1 1G 17 (3E 100)
Belgrave St. E1 5K 85
Belgrave Ter. IG8: Wfd G 3D 36
Belgrave Wlk. CR4: Mitc 3B 154
Belgrave Yd. SW1 2J 17 (3F 101)
(off Lwr. Belgrave St.)
BELGRAVIA 2H 17 (3E 100)
Belgravia Cl. EN5: Barn 3C 20
Belgravia Ct. SW1 2J 17 (3F 101)
(off Ebury St.)
Belgravia Gdns. BR1: Broml 6G 141
Belgravia Ho. SW1 1G 17 (3E 100)
(off Halkin Pl.)
Belgravia Ho. SW4 6H 119
Belgravia M. KT1: King T 4D 150
Belgravia Workshops N19 2J 65
(off Marlborough Rd.)
Belgrove St. WC1 1F 7 (3J 83)
Belham Wlk. SE5 1D 120
Belinda Rd. SW9 3B 120
Belitha Vs. N1 7K 65
THE BELL 3C 50
Bella Best Ho. SW1 5K 17 (5F 101)
(off Westmoreland Ter.)
Bellamy Cl. E14 2C 104
Bellamy Cl. HA8: Edg 2D 28
Bellamy Cl. UB10: Ick 3C 56
Bellamy Cl. W14 5H 99
Bellamy Ct. HA7: Stan 1B 42
Bellamy Dr. HA7: Stan 1B 42
Bellamy Ho. SW17 4B 136
Bellamy Ho. TW5: Hest 6E 94
Bellamy Rd. E4 6J 35
Bellamy Rd. EN2: Enf 2J 23
Bellamy's Ct. SE16 1K 103
(off Abbotshade Rd.)
Bellamy St. SW12 7F 119
Bel La. TW13: Hanw 3C 130
Bellarmine Cl. SE28 1K 107
Bellasis Av. SW2 2J 137
Bell Av. UB7: W Dray 4B 92
Bell Brook Ri. N11 4A 32
Bell Cl. HA4: Ruis 3H 57
Bell Cl. HA5: Pinn 2A 40
Bellclose Rd. UB7: W Dray 2A 92
Bell Ct. NW4 4E 44
Bell Dr. SW18 7G 117
Bellefields Rd. SW9 3K 119
Bellegrove Cl. DA16: Well 2K 125
Bellegrove Pde. DA16: Well 3K 125
Bellegrove Rd. DA16: Well 2H 125
Bellenden Rd. SE15 1F 121
Bellenden Rd. Retail Pk. 1G 121
Bellestaines Pleasaunce E4 2H 35
Belleville Ho. SE10 7D 104
(off Norman Rd.)
Belleville Rd. SW11 5C 118
Belle Vue UB6: G'frd 1H 77
Bellevue Ct. TW3: Houn 4E 112
Belle Vue Est. NW4 4F 45
Belle Vue La. WD23: B Hea 1C 26
Bellevue M. N11 5K 31
Bellevue Pde. SW17 1D 136
Belle Vue Pk. CR7: Thor H 3C 156
Bellevue Pl. E1 4J 85
Belle Vue Rd. E17 2F 51
Belle Vue Rd. NW4 4E 44
Bellevue Rd. DA6: Bex 5F 127
Bellevue Rd. KT1: King T 3E 150
(not continuous)
Bellevue Rd. N11 4K 31
Bellevue Rd. SW13 2C 116
Bellevue Rd. SW17 1C 136
Bellevue Rd. W13 4B 78
Bellew St. SW17 3A 136
Bell Farm Av. RM10: Dag 3J 73
Bellfield CR0: Sels 7A 170
Bellfield Av. HA3: Hrw W 6C 26
Bellfield Cl. SE3 7K 105
Bellflower Cl. E6 5C 88
Bell Foundry Cl. CR0: C'don 6D 156
Bell Gdns. E10 1C 68
(off Church Rd.)
Bellgate M. NW5 4F 65
BELL GREEN 4B 140
Bell Grn. SE26 4B 140
Bell Grn. La. SE26 5B 140
Bell Grn. Retail Pk. 3B 140
Bell Grn. Trade City SE6 3B 140
Bellhaven E15 6F 69
Bell Hill CR0: C'don 2C 168
Bell Ho. HA9: Wemb 3E 60
Bell Ho. SE10 6E 104
(off Haddo St.)
Bellhouse Cotts. UB3: Hayes 7G 75
Bell Ho. Rd. RM7: Rush G 1J 73
Bellina M. NW5 4F 65
Bell Ind. Est. W4 4J 97
Belling Cres. EN3: Pond E 5D 24
Bellingham N17 7C 34
(off Park La.)
BELLINGHAM 3D 140
Bellingham Ct. IG11: Bark 3B 90
Bellingham Grn. SE6 3C 140
Bellingham Grn. Pk. 3C 140
(off Bellingham Green)
Bellingham Leisure & Lifestyle Cen.
3D 140
Bellingham Rd. SE6 3D 140
Bellingham Trad. Est. SE6 3D 140
Bell Inn Yd. EC3 1F 15 (6D 84)
Bell La. E1 6J 9 (5F 85)
Bell La. E16 1H 105
Bell La. EN3: Enf H 1E 24
Bell La. EN3: Enf W 1E 24
Bell La. HA9: Wemb 2D 60
Bell La. NW4 4F 45
Bell La. TW1: Twick 1A 132
Bell La. TW14: Bedf 7F 111
Bellmaker Ct. E3 5C 86
Bell Mdw. SE19 5E 138
Bell Moor NW3 3A 64
Bello Cl. SE24 7B 120
Bellot Gdns. SE10 5G 105
(off Bellot St.)
Bellot St. SE10 5G 105
Bell Pde. BR4: W W'ck 2E 170
Bellring Cl. DA17: Belv 6G 109
Bell Rd. EN1: Enf 1J 23
Bell Rd. KT8: E Mos 5H 149
Bell Rd. TW3: Houn 3F 113
Bells All. SW6 2J 117
Bells Hill EN5: Barn 5A 20
Bellsize Ct. NW3 5B 64
Bell St. NW1 5C 4 (5C 82)
Bell St. SE18 1C 124
Belltrees Gro. SW16 5K 137
Bellview Ct. TW3: Houn 4F 113
Bell Vw. Mnr. HA4: Ruis 7F 39
Bell Water Ga. SE18 3E 106
Bellwether La. SW18 5K 117
(off Ryland Blvd.)
Bell Wharf La. EC4 3D 14 (7C 84)
Bellwood Rd. SE15 4K 121
Bell Yd. WC2 1J 13 (6A 84)
Bell Yd. M. SE1 7H 15 (2E 102)
Belmarsh Rd. SE28 2J 107
BELMONT 2A 42
Belmont Av. DA16: Well 3J 125
Belmont Av. EN4: Cockf 5J 21
Belmont Av. HA0: Wemb 1F 79
Belmont Av. KT3: N Mald 5C 152
Belmont Av. N13 5E 32
Belmont Av. N17 3C 48
Belmont Av. N9 1B 34
Belmont Av. UB2: S'hall 3C 94
Belmont Circ. HA3: Kenton 1B 42
Belmont Cl. E4 5A 36
Belmont Cl. EN4: Cockf 4J 21
Belmont Cl. IG8: Wfd G 4E 36
Belmont Cl. N20 1E 30
Belmont Cl. SW4 3G 119
Belmont Cl. UB8: Uxb 6A 56
Belmont Ct. N5 4C 66
Belmont Ct. NW11 5H 45
Belmont Gro. SE13 3F 123
Belmont Gro. W4 4K 97
Belmont Hall Ct. SE13 3F 123
Belmont Hill SE13 3F 123
Belmont La. BR7: Chst 5G 143
Belmont La. HA7: Stan 1C 42
Belmont Lodge HA3: Hrw W 7C 26
Belmont M. SW19 2F 135
Belmont Pde. BR7: Chst 5G 143
Belmont Pde. NW11 5H 45
Belmont Pk. SE13 4F 123
Belmont Pk. Cl. SE13 4G 123
Belmont Pk. Rd. E10 6D 50
Belmont Ri. SM2: Sutt 7H 165
Belmont Rd. BR3: Beck 2A 158
Belmont Rd. BR7: Chst 5F 143
Belmont Rd. DA8: Erith 7G 109
Belmont Rd. HA3: W'stone 3K 41
Belmont Rd. IG1: Ilf 3G 71
Belmont Rd. N15 4C 48
Belmont Rd. N17 4C 48
Belmont Rd. SE25 5H 157
Belmont Rd. SM6: W'gton 5F 167
Belmont Rd. SW4 3G 119
Belmont Rd. TW2: Twick 2H 131
Belmont Rd. W4 4K 97
Belmont St. NW1 7E 64
Belmont Ter. W4 4K 97
Belmore Av. UB4: Hayes 6J 75
Belmore Ho. N7 5H 65
Belmore La. N7 5H 65
Belmore St. SW8 1H 119
Beloe Cl. SW15 4C 116
Belsham St. E9 6J 67
Belsize Av. N13 6E 32
Belsize Av. NW3 6B 64
Belsize Av. W13 3B 96
Belsize Ct. SM1: Sutt 4K 165
Belsize Ct. Garages NW3 5B 64
(off Belsize La.)
Belsize Cres. NW3 5B 64
Belsize Gdns. SM1: Sutt 4K 165
Belsize Gro. NW3 6C 64
Belsize La. NW3 6B 64
Belsize M. NW3 6B 64
Belsize Pk. NW3 6B 64
Belsize Pk. Gdns. NW3 6B 64
Belsize Pk. M. NW3 6B 64
Belsize Pl. NW3 5B 64
Belsize Rd. HA3: Hrw W 7C 26
Belsize Rd. NW6 1K 81
Belsize Sq. NW3 6B 64
Belsize Ter. NW3 6B 64
Belson Rd. SE18 4D 106
Beltane Dr. SW19 3F 135
Belthorn Cres. SW12 7G 119
Belton Rd. DA14: Sidc 4A 144
Belton Rd. E11 4G 69
Belton Rd. E7 7K 69
Belton Rd. N17 3E 48
Belton Rd. NW2 6C 62
Belton Way E3 5C 86
Beltran Rd. SW6 2K 117
Beltwood Rd. DA17: Belv 4J 109
BELVEDERE 4G 109
Belvedere, The SE1 5H 13 (1K 101)
Belvedere, The SW10 1A 118
(off Chelsea Harbour)
Belvedere Av. IG5: Ilf 2F 53
Belvedere Av. SW19 5G 135
Belvedere Bldgs. SE1 7B 14 (2B 102)
Belvedere Bus. Pk. DA17: Belv 2H 109
Belvedere Cl. TW11: Tedd 5J 131
Belvedere Ct. DA17: Belv 3F 109
Belvedere Ct. N1 1E 84
(off De Beauvoir Cres.)
Belvedere Ct. N2 5B 46
Belvedere Ct. NW2 6F 63
(off Willesden La.)
Belvedere Ct. SW15 4E 116
Belvedere Dr. SW19 5G 135
Belvedere Gdns. KT8: W Mole 5D 148
Belvedere Gdns. SE1 6H 13 (2K 101)
Belvedere Gro. SW19 5G 135
Belvedere Ho. TW13: Felt 1J 129
(off Lemon Gro.)
Belvedere Ind. Est. DA17: Belv 1J 109
Belvedere Link Bus. Pk. DA8: Erith
3J 109
Belvedere M. SE15 3J 121
Belvedere M. SE3 7K 105
Belvedere Pl. SE1 7B 14 (2B 102)
Belvedere Pl. SW2 4K 119
Belvedere Rd. DA7: Bex 3F 127
Belvedere Rd. E10 1A 68
Belvedere Rd. SE1 7G 13 (2K 101)
Belvedere Rd. SE19 7F 139
Belvedere Rd. W7 3K 95
Belvedere Row Apts. W12 7E 80
(off Fountain Park Way)
Belvedere Sq. SW19 5G 135
Belvedere Strand NW9 2B 44
Belvedere Way HA3: Kenton 6E 42
Belvoir Cl. SE9 3C 142
Belvoir Ho. SW1 4B 18 (4G 101)
Belvoir Rd. SE22 7G 121
Belvue Bus. Cen. UB5: N'olt 7F 59
Belvue Cl. UB5: N'olt 7E 58
Belvue Rd. UB5: N'olt 7E 58
Belz Dr. N15 4E 48
Belz Ter. E5 7G 49
Bembridge Cl. NW6 7G 63
Bembridge Gdns. HA4: Ruis 2F 57
Bembridge Ho. KT2: King T 2G 151
(off Coombe Rd.)
Bembridge Ho. SE8 4B 104
(off Longshore)
Bembridge Ho. SW18 6K 117
(off Iron Mill Rd.)
Bemersyde Point E13 3K 87
(off Dongola Rd. W.)
Bemerton Est. N1 7J 65
Bemerton St. N1 1K 83
Bemish Rd. SW15 3F 117
Bempton Dr. HA4: Ruis 2K 57
Bemsted Rd. E17 3B 50
Benares Rd. SE18 4K 107
Benbow Ct. W6 3E 98
(off Benbow Rd.)
Benbow Ho. SE8 6C 104
(off Benbow St.)
Benbow M. E3 3B 86
(off Tredegar Sq.)
Benbow Rd. W6 3D 98
Benbow St. SE8 6C 104
Benbury Cl. BR1: Broml 5E 140
Bence Ho. SE8 4A 104
(off Rainsborough Av.)
Bench, The TW10: Ham 3C 132
Bench Fld. CR2: S Croy 6F 169
Bencroft Rd. SW16 7G 137
Bencurtis Pk. BR4: W W'ck 3F 171
Bendall Ho. NW1 5D 4 (5C 82)
(off Penfold St.)
Bendall M. NW1 5D 4 (5C 82)
(off Bell St.)
Bendemeer Rd. SW15 3F 117
Benden Ho. SE13 5E 122
(off Monument Gdns.)
Bendish Point SE28 2G 107
Bendish Rd. E6 7C 70
Bendmore Av. SE2 5A 108
Bendon Valley SW18 7K 117
Benedict Cl. BR6: Orp 3J 173
Benedict Cl. DA17: Belv 3E 108
Benedict Ct. RM6: Chad H 6F 55
Benedict Dr. TW14: Bedf 7F 111
Benedict Rd. CR4: Mitc 3B 154
Benedict Rd. SW9 3K 119
Benedicts Wharf IG11: Bark 1F 89
Benedict Way N2 3A 46
Benedict Wharf CR4: Mitc 3C 154
Benenden Grn. BR2: Broml 5J 159
Benenden Ho. SE17 5E 102
(off Mina Rd.)
Benett Gdns. SW16 2J 155
Ben Ezra Ct. SE17 4C 102
(off Asolando Dr.)
Benfleet Cl. SM1: Sutt 3A 166
Benfleet Ct. E8 1F 85
Benfleet Way N11 2K 31
Bengal Ct. EC3 1F 15 (6D 84)
(off Birchin La.)
Bengal Rd. IG1: Ilf 4F 71
Bengarth Dr. HA3: Hrw W 2H 41
Bengarth Rd. UB5: N'olt 1C 76
Bengeo Gdns. RM6: Chad H 6C 54
Bengeworth Rd. HA1: Harr 2A 60
Bengeworth Rd. SE5 3C 120
Ben Hale Cl. HA7: Stan 5G 27
Benham Cl. KT9: Chess 6C 162
Benham Cl. SW11 3B 118
Benham Gdns. TW4: Houn 5D 112
Benham Ho. SW10 7K 99
(off Coleridge Gdns.)
Benham Rd. W7 5J 77
Benham's Pl. NW3 4A 64
Benhill Av. SM1: Sutt 4K 165
(not continuous)
Benhill Rd. SE5 7D 102
Benhill Rd. SM1: Sutt 3A 166
Benhill Wood Rd. SM1: Sutt 3A 166
BENHILTON 2K 165
Benhilton Gdns. SM1: Sutt 3K 165
Benhurst Ct. SW16 5A 138
Benhurst La. SW16 5A 138
Benina Cl. IG2: Ilf 5K 53
Benin Ho. WC1 6G 7 (5K 83)
(off Procter St.)
Benin St. SE13 7F 123
Benjafield Cl. N18 4C 34
Benjamin Cl. E8 1G 85
Benjamin Ct. DA17: Belv 6F 109
Benjamin Ct. TW15: Ashf 7E 128
Benjamin Franklin House 4E 12 (1J 101)
(off Craven St.)
Benjamin M. SW12 7G 119
Benjamin St. EC1 5A 8 (5B 84)
Benjamin Truman Cl. E1 4G 85
Ben Jonson Ct. N1 2E 84
Ben Jonson Ho. EC2 5C 8 (5C 84)
(off Beech St.)
Ben Jonson Pl. EC2 5C 8 (5C 84)
(off Beech St.)
Ben Jonson Rd. E1 5K 85
Benkart M. SW15 6C 116
Benledi Rd. E14 6F 87
Benlow Works UB3: Hayes 2H 93
(off Silverdale Rd.)
Bennelong Cl. W12 7D 80
Bennerley Rd. SW11 5C 118
Bennet Cl. KT1: Hamp W 1C 150
Bennet M. N19 3H 65
(off Wedmore St.)
Bennets Ctyd. SW19 1A 154
Bennets Fld. Rd. UB11: Stock P 1D 92
Bennet's Hill EC4 2C 14 (7C 84)
Bennets Lodge EN2: Enf 3G 23
Bennet St. SW1 4A 12 (1G 101)
Bennett Cl. DA16: Well 2A 126
Bennett Cl. HA6: Nwood 1H 39
Bennett Cl. TW4: Houn 5C 112
Bennett Ct. N7 3K 65
Bennett Gro. SE13 1D 122
Bennett Ho. SW1 3D 18 (4H 101)
(off Page St.)
Bennett Pk. SE3 3H 123
Bennett Rd. E13 4A 88
Bennett Rd. N16 4E 66
Bennett Rd. RM6: Chad H 7E 54
Bennett Rd. SW9 2A 120
Bennetts Av. CR0: C'don 2A 170
Bennetts Av. UB6: G'frd 1J 77
Bennett's Castle La. RM8: Dag 2C 72
Bennetts Cl. CR4: Mitc 1F 155
Bennetts Cl. N17 6A 34
Bennetts Copse BR7: Chst 6C 142
Bennett St. W4 6A 98
Bennetts Way CR0: C'don 2A 170
Bennett's Yd. SW1 2D 18 (3H 101)
Benning Dr. RM8: Dag 1E 72
Benningholme Rd. HA8: Edg 6F 29
Bennington Cl. CR7: Thor H 4C 156
Bennington Rd. IG8: Wfd G 7B 36
Bennington Rd. N17 1E 48
Benn's All. TW12: Hamp 2F 149
Benn St. E9 6A 68
Benns Wlk. TW9: Rich 4E 114
(off Michelsdale Dr.)
Benrek Cl. IG6: Ilf 1G 53
Bensbury Cl. SW15 7D 116
Bensham Cl. CR7: Thor H 4C 156
Bensham Gro. CR7: Thor H 2C 156
Bensham La. CR0: C'don 7B 156
Bensham La. CR7: Thor H 5B 156
Bensham Mnr. Rd. CR7: Thor H 4C 156
Bensham Mnr. Rd. Pas. CR7: Thor H
4C 156
Bensley Cl. N11 5J 31
Ben Smith Way SE16 3G 103
Benson Av. E6 2A 88
Benson Cl. EN5: Barn 5C 20
Benson Cl. TW3: Houn 4E 112
Benson Cl. UB8: Hil 5A 74
Benson Ct. SW8 1J 119
(off Hartington Rd.)
Benson Ho. E2 3J 9 (4F 85)
(off Ligonier St.)
Benson Ho. SE1 5K 13 (1A 102)
(off Hatfields)
Benson Ho. W14 4H 99
(off Radnor Ter.)
Benson M. BR7: Chst 5E 142
Benson Quay E1 7J 85
Benson Rd. CR0: Wadd 3A 168
Benson Rd. SE23 1J 139
Benson St. IG11: Bark 3C 90
Bentall Cen., The 2D 150
Bentfield Gdns. SE9 3B 142
Bentfield Ho. NW9 3B 44
(off Heritage Av.)
Benthal Rd. N16 2G 67
Bentham Ct. N1 7C 66
(off Ecclesbourne Rd.)
Bentham Ho. SE1 3D 102
(off Falmouth Rd.)
Bentham Ho. SE18 3F 107
Bentham Rd. E9 6K 67
Bentham Rd. SE28 7B 90
Bentham Wlk. NW10 5J 61
Ben Tillet Cl. E16 1D 106
Ben Tillet Cl. IG11: Bark 7A 72
Ben Tillet Ho. N15 3B 48
Bentinck Cl. NW8 2C 82
Bentinck Ho. SW1 2D 18 (3H 101)
(off Monck St.)
Bentinck Ho. W12 7D 80
(off White City Est.)
Bentinck Mans. W1 7H 5 (6E 82)
(off Bentinck St.)
Bentinck M. W1 7H 5 (6E 82)
Bentinck Rd. UB7: Yiew 1A 92
Bentinck St. W1 7H 5 (6E 82)
Bentley Cl. SW19 3J 135
Bentley Cl. W7 1K 95
Bentley Ct. SE13 4E 122
(off Whitburn Rd.)
Bentley Dr. IG2: Ilf 6G 53
Bentley Dr. NW2 3H 63
Bentley Ho. E3 4C 86
(off Wellington Way)
Bentley Ho. SE5 1E 120
(off Peckham Rd.)
Bentley Lodge WD23: B Hea 2D 26
Bentley M. EN1: Enf 6J 23
Bentley Priory Local Nature Reserve
4D 26
Bentley Priory Mus. 3D 26
Bentley Rd. N1 6E 66
Bentley Way EN5: New Bar 4F 21
Bentley Way HA7: Stan 5F 27
Bentley Way IG8: Buck H 2D 36
Bentley Way IG8: Wfd G 2D 36
Benton Rd. IG1: Ilf 1H 71
Bentons La. SE27 4C 138
Benton's Ri. SE27 5D 138
Bentry Cl. RM8: Dag 2E 72
Bentry Rd. RM8: Dag 2E 72
Bentworth Ct. E2 3K 9 (4G 85)
(off Granby St.)
Bentworth Rd. W12 6D 80
Ben Uri Gallery 1K 81
Benville Ho. SW8 7K 101
(off Dorset Rd.)
Benwell Cen. TW16: Sun 1J 147
Benwell Ct. TW16: Sun 1J 147
Benwell Rd. N7 4A 66
Benwick Cl. SE16 4H 103
Benwick M. SE20 1J 157
Benwood Ct. SM1: Sutt 3A 166
Benworth St. E3 3B 86
Benyon Ct. N1 1E 84
(off De Beauvoir Est.)
Benyon Ho. EC1 1K 7 (3A 84)
(off Myddelton Pas.)
Benyon Rd. N1 1D 84
Benyon Wharf E8 1E 84
(off Kingsland Rd.)
Berberis Ct. IG1: Ilf 6F 71
Berberis Ho. E3 5C 86
(off Gale St.)
Berberis Ho. TW13: Felt 2J 129
Berberis Wlk. UB7: W Dray 4A 92
Berber Pde. SE18 1C 124
Berber Pl. E14 7C 86
Berber Rd. SW11 5D 118
Berberry Cl. HA8: Edg 4D 28
Bercta Rd. SE9 2G 143
Berebinder Ho. E3 2B 86
(off Tredegar Rd.)
Beregaria Ct. SE11 7K 19 (6A 102)
(off Kennington Pk. Rd.)
Berengers Ct. RM6: Chad H 7F 55
(off Whalebone La. Sth.)
Berengers Pl. RM9: Dag 6B 72
Berenger Twr. SW10 7B 100
(off Worlds End Est.)
Berenger Wlk. SW10 7B 100
(off Worlds End Est.)
Berens Ct. DA14: Sidc 4K 143
Berens Rd. NW10 3F 81
Berens Way BR7: Chst 3K 161
Beresford Av. HA0: Wemb 1F 79
Beresford Av. KT5: Surb 1H 163
Beresford Av. N20 2J 31
Beresford Av. TW1: Twick 6C 114
Beresford Av. W7 5H 77
Beresford Ct. E9 5A 68
(off Mabley St.)
Beresford Dr. BR1: Broml 3C 160
Beresford Dr. IG8: Wfd G 4F 37
Beresford Gdns. EN1: Enf 4K 23
Beresford Gdns. RM6: Chad H 5E 54
Beresford Gdns. TW4: Houn 5D 112
Beresford Rd. E17 1D 50
Beresford Rd. E4 1B 36
Beresford Rd. HA1: Harr 5H 41
Beresford Rd. KT2: King T 1F 151
Beresford Rd. KT3: N Mald 4J 151
Beresford Rd. N2 3C 46
Beresford Rd. N5 5D 66
Beresford Rd. N8 5A 48
Beresford Rd. SM2: Sutt 7H 165
Beresford Rd. UB1: S'hall 1B 94
Beresford Sq. SE18 4F 107
Beresford St. SE18 3F 107
Beresford Ter. N5 5C 66
Berestede Rd. W6 5B 98
Bere St. E1 7K 85
Bergen Ho. SE5 2C 120
(off Carew St.)

Bergenia Ho. TW13: Felt 1J 129
Bergen Sq. SE16 3A 104
Berger Cl. BR5: Pet W 6H 161
Berger Ct. E3 3E 86
(off Bullinder Way)
Berger Rd. E9 6K 67
Berghem M. W14 3F 99
Bergholt Av. IG4: Ilf 5C 52
Bergholt Cres. N16 7E 48
Bergholt M. NW1 7H 65
Berglen Ct. E14 6A 86
Bergman Ho. E17 4C 50
(off Hoe St.)
Berica Ct. IG6: Ilf 3G 53
Bering Sq. E14 5C 104
Bering Wlk. E16 6B 88
Berisford M. SW18 6A 118
Berkeley Av. DA7: Bex 1D 126
Berkeley Av. IG5: Ilf 2E 52
Berkeley Av. RM5: Col R 1J 55
Berkeley Av. TW4: Cran 1J 111
Berkeley Av. UB6: G'frd 6H 59
(not continuous)
Berkeley Cl. BR5: Pet W 7J 161
Berkeley Cl. HA4: Ruis 3J 57
Berkeley Cl. KT2: King T 7E 132
Berkeley Ct. BR2: Broml 4K 159
Berkeley Ct. CR0: C'don 4D 168
(off Coombe Rd.)
Berkeley Ct. KT6: Surb 7D 150
Berkeley Ct. N14 6B 22
Berkeley Ct. N3 1K 45
Berkeley Ct. NW1 4F 5 (4D 82)
(off Marylebone Rd.)
Berkeley Ct. NW10 4A 62
Berkeley Ct. NW11 7H 45
(off Ravenscroft Av.)
Berkeley Ct. SM6: W'gton 3G 167
Berkeley Ct. W5 7C 78
Berkeley Cres. EN4: E Barn 5G 21
Berkeley Dr. KT8: W Mole 3D 148
Berkeley Gdns. KT10: Clay 6A 162
Berkeley Gdns. KT12: Walt T 7H 147
Berkeley Gdns. N21 7J 23
Berkeley Gdns. W8 1J 99
Berkeley Ho. E3 3C 86
(off Wellington Way)
Berkeley Ho. SE8 5B 104
(off Grove St.)
Berkeley Ho. TW8: Bford 6D 96
(off Albany Rd.)
Berkeley M. TW16: Sun 3A 148
Berkeley M. W1 7F 5 (6D 82)
Berkeley Pl. SW19 6F 135
Berkeley Rd. E12 5C 70
Berkeley Rd. N15 6D 48
Berkeley Rd. N8 5H 47
Berkeley Rd. NW9 4G 43
Berkeley Rd. SW13 1C 116
Berkeley Rd. UB10: Hil 7E 56
Berkeleys, The SE25 4G 157
Berkeley Sq. W1 3K 11 (7F 83)
Berkeley St. W1 3K 11 (7F 83)
Berkeley Twr. E14 1B 104
(off Westferry Cir.)
Berkeley Wlk. N7 2K 65
(off Durham Rd.)
Berkeley Waye TW5: Hest 6B 94
Berkhampstead Rd. DA17: Belv 5G 109
Berkhamsted Av. HA9: Wemb 6F 61
Berkley Cl. TW2: Twick 3J 131
(off Wellesley Rd.)
Berkley Gro. NW1 7E 64
Berkley Rd. NW1 7D 64
Berkshire Ct. W7 4K 77
(off Copley Cl.)
Berkshire Gdns. N13 6F 33
Berkshire Gdns. N18 5C 34
Berkshire Ho. SE6 4C 140
Berkshire Rd. E9 6B 68
Berkshire Way CR4: Mitc 4J 155
Berley Rd. E17 1B 50
Berlin Ter. E15 5G 69
Bermans Way NW10 4A 62
BERMONDSEY 2G 103
Bermondsey Exchange SE1
7H 15 (3E 102)
(off Bermondsey St.)
Bermondsey Spa Gdns. 3F 103
Bermondsey Sq. SE1 3E 102
Bermondsey St. SE1 5G 15 (1E 102)
Bermondsey Trad. Est. SE16 5J 103
Bermondsey Wall E. SE16 2G 103
Bermondsey Wall W. SE16
6K 15 (2G 103)
Bermuda Way E1 5A 86
(off Dongola Rd.)
Bernal Cl. SE28 7D 90
Bernard Angell Ho. SE10 6F 105
(off Trafalgar Rd.)
Bernard Ashley Dr. SE7 5K 105
Bernard Av. W13 3B 96
Bernard Cassidy St. E16 5H 87
Bernard Gdns. SW19 5H 135
Bernard Hegarty Lodge E8 7G 67
(off Lansdowne Dr.)
Bernard Ho. E1 6J 9 (5F 85)
(off Toynbee St.)
Bernard Mans. WC1 4E 6 (4J 83)
(off Bernard St.)
Bernard Myers Ho. SE5 7E 102
(off Havil St.)
Bernard Rd. N15 5F 49
Bernard Rd. RM7: Rush G 7J 55
Bernard Rd. SM6: W'gton 4F 167
Bernard Shaw Ct. NW1 7G 65
(off St Pancras Way)
Bernard Shaw Ho. NW10 1K 79
(off Knatchbull Rd.)
Bernard St. WC1 4E 6 (4J 83)
Bernard Sunley Ho. SW9 7A 102
(off Sth. Island Pl.)
Bernays Cl. HA7: Stan 6H 27
Bernays Gro. SW9 4K 119
Bernel Dr. CR0: C'don 3B 170
Bernera Wlk. NW9 3B 44
Berne Rd. CR7: Thor H 5C 156
Berners Dr. W13 7A 78
Berners Ho. N1 2A 84
(off Barnsbury Est.)
Berners M. W1 6B 6 (5G 83)
Berners Pl. W1 7B 6 (6G 83)
Berners Rd. N1 1B 84
Berners Rd. N22 1A 48
Berners St. W1 6B 6 (5G 83)
Berner Ter. E1 6G 85
(off Fairclough St.)
Berney Ho. BR3: Beck 5A 158
Berney Rd. CR0: C'don 7D 156
Bernhard Baron Ho. E1 6G 85
(off Henriques St.)
Bernhardt Cres. NW8 3C 4 (4C 82)
Bernhart Cl. HA8: Edg 7D 28
Bernie Grant Arts Cen. 4F 49
Bernville Way HA3: Kenton 5F 43
Bernwell Rd. E4 3B 36
Berridge Cl. SM2: Sutt 6K 165
Berridge Grn. HA8: Edg 7B 28
Berridge M. NW6 5J 63
Berridge Rd. SE19 5D 138
Berriman Rd. N7 3K 65
Berrington Ho. W2 7J 81
(off Herrington Rd.)
Berriton Rd. HA2: Harr 1D 58
Berrybank Cl. E4 2K 35
Berry Cl. N21 1G 33
Berry Cl. RM10: Dag 5G 73
Berry Cotts. E14 6A 86
(off Maroon St.)
Berry Ct. TW4: Houn 5D 112
Berrydale Rd. UB4: Yead 4C 76
Berryfield Cl. BR1: Broml 1C 160
Berryfield Cl. E17 4D 50
Berryfield Rd. SE17 5B 102
Berry Hill HA7: Stan 4J 27
Berryhill SE9 4F 125
Berryhill Gdns. SE9 4F 125
Berry Ho. E1 4H 85
(off Headlam St.)
Berry Ho. SW11 2D 118
(off Culvert Rd.)
Berrylands KT5: Surb 6F 151
BERRYLANDS 6G 151
Berrylands SW20 3E 152
Berrylands Rd. KT5: Surb 6F 151
Berry La. SE21 4D 138
Berryman Cl. RM8: Dag 3C 72
Berryman's La. SE26 4K 139
Berrymead Gdns. W3 1J 97
Berrymede Rd. W4 3K 97
Berry Pl. EC1 2B 8 (3B 84)
Berryside Apts. N4 1C 66
(off Swan La.)
Berry St. EC1 3B 8 (4B 84)
Berry Way W5 3E 96
Bertal Rd. SW17 4B 136
Bertelli Pl. TW13: Felt 1K 129
Bertha Hollamby Ct. DA14: Sidc 5C 144
(off Sidcup Hill)
Bertha James Ct. BR2: Broml 4K 159
Berthons Gdns. E17 5F 51
(off Wood St.)
Berthon St. SE8 7C 104
Bertie Rd. NW10 6C 62
Bertie Rd. SE26 6K 139
Bertram Cotts. SW19 7J 135
Bertram Rd. EN1: Enf 4B 24
Bertram Rd. KT2: King T 7G 133
Bertram Rd. NW4 6C 44
Bertram St. N19 2F 65
Bertrand Ho. E16 6K 87
(off Russell Rd.)
Bertrand Ho. SW16 3J 137
(off Leigham Av.)
Bertrand St. SE13 3D 122
Bertrand Way SE28 7B 90
Bert Rd. CR7: Thor H 5C 156
Bert Way EN1: Enf 4A 24
Berwick Av. UB4: Yead 6B 76
Berwick Cl. HA7: Stan 6E 26
Berwick Cl. TW2: Whitt 1E 130
Berwick Ct. SE1 7D 14 (2C 102)
(off Swan St.)
Berwick Cres. DA15: Sidc 7J 125
Berwick Gdns. SM1: Sutt 3A 166
Berwick Ho. BR6: Orp 1K 173
Berwick Ho. N2 2B 46
Berwick Rd. DA16: Well 1B 126
Berwick Rd. E16 6K 87
Berwick Rd. N22 1B 48
Berwick St. W1 7B 6 (6G 83)
Berwick Way BR6: Orp 1K 173
Berwyn Av. TW3: Houn 1F 113
Berwyn Rd. SE24 1B 138
Berwyn Rd. TW10: Rich 4H 115
Beryl Av. E6 5C 88
Beryl Ho. SE18 5K 107
(off Spinel Cl.)
Beryl Rd. W6 5F 99
Berystede KT2: King T 7H 133
Besant Cl. NW2 3G 63
Besant Ct. N1 5D 66
Besant Ct. SE28 1B 108
(off Titmuss Av.)
Besant Ho. NW8 1A 82
(off Boundary Rd.)
Besant Pl. SE22 4F 121
Besant Rd. NW2 4G 63
Besant Wlk. N7 2K 65
Besant Way NW10 5J 61
Besford Ho. E2 2G 85
(off Pritchard's Rd.)
Besley St. SW16 6G 137
Bessant Dr. TW9: Kew 1H 115
Bessborough Gdns. SW1
5D 18 (5H 101)
Bessborough Pl. SW1 5D 18 (5H 101)
Bessborough Rd. HA1: Harr 1H 59
Bessborough Rd. SW15 1C 134
Bessborough St. SW1 5C 18 (5H 101)
Bessborough Vw. KT8: W Mole 4C 148
Bessemer Ct. NW1 7G 65
(off Rochester Sq.)
Bessemer Pk. Ind. Est. SE24 4B 120
Bessemer Pl. SE10 3H 105
Bessemer Rd. SE5 2C 120
Bessie Lansbury Cl. E6 6E 88
Bessingby Rd. HA4: Ruis 2K 57
Bessingham Wlk. SE4 4K 121
(off Aldersford Cl.)
Besson St. SE14 1J 121
Bessy St. E2 3J 85
Bestwood St. SE8 4K 103
Beswick M. NW6 6K 63
Beta Ct. CR0: C'don 1D 168
(off Sydenham Rd.)
Betam Rd. UB3: Hayes 2F 93
Beta Pl. SW4 4K 119
Betchworth Cl. SM1: Sutt 5B 166
Betchworth Rd. IG3: Ilf 2J 71
Betchworth Way CR0: New Ad 7E 170
Betham Rd. UB6: G'frd 3H 77
Bethany Waye TW14: Bedf 7G 111
Bethecar Rd. HA1: Harr 5J 41
Bethel Cl. NW4 5F 45
Bethell Av. E16 4H 87
Bethell Av. IG1: Ilf 7E 52
Bethel Rd. DA16: Well 3C 126
Bethersden Cl. BR3: Beck 7B 140
Bethersden Ho. SE17 5E 102
(off Kinglake Est.)
Bethlehem Cl. UB6: G'frd 2C 78
Bethlehem Ho. E14 7B 86
(off Limehouse C'way.)
BETHNAL GREEN 3H 85
Bethnal Green Cen. for Sports &
Performing Arts 2K 9 (3F 85)
Bethnal Grn. Rd. E1 3J 9 (4F 85)
Bethnal Grn. Rd. E2 3K 9 (4F 85)
Bethune Av. N11 4J 31
Bethune Rd. N16 7D 48
Bethune Rd. NW10 4K 79
Bethwin Rd. SE5 7B 102
Betjeman Cl. HA5: Pinn 4E 40
Betjeman Ct. UB7: Yiew 1A 92
Betjeman M. N5 4C 66
Betony Cl. CR0: C'don 1K 169
Betoyne Av. E4 4B 36
Betsham Ho. SE1 6E 14 (2D 102)
(off Newcomen St.)
BETSTYLE CIR. 4A 32
Betstyle Ho. N10 7K 31
Betstyle Rd. N11 4A 32
Bettenson Cl. BR7: Chst 5D 142
Better Gym East Village 6E 68
Better Gym Greenwich 2G 105
Better Gym Harrow 6J 41
(within St George's Shop. & Leisure Cen.)
Better Gym Pinner 3B 40
Better Gym Woolwich 3F 107
Betterton Dr. DA14: Sidc 2E 144
Betterton Ho. WC2 1F 13 (6J 83)
(off Betterton St.)
Betterton Rd. RM13: Rain 3K 91
Betterton St. WC2 1E 12 (6J 83)
Bettons Pk. E15 1G 87
Bettridge Rd. SW6 2H 117
Betts Cl. BR3: Beck 2A 158
Betts Ho. E1 7H 85
(off Betts St.)
Betts M. E17 6B 50
Betts Rd. E16 7K 87
Betts St. E1 7H 85
Betts Way KT6: Surb 1B 162
Betts Way SE20 1H 157
Betty Brooks Ho. E11 3F 69
Betty May Gray Ho. E14 4E 104
(off Pier St.)
Beulah Av. CR7: Thor H 2C 156
Beulah Cl. HA8: Edg 3C 28
Beulah Cres. CR7: Thor H 2C 156
Beulah Gro. CR0: C'don 6C 156
Beulah Hill SE19 6B 138
Beulah Path E17 5E 50
Beulah Rd. CR7: Thor H 3C 156
Beulah Rd. E17 5D 50
Beulah Rd. SM1: Sutt 4J 165
Beulah Rd. SW19 7H 135
Bevan Av. IG11: Bark 7A 72
Bevan Ct. CR0: Wadd 5A 168
Bevan Ct. E3 2C 86
(off Tredegar Rd.)
Bevan Ct. TW1: Twick 6D 114
Bevan Ho. IG11: Bark 7B 72
Bevan Ho. N1 1E 84
(off Halcomb St.)
Bevan Ho. WC1 5F 7 (5J 83)
(off Boswell St.)
Bevan M. W12 2C 98
Bevan Rd. EN4: Cockf 4J 21
Bevan Rd. SE2 5B 108
Bevans Ho. SW18 4A 118
(off Eltringham St.)
Bevan St. N1 1C 84
Bev Callender Cl. SW8 3F 119
Bevenden St. N1 1F 9 (3D 84)
Bevercote Wlk. DA17: Belv 6F 109
(off Osborne Rd.)
Beveree Stadium 1F 149
Beveridge Ct. N21 5D 22
(off Pennington Dr.)
Beveridge Ct. SE28 7B 90
(off Saunders Way)
Beveridge M. E1 5J 85
Beveridge Rd. NW10 7A 62
Beverley Av. DA15: Sidc 7K 125
Beverley Av. SW20 1B 152
Beverley Av. TW4: Houn 4D 112
Beverley Cl. EN1: Enf 4K 23
Beverley Cl. KT9: Chess 4C 162
Beverley Cl. N21 1H 33
Beverley Cl. SW11 4B 118
Beverley Cl. SW13 2C 116
Beverley Cotts. SW15 3A 134
Beverley Ct. HA2: Harr 3H 41
Beverley Ct. HA3: Kenton 4C 42
Beverley Ct. N14 7B 22
Beverley Ct. N2 4D 46
(off Western Rd.)
Beverley Ct. NW6 7A 64
(off Fairfax Rd.)
Beverley Ct. SE4 3B 122
(not continuous)
Beverley Ct. TW4: Houn 4D 112
Beverley Ct. W4 5J 97
Beverley Cres. IG8: Wfd G 7E 36
Beverley Dr. HA8: Edg 3G 43
Beverley Gdns. HA7: Stan 1A 42
Beverley Gdns. HA9: Wemb 1H 61
Beverley Gdns. KT4: Wor Pk 1C 164
Beverley Gdns. NW11 7G 45
Beverley Gdns. SW13 3B 116
Beverley Ho. BR1: Broml 5F 141
(off Brangbourne Rd.)
Beverley Hyrst CR0: C'don 2F 169
Beverley La. KT2: King T 7A 134
Beverley La. SW15 3B 134
Beverley Meads & Fishponds Wood
Nature Reserve 6B 134
Beverley M. E4 6A 36
Beverley Path SW13 2B 116
Beverley Rd. BR2: Broml 2C 172
Beverley Rd. CR4: Mitc 4H 155
Beverley Rd. DA7: Bex 2J 127
Beverley Rd. E4 6A 36
Beverley Rd. E6 3B 88
Beverley Rd. HA4: Ruis 2J 57
Beverley Rd. KT1: Hamp W 1C 150
Beverley Rd. KT3: N Mald 4C 152
Beverley Rd. KT4: Wor Pk 2E 164
Beverley Rd. RM9: Dag 4E 72
Beverley Rd. SE20 2H 157
Beverley Rd. SW13 3B 116
Beverley Rd. TW16: Sun 1H 147
Beverley Rd. UB2: S'hall 4C 94
Beverley Rd. W4 5B 98
Beverley Trad. Est. SM4: Mord 7F 153
Beverley Way KT3: N Mald 3C 152
Beverley Way SW20 1B 152
Beversbrook Rd. N19 3H 65
Beverstone Rd. CR7: Thor H 4A 156
Beverstone Rd. SW2 5K 119
Beverston M. W1 6E 4 (5D 82)
(off Up. Montagu St.)
Bevill Allen Cl. SW17 5D 136
Bevill Cl. SE25 3G 157
Bevin Cl. SE16 1A 104
Bevin Ct. WC1 1H 7 (3K 83)
Bevington Path SE1 7J 15 (2F 103)
(off Tanner St.)
Bevington Rd. BR3: Beck 2D 158
Bevington Rd. W10 5G 81
Bevington St. SE16 2G 103
Bevin Ho. E2 3J 85
(off Butler St.)
Bevin Ho. E3 3C 86
(off Alfred St.)
Bevin Rd. UB4: Yead 3J 75
Bevin Sq. SW17 3D 136
Bevin Way WC1 1J 7 (2A 84)
Bevis Marks EC3 7H 9 (6E 84)
Bewcastle Gdns. EN2: Enf 4D 22
Bew Ct. SE22 7G 121
Bewdley St. N1 7A 66
Bewick M. SE15 7H 103
Bewick St. SW8 2F 119
Bewley Ho. E1 7H 85
(off Bewley St.)
Bewley St. E1 7J 85
Bewley St. SW19 6A 136
Bewlys Rd. SE27 5B 138
Bexhill Cl. TW13: Felt 2C 130
Bexhill Rd. N11 5C 32
Bexhill Rd. SE4 6B 122
Bexhill Rd. SW14 3J 115
Bexhill Wlk. E15 1G 87
BEXLEY 7G 127
Bexley Gdns. N9 3J 33
Bexley Gdns. RM6: Chad H 5B 54
BEXLEYHEATH 4G 127
Bexleyheath Golf Course 5E 126
Bexleyheath Sports Club 4C 126
Bexley High St. DA5: Bexl 7G 127
Bexley Ho. SE4 4A 122
Bexley La. DA1: Cray 5K 127
Bexley La. DA14: Sidc 4C 144
Bexley Lawn Tennis, Squash &
Racketball Club 7G 127
Bexley Mus. Collection, The 6J 127
Bexley Music & Dance Cen.
4A 144
(off Station Rd.)
Bexley Rd. DA8: Erith 7J 109
(not continuous)
Bexley Rd. SE9 5F 125
Bexley Tourist Info. Cen. 4F 127
Beynon Rd. SM5: Cars 5D 166
Bezier Apts. EC2 3F 9 (4D 84)
BFI Southbank 4H 13 (1K 101)
(off Waterloo Rd.)
Bianca Ho. N1 1G 9 (2E 84)
(off Crondall St.)
Bianca Rd. SE15 6G 103
Bibsworth Rd. N3 2H 45
Bibury Cl. SE15 6E 102
(not continuous)
Bicester Rd. TW9: Rich 3G 115
Bickels Yd. SE1 7H 15 (2E 102)
Bickenhall Mans. W1 5F 5 (5D 82)
(off Bickenhall St.)
Bickenhall St. W1 5F 5 (5D 82)
Bickersteth Rd. SW17 6D 136
Bickerton Rd. N19 2G 65
BICKLEY 3C 160
Bickley Cres. BR1: Broml 4C 160
Bickley Pk. Rd. BR1: Broml 3C 160
Bickley Rd. BR1: Broml 2B 160
Bickley Rd. E10 7D 50
Bickley St. SW17 5C 136
Bicknell Ho. E1 6G 85
(off Ellen St.)
Bicknell Rd. SE5 3C 120
Bicknell Wy. SW17 2C 136
Bicknoller Rd. EN1: Enf 1K 23
Bicknor Rd. BR6: Orp 7J 161
Bicycle M. SW4 3H 119
Bidborough Cl. BR2: Broml 5H 159
Bidborough St. WC1 2E 6 (3J 83)
Biddenden Way SE9 4E 142
Biddenham Ho. SE16 4K 103
(off Plough Way)
Bidder St. E16 5G 87
(not continuous)
Biddesden Ho. SW3 4E 16 (4D 100)
(off Cadogan St.)
Biddestone Rd. N7 4K 65
Biddulph Ho. SE18 4D 106
Biddulph Mans. W9 3K 81
(off Elgin Av.)
Biddulph Rd. W9 3K 81
Bideford Av. UB6: G'frd 2B 78
Bideford Cl. HA8: Edg 1G 43
Bideford Cl. TW13: Hanw 3D 130
Bideford Gdns. EN1: Enf 7K 23
Bideford Rd. BR1: Broml 3H 141
Bideford Rd. DA16: Well 7B 108
Bideford Rd. EN3: Enf L 1G 25
Bideford Rd. HA4: Ruis 3K 57
Bidwell Gdns. N11 7B 32
Bidwell St. SE15 1H 121
Big Ben 7F 13 (2J 101)
Bigbury Cl. N17 7J 33
Biggerstaff Rd. E15 1E 86
Biggerstaff St. N4 2A 66
Biggin Av. CR4: Mitc 1D 154
Biggin Hill SE19 7B 138
Biggin Hill Cl. KT2: King T 5C 132
Biggin Way SE19 7B 138
Bigginwood Rd. SW16 7B 138
Biggs Ct. NW9 2A 44
(off Harvey Cl.)
Biggs Row SW15 3F 117
Biggs Sq. E9 6B 68
Big Hill E5 1H 67
Bigland St. E1 6H 85
Bignell Rd. SE18 5F 107
Bignold Rd. E7 4J 69
Bigsworth Ct. SE20 1H 157
Bigwood Ct. NW11 5K 45
Bigwood Rd. NW11 5K 45
Bilberry Ho. E3 5C 86
(off Watts Gro.)
Billet Cl. RM6: Chad H 3D 54
Billet Rd. E17 1K 49
Billet Rd. RM6: Chad H 3B 54
Billets Hart Cl. W7 2J 95
Bill Hamling Cl. SE9 2D 142
Billingford Cl. SE4 4K 121
Billing Ho. E1 6K 85
(off Bower St.)
Billinghurst Way SE10 3J 105
Billingley NW1 1G 83
(off Pratt St.)
Billing Pl. SW10 7K 99
Billing Rd. SW10 7K 99
Billings Cl. RM9: Dag 7C 72
Billingsgate Market 1D 104
Billing St. SW10 7K 99
Billington M. W3 1H 97
(off High St.)
Billington Rd. SE14 7K 103
Billinton Hill CR0: C'don 2D 168
Billiter St. EC3 1H 15 (6E 84)
Bill Nicholson Way N17 7A 34
(off High Rd.)
Billockby Cl. KT9: Chess 6F 163
Billson St. E14 4E 104
Bill Voisey Ct. E14 6A 86
(off Repton St.)
Bilsby Gro. SE9 4B 142
Bilsby Lodge HA9: Wemb 3J 61
(off Chalklands)
Bilton Cen., The UB6: G'frd 1B 78
Bilton Rd. UB6: G'frd 1A 78
Bilton Towers W1 1F 11 (6D 82)
(off Gt. Cumberland Pl.)
Bilton Way EN3: Enf L 1F 25
Bilton Way UB3: Hayes 2K 93
Bina Gdns. SW5 4A 100
Binbrook Ho. W10 5E 80
(off Sutton Way)
Bincote Rd. EN2: Enf 3E 22
Binden Rd. W12 3B 98
Bindon Grn. SM4: Mord 4K 153
Binfield Rd. CR2: S Croy 5F 169
Binfield Rd. SW4 1J 119
Bingfield St. N1 1J 83
(not continuous)
Bingham Ct. N1 7B 66
(off Halton Rd.)
Bingham Pl. W1 5G 5 (5E 82)
Bingham Point SE18 4F 107
(off Wilmount St.)
Bingham Rd. CR0: C'don 1G 169
Bingham St. N1 6D 66
Bingley Rd. E16 6A 88
Bingley Rd. TW16: Sun 7J 129
Bingley Rd. UB6: G'frd 4G 77
Binley Ho. SW15 6C 116
Binnacle Ho. E1 1H 103
(off Cobblestone Sq.)
Binney St. W1 1H 11 (6E 82)
Binnie Ho. SE1 3C 102
(off Bath Ter.)
Binnington Twr. BR2: Broml 6C 160
Binns Rd. W4 5A 98
Binns Ter. W4 5A 98
Binstead Cl. UB4: Yead 6C 76
Binyon Cres. HA7: Stan 5E 26
Bioko Ct. E1 5A 86
(off Ocean Est.)
Biraj Ho. E6 1D 88
Birbetts Rd. SE9 2D 142
Bircham Path SE4 4K 121
(off Aldersford Cl.)
Birchanger Rd. SE25 5G 157
Birch Av. N13 3H 33
Birch Av. UB7: Yiew 6B 74
Birch Cl. E16 5G 87
Birch Cl. IG9: Buck H 3G 37
Birch Cl. N19 2G 65
Birch Cl. RM7: Mawney 3H 55
Birch Cl. SE15 2G 121
Birch Cl. TW11: Tedd 5A 132
Birch Cl. TW17: Shep 2G 147
Birch Cl. TW3: Houn 2H 113
Birch Cl. TW8: Bford 7B 96
Birch Ct. N12 4E 30
Birch Ct. RM6: Chad H 6C 54
Birch Ct. SM1: Sutt 4A 166
Birch Ct. SM6: W'gton 4F 167
Birch Cres. UB10: Uxb 1B 74
Birchdale Gdns. RM6: Chad H 7D 54
Birchdale Rd. E7 5A 70
Birchdene Dr. SE28 1A 108
Birchdown Ho. E3 3D 86
(off Rainhill Way)
Birchen Cl. NW9 2K 61
Birchend Cl. CR2: S Croy 6D 168
Birchen Gro. NW9 2K 61
Birches, The BR2: Broml 4H 159
(off Durham Rd.)
Birches, The BR6: Farnb 4E 172
Birches, The E12 4C 70
Birches, The N21 6E 22
Birches, The SE5 2E 120
Birches, The SE7 6K 105
Birches, The TW4: Houn 7D 112
Birches Cl. CR4: Mitc 3D 154
Birches Cl. HA5: Pinn 5C 40
Birches Ct. N17 7B 34
Birchfield Ct. KT12: Walt T 7K 147
(off Grove Cres.)
Birchfield Ho. E14 7C 86
(off Birchfield St.)
Birchfield St. E14 7C 86
Birch Gdns. RM10: Dag 3J 73
Birch Grn. NW9 7F 29
Birch Gro. DA16: Well 4A 126
Birch Gro. E11 4G 69
Birch Gro. SE12 7H 123
Birch Gro. TW17: Shep 2G 147
Birch Gro. W3 1G 97
Birchgrove Ho. TW9: Kew 7H 97

Birch Hill CR0: C'don....5K 169
Birch Ho. N22....1A 48
....(off Acacia Rd.)
Birch Ho. SE14....1B 122
Birch Ho. SW2....6A 120
Birch Ho. UB7: W Dray....2B 92
....(off Park Lodge Av.)
Birch Ho. W10....4G 81
....(off Droop St.)
Birchington Cl. DA7: Bex....1H 127
Birchington Ct. NW6....1K 81
....(off West End La.)
Birchington Ho. E5....5H 67
Birchington Rd. KT5: Surb....7F 151
Birchington Rd. N8....6H 47
Birchington Rd. NW6....1J 81
Birchin La. EC3....1F 15 (6D 84)
Birchlands Av. SW12....7D 118
Birch Mead BR6: Farnb....2E 172
Birchmead Av. HA5: Pinn....4A 40
Birchmere Bus. Pk. SE28....2A 108
Birchmere Lodge SE16....5H 103
....(off Sherwood Gdns.)
Birchmere Row SE3....2H 123
Birchmore Hall N5....3C 66
Birchmore Wlk. N5....3C 66
....(not continuous)
Birch Pk. HA3: Hrw W....7B 26
Birch Rd. RM7: Mawney....3H 55
Birch Rd. TW13: Hanw....5B 130
Birch Row BR2: Broml....7E 160
Birchside Apts. NW6....2H 81
Birch Tree Av. BR4: W W'ck....5H 171
Birch Tree Way CR0: C'don....2H 169
Birch Va. Ct. NW8....3B 4 (4B 82)
....(off Pollitt Dr.)
Birch Vw. HA1: Harr....5H 41
Birchville Ct. WD23: B Hea....1D 26
Birch Wlk. CR4: Mitc....1F 155
Birch Wlk. DA8: Erith....6J 109
Birch Wlk. IG3: Ilf....4J 71
....(off Loxford La.)
Birchway UB3: Hayes....1J 93
Birchwood Apts. N4....7C 48
....(off Woodberry Gro.)
Birchwood Av. BR3: Beck....4B 158
Birchwood Av. DA14: Sidc....2B 144
Birchwood Av. N10....3E 46
Birchwood Av. SM6: W'gton....3E 166
Birchwood Cl. SM4: Mord....4K 153
Birchwood Ct. HA8: Edg....2J 43
Birchwood Ct. N13....5G 33
Birchwood Dr. DA2: Wilm....4K 145
Birchwood Dr. NW3....3K 63
Birchwood Gro. TW12: Hamp....6E 130
Birchwood Pde. DA2: Wilm....4K 145
Birchwood Pk. Golf Course....7J 145
Birchwood Rd. BR5: Pet W....4H 161
Birchwood Rd. DA2: Wilm....5K 145
Birchwood Rd. SW17....5F 137
Birdbrook Cl. RM10: Dag....7J 73
Birdbrook Ho. N1....7C 66
....(off Popham Rd.)
Birdbrook Rd. SE3....4A 124
Birdcage Wlk. SW1....7A 12 (2G 101)
Birdham Cl. BR1: Broml....5C 160
Birdhurst Av. CR2: S Croy....4D 168
Birdhurst Ct. SM6: W'gton....7G 167
....(off Woodcote Av.)
Birdhurst Gdns. CR2: S Croy....4D 168
Birdhurst Ri. CR2: S Croy....5E 168
Birdhurst Rd. CR2: S Croy....5E 168
Birdhurst Rd. SW18....5A 118
Birdhurst Rd. SW19....6C 136
Bird in Bush BMX Track....7H 103
....(off Bird in Bush Rd.)
Bird in Bush Rd. SE15....7G 103
Bird in Hand La. BR1: Broml....2B 160
Bird in Hand M. SE23....2J 139
....(off Bird-in-Hand Pas.)
Bird in Hand Pas. SE23....2J 139
Bird in Hand Path CR0: C'don....7D 156
....(off Sydenham Rd.)
Bird in Hand Yd. NW3....4A 64
Birdsall Ho. SE5....3E 120
Birds Farm Av. RM5: Col R....1H 55
Birdsfield La. E3....1B 86
Birdsmouth Ct. N15....4E 48
....(off Bathurst Sq.)
Bird St. W1....1H 11 (6E 82)
Bird Wlk. TW2: Whitt....1D 130
Birdwood Av. SE13....6F 123
Birdwood Cl. TW11: Tedd....4J 131
Birkbeck Av. UB6: G'frd....1G 77
Birkbeck Av. W3....7J 79
Birkbeck Ct. W3....1K 97
Birkbeck Gdns. IG8: Wfd G....2D 36
Birkbeck Gro. W3....2K 97
Birkbeck Hill SE21....1B 138
Birkbeck M. E8....5F 67
Birkbeck M. W3....1K 97
Birkbeck Pl. SE21....2C 138
Birkbeck Rd. BR3: Beck....2J 157
Birkbeck Rd. DA14: Sidc....3A 144
Birkbeck Rd. E8....5F 67
Birkbeck Rd. EN2: Enf....1J 23
Birkbeck Rd. IG2: Ilf....5H 53
Birkbeck Rd. N12....5F 31
Birkbeck Rd. N17....1F 49
Birkbeck Rd. N8....4J 47
Birkbeck Rd. NW7....5G 29
Birkbeck Rd. RM7: Rush G....1K 73
Birkbeck Rd. SW19....5K 135
Birkbeck Rd. W3....1K 97
Birkbeck Rd. W5....4C 96
Birkbeck St. E2....3H 85
Birkbeck Way UB6: G'frd....1H 77
Birkdale Av. HA5: Pinn....3E 40
Birkdale Cl. BR6: Orp....7H 161
Birkdale Cl. SE16....5H 103
Birkdale Cl. SE28....6D 90
Birkdale Ct. UB1: S'hall....6G 77
....(off Redcroft Rd.)
Birkdale Gdns. CR0: C'don....4K 169
Birkdale Ho. E14....6B 86
....(off Keymer Pl.)
Birkdale Rd. SE2....4A 108
Birkdale Rd. W5....4E 78
Birkenhead Av. KT2: King T....2F 151
Birkenhead St. WC1....1F 7 (3J 83)
Birkhall Rd. SE6....1F 141
Birkwood Cl. SW12....7H 119
Birley Lodge NW8....2B 82
....(off Acacia Rd.)
Birley Rd. N20....2F 31
Birley St. SW11....2E 118
Birling Rd. DA8: Erith....7K 109
Birnam Rd. N4....2K 65
Birnbeck Ct. EN5: Barn....4A 20
Birnbeck Ct. NW11....5H 45
Birrell Ho. SW9....2K 119
....(off Stockwell Rd.)
Birse Cres. NW10....3A 62
Birstall Rd. N15....5E 48
Birtwhistle Ho. E3....1B 86
....(off Parnell Rd.)
Biscay Ho. E1....4K 85
....(off Mile End Rd.)
Biscayne Av. E14....1F 105
Biscay Rd. W6....5F 99
Biscoe Cl. TW5: Hest....6E 94
Biscoe Way SE13....3F 123
Biscott Ho. E3....4D 86
Bisenden Rd. CR0: C'don....2E 168
Bisham Cl. SM5: Cars....1D 166
Bisham Gdns. N6....1E 64
Bishop Butt Cl. BR6: Orp....3K 173
Bishop Ct. TW9: Rich....3E 114
Bishop Duppas Pk. TW17: Shep....7G 147
Bishop Fox Way KT8: W Mole....4D 148
Bishop Ken Rd. HA3: W'stone....2K 41
Bishop King's Rd. W14....4G 99
Bishop Ramsey Cl. HA4: Ruis....7H 39
Bishop Rd. N14....7A 22
Bishop's Av. E13....1K 87
Bishop's Av. SW6....2F 117
Bishops Av. BR1: Broml....2A 160
Bishops Av. RM6: Chad H....6C 54
Bishops Av., The N2....7B 46
Bishop's Bri. Rd. W2....6K 81
Bishop's Cl. N19....3G 65
Bishop's Cl. SE9....2G 143
Bishop's Cl. SM1: Sutt....3J 165
Bishops Cl. E17....4D 50
Bishops Cl. EN1: Enf....2C 24
Bishops Cl. EN5: Barn....6A 20
Bishops Cl. TW10: Ham....3D 132
Bishops Cl. UB10: Hil....2C 74
Bishops Cl. W4....5J 97
Bishop's Ct. EC4....7B 8 (6B 84)
....(off Old Bailey)
Bishop's Ct. WC2....7J 7 (6A 84)
....(off Star Yd.)
Bishops Ct. CR0: C'don....2F 169
Bishops Ct. HA0: Wemb....4B 60
Bishops Ct. N2....5C 46
Bishops Ct. W2....6K 81
....(off Bishop's Bri. Rd.)
Bishopsdale Ho. NW6....1J 81
....(off Kilburn Vale)
Bishop's Dr. TW14: Bedf....6F 111
Bishops Dr. UB5: N'olt....1C 76
Bishopsford Ho. SM5: Cars....6C 154
Bishopsford Rd. SM4: Mord....7A 154
Bishopsgate EC2....1G 15 (6E 84)
Bishopsgate Arc. EC2....6H 9 (5E 84)
....(off Bishopsgate)
Bishopsgate Churchyard EC2
....6G 9 (5E 84)
Bishopsgate Plaza EC3....7H 9 (6E 84)
....(off Bishopsgate)
Bishops Grn. BR1: Broml....1A 160
Bishop's Gro. TW12: Hamp....4D 130
Bishops Gro. N2....6C 46
Bishops Gro. Cvn. Site TW12: Hamp
....4E 130
Bishop's Hall KT1: King T....2D 150
Bishops Hill KT12: Walt T....7J 147
Bishops Ho. SW8....7J 101
....(off Sth. Lambeth Rd.)
Bishop's Mans. SW6....2F 117
Bishops Mead SE5....7C 102
....(off Camberwell Rd.)
Bishop's Pk. Rd. SW6....2F 117
Bishops Pk. Rd. SW16....1J 155
Bishops Pl. SM1: Sutt....5A 166
Bishop's Rd. CR0: C'don....7B 156
Bishop's Rd. SW11....7C 100
Bishop's Rd. UB3: Hayes....6E 74
Bishops Rd. N6....6E 46
Bishops Rd. SW6....1G 117
Bishops Rd. W7....2J 95
Bishops Sq. E1....5H 9 (5E 84)
Bishop's Ter. SE11....3K 19 (4A 102)
Bishopsthorpe Rd. SE26....4K 139
Bishop St. N1....1C 84
Bishops Vw. Ct. N10....4F 47
Bishops Wlk. BR7: Chst....1G 161
Bishops Wlk. CR0: Addtn....5K 169
Bishops Wlk. HA5: Pinn....3C 40
Bishop's Way E2....2H 85
Bishops Wharf Ho. SW11....7C 100
....(off Parkgate Rd.)
Bishops Wood Almshouses E5....4H 67
....(off Lwr. Clapton Rd.)
Bishopswood Rd. N6....7D 46
Bishop Way NW10....7A 62
Bishop Wilfred Wood Cl. SE15....2G 121
Bishop Wilfred Wood Ct. E13....2A 88
....(off Pragel St.)
Bisley Cl. KT4: Wor Pk....1E 164
Bisley Pl. TW3: Houn....2F 113
Bison Ct. TW14: Felt....7K 111
Bison Dr....3E 94
Bispham Rd. NW10....3F 79
Bissagos Ct. E1....5A 86
....(off Ocean Est.)
Bissextile Ho. SE13....2D 122
Bisson Rd. E15....2E 86
Bittacy Av. E17....3F 51
Bittacy Bus. Cen. NW7....7B 30
Bittacy Cl. NW7....6A 30
Bittacy Ct. NW7....7B 30
Bittacy Hill NW7....6A 30
Bittacy Pk. Av. NW7....5A 30
Bittacy Ri. NW7....6K 29
Bittacy Rd. NW7....6A 30
Bittern Cl. UB4: Yead....5B 76
Bittern Ct. NW9....2A 44
Bittern Ct. SE8....6C 104
Bittern Ho. SE1....7C 14 (2C 102)
....(off Gt. Suffolk St.)
Bittern Pl. N22....2K 47
Bittern St. SE1....7C 14 (2C 102)
Bittoms, The KT1: King T....3D 150
Bittoms Ct. KT1: King T....3D 150
Bixley Cl. UB2: S'hall....4D 94
Blackall St. EC2....3G 9 (4E 84)
Blackberry Cl. E17....3D 50
Blackberry Cl. TW17: Shep....4G 147
Blackberry Ct. HA3: Kenton....7E 42
Blackberry Farm Cl. TW5: Hest....7C 94
Blackberry Fld. BR5: St P....7A 144
Blackbird Ct. NW9....3K 61
Blackbird Hill NW9....2J 61
Blackbird Yd. E2....1K 9 (3F 85)
Blackborne Rd. RM10: Dag....6G 73
Blackborough Ho. IG9: Buck H....2G 37
....(off Beatrice Ct.)
Blackbrook La. BR1: Broml....4E 160
Blackbrook La. BR2: Broml....5E 160
Black Bull Yd. EC1....5K 7 (5A 84)
....(off Hatton Wall)
Blackburn NW9....2B 44
Blackburne's M. W1....2G 11 (7E 82)
Blackburn Rd. NW6....6K 63
Blackburn Trad. Est. TW19: Stanw....6B 110
Blackburn Way TW4: Houn....5C 112
Blackbush Av. RM6: Chad H....5D 54
Blackbush Cl. SM2: Sutt....7K 165
Blackdown Cl. N2....2A 46
Blackdown Ter. SE18....1D 124
Blackett Apts. E3....4B 86
....(off Hamlets Way)
Blackett St. SW15....3F 117
Black Fan Cl. EN2: Enf....1H 23
BLACKFEN....6A 126
Blackfen Pde. DA15: Sidc....6A 126
Blackfen Rd. DA15: Sidc....5J 125
Blackford Cl. CR2: S Croy....7B 168
Blackford's Path SW15....7C 116
Blackfriars Bri. EC4....3A 14 (7B 84)
Blackfriars Ct. EC4....2A 14 (7B 84)
....(off New Bri. St.)
Black Friars La. EC4....1A 14 (6B 84)
....(not continuous)
Blackfriars Pas. EC4....2A 14 (7B 84)
Blackfriars Rd. SE1....7A 14 (2B 102)
Blackfriars Underpass EC4
....2K 13 (7A 84)
Black Gates HA5: Pinn....3D 40
BLACKHEATH....2H 123
Blackheath Av. SE10....7F 105
Blackheath Bus. Cen. SE10....1E 122
Blackheath Bus. Est. SE10....1E 122
....(off Blackheath Hill)
Blackheath Concert Halls....3H 123
Blackheath Gro. SE3....2H 123
Blackheath Hill SE10....1E 122
Blackheath Pk. SE3....3H 123
BLACKHEATH PARK....3J 123
Blackheath Ri. SE13....2E 122
....(not continuous)
Blackheath Rd. SE10....1D 122
Blackheath RUFC....7K 105
Blackheath Va. SE3....2G 123
BLACKHEATH VALE....2H 123
Blackheath Village SE3....2H 123
Black Horse Ct. SE1....3D 102
Blackhorse La. CR0: C'don....7G 157
Blackhorse La. E17....2K 49
Blackhorse M. E17....3K 49
Black Horse Pde. HA5: Eastc....5K 39
Blackhorse Rd. DA14: Sidc....4A 144
Blackhorse Rd. E17....4K 49
Blackhorse Rd. SE8....6A 104
BLACKHORSE ROAD....4K 49
Blacklands Dr. UB4: Hayes....4E 74
Blacklands Rd. SE6....4E 140
Blacklands Ter. SW3....4E 16 (4D 100)
Black Lion La. W6....4C 98
Black Lion M. W6....4C 98
Blackmans Yd. E2....4K 9 (4G 85)
Blackmore Av. UB1: S'hall....1H 95
Blackmore Dr. NW10....7H 61
Blackmore Ho. N1....1K 83
....(off Barnsbury Est.)
Blackmore Rd. IG9: Buck H....1H 37
Blackmore's Gro. TW11: Tedd....6A 132
Blackness La. BR2: Kes....7B 172
Black Path E10....7A 50
Blackpool Gdns. UB4: Hayes....4G 75
Blackpool Rd. SE15....2H 121
BLACK PRINCE INTERCHANGE....6H 127
Black Prince Rd. SE1....4G 19 (4K 101)
Black Prince Rd. SE11....4G 19 (4K 101)
Black Prince St. SE18....6A 108
Black Rod Cl. UB3: Hayes....3H 93
Blackshaw Rd. SW17....4A 136
Blacksmith Cl. RM6: Chad H....6C 54
Blacksmith Cl. TW16: Sun....3J 147
Blacksmiths Ho. E14....6F 87
....(off Valencia Cl.)
Blacksmiths Ho. E17....4C 50
....(off Gillards M.)
Blacks Rd. W6....5E 98
Blackstock M. N4....2B 66
Blackstock Rd. N4....2B 66
Blackstock Rd. N5....3B 66
Blackstone Est. E8....7G 67
Blackstone Ho. SW1....6A 18 (5G 101)
....(off Churchill Gdns.)
Blackstone Rd. NW2....5E 62
Black Swan Yd. SE1....6H 15 (2E 102)
Blackthorn Av. N7....6A 66
Blackthorn Av. UB7: W Dray....4C 92
Blackthorn Ct. E15....4F 69
....(off Hall Rd.)
Blackthorn Ct. TW5: Hest....7C 94
Blackthorne Av. CR0: C'don....1J 169
Blackthorne Ct. SE15....7F 103
....(off Cator St.)
Blackthorne Ct. TW15: Ashf....7E 128
Blackthorne Ct. UB1: S'hall....1F 95
....(off Dormer's Wells La.)
Blackthorne Cres. SL3: Poyle....5A 174
Blackthorne Dr. E4....4A 36
Blackthorne Ind. Est. SL3: Poyle....6A 174
Blackthorn Gro. DA7: Bex....3E 126
Blackthorn Ho. SE16....2A 104
....(off Blondin Way)
Blackthorn Rd. IG1: Ilf....5H 71
Blackthorn St. E3....4C 86
BLACKWALL....1E 104
Blackwall La. SE10....5G 105
Blackwall Trad. Est. E14....5F 87
BLACKWALL TUNNEL....1F 105
Blackwall Tunnel App. E14....7E 86
Blackwall Tunnel Northern App. E3
....2C 86
Blackwall Tunnel Southern App. SE10
....3G 105
Blackwall Way E14....1E 104
Blackwater Cl. E7....4H 69
Blackwater Cl. RM13: Rain....5K 91
Blackwater Ho. NW8....5B 4 (5B 82)
....(off Church St.)
Blackwater St. SE22....5F 121
Blackwell Cl. E5....4K 67
Blackwell Cl. HA3: Hrw W....7C 26
Blackwell Cl. N21....5D 22
Blackwell Gdns. HA8: Edg....4B 28
Blackwell Ho. SW4....6H 119
Blackwood Ho. E1....4H 85
....(off Collingwood St.)
Blackwood St. SE17....5D 102
Blade M. SW15....4H 117
Bladen Ho. E1....6K 85
....(off Dunelm St.)
Blades Ct. SW15....4H 117
Blades Ct. W6....5D 98
....(off Lower Mall)
Blades Ho. SE11....7J 19 (6A 102)
....(off Kennington Oval)
Bladindon Dr. DA5: Bexl....7C 126
Bladon Ct. SW16....6J 137
Bladon Gdns. HA2: Harr....6F 41
Blagdens Cl. N14....2C 32
Blagdens La. N14....2B 32
Blagdon Ct. W7....7J 77
Blagdon Rd. KT3: N Mald....4B 152
Blagdon Rd. SE13....6D 122
Blagdon Wlk. TW11: Tedd....6C 132
Blagrove Cres. HA4: Ruis....6K 39
Blagrove Rd. TW11: Hamp W....7B 132
Blagrove Rd. W10....5G 81
Blair Av. NW9....7A 44
Blair Cl. DA15: Sidc....5J 125
Blair Cl. N1....6C 66
Blair Cl. UB3: Harl....4J 93
Blair Ct. BR3: Beck....1D 158
Blair Ct. NW8....1B 82
Blair Ct. SE6....1H 141
Blairderry Rd. SW2....2J 137
Blairgowrie Ct. E14....6F 87
....(off Blair St.)
Blair Ho. SW9....2K 119
Blair St. E14....6E 86
Blake Av. IG11: Bark....1J 89
Blake Bldg. N8....3K 47
Blake Cl. DA16: Well....1J 125
Blake Cl. SM5: Cars....1C 166
Blake Cl. UB4: Hayes....2F 75
Blake Cl. W10....5E 80
Blake Ct. N21....5E 22
Blake Ct. NW6....3J 81
....(off Malvern Rd.)
Blake Ct. SE16....5H 103
....(off Stubbs Dr.)
Blakeden Dr. KT10: Clay....6A 162
Blake Gdns. SW6....1K 117
Blake Hall Cres. E11....1J 69
Blake Hall Rd. E11....7J 51
Blakehall Rd. SM5: Cars....6D 166
Blake Ho. E14....2C 104
....(off Admirals Way)
Blake Ho. SE1....1J 19 (3A 102)
Blake Ho. SE8....6C 104
....(off New King St.)
Blake M. TW9: Kew....1G 115
Blakemore Gdns. SW13....6D 98
Blakemore Rd. CR7: Thor H....5K 155
Blakemore Rd. SW16....3J 137
Blakemore Way DA17: Belv....3E 108
Blakeney Av. BR3: Beck....1B 158
Blakeney Cl. E8....5G 67
Blakeney Cl. N20....1F 31
Blakeney Cl. NW1....7H 65
Blakeney Rd. BR3: Beck....7B 140
Blakenham Rd. SW17....4D 136
Blaker Ct. SE7....7A 106
....(not continuous)
Blake Rd. CR0: C'don....2E 168
Blake Rd. CR4: Mitc....3C 154
Blake Rd. E16....4H 87
Blake Rd. N11....7B 32
Blaker Rd. E15....2E 86
Blakes Av. KT3: N Mald....5B 152
Blake's Grn. BR4: W W'ck....1E 170
Blakes La. KT3: N Mald....5B 152
Blakesley Av. W5....6C 78
Blakesley Ho. E12....3E 70
....(off Grantham Rd.)
Blakesley Wlk. SW20....2H 153
Blake's Rd. SE15....7E 102
Blakes Ter. KT3: N Mald....5C 152
Blakesware Gdns. N9....7J 23
Blake Twr. EC2....5C 8 (5C 84)
....(off Fann St.)
Blakewood Cl. TW13: Hanw....4A 130
Blakewood Ct. SE20....7H 139
....(off Anerley Pk.)
Blanchard Cl. SE9....3C 142
Blanchard Ho. TW1: Twick....6D 114
....(off Clevedon Rd.)
Blanchard Way E8....6G 67
Blanch Cl. SE15....7J 103
Blanchedowne SE5....4D 120
Blanche St. E16....4H 87
Blanchland Rd. SM4: Mord....5K 153
Blandfield Rd. SW12....7E 118
Blandford Av. BR3: Beck....2A 158
Blandford Av. TW2: Whitt....1F 131
Blandford Cl. CR0: Bedd....3J 167
Blandford Cl. N2....4A 46
Blandford Cl. RM7: Mawney....4H 55
Blandford Ct. N1....7E 66
....(off St Peter's Way)
Blandford Ct. NW6....7F 63
Blandford Cres. E4....7K 25
Blandford Ho. SW8....7K 101
....(off Richborne Ter.)
Blandford Rd. BR3: Beck....2J 157
Blandford Rd. TW11: Tedd....5H 131
Blandford Rd. UB2: S'hall....4E 94
Blandford Rd. W4....3A 98
Blandford Rd. W5....2D 96
Blandford Sq. NW1....4D 4 (4C 82)
Blandford St. W1....7F 5 (6D 82)
Blandford Waye UB4: Yead....6A 76
Bland Ho. SE11....5H 19 (5K 101)
....(off Vauxhall St.)
Bland St. SE9....4B 124
Blaney Cres. E6....3F 89
Blanmerle Rd. SE9....1F 143
Blann Cl. SE9....6B 124
Blantyre St. SW10....7B 100
Blantyre Twr. SW10....7B 100
....(off Worlds End Est.)
Blantyre Wlk. SW10....7B 100
....(off Worlds End Est.)
Blashford NW3....7D 64
....(off Adelaide Rd.)
Blashford St. SE13....7F 123
Blashill Ct. E14....7E 86
....(off Bullivant St.)
Blasker Wlk. E14....5D 104
Blaven Path E16....4H 87
Blawith Rd. HA1: Harr....4J 41
Blaxland Ho. W12....7D 80
....(off White City Est.)
Blaydon Cl. HA4: Ruis....7G 39
Blaydon Cl. N17....7C 34
Blaydon Ct. UB5: N'olt....6E 58
Blaydon Wlk. N17....7C 34
Blazer Ct. NW8....2B 4 (3B 82)
....(off St John's Wood Rd.)
Bleak Hill La. SE18....6K 107
Bleak Ho. La. W4....5K 97
....(off Chiswick High Rd.)
Blean Gro. SE20....7J 139
Bleasdale Av. UB6: G'frd....2A 78
Blechynden Ho. W10....6F 81
....(off Kingsdown Cl.)
Blechynden St. W10....7F 81
Bledlow Cl. NW8....4B 4 (4B 82)
Bledlow Cl. SE28....7C 90
Bledlow Ri. UB6: G'frd....2G 77
Bleeding Heart Yd. EC1....6K 7 (5A 84)
....(off Greville St.)
Blegborough Rd. SW16....6G 137
Blemundsbury WC1....5G 7 (5K 83)
....(off Dombey St.)
BLENDON....6D 126
Blendon Dr. DA5: Bexl....6D 126
Blendon Path BR1: Broml....7H 141
Blendon Rd. DA5: Bexl....6D 126
Blendon Row SE17....4D 102
....(off Orb St.)
Blendon Ter. SE18....5G 107
Blendworth Point SW15....1D 134
Blenheim Av. IG2: Ilf....6E 52
Blenheim Bus. Cen. CR4: Mitc....2D 154
....(off London Rd.)
Blenheim Cen., The....3F 113
Blenheim Cl. N21....1H 33
Blenheim Cl. RM7: Mawney....4J 55
Blenheim Cl. SE12....1K 141
Blenheim Cl. SM6: W'gton....7G 167
Blenheim Cl. SW20....3E 152
Blenheim Cl. UB6: G'frd....2H 77
Blenheim Ct. BR2: Broml....4H 159
Blenheim Ct. DA14: Sidc....3H 143
Blenheim Ct. HA3: Kenton....6A 42
Blenheim Ct. IG8: Wfd G....7E 36
Blenheim Ct. N19....2J 65
Blenheim Ct. N7....6J 65
Blenheim Ct. RM13: Rain....2K 91
....(off Lowen Rd.)
Blenheim Ct. SE10....5J 105
....(off Denham St.)
Blenheim Ct. SE16....1K 103
....(off King & Queen Wharf)
Blenheim Ct. SM2: Sutt....6A 166
Blenheim Cres. CR2: S Croy....7C 168
Blenheim Cres. HA4: Ruis....2F 57
Blenheim Cres. W11....7G 81
Blenheim Dr. DA16: Well....1K 125
Blenheim Gdns. HA9: Wemb....3E 60
Blenheim Gdns. KT2: King T....7H 133
Blenheim Gdns. NW2....6E 62
Blenheim Gdns. SM6: W'gton....6G 167
Blenheim Gdns. SW2....6K 119
Blenheim Gro. SE15....2G 121
Blenheim Ho. E16....1K 105
....(off Constable Av.)
Blenheim Ho. SE18....3G 107
Blenheim Ho. SW3....6D 16 (5C 100)
....(off Kings Rd.)
Blenheim Ho. TW3: Houn....3E 112
Blenheim Pde. UB10: Hil....4D 74
Blenheim Pk. Rd. CR2: S Croy....7C 168
Blenheim Pas. NW8....2A 82
Blenheim Pl. TW11: Tedd....5K 131
Blenheim Ri. N15....4F 49
Blenheim Rd. BR1: Broml....4C 160
Blenheim Rd. DA15: Sidc....1C 144
Blenheim Rd. E15....4G 69
Blenheim Rd. E17....3K 49
Blenheim Rd. E6....3B 88
Blenheim Rd. EN5: Barn....3A 20
Blenheim Rd. HA2: Harr....6F 41
Blenheim Rd. NW8....2A 82
Blenheim Rd. SE20....7J 139
Blenheim Rd. SM1: Sutt....3J 165
Blenheim Rd. SW20....3E 152
Blenheim Rd. UB5: N'olt....6F 59
Blenheim Rd. W4....3A 98
Blenheim Shop. Cen....7J 139
Blenheim St. W1....1J 11 (6F 83)
Blenheim Ter. NW8....2A 82
Blenheim Twr. SE14....7A 104
....(off Batavia Rd.)
Blenheim Way TW7: Isle....1A 114
Blenkarne Rd. SW11....6D 118
Bleriot Rd. TW5: Hest....7A 94
Blessbury Rd. HA8: Edg....1J 43
Blessington Cl. SE13....3F 123
Blessington Rd. SE13....3F 123
Blessing Way IG11: Bark....3C 90
Bletchingley Cl. CR7: Thor H....4B 156
Bletchley Ct. HA7: Stan....7K 27
....(off Hitchin Way)
Bletchley Ct. N1....1E 8 (2D 84)
....(off Bletchley St.)
Bletchley St. N1....1E 8 (2D 84)
Bletchmore Cl. UB3: Harl....5F 93
Bletsoe Wlk. N1....2C 84
Blick Ho. SE16....3J 103
....(off Neptune St.)
Blincoe Cl. SW19....2F 135
Bliss Cres. SE13....2D 122
Blissett St. SE10....1E 122
Bliss Ho. EN1: Enf....1B 24
Bliss M. W10....3G 81
Blisworth Cl. UB4: Yead....4C 76
Blisworth Ho. E2....1G 85
....(off Whiston Rd.)
Blithbury Rd. RM9: Dag....6B 72
Blithdale Rd. SE2....4A 108
Blithehale Ct. E2....3H 85
....(off Witham St.)
Blithfield St. W8....3K 99
Blockley Rd. HA0: Wemb....2B 60

Block Wharf – Bourne M.

Block Wharf E14 2C 104
(off Cuba St.)
Bloemfontein Av. W12 1D 98
Bloemfontein Rd. W12 7D 80
Bloemfontein Way W12 1D 98
Blomfield Ct. W9 3A 4 (4A 82)
(off Maida Vale)
Blomfield Mans. W12 1E 98
(off Stanlake Rd.)
Blomfield Rd. W9 5K 81
Blomfield St. EC2 6F 9 (5D 84)
Blomfield Vs. W2 5K 81
Blomville Rd. RM8: Dag 3E 72
Blondell Cl. UB7: Harm 2E 174
Blondel St. SW11 2E 118
Blondin Av. W5 4C 96
Blondin Pk. & Nature Area 4B 96
Blondin St. E3 2C 86
Blondin Way SE16 2A 104
Bloomberg Arc. EC4 1E 14 (6D 84)
Bloomberg Ct. SW1 4C 18 (4H 101)
(off Vauxhall Bri. Rd.)
Bloomburg St. SW1 4C 18 (4H 101)
Bloomfield Ct. E10 3D 68
(off Brisbane Rd.)
Bloomfield Ct. N6 6E 46
Bloomfield Cres. IG2: Ilf 6F 53
Bloomfield Ho. E1 5G 85
(off Old Montague St.)
Bloomfield Pl. W1 2K 11 (7F 83)
(off Bourdon St.)
Bloomfield Rd. BR2: Broml 5B 160
Bloomfield Rd. KT1: King T 4E 150
Bloomfield Rd. N6 6E 46
Bloomfield Rd. SE18 6F 107
Bloomfield Ter. SW1 5H 17 (5E 100)
Bloom Gro. SE27 3B 138
Bloomhall Rd. SE19 5D 138
Bloom Ho. E3 2D 86
(off Alameda Pl.)
Bloom Pk. Rd. SW6 7H 99
BLOOMSBURY 5E 6 (5J 83)
Bloomsbury Cl. NW7 7H 29
Bloomsbury Cl. W5 7F 79
Bloomsbury Ct. HA5: Pinn 3D 40
Bloomsbury Ct. TW5: Cran 1K 111
Bloomsbury Ct. WC1 6F 7 (5J 83)
(off Barter St.)
Bloomsbury Ho. SW4 6H 119
Bloomsbury Mans. BR1: Broml 1K 159
(off Widmore Rd.)
Bloomsbury M. IG8: Wfd G 6H 37
Bloomsbury Pl. SW18 5A 118
Bloomsbury Pl. WC1 6F 7 (5J 83)
Bloomsbury Sq. WC1 6F 7 (5J 83)
Bloomsbury St. WC1 6D 6 (5H 83)
Bloomsbury Theatre 3C 6 (4H 83)
(off Gordon St.)
Bloomsbury Way WC1 6E 6 (5J 83)
Blore Cl. SW8 1H 119
Blore Ct. W1 1C 12 (6H 83)
(off Berwick St.)
Blore Ho. SW10 7K 99
(off Coleridge Gdns.)
Blossom Av. HA2: Harr 2F 59
Blossom Cl. CR2: S Croy 5F 169
Blossom Cl. RM9: Dag 1F 91
Blossom Cl. W5 2E 96
Blossom Ct. SE15 7F 103
(off All Saints Walk)
Blossom Dr. BR6: Orp 2K 173
Blossom La. EN2: Enf 1H 23
Blossom Pl. SE28 3G 107
Blossom St. E1 4H 9 (4E 84)
Blossom Way UB10: Hil 7B 56
Blossom Way UB7: W Dray 4C 92
Blossom Waye TW5: Hest 6C 94
Blount M. UB10: Uxb 2A 74
Blount St. E14 6A 86
Bloxam Gdns. SE9 5C 124
Bloxhall Rd. E10 1B 68
Bloxham Cres. TW12: Hamp 7D 130
Bloxworth Cl. SM6: W'gton 3G 167
Blucher Rd. SE5 7C 102
Blue Anchor All. TW9: Rich 4E 114
Blue Anchor La. SE16 4G 103
Blue Anchor Yd. E1 2K 15 (7G 85)
Blue Ball Yd. SW1 5A 12 (1G 101)
Bluebell Apts. N4 1C 66
(off Swan La.)
Bluebell Av. E12 5B 70
Bluebell Cl. BR6: Farnb 2G 173
Bluebell Cl. E9 1J 85
Bluebell Cl. RM7: Rush G 2K 73
Bluebell Cl. SE26 4F 139
Bluebell Cl. SM6: W'gton 1F 167
Bluebell Cl. UB5: N'olt 6D 58
Bluebell Ct. NW9 1A 44
(off Heybourne Cres.)
Bluebell Ho. SE16 2A 104
(off Bondin Way)
Bluebell M. E4 5H 35
Bluebell Ter. UB7: W Dray 2B 92
Bluebell Way IG1: Ilf 6F 71
Blueberry Cl. IG8: Wfd G 6D 36
Bluebird Cl. SW20 2E 152
Bluebird Ho. IG11: Bark 3K 89
Bluebird La. RM10: Dag 7G 73
Bluebird Way SE28 2H 107
Blue Boar All. EC3 7J 9 (6F 85)
(off Aldgate High St.)
Blue Bldg. SE10 5H 105
(off Glenforth St.)
Blue Ct. N1 1D 84
(off Sherborne St.)
Blue Elephant Theatre 7C 102
(off Bethwin Rd.)
Bluefield Cl. TW12: Hamp 5E 130
Blue Fin Bldg. SE1 4B 14 (1B 102)
(off Summer St.)
Bluegate M. E1 7H 85
Bluegates KT17: Ewe 7C 164
Bluehouse Rd. E4 2B 36
Blue Lion Pl. SE1 7G 15 (3E 102)
Blueprint Apts. SW12 7F 119
(off Balham Gro.)
Blue Riband Ind. Est. CR0: C'don 2B 168
Blues St. E8 6F 67
Blue Water SW18 4K 117
Blumenthal Cl. TW7: Isle 7H 95
Blundell Cl. E8 5G 67
Blundell Rd. HA8: Edg 1K 43
Blundell St. N7 7J 65
Blunden Cl. RM8: Dag 1C 72
Blunden Ct. SW6 7J 99
(off Farm La.)
Blunt Rd. CR2: S Croy 5D 168
Blunts Av. UB7: Sip 7C 92
Blunts Rd. SE9 5E 124
Blurton Rd. E5 4J 67
Blydon Ct. N21 5E 22
(off Chaseville Pk. Rd.)
Blyth Cl. E14 4F 105
Blyth Cl. TW1: Twick 6K 113
Blyth Ct. BR1: Broml 1H 159
(off Blyth Rd.)
Blythe Cl. SE6 7B 122
Blythe Hill BR5: St P 1K 161
Blythe Hill SE6 7B 122
BLYTHE HILL 7B 122
Blythe Hill La. SE6 7B 122
Blythe Hill Pl. SE23 7A 122
Blythe Ho. SE11 7J 19 (6A 102)
Blythe M. W14 3F 99
Blythendale Ho. E2 2G 85
(off Mansford St.)
Blythe Rd. W14 3F 99
Blythe St. E2 3H 85
Blytheswood Pl. SW16 4K 137
Blythe Va. SE6 1B 140
Blyth Hill Pl. SE23 7A 122
(off Brockley Pk.)
Blyth Ho. DA8: Erith 5K 109
Blyth Rd. BR1: Broml 1H 159
Blyth Rd. E17 7B 50
Blyth Rd. SE28 7C 90
Blyth Rd. UB3: Hayes 2G 93
Blyth's Wharf E14 7A 86
Blythswood Rd. IG3: Ilf 1A 72
Blyth Wood Pk. BR1: Broml 1H 159
Blythwood Rd. HA5: Pinn 1B 40
Blythwood Rd. N4 7J 47
BMX Track, The London 6D 102
Boades M. NW3 4B 64
Boadicea St. N1 1K 83
Boakes Cl. NW9 4J 43
Boardman Av. E4 5J 25
Boardman Cl. EN5: Barn 5B 20
Boardwalk Pl. E14 1E 104
Boarley Ho. SE17 4E 102
(off Massinger St.)
Boatemah Wlk. SW9 2A 120
(off Peckford Pl.)
Boaters Av. TW8: Bford 7C 96
Boathouse, The E14 6C 86
Boathouse Cen., The W10 4F 81
(off Canal Cl.)
Boathouse Wlk. SE15 7F 103
(not continuous)
Boat La. E2 1F 85
Boat Lifter Way SE16 4A 104
Boat Quay E16 7A 88
Boatyard Apts. E14 5D 104
Bob Anker Cl. E13 3J 87
Bobbin Cl. SM6: W'gton 2E 166
Bobbin Cl. SW4 3G 119
Bobby Moore Way IG11: Bark 1G 89
Bobby Moore Way N10 7J 31
Bob Hope Theatre, The 6D 124
Bob Marley Way SE24 4A 120
Bockhampton Rd. KT2: King T 7F 133
Bocking St. E8 1H 85
Boddicott Cl. SW19 2G 135
Boddington Gdns. W3 2G 97
Boddington Ho. SE14 1J 121
(off Pomeroy St.)
Boddington Ho. SW13 6D 98
(off Wyatt Dr.)
Bodeney Ho. SE5 1E 120
(off Peckham Rd.)
Boden Ho. E1 5K 9 (5G 85)
(off Woodseer St.)
Bodiam Cl. EN1: Enf 2K 23
Bodiam Rd. SW16 7H 137
Bodiam Way NW10 3F 79
Bodicea M. TW4: Houn 6D 112
Bodington Ct. W12 2F 99
Bodium Ct. E17 1B 50
(off Thornbury Way)
Bodleian Ho. SE20 1G 157
Bodley Cl. KT3: N Mald 5A 152
Bodley Mnr. Way SW2 7A 120
Bodley Rd. KT3: N Mald 6K 151
Bodley Way SE17 4C 102
Bodmin Cl. HA2: Harr 3D 58
Bodmin Gro. SM4: Mord 5K 153
Bodmin St. SW18 1J 135
Bodnant Gdns. SW20 3C 152
Bodney Rd. E8 5H 67
Boeing Way UB2: S'hall 3K 93
Boevey Path DA17: Belv 5F 109
Bogart Ct. E14 7C 86
(off Premiere Pl.)
Bogey La. BR6: Downe 7E 172
Bognor Rd. DA16: Well 1D 126
Bohemia Pl. E8 6J 67
Bohn Rd. E1 5A 86
Bohun Gro. EN4: E Barn 6H 21
Boileau Pde. W5 6F 79
(off Boileau Rd.)
Boileau Rd. SW13 7C 98
Boileau Rd. W5 6F 79
Boiler Ho., The UB3: Hayes 2G 93
(off Material Wlk.)
Boisseau Ho. E1 5J 85
(off Stepney Way)
Bolanachi Bldg. SE16 3F 103
Bolander Gro. SW6 6J 99
Bolden St. SE8 2D 122
Boldero Pl. NW8 4C 4 (4C 82)
(off Gateforth St.)
Bolderwood Way BR4: W W'ck 2D 170
Boldmere Rd. HA5: Eastc 7A 40
Boleyn Av. EN1: Enf 1C 24
Boleyn Cl. E17 4C 50
Boleyn Ct. IG9: Buck H 1D 36
Boleyn Ct. KT8: E Mos 4H 149
(off Bridge Rd.)
Boleyn Dr. HA4: Ruis 2B 58
Boleyn Dr. KT8: W Mole 3D 148
Boleyn Gdns. BR4: W W'ck 2D 170
Boleyn Gdns. RM10: Dag 7J 73
Boleyn Gro. BR4: W W'ck 2E 170
Boleyn Ho. E16 1J 105
(off Southey M.)
Boleyn Rd. E6 2B 88
Boleyn Rd. E7 7J 69
Boleyn Rd. N16 5E 66
Boleyn Way EN5: New Bar 3F 21
Bolina Rd. SE16 5J 103
Bolinder Way E3 3K 35
Bolingbroke Cl. EN4: Cockf 3J 21
Bolingbroke Gro. SW11 4C 118
Bolingbroke Rd. W14 3F 99
Bolingbroke Wlk. SW11 1B 118
Bolingbroke Way UB3: Hayes 1F 93
Bolliger Ct. NW10 4J 79
Bollinder Pl. EC1 1C 8 (3C 84)
Bollo Bri. Rd. W3 3H 97
Bollo La. W3 2H 97
Bollo La. W4 4J 97
Bolney Ga. SW7 7C 10 (2C 100)
Bolney St. SW8 7K 101
Bolney Way TW13: Hanw 3C 130
Bolsover St. W1 4K 5 (4F 83)
Bolstead Rd. CR4: Mitc 1F 155
Bolster Gro. N22 7C 32
Bolt Ct. EC4 1K 13 (6A 84)
Bolt Ho. N1 1E 84
(off Phillipp St.)
Boltmore Cl. NW4 3F 45
Bolton Cl. KT9: Chess 6D 162
Bolton Cl. SE20 2G 157
Bolton Cres. SE11 7A 102
Bolton Cres. SE5 7B 102
Bolton Dr. SM4: Mord 7A 154
Bolton Gdns. BR1: Broml 6H 141
Bolton Gdns. NW10 2F 81
Bolton Gdns. SW5 5K 99
Bolton Gdns. TW11: Tedd 6A 132
Bolton Gdns. M. SW10 5A 100
Bolton Ho. SE10 5G 105
(off Trafalgar Rd.)
Bolton Ho. SE11 4B 102
(off George Mathers Rd.)
Bolton Pl. NW8 1K 81
(off Bolton Rd.)
Bolton Rd. E15 6H 69
Bolton Rd. HA1: Harr 4G 41
Bolton Rd. KT9: Chess 6D 162
Bolton Rd. N18 5A 34
Bolton Rd. NW10 1A 80
Bolton Rd. NW8 1K 81
Bolton Rd. W4 7J 97
Boltons, The HA0: Wemb 4K 59
Boltons, The IG8: Wfd G 4D 36
Boltons, The SW10 5A 100
Boltons Ct. SW5 5K 99
(off Old Brompton Rd.)
Bolton's La. UB3: Harl 1E 110
Boltons Pl. SW5 5A 100
Bolton St. W1 4K 11 (1F 101)
Bolton Studios SW10 5A 100
Bolton Wlk. N7 2K 65
(off Durham Rd.)
Bombay Ct. SE16 2J 103
(off St Marychurch St.)
Bombay St. SE16 4H 103
Bomer Cl. UB7: Sip 7C 92
Bomore Rd. W11 7G 81
Bonar Pl. BR7: Chst 7C 142
Bonar Rd. SE15 7G 103
Bonchester Cl. BR7: Chst 7E 142
Bonchurch Cl. SM2: Sutt 7K 165
Bonchurch Rd. W10 5G 81
Bonchurch Rd. W13 1B 96
Bond Cl. DA16: Well 2J 125
Bond Cl. UB7: Yiew 6B 74
Bond Ct. EC4 2E 14 (7D 84)
Bondfield Av. UB4: Yead 3J 75
Bondfield Rd. E6 5D 88
Bond Gdns. SM6: W'gton 4G 167
Bond Ho. NW6 2H 81
(off Rupert Rd.)
Bond Ho. SE14 7A 104
(off Goodwood Rd.)
Bond Ho. TW8: Bford 5D 96
Bonding Yd. Wlk. SE16 3A 104
Bond Rd. CR4: Mitc 2C 154
Bond Rd. KT6: Surb 2F 163
Bond St. E15 5G 69
Bond St. W4 4K 97
Bond St. W5 7D 78
Bondway SW8 7F 19 (6J 101)
Bonesgate Open Space Local Nature Reserve 6G 163
Boneta Rd. SE18 3D 106
Bonfield Rd. SE13 4E 122
Bonham Cl. DA17: Belv 5F 109
Bonham Gdns. RM8: Dag 2D 72
Bonham Ga. KT12: Walt T 7H 147
(off New Zealand Av.)
Bonham Ho. W11 1H 99
(off Boyne Ter. M.)
Bonham Rd. RM8: Dag 2D 72
Bonham Rd. SW2 5K 119
Bonheur Rd. W4 2K 97
Bonhill St. EC2 4F 9 (4D 84)
Boniface Gdns. HA3: Hrw W 7A 26
Boniface Rd. UB10: Ick 3D 56
Boniface Wlk. HA3: Hrw W 7A 26
Bonington Ho. EN1: Enf 5B 24
Bonita M. SE4 3K 121
Bon Marche M. SE27 4E 138
Bonner Hill Rd. KT1: King T 2F 151
Bonner Rd. E2 2J 85
Bonnersfield Cl. HA1: Harr 6K 41
Bonnersfield La. HA1: Harr 6K 41
(not continuous)
Bonner St. E2 2J 85
Bonnet St. E16 2K 105
Bonneville Gdns. SW4 6G 119
Bonnington Ct. UB5: N'olt 2B 76
(off Gallery Gdns.)
Bonnington Ho. N1 2K 83
Bonnington Sq. SW8 7G 19 (6K 101)
Bonny St. NW1 7G 65
Bonser Rd. TW1: Twick 2K 131
Bonsor Ho. SW8 1G 119
Bonsor St. SE5 7E 102
Bonville Gdns. NW4 4D 44
Bonville Rd. BR1: Broml 5H 141
Bonwick Ct. KT8: E Mos 5H 149
Bookbinders Cott. Homes N20 3J 31
Bookbinders Ct. E1 4H 85
(off Cudworth St.)
Booker Cl. E14 5B 86
Booker Rd. N18 5B 34
Bookham Ct. CR4: Mitc 3B 154
Book Ho. N1 1C 8 (2C 84)
Book M. WC2 1D 12 (6H 83)
Boone Ct. N9 3D 34
Boones Rd. SE13 4G 123
Boone St. SE13 4G 123
Boord St. SE10 3G 105
Boothby Ct. E4 3K 35
Boothby Rd. N19 2H 65
Booth Cl. E9 1H 85
Booth Cl. SE28 1B 108
Booth Ct. SE13 3D 122
Booth Dr. TW18: Staines 6A 128
Booth Ho. TW8: Bford 7C 96
(off High St.)
Booth La. EC4 2C 14 (7C 84)
(off Baynard St.)
Boothman Ho. HA3: Kenton 3D 42
Booth Rd. CR0: C'don 2B 168
Booth Rd. E16 2A 106
Booth Rd. NW9 2K 43
Booth's Pl. W1 6B 6 (5G 83)
Boot Pde. HA8: Edg 6B 28
(off High St.)
Boot St. N1 2G 9 (3E 84)
Bordars Rd. W7 5J 77
Bordars Wlk. W7 5J 77
Bordeaux Ho. E15 5G 69
(off Luxembourg M.)
Borden Av. EN1: Enf 6J 23
Border Cres. SE26 5H 139
Border Gdns. CR0: C'don 4D 170
Bordergate CR4: Mitc 1D 154
Border Rd. SE26 5H 139
Bordesley Rd. SM4: Mord 5K 153
Bordeston Ct. TW8: Bford 7C 96
(off The Ham)
Bordon Wlk. SW15 7C 116
Boreas Wlk. N1 1B 8 (2B 84)
(off Nelson Pl.)
Boreham Av. E16 6J 87
Boreham Cl. E11 1E 68
Boreham Rd. N22 2C 48
Boreman Ho. SE10 6E 104
(off Thames St.)
Borgard Rd. SE18 4D 106
Borkwood Pk. BR6: Orp 4K 173
Borkwood Way BR6: Orp 4J 173
Borland Rd. SE15 4J 121
Borland Rd. TW11: Tedd 7B 132
Borley Ct. TW19: Stanw 1A 128
Borneo St. SW15 3E 116
THE BOROUGH 7F 15 (2D 102)
Borough High St. SE1 7D 14 (2C 102)
Borough Hill CR0: Wadd 3B 168
Borough Mkt. SE1 5E 14 (1D 102)
(off Borough High St.)
Borough Rd. CR4: Mitc 2C 154
Borough Rd. KT2: King T 1G 151
Borough Rd. SE1 7A 14 (3B 102)
Borough Rd. TW7: Isle 1J 113
Borough Sq. SE1 7C 14 (2C 102)
(off McCoid Way)
Borrett Cl. SE17 5C 102
Borrodaile Rd. SW18 6K 117
Borrowdale NW1 2A 6 (3G 83)
(off Robert St.)
Borrowdale Av. HA3: W'stone 2A 42
Borrowdale Cl. IG4: Ilf 4C 52
Borrowdale Cl. N2 2A 46
Borrowdale Ct. EN2: Enf 1H 23
Borthwick M. E15 4G 69
Borthwick Rd. E15 4G 69
Borthwick Rd. NW9 6B 44
Borthwick St. SE8 5C 104
Borwick Av. E17 3B 50
Bosanquet Cl. UB8: Cowl 4A 74
Bosbury Rd. SE6 3E 140
Boscastle Rd. NW5 3F 65
Boscobel Cl. BR1: Broml 2D 160
Boscobel Ho. E8 6H 67
Boscobel Pl. SW1 3H 17 (4E 100)
Boscobel St. NW8 4B 4 (4B 82)
Bosco Cl. BR6: Orp 4K 173
Boscombe Av. E10 7F 51
Boscombe Cir. NW9 1K 43
Boscombe Cl. E5 5A 68
Boscombe Gdns. SW16 6J 137
Boscombe Ho. CR0: C'don 1D 168
(off Sydenham Rd.)
Boscombe Rd. KT4: Wor Pk 1E 164
Boscombe Rd. SW17 6E 136
Boscombe Rd. SW19 1K 153
Boscombe Rd. W12 1C 98
Bose Cl. N3 1G 45
Bosgrove E4 2K 35
Boss Ho. SE1 6J 15 (2F 103)
(off Boss St.)
Boss St. SE1 6J 15 (2F 103)
Bostall Heath SE2 5C 108
Bostall Hill SE2 5A 108
Bostall La. SE2 4B 108
Bostall Mnr. Way SE2 4B 108
Bostall Pk. Av. DA7: Bex 7E 108
Bostall Rd. BR5: St P 7B 144
Bostock Ho. TW5: Hest 6E 94
Boston Bus. Pk. W7 3J 95
Boston Ct. SE25 4F 157
Boston Ct. SM2: Sutt 7A 166
Boston Gdns. TW8: Bford 4A 96
Boston Gdns. W4 6A 98
Boston Gdns. W7 4A 96
Boston Gro. HA4: Ruis 6E 38
Boston Ho. SW5 4K 99
(off Collingham Rd.)
BOSTON MANOR 4A 96
Boston Manor House 5B 96
Boston Mnr. Rd. TW8: Bford 4B 96
Boston Pde. W7 3A 96
Boston Pk. Rd. TW8: Bford 5D 96
Boston Pl. NW1 4E 4 (4D 82)
Boston Rd. CR0: C'don 6K 155
Boston Rd. E17 6C 50
Boston Rd. E6 3C 88
Boston Rd. HA8: Edg 7D 28
Boston Rd. W7 1J 95
Bostonthorpe Rd. W7 2J 95
Boston Va. W7 4A 96
Bosun Cl. E14 2C 104
Boswell Ct. KT2: King T 1F 151
(off Clifton Rd.)
Boswell Ct. NW9 2A 44
(off Charcot Rd.)
Boswell Ct. W14 3F 99
(off Blythe Rd.)
Boswell Ct. WC1 5F 7 (5J 83)
Boswell Ho. WC1 5F 7 (5J 83)
(off Boswell St.)
Boswell Path UB3: Harl 4H 93
Boswell Rd. CR7: Thor H 4C 156
Boswell St. WC1 5F 7 (5J 83)
Boswood Ct. TW3: Houn 3D 112
Bosworth Cl. E17 1B 50
Bosworth Ho. W10 4G 81
(off Bosworth Rd.)
Bosworth Rd. EN5: New Bar 3D 20
Bosworth Rd. N11 6C 32
Bosworth Rd. RM10: Dag 3G 73
Bosworth Rd. W10 4G 81
Botanic Sq. E14 6G 87
Botany Bay La. BR7: Chst 3G 161
Botany Cl. EN4: E Barn 4H 21
Boteley Cl. E4 2A 36
Botham Cl. HA8: Edg 7D 28
Botha Rd. E13 5K 87
Bothwell Cl. E16 5H 87
Bothwell St. W6 6F 99
Botolph All. EC3 2G 15 (7E 84)
(off Botolph La.)
Botolph La. EC3 3G 15 (7E 84)
Botsford Rd. SW20 2G 153
Botts M. W2 6J 81
Botwell Comn. Rd. UB3: Hayes 7F 75
Botwell Cres. UB3: Hayes 6G 75
Botwell Green Sports & Leisure Cen. 1H 93
Botwell La. UB3: Hayes 7G 75
Boucher Cl. TW11: Tedd 5K 131
Bouchier Ho. N2 2B 46
(off The Grange)
Boughton Av. BR2: Hayes 7H 159
Boughton Ho. SE1 6E 14 (2D 102)
(off Tennis St.)
Boughton Rd. SE28 3J 107
Boulcott St. E1 6K 85
Boulevard, The IG8: Wfd G 6K 37
Boulevard, The SW17 2E 136
Boulevard, The SW18 4K 117
Boulevard, The SW6 1A 118
Boulevard Dr. NW9 2B 44
Boulevard Walkway E1 1K 15 (6G 85)
Boulogne Ho. SE1 7J 15 (3F 103)
(off St Saviour's Est.)
Boulogne Rd. CR0: C'don 6C 156
Boulter Cl. BR1: Broml 3E 160
Boulter Ho. SE14 1J 121
(off Kender St.)
Boulton Ho. TW8: Bford 5E 96
Boulton Rd. RM8: Dag 2E 72
Boultwood Rd. E6 6D 88
Bounces La. N9 2C 34
Bounces Rd. N9 2C 34
Boundaries Rd. SW12 2D 136
Boundaries Rd. TW13: Felt 1A 130
Boundary Av. E17 7B 50
Boundary Bus. Ct. CR4: Mitc 3B 154
Boundary Cl. EN5: Barn 1C 20
Boundary Cl. IG3: Ilf 4J 71
Boundary Cl. KT1: King T 3H 151
Boundary Cl. SE20 2G 157
Boundary Cl. UB2: S'hall 5E 94
Boundary Ct. N18 6A 34
(off Snells Pk.)
Boundary Ho. SE5 7C 102
Boundary Ho. W11 1F 99
(off Queensdale Cres.)
Boundary La. E13 3B 88
Boundary La. SE17 6C 102
Boundary Pas. E2 3J 9 (4F 85)
Boundary Rd. IG11: Bark King Edwards Rd. 1H 89
Boundary Rd. IG11: Bark The Clarksons 2G 89
Boundary Rd. DA15: Sidc 5J 125
Boundary Rd. E13 2A 88
Boundary Rd. E17 7B 50
Boundary Rd. HA5: Eastc 7B 40
Boundary Rd. HA9: Wemb 3E 60
Boundary Rd. N2 1B 46
Boundary Rd. N22 3B 48
Boundary Rd. N9 6D 24
Boundary Rd. NW8 1K 81
Boundary Rd. SM5: Cars 6F 167
Boundary Rd. SM5: W'gton 6F 167
Boundary Rd. SM6: W'gton 6F 167
Boundary Rd. SW19 6B 136
Boundary Row SE1 6A 14 (2B 102)
Boundary St. E2 2J 9 (3F 85)
Boundary Way CR0: Addtn 5C 170
Boundfield Rd. SE6 3G 141
BOUNDS GREEN 6C 32
Bounds Grn. Ct. N11 6C 32
(off Bounds Grn. Rd.)
Bounds Grn. Ind. Est. N11 6B 32
Bounds Grn. Rd. N11 6B 32
Bounds Grn. Rd. N22 7D 32
Bourbon Ho. SE6 5E 140
Bourbon La. W12 1F 99
Bourbon Rd. SW9 1A 120
Bourchier St. W1 2C 12 (7H 83)
Bourdon Pl. W1 2K 11 (7F 83)
(off Bourdon St.)
Bourdon Rd. SE20 2J 157
Bourdon St. W1 3J 11 (7F 83)
Bourke Cl. NW10 6A 62
Bourke Cl. SW4 6J 119
Bourlet Cl. W1 6A 6 (5G 83)
Bourn Av. EN4: E Barn 5G 21
Bourn Av. N15 4D 48
Bourn Av. UB8: Hil 4C 74
Bournbrook Rd. SE3 3B 124
Bourne, The N14 1C 32
Bourne Av. HA4: Ruis 5A 58
Bourne Av. N14 2D 32
Bourne Av. UB3: Harl 3E 92
Bournebrook Gro. RM7: Rush G 6K 55
Bourne Cir. UB3: Harl 3E 92
Bourne Cl. TW7: Isle 3J 113
Bourne Ct. E11 5J 51
Bourne Ct. HA4: Ruis 5K 57
Bourne Ct. IG8: Wfd G 3B 52
Bourne Ct. W4 6J 97
Bourne Dr. CR4: Mitc 2B 154
Bourne Est. EC1 5J 7 (5A 84)
Bourne Gdns. E4 4J 35
Bourne Hall Mus. 7B 164
Bourne Hill N13 2D 32
Bourne Hill Cl. N13 2E 32
Bourne Ho. IG9: Buck H 3G 37
Bourne Ho. TW15: Ashf 5C 128
Bourne Ind. Pk. DA1: Cray 5K 127
Bourne Mead DA5: Bexl 5K 127
Bournemead Av. UB5: N'olt 2J 75
Bournemead Cl. UB5: N'olt 3J 75
Bournemead Way UB5: N'olt 2K 75
Bourne M. W1 1H 11 (6E 82)

190 A-Z London

Bournemouth Cl. – Brangton Rd.

Bournemouth Cl. SE15 2G 121
Bournemouth Rd. SE15 2G 121
Bournemouth Rd. SW19 1J 153
Bourne Pde. DA5: Bexl 7H 127
Bourne Pl. W4 5K 97
Bourne Rd. BR2: Broml 4B 160
Bourne Rd. DA1: Cray 5K 127
Bourne Rd. DA5: Bexl 7H 127
Bourne Rd. DA5: Dart 7H 127
Bourne Rd. E7 3H 69
Bourne Rd. N8 6J 47
Bournes Ho. N15 6E 48
(off Chisley Rd.)
Bourneside Cres. N14 1C 32
Bourneside Gdns. SE6 5E 140
Bourne St. CR0: C'don 2B 168
Bourne St. SW1 4G 17 (4E 100)
Bourne Ter. W2 5K 81
Bourne Va. BR2: Hayes 1H 171
Bournevale Rd. SW16 4J 137
Bourne Vw. UB6: G'frd 6K 59
Bourne Way BR2: Hayes 2H 171
Bourne Way KT19: Ewe 4J 163
Bourne Way SM1: Sutt 5H 165
Bournewood Rd. SE18 7A 108
Bournville Rd. SE6 7C 122
Bournwell Cl. EN4: Cockf 3J 21
Bourton Cl. UB3: Hayes 1J 93
Bousfield Rd. SE14 2K 121
Boutflower Rd. SW11 4C 118
Boutique Hall SE13 4E 122
Bouton Pl. N1 7B 66
(off Waterloo Ter.)
Bouverie Gdns. HA3: Kenton 6D 42
Bouverie M. N16 2E 66
Bouverie Pl. W2 7B 4 (6B 82)
Bouverie Rd. HA1: Harr 6G 41
Bouverie Rd. N16 2E 66
Bouverie St. EC4 1K 13 (6A 84)
Boveney Cl. SE23 6K 121
Boveney Rd. SE23 7K 121
Bovet Ct. E1 5A 86
(off Ocean Est.)
Bovill Rd. SE23 7K 121
Bovingdon Av. HA9: Wemb 6G 61
Bovingdon Cl. N19 2G 65
Bovingdon La. NW9 1A 44
Bovingdon Rd. SW6 1K 117
Bovril Ct. SW6 7K 99
(off Fulham Rd.)
BOW 3B 86
Bowater Cl. NW9 5K 43
Bowater Cl. SW2 6J 119
Bowater Gdns. TW16: Sun 2A 148
Bowater Ho. EC1 4C 8 (4C 84)
(off Golden La. Est.)
Bowater Pl. SE3 7K 105
Bowater Rd. HA9: Wemb 3H 61
Bowater Rd. SE18 3B 106
Bow Bell Twr. E3 1C 86
(off Pancras Way)
Bow Bri. Est. E3 3D 86
Bow Brook, The E2 2K 85
(off Mace St.)
Bow Churchyard EC4 1D 14 (6C 84)
(off Bow La.)
BOW COMMON 5C 86
Bow Comn. La. E3 4B 86
Bow Creek Ecology Pk. 6G 87
Bowden Cl. TW14: Bedf 1G 129
Bowden Ho. E3 3D 86
(off Rainhill Way)
Bowden St. SE11 6K 19 (5A 102)
Bowditch SE8 4B 104
Bowdon Rd. E17 7C 50
Bowen Ct. SE16 4J 103
(off Debnams Rd.)
Bowen Dr. SE21 3E 138
Bowen Dr. SE7 5K 105
Bowen Rd. HA1: Harr 7G 41
Bowen St. E14 6D 86
Bower Av. SE10 1G 123
Bower Cl. RM5: Col R 1K 55
Bower Cl. UB5: N'olt 2A 76
Bower Ct. E4 1K 35
(off The Ridgeway)
Bowerdean St. SW6 1K 117
Bowerden Ct. NW10 2D 80
Bowerman Av. SE14 6A 104
Bowerman Ct. N19 2H 65
(off St John's Way)
Bower St. E1 6K 85
Bowers Wlk. E6 6D 88
Bowery Apts. W12 7E 80
(off Fountain Park Way)
Bowery Ct. RM10: Dag 6H 73
Bowes Cl. DA15: Sidc 6B 126
Bowe's Ho. IG11: Bark 7F 71
Bowes-Lyon Hall E16 1J 105
(off Wesley Av.)
BOWES PARK 6D 32
Bowes Rd. N11 5B 32
Bowes Rd. N13 5D 32
Bowes Rd. RM8: Dag 4C 72
Bowes Rd. W3 7A 80
Bow Exchange E3 5D 86
(off Yeo St.)
Bow Fair E3 2C 86
(off Fairfield Rd.)
Bowfell Rd. W6 6E 98
Bowford Av. DA7: Bex 1E 126
Bowhill Cl. SW9 7A 102
Bow Ho. N1 1E 84
(off Wilmer Gdns.)
Bowie Cl. SW4 7H 119
BOW INTERCHANGE 2D 86
Bowland Rd. IG8: Wfd G 6F 37
Bowland Rd. SW4 4H 119
Bowland Yd. SW1 7F 11 (2D 100)
(off Kinnerton St.)
Bow La. EC4 1D 14 (6C 84)
Bow La. N12 7F 31
Bow La. SM4: Mord 6G 153
Bowlby Ho. SE4 4K 121
(off Frendsbury Rd.)
Bowl Ct. EC2 4H 9 (4E 84)
Bowles Ct. N12 7H 31
Bowles Rd. SE1 6G 103
Bowley Cl. SE19 6F 139
Bowley Ho. SE16 3G 103
Bowley La. SE19 5F 139
Bowline Ct. SE10 4G 105
Bowline Ct. TW8: Bford 7C 96
(off Durham Wharf Dr.)
Bowling, The KT12: Walt T 7J 147
Bowling Cl. UB10: Uxb 1B 74
Bowling Grn. Cl. SW15 7D 116
Bowling Grn. Ct. HA9: Wemb 2F 61
Bowling Grn. Ho. SW10 7B 100
(off Riley St.)
Bowling Grn. La. EC1 3K 7 (4A 84)
Bowling Grn. Pl. SE1 6E 14 (2D 102)
Bowling Grn. Row SE18 3D 106
Bowling Grn. Sq. SW12 1E 136
Bowling Grn. St. SE11 7J 19 (6A 102)
Bowling Grn. Wlk. N1 1G 9 (3E 84)
Bow Locks E3 4E 86
Bowls Cl. HA7: Stan 5G 27
Bowman Av. E16 7H 87
Bowman Ho. N1 1E 84
(off Nuttall St.)
Bowman M. SW18 1H 135
Bowman's Bldgs. NW1 5C 4 (5C 82)
(off Penfold Pl.)
Bowmans Cl. W13 1B 96
Bowmans Lea SE23 7J 121
Bowmans Mdw. SM6: W'gton 3F 167
Bowman's M. E1 6G 85
Bowman's M. N7 3J 65
Bowman's Pl. N7 3J 65
Bowman Trad. Est. NW9 3G 43
Bowmead SE9 2D 142
Bowmore Wlk. NW1 7H 65
Bown Cl. HA2: Harr 3G 41
Bowness Cl. E8 6F 67
(off Beechwood Rd.)
Bowness Cres. SW15 5A 134
Bowness Dr. TW4: Houn 4C 112
Bowness Ho. SE15 7J 103
(off Hillbeck Cl.)
Bowness Rd. DA7: Bex 2H 127
Bowness Rd. SE6 7D 122
Bowood Rd. EN3: Enf H 2E 24
Bowood Rd. SW11 5E 118
Bow River Village E3 2E 86
(off Global App.)
Bow Rd. E3 3B 86
Bowrons Av. HA0: Wemb 7D 60
Bowry Ho. E14 5B 86
(off Wallwood St.)
Bowsley Ct. TW13: Felt 2J 129
Bowspirit Apts. SE8 7D 104
Bowsprit Point E14 3C 104
(off Westferry Rd.)
Bow St. E15 5G 69
Bow St. WC2 1F 13 (6J 83)
Bowstring Plaza E3 3B 86
(off St Clements Av.)
Bow Triangle Bus. Cen. E3 4C 86
(not continuous)
Bowyer Cl. E6 5D 88
Bowyer Ho. N1 1E 84
(off Whitmore Est.)
Bowyer Pl. SE5 7C 102
Bowyer Plaza E3 3B 86
(off St Clements Av.)
Bowyers Ct. TW1: Isle 4B 114
Bowyer St. SE5 7C 102
Boxall Rd. SE21 6E 120
Boxelder Cl. HA8: Edg 5D 28
Boxgrove Rd. SE2 3C 108
Box La. IG11: Bark 2B 90
Boxley Rd. SM4: Mord 4A 154
Boxley St. E16 1K 105
Boxmoor Ho. E2 1G 85
(off Whiston Rd.)
Boxmoor Ho. W11 1F 99
(off Queensdale Cres.)
Boxmoor Rd. HA3: Kenton 4B 42
Boxoll Rd. RM9: Dag 4F 73
Box Pk. 2D 168
Boxted Cl. IG9: Buck H 1H 37
Box Tree Ho. SE8 6A 104
Boxtree La. HA3: Hrw W 1G 41
Boxtree Rd. HA3: Hrw W 7C 26
Boxwood Cl. UB7: W Dray 2B 92
Boxworth Cl. N12 5G 31
Boxworth Gro. N1 1K 83
Boyce Ho. SW16 5G 137
Boyce Ho. W10 3H 81
(off Bruckner St.)
Boyce Way E13 4J 87
Boycroft Av. NW9 6J 43
Boyd Av. UB1: S'hall 1D 94
Boyd Bldg. E16 7G 89
(off Frobisher Yd.)
Boyd Cl. KT2: King T 7G 133
Boydell Ct. NW8 7B 64
(not continuous)
Boyden Ho. E17 3E 50
Boyd Rd. SW19 6B 136
Boyd St. E1 6G 85
Boyd Way SE3 4A 124
Boyfield St. SE1 7B 14 (2B 102)
Boyland Rd. BR1: Broml 5H 141
Boyle Av. HA7: Stan 6F 27
Boyle Cl. UB10: Uxb 2B 74
Boyle Farm Island KT7: T Ditt 6A 150
Boyle Farm Rd. KT7: T Ditt 6A 150
Boyle St. W1 2A 12 (7G 83)
Boyne Av. NW4 4F 45
Boyne Rd. RM10: Dag 3G 73
Boyne Rd. SE13 3E 122
Boyne Ter. M. W11 1H 99
Boyseland Ct. HA8: Edg 2D 28
Boyson Rd. SE17 6C 102
(not continuous)
Boyson Wlk. SE17 6D 102
Boyton Cl. E1 4J 85
Boyton Cl. N8 3J 47
Boyton Ho. NW8 2B 82
(off Wellington Rd.)
Boyton Rd. N8 3J 47
Brabant Ct. EC3 2G 15 (7E 84)
(off Philpot La.)
Brabant Rd. N22 2K 47
Brabazon Av. SM6: W'gton 7J 167
Brabazon Ct. SW1 5C 18 (5H 101)
(off Moreton St.)
Brabazon Rd. TW5: Hest 7A 94
Brabazon Rd. UB5: N'olt 2E 76
Brabazon St. E14 6D 86
Brabner Ho. E2 1K 9 (3G 85)
(off Wellington Row)
Brabourne Cl. SE19 5E 138
Brabourne Cres. DA7: Bex 6F 109
Brabourne Hgts. NW7 3F 29
Brabourne Ri. BR3: Beck 5E 158
Brabourn Gro. SE15 2J 121
Brabrook Ct. SM6: W'gton 4F 167
Brabstone Ho. UB6: G'frd 2K 77
Bracer Ho. N1 2E 84
(off Whitmore Est.)
Bracewell Av. UB6: G'frd 5K 59
Bracewell Rd. W10 5E 80
Bracewood Gdns. CR0: C'don 3F 169
Bracey M. N4 2J 65
Bracey St. N4 2J 65
Bracken, The E4 2K 35
Bracken Av. CR0: C'don 3D 170
Bracken Av. SW12 6E 118
Brackenbridge Dr. HA4: Ruis 3B 58
Brackenbridge Ho. HA4: Ruis 4C 58
(off Brackenhill)
Brackenbury N4 1A 66
(off Osborne Rd.)
Brackenbury Gdns. W6 3D 98
Brackenbury Rd. N2 3A 46
Brackenbury Rd. W6 3D 98
Bracken Cl. E6 5D 88
Bracken Cl. TW16: Sun 6H 129
Bracken Cl. TW2: Whitt 7E 112
Brackendale N21 2E 32
Brackendale Cl. TW3: Houn 1F 113
Brackendene DA2: Wilm 4K 145
Bracken End TW7: Isle 5H 113
Brackenfield Cl. E5 3H 67
Bracken Gdns. SW13 2C 116
Brackenhill HA4: Ruis 4C 58
Bracken Hill Cl. BR1: Broml 1H 159
Bracken Hill La. BR1: Broml 1H 159
Bracken Ho. E3 5C 86
(off Devons Rd.)
Bracken Ind. Est. IG6: Ilf 1J 53
Bracken M. E4 1K 35
Bracken M. RM7: Rom 6H 55
Brackens BR3: Beck 7C 140
Brackens, The EN1: Enf 7K 23
Brackenwood TW16: Sun 1J 147
Brackenwood Lodge EN5: New Bar 4D 20
(off Prospect Rd.)
Brackley Av. SE15 3J 121
Brackley Cl. SM6: W'gton 7J 167
Brackley Ct. NW8 3A 4 (4B 82)
(off Pollitt Dr.)
Brackley Rd. BR3: Beck 7B 140
Brackley Rd. W4 5A 98
Brackley Sq. IG8: Wfd G 7G 37
Brackley St. EC1 4D 8 (4C 84)
Brackley Ter. W4 5A 98
Bracklyn Ct. N1 2D 84
(not continuous)
Bracklyn St. N1 2D 84
Bracknell Cl. N22 1A 48
Bracknell Gdns. NW3 4K 63
Bracknell Ga. NW3 5K 63
Bracknell Way NW3 4K 63
Bracondale Rd. SE2 4A 108
Bradbeer Ho. E2 3J 85
(off Cornwall Av.)
Bradbourne Rd. DA5: Bexl 7G 127
Bradbourne St. SW6 2J 117
Bradbury Cl. UB2: S'hall 4D 94
Bradbury M. N16 5E 66
Bradbury St. N16 5E 66
Bradby Ho. NW8 2K 81
(off Hamilton Ter.)
Bradby's HA1: Harr 1J 59
(off High St.)
Braddock Cl. TW7: Isle 2K 113
Braddon Ct. EN5: Barn 3B 20
Braddon Rd. TW9: Rich 3F 115
Braddyll St. SE10 5G 105
Bradenham Av. DA16: Well 4A 126
Bradenham Cl. SE17 6D 102
Bradenham Rd. HA3: Kenton 4B 42
Bradenham Rd. UB4: Hayes 3G 75
Braden St. W9 4K 81
Bradfield Ct. NW1 7F 65
(off Hawley Rd.)
Bradfield Dr. IG11: Bark 5A 72
Bradfield Ho. IG8: Wfd G 6K 37
Bradfield Rd. E16 2J 105
Bradfield Rd. HA4: Ruis 5C 58
Bradford Cl. BR2: Broml 1D 172
Bradford Cl. N17 6A 34
Bradford Cl. SE26 4H 139
Bradford Dr. KT19: Ewe 6B 164
Bradford Ho. W14 3F 99
(off Spring Va. Ter.)
Bradford Rd. IG1: Ilf 1H 71
Bradford Rd. W3 2A 98
Bradfords Cl. IG9: Buck H 4G 37
Bradgate Rd. SE6 6D 122
Brading Cres. E11 2K 69
Brading Rd. CR0: C'don 6K 155
Brading Rd. SW2 7K 119
Brading Ter. W12 3C 98
Bradiston Rd. W9 3H 81
Bradley Cl. N7 6J 65
Bradley Gdns. W13 6B 78
Bradley Ho. E3 3D 86
(off Bromley High St.)
Bradley Ho. IG8: Wfd G 7D 36
Bradley Ho. SE16 4J 103
(off Raymouth Rd.)
Bradley M. SW17 1D 136
Bradley Rd. N22 2K 47
Bradley Rd. SE19 6C 138
Bradley Rd. SW4 6H 119
Bradley's Cl. N1 2A 84
Bradley Stone Rd. E6 5D 88
Bradman Ho. NW8 3A 82
(off Abercorn Pl.)
Bradman Row HA8: Edg 7D 28
Bradmead SW8 7F 101
Bradmore Ct. EN3: Enf H 3F 25
(off Enstone Rd.)
Bradmore Pk. Rd. W6 4D 98
Bradshaw Cl. SW19 6J 135
Bradshaw Cotts. E14 6A 86
(off Repton St.)
Bradshaw Dr. NW7 7A 30
Bradshawe Waye UB8: Hil 5B 74
Bradshaws Cl. SE25 3G 157
Bradstock Ho. E9 7K 67
Bradstock Rd. E9 6K 67
Bradstock Rd. KT17: Ewe 5C 164
Brad St. SE1 5K 13 (1A 102)
Bradwell Av. RM10: Dag 2G 73
Bradwell Cl. E18 4H 51
Bradwell Ho. NW6 1K 81
(off Mortimer Cres.)
Bradwell M. N18 4B 34
Bradwell Rd. IG9: Buck H 1H 37
Bradwell St. E1 3K 85
Brady Ct. RM8: Dag 1D 72
Brady Dr. BR1: Broml 3E 160
Brady Ho. SW8 1G 119
(off Corunna Rd.)
Bradymead E6 6E 88
Brady St. E1 4H 85
Braeburn Ct. BR6: Orp 2K 173
(off Blossom Dr.)
Braeburn Ct. EN4: E Barn 4G 21
Braeburn Ct. RM13: Rain 2K 91
(off Broadis Way)
Brae Ct. KT2: King T 1G 151
Braemar SW15 6F 117
Braemar Av. CR7: Thor H 3A 156
Braemar Av. DA7: Bex 4J 127
Braemar Av. HA0: Wemb 7D 60
Braemar Av. N22 1J 47
Braemar Av. NW10 3K 61
Braemar Av. SW18 2J 135
Braemar Av. SW19 2J 135
Braemar Cl. SE16 5H 103
(off Masters Dr.)
Braemar Ct. SE6 1H 141
(off Cumberland Pl.)
Braemar Gdns. BR4: W W'ck 1E 170
Braemar Gdns. DA15: Sidc 3H 143
Braemar Gdns. NW9 1K 43
Braemar Ho. W9 3A 82
(off Maida Vale)
Braemar Mans. SW7 3K 99
(off Cornwall Gdns.)
Braemar Rd. E13 4H 87
Braemar Rd. KT4: Wor Pk 3D 164
Braemar Rd. N15 5E 48
Braemar Rd. TW8: Bford 6D 96
Braeside BR3: Beck 5C 140
Braeside Av. SW19 1G 153
Braeside Cres. DA7: Bex 4J 127
Braeside Rd. SW16 7G 137
Braes St. N1 7B 66
Braesyde Cl. DA17: Belv 4F 109
Brafferton Rd. CR0: C'don 4C 168
Braganza St. SE17 5B 102
Bragg Cl. RM8: Dag 6B 72
Braham Ct. E2 4H 85
(off Three Colts La.)
Braham Ho. SE11 6H 19 (5K 101)
Braham St. E1 1K 15 (6F 85)
Braham St. Pk. 1K 15 (6F 85)
(off Half Moon Pas.)
Braid Av. W3 6A 80
Braid Cl. TW13: Hanw 2D 130
Braidwood Pas. EC1 5C 8 (5C 84)
(off Aldersgate St.)
Braidwood Rd. SE6 1F 141
Braidwood St. SE1 5G 15 (1E 102)
Brailey Ho. E10 1G 69
Brailsford Cl. CR4: Mitc 7C 136
Brailsford Rd. SW2 5A 120
Brainton Av. TW14: Felt 7K 111
Braintree Av. IG4: Ilf 4C 52
Braintree Ho. E1 4J 85
(off Malcolm Rd.)
Braintree Rd. HA4: Ruis 4K 57
Braintree Rd. RM10: Dag 3G 73
Braintree St. E2 3J 85
Braithwaite Av. RM7: Rush G 7G 55
Braithwaite Gdns. HA7: Stan 1C 42
Braithwaite Ho. E15 6F 69
(off Forrester Way)
Braithwaite Ho. EC1 3E 8 (4D 84)
(off Bunhill Row)
Braithwaite Rd. EN3: Brim 3G 25
Braithwaite St. E1 4J 9 (4F 85)
Braithwaite Twr. W2 5B 4 (5B 82)
(off Hall Pl.)
Bramah Grn. SW9 1A 120
(off Eythorne Rd.)
Bramah Ho. SW1 6J 17 (5F 101)
Bramah Rd. SW9 1A 120
Bramalea Cl. N6 6E 46
Bramall Cl. E15 5H 69
Bramall Ct. N7 6K 65
(off Watkinson Rd.)
Bramber WC1 2E 6 (3J 83)
(off Cromer St.)
Bramber Ct. TW8: Bford 4E 96
Bramber Ct. W14 6H 99
(off Bramber Rd.)
Bramber Ho. KT2: King T 1E 150
(off Seven Kings Way)
Bramber Rd. N12 5H 31
Bramber Rd. W14 6H 99
Brambleacres Cl. SM2: Sutt 7J 165
Bramblebury Rd. SE18 5G 107
Bramble Cl. BR3: Beck 5E 158
Bramble Cl. CR0: C'don 4C 170
Bramble Cl. HA7: Stan 7J 27
Bramble Cl. N15 4G 49
Bramble Cl. SE19 1D 156
Bramble Cl. TW17: Shep 3F 147
Bramble Cl. UB8: Hil 6B 74
Bramble Cft. DA8: Erith 4J 109
Brambledown Cl. BR4: W W'ck 5G 159
Brambledown Rd. CR2: Sande 7E 168
Brambledown Rd. SM5: Cars 7E 166
Brambledown Rd. SM6: W'gton 7E 166
Bramble Gdns. W12 7B 80
Bramble Ho. E3 5C 86
(off Devons Rd.)
Bramble La. TW12: Hamp 6D 130
Bramble M. SW17 2C 136
Brambles, The SM1: Sutt 2B 166
Brambles, The SW19 5H 135
(off Woodside)
Brambles, The UB7: W Dray 1E 174
Brambles Cl. TW7: Isle 7B 96
Brambles Farm Dr. UB10: Hil 3C 74
Bramblewood Cl. SM5: Cars 1C 166
Brambling Ct. SE8 6B 104
(off Abinger Gro.)
Bramblings, The E4 4A 36
Bramcote Av. CR4: Mitc 4D 154
Bramcote Ct. CR4: Mitc 4D 154
(off Bramcote Av.)
Bramcote Gro. SE16 5J 103
Bramcote Rd. SW15 4D 116
Bramdean Cres. SE12 1J 141
Bramdean Gdns. SE12 1J 141
Bramerton NW6 7F 63
(off Willesden La.)
Bramerton Rd. BR3: Beck 3B 158
Bramerton St. SW3 7C 16 (6C 100)
Bramfield Ct. N4 2C 66
(off Queen's Dr.)
Bramfield Rd. SW11 6C 118
Bramford Ct. N14 2C 32
Bramford Rd. SW18 4A 118
Bramham Gdns. KT9: Chess 4D 162
Bramham Gdns. SW5 5K 99
Bramhope La. SE7 6K 105
Bramlands Cl. SW11 3C 118
Bramley Av. TW17: Shep 3G 147
Bramley Bank Local Nature Reserve 6J 169
Bramley Cl. BR6: Farnb 1F 173
Bramley Cl. CR2: S Croy 5C 168
Bramley Cl. E17 2A 50
Bramley Cl. HA5: Eastc 3H 39
Bramley Cl. IG8: Wfd G 7F 37
Bramley Cl. N14 5A 22
Bramley Cl. NW7 3F 29
Bramley Cl. TW2: Whitt 6G 113
Bramley Cl. UB3: Hayes 7J 75
Bramley Ct. BR6: Orp 2K 173
(off Blossom Dr.)
Bramley Ct. CR4: Mitc 2B 154
Bramley Ct. DA16: Well 1B 126
Bramley Ct. E4 1K 35
(off The Ridgeway)
Bramley Ct. EN4: E Barn 4H 21
Bramley Ct. RM13: Rain 2K 91
(off Broadis Way)
Bramley Ct. UB1: S'hall 7G 77
(off Haldane Rd.)
Bramley Cres. IG2: Ilf 6E 52
Bramley Cres. SW8 7H 101
Bramley Hill CR2: S Croy 5B 168
Bramley Ho. SW15 6B 116
(off Tunworth Cres.)
Bramley Ho. TW4: Houn 4D 112
Bramley Ho. W10 6F 81
Bramley Hyrst CR2: S Croy 5C 168
Bramley Lodge HA0: Wemb 4D 60
Bramley Pde. N14 4C 22
Bramley Rd. N14 5A 22
Bramley Rd. SM1: Sutt 5B 166
Bramley Rd. SM2: Cheam 7F 165
Bramley Rd. W10 6F 81
Bramley Rd. W5 3C 96
Bramley Sports Ground 5K 21
Bramley Way BR4: W W'ck 2D 170
Bramley Way TW4: Houn 5D 112
Brampton WC1 6G 7 (5K 83)
(off Red Lion Sq.)
Brampton Cl. E5 2H 67
Brampton Ct. NW4 4D 44
Brampton Ct. RM7: Rush G 6K 55
(off Union Rd.)
Brampton Gro. HA3: Kenton 4A 42
Brampton Gro. HA9: Wemb 1G 61
Brampton Gro. NW4 4D 44
Brampton Ho. SE16 2J 103
(off Albatross Way)
Brampton La. NW4 4E 44
Brampton Pk. Rd. N22 3A 48
Brampton Rd. CR0: C'don 7F 157
Brampton Rd. DA7: Bex 3D 126
Brampton Rd. E6 3B 88
Brampton Rd. N15 5C 48
Brampton Rd. NW9 4G 43
Brampton Rd. SE2 6C 108
Brampton Rd. UB10: Hil 2D 74
Bramshaw Ri. KT3: N Mald 6A 152
Bramshaw Rd. E9 6K 67
Bramshill Gdns. NW5 3F 65
Bramshill Rd. NW10 2B 80
Bramshot Av. SE7 6J 105
Bramshurst NW8 1K 81
(off Abbey Rd.)
Bramston Rd. NW10 2C 80
Bramston Rd. SW17 3A 136
Bramwell Cl. TW16: Sun 2B 148
Bramwell Ho. SE1 3C 102
Bramwell Ho. SW1 6A 18 (5G 101)
(off Churchill Gdns.)
Bramwell M. N1 1K 83
Bramwell Way E16 1A 106
Brancaster Dr. NW7 7H 29
Brancaster Ho. E1 3K 85
(off Moody St.)
Brancaster Rd. E12 4D 70
Brancaster Rd. IG2: Ilf 6J 53
Brancaster Rd. SW16 3J 137
Brancepeth Gdns. IG9: Buck H 2D 36
Branch Hill NW3 3A 64
Branch Hill Ho. NW3 3K 63
Branch Pl. N1 1D 84
Branch Rd. E14 7A 86
Branch St. SE15 7E 102
Brancker Rd. HA3: Kenton 3D 42
Brancroft Way EN3: Brim 1F 25
Brand Av. UB10: Uxb 2A 74
Brand Cl. N4 1B 66
Brandesbury Sq. IG8: Wfd G 7K 37
Brandlehow Rd. SW15 4H 117
Brandon Ct. E16 4H 87
Brandon Est. SE17 6B 102
Brandon Ho. BR3: Beck 5D 140
(off Beckenham Hill Rd.)
Brandon Mans. W14 6G 99
(off Queen's Club Gdns.)
Brandon M. EC2 6E 8 (5D 84)
(off Moor La.)
Brandon M. SE17 4C 102
Brandon Rd. E17 4E 50
Brandon Rd. N7 7J 65
Brandon Rd. SM1: Sutt 4K 165
Brandon Rd. UB2: S'hall 5D 94
Brandon St. SE17 4C 102
(not continuous)
Brandram M. SE13 4G 123
(off Brandram Rd.)
Brandram Rd. SE13 3G 123
Brandrams Wharf SE16 2J 103
Brandreth Ct. HA1: Harr 6K 41
Brandreth Rd. E6 6D 88
Brandreth Rd. SW17 2F 137
Brandries, The SM6: Bedd 3H 167
Brands Ho. NW6 1H 81
(off Lincoln M.)
Brand St. SE10 7E 104
Brandville Gdns. IG6: Ilf 4F 53
Brandville Rd. UB7: W Dray 2A 92
Brandy Way SM2: Sutt 7J 165
Brangbourne Rd. BR1: Broml 5E 140
Brangton Rd. SE11 6H 19 (5K 101)

Brangwyn Ct. – Brighton Rd.

Brangwyn Ct. W14 ... 3G 99
(off Blythe Rd.)
Brangwyn Cres. SW19 ... 1A 154
Branksea St. SW6 ... 7G 99
Branksome Av. N18 ... 6A 34
Branksome Cl. TW11: Tedd ... 4H 131
Branksome Ho. SW8 ... 7K 101
(off Meadow Rd.)
Branksome Rd. SW19 ... 1J 153
Branksome Rd. SW2 ... 5J 119
Branksome Way HA3: Kenton ... 6F 43
Branksome Way KT3: N Mald ... 1J 151
Branksone Ct. N2 ... 3A 46
Brannan St. ... 1E 104
Brannigan Way HA8: Edg ... 4K 27
Bransby Rd. KT9: Chess ... 6E 162
Branscombe NW1 ... 1G 83
(off Plender St.)
Branscombe Ct. BR2: Broml ... 5H 159
Branscombe Gdns. N21 ... 7F 23
Branscombe St. SE13 ... 3D 122
Bransdale Cl. NW6 ... 1J 81
Bransgrove Rd. HA8: Edg ... 1F 43
Branston Cres. BR5: Pet W ... 1H 173
Branstone Rd. TW9: Kew ... 1F 115
Brants Wlk. W7 ... 4J 77
Brantwood Av. DA8: Erith ... 7J 109
Brantwood Av. TW7: Isle ... 4A 114
Brantwood Cl. E17 ... 3D 50
Brantwood Gdns. EN2: Enf ... 4D 22
Brantwood Gdns. IG4: Ilf ... 4C 52
Brantwood Ho. SE5 ... 7C 102
(off Wyndam Est.)
Brantwood Rd. CR2: S Croy ... 7C 168
Brantwood Rd. DA7: Bex ... 2H 127
Brantwood Rd. N17 ... 6B 34
Brantwood Rd. SE24 ... 5C 120
Branxholme Ct. BR1: Broml ... 1H 159
(off Highland Rd.)
Braque Bldg. SE1 ... 5C 14 (1C 102)
(off Union St.)
Brasenose Dr. SW13 ... 6E 98
Brasher Cl. UB6: G'frd ... 5H 59
Brassett Point E15 ... 1G 87
(off Abbey Rd.)
Brassey Cl. TW14: Felt ... 1J 129
Brassey Ho. E14 ... 4D 104
(off Cahir St.)
Brassey Rd. NW6 ... 6H 63
Brassey Sq. SW11 ... 3E 118
Brassie Av. W3 ... 6A 80
Brass Talley All. SE16 ... 2K 103
Brasted Cl. BR6: Orp ... 2K 173
Brasted Cl. DA6: Bex ... 5D 126
Brasted Cl. SE26 ... 4J 139
Brasted Lodge BR3: Beck ... 7C 140
Brathay NW1 ... 1B 6 (2G 83)
(off Ampthill Est.)
Brathway Rd. SW18 ... 7J 117
Bratley St. E1 ... 4G 85
Bratten Ct. CR0: C'don ... 6D 156
Braund Av. UB6: G'frd ... 4F 77
Braundton Av. DA15: Sidc ... 1K 143
Braunston Dr. UB4: Yead ... 4C 76
Braunston Ho. HA0: Wemb ... 1E 78
Bravington Cl. TW17: Shep ... 5B 146
Bravington Pl. W9 ... 4H 81
Bravington Rd. W9 ... 2H 81
Bravingtons Wlk. N1 ... 1F 7 (2J 83)
(off York Way)
Brawne Ho. SE17 ... 6B 102
(off Brandon Est.)
Braxfield Rd. SE4 ... 4A 122
Braxted Pk. SW16 ... 6K 137
Bray NW3 ... 7C 64
Brayards Rd. SE15 ... 2H 121
Brayards Rd. Est. SE15 ... 2H 121
(off Caulfield Rd.)
Braybourne Dr. TW7: Isle ... 7K 95
Braybrooke Gdns. SE19 ... 7E 138
Braybrook St. W12 ... 5B 80
Brayburne Av. SW4 ... 2G 119
Bray Ct. E2 ... 3K 85
(off Meath Cres.)
Bray Ct. SW16 ... 5J 137
Braycourt Av. KT12: Walt T ... 7K 147
Bray Cres. SE16 ... 2K 103
Braydon Rd. N16 ... 1G 67
Bray Dr. E16 ... 7H 87
Brayfield Ter. N1 ... 7A 66
Brayford Sq. E1 ... 6J 85
Bray Pas. E16 ... 7J 87
Bray Pl. SW3 ... 4E 16 (4D 100)
Bray Rd. NW7 ... 6A 30
Brays Gdns. SE13 ... 6E 122
Brays Gdns. SE6 ... 7D 122
Brayton Gdns. EN2: Enf ... 4C 22
Braywood Rd. SE9 ... 4H 125
Brazier Cres. UB5: N'olt ... 4D 76
Brazil Cl. CR0: Bedd ... 7J 155
Breacher Ho. Apts. IG11: Bark ... 4A 90
Breach La. RM9: Dag ... 3G 91
Bread St. EC4 ... 1D 14 (6C 84)
(not continuous)
Breakspear Crematorium ... 5E 38
Breakspear Ho. UB9: Hare ... 3A 38
Breakspear M. UB9: Hare ... 3A 38
Breakspear Rd. HA4: Ruis ... 7D 38
Breakspear Rd. Sth. UB10: Ick ... 3B 56
Breakspear Rd. Sth. UB9: Hare ... 1C 56
Breakspears Dr. BR5: St P ... 1K 161
Breakspears M. SE4 ... 2B 122
Breakspears Rd. SE4 ... 4B 122
(not continuous)
Breakwell Ct. W10 ... 4G 81
(off Wornington Rd.)
Bream Cl. N17 ... 4H 49
Bream Gdns. E6 ... 3E 88
Breamore Cl. SW15 ... 1C 134
Breamore Ct. IG3: Ilf ... 2A 72
Breamore Ho. SE15 ... 7G 103
(off Friary Est.)
Breamore Rd. IG3: Ilf ... 2K 71
Bream's Bldgs. EC4 ... 7J 7 (6A 84)
Bream St. E3 ... 7C 68
Breamwater Gdns. TW10: Ham ... 3B 132
Brearley Cl. HA8: Edg ... 7D 28
Brearley Cl. UB8: Uxb ... 6A 56
Breasley Cl. SW15 ... 4D 116
Breasy Pl. NW4 ... 4D 44
(off Burroughs Gdns.)
Brechin Pl. SW7 ... 4A 100
Brecknock Rd. N19 ... 4G 65
Brecknock Rd. N7 ... 5H 65
Brecknock Rd. Est. N19 ... 4G 65
Breckonmead BR1: Broml ... 2A 160
Brecon Cl. CR4: Mitc ... 3J 155
Brecon Cl. KT4: Wor Pk ... 2E 164
Brecon Grn. NW9 ... 6A 44
Brecon Ho. E3 ... 2B 86
(off Ordell Rd.)
Brecon Ho. UB5: N'olt ... 3D 76
(off Taywood Rd.)
Brecon Ho. W2 ... 6A 82
(off Hallfield Est.)
Brecon Lodge UB7: W Dray ... 2B 92
Brecon M. N7 ... 5H 65
Brecon Rd. EN3: Pond E ... 4D 24
Brecon Rd. W6 ... 6G 99
Brede Cl. E6 ... 3E 88
Bredel Ho. E14 ... 5C 86
(off St Paul's Way)
Brede M. E6 ... 3E 88
Bredgar SE13 ... 5D 122
Bredgar Rd. N19 ... 2G 65
Bredhurst Cl. SE20 ... 6J 139
Bredinghurst SE22 ... 7G 121
Bredin Ho. SW10 ... 7K 99
(off Coleridge Gdns.)
Bredon Rd. CR0: C'don ... 7F 157
Bree Ct. NW9 ... 3J 43
Breer St. SW6 ... 3K 117
Breezers Ct. E1 ... 7G 85
(off The Highway)
Breezer's Hill E1 ... 7G 85
Brember Rd. HA2: Harr ... 2G 59
Bremer M. E17 ... 4D 50
Bremner Rd. SW7 ... 1A 16 (3A 100)
Brenchley Cl. BR2: Broml ... 6H 159
Brenchley Cl. BR7: Chst ... 1E 160
Brenchley Gdns. SE23 ... 6J 121
Brenchley Rd. BR5: St P ... 2K 161
Brenda Rd. SW17 ... 2D 136
Brende Gdns. KT8: W Mole ... 4F 149
Brendon Av. NW10 ... 4A 62
Brendon Cl. UB3: Harl ... 7E 92
Brendon Ct. UB2: S'hall ... 4F 95
Brendon Gdns. HA2: Harr ... 4F 59
Brendon Gdns. IG2: Ilf ... 5J 53
Brendon Gro. N2 ... 2A 46
Brendon Rd. RM8: Dag ... 1F 73
Brendon Rd. SE9 ... 2H 143
Brendon St. W1 ... 7D 4 (6C 82)
Brendon Vs. N21 ... 1H 33
Brendon Way EN1: Enf ... 7K 23
Brenley Cl. CR4: Mitc ... 3E 154
Brenley Gdns. SE9 ... 4B 124
Brenley Ho. SE1 ... 6E 14 (2D 102)
(off Tennis St.)
Brennand Ct. N19 ... 3G 65
Brent Cl. DA5: Bexl ... 1E 144
Brentcot Cl. W13 ... 4B 78
Brent Ct. NW11 ... 7F 45
Brent Ct. W7 ... 7H 77
Brent Cres. NW10 ... 2F 79
BRENT CROSS ... 7E 44
Brent Cross Fly-Over NW4 ... 7F 45
Brent Cross Gdns. NW4 ... 6F 45
BRENT CROSS INTERCHANGE ... 6E 44
Brent Cross Shop. Cen. ... 7E 44
Brentfield NW10 ... 7H 61
Brentfield Cl. NW10 ... 6K 61
Brentfield Gdns. NW2 ... 7F 45
Brentfield Ho. NW10 ... 7K 61
Brentfield Rd. NW10 ... 6K 61
BRENTFORD ... 6D 96
Brentford Bus. Cen. TW8: Bford ... 7C 96
Brentford Cl. UB4: Yead ... 4B 76
Brentford Community Stadium ... 5F 97
BRENTFORD END ... 7B 96
Brentford FC ... 5F 97
Brentford Fountain Leisure Cen. ... 5G 97
Brentford Ho. TW1: Twick ... 7B 114
Brent Grn. NW4 ... 5E 44
Brent Grn. Wlk. HA9: Wemb ... 3J 61
Brentham Club ... 3C 78
Brentham Way W5 ... 4D 78
Brent Ho. E9 ... 6J 67
(off Brenthouse Rd.)
Brenthouse Rd. E9 ... 7J 67
Brenthurst Rd. NW10 ... 6B 62
Brent Lea TW8: Bford ... 7C 96
Brentmead Cl. W7 ... 7J 77
Brentmead Gdns. NW10 ... 2F 79
Brentmead Pl. NW11 ... 6F 45
Brent Mus. ... 6D 62
Brent New Ent. Cen. NW10 ... 6B 62
Brenton Ct. E9 ... 5A 68
(off Mabley St.)
Brenton St. E14 ... 6A 86
Brent Pk. Ind. Est. UB2: S'hall ... 3K 93
Brent Pk. Rd. NW4 ... 7D 44
Brent Pk. Rd. NW9 ... 7D 44
Brent Pl. EN5: Barn ... 5C 20
Brent Reservoir ... 1B 62
Brent Rd. CR2: Sels ... 7H 169
Brent Rd. E16 ... 6J 87
Brent Rd. SE18 ... 7F 107
Brent Rd. TW8: Bford ... 6C 96
Brent Rd. UB2: S'hall ... 3A 94
Brent Side TW8: Bford ... 6C 96
Brentside Cl. W13 ... 4A 78
Brentside Executive Cen. TW8:
Bford ... 6B 96
Brent Sth. Shop. Pk. ... 1E 62
Brent St. NW4 ... 4E 44
Brent Ter. NW2 ... 1E 62
(not continuous)
Brent Trad. Cen. NW10 ... 5A 62
Brentvale Av. HA0: Wemb ... 1F 79
Brentvale Av. UB1: S'hall ... 1H 95
Brent Valley Golf Course ... 7J 77
Brent Vw. Rd. NW9 ... 6C 44
Brentwaters Bus. Pk. TW8: Bford ... 7C 96
Brent Way HA9: Wemb ... 6H 61
Brent Way N3 ... 6D 30
Brent Way TW8: Bford ... 7D 96
Brentwick Gdns. TW8: Bford ... 4E 96
Brentwood Cl. SE9 ... 1G 143
Brentwood Ho. SE18 ... 7B 106
(off Portway Gdns.)
Brentwood Lodge NW4 ... 5F 45
(off Holmdale Gdns.)
Brereton Rd. N17 ... 7A 34
Bressay Dr. NW7 ... 7H 29
Bressenden Pl. SW1 ... 1K 17 (3F 101)
Bressey Av. EN1: Enf ... 1B 24
Bressey Gro. E18 ... 2H 51
Bresslaw Ct. E3 ... 5B 86
(off Wager St.)
Breton Highwalk EC2 ... 5D 8 (5C 84)
(off Golden La.)
Breton Ho. EC2 ... 5D 8 (5C 84)
(off Golden La.)
Breton Ho. SE1 ... 7J 15 (3F 103)
(off St Saviour's Est.)
Brett Cl. N16 ... 2E 66
Brett Cl. UB5: N'olt ... 3B 76
Brett Ct. N9 ... 2D 34
Brettell St. SE17 ... 5D 102
Brettenham Av. E17 ... 1C 50
Brettenham Rd. E17 ... 2C 50
Brettenham Rd. N18 ... 4B 34
Brett Gdns. RM9: Dag ... 7E 72
Brett Ho. Cl. SW15 ... 7F 117
Brettinghurst SE1 ... 5G 103
(off Avondale Sq.)
Brett Pas. E8 ... 5H 67
Brett Rd. E8 ... 5H 67
Brewers Bldgs. EC1 ... 1A 8 (3B 84)
(off Rawstorne St.)
Brewers Ct. W2 ... 5A 82
Brewer's Grn. SW1 ... 1C 18 (3H 101)
(off Buckingham Ga.)
Brewer's Hall Gdn. EC2 ... 6D 8 (5C 84)
(off Aldermanbury Sq.)
Brewers La. E20 ... 5D 68
Brewers La. TW9: Rich ... 5D 114
Brewer St. W1 ... 3B 12 (7G 83)
Brewery, The EC2 ... 5D 8 (5C 84)
Brewery, The RM1: Rom ... 5K 55
Brewery Cl. HA0: Wemb ... 5A 60
Brewery Ind. Est., The N1 ... 1D 8 (2C 84)
(off Wenlock Rd.)
Brewery La. TW1: Twick ... 7K 113
Brewery M. Cen. TW7: Isle ... 3A 114
Brewery Rd. BR2: Broml ... 1C 172
Brewery Rd. N7 ... 7J 65
Brewery Rd. SE18 ... 5H 107
Brewery Sq. EC1 ... 4B 8 (4B 84)
Brewery Sq. SE1 ... 6J 15 (2F 103)
(off Horselydown La.)
Brewery Wlk. RM1: Rom ... 5K 55
Brewhouse La. E1 ... 1H 103
Brewhouse La. SW15 ... 3G 117
Brewhouse Rd. SE18 ... 4D 106
Brewhouse Wlk. SE16 ... 1A 104
Brewhouse Yd. EC1 ... 3A 8 (4B 84)
Brewin Ter. UB4: Yead ... 5A 76
(off Larch Cres.)
Brewood Rd. RM8: Dag ... 6B 72
Brewster Gdns. W10 ... 5E 80
Brewster Ho. E14 ... 7B 86
(off Three Colt St.)
Brewster Ho. SE1 ... 4F 103
(off Dunton Rd.)
Brewster Pl. KT1: King T ... 2J 151
Brewster Rd. E10 ... 1D 68
Breyer Group Stadium, The ... 3D 68
(shown as Leyton Orient FC)
Brian Rd. RM6: Chad H ... 5C 54
Briant Ho. SE1 ... 2H 19 (3K 101)
(off Hercules Rd.)
Briants Cl. HA5: Pinn ... 2D 40
Briant St. SE14 ... 1K 121
Briar Av. SW16 ... 7K 137
Briarbank Rd. W13 ... 6A 78
Briar Cl. IG9: Buck H ... 2G 37
Briar Cl. N13 ... 3H 33
Briar Cl. N2 ... 3K 45
Briar Cl. TW12: Hamp ... 5D 130
Briar Cl. TW7: Isle ... 5K 113
Briar Ct. E3 ... 2C 86
(off Morville St.)
Briar Ct. SM3: Cheam ... 4E 164
Briar Ct. SW15 ... 4D 116
Briar Cres. UB5: N'olt ... 6F 59
Briardale HA8: Edg ... 4E 28
Briardale Gdns. NW3 ... 3J 63
Briarfield Av. N3 ... 2K 45
(not continuous)
Briarfield Cl. DA7: Bex ... 2G 127
Briar Gdns. BR2: Hayes ... 1H 171
Briaris Cl. N17 ... 7C 34
Briar La. BR4: Addtn ... 4D 170
Briar Rd. DA5: Bexl ... 3K 145
Briar Rd. HA3: Kenton ... 5C 42
Briar Rd. NW2 ... 4E 62
Briar Rd. SW16 ... 3J 155
Briar Rd. TW17: Shep ... 5B 146
Briar Rd. TW2: Twick ... 1J 131
Briars, The TW19: Stanw M ... 7B 174
Briars, The WD23: B Hea ... 1D 26
Briarswood Way BR6: Chels ... 5K 173
Briar Wlk. HA8: Edg ... 7D 28
Briar Wlk. SW15 ... 4D 116
Briar Wlk. W10 ... 4G 81
Briar Way UB7: W Dray ... 2C 92
Briar Wood Cl. BR2: Broml ... 2C 172
Briarwood Cl. NW9 ... 6J 43
Briarwood Cl. TW13: Felt ... 4G 129
Briarwood Ct. KT4: Wor Pk ... 1C 164
(off The Avenue)
Briarwood Dr. HA6: Nwood ... 2J 39
Briarwood Rd. KT17: Ewe ... 6C 164
Briarwood Rd. SW4 ... 5H 119
Briary Cl. NW3 ... 7C 64
Briary Ct. DA14: Sidc ... 5B 144
Briary Ct. E16 ... 6H 87
Briary Gdns. BR1: Broml ... 5K 141
Briary Gro. HA8: Edg ... 2H 43
Briary La. N9 ... 3A 34
Briary Lodge BR3: Beck ... 1E 158
Brickbarn Cl. SW10 ... 7A 100
(off King's Barn)
Brick Ct. EC4 ... 1J 13 (6A 84)
Brickett Cl. HA4: Ruis ... 5E 38
Brick Farm Cl. TW9: Kew ... 1H 115
Brickfield Cl. E9 ... 6J 67
Brickfield Cl. TW8: Bford ... 7C 96
Brickfield Cotts. BR7: Chst ... 5E 142
Brickfield Cotts. SE18 ... 6K 107
Brickfield Farm Gdns. BR6: Farnb
... 4G 173
Brickfield Ho. N1 ... 1E 84
(off Hertford Rd.)
Brickfield La. UB3: Harl ... 6F 93
Brickfield Rd. CR4: Mitc ... 3C 154
Brickfield Rd. CR7: Thor H ... 1B 156
Brickfield Rd. E3 ... 4D 86
Brickfield Rd. SW19 ... 4K 135
Brickfield Rd. SW4 ... 6H 119
(off Parkfield Rd.)
Brickfields HA2: Harr ... 2H 59
(not continuous)
Brickfields Way UB7: W Dray ... 3B 92
Brick Kiln One SE13 ... 3E 122
(off Station Rd.)
Brick Kiln Two SE13 ... 3E 122
(off Station Rd.)
Brick La. E1 ... 3K 9 (4F 85)
Brick La. E2 ... 2K 9 (3F 85)
Brick La. EN1: Enf ... 2C 24
Brick La. EN3: Enf H ... 2D 24
Brick La. HA7: Stan ... 7J 27
Brick La. UB5: N'olt ... 3D 76
Brick Lane Music Hall ... 1B 106
BRICKLAYER'S ARMS ... 4D 102
Bricklayers Arms Distribution Cen.
SE1 ... 4E 102
(not continuous)
Bricklayers St. SE11 ... 4J 19 (4A 102)
Brick St. W1 ... 5J 11 (1F 101)
Brickwall La. HA4: Ruis ... 1G 57
Brickwood Cl. SE26 ... 3H 139
Brickwood Rd. CR0: C'don ... 2E 168
Brideale Cl. SE15 ... 6F 103
Bride Ct. EC4 ... 1A 14 (6B 84)
(off Bride La.)
Bride La. EC4 ... 1A 14 (6B 84)
Bridel M. N1 ... 1B 84
(off Colebrook Row)
Brides M. N7 ... 6K 65
Brides Pl. N1 ... 7E 66
Bride St. N7 ... 6K 65
Bridewain St. SE1 ... 7J 15 (3F 103)
Bridewell Pl. E1 ... 1H 103
Bridewell Pl. EC4 ... 1A 14 (6B 84)
Bridford M. W1 ... 5K 5 (5F 83)
Bridge, The HA3: W'stone ... 4K 41
Bridge, The SW11 ... 7F 101
Bridge App. NW1 ... 7E 64
Bridge Av. W6 ... 4E 98
Bridge Av. W7 ... 5H 77
Bridge Av. Mans. W6 ... 5E 98
(off Bridge Av.)
Bridge Bus. Cen., The UB2: S'hall ... 2E 94
Bridge Cl. EN1: Enf ... 2C 24
Bridge Cl. KT12: Walt T ... 7H 147
Bridge Cl. TW11: Tedd ... 4K 131
Bridge Cl. W10 ... 6F 81
Bridge Ct. E10 ... 1B 68
Bridge Ct. E14 ... 7F 87
(off Newport Av.)
Bridge Ct. HA2: Harr ... 2G 59
Bridge Ct. KT12: Walt T ... 7H 147
(off Bridge St.)
Bridge Dr. N13 ... 4E 32
Bridge End E17 ... 1E 50
Bridge End Cl. KT2: King T ... 1G 151
Bridge End Cres. RM13: Rain ... 3J 91
Bridgefield Ho. W2 ... 6K 81
(off Queensway)
Bridgefield Rd. SM1: Sutt ... 6J 165
Bridgefoot SE1 ... 6F 19 (5J 101)
Bridgefoot TW16: Sun ... 1H 147
Bridge Gdns. KT8: E Mos ... 4H 149
Bridge Gdns. N16 ... 4D 66
Bridge Gdns. TW15: Ashf ... 7E 128
Bridge Ga. N21 ... 7H 23
Bridgehill Cl. HA0: Wemb ... 1D 78
Bridge Ho. CR0: C'don ... 3C 168
(off Surrey St.)
Bridge Ho. E9 ... 6K 67
(off Shepherds La.)
Bridge Ho. NW10 ... 2F 81
(off Chamberlayne Rd.)
Bridge Ho. NW3 ... 7E 64
(off Adelaide Rd.)
Bridge Ho. SE4 ... 4B 122
Bridge Ho. SM2: Sutt ... 6K 165
(off Bridge Rd.)
Bridge Ho. SW1 ... 5J 17 (5F 101)
(off Ebury Bri.)
Bridge Ho. UB7: W Dray ... 1A 92
Bridgehouse Ct. SE1 ... 6A 14 (2B 102)
(off Blackfriars Rd.)
Bridge Ho. Quay E14 ... 1E 104
Bridgeland Rd. E16 ... 7J 87
Bridgelands Cl. BR3: Beck ... 7B 140
Bridge La. NW11 ... 4G 45
Bridge La. SW11 ... 1C 118
Bridge Leisure Cen., The ... 4B 140
Bridgeman Ho. E9 ... 7J 67
(off Frampton Pk. Rd.)
Bridgeman Ho. W14 ... 4H 99
(off Radnor Ter.)
Bridgeman Rd. N1 ... 7K 65
Bridgeman Rd. TW11: Tedd ... 6A 132
Bridgeman St. NW8 ... 2C 82
Bridge Mdws. SE14 ... 6K 103
Bridge M. NW10 ... 6A 62
Bridgemount M. N4 ... 7K 47
BRIDGEN ... 7E 126
Bridgend Rd. SW18 ... 4A 118
Bridgenhall Rd. EN1: Enf ... 1A 24
Bridgen Ho. E1 ... 6H 85
(off Nelson St.)
Bridgen Rd. DA5: Bexl ... 7E 126
Bridge Pde. N21 ... 7H 23
(off Ridge Av.)
Bridgepark SW18 ... 5J 117
Bridge Pk. Community Leisure Cen.
... 7H 61
Bridge Pl. CR0: C'don ... 1D 168
Bridge Pl. SW1 ... 3K 17 (4F 101)
Bridgepoint Lofts E7 ... 7A 70
Bridgepoint Pl. N6 ... 1G 65
(off Hornsey La.)
Bridgeport Pl. E1 ... 1G 103
Bridge Rd. BR3: Beck ... 7B 140
Bridge Rd. DA7: Bex ... 2E 126
Bridge Rd. E11 ... 6F 51
Bridge Rd. E15 ... 7F 69
Bridge Rd. E17 ... 7B 50
Bridge Rd. E6 ... 7D 70
Bridge Rd. HA9: Wemb ... 3G 61
Bridge Rd. KT8: E Mos ... 4H 149
Bridge Rd. KT9: Chess ... 5E 162
Bridge Rd. N22 ... 1J 47
Bridge Rd. N9 ... 3B 34
Bridge Rd. NW10 ... 6A 62
Bridge Rd. SM2: Sutt ... 6K 165
Bridge Rd. SM6: W'gton ... 5F 167
Bridge Rd. TW1: Twick ... 6B 114
Bridge Rd. TW3: Houn ... 3H 113
Bridge Rd. TW3: Isle ... 3H 113
Bridge Rd. TW7: Isle ... 3H 113
Bridge Rd. UB2: S'hall ... 2D 94
Bridge Rd. Dpt. E15 ... 1G 87
Bridge Row CR0: C'don ... 1D 168
Bridges Av. KT8: E Mos ... 6H 149
Bridges Ct. Rd. SW11 ... 3B 118
Bridges Ho. SE5 ... 7D 102
(off Elmington Est.)
Bridgeside Lodge N1 ... 2C 84
(off Wharf Rd.)
Bridges La. CR0: Bedd ... 4J 167
Bridges Pl. SW6 ... 1H 117
Bridges Rd. HA7: Stan ... 5E 26
Bridges Rd. SW19 ... 6K 135
Bridges Rd. M. SW19 ... 6K 135
Bridge St. HA5: Pinn ... 3C 40
Bridge St. KT12: Walt T ... 7G 147
Bridge St. SW1 ... 7E 12 (2J 101)
Bridge St. TW9: Rich ... 5D 114
Bridge St. W4 ... 4K 97
Bridges Wharf SW11 ... 3B 118
Bridge Ter. E15 ... 7F 69
Bridge Theatre ... 5J 15 (1F 103)
(off Tower Bri. Rd.)
Bridgetown Cl. SE19 ... 5E 138
Bridge Vw. W6 ... 5E 98
Bridge Vw. Ct. SE1 ... 3E 102
(off Grange Rd.)
Bridge Wlk. IG1: Ilf ... 2F 71
(within The Exchange)
Bridge Wlk. SE8 ... 6D 104
(off Copperas St.)
Bridgewalk Hgts. SE1 ... 6F 15 (2D 102)
(off Weston St.)
Bridgewater Cl. BR7: Chst ... 3J 161
Bridgewater Gdns. HA8: Edg ... 2F 43
Bridgewater Highwalk EC2
... 5C 8 (5C 84)
(off Beech St.)
Bridgewater Ho. E14 ... 6G 87
(off Lookout Lane)
Bridgewater Rd. E15 ... 1E 86
Bridgewater Rd. HA0: Wemb ... 6C 60
Bridgewater Sq. EC2 ... 5C 8 (5C 84)
Bridgewater St. EC2 ... 5C 8 (5C 84)
Bridge Way N11 ... 3B 32
Bridge Way NW11 ... 5H 45
Bridge Way TW2: Whitt ... 7G 113
Bridge Way UB10: Ick ... 5D 56
Bridgeway HA0: Wemb ... 7E 60
Bridgeway IG11: Bark ... 7K 71
Bridgeway St. NW1 ... 2G 83
Bridge Wharf E2 ... 2K 85
Bridge Wharf N1 ... 2K 83
(off Calshot St.)
Bridge Wharf Rd. TW7: Isle ... 3B 114
Bridgewood Cl. SE20 ... 7H 139
Bridgewood Rd. KT4: Wor Pk ... 4C 164
Bridgewood Rd. SW16 ... 7H 137
Bridge Yd. SE1 ... 4F 15 (1D 102)
Bridgford St. SW18 ... 3A 136
Bridgman Rd. W4 ... 3J 97
Bridgnorth Ho. SE15 ... 6G 103
(off Friary Est.)
Bridgwater Ho. W2 ... 6A 82
(off Hallfield Est.)
Bridgwater Rd. HA4: Ruis ... 4J 57
Bridle Cl. KT1: King T ... 4D 150
Bridle Cl. KT19: Ewe ... 5K 163
Bridle Cl. TW16: Sun ... 3J 147
Bridle La. TW1: Twick ... 6B 114
Bridle La. W1 ... 2B 12 (7G 83)
Bridle M. E1 ... 6G 85
Bridle M. EN5: Barn ... 4C 20
Bridle Path CR0: Bedd ... 3J 167
Bridle Path, The IG8: Wfd G ... 7B 36
Bridlepath Way TW14: Bedf ... 7G 111
Bridle Rd. CR0: C'don ... 3C 170
Bridle Rd. CR2: Sande ... 7G 169
Bridle Rd. HA5: Eastc ... 6K 39
Bridle Rd. KT10: Clay ... 6B 162
Bridle Way BR6: Farnb ... 4G 173
Bridle Way CR0: C'don ... 5C 170
Bridle Way, The SM6: W'gton ... 4G 167
Bridlington Rd. N9 ... 7C 24
Bridport SE17 ... 5D 102
(off Cadiz St.)
Bridport Av. RM7: Rom ... 6H 55
Bridport Ho. N1 ... 1D 84
(off Bridport Pl.)
Bridport Ho. N18 ... 5A 34
(off College Gdns.)
Bridport Pl. N1 ... 1D 84
(not continuous)
Bridport Rd. CR7: Thor H ... 3A 156
Bridport Rd. N18 ... 5K 33
Bridport Rd. UB6: G'frd ... 1F 77
Bridport Ter. SW8 ... 1H 119
(off Deeley Rd.)
Bridstow Pl. W2 ... 6J 81
Brief St. SE5 ... 1B 120
Brierfield NW1 ... 1G 83
(off Arlington Rd.)
Brierley CR0: New Ad ... 6D 170
(not continuous)
Brierley Av. N9 ... 1D 34
Brierley Cl. SE25 ... 4G 157
Brierley Ct. W7 ... 7J 77
Brierley Rd. E11 ... 4F 69
Brierley Rd. SW12 ... 2G 137
Brierly Gdns. E2 ... 2J 85
Brigade Cl. HA2: Harr ... 2H 59
Brigade St. SE3 ... 2H 123
(off Tranquil Va.)
Brigadier Av. EN2: Enf ... 1H 23
Brigadier Hill EN2: Enf ... 1H 23
Brigadier Ho. NW9 ... 2B 44
(off Heritage Av.)
Briggeford Cl. E5 ... 2G 67
Briggs Cl. CR4: Mitc ... 1F 155
Briggs Ho. E2 ... 1K 9 (3F 85)
(off Chambord St.)
Bright Cl. DA17: Belv ... 4D 108
Brightfield Rd. SE12 ... 5G 123
Bright Ho. KT1: King T ... 3D 150
(off Kingston Hall Rd.)
Brightling Rd. SE4 ... 6B 122
Brightlingsea Pl. E14 ... 7B 86
Brightman Rd. SW18 ... 1B 136
Brighton Av. E17 ... 5B 50
Brighton Bldgs. SE1 ... 3E 102
(off Tower Bri. Rd.)
Brighton Cl. UB10: Hil ... 7D 56
Brighton Dr. UB5: N'olt ... 6E 58
Brighton Gro. SE14 ... 1A 122
Brighton Ho. SE5 ... 1D 120
(off Camberwell Grn.)
Brighton Rd. CR2: S Croy ... 5C 168

Brighton Rd. – Brookfield Cres.

Brighton Rd. E6 3E 88
(not continuous)
Brighton Rd. KT6: Surb 6C 150
Brighton Rd. N16 4E 66
Brighton Rd. N2 2A 46
Brighton Ter. SW9 4K 119
Brightside, The EN3: Enf H 1E 24
Brightside Rd. SE13 6F 123
Bright St. E14 5D 86
Brightwell Cl. CR0: C'don 1A 168
Brightwell Ct. N7 5K 65
(off Mackenzie Rd.)
Brightwell Cres. SW17 5D 136
Brightwen Gro. HA7: Stan 2F 27
Brig M. SE8 6C 104
Brigstock Ho. SE5 2C 120
Brigstock Rd. CR7: Thor H 5A 156
Brigstock Rd. DA17: Belv 4H 109
Brill Pl. NW1 1D 6 (2H 83)
Brim Hill N2 4A 46
Brimpsfield Cl. SE2 3B 108
(not continuous)
BRIMSDOWN 2G 25
Brimsdown Av. EN3: Enf H 2F 25
Brimsdown Ho. E3 4D 86
Brimsdown Ind. Est. EN3: Brim Lockfield Av. 1G 25
Brimsdown Ind. Est. EN3: Brim Stockingswater La. 2G 25
Brimstone Ho. E15 7G 69
(off Victoria St.)
Brindle Ga. DA15: Sidc 1J 143
Brindlewick Gdns. BR3: Beck 6C 140
Brindley Cl. DA7: Bex 3H 127
Brindley Cl. HA0: Wemb 1D 78
Brindley Ct. HA7: Stan 7J 27
Brindley Ho. W2 5J 81
(off Alfred Rd.)
Brindley St. SE14 1B 122
Brindley Way BR1: Broml 5J 141
Brindley Way UB1: S'hall 7F 77
Brindwood Rd. E4 3G 35
Brine Ho. E3 2A 86
(off St Stephen's Rd.)
Brinkburn Cl. HA8: Edg 3H 43
Brinkburn Cl. SE2 4A 108
Brinkburn Gdns. HA8: Edg 3G 43
Brinkley KT1: King T 2G 151
Brinkley Rd. KT4: Wor Pk 2D 164
Brinklow Cres. SE18 7F 107
Brinklow Ho. W2 5K 81
(off Torquay St.)
Brinkworth Rd. IG5: Ilf 3C 52
Brinkworth Way E9 6B 68
Brinsdale Rd. NW4 3F 45
Brinsley Ho. E1 6J 85
(off Tarling St.)
Brinsley Rd. HA3: Hrw W 2H 41
Brinsworth Cl. TW2: Twick 1H 131
Brinsworth Ho. TW2: Twick 2H 131
Brinton Wlk. SE1 5A 14 (1B 102)
(off Nicholson St.)
Brion Pl. E14 5E 86
Brisbane Av. SW19 1K 153
Brisbane Ho. W12 7D 80
(off White City Est.)
Brisbane Rd. E10 2D 68
Brisbane Rd. IG1: Ilf 7F 53
Brisbane Rd. W13 2A 96
Brisbane St. SE5 7D 102
Briscoe Cl. E11 2H 69
Briscoe M. TW2: Twick 2H 131
Briscoe Rd. SW19 6B 136
Briset Rd. SE9 3B 124
Briset St. EC1 4A 8 (4B 84)
Briset Way N7 2K 65
Bristol Av. NW9 2B 44
Bristol Cl. SM6: W'gton 7J 167
Bristol Cl. TW19: Stanw 6A 110
Bristol Cl. TW4: Houn 7E 112
Bristol Ct. TW19: Stanw 6A 110
Bristol Gdns. SW15 7E 116
Bristol Gdns. W9 4K 81
Bristol Ho. IG11: Bark 7A 72
(off Margaret Bondfield Av.)
Bristol Ho. SE11 2J 19 (3A 102)
(off Lambeth Wlk.)
Bristol Ho. SW1 5G 17 (5E 100)
(off Lwr. Sloane St.)
Bristol Ho. WC1 5F 7 (5J 83)
(off Southampton Row)
Bristol M. W9 4K 81
Bristol Pk. Rd. E17 4A 50
Bristol Rd. E7 6A 70
Bristol Rd. SM4: Mord 5A 154
Bristol Rd. UB6: G'frd 1F 77
Bristol Wlk. NW6 2J 81
(off Alpha Pl.)
Briston Gro. N8 6J 47
Briston M. NW7 7H 29
Bristow Ct. E8 1H 85
(off Triangle Rd.)
Bristowe Cl. SW2 6A 120
Bristow Rd. CR0: Bedd 4J 167
Bristow Rd. DA7: Bex 1E 126
Bristow Rd. SE19 5E 138
Bristow Rd. TW3: Houn 3G 113
Britannia Bldg. N1 1E 8 (3D 84)
(off Ebenezer St.)
Britannia Bus. Cen. NW2 4F 63
Britannia Cl. SW4 4H 119
Britannia Cl. UB5: N'olt 3B 76
Britannia Ct. KT2: King T 1D 150
(off Skerne Wlk.)
Britannia Ct. UB7: W Dray 3A 92
Britannia Ga. E16 1J 105
BRITANNIA JUNC. 1F 83
Britannia La. TW2: Whitt 7G 113
Britannia Leisure Cen. 1D 84
Britannia Rd. E14 4C 104
Britannia Rd. IG1: Ilf 3F 71
Britannia Rd. KT5: Surb 7F 151
Britannia Rd. N12 3F 31
Britannia Rd. SW6 7K 99
Britannia Row N1 1B 84
Britannia St. WC1 1G 7 (3K 83)
Britannia Wlk. N1 1E 8 (2D 84)
(not continuous)
Britannia Way NW10 4H 79
Britannia Way SW6 7K 99
(off Britannia Rd.)
Britannia Way TW19: Stanw 7A 110
Britannic Highwalk EC2 6E 8 (5D 84)
(off Moor La.)
British Gro. W4 5B 98
British Gro. Nth. W4 5B 98
British Gro. Pas. W4 5B 98
British Gro. Sth. W4 5B 98
British Legion Rd. E4 2C 36
British Mus. 6E 6 (5J 83)
British St. E3 3B 86
British Telecom Cen. 7C 8 (6C 84)
(off Newgate St.)
British Transport Police 6C 6 (5H 83)
(off Whitfield St.)
British Wharf Ind. Est. SE14 5K 103
Britley Ho. E14 6B 86
(off Copenhagen Pl.)
Brittain Ct. SE9 1C 142
Brittain Rd. RM8: Dag 3E 72
Brittany Ho. EN2: Enf 1H 23
Brittany Point SE11 4J 19 (4A 102)
(off Lollard Street)
Britten Cl. NW11 1K 63
Britten Ct. E15 2F 87
Brittenden Cl. BR6: Chels 6K 173
Brittenden Pde. BR6: Chels 6K 173
Britten Dr. UB1: S'hall 6E 76
Britten Ho. SW3 5C 16 (5C 100)
(off Britten St.)
Britten St. SW3 6C 16 (5C 100)
Britten Theatre 1A 16 (3B 100)
(off Prince Consort Rd.)
Brittidge Rd. NW10 7A 62
Britton Cl. SE6 7F 123
Britton St. EC1 4A 8 (4B 84)
Brixham Cres. HA4: Ruis 1J 57
Brixham Gdns. IG3: Ilf 5J 71
Brixham Rd. DA16: Well 1D 126
Brixham St. E16 1E 106
BRIXTON 4K 119
Brixton Hill SW2 7J 119
Brixton Hill Ct. SW2 5K 119
Brixton Hill Pl. SW2 7J 119
Brixton Oval SW2 4A 120
Brixton Recreation Cen. 3A 120
(off Brixton Sta. Rd.)
Brixton Rd. SE11 7J 19 (6A 102)
Brixton Rd. SW9 4A 120
Brixton Sta. Rd. SW9 3A 120
Brixton Water La. SW2 5K 119
Broadacre Cl. UB10: Ick 3D 56
Broadash Cl. SW16 3A 138
Broadbent Cl. N6 1F 65
Broadbent St. W1 2J 11 (7F 83)
Broadberry Ct. N18 6C 34
Broadbridge Cl. SE3 7J 105
Broad Comn. Est. N16 1G 67
(off Osbaldeston Rd.)
Broadcoombe CR2: Sels 7J 169
Broad Ct. WC2 1F 13 (6J 83)
Broadcroft Av. HA7: Stan 2D 42
Broadcroft Rd. BR5: Pet W 7H 161
Broadeaves Cl. CR2: S Croy 5E 168
Broadfield NW6 6K 63
Broadfield Cl. CR0: Wadd 2K 167
Broadfield Cl. NW2 3E 62
Broadfield Ct. HA2: Harr 1F 41
(off Broadfields)
Broadfield Ct. WD23: B Hea 2D 26
Broadfield La. NW1 7J 65
Broadfield Pde. HA8: Edg 3C 28
(off Glengall Rd.)
Broadfield Rd. SE6 7G 123
Broadfields HA2: Harr 2F 41
Broadfields KT8: E Mos 6J 149
Broadfields Av. HA8: Edg 4C 28
Broadfields Av. N21 6F 23
Broadfields Hgts. HA8: Edg 4C 28
Broadfield Sq. EN1: Enf 2C 24
Broadfields Way NW10 5B 62
Broadfield Way IG9: Buck H 3F 37
Broadford Ho. E1 4A 86
(off Commodore St.)
Broadgate EC2 6G 9 (5E 84)
(off Broadgate Circ.)
Broadgate Circ. EC2 6G 9 (5E 84)
Broadgate Circle 6G 9 (5E 84)
Broadgate Plaza EC2 5H 9 (5E 84)
Broadgate Rd. E16 6B 88
Broadgates Av. EN4: Had W 1E 20
Broadgates Ct. SE11 6K 19 (5A 102)
(off Cleaver St.)
Broadgates Rd. SW18 1B 136
Broadgate Twr. EC2 4H 9 (4E 84)
BROAD GREEN 7B 156
Broad Grn. Av. CR0: C'don 7B 156
Broadhead Apts. E3 3B 86
(off St Clements Av.)
Broadhead Strand NW9 1B 44
Broadheath Dr. BR7: Chst 5D 142
Broadhinton Rd. SW4 3F 119
Broadhurst Av. HA8: Edg 4C 28
Broadhurst Av. IG3: Ilf 4K 71
Broadhurst Cl. NW6 6A 64
Broadhurst Cl. TW10: Rich 5F 115
Broadhurst Gdns. HA4: Ruis 2A 58
Broadhurst Gdns. NW6 6K 63
Broadis Way RM13: Rain 2K 91
Broadlands E17 3A 50
Broadlands TW13: Hanw 3E 130
Broadlands Av. EN3: Enf H 3C 24
Broadlands Av. SW16 2J 137
Broadlands Av. TW17: Shep 6E 146
Broadlands Cl. EN3: Enf H 3D 24
Broadlands Cl. N6 7E 46
Broadlands Cl. SW16 2J 137
Broadlands Ct. TW9: Kew 7G 97
(off Kew Gdns. Rd.)
Broadlands Lodge N6 7D 46
Broadlands Rd. BR1: Broml 4K 141
Broadlands Rd. N6 7D 46
Broadlands Way KT3: N Mald 6B 152
Broad La. EC2 5G 9 (5E 84)
Broad La. N15 4F 49
Broad La. N17 4G 49
Broad La. N8 5K 47
Broad La. TW12: Hamp 7D 130
Broad Lawn SE9 2E 142
Broadlawns Ct. HA3: Hrw W 1K 41
Broadley St. NW8 5B 4 (5B 82)
Broadley Ter. NW1 4D 4 (4C 82)
Broadmayne SE17 5D 102
(off Portland St.)
Broadmead SE6 3C 140
Broadmead W14 4G 99
Broadmead Av. KT4: Wor Pk 7C 152
Broadmead Cen. IG8: Wfd G 7F 37
(off Navestock Cres.)
Broadmead Cl. HA5: Hat E 1C 40
Broadmead Cl. TW12: Hamp 6E 130
Broadmead Ct. IG8: Wfd G 6D 36
Broadmead Rd. IG8: Wfd G 6D 36
(not continuous)
Broadmead Rd. UB4: Yead 4C 76
Broadmead Rd. UB5: N'olt 4C 76
Broad Oak IG8: Wfd G 5E 36
Broad Oak TW16: Sun 6H 129
Broad Oak Cl. E4 5H 35
Broadoak Ct. SW9 3A 120
(off Gresham Rd.)
Broadoak Ho. NW6 1K 81
(off Mortimer Cres.)
Broadoak Rd. DA8: Erith 7K 109
Broadoaks KT6: Surb 2H 163
Broadoaks Way BR2: Broml 5H 159
Broad Pas. W3 1B 98
Broad Sanctuary SW1 7D 12 (2H 101)
Broadstone NW1 7H 65
(off Agar Gro.)
Broadstone Ho. SW8 7K 101
(off Dorset Rd.)
Broadstone Pl. W1 6G 5 (5E 82)
Broad St. RM10: Dag 7G 73
Broad St. TW11: Tedd 6K 131
Broad St. Av. EC2 6G 9 (5E 84)
Broad St. Mkt. RM10: Dag 7G 73
Broad St. Pl. EC2 6F 9 (5D 84)
(off Blomfield St.)
Broadview NW9 6G 43
Broadview Pl. E5 1J 67
Broadview Rd. SW16 7H 137
Broad Wlk. W1 Hyde Pk. 3F 11 (7D 82)
Broad Wlk. NW1 Regent's Pk. 1E 82
Broad Wlk. N21 2E 32
Broad Wlk. SE3 2A 124
Broad Wlk. TW5: Hest 1B 112
Broad Wlk. TW9: Kew 7F 97
Broadwalk E18 3H 51
Broadwalk HA2: Harr 5E 40
Broad Wlk., The KT8: E Mos 4K 149
Broad Wlk., The W8 1K 99
Broadwalk, The HA6: Nwood 2E 38
Broadwalk Ct. W8 1J 99
(off Palace Gdns. Ter.)
Broadwalk Ho. EC2 4G 9 (4E 84)
(off Appold St.)
Broadwalk Ho. SW7 2A 100
(off Hyde Pk. Ga.)
Broad Wlk. La. NW11 7H 45
Broadwalk Shop. Cen. Edgware 6C 28
Broadwall SE1 4K 13 (1A 102)
Broadwater Farm Est. N17 2D 48
Broadwater Gdns. BR6: Farnb 4F 173
Broadwater Rd. N17 1E 48
Broadwater Rd. SE28 3H 107
Broadwater Rd. SW17 4C 136
Broadway DA6: Bex 4E 126
(not continuous)
Broadway DA7: Bex 4H 127
Broadway E15 7F 69
Broadway IG11: Bark 1G 89
Broadway SW1 1C 18 (3H 101)
Broadway W13 1A 96
Broadway W7 1J 95
Broadway, The CR0: Bedd 4J 167
Broadway, The E13 2K 87
Broadway, The E4 6A 36
Broadway, The HA2: Harr 2H 59
Broadway, The HA3: W'stone 2J 41
Broadway, The HA6: Nwood 2J 39
Broadway, The HA7: Stan 5H 27
Broadway, The HA9: Wemb 3E 60
Broadway, The IG8: Wfd G 6E 36
Broadway, The KT7: T Ditt 7J 149
Broadway, The N11 5J 31
Broadway, The N14 1C 32
(off The Bourne)
Broadway, The N22 2A 48
Broadway, The N8 6J 47
Broadway, The N9 3B 34
Broadway, The NW7 5F 29
Broadway, The RM8: Dag 1F 73
Broadway, The SM1: Sutt 5A 166
Broadway, The SM3: Cheam 6G 165
Broadway, The SW13 2A 116
Broadway, The SW19 6H 135
Broadway, The UB1: S'hall 7B 76
Broadway, The UB6: G'frd 4G 77
Broadway, The W3 2G 97
(off Ridgeway Dr.)
Broadway, The W5 7D 78
Broadway Arc. W6 4E 98
(off Hammersmith B'way.)
Broadway Av. CR0: C'don 5D 156
Broadway Av. TW1: Twick 6B 114
Broadway Cen., The 4E 98
B'way. Chambers W6 4E 98
(off Hammersmith B'way.)
Broadway Cl. IG8: Wfd G 6E 36
Broadway Ct. BR3: Beck 3E 158
Broadway Ct. SW19 6J 135
Broadway Gdns. CR4: Mitc 4C 154
Broadway Gdns. IG8: Wfd G 6E 36
Broadway Ho. BR1: Broml High St. 3J 159
Broadway Ho. BR1: Broml 5F 141
(off Bromley Rd.)
Broadway Ho. E8 1H 85
(off Ada St.)
Broadway Mans. SW6 7J 99
(off Fulham Rd.)
Broadway Mkt. E8 1H 85
(not continuous)
Broadway Mkt. IG6: Ilf 1H 53
(not continuous)
Broadway Mkt. SW17 4D 136
Broadway Mkt. M. E8 1G 85
Broadway M. E5 7F 49
Broadway M. IG8: Ilf 6E 36
Broadway M. N13 5E 32
Broadway M. N21 1G 33
Broadway Pde. E4 6K 35
(off The Broadway)
Broadway Pde. HA2: Harr 5F 41
Broadway Pde. N8 6J 47
Broadway Pde. UB3: Hayes 1J 93
Broadway Pl. SW19 6H 135
Broadway Retail Pk. 4F 63
Broadway Shop. Cen. Bexleyheath 4G 127
Broadway Shop. Mall St James's Park 1C 18 (3H 101)
Broadway Sq. DA6: Bex 4F 127
Broadway Theatre Barking, The 1G 89
Broadway Theatre Catford, The 7D 122
Broadway Wlk. E14 2C 104
Broadwell Ct. TW5: Hest 1B 112
(off Springwell Rd.)
Broadwell Pde. NW6 6K 63
(off Broadhurst Gdns.)
Broadwick St. W1 2B 12 (7G 83)
Broadwood Av. HA4: Ruis 6F 39
Broadwood Ter. W8 4H 99
Broad Yd. EC1 4A 8 (4B 84)
Brocade Cl. SM6: W'gton 2F 167
Brocas Cl. NW3 7C 64
Brockbridge Ho. SW15 6B 116
Brockdene Dr. BR2: Kes 4B 172
Brockdish Av. IG11: Bark 5K 71
Brockenhurst KT8: W Mole 5D 148
Brockenhurst Av. KT4: Wor Pk 1A 164
Brockenhurst Gdns. IG1: Ilf 5G 71
Brockenhurst Gdns. NW7 5F 29
Brockenhurst M. N18 4B 34
Brockenhurst Rd. CR0: C'don 7H 157
Brockenhurst Way SW16 2H 155
Brocket Ho. SW8 2H 119
Brockham Cl. SW19 5H 135
Brockham Ct. CR2: S Croy 5C 168
Brockham Cres. CR0: New Ad 7F 171
Brockham Dr. IG2: Ilf 6F 53
Brockham Dr. SW2 7K 119
Brockham Ho. NW1 1G 83
(off Bayham Pl.)
Brockham Ho. SW2 7K 119
(off Brockham Dr.)
Brockham St. SE1 7D 14 (3C 102)
Brockhurst Cl. HA7: Stan 6E 26
Brockill Cres. SE4 4A 122
Brocklebank Ho. E16 1E 106
(off Glenister St.)
Brocklebank Retail Pk. 4K 105
Brocklebank Rd. SE7 4K 105
Brocklebank Rd. SW18 7A 118
Brocklehurst St. SE14 7K 103
Brocklesby Rd. SE25 4H 157
BROCKLEY 4K 121
Brockley Av. HA7: Stan 3K 27
Brockley Cl. HA7: Stan 4K 27
Brockley Cres. RM5: Col R 1J 55
Brockley Cross SE4 3A 122
Brockley Cross Bus. Cen. SE4 3A 122
Brockley Footpath SE15 3J 121
(not continuous)
Brockley Gdns. SE4 2B 122
Brockley Gro. SE4 5B 122
Brockley Hall Rd. SE4 5A 122
Brockley Hill HA7: Stan 1H 27
Brockley Jack Theatre 5A 122
Brockley M. SE4 5A 122
Brockley Pk. SE23 7A 122
Brockley Ri. SE23 1A 140
Brockley Rd. SE4 3B 122
Brockleyside HA7: Stan 4K 27
Brockley Vw. SE23 7A 122
Brockley Way SE4 5K 121
Brockman Ri. BR1: Broml 4F 141
Brockmer Ho. E1 7H 85
(off Crowder St.)
Brock Pl. E3 4D 86
Brock Rd. E13 5K 87
Brocks Dr. SM3: Cheam 3G 165
Brockshot Cl. TW8: Bford 5D 96
Brock St. NW1 3A 6 (4G 83)
(off Triton Sq.)
Brock St. SE15 3J 121
Brockway Cl. E11 2G 69
Brockweir E2 2J 85
(off Cyprus St.)
Brockwell Av. BR3: Beck 5D 158
Brockwell Cl. BR5: St M Cry 5K 161
Brockwell Ct. SW2 5A 120
Brockwell Ho. SE11 7H 19 (6K 101)
(off Vauxhall St.)
Brockwell Pk. 6B 120
Brockwell Pk. Gdns. SE24 7A 120
Brockwell Pk. Lido 6B 120
Brockwell Pk. Row SW2 7A 120
Brockwell Pas. SE24 6B 120
Brodia Rd. N16 3E 66
Brodick Ho. E3 2B 86
(off Saxon Rd.)
Brodie Ho. SE1 5F 103
(off Cooper's Rd.)
Brodie Rd. E4 1K 35
Brodie Rd. EN2: Enf 1H 23
Brodie St. SE1 5F 103
Brodlove La. E1 7K 85
Brodrick Gro. SE2 4B 108
Brodrick Rd. SW17 2C 136
Brody Ho. E1 6J 9 (5F 85)
(off Strype St.)
Brograve Gdns. BR3: Beck 2D 158
Broken Wharf EC4 2C 14 (7C 84)
Brokesley St. E3 3B 86
Broke Wlk. E8 1F 85
Bromar Rd. SE5 3E 120
Bromefield HA7: Stan 1C 42
Bromehead St. E1 6J 85
Bromell's Rd. SW4 4G 119
Brome Rd. SE9 3D 124
Bromfelde Rd. SW4 3H 119
Bromfelde Wlk. SW4 2H 119
Bromfield Ct. SE16 3G 103
(off Ben Smith Way)
Bromfield St. N1 1A 84
Bromhall Rd. RM8: Dag 6B 72
Bromhall Rd. RM9: Dag 6B 72
Bromhead Rd. E1 6J 85
(off Jubilee St.)
Bromhedge SE9 3D 142
Bromholm Rd. SE2 3B 108
Bromleigh Ct. SE23 2G 139
Bromleigh Ho. SE1 7J 15 (3F 103)
(off St Saviour's Est.)
BROMLEY 2J 159
BROMLEY 3D 86
Bromley Av. BR1: Broml 7G 141
Bromley Coll. BR1: Broml 1J 159
BROMLEY COMMON 7C 160
Bromley Comn. BR2: Broml 4A 160
Bromley Cres. BR2: Broml 3H 159
Bromley Cres. HA4: Ruis 4H 57
Bromley FC 5K 159
Bromley Gdns. BR2: Broml 3H 159
Bromley Golf Course 7C 160
Bromley Gro. BR2: Broml 2F 159
Bromley Hall Rd. E14 5E 86
Bromley High St. E3 3D 86
Bromley Hill BR1: Broml 6G 141
Bromley Ho. BR1: Broml 1J 159
(off North St.)
Bromley Ind. Cen. BR1: Broml 3B 160
Bromley La. BR7: Chst 7G 143
Bromley Little Theatre 1J 159
Bromley Pk. BR1: Broml 1H 159
BROMLEY PARK 1G 159
Bromley Pl. W1 5A 6 (5G 83)
Bromley Rd. BR1: Broml 4F 141
Bromley Rd. BR2: Broml 2F 159
Bromley Rd. BR3: Beck 1D 158
Bromley Rd. BR7: Chst 1F 161
Bromley Rd. E10 6D 50
Bromley Rd. E17 3C 50
Bromley Rd. N17 1F 49
Bromley Rd. N18 3J 33
Bromley Rd. SE6 1D 140
Bromley St. E1 5K 85
Bromley Tennis Cen. 3H 173
BROMPTON 2D 16 (3C 100)
Brompton Arc. SW3 7E 10 (2D 100)
(off Brompton Rd.)
Brompton Cemetery 6K 99
Brompton Cl. SE20 2G 157
Brompton Cl. TW4: Houn 5D 112
Brompton Cotts. SW10 6A 100
(off Hollywood Rd.)
Brompton Ct. BR1: Broml 1J 159
(off Tweedy Rd.)
Brompton Gro. N2 4C 46
Brompton M. N12 6F 31
Brompton Pk. Cres. SW6 6K 99
Brompton Pl. SW3 1D 16 (3C 100)
Brompton Rd. SW1 7E 10 (2D 100)
Brompton Rd. SW3 3C 16 (4C 100)
Brompton Rd. SW7 2C 16 (3C 100)
Brompton Sq. SW3 1C 16 (3C 100)
Brompton Ter. SE18 1D 124
Brompton Vs. SW6 6J 99
(off Lillie Rd.)
Bromwich Av. N6 2E 64
Bromyard Av. W3 7A 80
Bromyard Ho. SE15 7H 103
(off Commercial Way)
Bromyard Ho. W3 1B 98
Bron Ct. NW6 1J 81
BRONDESBURY 7H 63
Brondesbury Ct. NW2 6F 63
Brondesbury M. NW6 7J 63
BRONDESBURY PARK 1E 80
Brondesbury Pk. NW2 6E 62
Brondesbury Pk. NW6 7E 62
Brondesbury Pk. Mans. NW6 1G 81
(off Salusbury Rd.)
Brondesbury Rd. NW6 2H 81
Brondesbury Vs. NW6 2H 81
Bronhill Ter. N17 1G 49
Bronsart Rd. SW6 7G 99
Bronson Rd. SW20 2F 153
Bronte Cl. DA8: Erith 7H 109
Bronte Cl. E7 4J 69
Bronte Cl. IG2: Ilf 4E 52
Bronte Ct. W14 3F 99
(off Girdler's Rd.)
Bronte Ct. W3 2G 97
Bronte Ho. N16 5E 66
Bronte Ho. SW17 3B 136
(off Grosvenor Way)
Bronte Ho. SW4 7G 119
Bronti Cl. SE17 5C 102
Bronwen Ct. NW8 2A 4 (3B 82)
(off Grove End Rd.)
Bronze Age Way DA17: Belv 2H 109
Bronze Age Way DA8: Erith 4K 109
Bronze St. SE8 7C 104
Bronze Wlk. W12 7F 81
Brook Av. HA8: Edg 6C 28
Brook Av. HA9: Wemb 2F 61
Brook Av. RM10: Dag 7H 73
Brookbank Av. W7 5H 77
Brookbank Rd. SE13 3C 122
Brook Cl. HA4: Ruis 7G 39
Brook Cl. NW7 7B 30
Brook Cl. SW17 2E 136
Brook Cl. SW20 3D 152
Brook Cl. TW19: Stanw 7B 110
Brook Cl. W3 1G 97
Brook Ct. IG11: Bark Sebastian Ct. 1K 89
Brook Ct. IG11: Bark Spring Pl. 2G 89
Brook Ct. BR3: Beck 1B 158
Brook Ct. E11 3G 69
Brook Ct. E17 3A 50
Brook Ct. EC4 2E 14 (7D 84)
(off Laurence Pountney La.)
Brook Ct. HA8: Edg 5C 28
Brook Ct. SE12 3A 142
Brook Cres. E4 4H 35
Brook Cres. N9 4C 34
Brookdale N11 4B 32
Brookdale Rd. SE6 Catford B'way 7D 122
Brookdale Rd. SE6 Medusa Rd. 6D 122
Brookdale Rd. DA5: Bexl 6E 126
Brookdale Rd. E17 3C 50
Brookdales NW11 4G 45
Brookdene Rd. SE18 4J 107
Brook Dr. HA1: Harr 4G 41
Brook Dr. HA4: Ruis 7G 39
Brook Dr. SE11 2K 19 (3A 102)
Brooke Av. HA2: Harr 3G 59
Brooke Cl. WD23: Bush 1B 26
Brooke Ct. W10 2G 81
(off Kilburn La.)
Brooke Ho. SE14 1A 122
Brooke Ho. WD23: Bush 1B 26
Brookehowse Rd. SE6 2C 140
Brookend Rd. DA15: Sidc 1J 143
Brooke Rd. E17 4E 50
Brooke Rd. E5 3G 67
Brooke Rd. N16 3F 67
Brooke's Ct. EC1 6J 7 (5A 84)
Brooke's Mkt. EC1 5J 7 (5A 84)
(off Dorrington St.)
Brooke St. EC1 6J 7 (5A 84)
Brooke Way WD23: Bush 1B 26
Brookfield N6 3E 64
Brookfield Av. E17 4E 50
Brookfield Av. NW7 6J 29
Brookfield Av. SM1: Sutt 4B 166
Brookfield Av. W5 4D 78
Brookfield Ct. NW7 6J 29
Brookfield Ct. N12 4E 30
Brookfield Ct. UB6: G'frd 3G 77
Brookfield Cres. HA3: Kenton 5E 42
Brookfield Cres. NW7 6J 29

Brookfield Gdns. KT10: Clay 6A 162
Brookfield Pk. NW5 3F 65
Brookfield Path IG8: Wfd G 6B 36
Brookfield Rd. E9 6A 68
Brookfield Rd. N9 3B 34
Brookfield Rd. W4 2K 97
Brookfields EN3: Pond E 4E 24
Brookfields Av. CR4: Mitc 5C 154
Brook Gdns. E4 4J 35
Brook Gdns. KT2: King T 1J 151
Brook Gdns. SW13 3B 116
Brook Ga. W1 3F 11 (7D 82)
BROOK GREEN 4F 99
Brook Grn. W6 3F 99
Brook Grn. Flats W14 3F 99
(off Dunsany Rd.)
Brookhill Cl. EN4: E Barn 5H 21
Brookhill Cl. SE18 5F 107
Brookhill Rd. EN4: E Barn 5H 21
Brookhill Rd. SE18 6F 107
Brook Ho. E1 7G 85
(off Fletcher St.)
Brook Ho. W6 4E 98
(off Shepherd's Bush Rd.)
Brookhouse Gdns. E4 4B 36
Brook Ho's. NW1 2G 83
(off Cranleigh St.)
Brook Ind. Est. UB4: Yead 1B 94
Brooking Cl. RM8: Dag 3C 72
Brooking Rd. E7 5J 69
Brookland Cl. NW11 4J 45
Brookland Gth. NW11 4K 45
Brookland Hill NW11 4K 45
Brookland Ri. NW11 4J 45
Brooklands, The TW7: Isle 1H 113
Brooklands App. RM1: Rom 4K 55
Brooklands Av. DA15: Sidc 2H 143
Brooklands Av. SW19 2K 135
Brooklands Cl. RM7: Rom 4K 55
Brooklands Cl. TW16: Sun 1G 147
Brooklands Ct. CR4: Mitc 2B 154
Brooklands Ct. KT1: King T 4D 150
(off Surbiton Rd.)
Brooklands Ct. N21 5J 23
Brooklands Ct. NW6 7H 63
Brooklands Dr. UB6: G'frd 1C 78
Brooklands La. RM7: Rom 4K 55
(not continuous)
Brooklands Pk. SE3 3J 123
Brooklands Pas. SW8 1H 119
Brooklands Pl. TW12: Hamp H 5F 131
Brooklands Rd. KT7: T Ditt 1A 162
Brooklands Rd. RM7: Rom 4K 55
Brooklands Ter. TW16: Sun 4J 147
Brook La. BR1: Broml 6J 141
Brook La. DA5: Bex 6D 126
Brook La. DA5: Bexl 6D 126
Brook La. SE3 2K 123
Brook La. Bus. Cen. TW8: Bford 5D 96
Brook La. Nth. TW8: Bford 5D 96
(not continuous)
Brooklea Cl. NW9 1A 44
Brook Lodge NW11 5F 45
(off Nth. Circular Rd.)
Brook Lodge RM7: Rom 4K 55
(off Brooklands Rd.)
Brooklyn SE20 7G 139
Brooklyn Av. SE25 4H 157
Brooklyn Cl. SM5: Cars 2C 166
Brooklyn Ct. W12 1E 98
(off Frithville Gdns.)
Brooklyn Gro. SE25 4H 157
Brooklyn Rd. BR2: Broml 5B 160
Brooklyn Rd. SE25 4H 157
Brookman Ho. E3 2B 86
(off Mostyn Gro.)
Brookmarsh Ind. Est. SE10 7D 104
Brook Mead KT19: Ewe 6A 164
Brookmead CR0: Bedd 6G 155
Brookmead Av. BR1: Broml 5D 160
Brookmead Ind. Est. CR0: Bedd 6G 155
Brook Mdw. N12 3E 30
Brook Mdw. Cl. IG8: Wfd G 6B 36
Brookmead Rd. CR0: C'don 6G 155
Brook M. IG7: Chig 3K 37
Brook M. N13 5F 33
Brook M. Nth. W2 2A 10 (7A 82)
Brookmill Rd. SE8 1C 122
Brook Pde. IG7: Chig 3K 37
Brook Pk. Cl. N21 5G 23
Brook Pl. EN5: Barn 5D 20
Brook Retail Pk. South Ruislip 5B 58
Brook Ri. IG7: Chig 3K 37
Brook Rd. CR7: Thor H 4C 156
Brook Rd. IG2: Ilf 6J 53
Brook Rd. IG9: Buck H 2D 36
Brook Rd. IG9: Wfd G 2D 36
Brook Rd. KT6: Surb 2E 162
Brook Rd. N22 3K 47
Brook Rd. N8 4J 47
Brook Rd. NW2 2B 62
Brook Rd. TW1: Twick 6A 114
Brook Rd. Sth. TW8: Bford 6D 96
Brooks Apts. E3 5C 86
(off Geoff Cade Way)
Brooks Av. E6 4D 88
Brooksbank Ho. E9 6J 67
(off Retreat Pl.)
Brooksbank St. E9 6J 67
Brooksby Ho. N1 7A 66
(off Liverpool Rd.)
Brooksby M. N1 7A 66
Brooksby St. N1 7A 66
Brooksby's Wlk. E9 5K 67
Brooks Cl. SE9 2E 142
Brooks Ct. SW11 7G 101
Brookscroft E17 3D 50
Brookscroft Rd. E17 1D 50
(not continuous)
Brooks Farm 7D 50
Brookshill HA3: Hrw W 5C 26
Brookshill Av. HA3: Hrw W 5C 26
Brookshill Dr. HA3: Hrw W 5C 26
Brookshill Ga. HA3: Hrw W 5C 26
Brookside BR6: Orp 7K 161
Brookside EN4: E Barn 6H 21
Brookside N21 6E 22
Brookside SM5: Cars 5E 166
Brookside UB10: Uxb 7B 56
Brookside Cl. EN5: Barn 6B 20
Brookside Cl. HA2: Harr 4C 58
Brookside Cl. HA3: Kenton 5D 42
Brookside Cl. TW13: Felt 3J 129
Brookside Cres. KT4: Wor Pk 1C 164
Brookside Rd. N19 2G 65
Brookside Rd. N9 4C 34
(not continuous)
Brookside Rd. NW11 6G 45
Brookside Rd. UB4: Yead 7A 76
Brookside Sth. EN4: E Barn 7K 21
Brookside Wlk. N3 3G 45
Brookside Way CR0: C'don 6K 157
Brooks La. W4 6G 97
Brooks Lodge N1 2E 84
Brook's M. W1 2J 11 (7F 83)
Brook Sq. SE18 1C 124
Brooks Rd. E13 1J 87
Brooks Rd. W4 5G 97
Brook St. DA17: Belv 5H 109
Brook St. DA17: Erith 5H 109
Brook St. DA8: Erith 5H 109
Brook St. KT1: King T 2E 150
Brook St. N17 2F 49
Brook St. W1 2J 11 (7F 83)
Brook St. W2 2B 10 (7B 82)
Brooksville Av. NW6 1G 81
Brook Va. DA8: Erith 1H 127
Brookview Ct. EN1: Enf 5K 23
Brookview Rd. SW16 5G 137
Brookville Rd. SW6 7H 99
Brook Wlk. HA8: Edg 6E 28
Brook Wlk. N2 1B 46
Brook Way IG7: Chig 3K 37
Brookway SE3 3J 123
Brookwell Ho. E17 4K 49
Brookwood Av. SW13 2B 116
Brookwood Cl. BR2: Broml 4H 159
Brookwood Ho. SE1 7B 14 (2B 102)
(off Webber St.)
Brookwood Rd. SW18 1H 135
Brookwood Rd. TW3: Houn 2F 113
Broom Cl. BR2: Broml 6C 160
Broom Cl. TW11: Tedd 7D 132
Broomcroft Av. UB5: N'olt 3A 76
Broome Rd. TW12: Hamp 7D 130
Broome Way SE5 7D 102
Broomfield E17 7B 50
Broomfield NW1 7E 64
(off Ferdinand St.)
Broomfield TW16: Sun 1J 147
Broomfield Av. N13 5E 32
Broomfield Ct. N2 4C 46
Broomfield Ho. HA7: Stan 3F 27
(off Stanmore Hill)
Broomfield Ho. SE17 4E 102
(off Massinger St.)
Broomfield La. N13 4D 32
Broomfield Pl. W13 1B 96
Broomfield Rd. BR3: Beck 3A 158
Broomfield Rd. DA6: Bex 5G 127
Broomfield Rd. KT5: Surb 1F 163
Broomfield Rd. N13 5D 32
Broomfield Rd. RM6: Chad H 7D 54
Broomfield Rd. TW11: Tedd 6C 132
Broomfield Rd. TW9: Kew 1F 115
Broomfield Rd. W13 1B 96
Broomfield St. E14 5C 86
Broom Gdns. CR0: C'don 3C 170
Broomgrove Gdns. HA8: Edg 1G 43
Broomgrove Rd. SW9 2K 119
Broomhall Rd. CR2: Sande 7D 168
BROOM HILL 7K 161
Broomhill Ct. IG8: Wfd G 6D 36
Broomhill Ri. DA6: Bex 5G 127
Broomhill Rd. BR6: Orp 7K 161
Broomhill Rd. IG3: Ilf 2A 72
Broomhill Rd. IG8: Wfd G 6D 36
(not continuous)
Broomhill Rd. SW18 5J 117
Broomhill Wlk. IG8: Wfd G 7C 36
Broomhouse La. SW6 2J 117
Broomhouse Rd. SW6 2J 117
Broomloan La. SM1: Sutt 2J 165
Broom Lock TW11: Tedd 6C 132
Broom Mead DA6: Bex 6G 127
Broom Pk. TW11: Tedd 7D 132
Broom Rd. CR0: C'don 3C 170
Broom Rd. TW11: Tedd 5B 132
Broomsleigh Bus. Pk. SE26 5B 140
Broomsleigh St. NW6 5H 63
Broom Water TW11: Tedd 6C 132
Broom Water W. TW11: Tedd 5C 132
Broomwood Cl. CR0: C'don 5K 157
Broomwood Cl. DA5: Bexl 2K 145
Broomwood Rd. SW11 6D 118
Broseley Gro. SE26 5A 140
Brosse Way BR2: Broml 6C 160
Broster Gdns. SE25 3F 157
Brotherstone Wlk. TW9: Kew 1H 115
Brouard Ct. BR1: Broml 3J 159
Brougham Rd. E8 1G 85
Brougham Rd. W3 6J 79
Brougham St. SW11 2D 118
Brough Cl. KT2: King T 5D 132
Brough Cl. SW8 7J 101
Broughton Av. N3 3G 45
Broughton Av. TW10: Ham 3B 132
Broughton Ct. W13 7B 78
Broughton Dr. SW9 4A 120
Broughton Gdns. N6 6G 47
Broughton Pl. E17 1B 50
Broughton Rd. BR6: Orp 2H 173
Broughton Rd. CR7: Thor H 6A 156
Broughton Rd. SW6 2K 117
Broughton Rd. W13 7B 78
Broughton Rd. App. SW6 2K 117
Broughton St. SW8 2E 118
Broughton St. Ind. Est. SW11 2E 118
Brouncker Rd. W3 2J 97
Browells La. TW13: Felt 2K 129
(not continuous)
Brown Bear Ct. TW13: Hanw 4B 130
Brown Cl. SM6: W'gton 7J 167
Browne Ho. SE8 7C 104
(off Deptford Chu. St.)
Brownell Pl. W7 2K 95
Brownfield Area E14 6D 86
Brownfield St. E14 6D 86
Browngraves Rd. UB3: Harl 7E 92
Brown Hart Gdns. W1 2H 11 (7E 82)
Brownhill Rd. SE6 7D 122
Browning Apts. E3 4B 86
(off Hamlets Way)
Browning Av. KT4: Wor Pk 1D 164
Browning Av. SM1: Sutt 4C 166
Browning Av. W7 6K 77
Browning Cl. DA16: Well 1J 125
Browning Cl. E17 4E 50
Browning Cl. RM5: Col R 1F 55
Browning Cl. TW12: Hamp 4D 130
Browning Cl. W9 4A 4 (4A 82)
Browning Ct. W14 6H 99
(off Turneville Rd.)
Browning Ho. N16 4E 66
(off Shakspeare Wlk.)
Browning Ho. SE14 1A 122
(off Loring Rd.)
Browning Ho. W12 6E 80
(off Wood La.)
Browning M. W1 6J 5 (5F 83)
Browning Rd. E11 7H 51
Browning Rd. E12 5D 70
Browning St. SE17 5C 102
Browning Way TW5: Hest 1B 112
Brownlea Gdns. IG3: Ilf 2A 72
Brownlow Cl. EN4: E Barn 5G 21
Brownlow Ct. N11 6D 32
(off Brownlow Rd.)
Brownlow Ct. N2 5A 46
Brownlow Ho. SE16 2G 103
(off George Row)
Brownlow M. WC1 4H 7 (4K 83)
Brownlow Rd. CR0: C'don 4E 168
Brownlow Rd. E7 4J 69
Brownlow Rd. E8 1F 85
Brownlow Rd. N11 6D 32
Brownlow Rd. N3 7E 30
Brownlow Rd. NW10 7A 62
Brownlow Rd. W13 1A 96
Brownlow St. WC1 6H 7 (5K 83)
Brownrigg Rd. TW15: Ashf 4C 128
Brown's Bldgs. EC3 1H 15 (6E 84)
Brownsea Wlk. NW7 6A 30
Browns La. NW5 5F 65
Brownspring Dr. SE9 4F 143
Brown's Rd. KT5: Surb 7F 151
Browns Rd. E17 3C 50
Brown St. W1 7E 4 (6D 82)
Brownswell Rd. N2 2B 46
BROWNSWOOD PARK 2B 66
Brownswood Rd. N4 3B 66
Broxash Rd. SW11 6E 118
Broxbourne Av. E18 4K 51
Broxbourne Ho. E3 4D 86
(off Empson St.)
Broxbourne Rd. BR6: Orp 1K 173
Broxbourne Rd. E7 3J 69
Broxholme Cl. SE25 4D 156
Broxholme Ho. SW6 1K 117
(off Harwood Rd.)
Broxholm Rd. SE27 3A 138
Broxted Rd. SE6 2B 140
Broxwood Way NW8 1C 82
Bruce Av. TW17: Shep 6E 146
Bruce Castle Ct. N17 1F 49
(off Lordship La.)
Bruce Castle Mus. 1E 48
Bruce Castle Rd. N17 1F 49
Bruce Cl. DA16: Well 1B 126
Bruce Cl. W10 5F 81
Bruce Ct. DA15: Sidc 4K 143
Bruce Gdns. N20 3J 31
Bruce Gro. N17 1E 48
Bruce Hall M. SW17 4E 136
Bruce Ho. W10 5F 81
Bruce Rd. CR4: Mitc 7E 136
Bruce Rd. E3 3D 86
Bruce Rd. EN5: Barn 3B 20
Bruce Rd. HA3: W'stone 2J 41
Bruce Rd. NW10 7K 61
Bruce Rd. SE25 4D 156
Bruckner St. W10 3G 81
Brudenell Rd. SW17 3D 136
Brutts Mdw. UB5: N'olt 6C 58
Bruford Ct. SE8 6C 104
Bruges Pl. NW1 7G 65
(off Randolph St.)
Brumfield Rd. KT19: Ewe 5J 163
Brummel Cl. DA7: Bex 3J 127
Brumwell Av. SE18 5E 106
Brune Ho. E1 6J 9 (5F 85)
(off Bell La.)
Brunei Gallery 5D 6 (5H 83)
Brunel Bldg. W2 6A 4 (5B 82)
(off Nth. Wharf Rd.)
Brunel Cl. SE19 6F 139
Brunel Cl. TW5: Cran 7K 93
Brunel Cl. UB5: N'olt 3D 76
Brunel Ct. HA8: Edg 4A 28
Brunel Ct. SE16 2J 103
(off Canon Beck Rd.)
Brunel Ct. SW13 2B 116
(off Westfields Av.)
Brunel Est. W2 5J 81
Brunel Ho. BR2: Broml 6C 160
(off Wells Vw. Dr.)
Brunel Ho. E14 5D 104
(off Ship Yd.)
Brunel Ho. RM8: Dag 4A 72
Brunel Ho. SW10 7B 100
(off Cheyne Rd.)
Brunel M. W10 3F 81
Brunel Mus. 2J 103
Brunel Pl. UB1: S'hall 6F 77
Brunel Rd. E17 6A 50
Brunel Rd. IG8: Wfd G 5J 37
Brunel Rd. SE16 2J 103
Brunel Rd. W3 5A 80
Brunel Science Pk. UB8: Cowl 3A 74
Brunel St. E16 6H 87
Brunel University Indoor Athletics Cen. 3A 74
Brunel University Sports Pk. 4B 74
Brunel University Uxbridge Campus 3A 74
Brunel Wlk. N15 5E 48
Brunel Wlk. TW2: Whitt 7E 112
Brune St. E1 6J 9 (5F 85)
Brunlees Ho. SE1 3C 102
(off Bath Ter.)
Brunner Cl. NW11 5K 45
Brunner Ho. SE6 4E 140
Brunner Rd. E17 5A 50
Brunner Rd. W5 4D 78
Bruno Pl. NW9 2J 61
Brunswick Av. N11 3K 31
Brunswick Cen. 3E 6 (4J 83)
Brunswick Cl. DA6: Bex 4D 126
Brunswick Cl. HA5: Pinn 6C 40
Brunswick Cl. KT7: T Ditt 1A 162
Brunswick Cl. TW2: Twick 3H 131
Brunswick Cl. Est. EC1 2A 8 (3B 84)
Brunswick Ct. EC1 2A 8 (3B 84)
(off Tompion St.)
Brunswick Ct. EN4: E Barn 5G 21
Brunswick Ct. SE1 7H 15 (2E 102)
Brunswick Ct. SM1: Sutt 4K 165
Brunswick Ct. SW1 4D 18 (4H 101)
(off Regency St.)
Brunswick Cres. N11 3K 31
Brunswick Flats W11 6J 81
(off Westbourne Gro.)
Brunswick Gdns. IG6: Ilf 1G 53
Brunswick Gdns. W5 4E 78
Brunswick Gdns. W8 1J 99
Brunswick Gro. N11 3K 31
Brunswick Ho. E2 2F 85
(off Thurtle Rd.)
Brunswick Ho. N3 1H 45
Brunswick Ho. SE16 3A 104
(off Brunswick Quay)
Brunswick Ho. W6 5E 98
(off Parrs Way)
Brunswick Ind. Pk. N11 4A 32
Brunswick Mans. WC1 3F 7 (4J 83)
(off Handel St.)
Brunswick M. SW16 6H 137
Brunswick M. W1 7F 5 (6D 82)
BRUNSWICK PARK 3J 31
Brunswick Pk. SE5 1E 120
Brunswick Pk. Gdns. N11 2K 31
Brunswick Pk. Rd. N11 2K 31
Brunswick Pl. N1 2F 9 (3D 84)
Brunswick Pl. NW1 4H 5 (4E 82)
(not continuous)
Brunswick Pl. SE19 7G 139
Brunswick Quay SE16 3K 103
Brunswick Rd. DA6: Bex 4D 126
Brunswick Rd. E10 1E 68
Brunswick Rd. E14 6E 86
Brunswick Rd. EN3: Enf L 1H 25
Brunswick Rd. KT2: King T 1G 151
Brunswick Rd. N15 5E 48
Brunswick Rd. SM1: Sutt 4K 165
Brunswick Rd. W5 4D 78
Brunswick Sq. N17 6A 34
Brunswick Sq. WC1 3F 7 (4J 83)
(not continuous)
Brunswick St. E17 5E 50
Brunswick Ter. BR3: Beck 1D 158
Brunswick Vs. SE5 1E 120
Brunswick Way N11 4A 32
Brunton Pl. E14 6A 86
Brushfield St. E1 5H 9 (5E 84)
Brushwood Cl. E14 5D 86
Brussels Rd. SW11 4B 118
Bruton Cl. BR7: Chst 7D 142
Bruton La. W1 3K 11 (7F 83)
Bruton Pl. W1 3K 11 (7F 83)
Bruton Rd. SM4: Mord 4A 154
Bruton St. W1 3K 11 (7F 83)
Bruton Way W13 5A 78
Brutus Ct. SE11 4K 19 (4B 102)
(off Kennington La.)
Bryan Av. NW10 7D 62
Bryan Cl. TW16: Sun 7J 129
Bryan Ho. NW10 7D 62
Bryan Ho. SE16 2B 104
Bryan Rd. SE16 2B 104
Bryan's All. SW6 2K 117
Bryanston Av. TW2: Whitt 1F 131
Bryanston Cl. UB2: S'hall 4D 94
Bryanston Ct. W1 7E 4 (6D 82)
(off Seymour Pl.)
Bryanstone Ct. SM1: Sutt 3A 166
Bryanstone Rd. N8 5H 47
Bryanston Mans. W1 5E 4 (5D 82)
(off York St.)
Bryanston M. E. W1 6E 4 (5D 82)
Bryanston M. W. W1 6E 4 (5D 82)
Bryanston Pl. W1 6E 4 (5D 82)
Bryanston Sq. W1 7E 4 (6D 82)
Bryanston St. W1 1F 11 (6D 82)
Bryan St. N1 1K 83
Bryant Av. RM10: Dag 7J 73
Bryant Cl. EN5: Barn 5C 20
Bryant Ct. E2 1F 85
(off Whiston Rd.)
Bryant Ct. W3 1K 97
Bryant Ho. E3 2C 86
(off Thomas Fyre Dr.)
Bryant Rd. UB5: N'olt 3A 76
Bryant St. E15 7F 69
Bryant St. E2 1F 85
Bryantwood Rd. N7 5A 66
Brycedale Cres. N14 4C 32
Bryce Ho. SE14 6K 103
(off John Williams Cl.)
Bryce Rd. RM8: Dag 4C 72
Brydale Ho. SE16 4K 103
(off Rotherhithe New Rd.)
Bryden Cl. SE26 5A 140
Brydges Pl. WC2 3E 12 (7J 83)
Brydges Rd. E15 5F 69
Brydon Wlk. N1 1J 83
Bryer Ct. EC2 5C 8 (5C 84)
(off Bridgewater Sq.)
Bryett Rd. N7 3J 65
Bryher Ct. SE11 5J 19 (5A 102)
(off Sancroft St.)
Brymay Cl. E3 2C 86
Brymcourt W9 2K 81
Brynmaer Rd. SW11 1D 118
Bryn-y-mawr Rd. EN1: Enf 4A 24
Bryony Cl. UB8: Hil 5B 74
Bryony Rd. W12 7C 80
Bryony Way TW16: Sun 6J 129
Bubbling Well Sq. SW18 5K 117
(off Ryland Blvd.)
Buccleugh Ho. E5 7G 49
Buchanan Cl. N21 5E 22
Buchanan Ct. SE16 4K 103
(off Worgan St.)
Buchanan Gdns. NW10 2D 80
Buchan Ho. W3 2H 97
(off Hanbury Rd.)
Buchan Rd. SE15 3J 121
Bucharest Rd. SW18 7A 118
Buckden Cl. N2 4D 46
Buckden Cl. SE12 6J 123
Buckfast Ct. W13 7A 78
(off Romsey Rd.)
Buckfast Ho. N14 5B 22
Buckfast Rd. SM4: Mord 4K 153
Buckfast St. E2 3G 85
Buck Hill Wlk. W2 3B 10 (7B 82)
Buckhold Rd. SW18 6J 117
Buckhurst Av. SM5: Cars 1C 166
Buckhurst Ct. IG9: Buck H 1G 37
BUCKHURST HILL 2G 37
Buckhurst Hill Ho. IG9: Buck H 2E 36
Buckhurst Ho. N7 5H 65
Buckhurst St. E1 4H 85
Buckhurst St. E2 4H 85
Buckhurst Way IG9: Buck H 4G 37
Buckingham Arc. WC2 3F 13 (7J 83)
(off Strand)
Buckingham Av. CR7: Thor H 1A 156
Buckingham Av. DA16: Well 4J 125
Buckingham Av. KT8: W Mole 2F 149
Buckingham Av. N20 7F 21
Buckingham Av. TW14: Felt 6K 111
Buckingham Av. UB6: G'frd 1A 78
Buckingham Chambers SW1 3B 18 (4G 101)
(off Greencoat Pl.)
Buckingham Cl. BR5: Pet W 7J 161
Buckingham Cl. EN1: Enf 2K 23
Buckingham Cl. TW12: Hamp 5D 130
Buckingham Cl. W5 5C 78
Buckingham Ct. NW4 3C 44
Buckingham Ct. UB5: N'olt 2C 76
Buckingham Ct. W11 7J 81
(off Kensington Pk. Rd.)
Buckingham Ct. W7 4K 77
(off Copley Cl.)
Buckingham Dr. BR7: Chst 4G 143
Buckingham Gdns. CR7: Thor H 2A 156
Buckingham Gdns. HA8: Edg 7K 27
Buckingham Gdns. KT8: W Mole 2F 149
Buckingham Ga. SW1 1A 18 (3G 101)
Buckingham Gro. UB10: Hil 2C 74
Buckingham La. SE23 7A 122
Buckingham Mans. NW6 5K 63
(off West End La.)
Buckingham M. N1 6E 66
Buckingham M. NW10 2B 80
Buckingham M. SW1 1A 18 (3G 101)
(off Stafford Pl.)
Buckingham Palace 7K 11 (2F 101)
Buckingham Pal. Rd. SW1 4J 17 (4F 101)
Buckingham Pde. HA7: Stan 5H 27
Buckingham Pl. SW1 1A 18 (3G 101)
Buckingham Rd. CR4: Mitc 4J 155
Buckingham Rd. E10 3D 68
Buckingham Rd. E11 5A 52
Buckingham Rd. E15 5H 69
Buckingham Rd. E18 1H 51
Buckingham Rd. HA1: Harr 5H 41
Buckingham Rd. HA8: Edg 7A 28
Buckingham Rd. IG1: Ilf 2H 71
Buckingham Rd. KT1: King T 4F 151
Buckingham Rd. N1 6E 66
Buckingham Rd. N22 1J 47
Buckingham Rd. NW10 2B 80
Buckingham Rd. TW10: Ham 2D 132
Buckingham Rd. TW12: Hamp 4D 130
Buckingham St. WC2 3F 13 (7J 83)
Buckland Cl. NW7 4H 29
Buckland Ct. N1 2E 84
(off St John's Est.)
Buckland Ct. UB10: Ick 2E 56
Buckland Cres. NW3 7B 64
Buckland Ho. SW1 5J 17 (5F 101)
(part of Abbots Mnr.)
Buckland Ri. HA5: Pinn 1A 40
Buckland Rd. BR6: Orp 4J 173
Buckland Rd. E10 2E 68
Buckland Rd. KT9: Chess 5F 163
Bucklands Rd. TW11: Tedd 6C 132
Buckland St. N1 2D 84
Buckland's Wharf KT1: King T 2D 150
Buckland Wlk. SM4: Mord 4A 154
Buckland Wlk. W3 2J 97
Buckland Way KT4: Wor Pk 1E 164
Buck La. NW9 5K 43
Bucklebury NW1 3A 6 (4G 83)
(off Stanhope St.)
Buckleigh Av. SW20 3G 153
Buckleigh Rd. SW16 6H 137
Buckleigh Way SE19 7F 139
Buckler Ct. N7 5K 65
Buckler Gdns. SE9 3D 142
Bucklers All. SW6 6H 99
Bucklersbury EC4 1E 14 (6D 84)
Bucklersbury Pas. EC4 1E 14 (6D 84)
Buckler's Way SM5: Cars 3D 166
Buckles Ct. DA17: Belv 4D 108
Buckle St. E1 7K 9 (6F 85)
Buckley Cl. SE23 7H 121
Buckley Ct. NW6 7H 63
Buckley Ct. SE1 3F 103
Buckley Ho. W14 2G 99
(off Holland Pk. Av.)
Buckley Rd. NW6 7H 63
Buckmaster Cl. SW9 3A 120
(off Stockwell Pk. Rd.)
Buckmaster Ho. N7 4K 65
Buckmaster Rd. SW11 4C 118
Bucknall St. WC2 7E 6 (6J 83)
Bucknall Way BR3: Beck 4D 158
Bucknell Cl. SW2 4K 119
Buckner Rd. SW2 4K 119
Bucknill Ho. SW1 5J 17 (5F 101)
(off Ebury Bri. Rd.)
Buckrell Rd. E4 2A 36
Buckridge Ho. EC1 5J 7 (5A 84)
(off Portpool La.)
Buckshead Ho. W2 5J 81
(off Gt. Western Rd.)
Buckstone Cl. SE23 6J 121
Buckstone Rd. N18 5B 34
Buck St. NW1 7F 65
Buckters Rents SE16 1A 104
Buckthorne Rd. SE4 5A 122
Buckthorn Ho. DA15: Sidc 3K 143
(off Longlands Rd.)
Buckthorn Ho. E15 3G 87
(off Manor Rd.)
Buck Wlk. E17 4F 51
Buckwheat Ct. DA18: Erith 3D 108
Budd Cl. N12 4E 30
Buddings Circ. HA9: Wemb 3J 61
Buddleia Ho. TW13: Felt 1J 129
Budd's All. TW1: Twick 5C 114
Bude Cl. E17 5B 50
Budge La. CR4: Mitc 7D 154
Budleigh Cres. DA16: Well 1C 126
Budleigh Ho. SE15 7G 103
(off Bird in Bush Rd.)
Budoch Ct. IG3: Ilf 2A 72
Budoch Dr. IG3: Ilf 2A 72
Buer Rd. SW6 2G 117
Bugsby's Way SE10 4H 105

Bugsby's Way – Buttermere Ct.

Bugsby's Way SE7 4J 105
Buick Ho. E3 4C 86
(off Wellington Way)
Buick Ho. KT2: King T 2F 151
Building 50 SE18 3G 107
Bulbarrow NW8 1K 81
(off Abbey Rd.)
Bulganak Rd. CR7: Thor H 4C 156
Bulinga St. SW1 4E 18 (4J 101)
(off John Islip St.)
Bullace Row SE5 1D 120
Bull All. DA16: Well 3B 126
Bullard's Pl. E2 3K 85
Bullbanks Rd. DA17: Belv 4J 109
Bulleid Way SW1 4K 17 (4F 101)
Bullen Ho. E1 4H 85
(off Collingwood St.)
Bullen St. SW11 2C 118
Buller Cl. SE15 7G 103
Buller Rd. CR7: Thor H 2D 156
Buller Rd. IG11: Bark 7J 71
Buller Rd. N17 2G 49
Buller Rd. N22 2A 48
Buller Rd. NW10 3F 81
Bullers Cl. DA14: Sidc 5E 144
Bullers Wood Dr. BR7: Chst 7D 142
Bullescroft Rd. HA8: Edg 3B 28
Bullfinch Ho. NW9 6B 44
(off Perryfield Way)
Bullingham Mans. W8 2J 99
(off Pitt St.)
Bull Inn Ct. WC2 3F 13 (7J 83)
(off Strand)
Bullivant St. E14 7E 86
Bull La. BR7: Chst 7H 143
Bull La. N18 5K 33
Bull La. RM10: Dag 3H 73
Bullman Cl. DA7: Bex 3H 127
Bull Rd. E15 2H 87
Bullrush Cl. CR0: C'don 6E 156
Bullrush Cl. SM5: Cars 2C 166
Bull's All. SW14 2K 115
Bulls Bri. Cen. UB3: Hayes 3J 93
Bullsbridge Ind. Est. UB2: S'hall 4K 93
Bulls Bri. Rd. UB2: S'hall 4A 94
Bulls Bri. Rd. UB3: Hayes 3K 93
Bullsbrook Rd. UB4: Yead 1A 94
Bulls Gdns. SW3 3D 16 (4C 100)
Bulls Head Pas. EC3 1G 15 (6E 84)
(off Lime St. Pas.)
Bull Theatre, The 4C 20
Bull Yd. SE15 1G 121
Bulmer Gdns. HA3: Kenton 7D 42
Bulmer M. W11 7J 81
Bulmer Pl. W11 1J 99
Bulrush Ter. IG11: Bark 3C 90
Bulstrode Av. TW3: Houn 2D 112
Bulstrode Gdns. TW3: Houn 3E 112
Bulstrode Pl. W1 6H 5 (5E 82)
Bulstrode Rd. TW3: Houn 3E 112
Bulstrode St. W1 7H 5 (6E 82)
Bulwark Ct. E14 4E 104
(off Parkside Sq.)
Bulwer Ct. E11 1F 69
Bulwer Ct. Rd. E11 1F 69
Bulwer Gdns. EN5: New Bar 4F 21
Bulwer Rd. E11 7F 51
Bulwer Rd. EN5: New Bar 4E 20
Bulwer Rd. N18 4K 33
Bulwer St. W12 1E 98
Bunbury Ho. SE15 7G 103
(off Fenham Rd.)
Bunce's La. IG8: Wfd G 7C 36
Bungalow Rd. SE25 4E 156
Bungalows, The E10 6E 50
Bungalows, The HA2: Harr 4D 58
Bungalows, The IG6: Ilf 1J 53
Bungalows, The SM6: W'gton 5F 167
Bungalows, The SW16 7F 137
Bungalows, The UB4: Yead 4B 76
Bunhill Row EC1 3E 8 (4D 84)
Bunhouse Pl. SW1 5G 17 (5E 100)
Bunkers Hill DA14: Sidc 3F 145
Bunkers Hill DA17: Belv 4G 109
Bunkers Hill NW11 7A 46
Bunning Way N7 7J 65
Bunns La. NW7 6F 29
(not continuous)
Bunsen Ho. E3 2A 86
(off Grove Rd.)
Bunsen St. E3 2A 86
Buntingbridge Rd. IG2: Ilf 5H 53
Bunting Cl. CR4: Mitc 5D 154
Bunting Cl. N9 1E 34
Bunting Ct. NW9 2A 44
Bunting Ho. UB10: Ick 2E 56
(off Coyle Dr.)
Bunton St. SE18 3E 106
Bunwell Ho. E3 4B 86
(off William Whiffin Sq.)
Bunyan Ct. EC2 5C 8 (5C 84)
(off Fann St.)
Bunyan Rd. E17 3A 50
Buonaparte M. SW1 5C 18 (5H 101)
Burbage Cl. SE1 3D 102
Burbage Cl. UB3: Hayes 6F 75
Burbage Ho. N1 1D 84
(off Poole St.)
Burbage Ho. SE14 6K 103
(off Samuel Cl.)
Burbage Rd. SE21 7D 120
Burbage Rd. SE24 6C 120
Burberry Cl. KT3: N Mald 2A 152
Burbidge Rd. TW17: Shep 4C 146
Burbridge Gdns. UB10: Uxb 2A 74
Burbridge Way N17 2G 49
Burcham Cl. TW12: Hamp 7E 130
Burcham St. E14 6D 86
Burcharbro Rd. SE2 6D 108
Burchell Ct. WD23: Bush 1B 26
Burchell Ho. SE11 5H 19 (5K 101)
(off Jonathan St.)
Burchell Rd. E10 1D 68
Burchell Rd. SE15 1H 121
Burcher Gale Gro. SE15 7F 103
Burchetts Way TW17: Shep 6D 146
Burchett Way RM6: Chad H 6F 55
Burchwall Cl. RM5: Col R 1J 55
Burcote Rd. SW18 7B 118
Burden Cl. TW8: Bford 5C 96
Burden Ho. SW8 7J 101
(off Thorncroft St.)
Burdenshott Av. TW10: Rich 4H 115
Burden Way E11 2K 69
Burder Cl. N1 6E 66
Burder Rd. N1 6E 66
Burdett Av. SW20 1C 152
Burdett Cl. DA14: Sidc 5E 144
Burdett Cl. W7 1K 95
Burdett M. NW3 6B 64
Burdett M. W2 6K 81
Burdett Rd. CR0: C'don 6D 156
Burdett Rd. E14 5B 86
Burdett Rd. E3 4A 86
Burdett Rd. TW9: Rich 2F 115
Burdetts Rd. RM9: Dag 1F 91
Burdock Cl. CR0: C'don 1K 169
Burdock Rd. N17 3G 49
Burdock Ter. IG11: Bark 3C 90
Burdon La. SM2: Cheam 7G 165
Burdon Pk. SM2: Cheam 7H 165
Bure Ct. EN5: New Bar 5E 20
Burfield Cl. SW17 4B 136
Burford Cl. IG6: Ilf 4G 53
Burford Cl. RM8: Dag 3C 72
Burford Cl. UB10: Ick 4A 56
Burford Gdns. N13 3E 32
Burford Ho. TW8: Bford 5D 96
Burford Rd. BR1: Broml 4C 160
Burford Rd. E15 1F 87
Burford Rd. E6 3C 88
Burford Rd. KT4: Wor Pk 7B 152
Burford Rd. SE6 2B 140
Burford Rd. SM1: Sutt 2J 165
Burford Rd. TW8: Bford 5E 96
Burford Wlk. SW6 7A 100
Burford Way CR0: New Ad 6E 170
Burford Wharf Apts. E15 1F 87
(off Cam Rd.)
Burges Gro. SW13 7D 98
Burges Rd. E6 7C 70
Burgess Av. NW9 6K 43
Burgess Bus. Pk. SE5 7D 102
Burgess Cl. TW13: Hanw 4C 130
Burgess Ct. E6 7E 70
Burgess Ct. SE6 7C 122
Burgess Ct. UB1: S'hall 6F 77
(off Fleming Rd.)
Burgess Hill NW2 4J 63
Burgess Ho. SE5 7C 102
(off Bethwin Rd.)
Burgess Lofts SE5 7C 102
(off Bethwin Rd.)
Burgess M. SW19 6K 135
Burgess Pk. 6D 102
Burgess Rd. E15 4G 69
Burgess Rd. E6 7E 70
Burgess Rd. SM1: Sutt 4K 165
Burgess St. E14 5C 86
Burge St. SE1 3D 102
Burgh House 4B 64
Burghill Rd. SE26 4A 140
Burghley Av. KT3: N Mald 1K 151
Burghley Hall Cl. SW19 1G 135
Burghley Ho. SW19 3G 135
Burghley Pas. E11 1G 69
(off Burghley Rd.)
Burghley Pl. CR4: Mitc 5D 154
Burghley Rd. E11 1G 69
Burghley Rd. N8 3A 48
Burghley Rd. NW5 4F 65
Burghley Rd. SW19 4F 135
Burghley Twr. W3 7B 80
Burgh St. N1 2B 84
Burgoine Quay KT1: Hamp W 1D 150
Burgon St. EC4 1B 14 (6B 84)
Burgos Cl. CR0: Wadd 6A 168
Burgos Gro. SE10 1D 122
Burgoyne Ho. TW8: Bford 5D 96
(off Ealing Rd.)
Burgoyne Rd. N4 6B 48
Burgoyne Rd. SE25 4F 157
Burgoyne Rd. SW9 3K 119
Burgoyne Rd. TW16: Sun 6H 129
Burgundy Ct. HA4: Ruis 4A 58
Burgundy Ho. E20 5E 68
(off Liberty Bri. Rd.)
Burgundy Ho. EN2: Enf 1H 23
(off Bedale Rd.)
Burgundy Pl. W12 1F 99
Burham Cl. SE20 7J 139
Burhill Gro. HA5: Pinn 2C 40
Burke Cl. SW15 4A 116
Burke Lodge E13 3K 87
Burke St. E16 5H 87
(not continuous)
Burket Cl. UB2: S'hall 4C 94
Burland Rd. SW11 5D 118
Burleigh Av. DA15: Sidc 5K 125
Burleigh Av. SM6: W'gton 3E 166
Burleigh Cl. RM7: Mawney 4H 55
Burleigh Gdns. N14 1B 32
Burleigh Gdns. TW15: Ashf 5E 128
Burleigh Ho. SW3 7B 16 (6B 100)
(off Beaufort St.)
Burleigh Ho. W10 5G 81
(off St Charles Sq.)
Burleigh Ho. WC1 2G 7 (3K 83)
(off Westking Pl.)
Burleigh Pde. N14 1C 32
Burleigh Pl. SW15 5F 117
Burleigh Rd. EN1: Enf 4K 23
Burleigh Rd. SM3: Sutt 1G 165
Burleigh Rd. UB10: Hil 1D 74
Burleigh St. WC2 2G 13 (7K 83)
Burleigh Wlk. SE6 1E 140
Burleigh Way EN2: Enf 3J 23
Burley Cl. E4 5H 35
Burley Cl. SW16 2H 155
Burley Ho. E1 6K 85
(off Chudleigh St.)
Burley Rd. E16 6A 88
Burlington Arc. W1 3A 12 (7G 83)
Burlington Av. RM7: Rom 6H 55
Burlington Av. TW9: Kew 1G 115
Burlington Cl. BR6: Farnb 2F 173
Burlington Cl. E6 6C 88
Burlington Cl. HA5: Eastc 3K 39
Burlington Cl. TW14: Bedf 7F 111
Burlington Cl. W9 4J 81
Burlington Cnr. NW1 7G 65
(off Camden Rd.)
Burlington Ct. E1 7G 85
(off Cable St.)
Burlington Gdns. RM6: Chad H
7E 54
Burlington Gdns. SW6 2G 117
Burlington Gdns. W1 3A 12 (7G 83)
Burlington Gdns. W3 1J 97
Burlington Gdns. W4 5J 97
Burlington Ho. N15 6D 48
(off Tewkesbury Rd.)
Burlington Ho. SE16 2K 103
(off Province Dr.)
Burlington Ho. UB7: W Dray 2B 92
(off Park Lodge Av.)
Burlington La. W4 7J 97
Burlington M. SW15 5H 117
Burlington M. W3 1J 97
Burlington Pl. IG8: Wfd G 3E 36
Burlington Pl. SW6 2G 117
Burlington Ri. EN4: E Barn 1H 31
Burlington Rd. CR7: Thor H 2C 156
Burlington Rd. EN2: Enf 1J 23
Burlington Rd. KT3: N Mald 4B 152
Burlington Rd. N10 3E 46
Burlington Rd. N17 1G 49
Burlington Rd. SW6 2G 117
Burlington Rd. TW7: Isle 1H 113
Burlington Rd. W4 5J 97
Burma M. N16 4D 66
Burma Rd. N16 4D 66
Burmarsh NW5 6E 64
Burmarsh Ct. SE20 1J 157
Burma Ter. SE19 5E 138
Burmester Rd. SW17 3A 136
Burnaby Cres. W4 6J 97
Burnaby Gdns. W4 6H 97
Burnaby St. SW10 7A 100
Burnand Ho. W14 3F 99
(off Redan St.)
Burnbrae Cl. N12 6E 30
Burnbury Rd. SW12 1G 137
Burncroft Av. EN3: Enf H 2D 24
Burndell Way UB4: Yead 5B 76
Burne Jones Ho. W14 4G 99
Burnell Av. DA16: Well 2A 126
Burnell Av. TW10: Ham 5C 132
Burnell Bldg. NW2 2E 62
Burnell Gdns. HA7: Stan 2D 42
Burnell Ho. E20 5D 68
(off Peloton Av.)
Burnelli Bldg. SW11 7F 101
(off Sopwith Way)
Burnell Rd. SM1: Sutt 4K 165
Burnell Wlk. SE1 5F 103
(off Cadet Dr.)
Burnels Av. E6 3E 88
Burness Cl. N7 6K 65
Burne St. NW1 5C 4 (5C 82)
Burnett Cl. E9 5J 67
Burnett Ho. SE13 2E 122
(off Lewisham Hill)
Burnett Rd. IG6: Ilf 7K 37
Burney Av. KT5: Surb 5F 151
Burney St. SE10 7E 104
Burnfoot Av. SW6 1G 117
Burnham NW3 7C 64
Burnham Av. UB10: Ick 4E 56
Burnham Cl. EN1: Enf 1K 23
Burnham Cl. HA3: W'stone 4A 42
Burnham Cl. NW7 7H 29
Burnham Cl. SE1 4F 103
Burnham Ct. NW4 4E 44
(off Brent St.)
Burnham Ct. NW6 7A 64
(off Fairhazel Gdns.)
Burnham Ct. W2 7K 81
(off Moscow Rd.)
Burnham Cres. E11 4A 52
Burnham Dr. KT4: Wor Pk 2F 165
Burnham Est. E2 3J 85
(off Burnham St.)
Burnham Gdns. CR0: C'don 7F 157
Burnham Gdns. TW4: Cran 1K 111
Burnham Gdns. UB3: Harl 3F 93
Burnham Rd. DA14: Sidc 2E 144
Burnham Rd. E4 5G 35
Burnham Rd. RM7: Rom 3K 55
Burnham Rd. RM9: Dag 7B 72
Burnham Rd. SM4: Mord 4K 153
Burnham St. E2 3J 85
Burnham St. KT2: King T 1G 151
Burnham Way SE26 5B 140
Burnham Way W13 4B 96
Burnhill Cl. SE15 7H 103
Burnhill Ho. EC1 2C 8 (3C 84)
(off Norman St.)
Burnhill Rd. BR3: Beck 2C 158
Burnley Rd. NW10 5B 62
Burnley Rd. SW9 2K 119
Burnsall St. SW3 6D 16 (5C 100)
Burns Av. DA15: Sidc 6B 126
Burns Av. RM6: Chad H 7C 54
Burns Av. TW14: Felt 6J 111
Burns Av. UB1: S'hall 7E 76
Burns Cl. DA16: Well 1K 125
Burns Cl. E17 4E 50
Burns Cl. SW19 6B 136
Burns Cl. UB4: Hayes 5H 75
Burns Ho. E2 3J 85
(off Cornwall Av.)
Burns Ho. SE17 5B 102
(off Doddington Gro.)
Burnside Av. E4 6G 35
Burnside Cl. EN5: New Bar 3D 20
Burnside Cl. SE16 1K 103
Burnside Cl. TW1: Twick 6A 114
Burnside Ct. SM5: Cars 3E 166
Burnside Cres. HA0: Wemb 1D 78
Burnside Rd. RM8: Dag 2C 72
Burns Rd. HA0: Wemb 2E 78
Burns Rd. NW10 1B 80
Burns Rd. SW11 2D 118
Burns Rd. W13 2B 96
Burns Way TW5: Hest 2B 112
Burnt Ash Hgts. BR1: Broml 5K 141
Burnt Ash Hill SE12 6H 123
Burnt Ash La. BR1: Broml 7J 141
Burnt Ash Rd. SE12 5H 123
Burnthwaite M. SW6 7J 99
(off Burnthwaite Rd.)
Burnthwaite Rd. SW6 7H 99
BURNT OAK 1H 43
Burnt Oak Apts. E16 6J 87
(off Pacific Rd.)
Burnt Oak B'way. HA8: Edg 7B 28
Burnt Oak Flds. HA8: Edg 1J 43
Burnt Oak La. DA15: Sidc 6A 126
(not continuous)
Burntwood Cl. SW18 1C 136
Burntwood Grange Rd. SW18 1B 136
Burntwood La. SW17 3A 136
Burntwood Vw. SE19 5F 139
Buross St. E1 6H 85
Burpham Cl. UB4: Yead 5B 76
Burrage Ct. SE16 4K 103
(off Worgan St.)
Burrage Gro. SE18 4G 107
Burrage Pl. SE18 5F 107
Burrage Rd. SE18 5G 107
Burrard Ho. E2 2J 85
(off Bishop's Way)
Burrard Rd. E16 6K 87
Burrard Rd. NW6 5J 63
Burr Cl. DA7: Bex 3F 127
Burr Cl. E1 4K 15 (1G 103)
Burreed M. RM13: Rain 2J 91
Burrell Cl. CR0: C'don 6A 158
Burrell Cl. HA8: Edg 2C 28
Burrell Row BR3: Beck 2C 158
Burrell St. SE1 4A 14 (1B 102)
Burrells Wharf Sq. E14 5D 104
Burrell Towers E10 7C 50
Burrhill Ct. SE16 3K 103
(off Worgan St.)
Burritt Rd. KT1: King T 2G 151
Burroughs, The NW4 4D 44
Burroughs Club, The 4D 44
Burroughs Cotts. E14 5A 86
(off Halley St.)
Burroughs Gdns. NW4 4D 44
Burroughs Pde. NW4 4D 44
Burrow Ho. SW9 2A 120
(off Stockwell Pk. Rd.)
Burrow Rd. SE22 4E 120
Burrows M. SE1 6A 14 (2B 102)
Burrows Rd. NW10 3E 80
Burrow Wlk. SE21 7C 120
Burr Rd. SW18 1J 135
Bursar St. SE1 5G 15 (1E 102)
Bursdon Cl. DA15: Sidc 2K 143
Bursland Rd. EN3: Pond E 4E 24
Burslem St. E1 6G 85
Burstock Rd. SW15 4G 117
Burston Rd. SW15 5F 117
Burston Vs. SW15 5F 117
(off St John's Av.)
Burstow Rd. SW20 1G 153
Burtenshaw Rd. KT7: T Ditt 7A 150
Burtley Cl. N4 1C 66
Burton Bank N1 7D 66
(off Yeate St.)
Burton Cl. CR7: Thor H 3D 156
Burton Cl. KT9: Chess 7D 162
Burton Ct. KT7: T Ditt 6A 150
Burton Ct. SE20 2J 157
Burton Ct. SW3 5F 17 (5D 100)
(off Franklin's Row)
Burton Gdns. TW5: Hest 1D 112
Burton Gro. SE17 5D 102
Burtonhole Cl. NW7 4A 30
Burtonhole La. N12 4B 30
Burtonhole La. NW7 5K 29
Burton Ho. SE16 2H 103
(off Cherry Gdn. St.)
Burton La. SW9 2A 120
(not continuous)
Burton M. SW1 4H 17 (4E 100)
Burton Pl. WC1 2D 6 (3H 83)
Burton Ridge Ct. E3 2B 86
(off Festubert Pl.)
Burton Rd. SW9 Akerman Rd. 2B 120
Burton Rd. SW9 Evesham Wlk. 2A 120
Burton Rd. E18 3K 51
Burton Rd. KT2: King T 7E 132
Burton Rd. NW6 7H 63
Burtons Ct. E15 7F 69
Burton's Rd. TW12: Hamp H 4F 131
Burton St. WC1 2D 6 (3H 83)
Burtonwood Ho. N4 7D 48
Burtop Rd. Est. SW17 3A 136
Burt Rd. E16 1A 106
Burts Wharf DA17: Belv 7J 91
Burtt Ho. N1 1G 9 (3E 84)
(off Aske St.)
Burtwell La. SE27 4D 138
Burwash Ho. SE1 7F 15 (2D 102)
(off Kipling Est.)
Burwash Rd. SE18 5H 107
Burway Cl. CR2: S Croy 6E 168
Burwell KT1: King T 2G 151
(off Excelsior Cl.)
Burwell Av. UB6: G'frd 6J 59
Burwell Cl. E1 6H 85
Burwell Rd. E10 1A 68
Burwell Wlk. E3 4C 86
Burwood Av. BR2: Hayes 2K 171
Burwood Av. HA5: Eastc 5K 39
Burwood Cl. KT6: Surb 1G 163
Burwood Ho. EN4: Had W 1F 21
Burwood Pl. W2 7D 4 (6C 82)
Bury Av. HA4: Ruis 6E 38
Bury Av. UB4: Hayes 2G 75
Bury Cl. SE16 1K 103
Bury Ct. EC3 7H 9 (6E 84)
Buryfield Ct. SE8 4K 103
(off Lower Rd.)
Bury Gro. SM4: Mord 5K 153
Bury Hall Vs. N9 7A 24
Bury Pl. WC1 6E 6 (5J 83)
Bury Rd. N22 2A 48
Bury Rd. RM10: Dag 5H 73
Buryside Cl. IG2: Ilf 4K 53
Bury St. EC3 1H 15 (6E 84)
Bury St. HA4: Ruis 5E 38
Bury St. N9 7A 24
Bury St. SW1 4A 12 (1G 101)
Bury St. W. N9 7J 23
Bury Wlk. SW3 4C 16 (4C 100)
Busbridge Ho. E14 5C 86
(off Brabazon St.)
Busby Ho. SW16 4G 137
Busby M. NW5 6H 65
Busby Pl. NW5 6H 65
Busch Cl. TW7: Isle 1B 114
Bushbaby Cl. SE1 3E 102
Bushberry Rd. E9 6A 68
Bush Cl. IG2: Ilf 5H 53
Bush Cotts. SW18 5J 117
Bush Ct. N14 1C 32
Bush Ct. W12 2F 99
Bushell Cl. SW2 2K 137
Bushell Grn. WD23: B Hea 2C 26
Bushell St. E1 1G 103
Bushell Way BR7: Chst 5E 142
Bushey Av. BR5: Pet W 7H 161
Bushey Av. E18 3H 51
Bushey Cl. E4 3K 35
Bushey Cl. UB10: Ick 2C 56
Bushey Ct. SW20 3D 152
Bushey Down SW12 2F 137
BUSHEY HEATH 1C 26
Bushey Hill Rd. SE5 1E 120
Bushey La. SM1: Sutt 4J 165
Bushey Lees DA15: Sidc 6K 125
BUSHEY MEAD 2F 153
Bushey Rd. CR0: C'don 2C 170
Bushey Rd. E13 2A 88
Bushey Rd. N15 6E 48
Bushey Rd. SM1: Sutt 4J 165
(not continuous)
Bushey Rd. SW20 3D 152
Bushey Rd. UB10: Ick 2C 56
Bushey Rd. UB3: Harl 4G 93
Bushey Way BR3: Beck 6F 159
Bush Fair Ct. N14 6A 22
Bushfield Cl. HA8: Edg 2C 28
Bushfield Cres. HA8: Edg 2C 28
Bush Gro. HA7: Stan 1D 42
Bush Gro. NW9 7J 43
Bushgrove Rd. RM8: Dag 4D 72
Bush Hill N21 7H 23
Bush Hill Gdns. 7J 23
(off Bush Hill Road)
Bush Hill Pde. EN1: Enf 7J 23
Bush Hill Pde. N9 7J 23
BUSH HILL PARK 6A 24
Bush Hill Pk. Golf Course 5H 23
Bush Hill Rd. HA3: Kenton 6F 43
Bush Hill Rd. N21 6J 23
Bush Ind. Est. N19 3G 65
Bush Ind. Est. NW10 4K 79
Bush La. EC4 2E 14 (7D 84)
Bushmead Cl. N15 4F 49
Bushmoor Cres. SE18 7F 107
Bushnell Rd. SW17 2F 137
Bush Rd. E11 7H 51
Bush Rd. E8 1H 85
Bush Rd. IG9: Buck H 4G 37
Bush Rd. SE8 4K 103
Bush Rd. TW17: Shep 5B 146
Bush Rd. TW9: Kew 6F 97
Bush Theatre 2E 98
Bushway RM8: Dag 4D 72
Bushwood E11 7H 51
Bushwood Dr. SE1 4F 103
Bushwood Rd. TW9: Kew 6G 97
Bushy Ct. KT1: Hamp W 1C 150
(off Beverley Rd.)
Bushy Pk. 7H 131
Bushy Pk. Gdns. TW11: Tedd 5H 131
Bushy Pk. Rd. TW11: Tedd 7B 132
(not continuous)
Bushy Rd. TW11: Tedd 6K 131
Business Design Cen. 1A 84
(off Upper St.)
Buspace Studios W10 4G 81
(off Conlan St.)
Butcher Row E14 7K 85
Butchers M. UB3: Hayes 7H 75
(off Hemmen La.)
Butchers Rd. E16 6J 87
Bute Av. TW10: Ham 2E 132
Bute Ct. SM6: W'gton 5G 167
Bute Gdns. SM6: W'gton 5G 167
Bute Gdns. TW10: Ham 1E 132
Bute Gdns. W6 4F 99
Bute Gdns. W. SM6: W'gton 5G 167
Bute M. NW11 5A 46
Bute Rd. CR0: C'don 1A 168
Bute Rd. IG6: Ilf 5F 53
Bute Rd. SM6: W'gton 4G 167
Bute St. SW7 3A 16 (4B 100)
Bute Wlk. N1 6D 66
Butfield Ho. E9 6J 67
(off Stevens Av.)
Butler Av. HA1: Harr 7H 41
Butler Cl. HA8: Edg 2H 43
Butler Ct. HA0: Wemb 4A 60
Butler Ct. RM8: Dag 2G 73
(off Gosfield Rd.)
Butler Ct. SW11 1C 118
(off Hyde La.)
Butler Farm Cl. TW10: Ham 4D 132
Butler Ho. E14 6B 86
(off Burdett St.)
Butler Ho. E2 3J 85
(off Bacton St.)
Butler Ho. E3 5B 86
(off Geoffrey Chaucer Way)
Butler Ho. SW9 1B 120
(off Lothian Rd.)
Butler Pl. SW1 1C 18 (3H 101)
Butler Rd. HA1: Harr 7G 41
Butler Rd. NW10 7B 62
Butler Rd. RM8: Dag 4B 72
Butlers & Colonial Wharf SE1
6K 15 (2F 103)
(off Shad Thames)
Butlers Cl. TW4: Houn 3D 112
Butlers Dr. E4 1K 25
Butler St. E2 3J 85
Butler St. UB10: Hil 4D 74
Butlers Wharf SE1 5K 15 (1F 103)
Butlers Wharf W. SE1 5J 15 (1F 103)
(off Shad Thames)
Butley Ct. E3 2A 86
(off Ford St.)
Buttercup Cl. UB5: N'olt 6D 58
Butterfield Cl. N17 6H 33
Butterfield Cl. SE16 2H 103
Butterfield Cl. TW1: Twick 6K 113
Butterfields E17 5E 50
Butterfield Sq. E6 6D 88
Butterfly Apts. SW11 4C 118
(off Comyn Rd.)
Butterfly Ct. E6 3D 88
Butterfly Ct. N15 4E 48
(off Bathurst Sq.)
Butterfly Ct. NW9 1A 44
Butterfly La. SE9 6F 125
Butterfly Wlk. SE5 1D 120
(off Denmark Hill)
Butter Hill SM5: Cars 3E 166
Butter Hill SM6: W'gton 3E 166
Butteridges Cl. RM9: Dag 1F 91
Buttermere NW1 1K 5 (3F 83)
(off Augustus St.)
Buttermere Cl. E15 4F 69
Buttermere Cl. SE1 4F 103
Buttermere Cl. SM4: Mord 6F 153
Buttermere Cl. TW14: Felt 1H 129
Buttermere Ct. NW8 1B 82
(off Boundary Rd.)

Buttermere Dr. – Camden Sq.

Buttermere Dr. SW15 5G 117
Buttermere Ho. E3 3B 86
(off Mile End Rd.)
Buttermere Wlk. E8 6F 67
Butterwick W6 4F 99
Butterworth Gdns. IG8: Wfd G 6D 36
Butterworth Ter. SE17 5C 102
(off Sutherland Wlk.)
Buttery M. N14 3D 32
Buttesland St. N1 1F 9 (3D 84)
Buttfield Cl. RM10: Dag 6H 73
Buttmarsh Cl. SE18 5F 107
Button Lodge E17 4C 50
Buttonscroft Cl. CR7: Thor H 3C 156
Butts, The TW16: Sun 3A 148
Butts, The TW8: Bford 6C 96
Buttsbury Rd. IG1: Ilf 5G 71
Butts Cotts. TW13: Hanw 3C 130
Butts Cres. TW13: Hanw 3E 130
Buttsmead HA6: Nwood 1E 38
Butts Piece UB5: N'olt 2K 75
Butts Rd. BR1: Broml 5G 141
Buxhall Cres. E9 6B 68
Buxted Rd. E8 7F 67
Buxted Rd. N12 5H 31
Buxted Rd. SE22 4E 120
Buxton Cl. IG8: Wfd G 6G 37
Buxton Cl. N9 2D 34
Buxton Ct. E11 7H 51
Buxton Ct. N1 1D 8 (3C 84)
(off Thoresby St.)
Buxton Cres. SM3: Cheam 4G 165
Buxton Dr. E11 4G 51
Buxton Dr. KT3: N Mald 2K 151
Buxton Gdns. W3 7H 79
Buxton Ho. E11 4G 51
Buxton M. SW4 2H 119
Buxton Rd. CR7: Thor H 5B 156
Buxton Rd. DA8: Erith 7K 109
Buxton Rd. E15 5G 69
Buxton Rd. E17 4A 50
(not continuous)
Buxton Rd. E4 1A 36
Buxton Rd. E6 3C 88
Buxton Rd. IG2: Ilf 6J 53
Buxton Rd. N19 1H 65
Buxton Rd. NW2 6D 62
Buxton Rd. SW14 3A 116
Buxton St. E1 4K 9 (4F 85)
Buzzard Creek Ind. Est. IG11: Bark 5A 90
Buzz Bingo Bexleyheath 4H 127
Buzz Bingo Enfield 4B 24
Buzz Bingo Feltham 2K 129
Buzz Bingo Stratford 1F 87
Byam St. SW6 2A 118
Byards Ct. SE16 4K 103
(off Worgan St.)
Byards Cft. SW16 1H 155
Byas Ho. E3 3B 86
(off Benworth St.)
Byatt Wlk. TW12: Hamp 6C 130
Bychurch End TW11: Tedd 5K 131
Bycroft Rd. UB1: S'hall 4E 76
Bycroft St. SE20 7K 139
Bycullah Av. EN2: Enf 3G 23
Bycullah Rd. EN2: Enf 2G 23
Bye, The W3 6A 80
Byegrove Rd. SW19 6B 136
Byelands Cl. SE16 1K 103
Bye Way, The HA3: W'stone 1J 41
Byeway, The SW14 3J 115
Byeways TW2: Twick 3F 131
Byeways, The KT5: Surb 5G 151
Byfeld Gdns. SW13 1C 116
Byfield Cl. SE16 2B 104
Byfield Rd. TW7: Isle 3A 114
Byford Cl. E15 7G 69
Byford Ho. EN5: Barn 4A 20
Byford Ho. HA2: Harr 1E 58
Bygrove CR0: New Ad 6D 170
Bygrove St. E14 6D 86
(not continuous)
Byland Cl. N21 7E 22
Byland Cl. SE2 3B 108
Byland Cl. SM4: Mord 7A 154
Byne Rd. SE26 6J 139
Byne Rd. SM5: Cars 2C 166
Bynes Rd. CR2: S Croy 7D 168
Byng Pl. WC1 4C 6 (4H 83)
Byng Rd. EN5: Barn 2A 20
Byng St. E14 2C 104
Byron Av. DA7: Bex 3F 127
Byre Rd. N14 6A 22
Byrne Cl. CR0: C'don 6C 156
Byrne Rd. SW12 1F 137
Byron Av. E12 6C 70
Byron Av. E18 3H 51
Byron Av. KT3: N Mald 5C 152
Byron Av. NW9 4H 43
Byron Av. SM1: Sutt 4B 166
Byron Av. TW4: Cran 2J 111
Byron Av. E. SM1: Sutt 4B 166
Byron Cl. E8 1G 85
Byron Cl. KT12: Walt T 7C 148
Byron Cl. SE20 3H 157
Byron Cl. SE26 4A 140
Byron Cl. SE28 1C 108
Byron Cl. SW16 6J 137
Byron Cl. TW12: Hamp 4D 130
Byron Ct. E11 4K 51
(off Makepeace Rd.)
Byron Ct. EN2: Enf 2G 23
Byron Ct. HA1: Harr 6J 41
Byron Ct. NW6 7A 64
(off Fairfax Rd.)
Byron Ct. SE22 1G 139
Byron Ct. SW3 4D 16 (4C 100)
(off Elystan St.)
Byron Ct. W7 4A 96
(off Boston Rd.)
Byron Ct. W9 4J 81
(off Lanhill Rd.)
Byron Ct. WC1 3G 7 (4K 83)
(off Mecklenburgh Sq.)
Byron Dr. DA8: Erith 7H 109
Byron Dr. N2 6B 46
Byron Gdns. SM1: Sutt 4B 166
Byron Hill Rd. HA2: Harr 1H 59
Byron Ho. DA1: Cray 5K 127
Byron M. NW3 4C 64
Byron M. W9 4J 81
Byron Pde. UB10: Hil 4E 74
Byron Rd. E10 1D 68
Byron Rd. E17 3C 50
Byron Rd. HA0: Wemb 2C 60
Byron Rd. HA1: Harr 6J 41
Byron Rd. HA3: W'stone 2K 41
Byron Rd. NW2 2D 62
Byron Rd. NW7 5H 29
Byron Rd. W5 1F 97
Byron St. E14 6E 86
Byron Ter. N9 6D 24
Byron Ter. SE7 7A 106
Byron Way UB4: Hayes 4H 75
Byron Way UB5: N'olt 3C 76
Byron Way UB7: W Dray 4B 92
Bysouth Cl. IG5: Ilf 1F 53
Bysouth Cl. N15 4D 48
Bythorn St. SW9 3K 119
Byton Cl. RM7: Rush G 7J 55
Byton Rd. SW17 6D 136
Byward Av. TW14: Felt 6A 112
Byward St. EC3 3H 15 (7E 84)
Bywater Ho. SE18 3C 106
Bywater Pl. SE16 1A 104
Bywater St. SW3 5E 16 (5D 100)
Byway, The KT19: Ewe 4B 164
Byway, The SM2: Sutt 7B 166
Bywell Pl. E16 5H 87
Bywell Pl. W1 6A 6 (5G 83)
(off Wells St.)
Bywood Av. CR0: C'don 6J 157
Byworth Wlk. N19 1J 65

C

Cabanel Pl. SE11 4J 19 (4A 102)
Cabbell St. NW1 6C 4 (5C 82)
Cabinet Ct. NW2 3B 62
Cabinet Way E4 4G 35
Cable Ct. SE16 4A 104
(off Rope St.)
Cable Ho. WC1 1J 7 (3A 84)
(off Gt. Percy St.)
Cable Pl. SE10 1E 122
Cable St. E1 7G 85
Cable St. E16 2K 105
Cable Trade Pk. SE7 4A 106
Cable Wlk. SE10 4G 105
Cabot Cl. CR0: Wadd 3A 168
Cabot Ct. SE16 4K 103
(off Worgan St.)
Cabot Sq. E14 1C 104
Cabot Way E6 1B 88
Cabrail Ct. E14 5A 86
(off Aston Street)
Cab Rd. SE1 6J 13 (2A 102)
(off West Rd.)
Cabul Rd. SW11 2C 118
Caci Ho. W14 4H 99
(off Kensington Village)
Cactus Cl. SE15 2E 120
Cactus Wlk. W12 6B 80
Cadbury Cl. N20 1F 31
Cadbury Cl. TW16: Sun 7G 129
Cadbury Cl. TW7: Isle 1A 114
Cadbury Rd. TW16: Sun 7G 129
Cadbury Way SE16 3F 103
Caddington Cl. EN4: E Barn 5H 21
Caddington Rd. NW2 3G 63
Caddis Cl. HA7: Stan 7E 26
Cadell Cl. E2 1K 9 (2F 85)
Cade Rd. SE10 1F 123
Cader Rd. SW18 6A 118
Cadet Dr. SE1 4F 103
Cadet Ho. SE18 3F 107
Cadiz Ct. RM10: Dag 7K 73
Cadiz Rd. RM10: Dag 7J 73
Cadiz St. SE17 5C 102
Cadley Ter. SE23 2J 139
Cadman Cl. SW9 7B 102
Cadman Ct. W4 5H 97
(off Chaseley Dr.)
Cadmer Cl. KT3: N Mald 4A 152
Cadmium Sq. E2 3K 85
(off Palmer's Rd.)
Cadmore Ho. N1 7B 66
(off The Sutton Est.)
Cadmus Cl. SW4 3H 119
Cadmus Ct. SE16 4A 104
(off Seafarer Way)
Cadmus Ct. SW9 1A 120
(off Southey Rd.)
Cadnam Lodge E14 3E 104
(off Schooner Cl.)
Cadnam Point SW15 1D 134
Cadogan Cl. BR3: Beck 1F 159
Cadogan Cl. E9 7B 68
Cadogan Cl. HA2: Harr 4F 59
Cadogan Cl. TW11: Tedd 5J 131
Cadogan Ct. E9 7B 68
(off Cadogan Ter.)
Cadogan Ct. SM2: Sutt 6K 165
Cadogan Ct. SW3 4E 16 (4D 100)
(off Draycott Av.)
Cadogan Ct. Gdns. SW1 3G 17 (4E 100)
(off D'Oyley St.)
Cadogan Gdns. E18 3K 51
Cadogan Gdns. N21 5F 23
Cadogan Gdns. N3 1K 45
Cadogan Gdns. SW3 3F 17 (4D 100)
Cadogan Ga. SW1 3F 17 (4D 100)
Cadogan Hall 3G 17 (4E 100)
(off Sloane Ter.)
Cadogan Ho. IG8: Wfd G 7K 37
Cadogan Ho. SW3 7B 16 (6B 100)
(off Beaufort St.)
Cadogan La. SW1 2G 17 (3E 100)
Cadogan Mans. SW3 4F 17 (4D 100)
(off Cadogan Gdns.)
Cadogan Pl. SW1 1F 17 (3D 100)
Cadogan Rd. KT6: Surb 5D 150
Cadogan Rd. SE18 3G 107
Cadogan Sq. SW1 2F 17 (3D 100)
Cadogan St. SW3 4E 16 (4D 100)
Cadogan Ter. E9 6B 68
Cadoxton Av. N15 6F 49
Cadwal Apts. N1 7J 65
(off Caledonian Rd.)
Cadwallon Rd. SE9 2F 143
Caedmon Rd. N7 4K 65
Caerleon Cl. DA14: Sidc 5C 144
Caerleon Cl. KT10: Clay 7B 162
Caerleon Ter. SE2 4B 108
Caernafon Ho. HA7: Stan 5F 27
Caernarvon Cl. CR4: Mitc 3J 155
Caernarvon Dr. IG5: Ilf 1E 52
Caernarvon Ho. E16 1K 105
(off Audley Dr.)
Caernarvon Ho. W2 6A 82
(off Hallfield Est.)
Caesar Ct. E2 2K 85
(off Palmer's Rd.)
Caesars Wlk. CR4: Mitc 5D 154
Caesars Way TW17: Shep 6F 147
Cagney Cl. TW16: Sun 1J 147
Cagny Ho. SM1: Sutt 4K 165
Cahill St. EC1 4D 8 (4C 84)
Cahir St. E14 4D 104
Cain Ct. W5 5C 78
(off Castlebar M.)
Caine Ho. W3 2H 97
(off Hanbury Rd.)
Cain's La. TW14: Felt 5G 111
Caird St. W10 3G 81
Cairn Av. W5 1D 96
Cairncross M. N8 6J 47
Cairndale Cl. BR1: Broml 7H 141
Cairnfield Av. NW2 3A 62
Cairngorm Cl. TW11: Tedd 5A 132
Cairns Av. IG8: Wfd G 6H 37
Cairns Av. SW16 3G 155
Cairns M. SE18 1C 124
Cairns Pl. SW16 2G 155
Cairns Rd. SW11 5C 118
Cairn Way HA7: Stan 6E 26
Cairo New Rd. CR0: C'don 2B 168
Cairo Rd. E17 4C 50
Caisson Moor Ct. E3 4E 86
(off Navigation Rd.)
Caister Ho. N7 6K 65
Caistor Ho. E15 1H 87
(off Caistor Pk. Rd.)
Caistor M. SW12 7F 119
Caistor Pk. Rd. E15 1H 87
Caistor Rd. SW12 7F 119
Caithness Gdns. DA15: Sidc 6K 125
Caithness Ho. N1 1K 83
(off Twyford St.)
Caithness Rd. CR4: Mitc 7F 137
Caithness Rd. W14 3F 99
Caithness Wlk. CR0: C'don 2D 168
Calabria Rd. N5 6B 66
Calais Ga. SE5 1B 120
Calais St. SE5 1B 120
Calbourne Rd. SW12 7D 118
Calcott Ct. W14 3G 99
(off Blythe Rd.)
Calcott Wlk. SE9 4C 142
Calcraft Ho. E2 2J 85
(off Bonner Rd.)
Caldbeck Av. KT4: Wor Pk 2C 164
Caldecote KT1: King T 2G 151
(off Excelsior Cl.)
Caldecot Rd. SE5 2C 120
Caldecott Way E5 3K 67
Calder Av. UB6: G'frd 2K 77
Calder Cl. EN1: Enf 3K 23
Calder Ct. SE16 1B 104
Calder Gdns. HA8: Edg 3G 43
Calderon Ho. NW8 2C 82
(off Townshend Est.)
Calderon Pl. W10 5E 80
Calderon Rd. E11 4E 68
Calder Rd. SM4: Mord 5A 154
Caldervale Rd. SW4 5H 119
Calder Way SL3: Poyle 6A 174
Calderwood Pl. EN4: Had W 1E 20
Calderwood St. SE18 4E 106
Caldew Ct. NW7 7H 29
Caldew St. SE5 7D 102
Caldicote Grn. NW9 6A 44
Caldon Apts. CR0: C'don 2D 168
Caldon Ho. UB5: N'olt 4D 76
Caldwell Cl. SE18 5E 106
Caldwell Ho. SW13 7E 98
(off Trinity Chu. Rd.)
Caldwell St. SW9 7K 101
Caldy Rd. DA17: Belv 3H 109
Caldy Wlk. N1 7C 66
Caleb St. SE1 6D 14 (2C 102)
Caledonia Ct. IG11: Bark 2C 90
(off Keel Cl.)
Caledonia Ho. E14 6A 86
(off Salmon La.)
Caledonian Cl. IG3: Ilf 1B 72
Caledonian Ct. BR2: Broml 6C 160
(off Wells Vw. Dr.)
Caledonian Ct. UB5: N'olt 4C 76
Caledonian Point SE10 6D 104
(off Norman Rd.)
Caledonian Rd. N1 1F 7 (2J 83)
Caledonian Rd. N7 4K 65
Caledonian Sq. NW1 6H 65
Caledonian Wharf E14 4F 105
Caledonia Rd. TW19: Stanw 1A 128
Caledonia St. N1 1F 7 (3J 83)
Caledon Rd. E6 1D 88
Caledon Rd. SM6: W'gton 4E 166
Calendar M. KT6: Surb 6D 150
Cale St. SW3 5C 16 (5C 100)
Caletock Way SE10 5H 105
Calgarth NW1 1B 6 (2G 83)
(off Ampthill Est.)
Calgary Ct. RM7: Mawney 4H 55
Calgary Ct. SE16 2J 103
(off Canada Est.)
Calia Ho. E20 6E 68
(off Anthems Way)
Caliban Twr. N1 2E 84
(off Arden Est.)
Calico Av. SM6: W'gton 2E 166
Calico Ct. SE16 3G 103
(off Marine St.)
Calico Ho. E20 6E 68
(off Mirabelle Gdns.)
Calico Ho. EC4 1D 14 (6C 84)
(off Well Ct.)
Calico Ho. SE1 7G 15 (2E 102)
(off Long La.)
Calico Row SW11 3A 118
Calidore Cl. SW2 6K 119
California Bldg. SE13 1D 122
(off Deal's Gateway)
California Ct. WD23: B Hea 1C 26
(off High Rd.)
California La. WD23: B Hea 1C 26
California Rd. KT3: N Mald 4H 151
Callaby Ter. N1 6D 66
Callaghan Cl. SE13 4G 123
Callahan Cotts. E1 5J 85
(off Lindley St.)
Callander Rd. SE6 2D 140
Callanders, The WD23: B Hea 1D 26
Callard Av. N13 4G 33
Callard Cl. W2 4A 4 (4B 82)
Callcott Ct. NW6 7H 63
Callcott Rd. NW6 7H 63
Callcott St. W8 1J 99
Callendar Rd. SW7 1A 16 (3B 100)
Callender Ct. CR0: C'don 6C 156
(off Harry Cl.)
Callingham Cl. E14 5B 86
Callington M. TW2: Twick 2J 131
Callis Cl. SE18 3E 106
Callis Farm Cl. TW19: Stanw 6A 110
Callisons Pl. SE10 5G 105
Callis Rd. E17 6B 50
Calliston Ct. E16 5J 87
(off Hammersley Rd.)
Callonfield E17 4K 49
Callow St. SW3 7A 16 (6B 100)
Cally Pool & Gym 1K 83
Calmont Rd. BR1: Broml 6F 141
Calne Av. IG5: Ilf 1F 53
Calonne Rd. SW19 4F 135
Calshot Ho. N1 2K 83
(off Calshot St.)
Calshot Rd. TW6: H'row A 2C 110
Calshot St. N1 2K 83
Calshot Way EN2: Enf 3G 23
Calshot Way TW6: H'row A 2C 110
Calstock NW1 1G 83
(off Royal Coll. St.)
Calstock Ho. SE11 5K 19 (5A 102)
(off Kennings Way)
Calthorpe Gdns. HA8: Edg 5K 27
Calthorpe Gdns. SM1: Sutt 3A 166
Calthorpe St. WC1 3H 7 (4K 83)
Calton Av. SE21 6E 120
Calton Rd. EN5: New Bar 6F 21
Calverley Cl. BR3: Beck 6D 140
Calverley Ct. KT19: Ewe 4K 163
Calverley Cres. RM10: Dag 2G 73
Calverley Gdns. HA3: Kenton 7D 42
Calverley Gro. N19 1H 65
Calverley Rd. KT17: Ewe 6C 164
Calvert Av. E2 2H 9 (3E 84)
Calvert Cl. DA14: Sidc 6E 144
Calvert Cl. DA17: Belv 4G 109
Calvert Ct. TW9: Rich 4F 115
Calvert Dr. DA2: Wilm 2K 145
Calvert Ho. W12 7D 80
(off White City Est.)
Calvert M. RM8: Dag 1E 72
Calverton SE5 6E 102
(off Albany Rd.)
Calverton Pl. UB6: G'frd 6K 59
Calverton Rd. E6 1E 88
Calvert Rd. EN5: Barn 2A 20
Calvert Rd. SE10 5H 105
Calvert's Bldgs. SE1 5E 14 (1D 102)
Calvert St. NW1 1E 82
Calvin St. E1 4J 9 (4F 85)
Calydon Rd. SE7 5K 105
Calypso Cres. SE15 7F 103
Calypso Way SE16 3B 104
Camac Rd. TW2: Twick 1H 131
Camarthen Grn. NW9 5A 44
Cambalt Rd. SW15 5F 117
Cambay Ho. E1 4A 86
(off Harford St.)
Camber Ho. SE15 6J 103
Camberley Av. EN1: Enf 4K 23
Camberley Av. SW20 2D 152
Camberley Cl. SM3: Cheam 3F 165
Camberley Ho. NW1 1K 5 (2F 83)
(off Redhill St.)
Camberley Rd. TW6: H'row A 3C 110
Cambert Way SE3 4K 123
CAMBERWELL 1D 120
Camberwell Chu. St. SE5 1D 120
Camberwell Glebe SE5 1E 120
CAMBERWELL GREEN 1C 120
Camberwell Grn. SE5 1D 120
Camberwell Gro. SE5 1D 120
Camberwell Leisure Cen. 1D 120
Camberwell New Rd. SE5 6A 102
Camberwell Pas. SE5 1C 120
Camberwell Rd. SE5 6C 102
Camberwell Sta. Rd. SE5 1C 120
Camberwell Trad. Est. SE5 1B 120
Cambeys Rd. RM10: Dag 5H 73
Cambisgate SW19 5G 135
Cambium Apts. SW19 7F 117
(off Beatrice Pl.)
Cambium Apts. W8 3K 99
(off Beatrice Pl.)
Cambium Ho. HA9: Wemb 4G 61
(off Palace Arts Way)
Camborne Av. W13 2B 96
Camborne Cl. TW6: H'row A 3C 110
Camborne Cres. TW6: H'row A 3C 110
(off Camborne Rd.)
Camborne M. SW18 7J 117
Camborne M. W11 6G 81
Camborne Rd. CR0: C'don 7G 157
Camborne Rd. DA14: Sidc 3C 144
Camborne Rd. DA16: Well 2K 125
Camborne Rd. HA8: Edg 4A 28
Camborne Rd. SM2: Sutt 7J 165
Camborne Rd. SM4: Mord 5F 153
Camborne Rd. SW18 7J 117
Camborne Way TW5: Hest 1E 112
Cambourne Av. N9 7E 24
Cambourne Wlk. TW10: Rich 6D 114
Cambrai Ct. N13 3D 32
Cambray Rd. BR6: Orp 7K 161
Cambray Rd. SW12 1G 137
Cambria Cl. DA15: Sidc 1H 143
Cambria Cl. TW3: Houn 4E 112
Cambria Ct. E17 3A 50
Cambria Ct. TW14: Felt 7K 111
Cambria Gdns. TW19: Stanw 7A 110
(not continuous)
Cambria Ho. E14 6A 86
(off Salmon La.)
Cambria Ho. SE26 4G 139
(off High Level Dr.)
Cambrian Av. IG2: Ilf 5J 53
Cambrian Cl. SE27 3B 138
Cambrian Grn. NW9 5A 44
(off Snowdon Dr.)
Cambrian Rd. E10 7C 50
Cambrian Rd. TW10: Rich 6F 115
Cambria Rd. SE5 3C 120
Cambria St. SW6 7K 99
Cambridge Av. DA16: Well 4K 125
Cambridge Av. KT3: N Mald 3A 152
(not continuous)
Cambridge Av. NW6 2J 81
Cambridge Av. UB6: G'frd 5K 59
Cambridge Barracks Rd. SE18 4D 106
Cambridge Cir. WC2 1D 12 (6H 83)
Cambridge Cl. E17 6B 50
Cambridge Cl. EN4: E Barn 1K 31
Cambridge Cl. N22 1A 48
Cambridge Cl. NW10 3J 61
Cambridge Cl. SW20 1D 152
Cambridge Cl. TW4: Houn 4C 112
Cambridge Cl. UB7: Harm 2E 174
Cambridge Cotts. TW9: Kew 6G 97
Cambridge Ct. E2 2H 85
(off Cambridge Heath Rd.)
Cambridge Ct. N16 7E 48
(off Amhurst Pk.)
Cambridge Ct. NW6 2J 81
(not continuous)
Cambridge Ct. W2 6C 4 (5C 82)
(off Edgware Rd.)
Cambridge Ct. W6 4E 98
(off Shepherd's Bush Rd.)
Cambridge Cres. E2 2H 85
Cambridge Cres. TW11: Tedd 5A 132
Cambridge Dr. HA4: Ruis 2A 58
Cambridge Dr. SE12 5J 123
Cambridge Gdns. EN1: Enf 2B 24
Cambridge Gdns. KT1: King T 2G 151
Cambridge Gdns. N10 1E 46
Cambridge Gdns. N17 7J 33
Cambridge Gdns. N21 7J 23
Cambridge Gdns. NW6 2J 81
Cambridge Gdns. W10 6F 81
Cambridge Ga. NW1 3J 5 (4F 83)
Cambridge Ga. M. NW1 3K 5 (4F 83)
Cambridge Grn. SE9 1F 143
Cambridge Gro. SE20 1H 157
Cambridge Gro. W6 4D 98
Cambridge Gro. Rd. KT1: King T 3G 151
(not continuous)
Cambridge Heath Rd. E1 5H 85
Cambridge Heath Rd. E2 4J 85
Cambridge Ho. W13 6A 78
Cambridge Ho. W6 4D 98
(off Cambridge Gro.)
Cambridge Pde. EN1: Enf 1B 24
Cambridge Pk. E11 7J 51
Cambridge Pk. TW1: Twick 6C 114
Cambridge Pk. Ct. TW1: Twick 7D 114
Cambridge Pk. Rd. E11 7J 51
(off Lonsdale Rd.)
Cambridge Pas. E9 7J 67
Cambridge Pl. W8 2K 99
Cambridge Rd. BR1: Broml 7J 141
Cambridge Rd. CR4: Mitc 3G 155
Cambridge Rd. DA14: Sidc 4J 143
Cambridge Rd. E11 6H 51
Cambridge Rd. E4 1A 36
Cambridge Rd. HA2: Harr 5E 40
Cambridge Rd. IG11: Bark 7G 71
Cambridge Rd. IG3: Ilf 1J 71
Cambridge Rd. KT1: King T 2F 151
Cambridge Rd. KT12: Walt T 6K 147
Cambridge Rd. KT2: King T 2F 151
Cambridge Rd. KT3: N Mald 4K 151
Cambridge Rd. KT8: W Mole 4D 148
Cambridge Rd. NW6 2J 81
(not continuous)
Cambridge Rd. SE20 3H 157
Cambridge Rd. SM5: Cars 6C 166
Cambridge Rd. SW11 1D 118
Cambridge Rd. SW13 2B 116
Cambridge Rd. SW20 1C 152
Cambridge Rd. TW1: Twick 6D 114
Cambridge Rd. TW11: Tedd 4K 131
Cambridge Rd. TW12: Hamp 7D 130
Cambridge Rd. TW15: Ashf 7E 128
Cambridge Rd. TW4: Houn 4C 112
Cambridge Rd. TW9: Kew 7G 97
Cambridge Rd. UB1: S'hall 1D 94
Cambridge Rd. W7 2K 95
Cambridge Rd. Nth. W4 5H 97
Cambridge Rd. Sth. W4 5H 97
Cambridge Row SE18 5F 107
Cambridge Sq. W2 7C 4 (6C 82)
Cambridge St. SW1 4K 17 (4F 101)
Cambridge Ter. N9 7K 23
Cambridge Ter. NW1 2J 5 (3F 83)
Cambridge Ter. M. NW1 2K 5 (3F 83)
Cambridge Theatre 1E 12 (6J 83)
(off Earlham St.)
Cambstone Cl. N11 2K 31
Cambus Cl. UB4: Yead 5C 76
Cambus Rd. E16 5J 87
Cam Ct. SE15 6F 103
Camdale Rd. SE18 7K 107
Camden Arts Cen. 5K 63
Camden Av. TW13: Felt 1A 130
Camden Av. UB4: Yead 7B 76
Camden Cl. BR7: Chst 1G 161
Camden Cl. DA17: Belv 5G 109
Camden Ct. NW1 7G 65
(off Rousden St.)
Camden Gdns. CR7: Thor H 3B 156
Camden Gdns. NW1 7F 65
Camden Gdns. SM1: Sutt 5K 165
Camden Gro. BR7: Chst 6F 143
Camden High St. NW1 7F 65
Camden Hill Rd. SE19 6E 138
Camden Ho. SE8 5B 104
Camdenhurst St. E14 6A 86
Camden La. N7 5H 65
Camden Lock Market 7F 65
Camden Lock Pl. NW1 7F 65
Camden Markets 7F 65
Camden M. NW1 7G 65
Camden Pk. Rd. BR7: Chst 7D 142
Camden Pk. Rd. NW1 6H 65
Camden Pas. N1 2B 84
Camden People's Theatre 3A 6 (4G 83)
(off Hampstead Rd.)
Camden Rd. DA5: Bexl 1E 144
Camden Rd. E11 6K 51
Camden Rd. E17 6B 50
Camden Rd. N7 4J 65
Camden Rd. NW1 7G 65
Camden Rd. SM1: Sutt 5K 165
Camden Rd. SM5: Cars 4D 166
Camden Row HA5: Pinn 3A 40
Camden Row SE3 2G 123
Camden Sq. NW1 7H 65
(not continuous)
Camden Sq. SE15 1F 121

Camden St. – Cargrey Ho.

Camden St. NW1 7G 65
Camden Studios NW1 1G 83
(off Camden St.)
Camden Ter. NW1 6H 65
CAMDEN TOWN 1F 83
Camden Wlk. N1 1B 84
Camden Way BR7: Chst 7D 142
Camden Way CR7: Thor H 3B 156
Cameford Ct. SW2 7J 119
Camelford NW1 1G 83
(off Royal Coll. St.)
Camelford Ct. W11 6G 81
Camelford Ho. SE1 5F 19 (5J 101)
Camelford Wlk. W11 6G 81
Camel Gro. KT2: King T 5D 132
Camellia Cl. E10 2C 68
Camellia Ho. SE8 7B 104
(off Idonia St.)
Camellia Ho. SW11 7F 101
Camellia Ho. TW13: Felt 1J 129
(off Bedfont La.)
Camellia La. KT5: Surb 4H 151
Camellia Pl. TW2: Whitt 7F 113
Camellia St. SW8 7J 101
(not continuous)
Camelot Cl. SE28 2H 107
Camelot Cl. SW19 4H 135
Camelot Ho. NW1 6H 65
Camel Rd. E16 1C 106
Camera Pl. SW10 7A 16 (6B 100)
Camera Press Gallery, The
6J 15 (2F 103)
(off Queen Elizabeth St.)
Cameret Ct. W11 2F 99
(off Holland Rd.)
Cameron Cl. DA5: Bexl 3K 145
Cameron Cl. N18 4C 34
Cameron Cl. N20 2G 31
Cameron Cl. N22 7E 32
Cameron Cres. HA8: Edg 1H 43
Cameron Ho. BR1: Broml 1H 159
Cameron Ho. NW8 2C 82
(off St John's Wood Ter.)
Cameron Ho. SE5 7C 102
Cameron Pl. E1 6H 85
Cameron Pl. SW16 2A 138
Cameron Rd. BR2: Broml 5J 159
Cameron Rd. CR0: C'don 6B 156
Cameron Rd. IG3: Ilf 1J 71
Cameron Rd. SE6 2B 140
Cameron Sq. CR4: Mitc 1C 154
Cameron Ter. SE12 3K 141
Camerton Cl. E8 6F 67
Camgate Cen., The TW19: Stanw 6B 110
Camgate Mans. SE5 6C 102
(off Camberwell Rd.)
Camilla Cl. TW16: Sun 6H 129
Camilla Rd. SE16 4H 103
Camille Cl. SE25 3G 157
Camlan Rd. BR1: Broml 4H 141
Camlet St. E2 3J 9 (4F 85)
Camlet Way EN4: Barn 2D 20
Camlet Way EN4: Had W 2D 20
Camley St. N1 7H 65
Camley Street Natural Pk. 2J 83
Camley Street Natural Pk. Vis. Cen.
2H 83
Camm Gdns. KT1: King T 2F 151
Camm Gdns. KT7: T Ditt 7K 149
Camms Ter. RM10: Dag 5J 73
(off Cambeys Rd.)
Camomile Av. CR4: Mitc 1D 154
Camomile Rd. RM7: Rush G 2K 73
Camomile St. EC3 7H 9 (6E 84)
Camomile Way UB7: Yiew 6A 74
Campaign Ct. W9 4H 81
(off Chantry Cl.)
Campana Rd. SW6 1J 117
Campania Bldg. E1 7K 85
(off Jardine Rd.)
Campaspe Bus. Pk. TW16: Sun 5H 147
Campbell Av. IG6: Ilf 4F 53
Campbell Cl. HA4: Ruis 6J 39
Campbell Cl. SE18 1E 124
Campbell Cl. SW16 4H 137
Campbell Cl. TW2: Twick 1H 131
Campbell Ct. N17 1F 49
Campbell Ct. NW9 6J 43
Campbell Ct. SE22 1G 139
Campbell Ct. SW7 3A 100
(off Gloucester Rd.)
Campbell Cft. HA8: Edg 5B 28
Campbell Gordon Way NW2 4D 62
Campbell Ho. SW1 6A 18 (5G 101)
(off Churchill Gdns.)
Campbell Ho. W12 7D 80
(off White City Est.)
Campbell Ho. W2 5A 4 (5B 82)
(off Hall Pl.)
Campbell Ho. WC1 3C 6 (4H 83)
Campbell Rd. CR0: C'don 7B 156
Campbell Rd. E15 4H 69
Campbell Rd. E17 4B 50
Campbell Rd. E3 3C 86
Campbell Rd. E6 1C 88
Campbell Rd. KT8: E Mos 3J 149
Campbell Rd. N17 1F 49
Campbell Rd. TW2: Twick 2H 131
Campbell Rd. W7 7J 77
Campbell Wlk. N1 1J 83
(off Outram Pl.)
Campdale Rd. N7 3H 65
Campden Cres. HA0: Wemb 3B 60
Campden Cres. RM8: Dag 4B 72
Campden Gro. W8 2J 99
Campden Hill W8 2J 99
Campden Hill Ct. W8 2J 99
Campden Hill Gdns. W8 1J 99
Campden Hill Ga. W8 2J 99
Campden Hill Mans. W8 1J 99
(off Edge St.)
Campden Hill Pl. W11 1H 99
Campden Hill Rd. W8 1J 99
Campden Hill Sq. W8 1H 99
Campden Hill Towers W11 1J 99
Campden Ho. NW6 7B 64
(off Harben Rd.)
Campden Ho. W8 1J 99
(off Sheffield Ter.)
Campden Ho. Cl. W8 2J 99
Campden Ho's. W8 1J 99
Campden Ho. Ter. W8 1J 99
(off Kensington Chu. St.)
Campden Mans. W8 1J 99
(off Kensington Mall)
Campden Rd. CR2: S Croy 5E 168
Campden Rd. UB10: Ick 3B 56
Campden St. W8 1J 99
Campden Way RM8: Dag 4B 72
Campe Ho. N10 7K 31
Campen Cl. SW19 2G 135
Camperdown St. E1 1K 15 (6F 85)
Campfield Rd. SE9 7B 124
Campion Cl. CR0: C'don 4E 168
Campion Cl. E6 7D 88
Campion Cl. HA3: Kenton 6F 43
Campion Cl. RM7: Rush G 2K 73
Campion Cl. UB8: Hil 5B 74
Campion Ct. HA0: Wemb 2E 78
Campion Gdns. IG8: Wfd G 5D 36
Campion Ho. E14 6B 86
(off Frances Wharf)
Campion Ho. SE16 2A 104
(off Blondin Way)
Campion Pl. SE28 1A 108
Campion Rd. E10 7D 50
Campion Rd. SW15 4E 116
Campion Rd. TW7: Isle 1K 113
Campion Ter. NW2 3F 63
Campion Way HA8: Edg 4D 28
Camplin Rd. HA3: Kenton 5E 42
Camplin St. SE14 7K 103
Camp Rd. SW19 5D 134
Campsbourne, The N8 4J 47
Campsbourne Ho. N8 4J 47
(off Pembroke Rd.)
Campsbourne Pde. N8 4J 47
(off High St.)
Campsbourne Rd. N8 3J 47
(not continuous)
Campsey Gdns. RM9: Dag 7B 72
Campsey Rd. RM9: Dag 7B 72
Campsfield Ho. N8 3J 47
(off Campsfield Rd.)
Campsfield Rd. N8 3J 47
Campshill Pl. SE13 5E 122
Campshill Rd. SE13 5E 122
Campus Av. RM8: Dag 4A 72
Campus Ho. TW7: Isle 7J 95
Campus Rd. E17 6B 50
Campus Way NW4 3D 44
Camp Vw. SW19 5D 134
Cam Rd. E15 1F 87
Camrose Av. DA8: Erith 6H 109
Camrose Av. HA8: Edg 2E 42
Camrose Av. TW13: Felt 4A 130
Camrose Cl. CR0: C'don 7A 158
Camrose Cl. SM4: Mord 4J 153
Camrose St. SE2 5A 108
Camwal Ct. CR4: Mitc 2C 154
Canada Av. N18 6H 33
Canada Cres. W3 5J 79
Canada Est. SE16 3J 103
Canada Gdns. SE13 5E 122
Canada House 3A 104
(off Brunswick Quay)
Canada House 4D 12 (1H 101)
(off Trafalgar Sq.)
Canada Memorial 6A 12 (2G 101)
Canada Pl. E14 1D 104
(off Canada Sq.)
Canada Rd. W3 5J 79
Canada Sq. E14 1D 104
Canada St. SE16 2K 103
Canada Way W12 7D 80
Canada Wharf SE16 1B 104
Canadian Av. SE6 1D 140
Canal App. SE8 5A 104
Canal Blvd. NW1 6H 65
CANAL BRIDGE 6G 103
Canal Bldg. N1 2C 84
Canal Cl. E1 4A 86
Canal Cl. W10 4F 81
Canal Cotts. E3 1B 86
(off Parnell Rd.)
Canaletto EC1 1C 8 (3C 84)
(off City Rd.)
Canal Gro. SE15 6H 103
(off Yeoman St.)
Canal Market 7F 65
(off Castlehaven Rd.)
Canal Mill Apts. E2 1F 85
(off Boat La.)
Canal Path E2 1F 85
Canal Reach N1 1H 83
Canalside Activity Cen. 4F 81
Canalside Gdns. UB2: S'hall 4C 94
Canalside Sq. N1 1C 84
Canal Side Studios NW1 1H 83
(off St Pancras Way)
Canalside Studios N1 1E 84
(off Orsman Rd.)
Canalside Wlk. W2 6A 4 (5B 82)
Canal Wlk. CR0: C'don 6E 156
Canal Wlk. E17 3K 49
Canal Wlk. N1 1D 84
Canal Wlk. NW10 7J 61
(off Westend Cl.)
Canal Wlk. SE26 5J 139
Canal Way W10 4F 81
Canal Wharf E8 1E 84
(off Kingsland Rd.)
Canal Wharf UB6: G'frd 1A 78
Canal Yd. UB2: S'hall 4K 93
Canary Vw. SE10 6D 104
(off Dowells St.)
Canary Wharf Tower 1D 104
Canberra Cl. NW4 3C 44
Canberra Cl. RM10: Dag 1K 91
Canberra Cres. RM10: Dag 7K 73
Canberra Dr. UB4: N'olt 3B 76
Canberra Dr. UB5: N'olt 3A 76
Canberra Path E10 7D 50
(off Whitney Rd.)
Canberra Pl. TW9: Rich 3G 115
Canberra Rd. DA7: Bex 6D 108
Canberra Rd. E6 1D 88
Canberra Rd. SE7 6A 106
Canberra Rd. TW6: H'row A 3C 110
Canberra Rd. W13 1A 96
Canbury Av. KT2: King T 1F 151
Canbury Bus. Cen. KT2: King T 1E 150
Canbury Bus. Pk. KT2: King T 1E 150
(off Canbury Pk. Rd.)
Canbury Ct. KT2: King T 7D 132
Canbury M. SE26 3G 139
Canbury Pk. Rd. KT2: King T 1E 150
Canbury Pas. KT2: King T 1D 150
Cancell Rd. SW9 1A 120
Candahar Rd. SW11 2C 118
Candida Ct. NW1 7F 65
Candid Ho. NW10 3D 80
(off Trenmar Gdns.)
Candle Gro. SE15 3H 121
Candlelight Ct. E15 6H 69
(off Romford Rd.)
Candler M. TW1: Twick 7A 114
Candler St. N15 6D 48
Candle St. E1 5A 86
Candover Cl. UB7: Harm 3E 174
Candover St. W1 6A 6 (5G 83)
Candy St. E3 1B 86
Candy Wharf E3 4A 86
Caney M. NW2 2F 63
Canfield Dr. HA4: Ruis 5K 57
Canfield Gdns. NW6 7K 63
Canfield Ho. N15 6E 48
(off Albert Rd.)
Canfield Pl. NW6 6A 64
Canfield Rd. IG8: Wfd G 7H 37
Canford Av. UB5: N'olt 1D 76
Canford Cl. EN2: Enf 2F 23
Canford Gdns. KT3: N Mald 6A 152
Canford Pl. TW11: Tedd 6C 132
Canford Rd. SW11 5E 118
Canham Gdns. TW4: Houn 7D 112
Canham Rd. SE25 3E 156
Canham Rd. W3 2A 98
Canius Ho. CR0: C'don 3C 168
(off Scarbrook Rd.)
Canmore Gdns. SW16 7G 137
CANN HALL 4G 69
Cann Hall Rd. E11 4G 69
Cann Ho. W14 3G 99
(off Russell Rd.)
Canning Cres. N22 1K 47
Canning Cross SE5 2E 120
Canning Ho. W12 7D 80
(off Australia Rd.)
Canning Pas. W8 3A 100
Canning Pl. W8 3A 100
Canning Pl. M. W8 3A 100
(off Canning Pl.)
Canning Rd. CR0: C'don 2F 169
Canning Rd. E15 2G 87
Canning Rd. E17 4A 50
Canning Rd. HA3: W'stone 3J 41
Canning Rd. N5 3B 66
Canning Sq. EN1: Enf 1B 24
Cannington Rd. RM9: Dag 6C 72
CANNING TOWN 5G 87
CANNING TOWN 6H 87
Cannizaro Rd. SW19 6E 134
Cannock Ct. E17 2E 50
Cannock Ho. N4 7C 48
Cannonbury Av. HA5: Pinn 6B 40
Cannon Cl. SW20 3E 152
Cannon Cl. TW12: Hamp 6F 131
Cannon Ct. EC1 3A 8 (4B 84)
(off Brewhouse Yd.)
Cannon Dr. E14 7C 86
Cannon Hill N14 3D 32
Cannon Hill NW6 5J 63
Cannon Hill La. SW20 5F 153
Cannon Hill M. N14 3D 32
Cannon Ho. SE11 4H 19 (4K 101)
(off Beaufoy Wlk.)
Cannon La. HA5: Pinn 5C 40
Cannon La. NW3 3B 64
Cannon Pl. NW3 3B 64
Cannon Pl. SE7 5C 106
Cannon Retail Pk. 7A 90
Cannon Rd. DA7: Bex 1E 126
Cannon Rd. N14 3D 32
Cannon Rd. N17 6A 34
Cannon St. EC4 1C 14 (6C 84)
Cannon St. Rd. E1 6H 85
Cannon Trad. Est. HA9: Wemb 4H 61
Cannon Way KT8: W Mole 4E 148
Cannon Wharf Bus. Cen. SE8 4A 104
(off Pell St.)
Cannon Wharf Development SE8
4A 104
Cannon Workshops E14 7C 86
(off Cannon Dr.)
Canoe Wlk. E14 6B 86
Canon All. EC4 1C 14 (6C 84)
(off Queen's Head Pas.)
Canon Av. RM6: Chad H 5C 54
Canon Beck Rd. SE16 2J 103
Canonbie Rd. SE23 7J 121
CANONBURY 6C 66
Canonbury Bus. Cen. N1 1C 84
Canonbury Cotts. EN1: Enf 1K 23
Canonbury Ct. N1 7B 66
(off Hawes St.)
Canonbury Cres. N1 7C 66
Canonbury Gro. N1 7C 66
Canonbury Hgts. N1 6D 66
(off Dove Rd.)
Canonbury La. N1 7B 66
Canonbury Pk. Nth. N1 6C 66
Canonbury Pk. Sth. N1 6C 66
Canonbury Pl. N1 6B 66
(not continuous)
Canonbury Rd. EN1: Enf 1K 23
Canonbury Rd. N1 6B 66
Canonbury Sq. N1 7B 66
Canonbury St. N1 7C 66
Canonbury Vs. N1 7B 66
Canon Ho. W10 3H 81
(off Bruckner St.)
Canon Mohan Cl. N14 6K 21
Canon Rd. BR1: Broml 3A 160
Canon Row SW1 7E 12 (2J 101)
(not continuous)
Canon's Cl. N2 7B 46
Canons Cl. CR4: Mitc 4D 154
Canons Cl. HA8: Edg 6A 28
Canons Cnr. HA8: Edg 4K 27
Canons Ct. E15 4G 69
Canons Ct. HA8: Edg 6A 28
Canons Dr. HA8: Edg 6K 27
Canonsleigh Rd. RM9: Dag 7B 72
Canons Leisure Cen. Mitcham 4D 154
Canons Pk. 6J 27
CANONS PARK 7J 27
Canons Pk. Cl. HA8: Edg 7K 27
Canons Row HA8: Edg 4K 27
Canon St. N1 1C 84
Canon's Wlk. CR0: C'don 3K 169
Canons Way HA8: Edg 4A 28
Canopus Way TW19: Stanw 7A 110
Canrobert St. E2 2H 85
Cantelowes Rd. NW1 6H 65
Canterbury Av. DA15: Sidc 2B 144
Canterbury Av. IG1: Ilf 7C 52
Canterbury Cl. BR3: Beck 1D 158
Canterbury Cl. E6 6D 88
Canterbury Cl. KT4: Wor Pk 2F 165
Canterbury Cl. SE5 2C 120
(off Lilford Rd.)
Canterbury Cl. UB6: G'frd 5F 77
Canterbury Ct. CR2: S Croy 7C 168
(off St Augustine's Av.)
Canterbury Ct. NW6 2J 81
(off Canterbury Rd.)
Canterbury Ct. NW9 2A 44
Canterbury Ct. SE12 3K 141
Canterbury Ct. SE5 7A 102
Canterbury Ct. TW15: Ashf 4B 128
Canterbury Cres. SW9 3A 120
Canterbury Gro. SE27 4A 138
Canterbury Hall KT4: Wor Pk 7D 152
Canterbury Ho. CR0: C'don 1D 168
(off Sydenham Rd.)
Canterbury Ho. E3 3D 86
(off Bow Rd.)
Canterbury Ho. IG11: Bark 7A 72
(off Margaret Bondfield Av.)
Canterbury Ho. RM8: Dag 4A 72
(off Academy Way)
Canterbury Ho. SE1 1H 19 (3K 101)
Canterbury Ho. SE8 5C 104
(off Wharf St.)
Canterbury Ind. Pk. SE15 6J 103
Canterbury Pl. SE17 5B 102
Canterbury Rd. NW6 Carlton Va. 2H 81
Canterbury Rd. NW6 Princess Rd. 2J 81
Canterbury Rd. CR0: C'don 7K 155
Canterbury Rd. E10 7E 50
Canterbury Rd. HA1: Harr 5F 41
Canterbury Rd. HA2: Harr 5F 41
Canterbury Rd. SM4: Mord 7K 153
Canterbury Rd. TW13: Hanw 2C 130
Canterbury Ter. NW6 2J 81
Canter Way E1 1K 15 (6G 85)
Cantium Retail Pk. 6G 103
Cantley Gdns. IG2: Ilf 6G 53
Cantley Gdns. SE19 1F 157
Cantley Rd. W7 3A 96
Canto Ct. EC1 3D 8 (4C 84)
(off Old St.)
Canton St. E14 6C 86
Cantrell Rd. E3 4B 86
Cantwell Rd. SE18 7F 107
Canute Gdns. SE16 4K 103
Canvey St. SE1 4C 14 (1C 102)
Canyon Gdn. E3 3B 86
(off St Clements Av.)
Capa Taro Way HA2: Harr 3G 41
Cape Cl. IG11: Bark 7F 71
Cape Henry Ct. E14 7F 87
(off Jamestown Way)
Cape Ho. E16 1K 105
(off Cunningham Av.)
Cape Ho. E8 6F 67
(off Dalston La.)
Capel Av. SM6: W'gton 5K 167
Capel Cl. BR2: Broml 1C 172
Capel Cl. N20 3F 31
Capel Ct. EC2 1F 15 (6D 84)
(off Bartholomew La.)
Capel Ct. SE20 1J 157
Capel Cres. HA7: Stan 2F 27
Capel Gdns. HA5: Pinn 4D 40
Capel Gdns. IG3: Bark 4K 71
Capel Gdns. IG3: Ilf 4K 71
Capel Ho. E9 7J 67
(off Loddiges Rd.)
Capel Rd. E12 4B 70
Capel Rd. E7 4K 69
Capel Rd. EN4: E Barn 6H 21
Capener's Cl. SW1 7G 11 (2E 100)
(off Kinnerton St.)
Capern Rd. SW18 1A 136
Cape Rd. N17 3G 49
Cape Yd. E1 1G 103
Capital Bus. Cen. CR2: S Croy 7D 168
Capital Bus. Cen. HA0: Wemb 2D 78
Capital E. Apts. E16 7J 87
(off Western Gateway)
Capital Ho. SW15 5G 117
(off Plaza Gdns.)
Capital Ind. Est. CR4: Mitc 5D 154
Capital Ind. Est. DA17: Belv 3H 109
Capital Interchange Way TW8: Bford
5G 97
Capital Mill Apts. E2 1F 85
(off Whiston Rd.)
Capital Trad. Est. IG11: Bark 2H 89
Capital Wharf E1 1G 103
Capitol Bldg. SW11 6H 101
(off New Union Sq.)
Capitol Ind. Pk. NW9 3J 43
Capitol Wlk. SE23 2J 139
(off London Rd.)
Capitol Way NW9 3J 43
Capland Ho. NW8 3B 4 (4B 82)
(off Capland St.)
Capland St. NW8 3B 4 (4B 82)
Caple Ho. SW10 7A 100
(off King's Rd.)
Caple Rd. NW10 2B 80
Capper St. WC1 4B 6 (4G 83)
Caprea Cl. UB4: Yead 5B 76
Capricorn Cen. RM8: Dag 7F 55
Capricorn Ct. HA8: Edg 7B 28
(off Zodiac Cl.)
Capri Ho. E17 2B 50
Capri Ho. NW9 3B 44
(off Caversham Rd.)
Capri Rd. CR0: C'don 1F 169
Capstan Cl. RM6: Chad H 6B 54
Capstan Ct. E1 7J 85
(off Wapping Wall)
Capstan Ho. E14 Clove Cres. 7F 87
(off Clove Cres.)
Capstan Ho. E14 Stebondale St. 4E 104
(off Stebondale St.)
Capstan Ride EN2: Enf 2F 23
Capstan Rd. SE8 4B 104
Capstan Sq. E14 2E 104
Capstan Way SE16 1A 104
Capstone Rd. BR1: Broml 4H 141
Captain St. SE18 1C 124
(off Tellson Av.)
Capthorne Av. HA2: Harr 1C 58
Capuchin Cl. HA7: Stan 6G 27
Capulet M. E16 1J 105
Capulet Sq. E3 3D 86
(off Talwin St.)
Capworth St. E10 1C 68
Caradoc Cl. W2 6J 81
Caradoc Evans Cl. N11 5A 32
(off Springfield Rd.)
Caradoc St. SE10 5G 105
Caradon Cl. E11 1G 69
Caradon Way N15 4D 48
Caragh M. UB2: S'hall 4C 94
Cara Ho. N1 7A 66
(off Liverpool Rd.)
Cara Ho. NW9 3J 43
Caramel Ct. E3 2D 86
(off Taylor Pl.)
Caranday Vs. W11 1F 99
(off Norland Rd.)
Carat Ho. E14 5C 86
(off Ursula Gould Way)
Caravel Cl. E14 3C 104
Caravel Ho. E16 2K 105
(off Regalia Close)
Caravelle Gdns. UB5: N'olt 3B 76
Caravel M. SE8 6C 104
Caraway Apts. SE1 6K 15 (2F 103)
(off Cayenne Ct.)
Caraway Cl. E13 5K 87
Caraway Hgts. E14 7E 86
(off Poplar High St.)
Caraway Pl. SM6: W'gton 3F 167
Carberry Rd. SE19 6E 138
Carbery Av. W3 2F 97
Carbis Cl. E4 1A 36
Carbis Rd. E14 6B 86
Carbrooke Ho. E9 1J 85
(off Templecombe Rd.)
Carbuncle Pas. N17 2G 49
Carburton St. W1 5K 5 (5F 83)
Cardale St. E14 2E 104
Cardamon Bldg. SE1 6K 15 (2F 103)
(off Shad Thames)
Carden Ct. KT8: W Mole 4F 149
Carden Rd. SE15 3H 121
Cardiff Ho. SE15 6G 103
(off Friary Est.)
Cardiff Rd. EN3: Pond E 4C 24
Cardiff Rd. W7 3A 96
Cardiff St. SE18 7J 107
Cardigan Ct. W7 4K 77
(off Copley Cl.)
Cardigan Gdns. IG3: Ilf 2A 72
Cardigan Pl. SE3 2F 123
Cardigan Rd. E3 2B 86
Cardigan Rd. SW13 2C 116
Cardigan Rd. SW19 6A 136
Cardigan Rd. TW10: Rich 6E 114
Cardigan St. SE11 5J 19 (5A 102)
Cardigan Wlk. N1 7C 66
(off Ashby Gro.)
Cardinal Av. KT2: King T 5E 132
Cardinal Av. SM4: Mord 6G 153
Cardinal Bourne St. SE1 3D 102
Cardinal Cap All. SE1 4C 14 (1C 102)
Cardinal Cl. BR7: Chst 1J 161
Cardinal Cl. HA8: Edg 7D 28
Cardinal Cl. KT4: Wor Pk 4C 164
Cardinal Cl. SM4: Mord 6G 153
Cardinal Ct. E1 7G 85
(off Thomas More St.)
Cardinal Cres. KT3: N Mald 2J 151
Cardinal Hinsley Cl. NW10 2C 80
Cardinal Mans. SW1 3A 18 (4G 101)
(off Carlisle Pl.)
Cardinal Pl. SW1 1A 18 (3G 101)
(not continuous)
Cardinal Pl. SW15 4F 117
Cardinal Rd. HA4: Ruis 1B 58
Cardinal Rd. TW13: Felt 1K 129
Cardinals Wlk. TW12: Hamp 7G 131
Cardinals Wlk. TW16: Sun 6G 129
Cardinals Way N19 1H 65
Cardinal Wlk. SW1 2A 18 (3G 101)
(off Victoria St.)
Cardinal Way HA3: W'stone 3J 41
Cardine M. SE15 7H 103
Cardington Sq. TW4: Houn 4B 112
Cardington St. NW1 1B 6 (3G 83)
Cardinham Rd. BR6: Chels 4K 173
Cardozo Rd. N7 5J 65
Cardrew Av. N12 5G 31
Cardrew Cl. N12 5H 31
Cardrew Ct. N12 5G 31
Cardross Ho. W6 3D 98
(off Cardross St.)
Cardross St. W6 3D 98
Cardwell Rd. N7 4J 65
Cardwell Ter. N7 4J 65
(off Cardwell Rd.)
Career Ct. SE16 2K 103
(off Christopher Cl.)
Carew Cl. N7 2K 65
Carew Ct. RM6: Chad H 6B 54
(off Quarles Pk. Rd.)
Carew Ct. SE14 6K 103
(off Samuel Cl.)
Carew Ct. SM2: Sutt 7K 165
Carew Manor & Dovecote 3H 167
Carew Mnr. Cotts. SM6: Bedd 3H 167
Carew Rd. CR4: Mitc 2E 154
Carew Rd. CR7: Thor H 4B 156
Carew Rd. N17 2G 49
Carew Rd. SM6: W'gton 6G 167
Carew Rd. TW15: Ashf 6E 128
Carew Rd. W13 2C 96
Carew St. SE5 2C 120
Carey Ct. DA6: Bex 5H 127
Carey Ct. SE5 7C 102
Carey Gdns. SW8 1G 119
Carey La. EC2 7C 8 (6C 84)
Carey Mans. SW1 3C 18 (4H 101)
(off Rutherford St.)
Carey Pl. SW1 4C 18 (4H 101)
Carey Rd. RM9: Dag 4E 72
Carey St. WC2 1H 13 (6K 83)
Carey Way HA9: Wemb 4H 61
Carfax Ho. SE20 1G 157
Carfax Pl. SW4 4H 119
Carfax Rd. UB3: Harl 5H 93
Carfree Cl. N1 7A 66
Cargill Rd. SW18 1K 135
Cargo Point TW19: Stanw 6B 110
Cargreen Pl. SE25 4F 157
(off Cargreen Rd.)
Cargreen Rd. SE25 4F 157
Cargrey Ho. HA7: Stan 5H 27

A–Z London 197

Carholme Rd. – Cathcart Hill

Carholme Rd. SE23 1B 140
Carillon Ct. E1 5G 85 (off Greatorex St.)
Carillon Ct. W5 7D 78
Carina Ho. E20 5E 68 (off Cheering La.)
Carinthia Ct. SE16 4A 104 (off Plough Way)
Carisbrook N10 2F 47
Carisbrook Cl. EN1: Enf 1A 24
Carisbrooke Av. DA5: Bexl 1D 144
Carisbrooke Cl. HA7: Stan 2D 42
Carisbrooke Cl. TW4: Houn 7C 112
Carisbrooke Ct. SM2: Cheam 7H 165
Carisbrooke Ct. UB5: N'olt 1D 76 (off Eskdale Av.)
Carisbrooke Ct. W1 6H 5 (5E 82) (off Weymouth St.)
Carisbrooke Ct. W3 2J 97 (off Brouncker Rd.)
Carisbrooke Gdns. SE15 7F 103
Carisbrooke Ho. KT2: King T 1E 150 (off Seven Kings Way)
Carisbrooke Ho. TW10: Rich 5G 115
Carisbrooke Ho. UB7: W Dray 2B 92 (off Park Lodge Av.)
Carisbrooke Rd. BR2: Broml 4A 160
Carisbrooke Rd. CR4: Mitc 4H 155
Carisbrooke Rd. E17 4A 50
Carker's La. NW5 5F 65
Carlcott Cl. KT12: Walt T 7K 147
Carleton Av. KT8: E Mos 6H 149
Carleton Av. SM6: W'gton 7H 167
Carleton Cl. KT10: Esh 7H 149
Carleton Gdns. N19 5G 65
Carleton Ho. NW9 3B 44 (off Boulevard Dr.)
Carleton Rd. N19 5H 65
Carleton Rd. N7 5G 65
Carleton Vs. NW5 5G 65
Carlile Cl. E3 2B 86
Carlile Ho. SE1 3D 102 (off Tabard St.)
Carlile Pl. TW10: Rich 6F 115
Carlina Gdns. IG8: Wfd G 5E 36
Carlingford Gdns. CR4: Mitc 7D 136
Carlingford Rd. N15 3B 48
Carlingford Rd. NW3 4B 64
Carlingford Rd. SM4: Mord 6F 153
Carlisle Av. EC3 1H 15 (6E 84)
Carlisle Av. W3 6A 80
Carlisle Cl. HA5: Pinn 7C 40
Carlisle Cl. KT2: King T 1G 151
Carlisle Gdns. HA3: Kenton 7D 42
Carlisle Gdns. IG1: Ilf 6C 52
Carlisle Ho. IG1: Ilf 6C 52
Carlisle La. SE1 2H 19 (3K 101)
Carlisle Mans. SW1 3A 18 (4G 101) (off Carlisle Pl.)
Carlisle M. KT2: King T 1G 151
Carlisle Pl. N11 4A 32
Carlisle Pl. SW1 2A 18 (3G 101)
Carlisle Rd. E10 1C 68
Carlisle Rd. N4 7A 48
Carlisle Rd. NW6 1G 81
Carlisle Rd. NW9 3J 43
Carlisle Rd. SM1: Sutt 6H 165
Carlisle Rd. TW12: Hamp 7F 131
Carlisle St. W1 1C 12 (6H 83)
Carlisle Wlk. E8 6F 67
Carlisle Way SW17 5E 136
Carlos Pl. W1 3H 11 (7E 82)
Carlow St. NW1 2G 83
Carlson Ct. SW15 4H 117
Carlton Av. CR2: S Croy 7E 168
Carlton Av. HA3: Kenton 5B 42
Carlton Av. N14 5C 22
Carlton Av. TW14: Felt 6A 112
Carlton Av. UB3: Harl 4G 93
Carlton Av. E. HA9: Wemb 2D 60
Carlton Av. W. HA0: Wemb 2B 60
Carlton Cl. HA8: Edg 5B 28
Carlton Cl. KT9: Chess 6D 162
Carlton Cl. NW3 2J 63
Carlton Cl. UB5: N'olt 5G 59
Carlton Ct. IG6: Ilf 3H 53
Carlton Ct. N3 7D 30
Carlton Ct. SE20 1H 157
Carlton Ct. UB8: Cowl 5A 74
Carlton Ct. W9 2K 81 (off Maida Vale)
Carlton Cres. SM3: Cheam 4G 165
Carlton Dr. IG6: Ilf 3H 53
Carlton Dr. SW15 5F 117
Carlton Gdns. SW1 5C 12 (1H 101)
Carlton Gdns. W5 6C 78
Carlton Grn. DA14: Sidc 4K 143
Carlton Gro. SE15 1H 121
Carlton Hill NW8 2K 81
Carlton Ho. NW6 2J 81 (off Canterbury Ter.)
Carlton Ho. SE16 2K 103 (off Wolfe Cres.)
Carlton Ho. TW14: Felt 6H 111
Carlton Ho. TW3: Houn 6E 112
Carlton Ho. Ter. SW1 5C 12 (1H 101)
Carlton Lodge N4 7A 48 (off Carlton Rd.)
Carlton Mans. N16 1F 67
Carlton Mans. NW6 7J 63 (off West End La.)
Carlton Mans. W14 2G 99 (off Holland Pk. Gdns.)
Carlton Mans. W9 3K 81
Carlton M. NW6 5J 63 (off West Cotts.)
Carlton Pde. HA9: Wemb 2E 60
Carlton Pk. Av. SW20 2F 153
Carlton Rd. CR2: S Croy 6D 168
Carlton Rd. DA14: Sidc 5K 143
Carlton Rd. DA16: Well 3B 126
Carlton Rd. DA8: Erith 6H 109
Carlton Rd. E11 1H 69
Carlton Rd. E12 4B 70
Carlton Rd. E17 1A 50
Carlton Rd. KT12: Walt T 7K 147
Carlton Rd. KT3: N Mald 2A 152
Carlton Rd. N11 5K 31
Carlton Rd. N4 7A 48
Carlton Rd. SW14 3J 115
Carlton Rd. TW16: Sun 7H 129
Carlton Rd. W4 2K 97
Carlton Rd. W5 7C 78
Carlton Sq. E1 4K 85 (not continuous)
Carlton St. SW1 3C 12 (7H 83)
Carlton Ter. E11 5K 51 (not continuous)
Carlton Ter. E7 7A 70
Carlton Ter. N18 3J 33
Carlton Ter. SE26 3J 139
Carlton Twr. Pl. SW1 1F 17 (3D 100)
Carlton Towers SM5: Cars 3D 166
Carlton Va. NW6 2H 81
Carlton Vs. SW15 5G 117
Carlton Works, The SE15 7H 103 (off Asylum Rd.)
Carlwell St. SW17 5C 136
Carlyle Av. BR1: Broml 3B 160
Carlyle Av. UB1: S'hall 7D 76
Carlyle Cl. KT8: W Mole 2F 149
Carlyle Cl. N2 6A 46
Carlyle Ct. SW10 1A 118 (off Chelsea Harbour Dr.)
Carlyle Ct. SW6 1K 117 (off Imperial Rd.)
Carlyle Gdns. UB1: S'hall 7D 76
Carlyle Ho. KT8: W Mole 5E 148 (off Down St.)
Carlyle Ho. N16 3E 66
Carlyle Ho. SE5 7C 102 (off Bethwin Rd.)
Carlyle Ho. SW3 7B 16 (6B 100) (off Old Church St.)
Carlyle Mans. SW3 7C 16 (6C 100) (off Cheyne Wlk.)
Carlyle Mans. W8 1J 99 (off Kensington Mall)
Carlyle M. E1 4K 85
Carlyle Pl. SW15 4F 117
Carlyle Rd. CR0: C'don 2G 169
Carlyle Rd. E12 4C 70
Carlyle Rd. NW10 1K 79
Carlyle Rd. SE28 7B 90
Carlyle Rd. W5 4C 96
Carlyle's House 7C 16 (6C 100) (off Cheyne Row)
Carlyle Sq. SW3 6B 16 (5B 100)
Carly M. E2 3G 85 (off Barnet Gro.)
Carlyon Av. HA2: Harr 4D 58
Carlyon Cl. HA0: Wemb 1E 78
Carlyon Rd. HA0: Wemb 2E 78
Carlyon Rd. UB4: Yead 5A 76 (not continuous)
Carlys Cl. BR3: Beck 2K 157
Carmalt Gdns. SW15 4E 116
Carmarthen Ct. W7 4K 77 (off Copley Cl.)
Carmarthen Pl. SE1 6G 15 (2E 102)
Carmel Ct. HA9: Wemb 2H 61
Carmel Ct. W8 2K 99 (off Holland St.)
Carmelite Cl. HA3: Hrw W 1G 41
Carmelite Rd. HA3: Hrw W 1G 41
Carmelite St. EC4 2K 13 (7A 84)
Carmelite Wlk. HA3: Hrw W 1G 41
Carmelite Way HA3: Hrw W 2G 41
Carmel Lodge SW6 6J 99 (off Lillie Rd.)
Carmelo M. E1 5K 85 (off Maria Ter.)
Carmel Way TW9: Rich 2H 115
Carmen St. E14 6D 86
Carmichael Cl. HA4: Ruis 4J 57
Carmichael Cl. SW11 3B 118
Carmichael Ct. SW13 2B 116 (off Grove Rd.)
Carmichael Ho. E14 7E 86 (off Poplar High St.)
Carmichael M. SW18 7B 118
Carmichael Rd. SE25 5F 157
Carmine W2 6B 4 (5B 82) (off Nth. Wharf Rd.)
Carmine Ct. BR1: Broml 7H 141
Carmine Wharf E14 6B 86
Carminia Rd. SW17 2F 137
Carnaby St. W1 1A 12 (6G 83)
Carnac St. SE27 4D 138
Carnanton Rd. E17 1F 51
Carnarvon Av. EN1: Enf 3A 24
Carnarvon Dr. UB3: Harl 3E 92
Carnarvon Rd. E10 5E 50
Carnarvon Rd. E15 6H 69
Carnarvon Rd. E18 1H 51
Carnarvon Rd. EN5: Barn 3B 20
Carnation Cl. RM7: Rush G 2K 73
Carnation St. SE2 5B 108
Carnation Way SW8 7H 101
Carnbrook M. SE3 3B 124
Carnbrook Rd. SE3 3B 124
Carnecke Gdns. SE9 5C 124
Carnegie Cl. KT6: Surb 2F 163
Carnegie Pl. SW19 3F 135
Carnegie Rd. HA1: Harr 7K 41
Carnegie St. N1 1K 83
Carnell Apts. E14 6B 86 (off St Anne's Row)
Carney Pl. SW9 4A 120
Carnforth Cl. KT19: Ewe 6H 163
Carnforth Rd. SW16 7H 137 (not continuous)
Carnie Lodge SW17 3F 137
Carnival Ho. SE1 6K 15 (2F 103) (off Gainsford St.)
Carnoustie Cl. SE28 6D 90
Carnoustie Dr. N1 7K 65 (not continuous)
Carnwath Rd. SW6 3J 117
Caroe Ct. N9 1C 34
Carol Cl. NW4 4F 45
Carolean Cres. SE8 4A 104
Carole Ho. NW1 1D 82 (off Regent's Pk. Rd.)
Carolina Cl. E15 5G 69
Carolina Rd. CR7: Thor H 2B 156
Caroline Cl. CR0: C'don 4E 168
Caroline Cl. N10 2F 47
Caroline Cl. SW16 3K 137
Caroline Cl. TW7: Isle 7H 95
Caroline Cl. W2 7K 81
Caroline Ct. HA7: Stan 6F 27
Caroline Ct. SE6 4F 141
Caroline Ct. TW15: Ashf 6D 128
Caroline Gdns. E2 1H 9 (3E 84)
Caroline Gdns. SE15 7H 103 (not continuous)
Caroline Ho. W2 7K 81 (off Bayswater Rd.)
Caroline Ho. W6 5E 98 (off Queen Caroline St.)
Caroline Pl. SW11 2E 118
Caroline Pl. UB3: Harl 7G 93
Caroline Pl. W2 7K 81
Caroline Pl. M. W2 7K 81
Caroline Rd. SW19 7H 135
Caroline St. E1 6K 85
Caroline Ter. SW1 4G 17 (4E 100)
Caroline Wlk. W6 6G 99 (off Lillie Rd.)
Carol St. NW1 1G 83
Caronia Ct. SE16 4A 104 (off Plough Way)
Caro Pl. KT3: N Mald 4B 152
Carpenter Gdns. N21 2G 33
Carpenter Ho. E1 5K 85 (off Trafalgar Gdns.)
Carpenter Ho. E14 5C 86 (off Burgess St.)
Carpenter Ho. NW11 6A 46
Carpenters Arms Apts. SE1 4G 103 (off Welsford St.)
Carpenters Arms Path SE9 6E 124 (off Eltham High St.)
Carpenters Cl. EN5: New Bar 6E 20
Carpenters Ct. BR1: Broml 2B 160
Carpenters Ct. NW1 1G 83 (off Pratt St.)
Carpenters Ct. TW2: Twick 2J 131
Carpenters M. N7 5J 65
Carpenters Pl. SW4 4H 119
Carpenter's Rd. E15 7E 68
Carpenter's Rd. E20 6C 68
Carpenter St. W1 3J 11 (7F 83)
Carp Ho. E3 1B 86 (off Old Ford Rd.)
Carradale Ho. E14 6E 86 (off St Leonard's Rd.)
Carrara Cl. SE24 4A 120
Carrara Cl. SW9 4B 120
Carrara M. E8 6G 67 (off Dalston La.)
Carrara Wharf SW6 3G 117
Carr Cl. HA7: Stan 6F 27
Carre M. SE5 1B 120 (off Calais St.)
Carrera Twr. EC1 1C 8 (3C 84) (off Bollinder Pl.)
Carr Gro. SE18 4C 106
Carr Ho. DA1: Cray 5K 127
Carriage Dr. E. SW11 7E 100
Carriage Dr. Nth. SW11 Carriage Dr. E. 6E 100
Carriage Dr. Nth. SW11 The Parade 7D 100
Carriage Dr. Sth. SW11 1D 118 (not continuous)
Carriage Dr. W. SW11 7D 100
Carriage Ho. E15 6F 69 (off Leyton Rd.)
Carriage Ho. N4 2A 66
Carriage M. IG1: Ilf 2G 71
Carriage Pl. N16 3D 66
Carriage Pl. SW16 5G 137
Carriage St. SE18 3F 107
Carriage Way SE8 7C 104 (off Deptford High St.)
Carrick Cl. TW7: Isle 3A 114
Carrick Ct. E3 3E 86 (off Bolinder Way)
Carrick Dr. IG6: Ilf 1G 53
Carrick Gdns. N17 7K 33
Carrick Ho. N7 6K 65 (off Caledonian Rd.)
Carrick Ho. SE11 5K 19 (5A 102)
Carrick M. SE8 6C 104
Carrick Sq. TW8: Bford 7C 96 (off Narrowboat Av.)
Carrill Way DA17: Belv 3D 108
Carrington Av. TW3: Houn 5F 113
Carrington Cl. CR0: C'don 7A 158
Carrington Cl. KT2: King T 5J 133
Carrington Ct. SW11 4C 118 (off Barnard Rd.)
Carrington Gdns. E7 4J 69
Carrington Ho. W1 5J 11 (1F 101) (off Carrington St.)
Carrington Rd. TW10: Rich 4G 115
Carrington Sq. HA3: Hrw W 6B 26
Carrington St. W1 5J 11 (1F 101)
Carrock Ct. RM7: Rush G 6K 55 (off Union Rd.)
Carrol Cl. NW5 4F 65
Carroll Cl. E15 5H 69
Carroll Ho. W2 2A 10 (7B 82) (off Craven Ter.)
Carronade Ct. N7 5K 65
Carronade Pl. SE28 3G 107
Carron Cl. E14 6D 86
Carroun Rd. SW8 7K 101
Carroway La. UB6: G'frd 3H 77
Carrow Rd. RM9: Dag 7B 72
Carr Rd. E17 2B 50
Carr Rd. UB5: N'olt 6F 59
Carrs La. N21 5H 23
Carr St. E14 5A 86
CARSHALTON 4E 166
Carshalton Athletic FC 4C 166
CARSHALTON BEECHES 7C 166
Carshalton Boys Sports Coll. Cen. 2C 166
Carshalton Gro. SM1: Sutt 4B 166
CARSHALTON ON THE HILL 7E 166
Carshalton Pk. Rd. SM5: Cars 5D 166
Carshalton Pl. SM5: Cars 5E 166
Carshalton Rd. CR4: Mitc 4E 154
Carshalton Rd. SM1: Sutt 5A 166
Carshalton Rd. SM5: Cars 5C 166
Carslake Rd. SW15 6E 116
Carson Rd. E16 4J 87
Carson Rd. EN4: Cockf 4J 21
Carson Rd. SE21 2D 138
Carson Ter. W11 1G 99 (off Princes Pl.)
Carstairs Rd. SE6 3E 140
Carston Cl. SE12 5H 123
Carswell Cl. IG4: Ilf 4B 52
Carswell Rd. SE6 7E 122
Carter Cl. EN5: Barn 5B 20
Carter Cl. NW9 6K 43
Carter Ct. EC4 1B 14 (6B 84) (off Carter La.)
Carteret Ho. W12 7D 80 (off White City Est.)
Carteret St. SW1 7C 12 (2H 101)
Carteret Way SE8 4A 104
Carterhatch La. EN1: Enf 1A 24
Carterhatch Rd. EN3: Enf H 1D 24
Carter Ho. E1 6J 9 (5F 85) (off Brune St.)
Carter La. EC4 1B 14 (6B 84)
Carter Pl. SE17 5C 102
Carter Rd. E13 1K 87
Carter Rd. SW19 6B 136
Carters Cl. KT4: Wor Pk 2F 165
Carters Cl. NW5 5H 65 (off Torriano Av.)
Carters Hill Cl. SE9 1A 142
Carters La. SE23 2A 140
Carter Sq. E14 6D 86 (off Bowen St.)
Carter St. SE17 6C 102
Carter's Yd. SW18 5J 117
Carthew Rd. W6 3D 98
Carthew Vs. W6 3D 98
Carthusian Ct. EC1 5C 8 (5C 84) (off Carthusian St.)
Carthusian St. EC1 5C 8 (5C 84)
Cartier Circ. E14 1D 104
Carting La. WC2 3F 13 (7J 83)
Cart La. E4 1B 36
Cart Lodge M. CR0: C'don 1E 168
Cartmel NW1 1A 6 (3G 83) (off Harrington St.)
Cartmel Cl. N17 7C 34
Cartmel Ct. UB5: N'olt 6C 58
Cartmel Gdns. SM4: Mord 5A 154
Cartmel Rd. DA7: Bex 1G 127
Carton Ho. W11 7F 81 (off St Ann's Rd.)
Cartoon Mus. 7A 6 (6G 83)
Cartridge Pl. SE18 3F 107
Cartwright Gdns. WC1 2E 6 (3J 83)
Cartwright Ho. SE1 3C 102 (off County St.)
Cartwright Rd. RM9: Dag 7F 73
Cartwright St. E1 2K 15 (7F 85)
Cartwright Way SW13 7D 98
Carvel Ho. E14 5E 104 (off Manchester Rd.)
Carvell Ho. NW9 3B 44 (off Aerodrome Rd.)
Carver Cl. W4 3J 97
Carver Rd. SE24 6C 120
Carville Cres. TW8: Bford 4E 96
Carville Hall Pk. TW8: Bford 5E 96 (off Claypond La.)
Carville St. N4 2A 66
Cary Av. SE16 4A 104
Cary Rd. E11 4G 69
Carysfort Rd. N16 3D 66
Carysfort Rd. N8 5H 47
Casbeard St. N4 2C 66
Casby Ho. SE16 3G 103 (off Marine St.)
Cascade Av. N10 4G 47
Cascade Cl. IG9: Buck H 2G 37
Cascade Ct. SW11 7F 101
Cascade Rd. IG9: Buck H 2G 37
Cascades Ct. SW19 7H 135
Cascades Twr. E14 1B 104
Casel Ct. HA7: Stan 2F 27 (off Brightwen Gro.)
Casella Rd. SE14 7K 103
Casewick Rd. SE27 5A 138
Casey Av. UB5: N'olt 2D 76
Casey Cl. NW8 2C 4 (3C 82)
Casey Ct. SE14 1K 121 (off Besson St.)
Cashmere Ho. E8 1F 85 (off Pamela St.)
Casia Point E20 7E 68
Casimir Rd. E5 2J 67
Casings Way E3 7C 68
Casino Av. SE24 5C 120
Caspian St. SE5 7D 102
Caspian Wlk. E16 6B 88
Caspian Wharf E3 5D 86 (off Violet Rd.)
Cassander Pl. HA5: Pinn 1C 40 (off Holly Gro.)
Cassandra Cl. UB5: N'olt 4H 59
Casselden Rd. NW10 7K 61
Cassell Ho. SW9 2K 119 (off Stockwell Gdns. Est.)
Cass Ho. E9 6K 67 (off Harrowgate Rd.)
Cassia Ho. E1 6G 85 (off Piazza Wlk.)
Cassidy Rd. SW6 7J 99 (not continuous)
Cassilda Rd. SE2 4A 108
Cassilis Rd. E14 2C 104
Cassilis Rd. TW1: Twick 5B 114
Cassini Apts. E16 6J 87
Cassiobury Av. TW14: Felt 7H 111
Cassiobury Rd. E17 5A 50
Cassland Rd. CR7: Thor H 4D 156
Cassland Rd. E9 7K 67
Casslee Rd. SE6 7B 122
Cassocks Sq. TW17: Shep 7F 147
Casson Apts. E14 6C 86 (off Upper Nth. St.)
Casson Ho. E1 5K 9 (5G 85) (off Hanbury St.)
Casson Sq. SE1 5H 13 (1K 101)
Casson St. E1 5G 85
Castalia Sq. E14 2E 104
Castellain Mans. W9 4K 81 (off Castellain Rd.)
Castellain Rd. W9 4K 81
Castellane Cl. HA7: Stan 7E 26
Castell Ho. SE8 7C 104
Castello Av. SW15 5E 116
Castelnau SW13 1C 116
CASTELNAU 6D 98
Castelnau Gdns. SW13 6D 98
Castelnau Mans. SW13 6D 98 (off Castelnau)
Castelnau Row SW13 6D 98
Casterbridge NW6 1K 81 (off Abbey Rd.)
Casterbridge W11 6H 81 (off Dartmouth Cl.)
Casterbridge Rd. SE3 3J 123
Casterton St. E8 6H 67
Castile Rd. SE18 4E 106
Castillon Rd. SE6 2G 141
Casting Ho. SE14 6B 104
Castlands Rd. SE6 2B 140
Castleacre W2 1C 10 (6C 82) (off Hyde Pk. Cres.)
Castle Av. E4 5A 36
Castle Av. UB7: Yiew 7A 74
Castlebar Ct. W5 5C 78
Castlebar Hill W5 5B 78
Castlebar M. W5 5C 78
Castlebar Pk. W5 5B 78
Castlebar Rd. W5 5C 78
Castle Baynard St. EC4 2B 14 (7B 84)
Castlebrook Cl. SE11 4B 102
Castle Bus. Cen. TW12: Hamp 1F 149 (off Castle M.)
Castle Cen., The 4B 102
Castle Cinema, The 5K 67
Castle Climbing Cen., The 2C 66
Castle Cl. BR2: Broml 3G 159
Castle Cl. E9 5A 68
Castle Cl. SW19 3F 135
Castle Cl. TW16: Sun 7G 129
Castle Cl. W3 2H 97
Castlecombe Dr. SW19 7F 117
Castlecombe Rd. SE9 4C 142
Castle Ct. EC3 1F 15 (6D 84) (off Birchin La.)
Castle Ct. SE26 4A 140
Castle Ct. SW15 3G 117 (off Brewhouse La.)
Castleden Ho. NW3 7B 64 (off Hilgrove Rd.)
Castledine Rd. SE20 7H 139
Castle Dr. IG4: Ilf 6C 52
Castleford Av. SE9 1F 143
Castleford Cl. N17 6A 34
Castleford Ct. NW8 3B 4 (4B 82) (off Henderson Dr.)
Castlegate TW9: Rich 3F 115
Castle Green Leisure Cen. 1D 90
Castlehaven Rd. NW1 7F 65
Castle Hgts. RM9: Dag 1B 90
Castle Hill Av. CR0: New Ad 7D 170
Castle Hill Local Nature Reserve Chessington 6G 163
Castle Hill Pde. W13 7B 78 (off The Avenue)
Castle Ho. SM2: Sutt 6J 165
Castle Ho. SW8 7J 101 (off Sth. Lambeth Rd.)
Castle La. SW1 1A 18 (3G 101)
Castleleigh Ct. EN2: Enf 5J 23
Castlemaine SW11 2D 118
Castlemaine Av. CR2: S Croy 5F 169
Castlemaine Av. KT17: Ewe 7D 164
Castlemain St. E1 5H 85
Castle Mead SE5 7C 102
Castle M. HA1: Harr 4K 41
Castle M. N12 5F 31
Castle M. NW1 6F 65
Castle M. SW17 4C 136
Castle M. TW12: Hamp 1F 149 (not continuous)
Castle Pde. KT17: Ewe 7C 164
Castle Pl. NW1 6F 65
Castle Pl. W4 4A 98
Castle Point E13 2A 88 (off Boundary Rd.)
Castlereagh Ho. HA7: Stan 6G 27
Castlereagh St. W1 7E 4 (6D 82)
Castle Rd. EN3: Enf H 1F 25
Castle Rd. N12 5F 31
Castle Rd. NW1 6F 65
Castle Rd. RM9: Dag 1B 90
Castle Rd. TW7: Isle 2K 113
Castle Rd. UB2: S'hall 3D 94
Castle Rd. UB5: N'olt 6F 59
Castle Row W4 5K 97
Castle Sq. SE17 4C 102
Castle St. E13 2A 88
Castle St. E6 2A 88
Castle St. KT1: King T 2E 150
Castleton Av. DA7: Bex 1K 127
Castleton Av. HA9: Wemb 4E 60
Castleton Cl. CR0: C'don 6A 158
Castleton Gdns. HA9: Wemb 3E 60
Castleton Ho. E14 4E 104 (off Pier St.)
Castleton Rd. CR4: Mitc 4H 155
Castleton Rd. E17 2F 51
Castleton Rd. HA4: Ruis 1B 58
Castleton Rd. IG3: Ilf 1A 72
Castleton Rd. SE9 4B 142
Castletown Rd. W14 5G 99
Castleview Cl. N4 2C 66
Castleview Gdns. IG1: Ilf 6C 52
Castle Wlk. TW16: Sun 3A 148
Castle Way SW19 3F 135
Castle Way TW13: Hanw 4A 130
Castle Wharf E14 7G 87 (off Orchard Pl.)
Castlewood Dr. SE9 2D 124
Castlewood Rd. EN4: Cockf 3G 21
Castlewood Rd. N15 6G 49
Castlewood Rd. N16 6G 49
Castle Yd. N6 7E 46
Castle Yd. SE1 4B 14 (1B 102)
Castle Yd. TW10: Rich 5D 114
Castor La. E14 7D 86
Catalina Ho. E1 1K 15 (6G 85) (off Piazza Wlk.)
Catalina Rd. TW6: H'row A 2D 110
Catalpa Ct. SE13 6F 123
Caterham Av. IG5: Ilf 2D 52
Caterham High School Fitness Cen. 2D 52
Caterham Rd. SE13 3F 123
Catesby Ho. E9 7J 67 (off Frampton Pk. Rd.)
Catesby St. SE17 4D 102
CATFORD 7D 122
Catford B'way. SE6 7D 122
CATFORD GYRATORY 7D 122
Catford Hill SE6 1B 140
Catford Island SE6 7D 122
Catford M. SE6 7D 122
Catford Rd. SE6 7C 122
Catford Trad. Est. SE6 2D 140
Cathall Rd. E11 2F 69
Cathay Ho. SE16 2H 103
Cathay St. SE16 2H 103
Cathay Wlk. UB5: N'olt 2E 76 (off Brabazon Rd.)
Cathcart Dr. BR6: Orp 2J 173
Cathcart Hill N19 3G 65

Cathcart Ho. SW10 5A 100
(off Cathcart Rd.)
Cathcart Rd. SW10 6K 99
Cathcart St. NW5 6F 65
Cathedral Lodge EC1 5C 8 (5C 84)
(off Aldersgate St.)
Cathedral Mans. SW1 3A 18 (4G 101)
(off Vauxhall Bri. Rd.)
Cathedral Piazza SW1 2A 18 (3G 101)
Cathedral St. SE1 4E 14 (1D 102)
Cathedral Wlk. SW1 1A 18 (3G 101)
Catherall Rd. N5 3C 66
Catherine Cl. NW4 4D 44
Catherine Ct. IG2: Ilf 5G 53
Catherine Ct. N14 5B 22
Catherine Ct. SW19 5H 135
Catherine Ct. SW3 7A 16 (6B 100)
(off Callow St.)
Catherine Dr. TW16: Sun 6H 129
Catherine Dr. TW9: Rich 4E 114
Catherine Gdns. TW3: Houn 4H 113
Catherine Griffiths Ct. EC1 3K 7 (4A 84)
(off Northampton Rd.)
Catherine Gro. SE10 1D 122
Catherine Ho. E3 2C 86
(off Thomas Fyre Dr.)
Catherine Ho. N1 1E 84
(off Whitmore Est.)
Catherine Howard Ct. SE9 6H 125
Catherine of Aragon Ct. SE9 6G 125
Catherine Parr Ct. SE9 6H 125
Catherine Pl. HA1: Harr 5K 41
Catherine Pl. SW1 1A 18 (3G 101)
Catherine Rd. KT6: Surb 5D 150
Catherine St. WC2 2G 13 (7K 83)
Catherine Wheel All. E1 6H 9 (5E 84)
Catherine Wheel Rd. TW8: Bford 7D 96
Catherine Wheel Yd. SW1
5A 12 (1G 101)
(off Lit. St James's St.)
Catherwood Ct. N1 1E 8 (2D 84)
(off Murray Gro.)
Cat Hill EN4: E Barn 6H 21
Cathles Rd. SW12 6F 119
Cathnor Rd. W12 2D 98
Catkin Cl. E14 6F 87
Catlin Cres. TW17: Shep 5F 147
Catling Cl. SE23 3J 139
Catlin's La. HA5: Eastc 3K 39
Catlin St. SE16 5G 103
Cator La. BR3: Beck 1B 158
Cato Rd. SW4 3H 119
Cator Rd. SE26 6K 139
Cator Rd. SM5: Cars 5D 166
Cator St. SE15 Commercial Way 7F 103
Cator St. SE15 Ebley Cl. 6F 103
Cato St. W1 6D 4 (5C 82)
Catsey La. WD23: Bush 1B 26
Catsey Woods WD23: Bush 1B 26
Catterick Cl. N11 6K 31
Cattistock Rd. SE9 5C 142
Cattley Cl. EN5: Barn 4B 20
Catton St. WC1 6G 7 (5K 83)
Catwalk Pl. N15 6D 48
Caudwell Ter. SW18 6B 118
Caughley Ho. SE11 2J 19 (3A 102)
(off Lambeth Wlk.)
Caulfield Ct. NW1 7G 65
(off Baynes St.)
Caulfield Gdns. HA5: Pinn 2A 40
Caulfield Rd. E6 1C 88
Caulfield Rd. SE15 2H 121
Caulfield Rd. W3 3J 97
Causeway, The KT10: Clay 7A 162
Causeway, The KT9: Chess 4E 162
Causeway, The N2 4C 46
Causeway, The SM2: Sutt 7A 166
Causeway, The SM5: Cars 3E 166
Causeway, The SW18 5K 117
Causeway, The SW19 5E 134
Causeway, The TW11: Tedd 6K 131
Causeway, The TW14: Felt 4J 111
Causeway, The TW14: Houn 4J 111
Causeyware Rd. N9 7D 24
Causton Cotts. E14 6A 86
(off Galsworthy Av.)
Causton Ho. SE5 6C 102
Causton Ho. SW9 1K 119
Causton Rd. N6 7F 47
Causton Sq. RM10: Dag 7G 73
Causton St. SW1 4D 18 (4H 101)
Cautley Av. SW4 5G 119
Cavalier Cl. RM6: Chad H 4D 54
Cavalier Cl. SM6: W'gton 6G 167
Cavalier Ct. KT5: Surb 6F 151
Cavalier Gdns. UB3: Hayes 6F 75
Cavalier Ter. SE7 6A 106
Cavalry Cres. TW4: Houn 4B 112
Cavalry Gdns. SW15 5H 117
Cavalry Pl. E17 2K 49
Cavalry Sq. SW3 5F 17 (5D 100)
Cavan Pl. HA5: Hat E 1D 40
Cavatina Point SE8 6D 104
(off Copperas St.)
Cavaye Ho. SW10 7A 16 (6A 100)
(off Cavaye Pl.)
Cavaye Pl. SW10 6A 16 (5A 100)
Cavell Dr. EN2: Enf 2F 23
Cavell Ho. N1 1E 84
(off Colville Est.)
Cavell Rd. N17 7J 33
Cavell St. E1 5H 85
Cavendish Av. DA15: Sidc 7A 126
Cavendish Av. DA16: Well 3K 125
Cavendish Av. DA8: Erith 6J 109
Cavendish Av. HA1: Harr 4H 59
Cavendish Av. HA4: Ruis 5K 57
Cavendish Av. IG8: Wfd G 1K 51
Cavendish Av. KT3: N Mald 5C 152
Cavendish Av. N3 2J 45
Cavendish Av. NW8 1B 4 (2B 82)
Cavendish Av. W13 5A 78
Cavendish Cl. N18 5C 34
Cavendish Cl. NW6 6H 63
Cavendish Cl. NW8 1B 4 (3B 82)
Cavendish Cl. TW16: Sun 6H 129
Cavendish Cl. UB4: Hayes 5G 75
Cavendish Ct. EC3 7H 9 (6E 84)
(off Devonshire Sq.)
Cavendish Ct. SE6 1D 140
(off Bromley Rd.)
Cavendish Ct. SM6: W'gton 6F 167
Cavendish Ct. TW16: Sun 6H 129
Cavendish Dr. E11 1F 69
Cavendish Dr. HA8: Edg 6A 28
Cavendish Gdns. IG1: Ilf 1E 70
Cavendish Gdns. IG11: Bark 5J 71
Cavendish Gdns. RM6: Chad H 5E 54
Cavendish Gdns. SW4 6G 119
Cavendish Ho. CR0: C'don 1D 168
(off Tavistock Rd.)
Cavendish Ho. NW8 1B 4 (2B 82)
(off Wellington Rd.)
Cavendish Ho. NW9 3B 44
Cavendish Ho. SW1 2D 18 (3H 101)
(off Monck St.)
Cavendish Ho. UB7: W Dray 2B 92
(off Park Lodge Av.)
Cavendish Ho. W1 6A 6 (5G 83)
(off Mortimer St.)
Cavendish Mans. EC1 4J 7 (4A 84)
(off Rosebery Av.)
Cavendish Mans. NW6 5J 63
Cavendish M. Nth. W1 5K 5 (5F 83)
Cavendish M. Sth. W1 6K 5 (5F 83)
Cavendish Pde. SW4 6F 119
(off Clapham Comn. Sth. Side)
Cavendish Pde. TW4: Houn 2C 112
Cavendish Pl. BR1: Broml 4D 160
Cavendish Pl. NW2 6F 63
Cavendish Pl. SW4 5H 119
Cavendish Pl. W1 7K 5 (6F 83)
Cavendish Rd. CR0: C'don 1B 168
Cavendish Rd. E4 6K 35
Cavendish Rd. EN5: Barn 3A 20
Cavendish Rd. KT3: N Mald 4B 152
Cavendish Rd. N18 5C 34
Cavendish Rd. N4 6B 48
Cavendish Rd. NW6 7G 63
Cavendish Rd. SM2: Sutt 7A 166
Cavendish Rd. SW12 6F 119
Cavendish Rd. SW19 7B 136
Cavendish Rd. TW16: Sun 6H 129
Cavendish Rd. W4 1J 115
Cavendish Sq. W1 7J 5 (6F 83)
Cavendish St. N1 2D 84
Cavendish Ter. E3 3B 86
Cavendish Ter. TW13: Felt 2J 129
Cavendish Way BR4: W W'ck 1D 170
Cavenham Gdns. IG1: Ilf 3H 71
Caverleigh Pl. BR1: Broml 2A 160
Caverleigh Way KT4: Wor Pk 1C 164
Cave Rd. E13 3K 87
Cave Rd. TW10: Ham 4C 132
Caversham Av. N13 3F 33
Caversham Av. SM3: Cheam 2G 165
Caversham Ct. N11 3K 31
(off Brunswick Pk. Rd.)
Caversham Ho. KT1: King T 2E 150
(off Lady Booth Rd.)
Caversham Ho. N15 4C 48
(off Caversham Rd.)
Caversham Ho. SE15 6G 103
(off Haymerle Rd.)
Caversham M. SW3 7E 16 (6D 100)
(off Caversham St.)
Caversham Rd. KT1: King T 2F 151
Caversham Rd. N15 4C 48
Caversham Rd. NW5 6G 65
Caversham Rd. NW9 3C 44
Caversham St. SW3 7E 16 (6D 100)
Caverswall St. W12 6E 80
Caveside Cl. BR7: Chst 1E 160
Cavesson Ho. E20 5E 68
(off Ribbons Wlk.)
Cavour Ho. SE17 5B 102
(off Alberta Est.)
Cawdor Cres. W7 4A 96
Cawdor Wlk. E14 6E 86
Cawnpore St. SE19 5E 138
Cawston Ct. BR1: Broml 7H 141
Cawston M. SW16 5B 138
Caxton Ct. SW11 2C 118
Caxton Gro. E3 3C 86
Caxton Hall SW1 1C 18 (3H 101)
(off Caxton St.)
Caxton Ho. 7D 12 (2H 101)
(off Tothill St.)
Caxton M. TW8: Bford 6D 96
Caxton Pl. IG1: Ilf 3E 70
Caxton Rd. N22 2K 47
Caxton Rd. SW19 5A 136
Caxton Rd. UB2: S'hall 3B 94
Caxton Rd. W12 2F 99
Caxtons, The SW9 7B 102
(off Langton Rd.)
Caxton St. SW1 1B 18 (3G 101)
Caxton St. Nth. E16 6H 87
Caxton Trad. Est. UB3: Hayes 2G 93
Caxton Wlk. WC2 1D 12 (6H 83)
Cayenne Ct. SE1 6J 15 (2F 103)
Caygill Cl. BR2: Broml 4H 159
Cayley Rd. TW6: H'row A 3D 110
Cayley Rd. UB2: S'hall 3F 95
Cayton Pl. EC1 2E 8 (3D 84)
(off Cayton St.)
Cayton Rd. UB6: G'frd 2J 77
Cayton St. EC1 2E 8 (3D 84)
Cazenove Rd. E17 1C 50
Cazenove Rd. N16 2F 67
Cearns Ho. E6 1B 88
Ceasar Rd. BR3: Beck 4D 158
Cecil Av. EN1: Enf 4A 24
Cecil Av. HA9: Wemb 5F 61
Cecil Av. IG11: Bark 7H 71
Cecil Cl. KT9: Chess 4D 162
Cecil Cl. TW15: Ashf 7E 128
Cecil Cl. W5 5D 78
Cecil Ct. CR0: C'don 2F 169
Cecil Ct. EN2: Enf 4J 23
Cecil Ct. EN5: Barn 3A 20
Cecil Ct. NW6 7K 63
Cecil Ct. SW10 6A 100
(off Fawcett St.)
Cecil Ct. WC2 2E 12 (7J 83)
Cecile Pk. N8 6J 47
Cecil Gro. NW8 1C 82
Cecil Hepworth Playhouse, The 7H 147
(off Hepworth Way)
Cecil Ho. E17 1C 50
Cecilia Cl. N2 3A 46
Cecilia Rd. E8 5F 67
Cecil Manning Cl. UB6: G'frd 1A 78
Cecil Mans. SW17 2E 136
Cecil Pk. HA5: Pinn 4C 40
Cecil Pl. CR4: Mitc 5D 154
Cecil Rhodes Ho. NW1 2H 83
(off Goldington St.)
Cecil Rd. CR0: C'don 6J 155
Cecil Rd. E11 3H 69
Cecil Rd. E13 1J 87
Cecil Rd. E17 1C 50
Cecil Rd. EN2: Enf 3H 23
Cecil Rd. HA3: W'stone 3J 41
Cecil Rd. IG1: Ilf 4F 71
Cecil Rd. N10 2F 47
Cecil Rd. N14 1B 32
Cecil Rd. NW10 1A 80
Cecil Rd. NW9 3A 44
Cecil Rd. RM6: Chad H 7D 54
Cecil Rd. SM1: Sutt 6H 165
Cecil Rd. SW19 7K 135
Cecil Rd. TW15: Ashf 7E 128
Cecil Rd. TW3: Houn 2G 113
Cecil Rd. W3 5J 79
Cecil Rosen Ct. HA0: Wemb 3B 60
Cecil Rosen Ct. WD23: B Hea 1D 26
Cecil Sharp House 1E 82
(off Gloucester Av.)
Cecil Way BR2: Hayes 1J 171
Cedar Av. DA15: Sidc 7A 126
Cedar Av. EN3: Enf H 2D 24
Cedar Av. EN4: E Barn 7H 21
Cedar Av. HA4: Ruis 5A 58
Cedar Av. RM6: Chad H 5E 54
Cedar Av. TW2: Whitt 6F 113
Cedar Av. UB3: Hayes 6J 75
Cedar Av. UB7: Yiew 7B 74
Cedar Cl. BR2: Broml 3C 172
Cedar Cl. E3 1B 86
Cedar Cl. IG1: Ilf 5H 71
Cedar Cl. IG9: Buck H 2G 37
Cedar Cl. KT8: E Mos 4J 149
Cedar Cl. RM7: Rom 4J 55
Cedar Cl. SE21 1C 138
Cedar Cl. SM5: Cars 6D 166
Cedar Cl. SW15 4K 133
Cedar Copse BR1: Broml 2D 160
Cedar Ct. E11 5K 51
Cedar Ct. E18 1J 51
Cedar Ct. N1 7C 66
Cedar Ct. N10 2E 46
Cedar Ct. N11 5B 32
Cedar Ct. N20 1G 31
Cedar Ct. SE1 7G 15 (2E 102)
(off Royal Oak Yd.)
Cedar Ct. SE13 4F 123
Cedar Ct. SE7 6A 106
Cedar Ct. SE9 6C 124
Cedar Ct. SM2: Sutt 6A 166
Cedar Ct. SW19 3F 135
Cedar Ct. TW8: Bford 6C 96
Cedar Cres. BR2: Broml 3C 172
Cedarcroft Rd. KT9: Chess 4F 163
Cedar Dr. N2 4C 46
Cedar Gdns. SM2: Sutt 6A 166
Cedar Grange EN1: Enf 5K 23
Cedar Gro. DA5: Bexl 6D 126
Cedar Gro. UB1: S'hall 5E 76
Cedar Gro. W5 3E 96
Cedar Hgts. NW2 6H 63
Cedar Hgts. TW10: Ham 1E 132
Cedar Ho. CR0: New Ad 6D 170
Cedar Ho. E14 2E 104
(off Manchester Rd.)
Cedar Ho. E2 2H 85
(off Mowlem St.)
Cedar Ho. HA9: Wemb 4G 61
(off Engineers Way)
Cedar Ho. N22 1A 48
(off Acacia Rd.)
Cedar Ho. SE14 1K 121
Cedar Ho. SE16 2K 103
(off Woodland Cres.)
Cedar Ho. SW6 2A 118
(off Lensbury Av.)
Cedar Ho. TW16: Sun 7H 129
(off Spelthorne Gro.)
Cedar Ho. TW9: Kew 1H 115
Cedar Ho. UB4: Yead 4A 76
Cedar Ho. W8 3K 99
(off Marloes Rd.)
Cedarhurst BR1: Broml 7G 141
Cedarhurst Cotts. DA5: Bexl 7G 127
Cedarhurst Dr. SE9 5A 124
Cedarland Ter. SW20 7D 134
Cedar Lawn Av. EN5: Barn 5B 20
Cedar M. SE4 3B 122
Cedar M. SW15 5F 117
Cedar Mt. SE9 1B 142
Cedarne Rd. SW6 7K 99
Cedar Pk. IG7: Chig 4K 37
Cedar Pk. Gdns. RM6: Chad H 7D 54
Cedar Pk. Gdns. SW19 5D 134
Cedar Pk. Rd. EN2: Enf 1H 23
Cedar Pl. SE7 5A 106
Cedar Ri. N14 7K 21
Cedar Rd. BR1: Broml 2A 160
Cedar Rd. CR0: C'don 2D 168
Cedar Rd. EN2: Enf 1G 23
Cedar Rd. KT8: E Mos 4J 149
Cedar Rd. N17 1F 49
Cedar Rd. NW2 4E 62
Cedar Rd. RM7: Rom 4J 55
Cedar Rd. SM2: Sutt 6A 166
Cedar Rd. TW11: Tedd 5A 132
Cedar Rd. TW14: Bedf 1F 129
Cedar Rd. TW4: Cran 2A 112
Cedars, The E15 7H 69
Cedars, The E9 7K 67
(off Banbury Rd.)
Cedars, The IG9: Buck H 1D 36
Cedars, The SM6: W'gton 4G 167
Cedars, The TW11: Tedd 6K 131
Cedars, The W13 6C 78
Cedars Av. CR4: Mitc 4E 154
Cedars Av. E17 5C 50
Cedars Cl. NW4 3F 45
Cedars Cl. SE13 3F 123
Cedars Ct. N9 2K 33
Cedars Dr. UB10: Hil 2B 74
Cedars Ho. E17 3D 50
Cedarside Apts. NW6 2H 81
Cedars M. SW4 4F 119
(not continuous)
Cedars Rd. BR3: Beck 2A 158
Cedars Rd. CR0: Bedd 3J 167
Cedars Rd. E15 6G 69
Cedars Rd. KT1: Hamp W 1C 150
Cedars Rd. N21 2G 33
Cedars Rd. N9 2B 34
Cedars Rd. SM4: Mord 4J 153
Cedars Rd. SW13 2C 116
Cedars Rd. SW4 3F 119
Cedars Rd. W4 5J 97
Cedar Ter. TW9: Rich 4E 114
Cedar Tree Gro. SE27 5B 138
Cedar Vw. KT1: King T 3D 150
(off Milner Rd.)
Cedarville Gdns. SW16 6K 137
Cedar Way N1 7H 65
Cedar Way TW16: Sun 7G 129
Cedar Way Ind. Est. N1 7H 65
Cedarwood Pl. DA14: Sidc 2D 144
Cedra Ct. N16 1G 67
Cedric Chambers NW8 3A 4 (4B 82)
(off Northwick Cl.)
Cedric Rd. SE9 3G 143
Cedrus Av. UB1: S'hall 2B 94
Celadon Cl. EN3: Enf H 3F 25
Celandine Cl. E14 5C 86
Celandine Cl. E4 3J 35
Celandine Dr. E8 7F 67
Celandine Dr. SE28 1B 108
Celandine Gro. N14 5B 22
Celandine Way E15 3G 87
Celbridge M. W2 5K 81
Celebration Av. E20 5E 68
Celebration Way E4 6K 35
Celestial Gdns. SE13 4F 123
Celia Cres. TW15: Ashf 6A 128
Celia Ho. N1 2E 84
(off Arden Est.)
Celia Rd. N19 4G 65
Cellini St. SW8 7H 101
Celtic Av. BR2: Broml 3G 159
Celtic St. E14 5D 86
Cemetery La. SE7 6C 106
Cemetery La. TW17: Shep 7D 146
Cemetery Rd. E7 5H 69
Cemetery Rd. N17 7K 33
Cemetery Rd. SE2 7B 108
Cemetery Way E4 3H 35
Cenacle Cl. NW3 3J 63
Cena Ho. CR8: Kenley 6D 156
Cenotaph 6E 12 (2J 101)
Centaur Ct. TW8: Bford 5E 96
Centaurs Bus. Pk. TW7: Isle 6A 96
Centaur St. SE1 1H 19 (3K 101)
Centenary Rd. EN3: Brim 4G 25
Centenary Trad. Est. EN3: Brim 3G 25
Centennial Ct. WD6: E'tree 1H 27
Central Apts. HA9: Wemb 5E 60
Central Arc. TW15: Ashf 4B 128
(off Woodthorpe Rd.)
Central Av. DA16: Well 2K 125
Central Av. E11 2F 69
Central Av. EN1: Enf 2C 24
Central Av. HA5: Pinn 6D 40
Central Av. KT8: W Mole 4D 148
Central Av. N2 2B 46
Central Av. N9 3K 33
Central Av. SM6: W'gton 5J 167
Central Av. SW11 7D 100
Central Av. SW6 3A 118
Central Av. TW3: Houn 4G 113
Central Av. UB3: Hayes 1H 93
Central Bus. Cen. NW10 5A 62
Central Cir. NW4 5D 44
Central Ctyd. EC2 7H 9 (6E 84)
(off Cutlers Gdns.)
Central Criminal Court Old Bailey
7B 8 (6B 84)
Central Cross Apts. CR0: C'don 4C 168
(off South End)
Centrale Shop. Cen. 2C 168
Central Gallery IG1: Ilf 2F 71
(within The Exchange)
Central Gdns. SM4: Mord 5K 153
Central Hill SE19 5D 138
Central Ho. E15 2D 86
Central Ho. IG11: Bark 7G 71
Central Lawn RM8: Dag 1E 72
(off Ager Av.)
Central Mall SW18 6K 117
(within Southside Shop. Cen.)
Central Mans. NW4 5D 44
(off Watford Way)
Central Mill Apts. E8 1F 85
(off Samuel St.)
Central Pde. DA15: Sidc 3A 144
Central Pde. E17 4C 50
Central Pde. EN3: Enf H 2D 24
Central Pde. HA1: Harr 5K 41
Central Pde. IG2: Ilf 6H 53
Central Pde. KT6: Surb 6E 150
Central Pde. KT8: W Mole 4D 148
Central Pde. SE20 7K 139
(off High St.)
Central Pde. TW14: Felt 7A 112
Central Pde. TW5: Hest 7D 94
Central Pde. UB6: G'frd 3A 78
Central Pde. W3 2H 97
Central Pk. NW10 3J 79
Central Pk. Av. RM10: Dag 3H 73
Central Pk. Est. TW4: Houn 5B 112
Central Pk. Rd. E6 2B 88
Central Pl. SE25 5G 157
Central Rd. HA0: Wemb 5B 60
Central Rd. KT4: Wor Pk 1C 164
Central Rd. SM4: Mord 6J 153
Central St Giles Piazza WC2
7E 6 (6J 83)
(off St Giles High St.)
Central St Martins College of Art & Design Back Hill Site 4K 7 (4A 84)
(off Back Hill)
Central St Martins College of Art & Design Byam Shaw Campus 2H 65
Central School of Speech & Drama, The
7B 64
Central School Path SW14 3J 115
Central Sq. HA9: Wemb 5E 60
(off High Rd.)
Central Sq. KT8: W Mole 5D 148
Central Sq. NW11 6K 45
Central St. EC1 1C 8 (3C 84)
Central Ter. BR3: Beck 3K 157
Central Walkway N19 4H 65
(off Pleshey Rd.)
Central Way NW10 3J 79
Central Way SE28 1A 108
Central Way SM5: Cars 7C 166
Central Way TW14: Felt 5J 111
Central W. UB6: G'frd 4G 77
Centre, The KT12: Walt T 7J 147
Centre, The TW13: Felt 1K 129
Centre, The TW3: Houn 3F 113
Centre Av. W3 1K 97
Centre Comn. Rd. BR7: Chst 6G 143
Centre Ct. Shop. Cen. 6H 135
Centre for Wildlife Gardening Vis. Cen.
3F 121
Centre Hgts. NW3 7B 64
(off Finchley Rd.)
Centre Point SE1 5G 103
Centrepoint WC2 7D 6 (6H 83)
(off St Giles High St.)
Centre Point Ho. WC2 7D 6 (6H 83)
(off St Giles High St.)
Centre Rd. E11 2J 69
Centre Rd. E7 2J 69
Centre Rd. RM10: Dag 2H 91
Centre Sq. KT1: King T 2E 150
(off Eden Walk Shop. Cen.)
Centre St. E2 2H 85
Centre Vw. Apts. CR0: C'don 3C 168
(off Whitgift St.)
Centre Way E17 7K 35
Centre Way N9 2D 34
Centreway IG1: Ilf 2G 71
(off High Rd.)
Centreway Apts. IG1: Ilf 2G 71
(off Axon Pl.)
Centric Cl. NW1 1E 82
Centrillion Point CR0: C'don 4C 168
(off Mason's Av.)
Centro Ct. E6 4D 88
Centurian Sq. SE18 1C 124
Centurion Bldg. SW11 7J 17 (6F 101)
Centurion Cl. N7 7K 65
Centurion Ct. SE18 4E 106
Centurion Ct. SM6: W'gton 2F 167
Centurion Ho. UB3: Hayes 6F 75
Centurion La. E3 1B 86
Centurion Way DA18: Erith 3F 109
Century Cl. NW4 5F 45
Century Ct. NW8 2B 4 (3B 82)
(off Grove End Rd.)
Century Ho. HA9: Wemb 2F 61
Century Ho. SW15 4F 117
Century M. E5 4J 67
Century M. N5 3B 66
(off Conewood St.)
Century Plaza HA8: Edg 6B 28
(off Station Rd.)
Century Rd. E17 3A 50
Century Way BR3: Beck 6B 140
Century Yd. SE23 2J 139
(not continuous)
Cephas Av. E1 4J 85
Cephas Ho. E1 4J 85
(off Doveton St.)
Cephas St. E1 4J 85
Ceres Rd. SE18 4K 107
Cerise Apts. E3 1A 86
(off Gunmaker's La.)
Cerise Rd. SE15 1G 121
Cerne Cl. UB4: Yead 7A 76
Cerne Rd. SM4: Mord 6A 154
Cerney M. W2 2A 10 (7B 82)
(off Gloucester Ter.)
Cervantes Ct. W11 6G 81
(off Rushton M.)
Cervantes Ct. W2 6K 81
Cervantes Theatre 6B 14 (2B 102)
Cester St. E2 1G 85
Ceylon Ho. E1 7K 9 (6G 85)
(off Alie St.)
Ceylon Rd. W14 3F 99
Ceylon Wharf Apts. SE16 2J 103
(off St Marychurch St.)
Cezanne Rd. W3 7A 80
CFGS Community Performing Arts & Sports Cen. 3B 86
Chabot Dr. SE15 3H 121
Chadacre Av. IG5: Ilf 3D 52
Chadacre Ct. E15 1J 87
(off Vicars Cl.)
Chadacre Ho. SW9 4B 120
(off Loughborough Pk.)
Chadacre Rd. KT17: Ewe 6D 164
Chadbourn St. E14 5D 86
Chadbury Ct. NW7 1C 44
Chad Cres. N9 3D 34
Chadd Dr. BR1: Broml 3C 160
Chadd Grn. E13 1J 87
(not continuous)
Chadston Ho. N1 7B 66
(off Halton Rd.)
Chadswell WC1 2F 7 (3J 83)
(off Cromer St.)
Chadview Ct. RM6: Chad H 7D 54
Chadville Gdns. RM6: Chad H 5D 54
Chadway RM8: Dag 1C 72
Chadwell Av. RM6: Chad H 7B 54
CHADWELL HEATH 7D 54
Chadwell Heath Ind. Pk. RM8: Dag 1D 72
Chadwell Heath La. RM6: Chad H 4B 54
Chadwell Ho. SE17 5D 102
(off Inville Rd.)
Chadwell La. N8 3K 47
Chadwell St. EC1 1K 7 (3A 84)
Chadwick Av. E4 4A 36
Chadwick Av. N21 5E 22
Chadwick Av. SW19 6J 135
Chadwick Cl. SW15 7B 116
Chadwick Cl. TW11: Tedd 6A 132
Chadwick Cl. W7 5K 77
Chadwick Ct. E14 6C 86
(off Jonzen Wlk.)
Chadwick Gdns. UB8: Uxb 7A 56
Chadwick M. W4 6H 97
Chadwick Pl. KT6: Surb 7C 150
Chadwick Rd. E11 6G 51
Chadwick Rd. IG1: Ilf 3F 71
Chadwick Rd. NW10 1B 80
Chadwick Rd. SE15 2F 121
Chadwick St. SW1 2C 18 (3H 101)
Chadwick Way SE28 7D 90
Chadwin Rd. E13 5K 87
Chadworth Ho. EC1 2C 8 (3C 84)
(off Lever St.)
Chadworth Ho. N4 1C 66
Chaffinch Av. CR0: C'don 6K 157
Chaffinch Bus. Pk. BR3: Beck 4K 157
Chaffinch Cl. CR0: C'don 5K 157
Chaffinch Cl. KT6: Surb 3G 163
Chaffinch Cl. N9 1E 34
Chaffinch Rd. BR3: Beck 1A 158
Chafford Way RM6: Chad H 4C 54
Chagford Ho. E3 3D 86
(off Talwin St.)
Chagford St. NW1 4E 4 (4D 82)
Chailey Av. EN1: Enf 2A 24

Chailey Cl. – Charteris Community Sports Cen.

Chailey Cl. DA15: Sidc....6B 126
Chailey Cl. TW5: Hest....1B 112
Chailey Ind. Est. UB3: Hayes....2J 93
Chailey St. E5....3J 67
Chainmakers Ho. E14....6F 87
(off Blair St.)
Chalbury Wlk. N1....2K 83
Chalcombe Rd. SE2....3B 108
Chalcot Cl. SM2: Sutt....7J 165
Chalcot Cres. NW1....1D 82
Chalcot Gdns. NW3....6D 64
Chalcot M. SW16....3J 137
Chalcot Rd. NW1....7E 64
Chalcot Sq. NW1....7E 64
(not continuous)
Chalcott Gdns. KT6: Surb....1C 162
Chalcroft Rd. SE13....5G 123
Chaldon Ct. SE19....2D 156
Chaldon Path CR7: Thor H....4B 156
Chaldon Rd. SW6....7G 99
Chale Rd. SW2....6J 119
Chalet Cl. DA5: Bexl....4K 145
Chalet Cl. TW15: Ashf....6F 129
Chalet Ct. CR7: Thor H....5C 156
Chalet Est. NW7....4H 29
Chalfont Av. HA9: Wemb....6H 61
Chalfont Ct. HA1: Harr....6K 41
(off Northwick Pk. Rd.)
Chalfont Ct. NW1....4F 5 (4D 82)
(off Baker St.)
Chalfont Ct. NW9....3B 44
Chalfont Grn. N9....3K 33
Chalfont Ho. SE16....3H 103
(off Keetons Rd.)
Chalfont M. SW19....1H 135
Chalfont M. UB10: Hil....7D 56
Chalfont Rd. N9....3K 33
Chalfont Rd. SE25....3F 157
Chalfont Rd. UB3: Hayes....2J 93
Chalfont Wlk. HA5: Pinn....2A 40
Chalfont Way W13....3B 96
Chalford NW6....6A 64
(off Finchley Rd.)
Chalford Cl. KT8: W Mole....4E 148
Chalford Rd. SE21....4D 138
Chalford Wlk. IG8: Wfd G....1B 52
Chalgrove Av. SM4: Mord....5J 153
Chalgrove Cres. IG5: Ilf....2C 52
Chalgrove Gdns. N3....3G 45
Chalgrove Rd. N17....1H 49
Chalgrove Rd. SM2: Sutt....7B 166
Chalice Cl. SM6: W'gton....6H 167
Chalice Ct. N2....4C 46
Chalice Ct. SE19....6D 138
Chalkenden Cl. SE20....7H 139
CHALKER'S CORNER....3H 115
CHALK FARM....7E 64
Chalk Farm Pde. NW3....7E 64
(off Adelaide Rd.)
Chalk Farm Rd. NW1....7E 64
Chalk Hill Rd. W6....4F 99
Chalkhill Rd. HA9: Wemb....3H 61
Chalklands HA9: Wemb....3J 61
Chalk La. EN4: Cockf....3J 21
Chalkley Cl. CR4: Mitc....2D 154
Chalkmill Dr. EN1: Enf....3C 24
Chalk Pit Way SM1: Sutt....5A 166
Chalk Rd. DA8: Erith....6J 109
Chalk Rd. E13....5K 87
Chalkstone Cl. DA16: Well....1A 126
Chalkwell Ho. E1....6K 85
(off Pitsea St.)
Chalkwell Pk. Av. EN1: Enf....4K 23
Challenge Cl. NW10....1A 80
Challenge Ct. TW2: Twick....7J 113
Challenger Ho. E14....7A 86
(off Victory Pl.)
Challenge Rd. TW15: Ashf....3F 129
Challice Way SW2....1K 137
Challin St. SE20....1J 157
Challis Ho. SW11....2D 118
Challis Rd. TW8: Bford....5D 96
Challoner Cl. N2....2B 46
Challoner Ct. BR2: Broml....2F 159
Challoner Ct. W14....5H 99
(off Challoner St.)
Challoner Cres. W14....5H 99
Challoner Mans. W14....5H 99
(off Challoner St.)
Challoners Cl. KT8: E Mos....4H 149
Challoner St. W14....5H 99
Challoner Wlk. E1....6G 85
(off Christian St.)
Chalmers Ho. E17....5D 50
Chalmers Rd. TW15: Ashf....5D 128
Chalmers Rd. E. TW15: Ashf....4D 128
Chalmers Wlk. SE17....6B 102
(off Hillingdon St.)
Chalmers Way TW1: Isle....4B 114
Chalmers Way TW14: Felt....5K 111
Chaloner Ct. SE1....6E 14 (2D 102)
(off Tennis St.)
Chalsey Rd. SE4....4B 122
Chalton Dr. N2....6B 46
Chalton Ho. NW1....1C 6 (3H 83)
(off Chalton St.)
Chalton St. NW1....2G 83
(not continuous)
Chamberlain Cl. IG1: Ilf....3G 71
Chamberlain Cl. SE28....3H 107
Chamberlain Cl. UB3: Hayes....7H 75
Chamberlain Cotts. SE5....1D 120
Chamberlain Ct. SE16....4J 103
(off Silwood St.)
Chamberlain Cres. BR4: W W'ck....1D 170
Chamberlain Gdns. TW3: Houn....1G 113
Chamberlain Ho. E1....7J 85
(off Cable St.)
Chamberlain Ho. EC2....3G 9 (4E 84)
(off Blackall St.)
Chamberlain Ho. NW1....1D 6 (3H 83)
(off Ossulston St.)
Chamberlain Ho. SE1....7J 13 (2A 102)
(off Westminster Bri. Rd.)
Chamberlain La. HA5: Eastc....3J 39
Chamberlain Mews RM13: Rain....3J 91
Chamberlain Pl. E17....3A 50
Chamberlain Rd. N2....2A 46
Chamberlain Rd. W13....2A 96
Chamberlain St. NW1....7D 64
Chamberlain Wlk. TW13: Hanw....4C 130
Chamberlain Way HA5: Eastc....3K 39
Chamberlain Way KT6: Surb....7E 150
Chamberlayne Av. HA9: Wemb....3E 60
Chamberlayne Mans. NW10....3F 81
(off Chamberlayne Rd.)
Chamberlayne Rd. NW10....1E 80
Chamberlens Garages W6....4D 98
(off Dalling Rd.)
Chambers, The SW10....1A 118
(off Chelsea Harbour Dr.)
Chambers Av. DA14: Sidc....6E 144
Chambers Bus. Pk. UB7: Sip....6C 92
Chambers Gdns. N2....1B 46
Chambers La. NW10....7D 62
Chambers Pk. Hill SW20....7D 134
Chambers Pl. CR2: S Croy....7D 168
Chambers Rd. N7....4J 65
Chambers St. SE16....2G 103
Chamber St. E1....2K 15 (7F 85)
Chambers Wlk. HA7: Stan....5G 27
Chambers Wharf SE16....2G 103
Chambon Pl. W6....4C 98
Chambord Ho. E2....2K 9 (3F 85)
(off Chambord St.)
Chambord St. E2....2K 9 (3F 85)
Chamomile Ct. E17....6C 50
(off Yunus Khan Cl.)
Champa Cl. N17....2F 49
Champion Cres. SE26....4A 140
Champion Gro. SE5....3D 120
Champion Hill SE5....3D 120
Champion Hill Est. SE5....3E 120
Champion Hill Stadium....4E 120
Champion Ho. SE7....6A 106
(off Charlton Rd.)
Champion Pk. SE5....2D 120
Champion Rd. SE26....4A 140
Champions Wlk. E20....5E 68
Champions Way NW4....1D 44
Champions Way NW7....1D 44
Champlain Ho. W12....7D 80
(off White City Est.)
Champness Cl. E17....3K 49
Champness Cl. SE27....4D 138
Champness Rd. IG11: Bark....6K 71
Champneys Cl. SM2: Cheam....7H 165
Chancel Ct. W1....2C 12 (7H 83)
(off Old Compton St.)
Chancel Ind. Est. NW10....5B 62
Chancellor Gdns. CR2: S Croy....7B 168
Chancellor Gro. SE21....2C 138
Chancellor Ho. E1....1H 103
(off Green Bank)
Chancellor Ho. SW7....3A 100
(off Hyde Pk. Ga.)
Chancellor Pas. E14....1C 104
Chancellor Pl. NW9....2B 44
Chancellors Cl. BR3: Beck....7C 158
Chancellors Ct. WC1....5G 7 (5K 83)
(off Orde Hall St.)
Chancellor's Rd. W6....5E 98
Chancellor's St. W6....5E 98
Chancellors Wharf W6....5E 98
Chancellor Way RM8: Dag....4A 72
Chancelot Rd. SE2....4B 108
Chancel St. SE1....5A 14 (1B 102)
Chancery Bldg. SW11....7H 101
Chancery Bldgs. E1....7H 85
(off Lowood St.)
Chancerygate UB7: Yiew....1C 92
Chancerygate Bus. Cen. HA4: Ruis....4C 58
Chancery Ga. Bus. Pk. KT6: Surb....2F 163
Chancerygate Ind. Pk. DA14: Sidc 7D 144
Chancery La. BR3: Beck....2D 158
Chancery La. WC2....7J 7 (6A 84)
Chancery M. SW17....2C 136
Chance St. E1....3J 9 (4F 85)
Chance St. E2....3J 9 (4F 85)
Chanctonbury Cl. SE9....3F 143
Chanctonbury Gdns. SM2: Sutt....7K 165
Chanctonbury Way N12....4C 30
Chandaria Ct. CR0: C'don....3C 168
(off Church Rd.)
Chandler Av. E16....5J 87
Chandler Cl. TW12: Hamp....1E 148
Chandler Ct. TW14: Felt....6J 111
Chandler Ho. NW6....1H 81
(off Willesden La.)
Chandler Ho. WC1....4F 7 (4J 83)
(off Colonnade)
Chandlers Av. SE10....2H 105
Chandlers Cl. KT8: W Mole....5F 149
Chandlers Cl. TW14: Felt....7H 111
Chandlers Ct. SE12....1K 141
Chandlers Dr. DA8: Erith....4K 109
Chandlers M. E14....2C 104
Chandler St. E1....1H 103
Chandlers Way SW2....7A 120
Chandler Way SE15....6E 102
Chandlery, The SE1....1K 19 (3A 102)
(off Gerridge St.)
Chandlery Ho. E1....6G 85
(off Gower's Wlk.)
Chandon Lodge SM2: Sutt....7A 166
Chandos Av. E17....2C 50
Chandos Av. N14....3B 32
Chandos Av. N20....1F 31
Chandos Av. W5....4C 96
Chandos Cl. IG9: Buck H....2E 36
Chandos Ct. HA7: Stan....6G 27
Chandos Ct. HA8: Edg....7A 28
Chandos Ct. N14....2C 32
Chandos Cres. HA8: Edg....7A 28
Chandos Pde. HA8: Edg....7A 28
Chandos Pl. WC2....3E 12 (7J 83)
Chandos Rd. E15....5F 69
Chandos Rd. HA1: Harr....5G 41
Chandos Rd. HA5: Eastc....7B 40
Chandos Rd. N17....2E 48
Chandos Rd. N2....2B 46
Chandos Rd. NW10....4A 80
Chandos Rd. NW2....5E 62
Chandos St. W1....6K 5 (5F 83)
Chandos Way NW11....1K 63
Change All. EC3....1F 15 (6D 84)
Chanin M. NW2....5E 62
Channel 4 TV....2C 18 (3H 101)
(off Horseferry Rd.)
Channel Cl. TW5: Hest....1E 112
Channel Ga. Rd. NW10....3A 80
Channel Ho. SE16....2K 103
(off Water Gdns. Sq.)
Channel Islands Est. N1....6C 66
Channelsea Ho. E15....2F 87
Channelsea Path E15....1F 87
Channelsea Rd. E15....1F 87
Channon Ct. KT6: Surb....5E 150
(off Maple Rd.)
Chantrelle Ct. SE8....4A 104
(off Yeoman St.)
Chantress Cl. RM10: Dag....1J 91
Chantrey Ho. SW1....3J 17 (4F 101)
(off Eccleston St.)
Chantrey Rd. SW9....3K 119
Chantry, The E4....1K 35
Chantry, The UB8: Hil....3B 74
Chantry Cl. DA14: Sidc....5E 144
Chantry Cl. EN2: Enf....1H 23
Chantry Cl. HA3: Kenton....5F 43
Chantry Cl. SE2....3C 108
Chantry Cl. TW16: Sun....7J 129
Chantry Cl. UB7: Yiew....7A 74
Chantry Cl. W9....4J 81
Chantry Ct. SM5: Cars....3C 166
Chantry Cres. NW10....6B 62
Chantry Ho. KT1: King T....4E 150
Chantry La. BR2: Broml....5B 160
Chantry Pl. HA3: Hrw W....1F 41
Chantry Rd. HA3: Hrw W....1F 41
Chantry Rd. KT9: Chess....5F 163
Chantry Sq. W8....3K 99
Chantry St. N1....1B 84
Chantry Way CR4: Mitc....3B 154
Chant Sq. E15....7F 69
Chant St. E15....7F 69
(not continuous)
Chapel, The SW15....6G 117
Chapel Cl. DA1: Cray....5K 127
Chapel Cl. NW10....5B 62
Chapel Ct. E10....2D 68
(off Rosedene Ter.)
Chapel Ct. N2....3C 46
Chapel Ct. RM7: Rush G....6K 55
(off Bournebrook Gro.)
Chapel Ct. SE1....6E 14 (2D 102)
Chapel Ct. SE18....6A 108
Chapel Ct. UB3: Hayes....7H 75
CHAPEL END....1D 50
Chapel Farm Rd. SE9....3D 142
Chapel Ga. M. SW4....3J 119
(off Bedford Rd.)
Chapel Ga. Pl. BR7: Chst....6F 143
Chapel Hill DA1: Cray....5K 127
Chapel Ho. St. E14....5D 104
Chapelier Ho. SW18....4J 117
Chapel La. HA5: Pinn....3B 40
Chapel La. RM6: Chad H....7D 54
Chapel La. UB8: Hil....6C 74
Chapel Mkt. N1....2A 84
Chapel M. IG8: Wfd G....6K 37
Chapel Mill Rd. KT1: King T....3F 151
Chapelmount Rd. IG8: Wfd G....6J 37
Chapel Path E11....6K 51
(off Woodbine Pl.)
Chapel Pl. EC2....2G 9 (3E 84)
Chapel Pl. N1....2A 84
Chapel Pl. N17....7A 34
Chapel Pl. W1....1J 11 (6F 83)
Chapel Rd. DA7: Bex....4G 127
Chapel Rd. IG1: Ilf....3E 70
Chapel Rd. SE27....4B 138
Chapel Rd. TW1: Twick....7B 114
Chapel Rd. TW3: Houn....3F 113
Chapel Rd. W13....1B 96
Chapel Side W2....7K 81
Chapel Stones N17....1F 49
Chapel St. EN2: Enf....3H 23
Chapel St. NW1....6C 4 (5C 82)
Chapel St. SW1....1H 17 (3E 100)
Chapel Vw. CR2: Sels....6J 169
Chapel Wlk. CR0: C'don....2C 168
Chapel Wlk. NW4....4D 44
(not continuous)
Chapel Way N7....3K 65
Chapel Yd. SW18....5K 117
(off Wandsworth High St.)
Chaplin Cl. HA0: Wemb....6D 60
Chaplin Cl. SE1....6K 13 (2A 102)
Chaplin Ct. E3....4B 86
(off Joseph St.)
Chaplin Ct. SE14....1K 121
(off Besson St.)
Chaplin Ct. SE17....6B 102
(off Royal Rd.)
Chaplin Cres. TW16: Sun....6G 129
Chaplin Ho. DA14: Sidc....4A 144
(off Sidcup High St.)
Chaplin Ho. E17....4C 50
(off Hoe St.)
Chaplin Ho. N1....1D 84
(off Shepperton Rd.)
Chaplin Ho. W3....3J 97
(off All Saints Rd.)
Chaplin Rd. E15....2H 87
Chaplin Rd. HA0: Wemb....6C 60
Chaplin Rd. N17....3F 49
Chaplin Rd. NW2....6C 62
Chaplin Rd. RM9: Dag....7E 72
Chaplin Sq. N12....7G 31
Chapman Cl. UB7: W Dray....3B 92
Chapman Cres. HA3: Kenton....6E 42
Chapman Grn. N22....1A 48
Chapman Ho. E1....6H 85
(off Bigland St.)
Chapman Ho. NW9....3B 44
(off Aerodrome Rd.)
Chapman Pl. N4....2B 66
Chapman Rd. CR0: C'don....1A 168
Chapman Rd. DA17: Belv....5G 109
Chapman Rd. E9....6B 68
Chapman's La. DA17: Belv....4D 108
Chapman's La. SE2....4C 108
Chapmans Pk. Ind. Est. NW10....6B 62
Chapman Sq. SW19....2F 135
Chapman's Ter. N22....1B 48
Chapman St. E1....7H 85
Chapone Pl. W1....1C 12 (6H 83)
Chapter Chambers SW1....4C 18 (4H 101)
(off Chapter St.)
Chapter Cl. UB10: Hil....7B 56
Chapter Cl. W4....3J 97
Chapter Ho. E2....4G 85
(off Dunbridge St.)
Chapter Rd. NW2....5C 62
Chapter Rd. SE17....5B 102
Chapter St. SW1....4C 18 (4H 101)
Chapter Way SW19....1B 154
Chapter Way TW12: Hamp....4E 130
Chara Pl. W4....6K 97
Charcot Ho. SW15....6B 116
Charcot Rd. NW9....2A 44
Charcroft Ct. W14....2F 99
(off Minford Gdns.)
Charcroft Gdns. EN3: Pond E....4E 24
Chardin Ho. SW9....1A 120
(off Gosling Way)
Chardin Rd. W4....4A 98
Chardmore Rd. N16....1G 67
Chard Rd. TW6: H'row A....2D 110
Chardwell Cl. E6....6D 88
Charecroft Way W14....2F 99
Charfield Ct. W9....4K 81
(off Shirland Rd.)
Charford Rd. E16....5J 87
Chargeable La. E13....4H 87
Chargeable St. E16....4H 87
Chargrove Cl. SE16....2K 103
Charing Cl. BR6: Orp....4K 173
Charing Ct. BR2: Broml....2G 159
Charing Cross SW1....4E 12 (1J 101)
(off Whitehall)
Charing Cross Rd. WC2....1D 12 (6H 83)
Charing Cross Sports Club....6F 99
Charing Cross Theatre....4F 13 (1J 101)
(off Villiers St.)
Charing Cross Underground Shop. Cen.....3E 12 (7J 83)
(off The Strand)
Charing Ho. SE1....6K 13 (2A 102)
(off Windmill Wlk.)
Chariot Cl. E3....1C 86
Charis Ho. E3....3D 86
(off Grace St.)
Charlbert Ct. NW8....2C 82
(off Charlbert St.)
Charlbert St. NW8....2C 82
Charlbury Av. HA7: Stan....5J 27
Charlbury Gdns. IG3: Ilf....2K 71
Charlbury Gro. W5....6C 78
Charlbury Rd. UB10: Ick....3B 56
Charldane Rd. SE9....3F 143
Charlecote Gro. SE26....3H 139
Charlecote Rd. RM8: Dag....3E 72
Charlemont Rd. E6....4D 88
Charles II Pl. SW3....6E 16 (5D 100)
Charles II St. SW1....4C 12 (1H 101)
Charles Auffray Ho. E1....5J 85
(off Smithy St.)
Charles Babbage Cl. KT9: Chess....7C 162
Charles Baker Pl. SW17....1C 136
Charles Barry Cl. SW4....3G 119
Charles Bradlaugh Ho. N17....7C 34
(off Haynes Cl.)
Charles Burton Ct. E5....5A 68
(off Ashenden Rd.)
Charles Chu. Wlk. IG1: Ilf....6D 52
Charles Cl. DA14: Sidc....4B 144
Charles Clowes Wlk. SW11....7H 101
Charles Cobb Gdns. CR0: Wadd....5A 168
Charles Coveney Rd. SE15....1F 121
Charles Cres. HA1: Harr....7H 41
(not continuous)
Charles Cryer Studio Theatre, The....4E 166
Charles Darwin Ho. E16....6H 87
(off Minnie Baldock St.)
Charles Darwin Ho. E2....3H 85
(off Canrobert St.)
Charles Dickens Ho. E2....3G 85
(off Mansford St.)
Charles Dickens Mus., The....4H 7 (4K 83)
(off Doughty St.)
Charlesfield SE9....3A 142
Charles Flemwell M. E16....1J 105
Charles Gardner Ct. N1....1F 9 (3D 84)
(off Haberdasher St.)
Charles Grinling Wlk. SE18....4E 106
Charles Gro. N14....1B 32
Charles Haller St. SW2....7A 120
Charles Harrod Ct. SW13....6E 98
(off Somerville Av.)
Charles Hocking Ho. W3....2J 97
(off Bollo Bri. Rd.)
Charles Ho. N17....7A 34
(off Love La.)
Charles Ho. UB2: S'hall....2E 94
Charles Ho. W14....4H 99
Charles Lamb Ct. N1....2B 84
(off Gerrard Rd.)
Charles La. NW8....2C 82
Charles Lesser Ho. KT9: Chess....5D 162
Charles Mackenzie Ho. SE16....4G 103
(off Linsey St.)
Charlesmere Gdns. SE28....2J 107
(off Thames Reach)
Charles Nex M. SE21....2C 138
Charles Pl. E4....1A 36
Charles Pl. NW1....2B 6 (3G 83)
Charles Rd. E7....7A 70
Charles Rd. RM10: Dag....6K 73
Charles Rd. RM6: Chad H....6D 54
Charles Rd. SW19....1J 153
Charles Rd. W13....6A 78
Charles Rowan Ho. WC1....2J 7 (3A 84)
(off Margery St.)
Charles Sevright Way NW7....5A 30
Charles Simmons Ho. WC1....2H 7 (3K 83)
(off Margery St.)
Charles Sq. N1....2F 9 (3D 84)
Charles Sq. Est. N1....2F 9 (3D 84)
(off Pitfield St.)
Charles St. CR0: C'don....3C 168
Charles St. E16....1A 106
Charles St. EN1: Enf....5A 24
Charles St. N19....1J 65
Charles St. SW13....2A 116
Charles St. TW3: Houn....2D 112
Charles St. UB10: Hil....4D 74
Charles St. W1....4J 11 (1F 101)
Charles Talbot M. SE22....1H 139
Charleston Cl. TW13: Felt....3J 129
Charleston St. SE17....4C 102
Charles Townsend Ho. EC1....2A 8 (3B 84)
(off Skinner St.)
Charles Uton Ct. E8....4G 67
Charles Whincup Rd. E16....1K 105
Charlesworth Ho. E14....6C 86
(off Dod St.)
Charlesworth Pl. SW13....3A 116
Charleville Cir. SE26....5G 139
Charleville Ct. W14....5H 99
(off Charleville Rd.)
Charleville Mans. W14....5G 99
(off Charleville Rd.)
Charleville M. TW7: Isle....4B 114
Charleville Rd. W14....5G 99
CHARLIE BROWN'S RDBT.....2A 52
Charlie Chaplin Wlk. SE1....5H 13 (1K 101)
Charlieville Rd. DA8: Erith....7J 109
Charlmont Rd. SW17....6C 136
Charlotte Cl. DA6: Bex....5E 126
Charlotte Cl. IG6: Ilf....1G 53
Charlotte Ct. IG2: Ilf....6E 52
Charlotte Ct. N8....6H 47
Charlotte Ct. SE1....4E 102
(off Old Kent Rd.)
Charlotte Ct. W6....4C 98
Charlotte Despard Av. SW11....1E 118
Charlotte Ho. E16....1K 105
(off Fairfax M.)
Charlotte Ho. W6....5E 98
(off Queen Caroline St.)
Charlotte M. W1....5B 6 (5G 83)
Charlotte M. W10....6F 81
Charlotte M. W14....4G 99
Charlotte Pk. Av. BR1: Broml....3C 160
Charlotte Pl. NW9....5J 43
Charlotte Pl. SW1....4A 18 (4G 101)
Charlotte Pl. W1....6B 6 (5G 83)
Charlotte Rd. EC2....2G 9 (3E 84)
Charlotte Rd. RM10: Dag....6H 73
Charlotte Rd. SM6: W'gton....6G 167
Charlotte Rd. SW13....1B 116
Charlotte Row SW4....3G 119
Charlotte Sq. TW10: Rich....6F 115
Charlotte St. W1....5B 6 (5G 83)
Charlotte Ter. N1....1K 83
Charlow Cl. SW6....2A 118
CHARLTON....7B 106
CHARLTON....3E 146
Charlton Athletic FC....5A 106
Charlton Chu. La. SE7....5A 106
Charlton Cl. UB10: Ick....2D 56
Charlton Ct. E2....1F 85
Charlton Ct. NW5....5H 65
Charlton Cres. IG11: Bark....2K 89
Charlton Dene SE7....7A 106
Charlton Ga. Bus. Pk. SE7....4A 106
Charlton Ho. TW8: Bford....6E 96
Charlton King's Rd. NW5....5H 65
Charlton La. SE7....4B 106
Charlton La. TW17: Shep....3E 146
(not continuous)
Charlton Lido....7B 106
Charlton Pk. La. SE7....7B 106
Charlton Pk. Rd. SE7....6B 106
Charlton Pl. N1....2B 84
Charlton Riverside Pl. SE7....4K 105
Charlton Rd. HA3: Kenton....4D 42
Charlton Rd. HA9: Wemb....1F 61
Charlton Rd. N9....1E 34
Charlton Rd. NW10....1A 80
Charlton Rd. SE3....7J 105
Charlton Rd. SE7....6K 105
Charlton Rd. TW17: Shep....3E 146
Charlton Ter. SE11....4E 102
(off Caroline St.)
Charlton Way SE3....1G 123
Charlwood CR0: Sels....7B 170
Charlwood Cl. HA3: Hrw W....6D 26
Charlwood Ho. SW1....4C 18 (4H 101)
(off Vauxhall Bri. Rd.)
Charlwood Ho. TW9: Kew....7H 97
Charlwood Ho's. WC1....2F 7 (3J 83)
(off Midhope St.)
Charlwood Pl. SW1....4B 18 (4G 101)
Charlwood Rd. SW15....4F 117
Charlwood St. SW1....6A 18 (5G 101)
(not continuous)
Charlwood Ter. SW15....4F 117
Charmans Ho. SW8....7J 101
(off Wandsworth Rd.)
Charmeuse Ct. E2....2H 85
(off Silk Weaver Way)
Charmian Av. HA7: Stan....3D 42
Charmian Ho. N1....1G 9 (2E 84)
(off Crondall St.)
Charmille Av. NW9....1B 44
Charminster Av. SW19....2J 153
Charminster Ct. KT6: Surb....7D 150
Charminster Rd. KT4: Wor Pk....1F 165
Charminster Rd. SE9....4B 142
Charmouth Ct. TW10: Rich....5F 115
Charmouth Ho. SW8....7K 101
Charmouth Rd. DA16: Well....1C 126
Charnock Ho. W12....7D 80
(off White City Est.)
Charnock Rd. E5....3H 67
Charnwood Av. SW19....2J 153
Charnwood Cl. KT3: N Mald....4A 152
Charnwood Dr. E18....3K 51
Charnwood Gdns. E14....4C 104
Charnwood Pl. N20....3F 31
Charnwood Rd. SE25....5D 156
Charnwood Rd. UB10: Hil....2C 74
Charnwood St. E5....2H 67
Charrington Ct. RM1: Rush G....6K 55
Charrington Rd. CR0: C'don....2C 168
Charrington St. NW1....2H 83
(not continuous)
Charsley Rd. SE6....2D 140
Chart Cl. BR2: Broml....1G 159
Chart Cl. CR0: C'don....6J 157
Chart Cl. CR4: Mitc....4D 154
Charter Av. IG2: Ilf....1H 71
Charter Bldgs. SE10....1D 122
(off Catherine Gro.)
Charter Ct. KT3: N Mald....3A 152
Charter Ct. N22....1H 47
Charter Ct. N4....1A 66
Charter Ct. UB1: S'hall....1E 94
Charter Cres. TW4: Houn....4C 112
Charter Dr. DA5: Bexl....7E 126
Charter Ho. SM2: Sutt....6K 165
(off Mulgrave Rd.)
Charter Ho. WC2....1F 13 (6J 83)
(off Crown Ct.)
Charterhouse....4B 8 (4B 84)
Charterhouse Apts. SW18....4A 118
Charterhouse Av. HA0: Wemb....4C 60
Charterhouse Bldgs. EC1....4C 8 (4C 84)
Charterhouse M. EC1....5B 8 (5B 84)
Charterhouse Mus.....5B 8 (5B 84)
(within Charterhouse)
Charterhouse Rd. BR6: Chels....3K 173
Charterhouse Rd. E8....4G 67
Charterhouse Sq. EC1....5B 8 (5B 84)
Charterhouse St. EC1....6K 7 (5A 84)
Charteris Community Sports Cen.....1J 81

Charteris Rd. – Chesterfield Wlk.

Charteris Rd. IG8: Wfd G 7E 36
Charteris Rd. N4 1A 66
Charteris Rd. NW6 1H 81
Charter Quay KT1: King T 2D 150
(off Wadbrook St.)
Charter Rd. KT1: King T 3H 151
Charter Rd., The IG8: Wfd G 6B 36
Charters Cl. SE19 5E 138
Charter Sq. KT1: King T 2H 151
Charter St. E14 1E 104
Charter Way N14 6B 22
Charter Way N3 4H 45
Chartes Ho. SE1 7H 15 (3E 102)
(off Stevens St.)
Chartfield Av. SW15 5D 116
Chartfield Sq. SW15 5F 117
Chartham Ct. SW9 3A 120
(off Canterbury Cres.)
Chartham Gro. SE27 3B 138
Chartham Ho. SE1 7F 15 (3D 102)
(off Weston St.)
Chartham Rd. SE25 3H 157
Chart Hills Cl. SE28 6E 90
Chart Ho. CR4: Mitc 2D 154
Chart Ho. E14 5D 104
(off Burrells Wharf Sq.)
Chartley Av. HA7: Stan 6E 26
Chartley Av. NW2 3A 62
Charton Cl. DA17: Belv 6F 109
Chartres Ct. UB6: G'frd 2H 77
Chartridge SE17 6D 102
(off Westmoreland Rd.)
Chart St. N1 1F 9 (3D 84)
Chartwell Bus. Cen. BR1: Broml 3B 160
Chartwell Cl. CR0: C'don 1D 168
Chartwell Cl. SE9 2H 143
Chartwell Cl. UB6: G'frd 1F 77
Chartwell Ct. EN5: Barn 4B 20
Chartwell Ct. IG8: Wfd G 7D 36
Chartwell Ct. NW2 3C 62
Chartwell Ct. UB3: Hayes 7H 75
Chartwell Dr. BR6: Farnb 5H 173
Chartwell Gdns. SM3: Cheam 4G 165
Chartwell Ho. SW10 1A 118
Chartwell Ho. W11 1H 99
(off Ladbroke Rd.)
Chartwell Lodge BR3: Beck 7C 140
Chartwell Pl. HA2: Harr 2H 59
Chartwell Pl. SM3: Cheam 4G 165
Chartwell Way SE20 1H 157
Charville Ct. HA1: Harr 6K 41
(off Gayton Rd.)
Charville Ct. SE10 6F 105
(off Trafalgar Gro.)
Charville La. UB4: Hayes 3E 74
Charville La. W. UB10: Hil 3D 74
(not continuous)
Charwood SW16 4A 138
Chase, The UB10: Ick The Grove 5C 56
Chase, The BR1: Broml 3K 159
Chase, The DA7: Bex 3H 127
Chase, The E12 4B 70
Chase, The HA5: Eastc 6A 40
Chase, The HA5: Pinn 4D 40
Chase, The HA7: Stan 6F 27
Chase, The HA8: Edg 1H 43
Chase, The RM1: Rom 3K 55
Chase, The RM6: Chad H 6E 54
Chase, The RM7: Rush G 3K 73
Chase, The SM6: W'gton 5J 167
Chase, The SW16 7K 137
Chase, The SW20 1G 153
Chase, The SW4 3F 119
Chase, The TW16: Sun 1K 147
Chase Bank Ct. N14 6B 22
(off Avenue Rd.)
Chase Cen., The NW10 3K 79
Chase Ct. SW20 2G 153
Chase Ct. SW3 2E 16 (3D 100)
(off Beaufort Gdns.)
Chase Ct. TW7: Isle 2A 114
Chase Ct. Gdns. EN2: Enf 3H 23
Chase Cross Rd. RM5: Col R 1J 55
Chasefield Rd. SW17 4D 136
Chase Gdns. E4 4H 35
Chase Gdns. TW2: Whitt 7H 113
Chase Grn. EN2: Enf 3H 23
Chase Grn. Av. EN2: Enf 2G 23
Chase Hill EN2: Enf 3H 23
Chase Ho. NW6 3J 81
(off Hansel Rd.)
Chase La. IG2: Ilf 5H 53
Chase La. IG6: Ilf 5H 53
Chaseley Dr. W4 5H 97
Chaseley St. E14 6A 86
Chasemore Cl. CR4: Mitc 7D 154
Chasemore Gdns. CR0: Wadd 5A 168
Chasemore Ho. SW6 7G 99
(off Williams Cl.)
Chase Ridings EN2: Enf 2F 23
Chase Rd. N14 5B 22
Chase Rd. NW10 4K 79
Chase Rd. Trad. Est. NW10 4K 79
Chase Side EN2: Enf 3H 23
CHASE SIDE 1J 23
Chase Side N14 6K 21
Chase Side Av. EN2: Enf 2H 23
Chase Side Av. SW20 1G 153
Chase Side Cres. EN2: Enf 1H 23
Chase Side Pl. EN2: Enf 2H 23
Chaseville Pde. N21 5E 22
Chaseville Pk. Rd. N21 5D 22
Chase Way N14 2A 32
Chaseway Lodge E16 6J 87
(off Butchers Rd.)
Chaseways Vs. RM5: Col R 1F 55
Chasewood Av. EN2: Enf 2G 23
Chasewood Ct. NW7 5E 28
Chasewood Pk. HA1: Harr 3K 59
Chaston Pl. NW5 5E 64
(off Grafton Ter.)
Chater Ho. E2 3K 85
(off Roman Rd.)
Chatfield Rd. CR0: C'don 1B 168
Chatfield Rd. SW11 3A 118
Chatham Av. BR2: Hayes 7H 159
Chatham Cl. NW11 5J 45
Chatham Cl. SE18 3F 107
Chatham Cl. SM3: Sutt 7H 153
Chatham Ho. SM6: W'gton 5F 167
(off Melbourne Rd.)
Chatham Pl. E9 6J 67
Chatham Rd. E17 3A 50
Chatham Rd. E18 2H 51
Chatham Rd. KT1: King T 2G 151
Chatham Rd. SW11 6D 118
Chatham St. SE17 4D 102
Chatsfield Pl. W5 6E 78
Chats Palace Arts Cen. 5K 67
Chatsworth M. DA14: Sidc 4K 143
Chatsworth Av. BR1: Broml 4K 141
Chatsworth Av. DA15: Sidc 1A 144
Chatsworth Av. HA9: Wemb 5F 61
Chatsworth Av. NW4 2E 44
Chatsworth Av. SW20 1G 153
Chatsworth Cl. BR4: W W'ck 2H 171
Chatsworth Cl. NW4 2E 44
Chatsworth Cl. W4 6J 97
Chatsworth Ct. HA7: Stan 5H 27
Chatsworth Ct. SW16 3K 155
Chatsworth Ct. W8 4J 99
(off Pembroke Rd.)
Chatsworth Cres. TW3: Houn 4H 113
Chatsworth Dr. EN1: Enf 7B 24
Chatsworth Est. E5 4K 67
Chatsworth Gdns. HA2: Harr 1F 59
Chatsworth Gdns. KT3: N Mald 5B 152
Chatsworth Gdns. W3 1H 97
Chatsworth Ho. BR2: Broml 4J 159
(off Westmoreland Rd.)
Chatsworth Ho. E16 1K 105
(off Wesley Av.)
Chatsworth Ho. SE1 5J 15 (1F 103)
(off Duchess Wlk.)
Chatsworth Lodge W4 5K 97
(off Bourne Pl.)
Chatsworth Pde. BR5: Pet W 5G 161
Chatsworth Pl. CR4: Mitc 3D 154
Chatsworth Pl. TW11: Tedd 4A 132
Chatsworth Ri. W5 4F 79
Chatsworth Rd. CR0: C'don 4D 168
Chatsworth Rd. E15 5H 69
Chatsworth Rd. E5 3J 67
Chatsworth Rd. NW2 6E 62
Chatsworth Rd. SM3: Cheam 5F 165
Chatsworth Rd. UB4: Yead 4K 75
Chatsworth Rd. W4 6J 97
Chatsworth Rd. W5 4F 79
Chatsworth Way SE27 3B 138
Chattern Hill TW15: Ashf 4D 128
CHATTERN HILL 4D 128
Chattern Rd. TW15: Ashf 4E 128
Chatterton Ct. TW9: Kew 2F 115
Chatterton M. N4 3B 66
(off Chatterton Rd.)
Chatterton Rd. BR2: Broml 4B 160
Chatterton Rd. N4 3B 66
Chatto Rd. SW11 5D 118
Chaucer Av. TW4: Cran 2K 111
Chaucer Av. TW9: Rich 3G 115
Chaucer Av. UB4: Hayes 5J 75
Chaucer Cl. N11 5B 32
Chaucer Ct. BR2: Broml 5A 160
Chaucer Ct. EN5: New Bar 5E 20
Chaucer Ct. N16 4E 66
Chaucer Ct. SW17 3B 136
(off Lanesborough Way)
Chaucer Dr. SE1 4F 103
Chaucer Gdns. E1 6G 85
(off Piazza Wlk.)
Chaucer Gdns. SM1: Sutt 3J 165
Chaucer Grn. CR0: C'don 7H 157
Chaucer Ho. EN5: Barn 4A 20
Chaucer Ho. SM1: Sutt 3J 165
(off Chaucer Gdns.)
Chaucer Ho. SW1 6A 18 (5G 101)
(off Churchill Gdns.)
Chaucer Mans. W14 6G 99
(off Queen's Club Gdns.)
Chaucer Rd. DA15: Sidc 1C 144
Chaucer Rd. DA16: Well 1J 125
Chaucer Rd. E11 6J 51
Chaucer Rd. E17 2E 50
Chaucer Rd. E7 6J 69
Chaucer Rd. SE24 5A 120
Chaucer Rd. SM1: Sutt 4J 165
Chaucer Rd. TW15: Ashf 4A 128
Chaucer Rd. W3 1J 97
Chaucer Way SW19 6B 136
Chaulden Ho. EC1 2F 9 (3D 84)
(off Cranwood St.)
Chauncey Cl. N9 3B 34
Chaundrye Cl. SE9 6D 124
Chauntler Cl. E16 6K 87
Chaville Ct. N11 4K 31
Chaville Way N3 1J 45
Cheadle Ct. NW8 3B 4 (4B 82)
(off Henderson Dr.)
Cheadle Ho. E14 6B 86
(off Copenhagen Pl.)
CHEAM 6G 165
Cheam Comn. Rd. KT4: Wor Pk 2D 164
Cheam Leisure Cen. 4F 165
Cheam Mans. SM3: Cheam 7G 165
Cheam Pk. Way SM3: Cheam 6G 165
Cheam Rd. SM1: Sutt 6H 165
Cheam St. SE15 3J 121
CHEAM VILLAGE 6G 165
Cheapside EC2 7C 8 (6C 84)
Cheapside N13 4J 33
Cheapside N22 3A 48
Cheapside Pas. EC2 1C 14 (6C 84)
(off One New Change)
Cheddar Cl. N11 6J 31
Cheddar Waye UB4: Yead 6K 75
Cheddington Ho. E2 1G 85
(off Whiston Rd.)
Cheddington Rd. N18 3K 33
Chedworth Ho. N15 4D 48
(off West Grn. Rd.)
Cheering La. E20 5E 68
Cheesegrater, The 1G 15 (6E 84)
(off Leadenhall St.)
Cheeseman Cl. TW12: Hamp 6C 130
Cheesemans Ter. W14 5H 99
(not continuous)
Cheffery Ct. TW15: Ashf 6D 128
Cheldon Av. NW7 7A 30
Chelford Rd. BR1: Broml 5F 141
Chelmer Cres. IG11: Bark 2B 90
Chelmer Rd. E9 5K 67
Chelmsford Cl. E6 6D 88
Chelmsford Cl. W6 6F 99
Chelmsford Ct. N14 7C 22
(off Chelmsford Rd.)
Chelmsford Gdns. IG1: Ilf 7C 52
Chelmsford Ho. N7 4K 65
(off Holloway Rd.)
Chelmsford Rd. E11 1F 69
Chelmsford Rd. E17 6C 50
Chelmsford Rd. E18 1H 51
Chelmsford Rd. N14 7B 22
Chelmsford Sq. NW10 1E 80
Chelmsine Ct. HA4: Ruis 5E 38
CHELSEA 6C 16 (5C 100)
CHELSEA BRI. 7J 17 (6F 101)
Chelsea Bri. Rd. SW1 5G 17 (5E 100)
Chelsea Bri. Wharf SW11
7J 17 (6F 101)
Chelsea Cloisters SW3 4D 16 (4C 100)
Chelsea Cl. HA8: Edg 2G 43
Chelsea Cl. KT4: Wor Pk 7C 152
Chelsea Cl. NW10 1K 79
Chelsea Cl. TW12: Hamp H 5G 131
Chelsea Ct. BR1: Broml 3C 160
(off Holmdene Ct.)
Chelsea Ct. SW3 7F 17 (6D 100)
(off Embankment Gdns.)
Chelsea Cres. NW2 6H 63
Chelsea Cres. SW10 1A 118
Chelsea Emb. SW3 7C 16 (6C 100)
Chelsea Farm Ho. Studios SW10 6B 100
(off Cremorne Est.)
Chelsea FC 7K 99
Chelsea Flds. SW19 1B 154
Chelsea Gdns. SM3: Cheam 4G 165
Chelsea Gdns. SW1 6H 17 (5E 100)
Chelsea Gdns. W13 5K 77
Chelsea Ga. SW1 6H 17 (5E 100)
(off Ebury Bri. Rd.)
Chelsea Harbour SW10 1A 118
Chelsea Harbour Design Cen. SW10
1A 118
(off Chelsea Harbour Dr.)
Chelsea Harbour Dr. SW10 1A 118
Chelsea Lodge SW3 7F 17 (6D 100)
(off Tite St.)
Chelsea Mnr. Ct. SW3 7D 16 (6C 100)
Chelsea Mnr. Gdns. SW3 6D 16 (5C 100)
Chelsea Mnr. St. SW3 6C 16 (5C 100)
Chelsea Mnr. Studios SW3
6D 16 (5C 100)
(off Flood St.)
Chelsea Pk. Gdns. SW3 7A 16 (6B 100)
Chelsea Physic Gdn. 7E 16 (6D 100)
Chelsea Reach Twr. SW10 7B 100
(off Worlds End Est.)
Chelsea Sports Cen. 6D 16 (5C 100)
Chelsea Sq. SW3 5B 16 (5B 100)
Chelsea Studios SW6 7K 99
(off Fulham Rd.)
Chelsea Theatre, The 7A 100
Chelsea Towers SW3 7D 16 (6C 100)
(off Chelsea Mnr. Gdns.)
Chelsea Village SW6 7K 99
(off Fulham Rd.)
Chelsea Vista SW6 1A 118
Chelsea Wharf SW10 7B 100
(off Lots Rd.)
Chelsfield Av. N9 7E 24
Chelsfield Gdns. SE26 3J 139
Chelsfield Grn. N9 7E 24
(not continuous)
Chelsfield Ho. SE17 4E 102
(off Massinger St.)
Chelsfield Point E9 7K 67
(off Penshurst Rd.)
Chelsham Rd. CR2: S Croy 7D 168
Chelsham Rd. SW4 3H 119
Chelsiter Ct. DA14: Sidc 4K 143
Chelston App. HA4: Ruis 2J 57
Chelston Ct. E11 5K 51
Chelston Rd. HA4: Ruis 1J 57
Chelsworth Dr. SE18 6H 107
Cheltenham Av. TW1: Twick 7A 114
Cheltenham Cl. KT3: N Mald 3J 151
Cheltenham Cl. UB5: N'olt 6F 59
Cheltenham Ct. HA7: Stan 5H 27
(off Marsh La.)
Cheltenham Gdns. E6 2C 88
Cheltenham Ho. IG8: Wfd G 6K 37
Cheltenham Ho. UB3: Harl 3E 92
(off Skipton Dr.)
Cheltenham Pl. HA3: Kenton 4E 42
Cheltenham Pl. W3 1H 97
Cheltenham Rd. BR6: Chels 3K 173
Cheltenham Rd. E10 6E 50
Cheltenham Rd. SE15 4J 121
Cheltenham Ter. SW3 5F 17 (5D 100)
Chelverton Rd. SW15 4F 117
Chelwood N20 2G 31
Chelwood Cl. E4 6J 25
Chelwood Ct. CR2: S Croy 5C 168
Chelwood Ct. SW11 1B 118
(off Westbridge Rd.)
Chelwood Gdns. TW9: Kew 2G 115
Chelwood Gdns. Pas. TW9: Kew 2G 115
Chelwood Ho. W2 1B 10 (6B 82)
(off Gloucester Sq.)
Chelwood Wlk. SE4 4A 122
Chenappa Cl. E13 3J 87
Chenduit Way HA7: Stan 5E 26
Cheney Ct. SE23 1K 139
Cheney Row E17 1B 50
Cheneys Rd. E11 3G 69
Cheney St. HA5: Eastc 4A 40
Chenies, The BR6: Pet W 6J 161
Chenies, The NW1 2H 83
(off Pancras Rd.)
Chenies Ho. W2 7K 81
(off Moscow Rd.)
Chenies Ho. W4 7B 98
(off Corney Reach Way)
Chenies M. WC1 4C 6 (4H 83)
Chenies Pl. NW1 2H 83
Chenies St. WC1 5C 6 (5H 83)
Cheniston Gdns. W8 3K 99
Chenla SE13 2D 122
Chenneston Cl. TW16: Sun 1J 147
Cheping Ho. W10 7F 81
(off Shalfleet Dr.)
Chepstow Cl. SW15 5G 117
Chepstow Cnr. W2 6J 81
(off Chepstow Pl.)
Chepstow Ct. W11 7J 81
(off Chepstow Vs.)
Chepstow Cres. IG3: Ilf 6J 53
Chepstow Cres. W11 7J 81
Chepstow Gdns. UB1: S'hall 6D 76
Chepstow Pl. W2 6J 81
Chepstow Ri. CR0: C'don 3E 168
Chepstow Rd. CR0: C'don 3E 168
Chepstow Rd. W2 6J 81
Chepstow Rd. W7 3A 96
Chepstow Vs. W11 7H 81
Chequers IG9: Buck H 1E 36
Chequers, The HA5: Pinn 3B 40
Chequers Cl. BR5: St P 4K 161
Chequers Cl. NW9 3A 44
Chequers Ct. DA17: Belv 4G 109
Chequers Ct. EC1 4E 8 (4D 84)
(off Chequer St.)
Chequers Ho. NW8 3C 4 (4C 82)
(off Jerome Cres.)
Chequers La. RM9: Dag 4F 91
(not continuous)
Chequers Pde. N13 5H 33
Chequers Pde. RM9: Dag 1F 91
Chequers Pde. SE9 6D 124
(off Eltham High St.)
Chequer St. EC1 4D 8 (4C 84)
(not continuous)
Chequers Way N13 5G 33
Cherbury Cl. SE28 6D 90
Cherbury Ct. N1 1F 9 (2D 84)
(off St John's Est.)
Cherbury St. N1 2D 84
Cherchefelle M. HA7: Stan 5G 27
Cherimoya Gdns. KT8: W Mole 3F 149
Cherington Rd. W7 1J 95
Cheriton Av. BR2: Broml 5H 159
Cheriton Av. IG5: Ilf 2D 52
Cheriton Cl. EN4: Cockf 3J 21
Cheriton Cl. W5 5C 78
Cheriton Ct. SE12 7J 123
Cheriton Ct. SE25 5E 156
Cheriton Dr. SE18 7H 107
Cheriton Lodge HA4: Ruis 1H 57
Cheriton Sq. SW17 2E 136
Cherry Av. UB1: S'hall 1B 94
Cherry Blossom Cl. N13 5G 33
Cherry Cl. E17 5D 50
Cherry Cl. HA0: Wemb 3D 60
Cherry Cl. HA4: Ruis 3H 57
Cherry Cl. NW9 2A 44
Cherry Cl. SM4: Mord 4G 153
Cherry Cl. SM5: Cars 2D 166
Cherry Cl. SW2 7A 120
Cherry Cl. W5 3D 96
Cherrycot Hill BR6: Farnb 4G 173
Cherrycot Ri. BR6: Farnb 4G 173
Cherry Ct. HA5: Pinn 2B 40
Cherry Ct. IG6: Ilf 3F 53
Cherry Ct. W3 1A 98
Cherry Cres. TW8: Bford 7B 96
Cherrydown Av. E4 3G 35
Cherrydown Cl. E4 3H 35
Cherrydown Rd. DA14: Sidc 2D 144
Cherrydown Wlk. RM7: Mawney 2H 55
Cherry Gdn. Ho. SE16 2H 103
(off Cherry Gdn. St.)
Cherry Gdns. RM9: Dag 5F 73
Cherry Gdns. UB5: N'olt 7F 59
Cherry Gdn. St. SE16 2H 103
Cherry Gth. TW8: Bford 5D 96
Cherry Gro. UB3: Hayes 1K 93
Cherry Gro. UB8: Hil 5D 74
Cherry Hill EN5: New Bar 6E 20
Cherry Hill HA3: Hrw W 6E 26
Cherry Hill Gdns. CR0: Wadd 4K 167
Cherrylands Cl. NW9 2J 61
Cherry La. UB7: W Dray 4B 92
Cherry Laurel Wlk. SW2 6K 119
Cherry M. SW17 2C 136
Cherry Orchard SE7 6A 106
Cherry Orchard UB7: W Dray 2A 92
Cherry Orchard Gdns. CR0: C'don
1D 168
Cherry Orchard Gdns. KT8: W Mole
3D 148
Cherry Orchard Rd. BR2: Broml 2C 172
Cherry Orchard Rd. CR0: C'don 2D 168
Cherry Orchard Rd. KT8: W Mole 3E 148
Cherry Pk. La. E20 7E 68
Cherry Red Records Stadium 3H 151
Cherry Rd. EN3: Enf W 1D 24
Cherry St. RM7: Rom 5K 55
Cherry Tree Av. UB7: Yiew 6B 74
Cherry Tree Cl. E9 1J 85
Cherry Tree Cl. HA0: Wemb 4A 60
Cherry Tree Ct. NW1 7G 65
(off Camden Rd.)
Cherry Tree Ct. NW9 4J 43
Cherry Tree Ct. SE7 6A 106
Cherry Tree Dr. SW16 3J 137
Cherry Tree Hill N2 5C 46
Cherry Tree Ho. N22 7D 32
Cherry Tree Ri. IG9: Buck H 4F 37
Cherry Tree Rd. E15 5G 69
Cherry Tree Rd. N2 4D 46
Cherry Tree Ter. SE1 7H 15 (2E 102)
(off Whites Grounds)
Cherry Tree Wlk. BR3: Beck 4B 158
Cherry Tree Wlk. BR4: W W'ck 4H 171
Cherry Tree Wlk. EC1 4D 8 (4C 84)
Cherry Tree Way E13 4B 88
Cherry Tree Way HA7: Stan 6G 27
Cherry Wlk. BR2: Hayes 1J 171
Cherry Way KT19: Ewe 6K 163
Cherry Way TW17: Shep 4F 147
Cherrywood Cl. E3 3A 86
Cherrywood Cl. KT2: King T 7G 133
Cherrywood Ct. TW11: Tedd 5A 132
Cherrywood Dr. SW15 5F 117
Cherrywood La. SM4: Mord 4G 153
Cherrywood Lodge SE13 6F 123
(off Birdwood Av.)
Cherry Wood Way W5 5G 79
Chertsey Ct. SW14 3H 115
Chertsey Dr. SM3: Cheam 2G 165
Chertsey Ho. E2 2J 9 (3F 85)
(off Arnold Cir.)
CHERTSEY MEADS 7A 146
Chertsey Meads Local Nature Reserve
7A 146
Chertsey Rd. E11 2F 69
Chertsey Rd. IG1: Ilf 4H 71
Chertsey Rd. TW1: Twick 6K 113
Chertsey Rd. TW13: Felt 3G 129
Chertsey Rd. TW15: Ashf 7F 129
Chertsey Rd. TW16: Sun 6G 129
Chertsey Rd. TW17: Shep 7A 146
Chertsey Rd. TW2: Twick 2F 131
Chertsey St. SW17 5E 136
Chervil Cl. TW13: Felt 3J 129
Chervil M. SE28 1B 108
Cherwell Ct. KT19: Ewe 4J 163
Cherwell Ho. NW8 4B 4 (4B 82)
(off Church St. Est.)
Cherwell M. SW11 4C 118
Cherwell Way HA4: Ruis 6E 38
Cheryls Cl. SW6 1K 117
Cheseman St. SE26 3H 139
Chesfield Rd. KT2: King T 7E 132
Chesham Apts. E4 7J 35
Chesham Av. BR5: Pet W 6F 161
Chesham Cl. NW7 4F 29
Chesham Cl. RM7: Rom 4K 55
Chesham Cl. SW1 2G 17 (3E 100)
(off Lyall St.)
Chesham Cres. SE20 1J 157
Chesham Flats W1 2H 11 (7E 82)
(off Brown Hart Gdns.)
Chesham Ho. SE8 1C 122
(off Brookmill Rd.)
Chesham M. SW1 1G 17 (3E 100)
(off Belgrave M. W.)
Chesham Pl. SW1 2G 17 (3E 100)
(not continuous)
Chesham Rd. KT1: King T 2G 151
Chesham Rd. SE20 2J 157
Chesham Rd. SW19 5B 136
Chesham St. NW10 3K 61
Chesham St. SW1 2G 17 (3E 100)
Chesham Ter. W13 2B 96
Cheshire Cl. CR4: Mitc 3J 155
Cheshire Cl. E17 1D 50
Cheshire Cl. SE4 2B 122
Cheshire Ct. EC4 1K 13 (6A 84)
(off Fleet St.)
Cheshire Gdns. KT9: Chess 6D 162
Cheshire Ho. N18 4C 34
Cheshire Ho. SM4: Mord 7K 153
Cheshire Rd. N22 7E 32
Cheshire St. E2 3K 9 (4F 85)
Cheshir Ho. NW4 4E 44
Chesholm Rd. N16 3E 66
Cheshunt Ho. NW6 1K 81
(off Mortimer Cres.)
Cheshunt Rd. DA17: Belv 5G 109
Cheshunt Rd. E7 6K 69
Chesil Ct. E2 2J 85
Chesil Ct. SW3 7D 16 (6C 100)
Chesilton Rd. SW6 1H 117
Chesil Way UB4: Hayes 3H 75
Chesley Gdns. E6 2B 88
Chesney Ct. W9 4J 81
(off Shirland Rd.)
Chesney Cres. CR0: New Ad 7E 170
Chesney Ho. SE13 4F 123
(off Mercator Rd.)
Chesney St. SW11 1E 118
Chesnut Gro. N17 3F 49
Chesnut Rd. N17 3F 49
Chesnut Row N3 7D 30
(off Nether St.)
Chessell Cl. CR7: Thor H 4B 156
Chessholme Ct. TW16: Sun 7G 129
(off Scotts Av.)
Chessholme Rd. TW15: Ashf 6E 128
Chessing Ct. N2 3D 46
(off Fortis Grn.)
CHESSINGTON 5E 162
Chessington Av. DA7: Bex 7E 108
Chessington Av. N3 3G 45
Chessington Cl. KT19: Ewe 6J 163
Chessington Ct. HA5: Pinn 4D 40
Chessington Ct. N3 3H 45
(off Charter Way)
Chessington Hall Gdns. KT9: Chess
7D 162
Chessington Hill Pk. KT9: Chess 5G 163
Chessington Ho. SW8 2H 119
Chessington Lodge N3 3H 45
Chessington Mans. E10 7C 50
Chessington Mans. E11 7G 51
Chessington Pde. KT9: Chess 6D 162
Chessington Pk. KT9: Chess 4G 163
Chessington Rd. KT19: Ewe 6G 163
Chessington Sports Cen. 7D 162
Chessington Trade Pk. KT9: Chess
4G 163
Chessington Way BR4: W W'ck 2D 170
Chesson Rd. W14 6H 99
Chesswood Way HA5: Pinn 2B 40
Chestbrook Ct. EN1: Enf 5K 23
(off Forsyth Pl.)
Chester Av. TW10: Rich 6F 115
Chester Av. TW2: Whitt 1D 130
Chester Cl. SM1: Sutt 2J 165
Chester Cl. SW1 7J 11 (2F 101)
Chester Cl. SW13 3D 116
Chester Cl. TW10: Rich 6F 115
Chester Cl. TW15: Ashf 5F 129
Chester Cl. UB8: Hil 6D 74
Chester Cl. Nth. NW1 1J 5 (3F 83)
Chester Cl. Sth. NW1 2J 5 (3F 83)
Chester Cotts. SW1 4G 17 (4E 100)
(off Bourne St.)
Chester Ct. BR2: Broml 4H 159
(off Durham Rd.)
Chester Ct. NW1 1K 5 (3F 83)
(not continuous)
Chester Ct. SE5 7D 102
(off Lomond Gro.)
Chester Ct. SE8 5K 103
Chester Ct. W6 4F 99
(off Wolverton Gdns.)
Chester Cres. E8 5F 67
Chester Dr. HA2: Harr 6D 40
Chesterfield Cl. SE13 2F 123
Chesterfield Ct. KT5: Surb 5E 150
(off Cranes Pk.)
Chesterfield Dr. KT10: Hin W 2A 162
Chesterfield Flats EN5: Barn 5A 20
(off Bells Hill)
Chesterfield Gdns. N4 5B 48
Chesterfield Gdns. SE10 7F 105
Chesterfield Gdns. W1 4J 11 (1F 101)
Chesterfield Gro. SE22 5F 121
Chesterfield Hill W1 4J 11 (1F 101)
Chesterfield Ho. W1 4H 11 (1E 100)
(off Chesterfield Gdns.)
Chesterfield Lodge N21 7E 22
(off Church Hill)
Chesterfield M. N4 5B 48
Chesterfield M. TW15: Ashf 4A 128
Chesterfield Rd. E10 6E 50
Chesterfield Rd. EN5: Barn 5A 20
Chesterfield Rd. KT19: Ewe 7K 163
Chesterfield Rd. N3 6D 30
Chesterfield Rd. TW15: Ashf 4A 128
Chesterfield Rd. W4 6J 97
Chesterfield St. W1 4J 11 (1F 101)
Chesterfield Wlk. SE10 1F 123

Chesterfield Way – Church Cl.

Chesterfield Way SE15 7J 103
Chesterfield Way UB3: Hayes 2J 93
Chesterford Gdns. NW3 4K 63
Chesterford Ho. SE18 1B 124
(off Tellson Av.)
Chesterford Rd. E12 5D 70
Chester Gdns. EN3: Pond E 6C 24
Chester Gdns. SM4: Mord 6A 154
Chester Gdns. W13 6B 78
Chester Ga. NW1 Regent's Pk. 2J 5 (3F 83)
Chester Ho. N10 2F 47
Chester Ho. SE8 6B 104
Chester Ho. SW1 3J 17 (4F 101)
(off Eccleston Pl.)
Chester Ho. SW9 7A 102
(off Cranmer Rd.)
Chesterman Ct. W4 7A 98
(off Corney Reach Way)
Chester M. E17 2C 50
Chester M. SW1 1J 17 (3F 101)
Chester Pl. NW1 1J 5 (3F 83)
Chester Rd. DA15: Sidc 5J 125
Chester Rd. E11 6K 51
Chester Rd. E16 4G 87
Chester Rd. E17 5K 49
Chester Rd. E7 7B 70
Chester Rd. IG3: Ilf 1K 71
Chester Rd. IG7: Chig 3K 37
Chester Rd. N17 3D 48
Chester Rd. N19 2F 65
Chester Rd. N9 1C 34
Chester Rd. NW1 2H 5 (3E 82)
Chester Rd. SW19 6E 134
Chester Rd. TW4: Houn 3K 111
Chester Rd. TW6: H'row A 3C 110
Chester Row SW1 4G 17 (4E 100)
Chesters, The KT3: N Mald 1A 152
Chester Sq. SW1 3H 17 (4E 100)
Chester Sq. M. SW1 2J 17 (3F 101)
(off Chester Sq.)
Chester St. E2 4G 85
Chester St. SW1 1H 17 (3E 100)
Chester Ter. IG11: Bark 6H 71
Chester Ter. NW1 1J 5 (3F 83)
(not continuous)
Chesterton Cl. SW18 5J 117
Chesterton Cl. UB6: G'frd 2F 77
Chesterton Ct. W5 5D 78
Chesterton Dr. TW19: Stanw 1B 128
Chesterton Ho. CR0: C'don 4D 168
(off Heathfield Rd.)
Chesterton Ho. SW11 3B 118
(off Ingrave St.)
Chesterton Ho. W10 5G 81
(off Portobello Rd.)
Chesterton Rd. E13 3J 87
Chesterton Rd. W10 5F 81
Chesterton Sq. W8 4J 99
Chesterton Ter. E13 3J 87
Chesterton Ter. KT1: King T 2G 151
Chester Way SE11 4K 19 (4A 102)
Chesthunte Rd. N17 1C 48
Chestlands Ct. UB10: Hil 6C 56
Chestnut All. SW6 6H 99
Chestnut Apts. E3 2D 86
(off Alameda Pl.)
Chestnut Av. BR4: W W'ck 5G 171
Chestnut Av. E7 4K 69
Chestnut Av. HA0: Wemb 5B 60
Chestnut Av. HA6: Nwood 2H 39
Chestnut Av. HA8: Edg 6K 27
Chestnut Av. IG9: Buck H 3G 37
Chestnut Av. KT10: Esh 7H 149
Chestnut Av. KT19: Ewe 4A 164
Chestnut Av. KT8: E Mos 3K 149
Chestnut Av. N8 5J 47
Chestnut Av. SW14 3K 115
Chestnut Av. TW11: Tedd 2K 149
Chestnut Av. TW12: Hamp 7E 130
Chestnut Av. TW8: Bford 4D 96
Chestnut Av. UB7: Yiew 7B 74
Chestnut Av. Nth. E17 4F 51
Chestnut Av. Sth. E17 5E 50
Chestnut Cl. BR6: Chels 5K 173
Chestnut Cl. DA15: Sidc 1A 144
Chestnut Cl. IG9: Buck H 3G 37
Chestnut Cl. N14 5B 22
Chestnut Cl. N16 2D 66
Chestnut Cl. SE14 1B 122
Chestnut Cl. SE6 5E 140
Chestnut Cl. SM5: Cars 1D 166
Chestnut Cl. SW16 4A 138
Chestnut Cl. TW15: Ashf 4D 128
Chestnut Cl. TW16: Sun 6H 129
Chestnut Cl. UB3: Hayes 7G 75
Chestnut Cl. UB7: Harl 7D 92
Chestnut Cl. UB7: Sip 7D 92
Chestnut Ct. CR2: S Croy 4C 168
(off Bramley Hill)
Chestnut Ct. N8 5J 47
Chestnut Ct. SW6 6H 99
Chestnut Ct. TW13: Hanw 5B 130
Chestnut Ct. TW19: Stanw 1A 128
(off Mulberry Av.)
Chestnut Ct. W8 3K 99
(off Abbots Wlk.)
Chestnut Dr. DA7: Bex 3D 126
Chestnut Dr. E11 6J 51
Chestnut Dr. HA3: Hrw W 7E 26
Chestnut Dr. HA5: Pinn 6B 40
Chestnut Gro. CR2: Sels 7H 169
Chestnut Gro. CR4: Mitc 5H 155
Chestnut Gro. DA2: Wilm 4K 145
Chestnut Gro. EN4: E Barn 5J 21
Chestnut Gro. HA0: Wemb 5B 60
Chestnut Gro. KT3: N Mald 3K 151
Chestnut Gro. SE20 7H 139
Chestnut Gro. SW12 7E 118
Chestnut Gro. TW7: Isle 4A 114
Chestnut Gro. W5 3D 96
Chestnut Ho. E3 1B 86
(off Sycamore Av.)
Chestnut Ho. SW15 4B 116
Chestnut Ho. W4 4A 98
(off The Orchard)
Chestnut La. N20 1B 30
Chestnut M. SW14 4J 115
Chestnut Pl. SE26 4F 139
Chestnut Plaza E20 6E 68
(within Westfield Shop. Cen.)
Chestnut Ri. SE18 6H 107
Chestnut Ri. WD23: Bush 1A 26
Chestnut Rd. KT2: King T 7E 132
Chestnut Rd. SE27 3B 138
Chestnut Rd. SW20 2F 153
Chestnut Rd. TW15: Ashf 4D 128
Chestnut Rd. TW2: Twick 2J 131
Chestnuts, The BR3: Beck 3K 157
Chestnuts, The HA5: Hat E 1D 40
Chestnuts, The N5 4C 66
(off Highbury Grange)
Chestnuts, The UB10: Uxb 7A 56
Chestnuts Ho. E17 6D 50
(off Hoe St.)
Chestnut Ter. SM1: Sutt 4K 165
Chestnut Wlk. IG8: Wfd G 5D 36
Chestnut Wlk. TW17: Shep 4G 147
Chestnut Way TW13: Felt 3K 129
Cheston Av. CR0: C'don 2A 170
Chestwood Gro. UB10: Hil 7B 56
Chesworth Ct. E1 5J 85
(off Fulneck Pl.)
Chettle Cl. SE1 3D 102
(off Spurgeon St.)
Chettle Ct. N8 6A 48
Chetwode Ho. NW8 3C 4 (4C 82)
(off Grendon St.)
Chetwode Rd. SW17 3D 136
Chetwood Wlk. E6 5C 88
(off Greenwich Cres.)
Chetwynd Av. EN4: E Barn 1J 31
Chetwynd Dr. UB10: Hil 2B 74
Chetwynd Rd. NW5 4F 65
Chetwynd Vs. NW5 4F 65
(off Chetwynd Rd.)
Chevalier Cl. HA7: Stan 4K 27
Cheval Pl. SW7 1D 16 (3C 100)
Cheval St. E14 3C 104
Cheveney Wlk. BR2: Broml 3J 159
Chevening Rd. NW6 2F 81
Chevening Rd. SE10 5H 105
Chevening Rd. SE19 6D 138
Chevenings, The DA14: Sidc 3C 144
Cheverell Ho. E2 2G 85
(off Pritchard's Rd.)
Cheverton Rd. N19 1H 65
Chevet St. E9 5A 68
Chevington NW2 6H 63
Cheviot N17 7C 34
(off Northumberland Gro.)
Cheviot Cl. DA7: Bex 2K 127
Cheviot Cl. EN1: Enf 2J 23
Cheviot Cl. UB3: Harl 7F 93
Cheviot Ct. SE14 6J 103
(off Avonley Rd.)
Cheviot Ct. UB2: S'hall 4F 95
Cheviot Gdns. NW2 2F 63
Cheviot Gdns. SE27 4B 138
Cheviot Ga. NW2 2G 63
Cheviot Ho. E1 6H 85
(off Commercial Rd.)
Cheviot Rd. SE27 5A 138
Cheviot Way IG2: Ilf 4J 53
Chevron Cl. E16 6J 87
Chevy Rd. UB2: S'hall 2G 95
Chewton Rd. E17 4A 50
Cheylesmore Ho. SW1 6J 17 (5F 101)
(off Ebury Bri. Rd.)
Cheyne Av. E18 3H 51
Cheyne Av. TW2: Whitt 1D 130
Cheyne Cl. BR2: Broml 3C 172
Cheyne Cl. NW4 5E 44
Cheyne Ct. SW3 7E 16 (6D 100)
Cheyne Gdns. SW3 7D 16 (6C 100)
Cheyne Hill KT5: Surb 4F 151
Cheyne Ho. SW3 7E 16 (6D 100)
(off Chelsea Emb.)
Cheyne M. SW3 7D 16 (6C 100)
Cheyne Pk. Dr. BR4: W W'ck 3E 170
Cheyne Path W7 5K 77
Cheyne Pl. SW3 7E 16 (6D 100)
Cheyne Rd. TW15: Ashf 7F 129
Cheyne Row SW3 7C 16 (6C 100)
Cheyne Wlk. CR0: C'don 2G 169
Cheyne Wlk. N21 5G 23
Cheyne Wlk. NW4 6E 44
Cheyne Wlk. SW10 7B 100
Cheyne Wlk. SW3 7C 16 (6C 100)
(not continuous)
Cheyneys Av. HA8: Edg 6J 27
Chichele Gdns. CR0: C'don 4E 168
Chichele Rd. NW2 5F 63
Chicheley Gdns. HA3: Hrw W 7B 26
(not continuous)
Chicheley Rd. HA3: Hrw W 7B 26
Chicheley St. SE1 6H 13 (2K 101)
Chichester Av. HA4: Ruis 2F 57
Chichester Cl. E6 6C 88
Chichester Cl. SE3 7A 106
Chichester Cl. TW12: Hamp 6D 130
Chichester Ct. HA7: Stan 3E 42
Chichester Ct. HA8: Edg 6B 28
(off Whitchurch La.)
Chichester Ct. KT17: Ewe 7B 164
Chichester Ct. NW1 7G 65
(off Royal Coll. St.)
Chichester Ct. TW19: Stanw 1A 128
Chichester Ct. UB5: N'olt 1D 76
Chichester Gdns. IG1: Ilf 7C 52
Chichester Ho. NW6 2J 81
Chichester Ho. SW9 7A 102
(off Cranmer Rd.)
Chichester Lodge SE10 4J 105
(off Peartree Way)
Chichester M. SE27 4A 138
Chichester Rents WC2 7J 7 (6A 84)
(off Chancery La.)
Chichester Rd. CR0: C'don 3E 168
Chichester Rd. E11 3G 69
Chichester Rd. N9 1B 34
Chichester Rd. NW6 2J 81
Chichester Rd. W2 5K 81
Chichester St. SW1 6B 18 (5G 101)
Chichester Way E14 4F 105
Chichester Way TW14: Felt 7A 112
Chickenshed Theatre 5K 21
Chicksand Ho. E1 5K 9 (5G 85)
(off Chicksand St.)
Chicksand St. E1 6K 9 (5F 85)
(not continuous)
Chiddingfold N12 3D 30
Chiddingstone SE13 5E 122
Chiddingstone Av. DA7: Bex 7F 109
Chiddingstone St. SW6 2J 117
Chieveley Pde. DA7: Bex 3H 127
Chieveley Rd. DA7: Bex 4H 127
Chignell Pl. W13 1A 96
CHIGWELL 3K 37
Chigwell Ct. E9 6A 68
(off Ballance Rd.)
Chigwell Golf Course 4K 37
Chigwell Hill E1 7H 85
Chigwell Hurst Ct. HA5: Pinn 3B 40
Chigwell Pk. IG7: Chig 4K 37
Chigwell Pk. Dr. IG7: Chig 4K 37
Chigwell Ri. IG7: Chig 2K 37
Chigwell Rd. E18 3K 51
Chigwell Rd. IG8: Wfd G 6J 37
Chilcombe Ho. SW15 7C 116
(off Fontley Way)
Chilcot Cl. E14 6D 86
Chilcott Cl. HA0: Wemb 4C 60
Childebert Rd. SW17 2F 137
Childeric Rd. SE14 7A 104
Childerley KT1: King T 3G 151
(off Burritt Rd.)
Childerley St. SW6 1G 117
Childers, The IG8: Wfd G 5J 37
Childers St. SE8 6A 104
Child La. SE10 3H 105
Childs Ct. UB3: Hayes 7J 75
CHILD'S HILL 3H 63
Childs Hill Wlk. NW2 3H 63
(off Cricklewood La.)
Child's La. SE19 6E 138
Child's M. SW5 4J 99
(off Child's Pl.)
Child's Pl. SW5 4J 99
Child's St. SW5 4J 99
Child's Wlk. SW5 4J 99
(off Child's St.)
Childs Way NW11 5H 45
Chilham Cl. DA5: Bexl 7F 127
Chilham Cl. UB6: G'frd 2A 78
Chilham Ho. SE1 3D 102
Chilham Ho. SE15 6J 103
Chilham Rd. SE9 4C 142
Chilham Way BR2: Hayes 7J 159
Chilianwallah Memorial 7G 17 (6E 100)
Chillerton Rd. SW17 5E 136
Chillingford Ho. SW17 4A 136
Chillington Dr. SW11 4B 118
Chillingworth Gdns. TW1: Twick 3K 131
Chillingworth Rd. N7 5A 66
Chill La. N1 1H 83
Chilmark Gdns. KT3: N Mald 6C 152
Chilmark Rd. SW16 2H 155
Chiltern Av. TW2: Whitt 1E 130
Chiltern Cl. CR0: C'don 3E 168
Chiltern Cl. KT4: Wor Pk 1E 164
Chiltern Cl. UB10: Ick 2C 56
Chiltern Ct. BR2: Broml 2C 172
(off Gravel Rd.)
Chiltern Ct. EN5: New Bar 5F 21
Chiltern Ct. HA1: Harr 5H 41
Chiltern Ct. N10 2E 46
Chiltern Ct. NW1 4F 5 (4D 82)
(off Baker St.)
Chiltern Ct. SE14 7J 103
(off Avonley Rd.)
Chiltern Ct. UB8: Hil 4D 74
Chiltern Dene EN2: Enf 4E 22
Chiltern Dr. KT5: Surb 6G 151
Chiltern Gdns. BR2: Broml 4H 159
Chiltern Gdns. NW2 3F 63
Chiltern Hgts. N1 7K 65
(off Caledonian Rd.)
Chiltern Ho. N9 3B 34
Chiltern Ho. SE17 6D 102
(off Portland St.)
Chiltern Ho. W10 5G 81
(off Telford Rd.)
Chiltern Ho. W5 5E 78
Chiltern Rd. E3 4C 86
Chiltern Rd. HA5: Eastc 5A 40
Chiltern Rd. IG2: Ilf 5J 53
Chilterns, The BR1: Broml 2K 159
(off Murray Av.)
Chiltern St. W1 5G 5 (5E 82)
Chiltern Way IG8: Wfd G 3D 36
Chilthorne Cl. SE6 7B 122
Chilton Av. W5 4D 96
Chilton Ct. N22 7D 32
(off Truro Rd.)
Chilton Gro. SE8 4K 103
Chiltonian Ind. Est. SE12 6H 123
Chiltonian M. SE13 5F 123
Chilton Rd. HA8: Edg 6B 28
Chilton Rd. TW9: Rich 3G 115
Chiltons, The E18 2J 51
Chilton St. E2 3K 9 (4F 85)
Chilvers Cl. TW2: Twick 2J 131
Chilver St. SE10 5H 105
Chilworth Ct. SW19 1F 135
Chilworth Gdns. SM1: Sutt 3A 166
Chilworth M. W2 1A 10 (6B 82)
Chilworth Pl. IG11: Bark 4A 90
Chilworth St. W2 6A 82
Chimes Av. N13 5F 33
Chimes Ho. BR3: Beck 1A 158
Chimes Ter. N8 5J 47
Chimney Ct. E1 1H 103
(off Brewhouse La.)
China Ct. E1 1H 103
(off Asher Way)
China Hall M. SE16 3J 103
China M. SW2 7K 119
China Wlk. SE11 2J 19 (3A 102)
China Wharf SE1 6K 15 (2G 103)
Chinbrook Cres. SE12 3K 141
Chinbrook Rd. SE12 3K 141
Chinchilla Dr. TW4: Houn 2A 112
Chine, The HA0: Wemb 5B 60
Chine, The N10 4G 47
Chine, The N21 6G 23
Ching Ct. WC2 1E 12 (6J 83)
(off Monmouth St.)
Chingdale Rd. E4 3B 36
CHINGFORD 1K 35
Chingford Av. E4 3H 35
Chingford Golf Course 1B 36
Chingford Golf Range 1H 35
CHINGFORD GREEN 1A 36
CHINGFORD HATCH 4A 36
Chingford Ind. Cen. E4 5F 35
Chingford La. IG8: Wfd G 4B 36
Chingford Leisure Cen. 4K 35
CHINGFORD MOUNT 4H 35
Chingford Mt. Rd. E4 4H 35
Chingford Rd. E17 1D 50
Chingford Rd. E4 6H 35
Chingley Cl. BR1: Broml 6G 141
Chingstone Ter. E4 1K 35
Ching Way E4 6G 35
(not continuous)
Chinnery Cl. EN1: Enf 1A 24
Chinnock's Wharf E14 7A 86
(off Narrow St.)
Chinnor Cres. UB6: G'frd 2F 77
Chipka St. E14 2E 104
(not continuous)
Chipley St. SE14 6A 104
Chipmunk Gro. UB5: N'olt 3C 76
Chippendale All. UB8: Uxb 7A 56
Chippendale Ho. SW1 6K 17 (5F 101)
(off Churchill Gdns.)
Chippendale St. E5 3K 67
Chippenham KT1: King T 2F 151
(off Excelsior Cl.)
Chippenham Av. HA9: Wemb 5H 61
Chippenham Cl. HA5: Eastc 4H 39
Chippenham Gdns. NW6 3J 81
Chippenham M. W9 4J 81
Chippenham Rd. W9 4J 81
Chipperfield Ho. SW3 5C 16 (5C 100)
(off Cale St.)
Chipperfield Rd. BR5: St P 7A 144
(not continuous)
CHIPPING BARNET 4B 20
Chipping Cl. EN5: Barn 3B 20
Chipstead Av. CR7: Thor H 4B 156
Chipstead Cl. SE19 7F 139
Chipstead Cl. SM2: Sutt 7K 165
Chipstead Gdns. NW2 2D 62
Chipstead Rd. TW6: H'row A 3C 110
Chipstead St. SW6 1J 117
Chip St. SW4 3H 119
Chirk Cl. UB4: Yead 4C 76
Chisenhale Rd. E3 2A 86
Chisholm Ct. W6 5C 98
Chisholm Rd. CR0: C'don 2E 168
Chisholm Rd. TW10: Rich 6F 115
Chisledon Wlk. E9 6B 68
(off Osborne Rd.)
CHISLEHURST 6F 143
Chislehurst Av. N12 7F 31
Chislehurst Caves 1E 160
Chislehurst Golf Course 7F 143
Chislehurst Rd. BR1: Broml 2B 160
Chislehurst Rd. BR5: Pet W 4J 161
Chislehurst Rd. BR6: Orp 6J 161
Chislehurst Rd. BR6: Pet W 6J 161
Chislehurst Rd. BR6: St M Cry 6J 161
Chislehurst Rd. BR7: Chst 1C 160
Chislehurst Rd. DA14: Sidc 5A 144
Chislehurst Rd. TW10: Rich 5E 114
CHISLEHURST WEST 6E 142
Chislet Cl. BR3: Beck 7C 140
Chisley Rd. N15 6E 48
Chiswell Sq. SE3 2K 123
Chiswell St. EC1 5D 8 (5C 84)
Chiswell St. SE5 7D 102
(off Edmund St.)
CHISWICK 5K 97
CHISWICK BRI. 2J 115
Chiswick Cl. CR0: Bedd 3K 167
Chiswick Comn. Rd. W4 4K 97
Chiswick Community Sports Hall 7K 97
Chiswick Ct. HA5: Pinn 3D 40
Chiswick Ct. W4 4H 97
Chiswick High Rd. TW8: Bford 5G 97
Chiswick High Rd. W4 5G 97
Chiswick House & Gdns. 6K 97
Chiswick Ho. Grounds W4 6A 98
Chiswick La. W4 5A 98
Chiswick La. Sth. W4 6B 98
Chiswick Lifeboat Station 7B 98
Chiswick Mall W4 6B 98
Chiswick Mall W6 5C 98
Chiswick Pk. W4 4H 97
Chiswick Pier 7B 98
Chiswick Plaza W4 6J 97
Chiswick Quay W4 1J 115
Chiswick Rd. N9 2B 34
Chiswick Rd. W4 4J 97
CHISWICK RDBT. 5G 97
Chiswick Sq. W4 6A 98
Chiswick Staithe W4 1J 115
Chiswick Ter. W4 4J 97
(off Chiswick High Rd.)
Chiswick Village W4 6G 97
Chiswick Wharf W4 6B 98
Chitterfield Ga. UB7: Sip 7C 92
Chitty's La. RM8: Dag 2D 72
Chitty St. W1 5B 6 (5G 83)
Chivalry Rd. SW11 5C 118
Chivelston SW19 1F 135
Chivenor Gro. KT2: King T 5D 132
Chivers Pas. SW18 5K 117
Chivers Rd. E4 3J 35
Choats Mnr. Way RM9: Dag 2E 90
Choats Rd. IG11: Bark 2C 90
Choats Rd. RM9: Dag 3D 90
Chobham Academy Sports Cen. 5E 68
Chobham Gdns. SW19 2F 135
CHOBHAM MANOR 5D 68
Chobham Rd. E15 5F 69
Chocolate Factory 1, The N22 2K 47
(off Clarendon Rd.)
Chocolate Factory 2, The N22 2K 47
(off Coburg Rd.)
Chocolate Studios N1 1E 8 (3D 84)
(off Shepherdess Pl.)
Choice Vw. IG1: Ilf 2G 71
(off Axon Pl.)
Cholmeley Cl. N6 7F 47
Cholmeley Cres. N6 7F 47
Cholmeley Lodge N6 1F 65
Cholmeley Pk. N6 1F 65
Cholmley Gdns. NW6 5J 63
Cholmley Rd. KT7: T Ditt 6B 150
Cholmley Ter. KT7: T Ditt 7B 150
(off Portsmouth Rd.)
Cholmley Vs. KT7: T Ditt 6B 150
(off Portsmouth Rd.)
Cholmondeley Av. NW10 2C 80
Cholmondeley Wlk. TW9: Rich 5C 114
Choppin's Ct. E1 1H 103
Chopwell Cl. E15 7F 69
Chorleywood Cres. BR5: St P 2K 161
Choudhury Mans. N1 7J 65
(off Pembroke St.)
Choumert Gro. SE15 2G 121
Choumert M. SE15 2G 121
Choumert Rd. SE15 3F 121
Choumert Sq. SE15 2G 121
Chow Sq. E8 5F 67
Chrislea Cl. TW5: Hest 6D 94
Chrisp Ho. SE10 6G 105
(off Maze Hill)
Chrisp St. E14 5D 86
(not continuous)
Chris Pullen Way N7 6J 65
Christabel Cl. TW7: Isle 3J 113
Christabel Pankhurst Ct. SE5 7D 102
(off Brisbane St.)
Christchurch Av. DA8: Erith 6K 109
Christchurch Av. HA0: Wemb 6E 60
Christchurch Av. HA3: Kenton 4K 41
Christchurch Av. HA3: W'stone 4K 41
Christchurch Av. N12 6F 31
Christchurch Av. NW6 1F 81
Christchurch Av. TW11: Tedd 5A 132
Christchurch Cl. EN2: Enf 2H 23
Christchurch Cl. N12 7G 31
Christchurch Cl. SW19 7B 136
Christ Church Ct. NW10 1A 80
Christchurch Ct. EC4 7B 8 (6B 84)
(off Warwick La.)
Christchurch Ct. NW6 7G 63
(off Willesden La.)
Christchurch Ct. UB4: Yead 4A 76
(off Dunedin Way)
Christchurch Flats TW9: Rich 3E 114
Christchurch Gdns. HA3: W'stone 4A 42
Christchurch Grn. HA0: Wemb 6E 60
Christchurch Hill NW3 3B 64
Christchurch Ho. RM8: Dag 5B 72
Christchurch Ho. SW2 1K 137
(off Christchurch Rd.)
Christchurch La. EN5: Barn 2B 20
Christchurch Lodge EN4: Cockf 4J 21
Christchurch Pk. SM2: Sutt 7A 166
Christchurch Pas. NW3 Hampstead 3A 64
Christchurch Pas. EN5: Barn High Barnet 2B 20
Christchurch Path UB3: Harl 3E 92
Christchurch Pl. SW8 2H 119
Christ Chu. Rd. BR3: Beck 2C 158
Christ Chu. Rd. KT5: Surb 6F 151
Christchurch Rd. DA15: Sidc 4K 143
Christchurch Rd. IG1: Ilf 1F 71
Christchurch Rd. N8 6J 47
Christchurch Rd. SW14 5H 115
Christchurch Rd. SW19 7B 136
Christchurch Rd. SW2 1K 137
Christchurch Rd. TW6: H'row A 3C 110
Christchurch Sq. E9 1J 85
Christchurch St. SW3 7E 16 (6D 100)
Christchurch Ter. SW3 7E 16 (6D 100)
(off Christchurch St.)
Christchurch Way SE10 5G 105
Christian Ct. SE16 1B 104
Christian Flds. SW16 7A 138
Christian Pl. E1 6G 85
(off Burslem St.)
Christian St. E1 6G 85
Christie Ct. N19 2J 65
Christie Dr. CR0: C'don 5G 157
Christie Gdns. RM6: Chad H 6B 54
Christie Ho. E16 5J 87
(off Hammersley Rd.)
Christie Ho. SE10 5H 105
(off Blackwall La.)
Christie Ho. W12 6D 80
(off Du Cane Rd.)
Christie Rd. E9 6A 68
Christina Sq. N4 1B 66
Christina St. EC2 3G 9 (4E 84)
Christine Worsley Cl. N21 1G 33
Christopher Av. W7 3A 96
Christopher Bell Twr. E3 2C 86
(off Pancras Way)
Christopher Boones Ct. SE13 4F 123
(off Bessington Rd.)
Christopher Cl. DA15: Sidc 5K 125
Christopher Cl. SE16 2K 103
Christopher Ct. DA15: Sidc 2A 144
(off Station Rd.)
Christopher Ct. E1 6G 85
(off Leman St.)
Christopher Ct. TW15: Ashf 5A 128
Christopher Gdns. RM9: Dag 5D 72
Christopher Pl. N22 7D 32
(off Myddleton Rd.)
Christopher Pl. NW1 2D 6 (3H 83)
Christopher Rd. UB2: S'hall 4K 93
Christophers M. W11 1G 99
Christopher St. EC2 4F 9 (4D 84)
Chroma Mans. E20 6E 68
(off Penny Brookes St.)
Chronicle Av. NW9 3A 44
Chronicle Twr. N1 1C 8 (3C 84)
Chryssell Rd. SW9 7A 102
Chubworthy St. SE14 6A 104
Chudleigh DA14: Sidc 4B 144
Chudleigh Cres. IG3: Ilf 4J 71
Chudleigh Gdns. SM1: Sutt 3A 166
Chudleigh Rd. NW6 7F 63
Chudleigh Rd. SE4 5B 122
Chudleigh Rd. TW2: Twick 6J 113
Chudleigh St. E1 6K 85
Chudleigh Way HA4: Ruis 1J 57
Chulsa Rd. SE26 5H 139
Chumleigh Gdns. SE5 6E 102
(off Chumleigh St.)
Chumleigh St. SE5 6E 102
Chumleigh Wlk. KT5: Surb 4F 151
Church All. CR0: C'don 1A 168
Church App. SE21 3D 138
Church Av. BR3: Beck 1C 158
Church Av. DA14: Sidc 5A 144
Church Av. E4 6A 36
(not continuous)
Church Av. HA4: Ruis 1F 57
Church Av. HA5: Pinn 6C 40
Church Av. NW1 6F 65
Church Av. SW14 3K 115
Church Av. UB2: S'hall 3C 94
Church Av. UB5: N'olt 7D 58
Churchbank E17 4C 50
(off Eastfield Rd.)
Churchbury Cl. EN1: Enf 2K 23
Churchbury La. EN1: Enf 3J 23
Churchbury Rd. EN1: Enf 2K 23
Churchbury Rd. SE9 7B 124
Church Cloisters EC3 3G 15 (7E 84)
(off Lovat La.)
Church Cl. HA6: Nwood 1H 39
Church Cl. HA8: Edg 5D 28
Church Cl. N20 3H 31
Church Cl. TW3: Houn 2C 112

Church Cl. – Clarence Rd.

Church Cl. UB4: Hayes 5F 75
Church Cl. UB7: W Dray 3A 92
Church Cl. W8 2K 99
Church Ct. EC4 1J 13 (6A 84)
Church Ct. SE16 2B 104
(off Rotherhithe St.)
Church Ct. TW9: Rich 5D 114
Church Cres. E9 7K 67
Church Cres. N10 4F 47
Church Cres. N20 3H 31
Church Cres. N3 1H 45
Churchcroft Cl. SW12 7E 118
Churchdown BR1: Broml 4G 141
Church Dr. BR4: W W'ck 3G 171
Church Dr. HA2: Harr 6E 40
Church Dr. NW9 1K 61
Church Elm La. RM10: Dag 6G 73
Church End E17 4D 50
CHURCH END 1H 45
CHURCH END 7A 62
Church End NW4 3D 44
Church Entry EC4 1B 14 (6B 84)
(off Carter La.)
Church Est. Almshouses TW9: Rich 4F 115
(off Sheen Rd.)
Church Farm La. SM3: Cheam 6G 165
Churchfield Av. N12 6G 31
Churchfield Cl. HA2: Harr 4G 41
Churchfield Cl. UB3: Hayes 7H 75
Churchfield Ho. KT12: Walt T 7J 147
Churchfield Ho. W2 4A 4 (4B 82)
(off Hall Pl.)
Churchfield Mans. SW6 2H 117
(off New Kings Rd.)
Churchfield Pl. TW17: Shep 7D 146
Churchfield Rd. DA16: Well 3A 126
Churchfield Rd. KT12: Walt T 7J 147
Churchfield Rd. W13 1B 96
Churchfield Rd. W3 1J 97
Churchfield Rd. W7 2J 95
Churchfields E18 1J 51
Churchfields KT8: W Mole 3E 148
Churchfields SE10 6E 104
Churchfields Av. TW13: Hanw 3D 130
Churchfields Rd. BR3: Beck 2K 157
Churchfield Way N12 6F 31
Church Gdns. HA0: Wemb 4A 60
Church Gdns. W5 2D 96
Church Gth. N19 2H 65
(off St John's Gro.)
Church Ga. SW6 3G 117
Church Grn. SW9 1A 120
Church Grn. UB3: Hayes 6H 75
Church Gro. KT1: Hamp W 1C 150
Church Gro. SE13 5D 122
Church Hill DA1: Cray 4K 127
Church Hill E17 4C 50
Church Hill HA1: Harr 1J 59
Church Hill N21 7E 22
Church Hill SE18 3D 106
Church Hill SM5: Cars 5D 166
Church Hill SW19 5H 135
Church Hill Rd. E17 4D 50
Church Hill Rd. EN4: E Barn 6H 21
Church Hill Rd. KT6: Surb 5E 150
Church Hill Rd. SM3: Cheam 3F 165
Church Hill Wood BR5: St M Cry 5K 161
Church Ho. EC1 3B 8 (4B 84)
(off Compton St.)
Church Ho. SW1 1D 18 (3H 101)
(off Gt. Smith St.)
Church Hyde SE18 6J 107
Churchill Av. HA3: Kenton 6B 42
Churchill Av. UB10: Hil 3D 74
Churchill Cl. TW14: Felt 1H 129
Churchill Cl. UB10: Hil 3D 74
Churchill Ct. HA2: Harr Eastcote Av. 2F 59
Churchill Ct. HA2: Harr Montrose Ct. 5F 41
Churchill Ct. BR6: Farnb 5G 173
Churchill Ct. HA5: Hat E 1C 40
Churchill Ct. N4 7A 48
Churchill Ct. N9 1K 33
Churchill Ct. SE18 4D 106
Churchill Ct. UB5: N'olt 5E 58
(off Newmarket Av.)
Churchill Ct. W5 4F 79
Churchill Gdns. SW1 6A 18 (5G 101)
(off Churchill Gdns. Rd.)
Churchill Gdns. W3 6G 79
Churchill Gdns. Rd. SW1 6K 17 (5F 101)
Churchill Lodge IG6: Ilf 4G 53
Churchill Pl. E14 1D 104
Churchill Pl. HA1: Harr 4J 41
Churchill Rd. CR2: S Croy 7C 168
Churchill Rd. E16 6A 88
Churchill Rd. HA8: Edg 6A 28
Churchill Rd. NW2 6D 62
Churchill Rd. NW5 4F 65
Churchill Rd. UB10: Uxb 2A 74
Churchills M. IG8: Wfd G 6C 36
Churchill Ter. E4 4H 35
Churchill Theatre 2J 159
Churchill Wlk. E9 5J 67
Churchill War Rooms 6D 12 (2H 101)
Churchill Way BR1: Broml 2J 159
Churchill Way TW16: Sun 5J 129
Churchlands Way KT4: Wor Pk 2F 165
Church La. BR2: Broml 1C 172
Church La. BR7: Chst 1G 161
Church La. E11 1G 69
Church La. E17 4D 50
Church La. EN1: Enf 3J 23
Church La. HA3: W'stone 1K 41
Church La. HA5: Pinn 3C 40
Church La. KT7: T Ditt 6K 149
Church La. KT9: Chess 6F 163
Church La. N17 1E 48
Church La. N2 3B 46
Church La. N8 4K 47
Church La. N9 2B 34
Church La. NW9 6J 43
Church La. RM10: Dag 7J 73
Church La. SM6: Bedd 3H 167
(not continuous)
Church La. SW17 5D 136
Church La. SW19 1H 153
Church La. TW1: Twick 1A 132
Church La. TW10: Ham 1E 132
Church La. TW11: Tedd 5K 131
Church La. W5 2C 96
Churchley Rd. SE26 4H 139
Church Manorway DA17: Belv 2J 109
Church Manorway DA8: Erith 4K 109
Church Manorway SE2 5A 108
Church Mead SE5 7C 102
(off Camberwell Rd.)
Churchmead Cl. EN4: E Barn 6H 21
Church Mdw. KT6: Surb 2C 162
Churchmead Rd. NW10 6C 62
Churchmore Rd. SW16 1G 155
Church Mt. N2 5B 46
Church Paddock Ct. SM6: Bedd 3H 167
Church Pde. TW15: Ashf 4B 128
Church Pas. EN5: Barn Barnet 3B 20
Church Pas. KT6: Surb 5E 150
Church Pas. TW1: Twick 1B 132
Church Path SM6: Bedd Beddington 3H 167
Church Path CR0: C'don Croydon 2C 168
Church Path N5 Highbury 5B 66
Church Path N8 Hornsey 5K 47
(off Tottenham La.)
Church Path SW14 Mortlake 3K 115
(not continuous)
Church Path UB1: S'hall Southall 1E 94
Church Path UB2: S'hall Southall Grn. 3D 94
(not continuous)
Church Path W3 Sth. Acton 2J 97
(not continuous)
Church Path E17 Walthamstow 4D 50
Church Path NW10 Willesden 7A 62
Church Path N12 Woodside La. 3F 31
Church Path N12 Woodside Pk. Rd. 4F 31
Church Path CR4: Mitc 3C 154
(not continuous)
Church Path E11 5J 51
Church Path N17 7K 33
Church Path SW19 2H 153
Church Path W4 3J 97
Church Pl. CR4: Mitc 3C 154
Church Pl. SW1 3B 12 (7G 83)
Church Pl. UB10: Ick 3E 56
Church Pl. W5 2D 96
Church Ri. KT9: Chess 6F 163
Church Ri. SE23 2K 139
Church Rd. SW19 Courthorpe Rd. 5G 135
Church Rd. BR2: Broml Edison Rd. 2J 159
Church Rd. BR2: Broml Hazelwood Ho's. 3G 159
Church Rd. SW19 Reynolds Cl. 1B 154
Church Rd. BR2: Kes 7B 172
Church Rd. BR6: Farnb 5G 173
Church Rd. CR0: C'don 3C 168
(not continuous)
Church Rd. CR4: Mitc 2B 154
Church Rd. DA14: Sidc 4A 144
Church Rd. DA16: Well 2B 126
Church Rd. DA7: Bex 2F 127
Church Rd. DA8: Erith 5K 109
Church Rd. E10 1C 68
Church Rd. E12 5C 70
Church Rd. E17 2A 50
Church Rd. EN3: Pond E 6D 24
Church Rd. HA6: Nwood 1H 39
Church Rd. HA7: Stan 5G 27
Church Rd. IG11: Bark 6G 71
Church Rd. IG2: Ilf 6J 53
Church Rd. IG9: Buck H 1E 36
Church Rd. KT1: King T 2F 151
Church Rd. KT19: Ewe 7K 163
Church Rd. KT4: Wor Pk 1A 164
Church Rd. KT6: Surb 1C 162
Church Rd. KT8: E Mos 4H 149
Church Rd. N1 6C 66
Church Rd. N17 1E 48
(not continuous)
Church Rd. N6 6E 46
Church Rd. NW10 7A 62
Church Rd. NW4 4D 44
Church Rd. SE19 1E 156
Church Rd. SM3: Cheam 6G 165
Church Rd. SM6: Bedd 3H 167
Church Rd. SW13 2B 116
Church Rd. TW10: Ham 4D 132
Church Rd. TW10: Rich 5E 114
Church Rd. TW11: Tedd 4J 131
Church Rd. TW13: Hanw 5B 130
Church Rd. TW15: Ashf 3B 128
Church Rd. TW17: Shep 7D 146
Church Rd. TW5: Cran 5K 93
Church Rd. TW5: Hest 7E 94
Church Rd. TW7: Isle 1H 113
Church Rd. TW9: Rich 4E 114
Church Rd. UB2: S'hall 3D 94
Church Rd. UB3: Hayes 1H 93
Church Rd. UB5: N'olt 2B 76
Church Rd. UB7: W Dray 3A 92
Church Rd. UB8: Cowl 4A 74
Church Rd. W3 1J 97
Church Rd. W7 7H 77
Church Rd. Almshouses E10 2D 68
(off Church Rd.)
Church Rd. Ind. Est. E10 1C 68
Church Row BR7: Chst 1G 161
Church Row NW3 4A 64
Church Row SW18 5K 117
Church Row SW6 7K 99
(off Moore Pk. Rd.)
Church Row M. BR7: Chst 7G 143
Church Sq. TW17: Shep 7D 146
Church St. CR0: C'don 3B 168
Church St. E15 1G 87
Church St. E16 1F 107
Church St. EN2: Enf 3H 23
Church St. KT1: King T 2D 150
Church St. KT12: Walt T 7J 147
Church St. N9 7J 23
Church St. NW8 5B 4 (5B 82)
Church St. RM10: Dag 6H 73
Church St. SM1: Sutt 5K 165
Church St. TW1: Twick 1A 132
Church St. TW12: Hamp 1G 149
Church St. TW16: Sun 3K 147
Church St. TW7: Isle 3B 114
Church St. W2 5B 4 (5B 82)
(not continuous)
Church St. W4 6B 98
Church St. Est. NW8 4B 4 (4B 82)
Church St. Nth. E15 1G 87
Church St. Pas. E15 1G 87
(off Church St.)
Church Stretton Rd. TW3: Houn 5G 113
Church Ter. NW4 3D 44
Church Ter. SE13 3G 123
Church Ter. TW10: Rich 5D 114
Church Va. N2 3D 46
Church Va. SE23 2K 139
Church Vw. TW10: Rich 5E 114
Church Vw. Gro. SE26 6K 139
Churchview Rd. TW2: Twick 1H 131
Church Wlk. SW13 Barnes 1C 116
Church Wlk. N6 Dartmouth Pk. 3E 64
Church Wlk. EN2: Enf Enfield 3J 23
Church Wlk. NW4 Hendon 3E 44
Church Wlk. SW15 Putney 5D 116
Church Wlk. TW9: Rich Richmond 5D 114
Church Wlk. NW9 Wembley 2K 61
Church Wlk. KT12: Walt T 7J 147
(not continuous)
Church Wlk. KT7: T Ditt 6K 149
Church Wlk. N16 3D 66
(not continuous)
Church Wlk. NW2 3H 63
Church Wlk. SW16 2G 155
Church Wlk. SW20 3E 152
Church Wlk. TW8: Bford 6C 96
(not continuous)
Church Wlk. UB3: Hayes 6G 75
Churchward Ho. SE17 6B 102
(off Lorrimore Sq.)
Churchward Ho. W14 5H 99
(off Ivatt Pl.)
Church Way EN4: Cockf 4J 21
Church Way HA8: Edg 6B 28
Church Way N20 3H 31
Churchway NW1 1D 6 (3H 83)
(not continuous)
Churchwell Path E9 5J 67
Churchwood Gdns. IG8: Wfd G 4D 36
Churchyard Pas. SE5 2D 120
Churchyard Row SE11 4B 102
Churston Av. E13 1K 87
Churston Cl. SW2 1A 138
Churston Dr. SM4: Mord 5F 153
Churston Gdns. N11 6B 32
Churston Mans. WC1 4H 7 (4K 83)
(off Gray's Inn Rd.)
Churton Pl. SW1 4B 18 (4G 101)
Churton Pl. W4 6H 97
(off Chiswick Village)
Churton St. SW1 4B 18 (4G 101)
Chusan Pl. E14 6B 86
Chute Ho. SW9 2A 120
(off Stockwell Pk. Rd.)
Chuter Ede Ho. SW6 6H 99
(off Clem Attlee Ct.)
Chyngton Cl. DA15: Sidc 3K 143
Cibber Rd. SE23 2K 139
Cicada Rd. SW18 6A 118
Cicely Ct. CR0: Wadd 5A 168
Cicely Ho. NW8 2B 82
(off Cochrane St.)
Cicely Rd. SE15 1G 121
Cinderella Path NW11 1K 63
Cinderford Way BR1: Broml 4G 141
Ciné Lumière 3A 16 (4B 100)
(off Queensberry Pl.)
Cineworld Cinema Bexleyheath 4H 127
Cineworld Cinema Chelsea, Fulham Rd. 6A 16 (5A 100)
Cineworld Cinema Enfield 4B 24
Cineworld Cinema Feltham 2K 129
Cineworld Cinema Ilford 3F 71
(off Clements Rd.)
Cineworld Cinema Leicester Sq 2D 12 (7H 83)
(off Leicester Sq.)
Cineworld Cinema South Ruislip 4K 57
Cineworld Cinema The O2 1G 105
(within The O2)
Cineworld Cinema Wandsworth 5K 117
Cineworld Cinema Wembley 4G 61
Cineworld Cinema West India Quay 7C 86
Cineworld Cinema Wood Green 2A 48
(within Wood Green Shop. City)
Cinnabar Wharf Central E1 1G 103
(off Wapping High St.)
Cinnabar Wharf E. E1 1G 103
(off Wapping High St.)
Cinnabar Wharf W. E1 1G 103
(off Wapping High St.)
Cinnamon Cl. CR0: C'don 7J 155
Cinnamon Cl. SE15 7F 103
Cinnamon M. N13 2F 33
Cinnamon Row SW11 3A 118
Cinnamon St. E1 1H 103
Cinnamon Wharf SE1 6K 15 (2F 103)
(off Shad Thames)
Cintra Pk. SE19 7F 139
Cipher Ct. NW2 3C 62
Circa Apts. NW1 7E 64
Circle, The NW2 3A 62
Circle, The NW7 6E 28
Circle, The SE1 6K 15 (2F 103)
(off Queen Elizabeth St.)
Circle Gdns. SW19 2J 153
Circuits, The HA5: Pinn 4A 40
Circular Rd. N17 3F 49
Circular Way SE18 6D 106
Circus Lodge NW8 1A 4 (3B 82)
(off Circus Rd.)
Circus M. W1 5E 4 (5D 82)
(off Enford St.)
Circus Pl. EC2 6F 9 (5D 84)
Circus Rd. NW8 1A 4 (3B 82)
Circus Rd. E. SW11 7G 101
Circus Rd. N. SW11 7K 17 (6F 101)
Circus Rd. S. SW11 7F 101
Circus Rd. W. SW11 7F 101
Circus St. SE10 7E 104
Circus W. SW11 6F 101
Cirencester St. W2 5K 81
Cirrus Apts. E1 3K 9 (4F 85)
(off Bacon St.)
Cirrus Cl. SM6: W'gton 7J 167
Cissbury Ho. SE26 3G 139
Cissbury Ring Nth. N12 5C 30
Cissbury Ring Sth. N12 5C 30
Cissbury Rd. N15 5D 48
Citadel Pl. SE11 5G 19 (5K 101)
Citius Apts. E3 2C 86
(off Tredegar La.)
Citius Ct. E4 6K 35
Citius Wlk. E20 6E 68
Citizen Ho. N7 4A 66
Citizen Rd. N7 4A 66
Citrine Apts. E3 1A 86
(off Gunmaker's La.)
Citrus Ho. SE8 5B 104
(off Alverton St.)
City Apts. E1 7K 9 (6G 85)
(off White Church La.)
City Bus. Cen. SE16 3J 103
City Ct. CR0: C'don 7B 156
City Cross Bus. Pk. SE10 4G 105
City E. Bldg. E1 7H 85
(off Cable St.)
City Forum EC1 1C 8 (3C 84)
City Gdn. Row N1 1C 8 (3C 84)
City Gdn. Row N1 2B 84
City Ga. Ho. IG2: Ilf 6E 52
(off Eastern Av.)
City Gateway E1 7G 85
(off Ensign St.)
City Hall Southwark 5H 15 (1E 102)
City Harbour E14 3D 104
(off Selsdon Way)
City Hgts. E8 1F 85
(off Kingsland Rd.)
City Ho. BR2: Broml 6C 160
City Island E14 6G 87
City Island Way E14 6G 87
City Lights Ct. SE11 5K 19 (5A 102)
(off Bowden St.)
City M. IG6: Ilf 2G 53
City Mill Apts. E8 1F 85
(off Lovelace St.)
City Mill River Path E15 1E 86
City Nth. E. Twr. N4 2A 66
(off City Nth. Pl.)
City Nth. Pl. N4 2A 66
City Nth. W. Twr. N4 2A 66
CITY OF LONDON 1F 15 (6D 84)
City of London Almshouses SW9 4K 119
City of London Crematorium 3C 70
City of London Distillery 1A 14 (6B 84)
City of London Point N7 6H 65
(off York Way)
City of London Police Mus. 7D 8 (6C 84)
City of London Tourist Info. Cen. 1C 14 (6C 84)
City Pav. EC1 5A 8 (5B 84)
(off Britton St.)
City Pavilion Marks Gate, The 2F 55
City Pl. Ho. EC2 6E 8 (5D 84)
(off Basinghall St.)
Citypoint EC2 5E 8 (5D 84)
(off Ropemaker St.)
City Pride Development E14 1C 104
City Rd. EC1 1A 8 (2B 84)
City Twr. EC2 6E 8 (5D 84)
(off Basinghall St.)
City Twr. SW8 7E 18 (6J 101)
City University London Goswell Pl. 2B 8 (3B 84)
City University London Northampton Square Campus 2A 8 (3B 84)
City University London The Saddlers Sports Cen. 3B 8 (4B 84)
City Vw. IG1: Ilf 2G 71
(off Axon Pl.)
Cityview SE7 6A 106
City Vw. Apts. N1 7C 66
(off Essex Rd.)
City Vw. Apts. N4 7D 48
(off Devan Gro.)
City Vw. Ct. SE22 7G 121
City Wlk. SE1 7G 15 (2E 102)
City Wlk. Apts. EC1 2C 8 (3C 84)
(off Seward St.)
City Wharf Ho. KT7: T Ditt 6B 150
Civic Cnr. TW3: Houn 2F 113
Civic St. TW3: Houn 2E 112
Civic Way HA4: Ruis 5B 58
Civic Way IG6: Ilf 4G 53
Civil & Family Court Barnet 1J 45
Civil Justice Cen. Central London 4J 5 (4F 83)
(off Park Cres.)
Clabon M. SW1 2E 16 (3D 100)
Clack La. HA4: Ruis 1E 56
Clack St. SE16 2J 103
Clacton Rd. E17 6A 50
Clacton Rd. E6 3B 88
Clacton Rd. N17 2F 49
Claigmar Gdns. N3 1K 45
Claire Ct. HA5: Hat E 1D 40
Claire Ct. N12 3F 31
Claire Ct. NW2 6G 63
Claire Ct. WD23: B Hea 1C 26
Claire Gdns. HA7: Stan 5H 27
Claire Ho. IG1: Ilf 4F 71
Claire Pl. E14 3C 104
Clairvale Rd. TW5: Hest 1B 112
Clairview Rd. SW16 5F 137
Clairville Gdns. W7 1J 95
Clairville Point SE23 3K 139
(off Dacres Rd.)
Clamp Hill HA7: Stan 4C 26
Clancarty Rd. SW6 2J 117
Clandon Cl. KT17: Ewe 6B 164
Clandon Cl. W3 2H 97
Clandon Gdns. N3 3J 45
Clandon Ho. SE1 7B 14 (2B 102)
(off Webber St.)
Clandon Rd. IG3: Ilf 2J 71
Clandon St. SE8 2C 122
Clandon Ter. SW20 2F 153
Clanricarde Gdns. W2 7J 81
CLAPHAM 4G 119
CLAPHAM COMMON 3F 119
Clapham Comn. Northside SW4 4G 119
(off Rookery Rd.)
Clapham Comn. Nth. Side SW4 4D 118
Clapham Comn. Sth. Side SW4 6F 119
Clapham Comn. W. Side SW4 4D 118
(not continuous)
Clapham Cres. SW4 4H 119
Clapham High St. SW4 4H 119
CLAPHAM JUNCTION 3C 118
Clapham Leisure Cen. 3H 119
Clapham Mnr. Ct. SW4 3G 119
Clapham Mnr. St. SW4 3G 119
CLAPHAM PARK 5H 119
Clapham Pk. Est. SW4 6H 119
Clapham Pk. Rd. SW4 4G 119
Clapham Pk. Ter. SW2 5J 119
(off Lyham Rd.)
Clapham Picturehouse 4G 119
Clapham Rd. SW9 3J 119
Clapham Rd. Est. SW4 3J 119
Clap La. RM10: Dag 2H 73
Clap La. RM10: Rush G 2H 73
Claps Ga. La. E6 4E 88
Clapton Comn. E5 7F 49
(not continuous)
CLAPTON PARK 4K 67
Clapton Pk. Est. E5 4K 67
Clapton Pas. E5 5J 67
Clapton Sq. E5 5J 67
Clapton Ter. E5 1G 67
Clapton Way E5 4G 67
Clara Grant Ho. E14 3C 104
(off Mellish St.)
Clara Nehab Ho. NW11 5H 45
(off Leeside Cres.)
Clara Pl. SE18 4E 106
Clare Cl. N2 3A 46
Clare Cnr. SE9 7F 125
Clare Ct. W11 7G 81
(off Clarendon Rd.)
Clare Ct. WC1 2F 7 (3J 83)
(off Judd St.)
Claredale Ho. E2 2H 85
(off Claredale St.)
Claredale St. E2 2G 85
Clare Gdns. E7 4J 69
Clare Gdns. IG11: Bark 6K 71
Clare Gdns. W11 6G 81
Clare Ho. E16 7E 88
(off University Way)
Clare Ho. E3 1B 86
Clare Ho. HA8: Edg 2J 43
(off Burnt Oak B'way.)
Clare Ho. SE1 5F 103
(off Cooper's Rd.)
Clare La. N1 7C 66
Clare Lawn Av. SW14 5K 115
Clare Mkt. WC2 1H 13 (6K 83)
Clare M. SW6 7K 99
Claremont TW17: Shep 6D 146
(off Laleham Rd.)
Claremont Av. HA3: Kenton 5E 42
Claremont Av. KT3: N Mald 5C 152
Claremont Av. TW16: Sun 1K 147
Claremont Cl. BR6: Farnb 4E 172
Claremont Cl. E16 1E 106
Claremont Cl. N1 1K 7 (2A 84)
Claremont Cl. SW2 1J 137
Claremont Ct. E2 Cambridge Heath Rd. 2H 85
(off Cambridge Heath Rd.)
Claremont Ct. E2 Claredale St. 2G 85
(off Claredale St.)
Claremont Ct. W2 6K 81
(off Queensway)
Claremont Ct. W9 2H 81
(off Claremont Rd.)
Claremont Dr. TW17: Shep 6D 146
Claremont Gdns. IG3: Ilf 2J 71
Claremont Gdns. KT6: Surb 5E 150
Claremont Gro. IG8: Wfd G 6F 37
Claremont Gro. W4 7A 98
Claremont Ho. NW9 3B 44
Claremont Ho. SE16 2A 104
Claremont Ho. SM2: Sutt 7K 165
Claremont Pk. N3 1G 45
Claremont Rd. BR1: Broml 4C 160
Claremont Rd. CR0: C'don 1G 169
Claremont Rd. E11 3F 69
Claremont Rd. E17 2A 50
Claremont Rd. E7 5K 69
Claremont Rd. HA3: W'stone 2J 41
Claremont Rd. KT6: Surb 5E 150
Claremont Rd. N6 7G 47
Claremont Rd. NW2 7F 45
Claremont Rd. TW1: Twick 6B 114
Claremont Rd. TW11: Tedd 5K 131
Claremont Rd. W13 5A 78
Claremont Rd. W9 2G 81
Claremont Sq. N1 1J 7 (2A 84)
Claremont St. E16 2E 106
Claremont St. N18 6B 34
Claremont St. SE10 6D 104
Claremont Ter. KT7: T Ditt 7B 150
Claremont Vs. SE5 7D 102
(off Southampton Way)
Claremont Way NW2 1E 62
(not continuous)
Claremont Way Ind. Est. NW2 1E 62
Clarence Av. BR1: Broml 4C 160
Clarence Av. IG2: Ilf 6E 52
Clarence Av. KT3: N Mald 2J 151
Clarence Av. SW4 7H 119
Clarence Cl. EN4: E Barn 5G 21
Clarence Cl. WD23: B Hea 1E 26
Clarence Ct. NW7 5F 29
Clarence Ct. W6 4D 98
(off Cambridge Gro.)
Clarence Cres. DA14: Sidc 3B 144
Clarence Cres. SW4 6H 119
Clarence Gdns. NW1 2K 5 (3F 83)
Clarence Ga. IG8: Ilf 6K 37
Clarence Ga. IG8: Wfd G 6K 37
Clarence Ga. Gdns. NW1 4F 5 (4D 82)
(off Glentworth St.)
Clarence Ho. SE17 6D 102
(off Merrow St.)
Clarence House 6B 12 (2G 101)
(off St James's Pal.)
Clarence La. SW15 6A 116
Clarence M. E5 5H 67
Clarence M. SE16 1K 103
Clarence M. SW12 7F 119
Clarence Pk. Cres. HA7: Stan 3D 26
Clarence Pl. E5 5H 67
Clarence Rd. BR1: Broml 3B 160
Clarence Rd. CR0: C'don 7D 156
Clarence Rd. DA14: Sidc 3B 144
Clarence Rd. DA6: Bex 4E 126
Clarence Rd. E12 4A 70
Clarence Rd. E16 4G 87
Clarence Rd. E17 2K 49
Clarence Rd. E5 4H 67
Clarence Rd. EN3: Pond E 5C 24
Clarence Rd. N15 5C 48
Clarence Rd. N22 7D 32
Clarence Rd. NW6 7H 63
Clarence Rd. SE8 6D 104
Clarence Rd. SE9 2C 142
Clarence Rd. SM1: Sutt 5K 165
Clarence Rd. SM6: W'gton 5F 167
Clarence Rd. SW19 6K 135
Clarence Rd. TW11: Tedd 6K 131

A–Z London 203

Clarence Rd. – Close, The

Clarence Rd. TW9: Kew 1F 115
Clarence Rd. W4 5G 97
Clarence St. KT1: King T 2D 150
Clarence St. TW9: Rich 4E 114
Clarence St. UB2: S'hall 3B 94
Clarence Ter. NW1 3F 5 (4D 82)
Clarence Ter. TW3: Houn 4F 113
Clarence Wlk. SW4 2J 119
Clarence Way NW1 7F 65
Clarenden Pl. DA2: Wilm 5K 145
Clarendon Cl. BR5: St P 3K 161
Clarendon Cl. E9 7J 67
Clarendon Cl. W2 2C 10 (7C 82)
Clarendon Ct. BR3: Beck 1D 158
(off Albemarle Rd.)
Clarendon Ct. EC1 4D 8 (4C 84)
(off Brackley St.)
Clarendon Ct. NW11 4H 45
Clarendon Ct. NW2 7E 62
Clarendon Ct. TW5: Cran 1J 111
Clarendon Ct. TW9: Kew 1F 115
Clarendon Ct. W9 3A 4 (4A 82)
(off Maida Va.)
Clarendon Cres. TW2: Twick 3H 131
Clarendon Cross W11 7G 81
Clarendon Dr. SW15 4E 116
Clarendon Flats W1 1H 11 (6E 83)
(off Balderton St.)
Clarendon Gdns. HA9: Wemb 3D 60
Clarendon Gdns. IG1: Ilf 7D 52
Clarendon Gdns. NW4 3C 44
Clarendon Gdns. W9 4A 82
Clarendon Grn. BR5: St P 4K 161
Clarendon Gro. CR4: Mitc 3D 154
Clarendon Gro. NW1 1C 6 (3H 83)
Clarendon Ho. KT2: King T 1F 150
(off Cowleaze Rd.)
Clarendon Ho. NW1 1B 6 (2G 83)
(off Werrington St.)
Clarendon Ho. W2 2C 10 (7C 82)
(off Strathearn Pl.)
Clarendon Lodge W11 7G 81
(off Clarendon Rd.)
Clarendon M. DA5: Bexl 1H 145
Clarendon M. W2 2C 10 (7C 82)
Clarendon Path BR5: St P 4K 161
(not continuous)
Clarendon Pl. W2 2C 10 (7C 82)
Clarendon Ri. SE13 4E 122
Clarendon Rd. CR0: C'don 2B 168
Clarendon Rd. E11 1F 69
Clarendon Rd. E17 6D 50
Clarendon Rd. E18 3J 51
Clarendon Rd. HA1: Harr 6J 41
Clarendon Rd. N15 4C 48
Clarendon Rd. N18 6B 34
Clarendon Rd. N22 2K 47
Clarendon Rd. N8 3K 47
Clarendon Rd. SM6: W'gton 6G 167
Clarendon Rd. SW19 7C 136
Clarendon Rd. TW15: Ashf 4B 128
Clarendon Rd. UB3: Hayes 2H 93
Clarendon Rd. W11 7G 81
Clarendon Rd. W5 3E 78
Clarendon St. SW1 6K 17 (5F 101)
Clarendon Ter. W9 3A 4 (4A 82)
Clarendon Wlk. W11 6G 81
Clarendon Way BR5: St P 3K 161
Clarendon Way BR7: Chst 3K 161
Clarendon Way N21 6H 23
Clarens St. SE6 2B 140
Clare Pl. SW15 7B 116
Clare Point NW2 1F 63
(off Whitefield Av.)
Clare Rd. E11 6F 51
Clare Rd. NW10 7C 62
Clare Rd. SE14 1B 122
Clare Rd. TW19: Stanw 1A 128
Clare Rd. TW4: Houn 3D 112
Clare Rd. UB6: G'frd 6H 59
Clare St. E2 2H 85
Claret Gdns. SE25 3E 156
Clareville Ct. SW7 4A 16 (4A 100)
(off Clareville St.)
Clareville Gro. SW7 4A 16 (4A 100)
Clareville Gro. M. SW7 4A 16 (4A 100)
Clareville Rd. BR5: Farnb 2G 173
Clareville St. SW7 4A 100
Clare Way DA7: Bex 1E 126
Clarewood Ct. W1 6E 4 (5D 82)
(off Seymour Pl.)
Clarewood Wlk. SW9 4A 120
Clarges M. W1 4J 11 (1F 101)
Clarges St. W1 4K 11 (1F 101)
Claribel Rd. SW9 2B 120
Clarice Way SM6: W'gton 7J 167
Claridge Ct. SW6 2H 117
Claridge Rd. RM8: Dag 1D 72
Clarinet Ct. HA8: Edg 7C 28
Clarion Ho. E3 2A 86
(off Roman Rd.)
Clarion Ho. SW1 5B 18 (5G 101)
(off Moreton Pl.)
Clarion Ho. W1 1C 12 (6H 83)
(off St Anne's Ct.)
Clarissa Ho. E14 6D 86
(off Cordela St.)
Clarissa Rd. RM6: Chad H 7D 54
Clarissa St. E8 1F 85
Clarke Apts. E3 4B 86
(off Heath Pl.)
Clarke Av. TW3: Houn 2E 112
Clarke Cl. CR0: C'don 6C 156
Clarke Mans. IG11: Bark 7K 71
(off Upney La.)
Clarke M. N9 3C 34
Clarke Path N16 1G 67
Clarkes Av. KT4: Wor Pk 1F 165
Clarkes Dr. UB8: Hil 5A 74
Clarke's M. W1 5H 5 (5E 82)
Clark Gro. IG3: Ilf 4J 71
Clark Ho. SW10 7A 100
(off Coleridge Gdns.)
Clarks Mead WD23: Bush 1B 26
Clarkson Rd. E16 6H 87
Clarkson Row NW1 2G 83
(off Mornington Ter.)
Clarksons, The IG11: Bark 2G 89
Clarkson St. E2 3H 85
Clarks Rd. IG1: Ilf 2H 71
Clark St. E1 5H 85
(not continuous)
Clark Way TW5: Hest 7B 94
Clarnico La. E20 6C 68
Clarson Ho. SE5 7B 102
(off Midnight Av.)
Clarson Ho. SE8 6A 104
Classic Mans. E9 7H 67
(off Wells St.)
Classon Cl. UB7: W Dray 2A 92
Claude Av. NW9 1B 44
Claude Rd. E10 2E 68
Claude Rd. E13 1K 87
Claude Rd. SE15 2H 121
Claude St. E14 4C 104
Claudia Jones Ho. N17 1C 48
Claudia Jones Way SW2 6J 119
Claudia Pl. SW19 1G 135
Claudius Cl. HA7: Stan 3J 27
Claughton Rd. E13 2A 88
Clauson Av. UB5: N'olt 5F 59
Clavell St. SE10 6E 104
Claverdale Rd. SW2 7K 119
Clavering Av. SW13 6D 98
Clavering Cl. TW1: Twick 4A 132
Clavering Ho. SE13 4F 123
(off Blessington Rd.)
Clavering Pl. SW12 6E 118
Clavering Rd. E12 1B 70
Claverings Ind. Est. N9 2D 34
(off Centre Way)
Claverley Gro. N3 1K 45
Claverley Vs. N3 7E 30
Claverton St. SW1 6B 18 (5G 101)
Clave St. E1 1J 103
Claxton Gro. W6 5F 99
Claxton Path SE4 4K 121
(off Coston Wlk.)
Clay Av. CR4: Mitc 2F 155
Claybank Gro. SE13 3D 122
Claybourne M. SE19 7E 138
Claybridge Rd. SE12 4A 142
Claybrook Cl. N2 3B 46
Claybrook Rd. W6 6F 99
Claybury WD23: Bush 1A 26
Claybury B'way. IG5: Ilf 3C 52
Claybury Hall IG8: Wfd G 7J 37
Claybury M. IG5: Ilf 1D 52
Claybury Rd. IG8: Wfd G 7H 37
Clay Ct. E17 3F 51
Clay Ct. SE1 7G 15 (3E 102)
(off Long La.)
Claydon Dr. CR0: Bedd 4J 167
Claydon Ho. NW4 2F 45
(off Holders Hill Rd.)
Claydon Ho. SW10 1A 118
Claydown M. SE18 5E 106
Clayfarm Rd. SE9 2G 143
Claygate Common 7A 162
Claygate Cres. CR0: New Ad 6E 170
Claygate La. KT10: Clay 2A 162
Claygate La. KT10: Hin W 2A 162
Claygate La. KT7: T Ditt 1A 162
Claygate Rd. W13 3B 96
CLAYHALL 3C 52
Clayhall Av. IG5: Ilf 3C 52
Clayhall Ct. E3 2B 86
(off St Stephen's Rd.)
Clayhill KT5: Surb 5G 151
Clayhill Cres. SE9 4B 142
Claylands Pl. SW8 7A 102
Claylands Rd. SW8 7H 19 (6K 101)
Clay La. HA3: Kenton 4D 42
Clay La. HA8: Edg 2B 28
Clay La. TW19: Stanw 7B 110
Clay La. WD23: B Hea 1D 26
Claymill Ho. SE18 5G 107
Claymore Cl. SM4: Mord 7J 153
Clay Path E17 2C 50
Claypole Ct. E17 5C 50
(off Yunus Khan Cl.)
Claypole Dr. TW5: Hest 1C 112
Claypole Rd. E15 2E 86
Clayponds Av. TW8: Bford 4D 96
Clayponds Gdns. W5 4D 96
(not continuous)
Clayponds La. TW8: Bford 5E 96
(not continuous)
Clay St. W1 6F 5 (5D 82)
Clayton Av. HA0: Wemb 7E 60
Clayton Bus. Cen. UB3: Hayes 2G 93
Clayton Cl. E6 6D 88
Clayton Cres. N1 1J 83
Clayton Cres. TW8: Bford 5D 96
Clayton Dr. SE8 5A 104
Clayton Fld. NW9 7F 29
Clayton Ho. E9 7J 67
(off Frampton Pk. Rd.)
Clayton Ho. KT7: T Ditt 1B 162
Clayton Ho. SW13 7E 98
(off Trinity Chu. Rd.)
Clayton M. SE10 1F 123
Clayton Rd. KT9: Chess 4C 162
Clayton Rd. RM7: Rush G 1J 73
Clayton Rd. SE15 1G 121
Clayton Rd. TW7: Isle 3J 113
Clayton Rd. UB3: Hayes 2G 93
Clayton St. SE11 7J 19 (6A 102)
Clayton Ter. UB4: Yead 5C 76
Claytonville Ter. DA17: Belv 2J 109
Clay Wood Cl. BR6: Orp 7J 161
Clayworth Cl. DA15: Sidc 6B 126
Cleanthus Cl. SE18 1F 125
Cleanthus Rd. SE18 2F 125
(not continuous)
Clearbrook Way E1 6J 85
Clearwater Pl. KT6: Surb 6C 150
Clearwater Ter. W11 2F 99
Clearwater Yd. NW1 1F 83
(off Inverness St.)
Clearwell Dr. W9 4K 81
Cleave Av. BR6: Chels 6J 173
Cleave Av. UB3: Harl 4G 93
Cleaveland Rd. KT6: Surb 5D 150
Cleaverholme Cl. SE25 6H 157
Cleaver Ho. NW3 7D 64
(off Adelaide Rd.)
Cleaver Sq. SE11 5K 19 (5A 102)
Cleaver St. SE11 5K 19 (5A 102)
Cleaves Almshouses KT2: King T 2E 150
(off London Rd.)
Cleeve Ct. TW14: Bedf 1G 129
Cleevedale Place SW4 5G 119
Cleeve Hill SE23 1H 139
Cleeve Ho. E2 2H 9 (3E 84)
(off Calvert Av.)
Cleeve Pk. Gdns. DA14: Sidc 2B 144
Cleeve Way SM1: Sutt 1K 165
Cleeve Way SW15 7B 116
Cleeve Workshops E2 2H 9 (3E 84)
(off Boundary Rd.)
Clegg Ho. SE16 3J 103
(off Moodkee St.)
Clegg St. E1 1H 103
Clegg St. E13 2J 87
Cleland Ho. E2 2J 85
(off Sewardstone Rd.)
Clematis Apts. E3 3B 86
(off Merchant St.)
Clematis Gdns. IG8: Wfd G 5D 36
Clematis St. W12 7C 80
Clem Attlee Ct. SW6 6H 99
Clem Attlee Pde. SW6 6H 99
(off North End Rd.)
Clemence Rd. RM10: Dag 1J 91
Clemence St. E14 5B 86
Clement Av. SW4 4H 119
Clement Cl. NW6 7E 62
Clement Cl. W4 4K 97
Clement Danes Ho. W12 6D 80
Clement Gdns. UB3: Harl 4G 93
Clementhorpe Rd. RM9: Dag 6C 72
Clement Ho. SE8 4A 104
Clement Ho. W10 5E 80
(off Dalgarno Gdns.)
Clementina Ct. E3 4A 86
(off Copperfield Rd.)
Clementina Rd. E10 1B 68
Clementine Cl. W13 2B 96
Clementine Wlk. IG8: Wfd G 7D 36
Clement Rd. BR3: Beck 2K 157
Clement Rd. SW19 5G 135
Clement's Av. E16 7J 87
Clements Cl. N12 4E 30
Clements Ct. IG1: Ilf 3F 71
Clements Ct. TW4: Houn 4B 112
Clement's Inn WC2 1H 13 (6K 83)
Clements La. EC4 2F 15 (7D 84)
Clements La. IG1: Ilf 3F 71
Clements Pl. TW8: Bford 5D 96
Clements Rd. E6 7C 70
Clements Rd. IG1: Ilf 3F 71
Clements Rd. SE16 3G 103
Clemson Ho. E8 1F 85
Clendon Way SE18 4H 107
Clennam St. SE1 6D 14 (2C 102)
Clensham Ct. SM1: Sutt 2J 165
Clensham La. SM1: Sutt 2J 165
Clenston M. W1 7E 4 (6D 82)
Cleopatra Cl. HA7: Stan 3J 27
Cleopatra's Needle 3G 13 (7K 83)
Clephane Rd. N1 6C 66
Clephane Rd. Nth. N1 6C 66
Clere Pl. EC2 3F 9 (4D 84)
Clere St. EC2 3F 9 (4D 84)
Clerics Wlk. TW17: Shep 7F 147
CLERKENWELL 3K 7 (4A 84)
Clerkenwell Cl. EC1 3K 7 (4A 84)
(not continuous)
Clerkenwell Ct. N1 2B 84
(off Duncan St.)
Clerkenwell Grn. EC1 4K 7 (4A 84)
Clerkenwell Rd. EC1 4J 7 (4A 84)
Clerks Pl. EC3 7G 9 (6E 84)
Clermont Rd. E9 1J 85
Clevedon Cl. N16 3F 67
Clevedon Ct. CR2: S Croy 5E 168
Clevedon Ct. SW11 1C 118
(off Bolingbroke Wlk.)
Clevedon Gdns. TW5: Cran 1K 111
Clevedon Gdns. UB3: Harl 3F 93
Clevedon Ho. SM1: Sutt 4A 166
Clevedon Mans. NW5 4E 64
Clevedon Pas. N16 2F 67
Clevedon Rd. KT1: King T 2G 151
Clevedon Rd. SE20 1K 157
Clevedon Rd. TW1: Twick 6D 114
Cleve Ho. NW6 7K 63
Cleveland Av. SW20 2H 153
Cleveland Av. TW12: Hamp 7D 130
Cleveland Av. W4 4B 98
Cleveland Ct. W13 5B 78
Cleveland Gdns. KT4: Wor Pk 2A 164
Cleveland Gdns. N4 5C 48
Cleveland Gdns. NW2 2F 63
Cleveland Gdns. SW13 2B 116
Cleveland Gdns. W2 6A 82
Cleveland Gro. E1 4J 85
Cleveland Ho. N2 2B 46
(off The Grange)
Cleveland Mans. NW6 7H 63
(off Willesden La.)
Cleveland Mans. SW9 7A 102
(off Mowll St.)
Cleveland Mans. W9 4J 81
Cleveland M. W1 5A 6 (5G 83)
Cleveland Pk. TW19: Stanw 6A 110
Cleveland Pk. Av. E17 4C 50
Cleveland Pk. Cres. E17 4C 50
Cleveland Pl. SW1 4B 12 (1G 101)
Cleveland Ri. SM4: Mord 7F 153
Cleveland Rd. DA16: Well 2K 125
Cleveland Rd. E18 3J 51
Cleveland Rd. IG1: Ilf 3F 71
Cleveland Rd. KT3: N Mald 4A 152
Cleveland Rd. KT4: Wor Pk 2A 164
Cleveland Rd. N1 7D 66
Cleveland Rd. N9 7C 24
Cleveland Rd. SW13 2B 116
Cleveland Rd. TW7: Isle 4A 114
Cleveland Rd. W13 5A 78
Cleveland Rd. W4 3J 97
Cleveland Row SW1 5A 12 (1G 101)
Cleveland Sq. W2 6A 82
Cleveland St. W1 4K 5 (4F 83)
Cleveland Ter. W2 6A 82
Cleveland Way E1 4J 85
Cleveley Cl. SE7 4B 106
Cleveley Ct. SE16 4A 104
(off Ashton Reach)
Cleveley Cres. W5 2E 78
Cleveleys Rd. E5 3H 67
Cleverly Est. W12 1C 98
Cleve Rd. DA14: Sidc 3D 144
Cleve Rd. NW6 7J 63
Cleves Av. KT17: Ewe 7D 164
Cleves Ho. E16 1J 105
(off Southey M.)
Cleves Rd. E6 1B 88
Cleves Rd. TW10: Ham 3C 132
Cleves Wlk. IG6: Ilf 1G 53
Cleves Way HA4: Ruis 1B 58
Cleves Way TW12: Hamp 7D 130
Cleves Way TW16: Sun 6H 129
Clewer Ct. E10 1C 68
(off Leyton Grange Est.)
Clewer Cres. HA3: Hrw W 1H 41
Clewer Ho. SE2 2D 108
(off Wolvercote Rd.)
Cley Ho. SE4 4K 121
C&L Golf Course 7K 57
Clichy Est. E1 5J 85
Clichy Ho. E1 5J 85
(off Stepney Way)
Clifden M. E5 4K 67
Clifden Rd. E5 5J 67
Clifden Rd. TW1: Twick 1K 131
Clifden Rd. TW8: Bford 6D 96
Cliffe Ho. SE10 5H 105
(off Blackwall La.)
Cliffe Rd. CR2: S Croy 5D 168
Cliffe Wlk. SM1: Sutt 5A 166
(off Greyhound Rd.)
Clifford Av. BR7: Chst 6D 142
Clifford Av. IG5: Ilf 1F 53
Clifford Av. SM6: W'gton 4G 167
Clifford Av. SW14 3H 115
Clifford Cl. UB5: N'olt 1C 76
Clifford Ct. W2 5K 81
(off Westbourne Pk. Vs.)
Clifford Dr. SW9 4B 120
Clifford Gdns. NW10 2E 80
Clifford Gdns. UB3: Harl 4G 93
Clifford Gro. TW15: Ashf 4C 128
Clifford Haigh Ho. SW6 7F 99
Clifford Ho. BR3: Beck 6D 140
(off Calverley Cl.)
Clifford Ho. W14 4H 99
(off Edith Vs.)
Clifford Rd. E16 4H 87
Clifford Rd. E17 2E 50
Clifford Rd. EN5: New Bar 3E 20
Clifford Rd. HA0: Wemb 7D 60
Clifford Rd. N1 1E 84
Clifford Rd. N9 6D 24
Clifford Rd. SE25 4G 157
Clifford Rd. TW10: Ham 2D 132
Clifford Rd. TW4: Houn 3B 112
Clifford's Inn EC4 1J 13 (6A 84)
(off Fetter La.)
Clifford's Inn Pas. EC4 1J 13 (6A 84)
Clifford St. W1 3A 12 (7G 83)
Clifford Way NW10 4B 62
Cliff Rd. NW1 6H 65
Cliffsend Ho. SW9 1A 120
(off Cowley Rd.)
Cliff Ter. SE8 2C 122
Cliffview Rd. SE13 3C 122
Cliff Vs. NW1 6H 65
Cliff Wlk. E16 5H 87
Clifton Av. E17 3K 49
Clifton Av. HA7: Stan 2B 42
Clifton Av. HA9: Wemb 6F 61
Clifton Av. N3 1H 45
Clifton Av. TW13: Felt 3A 130
Clifton Av. W12 1B 98
Clifton Cl. BR6: Farnb 5G 173
Clifton Ct. BR3: Beck 1D 158
Clifton Ct. IG8: Wfd G 6D 36
Clifton Ct. KT5: Surb 7F 151
Clifton Ct. N4 2A 66
Clifton Ct. NW8 3A 4 (4B 82)
(off Maida Vale)
Clifton Ct. SE15 7H 103
Clifton Ct. TW19: Stanw 6A 110
Clifton Cres. SE15 7H 103
Clifton Est. SE15 1H 121
Clifton Gdns. EN2: Enf 4D 22
Clifton Gdns. N15 6F 49
Clifton Gdns. NW11 6H 45
Clifton Gdns. UB10: Hil 2D 74
Clifton Gdns. W4 4K 97
(not continuous)
Clifton Gdns. W9 4A 82
Clifton Ga. SW10 6A 100
Clifton Gro. E8 6G 67
Clifton Hill NW8 2K 81
Clifton Hill Studios NW8 2A 82
Clifton Ho. E11 2G 69
Clifton Ho. E2 3J 9 (4F 85)
(off Club Row)
Clifton M. SE25 4E 156
Clifton Pde. TW13: Felt 3A 130
Clifton Pk. Av. SW20 2E 152
Clifton Pl. SE16 2J 103
Clifton Pl. SW10 6A 100
(off Hollywood Rd.)
Clifton Pl. W2 1B 10 (6B 82)
Clifton Ri. SE14 7A 104
(not continuous)
Clifton Rd. DA14: Sidc 4J 143
Clifton Rd. DA16: Well 3C 126
Clifton Rd. E16 5G 87
Clifton Rd. E7 6B 70
Clifton Rd. HA3: Kenton 4F 43
Clifton Rd. IG2: Ilf 6H 53
Clifton Rd. KT2: King T 7F 133
Clifton Rd. N1 6C 66
Clifton Rd. N22 1G 47
Clifton Rd. N3 1A 46
Clifton Rd. N8 6H 47
Clifton Rd. NW10 2C 80
Clifton Rd. SE25 4E 156
Clifton Rd. SM6: W'gton 5F 167
Clifton Rd. SW19 6F 135
Clifton Rd. TW11: Tedd 4J 131
Clifton Rd. TW7: Isle 2J 113
Clifton Rd. UB2: S'hall 4C 94
Clifton Rd. UB6: G'frd 4G 77
Clifton Rd. W9 4A 82
Clifton St. EC2 4G 9 (4E 84)
Clifton Ter. N4 2A 66
Clifton Vs. W9 5A 82
Cliftonville Ct. SE12 1J 141
Clifton Wlk. W6 4D 98
(off King St.)
Clifton Way HA0: Wemb 1E 78
Clifton Way SE15 7H 103
Climsland Ho. SE1 4K 13 (1A 102)
Cline Rd. N11 6B 32
Clinger Ct. N1 1E 84
(off Hobbs Pl. Est.)
Clink Prison Mus. 4E 14 (1D 102)
(off Clink St.)
Clink St. SE1 4E 14 (1D 102)
Clink Wharf SE1 4E 14 (1D 102)
(off Clink St.)
Clinton Av. DA16: Well 4A 126
Clinton Av. KT8: E Mos 4G 149
Clinton Ho. KT6: Surb 7D 150
(off Lovelace Gdns)
Clinton Rd. E3 3A 86
Clinton Rd. E7 4J 69
Clinton Rd. N15 4D 48
Clinton Ter. SE8 6C 104
(off Watergate St.)
Clinton Ter. SM1: Sutt 4A 166
Clipper Apts. SE10 6E 104
(off Welland St.)
Clipper Cl. SE16 2K 103
Clipper Ho. E14 5E 104
(off Manchester Rd.)
Clipper Way SE13 4E 122
Clippesby Cl. KT9: Chess 6F 163
Clipstone M. W1 5A 6 (5G 83)
Clipstone Rd. TW3: Houn 3E 112
Clipstone St. W1 5K 5 (5F 83)
Clissold Cl. N2 3D 46
Clissold Ct. N4 2C 66
Clissold Cres. N16 3D 66
Clissold Leisure Cen. 3D 66
Clissold Rd. N16 3D 66
Clitheroe Av. HA2: Harr 1E 58
Clitheroe Rd. SW9 2J 119
Clitherow Av. W7 3A 96
Clitherow Ct. TW8: Bford 5C 96
Clitherow Pas. TW8: Bford 5C 96
Clitherow Rd. TW8: Bford 5B 96
Clitterhouse Cres. NW2 1E 62
Clitterhouse Rd. NW2 1E 62
Clive Av. N18 6B 34
Clive Ct. W9 4A 82
Cliveden Cl. N12 4F 31
Cliveden Ho. E16 1J 105
(off Fitzwilliam M.)
Cliveden Ho. SW1 3G 17 (4E 100)
(off Cliveden Pl.)
Cliveden Pl. SW1 3G 17 (4E 100)
Cliveden Pl. TW17: Shep 6E 146
Cliveden Rd. SW19 1H 153
Clivedon Ct. W13 5B 78
Clivedon Rd. E4 5B 36
Clive Ho. SE10 6E 104
(off Haddo St.)
Clive Lloyd Ho. N15 5C 48
(off Woodlands Pk. Rd.)
Clive Lodge NW4 6F 45
Clive Pas. SE21 3D 138
Clive Rd. DA17: Belv 4G 109
Clive Rd. EN1: Enf 4B 24
Clive Rd. SE21 3D 138
Clive Rd. SW19 6C 136
Clive Rd. TW1: Twick 4K 131
Clive Rd. TW14: Felt 6J 111
Clivesdale Dr. UB3: Hayes 1K 93
Clive Way EN1: Enf 4B 24
Cloak La. EC4 2D 14 (7C 84)
Clochar Ct. NW10 1B 80
Clock Ct. E11 4K 51
Clock Ho. E17 4F 51
(off Wood St.)
Clock Ho. E3 3E 86
Clockhouse, The SW19 3E 134
Clockhouse Av. IG11: Bark 1G 89
Clockhouse Cl. SW19 2E 134
Clockhouse Ct. BR3: Beck 2A 158
CLOCKHOUSE JUNC. 5E 32
Clockhouse La. RM5: Col R 1H 55
Clockhouse La. TW14: Bedf 3D 128
Clockhouse La. TW15: Ashf 4C 128
Clock Ho. Pde. E11 6K 51
Clockhouse Pde. N13 5F 33
Clockhouse Pl. SW15 6G 117
Clock Ho. Rd. BR3: Beck 3A 158
CLOCKHOUSE RDBT. East Bedfont 1D 128
Clock Pde. EN2: Enf 5J 23
Clock Pl. SE1 4B 102
(off Newington Butts)
Clock Twr. Ind. Est. TW7: Isle 3K 113
Clock Twr. M. N1 1C 84
Clock Twr. M. SE28 7B 90
Clock Twr. M. W7 1J 95
Clock Twr. Rd. TW7: Isle 3K 113
Clock Vw. Cres. N7 6J 65
(not continuous)
Clockwork Apts. EC4 1B 14 (6B 84)
(off Ludgate Sq.)
Clockwork M. E5 5K 67
Cloister Cl. TW11: Tedd 5B 132
Cloister Gdns. HA8: Edg 5D 28
Cloister Gdns. SE25 6H 157
Cloister Rd. NW2 3H 63
Cloister Rd. W3 5J 79
Cloisters, The E1 5J 9 (5F 85)
(off Commercial St.)
Cloisters, The SW9 1A 120
Cloisters Av. BR2: Broml 5D 160
Cloisters Bus. Cen. SW8 7F 101
(off Battersea Pk. Rd.)
Cloisters Ct. DA7: Bex 3H 127
Cloisters Mall KT1: King T 2E 150
Clonbrock Rd. N16 4E 66
Cloncurry St. SW6 2F 117
Clonmel Cl. HA2: Harr 2H 59
Clonmell Rd. N17 3D 48
Clonmel Rd. SW6 7H 99
Clonmel Rd. TW11: Tedd 4H 131
Clonmore St. SW18 1H 135
Cloonmore Av. BR6: Chels 4K 173
Clorane Gdns. NW3 3J 63
Close, The BR3: Beck 4A 158
Close, The BR5: Pet W 6J 161
Close, The CR4: Mitc 4D 154
Close, The DA14: Sidc 4B 144
Close, The DA5: Bexl 6G 127
Close, The E4 7K 35
Close, The EN4: E Barn 6J 21
Close, The HA0: Wemb 6E 60
Close, The HA2: Harr 2G 41
Close, The HA5: Eastc 7A 40
Close, The HA5: Pinn 7D 40
Close, The HA9: Wemb 3J 61
Close, The IG2: Ilf 6J 53
Close, The KT3: N Mald 2J 151
Close, The KT6: Surb 6E 150
Close, The N10 2F 47
Close, The N14 2C 32
Close, The N20 2C 30
Close, The RM6: Chad H 6E 54
Close, The SE25 6G 157
Close, The SE3 2F 123
Close, The SM3: Sutt 7H 153
Close, The SM5: Cars 7C 166

204 A–Z London

Close, The – Colmore Rd.

Close, The TW7: Isle 2H 113
Close, The TW9: Rich 3H 115
Close, The UB10: Hil 1C 74
Cloth Ct. EC1 6B 8 (5B 84)
(off Cloth Fair)
Cloth Fair EC1 6B 8 (5B 84)
Cloth Ho. EC1 5C 8 (5C 84)
(off Cloth St.)
Clothier St. E1 7H 9 (6E 84)
Cloth St. EC1 5C 8 (5C 84)
Clothworkers Rd. SE18 7H 107
Cloudesdale Rd. SW17 2F 137
Cloudeseley Cl. DA14: Sidc 4K 143
Cloudesley Ho. N1 1A 84
(off Cloudesley St.)
Cloudesley Mans. N1 1A 84
(off Cloudesley Pl.)
Cloudesley Pl. N1 1A 84
Cloudesley Rd. DA7: Bex 1F 127
Cloudesley Rd. N1 1A 84
(not continuous)
Cloudesley Sq. N1 1A 84
Cloudesley St. N1 1A 84
Cloud Way TW6: H'row A 3D 110
Clouston Cl. SM6: W'gton 5J 167
Clova Rd. E7 6H 69
Clove Cres. E14 7E 86
Clove Hitch Quay SW11 3A 118
Clovelly Av. NW9 4B 44
Clovelly Av. UB10: Ick 4E 56
Clovelly Cl. HA5: Eastc 3K 39
Clovelly Cl. UB10: Ick 4E 56
Clovelly Ct. NW2 5E 62
Clovelly Gdns. EN1: Enf 7K 23
Clovelly Gdns. RM7: Mawney 1H 55
Clovelly Gdns. SE19 1F 157
Clovelly Ho. W2 6A 82
(off Hallfield Est.)
Clovelly Rd. DA7: Bex 6E 108
Clovelly Rd. N8 4H 47
Clovelly Rd. TW3: Houn 2E 112
Clovelly Rd. W4 2K 97
Clovelly Rd. W5 2C 96
Clovelly Way BR6: St M Cry 6K 161
Clovelly Way E1 6J 85
Clovelly Way HA2: Harr 2D 58
Clover Cl. E11 2F 69
Clover Ct. E14 3D 104
(off Watergate Walk)
Cloverdale Ct. SM6: W'gton 6F 167
Cloverdale Gdns. DA15: Sidc 6K 125
Clover M. SW3 7F 17 (6D 100)
Clover Way SM6: W'gton 1E 166
Clove St. E13 4J 87
Clove St. RM9: Dag 3E 90
Clowders Rd. SE6 3B 140
Clowser Cl. SM1: Sutt 5A 166
Cloysters Grn. E1 4K 15 (1G 103)
Cloyster Wood HA8: Edg 7J 27
Club Gdns. Rd. BR2: Hayes 7J 159
Clubhouse, The E14 6C 86
Clubhouse La. UB10: Ick 4C 56
Club Row E1 3J 9 (4F 85)
Club Row E2 3J 9 (4F 85)
Clumps, The TW15: Ashf 4F 129
Clunbury Av. UB2: S'hall 5D 94
Clunbury St. N1 2D 84
Clunie Ho. SW1 1F 17 (3D 100)
(off Hans Pl.)
Cluny Est. SE1 7G 15 (3E 102)
Cluny M. SW5 4J 99
Cluny Pl. SE1 7G 15 (3E 102)
Cluse Ct. N1 2C 84
(off St Peters St.)
Cluster Ho. W3 1B 98
Clutton St. E14 5D 86
Clydach Rd. EN1: Enf 4A 24
Clyde Cir. N15 4E 48
Clyde Ct. NW1 2H 83
(off Hampden Cl.)
Clyde Flats SW6 7H 99
(off Rylston Rd.)
Clyde Ho. KT2: King T 1D 150
Clyde Ho. SW18 4J 117
(off Enterprise Way)
Clyde Pl. E10 7D 50
Clyde Rd. CR0: C'don 2F 169
Clyde Rd. N15 4E 48
(not continuous)
Clyde Rd. N22 1H 47
Clyde Rd. SM1: Sutt 5J 165
Clyde Rd. SM6: W'gton 6G 167
Clyde Rd. TW19: Stanw 1A 128
Clydesdale EN3: Pond E 4E 24
Clydesdale Av. HA7: Stan 3D 42
Clydesdale Cl. TW7: Isle 3K 113
Clydesdale Ct. N20 1G 31
Clydesdale Gdns. TW10: Rich 4H 115
Clydesdale Ho. DA18: Erith 2E 108
(off Kale Rd.)
Clydesdale Ho. W11 6H 81
(off Clydesdale Rd.)
Clydesdale Rd. W11 6H 81
Clydesdale Way DA17: Belv 2H 109
Clyde Sq. E14 6B 86
Clyde St. SE8 6B 104
Clyde Ter. SE23 2J 139
Clyde Va. SE23 2J 139
Clyde Way RM1: Rom 1K 55
Clyde Wharf E16 1J 105
Clydon Cl. DA8: Erith 6K 109
Clyfford Rd. HA4: Ruis 4H 57
Clymping Dene TW14: Felt 7K 111
Clynes Ho. E2 3K 85
(off Knottisford St.)
Clynes Ho. RM10: Dag 3G 73
(off Uvedale Rd.)
Clyston St. SW8 2G 119
Coach & Horses Yd. W1 2A 12 (7G 83)
Coach Ho. La. N5 4B 66
Coach Ho. La. SW19 4F 135
Coach Ho. M. SE1 7G 15 (3E 102)
(off Long La.)
Coach Ho. M. SE14 2K 121
Coach Ho. M. SE23 6K 121
Coach Ho. M. SM2: Sutt 6K 165
Coachhouse M. SE20 7H 139
Coach Ho. Yd. NW3 4A 64
(off Heath St.)
Coach Ho. Yd. SW18 4K 117
Coachmaker M. SW4 3J 119
(off Bedford Rd.)
Coachmaker M. W4 3K 97
(off Berrymede Rd.)
Coach Yd. M. N19 1J 65
Coalbrookdale Gates 7B 10 (2B 100)
Coaldale Wlk. SE21 7C 120
Coal Drops Yard 1J 83
Coalecroft Rd. SW15 4E 116
Coal La. SW9 4A 120
Coalmakers Wharf E14 6C 86
Coalport Ho. SE11 3J 19 (4A 102)
(off Walnut Tree Wlk.)
Coal Post Cl. BR6: Chels 6K 173
Coalstore Ct. E1 5A 86
Coatbridge Ho. N1 7K 65
(off Carnoustie Dr.)
Coates Av. SW18 6C 118
Coates Cl. CR7: Thor H 3C 156
Coates Hill Rd. BR1: Broml 2E 160
Coate St. E2 2G 85
Coates Wlk. TW8: Bford 6E 96
Cobalt SE28 2A 108
Cobalt Bldg., The EC2 5C 8 (5C 84)
(off Bridgewater Sq.)
Cobalt Cl. BR3: Beck 4K 157
Cobalt Cl. NW9 1B 44
Cobalt Ct. HA4: Ruis 4A 58
Cobalt Pl. SW11 1B 118
Cobalt Sq. SW8 7G 19 (6K 101)
(off Sth. Lambeth Rd.)
Cobalt Twr. SE14 6A 104
Cobbett Rd. SE9 3C 124
Cobbett Rd. TW2: Whitt 1E 130
Cobbetts Av. IG4: Ilf 5B 52
Cobbett St. SW8 7K 101
Cobble La. N1 7B 66
Cobble M. N5 3C 66
Cobble M. N6 1E 64
(off Highgate West Hill)
Cobble Path E17 5C 50
(off Cedars Av.)
Cobblestone Pl. CR0: C'don 1C 168
Cobblestone Sq. E1 1H 103
Cobbold Ct. SW1 3C 18 (4H 101)
(off Elverton St.)
Cobbold Ind. Est. NW10 6B 62
Cobbold M. W12 2B 98
Cobbold Rd. E11 3H 69
Cobbold Rd. NW10 6B 62
Cobbold Rd. W12 2A 98
Cobb's Ct. EC4 1B 14 (6B 84)
(off Carter La.)
Cobb's Hall SW6 6F 99
(off Fulham Pal. Rd.)
Cobb's Rd. TW4: Houn 4D 112
Cobbsthorpe Vs. SE26 4K 139
Cobb St. E1 6J 9 (5F 85)
Cobden Bldgs. WC1 1G 7 (3K 83)
(off King's Cross Rd.)
Cobden Ct. BR2: Broml 4A 160
Cobden Ho. E2 3G 85
(off Nelson Gdns.)
Cobden Ho. NW1 2G 83
(off Arlington Rd.)
Cobden M. SE26 5H 139
Cobden Rd. BR6: Farnb 4H 173
Cobden Rd. E11 3G 69
Cobden Rd. SE25 5G 157
Cobham Av. KT3: N Mald 5C 152
Cobham Cl. BR2: Broml 7C 160
Cobham Cl. DA15: Sidc 6B 126
Cobham Cl. EN1: Enf 3B 24
Cobham Cl. HA8: Edg 2H 43
Cobham Cl. SM6: W'gton 6J 167
Cobham Cl. SW11 6C 118
Cobham Ct. CR4: Mitc 2B 154
Cobham M. NW1 7H 65
Cobham Pl. DA6: Bex 5E 126
Cobham Rd. E17 1E 50
Cobham Rd. IG3: Ilf 2J 71
Cobham Rd. KT1: King T 2G 151
Cobham Rd. N22 3B 48
Cobham Rd. TW5: Hest 7A 94
Cobland Rd. SE12 4A 142
Coborn M. E3 3B 86
(off Coborn St.)
Coborn Rd. E3 2B 86
Coborn St. E3 3B 86
Cobourg Rd. SE5 6F 103
Cobourg St. NW1 2B 6 (3G 83)
Cobtree Ct. UB1: S'hall 6E 76
(off Fleming Rd.)
Coburg Cl. SW1 3B 18 (4G 101)
Coburg Cres. SW2 1K 137
Coburg Dwellings E1 6J 85
(off Hardinge St.)
Coburg Gdns. IG5: Ilf 2B 52
Coburg Rd. N22 3K 47
Cochrane Ct. NW8 1B 4 (2B 82)
(off Cochrane St.)
Cochrane Ct. E10 1C 68
(off Leyton Grange Est.)
Cochrane Ho. E14 2C 104
(off Admirals Way)
Cochrane M. NW8 2B 82
Cochrane Rd. SW19 7G 135
Cochrane St. NW8 2B 82
Cockburn Ho. SW1 6D 18 (5H 101)
(off Aylesford St.)
COCKCROW HILL 1D 162
Cockerell Rd. E17 7A 50
COCKFOSTERS 4J 21
Cockfosters Pde. EN4: Cockf 4K 21
Cock Hill E1 6H 9 (5E 84)
Cock La. EC1 6A 8 (5B 84)
Cockpit Steps SW1 7D 12 (2H 101)
(off Birdcage Wlk.)
Cockpit Theatre 4C 4 (4C 82)
(off Gateforth St.)
Cockpit Yd. WC1 5H 7 (5K 83)
Cocks Cres. KT3: N Mald 4B 152
Cocksett Av. BR6: Chels 6J 173
Cockspur Ct. SW1 4D 12 (1H 101)
Cockspur St. SW1 4D 12 (1H 101)
Cocksure La. DA14: Sidc 3G 145
Coda Cen., The SW6 7G 99
Coda Residences SW11 3B 118
(off York Place)
Code Ct. NW2 3C 62
Code St. E1 4K 9 (4F 85)
Codicote Ho. SE8 4K 103
(off Chilton Gro.)
Codling Cl. E1 1G 103
Codling Way HA0: Wemb 4D 60
Codrington Ct. E1 4H 85
Codrington Ct. SE16 7A 86
Codrington Hill SE23 7A 122
Codrington M. W11 6G 81
Cody Cl. HA3: Kenton 3D 42
Cody Cl. SM6: W'gton 7H 167
Cody Rd. E16 4F 87
Coe Av. SE25 6G 157
Coe's All. EN5: Barn 4B 20
Cofferdam Way SE8 7D 104
Coffey St. SE8 7C 104
Cogan Av. E17 1A 50
Coin St. SE1 4J 13 (1A 102)
(not continuous)
Coity Rd. NW5 6E 64
Cokers La. SE21 1D 138
Coke St. E1 6G 85
Colas M. NW6 1J 81
Colbeck M. SE6 7F 123
Colbeck M. SW7 4K 99
Colbeck Rd. HA1: Harr 7G 41
Colberg Pl. N16 7F 49
Colbert SE5 1E 120
(off Sceaux Gdns.)
Colborne Cl. KT17: Ewe 6B 164
Colborne Ho. E14 7C 86
(off E. India Dock Rd.)
Colborne Way KT4: Wor Pk 3E 164
Colbrook Av. UB3: Harl 3F 93
Colbrook Cl. UB3: Harl 3F 93
Colburn Way SM1: Sutt 3B 166
Colby M. SE19 5E 138
Colby Rd. KT12: Walt T 7J 147
Colby Rd. SE19 5E 138
Colchester Av. E12 4D 70
Colchester Dr. HA5: Pinn 5B 40
Colchester Ho. E3 2C 86
(off Parnell Rd.)
Colchester Rd. E10 7E 50
Colchester Rd. E17 6C 50
Colchester Rd. HA6: Nwood 2J 39
Colchester Rd. HA8: Edg 7D 28
Colclough Ct. CR0: C'don 6C 156
(off Simpson Cl.)
Coldbath Sq. EC1 3J 7 (4A 84)
Coldbath St. SE13 1D 122
COLDBLOW 1J 145
Cold Blow Cres. DA5: Bexl 1K 145
Cold Blow La. SE14 7K 103
(not continuous)
Cold Blows CR4: Mitc 3D 154
Coldershaw Rd. W13 1A 96
Coldershaw Rd. W7 1A 96
Coldfall Av. N10 2E 46
Coldham Ct. N22 1B 48
Coldharbour E14 2E 104
Coldharbour Crest SE9 3E 142
Coldharbour Ind. Est. SE5 2C 120
Coldharbour La. SE5 3C 120
Coldharbour La. SW9 4A 120
Coldharbour La. UB3: Hayes 1J 93
Coldharbour Leisure Cen. 2D 142
Coldharbour Pl. SE5 2C 120
Coldharbour Rd. CR0: Wadd 5A 168
Coldharbour Way CR0: Wadd 5A 168
Coldstream Gdns. SW18 6H 117
Colebeck M. N1 6B 66
Colebert Av. E1 4J 85
Colebert Ho. E1 4J 85
(off Colebert Av.)
Colebrook Cl. NW7 6A 30
Colebrook Cl. SW15 7F 117
Colebrook Ct. SW3 4D 16 (4C 100)
(off Makins St.)
Colebrooke Av. W13 6B 78
Colebrooke Ct. DA14: Sidc 3B 144
Colebrooke Dr. E11 7A 52
Colebrooke Pl. N1 1B 84
Colebrooke Ri. BR2: Broml 2G 159
Colebrooke Row N1 2B 84
Colebrook Ho. E14 6D 86
(off Ellesmere St.)
Colebrook Ho. SE18 7E 106
Colebrook Rd. SW16 1J 155
Colebrook Way N11 5A 32
Coleby Path SE5 7D 102
Colechurch Ho. SE1 5G 103
(off Avondale Sq.)
Cole Cl. SE28 1B 108
Cole Ct. TW1: Twick 7A 114
Coledale Dr. HA7: Stan 1C 42
Colefax Bldgs. E1 6G 85
(off Plumber's Row)
Coleford Rd. SW18 5A 118
Cole Gdns. TW5: Cran 7J 93
Colegrave Rd. E15 5F 69
Colegrove Rd. SE15 6F 103
Coleherne Ct. SW5 5K 99
Coleherne Mans. SW5 5K 99
(off Old Brompton Rd.)
Coleherne M. SW10 5K 99
Coleherne Rd. SW10 5K 99
Colehill Gdns. SW6 2G 117
Colehill La. SW6 1G 117
Cole Ho. SE1 7K 13 (2A 102)
(off Baylis Rd.)
Coleman Cl. SE25 2G 157
Coleman Ct. SW18 7J 117
Coleman Flds. N1 1C 84
Coleman Mans. N8 7J 47
Coleman Rd. DA17: Belv 4G 109
Coleman Rd. RM9: Dag 6E 72
Coleman Rd. SE5 7E 102
Colemans Heath SE9 3E 142
Coleman St. EC2 7E 8 (6D 84)
Coleman St. Bldgs. EC2 7E 8 (6D 84)
(off Coleman St.)
Colenso Dr. NW7 7H 29
Colenso Rd. E5 4J 67
Colenso Rd. IG2: Ilf 1J 71
COLE PARK 6A 114
Cole Pk. Gdns. TW1: Twick 5A 114
Cole Pk. Rd. TW1: Twick 6A 114
Cole Pk. Vw. TW1: Twick 6A 114
Colepits Wood Rd. SE9 5H 125
Coleraine Rd. N8 3A 48
Coleraine Rd. SE3 6H 105
Coleridge Av. E12 6C 70
Coleridge Av. SM1: Sutt 4C 166
Coleridge Cl. SW8 2F 119
Coleridge Ct. EN5: New Bar 5E 20
(off Station Rd.)
Coleridge Ct. N1 1C 84
(off Dibden St.)
Coleridge Ct. SW1 3C 18 (4H 101)
(off Regency St.)
Coleridge Ct. W14 3F 99
(off Blythe Rd.)
Coleridge Dr. HA4: Ruis 6K 39
Coleridge Gdns. NW6 7A 64
Coleridge Gdns. SW10 7K 99
Coleridge Ho. SE17 5C 102
(off Browning St.)
Coleridge Ho. SW1 6A 18 (5G 101)
(off Churchill Gdns.)
Coleridge La. N8 6J 47
Coleridge Rd. CR0: C'don 7J 157
Coleridge Rd. E17 4B 50
Coleridge Rd. N12 5F 31
Coleridge Rd. N4 2A 66
Coleridge Rd. N8 6H 47
Coleridge Rd. TW15: Ashf 4A 128
Coleridge Sq. SW10 7A 100
(off Coleridge Gdns.)
Coleridge Sq. W13 6A 78
Coleridge Wlk. NW11 4J 45
Coleridge Way UB4: Hayes 6J 75
Coleridge Way UB7: W Dray 4A 92
Cole Rd. TW1: Twick 6A 114
Colesburg Rd. BR3: Beck 3B 158
Coles Cres. HA2: Harr 2F 59
Coles Grn. WD23: B Hea 1B 26
Coles Grn. Ct. NW2 2C 62
Coles Grn. Rd. NW2 1C 62
Coleshill Flats SW1 4H 17 (4E 100)
(off Pimlico Rd.)
Coleshill Rd. TW11: Tedd 6J 131
Colestown St. SW11 2C 118
Cole St. SE1 7D 14 (2C 102)
Colesworth Ho. HA8: Edg 2J 43
(off Burnt Oak B'way.)
Colet Cl. N13 6G 33
Colet Ct. W6 4F 99
(off Hammersmith Rd.)
Colet Flats E1 6A 86
(off Troon St.)
Colet Gdns. W14 4F 99
Colet Ho. SE17 5B 102
(off Doddington Gro.)
Colette Ct. SE16 2K 103
(off Eleanor Cl.)
Coley St. WC1 4H 7 (4K 83)
Colfe & Hatcliffe Glebe SE13 5D 122
(off Lewisham High St.)
Colfe Rd. SE23 1A 140
Colfes Leisure Cen. 6J 123
Colgate Ct. EN5: Barn 5B 20
(off Leecroft Rd.)
Colham Av. UB7: Yiew 1A 92
COLHAM GREEN 5C 74
Colham Grn. Rd. UB8: Hil 5C 74
Colham Mill Rd. UB7: W Dray 2A 92
Colham Rd. UB8: Hil 4B 74
COLHAM RDBT. 6C 74
Colina M. N15 4B 48
Colina Rd. N15 5B 48
Colin Cl. BR4: W W'ck 3H 171
Colin Cl. CR0: C'don 3B 170
Colin Cl. NW9 4A 44
Colin Ct. SE6 7B 122
Colin Cres. NW9 4B 44
COLINDALE 3K 43
Colindale Av. NW9 3K 43
Colindale Bus. Pk. NW9 3J 43
Colindale Gdns. NW9 3B 44
Colindale Retail Pk. 4K 43
Colindeep Gdns. NW4 4C 44
Colindeep La. NW4 4C 44
Colindeep La. NW9 3A 44
Colin Dr. NW9 5B 44
Colinette Rd. SW15 4E 116
Colin Gdns. NW9 4B 44
Colin Pde. NW9 4A 44
Colin Pk. Rd. NW9 4A 44
Colin Pond Ct. RM6: Chad H 4D 54
Colin Rd. NW10 6C 62
Colinsdale N1 1B 84
(off Camden Wlk.)
Colinton Rd. IG3: Ilf 2B 72
Colin Winter Ho. E1 4J 85
(off Nicholas Rd.)
Coliseum Theatre London 3E 12 (7J 83)
(off St Martin's La.)
Coliston Pas. SW18 7J 117
(off Coliston Rd.)
Coliston Rd. SW18 7J 117
Collamore Av. SW18 1C 136
Collapit Cl. HA1: Harr 6F 41
Collard Pl. NW1 7F 65
Collards Almshouses E17 5E 50
(off Maynard Rd.)
Collection Pl. NW8 1K 81
(off Bolton Pl.)
College App. SE10 6E 104
College Av. HA3: Hrw W 1J 41
College Cl. E9 5J 67
College Cl. HA3: Hrw W 7D 26
College Cl. N18 5A 34
College Cl. TW2: Twick 1H 131
College Ct. EN3: Pond E 5D 24
College Ct. NW3 6B 64
(off College Cres.)
College Ct. SW3 6F 17 (5D 100)
(off West Rd.)
College Ct. W5 7E 78
College Ct. W6 5E 98
(off Queen Caroline St.)
College Ct. Rd. EN3: Pond E 5D 24
College Cres. NW3 6A 64
College Cross N1 7A 66
College Dr. HA4: Ruis 7J 39
College Dr. KT7: T Ditt 7J 149
College E. E1 6K 9 (5F 85)
College Flds. Bus. Cen. SW19 1C 154
College Gdns. E4 7J 25
College Gdns. EN2: Enf 1J 23
College Gdns. IG4: Ilf 5C 52
College Gdns. KT3: N Mald 5B 152
College Gdns. N18 5B 34
College Gdns. SE21 1E 138
College Gdns. SW17 2C 136
College Grn. SE19 7E 138
College Gro. NW1 1G 83
College Hall WC1 4C 6 (4H 83)
College Hill EC4 2D 14 (7C 84)
College Hill Rd. HA3: Hrw W 7D 26
College Ho. SW15 5F 117
College Ho. TW7: Isle 7J 95
College La. NW5 4F 65
College Mans. NW6 1G 81
(off Salusbury Rd.)
College M. N1 7A 66
(off College Cross)
College M. SW1 1E 18 (3J 101)
(off Gt. College St.)
College M. SW18 5K 117
College of Arms 2C 14 (7C 84)
(off Queen Victoria St.)
College Pde. NW6 1G 81
(off Salusbury Rd.)
COLLEGE PARK 3D 80
College Pk. Cl. SE13 4F 123
College Pk. Rd. N17 6A 34
College Pl. E17 4G 51
College Pl. NW1 1G 83
College Pl. SW10 7A 100
College Point E15 6H 69
College Rd. BR1: Broml 1J 159
College Rd. BR8: Hext 7K 145
College Rd. CR0: C'don 2D 168
College Rd. E17 5E 50
College Rd. EN2: Enf 2J 23
College Rd. HA1: Harr 6J 41
College Rd. HA3: Hrw W 1J 41
College Rd. HA9: Wemb 1D 60
College Rd. N17 6A 34
College Rd. N21 2F 33
College Rd. NW10 2E 80
College Rd. SE19 5F 139
College Rd. SE21 7E 120
College Rd. SW19 6B 136
College Rd. TW7: Isle 1K 113
College Rd. W13 6B 78
COLLEGE RDBT. Kingston upon Thames 3E 150
College Row E9 5K 67
(off Homerton Gro.)
College Slip BR1: Broml 1J 159
College St. EC4 2D 14 (7C 84)
College Ter. E3 3B 86
College Ter. N3 2H 45
College Vw. SE9 1B 142
College Wlk. KT1: King T 3E 150
College Way RM8: Dag 4A 72
College Way TW15: Ashf 4B 128
College Way UB3: Hayes 7J 75
College Yd. NW5 4F 65
College Yd. NW6 1G 81
Collendale Rd. E17 3K 49
Collent St. E9 6J 67
Collerston Ho. SE10 5H 105
(off Armitage Rd.)
Colless Rd. N15 5F 49
Collett Rd. SE16 3G 103
Collett Way UB2: S'hall 2F 95
Collier Cl. E6 7F 89
Collier Cl. KT19: Ewe 6G 163
Collier Dr. HA8: Edg 2G 43
COLLIER ROW 1H 55
Collier Row La. RM5: Col R 1H 55
Collier Row Rd. RM5: Col R 1F 55
Colliers Ct. CR0: C'don 4D 168
(off St Peter's Rd.)
Colliers Shaw BR2: Kes 4B 172
Collier St. N1 1G 7 (2K 83)
Colliers Water La. CR7: Thor H 5A 156
COLLIERS WOOD 7B 136
COLLIERS WOOD 7B 136
Colliford Ct. HA8: Edg 4A 28
(off King's Dr.)
Collindale Av. DA15: Sidc 1A 144
Collindale Av. DA8: Erith 7H 109
Collingbourne Rd. W12 1D 98
Collingham Gdns. SW5 4K 99
Collingham Pl. SW5 4K 99
Collingham Rd. SW5 4K 99
Collings Cl. N22 6E 32
Collington St. SE10 5F 105
Collingtree Rd. SE26 4J 139
Collingwood Av. KT5: Surb 1J 163
Collingwood Av. N10 3E 46
Collingwood Cl. SE20 1H 157
Collingwood Cl. TW2: Whitt 7E 112
Collingwood Ct. EN5: New Bar 5E 20
Collingwood Ct. W5 5F 79
Collingwood Ho. E1 4H 85
(off Darling Row)
Collingwood Ho. SE16 2H 103
(off Cherry Gdn. St.)
Collingwood Ho. SW1 6C 18 (5H 101)
(off Dolphin Sq.)
Collingwood Ho. W1 5A 6 (5G 83)
(off Clipstone St.)
Collingwood Rd. CR4: Mitc 3C 154
Collingwood Rd. E17 6C 50
Collingwood Rd. N15 4E 48
Collingwood Rd. SM1: Sutt 3J 165
Collingwood Rd. UB8: Hil 4D 74
Collingwood St. E1 4H 85
Collins Av. HA7: Stan 2E 42
Collins Bldg. NW2 2E 62
Collins Ct. E8 6G 67
Collins Dr. HA4: Ruis 2A 58
Collins Ho. E14 7E 86
(off Newby Pl.)
Collins Ho. SE10 5H 105
(off Armitage Rd.)
Collinson Ct. SE1 7C 14 (2C 102)
(off Gt. Suffolk St.)
Collinson Ho. SE15 7G 103
(off Peckham Pk. Rd.)
Collinson Ho. SE3 4K 123
(off Wallace Ct.)
Collinson St. SE1 7C 14 (2C 102)
Collinson Wlk. SE1 7C 14 (2C 102)
Collins Path TW12: Hamp 6D 130
Collins Rd. N5 4C 66
Collins Sq. SE3 2H 123
Collins St. SE3 2G 123
(not continuous)
Collin's Yd. N1 1B 84
Collinwood Av. EN3: Enf H 3D 24
Collinwood Gdns. IG5: Ilf 5D 52
Collis All. TW2: Twick 1J 131
Collison Pl. N16 1E 66
Coll's Rd. SE15 1J 121
Collyer Av. CR0: Bedd 4J 167
Collyer Pl. SE15 1G 121
Collyer Rd. CR0: Bedd 4J 167
Colman Ct. HA7: Stan 6G 27
Colman Ct. N12 6F 31
Colman Pde. EN1: Enf 3K 23
Colman Rd. E16 5A 88
Colmans Wharf E14 5D 86
(off Morris Rd.)
Colmar Cl. E1 4K 85
Colmer Pl. HA3: Hrw W 7C 26
Colmer Rd. SW16 1J 155
Colmore M. SE15 1H 121
Colmore Rd. EN3: Pond E 4D 24

A–Z London 205

Colnbrook Ct. – Cooden Cl.

Colnbrook Ct. SL3: Poyle 4A 174
Colnbrook St. SE1 3B 102
Colne Ct. KT19: Ewe 4J 163
Colne Ct. W7 6H 77
(off High La.)
Colne Ho. IG11: Bark 7F 71
Colne Ho. NW8 4B 4 (4B 82)
(off Penfold St.)
Colne Pk. Cvn. Site UB7: W Dray 1D 174
Colne Reach TW19: Stanw M 7A 174
Colne Rd. E5 4A 68
Colne Rd. N21 7J 23
Colne Rd. TW1: Twick 1K 131
Colne Rd. TW2: Twick 1J 131
Colne St. E13 3J 87
COLNEY HATCH 6J 31
Colney Hatch La. N10 7K 31
Colney Hatch La. N11 6J 31
Colnmore Ct. E2 3K 85
(off Meath Cres.)
Coln Trad. Est. SL3: Poyle 4A 174
Cologne Rd. SW11 4B 118
Coloma Ct. BR4: W W'ck 4G 171
Colombo Cen. 5A 14 (1B 102)
(off Colombo St.)
Colombo Rd. IG1: Ilf 1G 71
Colombo St. SE1 5A 14 (1B 102)
Colomb St. SE10 5G 105
Colonel's Wlk. EN2: Enf 3G 23
Colonial Av. TW2: Whitt 6G 113
Colonial Ct. N7 3K 65
Colonial Dr. W4 4J 97
Colonial Rd. TW14: Felt 7G 111
Colonnade WC1 4E 6 (4J 83)
Colonnade, The SE1 6J 13 (2A 102)
(off Waterloo Rd.)
Colonnade, The SE8 4B 104
Colonnade Gdns. W3 1B 98
Colonnades, The W2 6K 81
Colonnades Leisure Pk., The 6A 168
Colonnade Wlk. SW1 4J 17 (4F 101)
Colony Mans. SW5 5K 99
(off Earl's Ct. Rd.)
Colony M. N1 5D 66
(off Mildmay Gro. Nth.)
Colorado Apts. N8 3K 47
(off Gt. Amwell La.)
Colorado Bldg. SE13 1D 122
(off Deal's Gateway)
Colosseum Apts. E2 2K 85
(off Palmers Rd.)
Colosseum Ter. NW1 2K 5 (3F 83)
(off Albany St.)
Colour Ct. SW1 5B 12 (1G 101)
(off Marlborough Rd.)
Colour Ho. SE1 7H 15 (2E 102)
(off Bell Yd M.)
Colour House Theatre Merton 1A 154
Colroy Ct. NW11 5G 45
Colson Rd. CR0: C'don 2E 168
Colson Way SW16 4G 137
Colstead Ho. E1 6H 85
(off Watney Mkt.)
Colsterworth Rd. N15 4F 49
(not continuous)
Colston Av. SM5: Cars 4C 166
Colston Ct. SM5: Cars 4D 166
Colston Rd. E7 6B 70
Colston Rd. SW14 4J 115
Coltash Ct. EC1 3D 8 (4C 84)
(off Whitecross St.)
Colthurst Cres. N4 2B 66
Colthurst Dr. N9 3C 34
Coltman Ho. SE10 6E 104
(off Welland St.)
Coltman St. E14 5A 86
Coltness Cres. SE2 5B 108
Colton Gdns. N17 3C 48
Colton Rd. HA1: Harr 5J 41
Coltsfoot Dr. UB7: Yiew 6A 74
Columbas Dr. NW3 1B 64
Columbia Av. HA4: Ruis 1K 57
Columbia Av. HA8: Edg 1H 43
Columbia Av. KT4: Wor Pk 7B 152
Columbia Gdns. SW6 6J 99
(off One Lillie Sq.)
Columbia Gdns. Nth. SW6 6J 99
(off Rickett St.)
Columbia Gdns. Sth. SW6 6J 99
(off Rickett St.)
Columbia Ho. E3 4B 86
(off Hamlets Way)
Columbia Point SE16 3J 103
(off Canada Est.)
Columbia Rd. E13 4H 87
Columbia Rd. E2 1J 9 (3F 85)
Columbia Rd. Flower Market
1K 9 (3F 85)
(off Columbia Rd.)
Columbia Sq. SW14 4J 115
Columbia Wharf EN3: Pond E 6F 25
Columbine Av. CR2: S Croy 7B 168
Columbine Av. E6 5C 88
Columbine Way SE13 2E 122
Columbus Ct. SE16 1J 103
(off Rotherhithe St.)
Columbus Ctyd. E14 1C 104
Columbus Gdns. HA6: Nwood 1J 39
Colva Wlk. N19 2F 65
Colvern Ho. RM7: Rom 5J 55
Colverson Ho. E1 5J 85
(off Lindley St.)
Colvestone Cres. E8 5F 67
Colview Ct. SE9 1B 142
Colville Est. N1 1E 84
Colville Est. W. E2 2K 9 (3F 85)
(off Turin St.)
Colville Gdns. W11 6H 81
(not continuous)
Colville Ho. E2 2J 85
(off Waterloo Gdns.)
Colville Ho's. W11 6H 81
Colville Mans. E20 5D 68
(off Victory Pde.)
Colville M. W11 6H 81
Colville Pl. W1 6C 6 (5H 83)
Colville Rd. E11 3E 68
Colville Rd. E17 2A 50
Colville Rd. N9 1C 34
Colville Rd. W11 6H 81
Colville Rd. W3 3H 97
Colville Sq. W11 6H 81
Colville Ter. W11 6H 81
Colvin Cl. SE26 5J 139
Colvin Gdns. E11 4K 51
Colvin Gdns. E4 3K 35
Colvin Gdns. IG6: Ilf 1G 53
Colvin Ho. W10 6F 81
(off Kingsdown Cl.)
Colvin Rd. CR7: Thor H 5A 156
Colvin Rd. E6 7C 70
Colwall Gdns. IG8: Wfd G 5D 36
Colwell Cres. EN3: Pond E 5D 24
Colwell Ho. KT12: Walt T 7H 147
(off Hepworth Way)
Colwell Rd. SE22 5F 121
Colwick Cl. N6 7H 47
Colwith Rd. W6 6E 98
Colwood Gdns. SW19 7B 136
Colworth Gro. SE17 4C 102
Colworth Rd. CR0: C'don 1G 169
Colworth Rd. E11 6G 51
Colwyn Av. UB6: G'frd 2K 77
Colwyn Cl. SW16 5G 137
Colwyn Cres. TW3: Houn 1G 113
Colwyn Grn. NW9 6A 44
(off Snowdon Dr.)
Colwyn Ho. SE1 2J 19 (3A 102)
Colwyn Rd. NW2 3D 62
Colyer Cl. SE9 2F 143
Colyers Cl. DA8: Erith 1K 127
Colyers La. DA8: Erith 1J 127
Colyers Wlk. DA8: Erith 1K 127
Colyton Cl. DA16: Well 1D 126
Colyton Cl. HA0: Wemb 6C 60
Colyton La. SW16 5A 138
Colyton Rd. SE22 5H 121
Colyton Way N18 5B 34
Combe, The NW1 2K 5 (3F 83)
Combe Av. SE3 7H 105
Combedale Rd. SE10 5J 105
Combe Ho. W2 5J 81
(off Gt. Western Rd.)
Combemartin Rd. SW18 7G 117
Combe M. SE3 7H 105
Comber Cl. NW2 3D 62
Comber Gro. SE5 7C 102
Comber Ho. SE5 7C 102
Combermere Rd. SM4: Mord 6K 153
Combermere Rd. SW9 3K 119
Comberton KT1: King T 2G 151
(off Eureka Rd.)
Comberton Rd. E5 2H 67
Combeside SE18 7K 107
Combwell Cres. SE2 3A 108
Comedy Store 3C 12 (7H 83)
(off Oxendon St.)
Comely Bank Rd. E17 5E 50
Comeragh M. W14 5G 99
Comeragh Rd. W14 5G 99
Comer Cres. UB2: S'hall 2G 95
(off Windmill Av.)
Comerford Rd. SE4 4A 122
Comer Ho. EN5: New Bar 4F 21
Comet Cl. E12 4B 70
Comet Ho. UB3: Harl 7E 92
Comet Pl. SE8 7C 104
(not continuous)
Comet Rd. TW19: Stanw 7A 110
Comet St. SE8 7C 104
Comfort St. SE15 6E 102
Commander Av. NW9 3C 44
Commerce Pk. CR0: Wadd 2K 167
Commerce Rd. N22 1K 47
Commerce Rd. TW8: Bford 6C 96
Commerce Way CR0: Wadd 2K 167
Commercial Rd. E1 7K 9 (6G 85)
Commercial Rd. E14 6A 86
Commercial Rd. N18 5K 33
Commercial Rd. Ind. Est. N18 6A 34
Commercial St. E1 4J 9 (4F 85)
Commercial Way NW10 2H 79
Commercial Way SE10 4H 105
Commercial Way SE15 7F 103
Commercial Wharf E8 1E 84
(off Kingsland Rd.)
Commerell Pl. SE10 5H 105
Commerell St. SE10 5G 105
Commodity Quay E1 3K 15 (7F 85)
Commodore Ct. SE8 1C 122
(off Albyn Rd.)
Commodore Ho. E14 7E 86
(off Poplar High St.)
Commodore Ho. E16 2K 105
(off Royal Crest Av.)
Commodore Ho. SW18 3A 118
Commodore St. E1 4A 86
Common, The E15 6G 69
Common, The HA7: Stan 2D 26
Common, The UB2: S'hall 4A 94
Common, The UB7: W Dray 1D 174
Common, The W5 7E 78
(not continuous)
Commondale SW15 2E 116
Commonfield La. SW17 5C 136
Common La. KT10: Clay 7A 162
Common Mile Cl. SW4 5H 119
Common Rd. HA7: Stan 4C 26
Common Rd. KT10: Clay 6A 162
Common Rd. SW13 3D 116
Commonside BR2: Kes 4A 172
Commonside E. CR4: Mitc 3E 154
Commonside W. CR4: Mitc 3D 154
Commonwealth Av. UB3: Hayes 6F 75
Commonwealth Av. W12 7D 80
(not continuous)
Commonwealth Memorial Gates
6J 11 (2F 101)
Commonwealth Rd. N17 7B 34
Commonwealth Way SE2 5B 108
Community Cl. TW5: Cran 1K 111
Community Cl. UB10: Ick 3D 56
Community La. N7 5H 65
Community Rd. E15 5F 69
Community Rd. UB6: G'frd 1G 77
Como Rd. SE23 2A 140
Como St. RM7: Rom 5K 55
Compass Bus. Pk. KT9: Chess 4G 163
Compass Cl. HA8: Edg 4A 28
Compass Cl. TW15: Ashf 7E 128
Compass Ct. SE1 5J 15 (1F 103)
(off Shad Thames)
Compass Hill TW10: Rich 6D 114
Compass Ho. E1 1H 103
(off Raine St.)
Compass Ho. SW18 4K 117
Compass La. BR1: Broml 1J 159
(off North St.)
Compass Point E14 7B 86
(off Grenade St.)
Compass Theatre 3E 56
Compayne Gdns. NW6 7K 63
Compayne Mans. NW6 6K 63
(off Fairhazel Gdns.)
Compter Pas. EC2 1D 14 (6C 84)
(off Wood St.)
Compton Av. E6 2B 88
Compton Av. HA0: Wemb 4C 60
Compton Av. N1 6B 66
Compton Av. N6 7C 46
Compton Cl. E3 5C 86
Compton Cl. HA8: Edg 7D 28
Compton Cl. NW1 2K 5 (3F 83)
(off Robert St.)
Compton Cl. NW11 3F 63
Compton Cl. SE15 7G 103
Compton Cl. W13 6A 78
Compton Ct. SE19 6E 138
Compton Ct. SM1: Sutt 4A 166
Compton Cres. KT9: Chess 5E 162
Compton Cres. N17 7H 33
Compton Cres. UB5: N'olt 1B 76
Compton Cres. W4 6J 97
Compton Ho. E20 5D 68
(off Peloton Av.)
Compton Ho. SW10 1A 118
Compton Ho. SW11 1C 118
Compton Leisure Cen. 6H 31
Compton Pas. EC1 3B 8 (4B 84)
Compton Pl. WC1 3E 6 (4J 83)
Compton Ri. HA5: Pinn 5C 40
Compton Rd. CR0: C'don 1H 169
Compton Rd. N1 6B 66
Compton Rd. N21 1G 33
Compton Rd. NW10 3F 81
Compton Rd. SW19 6H 135
Compton Rd. UB3: Hayes 7G 75
Compton St. EC1 3A 8 (4B 84)
Compton Ter. N1 6B 66
Compton Ter. N21 1F 33
Compton Ter. N4 6C 48
Comreddy Cl. EN2: Enf 1G 23
Comus Ho. SE17 4E 102
(off Comus Pl.)
Comus Pl. SE17 4E 102
Comyn Rd. SW11 4C 118
Comyns, The WD23: B Hea 1B 26
Comyns Cl. E16 5H 87
Comyns Rd. RM9: Dag 7G 73
Conant Ho. SE11 7K 19 (6B 102)
(off St Agnes Pl.)
Conant M. E1 7G 85
Concanon Rd. SW2 4K 119
Concert Hall App. SE1 5H 13 (1K 101)
Concord Bus. Cen. W3 4H 79
Concord Cl. UB5: N'olt 3B 76
Concord Ct. KT1: King T 3F 151
(off Winery La.)
Concord Ct. W4 6A 98
Concorde Cl. TW3: Houn 2F 113
Concorde Cl. UB10: Uxb 2A 74
Concorde Dr. E6 5D 88
Concorde Way SE16 4K 103
Concord Ho. CR0: C'don 6B 156
Concord Ho. KT3: N Mald 3A 152
Concord Ho. N17 7A 34
(off Park La.)
Concordia Wharf E14 1E 104
(off Coldharbour)
Concord Rd. EN3: Pond E 5C 24
Concord Rd. W3 4H 79
Concord Ter. HA2: Harr 2F 59
(off Coles Cres.)
Concourse, The N9 2B 34
(within Edmonton Grn. Shop. Cen.)
Concourse, The NW9 1B 44
(off Quakers Course)
Condell Rd. SW8 1G 119
Conder St. E14 6A 86
Condor Ho. E13 1J 87
(off Brooks Rd.)
Condor Path UB5: N'olt 2E 76
(off Union Rd.)
Condor Way TW6: H'row A 3C 110
Condover Cres. SE18 7F 107
Condray Pl. SW11 7C 100
Conduit Av. SE10 1F 123
Conduit Ct. WC2 2E 12 (7J 83)
(off Floral St.)
Conduit La. CR0: C'don 5G 169
Conduit La. CR2: S Croy 5G 169
Conduit La. EN3: Pond E 6F 25
Conduit La. N18 5D 34
Conduit M. SE18 5F 107
Conduit M. W2 1A 10 (6B 82)
Conduit Pas. W2 1A 10 (6B 82)
(off Conduit Pl.)
Conduit Pl. W2 1A 10 (6B 82)
Conduit Rd. SE18 5F 107
Conduit St. W1 2K 11 (7F 83)
Conduit Way NW10 7J 61
Conewood St. N5 3B 66
Coney Acre SE21 1C 138
Coneybear Point SE10 4J 105
Coney Burrows E4 2B 36
Coney Gro. UB8: Hil 3C 74
Coneygrove Path UB5: N'olt 6C 58
(off Arnold Rd.)
CONEY HALL 3G 171
Coney Hall Pde. BR4: W W'ck 3G 171
Coney Hill Rd. BR4: W W'ck 2G 171
Coney Way SW8 6K 101
Conference Cl. E4 2K 35
Conference Rd. SE2 4C 108
Confluence Plaza SE13 3E 122
(off Station Rd.)
Congers Ho. SE8 7C 104
Congleton Gro. SE18 5G 107
Congo Dr. N9 3D 34
Congo Rd. SE18 5H 107
Congress Rd. SE2 4C 108
Congreve Ho. N16 5E 66
Congreve Rd. SE9 3D 124
Congreve St. SE17 4E 102
Congreve Wlk. E16 5B 88
(off Fulmer Rd.)
Conical Cnr. EN2: Enf 2H 23
Conifer Cl. BR6: Orp 4H 173
Conifer Ct. TW15: Ashf 5B 128
(off The Crescent)
Conifer Gdns. EN1: Enf 6K 23
Conifer Gdns. SM1: Sutt 2K 165
Conifer Gdns. SW16 3K 137
Conifer Ho. SE4 4B 122
(off Brockley Rd.)
Conifers Cl. TW11: Tedd 7B 132
Conifer Way HA0: Wemb 3C 60
Conifer Way UB3: Hayes 7J 75
Coniger Rd. SW6 2J 117
Coningham Ct. SW10 7A 100
(off King's Rd.)
Coningham M. W12 1C 98
Coningham Rd. W12 2D 98
Coningsby Av. NW9 2A 44
Coningsby Cotts. W5 2D 96
Coningsby Ct. CR4: Mitc 2E 154
Coningsby Gdns. E4 6J 35
Coningsby Rd. CR2: S Croy 7C 168
Coningsby Rd. N4 7B 48
Coningsby Rd. W5 2D 96
Conington Rd. SE13 2D 122
Conisbee Ct. N14 5B 22
Conisborough Cres. SE6 3E 140
Conisbrough NW1 1G 83
(off Bayham St.)
Coniscliffe Cl. BR7: Chst 1E 160
Coniscliffe Rd. N13 3H 33
Coniston NW1 1A 6 (3G 83)
(off Harrington St.)
Coniston Av. DA16: Well 3J 125
Coniston Av. IG11: Bark 7J 71
Coniston Av. UB6: G'frd 3B 78
Coniston Cl. DA7: Bex 1J 127
Coniston Cl. DA8: Erith 7K 109
Coniston Cl. IG11: Bark 7J 71
Coniston Cl. N20 3F 31
Coniston Cl. SW13 7B 98
Coniston Cl. SW20 6F 153
Coniston Cl. W4 7J 97
Coniston Ct. NW7 7B 30
(off Langstone Way)
Coniston Ct. SE16 2K 103
(off Eleanor Cl.)
Coniston Ct. SM6: W'gton 4F 167
Coniston Ct. TW15: Ashf 3A 128
Coniston Ct. W2 1D 10 (6C 82)
(off Kendal St.)
Conistone Way N7 7J 65
Coniston Gdns. HA5: Eastc 4J 39
Coniston Gdns. HA9: Wemb 1C 60
Coniston Gdns. IG4: Ilf 4C 52
Coniston Gdns. N9 1D 34
Coniston Gdns. NW9 5K 43
Coniston Gdns. SM2: Sutt 6B 166
Coniston Ho. E3 4B 86
(off Southern Gro.)
Coniston Ho. SE5 7C 102
(off Wyndham Rd.)
Coniston Rd. BR1: Broml 6G 141
Coniston Rd. CR0: C'don 7G 157
Coniston Rd. DA7: Bex 1J 127
Coniston Rd. N10 2F 47
Coniston Rd. N17 6B 34
Coniston Rd. TW2: Whitt 6F 113
Coniston Wlk. E9 5J 67
Coniston Way KT9: Chess 3E 162
Conlan St. W10 4G 81
Conley Rd. NW10 6A 62
Conley St. SE10 5G 105
Connaught Av. E4 7K 25
Connaught Av. EN1: Enf 2K 23
Connaught Av. EN4: E Barn 1J 31
Connaught Av. SW14 3J 115
Connaught Av. TW15: Ashf 4A 128
Connaught Av. TW4: Houn 4C 112
Connaught Bri. E16 1B 106
Connaught Bus. Cen. CR0: Wadd
6K 167
Connaught Bus. Cen. CR4. Mitc
5D 154
Connaught Bus. Cen. NW9 5B 44
Connaught Cl. E10 2A 68
Connaught Cl. EN1: Enf 2K 23
Connaught Cl. SM1: Sutt 2B 166
Connaught Cl. UB8: Hil 4E 74
Connaught Cl. W2 1D 10 (6C 82)
Connaught Club, The 1C 36
Connaught Ct. E17 4D 50
(off Orford Rd.)
Connaught Ct. W2 1E 10 (6D 82)
(off Connaught St.)
Connaught Dr. NW11 4J 45
Connaught Gdns. N10 5F 47
Connaught Gdns. N13 4G 33
Connaught Gdns. SM4: Mord 4A 154
Connaught Hall WC1 3D 6 (4H 83)
Connaught Hgts. E16 1B 106
(off Agnes George Wlk.)
Connaught Hgts. UB10: Hil 4E 74
(off Uxbridge Rd.)
Connaught Ho. NW10 3D 80
(off Trenmar Gdns.)
Connaught Ho. W1 3J 11 (7F 83)
(off Davies St.)
Connaught La. IG1: Ilf 2G 71
Connaught Lodge N4 7A 48
(off Connaught Rd.)
Connaught M. NW3 4C 64
Connaught M. SE18 5E 106
Connaught M. SW6 1G 117
Connaught Pl. W2 2E 10 (7D 82)
Connaught Rd. E11 1F 69
Connaught Rd. E16 1B 106
Connaught Rd. E17 5C 50
Connaught Rd. E4 1B 36
Connaught Rd. EN5: Barn 6A 20
Connaught Rd. HA3: W'stone 1K 41
Connaught Rd. IG1: Ilf 2H 71
Connaught Rd. KT3: N Mald 4A 152
Connaught Rd. N4 7A 48
Connaught Rd. NW10 1A 80
Connaught Rd. SM1: Sutt 2B 166
Connaught Rd. TW10: Rich 5F 115
Connaught Rd. TW11: Tedd 5H 131
Connaught Rd. W13 7B 78
CONNAUGHT RDBT. 7B 88
(off Victoria Dock Rd.)
Connaught Sq. W2 1E 10 (6D 82)
Connaught St. W2 1C 10 (6C 82)
Connaught Way N13 4G 33
Connaught Works E3 1A 86
(off Old Ford Rd.)
Connect La. IG6: Ilf 2G 53
Connell Ct. SE14 6K 103
(off Myers La.)
Connell Cres. W5 4F 79
Connersville Way CR0: Wadd 3A 168
Conniffe Ct. SE9 5F 125
Conningham Ct. SE9 5A 124
Connington Cres. E4 3A 36
Connolly Ct. RM7: Rush G 6K 55
(off Union Rd.)
Connor Cl. E11 7G 51
Connor Cl. IG6: Ilf 1G 53
Connor Ct. SW11 1F 119
Connor Rd. RM9: Dag 4F 73
Connor St. E9 1K 85
Conolly Dell W7 1J 95
(off Conolly Rd.)
Conolly Rd. W7 1J 95
Conrad Ct. NW9 2A 44
(off Needleman Cl.)
Conrad Ct. SE16 4A 104
(off Cary Av.)
Conrad Dr. KT4: Wor Pk 1E 164
Conrad Ho. E14 7A 86
(off Victory Pl.)
Conrad Ho. E16 1K 105
(off Wesley Av.)
Conrad Ho. E8 6G 67
Conrad Ho. N16 5E 66
(off Matthias Rd.)
Conrad Ho. SW8 7J 101
(off Wyvil Rd.)
Consfield Av. KT3: N Mald 4C 152
Consort Ct. W8 3K 99
(off Wright's La.)
Consort Ho. E14 5D 104
(off St Davids Sq.)
Consort Ho. SW6 2A 118
(off Lensbury Av.)
Consort Ho. W2 7K 81
(off Queensway)
Consort Lodge NW8 1D 82
(off Prince Albert Rd.)
Consort M. TW7: Isle 5H 113
Consort Pk. 2H 121
(off Gordon Road)
Consort Rd. SE15 1H 121
Cons St. SE1 6K 13 (2A 102)
Constable Av. E16 1K 105
Constable Cl. N11 5J 31
Constable Cl. NW11 6K 45
Constable Cl. UB4: Hayes 2E 74
Constable Ct. SE16 5H 103
(off Stubbs Dr.)
Constable Ct. W4 5H 97
(off Chaseley Dr.)
Constable Cres. N15 5G 49
Constable Gdns. HA8: Edg 1G 43
Constable Gdns. TW7: Isle 5H 113
Constable Ho. E14 2C 104
(off Cassilis Rd.)
Constable Ho. NW3 7D 64
Constable Ho. UB5: N'olt 2B 76
(off Gallery Gdns.)
Constable M. BR1: Broml 2K 159
Constable M. RM8: Dag 4B 72
Constable Wlk. SE21 3E 138
Constabulary Cl. UB7: W Dray 3A 92
Constance Allen Ho. W10 6F 81
(off Bridge Cl.)
Constance Cl. SW15 4K 133
Constance Cres. BR2: Hayes 7H 159
Constance Rd. CR0: C'don 7B 156
Constance Rd. EN1: Enf 6K 23
Constance Rd. SM1: Sutt 4A 166
Constance Rd. TW2: Whitt 7F 113
Constance St. E16 1C 106
Constant Ho. E14 7D 86
(off Harrow La.)
Constantine Ct. E1 6G 85
(off Fairclough St.)
Constantine Ho. NW9 3B 44
(off Boulevard Dr.)
Constantine Ho. UB3: Hayes 6F 75
Constantine Pl. UB10: Hil 1B 74
Constantine Rd. NW3 4C 64
Constellation Way TW6: H'row A
3D 110
Constitution Hill SW1 6J 11 (2F 101)
Constitution Ri. SE18 1E 124
Consul Av. RM13: Rain 3K 91
Consul Av. RM9: Dag 3J 91
Consul Av. RM9: Rain 3J 91
Consul Ho. E3 4C 86
(off Wellington Way)
Container City 1 E14 7G 87
Container City 2 E14 7G 87
Contemporary Applied Arts
5B 14 (1B 102)
(off Southwark St.)
Content St. SE17 4D 102
Contessa Cl. BR6: Farnb 5J 173
Contrail Way TW6: H'row A 3D 110
Convair Wlk. UB5: N'olt 3B 76
Convent Cl. BR3: Beck 7E 140
Convent Cl. EN5: Barn 2C 20
Convent Gdns. W11 6G 81
Convent Gdns. W5 4C 96
Convent Hill SE19 6C 138
Convent Rd. TW15: Ashf 5D 128
Convent Way UB2: S'hall 4A 94
Conway Cl. BR3: Beck 1A 158
Conway Cl. HA7: Stan 6F 27
Conway Cres. RM6: Chad H 6C 54
Conway Cres. UB6: G'frd 2J 77
Conway Dr. SM2: Sutt 6K 165
Conway Dr. TW15: Ashf 6E 128
Conway Dr. UB3: Harl 3E 92
Conway Gdns. CR4: Mitc 4J 155
Conway Gdns. EN2: Enf 1K 23
Conway Gdns. HA9: Wemb 7C 42
Conway Gro. W3 5K 79
Conway Ho. E14 4C 104
(off Cahir St.)
Conway Ho. SW3 6F 17 (5D 100)
(off Ormonde Ga.)
Conway M. W1 4A 6 (4G 83)
(off Conway St.)
Conway Rd. N14 3D 32
Conway Rd. N15 5B 48
Conway Rd. NW2 2E 62
Conway Rd. SE18 4H 107
Conway Rd. SW20 1E 152
Conway Rd. TW13: Hanw 5B 130
Conway Rd. TW4: Houn 7D 112
Conway St. W1 4A 6 (4G 83)
(not continuous)
Conway Wlk. TW12: Hamp 6D 130
Conybeare NW3 7C 64
Conyers Cl. IG8: Wfd G 6B 36
Conyer's Rd. SW16 5H 137
Conyer St. E3 2A 86
Cooden Cl. BR1: Broml 7K 141

Cook Ct. SE16 1J **103**
(off Rotherhithe St.)
Cook Ct. SE8 5A **104**
(off Evelyn St.)
Cooke Cl. SE2 3C **108**
Cookes Cl. E11 2H **69**
Cookes La. SM3: Cheam 6G **165**
Cooke St. IG11: Bark 1G **89**
(not continuous)
Cookham Cl. UB2: S'hall 3F **95**
Cookham Cres. SE16 2K **103**
Cookham Dene Cl. BR7: Chst 1H **161**
Cookham Ho. E2 3J **9** (4F **85**)
(off Montclare St.)
Cookham Rd. BR8: Swan 7G **145**
Cookhill Rd. SE2 2B **108**
Cook Rd. RM9: Dag 1E **90**
Cook's Cl. RM5: Col R 1J **55**
Cooks Cl. E14 1C **104**
(off Cabot Sq.)
Cookson Gro. DA8: Erith 7H **109**
Cook's Rd. E15 2D **86**
Cooks Rd. SE17 6B **102**
Coolfin Rd. E16 6J **87**
Coolgardie Av. E4 5A **36**
Coolgardie Av. IG7: Chig 3K **37**
Coolgardie Rd. TW15: Ashf 5E **128**
Coolhurst Rd. N8 6H **47**
Coolhurst Tennis & Squash Club
6H **47**
Cool Oak La. NW9 7A **44**
Coomassie Rd. W9 4H **81**
COOMBE 7J **133**
Coombe Av. CR0: C'don 4E **168**
Coombe Bank KT2: King T 1A **152**
Coombe Cl. HA8: Edg 2F **43**
Coombe Cl. TW3: Houn 4E **112**
Coombe Cnr. N21 1G **33**
Coombe Ct. CR0: C'don 4D **168**
(off Coombe Rd.)
Coombe Cres. TW12: Hamp 7D **130**
Coombe Dene BR2: Broml 4H **159**
(off Cumberland Rd.)
Coombe Dr. HA4: Ruis 1K **57**
Coombe End KT2: King T 7K **133**
Coombefield Cl. KT3: N Mald 5A **152**
Coombe Gdns. KT3: N Mald 4B **152**
Coombe Gdns. SW20 2C **152**
Coombe Hill Glade KT2: King T 7A **134**
Coombe Hill Golf Course 7K **133**
Coombe Hill Rd. KT2: King T 7A **134**
Coombe Ho. N7 5H **65**
Coombe Ho. Chase KT3: N Mald 1K **151**
Coombehurst Cl. EN4: Cockf 2J **21**
Coombe La. CR0: C'don 5H **169**
Coombe La. SW20 1B **152**
COOMBE LANE 1B **152**
Coombe La. Flyover SW20 1B **152**
Coombe La. W. KT2: King T 1H **151**
Coombe Lea BR1: Broml 3C **160**
Coombe Lodge SE7 6A **106**
Coombe Neville KT2: King T 7K **133**
Coombe Pk. KT2: King T 5J **133**
Coombe Pl. KT2: King T 5J **133**
Coomber Ho. SW6 3K **117**
(off Wandsworth Bri. Rd.)
Coombe Ridings KT2: King T 5J **133**
Coombe Ri. KT2: King T 1J **151**
Coombe Rd. CR0: C'don 4D **168**
Coombe Rd. KT2: King T 1G **151**
Coombe Rd. KT3: N Mald 2A **152**
Coombe Rd. N22 2A **48**
Coombe Rd. NW10 3K **61**
Coombe Rd. SE26 4H **139**
Coombe Rd. TW12: Hamp 6D **130**
Coombe Rd. W13 3B **96**
Coombe Rd. W4 5A **98**
Coomber Way CR0: Bedd 7H **155**
Coombes Rd. RM9: Dag 1F **91**
Coombe Wlk. SM1: Sutt 3K **165**
Coombewood Dr. RM6: Chad H 6F **55**
Coombe Wood Golf Course 7H **133**
Coombe Wood Local Nature Reserve
7B **134**
Coombe Wood Rd. KT2: King T 5J **133**
Coombrook Ct. SE16 2A **104**
(off Elgar St.)
Coombs St. N1 1B **8** (2B **84**)
Coomer M. SW6 6H **99**
Coomer Pl. SW6 6H **99**
Coomer Rd. SW6 6H **99**
Cooms Wlk. HA8: Edg 1J **43**
Coope Ct. RM7: Rush G 6K **55**
(off Union Rd.)
Cooperage, The SE1 6J **15** (2F **103**)
(off Gainsford St.)
Cooperage, The SW8 7K **101**
(off Regent's Bri. Gdns.)
Cooperage Cl. N17 6A **34**
Cooperage Yd. E15 2E **86**
Co-operative Ho. SE15 3G **121**
Cooper Av. E17 1A **50**
Cooper Cl. SE1 7K **13** (2A **102**)
Cooper Ct. SE18 6F **107**
Cooper Cres. SM5: Cars 3D **166**
Cooper Ho. NW8 4A **4** (4B **82**)
(off Lyons Pl.)
Cooper Ho. SE4 5K **121**
(off St Norbert Rd.)
Cooper Ho. TW4: Houn 3D **112**
Cooper Rd. CR0: Wadd 4B **168**
Cooper Rd. NW10 5C **62**
Cooper Rd. NW4 6F **45**
Coopersale Cl. IG8: Wfd G 7F **37**
Coopersale Rd. E9 5K **67**
Coopers Cl. E1 4J **85**
Coopers Cl. RM10: Dag 6H **73**
Coopers Ct. E3 4B **86**
(off Eric St.)
Coopers Ct. TW7: Isle 2K **113**
(off Woodlands Rd.)
Coopers Ct. W3 1J **97**
(off Church Rd.)
Cooper's La. SE12 2K **141**
Coopers La. E10 1D **68**
Coopers La. E20 5D **68**
Coopers La. NW1 2H **83**
Coopers Lodge SE1 6J **15** (2F **103**)
(off Tooley St.)
Coopers M. BR3: Beck 2C **158**
Cooper's Rd. SE1 5F **103**
Coopers Row EC3 2J **15** (7F **85**)
Cooper St. E16 5H **87**
Coopers Wlk. E15 5G **69**
Cooper's Yd. SE19 6E **138**

Coopers Yd. N1 7B **66**
(off Upper St.)
Coote Gdns. RM8: Dag 3F **73**
Coote Rd. DA7: Bex 1F **127**
Coote Rd. RM8: Dag 3F **73**
Cope Ho. EC1 2D **8** (3C **84**)
(off Bath St.)
Copeland Dr. E14 4C **104**
Copeland Ho. SE11 2J **19** (3A **102**)
(off Lambeth Wlk.)
Copeland Ho. SW17 4B **136**
Copeland Rd. E17 6D **50**
Copeland Rd. SE15 2G **121**
Copeman Cl. SE26 5J **139**
Copenhagen Ct. SE8 4A **104**
(off Pell St.)
Copenhagen Gdns. W4 2K **97**
Copenhagen Ho. N1 1K **83**
(off Barnsbury Est.)
Copenhagen Pl. E14 6B **86**
(not continuous)
Copenhagen St. N1 1J **83**
Cope Pl. W8 3J **99**
Copers Cope Rd. BR3: Beck 7B **140**
Cope St. SE16 4K **103**
Copford Cl. IG8: Wfd G 6H **37**
Copford Wlk. N1 1C **84**
(off Popham St.)
Copgate Path SW16 6K **137**
Copinger Wlk. HA8: Edg 1H **43**
Copland Av. HA0: Wemb 5D **60**
Copland Cl. HA0: Wemb 5C **60**
Copland M. HA0: Wemb 6E **60**
Copland Rd. HA0: Wemb 6E **60**
Copleston M. SE15 2F **121**
Copleston Pas. SE5 2F **121**
Copleston Rd. SE15 3F **121**
Copley Cl. SE17 6C **102**
Copley Cl. W7 4K **77**
Copley Dene BR1: Broml 1B **160**
Copley Pk. SW16 6K **137**
Copley Rd. HA7: Stan 5H **27**
Copley St. E1 5K **85**
Coppard Gdns. KT9: Chess 6C **162**
Coppelia Rd. SE3 4H **123**
Coppen Rd. RM8: Dag 7F **55**
Copperas St. SE8 6D **104**
Copper Beech Cl. IG5: Ilf 1E **52**
Copperbeech Cl. NW3 5B **64**
Copper Beeches Ct. TW7: Isle 1H **113**
Copper Box Arena 6C **68**
Copper Cl. N17 7C **34**
Copper Cl. SE19 7F **139**
Copper Ct. E5 2J **67**
Copperdale Rd. UB3: Hayes 2J **93**
Copperfield Av. UB8: Hil 5C **74**
Copperfield Dr. N15 4F **49**
Copperfield Ho. SE1 7K **15** (2G **103**)
(off Wolseley St.)
Copperfield Ho. W1 5H **5** (5E **82**)
(off Marylebone High St.)
Copperfield Ho. W11 1F **99**
(off St Ann's Rd.)
Copperfield M. E2 2G **85**
(off Claredale St.)
Copperfield M. N18 4K **33**
Copperfield Rd. E3 4A **86**
Copperfield Rd. SE28 6C **90**
Copperfields BR3: Beck 1E **158**
Copperfields HA1: Harr 7J **41**
Copperfields TW16: Sun 6H **129**
Copperfields Ct. W3 2G **97**
Copperfield St. SE1 6B **14** (2B **102**)
Copperfield Way BR7: Chst 6G **143**
Copperfield Way HA5: Pinn 4D **40**
Coppergate Cl. BR1: Broml 1K **159**
Copper La. N16 4D **66**
Copperlight Apts. SW18 5J **117**
(off Buckhold Rd.)
Coppermead Cl. NW2 3E **62**
Copper M. W4 3J **97**
Copper Mill Dr. TW7: Isle 2K **113**
Coppermill Hgts. N17 3H **49**
(off Daneland Wlk.)
Copper Mill La. SW17 4A **136**
Coppermill La. E17 6J **49**
Copper Row SE1 5J **15** (1F **103**)
(off Horselydown La.)
Copperwood Pl. SE10 1E **122**
Copperworks, The N1 2J **83**
(off Railway St.)
Coppetts Cen. 7J **31**
Coppetts Cl. N12 7H **31**
Coppetts Rd. N10 7J **31**
Coppetts Wood & Glebelands Local Nature Reserve 6J **31**
Coppice, The DA5: Bexl 3K **145**
Coppice, The EN2: Enf 4G **23**
Coppice, The EN5: New Bar 6E **20**
(off Great Nth. Rd.)
Coppice, The TW15: Ashf 6D **128**
Coppice, The UB7: Yiew 6A **74**
Coppice Cl. BR3: Beck 4D **158**
Coppice Cl. HA4: Ruis 6F **39**
Coppice Cl. HA7: Stan 6E **26**
Coppice Cl. SW20 3E **152**
Coppice Dr. SW15 6D **116**
Coppice Wlk. N20 3D **30**
Coppice Way E18 4H **51**
Coppies Gro. N11 4A **32**
Copping Cl. CR0: C'don 4E **168**
Coppins, The CR0: New Ad 6D **170**
Coppins, The HA3: Hrw W 6D **26**
Coppock Cl. SW11 2C **118**
Coppsfield KT8: W Mole 3E **148**
Copse, The E4 1C **36**
Copse, The N2 3D **46**
Copse Av. BR4: W W'ck 2D **170**
Copse Cl. HA6: Nwood 2E **38**
Copse Cl. SE7 6K **105**
Copse Glade KT6: Surb 7D **150**
Copse Hill SM2: Sutt 7K **165**
Copse Hill SW20 1C **152**
COPSE HILL 7C **134**
Copse Vw. CR2: Sels 7K **169**
Copsewood Cl. DA15: Sidc 6J **125**
Copse Wood Way HA6: Nwood 1D **38**
Coptain Ho. SW18 4J **117**
Coptefield Dr. DA17: Belv 3D **108**
Copthall Av. EC2 7F **9** (6D **84**)
(not continuous)
Copthall Bldgs. EC2 7F **9** (6D **84**)
(off Copthall Av.)
Copthall Cl. EC2 7E **8** (6D **84**)
Copthall Dr. NW7 7H **29**

Copthall Gdns. NW7 7H **29**
Copthall Gdns. TW1: Twick 1K **131**
Copthall Rd. E. UB10: Ick 2C **56**
Copthall Rd. W. UB10: Ick 2C **56**
Copthorne Av. BR2: Broml 2D **172**
Copthorne Av. SW12 7H **119**
Copthorne Chase TW15: Ashf 4B **128**
Copthorne Cl. TW17: Shep 6E **146**
Copthorne M. UB3: Harl 4G **93**
Coptic St. WC1 6E **6** (5J **83**)
Copt Pl. NW7 6B **30**
Copwood Cl. N12 4G **31**
Coral Apts. E16 7J **87**
(off Western Gateway)
Coral Cl. RM6: Chad H 3D **54**
Coral Ho. E1 4A **86**
(off Harford St.)
Coral Ho. NW10 3G **79**
Coraline Cl. UB1: S'hall 3D **76**
Coralline Wlk. SE2 3C **108**
Coral Mans. NW6 1J **81**
(off Kilburn High Rd.)
Coral Row SW11 3A **118**
Coral St. SE1 7K **13** (2A **102**)
Coram Ho. W4 5A **98**
(off Wood St.)
Coram Ho. WC1 3E **6** (4J **83**)
(off Herbrand St.)
Coram Mans. WC1 4G **7** (4K **83**)
(off Millman St.)
Coram St. WC1 4E **6** (4J **83**)
Coran Cl. N9 7E **24**
Corban Rd. TW3: Houn 3E **112**
Corbar Cl. EN4: Had W 1G **21**
Corbden Cl. SE15 1F **121**
Corben M. SW8 2G **119**
Corbet Cl. SM6: W'gton 2E **166**
Corbet Ct. EC3 1F **15** (6D **84**)
Corbet Ho. N1 2A **84**
(off Barnsbury Est.)
Corbet Ho. SE5 7C **102**
(off Wyndham Rd.)
Corbet Pl. E1 5J **9** (5F **85**)
Corbett Av. KT8: E Mos 6H **149**
Corbett Ct. SE26 4B **140**
Corbett Gro. N22 7D **32**
Corbett Ho. SW10 6A **100**
(off Cathcart Rd.)
Corbett Rd. E11 6A **52**
Corbett Rd. E17 3E **50**
Corbetts La. SE16 4J **103**
(not continuous)
Corbetts Pas. SE16 4J **103**
(off Corbetts La.)
Corbetts Wharf SE16 2H **103**
(off Bermondsey Wall E.)
Corbicum E11 7G **51**
Corbidge Ct. SE8 6D **104**
Corbiere Ct. SW19 6F **135**
Corbiere Ho. N1 1D **84**
(off De Beauvoir Est.)
Corbin Ho. E3 3D **86**
(off Bromley High St.)
Corbins La. HA2: Harr 3F **59**
Corbould Cl. SM5: Cars 6D **166**
Corbridge N17 7C **34**
Corbridge Cres. E2 2H **85**
Corby Cres. EN2: Enf 4D **22**
Corbylands Rd. DA15: Sidc 7J **125**
Corbyn St. N4 1J **65**
Corby Rd. NW10 2K **79**
Corby Way E3 4C **86**
Cordage Ho. E1 1H **103**
(off Cobblestone Sq.)
Cordelia Cl. SE24 4B **120**
Cordelia Gdns. TW19: Stanw 7A **110**
Cordelia Ho. N1 2E **84**
(off Arden Est.)
Cordelia Rd. TW19: Stanw 7A **110**
Cordelia St. E14 6D **86**
Cordell Ho. N15 5F **49**
(off Newton Rd.)
Cordingley Rd. HA4: Ruis 2F **57**
Cording St. E14 5D **86**
Cordwainer Ho. E8 1H **85**
Cordwainers Ct. E9 7J **67**
(off St Thomas's Sq.)
Cordwainers Wlk. E13 2J **87**
Cord Way E14 3C **104**
Cordwell Rd. SE13 5G **123**
Corefield Cl. N11 2K **31**
Corelli Ct. SE1 4H **103**
Corelli Ct. SW5 4J **99**
(off W. Cromwell Rd.)
Corelli Rd. SE3 2C **124**
Corfe Av. HA2: Harr 4E **58**
Corfe Cl. TW4: Houn 1C **130**
Corfe Cl. UB4: Yead 6A **76**
Corfe Ho. SW8 7K **101**
(off Dorset Rd.)
Corfe Twr. W3 2H **97**
Corfield Rd. N21 5E **22**
Corfield St. E2 3H **85**
Corfton Lodge W5 5E **78**
Corfton Rd. W5 6E **78**
Coriander Av. E14 6F **87**
Coriander Ct. SE1 6K **15** (2F **103**)
(off Gainsford St.)
Cories Cl. RM8: Dag 2D **72**
Corinium Cl. HA9: Wemb 4F **61**
Corinne Rd. N19 4G **65**
Corinthian Manorway DA8: Erith 4K **109**
Corinthian Rd. DA8: Erith 4K **109**
Corinthian Way TW19: Stanw 7A **110**
Corkers Path IG1: Ilf 2G **71**
Corker Wlk. N7 2K **65**
Cork Ho. SW19 4K **135**
Corkran Rd. KT6: Surb 7D **150**
Corkscrew Hill BR4: W W'ck 2E **170**
Cork Sq. E1 1H **103**
Cork St. W1 3A **12** (7G **83**)
Cork St. M. W1 3A **12** (7G **83**)
(off Cork St.)
Cork Tree Ho. SE27 5B **138**
(off Lakeview Rd.)
Cork Tree Retail Pk. 5F **35**
Cork Tree Way E4 5F **35**
Corlett St. NW1 5C **4** (5C **82**)
Cormont Rd. SE5 1B **120**
Cormorant Cl. E17 7F **35**
Cormorant Ct. SE8 6B **104**
(off Pilot Cl.)
Cormorant Lodge E1 1G **103**
(off Thomas More St.)
Cormorant Pl. SM1: Sutt 5H **165**

Cormorant Rd. E7 5H **69**
Cornbury Ho. SE8 6B **104**
(off Evelyn St.)
Cornbury Rd. HA8: Edg 7J **27**
Corner Ho. DA15: Sidc 3A **144**
Cornelia Dr. UB4: Yead 4A **76**
Cornelia Ho. TW1: Twick 6D **114**
(off Denton Rd.)
Cornelia St. N7 6K **65**
Cornell Bldg. E1 6G **85**
(off Coke St.)
Cornell Cl. DA14: Sidc 6E **144**
Cornell Ct. EN3: Enf H 3F **25**
Cornell Gdns. EN4: E Barn 5K **21**
Cornell Ho. HA2: Harr 3D **58**
Cornell Sq. SW8 1H **119**
Corner, The W5 1E **96**
Corner Ct. E2 4H **85**
(off Three Colts La.)
Cornercroft SM3: Cheam 5F **165**
(off Wickham Av.)
Corner Fielde SW2 1K **137**
Corner Grn. SE3 2J **123**
Corner Ho. NW6 2K **81**
(off Oxford Rd.)
Corner HOUSE Arts Cen., The 1F **163**
Corner Ho. St. WC2 4E **12** (1J **101**)
(off Northumberland St.)
Corner Mead NW9 7G **29**
Cornerside TW15: Ashf 7E **128**
Cornerstone Ho. CR0: C'don 7C **156**
Corney Reach Way W4 7A **98**
Corney Rd. W4 6A **98**
Cornfield Cl. UB8: Uxb 2A **74**
Cornflower La. CR0: C'don 1K **169**
Cornflower Ter. SE22 6H **121**
Cornford Cl. BR2: Broml 5J **159**
Cornford Gro. SW12 2F **137**
Cornforth La. NW7 4K **29**
Cornhill EC3 1F **15** (6D **84**)
Cornick Ho. SE16 3H **103**
(off Slippers Pl.)
Cornish Ct. N9 7C **24**
Cornish Gro. SE20 1H **157**
Cornish Ho. SE17 6B **102**
(off Brandon Est.)
Cornish Ho. TW8: Bford 5F **97**
Corn Mill Dr. BR6: Orp 7K **161**
Cornmill Ho. RM7: Rom 6J **55**
Cornmill Ho. SE8 5C **104**
(off Wharf St.)
Cornmill La. SE13 3E **122**
Cornmow Dr. NW10 5B **62**
Cornshaw Rd. RM8: Dag 1D **72**
Cornthwaite Rd. E5 3J **67**
Cornwall Av. DA16: Well 3J **125**
Cornwall Av. E2 3J **85**
Cornwall Av. KT10: Clay 7A **162**
Cornwall Av. N22 1J **47**
Cornwall Av. N3 7D **30**
Cornwall Av. UB1: S'hall 5D **76**
Cornwall Cl. IG11: Bark 6K **71**
Cornwall Ct. HA5: Hat E 1D **40**
Cornwall Ct. W7 4K **77**
(off Copley Cl.)
Cornwall Cres. W11 6G **81**
Cornwall Dr. BR5: St P 7C **144**
Cornwall Gdns. NW10 6D **62**
Cornwall Gdns. SE25 4F **157**
Cornwall Gdns. SW7 3K **99**
Cornwall Gdns. Wlk. SW7 3K **99**
Cornwall Gro. W4 5A **98**
Cornwall Ho. SW7 3K **99**
(off Cornwall Gdns.)
Cornwallis Av. N9 2C **34**
Cornwallis Av. SE9 2H **143**
Cornwallis Ct. SW8 1J **119**
(off Lansdowne Grn.)
Cornwallis Gro. N9 2C **34**
Cornwallis Ho. SE16 2H **103**
(off Cherry Gdn. St.)
Cornwallis Ho. W12 7D **80**
(off India Way)
Cornwallis Rd. SE18 Gunnery Ter.
3G **107**
Cornwallis Rd. SE18 Warren La. 3F **107**
Cornwallis Rd. E17 4K **49**
Cornwallis Rd. N19 2J **65**
Cornwallis Rd. N9 2C **34**
Cornwallis Rd. RM9: Dag 4D **72**
Cornwallis Sq. N19 2J **65**
Cornwallis Wlk. SE9 3D **124**
Cornwall Mans. SW10 7A **100**
(off Cremorne Rd.)
Cornwall Mans. W14 3F **99**
(off Blythe Rd.)
Cornwall Mans. W8 2K **99**
(off Kensington Ct.)
Cornwall M. Sth. SW7 3A **100**
Cornwall M. W. SW7 3K **99**
Cornwall Pl. E4 4J **25**
Cornwall Rd. CR0: C'don 2B **168**
Cornwall Rd. HA1: Harr 6G **41**
Cornwall Rd. HA4: Ruis 3H **57**
Cornwall Rd. HA5: Hat E 1D **40**
Cornwall Rd. N15 5D **48**
Cornwall Rd. N18 5B **34**
Cornwall Rd. N4 7A **48**
Cornwall Rd. SE1 4J **13** (1A **102**)
Cornwall Rd. SM2: Sutt 7H **165**
Cornwall Rd. TW1: Twick 7A **114**
Cornwall Sq. SE11 5K **19** (5B **102**)
(off Seaton Cl.)
Cornwall St. E1 7H **85**
Cornwall Ter. NW1 4F **5** (4D **82**)
Cornwall Ter. M. NW1 4F **5** (4D **82**)
(off Allsop Pl.)
Corn Way E11 3F **69**
Cornwell Gdns. E10 7C **50**
Cornwood Cl. N2 5B **46**
Cornwood Dr. E1 6J **85**
Cornworthy Rd. RM8: Dag 5C **72**
Corona Bldg. E14 1E **104**
(off Blackwall Way)
Corona Rd. SE12 7J **123**
Coronation Av. N16 4F **67**
Coronation Cl. DA5: Bexl 6D **126**
Coronation Cl. IG6: Ilf 4G **53**
Coronation Ct. DA8: Erith 7K **109**
Coronation Ct. E15 6H **69**
Coronation Ct. KT1: King T 4E **150**
(off Surbiton Rd.)
Coronation Ct. W10 5E **80**
(off Brewster Gdns.)
Coronation Rd. E13 3A **88**

Coronation Rd. NW10 3G **79**
Coronation Rd. UB3: Harl 4H **93**
Coronation Vs. NW10 4H **79**
Coronation Wlk. TW2: Whitt 1E **130**
Coroner's Court City of London
2E **14** (7D **84**)
Coroner's Court North London 4C **20**
Coroner's Court Poplar 7D **86**
(off Poplar High St.)
Coroner's Court South London 3D **168**
(off Barclay Rd.)
Coroner's Court Southwark
6E **14** (2D **102**)
Coroner's Court St Pancras 1H **83**
Coroner's Court West London 1A **118**
Coroner's Court Westminster
3D **18** (4H **101**)
Coronet Pde. HA0: Wemb 6E **60**
Coronet St. N1 2G **9** (3E **84**)
Corporate Dr. TW13: Felt 3K **129**
Corporate Ho. HA3: Hrw W 1H **41**
Corporation Av. TW4: Houn 4C **112**
Corporation Row EC1 3K **7** (4A **84**)
Corporation St. E15 2G **87**
Corporation St. N7 5J **65**
Corrance Rd. SW2 4J **119**
Corri Av. N14 4C **32**
Corrib Ct. N13 3E **32**
Corrib Dr. SM1: Sutt 5C **166**
Corrigan Cl. NW4 3E **44**
Corringham Ct. NW11 7J **45**
Corringham Ho. E1 6K **85**
(off Pitsea St.)
Corringham Rd. HA9: Wemb 2G **61**
Corringham Rd. NW11 7J **45**
Corringway NW11 7K **45**
Corringway W5 4G **79**
Corris Grn. NW9 5A **44**
Corry Dr. SW9 4B **120**
Corry Ho. E14 7D **86**
(off Wade's Pl.)
Corsair Cl. TW19: Stanw 7A **110**
Corsair Ho. E16 2A **106**
(off Starboard Way)
Corsair Rd. TW19: Stanw 7A **110**
Corscombe Cl. KT2: King T 5J **133**
Corsehill St. SW16 6G **137**
Corsellis Sq. TW1: Isle 4B **114**
(off Varley Dr.)
Corsham St. N1 2F **9** (3D **84**)
Corsica St. N5 6B **66**
Corsley Way E9 6B **68**
Cortayne Ct. TW2: Twick 2J **131**
Cortayne Rd. SW6 2H **117**
Cortis Rd. SW15 6D **116**
Cortis Ter. SW15 6D **116**
Cortland Cl. IG8: Wfd G 1A **52**
Corunna Rd. SW8 1G **119**
Corunna Ter. SW8 1G **119**
Corvette Sq. SE10 6F **105**
Corwell Gdns. UB8: Hil 6E **74**
Corwell La. UB8: Hil 6E **74**
Coryton Path W9 4H **81**
(off Ashmore Rd.)
Cosbycote Av. SE24 5C **120**
Cosdach Av. SM6: W'gton 7H **167**
Cosedge Cres. CR0: Wadd 5A **168**
Cosgrove Cl. N21 2H **33**
Cosgrove Cl. UB4: Yead 4B **76**
Cosgrove Ho. E2 1G **85**
(off Whiston Rd.)
Cosgrove Ho. HA0: Wemb 1E **78**
(off Hatton Rd.)
Cosmo Pl. WC1 5F **7** (5J **83**)
Cosmopolitan Ct. EN1: Enf 5B **24**
Cosmopolitan Way TW6: H'row A
3D **110**
Cosmur Cl. W12 3B **98**
Cossall Wlk. SE15 2H **121**
Cossar M. SW2 5A **120**
Cosser St. SE1 2J **19** (3A **102**)
Costa St. SE15 2G **121**
Costemonger Bldg. SE16 3F **103**
(off Arts La.)
Coster Av. N4 1C **66**
Costons Av. UB6: G'frd 3H **77**
Costons La. UB6: G'frd 3H **77**
(not continuous)
Coston Wlk. SE4 4K **121**
Cosway Mans. NW1 5D **4** (5C **82**)
(off Shroton St.)
Cosway St. NW1 5D **4** (5C **82**)
Cotall St. E14 5C **86**
Coteford Cl. HA5: Eastc 5J **39**
Coteford St. SW17 4D **136**
Cotelands CR0: C'don 3E **168**
Cotesbach Rd. E5 3J **67**
Cotes Ho. NW8 4C **4** (4C **82**)
(off Broadley St.)
Cotesmore Gdns. RM8: Dag 4C **72**
Cotford Rd. CR7: Thor H 4C **156**
Cotham St. SE17 4C **102**
Cotherstone Ct. E2 4H **85**
(off Three Colts La.)
Cotherstone Rd. SW2 1K **137**
Cotleigh Av. DA5: Bexl 2D **144**
Cotleigh Rd. NW6 7J **63**
Cotleigh Rd. RM7: Rom 6K **55**
Cotman Cl. NW11 6A **46**
Cotman Cl. SW15 6F **117**
Cotman Gdns. HA8: Edg 2G **43**
Cotman Ho. NW8 2C **82**
(off Townshend Est.)
Cotman Ho. UB5: N'olt 2B **76**
(off Academy Gdns.)
Cotman M. RM8: Dag 5C **72**
(off Highgrove Rd.)
Cotmans Cl. UB3: Hayes 1J **93**
Coton Dr. UB10: Ick 3E **56**
Coton Rd. DA16: Well 3A **126**
Cotsford Av. KT3: N Mald 5J **151**
Cotswold Cl. DA7: Bex 2K **127**
Cotswold Cl. KT10: Hin W 2A **162**
Cotswold Cl. KT2: King T 6J **133**
Cotswold Cl. N11 4K **31**
Cotswold Ct. EC1 3C **8** (4C **84**)
(off Gee St.)
Cotswold Ct. UB6: G'frd 2K **77**
(off Hodder Dr.)
Cotswold Gdns. E6 3B **88**
Cotswold Gdns. IG2: Ilf 7H **53**
Cotswold Gdns. NW2 2F **63**
Cotswold Ga. NW2 1G **63**
Cotswold Grn. EN2: Enf 4E **22**
Cotswold M. SW11 1B **118**

Cotswold Ri. – Cranwell Cl.

Cotswold Ri. BR6: St M Cry 6K **161**
Cotswold Rd. TW12: Hamp 5E **130**
Cotswold St. SE27 4B **138**
Cotswold Way EN2: Enf 3E **22**
Cotswold Way KT4: Wor Pk 2E **164**
Cottage Av. BR2: Broml 1C **172**
Cottage Cl. E1 4J **85**
(off Mile End Rd.)
Cottage Cl. HA2: Harr 2H **59**
Cottage Cl. HA4: Ruis 1F **57**
Cottage Fld. Cl. DA14: Sidc 1C **144**
Cottage Grn. SE5 7D **102**
Cottage Gro. KT6: Surb 6D **150**
Cottage Gro. SW9 3J **119**
Cottage Pl. SW3 2C **16** (3C **100**)
Cottage Rd. KT19: Ewe 7K **163**
Cottage Rd. N7 5K **65**
(not continuous)
Cottages, The UB10: Ick 2A **56**
Cottage St. E14 7D **86**
Cottage Wlk. N16 3F **67**
Cottenham Dr. SW20 7D **134**
Cottenham Pde. SW20 2D **152**
COTTENHAM PARK 1D **152**
Cottenham Pk. Rd. SW20 1C **152**
(not continuous)
Cottenham Pl. SW20 7D **134**
Cottenham Rd. E17 4B **50**
Cotterill Rd. KT6: Surb 2E **162**
Cottesbrook St. SE14 7A **104**
Cottesloe Ho. NW8 3C **4** (4C **82**)
(off Jerome Cres.)
Cottesloe M. SE1 1K **19** (3A **102**)
(off Emery St.)
Cottesmore Av. IG5: Ilf 2E **52**
Cottesmore Ct. W8 3K **99**
(off Stanford Rd.)
Cottesmore Gdns. W8 3K **99**
Cottesmore Ho. UB10: Ick 2E **56**
Cottimore Av. KT12: Walt T 7K **147**
Cottimore Cres. KT12: Walt T 7K **147**
Cottimore La. KT12: Walt T 7K **147**
Cottimore Ter. KT12: Walt T 7K **147**
Cottingham Chase HA4: Ruis 3J **57**
Cottingham Rd. SE20 7K **139**
Cottingham Rd. SW8 7K **101**
Cottington Rd. TW13: Hanw 4B **130**
Cottington St. SE11 5K **19** (5A **102**)
Cottle Way SE16 2H **103**
(off Paradise St.)
Cotton Apts. E1 5K **85**
(off Killick Way)
Cotton Av. W3 6K **79**
Cotton Cl. CR4: Mitc 3C **154**
Cotton Cl. E11 2G **69**
Cotton Cl. RM9: Dag 7C **72**
Cottongrass Cl. CR0: C'don 1K **169**
Cottonham Cl. N12 5G **31**
Cotton Hill BR1: Broml 4E **140**
Cotton Ho. SW2 7J **119**
Cotton Row SW11 3A **118**
Cottons App. RM7: Rom 5K **55**
Cottons Cen. SE1 4G **15** (1E **102**)
Cottons Ct. RM7: Rom 5K **55**
Cotton's Gdns. E2 1H **9** (3E **84**)
Cottons La. SE1 4F **15** (1D **102**)
Cotton St. E14 7E **86**
Cotton Way SM6: W'gton 2E **166**
Cottonwood Cl. BR6: Farnb 4F **173**
Cottonworks Ho. N7 3K **65**
(off Seven Sisters Rd.)
Cottrell Ct. SE10 4H **105**
(off Hop St.)
Cottrill Gdns. E8 6H **67**
Cotts Cl. W7 5K **77**
Couchmore Av. IG5: Ilf 2D **52**
Coulgate St. SE4 3A **122**
Coulson Cl. RM8: Dag 1C **72**
Coulson St. SW3 5E **16** (5D **100**)
Coulter Cl. UB4: Yead 4C **76**
Coulter Rd. W6 3D **98**
Coulthurst Ct. SW16 7J **137**
(off Heybridge Av.)
Councillor St. SE5 7C **102**
Counter Ct. SE1 5E **14** (1D **102**)
(off Borough High St.)
Counter Ho. E1 7G **85**
Counters Ct. W14 3G **99**
(off Holland Rd.)
Counter St. SE1 4G **15** (1E **102**)
Countess Rd. NW5 5G **65**
Countisbury Av. EN1: Enf 7A **24**
Country Way TW13: Hanw 6K **129**
County Court Brentford 6D **96**
County Court Bromley 1J **159**
County Court Central London
4K **5** (4F **83**)
(off Park Cres.)
County Court Clerkenwell & Shoreditch
3C **8** (4C **84**)
County Court Croydon 2D **168**
County Court Edmonton 6B **34**
County Court Kingston upon Thames
2D **150**
County Court Uxbridge 5H **75**
County Court Wandsworth 5G **117**
County Court West London 5F **99**
(off Talgarth Rd.)
County Court Willesden 2B **80**
County Gdns. TW7: Isle 4H **113**
County Ga. EN5: New Bar 6E **20**
County Ga. SE9 3G **143**
County Ground Beckenham, The
6C **140**
County Gro. SE5 1C **120**
County Hall Apts. SE1 7G **13** (2K **101**)
(off Westminster Bri. Rd.)
County Hall (Former) 6G **13** (2K **101**)
(off Westminster Bri. Rd.)
County Ho. BR3: Beck 1A **158**
County Ho. SW9 1A **120**
(off Brixton Rd.)
County Rd. CR7: Thor H 2B **156**
County Rd. E6 5F **89**
County St. SE1 3C **102**
Coupland Pl. SE18 5G **107**
Courage Stadium 5K **159**
Courcy Rd. N8 3A **48**
Courier Rd. RM9: Dag 4J **91**
Courland Gro. SW8 1H **119**
Courland St. SW8 1H **119**
Course, The SE9 3E **142**
Court, The HA4: Ruis 4C **58**
Court Annexe 7D **14** (2C **102**)
Courtauld Cl. SE28 1A **108**
Courtauld Gallery 2G **13** (7K **83**)
(off Strand)
Courtauld Ho. E2 1G **85**
(off Goldsmiths Row)
Courtauld Institute of Art, The
2G **13** (7K **83**)
(off Strand)
Courtauld Rd. N19 1J **65**
Court Av. DA17: Belv 5F **109**
Court Cl. HA3: Kenton 3E **42**
Court Cl. NW8 7B **64**
(off Boydell Ct.)
Court Cl. SM6: W'gton 7H **167**
Court Cl. TW2: Twick 3F **131**
Court Cl. Av. TW2: Twick 3F **131**
Court Cres. KT9: Chess 5D **162**
Court Downs Rd. BR3: Beck 2D **158**
Court Dr. CR0: Wadd 4K **167**
Court Dr. HA7: Stan 4K **27**
Court Dr. SM1: Sutt 4C **166**
Court Dr. UB10: Hil 1B **74**
Courtenay Av. HA3: Hrw W 7B **26**
Courtenay Av. N6 7C **46**
Courtenay Av. SM2: Sutt 7J **165**
Courtenay Dr. BR3: Beck 2F **159**
Courtenay Gdns. HA3: Hrw W 2G **41**
Courtenay Ho. CR0: C'don 7C **156**
(off Oakfield Rd.)
Courtenay M. E17 5A **50**
Courtenay Pl. E17 5A **50**
Courtenay Rd. E11 3H **69**
Courtenay Rd. E17 4K **49**
Courtenay Rd. HA9: Wemb 3D **60**
Courtenay Rd. KT4: Wor Pk 3E **164**
Courtenay Rd. SE20 6K **139**
Courtenay Sq. SE11 6J **19** (5A **102**)
Courtenay St. SE11 5J **19** (5A **102**)
Courtens M. HA7: Stan 7H **27**
Court Farm Av. KT19: Ewe 5K **163**
Court Farm La. UB5: N'olt 7E **58**
Court Farm Rd. SE9 2B **142**
Court Farm Rd. UB5: N'olt 7E **58**
Courtfield W5 5C **78**
Courtfield Av. HA1: Harr 5K **41**
Courtfield Cres. HA1: Harr 5K **41**
Courtfield Gdns. HA4: Ruis 2H **57**
Courtfield Gdns. SW5 4K **99**
Courtfield Gdns. W13 6A **78**
Courtfield Ho. EC1 5J **7** (5A **84**)
(off Baldwins Gdns.)
Courtfield M. SW5 4A **100**
Courtfield Ri. BR4: W W'ck 3F **171**
Courtfield Rd. SW7 4A **100**
Courtfield Rd. TW15: Ashf 6D **128**
Court Gdns. N1 6A **66**
Court Gdns. N7 6A **66**
Courtgate Cl. NW7 6G **29**
Courthill Rd. SE13 4E **122**
Courthope Ho. SE16 3J **103**
(off Lower Rd.)
Courthope Ho. SW8 7J **101**
(off Hartington Rd.)
Courthope Rd. NW3 4D **64**
Courthope Rd. SW19 5G **135**
Courthope Rd. UB6: G'frd 2H **77**
Courthope Vs. SW19 7G **135**
Courthouse, The SW1 2E **18** (3J **101**)
(off Horseferry Rd.)
Courthouse Gdns. N3 6D **30**
Courthouse La. N16 4F **67**
Courthouse Rd. N12 6E **30**
Courthouse Way SW18 5K **117**
Courtland Av. E4 2C **36**
Courtland Av. IG1: Ilf 2D **70**
Courtland Av. NW7 3E **28**
Courtland Av. SW16 7K **137**
Courtland Gro. SE28 6D **90**
Courtland Ho. SE20 1G **157**
Courtland Rd. E6 1C **88**
Courtlands KT12: Walt T 7J **147**
Courtlands TW10: Rich 5G **115**
Courtlands Av. BR2: Hayes 1G **171**
Courtlands Av. SE12 5K **123**
Courtlands Av. TW12: Hamp 6D **130**
Courtlands Av. TW9: Kew 2H **115**
Courtlands Cl. HA4: Ruis 7H **39**
Courtlands Dr. KT19: Ewe 6A **164**
Courtlands Rd. KT5: Surb 7G **151**
Court La. SE21 6E **120**
Court La. Gdns. SE21 7E **120**
Courtleet Dr. DA8: Erith 1H **127**
Courtleigh NW11 5H **45**
Courtleigh Gdns. NW11 4G **45**
Court Lodge DA17: Belv 5G **109**
Court Lodge SW1 4G **17** (4E **100**)
(off Sloane Sq.)
Courtman Rd. N17 7H **33**
Court Mead UB5: N'olt 3D **76**
Courtmead Cl. SE24 6C **120**
Court M. SE13 6G **123**
Courtnell St. W2 6J **81**
Courtney Cl. SE19 6E **138**
Courtney Ct. N7 5A **66**
Courtney Cres. SM5: Cars 7D **166**
Courtney Ho. NW4 3E **44**
(off Mulberry Cl.)
Courtney Ho. W14 3G **99**
(off Russell Rd.)
Courtney Pl. CR0: Wadd 3A **168**
Courtney Rd. CR0: Wadd 3A **168**
Courtney Rd. N7 5A **66**
Courtney Rd. SW19 7C **136**
Courtney Rd. TW6: H'row A 3C **110**
Courtney Way TW6: H'row A 2C **110**
Court Pde. HA0: Wemb 3B **60**
Courtrai Rd. SE23 6A **122**
Court Rd. SE25 2F **157**
Court Rd. SE9 6D **124**
Court Rd. UB10: Ick 5D **56**
Court Rd. UB2: S'hall 4D **94**
Court Royal SW15 5G **117**
Courtside N8 6H **47**
Courtside SE26 3H **139**
Court St. BR1: Broml 2J **159**
Court St. E1 5H **85**
Courtville Ho. W10 3G **81**
(off Third Av.)
Court Way NW9 4A **44**
Court Way TW2: Twick 7K **113**
Court Way W3 5J **79**
Courtway IG6: Ilf 3G **53**
Courtway IG8: Wfd G 5F **37**
Court Yd. SE9 6D **124**
Courtyard SW3 5E **16** (5D **100**)
(off Smith St.)
Courtyard, The BR2: Kes 6C **172**
Courtyard, The E2 1K **9** (3F **85**)
(off Ezra St.)
Courtyard, The EC3 1F **15** (6D **84**)
(within Royal Exchange)
Courtyard, The N1 7K **65**
Courtyard, The NW1 7E **64**
Courtyard, The SE14 1K **121**
(off Besson St.)
Courtyard, The SW3 7B **16** (6B **100**)
(off Trident Pl.)
Courtyard Apts. E1 3K **9** (4F **85**)
(off Sclater St.)
Courtyard Ho. SW6 2A **118**
(off Lensbury Av.)
Courtyard M. BR5: St P 7A **144**
Courtyard Theatre Hoxton 2G **9** (3E **84**)
Cousin La. EC4 3E **14** (7D **84**)
Cousins Cl. UB7: Yiew 7A **74**
Couthurst Rd. SE3 6K **105**
Coutts Av. KT9: Chess 5E **162**
Coutt's Cres. NW5 3E **64**
Couzens Ho. E3 5B **86**
(off Weatherley Cl.)
Coval Gdns. SW14 4H **115**
Coval La. SW14 4H **115**
Coval Pas. SW14 4J **115**
Coval Rd. SW14 4H **115**
Covelees Wall E6 6E **88**
Covell Ct. EN2: Enf 1E **22**
(off The Ridgeway)
Covell Ct. SE8 7C **104**
COVENT GARDEN 2F **13** (7J **83**)
Covent Gdn. WC2 2F **13** (7J **83**)
Covent Garden Piazza WC2 2F **13** (7J **83**)
(off Covent Garden)
Coventry Cl. E6 6D **88**
Coventry Cl. NW6 2J **81**
Coventry Hall SW16 5J **137**
Coventry Rd. E1 4H **85**
Coventry Rd. E2 4H **85**
Coventry Rd. IG1: Ilf 2F **71**
Coventry Rd. SE25 4G **157**
Coventry St. W1 3C **12** (7H **83**)
Coventry University London RM10: Dag
2H **73**
Coverack Cl. CR0: C'don 7A **158**
Coverack Cl. N14 6B **22**
Coverdale Cl. HA7: Stan 5G **27**
Coverdale Gdns. CR0: C'don 3F **169**
Coverdale Rd. N11 6K **31**
Coverdale Rd. NW2 7F **63**
Coverdale Rd. W12 2D **98**
Coverdales, The IG11: Bark 2H **89**
Coverham Ho. SE4 4K **121**
(off Billingford Cl.)
Coverley Cl. E1 5G **85**
Coverley Point SE11 4G **19** (4K **101**)
(off Tyers St.)
Covert, The BR6: Pet W 6J **161**
Covert, The HA6: Nwood 1E **38**
Covert, The SE19 7F **139**
(off Fox Hill)
Coverton Rd. SW17 5C **136**
Covert Way EN4: Had W 2F **21**
Covet Wood Cl. BR5: St M Cry 6K **161**
Covey Cl. SW19 2K **153**
Covey Rd. KT4: Wor Pk 2F **165**
Covington Gdns. SW16 7B **138**
Covington Way SW16 6K **137**
(not continuous)
Cowan Cl. E6 5C **88**
Cowbridge La. IG11: Bark 7F **71**
Cowbridge Rd. HA3: Kenton 4F **43**
Cowcross St. EC1 5A **8** (5B **84**)
Cowdenbeath Path N1 1K **83**
Cowden Rd. BR6: Orp 7K **161**
Cowden St. SE6 4C **140**
Cowdray Rd. UB10: Hil 1E **74**
Cowdrey Cl. EN1: Enf 2K **23**
Cowdrey M. SE6 4C **140**
Cowdrey Rd. SW19 5K **135**
Cowen Av. HA2: Harr 2H **59**
Cowgate Rd. UB6: G'frd 3H **77**
Cowick Rd. SW17 4D **136**
Cowings Mead UB5: N'olt 6C **58**
Cowland Av. EN3: Pond E 4D **24**
Cow La. UB6: G'frd 2H **77**
Cow Leaze E6 6E **88**
Cowleaze Rd. KT2: King T 1E **150**
Cowley La. E11 3G **69**
COWLEY PEACHEY 6A **74**
Cowley Pl. NW4 5E **44**
Cowley Rd. E11 5K **51**
Cowley Rd. IG1: Ilf 7D **52**
Cowley Rd. SW14 3A **116**
Cowley Rd. SW9 1A **120**
(not continuous)
Cowley Rd. W3 1B **98**
Cowley St. SW1 1E **18** (3J **101**)
Cowling Cl. W11 1G **99**
Cowper Av. E6 7C **70**
Cowper Av. SM1: Sutt 4B **166**
Cowper Cl. BR2: Broml 4B **160**
Cowper Cl. DA16: Well 5A **126**
Cowper Gdns. N14 6A **22**
Cowper Gdns. SM6: W'gton 6G **167**
Cowper Ho. SE17 5C **102**
(off Browning St.)
Cowper Ho. SW1 6D **18** (5H **101**)
(off Aylesford St.)
Cowper Rd. BR2: Broml 4B **160**
Cowper Rd. DA17: Belv 4G **109**
Cowper Rd. KT2: King T 5F **133**
Cowper Rd. N14 1A **32**
Cowper Rd. N16 5E **66**
Cowper Rd. N18 5B **34**
Cowper Rd. SW19 6A **136**
Cowper Rd. W3 1K **97**
Cowper Rd. W7 7K **77**
Cowper's Ct. EC3 1F **15** (6D **84**)
(off Birchin La.)
Cowper St. EC2 3F **9** (4D **84**)
Cowper Ter. W10 5F **81**
Cowslip Cl. UB10: Uxb 7A **56**
Cowslip Rd. E18 2K **51**
Cowthorpe Rd. SW8 1H **119**
Cox Ct. EN4: E Barn 4H **21**
Coxe Pl. HA3: W'stone 4A **42**
Cox Ho. W6 6G **99**
(off Field Rd.)
Cox La. KT19: Ewe 5H **163**
(not continuous)
Cox La. KT9: Chess 4F **163**
Coxmount Rd. SE7 5B **106**
Coxs Av. TW17: Shep 3G **147**
Coxson Way SE1 7J **15** (2F **103**)
Cox's Wlk. SE21 1G **139**
Coxwell Blvd. NW9 7G **29**
Coxwell Rd. SE18 5H **107**
Coxwell Rd. SE19 7E **138**
Coxwold Path KT9: Chess 7E **162**
Coyle Dr. UB10: Ick 2E **56**
Crabbs Cft. Cl. BR6: Farnb 5G **173**
Crab Hill BR3: Beck 7F **141**
Crabtree Av. HA0: Wemb 2E **78**
Crabtree Av. RM6: Chad H 4D **54**
Crabtree Cl. E2 2F **85**
Crabtree Ct. EN5: New Bar 4E **20**
Crabtree Hall SW6 7E **98**
(off Crabtree La.)
Crabtree La. SW6 7E **98**
(not continuous)
Crabtree Manorway Nth. DA17: Belv
2J **109**
Crabtree Manorway Nth. DA17: Erith
2J **109**
Crabtree Manorway Sth. DA17: Belv
3J **109**
Crabtree Pl. W1 6B **6** (5G **83**)
Crabtree Wlk. CR0: C'don 1G **169**
Crace St. NW1 1C **6** (3H **83**)
Craddock Rd. EN1: Enf 3A **24**
Craddock St. NW5 6E **64**
Cradford Ho. Nth. E2 3K **85**
Cradford Ho. Sth. E2 3K **85**
Cradley Rd. SE9 1H **143**
Craft M. E10 2D **68**
Crafts Council & Gallery 2A **84**
Cragie Ho. SE1 4F **103**
(off Balaclava Rd.)
Craig Dr. UB8: Hil 6D **74**
Craigen Av. CR0: C'don 1H **169**
Craigen Gdns. IG3: Ilf 4J **71**
Craigerne Rd. SE3 7K **105**
Craig Gdns. E18 2H **51**
Craigholm SE18 2E **124**
Craig Ho. E17 4C **50**
(off High St.)
Craigmore Ct. HA6: Nwood 1G **39**
Craigmuir Pk. HA0: Wemb 1F **79**
Craignair Rd. SW2 7A **120**
Craignish Av. SW16 2K **155**
Craig Pk. Rd. N18 4C **34**
Craig Rd. TW10: Ham 4C **132**
Craig's Ct. SW1 4E **12** (1J **101**)
Craigton Rd. SE9 4D **124**
Craigweil Cl. HA7: Stan 5J **27**
Craigweil Dr. HA7: Stan 5J **27**
Craigwell Av. TW13: Felt 3J **129**
Craik Ct. NW6 2H **81**
(off Carlton Vale)
Crail Row SE17 4D **102**
Crales Ho. SE18 3C **106**
Cramer St. W1 6H **5** (5E **82**)
Crammond Cl. W6 6G **99**
Cramond Ct. TW14: Bedf 1G **129**
Cramonde Ct. DA16: Well 2A **126**
Crampton Ho. SW8 1G **119**
Crampton Rd. SE20 6J **139**
Crampton St. SE17 4C **102**
Cranberry Cl. NW7 6G **29**
Cranberry Cl. UB5: N'olt 2B **76**
Cranberry Ent. Pk. N17 7A **34**
(off White Hart La.)
Cranberry La. E16 4G **87**
Cranborne Av. KT6: Surb 3G **163**
Cranborne Av. UB2: S'hall 4E **94**
Cranborne Rd. IG11: Bark 1H **89**
Cranborne Waye UB4: Yead 6K **75**
(not continuous)
Cranbourn All. WC2 2D **12** (7H **83**)
(off Cranbourn St.)
Cranbourne NW1 7H **65**
(off Agar Gro.)
Cranbourne Av. E11 4K **51**
Cranbourne Cl. SW16 3J **155**
Cranbourne Ct. SW11 7C **100**
(off Albert Bri. Rd.)
Cranbourne Dr. HA5: Pinn 5B **40**
Cranbourne Gdns. IG6: Ilf 3G **53**
Cranbourne Gdns. NW11 5G **45**
Cranbourne Rd. E12 5C **70**
Cranbourne Rd. E15 4E **68**
Cranbourne Rd. HA6: Nwood 3H **39**
Cranbourne Rd. N10 2F **47**
Cranbourn Ho. SE16 2H **103**
(off Marigold St.)
Cranbourn Pas. SE16 2H **103**
Cranbourn St. WC2 2D **12** (7H **83**)
CRANBROOK 1D **70**
Cranbrook NW1 1G **83**
(off Camden St.)
Cranbrook Castle Tennis Club 7D **52**
Cranbrook Cl. BR2: Hayes 6J **159**
Cranbrook Ct. CR2: S Croy 5E **168**
Cranbrook Ct. TW8: Bford 6C **96**
Cranbrook Dr. KT10: Esh 7G **149**
Cranbrook Dr. TW2: Whitt 1F **131**
Cranbrook Est. E2 2K **85**
Cranbrook La. N11 4A **32**
Cranbrook M. E17 5B **50**
Cranbrook Pk. N22 1A **48**
Cranbrook Ri. IG1: Ilf 6D **52**
Cranbrook Rd. CR7: Thor H 2C **156**
Cranbrook Rd. DA7: Bex 1F **127**
Cranbrook Rd. EN4: E Barn 6G **21**
Cranbrook Rd. IG1: Ilf 7E **52**
Cranbrook Rd. IG2: Ilf 5E **52**
Cranbrook Rd. IG6: Ilf 5F **53**
Cranbrook Rd. SE8 1C **122**
Cranbrook Rd. SW19 7G **135**
Cranbrook Rd. TW4: Houn 4D **112**
Cranbrook Rd. W4 5A **98**
Cranbrook St. E2 2K **85**
Cranbury Rd. SW6 2K **117**
Crandley Ct. SE8 4A **104**
(not continuous)
Crane Av. TW7: Isle 5A **114**
Crane Av. W3 7J **79**
Cranebank 2J **111**
Cranebank M. TW1: Twick 4A **114**
Cranebrook TW2: Twick 2G **131**
Crane Cl. HA2: Harr 3G **59**
Crane Cl. RM10: Dag 6G **73**
Crane Ct. EC4 1K **13** (6A **84**)
Crane Ct. KT19: Ewe 4J **163**
Crane Ct. SW14 4J **115**
Craneford Cl. TW2: Twick 7K **113**
Craneford Way TW2: Twick 7J **113**
Crane Gdns. UB3: Harl 4H **93**
Crane Gro. N7 6A **66**
Crane Hgts. N17 3H **49**
(off Waterside Way)
Crane Ho. E3 2A **86**
(off Roman Rd.)
Crane Ho. SE15 1F **121**
Crane Ho. TW13: Hanw 3E **130**
Crane Lodge Rd. TW5: Cran 6K **93**
Crane Mead SE16 5J **103**
Crane Mead Ct. TW1: Twick 7K **113**
Crane Pk. Island Nature Reserve
2D **130**
Crane Pk. Rd. TW2: Whitt 2F **131**
Crane Rd. TW19: Stanw 6C **110**
Crane Rd. TW2: Twick 1J **131**
Cranesbill Cl. NW9 3K **43**
Cranesbill Cl. SW16 2H **155**
Cranes Dr. KT5: Surb 4E **150**
Cranes Pk. KT5: Surb 4E **150**
Cranes Pk. Av. KT5: Surb 4E **150**
Cranes Pk. Cres. KT5: Surb 4F **151**
Crane St. SE10 5F **105**
Crane St. SE15 1F **121**
Craneswater UB3: Harl 7H **93**
Craneswater Pk. UB2: S'hall 5D **94**
Crane Way TW2: Whitt 7G **113**
Cranfield Cl. SE27 3C **138**
Cranfield Ct. W1 6D **4** (5C **82**)
(off Homer St.)
Cranfield Dr. NW9 7F **29**
Cranfield Ho. WC1 5E **6** (5J **83**)
(off Southampton Row)
Cranfield Rd. SE4 3B **122**
Cranfield Rd. E. SM5: Cars 7E **166**
Cranfield Rd. W. SM5: Cars 7E **166**
Cranfield Row SE1 1K **19** (3A **102**)
(off Gerridge St.)
Cranfield Wlk. SE3 3K **123**
CRANFORD 7J **93**
Cranford Av. N13 5D **32**
Cranford Av. TW19: Stanw 7A **110**
Cranford Cl. SW20 7D **134**
Cranford Cl. TW19: Stanw 7A **110**
Cranford Community College Sports Cen. 6K **93**
Cranford Cotts. E1 7K **85**
(off Cranford St.)
Cranford Dr. UB3: Harl 4H **93**
Cranford La. TW6: H'row A Bath Rd. 1H **111**
Cranford La. TW6: H'row A Elmdon Rd.
3H **111**
Cranford La. TW5: Cran 7K **93**
Cranford La. TW5: Hest 7K **93**
Cranford La. UB3: Cran 6F **93**
Cranford La. UB3: Harl 6F **93**
Cranford M. BR2: Broml 5C **160**
Cranford Pk. Rd. UB3: Harl 4H **93**
Cranford St. E1 7K **85**
Cranford Way N8 4K **47**
Cranhurst Rd. NW2 5E **62**
Cranleigh W11 1H **99**
(off Ladbroke Rd.)
Cranleigh Cl. BR6: Chels 3K **173**
Cranleigh Cl. DA5: Bexl 6H **127**
Cranleigh Cl. SE20 2H **157**
Cranleigh Ct. CR4: Mitc 3B **154**
Cranleigh Ct. TW9: Rich 3G **115**
Cranleigh Ct. UB1: S'hall 6D **76**
Cranleigh Gdns. HA3: Kenton 5E **42**
Cranleigh Gdns. IG11: Bark 7H **71**
Cranleigh Gdns. KT2: King T 6F **133**
Cranleigh Gdns. N21 5F **23**
Cranleigh Gdns. SE25 3E **156**
Cranleigh Gdns. SM1: Sutt 2K **165**
Cranleigh Gdns. UB1: S'hall 6D **76**
Cranleigh Gdns. Ind. Est. UB1: S'hall
6D **76**
Cranleigh Ho's. NW1 2G **83**
(off Cranleigh St.)
Cranleigh M. SW11 2C **118**
Cranleigh Rd. N15 5C **48**
Cranleigh Rd. SW19 3J **153**
Cranleigh Rd. TW13: Felt 4H **129**
Cranleigh St. NW1 2G **83**
Cranley Dene Ct. N10 4F **47**
Cranley Dr. HA4: Ruis 2H **57**
Cranley Dr. IG2: Ilf 7G **53**
CRANLEY GARDENS 4F **47**
Cranley Gdns. N10 4F **47**
Cranley Gdns. N13 3E **32**
Cranley Gdns. SM6: W'gton 7G **167**
Cranley Gdns. SW7 5A **16** (5A **100**)
Cranley M. SW7 5A **16** (5A **100**)
Cranley Pde. SE9 4C **142**
(off Beaconsfield Rd.)
Cranley Pl. SW7 4A **16** (4B **100**)
Cranley Rd. E13 5K **87**
Cranley Rd. IG2: Ilf 6G **53**
Cranmer Av. W13 3B **96**
Cranmer Cl. HA4: Ruis 1B **58**
Cranmer Cl. HA7: Stan 7H **27**
Cranmer Cl. SM4: Mord 6F **153**
Cranmer Ct. N3 2G **45**
Cranmer Ct. SW3 4D **16** (4C **100**)
Cranmer Ct. SW4 3H **119**
Cranmer Ct. TW12: Hamp H 5F **131**
Cranmere Ct. EN2: Enf 2F **23**
Cranmer Farm Cl. CR4: Mitc 4D **154**
Cranmer Gdns. RM10: Dag 4J **73**
Cranmer Ho. SW11 1C **118**
(off Surrey La. Est.)
Cranmer Ho. SW9 7A **102**
(off Cranmer Rd.)
Cranmer Rd. CR0: C'don 3B **168**
Cranmer Rd. CR4: Mitc 4D **154**
Cranmer Rd. E7 4K **69**
Cranmer Rd. HA8: Edg 3C **28**
Cranmer Rd. KT2: King T 5E **132**
Cranmer Rd. SW9 7A **102**
Cranmer Rd. TW12: Hamp H 5F **131**
Cranmer Rd. UB3: Hayes 6F **75**
Cranmer Ter. SW17 5B **136**
Cranmore Av. TW7: Isle 7G **95**
Cranmore Rd. BR1: Broml 3H **141**
Cranmore Rd. BR7: Chst 5D **142**
Cranmore Way N10 4G **47**
Cranston Cl. TW3: Houn 2C **112**
Cranston Cl. UB10: Ick 2F **57**
Cranston Est. N1 2D **84**
Cranston Gdns. E4 6J **35**
Cranston Rd. SE23 1A **140**
Cranswick Rd. SE16 5H **103**
Crantock Rd. SE6 2D **140**
Cranwell Cl. E3 4D **86**

208 A–Z London

Cranwell Gro. – Crossmead Av.

Cranwell Gro. TW17: Shep ... 4B 146
Cranwell Rd. TW6: H'row A ... 2D 110
Cranwich Av. N21 ... 7J 23
Cranwich Rd. N16 ... 7D 48
Cranwood Ct. EC1 ... 2F 9 (3D 84)
... (off Vince St.)
Cranwood St. EC1 ... 2F 9 (3D 84)
Cranworth Cres. E4 ... 1A 36
Cranworth Gdns. SW9 ... 1A 120
Craster Rd. SW2 ... 7K 119
Crathie Rd. SE12 ... 6K 123
Cravan Av. TW13: Felt ... 2J 129
Craven Av. UB1: S'hall ... 5D 76
Craven Av. W5 ... 7C 78
Craven Cl. N16 ... 7G 49
Craven Cl. UB4: Hayes ... 6J 75
Craven Cottage ... 2F 117
Craven Ct. NW10 ... 1A 80
Craven Ct. RM6: Chad H ... 6E 54
Craven Gdns. IG11: Bark ... 2J 89
Craven Gdns. IG6: Ilf ... 2H 53
Craven Gdns. SW19 ... 5J 135
Craven Hill W2 ... 7A 82
Craven Hill Gdns. W2 ... 7A 82
... (not continuous)
Craven Hill M. W2 ... 7A 82
Craven Ho. N2 ... 2B 46
... (off High Rd. E. Finchley)
Craven Lodge SW6 ... 1F 117
... (off Harbord St.)
Craven Lodge W2 ... 7A 82
... (off Craven Hill)
Craven M. SW11 ... 3E 118
Craven Pk. NW10 ... 1K 79
Craven Pk. M. NW10 ... 7A 62
Craven Pk. Rd. N15 ... 6F 49
Craven Pk. Rd. NW10 ... 1A 80
Craven Pas. WC2 ... 4E 12 (1J 101)
... (off Craven St.)
Craven Rd. CR0: C'don ... 1H 169
Craven Rd. KT2: King T ... 1F 151
Craven Rd. NW10 ... 1K 79
Craven Rd. W2 ... 2A 10 (7A 82)
Craven Rd. W5 ... 7C 78
Craven St. WC2 ... 4E 12 (1J 101)
Craven Ter. W2 ... 2A 10 (7A 82)
Craven Wlk. N16 ... 7G 49
Crawford Av. HA0: Wemb ... 5D 60
Crawford Bldgs. W1 ... 6D 4 (5C 82)
... (off Homer St.)
Crawford Cl. TW7: Isle ... 2J 113
Crawford Ct. NW9 ... 3A 44
... (off Charcot Rd.)
Crawford Est. SE5 ... 2C 120
Crawford Gdns. N13 ... 3G 33
Crawford Gdns. UB5: N'olt ... 3D 76
Crawford Mans. W1 ... 6D 4 (5C 82)
... (off Crawford St.)
Crawford M. SW20 ... 7D 134
Crawford M. W1 ... 6E 4 (5D 82)
Crawford Pas. EC1 ... 4J 7 (4A 84)
Crawford Pl. W1 ... 7D 4 (6C 82)
Crawford Rd. SE5 ... 1C 120
Crawford St. NW10 ... 7K 61
Crawford St. W1 ... 6D 4 (5C 82)
Crawley Rd. E10 ... 1D 68
Crawley Rd. EN1: Enf ... 7K 23
Crawley Rd. N22 ... 2C 48
Crawshay Rd. SW9 ... 1A 120
Crawthew Gro. SE22 ... 4F 121
Craybrooke Rd. DA14: Sidc ... 4B 144
Craybury End SE9 ... 2G 143
Crayfields Bus. Pk. BR5: St P ... 7C 144
Crayford Cl. E6 ... 6C 88
Crayford Ct. W3 ... 3J 97
... (off Bollo Bri. Rd.)
Crayford Ho. SE1 ... 7F 15 (2D 102)
... (off Long La.)
Crayford M. N7 ... 4J 65
Crayford Rd. N7 ... 4H 65
Crayford Stadium (Greyhound) ... 6K 127
Cray Ho. NW8 ... 5B 4 (5B 82)
... (off Penfold St.)
Crayke Hill KT9: Chess ... 7E 162
Crayle Ho. EC1 ... 3A 8 (4B 84)
... (off Malta St.)
Crayleigh Ter. DA14: Sidc ... 6C 144
Crayonne Cl. TW16: Sun ... 1G 147
Cray Rd. DA14: Sidc ... 6C 144
Cray Rd. DA17: Belv ... 6G 109
Cray Valley Rd. BR5: St M Cry ... 5K 161
Cray Wanderers FC ... 5K 159
Crayzee Barn ... 2F 145
Crealock Gro. IG8: Wfd G ... 5C 36
Crealock St. SW18 ... 6K 117
Creasy Est. SE1 ... 3E 102
Creative Ho. SW8 ... 7F 101
... (off Prince of Wales Dr.)
Creative Rd. SE8 ... 7D 104
Crebor St. SE22 ... 6G 121
Crecy Ct. SE11 ... 5J 19 (5A 102)
... (off Hotspur St.)
Credenhall Dr. BR2: Broml ... 1D 172
Credenhill Ho. SE15 ... 7H 103
Credenhill St. SW16 ... 6G 137
Crediton Hgts. NW10 ... 1F 81
... (off Okehampton Rd.)
Crediton Hill NW6 ... 5K 63
Crediton Rd. E16 ... 6J 87
Crediton Rd. NW10 ... 1F 81
Crediton Way KT10: Clay ... 5A 162
Credon Rd. E13 ... 2A 88
Credon Rd. SE16 ... 5H 103
Creechurch La. EC3 ... 1H 15 (6E 84)
... (not continuous)
Creechurch Pl. EC3 ... 1H 15 (6E 84)
... (off Creechurch La.)
Creed Ct. E1 ... 3A 86
Creed Ct. EC4 ... 1B 14 (6B 84)
... (off Ludgate Sq.)
Creed La. EC4 ... 1B 14 (6B 84)
Creed Pas. SE10 ... 5G 105
... (off Hoskins St.)
Creek, The TW16: Sun ... 5J 147
Creek Cotts. KT8: E Mos ... 4J 149
... (off Creek Rd.)
Creek Ho. W14 ... 3G 99
... (off Russell Rd.)
Creek La. SW18 ... 4J 117
CREEKMOUTH ... 4K 89
Creekmouth Ind. Pk. IG11: Bark ... 4K 89
Creek Rd. IG11: Bark ... 3K 89
Creek Rd. KT8: E Mos ... 4J 149
Creek Rd. SE10 ... 6D 104
Creek Rd. SE8 ... 6C 104
Creekside SE8 ... 7D 104
Creekside Foyer SE8 ... 6D 104
... (off Stowage)
Creek Way RM13: Rain ... 5K 91
Creeland Gro. SE6 ... 1B 140
Crefeld Cl. W6 ... 6G 99
Creffield Rd. W3 ... 7G 79
Creffield Rd. W5 ... 7F 79
Creighton Av. E6 ... 2B 88
Creighton Av. N10 ... 2D 46
Creighton Av. N2 ... 3C 46
Creighton Cl. W12 ... 7C 80
Creighton Rd. N17 ... 7K 33
Creighton Rd. NW6 ... 2F 81
Creighton Rd. W5 ... 3D 96
Cremer Bus. Cen. E2 ... 1J 9 (2F 85)
... (off Cremer St.)
Cremer Ho. SE8 ... 7C 104
... (off Deptford Chu. St.)
Cremer St. E2 ... 1J 9 (2F 85)
Cremorne Est. SW10 ... 6B 100
... (not continuous)
Cremorne Riverside Cen. ... 7B 100
Cremorne Rd. SW10 ... 7A 100
Creon Ct. SW9 ... 7A 102
... (off Caldwell St.)
Crescent EC3 ... 2J 15 (7F 85)
Crescent, The BR3: Beck ... 1C 158
Crescent, The BR4: W W'ck ... 6G 159
Crescent, The CR0: C'don ... 5D 156
Crescent, The DA14: Sidc ... 4K 143
Crescent, The DA5: Bexl ... 7C 126
Crescent, The E17 ... 6A 50
Crescent, The EN5: New Bar ... 2E 20
Crescent, The HA0: Wemb ... 2B 60
Crescent, The HA2: Harr ... 1G 59
Crescent, The IG2: Ilf ... 6E 52
Crescent, The KT3: N Mald ... 3J 151
Crescent, The KT6: Surb ... 5E 150
Crescent, The KT8: W Mole ... 4E 148
Crescent, The N11 ... 4J 31
Crescent, The NW2 ... 3D 62
Crescent, The SE8 ... 1C 122
... (off Seager Pl.)
Crescent, The SM1: Sutt ... 5B 166
Crescent, The SW13 ... 2B 116
Crescent, The SW19 ... 3J 135
Crescent, The TW15: Ashf ... 5B 128
Crescent, The TW17: Shep ... 7H 147
Crescent, The UB1: S'hall ... 2D 94
Crescent, The UB3: Harl ... 7E 92
Crescent, The W12 ... 1E 98
Crescent, The W3 ... 6A 80
Crescent Arc. SE10 ... 6E 104
... (off Creek Rd.)
Crescent Ct. KT6: Surb ... 5D 150
Crescent Ct. SW4 ... 5H 119
... (off Park Hill)
Crescent Ct. Bus. Cen. E16 ... 4F 87
Crescent Dr. BR5: Pet W ... 5F 161
Crescent E. EN4: Had W ... 1F 21
Crescent Gdns. HA4: Ruis ... 7K 39
Crescent Gdns. SW19 ... 3J 135
Crescent Gro. CR4: Mitc ... 4C 154
Crescent Gro. SW4 ... 4G 119
Crescent Ho. EC1 ... 4C 8 (4C 84)
... (off Golden La. Est.)
Crescent Ho. SE13 ... 2D 122
Crescent La. SW4 ... 4G 119
Crescent Mans. SW3 ... 4C 16 (4C 100)
... (off Fulham Rd.)
Crescent Mans. W11 ... 7G 81
... (off Elgin Cres.)
Crescent M. N22 ... 1J 47
Crescent Pde. UB10: Hil ... 3C 74
Crescent Pl. SW3 ... 3D 16 (4C 100)
Crescent Ri. EN4: E Barn ... 5H 21
Crescent Ri. N22 ... 1H 47
Crescent Ri. N3 ... 1H 45
Crescent Rd. BR1: Broml ... 7J 141
Crescent Rd. BR3: Beck ... 2D 158
Crescent Rd. DA15: Sidc ... 3K 143
Crescent Rd. E10 ... 2D 68
Crescent Rd. E13 ... 1J 87
Crescent Rd. E18 ... 1A 52
Crescent Rd. E4 ... 1B 36
Crescent Rd. E6 ... 1A 88
Crescent Rd. EN2: Enf ... 4G 23
Crescent Rd. EN4: E Barn ... 4G 21
Crescent Rd. KT2: King T ... 7G 133
Crescent Rd. N11 ... 4J 31
Crescent Rd. N15 ... 3B 48
Crescent Rd. N22 ... 1H 47
Crescent Rd. N3 ... 1H 45
Crescent Rd. N8 ... 6H 47
Crescent Rd. N9 ... 1B 34
Crescent Rd. RM10: Dag ... 3H 73
Crescent Rd. SE18 ... 5F 107
Crescent Rd. SW20 ... 1F 153
Crescent Rd. TW17: Shep ... 5E 146
Crescent Row EC1 ... 4C 8 (4C 84)
Crescent Stables SW15 ... 5G 117
Crescent St. N1 ... 7K 65
Crescent Way BR6: Orp ... 5J 173
Crescent Way N12 ... 6H 31
Crescent Way SE4 ... 3C 122
Crescent Way SW16 ... 6K 137
Crescent W. EN4: Had W ... 1F 21
Crescent Wood Rd. SE26 ... 3G 139
Cresford Rd. SW6 ... 1K 117
Crespigny Rd. NW4 ... 6D 44
Cressage Cl. UB1: S'hall ... 4E 76
Cressage Ho. TW8: Bford ... 6E 96
... (off Ealing Rd.)
Cressal Ho. E14 ... 3C 104
... (off Tiller Rd.)
Cresset Ho. E9 ... 6J 67
Cresset Rd. E9 ... 6J 67
Cresset St. SW4 ... 3H 119
Cressfield Cl. NW5 ... 5E 64
Cressida Rd. N19 ... 1G 65
Cressingham Gro. SM1: Sutt ... 4A 166
Cressingham Rd. HA8: Edg ... 6E 28
Cressingham Rd. SE13 ... 3E 122
Cressington Cl. N16 ... 5E 66
Cress M. BR1: Broml ... 5F 141
Cresswell Gdns. SW5 ... 5A 100
Cresswell Ho. HA9: Wemb ... 3E 60
Cresswell Ho. TW19: Stanw ... 6A 110
... (off Douglas Rd.)
Cresswell Pk. SE3 ... 3H 123
Cresswell Pl. SW10 ... 5A 100
Cresswell Rd. SE25 ... 4G 157
Cresswell Rd. TW1: Twick ... 6D 114
Cresswell Rd. TW13: Hanw ... 3C 130
Cresswell Way N21 ... 7F 23
Cressy Ct. E1 ... 5J 85
Cressy Ct. W6 ... 3D 98
Cressy Ho. SW15 ... 3D 116
Cressy Ho's. E1 ... 5J 85
... (off Hannibal Rd.)
Cressy Pl. E1 ... 5J 85
Cressy Rd. NW3 ... 5D 64
Crest, The KT5: Surb ... 5G 151
Crest, The N13 ... 4F 33
Crest, The NW4 ... 5E 44
Cresta Ct. W5 ... 4F 79
Cresta Ho. E3 ... 4C 86
... (off Dimson Cres.)
Cresta Ho. NW3 ... 7B 64
... (off Finchley Rd.)
Crestbrook Av. N13 ... 3G 33
Crestbrook Pl. N13 ... 3G 33
... (off Green Lanes)
Crest Ct. NW4 ... 5E 44
Crest Dr. EN3: Enf W ... 1D 24
Crested Ct. NW9 ... 7B 44
Crestfield St. WC1 ... 1F 7 (3J 83)
Crest Gdns. HA4: Ruis ... 3A 58
Creston Ho. SW11 ... 3B 118
... (off Gartons Way)
Creston Way KT4: Wor Pk ... 1F 165
Crest Rd. BR2: Hayes ... 7H 159
Crest Rd. CR2: Sels ... 7H 169
Crest Rd. NW2 ... 2B 62
Crest Vw. HA5: Pinn ... 4B 40
Crest Vw. Dr. BR5: Pet W ... 5F 161
Crest Wlk. E18 ... 2A 52
Crestway SW15 ... 6C 116
Crestwood Way TW4: Houn ... 5C 112
Creswell Dr. BR3: Beck ... 5D 158
Creswick Ct. W3 ... 7H 79
Creswick Rd. W3 ... 7H 79
Creswick Wlk. E3 ... 3C 86
Creswick Wlk. NW11 ... 4H 45
Creton St. SE18 ... 3E 106
Creukhorne Rd. NW10 ... 7A 62
Crewdson Rd. SW9 ... 7A 102
Crewe Pl. NW10 ... 3B 80
Crewkerne Ct. SW11 ... 1B 118
... (off Bolingbroke Wlk.)
Crews St. E14 ... 4C 104
Crewys Rd. NW2 ... 2H 63
Crewys Rd. SE15 ... 2H 121
Crichton Av. SM6: Bedd ... 5H 167
Crichton Ho. DA14: Sidc ... 6D 144
Crichton Rd. SM5: Cars ... 6D 166
Crichton St. SW8 ... 2G 119
Crick Ct. IG11: Bark ... 2G 89
... (off Spring Pl.)
Cricketers Arms Rd. EN2: Enf ... 2H 23
Cricketers Cl. DA8: Erith ... 5K 109
Cricketers Cl. KT9: Chess ... 4D 162
Cricketers Cl. N14 ... 7B 22
Cricketers Ct. SE11 ... 4B 102
... (off Kennington La.)
Cricketers M. SW18 ... 5K 117
Cricketers Ter. SM5: Cars ... 3C 166
Cricketers Wlk. SE26 ... 5J 139
Cricketfield Rd. E5 ... 4H 67
Cricket Grn. CR4: Mitc ... 3D 154
Cricket Ground Rd. BR7: Chst ... 1F 161
Cricket La. BR3: Beck ... 6A 140
Cricket La. TW12: Hamp H ... 6G 131
Crickett Ho. SE6 ... 7D 122
Cricklade Av. SW2 ... 2J 137
Cricklefield Pl. IG1: Ilf ... 2J 71
CRICKLEWOOD ... 4F 63
Cricklewood B'way. NW2 ... 3E 62
Cricklewood La. NW2 ... 4F 63
Cridland St. E15 ... 1H 87
Crieff Ct. TW11: Tedd ... 7C 132
Crieff Rd. SW18 ... 6A 118
Criffel Av. SW2 ... 2H 137
Crimscott St. SE1 ... 3E 102
Crimsworth Rd. SW8 ... 1H 119
Crinan St. N1 ... 2J 83
Cringle St. SW8 ... 7G 101
Crinoline M. E1 ... 6J 9 (5F 85)
Cripplegate St. EC2 ... 5C 8 (5C 84)
Cripps Cl. IG6: Ilf ... 3G 53
Cripps Grn. UB4: Yead ... 4K 75
Crispe Ho. IG11: Bark ... 2H 89
Crispe Ho. N1 ... 1K 83
... (off Barnsbury Est.)
Crispen Rd. TW13: Hanw ... 4C 130
Crispian Cl. NW10 ... 4A 62
Crispin Cl. CR0: Bedd ... 2J 167
Crispin Ct. SE17 ... 4E 102
Crispin Cres. CR0: Bedd ... 3H 167
Crispin Ind. Cen. N18 ... 5D 34
Crispin Lodge N11 ... 5J 31
Crispin M. NW11 ... 5H 45
Crispin Pl. E1 ... 5J 9 (5F 85)
Crispin Rd. HA8: Edg ... 6D 28
Crispin St. E1 ... 6J 9 (5F 85)
Crispin Way UB8: Hil ... 4B 74
Crisp Rd. W6 ... 5E 98
Cristie Ct. E16 ... 4H 87
Cristowe Rd. SW6 ... 2H 117
Criterion Bldgs. KT7: T Ditt ... 7B 150
... (off Portsmouth Rd.)
Criterion Ct. E8 ... 7F 67
... (off Middleton Rd.)
Criterion M. N19 ... 2H 65
Criterion M. SE24 ... 5B 120
... (off Shakespeare Rd.)
Criterion Theatre London
... 3C 12 (7H 83)
... (off Piccadilly Cir.)
CRITTALLS CORNER ... 7C 144
Crockerton Rd. SW17 ... 2D 136
Crockham Way SE9 ... 4E 142
Crocus Cl. CR0: C'don ... 1K 169
Crocus Fld. EN5: Barn ... 6C 20
Croft, The CR0: C'don ... 3F 169
Croft, The E4 ... 2B 36
Croft, The EN5: Barn ... 4B 20
Croft, The HA0: Wemb ... 5C 60
Croft, The HA4: Ruis ... 4A 58
Croft, The HA5: Pinn ... 7D 40
Croft, The HA8: Edg ... 7C 28
Croft, The NW10 ... 2B 80
Croft, The TW5: Hest ... 6C 94
Croft, The W5 ... 5E 78
Croft Av. BR4: W W'ck ... 1E 170
Croft Cl. BR7: Chst ... 5D 142
Croft Cl. DA17: Belv ... 5F 109
Croft Cl. NW7 ... 3F 29
Croft Cl. UB10: Hil ... 7C 56
Croft Cl. UB3: Harl ... 7E 92
Croft Ct. HA4: Ruis ... 1H 57
Croft Ct. SE13 ... 6E 122
Croft Ct. SM1: Sutt ... 2B 166
Croftdown Rd. NW5 ... 3E 64
Croft End Cl. KT9: Chess ... 3F 163
Crofters Cl. TW7: Isle ... 5H 113
Crofters Ct. SE8 ... 4A 104
... (off Croft St.)
Crofters Mead CR0: Sels ... 7B 170
Crofters Way NW1 ... 1H 83
Croft Gdns. HA4: Ruis ... 1H 57
Croft Gdns. W7 ... 2A 96
Croft Ho. E17 ... 4D 50
Croft Ho. NW9 ... 2B 44
Croft Ho. W10 ... 3G 81
... (off Third Av.)
Croft Lodge Cl. IG8: Wfd G ... 6E 36
Croft M. N12 ... 3F 31
CROFTON ... 2G 173
Crofton Albion Sports Ground ... 4J 123
Crofton Av. BR6: Farnb ... 2G 173
Crofton Av. DA5: Bexl ... 7D 126
Crofton Av. W4 ... 7J 97
Croftongate Way SE4 ... 5A 122
Crofton Gro. E4 ... 4A 36
Crofton Ho. SW3 ... 7C 16 (6C 100)
... (off Old Church St.)
Crofton La. BR5: Farnb ... 2H 173
Crofton La. BR5: Orp ... 2H 173
Crofton La. BR5: Pet W ... 2H 173
Crofton La. BR6: Pet W ... 7H 161
CROFTON PARK ... 5B 122
Crofton Pk. Rd. SE4 ... 6B 122
Crofton Rd. BR6: Farnb ... 3E 172
Crofton Rd. BR6: Orp ... 3E 172
Crofton Rd. E13 ... 4K 87
Crofton Rd. SE5 ... 1E 120
Crofton Roman Villa ... 2J 173
Crofton Ter. E5 ... 5A 68
Crofton Ter. TW9: Rich ... 4F 115
Crofton Way EN2: Enf ... 2F 23
Crofton Way EN5: New Bar ... 6E 20
Croft Rd. BR1: Broml ... 6J 141
Croft Rd. EN3: Enf H ... 1F 25
Croft Rd. SM1: Sutt ... 5C 166
Croft Rd. SW16 ... 1A 156
Croft Rd. SW19 ... 7A 136
Crofts, The TW17: Shep ... 4G 147
Crofts Ho. E2 ... 2G 85
... (off Teale St.)
Croftside, The SE25 ... 3G 157
Crofts La. N22 ... 7F 33
Crofts Rd. HA1: Harr ... 6A 42
Crofts St. E1 ... 3K 15 (7G 85)
Croft St. SE8 ... 4A 104
Crofts Vs. HA1: Harr ... 6A 42
Croft Way DA15: Sidc ... 3J 143
Croft Way TW10: Ham ... 3B 132
Croftway NW3 ... 4J 63
Crogsland Rd. NW1 ... 7E 64
Croham Cl. CR2: S Croy ... 7E 168
Croham Hurst Golf Course ... 6F 169
Croham Mnr. Rd. CR2: S Croy ... 7E 168
Croham Mt. CR2: S Croy ... 7E 168
Croham Pk. Av. CR2: S Croy ... 5E 168
Croham Rd. CR2: S Croy ... 5D 168
Croham Valley Rd. CR2: Sels ... 6G 169
Croindene Rd. SW16 ... 1J 155
Crokesley Ho. HA8: Edg ... 2J 43
... (off Burnt Oak B'way.)
Cromartie Rd. N19 ... 7H 47
Cromarty Ct. SW2 ... 5K 119
Cromarty Ho. E1 ... 5A 86
... (off Ben Jonson Rd.)
Cromarty Rd. HA8: Edg ... 2C 28
Cromberdale Ct. N17 ... 1G 49
... (off Spencer Rd.)
Crombie Cl. IG4: Ilf ... 5D 52
Crombie M. SW11 ... 2C 118
Crombie Rd. DA15: Sidc ... 1H 143
Crome Ho. UB5: N'olt ... 2C 76
... (off Parkfield Dr.)
Cromer Cl. UB8: Hil ... 6E 74
Cromer Hyde SM4: Mord ... 5K 153
Crome Rd. NW10 ... 6A 62
Cromer Pl. BR6: Orp ... 1J 173
Cromer Rd. E10 ... 7F 51
Cromer Rd. EN5: New Bar ... 4F 21
Cromer Rd. IG8: Wfd G ... 4D 36
Cromer Rd. N17 ... 2G 49
Cromer Rd. RM6: Chad H ... 6E 54
Cromer Rd. RM7: Rom ... 6J 55
Cromer Rd. SE25 ... 3H 157
Cromer Rd. SW17 ... 6E 136
Cromer Rd. TW6: H'row A ... 2C 110
Cromer St. WC1 ... 2E 6 (3J 83)
Cromer Ter. E8 ... 5G 67
Cromer Ter. RM6: Chad H ... 5B 54
Cromer Vs. Rd. SW18 ... 6H 117
Cromford Cl. BR6: Orp ... 3J 173
Cromford Path E5 ... 4K 67
Cromford Rd. SW18 ... 5J 117
Cromford Way KT3: N Mald ... 1K 151
Cromie Cl. N13 ... 3F 33
Cromlix Cl. BR7: Chst ... 2F 161
Crompton Ct. BR2: Broml ... 3J 159
... (off St Mark's Sq.)
Crompton Ct. SW3 ... 3C 16 (4C 100)
Crompton Ho. SE1 ... 3C 102
... (off County St.)
Crompton Ho. W2 ... 4A 4 (4B 82)
... (off Hall Pl.)
Crompton Pl. EN3: Enf L ... 1H 25
Crompton St. W2 ... 4A 4 (4B 82)
Cromwell Av. BR2: Broml ... 4K 159
Cromwell Av. KT3: N Mald ... 5B 152
Cromwell Av. N6 ... 1F 65
Cromwell Av. W6 ... 5D 98
Cromwell Cen. IG11: Bark ... 3A 90
Cromwell Cen. NW10 ... 3K 79
Cromwell Cen., The RM8: Dag ... 7F 55
... (off Coppen Rd.)
Cromwell Cl. BR2: Broml ... 4K 159
Cromwell Cl. E1 ... 1G 103
Cromwell Cl. KT12: Walt T ... 7K 147
Cromwell Cl. N2 ... 4B 46
Cromwell Cl. W3 ... 1J 97
... (not continuous)
Cromwell Cl. W4 ... 5H 97
... (off Harvard Rd.)
Cromwell Ct. EN3: Pond E ... 5E 24
Cromwell Cres. SW5 ... 4J 99
Cromwell Gdns. SW7 ... 2B 16 (3B 100)
Cromwell Gro. W6 ... 3E 98
Cromwell Highwalk EC2 ... 5D 8 (5C 84)
... (off Silk St.)
Cromwell Ho. CR0: C'don ... 3B 168
Cromwell Ho. SW11 ... 1E 118
... (off Charlotte Despard Av.)
Cromwell Ind. Est. E10 ... 1A 68
Cromwell Lodge DA6: Bex ... 5E 126
Cromwell Lodge E1 ... 4J 85
... (off Cleveland Gro.)
Cromwell Lodge IG11: Bark ... 5J 71
Cromwell Mans. SW5 ... 4J 99
... (off Cromwell Rd.)
Cromwell M. SW7 ... 3A 16 (4B 100)
Cromwell Pl. EC2 ... 5D 8 (5C 84)
... (off Silk St.)
Cromwell Pl. N6 ... 1F 65
Cromwell Pl. SW14 ... 3J 115
Cromwell Pl. SW7 ... 3B 16 (4B 100)
Cromwell Rd. BR3: Beck ... 2A 158
Cromwell Rd. CR0: C'don ... 7D 156
Cromwell Rd. E17 ... 5E 50
Cromwell Rd. E7 ... 7A 70
Cromwell Rd. HA0: Wemb ... 2E 78
Cromwell Rd. KT2: King T ... 1E 150
Cromwell Rd. KT4: Wor Pk ... 3K 163
Cromwell Rd. N10 ... 7K 31
... (not continuous)
Cromwell Rd. N3 ... 1A 46
Cromwell Rd. SW19 ... 5J 135
Cromwell Rd. SW5 ... 4J 99
Cromwell Rd. SW7 ... 4K 99
Cromwell Rd. SW9 ... 1A 120
Cromwell Rd. TW11: Tedd ... 6A 132
Cromwell Rd. TW13: Felt ... 1K 129
Cromwell Rd. TW3: Houn ... 4E 112
Cromwell Rd. UB3: Hayes ... 6F 75
Cromwell St. TW3: Houn ... 4E 112
Cromwell Twr. EC2 ... 5D 8 (5C 84)
... (off Silk St.)
Cromwell Trad. Cen. IG11: Bark ... 3J 89
Crondace Rd. SW6 ... 1J 117
Crondall Ct. N1 ... 1G 9 (2E 84)
... (off St John's Est.)
Crondall Ho. SW15 ... 7C 116
Crondall St. N1 ... 1F 9 (2D 84)
Crone Ct. NW6 ... 2H 81
... (off Denmark Rd.)
Cronin St. SE15 ... 7F 103
CROOKED BILLET ... 1C 50
Crooked Billet SW19 ... 6E 134
Crooked Billet Yd. E2 ... 1H 9 (3E 84)
... (off Kingsland Rd.)
Crooked Usage N3 ... 3G 45
Crooke Rd. SE8 ... 5A 104
Crookham Rd. SW6 ... 1H 117
Crook Log DA6: Bex ... 3D 126
Crook Log Leisure Cen. ... 3D 126
Crookston Rd. SE9 ... 3E 124
Croombs Rd. E16 ... 5A 88
Croom's Hill SE10 ... 7E 104
Croom's Hill Gro. SE10 ... 7E 104
Cropley Ct. N1 ... 2D 84
... (off Cropley St.)
Cropley St. N1 ... 2D 84
Croppath Rd. RM10: Dag ... 4G 73
Cropthorne Ct. W9 ... 3A 82
Crosbie Ho. E17 ... 3E 50
... (off Prospect Hill)
Crosby Cl. TW13: Hanw ... 3C 130
Crosby Ct. SE1 ... 6E 14 (2D 102)
Crosby Gdns. UB8: Uxb ... 7A 56
Crosby Ho. BR1: Broml ... 2J 159
... (off Elmfield Rd.)
Crosby Ho. E14 ... 3E 104
... (off Manchester Rd.)
Crosby Ho. E7 ... 6J 69
Crosby Rd. E7 ... 6J 69
Crosby Rd. RM10: Dag ... 2H 91
Crosby Row SE1 ... 7E 14 (2D 102)
Crosby Sq. EC3 ... 1G 15 (6E 84)
Crosby Wlk. E8 ... 6F 67
Crosby Wlk. SW2 ... 7A 120
Crosby Way SW2 ... 7A 120
Crosier Cl. SE3 ... 1C 124
Crosier Rd. UB10: Ick ... 4E 56
Crosier Way HA4: Ruis ... 3G 57
Crosland Pl. SW11 ... 3E 118
Cross Av. SE10 ... 6F 105
Crossbones Graveyard
... 5D 14 (1C 102)
... (off Redcross Way)
Crossbow Ho. N1 ... 1E 84
... (off Whitmore Est.)
Crossbow Ho. W13 ... 1B 96
... (off Sherwood Cl.)
Crossbrook Rd. SE3 ... 2C 124
Cross Cl. SE15 ... 2H 121
Cross Ct. SE28 ... 7B 90
... (off Titmuss Av.)
Cross Deep TW1: Twick ... 2K 131
Cross Deep Gdns. TW1: Twick ... 2K 131
Crossfield Ct. W10 ... 6F 81
... (off Cambridge Gdns.)
Crossfield Ho. W11 ... 7G 81
... (off Mary Pl.)
Crossfield Rd. N17 ... 3C 48
Crossfield Rd. NW3 ... 6B 64
Crossfield St. SE8 ... 7C 104
... (not continuous)
Crossford St. SW9 ... 2K 119
Cross Ga. HA8: Edg ... 3B 28
Crossgate UB6: G'frd ... 6B 60
Crossharbour Plaza E14 ... 3D 104
Cross Keys Cl. N9 ... 2B 34
Cross Keys Cl. W1 ... 6H 5 (5E 82)
Cross Keys Sq. EC1 ... 6C 8 (5C 84)
... (off Little Britain)
Cross Lances Rd. TW3: Houn ... 4F 113
Crossland Rd. CR7: Thor H ... 6B 156
Crosslands Av. UB2: S'hall ... 5D 94
Crosslands Av. W5 ... 1F 97
Crosslands Pde. UB2: S'hall ... 5E 94
Crosslands Rd. KT19: Ewe ... 6K 163
Cross La. DA5: Bexl ... 7F 127
Cross La. EC3 ... 3G 15 (7E 84)
... (not continuous)
Cross La. N8 ... 3K 47
... (not continuous)
Crossleigh Ct. SE14 ... 7B 104
... (off New Cross Rd.)
Crosslet St. SE17 ... 4D 102
Crosslet Va. SE10 ... 1D 122
Crossley St. N7 ... 6A 66
Crossmead SE9 ... 1D 142
Crossmead Av. UB6: G'frd ... 3E 76

A–Z London 209

Crossmount Ho. – Cygnet Ho.

Crossmount Ho. SE5 7C 102
(off Bowyer St.)
Crossness Footpath DA18: Erith 1F 109
Crossness La. SE2 7E 90
Crossness Nature Reserve 1G 109
Crossness Pumping Station, The 6E 90
Crossness Rd. IG11: Bark 3K 89
Crosspoint Ho. SE8 7C 104
(off Watson's St.)
Crossrail Pl. E14 1D 104
Crossrail Wlk. E14 1D 104
Cross Rd. BR2: Broml 2C 172
Cross Rd. CR0: C'don 1D 168
Cross Rd. DA14: Sidc 4B 144
Cross Rd. E4 1A 36
Cross Rd. EN1: Enf 4K 23
Cross Rd. HA1: Harr 4H 41
Cross Rd. HA2: Harr 3F 59
Cross Rd. HA3: W'stone 2A 42
Cross Rd. IG8: Wfd G 6J 37
Cross Rd. KT2: King T 7F 133
Cross Rd. N11 5A 32
Cross Rd. N22 7F 33
Cross Rd. RM6: Chad H 7C 54
Cross Rd. RM7: Mawney 4G 55
Cross Rd. SE5 2E 120
Cross Rd. SM1: Sutt 5B 166
Cross Rd. SW19 7J 135
Cross Rd. TW13: Hanw 4C 130
Cross St. N1 1B 84
Cross St. N18 5B 34
Cross St. SE5 3D 120
Cross St. SW13 2A 116
Cross St. TW12: Hamp H 5G 131
Crossthwaite Av. SE5 4D 120
Crosstrees Ho. E14 3C 104
(off Cassilis Rd.)
Crosswall EC3 2J 15 (7F 85)
Cross Way NW10 7C 62
Crossway BR5: Pet W 4H 161
Crossway EN1: Enf 7K 23
Crossway HA4: Ruis 4A 58
Crossway HA5: Pinn 2K 39
Crossway IG8: Wfd G 4F 37
Crossway N12 6G 31
Crossway N16 5E 66
Crossway NW9 4B 44
Crossway RM8: Dag 3C 72
Crossway SE28 6B 90
Crossway SW20 4E 152
Crossway UB3: Hayes 1J 93
Crossway W13 4A 78
Cross Way, The HA3: W'stone 2J 41
Crossway, The N22 7G 33
Crossway, The SE9 2B 142
Crossway, The UB10: Hil 2B 74
Crossway Ct. SE4 2A 122
Crossway Pde. N22 7G 33
(off The Crossway)
Crossways CR2: Sels 7A 170
Crossways N21 6H 23
Crossways SM2: Sutt 7B 166
Crossways TW16: Sun 7H 129
Crossways, The HA9: Wemb 2G 61
Crossways, The KT5: Surb 1H 163
Crossways, The TW5: Hest 7D 94
Crossways Rd. BR3: Beck 4C 158
Crossways Rd. CR4: Mitc 3F 155
Crossways Ter. E5 4J 67
Crosswell Cl. TW17: Shep 2E 146
Croston St. E8 1G 85
Crothall Cl. N13 3E 32
Crouch Av. IG11: Bark 2B 90
Crouch Cl. BR3: Beck 6C 140
Crouch Cft. SE9 3E 142
CROUCH END 7H 47
Crouch End Hill N8 7H 47
Crouch Hall Ct. N19 1J 65
Crouch Hall Rd. N8 6H 47
Crouch Hill N4 7J 47
Crouch Hill N8 6J 47
Crouchman's Cl. SE26 3F 139
Crouch Rd. NW10 7K 61
Crowborough Rd. SW17 6E 136
Crowden Way SE28 7C 90
Crowder Cl. N12 1A 46
Crowder St. E1 7H 85
Crowfield Ho. N5 4C 66
Crowfoot Cl. E9 5B 68
Crowfoot Cl. SE28 1J 107
Crowhurst Cl. SW9 2A 120
Crowhurst Ho. SW9 2K 119
(off Aytoun Rd.)
Crowland Av. UB3: Harl 4G 93
Crowland Gdns. N14 7D 22
Crowland Ho. NW8 1A 82
(off Springfield Rd.)
Crowland Rd. CR7: Thor H 4D 156
Crowland Rd. N15 5F 49
CROWLANDS 7H 55
Crowlands Av. RM7: Rom 5H 55
Crowlands Heath Golf Course 1H 73
Crowland Ter. N1 7D 66
Crowland Wlk. SM4: Mord 6K 153
Crow La. RM7: Rush G 7F 55
Crowley Cres. CR0: Wadd 5A 168
Crowley M. SW16 3G 155
Crowline Wlk. N1 6C 66
Crowmarsh Gdns. SE23 7J 121
Crown All. SE9 6D 124
(off Court Yd.)
Crown Apts. HA4: Ruis 1J 57
Crown Arc. KT1: King T 2D 150
Crownbourne Ct. SM1: Sutt 4K 165
(off St Nicholas Way)
Crown Bldgs. E4 1K 35
Crown Cl. E3 1C 86
Crown Cl. IG9: Buck H 1E 36
Crown Cl. KT12: Walt T 7A 148
Crown Cl. N22 1A 48
Crown Cl. NW6 6K 63
Crown Cl. NW7 2G 29
Crown Cl. UB3: Hayes 2H 93
Crown Cl. Bus. Cen. E3 1C 86
(off Crown Cl.)
Crown Cotts. RM5: Col R 1G 55
Crown Court Blackfriars 6B 14 (2B 102)
Crown Court Croydon 2D 168
Crown Court Harrow 3H 41
Crown Court Inner London 7C 14 (3C 102)
Crown Court Isleworth 1J 113
Crown Court Kingston upon Thames 3D 150
Crown Court Snaresbrook 5H 51
Crown Court Southwark 4G 15 (1E 102)
Crown Court Wood Green 1A 48
Crown Court Woolwich 2J 107
Crown Ct. EC2 1D 14 (6C 84)
(off Cheapside)
Crown Ct. N10 7K 31
Crown Ct. NW8 2D 4 (3C 82)
(off Park Rd.)
Crown Ct. SE12 6K 123
Crown Ct. WC2 1F 13 (6J 83)
Crown Dale SE19 6B 138
(not continuous)
Crowndale Ct. NW1 2H 83
(off Crowndale Rd.)
Crowndale Pl. E17 2E 50
Crowndale Rd. NW1 2G 83
Crown Dr. RM7: Rush G 6K 55
Crownfield Av. IG2: Ilf 6J 53
Crownfield Rd. E15 4F 69
Crowngate Ho. E3 2B 86
(off Hereford Rd.)
Crown Grn. M. HA9: Wemb 2E 60
Crown Hill CR0: C'don 2C 168
Crownhill Rd. IG8: Wfd G 7H 37
Crownhill Rd. NW10 1B 80
Crown Ho. KT3: N Mald 3J 151
Crown Ho. NW10 2G 79
Crown La. BR2: Broml 5B 160
Crown La. BR7: Chst 1G 161
Crown La. N14 1B 32
Crown La. SM4: Mord 4J 153
Crown La. SW16 5A 138
Crown La. Gdns. SW16 5A 138
Crown La. Spur BR2: Broml 6B 160
Crown Lodge SW3 4D 16 (4C 100)
(off Elystan St.)
Crown Mdw. Ct. BR2: Broml 6C 160
Crownmead Way RM7: Mawney 4H 55
Crown M. E1 5K 85
(off White Horse La.)
Crown M. E13 1A 88
Crown M. TW13: Felt 1K 129
Crown M. W6 4C 98
Crown Mill CR4: Mitc 5C 154
Crown Office Row EC4 2J 13 (7A 84)
Crown Pde. N14 1B 32
Crown Pde. SM4: Mord 3J 153
Crown Pas. KT1: King T 2D 150
(off Church St.)
Crown Pas. SW1 5B 12 (1G 101)
Crown Pl. EC2 5G 9 (5E 84)
Crown Pl. NW5 6F 65
Crown Pl. SE16 5H 103
Crown Point SE19 6B 138
Crown Point Pde. SE19 6B 138
(off Crown Dale)
Crown Reach SW1 6D 18 (5H 101)
Crown Rd. EN1: Enf 3B 24
Crown Rd. HA4: Ruis 5B 58
(not continuous)
Crown Rd. IG6: Ilf 4H 53
Crown Rd. KT3: N Mald 1J 151
Crown Rd. N10 7K 31
Crown Rd. SM1: Sutt 4K 165
Crown Rd. SM4: Mord 4K 153
Crown Rd. TW1: Twick 6B 114
Crown Sq. SE1 5J 15 (1F 103)
(off Duchess Wlk.)
Crownstone Ct. SW2 5A 120
Crownstone Rd. SW2 5A 120
Crown St. HA2: Harr 1H 59
Crown St. RM10: Dag 6J 73
(not continuous)
Crown St. SE5 7C 102
Crown St. W3 1H 97
Crown Ter. N14 1C 32
(off Crown La.)
Crown Ter. TW9: Rich 4F 115
Crown Trad. Cen. UB3: Hayes 2G 93
Crowntree Cl. TW7: Isle 6K 95
Crown Village Green 6C 160
(off Crown Lane)
Crown Wlk. HA9: Wemb 3F 61
Crown Way UB7: Yiew 1B 92
Crown Wharf E14 1E 104
(off Coldharbour)
Crown Wharf SE8 5B 104
(off Grove St.)
Crown Woods La. SE18 2F 125
Crown Woods Way SE9 5H 125
Crown Yd. E2 2H 85
Crown Yd. SW6 2J 117
Crown Yd. TW3: Houn 3G 113
Crowshott Av. HA7: Stan 2C 42
Crows Rd. E3 3F 87
Crows Rd. IG11: Bark 6F 71
Crowther Av. TW8: Bford 4E 96
Crowther Cl. SW6 6H 99
(off Bucklers All.)
Crowther Rd. SE25 5G 157
Crowthorne Cl. SW18 7H 117
Crowthorne Rd. W10 6F 81
Croxall Ho. KT12: Walt T 6A 148
Croxden Cl. HA8: Edg 3G 43
Croxden Wlk. SM4: Mord 6A 154
Croxford Gdns. N22 7G 33
Croxford Way RM7: Rush G 1K 73
Croxley Grn. BR5: St P 7B 144
Croxley Rd. W9 3H 81
Croxted Cl. SE21 7C 120
Croxted M. SE24 6C 120
Croxted Rd. SE21 7C 120
Croxted Rd. SE24 7C 120
Croxteth Ho. SW8 2H 119
Croyde Av. UB3: Harl 4G 93
Croyde Av. UB6: G'frd 3G 77
Croyde Cl. DA15: Sidc 7H 125
CROYDON 2C 168
Croydon N17 2D 48
(off Gloucester Rd.)
Croydon Airport Ind. Est. CR0: Wadd 6K 167
Croydon Airport Vis. Cen. 6A 168
Croydon Clocktower 3C 168
(off Katharine St.)
Croydon Crematorium 5K 155
Croydon Flyover, The CR0: C'don 4B 168
Croydon Gro. CR0: C'don 1B 168
Croydon Ho. SE1 6K 13 (2A 102)
(off Wootton St.)
Croydon Rd. BR2: Hayes 3A 172
Croydon Rd. BR2: Kes 3A 172
Croydon Rd. BR3: Beck 4K 157
Croydon Rd. BR4: Hayes 3G 171
Croydon Rd. BR4: W W'ck 3G 171
Croydon Rd. CR0: Bedd 4H 167
Croydon Rd. CR0: C'don 5G 155
Croydon Rd. CR0: Wadd 4H 167
Croydon Rd. CR4: Mitc 4E 154
Croydon Rd. E13 4H 87
Croydon Rd. SE20 2H 157
Croydon Rd. SM6: Bedd 4F 167
Croydon Rd. SM6: W'gton 4F 167
Croydon Rd. TW6: H'row A 2D 110
Croydon Rd. Ind. Est. BR3: Beck 4K 157
Croydon Sailing Club 2F 157
Croydon Sports Arena 5J 157
Croydon Valley Trade Pk. CR0: Bedd 7J 155
(off Therapia La.)
Croyland Rd. N9 1B 34
Croylands Dr. KT6: Surb 7E 150
Croysdale Av. TW16: Sun 3J 147
Crozier Ho. SW8 7K 101
(off Wilkinson St.)
Crozier Ter. E9 5K 67
(not continuous)
Crucible Cl. RM6: Chad H 6B 54
Crucifix La. SE1 6G 15 (2E 102)
Cruden Ho. E3 2B 86
(off Vernon Rd.)
Cruden Ho. SE17 6B 102
(off Brandon Est.)
Cruden St. N1 1B 84
Cruikshank Ho. NW8 2C 82
(off Townshend Rd.)
Cruikshank Rd. E15 4G 69
Cruikshank St. WC1 1J 7 (3A 84)
Crummock Gdns. NW9 5A 44
Crumpsall St. SE2 4C 108
Crundale Av. NW9 5G 43
Crunden Rd. CR2: S Croy 7D 168
Crusader Gdns. CR0: C'don 3E 168
Crusader Ind. Est. N4 6C 48
Crusoe M. N16 2D 66
Crusoe Rd. CR4: Mitc 7D 136
Crusoe Rd. DA8: Erith 5K 109
Crutched Friars EC3 2H 15 (7E 84)
Crutchley Rd. SE6 2G 141
Crystal Ct. E8 1H 85
Crystal Ct. N14 5B 22
Crystal Ct. SE19 5F 139
(off College Rd.)
Crystal Ho. SE18 5K 107
CRYSTAL PALACE 6F 139
Crystal Palace Athletics Stadium 6G 139
Crystal Pal. Cvn. Club Site SE19 5G 139
Crystal Palace Dinosaurs 6G 139
Crystal Palace FC 4E 156
Crystal Palace Indoor Bowling Club 1H 157
Crystal Palace Mus. 6F 139
Crystal Palace Nat. Sports Cen. 5G 139
Crystal Palace Pde. SE19 6F 139
Crystal Palace Pk. 5G 139
Crystal Palace Pk. Farm 6G 139
Crystal Palace Pk. Rd. SE26 5G 139
Crystal Palace Rd. SE22 6F 121
Crystal Palace Sta. Rd. SE19 6G 139
Crystal Pl. KT4: Wor Pk 2D 164
Crystal Ter. SE19 6D 138
Crystal Vw. Ct. BR1: Broml 4F 141
Crystal Way HA1: Harr 5K 107
Crystal Way RM8: Dag 1C 72
Crystal Wharf N1 2B 84
Cuba Dr. EN3: Enf H 2D 24
Cuba St. E14 2C 104
Cube North East London Gymnastic Club, The 4D 66
Cube Ho. SE16 3F 103
Cubitt Apts. SW11 3A 118
(off Chatfield Rd.)
Cubitt Bldg. SW1 6J 17 (5F 101)
Cubitt Ct. NW1 1A 6 (2G 83)
(off Park Village E.)
Cubitt Ho. SW4 6G 119
Cubitt Sq. UB2: S'hall 1G 95
Cubitt Steps E14 1C 104
Cubitt St. WC1 2H 7 (3K 83)
Cubitt Ter. SW4 3G 119
CUBITT TOWN 4E 104
Cuckoo Av. W7 4J 77
Cuckoo Dene W7 5H 77
Cuckoo Hall La. N9 7D 24
Cuckoo Hall Rd. N9 7D 24
Cuckoo Hill HA5: Eastc 3A 40
Cuckoo Hill HA5: Pinn 3A 40
Cuckoo Hill Dr. HA5: Pinn 3A 40
Cuckoo Hill Rd. HA5: Pinn 4A 40
Cuckoo La. W7 7J 77
Cuckoo Pound TW17: Shep 5G 147
Cudas Cl. KT19: Ewe 4B 164
Cuddington Av. KT4: Wor Pk 3B 164
Cudham St. SE6 7E 122
Cudweed Ct. E14 3D 104
(off Watergate Walk)
Cudworth Ho. SW8 1G 119
Cudworth St. E1 4H 85
Cuff Cres. SE9 6B 124
Cuffley Ho. W10 5E 80
(off Sutton Way)
Cuff Point E2 1J 9 (3F 85)
(off Columbia Rd.)
Culand Ho. SE17 4E 102
(off Congreve St.)
Culford Gdns. SW3 4F 17 (4D 100)
Culford Gro. N1 6E 66
Culford Mans. SW3 4F 17 (4D 100)
(off Culford Gdns.)
Culford M. N1 6E 66
Culford Rd. N1 7E 66
Culford Ter. N1 6E 66
(off Balls Pond Rd.)
Culgaith Gdns. EN2: Enf 4D 22
Culham Ho. E2 2J 9 (3F 85)
(off Palissy St.)
Culham Ho. W2 5J 81
(off Gt. Western Rd.)
Cullen Way NW10 4J 79
Culling Rd. DA17: Belv 3J 109
Culling Rd. SE16 3J 103
Cullington Cl. HA3: W'stone 4A 42
Cullingworth Rd. NW10 5C 62
Culloden Cl. SE16 5G 103
Culloden Cl. SE7 6K 105
Culloden Ho. SE14 7A 104
(off Batavia Rd.)
Culloden Rd. EN2: Enf 2G 23
Cullum St. EC3 2G 15 (7E 84)
Cullum Welch Ct. N1 1F 9 (3D 84)
(off Haberdasher St.)
Cullum Welch Ho. EC1 4C 8 (4C 84)
(off Golden La. Est.)
Culmington Pde. W13 1C 96
(off Uxbridge Rd.)
Culmington Rd. CR2: S Croy 7C 168
Culmington Rd. W13 1C 96
Culmore Rd. SE15 7H 103
Culmstock Rd. SW11 5E 118
Culpepper Cl. N18 5C 34
Culpepper Ct. SE11 3J 19 (4A 102)
(off Kennington Rd.)
Culross Cl. N15 4C 48
Culross Ho. W10 6F 81
(off Bridge Cl.)
Culross St. W1 3G 11 (7E 82)
Culsac Rd. KT6: Surb 2E 162
Culverden Rd. SW12 2G 137
Culver Gro. HA7: Stan 2C 42
Culverhouse WC1 6G 7 (5K 83)
(off Red Lion Sq.)
Culverhouse Gdns. SW16 3K 137
Culverlands Cl. HA7: Stan 4G 27
Culverley Rd. SE6 1D 140
Culvers Av. SM5: Cars 2D 166
Culvers Retreat SM5: Cars 1D 166
Culverstone Cl. BR2: Broml 6H 159
Culvers Way SM5: Cars 2D 166
Culvert Dr. E3 3E 86
Culvert Pl. SW11 2E 118
Culvert Rd. N15 5E 48
(not continuous)
Culvert Rd. SW11 2D 118
Culworth Ho. NW8 2C 82
(off Allitsen Rd.)
Culworth St. NW8 1C 4 (2C 82)
Culzean Cl. SE27 3B 138
Cumberland Av. DA16: Well 3J 125
Cumberland Av. NW10 3H 79
Cumberland Basin Primrose Hill 1E 82
Cumberland Basin NW1 1E 82
Cumberland Bus. Pk. NW10 3H 79
Cumberland Cl. E8 6F 67
Cumberland Cl. IG6: Ilf 1G 53
Cumberland Cl. SW20 7F 135
Cumberland Cl. TW1: Twick 6B 114
Cumberland Ct. CR0: C'don 1D 168
Cumberland Ct. DA16: Well 2J 125
Cumberland Ct. HA1: Harr 3J 41
(off Princes Dr.)
Cumberland Ct. SW1 5K 17 (5F 101)
(off Cumberland St.)
Cumberland Ct. W1 1F 11 (6D 82)
(off Gt. Cumberland Pl.)
Cumberland Cres. W14 4G 99
(not continuous)
Cumberland Dr. DA7: Bex 7E 108
Cumberland Dr. KT10: Hin W 2A 162
Cumberland Dr. KT9: Chess 3E 162
Cumberland Gdns. NW4 2G 45
Cumberland Gdns. WC1 1J 7 (3A 84)
Cumberland Ga. W1 2E 10 (7D 82)
Cumberland Ho. E16 1J 105
(off Wesley Av.)
Cumberland Ho. KT2: King T 7H 133
Cumberland Ho. N9 1D 34
(off Cumberland Rd.)
Cumberland Ho. SE28 2G 107
Cumberland Ho. W8 2K 99
(off Kensington Ct.)
Cumberland Mans. W1 7E 4 (6D 82)
(off George St.)
Cumberland Mkt. NW1 1K 5 (3F 83)
Cumberland M. SE11 6K 19 (5A 102)
Cumberland Mills Sq. E14 5F 105
Cumberland Pk. NW10 3C 80
Cumberland Pk. W3 7J 79
Cumberland Pl. NW1 1J 5 (3F 83)
Cumberland Pl. SE6 1H 141
Cumberland Pl. TW16: Sun 4J 147
Cumberland Rd. BR2: Broml 4G 159
Cumberland Rd. E12 4B 70
Cumberland Rd. E13 5K 87
Cumberland Rd. E17 2A 50
Cumberland Rd. HA1: Harr 5F 41
Cumberland Rd. HA7: Stan 3F 43
Cumberland Rd. N22 2K 47
Cumberland Rd. N9 1D 34
Cumberland Rd. SE25 6H 157
Cumberland Rd. SW13 1B 116
Cumberland Rd. TW9: Kew 7G 97
Cumberland Rd. W3 7J 79
Cumberland Rd. W7 2K 95
Cumberland St. SW1 5K 17 (5F 101)
Cumberland Ter. NW1 2F 83
Cumberland Ter. M. NW1 1J 5 (2F 83)
(off Cumberland Ter.)
Cumberland Vs. W3 7J 79
(off Cumberland Rd.)
Cumberland Wharf SE16 2J 103
(off Rotherhithe St.)
Cumberlow Av. SE25 3F 157
Cumbernauld Gdns. TW16: Sun 5H 129
Cumberton Rd. N17 1D 48
Cumbrae Gdns. KT6: Surb 2D 162
Cumbrian Gdns. NW2 2F 63
Cumbrian Way UB8: Uxb 7A 56
Cumming St. N1 2K 83
Cumnor Cl. SW9 2K 119
(off Robsart St.)
Cumnor Gdns. KT17: Ewe 6C 164
Cumnor Rd. SM2: Sutt 6A 166
Cunard Ct. HA7: Stan 2F 27
(off Brightwen Gro.)
Cunard Cres. N21 6J 23
Cunard Pl. EC3 1H 15 (6E 84)
Cunard Rd. NW10 3K 79
Cunard Wlk. SE16 4K 103
Cundy Rd. E16 6A 88
Cundy St. SW1 4H 17 (4E 100)
Cuneo M. NW7 5B 30
Cunliffe Pde. KT19: Ewe 4B 164
Cunliffe Rd. KT19: Ewe 4B 164
Cunliffe St. SW16 6G 137
Cunningham Av. E16 2K 105
Cunningham Cl. BR4: W W'ck 2D 170
Cunningham Cl. RM6: Chad H 5C 54
Cunningham Ct. E10 3D 68
(off Oliver Rd.)
Cunningham Ct. W9 4A 4 (4A 82)
(off Maida Vale)
Cunningham Dr. UB10: Ick 2E 56
Cunningham Ho. SE5 7D 102
(off Elmington Est.)
Cunningham Pk. HA1: Harr 5G 41
Cunningham Pl. NW8 3A 4 (4B 82)
Cunningham Rd. N15 4G 49
Cunnington St. W4 3J 97
Cupar Rd. SW11 1E 118
Cupola Cl. BR1: Broml 5K 141
Cureton St. SW1 4D 18 (4H 101)
Curfew Ho. IG11: Bark 1G 89
Curfew Tower, The 1G 89
Curie Ct. HA1: Harr 7B 42
Curie Gdns. NW9 2A 44
Curlew Cl. SE28 7D 90
Curlew Ct. KT6: Surb 3G 163
Curlew Ct. W13 4K 77
Curlew Ho. EN3: Pond E 5E 24
Curlew Ho. SE15 1F 121
Curlew Ho. SE4 4A 122
(off St Norbert Rd.)
Curlew St. SE1 6J 15 (2F 103)
Curlew St. SE18 1C 124
(off Tellson Av.)
Curlew Way UB4: Yead 5B 76
Curness St. SE13 4E 122
Curnick's La. SE27 4C 138
Curran Av. DA15: Sidc 5K 125
Curran Av. SM6: W'gton 3E 166
Curran Ho. SW3 4C 16 (4C 100)
(off Lucan Pl.)
Curran St. SE10 4J 105
Currey Rd. UB6: G'frd 6H 59
Curricle St. W3 1A 98
Currie Hill Cl. SW19 4H 135
Curry Ri. NW7 6A 30
Cursitor St. EC4 7J 7 (6A 84)
Curtain Pl. EC2 2H 9 (3E 84)
Curtain Rd. EC2 4G 9 (4E 84)
Curthwaite Gdns. EN2: Enf 4C 22
Curtis & Staub Health Club Golders Green 7H 45
Curtis Dr. W3 6K 79
Curtis Fld. Rd. SW16 4K 137
Curtis Ho. SE17 5D 102
(off Morecambe St.)
Curtis La. HA0: Wemb 6E 60
Curtis Rd. KT19: Ewe 4J 163
Curtis Rd. TW4: Houn 7D 112
Curtiss Ho. NW9 3B 44
Curtis St. SE1 4F 103
Curtis Way SE1 4F 103
Curtis Way SE28 7B 90
Curtlington Ho. HA8: Edg 2J 43
(off Burnt Oak B'way.)
Curve, The W12 7C 80
Curwen Av. E7 4K 69
Curwen Rd. W12 2C 98
Curzon Av. EN3: Pond E 5E 24
Curzon Av. HA7: Stan 1A 42
Curzon Cinema Bloomsbury 3E 6 (4J 83)
Curzon Cinema Mayfair 4J 11 (1F 101)
(off Curzon St.)
Curzon Cinema Richmond 5D 114
Curzon Cinema Soho 2D 12 (7H 83)
(off Shaftesbury Av.)
Curzon Cinema Victoria 1B 18 (3G 101)
(off Victoria St.)
Curzon Cl. BR6: Orp 4H 173
Curzon Ct. SW6 1A 118
(off Imperial Rd.)
Curzon Cres. IG11: Bark 2K 89
Curzon Cres. NW10 7A 62
Curzon Ga. W1 5H 11 (1E 100)
Curzon Pl. HA5: Eastc 5A 40
Curzon Rd. CR7: Thor H 6A 156
Curzon Rd. N10 2F 47
Curzon Rd. W5 4B 78
Curzon Sq. W1 5H 11 (1E 100)
Curzon St. W1 5H 11 (1E 100)
Cusack Cl. TW1: Tedd 4K 131
Custance Ho. N1 1E 8 (2D 84)
(off Provost St.)
Custance St. N1 1E 8 (3D 84)
Custom Ho. EC3 3G 15 (7E 84)
CUSTOM HOUSE 6A 88
Custom Ho. Reach SE16 2B 104
Custom Ho. Wlk. EC3 3G 15 (7E 84)
Cut, The SE1 6K 13 (2A 102)
Cutbush Ho. N7 5H 65
Cutcombe Rd. SE5 2C 120
Cuthberga Cl. IG11: Bark 7G 71
Cuthbert Bell Twr. E3 2C 86
(off Pancras Way)
Cuthbert Gdns. SE25 3E 156
Cuthbert Harrowing Ho. EC1 4C 8 (4C 84)
(off Golden La. Est.)
Cuthbert Ho. W2 5A 4 (5B 82)
(off Hall Pl.)
Cuthbert Rd. CR0: C'don 2B 168
Cuthbert Rd. E17 3E 50
Cuthbert Rd. N18 5B 34
Cuthbert St. W2 5A 4 (5B 82)
Cuthill Wlk. SE5 1D 120
Cutlers Gdns. EC2 6H 9 (5E 84)
Cutlers Gdns. Arc. EC2 7H 9 (6E 84)
(off Devonshire Sq.)
Cutlers Sq. E14 4C 104
Cutlers Ter. N1 6E 66
(off Balls Pond Rd.)
Cutler St. E1 7H 9 (6E 84)
Cutter Ho. DA8: Erith 4K 109
Cutter Ho. E16 2K 105
(off Admiralty Av.)
Cutter La. SE10 2G 105
Cutthroat All. TW10: Ham 2C 132
Cutty Sark 6E 104
Cutty Sark Gdns. SE10 6E 104
(off King William Wlk.)
Cutty Sark Hall SE10 6E 104
(off Welland St.)
Cuxton BR5: Pet W 5G 161
Cuxton Cl. DA6: Bex 5E 126
Cuxton Ho. SE17 5E 102
(off Mina Rd.)
Cyan Apts. E3 1A 86
(off Gunmaker's La.)
Cyclamen Cl. TW12: Hamp 6E 130
Cyclamen Way KT19: Ewe 5J 163
Cyclops M. E14 4C 104
Cygnet Av. TW14: Felt 7A 112
Cygnet Cl. NW10 5K 61
Cygnet Ho. CR0: C'don 1D 168
Cygnet Ho. SE15 6G 103

210 A–Z London

David Lloyd Leisure Kingston upon Thames – Department for Transport

David Lloyd Leisure Kingston upon Thames 2E 150
(within The Rotunda Cen.)
David Lloyd Leisure Purley 6K 167
David Lloyd Leisure Raynes Park 3F 153
David Lloyd Leisure Sidcup 5C 144
David Lloyd Leisure Sudbury Hill 5H 59
David M. SE10 7E 104
David M. W1 5F 5 (5D 82)
David Rd. RM8: Dag 2E 72
David Rd. SL3: Poyle 5A 174
Davidson Gdns. SW8 7J 101
Davidson La. HA1: Harr 7K 41
Davidson Rd. CR0: C'don 1E 168
Davidson Terraces E7 5K 69
(off Claremont Rd.)
David's Rd. SE23 1J 139
David St. E15 6F 69
David Twigg Cl. KT2: King T 1E 150
David Weir Leisure Cen. 7B 154
David Wildman La. NW7 6B 30
Davies Cl. CR0: C'don 6G 157
Davies La. E11 2G 69
Davies M. W1 2J 11 (7F 83)
Davies St. W1 1J 11 (6F 83)
Davies Wlk. TW7: Isle 1H 113
Da Vinci Ct. SE16 5H 103
(off Rossetti Rd.)
Da Vinci Lodge SE10 3H 105
(off W. Parkside)
Da Vinci Torre SE13 3D 122
(off Loampit Va.)
Davington Gdns. RM8: Dag 5B 72
Davington Rd. RM8: Dag 6B 72
Davinia Cl. IG8: Wfd G 6J 37
Davis Ho. W12 7D 80
(off White City Est.)
Davison Cl. SE13 1D 122
Davis Rd. KT9: Chess 4G 163
Davis Rd. W3 1B 98
Davis Rd. Ind. Pk. KT9: Chess 4G 163
Davis St. E13 2K 87
Davisville Rd. W12 2C 98
Davis Way DA14: Sidc 6E 144
Davmor Ct. TW8: Bford 5C 96
Dawburn Pl. TW5: Hest 7B 94
Dawes Av. TW7: Isle 5A 114
Dawes Cl. UB10: Uxb 2A 74
Dawes Ho. SE17 4D 102
(off Orb St.)
Dawe's Rd. UB10: Uxb 2A 74
Dawes Rd. SW6 7G 99
Dawes St. SE17 5D 102
Dawkins Ct. SE1 3D 102
Dawley Av. UB8: Hil 5E 74
Dawley Pde. UB3: Hayes 7E 74
Dawley Pk. UB3: Hayes 2F 93
Dawley Rd. UB3: Harl 7E 74
Dawley Rd. UB3: Hayes 7E 74
Dawlish Av. N13 4D 32
Dawlish Av. SW18 2K 135
Dawlish Av. UB6: G'frd 2A 78
Dawlish Dr. HA4: Ruis 2J 57
Dawlish Dr. HA5: Pinn 5C 40
Dawlish Dr. IG3: Ilf 4J 71
Dawlish Rd. E10 1E 68
Dawlish Rd. N17 3G 49
Dawlish Rd. NW2 6F 63
Dawnay Gdns. SW18 2B 136
Dawnay Rd. SW18 2A 136
Dawn Cl. TW4: Houn 3C 112
Dawn Cres. E15 1F 87
Dawpool Rd. NW2 2B 62
Daws Hill E4 2K 25
Daws La. NW7 5G 29
Dawson Av. IG11: Bark 7K 71
Dawson Cl. SE18 4G 107
Dawson Cl. UB3: Hayes 5F 75
Dawson Close DA1: Cray 5K 127
Dawson Ct. W3 3J 97
(off Palmerston Rd.)
Dawson Gdns. IG11: Bark 7K 71
Dawson Ho. E2 3J 85
(off Sceptre Rd.)
Dawson Pl. W2 7J 81
Dawson Rd. KT1: King T 3F 151
Dawson Rd. NW2 5E 62
Dawson St. E2 2F 85
Dawson Ter. N9 7D 24
Dax Ct. TW16: Sun 3A 148
Daybrook Rd. SW19 2K 153
Day Dr. RM8: Dag 1D 72
Day Ho. SE5 7C 102
(off Bethwin Rd.)
Daylesford Av. SW15 4C 116
Daymer Gdns. HA5: Eastc 4K 39
Daynor Ho. NW6 1J 81
(off Quex Ho.)
Daysbrook Rd. SW2 1K 137
Days La. DA15: Sidc 7J 125
Dayton Gro. SE15 1J 121
Deaconess Ct. N15 4F 49
(off Tottenham Grn. E.)
Deacon Est., The E4 6G 35
Deacon Ho. SE11 4H 19 (4K 101)
(off Black Prince Rd.)
Deacon M. N1 7D 66
Deacon Rd. KT2: King T 1F 151
Deacon Rd. NW2 5C 62
Deacons Cl. HA5: Pinn 2K 39
Deacons Ct. TW1: Twick 2K 131
Deacons Leas BR6: Orp 4H 173
Deacon's Ri. N2 5B 46
Deacons Ter. N1 6C 66
(off Harecourt Rd.)
Deacon St. SE17 4C 102
Deacons Wlk. TW12: Hamp 4E 130
Deacon Way IG8: Wfd G 7J 37
Deal Ct. NW9 2B 44
(off Hazel Cl.)
Deal Ct. UB1: S'hall 6G 77
(off Haldane Rd.)
Deal Ho. SE15 6K 103
(off Lovelinch La.)
Deal Ho. SE17 5E 102
(off Mina Rd.)
Deal M. W5 4D 96
Deal Porters Wlk. SE16 2K 103
Deal Porters Way SE16 3J 103
Deal Rd. SW17 6E 136
Deal's Gateway SE10 1C 122
Deal's Gateway SE13 1C 122
Deal St. E1 5G 85
Dealtry Rd. SW15 4E 116
Deal Wlk. SW9 7A 102
Dean Abbott Ho. SW1 3C 18 (4H 101)
(off Vincent St.)
Dean Bradley St. SW1 2E 18 (3J 101)
Dean Cl. E9 5J 67
Dean Cl. SE16 1K 103
Dean Cl. UB10: Hil 7B 56
Dean Ct. HA0: Wemb 3B 60
Dean Ct. HA8: Edg 6C 28
Dean Ct. RM7: Rom 5K 55
Dean Ct. SW8 7J 101
(off Thorncroft St.)
Dean Ct. W3 6K 79
Deancross St. E1 6J 85
Dean Dr. HA7: Stan 2E 42
Deane Av. HA4: Ruis 5A 58
Deane Ct. HA6: Nwood 1G 39
Deane Cft. Rd. HA5: Eastc 6A 40
Deanery Cl. N2 4C 46
Deanery M. W1 4H 11 (1E 100)
(off Deanery St.)
Deanery Rd. E15 6G 69
Deanery St. W1 4H 11 (1E 100)
Deane Way HA4: Ruis 6K 39
Dean Farrar St. SW1 1D 18 (3H 101)
Deanfield Gdns. CR0: C'don 4D 168
Dean Gdns. E17 4F 51
Deanhill Ct. SW14 4H 115
Deanhill Rd. SW14 4H 115
Dean Ho. E1 6J 85
(off Tarling St.)
Dean Ho. SE14 7A 104
(off New Cross Rd.)
Dean Path RM8: Bark 4A 72
Dean Rd. CR0: C'don 4D 168
Dean Rd. NW2 6E 62
Dean Rd. SE28 1A 108
Dean Rd. TW12: Hamp 5E 130
Dean Rd. TW3: Houn 5F 113
Dean Ryle St. SW1 3E 18 (4J 101)
Deansbrook Cl. HA8: Edg 7D 28
Deansbrook Rd. HA8: Edg 7C 28
Dean's Bldgs. SE17 4D 102
Deans Cl. CR0: C'don 3F 169
Deans Cl. HA8: Edg 6D 28
Deans Cl. W4 6H 97
Dean's Ct. EC4 1B 14 (6B 84)
Deanscroft Av. NW9 1J 61
Deans Dr. HA8: Edg 5E 28
Deans Dr. N13 6G 33
Deans Ga. Cl. SE23 3K 139
Deanshanger Ho. SE8 4K 103
(off Chilton Gro.)
Deans La. HA8: Edg 6D 28
Deans La. W4 6H 97
(off Deans Cl.)
Dean's M. W1 7K 5 (6F 83)
Deans Rd. SM1: Sutt 3K 165
Deans Rd. W7 1K 95
Dean Stanley St. SW1 2E 18 (3J 101)
Deanston Wharf E16 2K 105
(not continuous)
Dean St. E7 5J 69
Dean St. W1 7C 6 (6H 83)
Deans Way HA8: Edg 5D 28
Deansway N2 4B 46
Deansway N9 3K 33
Deanswood N11 6C 32
Dean's Yd. SW1 1D 18 (3H 101)
Dean Trench St. SW1 2E 18 (3J 101)
Dean Wlk. HA8: Edg 6D 28
Dean Way UB2: S'hall 2F 95
Dearne Cl. HA7: Stan 5F 27
De'Arn Gdns. CR4: Mitc 3C 154
Dearsley Ho. RM13: Rain 2K 91
Dearsley Rd. EN1: Enf 3B 24
Deauville Cl. E14 6F 87
Deauville Ct. SE16 2K 103
(off Eleanor Cl.)
Deauville Ct. SW4 6G 119
De Barowe M. N5 4B 66
Debdale Ho. E2 1G 85
(off Whiston Rd.)
Debden N17 2D 48
(off Gloucester Rd.)
Debden Cl. IG8: Wfd G 7G 37
Debden Cl. KT2: King T 5D 132
Debden Cl. NW9 1A 44
Debden Pl. UB10: Uxb 1A 74
De Beauvoir Ct. N1 7D 66
(off Northchurch Rd.)
De Beauvoir Cres. N1 1E 84
De Beauvoir Est. N1 1E 84
De Beauvoir Pl. N1 6E 66
De Beauvoir Rd. N1 1E 84
De Beauvoir Sq. N1 7E 66
DE BEAUVOIR TOWN 1E 84
De Beauvoir Wharf N1 1E 84
(off Hertford Rd.)
Debenham Ct. E8 1G 85
(off Pownall Rd.)
Debham Ct. NW2 3E 62
Deblin Dr. UB10: Uxb 2A 74
Debnams Rd. SE16 4J 103
De Bohun Av. N14 6A 22
Deborah Cl. TW7: Isle 1J 113
Deborah Ct. E18 3K 51
(off Victoria Rd.)
Deborah Cres. HA4: Ruis 7F 39
Deborah Lodge HA8: Edg 1H 43
Debrabant Cl. DA8: Erith 6K 109
De Brome Rd. TW13: Felt 1A 130
De Bruin Ct. E14 5E 104
(off Ferry St.)
Deburgh Rd. SW19 7A 136
Debussy NW9 2B 44
Decapod St. E15 5F 69
Decima St. SE1 7G 15 (3E 102)
Decima Studios SE1 3E 102
(off Decima St.)
Decimus Cl. CR7: Thor H 4D 156
Deck Cl. SE16 1K 103
De Coubertin St. E20 6E 68
Decoy Av. NW11 5G 45
De Crespigny Pk. SE5 2D 120
Dee Ct. W7 6H 77
(off Hobbayne Rd.)
Dee Ho. KT2: King T 1D 150
(off May Bate Av.)
Deeley Rd. SW8 1H 119
Deena Cl. W3 6F 79
Deen City Farm 2A 154
Deepak Ho. SW17 4H 135
Deepdale SW19 4F 135
Deepdale Av. BR2: Broml 4H 159
Deepdale Cl. N11 6K 31
Deepdale Ct. CR2: S Croy 4D 168
(off Birdhurst Av.)
Deep Dene W5 4F 79
Deepdene Av. CR0: C'don 3F 169
Deepdene Cl. E11 4J 51
Deepdene Ct. BR2: Broml 3G 159
Deepdene Ct. N21 6G 23
Deepdene Gdns. SW2 7K 119
Deepdene Mans. SW6 1H 117
(off Rostrevor Rd.)
Deepdene Point SE23 3K 139
Deepdene Rd. DA16: Well 3A 126
Deepdene Rd. SE5 4D 120
Deepwell Cl. TW7: Isle 1A 114
Deepwood La. UB6: G'frd 3H 77
Deerbrook Rd. SE24 1B 138
Deerdale Rd. SE24 4C 120
Deerfield Cl. NW9 5B 44
Deerfield Cotts. NW9 5B 44
Deerhurst Cl. TW13: Felt 4K 129
Deerhurst Ct. CR0: C'don 1B 168
(off Parson's Mead)
Deerhurst Cres. TW12: Hamp H 5G 131
Deerhurst Ho. SE15 6G 103
(off Haymerle Rd.)
Deerhurst Rd. NW2 6F 63
Deerhurst Rd. SW16 5K 137
Deering Ho. SE3 4A 124
Deerings Dr. HA5: Eastc 5J 39
Deerleap Gro. E4 5J 25
Dee Rd. TW9: Rich 4F 115
Deer Pk. Cl. KT2: King T 7H 133
Deer Pk. Gdns. CR4: Mitc 4B 154
Deer Pk. Rd. SW19 2K 153
Deer Pk. Way BR4: W W'ck 2H 171
Deeside Rd. SW17 3B 136
Dee St. E14 6E 86
Defence Cl. SE28 1J 107
Defiance Wlk. SE18 3D 106
Defiant Way SM6: W'gton 7J 167
Defoe Av. TW9: Kew 7G 97
Defoe Cl. SE16 2B 104
Defoe Cl. SW17 6C 136
Defoe Ho. EC2 5C 8 (5C 84)
(off Beech St.)
Defoe Pl. EC2 5C 8 (5C 84)
(off Beech St.)
Defoe Pl. SW17 4D 136
Defoe Rd. N16 3E 66
De Frene Rd. SE26 4K 139
Degema Rd. BR7: Chst 5F 143
Dehar Cres. NW9 7B 44
Dehavilland Cl. UB5: N'olt 3B 76
De Havilland Ct. N17 3H 49
De Havilland Dr. SE18 6F 107
De Havilland Rd. HA8: Edg 2G 43
De Havilland Rd. TW5: Hest 7A 94
Dehavilland Studios E5 2J 67
(off Theydon Rd.)
De Havilland Way TW19: Stanw 6A 110
Dekker Cl. RM5: Col R 1G 55
Dekker Ho. SE5 7D 102
(off Elmington Est.)
Dekker Rd. SE21 6E 120
Dekota HA9: Wemb 4G 61
(off Engineers Way)
Delacourt Rd. SE3 7K 105
Delafield Ho. E1 6G 85
(off Christian St.)
Delafield Rd. SE7 5K 105
Delaford Rd. SE16 5H 103
Delaford St. SW6 7G 99
Delahay Ho. SW3 7E 16 (6D 100)
(off Chelsea Emb.)
Delamare Ct. SE6 3D 140
Delamare Cres. CR0: C'don 6J 157
Delamere Ct. E17 2E 50
Delamere Gdns. NW7 6E 28
Delamere Rd. SW20 1F 153
Delamere Rd. UB4: Yead 7B 76
Delamere Rd. W5 2E 96
Delamere St. W2 5K 81
Delamere Ter. W2 5K 81
Delancey Pas. NW1 1F 83
(off Delancey St.)
Delancey St. NW1 1F 83
Delancey Studios NW1 1F 83
Delany Ho. SE10 6E 104
(off Thames St.)
Delarch Ho. SE1 7A 14 (2B 102)
(off Webber Row)
De Laune St. SE17 6K 19 (5B 102)
Delaware Mans. W9 4K 81
(off Delaware Rd.)
Delaware Rd. W9 4K 81
Delawyk Cres. SE24 6C 120
Delcombe Av. KT4: Wor Pk 1E 164
Delderfield Ho. RM1: Rom 2K 55
(off Portnoi Cl.)
Delft Ho. KT2: King T 7F 133
(off Acre Rd.)
Delft Way SE22 5E 120
Delhi Rd. EN1: Enf 7A 24
Delhi St. N1 1J 83
Delia St. SW18 7K 117
Delisle Rd. SE28 1J 107
Delius Gro. E15 2F 87
Dell, The DA5: Bexl 1K 145
Dell, The HA0: Wemb 5B 60
Dell, The HA5: Pinn 2B 40
Dell, The IG8: Wfd G 3E 36
Dell, The SE19 1F 157
Dell, The SE2 5A 108
Dell, The TW14: Felt 7K 111
Dell, The TW8: Bford 6C 96
Della Path E5 3G 67
Dellbow Rd. TW14: Felt 5K 111
Dell Cl. E15 1F 87
Dell Cl. IG8: Wfd G 3E 36
Dell Cl. SM6: W'gton 4G 167
Dell Farm Rd. HA4: Ruis 5F 39
Dellfield Cl. BR3: Beck 1E 158
Dell La. KT17: Ewe 5C 164
Dellors Cl. EN5: Barn 5A 20
Dellow Cl. IG2: Ilf 7H 53
Dellow Ho. E1 7H 85
(off Dellow St.)
Dellow St. E1 7H 85
Dell Rd. KT17: Ewe 6C 164
Dell Rd. UB7: W Dray 4B 92
Dells Cl. E4 7J 25
Dells Cl. TW11: Tedd 6K 131
Dell's M. SW1 4B 18 (4G 101)
(off Churton Pl.)
Dell Wlk. KT3: N Mald 2A 152
Dell Way W13 6C 78
Dellwood Gdns. IG5: Ilf 3E 52
Delmare Cl. SW9 4K 119
Delme Cres. SE3 2K 123
Delmerend Ho. SW3 5C 16 (5C 100)
(off Cale St.)
Delmey Cl. CR0: C'don 3F 169
Deloraine Ho. SE8 1C 122
Delorme St. W6 6F 99
Delroy Ct. N20 7F 21
Delta Bldg. E14 6E 86
(off Ashton St.)
Delta Bldg., The RM7: Rush G 6K 55
Delta Cen. HA0: Wemb 1F 79
Delta Cl. KT4: Wor Pk 3B 164
Delta Ct. NW2 2C 62
Delta Ct. SE8 6A 104
(off Trundleys Rd.)
Delta Gro. UB5: N'olt 3B 76
Delta Ho. N1 1E 8 (3D 84)
(off Nile St.)
Delta M. NW7 5B 30
Delta Pk. SW18 4K 117
Delta Pk. Ind. Est. EN3: Brim 3G 25
Delta Point CR0: C'don 1C 168
(off Wellesley Rd.)
Delta Point E2 3G 85
(off Delta St.)
Delta Rd. KT4: Wor Pk 3A 164
Delta St. E2 3G 85
De Luci Rd. DA8: Erith 5J 109
De Lucy St. SE2 4B 108
Delvan Cl. SE18 7E 106
Delvers Mead RM10: Dag 4J 73
Delverton Ho. SE17 5B 102
(off Delverton Rd.)
Delverton Rd. SE17 5B 102
Delvino Rd. SW6 1J 117
Demesne Rd. SM6: W'gton 4H 167
Demeta Cl. HA9: Wemb 3J 61
De Montfort Pde. SW16 3J 137
De Montfort Rd. SW16 3J 137
De Morgan Rd. SW6 3K 117
Dempsey Ct. SE6 7C 122
Dempster Cl. KT6: Surb 1C 162
Dempster Rd. SW18 5A 118
Den, The 5J 103
Denbar Pde. RM7: Rom 4J 55
Denberry Dr. DA14: Sidc 3B 144
Denbigh Cl. BR7: Chst 6D 142
Denbigh Cl. HA4: Ruis 2H 57
Denbigh Cl. SM1: Sutt 5H 165
Denbigh Cl. UB1: S'hall 6D 76
Denbigh Cl. W11 7H 81
Denbigh Ct. E6 3B 88
Denbigh Ct. W7 5K 77
(off Copley Cl.)
Denbigh Dr. UB3: Harl 2E 92
Denbigh Gdns. TW10: Rich 5F 115
Denbigh Ho. SW1 1F 17 (3D 100)
(off Hans Pl.)
Denbigh Ho. W11 7H 81
(off Westbourne Gro.)
Denbigh M. SW1 4A 18 (4G 101)
(off Denbigh St.)
Denbigh Pl. SW1 5A 18 (5G 101)
Denbigh Rd. E6 3B 88
Denbigh Rd. TW3: Houn 2F 113
Denbigh Rd. UB1: S'hall 6D 76
Denbigh Rd. W11 7H 81
Denbigh Rd. W13 7B 78
Denbigh St. SW1 4A 18 (4G 101)
(not continuous)
Denbigh Ter. W11 7H 81
Denbridge Rd. BR1: Broml 2D 160
Denbury Ho. E3 3D 86
(off Talwin St.)
Denby Ct. SE11 3H 19 (4K 101)
(off Lambeth Wlk.)
Dence Ho. E2 2K 9 (3G 85)
(off Turin St.)
Denchworth Ho. SW9 2A 120
Dencliffe TW15: Ashf 5C 128
Den Cl. BR3: Beck 3F 159
Dencora Cen., The EN3: Brim 3F 25
Dene, The CR0: C'don 4K 169
Dene, The HA9: Wemb 4E 60
Dene, The KT8: W Mole 5D 148
Dene, The W13 5B 78
Dene Av. DA15: Sidc 7B 126
Dene Av. TW3: Houn 3D 112
Dene Cl. BR2: Hayes 1H 171
Dene Cl. DA2: Wilm 4K 145
Dene Cl. E10 2D 68
Dene Cl. KT4: Wor Pk 2B 164
Dene Cl. SE4 3A 122
Dene Ct. CR2: S Croy 5C 168
(off Warham Rd.)
Dene Ct. W5 5C 78
Denecroft Cres. UB10: Hil 1D 74
Dene Gdns. HA7: Stan 5H 27
Dene Gdns. KT7: T Ditt 2A 162
Dene Ho. N14 7C 22
Denehurst Gdns. IG8: Wfd G 4E 36
Denehurst Gdns. NW4 6E 44
Denehurst Gdns. TW10: Rich 4G 115
Denehurst Gdns. TW2: Twick 7H 113
Denehurst Gdns. W3 1H 97
Dene Rd. IG9: Buck H 1G 37
Dene Rd. N11 1J 31
Denesmead SE24 5C 120
Denewood EN5: New Bar 5F 21
Denewood Rd. N6 6D 46
Denford St. SE10 5H 105
(off Glenforth St.)
Dengie Wlk. N1 1C 84
(off Basire St.)
Denham Cl. DA16: Well 3C 126
Denham Ct. NW6 7K 63
(off Fairfax Rd.)
Denham Ct. SE26 3H 139
(off Kirkdale)
Denham Ct. UB1: S'hall 7G 77
(off Baird Av.)
Denham Cres. CR4: Mitc 4D 154
Denham Dr. IG2: Ilf 6G 53
Denham Ho. UB7: W Dray 2B 92
(off Park Lodge Av.)
Denham Ho. W12 7D 80
(off White City Est.)
Denham Rd. N20 3J 31
Denham Rd. TW14: Felt 7A 112
Denham St. SE10 5J 105
Denham Way IG11: Bark 1J 89
Denholme Rd. W9 3H 81
Denison Cl. N2 3A 46
Denison Ho. E14 3D 104
Denison Rd. SW19 6B 136
Denison Rd. TW13: Felt 4H 129
Denison Rd. W5 4C 78
Deniston Av. DA5: Bexl 1E 144
Denis Way SW4 3H 119
Denland Ho. SW8 7K 101
(off Dorset Rd.)
Denleigh Gdns. KT7: T Ditt 6J 149
Denleigh Gdns. N21 1F 33
Denman Av. UB2: S'hall 1H 95
Denman Dr. KT10: Clay 5A 162
Denman Dr. NW11 5J 45
Denman Dr. TW15: Ashf 6D 128
Denman Dr. Nth. NW11 5J 45
Denman Dr. Sth. NW11 5J 45
Denman Ho. N16 2E 66
Denman Pl. W1 2C 12 (7H 83)
(off Denman St.)
Denman Rd. SE15 1F 121
Denman St. W1 3C 12 (7H 83)
Denmark Av. SW19 7G 135
Denmark Ct. SM4: Mord 6J 153
Denmark Gdns. SM5: Cars 3D 166
Denmark Gro. N1 2A 84
Denmark Hill SE5 1D 120
DENMARK HILL 3C 120
Denmark Hill Dr. NW9 3C 44
Denmark Hill Est. SE5 4D 120
Denmark Mans. SE5 2C 120
(off Coldharbour La.)
Denmark Path SE25 5H 157
Denmark Pl. E3 3C 86
Denmark Pl. WC2 7D 6 (6H 83)
Denmark Rd. BR1: Broml 1K 159
Denmark Rd. KT1: King T 3E 150
Denmark Rd. N8 4A 48
Denmark Rd. NW6 2H 81
Denmark Rd. SE25 5G 157
Denmark Rd. SE5 1C 120
Denmark Rd. SM5: Cars 3D 166
Denmark Rd. SW19 6F 135
Denmark Rd. TW2: Twick 3H 131
Denmark Rd. W13 7B 78
Denmark St. E11 3G 69
Denmark St. E13 5K 87
Denmark St. N17 1H 49
Denmark St. WC2 1D 12 (6H 83)
Denmark Ter. N2 3D 46
Denmead Ho. SW15 6B 116
Denmead Rd. CR0: C'don 1B 168
Denmore Ct. SM6: W'gton 5F 167
Dennan Rd. KT6: Surb 1F 163
Dennard Way BR6: Farnb 4F 173
Denner Rd. E4 2H 35
Denne Ter. E8 1F 85
Dennett Rd. CR0: C'don 1A 168
Dennett's Gro. SE14 2K 121
Dennett's Rd. SE14 1J 121
Denning Av. CR0: Wadd 4A 168
Denning Cl. NW8 1A 4 (3A 82)
Denning Cl. TW12: Hamp 5D 130
Denning M. SW12 6E 118
Denning Point E1 7K 9 (6F 85)
(off Commercial St.)
Denning Rd. NW3 4B 64
Dennington Cl. E5 2J 67
Dennington Pk. Rd. NW6 6J 63
Denningtons, The KT4: Wor Pk 2A 164
Dennis Av. HA9: Wemb 5F 61
Dennis Cl. TW15: Ashf 7F 129
Dennis Gdns. HA7: Stan 5H 27
Dennis Ho. E3 2B 86
(off Roman Rd.)
Dennis Ho. SM1: Sutt 4K 165
Dennis La. HA7: Stan 3G 27
Dennison Point E15 7E 68
Dennis Pde. N14 1C 32
Dennis Pk. Cres. SW20 1G 153
Dennis Reeve Cl. CR4: Mitc 1D 154
Dennis Rd. KT8: E Mos 4G 149
Dennis Severs' House 5H 9 (5E 84)
Denny Cl. E6 5C 88
Denny Cres. SE11 5K 19 (5A 102)
Denny Gdns. RM9: Dag 7B 72
Denny Rd. N9 1C 34
Denny St. SE11 5K 19 (5A 102)
Den Rd. BR2: Broml 3F 159
Densham Ho. NW8 1B 4 (2B 82)
(off Cochrane St.)
Densham Rd. E15 1G 87
Densole Cl. BR3: Beck 1A 158
Denstone Ho. SE15 6G 103
(off Haymerle Rd.)
Densworth Gro. N9 2D 34
Dent Ho. SE17 4E 102
(off Peacock St.)
Denton NW1 6E 64
Denton Ho. N1 7B 66
(off Halton Rd.)
Denton Rd. DA16: Well 7C 108
Denton Rd. DA5: Bexl 2K 145
Denton Rd. N18 4K 33
Denton Rd. N8 5K 47
Denton Rd. TW1: Twick 6D 114
Denton St. SW18 6K 117
Denton Ter. DA5: Bexl 2K 145
Denton Way E5 3K 67
Dents Rd. SW11 6D 118
Denver Cl. BR6: Pet W 6J 161
Denver Rd. N16 7E 48
Denwood SE23 3K 139
Denyer St. SW3 4D 16 (4C 100)
Denys Ho. EC1 5J 7 (5A 84)
(off Bourne Est.)
Denziloe Av. UB10: Hil 3D 74
Denzil Rd. NW10 5B 62
Deodar Rd. SW15 4G 117
Deodora Cl. N20 3H 31
Department for Business, Energy & Industrial Strategy 1D 18 (3H 101)
Department for Communities 1A 18 (3G 101)
(off Bressenden Pl.)
Department for Education 1D 18 (3H 101)
(off Gt. Smith St.)
Department for Energy & Climate Change 5E 12 (1J 101)
(off Whitehall Pl.)
Department for Transport 3D 18 (4H 101)

Dollis Rd. NW7 7B **30**
Dollis Valley Dr. EN5: Barn 6C **20**
Dollis Valley Way EN5: Barn 6C **20**
Dolman Cl. N3 2A **46**
Dolman Rd. W4 4K **97**
Dolman St. SW4 4K **119**
Dolomite Ct. HA4: Ruis 4A **58**
Dolphin Cl. KT6: Surb 5D **150**
Dolphin Cl. SE16 2K **103**
Dolphin Cl. SE28 6D **90**
Dolphin Ct. NW11 6G **45**
Dolphin Est. TW16: Sun 1G **147**
Dolphin Ho. SW18 4K **117**
Dolphin Ho. SW6 2A **118**
(off Lensbury Av.)
Dolphin Ho. TW16: Sun 1G **147**
(off Windmill Rd.)
Dolphin La. E14 7D **86**
Dolphin Rd. TW16: Sun 1G **147**
Dolphin Rd. UB5: N'olt 2D **76**
Dolphin Rd. Nth. TW16: Sun 1G **147**
Dolphin Rd. Sth. TW16: Sun 1G **147**
Dolphin Rd. W. TW16: Sun 1G **147**
Dolphin Sq. SW1 6B **18** (5G **101**)
Dolphin Sq. W4 7A **98**
Dolphin St. KT1: King T 2E **150**
Dolphin Twr. SE8 6B **104**
(off Abinger Gro.)
Dombey Ho. SE1 7K **15** (2G **103**)
(off Wolseley St.)
Dombey Ho. W11 1F **99**
(off St Ann's Rd.)
Dombey St. WC1 5G **7** (5K **83**)
(not continuous)
Domecq Ho. EC1 3B **8** (4B **84**)
(off Dallington St.)
Dome Hill Pk. SE26 4F **139**
Domelton Ho. SW18 6K **117**
(off Iron Mill Rd.)
Domett Cl. SE5 4D **120**
Domfe Pl. E5 4J **67**
Domingo St. EC1 3C **8** (4C **84**)
Dominica Cl. E13 2B **88**
Dominion Apts. E17 5B **50**
Dominion Bus. Pk. N9 2E **34**
Dominion Cen., The UB2: S'hall 2C **94**
Dominion Cl. TW3: Houn 2H **113**
Dominion Ct. E8 7F **67**
(off Middleton Rd.)
Dominion Ct. TW3: Houn 3H **113**
Dominion Dr. SE16 2K **103**
Dominion Ho. E14 5D **104**
(off St Davids Sq.)
Dominion Ho. EC1 6C **8** (5C **84**)
(off Bartholomew Cl.)
Dominion Ind. Est. UB2: S'hall 2C **94**
(off Feather Rd.)
Dominion Pde. HA1: Harr 5K **41**
Dominion Rd. CR0: C'don 7F **157**
Dominion Rd. UB2: S'hall 2C **94**
Dominion St. EC2 5F **9** (5D **84**)
Dominion Theatre 7D **6** (6H **83**)
(off Tottenham Ct. Rd.)
Dominion Wlk. E14 7F **87**
(off Fairmont Av.)
Domitian Pl. BR3: Beck 4D **158**
Domonic Dr. SE9 4F **143**
Domville Cl. N20 2G **31**
Domville Ct. SE17 5E **102**
(off Bagshot St.)
Donald Dr. RM6: Chad H 5C **54**
Donald Hunter Ho. E7 5K **69**
(off Woodgrange Rd.)
Donald Rd. CR0: C'don 7A **156**
Donald Rd. E13 1K **87**
Donaldson Rd. NW6 1H **81**
Donaldson Rd. SE18 1E **124**
Donald Woods Gdns. KT5: Surb 2H **163**
Donato Dr. SE15 6E **102**
Doncaster Dr. UB5: N'olt 5D **58**
Doncaster Gdns. N4 6C **48**
Doncaster Gdns. UB5: N'olt 5D **58**
Doncaster Rd. N9 7C **24**
Donegal Ho. E1 4H **85**
(off Cambridge Heath Rd.)
Donegal St. N1 2K **83**
Doneraile Ho. SW1 6J **17** (5F **101**)
(off Ebury Bri. Rd.)
Doneraile St. SW6 2F **117**
Dongola Rd. E1 5A **86**
Dongola Rd. E13 3K **87**
Dongola Rd. N17 3E **48**
Dongola Rd. W. E13 3K **87**
Don Gratton Ho. E1 5G **85**
(off Old Montague St.)
Donington Av. IG2: Ilf 5G **53**
Donington Av. IG6: Ilf 5G **53**
Donkey All. SE22 7G **121**
Donkey La. EN1: Enf 2B **24**
Donkey La. UB7: W Dray 1D **174**
Donkin Ho. SE16 4H **103**
(off Rennie Est.)
Donmar Warehouse Theatre 1E **12** (6J **83**)
(off Earlham St.)
Donnatt's Rd. SE14 1B **122**
Donne Ct. SE24 6C **120**
Donnefield Av. HA8: Edg 7K **27**
Donne Ho. E14 6C **86**
(off Dod St.)
Donne Ho. SE14 6K **103**
(off Samuel Cl.)
Donnelly Ct. SW6 7G **99**
(off Dawes Rd.)
Donnelly Ho. SE1 1J **19** (3A **102**)
(off McAuley Cl.)
Donne Pl. CR4: Mitc 4F **155**
Donne Pl. SW3 3D **16** (4C **100**)
Donne Rd. RM8: Dag 2C **72**
Donnington Ct. NW1 7F **65**
(off Castlehaven Rd.)
Donnington Ct. NW10 7D **62**
(off Donnington Rd.)
Donnington Mans. NW10 1E **80**
(off Donnington Rd.)
Donnington Rd. HA3: Kenton 5D **42**
Donnington Rd. KT4: Wor Pk 2C **164**
Donnington Rd. NW10 7D **62**
Donnybrook Ct. E3 1B **86**
(off Old Ford Rd.)
Donnybrook Rd. SW16 7G **137**
Donoghue Bus. Pk. NW2 3F **63**
Donoghue Cotts. E14 5A **86**
(off Galsworthy Av.)
Donoghue Ct. E3 4D **86**
(off Barry Blandford Way)

Donovan Av. N10 2F **47**
Donovan Ct. SW10 6A **16** (5B **100**)
(off Drayton Gdns.)
Donovan Ho. E1 7J **85**
(off Cable St.)
Donovan Pl. N21 5E **22**
Don Phelan Cl. SE5 1D **120**
Dons Ct. BR1: Broml 1H **159**
(off London Rd.)
Doone Cl. TW11: Tedd 6A **132**
Doon St. SE1 4J **13** (1A **102**)
Dora Ho. E14 6B **86**
(off Rhodeswell Rd.)
Dora Ho. W11 7F **81**
(off St Ann's Rd.)
Doral Way SM5: Cars 5D **166**
Doran Ct. E6 2D **88**
Dorando Cl. W12 7D **80**
Doran Gro. SE18 7J **107**
Doran Mnr. N2 5D **46**
(off Great Nth. Rd.)
Doran Wlk. E15 7E **68**
Dora Rd. SW19 5J **135**
Dora St. E14 6B **86**
Dora Way SW9 2A **120**
Dorchester Av. DA5: Bexl 1D **144**
Dorchester Av. HA2: Harr 6G **41**
Dorchester Av. N13 4H **33**
Dorchester Cl. BR5: St P 7B **144**
Dorchester Cl. KT10: Hin W 2A **162**
Dorchester Cl. UB5: N'olt 5F **59**
Dorchester Ct. E18 1H **51**
(off Buckingham Rd.)
Dorchester Ct. N1 7E **66**
(off Englefield Rd.)
Dorchester Ct. N10 3F **47**
Dorchester Ct. N14 7A **22**
Dorchester Ct. NW2 3F **63**
Dorchester Ct. SE24 5C **120**
Dorchester Ct. SW1 2F **17** (3D **100**)
(off Sloane St.)
Dorchester Dr. SE24 5C **120**
Dorchester Dr. TW14: Bedf 6G **111**
Dorchester Gdns. E4 4H **35**
Dorchester Gdns. NW11 4J **45**
Dorchester Gro. W4 5A **98**
Dorchester Ho. TW9: Kew 7H **97**
Dorchester M. KT3: N Mald 4K **151**
Dorchester M. TW1: Twick 6C **114**
Dorchester Rd. KT4: Wor Pk 1E **164**
Dorchester Rd. SM4: Mord 7K **153**
Dorchester Rd. UB5: N'olt 5F **59**
Dorchester Ter. NW2 3F **63**
(off Needham Ter.)
Dorchester Way HA3: Kenton 6F **43**
Dorchester Waye UB4: Yead 6K **75**
(not continuous)
Dorcis Av. DA7: Bex 2E **126**
Dordrecht Rd. W3 1A **98**
Dore Av. E12 5E **70**
Doreen Av. NW9 1K **61**
Doreen Capstan Ho. E11 3G **69**
(off Apollo Pl.)
Dore Gdns. SM4: Mord 7K **153**
Dorell Cl. UB1: S'hall 5D **76**
Dorey Ho. TW8: Bford 7C **96**
(off High St.)
Dorfman Theatre 4J **13** (1A **102**)
(within National Theatre)
Doria Rd. SW6 2H **117**
Doric Ho. E2 2K **85**
(off Mace St.)
Doric Way NW1 1C **6** (3H **83**)
Dorie M. N12 4E **30**
(off Ashbourne Cl.)
Dorien Rd. SW20 2F **153**
Doris Ashby Cl. UB6: G'frd 1A **78**
Doris Av. DA8: Erith 1J **127**
Doris Emmerton Ct. SW11 4A **118**
Doris Rd. E7 7J **69**
Doris Rd. TW15: Ashf 6F **129**
Dorking Cl. KT4: Wor Pk 2F **165**
Dorking Cl. SE8 6B **104**
Dorking Ct. N17 1G **49**
(off Hampden La.)
Dorking Ho. SE1 3D **102**
Dorlcote Rd. SW18 7C **118**
Dorly Cl. TW17: Shep 5G **147**
Dorman Pl. N9 2B **34**
Dormans Cl. HA6: Nwood 1F **39**
Dorman Wlk. NW10 5K **61**
Dorman Way NW8 1B **82**
Dorma Trad. Pk. E10 1K **67**
Dormay St. SW18 5K **117**
Dormer Cl. E15 6H **69**
Dormer Cl. EN5: Barn 5A **20**
Dormer's Av. UB1: S'hall 6E **76**
Dormers Ri. UB1: S'hall 7F **77**
DORMER'S WELLS 6E **76**
Dormer's Wells La. UB1: S'hall 6E **76**
Dormers Wells Leisure Cen. 6F **77**
Dormstone Ho. SE17 4E **102**
(off Congreve St.)
Dormywood HA4: Ruis 5H **39**
Dornberg Cl. SE3 7J **105**
Dornberg Rd. SE3 7K **105**
Dorncliffe Rd. SW6 2G **117**
Dorney NW3 7C **64**
Dorney Ri. BR5: St M Cry 4K **161**
Dorney Way TW4: Houn 5C **112**
Dornfell St. NW6 5H **63**
Dornoch Ho. E3 2B **86**
(off Anglo Rd.)
Dornton Rd. CR2: S Croy 5D **168**
Dornton Rd. SW12 2F **137**
Dorothy Av. HA0: Wemb 7E **60**
Dorothy Evans Cl. DA7: Bex 4H **127**
Dorothy Gdns. RM8: Dag 4B **72**
Dorothy Pettingell Ho. SM1: Sutt 3K **165**
(off Vermont Rd.)
Dorothy Rd. SW11 3D **118**
Dorothy Smith La. N17 7J **33**
Dorrell Pl. SW9 3A **120**
Dorrien Wlk. SW16 2H **137**
Dorrington Cl. IG11: Bark 7A **72**
Dorrington Ct. SE25 2E **156**
Dorrington Point E3 3D **86**
(off Bromley High St.)
Dorrington St. EC1 5J **7** (5A **84**)
Dorrington Way BR3: Beck 5E **158**
Dorrit Ho. W11 1F **99**
(off St Ann's Rd.)
Dorrit M. N18 5A **34**
Dorrit St. SE1 6D **14** (2C **102**)
Dorrit Way BR7: Chst 6G **143**

Dorryn Ct. SE26 5K **139**
Dors Cl. NW9 1K **61**
Dorset Av. DA16: Well 4K **125**
Dorset Av. RM1: Rom 4K **55**
Dorset Av. UB2: S'hall 4E **94**
Dorset Av. UB4: Hayes 3G **75**
Dorset Bldgs. EC4 1A **14** (6B **84**)
Dorset Cl. KT9: Chess 4D **162**
Dorset Cl. NW1 5E **4** (5D **82**)
Dorset Cl. UB4: Hayes 3G **75**
Dorset Ct. HA6: Nwood 1H **39**
Dorset Ct. N1 7E **66**
(off Hertford Rd.)
Dorset Ct. UB5: N'olt 3C **76**
Dorset Ct. W7 5K **77**
(off Copley Cl.)
Dorset Dr. HA8: Edg 6A **28**
Dorset Gdns. CR4: Mitc 4K **155**
Dorset Gdns. HA0: Wemb 5C **60**
Dorset Ho. NW1 4F **5** (4D **82**)
(off Gloucester Pl.)
Dorset Mans. SW6 6F **99**
(off Lillie Rd.)
Dorset M. N3 1J **45**
Dorset M. SW1 1J **17** (3F **101**)
Dorset Pl. E15 6F **69**
Dorset Ri. EC4 1A **14** (6B **84**)
Dorset Rd. BR3: Beck 3K **157**
Dorset Rd. CR4: Mitc 2C **154**
Dorset Rd. E7 7A **70**
Dorset Rd. HA1: Harr 6G **41**
Dorset Rd. N15 4D **48**
Dorset Rd. N22 1J **47**
Dorset Rd. SE9 2C **142**
Dorset Rd. SW19 1J **153**
Dorset Rd. SW8 7J **101**
Dorset Rd. TW15: Ashf 3A **128**
Dorset Rd. W5 3C **96**
Dorset Sq. NW1 4E **4** (4D **82**)
Dorset St. W1 6F **5** (5D **82**)
Dorset Way TW2: Twick 1H **131**
Dorset Way UB10: Hil 2B **74**
Dorset Waye TW5: Hest 7D **94**
Dorset Wharf W6 7E **98**
(off Rainville Rd.)
Dorsey Ho. N1 6B **66**
(off Canonbury Rd.)
Dorton Cl. SE15 7E **102**
Dorton Vs. UB7: Sip 7C **92**
Dorville Cres. W6 3D **98**
Dorville Rd. SE12 5H **123**
Dothill Rd. SE18 7G **107**
Douai Gro. TW12: Hamp 1G **149**
Doughty Ct. E1 1H **103**
(off Prusom St.)
Doughty Ho. SW10 6A **100**
(off Netherton Gro.)
Doughty M. WC1 4G **7** (4K **83**)
Doughty St. WC1 3G **7** (4K **83**)
Douglas Av. E17 1B **50**
Douglas Av. HA0: Wemb 7E **60**
Douglas Av. KT3: N Mald 4D **152**
Douglas Bader Ho. TW7: Isle 3H **113**
Douglas Cl. HA7: Stan 5F **27**
Douglas Cl. IG6: Ilf 7K **37**
Douglas Cl. SM6: W'gton 6J **167**
Douglas Ct. KT1: King T 4E **150**
(off Geneva Rd.)
Douglas Ct. N3 2K **45**
Douglas Ct. NW6 7J **63**
(off Quex Rd.)
Douglas Cres. UB4: Yead 4A **76**
Douglas Dr. CR0: C'don 3C **170**
Douglas Eyre Sports Cen. 5K **49**
Douglas Ho. KT6: Surb 1F **163**
Douglas Johnstone Ho. SW6 6H **99**
(off Clem Attlee Ct.)
Douglas Mans. TW3: Houn 3F **113**
Douglas M. NW2 3G **63**
Douglas Path E14 5E **104**
(off Manchester Rd.)
Douglas Rd. DA16: Well 1B **126**
Douglas Rd. E16 5J **87**
Douglas Rd. E4 1B **36**
Douglas Rd. IG3: Ilf 7A **54**
Douglas Rd. KT1: King T 2H **151**
Douglas Rd. KT6: Surb 2F **163**
Douglas Rd. N1 7C **66**
Douglas Rd. N22 1A **48**
Douglas Rd. NW6 1H **81**
Douglas Rd. TW19: Stanw 6A **110**
Douglas Rd. TW3: Houn 3F **113**
Douglas Rd. Nth. N1 6C **66**
Douglas Rd. Sth. N1 6C **66**
Douglas Robinson Ct. SW16 7J **137**
(off Streatham High Rd.)
Douglas Sq. SM4: Mord 6J **153**
Douglas St. SW1 4C **18** (4H **101**)
Douglas Ter. E17 1B **50**
Douglas Waite Ho. NW6 7J **63**
Douglas Way SE8 Stanley St. 7B **104**
Douglas Way SE8 Watsons St. 7C **104**
Doulton Ho. SE11 2H **19** (3K **101**)
(off Lambeth Wlk.)
Doulton M. NW6 6K **63**
Dounesforth Gdns. SW18 1K **135**
Douro Pl. W8 3K **99**
Douro St. E3 2C **86**
Douthwaite Sq. E1 1G **103**
Dove App. E6 5C **88**
Dove Cl. NW7 7G **29**
Dove Cl. SM6: W'gton 7K **167**
Dove Cl. UB5: N'olt 4B **76**
Dove Commercial Cen. NW5 5G **65**
Dovecot Cl. HA5: Eastc 5A **40**
Dovecote Av. N22 3A **48**
Dovecote Gdns. SW14 3K **115**
Dovecote Ho. SE16 2K **103**
(off Water Gdns. Sq.)
Dovecote M. UB9: Hare 3A **38**
Dove Ct. TW19: Stanw 7A **110**
Dovedale Av. HA3: Kenton 6C **42**
Dovedale Av. IG5: Ilf 2E **52**
Dovedale Bus. Est. SE15 2G **121**
(off Blenheim Gro.)
Dovedale Cl. DA16: Well 2A **126**
Dovedale Ri. CR4: Mitc 7D **136**
Dovedale Rd. SE22 5H **121**
Dovedon Cl. N14 2D **32**
Dovehouse Ct. UB5: N'olt 3B **76**
(off Delta Gro.)
Dove Ho. Gdns. E4 2H **35**
Dovehouse Mead IG11: Bark 2H **89**
Dovehouse St. SW3 5B **16** (5B **100**)
Dove M. SW5 4A **100**

Dove Pk. HA5: Hat E 1E **40**
Dover Cl. NW2 2F **63**
Dover Cl. RM5: Col R 2J **55**
Dover Ct. EC1 3A **8** (4B **84**)
(off St John St.)
Dover Ct. N1 7D **66**
(off Southgate Rd.)
Dovercourt Av. CR7: Thor H 5A **156**
Dovercourt Est. N1 6D **66**
Dovercourt Gdns. HA7: Stan 5K **27**
Dovercourt La. SM1: Sutt 3A **166**
Dovercourt Rd. SE22 6E **120**
Doverfield Rd. SW2 7J **119**
Dover Flats SE1 4E **102**
Dover Gdns. SM5: Cars 3D **166**
Dover Ho. N18 5A **34**
Dover Ho. SE15 6J **103**
Dover Ho. Rd. SW15 4C **116**
Doveridge Gdns. N13 4G **33**
Dove Rd. N1 6D **66**
Dove Row E2 1G **85**
Dover Pk. Dr. SW15 6D **116**
Dover Patrol SE3 2K **123**
Dover Rd. E12 2A **70**
Dover Rd. N9 2D **34**
Dover Rd. RM6: Chad H 6E **54**
Dover Rd. SE19 6D **138**
Dover St. W1 3K **11** (7F **83**)
Dover Ter. TW9: Rich 2F **115**
(off Sandycombe Rd.)
Dover Yd. W1 4A **12** (1G **101**)
(off Berkeley St.)
Doves Cl. BR2: Broml 2C **172**
Doves Yd. N1 1A **84**
Dovet Ct. SW9 1K **119**
Doveton Ho. E1 4J **85**
(off Doveton St.)
Doveton Rd. CR2: S Croy 5D **168**
Doveton St. E1 4J **85**
Dove Wlk. SW1 5G **17** (5E **100**)
Dovey Lodge N1 7A **66**
(off Bewdley St.)
Dovoll Ct. SE16 7K **15** (3G **103**)
(off Old Jamaica Rd.)
Dowanhill Rd. SE6 1F **141**
Dowd Cl. N11 2K **31**
Dowdeswell Cl. SW15 4A **116**
Dowding Dr. SE9 5A **124**
Dowding Ho. N6 7E **46**
(off Hillcrest)
Dowding Pl. HA7: Stan 6F **27**
Dowding Rd. UB10: Uxb 7B **56**
Dowdney Cl. NW5 5G **65**
Dowe Ho. SE3 3G **123**
Dowells St. SE10 6D **104**
Dower Av. SM6: W'gton 7F **167**
Dower Ct. SE16 4J **103**
(off Silwood Rd.)
Dowes Ho. SW16 3J **137**
Dowgate Hill EC4 2E **14** (7D **84**)
Dowland St. W10 3G **81**
Dowlas St. SE5 7E **102**
Dowler Ct. KT2: King T 1E **150**
Dowler Ho. E1 6G **85**
(off Burslem St.)
Dowlerville Rd. BR6: Chels 6K **173**
Dowletts Rd. RM8: Dag 1E **72**
Dowling Ho. DA17: Belv 3F **109**
Dowman Cl. SW19 7K **135**
Downage NW4 3E **44**
(not continuous)
Downalong WD23: B Hea 1C **26**
Downbank Av. DA7: Bex 1K **127**
Down Barns Rd. HA4: Ruis 3B **58**
Downbarton Ho. SW9 1A **120**
(off Gosling Way)
Downbury M. SW18 5J **117**
Down Cl. UB5: N'olt 2K **75**
Downderry Rd. BR1: Broml 3F **141**
Downe Cl. DA16: Well 7C **108**
Downend SE18 7F **107**
Downend Ct. SE15 6E **102**
(off Bibury Cl.)
Downe Rd. BR2: Kes 7C **172**
Downe Rd. CR4: Mitc 2D **154**
Downer's Cott. SW4 4G **119**
Downesbury NW3 6D **64**
(off Steele's Rd.)
Downes Cl. TW1: Twick 6B **114**
Downes Ct. N21 1F **33**
Downes Ho. CR0: Wadd 4B **168**
(off Violet La.)
Downe Ter. TW10: Rich 6E **114**
Downey Ho. E1 4K **85**
(off Globe Rd.)
Downfield KT4: Wor Pk 1B **164**
Downfield Cl. W9 4K **81**
Down Hall Rd. KT2: King T 1D **150**
DOWNHAM 5F **141**
Downham Cl. RM5: Col R 1G **55**
Downham Ct. N1 7D **66**
(off Downham Rd.)
Downham Ent. Cen. SE6 2H **141**
Downham Health & Leisure Cen. 4H **141**
Downham La. BR1: Broml 5F **141**
Downham Rd. N1 7D **66**
Downham Way BR1: Broml 5F **141**
Downham Wharf N1 1E **84**
(off Downham Rd.)
Downhills Av. N17 3D **48**
Downhills Pk. Rd. N17 3C **48**
Downhills Way N17 3C **48**
Downhurst Av. NW7 5E **28**
Downhurst Ct. NW4 3E **44**
Downie Wlk. SE18 5F **107**
(off Brumwell Av.)
Downing Cl. HA2: Harr 3G **41**
Downing Ct. WC1 4F **7** (4J **83**)
(off Grenville St.)
Downing Dr. UB6: G'frd 1H **77**
Downing Ho. W10 6F **81**
(off Cambridge Gdns.)
Downing Rd. RM9: Dag 7F **73**
Downings E6 6E **88**
Downing St. SW1 6E **12** (2J **101**)
Downland Cl. N20 1F **31**
Downland Ct. E11 2G **69**
Downleys Cl. SE9 2C **142**
Downman Rd. SE9 3C **124**
Down Pl. W6 4D **98**
Down Rd. TW11: Tedd 6B **132**
Downs, The SW20 7F **135**
Downs Av. BR7: Chst 5D **142**
Downs Av. HA5: Pinn 6C **40**

Downs Bri. Rd. BR3: Beck 1F **159**
Downs Ct. UB6: G'frd 3A **78**
Downs Ct. Pde. E8 5H **67**
(off Amhurst Rd.)
Downsell Rd. E15 4E **68**
Downsfield Rd. E17 6A **50**
Downshall Av. IG3: Ilf 6J **53**
Downs Hill BR3: Beck 7F **141**
Downshire Hill NW3 4B **64**
Downside TW1: Twick 3K **131**
Downside TW16: Sun 1J **147**
Downside Cl. SW19 6A **136**
Downside Cres. NW3 5C **64**
Downside Cres. W13 4A **78**
Downside Rd. SM2: Sutt 6B **166**
Downside Wlk. TW8: Bford 6D **96**
(off Windmill Rd.)
Downside Wlk. UB5: N'olt 3D **76**
Downs La. E5 4H **67**
Downs Pk. Rd. E5 5G **67**
Downs Pk. Rd. E8 5F **67**
Downs Rd. BR3: Beck 2D **158**
Downs Rd. CR7: Thor H 1C **156**
Downs Rd. E5 4G **67**
Downs Rd. EN1: Enf 4K **23**
Down St. KT8: W Mole 5E **148**
Down St. W1 5J **11** (1F **101**)
Down St. M. W1 5J **11** (1F **101**)
Downs Vw. TW7: Isle 1K **113**
Downsview Gdns. SE19 7B **138**
Downsview Rd. SE19 7C **138**
Downsway BR6: Orp 5J **173**
Downsway, The SM2: Sutt 7A **166**
Downton Av. SW2 2J **137**
Downtown Rd. SE16 2A **104**
Down Way UB5: N'olt 3K **75**
Downy Ho. W3 1A **98**
Dowrey St. N1 1A **84**
Dowsett Rd. N17 2F **49**
Dowson Cl. SE5 4D **120**
Dowson Ho. E1 6K **85**
(off Bower St.)
Doyce St. SE1 6C **14** (2C **102**)
Doyle Gdns. NW10 1C **80**
Doyle Ho. SW13 7E **98**
(off Trinity Chu. Rd.)
Doyle Rd. SE25 4G **157**
D'Oyley St. SW1 3G **17** (4E **100**)
Doynton St. N19 2F **65**
Draco Ga. SW15 3E **116**
Draco St. SE17 6C **102**
Dragmore St. SW4 6H **119**
Dragonfly Cl. E13 3K **87**
Dragonfly Cl. KT5: Surb 1J **163**
Dragonfly Ct. NW9 1A **44**
(off Heybourne Cres.)
Dragonfly Pl. SE4 3A **122**
Dragon Rd. SE15 6E **102**
Dragons Way EN5: Barn 5C **20**
Dragon Yd. WC1 7F **7** (6J **83**)
Dragoon Rd. SE8 5B **104**
Dragor Rd. NW10 4J **79**
Drake Cl. IG11: Bark 4A **90**
Drake Cl. SE16 2K **103**
Drake Ct. KT5: Surb 4E **150**
(off Cranes Pk. Av.)
Drake Ct. SE1 7D **14** (2C **102**)
(off Swan St.)
Drake Ct. SE19 5F **139**
Drake Ct. W12 2E **98**
(off Scott's Rd.)
Drake Cres. SE28 6C **90**
Drakefell Rd. SE14 2K **121**
Drakefell Rd. SE4 3A **122**
Drakefield Rd. SW17 3E **136**
Drake Hall E16 1K **105**
(off Wesley Av.)
Drake Ho. E1 5J **85**
(off Stepney Way)
Drake Ho. E14 7A **86**
(off Victory Pl.)
Drake Ho. SW1 7C **18** (6H **101**)
(off Dolphin Sq.)
Drakeland Ho. W9 4H **81**
(off Fernhead Rd.)
Drakeley Ct. N5 4B **66**
Drake M. BR2: Broml 4A **160**
Drake Rd. CR0: C'don 7K **155**
Drake Rd. CR4: Mitc 6E **154**
Drake Rd. HA2: Harr 2D **58**
Drake Rd. KT9: Chess 5G **163**
Drake Rd. SE4 3C **122**
Drakes, The SE8 6C **104**
Drakes Ct. SE23 1J **139**
Drakes Ctyd. NW6 7H **63**
Drakes Dr. HA6: Nwood 1D **38**
Drake St. EN2: Enf 1J **23**
Drake St. WC1 6G **7** (5K **83**)
Drakes Wlk. E6 1D **88**
Drakewood Rd. SW16 7H **137**
Draper Cl. DA17: Belv 4F **109**
Draper Cl. TW7: Isle 2H **113**
Draper Ct. BR1: Broml 4C **160**
Draper Ho. SE1 4B **102**
(off Newington Butts)
Draper Pl. N1 1B **84**
(off Dagmar Ter.)
Drapers Almshouses E3 3D **86**
(off Rainhill Way)
Drapers Cott. Homes NW7 4G **29**
(not continuous)
Draper's Ct. SW11 1E **118**
(off Battersea Pk. Rd.)
Drapers Gdns. EC2 7F **9** (6D **84**)
Drapers Rd. E15 4F **69**
Drapers Rd. EN2: Enf 2G **23**
Drapers Rd. N17 3F **49**
Drapers Yd. SW18 5K **117**
(off Ryland Blvd.)
Drappers Way SE16 4G **103**
Draven Cl. BR2: Hayes 7H **159**
Drawdock Rd. SE10 2F **105**
Drawell Cl. SE18 5J **107**
Drax Av. SW20 7C **134**
Draxmont SW19 6G **135**
Draycot Rd. E11 6K **51**
Draycot Rd. KT6: Surb 1G **163**
Draycott Av. HA3: Kenton 6B **42**
Draycott Av. SW3 3D **16** (4C **100**)
Draycott Cl. HA3: Kenton 6B **42**
Draycott Cl. NW2 3F **63**
Draycott Cl. SE5 7D **102**
(not continuous)
Draycott Ct. SW11 1C **118**
(off Westbridge Rd.)

Draycott M. – Durham Ri.

Draycott M. SW6 2H 117
(off Laurel Bank Gdns.)
Draycott Pl. SW3 4E 16 (4D 100)
Draycott Ter. SW3 3E 16 (4D 100)
Dray Ct. HA0: Wemb 5A 60
(off Brewery Cl.)
Drayford Cl. W9 4H 81
Dray Gdns. SW2 5K 119
Draymans M. SE15 2F 121
Draymans Way TW7: Isle 3K 113
Drayside M. UB2: S'hall 2D 94
Drayson M. W8 2J 99
Drayton Av. BR6: Farnb 1F 173
Drayton Av. W13 7A 78
Drayton Bri. Rd. W13 6K 77
Drayton Bri. Rd. W7 7K 77
Drayton Cl. IG1: Ilf 1H 71
Drayton Cl. TW4: Houn 5D 112
Drayton Ct. UB7: W Dray 4B 92
Drayton Gdns. N21 7G 23
Drayton Gdns. SW10 5A 100
Drayton Gdns. UB7: W Dray 2A 92
Drayton Gdns. W13 7A 78
Drayton Grn. W13 7A 78
Drayton Grn. Rd. W13 7B 78
Drayton Gro. W13 7A 78
Drayton Ho. E11 1F 69
Drayton Ho. SE5 7D 102
(off Elmington Rd.)
Drayton Pk. N5 4A 66
Drayton Pk. M. N5 5A 66
Drayton Rd. CR0: C'don 2B 168
Drayton Rd. E11 1F 69
Drayton Rd. N17 2E 48
Drayton Rd. NW10 1B 80
Drayton Rd. W13 7A 78
Drayton Waye HA3: Kenton 6B 42
Dray Wlk. E1 4K 9 (4F 85)
Dreadnought Cl. SW19 2B 154
Dreadnought St. SE10 3G 105
Dreadnought Wlk. SE10 6D 104
Drenon Sq. UB3: Hayes 7H 75
Dresden Cl. NW6 6K 63
Dresden Ho. SE11 3H 19 (4K 101)
(off Lambeth Wlk.)
Dresden Ho. SW11 2E 118
(off Dagnall St.)
Dresden Rd. N19 1G 65
Dressington Av. SE4 6C 122
Drewery Ct. SE3 3G 123
Drewett Ho. E1 6G 85
(off Christian St.)
Drew Gdns. UB6: G'frd 6K 59
Drew Ho. SE8 5C 104
Drew Ho. SW16 3J 137
Drew Rd. E16 1B 106
(not continuous)
Drewstead La. SW16 2H 137
Drewstead Rd. SW16 2H 137
Drey Ct. KT4: Wor Pk 2C 164
(off The Avenue)
Driffield Ct. NW9 1A 44
(off Pageant Av.)
Driffield Rd. E3 2A 86
Drift, The BR2: Broml 3B 172
Drift Ct. E16 7F 89
Driftway, The CR4: Mitc 1E 154
Driftway Ho. E3 2B 86
(off Stafford Rd.)
Drinkwater Ho. SE5 7D 102
(off Picton St.)
Drinkwater Rd. HA2: Harr 2F 59
Drive, The EN2: Enf Farr Rd 1J 23
Drive, The BR3: Beck 2C 158
Drive, The BR4: W W'ck 7F 159
Drive, The BR6: Orp 2K 173
Drive, The BR7: Chst 3K 161
Drive, The CR7: Thor H 4D 156
Drive, The DA14: Sidc 3B 144
Drive, The DA5: Bexl 6C 126
Drive, The DA8: Erith 7H 109
Drive, The E17 3D 50
Drive, The E18 4J 51
Drive, The E4 1A 36
Drive, The EN5: Barn 3B 20
Drive, The EN5: New Bar 6F 21
Drive, The HA2: Harr 7E 40
Drive, The HA6: Nwood 2G 39
Drive, The HA8: Edg 5B 28
Drive, The HA9: Wemb 2J 61
Drive, The IG1: Ilf 6C 52
Drive, The IG11: Bark 7K 71
Drive, The IG9: Buck H 1F 37
Drive, The KT10: Esh 7G 149
Drive, The KT19: Ewe 6B 164
Drive, The KT2: King T 7J 133
Drive, The KT6: Surb 7E 150
Drive, The N11 6B 32
Drive, The N3 7D 30
Drive, The N6 5D 46
Drive, The N7 6K 65
(not continuous)
Drive, The NW10 1B 80
Drive, The NW11 7G 45
Drive, The RM5: Col R 1J 55
Drive, The SM4: Mord 5A 154
Drive, The SW20 7E 134
Drive, The SW6 2G 117
Drive, The TW14: Felt 7A 112
Drive, The TW15: Ashf 7F 129
Drive, The TW3: Houn 2H 113
Drive, The TW7: Isle 2H 113
Drive, The UB10: Ick 4A 56
Drive, The W3 6J 79
Drive Ct. HA8: Edg 5B 28
Drive Mans. SW6 2G 117
(off Fulham Rd.)
Droitwich Cl. SE26 3G 139
Dromey Gdns. HA3: Hrw W 7E 26
Dromore Rd. SW15 6G 117
Dronfield Gdns. RM8: Dag 5C 72
Dron Ho. E1 5J 85
(off Adelina Gro.)
Droop St. W10 3F 81
Drovers Ct. KT1: King T 2E 150
(off Fairfield E.)
Drovers Pl. SE15 7J 103
Drovers Rd. CR2: S Croy 5D 168
Drovers Way N7 6J 65
Druce Rd. SE21 6E 120
Druid St. SE1 6H 15 (2E 102)
(not continuous)
Druids Way BR2: Broml 4F 159
Drumaline Ridge KT4: Wor Pk 2A 164
Drum Ct. N1 7J 65
(off Gifford St.)
Drummer Stagpole M. NW7 5B 30
Drummond Av. RM7: Rom 4K 55
Drummond Ct. N12 7H 31
Drummond Ct. W3 3J 97
(off Palmerston Rd.)
Drummond Cres. NW1 1C 6 (3H 83)
Drummond Dr. HA7: Stan 7E 26
Drummond Ga. SW1 5D 18 (5H 101)
Drummond Ho. E2 2G 85
(off Goldsmiths Row)
Drummond Ho. N2 2A 46
(off Font Hills)
Drummond Pl. TW1: Twick 7B 114
Drummond Rd. CR0: C'don 2C 168
Drummond Rd. E11 6A 52
Drummond Rd. RM7: Rom 4K 55
Drummond Rd. SE16 3H 103
Drummonds, The IG9: Buck H 2E 36
Drummonds Pl. TW9: Rich 4E 114
Drummond St. NW1 3A 6 (4G 83)
Drummond Way N1 7A 66
Druries HA1: Harr 1J 59
(off High St.)
Drury Cl. SW15 6C 116
Drury Cres. CR0: Wadd 2A 168
Drury Ho. SW8 1G 119
Drury La. WC2 7F 7 (6J 83)
Drury Lane Theatre Royal 1F 13 (6J 83)
(off Catherine St.)
Drury Rd. HA1: Harr 7G 41
Drury Way NW10 5K 61
Drury Way Ind. Est. NW10 5J 61
Dryad St. SW15 3F 117
Dryburgh Gdns. NW9 3G 43
Dryburgh Ho. SW1 5J 17 (5F 101)
(part of Abbots Mnr.)
Dryburgh Rd. SW15 3D 116
Dryden Av. W7 6K 77
Dryden Bldg. E1 6G 85
(off Commercial Rd.)
Dryden Cl. SW4 5H 119
Dryden Ct. SE11 4K 19 (4A 102)
Dryden Mans. W14 6G 99
(off Queen's Club Gdns.)
Dryden Rd. DA16: Well 1K 125
Dryden Rd. EN1: Enf 6K 23
Dryden Rd. HA3: W'stone 1K 41
Dryden Rd. SE10 4J 105
Dryden Rd. SW19 6A 136
Dryden St. WC2 1F 13 (6J 83)
Dryfield Cl. NW10 6J 61
Dryfield Rd. HA8: Edg 6D 28
Dryfield Wlk. SE8 6C 104
Dryhill Rd. DA17: Belv 6F 109
Dryland Av. BR6: Orp 4K 173
Drylands Rd. N8 6J 47
Drysdale Av. E4 7J 25
Drysdale Cl. HA6: Nwood 1G 39
Drysdale Dwellings E8 5F 67
(off Dunn St.)
Drysdale Pl. N1 1H 9 (3E 84)
Drysdale St. N1 1H 9 (3E 84)
Dublin Av. E8 1G 85
Dublin Ct. HA2: Harr 2H 59
(off Northolt Rd.)
Du Burstow Ter. W7 2J 95
Ducaine Apts. E3 3B 86
(off Merchant St.)
Ducal St. E2 2K 9 (3F 85)
Du Cane Cl. W12 6E 80
Du Cane Ct. SW17 1E 136
Du Cane Rd. W12 6B 80
Ducavel Ho. SW2 1K 137
Duchess Cl. N11 5A 32
Duchess Cl. SM1: Sutt 4A 166
Duchess Cres. HA7: Stan 3E 26
Duchess Dr. E13 4K 87
Duchess Gro. IG9: Buck H 2E 36
Duchess M. W1 6K 5 (5F 83)
Duchess M. W3 1G 97
Duchess of Bedford Ho. W8 2J 99
(off Duchess of Bedford's Wlk.)
Duchess of Bedford's Wlk. W8 2J 99
Duchess St. W1 6K 5 (5F 83)
Duchess Theatre 2G 13 (7K 83)
(off Catherine St.)
Duchess Wlk. SE1 5J 15 (1F 103)
Duchy Rd. EN4: Had W 1G 21
Duchy St. SE1 4K 13 (1A 102)
(not continuous)
Ducie St. SW4 4K 119
Duckett M. N4 6B 48
Duckett Rd. N4 6B 48
Duckett's Apts. E3 7B 68
(off Wick La.)
Duckett St. E1 4K 85
Duckham Ct. E14 4D 104
(off Nauticus Wlk.)
Ducking Stool Ct. RM1: Rom 4K 55
Duck La. W1 1C 12 (6H 83)
(off Broadwick St.)
Duck Lees La. EN3: Pond E 4F 25
Duck's Hill Rd. HA4: Ruis 4E 38
Duck's Hill Rd. HA6: Nwood 1D 38
DUCKS ISLAND 6A 20
Ducks Wlk. TW1: Twick 5C 114
Du Cros Dr. HA7: Stan 6J 27
Du Cros Rd. W3 1A 98
DUDDEN HILL 5D 62
Dudden Hill La. NW10 4B 62
Dudden Hill Pde. NW10 4B 62
Duddington Cl. SE9 4B 142
Dudley Av. HA3: Kenton 3C 42
Dudley Ct. NW11 4H 45
Dudley Ct. W1 1E 10 (6D 82)
(off Up. Berkeley St.)
Dudley Ct. WC2 7E 6 (6J 83)
Dudley Dr. HA4: Ruis 5K 57
Dudley Dr. SM4: Mord 1G 165
Dudley Gdns. HA2: Harr 1H 59
Dudley Gdns. W13 2B 96
Dudley M. SW2 6A 120
Dudley Pl. TW19: Stanw 6B 110
Dudley Pl. UB3: Harl 4F 93
Dudley Rd. E17 2C 50
Dudley Rd. HA2: Harr 2G 59
Dudley Rd. IG1: Ilf 4F 71
Dudley Rd. KT1: King T 3F 151
Dudley Rd. KT12: Walt T 6J 147
Dudley Rd. N3 2K 45
Dudley Rd. NW6 2G 81
Dudley Rd. SW19 6J 135
Dudley Rd. TW14: Bedf 1E 128
Dudley Rd. TW15: Ashf 5B 128
Dudley Rd. TW9: Rich 2F 115
Dudley Rd. UB2: S'hall 2B 94
Dudley St. W2 6A 4 (5B 82)
Dudlington Rd. E5 2J 67
Dudmaston M. SW3 5B 16 (5B 100)
(off Fulham Rd.)
Dudrich Cl. N11 6J 31
Dudrich M. EN2: Enf 1F 23
Dudrich M. SE22 5F 121
Dudsbury Rd. DA14: Sidc 6B 144
Dudset La. TW5: Cran 1J 111
Duett Ct. TW5: Hest 7C 94
Duffell Ho. SE11 6H 19 (5K 101)
(off Loughborough St.)
Dufferin Av. EC1 4E 8 (4D 84)
(off Dufferin St.)
Dufferin Ct. EC1 4E 8 (4D 84)
(off Dufferin St.)
Dufferin St. EC1 4D 8 (4C 84)
Duffield Cl. HA1: Harr 5K 41
Duffield Dr. N15 4F 49
Duff St. E14 6D 86
Duffy Av. HA2: Harr 3G 41
Dufour's Pl. W1 1B 12 (6G 83)
Dufton Dwellings E15 4G 69
(off High Rd. Leyton)
Dugard Way SE11 4B 102
Dugdale Cen. Enfield 4J 23
Dugdale Ct. NW10 3D 80
(off Harrow Rd.)
Duggan Dr. BR7: Chst 6C 142
Dugolly Av. HA9: Wemb 3H 61
Dujardin M. EN3: Pond E 6E 24
Duke Ct. TW3: Houn 4D 112
Duke Gdns. IG6: Ilf 4H 53
Duke Humphrey Rd. SE3 1G 123
Duke of Cambridge Cl. TW2: Whitt 6H 113
Duke of Clarence Ct. SE17 5C 102
(off Manor Pl.)
Duke of Edinburgh Rd. SM1: Sutt 2B 166
Duke of Wellington Av. SE18 3F 107
Duke of Wellington Pl. SW1 6H 11 (2E 100)
Duke of York Column 5D 12 (1H 101)
Duke of York Sq. SW3 5F 17 (5D 100)
Duke of York's Theatre 3E 12 (7J 83)
(off St Martin's La.)
Duke of York St. SW1 4B 12 (1G 101)
Duke Rd. IG6: Ilf 4H 53
Duke Rd. W4 5K 97
Duke's Av. HA8: Edg 6A 28
Duke's Av. N10 3F 47
Duke's Av. W4 5K 97
Dukes Av. HA1: Harr 4J 41
Dukes Av. HA2: Harr 6D 40
Dukes Av. KT2: King T 4D 132
Dukes Av. KT3: N Mald 3A 152
Dukes Av. N3 1K 45
Dukes Av. TW10: Ham 4C 132
Dukes Av. TW4: Houn 4C 112
Dukes Av. UB5: N'olt 7C 58
Dukes Cl. TW12: Hamp 5D 130
Dukes Cl. TW15: Ashf 4E 128
Dukes Ct. E6 1E 88
(not continuous)
Dukes Ct. SE13 2E 122
Dukes Ct. SW14 2K 115
Dukes Ct. W2 7K 81
(off Moscow Rd.)
Dukes Ga. W4 4J 97
Dukes Grn. Av. TW14: Felt 5J 111
Dukes Head Pas. TW12: Hamp 7G 131
Duke's Head Yd. N6 1F 65
Duke Shore Wharf E14 7B 86
Duke's Ho. SW1 3D 18 (4H 101)
(off Vincent Sq.)
Dukes La. W8 2K 99
Dukes La. Chambers W8 2K 99
(off Dukes La.)
Duke's La. Mans. W8 2K 99
(off Dukes La.)
Dukes Lodge W8 1H 99
(off Holland Wlk.)
Dukes Meadow Golf & Tennis 2K 115
Duke's Meadow Golf Course 2K 115
Duke's Meadows 2K 115
Duke's M. W1 7H 5 (6E 82)
(off Duke St.)
Dukes M. N10 3F 47
Dukes Orchard DA5: Bexl 1J 145
Duke's Pas. E17 4E 50
Duke's Pl. EC3 1H 15 (6E 84)
Dukes Point N6 1F 65
(off Dukes Head Yd.)
Dukes Ride UB10: Ick 4A 56
Duke's Rd. WC1 2D 6 (3H 83)
Dukes Rd. E6 1E 88
Dukes Rd. W3 4G 79
Dukesthorpe Rd. SE26 4K 139
Duke St. SM1: Sutt 4B 166
Duke St. TW9: Rich 4D 114
Duke St. W1 7H 5 (6E 82)
Duke St. Hill SE1 4F 15 (1D 102)
Duke St. Mans. W1 1H 11 (6E 82)
(off Duke St.)
Duke St. St James's SW1 4B 12 (1G 101)
Dukes Way BR4: W W'ck 3G 171
Dukes Way HA9: Wemb 5E 60
Duke's Yd. W1 2H 11 (7E 82)
Dulas St. N4 1K 65
Dulford St. W11 7G 81
Dulka Rd. SW11 5D 118
Dulverton NW1 1G 83
(off Royal College St.)
Dulverton Mans. WC1 4H 7 (4K 83)
(off Gray's Inn Rd.)
Dulverton Rd. HA4: Ruis 1J 57
Dulverton Rd. SE9 2G 143
DULWICH 2E 138
Dulwich & Sydenham Hill Golf Course 2F 139
Dulwich Bus. Cen. SE23 1K 139
Dulwich Comn. SE21 1E 138
Dulwich Comn. SE22 1G 139
Dulwich Hamlet FC 4E 120
Dulwich Lawn Cl. SE22 5F 121
Dulwich Leisure Cen. 4G 121
Dulwich Oaks, The SE21 3F 139
Dulwich Picture Gallery 7D 120
Dulwich Ri. Gdns. SE22 5F 121
Dulwich Rd. SE24 5A 120
Dulwich Upper Wood Nature Pk. 5F 139
Dulwich Village SE21 6D 120
DULWICH VILLAGE 7E 120
Dulwich Wood Av. SE19 4E 138
Dulwich Wood Pk. SE19 4E 138
Dumain Ct. SE11 4B 102
(off Opal St.)
Dumbarton Ct. SW2 6J 119
Dumbarton Rd. SW2 6J 119
Dumbleton Cl. KT1: King T 1H 151
Dumbreck Rd. SE9 4D 124
Dumont Rd. N16 3E 66
Dumpton Pl. NW1 7E 64
Dumsey Eyot KT16: Chert 7A 146
Dunally Pk. TW17: Shep 7F 147
Dunbar Av. BR3: Beck 4A 158
Dunbar Av. RM10: Dag 3G 73
Dunbar Av. SW16 2A 156
Dunbar Cl. UB4: Hayes 5K 75
Dunbar Ct. BR2: Broml 3H 159
(off Durham Rd.)
Dunbar Ct. SM1: Sutt 5B 166
Dunbar Gdns. RM10: Dag 5G 73
Dunbar Rd. E7 6J 69
Dunbar Rd. KT3: N Mald 4J 151
Dunbar Rd. N22 1A 48
Dunbar St. SE27 3C 138
Dunbar Twr. E8 6F 67
(off Dalston Sq.)
Dunbar Wharf E14 7B 86
(off Narrow St.)
Dunblane Cl. HA8: Edg 2C 28
Dunblane Rd. SE9 3C 124
Dunboe Pl. TW17: Shep 7E 146
Dunboyne Rd. NW3 5D 64
Dunbridge Ho. SW15 6B 116
Dunbridge St. E2 4G 85
Duncan Cl. EN5: New Bar 4F 21
Duncan Ct. E14 5E 86
(off Teviot St.)
Duncan Ct. N21 1G 33
Duncan Gro. W3 6A 80
Duncan Ho. E15 1F 87
Duncan Ho. NW3 7D 64
(off Fellows Rd.)
Duncan Ho. SW1 6B 18 (5G 101)
(off Dolphin Sq.)
Duncannon Ho. SW1 6D 18 (5H 101)
(off Lindsay Sq.)
Duncannon St. WC2 3E 12 (7J 83)
Duncan Rd. E8 1H 85
Duncan Rd. TW9: Rich 4E 114
Duncan St. N1 2B 84
Duncan Ter. N1 2B 84
(not continuous)
Dunch St. E1 6H 85
Dunchurch Ho. RM10: Dag 7G 73
Duncombe Hill SE23 7A 122
Duncombe Rd. N19 1H 65
Duncrievie Rd. SE13 6F 123
Duncroft SE18 7J 107
Dundalk Ho. E1 6J 85
(off Clark St.)
Dundalk Rd. SE4 3A 122
Dundas Ct. SE10 6D 104
(off Dowells St.)
Dundas Gdns. KT8: W Mole 3F 149
Dundas Ho. E2 2J 85
(off Bishop's Way)
Dundas Rd. SE15 2J 121
Dundas Rd. SW9 1A 120
Dundee Ct. E1 1H 103
(off Wapping High St.)
Dundee Ct. SE1 7G 15 (3E 102)
(off Long La.)
Dundee Ho. W9 3A 82
(off Maida Vale)
Dundee Rd. E13 2K 87
Dundee Rd. SE25 5H 157
Dundee St. E1 1H 103
Dundee Way EN3: Brim 3F 25
Dundee Wharf E14 7B 86
Dundela Gdns. KT4: Wor Pk 4D 164
Dundonald Cl. E6 6C 88
Dundonald Rd. NW10 1F 81
Dundonald Rd. SW19 7G 135
Dundry Ho. SE26 3G 139
Dunedin Ho. E16 1D 106
(off Manwood St.)
Dunedin M. SW2 1J 137
Dunedin Rd. E10 3D 68
Dunedin Rd. IG1: Ilf 1G 71
Dunedin Way UB4: Yead 4A 76
Dunelm Gro. SE27 3C 138
Dunelm St. E1 6K 85
Dunfield Gdns. SE6 5D 140
Dunfield Rd. SE6 5D 140
(not continuous)
Dunford Ct. HA5: Hat E 1D 40
Dunford Rd. N7 4K 65
Dungannon Ho. SW6 7J 99
(off Vanston Pl.)
Dungarvan Av. SW15 4C 116
Dunheved Cl. CR7: Thor H 6A 156
Dunheved Rd. Nth. CR7: Thor H 6A 156
Dunheved Rd. Sth. CR7: Thor H 6A 156
Dunheved Rd. W. CR7: Thor H 6A 156
Dunhill Point SW15 1C 134
Dunholme Grn. N9 3A 34
Dunholme La. N9 3A 34
Dunholme Rd. N9 3A 34
Dunkeld Rd. RM8: Dag 2B 72
Dunkeld Rd. SE25 4D 156
Dunkery Rd. SE9 4B 142
Dunkirk Ho. SE1 7F 15 (2D 102)
Dunkirk St. SE27 4C 138
Dunlace Rd. E5 4J 67
Dunleary Cl. TW4: Houn 7D 112
Dunley Dr. CR0: New Ad 7D 170
Dunlin Ho. SE16 4K 103
(off Tawny Way)
Dunloe Av. N17 3D 48
Dunloe Ct. E2 2F 85
Dunloe St. E2 2F 85
Dunlop Pl. SE16 3F 103
Dunmore Point E2 1J 9 (3F 85)
(off Gascoigne Pl.)
Dunmore Rd. NW6 1G 81
Dunmore Rd. SW20 1E 152
Dunmow Cl. RM6: Chad H 5C 54
Dunmow Cl. TW13: Hanw 3C 130
Dunmow Ho. SE11 5H 19 (5K 101)
(off Newburn St.)
Dunmow Rd. E15 4F 69
Dunmow Wlk. N1 1C 84
(off Popham St.)
Dunnage Cres. SE16 4A 104
(not continuous)
Dunnell Cl. TW16: Sun 1J 147
Dunnett Ho. E3 2B 86
(off Vernon Rd.)
Dunnico Ho. SE17 5E 102
(off East St.)
Dunn Mead NW9 7G 29
Dunnock Cl. N9 1E 34
Dunnock Dr. HA7: Stan 5E 26
Dunnock Ho. NW9 6B 44
Dunnock M. E5 3G 67
Dunnock Rd. E6 6C 88
Dunn St. E8 5F 67
Dunollie Pl. NW5 5G 65
Dunollie Rd. NW5 5G 65
Dunoon Gdns. SE23 7K 121
Dunoon Ho. N1 1K 83
(off Bemerton Est.)
Dunoon Rd. SE23 7J 121
Dunoran Home BR1: Broml 1C 160
Dunraven Dr. EN2: Enf 2F 23
Dunraven Rd. W12 1C 98
Dunraven St. W1 2F 11 (7D 82)
Dunsany Rd. W14 3F 99
Dunsfold Cl. SM2: Sutt 7K 165
(off Blackbush Cl.)
Dunsfold Way CR0: New Ad 7D 170
Dunsford Way SW15 6D 116
Dunsmore Cl. UB4: Yead 4B 76
Dunsmore Rd. KT12: Walt T 6K 147
Dunsmure Rd. N16 1E 66
Dunspring La. IG5: Ilf 2F 53
Dunstable M. W1 5H 5 (5E 82)
Dunstable Rd. KT8: W Mole 4D 148
Dunstable Rd. TW9: Rich 4E 114
Dunstall Rd. SW20 6D 134
Dunstall Way KT8: W Mole 3F 149
Dunstall Welling Est. DA16: Well 2B 126
Dunstan Cl. N2 3A 46
Dunstan Glade BR5: Pet W 6H 161
Dunstan Gro. SE20 7H 139
Dunstan Ho's. E1 5J 85
(off Stepney Grn.)
Dunstan M. EN1: Enf 3K 23
Dunstan Rd. NW11 1H 63
Dunstan's Gro. SE22 6H 121
Dunstan's Rd. SE22 7G 121
Dunster Av. SM4: Mord 1F 165
Dunster Cl. EN5: Barn 4A 20
Dunster Cl. RM5: Col R 2J 55
Dunster Ct. EC3 2G 15 (7E 84)
Dunster Dr. NW9 1J 61
Dunster Gdns. NW6 7H 63
Dunster Ho. SE6 3E 140
Dunsterville Way SE1 7F 15 (2D 102)
Dunster Way HA2: Harr 3C 58
Dunster Way SM6: W'gton 1E 166
Dunstone Ct. SE6 7C 122
Dunston Rd. E8 1F 85
Dunston Rd. SW11 2E 118
Dunston St. E8 1E 84
Dunton Cl. KT6: Surb 1E 162
Dunton Ct. SE23 2H 139
Dunton Rd. E10 7D 50
Dunton Rd. RM1: Rom 4K 55
Dunton Rd. SE1 5F 103
Duntshill Rd. SW18 1K 135
Dunvegan Cl. KT8: W Mole 4E 148
Dunvegan Rd. SE9 4D 124
Dunwich Ct. RM6: Chad H 5B 54
(off Glandford Way)
Dunwich Rd. DA7: Bex 1F 127
Dunworth M. W11 6H 81
Duplex Ride SW1 7F 11 (2D 100)
Dupont Rd. SW20 2F 153
Duppas Av. CR0: Wadd 4B 168
Duppas Cl. TW17: Shep 5F 147
Duppas Ct. CR0: C'don 3B 168
(off Duppas Hill Ter.)
Duppas Hill La. CR0: C'don 4B 168
Duppas Hill Rd. CR0: Wadd 4A 168
Duppas Hill Ter. CR0: C'don 3B 168
Duppas Rd. CR0: Wadd 3A 168
Dupree Rd. SE7 5K 105
Dura Den Cl. BR3: Beck 7D 140
Durand Gdns. SW9 1K 119
Durands Wlk. SE16 2B 104
Durand Way NW10 7J 61
Durants Pk. 3D 24
Durants Pk. Av. EN3: Pond E 4E 24
Durants Rd. EN3: Pond E 4D 24
Durant St. E2 2G 85
Durban Ct. E7 7B 70
Durban Gdns. RM10: Dag 7J 73
Durban Ho. W12 7D 80
(off White City Est.)
Durban Rd. BR3: Beck 2B 158
Durban Rd. E15 3G 87
Durban Rd. E17 1B 50
Durban Rd. IG2: Ilf 1J 71
Durban Rd. N17 6K 33
Durban Rd. SE27 4C 138
Durbin Rd. KT9: Chess 4E 162
Durdan Cotts. UB1: S'hall 6D 76
(off Denbigh Rd.)
Durdans Ho. NW1 7F 65
(off Farrier St.)
Durdans Rd. UB1: S'hall 6D 76
Durell Gdns. RM9: Dag 5D 72
Durell Ho. SE16 2K 103
(off Wolfe Cres.)
Durell Rd. RM9: Dag 5D 72
Durfey Pl. SE5 7D 102
Durford Cres. SW15 1D 134
Durham Av. BR2: Broml 4H 159
Durham Av. IG8: Buck H 5G 37
Durham Av. IG8: Wfd G 5G 37
Durham Av. TW5: Hest 5D 94
Durham Cl. SW20 2D 152
Durham Ct. NW6 2J 81
(off Kilburn Pk. Rd.)
Durham Ct. TW11: Tedd 4J 131
Durham Hill BR1: Broml 4H 141
Durham Ho. BR2: Broml 4G 159
Durham Ho. IG11: Bark 7A 72
(off Margaret Bondfield Av.)
Durham Ho. NW8 2D 4 (3C 82)
(off Lorne Cl.)
Durham Ho. RM10: Dag 5J 73
Durham Ho. St. WC2 3F 13 (7J 83)
(off John Adam St.)
Durham Pl. IG1: Ilf 4G 71
Durham Pl. SW3 6E 16 (5D 100)
Durham Ri. SE18 5G 107

Durham Rd. – Eckstein Rd.

Durham Rd. BR2: Broml....3H 159
Durham Rd. DA14: Sidc....5B 144
Durham Rd. E12....4B 70
Durham Rd. E16....4G 87
Durham Rd. HA1: Harr....5F 41
Durham Rd. N2....3C 46
Durham Rd. N7....2K 65
Durham Rd. N9....2B 34
Durham Rd. RM10: Dag....5J 73
Durham Rd. SW20....1D 152
Durham Rd. TW14: Felt....7A 112
Durham Rd. W5....3D 96
Durham Row E1....5A 86
Durham St. SE11....6G 19 (5K 101)
Durham Ter. W2....6K 81
Durham Wharf Dr. TW8: Bford....7C 96
Durham Yd. E2....3H 85
Durley Av. HA5: Pinn....7C 40
Durley Rd. N16....7E 48
Durlston Rd. E5....2G 67
Durlston Rd. KT2: King T....6E 132
Durnford Ho. SE6....3E 140
Durnford St. N15....5E 48
Durnford St. SE10....6E 104
Durning Rd. SE19....5D 138
Durnsford Av. SW19....2J 135
Durnsford Ct. EN3: Enf H....3F 25
(off Enstone Rd.)
Durnsford Rd. N11....1H 47
Durnsford Rd. SW19....2J 135
Durrant Ct. HA3: Hrw W....2J 41
Durrant Ho. EC1....5E 8 (5D 84)
(off Chiswell St.)
Durrant Way BR6: Farnb....5H 173
Durrell Rd. SW6....1H 117
Durrell Way TW17: Shep....6F 147
Durrels Ho. W14....4H 99
(off Warwick Gdns.)
Durrington Av. SW20....7E 134
Durrington Pk. Rd. SW20....1E 152
Durrington Rd. E5....4A 68
Durrington Twr. SW8....2G 119
Durrisdeer Ho. NW2....4H 63
(off Lyndale)
Dursley Cl. SE3....2A 124
Dursley Gdns. SE3....1B 124
Dursley Rd. SE3....2A 124
Durward Ho. W8....2K 99
(off Kensington Ct.)
Durward St. E1....5H 85
Durweston M. W1....5F 5 (5D 82)
(off York St.)
Durweston St. W1....6F 5 (5D 82)
Dury Falls Ct. RM5: Col R....2J 55
Dury Rd. EN5: Barn....1C 20
Dutch Barn Cl. TW19: Stanw....6A 110
Dutch Gdns. KT2: King T....6H 133
Dutch Yd. SW18....5J 117
Dutton St. SE10....1E 122
Duval Ho. N19....2H 65
(off Ashbrook Rd.)
Duval Ho. SW11....3C 118
Duxberry Av. TW13: Felt....3A 130
Duxberry Cl. BR2: Broml....5C 160
Duxford Ho. SE2....2D 108
(off Wolvercote Rd.)
DW Fitness Waldorf Hotel
....1G 13 (6K 83)
(off Tavistock St.)
Dyas Rd. TW16: Sun....1J 147
Dye Ho. La. E3....1C 86
Dyer Ho. TW12: Hamp....1F 149
Dyer's Bldgs. EC1....6J 7 (5A 84)
Dyers Hall Rd. E11....1G 69
Dyers Hall Rd. Sth. E11....2F 69
Dyers La. SW15....4D 116
Dykes Way BR2: Broml....3H 159
Dykewood Cl. DA5: Bexl....3K 145
Dylan Rd. DA17: Belv....3G 109
Dylan Rd. SE24....4B 120
Dylways SE5....4D 120
Dymchurch Cl. BR6: Orp....4J 173
Dymchurch Cl. IG5: Ilf....2E 52
Dymes Path SW19....2F 135
Dymock St. SW6....3K 117
Dyneley Rd. SE12....3A 142
Dyne Rd. NW6....7G 63
Dynevor Rd. N16....3E 66
Dynevor Rd. TW10: Rich....5E 114
Dynham Rd. NW6....7J 63
Dyott St. WC1....7D 6 (6H 83)
Dysart Av. KT2: King T....5C 132
Dysart St. EC2....4F 9 (4D 84)
Dyson Ct. HA0: Wemb....4A 60
Dyson Ct. NW2....1E 62
Dyson Dr. UB10: Uxb....1A 74
Dyson Ho. SE10....5H 105
(off Blackwall La.)
Dyson Rd. E11....6G 51
Dyson Rd. E15....6H 69
Dysons Rd. N18....5C 34

E

Eade Rd. N4....7C 48
Eagans Cl. N2....3B 46
Eagle Av. RM6: Chad H....6E 54
Eagle Cl. EN3: Pond E....4D 24
Eagle Cl. SE16....5J 103
Eagle Cl. SM6: W'gton....6J 167
Eagle Ct. E11....4J 51
Eagle Ct. EC1....5A 8 (5B 84)
Eagle Dr. NW9....2A 44
Eagle Dwellings EC1....2D 8 (3C 84)
(off City Rd.)
Eagle Hgts. SW11....3C 118
Eagle Hill SE19....6D 138
Eagle Ho. E1....4H 85
(off Headlam St.)
Eagle Ho. EC1....1E 8 (3D 84)
(off City Rd.)
Eagle Ho. N1....2D 84
(off Eagle Wharf Rd.)
Eagle Ho. M. SW4....5G 119
Eagle La. E11....4J 51
Eagle Lodge NW11....7H 45
Eagle Mans. N16....5F 67
(off Salcombe Rd.)
Eagle M. N1....6E 66
Eagle Pl. SW1....3B 12 (7G 83)
(off Piccadilly)
Eagle Pl. SW7....5A 100
Eagle Point EC1....1E 8 (3D 84)
(off City Rd.)
Eagle Rd. HA0: Wemb....7D 60
Eagle Rd. TW6: H'row A....3H 111
Eaglesfield Rd. SE18....1F 125
Eagle St. WC1....6G 7 (5K 83)
Eagle Ter. IG8: Wfd G....7E 36
Eagle Trad. Est. CR4: Mitc....6D 154
Eagle Wharf Ct. SE1....5J 15 (1F 103)
(off Lafone St.)
Eagle Wharf E. E14....7A 86
(off Narrow St.)
Eagle Wharf Rd. N1....2C 84
Eagle Wharf W. E14....7A 86
(off Narrow St.)
Eagle Works E. E1....4K 9 (4F 85)
(off Quaker St.)
Eagle Works W. E1....4J 9 (4F 85)
(off Quaker St.)
Eagling Cl. E3....3C 86
Ealdham Sq. SE9....4A 124
EALING....7D 78
Ealing B'way. Cen....7D 78
EALING COMMON....7F 79
Ealing Golf Course....3B 78
Ealing Grn. W5....1D 96
Ealing Lawn Tennis Club & Indoor Tennis Cen....7F 79
Ealing Pk. Gdns. W5....4C 96
Ealing Pk. Mans. W5....3D 96
(off Sth. Ealing Rd.)
Ealing Rd. HA0: Wemb....6E 60
Ealing Rd. TW8: Bford....5D 96
Ealing Rd. UB5: N'olt....1E 76
Ealing Squash & Fitness Club....6E 78
Ealing Studios....1D 96
Ealing Village W5....6E 78
Eamont Cl. HA4: Ruis....7D 38
Eamont Ct. NW8....2C 82
(off Eamont St.)
Eamont St. NW8....2C 82
Eardley Cres. SW5....5J 99
Eardley Point SE18....4F 107
(off Wilmount St.)
Eardley Rd. DA17: Belv....5G 109
Eardley Rd. SW16....5G 137
Earhart Ho. NW9....3C 44
(off East Dr.)
Earhart Way TW6: Cran....3J 111
Earhart Way TW6: H'row A....3J 111
Earl Cl. N11....5A 32
Earldom Rd. SW15....4E 116
Earle Gdns. KT2: King T....7E 132
Earle Ho. SW1....4D 18 (4H 101)
(off Montaigne Cl.)
Earlham Ct. E11....7H 51
Earlham Gro. E7....5H 69
Earlham Gro. N22....7E 32
Earlham St. WC2....1E 12 (6J 83)
Earl Ho. NW1....4D 4 (4C 82)
(off Lisson Gro.)
Earlom Ho. WC1....2J 7 (3A 84)
(off Margery St.)
Earl Ri. SE18....5H 107
Earl Rd. SW14....4J 115
Earlsbury Gdns. HA8: Edg....4B 28
EARL'S COURT....4K 99
Earl's Ct. Gdns. SW5....4K 99
Earl's Ct. Rd. SW5....4J 99
Earl's Ct. Rd. W8....3J 99
Earl's Ct. Sq. SW5....5K 99
Earls Cres. HA1: Harr....4J 41
Earlsdown Ho. IG11: Bark....2H 89
Earlsferry Way N1....7J 65
(not continuous)
EARLSFIELD....1A 136
Earlsfield Ho. KT2: King T....1D 150
(off Seven Kings Way)
Earlsfield Rd. SW18....1A 136
Earlshall Rd. SE9....4D 124
Earls Ho. TW9: Kew....7H 97
Earlsmead HA2: Harr....4D 58
Earlsmead Rd. N15....5F 49
Earlsmead Rd. NW10....3E 80
Earlsmead Stadium....4D 58
Earls Ter. W8....3H 99
Earlsthorpe M. SW12....6E 118
Earlsthorpe Rd. SE26....4K 139
Earlstoke St. EC1....1A 8 (3B 84)
Earlston Gro. E9....1H 85
Earl St. EC2....5F 9 (5D 84)
Earl's Wlk. RM8: Dag....4B 72
Earls Wlk. W8....3J 99
Earls Way SE1....5H 15 (1E 102)
(off Duchess Wlk.)
Earlswood Av. CR7: Thor H....5A 156
Earlswood Cl. SE10....6G 105
Earlswood Gdns. IG5: Ilf....3E 52
Earlswood St. SE10....5G 105
Early M. NW1....1F 83
Early Rivers Ho. E20....5E 68
(off Ellis Way)
Earnshaw Ho. EC1....3B 8 (4B 84)
(off Percival St.)
Earnshaw St. WC2....7D 6 (6H 83)
Earsby St. W14....4G 99
(not continuous)
Easby Cres. SM4: Mord....6K 153
Easebourne Rd. RM8: Dag....5C 72
Easedale Ho. TW7: Isle....5K 113
Eashing Point SW15....1D 134
(off Wanborough Dr.)
Easleys M. W1....7H 5 (6E 82)
East 10 Ent. Pk. E10....1A 68
EAST ACTON....7B 80
East Acton Arc. W3....6A 80
East Acton Ct. W3....7A 80
East Acton La. W3....1A 98
East Arbour St. E1....6K 85
East Av. E12....7C 70
East Av. E17....4D 50
East Av. SM6: W'gton....5K 167
East Av. UB1: S'hall....7D 76
East Av. UB3: Hayes....1H 93
East Bank N16....7E 48
Eastbank Cl. E17....5D 50
Eastbank Rd. TW12: Hamp H....5G 131
EAST BARNET....6H 21
East Barnet Rd. EN4: E Barn....4G 21
East Bay La. E20....5C 68
East Beckton District Cen....5D 88
EAST BEDFONT....7G 111
East Block SE1....6H 13 (2K 101)
(off York Rd.)
Eastbourne Av. W3....6K 79
Eastbourne Gdns. SW14....3J 115
Eastbourne M. W2....6A 82
Eastbourne Rd. E15....1G 87
Eastbourne Rd. E6....3E 88
(not continuous)
Eastbourne Rd. N15....6E 48
Eastbourne Rd. SW17....6E 136
Eastbourne Rd. TW13: Felt....2B 130
Eastbourne Rd. TW8: Bford....5C 96
Eastbourne Rd. W4....6J 97
Eastbourne Ter. W2....6A 82
Eastbournia Av. N9....3C 34
Eastbrook Av. N9....7D 24
Eastbrook Av. RM10: Dag....4J 73
Eastbrook Cl. RM10: Dag....4J 73
Eastbrook Dr. RM7: Rush G....3K 73
Eastbrookend Country Pk....3K 73
Eastbrookend Discovery Cen....4K 73
Eastbrook Rd. SE3....1K 123
Eastbury Av. EN1: Enf....1A 24
Eastbury Av. IG11: Bark....1J 89
Eastbury Ct. EN5: New Bar....5F 21
(off Lyonsdown Rd.)
Eastbury Ct. IG11: Bark....1J 89
Eastbury Gro. W4....5A 98
Eastbury Manor House....1K 89
Eastbury Rd. BR5: Pet W....6H 161
Eastbury Rd. E6....4E 88
Eastbury Rd. KT2: King T....7E 132
Eastbury Rd. RM7: Rom....6K 55
Eastbury Sq. IG11: Bark....1K 89
Eastbury Ter. E1....4K 85
East Carriage Ho. SE18....3F 107
(off Royal Carriage M.)
Eastcastle St. W1....7A 6 (6G 83)
Eastcheap EC3....2G 15 (7E 84)
East Churchfield Rd. W3....1K 97
Eastchurch Rd. TW6: H'row A....2G 111
East Cl. EN4: Cockf....4K 21
East Cl. UB6: G'frd....2G 77
East Cl. W5....4G 79
Eastcombe Av. SE7....6K 105
Eastcote BR6: Orp....1K 173
EASTCOTE....7K 39
Eastcote Av. HA2: Harr....2F 59
Eastcote Av. KT8: W Mole....5D 148
Eastcote Av. UB6: G'frd....5A 60
Eastcote Hockey & Badminton Club....6H 39
Eastcote Ind. Est. HA4: Ruis....7A 40
Eastcote La. HA2: Harr....4C 58
Eastcote La. UB5: N'olt....5D 58
(not continuous)
Eastcote La. Nth. UB5: N'olt....6D 58
Eastcote Pl. HA5: Eastc....6K 39
Eastcote Rd. DA16: Well....2H 125
Eastcote Rd. HA2: Harr....3G 59
Eastcote Rd. HA4: Ruis....7G 39
Eastcote Rd. HA5: Pinn....5B 40
Eastcote St. SW9....2K 119
Eastcote Vw. HA5: Pinn....4A 40
EASTCOTE VILLAGE....5K 39
Eastcott Cl. KT2: King T....5J 133
East Ct. HA0: Wemb....2C 60
East Cres. EN1: Enf....5A 24
East Cres. N11....4J 31
East Cft. Ho. HA2: Harr....2G 59
Eastcroft Rd. KT19: Ewe....7A 164
East Cross Route E9 Crowfoot Cl....5B 68
East Cross Route E9 Wansbeck Rd....7B 68
Eastdown Ct. SE13....4F 123
Eastdown Ho. E8....4G 67
Eastdown Pk. SE13....4F 123
East Dr. NW9....3C 44
East Dr. SM5: Cars....7C 166
East Duck Lees La. EN3: Pond E....4F 25
EAST DULWICH....4F 121
East Dulwich Est. SE22....3E 120
(off Albrighton Rd.)
East Dulwich Gro. SE22....5E 120
East Dulwich Rd. SE15....4G 121
East Dulwich Rd. SE22....4F 121
(not continuous)
East End Farm HA5: Pinn....3D 40
East End Rd. N2....3K 45
East End Rd. N3....2J 45
East End Way HA5: Pinn....3C 40
East Entrance RM10: Dag....2H 91
Easterbrook Pl. BR2: Hayes....7K 159
Eastern App. IG11: Bark....1A 90
Eastern Av. E11....6K 51
Eastern Av. HA5: Pinn....7B 40
Eastern Av. IG2: Ilf....6F 53
Eastern Av. IG4: Ilf....6C 52
Eastern Av. RM6: Chad H....4B 54
Eastern Av. E. RM1: Rom....3K 55
Eastern Av. Retail Pk. Romford....4J 55
Eastern Av. W. RM1: Rom....3K 55
Eastern Av. W. RM6: Chad H....4E 54
Eastern Av. W. RM7: Chad H....4G 55
Eastern Av. W. RM7: Mawney....4G 55
Eastern Av. W. RM7: Rom....4G 55
Eastern Bus. Pk. TW6: H'row A....2G 111
Eastern Ct. E15....6G 69
(off Gt. Eastern Rd.)
Eastern Gateway E16....7A 88
Eastern Ho. E2....3H 85
(off Bethnal Grn. Rd.)
Eastern Ind. Est. DA18: Erith....2G 109
Eastern Perimeter Rd. TW6: H'row A....2H 111
Eastern Quay Apts. E16....1K 105
(off Portsmouth M.)
Eastern Rd. E13....2K 87
Eastern Rd. E17....5E 50
Eastern Rd. N2....3D 46
Eastern Rd. N22....1J 47
Eastern Rd. SE4....4C 122
EASTERN RDBT....2G 71
Easternville Gdns. IG2: Ilf....6G 53
Eastern Way DA17: Belv....2H 109
Eastern Way DA18: Erith....7E 90
Eastern Way SE2....7E 90
Eastern Way SE28....2A 108
East Ferry Rd. E14....4D 104
Eastfield Gdns. RM10: Dag....4G 73
Eastfield Rd. E17....4C 50
Eastfield Rd. EN3: Enf W....1E 24
Eastfield Rd. N8....3J 47
Eastfield Rd. RM10: Dag....4G 73
Eastfield Rd. RM9: Dag....4F 73
Eastfields HA5: Eastc....5A 40
Eastfields Av. SW18....4J 117
Eastfields Rd. CR4: Mitc....2E 154
Eastfields Rd. W3....5J 79
Eastfield St. E14....5A 86
EAST FINCHLEY....4C 46
East Gdns. SW17....6C 136
Eastgate Bus. Pk. E10....1A 68
Eastgate Cl. SE28....6D 90
Eastglade HA5: Pinn....3D 40
East Gro. SE17....4C 102
EAST HAM....2D 88
East Ham & Barking By-Pass IG11: Bark....2H 89
Eastham Cl. EN5: Barn....5B 20
East Ham Leisure Cen....1D 88
East Ham Mnr. Way E6....6E 88
East Ham Nature Reserve....4D 88
East Ham Nature Reserve Vis. Cen....4D 88
East Handyside Canopy....1J 83
East Harding St. EC4....7K 7 (6A 84)
East Heath Rd. NW3....3A 64
East Hill HA9: Wemb....2G 61
East Hill SW18....5K 117
Eastholm NW11....4K 45
East Holme DA8: Erith....1K 127
Eastholme UB3: Hayes....1J 93
East India Bldgs. E14....7C 86
(off Saltwell St.)
East India Ct. SE16....2J 103
(off St Marychurch St.)
East India Dock Basin Local Nature Reserve....7G 87
East India Dock Ho. E14....6E 86
East India Dock Rd. E14....6C 86
East India Way CR0: C'don....1F 169
Eastlake Ho. NW8....4B 4 (4B 82)
(off Frampton St.)
Eastlake Rd. SE5....2C 120
Eastlands Cres. SE21....6F 121
East La. SE16 Chambers St....2G 103
East La. SE16 Scott Lidgett Cres....2G 103
East La. HA0: Wemb....3B 60
East La. HA9: Wemb....3D 60
East La. KT1: King T....3D 150
East La. Bus. Pk. HA9: Wemb....2D 60
Eastlea M. E16....4G 87
Eastleigh Av. HA2: Harr....2F 59
Eastleigh Cl. NW2....3A 62
Eastleigh Cl. SM2: Sutt....7K 165
Eastleigh Rd. DA7: Bex....3J 127
Eastleigh Rd. E17....2B 50
Eastleigh Wlk. SW15....7C 116
Eastleigh Way TW14: Felt....1J 129
East Lodge E16....1J 105
(off Wesley Av.)
East London Crematorium....3H 87
East London Gymnastic Cen....6D 88
Eastman Ho. SW4....6G 119
Eastman Rd. W3....2K 97
East Mead HA4: Ruis....3B 58
Eastmead Av. UB6: G'frd....3F 77
Eastmead Cl. BR1: Broml....2C 160
Eastmearn Rd. SE21....2C 138
EAST MOLESEY....4H 149
East Molesey Memorial Cricket Ground....3H 149
Eastmoor Pl. SE7....3B 106
Eastmoor St. SE7....3B 106
East Mt. St. E1....5H 85
(not continuous)
Eastney Rd. CR0: C'don....1B 168
Eastney St. SE10....5F 105
Eastnor Rd. SE9....1G 143
Eastone Apts. E1....6K 9 (5F 85)
(off Lolesworth Cl.)
Easton St. WC1....3J 7 (4A 84)
East Park Cl. RM6: Chad H....5E 54
East Parkside SE10....2G 105
East Park Wlk. E20....5E 68
East Pas. EC1....5C 8 (5C 84)
(off Cloth St.)
East Pl. SE27....4C 138
East Point SE1....5G 103
East Pole Cotts. N14....4C 22
East Poultry Av. EC1....6A 8 (5B 84)
East Ramp TW6: H'row A....1D 110
East Rd. DA16: Well....2B 126
East Rd. E15....1J 87
East Rd. EN3: Enf W....1D 24
East Rd. EN4: E Barn....1K 31
East Rd. HA1: Harr....7B 42
East Rd. HA8: Edg....1H 43
East Rd. KT2: King T....1E 150
East Rd. N1....2E 8 (3D 84)
East Rd. RM6: Chad H....5E 54
East Rd. RM7: Rush G....7K 55
East Rd. SW19....6A 136
East Rd. SW3....6G 17 (5E 100)
East Rd. TW14: Bedf....7F 111
East Rd. UB7: W Dray....4C 92
East Rochester Way DA15: Sidc....5J 125
East Rochester Way DA5: Bexl....6F 127
East Row E11....6J 51
East Row W10....4G 81
Eastry Av. BR2: Hayes....6H 159
Eastry Ho. SW8....7J 101
(off Hartington Rd.)
Eastry Ho. W11....7G 81
(off Walmer Rd.)
Eastry Rd. DA8: Erith....7G 109
EAST SHEEN....4J 115
East Sheen Av. SW14....5K 115
East Shop. Cen....7K 69
East Side W12....2E 98
(off Shepherd's Bush Mkt.)
Eastside Halls SW7....1B 16 (3B 100)
(off Prince's Gdns.)
Eastside M. E3....2C 86
(off Morville St.)
Eastside Rd. NW11....4H 45
East Smithfield E1....3K 15 (7F 85)
East Stand N5....3B 66
East St. BR1: Broml....2J 159
East St. DA7: Bex....4G 127
East St. IG11: Bark....1G 89
East St. SE17....5C 102
(not continuous)
East Surrey Gro. SE15....7F 103
East Tenter St. E1....1K 15 (6F 85)
East Ter. DA15: Sidc....1J 143
East Thamesmead Bus. Pk. DA18: Erith....2F 109
East Twr. E14....2D 104
(off Pan Peninsula Sq.)
East Twr. SW10....7B 100
East Towers HA5: Pinn....5B 40
East Va. W3....1B 98
East Vw. E4....5K 35
East Vw. EN5: Barn....2C 20
Eastview Av. SE18....7J 107
EAST VILLAGE....5E 68
Eastville Av. NW11....6H 45
East Wlk. EN4: E Barn....7K 21
East Wlk. UB3: Hayes....1J 93
East Way BR2: Hayes....7J 159
East Way CR0: C'don....2A 170
East Way E11....5K 51
East Way HA4: Ruis....1J 57
East Way UB3: Hayes....1J 93
Eastway E9....6B 68
(not continuous)
Eastway SM4: Mord....5F 153
Eastway SM6: W'gton....4G 167
Eastway Cres. HA2: Harr....2F 59
Eastwell Cl. BR3: Beck....7A 140
Eastwell Ho. SE1....7F 15 (3D 102)
(off Weston St.)
East Wick E20....5C 68
EAST WICKHAM....1C 126
Eastwood Cl. E18....2J 51
Eastwood Cl. N17....7C 34
Eastwood Cl. N7....5A 66
Eastwood Ho. E3....5C 86
(off Bow Comn. La.)
Eastwood Rd. E18....2J 51
Eastwood Rd. IG3: Ilf....1A 72
Eastwood Rd. N10....2E 46
Eastwood Rd. UB7: W Dray....2C 92
East Woodside DA5: Bexl....7E 126
Eastwood St. SW16....6G 137
easyGym Fulham....6H 99
Eatington Rd. E10....5F 51
Eaton Cl. HA7: Stan....4G 27
Eaton Cl. SW1....4G 17 (4E 100)
Eaton Ct. E18....2J 51
Eaton Ct. HA8: Edg....4B 28
Eaton Dr. KT2: King T....7G 133
Eaton Dr. RM5: Col R....1H 55
Eaton Dr. SW9....4B 120
Eaton Gdns. RM9: Dag....7E 72
Eaton Ga. SW1....3G 17 (4E 100)
Eaton Ho. E14....7B 86
(off Westferry Cir.)
Eaton Ho. SW11....1B 118
Eaton La. SW1....2K 17 (3F 101)
Eaton Mans. SW1....4G 17 (4E 100)
(off Bourne St.)
Eaton M. Nth. SW1....3G 17 (4E 100)
Eaton M. Sth. SW1....3H 17 (4E 100)
Eaton M. W. SW1....3H 17 (4E 100)
Eaton Pk. Rd. N13....2F 33
Eaton Pl. SW1....3G 17 (4E 100)
Eaton Ri. E11....5A 52
Eaton Ri. W5....5D 78
Eaton Rd. DA14: Sidc....2D 144
Eaton Rd. EN1: Enf....4K 23
Eaton Rd. NW4....5E 44
Eaton Rd. SM2: Sutt....6B 166
Eaton Rd. TW3: Houn....4H 113
Eaton Row SW1....2J 17 (3F 101)
Eatons Mead E4....2H 35
Eaton Sq. SW1....3G 17 (4E 100)
Eaton Ter. E3....3A 86
Eaton Ter. SW1....3G 17 (4E 100)
Eaton Ter. M. SW1....3G 17 (4E 100)
(off Eaton Ter.)
Eatonville Rd. SW17....2D 136
Eatonville Vs. SW17....2D 136
Ebb Ct. E16....7G 89
Ebbett Ct. W3....5K 79
Ebbisham Dr. SW8....7G 19 (6K 101)
Ebbisham Rd. KT4: Wor Pk....2E 164
Ebbsfleet Rd. NW2....5G 63
Ebenezer Ho. SE11....4K 19 (4B 102)
Ebenezer Mussel Ho. E2....2J 85
(off Patriot Sq.)
Ebenezer St. N1....1E 8 (3D 84)
Ebenezer Wlk. SW16....1G 155
Ebley Cl. SE15....6F 103
Ebner St. SW18....5K 117
Ebony Cres. EN4: E Barn....5K 21
Ebony Ho. E2....3G 85
(off Buckfast St.)
Ebor Cotts. SW15....3A 134
Ebor St. E1....3J 9 (4F 85)
Ebrington Rd. HA3: Kenton....6D 42
Ebsworth St. SE23....7K 121
Eburne Rd. N7....3J 65
Ebury Bri. SW1....5J 17 (5F 101)
Ebury Bri. Est. SW1....5J 17 (5F 101)
Ebury Bri. Rd. SW1....6H 17 (5E 100)
Ebury Cl. BR2: Kes....3C 172
Ebury M. N5....3C 66
Ebury M. SE27....3B 138
Ebury M. SW1....3J 17 (4F 101)
Ebury M. E. SW1....2J 17 (3F 101)
Ebury Sq. SW1....4H 17 (4E 100)
Ebury St. SW1....4H 17 (4E 100)
Ecclesbourne Apts. N1....7D 66
(off Ecclesbourne Rd.)
Ecclesbourne Cl. N13....5F 33
Ecclesbourne Gdns. N13....5F 33
Ecclesbourne Rd. CR7: Thor H....5C 156
Ecclesbourne Rd. N1....7C 66
Eccleshill BR2: Broml....4H 159
(off Durham Rd.)
Eccles Rd. SW11....4D 118
Eccleston Bri. SW1....3K 17 (4F 101)
Eccleston Cl. BR6: Orp....1H 173
Eccleston Cl. EN4: Cockf....4J 21
Eccleston Cres. RM6: Chad H....7B 54
Ecclestone Ct. HA9: Wemb....5E 60
Ecclestone M. HA9: Wemb....5E 60
Ecclestone Pl. HA9: Wemb....5F 61
Eccleston Ho. SW2....6A 120
Eccleston M. SW1....2H 17 (3E 100)
Eccleston Pl. SW1....3J 17 (4F 101)
Eccleston Rd. W13....7A 78
Eccleston Sq. SW1....4K 17 (4F 101)
(not continuous)
Eccleston Sq. M. SW1....4K 17 (4F 101)
Eccleston St. SW1....2J 17 (3F 101)
Eccleston Yd. SW1....3J 17 (4F 101)
(off Eccleston Pl.)
Echelforde Dr. TW15: Ashf....4C 128
Echo Ct. E16....2A 106
(off Admiralty Av.)
Echo Hgts. E4....1J 35
Eckford St. N1....2A 84
Eckington Cl. SE14....7K 103
Eckington Ho. N15....6D 48
(off Fladbury Rd.)
Eckington La. SE14....7K 103
Eckstein Rd. SW11....4C 118

216 A–Z London

Eclipse Bldg. N1 6A 66
(off Laycock St.)
Eclipse Ho. N22 2K 47
(off Station Rd.)
Eclipse Rd. E13 5K 87
Eco Va. SE23 6H 121
Ector Rd. SE6 2G 141
Edam Ct. DA15: Sidc 3A 144
Edans Ct. W12 2B 98
Edbrooke Rd. W9 4J 81
Eddington Ct. E16 6H 87
(off Silvertown Sq.)
Eddinton Cl. CR0: New Ad 6E 170
Eddisbury Ho. SE26 3G 139
Eddiscombe Rd. SW6 2H 117
Eddy Cl. RM7: Rom 6H 55
Eddystone Rd. SE4 5A 122
Eddystone Twr. SE8 5A 104
Eddystone Wlk. TW19: Stanw 7A 110
Ede Cl. TW3: Houn 3D 112
Edeleny Cl. N2 3A 46
Eden Apts. E14 4E 104
(off Glengarnock Av.)
Edenbridge Cl. SE16 5H 103
(off Masters Dr.)
Edenbridge Rd. E9 7K 67
Edenbridge Rd. EN1: Enf 6K 23
Eden Cl. DA5: Bexl 4K 145
Eden Cl. HA0: Wemb 1D 78
Eden Cl. NW3 2J 63
Eden Cl. W8 3J 99
Eden Ct. IG6: Ilf 1H 53
Edencourt Rd. SW16 6F 137
Edendale W3 7H 79
Edendale Rd. DA7: Bex 1K 127
Edenfield Gdns. KT4: Wor Pk 3B 164
Eden Gro. E17 5D 50
Eden Gro. N7 5K 65
Eden Gro. NW10 6D 62
Edenham Way W10 4H 81
Eden Ho. NW8 4C 4 (4C 82)
(off Church St.)
Eden Ho. SE16 2K 103
(off Water Gdns. Sq.)
Eden Ho. SE8 7C 104
(off Deptford High St.)
Edenhurst Av. SW6 3H 117
Eden Lodge NW6 7F 63
Eden M. KT2: King T 1G 151
Eden M. SW17 3A 136
EDEN PARK 5C 158
Eden Pk. Av. BR3: Beck 4A 158
Eden Rd. BR3: Beck 4A 158
Eden Rd. CR0: C'don 4D 168
Eden Rd. DA5: Bexl 4J 145
Eden Rd. E17 5D 50
Eden Rd. SE27 4B 138
Edensor Gdns. W4 7A 98
Edensor Rd. W4 7A 98
Eden St. KT1: King T 2D 150
Edenvale Cl. CR4: Mitc 7E 136
Edenvale Rd. CR4: Mitc 7E 136
Edenvale St. SW6 2A 118
Eden Wlk. KT1: King T 2E 150
Eden Walk Shop. Cen. 2E 150
Eden Way BR3: Beck 5B 158
Eden Way E3 1B 86
Ederline Av. SW16 3K 155
Edgar Ct. KT3: N Mald 2A 152
Edgar Ho. E11 7J 51
Edgar Ho. E9 5A 68
(off Homerton Rd.)
Edgar Ho. SW8 7J 101
(off Wyvil Rd.)
Edgar Kail Way SE22 4E 120
Edgarley Ter. SW6 1G 117
Edgar Myles Ho. E16 5H 87
(off Ordnance Rd.)
Edgar Rd. E3 3D 86
Edgar Rd. RM6: Chad H 7D 54
Edgar Rd. TW4: Houn 7D 112
Edgar Rd. UB7: Yiew 7A 74
Edgar Wallace Cl. SE15 7E 102
Edgar Wright Ct. SW6 7H 99
(off Dawes Rd.)
Edgcott Ho. W10 5E 80
(off Sutton Way)
Edge Finsbury, The 7C 48
Edge, The SE8 7B 104
(off Glenville Gro.)
Edge Apts. E15 7F 69
Edgeborough Way BR1: Broml 7B 142
Edgebury BR7: Chst 4F 143
Edgebury Wlk. BR7: Chst 4G 143
Edge Bus. Cen., The NW2 2D 62
Edgecombe Ho. SE5 2E 120
Edgecombe Ho. SW19 1G 135
Edgecoombe CR2: Sels 7J 169
Edgecoombe Cl. KT2: King T 7K 133
Edgecote Cl. W3 1J 97
Edgecot Gro. N15 5E 48
Edgecumbe Av. NW9 1B 44
Edgefield Av. IG11: Bark 7K 71
Edgefield Cl. BR3: Beck 6C 140
Edgefield Ct. IG11: Bark 7K 71
(off Edgefield Av.)
Edge Hill SE18 6F 107
Edge Hill SW19 7F 135
Edge Hill Av. N3 4J 45
Edge Hill Ct. DA14: Sidc 4K 143
Edge Hill Ct. SW19 7F 135
Edgehill Gdns. RM10: Dag 4G 73
Edgehill Ho. SW9 2B 120
Edgehill Rd. BR7: Chst 3G 143
Edgehill Rd. CR4: Mitc 1F 155
Edgehill Rd. W13 5C 78
Edgeley La. SW4 3H 119
Edgeley Rd. SW4 3H 119
Edgel St. SW18 4K 117
Edge Point Cl. SE27 5B 138
Edge St. W8 1J 99
Edgewood Dr. BR6: Chels 5K 173
Edgewood Grn. CR0: C'don 1K 169
Edgeworth Av. NW4 5C 44
Edgeworth Cl. NW4 5C 44
Edgeworth Ct. EN4: Cockf 4H 21
(off Fordham Rd.)
Edgeworth Cres. NW4 5C 44
Edgeworth Ho. NW8 1A 82
(off Boundary Rd.)
Edgeworth Rd. EN4: Cockf 4H 21
Edgeworth Rd. SE9 4A 124
Edge Youth Cen., The 4J 163
Edgington Rd. SW16 6H 137
Edgington Way DA14: Sidc 7C 144

Edgson Ho. SW1 5J 17 (5F 101)
(off Ebury Bri. Rd.)
EDGWARE 6B 28
EDGWARE BURY 1A 28
Edgwarebury Gdns. HA8: Edg 5B 28
Edgwarebury La. HA8: Edg 1A 28
(not continuous)
Edgware Ct. HA8: Edg 6B 28
Edgware Rd. NW2 1D 62
Edgware Rd. NW9 2J 43
Edgware Rd. W2 4A 4 (4B 82)
Edgware Way HA8: Edg 4A 28
Edgware Way NW7 4E 28
Edgware Way WD6: E'tree 1J 27
Edicule Sq. E3 3A 86
Edinburgh Cl. E2 2J 85
Edinburgh Cl. HA5: Pinn 7B 40
Edinburgh Cl. UB10: Ick 4D 56
Edinburgh Ct. DA8: Erith 7K 109
Edinburgh Ct. KT1: King T 3E 150
(off Watersplash Cl.)
Edinburgh Ct. SE16 1K 103
(off Rotherhithe St.)
Edinburgh Ct. SW20 5F 153
Edinburgh Dr. UB10: Ick 4D 56
Edinburgh Ga. SW1 6E 10 (2D 100)
Edinburgh Ho. NW4 3E 44
Edinburgh Ho. W9 3K 81
(off Maida Vale)
Edinburgh Rd. E13 2K 87
Edinburgh Rd. E17 5C 50
Edinburgh Rd. N18 5B 34
Edinburgh Rd. SM1: Sutt 2A 166
Edinburgh Rd. W7 2K 95
Edington NW5 6E 64
Edington Rd. EN3: Enf H 2D 24
Edington Rd. SE2 3B 108
Edison Bldg. E14 2C 104
Edison Cl. E17 5C 50
Edison Cl. UB7: W Dray 2B 92
Edison Ct. CR0: C'don 7B 156
(off Campbell Rd.)
Edison Ct. SE10 3H 105
(off Schoolbank Rd.)
Edison Ct. W3 2A 98
Edison Dr. HA9: Wemb 3E 60
Edison Dr. UB1: S'hall 6F 77
Edison Gro. SE18 7K 107
Edison Hgts. E1 3K 9 (4F 85)
(off Cygnet St.)
Edison Ho. HA9: Wemb 3J 61
(off Barnhill Rd.)
Edison Ho. SE1 4D 102
(off New Kent Rd.)
Edison M. SW18 6K 117
Edison Rd. BR2: Broml 2J 159
Edison Rd. DA16: Well 1K 125
Edison Rd. EN3: Brim 2G 25
Edison Rd. N8 6H 47
Edis St. NW1 1E 82
Ediswan Way EN3: Pond E 5D 24
Editha Mans. SW10 6A 100
(off Edith Gro.)
Edith Brinson Ho. E14 6F 87
(off Oban St.)
Edith Cavell Cl. N19 7J 47
Edith Cavell Ho. E14 6D 86
(off Sturry St.)
Edith Cavell Way SE18 1C 124
Edith Gdns. KT5: Surb 7H 151
Edith Gro. SW10 6A 100
Edith Ho. W6 5E 98
(off Queen Caroline St.)
Edithna St. SW9 3J 119
Edith Nesbit Wlk. SE9 5D 124
Edith Neville Cotts. NW1 1C 6 (3H 83)
(off Drummond Cres.)
Edith Ramsay Ho. E1 5A 86
(off Duckett St.)
Edith Rd. E15 5F 69
Edith Rd. E6 7B 70
Edith Rd. N11 7C 32
Edith Rd. RM6: Chad H 7D 54
Edith Rd. SE25 5D 156
Edith Rd. SW19 6K 135
Edith Rd. W14 4G 99
Edith Row SW6 1K 117
Edith St. E2 2G 85
Edith Summerskill Ho. SW6 7H 99
(off Clem Attlee Ct.)
Edith Ter. SW10 7A 100
Edith Vs. W14 4H 99
Edith Yd. SW10 7A 100
Edmansons Cl. N17 1F 49
Edmeston Cl. E9 6A 68
Edmond Ct. SE14 1J 121
Edmonds Ct. KT8: W Mole 5F 149
Edmonscote W13 5A 78
EDMONTON 3B 34
Edmonton Ct. SE16 3J 103
(off Canada Est.)
Edmonton Grn. Shop. Cen. 2B 34
Edmonton Leisure Cen. 3B 34
Edmund Gro. TW13: Hanw 2D 130
Edmund Halley Way SE10 2G 105
Edmund Ho. SE17 6B 102
Edmund Hurst Dr. E6 5F 89
Edmund Rd. CR4: Mitc 3C 154
Edmund Rd. DA16: Well 3A 126
Edmundsbury Ct. Est. SW9 4K 119
Edmunds Cl. UB4: Yead 5A 76
Edmund St. SE5 7D 102
Edmunds Wlk. N2 4C 46
Ednam Ho. SE15 6G 103
(off Haymerle Rd.)
Edna Rd. SW20 2F 153
Edna St. SW11 1C 118
Edred Ho. E9 4A 68
(off Lindisfarne Way)
Edrich Ho. SW4 1J 119
Edric Ho. SW1 3D 18 (4H 101)
(off Page St.)
Edrick Rd. HA8: Edg 6D 28
Edrick Wlk. HA8: Edg 6D 28
Edric Rd. SE14 7K 103
Edridge Rd. CR0: C'don 3C 168
Education Sq. E1 6G 85
(off Alder St.)
Edward VII Mans. NW10 3F 81
(off Chamberlayne Rd.)
Edward Alderton Theatre 3D 126
Edward Av. E4 6J 35
Edward Av. SM4: Mord 5B 154
Edward Bond Ho. WC1 2F 7 (3J 83)
(off Cromer St.)

Edward Clifford Ho. SE17 4D 102
(off Elsted St.)
Edward Cl. N9 7A 24
Edward Cl. NW2 4F 63
Edward Cl. TW12: Hamp H 5G 131
Edward Ct. E16 5J 87
Edward Dodd Ct. N1 1F 9 (3D 84)
(off Chart St.)
Edward Edward's Ho. SE1 5A 14 (1B 102)
(off Nicholson St.)
Edwardes Pl. W8 3H 99
Edwardes Sq. W8 3H 99
Edward Gro. EN4: E Barn 5G 21
Edward Heylin Ct. E15 2D 86
(off High St.)
Edward Heylyn Ho. E3 2C 86
(off Thomas Fyre Dr.)
Edward Ho. SE11 5H 19 (5K 101)
(off Newburn St.)
Edward Ho. W2 4A 4 (4B 82)
(off Hall Pl.)
Edward Kennedy Ho. W10 4G 81
(off Wornington Rd.)
Edward Mann Cl. E. E1 6K 85
(off Pitsea St.)
Edward Mann Cl. W. E1 6K 85
(off Pitsea St.)
Edward M. NW1 1K 5 (3F 83)
Edward Mills Way E14 6C 86
Edward Pl. SE8 6B 104
Edward Rd. BR1: Broml 7K 141
Edward Rd. BR7: Chst 5F 143
Edward Rd. CR0: C'don 7E 156
Edward Rd. E17 4K 49
Edward Rd. EN4: E Barn 5G 21
Edward Rd. HA2: Harr 3G 41
Edward Rd. RM6: Chad H 6E 54
Edward Rd. SE20 7K 139
Edward Rd. TW12: Hamp H 5G 131
Edward Rd. TW14: Felt 5F 111
Edward Rd. UB5: N'olt 2A 76
Edward's Av. HA4: Ruis 6K 57
Edwards Cl. KT4: Wor Pk 2F 165
Edward's Cotts. N1 6B 66
Edwards Ct. CR0: C'don 4E 168
(off South Pk. Hill Rd.)
Edwards Dr. N11 7C 32
Edward's La. N16 2E 66
Edwards Mans. IG11: Bark 7K 71
(off Upney La.)
Edwards M. N1 7B 66
Edwards M. W1 1G 11 (6E 82)
Edwards Pas. E1 5J 85
(off Trinity Grn.)
Edwards Pl. KT12: Walt T 7J 147
Edward Sq. N1 1K 83
Edward Sq. SE16 1A 104
Edwards Rd. DA17: Belv 4G 109
Edward St. E16 4J 87
(not continuous)
Edward St. SE14 7A 104
Edward St. SE8 6B 104
Edwards Way SE4 5C 122
Edwards Yd. HA0: Wemb 1E 78
Edward Temme Av. E15 7H 69
Edward Tyler Rd. SE12 2A 142
Edward Way TW15: Ashf 2B 128
Edwina Gdns. IG4: Ilf 5C 52
Edwin Arnold Ct. DA14: Sidc 4K 143
Edwin Av. E6 2E 88
(not continuous)
Edwin Cl. DA7: Bex 6F 109
Edwin Hall Pl. SE13 6F 123
Edwin Ho. SE15 7G 103
Edwin Pl. CR0: C'don 1E 168
(off Cross Rd.)
Edwin Rd. HA8: Edg 6E 28
Edwin Rd. TW1: Twick 1K 131
Edwin Rd. TW2: Twick 1J 131
Edwin's Mead E9 4A 68
Edwin Stray Ho. TW13: Hanw 2E 130
Edwin St. E1 4J 85
Edwin St. E16 5J 87
Edwin Ware Ct. HA5: Pinn 2A 40
Edwy Ho. E9 4B 68
(off Homerton Rd.)
Edwyn Cl. EN5: Barn 6A 20
Edwyn Ho. SW18 6K 117
(off Neville Gill Cl.)
Eel Brook Cl. SW6 1K 117
Eel Pie Island TW1: Twick 1A 132
Effie Pl. SW6 7J 99
Effie Rd. SW6 7J 99
Effingham Cl. SM2: Sutt 7K 165
Effingham Lodge KT1: King T 4D 150
Effingham Rd. CR0: C'don 7K 155
Effingham Rd. KT6: Surb 7B 150
Effingham Rd. N8 5A 48
Effingham Rd. SE12 5G 123
Effort St. SW17 5C 136
Effra Cl. SW19 6K 135
Effra Ct. SW2 5K 119
(off Brixton Hill)
Effra Pde. SW2 5A 120
Effra Rd. SW19 6K 135
Effra Rd. SW2 4A 120
Effra Rd. Retail Pk. 5A 120
Egan Way UB3: Hayes 7G 75
Egbert Ho. E9 5A 68
(off Homerton Rd.)
Egbert St. NW1 1E 82
Egbury Ho. SW15 6B 116
(off Tangley Gro.)
Eger Cl. N3 3K 45
Egeremont Rd. SE13 2D 122
Egerton Cl. DA17: Belv 5J 109
Egerton Cl. HA5: Eastc 4J 39
Egerton Ct. E11 7F 51
Egerton Cres. SW3 3D 16 (4C 100)
Egerton Dr. SE10 1D 122
Egerton Dr. TW7: Isle 3B 114
Egerton Gdns. IG3: Ilf 3K 71
Egerton Gdns. NW10 1E 80
Egerton Gdns. NW4 4D 44
Egerton Gdns. SW3 3C 16 (4C 100)
Egerton Gdns. W13 6B 78
Egerton Gdns. M. SW3 2D 16 (3C 100)
Egerton Pl. SW3 2D 16 (3C 100)
Egerton Rd. HA0: Wemb 7F 61
Egerton Rd. KT3: N Mald 4B 152
Egerton Rd. N16 7F 49
Egerton Rd. SE25 3E 156
Egerton Rd. TW2: Twick 7J 113
Egerton Ter. SW3 2D 16 (3C 100)
Egerton Way UB3: Harl 7D 92

Eggardon Ct. UB5: N'olt 6F 59
Egham Cl. SM3: Cheam 2G 165
Egham Cl. SW19 2G 135
Egham Cres. SM3: Cheam 3G 165
Egham Rd. E13 5K 87
Eglantine Rd. SW18 5A 118
Egleston Rd. SM4: Mord 6K 153
Egleton Ho. SW15 7C 116
Eglington Ct. SE17 6C 102
Eglington Rd. E4 1A 36
Eglinton Hill SE18 6F 107
Eglinton Rd. SE18 6E 106
Egliston M. SW15 3E 116
Egliston Rd. SW15 3E 116
Eglon M. NW1 7D 64
Egmont Av. KT6: Surb 1F 163
Egmont Ct. KT12: Walt T 7K 147
(off Egmont Rd.)
Egmont M. KT19: Ewe 4K 163
Egmont Rd. KT12: Walt T 7K 147
Egmont Rd. KT3: N Mald 4B 152
Egmont Rd. KT6: Surb 1F 163
Egmont Rd. SM2: Sutt 7A 166
Egmont St. SE14 7K 103
Egremont Ho. E20 5E 68
(off Medals Way)
Egremont Ho. SE13 2D 122
(off Russett Way)
Egremont Rd. SE27 3A 138
Egret Hgts. N17 3H 49
(off Waterside Way)
Egret Ho. SE16 4K 103
(off Tawny Way)
Egret Way UB4: Yead 5B 76
Eider Cl. E7 5H 69
Eider Cl. UB4: Yead 5B 76
Eider Ct. SE8 6B 104
(off Pilot Cl.)
Eighteenth Rd. CR4: Mitc 4J 155
Eighth Av. E12 4D 70
Eighth Av. UB3: Hayes 1J 93
Eileen Lenton Ct. N15 4F 49
(off Tottenham Grn. E.)
Eileen Rd. SE25 5D 156
Eindhoven Cl. SM5: Cars 1E 166
Einstein Ho. HA9: Wemb 3J 61
Eisenhower Dr. E6 5C 88
Ekarro Ho. SW8 1J 119
(off Guildford Rd.)
Elaine Gro. NW5 5E 64
Elam Cl. SE5 2B 120
Elam St. SE5 2B 120
Elan Ct. E1 5H 85
Eland Pl. CR0: Wadd 3B 168
Eland Rd. CR0: Wadd 3B 168
Eland Rd. SW11 3D 118
Elba Pl. SE17 4C 102
Elberon Av. CR0: Bedd 6G 155
Elbe St. SW6 2A 118
Elborough Rd. SE25 5G 157
Elborough St. SW18 1J 135
Elbourne Ct. SE16 3K 103
(off Worgan St.)
Elbourne Trad. Est. DA17: Belv 3H 109
Elbourn Ho. SW3 5C 16 (5C 100)
(off Cale St.)
Elbow Mdw. SL3: Poyle 4A 174
Elbury Dr. E16 6J 87
Elcho St. SW11 7C 100
Elcot Av. SE15 7H 103
Elden Ho. SW3 3C 16 (4C 100)
(off Sloane Av.)
Elden M. SW17 3C 136
Elder Av. N8 5J 47
Elderberry Gro. SE27 4C 138
Elderberry Rd. W5 2E 96
Elderberry Way E6 3D 88
Elder Cl. DA15: Sidc 1K 143
Elder Cl. N20 2E 30
Elder Cl. UB7: Yiew 7A 74
Elder Ct. WD23: B Hea 2D 26
Elderfield Ho. E14 7C 86
(off Pennyfields)
Elderfield Pl. SW17 4F 137
Elderfield Rd. E5 4K 67
Elderfield Wlk. E11 5K 51
Elderflower Way E15 7G 69
Elder Gdns. SE27 5C 138
Elder Ho. E15 3G 87
(off Manor Rd.)
Elder Ho. KT1: King T 1D 150
(off Water La.)
Elder Ho. SE16 3A 104
Elder Oak Cl. SE20 1H 157
Elder Oak Ct. SE20 1H 157
(off Anerley Rd.)
Elder Pl. CR2: S Croy 6B 168
Elder Rd. SE27 5C 138
Elderslie Cl. BR3: Beck 5C 158
Elderslie Rd. SE9 5E 124
Elder St. E1 4J 9 (4F 85)
(not continuous)
Elderton Rd. SE26 4A 140
Eldertree Pl. CR4: Mitc 1G 155
Eldertree Way CR4: Mitc 1G 155
Elder Wlk. N1 1B 84
(off Popham St.)
Elder Wlk. SE13 3E 122
Elderwood Pl. SE27 5C 138
Eldon Av. CR0: C'don 2J 169
Eldon Av. TW5: Hest 7E 94
Eldon Ct. NW6 1J 81
Eldon Gro. NW3 5B 64
Eldon Ho. NW9 3C 44
(off East Dr.)
Eldon Pk. SE25 4H 157
Eldon Rd. E17 4B 50
Eldon Rd. N22 1B 48
Eldon Rd. N9 1D 34
Eldon Rd. W8 3K 99
Eldons Pas. E1 7G 85
(off Cable St.)
Eldon St. EC2 6F 9 (5D 84)
Eldon Way NW10 3H 79
Eldred Rd. IG11: Bark 1J 89
Eldrick Ct. TW14: Bedf 1F 129
Eldridge Cl. TW14: Felt 1J 129
Eldridge Ct. RM10: Dag 6H 73
Eldridge Ct. SE16 3G 103
Eleanor Cl. N15 3F 49
Eleanor Cl. SE16 2K 103
Eleanor Ct. E2 1G 85
(off Whiston Rd.)
Eleanor Cres. NW7 5A 30
Eleanor Gdns. EN5: Barn 5A 20

Eleanor Gdns. RM8: Dag 2F 73
Eleanor Gro. SW13 3A 116
Eleanor Gro. UB10: Ick 3D 56
Eleanor Ho. W6 5E 98
(off Queen Caroline St.)
Eleanor Rathbone Ho. N6 7H 47
(off Avenue Rd.)
Eleanor Rd. E15 6H 69
Eleanor Rd. E8 6H 67
Eleanor Rd. N11 6D 32
Eleanor Rd. SW9 1A 120
Eleanor St. E3 3C 86
Eleanor Wlk. SE18 4C 106
Electra Av. TW6: H'row A 3H 111
Electra Bus. Pk. E16 5F 87
Electric Av. SW9 4A 120
Electric Blvd. SW11 7F 101
Electric Cinema Portobello 6H 81
Electric Cinema Shoreditch 3J 9 (4F 85)
(off Club Row)
Electric Empire, The SE14 1K 121
(off New Cross Rd.)
Electric Ho. E3 3C 86
(off Bow Rd.)
Electric La. SW9 4A 120
(not continuous)
Electric Pde. E18 2J 51
(off George La.)
Electric Pde. IG3: Ilf 2J 71
Electric Pde. KT6: Surb 6D 150
Elektron Twr. E14 7F 87
Eleonora Ter. SM1: Sutt 5A 166
(off Lind Rd.)
Elephant & Castle SE1 4B 102
ELEPHANT & CASTLE 3B 102
Elephant La. SE16 2J 103
Elephant Pk. Development SE17 4C 102
Elephant Rd. SE17 4C 102
Elers Rd. UB3: Harl 4F 93
Elers Rd. W13 2C 96
Eley Rd. N18 4E 34
Eley Rd. Retail Pk. 5D 34
Eleys Est. N18 4E 34
(not continuous)
Elfindale Rd. SE24 5C 120
Elfin Gro. TW11: Tedd 5K 131
Elfin Oak 1K 99
Elford Cl. SE3 4A 124
Elford M. SW4 5G 119
Elfort Rd. N5 4A 66
Elfrida Cl. IG8: Wfd G 7D 36
Elfrida Cres. SE6 4C 140
Elf Row E1 7J 85
Elfwine Rd. W7 5J 77
Elgal Cl. BR6: Farnb 5F 173
Elgar N8 3J 47
(off Boyton Cl.)
Elgar Av. KT5: Surb 1G 163
Elgar Av. NW10 6K 61
(not continuous)
Elgar Av. SW16 3J 155
Elgar Av. W5 2E 96
Elgar Cl. E13 2A 88
Elgar Cl. IG9: Buck H 2G 37
Elgar Cl. SE8 7C 104
Elgar Cl. UB10: Ick 2C 56
Elgar Ct. NW6 3J 81
Elgar Ct. W14 3G 99
(off Blythe Rd.)
Elgar Ho. NW6 7A 64
(off Fairfax Rd.)
Elgar Ho. SW1 6K 17 (5F 101)
(off Churchill Gdns.)
Elgar St. SE16 3A 104
Elgin Av. HA3: Kenton 2B 42
Elgin Av. TW15: Ashf 6E 128
Elgin Av. W12 2C 98
Elgin Av. W9 4H 81
Elgin Cl. W12 2D 98
Elgin Ct. CR2: S Croy 4C 168
(off Bramley Hill)
Elgin Ct. W9 4K 81
Elgin Cres. TW6: H'row A 2G 111
Elgin Cres. W11 7G 81
Elgin Dr. HA6: Nwood 1G 39
Elgin Est. W9 4J 81
(off Elgin Av.)
Elgin Ho. E14 6D 86
(off Ricardo St.)
Elgin Ho. RM6: Chad H 6F 55
(off High Rd.)
Elgin Mans. W9 3K 81
Elgin M. W11 6G 81
Elgin M. Nth. W9 3K 81
Elgin M. Sth. W9 3K 81
Elgin Rd. CR0: C'don 2F 169
Elgin Rd. IG3: Ilf 1J 71
Elgin Rd. N22 2G 47
Elgin Rd. SM1: Sutt 3A 166
Elgin Rd. SM6: W'gton 6G 167
Elgood Cl. W11 7G 81
Elgood Ho. NW8 2B 82
(off Wellington Rd.)
Elgood Ho. SE1 7E 14 (2D 102)
(off Tabard St.)
Elham Cl. BR1: Broml 7B 142
Elham Ho. E5 5H 67
Elia M. N1 1A 8 (2B 84)
Elias Pl. SW8 6A 102
Elia St. N1 2B 84
Elibank Rd. SE9 4D 124
Elim Est. SE1 7G 15 (3E 102)
Elim St. SE1 7F 15 (3D 102)
(not continuous)
Elim Way E13 3H 87
Eliot Bank SE23 2H 139
Eliot Cotts. SE3 2G 123
Eliot Ct. SW18 6K 117
Eliot Dr. HA2: Harr 2F 59
Eliot Gdns. SW15 4C 116
Eliot Hill SE13 2E 122
Eliot M. NW8 2A 82
Eliot Pk. SE13 2E 122
Eliot Pl. SE3 2G 123
Eliot Rd. RM9: Dag 4D 72
Eliot Va. SE3 2F 123
Elis David Almshouses CR0: C'don 3B 168
Elis Way E20 5E 68
Elizabethan Cl. TW19: Stanw 7A 110
Elizabethan Way TW19: Stanw 7A 110
Elizabeth Av. EN2: Enf 3G 23
Elizabeth Av. IG1: Ilf 2H 71
Elizabeth Av. N1 1C 84

Elizabeth Barnes Ct. – Ely Rd.

Elizabeth Barnes Ct. SW6 2K **117**
(off Marinefield Rd.)
Elizabeth Bates Ct. E1 5J **85**
(off Fulneck Pl.)
Elizabeth Blackwell Ho. N22 1A **48**
(off Progress Way)
Elizabeth Blount Ct. E14 6A **86**
(off Carr St.)
Elizabeth Bri. SW1 4J **17** (4F **101**)
Elizabeth Cl. E14 6D **86**
Elizabeth Cl. EN5: Barn 3A **20**
Elizabeth Cl. RM7: Mawney 1H **55**
Elizabeth Cl. SM1: Sutt 4H **165**
Elizabeth Cl. W9 4A **82**
Elizabeth Clyde Cl. N15 4E **48**
Elizabeth Cotts. TW9: Kew 1F **115**
Elizabeth Ct. BR1: Broml 1H **159**
(off Highland Rd.)
Elizabeth Ct. CR0: C'don 3E **168**
(off The Avenue)
Elizabeth Ct. E10 7D **50**
Elizabeth Ct. E4 5G **35**
Elizabeth Ct. IG8: Wfd G 7F **37**
Elizabeth Ct. KT2: King T 1E **150**
Elizabeth Ct. NW1 3D **4** (4C **82**)
(off Palgrave Gdns.)
Elizabeth Ct. SW1 2D **18** (3H **101**)
(off Milmans Ct.)
Elizabeth Ct. SW10 6B **100**
(off Milman's St.)
Elizabeth Ct. TW11: Tedd 5J **131**
Elizabeth Ct. TW16: Sun 3A **148**
(off Elizabeth Gdns.)
Elizabeth Croll Ho. WC1 1H **7** (3K **83**)
(off Penton Ri.)
Elizabeth Fry Apts. IG11: Bark 7G **71**
(off Kings Rd.)
Elizabeth Fry Ho. UB3: Harl 4H **93**
Elizabeth Fry M. E8 7H **67**
Elizabeth Fry Pl. SE18 1C **124**
Elizabeth Gdns. HA7: Stan 6H **27**
Elizabeth Gdns. TW16: Sun 3A **148**
Elizabeth Gdns. TW7: Isle 4A **114**
Elizabeth Gdns. W3 1B **98**
Elizabeth Garrett Anderson Ho.
DA17: Belv 3G **109**
(off Ambrooke Rd.)
Elizabeth Ho. E3 3D **86**
(off St Leonard's St.)
Elizabeth Ho. SE11 4K **19** (4A **102**)
(off Reedworth St.)
Elizabeth Ho. SM3: Cheam 6G **165**
(off Park La.)
Elizabeth Ho. W6 5E **98**
(off Queen Caroline St.)
Elizabeth Ind. Est. SE14 6K **103**
Elizabeth M. E10 1E **68**
Elizabeth M. E2 2G **85**
(off Kay St.)
Elizabeth M. HA1: Harr 6J **41**
Elizabeth M. NW3 6C **64**
Elizabeth Newcomen Ho. SE1
6E **14** (2D **102**)
(off Newcomen St.)
Elizabeth Newton Wy. SW17 3C **136**
Elizabeth Pl. N15 4D **48**
Elizabeth Ride N9 7C **24**
Elizabeth Rd. E6 1B **88**
Elizabeth Rd. N15 5E **48**
Elizabeth Sq. SE16 7A **86**
(off Sovereign Cres.)
Elizabeth St. SW1 3H **17** (4E **100**)
Elizabeth Ter. SE9 6D **124**
Elizabeth Way SE19 7D **138**
Elizabeth Way TW13: Hanw 4A **130**
Elkanette M. N20 2F **31**
Elkington Point SE11 4J **19** (4A **102**)
(off Lollard St.)
Elkington Rd. E13 4K **87**
Elkstone Rd. W10 5H **81**
Ella Cl. BR3: Beck 2C **158**
Ellacott M. SW16 2H **137**
Ellaline Rd. W6 6F **99**
Ella M. NW3 4D **64**
Ellanby Cres. N18 4C **34**
Elland Cl. EN5: New Bar 5G **21**
Elland Ho. E14 6B **86**
(off Copenhagen Pl.)
Elland Rd. SE15 4J **121**
Ella Rd. N8 7J **47**
Ellement Cl. HA5: Pinn 5B **40**
Ellena Ct. N14 3D **32**
(off Conway Rd.)
Ellenborough Ho. W12 7D **80**
(off White City Est.)
Ellenborough Pl. SW15 4C **116**
Ellenborough Rd. DA14: Sidc 5D **144**
Ellenborough Rd. N22 1C **48**
Ellenbridge Way CR2: Sande 7E **168**
Ellen Cl. BR1: Broml 3B **160**
Ellen Ct. E4 1K **35**
(off The Ridgeway)
Ellen Ct. N9 2D **34**
Ellen Julia Ct. E1 6J **85**
(off James Voller Way)
Ellen Phillips La. E2 2G **85**
Ellen St. E1 6G **85**
Ellen Terry Ct. NW1 7F **65**
(off Farrier St.)
Ellen Webb Dr. HA3: W'stone 3J **41**
Ellen Wilkinson Ho. E2 3K **85**
(off Usk St.)
Ellen Wilkinson Ho. RM10: Dag 3G **73**
Ellen Wilkinson Ho. SW6 6H **99**
(off Clem Attlee Ct.)
Elleray Rd. TW11: Tedd 6K **131**
Ellerby St. SW6 1F **117**
Ellerdale Cl. NW3 4A **64**
Ellerdale Rd. NW3 5A **64**
Ellerdale St. SE13 4D **122**
Ellerdine Rd. TW3: Houn 4G **113**
Ellerker Gdns. TW10: Rich 6E **114**
Ellerman Av. TW2: Whitt 1D **130**
Ellerslie Gdns. NW10 1C **80**
Ellerslie Rd. W12 1D **98**
Ellerslie Sq. Ind. Est. SW2 5J **119**
Ellerton Gdns. RM9: Dag 7C **72**
Ellerton Lodge N3 2J **45**
Ellerton Rd. KT6: Surb 2F **163**
Ellerton Rd. RM9: Dag 7C **72**
Ellerton Rd. SW13 1C **116**
Ellerton Rd. SW18 1B **136**
Ellerton Rd. SW20 7C **134**
Ellery Ho. SE17 4D **102**
Ellery Rd. SE19 7D **138**
Ellery St. SE15 2H **121**
Ellesmere Av. BR3: Beck 2E **158**
Ellesmere Av. NW7 3E **28**
Ellesmere Cl. E11 5H **51**
Ellesmere Cl. HA4: Ruis 7E **38**
Ellesmere Ct. SE12 1J **141**
Ellesmere Ct. W4 5K **97**
Ellesmere Gdns. IG4: Ilf 5C **52**
Ellesmere Gro. EN5: Barn 5C **20**
Ellesmere Ho. SW10 6A **100**
(off Fulham Rd.)
Ellesmere Mans. NW6 6A **64**
(off Canfield Gdns.)
Ellesmere Rd. E3 2A **86**
Ellesmere Rd. NW10 5C **62**
Ellesmere Rd. TW1: Twick 6C **114**
Ellesmere Rd. UB6: G'frd 4G **77**
Ellesmere Rd. W4 6K **97**
Ellesmere St. E14 6D **86**
Ellie M. E13 2A **88**
Ellie M. TW15: Ashf 2A **128**
Ellingfort Rd. E8 7H **67**
Ellingham Rd. E15 4F **69**
Ellingham Rd. KT9: Chess 6D **162**
Ellingham Rd. W12 2C **98**
Ellington Ct. N14 2C **32**
Ellington Ho. SE1 3C **102**
Ellington Ho. SE18 7E **106**
Ellington Rd. N10 4F **47**
Ellington Rd. TW13: Felt 4H **129**
Ellington Rd. TW3: Houn 2F **113**
Ellington St. N7 6A **66**
Elliot Cl. E15 7G **69**
Elliot Cl. IG8: Wfd G 6G **37**
Elliot Ho. SW17 3B **136**
(off Grosvenor Way)
Elliot Ho. W1 6D **4** (5C **82**)
(off Cato St.)
Elliot Rd. NW4 6D **44**
Elliott Av. HA4: Ruis 2K **57**
Elliott Cl. HA9: Wemb 3F **61**
Elliott Gdns. TW17: Shep 4C **146**
Elliott Rd. BR2: Broml 4B **160**
Elliott Rd. CR7: Thor H 4B **156**
Elliott Rd. HA7: Stan 6F **27**
Elliott Rd. SW9 1B **120**
Elliott Rd. W4 4A **98**
Elliott's Pl. N1 1B **84**
Elliott Sq. NW3 7C **64**
Elliotts Row SE11 4B **102**
Ellis Av. RM8: Dag 1E **72**
Ellis Cl. HA4: Eastc 6J **39**
Ellis Cl. HA8: Edg 6F **29**
Ellis Cl. NW10 6D **62**
Ellis Cl. SE9 2G **143**
Elliscombe Mt. SE7 6A **106**
Elliscombe Rd. SE7 6A **106**
Ellis Ct. E1 6J **85**
(off James Voller Way)
Ellis Ct. W7 5K **77**
Ellisfield Dr. SW15 7C **116**
Ellis Franklin Ct. NW8 2A **82**
(off Abbey Rd.)
Ellis Ho. SE17 5D **102**
(off Brandon St.)
Ellison Apts. E3 3C **86**
(off Merchant St.)
Ellison Gdns. UB2: S'hall 4D **94**
Ellison Ho. SE13 2D **122**
(off Lewisham Rd.)
Ellison Rd. DA15: Sidc 1H **143**
Ellison Rd. SW13 2B **116**
Ellison Rd. SW16 7H **137**
Ellis Rd. CR4: Mitc 6D **154**
Ellis Rd. UB2: S'hall 1G **95**
Ellis St. SW1 3G **17** (4E **100**)
Ellis Ter. SE11 7A **102**
Elliston Ho. SE18 4E **106**
(off Wellington St.)
Ellora Rd. SW16 5H **137**
Ellswood Ct. KT6: Surb 7D **150**
Ellsworth St. E2 3H **85**
Ellwood Ct. W9 4K **81**
(off Clearwell Dr.)
Elmar Rd. N15 4D **48**
Elm Av. HA4: Ruis 1J **57**
Elm Av. TW19: Stanw 2A **128**
Elm Av. W5 1E **96**
Elmbank N14 7D **22**
Elm Bank Dr. BR1: Broml 2B **160**
Elm Bank Gdns. SW13 2A **116**
Elmbank Way W7 5H **77**
Elmbourne Dr. DA17: Belv 4H **109**
Elmbourne Rd. SW17 3F **137**
Elmbridge Av. KT5: Surb 5H **151**
Elmbridge Cl. HA4: Ruis 6J **39**
Elmbridge Dr. HA4: Ruis 5H **39**
Elmbridge Wlk. E8 7G **67**
Elmbridge Xcel Leisure Complex 5K **147**
Elmbridge Xcel Sports Hub 5K **147**
Elmbrook Cl. TW16: Sun 1K **147**
Elmbrook Gdns. SE9 4C **124**
Elmbrook Rd. SM1: Sutt 4H **165**
Elm Cl. CR2: S Croy 6E **168**
Elm Cl. E11 6K **51**
Elm Cl. HA2: Harr 6F **41**
Elm Cl. IG9: Buck H 2G **37**
Elm Cl. KT5: Surb 7J **151**
Elm Cl. N19 2G **65**
Elm Cl. NW4 5F **45**
Elm Cl. RM7: Mawney 1H **55**
Elm Cl. SM5: Cars 1D **166**
Elm Cl. SW20 4E **152**
Elm Cl. TW2: Twick 2F **131**
Elm Cl. UB3: Hayes 6J **75**
Elmcote HA5: Pinn 2B **40**
Elm Cotts. CR4: Mitc 2D **154**
Elm Ct. CR4: Mitc 2D **154**
Elm Ct. EC4 1J **13** (6A **84**)
(off King's Bench Wlk.)
Elm Ct. EN4: E Barn 7H **21**
Elm Ct. KT8: W Mole 4F **149**
Elm Ct. SE1 7H **15** (2E **102**)
(off Royal Oak Yd.)
Elm Ct. SE13 3F **123**
Elm Ct. SW9 1A **120**
(off Cranworth Gdns.)
Elm Ct. TW16: Sun 7H **129**
(off Grangewood Dr.)
Elm Ct. W9 5J **81**
(off Admiral Wlk.)
Elmcourt Rd. SE27 2B **138**
Elm Cres. KT2: King T 1E **150**
Elm Cres. W5 1E **96**
Elmcroft N6 7G **47**
Elmcroft N8 5K **47**
Elmcroft Av. DA15: Sidc 7K **125**
Elmcroft Av. E11 5K **51**
Elmcroft Av. N9 6C **24**
Elmcroft Av. NW11 7H **45**
Elmcroft Cl. E11 4K **51**
Elmcroft Cl. KT9: Chess 3E **162**
Elmcroft Cl. TW14: Felt 6H **111**
Elmcroft Cl. W5 6D **78**
Elmcroft Cres. HA2: Harr 3E **40**
Elmcroft Cres. NW11 7G **45**
Elmcroft Dr. KT9: Chess 3E **162**
Elmcroft Dr. TW15: Ashf 5C **128**
Elmcroft Gdns. NW9 4G **43**
Elmcroft St. E5 4J **67**
Elmcroft Ter. UB8: Hil 6C **74**
Elmdale Rd. N13 5E **32**
Elmdene KT5: Surb 1J **163**
Elmdene Cl. BR3: Beck 6B **158**
Elmdene Rd. SE18 5F **107**
Elmdon Rd. TW4: Houn 2B **112**
Elmdon Rd. TW6: H'row A 3H **111**
Elm Dr. HA2: Harr 6F **41**
Elm Dr. TW16: Sun 2A **148**
Elmer Cl. EN2: Enf 3E **22**
Elmer Gdns. HA8: Edg 7C **28**
Elmer Gdns. TW7: Isle 3H **113**
Elmer Ho. NW8 5C **4** (5C **82**)
(off Penfold St.)
Elmer Rd. SE6 7E **122**
Elmers Dr. TW11: Tedd 6B **132**
ELMERS END 4A **158**
Elmers End Rd. BR3: Beck 2J **157**
Elmers End Rd. SE20 2J **157**
Elmerside Rd. BR3: Beck 4A **158**
Elmers Lodge BR3: Beck 4A **158**
Elmers Rd. SE25 7G **157**
Elmfield HA1: Harr 7K **41**
Elmfield Av. CR4: Mitc 1E **154**
Elmfield Av. N8 5J **47**
Elmfield Av. TW11: Tedd 5K **131**
Elmfield Cl. HA1: Harr 2J **59**
Elmfield Ct. DA16: Well 1B **126**
Elmfield Ho. N2 2B **46**
(off The Grange)
Elmfield Ho. NW8 2K **81**
(off Carlton Hill)
Elmfield Ho. W9 4J **81**
(off Goldney Rd.)
Elmfield Pk. BR1: Broml 3J **159**
Elmfield Rd. BR1: Broml 2J **159**
Elmfield Rd. E17 6K **49**
Elmfield Rd. E4 2K **35**
Elmfield Rd. N2 3B **46**
Elmfield Rd. SW17 2E **136**
Elmfield Rd. UB2: S'hall 3C **94**
Elmfield Way CR2: Sande 7F **169**
Elmfield Way W9 5J **81**
Elm Friars Wlk. NW1 7H **65**
Elm Gdns. CR4: Mitc 4H **155**
Elm Gdns. KT10: Clay 6A **162**
Elm Gdns. N2 3A **46**
Elmgate Av. TW13: Felt 3K **129**
Elmgate Gdns. HA8: Edg 5D **28**
Elm Grn. W3 6A **80**
Elmgreen Cl. E15 1G **87**
Elm Gro. BR6: Orp 1K **173**
Elm Gro. DA8: Erith 7K **109**
Elm Gro. HA2: Harr 7E **40**
Elm Gro. IG8: Wfd G 5C **36**
Elm Gro. KT2: King T 1E **150**
Elm Gro. N8 6J **47**
Elm Gro. NW2 4F **63**
Elm Gro. SE15 2F **121**
Elm Gro. SM1: Sutt 4K **165**
Elm Gro. SW19 7G **135**
Elm Gro. UB7: Yiew 7B **74**
Elmgrove Cres. HA1: Harr 5K **41**
Elmgrove Gdns. HA1: Harr 5A **42**
Elm Gro. Pde. SM6: W'gton 3E **166**
Elmgrove Point SE18 4H **107**
Elm Gro. Rd. SW13 1C **116**
Elm Gro. Rd. W5 2E **96**
Elmgrove Rd. CR0: C'don 7H **157**
Elmgrove Rd. HA1: Harr 5K **41**
Elm Hall Gdns. E11 5K **51**
(not continuous)
Elm Ho. E14 2E **104**
(off E. Ferry Rd.)
Elm Ho. E3 1B **86**
(off Sycamore Av.)
Elm Ho. KT2: King T 7F **133**
(off Elm Rd.)
Elm Ho. W10 4G **81**
(off Briar Wlk.)
Elmhurst DA17: Belv 6E **108**
Elmhurst Av. CR4: Mitc 7F **137**
Elmhurst Av. N2 3B **46**
Elmhurst Ct. CR0: C'don 4D **168**
Elmhurst Dr. E18 2J **51**
Elmhurst Lodge SM2: Sutt 7A **166**
Elmhurst Mans. SW4 3H **119**
Elmhurst Rd. E7 7K **69**
Elmhurst Rd. N17 2F **49**
Elmhurst Rd. SE9 2C **142**
Elmhurst St. SW4 3H **119**
Elmington Cl. DA5: Bexl 6H **127**
Elmington Est. SE5 7D **102**
Elmington Rd. SE5 7D **102**
Elmira St. SE13 3D **122**
Elm La. SE6 2B **140**
Elm Lawn Cl. UB8: Uxb 7A **56**
Elmlea Dr. UB3: Hayes 5G **75**
Elm Lea Trad. Est. N17 6C **34**
Elmlee Cl. BR7: Chst 6D **142**
Elmley Cl. E6 5C **88**
Elmley St. SE18 5H **107**
(not continuous)
Elm Lodge SW6 1E **116**
Elmore Cl. HA0: Wemb 2E **78**
Elmore Cl. HA3: Kenton 2B **42**
Elmore Dr. HA3: Kenton 2B **42**
Elmore Ho. N1 7D **66**
(off Elmore St.)
Elmore Ho. SW9 2B **120**
Elmore Rd. E11 3E **68**
Elmore Rd. EN3: Enf W 1E **24**
Elmore St. N1 7C **66**
Elm Pde. DA14: Sidc 4A **144**
Elm Pk. HA7: Stan 5G **27**
Elm Pk. SW2 6K **119**
Elm Pk. Av. N15 5F **49**
Elm Pk. Chambers SW10 6A **16** (5B **100**)
(off Fulham Rd.)
Elm Pk. Ct. HA5: Pinn 3A **40**
Elm Pk. Gdns. NW4 5F **45**
Elm Pk. Gdns. SW10 6A **16** (5B **100**)
Elm Pk. Ho. SW10 6A **16** (5B **100**)
Elm Pk. La. SW3 6A **16** (5B **100**)
Elm Pk. Mans. SW10 7A **16** (6A **100**)
Elm Pk. Rd. E10 1A **68**
Elm Pk. Rd. HA5: Pinn 2A **40**
Elm Pk. Rd. N21 7H **23**
Elm Pk. Rd. N3 7C **30**
Elm Pk. Rd. SE25 3F **157**
Elm Pk. Rd. SW3 7A **16** (6B **100**)
Elm Pas. EN5: Barn 4C **20**
Elm Pl. SW7 5A **16** (5B **100**)
Elm Pl. TW15: Ashf 5C **128**
Elm Quay Ct. SW11 7C **18** (6H **101**)
Elm Rd. BR3: Beck 2B **158**
Elm Rd. BR6: Chels 7K **173**
Elm Rd. CR7: Thor H 4D **156**
Elm Rd. DA14: Sidc 4A **144**
Elm Rd. E11 2F **69**
Elm Rd. E17 5E **50**
Elm Rd. E7 6H **69**
Elm Rd. EN5: Barn 4C **20**
Elm Rd. HA9: Wemb 5E **60**
Elm Rd. KT17: Ewe 6B **164**
Elm Rd. KT2: King T 1F **151**
Elm Rd. KT3: N Mald 2K **151**
Elm Rd. KT9: Chess 4E **162**
Elm Rd. N22 1B **48**
Elm Rd. RM7: Mawney 2H **55**
Elm Rd. SM6: W'gton 1E **166**
Elm Rd. SW14 3J **115**
Elm Rd. TW14: Bedf 1F **129**
Elm Rd. W. SM3: Sutt 7H **153**
Elm Row NW3 3A **64**
Elms, The CR0: C'don 1C **168**
(off Tavistock Rd.)
Elms, The E12 6B **70**
Elms, The KT10: Clay 7A **162**
Elms, The SW13 3B **116**
Elms, The TW15: Ashf 5C **128**
Elms Av. N10 3F **47**
Elms Av. NW4 5F **45**
Elmscott Gdns. N21 6H **23**
Elmscott Rd. BR1: Broml 5G **141**
Elms Ct. HA0: Wemb 4A **60**
Elms Cres. SW4 6G **119**
Elmsdale Rd. E17 4B **50**
Elms Gdns. HA0: Wemb 4A **60**
Elms Gdns. RM9: Dag 4F **73**
Elmshaw Rd. SW15 5C **116**
Elmshurst Cres. N2 4B **46**
Elmside CR0: New Ad 6D **170**
Elmside Rd. HA9: Wemb 3G **61**
Elms La. HA0: Wemb 3A **60**
Elmsleigh Av. HA3: Kenton 4B **42**
Elmsleigh Ct. SM1: Sutt 3K **165**
Elmsleigh Ho. TW2: Twick 2H **131**
(off Staines Rd.)
Elmsleigh Rd. TW2: Twick 2H **131**
Elmslie Cl. IG8: Wfd G 6J **37**
Elmslie Point E3 5B **86**
(off Leopold St.)
Elms M. W2 2A **10** (7B **82**)
Elms Pk. Av. HA0: Wemb 4A **60**
Elms Rd. HA3: Hrw W 7D **26**
Elms Rd. SW4 5G **119**
ELMSTEAD 6D **142**
Elmstead Av. BR7: Chst 5D **142**
Elmstead Av. HA9: Wemb 1E **60**
Elmstead Cl. KT19: Ewe 5A **164**
Elmstead Cl. N20 2D **30**
Elmstead Gdns. KT4: Wor Pk 3C **164**
Elmstead Glade BR7: Chst 6D **142**
Elmstead La. BR7: Chst 7C **142**
Elmstead Rd. DA8: Erith 1K **127**
Elmstead Rd. IG3: Ilf 2J **71**
Elmsted Cres. DA16: Well 6C **108**
Elmstone Rd. SW6 1J **117**
Elm St. WC1 4H **7** (4K **83**)
Elmsway TW15: Ashf 5C **128**
Elmsworth Av. TW3: Houn 2F **113**
Elm Ter. HA3: Hrw W 1H **41**
Elm Ter. NW2 3J **63**
Elm Ter. NW3 4C **64**
Elm Ter. SE9 6E **124**
Elmton Ct. NW8 3A **4** (4B **82**)
(off Cunningham Pl.)
Elm Tree Av. KT10: Esh 7H **149**
Elm Tree Cl. NW8 1A **4** (3B **82**)
Elm Tree Cl. TW15: Ashf 5D **128**
Elm Tree Cl. UB5: N'olt 2D **76**
Elm Tree Ct. NW8 1A **4** (3B **82**)
(off Elm Tree Rd.)
Elm Tree Ct. SE7 6A **106**
Elm Tree Rd. NW8 1A **4** (3B **82**)
Elmtree Rd. TW11: Tedd 4J **131**
Elm Vw. Ct. UB2: S'hall 4E **94**
Elm Vw. Ho. UB3: Harl 4F **93**
Elm Wlk. BR6: Farnb 3D **172**
Elm Wlk. NW3 2J **63**
Elm Wlk. SW20 4E **152**
Elm Way KT19: Ewe 5K **163**
Elm Way KT4: Wor Pk 3E **164**
Elm Way N11 6K **31**
Elm Way NW10 4A **62**
Elmwood Av. HA3: Kenton 5A **42**
Elmwood Av. N13 5D **32**
Elmwood Av. TW13: Felt 2J **129**
Elmwood Av. TW13: Hanw 2J **129**
Elmwood Cl. KT17: Ewe 7C **164**
Elmwood Cl. SM6: W'gton 2F **167**
Elmwood Ct. E10 1C **68**
(off Goldsmith Rd.)
Elmwood Ct. HA0: Wemb 3A **60**
Elmwood Ct. SW11 1F **119**
Elmwood Cres. NW9 4J **43**
Elmwood Dr. DA5: Bexl 7E **126**
Elmwood Dr. KT17: Ewe 6C **164**
Elmwood Gdns. W7 6J **77**
Elmwood Ho. NW10 2F **81**
(off All Souls Av.)
Elmwood Rd. CR0: C'don 7B **156**
Elmwood Rd. CR4: Mitc 3D **154**
Elmwood Rd. SE24 5D **120**
Elmwood Rd. W4 6J **97**
Elmworth Gro. SE21 2D **138**
Elnathan M. W9 4K **81**
Elphinstone Ct. SW16 6J **137**
Elphinstone Rd. E17 2B **50**
Elphinstone St. N5 4B **66**
Elrington Rd. E8 6G **67**
Elrington Rd. IG8: Wfd G 5D **36**
Elsa Cotts. E14 5A **86**
(off Halley St.)
Elsa Ct. BR3: Beck 1B **158**
Elsa Rd. DA16: Well 2B **126**
Elsa St. E1 5A **86**
Elsdale St. E9 6J **67**
Elsden M. E2 2J **85**
Elsden Rd. N17 1F **49**
Elsenham Rd. E12 5E **70**
Elsenham St. SW18 1H **135**
Elsham Rd. E11 3G **69**
Elsham Rd. W14 2G **99**
Elsham Ter. W14 3G **99**
(off Elsham Rd.)
Elsiedene Rd. N21 7H **23**
Elsie La. Ct. W2 5J **81**
(off Westbourne Pk. Vs.)
Elsiemaud Rd. SE4 5B **122**
Elsie Rd. SE22 4F **121**
Elsinore Av. TW19: Stanw 7A **110**
Elsinore Gdns. NW2 3G **63**
Elsinore Ho. N1 1A **84**
(off Denmark Gro.)
Elsinore Ho. SE5 2C **120**
(off Denmark Rd.)
Elsinore Ho. W6 5F **99**
(off Fulham Pal. Rd.)
Elsinore Rd. SE23 1A **140**
Elsinore Way TW9: Rich 3H **115**
Elsley Ct. HA9: Wemb 6H **61**
Elsley Rd. SW11 3D **118**
Elspeth Rd. HA0: Wemb 5E **60**
Elspeth Rd. SW11 4D **118**
Elsrick Av. SM4: Mord 5J **153**
Elstan Way CR0: C'don 7A **158**
Elstar Ct. RM13: Rain 2K **91**
(off Lowen Rd.)
Elstead Ct. SM3: Sutt 1G **165**
Elstead Ho. SW2 7K **119**
(off Redlands Way)
Elsted St. SE17 4D **102**
Elstow Cl. HA4: Ruis 7B **40**
Elstow Cl. SE9 5D **124**
(not continuous)
Elstow Gdns. RM9: Dag 1E **90**
Elstow Grange NW6 7F **63**
Elstow Rd. RM9: Dag 1E **90**
Elstree Gdns. DA17: Belv 4E **108**
Elstree Gdns. IG1: Ilf 5G **71**
Elstree Gdns. N9 1C **34**
Elstree Hill BR1: Broml 7G **141**
Elstree Hill Sth. WD6: E'tree 1H **27**
Elstree Rd. WD23: B Hea 1C **26**
Elswick Rd. SE13 2D **122**
Elswick St. SW6 2A **118**
Elsworth Cl. TW14: Bedf 1G **129**
Elsworthy KT7: T Ditt 6J **149**
Elsworthy Ct. NW3 7D **64**
(off Primrose Hill Rd.)
Elsworthy Ri. NW3 7C **64**
Elsworthy Rd. NW3 1C **82**
Elsworthy Ter. NW3 7C **64**
Elsynge Rd. SW18 5B **118**
ELTHAM 6D **124**
Eltham Cen. 5E **124**
Eltham Crematorium 4H **125**
Eltham Grn. SE9 5B **124**
Eltham Grn. Rd. SE9 4A **124**
Eltham High St. SE9 6D **124**
Eltham Hill SE9 5B **124**
Eltham Palace & Gdns. 7C **124**
Eltham Pal. Rd. SE9 6A **124**
ELTHAM PARK 4E **124**
Eltham Pk. Gdns. SE9 4E **124**
Eltham Rd. SE12 5H **123**
Eltham Rd. SE9 5A **124**
Eltham Warren Golf Course 5F **125**
Elthiron Rd. SW6 1J **117**
Elthorne Av. W7 2K **95**
Elthorne Ct. TW13: Felt 1A **130**
ELTHORNE HEIGHTS 5J **77**
Elthorne Pk. Rd. W7 2K **95**
Elthorne Rd. N19 2H **65**
Elthorne Rd. NW9 7K **43**
Elthorne Sports Cen. 3K **95**
Elthorne Way NW9 6K **43**
Elthruda Rd. SE13 6F **123**
Eltisley Rd. IG1: Ilf 4F **71**
Elton Av. EN5: Barn 5C **20**
Elton Av. HA0: Wemb 5B **60**
Elton Av. UB6: G'frd 6J **59**
Elton Cl. KT1: Hamp W 7C **132**
Elton Ho. E3 1B **86**
(off Candy St.)
Elton Pl. N16 5E **66**
Elton Rd. KT2: King T 1F **151**
Eltringham St. SW18 4A **118**
Eluna Apts. E1 7H **85**
(off Wapping La.)
Elvaston M. SW7 3A **100**
Elvaston Pl. SW7 3A **100**
Elveden Pl. NW10 2G **79**
Elveden Rd. NW10 2G **79**
Elvedon Rd. TW13: Felt 3H **129**
Elvendon Rd. N13 6D **32**
Elven M. SE15 1J **121**
Elver Gdns. E2 3G **85**
Elverson Rd. SE8 2D **122**
Elverton St. SW1 3C **18** (4H **101**)
Elvin Ct. NW9 7J **43**
Elvin Gdns. HA9: Wemb 4G **61**
Elvington Grn. BR2: Broml 5H **159**
Elvington La. NW9 1A **44**
Elvino Rd. SE26 5A **140**
Elvis Rd. NW2 6E **62**
Elwill Way BR3: Beck 4E **158**
Elwin St. E2 1K **9** (3G **85**)
Elwood Cl. EN5: New Bar 4F **21**
Elwood St. N5 3B **66**
Elworth Ho. SW8 7K **101**
(off Oval Pl.)
Elwyn Gdns. SE12 7J **123**
Ely Cl. KT3: N Mald 2B **152**
Ely Cotts. SW8 7K **101**
Ely Ct. EC1 6K **7** (5A **84**)
(off Ely Pl.)
Ely Ct. KT1: King T 2G **151**
Ely Gdns. IG1: Ilf 7C **52**
Ely Gdns. RM10: Dag 3J **73**
Ely Ho. SE15 7G **103**
(off Friary Est.)
Elyne Rd. N4 6A **48**
Ely Pl. EC1 6K **7** (5A **84**)
Ely Pl. IG8: Wfd G 6K **37**
Ely Rd. CR0: C'don 5D **156**
Ely Rd. E10 6E **50**
Ely Rd. TW4: Houn 3A **112**

Ely Rd. TW6: H'row A 2H 111 (off Esher Cres.)
Elysian Av. BR5: St M Cry 6K 161
Elysian M. N7 6K 65
Elysian Pl. CR2: S Croy 7C 168
Elysium Apts. E1 4J 85 (off Theven St.)
Elysium Pl. SW6 2H 117 (off Elysium St.)
Elysium St. SW6 2H 117
Elystan Bus. Cen. UB4: Yead 7A 76
Elystan Cl. SM6: W'gton 7G 167
Elystan Ho. SW3 4C 16 (4C 100) (off Elystan St.)
Elystan Pl. SW3 5D 16 (5C 100)
Elystan St. SW3 4C 16 (4C 100)
Elystan Wlk. N1 1A 84
Ely's Yd. E1 5K 9 (5F 85)
Emanuel Av. W3 6J 79
Emanuel Dr. TW12: Hamp 5D 130
Emanuel Ho. SW1 2C 18 (3H 101)
Embankment SW15 2F 117
Embankment, The TW1: Twick 1A 132
Embankment Galleries 2H 13 (7K 83) (within Somerset House)
Embankment Gdns. SW3 7F 17 (6D 100)
Embankment Pier WC2 4F 13 (1J 101)
Embankment Pl. WC2 4F 13 (1J 101)
Embassy Apts. SE5 2C 120 (off Coldharbour La.)
Embassy Ct. DA14: Sidc 3B 144
Embassy Ct. DA16: Well 3B 126
Embassy Ct. E2 4H 85 (off Brady St.)
Embassy Ct. N11 6C 32 (off Bounds Grn. Rd.)
Embassy Ct. NW8 1B 4 (2B 82) (off Wellington Rd.)
Embassy Ct. SM6: W'gton 6F 167
Embassy Ct. W5 7F 79
Embassy Gdns. BR3: Beck 1B 158
Embassy Ho. NW6 7K 63
Embassy Lodge N3 2H 45 (off Cyprus Rd.)
Embassy of United States of America 7D 18 (6H 101)
Embassy Theatre Central School of Speech & Drama 7B 64
Embassy Way SW11 6H 101
Emba St. SE16 2G 103
Ember Cl. BR5: Pet W 7G 161
Ember Ct. NW9 2B 44
Embercourt Rd. KT7: T Ditt 6J 149
Ember Farm Av. KT8: E Mos 6H 149
Ember Farm Way KT8: E Mos 6H 149
Ember Gdns. KT7: T Ditt 7J 149
Ember La. KT10: Esh 7H 149
Ember La. KT8: E Mos 6H 149
Emberton SE5 6E 102 (off Albany Rd.)
Emberton Ct. EC1 2A 8 (3B 84) (off Tompion St.)
Embleton Rd. SE13 4D 122
Embleton Wlk. TW12: Hamp 5D 130
Embroidery World Bus. Cen. IG8: Wfd G 2B 52
Embry Cl. HA7: Stan 4F 27
Embry Dr. HA7: Stan 6F 27
Embry Rd. SE9 4A 124
Embry Way HA7: Stan 5F 27
Emden Cl. UB7: W Dray 2C 92
Emden St. SW6 1K 117
Emerald Cl. E16 6B 88
Emerald Ct. HA4: Ruis 4A 58
Emerald Gdns. RM8: Dag 1G 73
Emerald Rd. NW10 1K 79
Emerald Sq. SW15 5C 116
Emerald Sq. UB2: S'hall 3B 94
Emerald St. WC1 5G 7 (5K 83)
Emerson Apts. N8 3K 47
Emerson Gdns. HA3: Kenton 6F 43
Emerson M. KT3: N Mald 4A 152
Emerson Rd. IG1: Ilf 7E 52
Emerson St. SE1 4C 14 (1C 102)
Emerton Cl. DA6: Bex 4E 126
Emery Hill St. SW1 2B 18 (3G 101)
Emery St. SE1 1K 19 (3A 102)
Emery Walker Trust 5C 98 (off Hammersmith Ter.)
Emes Rd. DA8: Erith 7J 109
Emilia Cl. EN3: Pond E 5C 24
Emily Bowes Ct. N17 3H 49
Emily Ct. SE1 7C 14 (2C 102) (off Sudrey St.)
Emily Duncan Pl. E7 4K 69
Emily Ho. W10 4G 81 (off Kensal Rd.)
Emily St. E16 6H 87 (off Jude St.)
Emirates Stadium 4A 66
Emlyn Gdns. W12 2A 98
Emlyn Rd. W12 2A 98
Emma Ho. RM1: Rom 4K 55
Emmanuel Ct. E10 7D 50
Emmanuel Ho. SE11 4J 19 (4A 102)
Emmanuel Rd. HA6: Nwood 1H 39
Emmanuel Rd. SW12 1G 137
Emma Rd. E13 2H 87
Emma St. E2 2H 85
Emmaus Way IG7: Chig 5K 37
Emmeline Ct. KT12: Walt T 7A 148
Emminster NW6 1K 81 (off Abbey Rd.)
Emmott Av. IG6: Ilf 5G 53
Emmott Cl. E1 4A 86
Emmott Cl. NW11 6A 46
Emms Pas. KT1: King T 2D 150
Emperor Ho. E20 5E 68 (off Napa Cl.)
Emperor Ho. SE4 3A 122 (off Dragonfly Pl.)
Emperor's Ga. SW7 3A 100
Emperor Way NW9 6B 44
Empingham Ho. SE8 4K 103 (off Chilton Gro.)
Empire Av. N18 5H 33
Empire Cinema Haymarket 3C 12 (7H 83) (off Haymarket)
Empire Cinema Sutton 5K 165
Empire Cinema Walthamstow 4C 50
Empire Cl. SE7 6K 105
Empire Ct. HA9: Wemb 3H 61
Empire Ho. N18 6J 33
Empire Ho. SW7 2C 16 (3C 100) (off Thurloe Pl.)
Empire M. SW16 5J 137
Empire Pde. HA9: Wemb 3G 61
Empire Pde. N18 6J 33
Empire Reach SE10 6D 104 (off Dowells St.)
Empire Rd. UB6: G'frd 1B 78
Empire Sq. N7 3J 65
Empire Sq. SE1 7E 14 (2D 102) (off Tabard St.)
Empire Sq. SE20 7K 139 (off High St.)
Empire Sq. E. SE1 7E 14 (2D 102) (off Long La.)
Empire Sq. Sth. SE1 7E 14 (2D 102) (off Sterry St.)
Empire Sq. W. SE1 7E 14 (2D 102) (off Tabard St.)
Empire Way HA9: Wemb 4F 61
Empire Wharf E3 1A 86 (off Old Ford Rd.)
Empire Wharf Rd. E14 4F 105
Empress App. SW6 5J 99
Empress Av. E12 2A 70
Empress Av. E4 7J 35
Empress Av. IG1: Ilf 2D 70
Empress Av. IG8: Wfd G 7C 36
Empress Dr. BR7: Chst 6F 143
Empress M. SE5 2C 120
Empress Pde. E4 7H 35
Empress Pl. SW6 5J 99
Empress State Bldg. SW6 5J 99
Empress St. SE17 6C 102
Empson St. E3 4D 86
Emslie Horniman Pleasance 4G 81 (off Bosworth Road)
Emsworth Cl. N9 1D 34
Emsworth Ct. SW16 3J 137
Emsworth Rd. IG6: Ilf 2F 53
Emsworth St. SW2 2K 137
EMT Ho. E6 5E 88
Emu Rd. SW8 2F 119
Enard Ho. E3 2B 86 (off Cardigan Rd.)
Ena Rd. SW16 3J 155
Enbrook St. W10 3G 81
Enclave, The SW13 2B 116
Enclave Ct. EC1 3B 8 (4B 84) (off Dallington St.)
Endale Cl. SM5: Cars 2D 166
Endeavour Ho. E14 2C 104 (off Cuba St.)
Endeavour Ho. SE16 4A 104 (off Ashton Reach)
Endeavour Sq. E20 7E 68
Endeavour Way CR0: Bedd 7J 155
Endeavour Way IG11: Bark 2A 90
Endeavour Way SW19 4K 135
Endell St. WC2 7E 6 (6J 83)
Enderby St. SE10 5F 105
Enderley Cl. HA3: Hrw W 2J 41
Enderley Rd. HA3: Hrw W 1J 41
Enders Cl. EN2: Enf 1F 23
Endersleigh Gdns. NW4 4C 44
Endlebury Rd. E4 2K 35
Endlesham Rd. SW12 7E 118
Endsleigh Ct. WC1 3D 6 (4H 83) (off Endsleigh St.)
Endsleigh Gdns. IG1: Ilf 2D 70
Endsleigh Gdns. KT6: Surb 6C 150
Endsleigh Gdns. WC1 3C 6 (4H 83)
Endsleigh Ind. Est. UB2: S'hall 4C 94
Endsleigh Pl. WC1 3C 6 (4H 83)
Endsleigh Rd. UB2: S'hall 4C 94
Endsleigh Rd. W13 7A 78
Endsleigh St. WC1 3C 6 (4H 83)
Endurance Way CR0: Bedd 7G 155
Endway KT5: Surb 7H 151
Endwell Rd. SE4 2A 122
Endymion Rd. N4 7A 48
Endymion Rd. SW2 6K 119
Energen Cl. NW10 6A 62
Énergie Fitness Old Street 3E 8 (4D 84)
Energy Cen., The N1 1G 9 (3E 84) (off Bowling Grn. Wlk.)
ENFIELD 3J 23
Enfield Bus. Cen. EN3: Enf H 2D 24
Enfield Cloisters N1 1G 9 (3E 84) (off Fanshaw St.)
Enfield Golf Course 4G 23
ENFIELD HIGHWAY 3D 24
Enfield Ho. SW9 2J 119 (off Stockwell Rd.)
Enfield Lock EN3: Enf L 1H 25
Enfield Mus. 4J 23 (off London Rd.)
Enfield Retail Pk. 3B 24
Enfield Rd. EN2: Enf 4C 22
Enfield Rd. N1 7E 66
Enfield Rd. TW6: H'row A 2G 111
Enfield Rd. TW8: Bford 5D 96
Enfield Rd. W3 2H 97
ENFIELD ROAD RDBT. 2G 111
ENFIELD TOWN 4J 23
Enfield Town FC 2A 24
Enfield Wlk. TW8: Bford 5D 96
Enford St. W1 5E 4 (5D 82)
Engadine Cl. CR0: C'don 3F 169
Engadine St. SW18 1H 135
Engate St. SE13 4E 122
Engel Pk. NW7 6K 29
Engine Ct. SW1 5B 12 (1G 101) (off Ambassador's Ct.)
Engineer Cl. SE18 6E 106
Engineers Row SE18 4E 106 (off Woolwich New Rd.)
Engineers Way HA9: Wemb 4G 61
Engineers Wharf UB5: N'olt 4D 76
England's La. NW3 6D 64
England Way KT3: N Mald 4H 151
Englefield NW1 2A 6 (3G 83) (off Clarence Gdns.)
Englefield Cl. BR5: St M Cry 5K 161
Englefield Cl. CR0: C'don 6C 156
Englefield Cl. EN2: Enf 2F 23
Englefield Cres. BR5: St M Cry 4K 161
Englefield Path BR5: St M Cry 4K 161
Englefield Rd. N1 7D 66
Engleheart Dr. TW14: Felt 6H 111
Engleheart Rd. SE6 7D 122
Englewood Rd. SW12 6F 119
English Grounds SE1 5G 15 (1E 102)
English St. E3 4B 86
Enid St. SE16 7K 15 (3F 103)
Enmore Av. SE25 5G 157
Enmore Gdns. SW14 5K 115
Enmore Rd. SE25 5G 157
Enmore Rd. SW15 4E 116
Enmore Rd. UB1: S'hall 4E 76
Ennerdale NW1 1A 6 (3G 83) (off Varndell St.)
Ennerdale Av. HA7: Stan 3C 42
Ennerdale Cl. SM1: Sutt 4H 165
Ennerdale Cl. TW14: Felt 1H 129
Ennerdale Ct. E11 7J 51 (off Cambridge Rd.)
Ennerdale Dr. NW9 5A 44
Ennerdale Gdns. HA9: Wemb 1C 60
Ennerdale Ho. E3 4B 86
Ennerdale Rd. DA7: Bex 1G 127
Ennerdale Rd. TW9: Kew 2F 115
Ennerdale Rd. TW9: Rich 2F 115
Ennersdale Rd. SE13 5F 123
Ennis Ho. E14 6D 86 (off Vesey Path)
Ennismore Av. UB6: G'frd 6J 59
Ennismore Av. W4 4B 98
Ennismore Gdns. KT7: T Ditt 6J 149
Ennismore Gdns. SW7 7C 10 (2C 100)
Ennismore Gdns. M. SW7 1C 16 (3C 100)
Ennismore M. SW7 1C 16 (3C 100)
Ennismore St. SW7 1C 16 (3C 100)
Ennis Rd. N4 1A 66
Ennis Rd. SE18 6G 107
Ennor Ct. SM3: Cheam 4E 164
Ensbury Ho. SW8 7K 101 (off Carroun Rd.)
Ensham Ho. SW17 5D 136
Ensign Cl. TW19: Stanw 1A 128
Ensign Cl. TW6: H'row A 3G 111
Ensign Dr. N13 3H 33
Ensign Ho. E14 2C 104 (off Admirals Way)
Ensign Ho. NW9 3C 44 (off East Dr.)
Ensign Ho. SW18 3A 118
Ensign St. E1 7G 85
Ensign St. SE3 4K 123
Ensign Way SM6: W'gton 7J 167
Ensign Way TW19: Stanw 1A 128
Enslin Rd. SE9 6E 124
Ensor M. SW7 5A 16 (5B 100)
Enstone Rd. EN3: Enf H 3F 25
Enstone Rd. UB10: Ick 3B 56
Enterprise Bus. Pk. E14 2D 104
Enterprise Cen., The BR3: Beck 5A 140 (off Cricket La.)
Enterprise Cl. CR0: C'don 1A 168
Enterprise Ho. E14 5D 104 (off St Davids Sq.)
Enterprise Ho. E4 7K 25
Enterprise Ho. E9 7J 67 (off Tudor Gro.)
Enterprise Ho. IG11: Bark 3K 89
Enterprise Ho. KT12: Walt T 7K 147
Enterprise Ind. Est. SE16 5J 103
Enterprise Row N15 5F 49
Enterprise Trad. Est. UB2: S'hall 2F 95
Enterprise Way NW10 3B 80
Enterprise Way SW18 4J 117
Enterprise Way TW11: Tedd 6K 131
Enterprize Way SE8 4B 104
Entertainment Av. SE10 1G 105
Envoy Av. TW6: H'row A 3H 111
Envoy Ho. NW9 3C 44 (off East Dr.)
ENVOY RDBT. 3H 111
Epcot M. NW10 3F 81
Epirus M. SW6 7J 99
Epirus Rd. SW6 7H 99
Epping Cl. E14 4C 104
Epping Cl. RM7: Mawney 3H 55
Epping Glade E4 6K 25
Epping New Rd. IG9: Buck H 3D 36
Epping Pl. N1 6A 66
Epping Way E4 6J 25
Epple Rd. SW6 1H 117
Epsom Cl. DA7: Bex 3H 127
Epsom Cl. UB5: N'olt 5D 58
Epsom Rd. CR0: Wadd 4A 168
Epsom Rd. E10 6E 50
Epsom Rd. IG3: Ilf 6K 53
Epsom Rd. SM3: Sutt 7H 153
Epsom Rd. SM4: Mord 6H 153
Epsom Sq. TW6: H'row A 2H 111
Epstein Ct. N1 1B 84 (off Gaskin St.)
Epstein Rd. SE28 1A 108
Epstein Sq. E14 6C 86 (off Upper Nth. St.)
Epworth Rd. TW7: Isle 7B 96
Epworth St. EC2 4F 9 (4D 84)
Equana Apts. SE8 5A 104 (off Evelyn St.)
Equiano Ho. SW9 1K 119 (off Lett Rd.)
Equinox Ct. IG2: Ilf 5F 53
Equinox Ho. IG11: Bark 6G 71 (off Wakering Rd.)
Equinox Sq. E14 6D 86
Equity M. W5 1D 96
Equity Sq. E2 2K 9 (3F 85) (off Shacklewell St.)
Erasmus St. SW1 4D 18 (4H 101)
Erconwald St. W12 6B 80
Erebus Dr. SE28 3G 107
Eresby Dr. BR3: Beck 1C 170
Eresby Ho. SW7 7D 10 (2C 100) (off Rutland Ga.)
Eresby Pl. NW6 7J 63
Erica Gdns. CR0: C'don 3D 170
Erica Ho. N22 1A 48 (off Acacia Rd.)
Erica Ho. SE4 3B 122
Erica St. W12 7C 80
Eric Clarke La. IG11: Bark 4F 89
Eric Cl. E7 4J 69
Ericcson Cl. SW18 5J 117
Eric Fletcher Ct. N1 7C 66 (off Essex Rd.)
Erickson Gdns. BR2: Broml 6C 160
Eric Liddell Sports Cen. 2B 142
Eric Rd. E7 4J 69
Eric Rd. NW10 6B 62
Eric Rd. RM6: Chad H 7D 54
Eric Shipman Ter. E13 4J 87 (off Balaam St.)
Ericson Ho. SE13 4F 123 (off Blessington Rd.)
Eric St. E3 4B 86 (not continuous)
Eric Wilkins Ho. SE1 5G 103 (off Old Kent Rd.)
Eridge Rd. W4 3K 97
Erin Cl. BR1: Broml 7G 141
Erin Cl. IG3: Ilf 6A 54
Erin Cl. SW6 7J 99
Erin Ct. NW2 6E 62
Erindale SE18 6H 107
Erindale Ter. SE18 6H 107
Erin M. N22 1B 48
Erin's Vs. SE14 1K 121 (off New Cross Rd.)
Erith Cres. RM5: Col R 1J 55
Erith Rd. DA8: Erith Picardy Rd. 5J 109
Erith Rd. DA8: Erith Watling St. 1J 127
Erith Rd. DA17: Belv 5G 109
Erith Rd. DA17: Erith 5G 109
Erith Rd. DA7: Bex 4H 127
Erith School Community Sports Cen. 7J 109
Erlanger Rd. SE14 1K 121
Erlesmere Gdns. W13 3A 96
Erlich Cotts. E1 5J 85 (off Sidney St.)
Ermine Cl. TW4: Houn 2A 112
Ermine Ho. E3 1B 86 (off Parnell Rd.)
Ermine Ho. N17 7A 34 (off Moselle St.)
Ermine M. E2 1F 85
Ermine Rd. N15 6F 49
Ermine Rd. SE13 4D 122
Ermine Side EN1: Enf 5B 24
Ermington Rd. SE9 2G 143
Ernald Av. E6 2C 88
Erncroft Way TW1: Twick 6K 113
Ernest Av. SE27 4B 138
Ernest Cl. BR3: Beck 5C 158
Ernest Cotts. KT17: Ewe 7B 164
Ernest Gdns. W4 6H 97
Ernest Gro. BR3: Beck 5B 158
Ernest Harriss Ho. W9 4J 81 (off Elgin Av.)
Ernest Rd. KT1: King T 2H 151
Ernest Shackleton Lodge SE10 4G 105 (off Christchurch Way)
Ernest Sq. KT1: King T 2H 151
Ernest St. E1 4K 85
Ernle Rd. SW20 7D 134
Ernshaw Pl. SW15 5G 117
Ernst Bldg. SE1 5C 14 (1C 102) (off Union St.)
Eros 3C 12 (7H 83)
Eros Ho. Shops SE6 7D 122 (off Brownhill Rd.)
Erpingham Rd. SW15 3E 116
Erridge Rd. SW19 2J 153
Errington Rd. W9 4H 81
Errol Gdns. KT3: N Mald 4C 152
Errol Gdns. UB4: Yead 4K 75
Errol St. EC1 4D 8 (4C 84)
Erskine Cl. SM1: Sutt 3C 166
Erskine Cres. N17 4H 49
Erskine Hill NW11 4J 45
Erskine Ho. SW1 6A 18 (5G 101) (off Churchill Gdns.)
Erskine M. NW3 7D 64 (off Erskine Rd.)
Erskine Rd. E17 4B 50
Erskine Rd. NW3 7D 64
Erskine Rd. SM1: Sutt 4B 166
Erwin Ho. NW9 3C 44 (off Commander Av.)
Erwood Rd. SE7 5C 106
Esam Way SW16 5A 138
Escot Rd. TW16: Sun 7G 129
Escott Gdns. SE9 4C 142
Escreet Gro. SE18 4E 106
Esher Av. KT12: Walt T 7J 147
Esher Av. RM7: Rom 6J 55
Esher Av. SM3: Cheam 3F 165
Esher Cl. DA5: Bexl 1E 144
Esher Cres. TW6: H'row A 2H 111
Esher Gdns. SW19 2F 135
Esher M. CR4: Mitc 3E 154
Esher Rd. IG3: Ilf 3J 71
Esher Rd. KT8: E Mos 6H 149
Eskdale NW1 1A 6 (2G 83) (off Stanhope St.)
Eskdale Av. UB5: N'olt 1D 76
Eskdale Cl. HA9: Wemb 2D 60
Eskdale Rd. DA7: Bex 2G 127
Esker Pl. E2 2H 85
Esk Ho. E3 4B 86 (off British St.)
Eskmont Ridge SE19 7D 138
Esk Rd. E13 4J 87
Esk Way RM1: Rom 1K 55
Esmar Cres. NW9 7C 44
Esmat Cl. E11 5K 51
Esmeralda Rd. SE1 4G 103
Esmond Ct. W8 3K 99 (off Thackeray St.)
Esmond Gdns. W4 4K 97
Esmond Rd. NW6 1H 81
Esmond Rd. W4 4K 97
Esmond St. SW15 4G 117
Esparto St. SW18 7K 117
Esprit Ct. E1 6J 9 (5F 85) (off Brune St.)
Esquiline La. CR4: Mitc 3F 155
Essan Ho. W5 5B 78
Essence E3 2B 86 (off Cardigan Rd.)
Essence Ct. HA9: Wemb 2F 61
Essenden Rd. CR2: S Croy 7E 168
Essenden Rd. DA17: Belv 5G 109
Essendine Mans. W9 3J 81
Essendine Rd. W9 3J 81
Essex Av. TW7: Isle 3J 113
Essex Cl. E17 4A 50
Essex Cl. HA4: Ruis 1B 58
Essex Cl. RM7: Mawney 4H 55
Essex Cl. SM4: Mord 7F 153
Essex Ct. EC4 1J 13 (6A 84) (off Brick Ct.)
Essex Ct. SW13 2B 116
Essex Ct. W6 3E 98 (off Hammersmith Gro.)
Essex Gdns. N4 6B 48
Essex Gro. SE19 6D 138
Essex Hall E17 1K 49
Essex Ho. E14 6D 86 (off Girauld St.)
Essex Mans. E11 7F 51
Essex M. SE19 6E 138
Essex Pk. N3 6E 30
Essex Pk. M. W3 1A 98
Essex Pl. W4 4J 97 (not continuous)
Essex Pl. Sq. W4 4K 97
Essex Rd. E10 6E 50
Essex Rd. E12 5C 70
Essex Rd. E17 6A 50
Essex Rd. E18 2K 51
Essex Rd. E4 1B 36
Essex Rd. EN2: Enf 4J 23
Essex Rd. IG11: Bark 7H 71
Essex Rd. N1 1B 84
Essex Rd. NW10 7A 62
Essex Rd. RM10: Dag 5J 73
Essex Rd. RM6: Chad H 7C 54
Essex Rd. RM7: Mawney 4H 55
Essex Rd. W3 7J 79
Essex Rd. W4 4K 97
Essex Rd. Sth. E11 7F 51
Essex St. E7 5J 69
Essex St. WC2 1J 13 (6A 84)
Essex Twr. SE20 1H 157 (off Jasmine Gro.)
Essex Vs. W8 2J 99
Essex Wharf E5 2K 67
Essian St. E1 5A 86
Essoldo Cl. HA3: Kenton 2B 42
Essoldo Way HA8: Edg 3F 43
Estate Way E10 1B 68
Estcourt Rd. SE25 6H 157
Estcourt Rd. SW6 7H 99
Estella Apts. E15 6F 69 (off Grove Cres. Rd.)
Estella Av. KT3: N Mald 4D 152
Estella Ho. W11 7F 81 (off St Ann's Rd.)
Estelle Rd. NW3 4D 64
Esterbrooke St. SW1 4C 18 (4H 101)
Este Rd. SW11 3C 118
Esther Anne Pl. N1 1B 84
Esther Cl. N21 7F 23
Esther M. BR1: Broml 1K 159 (off Freelands Rd.)
Esther Randall Ct. NW1 3K 5 (4F 83) (off Lit. Albany St.)
Esther Rd. E11 7G 51
Estoria Cl. SW2 7A 120
Estorick Collection of Modern Italian Art 6B 66
Estreham Rd. SW16 6H 137
Estridge Cl. TW3: Houn 4E 112
Estuary Cl. IG11: Bark 3B 90
Estuary Ho. E16 1B 106 (off Agnes George Wlk.)
Eswyn Rd. SW17 4D 136
Etal Ho. N1 7B 66 (off The Sutton Est.)
Etcetera Theatre 7F 65 (off Camden High St.)
Etchingham Ct. N3 7E 30
Etchingham Pk. Rd. N3 7E 30
Etchingham Rd. E15 4E 68
Eternit Wlk. SW6 1E 116
Etfield Gro. DA14: Sidc 5B 144
Ethan Dr. N2 3K 45
Ethelbert Cl. BR1: Broml 2J 159
Ethelbert Ct. BR1: Broml 3J 159 (off Ethelbert Rd.)
Ethelbert Gdns. IG2: Ilf 5D 52
Ethelbert Ho. E9 4A 68 (off Homerton Rd.)
Ethelbert Rd. BR1: Broml 3J 159
Ethelbert Rd. DA8: Erith 7J 109
Ethelbert Rd. SW20 1F 153
Ethelbert St. SW12 1F 137
Ethel Brooks Ho. SE18 6F 107
Ethelburga St. SW11 1C 118
Ethelburga Twr. SW11 1C 118 (off Rosenau Rd.)
Etheldene Av. N10 4G 47
Ethelden Rd. W12 1D 98
Ethelred Ct. HA3: Kenton 5G 43
Ethel Rd. E16 6K 87
Ethel Rd. TW15: Ashf 5A 128
Ethel St. SE17 4C 102
Etheridge Rd. NW4 7E 44 (not continuous)
Etherley Rd. N15 5C 48
Etherow St. SE22 7G 121
Etherstone Grn. SW16 4A 138
Etherstone Rd. SW16 4A 138
Ethnard Rd. SE15 6H 103
Ethos Sport Imperial 7B 10 (2B 100)
Ethronvi Rd. DA7: Bex 3E 126
Etloe Ho. E10 1C 68
Etloe Rd. E10 2C 68
Eton Av. EN4: E Barn 6H 21
Eton Av. HA0: Wemb 4B 60
Eton Av. KT3: N Mald 5K 151
Eton Av. N12 7F 31
Eton Av. NW3 7B 64
Eton Av. TW5: Hest 6D 94
Eton Cl. SW18 7K 117
Eton Coll. Rd. NW3 6D 64
Eton Ct. HA0: Wemb 4C 60
Eton Ct. NW3 7B 64
Eton Garages NW3 6C 64
Eton Gro. NW9 3G 43
Eton Gro. SE13 3G 123
Eton Hall NW3 6D 64
Eton Ho. N5 4B 66 (off Leigh Rd.)
Eton Ho. UB7: W Dray 2B 92
ETON MANOR 4D 68
Eton Mnr. Ct. E10 2C 68 (off Leyton Grange Est.)
Eton M. N1 7K 65
Eton Pl. NW3 7E 64
Eton Ri. NW3 6D 64
Eton Rd. IG1: Ilf 4G 71
Eton Rd. NW3 7D 64
Eton Rd. UB3: Harl 7H 93
Eton St. TW9: Rich 5E 114
Eton Vs. NW3 6D 64
Etta St. SE8 6A 104
Ettrick St. E14 6E 86 (not continuous)
Etwell Pl. KT5: Surb 6F 151
Eucalyptus M. SW16 6H 137

Euesden Cl. – Fairview Way

Euesden Cl. N9 3C 34
Eugene Cotter Ho. SE17 4D 102
(off Tatum St.)
Eugenia Rd. SE16 4J 103
Eugenie M. BR7: Chst 1F 161
Eureka Rd. KT1: King T 2G 151
Euro Cl. NW10 6C 62
Eurolink Bus. Cen. SW2 4A 120
Europa Pl. EC1 2C 8 (3C 84)
Europa Trade Pk. E16 4G 87
Europa Trad. Est. DA8: Erith 5K 109
European Bus. Cen. NW9 3J 43
(not continuous)
European Design Cen. NW9 3K 43
Europe Rd. SE18 3D 106
Euro Trade Cen. DA17: Belv 2J 109
Eustace Bldg. SW11 6F 101
Eustace Ho. SE11 3G 19 (4K 101)
(off Old Paradise St.)
Eustace Pl. SE18 4D 106
Eustace Rd. E6 3C 88
Eustace Rd. RM6: Chad H 7D 54
Eustace Rd. SW6 7J 99
Euston Cir. NW1 3A 6 (4G 83)
Euston Gro. NW1 2C 6 (3H 83)
(off Euston Sq.)
Euston Rd. CR0: C'don 1A 168
Euston Rd. N1 1E 6 (3J 83)
Euston Rd. NW1 4K 5 (4F 83)
Euston Sq. NW1 2C 6 (3H 83)
(not continuous)
Euston Sta. Colonnade NW1
2C 6 (3H 83)
Euston St. NW1 2B 6 (3G 83)
Euston Twr. NW1 3A 6 (4G 83)
EUSTON UNDERPASS 3A 6 (4G 83)
Eva Ct. CR2: S Croy 6E 168
Evan Cook Cl. SE15 1J 121
Evandale Rd. SW9 2A 120
Evangelist Ho. EC4 1A 14 (6B 84)
(off Black Friars La.)
Evangelist Rd. NW5 4F 65
Evan Ho. E16 5J 87
(off Exeter Rd.)
Evans Apts. E2 3K 85
Evans Cl. E8 6F 67
Evans Gro. TW13: Hanw 2E 130
Evans Ho. SW8 7H 101
(off Wandsworth Rd.)
Evans Ho. TW13: Hanw 2E 130
Evans Ho. W12 7D 80
(off White City Est.)
Evans Rd. SE6 2G 141
Evanston Av. E4 7K 35
Evanston Gdns. IG4: Ilf 6C 52
Eva Rd. RM6: Chad H 7C 54
Evedon Ho. N1 1E 84
(off Halcomb St.)
Evelina Ct. W6 3D 98
(off Vinery Way)
Evelina Mans. SE5 7D 102
Evelina Rd. SE15 3J 121
Evelina Rd. SE20 7J 139
Eveline Lowe Est. SE16 3G 103
Eveline Rd. CR4: Mitc 1D 154
Evelyn Av. HA4: Ruis 7G 39
Evelyn Av. NW9 4K 43
Evelyn Cl. TW2: Whitt 7F 113
Evelyn Ct. E3 5B 86
(off Burdett Rd.)
Evelyn Ct. E8 4G 67
Evelyn Ct. N1 1E 8 (2D 84)
(off Evelyn Wlk.)
Evelyn Cres. TW16: Sun 1H 147
Evelyn Denington Ct. N1 7B 66
(off The Sutton Est.)
Evelyn Denington Rd. E6 4C 88
Evelyn Dr. HA5: Pinn 1B 40
Evelyn Fox Ct. W10 5E 80
Evelyn Gdns. SW7 6A 16 (5A 100)
Evelyn Gdns. TW9: Rich 4E 114
Evelyn Gro. UB1: S'hall 6D 76
Evelyn Gro. W5 1F 97
Evelyn Ho. SE14 1A 122
(off Loring Rd.)
Evelyn Ho. W12 2B 98
(off Cobbold Rd.)
Evelyn Ho. W8 2K 99
(off Hornton Pl.)
Evelyn Mans. SW1 2A 18 (3G 101)
(off Carlisle Pl.)
Evelyn Mans. W14 6G 99
(off Queen's Club Gdns.)
Evelyn Rd. E16 1J 105
Evelyn Rd. E17 4E 50
Evelyn Rd. EN4: Cockf 4J 21
Evelyn Rd. SW19 5K 135
Evelyn Rd. TW10: Ham 3C 132
Evelyn Rd. TW9: Rich 3E 114
Evelyn Rd. W4 3K 97
Evelyns Cl. UB8: Hil 6C 74
Evelyn St. SE8 4A 104
Evelyn Ter. TW9: Rich 3E 114
Evelyn Wlk. N1 2D 84
Evelyn Way SM6: Bedd 4H 167
Evelyn Way TW16: Sun 1H 147
Evelyn Yd. W1 7C 6 (6H 83)
Eve Martin Ct. EC1 2B 8 (3B 84)
(off Goswell Road)
Evening Hill BR3: Beck 7E 140
Evenlode Ho. SE2 2C 108
Evenwood Cl. SW15 5G 117
Everall Ct. E4 6G 35
Everard Av. BR2: Hayes 1J 171
Everard Ct. N13 3E 32
Everard Ho. E1 6G 85
(off Boyd St.)
Everard Way HA9: Wemb 3E 60
Everatt Cl. SW18 6H 117
Everdon Rd. SW13 6C 98
Everest Logistic Pk. CR0: Bedd 7G 155
Everest Pl. E14 5E 86
Everest Rd. SE9 5D 124
Everest Rd. TW19: Stanw 7A 110
Everett Cl. HA5: Eastc 3H 39
Everett Cl. WD23: B Hea 1D 26
Everett Ho. SE17 5D 102
(off East St.)
Everett Wlk. DA17: Belv 5F 109
(off Osborne Rd.)
Everglade Ho. E17 2B 50
Everglades, The TW3: Houn 3G 113
Everglade Strand NW9 1B 44
Evergreen Apts. IG8: Wfd G 1H 51
(off High Rd. Woodford Grn.)
Evergreen Cl. SE20 7J 139
Evergreen Dr. UB10: Hil 2D 74
Evergreen Dr. UB7: W Dray 2B 92
Evergreen Sq. E8 7F 67
Evergreen Way UB3: Hayes 7H 75
Everilda St. N1 1K 83
Evering Rd. E5 3G 67
Evering Rd. N16 3F 67
Everington Rd. N10 2D 46
Everington St. W6 6F 99
Everitt Rd. NW10 3K 79
Everleigh St. N4 1K 65
Eve Rd. E11 4G 69
Eve Rd. E15 2G 87
Eve Rd. N17 3E 48
Eve Rd. TW7: Isle 4A 114
Eversfield Gdns. NW7 6F 29
Eversfield Rd. TW9: Kew 2F 115
Evershed Ho. E1 7K 9 (6F 85)
(off Old Castle St.)
Evershed Wlk. W4 3J 97
Eversholt Ct. EN5: New Bar 5F 21
Eversholt St. NW1 2G 83
Evershot Rd. N4 1K 65
Eversleigh Ct. N3 7C 30
Eversleigh Pl. BR3: Beck 6C 140
Eversleigh Rd. E6 1B 88
Eversleigh Rd. EN5: New Bar 5F 21
Eversleigh Rd. N3 7C 30
Eversleigh Rd. SW11 3D 118
Eversley Av. DA7: Bex 2K 127
Eversley Av. HA9: Wemb 2G 61
Eversley Cl. N21 6E 22
Eversley Cres. HA4: Ruis 2G 57
Eversley Cres. N21 6F 23
Eversley Cres. TW7: Isle 1H 113
Eversley Ho. E2 2K 9 (3G 85)
(off Gosset St.)
Eversley Mt. N21 6E 22
Eversley Pk. SW19 6D 134
Eversley Pk. Rd. N21 6E 22
Eversley Rd. KT5: Surb 4F 151
Eversley Rd. SE19 7D 138
Eversley Rd. SE7 6K 105
Eversley Way CR0: C'don 3C 170
Everthorpe Rd. SE15 3F 121
Everton Ct. HA7: Stan 3E 42
(off Honeypot La.)
Everton Dr. HA7: Stan 3E 42
Everton M. NW1 2A 6 (3G 83)
Everton Rd. CR0: C'don 1G 169
Everyman Cinema Baker St.
5F 5 (5D 82)
(off Baker St.)
Everyman Cinema Barnet 5D 20
Everyman Cinema Belsize Pk. 5C 64
Everyman Cinema King's Cross 1J 83
Everyman Cinema Muswell Hill 4F 47
Everyman on the Corner Cinema 1H 83
Everyman Screen on the Green Cinema
1B 84
(off Upper St.)
Evesham Av. E17 2C 50
Evesham Cl. SM2: Sutt 7J 165
Evesham Cl. UB6: G'frd 2F 77
Evesham Ct. TW10: Rich 6F 115
Evesham Ct. W13 1A 96
(off Tewkesbury Rd.)
Evesham Grn. SM4: Mord 6K 153
Evesham Ho. E2 2J 85
(off Old Ford Rd.)
Evesham Ho. NW8 1A 82
(off Abbey Rd.)
Evesham Ho. SW1 5K 17 (5F 101)
(part of Abbots Mnr.)
Evesham Rd. E15 7H 69
Evesham Rd. N11 5B 32
Evesham Rd. SM4: Mord 6K 153
Evesham St. W11 7F 81
Evesham Ter. KT6: Surb 6D 150
Evesham Wlk. SE5 2D 120
Evesham Wlk. SW9 2A 120
Evesham Way IG5: Ilf 3E 52
Evesham Way SW11 3E 118
Evette M. IG5: Ilf 1E 52
Evry Rd. DA14: Sidc 6C 144
Ewald Rd. SW6 2H 117
Ewanrigg Ter. IG8: Wfd G 5F 37
Ewart Gro. N22 1K 47
Ewart Ho. HA1: Harr 5A 42
Ewart Pl. E3 2B 86
Ewart Rd. SE23 7K 121
Ewe Cl. N7 6J 65
EWELL 7B 164
Ewell By-Pass KT17: Ewe 7C 164
Ewell Ct. Av. KT19: Ewe 5A 164
Ewellhurst Rd. IG5: Ilf 2C 52
Ewell Pk. Gdns. KT17: Ewe 7C 164
Ewell Pk. Way KT17: Ewe 6C 164
Ewell Rd. KT6: Surb Mount Holme 7B 150
Ewell Rd. KT6: Surb South Ter. 6E 150
Ewell Rd. SM3: Cheam 6F 165
Ewelme Rd. SE23 1J 139
Ewen Cres. SW2 7A 120
Ewen Henderson Ct. SE14 7A 104
(off Goodwood Rd.)
Ewen Ho. N1 1K 83
(off Barnsbury Est.)
Ewer St. SE1 5C 14 (1C 102)
Ewhurst Av. CR2: Sande 7F 169
Ewhurst Cl. E1 5J 85
Ewhurst Ct. CR4: Mitc 3B 154
Ewhurst Rd. SE4 6B 122
Exbury Ho. E9 7J 67
Exbury Ho. SW1 5C 18 (5H 101)
(off Rampayne St.)
Exbury Rd. SE6 2C 140
Excalibur Dr. SE6 2G 141
ExCeL 7K 87
Excel Ct. WC2 3D 12 (7H 83)
(off Whitcomb St.)
Excel Marina E16 7J 87
Excelsior Cl. KT1: King T 2G 151
Excelsior Gdns. SE13 2E 122
Excelsior Ind. Est. SE15 6J 103
Excel Waterfront E16 7K 87
Exchange, The CR0: C'don 3C 168
(off Surrey St.)
Exchange, The IG1: Ilf 2F 71
Exchange Apts. BR2: Broml 4K 159
(off Sparkes Cl.)
Exchange Arc. EC2 5H 9 (5E 84)
Exchange Bldg. E1 4J 9 (4F 85)
(off Commercial St.)
Exchange Cl. N11 2K 31
Exchange Ct. CR0: C'don 1C 168
(off Bedford Pk.)
Exchange Ct. WC2 3F 13 (7J 83)
Exchange Garages N13 4F 33
Exchange Gdns. SW8 6J 101
Exchange Ho. E17 6D 50
Exchange Ho. EC2 5H 9 (5E 84)
(off Exchange Sq.)
Exchange Ho. NW10 7D 62
Exchange Ho. SW1 4C 18 (4H 101)
(off Vauxhall Bri. Rd.)
Exchange Mans. NW11 7H 45
Exchange Pl. EC2 5G 9 (5E 84)
Exchange Sq. EC2 5G 9 (5E 84)
Exchange St. EC1 2C 8 (3C 84)
Exchange St. RM1: Rom 5K 55
Exchange Wlk. HA5: Pinn 7C 40
Exeforde Av. TW15: Ashf 4C 128
Exeter Cl. E6 6D 88
Exeter Ct. KT6: Surb 5E 150
(off Maple Rd.)
Exeter Ct. NW6 2J 81
(off Cambridge Rd.)
Exeter Gdns. IG1: Ilf 1C 70
Exeter Ho. E14 5E 86
(off St Ives Pl.)
Exeter Ho. IG11: Bark 7A 72
(off Margaret Bondfield Av.)
Exeter Ho. N1 1E 84
(off New Era Est.)
Exeter Ho. RM8: Dag 4A 72
Exeter Ho. SE15 6G 103
(off Friary Est.)
Exeter Ho. SW15 6E 116
Exeter Ho. TW13: Hanw 2D 130
(off Watermill Way)
Exeter Ho. W2 6A 82
(off Hallfield Est.)
Exeter Mans. NW2 6G 63
Exeter M. NW6 6K 63
Exeter M. SW6 7J 99
Exeter Pl. SE26 3G 139
Exeter Rd. CR0: C'don 7E 156
Exeter Rd. DA16: Well 2K 125
Exeter Rd. E16 5J 87
Exeter Rd. E17 5C 50
Exeter Rd. EN3: Pond E 3E 24
Exeter Rd. HA2: Harr 2C 58
Exeter Rd. N14 1A 32
Exeter Rd. N9 2D 34
Exeter Rd. NW2 5G 63
Exeter Rd. RM10: Dag 6H 73
Exeter Rd. TW13: Hanw 3D 130
Exeter Rd. TW6: H'row A 3F 111
Exeter St. WC2 2F 13 (7J 83)
Exeter Way SE14 7B 104
Exeter Way TW6: H'row A 2G 111
Exford Ct. SW11 1B 118
(off Bolingbroke Wlk.)
Exford Gdns. SE12 1K 141
Exford Rd. SE12 2K 141
Exhibition Cl. W12 7E 80
Exhibition Grounds HA9: Wemb 4H 61
Exhibition Rd. SW7 7B 10 (2B 100)
Exhibition Way HA9: Wemb 4G 61
Exit Rd. N2 2B 46
Exmoor Cl. IG6: Ilf 1G 53
Exmoor Ho. DA17: Belv 2H 109
Exmoor Ho. E3 2A 86
(off Gernon Rd.)
Exmoor St. W10 4F 81
Exmouth Ho. E14 4D 104
(off Cahir St.)
Exmouth Ho. EC1 3K 7 (4A 84)
(off Pine St.)
Exmouth Mkt. EC1 3J 7 (4A 84)
Exmouth M. NW1 2B 6 (3G 83)
Exmouth Pl. E8 7H 67
Exmouth Rd. DA16: Well 1C 126
Exmouth Rd. E17 5B 50
Exmouth Rd. HA4: Ruis 3A 58
Exmouth Rd. UB4: Hayes 3G 75
Exmouth St. E1 6J 85
Exning Rd. E16 4H 87
Exonbury NW8 1K 81
(off Abbey Rd.)
Exon St. SE17 5E 102
Explorer Av. TW19: Stanw 1A 128
Explorers Ct. E14 7F 87
(off Newport Av.)
Export Ho. SE1 7H 15 (2E 102)
(off Tower Bri. Rd.)
Express Dr. IG3: Ilf 1B 72
Express Ho. SE8 6A 104
(off Rolt St.)
Express Newspapers SE1 4A 14 (1B 102)
(off Blackfriars Rd.)
Express Wharf E14 2C 104
(off Hutchings St.)
Exton Gdns. RM8: Dag 5C 72
Exton Rd. NW10 7J 61
Exton St. SE1 5J 13 (1A 102)
Eyebright Cl. CR0: C'don 1K 169
Eyhurst Cl. NW2 2C 62
Eylewood Rd. SE27 5C 138
Eynella Rd. SE22 7F 121
Eynham Rd. W12 6E 80
Eynsford Cl. BR5: Pet W 7G 161
Eynsford Cres. DA5: Bexl 1C 144
Eynsford Ho. SE1 7E 14 (2D 102)
(off Crosby Row)
Eynsford Ho. SE15 6J 103
Eynsford Ho. SE17 4E 102
(off East St.)
Eynsford Rd. IG3: Ilf 2J 71
Eynsford Ter. UB7: Yiew 6B 74
Eynsham Dr. SE2 4A 108
Eynswood Dr. DA14: Sidc 5B 144
Eyot Gdns. W6 5B 98
Eyot Grn. W4 5B 98
Eyot Ho. SE16 3G 103
(off Frean St.)
Eyre Ct. NW8 2B 82
Eyre Rd. NW8 1A 4 (3A 82)
Eyre St. Hill EC1 4J 7 (4A 84)
Eysham Ct. EN5: New Bar 5E 20
Eythorne Rd. SW9 1A 120
Ezra St. E2 1K 9 (3F 85)

F

Faber Gdns. NW4 5C 44
Fabian Bell Twr. E3 2C 86
(off Pancras Way)
Fabian Rd. SW6 7H 99
Fabian St. E6 4D 88
Fable Apts. N1 1C 8 (3C 84)
Facade, The SE23 2J 139
Factory La. CR0: C'don 1A 168
Factory La. N17 2F 49
Factory Rd. E16 1B 106
Factory Yd. W7 1J 95
Faggs Rd. TW14: Felt 4H 111
Fairacre HA5: Eastc 4J 39
Fairacre KT3: N Mald 3A 152
Fairacre Ct. HA6: Nwood 1G 39
Fair Acres BR2: Broml 5J 159
Fair Acres CR0: Sels 7B 170
Fairacres HA4: Ruis 7H 39
Fairacres SW15 4B 116
Fairbairn Grn. SW9 1B 120
Fairbank Av. BR6: Farnb 2F 173
Fairbank Est. N1 1E 8 (2D 84)
Fairbanks Ct. HA0: Wemb 1E 78
Fairbanks Rd. N17 3F 49
Fairbourne Ho. UB3: Harl 3E 92
Fairbourne Rd. N17 3E 48
Fairbourne Rd. SW4 6H 119
Fairbriar Residence SW7 4A 100
(off Stanhope Gdns.)
Fairbridge Rd. N19 2H 65
Fairbrook Cl. N13 5F 33
Fairbrook Rd. N13 6F 33
Fairburn Ct. SW15 5G 117
Fairburn Ho. W14 5H 99
(off Ivatt Pl.)
Fairby Ho. SE1 4F 103
(off Longfield Est.)
Fairby Rd. SE12 5K 123
Fairchild Cl. SW11 2B 118
Fairchild Ho. E2 2H 85
(off Cambridge Cres.)
Fairchild Ho. E9 7J 67
(off Frampton Pk. Rd.)
Fairchild Ho. N1 1G 9 (3E 84)
(off Fanshaw St.)
Fairchild Ho. N3 1J 45
Fairchild Pl. EC2 4H 9 (4E 84)
(off Gt. Eastern St.)
Fairchild St. EC2 4H 9 (4E 84)
Fair Cl. WD23: Bush 1A 26
Fairclough Cl. UB5: N'olt 4D 76
Fairclough St. E1 6G 85
Faircroft Ct. TW11: Tedd 6A 132
FAIR CROSS 5J 71
Faircross Av. IG11: Bark 6G 71
Faircross Av. RM5: Col R 1K 55
Faircross Pde. IG11: Bark 5J 71
Fairdale Gdns. SW15 4D 116
Fairdale Gdns. UB3: Hayes 2J 93
Fairey Av. UB3: Harl 4H 93
Fairfax Cl. KT12: Walt T 7K 147
Fairfax Ct. NW6 7A 64
(off Fairfax Rd.)
Fairfax Gdns. SE3 1A 124
Fairfax Ho. KT1: King T 3F 151
(off Livesey Cl.)
Fairfax Mans. NW6 7A 64
(off Finchley Rd.)
Fairfax M. E16 1K 105
Fairfax M. N8 4B 48
Fairfax M. SW15 4E 116
Fairfax Pl. NW6 7A 64
Fairfax Pl. W14 3G 99
Fairfax Rd. N8 4A 48
Fairfax Rd. NW6 7A 64
Fairfax Rd. TW11: Tedd 6A 132
Fairfax Rd. W4 3A 98
Fairfax Way N10 7K 31
Fairfield E1 5J 85
(off Redman's Rd.)
Fairfield KT1: King T 2F 151
Fairfield N20 7G 21
Fairfield NW1 1G 83
(off Arlington Rd.)
Fairfield Av. HA4: Ruis 7E 38
Fairfield Av. HA8: Edg 6C 28
Fairfield Av. NW4 6D 44
Fairfield Av. TW2: Whitt 1F 131
Fairfield Cl. CR4: Mitc 7C 136
Fairfield Cl. DA15: Sidc 6K 125
Fairfield Cl. EN3: Pond E 4E 24
Fairfield Cl. KT19: Ewe 5A 164
Fairfield Cl. N12 4F 31
Fairfield Ct. HA4: Ruis 1F 57
Fairfield Ct. HA6: Nwood 2J 39
Fairfield Ct. NW10 1C 80
Fairfield Cres. HA8: Edg 6C 28
Fairfield Dr. HA2: Harr 3G 41
Fairfield Dr. SW18 5K 117
Fairfield Dr. UB6: G'frd 1C 78
Fairfield E. KT1: King T 2E 150
Fairfield Gdns. N8 5J 47
Fairfield Gro. SE7 6B 106
Fairfield Halls Croydon 3D 168
Fairfield Nth. KT1: King T 2E 150
Fairfield Path CR0: C'don 3D 168
Fairfield Pl. KT1: King T 3E 150
Fairfield Rd. BR1: Broml 7J 141
Fairfield Rd. BR3: Beck 2C 158
Fairfield Rd. BR5: Pet W 6H 161
Fairfield Rd. CR0: C'don 3D 168
Fairfield Rd. DA7: Bex 2F 127
Fairfield Rd. E17 2A 50
Fairfield Rd. E3 2C 86
Fairfield Rd. IG1: Ilf 6F 71
Fairfield Rd. IG8: Wfd G 6D 36
Fairfield Rd. KT1: King T 2E 150
Fairfield Rd. N18 4B 34
Fairfield Rd. N8 5J 47
Fairfield Rd. UB1: S'hall 6D 76
Fairfield Rd. UB7: Yiew 7A 74
Fairfields Cl. NW9 5J 43
Fairfields Cres. NW9 4J 43
Fairfield Sth. KT1: King T 2E 150
Fairfields Rd. TW3: Houn 3G 113
Fairfield St. SW18 5K 117
Fairfield Trade Pk. KT1: King T 3F 151
Fairfield Way EN5: Barn 5D 20
Fairfield Way KT19: Ewe 5A 164
Fairfield W. KT1: King T 2E 150
Fairfoot Rd. E3 4C 86
Fairford SE6 1C 140
Fairford Av. CR0: C'don 5K 157
Fairford Av. DA7: Bex 1K 127
Fairford Cl. CR0: C'don 5A 158
Fairford Ct. SM2: Sutt 7K 165
Fairford Gdns. KT4: Wor Pk 2B 164
Fairford Ho. SE11 4K 19 (4A 102)
Fairgreen EN4: Cockf 3J 21
Fairgreen Ct. EN4: Cockf 3J 21
Fairgreen E. EN4: Cockf 3J 21
Fairgreen Rd. CR7: Thor H 5B 156
Fairhall Ct. KT5: Surb 7F 151
Fairhaven Av. CR0: C'don 6K 157
Fairhaven Ct. CR2: S Croy 5C 168
(off Warham Rd.)
Fairhazel Gdns. NW6 6K 63
Fairhazel Mans. NW6 7A 64
(off Fairhazel Gdns.)
Fairholme TW14: Bedf 7F 111
Fairholme Cl. N3 4G 45
Fairholme Cres. UB4: Hayes 4H 75
Fairholme Gdns. N3 3G 45
Fairholme Rd. CR0: C'don 7A 156
Fairholme Rd. HA1: Harr 5K 41
Fairholme Rd. IG1: Ilf 7D 52
Fairholme Rd. SM1: Sutt 6H 165
Fairholme Rd. TW15: Ashf 5A 128
Fairholme Rd. W14 5G 99
Fairholt Cl. N16 1E 66
Fairholt Rd. N16 1D 66
Fairholt St. SW7 1D 16 (3C 100)
Fairland Ho. BR2: Broml 4K 159
Fairland Rd. E15 6H 69
Fairlands Av. CR7: Thor H 4K 155
Fairlands Av. IG9: Buck H 2D 36
Fairlands Av. SM1: Sutt 2J 165
Fairlands Ct. SE9 6E 124
Fairlane Rd. RM13: Rain 3J 91
Fairlawn KT2: King T 6J 133
Fairlawn SE7 7A 106
Fairlawn Av. DA7: Bex 2D 126
Fairlawn Av. N2 4C 46
Fairlawn Av. W4 4J 97
Fairlawn Cl. KT10: Clay 6A 162
Fairlawn Cl. KT2: King T 6J 133
Fairlawn Cl. N14 6B 22
Fairlawn Cl. TW13: Hanw 4D 130
Fairlawn Ct. SE7 7A 106
(not continuous)
Fairlawn Ct. W4 4J 97
Fairlawn Dr. IG8: Wfd G 7D 36
Fairlawnes SM6: W'gton 5F 167
Fairlawn Gdns. UB1: S'hall 7D 76
Fairlawn Gro. W4 4J 97
Fairlawn Mans. SE14 1K 121
Fairlawn Pk. SE26 5A 140
Fairlawn Rd. SW19 7H 135
Fairlawns HA5: Pinn 2B 40
Fairlawns TW1: Twick 6C 114
Fairlawns TW16: Sun 3J 147
Fairlead Ho. E14 3C 104
(off Alpha Gro.)
Fairleads Ho. E17 4K 49
(off Wickford Way)
Fairlea Pl. W5 4C 78
Fairlie Ct. E3 3D 86
(off Stroudley Wlk.)
Fairlie Gdns. SE23 7J 121
Fairlight TW12: Hamp H 5F 131
Fairlight Av. E4 2A 36
Fairlight Av. IG8: Wfd G 6D 36
Fairlight Av. NW10 2A 80
Fairlight Cl. E4 2A 36
Fairlight Cl. KT4: Wor Pk 4E 164
Fairlight Ct. NW10 2A 80
Fairlight Ct. UB6: G'frd 2G 77
Fairlight Rd. SW17 4B 136
Fairline Ct. BR3: Beck 2E 158
FAIRLOP 1J 53
Fairlop Ct. E11 1F 69
Fairlop Gdns. IG6: Ilf 1G 53
Fairlop Outdoor Activity Cen. 1K 53
Fairlop Rd. E11 7F 51
Fairlop Rd. IG6: Ilf 2G 53
Fairlop Waters Country Pk. 2K 53
Fairlop Waters Golf Course 1J 53
Fairmark Dr. UB10: Hil 6C 56
Fairmead BR1: Broml 4D 160
Fairmead KT5: Surb 1H 163
Fairmead Cl. BR1: Broml 4D 160
Fairmead Cl. KT3: N Mald 3K 151
Fairmead Cl. TW5: Hest 7B 94
Fairmead Ct. TW9: Rich 2H 115
Fairmead Cres. HA8: Edg 3D 28
Fairmead Gdns. IG4: Ilf 5C 52
Fairmead Ho. E9 4A 68
Fairmead Rd. CR0: C'don 7K 155
Fairmead Rd. N19 3H 65
Fairmile Av. SW16 5H 137
Fairmile Ho. TW11: Tedd 4A 132
Fairmont Av. E14 1F 105
Fairmont Cl. DA17: Belv 5F 109
Fairmont Ho. E3 4C 86
(off Wellington Way)
Fairmont Ho. SE16 2K 103
(off Needleman St.)
Fairmont M. NW2 2J 63
Fairmount Rd. RM13: Rain 3J 91
Fairmount Rd. SW2 6K 119
Fairoak Cl. BR5: Pet W 7F 161
Fairoak Dr. SE9 5H 125
Fairoak Gdns. RM1: Rom 2K 55
Fair Oak Pl. IG6: Ilf 2G 53
Fairseat Cl. WD23: B Hea 2D 26
Fairstead Lodge IG8: Wfd G 6D 36
(off Snakes La. W.)
Fairstead Wlk. N1 1C 84
(off Popham St.)
Fair St. SE1 6H 15 (2E 102)
Fair St. TW3: Houn 3G 113
Fairthorne Vs. SE7 5J 105
(off Felltram Way)
Fairthorn Rd. SE7 5J 105
Fairview HA4: Ruis 4A 58
Fairview Av. HA0: Wemb 6D 60
Fairview Cl. E17 1A 50
Fairview Cl. SE26 5A 140
Fairview Ct. NW4 2F 45
Fairview Ct. TW15: Ashf 5C 128
Fairview Cres. HA2: Harr 1E 58
Fairview Dr. BR6: Orp 4H 173
Fairview Dr. TW17: Shep 5B 146
Fairview Est. NW10 3J 79
Fairview Gdns. IG8: Wfd G 1K 51
Fairview Ho. SW2 7K 119
Fairview Ind. Pk. RM13: Rain 5K 91
Fairview Pl. SW2 7K 119
Fairview Rd. EN2: Enf 1F 23
Fairview Rd. N15 5F 49
Fairview Rd. SM1: Sutt 5B 166
Fairview Rd. SW16 1K 155
Fairview Vs. E4 7H 35
Fairview Way HA8: Edg 4B 28

Fairwall Ho. SE5 1E 120
Fairwater Av. DA16: Well 4A 126
Fairwater Dr. TW17: Shep 5E 146
Fairwater Ho. E16 2K 105
(off Bonnet St.)
Fairwater Ho. TW11: Tedd 4A 132
Fairway BR5: Pet W 5H 161
Fairway DA6: Bex 5E 126
Fairway IG8: Wfd G 5F 37
Fairway SW20 3E 152
Fairway, The BR1: Broml 5D 160
Fairway, The EN5: New Bar 6E 20
Fairway, The HA0: Wemb 3B 60
Fairway, The HA4: Ruis 4A 58
Fairway, The KT3: N Mald 1K 151
Fairway, The KT8: W Mole 3F 149
Fairway, The N13 3H 33
Fairway, The N14 6A 22
Fairway, The NW7 3E 28
Fairway, The UB10: Hil 3B 74
Fairway, The UB5: N'olt 6G 59
Fairway, The W3 6A 80
Fairway Av. NW9 3H 43
Fairway Cl. TW4: Houn Amberley Way 5A 112
Fairway Cl. TW4: Houn Islay Gdns. 5B 112
Fairway Cl. CR0: C'don 5A 158
Fairway Cl. KT10: Surb 3B 162
Fairway Cl. KT19: Ewe 4J 163
Fairway Cl. NW11 7A 46
Fairway Ct. E3 3E 86
(off Culvert Dr.)
Fairway Ct. EN5: New Bar 6E 20
Fairway Ct. NW7 3E 28
Fairway Ct. SE16 2K 103
(off Christopher Cl.)
Fairway Dr. SE28 6D 90
Fairway Dr. UB6: G'frd 7F 59
Fairway Gdns. BR3: Beck 6F 159
Fairway Gdns. IG1: Ilf 5G 71
Fairways E17 4E 50
Fairways HA7: Stan 2E 42
Fairways TW11: Tedd 7D 132
Fairways TW15: Ashf 6D 128
Fairways TW7: Isle 1H 113
Fairways Bus. Pk. E10 2A 68
Fairway Trad. Est. TW4: Houn 5A 112
Fairweather Cl. DA16: Well 5A 126
Fairweather Cl. N15 4E 48
Fairweather Ct. N13 3E 32
Fairweather Ho. N7 4J 65
Fairweather Rd. N16 6G 49
Fairwyn Rd. SE26 4A 140
Faith Ct. E3 2C 86
(off Lefevre Wlk.)
Faith Ct. SE1 5F 103
(off Cooper's Rd.)
Faith M. E12 4B 70
Fakenham Cl. NW7 7H 29
Fakenham Cl. UB5: N'olt 6D 58
Fakruddin St. E1 4G 85
Falcon WC1 5F 7 (5J 83)
(off Old Gloucester St.)
Falcon Av. BR1: Broml 4C 160
Falconberg M. W1 7C 6 (6H 83)
Falcon Cl. HA6: Nwood 1G 39
Falcon Cl. W4 6J 97
Falcon Ct. E18 3K 51
(off Albert Rd.)
Falcon Ct. EC4 1K 13 (6A 84)
Falcon Ct. EN5: New Bar 4F 21
Falcon Ct. HA4: Ruis 2G 57
Falcon Ct. N1 1B 8 (2B 84)
(off City Gdn. Row)
Falcon Cres. EN3: Pond E 5E 24
Falcondal Ct. NW10 3G 79
Falcon Dr. TW19: Stanw 6A 110
Falconer Ct. N17 7H 33
(off Compton Cres.)
Falconer Wlk. N7 2K 65
Falconet Ct. E1 1H 103
(off Wapping High St.)
Falcon Gro. SW11 3C 118
Falcon Highwalk EC2 6C 8 (5C 84)
(off Aldersgate St.)
Falcon Ho. BR1: Broml 1H 159
Falcon Ho. E14 5D 104
(off St Davids Sq.)
Falcon Ho. NW6 1K 81
(off Springfield Wlk.)
Falcon Ho. SW5 5K 99
(off Old Brompton Rd.)
Falcon La. SW11 3C 118
Falcon Lodge W9 5J 81
(off Admiral Wlk.)
Falcon Pk. Community Sports Cen. 2D 118
Falcon Pk. Ind. Est. NW10 4A 62
Falcon Point SE1 3B 14 (7B 84)
Falcon Rd. EN3: Pond E 5E 24
Falcon Rd. SW11 2C 118
Falcon Rd. TW12: Hamp 7D 130
Falconry Ct. KT1: King T 3E 150
(off Fairfield Sth.)
Falcon St. E13 4J 87
Falcon Ter. SW11 3C 118
Falcon Way E11 4J 51
Falcon Way E14 4D 104
Falcon Way HA3: Kenton 5E 42
Falcon Way NW9 2A 44
Falcon Way TW14: Felt 5K 111
Falcon Way TW16: Sun 2G 147
Falcon Wharf SW11 2B 118
FALCONWOOD 4K 125
FALCONWOOD 4H 125
Falconwood Av. DA16: Well 2H 125
Falconwood Ct. SE3 2H 123
(off Montpelier Row)
Falconwood Pde. DA16: Well 4J 125
Falconwood Rd. CR0: Sels 7B 170
Falcourt Cl. SM1: Sutt 5K 165
Falkirk Ct. SE16 1K 103
(off Rotherhithe St.)
Falkirk Ho. W9 2K 81
(off Maida Vale)
Falkirk St. N1 1H 9 (2E 84)
Falkland Av. N11 4A 32
Falkland Av. N3 7D 30
Falkland Ho. SE6 4E 140
Falkland Ho. W14 5H 99
(off Edith Vs.)
Falkland Ho. W8 3K 99
Falkland Pk. Av. SE25 3E 156
Falkland Pl. NW5 5G 65
Falkland Rd. EN5: Barn 2B 20
Falkland Rd. N8 4A 48
Falkland Rd. NW5 5G 65
Fallaize Av. IG1: Ilf 4F 71
Falling La. UB7: Yiew 7A 74
Falloden Way NW11 4J 45
Fallodon Ho. W11 5H 81
(off Tavistock Cres.)
FALLOW CORNER 7F 31
Fallow Ct. SE16 5G 103
(off Argyle Way)
Fallow Ct. Av. N12 7F 31
Fallowfield HA7: Stan 4F 27
Fallowfield Ct. HA7: Stan 3F 27
Fallowfields Dr. N12 6H 31
Fallowhurst Path N3 7E 31
Fallow Pl. TW11: Tedd 5J 131
Fallows Cl. N2 2B 46
Fallsbrook Rd. SW16 6F 137
Falman Cl. N9 1B 34
Falmer Rd. E17 3D 50
Falmer Rd. EN1: Enf 4K 23
Falmer Rd. N15 5C 48
Falmouth Av. E4 5A 36
Falmouth Cl. N22 7E 32
Falmouth Cl. SE12 5H 123
Falmouth Gdns. IG4: Ilf 4B 52
Falmouth Ho. HA5: Hat E 1D 40
Falmouth Ho. KT2: King T 1D 150
(off Skerne Rd.)
Falmouth Ho. SE11 5K 19 (5A 102)
(off Seaton Cl.)
Falmouth Ho. W2 2C 10 (7C 82)
(off Clarendon Pl.)
Falmouth Rd. SE1 3C 102
Falmouth St. E15 5F 69
Falmouth Wlk. SW15 6C 116
Falmouth Way E17 5B 50
Falstaff Bldg. E1 7H 85
(off Cannon St. Rd.)
Falstaff Cl. DA1: Cray 7K 127
Falstaff Ct. SE11 4B 102
(off Opal St.)
Falstaff Ho. N1 1G 9 (2E 84)
(off Regan Way)
Falstaff M. TW12: Hamp H 5H 131
(off High St.)
Fambridge Cl. SE26 4B 140
Fambridge Ct. RM7: Rom 5K 55
(off Marks Rd.)
Fambridge Rd. RM8: Dag 1G 73
Family Court East London 1C 104
Family Court West London 6J 111
Fancourt M. BR1: Broml 3E 160
Fane St. W14 6H 99
Fan Mus., The 7E 104
Fann St. EC1 4C 8 (4C 84)
Fann St. EC2 4C 8 (4C 84)
(not continuous)
Fanshawe Av. IG11: Bark 6G 71
Fanshawe Cres. RM9: Dag 5E 72
Fanshawe Rd. TW10: Ham 4C 132
Fanshaw St. N1 1G 9 (3E 84)
THE FANTAIL 3D 172
Fantail Cl. SE28 6C 90
Fanthorpe St. SW15 3E 116
Faraday Av. DA14: Sidc 2A 144
Faraday Cl. N7 6K 65
Faraday Ho. E14 7B 86
(off Brightlingsea Pl.)
Faraday Ho. HA9: Wemb 3J 61
Faraday Ho. SE1 7E 14 (2D 102)
(off Cole St.)
Faraday Ho. SW11 7K 17 (6F 101)
Faraday Lodge SE10 3H 105
Faraday Mans. W14 6G 99
(off Queen's Club Gdns.)
Faraday Mus., The 3A 12 (7G 83)
Faraday Pl. KT8: W Mole 4E 148
Faraday Rd. DA16: Well 3A 126
Faraday Rd. E15 6H 69
Faraday Rd. KT8: W Mole 4E 148
Faraday Rd. SW19 6J 135
Faraday Rd. UB1: S'hall 7F 77
Faraday Rd. W10 5G 81
Faraday Rd. W3 7J 79
Faraday Way CR0: Wadd 1K 167
Faraday Way SE18 3B 106
Fareham Rd. TW14: Felt 7A 112
Farewell Pl. CR4: Mitc 1C 154
Fari Ct. E17 4C 50
(off Tower M.)
Faringdon Av. BR2: Broml 7E 160
Faringford Rd. E15 7G 69
Farjeon Ho. NW6 7B 64
(off Hilgrove Rd.)
Farjeon Rd. SE3 1B 124
Farleigh Av. BR2: Hayes 7H 159
Farleigh Ct. CR2: S Croy 5C 168
Farleigh Ho. N1 7B 66
(off Halton Rd.)
Farleigh Pl. N16 4F 67
Farleigh Rd. N16 4F 67
Farley Ct. NW1 4F 5 (4D 82)
(off Allsop Pl.)
Farley Ct. W14 3H 99
Farley Dr. IG3: Ilf 1J 71
Farley Ho. SE26 3H 139
Farley M. SE6 7E 122
Farley Pl. SE25 4G 157
Farley Rd. CR2: Sels 7H 169
Farley Rd. SE6 7D 122
Farlington Pl. SW15 7D 116
Farlow Rd. SW15 3F 117
Farlton Rd. SW18 1K 135
Farman Gro. UB5: N'olt 3B 76
Farman Ter. HA3: Kenton 4D 42
Farm Av. HA0: Wemb 6C 60
Farm Av. HA2: Harr 7D 40
Farm Av. NW2 3G 63
Farm Av. SW16 4J 137
Farmborough Cl. HA1: Harr 7H 41
Farm Cl. BR4: W W'ck 3H 171
Farm Cl. IG9: Buck H 3F 37
Farm Cl. RM10: Dag 7J 73
Farm Cl. SM2: Sutt 7B 166
Farm Cl. SW6 7J 99
Farm Cl. TW17: Shep 7C 146
Farm Cl. UB1: S'hall 7F 77
Farm Cl. UB10: Ick 2D 56
Farmcote Rd. SE12 1J 141
Farm Ct. NW4 3C 44
Farmdale Rd. SE10 5J 105
Farmdale Rd. SM5: Cars 7C 166
Farm Dr. CR0: C'don 2B 170
Farm End HA6: Nwood 1D 38
Farmer Rd. E10 1D 68
Farmer's Rd. SE5 7B 102
Farmer St. W8 1J 99
Farmfield Rd. BR1: Broml 5G 141
Farm Ho. Ct. NW7 7H 29
Farmhouse Rd. SW16 7G 137
Farmilo Rd. E17 7B 50
Farmington Av. SM1: Sutt 3B 166
Farmlands EN2: Enf 1F 23
Farmlands HA5: Eastc 4J 39
Farmlands, The UB5: N'olt 6D 58
Farmland Wlk. BR7: Chst 5F 143
Farm La. CR0: C'don 2B 170
Farm La. N14 7A 22
Farm La. SW6 6J 99
Farmleigh N14 7B 22
Farm M. CR4: Mitc 2F 155
Farm Pl. W8 1J 99
Farm Rd. HA8: Edg 6C 28
Farm Rd. N21 1H 33
Farm Rd. NW10 1K 79
Farm Rd. SM2: Sutt 7B 166
Farm Rd. SM4: Mord 5K 153
Farm Rd. TW4: Houn 1C 130
Farmstead Ct. SM6: W'gton 5F 167
(off Melbourne Rd.)
Farmstead Rd. HA3: Hrw W 1H 41
Farmstead Rd. SE6 4D 140
Farm St. W1 3J 11 (7F 83)
Farm Va. DA5: Bexl 6H 127
Farm Vw. Ct. IG2: Ilf 4A 54
Farm Wlk. NW11 5H 45
Farm Way IG9: Buck H 4F 37
Farm Way KT4: Wor Pk 3E 164
Farmway RM8: Dag 3C 72
Farnaby Ho. W10 3H 81
(off Bruckner St.)
Farnaby Rd. BR1: Broml 7G 141
Farnaby Rd. BR2: Broml 7F 141
Farnaby Rd. SE9 4A 124
Farnan Av. E17 2C 50
Farnan Lodge SW16 5J 137
Farnan Rd. SW16 5J 137
FARNBOROUGH 5G 173
Farnborough Av. CR2: Sels 7K 169
Farnborough Av. E17 3A 50
Farnborough Cl. HA9: Wemb 2H 61
Farnborough Comn. BR6: Farnb 3D 172
Farnborough Cres. BR2: Hayes 1H 171
Farnborough Cres. CR2: Sels 7A 170
Farnborough Hill BR6: Chels 5H 173
Farnborough Hill BR6: Farnb 5H 173
Farnborough Ho. SW15 1C 134
Farnborough Way BR6: Chels 5G 173
Farnborough Way BR6: Farnb 5G 173
Farnborough Way SE15 7E 102
Farncombe St. SE16 2G 103
Farndale Av. N13 2G 33
Farndale Ct. SE18 7C 106
Farndale Cres. UB6: G'frd 3G 77
Farndale Ho. NW6 1K 81
(off Kilburn Vale)
Farnell M. SW5 5K 99
Farnell Pl. W3 7H 79
Farnell Rd. TW7: Isle 3H 113
Farnfield Ct. CR2: S Croy 5B 168
Farnham Cl. N20 7F 21
Farnham Ct. SM3: Cheam 6G 165
Farnham Ct. UB1: S'hall 7G 77
(off Redcroft Rd.)
Farnham Gdns. SW20 2D 152
Farnham Ho. NW1 4D 4 (4C 82)
(off Harewood Av.)
Farnham Ho. SE1 6C 14 (2C 102)
(off Union St.)
Farnham Pl. SE1 5B 14 (1B 102)
Farnham Rd. DA16: Well 2C 126
Farnham Rd. IG3: Ilf 7K 53
Farnham Royal SE11 6H 19 (5K 101)
Farningham Ct. SW16 7H 137
Farningham Ho. N4 7D 48
Farningham Rd. N17 7B 34
Farnley Ho. SW8 2H 119
Farnley Rd. E4 1B 36
Farnley Rd. SE25 4D 156
Farnsworth Ct. SE10 3H 105
(off West Parkside)
Farnsworth Dr. HA8: Edg 4K 27
Farnworth Ho. E14 4F 105
(off Manchester Rd.)
Faro Cl. BR1: Broml 2E 160
Faroe Rd. W14 3F 99
Farorna Wlk. EN2: Enf 1F 23
Farquhar Rd. SE19 5F 139
Farquhar Rd. SW19 3J 135
Farquharson Rd. CR0: C'don 1C 168
Farrance Rd. RM6: Chad H 7E 54
Farrance St. E14 6C 86
Farrans Ct. HA3: Kenton 7B 42
Farrant Av. N22 2A 48
Farrant Cl. BR6: Chels 7K 173
Farr Av. IG11: Bark 2A 90
Farrell Ho. E1 6J 85
(off Ronald St.)
Farren Rd. SE23 2A 140
Farrer Ct. TW1: Twick 7D 114
Farrer Ho. SE8 7C 104
Farrer M. N8 4G 47
Farrer Rd. HA3: Kenton 5E 42
Farrer Rd. N8 4G 47
Farrer's Pl. CR0: C'don 4K 169
Farrier Cl. BR1: Broml 3B 160
Farrier Cl. TW16: Sun 4J 147
Farrier Cl. UB8: Hil 6C 74
Farrier Ct. E1 5K 85
(off White Horse La.)
Farrier Ct. RM13: Rain 2K 91
(off Lowen Rd.)
Farrier Pl. SM1: Sutt 3K 165
Farrier Rd. UB5: N'olt 2E 76
Farriers Ho. EC1 4D 8 (4C 84)
(off Errol St.)
Farriers M. SE15 3J 121
Farriers M. SW9 4A 120
Farrier St. NW1 7F 65
Farriers Yd. W6 5F 99
(off Smiths Sq.)
Farrier Wlk. SW10 6A 100
Farringdon Ho. TW9: Kew 7H 97
Farringdon Ho. UB7: W Dray 2B 92
Farringdon La. EC1 4K 7 (4A 84)
Farringdon Rd. EC1 3J 7 (4A 84)
Farringdon St. EC4 6A 8 (5B 84)
Farrington Ct. BR1: Broml 2K 159
(off Widmore Rd.)
Farrington Pl. BR7: Chst 7H 143
Farrins Rents SE16 1A 104
Farrow Ho. NW9 3C 44
Farrow La. SE14 7J 103
Farrow Pl. SE16 3A 104
Farr Rd. EN2: Enf 1J 23
Farsby Ho. Apts. IG11: Bark 1G 89
(off Manwell La.)
Farthingale Wlk. E15 7F 69
Farthing All. SE1 7K 15 (2G 103)
Farthing Barn La. BR6: Downe 7E 172
Farthing Ct. NW7 7B 30
Farthing Flds. E1 1H 103
Farthings, The KT2: King T 1G 151
Farthings Cl. E4 3B 36
Farthings Cl. HA5: Eastc 6K 39
Farthing St. BR6: Downe 7D 172
FARTHING STREET 7D 172
Farwell Rd. DA14: Sidc 4B 144
Farwig La. BR1: Broml 1H 159
Fashion & Textile Mus. 6H 15 (2E 102)
Fashion St. E1 6K 9 (5F 85)
Fashoda Rd. BR2: Broml 4B 160
Fassett Rd. E8 6G 67
Fassett Rd. KT1: King T 4E 150
Fassett Sq. E8 6G 67
Fathom Ct. E16 7F 89
(off Basin App.)
Fauconberg Ct. W4 6J 97
(off Fauconberg Rd.)
Fauconberg Rd. W4 6J 97
Faulkner Cl. RM8: Dag 7D 54
Faulkner Ho. BR7: Chst 7H 143
Faulkner Ho. W6 6E 98
Faulkner M. E17 1A 50
Faulkners All. EC1 5A 8 (5B 84)
Faulkner St. SE14 1J 121
Fauna Cl. HA7: Stan 4J 27
Fauna Cl. RM6: Chad H 6C 54
Faunce Ho. SE17 6B 102
(off Doddington Gro.)
Faunce St. SE17 5B 102
Favart Rd. SW6 1J 117
Faversham Av. E4 1B 36
Faversham Av. EN1: Enf 6J 23
Faversham Ho. NW1 1G 83
(off Bayham Pl.)
Faversham Ho. SE17 5E 102
(off Kinglake St.)
Faversham Rd. BR3: Beck 2B 158
Faversham Rd. SE6 7B 122
Faversham Rd. SM4: Mord 6K 153
Fawcett Cl. SW11 2B 118
Fawcett Cl. SW16 5A 138
Fawcett Ct. SW10 6A 100
(off Fawcett St.)
Fawcett Est. E5 1G 67
Fawcett Rd. CR0: C'don 3C 168
Fawcett Rd. NW10 7B 62
Fawcett St. SW10 6A 100
Fawe Pk. M. SW15 4H 117
Fawe Pk. Rd. SW15 4H 117
Fawe St. E14 5D 86
Fawkham Ho. SE1 4F 103
(off Longfield Est.)
Fawley Lodge E14 4F 105
(off Millennium Dr.)
Fawley Rd. NW6 5K 63
Fawnbrake Av. SE24 5B 120
Fawn Hgts. IG9: Buck H 2E 36
(off Stag La.)
Fawn Rd. E13 2A 88
Fawns Mnr. Cl. TW14: Bedf 1E 128
Fawns Mnr. Rd. TW14: Bedf 1F 129
Fawood Av. NW10 7J 61
Faygate Cres. DA6: Bex 5G 127
Faygate Rd. SW2 2K 137
Fayland Av. SW16 5G 137
Fazeley Ct. W9 5J 81
(off Elmfield Way)
Fazeley Ho. UB5: N'olt 3D 76
(off Taywood Rd.)
Fearnley Cres. TW12: Hamp 5C 130
Fearnley Ho. SE5 2E 120
Fearns Ho. W13 1A 96
Fearon St. SE10 5J 105
Featherbed La. CR0: Sels 7B 170
Feather M. E1 5G 85
Feathers Pl. SE10 6F 105
Featherstone Av. SE23 2H 139
Featherstone Ct. UB2: S'hall 3B 94
Featherstone Ho. UB4: Yead 5A 76
Featherstone Ind. Est. UB2: S'hall 3C 94
(off Feather Rd.)
Featherstone M. SE22 4E 120
Featherstone Rd. NW7 6J 29
Featherstone Rd. UB2: S'hall 3C 94
Featherstone Sports Cen. 4B 94
Featherstone St. EC1 3E 8 (4D 84)
Featherstone Ter. UB2: S'hall 3C 94
Featley Rd. SW9 3B 120
Federal Rd. UB6: G'frd 1C 78
Federation Rd. SE2 4B 108
Fee Farm Rd. KT10: Clay 7A 162
Feeny Cl. NW10 4B 62
Felar Wlk. NW9 3B 44
Felbridge Av. HA7: Stan 2A 42
Felbridge Cl. SM2: Sutt 7K 165
Felbridge Cl. SW16 4A 138
Felbridge Ct. TW13: Felt 1K 129
(off High St.)
Felbridge Ct. UB3: Harl 6F 93
Felbridge Ho. SE22 3E 120
Felbridge Rd. IG3: Ilf 2K 71
Felday Rd. SE13 6D 122
Felden Cl. HA5: Hat E 1C 40
Felden St. SW6 1H 117
Feldman Cl. N16 1G 67
Feldspar Ct. EN3: Enf H 3F 25
(off Enstone Rd.)
Feldspar M. N13 5G 33
Felgate M. W6 4D 98
Felhampton Rd. SE9 2F 143
Felhurst Cres. RM10: Dag 4H 73
Feline Ct. EN4: E Barn 6H 21
Felix Av. N8 6J 47
Felix Ct. E17 5D 50
Felix Ct. NW9 2A 44
Felix Ho. E16 7E 88
(off University Way)
Felix La. TW17: Shep 6G 147
Felix Mnr. BR7: Chst 6J 143
Felix Neubergh Ho. EN1: Enf 4K 23
Felix Pl. SW2 5A 120
(off Talma Rd.)
Felix Point E14 6C 86
(off Upper Nth. St.)
Felix Rd. KT12: Walt T 6J 147
Felix Rd. W13 7A 78
Felixstowe Ct. E16 1F 107
Felixstowe Rd. N17 3F 49
Felixstowe Rd. N9 3B 34
Felixstowe Rd. NW10 3D 80
Felixstowe Rd. SE2 3B 108
Felix St. E2 2H 85
Fellbrigg Rd. SE22 5F 121
Fellbrigg St. E1 4H 85
Fellbrook TW10: Ham 3B 132
Fellmongers Path SE1 7J 15 (2F 103)
(off Tower Bri. Rd.)
Fellmongers Yd. CR0: C'don 3C 168
Fellowes Cl. UB4: Yead 4B 76
Fellowes Rd. SM5: Cars 3C 166
Fellows Ct. E2 2F 85
(not continuous)
Fellowship Cl. RM8: Dag 4A 72
Fellowship Ho. E6 2C 88
(off St Bartholomew's Rd.)
Fellows Rd. NW3 7B 64
Fell Rd. CR0: C'don 3C 168
Felltram M. SE7 5J 105
Felltram Way SE7 5J 105
Fell Wlk. HA8: Edg 1J 43
Felmersham Cl. SW4 4J 119
Felmingham Rd. SE20 2J 157
Felnex Av. SM6: W'gton 2E 166
Felnex Trad. Est. NW10 2K 79
Felnex Trad. Est. SM6: W'gton 2E 166
Felsberg Rd. SW2 6J 119
Fels Cl. RM10: Dag 3H 73
Fels Farm Av. RM10: Dag 3J 73
Felsham M. SW15 3F 117
(off Felsham Rd.)
Felsham Rd. SW15 3E 116
Felspar Cl. SE18 5K 107
Felstead Av. IG5: Ilf 1E 52
Felstead Cl. N13 5F 33
Felstead Gdns. E14 5E 104
Felstead Rd. E11 7J 51
Felstead Rd. E9 6B 68
Felstead St. E9 6B 68
Felstead Wharf E14 5E 104
Felsted Rd. E16 6B 88
FELTHAM 1K 129
Feltham Av. KT8: E Mos 4J 149
Felthambrook Ind. Est. TW13: Felt 3K 129
Felthambrook Way TW13: Felt 3K 129
Feltham Bus. Complex TW13: Felt 2K 129
Feltham Corporate Cen. TW13: Felt 3K 129
FELTHAMHILL 5H 129
Feltham Hill Rd. TW15: Ashf 5C 128
Feltham Rd. CR4: Mitc 2D 154
Feltham Rd. TW15: Ashf 4C 128
Felton Cl. BR5: Pet W 6F 161
Felton Gdns. IG11: Bark 1J 89
Felton Hall Ho. SE16 2G 103
(off George Row)
Felton Ho. N1 1D 84
(off Colville Est.)
Felton Lea DA14: Sidc 5K 143
Felton Rd. IG11: Bark 2J 89
Felton Rd. W13 2C 96
Felton St. N1 1D 84
Fenchurch Av. EC3 1G 15 (6E 84)
Fenchurch Bldgs. EC3 1H 15 (6E 84)
Fenchurch Ho. EC3 1J 15 (6F 85)
(off Minories)
Fenchurch M. E3 5B 86
(off St Paul's Way)
Fenchurch Pl. EC3 1H 15 (6E 84)
Fenchurch St. EC3 2G 15 (7E 84)
Fen Ct. EC3 1G 15 (6E 84)
Fendall Rd. KT19: Ewe 5J 163
Fendall St. SE1 3E 102
(not continuous)
Fendt Cl. E16 6H 87
Fendyke Rd. DA17: Belv 4D 108
Fenelon Pl. W14 4H 99
Fengate Cl. KT9: Chess 6D 162
Fen Gro. DA15: Sidc 5K 125
Fenham Rd. SE15 7G 103
Fenland Ho. E5 2J 67
Fen La. SW13 1D 116
Fenman Ct. N17 1H 49
Fenman Gdns. IG3: Ilf 1B 72
Fenn Cl. BR1: Broml 6J 141
Fennel Apts. SE1 5K 15 (1F 103)
(off Cayenne Ct.)
Fennel Cl. CR0: C'don 1K 169
Fennel Cl. E16 4G 87
Fennells Mead KT17: Ewe 7B 164
Fennell St. SE18 6E 106
Fenner Cl. SE16 4H 103
Fenner Ho. E1 1H 103
(off Watts St.)
Fenner Sq. SW11 3B 118
Fenn Ho. TW7: Isle 1B 114
Fennings Rd. SW4 6H 119
Fenning St. SE1 6G 15 (2E 102)
Fenn St. E9 5K 67
Fenstanton N4 1K 65
(off Marquis Rd.)
Fenstanton Av. N12 6G 31
Fen St. E16 7H 87
Fenswood Cl. DA5: Bexl 6G 127
Fentiman Rd. SW8 7F 19 (6J 101)
Fentiman Way HA2: Harr 2F 59
Fenton Cl. BR7: Chst 5D 142
Fenton Cl. E8 6F 67
Fenton Cl. SW9 2K 119
Fenton Ho. SE14 7A 104
Fenton Ho. TW5: Hest 6E 94
Fenton House 3A 64
(off Hampstead Gro.)
Fenton Pde. SE10 5H 105
(off Woolwich Rd.)
Fenton Rd. HA2: Harr 3G 41
Fenton Rd. N17 7H 33
Fentons Av. E13 3K 87
Fenton St. E1 6H 85
Fenwick Cl. SE18 6E 106
Fenwick Gro. SE15 3G 121
Fenwick Ho. EC1 6B 8 (5B 84)
(off Little Britain)
Fenwick Pl. CR2: S Croy 7B 168
Fenwick Pl. SW9 3J 119
Fenwick Rd. SE15 3G 121

Ferby Ct. – Fitzpatrick Rd.

Ferby Ct. DA14: Sidc 4K 143
(off Main Rd.)
Ferdinand Ct. SE6 7C 122
(off Adenmore Rd.)
Ferdinand Dr. SE15 7E 102
Ferdinand Ho. NW1 7E 64
(off Ferdinand Pl.)
Ferdinand Magellan Ct. E16 2K 105
(Ferdinand Magellan Court)
Ferdinand Pl. NW1 7E 64
Ferdinand St. NW1 7E 64
Ferguson Av. KT5: Surb 5F 151
Ferguson Cl. BR2: Broml 3F 159
Ferguson Cl. E14 4C 104
Ferguson Dr. W3 6K 79
Fergus Rd. N5 5B 66
Fergusson M. SW4 2J 119
Fergus St. SE10 3J 105
Ferial Ct. SE15 7G 103
(off Fenham Rd.)
Fermain Ct. E. N1 1E 84
(off Hertford Rd.)
Fermain Ct. Nth. N1 1E 84
(off De Beauvoir Est.)
Fermain Ct. W. N1 1E 84
(off De Beauvoir Est.)
Ferme Pk. Rd. N4 6K 47
Ferme Pk. Rd. N8 5J 47
Fermor Rd. SE23 1A 140
Fermoy Ho. W9 4H 81
(off Fermoy Rd.)
Fermoy Rd. UB6: G'frd 4F 77
Fermoy Rd. W9 4H 81
(not continuous)
Fern Av. CR4: Mitc 4H 155
Fernbank IG9: Buck H 1E 36
Fernbank Av. HA0: Wemb 4K 59
Fernbank Av. KT12: Walt T 7C 148
Fernbank M. SW12 6G 119
Fernbrook Av. DA15: Sidc 5J 125
Fernbrook Cres. SE13 6G 123
(off Leahurst Rd.)
Fernbrook Dr. HA2: Harr 7F 41
Fernbrook Rd. SE13 5G 123
Ferncliff Rd. E8 5G 67
Fern Cl. N1 2E 84
Fern Ct. DA7: Bex 4G 127
Fern Ct. RM7: Rom 5K 55
Fern Ct. SE14 2K 121
Ferncroft Av. HA4: Ruis 2A 58
Ferncroft Av. N12 6J 31
Ferncroft Av. NW3 3J 63
Ferndale BR1: Broml 2A 160
Ferndale Av. E17 5F 51
Ferndale Av. TW4: Houn 3C 112
Ferndale Cl. DA7: Bex 1E 126
Ferndale Community Sports Cen. 3K 119
Ferndale Cres. SM5: Cars 1D 166
Ferndale Rd. E11 2G 69
Ferndale Rd. E7 7K 69
Ferndale Rd. N15 6F 49
Ferndale Rd. RM5: Col R 2J 55
Ferndale Rd. SE25 5H 157
Ferndale Rd. SW4 4J 119
Ferndale Rd. SW9 4K 119
Ferndale Rd. TW15: Ashf 5A 128
Ferndale St. E6 7F 89
Ferndale Ter. HA1: Harr 4K 41
Ferndale Way BR6: Farnb 5H 173
Ferndell Av. DA5: Bexl 3K 145
Fern Dene W13 5B 78
Ferndene Rd. SE24 4C 120
Fernden Way RM7: Rom 6H 55
Ferndown HA6: Nwood 2J 39
Ferndown NW1 7H 65
(off Camley St.)
Ferndown Av. BR6: Orp 1H 173
Ferndown Cl. HA5: Pinn 1C 40
Ferndown Cl. SM2: Sutt 6B 166
Ferndown Ct. UB1: S'hall 6G 77
(off Haldane Rd.)
Ferndown Lodge E14 3E 104
(off Manchester Rd.)
Ferndown Rd. SE9 7B 124
Ferney Meade Way TW7: Isle 2A 114
Ferney Rd. EN4: E Barn 7K 21
Fern Gro. TW14: Felt 7K 111
Fernhall Dr. IG4: Ilf 5B 52
Fernham Rd. CR7: Thor H 3C 156
Fernhead Rd. W9 3H 81
Fernheath Way DA2: Wilm 5K 145
Fernhill Ct. E17 2F 51
Fernhill Gdns. KT2: King T 5D 132
Fern Hill Pl. BR6: Farnb 5G 173
Fernhill St. E16 1D 106
Fernholme Rd. SE15 5K 121
Fernhurst Gdns. HA8: Edg 6B 28
Fernhurst Rd. CR0: C'don 7H 157
Fernhurst Rd. SW6 1G 117
Fernhurst Rd. TW15: Ashf 4E 128
Fern La. TW5: Hest 5D 94
Fernlea Rd. CR4: Mitc 2E 154
Fernlea Rd. SW12 1F 137
Fernleigh Cl. CR0: Wadd 4A 168
Fernleigh Cl. W9 3H 81
Fernleigh Ct. HA2: Harr 2F 41
Fernleigh Ct. HA9: Wemb 2E 60
Fernleigh Ct. RM7: Rom 5J 55
Fernleigh Rd. N21 2F 33
Fernly Cl. HA5: Eastc 4J 39
Fernsbury St. WC1 2J 7 (3A 84)
Fernshaw Cl. SW10 6A 100
Fernshaw Mans. SW10 6A 100
(off Fernshaw Rd.)
Fernshaw Rd. SW10 6A 100
Fernside IG9: Buck H 1E 36
Fernside KT7: T Ditt 1B 162
Fernside NW11 2J 63
Fernside Av. NW7 3E 28
Fernside Av. TW13: Felt 4K 129
Fernside Ct. NW4 2F 45
Fernside Rd. SW12 1D 136
Ferns Rd. E15 6H 69
Fern St. E3 4C 86
Fernthorpe Rd. SW16 6G 137
Ferntower Rd. N5 5D 66
Fern Wlk. SE16 5G 103
Fern Wlk. TW15: Ashf 5A 128
Fernways IG1: Ilf 4F 71
Fernwood CR0: Sels 7A 170
Fernwood SW19 1H 135
Fernwood Av. HA0: Wemb 6C 60
Fernwood Av. SW16 4H 137
Fernwood Cl. BR1: Broml 2A 160
Fernwood Ct. N14 7B 22
Fernwood Cres. N20 3J 31
Fernwood Pl. KT10: Hin W 2A 162
Ferranti Cl. SE18 3B 106
Ferraro Cl. TW5: Hest 6E 94
Ferrers Av. SM6: Bedd 4H 167
Ferrers Av. UB7: W Dray 2A 92
Ferrers Rd. SW16 5H 137
Ferrestone Rd. N8 4K 47
Ferrey M. SW9 2A 120
Ferriby Cl. N1 7A 66
Ferric Cl. NW9 1B 44
Ferrier Ind. Est. SW18 4K 117
(off Ferrier St.)
Ferrier Point E16 5J 87
(off Forty Acre La.)
Ferrier St. SW18 4K 117
Ferring Cl. HA2: Harr 1G 59
Ferrings SE21 3E 138
Ferris Av. CR0: C'don 3B 170
Ferris Rd. SE22 4G 121
Ferron Rd. E5 3H 67
Ferrybridge Ho. SE11 2J 19 (3A 102)
(off Lambeth Wlk.)
Ferrydale Lodge NW4 4E 44
(off Parson St.)
Ferry Ho. E5 1H 67
(off Harrington Hill)
Ferry Island Retail Pk. 3G 49
Ferry La. N17 4G 49
Ferry La. SW13 6B 98
Ferry La. TW17: Shep 7C 146
Ferry La. TW8: Bford 6E 96
Ferry La. TW9: Kew 6F 97
Ferryman's Quay SW6 2A 118
Ferrymead Av. UB6: G'frd 3E 76
Ferrymead Dr. UB6: G'frd 2E 76
Ferrymead Gdns. UB6: G'frd 2G 77
Ferrymoor TW10: Ham 3B 132
Ferry Pl. SE18 3E 106
Ferry Quays TW8: Bford Ferry La. 6E 96
Ferry Quays TW8: Bford Point Wharf La. 7D 96
(off Point Wharf La.)
Ferry Rd. KT7: T Ditt 6B 150
Ferry Rd. KT8: W Mole 3E 148
Ferry Rd. SW13 7C 98
Ferry Rd. TW1: Twick 1B 132
Ferry Rd. TW11: Tedd 5B 132
Ferry Sq. TW8: Bford 7E 96
Ferry St. E14 5E 104
Ferry Wharf TW8: Bford 7E 96
Festing Rd. SW15 3F 117
Festival Cl. DA5: Bexl 1D 144
Festival Cl. UB10: Hil 1D 74
Festival Ct. E8 7F 67
(off Holly St.)
Festival Ct. SM1: Sutt 7K 153
Festival Wlk. SM5: Cars 4D 166
Festival Way E4 6K 35
Festive Mans. E20 5E 68
(off Napa Cl.)
Festive Wlk. SW15 2F 117
Festoon Way E16 7B 88
Festubert Pl. E3 2B 86
Festuca Ho. E20 5E 68
(off Mirabelle Gdns.)
Fetherstone Ct. RM6: Chad H 6F 55
(off High Rd.)
Fetherton Ct. IG11: Bark 2G 89
(off Spring Pl.)
Fetter La. EC4 1K 13 (6A 84)
Fetter La. Apts. EC4 1J 13 (6A 84)
(off Fetter La.)
Fettes Ho. NW8 2B 82
(off Wellington Rd.)
Fettle Ct. SE14 6A 104
(off Moulding La.)
Fews Lodge RM6: Chad H 4D 54
Ffinch St. SE8 7C 104
Fiador Apts. SE10 4G 105
(off Telegraph Av.)
Fidelis Ho. E1 6J 9 (5F 85)
(off Gun St.)
Fidgeon Cl. BR1: Broml 3E 160
Field Cl. BR1: Broml 2A 160
Field Cl. E4 6J 35
Field Cl. HA4: Ruis 1E 56
Field Cl. IG9: Buck H 3F 37
Field Cl. KT8: W Mole 5F 149
Field Cl. KT9: Chess 5C 162
Field Cl. NW2 2C 62
Field Cl. TW4: Cran 1K 111
Field Cl. UB10: Ick 2D 56
Field Cl. UB3: Harl 7E 92
FIELDCOMMON 7D 148
Fieldcommon La. KT12: Walt T 7C 148
Field Ct. SW19 3J 135
Field Ct. WC1 6H 7 (5K 83)
Field End HA4: Ruis 6A 58
Field End UB5: N'olt 6B 58
Fieldend TW1: Twick 4K 131
Fieldend Rd. SW16 1G 155
Field End Rd. HA4: Ruis 1B 58
Field End Rd. HA5: Eastc 5K 39
Fielder Apts. E3 4B 86
(off Heath Pl.)
Fielders Cl. EN1: Enf 4K 23
Fielders Cl. HA2: Harr 1G 59
Fielders Cres. IG11: Bark 4C 90
Fieldfare Rd. SE28 7C 90
Fieldgate La. CR4: Mitc 2C 154
Fieldgate Mans. E1 5G 85
(off Fieldgate St.)
Fieldgate St. E1 5G 85
Field Ho. NW6 3F 81
(off Harvist Rd.)
Field Ho. SM4: Mord 5K 153
(off School Ga. Dr.)
Fieldhouse Cl. E18 1J 51
Fieldhouse Rd. SW12 1G 137
Fielding Av. TW2: Twick 3G 131
Fielding Ct. WC2 1E 12 (6J 83)
(off Earlham St.)
Fielding Ho. NW8 1A 82
(off Ainsworth Way)
Fielding Ho. W4 6A 98
(off Devonshire Rd.)
Fielding La. BR2: Broml 4A 160
Fielding M. SW13 6D 98
Fielding Rd. W14 3F 99
Fielding Rd. W4 3K 97
Fieldings, The SE23 1J 139
Fielding St. SE17 6C 102
Fielding Ter. W5 7F 79
Fielding Wlk. W13 3B 96
Field La. TW11: Tedd 5A 132
Field La. TW8: Bford 7C 96
Field Maple M. RM5: Col R 1G 55
Field Mead NW7 7F 29
Field Mead NW9 7G 29
Fieldpark Gdns. CR0: C'don 1A 170
Field Pl. KT3: N Mald 6B 152
Field Pl. SW19 1B 154
Field Point E7 4J 69
Field Rd. E7 4H 69
Field Rd. N17 3D 48
Field Rd. TW14: Felt 6K 111
Field Rd. W6 5G 99
Fieldsend Rd. SM3: Cheam 5G 165
Fields Est. E8 7G 67
Fieldside Cl. BR6: Farnb 4G 173
Fieldside Rd. BR1: Broml 5F 141
Fields Pk. Cres. RM6: Chad H 5D 54
Field St. WC1 1G 7 (3K 83)
Fields Wlk. SW11 7F 101
Fieldsway Ho. N5 5A 66
Field Vw. TW13: Felt 4F 129
Fieldview SW18 1B 136
Field View Cl. DA14: Sidc 5G 145
Field Vw. Cl. RM7: Mawney 3G 55
Fieldview Cotts. N14 2C 32
(off Balaams La.)
Field Way HA4: Ruis 1E 56
Field Way NW10 7J 61
Field Way UB6: G'frd 1F 77
Fieldway BR5: Pet W 6H 161
Fieldway CR0: New Ad 7D 170
Fieldway RM8: Dag 3C 72
Fieldway Cres. N5 5A 66
Fiennes Cl. RM8: Dag 1C 72
Fiesta Dr. RM9: Dag 4J 91
Fifehead Cl. TW15: Ashf 6A 128
Fife Rd. E16 5J 87
Fife Rd. KT1: King T 2E 150
Fife Rd. N22 7G 33
Fife Rd. SW14 5J 115
Fife Ter. N1 2K 83
Fifield Path SE23 3K 139
Fifth Av. E12 4D 70
Fifth Av. UB3: Hayes 1H 93
Fifth Av. W10 3G 81
Fifth Cross Rd. TW2: Twick 2H 131
Fifth Way HA9: Wemb 4H 61
Figges Rd. CR4: Mitc 7E 136
Fight for Peace Academy 1E 106
Fig Tree Cl. NW10 1A 80
Figure Ct. SW3 6F 17 (5D 100)
(off West Rd.)
Filament Wlk. SW18 5J 117
(off Spectrum Way)
Filanco Ct. W7 1K 95
Filby Cl. DA8: Erith 7K 109
Filby Rd. KT9: Chess 6F 163
Filey Av. N16 1G 67
Filey Cl. SM2: Sutt 7A 166
Filey Waye HA4: Ruis 2J 57
Filigree Ct. SE16 1B 104
Fillebrook Av. EN1: Enf 2K 23
Fillebrook Rd. E11 1F 69
Filmer Chambers SW6 1G 117
(off Filmer Rd.)
Filmer Ho. SW6 1H 117
(off Filmer Rd.)
Filmer M. SW6 1H 117
Filmer Rd. SW6 1G 117
Filston Rd. DA8: Erith 5J 109
Filton Cl. NW9 1A 44
Filton Ct. SE14 7J 103
(off Farrow La.)
Finborough Ho. SW10 6A 100
(off Finborough Rd.)
Finborough Rd. SW10 5K 99
Finborough Rd. SW17 6D 136
Finborough Theatre, The 6K 99
(off Finborough Rd.)
Finchale Rd. SE2 3A 108
Fincham Cl. UB10: Ick 3E 56
Finch Av. SE27 4D 138
Finch Cl. EN5: Barn 5D 20
Finch Cl. NW10 6K 61
Finch Ct. DA14: Sidc 3B 144
Finchdean Ho. SW15 7B 116
Finch Dr. TW14: Felt 7B 112
Finch Gdns. E4 5H 35
Finch Ho. E3 1B 86
(off Jasmine Sq.)
Finch Ho. SE8 7D 104
(off Bronze St.)
Finchingfield Av. IG8: Wfd G 7F 37
Finch La. EC3 1F 15 (6D 84)
FINCHLEY 1J 45
Finchley Ct. N3 6E 30
Finchley Golf Course 6C 30
Finchley Ind. Est. N12 4F 31
Finchley La. NW4 4E 44
Finchley Lido Leisure Cen. 7G 31
Finchley Manor Club 1H 45
Finchley Pk. N12 4F 31
Finchley Pl. NW8 2B 82
Finchley Rd. NW11 4H 45
Finchley Rd. NW2 3J 63
Finchley Rd. NW3 4J 63
Finchley Rd. NW8 1B 82
Finchley Way N3 7D 30
Finch Lodge W9 5J 81
(off Admiral Wlk.)
Finch M. SE15 1F 121
Finch's Ct. E14 7D 86
Finch's Ct. M. E14 7D 86
(off Finch's Ct.)
Finden Rd. E7 5A 70
Findhorn Av. UB4: Yead 5K 75
Findhorn St. E14 6E 86
Findlay Ho. E3 3C 86
(off Trevithick Way)
Findon Cl. HA2: Harr 3F 59
Findon Cl. SW18 6J 117
Findon Rd. N9 1C 34
Findon Rd. W12 2C 98
Fine Bush La. UB9: Hare 6D 38
Fingal St. SE10 5H 105
Fingest Ho. NW8 3C 4 (4C 82)
(off Lilestone St.)
Finians Cl. UB10: Uxb 7B 56
Finland Rd. SE4 3A 122
Finland St. SE16 3A 104
Finlays Cl. KT9: Chess 5G 163
Finlay St. SW6 1F 117
Finley Ct. SE5 7C 102
(off Redcar St.)
Finmere Ho. N4 7C 48
Finnemore Ho. N1 1C 84
(off Britannia Row)
Finney La. TW7: Isle 1A 114
Finn Ho. N1 1F 9 (3D 84)
(off Bevenden St.)
Finnis St. E2 3H 85
Finnymore Rd. RM9: Dag 7E 72
FINSBURY 1J 7 (3A 84)
Finsbury Av. EC2 6F 9 (5D 84)
Finsbury Av. Sq. EC2 5G 9 (5E 84)
Finsbury Cir. EC2 6F 9 (5D 84)
Finsbury Cotts. N22 7D 32
Finsbury Est. EC1 2K 7 (3A 84)
Finsbury Ho. N22 1J 47
Finsbury Leisure Cen. 2C 8 (3C 84)
Finsbury Mkt. EC2 4G 9 (4E 84)
(not continuous)
FINSBURY PARK 1A 66
Finsbury Pk. Av. N4 6C 48
Finsbury Pk. Rd. N4 2B 66
Finsbury Pavement EC2 5F 9 (5D 84)
Finsbury Rd. N22 7E 32
(not continuous)
Finsbury Sq. EC2 4F 9 (4D 84)
Finsbury St. EC2 5E 8 (5D 84)
Finsbury Way DA5: Bexl 6F 127
Finsen Rd. SE5 4C 120
Finstock Rd. W10 6F 81
Finucane Ct. TW9: Rich 3F 115
(off Lwr. Mortlake Rd.)
Finucane Ri. WD23: B Hea 2B 26
Finwhale Ho. E14 3D 104
(off Glengall Gro.)
Fiona Ct. EN2: Enf 3G 23
Fiona Ct. NW6 2J 81
Firbank Cl. E16 5B 88
Firbank Cl. EN2: Enf 4H 23
Firbank Rd. SE15 2H 121
Fir Cl. KT12: Walt T 7J 147
Fircroft Gdns. HA1: Harr 3J 59
Fircroft Rd. KT9: Chess 4F 163
Fircroft Rd. SW17 2D 136
Fir Dene BR6: Farnb 3D 172
Firdene KT5: Surb 1J 163
Fire Bell All. KT6: Surb 6E 150
Firecrest Dr. NW3 3K 63
Firefly Cl. UB3: Hayes 7H 75
Firefly Cl. UB5: N'olt 3B 76
Firefly Gdns. E6 4C 88
Firehorn Ho. E15 3G 87
(off Teasel Way)
Firemans Flats N22 7D 32
Fire Station All. EN5: Barn 3B 20
Fire Station M. BR3: Beck 1C 158
Fire Station Sq. SE1 5H 15 (1E 102)
(off Abbots La.)
Firestone Ho. TW8: Bford 5E 96
Firethorn Cl. HA8: Edg 4D 28
Firewatch Ct. E1 5A 86
(off Candle St.)
Fir Gro. KT3: N Mald 6B 152
Firgrove Ct. SE6 7C 122
Fir Gro. Rd. SW9 2A 120
Firhill Rd. SE6 4C 140
Fir Ho. W10 4G 81
(off Droop St.)
Firle Ho. W10 5E 80
(off Sutton Way)
Firman Cl. KT3: N Mald 4A 152
Firmans Ct. E17 4F 51
Fir Rd. SM3: Sutt 1H 165
Fir Rd. TW13: Hanw 5B 130
Firs, The SE26 Border Rd. 5H 139
Firs, The SE26 Waverley Ct. 5J 139
Firs, The DA15: Sidc 2K 143
Firs, The DA5: Bexl 1K 145
Firs, The E6 7C 70
Firs, The HA8: Edg 4E 28
(off Stoneyfields La.)
Firs, The IG8: Wfd G 7F 37
Firs, The N20 1G 31
Firs, The W5 5D 78
Firs Av. N10 3E 46
Firs Av. N11 6J 31
Firs Av. SW14 4J 115
Firsby Av. CR0: C'don 1K 169
Firsby Rd. N16 1G 67
Firs Cl. CR4: Mitc 2F 155
Firs Cl. N10 4E 46
Firs Cl. SE23 7A 122
Firscroft N13 3H 33
Firs Dr. TW5: Cran 7K 93
Firs Ho. N22 1A 48
(off Acacia Rd.)
Firside Gro. DA15: Sidc 1K 143
Firs La. N13 3H 33
Firs La. N21 7H 23
Firs Pk. Av. N21 1J 33
Firs Pk. Gdns. N21 1H 33
First Av. DA7: Bex 7C 108
First Av. E12 4C 70
First Av. E13 3J 87
First Av. E17 5C 50
First Av. EN1: Enf 5A 24
First Av. HA9: Wemb 2D 60
First Av. KT12: Walt T 6K 147
First Av. KT19: Ewe 7A 164
First Av. KT8: W Mole 4D 148
First Av. N18 4D 34
First Av. NW4 4E 44
First Av. RM10: Dag 2H 91
First Av. RM6: Chad H 5C 54
First Av. SW14 3A 116
First Av. UB3: Hayes 1H 93
First Av. W10 4H 81
First Av. W3 1B 98
First Central Bus. Pk. NW10 3F 79
First Cl. KT8: W Mole 3G 149
First Cross Rd. TW2: Twick 2J 131
First Dr. NW10 7J 61
First St. SW3 3D 16 (4C 100)
First Way HA9: Wemb 4H 61
Firstway SW20 2E 152
Firs Wlk. IG8: Wfd G 5D 36
Firswood Av. KT19: Ewe 5A 164
Firth Gdns. SW6 1G 117
Firth Ho. E2 3G 85
(off Turin St.)
Fir Tree Av. UB7: W Dray 3C 92
Firtree Av. CR4: Mitc 2E 154
Fir Tree Cl. BR6: Chels 5K 173
Fir Tree Cl. KT19: Ewe 4B 164
Fir Tree Cl. RM1: Rom 3K 55
Fir Tree Cl. SW16 5G 137
Fir Tree Cl. W5 6E 78
Fir Tree Gdns. CR0: C'don 4C 170
Fir Tree Gro. SM5: Cars 7D 166
Firtree Ho. SE13 7F 123
(off Birdwood Av.)
Fir Tree Pl. TW15: Ashf 5C 128
Fir Tree Rd. TW4: Houn 4C 112
Fir Trees Cl. SE16 1A 104
Fir Tree Wlk. EN1: Enf 3J 23
Fir Tree Wlk. RM10: Dag 3J 73
Fir Wlk. SM3: Cheam 6F 165
Fisher Cl. CR0: C'don 1F 169
Fisher Cl. E9 5K 67
Fisher Cl. SE16 1K 103
Fisher Cl. UB6: G'frd 3E 76
Fisher Ho. E1 7J 85
(off Cable St.)
Fisher Ho. N1 1A 84
(off Barnsbury Est.)
Fisherman Cl. TW10: Ham 4B 132
Fishermans Dr. SE16 2K 103
Fisherman's Pl. W4 6B 98
Fisherman's Wlk. E14 1C 104
Fishermans Wlk. SE28 2J 107
Fisher Rd. HA3: W'stone 2K 41
Fisher's Cl. SW16 3H 137
Fishers Ct. SE14 1K 121
Fishersdene KT10: Clay 7A 162
Fisher's La. W4 4K 97
Fisher St. E16 5J 87
Fisher St. WC1 6G 7 (5K 83)
Fishers Way DA17: Belv 1J 109
Fishers Way HA0: Wemb 5B 60
Fishers Wood Gro. BR2: Broml 7C 160
Fisherton St. NW8 4A 4 (4B 82)
Fishguard Way E16 1F 107
Fishmongers Hall Wharf EC4 3E 14 (7D 84)
(off Swan La.)
Fishponds Rd. BR2: Kes 5B 172
Fishponds Rd. SW17 4C 136
Fish St. Hill EC3 3F 15 (7D 84)
Fish Wharf EC3 3F 15 (7D 84)
Fisk Cl. TW16: Sun 6H 129
Fiske Ct. IG11: Bark 2H 89
Fiske Ct. N17 1G 49
Fiske Ct. SM2: Sutt 7A 166
Fitch Ct. SW2 5A 120
Fitch Way RM13: Rain 3K 91
Fitness4Less Canning Town 5H 87
Fitness4Less Sutton 6J 165
Fitness First Angel 1A 8 (2B 84)
Fitness First Baker Street 6F 5 (5D 82)
Fitness First Beckenham 6C 140
Fitness First Berkeley Square 3K 11 (7F 83)
Fitness First Brixton 3A 120
Fitness First Camden 1F 83
Fitness First Clapham Junction 4C 118
Fitness First Covent Garden 3F 13 (7J 83)
(off Bedford St.)
Fitness First Fetter Lane 1K 13 (6A 84)
(off Fetter La.)
Fitness First Gracechurch Street 2G 15 (7E 84)
(off Gracechurch St.)
Fitness First Great Marlborough Street 1A 12 (6G 83)
(off Gt. Marlborough St.)
Fitness First Hammersmith 4E 98
Fitness First Harringay 6B 48
(off Arena Shop. Pk.)
Fitness First High Holborn 7G 7 (6K 83)
(off High Holborn)
Fitness First Highbury 3B 66
Fitness First Ilford 2G 71
Fitness First Kilburn 1H 81
Fitness First Kingly Street 2A 12 (7G 83)
(off Kingly St.)
Fitness First Leyton Mills 3E 68
Fitness First London Bridge 5F 15 (1D 102)
(off London Bri. St.)
Fitness First London Bridge, Cottons 4G 15 (1E 102)
(off Tooley St.)
Fitness First Paternoster Square 7B 8 (6B 84)
(off Paternoster Sq.)
Fitness First Queen Victoria Street 2C 14 (7C 84)
(off Queen Victoria St.)
Fitness First Streatham 2J 137
Fitness First Thomas More Square 7G 85
(off Thomas More Sq.)
Fitness First Tooting Bec 3E 136
Fittleton Gdns. E3 4D 86
Fitzalan Rd. N3 3G 45
Fitzalan St. SE11 3J 19 (4A 102)
Fitzclarence Ho. W11 2G 99
(off Holland Park Av.)
Fitzgeorge Av. KT3: N Mald 1K 151
Fitzgeorge Av. W14 4G 99
Fitzgerald Av. SW14 3A 116
Fitzgerald Ct. E10 1D 68
(off Leyton Grange Est.)
Fitzgerald Ho. E14 6D 86
(off E. India Dock Rd.)
Fitzgerald Ho. SW17 3B 136
Fitzgerald Ho. SW9 2A 120
Fitzgerald Ho. UB3: Hayes 1K 93
Fitzgerald Rd. E11 5J 51
Fitzgerald Rd. KT7: T Ditt 6A 150
Fitzgerald Rd. SW14 3K 115
Fitzhardinge Ho. W1 7G 5 (6E 82)
(off Portman Sq.)
Fitzhardinge St. W1 7G 5 (6E 82)
Fitzherbert Cl. IG8: Ilf 1C 52
Fitzherbert Cl. IG8: Wfd G 1C 52
Fitzherbert Wlk. UB1: S'hall 2H 95
Fitzhugh Gro. SW18 6B 118
Fitzjames Av. CR0: C'don 2G 169
Fitzjames Av. W14 4G 99
Fitzjohn Av. EN5: Barn 5B 20
Fitzjohn's Av. NW3 4A 64
Fitzmaurice Ho. SE16 4H 103
(off Rennie Est.)
Fitzmaurice Pl. W1 4K 11 (1F 101)
Fitzneal St. W12 6B 80
Fitzpatrick Rd. SW9 1B 120

222 A–Z London

Fitzrovia Apts. – Fortrose Cl.

Fitzrovia Apts. W1 ... 4K 5 (4F 83)
(off Bolsover St.)
FITZROY BRI. ... 1E 82
Fitzroy Bus. Pk. BR5: St P ... 7D 144
Fitzroy Cl. N6 ... 1D 64
Fitzroy Ct. CR0: C'don ... 7D 156
Fitzroy Ct. N6 ... 6G 47
Fitzroy Ct. W1 ... 4B 6 (4G 83)
(off Tottenham Ct. Rd.)
Fitzroy Cres. W4 ... 7K 97
Fitzroy Gdns. SE19 ... 7E 138
Fitzroy Ho. E14 ... 5B 86
(off Wallwood St.)
Fitzroy Ho. SE1 ... 5F 103
(off Cooper's Rd.)
Fitzroy House Mus. ... 4A 6 (4G 83)
Fitzroy M. W1 ... 4A 6 (4G 83)
(off Cleveland St.)
Fitzroy Pk. N6 ... 1D 64
Fitzroy Rd. NW1 ... 1E 82
Fitzroy Sq. W1 ... 4A 6 (4G 83)
Fitzroy St. W1 ... 4A 6 (4G 83)
(not continuous)
Fitzroy Yd. NW1 ... 1E 82
Fitzstephen Rd. RM8: Dag ... 5B 72
Fitzwarren Gdns. N19 ... 1G 65
Fitzwilliam Av. TW9: Rich ... 2F 115
Fitzwilliam Cl. N20 ... 1K 31
Fitzwilliam Hgts. SE23 ... 2J 139
Fitzwilliam Ho. TW9: Rich ... 4D 114
Fitzwilliam M. E16 ... 1J 105
Fitzwilliam Rd. SW4 ... 3G 119
Fitz Wygram Cl. TW12: Hamp H ... 5G 131
Five Acre NW9 ... 2B 44
Fiveacre Cl. CR7: Thor H ... 6A 156
Five Arches Bus. Pk. DA14: Sidc ... 5D 144
Five Bell All. E14 ... 6B 86
(off Three Colt St.)
Five Elms BR2: Hayes ... 3K 171
Five Elms Rd. BR2: Hayes ... 3K 171
Five Elms Rd. RM9: Dag ... 3F 73
Five Oaks M. BR1: Broml ... 3J 141
Fives Ct. SE11 ... 3B 102
FIVEWAYS New Eltham ... 2F 143
Five Ways Bus. Cen. TW13: Felt ... 3K 129
FIVEWAYS CORNER Croydon ... 4A 168
FIVEWAYS CORNER Hendon ... 1C 44
Fiveways Rd. SW9 ... 2A 120
Fixie Bldg. E17 ... 5B 50
(off Track St.)
Flack Ct. E10 ... 7D 50
Fladbury Rd. N15 ... 6D 48
Fladgate Rd. E11 ... 6G 51
Flag Cl. CR0: C'don ... 1K 169
Flagon Ct. CR0: C'don ... 4C 168
(off St Andrew's Rd.)
Flagship Ho. E16 ... 2K 105
(off Royal Crest Av.)
Flag Wlk. HA5: Eastc ... 6J 39
Flambard Rd. HA1: Harr ... 6A 42
Flamborough Ho. SE15 ... 1G 121
(off Clayton Rd.)
Flamborough Rd. HA4: Ruis ... 3J 57
Flamborough St. E14 ... 6A 86
Flamborough Wlk. E14 ... 6A 86
(off Flamborough St.)
Flamingo Ct. SE17 ... 5C 102
(off Crampton St.)
Flamingo Ct. SE8 ... 7C 104
(off Hamilton St.)
Flamingo Gdns. UB5: N'olt ... 3C 76
Flamstead Gdns. RM9: Dag ... 7C 72
Flamstead Ho. SW3 ... 5C 16 (5C 100)
(off Cale St.)
Flamstead Rd. RM9: Dag ... 7C 72
Flamsted Av. HA9: Wemb ... 6G 61
Flamsteed Rd. SE7 ... 5C 106
Flanaghan Apts. E3 ... 4B 86
(off Portia Way)
Flanchford Rd. W12 ... 3B 98
Flanders Ct. E17 ... 7A 50
Flanders Cres. SW17 ... 7D 136
Flanders Mans. W4 ... 4B 98
Flanders Rd. E6 ... 2D 88
Flanders Rd. W4 ... 4A 98
Flanders Way E9 ... 6K 67
Flandrian Cl. EN3: Enf L ... 1J 25
Flank St. E1 ... 2K 15 (7G 85)
Flannery Ct. SE16 ... 3H 103
Flansham Ho. E14 ... 6B 86
(off Clemence St.)
Flask Wlk. NW3 ... 4A 64
Flatford Ho. SE6 ... 4E 140
Flather Cl. SW16 ... 5G 137
Flat Iron Sq. SE1 ... 5D 14 (1C 102)
(off Southwark Bri. Rd.)
Flatiron Yd. SE1 ... 5D 14 (1C 102)
(off Ayres St.)
Flavell M. SE10 ... 5G 105
Flaxen Cl. E4 ... 3J 35
Flaxen Rd. E4 ... 3J 35
Flaxley Ho. SW1 ... 5J 17 (5F 101)
(part of Abbots Mnr.)
Flaxley Rd. SM4: Mord ... 7K 153
Flaxman Ct. DA17: Belv ... 5G 109
(off Hoddesdon Rd.)
Flaxman Ct. W1 ... 1C 12 (6H 83)
Flaxman Ct. WC1 ... 2D 6 (3H 83)
(off Flaxman Ter.)
Flaxman Ho. SE1 ... 3B 102
(off London Rd.)
Flaxman Ho. W4 ... 5A 98
(off Devonshire St.)
Flaxman Rd. SE5 ... 3B 120
Flaxman Sports Cen. ... 2C 120
Flaxman Ter. WC1 ... 2D 6 (3H 83)
Flaxton Rd. SE18 ... 1H 125
Flecker Cl. HA7: Stan ... 5E 26
Flecker Ho. SE5 ... 7D 102
(off Lomond Gro.)
Fleece Dr. N9 ... 4B 34
Fleece Rd. KT6: Surb ... 1C 162
Fleece Wlk. N7 ... 6J 65
Fleeming Cl. E17 ... 2B 50
Fleeming Rd. E17 ... 2B 50
Fleetbank Ho. EC4 ... 1K 13 (6A 84)
(off Salisbury Sq.)
Fleet Cl. HA4: Ruis ... 6E 38
Fleet Cl. KT8: W Mole ... 5D 148
Fleetfield WC1 ... 1F 7 (3J 83)
(off Birkenhead St.)
Fleet Ho. E14 ... 7A 86
(off Victory Pl.)
Fleet La. KT8: W Mole ... 6D 148
Fleet Pl. EC4 ... 7A 8 (6B 84)
Fleet Rd. IG11: Bark ... 1F 89
Fleet Rd. NW3 ... 5C 64
Fleetside KT8: W Mole ... 5D 148
Fleet Sq. WC1 ... 2G 7 (3K 83)
Fleet St. EC4 ... 1J 13 (6A 84)
Fleetway WC1 ... 1F 7 (3J 83)
(off Birkenhead St.)
Fleetway W. UB6: G'frd ... 2B 78
Fleetwood Cl. CR0: C'don ... 3F 169
Fleetwood Cl. E16 ... 5B 88
Fleetwood Cl. KT9: Chess ... 7D 162
Fleetwood Ct. E6 ... 5D 88
(off Evelyn Dennington Rd.)
Fleetwood Ct. TW19: Stanw ... 6A 110
(off Douglas Rd.)
Fleetwood Rd. KT1: King T ... 3H 151
Fleetwood Rd. NW10 ... 5C 62
Fleetwood Sq. KT1: King T ... 3H 151
Fleetwood St. N16 ... 2E 66
Fleming N8 ... 3J 47
(off Boyton Cl.)
Fleming Cl. SW10 ... 7A 16 (6A 100)
(off Winterton Pl.)
Fleming Cl. W9 ... 4J 81
Fleming Ct. CR0: Wadd ... 5A 168
Fleming Ct. W2 ... 5A 4 (5B 82)
(off St Mary's Sq.)
Fleming Dr. N21 ... 5E 22
Fleming Ho. HA9: Wemb ... 3J 61
(off Barnhill Rd.)
Fleming Ho. N4 ... 1C 66
Fleming Ho. SE16 ... 2G 103
(off George Row)
Fleming Ho. SW17 ... 3B 136
Fleming Lodge W9 ... 5J 81
(off Admiral Wlk.)
Fleming Mead CR4: Mitc ... 7C 136
Fleming M. IG11: Bark ... 2H 89
Fleming Rd. SE17 ... 6B 102
Fleming Rd. UB1: S'hall ... 6F 77
Fleming St. IG11: Bark ... 2H 89
Fleming Wlk. NW9 ... 3A 44
Fleming Way SE28 ... 7D 90
Fleming Way TW7: Isle ... 4K 113
Flemming Av. HA4: Ruis ... 1K 57
Flempton Rd. E10 ... 1A 68
Fletcher Bldgs. WC2 ... 1F 13 (6J 83)
(off Martlett Ct.)
Fletcher Cl. E6 ... 6F 89
Fletcher Ct. NW9 ... 3A 44
Fletcher Ho. N1 ... 1E 84
(off Nuttall St.)
Fletcher Ho. SE15 ... 7J 103
(off Clifton Way)
Fletcher La. E10 ... 7E 50
Fletcher Path SE8 ... 7C 104
Fletcher Rd. W4 ... 3J 97
Fletchers Cl. BR2: Broml ... 4K 159
Fletcher St. E1 ... 7G 85
Fletching Apts. E3 ... 4B 86
(off Siyah Gdn.)
Fletching Rd. E5 ... 3J 67
Fletching Rd. SE7 ... 6A 106
Fletton Rd. N11 ... 7D 32
Fleur de Lis St. E1 ... 4J 9 (4F 85)
Fleur Gates SW19 ... 7F 117
Flexmere Gdns. N17 ... 1D 48
Flexmere Rd. N17 ... 1D 48
Flight App. NW9 ... 2B 44
Flight Ho. N1 ... 1E 84
(off Phillipp St.)
Flimwell Cl. BR1: Broml ... 5G 141
Flinders Ho. E1 ... 1H 103
(off Green Bank)
Flint Cl. BR6: Chels ... 6K 173
Flint Cl. CR0: C'don ... 6K 155
Flint Cl. E15 ... 7H 69
Flintlock Cl. E1 ... 6H 85
Flintlock Cl. TW19: Stanw M ... 7B 174
Flintmill Cres. SE3 ... 2C 124
Flinton St. SE17 ... 5E 102
Flint St. SE17 ... 4D 102
Flip Out Brent Cross ... 1D 62
Flip Out East Ham ... 1C 88
Flip Out Wandsworth ... 1K 135
Flitcroft St. WC2 ... 1D 12 (6H 83)
Flitton Ho. N1 ... 7B 66
(off The Sutton Est.)
Floathaven Cl. SE28 ... 1A 108
Flock Mill Pl. SW18 ... 1K 135
Flockton St. SE16 ... 2G 103
Flodden Rd. SE5 ... 1C 120
Flood La. TW1: Twick ... 1A 132
Flood Pas. SE18 ... 3C 106
Flood St. SW3 ... 6D 16 (5C 100)
Flood Wlk. SW3 ... 7D 16 (6C 100)
Flora Cl. E14 ... 6D 86
Flora Cl. HA7: Stan ... 3K 27
Flora Gdns. RM6: Chad H ... 6C 54
Flora Gdns. W6 ... 4D 98
(off Albion Gdns.)
Flora Ho. E3 ... 1C 86
(off Garrison Rd.)
Floral Ct. WC2 ... 2E 12 (7J 83)
Floral Pl. N1 ... 5D 66
Floral St. WC2 ... 2E 12 (7J 83)
Flora St. DA17: Belv ... 5F 109
Florence Av. EN2: Enf ... 3H 23
Florence Av. SM4: Mord ... 5A 154
Florence Cantwell Wlk. N19 ... 7J 47
(off Jessie Blythe La.)
Florence Cl. KT12: Walt T ... 7K 147
Florence Cl. KT2: King T ... 5F 133
Florence Ct. E11 ... 4K 51
Florence Ct. N1 ... 7B 66
(off Florence St.)
Florence Ct. SW19 ... 6G 135
Florence Ct. W9 ... 3A 82
(off Maida Vale)
Florence Dr. EN2: Enf ... 3H 23
Florence Elson Cl. E12 ... 4E 70
Florence Gdns. RM6: Chad H ... 7C 54
Florence Gdns. W4 ... 6J 97
Florence Ho. KT2: King T ... 7F 133
(off Florence Rd)
Florence Ho. SE16 ... 5H 103
(off Rotherhithe New Rd.)
Florence Ho. W11 ... 7F 81
(off St Ann's Rd.)
Florence Mans. NW4 ... 5D 44
(off Vivian Av.)
Florence Mans. SW6 ... 1H 117
(off Rostrevor Rd.)
Florence Nightingale Mus. ... 7H 13 (2K 101)
Florence Rd. BR1: Broml ... 1J 159
Florence Rd. BR3: Beck ... 2A 158
Florence Rd. E13 ... 2J 87
Florence Rd. E6 ... 1A 88
Florence Rd. KT12: Walt T ... 7K 147
Florence Rd. KT2: King T ... 7F 133
Florence Rd. N4 ... 7K 47
(not continuous)
Florence Rd. SE14 ... 1B 122
Florence Rd. SE2 ... 4C 108
Florence Rd. SW19 ... 6K 135
Florence Rd. TW13: Felt ... 1K 129
Florence Rd. UB2: S'hall ... 4B 94
Florence Rd. W4 ... 3K 97
Florence Rd. W5 ... 7E 78
Florence Root Ho. IG4: Ilf ... 5C 52
Florence Sq. E3 ... 4D 86
Florence St. E16 ... 4H 87
Florence St. N1 ... 7B 66
Florence St. NW4 ... 4E 44
Florence Ter. SE14 ... 1B 122
Florence Ter. SW15 ... 3A 134
Florence Way SW12 ... 1D 136
Florey Lodge W9 ... 5J 81
(off Admiral Wlk.)
Florey Sq. N21 ... 5E 22
Florfield Pas. E8 ... 6H 67
(off Reading La.)
Florfield Rd. E8 ... 6H 67
Florian SE5 ... 1E 120
Florian Av. SM1: Sutt ... 4B 166
Florian Ct. E16 ... 5J 87
(off Hastings Rd.)
Florian Rd. SW15 ... 4G 117
Florida Cl. WD23: B Hea ... 2C 26
Florida Ct. BR2: Broml ... 4H 159
(off Westmoreland Rd.)
Florida Rd. CR7: Thor H ... 1B 156
Florida St. E2 ... 3G 85
Florin Ct. EC1 ... 5C 8 (5C 84)
(off Charterhouse Sq.)
Florin Ct. N18 ... 4K 33
Florin Ct. SE1 ... 7J 15 (2F 103)
(off Tanner St.)
Floris Pl. SW4 ... 3G 119
Floriston Av. UB10: Hil ... 7E 56
Floriston Cl. HA7: Stan ... 1B 42
Floriston Ct. UB5: N'olt ... 5F 59
Floriston Gdns. HA7: Stan ... 1B 42
Florys Ct. SW19 ... 1G 135
Floss St. SW15 ... 2E 116
Flotilla Ho. E16 ... 2K 105
(off Cable St.)
Flotilla Ho. SW18 ... 3A 118
Flounder Ho. SE8 ... 7D 104
(off Creative Rd.)
Flower & Dean Wlk. E1 ... 6K 9 (5F 85)
Flowerdown Ct. HA4: Eastc ... 6J 39
(off Lidgould Gro.)
Flower La. NW7 ... 5G 29
Flower M. NW11 ... 6G 45
Flower Pot Cl. N15 ... 6F 49
Flowers Av. HA4: Eastc ... 6J 39
Flowers Av. HA4: Ruis ... 6J 39
Flowers Cl. NW2 ... 3C 62
Flowersmead SW17 ... 2E 136
Flowers M. N19 ... 2G 65
Flower Wlk., The SW7 ... 2A 100
Floyd Rd. SE7 ... 5A 106
Floyer Cl. TW10: Rich ... 5F 115
Fludyer St. SE13 ... 4G 123
Flutemakers M. SW4 ... 5H 119
Flying Angel Ho. E16 ... 7K 87
(off Victoria Dock Rd.)
Flynn Ct. E14 ... 7C 86
(off Garford St.)
Foley Ho. E1 ... 6J 85
(off Tarling St.)
Foley St. W1 ... 6A 6 (5G 83)
Folgate St. E1 ... 5H 9 (5E 84)
(not continuous)
Foliot Ho. N1 ... 2K 83
(off Priory Grn. Est.)
Foliot St. W12 ... 6B 80
Folkestone Ct. UB5: N'olt ... 5F 59
(off Newmarket Av.)
Folkestone Ho. SE17 ... 5E 102
(off Upnor Way)
Folkestone Rd. E17 ... 4D 50
Folkestone Rd. E6 ... 2E 88
Folkestone Rd. N18 ... 4B 34
Folkingham La. NW9 ... 1K 43
Folkington Cnr. N12 ... 5C 30
Folland NW9 ... 2B 44
(off Hundred Acre)
Follett Ho. SW10 ... 7B 100
(off Worlds End Est.)
Follett St. E14 ... 6E 86
Follingham Ct. N1 ... 1H 9 (3E 84)
(off Drysdale Pl.)
Folly Brook & Darland's Lake Nature Reserve ... 3B 30
Folly La. E17 ... 1A 50
Folly La. E4 ... 6G 35
Folly M. W11 ... 6H 81
Folly Wall E14 ... 2E 104
Fonda Ct. E14 ... 7C 86
(off Premiere Pl.)
Fondant Ct. E3 ... 2D 86
(off Taylor Pl.)
Fontaine Ho. E17 ... 4C 50
(off Hoe St.)
Fontaine Rd. SW16 ... 7K 137
Fontarabia Rd. SW11 ... 4E 118
Fontayne Av. RM1: Rom ... 2K 55
Fontenelle SE5 ... 1E 120
Fontenoy Ho. SE11 ... 4B 102
(off Kennington La.)
Fontenoy Rd. SW12 ... 2F 137
Fonteyne Gdns. IG8: Wfd G ... 2B 52
Fonthill Cl. SE20 ... 2G 157
Fonthill Ho. SW1 ... 5K 17 (5F 101)
(part of Abbots Mnr.)
Fonthill Ho. W14 ... 3G 99
(off Russell Rd.)
Fonthill M. N4 ... 2K 65
Fonthill Rd. N4 ... 1K 65
Font Hills N2 ... 2A 46
Fontley Way SW15 ... 7C 116
Fontmell Cl. TW15: Ashf ... 5C 128
Fontmell Pk. TW15: Ashf ... 5B 128
Fontwell Cl. HA3: Hrw W ... 7D 26
Fontwell Cl. UB5: N'olt ... 6E 58
Fontwell Dr. BR2: Broml ... 5E 160
Football La. HA1: Harr ... 1K 59
Footpath, The SW15 ... 6C 116
FOOTS CRAY ... 6C 144
Foots Cray High St. DA14: Sidc ... 6C 144
Foots Cray La. DA14: Sidc ... 1C 144
Foots Cray Meadows ... 4D 144
Footscray Rd. SE9 ... 6E 124
Forber Ho. E2 ... 3J 85
(off Cornwall Av.)
Forbes Cl. NW2 ... 3C 62
Forbes Ho. E7 ... 5A 70
(off Romford Rd.)
Forbes Ho. W4 ... 5G 97
(off Stonehill Rd.)
Forbes St. E1 ... 6G 85
Forbes Way HA4: Ruis ... 2K 57
Forburg Rd. N16 ... 1G 67
Forbury Rd. SE13 ... 3G 123
Fordbridge Ct. TW15: Ashf ... 6A 128
Fordbridge Pk. TW16: Sun ... 6H 147
Fordbridge Rd. TW15: Ashf ... 6A 128
Fordbridge Rd. TW16: Sun ... 6G 147
Fordbridge Rd. TW17: Shep ... 6G 147
FORDBRIDGE RDBT. ... 6A 128
Ford Cl. CR7: Thor H ... 5B 156
Ford Cl. E3 ... 2A 86
Ford Cl. HA1: Harr ... 7H 41
Ford Cl. TW15: Ashf ... 6A 128
Ford Cl. TW17: Shep ... 4C 146
Forde Av. BR1: Broml ... 3A 160
Fordel Rd. SE6 ... 1E 140
Ford End IG8: Wfd G ... 6E 36
Fordgate Bus. Pk. DA17: Belv ... 2J 109
Fordham KT1: King T ... 2G 151
(off Excelsior Cl.)
Fordham Cl. EN4: Cockf ... 3H 21
Fordham Cl. KT4: Wor Pk ... 1D 164
Fordham Ho. SE14 ... 7A 104
(off Angus St.)
Fordham Rd. EN4: Cockf ... 3G 21
Fordham St. E1 ... 6G 85
Fordhook Av. W5 ... 1F 97
Ford Ho. EN5: New Bar ... 5E 20
Fordie Ho. SW1 ... 2F 17 (3D 100)
(off Sloane St.)
Ford Ind. Pk. RM9: Dag ... 4H 91
Fordingley Rd. W9 ... 3H 81
Fordington Ho. SE26 ... 3G 139
Fordington Rd. N6 ... 5D 46
Ford Lodge RM7: Rom ... 4K 55
Fordmill Rd. SE6 ... 2C 140
Ford Rd. E3 ... 2B 86
Ford Rd. RM10: Dag ... 7G 73
Ford Rd. RM9: Dag ... 7F 73
Ford Rd. TW15: Ashf ... 4B 128
Fords Gro. N21 ... 1H 33
Fords Pk. Rd. E16 ... 5J 87
Fords Pl. HA6: Nwood ... 2J 39
Ford Sq. E1 ... 5H 85
Ford St. E16 ... 6H 87
Ford St. E3 ... 1A 86
Fordview Ind. Est. RM13: Rain ... 3K 91
Fordwich Cl. BR6: Orp ... 7K 161
Fordwych Rd. NW2 ... 4G 63
Fordyce Rd. SE13 ... 6E 122
Fordyke Rd. RM8: Dag ... 2F 73
Foreign St. SE5 ... 2B 120
Foreland Ct. NW4 ... 1F 45
Foreland Ho. W11 ... 7G 81
(off Walmer Rd.)
Foreland St. SE18 ... 4H 107
Foreman Ct. TW1: Twick ... 1K 131
Foreman Ho. SE4 ... 4K 121
(off Billingford Cl.)
Foreshore SE8 ... 4D 104
Forest, The E11 ... 4G 51
Forest App. E4 ... 1B 36
Forest App. IG8: Wfd G ... 7D 36
Forest Av. E4 ... 1B 36
Forest Av. IG7: Chig ... 5K 37
Forest Bus. Pk. E10 ... 7K 49
Forest Cl. BR7: Chst ... 1E 160
Forest Cl. E11 ... 5J 51
Forest Cl. IG8: Wfd G ... 3E 36
Forest Cl. N10 ... 1F 47
Forest Cl. NW6 ... 7G 63
Forest Ct. E11 ... 4G 51
Forest Ct. E4 ... 1C 36
Forest Ct. N12 ... 5E 30
Forest Cft. SE23 ... 2H 139
FORESTDALE ... 7B 170
Forestdale N14 ... 4C 32
Forestdale Cen., The ... 7B 170
Forest Dene Ct. SM2: Sutt ... 6A 166
Forest Dr. BR2: Kes ... 4C 172
Forest Dr. BR3: Beck ... 7B 158
Forest Dr. E12 ... 3B 70
Forest Dr. IG8: Wfd G ... 7A 36
Forest Dr. TW16: Sun ... 7H 129
Forest Dr. E. E11 ... 7F 51
Forest Dr. W. E11 ... 7E 50
Forest Edge IG9: Buck H ... 4F 37
Forester Ho. E14 ... 7A 86
(off Victory Pl.)
Forester Rd. SE15 ... 3H 121
Foresters Cl. SM6: W'gton ... 7H 167
Foresters Cres. DA7: Bex ... 4H 127
Foresters Dr. E17 ... 4F 51
Foresters Dr. SM6: W'gton ... 7H 167
Forest Gdns. N17 ... 2F 49
Forest Ga. NW9 ... 4A 44
FOREST GATE ... 5J 69
Forest Gate Learning Zone ... 4J 69
(off Woodford Rd.)
Forest Ga. Retreat E7 ... 5J 69
(off Odessa Rd.)
Forest Glade E11 ... 6G 51
Forest Glade E4 ... 4B 36
Forest Gro. E8 ... 6F 67
Forest Hgts. IG9: Buck H ... 2D 36
FOREST HILL ... 2J 139
Forest Hill Bus. Cen. SE23 ... 2J 139
(off Clyde Va.)
Forest Hill Ind. Est. SE23 ... 2J 139
Forest Hill Pools ... 2J 139
Forest Hill Rd. SE22 ... 5H 121
Forest Hill Rd. SE23 ... 6J 121
Forest Hill School Sports Cen. ... 3K 139
Forestholme Cl. SE23 ... 2J 139
Forest Ind. Pk. IG6: Ilf ... 1J 53
Forest La. E15 ... 5G 69
Forest La. E7 ... 5H 69
Forest La. IG7: Chig ... 5K 37
Forest Lodge SE23 ... 3J 139
(off Dartmouth Rd.)
Forest Mt. Rd. IG8: Wfd G ... 7A 36
Forest Point E7 ... 5K 69
(off Windsor Rd.)
Fore St. EC2 ... 6D 8 (5C 84)
Fore St. HA5: Eastc ... 4H 39
Fore St. N18 ... 6A 34
Fore St. N9 ... 4B 34
Fore St. Av. EC2 ... 6E 8 (5D 84)
Forest Ridge BR2: Kes ... 4C 172
Forest Ridge BR3: Beck ... 3C 158
Forest Ri. E17 ... 3F 51
Forest Rd. E11 ... 7F 51
Forest Rd. E17 ... 3D 50
Forest Rd. E7 ... 4J 69
Forest Rd. E8 ... 6F 67
Forest Rd. IG6: Chig ... 2H 53
Forest Rd. IG6: Ilf ... 2H 53
Forest Rd. IG8: Wfd G ... 3D 36
Forest Rd. N17 ... 4J 49
Forest Rd. N9 ... 1C 34
Forest Rd. RM7: Mawney ... 3H 55
Forest Rd. SM3: Sutt ... 1J 165
Forest Rd. TW13: Felt ... 2A 130
Forest Rd. TW9: Kew ... 7G 97
Forest Side E4 ... 1C 36
Forest Side E7 ... 4K 69
Forest Side IG9: Buck H ... 1F 37
Forest Side KT4: Wor Pk ... 1B 164
Forest St. E7 ... 5J 69
Forest Ter. IG7: Chig ... 5K 37
Forest Trad. Est. E17 ... 3K 49
Forest Vw. E11 ... 7H 51
Forest Vw. E4 ... 7K 25
Forest Vw. Av. E10 ... 5F 51
Forest Vw. Rd. E12 ... 4C 70
Forest Vw. Rd. E17 ... 1E 50
Forest Wlk. N10 Bounds Grn. ... 1F 47
Forest Way BR5: St M Cry ... 5K 161
Forest Way DA15: Sidc ... 7H 125
Forest Way IG8: Wfd G ... 4E 36
Forest Way N19 ... 2G 65
Forfar Rd. N22 ... 1B 48
Forfar Rd. SW11 ... 1E 118
Forge Cl. BR2: Hayes ... 1J 171
Forge Cl. UB3: Harl ... 6F 93
Forge Cotts. W5 ... 1D 96
Forge Dr. KT10: Clay ... 7A 162
Forge La. HA6: Nwood ... 1G 39
Forge La. SM3: Cheam ... 7G 165
Forge La. TW10: Ham ... 1E 132
Forge La. TW13: Hanw ... 5C 130
Forge La. TW16: Sun ... 3J 147
Forge M. CR0: Addtn ... 5C 170
Forge M. TW16: Sun ... 3J 147
(off Forge La.)
Forge Pl. NW1 ... 6E 64
Forge Sq. E14 ... 4D 104
Forlong Path UB5: N'olt ... 6C 58
(off Cowings Mead)
Forman Pl. N16 ... 4F 67
Formation, The E16 ... 2F 107
(off Woolwich Mnr. Way)
Formby Av. HA7: Stan ... 3C 42
Formby Ct. N7 ... 5A 66
(off Morgan Rd.)
Formosa Ho. E1 ... 4A 86
(off Ernest St.)
Formosa St. W9 ... 4K 81
Formunt Cl. E16 ... 5H 87
Forres Gdns. NW11 ... 6J 45
Forrester Path SE26 ... 4J 139
Forresters Apts. IG11: Bark ... 7G 71
(off Linton Rd.)
Forrester Way E15 ... 6F 69
Forrest Gdns. SW16 ... 3K 155
Forris Av. UB3: Hayes ... 1H 93
Forset Ct. W2 ... 7D 4 (6C 82)
(off Edgware Rd.)
Forset St. W1 ... 7D 4 (6C 82)
(not continuous)
Forstal Cl. BR2: Broml ... 3J 159
Forster Cl. IG8: Wfd G ... 7A 36
Forster Ho. BR1: Broml ... 4F 141
Forster Ho. SW17 ... 3B 136
(off Grosvenor Way)
Forster Rd. BR3: Beck ... 3A 158
Forster Rd. E17 ... 6A 50
Forster Rd. N17 ... 3F 49
Forster Rd. SW2 ... 7J 119
Forsters Cl. RM6: Chad H ... 6F 55
Forsters Way UB4: Yead ... 6K 75
Forston Apts. SW11 ... 4C 118
(off Monarch Square)
Forston St. N1 ... 2C 84
Forsyte Cres. SE19 ... 1E 156
Forsyte Ho. SW3 ... 6D 16 (5C 100)
(off Chelsea Mnr. St.)
Forsythe Shades Ct. BR3: Beck ... 1E 158
Forsyth Gdns. SE17 ... 6B 102
Forsyth Ho. E9 ... 7J 67
(off Frampton Pk. Rd.)
Forsyth Ho. SW1 ... 5B 18 (5G 101)
(off Tachbrook St.)
Forsythia Cl. IG1: Ilf ... 5F 71
Forsyth Pl. EN1: Enf ... 5K 23
Forterie Gdns. IG3: Bark ... 3A 72
Forterie Gdns. IG3: Ilf ... 3A 72
Fortescue Av. E8 ... 7H 67
Fortescue Av. TW2: Twick ... 3G 131
Fortescue Rd. HA8: Edg ... 1K 43
Fortescue Rd. SW19 ... 7B 136
Fortess Gro. NW5 ... 5G 65
Fortess Rd. NW5 ... 5F 65
Fortess Wlk. NW5 ... 5F 65
Fortess Yd. NW5 ... 4F 65
Forte St. SE18 ... 1C 124
(off Tellson Av.)
Forthbridge Rd. SW11 ... 4E 118
Forth Ho. E3 ... 2B 86
(off Tredegar Rd.)
Fortis Cl. E16 ... 6A 88
Fortis Ct. N10 ... 3E 46
FORTIS GREEN ... 4D 46
Fortis Grn. N10 ... 3E 46
Fortis Grn. N2 ... 4C 46
Fortis Grn. Av. N2 ... 3D 46
Fortis Grn. Rd. N10 ... 3E 46
Fortismere Av. N10 ... 3E 46
Fortius Apts. E3 ... 2C 86
(off Tredegar La.)
Fortius Wlk. E20 ... 6E 68
Fortnam Rd. N19 ... 2H 65
Fortnum's Acre HA7: Stan ... 6E 26
Fort Rd. SE1 ... 4F 103
Fort Rd. UB5: N'olt ... 7E 58
Fortrose Cl. E14 ... 6F 87

A–Z London 223

Frimley Rd. – Garland Ho.

Frimley Rd. IG3: Ilf 3J 71
Frimley Rd. KT9: Chess 5D 162
Frimley St. E1 4K 85
(off Frimley Way)
Frimley Way E1 4K 85
Fringewood Cl. HA6: Nwood 1D 38
Frinstead Ho. W10 7F 81
(off Freston Rd.)
Frinsted Rd. DA8: Erith 7K 109
Frinton Ct. W13 5B 78
(off Hardwick Grn.)
Frinton Dr. IG8: Wfd G 7A 36
Frinton M. IG2: Ilf 6E 52
Frinton Rd. DA14: Sidc 2E 144
Frinton Rd. E6 3B 88
Frinton Rd. N15 6E 48
Frinton Rd. SW17 6E 136
Friston St. SW6 2K 117
Friswell Pl. DA6: Bex 4G 127
Fritham Cl. KT3: N Mald 6A 152
Frith Ct. NW7 7B 30
Frith Ho. NW8 4B 4 (4B 82)
(off Frampton St.)
Frith La. NW7 7B 30
Frith Rd. CR0: C'don 2C 168
Frith Rd. E11 4E 68
Frith St. W1 1C 12 (6H 83)
Frithville Ct. W12 1E 98
(off Frithville Gdns.)
Frithville Gdns. W12 1E 98
Frizlands La. RM10: Dag 2H 73
Frobisher Cl. HA5: Pinn 7B 40
Frobisher Ct. NW9 2A 44
Frobisher Ct. SE10 6F 105
(off Old Woolwich Rd.)
Frobisher Ct. SE23 2H 139
Frobisher Ct. SE8 5A 104
(off Evelyn St.)
Frobisher Ct. SM3: Cheam 7G 165
Frobisher Ct. W12 2E 98
(off Lime Gro.)
Frobisher Cres. EC2 5D 8 (5C 84)
(off Silk St.)
Frobisher Cres. TW19: Stanw 7A 110
Frobisher Gdns. E10 7D 50
Frobisher Gdns. TW19: Stanw 7A 110
Frobisher Ho. E1 1H 103
(off Watts St.)
Frobisher Ho. SW1 7C 18 (6H 101)
(off Dolphin Sq.)
Frobisher M. EN2: Enf 4J 23
Frobisher Pas. E14 1C 104
Frobisher Pl. SE15 1J 121
Frobisher Rd. E6 6D 88
Frobisher Rd. N8 4A 48
Frobisher St. SE10 6G 105
Frobisher Yd. E16 7G 89
Froebel Coll. 6B 116
Frog La. RM13: Rain 6K 91
Frogley Rd. SE22 4F 121
Frogmore SW18 5J 117
Frogmore Av. UB4: Hayes 4G 75
Frogmore Cl. SM3: Cheam 3F 165
Frogmore Ct. UB2: S'hall 4D 94
Frogmore Gdns. SM3: Cheam 4G 165
Frogmore Gdns. UB4: Hayes 4G 75
Frogmore Ind. Est. N5 5C 66
Frogmore Ind. Est. NW10 3J 79
Frogmore Ind. Est. UB3: Hayes 2G 93
Frognal NW3 4A 64
Frognal Av. DA14: Sidc 6A 144
Frognal Av. HA1: Harr 4K 41
Frognal Cl. NW3 5A 64
FROGNAL CORNER 6K 143
Frognal Ct. NW3 6A 64
Frognal Gdns. NW3 4A 64
Frognal La. NW3 5K 63
Frognal Pde. NW3 6A 64
Frognal Pl. DA14: Sidc 6A 144
Frognal Ri. NW3 3A 64
Frognal Way NW3 4A 64
Frogwell Cl. N15 6D 48
Froissart Rd. SE9 5B 124
Frome Ho. SE15 4H 121
Frome Rd. N22 3B 48
Frome St. N1 2C 84
Fromondes Rd. SM3: Cheam 5G 165
Fromows Cnr. W4 5J 97
Frontenac NW10 7D 62
Frontier Works N17 6K 33
Frost Ct. NW9 2A 44
(off Salk Cl.)
Frostic Wlk. E1 6K 9 (5G 85)
Froude St. SW8 2F 119
Fruen Rd. TW14: Felt 7H 111
Fryatt Rd. N17 7J 33
(not continuous)
Fryday Gro. M. SW12 7G 119
(off Weir Rd.)
Frye Ct. E3 3B 86
(off Benworth St.)
Frye Ho. E20 6E 68
(off Penny Brookes St.)
Fryent Cl. NW9 6G 43
Fryent Country Pk. 7G 43
Fryent Cres. NW9 6A 44
Fryent Flds. NW9 6A 44
Fryent Gro. NW9 6A 44
Fryent Way NW9 5G 43
Fryers Vw. SE4 4K 121
(off Frendsbury Rd.)
Fry Ho. E6 7A 70
Frying Pan All. E1 6J 9 (5F 85)
(off Bell La.)
Fry La. HA8: Edg 4A 28
Fry Rd. E6 7B 70
Fry Rd. NW10 1B 80
Frys Ct. SE10 6E 104
(off Durnford St.)
Fryston Av. CR0: C'don 2G 169
Fuchsia Cl. RM7: Rush G 2K 73
Fuchsia St. SE2 5B 108
Fulbeck Dr. NW9 1A 44
Fulbeck Ho. N7 6K 65
(off Sutterton St.)
Fulbeck Rd. N19 4G 65
Fulbeck Wlk. HA8: Edg 2C 28
Fulbeck Way HA2: Harr 2G 41
Fulbourn KT1: King T 2G 151
(off Eureka Rd.)
Fulbourne Rd. E17 1E 50
Fulbourne St. E1 5H 85
Fulbrook M. N19 4G 65
Fulcher Ho. N1 1E 84
(off Colville Est.)
Fulcher Ho. SE8 5B 104
Fulford Ho. KT19: Ewe 7K 163
Fulford Rd. KT19: Ewe 7K 163
Fulford St. SE16 2H 103
FULHAM 1G 117
Fulham B'way. SW6 7J 99
FULHAM BROADWAY 7J 99
Fulham B'way. Shop. Cen. 7J 99
Fulham Bus. Exchange SW6 1A 118
(off The Boulevard)
Fulham Cl. UB10: Hil 4E 74
Fulham Ct. SW6 1J 117
Fulham FC 1F 117
Fulham FC Training Ground KT3: N Mald 6C 152
Fulham High St. SW6 2G 117
Fulham Island SW6 7J 99
(off Farm La.)
Fulham Palace 2G 117
Fulham Pal. Rd. SW6 6F 99
Fulham Pal. Rd. W6 5E 98
Fulham Pk. Gdns. SW6 2H 117
Fulham Pk. Rd. SW6 2H 117
Fulham Pools Virgin Active 6G 99
Fulham Rd. SW10 7K 99
Fulham Rd. SW3 6A 16 (5B 100)
Fulham Rd. SW6 2G 117
(not continuous)
Fullbrooks Av. KT4: Wor Pk 1B 164
Fuller Cl. BR6: Chels 5K 173
Fuller Cl. E2 3K 9 (4G 85)
(off Cheshire St.)
Fuller Cl. WD23: Bush 1C 26
Fuller Ct. N8 5H 47
Fuller Rd. RM8: Dag 3B 72
Fullers Av. IG8: Wfd G 7C 36
Fullers Av. KT6: Surb 2F 163
Fullers Cl. RM5: Col R 1J 55
Fuller's Griffin Brewery 6B 98
Fullers La. RM5: Col R 1J 55
Fullers Rd. E18 7C 36
Fuller St. NW4 4E 44
Fullers Way Nth. KT6: Surb 3F 163
Fullers Way Sth. KT9: Chess 4E 162
Fuller's Wood CR0: C'don 5C 170
Fullerton Av. RM8: Dag 1E 72
Fullerton Ct. TW11: Tedd 6A 132
Fullerton Rd. CR0: C'don 7F 157
Fullerton Rd. SM5: Cars 7C 166
Fullerton Rd. SW18 5K 117
Fuller Way UB3: Harl 5H 93
Fullwell Av. IG5: Ilf 1D 52
Fullwell Av. IG6: Ilf 1F 53
FULLWELL CROSS 2G 53
FULLWELL CROSS 2H 53
Fullwell Cross Leisure Cen. 2G 53
Fullwell Pde. IG5: Ilf 1E 52
Fullwood's M. N1 1F 9 (3D 84)
Fulmar Ct. KT5: Surb 6F 151
Fulmar Ho. SE16 4K 103
(off Tawny Way)
Fulmead St. SW6 1K 117
Fulmer Cl. TW12: Hamp 5C 130
Fulmer Ho. NW8 4C 4 (4C 82)
(off Mallory St.)
Fulmer Ho. UB8: Uxb 6A 56
Fulmer Rd. E16 5B 88
Fulmer Way W13 3B 96
Fulneck Pl. E1 4J 85
Fulready Rd. E10 5F 51
Fulstone Cl. TW4: Houn 4D 112
Fulthorp Rd. SE3 2H 123
Fulton M. W2 7A 82
Fulton Rd. HA9: Wemb 3G 61
FULWELL 4H 131
Fulwell Ct. IG5: Ilf 1E 52
Fulwell Ct. UB1: S'hall 7G 77
(off Baird Av.)
Fulwell Golf Course 4H 131
Fulwell Pk. Av. TW2: Twick 2F 131
Fulwell Rd. TW11: Tedd 4H 131
Fulwood Av. HA0: Wemb 2F 79
Fulwood Cl. UB3: Hayes 6H 75
Fulwood Ct. HA3: Kenton 6A 42
Fulwood Gdns. TW1: Twick 6K 113
Fulwood Pl. WC1 6H 7 (5K 83)
Fulwood Wlk. SW19 1G 135
Funky Footprints Nature Reserve 6C 146
Furber St. W6 3D 98
Furham Feild HA5: Hat E 7A 26
Furley Ho. SE15 7G 103
(off Peckham Pk. Rd.)
Furley Rd. SE15 7G 103
Furlong Av. CR4: Mitc 3C 154
Furlong Cl. CR0: C'don 1H 169
Furlong Cl. SM6: W'gton 1F 167
Furlong Rd. N7 6A 66
Furlow Ho. NW9 3C 44
Furmage St. SW18 7K 117
Furneaux Av. SE27 5B 138
Furness Ho. SW1 5J 17 (5F 101)
(part of Abbots Mnr.)
Furness Rd. HA2: Harr 7F 41
Furness Rd. NW10 2C 80
Furness Rd. SM4: Mord 6K 153
Furness Rd. SW6 2K 117
Furnival Ct. E3 2C 86
(off Four Seasons Cl.)
Furnival Mans. W1 6A 6 (5G 83)
(off Wells St.)
Furnival St. EC4 7J 7 (6A 84)
Furrow Ho. E4 6K 35
Furrow La. E9 5J 67
Fursby Av. N3 6D 30
Fursecroft W1 7E 4 (6D 82)
(off George St.)
Furtherfield Cl. CR0: C'don 6A 156
Further Grn. Rd. SE6 7G 123
FURZEDOWN 5F 137
Furzedown Dr. SW17 5F 137
Furzedown Recreation Cen. 5F 137
Furzedown Rd. SW17 5F 137
Furze Farm Cl. RM6: Chad H 2E 54
Furzefield Cl. BR7: Chst 6F 143
Furzefield Rd. SE3 6K 105
Furzeground Way UB11: Stock P 1E 92
Furzeham Rd. UB7: W Dray 2A 92
Furze Rd. CR7: Thor H 3C 156
Furze St. E3 5C 86
Furzewood TW16: Sun 1J 147
Fusilier Mus., The 3J 15 (7F 85)
Fusiliers Way TW4: Houn 3A 112
(not continuous)
Fusion Apts. SE14 6A 104
(off Moulding La.)
Fye Foot La. EC4 2C 14 (7C 84)
(off Queen Victoria St.)
Fyfe Apts. N8 3K 47
Fyfe Way BR1: Broml 2J 159
Fyfield N4 2A 66
(off Six Acres Est.)
Fyfield Cl. BR2: Broml 4F 159
Fyfield Ct. E7 6J 69
Fyfield Ho. E6 1C 88
(off Ron Leighton Way)
Fyfield Rd. E17 3F 51
Fyfield Rd. EN1: Enf 3K 23
Fyfield Rd. IG8: Wfd G 7F 37
Fyfield Rd. SW9 3A 120
Fynes St. SW1 3C 18 (4H 101)

G

Gable Cl. HA5: Hat E 1E 40
Gable Ct. SE26 4H 139
Gable M. BR2: Broml 2C 172
Gables, The BR1: Broml 7K 141
Gables, The HA9: Wemb 3G 61
Gables, The IG11: Bark 6G 71
Gables, The N10 3E 46
(off Fortis Grn.)
Gables Av. TW15: Ashf 5B 128
Gables Cl. SE12 1J 141
Gables Cl. SE5 1E 120
Gables Lodge EN4: Had W 1F 21
Gabriel Cl. TW13: Hanw 4C 130
Gabriel Ct. E1 5A 86
(off Elsa Street)
Gabriel Ct. NW9 2A 44
Gabriel Ho. N1 1B 84
(off Islington Grn.)
Gabriel Ho. SE11 3G 19 (4K 101)
Gabriel Ho. SE16 3B 104
(off Odessa St.)
Gabrielle Cl. HA9: Wemb 3F 61
Gabrielle Ct. NW3 6B 64
Gabriel M. NW2 2H 63
Gabriel's M. BR3: Beck 1K 157
Gabriel St. SE23 7K 121
Gabriels Wharf SE1 4J 13 (1A 102)
Gad Cl. E13 3K 87
Gaddesden Av. HA9: Wemb 6F 61
Gaddesden Ho. EC1 2F 9 (3D 84)
(off Cranwood St.)
Gadebridge Ho. SW3 5C 16 (5C 100)
(off Cale St.)
Gade Cl. UB3: Hayes 1K 93
Gadesden Rd. KT19: Ewe 6J 163
Gadsbury Cl. NW9 6B 44
Gadsden Ho. W10 4G 81
(off Hazlewood Cres.)
Gadwall Cl. E16 6K 87
Gadwall Ho. NW9 6C 44
(off Perryfield Way)
Gadwall Way SE28 2H 107
Gage Brown Ho. W10 6F 81
(off Bridge Cl.)
Gage M. CR2: S Croy 5B 168
Gage Rd. E16 5G 87
Gage St. WC1 5F 7 (5J 83)
Gainford Ho. E2 3H 85
(off Ellsworth St.)
Gainford St. N1 1A 84
Gainsboro Gdns. UB6: G'frd 5J 59
Gainsborough Av. E12 5E 70
Gainsborough Cl. BR3: Beck 7C 140
Gainsborough Cl. KT10: Esh 7J 149
Gainsborough Ct. BR2: Broml 4A 160
Gainsborough Ct. KT19: Ewe 6B 164
Gainsborough Ct. N12 5E 30
Gainsborough Ct. SE16 5H 103
(off Stubbs Dr.)
Gainsborough Ct. SE21 2E 138
Gainsborough Ct. W12 2E 98
Gainsborough Ct. W4 5H 97
(off Chaseley Dr.)
Gainsborough Gdns. HA8: Edg 2F 43
Gainsborough Gdns. NW11 7H 45
Gainsborough Gdns. NW3 3B 64
Gainsborough Gdns. TW7: Isle 5H 113
Gainsborough Ho. E14 Cassilis Rd. 2C 104
(off Cassilis Rd.)
Gainsborough Ho. E14 Victory Pl. 7A 86
(off Victory Pl.)
Gainsborough Ho. EN1: Enf 5B 24
Gainsborough Ho. RM8: Dag 4B 72
(off Longbridge Rd.)
Gainsborough Ho. SW1 4D 18 (4H 101)
(off Erasmus St.)
Gainsborough Lodge HA1: Harr 5K 41
(off Hindes Rd.)
Gainsborough Mans. W14 6G 99
(off Queen's Club Gdns.)
Gainsborough M. SE26 3H 139
Gainsborough Rd. E11 7G 51
Gainsborough Rd. E15 3G 87
Gainsborough Rd. IG8: Wfd G 6H 37
Gainsborough Rd. KT3: N Mald 6K 151
Gainsborough Rd. N12 5E 30
Gainsborough Rd. RM8: Dag 4B 72
Gainsborough Rd. TW9: Rich 2F 115
Gainsborough Rd. UB4: Hayes 2E 74
Gainsborough Rd. W4 4B 98
Gainsborough Sq. DA6: Bex 3D 126
Gainsborough St. E9 6B 68
Gainsborough Studios E. N1 1D 84
(off Poole St.)
Gainsborough Studios Nth. N1 1D 84
(off Poole St.)
Gainsborough Studios Sth. N1 1D 84
(off Poole St.)
Gainsborough Studios W. N1 1D 84
(off Poole St.)
Gainsborough Ter. SM2: Sutt 7H 165
(off Belmont Ri.)
Gainsborough Twr. UB5: N'olt 2B 76
(off Academy Gdns.)
Gainsfield Ct. E11 3G 69
Gainsford Rd. E17 4B 50
Gainsford St. SE1 6J 15 (2F 103)
Gairloch Ho. NW1 7H 65
(off Stratford Vs.)
Gairloch Rd. SE5 2E 120
Gaisford St. NW5 6G 65
Gaitskell Ct. SW11 2C 118
Gaitskell Ho. E17 3D 50
Gaitskell Ho. E6 1B 88
Gaitskell Ho. SE17 6E 102
(off Villa St.)
Gaitskell Rd. SE9 1G 143
Gaitskell Way SE1 6D 14 (2C 102)
(off Weller St.)
Gala Bingo Surrey Quays 3K 103
Gala Bingo Tooting 5C 136
Gala Ct. CR7: Thor H 5A 156
Galahad M. E3 2B 86
Galahad Rd. BR1: Broml 4J 141
Galahad Rd. N9 3B 34
Galata Rd. SW13 7C 98
Galatea Sq. SE15 3H 121
Galaxy Bldg. E14 4C 104
(off Crews St.)
Galaxy Ho. EC2 3F 9 (4D 84)
(off Leonard St.)
Galba Ct. TW8: Bford 7D 96
Galbraith St. E14 3E 104
Galdana Av. EN5: New Bar 3F 21
Galeborough Av. IG8: Wfd G 7A 36
Gale Cl. CR4: Mitc 3B 154
Gale Cl. TW12: Hamp 6C 130
Galena Arches W6 4D 98
(off Galena Rd.)
Galena Hgts. E20 6E 68
(off Mirabelle Gdns.)
Galena Ho. SE18 5K 107
(off Grosmont Rd.)
Galena Rd. W6 4D 98
Galen Pl. WC1 6F 7 (5J 83)
Galesbury Rd. SW18 6A 118
Gales Gdns. E2 3H 85
Gale St. E3 5C 86
Gale St. RM9: Dag 5C 72
Gales Way IG8: Wfd G 7H 37
Galgate Cl. SW19 1F 135
Gallants Farm Rd. EN4: E Barn 7H 21
Galleon Cl. DA8: Erith 4K 109
Galleon Cl. SE16 2K 103
Galleon Ho. E14 4E 104
(off Glengarnock Av.)
Galleons Dr. IG11: Bark 3A 90
Galleons Vw. E14 2E 104
Galleria Ct. SE15 6F 103
Galleria Shop. Mall, The 2J 51
Galleries, The NW8 1A 4 (2A 82)
(off Abbey Rd.)
Gallery, The E20 6E 68
(within Westfield Shop. Cen.)
Gallery, The 1G 89
(off Clockhouse Av.)
Gallery, The SE14 7B 104
(off New Cross Rd.)
Gallery Apts. E1 6J 85
(off Commercial Rd.)
Gallery at London Glassblowing, The 6G 15 (2E 102)
(off Bermondsey St.)
Gallery By The Pool 3J 103
Gallery Ct. E17 2E 50
(off Fulbourne Rd.)
Gallery Ct. SE1 7E 14 (2D 102)
(off Pilgrimage St.)
Gallery Ct. SW10 6A 100
(off Gunter Gro.)
Gallery Gdns. UB5: N'olt 2B 76
Gallery Ho. E8 6H 67
(off Hackney Gro.)
Gallery Rd. SE21 1D 138
Galley, The E16 7F 89
Galleymead Rd. SL3: Poyle 4A 174
Galleywall Rd. SE16 4H 103
Galleywall Rd. Trad. Est. SE16 4H 103
Galleywood Ho. W10 5E 80
(off Sutton Way)
Galliard Cl. N9 6D 24
Galliard Ct. N9 6B 24
Galliard Rd. N9 1B 34
Gallia Rd. N5 5B 66
Gallica Ct. SM1: Sutt 1K 165
Gallions Cl. IG11: Bark 3A 90
Gallions Reach Shop. Pk. E6 5G 89
Gallions Rd. E16 7F 89
Gallions Rd. SE7 4K 105
(not continuous)
GALLIONS RDBT. 7F 89
Gallions Vw. Rd. SE28 2J 107
Gallipoli Pl. RM9: Dag 1B 90
Gallon Cl. SE7 4A 106
Gallop, The CR2: Sels 7H 169
Gallop, The SM2: Sutt 7B 166
Gallosson Rd. SE18 4J 107
Galloway Path CR0: C'don 4D 168
Galloway Rd. W12 1C 98
Gallus Cl. N21 6E 22
Galpins Rd. CR7: Thor H 5J 155
Galsworthy Av. E14 6A 86
Galsworthy Av. RM6: Chad H 7B 54
Galsworthy Cl. NW2 4G 63
Galsworthy Cl. SE28 1B 108
Galsworthy Cres. SE3 7A 106
Galsworthy Ho. W11 6G 81
(off Elgin Cres.)
Galsworthy Rd. KT2: King T 7H 133
Galsworthy Rd. NW2 4G 63
Galsworthy Ter. N16 3D 66
Galton Ct. NW9 3A 44
(off Joslin Av.)
Galton St. W10 3G 81
Galva Cl. EN4: Cockf 4K 21
Galvani Way CR0: Wadd 1K 167
Galveston Ho. E1 4A 86
(off Harford St.)
Galveston Rd. SW15 5H 117
Galway Cl. SE16 5H 103
(off Masters Dr.)
Galway Ho. E1 5K 85
(off White Horse La.)
Galway Ho. EC1 2D 8 (3C 84)
(off Galway St.)
Galway St. EC1 2D 8 (3C 84)
Gambado Beckenham 6C 140
Gambado Chelsea 1A 118
(off Station Ct.)
Gambetta St. SW8 2F 119
Gambia St. SE1 5B 14 (1B 102)
Gambier Ho. EC1 2D 8 (3C 84)
(off Mora St.)
Gambole Rd. SW17 4C 136
Games Rd. EN4: Cockf 3H 21
Gamlen Rd. SW15 4F 117
Gamma Ct. CR0: C'don 1D 168
(off Sydenham Rd.)
Gamuel Cl. E17 6C 50
Gander Grn. Cres. TW12: Hamp 1E 148
Gander Grn. La. SM1: Sutt 3H 165
Gander Grn. La. SM3: Cheam 2G 165
Gandhi Cl. E17 6C 50
Gandolfi St. SE15 6E 102
Ganley Ct. SW11 3B 118
(off Winstanley Est.)
Ganton St. W1 2A 12 (7G 83)
GANTS HILL 6E 52
GANTS HILL 6E 52
Gantshill Cres. IG2: Ilf 5E 52
Gap Rd. SW19 5J 135
Garage Rd. W3 6G 79
Garand Ct. N7 5K 65
Garbett Ho. SE17 6B 102
(off Doddington Gro.)
Garbutt Pl. W1 5H 5 (5E 82)
Garda Ho. SE10 4G 105
(off Cable Wlk.)
Garden Av. CR4: Mitc 7F 137
Garden Av. DA7: Bex 3F 127
Garden City HA8: Edg 6B 28
Garden Cl. E4 5H 35
Garden Cl. HA4: Ruis 2G 57
Garden Cl. KT3: N Mald 4A 152
Garden Cl. SE12 3K 141
Garden Cl. SM6: W'gton 5J 167
Garden Cl. SW15 7E 116
Garden Cl. TW12: Hamp 5D 130
Garden Cl. TW15: Ashf 6E 128
Garden Cl. UB5: N'olt 1C 76
Garden Ct. CR0: C'don 2F 169
Garden Ct. EC4 2J 13 (7A 84)
(off Fountain Ct.)
Garden Ct. HA7: Stan 5H 27
Garden Ct. N12 5E 30
Garden Ct. NW8 1A 4 (3B 82)
(off Garden Rd.)
Garden Ct. TW12: Hamp 5D 130
Garden Ct. TW9: Kew 1F 115
Garden Ct. W11 7G 81
(off Clarendon Rd.)
Garden Ct. W4 3J 97
Gardener Gro. TW13: Hanw 2D 130
Gardeners Cl. N11 2K 31
Gardeners Cl. SE9 3C 142
Gardeners Rd. CR0: C'don 1B 168
Garden Halls, The WC1 2E 6 (3J 83)
Garden Ho. N2 2B 46
(off The Grange)
Garden Ho. NW6 2K 81
(off Oxford Rd.)
Garden Ho. SW7 3K 99
(off Cornwall Gdns.)
Garden Ho's., The W6 6F 99
(off Bothwell St.)
Gardenia Rd. BR1: Broml 3E 160
Gardenia Rd. EN1: Enf 6K 23
Gardenia Way IG8: Wfd G 6D 36
Garden La. BR1: Broml 6K 141
Garden La. SW2 1K 137
Garden M. SE10 4G 105
Garden M. W2 7J 81
Garden Mus., The 2G 19 (3K 101)
Garden Pl. E8 1F 85
Garden Rd. BR1: Broml 7K 141
Garden Rd. KT12: Walt T 6K 147
Garden Rd. NW8 1A 4 (3A 82)
Garden Rd. SE20 1J 157
Garden Rd. TW9: Rich 3G 115
Garden Row SE1 3B 102
Garden Royal SW15 6F 117
Gardens, The BR3: Beck 1E 158
Gardens, The E5 7F 49
Gardens, The HA1: Harr 6G 41
Gardens, The HA5: Pinn 6D 40
Gardens, The N8 4J 47
(not continuous)
Gardens, The SE22 4G 121
Gardens, The TW14: Felt 5F 111
Garden Sq. SW1 6H 17 (5E 100)
Garden St. E1 5K 85
Garden Ter. SW1 5C 18 (5H 101)
Garden Ter. SW7 7D 10 (2C 100)
(off Trevor Pl.)
Garden Wlk. BR3: Beck 1B 158
Garden Wlk. EC2 2G 9 (3E 84)
Garden Way NW10 6J 61
Gardiner Av. NW2 5E 62
Gardiner Cl. EN3: Pond E 6E 24
Gardiner Cl. RM8: Dag 4D 72
Gardiner Ct. CR2: S Croy 6D 168
Gardiner Ho. SW11 1C 118
Gardner Cl. E11 6K 51
Gardner Ct. EC1 4A 8 (4B 84)
(off Brewery Sq.)
Gardner Ct. N5 4C 66
Gardner Ho. TW13: Hanw 2D 130
Gardner Ho. UB1: S'hall 7B 76
(off The Broadway)
Gardner Ind. Est. BR3: Beck 5B 140
Gardner Pl. TW14: Felt 6K 111
Gardner Rd. E13 4K 87
Gardners La. EC4 2C 14 (7C 84)
Gardnor Rd. NW3 4B 64
Gard St. EC1 1B 8 (3B 84)
Garendon Gdns. SM4: Mord 7K 153
Garendon Rd. SM4: Mord 7K 153
Garenne Ct. E4 1K 35
Gareth Cl. KT4: Wor Pk 2F 165
Gareth Ct. SW16 3H 137
Gareth Dr. N9 2B 34
Gareth Gro. BR1: Broml 4J 141
Garfield EN2: Enf 5J 23
(off London Rd.)
Garfield Ct. NW6 7G 63
(off Willesden La.)
Garfield M. SW11 3E 118
Garfield Rd. E13 4H 87
Garfield Rd. E4 1A 36
Garfield Rd. EN3: Pond E 4D 24
Garfield Rd. SW11 3E 118
Garfield Rd. SW19 5A 136
Garfield Rd. TW1: Twick 1A 132
Garford St. E14 7C 86
Garganey Ct. NW10 6K 61
(off Elgar Av.)
Garganey Wlk. SE28 7C 90
Garibaldi St. SE18 4J 107
Garland Cl. SE1 3C 102
Garland Ct. E14 7C 86
(off Premiere Pl.)
Garland Ct. SE17 4C 102
(off Wansey St.)
Garland Dr. TW3: Houn 2G 113
Garland Ho. KT2: King T 1E 150
(off Skerne Rd.)

A–Z London 225

Garland Ho. UB7: W Dray 2B 92
Garland Rd. HA7: Stan 1E 42
Garland Rd. SE18 7H 107
Garlands Ct. CR0: C'don 4D 168
(off Chatsworth Rd.)
Garlands Ho. NW8 2A 82
(off Carlton Hill)
Garlands La. HA1: Harr 1K 59
Garlick Hill EC4 2D 14 (7C 84)
Garlies Rd. SE23 3A 140
Garlinge Ho. SW9 1A 120
(off Gosling Way)
Garlinge Rd. NW2 6H 63
Garman Cl. N18 5J 33
Garman Rd. N17 7C 34
(not continuous)
Garnault M. EC1 2K 7 (3A 84)
(off Rosebery Av.)
Garnault Pl. EC1 2K 7 (3A 84)
Garnault Rd. EN1: Enf 1A 24
Garner Cl. RM8: Dag 1D 72
Garner Ct. TW19: Stanw 6A 110
(off Douglas Rd.)
Garner Rd. E17 1E 50
Garner St. E2 2G 85
Garnet Ho. E1 1J 103
(off Garnet St.)
Garnet Pl. UB7: Yiew 1A 92
Garnet Rd. CR7: Thor H 4C 156
Garnet Rd. NW10 6A 62
Garnet St. E1 7J 85
Garnett Cl. SE9 3D 124
Garnett Rd. NW3 5D 64
Garnett Way E17 1A 50
(off McEntee Av.)
Garnet Wlk. E6 5C 88
Garnham Cl. N16 2F 67
Garnham St. N16 2F 67
Garnies Cl. SE15 7F 103
Garrad's Rd. SW16 3H 137
Garrard Cl. BR7: Chst 5F 143
Garrard Cl. DA7: Bex 3G 127
Garrard Wlk. NW10 6A 62
Garratt Cl. CR0: Bedd 4J 167
Garratt Cl. CR7: Thor H 2C 156
Garratt Ct. SW18 7K 117
Garratt La. SW17 3A 136
Garratt La. SW18 6K 117
Garratt Rd. HA8: Edg 7B 28
Garratt Ter. SW17 4C 136
Garraway Ct. SW13 7E 98
(off Wyatt Dr.)
Garrett Cl. W3 5K 79
Garrett Ho. SE1 6A 14 (2B 102)
(off Burrows M.)
Garrett St. EC1 3D 8 (4C 84)
Garrick Av. NW11 6G 45
Garrick Cl. SW18 4A 118
Garrick Cl. TW9: Rich 5D 114
Garrick Cl. W5 4E 78
Garrick Ct. E8 7F 67
(off Jacaranda Gro.)
Garrick Cres. CR0: C'don 2E 168
Garrick Dr. NW4 2E 44
Garrick Dr. SE28 3H 107
Garrick Gdns. KT8: W Mole 3E 148
Garrick Ho. KT1: King T 4E 150
(off Surbiton Rd.)
Garrick Ho. W1 5J 11 (1F 101)
(off Carrington St.)
Garrick Ho. W4 6A 98
Garrick Ind. Cen. NW9 5B 44
Garrick Pk. NW4 2F 45
Garrick Rd. NW9 6B 44
Garrick Rd. TW9: Rich 2G 115
Garrick Rd. UB6: G'frd 4F 77
Garricks Ho. KT1: King T 2D 150
(off Wadbrook St.)
Garrick St. WC2 2E 12 (7J 83)
Garrick Theatre 3D 12 (7H 83)
(off Charing Cross Rd.)
Garrick Way NW4 4F 45
Garrick Yd. WC2 2E 12 (7J 83)
(off St Martin's La.)
Garrison Cl. SE18 7E 106
Garrison Cl. TW4: Houn 5D 112
Garrison La. KT9: Chess 7D 162
Garrison Rd. E3 1C 86
Garrison Sq. SW1 5H 17 (5E 100)
Garrowsfield EN5: Barn 6C 20
Garsdale Cl. N11 6K 31
Garsdale Ter. W14 5H 99
(off Aisgill Av.)
Garside Cl. SE28 3H 107
Garside Cl. TW12: Hamp 6F 131
Garside Ct. TW11: Hamp W 1C 150
Garsington M. SE4 3B 122
Garson Ho. W2 2A 10 (7B 82)
(off Gloucester Ter.)
Garston Ho. N1 7B 66
(off The Sutton Est.)
Garter Way SE16 2K 103
Garth, The HA3: Kenton 6F 43
Garth, The TW12: Hamp H 6F 131
Garth Cl. HA4: Ruis 1B 58
Garth Cl. KT2: King T 5F 133
Garth Cl. SM4: Mord 7F 153
Garth Ct. HA1: Harr 6K 41
(off Northwick Pk. Rd.)
Garth Ct. W4 5K 97
Garth Ho. NW2 2H 63
Garth M. W5 4E 78
Garthorne Rd. SE23 7K 121
Garthorne Road Nature Reserve 7K 121
Garth Rd. KT2: King T 5F 133
Garth Rd. NW2 2H 63
Garth Rd. SM4: Mord 6E 152
Garth Rd. W4 5K 97
Garth Rd. Ind. Cen., The SM4: Mord 1F 165
Garthside TW10: Ham 5E 132
Garthway N12 6H 31
Gartmoor Gdns. SW19 1H 135
Gartmore Rd. IG3: Ilf 2K 71
Garton Pl. SW18 6A 118
Gartons Cl. EN3: Pond E 4D 24
Gartons Way SW11 3A 118
Garvary Rd. E16 6K 87
Garway Ct. E3 2C 86
(off Matilda Gdns.)
Garway Rd. W2 6K 81
Garwood Cl. N17 1H 49
Gascoigne Cl. N17 1F 49
Gascoigne Gdns. IG8: Wfd G 7B 36
Gascoigne Pl. E2 2J 9 (3F 85)
(not continuous)

Gascoigne Rd. IG11: Bark 1G 89
Gascony Av. NW6 7J 63
Gascony Pl. W12 1F 99
Gascoyne Ho. E9 7A 68
Gascoyne Rd. E9 7K 67
Gaselee St. E14 1E 104
(off Baffin Way)
Gasholder Pk. 1H 83
Gaskarth Rd. HA8: Edg 1J 43
Gaskarth Rd. SW12 6F 119
Gaskell Ct. SE20 7K 139
Gaskell Rd. N6 6D 46
Gaskell St. SW4 2J 119
Gaskin St. N1 1B 84
Gaspar Cl. SW5 4K 99
Gaspar M. SW5 4K 99
Gassiot Rd. SW17 4D 136
Gassiot Way SM1: Sutt 3B 166
Gasson Ho. SE14 6K 103
(off John Williams Cl.)
Gastein Rd. W6 6F 99
Gastigny Ho. EC1 2D 8 (3C 84)
(off Pleydell Est.)
Gaston Bell Cl. TW9: Rich 3F 115
Gaston Bri. Rd. TW17: Shep 6F 147
Gaston Rd. CR4: Mitc 3E 154
Gaston Way TW17: Shep 5F 147
Gataker Ho. SE16 3H 103
(off Slippers Pl.)
Gataker St. SE16 3H 103
Gatcombe Ct. BR3: Beck 7C 140
Gatcombe Ho. SE22 3E 120
Gatcombe M. W5 7F 79
Gatcombe Rd. E16 1J 105
Gatcombe Rd. N19 3H 65
Gatcombe Way EN4: Cockf 3J 21
Gateacre Ct. DA14: Sidc 4B 144
Gate Cen., The TW8: Bford 7A 96
Gate Cinema 1J 99
(off Notting Hill Ga.)
Gatefold Bldg., The UB3: Hayes 3G 93
Gateforth St. NW8 4C 4 (4C 82)
Gate Hill Ct. W11 1H 99
(off Ladbroke Ter.)
Gate Ho. E3 1A 86
(off Gunmakers La.)
Gate Ho. N1 7D 66
(off Ufton Rd.)
Gate Ho. NW6 2K 81
(off Oxford Rd.)
Gatehouse Cl. KT2: King T 7J 133
Gatehouse Ct. TW15: Ashf 6E 128
Gatehouse Sq. SE1 4D 14 (1C 102)
(off Southwark Bri. Rd.)
Gateley Ho. SE4 4K 121
(off Coston Wlk.)
Gateley Rd. SW9 3K 119
Gate Lodge W9 5J 81
(off Admiral Wlk.)
Gately Ct. SE15 7F 103
Gate M. SW7 7D 10 (2C 100)
(off Rutland Ga.)
Gater Dr. EN2: Enf 1J 23
Gatesborough St. EC2 3G 9 (4E 84)
Gates Cnr. Cl. E18 1J 51
Gates Ct. SE17 5C 102
Gatesden WC1 1F 7 (3J 83)
Gates Grn. Rd. BR2: Kes 4J 171
Gates Grn. Rd. BR4: W W'ck 3H 171
Gateside Rd. SW17 3D 136
Gatestone Ct. SE19 6E 138
(off Central Hill)
Gatestone Rd. SE19 6E 138
Gate St. WC2 7G 7 (6K 83)
Gate Theatre, The 1J 99
(off Pembridge Rd.)
Gateway SE17 6C 102
Gateway Apts. E17 5C 50
Gateway Arc. N1 2B 84
(off Upper St.)
Gateway Bus. Cen. SE26 6A 140
Gateway Bus. Cen. SE28 3H 107
Gateway Ct. IG2: Ilf 6E 52
(off Parham Dr.)
Gateway Ho. IG11: Bark 1G 89
Gateway Ind. Est. NW10 3B 80
Gateway M. E8 5F 67
Gateway M. N11 6B 32
Gateway Retail Pk. 4F 89
Gateway Rd. E10 3D 68
Gateways KT6: Surb 5E 150
(off Surbiton Hill Rd.)
Gateways, The SW3 4D 16 (4C 100)
Gateways, The TW9: Rich 4D 114
(off Park La.)
Gateways Ct. SM6: W'gton 5F 167
Gatfield Gro. TW13: Hanw 2E 130
Gatfield Ho. TW13: Hanw 2D 130
Gathorne Rd. N22 2A 48
Gathorne St. E2 2K 85
Gatley Av. KT19: Ewe 5H 163
Gatliff Cl. SW1 6J 17 (5F 101)
(off Ebury Bri. Rd.)
Gatliff Rd. SW1 6J 17 (5F 101)
Gatling Rd. SE2 5A 108
Gatonby St. SE15 1F 121
Gatting Cl. HA8: Edg 7D 28
Gatting Way UB8: Uxb 6A 56
Gattis Wharf N1 2J 83
(off New Wharf Rd.)
Gatton Cl. SM2: Sutt 7K 165
Gatton Rd. SW17 4C 136
Gattons Way DA14: Sidc 4F 145
Gatward Cl. N21 6G 23
Gatward Grn. N9 2A 34
Gatward Pl. IG11: Bark 3K 89
Gatwick Ho. E14 6B 86
(off Clemence St.)
Gatwick Rd. SW18 7H 117
Gauden Cl. SW4 3H 119
Gauden Rd. SW4 2H 119
Gaudi Apts. N8 3K 47
(off Gt. Amwell La.)
Gaugin Ct. SE16 5H 103
(off Stubbs Dr.)
GAUGING LOCKS 7C 96
(off Tallow Rd.)
Gaugin Sq. E1 7G 85
Gaumont Pl. SW2 2J 137
Gaumont Ter. W12 2E 98
(off Lime Gro.)
Gaumont Twr. E8 6F 67
(off Dalston Sq.)
Gauntlet NW9 2B 44
(off Five Acre)

Gauntlet Cl. UB5: N'olt 7C 58
Gauntlett Ct. HA0: Wemb 5B 60
Gauntlett Rd. SM1: Sutt 5B 166
Gaunt St. SE1 3C 102
Gautrey Rd. SE15 2J 121
Gautrey Sq. E6 6D 88
Gavel St. SE17 4D 102
Gaverick M. E14 4C 104
Gavestone Cres. SE12 7A 124
Gavestone Rd. SE12 7K 123
Gaviller Pl. E5 4H 67
Gavina Cl. SM4: Mord 5C 154
Gavin Ho. SE18 4J 107
Gawain Wlk. N9 3B 34
Gawber St. E2 3J 85
Gawsworth Cl. E15 5H 69
Gawthorne Ct. E3 2C 86
Gay Cl. NW2 5D 62
Gaydon Ho. W2 5K 81
(off Bourne Ter.)
Gaydon La. NW9 1A 44
Gayfere Pl. SE25 2E 156
(off Grange Hill)
Gayfere Rd. IG5: Ilf 3D 52
Gayfere Rd. KT17: Ewe 5C 164
Gayfere St. SW1 2E 18 (3J 101)
Gayford Rd. W12 2B 98
Gay Gdns. RM10: Dag 4J 73
Gay Ho. N16 5E 66
Gayhurst SE17 6D 102
(off Hopwood Rd.)
Gayhurst Ct. UB5: N'olt 3A 76
Gayhurst Ho. NW8 3C 4 (4C 82)
(off Mallory St.)
Gayhurst Rd. E8 7G 67
Gaylor Rd. UB5: N'olt 5D 58
Gaymead NW8 1K 81
(off Abbey Rd.)
Gaynesford Rd. SE23 2K 139
Gaynesford Rd. SM5: Cars 7D 166
Gaynes Hill Rd. IG8: Wfd G 6H 37
Gay Rd. E15 2F 87
Gaysham Av. IG2: Ilf 5E 52
Gaysham Hall IG5: Ilf 3F 53
Gaysley Ho. SE11 4J 19 (4A 102)
(off Hotspur St.)
Gay St. SW15 3F 117
Gayton HA1: Harr 7J 41
(off Grove Hill)
Gayton Ct. HA1: Harr 6K 41
Gayton Cres. NW3 4B 64
Gayton Ho. E3 4C 86
(off Chiltern Rd.)
Gayton Rd. HA1: Harr 6K 41
Gayton Rd. NW3 4B 64
Gayton Rd. SE2 3C 108
Gayville Rd. SW11 6D 118
Gaywood Cl. SW2 1K 137
Gaywood Rd. E17 3C 50
Gaywood St. SE1 3B 102
Gaza St. SE17 5B 102
Gazelle Ho. E15 6G 69
Gean Ct. E11 4F 69
Gean Ct. N11 6B 32
(off Cline Rd.)
Geariesville Gdns. IG6: Ilf 4F 53
Gearing Cl. SW17 4E 136
Geary Rd. NW10 5C 62
Geary St. N7 5K 65
Geddes Pl. DA6: Bex 4G 127
(off Arnsberg Way)
Gedeney Rd. N17 1C 48
Gedling Ct. SE1 7K 15 (2F 103)
(off Sweeney Cres.)
Gedling Pl. SE1 7K 15 (3F 103)
Geere Rd. E15 1H 87
Gees Ct. W1 1H 11 (6E 82)
Gee St. EC1 3C 8 (4C 84)
Geffery's Ct. SE9 3C 142
Geffrye Ct. N1 1H 9 (2E 84)
Geffrye Est. N1 2E 84
Geffrye Mus. 2F 85
Geffrye St. E2 2F 85
Geldart Rd. SE15 7H 103
Geldeston Rd. E5 2G 67
Gellatly Rd. SE14 2J 121
Gell Cl. UB10: Ick 3B 56
Gelsthorpe Rd. RM5: Col R 1H 55
Gem Ct. SE10 7D 104
(off Merryweather Pl.)
Gemini Apts. E1 3K 9 (4F 85)
(off Sclater St.)
Gemini Bus. Cen. E16 4F 87
Gemini Bus. Est. SE14 5K 103
Gemini Bus. Pk. E6 5H 89
Gemini Ct. E1 7G 85
(off Vaughan Way)
Gemini Gro. UB5: N'olt 3C 76
Gemini Ho. E3 1C 86
(off Garrison Rd.)
Gemini Pl. TW15: Ashf 6G 129
Genas Cl. IG6: Ilf 1F 53
General Gordon Pl. SE18 4F 107
General Gordon Sq. SE18 4F 107
(off Woolwich New Rd.)
General Wolfe Rd. SE10 1F 123
Genesis Bus. Pk. NW10 2H 79
Genesis Cl. TW19: Stanw 1B 128
Genesta Rd. SE18 6F 107
Geneva Cl. TW17: Shep 2G 147
Geneva Ct. NW9 5B 44
Geneva Dr. SW9 4A 120
Geneva Gdns. RM6: Chad H 5E 54
Geneva Rd. CR7: Thor H 5C 156
Geneva Rd. KT1: King T 4E 150
Genever Cl. E4 5H 35
Genista Rd. N18 5C 34
Genoa Av. SW15 5E 116
Genoa Ho. E1 4K 85
(off Ernest St.)
Genoa Ho. SW18 3A 118
Genoa Rd. SE20 1J 157
Genotin Rd. EN1: Enf 3J 23
Genotin Ter. EN1: Enf 3J 23
Gentlemans Row EN2: Enf 3H 23
Gentry Gdns. E13 4J 87
Geoff Cade Way E3 5B 86
Geoffrey Chaucer Way E3 5B 86
Geoffrey Cl. SE5 2C 120
Geoffrey Ct. SE4 2B 122
Geoffrey Gdns. E6 2C 88
Geoffrey Ho. SE1 7F 15 (3D 102)
(off Pardoner St.)
Geoffrey Jones Ct. NW10 1C 80
Geoffrey Rd. SE4 3B 122

George V Av. HA5: Pinn 2D 40
George V Cl. HA5: Pinn 3E 40
George V Way UB6: G'frd 1B 78
George Beard Rd. SE8 4B 104
George Belt Ho. E2 3K 85
(off Smart St.)
George Comberton Wlk. E12 5E 70
George Ct. TW15: Ashf 4B 128
(off Church Rd.)
George Ct. UB3: Hayes 5H 75
George Ct. WC2 3F 13 (7J 83)
(off John Adam St.)
George Cres. N10 7K 31
George Davies Lodge IG6: Ilf 5G 53
(off Veronique Gdns.)
George Downing Est. N16 2F 67
George Eliot Ho. SE17 5C 102
(off Thrush St.)
George Eliot Ho. SW1 4B 18 (4G 101)
(off Vauxhall Bri. Rd.)
George Elliston Ho. SE1 5G 103
(off Old Kent Rd.)
George Eyre Ho. NW8 1B 4 (2B 82)
(off Cochrane St.)
George Furness Ho. NW10 6D 62
(off Grange Rd.)
George Gange Way HA3: W'stone 3J 41
George Gillett Ct. EC1 3D 8 (4C 84)
(off Banner St.)
George Groves Rd. SE20 1G 157
George Hilsdon Ct. E14 6A 86
(off Repton St.)
George Ho. NW6 2H 81
(off Albert Rd.)
George Hudson Twr. E15 2D 86
(off High St.)
George Inn Yd. SE1 5E 14 (1D 102)
George La. BR2: Hayes 1K 171
George La. E18 2J 51
George La. SE13 6D 122
George La. SE6 6D 122
George Lansbury Ho. E3 3B 86
(off Bow Rd.)
George Lansbury Ho. N22 1A 48
(off Progress Way)
George Lansbury Ho. NW10 7A 62
George Leybourne Ho. E1 7G 85
(off Fletcher St.)
George Lindgren Ho. SW6 7H 99
(off Clem Attlee Ct.)
George Loveless Ho. E2 1K 9 (3F 85)
(off Diss St.)
George Lowe Ct. W2 5K 81
(off Bourne Ter.)
George Mathers Rd. SE11 4B 102
George M. EN2: Enf 3J 23
George M. NW1 2B 6 (3G 83)
(off Drummond St.)
George M. SW9 2A 120
George Padmore Ho. E8 1G 85
(off Brougham Rd.)
George Peabody Ct. NW1 5C 4 (5C 82)
(off Burne St.)
George Peabody St. E13 2A 88
George Pl. N17 3E 48
George Potter Ho. SW11 2B 118
(off George Potter Way)
George Potter Way SW11 2B 118
George Rd. E4 6H 35
George Rd. KT2: King T 7H 133
George Rd. KT3: N Mald 4B 152
George Row SE16 2G 103
George Scott Ho. E1 6K 85
(off W. Arbour St.)
George Sq. SW19 3J 153
George's Rd. N7 5K 65
George's Sq. SW6 6H 99
(off North End Rd.)
George St. CR0: C'don 2C 168
George St. E14 1D 104
George St. IG11: Bark 7G 71
George St. TW3: Houn 2D 112
George St. TW9: Rich 5D 114
George St. UB2: S'hall 4C 94
George St. W1 7E 4 (6D 82)
George St. W7 1J 95
Georgetown Cl. SE19 5E 138
Georgette Pl. SE10 7E 104
George Vale Ho. E2 2G 85
(off Mansford St.)
George Vw. Ho. SW18 1K 135
(off Knaresborough Dr.)
Georgeville Gdns. IG6: Ilf 4F 53
George Walter Ct. SE16 4J 103
(off Millender Wlk.)
George Wyver Cl. SW19 7G 117
George Yd. EC3 1F 15 (6D 84)
George Yd. W1 2H 11 (7E 82)
Georgia Ct. SE16 3G 103
(off Priter Rd.)
Georgiana St. NW1 1G 83
Georgian Cl. BR2: Hayes 1K 171
Georgian Cl. HA7: Stan 7F 27
Georgian Cl. UB10: Ick 4A 56
Georgian Ct. CR0: C'don 1D 168
(off Cross Rd.)
Georgian Ct. E9 1J 85
Georgian Ct. EN5: New Bar 4F 21
Georgian Ct. HA9: Wemb 6G 61
Georgian Ct. N3 1H 45
Georgian Ct. NW4 5D 44
Georgian Ct. SW16 4J 137
Georgian Ho. E16 1J 105
(off Capulet M.)
Georgian Ho. N1 1E 84
(off Hertford Rd.)
Georgian Way HA1: Harr 2H 59
Georgia Rd. CR7: Thor H 1B 156
Georgia Rd. KT3: N Mald 4J 151
Georgina Gdns. E2 1K 9 (3F 85)
Geotgette Ct. SW18 5K 117
(off Courthouse Way)
Geraint Rd. BR1: Broml 4J 141
Geraldine Rd. SW18 5A 118
Geraldine Rd. W4 6H 97
Geraldine St. SE11 2K 19 (3B 102)
Gerald M. SW1 3H 17 (4E 100)
(off Gerald Rd.)
Gerald Pl. E8 6F 67
(off Dalston Sq.)
Gerald Rd. E16 4H 87
Gerald Rd. RM8: Dag 1F 73
Gerald Rd. SW1 3H 17 (4E 100)
Gerard Av. TW4: Houn 7E 112
Gerard Gdns. RM13: Rain 2K 91

Gerard Pl. E9 7K 67
Gerard Rd. HA1: Harr 6A 42
Gerard Rd. SW13 1B 116
Gerards Cl. SE16 5J 103
Gerards Pl. SW4 4H 119
Gerda Rd. SE9 2G 143
Germander Way E15 3G 87
Gernigan Ho. SW18 6B 118
Gernon Rd. E3 2A 86
Geron Way NW2 1D 62
Gerrard Gdns. HA5: Eastc 5J 39
Gerrard Ho. SE14 7J 103
(off Briant St.)
Gerrard Pl. W1 2D 12 (7H 83)
Gerrard Rd. N1 2B 84
Gerrards Cl. N14 5B 22
Gerrards Ct. W5 3D 96
Gerrard St. W1 2C 12 (7H 83)
Gerrard Way SE3 4A 124
Gerridge Ct. SE1 1K 19 (3A 102)
(off Gerridge St.)
Gerridge St. SE1 1K 19 (3A 102)
Gerry Raffles Sq. E15 6F 69
Gertrude Rd. DA17: Belv 4G 109
Gertrude St. SW10 6A 100
Gervase Cl. HA9: Wemb 3J 61
Gervase Rd. HA8: Edg 1J 43
Gervase St. SE15 7H 103
Gervis Ct. TW7: Isle 7G 95
Ghent St. SE6 2C 140
Ghent Way E8 6F 67
Gherkin, The 1H 15 (6E 84)
(off St Mary Axe)
Giant Arches Rd. SE24 7C 120
Giant Tree Hill WD23: B Hea 1C 26
Gibbfield Cl. RM6: Chad H 3E 54
Gibbings Ho. SE1 7B 14 (2B 102)
(off King James St.)
Gibbins Rd. E15 7E 68
Gibbon Ho. NW8 4B 4 (4B 82)
(off Fisherton St.)
Gibbon Rd. KT2: King T 1E 150
Gibbon Rd. SE15 2J 121
Gibbon Rd. W3 7A 80
Gibbons M. NW11 5H 45
Gibbon's Rents SE1 5G 15 (1E 102)
(off Magdalen St.)
Gibbons Rd. NW10 6A 62
Gibbon Wlk. SW15 4C 116
Gibbs Av. SE19 5D 138
Gibbs Cl. SE19 6D 138
Gibbs Grn. HA8: Edg 4D 28
Gibbs Grn. W14 5H 99
(not continuous)
Gibbs Ho. BR1: Broml 1H 159
(off Longfield)
Gibbs La. E2 2G 85
Gibb's Rd. N18 4D 34
Gibbs Sq. SE19 5D 138
Gibney Ter. BR1: Broml 4H 141
Gibraltar Wlk. E2 2K 9 (3F 85)
(off Shackwell St.)
Gibson Cl. E1 4J 85
Gibson Cl. KT9: Chess 5C 162
Gibson Cl. N21 6F 23
Gibson Cl. TW7: Isle 3J 113
Gibson Ct. SE9 5A 124
Gibson Gdns. N16 2F 67
Gibson Ho. SM1: Sutt 4J 165
Gibson M. TW1: Twick 6C 114
Gibson Rd. RM8: Dag 1C 72
Gibson Rd. SE11 4H 19 (4K 101)
Gibson Rd. SM1: Sutt 5K 165
Gibson Rd. UB10: Ick 4B 56
Gibsons Hill SW16 7A 138
(not continuous)
Gibsons Pl. TW8: Bford 6D 96
(off Sidney Gdns.)
Gibson Sq. N1 1A 84
Gibson Sq. Gdns. 1A 84
(off Gibson Sq.)
Gibson St. SE10 5G 105
Gideon Cl. DA17: Belv 4H 109
Gideon Cl. HA8: Edg 6B 28
Gideon M. W5 2D 96
Gideon Rd. SW11 3E 118
Gielgud Theatre 2C 12 (7H 83)
(off Shaftesbury Av.)
Giesbach Rd. N19 2H 65
Giffard Rd. N18 6K 33
Giffin Sq. Mkt. 7C 104
(off Giffin St.)
Giffin St. SE8 7C 104
Gifford Gdns. W7 5H 77
Gifford Ho. SE10 5F 105
(off Eastney St.)
Gifford Ho. SW1 6A 18 (5G 101)
(off Churchill Gdns.)
Gifford Rd. NW10 7A 62
Gifford St. N1 7J 65
Gift La. E15 1G 87
Giggs Hill BR5: St P 2K 161
GIGGSHILL 7A 150
Giggs Hill Gdns. KT7: T Ditt 1A 162
Giggs Hill Rd. KT7: T Ditt 7A 150
GILBERT BRI. 5D 8 (5C 84)
(off Wood St.)
Gilbert Cl. SE18 1D 124
Gilbert Cl. SW19 1K 153
(off Morden Rd.)
Gilbert Ct. W5 6F 79
(off Green Va.)
Gilbert Gro. HA8: Edg 1K 43
Gilbert Ho. E17 3E 50
Gilbert Ho. E2 3K 85
(off Usk St.)
Gilbert Ho. EC2 5D 8 (5C 84)
(off Wood St.)
Gilbert Ho. SE8 6C 104
Gilbert Ho. SW1 6K 17 (5F 101)
(off Churchill Gdns.)
Gilbert Ho. SW13 7D 98
(off Trinity Chu. Rd.)
Gilbert Ho. SW8 7J 101
(off Wyvil Rd.)
Gilbert Pl. WC1 6E 6 (5J 83)
Gilbert Rd. BR1: Broml 7J 141
Gilbert Rd. DA17: Belv 3G 109
Gilbert Rd. HA5: Pinn 4B 40
Gilbert Rd. SE11 4K 19 (4A 102)
Gilbert Rd. SW19 7A 136
Gilbert Scott Bldg. SW15 6G 117
Gilbert Scott Cl. HA0: Wemb 5D 60
Gilbert Scott Ho. W14 4H 99
(off Warwick La.)

Gilbert Sheldon Ho. W2 5B 4 (5B 82)
(off Edgware Rd.)
Gilbertson Ho. E14 3C 104
(off Mellish St.)
Gilbert St. E15 4G 69
Gilbert St. TW3: Houn 3G 113
Gilbert St. W1 1H 11 (6E 82)
Gilbert Way CR0: Wadd 2K 167
Gilbert White Cl. UB6: G'frd 1A 78
Gilbey Cl. UB10: Ick 4D 56
Gilbey Ho. NW1 7F 65
Gilbey Rd. SW17 4C 136
Gilbeys Yd. NW1 7E 64
Gilbourne Rd. SE18 6K 107
Gilby Ho. E9 6K 67
Gilda Av. EN3: Pond E 5F 25
Gilda Ct. NW7 1C 44
Gilda Cres. N16 1G 67
Gildea Cl. HA5: Hat E 1E 40
Gildea St. W1 6K 5 (5F 83)
Gilden Cres. NW5 5E 64
Gildersome St. SE18 6E 106
Gilders Rd. KT9: Chess 7F 163
Gilding Wy. 4D 94
Giles Coppice SE19 4F 139
Giles Cres. UB10: Uxb 1B 74
(off St Andrews Rd.)
Giles Ho. E15 6F 69
(off Forrester Way)
Giles Ho. W11 6J 81
(off Westbourne Gro.)
Gilesmead SE5 1D 120
Gilford Ho. IG1: Ilf 2F 71
(off Clements Rd.)
Gilfrid Cl. UB8: Hil 6D 74
Gilkes Cres. SE21 6E 120
Gilkes Pl. SE21 6E 120
Gillan Ct. SE12 3K 141
Gillan Grn. WD23: B Hea 2B 26
Gillards M. E17 4C 50
Gillards Way E17 4C 50
Gill Av. E16 6J 87
Gillender St. E14 4E 86
Gillender St. E3 4E 86
Gillespie Pk. Local Nature Reserve
3A 66
Gillespie Rd. N5 3A 66
Gillett Av. E6 2C 88
GILLETTE CORNER 7A 96
Gillett Ho. N8 3J 47
(off Campsfield Rd.)
Gillett Pl. N16 5E 66
Gillett Rd. CR7: Thor H 4D 156
Gillett Sq. N16 5E 66
(off Gillett St.)
Gillett St. N16 5E 66
Gillfoot NW1 1A 6 (2G 83)
(off Hampstead Rd.)
Gillham Ter. N17 6B 34
Gillian Ho. HA3: Hrw W 6D 26
Gillian Lynne Theatre 7F 7 (6J 83)
(off Parker St.)
Gillian Pk. Rd. SM3: Sutt 1H 165
Gillian St. SE13 5D 122
Gillies Ho. NW6 7B 64
(off Hilgrove Rd.)
Gillies St. NW5 5E 64
Gilling Ct. NW3 6C 64
Gillingham M. SW1 3A 18 (4G 101)
Gillingham Rd. NW2 3G 63
Gillingham Row SW1 3A 18 (4G 101)
Gillingham St. SW1 3A 18 (4G 101)
Gillings Ct. EN5: Barn 4B 20
(off Wood St.)
Gillison Wlk. SE16 3H 103
Gillis Sq. SW15 6C 116
Gillman Dr. E15 1H 87
Gillman Ho. E2 2G 85
(off Pritchard's Rd.)
Gillray Ho. SW10 6B 100
(off Ann La.)
Gill St. E14 6B 86
Gillum Cl. EN4: E Barn 1J 31
Gilman Ho. N1 7A 66
(off Drummond Way)
Gilmore Cl. UB10: Ick 3C 56
Gilmore Ct. N11 5J 31
Gilmore Cres. TW15: Ashf 5C 128
Gilmore Rd. SE13 4F 123
Gilmour Ho. NW9 2C 44
Gilpin Av. SW14 4K 115
Gilpin Cl. CR4: Mitc 2C 154
Gilpin Cl. W2 5A 4 (5A 82)
(off Porteus Rd.)
Gilpin Cres. N18 5A 34
Gilpin Cres. TW2: Whitt 7F 113
Gilpin Rd. E5 4A 68
Gilpin Way UB3: Harl 7F 93
Gilray Ho. W2 2A 10 (7B 82)
(off Gloucester Ter.)
Gilroy St. SE10 4J 105
Gilsland Pl. CR7: Thor H 4D 156
Gilsland Rd. CR7: Thor H 4D 156
Gilson Pl. N10 7J 31
Gilstead Rd. SW6 2K 117
Gilston Rd. SW10 5A 100
Gilton Rd. SE6 3G 141
Giltspur St. EC1 7B 8 (6B 84)
Gilwell Cl. E4 4J 25
Gilwell La. E4 4K 25
(not continuous)
Gilwell Pk. E4 3K 25
Ginger Apts. SE1 6K 15 (2F 103)
(off Cayenne Ct.)
Ginsburg Yd. NW3 4A 64
Gippeswyck Cl. HA5: Pinn 1B 40
Gipsy Hill SE19 4E 138
Gipsy La. SW15 3D 116
Gipsy Rd. DA16: Well 7D 108
Gipsy Rd. SE27 4C 138
Gipsy Rd. Gdns. SE27 4C 138
Giralda Cl. E16 5B 88
Giraud St. E14 6D 86
Girdler's Rd. W14 4F 99
Girdlestone Wlk. N19 2G 65
Girdwood Rd. SW18 7G 117
Girling Ho. N1 1E 84
(off Colville Est.)
Girling Way TW14: Felt 3J 111
Gironde Rd. SW6 7H 99
Girtin Ho. UB5: N'olt 2B 76
(off Academy Gdns.)
Girton Av. NW9 3G 43
Girton Cl. UB5: N'olt 6G 59
Girton Gdns. CR0: C'don 3C 170
Girton Rd. SE26 5K 139
Girton Rd. UB5: N'olt 6G 59
Girton Vs. W10 6F 81
Gisbourne Cl. SM6: Bedd 3H 167
Gisburn Ho. SE15 6G 103
(off Friary Est.)
Gisburn Rd. N8 4K 47
Gissing Wlk. N1 7A 66
Gittens Cl. BR1: Broml 4H 141
Given Wilson Wlk. E13 2H 87
Giverny Ho. SE16 2K 103
(off Water Gdns. Sq.)
Glacier Ho. SW11 7H 101
(off Ponton Rd.)
Glacier Pl. E2 2H 85
(off Clare St.)
Glacier Way HA0: Wemb 2D 78
Gladbeck Way EN2: Enf 4G 23
Gladding Rd. E12 4B 70
Glade, The BR1: Broml 2B 160
Glade, The BR4: W W'ck 3D 170
Glade, The CR0: C'don 5K 157
Glade, The E8 6G 67
Glade, The EN2: Enf 3F 23
Glade, The IG5: Ilf 1D 52
Glade, The IG8: Wfd G 3E 36
Glade, The KT17: Ewe 6C 164
Glade, The N12 3G 31
Glade, The N21 6E 22
Glade, The SE7 7A 106
Glade, The SM2: Cheam 7G 165
Glade, The W12 2D 98
(off Coningham Rd.)
Glade Apts. E14 4E 104
(off Stebondale St.)
Glade Cl. KT6: Surb 2D 162
Glade Ct. IG5: Ilf 1D 52
Glade Gdns. CR0: C'don 7A 158
Glade La. UB2: S'hall 2F 95
Glade Path SE1 7A 14 (2B 102)
(off Blackfriars Rd.)
Glades, The 2J 159
Glades, The KT6: Surb 7E 150
Gladeside CR0: C'don 6K 157
Gladeside N21 6E 22
Gladeside Cl. KT9: Chess 7D 162
Glade Wlk. E20 6D 68
Gladiator St. SE23 7A 122
Glading Ter. N16 3F 67
Gladioli Cl. TW12: Hamp 6E 130
Gladsaxe Ho. SM1: Sutt 4K 165
Gladsdale Dr. HA5: Eastc 4J 39
Gladsmuir Rd. EN5: Barn 2B 20
Gladsmuir Rd. N19 1G 65
Gladstone Av. E12 7C 70
Gladstone Av. N22 2A 48
Gladstone Av. TW14: Felt 6J 111
Gladstone Av. TW2: Twick 1H 131
Gladstone Ct. NW6 7A 64
(off Fairfax Rd.)
Gladstone Ct. SW1 4D 18 (4H 101)
(off Regency St.)
Gladstone Ct. Bus. Cen. SW8
1F 119
(off Pagden St.)
Gladstone Gdns. TW3: Houn 1G 113
Gladstone Ho. CR4: Mitc 2D 154
Gladstone Ho. E14 6C 86
(off E. India Dock Rd.)
Gladstone M. N22 2A 48
Gladstone M. NW6 7H 63
(off Cavendish Rd.)
Gladstone M. SE20 7J 139
Gladstone Pde. NW2 2E 62
Gladstone Pk. Gdns. NW2 4D 62
Gladstone Pl. E3 2B 86
Gladstone Pl. EN5: Barn 4A 20
Gladstone Pl. KT8: E Mos 5J 149
Gladstone Rd. BR6: Farnb 5G 173
Gladstone Rd. CR0: C'don 7D 156
Gladstone Rd. IG9: Buck H 1F 37
Gladstone Rd. KT1: King T 3G 151
Gladstone Rd. KT6: Surb 2D 162
Gladstone Rd. SW19 7J 135
Gladstone Rd. UB2: S'hall 2C 94
Gladstone Rd. W4 3K 97
Gladstone St. SE1 1K 19 (3B 102)
Gladstone St. SE27 5C 138
(off Bentons La.)
Gladstone Ter. SW8 1F 119
Gladstone Way HA3: W'stone 3J 41
Gladwell Rd. BR1: Broml 6J 141
Gladwell Rd. N8 6K 47
Gladwin Ho. NW1 1B 6 (2G 83)
(off Werrington St.)
Gladwyn Rd. SW15 3F 117
Gladys Ct. BR1: Broml 2H 141
Gladys Dimson Ho. E7 5H 69
Gladys Rd. NW6 7J 63
Glaisher St. SE8 6C 104
Glamis Ct. W3 2H 97
Glamis Cres. UB3: Harl 3E 92
Glamis Pl. E1 7J 85
Glamis Rd. E1 7J 85
Glamis Way UB5: N'olt 6G 59
Glamorgan Cl. CR4: Mitc 3J 155
Glamorgan Ct. W7 5K 77
(off Copley Cl.)
Glamorgan Rd. KT1: Hamp W 7C 132
Glandford Way RM6: Chad H 5B 54
Glanfield Rd. BR3: Beck 4B 158
Glanleam Rd. HA7: Stan 4J 27
Glanville M. HA7: Stan 5F 27
Glanville Rd. BR2: Broml 3K 159
Glanville Rd. SW2 5J 119
Glasbrook Av. TW2: Whitt 1D 130
Glasbrook Rd. SE9 7B 124
Glaserton Rd. N16 7E 48
Glasford St. SW17 6D 136
Glasfryn Ct. HA2: Harr 2H 59
(off Roxeth Hill)
Glasfryn Ho. HA2: Harr 2H 59
(off Roxeth Hill)
Glasgow Ho. W9 2K 81
(off Maida Vale)
Glasgow Rd. E13 2K 87
Glasgow Rd. N18 5C 34
Glasgow Ter. SW1 6A 18 (5G 101)
Glasier Ct. E15 7G 69
Glaskin M. E9 6A 68
Glass Blowers Ho. E14 6F 87
(off Valencia Cl.)
Glass Bldg., The NW1 1F 83
(off Jamestown Rd.)
Glasse Cl. W13 7A 78
Glass Foundry Yd. E13 5K 87
(off Denmark St.)
Glasshill St. SE1 6B 14 (2B 102)
Glass Ho. WC2 1E 12 (6J 83)
(off Shaftesbury Av.)
Glass Ho., The SE1 7G 15 (2E 102)
(off Royal Oak Yd.)
Glasshouse Cl. UB8: Hil 5D 74
Glasshouse Flds. E1 7K 85
(not continuous)
Glasshouse Gdns. E20 7E 68
Glasshouse Gdns. Development E20
7D 68
Glasshouse St. W1 3B 12 (7G 83)
Glasshouse Wlk. SE11 5F 19 (5J 101)
Glasshouse Yd. EC1 4C 8 (4C 84)
Glasslyn Rd. N8 5H 47
Glassmill La. BR2: Broml 2H 159
Glass Mill Leisure Cen. 3E 122
Glass St. E2 4H 85
Glassworks Studios E2 1H 9 (3E 84)
(off Basing Pl.)
Glass Yd. SE18 3E 106
Glastonbury Av. IG8: Wfd G 7G 37
Glastonbury Ct. SE14 7J 103
(off Farrow La.)
Glastonbury Ho. SE12 5H 123
(off Wantage Rd.)
Glastonbury Ho. SW1 5J 17 (5F 101)
(part of Abbots Mnr.)
Glastonbury Pl. E1 6J 85
Glastonbury Rd. N9 1B 34
Glastonbury Rd. SM4: Mord 7J 153
Glastonbury St. NW6 5H 63
Glaston Ct. W5 1D 96
(off Grange Rd.)
Glaucus St. E3 5D 86
Glazbury Rd. W14 4G 99
Glazebrook Cl. SE21 2D 138
Glazebrook Rd. TW11: Tedd 7K 131
Glebe, The BR7: Chst 1G 161
Glebe, The KT4: Wor Pk 1B 164
Glebe, The SE3 3G 123
Glebe, The SW16 4H 137
Glebe, The UB7: W Dray 4B 92
Glebe Av. CR4: Mitc 2C 154
Glebe Av. EN2: Enf 3G 23
Glebe Av. HA3: Kenton 4E 42
Glebe Av. HA4: Ruis 6K 57
Glebe Av. IG8: Wfd G 6D 36
Glebe Av. UB10: Ick 3E 56
Glebe Cl. UB10: Ick 4E 56
Glebe Cl. W4 5A 98
Glebe Cotts. TW13: Hanw 3E 130
(off Twickenham Rd.)
Glebe Ct. CR4: Mitc 3D 154
Glebe Ct. E3 3D 86
(off Rainhill Way)
Glebe Ct. HA7: Stan 5H 27
Glebe Ct. N13 3F 33
Glebe Ct. SE3 3G 123
Glebe Ct. W5 1D 96
Glebe Ct. W7 7H 77
Glebe Cres. HA3: Kenton 3E 42
Glebe Cres. NW4 4E 44
Glebe Farm Bus. Pk. BR2: Kes 7B 172
Glebe Gdns. KT3: N Mald 7A 152
Glebe Ho. SE16 3H 103
(off Slippers Pl.)
Glebe Ho. Dr. BR2: Hayes 1K 171
Glebe Hyrst SE19 4E 138
Glebe Knoll BR2: Broml 2H 159
Glebeland Gdns. TW17: Shep 6E 146
Glebelands E10 2D 68
Glebelands KT8: W Mole 5F 149
Glebelands Av. E18 2J 51
Glebelands Av. IG2: Ilf 7H 53
Glebelands Cl. N12 1B 46
Glebelands Cl. SE5 3E 120
Glebelands Rd. TW14: Felt 1J 129
Glebe La. HA3: Kenton 4E 42
Glebe M. DA15: Sidc 6K 125
Glebe Path CR4: Mitc 3D 154
Glebe Pl. SW3 7C 16 (6C 100)
Glebe Rd. BR1: Broml 1J 159
Glebe Rd. E8 7F 67
Glebe Rd. HA7: Stan 5H 27
Glebe Rd. N3 1A 46
Glebe Rd. N8 4K 47
Glebe Rd. NW10 6C 62
Glebe Rd. RM10: Dag 6H 73
Glebe Rd. SM2: Cheam 7G 165
Glebe Rd. SM5: Cars 6D 166
Glebe Rd. SW13 2C 116
Glebe Rd. UB3: Hayes 1H 93
Glebe Side TW1: Twick 6K 113
Glebe Sq. CR4: Mitc 3D 154
Glebe St. W4 5A 98
Glebe Ter. W4 5A 98
Glebe Way BR4: W W'ck 2E 170
Glebe Way IG8: Wfd G 5F 37
Glebe Way TW13: Hanw 3E 130
Gledhow Gdns. SW5 4A 100
Gledstanes Rd. W14 5G 99
Gledwood Av. UB4: Hayes 5H 75
Gledwood Ct. UB4: Hayes 5H 75
Gledwood Cres. UB4: Hayes 5H 75
Gledwood Dr. UB4: Hayes 5H 75
Gledwood Gdns. UB4: Hayes 5H 75
Gleed Av. WD23: B Hea 2C 26
Gleeson Dr. BR6: Chels 5K 173
Glegg Pl. SW15 4F 117
Glen, The BR2: Broml 2G 159
Glen, The BR6: Farnb 3D 172
Glen, The CR0: C'don 3K 169
Glen, The EN2: Enf 4G 23
Glen, The HA5: Eastc 5K 39
Glen, The HA5: Pinn 7C 40
Glen, The HA9: Wemb 4E 60
Glen, The UB2: S'hall 5D 94
Glenaffric Av. E14 4E 104
Glen Albyn Rd. SW19 2F 135
Glenallan Ho. W14 4H 99
(off North End Cres.)
Glenalla Rd. HA4: Ruis 7H 39
Glenalmond Ho. TW15: Ashf 3A 128
Glenalmond Rd. HA3: Kenton 4E 42
Glena Mt. SM1: Sutt 4A 166
Glenarm Rd. E5 4J 67
Glen Av. TW15: Ashf 4C 128
Glenavon Cl. KT10: Clay 6A 162
Glenavon Ct. KT4: Wor Pk 2D 164
Glenavon Lodge BR3: Beck 7C 140
Glenavon Rd. E15 7G 69
Glenbarr Cl. SE9 3F 125
Glenbow Rd. BR1: Broml 6G 141
Glenbrook Nth. EN2: Enf 4E 22
Glenbrook Rd. NW6 5J 63
Glenbrook Sth. EN2: Enf 4E 22
Glenbuck Ct. KT6: Surb 6E 150
Glenbuck Rd. KT6: Surb 6D 150
Glenburnie Rd. SW17 3D 136
Glencairn Dr. W5 4C 78
Glencairne Cl. E16 5B 88
Glencairn Rd. SW16 1J 155
Glencar Ct. SE19 6B 138
Glen Cl. TW17: Shep 4C 146
Glencoe Av. IG2: Ilf 7H 53
Glencoe Dr. RM10: Dag 4G 73
Glencoe Mans. SW9 7A 102
(off Mowll St.)
Glencoe Rd. UB4: Yead 5B 76
Glen Ct. BR1: Broml 7H 141
(off Bromley Av.)
Glen Ct. DA15: Sidc 4A 144
Glen Cres. IG8: Wfd G 6E 36
Glendale Av. HA8: Edg 4A 28
Glendale Av. N22 7F 33
Glendale Av. RM6: Chad H 7C 54
Glendale Cl. SE9 3E 124
Glendale Dr. SW19 5H 135
Glendale Gdns. HA9: Wemb 1D 60
Glendale M. BR3: Beck 1D 158
Glendale Rd. DA8: Erith 4J 109
Glendale Way SE28 7C 90
Glendall St. SW9 4K 119
Glendarvon St. SW15 3F 117
Glendevon Cl. HA8: Edg 3C 28
Glendish Rd. N17 1H 49
Glendor Gdns. NW7 4E 28
Glendower Gdns. SW14 3K 115
Glendower Pl. SW7 3A 16 (4B 100)
Glendower Rd. E4 1A 36
Glendower Rd. SW14 3K 115
Glendown Ho. E8 5G 67
Glendown Rd. SE2 5A 108
Glendun Ct. W3 7A 80
Glendun Rd. W3 7A 80
Gleneagle M. SW16 5H 137
Gleneagle Rd. SW16 5H 137
Gleneagles HA7: Stan 7G 27
Gleneagles W13 5B 78
(off Malvern Way)
Gleneagles Cl. BR6: Orp 1H 173
Gleneagles Cl. SE16 5H 103
Gleneagles Grn. BR6: Orp 1H 173
Gleneagles Twr. UB1: S'hall 6G 77
(off Fleming Rd.)
Gleneldon M. SW16 4J 137
Gleneldon Rd. SW16 4J 137
Glenelg Rd. SW2 5J 119
Glenesk Rd. SE9 3E 124
Glenfarg Rd. SE6 1E 140
Glenfield Cres. HA4: Ruis 7F 39
Glenfield Rd. SW12 1G 137
Glenfield Rd. TW15: Ashf 6D 128
Glenfield Rd. W13 2B 96
Glenfield Ter. W13 2B 96
Glenfinlas Way SE5 7B 102
Glenforth St. SE10 5H 105
Glengall Bus. Cen. SE15 6F 103
Glengall Gro. E14 3D 104
Glengall Pas. NW6 1J 81
(off Priory Pk. Rd.)
Glengall Rd. DA7: Bex 3E 126
Glengall Rd. HA8: Edg 3C 28
Glengall Rd. IG8: Wfd G 6D 36
Glengall Rd. NW6 1H 81
Glengall Rd. SE15 5F 103
Glengall Ter. SE15 6F 103
Glen Gdns. CR0: Wadd 3A 168
Glengariff Mans. SW9 7A 102
(off Sth. Island Pl.)
Glengarnock Av. E14 4E 104
Glengarry Rd. SE22 5E 120
Glenham Dr. IG2: Ilf 5F 53
Glenhead Cl. SE9 3F 125
Glenhill Cl. N3 2J 45
Glen Ho. E16 1E 106
(off Storey St.)
Glenhouse Rd. SE9 5E 124
Glenhurst BR3: Beck 1E 158
Glenhurst Av. DA5: Bexl 1F 145
Glenhurst Av. HA4: Ruis 7E 38
Glenhurst Av. NW5 4E 64
Glenhurst Ct. SE19 5F 139
Glenhurst Ri. SE19 7C 138
Glenhurst Rd. N12 5G 31
Glenhurst Rd. TW8: Bford 6C 96
Glenilla Rd. NW3 6C 64
Glenister Gdns. UB3: Hayes 2K 93
Glenister Ho. UB3: Hayes 1K 93
(off Avondale Dr.)
Glenister Pk. Rd. SW16 7H 137
Glenister Rd. SE10 5H 105
Glenister St. E16 1E 106
Glenkerry Ho. E14 6E 86
(off Burcham St.)
Glenlea Rd. SE9 5D 124
Glenloch Rd. EN3: Enf H 2D 24
Glenloch Rd. NW3 6C 64
Glenluce Rd. SE3 6J 105
Glenlyon Rd. SE9 5E 124
Glenmead IG9: Buck H 1F 37
Glenmere Av. NW7 7H 29
Glenmere Row SE12 6J 123
Glen M. E17 5B 50
Glenmill TW12: Hamp 5D 130
Glenmore Lawns W13 6A 78
Glenmore Lodge BR3: Beck 1D 158
Glenmore Pde. HA0: Wemb 1E 78
Glenmore Rd. DA16: Well 7K 107
Glenmore Rd. NW3 6C 64
Glenmore Way IG11: Bark 2A 90
Glenmount Path SE18 5G 107
Glennie Ct. SE22 1G 139
Glennie Rd. SE27 3A 138
Glenny Rd. IG11: Bark 6G 71
Glenorchy Cl. UB4: Yead 5C 76
Glenpark Ct. W13 7A 78
Glenparke Rd. E7 6K 69
Glenridding NW1 1B 6 (2G 83)
(off Ampthill Est.)
Glen Ri. IG8: Wfd G 6E 36
Glen Rd. E13 4A 88
Glen Rd. E17 5B 50
Glen Rd. KT9: Chess 4F 163
Glen Rd. End SM6: W'gton 7F 167
Glenrosa St. SW6 2A 118
Glenrose Ct. DA14: Sidc 5B 144
Glenrose Ct. SE1 7G 15 (3E 102)
(off Long La.)
Glenroy St. W12 6E 80
Glensdale Rd. SE4 3B 122
Glenshaw Mans. SW9 7A 102
(off Brixton Rd.)
Glenshiel Rd. SE9 5E 124
Glentanner Way SW17 3B 136
Glen Ter. E14 2E 104
(off Manchester Rd.)
Glentham Gdns. SW13 6D 98
Glentham Rd. SW13 6C 98
Glenthorne Av. CR0: C'don 1H 169
Glenthorne Cl. SM3: Sutt 1J 165
Glenthorne Cl. UB10: Hil 3C 74
Glenthorne Gdns. IG6: Ilf 3E 52
Glenthorne Gdns. SM3: Sutt 1J 165
Glenthorne M. W6 4D 98
Glenthorne Rd. E17 5A 50
Glenthorne Rd. KT1: King T 4F 151
Glenthorne Rd. N11 5J 31
Glenthorne Rd. W6 4D 98
Glenthorpe Av. SW15 4C 116
Glenthorpe Gdns. HA7: Stan 3E 26
Glenthorpe Rd. SM4: Mord 5F 153
Glenton M. SE15 2J 121
Glenton Rd. SE13 4G 123
Glentrammon Av. BR6: Chels 6K 173
Glentrammon Cl. BR6: Chels 5K 173
Glentrammon Gdns. BR6: Chels
6K 173
Glentrammon Rd. BR6: Chels 6K 173
Glentworth St. NW1 4F 5 (4D 82)
Glenure Rd. SE9 5E 124
Glenvern Ct. TW7: Isle 2A 114
(off White Lodge Cl.)
Glenview SE2 6D 108
Glenview Rd. BR1: Broml 2B 160
Glenville Av. EN2: Enf 1H 23
Glenville Gro. SE8 7B 104
Glenville M. SW18 7K 117
Glenville M. Ind. Est. SW18 7J 117
Glenville Rd. KT2: King T 1G 151
Glen Wlk. TW7: Isle 5H 113
(not continuous)
Glenwood Av. NW9 1A 62
Glenwood Cl. HA1: Harr 5K 41
Glenwood Ct. DA14: Sidc 4A 144
Glenwood Ct. E18 3J 51
Glenwood Gdns. IG2: Ilf 5E 52
Glenwood Gro. NW9 1J 61
Glenwood Rd. KT17: Ewe 6C 164
Glenwood Rd. N15 5B 48
Glenwood Rd. NW7 3F 29
Glenwood Rd. SE6 1B 140
Glenwood Rd. TW3: Houn 3H 113
Glenwood Way CR0: C'don 6K 157
Glenworth Av. E14 4F 105
Gliddon Dr. E5 4H 67
Gliddon Rd. W14 4G 99
Glimpsing Grn. DA18: Erith 3E 108
Glisson Rd. UB10: Hil 2C 74
Global App. E3 2E 86
Globe Apts. SE8 6B 104
(off Evelyn St.)
Globe Ho. E14 6G 87
Globe Pond Rd. SE16 1A 104
Globe Rd. E1 3J 85
Globe Rd. E15 5H 69
Globe Rd. E2 3J 85
Globe Rd. IG8: Wfd G 6F 37
Globe St. SE1 7E 14 (3D 102)
Globe Ter. E2 3J 85
GLOBE TOWN 3K 85
Globe Town Mkt. 3K 85
Globe Vw. EC4 2C 14 (7C 84)
(off High Timber St.)
Globe Wharf SE16 7K 85
Glossop Rd. CR2: Sande 7D 168
Gloster Ridley Ct. E14 6B 86
(off St Anne's Row)
Gloster Rd. KT3: N Mald 4A 152
Gloucester W14 4H 99
(off Kensington Village)
Gloucester Arc. SW7 4A 100
Gloucester Av. DA15: Sidc 2J 143
Gloucester Av. DA16: Well 4K 125
Gloucester Av. NW1 7E 64
Gloucester Cir. SE10 7E 104
Gloucester Cl. KT7: T Ditt 1A 162
Gloucester Cl. NW10 7K 61
Gloucester Ct. SE1 Rolls Rd. 5F 103
(off Rolls Rd.)
Gloucester Ct. SE1 Swan St.
7D 14 (3C 102)
(off Swan St.)
Gloucester Ct. CR4: Mitc 5J 155
Gloucester Ct. EC3 3H 15 (7E 84)
Gloucester Ct. HA1: Harr 3J 41
Gloucester Ct. NW11 7H 45
(off Golders Grn. Rd.)
Gloucester Ct. SE22 1G 139
Gloucester Ct. TW9: Kew 7G 97
Gloucester Ct. W7 5K 77
(off Copley Cl.)
Gloucester Cres. NW1 1F 83
Gloucester Dr. N4 2B 66
Gloucester Dr. NW11 4J 45
Gloucester Gdns. EN4: Cockf 4K 21
Gloucester Gdns. IG1: Ilf 7C 52
Gloucester Gdns. NW11 7H 45
Gloucester Gdns. SM1: Sutt 2K 165
Gloucester Gdns. W2 6A 82
Gloucester Ga. NW1 2F 83
(not continuous)
GLOUCESTER GA. BRI. 1F 83
(off Gloucester Gate)
Gloucester Ga. M. NW1 2F 83
Gloucester Gro. HA8: Edg 1K 43
Gloucester Ho. E16 1J 105
(off Gatcombe Rd.)
Gloucester Ho. NW6 2J 81
(off Cambridge Rd.)
Gloucester Ho. SW9 7A 102
Gloucester Ho. TW10: Rich 5G 115
Gloucester M. E10 7C 50
Gloucester M. W2 1A 10 (6A 82)
Gloucester M. W. W2 6A 82
Gloucester Pde. DA15: Sidc 5A 126
Gloucester Pde. UB3: Harl 3E 92

Gloucester Pk. Apts. – Graham Gdns.

Gloucester Pk. Apts. SW7 ....4A **100**
.... *(off Ashburn Pl.)*
Gloucester Pl. NW1 ....3E **4** (4D **82**)
Gloucester Pl. W1 ....5F **5** (5D **82**)
Gloucester Pl. M. W1 ....6F **5** (5D **82**)
Gloucester Rd. CR0: C'don 1D **168**
Gloucester Rd. DA17: Belv 5F **109**
Gloucester Rd. E10 ....7C **50**
Gloucester Rd. E11 ....5K **51**
Gloucester Rd. E12 ....3D **70**
Gloucester Rd. E17 ....2K **49**
Gloucester Rd. EN2: Enf 1H **23**
Gloucester Rd. EN5: New Bar 5E **20**
Gloucester Rd. HA1: Harr 5F **41**
Gloucester Rd. KT1: King T 2G **151**
Gloucester Rd. N17 ....2D **48**
Gloucester Rd. N18 ....5A **34**
Gloucester Rd. SW7 ....3A **100**
Gloucester Rd. TW11: Tedd 5J **131**
Gloucester Rd. TW12: Hamp 7F **131**
Gloucester Rd. TW13: Felt 1A **130**
Gloucester Rd. TW2: Twick 1G **131**
Gloucester Rd. TW4: Houn 4C **112**
Gloucester Rd. TW9: Kew 7G **97**
Gloucester Rd. W3 ....2J **97**
Gloucester Rd. W5 ....2C **96**
Gloucester Sq. E2 ....1G **85**
Gloucester Sq. W2 ....1B **10** (6B **82**)
.... (not continuous)
Gloucester St. SW1 ....6A **18** (5G **101**)
Gloucester Ter. N14 ....1C **32**
.... *(off Crown La.)*
Gloucester Ter. W2 ....6K **81**
Gloucester Wlk. W8 ....2J **99**
Gloucester Way EC1 ....2K **7** (3A **84**)
Glover Cl. SE2 ....4C **108**
Glover Dr. N18 ....6D **34**
Glover Ho. NW6 ....7A **64**
.... *(off Harben Rd.)*
Glover Ho. SE15 ....4H **121**
Glover Rd. HA5: Pinn 6B **40**
Glovers Gro. HA4: Ruis 7D **38**
Gloxinia Wlk. TW12: Hamp 6E **130**
Glycena Rd. SW11 ....3D **118**
Glyn Av. EN4: E Barn 4G **21**
Glyn Cl. SE25 ....2E **156**
Glyn Ct. HA7: Stan 6G **27**
Glyn Ct. SW16 ....3A **138**
Glyndale Grange SM2: Sutt 6K **165**
Glyndebourne Ct. UB5: N'olt 3A **76**
.... *(off Canberra Dr.)*
Glyndebourne Pk. BR6: Farnb
....2F **173**
Glynde M. SW3 ....2D **16** (3C **100**)
.... *(off Walton St.)*
Glynde Reach WC1 ....2F **7** (3J **83**)
.... *(off Harrison St.)*
Glynde Rd. DA7: Bex 3D **126**
Glynde St. SE4 ....6B **122**
Glyndon Rd. SE18 ....4G **107**
.... (not continuous)
Glyn Dr. DA14: Sidc 4B **144**
Glynfield Rd. NW10 ....7A **62**
Glyn Mans. W14 ....4G **99**
.... *(off Hammersmith Rd.)*
Glynne Rd. N22 ....2A **48**
Glyn Rd. E5 ....4K **67**
Glyn Rd. EN3: Pond E 4D **24**
Glyn Rd. KT4: Wor Pk 2F **165**
Glyn St. SE11 ....6G **19** (5K **101**)
Glynswood Pl. HA6: Nwood 1D **38**
Glynwood Ct. SE23 ....2J **139**
Goals Soccer Cen. Bexleyheath 3F **127**
Goals Soccer Cen. Chingford 6H **35**
Goals Soccer Cen. Dagenham 1D **90**
Goals Soccer Cen. Eltham 6A **124**
Goals Soccer Cen. Gillette Corner
....6K **95**
Goals Soccer Cen. Hayes 1A **94**
Goals Soccer Cen. Heathrow 4E **92**
Goals Soccer Cen. Ruislip 5B **58**
Goals Soccer Cen. Sutton 3F **165**
Goals Soccer Cen. Tolworth 2J **163**
Goals Soccer Cen. Wimbledon 3C **152**
Go Ape! Alexandra Palace 2H **47**
Go Ape! Battersea Park 1D **118**
Go Ape! Trent Park 3K **21**
Goater's All. SW6 ....7H **99**
.... *(off Dawes Rd.)*
GOAT HO. BRI. 3G **157**
Goat Rd. CR4: Cars 7D **154**
Goat Rd. CR4: Mitc 7D **154**
Goat Wharf TW8: Bford 6E **96**
Goby Ho. SE8 ....7D **104**
.... *(off Creative Rd.)*
Godalming Av. SM6: W'gton 5J **167**
Godalming Rd. E14 ....5D **86**
Godbold Rd. E15 ....4G **87**
Goddard Cl. TW17: Shep 3B **146**
Goddard Ct. HA3: Kenton 2A **42**
Goddard Ho. KT8: E Mos 5H **149**
Goddard Ho. SE11 ....4B **102**
.... *(off George Mathers Rd.)*
Goddard Pl. N19 ....3G **65**
Goddard Rd. BR3: Beck 4K **157**
Goddards Way IG1: Ilf 1H **71**
Goddarts Ho. E17 ....3C **50**
Goddington La. BR6: Chels 3K **173**
Godfree Ct. SE1 ....6E **14** (2D **102**)
.... *(off Long La.)*
Godfrey Av. TW2: Whitt 7H **113**
Godfrey Av. UB5: N'olt 1C **76**
Godfrey Hill SE18 ....4C **106**
Godfrey Ho. EC1 ....2E **8** (3D **84**)
.... *(off St Luke's Est.)*
Godfrey Pl. E2 ....2J **9** (3F **85**)
.... *(off Austin St.)*
Godfrey Rd. SE18 ....4D **106**
Godfrey St. E15 ....2E **86**
Godfrey St. SW3 ....5D **16** (5C **100**)
Godfrey Way TW4: Houn 7C **112**
Goding St. SE11 ....5F **19** (5J **101**)
Godley Cl. SE14 ....1J **121**
Godley Rd. SW18 ....1B **136**
Godliman St. EC4 ....1B **14** (6B **84**)
Godman Rd. SE15 ....2H **121**
Godolphin Cl. N13 ....6G **33**
Godolphin Ho. NW3 ....7C **64**
.... *(off Fellows Rd.)*
Godolphin Pl. W3 ....7K **79**
Godolphin Rd. W12 ....1D **98**
.... (not continuous)
Godson Rd. CR0: Wadd 3A **168**
Godson St. N1 ....2A **84**
Godson Yd. NW6 ....3J **81**
Godstone Ho. SE1 ....7F **15** (3D **102**)
.... *(off Pardoner St.)*
Godstone Rd. SM1: Sutt 4A **166**
Godstone Rd. TW1: Twick 6B **114**
Godstow Rd. SE2 ....2B **108**
Godward Sq. E1 ....4K **85**
Godwin Cl. E4 ....1K **25**
Godwin Cl. KT19: Ewe 6J **163**
Godwin Cl. N1 ....2C **84**
Godwin Ct. NW1 ....2G **83**
.... *(off Chalton St.)*
Godwin Ho. E2 ....2F **85**
.... *(off Thurtle Rd.)*
Godwin Ho. SE1 ....5J **15** (1F **103**)
.... *(off Duchess Wlk.)*
Godwin Rd. BR2: Broml 3A **160**
Godwin Rd. E7 ....4K **69**
Goffers Rd. SE3 ....1G **123**
Goffs Rd. TW15: Ashf 6F **129**
Goidel Cl. SM6: Bedd 4H **167**
Golborne Gdns. W10 ....4G **81**
.... (not continuous)
Golborne M. W10 ....5G **81**
Golborne Rd. W10 ....5G **81**
Golda Cl. EN5: Barn 6A **20**
Golda Ct. N3 ....2H **45**
Goldbeaters Gro. HA8: Edg 6F **29**
Goldbeaters Ho. W1 ....1D **12** (6H **83**)
.... *(off Manette St.)*
Goldcliff Cl. SM4: Mord 7J **153**
Goldcrest Cl. E16 ....5B **88**
Goldcrest Cl. SE28 ....7C **90**
Goldcrest M. N16 ....3G **67**
Goldcrest M. W5 ....5D **78**
Goldcrest Way CR0: New Ad 7F **171**
Goldcrest Way WD23: Bush 1B **26**
Golden Anchor Ho. SE10 ....3J **105**
.... *(off Latimer Square)*
Golden Bus. Pk. E10 ....1A **68**
Golden Ct. EN4: E Barn 4H **21**
Golden Ct. TW7: Isle 2H **113**
Golden Ct. TW9: Rich 5D **114**
Golden Cres. UB3: Hayes 1H **93**
Golden Cross M. W11 ....6H **81**
.... *(off Portobello Rd.)*
Golden Hinde 4E **14** (1D **102**)
Golden Hind Pl. SE8 ....4B **104**
.... *(off Grove St.)*
GOLDEN JUBILEE BRIDGES
....5G **13** (1K **101**)
.... *(off Belvedere Rd.)*
Golden La. BR4: W W'ck 3E **170**
Golden La. EC1 ....3C **8** (4C **84**)
Golden La. Campus EC1 ....4D **8** (4C **84**)
.... *(off Golden La.)*
Golden La. Est. EC1 ....4C **8** (4C **84**)
Golden Lane Sport & Fitness Cen.
....4C **8** (4C **84**)
.... *(off Golden La. Est.)*
Golden Mnr. W7 ....7J **77**
Golden M. SE20 ....1J **157**
Golden Mile Ho. TW8: Bford 5E **96**
.... *(off Clayponds La.)*
Golden Pde. E17 ....3E **50**
.... *(off Wood St.)*
Golden Plover Cl. E16 ....6J **87**
Golden Sq. W1 ....2B **12** (7G **83**)
Golden Yd. NW3 ....4A **64**
.... *(off Holly Mt.)*
Golders Cl. HA8: Edg 5C **28**
Golders Ct. NW11 ....7H **45**
Golders Gdns. NW11 ....7G **45**
GOLDERS GREEN 6G **45**
Golders Grn. Crematorium 7J **45**
Golders Grn. Cres. NW11 ....7H **45**
Golders Grn. Rd. NW11 ....6G **45**
Golderslea NW11 ....1J **63**
Golders Mnr. Dr. NW11 ....6F **45**
Golders Pk. Cl. NW11 ....1J **63**
Golders Ri. NW4 ....5F **45**
Golders Way NW11 ....7H **45**
Golderton NW4 ....4D **44**
.... *(off Prince of Wales Cl.)*
Goldfinch Ct. E3 ....2C **86**
.... *(off Four Seasons Cl.)*
Goldfinch Rd. SE28 ....3H **107**
Goldhawk Ho. NW9 ....2C **44**
Goldhawk M. W12 ....2D **98**
Goldhawk Rd. W12 ....3C **98**
Goldhawk Rd. W6 ....4B **98**
Goldhaze Cl. IG8: Wfd G 7F **37**
Gold Hill HA8: Edg 6E **28**
Goldhurst Ho. W6 ....6E **98**
Goldhurst Mans. NW6 ....6A **64**
.... *(off Goldhurst Ter.)*
Goldhurst Ter. NW6 ....7K **63**
Goldie Ho. N19 ....7H **47**
Golding Cl. KT9: Chess 6C **162**
Golding Cl. N18 ....6J **33**
Golding Ct. IG1: Ilf 3E **70**
Golding Ct. IG1: Ilf 3E **70**
Golding Ho. NW9 ....2C **44**
Golding St. E1 ....6G **85**
.... (not continuous)
Golding Ter. E1 ....6G **85**
.... *(off Rope Wlk. Gdns.)*
Golding Ter. SW11 ....2E **118**
Goldington Bldgs. NW1 ....1H **83**
.... *(off Royal College St.)*
Goldington Cres. NW1 ....2H **83**
Goldington St. NW1 ....2H **83**
Gold La. HA8: Edg 6E **28**
Goldman Cl. E2 ....3K **9** (4G **85**)
Goldney Rd. W9 ....4J **81**
Goldrill Dr. N11 ....2K **31**
Goldsboro' Rd. SW8 ....1H **119**
Goldsborough Cres. E4 ....2J **35**
Goldsborough Ho. E14 ....5D **104**
.... *(off St Davids Sq.)*
Goldsdown Cl. EN3: Enf H 2F **25**
Goldsdown Rd. EN3: Enf H 2E **24**
Goldsmid St. SE18 ....5J **107**
Goldsmith Av. E12 ....6C **70**
Goldsmith Av. NW9 ....5A **44**
Goldsmith Av. RM7: Rush G 7G **55**
Goldsmith Av. W3 ....7K **79**
Goldsmith Cl. HA2: Harr 1E **58**
Goldsmith Ct. WC2 ....7F **7** (6J **83**)
.... *(off Stukeley St.)*
Goldsmith Est. SE15 ....1G **121**
Goldsmith La. NW9 ....4H **43**
Goldsmith Rd. E10 ....1C **68**
Goldsmith Rd. E17 ....2K **49**
Goldsmith Rd. N11 ....5J **31**
Goldsmith Rd. SE15 ....1G **121**
Goldsmith Rd. W3 ....1K **97**
Goldsmith's Bldgs. W3 ....1K **97**
Goldsmiths Cl. W3 ....1K **97**
Goldsmiths Coll. 1A **122**
Goldsmith's Pl. NW6 ....1K **81**
.... *(off Springfield La.)*
Goldsmith's Row E2 ....2G **85**
Goldsmith's Sq. E2 ....2G **85**
Goldsmith St. EC2 ....7D **8** (6C **84**)
Goldsworthy Gdns. SE16 ....5J **103**
Goldthorpe NW1 ....1G **83**
.... *(off Camden St.)*
Goldwell Ho. SE22 ....3E **120**
.... *(off Quorn Rd.)*
Goldwell Rd. CR7: Thor H 4K **155**
Goldwing Cl. E16 ....6J **87**
Golf Cl. CR7: Thor H 1A **156**
Golf Cl. HA7: Stan 7H **27**
Golf Club Dr. KT2: King T 7K **133**
Golfe Rd. IG1: Ilf 3H **71**
Golf Kingdom Barking 5F **55**
Golf Rd. BR1: Broml 3E **160**
Golf Rd. W5 ....6F **79**
Golf Side TW2: Twick 3H **131**
Golfside Cl. KT3: N Mald 2A **152**
Golfside Cl. N20 ....3H **31**
Gollogly Ter. SE7 ....5A **106**
Gomer Gdns. TW11: Tedd 6A **132**
Gomer Pl. TW11: Tedd 6A **132**
Gomm Rd. SE16 ....3J **103**
Gomshall Av. SM6: W'gton 5J **167**
Gondar Gdns. NW6 ....5H **63**
Gonson St. SE8 ....6D **104**
Gonston Cl. SW19 ....2G **135**
Gonville Cres. UB5: N'olt 6F **59**
Gonville Rd. CR7: Thor H 5K **155**
Gonville St. SW6 ....3G **117**
Gooch Ho. E5 ....3H **67**
Gooch Ho. EC1 ....5J **7** (5A **84**)
.... *(off Portpool La.)*
Gooch Ho. SW11 ....7H **101**
.... *(off Malthouse Rd.)*
Goodall Ho. SE4 ....4K **121**
Goodall Rd. E11 ....3E **68**
Goodchild Rd. N4 ....1C **66**
Gooden Ct. HA1: Harr 3J **59**
Goodenough Rd. SW19 ....7H **135**
Goodey Rd. IG11: Bark 7K **71**
Goodfaith Ho. E14 ....7D **86**
.... *(off Simpson's Rd.)*
Goodge Pl. W1 ....6B **6** (5G **83**)
Goodge St. W1 ....6B **6** (5G **83**)
Goodhall Cl. HA7: Stan 6F **27**
Goodhall St. NW10 ....3B **80**
.... (not continuous)
Goodhart Pl. E14 ....7A **86**
Goodhart Way BR4: W W'ck 7G **159**
Goodhew Rd. CR0: C'don 6G **157**
Goodhope Ho. E14 ....7D **86**
.... *(off Poplar High St.)*
Gooding Cl. KT3: N Mald 4J **151**
Goodinge Cl. N7 ....6J **65**
Goodinge Rd. N7 ....6J **65**
Gooding Ho. SE7 ....5A **106**
Goodman Cres. CR0: C'don 6B **156**
Goodman Cres. SW2 ....2J **137**
Goodman Rd. E10 ....7E **50**
Goodman's Ct. E1 ....2J **15** (7F **85**)
Goodmans Ct. HA0: Wemb 4D **60**
Goodman's Stile E1 ....7K **9** (6G **85**)
Goodmans Yd. E1 ....2J **15** (7F **85**)
GOODMAYES 2A **72**
Goodmayes Av. IG3: Ilf 1A **72**
Goodmayes La. IG3: Ilf 4A **72**
Goodmayes Lodge RM8: Dag 4A **72**
Goodmayes Retail Pk. 1B **72**
Goodmayes Rd. IG3: Ilf 1A **72**
Goodrich Ct. W10 ....6F **81**
Goodrich Ho. E2 ....2J **85**
.... *(off Sewardstone Rd.)*
Goodrich Rd. SE22 ....6F **121**
Goodridge Ho. E4 ....7K **35**
Goodson Ho. SM4: Mord 7A **154**
.... *(off Green La.)*
Goodson Rd. NW10 ....7A **62**
Goodspeed Ho. E14 ....7D **86**
.... *(off Simpson's Rd.)*
Goods Way N1 ....2J **83**
Goodway Gdns. E14 ....6F **87**
Goodwill Dr. HA2: Harr 1E **58**
Goodwill Ho. E14 ....7D **86**
.... *(off Simpson's Rd.)*
Goodwin Cl. CR4: Mitc 3B **154**
Goodwin Cl. SE16 ....3F **103**
Goodwin Ct. EN4: E Barn 6H **21**
Goodwin Ct. N8 ....3J **47**
.... *(off Campsbourne Rd.)*
Goodwin Ct. SW19 ....7C **136**
Goodwin Dr. DA14: Sidc 3D **144**
Goodwin Gdns. CR0: Wadd 6B **168**
Goodwin Ho. N9 ....1D **34**
Goodwin Rd. CR0: Wadd 5B **168**
Goodwin Rd. N9 ....1E **34**
Goodwin Rd. W12 ....2C **98**
Goodwins Ct. WC2 ....2E **12** (7J **83**)
Goodwin St. N4 ....2A **66**
Goodwood Apts. E4 ....7J **35**
Goodwood Cl. HA7: Stan 5H **27**
Goodwood Cl. SM4: Mord 4J **153**
Goodwood Ct. W1 ....5K **5** (5F **83**)
.... *(off Devonshire St.)*
Goodwood Dr. UB5: N'olt 6E **58**
Goodwood Ho. SE14 ....7A **104**
.... *(off Goodwood Rd.)*
Goodwood Pde. BR3: Beck 4A **158**
Goodwood Rd. SE14 ....7A **104**
Goodwyn Av. NW7 ....5F **29**
Goodwyns Va. N10 ....1E **46**
Goodyear Ho. N2 ....2B **46**
.... *(off The Grange)*
Goodyear Pl. SE5 ....6C **102**
Goodyer Ho. SW1 ....5C **18** (5H **101**)
.... *(off Tachbrook St.)*
Goodyers Gdns. NW4 ....5F **45**
Goosander Way SE28 ....3H **107**
Gooseacre La. HA3: Kenton 5D **42**
Goose Grn. Trad. Est. SE22 ....4F **121**
Gooseley La. E6 Claps Ga. La. 4F **89**
Gooseley La. E6 Folkestone Rd. 3E **88**
Goosens Cl. SM1: Sutt 5A **166**
Goose Sq. E6 ....6D **88**
Gophir La. EC4 ....2E **14** (7D **84**)
Gopsall St. N1 ....1D **84**
Gordian Apts. SE10 ....4G **105**
.... *(off Cable Wlk.)*
Gordon Av. E4 ....6B **36**
Gordon Av. HA7: Stan 7E **26**
Gordon Av. SW14 ....4A **116**
Gordon Av. TW1: Twick 5A **114**
Gordonbrock Rd. SE4 ....5C **122**
Gordon Cl. E17 ....6C **50**
Gordon Cl. N19 ....1G **65**
Gordon Cotts. W8 ....2K **99**
.... *(off Dukes La.)*
Gordon Ct. HA8: Edg 5A **28**
Gordon Cres. CR0: C'don 1E **168**
Gordon Cres. UB3: Hayes 4J **93**
Gordondale Rd. SW19 ....2J **135**
Gordon Dr. TW17: Shep 7F **147**
Gordon Gdns. HA8: Edg 2H **43**
Gordon Gro. SE5 ....2B **120**
Gordon Hill EN2: Enf 1H **23**
Gordon Ho. E1 ....7J **85**
.... *(off Glamis Rd.)*
Gordon Ho. SW1 ....2B **18** (3G **101**)
.... *(off Greencoat Pl.)*
Gordon Ho. W5 ....3E **78**
Gordon Ho. Rd. NW5 ....4E **64**
Gordon Mans. W14 ....3F **99**
.... *(off Addison Gdns.)*
Gordon Mans. WC1 ....4C **6** (4H **83**)
.... *(off Torrington Pl.)*
Gordon Pl. W8 ....2J **99**
Gordon Rd. BR3: Beck 3B **158**
Gordon Rd. DA15: Sidc 5J **125**
Gordon Rd. DA17: Belv 4J **109**
Gordon Rd. E11 ....6J **51**
Gordon Rd. E15 ....4E **68**
Gordon Rd. E18 ....1K **51**
Gordon Rd. E4 ....1B **36**
Gordon Rd. EN2: Enf 1H **23**
Gordon Rd. HA3: W'stone 3J **41**
Gordon Rd. IG1: Ilf 3H **71**
Gordon Rd. IG11: Bark 1J **89**
Gordon Rd. KT2: King T 1F **151**
Gordon Rd. KT5: Surb 7F **151**
Gordon Rd. N11 ....7C **32**
Gordon Rd. N3 ....7C **30**
Gordon Rd. N9 ....2C **34**
Gordon Rd. RM6: Chad H 6F **55**
Gordon Rd. SE15 ....2H **121**
Gordon Rd. SM5: Cars 6D **166**
Gordon Rd. TW15: Ashf 3A **128**
Gordon Rd. TW17: Shep 6F **147**
Gordon Rd. TW3: Houn 4G **113**
Gordon Rd. TW9: Rich 2F **115**
Gordon Rd. UB2: S'hall 4C **94**
Gordon Rd. UB7: Yiew 7A **74**
Gordon Rd. W13 ....7B **78**
Gordon Rd. W4 ....6H **97**
Gordon Rd. W5 ....7C **78**
Gordon Sq. WC1 ....3C **6** (4H **83**)
Gordon Sq. Gdn. 3C **6** (4H **83**)
.... *(off Gordon Square)*
Gordon St. E13 ....3J **87**
Gordon St. WC1 ....3C **6** (4H **83**)
Gordon Way BR1: Broml 1J **159**
Gordon Way EN5: Barn 4C **20**
Gore Ct. NW9 ....5G **43**
Gorefield Ho. NW6 ....2J **81**
.... *(off Gorefield Pl.)*
Gorefield Pl. NW6 ....2J **81**
Gore Ho. N1 ....7A **66**
.... *(off Drummond Way)*
Gore Rd. E9 ....1J **85**
Gore Rd. SW20 ....2E **152**
GORESBROOK INTERCHANGE
....2F **91**
Goresbrook Rd. RM9: Dag 1B **90**
Gore St. SW7 ....3A **100**
Gorham Ho. SE16 ....2K **103**
.... *(off Wolfe Cres.)*
Gorham Pl. W11 ....7G **81**
Goring Cl. RM5: Col R 1J **55**
Goring Gdns. RM8: Dag 4C **72**
Goring Rd. N11 ....6D **32**
Goring Rd. RM10: Dag 6K **73**
Goring St. EC3 ....7H **9** (6E **84**)
.... *(off Houndsditch)*
Goring Way UB6: G'frd 2G **77**
Gorleston Rd. N15 ....5D **48**
Gorleston St. W14 ....4G **99**
.... (not continuous)
Gorman Rd. SE18 ....4D **106**
Gorringe Pk. Av. CR4: Mitc 7D **136**
Gorse Cl. E16 ....6J **87**
Gorsefield Ho. E14 ....7C **86**
.... *(off E. India Dock Rd.)*
Gorse Ri. SW17 ....5E **136**
Gorse Rd. CR0: C'don 4C **170**
Gorse Wlk. UB7: Yiew 6A **74**
Gorseway RM7: Rush G 1K **73**
Gorst Rd. NW10 ....4J **79**
Gorst Rd. SW11 ....6D **118**
Gorsuch Pl. E2 ....1J **9** (3F **85**)
Gorsuch St. E2 ....1J **9** (2F **85**)
Gosberton Rd. SW12 ....1D **136**
Gosbury Hill KT9: Chess 4E **162**
Gosfield Rd. RM8: Dag 2G **73**
Gosfield St. W1 ....5A **6** (5G **83**)
Gosford Gdns. IG4: Ilf 5D **52**
Gosford Ho. E3 ....2B **86**
.... *(off Tredegar Rd.)*
Goshawk Ct. NW9 ....7B **44**
Goshawk Gdns. UB4: Hayes 3G **75**
Goslett Yd. WC2 ....1D **12** (6H **83**)
Gosling Cl. UB6: G'frd 3E **76**
Gosling Ho. E1 ....7J **85**
.... *(off Sutton St.)*
Gosling Way SW9 ....1A **120**
Gospatrick Rd. N17 ....7H **33**
GOSPEL OAK 4E **64**
Gosport Rd. E17 ....5B **50**
Gosport Wlk. N17 ....4H **49**
Gossage Rd. SE18 ....5H **107**
Gossage Rd. UB10: Uxb 7B **56**
Gossamer Gdns. E2 ....2H **85**
Gosse Ct. N1 ....1E **84**
.... *(off Downham Rd.)*
Gosset St. E2 ....1K **9** (3F **85**)
Gosshill Rd. BR7: Chst 2E **160**
Gossington Cl. BR7: Chst 4F **143**
Gosterwood St. SE8 ....6A **104**
Gostling Rd. TW2: Whitt 1E **130**
Goston Gdns. CR7: Thor H 3A **156**
Goston Ga. SW8 ....1K **119**
.... *(off Hampson Way)*
Goswell Pl. EC1 ....2B **8** (3B **84**)
.... *(off Goswell Rd.)*
Goswell Rd. EC1 ....1A **8** (2B **84**)
Gothenburg Ct. SE8 ....4A **104**
.... *(off Bailey St.)*
Gothic Cotts. EN2: Enf 2H **23**
.... *(off Chase Grn. Av.)*
Gothic Ct. SE5 ....7C **102**
.... *(off Wyndham Rd.)*
Gothic Ct. UB3: Harl 6F **93**
Gothic Rd. TW2: Twick 2H **131**
Gottfried M. NW5 ....4G **65**
Goudhurst Rd. BR1: Broml 5G **141**
Gough Ho. KT1: King T 2E **150**
.... *(off Eden St.)*
Gough Ho. N1 ....1B **84**
.... *(off Windsor St.)*
Gough Rd. E15 ....4H **69**
Gough Rd. EN1: Enf 2C **24**
Gough Sq. EC4 ....7K **7** (6A **84**)
Gough St. WC1 ....4H **7** (4K **83**)
Gough Wlk. E14 ....6C **86**
Goulden Ho. SW11 ....2C **118**
Goulden Ho. App. SW11 ....2C **118**
Goulding Gdns. CR7: Thor H 2C **156**
Gouldman Ho. E1 ....4J **85**
.... *(off Wyllen Cl.)*
Gould Rd. TW14: Felt 7G **111**
Gould Rd. TW2: Twick 1J **131**
Gould's Grn. UB8: Hil 7D **74**
GOULDS GREEN 5D **74**
Gould Ter. E8 ....5H **67**
Gould Way HA8: Edg 7C **28**
Goulston St. E1 ....7J **9** (6F **85**)
Goulton Rd. E5 ....4H **67**
Gourley Pl. N15 ....5E **48**
Gourley St. N15 ....5E **48**
Gourock Rd. SE9 ....5E **124**
Govan St. E2 ....1G **85**
Gover Ct. SW4 ....2J **119**
Govett Av. TW17: Shep 5E **146**
Govier Cl. E15 ....7G **69**
Gowan Av. SW6 ....1G **117**
Gowan Ho. E2 ....2K **9** (3F **85**)
.... *(off Chambord St.)*
Gowan Rd. NW10 ....6D **62**
Gower Cl. SW4 ....6G **119**
Gower Ct. WC1 ....3C **6** (4H **83**)
Gower Ho. E17 ....3D **50**
Gower Ho. SE17 ....5C **102**
.... *(off Morecambe St.)*
Gower M. WC1 ....6C **6** (5H **83**)
Gower M. Mans. WC1 ....5D **6** (5H **83**)
.... *(off Gower M.)*
Gower Pl. WC1 ....3C **6** (4H **83**)
Gower Rd. E7 ....6J **69**
Gower Rd. TW7: Isle 6K **95**
Gower St. WC1 ....3B **6** (4G **83**)
Gower's Wlk. E1 ....6G **85**
Gowland Pl. BR3: Beck 2B **158**
Gowlett Rd. SE15 ....3G **121**
Gowlland Cl. CR0: C'don 7G **157**
Gowrie Rd. SW11 ....3E **118**
Graburn Way KT8: E Mos 3H **149**
Grace Av. DA7: Bex 2F **127**
Grace Bus. Cen. CR4: Mitc 6D **154**
Gracechurch St. EC3 ....2F **15** (7D **84**)
Grace Cl. HA8: Edg 7D **28**
Grace Cl. SE9 ....3B **142**
Grace Ct. CR0: C'don 3B **168**
.... *(off Waddon Rd.)*
Grace Ct. SM2: Sutt 7K **165**
Gracedale Rd. SW16 ....5F **137**
Gracefield Gdns. SW16 ....3J **137**
Gracehill E1 ....5J **85**
.... *(off Hannibal Rd.)*
Grace Ho. SE11 ....7H **19** (6K **101**)
.... *(off Vauxhall St.)*
Grace Jones Cl. E8 ....6G **67**
Grace M. BR3: Beck 6C **140**
Grace M. SE20 ....2J **157**
.... *(off Marlow Rd.)*
Grace Path SE26 ....4J **139**
Grace Pl. E3 ....3D **86**
Grace Rd. CR0: C'don 6C **156**
Graces All. E1 ....7G **85**
Grace's M. SE5 ....2D **120**
Graces M. NW8 ....2A **82**
Grace's Rd. SE5 ....2E **120**
Grace St. E3 ....3D **86**
Gradient, The SE26 ....4G **139**
Graduate Pl. SE1 ....7G **15** (3E **102**)
.... *(off Long La.)*
Graeme Rd. EN1: Enf 2J **23**
Graemesdyke Av. SW14 ....3H **115**
Grafton Chambers NW1 ....2D **6** (3H **83**)
.... *(off Grafton Pl.)*
Grafton Cl. KT4: Wor Pk 3A **164**
Grafton Cl. TW4: Houn 1C **130**
Grafton Cl. W13 ....6A **78**
Grafton Ct. TW14: Bedf 1F **129**
Grafton Cres. NW1 ....6F **65**
Grafton Gdns. N4 ....6C **48**
Grafton Gdns. RM8: Dag 2E **72**
Grafton Ho. E3 ....3C **86**
.... *(off Wellington Way)*
Grafton Ho. SE8 ....5B **104**
Grafton M. W1 ....4A **6** (4G **83**)
Grafton Pk. Rd. KT4: Wor Pk 2A **164**
Grafton Pl. NW1 ....2D **6** (3H **83**)
Grafton Rd. CR0: C'don 1A **168**
Grafton Rd. EN2: Enf 3E **22**
Grafton Rd. HA1: Harr 5G **41**
Grafton Rd. KT3: N Mald 3A **152**
Grafton Rd. KT4: Wor Pk 3K **163**
Grafton Rd. NW5 ....5E **64**
Grafton Rd. RM8: Dag 2E **72**
Grafton Rd. W3 ....7J **79**
Graftons, The NW2 ....3J **63**
Grafton Sq. SW4 ....3G **119**
Grafton St. W1 ....3K **11** (7F **83**)
Grafton Ter. NW5 ....5D **64**
Grafton Way KT8: W Mole 4D **148**
Grafton Way W1 ....4A **6** (4G **83**)
.... (not continuous)
Grafton Way WC1 ....4B **6** (4G **83**)
Grafton Yd. NW5 ....6F **65**
Graham Av. CR4: Mitc 1E **154**
Graham Av. W13 ....2B **96**
Graham Cl. CR0: C'don 2C **170**
Graham Ct. SE14 ....6K **103**
.... *(off Myers La.)*
Graham Ct. UB5: N'olt 5C **58**
GRAHAME PARK 1A **44**
Grahame Pk. Way NW7 ....7G **29**
Grahame Pk. Way NW9 ....2B **44**
Grahame White Ho. HA3: Kenton 3D **42**
Graham Gdns. KT6: Surb 1E **162**

Graham Ho. N9 .... 1D 34
(off Cumberland Rd.)
Graham Lodge NW4 .... 6D 44
Graham Mans. IG11: Bark 7A 72
(off Lansbury Av.)
Graham Rd. CR4: Mitc 1E 154
Graham Rd. DA6: Bex 4F 127
Graham Rd. E13 .... 4J 87
Graham Rd. E8 .... 6G 67
Graham Rd. HA3: W'stone 3J 41
Graham Rd. N15 .... 3B 48
Graham Rd. NW4 .... 6D 44
Graham Rd. SW19 .... 7H 135
Graham Rd. TW12: Hamp H 4E 130
Graham Rd. W4 .... 3K 97
Graham St. N1 .... 2B 84
Graham Ter. DA15: Sidc 6B 126
(off Westerham Dr.)
Graham Ter. SW1 .... 4G 17 (4E 100)
Grail Rd. SE6 .... 2G 141
Grainger Cl. UB5: N'olt 5F 59
Grainger Ct. SE5 .... 7C 102
Grainger Rd. N22 .... 1C 48
Grainger Rd. TW7: Isle 2K 113
Grainstore, The E16 .... 7J 87
Gramer Cl. E11 .... 2F 69
Gramophone La. UB3: Hayes 3G 93
Grampian Cl. BR6: St M Cry 6K 161
Grampian Cl. SM2: Sutt 7A 166
Grampian Cl. UB3: Harl 7F 93
Grampian Gdns. NW2 .... 1G 63
Grampians, The W6 .... 2F 99
(off Shepherd's Bush Rd.)
Gramsci Way SE6 .... 3D 140
Granada St. SW17 .... 5D 136
Granard Av. SW15 .... 5D 116
Granard Bus. Cen. NW7 .... 6F 29
Granard Ho. E9 .... 6K 67
Granard Rd. SW12 .... 7D 118
Granary Cl. N9 .... 7D 24
Granary Ct. E15 .... 6F 69
(off Millstone Cl.)
Granary Mans. SE28 .... 2G 107
Granary Rd. E1 .... 4H 85
Granary Sq. N1 .... 1J 83
Granary St. NW1 .... 1H 83
Granby Pl. SE1 .... 7J 13 (2A 102)
(off Lwr. Marsh)
Granby Rd. SE9 .... 2D 124
Granby St. E2 .... 3K 9 (4G 85)
(not continuous)
Granby Ter. NW1 .... 1A 6 (2G 83)
Grand Arc. N12 .... 5F 31
Grand Av. EC1 .... 5B 8 (5B 84)
(not continuous)
Grand Av. HA9: Wemb 5G 61
Grand Av. KT5: Surb 5H 151
Grand Av. N10 .... 4E 46
Grand Av. E. HA9: Wemb 5H 61
Grand Canal Apts. N1 .... 1E 84
(off De Beauvoir Cres.)
Grand Canal Av. SE16 .... 4A 104
Grand Courts RM8: Dag 3E 72
Grand Depot Rd. SE18 .... 5E 106
Grand Dr. SW20 .... 2E 152
Grand Dr. UB2: S'hall 2G 95
Granden Rd. SW16 .... 2J 155
Grandfield Ct. W4 .... 6K 97
Grandison Rd. KT4: Wor Pk 2E 164
Grandison Rd. SW11 .... 5D 118
Grand Junc. Wharf E2 .... 3K 85
Grand Junc. Wharf N1 .... 2C 84
Grand Pde. HA9: Wemb 2G 61
Grand Pde. KT6: Surb 1G 163
Grand Pde. N4 .... 5B 48
Grand Pde. SW14 .... 4J 115
(off Up. Richmond Rd. W.)
Grand Pde. M. SW15 .... 5G 117
Grand Regent Twr. E2 .... 3K 85
(off Palmer's Rd.)
Grandstand Way UB5: N'olt 5D 58
Grand Twr. SW15 .... 5G 117
(off Plaza Gdns.)
Grand Union Cen. W10 .... 4F 81
(off West Row)
Grand Union Cl. W9 .... 5H 81
Grand Union Cres. E8 .... 1G 85
Grand Union Ent. Pk. UB2: S'hall 3E 94
Grand Union Hgts. HA0: Wemb 1D 78
Grand Union Ho. N1 .... 1E 84
(off Hertford Rd.)
Grand Union Ind. Est. NW10 .... 2H 79
Grand Union Village UB5: N'olt 3D 76
Grand Union Wlk. NW1 .... 7F 65
(off Kentish Town Rd.)
Grand Union Way UB2: S'hall 2E 94
Grand Vitesse Ind. Cen. SE1
.... 5B 14 (1B 102)
(off Gt. Suffolk St.)
Grand Wlk. E1 .... 4A 86
Granfield St. SW11 .... 1B 118
Grange, The N20 Grangeview Rd. 1F 31
Grange, The N20 Oxford Gdns. 1G 31
Grange, The CR0: C'don 2B 170
Grange, The E17 .... 5A 50
(off Lynmouth Rd.)
Grange, The HA0: Wemb 7G 61
Grange, The KT3: N Mald 5B 152
Grange, The KT4: Wor Pk 4K 163
Grange, The N2 .... 2B 46
Grange, The SE1 .... 7J 15 (3F 103)
Grange, The SW19 .... 6F 135
Grange, The W13 .... 5C 78
Grange, The W14 .... 4H 99
Grange, The W3 .... 2H 97
Grange, The W4 .... 5H 97
Grange Av. EN4: E Barn 1H 31
Grange Av. HA7: Stan 2B 42
Grange Av. IG8: Wfd G 6D 36
Grange Av. N12 .... 5F 31
Grange Av. N20 .... 7B 20
Grange Av. SE25 .... 2E 156
Grange Av. TW2: Twick 2J 131
Grangecliffe Gdns. SE25 .... 2E 156
Grange Cl. DA15: Sidc 3A 144
Grange Cl. HA8: Edg 5D 28
Grange Cl. IG8: Wfd G 7D 36
Grange Cl. KT8: W Mole 4F 149
Grange Cl. TW5: Hest 6D 94
Grange Cl. UB3: Hayes 5G 75
Grange Ct. HA1: Harr 4K 59
Grange Ct. HA5: Pinn 3C 40
Grange Ct. NW10 .... 3A 62
(off Neasden La.)
Grange Ct. SM2: Sutt 7K 165
Grange Ct. SM6: W'gton 3F 167
Grange Ct. TW17: Shep 4C 146
Grange Ct. UB5: N'olt 2A 76
Grange Ct. WC2 .... 1H 13 (6K 83)
Grangecourt Rd. N16 .... 1E 66
Grange Cres. SE28 .... 6C 90
Grangedale Cl. HA6: Nwood 1G 39
Grange Dr. BR7: Chst 6C 142
Grange Farm Cl. HA2: Harr 2G 59
Grangefield NW1 .... 7H 65
(off Marquis Rd.)
Grange Gdns. HA5: Pinn 3C 40
Grange Gdns. N14 .... 1C 32
Grange Gdns. NW3 .... 3K 63
Grange Gdns. SE25 .... 2E 156
Grange Gro. N1 .... 6C 66
Grange Hill HA8: Edg 5D 28
Grange Hill SE25 .... 2E 156
Grangehill Pl. SE9 .... 3D 124
Grangehill Rd. SE9 .... 4D 124
Grange Ho. NW10 .... 7D 62
Grange Ho. SE1 .... 3F 103
Grange La. SE21 .... 2F 139
Grange Lodge SW19 .... 6F 135
Grange Mans. KT17: Ewe 7B 164
Grange M. N21 .... 6G 23
Grange M. TW13: Felt 4J 129
Grangemill Rd. SE6 .... 3C 140
Grangemill Way SE6 .... 2C 140
GRANGE PARK 6G 23
Grange Pk. W5 .... 1E 96
Grange Pk. Av. N21 .... 6H 23
Grange Pk. Pl. SW20 .... 7D 134
Grange Pk. Rd. CR7: Thor H 4D 156
Grange Pk. Rd. E10 .... 1D 68
Grange Pl. NW6 .... 7J 63
Grange Rd. BR6: Orp 2H 173
Grange Rd. CR7: Thor H 4D 156
Grange Rd. E10 .... 1C 68
Grange Rd. E13 .... 3H 87
Grange Rd. E17 .... 5A 50
(not continuous)
Grange Rd. HA1: Harr 5A 42
Grange Rd. HA2: Harr 2H 59
Grange Rd. HA8: Edg 6E 28
Grange Rd. IG1: Ilf 4F 71
Grange Rd. KT1: King T 3E 150
Grange Rd. KT8: W Mole 4F 149
Grange Rd. KT9: Chess 4E 162
Grange Rd. N17 .... 6B 34
Grange Rd. N18 .... 6B 34
Grange Rd. N6 .... 6E 46
Grange Rd. NW10 .... 6D 62
Grange Rd. SE1 .... 3E 102
Grange Rd. SE19 .... 2D 156
Grange Rd. SE25 .... 3D 156
Grange Rd. SM2: Sutt 7J 165
Grange Rd. SW13 .... 1C 116
Grange Rd. UB1: S'hall 2C 94
Grange Rd. UB3: Hayes 6G 75
Grange Rd. W4 .... 5H 97
Grange Rd. W5 .... 1D 96
Grange St. N1 .... 1D 84
Grange Va. SM2: Sutt 7K 165
Grange Vw. Rd. N20 .... 1F 31
Grange Wlk. SE1 .... 3E 102
Grange Wlk. M. SE1 .... 3E 102
(off Grange Wlk.)
Grangeway IG8: Wfd G 4F 37
Grangeway N12 .... 4E 30
Grangeway NW6 .... 7J 63
Grangeway, The N21 .... 6G 23
Grangeway Gdns. IG4: Ilf 5C 52
Grangewood DA5: Bexl 1F 145
Grangewood Cl. HA5: Eastc 5J 39
Grangewood Dr. TW16: Sun 7H 129
Grangewood La. BR3: Beck 6B 140
Grangewood St. E6 .... 1B 88
Grangewood Ter. SE25 .... 2D 156
Grange Yd. SE1 .... 3F 103
Granham Gdns. N9 .... 2A 34
Granite Apts. E15 .... 6G 69
Granite Apts. SE10 .... 5G 105
Granite St. SE18 .... 5K 107
Granleigh Rd. E11 .... 2G 69
Gransden Av. E8 .... 7H 67
Gransden Ho. SE8 .... 5B 104
Gransden Rd. W12 .... 2B 98
Grant Av. KT12: Walt T 5A 148
Grantbridge St. N1 .... 2B 84
Grantchester KT1: King T 2G 151
(off St Peters Rd.)
Grantchester Cl. HA1: Harr 3K 59
Grant Cl. DA17: Belv 5F 109
Grant Cl. N14 .... 7B 22
Grant Cl. N17 .... 2E 48
Grant Cl. TW17: Shep 6D 146
Grant Ct. E4 .... 1K 35
(off The Ridgeway)
Grant Ct. NW9 .... 2B 44
(off Hazel Cl.)
Grantham Cl. HA8: Edg 3K 27
Grantham Ct. KT2: King T 5D 132
Grantham Ct. RM6: Chad H 7F 55
Grantham Ct. SE16 .... 2K 103
(off Eleanor Cl.)
Grantham Gdns. RM6: Chad H 6F 55
Grantham Ho. E14 .... 6G 87
Grantham Ho. SE15 .... 6G 103
(off Friary Est.)
Grantham Ho. TW16: Sun 7G 129
Grantham Ho. UB5: N'olt 3D 76
(off Taywood Rd.)
Grantham Pl. W1 .... 5J 11 (1F 101)
Grantham Rd. E12 .... 4E 70
Grantham Rd. SW9 .... 2J 119
Grantham Rd. W4 .... 7A 98
Grant Ho. E17 .... 4C 50
(off High St.)
Grant Ho. SW9 .... 1K 119
(off Liberty St.)
Grantley Ho. SE14 .... 6K 103
(off Myers La.)
Grantley Rd. TW4: Cran 2A 112
Grantley St. E1 .... 3K 85
Grant Mus. of Zoology 4C 6 (4H 83)
Grantock Rd. E17 .... 1F 51
Granton Rd. DA14: Sidc 6C 144
Granton Rd. IG3: Ilf 1A 72
Granton Rd. SW16 .... 1G 155
Grant Pl. CR0: C'don 1F 169
Grant Rd. CR0: C'don 1F 169
Grant Rd. HA3: W'stone 3K 41
Grant Rd. SW11 .... 4B 118
Grants Cl. NW7 .... 7K 29
Grants Quay Wharf EC3 .... 3F 15 (7D 84)
Grant St. E13 .... 3J 87
Grant St. N1 .... 2A 84
Grant Ter. N16 .... 7G 49
(off Castlewood Rd.)
Grantully Rd. W9 .... 3K 81
Grant Way TW7: Isle 6A 96
Granville Arc. SW9 .... 4A 120
Granville Av. N9 .... 3D 34
Granville Av. TW13: Felt 2J 129
Granville Av. TW3: Houn 5E 112
Granville Cl. CR0: C'don 2E 168
Granville Ct. N1 .... 1E 84
Granville Ct. N4 .... 6K 47
Granville Ct. SE14 .... 7A 104
(off Nynehead St.)
Granville Gdns. SW16 .... 1K 155
Granville Gdns. W5 .... 1F 97
Granville Gro. SE13 .... 3E 122
Granville Ho. E14 .... 6C 86
(off E. India Dock Rd.)
Granville Mans. W12 .... 2E 98
(off Shepherd's Bush Grn.)
Granville M. DA14: Sidc 4A 144
Granville Pk. SE13 .... 3E 122
Granville Pl. HA5: Pinn 3B 40
Granville Pl. N12 .... 7F 31
Granville Pl. SW6 .... 7K 99
Granville Pl. W1 .... 1G 11 (6E 82)
Granville Point NW2 .... 2H 63
Granville Rd. DA14: Sidc 4A 144
Granville Rd. DA16: Well 3C 126
Granville Rd. E17 .... 6D 50
Granville Rd. E18 .... 2K 51
Granville Rd. EN5: Barn 4A 20
Granville Rd. IG1: Ilf 1F 71
Granville Rd. N12 .... 7F 31
Granville Rd. N13 .... 6E 32
Granville Rd. N22 .... 1B 48
Granville Rd. N4 .... 6K 47
Granville Rd. NW2 .... 2H 63
Granville Rd. NW6 .... 2J 81
(not continuous)
Granville Rd. SW18 .... 7H 117
Granville Rd. SW19 .... 7J 135
Granville Rd. UB10: Hil 6D 56
Granville Rd. UB3: Harl 4H 93
Granville Sq. SE15 .... 7E 102
Granville Sq. WC1 .... 2H 7 (3K 83)
Granville St. WC1 .... 2H 7 (3K 83)
Granwood Ct. TW7: Isle 1J 113
Grape St. WC2 .... 7E 6 (6J 83)
Graphite Apts., The N1 .... 1E 8 (2D 84)
(off Provost St.)
Graphite Point E2 .... 3K 85
(off Palmer's Rd.)
Graphite Sq. SE11 .... 5G 19 (5K 101)
Grapsome Cl. KT9: Chess 7C 162
Grasdene Rd. SE18 .... 7A 108
Grasgarth Cl. W3 .... 7J 79
Grasmere NW1 .... 2K 5 (3F 83)
(off Osnaburgh St.)
Grasmere Av. BR6: Farnb 3F 173
Grasmere Av. HA4: Ruis 7E 38
Grasmere Av. HA9: Wemb 7C 42
Grasmere Av. SW15 .... 4K 133
Grasmere Av. SW19 .... 3J 153
Grasmere Av. TW3: Houn 6F 113
Grasmere Av. W3 .... 7K 79
Grasmere Cl. TW14: Felt 1H 129
Grasmere Ct. N22 .... 6E 32
Grasmere Ct. SE26 .... 5G 139
Grasmere Ct. SM2: Sutt 6A 166
Grasmere Ct. SW13 .... 6C 98
(off Verdun Rd.)
Grasmere Gdns. BR6: Farnb 3F 173
Grasmere Gdns. HA3: W'stone 2A 42
Grasmere Gdns. IG4: Ilf 5D 52
Grasmere Point SE15 .... 7J 103
(off Old Kent Rd.)
Grasmere Rd. BR1: Broml 1H 159
Grasmere Rd. BR6: Farnb 3F 173
Grasmere Rd. DA7: Bex 2J 127
Grasmere Rd. E13 .... 2J 87
Grasmere Rd. N10 .... 1F 47
Grasmere Rd. N17 .... 6B 34
Grasmere Rd. SE25 .... 6H 157
Grasmere Rd. SW16 .... 5J 137
Grasshaven Way SE28 .... 1K 107
(not continuous)
Grassington Cl. N11 .... 6K 31
Grassington Rd. DA14: Sidc
.... 4A 144
Grassmount SE23 .... 2H 139
Grass Pk. N3 .... 1H 45
Grassway SM6: W'gton 4G 167
Grasvenor Av. EN5: Barn 5D 20
Gratton Rd. W14 .... 3G 99
Gratton Ter. NW2 .... 3F 63
Gravel Hill CR0: Addtn 6K 169
Gravel Hill DA6: Bex 4H 127
Gravel Hill N3 .... 2H 45
Gravel Hill Cl. DA6: Bex 5H 127
Gravel La. E1 .... 7J 9 (6F 85)
Gravel Pit La. SE9 .... 5F 125
Gravel Pit Way BR6: Orp 2K 173
Gravel Rd. BR2: Broml 3C 172
Gravel Rd. TW2: Twick 1J 131
Gravelwood Cl. BR7: Chst 3G 143
Gravely Ho. SE8 .... 4B 104
(off Chilton Gro.)
Gravenel Gdns. SW17 .... 5C 136
(off Nutwell St.)
Graveney Gro. SE20 .... 7J 139
Graveney Rd. SW17 .... 4C 136
Gravesend Rd. W12 .... 7C 80
Gravesham Way BR3: Beck 7B 158
Gray Av. RM8: Dag 1F 73
Gray Ct. E1 .... 5A 86
Gray Ct. HA5: Pinn 4C 40
Grayham Cres. KT3: N Mald 4K 151
Grayham Rd. KT3: N Mald 4K 151
Gray Ho. SE17 .... 5C 102
(off King & Queen St.)
Grayland Cl. BR1: Broml 1B 160
Grayling Cl. E16 .... 4G 87
Grayling Ct. W5 .... 1D 96
(off Grange Rd.)
Grayling Rd. N16 .... 2D 66
Grayling Sq. E2 .... 3G 85
(off Nelson Gdns.)
Grayscroft Rd. SW16 .... 7H 137
Grays Farm Rd. BR5: St P 7B 144
Grayshott Rd. SW11 .... 2E 118
Gray's Inn 5H 7 (5K 83)
Gray's Inn Bldgs. EC1 .... 4J 7 (4A 84)
(off Rosebery Av.)
Gray's Inn Pl. WC1 .... 6H 7 (5K 83)
Gray's Inn Rd. WC1 .... 1F 7 (3J 83)
Gray's Inn Sq. WC1 .... 5H 7 (5K 83)
Grays La. TW15: Ashf 4D 128
Grayson Ho. EC1 .... 2D 8 (3C 84)
(off Radnor St.)
Grays Rd. UB10: Uxb 7A 56
Grays Ter. E7 .... 6A 70
Grayston Ho. SE3 .... 4A 124
Gray St. SE1 .... 7K 13 (2A 102)
Grayswood Gdns. SW20 .... 2D 152
Grayswood Point SW15 .... 1C 134
Gray's Yd. W1 .... 1H 11 (6E 82)
(off James St.)
Graywood Ct. N12 .... 7F 31
Grazebrook Rd. N16 .... 2D 66
Grazeley Cl. DA6: Bex 5J 127
Grazeley Ct. SE19 .... 5E 138
Great Acre Ct. SW4 .... 4H 119
Great Amwell La. N8 .... 3K 47
Great Arthur Ho. EC1 .... 4C 8 (4C 84)
(off Golden La. Est.)
Great Bell All. EC2 .... 7E 8 (6D 84)
Great Benty UB7: W Dray 4A 92
Great Brownings SE21 .... 4F 139
Great Bushey Dr. N20 .... 1E 30
Great Cambridge Ind. Est. EN1: Enf
.... 5C 24
GREAT CAMBRIDGE JUNC. 4J 33
Great Cambridge Rd. EN1: Enf 6B 24
Great Cambridge Rd. N17 .... 6J 33
Great Cambridge Rd. N18 .... 4J 33
Great Cambridge Rd. N9 .... 3J 33
Great Castle St. W1 .... 7K 5 (6F 83)
Great Central Av. HA4: Ruis 5A 58
Great Central St. NW1 .... 5E 4 (5D 82)
Great Central Way HA9: Wemb 4J 61
Great Central Way NW10 .... 5A 62
Great Chapel St. W1 .... 7C 6 (6H 83)
Great Chart St. SW11 .... 4B 118
Great Chertsey Rd. TW13: Hanw 3D 130
Great Chertsey Rd. TW13: Twick 3D 130
Great Chertsey Rd. TW2: Twick 2F 131
Great Chertsey Rd. W4 .... 1J 115
(not continuous)
Great Church La. W6 .... 4F 99
Great College St. SW1 .... 1E 18 (3J 101)
Great Cft. WC1 .... 2F 7 (3J 83)
(off Cromer St.)
Great Cross Av. SE10 .... 7F 105
Great Cumberland M. W1 .... 1E 10 (6D 82)
Great Cumberland Pl. W1 .... 7E 4 (6D 82)
Great Dover St. SE1 .... 7D 14 (2C 102)
Greatdown Rd. W7 .... 4K 77
Great Eastern Ent. Cen. E14 .... 2D 104
Great Eastern Mkt. 6E 68
(within Westfield Shop. Cen.)
Great Eastern Rd. E15 .... 7F 69
Great Eastern St. EC2 .... 2G 9 (3E 84)
Great Eastern Wharf SW11 .... 7C 100
Great Elms Rd. BR2: Broml 4A 160
Greater London Ho. NW1 .... 2G 83
(off Hampstead Rd.)
Great Fld. NW9 .... 1A 44
Greatfield NW5 .... 5G 65
Greatfield Av. E6 .... 4D 88
Greatfield Cl. N19 .... 4G 65
Greatfield Cl. SE4 .... 4C 122
Greatfields Dr. UB8: Hil 5C 74
Greatfields Rd. IG11: Bark 1H 89
Great Fleete Way IG11: Bark 2C 90
Great Galley Cl. IG11: Bark 3B 90
Great Gatton Cl. CR0: C'don 7A 158
Great George St. SW1 .... 7D 12 (2H 101)
Great Guildford Bus. Sq. SE1
.... 5C 14 (1C 102)
Great Guildford St. SE1 .... 4C 14 (1C 102)
Great Hall SW11 .... 1E 118
(off Battersea Pk. Rd.)
Greatham Wlk. SW15 .... 1C 134
Great Harry Dr. SE9 .... 3E 142
Great James St. WC1 .... 5G 7 (5K 83)
Great Marlborough St. W1 .... 1A 12 (6G 83)
Great Maze Pond SE1 .... 6F 15 (2D 102)
Great Mill Apts. E2 .... 1F 85
(off Whiston Rd.)
Great Minster Ho. SW1 .... 3D 18 (4H 101)
(off Marsham St.)
Great Newport St. WC2 .... 2E 12 (7J 83)
Great New St. EC4 .... 7K 7 (6A 84)
(off New Fetter La.)
Great Nth. Leisure Pk. N12 .... 7G 31
Great Nth. Rd. EN5: Barn 2C 20
Great Nth. Rd. EN5: New Bar 5D 20
Great Nth. Rd. N2 .... 5C 46
Great Nth. Rd. N6 .... 5D 46
Great Nth. Way NW4 .... 2D 44
Greatorex Ho. E1 .... 5G 85
(off Greatorex St.)
Greatorex St. E1 .... 5G 85
Great Ormond St. WC1 .... 5F 7 (5J 83)
Great Owl Rd. IG7: Chig 3K 37
Great Pk. Cl. UB10: Hil 7C 56
Great Percy St. WC1 .... 1H 7 (3K 83)
Great Peter St. SW1 .... 2C 18 (3H 101)
Great Portland St. W1 .... 4K 5 (4F 83)
Great Pulteney St. W1 .... 2B 12 (7G 83)
Great Queen St. WC2 .... 1F 13 (6J 83)
Great Russell Mans. WC1 .... 6E 6 (5J 83)
(off Gt. Russell St.)
Great Russell St. WC1 .... 7D 6 (6H 83)
Great St Helen's EC3 .... 7G 9 (6E 84)
Great St Thomas Apostle EC4
.... 2D 14 (7C 84)
Great Scotland Yd. SW1 .... 5E 12 (1J 101)
Great Smith St. SW1 .... 1D 18 (3H 101)
Great Sth. W. Rd. TW14: Bedf 7E 110
Great Sth. W. Rd. TW14: Felt 7E 110
Great Sth. W. Rd. TW4: Houn 3K 111
Great Spilmans SE22 .... 5E 120
Great Strand NW9 .... 1B 44
Great Suffolk St. SE1 .... 5B 14 (1B 102)
Great Sutton St. EC1 .... 4B 8 (4B 84)
Great Swan All. EC2 .... 7E 8 (6D 84)
Great Thrift BR5: Pet W 4G 161
Great Titchfield St. W1 .... 4K 5 (4F 83)
Great Tower St. EC3 .... 2G 15 (7E 84)
Great Trinity La. EC4 .... 2D 14 (7C 84)
Great Turnstile WC1 .... 6H 7 (5K 83)
Great Turnstile Ho. WC1 .... 6H 7 (5K 83)
(off Great Turnstile)
Great Western Ind. Pk. UB2: S'hall 2F 95
Great Western Rd. W11 .... 5H 81
Great Western Rd. W2 .... 5H 81
Great Western Rd. W9 .... 5H 81
Great West Rd. W4 Cedars Rd. 5H 97
Great West Rd. W4 Dorchester Gro.
.... 6B 98
Great West Rd. TW5: Hest 2B 112
Great West Rd. TW7: Bford 7J 95
Great West Rd. TW7: Isle 7J 95
Great West Rd. TW8: Bford 7A 96
Great West Rd. W6 .... 5B 98
Great W. Trad. Est. TW8: Bford 6B 96
Great Winchester St. EC2 .... 7F 9 (6D 84)
Great Windmill St. W1 .... 2C 12 (7H 83)
Greatwood BR7: Chst 7E 142
Great Yd. SE1 .... 6H 15 (2E 102)
(off Crucifix La.)
Greaves Cl. IG11: Bark 7H 71
Greaves Cotts. E14 .... 5A 86
(off Maroon St.)
Greaves Pl. SW17 .... 4C 136
Greaves Twr. SW10 .... 7A 100
(off Worlds End Est.)
Grebe Av. UB4: Yead 6B 76
Grebe Cl. E17 .... 7F 35
Grebe Cl. E7 .... 5H 69
Grebe Cl. IG11: Bark 4A 90
Grebe Ct. E14 .... 2E 104
(off River Barge Cl.)
Grebe Ct. SE8 .... 6B 104
(off Dorking Cl.)
Grebe Ct. SM1: Sutt 5H 165
Grebe Ter. KT1: King T 3E 150
Grecian Cres. SE19 .... 6B 138
Greek Ct. W1 .... 1D 12 (6H 83)
Greek Orthodox Cathedral Kimisis
Panayias, The 1K 47
Greek Orthodox Cathedral of St Sophia
.... 7K 81
Greek St. W1 .... 1D 12 (6H 83)
Green, The BR1: Broml 3J 141
(not continuous)
Green, The BR2: Hayes 7J 159
Green, The BR5: St P 7B 144
Green, The CR0: Sels 7B 170
Green, The DA14: Sidc 4A 144
Green, The DA16: Well 4J 125
Green, The DA7: Bex 1G 127
Green, The E11 .... 6K 51
Green, The E15 .... 6G 69
Green, The E4 .... 1K 35
Green, The HA0: Wemb 2A 60
Green, The IG8: Wfd G 5D 36
Green, The IG9: Buck H 1E 36
Green, The KT3: N Mald 3K 151
Green, The N14 .... 2C 32
Green, The N17 .... 6H 33
Green, The N21 .... 7F 23
Green, The N9 .... 2B 34
Green, The SM1: Sutt 3K 165
Green, The SM4: Mord 4G 153
Green, The SM5: Cars 4E 166
Green, The SM6: W'gton 2E 166
Green, The SW14 .... 3J 115
Green, The SW19 .... 5F 135
Green, The TW13: Felt 2K 129
Green, The TW17: Shep 4G 147
Green, The TW2: Twick 1J 131
Green, The TW5: Hest 6E 94
Green, The TW9: Rich 5D 114
Green, The UB10: Ick 2E 56
Green, The UB2: S'hall 3C 94
Green, The UB7: W Dray 3A 92
Green, The W3 .... 6A 80
Green, The W5 .... 1D 96
Greenacre Cl. EN5: Barn 1C 20
Greenacre Cl. UB5: N'olt 5D 58
Greenacre Gdns. E17 .... 4E 50
Greenacre Pl. SM6: W'gton 2F 167
Greenacres N3 .... 2H 45
Greenacres SE9 .... 6E 124
Greenacres WD23: B Hea 2C 26
Green Acres CR0: C'don 3F 169
Green Acres DA14: Sidc 4A 144
Greenacres Av. UB10: Ick 3B 56
Greenacres Cl. BR6: Farnb 4G 173
Greenacres Dr. HA7: Stan 6G 27
Greenacres Ho. SW18 .... 1K 135
(off Knaresborough Dr.)
Greenacre Sq. SE16 .... 2K 103
Greenacre Wlk. N14 .... 3C 32
Greenan Ct. E2 .... 3K 85
(off Meath Cres.)
Green Arbour Ct. EC1 .... 7B 8 (6B 84)
(off Old Bailey)
Green Av. NW7 .... 4E 28
Green Av. W13 .... 3B 96
Greenaway Gdns. NW3 .... 4K 63
Greenaway Ho. NW8 .... 1A 82
(off Boundary Rd.)
Greenaway Ho. WC1 .... 2J 7 (3A 84)
(off Fernsbury St.)
Greenaway Ter. TW19: Stanw 1A 128
(off Victory Cl.)
Green Bank E1 .... 1H 103
Green Bank N12 .... 4E 30
Greenbank Av. HA0: Wemb 5A 60
Greenbank Cl. E4 .... 2K 35
Greenbank Ct. TW7: Isle 2K 113
(off Lanadron Cl.)
Greenbank Cres. NW4 .... 4G 45
Greenbank Lodge BR7: Chst 2E 160
(off Forest Cl.)
Greenbanks HA1: Harr 4J 59
Greenbanks Cl. SE13 .... 3D 122
Greenbay Rd. SE7 .... 7B 106
Greenberry St. NW8 .... 1C 4 (2C 82)
Greenbrook Av. EN4: Had W 1F 21
Green Cl. BR2: Broml 3G 159
Green Cl. NW11 .... 7A 46
Green Cl. NW9 .... 6J 43
Green Cl. SM5: Cars 2D 166
Green Cl. TW13: Hanw 5C 130
Greencoat Mans. SW1 .... 2B 18 (3G 101)
(off Greencoat Row)
Greencoat Pl. SW1 .... 3B 18 (4G 101)
Greencoat Row SW1 .... 2B 18 (3G 101)
Green Ct. TW16: Sun 6H 129
Greencourt Av. CR0: C'don 2H 169
Greencourt Av. HA8: Edg 1H 43
Greencourt Gdns. CR0: C'don 1H 169
Greencourt Ho. E1 .... 4K 85
(off Mile End Rd.)
Greencourt Rd. BR5: Pet W 5H 161
Greencrest Pl. NW2 .... 3C 62
Greencroft HA8: Edg 5D 28

Greencroft Av. – Grosvenor Rd.

Greencroft Av. HA4: Ruis 2A **58**
Greencroft Cl. E6 5B **88**
Greencroft Gdns. EN1: Enf 3K **23**
Greencroft Gdns. NW6 7K **63**
Greencroft Rd. TW5: Hest 1D **112**
Greendale NW7 4F **29**
Green Dale SE22 5E **120**
Green Dale SE5 4D **120**
Green Dale Cl. SE22 5E **120**
Green Dragon Ct. SE1 5E **14** (1D **102**)
(off Bedale St.)
Green Dragon Ho. CR0: C'don 3C **168**
(off High St.)
Green Dragon Ho. WC2 7F **7** (6J **83**)
(off Stukeley St.)
Green Dragon La. N21 6F **23**
Green Dragon La. TW8: Bford 5E **96**
Green Dragon Yd. E1 6K **9** (5G **85**)
Green Dr. UB1: S'hall 1E **94**
Greene Ct. SE14 6K **103**
(off Samuel Cl.)
Greene Ho. SE1 3D **102**
(off Burbage Cl.)
Green End KT9: Chess 4E **162**
Green End N21 2G **33**
Greenend Rd. W4 2A **98**
Greener Ct. CR0: C'don 6C **156**
(off Goodman Cres.)
Greener Ho. SW4 3H **119**
Green Farm Cl. BR6: Chels 5K **173**
Greenfell Mans. SE8 6D **104**
Green Ferry Way E17 4K **49**
Greenfield Av. KT5: Surb 7H **151**
Greenfield Ct. SE9 3C **142**
Greenfield Dr. BR1: Broml 2A **160**
Greenfield Dr. N2 4D **46**
Greenfield Gdns. BR5: Pet W 7H **161**
Greenfield Gdns. NW2 2G **63**
Greenfield Gdns. RM9: Dag 1D **90**
Greenfield Ho. SW19 1F **135**
Greenfield Pl. UB3: Hayes 7H **75**
Greenfield Rd. DA2: Wilm 5K **145**
Greenfield Rd. E1 5G **85**
Greenfield Rd. N15 5E **48**
Greenfield Rd. RM9: Dag 1C **90**
Greenfields UB1: S'hall 6E **76**
Greenfield Way HA2: Harr 3F **41**
GREENFORD 3E **76**
Greenford Av. UB1: S'hall 7D **76**
Greenford Av. W7 4J **77**
Greenford Bus. Cen. UB6: G'frd 7H **59**
Greenford Gdns. UB6: G'frd 3F **77**
GREENFORD GREEN 6J **59**
Greenford Ind. Est. UB6: G'frd 7F **59**
Greenford Pk. UB6: G'frd 7H **59**
Greenford Rd. HA1: Harr 4J **59**
Greenford Rd. SM1: Sutt 4K **165**
(not continuous)
Greenford Rd. UB1: S'hall 1G **95**
Greenford Rd. UB6: G'frd 1H **77**
GREENFORD RDBT. 2H **77**
Greenford Sports Cen. 3E **76**
Green Gdns. BR6: Farnb 5G **173**
Greengate UB6: G'frd 6B **60**
Greengate Lodge E13 2K **87**
(off Hollybush St.)
Greengate Pde. IG2: Ilf 6H **53**
Greengate St. E13 2K **87**
Greenhalgh Wlk. N2 4A **46**
Greenham Cl. SE1 7J **13** (2A **102**)
Greenham Cres. E4 6G **35**
Greenham Ho. E9 1J **85**
(off Templecombe Rd.)
Greenham Ho. TW7: Isle 3H **113**
Greenham Rd. N10 2E **46**
Greenhaven Dr. SE28 6B **90**
Green Hedges TW1: Twick 5C **114**
Greenheys Cl. HA6: Nwood 1G **39**
Greenheys Dr. E18 3H **51**
GREENHILL 5J **41**
Greenhill HA9: Wemb 2H **61**
Greenhill IG9: Buck H 1F **37**
Greenhill NW3 4B **64**
Greenhill SE18 5D **106**
Greenhill SM1: Sutt 2A **166**
Greenhill Ct. EN5: New Bar 5E **20**
Greenhill Ct. SE18 5D **106**
Greenhill Gdns. UB5: N'olt 2D **76**
Greenhill Gro. E12 4C **70**
Greenhill Pde. EN5: New Bar 5E **20**
Greenhill Pk. EN5: New Bar 5E **20**
Greenhill Pk. NW10 1A **80**
Greenhill Rd. HA1: Harr 6J **41**
Greenhill Rd. NW10 1A **80**
Greenhill's Rents EC1 5A **8** (5B **84**)
Greenhills Ter. N1 6D **66**
Greenhill Ter. SE18 5D **106**
Greenhill Ter. UB5: N'olt 2D **76**
Greenhill Way HA1: Harr 6J **41**
Greenhill Way HA9: Wemb 2H **61**
Greenhithe Cl. DA15: Sidc 7J **125**
Greenholm Rd. SE9 5F **125**
Green Hundred Rd. SE15 6G **103**
Greenhurst Rd. SE27 5A **138**
Greening St. SE2 4C **108**
Greenland Cres. UB2: S'hall 3A **94**
Greenland Ho. E1 4A **86**
(off Ernest St.)
Greenland M. SE8 5K **103**
Greenland Pl. NW1 1F **83**
Greenland Quay SE16 4K **103**
Greenland Rd. NW1 1G **83**
Greenlands KT19: Ewe 5H **163**
Greenlands La. NW4 1D **44**
Greenland St. NW1 1F **83**
Greenland Way CR0: Bedd 7H **155**
Green La. SM4: Mord Central Rd. 6J **153**
Green La. SM4: Mord Lwr. Morden La.
7E **152**
Green La. BR7: Chst 4F **143**
Green La. CR7: Thor H 1B **156**
Green La. HA1: Harr 3J **59**
Green La. HA7: Stan 4G **27**
Green La. HA8: Edg 4A **28**
(not continuous)
Green La. IG1: Ilf 2H **71**
Green La. IG3: Ilf 1B **72**
Green La. KT3: N Mald 5J **151**
Green La. KT4: Wor Pk 1C **164**
Green La. KT8: W Mole 5F **149**
Green La. NW4 4F **45**
Green La. RM8: Dag 1B **72**
Green La. SE20 7K **139**
Green La. SE9 1F **143**
Green La. SW16 7K **137**
Green La. TW13: Hanw 5C **130**
Green La. TW16: Sun 7H **129**
Green La. TW17: Shep 6E **146**
Green La. TW4: Houn 3K **111**
Green La. UB8: Hil 5E **74**
Green La. W7 2J **95**
Green La. Bus. Pk. SE9 2E **142**
Green La. Cotts. HA7: Stan 4G **27**
Green La. Gdns. CR7: Thor H 2C **156**
Green Lanes KT19: Ewe 7A **164**
Green Lanes N13 4F **33**
Green Lanes N15 3B **48**
Green Lanes N16 3C **66**
Green Lanes N21 2G **33**
Green Lanes N4 1C **66**
Green Lanes N8 3B **48**
Green Lanes Wlk. N4 1C **66**
Greenlaw Ct. W5 6D **78**
(off Mount Pk. Rd.)
Greenlaw Gdns. KT3: N Mald 7B **152**
Greenlawn La. TW8: Bford 4D **96**
Greenlawns N12 6E **30**
Green Lawns HA4: Ruis 1A **58**
Greenlaw St. SE18 3E **106**
Green Leaf Av. SM6: Bedd 4H **167**
Greenleaf Cl. SW2 7A **120**
Greenleafe Dr. IG6: Ilf 3F **53**
Greenleaf Rd. E17 3B **50**
Greenleaf Rd. E6 1A **88**
Greenleaf Wlk. UB1: S'hall 2C **94**
Greenleaf Way HA3: W'stone 3K **41**
Greenlea Pk. SW19 7B **136**
Green Leas KT1: King T 3E **150**
(off Mill St.)
Green Leas TW16: Sun 6H **129**
Green Leas Cl. TW16: Sun 6H **129**
Greenleaves Ct. TW15: Ashf 6D **128**
Greenlink Wlk. TW9: Kew 1H **115**
Green Man Gdns. W13 7A **78**
Green Man La. TW14: Felt 4J **111**
(not continuous)
Green Man La. W13 7A **78**
Green Man Pas. W13 7B **78**
(not continuous)
GREEN MAN RDBT. 7H **51**
Greenman St. N1 7C **66**
Greenmead DA18: Erith 3E **108**
Greenmead Cl. SE25 5G **157**
Green M. N1 1F **9** (3D **84**)
Green Moor Link N21 7G **23**
Greenmoor Rd. EN3: Enf H 2D **24**
Greenoak Cl. N20 1F **31**
Greenoak Pl. EN4: Cockf 2J **21**
Green Oaks UB2: S'hall 4B **94**
Greenoak Way SW19 4F **135**
Greenock Rd. SW16 1H **155**
Greenock Rd. W3 3H **97**
Greeno Cres. TW17: Shep 5C **146**
Green Pde. TW3: Houn 5F **113**
Green Pk. London 6K **11** (2F **101**)
Greenpark Ct. HA0: Wemb 7C **60**
Green Pk. Way UB6: G'frd 7J **59**
Green Pl. SE10 2G **105**
Green Point E15 6G **69**
Green Pond Cl. E17 3B **50**
Green Pond Rd. E17 3A **50**
Green Rd. N14 6A **22**
Green Rd. N20 3F **31**
Green Rd. Nth. EN3: Pond E 4F **25**
Greenrod Pl. TW8: Bford 5E **96**
(off Claypond La.)
Greenroof Way SE10 3H **105**
Green's Ct. W1 2C **12** (7H **83**)
(off Brewer St.)
Green's Ct. W11 1H **99**
(off Lansdowne M.)
Green's End SE18 4F **107**
Greenshank Cl. E17 7F **35**
Greenshank Ho. NW9 6B **44**
Greenshaw School Sports Cen. 2A **166**
Greenshields Ind. Est. E16 2J **105**
Greenside DA5: Bexl 1E **144**
Greenside RM8: Dag 1C **72**
Greenside Cl. N20 2G **31**
Greenside Cl. SE6 2F **141**
Greenside Rd. CR0: C'don 7A **156**
Greenside Rd. W12 3C **98**
Green Side Views CR4: Mitc 7E **154**
Greenslade Rd. IG11: Bark 7H **71**
Greenstead Av. IG8: Wfd G 7F **37**
Greenstead Cl. IG8: Wfd G 6F **37**
Greenstead Gdns. IG8: Wfd G 6F **37**
Greenstead Gdns. SW15 5D **116**
Greenstone M. E11 6J **51**
Green St. E13 7A **70**
Green St. E7 6K **69**
Green St. EN3: Brim 2D **24**
Green St. EN3: Enf H 2D **24**
Green St. TW16: Sun 1J **147**
Green St. W1 2G **11** (7E **82**)
GREEN STREET GREEN 6K **173**
Greenstreet Hill SE14 2K **121**
Green Ter. EC1 2K **7** (3A **84**)
Green Va. DA6: Bex 5D **126**
Green Va. W5 6F **79**
Greenvale Rd. SE9 4D **124**
Green Verges HA7: Stan 7J **27**
Green Vw. KT9: Chess 7F **163**
Greenview Av. BR3: Beck 6A **158**
Greenview Av. CR0: C'don 6A **158**
Greenview Cl. W3 1A **98**
Greenview Ct. TW15: Ashf 4B **128**
Greenview Dr. SW20 3E **152**
Green Wlk. HA4: Ruis 1H **57**
Green Wlk. IG10: Lough 1H **37**
Green Wlk. IG8: Wfd G 6H **37**
Green Wlk. NW4 5F **45**
Green Wlk. SE1 3E **102**
Green Wlk. TW12: Hamp 6D **130**
Green Wlk. UB2: S'hall 5E **94**
Green Wlk., The E4 1A **36**
Greenway BR7: Chst 5E **142**
Greenway E3 1C **86**
Greenway E6 4E **88**
Greenway HA3: Kenton 5E **42**
Greenway HA5: Pinn 2K **39**
Greenway IG8: Wfd G 5F **37**
Greenway N14 2D **32**
Greenway N20 2D **30**
Greenway RM8: Dag 2C **72**
Greenway SM6: W'gton 4G **167**
Greenway SW20 4E **152**
Greenway UB4: Yead 3J **75**
Green Way BR2: Broml 6C **160**
Green Way SE9 5B **124**
Green Way TW16: Sun 4J **147**
Greenway, The HA3: W'stone 1J **41**
Greenway, The HA5: Pinn 6D **40**
Greenway, The NW9 2K **43**
Greenway, The TW4: Houn 4D **112**
Greenway, The UB10: Ick 2D **56**
Greenway Av. E17 4F **51**
Greenway Cl. N11 6K **31**
Greenway Cl. N15 4F **49**
Greenway Cl. N20 2D **30**
Greenway Cl. N4 2C **66**
Greenway Cl. NW9 2K **43**
Greenway Ct. IG1: Ilf 1E **70**
Greenway Gdns. CR0: C'don 3B **170**
Greenway Gdns. HA3: W'stone 2J **41**
Greenway Gdns. NW9 2K **43**
Greenway Gdns. UB6: G'frd 3E **76**
Greenways BR3: Beck 3C **158**
Greenways, The TW1: Twick 6A **114**
Greenways Dr. TW4: Houn 4C **112**
Greenwell St. W1 4K **5** (4F **83**)
GREENWICH 7E **104**
Greenwich Bus. Pk. SE10 7D **104**
Greenwich Cen., The 5H **105**
(off Lambarde Sq.)
Greenwich Chu. St. SE10 6E **104**
Greenwich Ct. E1 6H **85**
(off Cavell St.)
Greenwich Cres. E6 5C **88**
GREENWICH FOOT TUNNEL 5E **104**
Greenwich Hgts. SE18 7C **106**
Greenwich High Rd. SE10 1D **122**
Greenwich Ho. SE13 6F **123**
Greenwich Mkt. SE10 6E **104**
GREENWICH MILLENNIUM VILLAGE
3H **105**
Greenwich Pk. 7F **105**
Greenwich Pk. St. SE10 6F **105**
Greenwich Peninsula Ecology Pk.
3J **105**
Greenwich Peninsula Golf Driving Range 2F **105**
Greenwich Picturehouse 7E **104**
Greenwich Quay SE8 6D **104**
Greenwich Shop. Pk. 4K **105**
Greenwich Sth. St. SE10 1D **122**
Greenwich Theatre 7E **104**
Greenwich Tourist Info. Cen. 6E **104**
Greenwich Vw. Pl. E14 3D **104**
Greenwich Yacht Club 3J **105**
Greenwood NW5 5G **65**
(off Osney Cres.)
Greenwood Av. EN3: Enf H 2F **25**
Greenwood Av. RM10: Dag 4H **73**
Greenwood Bus. Cen. CR0: C'don
7F **157**
Greenwood Cl. BR5: Pet W 6J **161**
Greenwood Cl. DA15: Sidc 2A **144**
Greenwood Cl. KT7: T Ditt 1A **162**
Greenwood Cl. SM4: Mord 4G **153**
Greenwood Cl. UB3: Hayes 1J **93**
Greenwood Cl. WD23: B Hea 1D **26**
Greenwood Dr. E4 5A **36**
Greenwood Gdns. IG6: Ilf 1G **53**
Greenwood Gdns. N13 3G **33**
Greenwood Ho. EC1 2J **7** (3A **84**)
(off Rosebery Av.)
Greenwood Ho. N22 1K **47**
Greenwood Ho. SE4 4K **121**
Greenwood La. TW12: Hamp H 5F **131**
Greenwood Mans. IG11: Bark 7A **72**
(off Lansbury Av.)
Greenwood Pk. KT2: King T 7A **134**
Greenwood Pl. NW5 5F **65**
Greenwood Rd. CR0: C'don 7B **156**
Greenwood Rd. CR4: Mitc 3H **155**
Greenwood Rd. DA5: Bexl 4K **145**
Greenwood Rd. E13 2H **87**
Greenwood Rd. E8 6G **67**
Greenwood Rd. KT7: T Ditt 1A **162**
Greenwood Rd. TW7: Isle 3K **113**
Greenwoods, The HA2: Harr 3G **59**
Greenwood Ter. NW10 1K **79**
Greenwood Theatre 6F **15** (2D **102**)
Green Wrythe Cres. SM5: Cars 1C **166**
Green Wrythe La. SM5: Cars 6B **154**
Green Yd. WC1 3H **7** (4K **83**)
Green Yd., The EC3 1G **15** (6E **84**)
(off Leadenhall Pl.)
Greer Rd. HA3: Hrw W 1G **41**
Greet Ho. SE1 7K **13** (2A **102**)
(off Frazier St.)
Greet St. SE1 5K **13** (1A **102**)
Greg Cl. E10 6E **50**
Gregor M. SE3 7J **105**
Gregory Cl. BR2: Broml 4G **159**
Gregory Cres. SE9 7B **124**
Gregory Pl. W8 2K **99**
Gregory Rd. RM6: Chad H 4D **54**
Gregory Rd. UB2: S'hall 3E **94**
Grehan M. SE14 7B **104**
Greig Cl. N8 5J **47**
Greig Ter. SE17 6B **102**
Grenaby Av. CR0: C'don 7D **156**
Grenaby Rd. CR0: C'don 7D **156**
Grenada Ho. E14 7B **86**
(off Limehouse C'way.)
Grenada Rd. SE7 7A **106**
Grenade St. E14 7B **86**
Grenadier St. E16 1E **106**
Grena Gdns. TW9: Rich 4F **115**
Grenard Cl. SE15 7G **103**
Grena Rd. TW9: Rich 4F **115**
Grendon Gdns. HA9: Wemb 2G **61**
Grendon Ho. E9 7J **67**
(off Shore Pl.)
Grendon Ho. N1 2K **83**
(off Calshot St.)
Grendon Lodge HA8: Edg 2D **28**
Grendon St. NW8 3C **4** (4C **82**)
Grenfell Ct. E3 4D **86**
(off Barry Blandford Way)
Grenfell Ct. NW7 6J **29**
Grenfell Gdns. HA3: Kenton 7E **42**
Grenfell Gdns. IG3: Ilf 5K **53**
Grenfell Ho. SE5 7C **102**
Grenfell Rd. CR4: Mitc 6D **136**
Grenfell Rd. W11 7F **81**
Grenfell Wlk. W11 7F **81**
Grenier Apts. SE15 7H **103**
Grennell Cl. SM1: Sutt 2B **166**
Grennell Rd. SM1: Sutt 2A **166**
Grenoble Gdns. N13 6F **33**
Grenville Cl. KT5: Surb 1J **163**
Grenville Cl. N3 1G **45**
Grenville Ct. W13 5B **78**
Grenville Gdns. IG8: Wfd G 1A **52**
Grenville Ho. E3 2A **86**
(off Arbery Rd.)
Grenville Ho. SE8 6C **104**
(off New King St.)
Grenville Ho. SW1 7C **18** (6H **101**)
(off Dolphin Sq.)
Grenville M. N19 1J **65**
Grenville M. SW7 4A **100**
Grenville M. TW12: Hamp H 5F **131**
Grenville Pl. NW7 5E **28**
Grenville Pl. SW7 3A **100**
Grenville Rd. N19 1J **65**
Grenville St. WC1 4F **7** (4J **83**)
Gresham Av. N20 4J **31**
Gresham Cl. DA5: Bexl 6E **126**
Gresham Cl. EN2: Enf 3H **23**
Gresham Dr. RM6: Chad H 5B **54**
Gresham Gdns. NW11 1G **63**
Gresham Lodge E17 5D **50**
Gresham Pl. E3 5C **86**
Gresham Pl. N19 2H **65**
Gresham Rd. BR3: Beck 2A **158**
Gresham Rd. E16 6K **87**
Gresham Rd. E6 2D **88**
Gresham Rd. HA8: Edg 6A **28**
Gresham Rd. NW10 5K **61**
Gresham Rd. SE25 4G **157**
Gresham Rd. SW9 3A **120**
Gresham Rd. TW12: Hamp 6E **130**
Gresham Rd. TW3: Houn 1G **113**
Gresham Rd. UB10: Hil 2C **74**
Gresham St. EC2 7C **8** (6C **84**)
Gresham Way SW19 3K **135**
Gresham Way Ind. Est. SW19 3K **135**
(off Gresham Way)
Gresley Cl. E17 6A **50**
Gresley Cl. N15 4D **48**
Gresley Rd. N19 1G **65**
Gressenhall Rd. SW18 6H **117**
Gresse St. W1 7C **6** (6H **83**)
Gresswell Cl. DA14: Sidc 3A **144**
Greswell St. SW6 1F **117**
Gretton Ho. E2 3J **85**
(off Globe Rd.)
Gretton Rd. N17 7A **34**
Greville Cl. TW1: Twick 7B **114**
Greville Ct. E5 3H **67**
(off Napoleon Rd.)
Greville Ct. HA1: Harr 4J **59**
Greville Hall NW6 2K **81**
Greville Ho. SW1 1F **17** (3D **100**)
(off Kinnerton St.)
Greville Lodge E13 1K **87**
Greville Lodge HA8: Edg 4C **28**
(off Broadhurst Av.)
Greville Lodge N12 5E **30**
Greville M. NW6 1K **81**
(off Greville Rd.)
Greville Pl. NW6 2K **81**
Greville Rd. E17 4E **50**
Greville Rd. NW6 2K **81**
Greville Rd. TW10: Rich 6F **115**
Greville St. EC1 6J **7** (5A **84**)
(not continuous)
Grey Cl. NW11 6A **46**
Greycoat Gdns. SW1 2C **18** (3H **101**)
(off Greycoat St.)
Greycoat Pl. SW1 2C **18** (3H **101**)
Greycoat St. SW1 2C **18** (3H **101**)
Greycot Rd. BR3: Beck 5C **140**
Grey Eagle St. E1 4J **9** (4F **85**)
Greyfell Cl. HA7: Stan 5G **27**
Greyfriars SE26 3G **139**
(off Wells Pk. Rd.)
Greyfriars Pas. EC1 7B **8** (6B **84**)
Greyhound Ct. WC2 2H **13** (7K **83**)
Greyhound Hill NW4 3C **44**
Greyhound La. SW16 6H **137**
Greyhound Mans. W6 6G **99**
(off Greyhound Rd.)
Greyhound Rd. N17 3E **48**
Greyhound Rd. NW10 3D **80**
Greyhound Rd. SM1: Sutt 5A **166**
Greyhound Rd. W14 6G **99**
Greyhound Rd. W6 6F **99**
Greyhound Ter. SW16 1G **155**
Greyhound Way DA1: Cray 5K **127**
Grey Ho. W12 7D **80**
(off White City Est.)
Greyladies Gdns. SE10 2E **122**
Greys Pk. Cl. BR2: Kes 5B **172**
Greystead Rd. SE23 7J **121**
Greystoke Av. HA5: Pinn 3E **40**
Greystoke Ct. W5 4E **78**
Greystoke Dr. HA4: Ruis 6D **38**
Greystoke Gdns. EN2: Enf 4C **22**
Greystoke Gdns. W5 4E **78**
Greystoke Ho. SE15 6G **103**
(off Peckham Pk. Rd.)
Greystoke Ho. W5 4E **78**
Greystoke Lodge W5 4E **79**
(off Hanger La.)
Greystoke Pk. Ter. W5 3D **78**
Greystoke Pl. EC4 7J **7** (6A **84**)
Greystone Gdns. HA3: Kenton 6C **42**
Greystone Gdns. IG6: Ilf 2G **53**
Greyswood St. SW16 6F **137**
Grey Turner Ho. W12 6C **80**
Grierson Ho. SW16 4G **137**
Grierson Rd. SE23 7K **121**
Griffen Ct. BR3: Beck 1D **158**
Griffin Cen. TW14: Felt 5K **111**
Griffin Cen., The KT1: King T 2D **150**
(off Market Pl.)
Griffin Cl. NW10 5D **62**
Griffin Ct. TW8: Bford 6E **96**
Griffin Ct. W4 5B **98**
Griffin Ho. CR0: C'don 7B **156**
Griffin Ho. E14 6D **86**
(off Ricardo St.)
Griffin Ho. N1 1E **84**
(off Halcomb St.)
Griffin Ho. W6 4F **99**
(off Hammersmith Rd.)
Griffin Mnr. Way SE28 3H **107**
Griffin M. SW12 1G **137**
Griffin Pk. 6D **96**
Griffin Rd. N17 2E **48**
Griffin Rd. SE18 5H **107**
Griffins Cl. N21 7J **23**
Griffin Way TW16: Sun 2J **147**
Griffith Cl. E17 1F **51**
Griffith Cl. RM8: Dag 7C **54**
Griffiths Cl. KT4: Wor Pk 2D **164**
Griffiths Rd. SW19 7J **135**
Griggs App. IG1: Ilf 2G **71**
Griggs Cl. IG3: Ilf 4J **71**
Griggs Ct. SE1 3E **102**
(off Grigg's Pl.)
Grigg's Pl. SE1 3E **102**
Griggs Rd. E10 6E **50**
Grilse Cl. N9 4C **34**
Grimaldi Ho. N1 2K **83**
(off Calshot St.)
Grimsby Gro. E16 2F **107**
Grimsby St. E2 4K **9** (4F **85**)
Grim's Ditch 5A **26**
Grim's Dyke Golf Course 5A **26**
Grimsel Path SE5 7B **102**
Grimshaw Cl. N6 7E **46**
Grimston Rd. SW6 2H **117**
Grimthorpe Ho. EC1 3A **8** (4B **84**)
(off Agdon St.)
Grimwade Av. CR0: C'don 3G **169**
Grimwade Cl. SE15 3J **121**
Grimwood Rd. TW1: Twick 7K **113**
Grindall Cl. CR0: Wadd 4B **168**
Grindall Ho. E1 4H **85**
(off Darling Row)
Grindal St. SE1 7J **13** (2A **102**)
Grindleford Av. N11 2K **31**
Grindley Gdns. CR0: C'don 6F **157**
Grindley Ho. E3 5B **86**
(off Leopold St.)
Grinling Pl. SE8 6C **104**
Grinstead Rd. SE8 5A **104**
Grisedale NW1 1A **6** (3G **83**)
(off Cumberland Mkt.)
Grittleton Av. HA9: Wemb 6H **61**
Grittleton Rd. W9 4J **81**
Grizedale Ter. SE23 2H **139**
Grocer's Hall Ct. EC2 1E **14** (6D **84**)
Grocer's Hall Gdns. EC2 1E **14** (6D **84**)
(off Prince's St.)
Grogan Cl. TW12: Hamp 6D **130**
Groombridge Cl. DA16: Well 5A **126**
Groombridge Ho. SE17 5E **102**
(off Upnor Way)
Groombridge Rd. E9 7K **67**
Groom Cl. BR2: Broml 4K **159**
Groom Cres. SW18 7B **118**
Groome Ho. SE11 4H **19** (4K **101**)
Groomfield Cl. SW17 4E **136**
Groom Pl. SW1 1H **17** (3E **100**)
Grooms Dr. HA5: Eastc 5J **39**
Grosmont Rd. SE18 5K **107**
Grosse Way SW15 6D **116**
Grosvenor Av. HA2: Harr 6F **41**
Grosvenor Av. N5 5C **66**
Grosvenor Av. SM5: Cars 6D **166**
Grosvenor Av. SW14 3A **116**
Grosvenor Av. TW10: Rich 5E **114**
Grosvenor Av. UB4: Hayes 2H **75**
Grosvenor Cotts. SW1 3G **17** (4E **100**)
Grosvenor Ct. E10 1D **68**
Grosvenor Ct. E14 6B **86**
(off Wharf La.)
Grosvenor Ct. N14 7B **22**
Grosvenor Ct. NW6 1F **81**
Grosvenor Ct. NW7 5E **28**
(off Hale La.)
Grosvenor Ct. SE5 6C **102**
Grosvenor Ct. SM2: Sutt 6K **165**
Grosvenor Ct. SM4: Mord 4J **153**
Grosvenor Ct. TW11: Tedd 6A **132**
Grosvenor Ct. W14 3F **99**
(off Irving Rd.)
Grosvenor Ct. W3 1G **97**
Grosvenor Ct. W5 7E **78**
(off The Grove)
Grosvenor Ct. Mans. W2 1E **10** (6D **82**)
(off Edgware Rd.)
Grosvenor Cres. NW9 4G **43**
Grosvenor Cres. SW1 7H **11** (2E **100**)
Grosvenor Cres. UB10: Hil 7D **56**
Grosvenor Cres. M. SW1 7G **11** (2E **100**)
Grosvenor Est. SW1 3D **18** (4H **101**)
Grosvenor Gdns. E6 3B **88**
Grosvenor Gdns. IG8: Wfd G 6D **36**
Grosvenor Gdns. KT2: King T 6D **132**
Grosvenor Gdns. N10 3G **47**
Grosvenor Gdns. N14 4C **22**
Grosvenor Gdns. NW11 6H **45**
Grosvenor Gdns. NW2 6E **62**
Grosvenor Gdns. SM6: W'gton 7G **167**
Grosvenor Gdns. SW1 1J **17** (3F **101**)
Grosvenor Gdns. SW14 3A **116**
Grosvenor Gdns. M. E. SW1
1K **17** (3F **101**)
(off Beeston Pl.)
Grosvenor Gdns. M. Nth. SW1
2J **17** (3F **101**)
(off Grosvenor Gdns.)
Grosvenor Gdns. M. Sth. SW1
2K **17** (3F **101**)
(off Ebury St.)
Grosvenor Ga. W1 3G **11** (7E **82**)
Grosvenor Hill SW19 6G **135**
Grosvenor Hill W1 2J **11** (7F **83**)
Grosvenor Hill Ct. W1 2J **11** (7F **83**)
(off Bourdon St.)
Grosvenor Ho. SM1: Sutt 5K **165**
(off West St.)
Grosvenor Pde. W5 1G **97**
(off Uxbridge Rd.)
Grosvenor Pk. SE5 7C **102**
Grosvenor Pk. Rd. E17 5C **50**
Grosvenor Pl. SW1 7H **11** (2E **100**)
Grosvenor Ri. E. E17 5D **50**
Grosvenor Rd. BR4: W W'ck 1D **170**
Grosvenor Rd. BR5: St M Cry 6J **161**
Grosvenor Rd. DA17: Belv 6G **109**
Grosvenor Rd. DA6: Bex 5D **126**
Grosvenor Rd. E10 1E **68**
Grosvenor Rd. E11 5K **51**
Grosvenor Rd. E6 1B **88**
Grosvenor Rd. E7 6K **69**
Grosvenor Rd. IG1: Ilf 3G **71**
Grosvenor Rd. N10 1F **47**
Grosvenor Rd. N3 7C **30**
Grosvenor Rd. N9 1C **34**
Grosvenor Rd. RM7: Rush G 7K **55**
Grosvenor Rd. RM8: Dag 1F **73**
Grosvenor Rd. SE25 4F **157**
Grosvenor Rd. SM6: W'gton 6F **167**
Grosvenor Rd. SW1 7J **17** (6F **101**)
Grosvenor Rd. TW1: Twick 1A **132**
Grosvenor Rd. TW10: Rich 5E **114**

230 A–Z London

Grosvenor Rd. – Half Moon Ct.

Grosvenor Rd. TW3: Houn ... 3D 112
Grosvenor Rd. TW8: Bford ... 6D 96
Grosvenor Rd. UB2: S'hall ... 3D 94
Grosvenor Rd. W4 ... 5H 97
Grosvenor Rd. W7 ... 1A 96
Grosvenor Sq. W1 ... 2H 11 (7E 82)
Grosvenor St. W1 ... 2J 11 (7F 83)
Grosvenor Studios SW1 ... 3G 17 (4E 100)
... (off Eaton Ter.)
Grosvenor Ter. SE5 ... 7C 102
Grosvenor Va. HA4: Ruis ... 2H 57
Grosvenor Vale Stadium ... 2H 57
Grosvenor Way E5 ... 2J 67
Grosvenor Way SW17 ... 3B 136
Grosvenor Wharf Rd. E14 ... 4F 105
Grotes Bldgs. SE3 ... 2G 123
Grote's Pl. SE3 ... 2G 123
Groton Rd. SW18 ... 2K 135
Grotto Ct. SE1 ... 6B 14 (2B 102)
Grotto Pas. W1 ... 5G 5 (5E 82)
Grotto Rd. TW1: Twick ... 2K 131
Grove, The BR4: W W'ck ... 3D 170
Grove, The DA14: Sidc ... 5E 144
Grove, The DA6: Bex ... 4D 126
Grove, The E15 ... 6G 69
Grove, The EN2: Enf ... 2F 23
Grove, The HA1: Harr ... 7J 41
Grove, The HA7: Stan ... 2F 27
Grove, The HA8: Edg ... 4C 28
Grove, The KT12: Walt T ... 7K 147
Grove, The N13 ... 4F 33
... (not continuous)
Grove, The N3 ... 1J 45
Grove, The N4 ... 7K 47
Grove, The N6 ... 1E 64
Grove, The N8 ... 5H 47
Grove, The NW11 ... 7G 45
Grove, The NW9 ... 5K 43
THE GROVE ... 1G 139
Grove, The TW1: Twick ... 6B 114
Grove, The TW11: Tedd ... 4A 132
Grove, The TW7: Isle ... 1J 113
Grove, The UB10: Ick ... 5C 56
Grove, The UB6: G'frd ... 6G 77
Grove, The W5 ... 1D 96
Grove Av. HA5: Pinn ... 4C 40
Grove Av. N10 ... 2G 47
Grove Av. N3 ... 7D 30
Grove Av. SM1: Sutt ... 6J 165
Grove Av. TW1: Twick ... 1K 131
Grove Av. W7 ... 7J 77
Grovebury Cl. DA8: Erith ... 6K 109
Grovebury Ct. DA6: Bex ... 5H 127
Grovebury Ct. N14 ... 7C 22
Grovebury Rd. SE2 ... 2B 108
Grove Cl. BR2: Hayes ... 2J 171
Grove Cl. KT1: King T ... 4F 151
Grove Cl. N14 ... 7B 22
Grove Cl. SE23 ... 1A 140
Grove Cl. TW13: Hanw ... 4C 130
Grove Cl. UB10: Ick ... 5C 56
Grove Cotts. SW3 ... 7D 16 (6C 100)
... (off Chelsea Mnr. St.)
Grove Cotts. W4 ... 6A 98
Grove Ct. EN5: Barn ... 3C 20
... (off Hadley Ridge)
Grove Ct. KT1: King T ... 3E 150
... (off Grove Cres.)
Grove Ct. KT8: E Mos ... 5H 149
Grove Ct. NW8 ... 1A 4 (3B 82)
... (off Grove End Rd.)
Grove Ct. SE15 ... 7E 102
... (off Peckham Rd.)
Grove Ct. SW10 ... 6A 16 (5A 100)
... (off Drayton Gdns.)
Grove Ct. TW3: Houn ... 4E 112
Grove Ct. W5 ... 1E 96
Grove Cres. E18 ... 2H 51
Grove Cres. KT1: King T ... 3E 150
Grove Cres. KT12: Walt T ... 7K 147
Grove Cres. NW9 ... 4J 43
Grove Cres. TW13: Hanw ... 4C 130
Grove Cres. Rd. E15 ... 6F 69
Grovedale Rd. N19 ... 2H 65
Grove Dwellings E1 ... 5J 85
Grove End E18 ... 2H 51
Grove End NW5 ... 4F 65
Grove End Gdns. NW8 ... 1A 4 (2B 82)
Grove End Ho. NW8 ... 2A 4 (3B 82)
... (off Grove End Rd.)
Grove End La. KT10: Esh ... 7H 149
Grove End Rd. NW8 ... 1A 4 (2B 82)
Grove Farm Retail Pk. ... 7C 54
Grovefield N11 ... 4A 32
... (off Coppies Gro.)
Grove Footpath KT5: Surb ... 4E 150
Grove Gdns. EN3: Enf W ... 1E 24
Grove Gdns. NW4 ... 5C 44
Grove Gdns. NW8 ... 2D 4 (3C 82)
Grove Gdns. RM10: Dag ... 3J 73
Grove Gdns. TW10: Rich ... 6F 115
Grove Gdns. TW11: Tedd ... 4A 132
Grove Grn. Rd. E11 ... 3E 68
Grove Hall Ct. E3 ... 2C 86
... (off Jebb St.)
Grove Hall Ct. NW8 ... 1A 4 (3A 82)
Grove Hill E18 ... 2H 51
Grove Hill HA1: Harr ... 7J 41
Grovehill Ct. BR1: Broml ... 6H 141
Grove Hill Rd. HA1: Harr ... 7K 41
Grove Hill Rd. SE5 ... 3E 120
Grove Ho. N3 ... 3F 45
Grove Ho. SW3 ... 7D 16 (6C 100)
... (off Chelsea Mnr. St.)
Grove Ho. Rd. N8 ... 4J 47
Groveland Av. SW16 ... 7K 137
Groveland Ct. EC4 ... 1D 14 (6C 84)
... (off Bow La.)
Groveland Rd. BR3: Beck ... 3B 158
Grovelands KT1: King T ... 4D 150
... (off Palace Rd.)
Grovelands KT8: W Mole ... 4E 148
Grovelands Cl. HA2: Harr ... 3F 59
Grovelands Cl. SE5 ... 2E 120
Grovelands Ct. N14 ... 7C 22
Grovelands Rd. BR5: St P ... 7A 144
Grovelands Rd. N13 ... 4E 32
Grovelands Rd. N15 ... 6G 49
Groveland Way KT3: N Mald ... 5J 151
Grove La. KT1: King T ... 4E 150
Grove La. SE5 ... 1D 120
Grove La. UB8: Hil ... 4B 74
Grove La. Ter. SE5 ... 2D 120
Groveley Rd. TW13: Felt ... 4J 129
Groveley Rd. TW16: Sun ... 5G 129
Grove Mans. W6 ... 2E 98
... (off Hammersmith Gro.)
Grove M. W6 ... 3E 98
Grove Mill Pl. SM5: Cars ... 3E 166
Grove Nature Reserve, The ... 4B 74
Grove Pk. E11 ... 6K 51
Grove Pk. NW9 ... 4J 43
GROVE PARK ... 3K 141
Grove Pk. SE5 ... 2E 120
GROVE PARK ... 1J 115
Grove Pk. Av. E4 ... 7J 35
GROVE PARK BRI. ... 7J 97
Grove Pk. Gdns. W4 ... 7H 97
Grove Pk. M. W4 ... 7J 97
Grove Pk. Nature Reserve ... 1H 141
Grove Pk. Rd. N15 ... 4E 48
Grove Pk. Rd. SE9 ... 3A 142
Grove Pk. Rd. W4 ... 7H 97
Grove Pk. Ter. W4 ... 7H 97
Grove Pas. E2 ... 2H 85
Grove Pl. IG11: Bark ... 7G 71
Grove Pl. NW3 ... 3B 64
Grove Pl. SE9 ... 6D 124
Grove Pl. SW12 ... 7F 119
Grove Pl. W3 ... 1J 97
Grover Ct. SE13 ... 2D 122
Grover Gdns. RM5: Col R ... 1F 55
Grover Ho. SE11 ... 6H 19 (5K 101)
Grove Rd. CR4: Mitc ... 3E 154
... (not continuous)
Grove Rd. CR7: Thor H ... 4A 156
Grove Rd. DA17: Belv ... 6F 109
Grove Rd. DA7: Bex ... 4J 127
Grove Rd. E11 ... 7H 51
Grove Rd. E17 ... 6D 50
Grove Rd. E18 ... 2H 51
Grove Rd. E3 ... 1K 85
Grove Rd. E4 ... 4K 35
Grove Rd. EN4: Cockf ... 3H 21
Grove Rd. HA5: Pinn ... 5D 40
Grove Rd. HA8: Edg ... 6B 28
Grove Rd. KT6: Surb ... 5D 150
Grove Rd. KT8: E Mos ... 4H 149
Grove Rd. N11 ... 5A 32
Grove Rd. N12 ... 5G 31
Grove Rd. N15 ... 5E 48
Grove Rd. NW2 ... 6E 62
Grove Rd. RM6: Chad H ... 7B 54
Grove Rd. SM1: Sutt ... 6J 165
Grove Rd. SW13 ... 2B 116
Grove Rd. SW19 ... 7A 136
Grove Rd. TW10: Rich ... 6F 115
Grove Rd. TW17: Shep ... 6E 146
Grove Rd. TW2: Twick ... 3H 131
Grove Rd. TW3: Houn ... 4E 112
Grove Rd. TW7: Isle ... 1J 113
Grove Rd. TW8: Bford ... 5C 96
Grove Rd. UB8: Uxb ... 7A 56
Grove Rd. W3 ... 1J 97
Grove Rd. W5 ... 7D 78
Groveside Cl. SM5: Cars ... 2C 166
Groveside Cl. W3 ... 5G 79
Groveside Ct. SW11 ... 2B 118
Groveside Rd. E4 ... 2B 36
Grovestile Waye TW14: Bedf ... 7F 111
Grove St. N18 ... 5A 34
Grove St. SE8 ... 4B 104
Grove Ter. NW5 ... 3F 65
Grove Ter. TW11: Tedd ... 4A 132
Grove Ter. UB1: S'hall ... 7E 76
Grove Ter. M. NW5 ... 3F 65
Grove Va. BR7: Chst ... 6E 142
Grove Va. SE22 ... 4F 121
Grove Vs. E14 ... 7D 86
Grove Way HA9: Wemb ... 5H 61
Grove Way KT10: Esh ... 7G 149
Grove Way UB8: Uxb ... 7A 56
Groveway RM8: Dag ... 3D 72
Groveway SW9 ... 1K 119
Grovewood TW9: Kew ... 1G 115
Grove Wood Cl. BR1: Broml ... 3E 160
Grovewood Pl. IG8: Wfd G ... 6J 37
Grummant Rd. SE15 ... 1F 121
Grundy St. E14 ... 6D 86
Gruneisen Rd. N3 ... 7E 30
Grunwick Cl. NW2 ... 5C 62
Gtec Ho. E15 ... 2F 87
... (off Canning Rd.)
Guardhouse Way NW7 ... 5A 30
Guardian Apts. E3 ... 4B 86
... (off Kevtar Gdn.)
Guardian Av. NW9 ... 3A 44
Guardian Ct. SE12 ... 5G 123
Guards Memorial ... 5D 12 (1H 101)
Guards' Mus., The ... 7B 12 (2G 101)
Gubyon Av. SE24 ... 5B 120
Guerin Sq. E3 ... 3B 86
Guernsey Cl. TW5: Hest ... 7E 94
Guernsey Gro. SE24 ... 7C 120
Guernsey Ho. EN3: Enf W ... 1E 24
... (off Eastfield Rd.)
Guernsey Ho. N1 ... 6C 66
... (off Channel Island Est.)
Guernsey Rd. E11 ... 1F 69
Guglielmo Marconi M. E3 ... 2B 86
Guibal Rd. SE12 ... 7K 123
Guildersfield Rd. SW16 ... 7J 137
Guildford Av. TW13: Felt ... 2H 129
Guildford Ct. SW8 ... 7J 101
... (off Guildford Rd.)
Guildford Gro. SE10 ... 1D 122
Guildford Rd. CR0: C'don ... 6D 156
Guildford Rd. E17 ... 1E 50
Guildford Rd. E6 ... 6D 88
Guildford Rd. IG3: Ilf ... 2J 71
Guildford Rd. SW8 ... 1J 119
Guildford Way SM6: W'gton ... 5J 167
Guildhall London ... 7D 8 (6C 84)
... (off Aldermanbury)
Guildhall Art Gallery ... 7E 8 (6D 84)
... (off Aldermanbury)
Guildhall Bldgs. EC2 ... 7E 8 (6D 84)
... (off Gresham St.)
Guildhall Coll. ... 6H 85
Guildhall Offices EC2 ... 7D 8 (6C 84)
... (off Basinghall St.)
Guildhall Yd. EC2 ... 7D 8 (6C 84)
Guildhouse St. SW1 ... 3A 18 (4G 101)
Guildown Av. N12 ... 4E 30
Guild Rd. SE7 ... 6B 106
Guildsway E17 ... 1B 50
Guilford Av. KT5: Surb ... 5F 151
Guilford Pl. WC1 ... 4G 7 (4K 83)
Guilford St. WC1 ... 4E 6 (4J 83)
Guilfoyle NW9 ... 2B 44
Guillemot Ct. SE8 ... 6B 104
... (off Alexandra Cl.)
Guillemot Pl. N22 ... 2K 47
Guinea Ct. E1 ... 2K 15 (7G 85)
... (off Royal Mint St.)
Guinea Point E14 ... 6A 86
... (off Repton St.)
Guinness Cl. E9 ... 7A 68
Guinness Cl. UB3: Harl ... 3F 93
Guinness Ct. CR0: C'don ... 2F 169
Guinness Ct. E1 ... 1J 15 (6F 85)
... (off Mansell St.)
Guinness Ct. EC1 ... 2D 8 (3C 84)
... (off Lever St.)
Guinness Ct. SE1 ... 6G 15 (2E 102)
... (off Snowsfields)
Guinness Ct. SW3 ... 4E 16 (4D 100)
Guinness Sq. SE1 ... 4E 102
Guinness Trust SW3 ... 4E 16 (4D 100)
... (off Cadogan St.)
Guinness Trust Bldgs. SE11
... 5B 102
Guinness Trust Bldgs. W6 ... 5E 98
... (off Fulham Pal. Rd.)
Guinness Trust Est., The N16 ... 1E 66
Guion Rd. SW6 ... 2H 117
Gulland Wlk. N1 ... 6C 66
... (off Church Rd.)
Gullane Ho. E3 ... 2B 86
... (off Shetland Rd.)
Gulliver Cl. UB5: N'olt ... 1D 76
Gulliver Rd. DA15: Sidc ... 2H 143
Gulliver's Ho. EC1 ... 4C 8 (4C 84)
... (off Goswell Rd.)
Gulliver St. SE16 ... 3A 104
Gullivers Wlk. SE8 ... 4B 104
Gulston Wlk. SW3 ... 4F 17 (4D 100)
... (off Blackland Ter.)
Gumleigh Rd. W5 ... 4C 96
Gumley Gdns. TW7: Isle ... 3A 114
Gumping Rd. BR5: Farnb ... 2G 173
Gundulf St. SE11 ... 4J 19 (4A 102)
Gundulph Rd. BR2: Broml ... 3A 160
Gun Ho. E1 ... 1H 103
... (off Wapping High St.)
Gunmakers La. E3 ... 1A 86
Gun M. IG9: Buck H ... 4G 37
Gunnel Ct. E3 ... 3E 86
... (off Bolinder Way)
Gunnell Cl. CR0: C'don ... 6G 157
Gunnell Cl. SE25 ... 6G 157
... (off Backley Gdns.)
Gunnell Cl. SE26 ... 4G 139
Gunner La. SE18 ... 5E 106
GUNNERSBURY ... 5H 97
Gunnersbury Av. W3 ... 3G 97
Gunnersbury Av. W4 ... 4G 97
Gunnersbury Av. W5 ... 1F 97
Gunnersbury Cl. W4 ... 5H 97
Gunnersbury Ct. W3 ... 2H 97
Gunnersbury Cres. W3 ... 2G 97
Gunnersbury Dr. W5 ... 2F 97
Gunnersbury Gdns. W3 ... 2G 97
Gunnersbury La. W3 ... 3G 97
Gunnersbury Mnr. W5 ... 1F 97
Gunnersbury M. W4 ... 5H 97
GUNNERSBURY PARK ... 3G 97
Gunnersbury Pk. Mus. ... 3G 97
Gunnersbury Triangle Nature Reserve
... 4J 97
Gunners Gro. E4 ... 3K 35
Gunners Rd. SW18 ... 2B 136
Gunnery Ter. SE18 ... 3G 107
Gunning St. SE18 ... 4J 107
Gunpowder Sq. EC4 ... 7K 7 (6A 84)
... (off E. Harding St.)
Gunstor Rd. N16 ... 4E 66
Gun St. E1 ... 6J 9 (5F 85)
Gunter Gro. HA8: Edg ... 1K 43
Gunter Gro. SW10 ... 6A 100
Gunter Hall Studios SW10 ... 6A 100
... (off Gunter Gro.)
Gunterstone Rd. W14 ... 4G 99
Gunthorpe St. E1 ... 6K 9 (5F 85)
Gunton M. SE13 ... 5F 123
Gunton Rd. E5 ... 3H 67
Gunton Rd. SW17 ... 6E 136
Gunwhale Cl. SE16 ... 1K 103
Gun Wharf E1 ... 1J 103
... (off Wapping High St.)
Gunyard M. SE18 ... 7C 106
Gurdon Ho. E14 ... 6C 86
... (off Dod St.)
Gurdon Rd. SE7 ... 5J 105
Gurdwara Way IG11: Bark ... 7F 71
Gurnard Cl. UB7: Yiew ... 7A 74
Gurnell Gro. W13 ... 4K 77
Gurnell Leisure Cen. ... 3K 77
Gurney Cl. E15 ... 5G 69
Gurney Cl. E17 ... 1K 49
Gurney Cl. IG11: Bark ... 6F 71
Gurney Cres. CR0: C'don ... 1K 167
Gurney Dr. N2 ... 4A 46
Gurney Ho. E2 ... 2G 85
... (off Goldsmiths Row)
Gurney Ho. UB3: Harl ... 5G 93
Gurney Rd. E15 ... 5G 69
Gurney Rd. SM5: Cars ... 4E 166
Gurney Rd. SW6 ... 3A 118
Gurney Rd. UB5: N'olt ... 3K 75
Gutenberg Ct. SE1 ... 3F 103
... (off Grange Rd.)
Guthridge Cl. E14 ... 5C 86
Guthrie Ct. SE1 ... 1K 19 (3A 102)
... (off Morley St.)
Guthrie St. SW3 ... 5B 16 (5B 100)
Gutter La. EC2 ... 1C 14 (6C 84)
Guyatt Gdns. CR4: Mitc ... 2E 154
Guy Barnett Gro. SE3 ... 3J 123
Guy Rd. SM6: Bedd ... 3H 167
Guyscliff Rd. SE13 ... 5E 122
Guys Retreat IG9: Buck H ... 1F 37
Guy St. SE1 ... 6F 15 (2D 102)
Guy St. Pk. ... 6F 15 (2D 102)
Guy Townsley Sq. E3 ... 5D 86
Gwalior Ho. N14 ... 6B 22
Gwalior Rd. SW15 ... 4F 117
Gwendolen Av. SW15 ... 4F 117
Gwendolen Cl. SW15 ... 5F 117
Gwendolen Ho. TW19: Stanw ... 1A 128
... (off Yeoman Dr.)
Gwendoline Av. E13 ... 1K 87
Gwendwr Rd. W14 ... 5G 99
Gweneth Cotts. HA8: Edg ... 6B 28
Gwen Morris Ho. SE5 ... 7C 102
Gwent Ct. SE16 ... 1K 103
... (off Rotherhithe St.)
Gwillim Cl. DA15: Sidc ... 5A 126
Gwilym Maries Ho. E2 ... 3H 85
... (off Blythe St.)
Gwydor Rd. BR3: Beck ... 3K 157
Gwydyr Rd. BR2: Broml ... 3H 159
Gwyn Cl. SW6 ... 7A 100
Gwynne Av. CR0: C'don ... 7K 157
Gwynne Cl. W4 ... 6B 98
Gwynne Ho. E1 ... 5H 85
... (off Turner St.)
Gwynne Ho. SW1 ... 5G 17 (5E 100)
... (off Lwr. Sloane St.)
Gwynne Ho. WC1 ... 2J 7 (3A 84)
... (off Lloyd Baker St.)
Gwynne Pk. Av. IG8: Wfd G ... 6J 37
Gwynne Pl. WC1 ... 2H 7 (3K 83)
Gwynne Rd. SW11 ... 2B 118
Gylcote Cl. SE5 ... 4D 120
Gyles Pk. HA7: Stan ... 1C 42
Gyllyngdune Gdns. IG3: Ilf ... 2K 71
Gym Bloomsbury, The ... 4E 6 (4J 83)
Gym Holborn Circus, The ... 7K 7 (6A 84)
... (off Thavie's Inn)
Gym Hounslow, The ... 3F 113
Gym Kingsbury, The ... 5G 43
Gym London Monument, The
... 3F 15 (7D 84)
Gym Walworth Road, The ... 5C 102
Gymnasium, The N1 ... 2J 83
GYPSY CORNER ... 5K 79

H

Haarlem Rd. W14 ... 3F 99
Haberdasher Est. N1 ... 1F 9 (3D 84)
Haberdasher Pl. N1 ... 1F 9 (3D 84)
Haberdashers Ct. SE14 ... 3K 121
Haberdasher St. N1 ... 1F 9 (3D 84)
Habitat Cl. SE15 ... 2H 121
Haccombe Rd. SW19 ... 6A 136
HACKBRIDGE ... 1E 166
Hackbridge Pk. Gdns. SM5: Cars
... 2D 166
Hackbridge Rd. SM6: W'gton ... 2E 166
Hackford Rd. SW9 ... 1K 119
Hackford Wlk. SW9 ... 1A 120
Hackington Cres. BR3: Beck ... 6C 140
HACKNEY ... 6H 67
Hackney City Farm ... 2G 85
Hackney Empire Theatre ... 6H 67
Hackney Fashion Hub E9 ... 6J 67
Hackney Gro. E8 ... 6H 67
Hackney Marshes Cen. ... 4B 68
Hackney Mus. ... 6H 67
Hackney Picturehouse ... 6H 67
... (off Mare St.)
Hackney Rd. E2 ... 1J 9 (3F 85)
Hackney University Technical Coll.
... 1H 9 (3E 84)
HACKNEY WICK ... 6A 68
HACKNEY WICK ... 6B 68
Hackworth Point E3 ... 3D 86
... (off Rainhill Way)
Hacon Sq. E8 ... 7H 67
... (off Mare St.)
Hadar Cl. N20 ... 1D 30
Hadden Rd. SE28 ... 3J 107
Hadden Way UB6: G'frd ... 6H 59
Haddington Rd. BR1: Broml ... 3F 141
Haddo Ho. SE10 ... 6D 104
... (off Haddo St.)
Haddon Cl. EN1: Enf ... 6B 24
Haddon Cl. KT3: N Mald ... 5B 152
Haddon Ct. NW4 ... 3E 44
Haddon Ct. W3 ... 7B 80
Haddonfield SE8 ... 4K 103
Haddon Gro. DA15: Sidc ... 7K 125
Haddon Rd. SM1: Sutt ... 4K 165
... (not continuous)
Haddo St. SE10 ... 6D 104
Haden Ct. N4 ... 2A 66
Haden La. N11 ... 4B 32
Hadfield Cl. UB1: S'hall ... 3D 76
Hadfield Ho. E1 ... 6G 85
... (off Ellen St.)
Hadleigh Cl. E1 ... 4J 85
Hadleigh Cl. HA2: Harr ... 4E 58
Hadleigh Cl. SW20 ... 2H 153
Hadleigh Ct. E4 ... 1B 36
Hadleigh Ct. NW2 ... 6E 62
Hadleigh Ho. E1 ... 4J 85
... (off Hadleigh Cl.)
Hadleigh Lodge IG8: Wfd G ... 6D 36
... (off Snakes La. W.)
Hadleigh Rd. N9 ... 7C 24
Hadleigh St. E2 ... 3J 85
Hadleigh Wlk. E6 ... 6C 88
HADLEY ... 3C 20
Hadley Cl. N21 ... 6F 23
Hadley Comn. EN5: Barn ... 2D 20
Hadley Comn. EN5: New Bar ... 2D 20
Hadley Ct. EN5: New Bar ... 3E 20
Hadley Ct. N16 ... 1G 67
Hadley Ct. SL3: Poyle ... 4A 174
... (off Coleridge Cres.)
Hadley Gdns. UB2: S'hall ... 5D 94
Hadley Gdns. W4 ... 5K 97
Hadley Grn. EN5: Barn ... 2C 20
Hadley Grn. Rd. EN5: Barn ... 2C 20
Hadley Grn. W. EN5: Barn ... 2C 20
Hadley Gro. EN5: Barn ... 2B 20
Hadley Highstone EN5: Barn ... 1C 20
Hadley M. EN5: Barn ... 3C 20
Hadley Pde. EN5: Barn ... 3B 20
... (off High St.)
Hadley Ridge EN5: Barn ... 3C 20
Hadley Rd. CR4: Mitc ... 4H 155
Hadley Rd. DA17: Belv ... 4F 109
Hadley Rd. EN2: Enf ... 1D 22
Hadley Rd. EN4: Had W ... 1K 21
Hadley Rd. EN5: New Bar ... 2E 20
Hadley St. NW1 ... 6F 65
... (not continuous)
Hadley Way N21 ... 6F 23
HADLEY WOOD ... 1F 21
Hadley Wood Golf Course ... 1H 21
Hadley Wood Nature Reserve ... 2F 21
Hadley Wood Rd. EN4: Cockf ... 2F 21
Hadley Wood Rd. EN5: Cockf ... 2F 21
Hadley Wood Rd. EN5: New Bar ... 2F 21
Hadlow Ho. SE17 ... 5E 102
... (off Kinglake Est.)
Hadlow Pl. SE19 ... 7G 139
Hadlow Rd. DA14: Sidc ... 4A 144
Hadlow Rd. DA16: Well ... 7C 108
Hadrian Cl. E3 ... 1C 86
... (off Garrison Rd.)
Hadrian Cl. TW19: Stanw ... 7A 110
Hadrian Ct. SM2: Sutt ... 7K 165
Hadrian Est. E2 ... 2G 85
Hadrian M. CR4: Mitc ... 3F 155
Hadrian M. N7 ... 7K 65
Hadrian Rd. BR3: Beck ... 5D 158
Hadrians Ride EN1: Enf ... 5A 24
Hadrian St. SE10 ... 5G 105
Hadrian Way TW19: Stanw ... 7A 110
... (not continuous)
Hadstock Ho. NW1 ... 1D 6 (3H 83)
... (off Ossulston St.)
Hadyn Pk. Ct. W12 ... 2C 98
... (off Curwen Rd.)
Hadyn Pk. Rd. W12 ... 2C 98
Hafer Rd. SW11 ... 4D 118
Hafton Rd. SE6 ... 1G 141
Haggard Rd. TW1: Twick ... 7B 114
Hagger Ct. E17 ... 3F 51
HAGGERSTON ... 7F 67
Haggerston Rd. E8 ... 7F 67
Haggerston Studios E8 ... 1F 85
... (off Kingsland Rd.)
Hague St. E2 ... 3G 85
Ha Ha Rd. SE18 ... 6D 106
Haider Cl. NW2 ... 2F 63
Haig Ho. E2 ... 1K 9 (2G 85)
... (off Shipton St.)
Haig Pl. SM4: Mord ... 6J 153
Haig Rd. HA7: Stan ... 5H 27
Haig Rd. UB8: Hil ... 5D 74
Haig Rd. E. E13 ... 3A 88
Haig Rd. W. E13 ... 3A 88
Haigville Gdns. IG6: Ilf ... 4F 53
Hailes Cl. CR0: Bedd ... 2H 167
Hailes Cl. SW19 ... 6A 136
Haileybury Av. EN1: Enf ... 6A 24
Hailey Rd. DA18: Erith ... 2G 109
Hailey Rd. Bus. Pk. DA18: Erith ... 2G 109
Hailing M. BR2: Broml ... 3K 159
... (off Wendover Rd.)
Hailsham Av. SW2 ... 2K 137
Hailsham Cl. KT6: Surb ... 7D 150
Hailsham Dr. HA1: Harr ... 3H 41
Hailsham Ho. NW8 ... 4C 4 (4C 82)
... (off Salisbury St.)
Hailsham Rd. SW17 ... 6E 136
Hailsham Ter. N18 ... 5J 33
Haimo Rd. SE9 ... 5B 124
Hainault Bri. Pde. IG1: Ilf ... 2F 71
... (off Hainault St.)
Hainault Ct. E17 ... 4F 51
... (off Forest Ri.)
Hainault Gore RM6: Chad H ... 5E 54
Hainault Rd. RM6: Chad H Forest Rd.
... 1B 54
Hainault Rd. RM6: Chad H Sylvan Av.
... 6F 55
Hainault Rd. E11 ... 1E 68
Hainault Rd. RM5: Col R ... 2J 55
Hainault Rd. RM5: Rom ... 2J 55
Hainault St. IG1: Ilf ... 2G 71
Hainault St. SE9 ... 1F 143
Haines Cl. N1 ... 7E 66
Haines Ho. SW11 ... 7H 101
... (off Ponton Rd.)
Haines St. SW11 ... 7G 101
Haines Wlk. SM4: Mord ... 7K 153
Hainford Cl. SE4 ... 4K 121
Haining Cl. W4 ... 5G 97
Hainthorpe Rd. SE27 ... 3B 138
Hainton Cl. E1 ... 6H 85
Halberd M. E5 ... 2H 67
Halbutt Gdns. RM9: Dag ... 3F 73
Halbutt St. RM9: Dag ... 4F 73
Halcomb St. N1 ... 1E 84
Halcot Av. DA6: Bex ... 5H 127
Halcrow St. E1 ... 5H 85
Halcyon EN1: Enf ... 5K 23
... (off Private Rd.)
Halcyon Cl. SW13 ... 3C 116
Halcyon Wharf E1 ... 1G 103
... (off Hermitage Wall)
Haldane Cl. N10 ... 7A 32
Haldane Pl. SW18 ... 1K 135
Haldane Rd. E6 ... 3B 88
Haldane Rd. SE28 ... 7D 90
Haldane Rd. SW6 ... 7H 99
Haldane Rd. UB1: S'hall ... 7G 77
Haldan Rd. E4 ... 6K 35
Haldon Rd. SW18 ... 6H 117
Hale, The E4 ... 7A 36
THE HALE ... 5E 28
Hale, The N17 ... 3G 49
Hale Cl. BR6: Farnb ... 4G 173
Hale Cl. E4 ... 3K 35
Hale Cl. HA8: Edg ... 5D 28
Hale Ct. HA8: Edg ... 5D 28
Hale Dr. NW7 ... 6D 28
HALE END ... 6B 36
Hale End Cl. HA4: Ruis ... 6J 39
Hale End Rd. E17 ... 1E 50
Hale End Rd. E4 ... 6A 36
Hale End Rd. IG8: Wfd G ... 7A 36
Halefield Rd. N17 ... 1H 49
Hale Gdns. N17 ... 4G 49
Hale Gdns. W3 ... 1G 97
Hale Gro. Gdns. NW7 ... 5F 29
Hale Ho. SW1 ... 5D 18 (5H 101)
... (off Lindsay Sq.)
Hale La. HA8: Edg ... 5C 28
Hale La. NW7 ... 5E 28
Hale Path SE27 ... 4B 138
Hale Rd. E6 ... 4C 88
Hale Rd. N17 ... 3G 49
Halesowen Rd. SM4: Mord ... 7K 153
Hales Prior N1 ... 1G 7 (2K 83)
... (off Calshot St.)
Hales St. SE8 ... 7C 104
Hale St. E14 ... 7D 86
Halesworth Cl. E5 ... 2J 67
Halesworth Rd. SE13 ... 3D 122
Hale Wlk. W7 ... 5J 77
Halewood Wy. RM13: Rain ... 3K 91
Haley Rd. NW4 ... 6E 44
Half Acre HA7: Stan ... 5H 27
Half Acre TW8: Bford ... 6D 96
Half Acre Rd. W7 ... 1J 95
Half Moon Ct. CR0: C'don ... 7B 156
Half Moon Ct. EC1 ... 6C 8 (5C 84)
... (off Bartholomew Cl.)

A–Z London 231

Half Moon Cres. – Hanson St.

Half Moon Cres. N1 2K 83
(not continuous)
Half Moon La. SE24 6C 120
Half Moon Pas. E1 1K 15 (6F 85)
(not continuous)
Half Moon St. W1 4K 11 (1F 101)
Halford Cl. HA8: Edg 2H 43
Halford Pl. W7 1K 95
Halford Rd. E10 5F 51
Halford Rd. SW6 6J 99
Halford Rd. TW10: Rich 5E 114
Halford Rd. UB10: Ick 4C 56
Halfway St. DA15: Sidc 7H 125
Haliburton Rd. TW1: Twick 5A 114
Haliday Ho. N1 6D 66
(off Mildmay St.)
Haliday Wlk. N1 6D 66
Halidon Cl. E9 5J 67
Halifax NW9 2B 44
Halifax Cl. TW11: Tedd 6J 131
Halifax Rd. EN2: Enf 2H 23
Halifax Rd. UB6: G'frd 1F 77
Halifax St. SE26 3H 139
Halifield Dr. DA17: Belv 3E 108
Haling Gro. CR2: S Croy 7C 168
Haling Pk. Gdns. CR2: S Croy 6B 168
Haling Pk. Rd. CR2: S Croy 5B 168
Haling Rd. CR2: S Croy 6D 168
Haliwell Ho. NW6 1K 81
(off Mortimer Cres.)
Halkett Ho. E2 1J 85
(off Waterloo Gdns.)
Halkin Arc. SW1 1F 17 (3D 100)
Halkin M. SW1 1G 17 (3E 100)
Halkin Pl. SW1 1G 17 (3E 100)
Halkin St. SW1 7H 11 (2E 100)
Hall, The SE3 3J 123
Hallam Cl. BR7: Chst 5D 142
Hallam Ct. W1 5K 5 (5F 83)
(off Hallam St.)
Hallam Gdns. HA5: Hat E 1C 40
Hallam Ho. SW1 6B 18 (5G 101)
(off Churchill Gdns.)
Hallam M. W1 5K 5 (5F 83)
Hallam Rd. N15 4B 48
Hallam Rd. SW13 3D 116
Hallam St. W1 5K 5 (5F 83)
Hallane Ho. SE27 5C 138
Hall Apts. E3 5B 86
(off Geoff Cade Way)
Hall Cl. W5 5E 78
Hall Ct. TW11: Tedd 5K 131
Hall Dr. SE26 5J 139
Hall Dr. W7 6J 77
Halley Gdns. SE13 4F 123
Halley Ho. E2 2G 85
(off Pritchards Rd.)
Halley Ho. SE10 5H 105
(off Armitage Rd.)
Halley Rd. E12 6B 70
Halley Rd. E7 6A 70
Halley St. E14 5A 86
Hall Farm Cl. HA7: Stan 4G 27
Hall Farm Dr. TW2: Whitt 7H 113
Hallfield Est. W2 6A 82
(not continuous)
Hall Gdns. E4 4G 35
Hall Ga. NW8 1A 4 (3B 82)
Halliards, The KT12: Walt T 6J 147
Halliday Ho. E1 6G 85
(off Christian St.)
Halliday Sq. UB2: S'hall 1H 95
Halliford Cl. TW17: Shep 4F 147
Halliford Rd. TW16: Sun 5H 147
Halliford Rd. TW17: Shep 5G 147
Halliford St. N1 7C 66
Hallingbury Ct. E17 3D 50
Halling Ho. SE1 7F 15 (2D 102)
(off Long La.)
Hallings Wharf Studios E15 1F 87
Hallington Ct. HA8: Edg 4A 28
(off Brannigan Way)
Halliwell Ct. SE22 5G 121
Halliwell Rd. SW2 6K 119
Halliwick Ct. Pde. N12 6J 31
(off Woodhouse Rd.)
Halliwick Rd. N10 1E 46
Hall La. E4 5F 35
Hall La. NW4 1C 44
Hall La. UB3: Harl 7F 93
HALL LANE 5E 34
Hallmark Ho. E14 5C 86
(off Ursula Gould Way)
Hallmark Trad. Est. HA9: Wemb 4J 61
Hallmead Rd. SM1: Sutt 3K 165
Hall Oak Wlk. NW6 6H 63
Hallowell Av. CR0: Bedd 4J 167
Hallowell Cl. CR4: Mitc 3E 154
Hallowell Gdns. CR7: Thor H 2C 156
Hallowfield Way CR4: Mitc 3B 154
Hallows Gro. TW16: Sun 5H 129
Hall Pl. W2 4A 4 (4B 82)
(not continuous)
Hall Place & Gdns. 6J 127
Hall Pl. Cres. DA5: Bexl 5J 127
Hall Place Sports Pavilion 6J 127
Hall Rd. E15 4F 69
Hall Rd. E6 1D 88
Hall Rd. NW8 3A 82
Hall Rd. RM6: Chad H 6C 54
Hall Rd. SM6: W'gton 7F 167
Hall Rd. TW7: Isle 5H 113
Hallside Rd. EN1: Enf 1A 24
Halls Ter. UB10: Hil 4D 74
Hall St. EC1 1B 8 (3B 84)
Hall St. N12 5F 31
Hallsville Rd. E16 6H 87
Hallswelle Pde. NW11 5H 45
Hallswelle Rd. NW11 5H 45
Hall Twr. W2 5B 4 (5B 82)
(off Hall Pl.)
Hall Vw. SE9 2B 142
Hallywell Cres. E6 5D 88
Halo E15 1E 86
Halons Rd. SE9 7E 124
Halpin Bldg. SE10 3J 105
(off Rennie Street)
Halpin Pl. SE17 4D 102
Halsbrook Rd. SE3 3A 124
Halsbury Cl. HA7: Stan 4G 27
Halsbury Ct. HA7: Stan 5G 27
Halsbury Ho. N7 4K 65
(off Biddestone Rd.)
Halsbury Rd. W12 1D 98
Halsbury Rd. E. UB5: N'olt 4G 59
Halsbury Rd. W. UB5: N'olt 5F 59
Halsend UB3: Hayes 1K 93
Halsey Ho. WC1 6G 7 (5K 83)
(off Red Lion Sq.)
Halsey M. SW3 3E 16 (4D 100)
Halsey St. SW3 3E 16 (4D 100)
Halsham Cres. IG11: Bark 5K 71
Halsmere Rd. SE5 1B 120
Halstead Cl. CR0: C'don 3C 168
Halstead Ct. E17 7B 50
Halstead Ct. N1 1F 9 (2D 84)
(off Murray Gro.)
Halstead Gdns. N21 1J 33
Halstead Rd. E11 5J 51
Halstead Rd. EN1: Enf 4K 23
Halstead Rd. N21 1H 33
Halston Cl. SW11 6D 118
Halstow Rd. NW10 3F 81
Halstow Rd. SE10 5J 105
Halsway UB3: Hayes 1J 93
Halton Cl. N11 6J 31
Halton Ct. SE3 3K 123
Halton Cross St. N1 1B 84
Halton Ho. N1 7B 66
(off Halton Rd.)
Halton Mans. N1 7B 66
Halton Pl. N1 1C 84
Halton Rd. N1 7B 66
Halt Robin La. DA17: Belv 4H 109
Halt Robin Rd. DA17: Belv 4G 109
(not continuous)
Halyard Ho. E14 3E 104
(off Manchester Rd.)
Halyard Pl. E16 2K 105
Halyard St. RM9: Dag 4E 90
HAM 3C 132
Ham, The TW8: Bford 7C 96
Hamara Ghar E13 1A 88
Hambalt Rd. SW4 5G 119
Hamble Cl. HA4: Ruis 2G 57
Hambledon SE17 6D 102
(off Villa St.)
Hambledon Cl. UB8: Hil 4D 74
Hambledon Ct. SE22 4E 120
Hambledon Ct. W5 7E 78
Hambledon Gdns. SE25 3F 157
Hambledon Pl. SE21 1E 138
Hambledon Rd. SW18 7H 117
Hambledown Rd. DA15: Sidc 7H 125
Hamble Dr. UB3: Hayes 7H 75
Hamblehyrst BR3: Beck 2D 158
Hamble St. SW6 3K 117
Hambleton Cl. KT4: Wor Pk 2E 164
Hamble Wlk. UB5: N'olt 2E 76
(off Brabazon Rd.)
Hambley Ho. SE16 4H 103
(off Camilla Rd.)
Hamblin Ho. UB1: S'hall 7C 76
(off The Broadway)
Hambridge Way SW2 7A 120
Hambro Av. BR2: Hayes 1J 171
Hambrook Rd. SE25 3H 157
Hambro Rd. SW16 6H 137
Hambrough Ho. UB4: Yead 5A 76
Hambrough Rd. UB1: S'hall 1C 94
Ham Cl. TW10: Ham 3C 132
(not continuous)
Ham Common 4E 132
Ham Comn. TW10: Ham 3D 132
Ham Ct. NW9 2A 44
Ham Cft. Cl. TW13: Felt 3J 129
Hamden Cres. RM10: Dag 3H 73
Hamel Cl. HA3: Kenton 4D 42
Hamella Ho. E9 5A 68
(off Sadler Pl.)
Hameway E6 3E 88
Ham Farm Rd. TW10: Ham 4D 132
Ham Flds. TW10: Ham 3B 132
Hamfrith Rd. E15 6H 69
Ham Ga. Av. TW10: Ham 3D 132
Ham House & Gdn. 1C 132
Hamilton Av. IG6: Ilf 4F 53
Hamilton Av. KT6: Surb 2G 163
Hamilton Av. N9 7B 24
Hamilton Av. RM1: Rom 2K 55
Hamilton Av. SM3: Cheam 2G 165
Hamilton Cl. EN4: Cockf 4H 21
Hamilton Cl. HA7: Stan 2D 26
Hamilton Cl. N17 3F 49
Hamilton Cl. NW8 2A 4 (3B 82)
Hamilton Cl. SE16 2A 104
Hamilton Cl. TW11: Tedd 6B 132
Hamilton Cl. TW13: Felt 5H 129
Hamilton Ct. CR0: C'don 1G 169
Hamilton Ct. SE6 1H 141
Hamilton Ct. SW15 3G 117
Hamilton Ct. TW3: Houn 4F 113
(off Hanworth Rd.)
Hamilton Ct. W5 7E 78
Hamilton Ct. W9 3A 82
(off Maida Vale)
Hamilton Cres. HA2: Harr 3D 58
Hamilton Cres. N13 4F 33
Hamilton Cres. TW3: Houn 5F 113
Hamilton Gdns. NW8 3A 82
Hamilton Hall NW8 2A 82
(off Hamilton Ter.)
Hamilton Ho. E14 St Davids Sq. 5D 104
(off St Davids Sq.)
Hamilton Ho. E14 Victory Pl. 7B 86
(off Victory Pl.)
Hamilton Ho. E3 3B 86
(off British St.)
Hamilton Ho. NW8 1A 4 (3B 82)
(off Hall Rd.)
Hamilton Ho. W4 6A 98
Hamilton Ho. W8 2K 99
(off Vicarage Ga.)
Hamilton La. N5 4B 66
Hamilton Lodge E1 4J 85
(off Cleveland Gro.)
Hamilton M. SW18 1J 135
Hamilton M. SW19 7J 135
Hamilton M. W1 6J 11 (2F 101)
Hamilton Pde. TW13: Felt 4H 129
Hamilton Pk. N5 4B 66
Hamilton Pk. W. N5 4B 66
Hamilton Pl. N19 3H 65
Hamilton Pl. TW16: Sun 7K 129
Hamilton Pl. W1 5H 11 (1E 100)
Hamilton Rd. CR7: Thor H 3D 156
Hamilton Rd. DA15: Sidc 4A 144
Hamilton Rd. DA7: Bex 2E 126
Hamilton Rd. E15 3G 87
Hamilton Rd. E17 2A 50
Hamilton Rd. EN4: Cockf 4H 21
Hamilton Rd. HA1: Harr 5J 41
Hamilton Rd. IG1: Ilf 4F 71
Hamilton Rd. N2 3A 46
Hamilton Rd. N9 7B 24
Hamilton Rd. NW10 5C 62
Hamilton Rd. NW11 7F 45
Hamilton Rd. SE27 4D 138
Hamilton Rd. SW19 7K 135
Hamilton Rd. TW13: Felt 4H 129
Hamilton Rd. TW2: Twick 1J 131
Hamilton Rd. TW8: Bford 6D 96
Hamilton Rd. UB1: S'hall 1D 94
Hamilton Rd. UB3: Hayes 7K 75
Hamilton Rd. W4 2A 98
Hamilton Rd. W5 7E 78
Hamilton Rd. Ind. Est. SE27 4D 138
Hamilton Rd. M. SW19 7K 135
Hamilton Sq. N12 6G 31
Hamilton Sq. SE1 6F 15 (2D 102)
Hamilton St. SE8 6C 104
Hamilton Ter. NW8 2K 81
Hamilton Way N13 4G 33
Hamilton Way N3 6D 30
Hamilton Way SM6: W'gton 7H 167
Ham Lands Nature Reserve 2A 132
Hamlea Cl. SE12 5J 123
Hamlet, The SE5 3D 120
Hamlet Cl. RM5: Col R 1G 55
Hamlet Cl. SE13 4G 123
Hamlet Cl. SE6 7D 122
Hamlet Ct. E3 3C 86
(off Tomlin's Gro.)
Hamlet Ct. EN1: Enf 5K 23
Hamlet Ct. SE11 5B 102
(off Opal St.)
Hamlet Ct. W6 4C 98
Hamlet Gdns. W6 4C 98
Hamlet Ind. Est. E9 7C 68
Hamlet Intl. Ind. Est. DA8: Erith 5K 109
Hamlet Lodge UB10: Hil 6D 56
Hamlet M. SE21 1D 138
Hamleton Ter. RM9: Dag 7C 72
(off Flamstead Rd.)
Hamlet Rd. RM5: Col R 1G 55
Hamlet Rd. SE19 7F 139
Hamlet Sq. NW2 3G 63
Hamlets Way E3 4B 86
Hamlet Way SE1 6F 15 (2D 102)
Hamlin Cres. HA5: Eastc 5A 40
Hamlyn Cl. HA8: Edg 3K 27
Hamlyn Gdns. SE19 7E 138
Hamlyn Ho. TW13: Felt 1K 129
Hammelton Ct. BR1: Broml 1H 159
(off London Rd.)
Hammelton Rd. BR1: Broml 1H 159
Hammerfield Ho. SW3 5D 16 (5C 100)
(off Cale St.)
Hammers La. NW7 5H 29
Hammersley Ho. SE14 7J 103
(off Pomeroy St.)
Hammersley Rd. E16 5J 87
HAMMERSMITH 4E 98
Hammersmith Apollo The Eventim Apollo 5E 98
HAMMERSMITH BRI. 6D 98
Hammersmith Bri. Rd. W6 5E 98
Hammersmith B'way. W6 4E 98
HAMMERSMITH BROADWAY 4E 98
Hammersmith Emb. W6 6E 98
Hammersmith Fitness & Squash Cen. 4F 99
(off Chalk Hill Rd.)
Hammersmith Flyover W6 5E 98
HAMMERSMITH FLYOVER 5E 98
Hammersmith Gro. W6 2E 98
Hammersmith Info. Cen. 4E 98
(within The Broadway Cen.)
Hammersmith Rd. W14 4F 99
Hammersmith Rd. W6 4F 99
Hammersmith Ter. W6 5C 98
Hammet Cl. UB4: Yead 5B 76
Hammett St. EC3 2J 15 (7F 85)
Hammond Av. CR4: Mitc 2F 155
Hammond Cl. EN5: Barn 5B 20
Hammond Cl. TW12: Hamp 1E 148
Hammond Cl. UB6: G'frd 5H 59
Hammond Ct. E10 2D 68
(off Leyton Grange Est.)
Hammond Ct. SE11 5J 19 (5A 102)
(off Hotspur St.)
Hammond Ho. E14 3C 104
(off Tiller Rd.)
Hammond Ho. SE14 7J 103
(off Lubbock St.)
Hammond Lodge W9 5J 81
(off Admiral Wlk.)
Hammond Rd. EN1: Enf 2C 24
Hammond Rd. UB2: S'hall 3C 94
Hammonds Cl. RM8: Dag 3C 72
Hammond St. NW5 6G 65
Hammond Way SE28 7B 90
Hamond Cl. CR2: S Croy 7B 168
Hamonde Cl. HA8: Edg 2C 28
Hamond Sq. N1 2E 84
Ham Pk. Rd. E15 7H 69
Ham Pk. Rd. E7 7J 69
Hampden Av. BR3: Beck 2A 158
Hampden Cl. NW1 2H 83
Hampden Ct. N10 7K 31
Hampden Gurney St. W1 1E 10 (6D 82)
Hampden Ho. SW9 2A 120
(off Overton Rd.)
Hampden La. N17 1F 49
Hampden Rd. BR3: Beck 2A 158
Hampden Rd. HA3: Hrw W 1G 41
Hampden Rd. KT1: King T 3G 151
Hampden Rd. N10 7K 31
Hampden Rd. N17 1G 49
Hampden Rd. N19 2H 65
Hampden Rd. N8 4A 48
Hampden Rd. RM5: Col R 1H 55
Hampden Sq. N14 1A 32
Hampden Way N14 1A 32
Hampshire Cl. N18 5C 34
Hampshire Hog La. W6 5D 98
Hampshire Rd. N22 7E 32
Hampshire St. NW5 6H 65
Hampson Way SW8 1K 119
HAMPSTEAD 4B 64
Hampstead Av. IG8: Wfd G 7K 37
Hampstead Cl. SE28 1B 108
Hampstead Cricket Club 5K 63
(off Lymington Rd.)
Hampstead Gdns. NW11 6J 45
Hampstead Gdns. RM6: Chad H 5B 54
HAMPSTEAD GARDEN SUBURB 5A 46
Hampstead Ga. NW3 5A 64
Hampstead Golf Course 7B 46
Hampstead Grn. NW3 5C 64
Hampstead Gro. NW3 3A 64
Hampstead Heath 2B 64
Hampstead Hgts. N2 3A 46
Hampstead High St. NW3 4B 64
Hampstead Hill Gdns. NW3 4B 64
Hampstead Ho. NW1 2A 6 (3G 83)
(off William Rd.)
Hampstead La. N6 7B 46
Hampstead La. NW3 1B 64
Hampstead Lodge NW1 5C 4 (5C 82)
(off Bell St.)
Hampstead M. BR3: Beck 4D 158
Hampstead Mus.
(off New End Sq.)
Hampstead Rd. NW1 2G 83
Hampstead Sq. NW3 3A 64
Hampstead Theatre 7B 64
Hampstead Wlk. E3 1B 86
Hampstead Way NW11 5H 45
Hampstead W. NW6 6J 63
HAMPTON 1F 149
Hampton & Richmond Borough FC 1F 149
Hampton Bus. Pk. TW13: Hanw 3C 130
Hampton Cl. N11 5A 32
Hampton Cl. NW6 3J 81
Hampton Cl. SW20 7E 134
HAMPTON COURT 3J 149
HAMPTON COURT 4J 149
Hampton Ct. N1 6B 66
Hampton Ct. N22 1G 47
Hampton Ct. SE14 7A 104
(off Batavia Rd.)
Hampton Ct. SE16 7K 85
(off King & Queen Wharf)
Hampton Ct. Av. KT8: E Mos 6H 149
HAMPTON CT. BRI. 4J 149
Hampton Ct. Cres. KT8: E Mos 3H 149
Hampton Ct. Est. KT7: T Ditt 4J 149
Hampton Ct. M. KT8: E Mos 4J 149
(off Feltham Av.)
Hampton Court Palace 4K 149
Hampton Court Palace Golf Course 5C 150
Hampton Ct. Pde. KT8: E Mos 4J 149
Hampton Ct. Rd. KT1: Hamp W 3B 150
Hampton Ct. Rd. KT8: E Mos 3K 149
Hampton Ct. Rd. TW12: E Mos 2G 149
Hampton Ct. Rd. TW12: Hamp 2G 149
Hampton Ct. Way KT8: E Mos 6J 149
Hampton Golf Course 3E 130
Hampton Grange BR1: Broml 7A 142
HAMPTON HILL 5G 131
Hampton Hill Bus. Pk. TW12: Hamp H 5G 131
(off High St.)
Hampton Hill Theatre 5G 131
Hampton Ho. DA7: Bex 2H 127
(off Erith Rd.)
Hampton Ho. SW8 7G 101
(off Ascalon St.)
Hampton La. TW13: Hanw 4C 130
Hampton M. EN3: Enf H 3D 24
Hampton M. NW10 3K 79
Hampton M. WD23: B Hea 1B 26
Hampton Open Air Pool 7G 131
Hampton Ri. HA3: Kenton 6E 42
Hampton Rd. CR0: C'don 6C 156
Hampton Rd. E11 1F 69
Hampton Rd. E4 5G 35
Hampton Rd. E7 5K 69
Hampton Rd. HA7: Stan 3D 26
Hampton Rd. IG1: Ilf 4G 71
Hampton Rd. KT4: Wor Pk 2C 164
Hampton Rd. TW11: Tedd 5H 131
Hampton Rd. TW12: Hamp H 5H 131
Hampton Rd. TW2: Twick 3H 131
Hampton Rd. E. TW13: Hanw 4D 130
Hampton Rd. Ind. Pk. CR0: C'don 6C 156
Hampton Rd. W. TW13: Hanw 3C 130
Hampton Sports & Fitness Cen. 5E 130
Hampton St. SE1 4C 102
Hampton St. SE17 4B 102
HAMPTON WICK 1C 150
Hampton Youth Project (Sports Hall) 6D 130
Ham Ridings TW10: Ham 5F 133
Hamshades Cl. DA15: Sidc 3K 143
Hamston Ho. W8 3K 99
(off Kensington Ct. Pl.)
Ham St. TW10: Ham 1B 132
Ham Vw. CR0: C'don 6A 158
Ham Yd. W1 2C 12 (7H 83)
Hanah Ct. SW19 7F 135
Hanameel St. E16 1K 105
Hana M. E5 4H 67
Hanbury Cl. NW4 3E 44
Hanbury Ct. HA1: Harr 6K 41
Hanbury Dr. E11 7H 51
Hanbury Dr. N21 5E 22
Hanbury Ho. E1 5G 85
(off Hanbury St.)
Hanbury Ho. SW8 7J 101
(off Regent's Bri. Gdns.)
Hanbury M. CR0: C'don 1A 170
Hanbury M. N1 1C 84
Hanbury Rd. N17 2H 49
Hanbury Rd. W3 2H 97
Hanbury St. E1 5K 9 (5F 85)
Hanbury Wlk. DA5: Bexl 3K 145
Hancock Nunn Ho. NW3 6D 64
(off Fellows Rd.)
Hancock Rd. E3 3E 86
Hancock Rd. SE19 6D 138
Handa Wlk. N1 6D 66
Hand Axe Yd. WC1 1F 7 (3J 83)
Hand Ct. WC1 6H 7 (5K 83)
Handcroft Rd. CR0: C'don 7B 156
Handel & Hendrix in London 2K 11 (7F 83)
(off Brook St.)
Handel Cl. HA8: Edg 6A 28
Handel Mans. SW13 7E 98
Handel Mans. WC1 3F 7 (4J 83)
(off Handel St.)
Handel Pde. HA8: Edg 7B 28
(off Whitchurch La.)
Handel Pl. NW10 6K 61
Handel St. WC1 3E 6 (4J 83)
Handel Way HA8: Edg 7B 28
Handen Rd. SE12 5G 123
Handforth Rd. IG1: Ilf 3F 71
Handforth Rd. SW9 7A 102
Handley Dr. SE3 3K 123
Handley Gro. NW2 3F 63
Handley Page Rd. IG11: Bark 4A 90
Handley Page Rd. SM6: W'gton 7K 167
Handley Rd. E9 7J 67
Handowe Cl. NW4 4C 44
Handside Cl. KT4: Wor Pk 1F 165
Hands Wlk. E16 6J 87
Handsworth Av. E4 6A 36
Handsworth Rd. N17 3D 48
Handyside St. N1 1H 83
Hanford Cl. SW18 1J 135
Hanford Row SW19 6E 134
Hanger Ct. W5 4F 79
Hanger Grn. W5 4G 79
HANGER HILL 4F 79
Hanger La. W5 2E 78
HANGER LANE 3E 78
Hanger Va. La. W5 6F 79
(not continuous)
Hanger Vw. Way W3 6G 79
Hanging Sword All. EC4 1K 13 (6A 84)
(off Whitefriars St.)
Hankey Ho. SE1 7E 14 (2D 102)
(off Hankey Pl.)
Hankey Pl. SE1 7F 15 (2D 102)
Hankins Ho. SE10 3J 105
(off Peartree Way)
Hankins La. NW7 2F 29
Hanley Gdns. N4 1K 65
Hanley Pl. BR3: Beck 7C 140
Hanley Rd. N4 1J 65
Hanmer Wlk. N7 2K 65
Hannaford Wlk. E3 4D 86
Hannah Barlow Ho. SW8 1K 119
Hannah Bldg. E1 6H 85
(off Watney St.)
Hannah Cl. BR3: Beck 3E 158
Hannah Cl. NW10 4J 61
Hannah Ct. E15 2H 87
Hannah Mary Way SE1 4G 103
Hannah M. SM6: W'gton 7G 167
Hannay Ho. SW15 6G 117
Hannay La. N8 7H 47
Hannay Wlk. SW16 2H 137
Hannell Rd. SW6 7G 99
Hannen Rd. SE27 3B 138
Hannibal Rd. E1 5J 85
Hannibal Rd. TW19: Stanw 7A 110
Hannibal Way CR0: Wadd 5K 167
Hannington Rd. SW4 3F 119
Hanno Cl. SM6: W'gton 7H 167
Hanover Av. E16 1J 105
Hanover Av. TW13: Felt 1J 129
Hanover Circ. UB3: Hayes 6E 74
Hanover Cl. SM3: Cheam 4G 165
Hanover Cl. TW15: Ashf 4A 128
Hanover Cl. TW9: Kew 7G 97
Hanover Ct. E8 1F 85
(off Stean St.)
Hanover Ct. HA4: Ruis 3J 57
Hanover Ct. NW9 3A 44
Hanover Ct. SE19 7G 139
(off Anerley Rd.)
Hanover Ct. SW15 4B 116
Hanover Ct. W12 1C 98
(off Uxbridge Rd.)
Hanover Dr. BR7: Chst 4G 143
Hanover Flats W1 2H 11 (7E 82)
(off Binney St.)
Hanover Gdns. IG6: Ilf 1G 53
Hanover Gdns. SE11 6A 102
Hanover Ga. NW1 2D 4 (3C 82)
Hanover Ga. Mans. NW1 3D 4 (4C 82)
Hanover Ho. E14 1B 104
(off Westferry Cir.)
Hanover Ho. NW8 1C 4 (2C 82)
(off St John's Wood High St.)
Hanover Ho. SE16 2K 103
(off Dominion Dr.)
Hanover Ho. SW9 3A 120
Hanover Mans. SW2 5A 120
(off Barnwell Rd.)
Hanover Mead NW11 5G 45
Hanover Pk. SE15 1G 121
Hanover Pl. E3 3B 86
Hanover Pl. WC2 1F 13 (6J 83)
Hanover Rd. N15 4F 49
Hanover Rd. NW10 7E 62
Hanover Rd. SW19 7A 136
Hanover Sq. W1 1K 11 (6F 83)
Hanover Steps W2 1D 10 (6C 82)
(off St George's Flds.)
Hanover St. CR0: C'don 3B 168
Hanover St. W1 1K 11 (6F 83)
Hanover Ter. NW1 2E 4 (3D 82)
Hanover Ter. TW7: Isle 1A 114
Hanover Ter. M. NW1 2D 4 (3C 82)
Hanover Trad. Est. N7 5J 65
Hanover Way DA6: Bex 3D 126
Hanover W. Ind. Est. NW10 3K 79
Hanover Yd. N1 2C 84
(off Noel Rd.)
Hansa Cl. UB2: S'hall 3A 94
Hansard M. W14 2F 99
Hansart Way EN2: Enf 1F 23
Hanscomb M. SW4 4G 119
Hans Ct. SW3 1E 16 (3D 100)
(off Hans Rd.)
Hans Cres. SW1 1E 16 (3D 100)
Hanselin Cl. HA7: Stan 5E 26
Hansel Rd. NW6 3J 81
Hansen Dr. N21 5E 22
Hanshaw Dr. HA8: Edg 1K 43
Hansler Ct. SW19 1G 135
(off Princes Way)
Hansler Gro. KT8: E Mos 4H 149
Hansler Rd. SE22 5F 121
Hansol Rd. DA6: Bex 5E 126
Hansom M. SE11 5H 19 (5K 101)
Hansom Ter. BR1: Broml 1K 159
(off Freelands Gro.)
Hanson Cl. BR3: Beck 6D 140
Hanson Cl. SW12 7F 119
Hanson Cl. SW14 3J 115
Hanson Cl. UB7: W Dray 3B 92
Hanson Ct. E17 6D 50
Hanson Gdns. UB1: S'hall 2C 94
Hanson Ho. E1 7G 85
(off Pinchin St.)
Hanson St. W1 5A 6 (5G 83)

232 A–Z London

Hans Pl. – Harvel Cres.

Hans Pl. SW1 ... 1F 17 (3D 100)
Hans Rd. SW3 ... 1E 16 (3D 100)
Hans St. SW1 ... 2F 17 (3D 100)
Hanway Pl. W1 ... 7C 6 (6H 83)
Hanway Rd. W7 ... 6H 77
Hanway St. W1 ... 7C 6 (6H 83)
HANWELL ... 1K 95
Hanwell Ho. W2 ... 5J 81
(off Gt. Western Rd.)
HANWORTH ... 4B 130
Hanworth Air Pk. Leisure Cen. ... 2B 130
Hanworth Ho. SE5 ... 7B 102
Hanworth Rd. TW12: Hamp ... 4D 130
Hanworth Rd. TW13: Felt ... 1K 129
Hanworth Rd. TW16: Sun ... 7J 129
(not continuous)
Hanworth Rd. TW3: Houn ... 5E 112
Hanworth Rd. TW4: Houn ... 1C 130
Hanworth Ter. TW3: Houn ... 4F 113
Hanworth Trad. Est. TW13: Hanw .. 3C 130
Hapgood Cl. UB6: G'frd ... 5H 59
Harad's Pl. E1 ... 7G 85
Harbans Ct. SL3: Poyle ... 4A 174
Harbard Cl. IG11: Bark ... 7F 71
Harben Pde. NW3 ... 7A 64
(off Finchley Rd.)
Harben Rd. NW6 ... 7A 64
Harberson Rd. E15 ... 1H 87
Harberson Rd. SW12 ... 1F 137
Harberton Rd. N19 ... 1G 65
Harbet Rd. E4 ... 6F 35
Harbet Rd. N18 ... 5F 35
Harbet Rd. W2 ... 6B 4 (5B 82)
Harbex Cl. DA5: Bexl ... 7H 127
Harbinger Rd. E14 ... 4D 104
Harbledown Ho. SE1 ... 7E 14 (2D 102)
(off Manciple St.)
Harbledown Rd. SW6 ... 1J 117
Harbord Cl. SE5 ... 2D 120
Harbord Ho. SE16 ... 4K 103
(off Cope St.)
Harbord Sq. ... 2E 104
Harbord St. SW6 ... 1F 117
Harborough Av. DA15: Sidc ... 7J 125
Harborough Ho. UB5: N'olt ... 3D 76
(off Taywood Rd.)
Harborough Rd. SW16 ... 4K 137
Harbour Av. SW10 ... 1A 118
Harbour Cl. CR4: Mitc ... 1E 154
Harbour Club Chelsea ... 2A 118
Harbour Club Kensington ... 4K 99
(off Point West)
Harbour Club Notting Hill ... 5J 81
Harbour Exchange Sq. E14 ... 2D 104
Harbour Reach SW6 ... 1A 118
Harbour Rd. SE5 ... 3C 120
Harbourside Ct. SE8 ... 4A 104
(off Plough Way)
Harbour Way E14 ... 2D 104
Harbour Yd. SW10 ... 1A 118
Harbridge Av. SW15 ... 7B 116
Harbury Rd. SM5: Cars ... 7C 166
Harbut Rd. SW11 ... 4B 118
Harbutt Rd. HA9: Wemb ... 4G 61
Harcombe Rd. N16 ... 3E 66
Harcourt Av. DA15: Sidc ... 6C 126
Harcourt Av. E12 ... 4D 70
Harcourt Av. HA8: Edg ... 3D 28
Harcourt Av. SM6: W'gton ... 4F 167
Harcourt Bldgs. EC4 ... 2J 13 (7A 84)
(off Middle Temple La.)
Harcourt Cl. TW7: Isle ... 3A 114
Harcourt Fld. SM6: W'gton ... 4F 167
Harcourt Ho. W1 ... 7J 5 (6F 83)
(off Cavendish Sq.)
Harcourt Lodge SM6: W'gton ... 4F 167
Harcourt Rd. CR7: Thor H ... 6K 155
Harcourt Rd. DA6: Bex ... 4E 126
Harcourt Rd. E15 ... 2H 87
Harcourt Rd. N22 ... 1H 47
Harcourt Rd. SE4 ... 3B 122
Harcourt Rd. SM6: W'gton ... 4F 167
Harcourt Rd. SW19 ... 7J 135
Harcourt St. W1 ... 6D 4 (5C 82)
Harcourt Ter. SW10 ... 5K 99
Hardcastle Cl. CR0: C'don ... 6G 157
Hardcastle Ho. SE14 ... 1A 122
(off Loring Rd.)
Hardcourts Cl. BR4: W W'ck ... 3D 170
Hardegray Cl. SM2: Sutt ... 7J 165
Hardel Ri. SW2 ... 1B 138
Hardel Wlk. SW2 ... 7A 120
Harden Ho. SE5 ... 2E 120
Harden's Manorway SE7 ... 3B 106
(not continuous)
Harders Rd. SE15 ... 2H 121
Hardess St. SE24 ... 3C 120
Hardie Cl. NW10 ... 5K 61
Hardie Rd. RM10: Dag ... 3J 73
Harding Cl. CR0: C'don ... 3F 169
Harding Cl. SE17 ... 6C 102
Harding Dr. RM8: Dag ... 1E 72
Hardinge Cl. UB8: Hil ... 5D 74
Hardinge Cres. SE18 ... 3G 107
Hardinge La. E1 ... 6J 85
(not continuous)
Hardinge Rd. N18 ... 6K 33
Hardinge Rd. NW10 ... 1D 80
Hardinge St. E1 Johnson St ... 7J 85
Hardinge St. E1 Steel's La ... 6J 85
Harding Ho. SW13 ... 6D 98
(off Wyatt Dr.)
Harding Ho. UB3: Hayes ... 6K 75
Harding Rd. DA7: Bex ... 2F 127
Harding's Cl. KT2: King T ... 1F 151
Hardings La. SE20 ... 6K 139
Hardington NW1 ... 7E 64
(off Belmont St.)
Hardman Rd. KT2: King T ... 2E 150
Hardman Rd. SE7 ... 5K 105
Hardwick Cl KT19: Eps ... 5H 163
Hardwick Cl. HA7: Stan ... 5H 27
Hardwick Ct. DA8: Erith ... 6K 109
Hardwicke Av. TW5: Hest ... 1E 112
Hardwicke M. WC1 ... 2H 7 (3K 83)
(off Lloyd Baker M.)
Hardwicke Rd. N13 ... 6D 32
Hardwicke Rd. TW10: Ham ... 4C 132
Hardwicke Rd. W4 ... 4K 97
Hardwicke St. IG11: Bark ... 1G 89
Hardwick Grn. W13 ... 5B 78
Hardwick Ho. NW8 ... 3D 4 (4C 82)
(off Lilestone St.)
Hardwick Pl. SW16 ... 7G 137
Hardwicks Sq. SW18 ... 5J 117
Hardwick St. EC1 ... 2K 7 (3A 84)
Hardwidge St. SE1 ... 6G 15 (2E 102)
Hardy Av. E16 ... 1J 105
Hardy Av. HA4: Ruis ... 5K 57
Hardy Cl. EN5: Barn ... 6B 20
Hardy Cl. HA5: Pinn ... 7B 40
Hardy Cl. SE16 ... 2K 103
Hardy Cotts. SE10 ... 6F 105
Hardy Ho. SW17 ... 3B 136
(off Grosvenor Way)
Hardy Ho. SW18 ... 7K 117
Hardy Ho. SW4 ... 7G 119
Hardying Ho. E17 ... 4A 50
Hardy Pas. N22 ... 1K 47
Hardy Rd. E4 ... 6G 35
Hardy Rd. SE3 ... 7H 105
Hardy Rd. SW19 ... 7K 135
Hardy's M. KT8: E Mos ... 4J 149
Hardy Way EN2: Enf ... 1F 23
Hare & Billet Rd. SE3 ... 1F 123
Harebell Dr. E6 ... 5E 88
Harebell Ter. IG11: Bark ... 3C 90
Harecastle Cl. UB4: Yead ... 4C 76
Hare Ct. EC4 ... 1J 13 (6A 84)
(off Church Ct.)
Harecourt Rd. N1 ... 6C 66
Harecroft La. UB10: Ick ... 3E 56
Haredale Ho. SE16 ... 2G 103
(off East La.)
Haredale Rd. SE24 ... 4C 120
Haredon Cl. SE23 ... 7K 121
Harefield Cl. EN2: Enf ... 1F 23
Harefield Grn. NW7 ... 6K 29
Harefield M. SE4 ... 3B 122
Harefield Rd. DA14: Sidc ... 3D 144
Harefield Rd. N8 ... 5H 47
Harefield Rd. SE4 ... 3B 122
Harefield Rd. SW16 ... 7K 137
Hare Marsh E2 ... 4G 85
Harepit Cl. CR2: S Croy ... 7B 168
Hare Pl. EC4 ... 1K 13 (6A 84)
(off Fleet St.)
Hare Row E2 ... 2H 85
Haresfield Rd. RM10: Dag ... 6G 73
Hare St. SE18 ... 3E 106
Hare Wlk. N1 ... 2E 84
(not continuous)
Harewood Av. NW1 ... 4D 4 (4C 82)
Harewood Av. NW7 ... 6A 30
Harewood Av. UB5: N'olt ... 7D 58
Harewood Cl. UB5: N'olt ... 7D 58
Harewood Dr. IG5: Ilf ... 2D 52
Harewood Pl. W1 ... 1K 11 (6F 83)
Harewood Rd. CR2: S Croy ... 6E 168
Harewood Rd. SW19 ... 6C 136
Harewood Rd. TW7: Isle ... 7K 95
Harewood Row NW1 ... 5D 4 (5C 82)
Harewood Ter. UB2: S'hall ... 4D 94
Harfield Gdns. SE5 ... 3E 120
Harfield Rd. TW16: Sun ... 2B 148
Harfleur Ct. SE11 ... 4B 102
(off Opal St.)
Harford Cl. E4 ... 7J 25
Harford Ho. SE5 ... 6C 102
(off Bethwin Rd.)
Harford Ho. W11 ... 5H 81
Harford M. N19 ... 3H 65
Harford Rd. E4 ... 7J 25
Harford St. E1 ... 4A 86
Harford Wlk. N2 ... 4B 46
Harfst Way BR8: Swan ... 7J 145
Hargood Cl. HA3: Kenton ... 6E 42
Hargood Rd. SE3 ... 1A 124
Hargrave Mans. N19 ... 2H 65
Hargrave Pk. N19 ... 2G 65
Hargrave Pl. N7 ... 5H 65
Hargrave Rd. N19 ... 2G 65
Hargraves Ho. W12 ... 7D 80
(off White City Est.)
Hargreaves Ct. E3 ... 3E 86
(off Bolinder Way)
Hargwyne St. SW9 ... 3K 119
Hari Cl. UB5: N'olt ... 5F 59
Haringey Independent Cinema ... 4C 48
Haringey Pk. N8 ... 6J 47
Haringey Pas. N8 ... 4A 48
Haringey Rd. N8 ... 4J 47
Harington Ter. N18 ... 3J 33
Harington Ter. N9 ... 3J 33
Harkett Cl. HA3: W'stone ... 2K 41
Harkett Ct. HA3: W'stone ... 2K 41
Harkness Ct. SM1: Sutt ... 1K 165
(off Cleeve Way)
Harkness Ho. E1 ... 6G 85
(off Christian St.)
Harland Av. CR0: C'don ... 3F 169
Harland Av. DA15: Sidc ... 3H 143
Harland Cl. SW19 ... 3K 153
Harland Rd. SE12 ... 1J 141
Harlands Gro. BR6: Farnb ... 4F 173
Harlech Gdns. HA5: Pinn ... 7B 40
Harlech Gdns. TW5: Hest ... 6A 94
Harlech Rd. N14 ... 3D 32
Harlech Twr. W3 ... 2J 97
Harlequin Av. TW8: Bford ... 6A 96
Harlequin Cl. IG11: Bark ... 4A 90
Harlequin Cl. TW7: Isle ... 5J 113
Harlequin Cl. UB4: Yead ... 5B 76
Harlequin Ct. E1 ... 7G 85
(off Thomas More St.)
Harlequin Ct. NW10 ... 6K 61
(off Mitchellbrook Way)
Harlequin Ct. W5 ... 7C 78
Harlequin FC ... 7J 113
Harlequin Ho. DA18: Erith ... 3E 108
(off Kale Rd.)
Harlequin Rd. TW11: Tedd ... 7B 132
Harlescott Rd. SE15 ... 4K 121
HARLESDEN ... 2B 80
Harlesden Gdns. NW10 ... 1B 80
Harlesden La. NW10 ... 1C 80
Harlesden Plaza NW10 ... 2B 80
Harlesden Rd. NW10 ... 1C 80
Harleston Cl. E5 ... 2J 67
Harley Cl. HA0: Wemb ... 6D 60
Harley Ct. E11 ... 7J 51
Harley Ct. HA1: Harr ... 4H 41
Harley Ct. N20 ... 3F 31
Harley Cres. HA1: Harr ... 4H 41
Harleyford BR1: Broml ... 1K 159
Harleyford Ct. SE11 ... 7H 19 (6K 101)
(off Harleyford Rd.)
Harleyford Mnr. W3 ... 1J 97
(off Edgecote Cl.)
Harleyford Rd. SE11 ... 7G 19 (6K 101)
Harleyford St. SE11 ... 7J 19 (6A 102)
Harley Gdns. BR6: Orp ... 4J 173
Harley Gdns. SW10 ... 5A 100
Harley Gro. E3 ... 3B 86
Harley Ho. E11 ... 7F 51
Harley Ho. E14 ... 6B 86
(off Frances Wharf)
Harley Ho. NW1 ... 4H 5 (4E 82)
(off Marylebone Rd.)
Harley Pl. W1 ... 6J 5 (5F 83)
Harley Rd. HA1: Harr ... 4H 41
Harley Rd. NW10 ... 2A 80
Harley Rd. NW3 ... 7B 64
Harley St. W1 ... 4J 5 (4F 83)
Harley Vs. NW10 ... 2A 80
Harling Ct. SE6 ... 6C 122
Harling Ct. SW11 ... 2D 118
Harlinger St. SE18 ... 3C 106
HARLINGTON ... 6F 93
Harlington Cl. UB3: Harl ... 7E 92
HARLINGTON CORNER ... 1F 111
Harlington Rd. DA7: Bex ... 3E 126
Harlington Rd. UB8: Hil ... 3C 74
Harlington Rd. E. TW13: Felt ... 1A 130
Harlington Rd. E. TW14: Felt ... 7K 111
Harlington Rd. W. TW14: Felt ... 6K 111
Harlington Sports Cen., The ... 4F 93
(off Pinkwell La.)
Harlington Young People's Cen. ... 4F 93
Harlow Mans. IG11: Bark ... 7F 71
(off Whiting Av.)
Harlow Rd. N13 ... 3J 33
Harlyn Dr. HA5: Eastc ... 3K 39
Harlynwood SE5 ... 7C 102
(off Wyndham Rd.)
Harman Av. IG8: Wfd G ... 6C 36
Harman Cl. E4 ... 4A 36
Harman Cl. NW2 ... 3G 63
Harman Cl. SE1 ... 5G 103
Harman Dr. DA15: Sidc ... 6K 125
Harman Dr. NW2 ... 3G 63
Harman Ri. IG3: Ilf ... 4J 71
Harman Rd. EN1: Enf ... 5A 24
HARMONDSWORTH ... 2E 174
Harmondsworth La. UB7: Harm ... 6A 92
Harmondsworth La. UB7: Sip ... 6A 92
Harmondsworth Moor Waterside ... 2C 174
Harmondsworth Moor Waterside Vis. Cen. ... 2C 174
Harmondsworth Rd. UB7: W Dray ... 5A 92
Harmon Ho. SE8 ... 4B 104
Harmont Ho. W1 ... 6J 5 (5F 83)
(off Harley St.)
Harmony Apts. BR1: Broml ... 2J 159
(off High St.)
Harmony Cl. NW11 ... 5G 45
(not continuous)
Harmony Cl. SM6: W'gton ... 7J 167
Harmony Pl. SE1 ... 5F 103
Harmony Pl. SE8 ... 6D 104
(off Dancers Way)
Harmony Ter. HA2: Harr ... 1F 59
Harmony Way BR1: Broml ... 2J 159
Harmony Way NW4 ... 4E 44
Harmood Gro. NW1 ... 7F 65
Harmood Ho. NW1 ... 7F 65
(off Harmood St.)
Harmood Pl. NW1 ... 7F 65
Harmood St. NW1 ... 6F 65
Harmsworth M. SE11 ... 2K 19 (3B 102)
Harmsworth St. SE17 ... 6K 19 (5B 102)
Harmsworth Way N20 ... 1C 30
Harold Av. DA17: Belv ... 5F 109
Harold Av. UB3: Hayes ... 3H 93
Harold Ct. SE16 ... 2K 103
(off Christopher Cl.)
Harold Est. SE1 ... 3E 102
Harold Gibbons Ct. SE7 ... 6A 106
Harold Ho. E2 ... 2K 85
(off Mace St.)
Harold Laski Ho. EC1 ... 2B 8 (3B 84)
(off Percival St.)
Harold Maddison Ho. SE17 ... 5B 102
(off Penton Pl.)
Harold Mugford Ter. E6 ... 6E 88
(off Pearl Cl.)
Harold Pinter Theatre ... 3C 12 (7H 83)
(off Panton St.)
Harold Pl. SE11 ... 6J 19 (5A 102)
Harold Rd. E11 ... 1G 69
Harold Rd. E13 ... 1K 87
Harold Rd. E4 ... 4K 35
Harold Rd. IG8: Wfd G ... 1J 51
Harold Rd. N15 ... 5F 49
Harold Rd. N8 ... 5K 47
Harold Rd. NW10 ... 3K 79
Harold Rd. SE19 ... 7D 138
Harold Rd. SM1: Sutt ... 4B 166
Haroldstone Rd. E17 ... 5K 49
Harold Wilson Ho. SE28 ... 1B 108
Harold Wilson Ho. SW6 ... 6H 99
(off Clem Attlee Ct.)
Harp All. EC4 ... 7A 8 (6B 84)
Harp Bus. Cen., The NW2 ... 2C 62
Harpenden Rd. E12 ... 2A 70
Harpenden Rd. SE27 ... 3B 138
Harpenmead Point NW2 ... 2H 63
Harper Cl. N14 ... 5B 22
Harper Ho. SW9 ... 3B 120
Harper M. SW17 ... 3A 136
Harper Rd. E6 ... 6D 88
Harper Rd. SE1 ... 7D 14 (3C 102)
Harper's Yd. N17 ... 1F 49
Harpers Yd. TW7: Isle ... 2J 113
(off Rennels Way)
Harp Island Cl. NW10 ... 2K 61
Harp La. EC3 ... 3G 15 (7E 84)
Harpley Sq. E1 ... 4K 85
Harpour Rd. IG11: Bark ... 6G 71
Harp Rd. W7 ... 4K 77
Harpsden St. SW11 ... 1E 118
Harpur M. WC1 ... 5G 7 (5K 83)
Harpur St. WC1 ... 5G 7 (5K 83)
Harraden Rd. SE3 ... 1A 124
Harrier Av. E11 ... 6K 51
Harrier Cen., The ... 6K 163
Harrier Ct. TW4: Houn ... 3C 112
Harrier M. SE28 ... 2H 107
Harrier Rd. NW9 ... 2A 44
Harriers Cl. W5 ... 7E 78
Harrier Way E6 ... 5D 88
Harries Rd. UB4: Yead ... 4A 76
Harriet Cl. E8 ... 1G 85
Harriet Ct. SE14 ... 7J 103
(off Pomeroy St.)
Harriet Gdns. CR0: C'don ... 2G 169
Harriet Ho. SW6 ... 7K 99
(off Wandon Rd.)
Harriet M. DA16: Well ... 2B 126
Harriet St. SW1 ... 7F 11 (2D 100)
Harriet Tubman Cl. SW2 ... 7K 119
Harriet Wlk. SW1 ... 7F 11 (2D 100)
Harriet Way WD23: Bush ... 1C 26
HARRINGAY ... 5B 48
Harringay Gdns. N8 ... 4B 48
Harringay Rd. N15 ... 5B 48
(not continuous)
Harrington Cl. CR0: Bedd ... 2J 167
Harrington Cl. NW10 ... 3K 61
Harrington Ct. CR0: C'don ... 2D 168
Harrington Ct. SW7 ... 3B 16 (4B 100)
(off Harrington Rd.)
Harrington Ct. W10 ... 3H 81
Harrington Gdns. SW7 ... 4K 99
Harrington Hill E5 ... 1H 67
Harrington Ho. NW1 ... 1A 6 (3G 83)
(off Harrington St.)
Harrington Ho. UB10: Ick ... 4D 56
Harrington Rd. E11 ... 1G 69
Harrington Rd. SE25 ... 4G 157
Harrington Rd. SW7 ... 3A 16 (4B 100)
Harrington Sq. NW1 ... 2G 83
Harrington St. NW1 ... 1A 6 (2G 83)
(not continuous)
Harrington Way SE18 ... 3B 106
Harriott Cl. SE10 ... 4H 105
Harriott Ho. E1 ... 5J 85
(off Jamaica St.)
Harris Bldgs. E1 ... 6G 85
(off Burslem St.)
Harris Cl. EN2: Enf ... 1G 23
Harris Cl. N11 ... 5J 31
Harris Cl. TW3: Houn ... 1E 112
Harris Ct. HA9: Wemb ... 3F 61
Harris Ho. E11 ... 1G 69
Harris Ho. E3 ... 3C 86
(off Alfred St.)
Harris Ho. SW9 ... 3A 120
(off St James's Cres.)
Harris Lodge SE6 ... 1E 140
Harrison Cl. N20 ... 1H 31
Harrison Cl. RM7: Mawney ... 3G 55
Harrison Ct. E18 ... 1J 51
(off Queen Mary Av.)
Harrison Dr. BR1: Broml ... 4E 160
Harrison Ho. E1 ... 6H 85
Harrison Ho. SE17 ... 5D 102
(off Brandon St.)
Harrison Rd. NW10 ... 1K 79
Harrison Rd. RM10: Dag ... 6H 73
Harrisons Ct. SE14 ... 6K 103
(off Myers La.)
Harrison's Ri. CR0: Wadd ... 3B 168
Harrison St. WC1 ... 2F 7 (3J 83)
Harrison Way TW17: Shep ... 5D 146
Harris Rd. DA7: Bex ... 1E 126
Harris Rd. RM9: Dag ... 5F 73
Harris Sports Cen. ... 5J 121
Harris St. E17 ... 7B 50
Harris St. SE5 ... 7D 102
Harris Way TW16: Sun ... 1G 147
Harrod Ct. NW9 ... 4J 43
Harrods ... 1E 16 (3D 100)
Harrogate Ct. N11 ... 6K 31
Harrogate Ct. SE12 ... 7J 123
Harrogate Ct. SE26 ... 3G 139
(off Droitwich Cl.)
Harrold Ho. NW3 ... 7B 64
Harrold Rd. RM8: Dag ... 5B 72
Harrovian Bus. Village HA1: Harr ... 7J 41
HARROW ... 6J 41
Harrow Arts Cen. ... 1E 40
Harrow Av. EN1: Enf ... 6A 24
Harroway Rd. SW11 ... 2B 118
Harrow Borough FC ... 4D 58
Harrowby Ho. W1 ... 7E 4 (6D 82)
(off Harrowby St.)
Harrowby St. W1 ... 7D 4 (6C 82)
Harrow Cl. KT9: Chess ... 7D 162
Harrow Club W10 ... 7F 81
Harrowdene Cl. HA0: Wemb ... 4D 60
Harrowdene Gdns. TW11: Tedd ... 6A 132
Harrowdene Rd. HA0: Wemb ... 3D 60
Harrow Dr. N9 ... 1A 34
Harrowes Meade HA8: Edg ... 3B 28
Harrow Flds. Gdns. HA1: Harr ... 3J 59
Harrow Gdns. KT8: E Mos ... 3H 149
Harrowgate Ho. E9 ... 6K 67
Harrowgate Rd. E9 ... 6A 68
Harrow Grn. E11 ... 3G 69
Harrow High School Sports Cen. ... 6A 42
Harrow Hill Golf Course ... 7K 41
Harrow La. E14 ... 7D 86
Harrow Leisure Cen. ... 3K 41
Harrow Lodge NW8 ... 3A 4 (4B 82)
(off Northwick Ter.)
Harrow Manorway SE2 ... 1C 108
Harrow Mnr. Way SE28 ... 7C 90
Harrow Mus. ... 3G 41
HARROW ON THE HILL ... 1J 59
Harrow Pk. HA1: Harr ... 2J 59
Harrow Pl. E1 ... 7H 9 (6E 84)
Harrow Rd. E11 ... 3G 69
Harrow Rd. E6 ... 1C 88
Harrow Rd. HA0: Wemb ... 4K 59
Harrow Rd. HA9: Wemb ... 5G 61
Harrow Rd. IG1: Ilf ... 4G 71
Harrow Rd. IG11: Bark ... 1J 89
Harrow Rd. NW10 ... 3D 80
Harrow Rd. SM5: Cars ... 6C 166
Harrow Rd. TW14: Bedf ... 2C 128
Harrow Rd. W10 ... 4G 81
Harrow Rd. W2 ... 5A 4 (5A 82)
(not continuous)
Harrow Rd. W9 ... 4H 81
HARROW ROAD ... 7H 61
HARROW RD. BRI. ... 5A 82
Harrow School Golf Course ... 2K 59
Harrow Sports Hall ... 7A 42
Harrow St. NW1 ... 5D 4 (5C 82)
(off Daventry St.)
Harrow Vw. HA1: Harr ... 4H 41
Harrow Vw. HA2: Harr ... 2G 41
Harrow Vw. UB10: Hil ... 3E 74
Harrow Vw. UB3: Hayes ... 6J 75
Harrow Vw. Rd. W5 ... 4B 78
Harrow Way TW17: Shep ... 2E 146
HARROW WEALD ... 1J 41
Harrow Weald Lawn Tennis Club ... 1J 41
Harrow Weald Pk. HA3: Hrw W ... 6C 26
Harry Cl. CR0: C'don ... 6C 156
Harry Cole Ct. SE17 ... 5D 102
(off Thurlow St.)
Harry Day M. SE27 ... 3C 138
Harry Hinkins Ho. SE17 ... 5C 102
(off Bronti Cl.)
Harry Lambourn Ho. SE15 ... 7H 103
(off Gervase St.)
Harry Zeital Way E5 ... 2J 67
Harston Wlk. E3 ... 4D 86
Hartcliff Ct. W7 ... 2K 95
Hart Cl. CR0: C'don ... 3B 168
Hart Ct. E6 ... 7E 70
Harte Rd. TW3: Houn ... 2D 112
Hartfield Av. UB5: N'olt ... 2K 75
Hartfield Cres. BR4: W W'ck ... 3J 171
Hartfield Cres. SW19 ... 7H 135
Hartfield Gro. SE20 ... 1J 157
Hartfield Ho. UB5: N'olt ... 2K 75
(off Hartfield Av.)
Hartfield Rd. BR4: W W'ck ... 4J 171
Hartfield Rd. KT9: Chess ... 5D 162
Hartfield Rd. SW19 ... 7H 135
Hartfield Ter. E3 ... 2C 86
Hartford Av. HA3: Kenton ... 3A 42
Hartford Rd. DA5: Bexl ... 6G 127
Hartford Rd. KT19: Ewe ... 6H 163
Hart Gro. UB1: S'hall ... 5E 76
Hart Gro. W5 ... 1G 97
Hart Gro. Ct. W5 ... 1G 97
Hartham Cl. N7 ... 5J 65
Hartham Cl. TW7: Isle ... 1A 114
Hartham Rd. N17 ... 2F 49
Hartham Rd. N7 ... 5J 65
Hartham Rd. TW7: Isle ... 1K 113
Harting Rd. SE9 ... 3C 142
Hartington Cl. BR6: Farnb ... 5G 173
Hartington Cl. HA1: Harr ... 4J 59
Hartington Ct. SW8 ... 1J 119
Hartington Ct. W4 ... 7H 97
Hartington Ho. SW1 ... 5D 18 (5H 101)
(off Drummond Ga.)
Hartington Rd. E16 ... 6K 87
Hartington Rd. E17 ... 6A 50
Hartington Rd. SW8 ... 1J 119
Hartington Rd. TW1: Twick ... 7B 114
Hartington Rd. UB2: S'hall ... 3C 94
Hartington Rd. W13 ... 7B 78
Hartington Rd. W4 ... 7H 97
Hartismere Rd. SW6 ... 7H 99
Hartlake Rd. E9 ... 6K 67
Hartland NW1 ... 1G 83
(off Royal College St.)
Hartland Cl. HA8: Edg ... 2B 28
Hartland Cl. N21 ... 6H 23
Hartland Ct. N11 ... 5J 31
(off Hartland Rd.)
Hartland Dr. HA4: Ruis ... 3K 57
Hartland Dr. HA8: Edg ... 2B 28
Hartland Rd. E15 ... 7H 69
Hartland Rd. N11 ... 5J 31
Hartland Rd. NW1 ... 7F 65
Hartland Rd. NW6 ... 2H 81
Hartland Rd. SM4: Mord ... 7J 153
Hartland Rd. TW12: Hamp H ... 4F 131
Hartland Rd. TW7: Isle ... 3A 114
Hartlands, The TW5: Cran ... 6K 93
Hartlands Cl. DA5: Bexl ... 6F 127
Hartland Way CR0: C'don ... 3A 170
Hartland Way SM4: Mord ... 7H 153
Hartlepool Ct. E16 ... 1F 107
Hartley Av. E6 ... 1C 88
Hartley Av. NW7 ... 5G 29
Hartley Cl. BR1: Broml ... 2D 160
Hartley Cl. NW7 ... 5G 29
Hartley Ho. SE1 ... 4F 103
(off Longfield Est.)
Hartley Rd. CR0: C'don ... 7C 156
Hartley Rd. DA16: Well ... 7C 108
Hartley Rd. E11 ... 1H 69
Hartley St. E2 ... 3J 85
(not continuous)
Hart Lodge EN5: Barn ... 3B 20
Hartmann Rd. E16 ... 1B 106
Hartnoll St. N7 ... 5K 65
Harton Cl. BR1: Broml ... 1B 160
Harton Lodge SE8 ... 1C 122
(off Harton St.)
Harton Rd. N9 ... 2C 34
Harton St. SE8 ... 1C 122
Hartop Point SW6 ... 7G 99
(off Pellant Rd.)
Hartsbourne Av. WD23: B Hea ... 2B 26
Hartsbourne Cl. WD23: B Hea ... 2C 26
Hartsbourne Country Club & Golf Course ... 2B 26
Hartsbourne Ct. UB1: S'hall ... 6G 77
(off Fleming Rd.)
Hartsbourne Pk. WD23: B Hea ... 2D 26
Hartsbourne Rd. WD23: B Hea ... 2C 26
Harts Gro. IG8: Wfd G ... 5D 36
Hartshill Cl. UB10: Hil ... 7D 56
Hartshorn All. EC3 ... 1H 15 (6E 84)
(off Leadenhall St.)
Hartshorn Gdns. E6 ... 4E 88
Hart's La. SE14 ... 1A 122
Harts La. IG11: Bark ... 6F 71
Hartslock Dr. SE2 ... 2D 108
Hartsmead Rd. SE9 ... 2D 142
Hart Sq. SM4: Mord ... 6J 153
Hart St. EC3 ... 2H 15 (7E 84)
Hartsway EN3: Pond E ... 4D 24
Hartswood Gdns. W12 ... 3B 98
Hartswood Grn. WD23: B Hea ... 2C 26
Hartswood Rd. W12 ... 2B 98
Hartsworth Cl. E13 ... 2H 87
Hartville Rd. SE18 ... 4J 107
Hartwell Cl. SW2 ... 1K 137
Hartwell Dr. E4 ... 6K 35
Hartwell Ho. SE7 ... 5K 105
(off Troughton Rd.)
Hartwell St. E8 ... 6F 67
Hart Wy. RM13: Rain ... 3J 91
Harvard Ct. NW6 ... 5K 63
Harvard Hill W4 ... 6H 97
Harvard Ho. SE17 ... 6B 102
(off Doddington Gro.)
Harvard La. W4 ... 5J 97
Harvard Rd. SE13 ... 5E 122
Harvard Rd. TW7: Isle ... 1J 113
Harvard Rd. W4 ... 5H 97
Harvel Cl. BR5: St P ... 3K 161
Harvel Cres. SE2 ... 5D 108

Harvest Bank Rd. BR4: W W'ck 3H **171**
Harvest Ct. RM13: Rain 2K **91**
(off Broadis Way)
Harvest Ct. TW17: Shep 4C **146**
Harvesters Cl. TW7: Isle 5H **113**
Harvest La. KT7: T Ditt 6A **150**
Harvest Rd. TW13: Felt 4J **129**
Harvey Cl. NW9 2A **44**
Harvey Ct. E17 5C **50**
Harvey Dr. TW12: Hamp 1F **149**
Harvey Gdns. E11 1H **69**
Harvey Gdns. SE7 5A **106**
Harvey Ho. E1 4H **85**
(off Brady St.)
Harvey Ho. N1 1D **84**
(off Colville Est.)
Harvey Ho. RM6: Chad H 4D **54**
Harvey Ho. SW1 6D **18** (5H **101**)
(off Aylesford St.)
Harvey Ho. TW8: Bford 5E **96**
Harvey Lodge W9 5J **81**
(off Admiral Wlk.)
Harvey M. N8 5K **47**
(off Harvey Rd.)
Harvey Rd. E11 1G **69**
Harvey Rd. IG1: Ilf 5F **71**
Harvey Rd. KT12: Walt T 7H **147**
Harvey Rd. N8 5K **47**
Harvey Rd. SE5 1D **120**
(not continuous)
Harvey Rd. TW4: Houn 7D **112**
Harvey Rd. UB10: Hil 2C **74**
Harvey Rd. UB5: N'olt 7A **58**
Harvey's Bldgs. WC2 3F **13** (7J **83**)
Harveys La. RM7: Rush G 2K **73**
Harvey St. N1 1D **84**
Harvil Ct. NW9 3A **44**
(off Mornington Cl.)
Harvill Rd. DA14: Sidc 5E **144**
Harvil Rd. UB10: Ick 1A **56**
Harvington Wlk. E8 7G **67**
Harvist Est. N7 4A **66**
Harvist Rd. NW6 2F **81**
Harwell Cl. HA4: Ruis 1F **57**
Harwell Pas. N2 4D **46**
Harwicke Ho. E3 3C **86**
(off Bow Rd.)
Harwood Av. BR1: Broml 2K **159**
Harwood Av. CR4: Mitc 3C **154**
Harwood Cl. HA0: Wemb 4D **60**
Harwood Cl. N12 6H **31**
Harwood Ct. N1 1D **84**
(off Colville Est.)
Harwood Ct. SW15 4E **116**
Harwood Dr. UB10: Hil 1B **74**
Harwood M. SW6 7J **99**
Harwood Point SE16 2B **104**
Harwood Rd. SW6 7J **99**
Harwoods Yd. N21 7F **23**
Harwood Ter. SW6 1K **117**
Hascombe Ter. SE5 2D **120**
(off Love Wlk.)
Haselbury Rd. N18 4K **33**
Haselbury Rd. N9 3K **33**
Haseley End SE23 7J **121**
Hasell Pk. Pl. BR2: Broml 2D **172**
Haselrigge Rd. SW4 4H **119**
Haseltine Rd. SE26 4B **140**
Haselwood Dr. EN2: Enf 4G **23**
Haskard Rd. RM9: Dag 4D **72**
Hasker St. SW3 3D **16** (4C **100**)
Haslam Av. SM3: Sutt 1G **165**
Haslam Cl. N1 7A **66**
Haslam Cl. UB10: Ick 2E **56**
Haslam Ct. N11 4A **32**
Haslam Ho. N1 7C **66**
(off Canonbury Rd.)
Haslam St. SE15 7F **103**
Haslemere Av. CR4: Mitc 2B **154**
Haslemere Av. EN4: E Barn 1J **31**
Haslemere Av. NW4 6F **45**
Haslemere Av. SW18 2K **135**
Haslemere Av. TW5: Cran 2A **112**
Haslemere Av. W13 3A **96**
Haslemere Av. W7 3A **96**
Haslemere Bus. Cen. EN1: Enf 4C **24**
Haslemere Cl. SM6: W'gton 5J **167**
Haslemere Cl. TW12: Hamp 5D **130**
Haslemere Gdns. N3 3H **45**
Haslemere Heathrow Est., The
TW4: Cran 2K **111**
Haslemere Ind. Est. SW18 2K **135**
Haslemere Rd. CR7: Thor H 5B **156**
Haslemere Rd. DA7: Bex 2F **127**
Haslemere Rd. IG3: Ilf 2K **71**
Haslemere Rd. N21 2G **33**
Haslemere Rd. N8 7H **47**
Hasler Cl. SE28 7B **90**
Haslers Wharf E3 1A **86**
(off Old Ford Rd.)
Haslett Rd. TW17: Shep 2G **147**
Hasluck Gdns. EN5: New Bar 6E **20**
Hassard St. E2 1K **9** (2F **85**)
Hassendean Rd. SE3 7K **105**
Hassett Rd. E9 6K **67**
Hassocks Cl. SE26 3H **139**
Hassocks Rd. SW16 1H **155**
Hassock Wood BR2: Kes 4B **172**
Hassop Rd. NW2 4F **63**
Hassop Wlk. SE9 4C **142**
Hasted Rd. SE7 5B **106**
Haste Hill Golf Course 2G **39**
Hastings Av. IG6: Ilf 4G **53**
Hastings Cl. EN5: New Bar 4F **21**
Hastings Cl. HA0: Wemb 4C **60**
Hastings Cl. SE15 7G **103**
Hastings Ct. TW11: Tedd 5H **131**
Hastings Dr. KT6: Surb 6C **150**
Hastings Ho. EN3: Enf H 2D **24**
Hastings Ho. SE18 4D **106**
(off Mulgrave Rd.)
Hastings Ho. W12 7D **80**
(off White City Est.)
Hastings Ho. W13 7B **78**
Hastings Ho. WC1 2E **6** (3J **83**)
(off Hastings St.)
Hastings Pl. CR0: C'don 1F **169**
(off Hastings Rd.)
Hastings Rd. BR2: Broml 1C **172**
Hastings Rd. CR0: C'don 1F **169**
Hastings Rd. E16 5J **87**
Hastings Rd. N11 5B **32**
Hastings Rd. N17 3D **48**
Hastings Rd. W13 7B **78**
Hastings St. SE18 3G **107**
Hastings St. WC1 2E **6** (3J **83**)
Hastingwood Ct. E17 5D **50**
Hastoe Cl. UB4: Yead 4C **76**
Hasty Cl. CR4: Mitc 1F **155**
Hat & Mitre Ct. EC1 4B **8** (4B **84**)
(off St John St.)
Hatch, The EN3: Enf H 1E **24**
Hatcham Mews Bus. Cen. SE14 1K **121**
(off Hatcham Pk. Rd.)
Hatcham Pk. M. SE14 1K **121**
Hatcham Pk. Rd. SE14 1K **121**
Hatcham Rd. SE15 6J **103**
Hatcham St. SE26 5B **140**
Hatchard Rd. N19 2H **65**
Hatchcroft NW4 3D **44**
HATCH END 1D **40**
Hatch End Lawn Tennis Club 6A **26**
Hatch End Swimming Pool 1E **40**
Hatchers M. SE1 7H **15** (2E **102**)
(off Bermondsey St.)
Hatchett Rd. TW14: Bedf 1E **128**
Hatchfield Ho. N15 6E **48**
(off Albert Rd.)
Hatch Gro. RM6: Chad H 4E **54**
Hatch La. E4 4A **36**
Hatch La. UB7: Harm 3E **174**
Hatch Pl. KT2: King T 5F **133**
Hatch Rd. SW16 2J **155**
Hatch Side IG7: Chig 5K **37**
Hatchwood Cl. IG8: Wfd G 4C **36**
Hatcliffe Almshouses SE10 5G **105**
(off Tuskar St.)
Hatcliffe Cl. SE3 3H **123**
Hatcliffe St. SE10 5H **105**
Hatfeild Cl. CR4: Mitc 4B **154**
Hatfeild Mead SM4: Mord 5J **153**
Hatfield Cl. IG6: Ilf 3F **53**
Hatfield Cl. SE14 7K **103**
Hatfield Ct. SE3 7J **105**
Hatfield Ct. UB5: N'olt 3A **76**
(off Canberra Dr.)
Hatfield Ho. EC1 4C **8** (4C **84**)
(off Golden La. Est.)
Hatfield Ho. SE10 7D **104**
Hatfield M. RM9: Dag 7E **72**
Hatfield Rd. E15 5G **69**
Hatfield Rd. RM9: Dag 6E **72**
Hatfield Rd. W13 1A **96**
Hatfield Rd. W4 2K **97**
Hatfields SE1 4K **13** (1A **102**)
Hathaway Cl. BR2: Broml 1D **172**
Hathaway Cl. HA4: Ruis 4H **57**
Hathaway Cl. HA7: Stan 5F **27**
Hathaway Cres. E12 6D **70**
Hathaway Gdns. RM6: Chad H 5D **54**
Hathaway Gdns. W13 5A **78**
Hathaway Ho. N1 1G **9** (2E **84**)
Hathaway Rd. CR0: C'don 7B **156**
Hatherleigh Cl. KT9: Chess 5D **162**
Hatherleigh Cl. NW7 6A **30**
Hatherleigh Cl. SM4: Mord 4J **153**
Hatherleigh Rd. HA4: Ruis 2J **57**
Hatherley Ct. W2 6K **81**
(off Hatherley Gro.)
Hatherley Cres. DA14: Sidc 2A **144**
Hatherley Gdns. E6 3B **88**
Hatherley Gdns. N8 6J **47**
Hatherley Gro. W2 6K **81**
Hatherley Ho. E17 4C **50**
Hatherley M. E17 4C **50**
Hatherley Rd. DA14: Sidc 4A **144**
Hatherley Rd. E17 4B **50**
Hatherley Rd. TW9: Kew 1F **115**
Hatherley St. SW1 4B **18** (4G **101**)
Hathern Gdns. SE9 4E **142**
Hatherop Rd. TW12: Hamp 7D **130**
Hathersage Ct. N1 5D **66**
Hathorne Cl. SE15 2H **121**
Hathway St. SE14 2K **121**
Hathway Ter. SE14 2K **121**
(off Hathway St.)
Hatley Av. IG6: Ilf 4G **53**
Hatley Cl. N11 5J **31**
Hatley Rd. N4 2K **65**
Hatteraick St. SE16 2J **103**
Hattersfield Cl. DA17: Belv 4F **109**
HATTON 4H **111**
Hatton Cl. SE18 7H **107**
HATTON CROSS 4H **111**
Hatton Cross Cen. TW6: H'row A 3H **111**
Hatton Gdn. EC1 5K **7** (5A **84**)
Hatton Gdns. CR4: Mitc 5D **154**
Hatton Grn. TW14: Felt 4J **111**
Hatton Gro. UB7: W Dray 2A **92**
Hatton Ho. E1 7G **85**
(off Hindmarsh Cl.)
Hatton Ho. KT1: King T 2F **151**
(off Victoria Rd.)
Hatton Pl. EC1 5K **7** (5A **84**)
Hatton Rd. CR0: C'don 1A **168**
Hatton Rd. HA0: Wemb 1E **78**
Hatton Rd. TW14: Bedf 7E **110**
Hatton Rd. TW14: Felt 7E **110**
Hatton Rd. Sth. TW14: Felt 4H **111**
Hatton Row NW8 4B **4** (4B **82**)
(off Hatton St.)
Hatton St. NW8 4B **4** (4B **82**)
Hatton Wlk. EN2: Enf 3J **23**
Hatton Wall EC1 5K **7** (5A **84**)
Haughmond N12 4E **30**
Haunch of Venison Yd. W1
1J **11** (6F **83**)
Hauteville Ct. Gdns. W6 3B **98**
(off South Side)
Havana Rd. SW19 2J **135**
Havanna Dr. NW11 5G **45**
Havannah St. E14 2C **104**
Havant Rd. E17 3E **50**
Havelock Cl. W12 7D **80**
Havelock Ct. UB2: S'hall 3D **94**
(off Havelock Rd.)
Havelock Ho. SE1 4F **103**
(off Fort Rd.)
Havelock Ho. SE23 1J **139**
Havelock Pl. HA1: Harr 6J **41**
Havelock Rd. BR2: Broml 4A **160**
Havelock Rd. CR0: C'don 2F **169**
Havelock Rd. DA17: Belv 4F **109**
Havelock Rd. HA3: W'stone 3J **41**
Havelock Rd. N17 2G **49**
Havelock Rd. SW19 5A **136**
Havelock Rd. UB2: S'hall 3C **94**
Havelock St. IG1: Ilf 2F **71**
Havelock St. N1 1J **83**
Havelock Ter. SW8 1F **119**
Havelock Ter. Arches SW8 1F **119**
(off Havelock Ter.)
Havelock Wlk. SE23 1J **139**
Haven, The TW16: Sun 7J **129**
Haven, The TW9: Rich 3G **115**
Haven Cl. DA14: Sidc 6C **144**
Haven Cl. SE9 3D **142**
Haven Cl. SW19 3F **135**
Haven Cl. UB4: Hayes 6G **75**
Haven Ct. BR3: Beck 2E **158**
Haven Ct. KT5: Surb 6F **151**
Haven Grn. W5 6D **78**
Haven Grn. Ct. W5 6D **78**
Havenhurst Ri. EN2: Enf 2F **23**
Haven La. W5 6E **78**
Haven Lodge EN1: Enf 6K **23**
(off Village Rd.)
Haven Lodge SE18 4F **107**
(off Vincent Rd.)
Haven M. E3 5B **86**
Haven M. N1 7A **66**
Haven Pl. W5 7D **78**
Havenpool NW8 1K **81**
(off Abbey Rd.)
Haven Rd. TW15: Ashf 4D **128**
Haven St. NW1 7F **65**
Haven Way SE1 3F **103**
Havenwood HA9: Wemb 3H **61**
Haverfield Gdns. TW9: Kew 7G **97**
Haverfield Rd. E3 3A **86**
Haverford Way HA8: Edg 1F **43**
Haverhill Rd. E4 1K **35**
Haverhill Rd. SW12 1G **137**
Havering NW1 7F **65**
(off Castlehaven Rd.)
Havering Dr. RM1: Rom 4K **55**
Havering Gdns. RM6: Chad H 5C **54**
Havering Mus. 5K **55**
Havering St. E1 6K **85**
Havering Way IG11: Bark 3B **90**
Haverley St. SE26 5B **140**
Haversham Cl. TW1: Twick 6D **114**
Haversham Ct. UB6: G'frd 6K **59**
Haversham Pl. N6 2D **64**
Haverstock Ct. HA1: Harr 7G **41**
Haverstock Hill NW3 5C **64**
Haverstock Pl. N1 1B **8** (3B **84**)
(off Haverstock St.)
Haverstock Rd. NW5 5E **64**
Haverstock St. N1 1B **8** (2B **84**)
Haverthwaite Rd. BR6: Orp 2H **173**
Havilland M. W12 2D **98**
Havil St. SE5 7E **102**
Havisham Apts. E15 6F **69**
(off Grove Cres. Rd.)
Havisham Ho. SE16 2G **103**
Havisham Pl. SE19 7B **138**
Hawarden Gro. SE24 7C **120**
Hawarden Hill NW2 3C **62**
Hawarden Rd. E17 4K **49**
Hawbridge Rd. E11 1F **69**
Hawbush Ct. RM6: Ilf 4B **54**
Hawes Ho. E17 4K **49**
Hawes La. BR4: W W'ck 1E **170**
Hawes Rd. BR1: Broml 1K **159**
(not continuous)
Hawes Rd. N18 6C **34**
Hawes St. N1 7B **66**
Haweswater Ho. TW7: Isle 5K **113**
Hawfinch Ho. NW9 7B **44**
Hawgood St. E3 5C **86**
Hawkdene E4 6J **25**
Hawke Ct. UB4: Yead 4A **76**
(off Perth Av.)
Hawke Ho. E1 4K **85**
(off Ernest St.)
Hawke Pk. Rd. N22 3B **48**
Hawke Pl. SE16 2K **103**
Hawker NW9 1B **44**
(off Everglade Strand)
Hawker Ct. E3 3E **86**
(off Bolinder Way)
Hawker Ct. KT1: King T 2F **151**
(off Church Rd.)
Hawke Rd. SE19 6D **138**
Hawker Pl. E17 2E **50**
Hawker Rd. CR0: Wadd 6A **168**
Hawkesbury Rd. SW15 5D **116**
Hawkesfield Rd. SE23 2A **140**
Hawkesley Cl. TW1: Twick 4A **132**
Hawkesley Ho. E17 6D **50**
Hawkes Rd. CR4: Mitc 1D **154**
Hawkes Rd. TW14: Felt 7J **111**
Hawkesworth Cl. HA6: Nwood 1G **39**
Hawkes Yd. KT7: T Ditt 6K **149**
Hawke Twr. SE14 6A **104**
Hawkewood Rd. TW16: Sun 3J **147**
Hawkfield Ct. TW7: Isle 2J **113**
Hawkhurst Gdns. KT9: Chess 4E **162**
Hawkhurst Rd. SW16 1H **155**
Hawkhurst Way BR4: W W'ck 2D **170**
Hawkhurst Way KT3: N Mald 5K **151**
Hawkinge N17 2D **48**
(off Gloucester Rd.)
Hawkins Cl. HA1: Harr 7H **41**
Hawkins Cl. NW7 5E **28**
Hawkins Ct. SE18 4C **106**
Hawkins Ho. SE8 6C **104**
(off New King St.)
Hawkins Ho. SW1 7B **18** (6G **101**)
(off Dolphin Sq.)
Hawkins Rd. NW10 7A **62**
Hawkins Rd. TW11: Tedd 6B **132**
Hawkins Ter. SE7 5C **106**
Hawkins Way SE6 5C **140**
Hawkley Gdns. SE27 2B **138**
Hawkridge Cl. RM6: Chad H 6C **54**
Hawksbrook La. BR3: Beck 6D **158**
Hawkshaw Cl. SW2 7J **119**
Hawkshead NW1 1A **6** (3G **83**)
(off Stanhope St.)
Hawkshead Cl. BR1: Broml 7G **141**
Hawkshead Rd. NW10 7B **62**
Hawkshead Rd. W4 2A **98**
Hawkslade Rd. SE15 5K **121**
Hawksley Rd. N16 3E **66**
Hawks M. SE10 7E **104**
Hawksmoor Cl. E6 6C **88**
Hawksmoor Cl. SE18 5J **107**
Hawksmoor Gro. BR2: Broml 6B **160**
Hawksmoor M. E1 7H **85**
Hawksmoor Pl. E2 3K **9** (4G **85**)
(off Cheshire St.)
Hawksmoor St. W6 6F **99**
Hawksmouth E4 7K **25**
Hawks Pas. KT1: King T 2F **151**
(off London Rd.)
Hawks Rd. KT1: King T 2F **151**
Hawkstone Rd. SE16 4J **103**
Hawksworth Ho. BR1: Broml 2J **159**
Hawkwell Ct. E4 3K **35**
Hawkwell Ho. RM8: Dag 1G **73**
Hawkwell Wlk. N1 1C **84**
(off Maldon Cl.)
Hawkwood Cres. E4 6J **25**
Hawkwood La. BR7: Chst 1G **161**
Hawkwood Mt. E5 1H **67**
Hawlands Dr. HA5: Pinn 7C **40**
Hawley Cl. TW12: Hamp 6D **130**
Hawley Cres. NW1 7F **65**
Hawley M. NW1 7F **65**
Hawley Rd. N18 5E **34**
Hawley Rd. NW1 7F **65**
(not continuous)
Hawley St. NW1 7F **65**
Hawley Way TW15: Ashf 5C **128**
Hawstead Rd. SE6 6D **122**
Hawsted IG9: Buck H 1E **36**
Hawthorn Av. CR7: Thor H 1B **156**
Hawthorn Av. E3 1B **86**
Hawthorn Av. N13 5D **32**
Hawthorn Cen., The HA1: Harr 5K **41**
Hawthorn Cl. BR5: Pet W 6H **161**
Hawthorn Cl. TW12: Hamp 5E **130**
Hawthorn Cl. TW5: Cran 7K **93**
Hawthorn Cotts. DA16: Well 3A **126**
(off Hook La.)
Hawthorn Ct. HA5: Pinn 2A **40**
(off Rickmansworth Rd.)
Hawthorn Ct. TW15: Ashf 7E **128**
Hawthorn Ct. TW9: Kew 1H **115**
Hawthorn Cres. IG5: Ilf 1D **52**
Hawthorn Cres. SW17 5E **136**
Hawthornden Cl. N12 6H **31**
Hawthorndene Cl. BR2: Hayes 2H **171**
Hawthorndene Rd. BR2: Hayes 2H **171**
Hawthorn Dr. BR4: W W'ck 4G **171**
Hawthorn Dr. HA2: Harr 6E **40**
Hawthorne Av. CR4: Mitc 2B **154**
Hawthorne Av. HA3: Kenton 6A **42**
Hawthorne Av. HA4: Ruis 6K **39**
Hawthorne Av. SM5: Cars 7E **166**
Hawthorne Cl. BR1: Broml 3D **160**
Hawthorne Cl. N1 6E **66**
Hawthorne Cl. SM1: Sutt 2A **166**
Hawthorne Ct. HA6: Nwood 2J **39**
Hawthorne Ct. W5 1E **96**
Hawthorne Cres. SE10 5H **105**
Hawthorne Cres. UB7: W Dray 2B **92**
Hawthorne Gro. NW9 7J **43**
Hawthorne Ho. N15 5G **49**
Hawthorne Ho. SW1 6B **18** (5G **101**)
(off Churchill Gdns.)
Hawthorne M. UB6: G'frd 6G **77**
Hawthorne Pl. UB3: Hayes 7H **75**
Hawthorne Rd. BR1: Broml 3C **160**
Hawthorne Rd. E17 3C **50**
Hawthorne Rd. N18 6A **34**
Hawthorne Way N9 2A **34**
Hawthorn Farm Av. UB5: N'olt 1C **76**
Hawthorn Gdns. W5 3D **96**
Hawthorn Gro. EN2: Enf 1J **23**
Hawthorn Gro. SE20 7H **139**
Hawthorn Hatch TW8: Bford 7B **96**
Hawthorn Ho. E15 6F **69**
(off Forrester Way)
Hawthorn Ho. SE16 2A **104**
(off Blondin Way)
Hawthorn M. NW7 1G **45**
Hawthorn Pl. DA8: Erith 5J **109**
Hawthorn Rd. DA6: Bex 4F **127**
Hawthorn Rd. IG9: Buck H 4G **37**
Hawthorn Rd. N8 3H **47**
Hawthorn Rd. NW10 7C **62**
Hawthorn Rd. SM1: Sutt 6C **166**
Hawthorn Rd. SM6: W'gton 7F **167**
Hawthorn Rd. TW13: Felt 1J **129**
Hawthorn Rd. TW8: Bford 7B **96**
Hawthorns CR2: S Croy 4C **168**
(off Bramley Hill)
Hawthorns IG8: Wfd G 3D **36**
Hawthorns, The KT17: Ewe 7B **164**
Hawthorns, The SL3: Poyle 4A **174**
Hawthorn Ter. DA15: Sidc 5K **125**
Hawthorn Wlk. W10 4G **81**
Hawthorn Way TW17: Shep 4F **147**
Hawtrey Av. UB5: N'olt 2B **76**
Hawtrey Dr. HA4: Ruis 7J **39**
Hawtrey Rd. NW3 7C **64**
Haxted Rd. BR1: Broml 1K **159**
Hay Cl. E15 7G **69**
Haycroft Gdns. NW10 1C **80**
Haycroft Rd. KT6: Surb 2D **162**
Haycroft Rd. SW2 5J **119**
Hay Currie St. E14 6D **86**
Hayday Rd. E16 5J **87**
(not continuous)
Hayden Ct. TW13: Felt 4G **129**
Hayden Piper Ho. SW3 7E **16** (6D **100**)
(off Caversham St.)
Haydens M. W3 6J **79**
Hayden's Pl. W11 6H **81**
Hayden Twr. SW8 7H **101**
Hayden Way RM5: Col R 2J **55**
Haydock Av. UB5: N'olt 6E **58**
Haydock Grn. UB5: N'olt 6E **58**
Haydock Grn. Flats UB5: N'olt 6E **58**
(off Haydock Grn.)
Haydon Cl. EN1: Enf 6K **23**
Haydon Cl. NW9 4J **43**
Haydon Ct. NW9 4J **43**
Haydon Dr. HA5: Eastc 4J **39**
Haydon Pk. Rd. SW19 5J **135**
Haydon Rd. RM8: Dag 2C **72**
Haydons Rd. SW19 5K **135**
Haydon St. EC3 2J **15** (7F **85**)
Haydon Wlk. E1 1K **15** (6F **85**)
Haydon Way SW11 4B **118**
Hay Dr. CR4: Mitc 2C **154**
HAYES Bromley 1J **171**
HAYES Uxbridge 6G **75**
Hayes & Yeading United FC 1A **94**
Hayes Bri. Retail Pk. 7A **76**
Hayes Chase BR4: W W'ck 6F **159**
Hayes Cl. BR2: Hayes 2J **171**
Hayes Ct. BR2: Hayes 3J **171**
Hayes Ct. HA0: Wemb 1E **78**
Hayes Ct. SE5 7C **102**
(off Camberwell New Rd.)
Hayes Ct. SW2 1J **137**
Hayes Cres. NW11 5H **45**
Hayes Cres. SM3: Cheam 4F **165**
HAYES END 4F **75**
Hayes End Cl. UB4: Hayes 4F **75**
Hayes End Dr. UB4: Hayes 4F **75**
Hayes End Rd. UB4: Hayes 4F **75**
Hayesens Ho. SW17 4A **136**
Hayesford Pk. Dr. BR2: Broml 5H **159**
Hayes Gdn. BR2: Hayes 1J **171**
Hayes Gro. SE22 3F **121**
Hayes Hill BR2: Hayes 1G **171**
Hayes Hill Rd. BR2: Hayes 1H **171**
Hayes La. BR2: Broml 5K **159**
Hayes La. BR2: Hayes 5K **159**
Hayes La. BR3: Beck 3E **158**
Hayes Mead Rd. BR2: Hayes 1G **171**
Hayes Metro Cen. UB4: Yead 7A **76**
Hayes M. SE8 1B **122**
Hayes Pk. Lodge UB4: Hayes 4F **75**
Hayes Pl. NW1 4D **4** (4C **82**)
Hayes Rd. BR2: Broml 4J **159**
Hayes Rd. UB2: S'hall 4K **93**
Hayes St. BR2: Hayes 1K **171**
HAYES TOWN 2H **93**
Hayes Way BR3: Beck 4E **158**
Hayes Wood Av. BR2: Hayes 1K **171**
Hayfield Pas. E1 4J **85**
Hayfield Yd. E1 4J **85**
Haygarth Pl. SW19 5F **135**
Haygreen Cl. KT2: King T 6H **133**
Hay Hill W1 3K **11** (7F **83**)
Hayhurst Ct. N1 1B **84**
(off Dibden St.)
Hayland Cl. NW9 4K **43**
Haylands Ct. TW8: Bford 6C **96**
Hay La. NW9 4J **43**
Hayles Bldgs. SE11 4B **102**
(off Elliotts Row)
Hayles St. SE11 4B **102**
Haylett Gdns. KT1: King T 4D **150**
Hayling Av. TW13: Felt 3J **129**
Hayling Cl. N16 5E **66**
Hayling Ct. SM3: Cheam 4E **164**
Hayling Way HA8: Edg 4A **28**
Haymaker Cl. UB10: Uxb 7B **56**
Hayman Cres. UB4: Hayes 2E **74**
Haymans Point SE11 4G **19** (4K **101**)
Hayman St. N1 7B **66**
Haymarket SW1 3C **12** (7H **83**)
Haymarket Arc. SW1 3C **12** (7H **83**)
(off Haymarket)
Haymarket Ct. E8 7F **67**
(off Jacaranda Gro.)
Haymarket Theatre Royal
3D **12** (7H **83**)
(off Haymarket)
Haymer Gdns. KT4: Wor Pk 3C **164**
Haymerle Ho. SE15 6G **103**
(off Haymerle Rd.)
Haymerle Rd. SE15 6G **103**
Hay M. NW3 6D **64**
Haymill Cl. UB6: G'frd 3K **77**
Hayne Ho. W11 1G **99**
(off Penzance Pl.)
Hayne Rd. BR3: Beck 2B **158**
Haynes Cl. N11 3K **31**
Haynes Cl. N17 7C **34**
Haynes Cl. SE3 3G **123**
Haynes Dr. N9 3C **34**
Haynes La. SE19 6E **138**
Haynes Rd. HA0: Wemb 7E **60**
Hayne St. EC1 5B **8** (5B **84**)
Haynt Wlk. SW20 3G **153**
Hayre Dr. UB2: S'hall 5C **94**
Hay's Ct. SE16 2J **103**
(off Rotherhithe St.)
Hay's Galleria SE1 4G **15** (1E **102**)
Hays La. SE1 4G **15** (1E **102**)
Haysleigh Gdns. SE20 2G **157**
Hay's M. W1 4J **11** (1F **101**)
Haysoms Cl. RM1: Rom 4K **55**
Haystall Cl. UB4: Hayes 2G **75**
Hay St. E2 1G **85**
Hayter Ct. E11 2K **69**
Hayter Rd. SW2 5J **119**
Hayton Cl. E8 6F **67**
Hayward Cl. DA1: Cray 5K **127**
Hayward Cl. SW19 7K **135**
Hayward Ct. SW9 2J **119**
(off Studley Rd.)
Hayward Gallery 4H **13** (1K **101**)
Hayward Gdns. SW15 6E **116**
Hayward Ho. N1 2A **84**
(off Penton St.)
Hayward M. SE4 5B **122**
Hayward Rd. KT7: T Ditt 1A **162**
Hayward Rd. N20 2F **31**
Haywards Cl. RM6: Chad H 5B **54**
Hayward's Pl. EC1 3A **8** (4B **84**)
Haywood Cl. HA5: Pinn 2B **40**
Haywood Lodge N11 6D **32**
(off York Rd.)
Haywood Ri. BR6: Orp 5J **173**
Haywood Rd. BR2: Broml 4B **160**
Hazel Av. UB7: W Dray 3C **92**
Hazel Bank SE25 2E **156**
Hazelbank KT5: Surb 1J **163**
Hazelbank Rd. SE6 2F **141**
Hazelbourne Rd. SW12 6F **119**
Hazelbury Cl. SW19 2J **153**
Hazelbury Grn. N9 3K **33**
Hazelbury La. N9 3K **33**
Hazel Cl. CR0: C'don 7K **157**
Hazel Cl. CR4: Mitc 4H **155**
Hazel Cl. N13 3J **33**
Hazel Cl. N19 2G **65**
Hazel Cl. NW9 2A **44**
Hazel Cl. SE15 2G **121**
(off Bournemouth Cl.)
Hazel Cl. TW2: Whitt 7G **113**
Hazel Cl. TW8: Bford 7B **96**
Hazel Ct. W5 7E **78**
Hazelcroft HA5: Hat E 6A **26**
Hazelcroft Cl. UB10: Hil 7B **56**
Hazeldean Rd. NW10 7K **61**
Hazeldene Dr. HA5: Pinn 3A **40**
Hazeldene Gdns. UB10: Hil 1E **74**
Hazeldene Rd. DA16: Well 2C **126**
Hazeldene Rd. IG3: Ilf 2B **72**
Hazeldon Rd. SE4 5A **122**
Hazeleigh Gdns. IG8: Wfd G 5H **37**
Hazel Gdns. HA8: Edg 4C **28**
Hazelgreen Cl. N21 1G **33**
Hazel Gro. BR6: Farnb 2F **173**
Hazel Gro. EN1: Enf 6B **24**

Hazel Gro. – Hepburn Gdns.

Hazel Gro. HA0: Wemb 1E 78
Hazel Gro. RM6: Chad H 3E 54
Hazel Gro. SE26 4K 139
Hazel Gro. TW13: Felt 1J 129
Hazel Ho. E3 1B 86
(off Barge La.)
Hazelhurst BR3: Beck 1F 159
Hazelhurst Ct. SE6 5E 140
(off Beckenham Hill Rd.)
Hazelhurst Rd. SW17 4A 136
Hazel La. IG6: Ilf 6K 37
Hazel La. SE10 5H 105
Hazel La. TW10: Ham 2E 132
Hazell Cres. RM5: Col R 1H 55
Hazellville Rd. N19 7H 47
Hazelmere Cl. TW14: Felt 6G 111
Hazelmere Cl. UB5: N'olt 2D 76
Hazelmere Ct. SW2 1K 137
Hazelmere Dr. UB5: N'olt 2D 76
Hazelmere Rd. BR5: Pet W 4G 161
Hazelmere Rd. NW6 1H 81
Hazelmere Rd. UB5: N'olt 2D 76
Hazelmere Wlk. UB5: N'olt 2D 76
(not continuous)
Hazelmere Way BR2: Hayes 6J 159
Hazel M. N22 3A 48
(off High Rd.)
Hazel Rd. E15 5G 69
Hazel Rd. NW10 3D 80
(not continuous)
Hazeltree La. UB5: N'olt 3C 76
Hazel Wlk. BR2: Broml 6E 160
Hazel Way E4 6G 35
Hazel Way SE1 4F 103
Hazelwood Av. SM4: Mord 4K 153
Hazelwood Cl. W5 2E 96
Hazelwood Ct. KT6: Surb 6E 150
Hazelwood Ct. N13 4F 33
(off Hazelwood La.)
Hazelwood Ct. NW10 3A 62
Hazelwood Cres. N13 4F 33
Hazelwood Dr. HA5: Pinn 2K 39
Hazelwood Dr. TW16: Sun 3J 147
Hazelwood Ho. SE8 4A 104
Hazelwood Ho. TW16: Sun 1J 147
Hazelwood Ho's. BR2: Broml 3G 159
Hazelwood La. N13 4F 33
Hazelwood Rd. E17 5A 50
Hazelwood Rd. EN1: Enf 6A 24
Hazelwood Sports Club 7H 23
Hazlebury Rd. SW6 2K 117
Hazledean Rd. CR0: C'don 2D 168
Hazledene Rd. W4 6J 97
Hazlemere Gdns. KT4: Wor Pk 1C 164
Hazlewell Rd. SW15 5E 116
Hazlewood Cl. E5 3A 68
Hazlewood Cl. HA2: Harr 4F 41
Hazlewood Cres. W10 4G 81
Hazlewood M. SW9 3J 119
Hazlewood Twr. W10 4G 81
(off Golborne Gdns.)
Hazlitt Cl. TW13: Hanw 4C 130
Hazlitt M. W14 3G 99
Hazlitt Rd. W14 3G 99
Heacham Av. UB10: Ick 3E 56
Headbourne Ho. E17 3A 50
(off Sutherland Rd.)
Headbourne Ho. SE1 7F 15 (3D 102)
Headcorn Pl. CR7: Thor H 4K 155
Headcorn Rd. BR1: Broml 5H 141
Headcorn Rd. CR7: Thor H 4K 155
Headcorn Rd. N17 7A 34
Headfort Pl. SW1 7H 11 (2E 100)
Headingley Dr. BR3: Beck 6C 140
Headington Ct. CR0: C'don 4C 168
(off Tanfield Rd.)
Headington Rd. SW18 2A 136
Headlam Rd. SW4 6H 119
(not continuous)
Headlam St. E1 4H 85
Headley App. IG2: Ilf 5F 53
Headley Av. SM6: W'gton 5K 167
Headley Cl. KT19: Ewe 6G 163
Headley Ct. SE26 5J 139
Headley Dr. CR0: New Ad 7D 170
Headley Dr. IG2: Ilf 6F 53
Headley M. SW18 5K 117
Head's M. W11 6J 81
HEADSTONE 4G 41
Headstone Dr. HA1: Harr 3H 41
Headstone Dr. HA3: W'stone 3J 41
Headstone Gdns. HA2: Harr 4G 41
Headstone La. HA2: Harr 4E 40
Headstone La. HA3: Hrw W 7A 26
Headstone Manor 3G 41
Headstone Pde. HA1: Harr 4H 41
Headstone Rd. HA1: Harr 5J 41
Head St. E1 6K 85
(not continuous)
Headway Cl. TW10: Ham 4C 132
Headway Gdns. E17 1C 50
Heald St. SE14 1C 122
Healey Ho. E3 4C 86
(off Wellington Way)
Healey Ho. SW9 7A 102
Healey St. NW1 6F 65
Healy Ct. EN5: Barn 6A 20
Healy Dr. BR6: Orp 4K 173
Hearne Rd. W4 6G 97
Hearn Pl. SW16 4A 138
Hearn Ri. UB5: N'olt 1B 76
Hearn's Bldgs. SE17 4D 102
Hearnshaw St. E14 6A 86
Hearn St. EC2 4H 9 (4E 84)
Hearnville Rd. SW12 1E 136
Heart, The KT12: Walt T 7J 147
Heartwell Av. E16 6H 87
Heath, The W7 1J 95
Heatham Pk. TW2: Twick 7K 113
Heath Av. DA7: Bex 6D 108
Heathbourne Rd. HA7: Stan 2D 26
Heathbourne Rd. WD23: B Hea 1D 26
Heath Brow NW3 3A 64
Heath Bus. Cen. TW3: Houn 4G 113
Heath Cl. CR2: S Croy 6B 168
Heath Cl. NW11 7K 45
Heath Cl. UB3: Harl 7F 93
Heath Cl. W5 4F 79
Heathcock Ct. WC2 3F 13 (7J 83)
(off Exchange Ct.)
Heathcote Av. IG5: Ilf 2D 52
Heathcote Ct. IG5: Ilf 1D 52
(not continuous)
Heathcote Ga. SW6 3J 117
Heathcote Gro. E4 3K 35
Heathcote Rd. TW1: Twick 6B 114
Heathcote St. WC1 3G 7 (4K 83)
Heath Ct. CR0: C'don 4D 168
(off Heathfield Rd.)
Heath Ct. SE9 1G 143
Heath Ct. TW4: Houn 4D 112
Heath Ct. UB8: Uxb 7A 56
Heath Cft. NW11 1K 63
Heathcroft W5 4F 79
(not continuous)
Heathcroft Av. TW16: Sun 7H 129
Heathcroft Gdns. E17 1F 51
Heathdale Av. TW4: Houn 3C 112
Heathdene Dr. DA17: Belv 4H 109
Heathdene Rd. SM6: W'gton 7F 167
Heathdene Rd. SW16 7K 137
Heath Dr. NW3 4K 63
Heath Dr. SW20 4E 152
Heathedge SE26 2H 139
Heath End Rd. DA5: Bexl 1K 145
Heather Av. RM1: Rom 2K 55
Heatherbank BR7: Chst 2E 160
Heatherbank SE9 2D 124
Heather Cl. E6 6E 88
Heather Cl. N7 3K 65
Heather Cl. RM1: Rom 1K 55
Heather Cl. SE13 7F 123
Heather Cl. SW8 3F 119
Heather Cl. TW12: Hamp 1D 148
Heather Cl. TW7: Isle 5H 113
Heather Cl. UB8: Hil 5B 74
Heather Ct. DA14: Sidc 6D 144
Heatherdale Cl. KT2: King T 6G 133
Heatherdene Cl. CR4: Mitc 4B 154
Heatherdene Cl. N12 7F 31
Heather Dr. EN2: Enf 2G 23
Heather Dr. RM1: Rom 2K 55
Heatherfold Way HA5: Eastc 3H 39
Heather Gdns. NW11 6G 45
Heather Gdns. RM1: Rom 2K 55
Heather Gdns. SM2: Sutt 6J 165
Heather Glen RM1: Rom 2K 55
Heather Ho. E14 6E 86
(off Dee St.)
Heatherlands TW16: Sun 6J 129
Heather La. UB7: Yiew 6A 74
Heatherlea Gro. KT4: Wor Pk 1D 164
Heatherley Ct. E5 3G 67
Heatherley Dr. IG5: Ilf 3C 52
Heather Pk. Dr. HA0: Wemb 7G 61
Heather Pk. Pde. HA0: Wemb 7F 61
(off Heather Pk. Dr.)
Heather Rd. E4 6G 35
Heather Rd. NW2 2C 62
Heather Rd. SE12 2J 141
Heathers, The TW19: Stanw 7B 110
Heatherset Gdns. SW16 7K 137
Heatherside Rd. DA14: Sidc 3C 144
Heatherside Rd. KT19: Ewe 7K 163
Heatherton Ter. N3 2K 45
Heather Wlk. HA8: Edg 5C 28
Heather Wlk. TW2: Whitt 7E 112
(off Stephenson Rd.)
Heather Wlk. W10 4G 81
Heather Way CR2: Sels 7K 169
Heather Way HA7: Stan 6E 26
Heather Way RM1: Rom 2K 55
Heatherwood Cl. E12 2A 70
Heatherwood Dr. UB4: Hayes 2F 75
Heathfield BR7: Chst 6G 143
Heathfield E4 3K 35
Heathfield HA1: Harr 7K 41
Heathfield Av. SW18 7B 118
Heathfield Cl. BR2: Kes 5A 172
Heathfield Cl. E16 5B 88
Heathfield Ct. DA8: Erith 1K 127
Heathfield Ct. E3 2C 86
(off Tredegar Rd.)
Heathfield Ct. SE14 7J 103
Heathfield Ct. SE20 7J 139
Heathfield Ct. TW15: Ashf 3A 128
Heathfield Ct. W4 5K 97
Heathfield Dr. CR4: Mitc 1C 154
Heathfield Gdns. CR0: C'don 4D 168
Heathfield Gdns. NW11 6F 45
Heathfield Gdns. SE3 2G 123
(off Baizdon Rd.)
Heathfield Gdns. SW18 6B 118
Heathfield Gdns. W4 5J 97
Heathfield Ho. SE3 2G 123
Heathfield La. BR7: Chst 6G 143
Heathfield Nth. TW2: Twick 7J 113
Heathfield Pk. NW2 6E 62
Heathfield Pk. Dr. RM6: Chad H 5B 54
Heathfield Ri. HA4: Ruis 7E 38
Heathfield Rd. BR1: Broml 7H 141
Heathfield Rd. BR2: Kes 5A 172
Heathfield Rd. CR0: C'don 4D 168
Heathfield Rd. DA6: Bex 4F 127
Heathfield Rd. SW18 6A 118
Heathfield Rd. W3 2H 97
Heathfields Ct. TW4: Houn 5C 112
Heathfield Sth. TW2: Twick 7K 113
Heathfield Sq. SW18 7B 118
Heathfield Ter. SE18 6J 107
Heathfield Ter. W4 5J 97
Heathfield Va. CR2: Sels 7K 169
Heath Gdns. TW1: Twick 1K 131
Heathgate NW11 6K 45
Heathgate Pl. NW3 5D 64
Heath Gro. SE20 7J 139
Heath Gro. TW16: Sun 7H 129
Heath Ho. DA15: Sidc 4K 143
Heath Hurst Rd. NW3 4C 64
Heathland Rd. N16 1E 66
Heathlands Cl. TW1: Twick 2K 131
Heathlands Cl. TW16: Sun 2J 147
Heathlands Way TW4: Houn 5C 112
Heath La. SE3 2F 123
(not continuous)
Heathlee Rd. SE3 4H 123
Heathley End BR7: Chst 6G 143
Heath Lodge WD23: B Hea 1D 26
Heathmans Rd. SW6 1H 117
Heath Mead SW19 3F 135
Heath Pk. Dr. BR1: Broml 3C 160
Heath Pas. NW3 2K 63
Heath Pl. E3 4B 86
Heathpool Ct. E1 4H 85
Heath Ri. BR2: Hayes 6H 159
Heath Ri. SW15 6F 117
Heath Rd. CR7: Thor H 3C 156
Heath Rd. DA5: Bexl 1J 145
Heath Rd. HA1: Harr 7G 41
Heath Rd. RM6: Chad H 7D 54
Heath Rd. SW8 2F 119
Heath Rd. TW1: Twick 1K 131
Heath Rd. TW2: Twick 1K 131
Heath Rd. TW3: Houn 4F 113
Heath Rd. TW3: Isle 4F 113
Heath Rd. TW7: Isle 4H 113
Heath Rd. UB10: Hil 4E 74
Heath Robinson Mus. 4B 40
Heathrow Blvd. UB7: Sip 7B 92
Heathrow Causeway Cen. TW4: Houn 3K 111
Heathrow Central Tourist Info. Cen. 3D 110
Heathrow Cl. UB7: Lford 4C 174
Heathrow Gateway TW4: Houn 7C 112
Heathrow Interchange UB4: Yead 1A 94
Heathrow Intl. Trad. Est. TW4: Houn 3K 111
Heathrow Prologis Pk. UB3: Harl 3D 92
Heath Royal SW15 6F 117
Heaths Cl. EN1: Enf 2K 23
Heath Side BR5: Pet W 1G 173
Heath Side NW3 4B 64
Heathside NW11 1J 63
Heathside SE13 2E 122
Heathside TW4: Houn 7D 112
Heathside Av. DA7: Bex 1E 126
Heathside Cl. IG2: Ilf 5H 53
Heathstan Rd. W12 6C 80
Heath St. NW3 4A 64
Heath Ter. RM6: Chad H 7D 54
Heath Vw. N2 4A 46
Heathview NW5 4E 64
Heath Vw. Cl. N2 4A 46
Heathview Dr. SE2 6D 108
Heathview Gdns. SW15 7E 116
Heathview Rd. CR7: Thor H 4A 156
Heath Vs. NW3 3B 64
Heath Vs. SE18 5K 107
Heathville Rd. N19 7J 47
Heathwall St. SW11 3D 118
Heath Way DA8: Erith 1J 127
Heathway CR0: C'don 3B 170
Heathway IG8: Wfd G 5F 37
Heathway RM10: Dag 3F 73
Heathway RM9: Dag 3F 73
HEATHWAY 1G 91
Heathway SE3 7J 105
Heathway UB2: S'hall 4B 94
Heathway Ct. NW3 2J 63
Heathway Ind. Est. RM10: Dag 4H 73
Heathwood Gdns. SE7 4C 106
Heathwood Point SE23 3K 139
Heathwood Wlk. DA5: Bexl 1K 145
Heaton Cl. E4 3K 35
Heaton Ho. SW10 6A 100
(off Fulham Rd.)
Heaton Rd. CR4: Mitc 7E 136
Heaton Rd. SE15 2H 121
Heaven Tree Cl. N1 6C 66
Heaver Rd. SW11 3B 118
Heavitree Cl. SE18 5H 107
Heavitree Rd. SE18 5H 107
(not continuous)
Hebden St. E2 1F 85
Hebden St. SW8 7H 101
Hebden Ter. N17 6K 33
Hebdon Rd. SW17 3C 136
Heber Mans. W14 6G 99
(off Queen's Club Gdns.)
Heber Rd. NW2 5F 63
Heber Rd. SE22 6F 121
Hebrides Ct. E1 5A 86
(off Ocean Est.)
Hebron Rd. W6 3E 98
Hecham Cl. E17 2A 50
Heckfield Pl. SW6 7J 99
Heckford Cl. SE18 5J 107
Heckford Ho. E14 6D 86
(off Grundy St.)
Heckford St. E1 7K 85
Heckford St. Bus. Cen. E1 7K 85
(off Heckford St.)
Hector NW9 1B 44
(off Five Acre)
Hector Cl. N9 2B 34
Hector Ct. SW9 7A 102
(off Caldwell St.)
Hector Ho. E2 2H 85
(off Old Bethnal Grn. Rd.)
Hector St. SE18 4J 107
Heddington Gro. N7 5K 65
Heddon Cl. TW7: Isle 4A 114
Heddon Ct. Av. EN4: Cockf 5J 21
Heddon Ct. Pde. EN4: Cockf 5K 21
Heddon Rd. EN4: Cockf 5J 21
Heddon St. W1 2A 12 (7G 83)
Hedera Pl. TW4: Houn 4D 112
Hedgegate Ct. W11 6H 81
(off Powis Ter.)
Hedge Hill EN2: Enf 1G 23
Hedge La. N13 3G 33
Hedgeley IG4: Ilf 4D 52
Hedgemans Rd. RM9: Dag 7D 72
Hedgemans Way RM9: Dag 6E 72
Hedgerley Gdns. UB6: G'frd 2G 77
Hedgerow Ct. E6 1D 88
(off Nelson St.)
Hedgers Gro. E9 6A 68
Hedger St. SE11 4B 102
Hedges Cl. TW14: Felt 6K 111
Hedge Wlk. SE6 5D 140
Hedgewood Gdns. IG5: Ilf 5E 52
Hedgley M. SE12 5H 123
Hedgley St. SE12 5H 123
Hedingham Cl. N1 7C 66
Hedingham Ho. KT2: King T 1E 150
(off Royal Quarter)
Hedingham Rd. RM8: Dag 5B 72
Hedley Cl. RM1: Rom 5K 55
Hedley Ho. E14 3E 104
(off Stewart St.)
Hedley Rd. TW2: Whitt 7E 112
Hedley Row N5 5D 66
Hedsor Ho. E2 3J 9 (4F 85)
(off Ligonier St.)
Heenan Cl. IG11: Bark 6G 71
Heene Rd. EN2: Enf 1J 23
Heer M. E2 2G 85
(off Hackney Rd.)
Hega Ho. E14 5E 86
(off Ullin St.)
Heidegger Cres. SW13 7D 98
Heigham Rd. E6 7C 70
Heighton Gdns. CR0: Wadd 5B 168
Heights, The BR3: Beck 7E 140
(not continuous)
Heights, The SE7 5A 106
Heights, The UB5: N'olt 5D 58
Heights Cl. SW20 7D 134
Heiron St. SE17 6B 102
Heldar Ct. SE1 7F 15 (2D 102)
Helder Gro. SE12 7H 123
Helder St. CR2: S Croy 6D 168
Heldmann Cl. TW3: Houn 4H 113
Helegan Cl. BR6: Chels 4K 173
Helena Cl. SW19 7F 117
Helena Ct. NW6 7K 63
(off Compayne Gdns.)
Helena Ct. W5 5D 78
Helena Pl. E9 1H 85
Helena Rd. E13 2H 87
Helena Rd. E17 5C 50
Helena Rd. NW10 5D 62
Helena Rd. W5 5D 78
Helena Sq. SE16 7A 86
(off Sovereign Cres.)
Helen Av. TW14: Felt 7K 111
Helen Cl. KT8: W Mole 4F 149
Helen Cl. N2 3A 46
Helen Gladstone Ho.
SE1 6A 14 (2B 102)
(off Surrey Row)
Helen Ho. E2 2H 85
(off Old Bethnal Grn. Rd.)
Helen Peele Cotts. SE16 3J 103
(off Lower Rd.)
Helenslea Av. NW11 1J 63
Helen's Pl. E2 3J 85
Helen St. SE18 4F 107
Helen Taylor Ho. SE16 3G 103
(off Evelyn Lowe Est.)
Helford Cl. HA4: Ruis 2G 57
Helgiford Gdns. TW16: Sun 7G 129
Heligan Ho. SE16 2K 103
(off Water Gdns. Sq.)
Helios, The 7E 80
Helios Rd. SM6: W'gton 1E 166
Helios Way EN5: Barn 5C 20
Heliport Ind. Est. SW11 2B 118
Helix Ct. W11 1F 99
(off Swanscombe Rd.)
Helix Gdns. SW2 6K 119
Helix Rd. SW2 6K 119
Helix Ter. SW19 2F 135
Hellings St. E1 1G 103
Helm, The E16 7F 89
Helme Cl. SW19 5H 135
Helmet Row EC1 3D 8 (4C 84)
Helmore Rd. IG11: Bark 7K 71
Helmsdale Apts. SW11 4C 118
(off Monarch Square)
Helmsdale Cl. UB4: Yead 4C 76
Helmsdale Ho. NW6 2K 81
(off Carlton Vale)
Helmsdale Rd. SW16 1H 155
Helmsley Pl. E8 7H 67
Helmsley St. E8 7H 67
Helperby Rd. NW10 7A 62
Helsby Ct. NW8 3A 4 (4B 82)
(off Pollitt Dr.)
Helsinki Sq. SE16 3A 104
Helston NW1 1G 83
(off Camden St.)
Helston Cl. HA5: Hat E 1D 40
Helston Ct. N15 5E 48
(off Culvert Rd.)
Helston Ho. SE11 5K 19 (5A 102)
(off Kennings Way)
Helvetia St. SE6 2B 140
Helwys Ct. E4 6J 35
Hemans St. SW8 7H 101
Hemans St. Est. SW8 7J 101
Hemberton Rd. SW9 3J 119
Hemery Rd. UB6: G'frd 5H 59
Hemingford Cl. N12 5G 31
Hemingford Rd. N1 1K 83
Hemingford Rd. SM3: Cheam 4E 164
Heming Rd. HA8: Edg 7C 28
Hemington Av. N11 5J 31
Hemingway Cl. NW5 4E 64
Hemlock Cl. SW16 2G 155
Hemlock Ho. SE16 3A 104
Hemlock Rd. W12 7B 80
(not continuous)
Hemmen La. UB3: Hayes 6H 75
Hemming Cl. TW12: Hamp 1E 148
Hemmings Cl. DA14: Sidc 2B 144
Hemmings Mead KT19: Ewe 6J 163
Hemming St. E1 4G 85
Hempstead Cl. IG9: Buck H 2D 36
Hempstead Rd. E17 3F 51
Hemp Wlk. SE17 4D 102
Hemsby Rd. KT9: Chess 6F 163
Hemstal Rd. NW6 7J 63
Hemsted Rd. DA8: Erith 7K 109
Hemswell Dr. NW9 1A 44
Hemsworth Ct. N1 2E 84
Hemsworth St. N1 2E 84
Hemus Pl. SW3 6D 16 (5C 100)
Hen & Chicken Ct. EC4 1J 13 (6A 84)
(off Fleet St.)
Hen & Chickens Theatre 6B 66
(off St Paul's Rd.)
Henchman St. W12 6B 80
Hendale Av. NW4 3D 44
Henderson Cl. NW10 6J 61
Henderson Ct. N12 4E 30
Henderson Ct. NW3 5B 64
(off Fitzjohn's Av.)
Henderson Ct. SE14 6K 103
(off Myers La.)
Henderson Dr. NW8 3A 4 (4B 82)
Henderson Ho. RM10: Dag 3G 73
(off Kershaw Rd.)
Henderson Rd. CR0: C'don 6D 156
Henderson Rd. E7 6A 70
Henderson Rd. N9 1C 34
Henderson Rd. SW18 7C 118
Henderson Rd. UB4: Yead 3J 75
Hendfield Ct. SM6: W'gton 6F 167
Hendham Rd. SW17 2C 136
HENDON 4E 44
Hendon Av. N3 1G 45
Hendon Crematorium 1F 45
Hendon FC 4D 58
Hendon Golf Course 7K 29
Hendon Hall Ct. NW4 3F 45
Hendon Ho. NW4 5F 45
Hendon La. N3 3G 45
Hendon Leisure Cen. 7F 45
Hendon Lodge NW4 3D 44
Hendon Pk. Mans. NW4 5E 44
Hendon Pk. Row NW11 6H 45
Hendon Rd. N9 2B 34
Hendon St. SE10 3H 105
Hendon Ter. TW15: Ashf 6F 129
Hendon Way NW2 7F 45
Hendon Way NW4 6D 44
Hendre Ho. SE1 4E 102
(off Hendre Rd.)
Hendren Cl. UB6: G'frd 5H 59
Hendre Rd. SE1 4E 102
Hendrick Av. SW12 7D 118
Heneage La. EC3 7H 9 (6E 84)
Heneage Pl. EC3 1H 15 (6E 84)
Heneage St. E1 5K 9 (5F 85)
Henfield Cl. DA5: Bexl 6G 127
Henfield Cl. N19 1G 65
Henfield Rd. SW19 1H 153
Hengelo Gdns. CR4: Mitc 4B 154
Hengest Av. KT10: Surb 3A 162
Hengist Rd. DA8: Erith 7H 109
Hengist Rd. SE12 7K 123
Hengist Way BR2: Broml 4G 159
Hengist Way SM6: W'gton 7H 167
Hengrave Rd. SE23 6J 121
Hengrove Ct. DA5: Bexl 1E 144
Henham Ct. RM5: Col R 1J 55
Henley Av. SM3: Cheam 3G 165
Henley Cl. SE16 2J 103
(off St Marychurch St.)
Henley Cl. TW7: Isle 1K 113
Henley Cl. UB6: G'frd 2G 77
Henley Ct. N14 7B 22
Henley Ct. NW2 6F 63
Henley Cross SE3 3K 123
Henley Dr. KT2: King T 7B 134
Henley Dr. SE1 4F 103
Henley Gdns. HA5: Eastc 3K 39
Henley Gdns. RM6: Chad H 5E 54
Henley Hgts. N1 7K 65
(off Caledonian Rd.)
Henley Ho. E2 3K 9 (4F 85)
(off Swanfield St.)
Henley Prior N1 1G 7 (2K 83)
(off Affleck St.)
Henley Rd. E16 2D 106
Henley Rd. IG1: Ilf 4G 71
Henley Rd. N18 4K 33
Henley Rd. NW10 1E 80
Henley St. SW11 2E 118
Henley Way TW13: Hanw 5B 130
Henlow Pl. TW10: Ham 2D 132
HENLYS CORNER 4H 45
HENLYS RDBT. 2A 112
Hennel Cl. SE23 3J 139
Hennessey M. RM8: Dag 1E 72
Hennessy Ct. E10 6E 50
Hennessy Rd. N9 2D 34
Henniker Gdns. E6 3B 88
Henniker M. SW3 7A 16 (6B 100)
Henniker Point E15 5G 69
(off Leytonstone Rd.)
Henniker Rd. E15 5F 69
Henningham Rd. N17 1D 48
Henning St. SW11 1C 118
Henrietta Barnet Wlk. NW11 6J 45
Henrietta Cl. SE8 6C 104
Henrietta Ct. TW1: Twick 7C 114
(off Richmond Rd.)
Henrietta Gdns. N21 1F 33
Henrietta Ho. N15 6E 48
(off St Ann's Rd.)
Henrietta Ho. W6 5E 98
(off Queen Caroline St.)
Henrietta M. WC1 3F 7 (4J 83)
Henrietta Pl. W1 1J 11 (6F 83)
Henrietta St. WC2 2F 13 (7J 83)
Henriques St. E1 6G 85
Henry Addlington Cl. E6 5F 89
Henry Chester Bldg. SW15 2E 116
Henry Cl. EN2: Enf 1K 23
Henry Cooper Way SE9 3B 142
Henry Ct. HA7: Stan 7J 27
Henry Darlot Dr. NW7 6A 30
Henry Dent Cl. SE5 3D 120
Henry Dickens Ct. W11 7F 81
Henry Doulton Dr. SW17 4E 136
Henry Hatch Ct. SM2: Sutt 7A 166
Henry Ho. SE1 5K 13 (1A 102)
Henry Ho. SW8 7J 101
(off Wyvil Rd.)
Henry Hudson Apts. SE10 5G 105
(off Banning St.)
Henry Jackson Rd. SW15 3F 117
Henry Macaulay Av. KT2: King T 1D 150
Henry Moore Ct. SW3 6C 16 (5C 100)
Henry Peters Dr. TW11: Tedd 5J 131
(off Somerset Gdns.)
Henry Purcell Ho. E16 1K 105
(off Evelyn Rd.)
Henry Rd. E6 2C 88
Henry Rd. EN4: E Barn 5G 21
Henry Rd. N4 1C 66
Henry Rd. SW9 1A 120
Henrys Av. IG8: Wfd G 5C 36
Henryson Rd. SE4 5C 122
Henry St. BR1: Broml 1K 159
Henry's Wlk. IG6: Ilf 1H 53
Henry Tate M. SW16 5K 137
Henry Tudor Ct. SE9 7G 125
Henry Wise Ho. SW1 4B 18 (4G 101)
(off Vauxhall Bri. Rd.)
Hensford Gdns. SE26 4H 139
Henshall Point E3 3D 86
(off Bromley High St.)
Henshall St. N1 6D 66
Henshawe Rd. RM8: Dag 3D 72
Henshaw St. SE17 4D 102
Henslowe Rd. SE22 5G 121
Henslow Ho. SE15 7G 103
(off Peckham Pk. Rd.)
Henson Av. NW2 5E 62
Henson Cl. BR6: Farnb 2F 173
Henson Path HA3: Kenton 3D 42
Henson Pl. UB5: N'olt 1A 76
Henson Rd. RM8: Dag 1E 72
Henstridge Pl. NW8 1C 82
Henty Cl. SW11 7C 100
Henty Wlk. SW15 5D 116
Henville Rd. BR1: Broml 1K 159
Henwick Rd. SE9 3B 124
Henwood Side IG8: Wfd G 6J 37
Hepburn Gdns. BR2: Hayes 1G 171

Hepburn M. – Highridge Pl.

Hepburn M. SW11 5D 118
Hepburn Pl. W3 7H 79
Hepdon M. SW17 5B 136
Hepple Cl. TW7: Isle 2B 114
Hepplestone Cl. SW15 6D 116
Hepscott Rd. E9 6C 68
Hepworth Ct. N1 1B 84
(off Gaskin St.)
Hepworth Ct. NW3 5C 64
Hepworth Ct. SM3: Sutt 1J 165
Hepworth Ct. SW1 6J 17 (5F 101)
Hepworth Gdns. IG11: Bark 5A 72
Hepworth Rd. SW16 7J 137
Hepworth Way KT12: Walt T 7H 147
Hera Av. EN5: Barn 5C 20
Heracles NW9 1B 44
(off Five Acre)
Hera Ct. E14 4C 104
(off Homer Dr.)
Herald Gdns. SM6: W'gton 2F 167
Herald's Pl. SE11 3K 19 (4B 102)
Herald St. E2 4H 85
Herbal Hill EC1 4K 7 (4A 84)
Herbal Hill Gdns. EC1 4K 7 (4A 84)
(off Herbal Hill)
Herbal Pl. EC1 4K 7 (4A 84)
(off Herbal Hill)
Herbert Ct. KT5: Surb 6F 151
(off Fulmar Cl.)
Herbert Cres. SW1 1F 17 (3D 100)
Herbert Gdns. NW10 2D 80
Herbert Gdns. RM6: Chad H 7D 54
Herbert Gdns. W4 6H 97
Herbert Ho. E1 7J 9 (6F 85)
(off Old Castle St.)
Herbert M. SW2 6A 120
Herbert Morrison Ho. SW6 6H 99
(off Clem Attlee Ct.)
Herbert Pl. SE18 6F 107
Herbert Pl. TW7: Isle 2H 113
Herbert Rd. BR2: Broml 5B 160
Herbert Rd. DA7: Bex 2E 126
Herbert Rd. E12 4C 70
Herbert Rd. E17 7B 50
Herbert Rd. IG3: Ilf 2J 71
Herbert Rd. KT1: King T 3F 151
Herbert Rd. N11 7D 32
Herbert Rd. N15 5F 49
Herbert Rd. NW9 6C 44
Herbert Rd. SE18 7E 106
(not continuous)
Herbert Rd. SW19 7H 135
(not continuous)
Herbert Rd. UB1: S'hall 1D 94
Herbert St. E13 2J 87
Herbert St. NW5 6E 64
Herbrand Est. WC1 3E 6 (4J 83)
Herbrand St. WC1 3E 6 (4J 83)
Hercies Rd. UB10: Hil 7B 56
Hercules Ct. SE14 6A 104
Hercules Ho. E14 6G 87
Hercules Pl. N7 3J 65
(not continuous)
Hercules Rd. SE1 2H 19 (3K 101)
Hercules St. N7 3J 65
Hercules Wharf E14 7G 87
(off Orchard Pl.)
Hercules Yd. N7 3J 65
Here E. E20 5C 68
Hereford Av. EN4: E Barn 1J 31
Hereford Bldgs. SW3 7B 16 (6B 100)
(off Old Church St.)
Hereford Ct. HA1: Harr 4J 41
Hereford Ct. SM2: Sutt 7J 165
Hereford Ct. W7 5K 77
(off Copley Cl.)
Hereford Gdns. HA5: Pinn 5C 40
Hereford Gdns. IG1: Ilf 7C 52
Hereford Gdns. SE13 5G 123
Hereford Gdns. TW2: Twick 1G 131
Hereford Ho. N18 5C 34
(off Cameron Cl.)
Hereford Ho. NW6 2J 81
(off Carlton Vale)
Hereford Ho. SW10 7K 99
(off Fulham Rd.)
Hereford Ho. SW3 1D 16 (3C 100)
(off Ovington Gdns.)
Hereford Mans. W2 6J 81
(off Hereford Rd.)
Hereford M. W2 6J 81
Hereford Pl. SE14 7B 104
Hereford Retreat SE15 7G 103
Hereford Rd. E11 5K 51
Hereford Rd. E3 2B 86
Hereford Rd. TW13: Felt 1A 130
Hereford Rd. W2 6J 81
Hereford Rd. W3 7H 79
Hereford Rd. W5 3C 96
Hereford Sq. SW7 4A 100
Hereford St. E2 4G 85
Hereford Way KT9: Chess 5C 162
Herent Dr. IG5: Ilf 4C 52
Herent Gdns. IG5: Ilf 4D 52
Hereward Gdns. N13 5F 33
Hereward Rd. SW17 4D 136
Herga Ct. HA1: Harr 3J 59
Herga Rd. HA3: W'stone 4K 41
Heriot Av. E4 2H 35
Heriot Rd. NW4 5E 44
Heriots Cl. HA7: Stan 4F 27
Heritage Av. NW9 3B 44
Heritage Cl. SW9 3B 120
Heritage Cl. TW16: Sun 1J 147
Heritage Ct. SE8 5K 103
Heritage Hill BR2: Kes 5A 172
Heritage La. NW6 6J 63
Heritage Pl. SW18 1A 136
Heritage Pl. TW8: Bford 5F 97
(off Heritage Wlk.)
Heritage Vw. HA1: Harr 3K 59
Heritage Wlk. TW8: Bford 5F 97
(off Kew Bri. Rd.)
Herlwyn Av. HA4: Ruis 2G 57
Herlwyn Gdns. SW17 4D 136
Her Majesty's Theatre 4C 12 (1H 101)
(off Haymarket)
Herm Cl. TW7: Isle 7G 95
Hermes Cl. EN5: Barn 5C 20
Hermes Cl. W9 4J 81
Hermes Ct. SW2 6K 119
Hermes Ct. SW9 1A 120
(off Southey Rd.)
Hermes St. N1 1J 7 (2A 84)
Hermes Wlk. UB5: N'olt 2E 76
Herm Ho. EN3: Enf W 1E 24
Herm Ho. N1 6C 66
(off Clifton Rd.)
Hermiston Av. N8 5J 47
Hermitage, The KT1: King T 4D 150
Hermitage, The SE13 2E 122
Hermitage, The SE23 1J 139
Hermitage, The SW13 1B 116
Hermitage, The TW10: Rich 5E 114
Hermitage, The TW13: Felt 3H 129
Hermitage, The UB8: Uxb 6A 56
Hermitage Basin 1G 103
(off Cromwell Cl.)
Hermitage Cl. E18 4H 51
Hermitage Cl. EN2: Enf 2G 23
Hermitage Cl. KT10: Clay 6A 162
Hermitage Cl. SE2 3C 108
Hermitage Cl. TW17: Shep 4C 146
Hermitage Ct. E1 1G 103
(off Knighten St.)
Hermitage Ct. E18 4J 51
Hermitage Ct. NW2 3J 63
Hermitage Gdns. NW2 3J 63
Hermitage Gdns. SE19 7C 138
Hermitage Ho. N1 2B 84
(off Gerrard Rd.)
Hermitage La. CR0: C'don 7G 157
Hermitage La. N18 5J 33
Hermitage La. NW2 3J 63
Hermitage La. SE25 6G 157
Hermitage La. SW16 7K 137
Hermitage Moorings E1 1G 103
Hermitage Path SW16 1J 155
Hermitage Rd. N15 6D 48
Hermitage Rd. N4 7B 48
Hermitage Rd. SE19 7C 138
Hermitage Row E8 5G 67
Hermitage St. W2 6A 4 (5B 82)
Hermitage Vs. SW6 6J 99
(off Lillie Rd.)
Hermitage Wlk. E18 4H 51
Hermitage Wall E1 1G 103
Hermitage Waterside E1 1G 103
(off Thomas More St.)
Hermitage Way HA7: Stan 1A 42
Hermit Pl. NW6 1K 81
Hermit Rd. E16 5H 87
Hermit St. EC1 1A 8 (3B 84)
Hermon Gro. UB3: Hayes 1J 93
Hermon Hill E11 5J 51
Hermon Hill E18 4K 51
Herndon Rd. SW18 5A 118
Herne Cl. NW10 5K 61
Herne Cl. UB3: Hayes 6H 75
Herne Ct. WD23: Bush 1C 26
Herne Ct. WD23: Bush 1B 26
Herne Hill SE24 6C 120
HERNE HILL 5C 120
Herne Hill Ho. SE24 6B 120
(off Railton Rd.)
Herne Hill Rd. SE24 3C 120
Herne Hill Velodrome 6D 120
Herne M. N18 4B 34
Herne Pl. SE24 5B 120
Herne Rd. KT6: Surb 2D 162
Heron Cl. E17 2B 50
Heron Cl. IG9: Buck H 1D 36
Heron Cl. NW10 6A 62
Heron Cl. SM1: Sutt 5H 165
Heron Ct. BR2: Broml 4A 160
Heron Ct. E14 3E 104
(off New Union Cl.)
Heron Ct. HA4: Ruis 2F 57
Heron Ct. KT1: King T 3E 150
Heron Ct. NW9 2A 44
Heron Ct. TW19: Stanw 1A 128
Heron Cres. DA14: Sidc 3J 143
Herondale Av. SW18 1B 136
Heron Dr. N4 2C 66
Herongate N1 1C 84
(off Ridgewell Cl.)
Herongate Rd. E12 2A 70
Heron Hill DA17: Belv 5F 109
Heron Ho. DA14: Sidc 3B 144
Heron Ho. E3 1B 86
(off Sycamore Av.)
Heron Ho. E6 7C 70
Heron Ho. NW8 1C 4 (2C 82)
(off Newcourt St.)
Heron Ho. SW11 7C 100
(off Searles Cl.)
Heron Ho. W13 4A 78
Heron Ind. Est. E15 2D 86
Heron Mead EN3: Enf L 1H 25
Heron M. IG1: Ilf 2F 71
Heron Pl. E16 1A 106
(off Bramwell Way)
Heron Pl. SE16 1A 104
Heron Pl. W1 7H 5 (6E 82)
(off Thayer St.)
Heron Quay E14 1C 104
Heron Rd. CR0: C'don 2E 168
Heron Rd. SE24 4C 120
Heron Rd. TW1: Twick 4A 114
Herons, The E11 6H 51
Heronsforde W13 6C 78
Heronsgate HA8: Edg 5B 28
Heron's Lea N6 6D 46
Heronslea Dr. HA7: Stan 5K 27
Heron's Pl. TW7: Isle 3B 114
Heron Sq. TW9: Rich 5D 114
Herons Ri. EN4: E Barn 4H 21
Heron Tower 7G 9 (6E 84)
(off Bishopsgate)
Heron Trad. Est. W3 5H 79
Heron Vw. TW8: Bford 7C 96
(off Commerce Rd.)
Heron Way SM6: W'gton 7H 167
Heron Way TW14: Felt 4J 111
Heronway IG8: Wfd G 4F 37
Herrick Ct. W3 3J 97
(off Bollo Bri. Rd.)
Herrick Ho. N16 4D 66
(off Howard Rd.)
Herrick Ho. SE5 7D 102
(off Elmington Est.)
Herrick Rd. N5 3C 66
Herrick St. SW1 4D 18 (4H 101)
Herries St. W10 2G 81
Herringham Rd. SE7 3A 106
Herron Ct. BR2: Broml 4H 159
Herrongate Cl. EN1: Enf 2A 24
Hersant Cl. NW10 1C 80
Herschell M. SE5 3C 120
Herschell Rd. SE23 7A 122
Hersham Cl. SW15 7C 116
Hershell Ct. SW14 4H 115
Hertford Av. SW14 5K 115
Hertford Cl. EN4: Cockf 3G 21
Hertford Ct. E6 3D 88
Hertford Ct. N13 3F 33
Hertford Grove RM7: Mawney 1G 55
Hertford Ho. UB5: N'olt 4D 76
Hertford Lock Ho. E3 1B 86
(off Parnell Rd.)
Hertford Pl. W1 4A 6 (4G 83)
Hertford Rd. EN3: Enf H 3D 24
Hertford Rd. EN3: Enf W 3D 24
Hertford Rd. EN4: Cockf 3F 21
Hertford Rd. IG11: Bark 7E 70
Hertford Rd. IG2: Ilf 6J 53
Hertford Rd. N1 1E 84
(not continuous)
Hertford Rd. N2 3C 46
Hertford Rd. N9 2C 34
Hertford St. W1 5J 11 (1F 101)
Hertford Wlk. DA17: Belv 5G 109
Hertford Way CR4: Mitc 4J 155
Hertford Wharf N1 1E 84
(off Hertford Rd.)
Hertslet Rd. N7 3K 65
Hertsmere Rd. E14 1C 104
Hertswood Ct. EN5: Barn 4B 20
Hervey Cl. N3 1J 45
Hervey Pk. Rd. E17 4A 50
Hervey Rd. SE3 1K 123
Hervey Way N3 1J 45
Hesa Rd. UB3: Hayes 6J 75
Hesewall Cl. SW4 2G 119
Hesketh Pl. W11 7G 81
Hesketh Rd. E7 3J 69
Heslop Rd. SW12 1D 136
Hesper M. SW5 4K 99
Hesperus Cres. E14 4D 104
Hessel Rd. W13 2A 96
Hessel St. E1 6H 85
Hestercombe Av. SW6 2G 117
Hesterman Way CR0: Wadd 1K 167
Hester Rd. N18 5B 34
Hester Rd. SW11 7C 100
Hester Ter. TW9: Rich 3G 115
Hestia Ho. SE1 7G 15 (2E 102)
(off City Wlk.)
HESTON 7E 94
Heston Av. TW5: Hest 6C 94
Heston Cen., The TW5: Cran 5A 94
Heston Community Sports Hall 7E 94
Heston Grange TW5: Hest 6D 94
Heston Grange La. TW5: Hest 6D 94
Heston Ho. SE8 1C 122
Heston Ind. Mall TW5: Hest 7D 94
Heston Phoenix Distribution Pk.
TW5: Hest 6A 94
Heston Pool 6D 94
Heston Rd. TW5: Hest 6E 94
HESTON SERVICE AREA 6B 94
Heston St. SE14 1C 122
Hetherington Rd. SW4 4J 119
Hetherington Rd. TW17: Shep 2E 146
Hetherington Way UB10: Ick 4A 56
Hethpool Ho. W2 4A 4 (4B 82)
(off Hall Pl.)
Hetley Gdns. SE19 7F 139
Hetley Rd. W12 1D 98
Heton Gdns. NW4 4D 44
Hevelius Cl. SE10 5H 105
Hever Cft. SE9 4E 142
Hever Gdns. BR1: Broml 2E 160
Heverham Rd. SE18 4J 107
Hever Ho. SE15 6K 103
(off Lovelinch Cl.)
Hever Pl. KT8: E Mos 3G 149
Heversham Ho. SE15 6J 103
Heversham Rd. DA7: Bex 2G 127
Hevingham Dr. RM6: Chad H 5C 54
Hevingham Vw. SE26 5H 139
Hewens Rd. UB10: Hil 4E 74
Hewens Rd. UB4: Hil 4E 74
Hewer St. W10 5F 81
Hewett Cl. HA7: Stan 4G 27
Hewett Rd. RM8: Dag 5D 72
Hewetts Quay IG11: Bark 1F 89
Hewett St. EC2 4H 9 (4E 84)
Hewish Rd. N18 4K 33
Hewison St. E3 2B 86
Hewitt Av. N22 2B 48
Hewitt Cl. CR0: C'don 3C 170
Hewitt Rd. N8 5A 48
Hewlett Ho. SW8 7F 101
(off Havelock Ter.)
Hewlett Rd. E3 2A 86
Hexagon, The N6 1D 64
Hexagon Bus. Cen. UB4: Yead 7A 76
Hexal Rd. SE6 3G 141
Hexham Gdns. TW7: Isle 7A 96
Hexham Gdns. UB5: N'olt 5D 58
Hexham Rd. EN5: New Bar 4E 20
Hexham Rd. SE27 2C 138
Hexham Rd. SM4: Mord 1K 165
Heybourne Cres. NW9 1A 44
Heybourne Rd. N17 7C 34
Heybridge NW1 6F 65
(off Lewis St.)
Heybridge Av. SW16 7J 137
Heybridge Dr. IG6: Ilf 2H 53
Heybridge Way E10 7A 50
Heydon Ct. BR4: W W'ck 2G 171
(off Deer Pk. Way)
Heydon Ho. SE14 1J 121
(off Kender St.)
Heyford Av. SW20 3H 153
Heyford Av. SW8 7J 101
Heyford Rd. CR4: Mitc 2C 154
Heyford Ter. SW8 7J 101
(off Old Sth. Lambeth Rd.)
Heygate St. SE17 4C 102
Heylyn Sq. E3 3B 86
Heynes Rd. RM8: Dag 4C 72
Heysham La. NW3 3K 63
Heysham Rd. N15 6D 48
Heythorp St. SW18 1H 135
Heythrop Dr. UB10: Ick 4B 56
Heywood Av. NW9 1A 44
Heywood Ct. HA7: Stan 5H 27
Heywood Ho. SE14 6K 103
(off Myers La.)
Heyworth Rd. E15 5H 69
Heyworth Rd. E5 4H 67
Hibbert Ho. E14 3C 104
(off Tiller Rd.)
Hibbert Rd. E17 7B 50
Hibbert Rd. HA3: W'stone 2K 41
Hibbert St. SW11 3B 118
Hibernia Gdns. TW3: Houn 4E 112
Hibernia Point SE2 2D 108
(off Wolvercote Rd.)
Hibernia Rd. TW3: Houn 4E 112
Hibiscus Cl. HA8: Edg 4D 28
Hibiscus Ho. E17 3D 50
Hibiscus Ho. TW13: Felt 1J 129
Hibiscus Lodge E15 7G 69
(off Glenavon Rd.)
Hichisson Rd. SE15 5J 121
Hicken Rd. SW2 5K 119
Hickes Ho. NW6 7B 64
Hickey's Almshouses TW9: Rich 4F 115
Hickin Cl. SE7 4B 106
Hickin St. E14 3E 104
Hickleton NW1 1G 83
(off Camden St.)
Hickling Ho. SE16 3H 103
(off Slippers Pl.)
Hickling Rd. IG1: Ilf 5F 71
Hickman Av. E4 6K 35
Hickman Cl. E16 5B 88
Hickman Rd. RM6: Chad H 7C 54
Hickman Wlk. SE18 5E 106
(off Brumwell Av.)
Hickmore Wlk. SW4 3H 119
Hickory Cl. N9 7B 24
Hicks Av. UB6: G'frd 3H 77
Hicks Bolton Ho. NW6 2H 81
(off Denmark Ho.)
Hicks Cl. SW11 3C 118
Hicks Ct. RM10: Dag 3H 73
Hicks Gallery 5J 135
Hicks Ho. SE16 3G 103
(off Spa Rd.)
Hicks St. SE8 5A 104
Hidcote Apts. SW11 4C 118
(off Danvers Av.)
Hidcote Gdns. SW20 3D 152
Hidden Cl. KT8: W Mole 4G 149
Hide E6 6E 88
Hide Pl. SW1 4C 18 (4H 101)
Hider Ct. SE3 7A 106
Hide Rd. HA1: Harr 4G 41
Hides St. N7 6K 65
Hide Twr. SW1 4C 18 (4H 101)
(off Regency St.)
Hierro Ct. E1 5A 86
(off Ocean Est.)
Higgins Ho. N1 1E 84
(off Colville Est.)
Higginson Ho. NW3 7D 64
(off Fellows Rd.)
Higgins Wlk. TW12: Hamp 6C 130
(off Abbott Cl.)
Higgs Ind. Est. SE24 3B 120
High Acres EN2: Enf 3G 23
HIGHAM HILL 2A 50
Higham Hill Rd. E17 1A 50
Higham M. UB5: N'olt 4D 76
Higham Path E17 3A 50
Higham Pl. E17 3A 50
Higham Rd. IG8: Wfd G 6D 36
Higham Rd. N17 3D 48
Highams, The E17 1E 50
Highams Ct. E4 3K 35
Highams Lodge Bus. Cen. E17 3K 49
HIGHAMS PARK 6A 36
Higham Sta. Av. E4 6H 35
Higham St. E17 3A 50
High Ashton KT2: King T 7H 133
Highbanks Cl. DA16: Well 7B 108
Highbanks Rd. HA5: Hat E 6A 26
Highbank Way N8 6A 48
HIGH BARNET 2A 20
Highbarrow Rd. CR0: C'don 1G 169
High Beech CR2: S Croy 7E 168
High Beech N21 6E 22
High Beeches DA14: Sidc 5E 144
High Birch Ct. EN4: E Barn 4H 21
(off Park Rd.)
High Bri. SE10 5F 105
Highbridge Ct. SE14 7J 103
(off Farrow La.)
Highbridge Rd. IG11: Bark 1F 89
High Bri. Wharf SE10 5F 105
(off High Bri.)
Highbrook Rd. SE3 3B 124
High Broom Cres. BR4: W W'ck 7D 158
HIGHBURY 4B 66
Highbury Av. CR7: Thor H 2A 156
Highbury Cl. BR4: W W'ck 2D 170
Highbury Cl. KT3: N Mald 4J 151
HIGHBURY CORNER 6B 66
Highbury Cres. N5 5A 66
Highbury Est. N5 5C 66
Highbury Gdns. IG3: Ilf 2J 71
Highbury Gdns. N7 5A 66
Highbury Grange N5 4C 66
Highbury Gro. N5 5B 66
Highbury Gro. Ct. N5 6C 66
Highbury Hill N5 3A 66
Highbury Leisure Cen. 6B 66
Highbury Mans. N1 7B 66
(off Upper St.)
Highbury New Pk. N5 5C 66
Highbury Pk. N5 3B 66
Highbury Pl. N5 6B 66
Highbury Quad. N5 3B 66
Highbury Rd. SW19 5G 135
Highbury Sq. N14 1B 32
Highbury Stadium Sq. N5 3B 66
Highbury Sta. Rd. N1 6A 66
Highbury Ter. N5 5B 66
Highbury Ter. M. N5 5B 66
High Cedar Dr. SW20 7E 134
Highclere Rd. KT3: N Mald 3K 151
Highclere St. SE26 4A 140
Highcliffe W13 5B 78
(off Clivedon Ct.)
Highcliffe Dr. SW15 6B 116
Highcliffe Gdns. IG4: Ilf 5C 52
Highcombe SE7 6K 105
Highcombe Cl. SE9 1B 142
High Coombe Pl. KT2: King T 6K 133
Highcroft NW9 5A 44
Highcroft Av. HA0: Wemb 7G 61
Highcroft Est. N19 7J 47
Highcroft Gdns. NW11 6H 45
Highcroft Rd. N19 7J 47
High Cross Cen., The N15 4G 49
High Cross Rd. N17 3G 49
Highcross Way SW15 1C 134
Highdaun Dr. SW16 4K 155
Highdown KT4: Wor Pk 2A 164
Highdown Rd. SW15 6D 116
High Dr. KT3: N Mald 1J 161
High Elms IG8: Wfd G 5D 36
High Elms Country Pk. 7H 173
High Elms Golf Course 7G 173
Highfield WD23: B Hea 2D 26
Highfield Av. BR6: Chels 5K 173
Highfield Av. DA8: Erith 6H 109
Highfield Av. HA5: Pinn 5D 40
Highfield Av. HA9: Wemb 3F 61
Highfield Av. NW11 7F 45
Highfield Av. NW9 5J 43
Highfield Av. UB6: G'frd 5J 59
Highfield Cl. HA6: Nwood 1G 39
Highfield Cl. KT6: Surb 1C 162
Highfield Cl. N22 1A 48
Highfield Cl. NW9 5J 43
Highfield Cl. SE13 6F 123
Highfield Ct. N14 6B 22
Highfield Ct. NW11 6G 45
Highfield Cres. HA6: Nwood 1G 39
Highfield Dr. BR2: Broml 4G 159
Highfield Dr. BR4: W W'ck 2D 170
Highfield Dr. KT19: Ewe 6B 164
Highfield Dr. UB10: Ick 4A 56
Highfield Gdns. NW11 6G 45
Highfield Hill SE19 7D 138
Highfield M. NW6 7K 63
(off Compayne Gdns.)
Highfield Rd. BR1: Broml 4D 160
Highfield Rd. BR7: Chst 3K 161
Highfield Rd. DA6: Bex 5F 127
Highfield Rd. HA6: Nwood 1G 39
Highfield Rd. IG8: Wfd G 7H 37
Highfield Rd. KT12: Walt T 7J 147
Highfield Rd. KT5: Surb 7J 151
Highfield Rd. N21 2G 33
Highfield Rd. NW11 6G 45
Highfield Rd. SM1: Sutt 5C 166
Highfield Rd. TW13: Felt 2J 129
Highfield Rd. TW16: Sun 5H 147
Highfield Rd. TW7: Isle 1K 113
Highfield Rd. W3 5H 79
Highfields SM1: Sutt 2J 165
Highfields Gro. N6 1D 64
High Foleys KT10: Clay 7B 162
High Gables BR2: Broml 2G 159
HIGHGATE 6E 46
Highgate Av. N6 7F 47
Highgate Cemetery 1E 64
Highgate Cl. N6 7E 46
Highgate Edge N2 5C 46
Highgate Golf Course 6C 46
Highgate Hgts. N6 6G 47
Highgate High St. N6 1E 64
Highgate Hill N19 1F 65
Highgate Hill N6 1F 65
Highgate Ho. SE26 3G 139
Highgate Rd. NW5 3E 64
Highgate Spinney N8 6H 47
Highgate Wlk. SE23 2J 139
Highgate W. Hill N6 1E 64
High Gro. BR1: Broml 1B 160
High Gro. SE18 7H 107
Highgrove Cl. BR7: Chst 1C 160
Highgrove Cl. N11 5K 31
Highgrove Ct. BR3: Beck 7C 140
Highgrove Ct. SM1: Sutt 6J 165
Highgrove Ho. HA4: Ruis 6J 39
Highgrove M. SM5: Cars 3D 166
Highgrove Pool & Fitness Cen. 6J 39
Highgrove Rd. RM8: Dag 5C 72
Highgrove Ter. E4 2A 36
Highgrove Way HA4: Ruis 6J 39
High Hill Est. E5 1H 67
High Hill Ferry E5 1H 67
High Holborn WC1 7E 6 (6J 83)
High Ho. M. N16 2E 66
Highland Av. RM10: Dag 3J 73
Highland Av. W7 6J 77
Highland Cotts. SM6: W'gton 4G 167
Highland Ct. BR1: Broml 1H 159
Highland Ct. E18 1K 51
Highland Cft. BR3: Beck 5D 140
Highland Dr. WD23: Bush 1A 26
Highland Pk. TW13: Felt 4H 129
Highland Rd. BR1: Broml 1H 159
Highland Rd. BR2: Broml 1H 159
Highland Rd. DA6: Bex 5G 127
Highland Rd. HA6: Nwood 2H 39
Highland Rd. SE19 6E 138
Highlands N20 2G 31
Highlands, The EN5: New Bar 4D 20
Highlands, The HA8: Edg 2H 43
Highlands Av. N21 5E 22
Highlands Av. W3 7J 79
Highlands Cl. N4 7J 47
Highlands Cl. TW3: Houn 1F 113
Highlands Ct. SE19 6E 138
Highlands Gdns. IG1: Ilf 1D 70
Highlands Heath SW15 7E 116
Highlands Rd. EN5: New Bar 5D 20
Highlands St. E15 2D 86
HIGHLANDS VILLAGE 5E 22
Highland Ter. SE13 3D 122
(off Algernon Rd.)
Highland Vw. Pk. Homes UB7: W Dray 1D 174
High La. W7 5H 77
Highlawn Hall HA1: Harr 3J 59
Highlea Cl. NW9 7F 29
High Level Dr. SE26 4G 139
Highlever Rd. W10 5E 80
High Mead BR4: W W'ck 2F 171
High Mead HA1: Harr 5J 41
Highmead SE18 7K 107
Highmead Cres. HA0: Wemb 7F 61
High Mdw. Cl. HA5: Eastc 4A 40
Highmeadow Cres. NW9 5K 43
High Meads Rd. E16 6B 88
Highmore Rd. SE3 7G 105
High Mt. NW4 6C 44
High Oaks EN2: Enf 1E 22
High Pde., The SW16 3J 137
High Pk. Av. TW9: Kew 1G 115
High Pk. Rd. TW9: Kew 1G 115
High Path SW19 1K 153
High Point N6 7E 46
High Point SE9 3F 143
High Ridge N10 1F 47
Highridge Pl. EN2: Enf 1E 22
(off Oak Av.)

Hogarth Ind. Est. – Hood Ho.

Hogarth Ind. Est. NW10 4C 80
Hogarth La. W4 6A 98
Hogarth Pl. SW5 4K 99
(off Hogarth Rd.)
Hogarth Rd. HA8: Edg 2G 43
Hogarth Rd. RM8: Dag 5B 72
Hogarth Rd. SW5 4K 99
HOGARTH RDBT. 6A 98
Hogarth's House 6A 98
(off Hogarth La.)
Hogarth Way TW12: Hamp 1G 149
Hog Hill Rd. RM5: Col R 1F 55
Hogsmill Ho. KT1: King T 3F 151
(off Vineyard Cl.)
Hogsmill La. KT1: King T 3F 151
Hogsmill Local Nature Reserve 5H 163
Hogsmill Wlk. KT1: King T 3E 150
(off Penrhyn Rd.)
Hogsmill Way KT19: Ewe 5J 163
Holbeach Cl. NW9 1A 44
Holbeach Gdns. DA15: Sidc 6J 125
Holbeach M. SW12 1F 137
Holbeach Rd. SE6 7C 122
Holbeck Rd. W13 1B 96
Holbeck Row SE15 7G 103
Holbein Ho. SW1 5G 17 (5E 100)
(off Holbein M.)
Holbein M. SW1 5G 17 (5E 100)
Holbein Pl. SW1 4G 17 (4E 100)
Holbein Ter. RM8: Dag 4C 72
(off Marlborough Rd.)
Holberton Gdns. NW10 3D 80
Holborn EC1 6J 7 (5A 84)
HOLBORN 7F 7 (6J 83)
Holborn Bars EC1 6J 7 (5A 84)
(off Holborn)
Holborn Cir. EC1 6K 7 (5A 84)
Holborn Cl. NW7 4G 29
Holborn Ho. W12 6D 80
Holborn Pl. WC1 6G 7 (5K 83)
Holborn Rd. E13 4K 87
Holborn Viaduct EC1 6A 8 (5B 84)
Holborn Way CR4: Mitc 2D 154
Holbrook Cl. EN1: Enf 1A 24
Holbrook Cl. N19 1F 65
Holbrooke Ct. N7 4J 65
Holbrooke Pl. TW10: Rich 5D 114
Holbrook Ho. BR7: Chst 1H 161
Holbrook La. BR7: Chst 7H 143
Holbrook Rd. E15 2H 87
Holbrook Way BR2: Broml 6D 160
Holburne Cl. SE3 1A 124
Holburne Gdns. SE3 1B 124
Holburne Rd. SE3 1A 124
Holcombe Hill NW7 3H 29
Holcombe Ho. SW9 3J 119
(off Landor Rd.)
Holcombe Pl. SE4 3A 122
(off St Asaph Rd.)
Holcombe Rd. IG1: Ilf 7E 52
Holcombe Rd. N17 3F 49
Holcombe St. W6 4D 98
Holcote Cl. DA17: Belv 3E 108
Holcroft Ct. W1 5A 6 (5G 83)
(off Clipstone St.)
Holcroft Ho. SW11 3B 118
Holcroft Rd. E9 7J 67
Holden Av. N12 5E 30
Holden Av. NW9 1J 61
Holdenby Rd. SE4 5A 122
Holden Cl. RM8: Dag 3B 72
Holden Ho. N1 1C 84
(off Prebend St.)
Holden Ho. SE8 7C 104
Holdenhurst Av. N12 7F 31
Holden Point E15 6F 69
(off Waddington St.)
Holden Rd. N12 5E 30
Holden St. SW11 2E 118
Holder Cl. N3 7E 30
Holdernesse Cl. TW7: Isle 1A 114
Holdernesse Rd. SW17 3D 136
Holderness Ho. SE5 3E 120
Holderness Way SE27 5B 138
HOLDERS HILL 2F 45
Holder's Hill Av. NW4 2F 45
HOLDERS HILL CIR. 7B 30
Holders Hill Cres. NW4 2F 45
Holders Hill Dr. NW4 3F 45
Holder's Hill Gdns. NW4 2G 45
Holders Hill Pde. NW7 1G 45
Holders Hill Rd. NW4 2F 45
Holders Hill Rd. NW7 1G 45
Holdron St. SE15 2H 121
Holford Ho. SE16 4H 103
(off Camilla Rd.)
Holford Ho. WC1 1H 7 (3K 83)
(off Gt. Percy St.)
Holford M. WC1 1J 7 (3A 84)
(off Cruikshank St.)
Holford Pl. WC1 1H 7 (3K 83)
Holford Rd. NW3 3A 64
Holford St. WC1 1H 7 (3K 83)
Holford Way SW15 6C 116
Holford Yd. WC1 1J 7 (2A 84)
(off Cruikshank St.)
Holgate Av. SW11 3B 118
Holgate Gdns. RM10: Dag 6G 73
Holgate Rd. RM10: Dag 5G 73
Holgate St. SE7 3B 106
Holinser Ter. W5 1D 96
Hollamby La. SE27 2B 138
Hollam Ho. N8 4K 47
Holland Av. SM2: Sutt 7J 165
Holland Av. SW20 1B 152
Holland Cl. BR2: Hayes 2H 171
Holland Cl. EN5: New Bar 7G 21
Holland Cl. HA7: Stan 5G 27
Holland Cl. RM7: Rom 5J 55
Holland Ct. E17 4E 50
(off Evelyn Rd.)
Holland Ct. KT6: Surb 7D 150
Holland Ct. NW7 6H 29
Holland Dr. SE23 3A 140
Holland Dwellings WC2 7F 7 (6J 83)
(off Newton St.)
Holland Gdns. SE9: Sidc 1H 143
Holland Gdns. TW8: Bford 6E 96
Holland Gdns. W14 3G 99
Hollandgreen Pl. W8 3J 99
Holland Gro. SW9 7A 102
Holland Ho. E4 4K 35
Holland Ho. NW10 2D 80
(off Holland Rd.)
Holland Pk. W11 1G 99
HOLLAND PARK 1H 99
Holland Pk. 2H 99
Holland Pk. Av. IG3: Ilf 6J 53
Holland Pk. Av. W11 2G 99
Holland Pk. Ct. W14 2G 99
(off Holland Pk. Gdns.)
Holland Pk. Gdns. W14 2G 99
Holland Pk. Mans. W14 1G 99
(off Holland Pk. Gdns.)
Holland Pk. M. W11 1G 99
Holland Pk. Rd. W14 3H 99
HOLLAND PARK RDBT. 2F 99
Holland Pk. Tennis Ground 1G 99
Holland Pk. Ter. W11 1G 99
(off Portland Rd.)
Holland Pk. Theatre (Open Air) 2H 99
Holland Pas. N1 1C 84
(off Basire St.)
Holland Pl. W8 2K 99
(off Kensington Chu. St.)
Holland Pl. Chambers W8 2K 99
(off Holland Pl.)
Holland Ri. Ho. SW9 7K 101
(off Clapham Rd.)
Holland Rd. E15 3G 87
Holland Rd. E6 1D 88
Holland Rd. HA0: Wemb 6D 60
Holland Rd. NW10 1C 80
Holland Rd. SE25 5G 157
Holland Rd. W14 2F 99
Hollands, The KT4: Wor Pk 1B 164
Hollands, The TW13: Hanw 4B 130
Holland St. SE1 4B 14 (1B 102)
Holland St. W8 2J 99
Holland Vs. Rd. W14 2G 99
Holland Wlk. W8 Kensington 1H 99
Holland Wlk. N19 Up. Holloway 1H 65
Holland Wlk. HA7: Stan 5F 27
Holland Wlk. N19 1H 65
(off Calverley Gro.)
Holland Way BR2: Hayes 2H 171
Hollar Rd. N16 3F 67
Hollen St. W1 7C 6 (6H 83)
Holles Cl. TW12: Hamp 6E 130
Holles Ho. SW9 2A 120
Holles St. W1 7K 5 (6F 83)
Holley Rd. W3 2A 98
Hollickwood Av. N12 6J 31
Holliday Sq. SW11 3B 118
(off Fowler Cl.)
Hollidge Way RM10: Dag 7H 73
Hollies, The E11 5J 51
(off New Wanstead)
Hollies, The HA3: W'stone 4A 42
Hollies, The N20 1G 31
Hollies Av. DA15: Sidc 2K 143
Hollies Cl. SW16 6A 138
Hollies Cl. TW1: Twick 2K 131
Hollies End NW7 5J 29
Hollies Rd. W5 4C 96
Hollies Way SW12 7E 118
Holligrave Rd. BR1: Broml 1J 159
Hollingbourne Av. DA7: Bex 1F 127
Hollingbourne Gdns. W13 5B 78
Hollingbourne Rd. SE24 5C 120
Hollingsworth Ct. KT6: Surb 7D 150
Hollingsworth Rd. CR0: C'don 6H 169
Hollington Ct. BR7: Chst 6F 143
Hollington Cres. KT3: N Mald 6B 152
Hollington Rd. E6 3D 88
Hollington Rd. N17 2G 49
Hollingworth Cl. KT8: W Mole 4D 148
Hollingworth Rd. BR5: Pet W 6F 161
Hollins Ho. N7 4J 65
Hollisfield WC1 2F 7 (3J 83)
(off Cromer St.)
Hollister Ho. NW6 3J 81
(off Kilburn Pk. Rd.)
Hollman Gdns. SW16 6B 138
Hollow, The IG8: Wfd G 4C 36
HOLLOWAY 3J 65
Holloway Cl. UB7: Harm 5A 92
Holloway Ho. NW2 3E 62
(off Stoll Cl.)
Holloway La. UB7: Harm 2E 174
Holloway La. UB7: W Dray 2E 174
Holloway Rd. E11 3F 69
Holloway Rd. E6 3D 88
Holloway Rd. N19 2H 65
Holloway Rd. N7 4K 65
Holloway St. TW3: Houn 3F 113
Hollowfield Wlk. UB5: N'olt 6C 58
Hollows, The TW8: Bford 6F 97
Holly Av. HA7: Stan 2E 42
Holly Av. KT12: Walt T 7B 148
Hollybank Cl. TW12: Hamp 5E 130
Hollyberry La. NW3 4A 64
Hollybrake Cl. BR7: Chst 7H 143
Hollybush Cl. E11 5J 51
Hollybush Cl. HA3: Hrw W 1J 41
Hollybush Gdns. E2 3H 85
Holly Bush Hill NW3 4A 64
Hollybush Hill E11 6H 51
Hollybush Ho. E2 3H 85
Holly Bush La. TW12: Hamp 7D 130
Hollybush Pl. E2 3H 85
Hollybush Rd. KT2: King T 5E 132
Holly Bush Steps NW3 4A 64
(off Holly Mt.)
Hollybush St. E13 3K 87
Holly Bush Va. NW3 4A 64
Hollybush Wlk. SW9 4B 120
Holly Cl. BR3: Beck 4E 158
Holly Cl. IG9: Buck H 3G 37
Holly Cl. KT19: Eps 7K 163
Holly Cl. SM6: W'gton 7F 167
Holly Cl. TW13: Hanw 5C 130
Holly Cl. TW16: Sun 3K 147
Holly Cott. M. UB8: Hil 5C 74
Holly Ct. DA14: Sidc 4B 144
(off Sidcup Hill)
Holly Ct. N15 4E 48
Holly Ct. SE10 3H 105
Holly Ct. SM2: Sutt 7J 165
Holly Cres. BR3: Beck 5B 158
Holly Cres. IG8: Wfd G 7A 36
Hollycroft Av. HA9: Wemb 2F 61
Hollycroft Av. NW3 3J 63
Hollycroft Cl. CR2: S Croy 5E 168
Hollycroft Cl. UB7: Sip 6C 92
Hollycroft Gdns. UB7: Sip 6C 92
Hollydale Cl. UB5: N'olt 4F 59
Hollydale Dr. BR2: Broml 3D 172
Hollydale Rd. SE15 1J 121
Hollydene BR2: Broml 1H 159
(off Beckenham La.)
Hollydene SE13 6F 123
Hollydene SE15 1H 121
Hollydown Way E11 3F 69
Holly Dr. E4 7J 25
Holly Farm Rd. UB2: S'hall 5C 94
Hollyfield Av. N11 5J 31
Hollyfield Rd. KT5: Surb 7F 151
Holly Gdns. DA7: Bex 4J 127
Holly Gdns. UB7: W Dray 2B 92
Holly Gro. HA5: Pinn 1C 40
Holly Gro. NW9 7J 43
Holly Gro. SE15 2F 121
Hollygrove WD23: Bush 1C 26
Hollygrove Cl. TW3: Houn 4D 112
Holly Hedge Ter. SE13 5F 123
Holly Hill N21 6E 22
Holly Hill NW3 4A 64
Holly Hill Rd. DA17: Belv 5H 109
Holly Hill Rd. DA17: Erith 5H 109
Holly Hill Rd. DA8: Erith 5J 109
Holly Ho. TW8: Bford 6C 96
Holly Ho. W10 4G 81
(off Hawthorn Wlk.)
Holly La. IG3: Ilf 2A 72
Holly Lodge HA1: Harr 5H 41
Holly Lodge W8 2J 99
(off Thornwood Gdns.)
Holly Lodge Gdns. N6 2E 64
Holly Lodge Mans. N6 2E 64
Hollymead SM5: Cars 3D 166
Holly M. SW10 6A 16 (5A 100)
Holly Mt. NW3 4A 64
Hollymount Cl. SE10 1E 122
Holly Pde. TW13: Felt 3H 129
(off High St.)
Holly Pk. N3 3H 45
Holly Pk. N4 7J 47
(not continuous)
Holly Pk. Est. N4 7K 47
Holly Pk. Gdns. N3 3J 45
Holly Pk. Rd. N11 5K 31
Holly Pk. Rd. W7 1K 95
Holly Pl. NW3 4A 64
(off Holly Berry La.)
Holly Rd. E11 7H 51
Holly Rd. TW1: Twick 1K 131
Holly Rd. TW12: Hamp H 6G 131
Holly Rd. TW3: Houn 4F 113
Holly Rd. W4 4K 97
Holly St. E8 7F 67
Holly Ter. N6 1E 64
Holly Tree Cl. SW19 1F 135
Holly Tree Cres. SM5: Cars 1D 166
Holly Tree Ho. SE4 3B 122
(off Brockley Rd.)
Hollytree Pde. DA14: Sidc 6C 144
(off Sidcup Hill)
Hollyview Cl. NW4 6C 44
Holly Village N6 2F 65
Holly Vs. W6 3D 98
(off Wellesley Av.)
Holly Wlk. EN2: Enf 3H 23
Holly Wlk. NW3 4A 64
Holly Way CR4: Mitc 4H 155
Hollywood Bowl Dagenham 1E 90
Hollywood Bowl Finchley 7G 31
Hollywood Bowl Surrey Quays 3K 103
Hollywood Bowl The O2 1G 105
Hollywood Bowl Tolworth 2H 163
Hollywood Ct. SW10 6A 100
(off Hollywood Rd.)
Hollywood Ct. W5 7F 79
Hollywood Gdns. UB4: Yead 6K 75
Hollywood M. SW10 6A 100
Hollywood Rd. E4 5F 35
Hollywood Rd. SW10 6A 100
Hollywood Way IG8: Wfd G 7A 36
Holman Ct. KT17: Ewe 7C 164
Holman Dr. UB2: S'hall 1H 95
Holman Ho. E2 3K 85
(off Roman Rd.)
Holman Hunt Ho. W6 5G 99
(off Field Rd.)
Holman Rd. KT19: Ewe 5J 163
Holman Rd. SW11 2B 118
Holmbank Dr. TW17: Shep 4G 147
Holmbridge Gdns. EN3: Pond E 4E 24
Holmbrook NW1 2G 83
(off Eversholt St.)
Holmbrook Dr. NW4 5F 45
Holmbury Ct. CR2: S Croy 5E 168
Holmbury Ct. SW17 3D 136
Holmbury Ct. SW19 7C 136
Holmbury Gdns. UB3: Hayes 1H 93
Holmbury Gro. CR0: Sels 7B 170
Holmbury Mnr. DA14: Sidc 4A 144
Holmbury Pk. BR1: Broml 7C 142
Holmbury Vw. E5 1H 67
Holmbush Rd. SW15 6G 117
Holmcote Gdns. N5 5C 66
Holm Ct. SE12 3K 141
Holmcroft Ho. E17 4D 50
Holmcroft Way BR2: Broml 5D 160
Holmdale Gdns. NW4 5F 45
Holmdale Rd. BR7: Chst 5G 143
Holmdale Rd. NW6 5J 63
Holmdale Ter. N15 6E 48
Holmdene N12 5E 30
Holmdene Av. HA2: Harr 3F 41
Holmdene Av. NW7 6H 29
Holmdene Av. SE24 5C 120
Holmdene Cl. BR3: Beck 2E 158
Holmdene Ct. BR1: Broml 3C 160
Holmead Rd. SW6 7K 99
Holmebury Cl. WD23: B Hea 2D 26
Holme Ct. TW7: Isle 3A 114
Holmefield Ho. W10 4G 81
(off Hazlewood Cres.)
Holme Ho. SE15 7H 103
(off Studholme St.)
Holme Lacey Rd. SE12 6H 123
Holme Rd. E6 2K 91
Holmeroak Av. RM13: Rain 1C 88
Holmes Av. E17 3B 50
Holmes Cl. SE22 4G 121
Holmesdale Av. SW14 3H 115
Holmesdale Cl. SE25 3F 157
Holmesdale Ho. NW6 1J 81
(off Kilburn Vale)
Holmesdale Rd. CR0: C'don 5D 156
Holmesdale Rd. DA7: Bex 2D 126
Holmesdale Rd. N6 7F 47
Holmesdale Rd. SE25 5D 156
Holmesdale Rd. TW11: Tedd 7C 132
Holmesdale Rd. TW9: Kew 1F 115
Holmesley Rd. SE23 6A 122
Holmes Pl. SW10 6A 100
Holmes Rd. NW5 5F 65
Holmes Rd. SW19 7A 136
Holmes Rd. TW1: Twick 2K 131
Holmes Ter. SE1 6J 13 (2A 102)
(off Waterloo Rd.)
Holmeswood SM2: Sutt 6K 165
Holmewood Ct. N22 2A 48
Holme Way HA7: Stan 6E 26
Holmewood Gdns. SW2 7K 119
Holmewood Rd. SE25 3E 156
Holmewood Rd. SW2 7K 119
Holmfield Av. NW4 5F 45
Holmfield Ct. NW3 5C 64
Holm Gro. UB10: Hil 7C 56
Holmhurst SE13 6F 123
Holmhurst Rd. DA17: Belv 5H 109
Holmlea Ct. CR0: C'don 4D 168
(off Chatsworth Rd.)
Holmleigh Ct. EN3: Pond E 4D 24
Holmleigh Rd. N16 1E 66
Holmleigh Rd. Est. N16 1E 66
Holm Oak Cl. SW15 6H 117
Holm Oak M. SW4 5J 119
Holmoaks Ho. BR3: Beck 2E 158
Holmsdale Ho. E14 7D 86
(off Poplar High St.)
Holmsdale Ho. N11 4A 32
(off Coppies Gro.)
Holmshaw Cl. SE26 4A 140
Holmside Rd. SW12 6E 118
Holmsley Cl. KT3: N Mald 6B 152
Holmsley Ho. SW15 7B 116
(off Tangley Gro.)
Holmstall Av. HA8: Edg 3J 43
Holmstall Pde. HA8: Edg 2J 43
Holmstead Ct. CR2: S Croy 5D 168
Holm Wlk. SE3 2J 123
Holmwood Cl. HA2: Harr 3G 41
Holmwood Cl. SM2: Cheam 7F 165
Holmwood Cl. UB5: N'olt 6F 59
Holmwood Gdns. N3 2J 45
Holmwood Gdns. SM6: W'gton 6F 167
Holmwood Gro. NW7 5E 28
Holmwood Rd. IG3: Ilf 2J 71
Holmwood Rd. KT9: Chess 5D 162
Holmwood Vs. SE7 5J 105
Holne Chase N2 6A 46
Holne Chase SM4: Mord 6H 153
Holness Rd. E15 6H 69
Holocaust Memorial Gdn., The 6F 11 (2D 100)
Holroyd Rd. SW15 4E 116
Holsgrove Ho. W3 1A 98
Holst Ct. SE1 1J 19 (3A 102)
(off Kennington Rd.)
Holstein Way DA18: Erith 3D 108
Holst Ho. W12 6D 80
(off Du Cane Rd.)
Holst Mans. SW13 6E 98
Holstock Rd. IG1: Ilf 2G 71
Holst Rd. W3 5J 79
Holsworth Cl. HA2: Harr 5G 41
Holsworthy Ho. E3 3D 86
(off Talwin St.)
Holsworthy Sq. WC1 4H 7 (4K 83)
(off Elm St.)
Holsworthy Way KT9: Chess 5C 162
Holt, The SM4: Mord 4J 153
Holt, The SM6: W'gton 4G 167
Holt Cl. BR7: Chst 5D 142
Holt Cl. DA14: Sidc 4E 144
Holt Cl. N10 4E 46
Holt Cl. SE28 7B 90
Holt Ct. SE10 6E 104
(off Horseferry Pl.)
Holt Gdns. SW17 3C 136
Holt Ho. SW2 6A 120
Holton St. E1 4K 85
Holt Rd. E16 1C 106
Holt Rd. HA0: Wemb 3B 60
Holtwhite Av. EN2: Enf 2H 23
Holtwhite's Hill EN2: Enf 1G 23
Holwell Pl. HA5: Pinn 4C 40
Holwood Est. BR2: Kes 6C 172
Holwood Pk. Av. BR6: Farnb 4D 172
Holwood Pl. SW4 4H 119
Holybourne Av. SW15 7C 116
Holycross Cl. SM4: Mord 7J 153
Holyhead Cl. E6 5D 88
Holyhead Ct. KT1: King T 4D 150
(off Anglesea Rd.)
Holyoake Ct. SE16 2B 104
Holyoake Ho. W5 4C 78
Holyoake Wlk. N2 3A 46
Holyoake Wlk. W5 4C 78
Holyoak Rd. SE11 4B 102
Holyport Rd. SW6 7F 99
Holyrood Av. HA2: Harr 4C 58
Holyrood Ct. NW1 1F 83
(off Gloucester Av.)
Holyrood Gdns. HA8: Edg 3H 43
Holyrood M. E16 1J 105
Holyrood Rd. EN5: New Bar 6F 21
Holyrood St. SE1 5G 15 (1E 102)
Holywell Cen. EC2 3G 9 (4E 84)
(off Phipp St.)
Holywell Cl. BR6: Chels 4K 173
Holywell Cl. SE16 5H 103
Holywell Cl. SE3 6J 105
Holywell Cl. TW19: Stanw 1A 128
Holywell La. EC2 3H 9 (4E 84)
Holywell Row EC2 4G 9 (4E 84)
Holywell Way TW19: Stanw 1A 128
Homan Ct. N12 4G 31
Homebush Ho. E4 7J 25
Homecedars Ho. WD23: B Hea 1C 26
Home Cl. SM5: Cars 2D 166
Home Cl. UB5: N'olt 3D 76
Home Ct. KT6: Surb 5D 150
Homecroft Rd. N22 1C 48
Homecroft Rd. SE26 5J 139
Home Farm Cl. KT7: T Ditt 7K 149
Home Farm Cl. TW17: Shep 4G 147
Homefarm Rd. W7 6J 77
Homefield SM4: Mord 4J 153
Homefield Av. IG2: Ilf 5J 53
Homefield Cl. NW10 6J 61
Homefield Cl. UB4: Yead 4B 76
Homefield Gdns. CR4: Mitc 2A 154
Homefield Gdns. N2 3B 46
Homefield Ho. SE23 3J 139
Homefield M. BR3: Beck 1C 158
Homefield Pk. SM1: Sutt 6K 165
Homefield Pl. CR0: C'don 2F 169
Homefield Rd. BR1: Broml 1A 160
Homefield Rd. HA0: Wemb 4A 60
Homefield Rd. HA8: Edg 6E 28
Homefield Rd. KT12: Walt T 7C 148
Homefield Rd. SW19 6F 135
Homefield Rd. W4 5B 98
Homefield St. N1 2E 84
Homefirs Ho. HA9: Wemb 3F 61
Home Gdns. RM10: Dag 3J 73
Homeheather Ho. IG4: Ilf 5D 52
Homelands Dr. SE19 7E 138
Home Lea BR6: Chels 5K 173
Homeleigh Ct. SW16 3J 137
Homeleigh Rd. SE15 5K 121
Home Mead HA7: Stan 1C 42
Home Mdw. M. SE22 5G 121
Homemead Rd. BR2: Broml 5D 160
Homemead Rd. CR0: C'don 6G 155
Home Pk. KT1: E Mos 5B 150
Home Pk. Ct. KT1: King T 4E 150
(off Palace Rd.)
Home Pk. Pde. KT1: Hamp W 2D 150
(off High St.)
Home Pk. Rd. SW19 4H 135
Home Pk. Ter. KT1: Hamp W 2D 150
(off Hampton Ct. Rd.)
Home Pk. Wlk. KT1: King T 4D 150
Homer Cl. DA7: Bex 1J 127
Homer Dr. E14 4C 104
Home Rd. SW11 2C 118
Homer Rd. CR0: C'don 6K 157
Homer Rd. E9 6A 68
Homer Row W1 6D 4 (5C 82)
Homersham Rd. KT1: King T 2G 151
Homer St. W1 6D 4 (5C 82)
HOMERTON 5K 67
Homerton Gro. E9 5K 67
Homerton High St. E9 5K 67
Homerton Rd. E9 5A 68
Homerton Row E9 5J 67
Homerton Ter. E9 6J 67
(not continuous)
Homesdale Cl. E11 5J 51
Homesdale Rd. BR1: Broml 3A 160
Homesdale Rd. BR2: Broml 4A 160
Homesdale Rd. BR5: Pet W 7J 161
Homesfield NW11 5J 45
Homestall Rd. SE22 5J 121
Homestead Ct. EN5: New Bar 5D 20
Homestead Paddock N14 5A 22
Homestead Pk. NW2 3B 62
Homestead Rd. RM8: Dag 2F 73
Homestead Rd. SW6 7H 99
Homesteads, The N11 4A 32
Homevale Cl. BR2: Hayes 7H 159
Homewalk Ho. SE26 4H 139
Homewaters Av. TW16: Sun 1H 147
Homewillow Cl. N21 6G 23
Homewood Cl. TW12: Hamp 6D 130
Homewood Cres. BR7: Chst 6J 143
Homewoods SW12 7G 119
Homildon Ho. SE26 3G 139
Honduras St. EC1 3C 8 (4C 84)
Honeybourne Rd. NW6 5K 63
Honeybourne Way BR5: Pet W 1H 173
Honeybrook Rd. SW12 7G 119
Honey Cl. RM10: Dag 6H 73
Honeycroft Hill UB10: Uxb 7A 56
Honeyden Rd. DA14: Sidc 6E 144
Honeyfield M. SE23 3K 139
Honeyghan Ct. SE17 5E 102
(off Sedan Way)
Honey Hill UB10: Uxb 7B 56
Honey La. EC2 1D 14 (6C 84)
(off Trump St.)
Honey La. Ho. SW10 6K 99
(off Finborough Rd.)
Honeyman Cl. NW6 7F 63
Honeymead N8 3J 47
(off Campsfield Rd.)
Honey M. RM7: Rom 5J 55
Honey M. SE27 4C 138
(off Norwood High St.)
Honey M. SE27 4C 138
Honeypot Bus. Cen. HA7: Stan 1E 42
Honeypot Cl. NW9 4F 43
Honeypot La. HA7: Stan 7J 27
Honeypot La. NW9 4F 43
Honeysett Rd. N17 2F 49
Honeysuckle Cl. UB1: S'hall 7C 76
Honeysuckle Ct. IG1: Ilf 6F 71
Honeysuckle Ct. IG9: Buck H 3G 37
Honeysuckle Gdns. CR0: C'don 7K 157
Honeysuckle Gdns. E17 3C 50
Honeysuckle La. N22 2C 48
Honeywell Rd. SW11 6D 118
Honeywood Ho. SE15 1G 121
(off Goldsmith Rd.)
Honeywood Mus. 5D 166
Honeywood Rd. NW10 2B 80
Honeywood Rd. TW7: Isle 4A 114
Honeywood Wlk. SM5: Cars 4D 166
Honister Cl. HA7: Stan 1B 42
Honister Gdns. HA7: Stan 7G 27
Honister Pl. HA7: Stan 1B 42
Honiton Gdns. NW7 7A 30
Honiton Gdns. SE15 2J 121
(off Gibbon Rd.)
Honiton Ho. EN3: Pond E 3E 24
Honiton Rd. DA16: Well 2K 125
Honiton Rd. NW6 2H 81
Honiton Rd. RM7: Rom 6K 55
Honley Rd. SE6 7D 122
Honnor Gdns. TW7: Isle 2H 113
HONOR OAK 6J 121
Honor Oak Crematorium 5K 121
Honor Oak Pk. SE23 6J 121
HONOR OAK PARK 7A 122
Honor Oak Ri. SE23 6J 121
Honor Oak Rd. SE23 1J 139
Honour Gdns. RM8: Dag 4A 72
Honour Lea Av. E20 5D 68
Hood Av. N14 6A 22
Hood Av. SW14 5J 115
Hood Cl. CR0: C'don 1B 168
Hoodcote Gdns. N21 7G 23
Hood Ct. EC4 1K 13 (6A 84)
(off Fleet St.)
Hood Ho. SE5 7D 102
(off Elmington Est.)
Hood Ho. SW1 6C 18 (5H 101)
(off Dolphin Sq.)

Hood Point – Hunters Gro.

Hood Point SE16 2B 104
(off Rotherhithe St.)
Hood Rd. SW20 7B 134
Hood Wlk. RM7: Mawney 1H 55
HOOK 4D 162
Hook, The EN5: New Bar 6G 21
Hooke Ct. SE10 1E 122
(off Winforton St.)
Hooke Ho. E3 2A 86
(off Gernon Rd.)
Hookers Rd. E17 3K 49
Hook Farm Rd. BR2: Broml 5B 160
Hookham Ct. SW8 1H 119
Hooking Grn. HA2: Harr 5F 41
HOOK JUNC. 3E 162
Hook La. DA16: Well 4K 125
Hook Ri. Nth. KT6: Surb 3E 162
Hook Ri. Sth. KT6: Surb 3E 162
Hook Ri. Sth. Ind. Pk. KT6: Surb 3F 163
Hook Rd. KT19: Eps 7J 163
Hook Rd. KT19: Ewe 7J 163
Hook Rd. KT6: Surb 2E 162
Hook Rd. KT9: Chess 5D 162
Hooks Cl. SE15 1H 121
Hooks Hall Dr. RM10: Dag 3J 73
Hookstone Way IG8: Wfd G 7G 37
Hook Wlk. HA8: Edg 6D 28
Hool Cl. NW9 5J 43
Hooper Dr. UB8: Hil 5D 74
Hooper Ho. TW15: Ashf 3A 128
Hooper Rd. E16 6J 87
Hooper's Ct. SW3 7E 10 (2D 100)
Hooper's M. W3 1J 97
Hoopers M. WD23: Bush 1A 26
Hooper Sq. E1 6G 85
(off Hooper St.)
Hooper St. E1 6G 85
Hoopers Yd. NW6 1H 81
(off Kimberley Rd.)
Hoop La. NW11 7H 45
Hop Ct. HA0: Wemb 5A 60
(off Brewery Cl.)
Hope Cl. IG8: Wfd G 6F 37
Hope Cl. N1 6C 66
Hope Cl. NW4 2E 44
Hope Cl. RM6: Chad H 4D 54
Hope Cl. SE12 3K 141
Hope Cl. SM1: Sutt 5A 166
Hope Cl. TW8: Bford 5E 96
Hope Ct. NW10 3F 81
(off Chamberlayne Rd.)
Hope Ct. SE1 5G 103
(off Avocet Cl.)
Hopedale Rd. SE7 6K 105
Hopefield Av. NW6 2G 81
Hope Gdns. W3 2H 97
Hope Ho. CR0: C'don 4E 168
(off Steep Hill)
Hope La. SE9 2F 143
Hope Pk. BR1: Broml 7H 141
Hopes Cl. TW5: Hest 6E 94
Hope Sq. EC2 6G 9 (5E 84)
(off Sun St. Pas.)
Hope St. E14 6G 87
Hope St. SW11 3B 118
Hopetown St. E1 6K 9 (5F 85)
Hopewell St. SE5 7D 102
Hopewell Yd. SE5 7D 102
(off Hopewell St.)
Hope Wharf SE16 2J 103
Hop Gdns. WC2 3E 12 (7J 83)
Hopgood St. W12 1E 98
Hopground Ho. E20 6E 68
(off De Coubertin St.)
Hopkins Cl. N10 7K 31
Hopkins Ho. E14 6C 86
(off Canton St.)
Hopkins M. E15 1H 87
Hopkinsons Pl. NW1 1E 82
Hopkins Rd. E10 7D 50
Hopkins St. W1 1B 12 (6G 83)
Hoppers Rd. N13 2F 33
Hoppers Rd. N21 2F 33
Hoppett Rd. E4 2B 36
Hopping La. N1 6B 66
Hoppingwood Av. KT3: N Mald 3A 152
Hoppner Rd. UB4: Hayes 2F 75
Hopps Ct. NW9 2A 44
(off Salk Cl.)
Hops Ho. E17 5B 50
(off Old Brewery Way)
Hop St. SE10 4H 105
Hopton Ct. BR2: Hayes 1K 171
Hopton Gdns. KT3: N Mald 6C 152
Hopton Rd. SE18 3F 107
Hopton Rd. SW16 5J 137
Hopton's Gdns. SE1 4B 14 (1B 102)
(off Hopton St.)
Hopton St. SE1 3A 14 (7B 84)
Hoptree Cl. N12 5E 30
Hopwood Cl. SW17 3A 136
Hopwood Rd. SE17 6D 102
Hopwood Wlk. E8 7G 67
Horace Av. RM7: Rush G 1J 73
Horace Bldg. SW11 7F 101
Horace Jones Ho. SE1 5J 15 (1F 103)
(off Duchess Wlk.)
Horace Rd. E7 4K 69
Horace Rd. IG6: Ilf 3G 53
Horace Rd. KT1: King T 3F 151
Horatio Ct. SE16 1J 103
(off Rotherhithe St.)
Horatio Ho. E2 1K 9 (2F 85)
(off Horatio St.)
Horatio Ho. W6 5F 99
(off Fulham Pal. Rd.)
Horatio Pl. E14 1E 104
(off Managers St.)
Horatio Pl. SW19 1J 153
Horatio St. E2 1K 9 (2F 85)
Horatius Way CR0: Wadd 5K 167
Horbury Cres. W11 7J 81
Horbury M. W11 7H 81
Horder Rd. SW6 1G 117
Hordle Prom. Sth. SE15 7F 103
(off Quarley Way)
Horizon Bldg. E14 7C 86
(off Hertsmere Rd.)
Horizon Bus. Cen. N9 2E 34
(off Goodwin Rd.)
Horizon Ct. SM2: Cheam 7G 165
(off Up. Mulgrave Rd.)
Horizon Ho. SW18 3A 118
(off Juniper Dr.)
Horizon Ind. Est. SE15 6G 103
Horle Wlk. SE5 2B 120
Horley Cl. DA6: Bex 5G 127
Horley Rd. SE9 4C 142
Hormead Rd. W9 4H 81
Hornbeam Cl. IG1: Ilf 5H 71
Hornbeam Cl. IG11: Bark 3A 90
Hornbeam Cl. IG9: Buck H 3G 37
Hornbeam Cl. NW7 3G 29
Hornbeam Cl. SE11 3J 19 (4A 102)
Hornbeam Cl. UB5: N'olt 5D 58
Hornbeam Cres. TW8: Bford 7B 96
Hornbeam Gdns. KT3: N Mald 6C 152
Hornbeam Gro. E4 3B 36
Hornbeam Ho. IG9: Buck H 3H 37
Hornbeam Ho. 2A 104
Hornbeam La. DA7: Bex 2J 127
Hornbeam M. SW17 2C 136
Hornbeam Rd. IG9: Buck H 3G 37
Hornbeam Rd. UB4: Yead 5A 76
Hornbeam Sq. E3 1B 86
Hornbeams Ri. N11 6K 31
Hornbeam Ter. SM5: Cars 1C 166
Hornbeam Wlk. TW10: Rich 2F 133
Hornbeam Way BR2: Broml 6E 160
Hornbean Ho. E15 3G 87
(off Manor Rd.)
Hornblower Cl. SE16 3A 104
Hornbuckle Cl. HA2: Harr 2H 59
Hornby Cl. NW3 7B 64
Hornby Ct. NW10 6B 62
Hornby Ho. SE11 7J 19 (6A 102)
(off Clayton St.)
Horncastle Cl. SE12 7J 123
Horncastle Rd. SE12 7J 123
Hornchurch N17 2D 48
(off Gloucester Rd.)
Hornchurch Cl. KT2: King T 4D 132
Horndean Cl. SW15 1C 134
Horndon Cl. RM5: Col R 1J 55
Horndon Grn. RM5: Col R 1J 55
Horndon Rd. RM5: Col R 1J 55
Horner Ho. N1 1E 84
(off Nuttall St.)
Horner La. CR4: Mitc 2B 154
Horne Rd. TW17: Shep 4C 146
Horner Sq. E1 5J 9 (5F 85)
(within Old Spitalfields Mkt.)
Hornet Way E6 5H 89
Horne Way SW15 2E 116
Hornfair Rd. SE7 6A 106
Horniman Dr. SE23 1H 139
Horniman Gdns. 1H 139
Horniman Mus. 1H 139
Horning Cl. SE9 4C 142
Horn La. IG8: Wfd G 6D 36
Horn La. SE10 5J 105
(not continuous)
Horn La. W3 7J 79
(not continuous)
Horn Link Way SE10 4J 105
HORN PARK 5K 123
Horn Pk. Cl. SE12 5K 123
Horn Pk. La. SE12 5K 123
Hornscroft Cl. IG11: Bark 7J 71
Horns End Pl. HA5: Eastc 4A 40
HORNSEY 4J 47
Hornsey Cricket Club 5H 47
Hornsey La. N6 1F 65
Hornsey La. Est. N19 7H 47
Hornsey La. Gdns. N6 7G 47
Hornsey Pk. Rd. N8 3K 47
Hornsey Ri. N19 7H 47
Hornsey Ri. Gdns. N19 7H 47
Hornsey Rd. N19 1J 65
Hornsey Rd. N7 2K 65
Hornsey St. N7 5K 65
HORNSEY VALE 5K 47
Hornshay St. SE15 6J 103
Horns Rd. IG2: Ilf 5G 53
Horns Rd. IG6: Ilf 4H 53
Hornton Ct. W8 2J 99
(off Kensington High St.)
Hornton Pl. W8 2K 99
Hornton St. W8 2J 99
Horsa Rd. DA8: Erith 7H 109
Horsa Rd. SE12 7A 124
Horse & Dolphin Yd. W1 2D 12 (7H 83)
(off Macclesfield St.)
Horsebridge Cl. RM9: Dag 1E 90
Horsecroft Rd. HA8: Edg 7E 28
Horse Fair KT1: King T 2D 150
Horseferry Pl. SE10 6E 104
Horseferry Rd. E14 7A 86
Horseferry Rd. SW1 2C 18 (3H 101)
Horseferry Rd. Est. SW1 2C 18 (3H 101)
(off Horseferry Rd.)
Horse Guards Av. SW1 5E 12 (1J 101)
Horse Guards Parade 5D 12 (1H 101)
Horse Guards Rd. SW1 5D 12 (1H 101)
Horse Leaze E6 6E 88
Horseley Ct. E1 5A 86
Horsell Rd. BR5: St P 7B 144
Horsell Rd. N5 5A 66
(not continuous)
Horselydown La. SE1 6J 15 (2F 103)
Horselydown Mans. SE1 6J 15 (2F 103)
(off Lafone St.)
Horsemongers M. SE1 7D 14 (2C 102)
(off Cole St.)
Horsenden Av. UB6: G'frd 5K 59
Horsenden Cres. UB6: G'frd 5K 59
Horsenden Hill Footgolf Cen. 6A 60
Horsenden Hill Golf Course 7A 60
Horsenden La. Nth. UB6: G'frd 6J 59
Horsenden La. Sth. UB6: G'frd 1A 78
Horse Ride SW1 5B 12 (1G 101)
Horseshoe Cl. E14 5E 104
Horseshoe Cl. NW2 2D 62
Horseshoe Ct. EC1 3B 8 (4B 84)
(off Brewhouse Yd.)
Horse Shoe Cres. UB5: N'olt 2E 76
Horseshoe Dr. UB8: Hil 6C 74
Horse Shoe Grn. SM1: Sutt 2K 165
Horseshoe La. EN2: Enf 3H 23
Horseshoe La. N20 1A 30
Horseshoe M. SW2 4J 119
Horseshoe Wharf SE1 4E 14 (1D 102)
(off Clink St.)
Horse Yd. N1 1B 84
(off Essex Rd.)
Horsfeld Gdns. SE9 5C 124
Horsfeld Rd. SE9 5B 124
Horsfield Ho. N1 7C 66
(off Northampton St.)
Horsford Rd. SW2 5K 119
Horsham Av. N12 5H 31
Horsham Ct. N17 1G 49
(off Lansdowne Rd.)
Horsham Rd. DA6: Bex 5G 127
Horsham Rd. TW14: Bedf 6E 110
Horsley Ct. SW1 4D 18 (4H 101)
(off Vincent St.)
Horsley Dr. CR0: New Ad 7E 170
Horsley Dr. KT2: King T 5D 132
Horsley Rd. BR1: Broml 1K 159
Horsley Rd. E4 2K 35
Horsley St. SE17 6D 102
Horsman Ho. SE5 6C 102
(off Bethwin Rd.)
Horsman St. SE5 6C 102
Horsmonden Cl. BR6: Orp 7K 161
Horsmonden Rd. SE4 5B 122
Horsnell Cl. SE5 7D 102
Hortensia Ho. SW10 7A 100
(off Gunter Gro.)
Hortensia Rd. SW10 7A 100
Horticultural Pl. W4 5K 97
Horton Av. NW2 4G 63
Horton Bri. Rd. UB7: Yiew 1B 92
Horton Cl. UB7: Yiew 1C 92
Horton Country Pk. Local Nature Reserve 7F 163
Horton Halls SW17 3B 136
Horton Ho. SE15 6J 103
Horton Ho. SW8 7K 101
Horton Ho. W6 5G 99
(off Field Rd.)
Horton Ind. Pk. UB7: Yiew 1B 92
Horton Pde. UB7: Yiew 1A 92
Horton Pk. Golf Course 7J 163
Horton Rd. E8 6H 67
Horton Rd. TW19: Stanw M 7A 174
Horton Rd. UB11: Stock P 1C 92
Horton Rd. UB7: Yiew 1A 92
Horton Rd. Ind. Est. UB7: Yiew 1B 92
Horton Way CR0: C'don 5K 157
Hortus Rd. E4 2K 35
Hortus Rd. UB2: S'hall 2D 94
Horwood Ho. E2 3H 85
(off Pott St.)
Horwood Ho. NW8 3D 4 (4C 82)
(off Paveley St.)
Hosack Rd. SW17 2E 136
Hoser Av. SE12 2J 141
Hosier La. EC1 6A 8 (5B 84)
Hoskins Cl. E16 6A 88
Hoskins Cl. UB3: Harl 5H 93
Hoskins St. SE10 5F 105
Hospital Bri. Rd. TW2: Twick 7F 113
Hospital Bri. Rd. TW2: Whitt 7F 113
HOSPITAL BRIDGE RDBT. 2F 131
Hospital Rd. E11 5F 51
Hospital Rd. E9 5K 67
Hospital Rd. TW3: Houn 3E 112
Hospital Way SE13 7F 123
Hotham Cl. KT8: W Mole 3E 148
Hotham Rd. SW15 3E 116
Hotham Rd. SW19 7A 136
Hotham Rd. M. SW19 7A 136
Hotham St. E15 1G 87
Hothfield Pl. SE16 3J 103
Hotspur Ind. Est. N17 6C 34
Hotspur Rd. UB5: N'olt 2E 76
Hotspur St. SE11 4J 19 (4A 102)
Houblon Rd. TW10: Rich 5E 114
Houghton Cl. E8 6F 67
Houghton Cl. TW12: Hamp 6C 130
Houghton Ct. EC1 4C 8 (4C 84)
(off Glasshouse Yd.)
Houghton Rd. N15 4F 49
Houghton Sq. SW9 2J 119
(off Clapham Rd.)
Houghton St. WC2 1H 13 (6K 83)
(not continuous)
Houlder Cres. CR0: Wadd 6B 168
Houlton Ho. SW3 5E 16 (5D 100)
(off Walpole St.)
Houlton Pl. E3 4B 86
(off Hamlets Way)
Houndsden Rd. N21 6E 22
Houndsditch EC3 7H 9 (6E 84)
Houndsfield Rd. N9 7C 24
HOUNSLOW 3F 113
Hounslow & District Indoor Bowls Club 2D 112
Hounslow Av. TW3: Houn 5F 113
Hounslow Cen. TW3: Houn 3F 113
Hounslow Gdns. TW3: Houn 5F 113
Hounslow Heath Local Nature Reserve 6C 112
Hounslow Rd. TW13: Hanw 4B 130
Hounslow Rd. TW14: Felt 1K 129
Hounslow Rd. TW2: Whitt 6F 113
Hounslow Urban Farm 5J 111
HOUNSLOW WEST 3C 112
Household Cavalry Mus., The 5D 12 (1H 101)
House Mill, The 3E 86
House of Illustration 1J 83
Houses of Parliament 1F 19 (3J 101)
Houston Bus. Pk. UB4: Yead 1A 94
Houston Pl. KT10: Esh 7J 149
Houston Rd. KT6: Surb 6B 150
Houston Rd. SE23 2A 140
Houstoun Ct. TW5: Hest 7D 94
Hove Av. E17 5B 50
Hoveden Rd. NW2 5G 63
Hove Gdns. SM1: Sutt 1K 165
Hove St. SE15 7J 103
(off Culmore Rd.)
Hoveton Rd. SE28 6C 90
Hoveton Way IG6: Ilf 1F 53
Howard Av. DA5: Bexl 1C 144
Howard Bldg. SW11 7J 17 (6F 101)
Howard Cl. N11 2K 31
Howard Cl. NW2 4G 63
Howard Cl. TW12: Hamp 7G 131
Howard Cl. TW16: Sun 6H 129
Howard Cl. W3 6H 79
Howard Cl. WD23: B Hea 1D 26
Howard Ct. IG11: Bark 1H 89
Howard Ho. E16 1K 105
(off Wesley Av.)
Howard Ho. SE8 6B 104
(off Evelyn St.)
Howard Ho. SW1 6B 18 (5G 101)
(off Dolphin Sq.)
Howard Ho. SW9 3B 120
(off Barrington Rd.)
Howard Ho. W1 4K 5 (4F 83)
(off Cleveland St.)
Howard M. N5 4B 66
Howard Rd. BR1: Broml 7J 141
Howard Rd. E11 3G 69
Howard Rd. E17 3C 50
Howard Rd. E6 2D 88
Howard Rd. HA7: Stan 1D 42
Howard Rd. IG1: Ilf 4F 71
Howard Rd. IG11: Bark 1H 89
Howard Rd. KT3: N Mald 3A 152
Howard Rd. KT5: Surb 6F 151
Howard Rd. N15 6E 48
Howard Rd. N16 4D 66
Howard Rd. NW2 4F 63
Howard Rd. SE20 1J 157
Howard Rd. SE25 5G 157
Howard Rd. TW7: Isle 3K 113
Howard Rd. UB1: S'hall 6F 77
Howards Cl. HA5: Pinn 2K 39
Howards Crest Cl. BR3: Beck 2E 158
Howard's La. SW15 4D 116
Howards Rd. E13 3J 87
Howard St. KT7: T Ditt 7B 150
Howard Wlk. N2 4A 46
Howard Way EN5: Barn 5A 20
Howarth Rd. SE2 5A 108
Howberry Cl. HA8: Edg 6J 27
Howberry Rd. CR7: Thor H 1D 156
Howberry Rd. HA7: Stan 6J 27
Howberry Rd. HA8: Edg 6J 27
Howbury Rd. SE15 3J 121
Howcroft Cres. N3 7D 30
Howcroft Ho. E3 3B 86
(off Benworth St.)
Howcroft La. UB6: G'frd 3H 77
Howden Cl. SE28 7D 90
Howden Rd. SE25 2F 157
Howden St. SE15 3G 121
Howe Cl. RM7: Mawney 1G 55
Howell Cl. RM6: Chad H 5D 54
Howell Ct. E10 7D 50
Howell Wlk. SE1 4B 102
Howerd Way SE18 1C 124
(not continuous)
Howes Cl. N3 3J 45
Howeth Ct. N11 6J 31
(off Ribblesdale Av.)
Howfield Pl. N17 3F 49
Howgate Rd. SW14 3K 115
Howick Pl. SW1 2B 18 (3G 101)
Howie St. SW11 7C 100
Howitt Cl. N16 4E 66
Howitt Cl. NW3 6C 64
Howitt Rd. NW3 6C 64
Howland Est. SE16 3J 103
Howland Ho. SW16 3J 137
Howland M. E. W1 5B 6 (5G 83)
Howland St. W1 5B 6 (5G 83)
Howland Way SE16 2A 104
Howlett Apts. N1 7J 65
(off Caledonian Rd.)
Howletts La. HA4: Ruis 5E 38
Howlett's Rd. SE24 6C 120
Howley Pl. W2 5A 82
Howley Rd. CR0: C'don 3B 168
Howsman Rd. SW13 6C 98
Howson Rd. SE4 4A 122
Howson Ter. TW10: Rich 6E 114
How's St. E2 2F 85
Howton Pl. WD23: B Hea 1C 26
HOXTON 2E 84
Hoxton Hall Theatre 2E 84
(off Hoxton St.)
Hoxton Mkt. N1 2G 9 (3E 84)
(off Coronet St.)
Hoxton Sq. N1 2G 9 (3E 84)
Hoxton St. N1 1E 84
Hoy Cl. NW9 3B 44
Hoylake Cres. UB10: Ick 2C 56
Hoylake Gdns. CR4: Mitc 3G 155
Hoylake Gdns. HA4: Ruis 1K 57
Hoylake Rd. W3 6A 80
Hoyland Cl. SE15 7H 103
Hoyle Rd. SW17 5C 136
Hoy St. E16 6H 87
HQS Wellington 3J 13 (7A 84)
(off Victoria Embankment)
Hub Westminster, The 1F 5 (2D 82)
Hubbard Ct. IG10: Lough 1H 37
Hubbard Dr. KT9: Chess 6D 162
Hubbard Ho. SW10 7B 100
(off World's End Pas.)
Hubbard Rd. SE27 4C 138
Hubbards Cl. UB8: Hil 6D 74
Hubbard St. E15 1G 87
Hubbard St. SE10 4J 105
Hubbinet Ind. Est. RM7: Mawney 3J 55
Huberd Ho. SE1 7F 15 (3D 102)
(off Manciple St.)
Hubert Gro. SW9 3J 119
Hubert Ho. NW8 4C 4 (4C 82)
(off Ashbridge St.)
Hubert Rd. E6 3B 88
Hucknall Ct. NW8 3A 4 (4B 82)
(off Cunningham Pl.)
Huddart St. E3 5B 86
(not continuous)
Huddleston Cl. E2 2J 85
Huddlestone Rd. E7 4H 69
Huddlestone Rd. NW2 6D 62
Huddleston Rd. N7 3G 65
Hudson NW9 1B 44
(off Five Acre)
Hudson Apts. N8 3K 47
Hudson Bldg. E1 5K 9 (5G 85)
(off Chicksand St.)
Hudson Cl. E15 1J 87
Hudson Cl. W12 7D 80
Hudson Ct. E14 5C 104
(off Maritime Quay)
Hudson Gdns. BR6: Chels 6K 173
Hudson Ho. SW10 7A 100
(off Hortensia Rd.)
Hudson Ho. W11 6G 81
(off Ladbroke Gro.)
Hudson Pl. SE18 5G 107
Hudson Rd. DA7: Bex 2F 127
Hudson Rd. UB3: Harl 6F 93
Hudson's Pl. SW1 3K 17 (4F 101)
Hudson Wlk. HA9: Wemb 4H 61
Hudson Way E16 7G 89
Hudson Way N9 3D 34
Hudson Way NW2 3F 63
Hugero Point SE10 3J 105
Huggin Ct. EC4 2D 14 (7C 84)
(off Huggin Hill)
Huggin Hill EC4 2D 14 (7C 84)
Huggins Ho. E3 3C 86
(off Alfred St.)
Huggins Pl. SW2 1K 137
Hughan Rd. E15 5F 69
Hugh Astor Ct. SE1 7B 14 (3B 102)
(off Keyworth St.)
Hugh Clark Ho. W13 1A 96
(off Singapore Rd.)
Hugh Cubitt Ho. N1 2K 83
(off Collier St.)
Hugh Dalton Av. SW6 6H 99
Hughenden Av. HA3: Kenton 5B 42
Hughenden Gdns. UB5: N'olt 3A 76
(not continuous)
Hughenden Ho. NW8 3C 4 (4C 82)
(off Jerome Cres.)
Hughenden Rd. KT4: Wor Pk 7C 152
Hughendon EN5: New Bar 4E 20
Hughendon Ct. UB3: Hayes 7H 75
(off Chamberlain Cl.)
Hughendon Ter. E15 4E 68
Hughes Cl. N12 5F 31
Hughes Ct. N7 5H 65
Hughes Ho. E2 3J 85
(off Sceptre Ho.)
Hughes Ho. E3 3C 86
(off Trevithick Way)
Hughes Ho. SE17 4B 102
(off Peacock St.)
Hughes Ho. SE5 1C 120
(off Flodden Rd.)
Hughes Ho. SE8 6C 104
(off Benbow St.)
Hughes Mans. E1 4G 85
Hughes Rd. TW15: Ashf 7E 128
Hughes Rd. UB3: Hayes 7K 75
Hughes Ter. SW9 3B 120
(off Styles Gdns.)
Hughes Wlk. CR0: C'don 7C 156
Hugh Gaitskell Cl. SW6 6H 99
Hugh Gaitskell Ho. N16 2F 67
Hugh Herland Ho. KT1: King T 3E 150
Hugh M. SW1 4K 17 (4F 101)
Hugh Platt Ho. E2 2H 85
(off Patriot Sq.)
Hugh St. SW1 4J 17 (4F 101)
Hugo Ho. SW1 1F 17 (3D 100)
(off Sloane St.)
Hugon Rd. SW6 3K 117
Hugo Rd. N19 4G 65
Huguenot Dr. N13 5F 33
Huguenot Pl. E1 5K 9 (5F 85)
Huguenot Pl. SW18 5A 118
Huguenot Sq. SE15 3H 121
Hullbridge M. N1 1D 84
Hull Cl. SE16 2K 103
Hull Pl. E16 1G 107
Hull St. EC1 2C 8 (3C 84)
Hulme Pl. SE1 7D 14 (2C 102)
Hulse Av. IG11: Bark 6H 71
Hulse Av. RM7: Mawney 1H 55
Hulse Ter. IG1: Ilf 6G 71
Hult Intl. Studios E1 6G 85
(off Alder St.)
Hult Twr. E1 6G 85
(off Alder St.)
Humber Ct. W7 6H 77
(off Hobbayne Rd.)
Humber Dr. W10 4F 81
Humber Rd. NW2 2D 62
Humber Rd. SE3 6H 105
Humberstone Rd. E13 3A 88
Humberton Cl. E9 5A 68
Humber Trad. Est. NW2 2D 62
Humbolt Rd. W6 6G 99
Hume Ct. N1 7B 66
(off Hawes St.)
Hume Ho. W11 1F 99
(off Queensdale Cres.)
Humes Av. W7 3J 95
Hume Ter. E16 5K 87
Hume Way HA4: Ruis 6J 39
Humphrey Cl. IG5: Ilf 1D 52
Humphrey St. SE1 5F 103
Humphries Cl. RM9: Dag 4F 73
Humphry Repton Way HA9: Wemb 4G 61
Hundred Acre NW9 2B 44
Hungerdown E4 1K 35
HUNGERFORD BRIDGE 4G 13 (1K 101)
Hungerford Ho. SW1 7B 18 (6G 101)
(off Churchill Gdns.)
Hungerford La. WC2 4E 12 (1J 101)
(off Craven St.)
Hungerford Rd. N7 6H 65
Hungerford St. E1 6H 85
Hunsdon Cl. RM9: Dag 6E 72
Hunsdon Rd. SE14 7K 103
Hunslett St. E2 3J 85
Hunstanton Ho. NW1 5D 4 (5C 82)
(off Cosway St.)
Hunston Rd. SM4: Mord 1K 165
Hunt Cl. W11 1F 99
Hunt Ct. N14 7A 22
Hunt Ct. RM7: Rush G 6K 55
(off Union Rd.)
Hunt Ct. UB5: N'olt 2B 76
(off Gallery Gdns.)
Hunter Cl. SE1 3D 102
Hunter Cl. SM6: W'gton 7J 167
Hunter Cl. SW12 1E 136
Hunter Ho. SE1 7B 14 (2B 102)
(off King James St.)
Hunter Ho. SW5 5J 99
(off Old Brompton Rd.)
Hunter Ho. SW8 7H 101
(off Fount St.)
Hunter Ho. TW13: Felt 1J 129
(off Hazel Gro.)
Hunter Ho. WC1 3E 6 (4J 83)
(off Hunter St.)
Hunterian Mus. 7H 7 (6K 83)
Hunter Lodge W9 5J 81
(off Admiral Wlk.)
Hunter Rd. CR7: Thor H 3D 156
Hunter Rd. IG1: Ilf 5F 71
Hunter Rd. SW20 1E 152
Hunters Cl. DA5: Bexl 3K 145
Hunters Ct. TW9: Rich 5D 114
Hunters Gro. BR6: Farnb 4G 173
Hunters Gro. HA3: Kenton 4C 42
Hunters Gro. UB3: Hayes 1J 93

Hunters Hall Rd. – Interchange, The

Hunters Hall Rd. RM10: Dag 4G **73**
Hunters Hill HA4: Ruis 3A **58**
Hunters Mdw. SE19 4E **138**
Hunter's Rd. KT9: Chess 3E **162**
Hunters Sq. RM10: Dag 4G **73**
Hunter St. WC1 3F **7** (4J **83**)
Hunter's Way CR0: C'don 4E **168**
Hunters Way EN2: Enf 1F **23**
Hunter Wlk. E13 2J **87**
Huntingdon Cl. CR4: Mitc 3J **155**
Huntingdon Cl. UB5: N'olt 6E **58**
Huntingdon Gdns. KT4: Wor Pk 3E **164**
Huntingdon Gdns. W4 7J **97**
Huntingdon Rd. N2 3C **46**
Huntingdon Rd. N9 2D **34**
Huntingdon St. E16 6H **87**
Huntingdon St. N1 7K **65**
Huntingfield CR0: Sels 7B **170**
Huntingfield Rd. SW15 4C **116**
Hunting Ga. Cl. EN2: Enf 3F **23**
Hunting Ga. Dr. KT9: Chess 7E **162**
Hunting Ga. M. SM1: Sutt 3K **165**
Hunting Ga. M. TW2: Twick 1J **131**
Hunting Pl. TW5: Hest 6D **94**
Huntings Farm IG1: Ilf 2J **71**
Huntings Rd. RM10: Dag 6G **73**
Huntington Cl. DA5: Bexl 1H **145**
Huntington Ho. SW11 7F **101**
(off Palmer Rd.)
Huntley Cl. SE10 5G **105**
Huntley Cl. TW19: Stanw 7A **110**
Huntley St. WC1 4B **6** (4G **83**)
Huntley Way SW20 2C **152**
Huntloe Ho. SE14 1J **121**
(off Kender St.)
Huntly Dr. N3 6D **30**
Huntly Rd. SE25 4E **156**
Hunton St. E1 5K **9** (5G **85**)
Hunt Rd. UB2: S'hall 3E **94**
Hunt's Cl. SE3 2J **123**
Hunt's Ct. WC2 3D **12** (7H **83**)
Huntshaw Ho. E3 3D **86**
(off Devons Rd.)
Hunts La. E15 2E **86**
Huntsmans Cl. TW13: Felt 4K **129**
Huntsman St. SE17 4E **102**
Hunts Mead EN3: Enf H 3E **24**
Hunts Mead Cl. BR7: Chst 7D **142**
Huntsmoor Rd. KT19: Ewe 5K **163**
Huntspill St. SW17 3A **136**
Hunts Slip Rd. SE21 3E **138**
Huntsworth M. NW1 3E **4** (4D **82**)
Hurdwick Ho. NW1 2G **83**
(off Harrington Sq.)
Hurdwick Pl. NW1 2G **83**
(off Hampstead Rd.)
Hurleston Ho. SE8 5B **104**
Hurley Ct. SW17 6E **136**
(off Mitcham Rd.)
Hurley Ct. W5 6C **78**
Hurley Cres. SE16 2K **103**
Hurley Ho. SE11 4K **19** (4B **102**)
Hurley Ho. UB7: W Dray 2B **92**
(off Park Lodge Av.)
Hurley Rd. UB6: G'frd 6F **77**
HURLINGHAM 3K **117**
Hurlingham Bus. Pk. SW6 3J **117**
Hurlingham Club, The 3J **117**
Hurlingham Ct. SW6 3H **117**
Hurlingham Gdns. SW6 3H **117**
Hurlingham Pk. 2H **117**
Hurlingham Retail Pk. 3K **117**
Hurlingham Rd. DA7: Bex 7F **109**
Hurlingham Rd. SW6 2H **117**
Hurlingham Sq. SW6 3J **117**
Hurlingham Yacht Club 3G **117**
Hurlock St. N5 3B **66**
Hurlstone Rd. SE25 5E **156**
Hurn Ct. TW4: Houn 2B **112**
Hurn Ct. Rd. TW4: Houn 2B **112**
Huron Cl. BR6: Chels 6J **173**
Huron Rd. SW17 2E **136**
Hurrell Dr. HA2: Harr 3G **41**
Hurren Cl. SE3 3G **123**
Hurricane Rd. SM6: W'gton 7J **167**
Hurricane Trad. Cen. NW9 1C **44**
Hurry Cl. E15 7G **69**
Hurst Av. E4 4H **35**
Hurst Av. N6 6G **47**
Hurstbourne KT10: Clay 6A **162**
Hurstbourne Gdns. IG11: Bark 6J **71**
Hurstbourne Ho. SW15 6B **116**
(off Tangley Gro.)
Hurstbourne Rd. SE23 1A **140**
Hurst Cl. BR2: Hayes 1H **171**
Hurst Cl. E4 3H **35**
Hurst Cl. KT9: Chess 5G **163**
Hurst Cl. NW11 6K **45**
Hurst Cl. UB5: N'olt 6D **58**
Hurstcombe IG9: Buck H 2D **36**
Hurst Ct. DA15: Sidc 2A **144**
Hurst Ct. E6 5B **88**
(off Tollgate Rd.)
Hurst Ct. IG8: Wfd G 6E **36**
(off Snakes La. W.)
Hurstcourt Rd. SM1: Sutt 2K **165**
Hurstdene Av. BR2: Hayes 1H **171**
Hurstdene Gdns. N15 7E **48**
Hurstfield BR2: Broml 5J **159**
Hurstfield Cres. UB4: Hayes 4G **75**
Hurstfield Rd. KT8: W Mole 3E **148**
Hurst Gro. KT12: Walt T 7H **147**
Hurst Ho. WC1 1H **7** (2K **83**)
(off Penton Ri.)
Hurst La. KT8: E Mos 4G **149**
Hurst La. SE2 5D **108**
Hurst La. Est. SE2 5D **108**
Hurstleigh Gdns. IG5: Ilf 1D **52**
Hurstmead Ct. HA8: Edg 4C **28**
HURST PARK 2G **149**
Hurst Pl. HA6: Nwood 1D **38**
Hurst Pool 3F **149**
Hurst Ri. EN5: New Bar 3D **20**
Hurst Rd. CR0: C'don 5D **168**
Hurst Rd. DA15: Bexl 2A **144**
Hurst Rd. DA15: Sidc 2A **144**
Hurst Rd. DA5: Bexl 1D **144**
Hurst Rd. DA8: Erith 1J **127**
Hurst Rd. E17 3D **50**
Hurst Rd. IG9: Buck H 1G **37**
Hurst Rd. KT12: Walt T 5A **148**
Hurst Rd. KT8: E Mos 3F **149**
Hurst Rd. KT8: W Mole 3F **149**
Hurst Rd. N21 1F **33**
Hurst Springs DA5: Bexl 1E **144**
Hurst St. SE24 6B **120**
Hurstview Grange CR2: S Croy 7E **168**
Hurst Vw. Rd. CR2: S Croy 7E **168**
Hurst Way CR2: S Croy 6E **168**
Hurstway Rd. W11 7F **81**
(off Hurstway Wlk.)
Hurstway Wlk. W11 7F **81**
Hurstwood Av. DA5: Bexl 1E **144**
Hurstwood Av. E18 4K **51**
Hurstwood Ct. N12 6H **31**
Hurstwood Ct. NW11 4H **45**
(off Finchley Rd.)
Hurstwood Dr. BR1: Broml 3D **160**
Hurstwood Rd. NW11 4G **45**
Hurtwood Rd. KT12: Walt T 7D **148**
Husborne Ho. SE8 4A **104**
(off Chilton Gro.)
Huson Cl. NW3 7C **64**
Hussain Cl. HA1: Harr 4K **59**
Hussars Cl. TW4: Houn 3C **112**
Husseywell Cres. BR2: Hayes 1J **171**
Hutchings St. E14 2C **104**
Hutchings Wlk. NW11 4K **45**
Hutchings Wharf E14 2C **104**
(off Hutchings St.)
Hutchins Cl. E15 7E **68**
Hutchinson Ct. RM6: Chad H 4D **54**
Hutchinson Ho. NW3 7D **64**
Hutchinson Ho. SE14 7J **103**
Hutchinson Ter. HA9: Wemb 3D **60**
Hutchins Rd. SE28 7A **90**
Hutton Cl. IG8: Wfd G 6E **36**
Hutton Cl. UB6: G'frd 5H **59**
Hutton Ct. N4 1K **65**
(off Victoria Rd.)
Hutton Ct. N9 7D **24**
(off Tramway Av.)
Hutton Ct. W5 5B **78**
Hutton Gdns. HA3: Hrw W 7B **26**
Hutton Gro. N12 5E **30**
Hutton La. HA3: Hrw W 7B **26**
Hutton M. SW15 5D **116**
Hutton Row HA8: Edg 7D **28**
Hutton St. EC4 1A **14** (6B **84**)
Hutton Wlk. HA3: Hrw W 7B **26**
Huxbear St. SE4 5B **122**
Huxley Cl. UB5: N'olt 2C **76**
Huxley Ct. RM6: Chad H 7B **54**
Huxley Gdns. NW10 3F **79**
Huxley Ho. NW8 4B **4** (4B **82**)
(off Fisherton St.)
Huxley Pde. N18 5J **33**
Huxley Pl. N13 3G **33**
Huxley Rd. DA16: Well 3K **125**
Huxley Rd. E10 2E **68**
Huxley Rd. N18 4J **33**
Huxley Sayze N18 5J **33**
Huxley Sth. N18 5J **33**
Huxley St. W10 3G **81**
Hyacinth Ct. IG1: Ilf 6F **71**
Hyacinth Cl. TW12: Hamp 6E **130**
Hyacinth Dr. UB10: Uxb 7A **56**
Hyacinth Ho. E17 3D **50**
(off Vine St.)
Hyacinth Rd. SW15 1C **134**
Hybrid Ho. W3 1A **98**
Hyde, The NW9 4A **44**
(not continuous)
THE HYDE 5B **44**
Hyde Cl. E13 2J **87**
Hyde Cl. EN5: Barn 3C **20**
Hyde Cl. TW15: Ashf 6G **129**
Hyde Ct. N20 3G **31**
Hyde Cres. NW9 5A **44**
Hyde Est. Rd. NW9 5B **44**
Hyde Farm M. SW12 1H **137**
Hydefield Cl. N21 1J **33**
Hydefield Ct. N9 2K **33**
Hyde Ho. E3 5C **86**
(off Furze St.)
Hyde Ho. TW3: Houn 3G **113**
Hyde Ho. UB8: Uxb 6A **56**
Hyde Ho. W13 1A **96**
(off Singapore Rd.)
Hyde Ind. Est., The NW9 5B **44**
Hyde La. SW11 1C **118**
Hyde Pk. 4E **10** (1D **100**)
Hyde Pk. Av. N21 2H **33**
HYDE PARK CORNER 6J **11** (2F **101**)
Hyde Pk. Cnr. W1 6H **11** (2E **100**)
Hyde Pk. Cres. W2 1C **10** (6C **82**)
Hyde Pk. Gdns. N21 1H **33**
Hyde Pk. Gdns. W2 2B **10** (7B **82**)
(not continuous)
Hyde Pk. Gdns. M. W2 2B **10** (7B **82**)
Hyde Pk. Ga. SW7 2A **100**
(not continuous)
Hyde Pk. Ga. M. SW7 2A **100**
Hyde Pk. Mans. NW1 6D **4** (5C **82**)
(off Cabbell St.)
Hyde Pk. Pl. W2 2D **10** (7C **82**)
Hyde Pk. Sq. W2 1C **10** (6C **82**)
Hyde Pk. Sq. M. W2 1C **10** (6C **82**)
(off Southwick Pl.)
Hyde Pk. St. W2 1C **10** (6C **82**)
Hyde Pk. Towers W2 7A **82**
Hyderabad Way E15 7G **69**
Hyde Rd. DA7: Bex 2F **127**
Hyde Rd. N1 1E **84**
Hyde Rd. TW10: Rich 5F **115**
Hydeside Gdns. N9 2A **34**
Hyde's Pl. N1 7B **66**
Hyde St. SE8 6C **104**
Hyde Ter. TW15: Ashf 6G **129**
Hydethorpe Av. N9 2A **34**
Hydethorpe Rd. SW12 1G **137**
Hyde Va. SE10 7E **104**
Hyde Wlk. SM4: Mord 7J **153**
Hyde Way N9 2A **34**
Hyde Way UB3: Harl 4H **93**
Hydon Ct. N11 5J **31**
Hydra Bldg., The EC1 2K **7** (3A **84**)
(off Hardwick St.)
Hylands Rd. E17 2F **51**
Hylton St. SE18 4K **107**
Hyndewood SE23 3K **139**
Hyndman Ho. RM10: Dag 3G **73**
(off Kershaw Rd.)
Hyndman St. SE15 6H **103**
Hynton Rd. RM8: Dag 2C **72**
Hyperion Ct. E16 5J **87**
(off Robertson Rd.)
Hyperion Ho. E3 2A **86**
(off Arbery Rd.)
Hyperion Ho. SW2 6K **119**
Hyrstdene CR2: S Croy 4B **168**
Hyson Rd. SE16 5H **103**
Hythe Av. DA7: Bex 7E **108**
Hythe Cl. N18 4B **34**
Hythe Ho. SE16 2J **103**
(off Swan Rd.)
Hythe Ho. W6 4E **98**
(off Shepherd's Bush Rd.)
Hythe Rd. CR7: Thor H 2D **156**
Hythe Rd. KT6: Surb 6E **150**
Hythe Rd. NW10 3B **80**
Hythe Rd. Ind. Est. NW10 3C **80**

I

Ian Bowater Ct. N1 1F **9** (3D **84**)
(off East Rd.)
Ian Ct. SE23 2J **139**
Ian Sq. EN3: Enf H 1E **24**
Ibberton Ho. SW8 7K **101**
(off Meadow Rd.)
Ibberton Ho. W14 3G **99**
(off Russell Rd.)
Ibbotson Av. E16 6H **87**
Ibbotson Ct. SL3: Poyle 4A **174**
Ibbott St. E1 4J **85**
Iberia Ho. N19 7H **47**
Iberian Av. SM6: Bedd 4H **167**
Ibex Ho. E15 5G **69**
(off Forest La.)
Ibis Ct. BR3: Beck 1F **159**
(off Albemarle Rd.)
Ibis Ct. SE8 6B **104**
(off Edward Pl.)
Ibis La. W4 1J **115**
Ibis Way UB4: Yead 6B **76**
Ibrox Ct. IG9: Buck H 2F **37**
Ibscott Cl. RM10: Dag 6J **73**
Ibsley Gdns. SW15 1C **134**
Ibsley Way EN4: Cockf 5H **21**
ICA Cinema 5D **12** (1H **101**)
(within ICA)
Icarus Ho. E3 3B **86**
(off British St.)
ICA Theatre 4D **12** (1H **101**)
(within ICA)
Iceland Rd. E3 1C **86**
Iceland Wharf SE16 4A **104**
Iceni Ct. E3 1B **86**
(off Parnell Rd.)
Iceni Ct. IG9: Buck H 1E **36**
Ice Wharf N1 2J **83**
Ice Wharf Marina N1 2J **83**
(off New Wharf Rd.)
Ice Works, The NW1 7F **65**
(off Jamestown Rd.)
Ickburgh Est. E5 2H **67**
Ickburgh Rd. E5 3H **67**
ICKENHAM 3D **56**
Ickenham Cl. HA4: Ruis 2F **57**
Ickenham Grn. UB10: Ick 1D **56**
Ickenham Rd. HA4: Ruis 2E **56**
Ickleton Rd. SE9 4C **142**
Icknield Dr. IG2: Ilf 5F **53**
Icknield Ho. SW3 5D **16** (5C **100**)
(off Cale St.)
Ickworth Pk. Rd. E17 4A **50**
Icon Apts. SE1 7G **15** (3E **102**)
(off Cluny Pl.)
Icona Point E15 1E **86**
(off Warton Rd.)
Icon College of Technology & Management 6G **85**
(off Adler St.)
Iconia Ho. BR2: Broml 4A **160**
Idaho Bldg. SE13 1D **122**
(off Deal's Gateway)
Ida Rd. N15 4D **48**
Ida St. E14 6E **86**
(not continuous)
Ide Mans. E1 7K **85**
(off Cable St.)
Iden Cl. BR2: Broml 3G **159**
Idlecombe Rd. SW17 6E **136**
Idmiston Rd. E15 4H **69**
Idmiston Rd. KT4: Wor Pk 7B **152**
Idmiston Rd. SE27 3C **138**
Idmiston Sq. KT4: Wor Pk 7B **152**
Idol La. EC3 3G **15** (7E **84**)
Idonia St. SE8 7C **104**
Iffley Cl. UB8: Uxb 7A **56**
Iffley Rd. W6 3D **98**
Ifield Ho. SE17 5E **102**
(off Madron St.)
Ifield Rd. SW10 6K **99**
Ifor Evans Pl. E1 4K **85**
Ightham Ho. BR3: Beck 7B **140**
(off Bethersden Cl.)
Ightham Ho. SE17 4E **102**
(off Beckway St.)
Ightham Rd. DA8: Erith 7G **109**
Ikon Ho. E1 7J **85**
(off Devonport St.)
Ilbert St. W10 3F **81**
Ilchester Gdns. W2 7K **81**
Ilchester Mans. W8 3J **99**
(off Abingdon Rd.)
Ilchester Pl. W14 3H **99**
Ilchester Rd. RM8: Dag 5B **72**
Ildersly Gro. SE21 2D **138**
Ilderton Rd. SE15 6J **103**
Ilderton Rd. SE16 5J **103**
Ilderton Wharf SE15 6J **103**
(off Rollins St.)
Ilex Cl. TW16: Sun 2A **148**
Ilex Rd. NW10 6B **62**
Ilex Way SW16 5A **138**
ILFORD 3F **71**
Ilford Bldg. IG1: Ilf 3E **70**
Ilford Golf Course 1D **70**
Ilford Hill IG1: Ilf 3E **70**
Ilford Ho. N1 6D **66**
(off Dove Rd.)
Ilford La. IG1: Ilf 3F **71**
Ilford Sports Club 2J **71**
Ilfracombe Flats SE1 6D **14** (2C **102**)
(off Marshalsea Rd.)
Ilfracombe Gdns. RM6: Chad H 7B **54**
Ilfracombe Rd. BR1: Broml 3H **141**
Iliffe St. SE17 5B **102**
Iliffe Yd. SE17 5B **102**
(off Crampton St.)
Ilkeston Ct. E5 4K **67**
(off Overbury St.)
Ilkley Cl. SE19 6D **138**
Ilkley Rd. E16 5A **88**
Illingworth Cl. CR4: Mitc 3B **154**
Illingworth Way EN1: Enf 5K **23**
Illumina Ho. SW18 5J **117**
(off Broomhill Rd.)
Ilmington Rd. HA3: Kenton 6D **42**
Ilminster Gdns. SW11 4C **118**
Ilsley Ct. SW8 2G **119**
Image Ct. RM7: Rush G 6K **55**
Images IG2: Ilf 6E **52**
Imani Mans. SW11 2B **118**
IMAX (BFI) 5J **13** (1A **102**)
Imber Cl. N14 7B **22**
Imber Court 7H **149**
Imber Cross KT7: T Ditt 6K **149**
Imber Gro. KT10: Esh 7H **149**
Imber Pk. Rd. KT10: Esh 7H **149**
Imber St. N1 1D **84**
Impact Bus. Pk. UB6: G'frd 2B **78**
Impact Ct. SE20 2H **157**
Impact Ho. CR0: C'don 3C **168**
Imperial Av. N16 4E **66**
Imperial Cl. HA2: Harr 6E **40**
Imperial Cl. NW2 5D **62**
Imperial College London Charing Cross Campus 6F **99**
Imperial College London Chelsea & Westminster Campus 6A **100**
(within Chelsea & Westminster Hospital)
Imperial College London Hamersmith Campus 6C **80**
Imperial College London Royal Brompton Campus, Emmanuel Kaye 6C **16** (5C **100**)
(off Manresa Rd.)
Imperial College London Royal Brompton Campus, Guy Scadding Bldg. 5B **16** (5B **100**)
(off Dovehouse St.)
Imperial College London St Mary's Campus 7B **4** (6B **82**)
(off Norfolk Pl.)
Imperial College London Sth. Kensington Campus 1A **16** (3B **100**)
Imperial College London Sth. Kensington Campus, Ennismore Gdns. M. 1B **16** (3B **100**)
(off Ennismore Gdns. M.)
Imperial College London Sth. Kensington Campus, Kensington Gore 1A **16** (3B **100**)
Imperial Coll. Rd. SW7 2A **16** (3B **100**)
Imperial Ct. HA2: Harr 7E **40**
Imperial Ct. N20 3F **31**
Imperial Ct. N6 6G **47**
Imperial Ct. NW8 2C **82**
(off Prince Albert Rd.)
Imperial Ct. SE11 6J **19** (5A **102**)
Imperial Cres. SW6 2A **118**
Imperial Dr. HA2: Harr 7E **40**
Imperial Gdns. CR4: Mitc 3F **155**
Imperial Gro. EN4: Had W 1E **20**
Imperial Hgts. E18 1J **51**
(off Queen Mary Av.)
Imperial Ho. E14 7B **86**
(off Victory Pl.)
Imperial Ho. E3 3A **86**
(off Grove Rd.)
Imperial M. E6 2B **88**
Imperial M. SW9 4K **119**
(off Brighton Ter.)
Imperial Pl. BR7: Chst 1E **160**
Imperial Rd. N22 7D **32**
Imperial Rd. SW6 1K **117**
Imperial Rd. TW14: Felt 7G **111**
Imperial Sq. SW6 1K **117**
Imperial St. E3 3E **86**
Imperial War Mus. London All Saints Annexe 2K 19 (3A 102)
(off Austral St.)
Imperial War Mus. London Main Museum 2K 19 (3A 102)
Imperial Way BR7: Chst 3G **143**
Imperial Way CR0: Wadd 6K **167**
Imperial Way HA3: Kenton 6E **42**
Imperial Wharf E2 2H **85**
(off Darwen Pl.)
Imperial Wharf SW6 2A **118**
Imperium Ho. E1 6H **85**
(off Cannon St. Rd.)
Imre Cl. W12 1D **98**
Inca Dr. SE9 7F **125**
Inca Ter. N15 3B **48**
Inchmery Rd. SE6 2D **140**
Inchwood BR4: Addtn 4D **170**
Independence Ho. SW19 1B **154**
(off Chapter Way)
Independent Ind. Est. UB7: Yiew 1A **92**
Independent Pl. E8 5F **67**
Independents Rd. SE3 3H **123**
Inderwick Rd. N8 5K **47**
Indescon Ct. E14 2D **104**
Indescon Sq. E14 2C **104**
India Gdns. UB5: N'olt 7A **58**
India House 2G 13 (7K 83)
(off Aldwych)
Indiana Bldg. SE13 1C **122**
(off Deal's Gateway)
India Pl. WC2 2G **13** (7K **83**)
(off Montreal Pl.)
India St. EC3 1J **15** (6F **85**)
India Way SW15 6C **116**
India Way W12 7D **80**
indigo at the O2 1G **105**
Indigo M. E14 7E **86**
Indigo M. N16 3D **66**
Indigo Wlk. N2 4D **46**
Indigo Wlk. N6 4D **46**
Indus Ct. SE15 7F **103**
(off Amstel Ct.)
Indus Rd. SE7 7A **106**
Infirmary Ct. SW3 7F **17** (6D **100**)
(off West Rd.)
Inforum M. SE15 7G **103**
Infrastructure Way IG11: Bark 3D **90**
Ingal Rd. E13 4J **87**
Ingate Pl. SW8 1F **119**
Ingatestone Rd. E12 1A **70**
Ingatestone Rd. IG8: Wfd G 7E **36**
Ingatestone Rd. SE25 4H **157**
Ingelow Ho. W8 2K **99**
(off Holland St.)
Ingelow Rd. SW8 2F **119**
Ingersoll Rd. EN3: Enf W 1D **24**
Ingersoll Rd. W12 1D **98**
Ingestre Pl. W1 1B **12** (6G **83**)
Ingestre Rd. E7 4J **69**
Ingestre Rd. NW5 4F **65**
Ingham Cl. CR2: Sels 7K **169**
Ingham Rd. CR2: Sels 7J **169**
Ingham Rd. NW6 4J **63**
Inglebert St. EC1 1J **7** (3A **84**)
Ingleborough St. SW9 2A **120**
Ingleby Dr. HA1: Harr 3H **59**
Ingleby Rd. IG1: Ilf 1F **71**
Ingleby Rd. N7 3J **65**
Ingleby Rd. RM10: Dag 6H **73**
Ingleby Way BR7: Chst 5E **142**
Ingleby Way SM6: W'gton 7H **167**
Ingle Cl. HA5: Pinn 3C **40**
Ingledene Cl. NW4 6C **44**
Ingledew Rd. SE18 5H **107**
Inglefield Sq. E1 1H **103**
(off Prusom St.)
Inglehurst Gdns. IG4: Ilf 5D **52**
Inglemere Rd. CR4: Mitc 7D **136**
Inglemere Rd. SE23 3K **139**
Ingle M. EC1 1J **7** (3A **84**)
Inglesham Wlk. E9 6B **68**
Ingleside SL3: Poyle 4A **174**
Ingleside Cl. BR3: Beck 7C **140**
Ingleside Gro. SE3 6H **105**
Inglethorpe St. SW6 1F **117**
Ingleton Av. DA16: Well 5A **126**
Ingleton Rd. N18 6B **34**
Ingleton Rd. SM5: Cars 7C **166**
Ingleton St. SW9 2A **120**
Ingleway N12 6G **31**
Inglewood BR7: Chst 6H **143**
Inglewood CR0: Sels 7A **170**
Inglewood Cl. E14 4C **104**
Inglewood Copse BR1: Broml 2C **160**
Inglewood Ct. BR1: Broml 7G **141**
Inglewood M. KT6: Surb 1G **163**
Inglewood M. SE27 5C **138**
(off Elder Rd.)
Inglewood Rd. DA7: Bex 4K **127**
Inglewood Rd. NW6 5J **63**
Inglis Rd. CR0: C'don 1F **169**
Inglis Rd. W5 7F **79**
Inglis St. SE5 1B **120**
Inglis Way NW7 6A **30**
Ingoldisthorpe Gro. SE15 6F **103**
Ingot Twr. E14 5C **86**
(off Ursula Gould Way)
Ingram Av. NW11 7A **46**
Ingram Cl. HA7: Stan 5H **27**
Ingram Cl. SE11 3H **19** (4K **101**)
Ingram Ct. CR0: C'don 1B **168**
Ingram Ho. E3 1A **86**
Ingram Rd. CR7: Thor H 1C **156**
Ingram Rd. N2 4C **46**
Ingram Way UB6: G'frd 1H **77**
Ingrave Rd. RM1: Rom 4K **55**
Ingrave St. SW11 3B **118**
Ingrebourne Apts. SW6 3K **117**
Ingrebourne Ct. E4 3J **35**
Ingrebourne Ho. BR1: Broml 5F **141**
(off Brangbourne Rd.)
Ingrebourne Ho. NW8 5B **4** (5B **82**)
(off Broadley St.)
Ingress St. W4 5A **98**
Inigo Jones Rd. SE7 7C **106**
Inigo Pl. WC2 2E **12** (7J **83**)
(off Bedford St.)
Ink Bldg. W10 5F **81**
Inkerman Rd. NW5 6F **65**
Inkerman Ter. W8 3J **99**
(off Allen St.)
Inks Grn. E4 5K **35**
Inkster Ho. SW11 3C **118**
Inkwell Cl. N12 3F **31**
Ink Works Ct. SE1 7H **15** (2E **102**)
(off Bell Yd. M.)
Inman Rd. NW10 1A **80**
Inman Rd. SW18 7A **118**
Inmans Row IG8: Wfd G 4D **36**
Inner Circ. NW1 2G **5** (3E **82**)
Inner Ct. SW3 7C **16** (6C **100**)
Innerd Ct. CR0: C'don 6C **156**
(off Harry Cl.)
Inner Pk. Rd. SW19 1F **135**
Inner Ring E. TW6: H'row A 3D **110**
Inner Ring W. TW6: H'row A 3C **110**
Inner Temple La. EC4 1J **13** (6A **84**)
(off Fleet St.)
Innes Cl. SW20 2G **153**
Innes Gdns. SW15 6D **116**
Innes St. SE15 7E **102**
Innes Yd. CR0: C'don 3C **168**
Innis Ho. SE17 5E **102**
(off East St.)
Inniskilling Rd. E13 2A **88**
Innova Ct. CR0: C'don 1E **168**
Innova Pas. E1 3K **9** (4F **85**)
(off Sclater St.)
Innovation Cen., The E14 2E **104**
(off Marsh Wall)
Innovation Cl. HA0: Wemb 1E **78**
Inns of Court & City Yeomanry Mus. 6H 7 (5K 83)
Insignia Point E20 5E **68**
Inskip Cl. E10 2D **68**
Inskip Rd. RM8: Dag 1D **72**
Insley Ho. E3 3D **86**
(off Bow Rd.)
Institute for Arts in Therapy & Education, The 1B 84
(off Britannia Row)
Institute of Archaeology Collections 3C 6 (4H 83)
Institute of Commonwealth Studies 5D 6 (5H 83)
(off Russell Sq.)
Institute of Contemporary Arts (ICA) 5D 12 (1H 101)
(off Carlton Ho. Ter.)
Institute of Germanic & Romance Studies 5D 6 (5H 83)
(off Russell Sq.)
Institute of Ophthalmology 2E 8 (3D 84)
(off Peerless St.)
Institute of Psychoanalysis, The 4J 81
(off Elgin Av.)
Institute Pl. E8 5H **67**
Integer Gdns. E11 7F **51**
Interchange, The NW1 7F **65**
(off Camden Lock Pl.)

240 A–Z London

Interface Ho. – Jennifer Ho.

Interface Ho. TW3: Houn 3E **112** *(off Staines Rd.)*
International Av. TW5: Cran 5A **94**
International Bus. Pk. E15 1F **87**
International Hall WC1 4F **7** (4J **83**) *(off Lansdowne Ter.)*
International Ho. E1 3K **15** (7F **85**) *(off St Katharine's Way)*
International Ho. TW8: Bford 5E **96** *(off Gt. West Rd.)*
INTERNATIONAL QUARTER, THE 6E **68**
International Sq. E20 6E **68** *(within Westfield Shop. Cen.)*
International Trad. Est. UB2: S'hall 3K **93**
International Way E20 6E **68**
International Way TW16: Sun 1G **147**
Inverary Pl. SE18 6H **107**
Inver Cl. E5 2J **67**
Inverclyde Gdns. RM6: Chad H 4D **54** (not continuous)
Inver Ct. W2 6K **81**
Inver Ct. W6 3C **98**
Inveresk Gdns. KT4: Wor Pk 3C **164**
Inverforth Cl. NW3 2A **64**
Inverforth Rd. N11 5A **32**
Invergarry Ho. NW6 2K **81** *(off Carlton Vale)*
Inverine Rd. SE7 5K **105**
Invermead Cl. W6 3C **98**
Invermore Pl. SE18 4G **107**
Inverness Av. EN1: Enf 1K **23**
Inverness Ct. SE6 1H **141**
Inverness Gdns. W8 1K **99**
Inverness M. E16 1G **107**
Inverness M. W2 7K **81**
Inverness Pl. W2 7K **81**
Inverness Rd. KT4: Wor Pk 1F **165**
Inverness Rd. N18 5C **34**
Inverness Rd. TW3: Houn 4D **112**
Inverness Rd. UB2: S'hall 4C **94**
Inverness St. NW1 1F **83**
Inverness Ter. W2 6K **81**
Inverton Rd. SE15 4K **121**
Invicta Cen., The IG11: Bark 1A **90**
Invicta Cl. BR7: Chst 5E **142**
Invicta Cl. E3 5C **86**
Invicta Cl. TW14: Felt 1H **129**
Invicta Gro. UB5: N'olt 3D **76**
Invicta Pde. DA14: Sidc 4B **144**
Invicta Plaza SE1 4A **14** (1B **102**)
Invicta Rd. SE3 7J **105**
Inville Rd. SE17 5D **102** (not continuous)
Inville Wlk. SE17 5D **102**
Invito IG2: Ilf 6E **52**
Inwen Ct. SE8 5A **104** (not continuous)
Inwood Av. TW3: Houn 3G **113**
Inwood Bus. Pk. TW3: Houn 4F **113**
Inwood Cl. CR0: C'don 2A **170**
Inwood Ct. NW1 7G **65** *(off Rochester Sq.)*
Inwood Ho. N1 1B **84** *(off Elliott's Pl.)*
Inwood Rd. TW3: Houn 4F **113**
Inworth St. SW11 2C **118**
Inworth Wlk. N1 1C **84** *(off Popham St.)*
IO Cen. SE18 3G **107** (not continuous)
Iona Cl. SE6 7C **122**
Iona Cl. SM4: Mord 7K **153**
Ion Ct. E2 2G **85**
Ionian Bldg. E14 7A **86** *(off Narrow St.)*
Ionian Ho. E1 4K **85** *(off Duckett St.)*
Ion Sq. E2 2G **85**
IO Trade Cen. CR0: Bedd 4K **167**
Ipsden Bldgs. SE1 6K **13** (2A **102**) *(off Windmill Wlk.)*
Ipswich Rd. SW17 6E **136**
Ira Ct. SE27 2B **138**
Ireland Cl. E6 5D **88**
Ireland Pl. N22 7D **32**
Ireland Yd. EC4 1B **14** (6B **84**)
Irene M. W7 1K **95** *(off Uxbridge Rd.)*
Irene Rd. BR6: Orp 7K **161**
Irene Rd. SW6 1J **117**
Ireton Cl. N10 7K **31**
Ireton Ho. SW15 5G **117** *(off Stamford Sq.)*
Ireton St. E3 4C **86**
Iris Av. DA5: Bexl 5E **126**
Iris Cl. CR0: C'don 1K **169**
Iris Cl. E6 5C **88**
Iris Cl. IG1: Ilf 5F **71**
Iris Cl. KT6: Surb 7F **151**
Iris Cl. N14 7C **22**
Iris Ct. SE14 1J **121** *(off Briant St.)*
Iris Cres. DA7: Bex 6F **109**
Iris Gdns. KT7: T Ditt 7J **149**
Iris M. TW4: Houn 6E **112**
Iris Rd. KT19: Ewe 5H **163**
Iris Wlk. HA8: Edg 4D **28**
Iris Way E4 6G **35**
Irkdale Av. EN1: Enf 1A **24**
Iron Bri. Cl. NW10 5A **62**
Ironbridge Cl. UB2: S'hall 1G **95**
Iron Bri. Ho. NW1 7D **64**
Iron Bri. Rd. Nth. UB11: Stock P 2C **92**
Iron Bri. Rd. Sth. UB7: W Dray 2C **92**
Iron Mill Pl. SW18 6K **117**
Iron Mill Rd. SW18 6K **117**
Ironmonger La. EC2 1D **14** (6C **84**)
Ironmonger Pas. EC1 2D **8** (3C **84**) *(off Ironmonger Row)*
Ironmonger Row EC1 2C **8** (3C **84**)
Ironmonger Row Baths 2D **8** (3C **84**) *(off Ironmonger Row)*
Ironmongers Pl. E14 4C **104**
Ironside Cl. SE16 2K **103**
Ironside Ct. CR2: S Croy 6D **168**
Ironside Ct. TW11: Hamp W 1C **150**
Ironside Ho. E9 4A **68**
Irons Way RM5: Col R 1J **55**
Iron Works E3 1C **86**
Ironworks, The N1 2J **83** *(off Albion Wlk.)*
Ironworks Way E13 2B **88**
Irvine Av. HA3: Kenton 3A **42**
Irvine Cl. E14 5D **86**
Irvine Cl. N20 2H **31**
Irvine Ct. W1 4B **6** (4G **83**) *(off Whitfield St.)*
Irvine Ho. N7 6K **65** *(off Caledonian Rd.)*
Irvine Way BR6: Orp 7K **161**
Irving Av. UB5: N'olt 1B **76**
Irving Gro. SW9 2K **119**
Irving Ho. SE17 5B **102** *(off Doddington Gro.)*
Irving Mans. W14 6G **99** *(off Queen's Club Gdns.)*
Irving M. N1 6C **66**
Irving Rd. W14 3F **99**
Irving St. WC2 3D **12** (7H **83**)
Irving Way NW9 5C **44**
Irwell Ct. W7 6H **77** *(off Hobbayne Rd.)*
Irwell Est. SE16 3J **103**
Irwin Av. SE18 7J **107**
Irwin Cl. NW7 5B **30**
Irwin Cl. UB10: Ick 3C **56**
Irwin Gdns. NW10 1D **80**
Isaac Way SE1 6D **14** (2C **102**) *(off Sanctuary St.)*
Isabel Hill Cl. TW12: Hamp 1F **149**
Isabella Cl. N14 7B **22**
Isabella Ct. TW10: Rich 6F **115** *(off Kingsmead)*
Isabella Dr. BR6: Farnb 4G **173**
Isabella Ho. SE11 5B **102** *(off Othello Cl.)*
Isabella Ho. W6 5E **98** *(off Queen Caroline St.)*
Isabella M. N1 6E **66**
Isabella Pl. KT2: King T 5F **133**
Isabella Plantation Gdn. 3H **133**
Isabella Rd. E9 5J **67**
Isabella St. SE1 5A **14** (1B **102**)
Isambard M. E14 3E **104**
Isambard Pl. SE16 1J **103**
Isambard Rd. 3E **94**
Isel Way SE22 5E **120**
Isham Rd. SW16 2J **155**
Isis Cl. HA4: Ruis 6E **38**
Isis Cl. SW15 4E **116**
Isis Ct. W4 7H **97**
Isis Ho. N18 6A **34**
Isis Ho. NW8 4B **4** (4B **82**) *(off Church St. Est.)*
Isis Ho. SE20 7G **139**
Isis St. SW18 2A **136**
Island, The KT7: T Ditt 6A **150**
Island, The UB7: Lford 3D **174**
Island Apts. N1 1C **84**
Island Barn Reservoir Sailing Club 6F **149**
Island Farm Av. KT8: W Mole 5D **148**
Island Farm Rd. KT8: W Mole 5D **148**
Island Ho. E3 3E **86**
Island Rd. CR4: Mitc 7D **136**
Island Rd. SE16 4K **103**
Island Row E14 6B **86**
Isla Rd. SE18 6G **107**
Islay Gdns. TW4: Houn 5B **112**
Islay Wlk. N1 6C **66** *(off Douglas Rd. Sth.)*
Isleden Ho. N1 1C **84** *(off Prebend St.)*
Isledon Rd. N7 3A **66**
ISLEDON VILLAGE 3A **66**
Islehurst Cl. BR7: Chst 1E **160**
ISLE OF DOGS 2D **104**
ISLEWORTH 3A **114**
Isleworth Ait Nature Reserve 3B **114**
Isleworth Bus. Complex TW7: Isle 2K **113**
Isleworth Prom. TW1: Twick 4B **114**
Isleworth Recreation Cen. 4K **113**
Isley Ct. E14 4E **86** *(off Teviot St.)*
Isley Ct. SW8 2G **119**
ISLINGTON 7B **66**
Islington Bus. Cen. N1 1C **84** *(off Coleman Flds.)*
Islington Crematorium 1D **46**
Islington Grn. N1 1B **84** (not continuous)
Islington High St. N1 2A **84** (not continuous)
Islington Mus. 2A **8** (3B **84**)
Islington Pk. M. N1 7B **66**
Islington Pk. St. N1 7A **66**
Islington Pl. N1 1A **84**
Islington Sq. N1 1B **84**
Islington Tennis Cen. 6J **65**
Islip Gdns. HA8: Edg 7E **28**
Islip Gdns. UB5: N'olt 7C **58**
Islip Mnr. Rd. UB5: N'olt 7C **58**
Islip St. NW5 5G **65**
Ismailia Rd. E7 7K **69**
Isobel Ho. HA1: Harr 5K **41**
Isobel Pl. N15 4F **49**
Isola Ct. N1 1C **84** *(off Popham Rd.)*
Isom Cl. E13 3K **87**
Issa Rd. TW3: Houn 4D **112**
Issigonis Ho. W3 1B **98** *(off Cowley Rd.)*
Istra Ho. E20 5E **68** *(off Logan Cl.)*
Itaska Cotts. WD23: B Hea 1D **26**
Ithell Ct. HA0: Wemb 5D **60**
Ivanhoe Cl. UB8: Cowl 5A **74**
Ivanhoe Dr. HA3: Kenton 3A **42**
Ivanhoe Ho. E3 2A **86** *(off Grove Rd.)*
Ivanhoe Rd. SE5 3F **121**
Ivanhoe Rd. TW4: Houn 3B **112**
Ivaro Cl. RM5: Col R 1J **55**
Ivatt Pl. W14 5H **99**
Ivatt Way N17 3B **48**
Iveagh Av. NW10 2G **79**
Iveagh Cl. E9 1K **85**
Iveagh Cl. HA6: Nwood 1D **38**
Iveagh Cl. NW10 2G **79**
Iveagh Ct. BR3: Beck 3E **158**
Iveagh Ct. E1 1J **15** (6F **85**) *(off Haydon St.)*
Iveagh Ho. SW10 7A **100** *(off King's Rd.)*
Iveagh Ho. SW9 2B **120**
Iveagh Ter. NW10 2G **79** *(off Iveagh Av.)*
Ivedon Rd. DA16: Well 2C **126**
Ive Farm Cl. E10 2C **68**
Ive Farm La. E10 2C **68**
Iveley Rd. SW4 2G **119**
Ivere Dr. EN5: New Bar 6E **20**
Iver Ho. N1 1E **84** *(off Halcomb St.)*
Iverhurst Cl. DA6: Bex 5D **126**
Iverna Ct. W8 3J **99**
Iverna Gdns. TW14: Felt 5F **111**
Iverna Gdns. W8 3J **99**
Iverson Rd. NW6 6H **63**
Ivers Way CR0: New Ad 7D **170**
Ives Rd. E16 5G **87**
Ives St. SW3 3D **16** (4C **100**)
Ivestor Ter. SE23 7J **121**
Ivimey St. E2 3G **85**
Ivinghoe Cl. EN1: Enf 1K **23**
Ivinghoe Ho. N7 5H **65**
Ivinghoe Rd. RM8: Dag 5B **72**
Ivo Pl. N19 3H **65**
Ivor Ct. N8 6J **47**
Ivor Ct. NW1 3E **4** (4D **82**) *(off Gloucester Pl.)*
Ivor Gro. SE9 1F **143**
Ivories, The N1 7C **66** *(off Northampton St.)*
Ivor Pl. NW1 4E **4** (4D **82**)
Ivor St. NW1 7G **65**
Ivory Ct. E18 1J **51**
Ivory Ct. TW13: Felt 1J **129**
Ivorydown BR1: Broml 4J **141**
Ivory Ho. E1 4K **15** (1F **103**)
Ivory Pl. W11 7G **81** *(off Treadgold St.)*
Ivory Sq. SW11 3A **118**
Ivybridge Cl. TW1: Twick 7A **114**
Ivybridge Cl. UB8: Uxb 3A **74**
Ivybridge Ct. BR7: Chst 1E **160** *(off Old Hill)*
Ivybridge Ct. NW1 7F **65** *(off Lewis St.)*
Ivybridge La. WC2 3F **13** (7J **83**)
Ivy Bri. Retail Pk. 5K **113**
Ivychurch Cl. SE20 7J **139**
Ivychurch La. SE17 5F **103**
Ivy Cl. HA2: Harr 4D **58**
Ivy Cl. HA5: Eastc 7A **40**
Ivy Cl. TW16: Sun 2A **148**
Ivy Cotts. E14 7E **86**
Ivy Cotts. UB10: Hil 3C **74**
Ivy Ct. SE16 5G **103** *(off Argyle Way)*
Ivy Cres. W4 4J **97**
Ivydale Rd. SE15 3K **121**
Ivydale Rd. SM5: Cars 2D **166**
Ivyday Gro. SW16 3K **137**
Ivydene KT8: W Mole 5D **148**
Ivydene Cl. SM1: Sutt 4A **166**
Ivydene Ct. IG9: Buck H 2F **37** *(off Queen's Rd.)*
Ivy Gdns. CR4: Mitc 3H **155**
Ivy Gdns. N8 6J **47**
Ivy Ho. Rd. UB10: Ick 3D **56**
Ivyhouse Rd. RM9: Dag 6D **72**
Ivy La. TW4: Houn 4D **112**
Ivy Lodge W11 1J **99** *(off Notting Hill Ga.)*
Ivymount Rd. SE27 3A **138**
Ivy Rd. E16 6J **87**
Ivy Rd. E17 6C **50**
Ivy Rd. KT6: Surb 1G **163**
Ivy Rd. N14 7B **22**
Ivy Rd. NW2 4E **62**
Ivy Rd. SE4 4B **122**
Ivy Rd. SW17 5C **136**
Ivy Rd. TW3: Houn 4F **113**
Ivy St. N1 2E **84**
Ivy Wlk. HA6: Nwood 1G **39**
Ivy Wlk. RM9: Dag 6E **72**
Ixworth Pl. SW3 5C **16** (5C **100**)
Izane Rd. DA6: Bex 4F **127**

J

Jacana Ct. E1 3K **15** (7F **85**) *(off Star Pl.)*
Jacaranda Cl. KT3: N Mald 3A **152**
Jacaranda Gro. E8 7F **67**
Jackass La. BR2: Kes 5K **171**
Jack Barnett Way N22 2K **47**
Jack Clow Rd. E15 2G **87**
Jack Cook Ho. IG11: Bark 7F **71**
Jack Cornwell St. E12 4E **70**
Jack Dash Way E6 4C **88**
Jack Dimmer Cl. SW16 2G **155**
Jackets La. HA6: Nwood 1D **38**
Jack Goodchild Way KT1: King T 3H **151**
Jack Jones Way RM9: Dag 1F **91**
Jacklin Grn. IG8: Wfd G 4D **36**
Jackman Ho. E1 1H **103** *(off Watts St.)*
Jackman M. NW2 3A **62**
Jackman St. E8 1H **85**
Jacks Farm Way E4 6K **35**
Jackson & Joseph Bldg. E1 5K **9** (5F **85**) *(off Princelet St.)*
Jackson Cl. E9 7J **67**
Jackson Cl. UB10: Uxb 7A **56**
Jackson Ct. E7 6K **69**
Jackson Ho. N11 5B **32**
Jackson Rd. BR2: Broml 2D **172**
Jackson Rd. EN4: E Barn 6H **21**
Jackson Rd. IG11: Bark 1H **89**
Jackson Rd. N7 4K **65**
Jackson Rd. UB10: Uxb 7A **56**
Jacksons La. N6 7E **46**
Jacksons Lane Theatre 6F **47** *(off Archway Rd.)*
Jacksons Pl. CR0: C'don 1D **168**
Jackson St. SE18 6E **106**
Jackson's Way CR0: C'don 3C **170**
Jackson Way UB2: S'hall 2F **95**
Jacks Pl. E1 5J **9** (5F **85**) *(off Corbet Pl.)*
Jack the Ripper Mus. 7G **85**
Jack Walker Ct. N5 4B **66**
Jacob Ho. DA18: Erith 2D **108** *(off Kale Rd.)*
Jacobin Lodge N7 5J **65**
Jacob Mans. E1 6H **85** *(off Commercial Rd.)*
Jacob M. HA7: Stan 2F **27**
Jacobs Cl. RM10: Dag 4H **73**
Jacobs Ct. E1 6G **85** *(off Plumber's Row)*
Jacobs Ho. E13 3A **88** *(off New City Rd.)*
Jacobs Island Ho. SE16 3F **103** *(off Spa Rd.)*
Jacobs M. SW15 4G **117**
Jacob St. SE1 6K **15** (2G **103**)
Jacob's Well M. W1 6H **5** (5E **82**)
Jacotts Ho. W10 4E **80** *(off Sutton Way)*
Jacquard Ct. SW18 5K **117** *(off Courthouse Way)*
Jacqueline Cl. UB5: N'olt 1C **76**
Jacqueline Creft Ter. N6 6E **46** *(off Grange Rd.)*
Jacqueline Ho. NW1 1D **82** *(off Regent's Pk. Rd.)*
Jacqueline Vs. E17 5E **50** *(off Shernhall St.)*
Jade Cl. E16 6B **88**
Jade Cl. NW2 7F **45**
Jade Cl. RM8: Dag 1C **72**
Jade Ter. NW6 7A **64**
Jaffe Rd. IG1: Ilf 1H **71**
Jaffray Rd. BR2: Broml 4B **160**
Jaggard Way SW12 7D **118**
Jagger Ho. SW11 1D **118** *(off Rosenau Rd.)*
Jago Cl. SE18 6G **107**
Jago Wlk. SE5 7D **102**
Jake Russell Wlk. E16 7A **88**
Jamaica Rd. CR7: Thor H 6B **156**
Jamaica Rd. SE1 7K **15** (2F **103**)
Jamaica Rd. SE16 3G **103**
Jamaica St. E1 6J **85**
James Allens School Swimming Pool 5E **120**
James Anderson Ct. E2 2E **84** *(off Kingsland Rd.)*
James Av. NW2 5E **62**
James Av. RM8: Dag 1F **73**
James Bedford Cl. HA5: Pinn 2A **40**
James Boswell Cl. SW16 4K **137**
James Brine Ho. E2 1K **9** (3F **85**) *(off Ravenscroft St.)*
James Campbell Ho. E2 2J **85** *(off Old Ford Rd.)*
James Clavell Sq. SE18 3F **107**
James Cl. E13 2J **87**
James Cl. NW11 6G **45**
James Collins Cl. W9 4H **81**
James Ct. HA6: Nwood 1H **39**
James Ct. N1 1C **84** *(off Raynor Pl.)*
James Ct. NW9 2A **44**
James Ct. UB5: N'olt 2C **76** *(off Church Rd.)*
James Docherty Ho. E2 2H **85** *(off Patriot Sq.)*
James Dudson Ct. NW10 7J **61**
James Est. CR4: Mitc 2D **154**
James Gdns. N22 7G **33**
James Hammett Ho. E2 1K **9** (3F **85**) *(off Ravenscroft St.)*
James Hill Ho. W10 4G **81** *(off Kensal Rd.)*
James Ho. E1 4A **86** *(off Solebay St.)*
James Ho. SE16 2K **103** *(off Wolfe Cres.)*
James Ho. SW8 7J **101** *(off Wyvil Rd.)*
James Ho. W10 4G **81**
James Joyce Wlk. SE24 4B **120**
James La. E10 7E **50**
James La. E11 6F **51**
James Leal Cen. Woodford 5G **37**
James Lighthill Ho. WC1 1H **7** (2K **83**) *(off Penton Ri.)*
James Lind Ho. SE8 4B **104** *(off Grove St.)*
James Middleton Ho. E2 3H **85** *(off Middleton St.)*
James Morgan M. N1 1C **84**
James Newman Ct. SE9 3E **142**
Jameson Cl. W3 2J **97**
Jameson Ct. E2 2J **85** *(off Russia La.)*
Jameson Ho. SE11 5G **19** (5K **101**) *(off Glasshouse Wlk.)*
Jameson Lodge N6 6G **47**
Jameson St. W8 1J **99**
James Pl. N17 1F **49**
James Riley Point E15 1E **86** *(off Carpenters Rd.)*
James's Cotts. TW9: Kew 7G **97**
James Stewart Ho. NW6 7H **63**
James St. EN1: Enf 5A **24**
James St. IG11: Bark 7G **71**
James St. TW3: Houn 3H **113**
James St. W1 7H **5** (6E **82**)
James St. WC2 2F **13** (7J **83**)
James Stroud Ho. SE17 5C **102** *(off Walworth Pl.)*
James Ter. SW14 3K **115** *(off Church Path)*
Jameston Lodge HA4: Ruis 1H **57**
Jamestown Rd. NW1 1F **83**
Jamestown Way E14 7F **87**
James Voller Way E1 6J **85**
James Yd. E4 6A **36**
Jam Factory, The SE1 3E **102** *(off Green Wlk.)*
Jamieson Ho. TW4: Houn 6D **112**
Jamilah Ho. E16 7E **88** *(off University Way)*
Jamuna Cl. E14 5A **86**
Jane Austen Hall E16 1K **105** *(off Wesley Av.)*
Jane Austen Ho. SW1 6A **18** (5G **101**) *(off Churchill Gdns.)*
Jane Seymour Ct. SE9 7H **125**
Jane St. E1 6H **85**
Janet Adegoke Swimming Pool 7C **80**
Janet St. E14 3C **104**
Janeway Pl. SE16 2H **103**
Janeway St. SE16 2G **103**
Janice M. IG1: Ilf 2F **71**
Jansen Wlk. SW11 3B **118**
Janson Cl. E15 5G **69**
Janson Cl. NW10 3A **62**
Janson Rd. E15 5G **69**
Jansons Rd. N15 3E **48**
Japan Cres. N4 7K **47**
Japan Rd. RM6: Chad H 6D **54**
Jaquard Ct. E2 2J **85** *(off Bishop's Way)*
Jardine Rd. E1 7K **85**
Jarman Ho. E1 5J **85** *(off Jubilee St.)*
Jarman Ho. SE16 4K **103** *(off Hawkstone Rd.)*
Jarret Ho. E3 3C **86** *(off Bow Rd.)*
Jarrett Cl. SW2 1B **138**
Jarrow Cl. SM4: Mord 5K **153**
Jarrow Rd. N17 4H **49**
Jarrow Rd. RM6: Chad H 6C **54**
Jarrow Rd. SE16 4J **103**
Jarrow Way E9 4B **68**
Jarvis Cl. EN5: Barn 5A **20**
Jarvis Cl. IG11: Bark 1H **89**
Jarvis Ho. SE15 1G **121** *(off Goldsmith Rd.)*
Jarvis Rd. CR2: S Croy 6D **168**
Jarvis Rd. SE22 4E **120**
Jashoda Ho. SE18 5E **106** *(off Connaught M.)*
Jasmin Cl. HA6: Nwood 1H **39**
Jasmin Ct. SE12 6J **123**
Jasmine Cl. BR6: Farnb 2F **173**
Jasmine Cl. IG1: Ilf 5F **71**
Jasmine Cl. UB1: S'hall 7C **76**
Jasmine Ct. SW19 5J **135**
Jasmine Gdns. CR0: C'don 3D **170**
Jasmine Gdns. HA2: Harr 2E **58**
Jasmine Gro. SE20 1H **157**
Jasmine Ho. SW18 3A **118**
Jasmine Rd. RM7: Rush G 2K **73**
Jasmine Sq. E3 1B **86** *(off Hawthorn Av.)*
Jasmine Ter. UB7: W Dray 2C **92**
Jasmine Way KT8: E Mos 4J **149**
Jasmin Lodge SE16 5H **103** *(off Sherwood Gdns.)*
Jasmin Rd. KT19: Ewe 5H **163**
Jason Ct. SW9 1A **120** *(off Southey Rd.)*
Jason Ct. W1 7H **5** (6E **82**) *(off Wigmore St.)*
Jason Wlk. SE9 4E **142**
Jasper Av. W7 2K **95**
Jasper Cl. EN3: Enf W 1D **24**
Jasper Pas. SE19 6F **139**
Jasper Rd. E16 6B **88**
Jasper Rd. SE19 5F **139**
Jasper Wlk. N1 1E **8** (3D **84**)
Java Ho. E14 6G **87**
Java Wharf SE1 6K **15** (2F **103**) *(off Shad Thames)*
Javelin Ct. HA7: Stan 5G **27** *(off William Dr.)*
Javelin Way UB5: N'olt 3B **76**
Jaycroft EN2: Enf 1F **23**
Jay Gdns. BR7: Chst 4D **142**
Jay Ho. E3 1B **86** *(off Hawthorn Av.)*
Jay M. SM5: Cars 3D **166**
Jay M. SW7 7A **10** (2A **100**)
Jays St. N1 1K **83**
Jazzfern Ter. HA0: Wemb 5A **60**
Jean Batten Cl. SM6: W'gton 7K **167**
Jean Brown Indoor Arena, The 1H **53**
Jean Darling Ho. SW10 6B **100** *(off Milman's St.)*
Jean Ho. SW17 5C **136**
Jeanne Ct. E14 5A **86** *(off Pechora Way)*
Jean Pardies Ho. E1 5J **85** *(off Jubilee St.)*
Jebb Av. SW2 6J **119** (not continuous)
Jebb St. E3 2C **86**
Jedburgh Rd. E13 3A **88**
Jedburgh St. SW11 4E **118**
Jeddo M. W12 2B **98**
Jeddo Rd. W12 2B **98**
Jeeyas Apts. E16 5H **87**
Jefferson Bldg. E14 2C **104**
Jefferson Cl. IG2: Ilf 5F **53**
Jefferson Cl. W13 3B **96**
Jefferson Ho. TW8: Bford 6E **96**
Jefferson Ho. UB7: W Dray 2B **92** *(off Park Lodge Av.)*
Jefferson Pl. BR2: Broml 6B **160**
Jefferson Plaza E3 4E **86** *(off Hannaford Wlk.)*
Jefferson Wlk. SE18 6E **106**
Jeffrey Row SE12 5K **123**
Jeffrey's Pl. NW1 7G **65**
Jeffreys Rd. EN3: Brim 4F **25**
Jeffreys Rd. SW4 2J **119**
Jeffrey's St. NW1 7G **65**
Jeffreys Wlk. SW4 2J **119**
Jeffs Cl. TW12: Hamp 6F **131**
Jeffs Rd. SM1: Sutt 4H **165**
Jeger Av. E2 1F **85**
Jeken Rd. SE9 4A **124**
Jelf Rd. SW2 5A **120**
Jelico Point SE16 2B **104** *(off Rotherhithe St.)*
Jellicoe Gdns. HA7: Stan 6E **26**
Jellicoe Ho. E2 1K **9** (2G **85**) *(off Ropley St.)*
Jellicoe Rd. E13 4J **87**
Jellicoe Rd. N17 7J **33**
Jemma Knowles Cl. SW2 1A **138** *(off Tulse Hill)*
Jemmett Cl. KT2: King T 1H **151**
Jemotts Ct. SE14 6K **103** *(off Myers La.)*
Jem Paterson Ct. HA1: Harr 4J **59**
Jengar Cl. SM1: Sutt 4K **165**
Jenkins La. IG11: Bark 2G **89**
Jenkinson Ho. E2 3K **85** *(off Usk St.)*
Jenkins Rd. E13 4K **87**
Jenner Av. W3 5K **79**
Jenner Cl. DA14: Sidc 4A **144**
Jenner Ct. N21 5D **22** *(off Pennington Dr.)*
Jenner Ho. WC1 3F **7** (4J **83**) *(off Hunter St.)*
Jenner Pl. SW13 6D **98**
Jenner Rd. N16 3F **67**
Jennett Rd. CR0: Wadd 3A **168**
Jennifer Ho. E14 6E **86**
Jennifer Ho. SE11 4K **19** (4A **102**) *(off Reedworth St.)*

Jennifer Rd. BR1: Broml 3H 141
Jenningsbury Ho. SW3 5D 16 (5C 100) *(off Cale St.)*
Jennings Cl. KT6: Surb 7C 150
Jennings Cl. RM8: Dag 1E 72
Jennings Ho. SE10 5F 105 *(off Old Woolwich Rd.)*
Jennings Rd. SE22 6F 121
Jennings Way EN5: Barn 3A 20
Jenningtree Way DA17: Belv 2J 109
Jenny Hammond Cl. E11 3H 69
Jensen Ho. E3 4C 86 *(off Wellington Way)*
Jenson Hgts. N1 7K 65 *(off Caledonian Rd.)*
Jenson Way SE19 7F 139
Jenton Av. DA7: Bex 1E 126
Jephson Ct. SW4 2J 119
Jephson Ho. SE17 6B 102 *(off Doddington Gro.)*
Jephson Rd. E7 7A 70
Jephson St. SE5 1D 120
Jephtha Rd. SW18 6J 117
Jeppos La. CR4: Mitc 4D 154
Jepson Ho. SW6 1K 117 *(off Pearscroft Rd.)*
Jerdan Ho. SW6 7J 99 *(off North End Rd.)*
Jerdan Pl. SW6 7J 99
Jeremiah St. E14 6D 86
Jeremy Bentham Ho. E2 3G 85 *(off Mansford St.)*
Jeremy's Grn. N18 4C 34
Jermyn St. SW1 4A 12 (1G 101)
Jermyn Street Theatre 3C 12 (7H 83) ***(off Jermyn St.)***
Jerningham Av. IG5: Ilf 2F 53
Jerningham Ct. SE14 1A 122
Jerningham Rd. SE14 2A 122
Jerome Cres. NW8 3C 4 (4C 82)
Jerome Ho. KT1: Hamp W 2D 150 *(off Old Bridge St.)*
Jerome Ho. NW1 5D 4 (5C 82) *(off Lisson Gro.)*
Jerome Ho. SW7 3A 16 (4B 100) *(off Glendower Pl.)*
Jerome Pl. KT1: King T 2D 150 *(off Wadbrook St.)*
Jerome St. E1 4J 9 (4F 85)
Jerome Twr. W3 2H 97
Jerrard St. SE13 3D 122
Jerrold St. N1 1H 9 (2E 84)
Jersey Av. HA7: Stan 2B 42
Jersey Dr. BR5: Pet W 6H 161
Jersey Ho. EN3: Enf W 1E 24 *(off Eastfield Rd.)*
Jersey Ho. N1 6C 66 *(off Jersey Rd.)*
Jersey Rd. E11 1F 69
Jersey Rd. E16 6A 88
Jersey Rd. IG1: Ilf 4F 71
Jersey Rd. N1 6C 66
Jersey Rd. SW17 6F 137
Jersey Rd. TW3: Houn 1F 113
Jersey Rd. TW5: Hest 1F 113
Jersey Rd. TW5: Isle 1F 113
Jersey Rd. TW7: Isle 7H 95
Jersey Rd. W7 2A 96
Jersey St. E2 3H 85
Jerusalem Pas. EC1 4A 8 (4B 84)
Jervis Ct. RM10: Dag 6H 73
Jervis Ct. SE10 1E 122 *(off Blissett St.)*
Jervis Ct. W1 1K 11 (6F 83) *(off Princes St.)*
Jervis Rd. SW6 6H 99
Jerviston Gdns. SW16 6A 138
Jerwood Space Art Gallery 6B 14 (2B 102) ***(off Union St.)***
Jesmond Av. HA9: Wemb 6F 61
Jesmond Cl. CR4: Mitc 3F 155
Jesmond Dene NW3 6A 64
Jesmond Rd. CR0: C'don 7F 157
Jesmond Way HA7: Stan 5K 27
Jessam Av. E5 1H 67
Jessamine Rd. W7 1K 95
Jessel Ho. SW1 3D 18 (4H 101) *(off Page St.)*
Jessel Ho. WC1 2E 6 (3J 83) *(off Judd St.)*
Jessel Mans. W14 6G 99 *(off Queen's Club Gdns.)*
Jesse Rd. E10 1E 68
Jessett Cl. DA8: Erith 4K 109
Jessica Rd. SW18 6A 118
Jessie Blythe La. N19 7J 47
Jessie Duffett Ho. SE5 7C 102 *(off Pitman St.)*
Jessie Wood Ct. SW9 7A 102 *(off Caldwell St.)*
Jessiman Ter. TW17: Shep 5C 146
Jesson Ho. SE17 4D 102 *(off Orb St.)*
Jessop Av. UB2: S'hall 4D 94
Jessop Ct. N1 2B 84
Jessop Ho. W4 4K 97 *(off Kirton Cl.)*
Jessop Lodge CR0: C'don 2C 168 *(off Tamworth Rd.)*
Jessop Pl. W7 3J 95
Jessop Rd. SE24 4B 120
Jessop Sq. E14 1C 104
Jessops Way CR0: Bedd 6G 155
Jessops Way CR0: Mitc 6G 155
Jessup Cl. SE18 4G 107
Jetstar Way UB5: N'olt 3C 76
Jevington Way SE12 1K 141
Jevons Ho. NW8 7B 64 *(off Hilgrove Rd.)*
Jewel Rd. E17 3C 50
Jewel Sq. E1 7H 85
Jewel Tower 1E 18 (3J 101) ***(off College M.)***
Jewish Mus. 1F 83
Jewry St. EC3 1J 15 (6F 85)
Jew's Row SW18 4K 117
Jews' Wlk. SE26 4H 139
Jeymer Av. NW2 5D 62
Jeymer Dr. UB6: G'frd 1F 77 (not continuous)
Jeypore Rd. SW18 7A 118
Jeypore Rd. Pas. SW18 6A 118
Jhumat Pl. IG1: Ilf 3E 70 *(off Roden St.)*
Jigger Mast Ho. SE18 3E 106
Jillian Cl. TW12: Hamp 7E 130
Jim Bradley Cl. SE18 4E 106
Jim Griffiths Ho. SW6 6H 99 *(off Clem Attlee Ct.)*
Jim Veal Dr. N7 6J 65
Joan Cres. SE9 7B 124
Joan Gdns. RM8: Dag 2E 72
Joanna Ho. W6 5E 98 *(off Queen Caroline St.)*
Joan Rd. RM8: Dag 2E 72
Joan St. SE1 5A 14 (1B 102)
Job Drain Pl. IG11: Bark 2A 90
Jocelin Ho. N1 1K 83 *(off Barnsbury Est.)*
Jocelyn Rd. TW9: Rich 3E 114
Jocelyn St. SE15 1G 121
Jockey's Flds. WC1 5H 7 (5K 83)
Jodane St. SE8 4B 104
Jodrell Cl. TW7: Isle 1A 114
Jodrell Rd. E3 1B 86
Joe Hunte Ct. SE27 5B 138
Joel St. HA5: Eastc 3J 39
Joel St. HA6: Nwood 2J 39
Johanna St. SE1 7J 13 (2A 102)
John Adams Ct. N9 2A 34
John Adam St. WC2 3F 13 (7J 83)
John Aird Ct. W2 5A 4 (5A 82) *(off Howley Pl.)*
John Archer Way SW18 6B 118
John Ashby Cl. SW2 6J 119
John Austin Cl. KT2: King T 1F 151
John Baird Ct. SE26 4J 139
John Barker Ct. NW6 7G 63
John Barnes Wlk. E15 6H 69
John Bell Twr. E. E3 2C 86 *(off Pancras Way)*
John Bell Twr. W. E3 2C 86 *(off Pancras Way)*
John Betts' Ho. W12 3B 98
John Bond Ho. E3 2B 86 *(off Wright's Rd.)*
John Bowles Ct. E1 7K 85 *(off Schoolhouse La.)*
John Bradshaw Rd. N14 1C 32
John Brent Ho. SE8 4K 103 *(off Haddonfield)*
John Buck Ho. NW10 1B 80
John Bull Pl. W4 4H 97
John Burns Dr. IG11: Bark 7J 71
John Campbell Rd. N16 5E 66
John Carpenter St. EC4 2A 14 (7B 84)
John Cartwright Ho. E2 3H 85 *(off Old Bethnal Grn. Rd.)*
John Crane St. SE17 6D 102
John Donne Way SE10 7D 104 *(off Norman Rd.)*
John Drinkwater Cl. E11 7H 51
John Fearon Wlk. W10 3G 81 *(off Dart St.)*
John Fielden Ho. E2 3H 85 *(off Canrobert St.)*
John Fisher St. E1 2K 15 (7G 85)
John Goddard Way TW13: Felt 2K 129
John Gooch Dr. EN2: Enf 1G 23
John Harrison Way SE10 3H 105
John Horner M. N1 2C 84
John Hunter Av. SW17 3C 136
John Islip St. SW1 4D 18 (4H 101)
John Kaye Ct. TW17: Shep 5C 146
John Keats Ho. N22 7E 32
John Keats Lodge EN2: Enf 1J 23
John Kennedy Ct. N1 6D 66 *(off Newington Grn. Rd.)*
John Kennedy Ho. SE16 4K 103 *(off Rotherhithe Old Rd.)*
John Knight Lodge SW6 7J 99
John Lamb Ct. HA3: W'stone 1J 41
John McDonald Ho. E14 3E 104 *(off Glengall Gro.)*
John McKenna Wlk. SE16 3G 103
John Masefield Ho. N15 6D 48 *(off Fladbury Rd.)*
John Maurice Cl. SE17 4D 102
John Nash M. E14 6A 86 *(off Commercial Rd.)*
John Newton Ct. DA16: Well 3B 126
Johnny Andrews Ho. E1 6K 85 *(off Boulcott St.)*
John Orwell Sports Cen. 1H 103
John Parker Cl. RM10: Dag 7H 73
John Parker Sq. SW11 3B 118
John Parry Ct. N1 2E 84 *(off Hare Wlk.)*
John Penn Ho. SE14 7B 104 *(off Amersham Va.)*
John Penn St. SE13 1D 122
John Penry Ho. SE1 5G 103 *(off Marlborough Gro.)*
John Perrin Pl. HA3: Kenton 7E 42
John Prince's St. W1 7K 5 (6F 83)
John Pritchard Ho. E1 4G 85 *(off Buxton St.)*
John Ratcliffe Ho. NW6 3J 81 *(off Chippenham Gdns.)*
John Rennie Wlk. E1 7H 85
John Riley Ho. E3 5B 86 *(off Geoffrey Chaucer Way)*
John Roll Way SE16 3G 103
John Ruskin St. SE5 7B 102
John's Av. NW4 4E 44
John Sayer Cl. IG11: Bark 3K 89
John's Cl. TW15: Ashf 4E 128
John Scurr Ho. E14 6A 86 *(off Ratcliffe La.)*
John Sessions Sq. E1 7K 9 (6G 85) *(off Alie St.)*
John Silkin La. SE8 5K 103
John's La. SM4: Mord 5A 154
John's M. WC1 4H 7 (4K 83)
John Smith Av. SW6 7H 99
John Smith M. E14 7F 87
Johnson Cl. E8 1G 85
Johnson Ct. SE9 4A 124
Johnson Ho. E2 3G 85 *(off Roberta St.)*
Johnson Ho. NW1 2G 83 *(off Cranleigh St.)*
Johnson Ho. NW3 7D 64 *(off Adelaide Rd.)*
Johnson Ho. SW1 4H 17 (4E 100) *(off Cundy St.)*
Johnson Ho. SW8 7H 101 *(off Wandsworth Rd.)*
Johnson Ho. W8 2J 99 *(off Campden Hill)*
Johnson Lock Ct. E1 5A 86
Johnson Lodge W9 5J 81 *(off Admiral Wlk.)*
Johnson Mans. W14 6G 99 *(off Queen's Club Gdns.)*
Johnson Rd. BR2: Broml 5B 160
Johnson Rd. CR0: C'don 7D 156
Johnson Rd. NW10 1K 79
Johnson Rd. TW5: Hest 7A 94
Johnsons Cl. SM5: Cars 2D 166
Johnson's Ct. EC4 1K 13 (6A 84)
Johnsons Dr. TW12: Hamp 1G 149
Johnsons Ind. Est. UB3: Hayes 2H 93
Johnson's Pl. SW1 6A 18 (5G 101)
Johnson St. E1 7J 85
Johnson St. UB2: S'hall 3A 94
Johnsons Way NW10 4H 79
John Spencer Sq. N1 6B 66
John's Pl. E1 6H 85
John's Ter. CR0: C'don 1E 168
Johnston Cl. SW9 1K 119
Johnston Ct. E10 3D 68
Johnstone Ho. SE13 3F 123 *(off Belmont Hill)*
Johnstone Rd. E6 3D 88
Johnston Rd. IG8: Wfd G 6D 36
Johnston Ter. NW2 3F 63
John Strachey Ho. SW6 6H 99 *(off Clem Attlee Ct.)*
John St. E15 1H 87
John St. EN1: Enf 5A 24
John St. SE25 4G 157
John St. TW3: Houn 2C 112
John St. WC1 4H 7 (4K 83)
John Strype Ct. E10 1D 68
John Trundle Ct. EC2 5C 8 (5C 84) *(off Aldersgate St.)*
John Trundle Highwalk EC2 5C 8 (5C 84) *(off Aldersgate St.)*
John Tucker Ho. E14 3C 104 *(off Mellish St.)*
John Watkin Cl. KT19: Eps 7H 163
John Wesley Cl. E6 3D 88
John Wesley Ct. TW1: Twick 1A 132
John Wesley Highwalk EC2 6C 8 (5C 84) *(off Aldersgate St.)*
John Wetherby Ct. E15 2D 86 *(off High St.)*
John Wetherby Ct. E. E15 2D 86 *(off High St.)*
John Wetherby Ct. W. E15 2D 86 *(off High St.)*
John Wheatley Ho. SW6 6H 99 *(off Clem Attlee Ct.)*
John Williams Cl. KT2: King T 1D 150
John Williams Cl. SE14 6K 103
John Wilson St. SE18 3E 106
John Woolley Cl. SE13 4G 123
Joiners Arms Yd. SE5 1D 120
Joiners M. E11 3G 69
Joiners Pl. N5 4D 66
Joiner St. SE1 5F 15 (1D 102)
Joiners Yd. N1 1F 7 (2J 83) *(off Caledonia St.)*
Jolles Ho. E3 3D 86 *(off Bromley High St.)*
Jolly M. SW16 2G 155
Jollys La. HA2: Harr 1H 59
Jollys La. UB4: Yead 5B 76
Jonathan St. SE11 5G 19 (5K 101)
Jones Ho. E14 6F 87 *(off Blair St.)*
Jones M. SW15 4G 117
Jones Rd. E13 4K 87
Jones St. W1 3J 11 (7F 83)
Jones Wlk. TW10: Rich 6F 115
Jonquil Gdns. TW12: Hamp 6E 130
Jonson Cl. CR4: Mitc 4F 155
Jonson Cl. UB4: Hayes 5J 75
Jonson Ho. SE1 3D 102 *(off Burbage Cl.)*
Jonzen Wlk. E14 6C 86
Jordan Cl. HA2: Harr 3D 58
Jordan Ct. SW15 4F 117
Jordan Ho. N1 1D 84 *(off Colville Est.)*
Jordan Ho. SE4 4K 121 *(off St Norbert Rd.)*
Jordan Rd. UB6: G'frd 1B 78
Jordans Cl. RM10: Dag 4H 73
Jordans Cl. TW7: Isle 1J 113
Jordans Ho. NW8 3B 4 (4B 82) *(off Capland St.)*
Jordans M. TW2: Twick 2J 131
Joscoyne Ho. E1 6H 85 *(off Philpot St.)*
Joseph Av. W3 6K 79
Joseph Cl. N4 2B 66
Joseph Conrad Ho. SW1 4B 18 (4G 101) *(off Tachbrook St.)*
Joseph Ct. N16 6E 48 *(off Amhurst Pk.)*
Joseph Grimaldi Pk. 1H 7 (2K 83)
Joseph Hardcastle Cl. SE14 7K 103
Josephine Av. SW2 5K 119
Joseph Irwin Ho. E14 7B 86 *(off Gill St.)*
Joseph Lister Ct. E7 7J 69
Joseph M. N7 6A 66 *(off Westbourne Rd.)*
Joseph M. SE15 5K 121
Joseph Powell Cl. SW12 6G 119
Joseph Priestley Ho. E2 3H 85 *(off Canrobert St.)*
Joseph Ray Rd. E11 2G 69
Joseph St. E3 4B 86
Joseph Trotter Cl. EC1 2K 7 (3A 84) *(off Finsbury Est.)*
Joshua Cl. CR2: S Croy 7B 168
Joshua Cl. N10 7A 32
Joshua Pedley M. E3 2C 86
Joshua St. E14 6E 86
Josiah Dr. UB10: Ick 2E 56
Joslin Av. NW9 3A 44
Joslings Cl. W12 7C 80
Joslyn Cl. EN3: Enf L 1H 25
Jossiline Ct. E3 2A 86 *(off Ford St.)*
Joubert Mans. SW3 5D 16 (5C 100) *(off Jubilee Pl.)*
Joubert St. SW11 2D 118
Jowett St. SE15 7F 103
Jowitt Ho. E2 3K 85 *(off Morpeth St.)*
Joyce Av. N18 5A 34
Joyce Butler Ho. N22 1K 47
Joyce Dawson Way SE28 7A 90
Joyce Latimore Ct. N9 3C 34 *(off Colthurst Dr.)*
Joyce Page Cl. SE7 6B 106
Joyce Wlk. SW2 6A 120
Joydens Wood 4H 145
JOYDENS WOOD 4K 145
Joydens Wood Rd. DA5: Bexl 4K 145
Joydon Dr. RM6: Chad H 6B 54
Joyners Cl. RM9: Dag 4F 73
Joy of Life Fountain 4G 11 (1E 100)
Joystone Ct. EN4: E Barn 4H 21 *(off Park Rd.)*
Jubb Powell Ho. N15 6E 48
Jubilee, The SE10 7D 104
Jubilee Av. E4 6K 35
Jubilee Av. RM7: Rom 5H 55
Jubilee Av. TW2: Whitt 1G 131
Jubilee Bldgs. NW8 1B 82
Jubilee Cl. HA5: Pinn 2A 40
Jubilee Cl. KT1: Hamp W 1C 150
Jubilee Cl. NW10 2A 80
Jubilee Cl. NW9 6K 43
Jubilee Cl. RM7: Rom 5H 55
Jubilee Country Pk. 4F 161
Jubilee Country Pk. Local Nature Reserve 5E 160
Jubilee Ct. BR4: W W'ck 1E 170
Jubilee Ct. E16 6H 87 *(off Silvertown Sq.)*
Jubilee Ct. E18 1J 51
Jubilee Ct. HA3: Kenton 7E 42
Jubilee Ct. N10 3E 46
Jubilee Ct. SE10 6D 104 *(off Dowells St.)*
Jubilee Ct. TW3: Houn 3F 113 *(off Bristow Rd.)*
Jubilee Cres. E14 3E 104
Jubilee Cres. N9 1B 34
Jubilee Dr. HA4: Ruis 4B 58
Jubilee Gdns. UB1: S'hall 5E 76
Jubilee Hall Gym 2F 13 (7J 83) ***(within Jubilee Hall)***
Jubilee Hgts. SE10 1E 122 *(off Parkside Av.)*
Jubilee Ho. HA7: Stan 5J 27
Jubilee Ho. SE11 4K 19 (4A 102) *(off Reedworth St.)*
Jubilee Ho. WC1 3G 7 (4K 83) *(off Gray's Inn Rd.)*
Jubilee La. W5 6E 78
Jubilee Lodge E18 2K 51
Jubilee Mans. E1 6J 85 *(off Jubilee St.)*
Jubilee Mkt. IG8: Wfd G 6F 37
Jubilee Mkt. WC2 2F 13 (7J 83) *(off Covent Garden)*
Jubilee Mkt. 2F 13 (7J 83) *(off Covent Gdn.)*
Jubilee Pde. IG8: Wfd G 6F 37
Jubilee Pl. SW3 5D 16 (5C 100)
Jubilee Pl. Shop. Mall 1D 104 *(off Bank St.)*
Jubilee Rd. SM3: Cheam 7F 165
Jubilee Rd. UB6: G'frd 1B 78
Jubilee St. E1 6J 85
Jubilee Vs. KT10: Esh 7H 149
Jubilee Walkway SE1 3A 14 (7B 84)
Jubilee Way DA14: Sidc 2A 144
Jubilee Way KT9: Chess 4G 163
Jubilee Way SW19 1K 153
Jubilee Way TW14: Felt 1J 129
Jubilee Way Training Track 3H 163
Jubilee Yd. SE1 6J 15 (2F 103) *(off Lafone St.)*
Judd Apts. N8 3K 47 *(off Gt. Amwell La.)*
Judd St. WC1 1E 6 (3J 83)
Jude St. E16 6H 87
Judge Heath La. UB3: Hayes 6E 74
Judge Heath La. UB8: Hil 6E 74
Judges Wlk. NW3 3A 64
Juer St. SW11 7C 100
Juett Lodge SE10 4J 105 *(off Peartree Way)*
Jules Thorn Av. EN1: Enf 4B 24
Julia Ct. E17 5D 50
Julia Gdns. IG11: Bark 2D 90
Julia Garfield M. E16 1K 105 (not continuous)
Juliana Cl. N2 2A 46
Julian Av. W3 7H 79
Julian Cl. EN5: New Bar 3E 20
Julian Ct. NW1 7G 65 *(off Rochester Sq.)*
Julian Hill HA1: Harr 2J 59
Julian Ho. SE21 4E 138
Julian Pl. E14 5D 104
Julian Taylor Path SE23 2H 139
Julia Scurr St. E3 5C 86
Julia St. NW5 4E 64
Julien Rd. W5 3C 96
Juliet Ho. N1 2E 84 *(off Arden Est.)*
Juliette Rd. E13 2J 87
Julius Caesar Way HA7: Stan 3J 27
Julius Ho. E14 6F 87 *(off E. India Dock Rd.)*
Julius Nyerere Cl. N1 1K 83 *(off Copenhagen St.)*
Junction App. SE13 3E 122
Junction App. SW11 3C 118
Junction M. W2 7C 4 (6C 82)
Junction Pl. W2 7B 4 (6B 82) *(off Praed St.)*
Junction Rd. CR2: S Croy 5D 168
Junction Rd. E13 2K 87
Junction Rd. HA1: Harr 6H 41 (not continuous)
Junction Rd. N17 3G 49
Junction Rd. N19 4G 65
Junction Rd. N9 1B 34
Junction Rd. TW15: Ashf 5E 128
Junction Rd. TW8: Bford 4D 96
Junction Rd. W5 4C 96
Junction Rd. E. RM6: Chad H 7E 54
Junction Rd. W. RM6: Chad H 7E 54
Junction Shop. Cen., The 4C 118
Jungle Falls Adventure Golf 4B 22
Juniper Cl. EN5: Barn 5A 20
Juniper Cl. HA2: Harr 2F 59
Juniper Cl. HA9: Wemb 5G 61
Juniper Cl. KT9: Chess 5F 163
Juniper Cl. TW13: Felt 3K 129
Juniper Ct. HA3: Hrw W 1K 41
Juniper Ct. HA6: Nwood 1J 39
Juniper Ct. KT8: W Mole 4F 149
Juniper Ct. RM6: Chad H 6B 54
Juniper Ct. TW3: Houn 4F 113 *(off Grove Rd.)*
Juniper Ct. W8 3K 99 *(off St Mary's Pl.)*
Juniper Cres. NW1 7E 64
Juniper Dr. SW18 4A 118
Juniper Gdns. SW16 1G 155
Juniper Gdns. TW16: Sun 6H 129
Juniper Ho. SE14 7J 103
Juniper Ho. TW9: Kew 1H 115
Juniper Ho. W10 4G 81 *(off Fourth Av.)*
Juniper La. E6 5C 88
Juniper Rd. IG1: Ilf 3E 70
Juniper St. E1 7J 85
Juniper Way UB3: Hayes 7F 75
Juno Ct. SW9 7A 102 *(off Caldwell St.)*
Juno Ent. Cen. SE14 6K 103
Juno Ho. E3 1C 86 *(off Garrison Rd.)*
Juno Way SE14 6K 103
Juno Way Ind. Est. SE14 6K 103
Jupiter Ct. E3 2C 86 *(off Four Seasons Cl.)*
Jupiter Ct. SW9 7A 102 *(off Caldwell St.)*
Jupiter Ct. UB5: N'olt 3B 76 *(off Seasprite Cl.)*
Jupiter Hgts. UB10: Uxb 1B 74
Jupiter Ho. E14 5D 104 *(off St Davids Sq.)*
Jupiter Ho. E16 6H 87 *(off Turner St.)*
Jupiter Ho. HA2: Harr 1E 58
Jupiter Way N7 6K 65
Jupiter Wy. SW17 3C 136
Jupp Rd. E15 7F 69
Jupp Rd. W. E15 1F 87
Jura Ho. SE16 4K 103 *(off Plough Way)*
Jurassic Encounter 3C 152
Jurston Ct. SE1 7K 13 (2A 102) *(off Gerridge St.)*
Justice Apts. E1 6K 85 *(off Aylward St.)*
Justice Wlk. SW3 7C 16 (6C 100)
Justin Cl. TW8: Bford 7D 96
Justines Pl. E2 3K 85
Justin Pl. N22 7E 32
Justin Plaza CR4: Mitc 4C 154
Justin Rd. E4 6G 35
Jute La. EN3: Brim 2F 25
Jutland Cl. N19 1J 65
Jutland Ho. SE5 2C 120
Jutland Rd. E13 4J 87
Jutland Rd. SE6 7E 122
Jutsums Av. RM7: Rom 6H 55
Jutsums Ct. RM7: Rom 6H 55
Jutsums La. RM7: Rom 6H 55
Jutsums La. RM7: Rush G 6H 55
Juxon Cl. HA3: Hrw W 1F 41
Juxon Ho. EC4 1B 14 (6B 84) *(off St Paul's Chyd.)*
Juxon St. SE11 3H 19 (4K 101)
JVC Bus. Pk. NW2 1C 62

K

Kaduna Cl. HA5: Eastc 5J 39
Kaine Pl. CR0: C'don 7A 158
Kaleidoscope Ho. E20 5E 68 *(off Mirabelle Gdns.)*
Kale Rd. DA18: Erith 2D 108
Kambala Rd. SW11 3B 118
Kamen Ho. SE1 5G 15 (1E 102) *(off Magdalen St.)*
Kamrans Pl. HA8: Edg 2F 43
Kane Ct. SE10 4J 105 *(off Peartree Way)*
Kangley Bri. Rd. SE26 6B 140
Kangley Bus. Cen. SE26 5B 140
Kanli M. SE6 3D 140
Kaplan Dr. N21 5E 22
Kapuvar Cl. SE15 2G 121
Karachi Ho. E15 6G 69 *(off Well St.)*
Kara Way NW2 4F 63
Karen Ct. BR1: Broml 1H 159
Karen Ter. E11 2H 69
Karenza Ct. HA9: Wemb 7C 42
Kariba Cl. N9 3D 34
Karim M. E17 4A 50
Karma Way HA2: Harr 1E 58
Karner Ho. E20 5D 68 *(off Logan Cl.)*
Karoline Gdns. UB6: G'frd 2H 77
Kashgar Rd. SE18 4K 107
Kashmir Rd. SE7 7B 106
Kassala Rd. SW11 1D 118
Katella Trad. Est. IG11: Bark 3J 89
Katharine Ho. CR0: C'don 3C 168 *(off Katharine St.)*
Katharine St. CR0: C'don 3C 168
Katherine Bell Twr. E3 2C 86 *(off Pancras Way)*
Katherine Cl. N4 7C 48
Katherine Cl. NW7 7K 29
Katherine Cl. SE16 1K 103
Katherine Ct. SE23 1H 139
Katherine Gdns. SE9 4B 124
Katherine Ho. W10 4G 81 *(off Portobello Rd.)*
Katherine Rd. E6 7B 70
Katherine Rd. E7 5A 70
Katherine Rd. TW1: Twick 1A 132
Katherine Sq. W11 1G 99
Kathleen Av. HA0: Wemb 7E 60
Kathleen Av. W3 5J 79
Kathleen Godfree Ct. SW19 6J 135
Kathleen Rd. SW11 3D 118
Katial Ho. EC1 1B 8 (3B 84) *(off Goswell Road)*
Kavan Gdns. TW5: Cran 7J 93
Kavsan Pl. TW5: Cran 7J 93
Kayani Av. N4 1C 66
Kayani Ho. E16 6K 87 *(off Burrard Rd.)*

Kepler Ho. – Kingsgate Bus. Cen.

Kepler Ho. SE10 5H 105
(off Armitage Rd.)
Kepler Rd. SW4 4J 119
Keppel Ho. SE8 5B 104
Keppel Ho. SW3 4C 16 (4C 100)
(off Elystan St.)
Keppel Rd. E6 7D 70
Keppel Rd. RM9: Dag 4E 72
Keppel Row SE1 5C 14 (1C 102)
Keppel St. WC1 5D 6 (5H 83)
Kepplestone M. BR3: Beck 2E 158
Kerbela St. E2 3K 9 (4G 85)
Kerbey St. E14 6D 86
Kerfield Cres. SE5 1D 120
Kerfield Pl. SE5 1D 120
Kerlin Vw. SW16 2G 155
Kerr Cl. CR2: Sels 7A 170
Kerridge Ct. N1 6E 66
(off Balls Pond Rd.)
Kerrier Ho. SW10 7A 100
(off Stadium St.)
Kerrington Ct. W10 4G 81
(off Wornington Rd.)
Kerrington Ct. W12 2E 98
(off Uxbridge Rd.)
Kerris Ho. SE11 5K 19 (5A 102)
(off Tavy Cl.)
Kerrison Pl. W5 1D 96
Kerrison Rd. E15 1F 87
Kerrison Rd. SW11 3C 118
Kerrison Rd. W5 1D 96
Kerrison Vs. W5 1D 96
Kerry Av. HA7: Stan 4H 27
Kerry Cl. E16 6K 87
Kerry Cl. N13 2E 32
Kerry Ct. HA7: Stan 4J 27
Kerry Ho. E1 6J 85
(off Sidney St.)
Kerry Path SE14 6B 104
Kerry Rd. SE14 6B 104
Kerscott Ho. E3 3D 86
(off Rainhill Way)
Kersey Gdns. SE9 4C 142
Kersfield Ho. SW15 6F 117
Kersfield Rd. SW15 6F 117
Kershaw Cl. SW18 6B 118
Kershaw Rd. RM10: Dag 3G 73
Kerslake Ms. 3D 106
Kersley M. SW11 1D 118
Kersley Rd. N16 2E 66
Kersley St. SW11 2D 118
Kerstin Cl. UB3: Hayes 7H 75
Kerswell Cl. N15 5E 48
Kerwick Cl. N7 7J 65
Keslake Mans. NW10 2F 81
(off Station Ter.)
Keslake Rd. NW6 2F 81
Kessock Cl. N17 5H 49
Kestlake Rd. DA5: Bexl 6C 126
KESTON 5A 172
Keston Av. BR2: Kes 5A 172
Keston Cl. DA16: Well 7C 108
Keston Cl. N18 3J 33
Keston Ct. DA5: Bexl 7F 127
Keston Ct. KT5: Surb 5F 151
(off Cranes Pk.)
Keston Gdns. BR2: Kes 4A 172
Keston Ho. SE17 5E 102
(off Kinglake Est.)
KESTON MARK 3C 172
KESTON MARK 4C 172
Keston Pk. Cl. BR2: Kes 3D 172
Keston Rd. CR7: Thor H 6A 156
Keston Rd. N17 3D 48
Keston Rd. SE15 3G 121
Keston Windmill 5B 172
Kestrel Av. E6 5C 88
Kestrel Av. SE24 5B 120
Kestrel Cl. KT2: King T 4D 132
Kestrel Cl. NW10 5K 61
Kestrel Cl. NW9 2A 44
Kestrel Ct. CR2: S Croy 6C 168
Kestrel Ct. E17 2K 49
Kestrel Ct. E3 2C 86
(off Four Seasons Cl.)
Kestrel Ct. HA4: Ruis 2G 57
Kestrel Ct. SM6: W'gton 5G 167
Kestrel Ho. EC1 1C 8 (3C 84)
(off Pickard St.)
Kestrel Ho. SE10 1E 122
(off Parkside Av.)
Kestrel Pl. SE14 6A 104
Kestrel Way CR0: New Ad 7F 171
Kestrel Way UB3: Hayes 2F 93
Keswick Av. SW15 5A 134
Keswick Av. SW19 2J 153
Keswick Av. TW17: Shep 3G 147
Keswick B'way. SW15 5H 117
(off Up. Richmond Rd.)
Keswick Cl. SM1: Sutt 4A 166
Keswick Ct. BR2: Broml 4H 159
Keswick Ct. SE13 5D 122
Keswick Ct. SE6 1H 141
Keswick Gdns. HA4: Ruis 6F 39
Keswick Gdns. HA9: Wemb 4E 60
Keswick Gdns. IG4: Ilf 4C 52
Keswick Ho. SE5 2C 120
Keswick M. W5 1E 96
Keswick Rd. BR4: W W'ck 2G 171
Keswick Rd. BR6: Orp 1K 173
Keswick Rd. DA7: Bex 1G 127
Keswick Rd. SW15 5G 117
Keswick Rd. TW2: Whitt 6G 113
Ketch St. IG11: Bark 1G 89
Kettering Ct. CR7: Thor H 4C 156
Kettering St. SW16 6G 137
Kett Gdns. SW2 5K 119
Kettlebaston Rd. E10 1B 68
Kettleby Ho. SW9 3B 120
(off Barrington Rd.)
Kettlewell Cl. N11 6K 31
Ketton Ho. W10 4E 80
(off Sutton Way)
Kevan Ct. E17 4C 50
Kevan Ho. SE5 7C 102
Kevelioc Rd. N17 1C 48
Kevin Cl. TW4: Houn 2B 112
Kevington Cl. BR5: St P 4K 161
Kevington Dr. BR5: St P 4K 161
Kevington Dr. BR7: Chst 4K 161
Kevtar Gdn. E3 3B 86
KEW 1G 115
KEW BRIDGE Bridge 6G 97
Kew Bri. Arches TW9: Kew 6G 97
Kew Bri. Ct. W4 5G 97
Kew Bri. Distribution Cen. TW8: Bford 5F 97
KEW BRIDGE JUNCTION Junction 5F 97
Kew Bri. Rd. TW8: Bford 6F 97
Kew Ct. KT2: King T 1F 150
Kew Cres. SM3: Cheam 3G 165
Kew Foot Rd. TW9: Rich 4E 114
Kew Gdns. 7E 96
Kew Gdns. Rd. TW9: Kew 7F 97
KEW GREEN 7G 97
Kew Grn. TW9: Kew 6F 97
Kew Mdw. Path TW9: Kew Clifford Av. 2J 115
Kew Mdw. Path TW9: Kew Magnolia Ct. 1H 115
Kew Palace 7E 96
Kew Retail Pk. Kew 1H 115
Kew Riverside Pk. TW9: Kew 7H 97
Kew Rd. TW9: Kew 6G 97
Kew Rd. TW9: Rich 6G 97
Key Cl. E1 4J 85
Keyes Ho. SW1 6C 18 (5H 101)
(off Dolphin Sq.)
Keyes Rd. NW2 5F 63
Keyham Ho. W2 5J 81
(off Westbourne Pk. Rd.)
Key Ho. SE11 7J 19 (6A 102)
Keymer Pl. E14 6B 86
Keymer Rd. SW2 2K 137
Keynes Cl. N2 4D 46
Keynes Ct. SE28 7B 90
(off Attlee Rd.)
Keynsham Av. IG8: Wfd G 4B 36
Keynsham Gdns. SE9 5C 124
Keynsham Rd. SE9 5B 124
Keynsham Rd. SM4: Mord 1K 165
Keynsham Wlk. SM4: Mord 1K 165
Keys Ct. CR0: C'don 3D 168
(off Beech Ho. Rd.)
Keyse Rd. SE1 3F 103
Keysham Av. TW5: Cran 1J 111
Keystone Cres. N1 1F 7 (2J 83)
Key W. Ct. IG7: Chig 4K 37
Keywood Dr. TW16: Sun 6J 129
Keyworth Cl. E5 4A 68
Keyworth Pl. SE1 7B 14 (3B 102)
(off Keyworth St.)
Keyworth St. SE1 7B 14 (3B 102)
Kezia M. SE8 5A 104
Kezia St. SE8 5A 104
Khalsa Ct. N22 1B 48
Khama Rd. SW17 4C 136
Khartoum Rd. E13 3K 87
Khartoum Rd. IG1: Ilf 5F 71
Khartoum Rd. SW17 4B 136
Khyber Rd. SW11 2C 118
Kia Oval, The 7H 19 (6K 101)
Kibble Cl. RM6: Chad H 7C 54
Kibworth St. SW8 7K 101
Kidabulous 1G 147
KIDBROOKE 2K 123
Kidbrooke Est. SE3 3A 124
Kidbrooke Gdns. SE3 2J 123
Kidbrooke Green Nature Reserve 3A 124
Kidbrooke Gro. SE3 1J 123
Kidbrooke La. SE9 4C 124
Kidbrooke Pk. Cl. SE3 1K 123
Kidbrooke Pk. Rd. SE3 1K 123
Kidbrooke Way SE3 2K 123
Kidderminster Pl. CR0: C'don 1B 168
Kidderminster Rd. CR0: C'don 1B 168
Kidderpore Av. NW3 4J 63
Kidderpore Gdns. NW3 4J 63
Kidd Pl. SE7 5C 106
Kidspace Croydon 6A 168
Kiebs Way SE17 5D 102
Kiffen St. EC2 3F 9 (4D 84)
Kilberry Cl. TW7: Isle 1H 113
Kilbrennan Ho. E14 6E 86
(off Findhorn St.)
KILBURN 2H 81
Kilburn Bri. NW6 1J 81
Kilburn Ga. NW6 2K 81
Kilburn High Rd. NW6 7H 63
Kilburn Ho. NW6 2H 81
(off Malvern Pl.)
Kilburn La. W10 3F 81
Kilburn La. W9 2G 81
Kilburn Pk. Rd. NW6 3J 81
Kilburn Pl. NW6 1J 81
Kilburn Priory NW6 1K 81
Kilburn Sq. NW6 1J 81
Kilburn Va. NW6 1K 81
Kilburn Va. Est. NW6 1K 81
(off Kilburn Vale)
Kilby Ct. SE10 3H 105
(off Greenroof Way)
Kildare Cl. HA4: Ruis 1A 58
Kildare Ct. W2 6J 81
(off Kildare Ter.)
Kildare Gdns. W2 6J 81
Kildare Rd. E16 5J 87
Kildare Ter. W2 6J 81
Kildare Wlk. E14 6C 86
Kildoran Rd. SW2 5J 119
Kildowan Rd. IG3: Ilf 1A 72
Kilgour Rd. SE23 6A 122
Kilkie St. SW6 2A 118
Killarney Rd. SW18 6A 118
Killburns Mill Cl. SM6: W'gton 2F 167
Killearn Rd. SE6 1F 141
Killester Gdns. KT4: Wor Pk 4D 164
Killick Ho. SM1: Sutt 4J 165
Killick M. SM3: Cheam 6G 165
Killick St. N1 2K 83
Killick Way E1 5K 85
Killieser Av. SW2 2J 137
Killigarth Ct. DA14: Sidc 4A 144
Killigrew Ho. TW16: Sun 7G 129
Killip Cl. E16 6H 87
Killoran Ho. E14 3E 104
(off Galbraith St.)
Killowen Av. UB5: N'olt 5G 59
Killowen Rd. E9 6K 67
Killyon Rd. SW8 2G 119
Killyon Ter. SW8 2G 119
Kilmaine Rd. SW6 7G 99
Kilmarnock Gdns. RM8: Dag 3C 72
Kilmarsh Rd. W6 4E 98
Kilmartin Av. SW16 3A 156
Kilmartin Rd. IG3: Ilf 2A 72
Kilmington Rd. SW13 6C 98
Kilmiston Av. TW17: Shep 6E 146
Kilmiston Ho. TW17: Shep 6E 146
Kilmore Ho. E14 6D 86
(off Vesey Path)
Kilmorey Gdns. TW1: Twick 5B 114
Kilmorey Rd. TW1: Twick 4B 114
Kilmorie Rd. SE23 1A 140
Kilmuir Ho. SW1 4H 17 (4E 100)
(off Bury St.)
Kiln Cinema 7H 63
Kiln Cl. UB3: Harl 6F 93
Kiln Ct. E14 7B 86
(off Newell St.)
Kilner Ho. E16 5K 87
(off Freemasons Rd.)
Kilner Ho. SE11 7J 19 (6A 102)
(off Clayton St.)
Kilner St. E14 5C 86
Kiln Ho. E1 5K 85
(off Duckett St.)
Kiln Ho. UB2: S'hall 3E 94
(off Lockwood Rd.)
Kiln M. SW17 5B 136
Kiln Pl. NW5 5E 64
Kilnside KT10: Clay 7A 162
Kiln Theatre 7H 63
Kilpatrick Way UB4: Yead 5C 76
Kilravock St. W10 3G 81
Kilronan W3 6K 79
Kilross Rd. TW14: Bedf 1F 129
Kilsby Wlk. RM9: Dag 6B 72
Kilsha Rd. KT12: Walt T 6A 148
Kimbell Gdns. SW6 1G 117
Kimbell Pl. SE3 4A 124
Kimber Ct. SE1 7G 15 (3E 102)
(off Long La.)
Kimberley Av. E6 2C 88
Kimberley Av. IG2: Ilf 7H 53
Kimberley Av. RM7: Rom 6J 55
Kimberley Av. SE15 2H 121
Kimberley Ct. NW6 1G 81
(off Kimberley Rd.)
Kimberley Dr. DA14: Sidc 2D 144
Kimberley Gdns. EN1: Enf 3A 24
Kimberley Gdns. N4 5B 48
Kimberley Ga. BR1: Broml 7G 141
Kimberley Ho. E14 3E 104
(off Galbraith St.)
Kimberley Rd. BR3: Beck 2K 157
Kimberley Rd. CR0: C'don 6B 156
Kimberley Rd. E11 2F 69
Kimberley Rd. E16 4H 87
Kimberley Rd. E17 1A 50
Kimberley Rd. E4 1B 36
Kimberley Rd. N17 2G 49
Kimberley Rd. N18 6C 34
Kimberley Rd. NW6 1G 81
Kimberley Rd. SW9 2J 119
Kimberley Wlk. KT12: Walt T 7K 147
Kimberley Way E4 1B 36
Kimber Pl. TW4: Houn Conway Rd. 7D 112
Kimber Pl. TW4: Houn Marryat Cl. 4D 112
Kimber Rd. SW18 7J 117
Kimble Ho. NW8 3D 4 (4C 82)
(off Lilestone St.)
Kimble Rd. SW19 6B 136
Kimbolton Cl. SE12 6H 123
Kimbolton Ct. SW3 4C 16 (4C 100)
(off Fulham Rd.)
Kimbolton Row SW3 4C 16 (4C 100)
(off Fulham Rd.)
Kimmeridge Gdns. SE9 4C 142
Kimmeridge Rd. SE9 4C 142
Kimmins Ct. SE16 7K 15 (3G 103)
(off Old Jamaica Rd.)
Kimpton Ho. SW15 7C 116
Kimpton Ind. Est. SM3: Sutt 2H 165
Kimpton Link Bus. Cen. SM3: Sutt 2H 165
Kimpton Pk. Way SM1: Sutt 2H 165
Kimpton Pk. Way SM3: Sutt 2G 165
Kimpton Rd. SE5 1D 120
Kimpton Rd. SM3: Sutt 2H 165
Kimpton Trade & Bus. Cen. SM3: Sutt 2H 165
Kinburn St. SE16 2K 103
Kincaid Rd. SE15 7H 103
Kincardine Gdns. W9 4J 81
(off Harrow Rd.)
Kincha Lodge KT2: King T 1F 151
(off Elm Rd.)
Kinch Gro. HA9: Wemb 7F 43
Kinder Cl. SE28 7D 90
Kinder Ho. N1 2D 84
(off Cranston Est.)
Kindersley Ho. E1 6G 85
(off Pinchin St.)
Kinder St. E1 6H 85
Kinderton Cl. N14 1B 32
Kindred Ho. CR0: C'don 3C 168
Kinefold Ho. N7 6J 65
(off York Way Est.)
Kinesis Gym & Fitness Cen. 4C 124
(off Well Hall Rd.)
Kinfauns Rd. IG3: Ilf 1A 72
Kinfauns Rd. SW2 2A 138
King Alfred Av. SE6 4C 140
(not continuous)
King & Queen Cl. SE9 4C 142
King & Queen St. SE17 5C 102
King & Queen Wharf SE16 7K 85
King Arthur Cl. SE15 7J 103
KING CHARLES I ISLAND 4E 12 (1J 101)
(end of Whitehall)
King Charles Ct. SE17 6B 102
(off Royal Rd.)
King Charles Cres. KT5: Surb 7F 151
King Charles Ho. SW6 7K 99
(off Wandon Rd.)
King Charles Rd. KT5: Surb 5F 151
King Charles's Ct. SE10 6E 104
(off Park Row)
King Charles St. SW1 6D 12 (2H 101)
King Charles Ter. E1 7H 85
(off Sovereign Cl.)
King Charles Wlk. SW19 1G 135
King Ct. E10 7D 50
Kingcup Cl. CR0: C'don 7K 157
King David La. E1 7J 85
Kingdom St. W2 5A 82
Kingdon Ho. E14 3E 104
(off Galbraith St.)
Kingdon Rd. NW6 6J 63
King Edward Bldg. EC1 7B 8 (6B 84)
(off King Edward St.)
King Edward Ct. HA9: Wemb 5E 60
(off Elm Rd.)
King Edward Dr. KT9: Chess 3E 162
King Edward Mans. E8 1H 85
(off Mare St.)
King Edward M. SW13 1C 116
King Edward Rd. E10 1E 68
King Edward Rd. E17 3A 50
King Edward Rd. EN5: New Bar 4D 20
King Edward's Gdns. W3 1G 97
King Edwards Gro. TW11: Tedd 6B 132
King Edwards Mans. SW6 7J 99
(off Fulham Rd.)
King Edward's Pl. W3 1G 97
King Edward's Rd. E9 1H 85
King Edward's Rd. EN3: Pond E 4E 24
King Edward's Rd. HA4: Ruis 1F 57
King Edward's Rd. N9 7C 24
King Edwards Rd. IG11: Bark 1H 89
King Edward St. EC1 7C 8 (6C 84)
King Edward the Third M. SE16 2H 103
King Edward Wlk. SE1 1K 19 (3A 102)
Kingfield Rd. W5 4D 78
Kingfield St. E14 4E 104
Kingfisher Av. E11 6K 51
Kingfisher Cl. HA3: Hrw W 7E 26
Kingfisher Cl. HA6: Nwood 1D 38
Kingfisher Cl. SE28 7C 90
Kingfisher Ct. CR0: C'don 3C 168
(off Wandle Rd.)
Kingfisher Ct. E14 2E 104
(off River Barge Cl.)
Kingfisher Ct. EN2: Enf 1E 22
Kingfisher Ct. KT8: E Mos 4J 149
Kingfisher Ct. SE1 7D 14 (2C 102)
(off Swan St.)
Kingfisher Ct. SM1: Sutt 5H 165
Kingfisher Ct. SW19 2F 135
Kingfisher Ct. TW3: Houn 5F 113
Kingfisher Ct. TW7: Isle 2H 113
Kingfisher Dr. TW10: Ham 4B 132
Kingfisher Hgts. E16 1A 106
(off Bramwell Way)
Kingfisher Hgts. N17 3H 49
(off Waterside Way)
Kingfisher Ho. SW18 3A 118
Kingfisher Ho. W14 3H 99
(off Melbury Rd.)
Kingfisher Leisure Cen. Kingston upon Thames 2E 150
Kingfisher M. SE13 4D 122
Kingfisher Pl. N22 2K 47
Kingfisher Sq. SE8 6B 104
(off Clyde St.)
Kingfisher St. E6 5C 88
Kingfisher Wlk. NW9 2A 44
Kingfisher Way BR3: Beck 5K 157
Kingfisher Way NW10 6K 61
King Frederick IX Twr. SE16 3B 104
King Gdns. CR0: Wadd 5B 168
King George IV Ct. SE17 5D 102
(off Dawes St.)
King George VI Av. CR4: Mitc 4D 154
King George VI Memorial 5C 12 (1H 101)
King George Av. E16 6A 88
King George Av. IG2: Ilf 5H 53
King George Cl. RM7: Mawney 3J 55
King George Cl. TW16: Sun 5G 129
King George Cres. HA0: Wemb 5D 60
King George M. SW17 5D 136
King George Sailing Club 6J 25
King George's Dr. UB1: S'hall 5D 76
King George's Field 3G 163
King George's Fld. 3J 103
(off Lower Road)
King George Sq. TW10: Rich 6F 115
King George's Trad. Est. KT9: Chess 4G 163
King George St. SE10 7E 104
King George Way E4 4J 25
Kingham Cl. SW18 7A 118
Kingham Cl. W11 2G 99
King Harolds Way DA17: Belv 6E 108
King Harolds Way DA7: Belv 7D 108
King Harolds Way DA7: Bex 7D 108
King Henry Lodge E4 4H 35
King Henry M. BR6: Chels 5K 173
King Henry M. HA2: Harr 1J 59
King Henry's Dr. CR0: New Ad 7D 170
King Henry's Reach W6 6E 98
King Henry's Rd. KT1: King T 3H 151
King Henry's Rd. NW3 7C 64
King Henry's Stairs E1 1H 103
King Henry St. N16 5E 66
King Henry's Wlk. N1 6E 66
King Henry Ter. E1 7H 85
(off Sovereign Cl.)
Kinghorn St. EC1 6C 8 (5C 84)
King Ho. W12 6D 80
Kingisholt Ct. NW10 3F 81
(off Wellington Rd.)
King James Ct. SE1 7B 14 (2B 102)
(off King James St.)
King James St. SE1 7B 14 (2B 102)
King John Ct. EC2 3H 9 (4E 84)
King John St. E1 5K 85
King John's Wlk. SE9 7C 124
Kinglake Est. SE17 5E 102
Kinglake St. SE17 5E 102
(not continuous)
Kinglet Cl. E7 6J 69
Kingly Ct. W1 2B 12 (7G 83)
(off Beak St.)
Kingly St. W1 1A 12 (6G 83)
Kingsand Rd. SE12 2J 141
Kings Arbour UB2: S'hall 5C 94
King's Arms All. TW8: Bford 6D 96
Kings Arms Ct. E1 5G 85
King's Arms Yd. SW18 5K 117
Kings Arms Yd. EC2 7E 8 (6D 84)
Kingsash Dr. UB4: Yead 4C 76
King's Av. IG9: Buck H Langfords 2G 37
King's Av. IG9: Buck H The Broadway 4F 37
King's Av. IG8: Wfd G 6E 36
King's Av. N10 3E 46
King's Av. SM5: Cars 7C 166
King's Av. TW16: Sun 5H 129
King's Av. UB6: G'frd 5F 77
Kings Av. BR1: Broml 6H 141
Kings Av. KT3: N Mald 4A 152
Kings Av. N21 1G 33
Kings Av. RM6: Chad H 6F 55
Kings Av. SW12 1H 137
Kings Av. SW4 7H 119
Kings Av. TW3: Houn 1F 113
Kings Av. W5 6D 78
King's Bench St. SE1 6B 14 (2B 102)
King's Bench Wlk. EC4 1K 13 (6A 84)
King's Blvd. N1 2J 83
Kingsbridge Av. W3 2F 97
Kingsbridge Ct. E14 3C 104
(off Dockers Tanner Rd.)
Kingsbridge Ct. NW1 7F 65
(off Castlehaven Rd.)
Kingsbridge Cres. UB1: S'hall 5D 76
Kingsbridge Dr. NW7 7A 30
Kingsbridge Rd. IG11: Bark 2H 89
Kingsbridge Rd. KT12: Walt T 7K 147
Kingsbridge Rd. SM4: Mord 6F 153
Kingsbridge Rd. UB2: S'hall 4D 94
Kingsbridge Rd. W10 6E 80
Kingsbridge Way UB4: Hayes 3G 75
Kingsbridge Wharf IG11: Bark 3J 89
KINGSBURY 5H 43
Kingsbury Circ. NW9 5G 43
KINGSBURY GREEN 6K 43
Kingsbury Rd. N1 6E 66
Kingsbury Rd. NW9 5G 43
Kingsbury Ter. N1 6E 66
Kingsbury Trad. Est. NW9 6K 43
Kings Chase KT8: E Mos 3G 149
Kings Chase Vw. EN2: Enf 2F 23
Kingsclere Cl. SW15 7C 116
Kingsclere Ct. N12 5H 31
Kingsclere Pl. EN2: Enf 2H 23
Kingscliffe Gdns. SW19 1H 135
King's Cl. DA1: Cray 4K 127
King's Cl. NW4 4F 45
Kings Cl. E10 7D 50
Kings Cl. KT12: Walt T 7K 147
Kings Cl. KT7: T Ditt 6A 150
Kings Cl. TW18: Staines 7A 128
King's Club, The 6E 134
Kings Coll. Ct. NW3 7C 64
King's College London Denmark Hill Campus 2D 120
King's College London Guy's Campus 5E 14 (1D 102)
(within Guy's Hospital)
King's College London Institute of Psychiatry, De Crespigny Park 2D 120
King's College London Maughan Library 7J 7 (6A 84)
King's College London St Thomas' Campus - Lambeth Pal. Rd. 2G 19 (3K 101)
(off Lambeth Pal. Rd.)
King's College London St Thomas' Campus - St Thomas' House 1G 19 (3K 101)
(off Lambeth Pal. Rd.)
King's College London Strand Campus 2H 13 (7K 83)
King's College London Waterloo Campus 5J 13 (1A 102)
King's Coll. Rd. NW3 7C 64
Kings Coll. Rd. HA4: Ruis 6H 39
King's College School of Medicine & Dentistry 2C 120
Kingscote Rd. CR0: C'don 7H 157
Kingscote Rd. KT3: N Mald 3K 151
Kingscote Rd. W4 3K 97
Kingscote St. EC4 2A 14 (7B 84)
King's Ct. E13 1K 87
King's Ct. SE1 6B 14 (2B 102)
Kings Ct. HA9: Wemb 2H 61
Kings Ct. IG9: Buck H 2G 37
Kings Ct. N7 7K 65
(off Caledonian Rd.)
Kings Ct. NW8 1D 82
(off Prince Albert Rd.)
Kings Ct. W6 4C 98
Kings Ct. Mans. SW6 1H 117
(off Fulham Rd.)
Kings Ct. M. KT8: E Mos 5H 149
Kings Ct. Nth. SW3 6C 16 (5C 100)
Kingscourt Rd. SW16 3H 137
Kings Ct. Sth. SW3 6C 16 (5C 100)
(off Chelsea Mnr. Gdns.)
King's Cres. N4 3C 66
Kings Cres. Est. N4 2C 66
Kingscroft SW4 6J 119
Kingscroft Rd. NW2 6H 63
KING'S CROSS 2J 83
King's Cross Bri. N1 1F 7 (3J 83)
(off Gray's Inn Rd.)
King's Cross Rd. WC1 1G 7 (3K 83)
King's Cross Sq. N1 1F 7 (3J 83)
(off Euston Rd.)
Kingsdale Gdns. W11 1F 99
Kingsdale Rd. SE18 7K 107
Kingsdale Rd. SE20 7K 139
Kingsdown Av. W13 2B 96
Kingsdown Av. W3 7A 80
Kingsdown Cl. SE16 5H 103
(off Masters Dr.)
Kingsdown Cl. W10 6F 81
Kingsdowne Rd. KT6: Surb 7E 150
Kingsdown Ho. E8 5G 67
Kingsdown Point SW2 2A 138
Kingsdown Rd. E11 3G 69
Kingsdown Rd. N19 2J 65
Kingsdown Rd. SM3: Cheam 5G 165
Kingsdown Way BR2: Hayes 7J 159
King's Dr. HA8: Edg 4A 28
Kings Dr. HA9: Wemb 2H 61
Kings Dr. KT5: Surb 7G 151
Kings Dr. KT7: T Ditt 7B 150
Kings Dr. TW11: Tedd 5H 131
Kingsend HA4: Ruis 1F 57
Kingsend Ct. HA4: Ruis 1G 57
Kings Farm E17 1D 50
Kings Farm Av. TW10: Rich 4G 115
Kingsfield Av. HA2: Harr 4F 41
Kingsfield Ho. SE9 3B 142
Kingsfield Rd. HA1: Harr 7H 41
Kingsfield Ter. HA1: Harr 7H 41
Kingsford St. NW5 5D 64
Kingsford Way E6 5D 88
King's Gdns. NW6 7J 63
Kings Gdns. IG1: Ilf 1H 71
Kings Gdns. KT12: Walt T 7K 147
Kings Gth. M. SE23 2J 139
Kingsgate HA9: Wemb 3J 61
Kingsgate Av. N3 3J 45
Kingsgate Bus. Cen. KT2: King T 1E 150
(off Kingsgate Rd.)

244 A–Z London

Kingsgate Cl. – Knoll Dr.

Kingsgate Cl. DA7: Bex 1E 126
Kingsgate Est. N1 6E 66
Kingsgate Ho. SW9 1A 120
Kingsgate Mans. WC1 6G 7 (5K 83) *(off Red Lion Sq.)*
Kings Ga. M. N8 5K 47 *(off Spencer Rd.)*
Kingsgate Pde. SW1 1B 18 (3G 101) *(off Victoria St.)*
Kingsgate Pl. NW6 7J 63
Kingsgate Rd. KT1: King T 1E 150
Kingsgate Rd. KT2: King T 1E 150
Kingsgate Rd. NW6 7J 63
Kings Ga. Wlk. SW1 1B 18 (3G 101) *(off Victoria St.)*
Kings Grange HA4: Ruis 1H 57
Kingsground SE9 7B 124
King's Gro. SE15 7H 103 (not continuous)
Kingsgrove Cl. DA14: Sidc 4K 143
Kings Hall Leisure Cen. 5J 67
Kings Hall M. SE13 3E 122
Kings Hall Rd. BR3: Beck 7A 140
Kings Head Hill E4 7J 25
Kingshead Ho. NW7 4J 29
Kings Head Pas. SW4 4H 119 *(off Clapham Pk. Rd.)*
Kings Head Theatre 1B 84 *(off Upper St.)*
King's Head Yd. SE1 5E 14 (1D 102)
King's Highway SE18 6J 107
Kingshill Av. HA3: Kenton 4B 42
Kingshill Av. KT4: Wor Pk 7C 152
Kingshill Av. UB4: Hayes 3G 75
Kingshill Av. UB4: Yead 3G 75
Kingshill Av. UB5: N'olt 3J 75
Kingshill Cl. UB4: Hayes 3J 75
Kingshill Ct. EN5: Barn 4B 20
Kingshill Dr. HA3: Kenton 2B 42
Kingshold Rd. E9 7J 67
Kingsholm Gdns. SE9 4B 124
King's Ho. SW10 7A 16 (6B 100) *(off King's Rd.)*
Kings Ho. SW8 7J 101 *(off Sth. Lambeth Rd.)*
King's Ho. Studios SW10 7A 16 (6B 100) *(off Lamont Rd. Pas.)*
Kingshurst Rd. SE12 7J 123
Kingside SE18 3C 106
Kings Keep BR2: Broml 2G 159
Kings Keep KT1: King T 4E 150
Kings Keep SW15 5F 117
KINGSLAND 6E 66
Kingsland NW8 1C 82
Kingsland Basin 1E 84
Kingsland Grn. E8 6E 66
Kingsland High St. E8 6F 67
Kingsland Pas. E8 6E 66
Kingsland Rd. E13 3A 88
Kingsland Rd. E2 1H 9 (3E 84)
Kingsland Rd. E8 1E 84
Kingsland Shop. Cen. 6F 67
Kings La. SM1: Sutt 6B 166
Kingslawn Cl. SW15 5D 116
Kingslee Ct. SM2: Sutt 7K 165
Kingsleigh Cl. TW8: Bford 6D 96
Kingsleigh Pl. CR4: Mitc 3D 154
Kingsleigh Wlk. BR2: Broml 4H 159
Kingsley Av. SM1: Sutt 4B 166
Kingsley Av. TW3: Houn 2G 113
Kingsley Av. UB1: S'hall 7E 76
Kingsley Av. W13 5A 78
Kingsley Cl. N2 5A 46
Kingsley Cl. RM10: Dag 4H 73
Kingsley Ct. DA6: Bex 4G 127
Kingsley Ct. HA8: Edg 3C 28
Kingsley Ct. KT4: Wor Pk 2B 164 *(off The Avenue)*
Kingsley Ct. NW2 6D 62
Kingsley Dr. KT4: Wor Pk 2B 164
Kingsley Flats SE1 4E 102 *(off Old Kent Rd.)*
Kingsley Gdns. E4 5H 35
Kingsley Ho. SW3 6B 100 *(off Beaufort St.)*
Kingsley Ho. W14 4G 99 *(off Avonmore Pl.)*
Kingsley Mans. W14 6G 99 *(off Greyhound Rd.)*
Kingsley M. BR7: Chst 6F 143
Kingsley M. E1 7H 85
Kingsley M. W8 3K 99
Kingsley Pl. N6 7E 46
Kingsley Rd. BR6: Chels 7K 173
Kingsley Rd. CR0: C'don 1A 168
Kingsley Rd. E17 2E 50
Kingsley Rd. E7 7J 69
Kingsley Rd. HA2: Harr 4G 59
Kingsley Rd. HA5: Pinn 4D 40
Kingsley Rd. IG6: Ilf 1G 53
Kingsley Rd. N13 4F 33
Kingsley Rd. NW6 1H 81
Kingsley Rd. SW19 5K 135
Kingsley Rd. TW3: Houn 1F 113
Kingsley St. SW11 3D 118
Kingsley Way N2 5A 46
Kingsley Wood Dr. SE9 3D 142
Kings Lodge HA4: Ruis 1G 57 *(off Pembroke Rd.)*
Kings Lodge N12 6F 31
Kingslyn Cres. SE19 1E 156
Kings Mall W6 4E 98
Kingsman Pde. SE18 3D 106
Kings Mans. SW3 7C 16 (6C 100) *(off Lawrence St.)*
Kingsman St. SE18 3D 106
Kingsmead EN5: New Bar 4D 20
Kingsmead TW10: Rich 6F 115
Kingsmead Av. CR4: Mitc 3G 155
Kingsmead Av. KT4: Wor Pk 2D 164
Kingsmead Av. KT6: Surb 2G 163
Kingsmead Av. N9 1C 34
Kingsmead Av. NW9 7K 43
Kingsmead Av. TW16: Sun 2A 148
Kingsmead Cl. DA15: Sidc 2A 144
Kingsmead Cl. KT19: Ewe 7K 163
Kingsmead Cl. TW11: Tedd 6B 132
Kingsmead Cotts. BR2: Broml 1C 172
Kingsmead Ct. N6 7H 47
Kingsmead Dr. UB5: N'olt 7D 58
Kingsmead Ho. E9 4A 68
Kingsmead Lodge SM2: Sutt 6B 166
Kingsmeadow 3G 151
Kingsmeadow Athletics Cen. 3G 151
Kingsmead Rd. SW2 2A 138
Kingsmead Way E9 4A 68
Kingsmere Cl. SW15 3F 117
Kingsmere Pk. NW9 1H 61
Kingsmere Pl. N16 1D 66
Kingsmere Rd. SW19 2F 135
King's M. SW4 5J 119
King's M. WC1 4H 7 (4K 83)
Kingsmill NW8 2B 82 *(off Kingsmill Ter.)*
Kingsmill Bus. Pk. KT1: King T 3F 151
Kingsmill Gdns. RM9: Dag 5F 73
Kingsmill Ho. SW3 5D 16 (5C 100) *(off Cale St.)*
Kingsmill Rd. RM9: Dag 5F 73
Kingsmill Ter. NW8 2B 82
Kingsnorth Ho. W10 6F 81
Kingsnympton Pk. KT2: King T 7H 133
Kings Oak RM7: Mawney 3G 55
King's Orchard SE9 6C 124
King's Paddock TW12: Hamp 1G 149
King's Pde. SM5: Cars 3D 166 *(off Wrythe La.)*
Kings Pde. N17 3F 49
Kings Pde. NW10 1E 80
Kings Pde. W12 3C 98
Kingspark Bus. Cen. KT3: N Mald 4J 151
Kingspark Ct. E18 3J 51
King's Pas. KT2: King T 1D 150
Kings Pas. E11 7G 51
Kings Pas. KT1: King T 2D 150
King's Pl. SE1 7D 14 (2C 102)
King's Pl. W4 5J 97
Kings Pl. IG9: Buck H 2F 37
Kings Place 2J 83
King Sq. EC1 2C 8 (3C 84)
Kings Quarter Apts. N1 1K 83 *(off Copenhagen St.)*
King's Quay SW10 1A 118 *(off Chelsea Harbour Dr.)*
Kings Reach Twr. SE1 4K 13 (1A 102) *(off Stamford St.)*
Kings Ride Ga. TW10: Rich 4G 115
Kingsridge SW19 2G 135
King's Rd. BR6: Orp 4K 173
King's Rd. E6 1A 88
King's Rd. KT2: King T 7E 132
King's Rd. KT6: Surb 1C 162
King's Rd. N17 1F 49
King's Rd. SW10 7A 100
King's Rd. SW19 6J 135
King's Rd. SW3 7A 16 (6B 100)
King's Rd. SW6 7K 99
King's Rd. TW11: Tedd 5H 131
King's Rd. UB7: W Dray 2B 92
Kings Rd. CR4: Mitc 3E 154
Kings Rd. E11 7G 51
Kings Rd. E4 1A 36
Kings Rd. EN5: Barn 3A 20
Kings Rd. HA2: Harr 2D 58
Kings Rd. IG11: Bark 7G 71
Kings Rd. N18 5B 34
Kings Rd. N22 1K 47
Kings Rd. NW10 7D 62
Kings Rd. SE25 3G 157
Kings Rd. SW14 3K 115
Kings Rd. TW1: Twick 6B 114
Kings Rd. TW10: Rich 6F 115
Kings Rd. TW13: Felt 1A 130
Kings Rd. W5 5D 78
King's Scholars' Pas. SW1 2A 18 (3G 101) *(off Carlisle Pl.)*
King Stairs Cl. SE16 2H 103
King's Ter. NW1 1G 83
King's Ter. TW7: Isle 4A 114
Kingsthorpe Rd. SE26 4K 139
Kingston Av. UB7: Yiew Ash Gro. 7B 74
Kingston Av. UB7: Yiew Whitethorn Av. 1B 92
Kingston Av. SM3: Cheam 3G 165
Kingston Av. TW14: Felt 6G 111
KINGSTON BRI. 2D 150
Kingston Bus. Cen. KT9: Chess 3E 162
Kingston By-Pass KT6: Surb 3D 162
Kingston Cl. RM6: Chad H 3E 54 (not continuous)
Kingston Cl. TW11: Tedd 6B 132
Kingston Cl. UB5: N'olt 1D 76
Kingston Crematorium 3G 151
Kingston Cres. BR3: Beck 1B 158
Kingston Gdns. CR0: Bedd 3J 167
Kingston Hall Rd. KT1: King T 3D 150
Kingston Hill KT2: King T 1G 151
Kingston Hill Av. RM6: Chad H 3E 54
Kingston Hill Pl. KT2: King T 4J 133
Kingston Ho. KT1: King T 4D 150 *(off Surbiton Rd.)*
Kingston Ho. NW1 1G 83 *(off Camden St.)*
Kingston Ho. NW6 7G 63
Kingston Ho. E. SW7 7C 10 (2C 100) *(off Prince's Ga.)*
Kingston Ho. Est. KT6: Surb 6B 150
Kingston Ho. Nth. SW7 7C 10 (2C 100) *(off Prince's Ga.)*
Kingston Ho. Sth. SW7 7C 10 (2C 100) *(off Ennismore Gdns.)*
Kingstonian FC 3G 163
Kingston La. TW11: Tedd 5A 132
Kingston La. UB7: W Dray 2B 92
Kingston La. UB8: Hil 3A 74
Kingston Lodge KT3: N Mald 4A 152
Kingston Mans. SW9 1K 119 *(off Clapham Rd.)*
Kingston Mus. 2E 150
Kingston Pl. HA3: Hrw W 7E 26
Kingston Rd. SW19 Norstead Pl. 1D 134
Kingston Rd. SW19 Rothesay Av. 1H 153
Kingston Rd. EN4: E Barn 5G 21
Kingston Rd. IG1: Ilf 4F 71
Kingston Rd. KT1: King T 3H 151
Kingston Rd. KT17: Ewe 7B 164
Kingston Rd. KT19: Ewe 3J 163
Kingston Rd. KT3: N Mald 3H 151
Kingston Rd. KT4: Wor Pk 3J 163
Kingston Rd. KT5: Surb 2H 163
Kingston Rd. N9 2B 34
Kingston Rd. SW15 2C 134
Kingston Rd. SW20 2F 153
Kingston Rd. TW11: Tedd 5B 132
Kingston Rd. TW15: Ashf 6A 128
Kingston Rd. UB2: S'hall 2D 94
Kingston Sq. SE19 5D 138
Kingston University Kingston Hill Campus 5K 133
Kingston University Knights Pk. Campus 3E 150
Kingston University Penrhyn Rd. Campus, Reg Bailey Bldg. 3D 150
Kingston University Penrhyn Road Campus 4E 150
Kingston University Roehampton Vale Cen. 3B 134
KINGSTON UPON THAMES 2D 150
Kingston upon Thames Tourist Info. Cen. 2D 150
Kingston Va. SW15 4K 133
KINGSTON VALE 4A 134
Kingstown St. NW1 1E 82 (not continuous)
King St. E13 4J 87
King St. EC2 7D 8 (6C 84)
King St. N17 1F 49
King St. N2 3B 46
King St. SW1 5B 12 (1G 101)
King St. TW1: Twick 1A 132
King St. TW9: Rich 5D 114
King St. UB2: S'hall 3C 94
King St. W3 1J 97
King St. W6 4C 98
King St. WC2 2E 12 (7J 83)
King St. Cloisters W6 4D 98 *(off King St.)*
King St. M. N2 3B 46
King St. Pde. TW1: Twick 1A 132 *(off King St.)*
Kings Wlk. Shop. Cen. Chelsea 5E 16 (5D 100)
Kingswater Pl. SW11 7C 100
King's Way CR0: Wadd 5K 167
Kings Way HA1: Harr 4J 41
Kingsway BR4: W W'ck 3G 171
Kingsway BR5: Pet W 5H 161
Kingsway EN3: Pond E 5C 24
Kingsway HA9: Wemb 4E 60
Kingsway IG8: Wfd G 5F 37
Kingsway KT3: N Mald 4E 152
Kingsway N12 6F 31
Kingsway SW14 3H 115
Kingsway TW19: Stanw 1A 128
Kingsway UB3: Hayes 5E 74
Kingsway WC2 7G 7 (6K 83)
Kingsway Bus. Pk. TW12: Hamp 1D 148
Kingsway Cres. HA2: Harr 4G 41
Kingsway Est. N18 6E 34
Kingsway Mans. WC1 5G 7 (5K 83) *(off Red Lion Sq.)*
Kingsway Pde. N16 3D 66 *(off Albion Rd.)*
Kingsway Pl. EC1 3K 7 (4A 84) *(off Sans Wlk.)*
Kingsway Rd. SM3: Cheam 7G 165
Kingswear Rd. HA4: Ruis 2J 57
Kingswear Rd. NW5 3F 65
King's Wharf SE10 6D 104 *(off Wood Wharf)*
Kings Wharf E8 1E 84 *(off Kingsland Rd.)*
Kingswood E2 2J 85 *(off Cyprus St.)*
Kingswood Av. BR2: Broml 3G 159
Kingswood Av. CR7: Thor H 5A 156
Kingswood Av. DA17: Belv 4F 109
Kingswood Av. NW6 1G 81
Kingswood Av. TW12: Hamp 6F 131
Kingswood Av. TW3: Houn 1D 112
Kingswood Cl. BR6: Orp 7J 161
Kingswood Cl. EN1: Enf 5K 23
Kingswood Cl. KT3: N Mald 6B 152
Kingswood Cl. KT6: Surb 7E 150
Kingswood Cl. N20 7F 21
Kingswood Cl. SW8 7J 101
Kingswood Cl. TW15: Ashf 5F 129
Kingswood Ct. E4 5H 35
Kingswood Ct. NW6 7J 63 *(off West End La.)*
Kingswood Ct. SE13 6F 123
Kingswood Ct. TW10: Rich 5F 115
Kingswood Dr. SE19 4E 138
Kingswood Dr. SM2: Sutt 7K 165
Kingswood Dr. SM5: Cars 1D 166
Kingswood Est. SE21 4E 138
Kingswood Hgts. E18 1J 51 *(off Queen Mary Av.)*
Kingswood M. N15 4B 48
Kingswood Pk. N3 2H 45
Kingswood Pl. SE13 4G 123
Kingswood Pl. UB4: Hayes 5G 75
Kingswood Rd. BR2: Broml 4F 159
Kingswood Rd. E11 7G 51
Kingswood Rd. HA9: Wemb 3G 61
Kingswood Rd. IG3: Ilf 1A 72
Kingswood Rd. SE20 6J 139
Kingswood Rd. SW19 7H 135
Kingswood Rd. SW2 6J 119
Kingswood Rd. W4 3J 97
Kingswood Ter. W4 3J 97
Kingswood Way SM6: W'gton 5J 167
Kingsworth Cl. BR3: Beck 5A 158
Kingsworthy Cl. KT1: King T 3F 151
Kings Yd. SW15 3E 116 *(off Lwr. Richmond Rd.)*
Kingthorpe Rd. NW10 7K 61
Kingthorpe Ter. NW10 6K 61
Kington Ho. NW6 1K 81 *(off Mortimer Cres.)*
Kingward Ho. E1 5G 85 *(off Hanbury St.)*
King Wardrobe Apts. EC4 1B 14 (6B 84) *(off Carter La.)*
Kingweston Cl. NW2 3G 63
King William IV Gdns. SE20 6J 139
King William La. SE10 5G 105
King William's Ct. SE10 6F 105 *(off Park Row)*
King William St. EC4 1F 15 (6D 84)
King William Wlk. SE10 6E 104 (not continuous)
Kingwood Gdns. E1 6G 85 *(off Piazza Wlk.)*
Kingwood Rd. SW6 1G 117
Kinlet Rd. SE18 1G 125
Kinloch Dr. NW9 7K 43
Kinloch St. N7 3K 65
Kinloss Ct. N3 4H 45
Kinloss Gdns. N3 3H 45
Kinloss Rd. SM5: Cars 7A 154
Kinnaird Av. BR1: Broml 6H 141
Kinnaird Av. W4 7J 97
Kinnaird Cl. BR1: Broml 6H 141
Kinnaird Ho. SE17 4D 102
Kinnaird Way IG8: Wfd G 6J 37
Kinnear Apts. N8 3K 47
Kinnear Rd. W12 2B 98
Kinnerton Pl. Nth. SW1 7F 11 (2D 100) *(off Kinnerton St.)*
Kinnerton Pl. Sth. SW1 7F 11 (2D 100) *(off Kinnerton St.)*
Kinnerton St. SW1 7G 11 (2E 100)
Kinnerton Yd. SW1 7G 11 (2E 100) *(off Kinnerton St.)*
Kinnoul Rd. W6 6G 99
Kino Bermondsey 7H 15 (3E 102) *(off Bermondsey Sq.)*
Kinross Av. KT4: Wor Pk 2C 164
Kinross Cl. HA3: Kenton 5F 43
Kinross Cl. HA8: Edg 2C 28
Kinross Cl. TW16: Sun 5H 129
Kinross Ct. BR1: Broml 1H 159 *(off Highland Rd.)*
Kinross Ct. SE6 1H 141
Kinross Dr. TW16: Sun 5H 129
Kinross Ho. N1 1K 83 *(off Bemerton Est.)*
Kinross Ter. E17 2B 50
Kinsale Cl. NW7 6A 30
Kinsale Rd. SE15 3G 121
Kinsella Gdns. SW19 5D 134
Kinsham Ho. E2 4G 85 *(off Ramsey St.)*
Kinsheron Pl. KT8: E Mos 4G 149
Kintore Way SE1 4F 103
Kintyre Cl. SW16 2K 155
Kintyre Ct. SW2 7J 119
Kintyre Ho. E14 1E 104 *(off Coldharbour)*
Kinveachy Gdns. SE7 5C 106
Kinver Ho. N19 2H 65
Kinver Rd. SE26 4J 139
Kipling Ct. W7 7K 77
Kipling Dr. SW19 6B 136
Kipling Est. SE1 7F 15 (2D 102)
Kipling Ho. N19 1J 65 *(off Charles St.)*
Kipling Ho. SE5 7D 102 *(off Elmington Est.)*
Kipling Pl. HA7: Stan 6E 26
Kipling Rd. DA7: Bex 1E 126
Kipling St. SE1 7F 15 (2D 102)
Kipling Ter. N9 3J 33
Kipling Twr. W3 3J 97 *(off Palmerston Rd.)*
Kippington Dr. SE9 1B 142
Kira Bldg. E3 3B 86
Kiran Apts. E1 6K 9 (5F 85) *(off Chicksand St.)*
Kirby Cl. KT19: Ewe 5B 164
Kirby Est. SE16 3H 103
Kirby Est. UB7: Yiew 7A 74
Kirby Gro. SE1 6G 15 (2E 102)
Kirby St. EC1 5K 7 (5A 84)
Kirby Way KT12: Walt T 6A 148
Kirby Way UB8: Hil 4B 74
Kirchen Rd. W13 7B 78
Kirkby Apts. E3 5B 86 *(off St Paul's Way)*
Kirkby Cl. N11 6K 31
Kirkdale SE26 2H 139
Kirkdale Cnr. SE26 4J 139
Kirkdale Rd. E11 1G 69
Kirkeby Ho. EC1 5J 7 (5A 84) *(off Leather La.)*
Kirkfield Cl. W13 1B 96
Kirkham Apts. IG11: Bark 7G 71 *(off Linton Rd.)*
Kirkham Rd. E6 6C 88
Kirkham St. SE18 6J 107
Kirk Ho. HA9: Wemb 3E 60
Kirkland Av. IG5: Ilf 2E 52
Kirkland Cl. DA15: Sidc 6J 125
Kirkland Dr. EN2: Enf 1H 23
Kirkland Ho. E14 St Davids Sq. 5D 104 *(off St Davids Sq.)*
Kirkland Ho. E14 Westferry Rd. 5D 104 *(off Westferry Rd.)*
Kirkland Ter. BR3: Beck 6C 140
Kirkland Wlk. E8 6F 67
Kirk La. SE18 6G 107
Kirkleas Rd. KT6: Surb 1E 162
Kirklees Rd. CR7: Thor H 5A 156
Kirklees Rd. RM8: Dag 5C 72
Kirkley Rd. SW19 1J 153
Kirkman Pl. W1 6C 6 (5H 83) *(off Tottenham Ct. Rd.)*
Kirkmichael Rd. E14 6E 86
Kirk Ri. SM1: Sutt 3K 165
Kirk Rd. E17 6B 50
Kirkside Rd. SE3 6J 105
Kirk's Place 5B 86
Kirkstall Av. N17 4D 48
Kirkstall Gdns. SW2 1J 137
Kirkstall Ho. SW1 5J 17 (5F 101) *(part of Abbots Mnr.)*
Kirkstall Rd. SW2 1H 137
Kirkstead Ct. E5 4K 67
Kirksted Rd. SM4: Mord 1K 165
Kirkstone NW1 1A 6 (3G 83) *(off Harrington St.)*
Kirkstone Way BR1: Broml 7G 141
Kirk St. WC1 4H 7 (4K 83) *(off Northington St.)*
Kirkton Rd. N15 4E 48
Kirkwall Pl. E2 3J 85
Kirkwood Pl. NW1 7E 64
Kirkwood Rd. SE15 2H 121
Kirn Rd. W13 7B 78
Kirrane Cl. KT3: N Mald 5B 152
Kirtley Ho. SW8 1G 119
Kirtley Rd. SE26 4A 140
Kirtling St. SW11 7G 101
Kirton Cl. W4 4K 97
Kirton Gdns. E2 2K 9 (3F 85) (not continuous)
Kirton Lodge SW18 6K 117
Kirton Rd. E13 2A 88
Kirton Wlk. HA8: Edg 7D 28
Kirwyn Way SE5 7B 102
Kitcat Ter. E3 3C 86
Kitchen Ct. E10 2D 68
Kitchener Ho. SE18 7E 106
Kitchener Rd. CR7: Thor H 3D 156
Kitchener Rd. E17 1D 50
Kitchener Rd. E7 6K 69
Kitchener Rd. N17 3E 48
Kitchener Rd. N2 3C 46
Kitchener Rd. RM10: Dag 6H 73
Kite Cl. SE2 2C 108
Kite Ho. SE1 4H 103
Kite Ho. SE3 4K 123
Kite Pl. E2 3G 85 *(off Warner Pl.)*
Kite Yd. SW11 1D 118 *(off Cambridge Rd.)*
Kitley Gdns. SE19 1F 157
Kitson Rd. SE5 7D 102
Kitson Rd. SW13 1C 116
Kittiwake Ct. SE1 7D 14 (2C 102) *(off Gt. Dover St.)*
Kittiwake Ct. SE8 6B 104 *(off Abinger Gro.)*
Kittiwake Pl. SM1: Sutt 5H 165
Kittiwake Rd. UB5: N'olt 3B 76
Kittiwake Way UB4: Yead 5B 76
Kitto Rd. SE14 2K 121
Kiver Rd. N19 2H 65
Klea Av. SW4 6G 119
Kleine Wharf N1 1E 84
Klein's Wharf E14 3C 104 *(off Westferry Rd.)*
Knapdale Cl. SE23 2H 139
Knapmill Rd. SE6 2C 140
Knapmill Way SE6 2D 140
Knapp Cl. NW10 6A 62
Knapp Rd. E3 4C 86
Knapp Rd. TW15: Ashf 4B 128
Knapton M. SW17 6E 136
Knaresborough Dr. SW18 1K 135
Knaresborough Pl. SW5 4K 99
Knatchbull Rd. NW10 1K 79
Knatchbull Rd. SE5 2B 120
Knebworth Av. E17 1C 50
Knebworth Cl. EN5: New Bar 4E 20
Knebworth Ho. SW8 2H 119
Knebworth Rd. N16 4E 66
Knee Hill SE2 4C 108
Knee Hill Cres. SE2 4C 108
Kneller Gdns. TW7: Isle 6H 113
Kneller Ho. UB5: N'olt 2B 76 *(off Academy Gdns.)*
Kneller Rd. KT3: N Mald 7A 152
Kneller Rd. SE4 4A 122
Kneller Rd. TW2: Whitt 6G 113
Knevett Ter. TW3: Houn 4E 112
Knight Cl. RM8: Dag 2C 72
Knight Ct. E4 1K 35 *(off The Ridgeway)*
Knight Ct. N15 5E 48
Knighten St. E1 1H 103
Knighthead Point E14 2C 104
Knight Ho. SE17 4E 102 *(off Tatum St.)*
Knightland Rd. E5 2H 67
Knightleas Ct. NW2 6E 62
Knightleys Ct. E10 1A 68 *(off Wellington Rd.)*
Knightley Wlk. SW18 4J 117
Knighton Cl. CR2: S Croy 7B 168
Knighton Cl. IG8: Wfd G 4E 36
Knighton Cl. RM7: Rom 6K 55
Knighton Dr. IG8: Wfd G 4D 36
Knighton Grn. IG9: Buck H 2E 36
Knighton La. IG9: Buck H 2E 36
Knighton Pk. Rd. SE26 5K 139
Knighton Pl. IG9: Buck H 2E 36 *(off Knighton La.)*
Knighton Rd. E7 3J 69
Knighton Rd. RM7: Rom 6J 55
Knightrider Ct. EC4 2C 14 (7C 84) *(off Knightrider St.)*
Knightrider St. EC4 1B 14 (6B 84)
Knights Arc. SW1 7E 10 (2D 100) *(off Knightsbridge)*
Knights Av. W5 2E 96
Knightsbridge SW1 7E 10 (2D 100)
Knightsbridge SW7 7E 10 (2D 100)
KNIGHTSBRIDGE 7C 10 (2C 100)
Knightsbridge Apts., The SW7 7E 10 (2D 100) *(off Knightsbridge)*
Knightsbridge Ct. BR2: Broml 6C 160 *(off Wells Vw. Dr.)*
Knightsbridge Ct. SW1 7F 11 (2D 100) *(off Sloane St.)*
Knightsbridge Gdns. RM7: Rom 5K 55
Knightsbridge Grn. SW1 7E 10 (2D 100) (not continuous)
Knights Cl. E9 5J 67
Knights Cl. KT8: W Mole 5D 148
Knights Community Stadium, The 4J 165
Knightscote Cl. UB9: Hare 2A 38
Knights Ct. BR1: Broml 3H 141
Knights Ct. KT1: King T 3E 150
Knights Ct. WD23: B Hea 1C 26
Knights Hill SE27 5B 138
Knight's Hill Sq. SE27 4B 138
Knight's Ho. SW10 7A 100 *(off Hortensia Rd.)*
Knight's Ho. W14 5H 99 *(off Baron's Ct. Rd.)*
Knights Ho. SW8 7J 101 *(off Sth. Lambeth Rd.)*
Knight's Pk. KT1: King T 3E 150
Knight's Pl. TW2: Twick 1J 131
Knight's Rd. E16 2J 105
Knights Rd. HA7: Stan 4H 27
Knights Twr. SE8 5C 104
Knight's Wlk. SE11 4K 19 (4B 102) (not continuous)
Knightswood Cl. HA8: Edg 2D 28
Knightswood Ct. N6 7H 47
Knightswood Ho. N12 6F 31
Knightwood Cres. KT3: N Mald 6A 152
Knivet Rd. SW6 6J 99
Knockholt Rd. SE9 5B 124
Knole, The SE9 4E 142
Knole Cl. CR0: C'don 6J 157
Knole Ct. UB5: N'olt 3A 76 *(off Broomcroft Av.)*
Knole Ga. DA15: Sidc 3J 143
Knoll, The BR2: Hayes 2J 171
Knoll, The BR3: Beck 1D 158
Knoll, The HA1: Harr 1K 59
Knoll, The HA5: Pinn 2B 40
Knoll, The W13 5C 78
Knoll Ct. SE19 5F 139 *(off Farquhar Rd.)*
Knoll Cres. HA6: Nwood 2G 39 (not continuous)
Knoll Dr. N14 7K 21

Knoll Ho. – Lane M.

Knoll Ho. NW8 .... 2A 82
(off Carlton Hill)
Knollmead KT5: Surb 1J 163
Knoll Ri. BR6: Orp 1K 173
Knoll Rd. DA14: Sidc 5B 144
Knoll Rd. DA5: Bexl 7G 127
Knoll Rd. SW18 .... 5A 118
Knolls Cl. KT4: Wor Pk 3D 164
Knollys Cl. SW16 .... 3A 138
Knolly's Ho. WC1 .... 3E 6 (4J 83)
(off Tavistock Pl.)
Knollys Rd. SW16 .... 3K 137
Knot Ho. SE1 .... 5J 15 (1F 103)
(off Brewery Sq.)
Knotley Way BR4: W W'ck 2D 170
Knottisford St. E2 .... 3J 85
Knotts Grn. M. E10 .... 6D 50
Knotts Grn. Rd. E10 .... 6D 50
Knowland M. CR7: Thor H 4D 156
Knowlden Ho. E1 .... 7J 85
(off Cable St.)
Knowle Av. DA7: Bex 7E 108
Knowle Cl. SW9 .... 3A 120
Knowledge Ct. SW16 .... 3K 155
Knowle Rd. BR2: Broml 2D 172
Knowle Rd. TW2: Twick 1J 131
Knowles Cl. UB7: Yiew 1A 92
Knowles Ct. HA1: Harr 6K 41
Knowles Hill Cres. SE13 .... 5F 123
Knowles Ho. SW18 .... 6K 117
(off Neville Gill Cl.)
Knowles Wlk. SW4 .... 3G 119
Knowles Wharf NW1 .... 1G 83
(off St Pancras Way)
Knowlton Grn. BR2: Broml 5H 159
Knowlton Ho. SW9 .... 1A 120
(off Cowley Rd.)
Knowl Wood La. BR6: Farnb 2E 172
Knowsley Av. UB1: S'hall 1F 95
Knowsley Rd. SW11 .... 2D 118
Knox Ct. SW4 .... 2J 119
Knox Rd. E7 .... 6H 69
Knox St. W1 .... 5E 4 (5D 82)
Knoyle Ho. W14 .... 3G 99
(off Russell Rd.)
Knoyle St. SE14 .... 6A 104
Koblenz Ho. N8 .... 3J 47
(off Newland Rd.)
Kohat Rd. SW19 .... 5K 135
Koops Mill M. SE1 .... 7K 15 (3F 103)
Korda Cl. TW17: Shep 3B 146
Kossuth St. SE10 .... 5G 105
Kotata Ho. E20 .... 6E 68
(off Ravens Wlk.)
Kotree Way SE1 .... 4G 103
Kramer M. SW5 .... 5J 99
Kreedman Wlk. E8 .... 5G 67
Kreisel Wlk. TW9: Kew 6F 97
Kristina Ct. SM2: Sutt 6J 165
(off Overton Rd.)
Krithia Rd. RM9: Dag 1B 90
Krupnik Pl. EC2 .... 3H 9 (4E 84)
(shown as Curtain Pl.)
Kuala Gdns. SW16 .... 1K 155
Kubrick Bus. Est. E7 .... 4K 69
(off Station App.)
Kuhn Way E7 .... 5J 69
Kurdish Mus. 4C 98
Kwame Ho. E16 .... 7F 89
(off University Way)
Kwesi M. SE27 .... 5A 138
Kydbrook Cl. BR5: Pet W 7G 161
Kyle Ho. NW6 .... 1J 81
Kylemore Cl. E6 .... 2B 88
Kylemore Rd. NW6 .... 7J 63
Kylestrome Ho. SW1 .... 4H 17 (4E 100)
(off Cundy St.)
Kymberley Rd. HA1: Harr 6J 41
Kymes Ct. HA2: Harr 2H 59
Kynance Gdns. HA7: Stan 1C 42
Kynance M. SW7 .... 3K 99
Kynance Pl. SW7 .... 3A 100
Kynaston Av. CR7: Thor H 5C 156
Kynaston Av. N16 .... 3F 67
Kynaston Cl. HA3: Hrw W 7C 26
Kynaston Cres. CR7: Thor H 5C 156
Kynaston Rd. BR1: Broml 5J 141
Kynaston Rd. CR7: Thor H 5C 156
Kynaston Rd. EN2: Enf 1J 23
Kynaston Rd. N16 .... 3E 66
Kynaston Wood HA3: Hrw W 7C 26
Kynersley Cl. SM5: Cars 3D 166
Kynoch Rd. N18 .... 4D 34
Kyrle Rd. SW11 .... 6E 118
Kyverdale Rd. N16 .... 7F 49

L

Laban Cen. 6D 104
Laban Wlk. SE8 .... 6D 104
(off Copperas St.)
Laboratory Spa & Health Club, The 3G 47
Laboratory Sq. SE18 .... 3F 107
Laburnham Cl. EN5: Barn 3C 20
Laburnum Av. N17 .... 7J 33
Laburnum Av. N9 .... 2A 34
Laburnum Av. SM1: Sutt 3C 166
Laburnum Av. UB7: Yiew 7B 74
Laburnum Cl. E4 .... 6G 35
Laburnum Cl. HA0: Wemb 1G 79
Laburnum Cl. N11 .... 6K 31
Laburnum Cl. SE15 .... 7J 103
Laburnum Ct. E2 .... 1F 85
Laburnum Ct. HA1: Harr 5F 41
Laburnum Ct. HA7: Stan 4H 27
Laburnum Ct. SE16 .... 2J 103
(off Albion St.)
Laburnum Cres. TW16: Sun 1K 147
Laburnum Gdns. CR0: C'don 7K 157
Laburnum Gdns. N21 .... 2H 33
Laburnum Gro. HA4: Ruis 6F 39
Laburnum Gro. KT3: N Mald 2K 151
Laburnum Gro. N21 .... 2H 33
Laburnum Gro. NW9 .... 7J 43
Laburnum Gro. TW3: Houn 4D 112
Laburnum Gro. UB1: S'hall 4D 76
Laburnum Ho. BR2: Broml 1F 159
Laburnum Ho. RM10: Dag 2G 73
Laburnum La. E2 .... 2F 85
Laburnum Lodge N3 .... 2H 45
Laburnum Pl. SE9 .... 5E 124
Laburnum Rd. CR4: Mitc 2E 154
Laburnum Rd. SW19 .... 7A 136
Laburnum Rd. UB3: Harl 4H 93
Laburnums, The E6 .... 4C 88
Laburnum St. E2 .... 1F 85
Laburnum Way BR2: Broml 7E 160
Laburnum Way TW19: Stanw 1B 128
Labyrinth Twr. E8 .... 6F 67
(off Dalston Sq.)
Lacebark Cl. DA15: Sidc 7K 125
Lace Cl. SM6: W'gton 2F 167
Lace Ct. E1 .... 5K 85
(off Master's St.)
Lacewing Cl. E13 .... 3J 87
Lacey Cl. N9 .... 2B 34
Lacey Dr. HA8: Edg 4K 27
Lacey Dr. RM8: Dag 3C 72
Lacey Dr. TW12: Hamp 1D 148
Lacey Gro. UB10: Uxb 2A 74
Lacey M. E3 .... 2C 86
Lacine Ct. SE16 .... 2K 103
(off Christopher Cl.)
Lackington St. EC2 .... 5F 9 (5D 84)
Lackland Ho. SE1 .... 5F 103
(off Rowcross St.)
Lacland Ho. SW10 .... 7B 100
(off Worlds End Est.)
Lacock Cl. SW19 .... 6A 136
Lacock Ct. W13 .... 1A 96
Lacon Ho. WC1 .... 5G 7 (5K 83)
(off Theobald's Rd.)
Lacon Rd. SE22 .... 4G 121
Lacrosse Way SW16 .... 1H 155
Lacy Rd. SW15 .... 4F 117
Ladas Rd. SE27 .... 4C 138
Ladbroke Ct. E1 .... 7K 9 (6F 85)
Ladbroke Cres. W11 .... 6G 81
Ladbroke Gdns. W11 .... 7H 81
Ladbroke Gro. W10 .... 4F 81
Ladbroke Gro. W11 .... 6G 81
Ladbroke Gro. Ho. W11 .... 7H 81
(off Ladbroke Gro.)
Ladbroke Grove Memorial 4F 81
Ladbroke M. W11 .... 1G 99
Ladbroke Rd. EN1: Enf 6A 24
Ladbroke Rd. W11 .... 1H 99
Ladbroke Sq. W11 .... 7H 81
Ladbroke Ter. W11 .... 7H 81
Ladbroke Wlk. W11 .... 1H 99
Ladbrook Cl. BR1: Broml 6G 141
Ladbrook Cl. HA5: Pinn 5D 40
Ladbrooke Cres. DA14: Sidc 3D 144
Ladbrook Rd. SE25 .... 4D 156
Ladderstile Ride KT2: King T 5H 133
Ladderswood Way N11 .... 5B 32
Ladlands SE22 .... 7G 121
Lady Anne Ct. E18 .... 1J 51
(off Queen Mary Av.)
Lady Aylesford Av. HA7: Stan 5F 27
Lady Booth Rd. KT1: King T 2E 150
Lady Craig Ct. UB8: Hil 5D 74
Ladycroft Gdns. BR6: Farnb 5G 173
Ladycroft Rd. SE13 .... 3D 122
Ladycroft Wlk. HA7: Stan 1D 42
Ladycroft Way BR6: Farnb 5G 173
Lady Dock Path SE16 .... 2A 104
Lady Elizabeth Ho. SW14 .... 3J 115
Ladyfern Ho. E3 .... 5C 86
(off Gail St.)
Lady Florence Ctyd. SE8 .... 7C 104
(off Reginald Sq.)
Lady Forsdyke Way KT19: Eps 7G 163
Ladygate La. HA4: Ruis 6D 38
Lady Hay KT4: Wor Pk 2B 164
Lady Jane Ct. KT2: King T 2F 151
(off Cambridge Rd.)
Lady Margaret Ho. SE17 .... 6D 102
(off Queen's Row)
Lady Margaret Rd. N19 .... 4G 65
Lady Margaret Rd. NW5 .... 5G 65
Lady Margaret Rd. UB1: S'hall 7D 76
Lady May Ho. SE5 .... 7C 102
(off Pitman St.)
Lady Micos Almshouses E1 .... 6J 85
(off Aylward St.)
Lady Sarah Cohen Ho. N11 .... 6J 31
(off Asher Loftus Way)
Lady Shaw Ct. N13 .... 2E 32
Ladyship Ter. SE22 .... 7G 121
Ladysmith Av. E6 .... 2C 88
Ladysmith Av. IG2: Ilf 7J 53
Ladysmith Cl. NW7 .... 7H 29
Ladysmith Rd. E16 .... 3H 87
Ladysmith Rd. EN1: Enf 3K 23
(not continuous)
Ladysmith Rd. HA3: W'stone 2J 41
Ladysmith Rd. N17 .... 2G 49
Ladysmith Rd. N18 .... 5C 34
Ladysmith Rd. SE9 .... 6E 124
Lady Somerset Rd. NW5 .... 4F 65
LADYWELL 5D 122
Ladywell Arena (Running Track) 6C 122
Ladywell Cl. SE4 .... 5C 122
Ladywell Hgts. SE4 .... 6B 122
Ladywell Rd. SE13 .... 5C 122
Ladywell St. E15 .... 1H 87
Ladywell Water Twr. SE4 .... 5C 122
Ladywood Av. BR5: Pet W 5J 161
Ladywood Rd. KT6: Surb 2G 163
Lafone Av. TW13: Felt 2A 130
Lafone St. SE1 .... 6J 15 (2F 103)
Lagado M. SE16 .... 1K 103
Lagare Apts. SE1 .... 6B 14 (2B 102)
(off Surrey Row)
Lagonda Ho. E3 .... 4C 86
(off Tidworth Rd.)
Lagonier Ho. EC1 .... 2D 8 (3C 84)
(off Ironmonger Row)
Laidlaw Dr. N21 .... 5E 22
Laing Dean UB5: N'olt 1A 76
Laing Ho. SE5 .... 7C 102
Laings Av. CR4: Mitc 2D 154
Lainlock Pl. TW3: Houn 1F 113
Lainson St. SW18 .... 7J 117
Lairdale Cl. SE21 .... 1C 138
Laird Ho. SE5 .... 7C 102
(off Redcar St.)
Lairs Cl. N7 .... 5J 65
Lait Ho. BR3: Beck 1D 158
Laitwood Rd. SW12 .... 1F 137
Lakanal SE5 .... 1E 120
(off Sceaux Gdns.)
Lake, The WD23: B Hea 1C 26
Lake Av. BR1: Broml 6J 141
Lake Bus. Cen. N17 .... 7B 34
Lake Cl. RM8: Dag 3D 72
Lake Cl. SW19 .... 5H 135
Lakedale Ct. IG11: Bark 4B 90
Lakedale Rd. SE18 .... 6J 107
Lake Dr. WD23: B Hea 2C 26
Lake Farm Country Pk. 1G 93
Lakefield Cl. SE20 .... 7H 139
Lakefield Rd. N22 .... 2B 48
Lake Gdns. RM10: Dag 5G 73
Lake Gdns. SM6: W'gton 3F 167
Lake Gdns. TW10: Ham 2B 132
Lakehall Gdns. CR7: Thor H 5B 156
Lakehall Rd. CR7: Thor H 5B 156
Lake Ho. SE1 .... 7C 14 (2C 102)
(off Southwark Bri. Rd.)
Lake Ho. Rd. E11 .... 3J 69
Lake House Rd. E11 .... 2J 69
Lakehurst Rd. KT19: Ewe 5A 164
Lakeland Cl. HA3: Hrw W 6C 26
Lakenham Pl. E3 .... 4B 86
Lakenheath N14 .... 5B 22
Laker Ct. SW4 .... 1J 119
Laker Ho. E16 .... 2K 105
Laker Ind. Est. BR3: Beck 5A 140
Lake Rd. CR0: C'don 2B 170
Lake Rd. E10 .... 7D 50
Lake Rd. RM6: Chad H 4D 54
Lake Rd. RM9: Dag 3H 91
Lake Rd. SW19 .... 5H 135
Laker Pl. SW15 .... 6G 117
Lakeside BR3: Beck 3D 158
Lakeside EN2: Enf 4C 22
Lakeside KT19: Ewe 6A 164
Lakeside KT2: King T 7H 133
Lakeside N3 .... 2K 45
Lakeside SM6: W'gton 4F 167
Lakeside W13 .... 6C 78
Lakeside Av. IG4: Ilf 4B 52
Lakeside Av. SE28 .... 1A 108
Lakeside Cl. DA15: Sidc 5C 126
Lakeside Cl. HA4: Ruis 4F 39
Lakeside Cl. SE25 .... 2G 157
Lakeside Ct. N4 .... 2C 66
Lakeside Cres. EN4: E Barn 5J 21
Lakeside Dr. BR2: Broml 3C 172
Lakeside Dr. NW10 .... 3F 79
Lakeside Ind. Est. SL3: Coln 2B 174
Lakeside Rd. N13 .... 4E 32
Lakeside Rd. SL0: Rich P 2B 174
Lakeside Rd. SL3: Coln 3A 174
Lakeside Rd. SL3: Rich P 3A 174
Lakeside Rd. W14 .... 3F 99
Lakeside Ter. EC2 .... 5D 8 (5C 84)
(off Silk St.)
Lakeside Way HA9: Wemb 4G 61
Lakes Rd. BR2: Kes 5A 172
Lakeswood Rd. BR5: Pet W 6F 161
Lake Vw. HA8: Edg 5A 28
Lakeview Ct. SE28 .... 7B 90
Lake Vw. Est. E3 .... 2K 85
Lakeview Rd. DA16: Well 4B 126
Lakeview Rd. SE27 .... 5A 138
Lake Vw. Ter. N18 .... 4A 34
(off Sweet Briar Wlk.)
Lakin Cl. SM5: Cars 4E 166
Lakis Cl. NW3 .... 4A 64
Laleham Av. NW7 .... 3E 28
Laleham Ct. SM1: Sutt 5A 166
Laleham Ho. E2 .... 3J 9 (4F 85)
(off Camlet St.)
Laleham Rd. SE6 .... 7E 122
Laleham Rd. TW17: Shep 4B 146
Lalor St. SW6 .... 2G 117
Lambarde Av. SE9 .... 4E 142
Lambarde Sq. SE10 .... 5H 105
Lambard Ho. SE10 .... 7E 104
(off Langdale Rd.)
Lamb Cl. UB5: N'olt 3C 76
Lamb Ct. E14 .... 7A 86
(off Narrow St.)
Lamberhurst Ho. SE15 .... 6J 103
Lamberhurst Rd. RM8: Dag 1F 73
Lamberhurst Rd. SE27 .... 4A 138
Lambert Av. TW9: Rich 3G 115
Lambert Ct. DA8: Erith 6J 109
(off Park Cres.)
Lambert Ho. SW11 .... 3B 118
(off Gartons Way)
Lambert Jones M. EC2 .... 5C 8 (5C 84)
(off Beech St.)
Lambert Lodge TW8: Bford 5D 96
(off Layton Rd.)
Lambert M. N12 .... 5F 31
(off Lambert Way)
Lambert Rd. E16 .... 6K 87
Lambert Rd. N12 .... 5G 31
Lambert Rd. SW2 .... 5J 119
Lambert's Pl. CR0: C'don 1D 168
Lamberts Rd. KT5: Surb 5E 150
Lambert St. N1 .... 7A 66
Lambert Wlk. HA9: Wemb 3E 60
Lambert Way N12 .... 5F 31
LAMBETH 2H 19 (3K 101)
Lambeth Bri. SW1 .... 3F 19 (4J 101)
Lambeth Crematorium 4A 136
Lambeth High St. SE1 .... 4G 19 (4K 101)
Lambeth Hill EC4 .... 2C 14 (7C 84)
Lambeth Palace 2G 19 (3K 101)
Lambeth Pal. Rd. SE1 .... 2G 19 (3K 101)
Lambeth Rd. CR0: C'don 7A 156
Lambeth Rd. SE1 .... 3G 19 (4K 101)
Lambeth Rd. SE11 .... 3H 19 (4K 101)
Lambeth Towers SE11 .... 2J 19 (3A 102)
(off Kennington Rd.)
Lambeth Wlk. SE11 .... 4H 19 (4K 101)
(not continuous)
Lambfold Ho. N7 .... 6J 65
(off North Rd.)
Lamb Ho. SE10 .... 6E 104
(off Haddo St.)
Lamb Ho. SE5 .... 7C 102
(off Elmington Est.)
Lambkins M. E17 .... 4E 50
Lamb La. E8 .... 7H 67
Lamble St. NW5 .... 5E 64
Lambley Rd. RM9: Dag 6B 72
Lambolle Pl. NW3 .... 6C 64
Lambolle Rd. NW3 .... 6C 64
Lamborne Pl. UB10: Ick 3D 56
Lambourn Cl. NW5 .... 4G 65
Lambourn Cl. W7 .... 2K 95
Lambourne Av. SW19 .... 4H 135
Lambourne Ct. IG8: Wfd G 7F 37
Lambourne Gdns. E4 .... 2H 35
Lambourne Gdns. EN1: Enf 2A 24
Lambourne Gdns. IG11: Bark 7K 71
Lambourne Gro. SE16 .... 5K 103
Lambourne Ho. NW8 .... 5B 4 (5B 82)
(off Broadley St.)
Lambourne Ho. SE20 .... 1G 157
Lambourne Pl. SE3 .... 1K 123
Lambourne Rd. E11 .... 7E 50
Lambourne Rd. IG11: Bark 7J 71
Lambourne Rd. IG3: Ilf 2J 71
Lambourn Gro. KT1: King T 2H 151
Lambourn Rd. SW4 .... 3F 119
Lambrook Ho. SE15 .... 1G 121
Lambrook Ter. SW6 .... 1G 117
Lamb's Bldgs. EC1 .... 4E 8 (4D 84)
Lamb's Cl. N9 .... 2B 34
Lamb's Conduit Pas. WC1 .... 5G 7 (5K 83)
Lamb's Conduit St. WC1 .... 4G 7 (4K 83)
(not continuous)
Lambscroft Av. SE9 .... 3A 142
Lambs Mdw. IG8: Wfd G 2B 52
Lamb's M. N1 .... 1B 84
Lambs Pas. EC1 .... 4E 8 (4D 84)
Lambs Ter. N9 .... 2J 33
Lamb St. E1 .... 5J 9 (5F 85)
Lamb's Wlk. EN2: Enf 2H 23
Lambton M. N19 .... 1J 65
(off Lambton Rd.)
Lambton Pl. W11 .... 7H 81
Lambton Rd. N19 .... 1J 65
Lambton Rd. SW20 .... 1E 152
Lamb Wlk. SE1 .... 7G 15 (2E 102)
Lamerock Rd. BR1: Broml 4H 141
Lamerton Rd. IG6: Ilf 2F 53
Lamerton St. SE8 .... 6C 104
Lamford Cl. N17 .... 7J 33
Lamington St. W6 .... 4D 98
Lamlash St. SE11 .... 4B 102
Lamley Ho. SE10 .... 7D 104
(off Ashburnham Pl.)
Lammas Av. CR4: Mitc 2E 154
Lammas Grn. SE26 .... 3H 139
Lammas Pk. Gdns. W5 .... 1C 96
Lammas Pk. Rd. W5 .... 2D 96
Lammas Rd. E10 .... 2A 68
Lammas Rd. E9 .... 7K 67
Lammas Rd. TW10: Ham 4C 132
Lammermoor Rd. SW12 .... 7F 119
Lamont Rd. SW10 .... 6B 100
Lamont Rd. Pas. SW10 .... 7A 16 (6B 100)
(off Lamont Rd.)
LAMORBEY 1K 143
Lamorbey Cl. DA15: Sidc 1K 143
Lamorbey Pk. 1B 144
Lamorna Cl. BR6: Orp 7K 161
Lamorna Cl. E17 .... 2E 50
Lamorna Gro. HA7: Stan 1D 42
Lampard Gro. N16 .... 1F 67
Lampern Sq. E2 .... 3G 85
Lampeter Cl. NW9 .... 6A 44
Lampeter Sq. W6 .... 6G 99
Lamplighter Cl. E1 .... 4J 85
Lampmead Rd. SE12 .... 5H 123
Lamp Office Ct. WC1 .... 4G 7 (4K 83)
(off Conduit St.)
Lamport Cl. SE18 .... 4D 106
LAMPTON 1F 113
Lampton Av. TW3: Houn 1F 113
Lampton Ct. TW3: Houn 1F 113
Lampton Ho. Cl. SW19 .... 4F 135
Lampton Pk. Rd. TW3: Houn 2F 113
Lampton Rd. TW3: Houn 2E 112
Lanacre Av. NW9 .... 1K 43
Lanadron Cl. TW7: Isle 2K 113
Lanain Ct. SE12 .... 7H 123
Lanark Cl. W5 .... 5C 78
Lanark Ct. UB5: N'olt 5E 58
(off Newmarket Av.)
Lanark Ho. SE1 .... 5G 103
(off Old Kent Rd.)
Lanark Mans. W12 .... 2E 98
(off Pennard Rd.)
Lanark Mans. W9 .... 4A 82
(off Lanark Rd.)
Lanark M. W9 .... 3A 82
Lanark Pl. W9 .... 3A 4 (4A 82)
Lanark Rd. W9 .... 2K 81
Lanark Sq. E14 .... 3D 104
Lanata Wlk. UB4: Yead 4B 76
(off Alba Cl.)
Lanbury Rd. SE15 .... 4K 121
Lancashire Ct. W1 .... 2J 11 (7F 83)
Lancaster Av. CR4: Mitc 5J 155
Lancaster Av. E18 .... 4K 51
Lancaster Av. EN4: Had W 1F 21
Lancaster Av. IG11: Bark 7J 71
Lancaster Av. SE27 .... 2B 138
Lancaster Av. SW19 .... 5F 135
Lancaster Cl. BR2: Broml 4H 159
Lancaster Cl. KT2: King T 5D 132
Lancaster Cl. N1 .... 7E 66
Lancaster Cl. N17 .... 7B 34
Lancaster Cl. NW9 .... 1B 44
Lancaster Cl. TW15: Ashf 4A 128
Lancaster Cl. TW19: Stanw 6A 110
Lancaster Cl. W2 .... 7K 81
(off St Petersburgh Pl.)
Lancaster Cotts. TW10: Rich 6E 114
Lancaster Ct. KT12: Walt T 7J 147
Lancaster Ct. SE27 .... 2B 138
Lancaster Ct. SM2: Sutt 7J 165
(off Mulgrave Rd.)
Lancaster Ct. SW6 .... 7H 99
Lancaster Ct. TW19: Stanw 1A 128
Lancaster Ct. W2 .... 2A 10 (7A 82)
(off Lancaster Ga.)
Lancaster Dr. E14 .... 1E 104
Lancaster Dr. NW3 .... 6C 64
Lancaster Gdns. BR1: Broml 5C 160
Lancaster Gdns. KT2: King T 5D 132
Lancaster Gdns. SW19 .... 5G 135
Lancaster Gdns. W13 .... 2B 96
Lancaster Ga. W2 .... 7A 82
Lancaster Gro. NW3 .... 6B 64
Lancaster Hall E16 .... 1J 105
(off Wesley Av.)
Lancaster Ho. E11 .... 2H 69
Lancaster Ho. EN2: Enf 1J 23
Lancaster Ho. RM8: Dag 4B 72
Lancaster Ho. TW7: Isle 7K 95
Lancaster House 6B 12 (2G 101)
(off Stable Yd. Rd.)
Lancaster Lodge W11 .... 6G 81
(off Lancaster Rd.)
Lancaster M. SW18 .... 5K 117
Lancaster M. TW10: Rich 6E 114
Lancaster M. W2 .... 2A 10 (7A 82)
Lancaster Pk. TW10: Rich 5E 114
Lancaster Pl. IG1: Ilf 5G 71
Lancaster Pl. SW19 .... 5F 135
Lancaster Pl. TW1: Twick 6A 114
Lancaster Pl. TW4: Houn 2A 112
Lancaster Pl. WC2 .... 2G 13 (7K 83)
Lancaster Rd. E11 .... 2G 69
Lancaster Rd. E17 .... 2K 49
Lancaster Rd. E7 .... 7J 69
Lancaster Rd. EN2: Enf 1J 23
Lancaster Rd. EN4: E Barn 5G 21
Lancaster Rd. HA2: Harr 5E 40
Lancaster Rd. N11 .... 6C 32
Lancaster Rd. N18 .... 5A 34
Lancaster Rd. N4 .... 7K 47
Lancaster Rd. NW10 .... 5C 62
Lancaster Rd. SE25 .... 2F 157
Lancaster Rd. SW19 .... 5F 135
Lancaster Rd. UB1: S'hall 7C 76
Lancaster Rd. UB5: N'olt 6G 59
Lancaster Rd. W11 .... 6G 81
Lancaster Rd. Ind. Est. EN4: E Barn 5G 21
Lancaster Stables NW3 .... 6C 64
Lancaster St. SE1 .... 7A 14 (2B 102)
Lancaster Ter. W2 .... 2A 10 (7B 82)
Lancaster Wlk. UB3: Hayes 6E 74
Lancaster Wlk. W2 .... 4A 10 (1A 100)
Lancaster Way KT4: Wor Pk 7D 152
Lancastrian Rd. SM6: W'gton 7J 167
Lancefield Ho. SE15 .... 4H 121
Lancefield St. W10 .... 3H 81
Lancell St. N16 .... 2E 66
Lancelot Av. HA0: Wemb 4D 60
Lancelot Cres. HA0: Wemb 4D 60
Lancelot Gdns. EN4: E Barn 7K 21
Lancelot Pl. SW7 .... 7E 10 (2D 100)
Lancelot Rd. DA16: Well 4A 126
Lancelot Rd. HA0: Wemb 4D 60
Lance Rd. HA1: Harr 7G 41
Lancer Sq. W8 .... 2K 99
(off Kensington Chu. St.)
Lancey Cl. SE7 .... 4C 106
Lanchester Ct. W2 .... 1E 10 (6D 82)
(off Seymour St.)
Lanchester Rd. N6 .... 5D 46
Lanchester Way SE14 .... 1J 121
Lancing Gdns. N9 .... 1A 34
Lancing Ho. CR0: C'don 4D 168
(off Coombe Rd.)
Lancing Rd. CR0: C'don 7K 155
Lancing Rd. IG2: Ilf 6H 53
Lancing Rd. TW13: Felt 2H 129
Lancing Rd. W13 .... 7B 78
Lancing St. NW1 .... 2C 6 (3H 83)
Lancresse Ct. N1 .... 1E 84
(off De Beauvoir Est.)
Landale Ho. SE16 .... 3J 103
(off Lower Rd.)
Landau Apts. SW6 .... 6J 99
Landau Ct. CR2: S Croy 5C 168
(off Warham Rd.)
Landcroft Rd. SE22 .... 5F 121
Landells Rd. SE22 .... 6F 121
Landford Rd. SW15 .... 3E 116
Landgrove Rd. SW19 .... 5J 135
Landing Waiters Ho. E14 .... 6F 87
(off New Village Av.)
Landin Ho. E14 .... 6C 86
(off Thomas Rd.)
Landleys Fld. N7 .... 5H 65
(off Long Mdw.)
Landmann Ho. SE16 .... 4H 103
(off Rennie Est.)
Landmann Point SE10 .... 3J 105
Landmann Way SE14 .... 5K 103
Landmark Arts Cen. 5B 132
Landmark Commercial Cen. N18 .... 6K 33
Landmark East Twr. E14 .... 2C 104
(off Marsh Wall)
Landmark Hgts. E5 .... 4A 68
Landmark Ho. W6 .... 5E 98
(off Hammersmith Bri. Rd.)
Landmark Pl. UB10: Hil 2D 74
Landmark Sq. E14 .... 2C 104
Landmark West Twr. E14 .... 2C 104
(off Marsh Wall)
Landon Pl. SW1 .... 1E 16 (3D 100)
Landon's Cl. E14 .... 1E 104
Landon Wlk. E14 .... 7D 86
Landon Way TW15: Ashf 6D 128
Landor Ho. SE5 .... 7D 102
(off Elmington Est.)
Landor Ho. W2 .... 5J 81
(off Westbourne Pk. Rd.)
Landor Rd. SW9 .... 3J 119
Landor Space 3J 119
Landor Wlk. W12 .... 2C 98
Landra Gdns. N21 .... 6G 23
Landrake NW1 .... 1G 83
(off Plender St.)
Landridge Dr. EN1: Enf 1C 24
Landridge Rd. SW6 .... 2H 117
Landrock Rd. N8 .... 6J 47
Landscape Rd. IG8: Wfd G 7E 36
Landsdown Cl. EN5: New Bar 4F 21
Landsdowne Ct. N19 .... 1J 65
(off Fairbridge Rd.)
Landseer Av. E12 .... 5E 70
Landseer Cl. HA8: Edg 2G 43
Landseer Cl. SW19 .... 1A 154
Landseer Ct. UB4: Hayes 2F 75
Landseer Ho. NW8 .... 3B 4 (4B 82)
(off Frampton St.)
Landseer Ho. SW1 .... 4D 18 (4H 101)
(off Herrick St.)
Landseer Ho. SW11 .... 1E 118
Landseer Ho. UB5: N'olt 2B 76
(off Parkfield Dr.)
Landseer Rd. EN1: Enf 5B 24
Landseer Rd. KT3: N Mald 7K 151
Landseer Rd. N19 .... 3J 65
(not continuous)
Landseer Rd. SM1: Sutt 6J 165
Landstead Rd. SE18 .... 7H 107
Landulph Ho. SE11 .... 5K 19 (5A 102)
(off Kennings Way)
Landward Ct. W1 .... 7D 4 (6C 82)
(off Harrowby St.)
Lane, The NW8 .... 2A 82
Lane, The SE3 .... 3J 123
Lane Cl. NW2 .... 3D 62
Lane End DA7: Bex 3H 127
Lane End SW15 .... 6F 117
Lane Gdns. WD23: B Hea 1D 26
Lane M. E12 .... 3D 70

Lanercost Cl. – Lawless Ho.

Lanercost Cl. SW2 2A 138
Lanercost Gdns. N14 7D 22
Lanercost Rd. SW2 2A 138
Lanesborough Ct. N1 1G 9 (3E 84)
(off Fanshaw St.)
Lanesborough Pl. SW1 6H 11 (2E 100)
(off Grosvenor Pl.)
Lanesborough Way SW17 3B 136
Laneside BR7: Chst 5F 143
Laneside HA8: Edg 5D 28
Laneside Av. RM8: Dag 7F 55
Laneway SW15 5D 116
Laney Ho. EC1 5J 7 (5A 84)
(off Leather La.)
Lanfranc Ct. HA1: Harr 3K 59
Lanfranc Rd. E3 2A 86
Lanfrey Pl. W14 5H 99
Langan Ho. E14 6B 86
(off Keymer Pl.)
Langbourne Av. N6 2E 64
Langbourne Ct. E17 6A 50
Langbourne Mans. N6 2E 64
Langbourne Pl. E14 5D 104
Langbourne Way KT10: Clay 6A 162
Langbrook Rd. SE3 3B 124
Langcroft Cl. SM5: Cars 3D 166
Langdale NW1 1A 6 (3G 83)
(off Stanhope St.)
Langdale Av. CR4: Mitc 3D 154
Langdale Cl. BR6: Farnb 3F 173
Langdale Cl. RM8: Dag 1C 72
Langdale Cl. SE17 6C 102
Langdale Cl. SW14 4H 115
Langdale Cres. DA7: Bex 7G 109
Langdale Dr. UB4: Hayes 2G 75
Langdale Gdns. UB6: G'frd 3B 78
Langdale Ho. SW1 6A 18 (5G 101)
(off Churchill Gdns.)
Langdale Pde. CR4: Mitc 3D 154
Langdale Rd. CR7: Thor H 4A 156
Langdale Rd. SE10 7E 104
Langdale St. E1 6H 85
Langdon Ct. EC1 1B 8 (2B 84)
(off City Rd.)
Langdon Ct. NW10 1A 80
Langdon Cres. E6 2E 88
Langdon Dr. NW9 1J 61
Langdon Ho. E14 6E 86
(off Ida St.)
Langdon Pk. TW11: Tedd 7C 132
Langdon Pk. Rd. N6 7G 47
Langdon Pl. SW14 3J 115
Langdon Rd. BR2: Broml 3K 159
Langdon Rd. E6 1E 88
Langdon Rd. SM4: Mord 5A 154
Langdons Ct. UB2: S'hall 3E 94
Langdon Shaw DA14: Sidc 5K 143
Langdon Wlk. SM4: Mord 5A 154
Langdon Way SE1 4G 103
Lange Rd. HA2: Harr 3G 41
Langford Cl. E8 5G 67
Langford Cl. N15 6E 48
Langford Cl. NW8 2A 82
Langford Cl. W3 2H 97
Langford Ct. NW8 2A 82
(off Abbey Rd.)
Langford Cres. EN4: Cockf 4J 21
Langford Gdn. 1K 117
(off Pearscroft Road)
Langford Grn. SE5 3E 120
Langford Ho. SE8 6C 104
Langford M. N1 7A 66
Langford M. SW11 4B 118
(off St John's Hill)
Langford Pl. DA14: Sidc 3A 144
Langford Pl. NW8 2A 82
Langford Rd. EN4: Cockf 4J 21
Langford Rd. IG8: Wfd G 6F 37
Langford Rd. SW6 2K 117
Langfords IG9: Buck H 2G 37
Langham Cl. BR2: Broml 2C 172
Langham Cl. N15 3B 48
(off Langham Rd.)
Langham Ct. HA4: Ruis 5K 57
Langham Ct. NW4 5F 45
Langham Ct. SW20 2E 152
Langham Dr. RM6: Chad H 6B 54
Langham Gdns. HA0: Wemb 2C 60
Langham Gdns. HA8: Edg 7D 28
Langham Gdns. N21 5F 23
Langham Gdns. TW10: Ham 4C 132
Langham Gdns. W13 7B 78
Langham Ho. E15 6F 69
(off Forrester Way)
Langham Ho. Cl. TW10: Ham 4D 132
Langham Mans. SW5 5K 99
(off Earl's Ct. Sq.)
Langham Pk. Pl. BR2: Broml 4H 159
Langham Pl. N15 3B 48
Langham Pl. W1 6K 5 (5F 83)
Langham Pl. W4 6A 98
Langham Rd. HA8: Edg 6D 28
Langham Rd. N15 3B 48
Langham Rd. SW20 1E 152
Langham Rd. TW11: Tedd 5B 132
Langham St. W1 6K 5 (5F 83)
Langhedge Cl. N18 6A 34
Langhedge La. N18 6A 34
Langhedge La. Ind. Est. N18 6A 34
Langholm Cl. SW12 7H 119
Langholme WD23: Bush 1B 26
Langhorn Dr. TW2: Twick 7J 113
Langhorne Ct. NW8 7B 64
(off Dorman Way)
Langhorne Rd. RM10: Dag 7G 73
Langhorne St. SE18 7D 106
Lang Ho. SW8 7J 101
(off Hartington Rd.)
Lang Ho. TW19: Stanw 1A 128
Langland Cres. HA7: Stan 2D 42
Langland Dr. HA5: Pinn 1C 40
Langland Gdns. CR0: C'don 2B 170
Langland Gdns. NW3 5K 63
Langland Ho. SE5 7D 102
(off Edmund St.)
Langler Rd. NW10 2E 80
Langley Av. HA4: Ruis 2K 57
Langley Av. KT4: Wor Pk 1F 165
Langley Av. KT6: Surb 1D 162
Langley Ct. WC2 2E 12 (7J 83)
Langley Cres. E11 7A 52
Langley Cres. HA8: Edg 3D 28
Langley Cres. RM9: Dag 7C 72
Langley Cres. UB3: Harl 7H 93
Langley Dr. E11 7K 51
Langley Dr. W3 2H 97
Langley Gdns. BR2: Broml 4A 160
Langley Gdns. BR5: Pet W 6F 161
Langley Gdns. RM9: Dag 7D 72
Langley Gro. KT3: N Mald 2A 152
Langley Ho. W2 5J 81
(off Alfred Rd.)
Langley La. SW8 7G 19 (6K 101)
Langley Mans. SW8 7G 19 (6K 101)
(off Langley La.)
Langley M. RM9: Dag 7D 72
Langley Pk. NW7 6F 29
Langley Pk. Golf Course 6F 159
Langley Pk. Rd. SM1: Sutt 5A 166
Langley Pk. Rd. SM2: Sutt 6A 166
Langley Pk. Sports Cen. 6E 158
Langley Rd. BR3: Beck 4A 158
Langley Rd. DA16: Well 6C 108
Langley Rd. KT6: Surb 7E 150
Langley Rd. SW19 1H 153
Langley Rd. TW7: Isle 2K 113
Langley Row EN5: Barn 1C 20
Langley St. WC2 1E 12 (6J 83)
Langley Way BR4: W W'ck 1F 171
Langmead Dr. WD23: B Hea 1D 26
Langmead Ho. E3 3D 86
(off Bruce Rd.)
Langmead St. SE27 4B 138
Langmore Ct. DA6: Bex 3D 126
Langmore Ho. E1 6G 85
(off Stutfield St.)
Langport Ct. KT12: Walt T 7A 148
Langport Ho. SW9 2B 120
Langridge M. TW12: Hamp 6D 130
Langroyd Rd. SW17 2D 136
Langside Av. SW15 4C 116
Langside Cres. N14 3C 32
Langstone M. UB1: S'hall 1E 94
Langstone Way NW7 7A 30
Langston Hughes Cl. SE24 4B 120
Lang St. E1 4J 85
Langthorn Ct. EC2 7E 8 (6D 84)
Langthorne Ct. BR1: Broml 4E 140
Langthorne Ho. E3 3B 86
(off Merchant St.)
Langthorne Ho. UB3: Harl 4G 93
Langthorne Rd. E11 3E 68
(not continuous)
Langthorne St. SW6 7F 99
Langton Av. E6 3E 88
Langton Av. N20 7F 21
Langton Cl. WC1 3H 7 (4K 83)
Langton Ho. SE11 3H 19 (4K 101)
(off Lambeth Wlk.)
Langton Pl. SW18 1J 135
Langton Ri. SE23 7H 121
Langton Rd. HA3: Hrw W 7B 26
Langton Rd. KT8: W Mole 4G 149
Langton Rd. NW2 3E 62
Langton Rd. SW9 7B 102
Langton St. SW10 6A 100
Langton Way CR0: C'don 3E 168
Langton Way SE3 1H 123
Langtry Ct. TW7: Isle 2K 113
Langtry Ho. KT2: King T 1G 151
(off London Rd.)
Langtry Pl. SW6 6J 99
Langtry Rd. NW8 1K 81
Langtry Rd. UB5: N'olt 2B 76
Langtry Wlk. NW8 1K 81
Langwood Chase TW11: Tedd 6C 132
Langworth Dr. UB4: Yead 6K 75
Lanhill Rd. W9 4J 81
Lanier Rd. SE13 6F 123
Lanigan Dr. TW3: Houn 5F 113
Lankaster Gdns. N2 1B 46
Lankers Dr. HA2: Harr 6D 40
Lankton Cl. BR3: Beck 1E 158
Lannock Rd. UB3: Hayes 1H 93
Lannoy Point SW6 7G 99
(off Pellant Rd.)
Lannoy Rd. SE9 1G 143
Lanrick Rd. E14 6F 87
Lanridge Rd. SE2 3D 108
Lansbury Av. IG11: Bark 7A 72
Lansbury Av. N18 5J 33
Lansbury Av. RM6: Chad H 5E 54
Lansbury Av. TW14: Felt 6K 111
Lansbury Cl. NW10 5J 61
Lansbury Ct. SE28 7B 90
(off Saunders Way)
Lansbury Dr. UB4: Hayes 2G 75
Lansbury Est. E14 6D 86
Lansbury Gdns. E14 6F 87
Lansbury Rd. EN3: Enf H 1E 24
Lansbury Way N18 5K 33
Lanscombe Wlk. SW8 1J 119
Lansdell Ho. SW2 6A 120
Lansdell Rd. CR4: Mitc 2E 154
Lansdowne Av. BR6: Farnb 1F 173
Lansdowne Av. DA7: Bex 7D 108
Lansdowne Cl. KT6: Surb 2H 163
Lansdowne Cl. SW20 7F 135
Lansdowne Cl. TW1: Twick 1K 131
Lansdowne Ct. IG5: Ilf 3C 52
Lansdowne Ct. KT4: Wor Pk 2C 164
Lansdowne Ct. W11 7G 81
(off Lansdowne Ri.)
Lansdowne Cres. W11 7G 81
Lansdowne Dr. E8 6G 67
Lansdowne Gdns. SW8 1J 119
Lansdowne Grn. SW8 1J 119
Lansdowne Gro. NW10 4A 62
Lansdowne Hill SE27 3B 138
Lansdowne Ho. W11 1H 99
(off Ladbroke Rd.)
Lansdowne La. SE7 6B 106
Lansdowne M. SE7 5B 106
Lansdowne M. W11 1H 99
Lansdowne Pl. SE1 3D 102
Lansdowne Pl. SE19 7F 139
Lansdowne Ri. W11 7G 81
Lansdowne Rd. BR1: Broml 7J 141
Lansdowne Rd. CR0: C'don 2D 168
Lansdowne Rd. E11 2H 69
Lansdowne Rd. E17 6C 50
Lansdowne Rd. E18 3J 51
Lansdowne Rd. E4 2H 35
Lansdowne Rd. HA1: Harr 7J 41
Lansdowne Rd. HA7: Stan 6H 27
Lansdowne Rd. IG3: Ilf 1K 71
Lansdowne Rd. KT19: Ewe 7J 163
Lansdowne Rd. N10 2G 47
Lansdowne Rd. N17 1F 49
Lansdowne Rd. N3 7D 30
Lansdowne Rd. SW20 7E 134
Lansdowne Rd. TW3: Houn 3F 113
Lansdowne Rd. UB8: Hil 6E 74
Lansdowne Rd. W11 7G 81
Lansdowne Row W1 4K 11 (1F 101)
Lansdowne Ter. WC1 4F 7 (4J 83)
Lansdowne Wlk. W11 1H 99
Lansdowne Way SW8 1H 119
Lansdowne Wood Cl. SE27 3B 138
Lansdowne Workshops SE7 5A 106
Lansdown Rd. DA14: Sidc 3B 144
Lansdown Rd. E7 7A 70
Lansfield Av. N18 4B 34
Lanson Apts. SW11 7F 101
Lantan Hgts. E20 7E 68
Lantern SE1 6C 14 (2C 102)
(off Lant St.)
Lantern Cl. BR6: Farnb 4F 173
Lantern Cl. HA0: Wemb 5D 60
Lantern Cl. SW15 4C 116
Lantern Ho. UB3: Harl 3E 92
(off Nine Acres Cl.)
Lanterns Way E14 2C 104
Lantern Way UB7: W Dray 2A 92
Lant Ho. SE1 7C 14 (2C 102)
(off Toulmin St.)
Lantry Ct. W3 1H 97
Lant St. SE1 6C 14 (2C 102)
Lanvanor Rd. SE15 2J 121
Lanward Apts. N1 7K 65
(off Caledonian Rd.)
Lanyard Ho. SE8 4B 104
Lapford Cl. W9 4H 81
Lapidge Dr. SW17 3B 136
Lapis Cl. NW10 3G 79
Lapis M. E15 1E 86
Lapponum Wlk. UB4: Yead 4B 76
Lapse Wood Wlk. SE23 1H 139
Lapstone Gdns. HA3: Kenton 6C 42
Lapwing Ct. KT6: Surb 3G 163
Lapwing Ct. SE1 7D 14 (2C 102)
(off Swan St.)
Lapwing Ter. E7 5B 70
Lapwing Twr. SE8 6B 104
(off Taylor Cl.)
Lapwing Way UB4: Yead 6B 76
Lapworth N11 4A 32
(off Coppies Gro.)
Lapworth Ct. W2 5K 81
(off Delamere Ter.)
Lara Cl. KT9: Chess 7E 162
Lara Cl. SE13 6E 122
Larbert Rd. SW16 7G 137
Larch Av. W3 1A 98
Larch Cl. E13 4K 87
Larch Cl. N11 7K 31
Larch Cl. N19 2G 65
Larch Cl. SE8 6B 104
Larch Cl. SW12 2F 137
Larch Ct. SE1 7G 15 (2E 102)
(off Royal Oak Yd.)
Larch Ct. W9 5J 81
(off Admiral Wlk.)
Larch Cres. KT19: Ewe 6H 163
Larch Cres. UB4: Yead 4A 76
Larch Dene BR6: Farnb 2E 172
Larch Dr. W4 5G 97
Larches, The N13 3H 33
Larches, The UB10: Hil 3D 74
Larches Av. SW14 4K 115
Larch Grn. NW9 1A 44
Larch Gro. DA15: Sidc 1K 143
Larch Ho. BR2: Broml 1G 159
Larch Ho. SE16 2J 103
(off Ainsty Est.)
Larch Ho. UB4: Yead 5A 76
Larch Ho. W10 4G 81
(off Rowan Wlk.)
Larch Rd. E10 2C 68
Larch Rd. NW2 4E 62
Larch Tree Way CR0: C'don 3C 170
Larchvale Ct. SM2: Sutt 7K 165
Larch Way BR2: Broml 7E 160
Larchwood Ho. UB7: W Dray 2B 92
(off Park Lodge Av.)
Larchwood Rd. SE9 2F 143
Larcombe Cl. CR0: C'don 4F 169
Larcombe Ct. SM2: Sutt 7K 165
(off Worcester Rd.)
Larcom St. SE17 4C 102
Larden Rd. W3 1A 98
Largewood Av. KT6: Surb 2G 163
Lariat Apts. SE10 4G 105
(off Cable Wlk.)
Larissa St. SE17 5D 102
Larkbere Rd. SE26 4A 140
Lark Ct. NW9 1A 44
(off Lanacre Av.)
Larken Cl. WD23: Bush 1B 26
Larken Dr. WD23: Bush 1B 26
Larkfield Av. HA3: Kenton 3B 42
Larkfield Cl. BR2: Hayes 2H 171
Larkfield Rd. DA14: Sidc 3K 143
Larkfield Rd. TW9: Rich 4E 114
Larkhall La. SW4 2H 119
Larkhall Ri. SW4 3G 119
(not continuous)
Larkham Cl. TW13: Felt 3G 129
Lark Row E2 1J 85
Larksfield Gro. EN1: Enf 1C 24
Larks Gro. IG11: Bark 7J 71
Larkshall Ct. RM7: Mawney 2J 55
Larkshall Cres. E4 4K 35
Larkshall Rd. E4 5K 35
Larkspur Cl. E6 5C 88
Larkspur Cl. HA4: Ruis 7E 38
Larkspur Cl. N17 7J 33
Larkspur Cl. NW9 5H 43
Larkspur Gro. HA8: Edg 4D 28
Larkspur Lodge DA14: Sidc 3B 144
Larkspur Rd. E17 3D 50
Larkspur Way KT19: Ewe 5J 163
Larkswood Ct. E4 5A 36
Larkswood Ri. HA5: Eastc 4A 40
Larkswood Rd. E4 4H 35
Lark Way SM5: Cars 7C 154
Larkway Cl. NW9 4K 43
Larkwood Av. SE10 1E 122
Larnach Rd. W6 6F 99
Larne Rd. HA4: Ruis 2H 57
La Rose La. N15 5C 48
Larpent Av. SW15 5E 116
Larson Wlk. E14 3C 104
Larwood Cl. UB6: G'frd 5H 59
Lascar Cl. TW3: Houn 3D 112
Lascar Wharf Bldg. E14 6A 86
(off Parnham St.)
Lascelles Av. HA1: Harr 7H 41
Lascelles Cl. E11 2F 69
Lascelles Ho. NW1 4D 4 (4C 82)
(off Harewood Av.)
Lascotts Rd. N22 6E 32
Laseron Ho. N15 4F 49
(off Tottenham Grn. E.)
Laserquest Romford 2F 55
Las Palmas Est. TW17: Shep 7E 146
Lassa Rd. SE9 5C 124
Lassell St. SE10 5F 105
Lasseter Pl. SE3 6H 105
Latchett Rd. E18 1K 51
Latchingdon Ct. E17 4K 49
Latchingdon Gdns. IG8: Wfd G 6H 37
Latchmere Cl. TW10: Ham 5E 132
Latchmere La. KT2: King T 6F 133
Latchmere La. TW10: Ham 5F 133
Latchmere Leisure Cen. 2D 118
Latchmere Pas. SW11 2C 118
Latchmere Pl. TW15: Ashf 2A 128
Latchmere Rd. KT2: King T 7E 132
Latchmere Rd. SW11 2D 118
Latchmere St. SW11 2D 118
Lateward Rd. TW8: Bford 6D 96
Latham Cl. E6 5C 88
Latham Cl. TW1: Twick 7A 114
Latham Ct. N11 6D 32
(off Brownlow Rd.)
Latham Ct. SW5 4J 99
(off W. Cromwell Rd.)
Latham Ct. UB5: N'olt 3B 76
(off Delta Gro.)
Latham Ho. E1 6K 85
(off Chudleigh St.)
Latham Rd. DA6: Bex 5G 127
Latham Rd. TW1: Twick 7K 113
Latham's Way CR0: Wadd 1K 167
Lathkill Cl. EN1: Enf 7B 24
Lathkill Ct. BR3: Beck 1B 158
Lathom Rd. E6 7C 70
Latimer Av. E6 1D 88
Latimer Cl. HA5: Pinn 1A 40
Latimer Cl. KT4: Wor Pk 4D 164
Latimer Ct. BR2: Broml 4H 159
(off Durham Rd.)
Latimer Gdns. HA5: Pinn 1A 40
Latimer Ho. E9 6K 67
Latimer Ho. W11 7H 81
(off Kensington Pk. Rd.)
Latimer Ind. Est. W10 6E 80
Latimer Pl. W10 6E 80
Latimer Rd. CR0: C'don 3B 168
Latimer Rd. E7 4K 69
Latimer Rd. EN5: New Bar 3E 20
Latimer Rd. N15 6E 48
Latimer Rd. SW19 6K 135
Latimer Rd. TW11: Tedd 5K 131
Latimer Rd. W10 5E 80
(not continuous)
Latimer Sq. SE10 3J 105
Latitude Apts. CR0: C'don 3D 168
(off Fairfield Rd.)
Latitude Ct. E16 7G 89
Latitude Ho. NW1 1F 83
(off Oval Rd.)
Latona Ct. SW9 7A 102
(off Caldwell St.)
Latona Rd. SE15 6G 103
La Tourne Gdns. BR6: Farnb 3G 173
Lattimer Pl. W4 7A 98
Latton Cl. KT12: Walt T 7C 148
Latvia Ct. SE17 5C 102
(off Macleod St.)
Latymer Ct. W6 4F 99
Latymer Gdns. N3 2G 45
Latymer Rd. N9 1A 34
Latymer Way N9 2K 33
Laubin Cl. TW1: Twick 4B 114
Lauder Cl. UB5: N'olt 2B 76
Lauder Ct. N14 7D 22
Lauderdale Dr. TW10: Ham 3D 132
Lauderdale Ho. SW9 1A 120
(off Gosling Way)
Lauderdale House Community Arts Cen. 1F 65
(within Lauderdale House)
Lauderdale Mans. W9 3K 81
(off Lauderdale Rd.)
Lauderdale Pde. W9 4K 81
Lauderdale Pl. EC2 5C 8 (5C 84)
(off Beech St.)
Lauderdale Rd. W9 3K 81
Lauderdale Twr. EC2 5C 8 (5C 84)
(off Beech St.)
Laud St. CR0: C'don 3C 168
Laud St. SE11 6G 19 (5K 101)
Laugan Wlk. SE17 5C 102
Laughton Rd. UB5: N'olt 1B 76
Launcelot Rd. BR1: Broml 4J 141
Launcelot St. SE1 7J 13 (2A 102)
Launceston Gdns. UB6: G'frd 1C 78
Launceston Pl. W8 3A 100
Launceston Rd. UB6: G'frd 1C 78
Launch St. E14 3E 104
Launders Ga. W3 2H 97
Laundress La. N16 3G 67
Laundry Cl. CR0: C'don 7D 156
Laundry La. N1 1C 84
Laundry M. SE23 7A 122
Laundry Rd. W6 6G 99
Launton Dr. DA6: Bex 5D 126
Laura Cl. E11 5A 52
Laura Cl. EN1: Enf 5K 23
Lauradale Rd. N2 4D 46
Laura Pl. E5 4J 67
Laura Ter. N4 2B 66
Laurel Apts. SE17 4E 102
(off Townsend St.)
Laurel Av. TW1: Twick 1K 131
Laurel Bank N12 4F 31
Laurel Bank Gdns. SW6 2H 117
Laurel Bank Rd. EN2: Enf 1H 23
Laurel Bank Vs. W7 2J 95
(off Lwr. Boston Rd.)
Laurel Cl. DA14: Sidc 3A 144
Laurel Cl. N19 2G 65
Laurel Cl. SW17 5C 136
Laurel Ct. CR2: S Croy 4E 168
(off South Pk. Hill Rd.)
Laurel Ct. HA0: Wemb 2E 78
Laurel Ct. SE1 3D 102
(off Garland Cl.)
Laurel Cres. CR0: C'don 3C 170
Laurel Cres. RM7: Rush G 1K 73
Laurel Dr. N21 7F 23
Laurel Gdns. BR1: Broml 4C 160
Laurel Gdns. E4 7J 25
Laurel Gdns. NW7 3E 28
Laurel Gdns. TW15: Ashf 5E 128
Laurel Gdns. TW4: Houn 4C 112
Laurel Gdns. W7 1J 95
Laurel Gro. SE20 7J 139
Laurel Gro. SE26 4K 139
Laurel Ho. BR2: Broml 1G 159
Laurel Ho. E3 1B 86
(off Hornbeam Sq.)
Laurel Ho. SE8 6B 104
Laurel La. UB7: W Dray 4A 92
Laurel Mnr. SM2: Sutt 7A 166
Laurel M. SE5 3C 120
(off Harbour Rd.)
Laurel Pk. HA3: Hrw W 7E 26
Laurel Rd. SW13 2C 116
Laurel Rd. SW20 1D 152
Laurel Rd. TW12: Hamp H 5H 131
Laurels, The BR1: Broml 1K 159
Laurels, The BR2: Broml 4J 159
Laurels, The IG9: Buck H 1F 37
Laurels, The NW10 1D 80
Laurels, The SW9 7B 102
(off Langton Rd.)
Laurels, The WD23: B Hea 2D 26
Laurel St. E8 6F 67
Laurel Vw. N12 3E 30
Laurel Way E18 4H 51
Laurel Way N20 3D 30
Laurence Calvert Cl. IG11: Bark 2J 89
Laurence Ct. E10 7D 50
Laurence Ct. W11 7G 81
(off Lansdowne Rd.)
Laurence M. W12 2C 98
Laurence Pountney Hill EC4 2E 14 (7D 84)
Laurence Pountney La. EC4 2E 14 (7D 84)
Laurence Rd. TW3: Houn 3G 113
Laurie Gro. SE14 1A 122
Laurie Ho. SE1 3B 102
(off St George's Rd.)
Laurie Ho. W8 1J 99
(off Airlie Gdns.)
Laurie Rd. W7 5J 77
Laurier Rd. CR0: C'don 7F 157
Laurier Rd. NW5 3F 65
Laurimel Cl. HA7: Stan 6G 27
Laurino Pl. WD23: B Hea 2B 26
Lauriston Ho. E9 7J 67
(off Lauriston Rd.)
Lauriston Rd. E9 7J 67
Lauriston Rd. SW19 6F 135
Lausanne Rd. N8 4A 48
Lausanne Rd. SE15 1J 121
Laval Ho. TW8: Bford 5E 96
(off Ealing Rd.)
Lavell St. N16 4D 66
Lavender Av. CR4: Mitc 1C 154
Lavender Av. KT4: Wor Pk 3E 164
Lavender Av. NW9 1J 61
Lavender Cl. BR2: Broml 6C 160
Lavender Cl. E4 4H 35
Lavender Cl. SM5: Cars 4F 167
Lavender Cl. SW3 7B 16 (6B 100)
Lavender Ct. KT8: W Mole 3F 149
Lavender Ct. SM2: Sutt 7A 166
Lavender Ct. TW14: Felt 6K 111
Lavender Gdns. EN2: Enf 1G 23
Lavender Gdns. HA3: Hrw W 6D 26
Lavender Gdns. SW11 4D 118
Lavender Gro. CR4: Mitc 1C 154
Lavender Gro. E8 7G 67
Lavender Hill EN2: Enf 1F 23
Lavender Hill SW11 4C 118
Lavender Ho. SE16 1K 103
(off Rotherhithe St.)
Lavender Ho. TW9: Kew 1H 115
Lavender M. KT6: Surb 5D 150
Lavender M. TW12: Hamp H 6G 131
Lavender Pl. IG1: Ilf 5F 71
Lavender Pond Nature Pk. 1A 104
Lavender Ri. UB7: W Dray 2C 92
Lavender Rd. CR0: C'don 6K 155
Lavender Rd. EN2: Enf 1J 23
Lavender Rd. KT19: Ewe 5H 163
Lavender Rd. SE16 1A 104
Lavender Rd. SM1: Sutt 4B 166
Lavender Rd. SM5: Cars 4E 166
Lavender Rd. SW11 3B 118
Lavender Rd. UB8: Hil 5B 74
Lavender Sq. SW9 1K 119
(off Printers Rd.)
Lavender St. E15 6G 69
Lavender Sweep SW11 4D 118
Lavender Ter. SW11 3C 118
Lavender Va. SM6: W'gton 6H 167
Lavender Wlk. CR4: Mitc 3E 154
Lavender Wlk. SW11 4D 118
Lavender Way CR0: C'don 6K 157
Lavendon Ho. NW8 3D 4 (4C 82)
(off Paveley St.)
Lavengro Rd. SE27 2C 138
Lavenham Rd. SW18 2H 135
Lavernock Rd. DA7: Bex 2G 127
Lavers Rd. N16 3E 66
Laverstoke Gdns. SW15 7B 116
Laverton M. SW5 4K 99
Laverton Pl. SW5 4K 99
Lavette Ho. E3 3C 86
(off Rainhill Way)
Lavidge Rd. SE9 2C 142
Lavina Gro. N1 2K 83
Lavington Cl. E9 6B 68
Lavington Rd. CR0: Bedd 3K 167
Lavington Rd. W13 1B 96
Lavington St. SE1 5B 14 (1B 102)
Lavisham Ho. BR1: Broml 5K 141
Lawdons Gdns. CR0: Wadd 4B 168
Lawes Ho. W10 3H 81
(off Lancefield St.)
Lawes Way IG11: Bark 3K 89
Lawford Rd. N1 7E 66
Lawford Rd. NW5 6G 65
Lawford Rd. W4 7J 97
Lawfords Wharf NW1 7G 65
(off Lyme St.)
Law Ho. IG11: Bark 2A 90
Lawless Ho. E14 7E 86
(off Bazely St.)

A–Z London 247

Lawless St. – Leslie Gro.

Lawless St. E14 7D 86
Lawley Ho. TW1: Twick 6D 114
Lawley Rd. N14 7A 22
Lawley St. E5 4J 67
Lawlor Cl. TW16: Sun 1K 147
Lawn, The UB2: S'hall 5E 94
Lawn Cl. BR1: Broml 6K 141
Lawn Cl. HA4: Ruis 3H 57
Lawn Cl. KT3: N Mald 2A 152
Lawn Cl. N9 7A 24
Lawn Cres. TW9: Kew 2G 115
Lawn Farm Gro. RM6: Chad H 4E 54
Lawnfield Ct. NW6 7F 63
(off Coverdale Rd.)
Lawn Gdns. W7 1J 95
Lawn Ho. Cl. E14 2E 104
Lawn La. SW8 7G 19 (6K 101)
Lawn Rd. BR3: Beck 7B 140
Lawn Rd. NW3 5D 64
Lawns, The DA14: Sidc 4B 144
Lawns, The E4 5H 35
Lawns, The HA5: Hat E 7A 26
Lawns, The SE19 1D 156
Lawns, The SE3 3H 123
Lawns, The SL3: Poyle 4A 174
Lawns, The SM2: Cheam 7G 165
Lawns, The SW19 5H 135
Lawns Ct. HA9: Wemb 2F 61
Lawnside SE3 4H 123
Lawns Way RM5: Col R 1J 55
Lawnswood EN5: Barn 5B 20
Lawn Ter. SE3 3G 123
Lawn Va. HA5: Pinn 2C 40
Lawrence Av. E12 4E 70
Lawrence Av. E17 1K 49
Lawrence Av. KT3: N Mald 6K 151
Lawrence Av. N13 4G 33
Lawrence Av. NW10 1K 79
Lawrence Av. NW7 4F 29
Lawrence Bldgs. N16 3F 67
Lawrence Campe Cl. N20 3G 31
Lawrence Cl. E3 3C 86
Lawrence Cl. N15 4E 48
Lawrence Cl. W12 7D 80
Lawrence Ct. N10 3G 47
Lawrence Ct. N16 3F 67
(off Smalley Rd. Est.)
Lawrence Ct. NW7 5F 29
Lawrence Ct. SE6 6C 122
Lawrence Ct. W3 3J 97
(off Stanley Rd.)
Lawrence Cres. HA8: Edg 2G 43
Lawrence Cres. RM10: Dag 3H 73
Lawrence Dr. UB10: Ick 4E 56
Lawrence Est. TW4: Houn 4A 112
Lawrence Gdns. NW7 3G 29
Lawrence Gro. UB10: Uxb 2A 74
Lawrence Hill E4 2H 35
Lawrence Ho. NW1 7F 65
(off Hawley Cres.)
Lawrence Ho. SW1 4D 18 (4H 101)
(off Cureton St.)
Lawrence La. EC2 1D 14 (6C 84)
Lawrence Mans. SW3 7C 16 (6C 100)
(off Lordship Pl.)
Lawrence M. SW15 4E 116
Lawrence M. SW8 7J 101
Lawrence Pde. TW7: Isle 3B 114
(off Lower Sq.)
Lawrence Pl. N1 1J 83
(off Brydon Wlk.)
Lawrence Rd. BR4: W W'ck 4J 171
Lawrence Rd. DA8: Erith 7H 109
Lawrence Rd. E13 1K 87
Lawrence Rd. E6 1C 88
Lawrence Rd. HA5: Pinn 6B 40
Lawrence Rd. N15 4E 48
Lawrence Rd. N18 4C 34
(not continuous)
Lawrence Rd. SE25 4F 157
Lawrence Rd. TW10: Ham 4C 132
Lawrence Rd. TW12: Hamp 7D 130
Lawrence Rd. TW4: Houn 4A 112
Lawrence Rd. UB4: Hayes 2E 74
Lawrence Rd. W5 4D 96
Lawrence St. E16 5H 87
Lawrence St. NW7 5G 29
Lawrence St. SW3 7C 16 (6C 100)
Lawrence Trad. Est. SE10 4G 105
Lawrence Way NW10 3J 61
Lawrence Weaver Cl. SM4: Mord 6J 153
Lawrence Yd. N15 4E 48
Lawrie Ho. SW19 5K 135
(off Durnsford Rd.)
Lawrie Pk. Av. SE26 5H 139
Lawrie Pk. Cres. SE26 5H 139
Lawrie Pk. Gdns. SE26 4H 139
Lawrie Pk. Rd. SE26 6H 139
Laws Cl. SE25 4D 156
Lawson Cl. E16 5A 88
Lawson Cl. IG1: Ilf 5H 71
Lawson Cl. SW19 3F 135
Lawson Ct. KT6: Surb 7D 150
Lawson Ct. N11 6B 32
(off Ring Way)
Lawson Ct. N4 1K 65
(off Lorne Rd.)
Lawson Gdns. HA5: Eastc 3K 39
Lawson Ho. SE18 6E 106
(off Nightingale Pl.)
Lawson Ho. W12 7D 80
(off White City Est.)
Lawson Rd. EN3: Enf H 1D 24
Lawson Rd. UB1: S'hall 4E 76
Lawson Ter. SE15 4J 121
Law St. SE1 3D 102
Lawton Rd. E10 1E 68
Lawton Rd. E3 3A 86
(not continuous)
Lawton Rd. EN4: Cockf 3G 21
Laxcon Cl. NW10 5K 61
Laxey Rd. BR6: Chels 6K 173
Laxfield Ct. E8 1G 85
(off Pownall Rd.)
Laxford Ho. SW1 4H 17 (4E 100)
(off Cundy St.)
Laxley Cl. SE5 7B 102
Laxton Ct. CR7: Thor H 4C 156
Laxton Pl. NW1 3K 5 (4F 83)
Layard Rd. CR7: Thor H 2D 156
Layard Rd. EN1: Enf 1A 24
Layard Rd. SE16 4H 103
Layard Sq. SE16 4H 103
Laybourne Ho. E14 2C 104
(off Admirals Way)
Laybrook Lodge E18 4H 51
Laycock St. N1 6A 66
Layer Gdns. W3 7G 79
Layfield Cl. NW4 7D 44
Layfield Cres. NW4 7D 44
Layfield Ho. SE10 5J 105
(off Kemsing Rd.)
Layfield Rd. NW4 7D 44
Layhams Rd. BR2: Kes 5H 171
Layhams Rd. BR4: W W'ck 4G 171
Laymarsh Cl. DA17: Belv 3F 109
Laymead Cl. UB5: N'olt 6C 58
Laystall Ct. WC1 4J 7 (4A 84)
(off Mt. Pleasant)
Laystall St. EC1 4J 7 (4A 84)
Layton Ct. TW8: Bford 5D 96
Layton Cres. CR0: Wadd 5A 168
Layton Pl. TW9: Kew 1G 115
Layton Rd. TW3: Houn 4F 113
Layton Rd. TW8: Bford 5D 96
Layton's La. TW16: Sun 2H 147
Layzell Wlk. SE9 1B 142
Lazar Wlk. N7 2K 65
Lazenby Ct. WC2 2E 12 (7J 83)
(off Floral St.)
Leabank Cl. HA1: Harr 3J 59
Leabank Sq. E9 6C 68
Leabank Vw. N15 6G 49
Lea Bon Ct. E15 1H 87
(off Plaistow Gro.)
Leabourne Rd. N16 7G 49
LEA BRIDGE 3K 67
Lea Bri. Ind. Cen. E10 1A 68
Lea Bri. Rd. E10 7C 50
Lea Bri. Rd. E17 5F 51
Lea Bri. Rd. E5 3J 67
Lea Cl. TW2: Whitt 7D 112
Lea Ct. E13 3J 87
Lea Ct. E4 2K 35
Lea Ct. N15 4G 49
Lea Cres. HA4: Ruis 4H 57
Leacroft Av. SW12 7D 118
Leacroft Cl. N21 2G 33
Leacroft Cl. UB7: Yiew 6A 74
Leadale Av. E4 2H 35
Leadale Rd. N15 6G 49
Leadale Rd. N16 6G 49
Leadbeaters Cl. N11 5J 31
Leadbetter Ct. NW10 7K 61
(off Melville Rd.)
Leadenhall Mkt. 1G 15 (6E 84)
Leadenhall Pl. EC3 1G 15 (6E 84)
Leadenhall St. EC3 1G 15 (6E 84)
Leadenham Ct. E3 4C 86
Leader Av. E12 5E 70
Leadings, The HA9: Wemb 3J 61
Leadmill La. E20 4D 68
Leaf Cl. HA6: Nwood 1F 39
Leaf Cl. KT7: T Ditt 5J 149
Leaf Gro. SE27 5A 138
Leaf Ho. HA1: Harr 5K 41
(off Catherine Pl.)
Leafield Cl. SW16 6B 138
Leafield La. DA14: Sidc 3F 145
Leafield Rd. SM1: Sutt 2J 165
Leafield Rd. SW20 3H 153
Leaf Wlk. N7 4H 65
Leafy Gro. BR2: Kes 5A 172
Leafy Oak Rd. SE12 4A 142
Leafy Way CR0: C'don 2F 169
Lea Gdns. HA9: Wemb 4F 61
Leagrave St. E5 3J 67
Lea Hall Gdns. E10 1C 68
Lea Hall Rd. E10 1C 68
Leaholme Way HA4: Ruis 6E 38
Lea Ho. NW8 4C 4 (4C 82)
(off Salisbury St.)
Leahurst Rd. SE13 5F 123
LEA INTERCHANGE 5C 68
Leake Ct. SE1 7H 13 (2K 101)
Leake St. SE1 6H 13 (2K 101)
(not continuous)
Lealand Rd. N15 6F 49
Leamington Av. BR1: Broml 5A 142
Leamington Av. BR6: Orp 4J 173
Leamington Av. E17 5C 50
Leamington Av. SM4: Mord 4G 153
Leamington Cl. BR1: Broml 4A 142
Leamington Cl. E12 5C 70
Leamington Cl. TW3: Houn 5G 113
Leamington Ct. SE3 6G 105
Leamington Cres. HA2: Harr 3C 58
Leamington Gdns. IG3: Ilf 2K 71
Leamington Ho. HA8: Edg 5A 28
Leamington Ho. W11 5H 81
(off Tavistock Rd.)
Leamington Pk. W3 5K 79
Leamington Pl. UB4: Hayes 4H 75
Leamington Rd. UB2: S'hall 4B 94
Leamington Rd. Vs. W11 5H 81
Leamore Ct. E2 3K 85
Leamore St. W6 4E 98
LEAMOUTH 7G 87
Leamouth Rd. E14 6F 87
Leamouth Rd. E6 5C 88
Leander Ct. E9 7K 67
(off Lauriston Rd.)
Leander Ct. KT6: Surb 7D 150
Leander Ct. NW9 1A 44
Leander Ct. SE8 1C 122
Leander Rd. CR7: Thor H 4K 155
Leander Rd. SW2 6K 119
Leander Rd. UB5: N'olt 2E 76
Lea Pk. Trad. Est. E10 7B 50
Learner Dr. HA2: Harr 2E 58
Lea Rd. BR3: Beck 2C 158
Lea Rd. EN2: Enf 1J 23
Lea Rd. UB2: S'hall 4C 94
Learoyd Gdns. E6 7E 88
Leary Ho. SE11 6H 19 (5K 101)
Leas Cl. KT9: Chess 7F 163
Leas Dale SE9 3E 142
Leas Grn. BR7: Chst 6K 143
Leaside Av. N10 3E 46
Leaside Bus. Cen. EN3: Brim 2G 25
Leaside Ct. UB10: Hil 3D 74
Leaside Mans. N10 3E 46
(off Fortis Grn.)
Leaside Rd. E5 1J 67
Leasowes Rd. E10 1C 68
Lea Sq. E3 1B 86
Leatherbottle Grn. DA18: Erith 3F 109
Leather Bottle La. DA17: Belv 4E 108
Leather Cl. CR4: Mitc 2E 154
Leatherdale St. E1 Portelet Rd. 3K 85
Leather Gdns. E15 1G 87
Leatherhead Cl. N16 7F 49
Leather La. EC1 5J 7 (5A 84)
(not continuous)
Leather Mkt., The SE1 7G 15 (2E 102)
(off Weston St.)
Leathermarket Ct. SE1 7G 15 (2E 102)
Leathermarket St. SE1 7G 15 (2E 102)
Leather Pl. SE1 3E 102
(off Crimscott St.)
Leather Rd. SE16 4K 103
Leathersellers Cl. EN5: Barn 3B 20
(off The Avenue)
Leather St. E1 7K 85
Leathsail Rd. HA2: Harr 3F 59
Leathwaite Rd. SW11 4D 118
Leathwell Rd. SE8 2D 122
Lea Va. DA1: Cray 4K 127
Lea Valley Bus. Pk. E10 2A 68
Lea Valley Rd. E4 6G 25
Lea Valley Rd. EN3: Pond E 5F 25
Lea Valley Trad. Est. N18 6E 34
Lea Valley Viaduct N18 5E 34
Leaveland Cl. BR3: Beck 4C 158
Leaver Gdns. UB6: G'frd 2H 77
Leavesden Rd. HA7: Stan 6F 27
Lea Vw. Ho. E5 1H 67
Leaway E10 1K 67
Lebanon Av. TW13: Hanw 5B 130
Lebanon Ct. TW1: Twick 7B 114
Lebanon Gdns. SW18 6J 117
Lebanon Pk. TW1: Twick 7B 114
Lebanon Rd. CR0: C'don 1E 168
Lebanon Rd. SW18 5J 117
Leben Ct. SM1: Sutt 6A 166
Lebus Ho. NW8 1C 4 (2C 82)
(off Cochrane St.)
Lebus St. N17 3H 49
Le Chateau CR0: C'don 3D 168
(off Chatsworth Rd.)
Lechmere App. IG8: Wfd G 2A 52
Lechmere Av. IG8: Wfd G 2B 52
Lechmere Rd. NW2 6D 62
Leckford Rd. SW18 2A 136
Leckhampton Pl. SW2 7A 120
Leckwith Av. DA7: Bex 6E 108
Lecky St. SW7 5A 16 (5B 100)
Leconfield Av. SW13 3B 116
Leconfield Ho. SE5 4E 120
Leconfield Rd. N5 4D 66
Leda Av. EN3: Enf W 1E 24
Leda Ct. SW9 7A 102
(off Caldwell St.)
Ledam Ho. EC1 5J 7 (5A 84)
(off Bourne Est.)
Leda Rd. SE18 3D 106
Ledbury Ho. SE22 3E 120
Ledbury Ho. W11 6H 81
(off Colville Rd.)
Ledbury M. Nth. W11 7J 81
Ledbury M. W. W11 7J 81
Ledbury Pl. CR0: C'don 4C 168
Ledbury Rd. CR0: C'don 4D 168
Ledbury Rd. W11 6H 81
Ledbury St. SE15 7G 103
Ledger M. E17 6C 50
Ledrington Rd. SE19 6G 139
Ledway Dr. HA9: Wemb 7F 43
LEE 6J 123
Lee Av. RM6: Chad H 6E 54
Lee Bri. SE13 3E 122
Leechcroft Av. DA15: Sidc 5K 125
Leechcroft Rd. SM6: W'gton 3E 166
Lee Chu. St. SE13 4G 123
Lee Cl. E17 1K 49
Lee Cl. EN5: New Bar 4F 21
Lee Conservancy Rd. E9 5B 68
Lee Ct. E3 4E 86
(off Navigation Rd.)
Lee Ct. SE13 4F 123
(off Lee High Rd.)
Leecroft Rd. EN5: Barn 5B 20
Leeds Ct. EC1 3A 8 (4B 84)
(off St John St.)
Leeds Pl. N4 1K 65
Leeds Rd. IG1: Ilf 1H 71
Leeds St. N18 5B 34
Leefern Rd. W12 2C 98
Leegate SE12 5H 123
LEE GREEN 5H 123
Lee Gro. IG7: Chig 2K 37
Lee High Rd. SE12 4H 123
Lee High Rd. SE13 3E 122
Leeke St. WC1 1G 7 (3K 83)
Leeland Rd. W13 1A 96
Leeland Ter. W13 1A 96
Leeland Way NW10 4B 62
Lee M. BR3: Beck 3A 158
Leemount Ho. NW4 4F 45
Lee Pk. SE3 4H 123
Lee Pk. Way N18 4E 34
Lee Pk. Way N9 4E 34
Leerdam Dr. E14 3E 104
Lee Rd. EN1: Enf 6B 24
Lee Rd. NW7 7A 30
Lee Rd. SE3 3H 123
Lee Rd. SW19 1K 153
Lee Rd. UB6: G'frd 1C 78
Lees, The CR0: C'don 2B 170
Lees Av. HA6: Nwood 1H 39
Lees Ct. W1 2G 11 (7E 82)
(off Lees Pl.)
Lees Ho. SE17 5D 102
(off Inville Rd.)
Leeside EN5: Barn 5B 20
Leeside Ct. SE16 1K 103
(off Rotherhithe St.)
Leeside Cres. NW11 6G 45
Leeside Ind. Est. N17 7D 34
Leeside Rd. N17 6C 34
Leeside Works N17 7D 34
Leeson Ho. TW1: Twick 7B 114
Leeson Rd. SE24 4A 120
Leesons Hill BR5: St P 3K 161
Leesons Hill BR7: Chst 3J 161
Leeson's Way BR5: St P 2K 161
Lees Pde. UB10: Hil 4D 74
Lees Pl. W1 2G 11 (7E 82)
Lees Rd. UB8: Hil 4D 74
Lee St. E8 1F 85
Lee Ter. SE13 3G 123
Lee Ter. SE3 3G 123
Lee Valley Athletics Cen. 1F 35
Lee Valley Golf Course 7F 25
Lee Valley Hockey & Tennis Cen. 4D 68
Lee Valley Ice Cen. 2K 67
Lee Valley Pk. 7E 34
Lee Valley Technopark N17 3G 49
Lee Valley VeloPark 5D 68
Leeve Ho. W10 3H 81
(off Lancefield St.)
Lee Vw. EN2: Enf 1G 23
Leeward Ct. E1 1G 103
Leeward Ct. SE8 4A 104
(off Yeoman St.)
Leeward Gdns. SW19 5G 135
Leeward Ho. N1 1E 84
(off Halcomb St.)
Leeway SE8 5B 104
Leeway Cl. HA5: Hat E 1D 40
Leeways, The SM3: Cheam 6G 165
Leewood Cl. SE12 6J 123
Lefa Bus. & Ind. Pk. DA14: Sidc 4C 144
Lefevre Wlk. E3 2C 86
Leff Ho. NW6 1G 81
Lefroy Ho. SE1 7C 14 (2C 102)
(off Southwark Bri. Rd.)
Lefroy Rd. W12 2B 98
Left Side N14 1C 32
(off Stationers Pde.)
Legacy Bldg. SW11 6H 101
Legacy Wharf E15 2D 86
Legard Rd. N5 3B 66
Legatt Rd. SE9 5B 124
Leggatt Rd. E15 2E 86
Legge St. SE13 5E 122
Leghorn Rd. NW10 2B 80
Leghorn Rd. SE18 5H 107
Legion Cl. N1 7A 66
Legion Ct. SM4: Mord 6J 153
Legion Rd. UB6: G'frd 1G 77
Legion Ter. E3 1B 86
Legion Way N12 7H 31
Leg O'Mutton Reservoir Local Nature Reserve 7B 98
Legon Av. RM7: Rush G 1J 73
Legrace Av. TW4: Houn 2B 112
Leicester Av. CR4: Mitc 4J 155
Leicester Cl. KT4: Wor Pk 4E 164
Leicester Ct. TW1: Twick 6D 114
(off Clevedon Rd.)
Leicester Ct. W9 5J 81
(off Elmfield Way)
Leicester Ct. WC2 2D 12 (7H 83)
(off Lisle St.)
Leicester Flds. 3D 12 (7H 83)
(off Leicester Sq.)
Leicester Gdns. IG3: Ilf 7J 53
Leicester Ho. N18 5C 34
(off Cavendish Cl.)
Leicester Ho. SW9 3B 120
(off Loughborough Rd.)
Leicester M. N2 3C 46
Leicester Pl. WC2 2D 12 (7H 83)
Leicester Rd. CR0: C'don 7E 156
Leicester Rd. E11 5K 51
Leicester Rd. EN5: New Bar 5E 20
Leicester Rd. N2 3C 46
Leicester Rd. NW10 7K 61
Leicester Sq. WC2 3D 12 (7H 83)
Leicester Square Theatre 2D 12 (7H 83)
(off Leicester Pl.)
Leicester St. WC2 2D 12 (7H 83)
Leigh, The KT2: King T 7A 134
Leigham Av. SW16 3J 137
Leigham Cl. SW16 3K 137
Leigham Ct. SM6: W'gton 6G 167
Leigham Ct. Rd. SW16 2J 137
Leigham Dr. TW7: Isle 7J 95
Leigham Hall Pde. SW16 3J 137
(off Streatham High Rd.)
Leigham Va. SW16 3K 137
Leigham Va. SW2 2A 138
Leigh Av. IG4: Ilf 4B 52
Leigh Cl. KT3: N Mald 4J 151
Leigh Cl. Ind. Est. KT3: N Mald 4K 151
Leigh Ct. HA2: Harr 1J 59
Leigh Ct. W14 4H 99
(off Avonmore Pl.)
Leigh Cres. CR0: New Ad 7D 170
Leigh Gdns. NW10 2E 80
Leigh Hunt Dr. N14 1C 32
Leigh Orchard Cl. SW16 3K 137
Leigh Pl. DA16: Well 2A 126
Leigh Pl. EC1 5J 7 (5A 84)
Leigh Pl. TW13: Felt 1A 130
Leigh Rd. E10 7E 50
Leigh Rd. E6 6E 70
Leigh Rd. N5 4B 66
Leigh Rd. TW3: Houn 4H 113
Leigh St. WC1 2E 6 (3J 83)
Leighton Av. E12 5E 70
Leighton Av. HA5: Pinn 3C 40
Leighton Cl. HA8: Edg 2G 43
Leighton Cres. NW5 5G 65
Leighton Gdns. CR0: C'don 1B 168
Leighton Gdns. NW10 2D 80
Leighton Gro. NW5 5G 65
Leighton Ho. SW1 4D 18 (4H 101)
(off Herrick St.)
Leighton House Mus. 3H 99
Leighton Mans. W14 6G 99
(off Greyhound Rd.)
Leighton Pl. NW5 5G 65
Leighton Rd. EN1: Enf 5A 24
Leighton Rd. HA3: Hrw W 2H 41
Leighton Rd. NW5 5G 65
Leighton Rd. W13 2A 96
Leighton St. CR0: C'don 1B 168
Leila Parnell Pl. SE7 6A 106
Leinster Av. SW14 3J 115
Leinster Gdns. W2 6A 82
Leinster M. EN5: Barn 3B 20
Leinster M. W2 7A 82
Leinster Pl. W2 6A 82
Leinster Rd. N10 4F 47
Leinster Sq. W2 6J 81
(not continuous)
Leinster Ter. W2 7A 82
Leirum St. N1 1K 83
Leisure Way N12 7G 31
Leisure W. 2K 129
Leitch Ho. NW8 7B 64
(off Hilgrove Rd.)
Leith Cl. NW9 1K 61
Leithcote Gdns. SW16 4K 137
Leithcote Path SW16 3K 137
Leith Hill BR5: St P 1K 161
Leith Hill Grn. BR5: St P 1K 161
Leith Mans. W9 3K 81
(off Grantully Rd.)
Leith Rd. N22 1B 48
Leith Towers SM2: Sutt 7K 165
Leith Yd. NW6 1J 81
(off Quex Rd.)
Lela Av. TW4: Houn 2A 112
Lelitia Cl. E8 1G 85
Lely Ho. UB5: N'olt 2B 76
(off Academy Gdns.)
Leman St. E1 7K 9 (6F 85)
Le Mare Ter. E3 5C 86
Lemark Cl. HA7: Stan 6H 27
Le May Av. SE12 3K 141
Lemmon Rd. SE10 6G 105
Lemna Rd. E11 7H 51
Le Moal Ho. E1 5J 85
(off Stepney Way)
Lemonade Bldg. IG11: Bark 7G 71
(off Ripple Rd.)
Lemon Gro. TW13: Felt 1J 129
Lemon Tree Ho. E3 3B 86
(off Bow Rd.)
Lemonwell Dr. SE9 5G 125
Lemsford Cl. N15 6G 49
Lemsford Ct. N4 2C 66
Lemuel St. SW18 6A 118
Lena Cres. N9 2D 34
Lena Gdns. W6 3E 98
Lena Kennedy Cl. E4 6K 35
Lenanton Steps E14 2C 104
(off Manilla St.)
Len Bishop Ct. E1 7K 85
(off Schoolhouse La.)
Len Clifton Ho. SE18 4D 106
(off Cambridge Barracks Rd.)
Lendal Ter. SW4 3H 119
Lendy Pl. TW16: Sun 4J 147
Lenelby Rd. KT6: Surb 1G 163
Len Freeman Pl. SW6 6H 99
Lenham Ho. SE1 7F 15 (3D 102)
(off Staple St.)
Lenham Rd. CR7: Thor H 2D 156
Lenham Rd. DA7: Bex 6F 109
Lenham Rd. SE12 4H 123
Lenham Rd. SM1: Sutt 4K 165
Lennard Av. BR4: W W'ck 2G 171
Lennard Cl. BR4: W W'ck 2G 171
Lennard Rd. BR2: Broml 1D 172
Lennard Rd. BR3: Beck 6A 140
Lennard Rd. CR0: C'don 1C 168
Lennard Rd. SE20 6K 139
Lennon Rd. NW2 5E 62
Lennox Gdns. CR0: Wadd 4B 168
Lennox Gdns. IG1: Ilf 1D 70
Lennox Gdns. NW10 4B 62
Lennox Gdns. SW1 2E 16 (3D 100)
Lennox Gdns. M. SW1 2E 16 (3D 100)
Lennox Ho. DA17: Belv 3G 109
(off Ambrooke Rd.)
Lennox Ho. TW1: Twick 6D 114
(off Clevedon Rd.)
Lennox Rd. E17 6B 50
Lennox Rd. N4 2K 65
Lennox Rd. SW9 1B 120
Lenor Cl. DA6: Bex 4E 126
Lensbury Av. SW6 2A 118
Lensbury Way SE2 3C 108
Lens Rd. E7 7A 70
Len Taylor Cl. UB4: Hayes 4G 75
Lenthall Ho. SW1 6B 18 (5G 101)
(off Churchill Gdns.)
Lenthall Rd. E8 7G 67
Lenthorp Rd. SE10 4H 105
Lentmead Rd. BR1: Broml 3H 141
Lenton Path SE18 6H 107
Lenton Ri. TW9: Rich 3E 114
Lenton St. SE18 4H 107
Lenton Ter. N4 2A 66
Len Williams Ct. NW6 2J 81
Leo Ct. TW8: Bford 7D 96
Leof Cres. SE6 5D 140
Leominster Rd. SM4: Mord 6A 154
Leominster Wlk. SM4: Mord 6A 154
Leonard Av. RM7: Rush G 1K 73
Leonard Av. SM4: Mord 5A 154
Leonard Cir. EC2 3F 9 (4D 84)
Leonard Ct. HA3: Hrw W 1J 41
Leonard Ct. W8 3J 99
Leonard Ct. WC1 3D 6 (4H 83)
Leonard Pl. N16 4E 66
Leonard Rd. E4 6H 35
Leonard Rd. E7 4J 69
Leonard Rd. N9 3A 34
Leonard Rd. SW16 1G 155
Leonard Rd. UB2: S'hall 3B 94
Leonard Robbins Path SE28 7B 90
(off Tawney Rd.)
Leonard St. E16 1C 106
Leonard St. EC2 3F 9 (4D 84)
Leon Ho. CR0: C'don 3C 168
Leonora Ho. W9 4A 82
(off Lanark Rd.)
Leonora Tyson M. SE21 2D 138
Leontine Cl. SE15 7G 103
Leopards Ct. EC1 5J 7 (5A 84)
(off Baldwins Gdns.)
Leopold Av. SW19 5H 135
Leopold Bldgs. E2 1J 9 (3F 85)
(off Columbia Rd.)
Leopold M. E9 1J 85
Leopold Rd. E17 5C 50
Leopold Rd. N18 5C 34
Leopold Rd. N2 3B 46
Leopold Rd. NW10 7A 62
Leopold Rd. SW19 4H 135
Leopold Rd. W5 1F 97
Leopold St. E3 5B 86
Leopold Ter. SW19 5H 135
Leo St. SE15 7H 103
Leo Yd. EC1 4B 8 (4B 84)
(off St John St.)
Leppoc Rd. SW4 5H 119
Leroy St. SE1 4E 102
Lerry Cl. W14 6H 99
Lerwick Ct. EN1: Enf 5K 23
Lescombe Cl. SE23 3A 140
Lescombe Rd. SE23 3A 140
Lescot Pl. BR2: Broml 6C 160
Lesley Cl. DA5: Bexl 7K 127
Lesley Ct. SW1 2C 18 (3H 101)
(off Strutton Ground)
Leslie Foster Cl. IG11: Bark 2K 89
Leslie Gdns. SM2: Sutt 6J 165
Leslie Gro. CR0: C'don 1E 168

Leslie Gro. Pl. – Lindisfarne Ct.

Leslie Gro. Pl. CR0: C'don 1E 168
Leslie Ho. SW8 7J 101
(off Wheatsheaf La.)
Leslie Pk. Rd. CR0: C'don 1E 168
Leslie Prince Ct. SE5 7D 102
Leslie Rd. E11 4E 68
Leslie Rd. E16 6K 87
Leslie Rd. N2 3B 46
Leslie Smith Sq. SE18 6E 106
Lesnes Abbey Woods 4D 108
Lesney Av. E20 5C 68
Lesney Farm Est. DA8: Erith 7K 109
Lesney Pk. DA8: Erith 6K 109
Lesney Pk. Rd. DA8: Erith 6K 109
Lessar Av. SW4 6G 119
Lessingham Av. IG5: Ilf 3E 52
Lessingham Av. SW17 4D 136
Lessing St. SE23 7A 122
Lessington Av. RM7: Rom 6J 55
Lessness Av. DA7: Bex 7D 108
LESSNESS HEATH 5G 109
Lessness Pk. DA17: Belv 5F 109
Lessness Rd. DA17: Belv 6G 109
Lessness Rd. SM4: Mord 6A 154
Lester Av. E15 4G 87
Lester Ct. E3 3D 86
(off Bruce Rd.)
Lestock Cl. SE25 3G 157
(off Manor Rd.)
Leswin Pl. N16 3F 67
Leswin Rd. N16 3F 67
Letchford Gdns. NW10 3C 80
Letchford Ho. E3 2C 86
(off Thomas Fyre Dr.)
Letchford M. NW10 3C 80
Letchford Ter. HA3: Hrw W 1F 41
Letchmore Ho. W10 4E 80
(off Sutton Way)
Letchworth Av. TW14: Felt 7H 111
Letchworth Cl. BR2: Broml 5J 159
Letchworth Dr. BR2: Broml 5J 159
Letchworth Rd. HA7: Stan 7K 27
Letchworth St. SW17 4D 136
Lethbridge Cl. SE10 1E 122
Letterstone Rd. SW6 7H 99
Lettice St. SW6 1H 117
Lett Rd. E15 7F 69
Lett Rd. SW9 1K 119
Lettsom St. SE5 2E 120
Lettsom Wlk. E13 2J 87
Leucha Rd. E17 5A 50
Levana Cl. SW19 1G 135
Levant Ho. E1 4K 85
(off Ernest St.)
Levehurst Ho. SE27 5C 138
Levendale Rd. SE23 2A 140
Levenhurst Way SW4 2J 119
Leven Rd. E14 5E 86
Leven Way UB3: Hayes 6G 75
Leverett St. SW3 3D 16 (4C 100)
Leverholme Gdns. SE9 4E 142
Leverington Pl. N1 2F 9 (3D 84)
Leverson St. SW16 6G 137
Leverstock Ho. SW3 5D 16 (5C 100)
(off Cale St.)
Lever St. EC1 2B 8 (3B 84)
Leverton Cl. N22 1K 47
Leverton Pl. NW5 5G 65
Leverton St. NW5 5G 65
Levett Building, The EC1 6B 8 (5B 84)
(off Little Britain)
Levett Gdns. IG3: Ilf 4K 71
Levett Rd. IG11: Bark 6J 71
Levett Sq. TW9: Kew 7H 97
Levine Gdns. IG11: Bark 2D 90
Levison Way N19 1H 65
Levita Ho. NW1 1D 6 (3H 83)
(off Ossulston St.)
Levyne Ct. EC1 3J 7 (4A 84)
(off Pine St.)
Lewen Cl. CR0: C'don 1D 168
Lewes Cl. UB5: N'olt 6E 58
Lewes Ct. CR4: Mitc 3D 154
(off Chatsworth Pl.)
Lewesdon Cl. SW19 1F 135
Lewes Ho. SE1 6H 15 (2E 102)
(off Druid St.)
Lewes Ho. SE15 6G 103
(off Friary Est.)
Lewes Rd. BR1: Broml 2B 160
Lewes Rd. N12 5H 31
Leweston Pl. N16 7F 49
Lew Evans Ho. SE22 5G 121
Lewey Ho. E3 4B 86
(off Joseph St.)
Lewgars Av. NW9 6J 43
Lewing Cl. BR6: Orp 1J 173
Lewington Apts. SE16 4J 103
(off Alpine Rd.)
Lewington Cen. SE16 4J 103
(off Alpine Rd.)
Lewin Rd. DA6: Bex 4E 126
Lewin Rd. SW14 3K 115
Lewin Rd. SW16 6H 137
Lewin Ter. TW14: Bedf 7F 111
Lewis Av. E17 1C 50
Lewis Cl. N14 7B 22
Lewis Ct. SE16 5H 103
(off Stubbs Dr.)
Lewis Cres. NW10 5K 61
Lewis Cubitt Pk. 1J 83
Lewis Cubitt Sq. N1 1J 83
Lewis Cubitt Wlk. N1 1J 83
Lewis Gdns. N16 6F 49
Lewis Gdns. N2 2B 46
Lewis Gro. SE13 3E 122
LEWISHAM 3E 122
Lewisham Cen. 4E 122
Lewisham Hgts. SE23 1J 139
Lewisham High St. SE13 3E 122
(not continuous)
Lewisham Hill SE13 2E 122
Lewisham Indoor Bowls Cen. 5B 140
Lewisham Lions Cen. 5J 103
Lewisham Model Mkt. 4E 122
(off Lewisham High St.)
Lewisham Pk. SE13 5E 122
Lewisham Rd. SE13 1D 122
Lewisham St. SW1 7D 12 (2H 101)
Lewisham Way SE14 1B 122
Lewisham Way SE4 1B 122
Lewis Ho. E14 1E 104
(off Coldharbour)
Lewis Ho. N1 6B 66
(off Canonbury Rd.)
Lewis M. BR7: Chst 5D 142
Lewis Pl. E8 5G 67
Lewis Rd. CR4: Mitc 2B 154
Lewis Rd. DA14: Sidc 3C 144
Lewis Rd. DA16: Well 3C 126
Lewis Rd. SM1: Sutt 4K 165
Lewis Rd. TW10: Rich 5D 114
Lewis Rd. UB1: S'hall 2C 94
Lewis Silkin Ho. SE15 6J 103
(off Lovelinch Cl.)
Lewis Sports & Leisure Cen. 1F 157
Lewis St. NW1 6F 65
(not continuous)
Lewiston Cl. KT4: Wor Pk 7D 152
Lewis Way RM10: Dag 6H 73
Lexden Dr. RM6: Chad H 6B 54
Lexden Rd. CR4: Mitc 4H 155
Lexden Rd. W3 7H 79
Lexham Gdns. W8 4J 99
Lexham Gdns. M. W8 3K 99
Lexham Ho. W8 4K 99
(off Lexham Gdns.)
Lexham M. W8 4J 99
Lexham Wlk. W8 3K 99
Lexington Apts. EC1 3E 8 (4D 84)
Lexington Bldg. E3 2C 86
Lexington Ho. UB7: W Dray 2B 92
(off Park Lodge Av.)
Lexington Pl. KT1: Hamp W 7D 132
Lexington St. W1 2B 12 (7G 83)
Lexington Way EN5: Barn 4A 20
Lexton Gdns. SW12 1H 137
Leyborne Av. W13 2B 96
Leyborne Pk. TW9: Kew 1G 115
Leybourne Cl. BR2: Broml 6J 159
Leybourne Ho. E14 6B 86
(off Dod St.)
Leybourne Ho. SE15 6J 103
Leybourne Rd. E11 1H 69
Leybourne Rd. NW1 7F 65
Leybourne Rd. NW9 5G 43
Leybourne Rd. UB10: Hil 1E 74
Leybourne St. NW1 7F 65
Leybridge Ct. SE12 5J 123
Leyburn Cl. E17 4D 50
Leyburn Gdns. CR0: C'don 2E 168
Leyburn Gro. N18 6B 34
Leyburn Rd. N18 6B 34
Leydenhatch La. BR8: Swan 7J 145
Leyden Mans. N19 7J 47
Leyden St. E1 6J 9 (5F 85)
Leydon Cl. SE16 1K 103
Leyes Rd. E16 6B 88
Leyfield KT4: Wor Pk 1A 164
Ley Ho. SE1 7C 14 (2C 102)
(off Scovell Rd.)
Leyland Av. EN3: Enf H 2F 25
Leyland Ct. SE15 7F 103
(off Shield Street)
Leyland Gdns. IG8: Wfd G 5F 37
Leyland Ho. E14 7D 86
(off Hale St.)
Leyland Rd. SE12 5J 123
Leylands SW18 6H 117
Leylands La. TW19: Stanw M 7A 174
(not continuous)
Leylang Rd. SE14 7K 103
Leys, The HA3: Kenton 6F 43
Leys, The N2 4A 46
Leys Av. RM10: Dag 1J 91
Leys Cl. HA1: Harr 5H 41
Leys Cl. RM10: Dag 7J 73
Leys Ct. SW9 2A 120
Leysdown Av. DA7: Bex 4J 127
Leysdown Ho. SE17 5E 102
(off Madron St.)
Leysdown Rd. SE9 2C 142
Leysfield Rd. W12 3C 98
Leys Gdns. EN4: Cockf 5K 21
Leyspring Rd. E11 1H 69
Leys Rd. E. EN3: Enf H 1F 25
Leys Rd. W. EN3: Enf H 1F 25
Leys Sq. N3 1K 45
Ley St. IG1: Ilf 2F 71
Ley St. IG2: Ilf 1H 71
Leyswood Dr. IG2: Ilf 5J 53
Leythe Rd. W3 2J 97
LEYTON 2E 68
Leyton Bus. Cen. E10 2C 68
Leyton Ct. SE23 1J 139
Leyton Grange E10 1C 68
Leyton Grn. Rd. E10 6E 50
Leyton Grn. Twr. E10 6E 50
(off Leyton Grn. Rd.)
Leyton Ho. E2 2J 9 (3F 85)
(off Calvert Av.)
Leyton Ind. Village E10 7K 49
Leyton Leisure Cen. 7E 50
Leyton Link Est. E10 7A 50
Leyton Mnr. Pk. 7D 50
Leyton Mills E10 3E 68
Leyton Orient FC 3D 68
Leyton Pk. Rd. E10 3E 68
Leyton Rd. E15 5E 68
Leyton Rd. SW19 7A 136
LEYTONSTONE 1G 69
Leytonstone Ho. E11 7H 51
(off Hanbury Dr.)
Leytonstone Leisure Cen. 2G 69
Leytonstone Rd. E15 6G 69
Leyton Way E11 7G 51
Leywick St. E15 2G 87
Lezayre Rd. BR6: Chels 6K 173
Lianne Gro. SE9 3A 142
Liardet St. SE14 6A 104
Libari Mans. E20 5E 68
(off Victory Pde.)
Liberia Rd. N5 6B 66
Liberty Av. SW19 1B 154
Liberty Bri. Rd. E15 5E 68
Liberty Bri. Rd. E20 5E 68
Liberty Cen. HA0: Wemb 1F 79
Liberty Cl. KT4: Wor Pk 1E 164
Liberty Cl. N18 4A 34
Liberty Ct. BR1: Broml 3B 160
Liberty Ct. IG11: Bark 2K 89
Liberty Ho. CR7: Thor H 5A 156
(off Thornton Rd.)
Liberty Ho. E1 7G 85
(off Ensign St.)
Liberty Ho. E13 2J 87
Liberty M. N22 1B 48
Liberty M. SW12 6F 119
Liberty Point CR0: C'don 7G 157
(off Blackhorse La.)
Liberty St. SW9 1K 119
Libra Mans. E3 2B 86
(off Libra Rd.)
Libra Rd. E13 2J 87
Libra Rd. E3 1B 86
Library & Mus. of Freemasonry, The
1F 13 (6J 83)
(off Gt. Queen St.)
Library Ct. N17 3F 49
Library Mans. W12 2E 98
(off Pennard Rd.)
Library M. TW12: Hamp H 6G 131
Library Pde. NW10 1A 80
(off Craven Pk. Rd.)
Library Pl. E1 7H 85
Library Sq. E1 4A 86
Library St. SE1 7A 14 (2B 102)
Library Way TW2: Whitt 7G 113
Libro Ct. E4 4H 35
Lichfield Cl. EN4: Cockf 3J 21
Lichfield Ct. KT6: Surb 5E 150
(off Claremont Rd.)
Lichfield Ct. TW9: Rich 5E 114
Lichfield Gdns. TW9: Rich 4E 114
Lichfield Gro. N3 1J 45
Lichfield La. TW2: Whitt 1G 131
Lichfield Rd. E3 3A 86
Lichfield Rd. E6 3B 88
Lichfield Rd. HA6: Nwood 3J 39
Lichfield Rd. IG8: Wfd G 4B 36
Lichfield Rd. N9 2B 34
Lichfield Rd. NW2 4G 63
Lichfield Rd. RM8: Dag 4B 72
Lichfield Rd. TW4: Houn 3A 112
Lichfield Rd. TW9: Kew 1F 115
Lichfield Ter. TW9: Rich 5E 114
(off Sheen Rd.)
Lichlade Cl. BR6: Orp 4K 173
Lickey Ho. W14 6H 99
(off North End Rd.)
Lidbury Gro. NW7 5B 30
Lidcote Gdns. SW9 2K 119
Liddall Way UB7: Yiew 1B 92
Liddell Cl. HA3: Kenton 3D 42
Liddell Gdns. NW10 2E 80
Liddell Pl. NW6 6J 63
Liddell Rd. NW6 6J 63
Liddiard Ho. W11 7G 81
(off Lansdowne Rd.)
Lidding Rd. HA3: Kenton 5D 42
Liddington Rd. E15 1H 87
Liddon Rd. BR1: Broml 3A 160
Liddon Rd. E13 3K 87
Liden Cl. E17 7B 50
Lidfield Rd. N16 4D 66
Lidgate Rd. SE15 7F 103
Lidgould Gro. HA4: Ruis 6J 39
Lidiard Rd. SW18 2A 136
Lidlington Pl. NW1 2G 83
Lido Sq. N17 2D 48
Lidyard Rd. N19 1G 65
Lifeboat Station Chiswick 7B 98
Lifestyle Club @ Charlton, The 7B 106
Liffler Rd. SE18 5J 107
Liffords Pl. SW13 2B 116
Lifford St. SW15 4F 117
Lightcliffe Rd. N13 4F 33
Lighterage Ct. TW8: Bford 6E 96
Lighter Cl. SE16 4A 104
Lighterman Ho. E14 7E 86
Lighterman M. E1 6K 85
Lighterman Point E14 6F 87
(off New Village Av.)
Lightermans Rd. E14 2C 104
Lightermans Wlk. SW18 4J 117
Lightfoot Rd. N8 5J 47
Lightfoot Vs. N1 7A 66
(off Augustas La.)
Light Horse Ct. SW3 6G 17 (5E 100)
(off Royal Hospital Rd.)
Lighthouse Apts. E1 6J 85
(off Commercial Rd.)
Lighthouse Vw. SE10 1G 105
Lightley Cl. HA0: Wemb 1E 78
Ligonier St. E2 3J 9 (4F 85)
Lilac Cl. E4 6G 35
Lilac Ct. E13 1A 88
Lilac Ct. TW11: Tedd 4K 131
Lilac Gdns. CR0: C'don 3C 170
Lilac Gdns. RM7: Rush G 1K 73
Lilac Gdns. UB3: Hayes 6G 75
Lilac Gdns. W5 3D 96
Lilac Ho. SE4 3C 122
Lilac La. E2 3K 85
Lilac M. N22 3A 48
(off High Rd.)
Lilac Pl. SE11 4G 19 (4K 101)
Lilac Pl. UB7: Yiew 7B 74
Lilac St. W12 7C 80
Lilah M. BR2: Broml 2G 159
Lilburne Gdns. SE9 5C 124
Lilburne Rd. SE9 5C 124
Lilburne Wlk. NW10 6J 61
Lile Cres. W7 5J 77
Lilestone Ho. NW8 3B 4 (4B 82)
(off Frampton St.)
Lilestone St. NW8 3C 4 (4C 82)
Lilford Ho. SE5 2C 120
Lilford Rd. SE5 2B 120
Lilian Barker Cl. SE12 5J 123
Lilian Board Way UB6: G'frd 5H 59
Lilian Cl. N16 3E 66
Lilian Gdns. IG8: Wfd G 1K 51
Lilian Knowles Ho. E1 6J 9 (5F 85)
(off Crispin St.)
Lilian Rd. SW16 1G 155
Lilium M. E10 7C 50
Lillechurch Rd. RM8: Dag 6B 72
Lilleshall Rd. SM4: Mord 6B 154
Lilley Cl. E1 1G 103
Lilley La. NW7 5E 28
Lillian Av. W3 2G 97
Lillian Rd. SW13 6C 98
Lillie Bri. Dpt. W14 5H 99
(off Aisgill Av.)
Lillie Mans. SW6 6G 99
(off Lillie Rd.)
Lillie Rd. SW6 6G 99
Lillie Road Fitness Cen. 7F 99
Lillieshall Rd. SW4 3F 119
Lillie Sq. SW6 6J 99
Lillie Yd. SW6 6J 99
Lillingston Ho. N7 4A 66
Lillington Gdns. Est. SW1 4B 18 (4G 101)
(off Vauxhall Bri. Rd.)
Lilliput Av. UB5: N'olt 1C 76
Lilliput Ct. SE12 5K 123
Lilliput Rd. E15 1G 87
Lilliput Rd. RM7: Rush G 7K 55
Lily Cl. HA5: Pinn 2A 40
Lily Cl. W14 4F 99
Lily Gdns. HA0: Wemb 2C 78
Lily M. SE11 4B 102
Lily Nichols Ho. E16 1B 106
(off Connaught Rd.)
Lily Pl. EC1 5K 7 (5A 84)
Lily Rd. E17 6C 50
Lilyville Rd. SW6 1H 117
Lily Way N13 5D 32
Limasol St. SE16 3F 103
Limborough Ho. E14 5C 86
(off Thomas Rd.)
Limbourne Av. RM8: Dag 7F 55
Limburg Rd. SW11 4C 118
Lime Av. UB7: Yiew 7B 74
Limeburner La. EC4 1A 14 (6B 84)
Lime Cl. BR1: Broml 4C 160
Lime Cl. E1 1G 103
Lime Cl. HA3: W'stone 2A 42
Lime Cl. HA5: Eastc 3H 39
Lime Cl. IG9: Buck H 2G 37
Lime Cl. RM7: Rom 4J 55
Lime Cl. SM5: Cars 2D 166
Lime Ct. CR4: Mitc 2B 154
Lime Ct. E11 2G 69
(off Trinity Cl.)
Lime Ct. E17 5E 50
Lime Ct. HA1: Harr 6K 41
(off Gayton Rd.)
Lime Ct. HA4: Ruis 7K 39
Lime Ct. SE9 2F 143
Lime Cres. TW16: Sun 2A 148
Limecroft Cl. KT19: Ewe 7K 163
Limedene Cl. HA5: Pinn 1B 40
Lime Gro. BR6: Farnb 2F 173
Lime Gro. DA15: Sidc 6K 125
Lime Gro. E4 6G 35
Lime Gro. HA4: Ruis 6K 39
Lime Gro. KT3: N Mald 3K 151
Lime Gro. N20 1C 30
Lime Gro. TW1: Twick 6K 113
Lime Gro. UB3: Hayes 7F 75
Lime Gro. W12 2E 98
Limeharbour E14 3D 104
Lime Ho. TW9: Kew 1H 115
LIMEHOUSE 6B 86
Limehouse C'way. E14 7B 86
Lime Ho. Ct. E14 6B 86
(off Wharf La.)
Limehouse Ct. E14 6C 86
Limehouse Cut E14 5D 86
(off Morris Rd.)
Limehouse Flds. Est. E14 5A 86
Limehouse Link E14 6A 86
Limehouse Lodge E5 2J 67
(off Harry Zeital Way)
Lime Kiln Dr. SE7 6K 105
Limekiln Pl. SE19 7F 139
Limekiln Wharf E14 7B 86
Limelight Ho. SE11 4B 102
(off Dugard Way)
Lime Lodge TW16: Sun 7H 129
(off Forest Dr.)
Lime Quay E14 4E 86
Limerick Cl. SW12 7G 119
Limerick M. N2 3C 46
Lime Rd. TW9: Rich 4F 115
Lime Row DA18: Erith 3F 109
Limerston St. SW10 6A 100
Limes, The BR2: Broml 2C 172
Limes, The KT8: W Mole 4F 149
Limes, The SW18 6J 117
Limes, The W2 7J 81
Limes Av. CR0: Wadd 3A 168
Limes Av. E11 4K 51
Limes Av. N12 4F 31
Limes Av. NW11 7G 45
Limes Av. NW7 6F 29
Limes Av. SE20 7H 139
Limes Av. SM5: Cars 1D 166
Limes Av. SW13 2B 116
Limes Av., The N11 5A 32
Limes Cl. N11 5B 32
Limes Cl. TW15: Ashf 5C 128
Limes Ct. BR3: Beck 2D 158
Limes Ct. NW6 7G 63
(off Brondesbury Pk.)
Limesdale Gdns. HA8: Edg 2J 43
Limes Fld. Rd. SW13 3A 116
Limesford Rd. SE15 4K 121
Limes Gdns. SW18 6J 117
Limes Gro. SE13 4E 122
Limes Pl. CR0: C'don 7D 156
Limes Rd. BR3: Beck 2D 158
Limes Rd. CR0: C'don 7D 156
Limes Row BR6: Farnb 5F 173
Limestone Wlk. DA18: Erith 2D 108
Lime St. E17 4A 50
Lime St. EC3 2G 15 (7E 84)
Lime St. Pas. EC3 1G 15 (6E 84)
Lime St. Sq. EC3 1G 15 (6E 84)
Limes Wlk. SE15 4J 121
Limes Wlk. W5 2D 96
Lime Ter. W7 7J 77
Lime Tree Av. KT10: Esh 7H 149
Lime Tree Av. KT7: T Ditt 7J 149
Lime Tree Cl. E18 4A 52
Limetree Cl. SW2 1K 137
Lime Tree Ct. CR2: S Croy 6C 168
Lime Tree Ct. E3 5C 86
(off Whitehorn St.)
Lime Tree Ct. SE17 5C 102
(off Walworth Rd.)
Lime Tree Gro. CR0: C'don 3B 170
Lime Tree Pl. CR4: Mitc 1F 155
Lime Tree Rd. TW5: Hest 1F 113
Limetree Ter. DA16: Well 3A 126
Limetree Ter. SE6 1B 140
Lime Tree Wlk. BR4: W W'ck 4H 171
Lime Tree Wlk. EN2: Enf 1H 23
Lime Tree Wlk. WD23: B Hea 1D 26
Limetree Wlk. SW17 5E 136
Lime View Apts. E14 6A 86
(off Commerical Rd.)
Lime Wlk. E15 1G 87
Lime Wlk. KT8: E Mos 4K 149
Limewood Cl. BR3: Beck 5E 158
Limewood Cl. E17 4B 50
Limewood Cl. W13 6B 78
Limewood Ct. IG4: Ilf 5D 52
Limewood M. SE20 7G 139
(off Lullington Rd.)
Limewood Rd. DA8: Erith 7J 109
Limpsfield Av. CR7: Thor H 5K 155
Limpsfield Av. SW19 2F 135
Limscott Ho. E3 3D 86
(off Bruce Rd.)
Linacre Cl. SE15 3H 121
Linacre Ct. W6 5F 99
Linacre Rd. NW2 6D 62
Linale Ho. N1 1E 8 (2D 84)
(off Murray Gro.)
Linberry Wlk. SE8 4B 104
Linchmere Rd. SE12 7H 123
Lincoln Apts. W12 7E 80
(off Fountain Park Way)
Lincoln Av. N14 3B 32
Lincoln Av. RM7: Rush G 2K 73
Lincoln Av. SW19 3F 135
Lincoln Av. TW2: Twick 2G 131
Lincoln Cl. HA2: Harr 5D 40
Lincoln Cl. SE25 6G 157
Lincoln Cl. UB6: G'frd 1G 77
Lincoln Ct. CR2: S Croy 5C 168
(off Warham Rd.)
Lincoln Ct. IG2: Ilf 6G 53
Lincoln Ct. N16 7D 48
Lincoln Ct. SE12 3K 141
Lincoln Cres. EN1: Enf 5K 23
Lincoln Gdns. IG1: Ilf 7C 52
Lincoln Grn. Rd. BR5: St M Cry 5K 161
Lincoln Ho. SE5 7A 102
Lincoln Ho. SW3 7E 10 (2D 100)
Lincoln Ho. TW8: Bford 5D 96
(off Ealing Rd.)
Lincoln M. N15 4C 48
Lincoln M. NW6 1H 81
Lincoln M. SE21 2D 138
Lincoln Pde. HA9: Wemb 1E 60
Lincoln Pde. N2 3C 46
(off Lincoln Rd.)
Lincoln Plaza E14 2D 104
(off Lightermans Rd.)
Lincoln Rd. CR4: Mitc 5J 155
Lincoln Rd. DA14: Sidc 5B 144
Lincoln Rd. E13 4K 87
Lincoln Rd. E18 1J 51
Lincoln Rd. E7 6B 70
Lincoln Rd. EN1: Enf 4K 23
Lincoln Rd. EN3: Pond E 5C 24
Lincoln Rd. HA0: Wemb 6D 60
Lincoln Rd. HA2: Harr 5D 40
Lincoln Rd. HA6: Nwood 3H 39
Lincoln Rd. KT3: N Mald 3J 151
Lincoln Rd. KT4: Wor Pk 1D 164
Lincoln Rd. N2 3C 46
Lincoln Rd. SE25 3H 157
Lincoln Rd. TW13: Hanw 3D 130
Lincolns, The NW7 3G 29
Lincoln's Inn Flds. WC2 7G 7 (6K 83)
Lincoln's Inn Hall 7H 7 (6K 83)
Lincoln St. E11 2G 69
Lincoln St. SW3 4E 16 (4D 100)
Lincoln Ter. SM2: Sutt 7J 165
Lincoln Way EN1: Enf 5C 24
Lincoln Way TW16: Sun 1G 147
Lincombe Rd. BR1: Broml 3H 141
Lindal Ct. E18 1H 51
Lindal Cres. EN2: Enf 4D 22
Lindale Cl. IG4: Ilf 5D 52
Lindales, The N17 6B 34
(off Grasmere Rd.)
Lindal Rd. SE4 5B 122
Lindbergh Rd. SM6: W'gton 7J 167
Linden Av. CR7: Thor H 4B 156
Linden Av. EN1: Enf 1B 24
Linden Av. HA4: Ruis 1J 57
Linden Av. HA9: Wemb 5F 61
Linden Av. NW10 2F 81
Linden Av. TW3: Houn 5F 113
Linden Cl. HA4: Ruis 1J 57
Linden Cl. HA7: Stan 5G 27
Linden Cl. KT7: T Ditt 7K 149
Linden Cl. N14 6B 22
Linden Ct. DA14: Sidc 4J 143
Linden Ct. SE20 7H 139
(off Anerley Pk.)
Linden Ct. W12 1E 98
Linden Cres. IG8: Wfd G 6E 36
Linden Cres. KT1: King T 2F 151
Linden Cres. UB6: G'frd 6K 59
Lindenfield BR7: Chst 2F 161
Linden Gdns. EN1: Enf 1B 24
Linden Gdns. W2 7J 81
Linden Gdns. W4 5A 98
Linden Gro. KT3: N Mald 3A 152
Linden Gro. SE15 3H 121
Linden Gro. SE26 6J 139
Linden Gro. TW11: Tedd 5K 131
Linden Ho. SE8 6B 104
(off Abinger Gro.)
Linden Ho. TW12: Hamp 6E 130
Linden Lawns HA9: Wemb 4F 61
Linden Lea N2 5A 46
Linden Leas BR4: W W'ck 2F 171
Linden Mans. N6 1F 65
(off Hornsey La.)
Linden M. N1 5D 66
Linden M. W2 7J 81
Linden Pl. CR4: Mitc 4C 154
Linden Rd. N10 4F 47
Linden Rd. N11 2J 31
Linden Rd. N15 4C 48
Linden Rd. TW12: Hamp 7E 130
Lindens, The CR0: New Ad 6E 170
Lindens, The E17 4D 50
(off Prospect Hill)
Lindens, The N12 5G 31
Lindens, The W4 1J 115
Linden St. RM7: Rom 4K 55
Linden Wlk. N19 2G 65
Linden Way N14 6B 22
Linden Way TW17: Shep 5E 146
Linder's Field Local Nature
Reserve 1G 37
Lindeth Cl. HA7: Stan 6G 27
Lindfield Gdns. NW3 5K 63
Lindfield Rd. CR0: C'don 6F 157
Lindfield Rd. W5 4C 78
Lindfield St. E14 6C 86
Lindhill Cl. EN3: Enf H 2E 24
Lindholme Ct. NW9 1A 44
(off Pageant Av.)
Lindie Gdns. UB8: Uxb 7A 56
Lindisfarne Ct. HA8: Edg 4A 28

Lindisfarne Rd. – Lofting Ho.

Lindisfarne Rd. RM8: Dag 3C 72
Lindisfarne Rd. SW20 7C 134
Lindisfarne Way E9 4A 68
Lindley Ct. KT1: Hamp W 1C 150
Lindley Est. SE15 7G 103
Lindley Ho. E1 5J 85
(off Lindley St.)
Lindley Ho. SE15 7G 103
(off Peckham Pk. Rd.)
Lindley Pl. TW9: Kew 1G 115
Lindley Rd. E10 2E 68
Lindley St. E1 5J 85
Lindop Ho. E1 4A 86
(off Mile End Rd.)
Lindore Rd. SW11 4D 118
Lindores Rd. SM5: Cars 7A 154
Lindo St. SE15 2J 121
Lind Rd. SM1: Sutt 5A 166
Lindrop St. SW6 2A 118
Lindsay Cl. KT9: Chess 7E 162
Lindsay Cl. TW19: Stanw 5A 110
Lindsay Cl. CR0: C'don 4D 168
(off Eden Rd.)
Lindsay Ct. SE13 3D 122
(off Loampit Va.)
Lindsay Ct. SW11 1B 118
(off Battersea High St.)
Lindsay Dr. HA3: Kenton 6E 42
Lindsay Dr. TW17: Shep 6F 147
Lindsay Ho. SW7 3A 100
(off Gloucester Rd.)
Lindsay Rd. KT4: Wor Pk 2D 164
Lindsay Rd. TW12: Hamp H 4F 131
Lindsay Sq. SW1 5D 18 (5H 101)
Lindsell St. SE10 1E 122
Lindsey Cl. BR1: Broml 3B 160
Lindsey Cl. CR4: Mitc 4J 155
Lindsey Ct. N13 3F 33
(off Green Lanes)
Lindsey Gdns. TW14: Bedf 7F 111
Lindsey Ho. W5 4D 96
Lindsey M. N1 7C 66
Lindsey Rd. RM8: Dag 4C 72
Lindsey St. EC1 5B 8 (5B 84)
Lind St. SE8 2C 122
Lindum Rd. TW11: Tedd 7C 132
Lindway SE27 5B 138
Lindwood Cl. E6 6D 88
Linear Pk. 6H 101
Linen Ho., The W10 2G 81
Linen M. W12 2B 98
Liner Ho. E16 2A 106
Linfield WC1 2G 7 (3K 83)
(off Sidmouth St.)
Linfield Cl. NW4 3E 44
Linford Christie Stadium 5C 80
Linford Ho. E16 5J 87
(off Hammersley Rd.)
Linford Ho. E2 1G 85
(off Whiston Rd.)
Linford Rd. E17 3E 50
Linford St. SW8 1G 119
Linford St. Bus. Est. SW8 1G 119
(off Linford St.)
Lingard Av. NW9 2A 44
Lingard Ho. E14 3E 104
(off Marshfield St.)
Lingards Rd. SE13 4E 122
Lingey Cl. DA15: Sidc 2K 143
Lingfield Apts. E4 7J 35
Lingfield Av. KT1: King T 4E 150
Lingfield Cl. EN1: Enf 6K 23
Lingfield Cl. HA6: Nwood 1G 39
Lingfield Cl. UB5: N'olt 2E 76
Lingfield Cres. SE9 4H 125
Lingfield Gdns. N9 7C 24
Lingfield Ho. SE1 7B 14 (2B 102)
(off Lancaster St.)
Lingfield Rd. KT4: Wor Pk 3E 164
Lingfield Rd. SW19 5F 135
Lingham Ct. SW9 2J 119
Lingham St. SW9 2J 119
Lingholm Way EN5: Barn 5A 20
Ling Rd. DA8: Erith 6J 109
Ling Rd. E16 5J 87
Lingrove Gdns. IG9: Buck H 2E 36
Lings Coppice SE21 2D 138
Lingwell Rd. SW17 3C 136
Lingwood DA7: Bex 2H 127
Lingwood Ct. N2 3C 46
(off Norfolk Cl.)
Lingwood Gdns. TW7: Isle 7J 95
Lingwood Rd. E5 7G 49
Linhope St. NW1 3E 4 (4D 82)
Link, The EN3: Enf H 1F 25
Link, The HA0: Wemb 1C 60
Link, The HA5: Eastc 7A 40
Link, The NW2 1C 62
Link, The SE9 3E 142
(off William Barefoot Dr.)
Link, The UB5: N'olt 5D 58
Link, The W3 6H 79
Linkenholt Mans. W6 4B 98
(off Stamford Brook Av.)
Linkfield BR2: Hayes 6J 159
Linkfield KT8: W Mole 3F 149
Linkfield Rd. TW7: Isle 2K 113
Link Ho. E3 3D 86
Link Ho. W10 6F 81
(off Kingsdown Cl.)
Link La. SM6: W'gton 6H 167
Linklea Cl. NW9 7F 29
Link Rd. E1 2K 15 (7G 85)
Link Rd. N11 4K 31
Link Rd. RM9: Dag 2H 91
Link Rd. SM6: W'gton 1E 166
Link Rd. TW14: Felt 7H 111
Links, The E17 4A 50
Links Av. SM4: Mord 4J 153
Linkscroft Av. TW15: Ashf 6D 128
Links Dr. N20 1D 30
Links Gdns. SW16 7A 138
Linkside KT3: N Mald 2A 152
Linkside N12 6D 30
Linkside Cl. EN2: Enf 3E 22
Linkside Gdns. EN2: Enf 3E 22
Links Rd. BR4: W W'ck 1E 170
Links Rd. IG8: Wfd G 5D 36
Links Rd. NW2 2B 62
Links Rd. SW17 6E 136
Links Rd. TW15: Ashf 5A 128
Links Rd. W3 6G 79
Links Side EN2: Enf 3E 22
Link St. E9 6J 67
Links Vw. N3 7C 30
Linksview N2 5D 46
(off Great Nth. Rd.)
Links Vw. Cl. HA7: Stan 7F 27
Linksview Ct. TW12: Hamp H 4H 131
Links Vw. Rd. CR0: C'don 3C 170
Links Vw. Rd. TW12: Hamp H 5G 131
Links Way BR3: Beck 6C 158
Linksway HA6: Nwood 1E 38
Linksway NW4 2F 45
Links Yd. E1 5K 9 (5G 85)
(off Spelman St.)
Link Way BR2: Broml 7C 160
Link Way HA5: Pinn 1B 40
Link Way TW10: Ham 2B 132
Linkway N4 7C 48
Linkway RM8: Dag 4C 72
Linkway SW20 3D 152
Linkway, The EN5: Barn 6E 20
Linkwood Wlk. NW1 7H 65
Linley Ct. SM1: Sutt 4A 166
Linley Cres. RM7: Mawney 3H 55
Linley Rd. N17 2E 48
Linnell Cl. NW11 6K 45
Linnell Dr. NW11 6K 45
Linnell Ho. E1 5J 9 (5F 85)
(off Folgate St.)
Linnell Ho. NW8 1A 82
(off Ainsworth Way)
Linnell Rd. N18 5B 34
Linnell Rd. SE5 2E 120
Linnet Cl. N9 1E 34
Linnet Cl. SE28 7C 90
Linnet Cl. WD23: Bush 1B 26
Linnet Ct. SW15 6E 116
Linnet M. SW12 7E 118
Linnett Cl. E4 4K 35
Linom Rd. SW4 4J 119
Linscott Rd. E5 4J 67
Linsdell Rd. IG11: Bark 1G 89
Linsey Ct. E10 1C 68
(off Grange Rd.)
Linsey St. SE16 4G 103
(not continuous)
Linslade Cl. HA5: Eastc 4K 39
Linslade Cl. TW4: Houn 5C 112
Linslade Ho. E2 1G 85
Linslade Ho. NW8 3D 4 (4C 82)
(off Paveley St.)
Linslade Rd. BR6: Chels 6K 173
Linstead St. NW6 7J 63
Linstead Way SW18 7G 117
Linsted Ct. SE9 6J 125
Lintaine Cl. W6 6G 99
Linthorpe Av. HA0: Wemb 6C 60
Linthorpe Rd. EN4: Cockf 3H 21
Linthorpe Rd. N16 7E 48
Linton Cl. CR4: Mitc 7D 154
Linton Cl. DA16: Well 1B 126
Linton Cl. SE7 5A 106
Linton Ct. NW1 7G 65
(off Agar Gro.)
Linton Ct. RM1: Rom 2K 55
Linton Gdns. E6 6C 88
Linton Gro. SE27 5B 138
Linton Ho. E3 5C 86
(off St Paul's Way)
Linton Rd. IG11: Bark 7G 71
Linton St. N1 1C 84
(not continuous)
Lintott Ct. TW19: Stanw 6A 110
Linver Rd. SW6 2J 117
Linwood Cl. SE5 2F 121
Linwood Cres. EN1: Enf 1B 24
Linzee Rd. N8 4J 47
Lion Apts. SE16 5H 103
(off Rotherhithe New Rd.)
Lion Av. TW1: Twick 1K 131
Lion Cl. SE4 6C 122
Lion Cl. TW17: Shep 3A 146
Lion Ct. E1 7K 85
(off The Highway)
Lion Ct. N1 1K 83
(off Copenhagen St.)
Lion Ct. SE1 5H 15 (1E 102)
(off Magdalen St.)
Lionel Gdns. SE9 5B 124
Lionel Mans. W14 3F 99
(off Haarlem Rd.)
Lionel M. W10 5G 81
Lionel Rd. SE9 5B 124
Lionel Rd. Nth. TW8: Bford 3E 96
Lionel Rd. Sth. TW8: Bford 5F 97
Liongate Ent. Pk. CR4: Mitc 4B 154
Lion Ga. Gdns. TW9: Rich 3F 115
Lion Ga. M. SW18 7J 117
Liongate M. KT8: E Mos 3K 149
Lion Head Ct. CR0: C'don 4C 168
(off St Andrew's Rd.)
Lion Mills E2 2G 85
Lion Pk. Av. KT9: Chess 4G 163
Lion Rd. CR0: C'don 5C 156
Lion Rd. DA6: Bex 4E 126
Lion Rd. E6 5D 88
Lion Rd. N9 2B 34
Lion Rd. TW1: Twick 1K 131
Lions Cl. SE9 3A 142
Lion Way TW8: Bford 7D 96
Lion Wharf Rd. TW7: Isle 3B 114
Lion Yd. SW4 4H 119
Liphook Cres. SE23 7J 121
Lipton Cl. N14 7A 22
Lipton Cl. SE28 7C 90
Lipton Rd. E1 6K 85
Lisbon Av. TW2: Twick 2G 131
Lisbon Cl. E17 2B 50
Lisburne Rd. NW3 4D 64
Lisford St. SE15 1F 121
Lisgar Ter. W14 4H 99
Liskeard Cl. BR7: Chst 6G 143
Liskeard Gdns. SE3 1J 123
Liskeard Ho. SE11 5K 19 (5A 102)
(off Kennings Way)
Lisle Cl. SW17 4F 137
Lisle Ct. NW2 3G 63
Lisle St. WC2 2D 12 (7H 83)
Lismore SW19 5H 135
(off Woodside)
Lismore Blvd. NW9 3B 44
Lismore Cir. NW5 5E 64
Lismore Cl. TW7: Isle 2A 114
Lismore Rd. CR2: S Croy 6E 168
Lismore Rd. N17 3D 48
Lismore Wlk. N1 6C 66
(off Clephane Rd. Nth.)
Lissant Cl. KT6: Surb 7D 150
Lisselton Ho. NW4 4F 45
(off Belle Vue Est.)
Lissenden Gdns. NW5 4E 64
(not continuous)
Lissenden Mans. NW5 4E 64
Lisson Grn. Est. NW8 3C 4 (4C 82)
(off Tresham Cres.)
Lisson Gro. NW1 4C 4 (4C 82)
Lisson Gro. NW8 3B 4 (4B 82)
LISSON GROVE 5D 4 (5C 82)
Lisson Ho. NW1 5C 4 (5C 82)
(off Lisson St.)
Lisson St. NW1 5C 4 (5C 82)
Lister Cl. CR4: Mitc 1C 154
Lister Cl. W3 5K 79
Lister Ct. HA1: Harr 7B 42
Lister Ct. N16 2E 66
Lister Ct. NW9 2A 44
Lister Gdns. N18 5H 33
Listergate Ct. SW15 4E 116
Lister Ho. E1 5G 85
(off Lomas St.)
Lister Ho. HA9: Wemb 3J 61
(off Barnhill Rd.)
Lister Ho. UB3: Harl 4G 93
Lister Lodge W9 5J 81
(off Admiral Wlk.)
Lister Rd. E11 1G 69
Lister Wlk. SE28 7D 90
Liston Rd. N17 1G 49
Liston Rd. SW4 3G 119
Liston Way IG8: Wfd G 7F 37
Listowel Cl. SW9 7A 102
Listowel Rd. RM10: Dag 3G 73
Listria Pk. N16 2E 66
Litcham Ho. E1 3K 85
(off Longnor Rd.)
Litchfield Av. E15 6G 69
Litchfield Av. SM4: Mord 7H 153
Litchfield Ct. E17 6C 50
Litchfield Gdns. NW10 6C 62
Litchfield Rd. SM1: Sutt 4A 166
Litchfield St. WC2 2D 12 (7H 83)
Litchfield Way NW11 5K 45
Lithgow's Rd. TW6: H'row A 4G 111
Lithos Rd. NW3 6K 63
Litten Nature Reserve 3G 77
Little Acre BR3: Beck 3C 158
Little Albany St. NW1 3K 5 (4F 83)
(off Longford St.)
Little Angel Theatre 1B 84
(off Dagmar Ter.)
Little Argyll St. W1 1A 12 (6G 83)
Little Benty UB7: W Dray 1E 174
Little Birches DA15: Sidc 2J 143
Little Boltons, The SW10 5K 99
Little Boltons, The SW5 5K 99
Little Bornes SE21 4E 138
Littlebourne SE13 7G 123
Littlebourne Ho. SE17 5E 102
(off Upnor Way)
Little Brights Rd. DA17: Belv 2H 109
Little Britain EC1 6B 8 (5B 84)
Littlebrook Cl. CR0: C'don 6K 157
Little Brownings SE23 2H 139
Littlebury Rd. SW4 3H 119
Little Bury St. N9 1J 33
Little Cedars N12 4F 31
Little Chelsea Ho. SW10 6A 100
(off Edith Gro.)
Little Chester St. SW1 1J 17 (3F 101)
Little Cloisters SW1 1E 18 (3J 101)
Little College La. EC4 2E 14 (7D 84)
(off College St.)
Little College St. SW1 1E 18 (3J 101)
Littlecombe SE7 6K 105
Littlecombe Cl. SW15 6F 117
Little Comn. HA7: Stan 3F 27
Littlecote Cl. SW19 7G 117
Littlecote Pl. HA5: Hat E 1C 40
Little Cottage Pl. SE10 7D 104
Little Ct. BR4: W W'ck 2G 171
Littlecroft SE9 3E 124
Littledale SE2 6A 108
Little Dean's Yd. SW1 1E 18 (3J 101)
(off Dean's Yd.)
Little Dimocks SW12 2F 137
Little Dorrit Ct. SE1 6D 14 (2C 102)
LITTLE EALING 3D 96
Little Ealing La. W5 4C 96
Little Edward St. NW1 1K 5 (3F 83)
Little Elms UB3: Harl 7F 93
Little Essex St. WC2 2J 13 (7A 84)
(off Essex St.)
Little Ferry Rd. TW1: Twick 1B 132
Littlefield Cl. KT1: King T 2E 150
Littlefield Cl. N19 4G 65
Littlefield Ho. KT1: King T 2E 150
(off Littlefield Cl.)
Littlefield Rd. HA8: Edg 7D 28
Little Friday Rd. E4 2B 36
Little Gearies IG6: Ilf 4F 53
Little George St. SW1 7E 12 (2J 101)
Little Grange UB6: G'frd 3A 78
Little Grn. TW9: Rich 4D 114
Little Green St. NW5 4F 65
Littlegrove EN4: E Barn 6H 21
Little Halliards KT12: Walt T 6J 147
Little Heath RM6: Chad H 4B 54
Little Heath SE7 6C 106
LITTLE HEATH 5B 54
Little Heath Rd. DA7: Bex 1F 127
Littleheath Rd. CR2: Sels 7H 169
Little Holland House 7D 166
Little Holt E11 5J 51
LITTLE ILFORD 5D 70
Little Ilford La. E12 4D 70
Littlejohn Rd. W7 6K 77
Little Larkins EN5: Barn 6B 20
Little London Cl. UB8: Hil 5D 74
Little London Ct. SE1 7K 15 (2F 103)
(off Wolseley St.)
Little Marlborough St. W1
1A 12 (6G 83)
(off Kingly St.)
Littlemede SE9 3D 142
Littlemoor Rd. IG1: Ilf 3H 71
Littlemore Rd. SE2 2A 108
Little Moss La. HA5: Pinn 2C 40
Little Newport St. WC2 2D 12 (7H 83)
Little New St. EC4 7K 7 (6A 84)
Little Oaks Cl. TW17: Shep 4B 146
Little Orchard Cl. HA5: Pinn 2C 40
Little Park Dr. TW13: Felt 2C 130
Little Park Gdns. EN2: Enf 3H 23
Little Pluckett's Way IG9: Buck H 1G 37
Little Portland St. W1 7A 6 (6G 83)
Little Potters WD23: Bush 1C 26
Little Queen's Rd. TW11: Tedd 6K 131
Little Redlands BR1: Broml 2C 160
Little Rd. UB3: Hayes 2H 93
Littlers Cl. SW19 1B 154
Little Russell St. WC1 6E 6 (5J 83)
Little St James's St. SW1
5A 12 (1G 101)
Little St Leonard's SW14 3J 115
Little Sanctuary SW1 7D 12 (2H 101)
Little Smith St. SW1 1D 18 (3H 101)
Little Somerset St. E1 1J 15 (6F 85)
Little South St. SE5 1E 120
LITTLE STANMORE 7A 28
Littlestone Cl. BR3: Beck 6C 140
Little Strand NW9 2B 44
Little Thames Wlk. SE8 6D 104
(off Dancers Way)
Little Thrift BR5: Pet W 4G 161
Little Titchfield St. W1 6A 6 (5G 83)
LITTLETON Staines 3C 146
Littleton Av. E4 1C 36
LITTLETON COMMON 7E 128
Littleton Cres. HA1: Harr 2K 59
Littleton Ho. SW1 6A 18 (5G 101)
(off Lupus St.)
Littleton La. TW17: Shep 7A 146
Littleton Rd. HA1: Harr 2K 59
Littleton Rd. TW15: Ashf 7E 128
Littleton St. SW18 2A 136
Little Trinity La. EC4 2D 14 (7C 84)
Little Turnstile WC1 6G 7 (5K 83)
LITTLE VENICE 5A 82
Little Venice Sports Cen. 5A 4 (5B 82)
Littlewood SE13 6E 122
Littlewood Cl. W13 3B 96
Little Wood St. KT1: King T 2D 150
Littleworth Bus. Cen. DA5: Bexl 1H 145
Livermere Ct. E8 1F 85
(off Queensbridge Rd.)
Livermere Rd. E8 1F 85
Liverpool Gro. SE17 5C 102
Liverpool Rd. CR7: Thor H 3C 156
Liverpool Rd. E10 6E 50
Liverpool Rd. E16 5G 87
Liverpool Rd. KT2: King T 7G 133
Liverpool Rd. N1 7A 66
Liverpool Rd. N7 5A 66
Liverpool Rd. W5 2D 96
Liverpool St. EC2 6G 9 (5E 84)
Livery Stables Cl. BR2: Broml 3B 172
Livesey Cl. KT1: King T 3F 151
Livesey Cl. SE28 3G 107
Livesey Pl. SE15 6G 103
Livingstone Ct. E10 6E 50
Livingstone Ct. EN5: Barn 2B 20
(off Church La.)
Livingstone Ct. HA3: W'stone 3K 41
Livingstone Ho. NW10 7K 61
Livingstone Ho. SE5 7C 102
(off Wyndham Rd.)
Livingstone Lodge W9 5J 81
(off Admiral Wlk.)
Livingstone Mans. W14 6G 99
(off Queen's Club Gdns.)
Livingstone Pl. E14 5E 104
Livingstone Rd. CR7: Thor H 2C 156
Livingstone Rd. E17 6D 50
Livingstone Rd. N13 6D 32
Livingstone Rd. SW11 3B 118
Livingstone Rd. TW3: Houn 4G 113
Livingstone Rd. UB1: S'hall 7B 76
LivingWell Health Club London
Heathrow Hilton 6E 110
LivingWell Health Club Wembley 4G 61
Livonia St. W1 1B 12 (6G 83)
Lizard St. EC1 2D 8 (3C 84)
Lizban St. SE3 7K 105
Lizmans Ter. W8 3J 99
(off Earl's Ct. Rd.)
Llandovery Ho. E14 2E 104
(off Chipka St.)
Llanelly Rd. NW2 2H 63
Llanover Rd. HA9: Wemb 3D 60
Llanover Rd. SE18 6E 106
Llanthony Rd. SM4: Mord 5B 154
Llanvanor Rd. NW2 2H 63
Llewellyn Ct. SE20 1J 157
Llewellyn Mans. W14 4G 99
(off Hammersmith Rd.)
Llewellyn St. SE16 2G 103
Lloyd Av. SW16 1J 155
Lloyd Baker St. WC1 2H 7 (3K 83)
(not continuous)
Lloyd Ct. HA5: Pinn 5B 40
Lloyd Ct. SW11 2D 118
(off Roydon Cl.)
Lloyd Ho. BR3: Beck 6D 140
Lloyd Ho. CR0: C'don 1D 168
(off Tavistock Rd.)
Lloyd M. EN3: Enf L 1H 25
Lloyd Pk. 2C 50
Lloyd Pk. Av. CR0: C'don 4F 169
Lloyd Pk. Ho. E17 3C 50
Lloyd Rd. E17 4K 49
Lloyd Rd. E6 1D 88
Lloyd Rd. KT4: Wor Pk 3E 164
Lloyd Rd. RM9: Dag 7F 73
Lloyd's Av. EC3 1H 15 (6E 84)
Lloyd's Building 1G 15 (6E 84)
Lloyd's Pl. SE3 2G 123
Lloyd Sq. WC1 1J 7 (3A 84)
Lloyd's Row EC1 2K 7 (3A 84)
Lloyd St. WC1 1J 7 (3A 84)
Lloyds Way BR3: Beck 5A 158
Lloyds Wharf SE1 7K 15 (2F 103)
(off Mill St.)
Lloyd Thomas Ct. N22 7E 32
Lloyd Vs. E6 4C 88
Lloyd Vs. SE4 2C 122
Loader M. SW2 6K 119
Loampit Hill SE13 2C 122
Loampit Rd. DA8: Erith 6J 109
Loampit Va. SE13 3D 122
LOAMPIT VALE 3E 122
Loanda Cl. E8 1F 85
Loats Rd. SW2 6J 119
Lobelia Cl. E6 5C 88
Locarno Ct. SW16 5G 137
Locarno Rd. UB6: G'frd 4H 77
Locarno Rd. W3 1J 97
Lochaber Rd. SE13 4G 123
Lochaline St. W6 6E 98
Lochan Cl. UB4: Yead 4C 76
Loch Cres. HA8: Edg 4A 28
Lochinvar St. SW12 7F 119
Lochleven Ho. N2 2B 46
(off The Grange)
Lochmere Cl. DA8: Erith 6H 109
Lochmore Ho. SW1 4H 17 (4E 100)
(off Cundy St.)
Lochnagar St. E14 5E 86
Lockbridge Ct. W9 5J 81
(off Woodfield Rd.)
Lock Bldg., The E15 2E 86
Lock Chase SE3 3G 123
Lock Cl. UB2: S'hall 2G 95
Lock Cotts. UB1: S'hall 2H 95
Lock Ct. E5 2K 67
Locke Apts. CR0: C'don 2D 168
Locke Hgts. N1 7K 65
(off Caledonian Rd.)
Locke Ho. SW8 1G 119
(off Wadhurst Rd.)
Lockes End E17 4E 50
Lockesfield Pl. E14 5D 104
Lockesley Dr. BR5: St M Cry 6K 161
Lockesley Sq. KT6: Surb 6D 150
Locket Rd. HA3: W'stone 3J 41
Locket Rd. M. HA3: W'stone 2J 41
Lockfield Av. EN3: Brim 2F 25
Lockgate Cl. E9 5B 68
Lockhart Cl. EN3: Pond E 5C 24
Lockhart Cl. N7 6K 65
Lockhart St. E3 4B 86
Lockhouse, The NW1 1E 82
Lockhurst St. E5 4K 67
Lockie Pl. SE25 3G 157
Lockier Wlk. HA9: Wemb 3D 60
Lockington Rd. SW8 1F 119
Lock Keepers Hgts. SE16 3K 103
(off Brunswick Quay)
Lockmead Rd. N15 6G 49
Lockmead Rd. SE13 3E 122
Lock M. NW1 6H 65
(off Northpoint Sq.)
Lock Mill Apts. E2 1F 85
(off Whiston Rd.)
Lock Rd. TW10: Ham 4C 132
LOCKSBOTTOM 3E 172
Locksfields SE17 4D 102
(off Catesby St.)
Lockside E14 7A 86
(off Narrow St.)
Lock Side Way E16 7G 89
Locks La. CR4: Mitc 1E 154
Locksley Est. E14 6B 86
Locksley Ho. E15 6F 69
(off Forrester Way)
Locksley St. E14 5B 86
Locksmeade Rd. TW10: Ham 4C 132
Locksons Cl. E14 5D 86
Lockswood Cl. EN4: Cockf 4J 21
Lockton St. W10 7F 81
(off Bramley Rd.)
Lock Vw. Ct. E14 7A 86
(off Narrow St.)
Lockwell Rd. RM10: Dag 3G 73
Lockwood Cl. SE26 4K 139
Lockwood Ho. E5 2J 67
Lockwood Ho. SE11 7J 19 (6A 102)
Lockwood Ind. Pk. N17 3H 49
Lockwood Pl. E4 6H 35
Lockwood Rd. UB2: S'hall 3E 94
Lockwood Sq. SE16 3H 103
Lockwood Way E17 2K 49
Lockwood Way KT9: Chess 5G 163
Lockworks Ho. E17 4K 49
(off Wickford Way)
Lockyer Est. SE1 7F 15 (2D 102)
(off Kipling St.)
Lockyer Ho. SE10 5H 105
(off Armitage Rd.)
Lockyer Ho. SW15 3F 117
Lockyer Ho. SW8 7H 101
(off Wandsworth Rd.)
Lockyer M. EN3: Enf L 1J 25
Lockyer St. SE1 7F 15 (2D 102)
Locomotive Dr. TW14: Felt 1J 129
Locton Grn. E3 1B 86
Loddiges Ho. E9 7J 67
Loddiges Rd. E9 7J 67
Loddon Ho. NW8 4B 4 (4B 82)
(off Church St. Est.)
Loder St. SE15 7J 103
Lodge, The W12 2F 99
(off Richmond Way)
Lodge Av. CR0: Wadd 3A 168
Lodge Av. HA3: Kenton 4E 42
Lodge Av. RM8: Dag 6B 72
Lodge Av. RM9: Dag 1A 90
Lodge Av. SW14 3A 116
LODGE AVENUE FLYOVER JUNC. 1A 90
Lodge Cl. HA8: Edg 6A 28
Lodge Cl. N18 5H 33
Lodge Cl. SM6: W'gton 1E 166
Lodge Cl. TW7: Isle 1B 114
Lodge Ct. HA0: Wemb 5E 60
(off Station Gro.)
Lodge Dr. N13 4F 33
Lodge Gdns. BR3: Beck 5B 158
Lodge Hill DA16: Well 7B 108
Lodge Hill IG4: Ilf 4C 52
Lodge Hill SE2 7B 108
Lodgehill Pk. Cl. HA2: Harr 2F 59
Lodge La. CR0: New Ad 6C 170
Lodge La. DA5: Bexl 6D 126
Lodge La. N12 5F 31
Lodge M. N5 4C 66
Lodge Pl. SM1: Sutt 5K 165
Lodge Rd. BR1: Broml 7A 142
Lodge Rd. CR0: C'don 6B 156
Lodge Rd. NW4 4E 44
Lodge Rd. NW8 2B 4 (3B 82)
Lodge Rd. SM6: W'gton 5F 167
Lodge Vs. IG8: Wfd G 6C 36
Lodge Way TW15: Ashf 2A 128
Lodge Way TW17: Shep 2E 146
Lodore Gdns. NW9 5A 44
Lodore Grn. UB10: Ick 3A 56
Lodore St. E14 6E 86
Loft, The W12 1F 99
Loft Ho. E1 7J 9 (6F 85)
(off Middlesex St.)
Lofthouse Pl. KT9: Chess 6C 162
Loftie St. SE16 2G 103
Lofting Ho. N1 7A 66
(off Liverpool Rd.)

250 A–Z London

Lysons Wlk. – Malvern Rd.

Lysons Wlk. SW15 4C 116
Lytchet Rd. BR1: Broml 7J 141
Lytchet Way EN3: Enf H 1D 24
Lytchgate Cl. CR2: S Croy 7E 168
Lytcott Dr. KT8: W Mole 3D 148
Lytcott Gro. SE22 5E 120
Lytham Cl. SE28 6E 90
Lytham Gro. W5 3F 79
Lytham St. SE17 5D 102
Lyttelton Cl. NW3 7C 64
Lyttelton Ct. N2 5A 46
Lyttelton Ho. E9 7J 67
(off Well St.)
Lyttelton Rd. E10 3D 68
Lyttelton Rd. N2 5A 46
Lyttelton Theatre 4J 13 (1A 102)
(within National Theatre)
Lyttleton Ct. UB4: Yead 4A 76
(off Dunedin Way)
Lyttleton Rd. N8 3A 48
Lytton Av. N13 2F 33
Lytton Cl. N2 6B 46
Lytton Cl. UB5: N'olt 7D 58
Lytton Ct. WC1 6F 7 (5J 83)
(off Barter St.)
Lytton Gdns. SM6: Bedd 4H 167
Lytton Gro. SW15 5F 117
Lytton Rd. E11 7G 51
Lytton Rd. EN5: New Bar 4F 21
Lytton Rd. HA5: Pinn 1C 40
Lytton Strachey Path SE28 7B 90
Lytton Ter. E12 6D 70
Lyveden Rd. SE3 7K 105
Lyveden Rd. SW17 6D 136

M

Mabbett Ho. SE18 6E 106
(off Nightingale Pl.)
Mabel Evetts Ct. UB3: Hayes 7K 75
Maberley Cres. SE19 7G 139
Maberley Rd. BR3: Beck 3K 157
Maberley Rd. SE19 1F 157
Mabledon Pl. WC1 2D 6 (3H 83)
Mablethorpe Rd. SW6 7G 99
Mabley St. E9 5A 68
Mablin Lodge IG9: Buck H 1F 37
McAdam Dr. EN2: Enf 2G 23
McAllister Gro. IG11: Bark 3A 90
Macaret Cl. N20 7E 20
Macarthur Cl. DA8: Erith 5K 109
Macarthur Cl. E7 6J 69
Macarthur Cl. HA9: Wemb 6H 61
Macarthur Ter. SE7 6B 106
Macartney Ho. SE10 7F 105
(off Chesterfield Wlk.)
Macartney Ho. SW9 1A 120
(off Gosling Way)
Macaulay Ct. SW4 3F 119
Macaulay Rd. E6 2B 88
Macaulay Rd. SW4 3F 119
Macaulay Sq. SW4 4F 119
Macaulay Wlk. SW9 1K 119
(off Lett Rd.)
Macaulay Way SE28 1B 108
McAuley Cl. SE1 1J 19 (3A 102)
McAuley Cl. SE9 5F 125
Macauley Ho. W10 5G 81
(off Portobello Rd.)
Macauley M. SE13 2E 122
McAusland Ho. E3 2B 86
(off Wright's Rd.)
Macbean St. SE18 3F 107
Macbeth Ho. N1 2E 84
Macbeth St. W6 5D 98
McBride Ho. E3 2B 86
(off Libra Rd.)
McCabe Ct. E16 5H 87
(off Barking Rd.)
McCall Cl. SW4 2J 119
McCall Cres. SE7 5C 106
McCall Ho. N7 4J 65
McCarthy Rd. TW13: Hanw 5B 130
Macclesfield Apts. N1 1D 84
(off Branch Pl.)
Macclesfield Ho. EC1 2C 8 (3C 84)
(off Central St.)
Macclesfield Rd. EC1 1C 8 (3C 84)
Macclesfield Rd. SE25 5J 157
Macclesfield St. W1 2D 12 (7H 83)
McCoid Way SE1 7C 14 (2C 102)
McCrone M. NW3 6B 64
McCullum Rd. E3 1B 86
McDermott Cl. SW11 3C 118
McDermott Rd. SE15 3G 121
Macdonald Av. RM10: Dag 3H 73
Macdonald Ho. SW11 2E 118
(off Dagnall St.)
McDonald Ho. NW6 3J 81
(off Malvern Rd.)
Macdonald Rd. E17 2E 50
(not continuous)
Macdonald Rd. E7 4J 69
Macdonald Rd. N11 5J 31
Macdonald Rd. N19 2G 65
McDonough Cl. KT9: Chess 4E 162
McDougall Ct. TW9: Rich 2G 115
McDowall Cl. E16 5H 87
McDowall Rd. SE5 1C 120
Macduff Rd. SW11 1E 118
Mace Cl. E1 1H 103
Mace Ho. TW7: Isle 1B 114
McEntee Av. E17 1A 50
Mace St. E2 2K 85
McEwan Ho. E3 2B 86
(off Roman Rd.)
McEwen Way E15 1F 87
(off Rokeby St.)
Macey Ho. SW11 1C 118
Macey St. SE10 6E 104
(off Thames St.)
McFadden Ct. E10 3D 68
(off Buckingham Rd.)
Macfarland Gro. SE15 7E 102
Macfarlane La. TW7: Isle 6K 95
Macfarlane Rd. W12 1E 98
Macfarren Pl. NW1 4H 5 (4E 82)
Macfarron Ho. W10 3G 81
(off Parry Rd.)
McGlashon Ho. E1 4K 9 (4G 85)
(off Hunton St.)
McGrath Rd. E15 5H 69
McGregor Ct. N1 1H 9 (3E 84)
(off Hoxton St.)
Macgregor Rd. E16 5A 88
McGregor Rd. W11 6H 81
Machell Rd. SE15 3J 121
McIndoe Ct. N1 1D 84
(off Sherborne St.)
McIntosh Cl. RM1: Rom 3K 55
McIntosh Cl. SM6: W'gton 7J 167
Macintosh Ho. W1 5H 5 (5E 82)
(off Beaumont St.)
McIntosh Ho. SE16 4J 103
(off Millender Wlk.)
McIntosh Ho. SE20 1G 157
McIntosh Rd. RM1: Rom 3K 55
McIntyre Ct. SE18 4C 106
(off Prospect Va.)
Mackay Ho. W12 7D 80
(off White City Est.)
Mackay Rd. SW4 3F 119
McKay Rd. SW20 7D 134
McKay Trad. Est. SL3: Poyle 5A 174
McKeever Ho. E16 5J 87
(off Hammersley Rd.)
McKellar Cl. WD23: B Hea 2B 26
McKenna Ho. E3 2B 86
(off Wright's Rd.)
Mackennal St. NW8 2C 82
Mackenzie Cl. W12 7D 80
Mackenzie Ho. N8 4J 47
(off Pembroke Rd.)
Mackenzie Ho. NW2 3C 62
Mackenzie Rd. BR3: Beck 2J 157
Mackenzie Rd. N7 6K 65
Mackenzie Wlk. E14 1C 104
McKerrell Rd. SE15 1G 121
Mackeson Rd. NW3 4D 64
Mackie Rd. SW2 7A 120
McKillop Way DA14: Sidc 7C 144
Mackintosh La. E9 5K 67
Mackintosh St. BR2: Broml 6B 160
Macklin St. WC2 7F 7 (6J 83)
Mackonochie Ho. EC1 5J 7 (5A 84)
(off Baldwins Gdns.)
Mackrow Wlk. E14 7E 86
Mack's Rd. SE16 4G 103
Mackworth Ho. NW1 1A 6 (3G 83)
(off Augustus St.)
Mackworth St. NW1 1A 6 (3G 83)
McLaren Ho. SE1 7A 14 (3B 102)
(off St Georges Cir.)
Maclaren M. SW15 4E 116
Maclean Rd. SE23 6A 122
McLeod Ct. SE22 1G 139
Macleod Rd. N21 5D 22
McLeod Rd. SE2 4B 108
McLeod's M. SW7 4K 99
Macleod St. SE17 5C 102
Maclise Ho. SW1 4E 18 (4J 101)
(off Marsham St.)
Maclise Rd. W14 3G 99
Macmillan Ct. HA2: Harr 1E 58
Macmillan Ct. UB6: G'frd 4H 77
Macmillan Ho. NW8 2D 4 (3C 82)
(off Lorne Cl.)
McMillan Ho. SE14 1A 122
McMillan Ho. SE4 3A 122
(off Arica Rd.)
McMillan St. SE8 6C 104
McMillan Student Village SE8 6C 104
Macmillan Way SW17 4F 137
McNair Rd. UB2: S'hall 3F 95
Macnamara Ho. SW10 7B 100
(off Worlds End Est.)
McNeil Rd. SE5 2E 120
McNicol Dr. NW10 2J 79
Macoma Rd. SE18 6H 107
Macoma Ter. SE18 6H 107
Maconochies Rd. E14 5D 104
MacOwan Theatre 4J 99
Macquarie Way E14 4D 104
McRae La. CR4: Mitc 7D 154
Macready Ho. W1 6D 4 (5C 82)
(off Crawford St.)
Macready Pl. N7 4J 65
(not continuous)
Mcready Rd. N20 2G 31
Macrea Ho. E3 3B 86
(off Bow Rd.)
Macroom Ho. W9 3H 81
(off Macroom Rd.)
Macroom Rd. W9 3H 81
Macs Ho. E17 3D 50
Mac's Pl. EC4 7K 7 (6A 84)
(off Greystoke Pl.)
Madame Tussaud's 4G 5 (4E 82)
Mada Rd. BR6: Farnb 3F 173
Maddams St. E3 4D 86
Madderfields Ct. N11 1H 47
Maddison Cl. N2 2A 46
Maddison Cl. TW11: Tedd 6K 131
Maddison Ct. E16 5J 87
(off Hastings Rd.)
Maddocks Cl. DA14: Sidc 5E 144
Maddocks Ho. E1 7H 85
(off Cornwall St.)
Maddock Way SE17 6B 102
Maddox St. W1 2K 11 (7F 83)
Madeira Av. BR1: Broml 7G 141
Madeira Gro. IG8: Wfd G 6F 37
Madeira Rd. CR4: Mitc 4D 154
Madeira Rd. E11 1F 69
Madeira Rd. N13 4G 33
Madeira Rd. SW16 5J 137
Madeira St. E14 5D 86
Madeira Twr. SW11 7H 101
Madeleine Cl. RM6: Chad H 6C 54
Madeleine Ct. HA7: Stan 7K 27
(off Letchworth Rd.)
Madeley Rd. W5 6D 78
Madeline Gro. IG1: Ilf 5H 71
Madeline Rd. SE20 7G 139
Madge Gill Way E6 1C 88
(off High St. Nth.)
Madge Hill W7 7J 77
Madinah Rd. E8 6G 67
Madison, The SE1 6E 14 (2D 102)
(off Long La.)
Madison Bldg. SE10 1D 122
(off Blackheath Rd.)
Madison Cl. SM2: Sutt 7B 166
Madison Ct. RM10: Dag 6H 73
Madison Cres. DA7: Bex 7C 108
Madison Gdns. BR2: Broml 3H 159
Madison Gdns. DA7: Bex 7C 108
Madison Ho. E14 7B 86
(off Victory Pl.)
Madison Way E20 5D 68
Madoc Cl. NW2 2J 63
Madras Pl. N7 6A 66
Madras Rd. IG1: Ilf 4F 71
Madrid Rd. SW13 1C 116
Madrigal La. SE5 7B 102
Madron St. SE17 5E 102
Mafeking Av. E6 2C 88
Mafeking Av. IG2: Ilf 7H 53
Mafeking Av. TW8: Bford 6E 96
Mafeking Rd. E16 4H 87
Mafeking Rd. EN1: Enf 3A 24
Mafeking Rd. N17 2G 49
Magazine Ga. W2 4D 10 (1C 100)
Magdala Av. N19 2G 65
Magdala Rd. CR2: S Croy 7D 168
Magdala Rd. TW7: Isle 3A 114
Magdalene Cl. SE15 2H 121
Magdalene Gdns. E6 4E 88
Magdalene Gdns. N20 1J 31
Magdalene Rd. TW17: Shep 4B 146
Magdalen Ho. E16 1K 105
(off Keats Av.)
Magdalen M. NW3 6A 64
(off Frognal)
Magdalen Pas. E1 2K 15 (7F 85)
Magdalen Rd. SW18 1A 136
Magdalen St. SE1 5G 15 (1E 102)
Magee St. SE11 7J 19 (6A 102)
Magellan Blvd. E16 7G 89
Magellan Ct. NW10 7K 61
(off Brentfield Rd.)
Magellan Ho. E1 4K 85
(off Ernest St.)
Magellan Pl. E14 4C 104
Magic Circle 3B 6 (4G 83)
(off Stephenson Way)
Magistrates' Court Barkingside 3G 53
Magistrates' Court Belmarsh 2J 107
Magistrates' Court Bexley 4G 127
Magistrates' Court Bromley 1H 159
Magistrates' Court City of London
1E 14 (6D 84)
(off Queen Victoria St.)
Magistrates' Court Croydon 3D 168
Magistrates' Court Ealing 1A 96
(off Green Man La.)
Magistrates' Court Hendon 6B 44
Magistrates' Court Highbury Corner
6A 66
Magistrates' Court Lavender Hill 3D 118
Magistrates' Court Stratford 7F 69
Magistrates' Court Thames 3C 86
Magistrates' Court Westminster
5D 4 (5C 82)
Magistrates' Court Willesden 6B 62
Magistrates' Court Wimbledon 6J 135
Magna Sq. SW14 3J 115
(off Moore Cl.)
Magnaville Rd. WD23: B Hea 1D 26
Magnet Rd. HA9: Wemb 2D 60
Magnin Cl. E8 1G 85
Magnolia Cl. E10 2C 68
Magnolia Cl. KT2: King T 6H 133
Magnolia Ct. HA3: Kenton 7F 43
Magnolia Ct. SM2: Sutt 7J 165
(off Grange Rd.)
Magnolia Ct. SM6: W'gton 5F 167
Magnolia Ct. TW13: Felt 1J 129
(off Plum Cl.)
Magnolia Ct. TW9: Kew 1H 115
Magnolia Ct. UB10: Hil 6D 56
Magnolia Ct. UB5: N'olt 4C 76
Magnolia Gdns. E10 2C 68
Magnolia Gdns. HA8: Edg 4D 28
Magnolia Ho. SE8 6B 104
(off Evelyn St.)
Magnolia Ho. TW16: Sun 7H 129
Magnolia Lodge E4 3J 35
Magnolia Lodge W8 3K 99
(off St Mary's Ga.)
Magnolia Pl. HA2: Harr 2H 41
Magnolia Pl. SW4 5J 119
Magnolia Pl. W5 5D 78
Magnolia Rd. W4 6H 97
Magnolia St. UB7: W Dray 1E 174
Magnolia Way KT19: Ewe 5J 163
Magnolia Wharf W4 6G 97
Magpie All. EC4 1K 13 (6A 84)
Magpie Cl. E7 5H 69
Magpie Cl. EN1: Enf 1B 24
Magpie Cl. NW9 2A 44
Magpie Hall Cl. BR2: Broml 6C 160
Magpie Hall La. BR2: Broml 5D 160
Magpie Hall Rd. WD23: B Hea 2D 26
Magpie Ho. E3 1B 86
(off Sycamore Av.)
Magpie Pl. SE14 6A 104
Magri Wlk. E1 5J 85
Maguire Apts. E3 5B 86
(off Geoff Cade Way)
Maguire Dr. TW10: Ham 4C 132
Maguire St. SE1 6K 15 (2F 103)
Maha Bldg. E3 3C 86
(off Merchant St.)
Mahatma Gandhi Ind. Est. SE24 4B 120
Mahlon Av. HA4: Ruis 5K 57
(not continuous)
Mahogany Cl. SE16 1A 104
Mahon Cl. EN1: Enf 1A 24
Mahoney Ho. SE14 1B 122
(off Heald St.)
Maibeth Gdns. BR3: Beck 4A 158
Maida Av. E4 7J 25
Maida Av. W2 5A 82
MAIDA HILL 4H 81
Maida Rd. DA17: Belv 3G 109
Maida Va. W9 2K 81
MAIDA VALE 4K 81
Maida Way E4 7J 25
Maiden Erlegh Av. DA5: Bexl 1E 144
Maiden La. NW1 7H 65
Maiden La. SE1 5D 14 (1C 102)
Maiden La. WC2 3F 13 (7J 83)
Maiden Pl. NW5 3G 65
Maiden Rd. E15 7G 69
Maidenstone Hill SE10 1E 122
Maids of Honour Row TW9: Rich 5D 114
Maidstone Av. RM5: Col R 2J 55
Maidstone Bldgs. M. SE1
5D 14 (1C 102)
Maidstone Ho. E14 6D 86
(off Carmen St.)
Maidstone Rd. DA14: Sidc 6D 144
Maidstone Rd. DA14: Swan 6D 144
Maidstone Rd. N11 6B 32
Mailcoach Yd. E2 1H 9 (3E 84)
Main Av. EN1: Enf 5A 24
Main Dr. HA9: Wemb 3D 60
Maine Twr. E14 2D 104
Main Mill SE10 7D 104
(off Greenwich High St.)
Mainridge Rd. BR7: Chst 4E 142
Main Rd. DA14: Sidc 3H 143
Main St. TW13: Hanw 5B 130
Mainwaring Ct. CR4: Mitc 2E 154
Mais Ho. SE26 2H 139
Maismore St. SE15 6G 103
Maisonettes, The SM1: Sutt 5H 165
Maison Ho. N20 1F 31
Maitland Cl. SE10 7D 104
Maitland Cl. TW4: Houn 3D 112
Maitland Ct. W2 2A 10 (7B 82)
(off Lancaster Ter.)
Maitland Ho. E2 2J 85
(off Waterloo Gdns.)
Maitland Ho. SW1 7A 18 (6G 101)
(off Churchill Gdns.)
Maitland Pk. Est. NW3 6D 64
Maitland Pk. Rd. NW3 6D 64
Maitland Pk. Vs. NW3 6D 64
Maitland Pl. E5 4H 67
Maitland Rd. E15 6H 69
Maitland Rd. SE26 6K 139
Maitland Yd. W13 1A 96
Maize Row E14 7B 86
Majendie Rd. SE18 5H 107
Majestic Way CR4: Mitc 2D 154
Major Cl. SW9 3B 120
Major Draper St. SE18 3F 107
Major Rd. E15 5F 69
Major Rd. SE16 3G 103
Makepeace Av. N6 2E 64
Makepeace Mans. N6 2E 64
Makepeace Rd. E11 4J 51
Makepeace Rd. UB5: N'olt 2C 76
Makers' Yd. E20 6C 68
Makinen Ho. IG9: Buck H 1F 37
Makins St. SW3 4D 16 (4C 100)
Malabar Ct. W12 7D 80
(off India Way)
Malabar St. E14 2C 104
Malam Ct. SE11 4J 19 (4A 102)
Malam Gdns. E14 7D 86
Malbrook Rd. SW15 4D 116
Malcolm Cl. SE20 7J 139
Malcolm Ct. E7 6H 69
Malcolm Ct. HA7: Stan 5H 27
Malcolm Ct. NW4 6C 44
Malcolm Cres. NW4 6C 44
Malcolm Dr. KT6: Surb 1E 162
Malcolm Ho. N1 2E 84
(off Arden Est.)
Malcolm Pl. E2 4J 85
Malcolm Rd. E1 4J 85
Malcolm Rd. SE20 7J 139
Malcolm Rd. SE25 6G 157
Malcolm Rd. SW19 6G 135
Malcolm Rd. UB10: Ick 4B 56
Malcolm Sargent Ho. E16 1K 105
(off Evelyn Rd.)
Malcolmson Ho. SW1 6C 18 (5H 101)
(off Aylesford St.)
Malcolms Way N14 5B 22
Malcolm Way E11 5J 51
Malden Av. SE25 4H 157
Malden Av. UB6: G'frd 5J 59
Malden Ct. KT3: N Mald 3D 152
Malden Ct. N4 6C 48
Malden Cres. NW1 6E 64
Malden Golf Course 2A 152
MALDEN GREEN 1C 164
Malden Grn. Av. KT4: Wor Pk 1B 164
Malden Grn. M. KT4: Wor Pk 1C 164
Malden Hill KT3: N Mald 3B 152
Malden Hill Gdns. KT3: N Mald 3B 152
MALDEN JUNC. 5B 152
Malden Pk. KT3: N Mald 6B 152
Malden Pl. NW5 5E 64
Malden Rd. KT3: N Mald 5A 152
Malden Rd. KT4: Wor Pk 7B 152
Malden Rd. NW5 5D 64
Malden Rd. SM3: Cheam 4F 165
Malden Way KT3: N Mald 7K 151
Maldon & District Society of Model Engineers 1A 162
Maldon Cl. E15 5G 69
Maldon Cl. N1 1C 84
Maldon Cl. SE5 3E 120
Maldon Ct. E6 1E 88
Maldon Ct. SM6: W'gton 5G 167
Maldon Rd. N9 3A 34
Maldon Rd. RM7: Rush G 7J 55
Maldon Rd. SM6: W'gton 5F 167
Maldon Rd. W3 7J 79
Maldon Wlk. IG8: Wfd G 6F 37
Malet Pl. WC1 4C 6 (4H 83)
Malet St. WC1 4C 6 (4H 83)
Maley Av. SE27 2B 138
Malford Ct. E18 2J 51
Malford Gro. E18 4H 51
Malfort Rd. SE5 3E 120
Malham Cl. N11 6K 31
Malham Rd. SE23 1K 139
Malham Rd. Ind. Est. SE23 1K 139
Malham Ter. N18 5C 34
Malibu Ct. SE26 3H 139
Mall, The BR1: Broml 3J 159
Mall, The CR0: C'don 2C 168
Mall, The DA6: Bex 4G 127
Mall, The E15 7F 69
Mall, The HA3: Kenton 6F 43
Mall, The KT6: Surb 5D 150
Mall, The N14 3D 32
Mall, The RM10: Dag 6G 73
Mall, The SW1 6B 12 (2G 101)
Mall, The SW14 5J 115
Mall, The TW8: Bford 6D 96
Mall, The W5 7E 78
Mallams M. SW9 3B 120
Mallard Cl. E9 6B 68
Mallard Cl. EN5: New Bar 6G 21
Mallard Cl. NW6 2J 81
Mallard Cl. TW2: Whitt 7E 112
Mallard Cl. W7 2J 95
Mallard Ct. E17 3F 51
Mallard Ho. NW8 2C 82
(off Bridgeman St.)
Mallard Ho. SW6 1A 118
(off Station Ct.)
Mallard Path SE28 3H 107
Mallard Pl. N22 2K 47
Mallard Pl. TW1: Twick 3A 132
Mallard Point E3 3D 86
(off Rainhill Way)
Mallards E11 7J 51
(off Blake Hall Rd.)
Mallards Rd. IG11: Bark 4A 90
Mallards Rd. IG8: Wfd G 7E 36
Mallard Wlk. BR3: Beck 5K 157
Mallard Wlk. DA14: Sidc 6C 144
Mallard Way NW9 7J 43
Mallard Way SM6: W'gton 7G 167
Mall Chambers W8 1J 99
(off Kensington Mall)
Mallet Dr. UB5: N'olt 5D 58
Mallet Rd. SE13 6F 123
Mall Galleries 4D 12 (1H 101)
(off The Mall)
Malling SE13 5D 122
Malling Cl. CR0: C'don 6J 157
Malling Gdns. SM4: Mord 6A 154
Malling Way BR2: Hayes 7H 159
Mallinson Rd. CR0: Bedd 3H 167
Mallinson Rd. SW11 5C 118
Mallinson Sports Cen. 7D 46
Mallon Gdns. E1 7K 9 (6F 85)
(off Commercial St.)
Mallord St. SW3 7B 16 (6B 100)
Mallory Bldgs. EC1 4A 8 (4B 84)
(off St John St.)
Mallory Cl. E14 5D 86
Mallory Cl. SE4 4A 122
Mallory Ct. N17 6A 34
(off Cannon Rd.)
Mallory Ct. SE12 7K 123
Mallory Gdns. EN4: E Barn 7K 21
Mallory St. NW8 3C 4 (4C 82)
Mallory Way SE3 4K 123
Mallow Cl. CR0: C'don 1K 169
Mallow Mead NW7 7B 30
Mallows, The UB10: Ick 3D 56
Mallow St. EC1 3E 8 (4D 84)
Mall Rd. W6 5D 98
Mall Vs. W6 5D 98
(off Mall Rd.)
Malmains Cl. BR3: Beck 4F 159
Malmains Way BR3: Beck 4E 158
Malmesbury E2 2J 85
(off Cyprus St.)
Malmesbury Cl. HA5: Eastc 4H 39
Malmesbury Rd. E16 5G 87
Malmesbury Rd. E18 1H 51
Malmesbury Rd. E3 3B 86
Malmesbury Rd. SM4: Mord 7A 154
Malmesbury Ter. E16 5H 87
Malmo Twr. SE8 4A 104
Malmsey Ho. SE11 5H 19 (5K 101)
Malmsmead Ho. E9 5B 68
(off Homerton Rd.)
Malory Cl. BR3: Beck 2A 158
Malpas Dr. HA5: Pinn 5B 40
Malpas Rd. E8 5H 67
Malpas Rd. RM9: Dag 6D 72
Malpas Rd. SE4 2B 122
Malswick Ct. SE15 7E 102
(off Tower Mill Rd.)
Malta Rd. E10 1C 68
Malta St. EC1 3B 8 (4B 84)
Maltby Cl. BR6: Orp 1K 173
Maltby Dr. EN1: Enf 1C 24
Maltby Ho. SE1 7J 15 (3F 103)
(off Maltby St.)
Maltby Ho. SE3 4A 124
Maltby Rd. KT9: Chess 6G 163
Maltby St. SE1 7J 15 (2F 103)
Malt Ho. E17 5B 50
(off Old Brewery Way)
Malthouse Ct. TW8: Bford 6E 96
(off High St.)
Malthouse Dr. TW13: Hanw 5B 130
Malthouse Dr. W4 6B 98
Malthouse Pas. SW13 2B 116
(off Clevelands Gdns.)
Malt Ho. Pl. RM1: Rom 5K 55
Malthouse Rd. SW11 7H 101
Malthus Path SE28 1C 108
Malting Ho. E14 7B 86
(off Oak La.)
Maltings, The BR6: Orp 1K 173
Maltings, The W4 5G 97
(off Spring Gro.)
Maltings Cl. E3 3E 86
Maltings Cl. SW13 2B 116
Maltings Lodge W4 6A 98
(off Corney Reach Way)
Maltings M. DA15: Sidc 3A 144
Maltings Pl. SE1 6H 15 (2E 102)
(off Roper La.)
Maltings Pl. SW6 1K 117
Malting Way TW7: Isle 3K 113
Malton M. SE18 6J 107
Malton M. W10 6G 81
Malton Rd. W10 6G 81
Malton St. SE18 6J 107
Malt St. SE1 6G 103
Malva Cl. SW18 5K 117
Malvern Av. DA7: Bex 7E 108
Malvern Av. E4 7A 36
Malvern Av. HA2: Harr 3C 58
Malvern Cl. CR4: Mitc 3G 155
Malvern Cl. KT6: Surb 1E 162
Malvern Cl. SE20 2G 157
Malvern Cl. UB10: Ick 2C 56
Malvern Cl. W10 5H 81
Malvern Ct. SM2: Sutt 7J 165
Malvern Ct. SW7 3B 16 (4B 100)
(off Onslow Sq.)
Malvern Ct. W12 2C 98
(off Hadyn Pk. Rd.)
Malvern Dr. IG3: Bark 4K 71
Malvern Dr. IG3: Ilf 4K 71
Malvern Dr. IG8: Wfd G 5F 37
Malvern Dr. TW13: Hanw 5B 130
Malvern Gdns. HA3: Kenton 4E 42
Malvern Gdns. NW2 2G 63
Malvern Ho. N16 1F 67
Malvern Ho. SE17 5C 102
(off Liverpool Gro.)
Malvern M. NW6 3J 81
Malvern Pl. NW6 3H 81
Malvern Rd. CR7: Thor H 4A 156
Malvern Rd. E11 2G 69
Malvern Rd. E6 1C 88
Malvern Rd. E8 7G 67
Malvern Rd. KT6: Surb 2E 162

A–Z London 253

Malvern Rd. – Margin Dr.

Malvern Rd. N17 3G 49
Malvern Rd. N8 3A 48
Malvern Rd. NW6 2H 81
(not continuous)
Malvern Rd. TW12: Hamp 7C 130
Malvern Rd. UB3: Harl 7G 93
Malvern Ter. N1 1A 84
Malvern Ter. N9 1A 34
Malvern Way W13 5B 78
Malwood Rd. SW12 6F 119
Malyons, The TW17: Shep 6F 147
Malyons Rd. SE13 6D 122
Malyons Ter. SE13 5D 122
Managers St. E14 1E 104
Manatee Pl. SM6: Bedd 3H 167
Manaton Cl. SE15 3H 121
Manaton Cres. UB1: S'hall 6E 76
Manbey Gro. E15 6G 69
Manbey M. E15 6G 69
Manbey Pk. Rd. E15 6G 69
Manbey Rd. E15 6G 69
Manbey St. E15 6G 69
Manbre Rd. W6 6E 98
Manbrough Av. E6 3D 88
Manby Wlk. E17 5A 50
Manchester Ct. E16 6K 87
(off Garvary Rd.)
Manchester Dr. W10 4G 81
Manchester Gro. E14 5E 104
Manchester Ho. SE17 5C 102
(off East St.)
Manchester M. W1 6G 5 (5E 82)
(off Manchester St.)
Manchester Rd. CR7: Thor H 3C 156
Manchester Rd. E14 5E 104
Manchester Rd. N15 6D 48
Manchester Sq. W1 7G 5 (6E 82)
Manchester St. W1 6G 5 (5E 82)
Manchester Way RM10: Dag 4H 73
Manchuria Rd. SW11 6E 118
Manciple St. SE1 7E 14 (2D 102)
Mancroft Ct. NW8 1B 82
(off St John's Wood Pk.)
Mandalay Rd. SW4 5G 119
Mandara Pl. SE8 4A 104
(off Yeoman St.)
Mandarin Ct. NW10 6K 61
(off Mitchellbrook Way)
Mandarin Ct. SE8 6B 104
Mandarin St. E14 7C 86
Mandarin Way UB4: Yead 6B 76
Mandarin Wharf N1 1E 84
(off De Beauvoir Cres.)
Mandela Cl. NW10 7J 61
Mandela Cl. W12 7D 80
Mandela Ho. E2 2J 9 (3F 85)
(off Virginia Rd.)
Mandela Ho. SE5 2B 120
Mandela Rd. E16 6J 87
Mandela St. NW1 1G 83
Mandela St. SW9 7A 102
(not continuous)
Mandela Way SE1 4E 102
Mandeley M. E11 1H 69
Mandel Ho. SW18 4J 117
Manderley W14 3H 99
(off Oakwood La.)
Mandeville Cl. SE3 7H 105
Mandeville Cl. SW20 7G 135
Mandeville Ct. E4 5F 35
Mandeville Dr. KT6: Surb 1D 162
Mandeville Ho. SE1 5F 103
(off Rolls Rd.)
Mandeville Ho. SW4 5G 119
Mandeville M. SW4 4J 119
Mandeville Pl. W1 7H 5 (6E 82)
Mandeville Rd. N14 2A 32
Mandeville Rd. TW17: Shep 5C 146
Mandeville Rd. TW7: Isle 2A 114
Mandeville Rd. UB5: N'olt 7E 58
Mandeville St. E5 3A 68
Mandrake Rd. SW17 3D 136
Mandrake Way E15 7G 69
Mandrell Rd. SW2 5J 119
Manesty Ct. N14 7C 22
(off Ivy Rd.)
Manet Gdns. W3 7A 80
Manette St. W1 1D 12 (6H 83)
Manfred Rd. SW15 5H 117
Manger Rd. N7 6J 65
Mangold Way DA18: Erith 3D 108
Manhattan Bldg. E3 2C 86
Manhattan Bus. Pk. W5 3E 78
Manhattan Loft Gdns. E20 6E 68
Manilla Ct. RM6: Chad H 6B 54
(off Quarles Pk. Rd.)
Manilla St. E14 2C 104
Manilla Wlk. SE10 4G 105
Manister Rd. SE2 3A 108
Manitoba Ct. SE16 2J 103
(off Canada Est.)
Manitoba Gdns. BR6: Chels 6K 173
Manley Ct. N16 3F 67
Manley Ho. SE11 4J 19 (4A 102)
Manley St. NW1 1E 82
Manna Ho. E20 6E 68
(off Glade Wlk.)
Mannan Ho. E3 2B 86
(off Roman Rd.)
Mann Cl. CR0: C'don 3C 168
Manneby Prior N1 1H 7 (2K 83)
(off Cumming St.)
Mannequin Ho. E17 3K 49
Manning Ct. SE28 1B 108
(off Titmuss Av.)
Manningford Cl. EC1 1A 8 (3B 84)
Manning Gdns. CR0: C'don 7H 157
Manning Gdns. HA3: Kenton 7D 42
Manning Ho. W11 6G 81
(off Westbourne Pk. Rd.)
Manning Pl. TW10: Rich 6F 115
Manning Rd. E17 5A 50
Manning Rd. RM10: Dag 6G 73
Manningtree Cl. SW19 1G 135
Manningtree Rd. HA4: Ruis 4K 57
Manningtree St. E1 7K 9 (6G 85)
Mannin Rd. RM6: Chad H 7B 54
Mannock Cl. NW9 3K 43
Mannock M. E18 1A 52
Mannock Rd. N22 3B 48
Mann's Cl. TW7: Isle 5K 113
Manns Rd. HA8: Edg 6B 28
Manns Ter. SE27 3C 138
Manny Shinwell Ho. SW6 6H 99
(off Clem Attlee Ct.)
Manoel Rd. TW2: Twick 2G 131
Manor, The IG8: Wfd G 7K 37
Manor Av. SE4 2B 122
Manor Av. TW4: Houn 3B 112
Manor Av. UB5: N'olt 7D 58
Manorbrook SE3 4J 123
MANOR CIRCUS 3G 115
Manor Cl. DA1: Cray 4K 127
Manor Cl. E17 2A 50
Manor Cl. EN5: Barn 4B 20
Manor Cl. HA4: Ruis 1H 57
Manor Cl. KT4: Wor Pk 1A 164
Manor Cl. NW7 5E 28
Manor Cl. NW9 5H 43
Manor Cl. RM10: Dag 6K 73
Manor Cl. SE28 7C 90
Manor Cotts. HA6: Nwood 1H 39
Manor Cotts. N2 2A 46
(off Manor Cotts. App.)
Manor Cotts. App. N2 2A 46
Manor Ct. BR4: W W'ck 1D 170
Manor Ct. DA7: Bex 4H 127
Manor Ct. E10 1D 68
Manor Ct. E4 1B 36
Manor Ct. HA1: Harr 6K 41
Manor Ct. HA9: Wemb 5E 60
Manor Ct. IG11: Bark 7K 71
Manor Ct. KT2: King T 1G 151
Manor Ct. KT8: W Mole 4E 148
Manor Ct. N14 2C 32
Manor Ct. N2 5D 46
Manor Ct. N20 3J 31
(off York Way)
Manor Ct. SM5: Cars 3E 166
Manor Ct. SW16 3J 137
Manor Ct. SW2 5K 119
Manor Ct. SW3 6D 16 (5C 100)
(off Hemus Pl.)
Manor Ct. SW6 1K 117
Manor Ct. TW2: Twick 2G 131
Manor Ct. W3 4G 97
Manor Ct. Rd. W7 7J 77
Manor Cres. KT5: Surb 6G 151
Manor Dene SE28 6C 90
Manordene Cl. KT7: T Ditt 1A 162
Manordene Rd. SE28 6C 90
Manor Dr. HA9: Wemb 4F 61
Manor Dr. KT10: Hin W 2A 162
Manor Dr. KT19: Ewe 6A 164
Manor Dr. KT5: Surb 6F 151
Manor Dr. N14 1A 32
Manor Dr. N20 4J 31
Manor Dr. NW7 5E 28
Manor Dr. TW13: Hanw 5B 130
Manor Dr. TW16: Sun 2J 147
Manor Dr., The KT4: Wor Pk 1A 164
Manor Dr. Nth. KT3: N Mald 7K 151
Manor Dr. Nth. KT4: Wor Pk 1K 151
Manor Est. SE16 4H 103
Manor Farm Ruislip 7G 39
Manor Farm Av. TW17: Shep 6D 146
Manor Farm Cl. KT4: Wor Pk 1A 164
Manor Farm Ct. E6 3D 88
Manor Farm Dr. E4 3B 36
Manor Farm Rd. HA0: Wemb 2D 78
Manor Farm Rd. SW16 2A 156
Manorfield Cl. N19 4G 65
(off Fulbrook M.)
Manor Flds. SW15 6F 117
Manorfields Cl. BR7: Chst 3K 161
Manor Gdns. CR2: S Croy 6F 169
Manor Gdns. HA4: Ruis 5A 58
Manor Gdns. N7 3J 65
Manor Gdns. SW20 2H 153
Manor Gdns. TW12: Hamp 7F 131
Manor Gdns. TW16: Sun 1J 147
Manor Gdns. TW9: Rich 4F 115
Manor Gdns. W3 4G 97
Manor Gdns. W4 5A 98
Manor Ga. UB5: N'olt 7C 58
Manorgate Rd. KT2: King T 1G 151
Manor Gro. BR3: Beck 2D 158
Manor Gro. SE15 6J 103
Manor Gro. TW9: Rich 4G 115
Manor Hall Av. NW4 2F 45
Manor Hall Gdns. NW4 2F 45
Manorhall Gdns. E10 1C 68
Manor Ho. NW1 5D 4 (5C 82)
(off Lisson Gro.)
Manor Ho. UB2: S'hall 3C 94
MANOR HOUSE 7C 48
MANOR HOUSE 7D 48
Manor Ho. Ct. TW17: Shep 7D 146
Manor Ho. Ct. W9 4A 82
(off Warrington Gdns.)
Manor Ho. Dr. HA6: Nwood 1D 38
Manor Ho. Dr. NW6 7F 63
Manor Ho. Est. HA7: Stan 6G 27
Manor Ho. Gdn. E11 6K 51
Manor Ho. Way TW7: Isle 3B 114
Manor La. SE12 5G 123
Manor La. SE13 5G 123
Manor La. SM1: Sutt 5A 166
Manor La. TW13: Felt 2J 129
Manor La. TW16: Sun 2J 147
Manor La. UB3: Harl 6F 93
Manor La. Ter. SE13 4G 123
Manor Lodge NW6 7F 63
(off Willesden La.)
Manor M. NW6 2J 81
(off Cambridge Av.)
Manor M. SE4 2B 122
Manor Mt. SE23 1J 139
Manor Pde. HA1: Harr 6K 41
Manor Pde. N16 2F 67
Manor Pde. NW10 2B 80
(off High St. Harlesden)
Manor Pk. BR7: Chst 2H 161
MANOR PARK 4B 70
Manor Pk. SE13 4F 123
Manor Pk. TW13: Felt 2J 129
Manor Pk. TW9: Rich 4F 115
Manor Pk. Cl. BR4: W W'ck 1D 170
Manor Pk. Crematorium 4A 70
Manor Pk. Cres. HA8: Edg 6B 28
Manor Pk. Dr. HA2: Harr 3F 41
Manor Pk. Gdns. HA8: Edg 5B 28
Manor Pk. Pde. SE13 4F 123
(off Lee High Rd.)
Manor Pk. Rd. BR4: W W'ck 1D 170
Manor Pk. Rd. BR7: Chst 1G 161
Manor Pk. Rd. E12 4B 70
(not continuous)
Manor Pk. Rd. N2 3A 46
Manor Pk. Rd. NW10 1B 80
Manor Pk. Rd. SM1: Sutt 5A 166
Manor Pl. BR1: Broml 1C 160
Manor Pl. BR7: Chst 2H 161
Manor Pl. CR4: Mitc 3G 155
Manor Pl. KT12: Walt T 7H 147
(not continuous)
Manor Pl. SE17 5B 102
Manor Pl. SM1: Sutt 4K 165
Manor Pl. TW14: Felt 1J 129
Manor Rd. BR3: Beck 2D 158
Manor Rd. BR4: W W'ck 2D 170
Manor Rd. CR4: Mitc 4G 155
Manor Rd. DA1: Cray 4K 127
Manor Rd. DA15: Sidc 3K 143
Manor Rd. DA5: Bexl 1H 145
Manor Rd. E10 7C 50
Manor Rd. E15 2G 87
Manor Rd. E16 4G 87
Manor Rd. E17 2A 50
Manor Rd. EN2: Enf 2H 23
Manor Rd. EN5: Barn 4B 20
Manor Rd. HA1: Harr 6A 42
Manor Rd. HA4: Ruis 1F 57
Manor Rd. IG11: Bark 6K 71
Manor Rd. IG8: Wfd G 6J 37
Manor Rd. KT12: Walt T 7H 147
Manor Rd. KT8: E Mos 4H 149
Manor Rd. N16 2D 66
Manor Rd. N17 1G 49
Manor Rd. N22 6D 32
Manor Rd. RM10: Dag 6J 73
Manor Rd. RM6: Chad H 6D 54
Manor Rd. SE25 4G 157
Manor Rd. SM2: Cheam 7H 165
Manor Rd. SM6: W'gton 4F 167
Manor Rd. SW20 2H 153
Manor Rd. TW11: Tedd 5A 132
(not continuous)
Manor Rd. TW15: Ashf 5B 128
Manor Rd. TW2: Twick 2G 131
Manor Rd. TW9: Rich 4G 115
Manor Rd. UB3: Hayes 6J 75
Manor Rd. W13 7A 78
Manor Rd. Ho. HA1: Harr 6A 42
Manor Rd. Nth. KT7: T Ditt 2A 162
Manor Rd. Nth. SM6: W'gton 4F 167
Manorside EN5: Barn 4B 20
Manorside Cl. SE2 4C 108
Manor Sq. RM8: Dag 2C 72
Manor Va. TW8: Bford 5C 96
Manor Vw. N3 2K 45
Manorway EN1: Enf 7K 23
Manorway IG8: Wfd G 5F 37
Manor Way BR2: Broml 6C 160
Manor Way BR3: Beck 2C 158
Manor Way BR5: Pet W 4G 161
Manor Way CR2: S Croy 6E 168
Manor Way CR4: Mitc 3G 155
Manor Way DA5: Bexl 1G 145
Manor Way DA7: Bex 3K 127
Manor Way E4 4A 36
Manor Way HA2: Harr 4F 41
Manor Way HA4: Ruis 7G 39
Manor Way KT4: Wor Pk 1A 164
Manor Way NW9 4A 44
Manor Way RM13: Rain 4K 91
Manor Way SE23 7J 121
Manor Way SE3 4H 123
Manor Way UB2: S'hall 4B 94
Manor Way, The SM6: W'gton 4F 167
Manor Way Bus. Cen. RM13: Rain 5K 91
Manor Waye UB8: Uxb 1A 74
Manpreet Ct. E12 5D 70
Manresa Rd. SW3 6C 16 (5C 100)
Mansard Beeches SW17 5E 136
Mansard Cl. HA5: Pinn 3B 40
Mansbridge Ho. SW8 1F 119
(off Patcham Ter.)
Manse Cl. UB3: Harl 6F 93
Mansel Gro. E17 1C 50
Mansell Rd. UB6: G'frd 5F 77
Mansell Rd. W3 2K 97
Mansell St. E1 1K 15 (6F 85)
Mansel Rd. SW19 6G 135
Manser Ct. RM13: Rain 3K 91
Mansergh Cl. SE18 7C 106
Manse Rd. N16 3F 67
Manser Rd. RM13: Rain 3K 91
Mansfield Av. EN4: E Barn 6J 21
Mansfield Av. HA4: Ruis 1K 57
Mansfield Av. N15 4D 48
Mansfield Cl. N9 6B 24
Mansfield Ct. E2 1F 85
(off Whiston Rd.)
Mansfield Ct. SE15 7F 103
(off Sumner Rd.)
Mansfield Dr. UB4: Hayes 4G 75
Mansfield Hgts. N2 5C 46
Mansfield Hill E4 7J 25
Mansfield Ho. N1 1E 84
(off Halcomb St.)
Mansfield M. W1 6J 5 (5F 83)
Mansfield Pl. CR2: S Croy 6D 168
Mansfield Pl. NW3 4A 64
Mansfield Rd. CR2: S Croy 6D 168
Mansfield Rd. E11 6K 51
Mansfield Rd. E17 4B 50
Mansfield Rd. IG1: Ilf 2E 70
Mansfield Rd. KT9: Chess 5C 162
Mansfield Rd. NW3 5D 64
Mansfield Rd. W3 4H 79
Mansfield St. W1 6J 5 (5F 83)
Mansford St. E2 2G 85
Manship Rd. CR4: Mitc 7E 136
Mansion Cl. SW9 1A 120
(not continuous)
Mansion Gdns. NW3 3K 63
Mansion House London 1E 14 (6D 84)
Mansion Ho. Dr. HA7: Stan 2D 26
Mansion Ho. Pl. EC4 1E 14 (6D 84)
Mansion Ho. St. EC4 1E 14 (6D 84)
(off Poultry)
Mansion Lock Ho. NW1 7F 65
(off Hawley Cres.)
Mansions, The SW5 Earl's Ct. Rd. 5K 99
Mansions, The SW5 Old Brompton Rd.
5K 99
(off Old Brompton Rd.)
Mansion Vw. E15 1F 87
(off High St.)
Manson Ho. N1 7A 66
(off Drummond Way)
Manson M. SW7 4A 16 (4B 100)
Manson Pl. SW7 4A 16 (4B 100)
Mansted Gdns. RM6: Chad H 7C 54
Manston N17 2D 48
(off Adams Rd.)
Manston NW1 7G 65
(off Agar Gro.)
Manston Av. UB2: S'hall 4E 94
Manston Cl. SE20 1J 157
Manston Ct. E17 1B 50
Manstone Rd. NW2 5G 63
Manston Gro. KT2: King T 5D 132
Manston Ho. W14 3G 99
(off Russell Rd.)
Manthorpe Rd. SE18 5G 107
Mantilla Rd. SW17 4E 136
Mantle Ct. SW18 6K 117
(off Mapleton Rd.)
Mantle Rd. SE4 3A 122
Mantlet Cl. SW16 7G 137
Mantle Way E15 7G 69
Manton Av. W7 2K 95
Manton Cl. UB3: Hayes 7G 75
Manton Rd. SE2 4A 108
Manton Way EN3: Enf L 1J 25
Mantua St. SW11 3B 118
Mantus Cl. E1 4J 85
Mantus Rd. E1 4J 85
Manuka Cl. W7 1A 96
Manuka Hgts. E20 5E 68
(off Napa Cl.)
Manus Way N20 2F 31
Manville Gdns. SW17 3F 137
Manville Rd. SW17 2E 136
Manwell La. IG11: Bark 4A 90
Manwood Rd. SE4 5B 122
Manwood St. E16 1D 106
Manygate La. TW17: Shep 7E 146
Manygate Pk. TW17: Shep 6F 147
(off Mitre Cl.)
Manygates SW12 2F 137
Mapesbury Ct. NW2 5G 63
Mapesbury M. NW4 6C 44
Mapesbury Rd. NW2 7G 63
Mapeshill Pl. NW2 6E 62
Mapes Ho. NW6 7G 63
Mape St. E2 4H 85
(not continuous)
Maple Av. E4 5G 35
Maple Av. HA2: Harr 2F 59
Maple Av. UB7: Yiew 7A 74
Maple Av. W3 1A 98
Maple Cl. BR5: Pet W 5H 161
Maple Cl. CR4: Mitc 1F 155
Maple Cl. HA4: Ruis 6K 39
Maple Cl. IG9: Buck H 3G 37
Maple Cl. N16 6G 49
Maple Cl. N3 6D 30
Maple Cl. SW4 6H 119
Maple Cl. TW12: Hamp 6D 130
Maple Cl. UB4: Yead 3B 76
Maple Ct. CR0: C'don Lwr. Coombe St.
4C 168
(off Lwr. Coombe St.)
Maple Ct. CR0: C'don The Waldrons
4C 168
(off The Waldrons)
Maple Ct. E3 2C 86
(off Four Seasons Cl.)
Maple Ct. E6 5E 88
Maple Ct. KT3: N Mald 3K 151
Maple Ct. SE6 1D 140
Maple Ct. TW15: Ashf 7F 129
Maple Cres. DA15: Sidc 6A 126
Maplecroft Cl. E6 6B 88
Mapledale Av. CR0: C'don 2G 169
Mapledene BR7: Chst 6G 143
Mapledene Est. E8 7G 67
Mapledene Rd. E8 7F 67
Maple Gdns. HA8: Edg 7F 29
Maple Gdns. TW19: Stanw 2A 128
Maple Gro. NW9 7J 43
Maple Gro. TW8: Bford 7B 96
Maple Gro. UB1: S'hall 5D 76
Maple Gro. W5 3D 96
Maple Gro. Bus. Cen. TW4: Houn
4A 112
Maple Ho. E17 3D 50
Maple Ho. HA9: Wemb 4G 61
(off Empire Way)
Maple Ho. KT1: King T 5E 150
(off Maple Rd.)
Maple Ho. N19 3G 65
Maple Ho. SE8 7B 104
(off Idonia St.)
Maple Ho. TW9: Kew 1H 115
Maplehurst BR2: Broml 2G 159
Maplehurst Cl. KT1: King T 4E 150
Maple Ind. Est. TW13: Felt 3J 129
Maple Leaf Dr. DA15: Sidc 1K 143
Mapleleafe Gdns. IG6: Ilf 3F 53
Maple Leaf Sq. SE16 2K 103
Maple Lodge W8 3K 99
(off Abbots Wlk.)
Maple M. NW6 2K 81
Maple M. SE16 2K 103
Maple M. SW16 5K 137
Maple Pl. N17 7B 34
Maple Pl. UB7: Yiew 1A 92
Maple Pl. W1 4B 6 (4G 83)
Maple Rd. E11 6G 51
Maple Rd. KT6: Surb 6D 150
Maple Rd. SE20 1H 157
Maple Rd. UB4: Yead 3A 76
Maples, The KT1: Hamp W 7C 132
Maples, The KT10: Clay 7A 162
Maples Pl. E1 5H 85
Maplestead Rd. RM9: Dag 1B 90
Maplestead Rd. SW2 7K 119
Maple St. E2 2H 85
Maple St. RM7: Rom 4J 55
Maple St. W1 5A 6 (5G 83)
Maplethorpe Rd. CR7: Thor H 4A 156
Mapleton Cl. BR2: Broml 6J 159
Mapleton Cres. EN3: Enf W 1D 24
Mapleton Cres. SW18 6K 117
Mapleton Rd. E4 3K 35
Mapleton Rd. EN1: Enf 2C 24
Mapleton Rd. SW18 6J 117
(not continuous)
Maple Tree Pl. SE3 1C 124
Maple Wlk. W10 3F 81
Maple Way SE16 2A 104
Maple Way TW13: Felt 3J 129
Maplewood Apts. N4 7C 48
(off Katherine Cl.)
Maplewood Ct. TW15: Ashf 4A 128
Maplin Cl. N21 6E 22
Maplin Ho. SE2 2D 108
(off Wolvercote Rd.)
Maplin Rd. E16 6J 87
Maplin St. E3 3B 86
Mapperley Cl. E11 6H 51
Mapperley Dr. IG8: Wfd G 7B 36
Marabou Cl. E12 5C 70
Mara Ho. E20 5D 68
(off Victory Pde.)
Maran Way DA18: Erith 2D 108
Maraschino Apartment CR0: C'don
1D 168
(off Cherry Orchard Rd.)
Marathon Ho. NW1 5E 4 (5D 82)
(off Marylebone Rd.)
Marathon Way SE28 2K 107
Marbaix Gdns. TW7: Isle 1H 113
Marban Rd. W9 3H 81
Marble Arch W1 2E 10 (7D 82)
Marble Arch 2F 11 (7D 82)
(off Cumberland Ga.)
MARBLE ARCH 2E 10 (6D 82)
Marble Arch Apts. W1 7E 4 (6D 82)
(off Harrowby St.)
Marble Cl. W3 1H 97
Marble Dr. NW2 1F 63
Marble Hill Cl. TW1: Twick 7B 114
Marble Hill Gdns. TW1: Twick 7B 114
Marble Hill House 7C 114
Marble Ho. SE18 5K 107
Marble Ho. W9 4H 81
Marble Quay E1 4K 15 (1G 103)
Marbles Ho. SE5 6C 102
(off Grosvenor Ter.)
Marbrook Ct. SE12 3A 142
Marcella Rd. SW9 2A 120
Marcellina Way BR6: Orp 3J 173
March NW9 1B 44
(off Long Mead)
Marchant Cl. NW7 6F 29
Marchant Ho. N1 1E 84
(off Halcomb St.)
Marchant Rd. E11 2F 69
Marchant St. SE14 6A 104
Marchbank Rd. W14 6H 99
March Ct. SW15 4D 116
Marchmont Gdns. TW10: Rich 5F 115
Marchmont Rd. SM6: W'gton 7G 167
Marchmont Rd. TW10: Rich 5F 115
Marchmont St. WC1 3E 6 (4J 83)
March Rd. TW1: Twick 7A 114
Marchside Cl. TW5: Hest 1B 112
Marchwood Cl. SE5 7E 102
Marchwood Cres. W5 6C 78
Marcia Ct. SE1 4E 102
(off Marcia Rd.)
Marcia Rd. SE1 4E 102
Marcilly Rd. SW18 5B 118
Marco Dr. HA5: Hat E 1D 40
Marcon Ct. E8 5H 67
(off Amhurst Rd.)
Marconi Pl. N11 4A 32
Marconi Rd. E10 1C 68
Marconi Way UB1: S'hall 6F 77
Marcon Pl. E8 6H 67
Marco Rd. W6 3E 98
Marcourt Lawns W5 4E 78
Marcus Ct. E15 1G 87
Marcus Garvey M. SE22 6H 121
Marcus Garvey Way SE24 4A 120
Marcus St. E15 1H 87
Marcus St. SW18 6K 117
Marcus Ter. SW18 6K 117
Mardale Ct. NW7 7H 29
Mardale Dr. NW9 5K 43
Mardell Rd. CR0: C'don 5K 157
Marden Av. BR2: Hayes 6J 159
Marden Cres. CR0: C'don 6K 155
Marden Cres. DA5: Bexl 5J 127
Marden Ho. E8 5H 67
Marden Rd. CR0: C'don 6K 155
Marden Rd. N17 2E 48
Marden Sq. SE16 3H 103
Marder Rd. W13 2A 96
Mardyke Cl. RM13: Rain 2J 91
Mardyke Ho. SE17 4D 102
(off Mason St.)
Marechal Niel Av. DA15: Sidc 3H 143
Marechal Niel Pde. DA14: Sidc 3H 143
(off Main Rd.)
Maresby Ho. E4 2J 35
Maresfield CR0: C'don 3E 168
Maresfield Gdns. NW3 5A 64
Mare St. E8 5H 67
Marfleet Cl. SM5: Cars 2C 166
Margaret Av. E4 6J 25
Margaret Bondfield Av. IG11: Bark
7A 72
Margaret Bondfield Ho. E3 2A 86
(off Driffield Rd.)
Margaret Ct. EN4: E Barn 4G 21
Margaret Ct. W1 7A 6 (6G 83)
(off Margaret St.)
Margaret Gardner Dr. SE9 2D 142
Margaret Herbison Ho. SW6 6H 99
(off Clem Attlee Ct.)
Margaret Ho. W6 5E 98
(off Queen Caroline St.)
Margaret Ingram Cl. SW6 6H 99
Margaret Lockwood Cl. KT1: King T
4F 151
Margaret McMillan Ho. E16 6A 88
Margaret McMillan Pk. 7B 104
Margaret Rd. DA5: Bexl 6D 126
Margaret Rd. E11 6G 51
Margaret Rd. EN4: E Barn 4G 21
Margaret Rd. N16 1F 67
Margaret Rutherford Pl. SW12 1G 137
Margarets Ct. HA8: Edg 5C 28
Margaret St. W1 7K 5 (6F 83)
Margaretta Ter. SW3 7C 16 (6C 100)
Margaretting Rd. E12 1A 70
Margaret Way IG4: Ilf 6C 52
Margaret White Ho. NW1 1C 6 (3H 83)
(off Chalton St.)
Margate Rd. SW2 5J 119
Margerie Ct. E2 2H 85
(off Esker Pl.)
Margery Fry Ct. N7 3J 65
Margery Pk. Rd. E7 6J 69
Margery Rd. RM8: Dag 3D 72
Margery St. WC1 2J 7 (3A 84)
Margery Ter. E7 6J 69
(off Margery Pk. Rd.)
Margin Dr. SW19 5F 135

254 A–Z London

Margravine Gdns. – Maryville

Margravine Gdns. W6 5F **99**
Margravine Rd. W6 5F **99**
Marham Dr. NW9 1A **44**
Marham Gdns. SM4: Mord 6A **154**
Marham Gdns. SW18 1C **136**
Mar Ho. NW9 3K **43**
Maria Cl. SE1 4H **103**
Maria Ct. SE25 2E **156**
Marian Cl. UB4: Yead 4B **76**
Marian Ct. E9 5J **67**
Marian Ct. SM1: Sutt 5K **165**
Marian Gdns. BR1: Broml 7A **142**
Marian M. EN2: Enf 1F **23**
Marianne Cl. SE5 1E **120**
Marianne North Gallery **2F 115**
Marian Pl. E2 2H **85**
Marian Rd. SW16 1G **155**
Marian St. E2 2H **85**
Marian Way NW10 7B **62**
Maria Ter. E1 5K **85**
Maria Theresa Cl. KT3: N Mald 5K **151**
Maribor SE10 7E **104**
(off Burney St.)
Maricas Av. HA3: Hrw W 1H **41**
Marie Curie SE5 1F **121**
Marie Lloyd Gdns. N19 7J **47**
Marie Lloyd Ho. N1 1E **8** (2D **84**)
(off Murray Gro.)
Marie Lloyd Wlk. E8 6F **67**
Marien Ct. E4 5A **36**
Mariette Way SM6: W'gton 7J **167**
Marigold All. SE1 3A **14** (7B **84**)
Marigold Cl. UB1: S'hall 7C **76**
Marigold Rd. N17 7D **34**
Marigold St. SE16 2H **103**
Marigold Way CR0: C'don 1K **169**
Marina App. UB4: Yead 5C **76**
Marina Av. KT3: N Mald 5D **152**
Marina Cl. BR2: Broml 3J **159**
Marina Ct. E3 3B **86**
(off Alfred St.)
Marina Dr. DA16: Well 2J **125**
Marina Gdns. RM7: Rom 5J **55**
Marina One N1 2J **83**
(off New Wharf Rd.)
Marina Pl. KT1: Hamp W 1D **150**
Marina Point E14 3D **104**
(off Lanark Sq.)
Marina Point SW6 2A **118**
Marina Way TW11: Tedd 7D **132**
Marine Ct. E11 2G **69**
Marine Dr. IG11: Bark 4A **90**
Marine Dr. SE18 4D **106**
Marinefield Rd. SW6 2K **117**
Marinel Ho. SE5 7C **102**
Mariner Bus. Cen. CR0: Wadd 5A **168**
Mariner Gdns. TW10: Ham 3C **132**
Mariner Rd. E12 4E **70**
Mariners Cl. EN4: E Barn 5G **21**
Mariners M. E14 4F **105**
Mariners Pl. SE16 4A **104**
(off Plough Way)
Marine St. SE16 3G **103**
Marine Twr. SE8 6B **104**
(off Abinger Gro.)
Marion Av. TW17: Shep 5D **146**
Marion Gro. IG8: Wfd G 5B **36**
Marion Ho. NW1 1D **82**
(off Regent's Pk. Rd.)
Marion M. SE21 3D **138**
Marion Rd. CR7: Thor H 5C **156**
Marion Rd. NW7 5H **29**
Marischal Rd. SE13 3F **123**
Maritime Ho. SE18 4F **107**
Maritime Quay E14 5C **104**
Maritime St. E3 4B **86**
Maritime St. SE16 3K **103**
Marius Mans. SW17 2E **136**
Marius Rd. SW17 2E **136**
Marjorie Gro. SW11 4D **118**
Marjorie M. E1 6K **85**
Mark Av. E4 6J **25**
Mark Cl. DA7: Bex 1E **126**
Mark Cl. UB1: S'hall 7F **77**
Marke Cl. BR2: Kes 4C **172**
Market, The SM1: Sutt 1A **166**
Market, The SM5: Cars 1A **166**
Market App. W12 2E **98**
Market Chambers EN2: Enf 3J **23**
(off Church St.)
Market Ct. W1 7A **6** (6G **83**)
(off Market Pl.)
Market Dr. W4 7A **98**
Market Est. N7 6J **65**
Market Hall N22 2A **48**
Market Hill SE18 3E **106**
Market La. HA8: Edg 1J **43**
Market La. W12 2E **98**
Market Link RM1: Rom 4K **55**
Market M. W1 5J **11** (1F **101**)
Market Pde. BR1: Broml 1J **159**
(off East St.)
Market Pde. DA14: Sidc 4B **144**
Market Pde. E10 6E **50**
(off High Rd. Leyton)
Market Pde. E17 3B **50**
(off Higham Hill Rd.)
Market Pde. N16 1G **67**
(off Oldhill St.)
Market Pde. N9 2B **34**
(off Winchester Rd.)
Market Pde. SE25 4G **157**
Market Pde. TW13: Hanw 3C **130**
Market Pav. E10 3C **68**
Market Pl. DA6: Bex 4G **127**
Market Pl. EN2: Enf 3J **23**
Market Pl. KT1: King T 2D **150**
Market Pl. N2 3B **46**
Market Pl. SE16 4G **103**
(not continuous)
Market Pl. TW8: Bford 7C **96**
Market Pl. UB1: S'hall 1D **94**
Market Pl. W1 7A **6** (6G **83**)
Market Pl. W3 1J **97**
Market Pl., The NW11 4A **46**
Market Rd. N7 6J **65**
Market Rd. TW9: Rich 3G **115**
Market Row SW9 4A **120**
Market Sq. BR1: Broml 2J **159**
(not continuous)
Market Sq. E14 6D **86**
Market Sq. KT1: King T 2D **150**
(off Market Pl.)
Market Sq., The N9 2C **34**
(within Edmonton Grn. Shop. Cen.)
Market St. E1 5J **9** (5F **85**)
Market St. E6 2D **88**
Market St. SE18 4E **106**
Market Ter. TW8: Bford 6E **96**
(off Albany Rd.)
Market Trad. Est. UB2: S'hall 4K **93**
Market Way E14 6D **86**
Market Way HA0: Wemb 5E **60**
Market Yd. SE8 7C **104**
Market Yd. M. SE1 7G **15** (2E **102**)
Markfield Beam Engine & Mus. **5G 49**
Markfield Gdns. E4 7J **25**
Markfield Rd. N15 4G **49**
Markham Ho. RM10: Dag 3G **73**
(off Uvedale Rd.)
Markham Pl. SW3 5E **16** (5D **100**)
Markham Sq. SW3 5E **16** (5D **100**)
Markham St. SE17 5E **102**
Markham St. SW3 5D **16** (5C **100**)
Markhole Cl. TW12: Hamp 7D **130**
Mark Ho. E2 2K **85**
(off Sewardstone Rd.)
Markhouse Av. E17 6A **50**
Markhouse Pas. E17 6B **50**
(off Downsfield Rd.)
Markhouse Rd. E17 6B **50**
Markland Ho. W10 7F **81**
(off Darfield Way)
Mark La. EC3 2H **15** (7E **84**)
Mark Lodge EN4: Cockf 4H **21**
(off Edgeworth Rd.)
Markmanor Av. E17 7A **50**
Mark Rd. N22 2B **48**
Marksbury Av. TW9: Rich 3G **115**
MARKS GATE 1E 54
Mark Sq. EC2 3G **9** (4E **84**)
Marks Rd. RM7: Rom 5J **55**
(not continuous)
Markstone Ho. SE1 7A **14** (2B **102**)
(off Lancaster St.)
Mark St. E15 7G **69**
Mark St. EC2 3G **9** (4E **84**)
Mark Twain Dr. NW2 4D **62**
Mark Wade Cl. E12 1B **70**
Markway TW16: Sun 2A **148**
Markwell Cl. SE26 4H **139**
Markyate Ho. W10 4E **80**
(off Sutton Way)
Markyate Rd. RM8: Dag 5B **72**
Marland Ho. SW1 1F **17** (3D **100**)
(off Sloane St.)
Marlands Rd. IG5: Ilf 3C **52**
Marlborough SW19 1F **135**
(off Inner Pk. Rd.)
Marlborough W9 3A **82**
(off Maida Vale)
Marlborough Av. E8 1G **85**
(not continuous)
Marlborough Av. HA4: Ruis 6E **38**
Marlborough Av. HA8: Edg 3C **28**
Marlborough Av. N14 3B **32**
Marlborough Cl. BR6: Orp 6K **161**
Marlborough Cl. N20 3J **31**
Marlborough Cl. SE17 4C **102**
Marlborough Cl. SW19 6C **136**
Marlborough Ct. CR2: S Croy 4E **168**
(off Birdhurst Rd.)
Marlborough Ct. EN1: Enf 5K **23**
Marlborough Ct. HA1: Harr 4H **41**
Marlborough Ct. HA6: Nwood 1H **39**
Marlborough Ct. IG9: Buck H 2F **37**
Marlborough Ct. N17 1G **49**
(off Kemble Rd.)
Marlborough Ct. SM6: W'gton 7G **167**
Marlborough Ct. W1 2A **12** (7G **83**)
(off Carnaby St.)
Marlborough Ct. W8 4J **99**
(off Pembroke Rd.)
Marlborough Cres. UB3: Harl 7F **93**
Marlborough Cres. W4 3K **97**
Marlborough Dr. IG5: Ilf 3C **52**
Marlborough Flats SW3 3D **16** (4C **100**)
(off Walton St.)
Marlborough Gdns. KT6: Surb 7D **150**
Marlborough Gdns. N20 3J **31**
Marlborough Ga. Ho. W2 2A **10** (7B **82**)
(off Elms M.)
Marlborough Gro. SE1 5G **103**
Marlborough Hill HA1: Harr 4H **41**
Marlborough Hill NW8 2A **82**
Marlborough Ho. E16 1J **105**
(off Hardy Av.)
Marlborough Ho. UB7: W Dray 2B **92**
(off Park Lodge Av.)
Marlborough House **5B 12 (1G 101)**
Marlborough La. SE7 6A **106**
Marlborough Lodge NW8 2A **82**
(off Hamilton Ter.)
Marlborough Mans. NW6 5K **63**
(off Canon Hill)
Marlborough M. SW2 4K **119**
Marlborough Pde. UB10: Hil 4D **74**
Marlborough Pk. Av. DA15: Sidc 7A **126**
Marlborough Pl. NW8 2A **82**
Marlborough Rd. BR2: Broml 4A **160**
Marlborough Rd. CR2: S Croy 7C **168**
Marlborough Rd. DA7: Bex 3D **126**
Marlborough Rd. E15 4G **69**
Marlborough Rd. E18 2J **51**
Marlborough Rd. E4 6J **35**
Marlborough Rd. E7 7A **70**
Marlborough Rd. N19 2H **65**
Marlborough Rd. N22 7D **32**
Marlborough Rd. N9 1B **34**
Marlborough Rd. RM7: Mawney 4G **55**
Marlborough Rd. RM8: Dag 4B **72**
Marlborough Rd. SE18 3F **107**
Marlborough Rd. SE28 3G **107**
Marlborough Rd. SM1: Sutt 3J **165**
Marlborough Rd. SW1 5B **12** (1G **101**)
Marlborough Rd. SW19 6C **136**
Marlborough Rd. TW10: Rich 6F **115**
Marlborough Rd. TW12: Hamp 6E **130**
Marlborough Rd. TW13: Felt 2B **130**
Marlborough Rd. TW15: Ashf 5A **128**
Marlborough Rd. TW7: Isle 1B **114**
Marlborough Rd. UB10: Hil 4D **74**
Marlborough Rd. UB2: S'hall 3A **94**
Marlborough Rd. W4 5J **97**
Marlborough Rd. W5 2D **96**
Marlborough St. SW3 4C **16** (4C **100**)
Marlborough Yd. N19 2H **65**
Marlbury NW8 1K **81**
(off Abbey Rd.)
Marler Rd. SE23 1A **140**
Marley Av. DA7: Bex 6D **108**
Marley Cl. N15 4B **48**
Marley Cl. UB6: G'frd 3E **76**
Marley Ho. E16 7F **89**
(off University Way)
Marley Ho. W11 7F **81**
(off St Ann's Rd.)
Marley St. SE16 4K **103**
Marley Wlk. NW2 5E **62**
Marl Fld. Cl. KT4: Wor Pk 1C **164**
Marlin Cl. TW16: Sun 6G **129**
Marling Ct. TW12: Hamp 6D **130**
Marlingdene Cl. TW12: Hamp 6E **130**
MARLING PARK 7D 130
Marlings Cl. BR7: Chst 4J **161**
Marlings Pk. Av. BR7: Chst 4J **161**
Marlin Pk. TW14: Felt 5K **111**
Marlins Cl. SM1: Sutt 5A **166**
Marloes Cl. HA0: Wemb 4D **60**
Marloes Rd. W8 3K **99**
Marlow Cl. SE20 3H **157**
Marlow Ct. N14 7B **22**
Marlow Ct. NW6 7F **63**
Marlow Ct. NW9 3B **44**
Marlow Cres. TW1: Twick 6K **113**
Marlow Dr. SM3: Cheam 2F **165**
Marlowe Cl. BR7: Chst 6H **143**
Marlowe Cl. IG6: Ilf 1G **53**
Marlowe Ct. SE19 5F **139**
Marlowe Ct. SW3 4D **16** (4C **100**)
(off Petyward)
Marlowe Gdns. SE9 6E **124**
Marlowe Ho. IG8: Wfd G 7K **37**
Marlowe Ho. KT1: King T 4D **150**
(off Portsmouth Rd.)
Marlowe Path SE8 6C **104**
Marlowe Rd. E17 4E **50**
Marlowes, The DA1: Cray 4K **127**
Marlowes, The NW8 1B **82**
Marlowe Sq. CR4: Mitc 4G **155**
Marlowe Way CR0: Bedd 2J **167**
Marlow Gdns. UB3: Harl 3F **93**
Marlow Ho. E2 2J **9** (3F **85**)
(off Calvert Av.)
Marlow Ho. KT5: Surb 5E **150**
(off Cranes Pk.)
Marlow Ho. SE1 7J **15** (3F **103**)
(off Abbey St.)
Marlow Ho. TW11: Tedd 4A **132**
Marlow Ho. W2 6K **81**
(off Hallfield Est.)
Marlow Rd. E6 3D **88**
Marlow Rd. RM8: Dag 1E **72**
Marlow Rd. SE20 3H **157**
Marlow Rd. UB2: S'hall 3D **94**
Marlow Way SE16 2K **103**
Marlow Workshops E2 2J **9** (3F **85**)
(off Virginia Rd.)
Marl Rd. SW18 4A **118**
Marlston NW1 2K **5** (3F **83**)
(off Munster Sq.)
Marlton St. SE10 5H **105**
Marlu Ct. SE14 1K **121**
(off Hatcham Pk. M.)
Marlu Ho. SE14 1K **121**
(off Hatcham Pk. M.)
Marlwood Cl. DA15: Sidc 2J **143**
Marmadon Rd. SE18 4K **107**
Marmara Apts. E16 7J **87**
(off Western Gateway)
Marmion App. E4 4H **35**
Marmion Av. E4 4G **35**
Marmion Cl. E4 4G **35**
Marmion M. SW11 3E **118**
Marmion Rd. SW11 4E **118**
Marmont Rd. SE15 1G **121**
Marmora Rd. SE22 6J **121**
Marmot Rd. TW4: Houn 3B **112**
Marne Av. DA16: Well 3A **126**
Marne Av. N11 4A **32**
Marnell Way TW4: Houn 3B **112**
Marne Rd. RM9: Dag 1B **90**
Marner Point E3 4E **86**
Marne St. W10 3G **81**
Marney Rd. SW11 4E **118**
Marnfield Cres. SW2 1A **138**
Marnham Av. NW2 4G **63**
Marnham Ct. HA0: Wemb 5C **60**
Marnham Cres. UB6: G'frd 3F **77**
Marnock Ho. SE17 5D **102**
(off Brandon St.)
Marnock Rd. SE4 5B **122**
Maroon St. E14 5A **86**
Maroons Way SE6 5C **140**
Marqueen Ct. W8 2K **99**
(off Kensington Chu. St.)
Marqueen Towers SW16 7K **137**
Marquess Hgts. E18 1K **51**
Marquess Rd. N1 6D **66**
Marquis Cl. HA0: Wemb 7F **61**
Marquis Ct. IG11: Bark 5J **71**
Marquis Ct. KT1: King T 4D **150**
(off Anglesea Rd.)
Marquis Ct. N4 1K **65**
(off Marquis Rd.)
Marquis Ct. TW19: Stanw 1A **128**
Marquis Rd. N22 6E **32**
Marquis Rd. N4 1K **65**
Marquis Rd. NW1 6H **65**
Marrabon Cl. DA15: Sidc 1A **144**
Marrick Cl. SW15 4C **116**
Marrick Ho. NW6 1K **81**
(off Mortimer Cres.)
Marriett Ho. SE6 4E **140**
Marriner Ct. UB3: Hayes 7G **75**
(off Barra Hall Rd.)
Marriott Cl. TW14: Felt 6F **111**
Marriott Rd. E15 1G **87**
Marriott Rd. EN5: Barn 3A **20**
Marriott Rd. N10 1D **46**
Marriott Rd. N4 1K **65**
Marriotts Cl. NW9 6B **44**
Marryat Cl. TW4: Houn 4D **112**
Marryat Ho. SW1 6A **18** (5G **101**)
(off Churchill Gdns.)
Marryat Pl. SW19 4G **135**
Marryat Rd. SW19 5F **135**
Marryat Sq. SW6 1G **117**
Marsala Rd. SE13 4D **122**
Marsalis Ho. E3 3C **86**
(off Rainhill Way)
Marsault Ct. TW9: Rich 4E **114**
(off Kew Foot Rd.)
Marsden Rd. N9 2C **34**
Marsden Rd. SE15 3F **121**
Marsden St. NW5 6E **64**
Marsden Way BR6: Orp 4K **173**
Marshall Bldg. W2 6A **4** (5B **82**)
(off Hermitage St.)
Marshall Cl. HA1: Harr 7H **41**
Marshall Cl. SW18 6A **118**
Marshall Cl. TW4: Houn 5D **112**
Marshall Ct. NW6 7F **63**
(off Coverdale Rd.)
Marshall Ct. SE20 7H **139**
(off Anerley Pk.)
Marshall Dr. UB4: Hayes 5H **75**
Marshall Est. NW7 4H **29**
Marshall Ho. N1 2D **84**
(off Cranston Est.)
Marshall Ho. SE1 3E **102**
(off Page's Wlk.)
Marshall Ho. SE17 5D **102**
(off East St.)
Marshall Path SE28 7B **90**
Marshall Rd. E10 3D **68**
Marshall Rd. N17 1D **48**
Marshalls Cl. N11 4A **32**
Marshalls Dr. RM1: Rom 3K **55**
Marshalls Gro. SE18 4C **106**
Marshall's Pl. SE16 3F **103**
Marshall's Rd. SM1: Sutt 4K **165**
Marshalls Rd. RM7: Rom 4K **55**
Marshall St. NW10 7K **61**
Marshall St. W1 1B **12** (6G **83**)
Marshall Street Leisure Cen.
1B 12 (6G 83)
Marshalsea Rd. SE1 6D **14** (2C **102**)
Marsham Cl. BR7: Chst 5F **143**
Marsham Ct. SW1 3D **18** (4H **101**)
Marsham St. SW1 2D **18** (3H **101**)
Marsh Av. CR4: Mitc 2D **154**
Marshbrook Cl. SE3 3B **124**
Marsh Cen., The E1 7K **9** (6F **85**)
(off Whitechapel High St.)
Marsh Cl. NW7 3G **29**
Marsh Ct. E8 6G **67**
Marsh Ct. SE17 5D **102**
(off Thurlow St.)
Marsh Ct. SW19 1A **154**
Marsh Dr. NW9 6B **44**
Marsh Farm Rd. TW2: Twick 1K **131**
Marshfield St. E14 3E **104**
Marshgate Bus. Cen. E15 1E **86**
Marshgate La. E15 1D **86**
Marshgate La. E20 6C **68**
Marshgate Path SE28 3G **107**
Marsh Grn. Rd. RM10: Dag 1G **91**
Marsh Hall HA9: Wemb 3F **61**
Marsh Hill E9 5A **68**
Marsh Ho. SW1 6D **18** (5H **101**)
(off Aylesford St.)
Marsh Ho. SW8 1G **119**
Marsh La. E10 2B **68**
Marsh La. HA7: Stan 5H **27**
Marsh La. N17 7C **34**
Marsh La. NW7 3F **29**
Marsh Rd. HA0: Wemb 3D **78**
Marsh Rd. HA5: Pinn 4C **40**
Marshside Cl. N9 1D **34**
Marsh St. E14 4D **104**
Marsh Wall E14 1C **104**
Marsh Way RM13: Rain 3K **91**
Marshwood Apts. SW11 4C **118**
(off Eckstein Road)
Marshwood Ho. NW6 1J **81**
(off Kilburn Vale)
Marsland Cl. SE17 5B **102**
Marsom Ho. N1 1E **8** (2D **84**)
(off Provost St.)
Marston Av. KT9: Chess 6E **162**
Marston Av. RM10: Dag 2G **73**
Marston Cl. NW6 7A **64**
Marston Cl. RM10: Dag 3G **73**
Marston Ho. SW9 2A **120**
Marston Rd. IG5: Ilf 1C **52**
Marston Rd. TW11: Tedd 5B **132**
Marston Way SE19 7B **138**
Marsworth Av. HA5: Pinn 1B **40**
Marsworth Cl. UB4: Yead 5C **76**
Marsworth Ho. E2 1G **85**
(off Whiston Rd.)
Marsworth Ho. HA0: Wemb 1E **78**
Martaban Rd. N16 2F **67**
Martara M. SE17 5C **102**
Marta Rose Ct. SE20 2H **157**
(off Wadhurst Cl.)
Martello St. E8 7H **67**
Martello Ter. E8 7H **67**
Martell Rd. SE21 3D **138**
Martel Pl. E8 6F **67**
Marten Rd. E17 2C **50**
Martens Av. DA7: Bex 4H **127**
Martens Cl. DA7: Bex 4J **127**
Martham Cl. IG6: Ilf 1F **53**
Martham Cl. SE28 7D **90**
Martha Rd. E15 6G **69**
Martha's Bldgs. EC1 3E **8** (4D **84**)
Martha St. E1 6J **85**
Marthorne Cres. HA3: Hrw W 2H **41**
Martin Bowes Rd. SE9 3D **124**
Martinbridge Trad. Est. EN1: Enf 5B **24**
Martin Cl. N9 1E **34**
Martin Cl. UB10: Uxb 2A **74**
Martin Ct. CR2: S Croy 5E **168**
(off Birdhurst Rd.)
Martin Ct. E14 2E **104**
(off River Barge Cl.)
Martin Cres. CR0: C'don 1A **168**
Martindale SW14 5J **115**
Martindale Av. BR6: Chels 5K **173**
Martindale Av. E16 7J **87**
Martindale Ho. E14 7D **86**
(off Poplar High St.)
Martin Dale Ind. Est. EN1: Enf 3C **24**
Martindale Rd. SW12 7F **119**
Martindale Rd. TW4: Houn 3C **112**
Martin Dene DA6: Bex 5F **127**
Martin Dr. UB5: N'olt 5D **58**
Martineau Dr. TW1: Twick 4B **114**
Martineau Est. E1 7J **85**
Martineau Ho. SW1 6A **18** (5G **101**)
(off Churchill Gdns.)
Martineau M. N5 4B **66**
Martineau Rd. N5 4B **66**
Martineau Sq. E1 7G **85**
Martingale Cl. TW16: Sun 4J **147**
Martingale Ho. E1 1H **103**
(off Raine St.)
Martingales Cl. TW10: Ham 3D **132**
Martin Gdns. RM8: Dag 4C **72**
Martin Gro. SM4: Mord 3J **153**
Martin Ho. E3 1B **86**
(off Old Ford Rd.)
Martin Ho. SE1 3C **102**
Martin Ho. SW8 7J **101**
(off Wyvil Rd.)
Martin Kinggett Gdns. RM9: Dag 1E **90**
Martin La. EC4 2F **15** (7D **84**)
(not continuous)
Martin Ri. DA6: Bex 5F **127**
Martin Rd. RM8: Dag 4C **72**
Martins, The HA9: Wemb 3F **61**
Martins, The SE26 5H **139**
Martins Cl. BR4: W W'ck 1F **171**
Martin's Mt. EN5: New Bar 4D **20**
Martins Pl. SE28 1J **107**
Martin's Rd. BR2: Broml 2G **159**
Martin St. SE28 1J **107**
Martins Wlk. N22 Noel Pk. 3A **48**
Martins Wlk. N10 1E **46**
Martins Wlk. SE28 1J **107**
Martin Way SM4: Mord 3G **153**
Martin Way SW20 2F **153**
Martlesham N17 2E **48**
(off Adams Rd.)
Martlesham Wlk. NW9 2A **44**
Martlet Gro. UB5: N'olt 3B **76**
Martlett Ct. WC2 1F **13** (6J **83**)
Martley Dr. IG2: Ilf 5F **53**
Martock Cl. HA3: W'stone 4A **42**
Martock Gdns. N11 5J **31**
Marton Cl. SE6 3C **140**
Marton Rd. N16 2E **66**
Martynside NW9 1B **44**
Martys Yd. NW3 4B **64**
Marula Ho. E1 6G **85**
(off Boulevard Walkway)
Marvell Av. UB4: Hayes 5J **75**
Marvell Ct. RM6: Chad H 6B **54**
(off Quarles Pk. Rd.)
Marvell Ho. SE5 7D **102**
(off Camberwell Rd.)
Marvels Cl. SE12 2K **141**
Marvels La. SE12 2K **141**
Marville Rd. SW6 7H **99**
Marvin St. E8 6H **67**
Marwell Cl. BR4: W W'ck 2H **171**
Marwood Cl. DA16: Well 3B **126**
Marwood Dr. NW7 7A **30**
Marwood Sq. N10 4E **46**
Mary Adelaide Cl. SW15 4A **134**
Mary Ann Gdns. SE8 6C **104**
Maryatt Av. HA2: Harr 2F **59**
Marybank SE18 4D **106**
Mary Bayly Ho. W11 1G **99**
(off Wilsham St.)
Mary Boast Wlk. SE5 2D **120**
Mary Cl. HA7: Stan 4F **43**
Mary Datchelor Cl. SE5 1D **120**
Mary Datchelor Ho. SE5 1D **120**
(off Grove La.)
Maryfield Cl. DA5: Bexl 3K **145**
Mary Flux Ct. SW5 5K **99**
(off Bramham Gdns.)
Mary Grn. NW8 1K **81**
Mary Holben Ho. SW16 5G **137**
Mary Ho. W6 5E **98**
(off Queen Caroline St.)
Mary Jones Ct. E14 7C **86**
(off Garford St.)
Maryland Ind. Est. E15 5G **69**
Maryland Pk. E15 5G **69**
(not continuous)
Maryland Point E15 6G **69**
(off The Grove)
Maryland Rd. CR7: Thor H 1B **156**
Maryland Rd. E15 5F **69**
Maryland Rd. N22 6E **32**
Maryland Sq. E15 5G **69**
Marylands Rd. W9 4J **81**
(not continuous)
Maryland St. E15 5F **69**
Maryland Wlk. N1 1C **84**
(off Popham St.)
Maryland Way TW16: Sun 2J **147**
Mary Lawrenson Pl. SE3 7J **105**
MARYLEBONE 5H 5 (5E 82)
Marylebone Cricket Club **1B 4 (3B 82)**
(shown as Lord's)
Marylebone Fly-Over W2 6B **4** (5B **82**)
MARYLEBONE FLYOVER 6C **4** (5C **82**)
Marylebone Gdns. TW9: Rich 4G **115**
Marylebone High St. W1 5H **5** (5E **82**)
Marylebone La. W1 6H **5** (5E **82**)
Marylebone M. W1 6J **5** (5F **83**)
Marylebone Pas. W1 7B **6** (6G **83**)
Marylebone Rd. NW1 5D **4** (5C **82**)
Marylebone St. W1 6H **5** (5E **82**)
Mary Le Bow Way E3 5D **86**
Marylee Way SE11 4H **19** (4K **101**)
Mary Macarthur Ho. E2 3K **85**
(off Warley St.)
Mary Macarthur Ho. RM10: Dag 3G **73**
(off Wythenshawe Rd.)
Mary Macarthur Ho. W6 6G **99**
Mary Neuner Rd. N22 3K **47**
Mary Neuner Rd. N8 3K **47**
Maryon Gro. SE7 4C **106**
Maryon Ho. NW6 7A **64**
(off Goldhurst Ter.)
Maryon M. NW3 4C **64**
Maryon Rd. SE18 4C **106**
Maryon Rd. SE7 4C **106**
Mary Peters Dr. UB6: G'frd 5H **59**
Mary Pl. W11 7G **81**
Mary Rose Cl. TW12: Hamp 1E **148**
Mary Rose Mall E6 5D **88**
Mary Rose Sq. SE16 4A **104**
(off Cary Av.)
Maryrose Way N20 1G **31**
Marys Ct. NW1 3D **4** (4C **82**)
(off Palgrave Gdns.)
Mary Seacole Cl. E8 1F **85**
Mary Seacole Ho. W6 3C **98**
(off Invermead Cl.)
Mary Smith Ct. SW5 4J **99**
(off Trebovir Rd.)
Marysmith Ho. SW1 5D **18** (5H **101**)
(off Cureton St.)
Mary's Ter. TW1: Twick 7A **114**
Mary St. E16 5H **87**
Mary St. N1 1C **84**
Mary Ter. NW1 1F **83**
Maryville DA16: Well 2K **125**

Mary Wallace Theatre Twickenham – Meard St.

Mary Wallace Theatre Twickenham 1A 132
Mary Wharrie Ho. NW3 7D 64
(off Fellows Rd.)
Marzell Ho. W14 5H 99
(off North End Rd.)
Marzena Ct. TW3: Houn 6G 113
Masbro' Rd. W14 3F 99
Mascalls Ct. SE7 6A 106
Mascalls Rd. SE7 6A 106
Mascotte Rd. SW15 4F 117
Mascotts Cl. NW2 3D 62
Masefield Av. HA7: Stan 5E 26
Masefield Av. UB1: S'hall 7E 76
Masefield Ct. EN5: New Bar 4F 21
Masefield Ct. KT6: Surb 7D 150
Masefield Cres. N14 5B 22
Masefield Gdns. E6 4E 88
Masefield Ho. NW6 3J 81
(off Stafford Rd.)
Masefield La. UB4: Yead 4K 75
Masefield Rd. TW12: Hamp 4D 130
Masefield Vw. BR6: Farnb 3G 173
Masefield Way TW19: Stanw 1B 128
Masey M. SW2 5A 120
Masham Ho. DA18: Erith 2D 108
(off Kale Rd.)
Mashie Rd. W3 6A 80
Mashiters Hill RM1: Rom 1K 55
Masjid La. E14 5B 86
Maskall Cl. SW2 1A 138
Maskani Wlk. SW16 7G 137
Maskell Rd. SW17 3A 136
Maskelyne Cl. SW11 1C 118
Mason Cl. DA7: Bex 3H 127
Mason Cl. E16 7J 87
Mason Cl. SE16 5G 103
Mason Cl. SW20 1F 153
Mason Cl. TW12: Hamp 1D 148
Mason Ho. E9 7J 67
(off Frampton Pk. Rd.)
Mason Ho. SE1 4G 103
(off Simms Rd.)
Mason Rd. IG8: Wfd G 4B 36
Mason Rd. SM1: Sutt 5K 165
Masonry Ho. SE14 1K 121
(off Fishers Ct.)
Mason's Arms M. W1 1K 11 (6F 83)
Mason's Av. CR0: C'don 3C 168
Mason's Av. EC2 7E 8 (6D 84)
Masons Av. HA3: W'stone 4K 41
Masons Grn. La. W3 4G 79
Masons Grn. La. W5 4G 79
Masons Hill BR1: Broml 3J 159
Masons Hill BR2: Broml 3K 159
Masons Hill SE18 4F 107
Masons Pl. CR4: Mitc 1D 154
Masons Pl. EC1 1C 8 (3C 84)
Mason St. SE17 4D 102
Mason's Yd. SW1 4B 12 (1G 101)
Mason's Yd. SW19 5F 135
Masons Yd. EC1 1B 8 (3B 84)
Massey Cl. N11 5A 32
Massey Ct. E6 1A 88
(off Florence Rd.)
Massie Rd. E8 6G 67
Massingberd Way SW17 4F 137
Massinger St. SE17 4E 102
Massingham St. E1 4K 85
Masson Av. HA4: Ruis 6A 58
Masson Ho. TW8: Bford 6F 97
Mast, The E16 7G 89
Mast Ct. SE16 4A 104
(off Boat Lifter Way)
Master Gunner Pl. SE18 7C 106
Masterhead Ho. E16 2K 105
(off Royal Crest Av.)
Masterman Ho. SE5 7D 102
(off Elmington Est.)
Masterman Rd. E6 3C 88
Masters Cl. SW16 6G 137
Masters Dr. SE16 5H 103
Masters Lodge E1 6J 85
(off Johnson St.)
Masters St. E1 5K 85
Mast Ho. Ter. E14 4C 104
(not continuous)
Mastmaker Ct. E14 2C 104
Mastmaker Rd. E14 2C 104
Mast Quay SE18 3D 106
Mast St. IG11: Bark 1H 89
MASWELL PARK 5G 113
Maswell Pk. Cres. TW3: Houn 5G 113
Maswell Pk. Rd. TW3: Houn 5F 113
Matcham Ct. TW1: Twick 6D 114
(off Clevedon Rd.)
Matcham Rd. E11 3G 69
Match Ct. E3 2C 86
(off Blondin St.)
Matching Ct. E3 3B 86
(off Merchant St.)
Matchless Dr. SE18 7E 106
Material Store, The UB3: Hayes 3G 93
(off Material Wlk.)
Material Wlk. UB3: Hayes 2G 93
Matfield Cl. BR2: Broml 5J 159
Matfield Rd. DA17: Belv 6G 109
Matha Ct. BR1: Broml 1A 160
Matham Gro. SE22 4F 121
Matham Rd. KT8: E Mos 5H 149
Matheson Lang Ho. SE1 7J 13 (2A 102)
(off Baylis Rd.)
Matheson Rd. W14 4H 99
Mathews Av. E6 2E 88
Mathews Pk. Av. E15 6H 69
Mathews Yd. WC2 1E 12 (6J 83)
Mathieson Ct. SE1 7B 14 (2B 102)
(off King James St.)
Mathison Ho. SW10 7A 100
(off Coleridge Gdns.)
Matilda Cl. SE19 7D 138
Matilda Gdns. E3 2C 86
Matilda Ho. E1 4K 15 (1G 103)
(off St Katherine's Way)
Matilda St. N1 1K 83
Matisse Ct. EC1 3E 8 (4D 84)
(off Featherstone St.)
Matisse Rd. TW3: Houn 3F 113
Matlock Cl. EN5: Barn 5A 20
Matlock Cl. SE24 4C 120
Matlock Ct. NW8 2A 82
(off Abbey Rd.)
Matlock Ct. SE5 4D 120
Matlock Ct. W11 7J 81
(off Kensington Pk. Rd.)
Matlock Cres. SM3: Cheam 4G 165
Matlock Gdns. SM3: Cheam 4G 165
Matlock Ho. E15 6F 69
(off Forrester Way)
Matlock Pl. SM3: Cheam 4G 165
Matlock Rd. E10 6E 50
Matlock St. E14 6A 86
Matlock Way KT3: N Mald 1K 151
Maton Ho. SW6 7H 99
(off Estcourt Rd.)
Matrimony Pl. SW8 2G 119
Matson Ct. IG8: Wfd G 7B 36
Matson Ho. SE16 3H 103
Matthew Cl. W10 4F 81
Matthew Ct. CR4: Mitc 5H 155
Matthew Ct. E17 3E 50
Matthew Parker St. SW1 7D 12 (2H 101)
Matthews Cl. HA9: Wemb 3G 61
Matthews Ho. E14 5C 86
(off Burgess St.)
Matthews Rd. UB6: G'frd 5H 59
Matthews St. SW11 2D 118
Matthews Wlk. E17 1C 50
(off Chingford Rd.)
Matthews Yd. CR0: C'don 3C 168
(off Surrey St.)
Matthias Apts. N1 7D 66
(off Northchurch Rd.)
Matthias Ct. TW10: Rich 5E 114
Matthias Rd. N16 5E 66
Mattison Rd. N4 6A 48
Mattock La. W13 1B 96
Mattock La. W5 1C 96
Maud Cashmore Way SE18 3D 106
Maud Chadburn Pl. SW4 6F 119
Maude Ho. E2 1K 9 (2G 85)
(off Ropley St.)
Maude Rd. E17 5A 50
Maude Rd. SE5 1E 120
Maudesville Cotts. W7 1J 95
Maude Ter. E17 5A 50
Maud Gdns. E13 1H 87
Maud Gdns. IG11: Bark 2K 89
Maudlins Grn. E1 4K 15 (1G 103)
Maud Rd. E10 3E 68
Maud Rd. E13 2H 87
Maudslay Rd. SE9 3D 124
Maudsley Ho. TW8: Bford 5E 96
Maud St. E16 5H 87
Maud Wilkes Cl. NW5 5G 65
Maugham Way W3 3J 97
Mauleverer Rd. SW2 5J 119
Maundeby Wlk. NW10 6A 62
Maunder Rd. W7 1K 95
Maunsel St. SW1 3C 18 (4H 101)
Maureen Campbell Ct. TW17: Shep 5D 146
(off Harrison Way)
Maureen Ct. BR3: Beck 2J 157
Maurer Ct. SE10 3H 105
Mauretania Bldg. E1 7K 85
(off Jardine Rd.)
Maurice Av. N22 2B 48
Maurice Browne Av. NW7 6A 30
Maurice Ct. E1 3K 85
Maurice Ct. N22 1K 47
Maurice Ct. TW8: Bford 7D 96
Maurice Drummond Ho. SE10 1D 122
(off Catherine Gro.)
Maurice St. W12 6D 80
Maurice Wlk. NW11 4A 46
Maurier Cl. UB5: N'olt 1A 76
Mauritius Rd. SE10 4G 105
Maury Rd. N16 2G 67
Mauveine Gdns. TW3: Houn 4E 112
Mavelstone Cl. BR1: Broml 1C 160
Mavelstone Rd. BR1: Broml 1B 160
Maverton Rd. E3 1C 86
Mavery Ct. BR1: Broml 7H 141
(off Bromley Av.)
Mavis Av. KT19: Ewe 5A 164
Mavis Cl. KT19: Ewe 5A 164
Mavis Wlk. E6 5C 88
(off Greenwich Cres.)
Mavor Ho. N1 1K 83
(off Barnsbury Est.)
Mawbey Ho. SE1 5G 103
Mawbey Pl. SE1 5F 103
Mawbey Rd. SE1 5F 103
Mawbey St. SW8 7J 101
Mawdley Ho. SE1 7A 14 (2B 102)
(off Webber Row)
MAWNEY 3H 55
Mawney Cl. RM7: Mawney 2H 55
Mawney Rd. RM7: Mawney 2H 55
Mawney Rd. RM7: Rom 2H 55
Mawson Cl. SW20 2G 153
Mawson Ct. N1 1D 84
(off Gopsall St.)
Mawson Ho. EC1 5J 7 (5A 84)
(off Baldwins Gdns.)
Mawson La. W4 6B 98
Maxden Ct. SE15 3F 121
Maxey Gdns. RM9: Dag 4E 72
Maxey Rd. RM9: Dag 4E 72
Maxey Rd. SE18 4G 107
Maxfield Cl. N20 7F 21
Maxilla Wlk. W10 6F 81
Maxim Apts. BR2: Broml 4K 159
(off Tiger La.)
Maximfeldt Rd. DA8: Erith 5K 109
Maxim Rd. DA8: Erith 4K 109
Maxim Rd. N21 6F 23
Maxted Pk. HA1: Harr 7J 41
Maxted Rd. SE15 3F 121
Maxwell Cl. CR0: Wadd 1J 167
Maxwell Cl. UB3: Hayes 7J 75
Maxwell Ct. SE22 1G 139
Maxwell Ct. SW4 5H 119
Maxwell Gdns. BR6: Orp 3K 173
Maxwell Rd. DA16: Well 3K 125
Maxwell Rd. HA6: Nwood 1F 39
Maxwell Rd. RM7: Rush G 6K 55
Maxwell Rd. SW6 7K 99
Maxwell Rd. TW15: Ashf 6E 128
Maxwell Rd. UB7: W Dray 4B 92
Maxwelton Av. NW7 5E 28
Maxwelton Cl. NW7 5E 28
Maya Angelou Ct. E4 4K 35
Maya Apts. E20 5E 68
(off Victory Pde.)
Maya Cl. SE15 2H 121
Mayall Cl. EN3: Enf L 1H 25
Mayall Rd. SE24 5B 120
Maya Pl. N11 7C 32
Maya Rd. N2 4A 46
Maybank Av. E18 2K 51
Maybank Av. HA0: Wemb 5K 59
Maybank Gdns. HA5: Eastc 5J 39
Maybank Rd. E18 1K 51
May Bate Av. KT2: King T 1D 150
Maybells Commercial Est. IG11: Bark 2D 90
Mayberry Ct. BR3: Beck 7B 140
(off Copers Cope Rd.)
Mayberry Pl. KT5: Surb 7F 151
Maybourne Cl. SE26 6H 139
Maybury Cl. BR5: Pet W 5F 161
Maybury Cl. EN1: Enf 1C 24
Maybury Ct. CR2: S Croy 5B 168
(off Haling Pk. Rd.)
Maybury Ct. HA1: Harr 6H 41
Maybury Ct. W1 6H 5 (5E 82)
(off Marylebone St.)
Maybury Gdns. NW10 6D 62
Maybury M. N6 7G 47
Maybury Rd. E13 4A 88
Maybury Rd. IG11: Bark 2K 89
Maybury St. SW17 5C 136
Maychurch Cl. HA7: Stan 7J 27
May Cl. KT9: Chess 6F 163
May Ct. SW19 1A 154
(off Pincott Rd.)
Maycroft HA5: Pinn 2K 39
Maycross Av. SM4: Mord 4H 153
Mayday Gdns. SE3 2C 124
Mayday Rd. CR7: Thor H 6B 156
Maydeb Ct. RM6: Chad H 6F 55
Maydew Ho. SE16 4J 103
(off Abbeyfield Est.)
Maydwell Ho. E14 5C 86
(off Thomas Rd.)
Mayerne Rd. SE9 5B 124
Mayesbrook Pk. Arena 5A 72
Mayesbrook Rd. IG11: Bark 1K 89
Mayesbrook Rd. IG3: Ilf 3A 72
Mayesbrook Rd. RM8: Dag 3B 72
Mayes Cl. CR0: New Ad 7F 171
Mayesford Rd. RM6: Chad H 7C 54
Mayes Rd. N22 2K 47
Mayeswood Rd. SE12 4A 142
MAYFAIR 3J 11 (7F 83)
Mayfair Av. DA7: Bex 1D 126
Mayfair Av. IG1: Ilf 2D 70
Mayfair Av. KT4: Wor Pk 1C 164
Mayfair Av. RM6: Chad H 6D 54
Mayfair Av. TW2: Whitt 7G 113
Mayfair Cl. BR3: Beck 1D 158
Mayfair Cl. KT6: Surb 1E 162
Mayfair Ct. HA8: Edg 5A 28
Mayfair Gdns. IG8: Wfd G 7D 36
Mayfair Gdns. N17 6H 33
Mayfair M. NW1 7D 64
(off Regents Pk. Rd.)
Mayfair M. SW12 1F 137
Mayfair Pl. W1 4K 11 (1F 101)
Mayfair Row W1 5J 11 (1F 101)
Mayfair Ter. N14 7C 22
Mayfield DA7: Bex 3F 127
Mayfield Av. BR6: Orp 1K 173
Mayfield Av. HA3: Kenton 5B 42
Mayfield Av. IG8: Wfd G 6D 36
Mayfield Av. N12 4F 31
Mayfield Av. N14 2C 32
Mayfield Av. W13 3B 96
Mayfield Av. W4 4A 98
Mayfield Cl. E8 6F 67
Mayfield Cl. KT7: T Ditt 1B 162
Mayfield Cl. SE20 1H 157
Mayfield Cl. SW4 5H 119
Mayfield Cl. TW15: Ashf 6D 128
Mayfield Cl. UB10: Hil 3D 74
Mayfield Cres. CR7: Thor H 4K 155
Mayfield Cres. N9 6C 24
Mayfield Dr. HA5: Pinn 4D 40
Mayfield Gdns. NW4 6F 45
Mayfield Gdns. W7 6H 77
Mayfield Ho. E2 2H 85
(off Cambridge Heath Rd.)
Mayfield Mans. SW15 5H 117
Mayfield Rd. BR1: Broml 5C 160
Mayfield Rd. CR7: Thor H 4K 155
Mayfield Rd. DA17: Belv 4J 109
Mayfield Rd. E13 4H 87
Mayfield Rd. E17 2A 50
Mayfield Rd. E4 2K 35
Mayfield Rd. E8 7F 67
Mayfield Rd. EN3: Enf H 2E 24
Mayfield Rd. N8 5K 47
Mayfield Rd. RM8: Dag 1C 72
Mayfield Rd. SM2: Sutt 6B 166
Mayfield Rd. SW19 1H 153
Mayfield Rd. W12 2A 98
Mayfield Rd. W3 7H 79
Mayfield Rd. Flats N8 6K 47
Mayfields HA9: Wemb 2G 61
Mayfields Cl. HA9: Wemb 2G 61
Mayfield Vs. DA14: Sidc 6C 144
Mayflower Cl. HA4: Ruis 6E 38
Mayflower Cl. SE16 4K 103
Mayflower Ho. E14 2C 104
(off Westferry Rd.)
Mayflower Ho. IG11: Bark 1H 89
(off Westbury Rd.)
Mayflower Rd. SW9 3J 119
Mayflower St. SE16 2J 103
Mayfly Cl. HA5: Eastc 7A 40
Mayfly Gdns. UB5: N'olt 3B 76
Mayford NW1 2G 83
(not continuous)
Mayford Cl. BR3: Beck 3K 157
Mayford Cl. SW12 7D 118
Mayford Rd. SW12 7D 118
May Gdns. HA0: Wemb 3C 78
Maygood Ho. N1 2K 83
(off Maygood St.)
Maygood St. N1 2A 84
Maygrove Rd. NW6 6H 63
Mayhew Cl. E4 3H 35
Mayhew Ct. SE5 4D 120
Mayhill Ct. SE15 7E 102
(off Tower Mill Rd.)
Mayhill Rd. EN5: Barn 6B 20
Mayhill Rd. SE7 6K 105
May Ho. E3 2C 86
(off Thomas Fyre Dr.)
Mayland Mans. IG11: Bark 7F 71
(off Whiting Av.)
Maylands Dr. DA14: Sidc 3D 144
Maylands Ho. SW3 4D 16 (4C 100)
(off Cale St.)
May La. HA3: Kenton 7F 43
Maylie Ho. SE16 2H 103
(off Marigold St.)
Maynard Cl. N15 5E 48
Maynard Cl. SW6 7K 99
Maynard Path E17 5E 50
Maynard Rd. E17 5E 50
Maynards Quay E1 7J 85
Mayne Ct. SE26 5H 139
Maynooth Gdns. SM5: Cars 7D 154
Mayo Ct. W13 3B 96
Mayo Ho. E1 5J 85
(off Lindley St.)
Mayola Rd. E5 4J 67
Mayo Rd. CR0: C'don 5D 156
Mayo Rd. KT12: Walt T 7J 147
Mayo Rd. NW10 6A 62
Mayor's & City of London Court, The 7E 8 (6D 84)
(off Basinghall St.)
Mayow Rd. SE23 3K 139
Mayow Rd. SE26 4K 139
Mayplace Cl. DA7: Bex 3H 127
Mayplace La. SE18 6F 107
(not continuous)
Mayplace Rd. E. DA1: Cray 4K 127
Mayplace Rd. E. DA7: Bex 3H 127
Mayplace Rd. W. DA7: Bex 4G 127
MAYPOLE 1K 145
Maypole Ct. UB2: S'hall 2D 94
(off Merrick Rd.)
May Rd. E13 2J 87
May Rd. E4 6H 35
May Rd. TW2: Twick 1J 131
Mayroyd Av. KT6: Surb 2G 163
May's Bldgs. M. SE10 7E 104
May's Ct. SE10 7F 105
Mays Ct. WC2 3E 12 (7J 83)
Mays Hill Rd. BR2: Broml 2G 159
Mays La. EN5: Ark 1J 29
Mays La. EN5: Barn 1J 29
Maysoule Rd. SW11 4B 118
Mays Rd. TW11: Tedd 5H 131
Mayston M. SE10 5J 105
(off Ormiston Rd.)
May St. W14 Kelway Ho. 5H 99
May St. W14 Orchard Sq. 5H 99
Mayswood Gdns. RM10: Dag 6J 73
Maythorne Cotts. SE13 5F 123
Mayton St. N7 3K 65
Maytree Cl. HA8: Edg 3D 28
Maytree Ct. CR4: Mitc 3E 154
Maytree Ct. UB5: N'olt 3C 76
Maytree Gdns. W5 2D 96
May Tree Ho. SE4 3B 122
(off Wickham Rd.)
Maytree La. HA7: Stan 7F 27
Maytree Wlk. SW2 2A 138
Mayville Est. N16 5E 66
Mayville Rd. E11 2G 69
(not continuous)
Mayville Rd. IG1: Ilf 5F 71
May Wlk. E13 2K 87
Mayward Ho. SE5 1E 120
(off Peckham Rd.)
Maywood Cl. BR3: Beck 7D 140
May Wynne Ho. E16 7K 87
(off Murray Sq.)
Mazal Ct. KT8: W Mole 4F 149
Maze Hill SE10 6G 105
Maze Hill SE3 7H 105
Maze Hill Lodge SE10 6F 105
(off Park Vista)
Mazenod Av. NW6 7J 63
Maze Rd. TW9: Kew 7G 97
MCC Cricket Mus. & Tours 2A 4 (3B 82)
Mead, The BR3: Beck 1E 158
Mead, The BR4: W W'ck 1F 171
Mead, The N2 2A 46
Mead, The SM6: W'gton 6H 167
Mead, The UB10: Ick 2C 56
Mead, The W13 5B 78
Meadbank Studios SW11 7C 100
(off Parkgate Rd.)
Mead Cl. HA3: Hrw W 1H 41
Mead Cl. NW1 6E 64
Mead Ct. NW9 5J 43
Mead Cres. E4 4K 35
Mead Cres. SM1: Sutt 3C 166
Meadcroft Rd. SE11 7K 19 (6B 102)
(not continuous)
Meadcroft Rd. SE17 6B 102
Meade Cl. W4 6G 97
Meade Ho. E14 6G 87
(off Lyell St.)
Meade M. SW1 5D 18 (5H 101)
(off Causton St.)
Meader Ct. SE14 7K 103
Mead Fld. HA2: Harr 3D 58
Meadfield HA8: Edg 2C 28
(not continuous)
Meadfield Grn. HA8: Edg 2C 28
Meadfoot Rd. SW16 7G 137
Meadgate Av. IG8: Wfd G 5H 37
Mead Gro. RM6: Chad H 3D 54
Mead Ho. W11 1H 99
(off Ladbroke Rd.)
Mead Ho. La. UB4: Hayes 4F 75
Meadhurst Club 5H 129
Meadhurst Pk. TW16: Sun 6G 129
Meadlands Dr. TW10: Ham 2D 132
Mead Lodge W4 2K 97
Meadow, The BR7: Chst 6G 143
Meadow, The N10 3E 46
Meadow Av. CR0: C'don 6K 157
Meadow Bank N21 6E 22
Meadowbank KT5: Surb 6F 151
Meadowbank NW3 7D 64
Meadowbank SE3 3H 123
Meadowbank Cl. SW6 7E 98
Meadowbank Cl. TW7: Isle 1J 113
Meadowbank Gdns. TW5: Cran 1J 111
Meadowbank Rd. NW9 7K 43
Meadowbridge Ct. CR0: C'don 5D 156
(off Princess Rd.)
Meadowbrook Cl. SL3: Poyle 4A 174
Meadowbrook Ct. TW7: Isle 3J 113
Meadow Cl. BR7: Chst 5F 143
Meadow Cl. DA6: Bex 5F 127
Meadow Cl. E4 1J 35
Meadow Cl. E9 6B 68
Meadow Cl. EN3: Enf W 1F 25
Meadow Cl. EN5: Barn 6C 20
Meadow Cl. HA4: Ruis 6H 39
Meadow Cl. IG11: Bark 7A 72
Meadow Cl. KT10: Hin W 3A 162
Meadow Cl. SE6 5C 140
Meadow Cl. SM1: Sutt 2A 166
Meadow Cl. SW20 4E 152
Meadow Cl. TW10: Ham 1E 132
Meadow Cl. TW4: Houn 6E 112
Meadow Cl. UB5: N'olt 2E 76
Meadow Ct. E16 1A 106
(off Booth Rd.)
Meadow Ct. N1 2E 84
Meadow Ct. TW3: Houn 6F 113
Meadowcourt Rd. SE3 4H 123
Meadowcroft BR1: Broml 3D 160
Meadowcroft W4 5G 97
(off Brooks Rd.)
Meadowcroft Cl. E10 7D 50
Meadowcroft Cl. N13 2F 33
Meadowcroft M. E1 7G 85
(off Cable St.)
Meadowcroft M. SE6 6D 122
Meadowcroft Rd. N13 2F 33
Meadow Dr. N10 3F 47
Meadow Dr. NW4 2E 44
Meadowford Cl. SE28 7A 90
Meadow Gdns. HA8: Edg 6C 28
Meadow Gth. NW10 7J 61
Meadow Ga. HA2: Harr 3F 59
Meadowgate Cl. NW7 5G 29
Meadow Hill KT3: N Mald 6A 152
Meadow La. SE12 3K 141
Meadowlark Ho. NW9 7B 44
Meadowlea Cl. UB7: Harm 2E 174
Meadow M. SW8 6K 101
Meadow Pl. SW8 7J 101
Meadow Pl. W4 7A 98
Meadow Rd. BR2: Broml 2G 159
Meadow Rd. HA5: Pinn 4B 40
Meadow Rd. IG11: Bark 7K 71
Meadow Rd. RM7: Rush G 1J 73
Meadow Rd. RM9: Dag 6F 73
Meadow Rd. SM1: Sutt 4C 166
Meadow Rd. SW19 7A 136
Meadow Rd. SW8 7K 101
Meadow Rd. TW13: Felt 2C 130
Meadow Rd. TW15: Ashf 5F 129
Meadow Rd. UB1: S'hall 7D 76
Meadow Row SE1 3C 102
Meadows, The E4 4A 36
Meadows Cl. E10 2C 68
Meadows Ct. DA14: Sidc 6B 144
Meadows End TW16: Sun 1J 147
Meadowside SE3 4A 124
Meadowside SE9 4A 124
Meadowside TW1: Twick 7D 114
Meadow Stile CR0: C'don 3C 168
Meadows Way SE4 3A 122
Meadowsweet Cl. E16 5B 88
Meadowsweet Cl. SW20 4E 152
Meadow Vw. DA15: Sidc 7B 126
Meadow Vw. HA1: Harr 1J 59
Meadow Vw. TW19: Stanw M 7A 174
Meadow Vw. Rd. CR7: Thor H 5B 156
Meadow Vw. Rd. SW20 4E 152
Meadow Vw. Rd. UB4: Hayes 4F 75
Meadowview Rd. DA5: Bexl 6E 126
Meadowview Rd. KT19: Ewe 7A 164
Meadowview Rd. SE6 5B 140
Meadow Wlk. E18 4J 51
Meadow Wlk. KT17: Ewe 7B 164
Meadow Wlk. KT19: Ewe 6A 164
Meadow Wlk. RM9: Dag 6F 73
Meadow Wlk. SM6: W'gton 3F 167
Meadow Way BR6: Farnb 3E 172
Meadow Way HA4: Ruis 6K 39
Meadow Way HA9: Wemb 4D 60
Meadow Way KT9: Chess 5E 162
Meadow Way NW9 5K 43
Meadow Way, The HA3: Hrw W 1J 41
Meadow Waye TW5: Hest 6C 94
Meadow Works EN5: New Bar 6E 20
Mead Path SW17 4A 136
Mead Pl. CR0: C'don 1C 168
Mead Pl. E9 6J 67
Mead Plat NW10 6J 61
Mead Rd. BR7: Chst 6G 143
Mead Rd. HA8: Edg 6B 28
Mead Rd. TW10: Ham 3C 132
Mead Row SE1 1J 19 (3A 102)
Meads, The HA8: Edg 6E 28
Meads, The SM3: Cheam 3G 165
Meads, The SM4: Mord 5C 154
Meads, The UB8: Cowl 4A 74
Meads Ct. E15 6H 69
Meadside Cl. BR3: Beck 1A 158
Meads La. IG3: Ilf 7J 53
Meads Rd. EN3: Enf H 1F 25
Meads Rd. N22 2B 48
Mead Ter. HA9: Wemb 4D 60
Meadvale Rd. CR0: C'don 7F 157
Meadvale Rd. W5 4B 78
Mead Way BR2: Hayes 6H 159
Mead Way CR0: C'don 2A 170
Mead Way HA4: Ruis 6F 39
Meadway BR3: Beck 1E 158
Meadway EN5: Barn 4D 20
Meadway EN5: New Bar 4D 20
Meadway IG3: Bark 4J 71
Meadway IG3: Ilf 4J 71
Meadway IG8: Wfd G 5F 37
Meadway KT5: Surb 1J 163
Meadway N14 2C 32
Meadway NW11 6J 45
Meadway SW20 4E 152
Meadway TW15: Ashf 4C 128
Meadway TW2: Twick 1H 131
Meadway, The IG9: Buck H 1G 37
Meadway, The SE3 2F 123
Meadway Cl. EN5: Barn 4D 20
Meadway Cl. HA5: Hat E 6A 26
Meadway Cl. NW11 6K 45
Meadway Ct. RM8: Dag 2F 73
Meadway Ct. TW11: Tedd 5C 132
Meadway Ct. W5 4F 79
Meadway Gdns. HA4: Ruis 6F 39
Meadway Ga. NW11 6J 45
Meaford Way SE20 7H 139
Meakin Est. SE1 3E 102
Meander Ho. E20 5D 68
(off Logan Cl.)
Meanley Rd. E12 4C 70
Meard St. W1 1C 12 (6H 83)
(not continuous)

256 A–Z London

Meyrick Rd. – Minson Rd.

Meyrick Rd. SW11 ......3B 118
MFA Bowl Lewisham 3E 122
Miah Ter. E1 ......1G 103
Miall Wlk. SE26 ......4A 140
Mia M. N13 ......5F 33
Mica Ho. N1 ......7A 66
Micawber Av. UB8: Hil 4C 74
Micawber Ct. N1 ......1D 8 (3C 84)
(off Windsor Ter.)
Micawber Ho. SE16 ......2G 103
(off Llewellyn St.)
Micawber St. N1 ......1D 8 (3C 84)
Michael Cliffe Ho. EC1 ......2A 8 (3B 84)
(off Finsbury Est.)
Michael Cl. E3 ......4B 86
Michael Edwards Studio Theatre, The 6E 104
(within Cutty Sark)
Michael Faraday Ho. SE17 ......5E 102
(off Beaconsfield Rd.)
Michael Gaynor Cl. W7 ......1K 95
Michael Haines Ho. SW9 ......7A 102
(off Sth. Island Pl.)
Michael Manley Ind. Est. SW8 ......1G 119
Michaelmas Cl. SW20 ......3E 152
Michael Rd. E11 ......1G 69
Michael Rd. SE25 ......3E 156
Michael Rd. SW6 ......1K 117
Michael Robbins Way NW7 ......5B 30
Michaels Cl. SE13 ......4G 123
Michael Stewart Ho. SW6 ......6H 99
(off Clem Attlee Ct.)
Michelangelo Ct. SE16 ......5H 103
(off Stubbs Dr.)
Micheldever Rd. SE12 ......6G 123
Michelham Gdns. TW1: Twick 3K 131
Michelle Ct. BR1: Broml 1H 159
(off Blyth Rd.)
Michelle Ct. N12 ......5F 31
Michelle Ct. W3 ......7K 79
Michelsdale Dr. TW9: Rich 4E 114
Michelson Ho. SE11 ......4H 19 (4K 101)
(off Black Prince Rd.)
Michel's Row TW9: Rich 4E 114
(off Michelsdale Dr.)
Michel Wlk. SE18 ......5F 107
Michigan Av. E12 ......4D 70
Michigan Bldg. E14 ......1F 105
(off Biscayne Av.)
Michigan Ho. E14 ......3C 104
Mickleham Down N12 ......4C 30
Mickledore NW1 ......1B 6 (2G 83)
(off Ampthill Est.)
Mickleham Cl. BR5: St P 2K 161
Mickleham Gdns. SM3: Cheam 6G 165
Mickleham Rd. BR5: St P 1K 161
Mickleham Way CR0: New Ad 7F 171
Micklethwaite Rd. SW6 ......6J 99
Mickleton Ho. W2 ......5J 81
(off Westbourne Pk. Rd.)
Midas Bus. Cen. RM10: Dag 4H 73
Midas Metropolitan Ind. Est. SM4: Mord 7E 152
MID BECKTON 5D 88
Midcroft HA4: Ruis 1G 57
Middle Dartrey Wlk. SW10 ......7A 100
(off Worlds End Est.)
Middle Dene NW7 ......3E 28
Middlefield NW8 ......1B 82
Middlefielde W13 ......5B 78
Middlefield Gdns. IG2: Ilf 6F 53
Middle Grn. Cl. KT5: Surb 6F 151
Middleham Gdns. N18 ......6B 34
Middleham Rd. N18 ......6B 34
Middle La. N8 ......5J 47
Middle La. TW11: Tedd 6K 131
Middle La. M. N8 ......5J 47
Middle Mill Halls of Residence KT1: King T 3F 151
Middle New St. EC4 ......7K 7 (6A 84)
(off Pemberton Row)
Middle Pk. Av. SE9 ......6B 124
Middle Path HA2: Harr 1H 59
Middle Rd. E13 ......2J 87
Middle Rd. EN4: E Barn 6H 21
Middle Rd. HA2: Harr 2H 59
Middle Rd. SW16 ......2H 155
Middle Row W10 ......4G 81
Middlesborough Rd. N18 ......6B 34
Middlesex Bldg., The E1 ......6H 9 (5E 84)
(off Artillery La.)
Middlesex Bus. Cen. UB2: S'hall 2E 94
Middlesex CCC 1B 4 (3B 82)
Middlesex Cl. UB1: S'hall 4F 77
Middlesex Ct. HA1: Harr 5K 41
Middlesex Ct. TW8: Bford 5C 96
(off Glenhurst Rd.)
Middlesex Ct. W4 ......4B 98
Middlesex Filter Beds Nature Reserve 3K 67
Middlesex Guildhall 7E 12 (2J 101)
(off Lit. George St.)
Middlesex Ho. HA0: Wemb 1D 78
Middlesex Pl. E9 ......6J 67
(off Elsdale St.)
Middlesex Rd. CR4: Mitc 5J 155
Middlesex St. E1 ......6H 9 (5E 84)
Middlesex University Archway Campus 1G 65
Middlesex University Hendon Campus 4D 44
Middlesex Wharf E5 ......2J 67
Middle St. CR0: C'don 2C 168
(not continuous)
Middle St. EC1 ......5C 8 (5C 84)
Middle Temple Hall 2J 13 (7A 84)
Middle Temple La. EC4 ......1J 13 (6A 84)
Middleton Av. DA14: Sidc 6B 144
Middleton Av. E4 ......4G 35
Middleton Av. UB6: G'frd 2H 77
Middleton Cl. E4 ......3G 35
Middleton Dr. HA5: Eastc 3J 39
Middleton Dr. SE16 ......2K 103
Middleton Gdns. IG2: Ilf 6F 53
Middleton Green 3H 85
(off Old Bethnal Green Road)
Middleton Gro. IG11: Bark 3A 90
Middleton Gro. N7 ......5J 65
Middleton Ho. E8 ......7G 67
Middleton Ho. SE1 ......3D 102
(off Burbage Cl.)
Middleton Ho. SW1 ......4D 18 (4H 101)
(off Causton St.)
Middleton M. N7 ......5J 65
Middleton Pl. W1 ......6A 6 (5G 83)
(off Langham St.)
Middleton Rd. E8 ......7F 67
Middleton Rd. NW11 ......7J 45
Middleton Rd. SM4: Cars 6K 153
Middleton Rd. SM4: Mord 6K 153
Middleton Rd. SM5: Cars 7B 154
Middleton Rd. UB3: Hayes 5F 75
Middleton St. E2 ......3H 85
Middleton Way SE13 ......4F 123
Middle Way DA18: Erith 3E 108
Middle Way SW16 ......2H 155
Middle Way UB4: Yead 4A 76
Middleway NW11 ......5K 45
Middle Way, The HA3: W'stone 2K 41
Middle Yd. SE1 ......4G 15 (1E 102)
Midfield Av. DA7: Bex 3J 127
Midfield Pde. DA7: Bex 3J 127
Midfield Way BR5: St P 7A 144
Midford Ho. NW4 ......4E 44
(off Belle Vue Est.)
Midford Pl. W1 ......4B 6 (4G 83)
Midholm HA9: Wemb 1G 61
Midholm NW11 ......4K 45
Midholm Cl. NW11 ......4K 45
Midholm Rd. CR0: C'don 2A 170
Midhope Ho. WC1 ......2F 7 (3J 83)
(off Midhope St.)
Midhope St. WC1 ......2F 7 (3J 83)
Midhurst SE26 ......6J 139
Midhurst Av. CR0: C'don 7A 156
Midhurst Av. N10 ......3E 46
Midhurst Gdns. UB10: Hil 1E 74
Midhurst Hill DA6: Bex 6G 127
Midhurst Ho. E14 ......6B 86
(off Salmon La.)
Midhurst Pde. N10 ......3E 46
(off Fortis Grn.)
Midhurst Rd. W13 ......2A 96
Midhurst Way E5 ......4G 67
Midland Goods Shed N1 ......1J 83
(off Handyside St.)
Midland Pde. NW6 ......6K 63
Midland Pl. E14 ......5E 104
Midland Rd. E10 ......7E 50
Midland Rd. NW1 ......2H 83
Midland Ter. NW10 ......4A 80
Midland Ter. NW2 ......3F 63
Midleton Rd. KT3: N Mald 3J 151
Midlothian Rd. E3 ......4B 86
(off Burdett Rd.)
Midmoor Rd. SW12 ......1G 137
Midmoor Rd. SW19 ......1F 153
Midnight Av. SE5 ......7B 102
Midship Cl. SE16 ......1K 103
Midship Point E14 ......2C 104
(off The Quarterdeck)
Midstrath Rd. NW10 ......4A 62
Midsummer Av. TW4: Houn 4D 112
Midway SM3: Sutt 7H 153
Midway Ho. EC1 ......1B 8 (3B 84)
(off Manningford Cl.)
Midwinter Cl. DA16: Well 3A 126
Midwood Cl. NW2 ......3D 62
Miers Cl. E6 ......1E 88
Mighell Av. IG4: Ilf 5B 52
Mikardo Ct. E14 ......7E 86
(off Poplar High St.)
Milan Ct. N11 ......1H 47
Milan Rd. UB1: S'hall 2D 94
Milborne Gro. SW10 ......5A 100
Milborne St. E9 ......6J 67
Milborough Cres. SE12 ......6G 123
Milbourne Ho. KT1: King T 1G 151
(off Coombe Rd.)
Milbourne Pl. KT19: Ewe 4K 163
Milburn Dr. UB7: Yiew 7A 74
Milcote St. SE1 ......7A 14 (2B 102)
Mildenhall Rd. E5 ......4J 67
Mildmay Av. N1 ......6D 66
Mildmay Gro. Nth. N1 ......5D 66
Mildmay Gro. Sth. N1 ......5D 66
Mildmay Pk. N1 ......5D 66
Mildmay Pl. N16 ......5E 66
Mildmay Rd. IG1: Ilf 3F 71
Mildmay Rd. N1 ......5D 66
Mildmay Rd. RM7: Rom 5J 55
Mildmay St. N1 ......6D 66
Mildred Av. UB3: Harl 4F 93
Mildred Av. UB5: N'olt 5F 59
Mildred Ct. CR0: C'don 1G 169
Mildred Rd. DA8: Erith 5K 109
Mildrose Ct. NW6 ......3J 81
(off Malvern M.)
Mildura Ct. N8 ......4K 47
MILE END 4B 86
Mile End, The E17 ......1K 49
Mile End Climbing Wall 3A 86
Mile End Pk. 2A 86
Mile End Pk. Leisure Cen. 5A 86
Mile End Pl. E1 ......4K 85
Mile End Rd. E1 ......5J 85
Mile End Rd. E3 ......5J 85
Mile End Stadium 5B 86
Mile Rd. SM6: Bedd 1F 167
(not continuous)
Mile Rd. SM6: W'gton 1F 167
(not continuous)
Miles Bldgs. NW1 ......5C 4 (5C 82)
(off Penfold Pl.)
Miles Cl. SE28 ......1H 107
Miles Ct. CR0: C'don 2B 168
(off Cuthbert Rd.)
Miles Ct. E1 ......6H 85
(off Tillman St.)
Miles Dr. SE28 ......1J 107
Miles Ho. SE10 ......5G 105
(off Tuskar St.)
Miles Lodge E15 ......5F 69
(off Colegrave Rd.)
Miles Lodge HA1: Harr 5H 41
Milespit Hill NW7 ......5J 29
Miles Pl. KT5: Surb 4F 151
Miles Pl. NW8 ......5B 4 (5B 82)
(off Broadley St.)
Miles Rd. CR4: Mitc 3C 154
Miles Rd. N8 ......3J 47
Miles St. SW8 ......7E 18 (6J 101)
(not continuous)
Milestone Cl. N9 ......2B 34
Milestone Cl. SM2: Sutt 6B 166
Milestone Ct. E10 ......7D 50
MILESTONE GREEN 4J 115
Milestone Ho. KT1: King T 3D 150
(off Surbiton Rd.)
Milestone Rd. SE19 ......6F 139
Miles Way N20 ......2H 31
Milfoil St. W12 ......7C 80
Milford Cl. SE2 ......6E 108
Milford Ct. UB1: S'hall 1E 94
Milford Gdns. CR0: C'don 5J 157
Milford Gdns. HA0: Wemb 4D 60
Milford Gdns. HA8: Edg 7B 28
Milford Gro. SM1: Sutt 4A 166
Milford La. WC2 ......2J 13 (7A 84)
Milford M. SW16 ......3K 137
Milford Rd. UB1: S'hall 7E 76
Milford Rd. W13 ......1B 96
Milford Towers SE6 ......7D 122
Milk St. BR1: Broml 6K 141
Milk St. E16 ......1F 107
Milk St. EC2 ......7D 8 (6C 84)
Milkwell Gdns. IG8: Wfd G 7E 36
Milkwell Yd. SE5 ......1C 120
Milkwood Rd. SE24 ......5B 120
Milk Yd. E1 ......7J 85
Millais Av. E12 ......5E 70
Millais Ct. UB5: N'olt 2B 76
(off Academy Gdns.)
Millais Cres. KT19: Ewe 5A 164
Millais Gdns. HA8: Edg 2G 43
Millais Ho. SW1 ......4E 18 (4J 101)
(off Marsham St.)
Millais Rd. E11 ......4E 68
Millais Rd. EN1: Enf 5A 24
Millais Rd. KT3: N Mald 7A 152
Millais Way KT19: Ewe 4J 163
Millard Cl. N16 ......5E 66
Millard Rd. SE8 ......5B 104
Millard Ter. RM10: Dag 6G 73
Millbank SM6: W'gton 5H 167
Millbank SW1 ......2E 18 (3J 101)
Millbank Ct. SW1 ......3E 18 (4J 101)
(off John Islip St.)
Millbank Twr. SW1 ......4E 18 (4J 101)
Millbank Way SE12 ......5J 123
Millbourne Rd. TW13: Hanw 4C 130
Mill Bri. EN5: Barn 6C 20
Millbroke M. IG8: Wfd G 6B 36
Millbrook Av. DA16: Well 4H 125
Millbrooke Ct. SW15 ......5G 117
(off Keswick Rd.)
Millbrook Gdns. RM6: Chad H 6F 55
Millbrook Ho. SE15 ......6G 103
(off Peckham Pk. Rd.)
Millbrook Pk. NW7 ......6B 30
Millbrook Pas. SW9 ......3B 120
Millbrook Pl. NW1 ......2G 83
(off Hampstead Rd.)
Millbrook Rd. N9 ......1C 34
Millbrook Rd. SW9 ......3B 120
Mill Cl. NW7 ......1G 45
Mill Cl. SM5: Cars 2E 166
Mill Cnr. EN5: Barn 1C 20
Mill Ct. E10 ......3E 68
Mill Ct. E5 ......2J 67
Mill Ct. SE28 ......7B 90
(off Titmuss Av.)
Millcroft Ho. SE6 ......4E 140
(off Melfield Gdns.)
Mill Dr. HA4: Ruis 7F 39
Millender Wlk. SE16 ......4J 103
(off New Rotherhithe Rd.)
MILLENNIUM BRIDGE Southwark 3C 14 (7C 84)
Millennium Bri. Ho. EC4 ......2C 14 (7C 84)
(off Up. Thames St.)
Millennium Bus. Cen. NW2 ......2D 62
Millennium Cl. E16 ......6K 87
Millennium Dr. E14 ......4F 105
Millennium Ho. E17 ......5K 49
Millennium Ho. SW15 ......5G 117
(off Plaza Gdns.)
Millennium Pl. E2 ......2H 85
Millennium Sq. SE1 ......6K 15 (2F 103)
Millennium Way SE10 ......2G 105
Miller Av. EN3: Enf L 1H 25
Miller Cl. BR1: Broml 5K 141
Miller Cl. CR4: Mitc 7D 154
Miller Cl. HA5: Pinn 2A 40
Miller Cl. RM5: Col R 1G 55
Miller Ct. DA7: Bex 3J 127
Miller Ho. E1 ......5K 85
(off Shandy St.)
Miller Ho. W10 ......4H 81
(off Harrow Rd.)
Miller Rd. CR0: C'don 1K 167
Miller Rd. SW19 ......6B 136
Miller's Av. E8 ......5F 67
Millers Cl. NW7 ......4H 29
Millers Ct. HA0: Wemb 7E 60
(off Vicars Bri. Cl.)
Millers Grn. Cl. EN2: Enf 3G 23
Miller's House Visitor Cen. 3E 86
(off Three Mill La.)
Millers Mdw. Cl. SE3 ......4H 123
Millers Row E20 ......5D 68
Miller's Ter. E8 ......5F 67
Miller St. NW1 ......2G 83
(not continuous)
Millers Way W6 ......2E 98
Millers Wharf Ho. E1 ......5K 15 (1G 103)
(off St Katherine's Way)
Millers Yd. N3 ......1K 45
Miller Wlk. SE1 ......5K 13 (1A 102)
Milles Sq. SW9 ......4A 120
Millet Rd. UB6: G'frd 2F 77
Mill Farm Av. TW16: Sun 7G 129
Mill Farm Bus. Pk. TW4: Houn 7C 112
Mill Farm Cl. HA5: Pinn 2A 40
Mill Farm Cres. TW4: Houn 1C 130
Millfield KT1: King T 3F 151
Millfield N4 ......2A 66
Millfield TW16: Sun 1F 147
Millfield Av. E17 ......1A 50
Millfield La. N6 ......1C 64
Millfield Pl. N6 ......2E 64
Millfield Rd. HA8: Edg 2J 43
Millfield Rd. TW4: Houn 1C 130
Millfields Rd. E5 ......4J 67
Millfield Theatre 4J 33
Mill Gdns. SE26 ......3H 139
Mill Grn. CR4: Mitc 7E 154
Mill Grn. Rd. CR4: Mitc 7D 154
Millgrove St. SW11 ......1E 118
Millharbour E14 ......2D 104
Millhaven Cl. RM6: Chad H 6B 54
MILL HILL 5F 29
Mill Hill SW13 ......2C 116
Mill Hill Cir. NW7 ......5G 29
MILL HILL CIR. 5G 29
Mill Hill Golf Course 2F 29
Mill Hill Gro. W3 ......1J 97
Mill Hill Ind. Est. NW7 ......6G 29
Mill Hill Old Railway Nature Reserve 6D 28
Mill Hill Rd. SW13 ......2C 116
Mill Hill Rd. W3 ......2H 97
Mill Hill School Sports Cen. 4H 29
Mill Hill Ter. W3 ......1H 97
Mill Ho. IG8: Wfd G 5C 36
Millhouse Pl. SE27 ......4B 138
Millicent Fawcett Ct. N17 ......1F 49
Millicent Gro. N13 ......5G 33
Millicent Preston Ho. IG11: Bark 1H 89
(off Ripple Rd.)
Millicent Rd. E10 ......1B 68
Milligan St. E14 ......7B 86
Milliner Ho. SW10 ......7A 100
(off Hortensia Rd.)
Milliners Ho. SE1 ......7H 15 (2E 102)
(off Bermondsey St.)
Milliners Ho. SW18 ......4J 117
Milling Rd. HA8: Edg 7E 28
Millington Ho. N16 ......3D 66
Millington Rd. UB3: Harl 3G 93
Mill La. CR0: Wadd 3K 167
Mill La. E4 ......3J 25
Mill La. IG8: Wfd G 5C 36
Mill La. KT17: Ewe 7B 164
Mill La. NW6 ......5H 63
Mill La. RM6: Chad H 6E 54
Mill La. SE18 ......5E 106
Mill La. SE8 ......1C 122
(off Deptford Bri.)
Mill La. SM5: Cars 4D 166
Mill La. Trad. Est. CR0: Wadd 3K 167
Millman Ct. WC1 ......4G 7 (4K 83)
(off Millman St.)
Millman M. WC1 ......4G 7 (4K 83)
Millman Pl. WC1 ......4H 7 (4K 83)
(off Millman St.)
Millman Rd. E16 ......7D 88
Millman St. WC1 ......4G 7 (4K 83)
Millmark Gro. SE14 ......2A 122
Millmarsh La. EN3: Brim 2F 25
Millmead Ind. Cen. N17 ......2H 49
Mill Mead Rd. N17 ......3H 49
MILL MEADS 2F 87
Mill Pl. BR7: Chst 1E 160
Mill Pl. E14 ......6A 86
Mill Pl. KT1: King T 3F 151
Mill Plat TW7: Isle 2A 114
(not continuous)
Mill Plat Av. TW7: Isle 2A 114
Mill Pond Cl. SW8 ......7H 101
Millpond Est. SE16 ......2H 103
Millpond Pl. SM5: Cars 3E 166
Mill Ridge HA8: Edg 5A 28
Mill River Trad. Est. EN3: Pond E 3F 25
Mill Rd. DA8: Erith 7J 109
Mill Rd. E16 ......1K 105
Mill Rd. IG1: Ilf 3E 70
Mill Rd. SW19 ......7A 136
Mill Rd. TW2: Twick 2G 131
Mill Row DA5: Bexl 1H 145
Mill Row N1 ......1E 84
Mills Cl. UB10: Hil 2C 74
Mills Ct. EC2 ......2G 9 (3E 84)
(off Curtain Rd.)
Mills Gro. E14 ......6E 86
Mills Gro. NW4 ......3F 45
Millshott Cl. SW6 ......1E 116
Mills Ho. SW8 ......1G 119
(off Thessaly Rd.)
Millside SM5: Cars 2D 166
Millside Pl. TW7: Isle 2B 114
Millson Cl. N20 ......2G 31
Mills Row W4 ......4K 97
Millstone Cl. E15 ......6F 69
Millstream Cl. N13 ......5F 33
Millstream Ho. SE16 ......2H 103
(off Jamaica Rd.)
Millstream Rd. SE1 ......7J 15 (2F 103)
Mill St. KT1: King T 3E 150
Mill St. SE1 ......7K 15 (2F 103)
Mill St. W1 ......2K 11 (7F 83)
Mills Yd. SW6 ......3K 117
Mill Trad. Est., The NW10 ......3J 79
Mill Va. BR2: Broml 2H 159
Mill Vw. Cl. KT17: Ewe 7B 164
Mill Vw. Gdns. CR0: C'don 3K 169
MILLWALL 4D 104
Millwall Dock Rd. E14 ......3C 104
Millwall FC 5J 103
Millwall Pk. 4E 104
Mill Way TW14: Felt 5K 111
Millway NW7 ......4F 29
Millway Gdns. UB5: N'olt 6D 58
Millwood Rd. TW3: Houn 5G 113
Millwood St. W10 ......5G 81
Mill Yd. E1 ......7G 85
Mill Yd. Ind. Est. HA8: Edg 1H 43
Milman Cl. HA5: Pinn 3B 40
Milman Rd. NW6 ......2F 81
Milman's Ho. SW10 ......6B 100
(off Milman's St.)
Milman's St. SW10 ......6B 100
Milne Ct. E18 ......1J 51
Milne Gdns. SE9 ......5C 124
Milne Ho. SE18 ......4D 106
(off Ogilby St.)
Milner Ct. SE15 ......7F 103
(off Colegrove Rd.)
Milner Dr. TW2: Whitt 7H 113
Milner Pl. N1 ......1A 84
Milner Pl. SE1 ......6H 13 (2B 102)
Milner Pl. SM5: Cars 4E 166
Milner Rd. CR7: Thor H 3D 156
Milner Rd. E15 ......3G 87
Milner Rd. KT1: King T 3D 150
Milner Rd. RM8: Dag 2C 72
Milner Rd. SM4: Mord 5B 154
Milner Rd. SW19 ......1K 153
Milner Sq. N1 ......7B 66
Milner St. SW3 ......3E 16 (4D 100)
Milner Wlk. SE9 ......2H 143
Milnthorpe Rd. W4 ......6K 97
Milo Gdns. SE22 ......6F 121
Milo Rd. SE22 ......6F 121
Milrood Ho. E1 ......5K 85
(off Stepney Grn.)
Milroy Wlk. SE1 ......4A 14 (1B 102)
Milson Rd. W14 ......3F 99
Milstead Ho. E5 ......5H 67
Milton Av. CR0: C'don 7D 156
Milton Av. E6 ......7B 70
Milton Av. EN5: Barn 5C 20
Milton Av. N6 ......7G 47
Milton Av. NW10 ......1J 79
Milton Av. NW9 ......3J 43
Milton Av. SM1: Sutt 3B 166
Milton Cl. N2 ......5A 46
Milton Cl. SE1 ......4F 103
Milton Cl. SM1: Sutt 3B 166
Milton Cl. UB4: Hayes 6J 75
Milton Ct. E17 ......4C 50
Milton Ct. EC2 ......5E 8 (5D 84)
Milton Ct. RM6: Chad H 7C 54
Milton Ct. SE14 ......6B 104
(not continuous)
Milton Ct. SW18 ......5J 117
Milton Ct. TW2: Twick 3J 131
Milton Ct. UB10: Ick 3D 56
Milton Court Concert Hall 5E 8 (5D 84)
(off Milton Ct.)
Milton Ct. Rd. SE14 ......6A 104
Milton Cres. IG2: Ilf 7F 53
Milton Dr. TW17: Shep 4A 146
Milton Gdn. Est. N16 ......4D 66
Milton Gdns. TW19: Stanw 1B 128
Milton Gro. N11 ......5B 32
Milton Gro. N16 ......4D 66
Milton Ho. E17 ......4C 50
Milton Ho. E2 ......3J 85
(off Roman Rd.)
Milton Ho. SE5 ......7D 102
(off Elmington Est.)
Milton Ho. SM1: Sutt 3J 165
Milton Lodge DA14: Sidc 4A 144
Milton Lodge TW1: Twick 7K 113
Milton Mans. W14 ......6G 99
(off Queen's Club Gdns.)
Milton Pk. N6 ......7G 47
Milton Pl. N7 ......5A 66
(off Eastwood Cl.)
Milton Rd. CR0: C'don 7D 156
Milton Rd. CR4: Mitc 7E 136
Milton Rd. DA16: Well 1K 125
Milton Rd. DA17: Belv 4G 109
Milton Rd. E17 ......4C 50
Milton Rd. HA1: Harr 4J 41
Milton Rd. N15 ......4B 48
Milton Rd. N6 ......7G 47
Milton Rd. NW7 ......5H 29
Milton Rd. NW9 ......7C 44
Milton Rd. SE24 ......5B 120
Milton Rd. SM1: Sutt 3J 165
Milton Rd. SM6: W'gton 6G 167
Milton Rd. SW14 ......3K 115
Milton Rd. SW19 ......6A 136
Milton Rd. TW12: Hamp 7E 130
Milton Rd. UB10: Ick 4D 56
Milton Rd. W3 ......1K 97
Milton Rd. W7 ......7K 77
Milton St. EC2 ......5E 8 (5D 84)
Milton Way UB7: W Dray 4B 92
Milverton Dr. UB10: Ick 4E 56
Milverton Gdns. IG3: Ilf 2K 71
Milverton Ho. SE6 ......3A 140
Milverton Pl. BR1: Broml 5A 142
Milverton Rd. NW6 ......7E 62
Milverton St. SE11 ......6K 19 (5A 102)
Milverton Way SE9 ......4E 142
Milward St. E1 ......5H 85
Milward Wlk. SE18 ......6E 106
Mimosa Cl. CR4: Mitc 7D 154
Mimosa Ho. E20 ......5E 68
(off Liberty Bri. Rd.)
Mimosa Ho. UB4: Yead 5A 76
Mimosa Lodge NW10 ......5B 62
Mimosa Rd. UB4: Yead 5A 76
Mimosa St. SW6 ......1H 117
Minard Rd. SE6 ......7G 123
Mina Rd. SE17 ......5E 102
Mina Rd. SW19 ......1J 153
Mina Ter. N9 ......7B 24
Minchenden Ct. N14 ......2C 32
Minchenden Cres. N14 ......3B 32
Minchin Ho. E14 ......6C 86
(off Dod St.)
Mincing La. EC3 ......2G 15 (7E 84)
Minden Gdns. IG11: Bark 3B 90
Minden Rd. SE20 ......1H 157
Minden Rd. SM3: Sutt 2G 165
Minehead Rd. HA2: Harr 3E 58
Minehead Rd. SW16 ......5K 137
Mineral Cl. EN5: Barn 6A 20
Mineral St. SE18 ......4J 107
Minera M. SW1 ......3G 17 (4E 100)
Minerva Cl. DA14: Sidc 3J 143
Minerva Cl. SW9 ......7A 102
Minerva Cl. TW19: Stanw M 7B 174
Minerva Ct. EC1 ......4K 7 (4A 84)
(off Bowling Grn. La.)
Minerva Lodge N7 ......6K 65
Minerva Rd. E4 ......7J 35
Minerva Rd. KT1: King T 2F 151
Minerva Rd. NW10 ......4J 79
Minerva St. E2 ......2H 85
Minerva Wlk. EC1 ......7B 8 (6B 84)
Minerva Way EN5: Barn 5C 20
Minet Av. NW10 ......2A 80
Minet Country Pk. 2A 94
Minet Dr. UB3: Hayes 1J 93
Minet Gdns. NW10 ......2A 80
Minet Gdns. UB3: Hayes 1K 93
Minet Rd. SW9 ......2B 120
Minford Gdns. W14 ......2F 99
Minford Ho. W14 ......2F 99
(off Minford Gdns.)
Mingard Wlk. N7 ......2K 65
Ming St. E14 ......7C 86
Minimax Cl. TW14: Felt 6J 111
Minima Yacht Club 3D 150
(off High St.)
Ministry Way SE9 ......2D 142
Miniver Pl. EC4 ......2D 14 (7C 84)
(off Garlick Hill)
Mink Ct. TW4: Houn 2A 112
Minnie Baldock St. E16 ......6H 87
Minniedale KT5: Surb 5F 151
Minnow St. SE17 ......4E 102
Minnow Wlk. SE17 ......4E 102
Minories EC3 ......1J 15 (6F 85)
Minotaur Dr. EN5: Barn 5C 20
Minshaw Ct. DA14: Sidc 4K 143
Minshill St. SW8 ......1H 119
Minshull Pl. BR3: Beck 7C 140
Minson Rd. E9 ......1K 85

Minstead Gdns. – Morden Rd. M.

Minstead Gdns. SW15 ... 7B 116
Minstead Way KT3: N Mald ... 6A 152
Minster Av. SM1: Sutt ... 2J 165
Minster Ct. EC3 ... 2H 15 (7E 84)
(off Mincing La.)
Minster Ct. W5 ... 4E 78
Minster Dr. CR0: C'don ... 4E 168
Minster Gdns. KT8: W Mole ... 4D 148
Minsterley Av. TW17: Shep ... 4G 147
Minster Pavement EC3 ... 2H 15 (7E 84)
(off Mincing La.)
Minster Rd. BR1: Broml ... 7K 141
Minster Rd. NW2 ... 5G 63
Minster Wlk. N8 ... 4J 47
Minstrel Gdns. KT5: Surb ... 4F 151
Mint Bus. Pk. E16 ... 5K 87
Mint Cl. UB10: Hil ... 3D 74
Mintern Cl. N13 ... 3G 33
Minterne Av. UB2: S'hall ... 4E 94
Minterne Rd. HA3: Kenton ... 5F 43
Minterne Waye UB4: Yead ... 6A 76
Mintern St. N1 ... 2D 84
Minter Rd. IG11: Bark ... 4A 90
Minton Apts. SW8 ... 7J 101
Minton Ho. SE11 ... 3J 19 (4A 102)
(off Walnut Tree Wlk.)
Minton M. NW6 ... 6K 63
Mint Rd. SM6: W'gton ... 4F 167
Mint St. E2 ... 4H 85
(off Three Colts La.)
Mint St. SE1 ... 6C 14 (2C 102)
Mint Wlk. CR0: C'don ... 3C 168
Mirabelle Gdns. E20 ... 5E 68
Mirabel Rd. SW6 ... 7H 99
Mira Ho. E20 ... 5E 68
(off Prize Wlk.)
Miranda Cl. E1 ... 5J 85
Miranda Ct. W3 ... 6F 79
Miranda Ho. N1 ... 1G 9 (2E 84)
(off Crondall St.)
Miranda Rd. N19 ... 1G 65
Mirfield St. SE7 ... 4B 106
Miriam Rd. SE18 ... 5J 107
Mirravale Trad. Est. RM8: Dag ... 7E 54
Mirren Cl. HA2: Harr ... 4D 58
Mirror Path SE9 ... 3A 142
Misbourne Rd. UB10: Hil ... 1C 74
Missenden SE17 ... 5D 102
(off Roland Way)
Missenden Cl. TW14: Felt ... 1H 129
Missenden Gdns. SM4: Mord ... 6A 154
Missenden Ho. NW8 ... 3C 4 (4C 82)
(off Jerome Cres.)
Mission, The E14 ... 6B 86
(off Commercial Rd.)
Mission Gro. E17 ... 5A 50
Mission Pl. SE15 ... 1G 121
Mission Sq. TW8: Bford ... 6E 96
Missouri Ct. HA5: Eastc ... 6A 40
Mistletoe Cl. CR0: C'don ... 1K 169
Mistral SE5 ... 1E 120
Misty's Fld. KT12: Walt T ... 7A 148
Mitali Pas. E1 ... 6G 85
MITCHAM ... 3D 154
Mitcham Gdn. Village CR4: Mitc ... 5E 154
Mitcham Golf Course ... 5E 154
Mitcham Ho. SE5 ... 1C 120
Mitcham Ind. Est. CR4: Mitc ... 1E 154
Mitcham La. SW16 ... 6G 137
Mitcham Pk. CR4: Mitc ... 4C 154
Mitcham Rd. CR0: C'don ... 6J 155
Mitcham Rd. E6 ... 3C 88
Mitcham Rd. IG3: Ilf ... 7K 53
Mitcham Rd. SW17 ... 5D 136
Mitchell NW9 ... 1B 44
(off Quakers Course)
Mitchellbrook Way NW10 ... 6K 61
Mitchell Cl. DA17: Belv ... 3J 109
Mitchell Cl. RM8: Dag ... 3C 72
Mitchell Cl. SE2 ... 4C 108
Mitchell Ho. N1 ... 7B 66
(off College Cross)
Mitchell Ho. W12 ... 7D 80
(off White City Est.)
Mitchell Rd. BR6: Orp ... 4K 173
Mitchell Rd. N13 ... 5H 33
Mitchell's Pl. SE21 ... 6E 120
(off Aysgarth Rd.)
Mitchell St. EC1 ... 3C 8 (4C 84)
(not continuous)
Mitchell Wlk. E6 Allhallows Rd. ... 5C 88
(off Allhallows Rd.)
Mitchell Wlk. E6 Elmley Cl. ... 5D 88
Mitchell Way BR1: Broml ... 1J 159
Mitchell Way NW10 ... 6J 61
Mitchison Ct. TW16: Sun ... 1J 147
(off Downside)
Mitchison Rd. N1 ... 6D 66
Mitchley Rd. N17 ... 3G 49
Mitford Bldgs. SW6 ... 7J 99
(off Dawes Rd.)
Mitford Cl. KT9: Chess ... 6C 162
Mitford Rd. N19 ... 2J 65
Mitre, The E14 ... 7B 86
Mitre Av. E17 ... 3C 50
Mitre Bri. Ind. Pk. W10 ... 4D 80
(not continuous)
Mitre Cl. BR2: Broml ... 2H 159
Mitre Cl. SM2: Sutt ... 7A 166
Mitre Cl. TW17: Shep ... 6F 147
Mitre Ho. SW3 ... 5E 16 (5D 100)
(off King's Rd.)
Mitre Pas. EC3 ... 1H 15 (6E 84)
(off Mitre Sq.)
Mitre Pas. SE10 ... 2G 105
Mitre Rd. E15 ... 2G 87
Mitre Rd. SE1 ... 6K 13 (2A 102)
Mitre Sq. EC3 ... 1H 15 (6E 84)
Mitre St. EC3 ... 1H 15 (6E 84)
Mitre Way W10 ... 4D 80
Mitre Yd. SW3 ... 3D 16 (4C 100)
Mitten Ho. SE8 ... 7D 104
(off Creative Rd.)
Mizen Ct. E14 ... 2C 104
(off Alpha Gro.)
Mizzen Mast Ho. SE18 ... 3D 106
Mizzen St. IG11: Bark ... 1H 89
Moat, The KT3: N Mald ... 1A 152
Moat Cl. BR6: Chels ... 6K 173
Moat Ct. DA15: Sidc ... 3K 143
Moat Ct. SE9 ... 6D 124
Moat Cres. N3 ... 3K 45
Moat Cft. DA16: Well ... 3C 126
Moat Dr. E13 ... 2A 88
Moat Dr. HA1: Harr ... 4G 41
Moat Dr. HA4: Ruis ... 7G 39
Moat Farm Rd. UB5: N'olt ... 6D 58
Moatfield NW6 ... 7G 63
Moatlands Ho. WC1 ... 2F 7 (3J 83)
(off Cromer St.)
Moat La. KT8: E Mos ... 3K 149
Moat Lodge, The HA2: Harr ... 2J 59
Moat Pl. SW9 ... 3K 119
Moat Pl. W3 ... 6H 79
Moat Side EN3: Pond E ... 4E 24
Moat Side TW13: Hanw ... 4A 130
Moat St. SW11 ... 7G 101
Moberly Rd. SW4 ... 7H 119
Moberly Sports Cen. ... 3F 81
Mobil Ct. WC2 ... 1H 13 (6K 83)
(off Clement's Inn)
MOBY DICK ... 4E 54
Mocatta Ho. E1 ... 4H 85
(off Brady St.)
Mocha Ct. E3 ... 2D 86
(off Taylor Pl.)
MoDA ... 2B 44
Modbury Gdns. NW5 ... 6E 64
Modder Pl. SW15 ... 4F 117
Model Cotts. SW14 ... 4J 115
Model Cotts. W13 ... 2B 96
Model Farm Cl. SE9 ... 3C 142
Modena Ho. E14 ... 6G 87
(off Lyell St.)
Modern Ct. EC4 ... 7A 8 (6B 84)
(off Farringdon St.)
Modling Ho. E2 ... 2K 85
(off Mace St.)
Moelwyn N7 ... 5H 65
Moelyn M. HA1: Harr ... 5A 42
Moffat Ct. SW19 ... 5J 135
Moffat Ho. SE5 ... 7C 102
Moffat Rd. CR7: Thor H ... 2C 156
Moffat Rd. N13 ... 6D 32
Moffat Rd. SW17 ... 4D 136
Mogden La. TW7: Isle ... 5K 113
Mogul Bldg. E15 ... 5E 68
(off Property Row)
Mohammedi Pk. UB5: N'olt ... 1E 76
Mohawk Ho. E3 ... 2A 86
(off Gernon Rd.)
Mohmmad Khan Rd. E11 ... 1H 69
Moineau NW9 ... 1B 44
(off Long Mead)
Moira Cl. N17 ... 2E 48
Moira Ho. SW9 ... 1A 120
(off Gosling Way)
Moira Rd. SE9 ... 4D 124
Mokswell Ct. N10 ... 1E 46
Molasses Ho. SW11 ... 3A 118
(off Clove Hitch Quay)
Molasses Row SW11 ... 3A 118
Mole Abbey Gdns. KT8: W Mole ... 3F 149
Mole Ct. KT19: Ewe ... 4J 163
Mole Ho. NW8 ... 4B 4 (4B 82)
(off Church St. Est.)
Molember Ct. KT8: E Mos ... 4J 149
Molember Rd. KT8: E Mos ... 5J 149
Mole Pl. KT8: W Mole ... 4F 149
Molescroft SE9 ... 3G 143
Molesey Av. KT8: W Mole ... 5D 148
Molesey Dr. SM3: Cheam ... 2G 165
Molesey Heath Local Nature Reserve ... 6E 148
Molesey Pk. Av. KT8: W Mole ... 5F 149
Molesey Pk. Cl. KT8: E Mos ... 5G 149
Molesey Pk. Rd. KT8: E Mos ... 5F 149
Molesey Pk. Rd. KT8: W Mole ... 5F 149
Molesey Rd. KT8: W Mole ... 6D 148
Molesford Rd. SW6 ... 1J 117
Molesham Cl. KT8: W Mole ... 3F 149
Molesham Way KT8: W Mole ... 3F 149
Molesworth Ho. SE17 ... 6B 102
(off Brandon Est.)
Molesworth St. SE13 ... 4E 122
Moliner Ct. BR3: Beck ... 7C 140
Mollis Ho. E3 ... 5C 86
(off Gale St.)
Mollison Dr. SM6: W'gton ... 7H 167
Mollison Sq. SM6: W'gton ... 7H 167
(off Mollison Dr.)
Mollison Way HA8: Edg ... 2F 43
Molly Huggins Cl. SW12 ... 7G 119
Molten Ct. SE14 ... 6B 104
(off Moulding La.)
Molton Ho. N1 ... 1K 83
(off Barnsbury Est.)
Molyneux Dr. SW17 ... 4F 137
Molyneux St. W1 ... 6D 4 (5C 82)
Monarch Cl. BR4: W W'ck ... 4H 171
Monarch Cl. TW14: Felt ... 7G 111
Monarch Ct. HA7: Stan ... 7J 27
(off Howard Rd.)
Monarch Ct. N2 ... 5B 46
Monarch Dr. E16 ... 5B 88
Monarch Dr. UB3: Hayes ... 7H 75
Monarch Ho. W8 ... 3J 99
(off Kensington High St.)
Monarch M. E17 ... 6D 50
Monarch M. SW16 ... 5A 138
Monarch Pde. CR4: Mitc ... 2D 154
Monarch Pl. IG9: Buck H ... 2F 37
Monarch Point SW6 ... 2A 118
Monarch Rd. DA17: Belv ... 3G 109
Monarch Sq. SW11 ... 4C 118
Monarchs Way HA4: Ruis ... 1F 57
Monarch Way IG2: Ilf ... 6H 53
Mona Rd. SE15 ... 2J 121
Monastery Gdns. EN2: Enf ... 2J 23
Mona St. E16 ... 5H 87
Monaveen Gdns. KT8: W Mole ... 3F 149
Monck Ho. SE1 ... 7D 14 (2C 102)
(off Cole St.)
Moncks Row SW18 ... 6H 117
Monck St. SW1 ... 2D 18 (3H 101)
Monckton Ct. W14 ... 3H 99
(off Strangways Ter.)
Monclar Rd. SE5 ... 4D 120
Moncorvo Cl. SW7 ... 7C 10 (2C 100)
Moncrieff Cl. E6 ... 6C 88
Moncrieff Pl. SE15 ... 2G 121
Moncrieff St. SE15 ... 2G 121
Monday All. N16 ... 2F 67
(off High St.)
Mondial Way UB3: Harl ... 7E 92
Mondragon Ho. SW8 ... 1J 119
(off Guildford Rd.)
Monega Rd. E12 ... 6B 70
Monega Rd. E7 ... 6A 70
Monet Ct. SE16 ... 5H 103
(off Stubbs Dr.)
Moneyer Ho. N1 ... 1E 8 (3D 84)
(off Provost St.)
Mongers Almshouses E9 ... 7K 67
(off Church Cres.)
Monica Ct. EN1: Enf ... 5K 23
Monica James Ho. DA14: Sidc ... 3A 144
Monica Shaw Ct. NW1 ... 1D 6 (2H 83)
(off Purchese St.)
Monier Rd. E3 ... 7C 68
Monivea Rd. BR3: Beck ... 7B 140
Monk Ct. W12 ... 1C 98
Monk Dr. E16 ... 7J 87
MONKEN HADLEY ... 2C 20
Monkfrith Av. N14 ... 6A 22
Monkfrith Cl. N14 ... 7A 22
Monkfrith Way N14 ... 7K 21
Monkham's Av. IG8: Wfd G ... 5E 36
Monkham's Dr. IG8: Wfd G ... 5E 36
Monkham's La. IG8: Wfd G ... 5D 36
Monkham's La. IG9: Buck H ... 3E 36
Monkleigh Rd. SM4: Mord ... 3G 153
Monks Av. EN5: New Bar ... 6F 21
Monks Av. KT8: W Mole ... 5D 148
Monks Cl. EN2: Enf ... 2H 23
Monks Cl. HA2: Harr ... 2F 59
Monks Cl. HA4: Ruis ... 4B 58
Monks Cl. SE2 ... 4D 108
Monks Cres. KT12: Walt T ... 7K 147
Monksdene Gdns. SM1: Sutt ... 3K 165
Monks Dr. W3 ... 5G 79
Monksfarm Pl. SE2 ... 2B 108
MONKS ORCHARD ... 7A 158
Monks Orchard Rd. BR3: Beck ... 1C 170
Monks Pk. HA9: Wemb ... 6H 61
Monks Pk. Gdns. HA9: Wemb ... 7H 61
Monks Rd. EN2: Enf ... 2G 23
Monk St. SE18 ... 4E 106
Monks Way BR3: Beck ... 6C 158
Monks Way BR5: Farnb ... 1G 173
Monks Way NW11 ... 4H 45
Monks Way UB7: Harm ... 6A 92
Monkswood Gdns. IG5: Ilf ... 3E 52
Monkton Ho. E5 ... 5H 67
Monkton Ho. SE16 ... 2K 103
(off Wolfe Cres.)
Monkton Rd. DA16: Well ... 2K 125
Monkton St. SE11 ... 3K 19 (4A 102)
Monkville Av. NW11 ... 4H 45
Monkville Pde. NW11 ... 4H 45
Monkwell Sq. EC2 ... 6D 8 (5C 84)
Monmouth Av. E18 ... 3K 51
Monmouth Av. KT1: Hamp W ... 7C 132
Monmouth Cl. CR4: Mitc ... 4J 155
Monmouth Cl. DA16: Well ... 4A 126
Monmouth Cl. W4 ... 3J 97
Monmouth Ct. W7 ... 5K 77
(off Copley Cl.)
Monmouth Gro. TW8: Bford ... 4E 96
Monmouth Pl. W2 ... 6K 81
(off Monmouth Rd.)
Monmouth Rd. E6 ... 3D 88
Monmouth Rd. N9 ... 2C 34
Monmouth Rd. RM9: Dag ... 5F 73
Monmouth Rd. UB3: Harl ... 4G 93
Monmouth Rd. W2 ... 6J 81
Monmouth St. WC2 ... 1E 12 (6J 83)
Monnery Rd. N19 ... 3G 65
Monnow Rd. SE1 ... 5G 103
Mono La. TW13: Felt ... 2K 129
Monolulu Ct. SE17 ... 5D 102
(off East St.)
Monoux Almshouses E17 ... 4D 50
Monoux Gro. E17 ... 1C 50
Monro Ct. E16 ... 4H 87
Monroe Cres. EN1: Enf ... 1C 24
Monroe Dr. SW14 ... 5H 115
Monroe Ho. NW8 ... 2D 4 (3C 82)
(off Lorne Cl.)
Monro Gdns. HA3: Hrw W ... 7D 26
Monro Way E5 ... 4G 67
Monsell Ct. N4 ... 3B 66
Monsell Rd. N4 ... 3A 66
Monsey Pl. E1 ... 4A 86
Monson Rd. NW10 ... 2C 80
Monson Rd. SE14 ... 7K 103
Mons Way BR2: Broml ... 6C 160
Montacute Rd. CR0: New Ad ... 7E 170
Montacute Rd. SE6 ... 7B 122
Montacute Rd. SM4: Mord ... 6B 154
Montagu Ct. W1 ... 6F 5 (5D 82)
(off Montagu Pl.)
Montagu Cres. N18 ... 4C 34
Montague Av. SE4 ... 4B 122
Montague Av. W7 ... 1K 95
Montague Cl. EN5: Barn ... 4C 20
Montague Cl. KT12: Walt T ... 7K 147
Montague Cl. SE1 ... 4E 14 (1D 102)
Montague Ct. DA15: Sidc ... 3A 144
Montague Ct. N7 ... 7A 66
(off St Clements St.)
Montague Gdns. W3 ... 7G 79
Montague Ho. E16 ... 1K 105
(off Wesley Av.)
Montague Ho. IG3: Ilf ... 1A 72
Montague Ho. N1 ... 1E 84
(off Halcomb St.)
Montague M. E3 ... 3B 86
(off Tredegar Ter.)
Montague M. SE20 ... 6J 139
Montague Pas. UB8: Uxb ... 7A 56
Montague Pl. WC1 ... 5D 6 (5H 83)
Montague Rd. CR0: C'don ... 1B 168
Montague Rd. E11 ... 2H 69
Montague Rd. E8 ... 5G 67
Montague Rd. N15 ... 4G 49
Montague Rd. N8 ... 5K 47
Montague Rd. SW19 ... 7K 135
Montague Rd. TW10: Rich ... 6E 114
Montague Rd. TW3: Houn ... 3F 113
Montague Rd. UB2: S'hall ... 4C 94
Montague Rd. UB8: Uxb ... 7A 56
Montague Rd. W13 ... 6B 78
Montague Rd. W7 ... 1K 95
Montague Sq. SE15 ... 7J 103
Montague St. EC1 ... 6C 8 (5C 84)
Montague St. WC1 ... 5E 6 (5J 83)
Montague Ter. BR2: Broml ... 4H 159
Montague Walks HA0: Wemb ... 1F 79
Montague Waye UB2: S'hall ... 3C 94
Montagu Gdns. N18 ... 4C 34
Montagu Gdns. SM6: W'gton ... 4G 167
Montagu Ind. Est. N18 ... 4D 34
Montagu Mans. W1 ... 5F 5 (5D 82)
Montagu M. Nth. W1 ... 6F 5 (5D 82)
Montagu M. Sth. W1 ... 7F 5 (6D 82)
Montagu M. W. W1 ... 7F 5 (6D 82)
Montagu Pl. W1 ... 6E 4 (5D 82)
Montagu Rd. N18 ... 5C 34
Montagu Rd. N9 ... 3D 34
Montagu Rd. NW4 ... 6C 44
Montagu Row W1 ... 6F 5 (5D 82)
Montagu Sq. W1 ... 6F 5 (5D 82)
Montagu St. W1 ... 7F 5 (6D 82)
Montaigne Cl. SW1 ... 4D 18 (4H 101)
Montalt Rd. IG8: Wfd G ... 4C 36
Montana HA9: Wemb ... 4G 61
(off Exhibition Way)
Montana Bldg. SE13 ... 1D 122
(off Deal's Gateway)
Montana Gdns. SE26 ... 5B 140
Montana Gdns. SM1: Sutt ... 5A 166
Montana Rd. SW17 ... 3E 136
Montana Rd. SW20 ... 1E 152
Montanaro Ct. N1 ... 1C 84
(off Coleman Flds.)
Montbelle Rd. SE9 ... 3F 143
Montcalm Cl. BR2: Hayes ... 6J 159
Montcalm Cl. UB4: Yead ... 3K 75
Montcalm Ho. E14 ... 4B 104
Montcalm Rd. SE7 ... 7B 106
Montclare St. E2 ... 3J 9 (4F 85)
Monteagle Av. IG11: Bark ... 6G 71
Monteagle Ct. N1 ... 2E 84
Monteagle Way E5 ... 3G 67
Monteagle Way SE15 ... 3H 121
Montefiore Ct. N16 ... 1F 67
Montefiore St. SW8 ... 2F 119
Montego Cl. SE24 ... 4A 120
Montem Rd. KT3: N Mald ... 4A 152
Montem Rd. SE23 ... 7B 122
Montem St. N4 ... 1K 65
Montenotte Rd. N8 ... 5G 47
Monterey Apts. N15 ... 5D 48
Monterey Cl. DA5: Bexl ... 2J 145
Monterey Cl. NW7 ... 5F 29
(off The Broadway)
Monterey Cl. UB10: Hil ... 7C 56
Monterey Studios W10 ... 2G 81
Montesole Ct. HA5: Pinn ... 2A 40
Montevetro SW11 ... 1B 118
Montfichet Rd. E20 ... 7E 68
Montford Pl. E15 ... 2E 86
Montford Pl. SE11 ... 6J 19 (5A 102)
Montford Rd. TW16: Sun ... 4J 147
Montfort Ho. E14 ... 3E 104
(off Galbraith St.)
Montfort Ho. E2 ... 3J 85
(off Victoria Pk. Sq.)
Montfort Pl. SW19 ... 1F 135
Montgolfier Wlk. UB5: N'olt ... 3C 76
Montgomerie M. SE23 ... 7J 121
Montgomery Cl. CR4: Mitc ... 4J 155
Montgomery Cl. DA15: Sidc ... 6K 125
Montgomery Ct. CR2: S Croy ... 5E 168
(off Birdhurst Rd.)
Montgomery Ct. W4 ... 7J 97
Montgomery Gdns. SM2: Sutt ... 7B 166
Montgomery Ho. UB5: N'olt ... 3D 76
(off Taywood Rd.)
Montgomery Ho. W2 ... 6A 4 (5B 82)
(off Harrow Rd.)
Montgomery Lodge E1 ... 4J 85
(off Cleveland Gro.)
Montgomery Rd. HA8: Edg ... 6A 28
Montgomery Rd. W4 ... 4J 97
Montgomery Sq. E14 ... 1D 104
Montgomery St. E14 ... 1D 104
Montholme Rd. SW11 ... 6D 118
Monthope Rd. E1 ... 6K 9 (5G 85)
Montolieu Gdns. SW15 ... 5D 116
Montpelier Av. DA5: Bexl ... 7D 126
Montpelier Av. W5 ... 5C 78
Montpelier Cl. UB10: Hil ... 1C 74
Montpelier Ct. BR2: Broml ... 4H 159
(off Westmoreland Rd.)
Montpelier Ct. W5 ... 5D 78
Montpelier Gdns. E6 ... 3B 88
Montpelier Gdns. RM6: Chad H ... 7C 54
Montpelier Gro. NW5 ... 5G 65
Montpelier M. SW7 ... 1D 16 (3C 100)
Montpelier Pl. E1 ... 6J 85
Montpelier Pl. SW7 ... 1D 16 (3C 100)
Montpelier Ri. HA9: Wemb ... 1D 60
Montpelier Ri. NW11 ... 7G 45
(not continuous)
Montpelier Rd. N3 ... 1A 46
Montpelier Rd. SE15 ... 1H 121
Montpelier Rd. SM1: Sutt ... 4A 166
Montpelier Rd. W5 ... 5D 78
Montpelier Row SE3 ... 2H 123
Montpelier Row TW1: Twick ... 7C 114
Montpelier Sq. SW7 ... 7D 10 (2C 100)
Montpelier St. SW7 ... 1D 16 (3C 100)
Montpelier Ter. SW7 ... 7D 10 (2C 100)
Montpelier Va. SE3 ... 2H 123
Montpelier Wlk. SW7 ... 1D 16 (3C 100)
Montpelier Way NW11 ... 7G 45
Montpellier Ct. KT12: Walt T ... 6J 147
Montrave Rd. SE20 ... 6J 139
Montreal Ho. SE16 ... 2K 103
(off Maple M.)
Montreal Ho. UB4: Yead ... 3K 75
(off Ayles Rd.)
Montreal Pl. WC2 ... 2G 13 (7K 83)
Montreal Rd. IG1: Ilf ... 7G 53
Montrell Rd. SW2 ... 1J 137
Montrose Av. DA15: Sidc ... 7A 126
Montrose Av. DA16: Well ... 3H 125
Montrose Av. HA8: Edg ... 2J 43
Montrose Av. NW6 ... 2G 81
Montrose Av. TW2: Whitt ... 7F 113
Montrose Cl. DA16: Well ... 3K 125
Montrose Cl. IG8: Wfd G ... 4D 36
Montrose Cl. TW15: Ashf ... 6E 128
Montrose Ct. HA1: Harr ... 5F 41
Montrose Ct. NW11 ... 4H 45
Montrose Ct. NW9 ... 3K 43
Montrose Ct. SE6 ... 2H 141
Montrose Ct. SW7 ... 7B 10 (2B 100)
Montrose Cres. HA0: Wemb ... 6E 60
Montrose Cres. N12 ... 6F 31
Montrose Gdns. CR4: Mitc ... 2D 154
Montrose Gdns. SM1: Sutt ... 2K 165
Montrose Ho. E14 ... 3C 104
Montrose Ho. SW1 ... 7H 11 (2E 100)
(off Montrose Pl.)
Montrose Pl. SW1 ... 7H 11 (2E 100)
Montrose Rd. HA3: W'stone ... 2J 41
Montrose Rd. TW14: Bedf ... 6F 111
Montrose Wlk. HA7: Stan ... 6G 27
Montrose Way SE23 ... 1K 139
Montserrat Av. IG8: Wfd G ... 7A 36
Montserrat Cl. SE19 ... 5D 138
Montserrat Rd. SW15 ... 4G 117
Monument, The ... 2F 15 (7D 84)
Monument Gdns. SE13 ... 5E 122
Monument St. EC3 ... 2F 15 (7D 84)
Monument Way N15 ... 3F 49
Monument Way N17 ... 3F 49
Monza St. E1 ... 7J 85
Moodkee St. SE16 ... 3J 103
Moody Rd. SE15 ... 1F 121
Moody St. E1 ... 3K 85
Moon Ct. SE12 ... 4J 123
Moon Ho. HA1: Harr ... 4J 41
Moon La. EN5: Barn ... 3C 20
Moonlight Dr. SE23 ... 7H 121
Moonraker Point SE1 ... 6C 14 (2C 102)
(off Pocock St.)
Moon St. N1 ... 1B 84
Moorcroft HA8: Edg ... 1H 43
Moorcroft Gdns. BR2: Broml ... 5C 160
Moorcroft La. UB8: Hil ... 5C 74
Moorcroft Rd. SW16 ... 3J 137
Moorcroft Way HA5: Pinn ... 5C 40
Moordown SE18 ... 7F 107
Moore Cl. CR4: Mitc ... 2F 155
Moore Cl. SW14 ... 3J 115
Moore Ct. HA0: Wemb ... 6E 60
Moore Ct. HA7: Stan ... 1D 42
Moore Ct. N1 ... 1B 84
(off Gaskin St.)
Moore Cres. RM9: Dag ... 1B 90
Moorefield Rd. N17 ... 2F 49
Moorehead Way SE3 ... 3J 123
Moore Ho. E1 ... 7J 85
(off Cable St.)
Moore Ho. E14 ... 2C 104
Moore Ho. E2 ... 3J 85
(off Roman Rd.)
Moore Ho. N8 ... 4J 47
(off Pembroke Rd.)
Moore Ho. SE10 ... 5H 105
(off Armitage Rd.)
Moore Ho. SW1 ... 6J 17 (5F 101)
(off Gatliff Rd.)
Mooreland Rd. BR1: Broml ... 7H 141
Moore Pk. Rd. SW6 ... 7J 99
Moore Rd. SE19 ... 6C 138
Moore St. SW3 ... 3E 16 (4D 100)
Moore Wlk. E7 ... 4J 69
Moorey Cl. E15 ... 1H 87
Moorfield Av. W5 ... 4D 78
Moorfield Rd. EN3: Enf H ... 1D 24
Moorfield Rd. KT9: Chess ... 5E 162
Moorfields EC2 ... 6E 8 (5D 84)
Moorfields Highwalk EC2 ... 6E 8 (5D 84)
(off New Union St.)
Moorgate EC2 ... 7E 8 (6D 84)
Moorgate Pl. EC2 ... 7E 8 (6D 84)
(off Moorgate)
Moorgreen Ho. EC1 ... 1A 8 (3B 84)
(off Wynyatt St.)
Moorhen Dr. NW9 ... 6B 44
Moorhen Ho. E3 ... 1B 86
(off Old Ford Rd.)
Moorhouse NW9 ... 1B 44
Moorhouse Rd. HA3: Kenton ... 3D 42
Moorhouse Rd. W2 ... 6J 81
Moorings, The E16 ... 5A 88
(off Prince Regent La.)
Moorings Ho. TW8: Bford ... 7C 96
MOOR JUNC. ... 3C 174
Moorland Cl. RM5: Col R ... 1H 55
Moorland Cl. TW2: Whitt ... 7E 112
Moorland Rd. SW9 ... 4B 120
Moorland Rd. UB7: Harm ... 2D 174
Moorlands UB5: N'olt ... 1C 76
Moorlands Av. NW7 ... 6J 29
Moor La. EC2 ... 6E 8 (5D 84)
(not continuous)
Moor La. KT9: Chess ... 4E 162
Moor La. UB7: Harm ... 2D 174
Moormead Dr. KT19: Ewe ... 5A 164
Moor Mead Rd. TW1: Twick ... 6A 114
Moor Pk. Gdns. KT2: King T ... 7A 134
Moor Pl. EC2 ... 6E 8 (5D 84)
Moorside Rd. BR1: Broml ... 3G 141
Moor St. W1 ... 1D 12 (6H 83)
Moot Ct. NW9 ... 5G 43
Moran Ho. E1 ... 1H 103
(off Wapping La.)
Morant Pl. N22 ... 1K 47
Morant St. E14 ... 7C 86
Mora Rd. NW2 ... 4E 62
Mora St. EC1 ... 2D 8 (3C 84)
Morat St. SW9 ... 1K 119
Moravian Cl. SW10 ... 7A 16 (6B 100)
Moravian Pl. SW10 ... 6B 100
Moravian St. E2 ... 2J 85
Moray Av. UB3: Hayes ... 1H 93
Moray Cl. HA8: Edg ... 2C 28
Moray Cl. RM1: Rom ... 1K 55
Moray Ct. CR2: S Croy ... 5C 168
(off Warham Rd.)
Moray Ho. E1 ... 4A 86
(off Harford St.)
Moray M. N7 ... 2K 65
Moray Rd. N4 ... 2K 65
Moray Way RM1: Rom ... 1K 55
Mordaunt Gdns. RM9: Dag ... 7E 72
Mordaunt Ho. NW10 ... 1K 79
(off Stracey Rd.)
Mordaunt Rd. NW10 ... 1K 79
Mordaunt St. SW9 ... 3K 119
MORDEN ... 3K 153
Morden Ct. SM4: Mord ... 4K 153
Morden Ct. Pde. SM4: Mord ... 4K 153
Morden Gdns. CR4: Mitc ... 4B 154
Morden Gdns. UB6: G'frd ... 5K 59
Morden Hall Pk. ... 3A 154
Morden Hall Rd. SM4: Mord ... 3K 153
Morden Hill SE13 ... 2E 122
Morden Ho. SM4: Mord ... 4J 153
Morden La. SE13 ... 2E 122
Morden Leisure Cen. ... 5H 153
MORDEN PARK ... 6G 153
Morden Rd. CR4: Mitc ... 4A 154
Morden Rd. RM6: Chad H ... 7E 54
Morden Rd. SE3 ... 2J 123
Morden Rd. SM4: Mord ... 4A 154
Morden Rd. SW19 ... 1K 153
Morden Rd. M. SE3 ... 2J 123

Neville Cl. NW1 2H 83
Neville Cl. NW6 2H 81
Neville Cl. SE15 1G 121
Neville Cl. TW3: Houn 2F 113
Neville Cl. W3 2J 97
Neville Ct. NW8 1A 4 (2B 82) *(off Abbey Rd.)*
Neville Dr. N2 6A 46
Neville Gdns. RM8: Dag 3D 72
Neville Gill Cl. SW18 6J 117
Neville Ho. N11 4K 31
Neville Ho. N22 1K 47 *(off Neville Pl.)*
Neville Ho. NW6 2H 81 *(off Denmark Rd.)*
Neville Ho. Yd. KT1: King T 2E 150
Neville Pl. N22 1K 47
Neville Rd. CR0: C'don 7D 156
Neville Rd. E7 7J 69
Neville Rd. IG6: Ilf 1G 53
Neville Rd. KT1: King T 2G 151
Neville Rd. NW6 2H 81
Neville Rd. RM8: Dag 3D 72
Neville Rd. TW10: Ham 3C 132
Neville Rd. W5 4D 78
Nevilles Ct. NW2 3C 62
Neville St. SW7 5A 16 (5B 100)
Neville Ter. SW7 5A 16 (5B 100)
Neville Wlk. SM5: Cars 7C 154
Nevill La. EC4 7K 7 (6A 84) *(off New Fetter La.)*
Nevill Rd. N16 4E 66
Nevin Dr. E4 1J 35
Nevin Ho. UB3: Harl 3E 92
Nevinson Cl. SW18 6B 118
Nevis Cl. E13 2K 87
Nevis Rd. SW17 2E 136
Nevitt Ho. N1 2D 84 *(off Cranston Est.)*
New Acres Rd. SE28 2J 107
Newall Cl. UB10: Uxb 1B 74
Newall Ho. SE1 3C 102 *(off Bath Ter.)*
Newall Rd. TW6: H'row A 1E 110
Newark Cres. NW10 3K 79
Newark Ho. SW9 2B 120
Newark Knok E6 6E 88
Newark Rd. CR2: S Croy 6D 168
Newark St. E1 5H 85 (not continuous)
Newark Way NW4 4C 44
New Ash Cl. N2 3B 46
New Atlas Wharf E14 3C 104 *(off Arnhem Pl.)*
New Baltic Wharf SE8 5A 104 *(off Evelyn St.)*
New Barn Cl. SM6: W'gton 6K 167
NEW BARNET 4G 21
New Barnet Leisure Cen. EN4: E Barn 4G 21
New Barn Rd. BR8: Swan 7K 145
New Barns Av. CR4: Mitc 4H 155
New Barn St. E13 4J 87
New Barns Way IG7: Chig 3K 37
Newbeck Ct. BR3: Beck 7B 140
NEW BECKENHAM 6B 140
New Bentham Ct. N1 7C 66 *(off Ecclesbourne Rd.)*
Newberry M. SW4 4J 119
Newbery Ho. N1 7C 66 *(off Northampton St.)*
Newbold Cotts. E1 6J 85
Newbolt Av. SM3: Cheam 5E 164
Newbolt Ho. SE17 5D 102 *(off Brandon St.)*
Newbolt Rd. HA7: Stan 5E 26
New Bond St. W1 1J 11 (6F 83)
Newborough Grn. KT3: N Mald 4K 151
New Brent St. NW4 5E 44
Newbridge Point SE23 3K 139 *(off Windrush La.)*
New Bri. St. EC4 1A 14 (6B 84)
New Broad St. EC2 6G 9 (5E 84)
New B'way. TW12: Hamp H 5H 131
New B'way. UB10: Hil 3D 74
New B'way. W5 7D 78
New Broadway Bldgs. W5 7D 78
Newburgh Rd. W3 1J 97
Newburgh St. W1 1B 12 (6G 83)
New Burlington M. W1 2A 12 (7G 83)
New Burlington Pl. W1 2A 12 (7G 83)
New Burlington St. W1 2A 12 (7G 83)
Newburn Ho. SE11 5H 19 (5K 101) *(off Newburn St.)*
Newburn St. SE11 6H 19 (5K 101)
Newbury Cl. RM10: Dag 2G 73
Newbury Cl. UB5: N'olt 6D 58
Newbury Ct. DA14: Sidc 4K 143
Newbury Ct. E5 5A 68 *(off Daubeney Rd.)*
Newbury Gdns. KT19: Ewe 4B 164
Newbury Ho. N22 1J 47
Newbury Ho. SW9 2B 120
Newbury Ho. W2 6K 81 *(off Hallfield Est.)*
Newbury M. NW5 6E 64
NEWBURY PARK 5H 53
Newbury Rd. BR2: Broml 3J 159
Newbury Rd. E4 6K 35
Newbury Rd. IG2: Ilf 6J 53
Newbury Rd. TW6: H'row A 1B 110
Newbury St. EC1 5C 8 (5C 84)
Newbury Way UB5: N'olt 6C 58
New Bus. Cen., The NW10 3B 80
New Butt La. SE8 7C 104
New Butt La. Nth. SE8 7C 104 *(off Hales St.)*
Newby NW1 2A 6 (3G 83) *(off Robert St.)*
Newby Cl. EN1: Enf 2K 23
Newby Ho. E14 7E 86 *(off Newby Pl.)*
Newby Pl. E14 7E 86
Newby St. SW8 3F 119
New Caledonian Mkt. 7H 15 (3E 102) *(off Bermondsey Sq.)*
New Caledonian Wharf SE16 3B 104
Newcastle Cl. EC4 7A 8 (6B 84)
Newcastle Ct. EC4 2D 14 (7C 84) *(off College Hill)*
Newcastle Ho. W1 5G 5 (5E 82) *(off Luxborough St.)*
Newcastle Pl. W2 5B 4 (5B 82)
Newcastle Row EC1 3K 7 (4A 84)
New Cavendish St. W1 6H 5 (5E 82)

New Century Ho. E16 6H 87 *(off Jude St.)*
New Change EC4 1C 14 (6C 84)
New Change Pas. EC4 1C 14 (6C 84) *(off New Change)*
New Chapel Sq. TW13: Felt 1K 129
New Charles St. EC1 1B 8 (3B 84)
NEW CHARLTON 4A 106
New Chiswick Pool 7A 98
New Church Rd. SE5 7C 102 (not continuous)
New City Rd. E13 3A 88
New Claremont Apts. SE1 4F 103 *(off Setchell Rd.)*
New Clocktower Pl. N7 6J 65
New Cl. SW19 3A 154
New Cl. TW13: Hanw 5C 130
New Colebrooke Ct. SM5: Cars 7D 166
New College Ct. NW3 6A 64 *(off College Cres.)*
New College M. N1 7A 66
New College Pde. NW3 6B 64 *(off Finchley Rd.)*
Newcombe Gdns. SW16 4J 137
Newcombe Gdns. TW4: Houn 4D 112
Newcombe Ho. E5 3H 67
Newcombe Pk. HA0: Wemb 1F 79
Newcombe Pk. NW7 5F 29
Newcombe Ri. UB7: Yiew 6A 74
Newcombe St. W8 1J 99
Newcomen Rd. E11 3H 69
Newcomen Rd. SW11 3B 118
Newcomen St. SE1 6E 14 (2D 102)
New Compton St. WC2 1D 12 (6H 83)
New Concordia Wharf SE1 6K 15 (2G 103)
New Ct. EC4 2J 13 (7A 84) *(off Fountain Ct.)*
New Ct. UB5: N'olt 5F 59
Newcourt Ho. E2 3H 85 *(off Pott St.)*
Newcourt St. NW8 1C 4 (2C 82)
New Covent Garden Market 7H 101
New Covent Rd. SW8 7G 101
New Crane Pl. E1 1J 103
New Crane Wharf E1 1J 103 *(off New Crane Pl.)*
New Cres. Yd. NW10 2B 80
Newcroft Cl. UB8: Hil 5B 74
Newcroft Ho. CR0: C'don 2F 169 *(off Homefield Pl.)*
NEW CROSS 1B 122
NEW CROSS 7B 104
NEW CROSS GATE 1K 121
NEW CROSS GATE 1K 121
New Cross Rd. SE14 7J 103
Newdales Cl. N9 2B 34
Newdene Av. UB5: N'olt 2B 76
Newdigate Ho. E14 6B 86 *(off Norbiton Rd.)*
New Diorama Theatre 3K 5 (4F 83)
New Drum St. E1 7K 9 (6F 85) *(off Aldgate Pl.)*
Newell St. E14 6B 86
NEW ELTHAM 2G 143
New End NW3 3A 64
New End Sq. NW3 4B 64
New England Ind. Est. IG11: Bark 2G 89
Newent Cl. SE15 7E 102
Newent Cl. SM5: Cars 1D 166
New Era Est. N1 1E 84 *(off Halcomb St.)*
New Era Ho. N1 1E 84 *(off Halcomb St.)*
New Farm Av. BR2: Broml 4J 159
New Farm La. HA6: Nwood 1G 39
New Ferry App. SE18 3E 106
New Festival Av. E14 6C 86
New Fetter La. EC4 7K 7 (6A 84)
Newfield Cl. TW12: Hamp 1E 148
Newfield Ri. NW2 3C 62
New Forest La. IG7: Chig 6K 37
Newgale Gdns. HA8: Edg 1F 43
New Gdn. Dr. UB7: W Dray 2A 92
Newgate CR0: C'don 1C 168
Newgate Cl. TW13: Hanw 2C 130
Newgate St. E4 3B 36 (not continuous)
Newgate St. EC1 7B 8 (6B 84)
New Globe Wlk. SE1 4C 14 (1C 102)
New Goulston St. E1 7J 9 (6F 85)
New Grn. Pl. SE19 6E 138
New Gun Wharf E3 1A 86 *(off Gunmaker's La.)*
Newhall Ct. N1 1C 84 *(off Popham Rd.)*
Newham Academy of Music 1C 88
Newham City Farm 6B 88
Newham Dockside E16 7C 88
Newham Leisure Cen. 4A 88
Newham's Row SE1 7H 15 (3E 102)
Newham Way E16 5H 87
Newham Way E6 4B 88
Newhaven Cl. UB3: Harl 4H 93
Newhaven Cres. TW15: Ashf 5F 129
Newhaven Gdns. SE9 4B 124
Newhaven La. E16 4H 87
Newhaven Rd. SE25 5D 156
New Heston Rd. TW5: Hest 7D 94
New Hope Ct. NW10 3D 80
New Horizons Ct. TW8: Bford 6A 96
Newhouse Av. RM6: Chad H 3D 54
Newhouse Cl. KT3: N Mald 7A 152
Newhouse Wlk. SM4: Mord 7A 154
Newick Cl. DA5: Bexl 6H 127
Newick Rd. E5 4H 67
Newing Grn. BR1: Broml 7B 142
NEWINGTON 3C 102
Newington Barrow Way N7 3K 65
Newington Butts SE1 4B 102
Newington Butts SE11 4B 102
Newington C'way. SE1 3B 102
Newington Ct. N16 4C 66 *(off Green Lanes)*
Newington Ct. Bus. Cen. SE1 7C 14 (3C 102) *(off Newington C'way.)*
Newington Grn. N1 5D 66
Newington Grn. N16 5D 66
Newington Grn. Community Gdns. 5D 66 *(off Newington Grn.)*
Newington Grn. Mans. N16 5D 66
Newington Grn. Rd. N1 6D 66
Newington Ind. Est. SE17 4B 102

New Inn B'way. EC2 3H 9 (4E 84)
New Inn Pas. WC2 1H 13 (6K 83) *(off Houghton St.)*
New Inn Sq. EC2 3H 9 (4E 84) *(off Bateman's Row)*
New Inn St. EC2 3H 9 (4E 84)
New Inn Yd. EC2 3H 9 (4E 84)
New Jubilee Ct. IG8: Wfd G 7D 36
New Jubilee Wharf E1 1J 103 *(off Wapping Wall)*
New Kelvin Av. TW11: Tedd 6J 131
New Kent Rd. SE1 3C 102
New Kings Rd. SW6 2H 117
New King St. SE8 6C 104
Newland Ct. EC1 3E 8 (4D 84) *(off St Luke's Est.)*
Newland Ct. HA9: Wemb 2G 61
Newland Dr. EN1: Enf 1C 24
Newland Gdns. W13 2A 96
Newland Ho. N8 3J 47 *(off Newland Rd.)*
Newland Ho. SE14 6K 103 *(off John Williams Cl.)*
Newland Rd. N8 3J 47
Newlands HA1: Harr 1J 59
NEWLANDS 3K 27
Newlands NW1 1A 6 (3G 83) *(off Harrington St.)*
NEWLANDS 5K 121
Newlands, The KT7: T Ditt 7J 149
Newlands, The SM6: W'gton 7G 167
Newlands Av. KT7: T Ditt 7J 149
Newlands Cl. HA0: Wemb 6C 60
Newlands Cl. HA8: Edg 3K 27
Newlands Cl. UB2: S'hall 5C 94
Newlands Ct. SE9 6E 124
Newlands Dr. SL3: Poyle 6A 174
Newlands Pk. SE26 6J 139
Newlands Pl. EN5: Barn 5A 20
Newlands Quay E1 7J 85
Newlands Rd. IG8: Wfd G 2C 36
Newlands Rd. SW16 2J 155
Newland St. E16 1C 106
Newlands Way KT9: Chess 5C 162
Newlands Woods CR0: Sels 7B 170
Newling Cl. E6 6D 88
New Lion Way SE17 4C 102
New London Performing Arts Cen. 4F 47
New London St. EC3 2H 15 (7E 84) *(off Hart St.)*
New Lydenburg Commercial Est. SE7 3A 106
New Lydenburg St. SE7 3A 106
Newlyn NW1 1G 83 *(off Plender St.)*
Newlyn Cl. BR6: Chels 4K 173
Newlyn Cl. UB8: Hil 5C 74
Newlyn Gdns. HA2: Harr 7D 40
Newlyn Ho. HA5: Hat E 1D 40
Newlyn Rd. DA16: Well 2K 125
Newlyn Rd. EN5: Barn 4C 20
Newlyn Rd. N17 1F 49
NEW MALDEN 4A 152
Newman Av. HA2: Harr 3G 41
Newman Cl. NW10 6D 62
Newman Cl. SE26 4J 139
Newman Ct. BR1: Broml 1J 159 *(off North St.)*
Newman Ct. TW15: Ashf 6D 128
Newman Ho. SE1 3B 102
Newman Pas. W1 6B 6 (5G 83) *(off Star Yd.)*
Newman Rd. BR1: Broml 1J 159
Newman Rd. CR0: C'don 1K 167
Newman Rd. E13 3K 87
Newman Rd. E17 5K 49
Newman Rd. UB3: Hayes 7K 75
Newman Rd. Ind. Est. CR0: C'don 7K 155
Newman's Ct. EC3 1F 15 (6D 84) *(off Cornhill)*
Newmans La. KT6: Surb 6D 150
Newman's Row WC2 6H 7 (5K 83)
Newman St. W1 6B 6 (5G 83)
Newman's Way EN4: Had W 1F 21
Newmarket Av. UB5: N'olt 5E 58
Newmarket Grn. SE9 7B 124
Newmarsh Rd. SE28 1K 107
Newmill Ho. E3 4E 86
New Mill Rd. SW11 6H 101
Newminster Rd. SM4: Mord 6A 154
New Mt. St. E15 7F 69
Newnes Path SW15 4D 116
Newnham Av. HA4: Ruis 1A 58
Newnham Cl. CR7: Thor H 2C 156
Newnham Cl. UB5: N'olt 6G 59
Newnham Gdns. UB5: N'olt 6G 59
Newnham Grn. N22 1A 48
Newnham Lodge DA17: Belv 5G 109 *(off Erith Rd.)*
Newnham M. N22 7F 33
Newnham Rd. N22 1K 47
Newnhams Cl. BR1: Broml 3D 160
Newnham Ter. SE1 1J 19 (3A 102)
Newnham Way HA3: Kenton 5E 42
New Nth. Pl. EC2 3G 9 (4E 84)
New Nth. Rd. N1 7C 66
New Nth. St. WC1 5G 7 (5K 83)
Newnton Cl. N4 7D 48
New Oak Rd. N2 2A 46
New Orleans Wlk. N19 7H 47
New Oxford St. WC1 7D 6 (6H 83)
New Pde. TW15: Ashf 4B 128
New Pde. UB7: Yiew 1A 92
New Paragon Wlk. SE17 4D 102
New Pk. Av. N13 3H 33
New Pk. Cl. UB5: N'olt 6C 58
New Pk. Est. N18 5D 34
New Pk. Ho. N13 4E 32
New Pk. Pde. SW2 7J 119 *(off New Pk. Rd.)*
New Pk. Rd. SW2 1H 137
New Pk. Rd. TW15: Ashf 5E 128
New Pl. CR0: Addtn 6C 170
New Pl. Sq. SE16 3H 103
New Plaistow Rd. E15 1G 87
New Pond Pde. HA4: Ruis 3J 57
Newport Av. E13 4K 87
Newport Av. E14 7F 87
Newport Ct. WC2 2D 12 (7H 83)
Newport Ho. E3 3A 86 *(off Strahan Rd.)*

Newport Lodge EN1: Enf 5K 23 *(off Village Rd.)*
Newport Pl. WC2 2D 12 (7H 83)
Newport Rd. E10 2E 68
Newport Rd. E17 4A 50
Newport Rd. SW13 1C 116
Newport Rd. TW6: H'row A 1C 110
Newport Rd. UB4: Hayes 5F 75
Newport Rd. W3 2J 97
Newport St. SE11 4G 19 (4K 101)
Newport Street Gallery 3H 19 (4K 101)
New Priory Ct. NW6 7J 63 *(off Mazenod Av.)*
New Providence Wharf E14 1F 105
Newquay Cres. HA2: Harr 2C 58
Newquay Ho. SE11 5J 19 (5A 102)
Newquay Rd. SE6 2D 140
New Quebec St. W1 1F 11 (6D 82)
New Ride SW7 6D 10 (2C 100)
New River Av. N8 3K 47
New River Ct. N5 4C 66
New River Cres. N13 4G 33
New River Head EC1 2K 7 (3A 84)
New River Sports & Fitness Cen. 7G 33
New River Wlk. N1 6C 66 (not continuous)
New River Way N4 7D 48
New Rd. NW7 Bittacy Ct. 7B 30
New Rd. CR4: Mitc 1D 166
New Rd. DA16: Well 2B 126
New Rd. E1 5H 85
New Rd. E4 4J 35
New Rd. HA1: Harr 4K 59
New Rd. IG3: Ilf 2J 71
New Rd. KT2: King T 7G 133
New Rd. KT8: W Mole 4E 148
New Rd. N17 1F 49
New Rd. N22 1C 48
New Rd. N8 5J 47
New Rd. N9 2C 34
New Rd. RM10: Dag 2G 91
New Rd. RM9: Dag 2G 91
New Rd. SE2 4D 108
New Rd. TW10: Ham 4C 132
New Rd. TW13: Hanw 5C 130
New Rd. TW14: Bedf 6F 111
New Rd. TW14: Felt 1K 129
New Rd. TW17: Shep 3C 146
New Rd. TW3: Houn 4F 113
New Rd. TW8: Bford 6D 96
New Rd. UB3: Harl 7E 92
New Rd. UB8: Hil 7E 74
New Rd. Hill BR2: Kes 7C 172
New Rd. Hill BR6: Downe 7D 172
New Rochford St. NW5 5D 64
New Row NW2 3E 62
New Row WC2 2E 12 (7J 83)
Newry Rd. TW1: Twick 5A 114
Newsam Av. N15 5D 48
New Scotland Yard 6E 12 (2J 101) *(off Victoria Emb.)*
Newsholme Dr. N21 5E 22
NEW SOUTHGATE 5A 32
New Southgate Crematorium 3A 32
New Southgate Ind. Est. N11 5B 32
New Spitalfields Mkt. E10 3C 68
New Spring Gdns. Wlk. SE11 6F 19 (5J 101)
New Sq. TW14: Bedf 1E 128
New Sq. WC2 7J 7 (6A 84)
New Sq. Pk. TW14: Bedf 1E 128
New Sq. Pas. WC2 7J 7 (6A 84) *(off Star Yd.)*
Newstead Av. BR6: Orp 3H 173
Newstead Cl. N12 6H 31
Newstead Ct. UB5: N'olt 3C 76
Newstead Ho. N1 2A 84 *(off Tolpuddle St.)*
Newstead Rd. SE12 7H 123
Newstead Wlk. SM5: Cars 7A 154
Newstead Way SW19 4F 135
New St. EC2 6H 9 (5E 84)
New St. Hill BR1: Broml 5K 141
New St. Sq. EC4 7K 7 (6A 84) (not continuous)
Newton Av. N10 1E 46
Newton Av. W3 2J 97
Newton Cl. E17 6A 50
Newton Cl. HA2: Harr 2E 58
Newton Ct. E3 5C 86
Newton Ct. NW6 7A 64 *(off Fairfax Rd.)*
Newton Ct. SW17 3B 136 *(off Grosvenor Way)*
Newton Ct. W8 2J 99 *(off Kensington Chu. St.)*
Newton Gro. W4 4A 98
Newton Ho. E1 7H 85 *(off Cornwall St.)*
Newton Ho. E17 3D 50 *(off Prospect Hill)*
Newton Ho. EN3: Enf H 3E 24
Newton Ho. NW8 1K 81 *(off Abbey Rd.)*
Newton Ho. SE20 7K 139
Newton Ind. Est. RM6: Chad H 4D 54
Newton Lodge SE10 3H 105 *(off Teal St.)*
Newton Mans. W14 6G 99 *(off Queen's Club Gdns.)*
Newton Pk. Pl. BR7: Chst 7D 142
Newton Pl. E14 4C 104
Newton Rd. DA16: Well 3A 126
Newton Rd. E15 5F 69
Newton Rd. HA0: Wemb 7F 61
Newton Rd. HA3: Hrw W 2J 41
Newton Rd. N15 5G 49
Newton Rd. NW2 4E 62
Newton Rd. SW19 7G 135
Newton Rd. TW7: Isle 2K 113
Newton Rd. W2 6K 81
Newton St. WC2 7F 7 (6J 83)
Newton's Yd. SW18 5J 117
Newton Ter. BR2: Broml 6B 160
Newton Wlk. HA8: Edg 1H 43
Newton Way N18 5H 33
New Tower Bldgs. E1 1H 103
Newtown St. SW11 1F 119
New Trinity Rd. N2 3B 46
New Turnstile WC1 6G 7 (5K 83) *(off High Holborn)*
New Union Cl. E14 3E 104
New Union Sq. SW11 6H 101
New Union St. EC2 5E 8 (5D 84)
New Village Av. E14 6F 87

New Wanstead E11 6H 51
New Warren La. SE18 3F 107
New Way Rd. NW9 4A 44
New Wharf Rd. N1 2J 83
New Willow Ho. E13 2J 87 *(off Plaistow Rd.)*
NEWYEARS GREEN 7B 38
New Years Grn. La. UB9: Hare 6A 38
New Zealand Av. KT12: Walt T 7H 147
New Zealand Way W12 7D 80
Nexus Apts. BR1: Broml 3K 159 *(off Elmfield Rd.)*
Nexus Cl. TW14: Felt 5J 111
Nexus Ct. E11 1G 69
Nexus Ct. NW6 3J 81
Niagara Av. W5 4C 96
Niagara Cl. N1 2C 84
Niagra Ct. SE16 3J 103 *(off Canada Est.)*
Nibthwaite Rd. HA1: Harr 5J 41
Nice Bus. Pk. SE15 6H 103
Nicholas Cl. UB6: G'frd 2F 77
Nicholas Ct. E13 3K 87
Nicholas Ct. N7 5K 65
Nicholas Ct. SE12 1J 141
Nicholas Ct. W4 6A 98 *(off Corney Reach Way)*
Nicholas Gdns. W5 2D 96
Nicholas La. EC4 2F 15 (7D 84) (not continuous)
Nicholas M. W4 6A 98
Nicholas Pas. EC4 2F 15 (7D 84) *(off Nicholas La.)*
Nicholas Rd. CR0: Bedd 4J 167
Nicholas Rd. E1 4J 85
Nicholas Rd. RM8: Dag 2F 73
Nicholas Rd. W11 7F 81
Nicholas Stacey Ho. SE7 5K 105 *(off Frank Burton Cl.)*
Nicholas Way HA6: Nwood 1E 38
Nicholay Rd. N19 1H 65 (not continuous)
Nichol Cl. N14 1C 32
Nicholes Rd. TW3: Houn 4E 112
Nichol La. BR1: Broml 7J 141
Nicholl Ct. SE27 1K 137
Nicholl Ho. N4 1C 66
Nicholls Av. UB8: Hil 4C 74
Nichollsfield Wlk. N7 5K 65
Nicholls M. SW16 4J 137
Nicholls Point E15 1J 87 *(off Park Gro.)*
Nicholl St. E2 1G 85
Nichols Cl. KT9: Chess 6C 162
Nichols Cl. N4 1A 66 *(off Osborne Rd.)*
Nichols Ct. E2 1J 9 (2F 85)
Nichols Grn. W5 5E 78
Nicholson Ct. E17 4K 49
Nicholson Ct. N17 3F 49
Nicholson Ho. SE17 5D 102
Nicholson M. KT1: King T 4E 150
Nicholson Rd. CR0: C'don 1F 169
Nicholson Sq. E3 3E 86 *(off Bolinder Way)*
Nicholson St. SE1 5A 14 (1B 102)
Nicholson Wlk. UB10: Uxb 1A 74
Nickelby Apts. E15 6F 69 *(off Grove Cres. Rd.)*
Nickelby Cl. SE28 6C 90
Nickleby Cl. UB8: Hil 6D 74
Nickleby Ho. SE16 7K 15 (2G 103) *(off Parkers Row)*
Nickleby Ho. W11 1F 99 *(off St Ann's Rd.)*
Nickols Wlk. SW18 4K 117
Nicola Cl. CR2: S Croy 6C 168
Nicola Cl. HA3: Hrw W 2H 41
Nicola Ter. DA7: Bex 1E 126
Nicol Cl. TW1: Twick 6B 114
Nicoll Cir. NW7 6B 30
Nicoll Ct. N10 7A 32
Nicoll Ct. NW10 1A 80
Nicoll Pl. NW4 6D 44
Nicoll Rd. NW10 1A 80
Nicolson NW9 1A 44
Nicolson Dr. WD23: B Hea 1B 26
Nicosia Rd. SW18 7C 118
Niederwald Rd. SE26 4A 140
Nield Rd. UB3: Hayes 2H 93
Nigel Cl. UB5: N'olt 1C 76
Nigel Ct. N3 7E 30
Nigel Fisher Way KT9: Chess 7C 162
Nigel Ho. EC1 5J 7 (5A 84) *(off Portpool La.)*
Nigel M. IG1: Ilf 4F 71
Nigel Playfair Av. W6 4D 98
Nigel Rd. E7 5A 70
Nigel Rd. SE15 3G 121
Nigeria Rd. SE7 7A 106
Nighthawk NW9 1B 44
Nightingale Av. E4 5B 36
Nightingale Av. HA1: Harr 7B 42
Nightingale Cl. E4 4A 36
Nightingale Cl. HA5: Eastc 5A 40
Nightingale Cl. SM5: Cars 2E 166
Nightingale Cl. W4 6J 97
Nightingale Ct. BR2: Broml 2G 159
Nightingale Ct. E14 2E 104 *(off Ovex Cl.)*
Nightingale Ct. HA1: Harr 6K 41
Nightingale Ct. N4 2K 65 *(off Tollington Pk.)*
Nightingale Ct. SM1: Sutt 5A 166
Nightingale Dr. KT19: Ewe 6H 163
Nightingale Gro. SE13 5F 123
Nightingale Hgts. SE18 6F 107
Nightingale Ho. E1 1G 103 *(off Thomas More St.)*
Nightingale Ho. E2 1E 84 *(off Kingsland Rd.)*
Nightingale Ho. NW8 4C 4 (4C 82) *(off Samford St.)*
Nightingale Ho. SE18 5E 106 *(off Connaught M.)*
Nightingale Ho. UB7: W Dray 2B 92
Nightingale Ho. W12 6E 80 *(off Du Cane Rd.)*
Nightingale La. BR1: Broml 2A 160
Nightingale La. E11 4K 51
Nightingale La. N8 4J 47
Nightingale La. SW12 7D 118
Nightingale La. SW4 6F 119
Nightingale La. TW10: Rich 7E 114

Nightingale Lodge – Northumberland Gro.

Nightingale Lodge W9 5J **81**
(off Admiral Wlk.)
Nightingale M. E11 5J **51**
Nightingale M. E3 2K **85**
Nightingale M. KT1: King T 3D **150**
(off South La.)
Nightingale M. SE11 3K **19** (4B **102**)
Nightingale Pl. SE18 6E **106**
Nightingale Pl. SW10 6A **100**
Nightingale Rd. BR5: Pet W 6G **161**
Nightingale Rd. E5 3H **67**
Nightingale Rd. KT12: Walt T 7A **148**
Nightingale Rd. KT8: W Mole 5F **149**
Nightingale Rd. N1 6C **66**
Nightingale Rd. N22 1J **47**
Nightingale Rd. N9 6D **24**
Nightingale Rd. NW10 2B **80**
Nightingale Rd. SM5: Cars 3D **166**
Nightingale Rd. TW12: Hamp 5E **130**
Nightingale Rd. W7 1K **95**
Nightingales, The TW19: Stanw 1B **128**
Nightingale Sq. SW12 7E **118**
Nightingale Va. SE18 6E **106**
Nightingale Wlk. N1 6C **66**
Nightingale Wlk. SW4 6F **119**
Nightingale Way E6 5C **88**
Nihill Pl. CR0: C'don 1F **169**
Nile Cl. N16 3F **67**
Nile Dr. N9 2D **34**
Nile Ho. N1 1E **8** (3D **84**)
(off Nile St.)
Nile Path SE18 6E **106**
Nile Rd. E13 2A **88**
Nile St. N1 1D **8** (3C **84**)
Nile Ter. SE15 5F **103**
Nimegen Way SE22 5E **120**
Nimmo Dr. WD23: B Hea 1C **26**
Nimrod NW9 1A **44**
Nimrod Cl. UB5: N'olt 3B **76**
Nimrod Ho. E16 5K **87**
(off Vanguard Cl.)
Nimrod Pas. N1 6E **66**
Nimrod Rd. SW16 6F **137**
Nina Mackay Cl. E15 1G **87**
Nine Acres Cl. E12 5C **70**
Nine Acres Cl. UB3: Harl 3E **92**
NINE ELMS 7G **101**
Nine Elms Cl. TW14: Felt 1H **129**
Nine Elms La. SW11 7G **101**
Nine Elms La. SW8 7D **18** (6H **101**)
Nineteenth Rd. CR4: Mitc 4J **155**
Ninhams Wood BR6: Farnb 4E **172**
Ninth Av. UB3: Hayes 7J **75**
Nipper All. KT1: King T 2E **150**
(off Clarence St.)
Nipponzan Myohoji Peace Pagoda 6D **100**
Nisbet Ho. E9 5K **67**
Nisbett Wlk. DA14: Sidc 4A **144**
Nita Ct. SE12 1J **141**
Nithdale Rd. SE18 7F **107**
Nithsdale Gro. UB10: Ick 3E **56**
Niton Cl. EN5: Barn 6A **20**
Niton Rd. TW9: Rich 3G **115**
Niton St. SW6 7F **99**
Niveda Cl. W12 2C **98**
Noah Cl. EN3: Enf W 1D **24**
Noah's Yd. N1 1F **7** (2J **83**)
Nobel Cl. NW9 2K **43**
Nobel Dr. UB3: Harl 1F **111**
Nobel Ho. SE5 2C **120**
Nobel Rd. N18 4D **34**
Noble Cnr. TW5: Hest 1E **112**
Noble Ct. CR4: Mitc 2B **154**
Noble Ct. E1 7H **85**
Noblefield Hgts. N2 5C **46**
Noble M. N16 3D **66**
(off Albion Rd.)
Noble St. EC2 7C **8** (6C **84**)
Noble Yd. N1 1B **84**
(off Camden Pas.)
Nocavia Ho. SW6 2A **118**
(off Townmead Rd.)
Noel NW9 1A **44**
Noel Ct. CR0: C'don 7D **156**
Noel Ct. TW4: Houn 3D **112**
Noel Coward Ho. SW1 4B **18** (4G **101**)
(off Vauxhall Bri. Rd.)
Noel Coward Theatre 2E **12** (7J **83**)
(off St Martin's La.)
Noel Ho. NW6 7B **64**
(off Harben Rd.)
NOEL PARK 2B **48**
Noel Pk. Rd. N22 2A **48**
Noel Rd. E6 4C **88**
Noel Rd. N1 2B **84**
Noel Rd. W3 7G **79**
Noel Sq. RM8: Dag 4C **72**
Noel Sq. TW11: Tedd 5K **131**
Noel St. W1 1B **12** (6G **83**)
Noel Ter. DA14: Sidc 4B **144**
Noel Ter. SE23 2J **139**
Noko W10 3F **81**
Nolands Cl. RM5: Col R 2J **55**
Nolan Mans. E20 5D **68**
(off Honour Lea Av.)
Nolan Way E5 4G **67**
Noll Ho. N7 2K **65**
(off Tomlins Wlk.)
Nolton Pl. HA8: Edg 1F **43**
Nonsuch Abbeyfield KT17: Ewe 7B **164**
Nonsuch Ho. SW19 1B **154**
(off Chapter Way)
Nonsuch Pl. SM3: Cheam 7F **165**
(off Ewell Rd.)
Nook Apts. E1 1K **15** (6F **85**)
(off Scarborough St.)
Nora Gdns. NW4 4F **45**
Nora Leverton Ct. NW1 7G **65**
(off Randolph St.)
NORBITON 2G **151**
Norbiton Av. KT1: King T 1G **151**
Norbiton Comn. Rd. KT1: King T 3H **151**
Norbiton Hall KT2: King T 2F **151**
Norbiton Ho. NW1 1G **83**
(off Camden St.)
Norbiton Rd. E14 6B **86**
Norbreck Gdns. NW10 3F **79**
Norbreck Pde. NW10 3E **78**
Norbroke St. W12 7B **80**
Norburn St. W10 5G **81**
NORBURY 1K **155**
Norbury Av. CR7: Thor H 1A **156**
Norbury Av. SW16 1K **155**
Norbury Av. TW3: Houn 4H **113**
Norbury Cl. SW16 1A **156**
Norbury Ct. Rd. SW16 3J **155**
Norbury Cres. SW16 1K **155**
Norbury Cross SW16 3J **155**
Norbury Gdns. RM6: Chad H 5D **54**
Norbury Gro. NW7 3F **29**
Norbury Hill SW16 7A **138**
Norbury Ri. SW16 3J **155**
Norbury Rd. CR7: Thor H 2C **156**
Norbury Rd. E4 5H **35**
Norbury Rd. TW13: Felt 3H **129**
Norbury Trad. Est. SW16 2K **155**
Norcombe Gdns. HA3: Kenton 6C **42**
Norcombe Ho. N19 3H **65**
(off Wedmore St.)
Norcott Cl. UB4: Yead 4A **76**
Norcott Rd. N16 2G **67**
Norcroft Gdns. SE22 7G **121**
Norcutt Rd. TW2: Twick 1J **131**
Nordenfeldt Rd. DA8: Erith 5K **109**
Norden Ho. E2 3H **85**
(off Pott St.)
Norfield Rd. DA2: Wilm 4J **145**
Norfolk Apts. E4 7J **35**
Norfolk Av. N13 6G **33**
Norfolk Av. N15 6F **49**
Norfolk Cl. EN4: Cockf 4K **21**
Norfolk Cl. N13 6G **33**
Norfolk Cl. N2 3C **46**
Norfolk Cl. TW1: Twick 6B **114**
Norfolk Ct. EN5: Barn 4B **20**
Norfolk Ct. RM6: Chad H 5B **54**
(off Norwich Cres.)
Norfolk Cres. DA15: Sidc 7J **125**
Norfolk Cres. W2 7C **4** (6C **82**)
Norfolk Gdns. DA7: Bex 1F **127**
Norfolk Ho. BR2: Broml 4H **159**
(off Westmoreland Rd.)
Norfolk Ho. EC4 2C **14** (7C **84**)
(off Trig La.)
Norfolk Ho. SE20 1J **157**
Norfolk Ho. SE8 1C **122**
(off Brookmill Rd.)
Norfolk Ho. SW1 3D **18** (4H **101**)
(off Page St.)
Norfolk Ho. Rd. SW16 3H **137**
Norfolk Mans. SW11 1D **118**
(off Prince of Wales Dr.)
Norfolk M. W10 5G **81**
(off Blagrove Rd.)
Norfolk Pl. DA16: Well 2A **126**
Norfolk Pl. W2 7B **4** (6B **82**)
(not continuous)
Norfolk Rd. CR7: Thor H 3C **156**
Norfolk Rd. E17 2K **49**
Norfolk Rd. E6 1D **88**
Norfolk Rd. EN3: Pond E 6C **24**
Norfolk Rd. EN5: New Bar 3D **20**
Norfolk Rd. HA1: Harr 5F **41**
Norfolk Rd. IG11: Bark 7J **71**
Norfolk Rd. IG3: Ilf 1J **71**
Norfolk Rd. NW10 7A **62**
Norfolk Rd. NW8 1B **82**
Norfolk Rd. RM10: Dag 5H **73**
Norfolk Rd. RM7: Rom 6J **55**
Norfolk Rd. SW19 7C **136**
Norfolk Rd. TW13: Felt 1A **130**
Norfolk Row SE1 3G **19** (4K **101**)
Norfolk Sq. W2 1B **10** (6B **82**)
Norfolk Sq. M. W2 1B **10** (6B **82**)
(off London St.)
Norfolk St. E7 5J **69**
Norfolk Ter. W6 5G **99**
Norgrove St. SW12 7E **118**
Norhyrst Av. SE25 3F **157**
Norland Ho. W11 1F **99**
(off Queensdale Cres.)
Norland Pl. W11 1G **99**
Norland Rd. W11 1F **99**
(not continuous)
Norlands Cres. BR7: Chst 1F **161**
Norlands Ga. BR7: Chst 1F **161**
Norland Sq. W11 1G **99**
Norland Sq. Mans. W11 1G **99**
(off Norland Sq.)
Norlem Ct. SE8 4A **104**
(off Seafarer Way)
Norley Va. SW15 1C **134**
Norlington Rd. E10 1E **68**
Norlington Rd. E11 1F **69**
Norman Av. N22 1B **48**
Norman Av. TW1: Twick 7C **114**
Norman Av. TW13: Hanw 2C **130**
Norman Av. UB1: S'hall 7C **76**
Norman Butler Ho. W10 4G **81**
(off Ladbroke Gro.)
Normanby Cl. SW15 5H **117**
Normanby Rd. NW10 4B **62**
Norman Cl. BR6: Farnb 3G **173**
Norman Cl. N22 1C **48**
Norman Cl. RM5: Col R 1H **55**
Norman Ct. IG2: Ilf 7H **53**
Norman Ct. IG8: Wfd G 5E **36**
Norman Ct. N3 1J **45**
(off Nether St.)
Norman Ct. N4 7A **48**
Norman Ct. NW10 7C **62**
Norman Ct. W13 1B **96**
(off Kirkfield Cl.)
Norman Cres. HA5: Pinn 1A **40**
Norman Cres. TW5: Hest 7B **94**
Normand Gdns. W14 6G **99**
(off Greyhound Rd.)
Normand Mans. W14 6G **99**
(off Normand M.)
Normand M. W14 6G **99**
Normand Rd. W14 6H **99**
Normandy Av. EN5: Barn 5C **20**
Normandy Cl. SE26 3A **140**
Normandy Dr. UB3: Hayes 6E **74**
Normandy Ho. E14 2E **104**
(off Plevna St.)
Normandy Ho. EN2: Enf 1H **23**
Normandy Pl. W12 1F **99**
Normandy Rd. SW9 1A **120**
Normandy Ter. E16 6K **87**
Normandy Way DA8: Erith 1K **127**
Norman Gro. E3 2A **86**
Norman Hay Trad. Est., The UB7: Sip 7B **92**
Norman Ho. SE1 7H **15** (3E **102**)
(off Riley Rd.)
Norman Ho. SW8 7J **101**
(off Wyvil Rd.)
Norman Ho. TW13: Hanw 2D **130**
(off Watermill Way)
Normanhurst TW15: Ashf 5C **128**
Normanhurst Av. DA7: Bex 1D **126**
Normanhurst Dr. TW1: Twick 5A **114**
Normanhurst Rd. SW2 2K **137**
Norman Leddy Memorial Gdns. 6H **75**
Norman Pk. Athletics Track 6K **159**
Norman Park Community Sports Centre BR2: Broml 6K **159**
Norman Park Community Sports Centre BR2: Hayes 6K **159**
Norman Rd. CR7: Thor H 5B **156**
Norman Rd. DA17: Belv 3H **109**
(not continuous)
Norman Rd. E11 2F **69**
Norman Rd. E6 4D **88**
Norman Rd. IG1: Ilf 5F **71**
Norman Rd. N15 5F **49**
Norman Rd. SE10 7D **104**
Norman Rd. SM1: Sutt 5J **165**
Norman Rd. SW19 7A **136**
Norman Rd. TW15: Ashf 6F **129**
Norman's Cl. NW10 6K **61**
Normans Cl. UB8: Hil 5B **74**
Normansfield Av. TW11: Tedd 7C **132**
Normanshire Dr. E4 4H **35**
Norman's Mead NW10 6K **61**
Norman St. EC1 2C **8** (3C **84**)
Norman Ter. NW6 5H **63**
Normanton Av. SW19 2J **135**
Normanton Ct. CR2: S Croy 5E **168**
(off Croham Rd.)
Normanton Pk. E4 2B **36**
Normanton Rd. CR2: S Croy 5E **168**
Normanton St. SE23 2K **139**
Norman Way N14 2D **32**
Norman Way W3 5H **79**
Normington Cl. SW16 5A **138**
Norrice Lea N2 5B **46**
Norris NW9 1B **44**
(off Withers Mead)
Norris Ho. E9 1J **85**
(off Handley Rd.)
Norris Ho. N1 1E **84**
(off Colville Est.)
Norris Ho. SE8 5B **104**
(off Grove St.)
Norris Ho. TW7: Isle 2A **114**
Norris St. SW1 3C **12** (7H **83**)
Norroy Rd. SW15 4F **117**
Norry's Cl. EN4: Cockf 4J **21**
Norry's Rd. EN4: Cockf 4J **21**
Norseman Cl. IG3: Ilf 1B **72**
Norseman Way UB6: G'frd 1F **77**
Norstead Pl. SW15 2C **134**
North Access Rd. E17 6K **49**
North Acre NW9 1A **44**
NORTH ACTON 4K **79**
North Acton Bus. Pk. W3 5K **79**
North Acton Rd. NW10 2K **79**
Northall Rd. DA7: Bex 2J **127**
Northampton Gro. N1 5D **66**
Northampton Pk. N1 6C **66**
Northampton Rd. CR0: C'don 2G **169**
Northampton Rd. EC1 3K **7** (4A **84**)
Northampton Rd. EN3: Pond E 4F **25**
Northampton Row EC1 3K **7** (4A **84**)
(off Rosoman Pl.)
Northampton Sq. EC1 2A **8** (3B **84**)
Northampton St. N1 7C **66**
Northanger Rd. SW16 6J **137**
North Audley St. W1 2G **11** (7E **82**)
North Av. HA2: Harr 6F **41**
North Av. N18 4B **34**
North Av. SM5: Cars 7E **166**
North Av. TW9: Kew 1G **115**
North Av. UB1: S'hall 7D **76**
North Av. UB3: Hayes 7J **75**
North Av. W13 5B **78**
Northaw Ho. W10 4E **80**
(off Sutton Way)
North Bank NW8 2C **4** (3C **82**)
Northbank Rd. E17 2E **50**
NORTH BECKTON 5D **88**
North Birkbeck Rd. E11 3F **69**
North Block SE1 6H **13** (2K **101**)
(off Chicheley St.)
Northborough Rd. SW16 3H **155**
Northbourne BR2: Hayes 7J **159**
Northbourne Rd. SW4 5H **119**
Northbrook Dr. HA6: Nwood 1G **39**
Northbrook Rd. CR0: C'don 5D **156**
Northbrook Rd. EN5: Barn 6B **20**
Northbrook Rd. IG1: Ilf 2E **70**
Northbrook Rd. N22 7D **32**
Northbrook Rd. SE13 5G **123**
Northburgh St. EC1 4B **8** (4B **84**)
Northbury Cl. IG11: Bark 7G **71**
North Carriage Dr. W2 2D **10** (7C **82**)
(off Bayswater Rd.)
NORTH CHEAM 3E **164**
Northchurch SE17 5D **102**
(not continuous)
Northchurch Ho. E2 1G **85**
(off Whiston Rd.)
Northchurch Rd. HA9: Wemb 6G **61**
Northchurch Rd. N1 7D **66**
(not continuous)
Northchurch Ter. N1 7E **66**
North Circular Rd. E12 3E **70**
North Circular Rd. E18 2A **52**
North Circular Rd. E4 6G **35**
North Circular Rd. IG1: Ilf 2D **70**
North Circular Rd. IG11: Bark 7E **70**
North Circular Rd. N12 1B **46**
North Circular Rd. N13 5F **33**
North Circular Rd. N3 3J **45**
North Circular Rd. NW10 2F **79**
North Circular Rd. NW11 7F **45**
North Circular Rd. NW2 3A **62**
North Circular Rd. NW4 7E **44**
Northcliffe Cl. KT4: Wor Pk 3A **164**
Northcliffe Dr. N20 1C **30**
North Cl. DA6: Bex 4D **126**
North Cl. RM10: Dag 1G **91**
North Cl. SM4: Mord 4G **153**
North Cl. TW14: Bedf 6F **111**
North Colonnade, The E14 1C **104**
(not continuous)
North Comn. Rd. UB8: Uxb 5A **56**
North Comn. Rd. W5 7E **78**
Northcote HA5: Pinn 2A **40**
Northcote Av. KT5: Surb 7H **151**
Northcote Av. TW7: Isle 5A **114**
Northcote Av. UB1: S'hall 7C **76**
Northcote Av. W5 7E **78**
Northcote Rd. CR0: C'don 6D **156**
Northcote Rd. DA14: Sidc 4J **143**
Northcote Rd. E17 4A **50**
Northcote Rd. KT3: N Mald 3J **151**
Northcote Rd. NW10 7A **62**
Northcote Rd. SW11 5C **118**
Northcote Rd. TW1: Twick 5A **114**
Northcott Av. N22 1J **47**
North Countess Rd. E17 2B **50**
North Ct. BR1: Broml 1K **159**
(off Palace Gro.)
North Ct. SE24 3B **120**
North Ct. SW1 2E **18** (3J **101**)
(off Gt. Peter St.)
North Ct. W1 5B **6** (5G **83**)
NORTH CRAY 5E **144**
North Cray Rd. DA14: Sidc 6E **144**
North Cray Rd. DA5: Bexl 1H **145**
North Cray Woods 4D **144**
North Cres. E16 4F **87**
North Cres. N3 2H **45**
North Cres. WC1 5C **6** (5H **83**)
Northcroft Ct. W12 2C **98**
Northcroft Rd. KT19: Ewe 7A **164**
Northcroft Rd. W13 2B **96**
North Crofts SE23 1H **139**
Northcroft Ter. W13 2B **96**
North Cross Rd. IG6: Ilf 4G **53**
North Cross Rd. SE22 5F **121**
Northdale Ct. SE25 3F **157**
North Dene NW7 3E **28**
North Dene TW3: Houn 1F **113**
Northdene Gdns. N15 6F **49**
Northdown Cl. HA4: Ruis 3H **57**
Northdown Gdns. IG2: Ilf 5J **53**
Northdown Rd. DA16: Well 2B **126**
Northdown St. N1 2J **83**
North Dr. BR3: Beck 4D **158**
North Dr. BR6: Orp 4J **173**
North Dr. HA4: Ruis 7G **39**
North Dr. SW16 4G **137**
North Dr. TW3: Houn 2G **113**
North E. Surrey Crematorium 6E **152**
NORTH END 2A **64**
North End CR0: C'don 2C **168**
North End IG9: Buck H 1F **37**
North End NW3 2A **64**
North End Av. NW3 2A **64**
North End Cres. W14 4H **99**
North End Ho. W14 4G **99**
North End Pde. W14 4G **99**
(off North End Rd.)
North End Rd. HA9: Wemb 3G **61**
North End Rd. NW11 1G **63**
North End Rd. SW6 6H **99**
North End Rd. W14 4G **99**
North End Way NW3 2A **64**
Northern Av. N9 2K **33**
Northernhay Wlk. SM4: Mord 4G **153**
Northern Hgts. N8 7H **47**
(off Crescent Rd.)
Northern Perimeter Rd. TW6: H'row A 1D **110**
Northern Perimeter Rd. (W.) TW6: H'row A 4E **174**
Northern Rd. E13 2K **87**
Northesk Ho. E1 4H **85**
(off Tent St.)
North Eyot Gdns. W6 5B **98**
Northey St. E14 7A **86**
NORTH FELTHAM 6K **111**
North Feltham Trad. Est. TW14: Felt 5K **111**
Northfield Av. HA5: Pinn 4B **40**
Northfield Av. W13 1B **96**
Northfield Av. W5 3C **96**
Northfield Cl. BR1: Broml 1C **160**
Northfield Cl. UB3: Harl 3H **93**
Northfield Cres. SM3: Cheam 4G **165**
Northfield Gdns. RM9: Dag 4F **73**
Northfield Ho. SE15 6G **103**
Northfield Pde. UB3: Harl 3G **93**
Northfield Pk. UB3: Harl 3H **93**
Northfield Path RM9: Dag 4F **73**
Northfield Recreation Ground W5 4B **96**
Northfield Rd. E6 7D **70**
Northfield Rd. EN3: Pond E 5C **24**
Northfield Rd. EN4: Cockf 3H **21**
Northfield Rd. N16 7E **48**
Northfield Rd. RM9: Dag 4F **73**
Northfield Rd. TW5: Hest 6B **94**
Northfield Rd. W13 2B **96**
Northfields SW18 4J **117**
NORTHFIELDS 3B **96**
Northfields Ind. Est. HA0: Wemb 1G **79**
Northfields Prospect Bus. Cen. SW18 4J **117**
Northfields Rd. W3 5H **79**
NORTH FINCHLEY 5F **31**
Northfleet Ho. SE1 6E **14** (2D **102**)
(off Tennis St.)
Northflock St. SE16 2G **103**
North Gdn. E14 1B **104**
North Gdns. SW19 7B **136**
North Ga. NW8 1C **4** (2C **82**)
(off Prince Albert Rd.)
Northgate HA6: Nwood 1E **38**
Northgate Bus. Cen. EN1: Enf 3C **24**
Northgate Ct. SW9 3A **120**
Northgate Dr. NW9 6A **44**
Northgate Ho. E14 7C **86**
(off E. India Dock Rd.)
Northgate Ind. Pk. RM5: Col R 1F **55**
Northgate Rd. IG11: Bark 3C **90**
North Gates N12 1A **46**
(off Bow La.)
North Glade, The DA5: Bexl 7F **127**
North Gower St. NW1 2B **6** (3G **83**)
North Grn. NW9 7F **29**
North Gro. N15 5D **48**
North Gro. N6 7E **46**
NORTH HARROW 5F **41**
North Hatton Rd. TW6: H'row A 1F **111**
North Hill N6 6D **46**
North Hill Av. N6 6E **46**
NORTH HILLINGDON 7E **56**
North Ho. SE8 5B **104**
North Hyde Gdns. UB3: Harl 4J **93**
North Hyde Gdns. UB3: Hayes 4J **93**
North Hyde La. TW5: Hest 5C **94**
North Hyde La. UB2: S'hall 5B **94**
North Hyde Rd. UB3: Harl 3G **93**
North Hyde Rd. UB3: Hayes 3G **93**
North Hyde Wharf UB2: S'hall 4A **94**
Northiam N12 4D **30**
Northiam WC1 2F **7** (3J **83**)
(off Cromer St.)
Northiam St. E9 1H **85**
Northington St. WC1 4H **7** (4K **83**)
NORTH KENSINGTON 5E **80**
Northlands Av. BR6: Orp 4J **173**
Northlands St. SE5 2C **120**
North La. TW11: Tedd 6K **131**
Northleigh Ho. E3 3D **86**
(off Powis Rd.)
North Lodge E16 1K **105**
(off Wesley Av.)
North Lodge EN5: New Bar 5F **21**
North Lodge Cl. SW15 5F **117**
North London Bus. Pk. N11 2K **31**
North Mall N9 2C **34**
(within Edmonton Grn. Shop. Cen.)
North Mall SW18 5K **117**
(off Southside Shop. Cen.)
North M. WC1 4H **7** (4K **83**)
North Middlesex Golf Course 3G **31**
North Mill Apts. E8 1F **85**
(off Lovelace St.)
North Mt. N20 2F **31**
(off High Rd.)
Northolm HA8: Edg 4E **28**
Northolme Gdns. HA8: Edg 1G **43**
Northolme Ri. BR6: Orp 2J **173**
Northolme Rd. N5 4C **66**
Northolt N17 2E **48**
(off Griffin Rd.)
NORTHOLT 7E **58**
Northolt Av. HA4: Ruis 5K **57**
Northolt Gdns. UB6: G'frd 5K **59**
Northolt Golf Course 2C **76**
Northolt Leisure Cen. 6E **58**
Northolt Rd. HA2: Harr 4F **59**
Northolt Rd. TW6: H'row A 1A **110**
(not continuous)
Northolt Trad. Est. UB5: N'olt 7F **59**
Northover BR1: Broml 3H **141**
North Pde. HA8: Edg 2G **43**
North Pde. KT9: Chess 5F **163**
North Pde. UB1: S'hall 6E **76**
(off North Rd.)
North Pk. SE9 6D **124**
North Pas. SW18 5J **117**
North Pl. CR4: Mitc 7D **136**
North Pl. TW11: Tedd 6K **131**
North Point N8 5K **47**
Northpoint Cl. SM1: Sutt 3A **166**
Northpoint Ho. N1 6D **66**
(off Essex Rd.)
Northpoint Sq. NW1 6H **65**
North Pole La. BR2: Kes 6H **171**
North Pole Rd. W10 5E **80**
Northport St. N1 1D **84**
North Quay Pl. E14 7D **86**
North Ride W2 3C **10** (7C **82**)
North Ri. W2 1D **10** (6C **82**)
North Rd. BR1: Broml 1K **159**
North Rd. BR4: W W'ck 1D **170**
North Rd. DA17: Belv 3H **109**
North Rd. HA1: Harr 7A **42**
North Rd. HA8: Edg 1H **43**
North Rd. IG3: Ilf 2J **71**
North Rd. KT6: Surb 6D **150**
North Rd. N6 7E **46**
North Rd. N7 6J **65**
North Rd. N9 1C **34**
North Rd. RM6: Chad H 5E **54**
North Rd. SE18 4J **107**
North Rd. SW19 6A **136**
North Rd. TW14: Bedf 6F **111**
North Rd. TW8: Bford 6F **96**
North Rd. TW9: Kew 3G **115**
North Rd. TW9: Rich 3G **115**
North Rd. UB1: S'hall 6E **76**
North Rd. UB3: Hayes 5F **75**
North Rd. UB7: W Dray 3B **92**
North Rd. W5 3D **96**
Northrop Rd. TW6: H'row A 1G **111**
North Row W1 2F **11** (7D **82**)
North Row Bldgs. W1 2G **11** (7E **82**)
(off North Row)
North Several SE3 2F **123**
NORTH SHEEN 3G **115**
Northside Rd. BR1: Broml 1J **159**
Northside Studios E8 1H **85**
(off Andrew's Rd.)
North Side Wandsworth Comn. SW18 5B **118**
Northspur Rd. SM1: Sutt 3J **165**
North Sq. N9 2C **34**
(off New Rd.)
North Sq. NW11 5J **45**
North Stand N5 3B **66**
Northstead Rd. SW2 2A **138**
North St. BR1: Broml 1J **159**
North St. DA7: Bex 4G **127**
North St. E13 2K **87**
North St. IG11: Bark 6F **71**
North St. NW4 5E **44**
North St. RM1: Rom 3K **55**
North St. RM5: Rom 3K **55**
North St. SM5: Cars 3D **166**
North St. SW4 3G **119**
North St. TW7: Isle 3A **114**
North St. Pas. E13 2K **87**
North Tenter St. E1 1K **15** (6F **85**)
North Ter. SW3 2C **16** (3C **100**)
North Ter. WC2 4D **12** (1H **101**)
(off Trafalgar Sq.)
Northumberland All. EC3 1H **15** (6E **84**)
(not continuous)
Northumberland Av. DA16: Well 4H **125**
Northumberland Av. E12 1A **70**
Northumberland Av. EN1: Enf 1C **24**
Northumberland Av. TW7: Isle 1K **113**
Northumberland Av. WC2 4E **12** (1J **101**)
Northumberland Cl. DA8: Erith 7J **109**
Northumberland Cl. TW19: Stanw 6A **110**
Northumberland Cres. TW14: Felt 6G **111**
Northumberland Gdns. BR1: Broml 4E **160**
Northumberland Gdns. CR4: Mitc 5H **155**
Northumberland Gdns. N9 3A **34**
Northumberland Gdns. TW7: Isle 7A **96**
Northumberland Gro. N17 7C **34**

A–Z London 263

O

Oakmead Rd. – Olive Rd.

Oakmead Rd. SW12 1E 136
Oakmede EN5: Barn 4A 20
Oakmere Rd. SE2 6A 108
Oakmont Pl. BR6: Orp 1H 173
Oak Pk. Gdns. SW19 1F 135
Oak Pk. M. N16 3F 67
Oak Pl. SW18 5K 117
Oakridge Dr. N2 3B 46
Oakridge La. BR1: Broml 5F 141
Oakridge Rd. BR1: Broml 4F 141
Oak Ri. IG9: Buck H 3G 37
Oak Rd. DA8: Erith Mill Rd. 7J 109
Oak Rd. BR6: Chels 7K 173
Oak Rd. KT3: N Mald 2K 151
Oak Rd. W5 7D 78
Oak Row SW16 2G 155
Oaks, The BR2: Broml 6E 160
Oaks, The EN2: Enf 3G 23
Oaks, The HA4: Ruis 7F 39
Oaks, The IG8: Wfd G 6B 36
Oaks, The N12 4E 30
Oaks, The NW10 7D 62
Oaks, The NW6 7F 63
(off Brondesbury Pk.)
Oaks, The SE18 5G 107
Oaks, The SM4: Mord 4G 153
Oaks, The TW13: Felt 2B 130
Oaks, The UB4: Hayes 2E 74
Oaks Av. KT4: Wor Pk 3D 164
Oaks Av. RM5: Col R 2J 55
Oaks Av. SE19 5E 138
Oaks Av. TW13: Felt 2C 130
Oaks Cvn. Pk., The KT9: Chess 3C 162
Oaksford Av. SE26 3H 139
Oaks Gro. E4 2B 36
Oakshade Rd. BR1: Broml 4F 141
Oakshaw Rd. SW18 7K 117
Oakshott Ct. NW1 1C 6 (2H 83)
(not continuous)
Oakside Ct. IG6: Ilf 2H 53
Oakside Ter. NW10 3K 61
Oaks La. CR0: C'don 3H 169
Oaks La. IG2: Ilf 5J 53
Oaks Pavilion M. SE19 5E 138
Oak Sq. SW9 2K 119
Oaks Rd. CR0: C'don 5H 169
Oak St. RM7: Rom 5J 55
Oaks Way KT6: Surb 1D 162
Oaks Way SM5: Cars 7D 166
Oakthorpe Ct. N13 5H 33
Oakthorpe Est. N13 5H 33
Oakthorpe Rd. N13 5F 33
Oaktree Av. N13 3G 33
Oak Tree Cl. HA7: Stan 7H 27
Oak Tree Cl. KT19: Ewe 6H 163
Oak Tree Cl. W5 6C 78
Oak Tree Ct. UB5: N'olt 2A 76
Oak Tree Ct. W3 7H 79
Oak Tree Dell NW9 5J 43
Oak Tree Dr. N20 1E 30
Oak Tree Gdns. BR1: Broml 5K 141
Oaktree Gdns. SE9 3F 143
Oaktree Gro. IG1: Ilf 5H 71
Oak Tree Ho. W9 4J 81
(off Shirland Rd.)
Oak Tree M. NW2 6C 62
Oak Tree Rd. NW8 2C 4 (3C 82)
Oakum Sq. E11 3F 69
Oakview Apts. SM1: Sutt 4B 166
Oakview Gdns. N2 4B 46
Oakview Gro. CR0: C'don 1A 170
Oakview Lodge NW11 7H 45
(off Beechcroft Av.)
Oakview Rd. SE6 5D 140
Oak Village NW5 4E 64
Oak Vs. NW11 6H 45
(off Hendon Pk. Row)
Oakville Ho. SE16 2K 103
(off Dominion Dr.)
Oak Wlk. SM6: W'gton 1E 166
(off Helios Rd.)
Oak Way CR0: C'don 6K 157
Oak Way N14 7A 22
Oak Way TW14: Felt 1G 129
Oak Way W3 1A 98
Oakway BR2: Broml 2F 159
Oakway SW20 4E 152
Oakway Cl. DA5: Bexl 6E 126
Oakways SE9 6F 125
OAKWOOD 4C 22
Oakwood SM6: W'gton 7F 167
Oakwood Av. BR2: Broml 3K 159
Oakwood Av. BR3: Beck 2E 158
Oakwood Av. CR4: Mitc 2B 154
Oakwood Av. N14 7C 22
Oakwood Av. UB1: S'hall 7E 76
Oakwood Bus. Pk. NW10 4K 79
Oakwood Cl. BR7: Chst 6D 142
Oakwood Cl. IG8: Wfd G 6H 37
Oakwood Cl. N14 6B 22
Oakwood Cl. SE13 6F 123
Oakwood Ct. E6 1C 88
Oakwood Ct. HA1: Harr 6H 41
Oakwood Ct. W14 3H 99
Oakwood Cres. N21 6D 22
Oakwood Cres. UB6: G'frd 6A 60
Oakwood Dr. DA7: Bex 4J 127
Oakwood Dr. HA8: Edg 6D 28
Oakwood Dr. SE19 6D 138
Oakwood Gdns. BR6: Farnb 2G 173
Oakwood Gdns. IG3: Ilf 2K 71
Oakwood Gdns. SM1: Sutt 2J 165
Oakwood Ho. E9 6J 67
(off Frampton Pk. Rd.)
Oakwood La. W14 3H 99
Oakwood Lodge N14 6B 22
(off Avenue Rd.)
Oakwood Mans. W14 3H 99
(off Oakwood Ct.)
Oakwood Pde. N14 5B 22
Oakwood Pk. Rd. N14 7C 22
Oakwood Pl. CR0: C'don 6A 156
Oakwood Rd. BR6: Farnb 2G 173
Oakwood Rd. CR0: C'don 6A 156
Oakwood Rd. HA5: Pinn 2K 39
Oakwood Rd. NW11 4J 45
Oakwood Rd. SW20 1C 152
Oakwood Vw. N14 6C 22
Oakworth Rd. W10 5E 80
Oarsman Pl. KT8: E Mos 4J 149
Oasis, The BR1: Broml 2A 160
Oasis Sports Cen. 7E 6 (6J 83)
Oast Ct. E14 7B 86
(off Newell St.)
Oast Lodge W4 7A 98
(off Corney Reach Way)
Oates Cl. BR2: Broml 3F 159
Oatfield Ho. N15 6E 48
(off Perry Ct.)
Oatfield Rd. BR6: Orp 1K 173
Oatland Ri. E17 2A 50
Oatlands Rd. EN3: Enf H 1D 24
Oat La. EC2 7C 8 (6C 84)
Oatwell Ho. SW3 5D 16 (5C 100)
(off Cale St.)
Oban Cl. E13 4A 88
Oban Ho. E14 6F 87
(off Oban St.)
Oban Ho. IG11: Bark 2H 89
Oban Rd. E13 3A 88
Oban Rd. SE25 4D 156
Oban St. E14 6F 87
Oberon Cl. E6 7B 70
Oberon Ho. N1 2E 84
(off Arden Est.)
Oberon Way TW17: Shep 3A 146
Oberstein Rd. SW11 4B 118
Oborne Cl. SE24 5B 120
O'Brien Ho. E2 3K 85
(off Roman Rd.)
Observatory Gdns. W8 2J 99
Observatory M. E14 4F 105
Observatory Rd. SW14 4J 115
Observatory Rd. SW7 2A 16 (3B 100)
Observer Cl. NW9 3A 44
O'Callaghan Way SE17 4C 102
Occupation La. SE18 1F 125
Occupation La. W5 4D 96
Occupation Rd. KT19: Ewe 7K 163
Occupation Rd. SE17 5C 102
Occupation Rd. W13 2B 96
Ocean Est. E1 Ben Jonson Rd. 5A 86
Ocean Est. E1 Ernest St. 4K 85
Oceanis Apts. E16 7J 87
(off Seagull La.)
Ocean St. E1 5K 85
Ocean Wharf E14 2B 104
Ockbrook E1 5J 85
(off Hannibal Rd.)
Ockendon M. N1 6D 66
Ockendon Rd. N1 6D 66
Ockham Bldg. SE16 3F 103
(off Arts La.)
Ockham Dr. BR5: St P 7A 144
Ockham Dr. UB6: G'frd 7G 59
Ockley Ct. DA14: Sidc 3J 143
Ockley Ct. SM1: Sutt 4A 166
Ockley Rd. CR0: C'don 7K 155
Ockley Rd. SW16 4J 137
Octagon, The SW10 7K 99
(off Coleridge Gdns.)
Octagon Arc. EC2 6G 9 (5E 84)
Octagon Ct. SE16 1K 103
(off Rotherhithe St.)
Octavia Cl. CR4: Mitc 5C 154
Octavia Ho. SW1 2C 18 (3H 101)
(off Medway St.)
Octavia Ho. W10 4G 81
Octavia M. W9 4H 81
Octavia Rd. TW7: Isle 3J 113
Octavia St. SW11 1C 118
Octavia Way SE28 7B 90
Octavius St. SE8 7C 104
October Pl. NW4 3F 45
Odard Rd. KT8: W Mole 4E 148
Oddmark Ho. IG11: Bark 2H 89
Odelia Ct. E15 1E 86
(off Biggerstaff Rd.)
Odell Ct. IG11: Bark 7K 71
Odell Ho. E14 6C 86
(off New Festival Av.)
Odell Wlk. SE13 3E 122
Odeon, The IG11: Bark 7H 71
Odeon Cinema Beckenham 2C 158
Odeon Cinema Camden Town 1F 83
(off Parkway)
Odeon Cinema Covent Gdn. 1D 12 (6H 83)
(off Shaftesbury Av.)
Odeon Cinema Edmonton 7E 24
Odeon Cinema Greenwich 4H 105
Odeon Cinema Haymarket, Panton St. 3D 12 (7H 83)
(off Panton St.)
Odeon Cinema Holloway 3J 65
Odeon Cinema IMAX (BFI) 5J 13 (1A 102)
Odeon Cinema Kingston upon Thames 2E 150
(within The Rotunda Cen.)
Odeon Cinema Leicester Sq. 3D 12 (7H 83)
(off Leicester Sq.)
Odeon Cinema Putney 3G 117
Odeon Cinema Richmond upon Thames, Hill Street 5D 114
Odeon Cinema Richmond upon Thames, Red Lion Street 5D 114
Odeon Cinema South Woodford 2J 51
Odeon Cinema Streatham 3J 137
Odeon Cinema Surrey Quays 3K 103
Odeon Cinema Swiss Cottage 7B 64
Odeon Cinema Tottenham Ct. Rd. 6C 6 (5H 83)
(off Tottenham Ct. Rd.)
Odeon Cinema Whiteleys 6K 81
Odeon Cinema Wimbledon 6H 135
Odeon Ct. E16 5J 87
Odeon Ct. NW10 1A 80
(off St Albans Rd.)
Odeon Pde. N7 3J 65
(off Holloway Rd.)
Odeon Pde. SE9 4C 124
(off Well Hall Rd.)
Odeon Pde. UB6: G'frd 6B 60
(off Allendale Rd.)
Odessa Rd. E7 3H 69
Odessa Rd. NW10 2C 80
Odessa St. SE16 2B 104
Odessa Wharf SE16 3B 104
(off Odessa St.)
Odessey Ho. E15 6F 69
(off Leyton Rd.)
Odette Duval Ho. E1 5J 85
(off Stepney Way)
Odger St. SW11 2D 118
Odhams Wlk. WC2 1F 13 (6J 83)
Odin Ho. SE5 2C 120
O'Donnell Ct. WC1 3F 7 (4J 83)
O'Driscoll Ho. W12 6D 80
Odyssey Bus. Pk. HA4: Ruis 5K 57
Offa's Mead E9 4B 68
Offenbach Ho. E2 2K 85
(off Mace St.)
Offenham Rd. SE9 4D 142
Offenham Rd. SW9 1A 120
Offers Ct. KT1: King T 3F 151
Offerton Rd. SW4 3G 119
Offham Ho. SE17 4E 102
(off Beckway St.)
Offham Slope N12 5C 30
Offley Pl. TW7: Isle 2H 113
Offley Rd. SW9 7A 102
Offord Cl. N17 6B 34
Offord Rd. N1 7K 65
Offord St. N1 7K 65
Ogden Ho. TW13: Hanw 3C 130
Ogilby St. SE18 4D 106
Ogilvie Ho. E1 6K 85
(off Stepney C'way.)
Oglander Rd. SE15 4F 121
Ogle St. W1 5A 6 (5G 83)
Oglethorpe Rd. RM10: Dag 3F 73
O'Gorman Ho. SW10 7A 100
(off King's Rd.)
O'Grady Ho. E17 3D 50
Ohio Bldg. SE13 1D 122
(off Deal's Gateway)
Ohio Rd. E13 4H 87
Oil Mill La. W6 5C 98
Okeburn Rd. SW17 5E 136
Okehampton Cl. N12 5G 31
Okehampton Cres. DA16: Well 1B 126
Okehampton Rd. NW10 1E 80
Olaf Ct. W8 2J 99
(off Kensington Chu. St.)
Olaf St. W11 7F 81
Old Abbey La. SE16 3F 103
(off Vauban St.)
Oldacre M. SW12 7E 118
Old Aeroworks, The NW8 4B 4 (4B 82)
(off Hatton St.)
Old Bailey EC4 1B 14 (6B 84)
Old Bailey 7B 8 (6B 84)
Old Barge Ho. All. SE1 3K 13 (7A 84)
(off Barge Ho. St.)
Old Barn Cl. SM2: Cheam 7G 165
Old Barn Way DA7: Bex 3K 127
Old Barracks W8 2K 99
Old Barrack Yd. SW1 7G 11 (2E 100)
(not continuous)
Old Barrowfield E15 1G 87
Old Bellgate Pl. E14 3C 104
Oldberry Rd. HA8: Edg 6E 28
Old Bethnal Grn. Rd. E2 3G 85
OLD BEXLEY 7H 127
Old Bexley Bus. Pk. DA5: Bexl 7H 127
Old Bexley La. DA5: Bexl 2K 145
Old Bexley La. DA5: Dart 2K 145
Old Billingsgate Mkt. EC3 3G 15 (7E 84)
(off Lwr. Thames St.)
Old Billingsgate Wlk. EC3 3G 15 (7E 84)
Old Bond St. W1 3A 12 (7G 83)
Oldborough Rd. HA0: Wemb 3C 60
OLD BRENTFORD 7D 96
Old Brewer's Yd. WC2 1E 12 (6J 83)
Old Brewery M. NW3 4B 64
Old Brewery Way E17 5B 50
Old Bri. Cl. UB5: N'olt 2E 76
Old Bridge St. KT1: Hamp W 2D 150
Old Broad St. EC2 7F 9 (6D 84)
Old Bromley Rd. BR1: Broml 5F 141
Old Brompton Rd. SW5 5J 99
Old Brompton Rd. SW7 5A 100
Old Bldgs. WC2 7J 7 (6A 84)
(off Chancery La.)
Old Burlington St. W1 3A 12 (7G 83)
Oldbury Ct. E9 5A 68
(off Mabley St.)
Oldbury Ho. W2 5K 81
(off Harrow Rd.)
Oldbury Pl. W1 5H 5 (5E 82)
Oldbury Rd. EN1: Enf 2B 24
Old Canal M. SE15 5F 103
(off Trafalgar Av.)
Old Castle St. E1 7J 9 (6F 85)
Old Cavendish St. W1 7J 5 (6F 83)
Old Change Ct. EC4 1C 14 (6C 84)
(off Distaff La.)
Old Chapel Pl. SW9 2A 120
Old Charlton Rd. TW17: Shep 5E 146
Old Chelsea M. SW3 7C 16 (6C 100)
Old Chiswick Yd. W4 6A 98
(off Pumping Sta. Rd.)
Old Church Ct. N11 5A 32
Oldchurch Gdns. RM7: Rush G 7K 55
Old Church La. HA7: Stan 5G 27
Old Church La. NW9 2K 61
Old Church La. UB6: G'frd 3A 78
Oldchurch Ri. RM7: Rush G 7K 55
Old Church Rd. E1 6K 85
Old Church Rd. E4 4H 35
Oldchurch Rd. RM7: Rush G 7K 55
Old Church St. SW3 6B 16 (5B 100)
Old Claygate La. KT10: Clay 6A 162
Old Clem Sq. SE18 6E 106
(off Woolwich Comn.)
Old Coal Yd. SE28 4H 107
Old College Ct. DA17: Belv 5H 109
Old Compton St. W1 2C 12 (7H 83)
Old Cople La. SE19 5F 139
Old Cote Dr. TW5: Hest 6E 94
Old Ct. Ho. W8 2K 99
(off Old Court Pl.)
Old Ct. Pl. W8 2K 99
Old Ctyd., The BR1: Broml 1K 159
Old Curiosity Shop 1H 13 (6K 83)
(off Portsmouth St.)
Old Dairy N15 6E 48
Old Dairy Gro. UB2: S'hall 5E 94
Old Dairy La. HA4: Ruis 4K 57
Old Dairy M. NW5 6F 65
Old Dairy M. SW12 1E 136
Old Dairy M. SW4 4J 119
(off Tintern St.)
Old Dairy Sq. N21 7F 23
(off Wade Hill)
Old Deer Pk. 2C 114
Old Deer Pk. Gdns. TW9: Rich 3E 114
Old Devonshire Rd. SW12 7F 119
Old Dock Cl. TW9: Kew 6G 97
Old Dover Rd. SE3 7J 105
Oldegate Ho. E6 7B 70
Old Farm Av. DA15: Sidc 1H 143
Old Farm Av. N14 7B 22
Old Farm Cl. SW17 2C 136
Old Farm Cl. TW4: Houn 4D 112
Old Farm La. SW19 5K 135
Old Farm Pas. TW12: Hamp 1G 149
Old Farm Pl. DA15: Sidc 2K 143
Old Farm Rd. N2 1B 46
Old Farm Rd. TW12: Hamp 6D 130
Old Farm Rd. E. DA15: Sidc 2A 144
Old Farm Rd. W. DA15: Sidc 2K 143
Oldfield Cl. BR1: Broml 4D 160
Oldfield Cl. HA7: Stan 5F 27
Oldfield Cl. UB6: G'frd 5J 59
Oldfield Ct. KT5: Surb 4F 151
(off Cranes Pk. Cres.)
Oldfield Farm Gdns. UB6: G'frd 1H 77
Oldfield Gro. SE16 4K 103
Oldfield Ho. W4 5A 98
(off Devonshire Rd.)
Oldfield La. Nth. UB6: G'frd 2H 77
Oldfield La. Sth. UB6: G'frd 4G 77
Oldfield M. N6 7G 47
Oldfield Rd. BR1: Broml 4D 160
Oldfield Rd. DA7: Bex 2E 126
Oldfield Rd. N16 3E 66
Oldfield Rd. NW10 7B 62
Oldfield Rd. SW19 6G 135
Oldfield Rd. TW12: Hamp 1D 148
Oldfield Rd. W3 2B 98
Oldfields Cir. UB5: N'olt 6G 59
Oldfields Rd. SM1: Sutt 3H 165
Old Fire Sta., The SE18 7F 107
Old Fish St. Hill EC4 2C 14 (7C 84)
(off Queen Victoria St.)
Old Fleet La. EC4 7A 8 (6B 84)
Old Fold Cl. EN5: Barn 1C 20
Old Fold La. EN5: Barn 1C 20
Old Fold Manor Golf Course 1B 20
OLD FORD 1B 86
OLD FORD 1C 86
Old Ford Rd. E2 3J 85
Old Ford Rd. E3 2A 86
Old Ford Trading Cen. E3 1C 86
(off Maverton Rd.)
Old Forge Cl. HA7: Stan 4F 27
Old Forge Cres. TW17: Shep 6D 146
Old Forge M. W12 2D 98
Old Forge Rd. EN1: Enf 1A 24
Old Forge Rd. N19 2H 65
Old Forge Way DA14: Sidc 4B 144
Old Gloucester St. WC1 5F 7 (5J 83)
Old Goods Yd., The W2 5A 82
Old Hall Cl. HA5: Pinn 1C 40
Old Hall Dr. HA5: Pinn 1C 40
Oldham Ter. W3 1J 97
(not continuous)
Old Hatch Mnr. HA4: Ruis 7H 39
Old Highwayman Pl. SW15 1D 134
Old Hill BR6: Downe 6H 173
Old Hill BR7: Chst 1E 160
Oldhill St. N16 1G 67
Old Homesdale Rd. BR2: Broml 4A 160
Old Hospital Cl. SW12 1D 136
Old Ho. Cl. SW19 5G 135
Old Ho. Gdns. TW1: Twick 6C 114
Old Howlett's La. HA4: Ruis 6F 39
OLD ISLEWORTH 3B 114
Old Jamaica Bus. Est. SE16 7K 15 (3F 103)
Old Jamaica Rd. SE16 7K 15 (3G 103)
Old James St. SE15 3H 121
Old Jewry EC2 1E 14 (6D 84)
Old Kenton La. NW9 5H 43
Old Kent Rd. SE1 4E 102
Old Kent Rd. SE15 6G 103
Old Kingston Rd. KT4: Wor Pk 2J 163
Old Laundry, The BR7: Chst 1G 161
Old Library Ct. HA4: Ruis 2J 57
Old Library Ho. E3 2A 86
(off Roman Rd.)
Old Lodge Pl. TW1: Twick 6B 114
Old Lodge Way HA7: Stan 5F 27
Old London Rd. DA14: Sidc 7G 145
Old London Rd. DA14: Swan 7G 145
Old London Rd. KT2: King T 2E 150
Old Lyonian Sports Club 5G 41
Old Maidstone Rd. DA14: Sidc 7F 145
OLD MALDEN 1A 164
Old Malden La. KT4: Wor Pk 2K 163
Old Mnr. Ct. NW8 2A 82
Old Mnr. Dr. TW7: Isle 6G 113
Old Mnr. Ho. M. TW17: Shep 3C 146
Old Mnr. Rd. UB2: S'hall 4B 94
Old Mnr. Way BR7: Chst 5D 142
Old Mnr. Way DA7: Bex 2K 127
Old Manor Yd. SW5 4K 99
Old Mkt. Ct. SM1: Sutt 4K 165
Old Mkt. Sq. E2 1J 9 (3F 85)
Old Marylebone Rd. NW1 6D 4 (5C 82)
Oldmead Ho. RM10: Dag 6H 73
Old M. HA1: Harr 5J 41
Old Mill Ct. E18 3A 52
Old Mill Pl. RM7: Rom 6K 55
Old Mill Rd. SE18 6H 107
Old Mitre Ct. EC4 1K 13 (6A 84)
Old Montague St. E1 6K 9 (5G 85)
Old Nichol St. E2 3J 9 (4F 85)
Old North St. WC1 5G 7 (5K 83)
(off Theobald's Rd.)
Old Nursery Ct. E2 2F 85
(off Dawson St.)
Old Nursery Pl. TW15: Ashf 5D 128
Old Oak Cl. KT9: Chess 4F 163
OLD OAK COMMON 5A 80
Old Oak Comn. La. NW10 5A 80
Old Oak Comn. La. W3 5A 80
Old Oak La. NW10 3A 80
Old Oak Rd. W3 7B 80
Old Operating Theatre Mus. & Herb Garret, The 5F 15 (1D 102)
(off St Thomas St.)
Old Orchard TW16: Sun 2A 148
Old Orchard, The NW3 4D 64
Old Orchard Cl. EN4: Had W 1G 21
Old Orchard Cl. UB8: Hil 6C 74
Old Palace La. TW9: Rich 5C 114
Old Palace Rd. CR0: C'don 3B 168
Old Palace Ter. TW9: Rich 5D 114
Old Palace Yd. SW1 1E 18 (3J 101)
Old Palace Yd. TW9: Rich 5C 114
Old Paradise St. SE11 3G 19 (4K 101)
Old Pk. Av. EN2: Enf 4H 23
Old Pk. Av. SW12 6E 118
Old Pk. Gro. EN2: Enf 4H 23
Old Pk. La. W1 5J 11 (1F 101)
Old Pk. M. TW5: Hest 7D 94
Old Pk. Ridings N21 6G 23
Old Pk. Rd. EN2: Enf 3G 23
Old Pk. Rd. N13 4E 32
Old Pk. Rd. SE2 5A 108
Old Pk. Rd. Sth. EN2: Enf 4G 23
Old Pk. Vw. EN2: Enf 3F 23
Old Pearson St. SE10 7D 104
Old Perry St. BR7: Chst 6J 143
Old Police Sta., The SW17 2D 136
Old Police Station M. SE20 7K 139
Old Post Office La. SE3 3K 123
Old Post Office Wlk. KT6: Surb 6D 150
(off Victoria Rd.)
Old Pound Cl. TW7: Isle 1A 114
Old Pye St. SW1 1C 18 (3H 101)
Old Pye St. Est. SW1 2C 18 (3H 101)
(off Old Pye St.)
Old Quebec St. W1 1F 11 (6D 82)
(not continuous)
Old Queen St. SW1 7D 12 (2H 101)
Old Rectory Gdns. HA8: Edg 6B 28
Old Redding HA3: Hrw W 5A 26
Old Red Lion Theatre 1K 7 (2A 84)
(off St John St.)
Oldridge Rd. SW12 7E 118
Old Rd. DA1: Cray 5K 127
Old Rd. EN3: Enf H 1D 24
Old Rd. SE13 4G 123
Old Rope Wlk. TW16: Sun 3K 147
Old Royal Free Pl. N1 1A 84
Old Royal Free Sq. N1 1A 84
Old Royal Naval College 5F 105
Old Ruislip Rd. UB5: N'olt 2A 76
Old School, The WC1 5H 7 (5K 83)
(off Princeton St.)
Old School Cl. BR3: Beck 2K 157
Old School Cl. SE10 3G 105
Old School Cl. SW19 2J 153
Old School Ct. N17 3F 49
Old School Cres. E7 6J 69
Old School Pl. CR0: Wadd 4A 168
Old School Rd. UB8: Hil 4B 74
Old Schools La. KT17: Ewe 7B 164
Old School Sq. E14 6C 86
(off Pelling St.)
Old School Sq. KT7: T Ditt 6K 149
Old School Ter. SM3: Cheam 7F 165
Old Seacoal La. EC4 7A 8 (6B 84)
Old Sessions Ho., The EC1 4A 8 (4B 84)
Old Slade La. SL3: Coln 1A 174
Old Sth. Cl. HA5: Pinn 1B 40
Old Sth. Lambeth Rd. SW8 7J 101
Old Speech Room Gallery 1J 59
Old Spitalfields Market 5J 9 (5F 85)
Old Sq. WC2 7H 7 (6K 83)
Old Stable M. N5 3C 66
Old Stable Row SE18 4E 106
(off Woolwich New Rd.)
Old Stables Ct. SE5 1C 120
(off Camberwell New Rd.)
Old Station Gdns. TW11: Tedd 6A 132
(off Victoria Rd.)
Old Station Ho. SE17 5C 102
Old Station Pas. TW9: Rich 4D 114
(off Little Green)
Old Station Rd. UB3: Harl 3H 93
Old Sta. Way SW4 3H 119
(off Voltaire Rd.)
Old Station Way SW4 3H 119
(Off Voltaire Road)
Old Station Yd., The E17 4E 50
Oldstead Rd. BR1: Broml 4E 140
Old Stockley Rd. UB7: W Dray 2D 92
Old St. E13 2K 87
Old St. EC1 3C 8 (4C 84)
OLD STREET 3F 9 (4D 84)
Old St. Yd. EC1 3E 8 (4D 84)
(off City Rd.)
Old Studio Cl. CR0: C'don 7D 156
Old Sungate Cotts. RM5: Col R 1F 55
Old Sun Wharf E14 7A 86
(off Narrow St.)
Old Swan Wharf SW11 1B 118
Old Swan Yd. SM5: Cars 4D 166
Old Theatre Ct. SE1 4D 14 (1C 102)
(off Porter St.)
Old Town CR0: C'don 3B 168
Old Town SW4 3G 119
Old Town Hall Apts. SE16 3F 103
Old Tramyard SE18 4J 107
Old Twelve Cl. W7 4J 77
Old Vic Theatre, The 6K 13 (2A 102)
(off The Cut)
Old Vinyl Factory, The UB3: Hayes 2G 93
Old Watercress Wlk. SM5: Cars 4E 166
Old Willow Cl. E3 3C 86
Old Woolwich Rd. SE10 6F 105
Old York Rd. SW18 5K 117
Oleander Cl. BR6: Farnb 5H 173
Oleander Ho. SE15 5F 103
O'Leary Sq. E1 5J 85
Olga St. E3 2A 86
Olinda Rd. N16 6F 49
Oliphant St. E14 7E 86
(off Bullivant St.)
Oliphant St. W10 3F 81
Olive Blythe Ho. W10 4G 81
(off Ladbroke Gro.)
Olive Ct. E5 2J 67
(off Woodmill Rd.)
Olive Ct. N1 1A 84
(off Liverpool Rd.)
Olive Gro. N15 4C 48
Olive Haines Lodge SW15 5H 117
Olive Ho. EC1 3K 7 (4A 84)
(off Bowling Grn. La.)
Oliver Av. SE25 3F 157
Oliver Bus. Pk. NW10 2J 79
Oliver Cl. W4 6H 97
Oliver Ct. SE18 4G 107
Oliver Gdns. E6 5C 88
Oliver Goldsmith Est. SE15 1G 121
Oliver Gro. SE25 4F 157
Oliver Ho. SE14 7B 104
(off New Cross Rd.)
Oliver Ho. SE16 2G 103
(off George Row)
Oliver Ho. SW8 7J 101
(off Wyvil Rd.)
Oliver M. SE15 2G 121
Olive Rd. E13 3A 88
Olive Rd. NW2 4D 62
Olive Rd. SW19 7A 136

Oster Ter. – Papworth Way

Oster Ter. E17 5K 49
Ostlers Dr. TW15: Ashf 5E 128
Ostliffe Rd. N13 5H 33
Ostro Twr. E14 2D 104
Oswald Bldg. SW11 6F 101
Oswald Rd. UB1: S'hall 1C 94
Oswald's Mead E9 4A 68
Oswald St. E5 3K 67
Oswald Ter. NW2 3E 62
Osward CR0: Sels 7B 170
(not continuous)
Osward Pl. N9 2C 34
Osward Rd. SW17 2D 136
Oswell Ho. E1 1H 103
(off Farthing Flds.)
Oswin St. SE11 4B 102
Oswyth Rd. SE5 2E 120
Otford Cl. BR1: Broml 3E 160
Otford Cl. DA5: Bexl 6H 127
Otford Cl. SE20 1J 157
Otford Cres. SE4 6B 122
Otford Ho. SE1 7F 15 (2D 102)
(off Staple St.)
Otford Ho. SE15 6J 103
(off Lovelinch Cl.)
Othello Cl. SE11 5K 19 (5B 102)
Other Place Theatre, The
1A 18 (3G 101)
(off Palace St.)
Otho Ct. TW8: Bford 7D 96
Otley App. IG2: Ilf 6F 53
Otley Dr. IG2: Ilf 5F 53
Otley Ho. N5 3A 66
Otley Rd. E16 6A 88
Otley Ter. E5 3K 67
Ottawa Gdns. RM10: Dag 7K 73
Ottawa Ho. SE16 2J 103
(off Province Dr.)
Ottawa Ho. UB4: Yead 3K 75
(off Ayles Rd.)
Ottaway St. E5 3G 67
Otterbourne Rd. CR0: C'don 2C 168
Otterbourne Rd. E4 3A 36
Otterburn Gdns. TW7: Isle 7A 96
Otterburn Ho. SE5 7C 102
(off Sultan St.)
Otterburn St. SW17 6D 136
Otter Cl. E15 1E 86
Otterden Cl. BR6: Orp 3J 173
Otterden St. SE6 4C 140
Otterden Ter. SE1 4F 103
(off Lynton Rd.)
Otter Dr. SM5: Cars 1D 166
Otterfield Rd. UB7: Yiew 7A 74
Otter Rd. UB6: G'frd 4G 77
Otter Way UB7: Yiew 1A 92
Ottley Dr. SE3 4A 124
Otto Cl. SE26 3H 139
Otto Dr. UB2: S'hall 3E 94
Otto St. SE17 6B 102
Ott's Yd. N19 4G 65
(off Southcote Rd.)
Otway Gdns. WD23: Bush 1D 26
Oulton Cl. E5 2J 67
Oulton Cl. SE28 6C 90
Oulton Cres. IG11: Bark 5K 71
Oulton Rd. N15 5D 48
Our Lady's Cl. SE19 6D 138
Ouseley Rd. SW12 1D 136
Outer Circ. NW1 1D 4 (2C 82)
Outgate Rd. NW10 7B 62
Outram Pl. N1 1J 83
Outram Rd. CR0: C'don 2F 169
Outram Rd. E6 1C 88
Outram Rd. N22 1H 47
Outwich St. EC3 7H 9 (6E 84)
(off Camomile St.)
Outwood Ho. SW2 7K 119
(off Deepdene Gdns.)
Oval Surrey CCC, The 7H 19 (6K 101)
Oval, The DA15: Sidc 7A 126
Oval, The E2 2H 85
Oval Ct. HA8: Edg 7D 28
Oval Ho. CR0: C'don 1E 168
(off Oval Rd.)
Oval Mans. SE11 7H 19 (6K 101)
Oval Pl. SW8 7K 101
Oval Rd. CR0: C'don 2D 168
Oval Rd. NW1 1F 83
Oval Rd. Nth. RM10: Dag 1H 91
Oval Rd. Sth. RM10: Dag 2H 91
Oval Way SE11 6H 19 (5K 101)
Ovanna M. N1 6E 66
Overbrae BR3: Beck 6C 140
Overbrook Wlk. HA8: Edg 7B 28
(not continuous)
Overbury Av. BR3: Beck 3D 158
Overbury Rd. N15 6D 48
Overbury St. E5 4K 67
Overcliff Rd. SE13 3C 122
Overcourt Cl. DA15: Sidc 6B 126
Overdale Av. KT3: N Mald 2J 151
Overdale Rd. W5 3C 96
Overdown Rd. SE6 4C 140
Overhill Rd. SE22 7G 121
Overhill Way BR3: Beck 5F 159
Overlea Rd. E5 7G 49
Overmead DA15: Sidc 7H 125
Oversley Ho. W2 5J 81
(off Alfred Rd.)
Overstand Cl. BR3: Beck 5C 158
Overstone Gdns. CR0: C'don 7B 158
Overstone Ho. E14 6C 86
(off E. India Dock Rd.)
Overstone Rd. W6 3E 98
Overstrand Mans. SW11 1D 118
Overton Cl. NW10 6J 61
Overton Cl. TW7: Isle 1K 113
Overton Ct. E11 7J 51
Overton Ct. SM2: Sutt 7J 165
Overton Dr. E11 7J 51
Overton Dr. RM6: Chad H 7C 54
Overton Ho. SW15 7B 116
(off Tangley Gro.)
Overton Rd. E10 1A 68
Overton Rd. N14 5D 22
Overton Rd. SE2 3C 108
Overton Rd. SM2: Sutt 6J 165
Overton Rd. SW9 2A 120
Overton Rd. E. SE2 3D 108
Overton's Yd. CR0: C'don 3C 168
Overy Ho. SE1 7A 14 (2B 102)
Ovesdon Av. HA2: Harr 1D 58
Ovett Cl. SE19 6E 138
Ovex Cl. E14 2E 104
Ovington Ct. SW3 2D 16 (3C 100)
(off Brompton Rd.)
Ovington Gdns. SW3 2D 16 (3C 100)
Ovington M. SW3 2D 16 (3C 100)
(off Ovington Gdns.)
Ovington Sq. SW3 2D 16 (3C 100)
Ovington St. SW3 3D 16 (4C 100)
Owen Cl. UB5: N'olt Arnold Rd.
6C 58
Owen Cl. UB5: N'olt Attlee Rd.
3K 75
Owen Cl. CR0: C'don 6D 156
Owen Cl. SE28 1C 108
Owen Cl. TW16: Sun 1G 147
Owen Gdns. IG8: Wfd G 6H 37
Owen Ho. TW1: Twick 7B 114
Owen Ho. TW14: Felt 7J 111
Owenite St. SE2 4B 108
Owen Mans. W14 6G 99
(off Queen's Club Gdns.)
Owen Rd. N13 5H 33
Owen Rd. UB4: Yead 3K 75
Owens M. E11 2G 69
Owen's Row EC1 1A 8 (3B 84)
Owen St. EC1 1A 8 (2B 84)
Owens Way SE23 7A 122
Owen Wlk. SE20 1G 157
Owen Way NW10 6J 61
Owgan Cl. SE5 7D 102
Oxberry Av. SW6 2G 117
Oxborough Ho. SW18 4A 118
(off Eltringham St.)
Oxendon St. SW1 3C 12 (7H 83)
Oxenford St. SE15 3F 121
Oxenham Ho. SE8 6C 104
(off Benbow St.)
Oxenholme NW1 1B 6 (2G 83)
(off Hampstead Rd.)
Oxenpark Av. HA9: Wemb 7E 42
Oxestall's Rd. SE8 5A 104
Oxford & Cambridge Mans. NW1
6D 4 (5C 82)
(off Old Marylebone Rd.)
Oxford Av. N14 1B 32
Oxford Av. SW20 2G 153
Oxford Av. TW5: Hest 5E 94
Oxford Av. UB3: Harl 7H 93
Oxford Cir. W1 1A 12 (6G 83)
(off Oxford St.)
Oxford Cir. Av. W1 1A 12 (6G 83)
Oxford Cl. CR4: Mitc 3G 155
Oxford Cl. N9 2C 34
Oxford Cl. TW15: Ashf 7E 128
Oxford Ct. EC4 2E 14 (7D 84)
(off Cannon St.)
Oxford Ct. KT6: Surb 5E 150
(off Avenue Elmers)
Oxford Ct. TW13: Hanw 4B 130
Oxford Ct. W3 6G 79
Oxford Ct. W4 5H 97
Oxford Ct. W7 5K 77
(off Copley Cl.)
Oxford Ct. W9 5J 81
(off Elmfield Way)
Oxford Cres. KT3: N Mald 6K 151
Oxford Dr. HA4: Ruis 2A 58
Oxford Dr. SE1 5G 15 (1E 102)
Oxford Gdns. N20 1G 31
Oxford Gdns. N21 7H 23
Oxford Gdns. W10 6E 80
Oxford Gdns. W4 5G 97
Oxford Ga. W6 4F 99
Oxford Ho. BR2: Broml 6B 160
(off Wells Vw. Dr.)
Oxford Ho. E3 5B 86
(off William Whiffin Sq.)
Oxford Ho. NW6 2J 81
(off Oxford Rd.)
Oxford Ho. RM8: Dag 4A 72
Oxford M. DA5: Bexl 7G 127
Oxford Pl. NW10 3K 61
(off Press Rd.)
Oxford Rd. DA14: Sidc 5B 144
Oxford Rd. E15 6F 69
(not continuous)
Oxford Rd. EN3: Pond E 5C 24
Oxford Rd. HA1: Harr 6G 41
Oxford Rd. HA3: W'stone 3K 41
Oxford Rd. IG1: Ilf 5G 71
Oxford Rd. IG8: Wfd G 5G 37
Oxford Rd. N4 1A 66
Oxford Rd. N9 2C 34
Oxford Rd. NW6 2J 81
Oxford Rd. SE19 6D 138
Oxford Rd. SM5: Cars 6C 166
Oxford Rd. SM6: W'gton 5G 167
Oxford Rd. SW15 4G 117
Oxford Rd. TW11: Tedd 5H 131
Oxford Rd. W5 7D 78
Oxford Rd. Nth. W4 5H 97
Oxford Rd. Sth. W4 5G 97
Oxford Row TW16: Sun 3A 148
Oxford Sq. W2 1C 10 (6C 82)
Oxford St. W1 1G 11 (6E 82)
Oxford Ter. NW6 2K 81
(off Oxford Rd.)
Oxford Wlk. UB1: S'hall 1D 94
Oxford Way TW13: Hanw 4B 130
Oxgate Cen. NW2 2D 62
Oxgate Ct. NW2 2C 62
Oxgate Ct. Pde. NW2 2C 62
Oxgate Gdns. NW2 3D 62
Oxgate La. NW2 2D 62
Oxgate Pde. NW2 2C 62
Oxhawth Cres. BR2: Broml 5E 160
Oxhey La. HA3: Hrw W 5A 26
Oxleas E6 6F 89
Oxleas Cl. DA16: Well 2H 125
Oxleay Rd. HA2: Harr 1E 58
Oxleigh Cl. KT3: N Mald 5A 152
Oxley Cl. SE1 5F 103
Oxley Sq. E3 4D 86
(off Truman Wlk.)
Oxleys Rd. NW2 3D 62
Oxlip Cl. CR0: C'don 1K 169
Oxlow La. RM10: Dag 4G 73
Oxlow La. RM9: Dag 4F 73
Oxonian St. SE22 4F 121
Oxo Tower Wharf 3K 13 (7A 84)
Oxted Cl. CR4: Mitc 3B 154
Oxtoby Way SW16 1H 155
Oxygen, The E16 7J 87
OYO Bus. Units DA17: Belv 2J 109
OYO Bus. Units RM9: Dag 4F 91
Oystercatcher Cl. E16 6K 87
Oyster Cl. EN5: Barn 6B 20
Oyster Ct. SE17 4C 102
(off Crampton St.)
Oyster M. E7 6B 70
Oyster Row E1 6J 85
Oyster Wharf SW11 2B 118
Ozolins Way E16 6J 87

P

Pablo Neruda Cl. SE24 4B 120
Pace Pl. E1 6H 85
Pacific Bldg. E15 5F 69
(off Property Row)
Pacific Cl. TW14: Felt 1H 129
Pacific Ct. E1 5J 85
Pacific Ho. E1 4K 85
(off Ernest St.)
Pacific M. SW9 4A 120
Pacific Rd. E16 6J 87
Pacific Wharf SE16 1K 103
Packenham Ho. E2 1K 9 (3F 85)
(off Wellington Row)
Packenham Ho. W10 7F 81
(off Shalfleet Dr.)
Packham Ct. KT4: Wor Pk 3E 164
Packington Rd. W3 3J 97
Packington Sq. N1 1C 84
(not continuous)
Packington St. N1 1B 84
Packmores Rd. SE9 5H 125
Packwell Pl. TW5: Hest 6A 94
Padbury SE17 5E 102
(off Bagshot St.)
Padbury Cl. TW14: Bedf 1F 129
Padbury Ct. E2 2K 9 (3F 85)
Padbury Ho. NW8 3D 4 (4C 82)
(off Tresham Cres.)
Padbury Oaks UB7: Lford 4C 174
Paddenswick Rd. W6 3C 98
PADDINGTON 7A 4 (6B 82)
Paddington Cl. UB4: Yead 4B 76
Paddington Ct. W7 5K 77
(off Copley Cl.)
Paddington Gdns. W2 6A 4 (5B 82)
Paddington Grn. W2 5A 4 (5B 82)
Paddington Sports Club 4K 81
Paddington St. W1 5G 5 (5E 82)
Paddock, The N10 3E 46
Paddock, The NW9 5G 43
Paddock, The UB10: Ick 4D 56
Paddock Cl. BR6: Farnb 4F 173
Paddock Cl. KT4: Wor Pk 1A 164
Paddock Cl. SE26 4K 139
Paddock Cl. SE3 2J 123
Paddock Cl. UB5: N'olt 2E 76
Paddock Gdns. SE19 6E 138
Paddock Lodge EN1: Enf 5K 23
(off Village Rd.)
Paddock Mobile Home Pk. BR2: Kes
7C 172
Paddock Pas. SE19 6E 138
(off Paddock Gdns.)
Paddock Rd. DA6: Bex 4E 126
Paddock Rd. HA4: Ruis 3B 58
Paddock Rd. NW2 3C 62
Paddocks, The CR0: Addtn 6C 170
Paddocks, The EN4: Cockf 3J 21
Paddocks, The HA9: Wemb 2H 61
Paddocks, The W5 3D 96
(off Popes La.)
Paddocks Cl. HA2: Harr 4F 59
Paddocks Grn. NW9 1H 61
Paddock Way BR7: Chst 7H 143
Paddock Way SW15 7E 116
Padelford La. HA7: Stan 2F 27
Padfield Ct. HA9: Wemb 3F 61
Padfield Rd. SE5 3C 120
Padley Cl. KT9: Chess 5F 163
Padnall Ct. RM6: Chad H 3D 54
Padnall Rd. RM6: Chad H 3D 54
Padstone Ho. E3 3D 86
(off Talwin St.)
Padstow Cl. BR6: Chels 4K 173
Padstow Ho. E14 7B 86
(off Three Colt St.)
Padstow Rd. EN2: Enf 1G 23
Padstow Wlk. TW14: Felt 1H 129
Padua Rd. SE20 1J 157
Pagden St. SW8 1F 119
Pageant Av. NW9 1K 43
Pageant Cres. SE16 1A 104
Pageantmaster Ct. EC4 1A 14 (6B 84)
(off Ludgate Hill)
Pageant Wlk. CR0: C'don 3E 168
Page Av. HA9: Wemb 3J 61
Page Cl. HA3: Kenton 6F 43
Page Cl. RM9: Dag 5E 72
Page Cl. TW12: Hamp 6C 130
Page Ct. NW7 7J 29
Page Cres. CR0: Wadd 5B 168
Page Grn. Rd. N15 5G 49
Page Grn. Ter. N15 5F 49
Page Heath La. BR1: Broml 3B 160
Page Heath Vs. BR1: Broml 3B 160
Page High N22 2A 48
(off Lymington Av.)
Page Ho. SE10 6E 104
(off Welland St.)
Pagehurst Rd. CR0: C'don 7H 157
Page Mdw. NW7 7J 29
Page M. SW11 2E 118
Page Rd. TW14: Bedf 6F 111
Pages Hill N10 2E 46
Pages La. N10 2E 46
Page St. NW7 1C 44
Page St. SW1 3D 18 (4H 101)
Page's Wlk. SE1 4E 102
Pages Yd. W4 6B 98
Paget Av. SM1: Sutt 3B 166
Paget Cl. TW12: Hamp H 4H 131
Paget Gdns. BR7: Chst 1F 161
Paget Ho. E2 2J 85
(off Bishop's Way)
Paget La. TW7: Isle 3H 113
Paget Pl. KT2: King T 6J 133
Paget Pl. KT7: T Ditt 1A 162
Paget Ri. SE18 6E 106
Paget Rd. IG1: Ilf 4F 71
Paget Rd. N16 1D 66
Paget Rd. UB10: Hil 4E 74
Paget St. EC1 1A 8 (3B 84)
Paget Ter. SE18 6F 107
Pagham Ho. W10 4E 80
(off Sutton Way)
Pagin Ho. N15 5E 48
(off Braemar Rd.)
Pagitts Gro. EN4: Had W 1E 20
Pagnell St. SE14 7B 104
Pagoda Av. TW9: Rich 3F 115
Pagoda Gdns. SE3 2F 123
Pagoda Gro. SE27 2C 138
Paignton Rd. HA4: Ruis 3J 57
Paignton Rd. N15 6E 48
Paines Cl. HA5: Pinn 3C 40
Paines La. HA5: Pinn 1C 40
Pain's Cl. CR4: Mitc 2F 155
Painsthorpe Rd. N16 3E 66
Painted Hall Greenwich 6E 104
Painters M. SE16 4G 103
Painters Rd. IG2: Ilf 3K 53
Paisley Rd. N22 1B 48
Paisley Rd. SM5: Cars 1B 166
Paisley Ter. SM5: Cars 7B 154
Pakefield M. SW2 1K 137
Pakeman Ho. SE1 6B 14 (2B 102)
(off Surrey Row)
Pakeman St. N7 3K 65
Pakenham Cl. SW12 1E 136
Pakenham St. WC1 2H 7 (3K 83)
Pakington Ho. SW9 2J 119
(off Stockwell Gdns. Est.)
Palace Arts Way HA9: Wemb 4G 61
Palace Av. W8 2K 99
Palace Cl. E9 6B 68
Palace Ct. BR1: Broml 1K 159
(off Palace Gro.)
Palace Ct. HA3: Kenton 6E 42
Palace Ct. NW3 5K 63
Palace Ct. W2 7K 81
(not continuous)
Palace Ct. Gdns. N10 3G 47
Palace Exchange 4J 23
Palace Gdns. IG9: Buck H 1G 37
Palace Gdns. M. W8 1K 99
Palace Gdns. Shop. Cen. 4J 23
Palace Gdns. Ter. W8 1J 99
Palace Ga. W8 2A 100
Palace Gates M. N8 4J 47
(off The Campsbourne)
Palace Gates Rd. N22 1H 47
Palace Grn. CR0: Sels 7B 170
Palace Grn. W8 1K 99
Palace Gro. BR1: Broml 1K 159
Palace Gro. SE19 7F 139
Palace Mans. KT1: King T 4D 150
(off Palace Rd.)
Palace Mans. W14 4G 99
(off Hammersmith Rd.)
Palace M. E17 4B 50
Palace M. SW1 4H 17 (4E 100)
(off Eaton Ter.)
Palace M. SW6 7H 99
Palace Pde. E17 4B 50
Palace Pl. SW1 1A 18 (3G 101)
Palace Pl. Mans. W8 2K 99
(off Kensington Ct.)
Palace Rd. BR1: Broml 1K 159
Palace Rd. HA4: Ruis 4C 58
Palace Rd. KT1: King T 4D 150
Palace Rd. KT8: E Mos 3G 149
Palace Rd. N11 7D 32
Palace Rd. N8 5H 47
(not continuous)
Palace Rd. SE19 7F 139
Palace Rd. SW2 1K 137
Palace Sq. SE19 7F 139
Palace St. SW1 1A 18 (3G 101)
Palace Superbowl 4C 102
(within Elephant & Castle Shop. Cen.)
Palace Theatre London
1D 12 (6H 83)
(off Shaftesbury Av.)
Palace Vw. BR1: Broml 3K 159
(not continuous)
Palace Vw. CR0: C'don 4B 170
Palace Vw. SE12 2J 141
Palace Vw. Rd. E4 5J 35
Palace Wharf W6 7E 98
(off Rainville Rd.)
Palamos Rd. E10 1C 68
Palatine Av. N16 4E 66
Palatine Rd. N16 4E 66
Palazzo Apts. N1 7E 66
(off Ardleigh Rd.)
Palemead Cl. SW6 1F 117
Palermo Rd. NW10 2C 80
Palestine Gro. SW19 1B 154
Palestra Ho. SE1 5A 14 (1B 102)
(off Blackfriars Rd.)
Palewell Comn. Dr. SW14 5K 115
Palewell Pk. SW14 5K 115
Palfrey Pl. SW8 7K 101
Palgrave Av. UB1: S'hall 7E 76
Palgrave Ct. TW11: Hamp W 7C 132
Palgrave Gdns. NW1 3D 4 (4C 82)
Palgrave Ho. SE5 7C 102
(off Wyndham Est.)
Palgrave Ho. TW2: Whitt 7G 113
Palgrave Rd. W12 3B 98
Palissy St. E2 2J 9 (3F 85)
(not continuous)
Palladian Gdns. W4 6A 98
Palladino Ho. SW17 5C 136
(off Laurel Cl.)
Palladio Ct. SW18 6K 117
(off Mapleton Cres.)
Palladium Ct. E8 7F 67
(off Queensbridge Rd.)
Pallant Ho. SE1 3D 102
(off Tabard St.)
Pallant Way BR6: Farnb 3E 172
Pallet Way SE18 1C 124
Palliser Ct. W14 5G 99
(off Palliser Rd.)
Palliser Ho. E1 4K 85
(off Ernest St.)
Palliser Ho. SE10 6F 105
(off Trafalgar Rd.)
Palliser Rd. W14 5G 99
Pallister Ter. SW15 3B 134
Pall Mall SW1 5B 12 (1G 101)
Pall Mall E. SW1 4D 12 (1H 101)
Pall Mall Pl. SW1 5B 12 (1G 101)
(off Pall Mall)
Palmadium Cl. N13 3F 33
Palmar Cres. DA7: Bex 3G 127
Palmar Rd. DA7: Bex 2G 127
Palm Av. DA14: Sidc 6D 144
Palm Cl. E10 3D 68
Palm Ct. SE15 7F 103
(off Garnies Cl.)
Palmeira Rd. DA7: Bex 3D 126
Palmer Av. SM3: Cheam 4E 164
Palmer Cl. BR4: W W'ck 3F 171
Palmer Cl. TW5: Hest 1E 112
Palmer Cl. UB5: N'olt 6C 58
Palmer Cres. KT1: King T 3E 150
Palmer Dr. BR1: Broml 4F 161
Palmer Gdns. EN5: Barn 5A 20
Palmer Ho. SE14 7K 103
(off Lubbock St.)
Palmer Pl. N7 5A 66
Palmer Rd. E13 4K 87
Palmer Rd. RM8: Dag 1D 72
Palmer Rd. SW11 7F 101
Palmer's Ct. N11 5B 32
(off Palmer's Rd.)
PALMERS GREEN 3F 33
Palmers Gro. KT8: W Mole 4E 148
Palmers La. EN1: Enf 1C 24
Palmers La. EN3: Enf H 1D 24
Palmers Pas. SW14 3J 115
(off Little St Leonard's)
Palmer's Rd. E2 2K 85
Palmer's Rd. N11 5B 32
Palmers Rd. SW14 3J 115
Palmers Rd. SW16 2K 155
Palmerston Cen. HA3: W'stone 3K 41
Palmerston Ct. E3 2K 85
(off Old Ford Rd.)
Palmerston Ct. IG9: Buck H 1F 37
Palmerston Ct. KT6: Surb 7D 150
Palmerston Cres. N13 5E 32
Palmerston Cres. SE18 6G 107
Palmerston Gro. SW19 7J 135
Palmerston Ho. SE1 7J 13 (2A 102)
(off Westminster Bri. Rd.)
Palmerston Ho. W8 1J 99
(off Kensington Pl.)
Palmerston Mans. W14 6G 99
(off Queen's Club Gdns.)
Palmerston Rd. BR6: Farnb 4G 173
Palmerston Rd. CR0: C'don 5D 156
Palmerston Rd. E17 3B 50
Palmerston Rd. E7 6K 69
Palmerston Rd. HA3: W'stone 3J 41
Palmerston Rd. IG9: Buck H 2E 36
Palmerston Rd. N22 7E 32
Palmerston Rd. NW6 7H 63
(not continuous)
Palmerston Rd. SM1: Sutt 5A 166
Palmerston Rd. SM5: Cars 4D 166
Palmerston Rd. SW14 4J 115
Palmerston Rd. SW19 7J 135
Palmerston Rd. TW2: Twick 6J 113
Palmerston Rd. TW3: Houn 1G 113
Palmerston Rd. W3 3J 97
Palmerston Way SW8 7F 101
Palmer St. SW1 1C 18 (3H 101)
(not continuous)
Palmers Wharf KT1: King T 2D 150
(off Emms Pas.)
Palm Gro. W5 3E 96
Palm Rd. RM7: Rom 5J 55
Palomino Cl. UB4: Hayes 2F 75
Palyn Ho. EC1 2D 8 (3C 84)
(off Radnor St.)
Pamela Ct. N12 6E 30
Pamela Gdns. HA5: Eastc 5K 39
Pamela St. E8 1F 85
Pams Way KT19: Ewe 5K 163
Panama Ho. E1 5K 85
(off Beaumont Sq.)
Panavia Ct. NW9 2B 44
Pancras La. EC4 1D 14 (6C 84)
Pancras Rd. N1 2J 83
Pancras Rd. NW1 2H 83
Pancras Sq. N1 2J 83
Pancras Square Leisure Cen. 2J 83
Pancras Way E3 2C 86
Pandangle Ho. E8 1F 85
(off Kingsland Rd.)
Pandian Way NW1 6H 65
Pandora Ct. E16 5J 87
(off Robertson Rd.)
Pandora Rd. NW6 6J 63
Panfield M. IG2: Ilf 6E 52
Panfield Rd. SE2 3A 108
Pangbourne NW1 2A 6 (3G 83)
(off Stanhope St.)
Pangbourne Av. W10 5E 80
Pangbourne Dr. HA7: Stan 5J 27
Panhard Pl. UB1: S'hall 7F 77
Pank Av. EN5: New Bar 5F 21
Pankhurst Av. E16 1K 105
Pankhurst Av. E3 5D 86
Pankhurst Cl. SE14 7K 103
Pankhurst Cl. TW7: Isle 3K 113
Pankhurst Green 6E 36
(off Snakes Lane West)
Pankhurst Ho. W12 6D 80
Pankhurst Rd. KT12: Walt T 7A 148
Panmuir Rd. SW20 1D 152
Panmure Cl. N5 4B 66
Panmure Ct. SE26 3H 139
Panmure Ct. UB1: S'hall 6G 77
(off Osborne Rd.)
Panmure Rd. SE26 3H 139
Pannells Ct. TW5: Hest 6E 94
Panorama Ct. N6 6G 47
Panoramic Twr. E14 6D 86
(off Burcham St.)
Pan Peninsula Sq. E14 2D 104
Pansy Gdns. W12 7C 80
Panther Dr. NW10 5K 61
Pantiles, The BR1: Broml 3C 160
Pantiles, The DA7: Bex 7F 109
Pantiles, The NW11 4H 45
Pantiles, The WD23: B Hea 1C 26
Pantiles Cl. N13 5G 33
Panton Cl. CR0: C'don 1B 168
Panton St. SW1 3C 12 (7H 83)
Panyer All. EC1 7C 8 (6C 84)
(off Newgate St.)
Panyers Gdns. RM10: Dag 3H 73
Papavero M. IG2: Ilf 5K 53
Paper Bldgs. EC4 2K 13 (7A 84)
(off King's Bench Wlk.)
Papermill Cl. SM5: Cars 4E 166
Papermill Pl. E17 2A 50
Paper Mill Wharf E14 7A 86
Papillons Wlk. SE3 2J 123
Papworth Gdns. N7 5K 65
Papworth Way SW2 7A 120

A–Z London 267

Parnell Rd. – Pembroke M.

Parnell Rd. E3 .... 1B 86
Parnell Way HA3: Stan 1B 42
Parnham Cl. BR1: Broml 3F 161
Parnham St. E14 .... 6A 86
(not continuous)
Parolles Rd. N19 .... 1G 65
Paroma Rd. DA17: Belv 4G 109
Parr Cl. N18 .... 4C 34
Parr Cl. N9 .... 4C 34
Parr Ct. N1 .... 2D 84
(off New North Rd.)
Parr Ct. TW13: Hanw 4A 130
Parr Ho. E16 .... 1K 105
(off Beaulieu Av.)
Parrington Ho. SW4 .... 6H 119
Parr Rd. E6 .... 1B 88
Parr Rd. HA7: Stan 1D 42
Parrs Cl. CR2: Sande 7D 168
Parrs Pl. TW12: Hamp 7E 130
Parr St. N1 .... 2D 84
Parrs Way W6 .... 6E 98
Parry Av. E6 .... 6D 88
Parry Cl. KT17: Ewe 7D 164
Parry Ho. E1 .... 1H 103
(off Green Bank)
Parry Pl. SE18 .... 4F 107
Parry Rd. SE25 .... 3E 156
Parry Rd. W10 .... 3G 81
Parry St. SW8 .... 7F 19 (6J 101)
Parsifal Rd. NW6 .... 5J 63
Parsley Gdns. CR0: C'don 1K 169
Parsloes Av. RM9: Dag 4D 72
Parsonage Cl. UB3: Hayes 6H 75
Parsonage Gdns. EN2: Enf 2H 23
Parsonage La. DA14: Sidc 4F 145
Parsonage La. EN1: Enf 2J 23
Parsonage La. EN2: Enf 2H 23
Parsonage Manorway DA17: Belv 6G 109
Parsonage St. E14 .... 4E 104
Parsons Cl. SM1: Sutt 3K 165
Parson's Cres. HA8: Edg 3B 28
Parsons Ga. M. SW6 .... 2J 117
Parson's Grn. SW6 .... 1J 117
PARSONS GREEN 2H 117
Parson's Grn. La. SW6 .... 1J 117
Parson's Gro. HA8: Edg 3B 28
Parsons Hill SE18 .... 3E 106
(off Powis St.)
Parsons Ho. W2 .... 4A 4 (4B 82)
(off Hall Pl.)
Parsons Lodge NW6 .... 7K 63
(off Priory Rd.)
Parson's Mead CR0: C'don 1B 168
Parsons Mead KT8: E Mos 3G 149
Parsons M. SW18 .... 5A 118
Parson's Rd. E13 .... 2A 88
Parson St. NW4 .... 4E 44
Parthenia Dr. TW7: Isle 3A 114
Parthenia Rd. SW6 .... 1J 117
Partingdale La. NW7 .... 5A 30
Partington Cl. N19 .... 1H 65
Partridge Cl. E16 .... 5B 88
Partridge Cl. HA7: Stan 4K 27
Partridge Cl. UB10: Uxb 1B 74
Partridge Cl. WD23: Bush 1B 26
Partridge Ct. EC1 .... 3A 8 (4B 84)
(off Cyrus St.)
Partridge Dr. BR6: Farnb 3G 173
Partridge Grn. SE9 .... 3E 142
Partridge Ho. E3 .... 2B 86
(off Stafford Rd.)
Partridge Rd. DA14: Sidc 3J 143
Partridge Rd. TW12: Hamp 6D 130
Partridge Sq. E6 .... 5C 88
Partridge Way N22 .... 1J 47
Pasadena Cl. UB3: Hayes 2J 93
Pasadena Cl. Trad. Est. UB3: Hayes 2K 93
Pascal Dr. RM10: Dag 7J 73
Pascall Ho. SE17 .... 6C 102
(off Draco St.)
Pascal M. SE19 .... 7G 139
Pascal Rd. UB1: S'hall 6F 77
Pascal St. SW8 .... 7H 101
Pascoe Rd. SE13 .... 5F 123
Pasley Cl. SE17 .... 5B 102
Pasquier Rd. E17 .... 3A 50
Passage, The TW9: Rich 5E 114
Passey Pl. SE9 .... 6D 124
Passfield Dr. E14 .... 5D 86
Passfield Hall WC1 .... 3D 6 (4H 83)
(off Endsleigh Pl.)
Passfield Path SE28 .... 7B 90
Passfields SE6 .... 3D 140
Passfields W14 .... 5H 99
(off Star Rd.)
Passing All. EC1 .... 5B 8 (5B 84)
(off St John St.)
Passingham Ho. TW5: Hest 6E 94
Passmore Ct. E14 .... 6C 86
(off New Festival Av.)
Passmore Edwards Ho. N11 .... 6C 32
Passmore Gdns. N11 .... 6C 32
Passmore Ho. E2 .... 1F 85
(off Kingsland Rd.)
Passmore St. SW1 .... 5G 17 (5E 100)
Pastel Ct. E1 .... 5K 85
(off Shandy St.)
Pasteur Cl. NW9 .... 2A 44
Pasteur Ct. HA1: Harr 1B 60
Pasteur Gdns. N18 .... 5G 33
Paston Cl. E5 .... 3K 67
Paston Cl. SM6: W'gton 3G 167
Paston Cres. SE12 .... 7K 123
Pastor Ct. N6 .... 6G 47
Pastor St. SE11 .... 4B 102
Pasture Cl. HA0: Wemb 3B 60
Pasture Rd. HA0: Wemb 2B 60
Pasture Rd. RM9: Dag 5F 73
Pasture Rd. SE6 .... 1H 141
Pastures, The N20 .... 1C 30
Pastures Mead UB10: Hil 6C 56
Pastures Path E11 .... 1H 69
Patcham Ter. SW8 .... 1F 119
Patch Cl. UB10: Uxb 1B 74
Patching Way UB4: Yead 5C 76
Patent Ho. E14 .... 5D 86
(off Morris Rd.)
Paternoster La. EC4 .... 1B 14 (6B 84)
Paternoster Row EC4 .... 1C 14 (6C 84)
Paternoster Sq. EC4 .... 1B 14 (6B 84)
Paterson Ct. EC1 .... 2E 8 (3D 84)
(off St Luke's Est.)
Pater St. W8 .... 3J 99
Pates Mnr. Dr. TW14: Bedf 7F 111
Path, The SW19 .... 1K 153
Pathfield Rd. SW16 .... 6H 137
Patience Rd. SW11 .... 2C 118
Patina Mans. E20 .... 5E 68
(off Mirabelle Gdns.)
Patio Cl. SW4 .... 6H 119
Patmore Est. SW8 .... 1G 119
Patmore Ho. N16 .... 5E 66
Patmore St. SW8 .... 1G 119
Patmos Lodge SW9 .... 1B 120
(off Elliott Rd.)
Patmos Rd. SW9 .... 7B 102
Paton Cl. E3 .... 3C 86
Paton Ho. SW9 .... 2K 119
(off Stockwell Rd.)
Paton St. EC1 .... 2C 8 (3C 84)
Patricia Ct. BR7: Chst 1H 161
Patricia Ct. DA16: Well 7B 108
Patrick Coman Ho. EC1 .... 2A 8 (3B 84)
(off St John St.)
Patrick Connolly Gdns. E3 .... 3D 86
Patrick Ct. SE1 .... 7B 14 (2B 102)
(off Webber St.)
Patrick Cres. RM8: Dag 1E 72
Patrick Pas. SW11 .... 2C 118
Patrick Rd. E13 .... 3A 88
Patriot Sq. E2 .... 2H 85
Patrol Pl. SE6 .... 6D 122
Patroni Ct. E15 .... 3G 87
(off Durban Rd.)
Pat Shaw Ho. E1 .... 4K 85
(off Globe Rd.)
Patshull Pl. NW5 .... 6G 65
Patshull Rd. NW5 .... 6G 65
Patten All. TW10: Rich 5D 114
Pattenden Rd. SE6 .... 1B 140
Patten Ho. N4 .... 1C 66
Patten Rd. SW18 .... 7C 118
Patterdale NW1 .... 2K 5 (3F 83)
(off Osnaburgh St.)
Patterdale Cl. BR1: Broml 6H 141
Patterdale Rd. SE15 .... 7J 103
Pattern Ho. EC1 .... 3A 8 (4B 84)
Patterson Ct. SE19 .... 7F 139
Patterson Rd. SE19 .... 6F 139
Pattina Wlk. SE16 .... 1A 104
(off Silver Wlk.)
Pattison Ho. E1 .... 6K 85
(off Wellesley St.)
Pattison Ho. SE1 .... 6D 14 (2C 102)
(off Redcross Way)
Pattison Rd. NW2 .... 3J 63
Pattison Wlk. SE18 .... 5G 107
Paul Byrne Ho. N2 .... 3A 46
Paul Cl. E15 .... 1G 87
Paul Ct. N18 .... 4B 34
(off Fairfield Rd.)
Paul Ct. RM7: Rom 5J 55
Paul Daisley Ct. NW6 .... 7G 63
(off Christchurch Av.)
Paulet Rd. SE5 .... 2B 120
Paulet Way NW10 .... 7A 62
Paul Gdns. CR0: C'don 2F 169
Paulhan Rd. HA3: Kenton 4D 42
Paul Ho. W10 .... 4G 81
(off Ladbroke Gro.)
Paulin Dr. N21 .... 7F 23
Pauline Cres. TW2: Whitt 1G 131
Pauline Ho. E1 .... 5G 85
(off Old Montague St.)
Paul Julius Cl. E14 .... 7F 87
Paul Robeson Cl. E6 .... 3E 88
Paul Robeson Ho. WC1 .... 1H 7 (2K 83)
(off Penton Ri.)
Paul Robeson Theatre, The 3F 113
Paul St. E15 .... 1G 87
Paul St. EC2 .... 4F 9 (4D 84)
Paul's Wlk. EC4 .... 2C 14 (7C 84)
Paultons Ho. SW3 .... 7B 16 (6B 100)
(off Paultons Sq.)
Paultons Sq. SW3 .... 7B 16 (6B 100)
Paultons St. SW3 .... 7B 16 (6B 100)
Pauntley St. N19 .... 1G 65
Pavan Ct. E2 .... 3J 85
(off Sceptre Rd.)
Paved Ct. TW9: Rich 5D 114
Paveley Ct. NW7 .... 7B 30
(off Langstone Way)
Paveley Dr. SW11 .... 7C 100
Paveley Ho. N1 .... 2K 83
(off Priory Grn. Est.)
Paveley St. NW8 .... 2C 4 (3C 82)
Pavement, The E11 .... 1E 68
(off Hainault Rd.)
Pavement, The SW19 .... 6H 135
(off Worple Rd.)
Pavement, The SW4 .... 4G 119
Pavement, The TW11: Tedd 7B 132
Pavement, The TW7: Isle 3A 114
(off South St.)
Pavement, The W5 .... 3E 96
Pavement M. RM6: Chad H 7D 54
Pavement Sq. CR0: C'don 1G 169
Pavers Way E3 .... 2K 85
Pavet Cl. RM10: Dag 6H 73
Pavilion, The SW8 .... 7H 101
Pavilion Apts. NW8 .... 2B 4 (3B 82)
Pavilion Ct. NW6 .... 3J 81
(off Stafford Rd.)
Pavilion La. BR3: Beck 6B 140
Pavilion Leisure Cen. 2J 159
Pavilion Lodge HA2: Harr 1H 59
Pavilion M. N3 .... 3J 45
Pavilion Pde. W12 .... 6E 80
(off Wood La.)
Pavilion Pl. KT8: W Mole 3G 149
Pavilion Rd. IG1: Ilf 7D 52
Pavilion Rd. SW1 .... 1F 17 (3D 100)
Pavilion Rd. SW3 .... 3F 17 (4D 100)
Pavilion Rd. TW11: Tedd 7K 131
Pavilion Sports & Fitness Club, The 3G 149
Pavilion Sq. SW17 .... 3D 136
Pavilion St. E13 .... 2A 88
Pavilion St. SW1 .... 2F 17 (3D 100)
Pavilion Ter. IG2: Ilf 5J 53
Pavilion Ter. W12 .... 6E 80
(off Wood La.)
Pavilion Wlk. E10 .... 2C 68
Pavilion Way HA4: Ruis 2A 58
Pavilion Way HA8: Edg 7C 28
Pavilion Way SE10 .... 2G 105
Pavillion Ho. SE16 .... 2K 103
(off Water Gdns. Sq.)
Pavillion M. N4 .... 2K 65
(off Tollington Pl.)
Pawleyne Cl. SE20 .... 7J 139
Pawsey Cl. E13 .... 1K 87
Pawsons Rd. CR0: C'don 6C 156
Paxfold HA7: Stan 5J 27
Paxford Rd. HA0: Wemb 2B 60
Paxton Cl. KT12: Walt T 7A 148
Paxton Cl. TW9: Kew 2F 115
Paxton Ct. CR4: Mitc 2D 154
(off Armfield Cres.)
Paxton Ct. N7 .... 6A 66
(off Westbourne Rd.)
Paxton Ct. SE12 .... 3A 142
Paxton Ct. SE26 .... 4A 140
(off Adamsrill Rd.)
Paxton Ho. SE17 .... 5D 102
(off Morecambe St.)
Paxton Ho. SE25 .... 4F 157
Paxton M. SE19 .... 7E 138
(off Westow St.)
Paxton Pl. SE27 .... 4E 138
Paxton Point SE10 .... 7D 104
Paxton Rd. BR1: Broml 7J 141
Paxton Rd. SE23 .... 3A 140
Paxton Rd. W4 .... 6A 98
Paxton Ter. SW1 .... 7K 17 (6F 101)
Paymal Ho. E1 .... 5J 85
(off Stepney Way)
Payne Cl. IG11: Bark 7J 71
Payne Ho. N1 .... 1K 83
(off Barnsbury Est.)
Paynell Ct. SE3 .... 3G 123
Payne Rd. E3 .... 2D 86
Paynesfield Av. SW14 .... 3K 115
Paynesfield Rd. WD23: B Hea 1E 26
Payne St. SE8 .... 7B 104
Paynes Wlk. W6 .... 6G 99
Payzes Gdns. IG8: Wfd G 6C 36
Peaberry Ct. NW4 .... 3C 44
Peabody Av. SW1 .... 5J 17 (5F 101)
Peabody Bldgs. E1 .... 2K 15 (7G 85)
(off John Fisher St.)
Peabody Bldgs. EC1 .... 4D 8 (4C 84)
(off Banner St.)
Peabody Bldgs. SW3 .... 7C 16 (6C 100)
(off Cheyne Row)
Peabody Cl. CR0: C'don 1J 169
Peabody Cl. SE10 .... 1D 122
Peabody Cl. SW1 .... 6J 17 (5F 101)
Peabody Cotts. N17 .... 1E 48
Peabody Ct. EC1 .... 4D 8 (4C 84)
(off Roscoe St.)
Peabody Ct. SE5 .... 1D 120
(off Kimpton Rd.)
Peabody Est. SE1 Duchy St. 5K 13 (1A 102)
Peabody Est. EC1 Dufferin St. 4D 8 (4C 84)
(off Dufferin St.)
Peabody Est. EC1 Farringdon La. 4K 7 (4A 84)
(off Farringdon La.)
Peabody Est. SE1 Marshalsea Rd. 6D 14 (2C 102)
(off Marshalsea Rd.)
Peabody Est. SE1 Southwark St. 4C 14 (1C 102)
Peabody Est. E1 .... 7K 85
(off Brodlove La.)
Peabody Est. E2 .... 2H 85
(off Minerva St.)
Peabody Est. N1 .... 1C 84
Peabody Est. SE24 .... 7B 120
Peabody Est. SE5 .... 1D 120
(off Camberwell Grn.)
Peabody Est. SW1 .... 3B 18 (4G 101)
(off Vauxhall Bri. Rd.)
Peabody Est. SW11 .... 4C 118
Peabody Est. SW3 .... 7D 16 (6C 100)
Peabody Est. SW6 .... 6J 99
(off Lillie Rd.)
Peabody Est. W10 .... 5E 80
Peabody Est. W6 .... 5E 98
Peabody Hill SE21 .... 1B 138
Peabody Ho. N1 .... 1C 84
(off Greenman St.)
Peabody Sq. N1 .... 1C 84
(off Peabody Est.)
Peabody Sq. SE1 .... 7A 14 (2B 102)
(not continuous)
Peabody Ter. EC1 .... 4K 7 (4A 84)
(off Farringdon La.)
Peabody Twr. EC1 .... 4D 8 (4C 84)
(off Golden La.)
Peabody Trust SE17 .... 4D 102
Peabody Yd. N1 .... 1C 84
Peace Cl. N14 .... 5A 22
Peace Cl. SE25 .... 4E 156
Peace Cl. UB6: G'frd 1H 77
Peace Ct. SE1 .... 5G 103
(off Harmony Pl.)
Peace Gro. HA9: Wemb 3H 61
Peace St. SE18 .... 6E 106
Peaches Cl. SM2: Cheam 7G 165
Peachey Ho. SW18 .... 4A 118
(off Eltringham St.)
Peach Gro. E11 .... 3F 69
Peach Rd. TW13: Felt 1J 129
Peach Rd. W10 .... 3F 81
Peach Tree Av. UB7: Yiew 6B 74
Peachtree Cl. EN1: Enf 2B 24
Peachtree Cl. IG6: Ilf 1F 53
Peachum Rd. SE3 .... 6H 105
Peachwalk M. E3 .... 2K 85
Peachy Cl. HA8: Edg 6B 28
Peacock Av. TW14: Bedf 1F 129
Peacock Cl. E4 .... 7G 35
Peacock Cl. NW7 .... 5B 30
Peacock Cl. RM8: Dag 1C 72
Peacock Ho. SE5 .... 1E 120
(off St Giles Rd.)
Peacock Ind. Est. N17 .... 7A 34
Peacock Pl. N1 .... 6A 66
Peacock St. SE17 .... 4B 102
Peacock Theatre 1G 13 (6K 83)
(off Portugal St.)
Peacock Wlk. N6 Highgate 7F 47
Peacock Yd. SE17 .... 5B 102
(off Iliffe St.)
Peak, The SE26 .... 3J 139
Peaketon Av. IG4: Ilf 4B 52
Peak Hill SE26 .... 4J 139
Peak Hill Av. SE26 .... 4J 139
Peak Hill Gdns. SE26 .... 4J 139
Peal Gdns. W13 .... 4A 78
Peall Rd. CR0: C'don 6K 155
Peall Rd. Ind. Est. CR0: C'don 6K 155
Pearce Cl. CR4: Mitc 2E 154
Pearcefield Av. SE23 .... 1J 139
Pearce Ho. SW1 .... 4D 18 (4H 101)
(off Causton St.)
Pear Cl. NW9 .... 4K 43
Pear Cl. SE14 .... 7A 104
Pear Ct. SE15 .... 7F 103
(off Thruxton Way)
Pearcroft Rd. E11 .... 2F 69
Peardon St. SW8 .... 2F 119
Peareswood Gdns. HA7: Stan 1D 42
Pearfield Rd. SE23 .... 3A 140
Pearing Cl. KT4: Wor Pk 2F 165
Pearl Cl. CR7: Thor H 2D 156
Pearl Cl. E6 .... 6E 88
Pearl Cl. NW2 .... 7F 45
Pearl Rd. E17 .... 3C 50
Pearl St. E1 .... 1H 103
Pearmain Cl. TW17: Shep 5D 146
Pearmain Ct. W6 .... 3D 98
(off Vinery Way)
Pearman St. SE1 .... 1K 19 (3A 102)
Pear M. SW17 .... 2C 136
Pear Pl. SE1 .... 6J 13 (2A 102)
Pear Rd. E11 .... 3F 69
Pears Av. TW17: Shep 3G 147
Pearscroft Ct. SW6 .... 1K 117
Pearscroft Rd. SW6 .... 1K 117
Pearse St. SE15 .... 6E 102
Pearson Cl. EN5: New Bar 3E 20
Pearson Cl. SE5 .... 1C 120
(off Camberwell New Rd.)
Pearson M. SW4 .... 3H 119
(off Edgeley Rd.)
Pearson's Av. SE14 .... 1C 122
Pearson Sq. W1 .... 6A 6 (5G 83)
Pearson St. E2 .... 2F 85
Pearson Way CR4: Mitc 1E 154
Pears Rd. TW3: Houn 3G 113
Peartree SE26 .... 5A 140
Pear Tree Av. UB7: Yiew 6B 74
Peartree Av. SW17 .... 3A 136
Pear Tree Cl. BR2: Broml 5B 160
Pear Tree Cl. CR4: Mitc 2C 154
Pear Tree Cl. E2 .... 1F 85
Pear Tree Cl. KT19: Eps 7K 163
Pear Tree Cl. KT9: Chess 5G 163
Peartree Cl. DA8: Erith 1K 127
Pear Tree Ct. E18 .... 1K 51
Pear Tree Ct. EC1 .... 4K 7 (4A 84)
Pear Tree Ct. SE26 .... 3B 140
Peartree Gdns. RM7: Mawney 2H 55
Peartree Gdns. RM8: Dag 4B 72
Pear Tree Ho. SE4 .... 3B 122
Pear Tree La. RM13: Rain 2K 91
Peartree La. E1 .... 7J 85
Pear Tree Rd. TW15: Ashf 5E 128
Peartree Rd. EN1: Enf 3K 23
Peartrees UB7: Yiew 7A 74
Pear Tree St. EC1 .... 3C 8 (4C 84)
Peartree Way SE10 .... 4J 105
Peary Ho. NW10 .... 7K 61
Peary Pl. E2 .... 3J 85
Peasmead Ter. E4 .... 4K 35
Peatfield Cl. DA15: Sidc 3J 143
Pebble Way W3 .... 1H 97
(off Steyne Rd.)
Pebworth Rd. HA1: Harr 2A 60
Pechora Way E14 .... 5A 86
Peckarmans Wood SE26 .... 3G 139
Peckett Sq. N5 .... 4C 66
Peckford Pl. SW9 .... 2A 120
PECKHAM 1G 121
Peckham Gro. SE15 .... 7E 102
Peckham High St. SE15 .... 1G 121
Peckham Hill St. SE15 .... 7G 103
Peckham Pk. Rd. SE15 .... 7G 103
Peckhamplex 2G 121
Peckham Pulse Leisure Cen. 1G 121
Peckham Rd. SE15 .... 1F 121
Peckham Rd. SE5 .... 1E 120
Peckham Rye SE15 .... 3G 121
Peckham Rye SE22 .... 4G 121
Peckham Sq. SE15 .... 1G 121
Pecks Yd. E1 .... 5J 9 (5F 85)
(off Hanbury St.)
Peckwater St. NW5 .... 5G 65
Pedlar's Wlk. N7 .... 5K 65
Pedley Rd. RM8: Dag 1C 72
Pedley St. E1 .... 4G 85
Pedro St. E5 .... 3K 67
Pedworth Gdns. SE16 .... 4J 103
Peebles Ct. UB1: S'hall 6G 77
(off Haldane Rd.)
Peebles Ho. NW6 .... 2K 81
(off Carlton Vale)
Peek Cres. SW19 .... 5F 135
Peel Cl. E4 .... 2J 35
Peel Cl. N9 .... 3B 34
Peel Dr. IG5: Ilf 3C 52
Peel Dr. NW9 .... 3B 44
Peel Gro. E2 .... 2J 85
Peel Pas. W8 .... 1J 99
Peel Pl. IG5: Ilf 2C 52
Peel Pl. SE18 .... 1D 124
Peel Pl. SW6 .... 6J 99
Peel Pct. NW6 .... 2J 81
Peel Rd. BR6: Farnb 5G 173
Peel Rd. E18 .... 1H 51
Peel Rd. HA3: W'stone 3K 41
Peel Rd. HA9: Wemb 3D 60
Peel Sq. NW9 .... 3C 44
Peel St. W8 .... 1J 99
Peel Way UB8: Hil 5A 74
Peerglow Est. EN3: Pond E 5D 24
Peerless St. EC1 .... 2E 8 (3D 84)
Pegamoid Rd. N18 .... 3D 34
Pegasus Cl. N16 .... 4D 66
Pegasus Ct. KT1: King T 3D 150
Pegasus Ct. N21 .... 7H 23
Pegasus Ct. NW10 .... 3D 80
(off Trenmar Gdns.)
Pegasus Ct. TW8: Bford 5F 97
Pegasus Ct. W3 .... 6J 79
(off Horn La.)
Pegasus Ho. E1 .... 4K 85
(off Beaumont Sq.)
Pegasus Ho. E13 .... 3K 87
Pegasus Pl. SE11 .... 7J 19 (6A 102)
Pegasus Pl. SW6 .... 1J 117
Pegasus Rd. CR0: Wadd 6A 168
Pegasus Way N11 .... 6A 32
Peggotty Way UB8: Hil 6D 74
Pegg Rd. TW5: Hest 7B 94
Pegler Sq. SE3 .... 3K 123
Pegley Gdns. SE12 .... 2J 141
Pegswood Ct. E1 .... 7G 85
(off Cable St.)
Pegwell St. SE18 .... 7J 107
Pekin Cl. E14 .... 6C 86
(off Pekin St.)
Pekin St. E14 .... 6C 86
Pelabon Ho. TW1: Twick 6D 114
(off Clevedon Rd.)
Peldon Cl. IG8: Wfd G 7F 37
Peldon Ct. TW9: Rich 4F 115
Peldon Pas. TW10: Rich 4F 115
Peldon Wlk. N1 .... 1B 84
(off Popham St.)
Pelham Av. IG11: Bark 1K 89
Pelham Cl. SE5 .... 3E 120
Pelham Cotts. DA5: Bexl 1H 145
Pelham Ct. DA14: Sidc 3A 144
Pelham Ct. SW3 .... 4C 16 (4C 100)
(off Fulham Rd.)
Pelham Cres. SW7 .... 4C 16 (4C 100)
Pelham Ho. SW1 .... 2D 18 (3H 101)
(off Gt. Peter St.)
Pelham Ho. W14 .... 4H 99
(off Mornington Av.)
Pelham Pl. SW7 .... 3C 16 (4C 100)
Pelham Pl. W13 .... 4K 77
Pelham Rd. BR3: Beck 2J 157
Pelham Rd. DA7: Bex 3G 127
Pelham Rd. E18 .... 3K 51
Pelham Rd. IG1: Ilf 2H 71
Pelham Rd. N15 .... 4F 49
Pelham Rd. N22 .... 2A 48
Pelham Rd. SW19 .... 7J 135
Pelham St. SW7 .... 3B 16 (4B 100)
Pelican Dr. HA2: Harr 2F 59
Pelican Est. SE15 .... 1F 121
Pelican Ho. SE5 .... 1F 121
Pelican Ho. SE8 .... 4B 104
Pelican Pas. E1 .... 4J 85
Pelican Wlk. SW9 .... 4B 120
Pelican Wharf E1 .... 1J 103
(off Wapping Wall)
Pelier St. SE17 .... 6C 102
Pelinore Rd. SE6 .... 2G 141
Pella Ho. SE11 .... 5H 19 (5K 101)
Pellant Rd. SW6 .... 7G 99
Pellatt Gro. N22 .... 1A 48
Pellatt Rd. HA9: Wemb 2D 60
Pellatt Rd. SE22 .... 5F 121
Pellerin Rd. N16 .... 5E 66
Pellew Ho. E1 .... 4H 85
(off Somerford St.)
Pellings Cl. BR2: Broml 3G 159
Pelling St. E14 .... 6C 86
Pellipar Cl. N13 .... 3F 33
Pellipar Gdns. SE18 .... 5D 106
Pellipar Rd. SE18 .... 5D 106
Pellow Cl. EN5: Barn 6C 20
Pell St. SE8 .... 4A 104
Pelly Rd. E13 .... 1J 87
(not continuous)
Peloton Av. E20 .... 5D 68
Pelter St. E2 .... 1J 9 (3F 85)
Pelton Rd. SE10 .... 5G 105
Pembar Av. E17 .... 3A 50
Pemberley Chase KT19: Ewe 5H 163
Pemberley Cl. KT19: Ewe 5H 163
Pemberley Ho. KT19: Ewe 5H 163
(off Pemberley Chase)
Pember Rd. NW10 .... 3F 81
Pemberton Cl. TW19: Stanw 1A 128
Pemberton Ct. E1 .... 3K 85
(off Portelet Rd.)
Pemberton Ct. EN1: Enf 3K 23
Pemberton Gdns. N19 .... 3G 65
Pemberton Gdns. RM6: Chad H 5E 54
Pemberton Ho. SE26 .... 4G 139
(off High Level Dr.)
Pemberton Pl. E8 .... 7H 67
Pemberton Rd. KT8: E Mos 4G 149
Pemberton Rd. N4 .... 5A 48
Pemberton Row EC4 .... 7K 7 (6A 84)
Pemberton Ter. N19 .... 3G 65
Pembridge Av. TW2: Whitt 1D 130
Pembridge Cres. W11 .... 7J 81
Pembridge Gdns. W2 .... 7J 81
Pembridge M. W11 .... 7J 81
Pembridge Pl. SW15 .... 5J 117
Pembridge Pl. W2 .... 7J 81
Pembridge Rd. W11 .... 7J 81
Pembridge Sq. W2 .... 7J 81
Pembridge Studios W11 .... 7J 81
(off Pembridge Vs.)
Pembridge Vs. W11 .... 7J 81
Pembridge Vs. W2 .... 6J 81
Pembroke W14 .... 4H 99
(off Kensington Village)
Pembroke Av. EN1: Enf 1C 24
Pembroke Av. HA3: Kenton 3A 42
Pembroke Av. HA5: Pinn 1B 58
Pembroke Av. KT5: Surb 5H 151
Pembroke Av. N1 .... 1J 83
Pembroke Bldgs. NW10 .... 3C 80
Pembroke Bus. Cen. BR8: Swan 7K 145
Pembroke Cen., The HA4: Ruis 1H 57
Pembroke Cl. SW1 .... 7H 11 (2E 100)
Pembroke Cotts. W8 .... 3J 99
(off Pembroke Sq.)
Pembroke Ct. W7 .... 6K 77
(off Copley Cl.)
Pembroke Ct. W8 .... 3J 99
(off Sth. Edwardes Sq.)
Pembroke Gdns. HA4: Ruis 1H 57
Pembroke Gdns. RM10: Dag 3H 73
Pembroke Gdns. SW14 .... 4H 115
Pembroke Gdns. W8 .... 4H 99
Pembroke Gdns. Cl. W8 .... 3J 99
Pembroke Hall NW4 .... 3E 44
(off Mulberry Cl.)
Pembroke Ho. RM8: Dag 5A 72
Pembroke Ho. SW1 .... 2G 17 (3E 100)
(off Chesham St.)
Pembroke Ho. W2 .... 6K 81
(off Hallfield Est.)
Pembroke Ho. W3 .... 2J 97
(off Park Rd. E.)
Pembroke Lodge HA7: Stan 6J 27
Pembroke Mans. NW6 .... 6A 64
(off Canfield Gdns.)
Pembroke M. E3 .... 3A 86
Pembroke M. N10 .... 1E 46

Pembroke M. – Phillimore Gdns.

Pembroke M. W8 3J 99
Pembroke Pde. DA8: Erith 5J 109
Pembroke Pl. HA8: Edg 7B 28
Pembroke Pl. TW7: Isle 2J 113
Pembroke Pl. W8 3J 99
Pembroke Rd. BR1: Broml 2A 160
Pembroke Rd. CR4: Mitc 2E 154
Pembroke Rd. DA8: Erith 5J 109
Pembroke Rd. E17 5D 50
Pembroke Rd. E6 5D 88
Pembroke Rd. HA4: Ruis 1G 57
Pembroke Rd. HA9: Wemb 3D 60
Pembroke Rd. IG3: Ilf 1K 71
Pembroke Rd. N10 1E 46
Pembroke Rd. N13 3H 33
Pembroke Rd. N15 5F 49
Pembroke Rd. N8 4J 47
Pembroke Rd. SE25 4E 156
Pembroke Rd. UB6: G'frd 4F 77
Pembroke Rd. W8 4H 99
Pembroke Sq. W8 3J 99
Pembroke St. N1 7J 65
(not continuous)
Pembroke Studios W8 3H 99
Pembroke Ter. NW8 1B 82
(off Queen's Ter.)
Pembroke Vs. TW9: Rich 4D 114
Pembroke Vs. W8 4J 99
Pembroke Wlk. W8 4J 99
Pembroke Way UB3: Harl 3E 92
Pembrook M. SW11 4B 118
Pembry Cl. SW9 1A 120
Pembury Av. KT4: Wor Pk 1C 164
Pembury Cl. BR2: Hayes 7H 159
Pembury Cl. E5 5H 67
Pembury Ct. UB3: Harl 6F 93
Pembury Cres. DA14: Sidc 2E 144
Pembury Pl. E5 5H 67
Pembury Rd. DA7: Bex 7E 108
Pembury Rd. E5 5H 67
Pembury Rd. N17 1F 49
Pembury Rd. SE25 4G 157
Pemdevon Rd. CR0: C'don 7A 156
Pemell Cl. E1 4J 85
Pemell Ho. E1 4J 85
(off Pemell Cl.)
Pemerich Cl. UB3: Harl 5H 93
Pempath Pl. HA9: Wemb 2D 60
Penally Pl. N1 1D 84
Penang Ho. E1 1H 103
(off Prusom St.)
Penang St. E1 1H 103
Penard Rd. UB2: S'hall 3F 95
Penarth Cen. SE15 6J 103
Penarth Ct. SM2: Sutt 7A 166
Penarth St. SE15 6J 103
Penberth Rd. SE6 2E 140
Penbury Rd. UB2: S'hall 4D 94
Pencombe M. W11 7H 81
Pencraig Way SE15 6H 103
Pendall Cl. EN4: E Barn 4H 21
Penda Rd. DA8: Erith 7H 109
Pendarves Rd. SW20 1E 152
Penda's Mead E9 4A 68
Pendell Av. UB3: Harl 7H 93
Pendennis Ho. SE8 4A 104
Pendennis Rd. N17 3D 48
Pendennis Rd. SW16 4J 137
Penderel Rd. TW3: Houn 5E 112
Penderry Ri. SE6 2F 141
Penderyn Way N7 4H 65
Pendlebury Ct. KT5: Surb 4E 150
(off Cranes Pk.)
Pendle Ct. UB10: Hil 1D 74
Pendle Ho. SE26 3G 139
Pendle Rd. SW16 6F 137
Pendlestone Rd. E17 5D 50
Pendlewood Cl. W5 5C 78
Pendley Ho. E2 1G 85
(off Whiston Rd.)
Pendolino Way NW10 7G 61
Pendragon Rd. BR1: Broml 3H 141
Pendragon Wlk. NW9 6A 44
Pendrell Ho. WC2 1D 12 (6H 83)
(off New Compton St.)
Pendrell Rd. SE4 2A 122
Pendrell St. SE18 6H 107
Pendula Dr. UB4: Yead 4B 76
Pendulum M. E8 5F 67
Penerley Rd. SE6 1D 140
Penfield Ct. NW9 3A 44
(off Tanner Cl.)
Penfield Lodge W9 5J 81
(off Admiral Wlk.)
Penfields Ho. N7 6J 65
(off York Way Est.)
Penfold Cl. CR0: Wadd 3A 168
Penfold La. DA5: Bexl 2D 144
(not continuous)
Penfold Pl. NW1 5C 4 (5C 82)
Penfold Rd. N9 1E 34
Penfold St. NW1 5C 4 (5C 82)
Penfold St. NW8 4B 4 (4B 82)
Penford Gdns. SE9 3B 124
Penford St. SE5 2B 120
Pengarth Rd. DA5: Bexl 5D 126
PENGE 7J 139
Penge Ho. SW11 3B 118
Penge La. SE20 7J 139
Pengelly Apts. E14 5D 104
(off Bartlett M.)
Penge Rd. E13 1A 88
Penge Rd. SE20 3G 157
Penge Rd. SE25 3G 157
Penhale Cl. BR6: Chels 4K 173
Penhall Rd. SE7 4B 106
Penhill Rd. DA5: Bexl 6C 126
Penhurst Mans. SW6 1H 117
(off Rostrevor Rd.)
Penhurst Pl. SE1 2H 19 (3K 101)
(off Carlisle La.)
Penhurst Rd. IG6: Ilf 1F 53
Penifather La. UB6: G'frd 3H 77
Peninsula Apts. N1 1C 84
(off Basire St.)
Peninsula Apts. W2 6B 4 (5B 82)
(off Praed St.)
Peninsula Ct. E14 3D 104
(off E. Ferry Rd.)
Peninsula Ct. N1 1C 84
(off Basire St.)
Peninsula Hgts. SE1 5F 19 (5J 101)
Peninsular Cl. NW7 5B 30
Peninsular Cl. TW14: Felt 6F 111
Peninsular Pk. 4J 105
Peninsular Pk. Rd. SE7 4J 105
Peninsula Sq. SE10 2G 105
Penistone Rd. SW16 7J 137
Penketh Dr. HA1: Harr 3H 59
Penley Ct. WC2 2H 13 (7K 83)
Penmayne Ho. SE11 5K 19 (5A 102)
(off Kennings Way)
Penmon Rd. SE2 3A 108
Pennack Rd. SE15 6F 103
Penn Almshouses SE10 1E 122
(off Greenwich Sth. St.)
Pennant M. W8 4K 99
Pennant Ter. E17 2B 50
Pennard Mans. W12 2E 98
(off Goldhawk Rd.)
Pennard Rd. W12 2E 98
Pennards, The TW16: Sun 3A 148
Penn Cl. HA3: Kenton 4C 42
Penn Cl. UB6: G'frd 2F 77
Penn Ct. NW9 3K 43
Penner Cl. SW19 2G 135
Penners Gdns. KT6: Surb 7E 150
Pennethorne Cl. E9 1J 85
Pennethorne Ho. SW11 3B 118
Pennethorne Rd. SE15 7H 103
Penn Gdns. BR7: Chst 2F 161
Penn Gdns. RM5: Col R 1G 55
Penn Ho. NW8 4C 4 (4C 82)
(off Mallory St.)
Pennine Dr. NW2 2F 63
Pennine Ho. N9 3B 34
(off Plevna Rd.)
Pennine La. NW2 2G 63
Pennine Pde. NW2 2G 63
Pennine Way DA7: Bex 1K 127
Pennine Way UB3: Harl 7F 93
Pennington Cl. SE27 4D 138
Pennington Ct. SE16 1A 104
Pennington Dr. N21 5D 22
Pennington Lodge KT5: Surb
5E 150
(off Cranes Dr.)
Pennington St. E1 7H 85
Pennington Way SE12 2K 141
Penniston Cl. N17 2C 48
Penniwell Cl. HA8: Edg 4A 28
Penn La. DA5: Bexl 5D 126
Penn Rd. N7 5J 65
Penn St. N1 1D 84
Penny Brookes St. E20 6E 68
Penny Ct. E4 3B 36
Pennycroft CR0: Sels 7A 170
Penny Farthing M. TW12: Hamp H
6G 131
Pennyfather La. EN2: Enf 3H 23
Pennyfields E14 7C 86
(not continuous)
Penny Flds. Ho. SE8 1B 122
(off Francis Harvey Way)
Pennyford Ct. NW8 3A 4 (4B 82)
(off St John's Wood Rd.)
Penny La. TW17: Shep 7G 147
Penny M. SW12 7F 119
Pennymoor Wlk. W9 4H 81
(off Fernhead Rd.)
Penny Rd. NW10 3H 79
Penny Royal SM6: W'gton 6H 167
Pennyroyal Av. E6 6E 88
Pennyroyal Dr. UB7: W Dray 2B 92
Penpoll Rd. E8 6H 67
Penpool La. DA16: Well 3B 126
Penrhyn Av. E17 1B 50
Penrhyn Cres. E17 1C 50
Penrhyn Cres. SW14 4J 115
Penrhyn Gdns. KT1: King T 4D 150
Penrhyn Gro. E17 1C 50
Penrhyn Rd. KT1: King T 4E 150
Penrith Cl. BR3: Beck 1D 158
Penrith Cl. SW15 5G 117
Penrith Cl. UB8: Uxb 7A 56
Penrith Pl. SE27 2B 138
Penrith Rd. CR7: Thor H 2C 156
Penrith Rd. KT3: N Mald 4K 151
Penrith Rd. N15 5D 48
Penrith St. SW16 6G 137
Penrose Ct. SW12 1E 136
Penrose Gdns. NW3 4J 63
Penrose Gro. SE17 5C 102
Penrose Ho. N21 5E 22
Penrose Ho. SE17 5C 102
Penrose St. SE17 5C 102
Penrose Way SE10 1G 105
Penryn Ho. SE11 5K 19 (5B 102)
(off Seaton Cl.)
Penryn St. NW1 2H 83
Penry St. SE1 4E 102
Pensbury Pl. SW8 2G 119
Pensbury St. SW8 2G 119
Pensford Av. TW9: Kew 2G 115
Penshurst NW5 6E 64
Penshurst Av. DA15: Sidc 6A 126
Penshurst Gdns. HA8: Edg 5C 28
Penshurst Grn. BR2: Broml 5H 159
Penshurst Ho. SE15 6J 103
(off Lovelinch Cl.)
Penshurst Rd. CR7: Thor H 5B 156
Penshurst Rd. DA7: Bex 1F 127
Penshurst Rd. E9 7K 67
Penshurst Rd. N17 7A 34
Penshurst Wlk. BR2: Broml 5H 159
Penshurst Way SM2: Sutt 7J 165
Pensilver Cl. EN4: E Barn 4H 21
Penstemon Cl. N3 6D 30
Penstock Footpath N8 3K 47
Pentagram Yd. W11 6J 81
(off Needham Rd.)
Pentavia Retail Pk. 7G 29
Pentelow Gdns. TW14: Felt 6J 111
Pentire Rd. E17 1F 51
Pentland Av. HA8: Edg 2C 28
Pentland Av. TW17: Shep 5C 146
Pentland Cl. N9 2D 34
Pentland Cl. NW11 2G 63
Pentland Gdns. SW18 6A 118
Pentland Pl. UB5: N'olt 1C 76
Pentland Rd. NW6 3J 81
Pentlands Cl. CR4: Mitc 3F 155
Pentland St. SW18 6A 118
Pentland Way UB10: Ick 3E 56
Pentlow St. SW15 3E 116
Pentlow Way IG9: Buck H 1H 37
Pentney Rd. E4 1A 36
Pentney Rd. SW12 1G 137
Pentney Rd. SW19 1G 153
Penton Gro. N1 2A 84
Penton Ho. N1 1J 7 (2A 84)
(off Pentonville Rd.)
Penton Ho. SE2 1D 108
Penton Pl. SE17 5B 102
Penton Ri. WC1 1H 7 (3K 83)
Penton St. N1 2A 84
PENTONVILLE 2K 83
Pentonville Rd. N1 1F 7 (2J 83)
Pentrich Av. EN1: Enf 1B 24
Pentridge St. SE15 7F 103
Pentyre Av. N18 5J 33
Penwerris Av. TW7: Isle 7G 95
Penwerris Ct. TW5: Hest 7G 95
Penwith Rd. SW18 2J 135
Penwood Ct. HA5: Pinn 4D 40
Penwood Ho. SW15 6B 116
Penwortham Ct. N22 2A 48
(off Mayes Rd.)
Penwortham Rd. SW16 6F 137
Penylan Pl. HA8: Edg 7B 28
Penywern Rd. SW5 5J 99
Penzance Pl. W11 1G 99
Penzance St. W11 1G 99
Peony Ct. IG8: Wfd G 7B 36
Peony Ct. SW10 7A 16 (6A 100)
Peony Dr. CR4: Mitc 7D 154
Peony Gdns. W12 7C 80
Peperfield WC1 2G 7 (3K 83)
(off Cromer St.)
Pepler Ho. W10 4G 81
(off Wornington Rd.)
Pepler M. SE5 5F 103
Peploe Rd. NW6 2F 81
Peplow Cl. UB7: Yiew 1A 92
Pepper Cl. E6 5D 88
Peppercorn Cl. CR7: Thor H 2D 156
Peppermead Sq. SE13 5C 122
Peppermint Cl. CR0: C'don 7J 155
Peppermint Pl. E11 3G 69
Pepper St. E14 3D 104
Pepper St. SE1 6C 14 (2C 102)
Peppie Cl. N16 2E 66
Pepys Cl. UB10: Ick 4D 56
Pepys Cres. E16 1J 105
Pepys Cres. EN5: Barn 5A 20
Pepys Ho. E2 3J 85
(off Kirkwall Pl.)
Pepys Ri. BR6: Orp 1K 173
Pepys Rd. SE14 1K 121
Pepys Rd. SW20 1E 152
Pepys St. EC3 2H 15 (7E 84)
Perceval Av. NW3 5C 64
Perceval Ct. UB5: N'olt 5E 58
Perceval Ho. W5 7C 78
Percheron Cl. TW7: Isle 3K 113
Perch St. E8 4F 67
Percival Av. NW9 2B 44
Percival Ct. N17 7A 34
Percival Gdns. RM6: Chad H 6C 54
Percivall Ho. EC1 6B 8 (5B 84)
(off Bartholomew Cl.)
Percival M. SE11 7G 19 (6K 101)
Percival Rd. BR6: Farnb 2F 173
Percival Rd. EN1: Enf 4A 24
Percival Rd. SW14 4J 115
Percival Rd. TW13: Felt 2H 129
Percival St. EC1 3A 8 (4B 84)
Percival Way KT19: Ewe 4K 163
Percy Av. TW15: Ashf 5C 128
Percy Bilton Ct. TW5: Hest 1F 113
(off Skinners La.)
Percy Bryant Rd. TW16: Sun 7G 129
Percy Bush Rd. UB7: W Dray 3B 92
Percy Cir. WC1 1H 7 (3K 83)
Percy Gdns. EN3: Pond E 5E 24
Percy Gdns. KT4: Wor Pk 1K 163
Percy Gdns. TW7: Isle 3A 114
Percy Gdns. UB4: Hayes 3G 75
Percy Laurie Ho. SW15 4F 117
(off Nursery Cl.)
Percy M. W1 6C 6 (5H 83)
(off Rathbone Pl.)
Percy Rd. CR4: Mitc 7E 154
Percy Rd. DA7: Bex 2E 126
Percy Rd. E11 7G 51
Percy Rd. E16 5G 87
Percy Rd. IG3: Ilf 7A 54
Percy Rd. N12 5F 31
Percy Rd. N21 7H 23
Percy Rd. RM7: Mawney 3H 55
Percy Rd. SE20 1K 157
Percy Rd. SE25 5G 157
Percy Rd. TW12: Hamp 7E 130
Percy Rd. TW2: Whitt 1F 131
Percy Rd. TW7: Isle 4A 114
Percy Rd. W12 2C 98
Percy St. W1 6C 6 (5H 83)
Percy Ter. BR1: Broml 3F 161
Percy Way TW2: Whitt 1G 131
Percy Yd. WC1 1H 7 (3K 83)
Peregrine Cl. NW10 5K 61
Peregrine Ct. DA16: Well 1K 125
Peregrine Ct. SE8 6C 104
(off Edward St.)
Peregrine Ct. SW16 4K 137
Peregrine Gdns. CR0: C'don 2A 170
Peregrine Ho. EC1 1B 8 (3B 84)
(off Hall St.)
Peregrine Rd. N17 7H 33
Peregrine Rd. TW16: Sun 2H 147
Peregrine Way SW19 7E 134
Perendale Dr. TW17: Shep 1E 146
Perham Rd. W14 5G 99
Peridot Ct. E2 2J 9 (3F 85)
(off Virginia Rd.)
Peridot St. E6 5C 88
Perifield SE21 1C 138
Perilla Ho. E1 6G 85
(off Boulevard Walkway)
Perimeade Rd. UB6: G'frd 2C 78
Periton Rd. SE9 4B 124
PERIVALE 1C 78
Perivale Gdns. W13 4B 78
Perivale Grange UB6: G'frd 3A 78
Perivale La. UB6: G'frd 3A 78
Perivale Lodge UB6: G'frd 3A 78
(off Perivale La.)
Perivale New Bus. Cen. UB6: G'frd
2C 78
Perivale Pk. UB6: G'frd 2B 78
Perivale Pk. Athletics Track 3J 77
Perivale Pk. Golf Course 3J 77
Perivale Wood Local Nature
Reserve 1K 77
Periwood Cres. UB6: G'frd 1A 78
Perkin Cl. HA0: Wemb 5B 60
Perkin Cl. TW3: Houn 4E 112
Perkins Ct. TW15: Ashf 5B 128
Perkins Gdns. UB10: Ick 2E 56
Perkins Ho. E14 5B 86
(off Wallwood St.)
Perkin's Rents SW1 2C 18 (3H 101)
Perkins Rd. IG2: Ilf 5H 53
Perkins Sq. SE1 4D 14 (1C 102)
Perks Cl. SE3 3G 123
Perkyn Sq. N17 3H 49
Perley Ho. E3 5B 86
(off Weatherley Cl.)
Perpins Rd. SE9 6J 125
Perran Rd. SW2 1B 138
Perran Wlk. TW8: Bford 5E 96
Perren St. NW5 6F 65
Perrers Rd. W6 4D 98
Perrin Apts. N1 7J 65
(off Caledonian Rd.)
Perrin Cl. TW15: Ashf 5B 128
Perrin Cl. WD23: B Hea 1D 26
Perrin Ct. TW15: Ashf 4C 128
Perring Est. E3 5C 86
(off Gale St.)
Perrin Ho. NW6 3J 81
Perrin Rd. HA0: Wemb 4B 60
Perrin's Ct. NW3 4A 64
Perrin's La. NW3 4A 64
Perrin's Wlk. NW3 4A 64
Perronet Ho. SE1 3B 102
(off Princess St.)
Perrott St. SE18 4G 107
Perry Av. W3 6K 79
Perry Cl. IG2: Ilf 6H 53
Perry Cl. RM13: Rain 2K 91
Perry Cl. UB8: Hil 6D 74
Perry Ct. E14 5C 104
(off Maritime Quay)
Perry Ct. KT2: King T 2E 150
(off Old London Rd.)
Perry Ct. N15 6E 48
Perryfield Way NW9 6B 44
Perryfield Way TW10: Ham 3B 132
Perry Gdns. N9 3J 33
Perry Gth. UB5: N'olt 1A 76
Perry Hall Rd. BR6: St M Cry 6K 161
Perry Hill SE6 3B 140
Perry How KT4: Wor Pk 1B 164
Perry Lodge E12 1B 70
Perryman Ho. IG11: Bark 1G 89
(off The Shaftesburys)
Perrymans Farm Rd. IG2: Ilf 6H 53
Perry Mead EN2: Enf 2G 23
Perrymead St. SW6 1J 117
Perryn Ct. TW1: Twick 6A 114
Perryn Ho. W3 7A 80
Perryn Rd. SE16 3H 103
Perryn Rd. W3 1K 97
Perry Ri. SE23 3A 140
Perry Rd. RM9: Dag 5F 91
Perry's Pl. W1 7C 6 (6H 83)
Perry St. BR7: Chst 6H 143
Perry St. Gdns. BR7: Chst 6J 143
Perry St. Shaw BR7: Chst 7J 143
Perry Va. SE23 2J 139
Persant Rd. SE6 2G 141
Perseverance Pl. SW9 7A 102
Perseverance Pl. TW9: Rich 4E 114
Perseverance Works E2 1H 9 (3E 84)
(off Kingsland Rd.)
Pershore Cl. IG2: Ilf 5F 53
Pershore Gro. SM5: Cars 6B 154
Pershore Ho. W13 1A 96
(off Singapore Rd.)
Pert Cl. N10 7A 32
Perth Av. NW9 7K 43
Perth Av. UB4: Yead 4A 76
Perth Cl. SE5 4D 120
Perth Cl. SW20 2B 152
Perth Cl. UB5: N'olt 5E 58
Perth Ho. N1 7K 65
(off Bemerton Est.)
Perth Rd. BR3: Beck 2E 158
Perth Rd. E10 1A 68
Perth Rd. E13 2K 87
Perth Rd. IG11: Bark 2H 89
Perth Rd. IG2: Ilf 6E 52
Perth Rd. N22 1B 48
Perth Rd. N4 1A 66
Perth Ter. IG2: Ilf 7G 53
Peruvian Wharf E16 1J 105
Perwell Av. HA2: Harr 1D 58
Perystreete SE23 2J 139
Petavel Rd. TW11: Tedd 6J 131
Peter Av. NW10 7D 62
Peter Best Ho. E1 6H 85
(off Nelson St.)
Peterboat Cl. SE10 4G 105
Peterborough Ct. EC4 7K 7 (6A 84)
Peterborough Gdns. IG1: Ilf 7C 52
Peterborough M. SW6 2J 117
Peterborough Rd. E10 5E 50
Peterborough Rd. HA1: Harr 1J 59
Peterborough Rd. SM5: Cars 6C 154
Peterborough Rd. SW6 2J 117
Peterborough Vs. SW6 1K 117
Peter Butler Ho. SE1 7K 15 (2G 103)
(off Wolseley St.)
Peterchurch Ho. SE15 6H 103
(off Commercial Way)
Peter Collinson Va. NW7 5B 30
Petergate SW11 4A 118
Peter Harrison Planetarium 7F 105
Peterhead Ct. UB1: S'hall 6G 77
(off Osborne Rd.)
Peter Heathfield Ho. E15 1F 87
(off Wise Rd.)
Peter Hills Ho. SE16 4G 103
(off Alexis St.)
Peter Ho. SW8 7J 101
(off Luscombe Way)
Peter James Bus. Cen. UB3: Hayes
2J 93
Peter James Ent. Cen. NW10 3J 79
Peter Kennedy Ct. CR0: C'don 6B 158
Peterley Bus. Cen. E2 2H 85
Peter Lyell Ct. HA4: Ruis 2K 57
Peter May Sports Cen. 7K 35
Peter Pan Statue 4A 10 (1B 100)
Peters Cl. DA16: Well 2J 125
Peters Cl. HA7: Stan 6J 27
Peters Cl. RM8: Dag 1D 72
Peters Ct. W2 6K 81
(off Porchester Rd.)
Petersfield Cl. N18 5H 33
Petersfield Ri. SW15 1D 134
Petersfield Rd. W3 2J 97
Petersgate KT2: King T 6J 133
(off Warren Rd.)
PETERSHAM 1E 132
Petersham Cl. SM1: Sutt 5J 165
Petersham Cl. TW10: Ham 2D 132
Petersham Dr. BR5: St P 2K 161
Petersham Gdns. BR5: St P 2K 161
Petersham Ho. SW7 3A 16 (4B 100)
(off Kendrick M.)
Petersham La. SW7 3A 100
Petersham M. SW7 3A 100
Petersham Pl. SW7 3A 100
Petersham Rd. TW10: Ham 6D 114
Petersham Rd. TW10: Rich 6D 114
Petersham Ter. CR0: Bedd 3J 167
(off Richmond Grn.)
Peter's Hill EC4 2C 14 (7C 84)
Peter Shore Ct. E1 5K 85
(off Beaumont Sq.)
Peter's La. EC1 5A 8 (5B 84)
(not continuous)
Peter's Path SE26 4H 139
Peterstone Rd. SE2 2B 108
Peterstow Cl. SW19 2G 135
Peter St. W1 2C 12 (7H 83)
Peterwood Pk. CR0: Wadd 2K 167
Peterwood Way CR0: Wadd 2K 167
Petherton Ct. HA1: Harr 6K 41
(off Gayton Rd.)
Petherton Ct. NW10 1F 81
(off Tiverton Rd.)
Petherton Rd. N5 5C 66
Petiver Cl. E9 7J 67
Petley Rd. W6 6F 99
Peto Pl. NW1 3K 5 (4F 83)
Peto St. Nth. E16 6H 87
Petra Way E16 5H 87
Petrie Cl. NW2 6G 63
Petrie Ho. SE18 6E 106
(off Woolwich Comn.)
Petrie Mus. of Egyptian Archaeology
4C 6 (4H 83)
Petros Gdns. NW3 6K 63
Pettacre Cl. SE28 3G 107
Petticoat Lane Market 6H 9 (5E 84)
Petticoat Sq. E1 7J 9 (6F 85)
Petticoat Twr. E1 7J 9 (6F 85)
(off Petticoat Sq.)
Pettits Cl. RM1: Rom 2K 55
Pettits La. Nth. RM1: Rom 1K 55
Pettits Pl. RM10: Dag 5G 73
Pettits Rd. RM10: Dag 5G 73
Pettiward Cl. SW15 4E 116
Pettley Gdns. RM7: Rom 5K 55
Pettman Cres. SE28 3H 107
Pettsgrove Av. HA0: Wemb 5C 60
Pett's Hill UB5: N'olt 5F 59
Petts La. TW17: Shep 4C 146
PETTS WOOD 5H 161
Petts Wood Rd. BR5: Pet W 5G 161
Petty France SW1 1B 18 (3G 101)
Petty Wales EC3 3H 15 (7E 84)
Petworth Cl. UB5: N'olt 7D 58
Petworth Gdns. SW20 3D 152
Petworth Gdns. UB10: Hil 1E 74
Petworth Rd. DA6: Bex 5G 127
Petworth Rd. N12 5H 31
Petworth St. SW11 1C 118
Petyt Pl. SW3 7C 16 (6C 100)
Petyward SW3 4D 16 (4C 100)
Pevensey Av. EN1: Enf 2K 23
Pevensey Av. N11 5C 32
Pevensey Cl. TW7: Isle 7G 95
Pevensey Ct. SW16 3A 138
Pevensey Ct. W3 2H 97
Pevensey Ho. E1 5K 85
(off Ben Jonson Rd.)
Pevensey Rd. E7 4H 69
Pevensey Rd. SW17 4B 136
Pevensey Rd. TW13: Felt 1C 130
Peverel E6 6E 88
Peverel Ho. RM10: Dag 2G 73
Peverett Cl. N11 5A 32
Peveril Dr. TW11: Tedd 5H 131
Peveril Ho. SE1 3D 102
(off Rephidim St.)
Pewsey Cl. E4 5H 35
Peyton Pl. SE10 7E 104
Pharamond NW2 6F 63
Pharaoh Cl. CR4: Mitc 7D 154
Pheasant Cl. E16 6K 87
Pheasantry Ho. SW3 5D 16 (5C 100)
(off Jubilee Pl.)
Pheasantry Welcome Cen., The 1K 149
Pheasant Sq. NW9 6B 44
Phelps La. NW7 5B 30
Phelps Lodge N1 1K 83
Phelp St. SE17 6D 102
Phelps Way UB3: Harl 4H 93
Phene St. SW3 7D 16 (6C 100)
Philadelphia Ct. SW10 7A 100
(off Uverdale Rd.)
Philbeach Gdns. SW5 5J 99
Phil Brown Pl. SW8 3F 119
(off Daley Thompson Way)
Philchurch Pl. E1 6G 85
Philia Ho. NW1 7G 65
(off Farrier St.)
Philimore Cl. SE18 5J 107
Philip Av. RM7: Rush G 1K 73
Philip Cl. RM7: Rush G 1K 73
Philip Ct. W2 5A 4 (5B 82)
(off Hall Pl.)
Philip Gdns. CR0: C'don 2B 170
Philip Ho. NW6 1K 81
(off Mortimer Pl.)
Philip Jones Ct. N4 1K 65
Philip La. N15 4D 48
Philip Mole Ho. W9 4J 81
(off Chippenham Rd.)
Philipot Path SE9 6D 124
Philippa Gdns. SE9 5B 124
Philip Rd. N15 4D 48
Philips Cl. SM5: Cars 1E 166
Philip Sq. SW8 2F 119
Philip St. E13 4J 87
Philip Wlk. SE15 3G 121
(not continuous)
Phillimore Ct. W8 2J 99
(off Kensington High St.)
Phillimore Gdns. NW10 1E 80
Phillimore Gdns. W3 1G 97

270 A-Z London

Phillimore Gdns. – Plover Way

Phillimore Gdns. W8 ... 2J 99
Phillimore Gdns. Cl. W8 ... 3J 99
Phillimore Pl. W8 ... 2J 99
Phillimore Ter. W8 ... 3J 99
(off Allen St.)
Phillimore Wlk. W8 ... 3J 99
Phillip Ho. E1 ... 6K 9 (5F 85)
(off Heneage St.)
Phillipp St. N1 ... 1E 84
Phillipps Ct. HA8: Edg ... 6B 28
Philpot La. EC3 ... 2G 15 (7E 84)
Philpot Path IG1: Ilf ... 3G 71
Philpots Cl. UB7: Yiew ... 7A 74
Philpot Sq. SW6 ... 3K 117
Philpot St. E1 ... 6H 85
Phineas Pett Rd. SE9 ... 3C 124
Phipps Bri. Rd. CR4: Mitc ... 3B 154
Phipps Bri. Rd. SW19 ... 2A 154
Phipps Hatch La. EN2: Enf ... 1H 23
Phipps Ho. SE7 ... 5K 105
(off Woolwich Rd.)
Phipps Ho. W12 ... 7D 80
(off White City Est.)
Phipp's M. SW1 ... 2K 17 (3F 101)
(off Buckingham Palace Rd.)
Phipp St. EC2 ... 3G 9 (4E 84)
Phoebeth Rd. SE4 ... 5C 122
Phoebe Wlk. E16 ... 6K 87
Phoenix Av. SE10 ... 2G 105
Phoenix Cen. ... 7J 167
Phoenix Cinema East Finchley ... 4C 46
Phoenix Cl. BR4: W W'ck ... 2F 171
Phoenix Cl. CR4: Mitc ... 3B 154
Phoenix Cl. E17 ... 2B 50
Phoenix Cl. E8 ... 1F 85
Phoenix Cl. W12 ... 7D 80
Phoenix Ct. CR2: S Croy ... 5F 169
Phoenix Ct. E1 ... 4H 85
(off Buckhurst St.)
Phoenix Ct. E14 ... 4C 104
Phoenix Ct. E4 ... 3J 35
Phoenix Ct. KT3: N Mald ... 3B 152
Phoenix Ct. NW1 ... 1D 6 (2H 83)
(off Purchese St.)
Phoenix Ct. SE14 ... 6A 104
(off Chipley St.)
Phoenix Ct. TW13: Felt ... 4G 129
Phoenix Ct. TW3: Houn ... 3E 112
Phoenix Ct. TW4: Houn ... 5B 112
Phoenix Ct. TW8: Bford ... 5E 96
Phoenix Dr. BR2: Kes ... 4B 172
Phoenix Fitness Cen. ... 7C 80
Phoenix Hgts. E. E14 ... 2C 104
(off Byng St.)
Phoenix Hgts. W. E14 ... 2C 104
(off Mastmaker Ct.)
Phoenix Ind. Est. HA1: Harr ... 4K 41
Phoenix Lodge Mans. W6 ... 4F 99
(off Brook Grn.)
Phoenix Pk. NW2 ... 2C 62
Phoenix Pl. WC1 ... 3H 7 (4K 83)
Phoenix Point SE28 ... 1C 108
Phoenix Rd. NW1 ... 1C 6 (3H 83)
Phoenix Rd. SE20 ... 6J 139
Phoenix St. WC2 ... 1D 12 (6H 83)
Phoenix Theatre ... 1D 12 (6H 83)
(off Charing Cross Rd.)
Phoenix Trad. Est. UB6: G'frd ... 1C 78
Phoenix Trad. Pk. TW8: Bford ... 5D 96
Phoenix Way E16 ... 5H 87
(off Barking Rd.)
Phoenix Way SW18 ... 5A 118
Phoenix Way TW5: Hest ... 6B 94
Phoenix Wharf E1 ... 1H 103
(off Wapping High St.)
Phoenix Wharf Rd. SE1 ... 7J 15 (2F 103)
(off Tanner St.)
Phoenix Works HA5: Hat E ... 1D 40
Phoenix Yd. WC1 ... 2H 7 (3K 83)
(off King's Cross Rd.)
Photographers' Gallery ... 1A 12 (6G 83)
(off Ramillies St.)
Phyllis Av. KT3: N Mald ... 5D 152
Phyllis Hodges Ho. NW1 ... 1C 6 (2H 83)
(off Aldenham St.)
Phyllis Ho. CR0: Wadd ... 4B 168
(off Ashley La.)
Phyppe Way E17 ... 5F 51
Physical Energy Statue ... 5A 10 (1A 100)
Physic Pl. SW3 ... 7E 16 (6D 100)
Piano La. N16 ... 3D 66
Piano Works IG11: Bark ... 7G 71
(off Ripple Rd.)
Piano Yd. NW5 ... 5F 65
Piazza, The UB8: Uxb ... 7A 56
Piazza, The WC2 ... 2F 13 (7J 83)
(off Covent Gdn.)
Piazza Wlk. E1 ... 1K 15 (6G 85)
Picardy Ho. EN2: Enf ... 1H 23
Picardy Manorway DA17: Belv ... 3H 109
Picardy Rd. DA17: Belv ... 5G 109
Picardy St. DA17: Belv ... 3G 109
Piccadilly W1 ... 5J 11 (1F 101)
Piccadilly Arc. SW1 ... 4A 12 (1G 101)
(off Piccadilly)
Piccadilly Circus ... 3C 12 (7H 83)
Piccadilly Ct. N7 ... 6K 65
(off Caledonian Rd.)
Piccadilly Pl. W1 ... 3B 12 (7G 83)
(off Piccadilly)
Piccadilly Theatre ... 2B 12 (7G 83)
(off Denman St.)
Pickard Cl. N14 ... 1C 32
Pickard Gdns. E3 ... 5B 86
Pickard St. EC1 ... 1B 8 (3B 84)
Pickering Av. E6 ... 2E 88
Pickering Cl. E9 ... 7K 67
Pickering Gdns. CR0: C'don ... 6F 157
Pickering Gdns. N11 ... 6K 31
Pickering Ho. W2 ... 6A 82
(off Hallfield Est.)
Pickering Ho. W5 ... 4C 96
(off Windmill Rd.)
Pickering La. BR5: Farnb ... 1H 173
Pickering M. W2 ... 6K 81
Pickering Pl. SW1 ... 5B 12 (1G 101)
(off St James's St.)
Pickering Rd. IG11: Bark ... 6G 71
Pickering St. N1 ... 1B 84
Pickets Cl. WD23: B Hea ... 1C 26
Pickets St. SW12 ... 7F 119
Pickett Cft. HA7: Stan ... 1D 42
Picketts Lock La. N9 ... 2D 34
Picketts Lock La. Ind. Est. N9 ... 2F 35
Picketts Ter. SE22 ... 5G 121
Pickford Cl. DA7: Bex ... 2E 126
Pickford La. DA7: Bex ... 2E 126
Pickford Rd. DA7: Bex ... 3E 126
Pickfords Wharf N1 ... 1C 8 (2C 84)
Pickfords Wharf SE1 ... 4E 14 (1D 102)
Pickhurst Grn. BR2: Hayes ... 7H 159
Pickhurst La. BR2: Hayes ... 7H 159
Pickhurst La. BR4: W W'ck ... 5G 159
Pickhurst Mead BR2: Hayes ... 7H 159
Pickhurst Pk. BR2: Broml ... 5G 159
Pickhurst Ri. BR4: W W'ck ... 7E 158
Pickle M. SW9 ... 7A 102
Pickle Sq. SE1 ... 3E 102
(off The Tannery)
Pickwick Cl. TW4: Houn ... 5C 112
Pickwick Ct. SE9 ... 1C 142
Pickwick Ho. SE16 ... 2G 103
(off George Row)
Pickwick Ho. W11 ... 1F 99
(off St Ann's Rd.)
Pickwick M. N18 ... 4K 33
Pickwick Pl. HA1: Harr ... 7J 41
Pickwick Rd. SE21 ... 7D 120
Pickwick St. SE1 ... 7C 14 (2C 102)
Pickwick Way BR7: Chst ... 6G 143
Pickworth Cl. SW8 ... 7J 101
Picton Pl. KT6: Surb ... 1G 163
Picton Pl. W1 ... 1H 11 (6E 82)
Picton St. SE5 ... 7D 102
Picture Ho. SW16 ... 2J 137
Picturehouse Central ... 2C 12 (7H 83)
(off Shaftesbury Av.)
Picture Ho. M. E17 ... 4F 51
Pied Bull Ct. WC1 ... 6F 7 (5J 83)
(off Bury Pl.)
Pied Bull Yd. N1 ... 1B 84
(off Theberton St.)
Pied Bull Yd. WC1 ... 6E 6 (5J 83)
(off Bury Pl.)
Piedmont Rd. SE18 ... 5H 107
(not continuous)
PIELD HEATH ... 4B 74
Pield Heath Av. UB8: Hil ... 4C 74
Pield Heath Rd. UB8: Cowl ... 4A 74
Pield Heath Rd. UB8: Hil ... 4A 74
Pierce Campion Ct. E17 ... 3B 50
Pier Head E1 ... 1H 103
(not continuous)
Pierhead Wharf E1 ... 1H 103
(off Wapping High St.)
Pier Ho. SW3 ... 7D 16 (6C 100)
Pieris Ho. TW13: Felt ... 2J 129
(off High St.)
Piermont Grn. SE22 ... 5H 121
Piermont Pl. BR1: Broml ... 2C 160
Piermont Rd. SE22 ... 5H 121
Pier Pde. E16 ... 1E 106
(off Pier Rd.)
Pierpoint Bldg. E14 ... 2B 104
Pierrepoint Rd. W3 ... 7H 79
Pierrepont Arc. N1 ... 2B 84
(off Islington High St.)
Pierrepont Row N1 ... 2B 84
(off Camden Pas.)
Pier Rd. E16 ... 1E 106
Pier Rd. TW14: Felt ... 5K 111
Pier St. E14 ... 4E 104
(not continuous)
Pier Ter. SW18 ... 4K 117
Pier Wlk. SE10 ... 2G 105
Pier Way SE28 ... 2G 107
Pietra Lara Bldg. EC1 ... 3C 8 (4C 84)
(off Pear Tree St.)
Pigeon La. TW12: Hamp ... 4E 130
Piggott Ho. E2 ... 2K 85
(off Sewardstone Rd.)
Pigott St. E14 ... 6C 86
Pike Cl. BR1: Broml ... 5K 141
Pike Cl. UB10: Uxb ... 1B 74
Pike Cres. TW15: Ashf ... 4B 128
Pikemans Ct. SW5 ... 4J 99
(off W. Cromwell Rd.)
Pike Rd. NW7 ... 4E 28
Pike's End HA5: Eastc ... 4K 39
Pikestone Cl. UB4: Yead ... 4C 76
Pikethorne SE23 ... 2K 139
Pilgrimage St. SE1 ... 7E 14 (2D 102)
Pilgrim Cl. SM4: Mord ... 7K 153
Pilgrim Hill SE27 ... 4C 138
Pilgrim Ho. SE1 ... 3D 102
(off Tabard St.)
Pilgrim Ho. SE16 ... 2J 103
(off Brunel Rd.)
Pilgrims Cloisters SE5 ... 7E 102
(off Sedgmoor Pl.)
Pilgrims Cl. N13 ... 4E 32
Pilgrims Cl. UB5: N'olt ... 5G 59
Pilgrims Cnr. NW6 ... 2J 81
(off Chichester Rd.)
Pilgrims Ct. EN1: Enf ... 2J 23
Pilgrim's La. NW3 ... 4B 64
Pilgrims M. E14 ... 7G 87
Pilgrim's Pl. NW3 ... 4B 64
Pilgrims Ri. EN4: E Barn ... 5H 21
Pilgrim St. EC4 ... 1A 14 (6B 84)
Pilgrim's Way HA9: Wemb ... 1H 61
Pilgrims Way CR2: S Croy ... 6F 169
Pilgrims Way E6 ... 1C 88
Pilgrims Way N19 ... 1H 65
Pilkington Rd. BR6: Farnb ... 3G 173
Pilkington Rd. SE15 ... 2H 121
Pill Box Studios E2 ... 4H 85
(off Coventry Rd.)
Pillfold Ho. SE11 ... 3G 19 (4K 101)
(off Old Paradise St.)
Pillions La. UB4: Hayes ... 4F 75
Pilot Cl. SE8 ... 6B 104
Pilot Ind. Cen. NW10 ... 4K 79
Pilot Wlk. SE10 ... 2H 105
Pilsdon Cl. SW19 ... 1F 135
Pilton Est., The CR0: C'don ... 2B 168
Pilton Gdns. SM4: Mord ... 6K 153
Pilton Pl. SE17 ... 5C 102
Pimento Ct. W5 ... 3D 96
PIMLICO ... 6A 18 (5G 101)
Pimlico Ho. SW1 ... 5J 17 (5F 101)
(off Ebury Bri. Rd.)
Pimlico Rd. SW1 ... 5G 17 (5E 100)
Pimlico Sq. SW1 ... 5G 17 (5E 100)
Pimp Hall Nature Reserve ... 2A 36
Pinchbeck Rd. BR6: Chels ... 6K 173
Pinchin & Johnsons Yd. E1 ... 7G 85
(off Pinchin St.)
Pinchin St. E1 ... 7G 85
Pincombe Ho. SE17 ... 5D 102
(off Orb St.)
Pincott Pl. SE4 ... 3K 121
Pincott Rd. DA6: Bex ... 5G 127
Pincott Rd. SW19 ... 7A 136
Pindar St. EC2 ... 5G 9 (5E 84)
Pindock M. W9 ... 4K 81
Pindoria M. E1 ... 4J 9 (4F 85)
(off Quaker St.)
Pineapple Ct. SW1 ... 1A 18 (3G 101)
(off Castle La.)
Pine Av. BR4: W W'ck ... 1D 170
Pine Av. E15 ... 5F 69
Pine Cl. E10 ... 2D 68
Pine Cl. HA7: Stan ... 4G 27
Pine Cl. N14 ... 7B 22
Pine Cl. N19 ... 2G 65
Pine Cl. SE20 ... 1J 157
Pine Coombe CR0: C'don ... 4K 169
Pine Ct. N21 ... 5E 22
Pine Ct. UB5: N'olt ... 4C 76
Pinecrest Gdns. BR6: Farnb ... 4F 173
Pinecroft Ct. DA16: Well ... 7A 108
Pinecroft Cres. EN5: Barn ... 4B 20
Pinedene SE15 ... 1H 121
Pinefield Cl. E14 ... 7C 86
Pine Gdns. HA4: Ruis ... 1K 57
Pine Gdns. KT5: Surb ... 6G 151
Pine Glade BR6: Farnb ... 4D 172
Pine Gro. N20 ... 1C 30
Pine Gro. N4 ... 2J 65
Pine Gro. SW19 ... 5H 135
Pine Ho. E3 ... 1A 86
(off Barge La.)
Pine Ho. SE16 ... 2J 103
(off Ainsty Est.)
Pine Ho. W10 ... 4G 81
(off Droop St.)
Pinehurst Ct. W11 ... 6H 81
(off Colville Gdns.)
Pinehurst Wlk. BR6: Orp ... 1H 173
Pinelands Cl. SE3 ... 7H 105
Pinemartin Cl. NW2 ... 3E 62
Pine M. NW10 ... 2F 81
(off Clifford Gdns.)
Pine Needle La. HA6: Nwood ... 1H 39
Pine Pl. UB4: Hayes ... 4H 75
Pine Ridge SM5: Cars ... 7E 166
Pineridge Ct. EN5: Barn ... 4A 20
Pine Rd. N11 ... 2K 31
Pine Rd. NW2 ... 4E 62
Pines, The IG8: Wfd G ... 3C 36
Pines, The KT9: Chess ... 3E 162
Pines, The N14 ... 5B 22
Pines, The SE19 ... 6B 138
Pines, The TW16: Sun ... 3J 147
Pines Rd. BR1: Broml ... 2C 160
Pine St. EC1 ... 3K 7 (4A 84)
Pine Tree Cl. TW2: Whitt ... 7F 113
Pine Tree Cl. TW5: Cran ... 1K 111
Pine Tree Lodge BR2: Broml ... 4H 159
Pine Trees Dr. UB10: Ick ... 4A 56
Pine Tree Way SE13 ... 3D 122
Pineview Ct. E4 ... 1K 35
Pine Wlk. KT5: Surb ... 6G 151
Pine Wood TW16: Sun ... 1J 147
Pinewood Av. DA15: Sidc ... 1J 143
Pinewood Av. HA5: Hat E ... 6A 26
Pinewood Av. UB8: Hil ... 6B 74
Pinewood Cl. BR6: Orp ... 1H 173
Pinewood Cl. CR0: C'don ... 3A 170
Pinewood Cl. HA5: Hat E ... 6A 26
Pinewood Ct. EN2: Enf ... 3G 23
Pinewood Ct. SW4 ... 6H 119
Pinewood Dr. BR6: Orp ... 5J 173
Pinewood Gdns. TW11: Tedd ... 5B 132
Pinewood Gro. W5 ... 6C 78
Pinewood Lodge WD23: B Hea ... 1C 26
Pinewood Pl. KT19: Ewe ... 4K 163
Pinewood Rd. BR2: Broml ... 4J 159
Pinewood Rd. SE2 ... 6D 108
Pinewood Rd. TW13: Felt ... 3K 129
Pinfold Rd. SW16 ... 4J 137
Pinglestone Cl. UB7: Harm ... 7A 92
Pinkcoat Cl. TW13: Felt ... 3K 129
Pinkerton Pl. SW16 ... 4H 137
Pinkham Mans. W4 ... 5G 97
Pinkham Way N11 ... 7K 31
Pinkwell Av. UB3: Harl ... 4F 93
Pinkwell La. UB3: Harl ... 4E 92
Pinley Gdns. RM9: Dag ... 1B 90
Pinnace Ho. E14 ... 3E 104
(off Manchester Rd.)
Pinnacle, The ... 1G 15 (6E 84)
(off Bishopsgate)
Pinnacle, The RM6: Chad H ... 6E 54
(off High Rd.)
Pinnacle Apts. CR0: C'don ... 1C 168
(off Saffron Central Sq.)
Pinnacle Cl. N10 ... 3F 47
Pinnacle Hill DA7: Bex ... 4H 127
Pinnacle Hill Nth. DA7: Bex ... 4H 127
Pinnacle Ho. EN1: Enf ... 3K 23
(off Colman Pde.)
Pinnacle Ho. NW9 ... 2B 44
(off Heritage Av.)
Pinnacle Ho. SW18 ... 4A 118
Pinnacle Pl. HA7: Stan ... 4G 27
Pinnacle Way E14 ... 6A 86
(off Commercial Rd.)
Pinnata Cl. EN2: Enf ... 1H 23
Pinnell Rd. SE9 ... 4B 124
PINNER ... 4C 40
Pinner Ct. HA5: Pinn ... 4E 40
Pinner Ct. NW8 ... 3A 4 (4B 82)
(off St John's Wood Rd.)
PINNER GREEN ... 2A 40
Pinner Grn. HA5: Pinn ... 2A 40
Pinner Gro. HA5: Pinn ... 4C 40
Pinner Hill HA5: Pinn ... 1K 39
Pinner Hill Farm HA5: Pinn ... 1K 39
Pinner Hill Rd. HA5: Pinn ... 1K 39
Pinner Pk. HA5: Pinn ... 2E 40
Pinner Pk. ... 1E 40
Pinner Pk. Av. HA2: Harr ... 3F 41
Pinner Pk. Gdns. HA2: Harr ... 2G 41
Pinner Rd. HA5: Pinn Nower Hill ... 4D 40
Pinner Rd. HA1: Harr ... 5F 41
Pinner Rd. HA2: Harr ... 4E 40
Pinner Rd. HA6: Nwood ... 1H 39
Pinner Rd. HA6: Pinn ... 1H 39
Pinners Cl. SM5: Cars ... 2C 166
Pinner Vw. HA1: Harr ... 4G 41
Pinner Vw. HA2: Harr ... 3G 41
PINNERWOOD PARK ... 1A 40
Pinn Way HA4: Ruis ... 7F 39
Pintail Cl. E6 ... 5C 88
Pintail Ct. SE8 ... 6B 104
(off Pilot Cl.)
Pintail Rd. IG8: Wfd G ... 7E 36
Pintail Way UB4: Yead ... 5B 76
Pintail Wy. SE2 ... 2C 108
Pinter Ho. SW9 ... 2J 119
(off Grantham Rd.)
Pintle Pl. E3 ... 3E 86
Pinto Twr. SW8 ... 7J 101
Pinto Way SE3 ... 4K 123
Pioneer Cen., The SE15 ... 1J 121
Pioneer Cl. E14 ... 5D 86
Pioneer Ct. E16 ... 5J 87
(off Hammersley Rd.)
Pioneer Ho. WC1 ... 1G 7 (3K 83)
(off Britannia St.)
Pioneer Point IG1: Ilf ... 3F 71
Pioneers Ind. Pk. CR0: Bedd ... 1J 167
Pioneer St. SE15 ... 1G 121
Pioneer Way W12 ... 6D 80
Piper Bldg., The SW6 ... 3K 117
Piper Cl. N7 ... 6K 65
Piper Rd. KT1: King T ... 3G 151
Piper's Gdns. CR0: C'don ... 7A 158
Pipers Grn. NW9 ... 5J 43
Pipers Grn. La. HA8: Edg ... 3K 27
(not continuous)
Pipers Ho. SE10 ... 5F 105
(off Collington St.)
Piper Way IG1: Ilf ... 1H 71
Pipewell Rd. SM5: Cars ... 6C 154
Pipit Dr. SW15 ... 6E 116
Pippenhall SE9 ... 6F 125
Pippin Cl. CR0: C'don ... 1B 170
Pippin Cl. NW2 ... 3C 62
Pippin Cl. TW13: Hanw ... 3D 130
Pippin Ct. SW8 ... 7G 19 (6K 101)
(off Vauxhall Gro.)
Pippin Ho. W10 ... 7F 81
(off Freston Rd.)
Pippin Mans. E20 ... 5E 68
(off Mirabelle Gdns.)
Pippins Cl. UB7: W Dray ... 3A 92
Pippins Ct. TW15: Ashf ... 6D 128
Pique M. E1 ... 7K 85
(off Glasshouse Flds.)
Piquet Rd. SE20 ... 2J 157
Pirbright Cres. CR0: New Ad ... 6E 170
Pirbright Rd. SW18 ... 1H 135
Pirie Cl. SE5 ... 3D 120
Pirie St. E16 ... 1K 105
Pirin Ct. E4 ... 4H 35
Pisces Ct. HA8: Edg ... 7B 28
Pissarro Ho. N1 ... 7A 66
(off Augustas La.)
Pitcairn Cl. RM7: Mawney ... 4G 55
Pitcairn Ho. E9 ... 7J 67
Pitcairn Rd. CR4: Mitc ... 7D 136
Pitcairn's Path HA2: Harr ... 3G 59
Pitcher La. TW15: Ashf ... 4B 128
Pitchford St. E15 ... 7F 69
Pitfield Cres. SE28 ... 1A 108
Pitfield Est. N1 ... 1G 9 (3E 84)
Pitfield St. N1 ... 2G 9 (3E 84)
Pitfield Way EN3: Enf H ... 1D 24
Pitfield Way NW10 ... 6J 61
Pitfold Cl. SE12 ... 6K 123
Pitfold Rd. SE12 ... 6J 123
Pitlake CR0: C'don ... 2B 168
Pitlochry Ho. SE27 ... 2B 138
(off Elmcourt Rd.)
Pitman Bldg. SE16 ... 7K 15 (3G 103)
(off Old Jamaica Rd.)
Pitman Ho. SE8 ... 1C 122
Pitman St. SE5 ... 7C 102
Pitmaston Ho. SE13 ... 2E 122
(off Lewisham Rd.)
Pitmaston Rd. SE13 ... 2E 122
Pitsea Pl. E1 ... 6K 85
Pitsea St. E1 ... 6K 85
Pitshanger La. W5 ... 4B 78
Pitshanger Manor House & Gallery ... 1D 96
Pitt Cres. SW19 ... 4K 135
Pittman Gdns. IG1: Ilf ... 5G 71
Pitt Rd. BR6: Farnb ... 4G 173
Pitt Rd. CR0: C'don ... 5C 156
Pitt Rd. CR7: Thor H ... 5C 156
Pitt's Head M. W1 ... 5H 11 (1E 100)
Pittsmead Av. BR2: Hayes ... 7J 159
Pitt St. W8 ... 2J 99
Pittville Gdns. SE25 ... 3G 157
Pitwell M. E8 ... 6G 67
Pixfield Ct. BR2: Broml ... 2H 159
(off Beckenham La.)
Pixley St. E14 ... 6B 86
Pixton Way CR0: Sels ... 7A 170
Place London, The ... 2D 6 (3H 83)
Place, The SE1 ... 5F 15 (1D 102)
Place Farm Av. BR6: Orp ... 1H 173
Plaisterers Highwalk EC2 ... 6C 8 (5C 84)
(off London Wall)
PLAISTOW ... 7J 141
PLAISTOW ... 2J 87
Plaistow Gro. BR1: Broml ... 7K 141
Plaistow Gro. E15 ... 1H 87
Plaistow La. BR1: Broml ... 7J 141
Plaistow Pk. Rd. E13 ... 2K 87
(not continuous)
Plaistow Rd. E13 ... 2J 87
Plaistow Rd. E15 ... 1H 87
Plaistow Wharf E16 ... 2J 105
Plaistow Ct. NW9 ... 2A 44
Plane Ho. BR2: Broml ... 2G 159
Plane St. SE26 ... 3H 139
Planetree Ct. W6 ... 4F 99
(off Brook Grn.)
Plane Tree Cres. TW13: Felt ... 3K 129
Plane Tree Ho. SE8 ... 6A 104
(off Etta St.)
Plane Tree Ho. W8 ... 2H 99
(off Duchess of Bedford's Wlk.)
Plane Tree M. SW17 ... 2C 136
Planetree Path E17 ... 4C 50
(off Selborne Rd.)
Plane Tree Wlk. N2 ... 3C 46
Plane Tree Wlk. SE19 ... 6E 138
Plantagenet Cl. KT4: Wor Pk ... 4K 163
Plantagenet Gdns. RM6: Chad H ... 7D 54
Plantagenet Ho. SE18 ... 3D 106
(off Leda Rd.)
Plantagenet Pl. RM6: Chad H ... 7D 54
Plantagenet Rd. EN5: New Bar ... 4F 21
Plantain Gdns. E11 ... 3F 69
(off Hollydown Way)
Plantain Pl. SE1 ... 6E 14 (2D 102)
Plantation, The SE3 ... 2J 123
Plantation Cl. SW4 ... 5J 119
Plantation La. EC3 ... 2G 15 (7E 84)
(off Rood La.)
Plantation Pl. EC3 ... 2G 15 (7E 84)
(off Mincing La.)
Plantation Wharf SW11 ... 3A 118
Plants & People Exhibition ... 7F 97
Plasel Ct. E13 ... 1K 87
(off Pawsey Cl.)
PLASHET ... 6C 70
Plashet Gro. E6 ... 1A 88
Plashet Rd. E13 ... 1J 87
Plassy Rd. SE6 ... 7D 122
Plate Ho. E14 ... 5D 104
(off Burrells Wharf Sq.)
Platform Theatre ... 1J 83
Platina St. EC2 ... 3F 9 (4D 84)
(off Tabernacle St.)
Platinum Ct. E1 ... 4J 85
(off Cephas Av.)
Platinum Ct. RM7: Mawney ... 3H 55
Platinum Jubilee Cl. BR6: Orp ... 1J 173
Platinum M. N15 ... 5F 49
Plato Rd. SW2 ... 4J 119
Platt, The SW15 ... 3F 117
Platt Halls NW9 ... 2B 44
Platt's Eyot TW12: Hamp ... 2E 148
Platt's La. NW3 ... 4J 63
Platts Rd. EN3: Enf H ... 1D 24
Platt St. NW1 ... 2H 83
Plawsfield Rd. BR3: Beck ... 1K 157
Plaxdale Ho. SE17 ... 4E 102
(off Congreve St.)
Plaxtol Cl. BR1: Broml ... 1A 160
Plaxtol Rd. DA8: Erith ... 7G 109
Plaxton Ct. E11 ... 3H 69
Playfair Ho. E14 ... 6C 86
(off Saracen St.)
Playfair Mans. W14 ... 6G 99
(off Queen's Club Gdns.)
Playfair St. W6 ... 5E 98
Playfield Av. RM5: Col R ... 1J 55
Playfield Cres. SE22 ... 5F 121
Playfield Rd. HA8: Edg ... 2J 43
Playford Rd. N4 ... 2K 65
(not continuous)
Playgreen Way SE6 ... 3C 140
Playground Cl. BR3: Beck ... 2K 157
Playground Gdns. E2 ... 2J 9 (3F 85)
(off Rochelle St.)
Playhouse Ct. SE1 ... 5C 14 (1C 102)
(off Southwark Bri. Rd.)
Playhouse Theatre London ... 4F 13 (1J 101)
(off Northumberland Av.)
Playhouse Yd. EC4 ... 1A 14 (6B 84)
Plaza Bus. Cen. EN3: Brim ... 2G 25
Plaza Gdns. SW15 ... 5G 117
Plaza Hgts. E10 ... 3E 68
Plaza Pde. HA0: Wemb ... 6E 60
(off Ealing Rd.)
Plaza Pde. NW6 ... 2K 81
Plaza Wlk. NW9 ... 3J 43
Pleasance, The SW15 ... 4D 116
Pleasance Rd. SW15 ... 5D 116
Pleasance Theatre London ... 6J 65
(off Carpenters M.)
Pleasant Gro. CR0: C'don ... 3B 170
Pleasant Pl. N1 ... 7B 66
Pleasant Row NW1 ... 1F 83
Pleasant Vw. DA8: Erith ... 5K 109
Pleasant Vw. Pl. BR6: Farnb ... 5F 173
Pleasant Way HA0: Wemb ... 2C 78
Pleasaunce Mans. SE10 ... 5J 105
(off Halstow Rd.)
Plender Ct. NW1 ... 1G 83
(off College Pl.)
Plender St. NW1 ... 1G 83
Pleshey Rd. N7 ... 4H 65
Plesman Way SM6: W'gton ... 7J 167
Plessey Bldg. E14 ... 6C 86
(off Dod St.)
Plevna Cres. N15 ... 6E 48
Plevna Rd. N9 ... 3B 34
Plevna Rd. TW12: Hamp ... 1F 149
Plevna St. E14 ... 3E 104
Pleydell Av. SE19 ... 7F 139
Pleydell Av. W6 ... 4B 98
Pleydell Ct. EC4 ... 1K 13 (6A 84)
(off Pleydell St.)
Pleydell Est. EC1 ... 2D 8 (3C 84)
(off Radnor St.)
Pleydell Gdns. SE19 ... 6F 139
(off Anerley Hill)
Pleydell Ho. EC4 ... 1K 13 (6A 84)
(off Pleydell St.)
Pleydell St. EC4 ... 1K 13 (6A 84)
(off Bouverie St.)
Plimley Pl. W12 ... 2F 99
(off Shepherd's Bush Pl.)
Plimsoll Cl. E14 ... 6D 86
Plimsoll Rd. N4 ... 3A 66
Plough Cl. NW10 ... 3D 80
Plough Ct. EC3 ... 2F 15 (7D 84)
Plough Ct. RM13: Rain ... 2K 91
(off Broadis Way)
Plough Farm Cl. HA4: Ruis ... 6F 39
Plough La. CR8: Purl ... 7J 167
Plough La. SE22 ... 6F 121
Plough La. SM6: Bedd ... 4J 167
Plough La. SW17 ... 4A 136
Plough La. SW19 ... 5K 135
Plough La. TW11: Tedd ... 5A 132
Plough La. Cl. SM6: Bedd ... 5J 167
Ploughmans Cl. NW1 ... 1H 83
Ploughmans End TW7: Isle ... 5H 113
Ploughmans Wlk. N2 ... 2A 46
(off Long La.)
Plough M. SW11 ... 4B 118
Plough Pl. EC4 ... 7K 7 (6A 84)
Plough Rd. KT19: Ewe ... 7K 163
Plough Rd. SW11 ... 3B 118
Plough St. E1 ... 7K 9 (6F 85)
(off Buckle St.)
Plough Ter. SW11 ... 4B 118
Plough Way SE16 ... 4K 103
Plough Yd. EC2 ... 4H 9 (4E 84)
Plover Ho. SW9 ... 7A 102
(off Brixton Rd.)
Plover Way SE16 ... 3A 104
Plover Way UB4: Yead ... 6B 76

A–Z London 271

Plowden Bldgs. – Poynings Rd.

Plowden Bldgs. EC4 2J 13 (7A 84)
(off Middle Temple La.)
Plowden Rd. SE3 3K 123
Plowman Cl. N18 5J 33
Plowman Way RM8: Dag 1C 72
Plumber's Row E1 5G 85
Plumbridge St. SE10 1E 122
Plum Cl. TW13: Felt 1J 129
Plume Ho. SE10 6D 104
(off Creek Rd.)
Plum Gth. TW8: Bford 4D 96
Plum La. RM13: Rain 2K 91
Plum La. SE18 7F 107
Plummer La. CR4: Mitc 2D 154
Plummer Rd. SW4 7H 119
Plum M. SW17 3C 136
Plumpton Cl. UB5: N'olt 6E 58
Plumpton Way SM5: Cars 3C 166
PLUMSTEAD 4J 107
PLUMSTEAD COMMON 6F 107
Plumstead Comn. Rd. SE18 6F 107
Plumstead High St. SE18 4H 107
Plumstead Rd. SE18 4F 107
(not continuous)
Plumtree Cl. RM10: Dag 6H 73
Plumtree Cl. SM6: W'gton 7H 167
Plumtree Ct. EC4 7A 8 (6B 84)
Plum Tree M. SW16 6J 137
Plymen Ho. KT8: W Mole 5E 148
Plymouth Ct. KT5: Surb 4E 150
(off Cranes Pk. Av.)
Plymouth Ho. IG11: Bark 7A 72
(off Margaret Bondfield Av.)
Plymouth Ho. SE10 1D 122
(off Devonshire Dr.)
Plymouth Rd. BR1: Broml 1K 159
Plymouth Rd. E16 5J 87
Plymouth Ter. NW2 6E 62
(off Sidmouth Rd.)
Plymouth Wharf E14 4F 105
Plympton Av. NW6 7H 63
Plympton Cl. DA17: Belv 3E 108
Plympton Pl. NW8 4C 4 (4C 82)
Plympton Rd. NW6 7H 63
Plympton St. NW8 4C 4 (4C 82)
Plymstock Rd. DA16: Well 7C 108
Pocklington Cl. NW9 2A 44
Pocklington Cl. W12 3C 98
(off Ashchurch Pk. Vs.)
Pocklington Lodge W12 3C 98
Pocock Av. UB7: W Dray 3B 92
Pocock St. SE1 6A 14 (2B 102)
Podmore Rd. SW18 4A 118
Poet Ct. E1 5K 85
(off Shandy St.)
Poets Ct. SE25 4G 157
Poets Ct. W3 1J 97
Poet's Rd. N5 5D 66
Poets Way HA1: Harr 4J 41
Point, The E17 4C 50
(off Tower M.)
Point, The HA4: Ruis 4J 57
Point, The W2 6A 4 (5B 82)
(off Nth. Wharf Rd.)
Pointalls Cl. N3 2A 46
Point Cl. SE10 1E 122
Pointer Cl. SE28 6D 90
Pointers Cl. E14 5D 104
Pointers Cotts. TW10: Ham 2C 132
Point Hill SE10 7E 104
Point Pl. HA9: Wemb 7H 61
Point Pleasant SW18 4J 117
Point Ter. E7 5K 69
(off Claremont Rd.)
Point W. SW7 4K 99
Point Wharf TW8: Bford 7E 96
Point Wharf La. TW8: Bford 7D 96
Poland St. W1 7B 6 (6G 83)
Polar Pk. UB7: Harm 7B 92
Poldo Ho. SE10 4G 105
(off Cable Wlk.)
Polebrook Rd. SE3 3A 124
Pole Cat All. BR2: Hayes 2H 171
Polecroft La. SE6 2B 140
Polehamptons, The TW12: Hamp 7G 131
Pole Hill Rd. E4 7K 25
Pole Hill Rd. UB10: Hil 4D 74
Pole Hill Rd. UB4: Hayes 2E 74
Polesden Gdns. SW20 2D 152
Polesworth Ho. W2 5J 81
(off Alfred Rd.)
Polesworth Rd. RM9: Dag 7D 72
Police Sta. La. WD23: Bush 1A 26
Police Support HQ 3H 19 (4K 101)
POLISH WAR MEMORIAL 7A 58
Polka Theatre for Children 6K 135
Pollard Cl. E16 7J 87
Pollard Cl. N7 4K 65
Pollard Ho. KT4: Wor Pk 4E 164
Pollard Ho. N1 1G 7 (2K 83)
(off Northdown St.)
Pollard Ho. SE16 3F 103
(off Spa Rd.)
Pollard Rd. N20 2H 31
Pollard Rd. SM4: Mord 5B 154
Pollard Row E2 3G 85
Pollards Cres. SW16 3J 155
Pollards Hill E. SW16 3K 155
Pollards Hill Nth. SW16 3J 155
Pollards Hill Sth. SW16 3J 155
Pollards Hill W. SW16 3K 155
Pollard St. E2 3G 85
Pollards Wood Rd. SW16 3J 155
Pollard Wlk. DA14: Sidc 6C 144
Pollen St. W1 1A 12 (6G 83)
Pollitt Dr. NW8 3A 4 (4B 82)
Pollock Ho. W10 4G 81
(off Kensal Rd.)
Pollock's Toy Mus. Pollocks
5B 6 (5G 83)
Polo M. BR7: Chst 5H 143
Polperro Cl. BR6: St M Cry 6K 161
Polperro Ho. W2 5J 81
(off Westbourne Pk. Rd.)
Polperro M. SE11 3K 19 (4B 102)
Polsted Rd. SE6 7B 122
Polthorne Est. SE18 4H 107
(off Polthorne Gro.)
Polthorne Gro. SE18 4G 107
Polworth Rd. SW16 5J 137
Polychrome Ct. SE1 7A 14 (2B 102)
(off Waterloo Rd.)
Polydamas Cl. E3 2C 86
Polygon, The NW8 1B 82
(off Avenue Rd.)
Polygon, The SW4 4G 119
Polygon Bus. Cen. SL3: Poyle 5A 174
Polygon Rd. NW1 1C 6 (2H 83)
(not continuous)
Polytechnic St. SE18 4E 106
Pomell Way E1 7K 9 (6F 85)
Pomeroy Cl. TW1: Twick 4B 114
Pomeroy Ho. E2 2K 85
(off St James's Av.)
Pomeroy Ho. W11 6G 81
(off Lancaster Rd.)
Pomeroy St. SE14 7J 103
Pomfret Pl. E14 7E 86
(off Bullivant St.)
Pomfret Rd. SE5 3B 120
Pomoja La. N19 2J 65
Pomona Ho. SE8 4A 104
(off Evelyn St.)
Pomona Pl. E17 2E 50
Pompadour Way IG11: Bark 2B 90
Pond Cl. N12 6H 31
Pond Cl. SE3 2J 123
Pond Cott. La. BR4: W W'ck 1C 170
Pond Cotts. SE21 1E 138
PONDERS END 5D 24
Ponders End Ind. Est. EN3: Pond E
5F 25
Ponder St. N7 7K 65
Pond Farm Est. E5 3J 67
Pondfield Ho. SE27 5C 138
Pondfield Rd. BR2: Hayes 1G 171
Pondfield Rd. BR6: Farnb 3F 173
Pondfield Rd. RM10: Dag 5H 73
Pond Grn. HA4: Ruis 2G 57
Pond Hill Gdns. SM3: Cheam 6G 165
Pond Ho. HA7: Stan 6G 27
Pond Ho. SW3 4C 16 (4C 100)
Pond Lees Cl. RM10: Dag 7K 73
Pond Mead SE21 6D 120
Pond Path BR7: Chst 6F 143
Pond Pl. SW3 4C 16 (4C 100)
Pond Rd. E15 2G 87
Pond Rd. SE3 2H 123
Pondside Av. KT4: Wor Pk 1E 164
Pondside Cl. UB3: Harl 6F 93
Pond Sq. N6 1E 64
Pond St. NW3 5C 64
Pond Way TW11: Tedd 6C 132
Pondwood Ri. BR6: Orp 7J 161
Ponler St. E1 6H 85
Ponsard Rd. NW10 3D 80
Ponsford St. E9 6J 67
Ponsonby Ho. E2 2J 85
(off Bishop's Way)
Ponsonby Pl. SW1 5D 18 (5H 101)
Ponsonby Rd. SW15 7D 116
Ponsonby Ter. SW1 5D 18 (5H 101)
Ponsonby Vs. E2 2J 85
(off Lark Row)
Pontefract Ct. UB5: N'olt 5F 59
(off Newmarket Av.)
Pontefract Rd. BR1: Broml 5H 141
Pontes Av. TW3: Houn 4D 112
Pontifex Apts. SE1 4E 14 (1D 102)
(off Stoney St.)
Ponton Rd. SW11 6H 101
Pontoon Reach E16 1B 106
Pont St. SW1 2E 16 (3D 100)
Pont St. M. SW1 2E 16 (3D 100)
Pontypool Pl. SE1 6A 14 (2B 102)
Pooja Ct. NW1 7G 65
(off Agar Gro.)
Pool Cl. BR3: Beck 5C 140
Pool Cl. KT8: W Mole 5D 148
Pool Ct. SE6 2C 140
Poole Cl. HA4: Ruis 2G 57
Poole Ct. N1 7E 66
(off St Peter's Way)
Poole Ct. TW4: Houn 2C 112
Poole Ct. Rd. TW4: Houn 2C 112
Poole Ho. SE11 2J 19 (3A 102)
(off Lambeth Wlk.)
Poole La. TW19: Stanw 7B 110
POOL END 5C 146
Pool End Cl. TW17: Shep 5C 146
Poole Rd. E9 6K 67
Poole Rd. KT19: Ewe 6K 163
Pooles Bldgs. WC1 4J 7 (4A 84)
(off Mt. Pleasant)
Pooles Cotts. TW10: Ham 2D 132
Pooles La. RM9: Dag 2E 90
Pooles La. SW10 7A 100
Pooles Pk. N4 2A 66
Poole St. N1 1D 84
Poole Way UB4: Hayes 3G 75
Pooley Dr. SW14 3J 115
Pooley Ho. E1 3K 85
Pooley Ho. E18 1J 51
Pool Ho. NW8 5B 4 (5B 82)
(off Penfold St.)
Poolmans St. SE16 2K 103
Pool Rd. HA1: Harr 7H 41
Pool Rd. KT8: W Mole 5D 148
Poolsford Rd. NW9 4A 44
Poolside Manor 1H 45
Pools on the Pk. 4D 114
Pool St. E20 7E 68
Poonah St. E1 6J 85
Pope Cl. SW19 6B 136
Pope Cl. TW14: Felt 1H 129
Pope Ho. SE16 4H 103
(off Manor Est.)
Pope Ho. SE5 7D 102
(off Elmington Est.)
Pope Rd. BR2: Broml 5B 160
Popes Av. TW2: Twick 2J 131
Popes Ct. TW2: Twick 2J 131
Popes Dr. N3 1J 45
Popes Gro. CR0: C'don 3B 170
Popes Gro. TW1: Twick 2K 131
Popes Gro. TW2: Twick 2K 131
Pope's Head All. EC3 1F 15 (6D 84)
Popes La. W5 3D 96
Pope's Rd. SW9 3A 120
Pope St. SE1 7H 15 (2E 102)
Popham Cl. TW13: Hanw 3D 130
Popham Gdns. TW9: Rich 3G 115
Popham Rd. N1 1C 84
Popham St. N1 1B 84
(not continuous)
Pop in Commercial Cen. HA9: Wemb
5H 61
Popinjays Row SM3: Cheam 5F 165
(off Netley Cl.)
POPLAR 7D 86
Poplar Av. BR6: Farnb 2F 173
Poplar Av. CR4: Mitc 1D 154
Poplar Av. UB2: S'hall 3F 95
Poplar Av. UB7: Yiew 7B 74
Poplar Baths Leisure Cen. 7D 86
Poplar Bath St. E14 6D 86
Poplar Bus. Pk. E14 7E 86
Poplar Cl. E9 5B 68
Poplar Cl. HA5: Pinn 1B 40
Poplar Cl. SL3: Poyle 4A 174
Poplar Ct. SW19 5J 135
Poplar Ct. TW1: Twick 6C 114
Poplar Ct. UB5: N'olt 2A 76
Poplar Cres. KT19: Ewe 6J 163
Poplar Farm Cl. KT19: Ewe 6J 163
Poplar Gdns. KT3: N Mald 2K 151
Poplar Gro. HA9: Wemb 3J 61
Poplar Gro. KT3: N Mald 2K 151
Poplar Gro. N11 6K 31
Poplar Gro. W6 2E 98
Poplar High St. E14 7D 86
Poplar Ho. SE16 2K 103
(off Woodland Cres.)
Poplar Ho. SE4 4B 122
(off Wickham Rd.)
Poplar M. W12 1E 98
Poplar Mt. DA17: Belv 4H 109
Poplar Pl. SE28 7C 90
Poplar Pl. UB3: Hayes 7J 75
Poplar Pl. W2 7K 81
Poplar Rd. KT10: Surb 3B 162
Poplar Rd. SE24 4C 120
Poplar Rd. SM3: Sutt 1H 165
Poplar Rd. SW19 2J 153
Poplar Rd. TW15: Ashf 5E 128
Poplar Rd. Sth. SW19 3J 153
Poplars, The N14 5A 22
Poplars Av. NW2 6E 62
Poplars Cl. HA4: Ruis 1G 57
Poplars Rd. E17 6D 50
Poplar St. RM7: Rom 4J 55
Poplar Vw. HA9: Wemb 2D 60
Poplar Wlk. CR0: C'don 2C 168
Poplar Wlk. SE24 3C 120
(not continuous)
Poplar Way IG6: Ilf 4G 53
Poplar Way TW13: Felt 3J 129
Poppins Cl. KT12: Walt T 5A 148
Poppins Ct. EC4 1A 14 (6B 84)
Poppleton Rd. E11 6G 51
Poppy Cl. DA17: Belv 3H 109
Poppy Cl. EN5: New Bar 6F 21
Poppy Cl. SM6: W'gton 1E 166
Poppy Cl. UB5: N'olt 6D 58
Poppy Cl. UB7: W Dray 3B 92
Poppy Dr. EN3: Pond E 4C 24
Poppy La. CR0: C'don 7J 157
Poppy M. SE22 5G 121
Poppy Pl. SE13 6F 123
Porchester Cl. SE5 4C 120
Porchester Ct. W2 7K 81
(off Porchester Gdns.)
Porchester Gdns. W2 7K 81
Porchester Gdns. M. W2 6K 81
Porchester Ga. W2 7K 81
(off Bayswater Rd.)
Porchester Ho. E1 6H 85
(off Philpot St.)
Porchester Leisure Cen. 6K 81
Porchester Mead BR3: Beck 6D 140
Porchester Pl. W2 1D 10 (6C 82)
Porchester Rd. KT1: King T 2H 151
Porchester Rd. W2 6K 81
Porchester Sq. W2 6K 81
Porchester Sq. M. W2 6K 81
Porchester Ter. W2 7A 82
Porchester Ter. Nth. W2 6K 81
Porch Way N20 3J 31
Porcupine Cl. SE9 2C 142
Porden Rd. SW2 4K 119
Porlock Av. HA2: Harr 1G 59
Porlock Ho. SE26 3G 139
Porlock Rd. EN1: Enf 7A 24
Porlock St. SE1 6F 15 (2D 102)
Porrington Cl. BR7: Chst 1D 160
Portal Cl. HA4: Ruis 4J 57
Portal Cl. SE27 3A 138
Portal Cl. UB10: Uxb 7A 56
Portal Way W3 5K 79
Portbury Cl. SE15 1G 121
Port Cres. E13 4K 87
Portcullis Ho. SW1 7E 12 (2J 101)
(off Bridge St.)
Portcullis Lodge Rd. EN1: Enf 3J 23
Port East Apts. E14 7C 86
(off Hertsmere Rd.)
Portelet Ct. N1 1E 84
(off De Beauvoir Est.)
Portelet Rd. E1 3K 85
Porten Ho's. W14 3G 99
(off Porten Rd.)
Porten Rd. W14 3G 99
Porter Rd. E6 6D 88
Porters & Walters Almshouses N22 7E 32
(off Nightingale Rd.)
Porters Av. RM8: Dag 6B 72
Porters Av. RM9: Dag 6B 72
Porters Lodge, The SW10 7A 100
(off Coleridge Gdns.)
Porters M. RM9: Dag 6B 72
Porter Sq. N19 1J 65
Porter St. SE1 4D 14 (1C 102)
Porter St. W1 5F 5 (5D 82)
Porters Wlk. E1 7H 85
Porters Way N12 6H 31
Porters Way UB7: W Dray 3B 92
Porteus Pl. SW4 3G 119
Porteus Rd. W2 5A 4 (5A 82)
Portfleet Pl. N1 1E 84
(off De Beauvoir Rd.)
Portgate Cl. W9 4H 81
Porthallow Cl. BR6: Chels 4K 173
Porthcawe Rd. SE26 4A 140
Porthkerry Av. DA16: Well 4A 126
Port Ho. E14 5D 104
(off Burrells Wharf Sq.)
Portia Ct. IG11: Bark 7A 72
Portia Ct. SE11 5B 102
(off Opal St.)
Portia Way E3 4B 86
Porticos, The SW3 7A 16 (6B 100)
(off King's Rd.)
Portinscale Rd. SW15 5G 117
Portishead Ho. W2 5J 81
(off Westbourne Pk. Rd.)
Portland Av. DA15: Sidc 6A 126
Portland Av. KT3: N Mald 7B 152
Portland Av. N16 7F 49
Portland Cl. KT4: Wor Pk 7D 152
Portland Cl. RM6: Chad H 5E 54
Portland Commercial Est. IG11: Bark
2C 90
Portland Cotts. CR0: Bedd 7H 155
Portland Ct. N1 7E 66
(off St Peter's Way)
Portland Ct. SE1 7E 14 (3D 102)
(off Gt. Dover St.)
Portland Ct. SE14 6A 104
(off Whitcher Cl.)
Portland Cres. HA7: Stan 2D 42
Portland Cres. SE9 2C 142
Portland Cres. TW13: Felt 4F 129
Portland Cres. UB6: G'frd 4F 77
Portland Dr. EN2: Enf 1K 23
Portland Gdns. N4 6B 48
Portland Gdns. RM6: Chad H 5D 54
Portland Gro. SW8 1K 119
Portland Ho. SW1 2A 18 (3G 101)
(off Bressenden Pl.)
Portland Ho. SW15 5F 117
Portland Mans. W14 4H 99
(off Addison Bri. Pl.)
Portland M. W1 1B 12 (6G 83)
Portland Pl. SE25 4G 157
(off Sth. Norwood Hill)
Portland Pl. W1 5J 5 (5F 83)
Portland Ri. N4 1B 66
(not continuous)
Portland Rd. BR1: Broml 4A 142
Portland Rd. CR4: Mitc 2C 154
Portland Rd. KT1: King T 3E 150
Portland Rd. N15 4F 49
Portland Rd. SE25 4G 157
Portland Rd. SE9 2C 142
Portland Rd. TW15: Ashf 3A 128
Portland Rd. UB2: S'hall 3D 94
Portland Rd. UB4: Hayes 3G 75
Portland Rd. W11 7G 81
Portland Sq. E1 1H 103
Portland St. SE17 5D 102
Portland Ter. HA8: Edg 7B 28
Portland Ter. TW9: Rich 4D 114
Portland Wlk. SE17 6D 102
Portman Av. SW14 3K 115
Portman Cl. DA5: Bexl 1K 145
Portman Cl. DA7: Bex 3E 126
Portman Cl. W1 7F 5 (6D 82)
Portman Dr. IG8: Wfd G 2B 52
Portman Gdns. NW9 2K 43
Portman Gdns. UB10: Hil 7C 56
Portman Ga. NW1 4D 4 (4C 82)
Portman Mans. W1 5F 5 (5D 82)
(off Chiltern St.)
Portman M. Sth. W1 1G 11 (6E 82)
Portman Pl. E2 3J 85
Portman Rd. KT1: King T 2F 151
Portman Sq. W1 7G 5 (6E 82)
Portman St. W1 1G 11 (6E 82)
Portman Towers W1 7F 5 (6D 82)
Portmeadow Wlk. SE2 2D 108
Portmeers Cl. E17 6B 50
Portnall Ho. W9 3H 81
(off Portnall Rd.)
Portnall Rd. W9 2H 81
Portnoi Cl. RM1: Rom 2K 55
Portobello Ct. W11 6H 81
Portobello Grn. W10 5G 81
(off Portobello Rd.)
Portobello Ho. BR2: Broml 6B 160
Portobello Lofts W10 4G 81
(off Kensal Rd.)
Portobello Mkt. 6H 81
Portobello M. W11 7J 81
Portobello Rd. W10 5G 81
Portobello Rd. W11 6H 81
Portobello Road Market 7H 81
(off Portobello Rd.)
Porton Ct. KT6: Surb 6C 150
Portpool La. EC1 5J 7 (5A 84)
Portree Cl. N22 7E 32
Portree St. E14 6F 87
Portrush Ct. UB1: S'hall 6G 77
(off Whitecote Rd.)
Portsdown HA8: Edg 5B 28
Portsdown Av. NW11 6H 45
Portsdown M. NW11 6H 45
Portsea Hall W2 1E 10 (6D 82)
(off Portsea Pl.)
Portsea M. W2 1D 10 (6C 82)
(off Portsea Pl.)
Portsea Pl. W2 1D 10 (6C 82)
Portslade Rd. SW8 2G 119
Portsmouth Av. KT7: T Ditt 7A 150
Portsmouth M. E16 1K 105
Portsmouth Rd. KT1: King T 4D 150
Portsmouth Rd. KT6: Surb 6B 150
Portsmouth Rd. KT7: T Ditt 7A 150
Portsmouth Rd. SW15 7D 116
Portsmouth St. WC2 1G 13 (6K 83)
Portsoken Pav. EC3 1J 15 (6F 85)
(off Aldgate Sq.)
Portsoken St. E1 2J 15 (7F 85)
Portswood Pl. SW15 6B 116
Portugal Gdns. TW2: Twick 2G 131
Portugal St. WC2 1G 13 (6K 83)
Portway E15 1H 87
Portway Gdns. SE18 7B 106
Pory Ho. SE11 4H 19 (4K 101)
Poseidon Ct. E14 4C 104
(off Homer Dr.)
Postal Cl. DA5: Bexl 7H 127
Postal Mus., The 3H 7 (4K 83)
Postern, The EC2 6D 8 (5C 84)
(off Wood St.)
Postern Grn. EN2: Enf 2F 23
Post La. TW2: Twick 1H 131
Postmark Development EC1
3H 7 (4K 83)
Postmasters Lodge HA5: Pinn 7C 40
Postmill Cl. CR0: C'don 3J 169
Post Office All. W4 6H 97
(off Thames Rd.)
Post Office App. E7 5K 69
Post Office Ct. EC3 1F 15 (6D 84)
(off King William St.)
Post Office Way SW11 7H 101
Post Rd. UB2: S'hall 3F 95
Postway M. IG1: Ilf 3F 71
(not continuous)
Potager Pl. CR0: Bedd 3H 167
Potier St. SE1 3D 102
Potter Cl. CR4: Mitc 2F 155
Potter Cl. SE15 7E 102
Potter Cl. SE2 5A 108
Potter Ho. E1 5K 85
(off Beaufort Gdns.)
Potteries, The EN5: Barn 5D 20
Potterne Cl. SW19 7F 117
Potters Cl. CR0: C'don 1A 170
Potters Ct. SM1: Sutt 6H 165
(off Rosebery Rd.)
Pottersfield EN1: Enf 4K 23
(off Lincoln Rd.)
Potters Flds. SE1 5H 15 (1E 102)
Potters Gro. KT3: N Mald 4J 151
Potters Hgts. Cl. HA5: Pinn 1K 39
Potter's La. SW16 6H 137
Potters La. EN5: New Bar 4D 20
Potters Lodge E14 5E 104
(off Ferry St.)
Potter's Rd. EN5: New Bar 4E 20
Potters Rd. SW6 2A 118
Potters Rd. UB2: S'hall 3E 94
Potters Row E20 5D 68
(off Keirin Rd.)
Potter St. HA5: Pinn 1K 39
Potter St. HA6: Nwood 1J 39
Pottery Café 1H 117
(off Fulham Rd.)
Pottery Cl. SE25 3G 157
Pottery Ga. N11 6C 32
Pottery La. W11 1G 99
Pottery M. SW6 2H 117
Pottery Rd. DA5: Bexl 2J 145
Pottery Rd. TW8: Bford 6E 96
Pottery St. SE16 2H 103
Pott St. E2 3H 85
Poulett Gdns. TW1: Twick 1A 132
Poulett Rd. E6 2D 88
Poulter Pk. 6C 154
Poulters Wood BR2: Kes 5B 172
Poulton Av. SM1: Sutt 3B 166
Poulton Cl. E8 6H 67
Poulton Ho. W3 5K 79
(off Victoria Rd.)
Poultry EC2 1E 14 (6D 84)
Pound Cl. BR6: Orp 2H 173
Pound Cl. KT6: Surb 1C 162
Pound Ct. Dr. BR6: Orp 2H 173
Pound Farm Cl. KT10: Esh 7H 149
Pound Grn. DA5: Bexl 7G 127
Pound La. NW10 6C 62
Pound Pk. Rd. SE7 4B 106
Pound Path E3 2K 85
(off Stoneway Wlk.)
Pound Pl. SE9 6E 124
Pound St. SM5: Cars 5D 166
Pound Way BR7: Chst 7G 143
Pountney Rd. SW11 3E 118
POVEREST 4K 161
Poverest Rd. BR5: St M Cry 5K 161
Povey Ho. SE17 4E 102
(off Beckway St.)
Powder Mill La. TW2: Whitt 7D 112
Powell Cl. HA8: Edg 6A 28
Powell Cl. KT9: Chess 5D 162
Powell Ct. CR2: S Croy 4B 168
(off Bramley Hill)
Powell Ct. E17 3D 50
Powell Dr. E4 4J 25
Powell Gdns. RM10: Dag 4G 73
Powell Ho. EN1: Enf 4K 23
(off Dunstan M.)
Powell Ho. W2 2A 10 (7B 82)
(off Gloucester Ter.)
Powell Rd. E5 3H 67
Powell Rd. IG9: Buck H 1F 37
Powell's Wlk. W4 6A 98
Powergate Bus. Pk. NW10 3K 79
Powerhouse, The 2G 93
Powerhouse La. UB3: Hayes 2G 93
Powerleague Battersea 7G 101
Powerleague Colney Hatch 7K 31
Powerleague Croydon 6K 167
Powerleague Ilford 1K 53
Powerleague Mill Hill 7J 29
Powerleague Newham 3G 89
Powerleague Tottenham 6C 34
Powerleague Wembley 4G 61
Power Rd. W4 4G 97
Powers Ct. TW1: Twick 7D 114
Powerscroft Rd. DA14: Sidc 6C 144
(not continuous)
Powerscroft Rd. E5 4J 67
Powis Ct. W11 6H 81
(off Powis Gdns.)
Powis Ct. WD23: B Hea 1C 26
(off Rutherford Way)
Powis Gdns. NW11 7H 45
Powis Gdns. W11 6H 81
Powis Ho. WC2 7F 7 (6J 83)
(off Macklin St.)
Powis M. W11 6H 81
Powis Pl. WC1 4F 7 (4J 83)
Powis Rd. E3 3D 86
Powis Sq. W11 6H 81
(not continuous)
Powis St. SE18 3E 106
Powis Ter. W11 6H 81
Powlesland Ct. E1 6A 86
(off White Horse Rd.)
Powlett Ho. NW1 6F 65
(off Powlett Pl.)
Powlett Pl. NW1 7E 64
Pownall Gdns. TW3: Houn 4F 113
Pownall Rd. E8 1F 85
Pownall Rd. TW3: Houn 4F 113
Pownell Ter. SE11 6A 102
Pownsett Ter. IG1: Ilf 5G 71
Powster Rd. BR1: Broml 5J 141
Powys Cl. DA7: Bex 6D 108
Powys Ct. N11 5D 32
Powys La. N13 4D 32
Powys La. N14 4D 32
POYLE 4A 174
Poyle Ind. Est. SL3: Poyle 6A 174
Poyle New Cotts. SL3: Poyle 5A 174
Poyle Technical Cen. SL3: Poyle 5A 174
Poyle Trad. Est. SL3: Poyle 6A 174
Poynders Ct. SW4 6G 119
Poynders Gdns. SW4 7G 119
Poynders Pde. SW4 6H 119
Poynders Rd. SW4 6G 119
Poynings, The SL0: Rich P 1A 174
Poynings Rd. N19 3G 65

Providence Twr. – Queen's Ter. Cotts.

Providence Twr. E14 ... 7F **87**
(off Fairmont Av.)
Providence Twr. SE16 ... 2G **103**
(off Bermondsey Wall W.)
Providence Yd. E2 ... 1K **9** (3G **85**)
(off Ezra St.)
Provident Ind. Est. UB3: Hayes ... 2J **93**
Province Dr. SE16 ... 2J **103**
Province Sq. E14 ... 1E **104**
(off Blackwall Way)
Provincial Ter. SE20 ... 7K **139**
Provost Ct. NW3 ... 6D **64**
(off Eton Rd.)
Provost Est. N1 ... 1E **8** (2D **84**)
(off Provost St.)
Provost Rd. NW3 ... 7D **64**
Provost St. N1 ... 1E **8** (2D **84**)
Provost Way RM8: Dag ... 4A **72**
Prowse Av. WD23: B Hea ... 1B **26**
Prowse Ct. N18 ... 5B **34**
(off Lord Graham M.)
Prowse Pl. NW1 ... 7G **65**
Proyers Path HA1: Harr ... 7B **42**
Prudence La. BR6: Farnb ... 4E **172**
Pruden Cl. N14 ... 2B **32**
Prudent Pas. EC2 ... 1D **14** (6C **84**)
(off King St.)
Prusom's Island E1 ... 1J **103**
(off Wapping High St.)
Prusom St. E1 ... 1H **103**
Pryce Ho. E3 ... 3C **86**
(off Campbell Rd.)
Puccinia Ct. TW19: Stanw ... 1A **128**
(off Yeoman Dr.)
Pucknells Cl. BR8: Swan ... 7J **145**
Pudding La. EC3 ... 3F **15** (7D **84**)
Pudding Mill La. E15 ... 1D **86**
Puddle Dock EC4 ... 2A **14** (7B **84**)
(not continuous)
Puffin Cl. BR3: Beck ... 5K **157**
Puffin Cl. IG11: Bark ... 3B **90**
Pugin Cl. SW19 ... 4K **135**
Pugin Ct. N1 ... 7A **66**
(off Liverpool Rd.)
Pulborough Rd. SW18 ... 7H **117**
Pulborough Way TW4: Houn ... 4A **112**
Pulford Rd. N15 ... 6D **48**
Pulham Av. N2 ... 4A **46**
Pulham Ho. SW8 ... 7K **101**
(off Dorset Rd.)
Pullen's Bldgs. SE17 ... 5B **102**
(off Iliffe St.)
Puller Rd. EN5: Barn ... 2B **20**
Pulleyns Av. E6 ... 3C **88**
Pullman Ct. SW2 ... 1J **137**
Pullman Gdns. SW15 ... 6E **116**
Pullman M. SE12 ... 3K **141**
Pullman Pl. SE9 ... 5C **124**
Pulross Rd. SW9 ... 3K **119**
Pulse Apts. NW6 ... 5K **63**
(off Lymington Rd.)
Pulse Ct. RM7: Rush G ... 6K **55**
Pulsford Cl. TW1: Twick ... 7K **113**
Pulteney Cl. E3 ... 1B **86**
Pulteney Cl. TW7: Isle ... 3A **114**
Pulteney Gdns. E18 ... 3J **51**
Pulteney Rd. E18 ... 3K **51**
Pulteney Ter. N1 ... 1K **83**
(not continuous)
Pultney St. N1 ... 1K **83**
Pulton Ho. SE4 ... 4A **122**
(off Turnham Rd.)
Pulton Pl. SW6 ... 7J **99**
Puma Ct. E1 ... 5J **9** (5F **85**)
Pump All. TW8: Bford ... 7D **96**
Pump Cl. UB5: N'olt ... 2E **76**
Pump Ct. EC4 ... 1J **13** (6A **84**)
Pumphandle Path N2 ... 2B **46**
(off Oak La.)
Pump Ho. SE25 ... 4F **157**
Pumphouse, The N8 ... 4K **47**
Pump Ho. Cl. BR2: Broml ... 2G **159**
Pump Ho. Cl. SE16 ... 2J **103**
Pump Ho. Cres. TW8: Bford ... 5E **96**
Pump House Gallery ... 7E **100**
Pump Ho. La. SW11 ... 7C **101**
Pump Ho. M. E1 ... 7G **85**
(off Hooper St.)
Pumping Ho. E14 ... 7F **87**
(off Naval Row)
Pumping Station Rd. W4 ... 7A **98**
Pump La. SE14 ... 7J **103**
Pump La. UB3: Hayes ... 2J **93**
Pump Pail Nth. CR0: C'don ... 3C **168**
Pump Pail Sth. CR0: C'don ... 3C **168**
Punchard Cres. EN3: Enf L ... 1J **25**
Punderson's Gdns. E2 ... 3H **85**
Punjab La. UB1: S'hall ... 1D **94**
Purbeck Av. KT3: N Mald ... 6B **152**
Purbeck Dr. NW2 ... 2F **63**
Purbeck Gdns. SE26 ... 5B **140**
Purbeck Ho. SW8 ... 7K **101**
(off Bolney St.)
Purbrook Est. SE1 ... 7H **15** (2E **102**)
Purbrook St. SE1 ... 7H **15** (3E **102**)
Purcell Cres. SW6 ... 7F **99**
Purcell Ho. EN1: Enf ... 1B **24**
Purcell Ho. SW10 ... 6B **100**
(off Milman's St.)
Purcell Mans. W14 ... 6G **99**
(off Queen's Club Gdns.)
Purcell M. NW10 ... 7A **62**
Purcell Rd. UB6: G'frd ... 5F **77**
Purcell Room ... 4H **13** (1K **101**)
(in Southbank Cen.)
Purcells Av. HA8: Edg ... 5B **28**
Purcell St. N1 ... 2E **84**
Purchese St. NW1 ... 2H **83**
Purday Ho. W10 ... 3G **81**
(off Bruckner St.)
Purdon Ho. SE15 ... 1G **121**
(off Oliver Goldsmith Est.)
Purdy Ct. KT4: Wor Pk ... 2C **164**
Purdy St. E3 ... 4D **86**
PureGym Aldgate ... 7J **9** (6F **85**)
(off Houndsditch)
PureGym Bayswater ... 7K **81**
(off Moscow Pl.)
PureGym Canary Wharf ... 7C **86**
PureGym Croydon ... 2C **168**
(off Crown Hill)
PureGym East India Dock ... 7E **86**
(off Clove Cres.)
PureGym Edgware ... 6B **28**
PureGym Finchley ... 2K **45**
PureGym Hallam St. ... 5K **5** (5F **83**)
(off Hallam St.)
PureGym Hammersmith Palais ... 4E **98**
PureGym Holborn ... 5G **7** (5K **83**)
(off Theobald's Rd.)
PureGym Limehouse ... 6A **86**
PureGym London Wall ... 6E **8** (5D **84**)
(off London Wall)
PureGym Marylebone, Balcombe St.
... 5E **4** (5D **82**)
PureGym Muswell Hill ... 4F **47**
PureGym New Barnet ... 4G **21**
PureGym Northolt ... 1E **76**
PureGym Piccadilly ... 4C **12** (1H **101**)
(off Regent St.)
PureGym Putney ... 4G **117**
PureGym South Kensington
... 3C **16** (4C **100**)
PureGym Southgate ... 1C **32**
PureGym St Pauls ... 6C **8** (5C **84**)
(off Little Britain)
PureGym Sydenham ... 4J **139**
PureGym Tower Hill ... 2J **15** (7F **85**)
(off America Sq.)
PureGym Wembley ... 5E **60**
Purelake M. SE13 ... 3F **123**
(off Marischal Rd.)
Purkis Cl. UB8: Hil ... 7E **74**
Purland Cl. RM8: Dag ... 1F **73**
Purland Rd. SE28 ... 2K **107**
(not continuous)
Purleigh Av. IG8: Wfd G ... 6H **37**
Purley Av. NW2 ... 2G **63**
Purley Cl. IG5: Ilf ... 2E **52**
Purley Pl. N1 ... 7B **66**
Purley Rd. CR2: S Croy ... 7D **168**
Purley Rd. N9 ... 3K **33**
Purley Vw. Ter. CR2: S Croy ... 7D **168**
(off Sanderstead Rd.)
Purley Way CR0: C'don ... 7K **155**
Purley Way CR0: Wadd ... 7K **155**
Purley Way Cen., The ... 2A **168**
Purley Way Cres. CR0: C'don ... 7K **155**
Purneys Rd. SE9 ... 4B **124**
Purrett Rd. SE18 ... 5K **107**
Purser Ho. SW2 ... 6A **120**
Pursers Cross Rd. SW6 ... 1H **117**
Pursewardens Cl. W13 ... 1C **96**
Pursley Rd. NW7 ... 7J **29**
Purves Rd. NW10 ... 3D **80**
Purvis Ho. CR0: C'don ... 7D **156**
Pusey Ho. E14 ... 6C **86**
(off Saracen St.)
Puteaux Ho. E2 ... 2K **85**
(off Mace St.)
PUTNEY ... 4F **117**
Putney Arts Theatre ... 4F **117**
PUTNEY BRI. ... 3G **117**
Putney Bri. App. SW6 ... 3G **117**
Putney Bri. Rd. SW15 ... 4G **117**
Putney Bri. Rd. SW18 ... 4J **117**
Putney Comn. SW15 ... 3E **116**
Putney Exchange (Shop. Cen.) ... 4F **117**
Putney Gdns. RM6: Chad H ... 5B **54**
Putney Heath SW15 ... 7D **116**
PUTNEY HEATH ... 6E **116**
Putney Heath La. SW15 ... 6F **117**
Putney High St. SW15 ... 4F **117**
Putney Hill SW15 ... 7F **117**
(not continuous)
Putney Leisure Cen. ... 4E **116**
Putney Pk. Av. SW15 ... 4C **116**
Putney Pk. La. SW15 ... 4D **116**
(not continuous)
PUTNEY VALE ... 3C **134**
Putney Va. Crematorium ... 2D **134**
Putney Wharf SW15 ... 3G **117**
Putt in the Pk. ... 4H **117**
Pycroft Way N9 ... 4A **34**
Pyecombe Cnr. N12 ... 4C **30**
Pylbrook Rd. SM1: Sutt ... 3J **165**
Pylon Way CR0: Bedd ... 1J **167**
Pym Cl. EN4: E Barn ... 5G **21**
Pymers Mead SE21 ... 1C **138**
Pymmes Brook Dr. EN4: E Barn ... 4H **21**
Pymmes Brook Ho. N10 ... 7K **31**
Pymmes Cl. N13 ... 5E **32**
Pymmes Cl. N17 ... 1H **49**
Pymmes Gdns. Nth. N9 ... 3A **34**
Pymmes Gdns. Sth. N9 ... 3A **34**
Pymmes Grn. Rd. N11 ... 4A **32**
Pymmes Rd. N13 ... 6D **32**
Pynchester Cl. UB10: Ick ... 2C **56**
Pyne Rd. KT6: Surb ... 1G **163**
Pyne Ter. SW19 ... 1G **135**
(off Windlesham Gro.)
Pynfolds SE16 ... 2H **103**
Pynham Cl. SE2 ... 3B **108**
Pynnacles Cl. HA7: Stan ... 5G **27**
Pynnersmead SE24 ... 5C **120**
Pyramid Ct. KT1: King T ... 2F **151**
(off Cambridge Rd.)
Pyramid Ho. TW4: Houn ... 2C **112**
Pyrland Rd. N5 ... 5D **66**
Pyrland Rd. TW10: Rich ... 6F **115**
Pyrmont Gro. SE27 ... 3B **138**
Pyrmont Rd. W4 ... 6G **97**
Pytchley Cres. SE19 ... 6C **138**
Pytchley Rd. SE22 ... 3E **120**

Q

Q Bldg., The E15 ... 6G **69**
(off The Grove)
QPR Training Academy & Sports Complex ... 3H **95**
Quad Ct. SE1 ... 3E **102**
(off Grigg's Pl.)
Quadrangle, The E15 ... 6G **69**
Quadrangle, The SE24 ... 5C **120**
Quadrangle, The SW10 ... 1A **118**
Quadrangle, The SW6 ... 7G **99**
Quadrangle, The W2 ... 7C **4** (6C **82**)
Quadrangle Cl. SE1 ... 4E **102**
Quadrangle M. HA7: Stan ... 7H **27**
Quadrant, The DA7: Bex ... 7D **108**
Quadrant, The HA2: Harr ... 3H **41**
Quadrant, The HA8: Edg ... 6B **28**
(off Manor Pk. Cres.)
Quadrant, The SM2: Sutt ... 6A **166**
Quadrant, The SW20 ... 1G **153**
Quadrant, The TW9: Rich ... 4D **114**
Quadrant, The W10 ... 3F **81**
Quadrant Arc. W1 ... 3B **12** (7G **83**)
(off Regent St.)
Quadrant Bus. Cen. NW6 ... 1G **81**
Quadrant Cl. NW4 ... 5D **44**
Quadrant Ct. HA9: Wemb ... 4F **61**
Quadrant Gro. NW5 ... 5D **64**
Quadrant Ho. E1 ... 7G **85**
(off Nesham St.)
Quadrant Ho. E15 ... 3G **87**
(off Durban Rd.)
Quadrant Ho. SE1 ... 4A **14** (1B **102**)
(off Burrell St.)
Quadrant Rd. CR7: Thor H ... 4B **156**
Quadrant Rd. TW9: Rich ... 4D **114**
Quadrant Wlk. E14 ... 3D **104**
(off Lanterns Way)
Quad Rd. HA9: Wemb ... 3D **60**
Quaggy Wlk. SE3 ... 4J **123**
Quain Mans. W14 ... 6G **99**
(off Queen's Club Gdns.)
Quainton St. NW10 ... 3K **61**
Quaker Ct. E1 ... 4J **9** (4F **85**)
(off Quaker St.)
Quaker Ct. EC1 ... 3D **8** (4C **84**)
(off Banner St.)
Quaker La. UB2: S'hall ... 3E **94**
Quakers Course NW9 ... 1B **44**
Quakers La. TW7: Isle ... 7A **96**
Quakers Pl. E7 ... 5B **70**
Quaker St. E1 ... 4J **9** (4F **85**)
Quakers Wlk. N21 ... 5J **23**
Quality Ct. WC2 ... 7J **7** (6A **84**)
(off Chancery La.)
Quant Bldg. E17 ... 4C **50**
Quantock Cl. UB3: Harl ... 7F **93**
Quantock Dr. KT4: Wor Pk ... 2E **164**
Quantock Gdns. NW2 ... 2F **63**
Quantock Ho. N16 ... 1F **67**
Quantock M. SE15 ... 2G **121**
Quantum Ct. E1 ... 7J **85**
(off King David La.)
Quarles Pk. Rd. RM6: Chad H ... 6B **54**
Quarrendon St. SW6 ... 2J **117**
Quarr Rd. SM5: Cars ... 6B **154**
Quarry Pk. Rd. SM1: Sutt ... 6H **165**
Quarry Ri. SM1: Sutt ... 6H **165**
Quarry Rd. SW18 ... 6A **118**
Quarterdeck, The E14 ... 2C **104**
Quarter Ho. SW18 ... 4A **118**
Quartermaster La. NW7 ... 5B **30**
Quarters Apts. CR0: C'don ... 2D **168**
(off Wellesley Rd.)
Quartz Apts. SE14 ... 6A **104**
(off Moulding La.)
Quartz Ho. HA2: Harr ... 1E **58**
Quastel Ho. SE1 ... 7E **14** (2D **102**)
(off Long La.)
Quatre Ports E4 ... 5A **36**
Quay Ho. E14 ... 2C **104**
(off Admirals Way)
Quayle Cres. N20 ... 2F **31**
Quayle Rd. IG11: Bark ... 2F **89**
Quayside Cotts. E1 ... 4K **15** (1G **103**)
(off Mews St.)
Quayside Ct. SE16 ... 1K **103**
(off Abbotshade Rd.)
Quayside Ho. E14 ... 1B **104**
Quayside Ho. E16 ... 6H **87**
(off Tarling Rd.)
Quayside Ho. TW8: Bford ... 6F **97**
Quayside Ho. W10 ... 4G **81**
Quayside Wlk. KT1: King T ... 2D **150**
(off Wadbrook St.)
Quay Vw. Apts. E14 ... 3C **104**
(off Arden Cres.)
Quebec M. W1 ... 1F **11** (6D **82**)
Quebec Rd. IG1: Ilf ... 7F **53**
Quebec Rd. IG2: Ilf ... 7G **53**
Quebec Rd. UB4: Yead ... 6A **76**
Quebec Way SE16 ... 2K **103**
Quebec Wharf E14 ... 6B **86**
Quebec Wharf E8 ... 1E **84**
(off Kingsland Rd.)
Quedgeley Ct. SE15 ... 6F **103**
(off Ebley Cl.)
Queen Adelaide Ct. SE20 ... 6J **139**
Queen Adelaide Rd. SE20 ... 6J **139**
Queen Alexandra Mans. WC1
... 2E **6** (3J **83**)
(off Bidborough St.)
Queen Alexandra's Ct. SW19 ... 5H **135**
Queen Anne Av. BR2: Broml ... 3H **159**
Queen Anne Ga. DA7: Bex ... 3D **126**
Queen Anne Ho. E16 ... 1J **105**
(off Hardy Av.)
Queen Anne M. W1 ... 6J **5** (5F **83**)
Queen Anne Rd. E9 ... 6K **67**
Queen Anne's Cl. TW2: Twick ... 3H **131**
Queen Anne's Ct. SE10 ... 5F **105**
(off Park Row)
Queen Anne's Gdns. CR4: Mitc ... 3D **154**
Queen Anne's Gdns. EN1: Enf ... 6K **23**
Queen Anne's Gdns. W4 ... 3A **98**
Queen Anne's Gdns. W5 ... 2E **96**
Queen Anne's Ga. SW1 ... 7C **12** (2H **101**)
Queen Anne's Gro. EN1: Enf ... 7J **23**
Queen Anne's Gro. W4 ... 3A **98**
Queen Anne's Gro. W5 ... 2E **96**
Queen Anne's Pl. EN1: Enf ... 6K **23**
Queen Annes Sq. SE1 ... 4G **103**
(off Monnow Rd.)
Queen Anne St. W1 ... 7J **5** (6F **83**)
Queen Anne Ter. E1 ... 7H **85**
(off Sovereign Cl.)
Queenborough Gdns. BR7: Chst ... 6H **143**
Queenborough Gdns. IG2: Ilf ... 4E **52**
Queen Caroline's Temple
... 5A **10** (1B **100**)
Queen Caroline St. W6 ... 5E **98**
Queen Catherine Ho. SW6 ... 7K **99**
(off Wandon Rd.)
Queen Charlotte's Cottage ... 2D **114**
Queen Ct. WC1 ... 4F **7** (4J **83**)
(off Queen Sq.)
Queen Elizabeth II Stadium ... 2A **24**
Queen Elizabeth Bldgs.
EC4 ... 2J **13** (7A **84**)
(off Middle Temple La.)
Queen Elizabeth Ct. EN5: Barn ... 3D **20**
Queen Elizabeth Gdns. SM4: Mord
... 4J **153**
Queen Elizabeth Hall ... 4H **13** (1K **101**)
Queen Elizabeth Ho. SW12 ... 7E **118**
Queen Elizabeth Leisure Cen. ... 4C **20**
Queen Elizabeth II Conference Cen.
... 7D **12** (2H **101**)
Queen Elizabeth Olympic Pk. ... 7D **68**
Queen Elizabeth Rd. E17 ... 3A **50**
Queen Elizabeth Rd. KT2: King T ... 2F **151**
Queen Elizabeth's Cl. N16 ... 2D **66**
Queen Elizabeth's Coll. SE10 ... 7E **104**
Queen Elizabeth's Dr. CR0: New Ad
... 7F **171**
Queen Elizabeth's Dr. N14 ... 1D **32**
Queen Elizabeth's Hunting Lodge ... 1C **36**
Queen Elizabeth St. SE1 ... 6H **15** (2E **102**)
Queen Elizabeth's Wlk. N16 ... 1D **66**
Queen Elizabeth's Wlk. SM6: Bedd
... 4H **167**
Queen Elizabeth Wlk. SW13 ... 1C **116**
Queenhithe EC4 ... 2D **14** (7C **84**)
Queen Isabella Way EC1 ... 7B **8** (6B **84**)
(off King Edward St.)
Queen Margaret Flats E2 ... 3H **85**
(off St Jude's Rd.)
Queen Margaret's Gro. N1 ... 5E **66**
Queen Mary Av. E18 ... 1J **51**
Queen Mary Av. SM4: Mord ... 5F **153**
Queen Mary Cl. KT6: Surb ... 3G **163**
Queen Mary Ct. TW19: Stanw ... 1A **128**
Queen Mary Ho. E16 ... 1K **105**
(off Wesley Av.)
Queen Mary Ho. E18 ... 1K **51**
Queen Mary Rd. SE19 ... 6B **138**
Queen Mary Rd. TW17: Shep ... 2E **146**
Queen Mary's Av. SM5: Cars ... 7D **166**
Queen Marys Bldgs. SW1
... 3B **18** (4G **101**)
(off Stillington St.)
Queen Mary's Ct. SE10 ... 6F **105**
(off Park Row)
Queen Mary's Ho. SW15 ... 6C **116**
Queen Mary University of London Charterhouse Sq. ... 4B **8** (4B **84**)
Queen Mary University of London Lincoln's Inn Flds. Campus
... 7G **7** (6K **83**)
(off Remnant St.)
Queen Mary University of London Mile End Campus ... 4A **86**
Queen Mary University of London W. Smithfield Campus ... 6B **8** (5B **84**)
(off Giltspur St.)
Queen Mother Sports Cen., The
... 3A **18** (4G **101**)
(off Vauxhall Bri. Rd.)
Queen of Denmark Ct. SE16 ... 3B **104**
Queens Acre SM3: Cheam ... 7F **165**
Queen's Av. UB6: G'frd ... 6F **77**
Queens Av. HA7: Stan ... 3C **42**
Queens Av. IG8: Wfd G ... 5E **36**
Queens Av. N10 ... 3E **46**
Queens Av. N20 ... 2G **31**
Queens Av. N21 ... 1G **33**
Queens Av. N3 ... 7J **31**
Queens Av. TW13: Hanw ... 4A **130**
Queensberry Ho. TW9: Rich ... 5C **114**
Queensberry M. W. SW7 ... 3A **16** (4B **100**)
Queensberry Pl. E12 ... 5B **70**
Queensberry Pl. SW7 ... 3A **16** (4B **100**)
Queensberry Pl. TW9: Rich ... 5D **114**
(off Friars La.)
Queensberry Way SW7 ... 3A **16** (4B **100**)
Queensborough Ct. N3 ... 4H **45**
(off Tillingbourne Gdns.)
Queensborough M. W2 ... 7A **82**
Queensborough Pas. W2 ... 7A **82**
(off Queensborough M.)
Queensborough Studios W2 ... 7A **82**
(off Queensborough M.)
Queensborough Ter. W2 ... 7K **81**
Queensbridge Ct. E2 ... 1F **85**
(off Queensbridge Rd.)
Queensbridge Pk. TW7: Isle ... 5J **113**
Queensbridge Rd. E2 ... 1F **85**
Queensbridge Rd. E8 ... 6F **67**
Queensbridge Sports & Community Cen. ... 7F **67**
QUEENSBURY ... 3E **42**
Queensbury Circ. Pde. HA3: Kenton
... 3E **42**
Queensbury Circ. Pde. HA7: Kenton
... 3E **42**
Queensbury Rd. HA0: Wemb ... 2F **79**
Queensbury Rd. NW9 ... 7K **43**
Queensbury Sta. Pde. HA8: Edg ... 3F **43**
Queensbury St. N1 ... 7C **66**
Queen's Cir. SW11 ... 7F **101**
Queens Cl. HA8: Edg ... 5B **28**
Queens Cl. SM6: W'gton ... 5F **167**
Queen's Club Gdns. W14 ... 6G **99**
Queen's Club (Tennis Courts), The
... 5G **99**
Queens Club Ter. W14 ... 6H **99**
(off Normand Rd.)
Queen's Ct. NW8 ... 2B **82**
(off Queen's Ter.)
Queens Ct. CR2: S Croy ... 5C **168**
(off Warham Rd.)
Queens Ct. CR7: Thor H ... 5A **156**
Queens Ct. E11 ... 7G **51**
Queens Ct. HA3: Kenton ... 2B **42**
Queens Ct. IG9: Buck H ... 2G **37**
Queens Ct. NW11 ... 5H **45**
Queens Ct. NW6 ... 5K **63**
Queens Ct. SE16 ... 7K **15** (3F **103**)
(off Old Jamaica Rd.)
Queens Ct. SE23 ... 2J **139**
Queens Ct. TW10: Rich ... 6F **115**
Queens Ct. W2 ... 7K **81**
(off Queensway)
Queenscourt HA9: Wemb ... 4E **60**
Queen's Cres. NW5 ... 6E **64**
Queen's Cres. TW10: Rich ... 5F **115**
Queenscroft Rd. SE9 ... 5B **124**
Queensdale Cres. W11 ... 1F **99**
(not continuous)
Queensdale Pl. W11 ... 1G **99**
Queensdale Rd. W11 ... 1F **99**
Queensdale Wlk. W11 ... 1G **99**
Queen's Diamond Jubilee Galleries, The
... 1E **18** (3J **101**)
Queensdown Rd. E5 ... 4H **67**
Queens Dr. KT5: Surb ... 7G **151**
Queen's Dr. KT7: T Ditt ... 6A **150**
Queen's Dr. N4 ... 2B **66**
Queens Dr. E10 ... 7C **50**
Queens Dr. W3 ... 6F **79**
Queens Dr. W5 ... 6F **79**
Queen's Elm Pde. SW3 ... 5B **16** (5B **100**)
(off Old Church St.)
Queen's Elm Sq. SW3 ... 6B **16** (5B **100**)
Queensferry Wlk. N17 ... 4H **49**
Queensfield Ct. SM3: Cheam ... 4E **164**
Queen's Gallery ... 7K **11** (2F **101**)
Queen's Gdns. NW4 ... 5E **44**
Queen's Gdns. RM13: Rain ... 2K **91**
Queen's Gdns. TW5: Hest ... 1C **112**
Queen's Gdns. W2 ... 7A **82**
Queen's Gdns. W5 ... 4C **78**
Queen's Ga. SW7 ... 7A **10** (2A **100**)
Queensgate Ct. N12 ... 5E **30**
Queens Ga. Gdns. SW7 ... 3A **100**
Queens Ga. Gdns. BR7: Chst ... 1H **161**
Queens Ga. Gdns. SW15 ... 4D **116**
Queensgate Ho. E3 ... 2B **86**
(off Hereford Rd.)
Queen's Ga. M. SW7 ... 3A **100**
Queensgate M. BR3: Beck ... 1A **158**
Queen's Ga. Pl. SW7 ... 3A **100**
Queensgate Pl. NW6 ... 7J **63**
Queen's Ga. Pl. M. SW7 ... 2A **16** (3A **100**)
Queen's Ga. Ter. SW7 ... 3A **100**
Queens Ga. Vs. E9 ... 7A **68**
Queen's Gro. NW8 ... 1B **82**
Queens Gro. Rd. E4 ... 1A **36**
Queen's Gro. Studios NW8 ... 1B **82**
Queen's Head Pas. EC4 ... 7C **8** (6C **84**)
Queen's Head St. N1 ... 1B **84**
Queen's Head Yd. SE1 ... 5E **14** (1D **102**)
(off Borough High St.)
Queens Ho. SE17 ... 6D **102**
(off Merrow St.)
Queens Ho. SW8 ... 7J **101**
(off Sth. Lambeth Rd.)
Queens Ho. TW11: Tedd ... 6K **131**
Queens Ho. W2 ... 7K **81**
(off Queensway)
Queen's House, The ... 6F **105**
(within National Maritime Mus.)
Queenshurst Sq. KT2: King T ... 1E **150**
Queen's Ice & Bowl ... 7K **81**
Queen's Keep TW1: Twick ... 6C **114**
Queensland Av. N18 ... 6H **33**
Queensland Av. SW19 ... 1K **153**
Queensland Cl. E17 ... 2B **50**
Queensland Ho. E16 ... 1E **106**
(off Rymill St.)
Queensland Rd. N7 ... 4A **66**
Queens La. N10 ... 3F **47**
Queen's Mans. W6 ... 4F **99**
(off Brook Grn.)
Queen's Mkt. E13 ... 1A **88**
Queens Mead HA8: Edg ... 6A **28**
Queensmead NW8 ... 1B **82**
Queens Mead Rd. BR2: Broml
... 2H **159**
Queensmead Sports Cen. ... 5B **58**
Queensmere Cl. SW19 ... 2F **135**
Queensmere Ct. SW13 ... 7B **98**
Queensmere Rd. SW19 ... 2F **135**
Queen's M. W2 ... 7K **81**
Queensmill Rd. SW6 ... 7F **99**
Queen's Pde. N11 ... 5J **31**
(off Friern Barnet Rd.)
Queen's Pde. NW2 ... 6E **62**
(off Willesden La.)
Queens Pde. N8 ... 4B **48**
Queens Pde. NW4 ... 5E **44**
(off Queens Rd.)
Queens Pde. W5 ... 6F **79**
Queen's Pde. Cl. N11 ... 5J **31**
QUEENS PARK ... 2G **81**
Queens Pk. Ct. W10 ... 3F **81**
Queen's Pk. Gdns. TW13: Felt ... 3H **129**
Queen's Pk. Rangers FC ... 1D **98**
Queens Pas. BR7: Chst ... 6F **143**
Queens Pl. SM4: Mord ... 4J **153**
Queen's Prom. KT1: King T ... 4D **150**
Queen's Prom. KT1: Surb ... 4D **150**
Queen Sq. WC1 ... 4F **7** (4J **83**)
Queen Sq. Pl. WC1 ... 4F **7** (4J **83**)
(off Queen Sq.)
Queen's Quay EC4 ... 2D **14** (7C **84**)
(off Up. Thames St.)
Queens Reach KT1: King T ... 2D **150**
Queens Reach KT8: E Mos ... 4J **149**
Queens Ride SW13 ... 3C **116**
Queens Ri. TW10: Rich ... 6F **115**
Queen's Rd. CR4: Mitc ... 3B **154**
Queen's Rd. DA16: Well ... 2B **126**
Queen's Rd. E17 ... 6B **50**
Queen's Rd. EN1: Enf ... 4K **23**
Queen's Rd. IG9: Buck H ... 2E **36**
Queen's Rd. KT7: T Ditt ... 5K **149**
Queen's Rd. SE14 ... 1J **121**
Queen's Rd. SE15 ... 1H **121**
Queen's Rd. SW14 ... 3K **115**
Queen's Rd. TW10: Rich ... 7F **115**
Queen's Rd. TW11: Tedd ... 6K **131**
Queen's Rd. TW12: Hamp H ... 4F **131**
Queen's Rd. TW13: Felt ... 1K **129**
Queen's Rd. TW3: Houn ... 3F **113**
Queen's Rd. W5 ... 6E **78**
Queens Rd. BR1: Broml ... 2J **159**
Queens Rd. BR3: Beck ... 2A **158**
Queens Rd. BR7: Chst ... 6F **143**
Queens Rd. CR0: C'don ... 6B **156**
Queens Rd. E11 ... 7F **51**
Queens Rd. E13 ... 1K **87**
Queens Rd. EN5: Barn ... 3A **20**
Queens Rd. IG11: Bark ... 6G **71**
Queens Rd. KT2: King T ... 7G **133**
Queens Rd. KT3: N Mald ... 4B **152**
Queens Rd. N11 ... 7D **32**
Queens Rd. N3 ... 1A **46**
Queens Rd. N9 ... 3C **34**
Queens Rd. NW4 ... 5E **44**
Queens Rd. SM4: Mord ... 4J **153**
Queens Rd. SM6: W'gton ... 5F **167**
Queens Rd. SW19 ... 6H **135**
Queens Rd. TW1: Twick ... 1A **132**
Queens Rd. UB2: S'hall ... 2B **94**
Queens Rd. UB3: Hayes ... 6G **75**
Queens Rd. UB7: W Dray ... 2B **92**
Queens Rd. Est. EN5: Barn ... 3A **20**
Queens Rd. W. E13 ... 2J **87**
Queens Row SE17 ... 6D **102**
Queens St. TW15: Ashf ... 4B **128**
Queen's Ter. E13 ... 1K **87**
Queen's Ter. NW8 ... 1B **82**
Queens Ter. E1 ... 4J **85**
(off Cephas St.)
Queens Ter. KT7: T Ditt ... 6A **150**
(off Queens Dr.)
Queens Ter. TW7: Isle ... 4A **114**
Queen's Ter. Cotts. W7 ... 2J **95**

274 A–Z London

Queen's Theatre London – Ravensbourne Ho.

Queen's Theatre London 2C 12 (7H 83)
(off Shaftesbury Av.)
Queensthorpe M. SE26 4K 139
Queensthorpe Rd. SE26 4K 139
Queen's Tower 1A 16 (3B 100)
(within Imperial College London)
Queenstown M. SW8 2F 119
Queenstown Rd. SW11 7J 17 (6F 101)
Queenstown Rd. SW8 1F 119
Queen St. CR0: C'don 4C 168
Queen St. DA7: Bex 3F 127
Queen St. EC4 2D 14 (7C 84)
(not continuous)
Queen St. N17 6K 33
Queen St. RM7: Rom 6K 55
Queen St. W1 4J 11 (1F 101)
Queen St. Pl. EC4 3D 14 (7C 84)
Queensville Rd. SW12 7H 119
Queen's Wlk. SW1 Green Pk.
5A 12 (1G 101)
Queen's Wlk. N5 Highbury 5B 66
Queen's Wlk. W5 4C 78
Queens Wlk. E4 1A 36
Queens Wlk. HA1: Harr 4J 41
Queens Wlk. HA4: Ruis 2A 58
Queens Wlk. NW9 2J 61
Queen's Wlk., The SE1 4H 13 (1K 101)
Queens Wlk. Ter. HA4: Ruis 3A 58
Queens Way NW4 5E 44
Queens Way TW13: Hanw 4A 130
Queensway BR4: W W'ck 3G 171
Queensway BR5: Pet W 5G 161
Queensway CR0: Wadd 6K 167
Queensway EN3: Pond E 4C 24
Queensway TW16: Sun 2K 147
Queensway W2 6K 81
Queensway Bus. Cen. EN3: Pond E 4C 24
Queensway Ind. Est. EN3: Pond E 4D 24
Queensway M. SE6 4E 140
(off Whitefoot La.)
Queenswell Av. N20 3H 31
Queenswood Av. CR7: Thor H 5A 156
Queenswood Av. E17 1E 50
Queenswood Av. SM6: Bedd 4H 167
Queenswood Av. TW12: Hamp 6F 131
Queenswood Av. TW3: Houn 2D 112
Queenswood Ct. KT2: King T 1G 151
Queenswood Ct. SE27 4D 138
Queenswood Ct. SW4 5J 119
Queenswood Gdns. E11 1K 69
Queenswood Pk. N3 2G 45
Queens Wood Rd. N10 6F 47
Queenswood Rd. DA15: Sidc 5K 125
Queenswood Rd. SE23 3K 139
Queen's Yd. WC1 5B 6 (5G 83)
Queens Yd. E9 6C 68
QUEEN VICTORIA 4F 165
Queen Victoria Av. HA0: Wemb 7D 60
Queen Victoria Memorial
7A 12 (2G 101)
Queen Victoria Seaman's Rest E14 6D 86
(off E. India Dock Rd.)
Queen Victoria Statue 1K 99
Queen Victoria St. EC4 2A 14 (7B 84)
Queen Victoria Ter. E1 7H 85
(off Sovereign Cl.)
Quemerford Rd. N7 5K 65
Quendon Ho. W10 4E 80
(off Sutton Way)
Quenington Ct. SE15 6F 103
Quentin Ho. SE1 6A 14 (2B 102)
(off Chaplin Cl.)
Quentin Pl. SE13 3G 123
Quentin Rd. SE13 3G 123
Quernmore Cl. BR1: Broml 6J 141
Quernmore Rd. BR1: Broml 6J 141
Quernmore Rd. N4 6A 48
Querrin St. SW6 2A 118
Quest, The W11 7G 81
(off Clarendon Rd.)
Quested Ct. E8 5H 67
(off Brett Rd.)
Questors Theatre, The 7C 78
Quex Ct. NW6 1K 81
(off West End La.)
Quex M. NW6 1J 81
Quex Rd. NW6 1J 81
Quiberon Ct. E13 1J 87
(off Pelly Rd.)
Quiberon Ct. TW16: Sun 3J 147
Quick Rd. W4 5A 98
Quicks Rd. SW19 7K 135
Quick St. N1 2B 84
Quick St. M. N1 2B 84
Quickswood NW3 7C 64
Quiet Nook BR2: Hayes 3B 172
Quill Ho. E2 3K 9 (4G 85)
(off Cheshire St.)
Quill La. SW15 4F 117
Quill St. N4 3A 66
Quill St. W5 3E 78
Quilp St. SE1 6C 14 (2C 102)
(not continuous)
Quilters Pl. SE9 1G 143
Quilter St. E2 1K 9 (3G 85)
Quilter St. SE18 5K 107
Quilting Ct. SE16 2K 103
(off Garter Way)
Quince Ho. SE13 2D 122
(off Quince Rd.)
Quince Rd. SE13 2D 122
Quinn Cl. E2 2J 85
Quinnell Cl. SE18 5K 107
Quintain Ho. KT1: King T 2D 150
(off Wood St.)
Quintet, The KT12: Walt T 7J 147
Quintin Av. SW20 1H 153
Quintin Cl. HA5: Eastc 4K 39
Quinton Cl. BR3: Beck 3E 158
Quinton Cl. SM6: W'gton 4F 167
Quinton Cl. TW5: Cran 7K 93
Quinton Ct. SE16 4A 104
(off Plough Way)
Quinton Ho. SW8 7J 101
(off Wyvil Rd.)
Quinton Rd. KT7: T Ditt 1A 162
Quinton St. SW18 2A 136
Quixley St. E14 7F 87
Quorn Rd. SE22 4E 120

R

Rabbit Row W8 1J 99
Rabbits Rd. E12 4C 70
Rabournmead Dr. UB5: N'olt 5C 58
Raby Rd. KT3: N Mald 4K 151
Raby St. E14 6A 86
Raccoon Way TW4: Houn 2A 112
Rachel Cl. IG6: Ilf 3H 53
Racine SE5 1E 120
(off Sceaux Gdns.)
Rackham Cl. DA16: Well 2B 126
Rackham M. SW16 6G 137
Rackstraw Ho. NW3 7D 64
Racton Rd. SW6 6J 99
RADA Chenies St. 5C 6 (5H 83)
(off Chenies St.)
RADA Gower St. 5D 6 (5H 83)
(off Gower St.)
RADA Studios 5C 6 (5H 83)
(off Chenies St.)
Radbourne Av. W5 4C 96
Radbourne Cl. E5 4K 67
Radbourne Ct. HA3: Kenton 6B 42
Radbourne Cres. E17 2F 51
Radbourne Rd. SW12 7G 119
Radcliff Ct. E3 4B 86
(off Jospeh St.)
Radcliffe Av. EN2: Enf 1H 23
Radcliffe Av. NW10 2C 80
Radcliffe Gdns. SM5: Cars 7C 166
Radcliffe Ho. SE16 4H 103
(off Anchor St.)
Radcliffe Ho. SE20 1G 157
Radcliffe M. TW12: Hamp H 5G 131
Radcliffe Path SW8 2F 119
Radcliffe Rd. CR0: C'don 2F 169
Radcliffe Rd. HA3: W'stone 2A 42
Radcliffe Rd. N21 1G 33
Radcliffe Rd. SE1 3E 102
Radcliffe Sq. SW15 6F 117
Radcliffe Way UB5: N'olt 3B 76
Radcot Point SE23 3K 139
Radcot St. SE11 6K 19 (5A 102)
Raddington Rd. W10 5G 81
Raddon Twr. E8 6F 67
(off Dalston Sq.)
Radfield Way DA15: Sidc 7H 125
Radford Ct. SE15 7H 103
(off Old Kent Rd.)
Radford Est. NW10 3A 80
Radford Ho. E14 5D 86
(off St Leonard's Rd.)
Radford Ho. N7 5K 65
Radford Rd. SE13 6E 122
Radford Way IG11: Bark 3K 89
Radio La. RM8: Dag 3B 72
Radipole Rd. SW6 1H 117
Radisson Ct. SE1 7G 15 (3E 102)
(off Long La.)
Radius Apts. N1 1G 7 (2K 83)
(off Omega Pl.)
Radius Pk. TW14: Felt 4H 111
Radland Rd. E16 6H 87
Radleigh Pl. BR3: Beck 6C 140
Radlet Av. SE26 3H 139
Radlett Cl. E7 6H 69
Radlett Pl. NW8 1C 82
Radley Av. IG3: Bark 4A 72
Radley Av. IG3: Ilf 4A 72
Radley Cl. TW14: Felt 1H 129
Radley Ct. SE16 2K 103
Radley Gdns. HA3: Kenton 4E 42
Radley Ho. NW1 3E 4 (4D 82)
(off Gloucester Pl.)
Radley Ho. SE2 2D 108
(off Wolvercote Rd.)
Radley M. W8 3J 99
Radley Rd. N17 2E 48
Radley's La. E18 2J 51
Radleys Mead RM10: Dag 6H 73
Radley Sq. E5 2J 67
Radley Ter. E16 5H 87
(off Hermit Rd.)
Radlix Rd. E10 1C 68
Radnor Av. DA16: Well 5B 126
Radnor Av. HA1: Harr 5J 41
Radnor Cl. BR7: Chst 6J 143
Radnor Cl. CR4: Mitc 4J 155
Radnor Ct. HA3: Hrw W 1K 41
Radnor Ct. W7 6K 77
(off Copley Cl.)
Radnor Cres. IG4: Ilf 5D 52
Radnor Cres. SE18 7A 108
Radnor Gdns. EN1: Enf 1K 23
Radnor Gdns. TW1: Twick 2K 131
Radnor Gro. UB10: Hil 2C 74
Radnor Ho. EC1 2D 8 (3C 84)
(off Radnor St.)
Radnor Ho. SW16 2K 155
Radnor Lodge W2 1B 10 (6B 82)
(off Sussex Pl.)
Radnor M. W2 1B 10 (6B 82)
Radnor Pl. W2 1C 10 (6C 82)
Radnor Rd. HA1: Harr 5H 41
Radnor Rd. NW6 1G 81
Radnor Rd. SE15 7G 103
Radnor Rd. TW1: Twick 2K 131
Radnor St. EC1 2D 8 (3C 84)
Radnor Ter. SM2: Sutt 7J 165
Radnor Ter. W14 4H 99
Radnor Wlk. CR0: C'don 6A 158
Radnor Wlk. E14 4C 104
(off Barnsdale Av.)
Radnor Wlk. SW3 6D 16 (5C 100)
Radnor Way NW10 4H 79
Radstock Av. HA3: Kenton 3A 42
Radstock Cl. N11 6K 31
Radstock St. SW11 7C 100
(not continuous)
Radway Ho. W2 5J 81
(off Alfred Rd.)
Raeburn Av. KT5: Surb 1H 163
Raeburn Cl. KT1: Hamp W 7D 132
Raeburn Cl. NW11 6A 46
Raeburn Ho. UB5: N'olt 2B 76
(off Academy Gdns.)
Raeburn Rd. DA15: Sidc 6J 125
Raeburn Rd. HA8: Edg 1G 43
Raeburn Rd. UB4: Hayes 2F 75
Raeburn St. SW2 4J 119
RAF Bomber Command Memorial
6J 11 (2F 101)
Raffles Ho. NW4 4D 44
Rafford Way BR1: Broml 2K 159
RAF Mus. London 2C 44
RAF Uxbridge, Battle of Britain
Bunker 1B 74
Ragged School Mus. 5A 86
Raggleswood BR7: Chst 1E 160
Raglan Cl. TW4: Houn 5D 112
Raglan Ct. CR2: S Croy 5B 168
Raglan Ct. E17 5E 50
Raglan Ct. HA9: Wemb 4F 61
Raglan Ct. SE12 5J 123
Raglan Rd. BR2: Broml 4A 160
Raglan Rd. DA17: Belv 4F 109
Raglan Rd. E17 5E 50
Raglan Rd. EN1: Enf 7A 24
Raglan Rd. SE18 5G 107
Raglan St. NW5 6F 65
Raglan Ter. HA2: Harr 4F 59
Raglan Way UB5: N'olt 6G 59
Ragley Cl. W3 2J 97
Ragwort Ct. SE26 5H 139
Rahere Ct. E1 4A 86
(off Toby La.)
Raider Cl. RM7: Mawney 1G 55
Railey M. NW5 5G 65
Railshead Rd. TW1: Isle 4B 114
Railshead Rd. TW7: Isle 4B 114
Railton Rd. SE24 4A 120
Railway App. HA1: Harr 4K 41
Railway App. HA3: Harr 4K 41
Railway App. N4 6A 48
Railway App. SE1 4F 15 (1D 102)
Railway App. SM6: W'gton 5F 167
Railway App. TW1: Twick 7A 114
Railway Arches E1 Barnardo St. 6K 85
(off Barnardo St.)
Railway Arches E1 Chapman St. 7H 85
(off Chapman St.)
Railway Arches E2 Cremer St.
1J 9 (2F 85)
(off Cremer St.)
Railway Arches E2 Geffrye St. 2F 85
(off Geffrye St.)
Railway Arches E2 Laburnum St. 1F 85
(off Laburnum St.)
Railway Arches E8 Martello Ter. 7H 67
(off Martello Ter.)
Railway Arches E8 Mentmore Ter. 7H 67
(off Mentmore Ter.)
Railway Arches E10 1E 68
Railway Arches E11 1F 69
(off Grove Grn. Rd.)
Railway Arches E16 1J 105
Railway Arches E3 4B 86
(off Cantrell Rd.)
Railway Arches E7 4J 69
(off Winchelsea Rd.)
Railway Arches W12 2E 98
(off Shepherd's Bush Mkt.)
Railway Arches W6 3E 98
Railway Av. SE16 2J 103
(not continuous)
Railway Children Wlk. BR1: Broml
2J 141
Railway Cotts. E15 2G 87
(off Baker's Row)
Railway Cotts. SW19 4K 135
Railway Cotts. W6 2E 98
(off Sulgrave Rd.)
Railway Fields Local Nature Reserve
6B 48
Railway Gro. SE14 7B 104
Railway M. W10 6G 81
Railway Pas. TW11: Tedd 6A 132
Railway Pl. DA17: Belv 3G 109
Railway Ri. SE22 4E 120
Railway Rd. TW11: Tedd 4J 131
Railway Side SW13 3A 116
Railway Sidings Rd. SE16 3G 103
Railway Sta. Bri. E7 5K 69
Railway St. N1 2J 83
Railway St. RM6: Chad H 7C 54
Railway Ter. E17 1E 50
Railway Ter. SE13 5D 122
Railway Ter. TW13: Felt 1J 129
Railway Wharf KT1: King T 1D 150
(off Thames Side)
Rainbird Cl. HA0: Wemb 2C 78
Rainborough Cl. NW10 6J 61
Rainbow Av. E14 5D 104
Rainbow Ct. SE14 6A 104
(off Chipley St.)
Rainbow Ind. Est. SW20 2D 152
Rainbow Ind. Est. UB7: Yiew 7A 74
Rainbow Quay SE16 3A 104
(not continuous)
Rainbow St. SE5 7E 102
Raine Gdns. IG8: Wfd G 4D 36
Rainer Apartment CR0: C'don 1D 168
(off Cherry Orchard Rd.)
Raines Ct. N16 2F 67
Raine St. E1 1H 103
Rainham Cl. SE9 6J 125
Rainham Cl. SW11 6C 118
Rainham Ho. NW1 1G 83
(off Bayham Pl.)
Rainham Rd. NW10 3E 80
Rainham Rd. Nth. RM10: Dag 2G 73
Rainham Rd. Sth. RM10: Dag 4H 73
Rainhill Way E3 3C 86
Rainsborough Av. SE8 4A 104
Rainsborough Ho. SW15 5G 117
(off Stamford Sq.)
Rainsborough Sq. SW6 6J 99
Rainsford Cl. HA7: Stan 5H 27
Rainsford Rd. NW10 3G 79
Rainsford St. W2 7C 4 (6C 82)
Rainton Rd. SE7 5J 105
Rainville Rd. W6 6E 98
Raisins Hill HA5: Eastc 3A 40
Raith Av. N14 3C 32
Rajsee Apts. E2 3G 85
(off Bethnal Grn. Rd.)
Raleana Rd. E14 1E 104
Raleigh Av. SM6: Bedd 4H 167
Raleigh Av. UB4: Yead 5K 75
Raleigh Cl. HA4: Ruis 2H 57
Raleigh Cl. HA5: Pinn 7B 40
Raleigh Cl. NW4 5E 44
Raleigh Ct. BR3: Beck 1D 158
Raleigh Ct. SE16 1K 103
(off Clarence M.)
Raleigh Ct. SE8 5A 104
(off Evelyn St.)
Raleigh Ct. SM6: W'gton 6F 167
Raleigh Ct. W12 2E 98
(off Scott's Rd.)
Raleigh Ct. W13 5B 78
Raleigh Dr. KT5: Surb 1J 163
Raleigh Dr. N20 3H 31
Raleigh Gdns. CR4: Mitc 3D 154
(not continuous)
Raleigh Gdns. SW2 6K 119
Raleigh Ho. BR1: Broml 1J 159
(off Hammelton Rd.)
Raleigh Ho. CR0: C'don 7K 155
(off Mitcham Rd.)
Raleigh Ho. E14 2D 104
(off Admirals Way)
Raleigh Ho. SW1 7C 18 (6H 101)
(off Dolphin Sq.)
Raleigh M. BR6: Chels 5K 173
Raleigh M. N1 1B 84
(off Packington St.)
Raleigh Rd. EN2: Enf 4J 23
Raleigh Rd. N8 4A 48
Raleigh Rd. SE20 7K 139
Raleigh Rd. TW13: Felt 3H 129
Raleigh Rd. TW9: Rich 3F 115
Raleigh Rd. UB2: S'hall 5C 94
Raleigh St. N1 1B 84
Raleigh Way N14 1C 32
Raleigh Way TW13: Hanw 5A 130
Rale La. E4 1A 36
Rally Bldg. E17 5B 50
Ralph Bayer Ct. E3 5C 86
(off Geoff Cade Way)
Ralph Brook Ct. N1 1F 9 (3D 84)
(off Chart St.)
Ralph Ct. W2 6K 81
(off Queensway)
Ralph Perring Ct. BR3: Beck
4C 158
Ralston St. SW3 6E 16 (5D 100)
Ramac Ind. Est. SE7 4K 105
Rama Cl. SW16 7J 137
Rama Ct. HA1: Harr 2J 59
Ramac Way SE7 4K 105
Rama La. SE19 7F 139
Ramar Ho. E1 5K 9 (5G 85)
(off Hanbury St.)
Rambert 4J 13 (1A 102)
(off Upper Ground)
Rambler Cl. SW16 4G 137
Rame Cl. SW17 5E 136
Ramilles Cl. SW2 6J 119
Ramillies Pl. W1 1A 12 (6G 83)
Ramillies Rd. DA15: Sidc 6B 126
Ramillies Rd. NW7 2F 29
Ramillies Rd. W4 4K 97
Ramillies St. W1 1A 12 (6G 83)
Ramones Ter. CR4: Mitc 4J 155
(off Yorkshire Rd.)
Rampart St. E1 6H 85
Ram Pas. KT1: King T 2D 150
Rampayne St. SW1 5C 18 (5H 101)
Ram Pl. E9 6J 67
Rampton Cl. E4 3H 35
Ram Quarter SW18 5K 117
Ramsay Ho. NW8 2C 82
(off Townshend Est.)
Ramsay M. SW3 7C 16 (6C 100)
Ramsay Rd. E7 4G 69
Ramsay Rd. W3 3J 97
Ramscroft Cl. N9 7K 23
Ramsdale Rd. SW17 5E 136
Ramsden Dr. RM5: Col R 1G 55
Ramsden Rd. DA8: Erith 7K 109
Ramsden Rd. N11 5J 31
Ramsden Rd. SW12 6E 118
Ramsey Cl. NW9 6B 44
Ramsey Cl. UB6: G'frd 5H 59
Ramsey Ct. CR0: C'don 2B 168
(off Church St.)
Ramsey Ho. SW9 7A 102
Ramsey Rd. CR7: Thor H 6K 155
Ramsey St. E2 4G 85
Ramsey Wlk. N1 6D 66
Ramsey Way N14 7B 22
Ramsfort Ho. SE16 4H 103
(off Camilla Rd.)
Ramsgate Cl. E16 1K 105
Ramsgate St. E8 6F 67
Ramsgill App. IG2: Ilf 4K 53
Ramsgill Dr. IG2: Ilf 5K 53
Rams Gro. RM6: Chad H 4E 54
Ram St. SW18 5K 117
Ram Twr. SW18 5K 117
Ramulis Dr. UB4: Yead 4B 76
Ramuswood Av. BR6: Chels 5J 173
Rancliffe Gdns. SE9 4C 124
Rancliffe Rd. E6 2C 88
Randall Av. NW2 2A 62
Randall Cl. DA8: Erith 6J 109
Randall Cl. SW11 1C 118
Randall Ct. NW7 7H 29
Randall Pl. SE10 7E 104
Randall Rd. SE11 5G 19 (5K 101)
Randall Row SE11 4G 19 (4K 101)
Randalls Rents SE16 3B 104
(off Gulliver St.)
Randell's Rd. N1 1J 83
Randisbourne Gdns. SE6 3D 140
Randle Rd. TW10: Ham 4C 132
Randlesdown Rd. SE6 4C 140
(not continuous)
Randolph App. E16 6A 88
Randolph Av. W9 2K 81
Randolph Cl. DA7: Bex 3J 127
Randolph Cl. KT2: King T 5J 133
Randolph Ct. NW8 1A 82
Randolph Cres. W9 4A 82
Randolph Gdns. NW6 2K 81
Randolph Gro. RM6: Chad H 5C 54
Randolph M. W9 4A 82
Randolph Rd. BR2: Broml 1D 172
Randolph Rd. E17 5D 50
Randolph Rd. UB1: S'hall 2D 94
Randolph Rd. W9 4A 82
Randolph St. NW1 7G 65
Randon Cl. HA2: Harr 2F 41
Ranelagh Av. SW13 2C 116
Ranelagh Av. SW6 3H 117
Ranelagh Bri. W2 5K 81
Ranelagh Cl. HA8: Edg 4B 28
Ranelagh Cotts. SW1 5J 17 (5F 101)
(off Ebury Bri. Rd.)
Ranelagh Dr. HA8: Edg 4B 28
Ranelagh Dr. TW1: Twick 4B 114
Ranelagh Gdns. E11 5A 52
Ranelagh Gdns. IG1: Ilf 1D 70
Ranelagh Gdns. SW6 3G 117
(not continuous)
Ranelagh Gdns. W4 7J 97
Ranelagh Gdns. W6 4B 98
Ranelagh Gdns. Mans. SW6 3G 117
(off Ranelagh Gdns.)
Ranelagh Gro. SW1 5H 17 (5E 100)
Ranelagh Ho. SW3 5E 16 (5D 100)
(off Elystan Pl.)
Ranelagh M. W5 2D 96
Ranelagh Pl. KT3: N Mald 5A 152
Ranelagh Rd. E11 4G 69
Ranelagh Rd. E15 2G 87
Ranelagh Rd. E6 1E 88
Ranelagh Rd. HA0: Wemb 6D 60
Ranelagh Rd. N17 3E 48
Ranelagh Rd. N22 1K 47
Ranelagh Rd. NW10 2B 80
Ranelagh Rd. SW1 6B 18 (5G 101)
Ranelagh Rd. UB1: S'hall 1B 94
Ranelagh Rd. W5 2D 96
Ranfurly Rd. SM1: Sutt 2J 165
Rangbourne Ho. N7 5J 65
Rangefield Rd. BR1: Broml 5G 141
Rangemoor Rd. N15 5F 49
Ranger's House 1F 123
Ranger's Rd. E4 1B 36
Rangers Sq. SE10 1F 123
Range Way TW17: Shep 7C 146
Rangeworth Pl. DA15: Sidc 3K 143
Rangoon St. EC3 1J 15 (6F 85)
(off Crutched Friars)
Rankin Cl. NW9 3A 44
Rankine Ho. SE1 3C 102
(off Bath Ter.)
Ranleigh Gdns. DA7: Bex 7F 109
Ranmere St. SW12 1F 137
Ranmoor Cl. HA1: Harr 4H 41
Ranmoor Gdns. HA1: Harr 4H 41
Ranmore Av. CR0: C'don 3F 169
Ranmore Ct. KT6: Surb 5D 150
Ranmore Path BR5: St M Cry 4K 161
Rannoch Cl. HA8: Edg 2C 28
Rannoch Rd. W6 6E 98
Rannock Av. NW9 7K 43
Ransome's Dock Bus. Cen. SW11 7C 100
Ransom Rd. SE7 4A 106
Ranston St. NW1 5C 4 (5C 82)
Ranulf Rd. NW2 4H 63
Ranwell Cl. E3 1B 86
Ranwell Ho. E3 1B 86
(off Ranwell Cl.)
Ranworth Rd. N9 2D 34
Ranyard Cl. KT9: Chess 3F 163
Raphael Cl. KT1: King T 4D 150
Raphael Ct. SE16 5H 103
(off Stubbs Dr.)
Raphael Dr. KT7: T Ditt 7K 149
Raphael Ho. IG1: Ilf 2G 71
Raphael St. SW7 7E 10 (2D 100)
Raphen Apts. E3 2A 86
(off Medway Rd.)
Rapley Ho. E2 2K 9 (3G 85)
(off Turin St.)
Raquel Ct. SE1 6G 15 (2E 102)
(off Snowfields)
Rashleigh Ct. SW8 2F 119
Rashleigh Ho. WC1 2E 6 (3J 83)
(off Thanet St.)
Rashleigh St. SW8 2F 119
(off Peardon St.)
Rasper Rd. N20 2F 31
Rastell Av. SW2 2H 137
RATCLIFF 5A 86
Ratcliffe Cl. SE12 7J 123
Ratcliffe Ct. SE1 7D 14 (2C 102)
(off Gt. Dover St.)
Ratcliffe Cross St. E1 6K 85
Ratcliffe Ho. E14 6A 86
(off Barnes St.)
Ratcliffe La. E14 6A 86
Ratcliffe Orchard E1 7K 85
Ratcliff Rd. E7 5A 70
Rathbone Ho. E16 6H 87
(off Rathbone St.)
Rathbone Ho. NW6 1J 81
Rathbone Mkt. E16 5H 87
Rathbone Pl. W1 6C 6 (5H 83)
Rathbone Sq. CR0: C'don 4C 168
Rathbone Sq. W1 7B 6 (6G 83)
Rathbone St. E16 6H 87
Rathbone St. W1 6B 6 (5G 83)
Rathcoole Av. N8 5K 47
Rathcoole Gdns. N8 5K 47
Rathfern Rd. SE6 1B 140
Rathgar Av. W13 1B 96
Rathgar Cl. N3 2H 45
Rathgar Rd. SW9 3B 120
Rathmell Dr. SW4 6H 119
Rathmore Rd. SE7 5K 105
Rathnew Ct. E2 3K 85
(off Meath Cres.)
Rathore Cl. RM6: Chad H 5D 54
Rattray Ct. SE6 2H 141
Rattray Rd. SW2 4A 120
Raul Rd. SE15 2G 121
Raveley St. NW5 4G 65
(not continuous)
Ravel Ho. SW11 3B 118
(off York Place)
Raven Cl. NW9 2A 44
Raven Cl. RM7: Rush G 7G 55
Ravendale Rd. TW16: Sun 2H 147
Ravenet St. SW11 1F 119
(not continuous)
Ravenet St. SW8 1F 119
Ravenfield Rd. SW17 3D 136
Ravenhill Rd. E13 2A 88
Raven Ho. SE16 4K 103
(off Tawny Way)
Ravenings Pde. IG3: Ilf 1A 72
Ravenna Rd. SW15 5F 117
Ravenor Ct. UB6: G'frd 4F 77
Ravenor Pk. Rd. UB6: G'frd 3F 77
Raven Rd. E18 2A 52
Raven Row E1 5H 85
Raven Row Contemporary Art Cen.
6J 9 (5F 85)
Ravensbourne Apts. SW6 3A 118
(off Central Av.)
Ravensbourne Av. BR2: Broml 7F 141
Ravensbourne Av. BR3: Beck 7F 141
Ravensbourne Av. TW19: Stanw 1A 128
Ravensbourne Ct. SE6 7C 122
Ravensbourne Gdns. IG5: Ilf 1E 52
Ravensbourne Gdns. W13 5B 78
Ravensbourne Ho. BR1: Broml 5F 141
Ravensbourne Ho. E15 6F 69
(off Forrester Way)

A–Z London 275

Ravensbourne Ho. NW8 5C 4 (5C 82)
(off Broadley St.)
Ravensbourne Mans. SE8 6C 104
(off Berthon St.)
Ravensbourne Pk. SE6 7C 122
Ravensbourne Pk. Cres. SE6 7B 122
Ravensbourne Pl. SE13 2D 122
Ravensbourne Pl. SE8 1C 122
Ravensbourne Rd. BR1: Broml 3J 159
Ravensbourne Rd. SE6 7B 122
Ravensbourne Rd. TW1: Twick 6C 114
Ravensbourne Ter. TW19: Stanw 1A 128
Ravensbury Av. SM4: Mord 5A 154
Ravensbury Ct. CR4: Mitc 4B 154
(off Ravensbury Gro.)
Ravensbury Gro. CR4: Mitc 4B 154
Ravensbury La. CR4: Mitc 4B 154
Ravensbury Path CR4: Mitc 4B 154
Ravensbury Rd. BR5: St P 3K 161
Ravensbury Rd. SW18 2K 135
Ravensbury Ter. SW18 2K 135
Ravenscar NW1 1G 83
(off Bayham St.)
Ravenscar Rd. BR1: Broml 4G 141
Ravenscar Rd. KT6: Surb 2F 163
Ravens Cl. BR2: Broml 2H 159
Ravens Cl. EN1: Enf 2K 23
Ravens Cl. KT6: Surb 6D 150
Ravens Ct. KT1: King T 5D 150
(off Uxbridge Rd.)
Ravenscourt TW16: Sun 1H 147
Ravenscourt Av. W6 4C 98
Ravenscourt Cl. HA4: Ruis 7E 38
Ravenscourt Gdns. W6 4C 98
Ravenscourt Pk. EN5: Barn 4A 20
Ravenscourt Pk. W6 3C 98
Ravenscourt Pk. Mans. W6 3D 98
(off Paddenswick Rd.)
Ravenscourt Pl. W6 4D 98
Ravenscourt Rd. W6 4D 98
Ravenscourt Sq. W6 3C 98
Ravenscraig Rd. N11 4B 32
Ravenscroft Av. HA9: Wemb 1E 60
Ravenscroft Av. NW11 7H 45
(not continuous)
Ravenscroft Cl. E16 5J 87
Ravenscroft Cotts. EN5: New Bar 4D 20
Ravenscroft Cres. SE9 3D 142
Ravenscroft Pk. EN5: Barn 3A 20
Ravenscroft Rd. BR3: Beck 2J 157
Ravenscroft Rd. E16 5J 87
Ravenscroft Rd. W4 4J 97
Ravenscroft St. E2 1K 9 (2F 85)
Ravensdale Av. N12 4F 31
Ravensdale Gdns. SE19 7D 138
Ravensdale Gdns. TW4: Houn 3C 112
Ravensdale Ind. Est. N16 6G 49
Ravensdale Mans. N8 6J 47
(off Haringey Pk.)
Ravensdale Rd. N16 7F 49
Ravensdale Rd. TW4: Houn 3C 112
Ravens Dene BR7: Chst 5D 142
Ravensdon St. SE11 6K 19 (5A 102)
Ravensfield Cl. RM9: Dag 4D 72
Ravensfield Gdns. KT19: Ewe 5A 164
Ravens Ga. M. BR2: Broml 2G 159
Ravenshaw St. NW6 5H 63
Ravenshill BR7: Chst 1F 161
Ravenshurst Av. NW4 4E 44
Ravenside KT1: King T 5D 150
(off Portsmouth Rd.)
Ravenside Cl. N18 5E 34
Ravenside Retail Pk. London 5E 34
Ravenslea Rd. SW12 7D 118
Ravensleigh Gdns. BR1: Broml 5K 141
Ravensmead Rd. BR2: Broml 7F 141
Ravensmede Way W4 4B 98
Ravens M. SE12 5J 123
Ravenstone SE17 5E 102
Ravenstone Rd. N8 3A 48
Ravenstone Rd. NW9 6B 44
Ravenstone St. SW12 1E 136
Ravens Wlk. E20 6D 68
Ravens Way SE12 5J 123
Ravenswood DA5: Bexl 1E 144
Ravenswood Av. BR4: W W'ck 1E 170
Ravenswood Av. KT6: Surb 2F 163
Ravenswood Ct. KT2: King T 6H 133
Ravenswood Ct. W3 3J 97
(off Bassington Rd.)
Ravenswood Cres. BR4: W W'ck 1E 170
Ravenswood Cres. HA2: Harr 2D 58
Ravenswood Gdns. TW7: Isle 1J 113
Ravenswood Ind. Est. E17 4E 50
Ravenswood Rd. CR0: Wadd 3B 168
Ravenswood Rd. E17 4E 50
Ravenswood Rd. SW12 7F 119
Ravensworth Ct. SW6 7J 99
(off Fulham Rd.)
Ravensworth Rd. NW10 3D 80
Ravensworth Rd. SE9 3D 142
Raven Wharf SE1 6J 15 (2F 103)
(off Lafone St.)
Ravey St. EC2 3G 9 (4E 84)
Ravine Gro. SE18 6J 107
Ravine Way SW11 6H 101
Rav Pinter Cl. N16 7E 48
Rawchester Cl. SW18 1H 135
Rawlings Cl. BR3: Beck 5E 158
Rawlings Cl. BR6: Chels 5K 173
Rawlings Cres. HA9: Wemb 3H 61
Rawlings St. SW3 3E 16 (4D 100)
Rawlins Cl. CR2: Sels 7B 170
Rawlins Cl. N3 3G 45
Rawlinson Ct. NW2 7E 44
Rawlinson Ho. SE13 4F 123
(off Mercator Rd.)
Rawlinson Ter. N17 3F 49
Rawnsley Av. CR4: Mitc 5B 154
Rawreth Wlk. N1 1C 84
(off Basire St.)
Rawson St. SW11 1E 118
(not continuous)
Rawsthorne Cl. E16 1D 106
Rawsthorne Ct. TW4: Houn 4D 112
Rawstone Wlk. E13 2J 87
Rawstorne Pl. EC1 1A 8 (3B 84)
Rawstorne St. EC1 1A 8 (3B 84)
(not continuous)
Raybell Ct. TW7: Isle 2K 113
Rayburne Ct. IG9: Buck H 1F 37
Rayburne Ct. W14 3G 99
Ray Cl. KT9: Chess 6C 162
Raydean Rd. EN5: New Bar 5E 20
Raydons Gdns. RM9: Dag 5E 72
Raydons Rd. RM9: Dag 5E 72
Raydon St. N19 2F 65
Rayfield Cl. BR2: Broml 6C 160
Rayford Av. SE12 7H 123
Ray Gdns. HA7: Stan 5G 27
Ray Gdns. IG11: Bark 2A 90
Ray Gunter Ho. SE17 5B 102
(off Marsland Cl.)
Ray Ho. N1 1E 84
(off Colville Est.)
Ray Ho. W10 6F 81
(off Cambridge Gdns.)
Rayleas Cl. SE18 1F 125
Rayleigh Av. TW11: Tedd 6J 131
Rayleigh Cl. N13 3J 33
Rayleigh Ct. KT1: King T 2G 151
Rayleigh Ct. N22 1C 48
Rayleigh Ri. CR2: S Croy 6E 168
Rayleigh Rd. E16 1K 105
Rayleigh Rd. IG8: Wfd G 6F 37
Rayleigh Rd. N13 3H 33
Rayleigh Rd. SW19 1H 153
Ray Lodge Rd. IG8: Wfd G 6F 37
Ray Massey Way E6 1C 88
(off High St. Nth.)
Raymead Av. CR7: Thor H 5A 156
Raymead Pas. CR7: Thor H 5A 156
(off Raymead Av.)
Raymede Towers W10 5F 81
(off Treverton St.)
Raymere Gdns. SE18 7H 107
Raymond Av. E18 3H 51
Raymond Av. W13 3A 96
Raymond Bldgs. WC1 5H 7 (5K 83)
Raymond Chadburn Ho. E7 4K 69
Raymond Cl. SE26 5J 139
Raymond Cl. SL3: Poyle 4A 174
Raymond Ct. N10 7A 32
Raymond Postgate Ct. SE28 7B 90
Raymond Rd. BR3: Beck 4A 158
Raymond Rd. E13 1A 88
Raymond Rd. IG2: Ilf 7H 53
Raymond Rd. SW19 6G 135
Raymond Way KT10: Clay 6A 162
Raymouth Rd. SE16 4H 103
Raynald Ho. SW16 3J 137
Rayne Ct. E18 4H 51
Rayne Ho. SW12 6E 118
Rayne Ho. W9 4K 81
(off Delaware Rd.)
Rayner Cl. SM5: Cars 5D 166
Rayner Ct. W12 2E 98
(off Bamborough Gdns.)
Rayners Cl. HA0: Wemb 5D 60
Rayners Cres. UB5: N'olt 3K 75
Rayners Gdns. UB5: N'olt 2K 75
Rayners La. HA2: Harr 1E 58
Rayners La. HA5: Pinn 5D 40
RAYNERS LANE 1D 58
Rayners Rd. SW15 5G 117
Rayners Ter. E14 6A 86
(off Carr St.)
Rayner Towers E10 7C 50
(off Albany Rd.)
Raynes Av. E11 7A 52
RAYNES PARK 4E 152
RAYNES PARK BRI. 2E 152
Raynes Pk. School Sports Cen. 3D 152
Raynham W2 7C 4 (6C 82)
(off Norfolk Cres.)
Raynham Av. N18 6B 34
Raynham Ho. E1 4K 85
(off Harpley Sq.)
Raynham Rd. N18 5B 34
Raynham Rd. W6 4D 98
Raynham Ter. N18 5B 34
Raynor Cl. UB1: S'hall 1D 94
Raynor Pl. N1 7C 66
Raynton Cl. HA2: Harr 1C 58
Raynton Cl. UB4: Hayes 4H 75
Raynton Dr. UB4: Hayes 4H 75
Rayon Cl. SM6: W'gton 2E 166
Ray Rd. KT8: W Mole 5F 149
Rays Av. N18 4D 34
Rays Rd. BR4: W W'ck 7E 158
Rays Rd. N18 4D 34
Ray St. EC1 4K 7 (4A 84)
RAY ST. BRI. 4K 7 (4A 84)
(off Farringdon Rd.)
Ray Wlk. N7 2K 65
Raywood Cl. UB3: Harl 7E 92
Raywood Mans. E20 6E 68
(off West Pk. Wlk.)
Razia M. E12 5D 70
Reachview Cl. NW1 7G 65
Read Cl. KT7: T Ditt 7A 150
Read Ct. E17 6C 50
Reade Ct. W3 3J 97
(off Stanley Rd.)
Reader Ho. SE5 1C 120
(off Badsworth Rd.)
Read Ho. SE11 7J 19 (6A 102)
(off Clayton St.)
Read Ho. SE20 7H 139
(off Anerley Pk.)
Reading Cl. SE22 6G 121
Reading Ho. SE15 6G 103
(off Friary Est.)
Reading Ho. W2 6A 82
(off Hallfield Est.)
Reading La. E8 6H 67
Reading Rd. SM1: Sutt 5A 166
Reading Rd. UB5: N'olt 5F 59
Readman Ct. SE20 1H 157
Reads Cl. IG1: Ilf 3F 71
Ream Apts. SE23 2J 139
(off Clyde Ter.)
Reapers Cl. NW1 1H 83
Reapers Way TW7: Isle 5H 113
Reardon Ct. N21 2G 33
Reardon Ho. E1 1H 103
(off Reardon St.)
Reardon Path E1 1H 103
(not continuous)
Reardon St. E1 1H 103
Reaston St. SE14 7K 103
Rebecca Ct. DA14: Sidc 4B 144
Rebecca Ho. E3 4B 86
(off Brokesley St.)
Rebecca Ho. N12 4E 30
(off Woodside Pk. Rd.)
Reckitt Rd. W4 5A 98
Record St. SE15 6J 103
Record Wlk. UB3: Hayes 2G 93
Recovery St. SW17 5C 136
Recreation Av. RM7: Rom 5J 55
Recreation Rd. BR2: Broml 2H 159
Recreation Rd. DA15: Sidc 3J 143
Recreation Rd. SE26 4K 139
Recreation Rd. UB2: S'hall 4C 94
Recreation Way CR4: Mitc 3H 155
Rector St. N1 1C 84
Rectory Bus. Cen. DA14: Sidc 4B 144
Rectory Chambers SW3 7C 16 (6C 100)
(off Old Church St.)
Rectory Cl. DA14: Sidc 4B 144
Rectory Cl. E4 3H 35
Rectory Cl. HA7: Stan 5G 27
Rectory Cl. KT6: Surb 1C 162
Rectory Cl. N3 1H 45
Rectory Cl. SW20 3E 152
Rectory Cl. TW17: Shep 3C 146
Rectory Ct. E18 1H 51
Rectory Ct. SM6: W'gton 4G 167
Rectory Ct. TW13: Felt 4A 130
Rectory Cres. E11 6A 52
(not continuous)
Rectory Farm 1A 112
Rectory Farm Rd. EN2: Enf 1E 22
(not continuous)
Rectory Field 7K 105
Rectory Fld. Cres. SE7 7A 106
Rectory Gdns. BR3: Beck 1C 158
(off Rectory Rd.)
Rectory Gdns. N8 4J 47
Rectory Gdns. SW4 3G 119
Rectory Gdns. UB5: N'olt 1D 76
Rectory Grn. BR3: Beck 1B 158
Rectory Gro. CR0: C'don 2B 168
Rectory Gro. SW4 3G 119
Rectory Gro. TW12: Hamp 4D 130
Rectory La. DA14: Sidc 4B 144
Rectory La. HA7: Stan 5G 27
Rectory La. HA8: Edg 6B 28
Rectory La. KT6: Surb 1B 162
Rectory La. SM6: W'gton 4G 167
Rectory La. SW17 6E 136
Rectory Orchard SW19 4G 135
Rectory Pk. Av. UB5: N'olt 3D 76
Rectory Pl. SE18 4E 106
Rectory Rd. BR2: Kes 7B 172
Rectory Rd. BR3: Beck 1C 158
Rectory Rd. E12 5D 70
Rectory Rd. E17 4D 50
Rectory Rd. N16 2F 67
Rectory Rd. RM10: Dag 6H 73
Rectory Rd. SM1: Sutt 3J 165
Rectory Rd. SW13 2C 116
Rectory Rd. TW4: Cran 2A 112
Rectory Rd. UB2: S'hall 3D 94
Rectory Rd. UB3: Hayes 6J 75
Rectory Rd. W3 1H 97
Rectory Sq. E1 5K 85
Rectory Way UB10: Ick 2D 56
Reculver Ho. SE15 6J 103
(off Lovelinch Cl.)
Reculver M. N18 4B 34
Reculver Rd. SE16 5K 103
Red Anchor Cl. SW3 7B 16 (6B 100)
Redan Pl. W2 6K 81
Redan St. W14 3F 99
Redan Ter. SE5 2B 120
Red Barracks Rd. SE18 4D 106
Redberry Gro. SE26 3J 139
Redbourne Av. N3 1J 45
Redbourne Dr. SE28 6D 90
(not continuous)
Redbourne Ho. E14 6B 86
(off Norbiton Rd.)
Redbourn Ho. W10 4E 80
(off Sutton Way)
REDBRIDGE 6C 52
Redbridge Ent. Cen. IG1: Ilf 2G 71
Redbridge Foyer IG1: Ilf 2G 71
(off Sylvan Rd.)
Redbridge Gdns. SE5 7E 102
Redbridge Ho. E16 7F 89
(off University Way)
Redbridge La. E. IG4: Ilf 6B 52
Redbridge La. W. E11 6K 51
REDBRIDGE RDBT. 6B 52
Redbridge Sports & Leisure Cen. 1H 53
Redburn Ind. Est. EN3: Pond E 6E 24
Redburn St. SW3 7E 16 (6D 100)
Redcar Cl. UB5: N'olt 5F 59
Redcar St. SE5 7C 102
Redcastle Cl. E1 7J 85
Red Cedars Rd. BR6: Orp 7J 161
Redchurch St. E2 3J 9 (4F 85)
Redcliffe Cl. SW5 5K 99
(off Old Brompton Rd.)
Redcliffe Ct. E5 3H 67
(off Napoleon Rd.)
Redcliffe Gdns. IG1: Ilf 1E 70
Redcliffe Gdns. SW10 5K 99
Redcliffe Gdns. SW5 5K 99
Redcliffe Gdns. W4 7H 97
Redcliffe M. SW10 5K 99
Redcliffe Pl. SW10 6A 100
Redcliffe Rd. SW10 5A 100
Redcliffe Sq. SW10 5K 99
Redcliffe St. SW10 6K 99
Redclose Av. SM4: Mord 5J 153
Redclyffe Rd. E6 1A 88
Redclyf Ho. E1 4J 85
(off Cephas St.)
Redcourt CR0: C'don 3E 168
Red Cow La. EC1 3C 8 (4C 84)
Redcroft Rd. UB1: S'hall 7G 77
Red Cross Cotts. SE1 6D 14 (2C 102)
(off Ayres St.)
Redcross Way SE1 6D 14 (2C 102)
Redding Ho. SE18 3C 106
Reddings, The NW7 3G 29
Reddings Cl. NW7 4G 29
Reddins Rd. SE15 6G 103
Reddons Rd. BR3: Beck 7A 140
Redenham Ho. SW15 7C 116
(off Ellisfield Dr.)
Rede Pl. W2 6J 81
Redesdale Gdns. TW7: Isle 7A 96
Redesdale St. SW3 7D 16 (6C 100)
Redfern Av. TW4: Houn 7E 112
Redfern Ho. E13 1H 87
(off Redriffe Rd.)
Redfern Ho. NW8 1B 82
(off Dorman Way)
Redfern Rd. NW10 7A 62
Redfern Rd. SE6 7E 122
Redfield La. SW5 4J 99
Redfield M. SW5 4K 99
Redford Av. CR7: Thor H 4K 155
Redford Av. SM6: W'gton 6J 167
Redford Cl. TW13: Felt 2H 129
Redford Wlk. N1 1C 84
(off Popham St.)
Redgate Dr. BR2: Hayes 2K 171
Redgate Ter. SW15 6F 117
Redgrave Cl. CR0: C'don 6F 157
Redgrave Rd. SW15 3F 117
Redgrave Ter. E2 3G 85
(off Derbyshire St.)
Red Hill BR7: Chst 5F 143
Redhill Ct. SW2 2A 138
Redhill Dr. HA8: Edg 2H 43
Redhill St. NW1 1K 5 (2F 83)
Red House 4E 126
Red Ho. La. DA6: Bex 4D 126
Redhouse Rd. CR0: C'don 6H 155
Red Ho. Sq. N1 7C 66
Redif Ho. RM10: Dag 4H 73
Redington Gdns. NW3 4K 63
Redington Ho. N1 2K 83
(off Priory Grn. Est.)
Redington Rd. NW3 3K 63
Redknap Ho. TW10: Ham 3C 132
Redland Gdns. KT8: W Mole 4D 148
Redlands N15 4D 48
Redlands TW11: Tedd 6A 132
Redlands, The BR3: Beck 2D 158
Redlands Ct. BR1: Broml 7H 141
Redlands Rd. EN3: Enf H 1F 25
Redlands Way SW2 7K 119
Red La. KT10: Clay 6A 162
Redleaf Cl. DA17: Belv 6G 109
Redleaves Av. TW15: Ashf 6D 128
Redlees Cl. TW7: Isle 4A 114
Red Leys UB8: Uxb 7A 56
Red Lion Bus. Pk. KT6: Surb 3F 163
Red Lion Cl. SE17 6D 102
(off Red Lion Row)
Red Lion Ct. EC4 1K 13 (6A 84)
Red Lion Ct. SE1 4D 14 (1C 102)
Red Lion Ct. TW3: Houn 3F 113
(off Alexandra Rd.)
Red Lion Hill N2 2B 46
(not continuous)
Red Lion La. SE18 7E 106
Red Lion Pde. HA5: Pinn 3C 40
Red Lion Pl. SE18 1E 124
Red Lion Rd. KT6: Surb 2F 163
Red Lion Row SE17 6C 102
Red Lion Sq. SW18 5J 117
Red Lion Sq. WC1 6G 7 (5K 83)
Red Lion St. TW9: Rich 5D 114
Red Lion St. WC1 5G 7 (5K 83)
Red Lion Wlk. TW3: Houn 3F 113
(off High St.)
Red Lion Yd. W1 4J 11 (1F 101)
(off Waverton St.)
Red Lodge BR4: W W'ck 1E 170
Red Lodge Cres. DA5: Bexl 3K 145
Red Lodge Rd. BR4: W W'ck 1E 170
Red Lodge Rd. DA5: Bexl 3K 145
Redlynch Ct. W14 2G 99
(off Addison Cres.)
Redlynch Ho. SW9 1A 120
(off Gosling Way)
Redman Cl. UB5: N'olt 2A 76
Redman Ho. EC1 5J 7 (5A 84)
(off Bourne Est.)
Redman Ho. SE1 7D 14 (2C 102)
(off Borough High St.)
Redman's Rd. E1 5J 85
Redmead La. E1 1G 103
Redmead Rd. UB3: Harl 4G 93
Redmill Ho. E1 4H 85
(off Headlam St.)
Redmond Ho. N1 1K 83
(off Barnsbury Est.)
Redmore Rd. W6 4D 98
Red Oak Cl. BR6: Farnb 3F 173
Red Oak Cl. CR0: C'don 2C 170
Redo Ho. E12 5E 70
(off Dore Av.)
Red Path E9 6A 68
Redpath Way SE10 2G 105
Red Pl. W1 2G 11 (7E 82)
Redpoll Way DA18: Erith 3D 108
Red Post Hill SE21 5D 120
Red Post Hill SE24 4D 120
Red Post Ho. E6 7B 70
Redriffe Rd. E13 1H 87
Redriff Est. SE16 3B 104
Redriff Rd. RM7: Mawney 2H 55
Redriff Rd. SE16 4K 103
Redroofs Cl. BR3: Beck 1D 158
Redrose Trad. Cen. EN4: E Barn 5G 21
RED ROVER 4C 116
Redrup Ho. SE14 6K 103
(off John Williams Cl.)
Redruth Cl. N22 7E 32
Redruth Gdns. KT10: Clay 7A 162
Redruth Ho. SM2: Sutt 7K 165
Redruth Rd. E9 1J 85
Redsan Cl. CR2: S Croy 7D 168
Redshank Ho. SE1 5F 103
(off Avocet Cl.)
Red Sq. N16 3D 66
Redstart Cl. E6 5C 88
Redstart Cl. SE14 7A 104
Redstart Mans. IG1: Ilf 3E 70
(off Mill Rd.)
Redston Rd. N8 4H 47
Redvers Rd. N22 2A 48
Redvers St. N1 1H 9 (3E 84)
Redwald Rd. E5 4K 67
Redway Dr. TW2: Whitt 7G 113
Redwing Ct. SE1 7D 14 (2C 102)
(off Swan St.)
Redwing M. SE5 2C 120
Redwing Path SE28 2H 107
Redwing Rd. SM6: W'gton 7J 167
Redwood Cl. DA15: Sidc 1A 144
Redwood Cl. E3 2C 86
Redwood Cl. N14 7C 22
Redwood Cl. SE16 1A 104
Redwood Cl. UB10: Hil 2D 74
Redwood Ct. KT6: Surb 7D 150
Redwood Ct. N19 7H 47
Redwood Ct. NW6 7G 63
Redwood Ct. UB5: N'olt 3C 76
Redwood Est. TW5: Cran 6K 93
Redwood Gdns. E4 6J 25
Redwood Gro. W5 3B 96
Redwood Ho. EC1 1C 8 (3C 84)
(off Bollinder Pl.)
Redwood Ho. HA9: Wemb 4G 61
(off Empire Way)
Redwood Mans. W8 3K 99
(off Chantry Sq.)
Redwood M. SW4 3F 119
Redwood M. TW15: Ashf 7F 129
(off Staines Rd. W.)
Redwoods SW15 1C 134
Redwoods Cl. IG9: Buck H 2E 36
Redwood Wlk. KT6: Surb 1D 162
Redwood Way EN5: Barn 5A 20
Reece M. SW7 3A 16 (4B 100)
Reed Av. BR6: Orp 3J 173
Reed Cl. E16 5J 87
Reed Cl. SE12 5J 123
Reede Gdns. RM10: Dag 5H 73
Reede Rd. RM10: Dag 6G 73
Reede Way RM10: Dag 6H 73
Reedham Cl. N17 4H 49
Reedham St. SE15 2G 121
Reedholm Vs. N16 4D 66
Reed Ho. SW19 4K 135
Reed Pl. SW4 4H 119
Reed Rd. N17 2F 49
Reedsfield Cl. TW15: Ashf 3D 128
Reedsfield Rd. TW15: Ashf 4D 128
Reed's Pl. NW1 7G 65
Reedworth St. SE11 4K 19 (4A 102)
Reef Ho. E14 3E 104
(off Manchester St.)
Reef St. RM9: Dag 3E 90
Reenglass Rd. HA7: Stan 4J 27
Rees Dr. HA7: Stan 4K 27
Rees Gdns. CR0: C'don 6F 157
Reesland Cl. E12 6E 70
Rees St. N1 1C 84
Reets Farm Cl. NW9 6A 44
Reeves Av. NW9 7K 43
Reeves Cnr. CR0: C'don 2B 168
Reeves Ho. SE1 7K 13 (2A 102)
(off Baylis Rd.)
Reeves M. W1 3G 11 (7E 82)
Reeves Rd. E3 4D 86
Reeves Rd. SE18 6F 107
Reference Ho. NW9 3B 44
Reflection, The E16 2F 107
(off Woolwich Mnr. Way)
Reflection Ho. E2 4G 85
(off Cheshire St.)
Reflex Apts. BR2: Broml 4K 159
(off Wheeler Pl.)
Reform Row N17 2F 49
Reform St. SW11 2D 118
Regal Bldg. W10 3F 81
Regal Cl. E1 5G 85
Regal Cl. W5 5D 78
Regal Ct. CR4: Mitc 3D 154
Regal Ct. N18 5A 34
Regal Ct. NW6 2H 81
(off Malvern Rd.)
Regal Ct. SW6 7J 99
(off Dawes Rd.)
Regal Cres. SM6: W'gton 3F 167
Regal Dr. N11 5A 32
Regal Ho. IG2: Ilf 6H 53
Regal Ho., The SW6 2A 118
Regalia Cl. E16 2K 105
Regalia Point E2 3K 85
(off Palmer's Rd.)
Regal La. NW1 1E 82
Regal Pl. E3 3D 86
Regal Pl. SW6 7K 99
Regal Row SE15 1J 121
Regal Way HA3: Kenton 6E 42
Regal Wharf Apts. N1 1E 84
(off De Beauvoir Cres.)
Regal Wk. DA6: Bex 4G 127
Regan Ho. N18 6A 34
Regan Way N1 2E 84
Regatta Ho. TW11: Tedd 4A 132
Regatta La. W6 6E 98
Regatta Point E14 2C 104
(off Westferry Rd.)
Regatta Point TW8: Bford 6F 97
Regency Cl. TW12: Hamp 5D 130
Regency Cl. W5 6E 78
Regency Ct. BR2: Broml 6B 160
Regency Ct. E18 2J 51
Regency Ct. E3 2B 86
(off Norman Gro.)
Regency Ct. E9 1J 85
(off Park Cl.)
Regency Ct. EN1: Enf 5J 23
Regency Ct. HA7: Stan 7J 27
(off Unwin Way)
Regency Ct. SE8 7B 104
(off Glenville Gro.)
Regency Ct. SM1: Sutt 4A 166
Regency Ct. TW11: Tedd 6B 132
Regency Cres. NW4 2F 45
Regency Dr. HA4: Ruis 1G 57
Regency Gdns. KT12: Walt T 7A 148
Regency Ho. E16 1J 105
(off Pepys Cres.)
Regency Ho. N3 2H 45
Regency Ho. SW1 3D 18 (4H 101)
(off Regency St.)
Regency Ho. SW6 1A 118
(off The Boulevard)
Regency Lawn NW5 3F 65
Regency Lodge IG9: Buck H 2G 37
Regency Lodge NW3 7B 64
(off Adelaide Rd.)
Regency M. BR3: Beck 1E 158
Regency M. NW10 6C 62
Regency M. SW9 7B 102
Regency M. TW7: Isle 5J 113
Regency Pde. NW3 7B 64
(off Finchley Rd.)
Regency Pl. SW1 3D 18 (4H 101)
Regency St. NW10 4A 80
Regency St. SW1 3D 18 (4H 101)
Regency Ter. SW7 5A 16 (5B 100)
(off Fulham Rd.)
Regency Wlk. CR0: C'don 6B 158
Regency Wlk. TW10: Rich 5E 114
(off The Vineyard)
Regency Way DA6: Bex 3D 126
Regeneration House 1J 83
Regeneration Rd. SE16 4K 103
Regent Av. UB10: Hil 7D 56
Regent Bus. Cen. UB3: Hayes 2K 93

Regent Cl. – Riggindale Rd.

Regent Cl. HA3: Kenton 6E 42
Regent Cl. N12 5F 31
Regent Cl. TW4: Cran 1K 111
Regent Ct. N20 2G 31
Regent Ct. N3 7E 30
Regent Ct. NW6 7H 63
(off Cavendish Rd.)
Regent Ct. NW8 2C 4 (3C 82)
(off North Bank)
Regent Ct. W6 3D 98
(off Vinery Way)
Regent Ct. W8 3K 99
(off Wright's La.)
Regent Gdns. IG3: Ilf 7A 54
Regent Ho. W14 4G 99
(off Windsor Way)
Regent Pde. SM2: Sutt 6A 166
Regent Pl. CR0: C'don 1F 169
Regent Pl. SW19 5A 136
Regent Pl. W1 2B 12 (7G 83)
Regent Rd. KT5: Surb 5F 151
Regent Rd. SE24 6B 120
Regents Av. N13 5F 33
Regent's Bri. Gdns. SW8 7J 101
Regents Canal Ho. E14 6A 86
(off Commercial Rd.)
Regents Cl. CR2: S Croy 6E 168
Regents Cl. HA8: Edg 4K 27
Regents Cl. UB4: Hayes 5H 75
Regents Ct. BR1: Broml 7H 141
Regents Ct. E8 1G 85
Regents Ct. HA5: Pinn 2B 40
Regents Ct. KT2: King T 1E 150
(off Sopwith Way)
Regents Dr. BR2: Kes 5B 172
Regents Dr. IG8: Wfd G 6K 37
Regents Ga. Ho. E14 7A 86
(off Horseferry Rd.)
Regents Ho. E3 5C 86
(off Bow Common La.)
Regents M. NW8 2A 82
Regent's Pk. 1E 4 (2D 82)
REGENT'S PARK 2K 5 (3F 83)
Regent's Pk. Barracks 1K 5 (2F 83)
(off Albany St.)
Regents Pk. Est. NW1 1A 6 (3G 83)
(off Robert St.)
Regent's Pk. Gdns. M. NW1 1D 82
Regent's Pk. Ho. NW8 2D 4 (3C 82)
(off Park Rd.)
Regent's Pk. Open Air Theatre
2G 5 (3E 82)
Regent's Pk. Rd. NW1 7D 64
(not continuous)
Regents Pk. Rd. N3 3H 45
Regent's Pk. Ter. NW1 1F 83
Regent's Pl. SE3 2J 123
Regents Pl. NW1 3A 6 (4G 83)
Regent's Pl. Plaza NW1 3A 6 (4G 83)
Regents Plaza NW6 2K 81
(off Kilburn High Rd.)
Regent Sq. DA17: Belv 4H 109
Regent Sq. E3 3D 86
Regent Sq. WC1 2F 7 (3J 83)
Regent's Row E8 1G 85
Regents Studios E8 1H 85
Regent St. NW10 3F 81
Regent St. SW1 3C 12 (7H 83)
Regent St. W1 7K 5 (6F 83)
Regent St. W4 5G 97
Regent Street Cinema 7K 5 (6F 83)
Regent's University London
3F 5 (4D 82)
Regents Wharf E2 1H 85
(off Wharf Pl.)
Regents Wharf N1 2K 83
Regent Ter. SW8 6J 101
Regiment Hill NW7 6B 30
Regina Cl. EN5: Barn 3A 20
Regina Ho. SE20 1K 157
Reginald Ellingworth St. RM9: Dag
1B 90
Reginald Pl. SE8 7C 104
(off Deptford High St.)
Reginald Rd. E7 7J 69
Reginald Rd. HA6: Nwood 1H 39
Reginald Rd. SE8 7C 104
Reginald Sorenson Ho. E11 7F 51
Reginald Sq. SE8 7C 104
Regina Point SE16 3J 103
(off Canada Est.)
Regina Rd. N4 1K 65
Regina Rd. SE25 3G 157
Regina Rd. UB2: S'hall 4C 94
Regina Rd. W13 1A 96
Regina Ter. W13 1B 96
Regis Ct. CR4: Mitc 1C 154
Regis Ct. N8 4K 47
Regis Ct. NW1 5E 4 (5D 82)
(off Melcombe Pl.)
Regis Ho. W1 5H 5 (5E 82)
(off Beaumont St.)
Regis Pl. SW2 4K 119
Regis Rd. NW5 5F 65
Regnart Bldgs. NW1 2B 6 (3G 83)
(off Euston St.)
Regnas Ho. E15 6H 69
(off Carnarvon Rd.)
Regnolruf Ct. KT12: Walt T 7J 147
Regnum Apts. E1 4J 9 (4F 85)
(off Wheler St.)
Reid Bldg. E3 4B 86
(off Eric St.)
Reid Cl. HA5: Eastc 4J 39
Reid Cl. UB3: Hayes 6G 75
Reidhaven Rd. SE18 4J 107
Reigate Av. SM1: Sutt 1J 165
Reigate Rd. BR1: Broml 3H 141
Reigate Rd. IG3: Ilf 2K 71
Reigate Way SM6: W'gton 5J 167
Reighton Rd. E5 3G 67
Reindeer Cl. E13 1J 87
Reinickendorf Av. SE9 6G 125
Reis Pl. N15 4F 49
(off Blenheim Ri.)
Reizel Cl. N16 1F 67
Relay Rd. W12 7F 81
Relf Rd. SE15 3G 121
Reliance Arc. SW9 4A 120
Reliance Wharf N1 1E 84
Relko Gdns. SM1: Sutt 5B 166
Relton M. SW7 1D 16 (3C 100)
Rembrandt Cl. E14 3F 105
Rembrandt Cl. SW1 5G 17 (5E 100)
(off Graham Ter.)
Rembrandt Ct. KT19: Ewe 6B 164
Rembrandt Ct. SE16 5H 103
(off Stubbs Dr.)
Rembrandt Rd. HA8: Edg 2G 43
Rembrandt Rd. SE13 4G 123
Reminder La. SE10 3H 105
(not continuous)
Remington Rd. E6 6C 88
Remington Rd. N15 6D 48
Remington St. N1 1B 8 (2B 84)
Remnant St. WC2 7G 7 (6K 83)
Remsted Ho. NW6 1K 81
(off Mortimer Cres.)
Remus Bldg., The EC1 2K 7 (3A 84)
(off Hardwick St.)
Remus Rd. E3 7C 68
Renaissance Ct. SM1: Sutt 1A 166
Renaissance Ct. TW3: Houn 3G 113
(off Prince Regent Rd.)
Renaissance Sq. W4 6A 98
Renaissance Wlk. SE10 3H 105
(off Teal St.)
Renbold Ho. SE10 1E 122
(off Blissett St.)
Rendalls HA1: Harr 1J 59
(off Grove Hill)
Rendel Apts. E16 7G 89
(off Lock Side Way)
Rendle Cl. CR0: C'don 5F 157
Rendle Ho. W10 4G 81
(off Wornington Rd.)
Rendlesham Rd. E5 4G 67
Rendlesham Rd. EN2: Enf 1G 23
Renforth St. SE16 3J 103
Renfree Way TW17: Shep 7C 146
Renfrew Cl. E6 7E 88
Renfrew Ct. TW4: Houn 2C 112
Renfrew Ho. E17 2B 50
Renfrew Ho. NW6 2K 81
(off Carlton Vale)
Renfrew Rd. KT2: King T 7H 133
Renfrew Rd. SE11 3K 19 (4B 102)
Renfrew Rd. TW4: Houn 2B 112
Renmuir St. SW17 6D 136
Rennell St. SE13 3E 122
Rennels Way TW7: Isle 2J 113
Renness Rd. E17 3A 50
Rennets Cl. SE9 5J 125
Rennets Wood Rd. SE9 5H 125
Rennie Cotts. E1 4J 85
(off Pemell Cl.)
Rennie Ct. SE1 4A 14 (1B 102)
(off Upper Ground)
Rennie Est. SE16 4H 103
Rennie Ho. SE1 3C 102
(off Bath Ter.)
Rennie St. SE1 4A 14 (1B 102)
(not continuous)
Rennie St. SE10 3J 105
Rennie St. 3J 105
Renoir Ct. SE16 5H 103
(off Stubbs Dr.)
Renovation, The E16 2F 107
(off Woolwich Mnr. Way)
Renown Cl. CR0: C'don 1B 168
Renown Cl. RM7: Mawney 1G 55
Rensburg Rd. E17 5K 49
Renshaw Cl. DA17: Belv 6F 109
Renshaw Cl. SE6 7C 122
Renters Av. NW4 6E 44
Renton Cl. SW2 6K 119
Renwick Dr. BR2: Broml 6B 160
Renwick Ind. Est. IG11: Bark 2B 90
Renwick Rd. IG11: Bark 4B 90
Repens Way UB4: Yead 4B 76
Rephidim St. SE1 3E 102
Replingham Rd. SW18 1H 135
Reporton Rd. SW6 7G 99
Repository Rd. SE18 6D 106
Repton Av. HA0: Wemb 4C 60
Repton Av. UB3: Harl 4F 93
Repton Cl. SM5: Cars 5C 166
Repton Ct. BR1: Broml 6B 142
Repton Ct. BR3: Beck 1D 158
Repton Gro. IG5: Ilf 1D 52
Repton Ho. E16 2K 105
(off Royal Crest Av.)
Repton Ho. E4 6K 35
Repton Ho. SW1 4B 18 (4G 101)
(off Charlwood St.)
REPTON PARK 7K 37
Repton Rd. BR6: Chels 3K 173
Repton Rd. HA3: Kenton 4F 43
Repton St. E14 6A 86
Repulse Cl. RM5: Col R 1G 55
Reservoir Cl. CR7: Thor H 3D 156
Reservoir Rd. HA4: Ruis 4E 38
Reservoir Rd. N14 5B 22
Reservoir Rd. SE4 2A 122
Reservoir Studios E1 6K 85
(off Cable St.)
Reservoir Way NW10 7C 62
Resham Cl. UB2: S'hall 3A 94
Residence Twr. N4 7C 48
(off Goodchild Rd.)
Resolution Plaza E1 7K 9 (6F 85)
(off Old Castle St.)
Resolution Wlk. SE18 3D 106
Resolution Way SE8 7C 104
(off Deptford High St.)
Restell Cl. SE3 6G 105
Restmor Way SM6: W'gton
2E 166
Reston Pl. SW7 2A 100
Restons Cres. SE9 6H 125
Restoration Sq. SW11 1B 118
Restormel Cl. TW3: Houn 5E 112
Restormel Ho. SE11 4K 19 (4A 102)
(off Chester Way)
Retcar Pl. N19 2F 65
Retford St. N1 1H 9 (2E 84)
Retingham Way E4 2J 35
Retles Ct. HA1: Harr 7J 41
Retreat, The CR7: Thor H 4D 156
Retreat, The HA2: Harr 7E 40
Retreat, The KT4: Wor Pk 2D 164
Retreat, The KT5: Surb 6F 151
Retreat, The NW9 5K 43
Retreat, The SW14 3A 116
Retreat Cl. HA3: Kenton 5C 42
Retreat Ho. E9 6J 67
Retreat Mobile Home Pk., The
IG9: Buck H 2D 36
Retreat Pl. E9 6J 67
Retreat Rd. TW9: Rich 5D 114
Reubens Ct. W4 5H 97
(off Chaseley Dr.)
Reuters Plaza E14 1D 104
(off The South Colonnade)
Reveley Sq. SE16 2A 104
Revell Ri. SE18 6K 107
Revell Rd. KT1: King T 2H 151
Revell Rd. SM1: Sutt 6H 165
Revelon Rd. SE4 4A 122
Revelstoke Rd. SW18 2H 135
Reventlow Rd. SE9 1G 143
Reverdy Rd. SE1 4G 103
Reverend Cl. HA2: Harr 3F 59
Revesby Rd. SM5: Cars 6B 154
Review Lodge RM10: Dag 1H 91
Review Rd. NW2 2B 62
Review Rd. RM10: Dag 1H 91
Revolution Karting 5B 86
Rewell St. SW6 7A 100
Rewley Rd. SM5: Cars 6B 154
Rex Av. TW15: Ashf 6C 128
Rex Cl. RM5: Col R 1H 55
Rex Pl. W1 3H 11 (7E 82)
Reydon Av. E11 5A 52
Reynard Cl. BR1: Broml 3E 160
Reynard Cl. SE4 3A 122
Reynard Dr. SE19 7F 139
Reynard Pl. SE14 6A 104
Reynardson Rd. N17 7H 33
Reynard Way TW8: Bford 5C 96
Reynolah Gdns. SE7 5K 105
Reynolds Av. E12 5E 70
Reynolds Av. KT9: Chess 7F 162
Reynolds Av. RM6: Chad H 7C 54
Reynolds Cl. NW11 7K 45
Reynolds Cl. SM5: Cars 1D 166
Reynolds Cl. SW19 1B 154
Reynolds Ct. RM6: Chad H 3D 54
Reynolds Dr. HA8: Edg 3F 43
Reynolds Ho. E2 2J 85
(off Approach Rd.)
Reynolds Ho. NW8 2B 82
(off Wellington Rd.)
Reynolds Ho. SW1 4D 18 (4H 101)
(off Erasmus St.)
Reynolds Pl. SE3 7K 105
Reynolds Pl. TW10: Rich 6F 115
Reynolds Rd. KT3: N Mald 7K 151
Reynolds Rd. SE15 4J 121
Reynolds Rd. UB4: Yead 4A 76
Reynolds Rd. W4 3J 97
Reynolds Sports Cen. 2G 97
Reynolds Way CR0: C'don 4E 168
Rheidol M. N1 2C 84
Rheidol Ter. N1 1C 84
Rheingold Way SM6: W'gton 7J 167
Rhein Ho. N8 3J 47
(off Campsfield Rd.)
Rheola Cl. N17 1F 49
Rhoda St. E2 3K 9 (4F 85)
Rhodes Av. N22 1G 47
Rhodes Ho. N1 1E 8 (3D 84)
(off Provost St.)
Rhodesia Rd. E11 2F 69
Rhodesia Rd. SW9 2J 119
Rhodes Moorhouse Ct. SM4: Mord
6J 153
Rhodes St. N7 5K 65
Rhodeswell Rd. E14 5A 86
(not continuous)
Rhodium Ct. E14 5C 86
(off Thomas Rd.)
Rhodrons Av. KT9: Chess 5E 162
Rhondda Gro. E3 3A 86
RHS Lawrence Hall 2C 18 (3H 101)
RHS Lindley Hall 3C 18 (4H 101)
(off Vincent Sq.)
Rhyl Rd. UB6: G'frd 2K 77
Rhyl St. NW5 6E 64
Rhys Av. N11 7C 32
Rialto Rd. CR4: Mitc 2E 154
Ribble Cl. IG8: Wfd G 6F 37
Ribblesdale Av. N11 6K 31
Ribblesdale Av. UB5: N'olt 6F 59
Ribblesdale Ho. NW6 1J 81
(off Kilburn Vale)
Ribblesdale Rd. N8 4K 47
Ribblesdale Rd. SW16 6F 137
Ribbon Dance M. SE5 1D 120
Ribbons Wlk. E20 5E 68
Ribchester Av. UB6: G'frd 3K 77
Ribston Cl. BR2: Broml 1D 172
Ricardo Path SE28 1C 108
Ricardo St. E14 6D 86
Ricards Rd. SW19 5H 135
Riccall Ct. NW9 1A 44
(off Pageant Av.)
Rice Pde. BR5: Pet W 5H 161
Riceyman Ho. WC1 2J 7 (3A 84)
(off Lloyd Baker St.)
Richard Anderson Ct. SE14 7K 103
(off Monson Rd.)
Richard Burbidge Mans. SW13 6E 98
(off Brasenose Dr.)
Richard Burton Ct. IG9: Buck H 2F 37
(off Palmerston Rd.)
Richard Challoner Sports Cen. 7K 151
Richard Cl. SE18 4C 106
Richard Fell Ho. E12 4E 70
(off Walton Rd.)
Richard Fielden Ho. E1 3A 86
Richard Ho. SE16 4J 103
(off Silwood St.)
Richard Ho. Dr. E16 6B 88
Richard Neale Ho. E1 7H 85
(off Cornwall St.)
Richard Neve Ho. SE18 4J 107
(off Plumstead High St.)
Richard Robert Residence, The
E15 6F 69
(off Salway Rd.)
Richard Ryan Pl. RM9: Dag 1E 90
Richards Av. RM7: Rom 6J 55
Richards Cl. HA1: Harr 5A 42
Richards Cl. UB10: Hil 1C 74
Richards Cl. UB3: Harl 6F 93
Richards Cl. WD23: Bush 1C 26
Richards Fld. KT19: Ewe 7K 163
Richard Sharples Ct. SM2: Sutt
7A 166
Richardson Cl. E8 1F 85
Richardson Ct. SW4 2J 119
(off Studley Rd.)
Richardson Gdns. RM10: Dag 6H 73
Richardson Rd. E15 2G 87
Richardson's M. W1 4A 6 (4G 83)
(off Warren St.)
Richard's Pl. SW3 3D 16 (4C 100)
Richards Pl. E17 3C 50
Richard St. E1 6H 85
Richard Tress Way E3 4B 86
Richbell WC1 5G 7 (5K 83)
(off Boswell St.)
Richbell Pl. WC1 5G 7 (5K 83)
Richborne Ter. SW8 7K 101
Richborough Ho. SE15 6J 103
(off Sharratt St.)
Richborough Rd. NW2 4G 63
Richbourne Ct. W1 7D 4 (6C 82)
(off Harrowby St.)
Richens Cl. TW3: Houn 2H 113
Riches Rd. IG1: Ilf 2G 71
Richfield Rd. WD23: Bush 1B 26
Richford Ga. W6 3E 98
Richford Rd. E15 1H 87
Richford St. W6 2E 98
Rich Ind. Est. SE1 4E 102
Rich Ind. Est. SE15 6H 103
Richland Ho. SE15 1G 121
(off Goldsmith Rd.)
Richlands Av. KT17: Ewe 4C 164
Rich La. SW5 5K 99
Richman Ho. SE8 5B 104
(off Grove St.)
Richmix Sq. E1 3K 9 (4F 85)
(off Bethnal Grn. Rd.)
RICHMOND 5D 114
Richmond, The American International University in London Kensington Campus, Ansdell Street 3K 99
(off Ansdell St.)
Richmond, The American International University in London Kensington Campus, St Albans Grove 3K 99
Richmond, The American International University in London Kensington Campus, Young Street 2K 99
Richmond, The American International University in London Richmond Hill Campus 7E 114
Richmond & London Scottish RUFC
3D 114
Richmond Athletic Ground 3D 114
Richmond Av. E4 5A 36
Richmond Av. N1 1K 83
Richmond Av. NW10 6E 62
Richmond Av. SW20 1G 153
Richmond Av. TW14: Felt 6G 111
Richmond Av. UB10: Hil 6D 56
RICHMOND BRI. 6D 114
Richmond Bldgs. W1 1C 12 (6H 83)
RICHMOND CIRCUS 4E 114
Richmond Cl. E17 6B 50
Richmond Cotts. W14 4G 99
(off Hammersmith Rd.)
Richmond Ct. CR4: Mitc 3B 154
Richmond Ct. E8 7H 67
(off Mare St.)
Richmond Ct. HA9: Wemb 3F 61
Richmond Ct. N11 6K 31
(off Pickering Gdns.)
Richmond Ct. NW6 7F 63
(off Willesden La.)
Richmond Ct. SW1 7F 11 (2D 100)
(off Sloane St.)
Richmond Ct. W14 4G 99
(off Hammersmith Rd.)
Richmond Cres. E4 5A 36
Richmond Cres. N1 1K 83
Richmond Cres. N9 1B 34
Richmond Cricket Ground 3E 114
Richmond Dr. IG8: Wfd G 7K 37
Richmond Dr. TW17: Shep 6F 147
Richmond FC 3D 114
Richmond Gdns. HA3: Hrw W 7E 26
Richmond Gdns. NW4 5C 44
Richmond Golf Course Surrey 2E 132
Richmond Grn. CR0: Bedd 3J 167
Richmond Gro. KT5: Surb 6F 151
Richmond Gro. N1 7B 66
(not continuous)
Richmond Hill TW10: Rich 6E 114
Richmond Hill Ct. TW10: Rich 6E 114
Richmond Ho. E3 5C 86
(off Bow Common La.)
Richmond Ho. NW1 1K 5 (2F 83)
(off Park Village E.)
Richmond Ho. SE17 5D 102
(off Portland St.)
Richmond Mans. SW5 5K 99
(off Old Brompton Rd.)
Richmond Mans. TW1: Twick 6D 114
Richmond M. SE6 1D 140
Richmond M. TW11: Tedd 5K 131
Richmond M. W1 1C 12 (6H 83)
Richmond Olympus Gym & Squash Club Richmond 4D 114
Richmond Pde. TW1: Twick 6C 114
(off Richmond Rd.)
Richmond Pk. 1G 133
Richmond Pk. Golf Course 7A 116
Richmond Pk. Rd. KT2: King T 1E 150
Richmond Pk. Rd. SW14 5J 115
Richmond Pl. SE18 4G 107
Richmond Rd. CR0: Bedd 3J 167
Richmond Rd. CR7: Thor H 3B 156
Richmond Rd. E11 2F 69
Richmond Rd. E4 1A 36
Richmond Rd. E7 5K 69
Richmond Rd. E8 7F 67
Richmond Rd. EN5: New Bar 5E 20
Richmond Rd. IG1: Ilf 3G 71
Richmond Rd. KT2: King T 5D 132
Richmond Rd. N11 6D 32
Richmond Rd. N15 6E 48
Richmond Rd. N2 2A 46
Richmond Rd. SW20 1D 152
Richmond Rd. TW1: Twick 7B 114
Richmond Rd. TW7: Isle 3A 114
Richmond Rd. W5 2E 96
Richmond St. E13 2J 87
Richmond Ter. SW1 6E 12 (2J 101)
Richmond Theatre 4D 114
Richmond Way E11 2J 69
Richmond Way W12 2F 99
Richmond Way W14 3F 99
Richmount Gdns. SE3 3J 123
Rich St. E14 7B 86
Rickard Cl. NW4 4D 44
Rickard Cl. SW2 1A 138
Rickard Cl. UB7: W Dray 3A 92
Rickards Cl. KT6: Surb 2E 162
Rickett St. SW6 6J 99
Rickman Ho. E1 3J 85
(off Rickman St.)
Rickman St. E1 4J 85
Rickmansworth Rd. HA5: Pinn 2K 39
Rick Roberts Way E15 1E 86
Rickthorne Rd. N19 2J 65
Rickyard Path SE9 4C 124
Riddell Ct. SE5 5F 103
(off Albany Rd.)
Ridding La. UB6: G'frd 5K 59
Riddons Rd. SE12 3A 142
Ride, The EN3: Pond E 3D 24
Ride, The TW8: Bford 5B 96
Rideout St. SE18 4D 106
Rider Cl. DA15: Sidc 6J 125
Riders Twr. E17 5B 50
(off Track St.)
Rideway Dr. W3 3G 97
Ridgdale St. E3 2D 86
Ridge, The BR6: Orp 2H 173
Ridge, The DA5: Bexl 7F 127
Ridge, The KT5: Surb 5G 151
Ridge, The TW2: Whitt 7H 113
Ridge Av. N21 7H 23
Ridgebrook Rd. SE3 3B 124
Ridge Cl. NW4 2F 45
Ridge Cl. NW9 4K 43
Ridge Cl. SE28 2H 107
Ridge Ct. SE22 7G 121
Ridge Crest EN2: Enf 1E 22
Ridgecroft Cl. DA5: Bexl 1J 145
Ridge Hill NW11 1G 63
Ridgemead Cl. N14 2D 32
Ridgemont Gdns. HA8: Edg 4D 28
Ridgemount Av. CR0: C'don 1K 169
Ridgemount Cl. SE20 7H 139
Ridgemount Gdns. EN2: Enf 3G 23
Ridge Rd. CR4: Mitc 7F 137
Ridge Rd. N21 1H 33
Ridge Rd. N8 6K 47
Ridge Rd. NW2 3H 63
Ridge Rd. SM3: Sutt 1G 165
(not continuous)
Ridges Yd. CR0: C'don 3B 168
Ridgeview Cl. EN5: Barn 6A 20
Ridgeview Rd. N20 3E 30
Ridge Way SE19 6E 138
Ridge Way TW13: Hanw 3C 130
Ridgeway BR2: Hayes 2J 171
Ridgeway IG8: Wfd G 4F 37
Ridgeway, The CR0: Wadd 3K 167
Ridgeway, The E4 2J 35
Ridgeway, The HA2: Harr 5D 40
(not continuous)
Ridgeway, The HA3: Kenton 6C 42
Ridgeway, The HA4: Ruis 7J 39
Ridgeway, The HA7: Stan 6H 27
Ridgeway, The KT12: Walt T 7H 147
Ridgeway, The N11 4J 31
Ridgeway, The N14 2D 32
Ridgeway, The N3 7E 30
Ridgeway, The NW11 7G 45
Ridgeway, The NW7 3H 29
Ridgeway, The NW9 4K 43
Ridgeway, The W3 3G 97
Ridgeway Av. EN4: E Barn 6J 21
Ridgeway Cres. BR6: Orp 3J 173
Ridgeway Cres. Gdns. BR6: Orp 2J 173
Ridgeway Dr. BR1: Broml 4K 141
Ridgeway E. DA15: Sidc 5K 125
Ridgeway Gdns. IG4: Ilf 5C 52
Ridgeway Gdns. N6 7G 47
Ridgeway Rd. TW7: Isle 7J 95
Ridgeway Rd. Nth. TW7: Isle 6J 95
Ridgeway Wlk. UB5: N'olt 6C 58
(off Cowings Mead)
Ridgeway W. DA15: Sidc 5J 125
Ridgewell Cl. N1 1C 84
Ridgewell Cl. RM10: Dag 1H 91
Ridgewell Cl. SE26 4B 140
Ridgmount Gdns. WC1 5C 6 (5H 83)
Ridgmount Pl. WC1 5C 6 (5H 83)
Ridgmount Rd. SW18 5K 117
Ridgmount St. WC1 5C 6 (5H 83)
Ridgway SW19 7E 134
Ridgway TW10: Rich 6E 114
Ridgway, The SM2: Sutt 7B 166
Ridgway Ct. SW19 6F 135
Ridgway Gdns. SW19 7F 135
Ridgway Pl. SW19 6G 135
Ridgway Rd. SW9 3B 120
Ridgwell Rd. E16 5A 88
Riding, The NW11 7H 45
Riding Ho. St. W1 6K 5 (5F 83)
Ridings, The E11 5J 51
Ridings, The EN4: E Barn 7G 21
Ridings, The KT17: Ewe 7B 164
Ridings, The KT5: Surb 5G 151
Ridings, The TW16: Sun 1J 147
Ridings, The W5 4F 79
Ridings Av. N21 4G 23
Ridings Cl. N6 7G 47
Ridings La. UB4: Hayes 2F 75
Ridler Rd. EN1: Enf 1K 23
Ridley Av. W13 3B 96
Ridley Cl. IG11: Bark 7K 71
Ridley Ct. SW16 6J 137
Ridley Ho. SW1 2D 18 (3H 101)
(off Monck St.)
Ridley Rd. BR2: Broml 3H 159
Ridley Rd. DA16: Well 1B 126
Ridley Rd. E7 4A 70
Ridley Rd. E8 5F 67
Ridley Rd. NW10 2C 80
Ridley Rd. SW19 7K 135
Ridsdale Rd. SE20 7H 139
Riefield Rd. SE9 4G 125
Riesco Dr. CR0: C'don 6J 169
Riffel Rd. NW2 5E 62
Rifle Club SW17 3K 135
Rifle St. E14 5D 86
Riga M. E1 7K 9 (6G 85)
(off Commercial Rd.)
Rigault Rd. SW6 2G 117
Rigby Cl. CR0: Wadd 3A 168
Rigby La. UB3: Hayes 2E 92
Rigby M. IG1: Ilf 2E 70
Rigden St. E14 6D 86
Rigeley Rd. NW10 3C 80
Rigg App. E10 1K 67
Rigge Pl. SW4 4H 119
Riggindale Rd. SW16 5H 137

A–Z London 277

Rodney Pl. E17 2A 50
Rodney Pl. SW17 4C 102
Rodney Pl. SW19 1A 154
Rodney Point SE16 2B 104
(off Rotherhithe St.)
Rodney Rd. CR4: Mitc 3C 154
Rodney Rd. E11 4K 51
Rodney Rd. KT3: N Mald 5A 152
Rodney Rd. SE17 4C 102
(not continuous)
Rodney Rd. TW2: Whitt 6E 112
Rodney St. N1 2K 83
Rodney Way RM7: Mawney 1H 55
Rodney Way SL3: Poyle 4A 174
Rodway Rd. BR1: Broml 1K 159
Rodway Rd. SW15 7C 116
Rodwell Cl. HA4: Ruis 1A 58
Rodwell Pl. HA8: Edg 6B 28
Rodwell Pl. RM10: Dag 6J 73
Rodwell Rd. SE22 6F 121
Roe NW9 7G 29
Roebourne Way E16 1E 106
Roebuck Cl. N17 6A 34
Roebuck Cl. TW13: Felt 4K 129
Roebuck Hgts. IG9: Buck H 1F 37
Roebuck La. IG9: Buck H 1F 37
Roebuck Rd. KT9: Chess 5G 163
Roedean Av. EN3: Enf H 1D 24
Roedean Cl. EN3: Enf H 1D 24
Roedean Cres. SW15 6A 116
Roe End NW9 4J 43
ROE GREEN 4J 43
Roe Grn. NW9 5J 43
ROEHAMPTON 7C 116
Roehampton Cl. SW15 4C 116
Roehampton Dr. BR7: Chst 6G 143
Roehampton Ga. SW15 6A 116
Roehampton Golf Course 4B 116
Roehampton High St. SW15 7C 116
Roehampton Ho. RM8: Dag 5A 72
Roehampton La. SW15 4C 116
ROEHAMPTON LANE 1D 134
Roehampton Sport & Fitness Cen. 7C 116
Roehampton University Digby Stuart College 5C 116
Roehampton University Main Site 5C 116
Roehampton University Southlands College 5C 116
Roehampton University Whitelands Site 7C 116
Roehampton Va. SW15 3B 134
Roe La. NW9 4H 43
Roesel Pl. BR5: Pet W 5F 161
Roe Way SM6: W'gton 6J 167
Roffe Gdns. RM8: Dag 1E 72
Roffey St. E14 2E 104
Roffo Ct. SE17 6D 102
(off Boundary La.)
Rogan Ho. SW8 1F 119
(off St Joseph's Ct.)
Rogate Ho. E5 3G 67
Roger Dowley Ct. E2 2J 85
Roger Harriss Almshouses E15 1H 87
(off Gift La.)
Roger Reede's Almshouses RM1: Rom 4K 55
Rogers Ct. E14 7C 86
(off Premiere Pl.)
Rogers Est. E2 3J 85
(not continuous)
Rogers Gdns. RM10: Dag 5G 73
Roger's Ho. RM10: Dag 3G 73
Rogers Ho. SW1 3D 18 (4H 101)
(off Page St.)
Rogers Rd. E16 6H 87
Rogers Rd. RM10: Dag 5G 73
Rogers Rd. SW17 4B 136
Rogers Ruff HA6: Nwood 1E 38
Roger St. WC1 4H 7 (4K 83)
Rogers Wlk. N12 3E 30
Rohere Ho. EC1 1C 8 (3C 84)
Rojack Rd. SE23 1K 139
Rokeby Gdns. IG8: Wfd G 1J 51
Rokeby Ho. SW12 7F 119
(off Lochinvar St.)
Rokeby Ho. WC1 4G 7 (4K 83)
(off Lamb's Conduit St.)
Rokeby Pl. SW20 7D 134
Rokeby Rd. HA1: Harr 3H 41
Rokeby Rd. SE4 2B 122
Rokeby St. E15 1F 87
Rokell Ho. BR3: Beck 5D 140
(off Beckenham Hill Rd.)
Roker Pk. Av. UB10: Ick 4A 56
Rokesby Cl. DA16: Well 2H 125
Rokesby Pl. HA0: Wemb 5D 60
Rokesly Av. N8 5J 47
Rokewood Apts. BR3: Beck 1C 158
Roland Gdns. SW10 6A 16 (5A 100)
Roland Gdns. SW7 5A 100
Roland Ho. SW7 5A 16 (5A 100)
(off Old Brompton Rd.)
Roland Mans. SW7 5A 100
(off Old Brompton Rd.)
Roland M. E1 5K 85
Roland Rd. E17 4F 51
Roland Way KT4: Wor Pk 2B 164
Roland Way SE17 5D 102
Roland Way SW7 5A 100
Roles Gro. RM6: Chad H 4D 54
Rolfe Cl. EN4: E Barn 4H 21
Rolfe Ter. SE18 5F 107
Rolinsden Way BR2: Kes 5B 172
Rolland Ho. W7 5J 77
Rollerbowl 2F 55
Rollesby Rd. KT9: Chess 6G 163
Rollesby Way SE28 6C 90
Rolleston Av. BR5: Pet W 6F 161
Rolleston Cl. BR5: Pet W 7F 161
Rolleston Rd. CR2: S Croy 7D 168
Roll Gdns. IG2: Ilf 5E 52
Rolling Mills M. E14 6A 86
Rollins Ho. SE15 6J 103
(off Rollins St.)
Rollins St. SE15 6J 103
Rollit Cres. TW3: Houn 5E 112
Rollit St. N7 5A 66
Rolls Bldgs. EC4 7J 7 (6A 84)
Rollscourt Av. SE24 5C 120
Rolls Pk. Av. E4 5J 35
Rolls Pk. Rd. E4 5J 35
Rolls Pas. EC4 7J 7 (6A 84)
(off Chancery La.)
Rolls Rd. SE1 5F 103
Rolls Royce Cl. SM6: W'gton 7J 167
Rolt St. SE8 6A 104
(not continuous)
Rolvenden Gdns. BR1: Broml 7B 142
Rolvenden Pl. N17 1G 49
Roma Corte SE13 3D 122
(off Elmira St.)
Romana Ct. CR0: C'don 2F 169
Roman Apts. E8 7H 67
(off Silesia Bldgs.)
Roman Cl. RM13: Rain 2K 91
Roman Cl. TW14: Felt 5A 112
Roman Cl. W3 2H 97
Roman Ct. N7 6K 65
Romanfield Rd. SW2 7K 119
Roman Ho. EC2 6D 8 (5C 84)
(off Wood St.)
Roman Ho. RM13: Rain 2K 91
Romanhurst Av. BR2: Broml 4G 159
Romanhurst Gdns. BR2: Broml 4G 159
Roman Ind. Est. CR0: C'don 7E 156
Roman Ri. SE19 6D 138
Roman Rd. NW2 Edgware Rd. 3E 62
Roman Rd. NW2 Temple Rd. 3E 62
Roman Rd. E2 3J 85
Roman Rd. E3 2A 86
Roman Rd. E6 4B 88
Roman Rd. IG1: Ilf 6F 71
Roman Rd. N10 7A 32
Roman Rd. W4 4A 98
Roman Rd. Mkt. 1B 86
(off Roman Rd.)
Roman Sq. SE28 1A 108
Roman Way BR3: Beck 5D 158
Roman Way CR0: C'don 2B 168
Roman Way EN1: Enf 5A 24
Roman Way N7 6K 65
Roman Way SE15 7J 103
Roman Way Ind. Est. N7 7K 65
(off Roman Way)
Romany Gdns. E17 1A 50
Romany Gdns. SM3: Sutt 7J 153
Romany Ri. BR5: Farnb 1G 173
Roma Read Cl. SW15 7D 116
Roma Rd. E17 3A 50
Romayne Ho. SW4 3H 119
Romberg Rd. SW17 3E 136
Romborough Gdns. SE13 5E 122
Romborough Way SE13 5E 122
Romero Cl. SW9 3K 119
Romeyn Rd. SW16 3K 137
Romford Greyhound Stadium 6J 55
Romford Rd. E12 5B 70
Romford Rd. E15 6G 69
Romford Rd. E7 6H 69
Romford St. E1 5G 85
Romilly Ho. W11 7G 81
(off Wilsham St.)
Romilly Rd. N4 2B 66
Romilly St. W1 2D 12 (7H 83)
Romily Ct. SW6 2H 117
Rommany Rd. SE27 4D 138
(not continuous)
Romney Cl. HA2: Harr 7E 40
Romney Cl. KT9: Chess 4E 162
Romney Cl. N17 1H 49
Romney Cl. NW11 1A 64
Romney Cl. SE14 7J 103
Romney Cl. TW15: Ashf 5E 128
Romney Ct. NW3 6C 64
Romney Ct. UB5: N'olt 2B 76
(off Parkfield Dr.)
Romney Ct. W12 2F 99
(off Shepherd's Bush Grn.)
Romney Dr. BR1: Broml 7B 142
Romney Dr. HA2: Harr 7E 40
Romney Gdns. DA7: Bex 1F 127
Romney Ho. SW1 2D 18 (3H 101)
(off Marsham St.)
Romney M. W1 5G 5 (5E 82)
Romney Pde. UB4: Hayes 2F 75
Romney Rd. KT3: N Mald 6K 151
Romney Rd. SE10 6F 105
Romney Rd. UB4: Hayes 2F 75
Romney Row NW2 2F 63
(off Brent Ter.)
Romney St. SW1 2E 18 (3J 101)
Romola Rd. SE24 1B 138
Romsey Cl. BR6: Farnb 4F 173
Romsey Gdns. RM9: Dag 1D 90
Romsey Rd. RM9: Dag 1D 90
Romsey Rd. W13 7A 78
Romside Pl. RM7: Rom 4K 55
Romulus Ct. TW8: Bford 7D 96
Romulus Dr. BR3: Beck 5D 158
Ronald Av. E15 3G 87
Ronald Buckingham Ct. SE16 2J 103
(off Kenning St.)
Ronald Cl. BR3: Beck 4B 158
Ronald Ct. EN5: New Bar 3E 20
Ronaldshay N4 7A 48
Ronalds Rd. BR1: Broml 1J 159
Ronalds Rd. N5 5A 66
(not continuous)
Ronaldstone Rd. DA15: Sidc 6J 125
Ronald St. E1 6J 85
Rona Rd. NW3 4E 64
Ronart St. HA3: W'stone 3K 41
Rona Wlk. N1 6D 66
Rondel Ct. DA5: Bexl 6E 126
Rondu Rd. NW2 5G 63
Ronelean Rd. KT6: Surb 2F 163
Ron Grn. Ct. DA8: Erith 6K 109
Ron Leighton Way E6 1C 88
Ronnie La. E12 4E 70
(not continuous)
Ron Todd Cl. RM10: Dag 1G 91
Ronver Rd. SE12 7H 123
Rood La. EC3 2G 15 (7E 84)
Roof Ter. Apts., The EC1 4B 8 (4B 84)
(off Gt. Sutton St.)
Rookby Ct. N21 2G 33
Rook Cl. HA9: Wemb 3H 61
Rookeries Cl. TW13: Felt 3K 129
Rookery Cl. NW9 5B 44
Rookery Ct. E10 3D 68
Rookery Cres. RM10: Dag 7H 73
Rookery Dr. BR7: Chst 1E 160
Rookery La. BR2: Broml 6B 160
Rookery Rd. SW4 4G 119
Rookery Way NW9 5B 44
Rooke Way SE10 5H 105
Rookfield Av. N10 4G 47
Rookfield Cl. N10 4G 47
Rooksmead Rd. TW16: Sun 2H 147
Rooks Ter. UB7: W Dray 2A 92
Rookstone Rd. SW17 5D 136
Rook Wlk. E6 6B 88
Rookwood Av. KT3: N Mald 4C 152
Rookwood Av. SM6: Bedd 4H 167
Rookwood Gdns. E4 2C 36
Rookwood Rd. N16 7F 49
Rookwood Way E3 7C 68
Roosevelt Memorial 2H 11 (7E 82)
Roosevelt Way RM10: Dag 6K 73
Rootes Dr. W10 5F 81
Ropemaker Rd. SE16 2A 104
Ropemaker's Flds. E14 7B 86
Ropemaker St. EC2 5E 8 (5D 84)
Roper Cres. TW16: Sun 1J 147
Roper La. SE1 7H 15 (2E 102)
Ropers Av. E4 5J 35
Ropers Orchard SW3 7C 16 (6C 100)
(off Danvers St.)
Roper St. SE9 5D 124
Ropers Wlk. SW2 7A 120
Roper Way CR4: Mitc 2E 154
Ropery Bus. Pk. SE7 4A 106
Ropery St. E3 4B 86
Rope St. SE16 4A 104
Rope Ter. E16 2K 105
Rope Wlk. TW16: Sun 3A 148
Ropewalk Gdns. E1 6G 85
Ropewalk M. E8 7G 67
Ropeworks, The IG11: Bark 1G 89
Ropley St. E2 1K 9 (2G 85)
Rosa Alba M. N5 4C 66
Rosa Av. TW15: Ashf 4C 128
Rosalind Ct. NW7 4K 29
Rosalind Ct. IG11: Bark 7A 72
(off Meadow Rd.)
Rosalind Ho. N1 2E 84
(off Arden Est.)
Rosaline Rd. SW6 7G 99
Rosaline Ter. SW6 7G 99
(off Rosaline Rd.)
Rosa M. E17 3B 50
Rosamond St. SE26 3H 139
Rosamund Cl. CR2: S Croy 4D 168
Rosamun St. UB2: S'hall 4C 94
Rosa Parks Ho. SE17 4C 102
(off Munton Rd.)
Rosary Cl. TW3: Houn 2C 112
Rosary Gdns. SW7 4A 100
Rosary Gdns. TW15: Ashf 4D 128
Rosaville Rd. SW6 7H 99
Roscoe St. EC1 4D 8 (4C 84)
(not continuous)
Roscoe St. Est. EC1 4D 8 (4C 84)
Roscoff Cl. HA8: Edg 1J 43
Rosea Apts. SW11 4C 118
(off Danvers Av.)
Roseacre Cl. SM1: Sutt 2A 166
Roseacre Cl. TW17: Shep 5C 146
Roseacre Cl. W13 5B 78
Roseacre Rd. DA16: Well 3B 126
Rose All. EC2 6H 9 (5E 84)
(off Bishopsgate)
Rose All. SE1 4D 14 (1C 102)
Rose & Crown Ct. EC2 7C 8 (6C 84)
(off Foster La.)
Rose & Crown M. TW7: Isle 1A 114
Rose & Crown Yd. SW1 5B 12 (1G 101)
Rose Apts. SE11 7K 19 (6A 102)
(off St Agnes Pl.)
Roseary Cl. UB7: W Dray 1E 174
Rose Av. CR4: Mitc 1D 154
Rose Av. E18 2K 51
Rose Av. SM4: Mord 5A 154
Rosebank SE20 7H 139
Rosebank SW6 7E 98
Rosebank W3 6K 79
Rosebank Av. HA0: Wemb 4K 59
Rosebank Cl. N12 5H 31
Rosebank Cl. TW11: Tedd 6A 132
Rosebank Gdns. E3 2B 86
Rosebank Gdns. W3 6K 79
Rosebank Gdns. Nth. E3 2B 86
Rosebank Gro. E17 3B 50
Rosebank Rd. E17 6D 50
Rosebank Rd. W7 2J 95
Rosebank Vs. E17 4C 50
Rosebank Wlk. NW1 7H 65
Rosebank Wlk. SE18 4C 106
Rosebank Way W3 6K 79
Rose Bates Dr. NW9 4G 43
Rosebay Dr. N17 2F 49
Rosebay Ho. E3 5C 86
(off Hawgood St.)
Roseberry Dr. HA8: Edg 2C 28
Roseberry Gdns. BR6: Orp 3J 173
Roseberry Gdns. N4 6B 48
Roseberry Mans. N1 1J 83
(off Tapper Wlk.)
Roseberry M. SW2 6J 119
Roseberry Pl. E8 6F 67
Roseberry St. SE16 4H 103
Rosebery Av. CR7: Thor H 2C 156
Rosebery Av. DA15: Sidc 7J 125
Rosebery Av. E12 6C 70
Rosebery Av. EC1 4J 7 (4A 84)
Rosebery Av. HA2: Harr 4C 58
Rosebery Av. KT3: N Mald 2B 152
Rosebery Av. N17 2G 49
Rosebery Cl. SM4: Mord 6F 153
Rosebery Ct. EC1 4J 7 (4A 84)
(off Rosebery Av.)
Rosebery Ct. W1 4J 11 (1F 101)
(off Charles St.)
Rosebery Gdns. N8 5J 47
Rosebery Gdns. SM1: Sutt 4K 165
Rosebery Gdns. W13 6A 78
Rosebery Ho. E2 2J 85
(off Sewardstone Rd.)
Rosebery Ind. Pk. N17 2H 49
Rosebery M. N10 2G 47
Rosebery Pl. NW7 7G 29
Rosebery Rd. KT1: King T 2H 151
Rosebery Rd. N10 2G 47
Rosebery Rd. SM1: Sutt 6H 165
Rosebery Rd. SW2 6J 119
Rosebery Rd. TW3: Houn 5G 113
Rosebery Rd. WD23: Bush 1A 26
Rosebery Sq. EC1 4J 7 (4A 84)
(off Rosebery Av.)
Rosebery Sq. KT1: King T 2H 151
Rosebine Av. TW2: Twick 7H 113
Rosebud M. SE16 3H 103
Rosebury Rd. SW6 2K 117
Rosebury Sq. IG8: Wfd G 7K 37
Rosebury Va. HA4: Ruis 2J 57
Rose Bush Ct. NW3 5D 64
Rose Ct. E1 6J 9 (5F 85)
(off Wentworth St.)
Rose Ct. E8 7F 67
(off Richmond Rd.)
Rose Ct. HA0: Wemb 2E 78
(off Vicars Bri. Cl.)
Rose Ct. HA2: Harr 2G 59
Rose Ct. N1 1B 84
(off Collin's Yd.)
Rose Ct. SE8 4K 103
Rosecourt Rd. CR0: C'don 6K 155
Rosecrest Ct. N15 4F 49
Rosecroft N14 2D 32
Rosecroft Av. NW3 3J 63
Rosecroft Gdns. NW2 3C 62
Rosecroft Gdns. TW2: Twick 1H 131
Rosecroft Rd. UB1: S'hall 4E 76
Rosecroft Wlk. HA0: Wemb 5D 60
Rosecroft Wlk. HA5: Pinn 5B 40
Rose Dale BR6: Farnb 2F 173
Rosedale Av. UB3: Hayes 5F 75
Rosedale Cl. HA7: Stan 6G 27
Rosedale Cl. SE2 3B 108
Rosedale Cl. W7 2K 95
Rosedale Ct. HA1: Harr 4K 59
Rosedale Ct. N5 4B 66
Rosedale Dr. RM9: Dag 7B 72
Rosedale Gdns. RM9: Dag 7B 72
Rosedale Ho. N16 1D 66
Rosedale Pl. CR0: C'don 7K 157
Rosedale Rd. E7 5A 70
Rosedale Rd. KT17: Ewe 5C 164
Rosedale Rd. RM1: Rom 2J 55
Rosedale Rd. RM9: Dag 7B 72
Rosedale Rd. TW9: Rich 3E 114
Rosedale Ter. W6 3D 98
(off Dalling Rd.)
Rosedene NW6 1F 81
Rosedene Av. CR0: C'don 7J 155
Rosedene Av. SM4: Mord 5J 153
Rosedene Av. SW16 3K 137
Rosedene Av. UB6: G'frd 3E 76
Rosedene Ct. HA4: Ruis 1G 57
Rosedene Gdns. IG2: Ilf 4E 52
Rosedene Ter. E10 2D 68
Rosedew Rd. W6 6F 99
Rose End KT4: Wor Pk 1F 165
Rosefield Cl. SM5: Cars 5C 166
Rosefield Gdns. E14 7C 86
Roseford Ct. W12 2F 99
(off Shepherd's Bush Grn.)
Rose Gdn. Cl. HA8: Edg 6K 27
Rose Gdns. TW13: Felt 2J 129
Rose Gdns. UB1: S'hall 4E 76
Rose Gdns. W5 3D 96
Rosegate Ho. E3 2B 86
(off Hereford Rd.)
Rose Glen NW9 4K 43
Rose Glen RM7: Rush G 1K 73
Rosehart M. W11 6J 81
Rose Hatch Av. RM6: Chad H 3D 54
Roseheath Rd. TW4: Houn 5D 112
Rose Hill SM1: Sutt 2K 165
Rosehill KT10: Clay 6A 162
ROSEHILL 7A 154
Rosehill TW12: Hamp 1E 148
Rosehill Av. SM1: Sutt 1A 166
Rosehill Ct. SM4: Mord 7A 154
(off St Helier Av.)
Rosehill Ct. Pde. SM4: Mord 7A 154
(off St Helier Av.)
Rosehill Gdns. SM1: Sutt 2K 165
Rosehill Gdns. UB6: G'frd 5K 59
Rose Hill Pk. W. SM1: Sutt 1A 166
Rosehill Rd. SW18 6A 118
ROSE HILL RDBT. 7A 154
Rose Joan M. NW6 4J 63
Rosekey Ct. SE8 7B 104
(off Baildon St.)
Roseland Cl. N17 7J 33
Rose La. RM6: Chad H 3D 54
Rose Lawn WD23: B Hea 1B 26
Roseleigh Av. N5 4B 66
Roseleigh Cl. TW1: Twick 6D 114
Rose Lipman Bldg. 1E 84
Rosemary Av. EN2: Enf 1K 23
Rosemary Av. KT8: W Mole 3E 148
Rosemary Av. N3 2K 45
Rosemary Av. N9 1C 34
Rosemary Av. TW4: Houn 2B 112
Rosemary Branch Theatre 1D 84
(off Rosemary St.)
Rosemary Cl. CR0: C'don 6J 155
Rosemary Cl. UB8: Hil 5C 74
Rosemary Ct. SE15 7E 102
Rosemary Ct. SE8 6B 104
(off Dorking Cl.)
Rosemary Dr. E14 6F 87
Rosemary Dr. IG4: Ilf 5B 52
Rosemary Gdns. KT9: Chess 4E 162
Rosemary Gdns. RM8: Dag 1F 73
Rosemary Gdns. SW14 3J 115
Rosemary Ho. N1 1D 84
(off Colville Est.)
Rosemary Ho. NW10 1D 80
(off Uffington Rd.)
Rosemary La. SW14 3J 115
Rosemary Rd. DA16: Well 1K 125
Rosemary Rd. SE15 7F 103
Rosemary Rd. SW17 3A 136
Rosemary St. N1 1D 84
Rosemary Works N1 1D 84
(off Branch Pl.)
Rosemead Av. CR4: Mitc 3G 155
Rosemead Av. HA9: Wemb 5E 60
Rosemead Av. TW13: Felt 2H 129
Rosemead Cl. KT6: Surb 1G 163
Rosemere Pl. BR2: Broml 4G 159
Rose M. N18 4C 34
Rosemont Av. N12 6F 31
Rosemont Ct. W3 1H 97
(off Rosemont Rd.)
Rosemont Rd. HA0: Wemb 1E 78
Rosemont Rd. KT3: N Mald 3J 151
Rosemont Rd. NW3 6A 64
Rosemont Rd. TW10: Rich 6E 114
Rosemont Rd. W3 7H 79
Rosemoor Ho. W13 1A 96
(off Broadway)
Rosemoor St. SW3 4E 16 (4D 100)
Rosemount SM6: W'gton 6G 167
(off Clarendon Rd.)
Rosemount Cl. IG8: Wfd G 6J 37
Rosemount Dr. BR1: Broml 4D 160
Rosemount Point SE23 3K 139
Rosemount Rd. W13 6A 78
Rosenau Cres. SW11 1D 118
Rosenau Rd. SW11 1C 118
Rosenburg Rd. W3 2H 97
Rosendale Rd. SE21 7C 120
Rosendale Rd. SE24 7C 120
Roseneath Av. N21 1G 33
Roseneath Pl. SW16 4K 137
(off Curtis Fld. Rd.)
Roseneath Rd. SW11 6E 118
Roseneath Wlk. EN1: Enf 4K 23
Rosen's Wlk. HA8: Edg 3C 28
Rosenthal Rd. SE6 6D 122
Rosenthorpe Rd. SE15 5K 121
Rose Pk. Cl. UB4: Yead 5A 76
Rosepark Ct. IG5: Ilf 2D 52
Rose Pl. N8 6J 47
Rose Playhouse 4D 14 (1C 102)
(off Park St.)
Roserton St. E14 2E 104
Rosery, The CR0: C'don 6K 157
Roses, The IG8: Wfd G 7C 36
Rose Sq. SW3 5B 16 (5B 100)
Rose Stapleton Ter. SE1 3E 102
(off Page's Wlk.)
Rose St. EC4 7B 8 (6B 84)
Rose St. WC2 2E 12 (7J 83)
(not continuous)
Rose Theatre Kingston 2D 150
Rose Theatre Sidcup 1B 144
Rosethorn Cl. SW12 7H 119
Rose Tree M. IG8: Wfd G 6H 37
Rosetree Pl. TW12: Hamp 7E 130
Rosetta Cl. SW8 7J 101
(off Kenchester Cl.)
Rosetta Ct. SE19 7E 138
Rosetti Ter. RM8: Dag 4B 72
(off Marlborough Rd.)
Roseveare Rd. SE12 4A 142
Roseville N21 1F 33
(off The Green)
Roseville Av. TW3: Houn 5E 112
Roseville Rd. UB3: Harl 5J 93
Rosevine Rd. SW20 1E 152
Rose Wlk. BR4: W W'ck 2E 170
Rose Wlk. KT5: Surb 5H 151
Rose Way HA8: Edg 4D 28
Rose Way SE12 5J 123
Roseway SE21 6D 120
Rosewell Cl. SE20 7H 139
Rosewood KT7: T Ditt 2A 162
Rosewood Av. UB6: G'frd 5A 60
Rosewood Cl. DA14: Sidc 3C 144
Rosewood Ct. BR1: Broml 1A 160
Rosewood Ct. E11 4F 69
Rosewood Ct. KT2: King T 7G 133
Rosewood Ct. RM6: Chad H 5C 54
Rosewood Dr. TW17: Shep 5B 146
Rosewood Gdns. SE13 2E 122
Rosewood Gro. SM1: Sutt 2A 166
Rosewood Ho. SW8 7G 19 (6K 101)
Rosewood Sq. W12 6C 80
Rosher Cl. E15 7F 69
Roshni Ho. SW17 6C 136
Rosina St. E9 6K 67
Rosing Apts. BR2: Broml 4A 160
(off Homesdale Rd.)
Roskeen Ct. SW20 7E 134
Roskell Rd. SW15 3F 117
Rosler Bldg. SE1 5C 14 (1C 102)
(off Ewer St.)
Roslin Ho. E1 7K 85
(off Brodlove La.)
Roslin Rd. W3 3H 97
Roslin Way BR1: Broml 5J 141
Roslyn Cl. CR4: Mitc 2B 154
Roslyn Rd. N15 5D 48
Rosmead Rd. W11 7G 81
Rosoman Pl. EC1 3K 7 (4A 84)
Rosoman St. EC1 2K 7 (3A 84)
Rossall Cres. NW10 3F 79
Ross Apts. E16 7J 87
(off Seagull La.)
Ross Av. RM8: Dag 1F 73
Ross Cl. HA3: Hrw W 7B 26
Ross Cl. UB3: Harl 4F 93
Ross Cl. UB5: N'olt 4H 59
Ross Ct. E5 4H 67
(off Napoleon Rd.)
Ross Ct. NW9 3A 44
Ross Ct. SW15 7F 117
Ross Ct. W13 5B 78
(off Cleveland Rd.)
Rosscourt Mans. SW1 1K 17 (3F 101)
(off Buckingham Pal. Rd.)
Rossdale SM1: Sutt 5C 166
Rossdale Dr. N9 6D 24
Rossdale Dr. NW9 1J 61
Rossdale Rd. SW15 4E 116
Rosse Gdns. SE13 6F 123
Rosse M. SE3 1K 123
Rossendale St. E5 2H 67
Rossendale Way NW1 7G 65
Rossetti CR0: C'don 1C 168
(off Saffron Central Sq.)
Rossetti Ct. WC1 5C 6 (5H 83)
(off Ridgmount Pl.)
Rossetti Gdn. Mans. SW3 7E 16 (6D 100)
(off Flood St.)
Rossetti Ho. SW1 4D 18 (4H 101)
(off Erasmus St.)
Rossetti M. NW8 1B 82
Rossetti Rd. SE16 5H 103
Rossetti Studios SW3 7D 16 (6C 100)
(off Flood St.)
Ross Haven Pl. HA6: Nwood 1H 39
Ross Ho. E1 1H 103
(off Prusom St.)
Rossignol Gdns. SM5: Cars 2E 166
Rossindel Rd. TW3: Houn 5E 112
Rossington Cl. EN1: Enf 1C 24
Rossington St. E5 2G 67
Rossiter Cl. SE19 7C 138
Rossiter Flds. EN5: Barn 6B 20
Rossiter Gro. SW9 3A 120
Rossiter Rd. SW12 1F 137
Rossland Cl. DA6: Bex 5H 127
Rosslyn Av. E4 2C 36
Rosslyn Av. EN4: E Barn 6H 21
Rosslyn Av. RM8: Dag 7F 55
Rosslyn Av. SW13 3A 116

Rosslyn Av. – Rushcutters Ct.

Rosslyn Av. TW14: Felt 6J 111
Rosslyn Cl. BR4: W W'ck 3H 171
Rosslyn Cl. TW16: Sun 6G 129
Rosslyn Cl. UB3: Hayes 5F 75
Rosslyn Cres. HA1: Harr 4K 41
Rosslyn Cres. HA9: Wemb 4E 60
Rosslyn Gdns. HA9: Wemb 3E 60
Rosslyn Hill NW3 4B 64
Rosslyn Mans. NW6 7A 64
(off Goldhurst Ter.)
Rosslyn M. NW3 4B 64
Rosslyn Pk. M. NW3 5B 64
Rosslyn Rd. E17 4E 50
Rosslyn Rd. IG11: Bark 7H 71
Rosslyn Rd. TW1: Twick 6C 114
Rossmore Cl. EN3: Pond E 4E 24
Rossmore Cl. NW1 4D 4 (4C 82)
(off Rossmore Rd.)
Rossmore Ct. NW1 3E 4 (4D 82)
Rossmore Rd. NW1 4D 4 (4C 82)
Ross Pde. SM6: W'gton 6F 167
Ross Rd. SE25 3D 156
Ross Rd. SM6: W'gton 5G 167
Ross Rd. TW2: Whitt 1F 131
Ross Wlk. SE27 3D 138
Ross Way E14 6A 86
Ross Way SE9 3C 124
Rosswood Gdns. SM6: W'gton 6G 167
Rostella Rd. SW17 4B 136
Rostrevor Av. N15 6F 49
Rostrevor Gdns. UB2: S'hall 5C 94
Rostrevor Gdns. UB3: Hayes 1G 93
Rostrevor Mans. SW6 1H 117
(off Rostrevor Rd.)
Rostrevor M. SW6 1H 117
Rostrevor Rd. SW19 5J 135
Rostrevor Rd. SW6 1H 117
Roswell Apts. E3 5B 86
(off Joseph St.)
Rotary St. SE1 7B 14 (3B 102)
Rothay NW1 1K 5 (3F 83)
(off Albany St.)
Rothbury Cotts. SE10 4G 105
(off Maritius Rd.)
Rothbury Gdns. TW7: Isle 7A 96
Rothbury Rd. E9 7B 68
Rothbury Wlk. N17 7B 34
Rotheley Ho. E9 7J 67
(off Balcorne St.)
Rotherfield Ct. N1 7D 66
(off Rotherfield St.)
Rotherfield Rd. SM5: Cars 4E 166
Rotherfield St. N1 7C 66
Rotherham Wlk. SE1 5A 14 (1B 102)
(off Nicholson St.)
Rotherhill Av. SW16 6H 137
ROTHERHITHE 2J 103
Rotherhithe Bus. Est. SE16 4H 103
Rotherhithe New Rd. SE16 5H 103
Rotherhithe Old Rd. SE16 4K 103
Rotherhithe Sands Film Studios 2J 103
(off Tunnel Rd.)
Rotherhithe St. SE16 2J 103
ROTHERHITHE TUNNEL 1K 103
Rother Ho. SE15 4H 121
Rotherwick Hill W5 4F 79
Rotherwick Ho. E1 7G 85
(off Thomas More St.)
Rotherwick Rd. NW11 7J 45
Rotherwood Cl. SW20 1G 153
Rotherwood Rd. SW15 3F 117
Rothery St. N1 1B 84
(off St Marys Path)
Rothery Ter. SW9 7B 102
(off Foxley Rd.)
Rothesay Av. SW20 2G 153
Rothesay Av. TW10: Rich 4H 115
Rothesay Av. UB6: G'frd 6G 59
(not continuous)
Rothesay Ct. SE11 7J 19 (6A 102)
(off Harleyford St.)
Rothesay Ct. SE12 3K 141
Rothesay Ct. SE6 2H 141
(off Cumberland Pl.)
Rothesay Rd. SE25 4D 156
Rothley Ct. NW8 3A 4 (4B 82)
(off St John's Wood Rd.)
Rothsay Rd. E7 7A 70
Rothsay St. SE1 3E 102
Rothsay Wlk. E14 4C 104
(off Charnwood Gdns.)
Rothschild Ho. TW8: Bford 6F 97
Rothschild Rd. W4 4J 97
Rothschild St. SE27 4B 138
Roth Wlk. N7 2K 65
Rothwell Ct. HA1: Harr 5K 41
Rothwell Gdns. RM9: Dag 7C 72
Rothwell Ho. TW5: Hest 6E 94
Rothwell Rd. RM9: Dag 1C 90
Rothwell St. NW1 1D 82
Rotten Row NW3 Hampstead Heath 1A 64
Rotten Row SW7 Hyde Pk. 6B 10 (2B 100)
Rotterdam Dr. E14 3E 104
Rotunda, The RM7: Rom 5K 55
(off Yew Tree Gdns.)
Rotunda, The SW10 7A 100
Rotunda Cen., The 2E 150
Rotunda Ct. BR1: Broml 5K 141
(off Burnt Ash La.)
Rouel Rd. SE16 4G 103
Rougemont Av. SM4: Mord 6J 153
Roundabout Ho. HA6: Nwood 1J 39
Roundacre SW19 2F 135
Roundaway Rd. IG5: Ilf 1D 52
Roundel Cl. SE4 4B 122
Round Gro. CR0: C'don 7K 157
Roundhay Cl. SE23 2K 139
Roundhedge Way EN2: Enf 1E 22
Round Hill SE26 2J 139
(not continuous)
Roundhill Dr. EN2: Enf 4E 22
Roundhouse, The 7E 64
Roundhouse La. E20 6E 68
(off International Way)
ROUNDSHAW 7J 167
Roundshaw Downs Local Nature Reserve 7K 167
Roundtable Rd. BR1: Broml 3H 141
Roundtree Rd. HA0: Wemb 5B 60
Roundway, The N17 1C 48
Roundways HA4: Ruis 3H 57
Roundwood BR7: Chst 2F 161
Roundwood Av. UB11: Stock P 1E 92
Roundwood Cl. HA4: Ruis 7F 39
Roundwood Ct. E2 3K 85
Roundwood Rd. NW10 6B 62
Rounton Rd. E3 4C 86
Roupell Ho. KT2: King T 7F 133
(off Florence Rd.)
Roupell Rd. SW2 1K 137
Roupell St. SE1 5K 13 (1A 102)
Rousden St. NW1 7G 65
Rouse Gdns. SE21 4E 138
Rous Rd. IG9: Buck H 1H 37
Routemaster Cl. E13 3K 87
Routh Ct. TW14: Bedf 1F 129
Routh Rd. SW18 7C 118
Routh St. E6 5D 88
Rover Ho. N1 1E 84
(off Whitmore Est.)
Rowallan Rd. SW6 7G 99
Rowallen Pde. RM8: Dag 1C 72
Rowan N10 2F 47
Rowan Av. E4 6G 35
Rowan Av. NW9 7G 29
Rowan Cl. HA0: Wemb 3A 60
Rowan Cl. HA7: Stan 6E 26
Rowan Cl. IG1: Ilf 5H 71
Rowan Cl. KT3: N Mald 2A 152
Rowan Cl. SW16 1G 155
Rowan Cl. W5 2E 96
Rowan Ct. E13 2K 87
(off High St.)
Rowan Ct. SE15 7F 103
(off Garnies Cl.)
Rowan Ct. SW11 6D 118
Rowan Cres. SW16 1G 155
Rowan Dr. NW9 3C 44
Rowan Gdns. CR0: C'don 3F 169
Rowan Ho. BR2: Broml 2G 159
Rowan Ho. DA14: Sidc 3K 143
Rowan Ho. E3 1B 86
(off Hornbeam Sq.)
Rowan Ho. IG1: Ilf 5H 71
Rowan Ho. SE16 2K 103
(off Woodland Cres.)
Rowan Lodge W8 3K 99
(off Chantry Sq.)
Rowan Pl. UB3: Hayes 7H 75
Rowan Rd. DA7: Bex 3E 126
Rowan Rd. SW16 2G 155
Rowan Rd. TW8: Bford 7B 96
Rowan Rd. UB7: W Dray 1E 174
Rowan Rd. W6 4F 99
Rowans, The N13 3G 33
Rowans, The TW16: Sun 5H 129
Rowans Tenpin 2A 66
Rowan Ter. SW19 7G 135
Rowan Ter. W6 4F 99
Rowantree Cl. N21 1J 33
Rowantree Rd. EN2: Enf 2G 23
Rowantree Rd. N21 1J 33
Rowan Wlk. BR2: Broml 3D 172
Rowan Wlk. EN5: New Bar 5E 20
Rowan Wlk. N19 2G 65
Rowan Wlk. N2 5A 46
Rowan Wlk. W10 4G 81
Rowan Way RM6: Chad H 3C 54
Rowanwood Av. DA15: Sidc 1A 144
Rowanwood M. EN2: Enf 2G 23
Rowben Cl. N20 1E 30
Rowberry Cl. SW6 7E 98
Rowcross St. SE1 5F 103
Rowdell Rd. UB5: N'olt 1E 76
Rowden Pde. E4 6H 35
(off Chingford Rd.)
Rowden Pk. Gdns. E4 7H 35
Rowden Rd. BR3: Beck 1A 158
Rowden Rd. E4 6J 35
Rowden Rd. KT19: Ewe 4H 163
Rowditch La. SW11 2E 118
Rowdon Av. NW10 7D 62
Rowdown Cres. CR0: New Ad 7F 171
Rowdowns Rd. RM9: Dag 1F 91
Rowe Gdns. IG11: Bark 2K 89
Rowe Ho. E9 6J 67
Rowe La. E9 5J 67
Rowell Dr. HA2: Harr 3G 41
Rowena Cres. SW11 2C 118
Rowenhurst Mans. NW6 6A 64
(off Canfield Gdns.)
Rowe Wlk. HA2: Harr 3E 58
Rowfant Rd. SW17 1E 136
Rowhill Rd. E5 4H 67
Rowington Cl. W2 5K 81
Rowland Av. HA3: Kenton 3C 42
Rowland Ct. E16 4H 87
Rowland Gro. SE26 3H 139
(not continuous)
Rowland Hill Almshouses TW15: Ashf 5C 128
(off Feltham Hill Rd.)
Rowland Hill Av. N17 7J 33
Rowland Hill Ho. SE1 6A 14 (2B 102)
Rowland Hill St. NW3 5C 64
Rowlands Av. HA5: Hat E 5A 26
Rowlands Cl. N6 6E 46
Rowlands Cl. NW7 7H 29
Rowlands Rd. RM8: Dag 2F 73
Rowland Way SW19 1K 153
Rowland Way TW15: Ashf 7F 129
Rowley Av. DA15: Sidc 7B 126
Rowley Cl. HA0: Wemb 7F 61
Rowley Ct. EN1: Enf 5K 23
(off Wellington Rd.)
Rowley Gdns. N4 7C 48
Rowley Ho. SE8 5C 104
(off Watergate St.)
Rowley Ind. Pk. W3 3H 97
Rowley Rd. N15 5C 48
Rowley Way NW8 1K 81
Rowlheys Pl. UB7: W Dray 3A 92
Rowlls Rd. KT1: King T 3F 151
Rowney Gdns. RM9: Dag 6C 72
Rowney Rd. RM9: Dag 6B 72
Rowntree Clifford Cl. E13 4J 87
Rowntree Cl. NW6 6J 63
Rowntree M. E17 1B 50
Rowntree Path SE28 1B 108
Rowntree Rd. TW2: Twick 1J 131
Rowse Cl. E15 1E 86
Rowsley Av. NW4 3E 44
Rowstock Gdns. N7 5H 65
Rowton Rd. SE18 7G 107
Roxborough Av. HA1: Harr 7H 41
Roxborough Av. TW7: Isle 7K 95
Roxborough Hgts. HA1: Harr 6J 41
(off College Rd.)
Roxborough Pk. HA1: Harr 7J 41
Roxborough Rd. HA1: Harr 5H 41
Roxbourne Cl. UB5: N'olt 6B 58
Roxbourne Pk. Miniature Railway 2B 58
Roxburghe Mans. W8 2K 99
(off Kensington Ct.)
Roxburgh Pl. BR1: Broml 1C 160
Roxburgh Rd. SE27 5B 138
Roxburn Way HA4: Ruis 3H 57
Roxby Pl. SW6 6J 99
ROXETH 2H 59
Roxeth Ct. TW15: Ashf 5C 128
Roxeth Grn. Av. HA2: Harr 3F 59
Roxeth Grn. Av. UB5: N'olt 5E 58
Roxeth Gro. HA2: Harr 4F 59
Roxeth Hill HA2: Harr 2H 59
Roxford Cl. TW17: Shep 5G 147
Roxford Ho. E3 4D 86
(off Devas St.)
Roxley Rd. SE13 6D 122
Roxton Gdns. CR0: Addtn 5C 170
Roxwell NW1 6F 65
(off Hartland Rd.)
Roxwell Rd. IG11: Bark 2A 90
Roxwell Rd. W12 2C 98
Roxwell Trad. Pk. E10 7A 50
Roxwell Way IG8: Wfd G 7F 37
Roxy Av. RM6: Chad H 7C 54
Royal Academy of Arts (Burlington House) 3A 12 (7G 83)
Royal Academy of Music Mus. 4H 5 (4E 82)
(off Marylebone Rd.)
Royal Air Force Memorial 5F 13 (1J 101)
Royal Albert Hall 7A 10 (2B 100)
ROYAL ALBERT RDBT. 7C 88
(on Royal Albert Way)
Royal Albert Way E16 7B 88
Royal Anglian Way RM8: Dag 1E 72
Royal Arc. W1 3A 12 (7G 83)
(off Old Bond St.)
Royal Archer SE14 7K 103
(off Egmont St.)
ROYAL ARSENAL WEST 3F 107
Royal Av. KT4: Wor Pk 2A 164
Royal Av. SW3 5E 16 (5D 100)
Royal Av. Ho. SW3 5E 16 (5D 100)
(off Royal Av.)
Royal Belgrave Ho. SW1 4K 17 (4F 101)
(off Hugh St.)
Royal Blackheath Golf Course 7D 124
Royal Borough of Kensington & Chelsea Cemetery, The 1K 95
Royal Botanic Gdns. Kew 1E 114
Royal Brass Foundry 3F 107
Royal Carriage M. SE18 3F 107
Royal Cir. SE27 3A 138
Royal Cl. BR6: Farnb 4F 173
Royal Cl. IG3: Ilf 7A 54
Royal Cl. KT4: Wor Pk 2A 164
Royal Cl. N16 1E 66
Royal Cl. SE8 6B 104
Royal Cl. SW19 3F 135
Royal Cl. UB8: Hil 6B 74
Royal College of Music 1A 16 (3B 100)
Royal College of Nursing 7K 5 (6F 83)
(off Dean's M.)
Royal College of Physicians Mus. 3K 5 (4F 83)
Royal Coll. St. NW1 7G 65
Royal Connaught Apts. E16 1B 106
(off Connaught Rd.)
Royal Ct. EC3 1F 15 (6D 84)
(off Cornhill)
Royal Ct. EN1: Enf 6K 23
Royal Ct. HA4: Ruis 6J 39
Royal Ct. SE16 3B 104
Royal Ct. SE9 1D 142
Royal Courts of Justice 1H 13 (6K 83)
(off Strand)
Royal Court Theatre London 4G 17 (4E 100)
(off Sloane Sq.)
Royal Cres. HA4: Ruis 4C 58
Royal Cres. IG2: Ilf 6H 53
Royal Cres. W11 1F 99
Royal Cres. M. W11 1F 99
Royal Crest Av. E16 2K 105
Royal Docks Rd. E6 6F 89
Royal Docks Rd. IG11: Bark 4F 89
Royal Dr. N11 5K 31
(not continuous)
Royal Duchess M. SW12 7F 119
Royale Leisure Pk. W3 4G 79
Royal Engineers Way NW7 6B 30
Royal Exchange 1F 15 (6D 84)
Royal Exchange Av. EC3 1F 15 (6D 84)
(off Threadneedle St.)
Royal Exchange Bldgs. EC3 1F 15 (6D 84)
(off Threadneedle St.)
Royal Festival Hall 5H 13 (1K 101)
Royal Gdns. W7 3A 96
Royal Geographical Society 7A 10 (2B 100)
(off Kensington Gore)
Royal George M. SE5 4D 120
Royal Herbert Pavilions SE18 1D 124
Royal Hill SE10 7E 104
Royal Hill Ct. SE10 7E 104
(off Greenwich High St.)
Royal Holloway (University of London) Gower Street 5D 6 (5H 83)
(off Gower St.)
Royal Hospital Chelsea 6G 17 (5E 100)
Royal Hospital Chelsea Great Hall 6F 17 (5D 100)
Royal Hospital Chelsea Mus. 6G 17 (5E 100)
Royal Hospital Rd. SW3 7E 16 (6D 100)
Royal Institution 3A 12 (7G 83)
Royal La. UB7: Yiew 6B 74
Royal La. UB8: Hil 5B 74
Royal Langford Apts. NW6 2K 81
(off Greville Rd.)
Royal London Bldgs. SE15 6H 103
(off Old Kent Rd.)
Royal London Est., The N17 6C 34
Royal London Hospital Archives & Mus. 5H 85
(off Newark St.)
Royal London Ind. Est. NW10 2K 79
Royal M. KT8: E Mos 3J 149
Royal M. SW1 1K 17 (3F 101)
Royal Mews, The 7K 11 (2F 101)
Royal Mid-Surrey Golf Course 3D 114
Royal Mint Ct. EC3 3K 15 (7F 85)
Royal Mint Pl. E1 2K 15 (7G 85)
Royal Mint St. E1 2K 15 (7F 85)
Royal Naval Pl. SE14 7B 104
Royal Oak Ct. N1 1G 9 (3E 84)
(off Pitfield St.)
Royal Oak M. TW11: Tedd 5A 132
Royal Oak Pl. SE22 6H 121
Royal Oak Rd. DA6: Bex 5F 127
(not continuous)
Royal Oak Rd. E8 6H 67
Royal Oak Yd. SE1 7G 15 (2E 102)
Royal Observatory Greenwich 7G 105
Royal Opera Arc. SW1 4C 12 (1H 101)
Royal Opera House 1F 13 (6J 83)
Royal Orchard Cl. SW18 7G 117
Royal Pde. BR7: Chst 7G 143
Royal Pde. RM10: Dag 6H 73
Royal Pde. SE3 2H 123
Royal Pde. SW6 7G 99
Royal Pde. TW9: Kew 1G 115
(off Station App.)
Royal Pde. W5 3E 78
Royal Pde. M. BR7: Chst 7G 143
(off Royal Pde.)
Royal Pde. M. SE3 2H 123
(off Royal Pde.)
Royal Pl. SE10 7E 104
Royal Quarter KT2: King T 1E 150
Royal Quay Rd. E16 7F 89
Royal Rd. DA14: Sidc 3D 144
Royal Rd. E16 6B 88
Royal Rd. SE17 7K 19 (6B 102)
Royal Rd. TW11: Tedd 5H 131
Royal Route HA9: Wemb 4F 61
Royal St. SE1 1H 19 (3K 101)
Royal Thames Wlk. KT7: T Ditt 1A 162
Royal Twr. Lodge E1 3K 15 (7G 85)
(off Cartwright St.)
Royalty Mans. W1 1C 12 (6H 83)
(off Meard St.)
Royalty M. W1 1C 12 (6H 83)
Royalty Studios W11 6G 81
(off Lancaster Rd.)
Royal Veterinary Coll. Camden Town 1H 83
Royal Victoria Dock E16 7K 87
Royal Victoria Gdns. SE16 4A 104
(off Whiting Way)
Royal Victoria Patriotic Bldg. SW18 6B 118
Royal Victoria Pl. E16 1K 105
Royal Victoria Sq. E16 7K 87
Royal Victor Pl. E3 2K 85
Royal Wlk. SM6: W'gton 2F 167
Royal Westminster Lodge SW1 3C 18 (4H 101)
(off Elverton St.)
Royal Wharf E16 2K 105
Royal Wharf Wlk. E16 2K 105
Royal Wimbledon Golf Course 5D 134
Royce Av. NW9 2C 44
Roycraft Av. IG11: Bark 2K 89
Roycroft Av. IG11: Bark 2K 89
Roycroft Cl. E18 1K 51
Roycroft Cl. SW2 1A 138
Roydene Rd. SE18 6J 107
Roydon Cl. IG10: Lough 1H 37
Roydon Cl. SW11 2D 118
Roy Gdns. IG2: Ilf 4J 53
Roy Gro. TW12: Hamp 6F 131
Royle Bldg. N1 2C 84
(off Wenlock Rd.)
Royle Cres. W13 4A 78
Royley Ho. EC1 3D 8 (4C 84)
(off Old St.)
Roymount Ct. TW2: Twick 3J 131
Roy Rd. HA6: Nwood 1H 39
Roy Sq. E14 7A 86
Royston Av. E4 5H 35
Royston Av. SM1: Sutt 3B 166
Royston Av. SM6: Bedd 4H 167
Royston Cl. KT12: Walt T 7J 147
Royston Cl. TW5: Cran 1K 111
Royston Ct. E13 1J 87
(off Stopford Rd.)
Royston Ct. SE24 6C 120
Royston Ct. TW9: Kew 1F 115
Royston Ct. W8 1J 99
(off Kensington Chu. St.)
Royston Gdns. IG1: Ilf 6B 52
Royston Ho. N11 4J 31
Royston Ho. SE15 6H 103
(off Friary Est.)
Royston Pde. IG1: Ilf 6B 52
Royston Rd. SE20 1K 157
Royston Rd. TW10: Rich 5E 114
Roystons, The KT5: Surb 5H 151
Royston St. E2 2J 85
Rozel Ct. N1 1E 84
Rozel Rd. SW4 3G 119
Rozel Ter. CR0: C'don 3C 168
(off Church Rd.)
RQ33 SW18 4J 117
Rubastic Rd. UB2: S'hall 3A 94
Rubens Gdns. SE22 7G 121
(off Lordship La.)
Rubens Pl. SW4 4J 119
Rubens Rd. UB5: N'olt 2A 76
Rubens St. SE6 2B 140
Rubicon Ct. N1 1J 83
Ruby Cl. E5 3K 67
Ruby Ct. E15 1E 86
(off Warton Rd.)
Ruby Ct. RM8: Dag 1G 73
(off Emerald Gdns.)
Ruby M. N13 5D 32
Ruby Rd. E17 3C 50
Ruby St. NW10 7J 61
Ruby St. SE15 6H 103
Ruby Triangle SE15 6H 103
Ruby Way NW9 1B 44
Ruckholt Cl. E10 3D 68
Ruckholt Rd. E10 4C 68
Rucklidge Av. NW10 2B 80
Rucklidge Pas. NW10 2B 80
(off Rucklidge Av.)
Rudall Cres. NW3 4B 64
Rudbeck Ho. SE15 7G 103
(off Peckham Pk. Rd.)
Ruddington Cl. E5 4A 68
Ruddock Cl. HA8: Edg 7D 28
Ruddstreet Cl. SE18 4F 107
Ruddy Way NW7 6G 29
Rudge Ho. SE16 3G 103
(off Jamaica Rd.)
Rudgwick Ct. SE18 4C 106
(off Woodville St.)
Rudgwick Ter. NW8 1C 82
Rudland Rd. DA7: Bex 3H 127
Rudloe Rd. SW12 7G 119
Rudolph Rd. E13 2H 87
Rudolph Rd. NW6 2J 81
Rudstone Ho. E3 3D 86
(off Bromley High St.)
Rudyard Ct. SE1 7F 15 (2D 102)
(off Long La.)
Rudyard Gro. NW7 6D 28
Ruegg Ho. SE18 6E 106
(off Woolwich Comn.)
Ruffell M. RM6: Rom 4C 54
Ruffetts, The CR2: Sels 7H 169
Ruffetts Cl. CR2: Sels 7H 169
Ruffle Cl. UB7: W Dray 2A 92
Rufford Cl. HA3: Kenton 6A 42
Rufford St. N1 1J 83
Rufford St. M. N1 7J 65
Rufford Twr. W3 1H 97
Rufforth Ct. NW9 1A 44
(off Pageant Av.)
Rufus Bus. Cen. SW18 2K 135
Rufus Cl. HA4: Ruis 3C 58
Rufus Ho. SE1 7J 15 (3F 103)
(off St Saviour's Est.)
Rufus St. N1 2G 9 (3E 84)
Rugby Av. HA0: Wemb 5B 60
Rugby Av. N9 1A 34
Rugby Av. UB6: G'frd 6H 59
Rugby Cl. HA1: Harr 4J 41
Rugby Gdns. RM9: Dag 6C 72
Rugby Mans. W14 4G 99
(off Bishop King's Rd.)
Rugby Rd. NW9 4H 43
Rugby Rd. RM9: Dag 7B 72
Rugby Rd. TW1: Twick 5J 113
Rugby Rd. W4 2A 98
Rugby St. WC1 4G 7 (4K 83)
Rugg St. E14 7C 86
Rugless Ho. E14 2E 104
(off E. Ferry Rd.)
Rugmere NW1 7E 64
(off Ferdinand St.)
RUISLIP 1G 57
Ruislip Cl. UB6: G'frd 4F 77
RUISLIP COMMON 4E 38
Ruislip Ct. HA4: Ruis 2H 57
RUISLIP GARDENS 3J 57
Ruislip Golf Course 2E 56
Ruislip Lido 4F 39
Ruislip Lido Railway 4F 39
Ruislip Lido Woodlands Cen. 4F 39
RUISLIP MANOR 2J 57
Ruislip Rd. UB5: N'olt 1A 76
Ruislip Rd. UB6: G'frd 3E 76
Ruislip Rd. E. UB6: G'frd 4H 77
Ruislip Rd. E. W13 4K 77
Ruislip Rd. E. W7 4J 77
Ruislip Social Club 2H 57
(off Cranley Dr.)
Ruislip St. SW17 4D 136
Ruislip Woods 3E 38
Rumball Ho. SE5 7E 102
(off Harris St.)
Rumbold Rd. SW6 7K 99
Rum Cl. E1 7J 85
Rumford Ho. SE1 3C 102
(off Tiverton St.)
Rumsey Cl. TW12: Hamp 6D 130
Rumsey M. N4 3B 66
Rumsey Rd. SW9 3K 119
Runacres Ct. SE17 5C 102
Runbury Circ. NW9 2K 61
Runcie Ct. IG6: Ilf 4H 53
Runcorn Cl. N17 4H 49
Runcorn Pl. W11 7G 81
Rundell Cres. NW4 5D 44
Rundell Twr. SW8 1K 119
Runes Cl. CR4: Mitc 4B 154
Runnel Ct. IG11: Bark 2G 89
(off Spring Pl.)
Runnelfield HA1: Harr 3J 59
Running Horse Yd. TW8: Bford 6E 96
Runnymede SW19 1A 154
Runnymede Cl. TW2: Whitt 6F 113
Runnymede Ct. SM6: W'gton 6F 167
Runnymede Ct. SW15 1C 134
Runnymede Cres. SW16 1H 155
Runnymede Gdns. TW2: Whitt 6F 113
Runnymede Gdns. UB6: G'frd 2J 77
Runnymede Ho. E9 4A 68
Runnymede Rd. TW2: Whitt 6F 113
Runway, The HA4: Ruis 5K 57
Runway Cl. NW9 2B 44
Rupack St. SE16 2J 103
Rupert Av. HA9: Wemb 5E 60
Rupert Ct. KT8: W Mole 4E 148
(off St Peter's Rd.)
Rupert Ct. W1 2C 12 (7H 83)
Rupert Gdns. SW9 2B 120
Rupert Ho. SE11 4K 19 (4A 102)
Rupert Ho. SW5 4J 99
(off Nevern Sq.)
Rupert Rd. N19 3H 65
(not continuous)
Rupert Rd. NW6 2H 81
Rupert Rd. W4 3A 98
Rupert St. W1 2C 12 (7H 83)
Rural Way SW16 7F 137
Rusbridge Cl. E8 5G 67
Ruscoe Rd. E16 6H 87
Ruscombe NW1 1F 83
(off Delancey St.)
Ruscombe Way TW14: Felt 7H 111
Ruscus Rd. E17 1C 50
Rush, The SW19 1H 153
(off Watery La.)
Rusham Rd. SW12 6D 118
Rushbridge Cl. CR0: C'don 6C 156
Rushbrook Cres. E17 1B 50
Rushbrook Rd. SE9 2G 143
Rushbury Ct. TW12: Hamp 1E 148
Rush Comn. M. SW2 7K 119
Rushcroft Rd. E4 7J 35
Rushcroft Rd. SW2 4A 120
Rushcutters Ct. SE16 4A 104
(off Boat Lifter Way)

280 A-Z London

St Barnabas Rd. – St Margaret's

St Barnabas Rd. IG8: Wfd G 1K **51**
St Barnabas Rd. SM1: Sutt 5B **166**
St Barnabas St. SW1 5H **17** (5E **100**)
St Barnabas Ter. E9 5K **67**
St Barnabas Vs. SW8 1J **119**
St Bartholomew's Cl. SE26 4H **139**
St Bartholomew's Ct. E6 2C **88**
(off St Bartholomew's Rd.)
St Bartholomew's Hospital Mus. 6B **8** (5B **84**)
(in St Bartholomew's Hospital)
St Bartholomew's Rd. E6 2D **88**
St Benedict's Cl. SW17 5E **136**
St Benet's Cl. SW17 2C **136**
St Benet's Gro. SM5: Cars 7A **154**
St Benet's Pl. EC3 2F **15** (7D **84**)
St Bernards CR0: C'don 3E **168**
St Bernard's Cl. SE27 4D **138**
St Bernards Ho. E14 3E **104**
(off Galbraith St.)
St Bernard's Rd. E6 1B **88**
St Blaise Av. BR1: Broml 2K **159**
St Botolph Row EC3 1J **15** (6F **85**)
St Botolphs E1 7J **9** (6F **85**)
(off St Botolph St.)
St Botolph St. EC3 7J **9** (6F **85**)
St Brelades Ct. N1 1E **84**
St Bride's Av. EC4 1A **14** (6B **84**)
(off Bride La.)
St Bride's Av. HA8: Edg 1F **43**
St Brides Cl. DA18: Erith 2D **108**
St Bride's Crypt Mus. 1A **14** (6B **84**)
(off Fleet St.)
St Bride's Ho. E3 2C **86**
(off Ordell Rd.)
St Bride's Pas. EC4 1A **14** (6B **84**)
(off Salisbury Ct.)
St Bride St. EC4 7A **8** (6B **84**)
St Catherine's Apts. E3 3D **86**
(off Bow Rd.)
St Catherine's Cl. SW17 2C **136**
St Catherine's Cl. SW20 5E **152**
St Catherines Cl. KT9: Chess 6D **162**
St Catherine's Ct. W4 3A **98**
St Catherines Ct. TW13: Felt 1J **129**
St Catherine's Dr. SE14 2K **121**
St Catherine's Farm Ct. HA4: Ruis 6E **38**
St Catherines M. SW3 3E **16** (4D **100**)
St Catherine's Rd. E4 2H **35**
St Catherine's Rd. HA4: Ruis 6F **39**
St Cecilia Pl. SE3 5J **105**
St Cecilia's Cl. SM3: Sutt 1G **165**
St Chads Cl. KT6: Surb 7C **150**
St Chad's Gdns. RM6: Chad H 7E **54**
St Chad's Pl. WC1 1F **7** (3J **83**)
St Chad's Rd. RM6: Chad H 7E **54**
St Chad's St. WC1 1F **7** (3J **83**)
(not continuous)
St Charles Pl. W10 5G **81**
St Charles Sq. W10 5F **81**
St Chloe's Ho. E3 2C **86**
(off Ordell Rd.)
St Christopher Rd. UB8: Cowl 6A **74**
St Christopher's Cl. TW7: Isle 1J **113**
St Christophers Dr. UB3: Hayes 7K **75**
St Christopher's Gdns. CR7: Thor H 3A **156**
St Christopher's Ho. NW1 1B **6** (2G **83**)
(off Bridgeway St.)
St Christopher's M. SM6: W'gton 5G **167**
St Christopher's Pl. W1 7H **5** (6E **82**)
St Clair Cl. IG5: Ilf 2D **52**
St Clair Dr. KT4: Wor Pk 3D **164**
St Clair Ho. E3 3B **86**
(off British St.)
St Clair Rd. E13 2K **87**
St Clair's Rd. CR0: C'don 2E **168**
St Clare Bus. Pk. TW12: Hamp H 6G **131**
St Clare St. EC3 1J **15** (6F **85**)
St Clements Av. E3 3B **86**
St Clement's Ct. EC4 2F **15** (7D **84**)
(off Clements La.)
St Clement's Ct. N7 6A **66**
St Clements Ct. SE14 6K **103**
(off Myers La.)
St Clements Ct. W11 7F **81**
(off Stoneleigh St.)
St Clement's Development E3 3B **86**
St Clement's Hgts. SE26 4G **139**
St Clements Ho. E1 6J **9** (5F **85**)
(off Leyden St.)
St Clement's La. WC2 1H **13** (6K **83**)
St Clements Mans. SW6 6F **99**
(off Lillie Rd.)
St Clements St. N7 6A **66**
St Clements Yd. SE22 4F **121**
St Cloud Rd. SE27 4C **138**
St Columba's Ct. E15 4G **69**
(off Janson Rd.)
St Columbas Ho. E17 4D **50**
St Columb's Ho. W10 5G **81**
(off Blagrove Rd.)
St Crispin's Cl. NW3 4C **64**
St Crispin's Cl. UB1: S'hall 6D **76**
St Cross St. EC1 5K **7** (5A **84**)
St Cuthbert's Rd. NW2 6H **63**
St Cuthberts Rd. N13 6F **33**
St Cyprian's St. SW17 4D **136**
St David Cl. UB8: Cowl 5A **74**
St David's Cl. BR4: W W'ck 7D **158**
St David's Cl. HA9: Wemb 3J **61**
St Davids Cl. SE16 5H **103**
(off Masters Dr.)
St David's Ct. BR1: Broml 3F **161**
St David's Ct. E17 3E **50**
St Davids Ct. TW15: Ashf 2B **128**
St David's Dr. HA8: Edg 1F **43**
St Davids M. E18 1J **51**
St Davids M. E3 3A **86**
(off Morgan St.)
St David's Pl. NW4 7D **44**
St Davids Sq. E14 5D **104**
St Denis Rd. SE27 4D **138**
St Dionis Rd. SW6 2H **117**
St Domingo Ho. SE18 3D **106**
(off Leda Rd.)
St Donatt's Rd. SE14 1B **122**
ST DUNSTAN'S 6H **165**
St Dunstan's All. EC3 3G **15** (7E **84**)
(off St Dunstans Hill)
St Dunstans Av. W3 7K **79**
St Dunstan's Cl. UB3: Harl 5H **93**
St Dunstan's Ct. EC4 1K **13** (6A **84**)
St Dunstan's Enterprises 1C **140**
St Dunstan's Gdns. W3 7K **79**
St Dunstan's Hill SM1: Sutt 5G **165**
St Dunstans Hill EC3 3G **15** (7E **84**)
St Dunstan's Ho. WC2 7J **7** (6A **84**)
(off Chancery La.)
St Dunstan's La. BR3: Beck 6E **158**
St Dunstan's La. EC3 3G **15** (7E **84**)
St Dunstans M. E1 5A **86**
(off White Horse Rd.)
St Dunstan's Rd. E7 6K **69**
St Dunstan's Rd. SE25 4F **157**
St Dunstan's Rd. TW13: Felt 3H **129**
St Dunstan's Rd. TW4: Cran 2K **111**
(not continuous)
St Dunstan's Rd. W6 5F **99**
St Dunstan's Rd. W7 2J **95**
St Edmund's Av. HA4: Ruis 6F **39**
St Edmund's Cl. NW8 1D **82**
St Edmund's Cl. SW17 2C **136**
St Edmunds Cl. DA18: Erith 2D **108**
St Edmund's Ct. NW8 1D **82**
(off St Edmund's Ter.)
St Edmunds Ct. CR0: C'don 2B **168**
St Edmunds Dr. HA7: Stan 1A **42**
St Edmund's La. TW2: Whitt 7F **113**
St Edmund's Rd. IG1: Ilf 6D **52**
St Edmund's Rd. N9 7B **24**
St Edmunds Sq. SW13 6E **98**
St Edmund's Ter. NW8 1C **82**
St Edward's Cl. NW11 6J **45**
St Edwards Ct. NW11 6J **45**
St Edwards Way RM1: Rom 5K **55**
St Egberts Way E4 1K **35**
St Elmo Rd. W12 1B **98**
St Elmos Rd. SE16 2A **104**
St Erkenwald M. IG11: Bark 1H **89**
St Erkenwald Rd. IG11: Bark 1H **89**
St Ermin's Hill SW1 1C **18** (3H **101**)
(off Broadway)
St Ervan's Rd. W10 5H **81**
St Eugene Ct. NW6 1G **81**
(off Salusbury Rd.)
St Faith's Cl. EN2: Enf 1H **23**
St Faith's Rd. SE21 1B **138**
St Fidelis Rd. DA8: Erith 4K **109**
St Fillans Rd. SE6 1E **140**
St Francis Cl. BR5: Pet W 6J **161**
St Francis' Ho. NW1 2H **83**
(off Bridgeway St.)
St Francis Pl. SW12 6F **119**
St Francis Rd. DA8: Erith 4K **109**
St Francis Rd. SE22 4E **120**
St Francis Way IG1: Ilf 4H **71**
St Frideswide's M. E14 6E **86**
St Gabriel's Cl. E11 2K **69**
St Gabriel's Cl. E14 5D **86**
St Gabriels Ct. N11 7C **32**
St Gabriels Mnr. SE5 1B **120**
(off Cormont Rd.)
St Gabriels Rd. NW2 5F **63**
St Gabriel Wlk. SE1 4B **102**
(off Elephant & Castle)
St George's Antiochian Orthodox Cathedral 1K **5** (3F **83**)
St George's Av. E7 7K **69**
St George's Av. N7 4H **65**
St George's Av. NW9 4K **43**
St George's Av. UB1: S'hall 7D **76**
St George's Av. W5 2D **96**
St George's Bldgs. SE1 3B **102**
(off St George's Rd.)
St George's Cir. SE1 1K **19** (3B **102**)
St George's Cl. HA0: Wemb 3A **60**
St George's Cl. NW11 6H **45**
St George's Cl. SW8 1G **119**
St Georges Cl. SE28 6D **90**
St George's Ct. E6 4D **88**
St George's Ct. SE1 3B **102**
(off Garden Row)
St George's Ct. SW1 5A **18** (5G **101**)
(off St George's Dr.)
St George's Ct. SW15 4H **117**
St George's Ct. SW3 3C **16** (4C **100**)
(off Brompton Rd.)
St George's Ct. SW7 3A **100**
St Georges Ct. E17 5F **51**
St Georges Ct. EC4 7A **8** (6B **84**)
St Georges Ct. HA3: Kenton 6A **42**
(off Kenton Rd.)
St George's Dr. SW1 4K **17** (4F **101**)
St George's Dr. UB10: Ick 3B **56**
ST GEORGE'S FIELD 2D **10** (7C **82**)
St George's Flds. W2 1D **10** (6C **82**)
St George's Gdns. KT6: Surb 2H **163**
St George's Gro. SW17 3B **136**
St George's Ho. NW1 2H **83**
(off Bridgeway St.)
St Georges Ho. SW11 1E **118**
(off Charlotte Despard Av.)
St George's Ind. Est. KT2: King T 5D **132**
St George's Ind. Est. N22 7G **33**
St George's La. EC3 2F **15** (7D **84**)
(off Pudding La.)
St George's Leisure Cen. 7H **85**
St George's Mans. SW1 5D **18** (5H **101**)
(off Causton St.)
St George's M. NW1 7D **64**
St George's M. SE1 1K **19** (3A **102**)
(off Westminster Bri. Rd.)
St George's M. SE8 4B **104**
St Georges Pde. SE6 2B **140**
(off Perry Hill)
St George's Path SE4 4C **122**
(off Adelaide Av.)
St George's Pl. TW1: Twick 1A **132**
St George's Rd. BR1: Broml 2D **160**
St George's Rd. BR3: Beck 1D **158**
St George's Rd. BR5: Pet W 6H **161**
St George's Rd. CR4: Mitc 3F **155**
St George's Rd. DA14: Sidc 6D **144**
St George's Rd. E10 3E **68**
St George's Rd. E7 7K **69**
St George's Rd. EN1: Enf 1A **24**
St George's Rd. IG1: Ilf 7D **52**
St George's Rd. KT2: King T 7G **133**
St George's Rd. N13 3E **32**
St George's Rd. NW11 6H **45**
St George's Rd. RM9: Dag 5E **72**
St George's Rd. SE1 1K **19** (3A **102**)
St George's Rd. SM6: W'gton 5F **167**
St George's Rd. SW19 7H **135**
(not continuous)
St George's Rd. TW1: Twick 5B **114**
St George's Rd. TW13: Hanw 4B **130**
St George's Rd. W4 2K **97**
St George's Rd. W7 1K **95**
St Georges Rd. TW9: Rich 3F **115**
St George's Rd. W. BR1: Broml 1C **160**
St George's Shop. & Leisure Cen. 6J **41**
St George's Sq. E7 7K **69**
St George's Sq. KT3: N Mald 3A **152**
St George's Sq. SE8 4B **104**
(not continuous)
St George's Sq. SW1 5C **18** (5H **101**)
St Georges Sq. E14 7A **86**
St George's Sq. M. SW1 6C **18** (5H **101**)
St George's Ter. E6 3C **88**
(off Masterman Rd.)
St George's Ter. NW1 7D **64**
St George's Ter. SE15 7G **103**
(off Peckham Hill St.)
St George St. W1 2K **11** (7F **83**)
St George's University of London 5B **136**
St George's Wlk. CR0: C'don 3C **168**
St George's Way SE15 6E **102**
St George's Wharf SE1 6K **15** (2F **103**)
(off Shad Thames)
St George Wharf SW8 7E **18** (6J **101**)
St Gerards Cl. SW4 5G **119**
St German's Pl. SE3 1J **123**
St German's Rd. SE23 1A **140**
St Giles Av. RM10: Dag 7H **73**
St Giles Av. UB10: Ick 4E **56**
St Giles Churchyard EC2 6D **8** (5C **84**)
St Giles Cir. W1 7D **6** (6H **83**)
St Giles Cl. BR6: Farnb 5H **173**
St Giles Cl. RM10: Dag 7H **73**
St Giles Cl. TW5: Hest 7C **94**
St Giles High St. WC2 7D **6** (6H **83**)
St Giles Ho. EN5: New Bar 4F **21**
St Giles Ho. SE5 1E **120**
St Giles Rd. SE5 7E **102**
St Giles Sq. WC2 7D **6** (6H **83**)
St Giles Ter. EC2 6D **8** (5C **84**)
(off Wood St.)
St Giles Twr. SE5 1E **120**
(off Gables Cl.)
St Gilles Ho. E2 2K **85**
(off Mace St.)
St Gothard Rd. SE27 4D **138**
(not continuous)
St Gregory Cl. HA4: Ruis 4A **58**
St Helena Ho. WC1 2J **7** (3A **84**)
(off Margery St.)
St Helena Rd. SE16 4K **103**
St Helena St. WC1 2J **7** (3A **84**)
St Helena Ter. TW9: Rich 5D **114**
St Helens KT7: T Ditt 7K **149**
St Helen's Cl. KT4: Wor Pk 1C **164**
St Helen's Cres. SW16 1K **155**
St Helen's Gdns. W10 5F **81**
St Helen's Pl. EC3 7G **9** (6E **84**)
St Helens Pl. E10 7A **50**
St Helen's Rd. DA18: Erith 2D **108**
St Helen's Rd. IG1: Ilf 6D **52**
St Helen's Rd. SW16 1K **155**
St Helen's Rd. W13 1B **96**
ST HELIER 7C 154
St Helier Av. SM4: Mord 7A **154**
St Helier Ct. N1 1E **84**
(off De Beauvoir Est.)
St Helier Ct. SE16 2K **103**
(off Poolmans St.)
St Helier's Av. TW3: Houn 5E **112**
St Helier's Rd. E10 6E **50**
St Henera's Ct. BR1: Broml 3E **160**
(off Brady Dr.)
St Hilary's Ct. BR1: Broml 3F **161**
St Hilda's Av. TW15: Ashf 5A **128**
St Hilda's Cl. NW6 7F **63**
St Hilda's Cl. SW17 2C **136**
St Hilda's Rd. SW13 6D **98**
St Hilda's Wharf E1 1J **103**
(off Wapping High St.)
St Hubert's Ho. E14 3C **104**
(off Janet St.)
St Hughes Cl. SW17 2C **136**
St Hugh's Rd. SE20 1H **157**
St Ives Pl. E14 5E **86**
St Ivian Ct. N10 2E **46**
St James Apts. E17 5A **50**
(off Pretoria Av.)
St James Av. N20 3H **31**
St James Av. SM1: Sutt 5J **165**
St James Av. W13 1A **96**
St James Cl. EN4: E Barn 4G **21**
St James Cl. HA4: Ruis 2A **58**
St James Cl. KT3: N Mald 5B **152**
St James Cl. N20 3H **31**
St James Ct. CR0: C'don 7B **156**
St James Ct. E12 2A **70**
St James Ct. E2 3G **85**
(off Bethnal Grn. Rd.)
St James Ct. SE3 1K **123**
St James' Ct. SW1 1B **18** (3G **101**)
St James Gdns. RM6: Chad H 4B **54**
St James' Gdns. HA0: Wemb 7D **60**
St James Ga. IG9: Buck H 1F **37**
St James Gro. SW11 2D **118**
St James Hall N1 1C **84**
(off Prebend St.)
St James Ind. M. SE1 5G **103**
St James Mans. SE1 1J **19** (3A **102**)
(off McAuley Cl.)
St James' Mans. NW6 7J **63**
(off West End La.)
St James M. E14 3E **104**
St James M. E17 5A **50**
St James Path E17 5A **50**
St James Residences W1 2C **12** (7H **83**)
(off Brewer St.)
St James Rd. CR4: Mitc 7E **136**
St James Rd. SM1: Sutt 5J **165**
St James Rd. SM5: Cars 3C **166**
St James' Rd. E15 5H **69**
St James' Rd. KT6: Surb 6D **150**
St James' Rd. N9 2C **34**
St James's SE14 1A **122**
ST JAMES'S 5C 12 (1H 101)
St James's App. EC2 4G **9** (4E **84**)
St James's Av. BR3: Beck 3A **158**
St James's Av. E2 2J **85**
St James's Av. TW12: Hamp H 5G **131**
St James's Chambers SW1 4B **12** (1G **101**)
(off Jermyn St.)
St James's Cl. NW8 1D **82**
(off St James's Ter. M.)
St James's Cl. SE18 5G **107**
St James's Cl. SW17 2D **136**
St James's Cotts. TW9: Rich 5D **114**
St James's Ct. HA1: Harr 6A **42**
St James's Ct. KT1: King T 3E **150**
St James's Ct. N18 5B **34**
(off Fore St.)
St James's Cres. SW9 3A **120**
St James's Dr. SW12 1D **136**
St James's Dr. SW17 1D **136**
St James's Gdns. W11 1G **99**
(not continuous)
St James's Ho. SE1 4G **103**
(off Strathnairn St.)
St James's La. N10 4F **47**
St James's Mkt. SW1 3C **12** (7H **83**)
St James's Palace 6B **12** (2G **101**)
St James's Pk. CR0: C'don 7C **156**
St James's Pk. 6C **12** (2H **101**)
St James's Pas. EC3 1H **15** (6E **84**)
(off Duke's Pl.)
St James's Pl. SW1 5A **12** (1G **101**)
St James's Rd. CR0: C'don 7B **156**
St James's Rd. KT1: King T 2D **150**
St James's Rd. SE1 6G **103**
St James's Rd. SE16 3G **103**
St James's Rd. TW12: Hamp H 5F **131**
St James's Sq. SW1 4B **12** (1G **101**)
St James's St. E17 5A **50**
St James's St. SW1 4A **12** (1G **101**)
St James's Ter. NW8 1D **82**
(off Prince Albert Rd.)
St James's Ter. M. NW8 1D **82**
St James St. W6 5E **98**
St James's Wlk. EC1 3A **8** (4B **84**)
St James Ter. SW12 1E **136**
St James Way DA14: Sidc 5E **144**
St Jeromes Gro. UB3: Hayes 6E **74**
St Joan's Ho. NW1 1C **6** (3H **83**)
(off Phoenix Rd.)
St Joan's Rd. N9 2A **34**
St John Fisher Rd. DA18: Erith 3D **108**
ST JOHNS 2C 122
St John's Av. N11 5J **31**
St John's Av. NW10 1B **80**
St John's Av. SW15 5F **117**
St Johns Chu. Rd. E9 5J **67**
St John's Cl. HA9: Wemb 5E **60**
St John's Cl. N20 3F **31**
(off Rasper Rd.)
St John's Cl. SW6 7J **99**
St Johns Cl. N14 6B **22**
St John's Cotts. SE20 7J **139**
St John's Ct. DA8: Erith 4K **109**
St John's Ct. E1 1H **103**
(off Scandrett St.)
St John's Ct. HA1: Harr 6K **41**
St John's Ct. HA6: Nwood 1G **39**
(off Murray Rd.)
St John's Ct. IG9: Buck H 1E **36**
St John's Ct. KT1: King T 4E **150**
(off Beaufort Rd.)
St John's Ct. N4 2B **66**
St John's Ct. SE13 2E **122**
St John's Ct. TW7: Isle 2K **113**
St John's Ct. W6 4D **98**
(off Glenthorne Rd.)
St Johns Ct. SW10 7A **100**
(off Ashburnham Rd.)
St John's Cres. SW9 3A **120**
St Johns Dr. SW18 1K **135**
St John's Est. N1 1F **9** (2D **84**)
St John's Est. SE1 6J **15** (2F **103**)
(off Fair St.)
St John's Gdns. W11 7G **81**
St John's Gate 4A **8** (4B **84**)
(off St John's La.)
St John's Gro. N19 2G **65**
St John's Gro. SW13 2B **116**
St John's Gro. TW9: Rich 4E **114**
St John's Hill SW11 5B **118**
St John's Hill Gro. SW11 4B **118**
St John's Ho. E14 4E **104**
(off Pier St.)
St Johns Ho. SE17 6D **102**
(off Lytham St.)
St John's La. EC1 4A **8** (4B **84**)
St John's Lodge NW3 7C **64**
(off King Henry's Rd.)
St John's Mans. EC1 1A **8** (3B **84**)
(off St John St.)
St John's M. KT1: Hamp W 2C **150**
St John's M. W11 6J **81**
St John Smith Square 2E **18** (3J **101**)
(off Smith Sq.)
St John's Pde. W13 1B **96**
St Johns Pde. DA14: Sidc 4A **144**
(off Sidcup High St.)
St John's Pk. SE3 7H **105**
St John's Pk. Mans. N19 3G **65**
St John's Pas. SW19 6G **135**
St John's Path EC1 4A **8** (4B **84**)
(off Britton St.)
St Johns Pathway SE23 1J **139**
St John's Pl. EC1 4A **8** (4B **84**)
St John's Rd. BR5: Pet W 6H **161**
St John's Rd. CR0: C'don 3B **168**
St John's Rd. DA14: Sidc 4B **144**
(not continuous)
St John's Rd. DA16: Well 3B **126**
St John's Rd. DA8: Erith 5K **109**
St John's Rd. E16 6J **87**
St John's Rd. E17 2D **50**
St John's Rd. E4 4J **35**
St John's Rd. E6 1C **88**
St John's Rd. HA1: Harr 6K **41**
St John's Rd. HA9: Wemb 4D **60**
St John's Rd. IG11: Bark 1J **89**
St John's Rd. IG2: Ilf 7H **53**
St John's Rd. KT1: Hamp W 2C **150**
St John's Rd. KT3: N Mald 3J **151**
St John's Rd. KT8: E Mos 4H **149**
St John's Rd. N15 6E **48**
St John's Rd. NW11 6H **45**
St John's Rd. SE20 6J **139**
St John's Rd. SM1: Sutt 2K **165**
St John's Rd. SM5: Cars 3C **166**
St John's Rd. SW11 4C **118**
St John's Rd. SW19 7G **135**
St John's Rd. TW13: Hanw 4C **130**
St John's Rd. TW7: Isle 2K **113**
St John's Rd. TW9: Rich 4E **114**
St John's Rd. UB2: S'hall 3C **94**
St John's Sq. EC1 4A **8** (4B **84**)
St John's Ter. E7 6K **69**
St John's Ter. SE18 6G **107**
St John's Ter. SW15 3A **134**
(off Kingston Va.)
St John's Ter. W10 4F **81**
St John St. EC1 1K **7** (2A **84**)
St John's Va. SE8 2C **122**
St John's Vs. N11 5J **31**
(off Friern Barnet Rd.)
St John's Vs. N19 2H **65**
St John's Vs. W8 3K **99**
(off St Mary's Pl.)
St John's Way N19 2G **65**
ST JOHN'S WOOD 2B 82
St John's Wood Ct. NW8 2B **4** (3B **82**)
(off St John's Wood Rd.)
St John's Wood High St. NW8 2B **82**
St John's Wood Pk. NW8 1B **82**
St John's Wood Rd. NW8 3A **4** (4B **82**)
St John's Wood Ter. NW8 2B **82**
St Josephs Almshouses W6 4F **99**
(off Brook Grn.)
St Joseph's Cl. BR6: Orp 4K **173**
St Joseph's Cl. W10 5G **81**
St Joseph's College Sports Cen. 6B **138**
St Joseph's Cotts. SW3 4E **16** (4D **100**)
(off Cadagon St.)
St Josephs Ct. SE2 6D **108**
St Josephs Ct. SE7 6K **105**
St Joseph's Dr. UB1: S'hall 1C **94**
St Joseph's Flats NW1 1C **6** (3H **83**)
(off Drummond Cres.)
St Joseph's Gro. NW4 4D **44**
St Joseph's Ho. W6 4F **99**
(off Brook Grn.)
St Joseph's Rd. N9 7C **24**
St Joseph's St. SW8 1F **119**
St Joseph's Va. SE3 3F **123**
St Judes Ct. IG8: Wfd G 7H **37**
St Jude's Rd. E2 2H **85**
St Jude St. N16 5E **66**
St Julian's Cl. SW16 4A **138**
St Julian's Farm Rd. SE27 4A **138**
St Julian's Rd. NW6 1J **81**
St Katharine Docks 3K **15** (7F **85**)
(off St Katharine's Way)
St Katharine's Pct. NW1 2F **83**
St Katharine's Way E1 4K **15** (1F **103**)
(not continuous)
St Katharine's Yacht Haven 4K **15** (1F **103**)
(off St Katharine's Way)
St Katherine's Rd. DA18: Erith 2D **108**
St Katherine's Row EC3 2H **15** (7E **84**)
(off Fenchurch St.)
St Katherines Wlk. W11 1F **99**
St Keverne Rd. SE9 4C **142**
St Kilda Rd. BR6: Orp 1K **173**
St Kilda Rd. W13 1A **96**
St Kilda's Rd. HA1: Harr 6J **41**
St Kilda's Rd. N16 1D **66**
St Kitts Ter. SE19 5E **138**
St Laurence Cl. NW6 1F **81**
St Lawrence Bus. Cen. TW13: Felt 2K **129**
St Lawrence Cl. HA8: Edg 7A **28**
St Lawrence Cotts. E14 1E **104**
(off St Lawrence St.)
St Lawrence Ct. N1 7D **66**
St Lawrence Dr. HA5: Eastc 5K **39**
St Lawrence Ho. SE1 7H **15** (3E **102**)
(off Purbrook St.)
St Lawrence St. E14 1E **104**
St Lawrence Ter. W10 5G **81**
St Lawrence Way SW9 1A **120**
St Leger Ct. NW6 7F **63**
(off Coverdale Rd.)
St Leonard M. N1 2E **84**
(off Hoxton St.)
St Leonard's Av. E4 6A **36**
St Leonard's Av. HA3: Kenton 5C **42**
St Leonard's Cl. DA16: Well 3A **126**
St Leonard's Ct. N1 1F **9** (3D **84**)
(off New North Rd.)
St Leonards Ct. SW14 3J **115**
St Leonard's Gdns. IG1: Ilf 5G **71**
St Leonard's Gdns. TW5: Hest 7C **94**
St Leonard's Ri. BR6: Orp 4J **173**
St Leonard's Rd. CR0: Wadd 3B **168**
St Leonard's Rd. E14 5D **86**
(not continuous)
St Leonard's Rd. KT6: Surb 5D **150**
St Leonard's Rd. KT7: T Ditt 6A **150**
St Leonard's Rd. NW10 4K **79**
St Leonard's Rd. SW14 3H **115**
St Leonard's Rd. W13 7C **78**
(not continuous)
St Leonards Sq. KT6: Surb 5D **150**
St Leonards Sq. NW5 6E **64**
St Leonard's St. E3 3D **86**
St Leonard's Studios SW3 6E **16** (5D **100**)
(off Smith St.)
St Leonard's Ter. SW3 6E **16** (5D **100**)
St Leonard's Wlk. SW16 7K **137**
St Loo Av. SW3 7D **16** (6C **100**)
St Loo Ct. SW3 7D **16** (6C **100**)
(off St Loo Av.)
St Louis Rd. SE27 4D **138**
St Loy's Rd. N17 2E **48**
St Lucia Dr. E15 1H **87**
St Luke Cl. UB8: Cowl 6A **74**
ST LUKE'S 3D 8 (4C 84)
St Luke's Av. EN2: Enf 1J **23**
St Luke's Av. IG1: Ilf 5F **71**
St Luke's Av. SW4 4H **119**
St Luke's Cl. EC1 3D **8** (4C **84**)
St Luke's Cl. SE25 6H **157**
St Lukes Ct. E10 7D **50**
(off Capworth St.)
St Lukes Ct. W11 6H **81**
(off St Luke's Rd.)
St Luke's Est. EC1 2E **8** (3D **84**)
St Luke's M. W11 6H **81**
St Lukes M. E14 2C **104**
(off Strafford St.)
St Luke's Pas. KT2: King T 1F **151**
St Luke's Path IG1: Ilf 5F **71**
St Luke's Rd. UB10: Uxb 1A **74**
St Luke's Rd. W11 5H **81**
St Luke's Sq. E16 6H **87**
St Luke's St. SW3 5C **16** (5C **100**)
St Luke's Yd. W9 2H **81**
(not continuous)
St Malo Av. N9 3D **34**
St Margaret's KT2: King T 5J **133**

282 A–Z London

St Margarets – Saltcoats Rd.

ST MARGARETS 6B 114
St Margaret's Av. DA15: Sidc 3H 143
St Margaret's Av. N17 1G 49
St Margaret's Av. HA2: Harr 3G 59
St Margaret's Av. N15 4B 48
St Margaret's Av. N20 1F 31
St Margaret's Av. SM3: Cheam 3G 165
St Margaret's Av. TW15: Ashf 5D 128
St Margarets Av. UB8: Hil 4C 74
St Margarets Bus. Cen. TW1: Twick 6B 114
St Margarets Cl. EC2 7E 8 (6D 84)
St Margaret's Ct. N11 4K 31
St Margarets Ct. SE1 5D 14 (1C 102)
St Margarets Ct. SW15 4D 116
St Margaret's Cres. SW15 5D 116
St Margaret's Dr. TW1: Twick 5B 114
St Margaret's Gro. E11 3H 69
St Margaret's Gro. SE18 6G 107
St Margaret's Gro. TW1: Twick 6A 114
St Margaret's Ho. NW1 1C 6 (2H 83)
(off Polygon Rd.)
St Margaret's La. W8 3K 99
St Margaret's M. KT2: King T 5J 133
St Margaret's Pas. SE13 3G 123
(not continuous)
St Margarets Path SE18 5G 107
St Margaret's Rd. E12 2A 70
St Margaret's Rd. HA4: Ruis 6F 39
St Margaret's Rd. HA8: Edg 5C 28
St Margaret's Rd. N17 3E 48
St Margaret's Rd. NW10 3E 80
St Margaret's Rd. W7 2J 95
St Margarets Rd. BR3: Beck 4K 157
St Margarets Rd. SE4 4B 122
(not continuous)
St Margarets Rd. TW1: Twick 6B 114
St Margarets Rd. TW7: Isle 4B 114
St Margarets Rd. TW7: Twick 4B 114
ST MARGARETS RDBT. 6B 114
St Margaret's Sports Cen. 1A 26
St Margaret's Ter. SE18 5G 107
St Margaret St. SW1 7E 12 (2J 101)
St Mark's Cl. EN5: New Bar 3E 20
St Mark's Cl. SE10 7E 104
St Mark's Cl. W11 6G 81
St Marks Cl. HA1: Harr 7B 42
St Marks Cl. SW6 1J 117
St Marks Ct. NW8 2A 82
(off Abercorn Pl.)
St Marks Ct. W7 2J 95
(off Lwr. Boston Rd.)
St Mark's Cres. NW1 1E 82
St Mark's Ga. E9 7B 68
St Mark's Gro. SW10 7K 99
St Mark's Hill KT6: Surb 6E 150
St Marks Ho. SE17 6D 102
(off Lytham St.)
St Marks Ind. Est. E16 1B 106
St Mark's Pl. RM10: Dag 6G 73
St Mark's Pl. SW19 6H 135
St Mark's Pl. W11 6G 81
St Mark's Ri. E8 5F 67
St Mark's Rd. BR2: Broml 3J 159
St Mark's Rd. SE25 4G 157
St Mark's Rd. TW11: Tedd 7B 132
St Mark's Rd. W10 6F 81
St Mark's Rd. W11 6G 81
St Mark's Rd. W5 1E 96
St Mark's Rd. W7 2J 95
St Marks Rd. CR4: Mitc 2D 154
St Marks Rd. EN1: Enf 6A 24
St Mark's Sq. BR2: Broml 3J 159
St Mark's Sq. NW1 1E 82
St Mark St. E1 1K 15 (6F 85)
St Mark's Vs. N4 2K 65
(off Moray Rd.)
St Martin-in-the-Fields Chu. Path WC2 3E 12 (7J 83)
(off St Martin's Pl.)
St Martin's Almshouses NW1 1G 83
St Martin's App. HA4: Ruis 7G 39
St Martin's Av. E6 2B 88
St Martin's Cl. DA18: Erith 2D 108
St Martin's Cl. EN1: Enf 1C 24
St Martin's Cl. NW1 1G 83
St Martin's Ct. EC4 7C 8 (6C 84)
(off Newgate St.)
St Martin's Ct. WC2 2E 12 (7J 83)
St Martins Ct. N1 1E 84
(off De Beauvoir Est.)
St Martin's Ctyd. WC2 2E 12 (7J 83)
(off Up. St Martin's La.)
St Martins Est. SW2 1A 138
St Martin's Ho. NW1 1C 6 (2H 83)
(off Polygon Rd.)
St Martin's La. BR3: Beck 5D 158
St Martin's La. WC2 2E 12 (7J 83)
St Martin's Le-Grand EC1 7C 8 (6C 84)
St Martin's Pl. WC2 3E 12 (7J 83)
St Martin's Rd. N9 2C 34
St Martin's Rd. SW9 2K 119
St Martin's St. WC2 3D 12 (7H 83)
(not continuous)
St Martin's Theatre 2E 12 (7J 83)
(off West St.)
St Martins Way SW17 3A 136
St Mary Abbot's Ct. W14 3H 99
(off Warwick Gdns.)
St Mary Abbot's Pl. W8 3H 99
St Mary Abbot's Ter. W14 3H 99
St Mary at Hill EC3 3G 15 (7E 84)
St Mary Av. SM6: W'gton 3E 166
St Mary Axe EC3 1G 15 (6E 84)
St Marychurch St. SE16 2J 103
St Mary Graces Ct. E1 2K 15 (7F 85)
St Marylebone Cl. NW10 1A 80
St Marylebone Crematorium 3K 45
St Mary le-Park Ct. SW11 7C 100
(off Parkgate Rd.)
St Mary Magdalene Cres. SE18 3E 106
St Mary Magdalene Gdns. N7 6K 65
St Mary Newington Cl. SE17 5E 102
(off Surrey Sq.)
St Mary Rd. E17 4C 50
St Mary's IG11: Bark 1H 89
St Mary's App. E12 5D 70
St Mary's Av. BR2: Broml 3G 159
St Mary's Av. E11 7K 51
St Mary's Av. N3 2G 45
St Mary's Av. TW11: Tedd 6K 131
St Mary's Av. Central UB2: S'hall 4F 95
St Mary's Av. Nth. UB2: S'hall 4F 95
St Mary's Av. Sth. UB2: S'hall 4F 95
St Mary's Cl. KT17: Ewe 7B 164
St Mary's Cl. KT9: Chess 7F 163
St Mary's Cl. N17 1G 49
St Mary's Cl. TW16: Sun 4J 147
St Mary's Community Gdn. 2F 85
(off Appleby St.)
St Mary's Copse KT4: Wor Pk 2A 164
St Mary's Ct. E3 3D 86
(off Bow Rd.)
St Mary's Ct. E6 4D 88
St Mary's Ct. KT3: N Mald 3A 152
St Mary's Ct. SE7 7B 106
St Mary's Ct. SM6: W'gton 4G 167
St Mary's Ct. W5 2D 96
St Mary's Ct. W6 3B 98
St Mary's Cres. NW4 3D 44
St Mary's Cres. TW7: Isle 7H 95
St Mary's Cres. UB3: Hayes 7H 75
St Mary's Dr. TW14: Bedf 7E 110
St Mary's Est. SE16 2J 103
(off Elephant La.)
St Mary's Flats NW1 1C 6 (3H 83)
(off Drummond Cres.)
St Mary's Gdns. SE11 3K 19 (4A 102)
St Mary's Ga. W8 3K 99
St Mary's Grn. N2 2A 46
St Mary's Gro. N1 6B 66
St Mary's Gro. SW13 3D 116
St Mary's Gro. TW9: Rich 4F 115
St Mary's Gro. W4 6H 97
St Mary's Ho. N1 1B 84
(off St Mary's Path)
St Mary's Mans. W2 5A 4 (5B 82)
St Mary's M. NW6 7K 63
St Marys M. TW10: Ham 2C 132
St Mary's Path N1 1B 84
St Mary's Pl. SE9 6E 124
St Mary's Pl. W5 2D 96
St Mary's Pl. W8 3K 99
St Mary's Rd. KT6: Surb St Chads Cl. 7C 150
St Mary's Rd. KT6: Surb Victoria Rd. 6D 150
St Mary's Rd. DA5: Bexl 1J 145
St Mary's Rd. E10 3E 68
St Mary's Rd. E13 2K 87
St Mary's Rd. EN4: E Barn 7J 21
St Mary's Rd. IG1: Ilf 2G 71
St Mary's Rd. KT4: Wor Pk 2A 164
St Mary's Rd. KT8: E Mos 5H 149
St Mary's Rd. N8 4J 47
St Mary's Rd. N9 1C 34
(not continuous)
St Mary's Rd. NW10 1A 80
St Mary's Rd. NW11 7G 45
St Mary's Rd. SE15 1J 121
St Mary's Rd. SE25 3E 156
St Mary's Rd. SW19 5G 135
St Mary's Rd. UB3: Hayes 7H 75
St Marys Rd. W5 2D 96
St Mary's Sq. W2 5A 4 (5B 82)
St Mary's Sq. W5 2D 96
St Mary's Ter. W2 5A 4 (5B 82)
St Mary's Twr. EC1 4D 8 (4C 84)
(off Fortune St.)
St Mary St. SE18 4D 106
St Mary's University Coll. 3K 131
St Mary's University College Sports Cen. 4K 131
St Mary's Vw. HA3: Kenton 5C 42
St Mary's Wlk. SE11 3K 19 (4A 102)
St Mary's Wlk. UB3: Hayes 7H 75
St Mary's Way IG7: Chig 5K 37
St Matthew Cl. UB8: Cowl 6A 74
St Matthew's Av. KT6: Surb 1E 162
St Matthew's Ct. TW15: Ashf 4C 128
(off Feltham Rd.)
St Matthews Ct. E10 7D 50
St Matthews Ct. N10 2E 46
St Matthews Ct. SE1 3C 102
(off Meadow Row)
St Matthew's Dr. BR1: Broml 3D 160
St Matthews Ho. SE17 6D 102
(off Phelp St.)
St Matthew's Lodge NW1 2G 83
(off Oakley Sq.)
St Matthew's Rd. SW2 4K 119
St Matthew's Rd. W5 1E 96
St Matthew's Row E2 3G 85
St Matthew St. SW1 2C 18 (3H 101)
St Matthias Cl. NW9 5B 44
St Maur Rd. SW6 1H 117
St Meddens BR7: Chst 7H 143
St Mellion Cl. SE28 6D 90
St Merryn Cl. SE18 7H 107
St Merryn Ct. BR3: Beck 7C 140
St Michael's All. EC3 1F 15 (6D 84)
St Michael's Av. HA9: Wemb 6G 61
St Michael's Av. N9 7D 24
St Michael's Cl. BR1: Broml 3C 160
St Michael's Cl. DA18: Erith 2D 108
St Michael's Cl. KT4: Wor Pk 2B 164
St Michael's Cl. N12 5H 31
St Michael's Cl. N3 2H 45
St Michaels Cl. E16 5B 88
St Michael's Ct. CR0: C'don 1C 168
(off Poplar Wlk.)
St Michael's Ct. SE1 7D 14 (2C 102)
(off Trinity St.)
St Michaels Ct. E14 5E 86
(off St Leonard's Rd.)
St Michael's Cres. HA5: Pinn 6C 40
St Michael's Flats NW1 1C 6 (2H 83)
(off Aldenham St.)
St Michael's Gdns. W10 5G 81
St Michael's M. SW1 4G 17 (4E 100)
St Michael's Ri. DA16: Well 1B 126
St Michael's Rd. CR0: C'don 1C 168
St Michael's Rd. DA16: Well 3B 126
St Michael's Rd. NW2 4E 62
St Michael's Rd. SM6: W'gton 6G 167
St Michael's Rd. SW9 2K 119
St Michael's Rd. TW15: Ashf 5C 128
St Michael's St. W2 7B 4 (6B 82)
St Michael's Ter. N22 1J 47
St Michaels Ter. N6 1E 64
(off South Gro.)
St Mildred's Ct. EC2 1E 14 (6D 84)
St Mildreds Rd. SE12 7H 123
St Mildreds Rd. SE6 7G 123
St Mirren Ct. EN5: New Bar 5F 21
St Nicholas Cen. 5K 165
St Nicholas Cl. UB8: Cowl 6A 74
St Nicholas Ct. KT1: King T 4E 150
(off Surbiton Rd.)
St Nicholas Dr. TW17: Shep 7C 146
St Nicholas' Flats NW1 1C 6 (2H 83)
(off Werrington St.)
St Nicholas Glebe SW17 5E 136
St Nicholas Ho. SE8 6C 104
(off Deptford Grn.)
St Nicholas M. KT7: T Ditt 6K 149
St Nicholas Rd. KT7: T Ditt 6K 149
St Nicholas Rd. SE18 5K 107
St Nicholas Rd. SM1: Sutt 5K 165
St Nicholas St. SE8 1B 122
St Nicholas Way SM1: Sutt 4K 165
St Nicolas La. BR7: Chst 1C 160
St Ninian's Ct. N20 3J 31
St Norbert Grn. SE4 4A 122
St Norbert Rd. SE4 5K 121
St Olaf Ho. SE1 4F 15 (1D 102)
(off Tooley St.)
St Olaf's Rd. SW6 7G 99
St Olaf Stairs SE1 4F 15 (1D 102)
(off Tooley St.)
St Olave's Ct. EC2 1E 14 (6D 84)
St Olave's Est. SE1 6H 15 (2E 102)
St Olave's Gdns. SE11 3J 19 (4A 102)
St Olaves Ho. SE11 3J 19 (4A 102)
(off Walnut Tree Wlk.)
St Olave's Mans. SE11 3J 19 (4A 102)
(off Walnut Tree Wlk.)
St Olave's Rd. E6 1E 88
St Olaves Wlk. SW16 2G 155
St Olav's Sq. SE16 2J 103
St Onge Pde. EN1: Enf 3J 23
(off Southbury Rd.)
St Oswald's Pl. SE11 5G 19 (5K 101)
St Oswald's Rd. SW16 1B 156
St Oswalds Studios SW6 6J 99
(off Sedlescombe Rd.)
St Oswulf St. SW1 4D 18 (4H 101)
St Owen Ho. SE1 3E 102
(off St Saviour's Est.)
ST PANCRAS 2F 7 (3J 83)
St Pancras Commercial Cen. NW1 1G 83
(off Pratt St.)
St Pancras Ct. N2 2B 46
St Pancras Gdns. NW1 2H 83
(off Pancras Rd.)
St Pancras Gdns. 2H 83
St Pancras Way NW1 7G 65
St Patrick's Ct. IG8: Wfd G 7B 36
St Paul Cl. UB8: Cowl 5A 74
St Paulinus Ct. DA1: Cray 4K 127
(off Manor Rd.)
St Paul's All. EC4 1B 14 (6B 84)
(off St Paul's Chyd.)
St Paul's Av. HA3: Kenton 4F 43
St Paul's Av. NW2 6E 62
St Paul's Av. SE16 1K 103
St Paul's Bldgs. EC1 3B 8 (4B 84)
(off Dallington St.)
St Paul's Cathedral 1C 14 (6C 84)
St Paul's Churchyard EC4 1B 14 (6B 84)
St Paul's Cl. KT9: Chess 4D 162
St Paul's Cl. SM5: Cars 1C 166
St Paul's Cl. TW15: Ashf 5E 128
St Paul's Cl. TW3: Houn 2C 112
St Paul's Cl. UB3: Harl 5F 93
St Paul's Cl. W5 2F 97
St Pauls Cl. SE7 5B 106
St Paul's Ct. TW4: Houn 3C 112
St Pauls Ct. SW4 5H 119
St Pauls Ctyd. SE8 7C 104
(off Crossfield St.)
St Paul's Cray Rd. BR7: Chst 1H 161
St Paul's Cres. NW1 7H 65
(not continuous)
St Paul's Dr. E15 5F 69
St Pauls Ho. SE8 7C 104
(off Market Yd.)
St Paul's M. NW1 7H 65
St Paul's Pl. N1 6D 66
St Paul's Ri. N13 6G 33
St Paul's Rd. CR7: Thor H 3C 156
St Paul's Rd. DA8: Erith 7J 109
St Paul's Rd. IG11: Bark 1G 89
St Paul's Rd. N1 6B 66
St Paul's Rd. N17 7B 34
St Paul's Rd. TW8: Bford 6D 96
St Paul's Rd. TW9: Rich 3F 115
St Paul's Shrubbery N1 6D 66
St Paul's Sq. BR2: Broml 2H 159
St Paul's Studios W14 5G 99
(off Talgarth Rd.)
St Pauls Ter. SE17 6B 102
St Paul St. N1 1C 84
(not continuous)
St Pauls Vw. Apts. EC1 2J 7 (3A 84)
(off Amwell St.)
St Paul's Wlk. KT2: King T 7G 133
St Paul's Way E3 5B 86
St Paul's Way N3 7E 30
St Paul's Wood Hill BR5: St P 2J 161
St Peter's All. EC3 1F 15 (6D 84)
(off Gracechurch St.)
St Peter's Av. E17 4G 51
St Peter's Av. E2 2G 85
St Peter's Av. N18 4B 34
St Petersburgh M. W2 7K 81
St Petersburgh Pl. W2 7K 81
St Peter's Cen. E1 1H 103
(off Reardon St.)
St Peter's Chu. Ct. N1 1B 84
(off St Peter's St.)
St Peter's Cl. BR7: Chst 7H 143
St Peter's Cl. E2 2G 85
St Peter's Cl. HA4: Ruis 2B 58
St Peter's Cl. IG2: Ilf 4J 53
St Peter's Cl. SW17 2C 136
St Peters Cl. WD23: B Hea 1C 26
St Peter's Ct. NW4 5E 44
St Peter's Ct. WC1 2F 7 (3J 83)
(off Seaford St.)
St Peters Ct. E1 4J 85
(off Cephas St.)
St Peters Ct. KT8: W Mole 4E 148
St Peters Ct. SE12 5H 123
St Peter's Gdns. SE27 3A 138
St Peter's Gro. W6 4C 98
St Peter's Ho. WC1 2F 7 (3J 83)
(off Regent Sq.)
St Peters Ho. SE17 6D 102
St Peters M. N4 5B 48
St Peters M. N8 5A 48
St Peter's Path E17 3G 51
St Peters Pl. W9 4K 81
St Peter's Rd. CR0: C'don 4D 168
St Peter's Rd. KT1: King T 2G 151
St Peter's Rd. KT8: W Mole 4E 148
St Peter's Rd. N9 1C 34
St Peter's Rd. TW1: Twick 5B 114
St Peter's Rd. UB1: S'hall 5E 76
St Peter's Rd. W6 5C 98
St Peters Rd. UB8: Cowl 5A 74
St Peter's Sq. E2 2G 85
St Peter's Sq. W6 4B 98
St Peter's St. CR2: S Croy 5D 168
St Peter's St. N1 1B 84
St Peter's St. M. N1 2B 84
(off St Peters St.)
St Peter's Ter. SW6 7H 99
St Peter's Vs. W6 4C 98
St Peter's Way N1 7E 66
St Peter's Way W5 5D 78
St Peters Way UB3: Harl 5F 93
St Peter's Wharf W4 5C 98
St Philip Ho. WC1 2J 7 (3A 84)
(off Lloyd Baker St.)
St Philip's Av. KT4: Wor Pk 2D 164
St Philip's Ga. KT4: Wor Pk 2D 164
St Philip Sq. SW8 2F 119
St Philip's Rd. E8 6G 67
St Philips Rd. KT6: Surb 6D 150
St Philip St. SW8 2F 119
St Philip's Way N1 1C 84
St Quentin Ho. SW18 6B 118
St Quentin Rd. DA16: Well 3K 125
St Quintin Av. W10 5E 80
St Quintin Gdns. W10 5E 80
St Quintin Ho. W10 5F 81
(off Princess Louise Wlk.)
St Quintin Rd. E13 3K 87
St Quintin Vw. W10 5E 80
St Raphael's Way NW10 5J 61
St Regis Cl. N10 2F 47
St Regis Hgts. NW3 3K 63
St Richard's Ho. NW1 1C 6 (3H 83)
(off Eversholt St.)
St Ronan's Cl. EN4: Had W 1G 21
St Ronan's Cres. IG8: Wfd G 7D 36
St Rule St. SW8 2G 119
St Saviours Cl. HA1: Harr 5J 41
St Saviours Ct. N22 2H 47
St Saviour's Est. SE1 7J 15 (2F 103)
St Saviour's Rd. CR0: C'don 6B 156
St Saviour's Rd. SW2 5K 119
St Saviour's Wharf SE1 Mill St. 6K 15 (2F 103)
(off Mill St.)
St Saviour's Wharf SE1 Shad Thames 6K 15 (2F 103)
(off Shad Thames)
Saints Cl. SE27 4B 138
Saints Dr. E7 5B 70
St Silas Pl. NW5 6E 64
St Simon's Av. SW15 5E 116
Saints M. CR4: Mitc 3C 154
St Stephen's Av. E17 5E 50
St Stephen's Av. W12 1D 98
(not continuous)
St Stephen's Av. W13 6B 78
St Stephen's Cl. E17 5D 50
St Stephen's Cl. NW8 1C 82
St Stephen's Cl. UB1: S'hall 5E 76
St Stephens Cl. NW5 5D 64
(off Malden Rd.)
St Stephen's Ct. EN1: Enf 6K 23
(off Park Av.)
St Stephens Ct. N8 6K 47
St Stephens Ct. W13 6B 78
St Stephen's Cres. CR7: Thor H 3A 156
St Stephen's Cres. W2 6J 81
St Stephen's Gdns. SW15 5H 117
St Stephen's Gdns. TW1: Twick 6C 114
St Stephen's Gdns. W2 6J 81
(not continuous)
St Stephens Gro. SE13 3E 122
St Stephens Ho. SE17 6D 102
(off Lytham St.)
St Stephen's M. W2 5J 81
St Stephens Pde. E7 7A 70
St Stephen's Pas. TW1: Twick 6C 114
St Stephen's Rd. E17 5D 50
St Stephen's Rd. E3 1A 86
St Stephen's Rd. E6 7A 70
St Stephen's Rd. EN5: Barn 5A 20
St Stephen's Rd. TW3: Houn 6E 112
St Stephen's Rd. UB7: Yiew 1A 92
St Stephen's Rd. W13 6B 78
St Stephen's Row EC4 1E 14 (6D 84)
(off Walbrook)
St Stephen's Ter. SW8 7K 101
St Stephen's Wlk. SW7 4A 100
(off Southwell Gdns.)
St Swithins La. EC4 2E 14 (7D 84)
St Swithun's Rd. SE13 6F 123
St Theresa's Cl. E9 4C 68
St Theresa's Rd. TW14: Felt 4H 111
St Thomas Cl. KT6: Surb 1F 163
St Thomas Ct. DA5: Bexl 7G 127
St Thomas Ct. E10 7D 50
(off Lake Rd.)
St Thomas Ct. HA5: Pinn 1C 40
St Thomas Ct. NW1 7G 65
(off Wrotham Rd.)
St Thomas Dr. BR5: Farnb 1G 173
St Thomas' Dr. HA5: Pinn 1C 40
St Thomas Gdns. IG1: Ilf 6G 71
St Thomas Ho. E1 6K 85
(off W. Arbour St.)
St Thomas M. SW18 5J 117
St Thomas Rd. DA17: Belv 2J 109
St Thomas Rd. E16 6J 87
St Thomas Rd. N14 7C 22
St Thomas Rd. W4 6J 97
St Thomas's Gdns. NW5 6E 64
St Thomas's M. SE7 4C 106
St Thomas's Pl. E9 7J 67
St Thomas's Rd. N4 2A 66
St Thomas's Rd. NW10 1A 80
St Thomas's Sq. E9 7J 67
St Thomas St. SE1 5F 15 (1D 102)
St Thomas's Way SW6 7H 99
St Timothys M. BR1: Broml 1K 159
St Ursula Gro. HA5: Pinn 5B 40
St Ursula Rd. UB1: S'hall 6E 76
St Valery Pl. TW5: Hest 7B 94
St Vincent Cl. SE27 5B 138
St Vincent De Paul Ho. E1 5J 85
(off Jubilee St.)
St Vincent Ho. SE1 3F 103
(off St Saviour's Est.)
St Vincent Rd. TW2: Whitt 6G 113
St Vincent's La. NW7 4K 29
St Vincent St. W1 6H 5 (5E 82)
St Wilfrid's Cl. EN4: E Barn 5H 21
St Wilfrid's Rd. EN4: E Barn 5G 21
St Williams Ct. N1 7J 65
St Winefride's Av. E12 5D 70
St Winifred's Rd. TW11: Tedd 6B 132
Sakura Dr. N22 1H 47
Salamanca Pl. IG11: Bark 2B 90
Salamanca Pl. SE1 4G 19 (4K 101)
Salamanca Sq. SE1 4G 19 (4K 101)
(off Salamanca Pl.)
Salamanca St. SE1 4G 19 (4K 101)
Salamanca St. SE11 4G 19 (4K 101)
Salamander Cl. KT2: King T 5C 132
Salamander Quay KT1: Hamp W 1D 150
Salcombe Ct. E14 5E 86
(off St Ives Pl.)
Salcombe Dr. RM6: Chad H 6F 55
Salcombe Dr. SM4: Mord 1F 165
Salcombe Gdns. NW7 6K 29
Salcombe Rd. E17 7B 50
Salcombe Rd. N16 5E 66
Salcombe Rd. TW15: Ashf 3A 128
Salcombe Vs. TW10: Rich 5E 114
Salcombe Way HA4: Ruis 2J 57
Salcombe Way UB4: Hayes 3F 75
Salcott Rd. CR0: Bedd 3J 167
Salcott Rd. SW11 5C 118
Salehurst Cl. HA3: Kenton 5E 42
Salehurst Rd. SE4 6B 122
Salem Pl. CR0: C'don 3C 168
Salem Rd. W2 7K 81
Salento Cl. N3 7D 30
Sale Pl. W2 6C 4 (5C 82)
Sale St. E2 4G 85
Salford Ho. E14 4E 104
(off Seyssel St.)
Salford Rd. SW2 1H 137
Salhouse Cl. SE28 6C 90
Salisbury Av. IG11: Bark 7H 71
Salisbury Av. N3 3H 45
Salisbury Av. SM1: Sutt 6H 165
Salisbury Cl. KT4: Wor Pk 3B 164
Salisbury Cl. SE17 4D 102
Salisbury Ct. E9 5A 68
(off Mabley St.)
Salisbury Ct. EC4 1A 14 (6B 84)
Salisbury Ct. EN2: Enf 4J 23
(off London Rd.)
Salisbury Ct. SE16 3G 103
(off Stork's Rd.)
Salisbury Ct. SM5: Cars 5D 166
Salisbury Ct. UB5: N'olt 5F 59
(off Newmarket Av.)
Salisbury Gdns. IG9: Buck H 2G 37
Salisbury Gdns. SW19 7G 135
Salisbury Hall Gdns. E4 6H 35
Salisbury Ho. E14 6D 86
(off Hobday St.)
Salisbury Ho. EC2 6F 9 (5D 84)
(off London Wall)
Salisbury Ho. HA7: Stan 6F 27
Salisbury Ho. N1 1B 84
(off St Mary's Path)
Salisbury Ho. SM6: W'gton 5F 167
Salisbury Ho. SW1 5D 18 (5H 101)
(off Drummond Ga.)
Salisbury Ho. SW9 7A 102
(off Cranmer Rd.)
Salisbury Mans. N15 5B 48
Salisbury M. SW6 7H 99
Salisbury Pas. SW6 7H 99
(off Dawes Rd.)
Salisbury Pavement SW6 7H 99
(off Dawes Rd.)
Salisbury Pl. SW9 7B 102
Salisbury Pl. W1 5E 4 (5D 82)
Salisbury Prom. N8 5B 48
Salisbury Rd. BR2: Broml 5C 160
Salisbury Rd. DA5: Bexl 1G 145
Salisbury Rd. E10 2E 68
Salisbury Rd. E12 5B 70
Salisbury Rd. E17 5E 50
Salisbury Rd. E4 3H 35
Salisbury Rd. E7 6J 69
Salisbury Rd. EN5: Barn 3B 20
Salisbury Rd. HA1: Harr 5H 41
Salisbury Rd. HA5: Eastc 4J 39
Salisbury Rd. IG3: Ilf 2J 71
Salisbury Rd. KT3: N Mald 3K 151
Salisbury Rd. KT4: Wor Pk 4K 163
Salisbury Rd. N22 1B 48
Salisbury Rd. N4 5B 48
Salisbury Rd. N9 3B 34
Salisbury Rd. RM10: Dag 6H 73
Salisbury Rd. SE25 6G 157
Salisbury Rd. SM5: Cars 6D 166
Salisbury Rd. SW19 7G 135
Salisbury Rd. TW13: Felt 1A 130
Salisbury Rd. TW4: Houn 3A 112
Salisbury Rd. TW6: H'row A 6E 110
(not continuous)
Salisbury Rd. TW9: Rich 4E 114
Salisbury Rd. UB2: S'hall 4C 94
Salisbury Rd. W13 2B 96
Salisbury Sq. EC4 1K 13 (6A 84)
Salisbury St. NW8 4C 4 (4C 82)
Salisbury St. W3 2J 97
Salisbury Ter. SE15 3J 121
Salisbury Wlk. N19 2G 65
Salix Cl. TW16: Sun 7K 129
Salix Ct. N3 6D 30
Salix La. IG8: Wfd G 1C 52
Salk Cl. NW9 2A 44
Salliesfield TW2: Whitt 6H 113
Sally Murray Cl. E12 4E 70
Salmen Rd. E13 2H 87
Salmond Cl. HA7: Stan 6F 27
Salmon La. E14 6A 86
Salmon M. NW6 5J 63
Salmon Rd. DA17: Belv 5G 109
Salmons Rd. KT9: Chess 6E 162
Salmons Rd. N9 1B 34
Salmon St. E14 6B 86
Salmon St. NW9 1H 61
Salomons Rd. E13 5A 88
Salop Rd. E17 6K 49
Salsabil Apts. E3 4B 86
Saltash Cl. SM1: Sutt 4H 165
Saltash Rd. DA16: Well 1C 126
Saltash Rd. IG6: Ilf 1H 53
Saltcoats Rd. W4 2A 98

A–Z London 283

Saltcroft Cl. HA9: Wemb 1H 61
Saltdene N4 1K 65
Salter Cl. HA2: Harr 4D 58
Salterford Rd. SW17 6E 136
Saltern Ct. IG11: Bark 3B 90
(off Galleons Dr.)
Salter Rd. SE16 1K 103
Salters Ct. EC4 1D 14 (6C 84)
(off Bow La.)
Salter's Hall Ct. EC4 2E 14 (7D 84)
(off Cannon St.)
Salter's Hill SE19 5D 138
Salters Rd. E17 4F 51
Salters Rd. W10 4F 81
Salters Row N1 6D 66
(off Tilney Gdns.)
Salter St. E14 7B 86
(not continuous)
Salter St. NW10 3C 80
Salterton Rd. N7 3K 65
Salt Hill Cl. UB8: Uxb 5A 56
Salting St. IG11: Bark 1H 89
Saltley Cl. E6 6C 88
Salton Cl. N3 2J 45
Salton Sq. E14 6B 86
Saltoun Rd. SW2 4A 120
Saltram Cl. N15 4F 49
Saltram Cres. W9 3H 81
Saltwell St. E14 7C 86
Saltwood Gro. SE17 5D 102
Saltwood Ho. SE15 6J 103
(off Lovelinch Cl.)
Salusbury Rd. NW6 1G 81
Salus Ct. CR0: C'don 4C 168
(off Parker Rd.)
Salutation Rd. SE10 4G 105
Salvador SW17 5D 136
Salvia Gdns. UB6: G'frd 2A 78
Salvin Rd. SW15 3F 117
Salway Cl. IG8: Wfd G 7D 36
Salway Pl. E15 6F 69
Salway Rd. E15 6F 69
Samantha Cl. E17 7B 50
Samara Dr. UB1: S'hall 2C 94
Samaras Mans. E20 5E 68
(off Liberty Bri. Rd.)
Sam Bartram Cl. SE7 5A 106
Sambourne Family Home, The 3J 99
(off Stafford Ter.)
Sambroke Sq. EN4: E Barn 4G 21
Sambrooke Ct. EN1: Enf 6K 23
Sambrook Ho. E1 5J 85
(off Jubilee St.)
Sambrook Ho. SE11 4J 19 (4A 102)
(off Hotspur St.)
Sambruck M. SE6 1D 140
Samels Ct. W6 5C 98
Samford Ho. N1 1A 84
(off Barnsbury Est.)
Samford St. NW8 4B 4 (4B 82)
Samira Cl. E17 6C 50
Sam King Wlk. SE5 7D 102
(off Edmund St.)
Sam Manners Ho. SE10 5G 105
(off Tuskar St.)
Sam March Ho. E14 6F 87
(off Blair St.)
Sammi Ct. CR7: Thor H 4C 156
Samos Rd. SE20 2H 157
Samphire Hgts. E20 5E 68
(off Napa Cl.)
Sampson Av. EN5: Barn 5A 20
Sampson Cl. DA17: Belv 3D 108
Sampson Ct. TW17: Shep 5E 146
Sampson Ho. SE1 4A 14 (1B 102)
Sampson St. E1 1G 103
Samson St. E13 2A 88
Samuda Est. E14 3E 104
Samuel Cl. E8 1F 85
Samuel Cl. HA7: Stan 2F 27
Samuel Cl. SE14 6K 103
Samuel Cl. SE18 4C 106
Samuel Ct. N1 2G 9 (3E 84)
(off Pitfield St.)
Samuel Ferguson Pl. IG11: Bark 2K 89
Samuel Gray Gdns. KT2: King T 1D 150
Samuel Johnson Cl. SW16 4K 137
Samuel Jones Ct. SE15 7E 102
Samuel Lewis Bldgs. N1 6A 66
Samuel Lewis Trust Dwellings
E8 5G 67
(off Amhurst Rd.)
Samuel Lewis Trust Dwellings
N16 6E 48
Samuel Lewis Trust Dwellings
SW3 4C 16 (4C 100)
Samuel Lewis Trust Dwellings
SW6 7J 99
(off Vanston Pl.)
Samuel Lewis Trust Dwellings
W1 44H 99
(off Lisgar Ter.)
Samuel Lewis Trust Est. SE5 1C 120
(off Warner Rd.)
Samuel Richardson Ho. W14 4H 99
(off North End Cres.)
Samuel's Cl. W6 4E 98
Samuelson Pl. TW7: Isle 2J 113
Samuel St. E8 1F 85
Samuel St. SE15 7F 103
Samuel St. SE18 4D 106
Samuel Wallis Lodge SE10 4G 105
(off Banning St.)
Samuel Wallis Lodge SE3 3H 123
(off Banning St.)
Sanchia Ct. E2 3G 85
(off Wellington Row)
Sancroft Cl. NW2 3D 62
Sancroft Ho. SE11 5H 19 (5K 101)
(off Sancroft St.)
Sancroft Rd. HA3: W'stone 2K 41
Sancroft St. SE11 5H 19 (5K 101)
Sanctuary, The DA5: Bexl 6D 126
Sanctuary, The SM4: Mord 6J 153
Sanctuary, The SW1 1D 18 (3H 101)
(off Broad Sanctuary)
Sanctuary M. E8 6F 67
Sanctuary Rd. TW6: H'row A 6C 110
Sanctuary St. SE1 7D 14 (2C 102)
Sandale Cl. N16 3D 66
Sandall Cl. W5 4E 78
Sandall Ho. E3 2A 86
Sandall Rd. NW5 6G 65
Sandall Rd. W5 4E 78
Sandal Rd. KT3: N Mald 5K 151
Sandal Rd. N18 5B 34
Sandal St. E15 1G 87
Sandalwood Cl. E1 4A 86
Sandalwood Dr. HA4: Ruis 7E 38
Sandalwood Ho. DA15: Sidc 2K 143
Sandalwood Mans. W8 3K 99
(off Stone Hall Gdns.)
Sandalwood Rd. TW13: Felt 3K 129
Sandbach Pl. SE18 4G 107
Sandbanks TW14: Felt 1G 129
Sandbourne NW8 1K 81
(off Abbey Rd.)
Sandbourne W11 6J 81
(off Dartmouth Cl.)
Sandbourne Av. SW19 2K 153
Sandbourne Rd. SE4 2A 122
Sandbrook Cl. NW7 6E 28
Sandbrook Rd. N16 3E 66
Sandby Ct. NW10 3D 80
(off Plough Cl.)
Sandby Grn. SE9 3C 124
Sandby Ho. NW6 1J 81
Sandcliff Rd. DA8: Erith 4K 109
Sandcroft Cl. N13 6G 33
Sandell's Av. TW15: Ashf 4E 128
Sandell St. SE1 6J 13 (2A 102)
Sanderling Ct. SE28 7C 90
Sanderling Ct. SE8 6B 104
(off Abinger Gro.)
Sanderling Lodge E1 3K 15 (7F 85)
(off Star Pl.)
Sanders Cl. TW12: Hamp H 5G 131
Sanders Ho. WC1 1J 7 (3A 84)
(off Gt. Percy St.)
Sanders La. NW7 Bittacy Ri 7K 29
Sanders La. NW7 Grants Cl. 7A 30
Sanders La. TW4: Houn 5D 112
Sanderson Bldg. NW2 2E 62
Sanderson Cl. NW5 4F 65
Sanderson Ho. E16 5J 87
(off Hammersley Rd.)
Sanderson Ho. SE8 5B 104
(off Grove St.)
Sandersons La. W4 5K 97
(off Chiswick High Rd.)
Sanderson Sq. BR1: Broml 3E 160
Sanderstead Av. NW2 2G 63
Sanderstead Cl. SW12 7G 119
Sanderstead Rd. CR2: S Croy 7D 168
Sanderstead Rd. CR2: Sande 7D 168
Sanderstead Rd. E10 1A 68
Sanders Way N19 1H 65
Sandes Ct. CR7: Thor H 3C 156
Sandfield WC1 2F 7 (3J 83)
(off Cromer St.)
Sandfield Gdns. CR7: Thor H 3B 156
Sandfield Pas. CR7: Thor H 3C 156
Sandfield Pl. CR7: Thor H 3C 156
Sandfield Rd. CR7: Thor H 3B 156
Sandford Av. N22 1C 48
Sandford Cl. E6 4D 88
Sandford Ct. EN5: New Bar 3E 20
Sandford Ct. N16 1E 66
Sandford Rd. BR2: Broml 3J 159
Sandford Rd. DA7: Bex 4E 126
Sandford Rd. E6 3C 88
Sandford St. SW6 7K 99
Sandgate Cl. RM7: Rush G 7J 55
Sandgate Ho. E5 5H 67
Sandgate Ho. W5 5C 78
Sandgate La. SW18 1C 136
Sandgate Rd. DA16: Well 7C 108
Sandgate St. SE15 6H 103
Sandgate Trad. Est. SE15 6H 103
(off Sandgate St.)
Sandham Ct. SW4 1J 119
Sandham Point SE18 4F 107
(off Vincent Rd.)
Sandhills SM6: Bedd 4H 167
Sandhills, The SW10 7A 16 (6A 100)
(off Limerston St.)
Sandhills Mdw. TW17: Shep 7E 146
Sandhurst Av. HA2: Harr 6F 41
Sandhurst Av. KT5: Surb 7H 151
Sandhurst Cl. CR2: Sande 7E 168
Sandhurst Cl. NW9 3G 43
Sandhurst Ct. SW2 4J 119
Sandhurst Dr. IG3: Bark 4K 71
Sandhurst Dr. IG3: Ilf 4K 71
Sandhurst Ho. E1 5J 85
(off Wolsy St.)
Sandhurst Ho. E17 1B 50
(off Robinswood Gdns.)
Sandhurst Mkt. SE6 1E 140
(off Sandhurst Rd.)
Sandhurst Rd. BR6: Chels 3K 173
Sandhurst Rd. DA15: Sidc 3K 143
Sandhurst Rd. DA5: Bexl 5D 126
Sandhurst Rd. N9 6D 24
Sandhurst Rd. NW9 3G 43
Sandhurst Rd. SE6 1F 141
Sandhurst Way CR2: Sande 7E 168
Sandifer Dr. NW2 3F 63
Sandiford Rd. SM3: Sutt 2H 165
Sandiland Cres. BR2: Hayes 2H 171
Sandilands CR0: C'don 2G 169
Sandilands Rd. SW6 1K 117
Sandison St. SE15 3G 121
Sandland St. WC1 6H 7 (5K 83)
Sandling Ri. SE9 3E 142
Sandlings, The N22 2A 48
Sandlings Cl. SE15 2H 121
Sandmartin Way SM6: W'gton
1E 166
Sandmere Rd. SW4 4J 119
Sandon Cl. KT10: Esh 7H 149
Sandover Ho. SE16 3G 103
(off Spa Rd.)
Sandow Cres. UB3: Hayes 3H 93
Sandown Av. RM10: Dag 6J 73
Sandown Cl. TW5: Cran 1J 111
Sandown Ct. HA7: Stan 5H 27
Sandown Ct. RM10: Dag 6J 73
(off Sandown Av.)
Sandown Ct. SE26 3H 139
Sandown Ct. SM2: Sutt 7K 165
Sandown Dr. SM5: Cars 7E 166
Sandown Rd. SE25 5H 157
Sandown Way UB5: N'olt 6C 58
Sandpiper Cl. E17 7E 34
Sandpiper Cl. SE16 2B 104
Sandpiper Ct. E1 7G 85
(off Thomas More St.)
Sandpiper Ct. E14 3E 104
(off New Union Cl.)
Sandpiper Ct. SE8 6C 104
(off Edward Pl.)
Sandpiper Dr. HA2: Harr 2F 59
Sandpiper Rd. SM1: Sutt 5H 165
Sandpiper Ter. IG5: Ilf 3F 53
Sandpit Pl. SE7 5C 106
Sandpit Rd. BR1: Broml 5G 141
Sandpits Rd. CR0: C'don 4K 169
Sandpits Rd. TW10: Ham 2D 132
Sandra Cl. KT8: E Mos 4H 149
Sandra Cl. N22 1C 48
Sandra Cl. TW3: Houn 5F 113
Sandra Ct. CR4: Mitc 6D 136
Sandridge Cl. HA1: Harr 4J 41
Sandridge St. N19 2G 65
Sandringham Av. SW20 1G 153
Sandringham Bldgs. SE17 4D 102
(off Balfour St.)
Sandringham Cl. EN1: Enf 2K 23
Sandringham Cl. IG6: Ilf 3G 53
Sandringham Cl. SW19 1F 135
Sandringham Ct. DA15: Sidc 6K 125
Sandringham Ct. KT2: King T 1E 150
(off Skerne Wlk.)
Sandringham Ct. SE16 1K 103
(off King & Queen Wharf)
Sandringham Ct. UB10: Hil 4E 74
Sandringham Ct. W1 1B 12 (6G 83)
(off Dufour's Pl.)
Sandringham Ct. W9 3A 82
(off Maida Vale)
Sandringham Cres. HA2: Harr 2E 58
Sandringham Dr. DA16: Well 2J 125
Sandringham Dr. DA2: Wilm 2K 145
Sandringham Flats WC2 2D 12 (7H 83)
(off Charing Cross Rd.)
Sandringham Gdns. IG6: Ilf 3G 53
Sandringham Gdns. KT8: W Mole
4E 148
Sandringham Gdns. N12 6G 31
Sandringham Gdns. N8 6J 47
Sandringham Gdns. TW5: Cran 1J 111
Sandringham Ho. SE1 5H 15 (1E 102)
(off Potters Flds.)
Sandringham Ho. W14 4G 99
(off Windsor Way)
Sandringham M. TW12: Hamp 1D 148
Sandringham M. W5 7D 78
Sandringham Rd. BR1: Broml 5J 141
Sandringham Rd. CR7: Thor H 5C 156
Sandringham Rd. E10 6F 51
Sandringham Rd. E7 5A 70
Sandringham Rd. E8 5F 67
Sandringham Rd. IG11: Bark 5K 71
Sandringham Rd. KT4: Wor Pk 3C 164
Sandringham Rd. N22 3C 48
Sandringham Rd. NW11 7G 45
Sandringham Rd. NW2 6D 62
Sandringham Rd. TW6: H'row A 5A 110
Sandringham Rd. UB5: N'olt 7E 58
Sandrock Pl. CR0: C'don 4K 169
Sandrock Rd. SE13 3C 122
SANDS END 1A 118
Sand's End La. SW6 1K 117
Sandstone La. E16 7K 87
Sandstone Pl. N19 2F 65
Sandstone Rd. SE12 2K 141
Sands Way IG8: Wfd G 6J 37
Sandtoft Rd. SE7 6K 105
Sandwell Cres. NW6 6J 63
Sandwich Ho. SE16 2J 103
(off Swan Rd.)
Sandwich Ho. WC1 2E 6 (3J 83)
(off Sandwich St.)
Sandwich Ms. SE9 1H 143
Sandwich St. WC1 2E 6 (3J 83)
Sandwick Cl. NW7 7H 29
Sandy Bury BR6: Orp 3H 173
Sandycombe Rd. TW14: Felt 1J 129
Sandycombe Rd. TW9: Kew 3F 115
Sandycombe Rd. TW9: Rich 3F 115
Sandycoombe Rd. TW1: Twick 6C 114
Sandycroft SE2 6A 108
Sandy Dr. TW14: Felt 1G 129
Sandy Hill Av. SE18 5F 107
Sandy Hill Rd. SE18 5F 107
Sandy Hill Rd. SM6: W'gton 7G 167
Sandyhill Rd. IG1: Ilf 4F 71
Sandy Ho. IG11: Bark 4A 90
Sandy La. BR6: Orp 7K 161
Sandy La. CR4: Mitc 1E 154
Sandy La. DA14: Sidc 7D 144
Sandy La. HA3: Kenton 6F 43
Sandy La. KT1: Hamp W 1C 150
Sandy La. KT12: Walt T 6K 147
Sandy La. SM2: Cheam 7G 165
Sandy La. SM6: W'gton 6H 167
Sandy La. TW10: Ham 2C 132
Sandy La. TW11: Hamp W 7A 132
Sandy La. TW11: Tedd 7A 132
Sandy La. Nth. SM6: W'gton 6H 167
Sandymount Av. HA7: Stan 5H 27
Sandy Ridge BR7: Chst 6E 142
Sandy Rd. DA8: Erith 5J 109
Sandy Rd. NW3 2K 63
Sandys Row E1 6H 9 (5E 84)
Sandy Way CR0: C'don 3B 170
Sandy Way KT12: Walt T 7H 147
Sanford La. N16 3F 67
Sanford St. SE14 6A 104
Sanford Ter. N16 3F 67
Sanford Wlk. N16 2F 67
Sanford Wlk. SE14 6A 104
Sangam Cl. UB2: S'hall 3C 94
Sanger Av. KT9: Chess 5E 162
Sangley Rd. SE25 4E 156
Sangley Rd. SE6 7D 122
Sangora Rd. SW11 4B 118
Sankey Ho. E2 2J 85
(off St James's Av.)
Sansom Rd. E11 2H 69
Sansom St. SE5 1D 120
Sans Wlk. EC1 3K 7 (4A 84)
Santa Maria Ct. E1 5A 86
(off Ocean Est.)
Sant Ho. SE17 4C 102
(off Browning St.)
Santiago Ct. E1 5A 86
(off Ocean Est.)
Santina Apartment CR0: C'don 1D 168
(off Cherry Orchard Rd.)
Santley Ho. SE1 7K 13 (2A 102)
Santley St. SW4 4K 119
Santos Rd. SW18 5J 117
Santway, The HA7: Stan 5D 26
Sapcote Trad. Cen. NW10 6B 62
Saperton Wlk. SE11 3H 19 (4K 101)
(off Juxon St.)
Saphire Ct. E15 1E 86
(off Warton Rd.)
Saphora Cl. BR6: Farnb 5H 173
Sapperton Ct. EC1 3C 8 (4C 84)
(off Gee St.)
Sapperton Ho. W2 5J 81
(off Westbourne Pk. Rd.)
Sapphire Cl. E6 6E 88
Sapphire Cl. RM8: Dag 1C 72
Sapphire Ct. E1 7G 85
(off Cable St.)
Sapphire Rd. NW10 7J 61
Sapphire Rd. SE8 4A 104
Saracen Cl. CR0: C'don 6D 156
Saracens FC 7K 29
Saracens Head Yd. EC3 1J 15 (6F 85)
(off Jewry St.)
Saracen St. E14 6C 86
Sarah Ct. UB5: N'olt 1D 76
Sarah Ho. E1 6H 85
(off Commercial Rd.)
Sarah Swift Ho. SE1 6F 15 (2D 102)
(off Kipling St.)
Sara La. Ct. N1 2E 84
(off Stanway St.)
Saratoga Rd. E5 4J 67
Sara Turnbull Ho. SE18 4D 106
Saravia Ct. SE13 6G 123
Sardinia St. WC2 1G 13 (6K 83)
Sarita Cl. HA3: Hrw W 2H 41
Sarjant Path SW19 2F 135
(off Blincoe Cl.)
Sarjeant Ct. BR4: W W'ck 2F 171
(off Bencurtis Pk.)
Sark Cl. TW5: Hest 7E 94
Sark Ho. EN3: Enf W 1E 24
Sark Twr. SE28 2G 107
Sark Wlk. E16 6K 87
Sarnes Ct. N11 4A 32
(off Oakleigh Rd. Sth.)
Sarnesfield Ho. SE15 6H 103
(off Pencraig Way)
Sarnesfield Rd. EN2: Enf 4J 23
Sarratt Ho. W10 5E 80
(off Sutton Way)
Sarre Rd. NW2 5H 63
Sarsen Av. TW3: Houn 2E 112
Sarsfeld Rd. SW12 2D 136
Sarsfield Rd. UB6: G'frd 2B 78
Sartor Rd. SE15 4K 121
Sarum Ho. W11 7H 81
(off Portobello Rd.)
Sarum Ter. E3 4B 86
Saskia M. SE15 2H 121
Sassoon NW9 1B 44
Satanita Cl. E16 6B 88
Satchell Mead NW9 1B 44
Satchwell Rd. E2 2K 9 (3G 85)
Satchwell St. E2 2K 9 (3G 85)
Satin Ho. E1 1K 15 (6G 85)
(off Piazza Wlk.)
Sattar M. N16 3D 66
Saturn Ho. E15 1F 87
(off High St.)
Saturn Ho. E3 1C 86
(off Garrison Rd.)
Sauls Grn. E11 3G 69
Saundby La. SE3 4K 123
Saunders Apts. E3 3C 86
(off Marchant St.)
Saunders Cl. E14 7B 86
(off Limehouse C'way.)
Saunders Cl. IG1: Ilf 1H 71
Saunders Ho. SE16 2K 103
(off Quebec Way)
Saunders Ness Rd. E14 5E 104
Saunders Rd. SE18 5K 107
Saunders Rd. UB10: Uxb 7B 56
Saunders St. SE11 3J 19 (4A 102)
Saunders Way SE28 7B 90
Saunderton Rd. HA0: Wemb 5B 60
Saunton Av. UB3: Harl 7H 93
Saunton Ct. UB1: S'hall 7G 77
(off Haldane Rd.)
Savage Gdns. E6 6D 88
Savage Gdns. EC3 2H 15 (7E 84)
(not continuous)
Savannah Cl. SE15 7F 103
Savera Cl. UB2: S'hall 3A 94
Savernake Ct. HA7: Stan 6G 27
Savernake Ho. N4 7C 48
Savernake Rd. N9 6B 24
Savernake Rd. NW3 4D 64
Savery Dr. KT6: Surb 7B 150
Savile Cl. KT3: N Mald 5A 152
Savile Cl. KT7: T Ditt 1A 162
Savile Gdns. CR0: C'don 2F 169
Savile Row W1 2A 12 (7G 83)
Saville Cres. TW15: Ashf 6F 129
Saville Rd. E16 1C 106
Saville Rd. RM6: Chad H 6F 55
Saville Rd. TW1: Twick 1K 131
Saville Rd. W4 3K 97
Saville Row BR2: Hayes 1H 171
Saville Row EN3: Enf H 2E 24
Savill Gdns. SW20 3C 152
Savill Ho. E16 1F 107
(off Robert St.)
Savill Ho. SW4 6H 119
Savill Row IG8: Wfd G 6C 36
Savin Lodge SM2: Sutt 7A 166
(off Walnut M.)
Savona Cl. SW19 7F 135
Savona Ho. SW8 7G 101
(off Savona St.)
Savona St. SW8 7G 101
Savoy Av. UB3: Harl 5G 93
Savoy Bldgs. WC2 3G 13 (7K 83)
(off Strand)
SAVOY CIRCUS 7B 80
Savoy Cl. E15 1G 87
Savoy Cl. HA8: Edg 5B 28
Savoy Ct. HA2: Harr 5F 41
Savoy Ct. NW3 3A 64
Savoy Ct. SW5 4J 99
(off Cromwell Rd.)
Savoy Ct. WC2 3G 13 (7K 83)
Savoy Hill WC2 3G 13 (7K 83)
Savoy M. SW9 3J 119
Savoy Pde. EN1: Enf 3K 23
Savoy Pl. W12 1F 99
Savoy Pl. WC2 3F 13 (7J 83)
Savoy Row WC2 3G 13 (7K 83)
(off Savoy St.)
Savoy Steps WC2 3G 13 (7K 83)
(off Savoy St.)
Savoy St. WC2 2G 13 (7K 83)
Savoy Theatre 3F 13 (7J 83)
(off Strand)
Savoy Way WC2 3G 13 (7K 83)
(off Savoy Hill)
Sawbill Cl. UB4: Yead 5B 76
Sawkins Cl. SW19 2G 135
Sawley Rd. W12 1C 98
Saw Mill Way N16 6G 49
Sawmill Yd. E3 1A 86
Sawtry Cl. SM5: Cars 7C 154
Sawyer Cl. N9 2B 34
Sawyer Ct. NW10 7K 61
Sawyers Apts. SW11 4C 118
(off Danvers Avenue)
Sawyers Cl. RM10: Dag 6J 73
Sawyer's Hill TW10: Rich 7F 115
Sawyers Lawn W13 6A 78
Sawyer St. SE1 6C 14 (2C 102)
Saxby Rd. SW2 7J 119
Saxham Rd. IG11: Bark 2J 89
Saxlingham Rd. E4 3A 36
Saxon Av. TW13: Hanw 2C 130
Saxonbury Av. TW16: Sun 3K 147
Saxonbury Cl. CR4: Mitc 3B 154
Saxonbury Ct. N7 5J 65
Saxonbury Gdns. KT6: Surb 1C 162
Saxon Bus. Cen. SW19 2A 154
Saxon Chase N8 6K 47
Saxon Cl. E17 7C 50
Saxon Cl. KT6: Surb 6D 150
Saxon Cl. UB8: Hil 5B 74
Saxon Ct. N1 1J 83
Saxon Dr. W3 6G 79
Saxonfield Cl. SW2 7K 119
Saxon Gdns. UB1: S'hall 7C 76
Saxon Hall W2 7K 81
(off Palace Ct.)
Saxon Ho. E1 6K 9 (5F 85)
(off Thrawl St.)
Saxon Ho. KT1: King T 4F 151
Saxon Ho. SM6: W'gton 1E 166
(off London Rd.)
Saxon Ho. TW13: Hanw 2D 130
Saxon Lea Ct. E3 2B 86
(off Saxon Rd.)
Saxon Lodge CR0: C'don 1C 168
(off Tavistock Rd.)
Saxon Rd. BR1: Broml 7H 141
Saxon Rd. E3 2B 86
Saxon Rd. E6 4D 88
Saxon Rd. HA9: Wemb 3J 61
Saxon Rd. IG1: Ilf 6F 71
Saxon Rd. KT2: King T 1E 150
Saxon Rd. N22 1B 48
Saxon Rd. SE25 5D 156
Saxon Rd. TW15: Ashf 6F 129
Saxon Rd. UB1: S'hall 7C 76
Saxon Ter. SE6 2B 140
Saxon Wlk. DA14: Sidc 6C 144
Saxon Way N14 6C 22
Saxon Way UB7: Harm 2D 174
Saxon Way Ind. Est. UB7: Harm 2D 174
Saxony Pde. UB3: Hayes 5E 74
Saxton Cl. SE13 3F 123
Saxton Pl. KT8: W Mole 4D 148
Sayers Ct. W5 2D 96
Sayers Ho. N2 2B 46
(off The Grange)
Sayer St. SE17 4C 102
Sayer's Wlk. TW10: Rich 7F 115
Sayesbury La. N18 5B 34
Sayes Ct. SE8 6B 104
Sayes Ct. St. SE8 6B 104
Scadbury Pk. 7K 143
Scads Hill Cl. BR6: Pet W 6K 161
Scafell NW1 1A 6 (3G 83)
(off Stanhope St.)
Scala 1F 7 (3J 83)
(off Pentonville Rd.)
Scala St. W1 5B 6 (5G 83)
Scales Rd. N17 3F 49
Scalpel, The 1H 15 (6E 84)
(off Leadenhall St.)
Scampston M. W10 6F 81
Scandrett St. E1 1H 103
Scarab Cl. E16 7H 87
Scarba Wlk. N1 6D 66
(off Essex Rd.)
Scarborough Rd. E11 1F 69
Scarborough Rd. N4 7A 48
Scarborough Rd. N9 7D 24
Scarborough Rd. TW6: H'row A
6E 110
Scarborough St. E1 1K 15 (6F 85)
Scarbrook Rd. CR0: C'don 3C 168
Scarle Rd. HA0: Wemb 6D 60
Scarlet Cl. E20 5D 68
Scarlet Rd. SE6 3G 141
Scarlette Mnr. Way SW2 7A 120
Scarlet Wlk. EN3: Pond E 5E 24
Scarsbrook Rd. SE3 3B 124
Scarsdale Pl. W8 3K 99
Scarsdale Rd. HA2: Harr 3G 59
Scarsdale Studios W8 3J 99
(off Stratford Rd.)
Scarsdale Vs. W8 3J 99
Scarth Rd. SW13 3B 116
Scawen Cl. SM5: Cars 4E 166
Scawen Rd. SE8 5A 104
Scawfell St. E2 2F 85
Scaynes Link N12 4D 30
Sceaux Gdns. SE5 1E 120
Scena Way SE5 7C 102
Sceptre Ct. EC3 3J 15 (7F 85)
(off Tower Hill)
Sceptre Ho. E1 4J 85
(off Malcolm Rd.)
Sceptre Rd. E2 3J 85
Schafer Ho. NW1 2A 6 (3G 83)
Schofield Wlk. SE3 7J 105
Scholars Cl. EN5: Barn 4B 20
Scholars Ho. NW6 1J 81
(off Glengall Rd.)
Scholars Pl. N16 3E 66
Scholars Rd. E4 1A 36
Scholars Rd. SW12 1G 137
Scholars Vw. KT7: T Ditt 7J 149
Scholars Way RM8: Dag 4A 72
Scholefield Rd. N19 2H 65
Scholey Ho. SW11 3C 118

Schomberg Ho. – Shackleton Ho.

Schomberg Ho. SW1 ... 3D 18 (4H 101)
... *(off Page St.)*
Schonfeld Sq. N16 ... 2D 66
School All. TW1: Twick ... 1A 132
School App. E2 ... 1H 9 (3E 84)
... *(off Kingsland Rd.)*
School App. UB4: Hayes ... 4H 75
Schoolbank Rd. SE10 ... 3H 105
Schoolbell M. E3 ... 2A 86
Schoolgate Dr. SM4: Mord ... 5K 153
School Ho. SE1 ... 4E 102
... *(off Page's Wlk.)*
School Ho. La. NW7 ... 6B 30
School Ho. La. TW11: Tedd ... 7B 132
Schoolhouse La. E1 ... 7K 85
Schoolhouse Yd. SE18 ... 5F 107
School La. DA16: Well ... 3B 126
School La. HA5: Pinn ... 4C 40
School La. KT1: Hamp W ... 1C 150
School La. KT6: Surb ... 1F 163
School La. SE23 ... 2H 139
School La. TW17: Shep ... 6D 146
School La. WD23: Bush ... 1A 26
School M. E1 ... 7H 85
... *(off Hawksmoor M.)*
School Nook E5 ... 2K 67
School of Oriental & African Studies
Vernon Sq. Campus ... 1H 7 (3K 83)
School of Pharmacy, The ... 3F 7 (4J 83)
... *(off Brunswick Sq.)*
School Pas. KT1: King T ... 2F 151
School Pas. UB1: S'hall ... 7D 76
School Rd. BR7: Chst ... 1G 161
School Rd. E12 ... 4D 70
School Rd. KT1: Hamp W ... 1C 150
School Rd. KT8: E Mos ... 4H 149
School Rd. NW10 ... 4K 79
School Rd. RM10: Dag ... 1G 91
School Rd. TW12: Hamp H ... 6G 131
School Rd. TW15: Ashf ... 6D 128
School Rd. TW3: Houn ... 3G 113
School Rd. UB7: Harm ... 2E 174
School Rd. Av. TW12: Hamp H ... 6G 131
SCHOOL ROAD JUNC. ... 7D 128
School Sq. SE10 ... 3H 105
School Wlk. TW16: Sun ... 4H 147
School Way N12 ... 6G 31
School Way RM8: Dag ... 3C 72
Schooner Cl. E14 ... 3F 105
Schooner Cl. IG11: Bark ... 3B 90
Schooner Cl. SE16 ... 2K 103
Schooner Ct. E16 ... 2K 105
Schubert Rd. SW15 ... 5H 117
Schurlock Pl. TW2: Twick ... 2J 131
Schwartz Wharf E9 ... 7C 68
Science Mus. ... 2A 16 (3B 100)
Sclater St. E1 ... 3K 9 (4F 85)
Scoble Pl. N16 ... 4F 67
Scoles Cres. SW2 ... 1B 138
Scoop, The ... 5H 15 (1E 102)
Scope Way KT1: King T ... 4E 150
Score Complex Leyton, The ... 3D 68
Scoresby St. SE1 ... 5A 14 (1B 102)
Scorton Av. UB6: G'frd ... 2A 78
Scorton Ho. N1 ... 2E 84
... *(off Whitmore Est.)*
Scotch Comn. W13 ... 5A 78
SCOTCH HOUSE ... 7F 11 (2D 100)
Scoter Cl. IG8: Wfd G ... 7E 36
Scoter Ct. SE8 ... 6B 104
... *(off Abinger Gro.)*
Scot Gro. HA5: Pinn ... 1B 40
Scotia Bldg. E1 ... 7K 85
... *(off Jardine Rd.)*
Scotia Ct. SE16 ... 2J 103
... *(off Canada Est.)*
Scotia Rd. SW2 ... 7A 120
Scotland Grn. N17 ... 2F 49
Scotland Grn. Rd. EN3: Pond E ... 5E 24
Scotland Grn. Rd. Nth. EN3: Pond E ... 4E 24
Scotland Pl. SW1 ... 4E 12 (1J 101)
Scotland Rd. IG9: Buck H ... 1F 37
Scotney Cl. BR6: Farnb ... 4E 172
Scotney Ho. E9 ... 6J 67
Scots Cl. TW19: Stanw ... 1A 128
Scotsdale Cl. BR5: Pet W ... 4J 161
Scotsdale Cl. SM3: Cheam ... 7G 165
Scotsdale Rd. SE12 ... 5K 123
Scotson Ho. SE11 ... 4J 19 (4A 102)
... *(off Marylee Way)*
Scotswood St. EC1 ... 3K 7 (4A 84)
Scotswood Wlk. N17 ... 7B 34
Scott Av. SW15 ... 6G 117
Scott Cl. KT19: Ewe ... 5J 163
Scott Cl. SW16 ... 1K 155
Scott Cl. UB7: W Dray ... 4B 92
Scott Ct. W3 ... 2K 97
Scott Cres. HA2: Harr ... 1F 59
Scott Ellis Gdns. NW8 ... 2A 4 (3B 82)
Scottes La. RM8: Dag ... 1D 72
Scott Farm Cl. KT7: T Ditt ... 1B 162
Scott Gdns. TW5: Hest ... 7B 94
Scott Ho. DA17: Belv ... 5F 109
Scott Ho. E13 ... 2J 87
... *(off Queens Rd. W.)*
Scott Ho. E14 ... 2C 104
... *(off Admirals Way)*
Scott Ho. N18 ... 5B 34
... *(off Woolmer Rd.)*
Scott Ho. N7 ... 6K 65
... *(off Caledonian Rd.)*
Scott Ho. NW10 ... 7K 61
... *(off Stonebridge Pk.)*
Scott Ho. NW8 ... 4C 4 (4C 82)
... *(off Broadley St.)*
Scott Ho. SE8 ... 5B 104
... *(off Grove St.)*
Scott Lidgett Cres. SE16 ... 2G 103
Scott Rd. HA8: Edg ... 2H 43
Scott Russell Pl. E14 ... 5D 104
Scotts Av. BR2: Broml ... 2F 159
Scotts Av. TW16: Sun ... 7G 129
Scotts Ct. W12 ... 2E 98
... *(off Scott's Rd.)*
Scotts Dr. TW12: Hamp ... 7F 131
Scotts Farm Rd. KT19: Ewe ... 6J 163
Scott's La. BR2: Broml ... 3F 159
Scotts Pas. SE18 ... 4F 107
Scott's Rd. E10 ... 1E 68
Scott's Rd. UB2: S'hall ... 3A 94
Scott's Rd. W12 ... 2D 98
Scotts Rd. BR1: Broml ... 7J 141
Scott's Sufferance Wharf SE1
... 7K 15 (2F 103)
... *(off Mill St.)*
Scotts Ter. SE9 ... 2C 142
Scott St. E1 ... 4H 85
Scotts Way TW16: Sun ... 7G 129
Scott's Yd. EC4 ... 2E 14 (7D 84)
Scott Trimmer Way TW3: Houn ... 2C 112
Scottwell Dr. NW9 ... 5B 44
Scoulding Ho. E14 ... 3C 104
... *(off Mellish St.)*
Scoulding Rd. E16 ... 6J 87
Scouler St. E14 ... 7E 86
Scout App. NW10 ... 4A 62
Scout La. SW4 ... 3G 119
Scout Pk. N11 ... 7C 32
Scout Way NW7 ... 4E 28
Scovell Cres. SE1 ... 7C 14 (2C 102)
... *(off McCoid Way)*
Scovell Rd. SE1 ... 7C 14 (2C 102)
Scrattons Farm Eco-Park ... 2E 90
Scrattons Ter. IG11: Bark ... 2D 90
Screenworks N5 ... 5C 66
Scrimgoeur Pl. N4 ... 1C 66
Scriven Ct. E8 ... 1F 85
Scriven St. E8 ... 1F 85
Scrooby St. SE6 ... 6D 122
Scrope Ho. EC1 ... 5J 7 (5A 84)
... *(off Bourne Est.)*
Scrubs La. NW10 ... 3C 80
Scrubs La. W10 ... 5D 80
Scrutton Cl. SW12 ... 7H 119
Scrutton St. EC2 ... 4G 9 (4E 84)
Scudamore La. NW9 ... 4J 43
Sculpture Ho. E1 ... 5K 85
... *(off Duckett St.)*
Scutari Rd. SE22 ... 5J 121
Scylla Cres. TW6: H'row A ... 7D 110
... (not continuous)
Scylla Rd. SE15 ... 3G 121
... (not continuous)
Scylla Rd. TW6: H'row A ... 6D 110
Seaborne Wharf E3 ... 5C 86
... *(off Invicta Cl.)*
Seabright St. E2 ... 3H 85
Seabrook Dr. BR4: W W'ck ... 2G 171
Seabrook Gdns. RM7: Rush G ... 7G 55
Seabrook Rd. RM8: Dag ... 3D 72
Seaburn Cl. RM13: Rain ... 2K 91
Seacole Cl. W3 ... 6K 79
Seacole Lodge N21 ... 5E 22
... *(off Pennington Dr.)*
Seacole Wk. SW17 ... 2C 136
Sea Containers Ho. SE1 ... 3K 13 (7A 84)
... *(off Upper Ground)*
Seacon Twr. E14 ... 2B 104
Seacourt Rd. SE2 ... 2D 108
Seafarer Way SE16 ... 4A 104
Seafield Rd. N11 ... 4C 32
Seaford Cl. HA4: Ruis ... 1F 57
Seaford Ho. SE16 ... 2J 103
... *(off Swan Rd.)*
Seaford Rd. E17 ... 3D 50
Seaford Rd. EN1: Enf ... 4K 23
Seaford Rd. N15 ... 5D 48
Seaford Rd. TW6: H'row A ... 5A 110
Seaford Rd. W13 ... 1B 96
Seaford St. WC1 ... 2F 7 (3J 83)
Seaforth Av. KT3: N Mald ... 5D 152
Seaforth Cres. N5 ... 5C 66
Seaforth Gdns. IG8: Wfd G ... 5F 37
Seaforth Gdns. KT19: Ewe ... 4B 164
Seaforth Gdns. N21 ... 7E 22
Seaforth Pl. SW1 ... 1B 18 (3G 101)
... *(off Buckingham Ga.)*
Seager Pl. SE8 ... 1C 122
... *(off Deptford Bri.)*
Seagrave Cl. E1 ... 5K 85
Seagrave Lodge SW6 ... 6J 99
... *(off Seagrave Rd.)*
Seagrave Rd. SW6 ... 6J 99
Seagry Rd. E11 ... 7J 51
Seagull Cl. IG11: Bark ... 3A 90
Seagull La. E16 ... 7J 87
Seahorse Sailing Club ... 2K 61
Sealand Rd. TW6: H'row A ... 6C 110
Sealand Wlk. UB5: N'olt ... 3B 76
Seal Ho. SE1 ... 7F 15 (3D 102)
... *(off Weston St.)*
Sea Life London ... 6G 13 (2K 101)
Seal St. E8 ... 4F 67
Searle Ho. NW8 ... 1C 82
... *(off Cecil Gro.)*
Searle Ho. SW11 ... 1E 118
... *(off Macduff Rd.)*
Searle Pl. N4 ... 1K 65
Searles Cl. SW11 ... 7C 100
Searles Dr. E6 ... 5F 89
Searles Rd. SE1 ... 4D 102
Searson Ho. SE17 ... 4B 102
... *(off Canterbury Pl.)*
Sears St. SE5 ... 7D 102
Seasalter Ho. SW9 ... 1A 120
... *(off Gosling Way)*
Seasons Cl. W7 ... 1K 95
Seasons Ho. E20 ... 6E 68
... *(off Mirabelle Gdns.)*
Seasprite Cl. UB5: N'olt ... 3B 76
Seaton Av. IG3: Ilf ... 5K 71
Seaton Cl. E13 ... 4J 87
Seaton Cl. SE11 ... 5K 19 (5A 102)
Seaton Cl. SW15 ... 1D 134
Seaton Cl. TW2: Whitt ... 6H 113
Seaton Dr. TW15: Ashf ... 2A 128
Seaton Gdns. HA4: Ruis ... 3H 57
Seaton Point E5 ... 4G 67
Seaton Rd. CR4: Mitc ... 2C 154
Seaton Rd. DA16: Well ... 7C 108
Seaton Rd. HA0: Wemb ... 2E 78
Seaton Rd. TW2: Whitt ... 6G 113
Seaton Rd. UB3: Harl ... 4F 93
Seaton Sq. NW7 ... 7A 30
Seaton St. N18 ... 5B 34
Seawall Ct. IG11: Bark ... 2G 89
... *(off Dock Rd.)*
Sebastian Ct. IG11: Bark ... 1K 89
Sebastian Ho. N1 ... 1G 9 (2E 84)
... *(off Hoxton St.)*
Sebastian St. EC1 ... 2B 8 (3B 84)
Sebastopol Rd. N9 ... 4B 34
Sebbon St. N1 ... 7B 66
Sebergham Gro. NW7 ... 7H 29
Sebert Rd. E7 ... 5K 69
Sebright Ho. E2 ... 2G 85
... *(off Coate St.)*
Sebright Pas. E2 ... 2G 85
Sebright Rd. EN5: Barn ... 2A 20
Secker Cres. HA3: Hrw W ... 1G 41
Secker Ho. SW9 ... 2B 120
... *(off Loughborough Est.)*
Secker St. SE1 ... 5J 13 (1A 102)
Second Av. E12 ... 4C 70
Second Av. E13 ... 3J 87
Second Av. E17 ... 5C 50
Second Av. EN1: Enf ... 5A 24
Second Av. HA9: Wemb ... 2D 60
Second Av. KT12: Walt T ... 6K 147
Second Av. N18 ... 4D 34
Second Av. NW4 ... 4F 45
Second Av. RM10: Dag ... 2H 91
Second Av. RM6: Chad H ... 5C 54
Second Av. SW14 ... 3A 116
Second Av. UB3: Hayes ... 1H 93
Second Av. W10 ... 4G 81
Second Av. W3 ... 1B 98
Second Cl. KT8: W Mole ... 4G 149
Second Cross Rd. TW2: Twick ... 2J 131
Second Way HA9: Wemb ... 4H 61
Sedan Way SE17 ... 5E 102
Sedcombe Cl. DA14: Sidc ... 4B 144
Sedcote Rd. EN3: Pond E ... 5D 24
Sedding St. SW1 ... 3G 17 (4E 100)
Sedding Studios SW1 ... 3G 17 (4E 100)
... *(off Sedding St.)*
Seddon Highwalk EC2 ... 5C 8 (5C 84)
... *(off Aldersgate St.)*
Seddon Ho. EC2 ... 5C 8 (5C 84)
... *(off Aldersgate St.)*
Seddon Rd. SM4: Mord ... 5B 154
Seddon St. WC1 ... 2G 7 (3K 83)
Sedgebrook Rd. SE3 ... 2B 124
Sedgecombe Av. HA3: Kenton ... 5C 42
Sedgefield Ct. UB5: N'olt ... 5F 59
... *(off Newmarket Av.)*
Sedgeford Rd. W12 ... 1B 98
Sedge Gdns. IG11: Bark ... 3A 90
Sedgehill Rd. SE6 ... 4C 140
Sedgemere Av. N2 ... 3A 46
Sedgemere Rd. SE2 ... 3C 108
Sedgemoor Dr. RM10: Dag ... 4G 73
Sedge Rd. N17 ... 7D 34
Sedgeway SE6 ... 1H 141
Sedgewood Cl. BR2: Hayes ... 7H 159
Sedgmoor Pl. SE5 ... 7E 102
Sedgwick Av. UB10: Hil ... 7D 56
Sedgwick Ho. E3 ... 5C 86
... *(off Gale St.)*
Sedgwick Rd. E10 ... 2E 68
Sedgwick St. E9 ... 5K 67
Sedleigh Rd. SW18 ... 6H 117
Sedlescombe Rd. SW6 ... 6J 99
Sedley Cl. EN1: Enf ... 1C 24
Sedley Ct. SE26 ... 2H 139
Sedley Ho. SE11 ... 5H 19 (5K 101)
... *(off Newburn St.)*
Sedley Pl. W1 ... 1J 11 (6F 83)
Sedona Ho. E20 ... 6D 68
... *(off Victory Pde.)*
Sedum Cl. NW9 ... 5H 43
Sedum M. EN2: Enf ... 3F 23
Seeley Dr. SE21 ... 4E 138
Seelig Av. NW9 ... 7C 44
Seely Rd. SW17 ... 6E 136
Seetha Ho. IG1: Ilf ... 2H 71
... *(off High Rd.)*
Seething La. EC3 ... 2H 15 (7E 84)
SEETHING WELLS ... 6C 150
Seething Wells La. KT6: Surb ... 6C 150
Sefton Av. HA3: Hrw W ... 2H 41
Sefton Av. NW7 ... 5E 28
Sefton Cl. BR5: St M Cry ... 4K 161
Sefton Ct. EN2: Enf ... 2G 23
Sefton Ct. TW3: Houn ... 1F 113
Sefton Rd. BR5: St M Cry ... 4K 161
Sefton Rd. CR0: C'don ... 1G 169
Sefton St. SW15 ... 3E 116
Segal Cl. SE23 ... 7A 122
Sekforde St. EC1 ... 4A 8 (4B 84)
Sekhon Ter. TW13: Hanw ... 3E 130
Selan Gdns. UB4: Yead ... 5K 75
Selbie Av. NW10 ... 5B 62
Selborne Av. DA5: Bexl ... 1E 144
Selborne Av. E12 ... 4E 70
Selborne Gdns. NW4 ... 4C 44
Selborne Gdns. UB6: G'frd ... 2A 78
Selborne Rd. CR0: C'don ... 3E 168
Selborne Rd. DA14: Sidc ... 4B 144
Selborne Rd. E17 ... 5B 50
Selborne Rd. IG1: Ilf ... 2E 70
Selborne Rd. KT3: N Mald ... 2A 152
Selborne Rd. N14 ... 3D 32
Selborne Rd. N22 ... 1K 47
Selborne Rd. SE5 ... 2D 120
Selborne Wlk. E17 ... 5B 50
Selborne Wlk. Shop. Cen. ... 4B 50
Selbourne Av. KT6: Surb ... 2F 163
Selbourne Av. TW3: Houn ... 3G 113
Selbourne Ho. SE1 ... 7E 14 (2D 102)
... *(off Gt. Dover St.)*
Selby Chase HA4: Ruis ... 2K 57
Selby Cl. BR7: Chst ... 6E 142
Selby Cl. E6 ... 5C 88
Selby Cl. KT9: Chess ... 7E 162
Selby Gdns. UB1: S'hall ... 4E 76
Selby Grn. SM5: Cars ... 7C 154
Selby Rd. E11 ... 3G 69
Selby Rd. E13 ... 5K 87
Selby Rd. N17 ... 7K 33
Selby Rd. SE20 ... 2G 157
Selby Rd. SM5: Cars ... 7C 154
Selby Rd. TW15: Ashf ... 6E 128
Selby Rd. W5 ... 4B 78
Selby Sq. W10 ... 3G 81
... *(off Dowland St.)*
Selby St. E1 ... 4G 85
Selcroft Ho. SE10 ... 5H 105
... *(off Glenister Rd.)*
Selden Ho. SE15 ... 2J 121
... *(off Selden Rd.)*
Selden Rd. SE15 ... 2J 121
Selden Wlk. N7 ... 2K 65
Seldon Ho. SW1 ... 6A 18 (5G 101)
... *(off Churchill Gdns.)*
Seldon Ho. SW8 ... 7G 101
... *(off Stewart's Rd.)*
Selfridges ... 1H 11 (6E 82)
... *(off Oxford St.)*
SELHURST ... 6E 156
Selhurst Cl. SW19 ... 1F 135
Selhurst New Rd. SE25 ... 6E 156
Selhurst Pk. ... 4E 156
Selhurst Pl. SE25 ... 6E 156
Selhurst Rd. N9 ... 3J 33
Selhurst Rd. SE25 ... 6E 156
Selig Ct. NW11 ... 7G 45
Selina Ho. NW8 ... 3B 4 (4B 82)
... *(off Frampton St.)*
Selinas La. RM8: Dag ... 7E 54
Selkirk Ho. N1 ... 1K 83
... *(off Bingfield St.)*
Selkirk Rd. SW17 ... 4C 136
Selkirk Rd. TW2: Twick ... 2G 131
Sellers Hall Cl. N3 ... 7D 30
Sellincourt Rd. SW17 ... 5C 136
Sellindge Cl. BR3: Beck ... 7B 140
Sellons Av. NW10 ... 1B 80
Sellwood Dr. EN5: Barn ... 5A 20
Selman Ho. E9 ... 6A 68
Selsdon Av. CR2: S Croy ... 6D 168
Selsdon Cl. KT6: Surb ... 5E 150
Selsdon Cl. RM5: Col R ... 1J 55
Selsdon Pk. Rd. CR0: Sels ... 7B 170
Selsdon Pk. Rd. CR2: Sels ... 7K 169
Selsdon Rd. CR2: S Croy ... 5D 168
Selsdon Rd. E11 ... 7J 51
Selsdon Rd. E13 ... 1A 88
Selsdon Rd. NW2 ... 2B 62
Selsdon Rd. SE27 ... 3A 138
Selsdon Way E14 ... 3D 104
Selsea Pl. N16 ... 5E 66
Selsey WC1 ... 2F 7 (3J 83)
... *(off Tavistock Pl.)*
Selsey Cres. DA16: Well ... 1D 126
Selsey St. E14 ... 5C 86
Selvage La. NW7 ... 5E 28
Selway Cl. HA5: Eastc ... 4K 39
Selway Ho. SW8 ... 1J 119
... *(off Sth. Lambeth Rd.)*
Selwood Pl. SW7 ... 5A 16 (5B 100)
Selwood Rd. CR0: C'don ... 2H 169
Selwood Rd. KT9: Chess ... 4D 162
Selwood Rd. SM3: Sutt ... 1H 165
Selwood St. SW2 ... 7A 120
Selwood Ter. SW7 ... 5A 16 (5B 100)
Selworthy Cl. E11 ... 5J 51
Selworthy Ho. SW11 ... 1B 118
... *(off Battersea Church Rd.)*
Selworthy Rd. SE6 ... 3B 140
Selwyn Av. E4 ... 6K 35
Selwyn Av. IG3: Ilf ... 6K 53
Selwyn Av. TW9: Rich ... 3E 114
Selwyn Cl. TW4: Houn ... 4C 112
Selwyn Ct. E17 ... 5C 50
... *(off Yunus Khan Cl.)*
Selwyn Ct. HA8: Edg ... 7C 28
Selwyn Ct. HA9: Wemb ... 3J 61
Selwyn Ct. SE3 ... 3H 123
Selwyn Ct. TW10: Rich ... 5F 115
... *(off Church Rd.)*
Selwyn Cres. DA16: Well ... 3B 126
Selwyn Rd. E13 ... 1K 87
Selwyn Rd. E3 ... 2B 86
Selwyn Rd. KT3: N Mald ... 5K 151
Selwyn Rd. NW10 ... 7A 62
Semley Ga. E9 ... 6B 68
... (not continuous)
Semley Ho. SW1 ... 4J 17 (4F 101)
... *(off Semley Pl.)*
Semley Pl. SW1 ... 4H 17 (4E 100)
Semley Rd. SW16 ... 2J 155
Senate St. SE15 ... 2J 121
Senators Lodge E3 ... 2A 86
... *(off Roman Rd.)*
Senator Wlk. SE28 ... 3H 107
Sendall Ct. SW11 ... 3B 118
... *(off Winstanley Rd.)*
Seneca Rd. CR7: Thor H ... 4C 156
Sener Ct. CR2: S Croy ... 6C 168
Senga Rd. SM6: W'gton ... 1E 166
Senhouse Rd. SM3: Cheam ... 3F 165
Senior St. W2 ... 5K 81
Senlac Rd. SE12 ... 1K 141
Sennen Rd. EN1: Enf ... 7A 24
Sennen Wlk. SE9 ... 3C 142
Senrab St. E1 ... 6K 85
Sentamu Cl. SE24 ... 1B 138
Sentinel Bldg. E15 ... 5F 69
... *(off Property Row)*
Sentinel Cl. UB5: N'olt ... 4C 76
Sentinel Sq. NW4 ... 4E 44
September Ct. UB1: S'hall ... 1F 95
... *(off Dormer's Wells La.)*
September Way HA7: Stan ... 6G 27
Septimus Pl. EN1: Enf ... 5B 24
Sequoia Cl. WD23: B Hea ... 1C 26
Sequoia Gdns. BR6: Orp ... 7K 161
Sequoia Pk. HA5: Hat E ... 6A 26
Serap Ct. CR0: C'don ... 4D 168
... *(off Dean Rd.)*
Seraph Ct. EC1 ... 1C 8 (3C 84)
... *(off Moreland St.)*
Serbin Cl. E10 ... 7E 50
Serenaders Rd. SW9 ... 2A 120
Serenity Apts. E17 ... 5D 50
Serenity Apts. SW11 ... 4C 118
... *(off Monarch Sq.)*
Serenity Cl. HA2: Harr ... 2F 59
Seren Pk. Gdns. SE3 ... 6G 105
Sergeant Ind. Est. SW18 ... 6K 117
Serica Ct. SE10 ... 7E 104
Serjeants Inn EC4 ... 1K 13 (6A 84)
Serlby Ct. W14 ... 3H 99
... *(off Somerset Sq.)*
Serle St. WC2 ... 7H 7 (6K 83)
Sermon La. EC4 ... 1C 14 (6C 84)
... *(off Carter La.)*
Serpentine, The ... 5C 10 (1C 100)
Serpentine Cl. RM6: Chad H ... 7C 54
Serpentine Ct. SE16 ... 2K 103
... *(off Christopher Cl.)*
Serpentine Gallery ... 6B 10 (2B 100)
Serpentine Lido, The ... 5C 10 (1C 100)
Serpentine Rd. W2 ... 5C 10 (1C 100)
Serpentine Sackler Gallery
... 4B 10 (1B 100)
Serviden Dr. BR1: Broml ... 1B 160
Servite Ho. BR3: Beck ... 1B 158
Servite Ho. KT4: Wor Pk ... 2B 164
... *(off The Avenue)*
Servite Ho. N14 ... 5A 22
... *(off Bramley Rd.)*
Servius Ct. TW8: Bford ... 7D 96
Setchell Rd. SE1 ... 4F 103
Setchell Way SE1 ... 4F 103
Seth St. SE16 ... 2J 103
Seton Gdns. RM9: Dag ... 7C 72
Settle Point E13 ... 2J 87
Settlers Ct. E14 ... 7F 87
Settles St. E1 ... 5G 85
Settrington Rd. SW6 ... 2K 117
Seven Acres SM5: Cars ... 2C 166
Seven Dials WC2 ... 1E 12 (6J 83)
Seven Dials Ct. WC2 ... 1E 12 (6J 83)
... *(off Shorts Gdns.)*
Sevenex Pde. HA9: Wemb ... 5E 60
Seven Islands Leisure Cen. ... 3J 103
SEVEN KINGS ... 1K 71
Seven Kings Rd. IG3: Ilf ... 1J 71
Seven Kings Way KT2: King T ... 1E 150
Sevenoaks Cl. DA7: Bex ... 4H 127
Sevenoaks Ct. HA6: Nwood ... 1E 38
Sevenoaks Rd. BR6: Chels ... 5K 173
Sevenoaks Rd. BR6: Orp ... 5K 173
Sevenoaks Rd. BR6: Prat B ... 7K 173
Sevenoaks Rd. SE4 ... 6A 122
Sevenoaks Way BR5: St P ... 7C 144
Sevenoaks Way DA14: Sidc ... 7C 144
Seven Sea Gdns. E3 ... 5D 86
Sevenseas Rd. TW6: H'row A ... 6E 110
SEVEN SISTERS ... 5F 49
Seven Sisters Rd. N15 ... 6D 48
Seven Sisters Rd. N4 ... 2A 66
Seven Sisters Rd. N7 ... 3K 65
Seven Stars Cnr. W12 ... 3C 98
Seven Stars Yd. E1 ... 5K 9 (5F 85)
... *(off Brick La.)*
Seventeen SM1: Sutt ... 6A 166
... *(off Sutton Ct. Rd.)*
Seventh Av. E12 ... 4D 70
Seventh Av. UB3: Hayes ... 1J 93
Seven Ways Pde. IG2: Ilf ... 5E 52
Severin Ct. SE17 ... 5E 102
... *(off East St.)*
Severnake Cl. E14 ... 4C 104
Severn Av. W10 ... 3G 81
Severn Ct. KT2: King T ... 1D 150
... *(off John Williams Cl.)*
Severn Dr. KT10: Hin W ... 2A 162
Severn Ho. SW18 ... 4J 117
... *(off Enterprise Way)*
Severn Way NW10 ... 5B 62
Severus Ho. UB3: Hayes ... 6F 75
Severus Pl. BR3: Beck ... 5D 158
Severus Rd. SW11 ... 4C 118
Seville Ho. E1 ... 1G 103
... *(off Wapping High St.)*
Seville M. N1 ... 7E 66
Seville St. SW1 ... 7F 11 (2D 100)
Sevington Rd. NW4 ... 6D 44
Sevington St. W9 ... 4K 81
Seward Rd. BR3: Beck ... 2K 157
Seward Rd. W7 ... 2A 96
SEWARDSTONE ... 1K 25
Sewardstone Cl. E4 ... 1K 25
Sewardstone Gdns. E4 ... 5J 25
Sewardstone Rd. E2 ... 2J 85
Sewardstone Rd. E4 ... 7J 25
Seward St. EC1 ... 2B 8 (3B 84)
Sewdley St. E5 ... 3K 67
Sewell Rd. SE2 ... 3A 108
Sewell St. E13 ... 3J 87
Sextant Av. E14 ... 4F 105
Sexton Ct. E14 ... 7F 87
... *(off Newport Av.)*
Sextons Ho. SE10 ... 6E 104
... *(off Bardsley La.)*
Seymer Rd. RM1: Rom ... 3K 55
Seymore M. SE14 ... 7B 104
... *(off New Cross Rd.)*
Seymour Av. N17 ... 2G 49
Seymour Av. SM4: Mord ... 7F 153
Seymour Cl. HA5: Hat E ... 1D 40
Seymour Cl. KT8: E Mos ... 5G 149
Seymour Ct. E4 ... 2C 36
Seymour Ct. KT1: Hamp W ... 1D 150
Seymour Ct. N10 ... 2E 46
Seymour Ct. N21 ... 6E 22
Seymour Ct. NW2 ... 2D 62
Seymour Dr. BR2: Broml ... 1D 172
Seymour Gdns. HA4: Ruis ... 1B 58
Seymour Gdns. IG1: Ilf ... 1D 70
Seymour Gdns. KT5: Surb ... 5F 151
Seymour Gdns. SE4 ... 3A 122
Seymour Gdns. TW1: Twick ... 7B 114
Seymour Gdns. TW13: Hanw ... 4A 130
Seymour Ho. E16 ... 1J 105
... *(off De Quincey M.)*
Seymour Ho. NW1 ... 1D 6 (3H 83)
... *(off Churchway)*
Seymour Ho. SM2: Sutt ... 6K 165
... *(off Mulgrave Rd.)*
Seymour Ho. WC1 ... 3E 6 (4J 83)
... *(off Tavistock Pl.)*
Seymour Leisure Cen. ... 6E 4 (5D 82)
Seymour M. W1 ... 7G 5 (6E 82)
Seymour Pl. SE25 ... 4H 157
Seymour Pl. W1 ... 6E 4 (5D 82)
Seymour Rd. CR4: Mitc ... 7E 154
Seymour Rd. E10 ... 1B 68
Seymour Rd. E4 ... 1J 35
Seymour Rd. E6 ... 2B 88
Seymour Rd. KT1: Hamp W ... 1D 150
Seymour Rd. KT8: E Mos ... 5G 149
Seymour Rd. KT8: W Mole ... 5G 149
Seymour Rd. N3 ... 7E 30
Seymour Rd. N8 ... 5A 48
Seymour Rd. N9 ... 2C 34
Seymour Rd. SM5: Cars ... 5E 166
Seymour Rd. SW18 ... 7H 117
Seymour Rd. SW19 ... 3F 135
Seymour Rd. TW12: Hamp H ... 5G 131
Seymour Rd. W4 ... 4J 97
Seymour St. SE18 ... 3G 107
Seymour St. W1 ... 1E 10 (6D 82)
Seymour St. W2 ... 1E 10 (6D 82)
Seymour Ter. SE20 ... 1H 157
Seymour Vs. SE20 ... 1H 157
Seymour Wlk. SW10 ... 6A 100
Seymour Way TW16: Sun ... 7H 129
Seyssel St. E14 ... 4E 104
Shaa Rd. W3 ... 7K 79
Shabana Rd. W12 ... 1D 98
Shacklegate La. TW11: Tedd ... 4J 131
Shackleton Cl. SE23 ... 2H 139
Shackleton Ct. E14 ... 5C 104
... *(off Maritime Quay)*
Shackleton Ct. TW19: Stanw ... 6A 110
... *(off Whitley Cl.)*
Shackleton Ct. W12 ... 2D 98
... *(off Scott's Rd.)*
Shackleton Ho. CR0: Wadd ... 1K 167
Shackleton Ho. E1 ... 1J 103
... *(off Prusom St.)*

A–Z London 285

Shackleton Ho. – Ship St.

Shackleton Ho. NW10 7K 61
Shackleton Rd. UB1: S'hall 7D 76
Shackleton Way E16 7G 89
SHACKLEWELL 4F 67
Shacklewell Grn. E8 4F 67
Shacklewell Ho. E8 4F 67
Shacklewell La. E8 5F 67
Shacklewell La. N16 4F 67
Shacklewell Rd. N16 4F 67
Shacklewell Row E8 4F 67
Shacklewell St. E2 2K 9 (3F 85)
Shadbolt Av. E4 5F 35
Shadbolt Cl. KT4: Wor Pk 2B 164
Shad Thames SE1 Anchor Brewhouse 5J 15 (1F 103)
Shad Thames SE1 Jamaica Rd. 7K 15 (2F 103)
SHADWELL 7H 85
Shadwell Ct. UB5: N'olt 2D 76
Shadwell Dr. UB5: N'olt 3D 76
Shadwell Gdns. E1 7J 85
Shadwell Pierhead E1 7J 85
Shadwell Pl. E1 7J 85
(off Sutton St.)
Shady Bush Cl. WD23: Bush 1B 26
Shaef Way TW11: Tedd 7A 132
Shafter Rd. RM10: Dag 6J 73
Shaftesbury Av. EN3: Enf H 2E 24
Shaftesbury Av. EN5: New Bar 4F 21
Shaftesbury Av. HA2: Harr 1F 59
Shaftesbury Av. HA3: Kenton 5D 42
Shaftesbury Av. TW14: Felt 6J 111
Shaftesbury Av. UB2: S'hall 4E 94
Shaftesbury Av. W1 3C 12 (7H 83)
Shaftesbury Av. WC1 7E 6 (6J 83)
Shaftesbury Av. WC2 7E 6 (6J 83)
Shaftesbury Barnet Harriers 1E 44
Shaftesbury Cen. W10 4F 81
(off Barlby Rd.)
Shaftesbury Circ. HA2: Harr 1G 59
Shaftesbury Ct. E6 6E 88
(off Sapphire Cl.)
Shaftesbury Ct. N1 2D 84
(off Shaftesbury St.)
Shaftesbury Ct. SE1 3D 102
(off Alderney M.)
Shaftesbury Ct. SE5 4D 120
Shaftesbury Ct. SW16 3H 137
Shaftesbury Gdns. NW10 4A 80
Shaftesbury Lodge E14 6D 86
(off Upper Nth. St.)
Shaftesbury M. SW4 5G 119
Shaftesbury M. W8 3J 99
Shaftesbury Pde. HA2: Harr 1G 59
Shaftesbury Pl. EC2 6C 8 (5C 84)
(off London Wall)
Shaftesbury Pl. W14 4H 99
(off Warwick Rd.)
Shaftesbury Point E13 2J 87
(off High St.)
Shaftesbury Rd. BR3: Beck 2B 158
Shaftesbury Rd. E10 1C 68
Shaftesbury Rd. E17 6D 50
Shaftesbury Rd. E4 1A 36
Shaftesbury Rd. E7 7A 70
Shaftesbury Rd. N18 6K 33
Shaftesbury Rd. N19 1J 65
Shaftesbury Rd. SM5: Cars 7B 154
Shaftesbury Rd. TW9: Rich 3E 114
Shaftesbury Row SE8 7C 104
(off Speedwell St.)
Shaftesburys, The IG11: Bark 2G 89
Shaftesbury St. N1 2C 84
(not continuous)
Shaftesbury Theatre London 7E 6 (6J 83)
(off Shaftesbury Av.)
Shaftesbury Vs. W8 3J 99
(off Allen St.)
Shaftesbury Way TW2: Twick 3H 131
Shaftesbury Waye UB4: Yead 5A 76
Shafto M. SW1 2E 16 (3D 100)
Shafton M. E9 1K 85
Shafton Rd. E9 1K 85
Shafts Ct. EC3 1G 15 (6E 84)
Shaftswood Ct. SW17 3D 136
(off Lynwood Rd.)
Shahjalal Ho. E2 2G 85
(off Pritchards Rd.)
Shakespeare Av. N11 5B 32
Shakespeare Av. NW10 1K 79
Shakespeare Av. TW14: Felt 6J 111
Shakespeare Av. UB4: Hayes 6J 75
(not continuous)
Shakespeare Av. UB4: Yead 4K 75
Shakespeare Av. UB4: Yead 6J 75
(not continuous)
Shakespeare Cl. HA3: Kenton 7G 43
Shakespeare Ct. EN5: New Bar 3E 20
Shakespeare Ct. HA3: Kenton 6F 43
Shakespeare Ct. NW6 7A 64
(off Fairfax Rd.)
Shakespeare Cres. E12 6D 70
Shakespeare Dr. HA3: Kenton 6F 43
Shakespeare Gdns. N2 4D 46
Shakespeare Ho. E9 7J 67
(off Lyme Gro.)
Shakespeare Ho. N14 2C 32
Shakespeare Rd. DA7: Bex 1E 126
Shakespeare Rd. E17 2K 49
Shakespeare Rd. N3 1J 45
Shakespeare Rd. NW10 1K 79
Shakespeare Rd. NW7 4G 29
Shakespeare Rd. SE24 5B 120
Shakespeare Rd. W3 1J 97
Shakespeare Rd. W7 7K 77
Shakespeare's Globe & Exhibition 4C 14 (1C 102)
Shakespeare Twr. EC2 5C 8 (5C 84)
(off Beech St.)
Shakespeare Way TW13: Hanw 4A 130
Shakspeare M. N16 4E 66
Shakspeare Wlk. N16 4E 66
Shalbourne Sq. E9 6B 68
Shalcomb St. SW10 7A 16 (6A 100)
Shalden Ho. SW15 6B 116
Shaldon Dr. HA4: Ruis 3A 58
Shaldon Dr. SM4: Mord 5G 153
Shaldon Rd. HA8: Edg 2F 43
Shalfleet Dr. W10 7F 81
Shalford Cl. BR6: Farnb 4G 173
Shalford Ct. N1 2B 84
Shalford Ho. SE1 3D 102
Shalimar Gdns. W3 7J 79
Shalimar Rd. W3 7J 79
Shallons Rd. SE9 4F 143
Shalstone Rd. SW14 3H 115
Shalston Vs. KT6: Surb 6F 151
Shamrock Ho. SE26 4G 139
(off Talisman Sq.)
Shamrock Rd. CR0: C'don 6K 155
Shamrock St. SW4 3H 119
Shamrock Way N14 1A 32
Shandon Rd. SW4 6G 119
Shand St. SE1 6H 15 (2E 102)
Shandy St. E1 5K 85
Shan Ho. WC1 4G 7 (4K 83)
(off Millman St.)
Shanklin Ho. E17 2B 50
Shanklin Rd. N15 4G 49
Shanklin Rd. N8 5H 47
Shannon Cl. NW2 3F 63
Shannon Cl. UB2: S'hall 5B 94
Shannon Commercial Cen. KT3: N Mald 4C 152
SHANNON CORNER 4C 152
Shannon Cnr. Retail Pk. 4C 152
Shannon Ct. CR0: C'don 1C 168
(off Tavistock Rd.)
Shannon Ct. N16 3E 66
Shannon Ct. SE15 7F 103
(off Garnies Cl.)
Shannon Gro. SW9 4K 119
Shannon Pl. NW8 2C 82
Shannon Way BR3: Beck 6D 140
Shanti Ct. SW18 1J 135
Shap Cres. SM5: Cars 1D 166
Shapland Way N13 5E 32
Shapwick Cl. N11 5J 31
Shard, The 5F 15 (1D 102)
Shardcroft Av. SE24 5B 120
Shardeloes Rd. SE14 2B 122
Shardeloes Rd. SE4 3B 122
Shard's Sq. SE15 6G 103
Sharland Cl. CR7: Thor H 6A 156
Sharman Ct. DA14: Sidc 4A 144
Sharman Way E3 5D 86
Sharnbrooke Cl. DA16: Well 3C 126
Sharnbrook Ho. W14 6J 99
Sharon Cl. KT6: Surb 1C 162
Sharon Ct. CR2: S Croy 5C 168
(off Warham Rd.)
Sharon Gdns. E9 1J 85
Sharon Rd. EN3: Enf H 2F 25
Sharon Rd. W4 5K 97
Sharpe Cl. W7 5K 77
Sharp Ho. SW8 3F 119
Sharp Ho. TW1: Twick 6D 114
Sharpleshall St. NW1 7D 64
Sharpley Ct. SE1 6B 14 (2B 102)
(off Pocock St.)
Sharpness Cl. UB4: Yead 5C 76
Sharp's La. HA4: Ruis 7F 39
Sharratt St. SE15 6J 103
Sharsted St. SE17 6K 19 (5B 102)
Sharvel La. UB5: N'olt 1J 75
Sharwood WC1 1H 7 (2K 83)
(off Penton Ri.)
Shaver's Pl. SW1 3C 12 (7H 83)
(off Coventry St.)
Shaw, The BR7: Chst 7G 143
Shaw Av. IG11: Bark 2E 90
Shawbrooke Rd. SE9 5A 124
Shawbury Cl. NW9 1A 44
Shawbury Rd. SE22 5F 121
Shaw Cl. SE28 1B 108
Shaw Cl. TW19: Stanw 1A 128
Shaw Cl. WD23: B Hea 2D 26
Shaw Ct. SM4: Mord 7A 154
Shaw Cres. E14 5A 86
Shaw Dr. KT12: Walt T 7A 148
Shawfield Ct. UB7: W Dray 3A 92
Shawfield Pk. BR1: Broml 2B 160
Shawfield St. SW3 6D 16 (5C 100)
Shawford Ct. SW15 7C 116
Shawford Rd. KT19: Ewe 6K 163
Shaw Gdns. IG11: Bark 2E 90
Shaw Ho. DA17: Belv 5F 109
Shaw Ho. E16 1E 106
(off Claremont St.)
Shaw Path BR1: Broml 3H 141
Shaw Pl. N2 3E 46
Shaw Rd. BR1: Broml 3H 141
Shaw Rd. EN3: Enf H 1E 24
Shaw Rd. SE22 4E 120
Shaws Cotts. SE23 3A 140
Shaw Sq. E17 1A 50
Shaw Theatre 1D 6 (3H 83)
Shaw Way SM6: W'gton 7J 167
Shead Ct. E1 6H 85
(off James Voller Way)
Shearing Dr. SM5: Cars 7A 154
Shearling Way N7 6J 65
Shearman Rd. SE3 4H 123
THE SHEARS 7G 129
Shears Ct. TW16: Sun 7G 129
Shears La. SW16 7J 137
Shearsmith Ho. E1 7G 85
(off Hindmarsh Cl.)
Shears Way TW16: Sun 1G 147
Shearwater Cl. IG11: Bark 3A 90
Shearwater Ct. E1 3K 15 (7G 85)
(off Star Pl.)
Shearwater Ct. SE8 6B 104
(off Abinger Gro.)
Shearwater Dr. NW9 7C 44
Shearwater Rd. SM1: Sutt 5H 165
Shearwater Way UB4: Yead 6B 76
Sheath Cotts. KT7: T Ditt 6B 150
(off Ferry Rd.)
Sheaveshill Av. NW9 4A 44
Sheaveshill Ct. NW9 4K 43
Sheaveshill Pde. NW9 4A 44
(off Sheaveshill Av.)
Sheba Ct. N17 6B 34
(off Altair Cl.)
Sheba Pl. E1 4K 9 (4F 85)
Sheen Comn. Dr. TW10: Rich 4G 115
Sheen Ct. TW10: Rich 4G 115
Sheen Ct. Rd. TW10: Rich 4G 115
Sheendale Rd. TW9: Rich 4F 115
Sheenewood SE26 4H 139
Sheen Ga. Gdns. SW14 4J 115
Sheengate Mans. SW14 4K 115
Sheen Gro. N1 1A 84
Sheen La. SW14 5J 115
Sheen Pk. TW9: Rich 4F 115
Sheen Rd. BR5: St M Cry 4K 161
Sheen Rd. TW10: Rich 4G 115
Sheen Rd. TW9: Rich 5E 114
Sheen Way SM6: W'gton 5K 167
Sheen Wood SW14 5J 115
Sheepcote Cl. TW5: Cran 7J 93
Sheepcote La. SW11 2D 118
Sheepcote Rd. HA1: Harr 6K 41
Sheepcotes Rd. RM6: Chad H 4E 54
Sheephouse Way KT3: N Mald 1K 163
Sheep La. E8 1H 85
Sheep Wlk. TW17: Shep 7B 146
Sheep Wlk. M. SW19 6F 135
Sheerness M. E16 2F 107
Sheerwater Rd. E16 5B 88
Sheffield Rd. TW6: H'row A 6E 110
Sheffield Sq. E3 3B 86
Sheffield St. WC2 1G 13 (6K 83)
Sheffield Ter. W8 1J 99
Sheffield Way TW6: H'row A 5F 111
Shelbourne Cl. HA5: Pinn 3D 40
Shelbourne Pl. BR3: Beck 7B 140
Shelbourne Rd. N17 2H 49
Shelburne Dr. TW4: Houn 6E 112
Shelburne Rd. N7 4K 65
Shelbury Cl. DA14: Sidc 3A 144
Shelbury Rd. SE22 5H 121
Sheldon Av. IG5: Ilf 2F 53
Sheldon Av. N2 6D 46
Sheldon Av. N6 7C 46
Sheldon Cl. SE12 5K 123
Sheldon Cl. SE20 1H 157
Sheldon Ct. EN5: New Bar 4E 20
Sheldon Ct. RM7: Rush G 6K 55
(off Union Rd.)
Sheldon Ct. SW8 7J 101
(off Lansdowne Grn.)
Sheldon Ho. N1 1E 84
(off Kingsland Rd.)
Sheldon Pl. E2 2G 85
(not continuous)
Sheldon Rd. DA7: Bex 1F 127
Sheldon Rd. N18 4K 33
Sheldon Rd. NW2 4F 63
Sheldon Rd. RM9: Dag 7E 72
Sheldon Sq. W2 5A 82
Sheldon St. CR0: C'don 3C 168
Sheldrake Cl. E16 1D 106
Sheldrake Ho. SE16 4K 103
(off Tawny Way)
Sheldrake Pl. W8 2J 99
Sheldrick Cl. SW19 2B 154
Shelduck Cl. E15 5H 69
Shelduck Ct. SE8 6B 104
(off Pilot Cl.)
Sheldwich Ter. BR2: Broml 6C 160
Shelford KT1: King T 2G 151
Shelford Pl. N16 3D 66
Shelford Ri. SE19 7F 139
Shelgate Rd. SW11 5C 118
Shell Cl. BR2: Broml 6C 160
Shellduck Cl. NW9 2A 44
Shelley N8 3J 47
(off Boyton Rd.)
Shelley Av. E12 6C 70
Shelley Av. UB6: G'frd 3H 77
Shelley Cl. BR6: Orp 3J 173
Shelley Cl. HA8: Edg 4B 28
Shelley Cl. SE15 2H 121
Shelley Cl. UB4: Hayes 5J 75
Shelley Cl. UB6: G'frd 3H 77
Shelley Ct. E10 7D 50
(off Skelton's La.)
Shelley Ct. E11 4K 51
(off Makepeace Rd.)
Shelley Ct. N19 1K 65
Shelley Ct. SW3 7F 17 (6D 100)
(off Tite St.)
Shelley Cres. TW5: Hest 1B 112
Shelley Cres. UB1: S'hall 6D 76
Shelley Dr. DA16: Well 1J 125
Shelley Gdns. HA0: Wemb 2C 60
Shelley Ho. E2 3J 85
(off Cornwall Av.)
Shelley Ho. N16 4E 66
Shelley Ho. SE17 5C 102
(off Browning St.)
Shelley Ho. SW1 7A 18 (6G 101)
(off Churchill Gdns.)
Shelley Lodge EN2: Enf 1J 23
Shelley Pl. N1 1B 84
Shelley Rd. NW10 1K 79
Shelley Way SW19 5B 136
Shellfield Cl. TW19: Stanw M 7B 174
Shellness Rd. E5 5H 67
Shell Rd. SE13 3D 122
Shell Twr. SE1 6H 13 (2K 101)
(off Milner Pl.)
Shellwood Rd. SW11 2D 118
Shelmerdine Cl. E3 5C 86
Shelson Av. TW13: Felt 3H 129
Shelson Pde. TW13: Felt 3H 129
Shelton Rd. SW19 1J 153
Shelton St. WC2 1E 12 (6J 83)
(not continuous)
Shene Ho. EC1 5J 7 (5A 84)
(off Bourne Est.)
Shene Sports & Fitness Cen. 4A 116
Shenfield Ho. SE18 1B 124
(off Portway Gdns.)
Shenfield Rd. IG8: Wfd G 7E 36
Shenfield St. N1 1H 9 (2E 84)
(not continuous)
Shenley Av. HA4: Ruis 2H 57
Shenley Rd. SE5 1E 120
Shenley Rd. TW5: Hest 1C 112
Shenstone W13 1C 96
Shenstone Cl. DA1: Cray 4K 127
Shenstone Ho. SW16 5G 137
Shepheard's Ho. BR7: Chst 1H 161
Shepherd Cl. TW13: Hanw 4C 130
Shepherdess Pl. N1 1D 8 (3C 84)
Shepherdess Wlk. N1 2C 84
Shepherd Ho. E14 6D 86
(off Annabel Cl.)
Shepherd Ho. E16 7F 89
(off University Way)
Shepherd Mkt. W1 4J 11 (1F 101)
SHEPHERD'S BUSH 2E 98
Shepherd's Bush Empire Theatre 2E 98
Shepherd's Bush Grn. W12 2E 98
Shepherd's Bush Mkt. W12 2E 98
(not continuous)
Shepherd's Bush Pl. W12 2F 99
Shepherd's Bush Rd. W6 4E 98
Shepherd's Cl. BR6: Orp 3K 173
Shepherd's Cl. N6 6F 47
Shepherds Cl. HA7: Stan 5F 27
(not continuous)
Shepherds Cl. RM6: Chad H 5D 54
Shepherds Cl. TW17: Shep 6D 146
Shepherds Cl. W1 2G 11 (7E 82)
(off Lees Pl.)
Shepherds Ct. W12 2F 99
(off Shepherd's Bush Grn.)
Shepherds Grn. BR7: Chst 7H 143
Shepherd's Hill N6 6F 47
Shepherds La. E9 6K 67
Shepherds La. SE28 1J 107
Shepherds Leas SE9 4G 125
Shepherd's Path NW3 5B 64
(off Lyndhurst Rd.)
Shepherds Path UB5: N'olt 6C 58
(off Arnold Rd.)
Shepherds Pl. W1 2G 11 (7E 82)
Shepherd St. W1 5J 11 (1F 101)
Shepherd's Wlk. NW3 5B 64
Shepherds Wlk. NW2 2C 62
Shepherds Wlk. WD23: B Hea 2C 26
Shepherds Way CR2: Sels 7K 169
Shepiston La. UB3: Harl 4D 92
Shepley Cl. SM5: Cars 3E 166
Sheppard Cl. EN1: Enf 1C 24
Sheppard Cl. KT1: King T 4E 150
Sheppard Dr. SE16 5H 103
Sheppard Ho. E2 2G 85
(off Warner Pl.)
Sheppard Ho. SW2 1A 138
Sheppards Coll. BR1: Broml 1J 159
(off London Rd.)
Sheppard St. E16 4H 87
SHEPPERTON 6D 146
Shepperton Bus. Pk. TW17: Shep 5E 146
Shepperton Ct. TW17: Shep 6D 146
Shepperton Ct. Dr. TW17: Shep 5D 146
Shepperton Film Studios 3B 146
SHEPPERTON GREEN 4C 146
Shepperton Marina TW17: Shep 6G 147
Shepperton Rd. BR5: Pet W 6G 161
Shepperton Rd. N1 1C 84
Shepperton South Studios TW17: Shep 4A 146
Sheppey Gdns. RM9: Dag 7C 72
Sheppey Rd. RM9: Dag 7B 72
Shepton Ho's. E2 3J 85
(off Welwyn St.)
Sherard Ct. N7 3J 65
Sherard Ho. E9 7J 67
(off Frampton Pk. Rd.)
Sherard Rd. SE9 5C 124
Sheraton Bus. Cen. UB6: G'frd 2B 78
Sheraton Ho. SW1 7K 17 (6F 101)
(off Churchill Gdns.)
Sheraton St. W1 1C 12 (6H 83)
Sherborne NW1 7G 65
(off Agar Gro.)
Sherborne Av. EN3: Enf H 2D 24
Sherborne Av. UB2: S'hall 4E 94
Sherborne Cl. SL3: Poyle 4A 174
Sherborne Cl. UB4: Yead 6A 76
Sherborne Cres. SM5: Cars 7C 154
Sherborne Gdns. NW9 3G 43
Sherborne Gdns. W13 5B 78
Sherborne Ho. SW1 5K 17 (5F 101)
(part of Abbots Mnr.)
Sherborne Ho. SW8 7K 101
(off Bolney St.)
Sherborne La. EC4 2E 14 (7D 84)
Sherborne Rd. BR5: St M Cry 4K 161
Sherborne Rd. KT9: Chess 5E 162
Sherborne Rd. SM3: Sutt 2J 165
Sherborne Rd. TW14: Bedf 1F 129
(not continuous)
Sherborne St. N1 1D 84
Sherboro Rd. N15 6F 49
Sherbourne Ct. SM2: Sutt 6A 166
Sherbourne Ct. SW5 4K 99
(off Cromwell Rd.)
Sherbourne Gdns. TW17: Shep 7G 147
Sherbourne Pl. HA7: Stan 6F 27
Sherbrooke Cl. DA6: Bex 4G 127
Sherbrooke Ho. E2 2J 85
(off Bonner Rd.)
Sherbrooke Ho. SW1 2D 18 (3H 101)
(off Monck St.)
Sherbrooke Rd. SW6 7G 99
Sherbrooke Ter. SW6 7G 99
(off Sherbrooke Rd.)
Sherbrooke Way KT4: Wor Pk 7D 152
Sherbrook Gdns. N21 7G 23
Sherbrook Ho. SE16 2J 103
(off Albatross Way)
Shere Cl. KT9: Chess 5D 162
Sheredan Rd. E4 5A 36
Shere Ho. SE1 7E 14 (3D 102)
(off Gt. Dover St.)
Shere Rd. IG2: Ilf 5E 52
Sherfield Cl. KT3: N Mald 4H 151
Sherfield Gdns. SW15 6B 116
Sherfield M. UB3: Hayes 6G 75
Sheridan Bldgs. WC2 1F 13 (6J 83)
(off Martlett Ct.)
Sheridan Cl. UB10: Hil 4E 74
Sheridan Ct. CR0: C'don 4E 168
(off Coombe Rd.)
Sheridan Ct. HA1: Harr 6H 41
Sheridan Ct. NW6 7A 64
(off Belsize Rd.)
Sheridan Ct. SW5 4K 99
(off Barkston Gdns.)
Sheridan Ct. TW4: Houn 5C 112
Sheridan Ct. UB5: N'olt 5F 59
Sheridan Ct. W7 7K 77
(off Milton Rd.)
Sheridan Cres. BR7: Chst 2F 161
Sheridan Gdns. HA3: Kenton 6D 42
Sheridan Hgts. E1 6H 85
(off Watney St.)
Sheridan Ho. SE11 4K 19 (4A 102)
(off Wincott St.)
Sheridan Lodge BR2: Broml 4A 160
(off Homesdale Rd.)
Sheridan M. E11 6K 51
Sheridan Pl. BR1: Broml 2B 160
Sheridan Pl. SW13 3B 116
Sheridan Pl. TW12: Hamp 1F 149
Sheridan Rd. DA17: Belv 4G 109
Sheridan Rd. DA7: Bex 3E 126
Sheridan Rd. E12 5C 70
Sheridan Rd. E7 3H 69
Sheridan Rd. SW19 1H 153
Sheridan Rd. TW10: Ham 3C 132
Sheridan Ter. UB5: N'olt 5F 59
Sheridan Wlk. NW11 6J 45
Sheridan Wlk. SM5: Cars 5D 166
Sheridan Way BR3: Beck 1B 158
Sheriden Pl. HA1: Harr 7J 41
Sheringham NW8 1B 82
Sheringham Av. E12 4D 70
Sheringham Av. N14 5C 22
Sheringham Av. RM7: Rom 6J 55
Sheringham Av. TW2: Whitt 1D 130
Sheringham Ct. TW13: Felt 3J 129
(off Sheringham Av.)
Sheringham Ct. UB3: Hayes 2H 93
Sheringham Dr. IG11: Bark 5K 71
Sheringham Ho. NW1 5C 4 (5C 82)
(off Lisson St.)
Sheringham Rd. N7 6K 65
Sheringham Rd. SE20 3J 157
Sheringham Twr. UB1: S'hall 7F 77
Sherington Av. HA5: Hat E 7A 26
Sherington Rd. SE7 6K 105
Sherland Rd. TW1: Twick 1K 131
Sherleys Ct. HA4: Ruis 2G 57
Sherlies Av. BR6: Orp 2J 173
Sherlock Cl. SW16 2K 155
Sherlock Ct. NW8 1B 82
(off Dorman Way)
Sherlock Holmes Mus. 4F 5 (4D 82)
(off Baker St.)
Sherlock M. W1 5G 5 (5E 82)
Sherman Av. KT12: Walt T 5A 148
Sherman Gdns. RM6: Chad H 6C 54
Sherman Ho. E14 6E 86
(off Dee St.)
Sherman Ho. UB3: Harl 3E 92
(off Nine Acres Cl.)
Sherman Rd. BR1: Broml 1J 159
Shernhall St. E17 3E 50
Sherrard Rd. E12 5B 70
Sherrard Rd. E7 6A 70
Sherrards Way EN5: Barn 5D 20
Sherren Ho. E1 4J 85
Sherrick Grn. Rd. NW10 5D 62
Sherriff Ct. NW6 6J 63
(off Sherriff Rd.)
Sherriff Rd. NW6 6J 63
Sherringham Av. N17 2G 49
Sherringham Av. TW13: Felt 3J 129
Sherringham Ct. E16 6H 87
(off Silvertown Sq.)
Sherrington Ct. E16 5H 87
(off Rathbone St.)
Sherrin Rd. E10 4D 68
Sherrock Gdns. NW4 4D 44
Sherry M. IG11: Bark 7H 71
Sherston Ct. SE1 4B 102
(off Newington Butts)
Sherston Ct. WC1 2J 7 (3A 84)
(off Attneave St.)
Sherwin Ho. SE11 7J 19 (6A 102)
(off Kennington Rd.)
Sherwin Rd. SE14 1K 121
Sherwood KT6: Surb 2D 162
Sherwood NW6 7G 63
Sherwood Av. E18 3K 51
Sherwood Av. HA4: Ruis 6G 39
Sherwood Av. SW16 7H 137
Sherwood Av. UB4: Yead 4K 75
Sherwood Av. UB6: G'frd 6J 59
Sherwood Cl. DA5: Bexl 6C 126
Sherwood Cl. E17 2B 50
Sherwood Cl. SW13 3D 116
Sherwood Cl. W13 1B 96
Sherwood Ct. CR2: S Croy 5C 168
(off Nottingham Rd.)
Sherwood Ct. HA2: Harr 2F 59
Sherwood Ct. SW11 3A 118
Sherwood Ct. W1 6E 4 (5D 82)
(off Bryanston Pl.)
Sherwood Gdns. E14 4C 104
Sherwood Gdns. IG11: Bark 7H 71
Sherwood Gdns. SE16 5G 103
Sherwood Pk. Av. DA15: Sidc 7A 126
Sherwood Pk. Rd. CR4: Mitc 4G 155
Sherwood Pk. Rd. SM1: Sutt 5J 165
Sherwood Rd. CR0: C'don 7H 157
Sherwood Rd. DA16: Well 2J 125
Sherwood Rd. HA2: Harr 2G 59
Sherwood Rd. IG6: Ilf 4H 53
Sherwood Rd. NW4 3E 44
Sherwood Rd. SW19 7H 135
Sherwood Rd. TW12: Hamp H 5G 131
Sherwood St. N20 3G 31
Sherwood St. W1 2B 12 (7G 83)
Sherwood Ter. E16 6A 88
(off Bingley Rd.)
Sherwood Ter. N20 3G 31
Sherwood Way BR4: W W'ck 2E 170
Shetland Ho. DA17: Belv 2H 109
Shetland Rd. E3 2B 86
Shetland Rd. TW6: H'row A 6E 110
Shield Dr. TW8: Bford 6A 96
Shieldhall St. SE2 4C 108
Shield Rd. TW15: Ashf 4E 128
Shield St. SE15 7F 103
Shifford Path SE23 3K 139
Shillaker Ct. W3 1B 98
Shillibeer Pl. W1 6D 4 (5C 82)
(off Harcourt St.)
Shillingford Cl. NW7 7A 30
Shillingford Ho. E3 3D 86
(off Talwin St.)
Shillingford St. N1 7B 66
Shilling Pl. W7 2A 96
Shillingshaw Lodge E16 6J 87
(off Butchers Rd.)
Shillingstone Ho. W14 3G 99
(off Russell Rd.)
Shillington St. Open Space 3C 118
Shinfield St. W12 6E 80
Shinglewell Rd. DA8: Erith 7G 109
Shingly Pl. E4 1K 35
Shinners Cl. SE25 5G 157
Ship All. W4 6G 97
Ship & Mermaid Row SE1 6F 15 (2D 102)
Shipbuilding Way E13 2B 88
Shipka Rd. SW12 1F 137
Shiplake Ho. E2 2J 9 (3F 85)
(off Arnold Cir.)
Ship La. SW14 3J 115
Shipman Rd. E16 6K 87
Shipman Rd. SE23 2K 139
Ship St. SE8 1C 122

286 A–Z London

Ship Tavern Pas. – Skua Ct.

Ship Tavern Pas. EC3 ......2G 15 (7E 84)
Shipton Cl. RM8: Dag 3D 72
Shipton Ho. E2 ......1K 9 (2F 85)
(off Shipton St.)
Shipton Rd. UB10: Ick 4B 56
Shipton St. E2 ......1K 9 (2F 85)
Shipwright Rd. SE16 ......2A 104
Shipwright St. E16 ......2K 105
Shipwright Yd. SE1 ......5G 15 (1E 102)
Ship Yd. E14 ......5D 104
Shirburn Cl. SE23 ......7J 121
Shirebrook Rd. SE3 ......3B 124
Shire Ct. DA18: Erith 3D 108
Shire Ct. KT17: Ewe 7B 164
Shirehall Cl. NW4 ......6F 45
Shirehall Gdns. NW4 ......6F 45
Shirehall La. NW4 ......6F 45
Shirehall Pk. NW4 ......5F 45
Shire Horse Way TW7: Isle 3K 113
Shire Ho. E3 ......3D 86
(off Talwin St.)
Shire Ho. EC1 ......4D 8 (4C 84)
(off Lambs Pas.)
Shire La. BR2: Kes 7C 172
Shire La. BR6: Chels 7F 173
(not continuous)
Shire La. BR6: Downe 7F 173
(not continuous)
Shire London Golf Course, The 1A 20
Shire M. TW2: Whitt 6G 113
Shire Pl. SW18 ......7A 118
Shire Pl. TW8: Bford 7D 96
Shires, The TW10: Ham 4E 132
Shirland M. W9 ......3H 81
Shirland Rd. W9 ......3H 81
Shirlbutt St. E14 ......7D 86
SHIRLEY 2K 169
Shirley Av. CR0: C'don 1J 169
Shirley Av. DA5: Bexl 7D 126
Shirley Av. SM1: Sutt 4B 166
Shirley Chu. Rd. CR0: C'don 3K 169
Shirley Cl. E17 ......5D 50
Shirley Cl. TW3: Houn 5G 113
Shirley Ct. SW16 ......7J 137
Shirley Cres. BR3: Beck 4A 158
Shirley Dr. TW3: Houn 5G 113
Shirley Gdns. IG11: Bark 6J 71
Shirley Gdns. W7 ......1K 95
Shirley Gro. N9 ......7D 24
Shirley Gro. SW11 ......3E 118
Shirley Hgts. SM6: W'gton 7G 167
Shirley Hills Rd. CR0: C'don 5J 169
Shirley Ho. SE5 ......7D 102
(off Picton St.)
Shirley Ho. Dr. SE7 ......7A 106
SHIRLEY OAKS 1K 169
Shirley Oaks Rd. CR0: C'don 1K 169
Shirley Pk. CR0: C'don 2J 169
Shirley Pk. Golf Course 2H 169
Shirley Pk. Rd. CR0: C'don 1H 169
Shirley Rd. CR0: C'don 7H 157
Shirley Rd. DA15: Sidc 3J 143
Shirley Rd. E15 ......7G 69
Shirley Rd. EN2: Enf 3H 23
Shirley Rd. SM6: W'gton 7G 167
Shirley Rd. W4 ......2K 97
Shirley Sherwood Gallery of Botanical Art, The 2F 115
Shirley St. E16 ......6H 87
Shirley Way CR0: C'don 3A 170
Shirley Windmill 3J 169
Shirlock Rd. NW3 ......4D 64
Shirwell Cl. NW7 ......7A 30
Shobden Rd. N17 ......1D 48
Shobroke Cl. NW2 ......3E 62
Shoebury Rd. E6 ......7D 70
Shoelands Ct. NW9 ......3K 43
Shoe La. EC4 ......7K 7 (6A 84)
Sholto Rd. TW6: H'row A 5B 110
Shona Ho. E13 ......5A 88
Shooters Av. HA3: Kenton 4C 42
Shooters Hill DA16: Well 2G 125
Shooters Hill SE18 ......1D 124
SHOOTERS HILL 1E 124
Shooters Hill Golf Course 1G 125
Shooters Hill Rd. SE10 ......1F 123
Shooters Hill Rd. SE18 ......1B 124
Shooters Hill Rd. SE3 ......7A 106
Shooters Rd. EN2: Enf 1G 23
Shoot Up Hill NW2 ......5G 63
Shopping Hall, The E6 ......1C 88
Shore Bus. Cen. E9 ......7J 67
Shore Cl. TW12: Hamp 6C 130
Shore Cl. TW14: Felt 7J 111
Shorediche Cl. UB10: Ick 3B 56
SHOREDITCH 1G 9 (3E 84)
Shoreditch Ct. E8 ......7F 67
(off Queensbridge Rd.)
Shoreditch High St. E1 ......4H 9 (4E 84)
Shoreditch Ho. BR2: Broml 6C 160
Shoreditch Ho. N1 ......2F 9 (3D 84)
(off Charles Sq.)
Shore Gro. TW13: Hanw 2E 130
Shoreham Cl. CR0: C'don 6J 157
Shoreham Cl. DA5: Bexl 1D 144
Shoreham Cl. SW18 ......5K 117
Shoreham Rd. E. TW6: H'row A 5A 110
Shoreham Rd. W. TW6: H'row A 5A 110
Shoreham Way BR2: Hayes 6J 159
Shore Ho. SW8 ......3F 119
Shore M. E9 ......7J 67
(off Shore Rd.)
Shore Pl. E9 ......7J 67
Shore Point IG9: Buck H 2E 36
Shore Rd. E9 ......7J 67
Shore Way SW9 ......2A 120
(off Crowhurst Cl.)
Shorncliffe Rd. SE1 ......5F 103
Shorndean St. SE6 ......1E 140
Shorne Cl. DA15: Sidc 6B 126
Shornefield Cl. BR1: Broml 3E 160
Shornells Way SE2 ......4C 108
Shorrold's Rd. SW6 ......7H 99
Short Blue Pl. IG11: Bark 7G 71
Shortcroft Rd. KT17: Ewe 7B 164
Shortcrofts Rd. RM9: Dag 6F 73
Shorter St. E1 ......2J 15 (7F 85)
Shortgate N12 ......4C 30
Short Hedges TW3: Houn 1E 112
Short Hill HA1: Harr 1J 59
SHORTLANDS 2G 159
Shortlands UB3: Harl 6F 93
Shortlands W6 ......4F 99
Shortlands Cl. DA17: Belv 3F 109
Shortlands Cl. N18 ......3J 33
Shortlands Gdns. BR2: Broml 2G 159
Shortlands Golf Course 1G 159
Shortlands Gro. BR2: Broml 3F 159
Shortlands Rd. BR2: Broml 3F 159
Shortlands Rd. E10 ......7D 50
Shortlands Rd. KT2: King T 7F 133
Short La. TW19: Stanw 7B 110
Short Path SE18 ......6F 107
Short Rd. E11 ......2G 69
Short Rd. TW6: H'row A 6A 110
Short Rd. W4 ......6A 98
Shorts Cft. NW9 ......4H 43
Shorts Gdns. WC2 ......1E 12 (6J 83)
Shorts Rd. SM5: Cars 4C 166
Short St. NW4 ......4E 44
(off Foster St.)
Short St. SE1 ......6K 13 (2A 102)
Short Wall E15 ......3E 86
Short Way SE9 ......3C 124
Short Way TW2: Whitt 7G 113
Shortway N12 ......6H 31
Shotfield SM6: W'gton 6F 167
Shott Cl. SM1: Sutt 5A 166
Shottendane Rd. SW6 ......1J 117
Shottery Cl. SE9 ......3C 142
Shottfield Av. SW14 ......4A 116
Shottsford W2 ......6J 81
(off Talbot Rd.)
Shoulder of Mutton All. E14 ......7A 86
Shouldham St. W1 ......6D 4 (5C 82)
Showcase Cinema Barking 3H 89
Showers Way UB3: Hayes 1J 93
Shrapnel Cl. SE18 ......7C 106
Shrapnel Rd. SE9 ......3D 124
Shrek's Adventure! 6G 13 (2K 101)
Shrewsbury Av. HA3: Kenton 4E 42
Shrewsbury Av. SW14 ......4J 115
Shrewsbury Cl. KT6: Surb 2E 162
Shrewsbury Ct. EC1 ......4D 8 (4C 84)
(off Whitecross St.)
Shrewsbury Ho. SW3 ......7C 16 (6C 100)
(off Cheyne Wlk.)
Shrewsbury Ho. SW8 ......7H 19 (6K 101)
(off Kennington Oval)
Shrewsbury La. SE18 ......1F 125
Shrewsbury M. W2 ......5J 81
(off Chepstow Rd.)
Shrewsbury Rd. BR3: Beck 3A 158
Shrewsbury Rd. E7 ......5B 70
Shrewsbury Rd. N11 ......6B 32
Shrewsbury Rd. NW10 ......1K 79
Shrewsbury Rd. SM5: Cars 6C 154
Shrewsbury Rd. TW6: H'row A 6E 110
(not continuous)
Shrewsbury Rd. W2 ......6J 81
Shrewsbury St. W10 ......4E 80
Shrewsbury Wlk. TW7: Isle 3A 114
(off Magdala Rd.)
Shrewton Rd. SW17 ......7D 136
Shroffold Rd. BR1: Broml 4G 141
Shropshire Cl. CR4: Mitc 4J 155
Shropshire Ct. W7 ......6K 77
(off Copley Cl.)
Shropshire Ho. N18 ......5C 34
(off Cavendish Cl.)
Shropshire Pl. WC1 ......4B 6 (4G 83)
Shropshire Rd. N22 ......7E 32
Shroton St. NW1 ......5C 4 (5C 82)
Shrubberies, The E18 ......2J 51
Shrubbery, The E11 ......5K 51
Shrubbery, The KT6: Surb 1E 162
Shrubbery Cl. N1 ......1C 84
Shrubbery Gdns. N21 ......7G 23
Shrubbery Rd. N9 ......3B 34
Shrubbery Rd. SW16 ......4J 137
Shrubbery Rd. UB1: S'hall 1D 94
Shrubland Gro. KT4: Wor Pk 3E 164
Shrubland Rd. E10 ......7C 50
Shrubland Rd. E17 ......5C 50
Shrubland Rd. E8 ......1F 85
Shrublands Av. CR0: C'don 3C 170
Shrublands Cl. N20 ......1G 31
Shrublands Cl. SE26 ......3J 139
Shrubsall Cl. SE9 ......1C 142
Shuna Wlk. N1 ......6D 66
Shurland Av. EN4: E Barn 6G 21
Shurland Gdns. SE15 ......7F 103
Shurlock Dr. BR6: Farnb 4G 173
Shushan Cl. N16 ......7E 48
Shuters Sq. W14 ......5H 99
Shuttle Cl. DA15: Sidc 7K 125
Shuttlemead DA5: Bexl 7F 127
Shuttle St. E1 ......4K 9 (4G 85)
Shuttleworth Rd. SW11 ......2C 118
Siamese M. N3 ......1J 45
Siani M. N8 ......4B 48
Sibella Rd. SW4 ......2H 119
Sibley Cl. BR1: Broml 5C 160
Sibley Cl. DA6: Bex 5E 126
Sibley Ct. BR2: Broml 2F 159
Sibley Ct. UB8: Hil 5E 74
Sibley Gro. E12 ......7C 70
Sibthorpe Rd. SE12 ......6K 123
Sibthorp Rd. CR4: Mitc 2D 154
Sibton Rd. SM5: Cars 7C 154
Sicilian Av. WC1 ......6F 7 (5J 83)
(off Vernon Pl.)
Sickle Cnr. RM9: Dag 4H 91
Sidbury St. SW6 ......1G 117
SIDCUP 4A 144
Sidcup By-Pass BR7: Chst 3H 143
Sidcup Family Golf 3G 143
Sidcup Golf Course 1B 144
Sidcup High St. DA14: Sidc 4A 144
Sidcup Hill DA14: Sidc 4B 144
Sidcup Hill Gdns. DA14: Sidc 5C 144
Sidcup Leisure Cen. 2A 144
Sidcup Pl. DA14: Sidc 5A 144
Sidcup Place 5A 144
Sidcup Rd. SE12 ......6A 124
Sidcup Rd. SE9 ......1D 142
Sidcup Technology Cen. DA14: Sidc 5D 144
Siddeley Dr. TW4: Houn 3C 112
Siddeley Rd. E17 ......2E 50
Siddons La. NW1 ......4F 5 (4D 82)
Siddons Rd. CR0: Wadd 3A 168
Siddons Rd. N17 ......1G 49
Siddons Rd. SE23 ......2A 140
Sidewood Rd. SE9 ......1H 143
Sidford Ho. SE1 ......2J 19 (3A 102)
(off Cosser St.)
Sidford Pl. SE1 ......2J 19 (3A 102)
Sidgwick Ho. SW9 ......2K 119
(off Stockwell Rd.)
Sidi Ct. N15 ......3B 48
Sidings, The E11 ......1E 68
Sidings Apts., The E16 ......2E 106
Sidings M. N7 ......3A 66
Siding St. E20 ......1D 86
Sidlaw Ho. N16 ......1F 67
Sidmouth Av. TW7: Isle 2J 113
Sidmouth Dr. HA4: Ruis 3J 57
Sidmouth Ho. SE15 ......7G 103
(off Lindsey Est.)
Sidmouth Ho. W1 ......7D 4 (6C 82)
(off Cato St.)
Sidmouth M. WC1 ......2G 7 (3K 83)
Sidmouth Pde. NW2 ......7E 62
Sidmouth Rd. DA16: Well 7C 108
Sidmouth Rd. E10 ......3E 68
Sidmouth Rd. NW2 ......7E 62
Sidmouth St. WC1 ......2F 7 (3J 83)
Sidney Av. N13 ......5E 32
Sidney Boyd Ct. NW6 ......7J 63
Sidney Elson Way E6 ......2E 88
Sidney Est. E1 Bromhead St. 6J 85
Sidney Est. E1 Lindley St. 5J 85
Sidney Gdns. TW8: Bford 6D 96
Sidney Godley (VC) Ho. E2 ......3J 85
(off Digby St.)
Sidney Gro. EC1 ......1A 8 (2B 84)
Sidney Ho. E2 ......2K 85
(off Old Ford Rd.)
Sidney Miller Ct. W3 ......1H 97
(off Crown St.)
Sidney Rd. BR3: Beck 2A 158
Sidney Rd. E7 ......3J 69
Sidney Rd. HA2: Harr 3G 41
Sidney Rd. KT12: Walt T 7J 147
Sidney Rd. N22 ......7E 32
Sidney Rd. SE25 ......5G 157
Sidney Rd. SW9 ......2K 119
Sidney Rd. TW1: Twick 6A 114
Sidney Sq. E1 ......5J 85
Sidney St. E1 ......5H 85
(not continuous)
Sidney Webb Ho. SE1 ......3D 102
(off Tabard St.)
Sidonie Apts. SW11 ......4C 118
(off Danvers Av.)
Sidworth St. E8 ......7H 67
Siebert Rd. SE3 ......6J 105
Siege Ho. E1 ......6H 85
(off Sidney St.)
Siemens Brothers Way E16 ......7J 87
Siemens Rd. SE18 ......3B 106
Sienna SE28 ......3A 108
Sienna Alto SE13 ......3E 122
(off Cornmill La.)
Sienna Cl. KT9: Chess 6D 162
Sienna Ho. E20 ......6D 68
(off Victory Pde.)
Sienna Ter. NW2 ......2C 62
Sigdon Pas. E8 ......5G 67
Sigdon Rd. E8 ......5G 67
Sigers, The HA5: Eastc 6K 39
Sigmund Freud Statue 6B 64
Signal Ho. E8 ......7H 67
(off Martello Ter.)
Signal Ho. SE1 ......7C 14 (2C 102)
(off Gt. Suffolk St.)
Signal Wlk. E4 ......6K 35
Signmakers Yd. NW1 ......1F 83
(off Delancey St.)
Sigrist Sq. KT2: King T 1E 150
Sikorski Mus. 7B 10 (2B 100)
Silbury Av. CR4: Mitc 1C 154
Silbury Ho. SE26 ......3G 139
Silbury St. N1 ......1E 8 (3D 84)
Silchester Ct. CR7: Thor H 4A 156
Silchester Ct. TW15: Ashf 2A 128
Silchester Rd. W10 ......6F 81
Silecroft Rd. DA7: Bex 1G 127
Silesia Bldgs. E8 ......7H 67
Silex St. SE1 ......7B 14 (2B 102)
Silicon Bus. Cen. UB6: G'frd 2C 78
Silicon M. E3 ......1C 86
Silicon Way N1 ......2F 9 (3D 84)
(off Corsham St.)
Silk Cl. SE12 ......5J 123
Silk Ct. E2 ......3G 85
(off Squirries St.)
Silkfield Rd. NW9 ......5A 44
Silk Ho. E1 Leman St. 1K 15 (6G 85)
(off Leman St.)
Silk Ho. E1 Trafalgar Gdns. 5K 85
(off Trafalgar Gdns.)
Silk Ho. E2 ......2F 85
(off How's St.)
Silk Ho. NW9 ......3K 43
Silkin M. SE15 ......7G 103
Silk M. SE11 ......6K 19 (5A 102)
(off Kennington Rd.)
Silk Mills Pas. SE13 ......2D 122
Silk Mills Path SE13 ......2E 122
(not continuous)
Silk Mills Sq. E9 ......6B 68
Silk Rd. SM6: W'gton 2E 166
Silks Ct. E11 ......1H 69
Silkstream Pde. HA8: Edg 1J 43
Silkstream Rd. HA8: Edg 1J 43
Silk St. EC2 ......5D 8 (5C 84)
Silk Weaver Way E2 ......2H 85
Sillitoe Ho. N1 ......1D 84
(off Colville Est.)
Silsoe Ho. NW1 ......2F 83
Silsoe Rd. N22 ......2K 47
Silverbeck Way TW19: Stanw M 7B 174
Silver Birch Av. E4 ......5G 35
Silver Birch Cl. DA2: Wilm 4K 145
Silver Birch Cl. N11 ......6K 31
Silver Birch Cl. SE28 ......1A 108
Silver Birch Cl. SE6 ......3B 140
Silver Birch Cl. UB10: Ick 4A 56
Silver Birch Gdns. E6 ......4D 88
Silverbirch Wlk. NW3 ......6D 64
Silverburn Ho. SW9 ......1B 120
(off Lothian Rd.)
Silvercliffe Gdns. EN4: E Barn 4H 21
Silver Cl. HA3: Hrw W 7C 26
Silver Cl. SE14 ......7A 104
Silver Cres. W4 ......4H 97
Silverdale EN2: Enf 4D 22
Silverdale NW1 ......1A 6 (3G 83)
(off Harrington St.)
Silverdale SE26 ......4J 139
Silverdale Av. IG2: Ilf 5J 53
Silverdale Cen., The HA0: Wemb 1F 79
Silverdale Cl. SM1: Sutt 4H 165
Silverdale Cl. UB5: N'olt 5D 58
Silverdale Cl. W7 ......1J 95
Silverdale Ct. EC1 ......3B 8 (4B 84)
(off Goswell Rd.)
Silverdale Dr. SE9 ......2C 142
Silverdale Dr. TW16: Sun 2K 147
Silverdale Factory Cen. UB3: Hayes 3J 93
Silverdale Gdns. UB3: Hayes 2J 93
Silverdale Ind. Est. UB3: Hayes 2J 93
Silverdale Rd. BR5: Pet W 4G 161
Silverdale Rd. DA7: Bex 2H 127
Silverdale Rd. E4 ......6A 36
Silverdale Rd. UB3: Hayes 2H 93
Silverdene N12 ......6E 30
(off Thyra Gro.)
Silvergate KT19: Ewe 5J 163
Silverhall St. TW7: Isle 3A 114
Silverholme Cl. HA3: Kenton 7E 42
Silver Jubilee Way TW4: Cran 2K 111
Silverland St. E16 ......1D 106
Silver La. BR4: W W'ck 2F 171
Silverleigh Rd. CR7: Thor H 4K 155
Silver Mead E18 ......1J 51
Silvermere Dr. N18 ......6E 34
Silvermere Rd. SE6 ......7D 122
Silver Pl. W1 ......1B 12 (6G 83)
Silver Rd. SE13 ......3D 122
Silver Rd. W12 ......7F 81
Silvers IG9: Buck H 1F 37
(off Palmerston Rd.)
Silver Spring Cl. DA8: Erith 6H 109
Silverston Way HA7: Stan 6H 27
Silver St. EN1: Enf 3J 23
Silver St. N18 ......4J 33
Silverthorn NW8 ......1K 81
(off Abbey Rd.)
Silverthorne Loft Apts. SE5 ......6D 102
(off Albany Rd.)
Silverthorne Rd. SW8 ......2F 119
Silverthorn Gdns. E4 ......2H 35
Silverton Rd. W6 ......6F 99
SILVERTOWN 1A 106
Silvertown Quay Development E16 ......1A 106
Silvertown Sq. E16 ......6H 87
Silvertown Viaduct E16 ......6H 87
Silvertown Way E16 Clarkson Rd. 6G 87
Silvertown Way E16 Hanover Av. 1J 105
Silvertree La. UB6: G'frd 3H 77
Silver Wlk. SE16 ......1A 104
Silver Way RM7: Mawney 3H 55
Silver Way UB10: Hil 2D 74
Silver Wing Ind. Est. CR0: Wadd 6K 167
Silverwood Cl. BR3: Beck 7C 140
Silverwood Cl. HA6: Nwood 1E 38
Silverwood Pl. SE10 ......1E 122
Silverworks Cl. NW9 ......3K 43
Silvester Ho. E1 ......6H 85
(off Varden St.)
Silvester Ho. E2 ......3J 85
(off Sceptre Rd.)
Silvester Ho. W11 ......6H 81
(off Basing St.)
Silvester Rd. SE22 ......5F 121
Silvester St. SE1 ......7E 14 (2D 102)
Silvocea Way E14 ......6F 87
Silwood Est. SE16 ......4J 103
Silwood St. SE16 ......4J 103
(off Rotherhithe New Rd.)
Simkins Cl. SW2 ......4J 119
Simla Ct. N7 ......7J 65
(off Brewery Rd.)
Simla Ho. SE1 ......7F 15 (2D 102)
(off Kipling Est.)
Simmonds Ct. SW5 ......4K 99
(off Earl's Ct. Gdns.)
Simmonds Ho. TW8: Bford 5E 96
(off Clayponds La.)
Simmons Cl. KT9: Chess 6C 162
Simmons Cl. N20 ......2H 31
Simmons Dr. RM8: Dag 3E 72
Simmons La. E4 ......2A 36
Simmons Way N20 ......2H 31
Simms Cl. SM5: Cars 2C 166
Simms Gdns. N2 ......2A 46
Simms Rd. SE1 ......4G 103
Simnel Rd. SE12 ......7K 123
Simon Cl. W11 ......7H 81
Simon Ct. W9 ......3J 81
(off Saltram Cres.)
Simonds Rd. E10 ......2C 68
Simone Cl. BR1: Broml 1B 160
Simone Ct. SE26 ......3J 139
Simons Ct. N16 ......2F 67
Simons Wlk. E15 ......5F 69
Simpson Cl. CR0: C'don 5C 156
Simpson Cl. N21 ......5D 22
Simpson Dr. W3 ......6K 79
Simpson Ho. NW8 ......3C 4 (4C 82)
Simpson Ho. SE11 ......6H 19 (5K 101)
Simpson Rd. TW10: Ham 4C 132
Simpson Rd. TW4: Houn 6D 112
Simpson's Rd. BR1: Broml 3J 159
Simpson's Rd. E14 ......7D 86
Simpson St. SW11 ......2C 118
Simpson Way KT6: Surb 6C 150
Simrose Ct. SW18 ......5J 117
Sim St. N4 ......2C 66
Sims Wlk. SE3 ......4H 123
Sinclair Ct. CR0: C'don 2E 168
Sinclair Dr. SM2: Sutt 7K 165
Sinclair Gdns. W14 ......2F 99
Sinclair Gro. NW11 ......6F 45
Sinclair Ho. E15 ......6F 69
(off Leyton Rd.)
Sinclair Ho. WC1 ......2E 6 (3J 83)
(off Sandwich St.)
Sinclair Mans. W12 ......2F 99
(off Richmond Way)
Sinclair Pl. SE4 ......6C 122
Sinclair Rd. E4 ......5G 35
Sinclair Rd. W14 ......2F 99
Sinclairs Ho. E3 ......2B 86
(off St Stephen's Rd.)
Sinclare Cl. EN1: Enf 1A 24
Sindercombe M. W12 ......3C 98
Singapore Rd. W13 ......1A 96
Singer M. SW4 ......2J 119
Singer St. EC2 ......2F 9 (3D 84)
Singleton Cl. CR0: C'don 7C 156
Singleton Cl. SW17 ......7D 136
Singleton Rd. RM9: Dag 5F 73
Singleton Scarp N12 ......5D 30
Sinnott Rd. E17 ......1K 49
Siobhan Davies Dance Studios 3B 102
(off St George's Rd.)
Sion Ct. TW1: Twick 1B 132
Sion Rd. TW1: Twick 1B 132
Sippets Ct. IG1: Ilf 1H 71
SIPSON 6C 92
Sipson Cl. UB7: Sip 6C 92
Sipson La. UB3: Harl 6D 92
Sipson La. UB7: Sip 6C 92
Sipson Rd. UB7: Sip 3B 92
(not continuous)
Sipson Rd. UB7: W Dray 3B 92
(not continuous)
Sipson Way UB7: Sip 7C 92
Sir Abraham Dawes Cotts. SW15 ......4G 117
Sir Alexander Cl. W3 ......1B 98
Sir Alexander Rd. W3 ......1B 98
Sir Christopher France Ho. E1 ......3A 86
Sir Cyril Black Way SW19 ......7J 135
Sirdar Rd. CR4: Mitc 6E 136
Sirdar Rd. N22 ......3B 48
Sirdar Rd. W11 ......7F 81
Sireen Apts. E3 ......4B 86
Sir Francis Drake Ct. SE10 ......5F 105
Sirinham Point SW8 ......7H 19 (6K 101)
(off Meadow Rd.)
Sirius Bldg. E1 ......7K 85
(off Jardine Rd.)
Sirius Ho. SE16 ......4A 104
(off Seafarer Way)
Sir James Black Ho. SE5 ......2D 120
(off Coldharbour La.)
Sir John Kirk Cl. SE5 ......7C 102
Sir John Lyon Ho. EC4 ......2C 14 (7C 84)
(off High Timber St.)
Sir John Morden Wlk. SE3 ......2J 123
Sir John Soane's Mus. 7G 7 (6K 83)
Sir Nicholas Garrow Ho. W10 ......4G 81
(off Kensal Rd.)
Sirocco Twr. E14 ......2D 104
Sir Oswald Stoll Mans. SW6 ......7K 99
(off Fulham Rd.)
Sir Simon Milton Sq. SW1 ......2K 17 (3F 101)
SIR STEVE REDGRAVE BRIDGE 7F 89
Sir Walter Raleigh Ct. SE10 ......5G 105
Sir William Powell's Almshouses SW6 ......2G 117
Sise La. EC4 ......1E 14 (6D 84)
Siskin Ho. SE16 ......4K 103
(off Tawny Way)
Siskin Pl. UB4: Yead 5A 76
Sisley Rd. IG11: Bark 1J 89
Sispara Gdns. SW18 ......6H 117
Sissinghurst Cl. BR1: Broml 5G 141
Sissinghurst Ho. SE15 ......6J 103
(off Sharratt St.)
Sissinghurst Rd. CR0: C'don 7G 157
Sissulu Ct. E6 ......1A 88
Sister Mabel's Way SE15 ......7G 103
Sisters Av. SW11 ......3D 118
Sisters Cl. DA5: Bexl 3J 145
Sistova Rd. SW12 ......1F 137
Sisulu Pl. SW9 ......3A 120
Sitarey Ct. W12 ......1D 98
Sitka Ho. SE16 ......2A 104
Sittingbourne Av. EN1: Enf 6J 23
Sitwell Gro. HA7: Stan 5E 26
Siverst Cl. UB5: N'olt 6F 59
Sivill Ho. E2 ......1K 9 (3F 85)
(off Columbia Rd.)
Siviter Way RM10: Dag 7H 73
Siward Rd. BR2: Broml 3K 159
Siward Rd. N17 ......1D 48
Siward Rd. SW17 ......3A 136
Six Acres Est. N4 ......2K 65
Six Bridges Ind. Est. SE1 ......5G 103
(not continuous)
Sixpenny Ct. IG11: Bark 6G 71
Sixth Av. E12 ......4D 70
Sixth Av. UB3: Hayes 1H 93
Sixth Av. W10 ......3G 81
Sixth Cross Rd. TW2: Twick 3G 131
Siyah Gdn. E3 ......3B 86
Skardu Rd. NW2 ......5G 63
Skeena Hill SW18 ......7G 117
Skeffington Rd. E6 ......1D 88
Skeffington St. SE18 ......3G 107
Skeggs Ho. E14 ......3E 104
(off Glengall St.)
Skegness Ho. N7 ......7K 65
(off Sutterton St.)
Skelbrook St. SW18 ......2A 136
Skelgill Rd. SW15 ......4H 117
Skelley Rd. E15 ......7H 69
Skelton Cl. E8 ......6F 67
Skelton Lodge SE10 ......3J 105
(off Billinghurst Way)
Skelton Rd. E7 ......6J 69
Skelton's La. E10 ......7D 50
Skelwith Rd. W6 ......6E 98
Skenfrith Ho. SE15 ......6H 103
(off Commercial Way)
Skerne Rd. KT2: King T 1D 150
Skerne Wlk. KT2: King T 1D 150
Sketch Apts. E1 ......5K 85
(off Shandy St.)
Sketchley Gdns. SE16 ......5K 103
Sketty Rd. EN1: Enf 3A 24
Skieasy 2K 115
Skiers St. E15 ......1G 87
Skiffington Cl. SW2 ......1A 138
Skillen Lodge HA5: Pinn 1B 40
Skinner Ct. E3 ......4D 86
(off Barry Blandford Way)
Skinner Pl. SW1 ......4G 17 (4E 100)
(off Bourne St.)
Skinners Ct. N13 ......3F 33
Skinners La. EC4 ......2D 14 (7C 84)
Skinners La. TW5: Hest 1F 113
Skinner's Row SE10 ......1D 122
Skinner St. EC1 ......2K 7 (3A 84)
Skip La. UB9: Hare 1A 56
Skipper Ct. IG11: Bark 1G 89
Skipsea Ho. SW18 ......6C 118
Skipsey Av. E6 ......3D 88
Skipton Cl. N11 ......6K 31
Skipton Dr. UB3: Harl 3E 92
Skipton Ho. SE4 ......4A 122
Skipwith Ho. EC1 ......5J 7 (5A 84)
(off Bourne Est.)
Skipworth Rd. E9 ......1J 85
Skua Ct. SE8 ......6B 104
(off Dorking Cl.)

A–Z London 287

Skye La. HA8: Edg....4A 28
Sky Gdn. Wlk. EC3....2G 15 (7E 84)
(off Philpot La.)
Skylark Ct. RM13: Rain....2K 91
Skylark Ct. SE1....7D 14 (2C 102)
(off Swan St.)
Skylark Ct. SW15....6E 116
Skyline Apts. N4....7D 48
(off Devan Gro.)
Skyline Ct. CR0: C'don....3D 168
(off Park La.)
Skyline Ct. SE1....3F 103
Skyline Plaza Bldg. E1....6G 85
(off Commercial Rd.)
Skylines E14....2E 104
Skylines Village E14....2E 104
Sky Peals Rd. IG8: Wfd G....7A 36
Skyport Dr. UB7: Harm....3E 174
Sky Studios E16....2E 106
Skyvan Cl. TW6: H'row A....5E 110
Skyview Apts. CR0: C'don....2C 168
(off Park St.)
Sky View Twr. E15....2D 86
(off High Street)
Skyway 14 SL3: Poyle....6A 174
Slade, The SE18....6J 107
Sladebrook Rd. SE3....3B 124
Slade Ct. EN5: New Bar....3E 20
Sladedale Rd. SE18....5J 107
Slade Ho. TW4: Houn....6D 112
Sladen Pl. E5....4H 67
Slades Cl. EN2: Enf....3F 23
Slades Dr. BR7: Chst....3G 143
Slades Gdns. EN2: Enf....2F 23
Slades Hill EN2: Enf....3F 23
Slades Ri. EN2: Enf....3F 23
Slade Twr. E10....2C 68
(off Leyton Grange Est.)
Slade Wlk. SE17....6B 102
Slade Way CR4: Mitc....1E 154
Slagrove Pl. SE13....5C 122
Slaidburn St. SW10....6A 100
Slaithwaite Rd. SE13....4E 122
Slaney Ct. NW10....7E 62
Slaney Pl. N7....5A 66
Slate Ho. E14....6B 86
(off Keymer Pl.)
Slater Cl. SE18....5E 106
Slater M. SW4....3G 119
(off Grafton Sq.)
Slatter NW9....7G 29
Slattery Rd. TW13: Felt....1B 130
Sleaford Ho. E3....4C 86
(off Fern St.)
Sleaford Ind. Est. SW8....7G 101
Sleaford St. SW8....7G 101
Sleat Ho. E3....2B 86
(off Saxon Rd.)
Sledmere Ct. TW14: Bedf....1G 129
Sleigh Ho. E2....3J 85
(off Bacton St.)
Slide, The....7D 68
Slievemore Cl. SW4....3H 119
Sligo Ho. E1....4K 85
(off Beaumont Gro.)
Slindon Ct. N16....3F 67
Slingsby Pl. WC2....2E 12 (7J 83)
Slippers Pl. SE16....3H 103
Slipway Ho. E14....5D 104
(off Burrells Wharf Sq.)
Sloane Av. SW3....4C 16 (4C 100)
Sloane Av. Mans. SW3....4E 16 (4D 100)
Sloane Ct. TW7: Isle....1J 113
Sloane Ct. E. SW3....5G 17 (5E 100)
Sloane Ct. W. SW3....5G 17 (5E 100)
Sloane Gdns. BR6: Farnb....3G 173
Sloane Gdns. SW1....4G 17 (4E 100)
Sloane Ga. Mans. SW1....3G 17 (4E 100)
(off D'Oyley St.)
Sloane Ho. E9....7J 67
(off Loddiges Rd.)
Sloane M. N8....5J 47
Sloane Sq. SW1....4G 17 (4E 100)
Sloane St. SW1....7F 11 (2D 100)
Sloane Ter. SW1....3G 17 (4E 100)
Sloane Ter. Mans. SW1....3G 17 (4E 100)
(off Sloane Ter.)
Sloane Wlk. CR0: C'don....6B 158
Slocum Cl. SE28....7C 90
Slough La. NW9....5J 43
Sly St. E1....6H 85
Smaldon Cl. UB7: W Dray....3C 92
Smallberry Av. TW7: Isle....2K 113
Smallbrook M. W2....1A 10 (6B 82)
Smalley Cl. N16....3F 67
Smalley Rd. Est. N16....3F 67
(off Smalley Cl.)
Smallwood Rd. SW17....4B 136
Smarden Cl. DA17: Belv....5G 109
Smarden Gro. SE9....4D 142
Smart's Pl. N18....5B 34
Smart's Pl. WC2....7F 7 (6J 83)
Smart St. E2....3K 85
Smead Way SE13....3D 122
Smeaton Cl. KT9: Chess....6D 162
Smeaton Ct. SE1....3C 102
Smeaton Rd. IG8: Wfd G....5J 37
Smeaton Rd. SW18....7J 117
Smeaton St. E1....1H 103
Smedley St. SW4....2H 119
Smedley St. SW8....2H 119
Smeed Rd. E3....7C 68
Smikle Ct. SE14....1K 121
(off Hatcham Pk. M.)
Smiles Pl. SE13....2E 122
Smith Cl. SE16....1K 103
Smithfield Ct. E1....7G 85
(off Cable St.)
Smithfield Market....6A 8 (5B 84)
(off West Smithfield)
Smithfield Sq. N8....4J 47
Smithfield St. EC1....6A 8 (5B 84)
Smith Hill TW8: Bford....6E 96
Smithies Rd. SE2....4B 108
Smith's Ct. W1....2C 12 (7H 83)
(off Gt. Windmill St.)
Smithson Rd. N17....1D 48
Smiths Point E13....1J 87
(off Brooks Rd.)
Smith Sq. SW1....2E 18 (3J 101)
Smiths Sq. W6....5F 99
Smith St. KT5: Surb....6F 151
Smith St. SW3....5E 16 (5D 100)
Smiths Yd. CR0: C'don....3C 168
(off St George's Wlk.)
Smiths Yd. SW18....2A 136
Smith Ter. SW3....6E 16 (5D 100)
Smithwood Cl. SW19....1G 135
Smithy La. TW3: Houn....3F 113
Smithy St. E1....5J 85
Smock Wlk. CR0: C'don....6C 156
Smokehouse Yd. EC1....5B 8 (5B 84)
(off St John St.)
Smoothfield Ct. TW3: Houn....4E 112
Smugglers Way SW18....4K 117
Smugglers Yd. W12....1D 98
(off Devonport Rd.)
Smyrk's Rd. SE17....5E 102
Smyrna Mans. NW6....7J 63
(off Smyrna Rd.)
Smyrna Rd. NW6....7J 63
Smythe Cl. N9....3B 34
Smythe St. E14....7D 86
Snakes La. N14....3A 22
Snakes La. E. IG8: Buck H....6F 37
Snakes La. E. IG8: Wfd G....6F 37
Snakes La. W. IG8: Wfd G....5D 36
Snakey La. TW13: Felt....4J 129
SNARESBROOK....5J 51
Snaresbrook Dr. HA7: Stan....4J 27
Snaresbrook Hall E18....4J 51
Snaresbrook Ho. E18....4H 51
Snaresbrook Rd. E11....4G 51
Snarsgate St. W10....5E 80
Sneath Av. NW11....7H 45
Snells Pk. N18....6A 34
Sneyd Rd. NW2....4E 62
Snowberry Cl. E15....4F 69
Snowberry Cl. EN5: Barn....3C 20
Snowbury Rd. SW6....2K 117
Snowden Av. UB10: Hil....2D 74
Snowden St. EC2....4G 9 (4E 84)
Snowdon Aviary....1D 82
(in London Zoo)
Snowdon Cres. UB3: Harl....3E 92
Snowdon Dr. NW9....6A 44
Snowdon Rd. TW6: H'row A....6E 110
Snowdown Cl. SE20....1K 157
Snowdrop Cl. TW12: Hamp....6E 130
Snowdrop Ct. RM13: Rain....2J 91
Snowdrop M. HA5: Pinn....2A 40
Snow Hill EC1....6A 8 (5B 84)
Snow Hill Ct. EC1....7B 8 (6B 84)
Snowman Ho. NW6....1K 81
Snowsfields SE1....6F 15 (2D 102)
Snowshill Rd. E12....5C 70
Snowy Fielder Waye TW7: Isle....2B 114
Soames Pl. EN4: Had W....2E 20
Soames St. SE15....3F 121
Soames Wlk. KT3: N Mald....1A 152
Soane Cl. W5....2D 96
Soane Ct. NW1....7G 65
(off St Pancras Way)
Soane Ho. SE17....5D 102
(off Roland Way)
Soane Sq. HA7: Stan....3D 26
Soap Ho. La. TW8: Bford....7E 96
Sobell Leisure Cen....3K 65
Sobraon Ho. KT2: King T....7F 133
(off Elm Rd.)
Socket La. BR2: Hayes....6K 159
Soda Studios E8....1F 85
(off Kingsland Rd.)
SOHO....1B 12 (6G 83)
Soho Ho. W12....7E 80
Soho Sq. W1....7C 6 (6H 83)
Soho St. W1....7C 6 (6H 83)
Soho Theatre....1C 12 (6H 83)
(off Dean St.)
Sojourner Truth Cl. E8....6H 67
Sola Ct. CR0: C'don....1D 168
(off Sydenham Rd.)
Solander Gdns. E1 Cable St....7H 85
(off Cable St.)
Solander Gdns. E1 The Highway....7J 85
Solar Ct. N3....7E 30
Solar Ct. SE16....2G 103
(off Chambers St.)
Solar Ho. E15....6G 69
(off Romford Rd.)
Solar Ho. E6....5E 88
Solarium Ct. SE1....4F 103
(off Alscot Rd.)
Soldene Ct. N7....6K 65
Solebay St. E1....4A 86
Solent Ct. SW16....2K 155
Solent Ho. E1....5A 86
(off Ben Jonson Rd.)
Solent Ri. E13....3J 87
Solent Rd. NW6....5J 63
Soley M. WC1....1J 7 (3A 84)
Solna Av. SW15....5E 116
Solna Rd. N21....1J 33
Solomon Av. N9....4B 34
Solomons Ct. N12....7F 31
Solomon's Pas. SE15....4H 121
Solomon Way E1....5A 86
Solon New Rd. SW4....4J 119
Solon New Rd. Est. SW4....4J 119
Solon Rd. SW2....4J 119
Solway Cl. E8....6F 67
(off Queensbridge Rd.)
Solway Cl. TW4: Houn....3C 112
Solway Ho. E1....4K 85
(off Ernest St.)
Solway Rd. N22....1B 48
Solway Rd. SE22....4G 121
Somaford Gro. EN4: E Barn....6G 21
Somali Rd. NW2....5H 63
Sombourne Ho. SW15....7C 116
(off Fontley Way)
Somerby Rd. IG11: Bark....7H 71
Somercoates Cl. EN4: Cockf....3H 21
Somer Ct. SW6....6J 99
(off Anselm Rd.)
Somerfield Rd. N4....2B 66
(not continuous)
Somerfield St. SE16....5K 103
Somerford Cl. HA5: Eastc....4J 39
Somerford Gro. N16....4F 67
Somerford Gro. N17....7B 34
(not continuous)
Somerford Gro. Est. N16....4F 67
Somerford St. E1....4H 85
Somerford Way SE16....2A 104
Somerhill Av. DA15: Sidc....7B 126
Somerhill Rd. DA16: Well....2B 126
Somerleyton Pas. SW9....4B 120
Somerleyton Rd. SW9....4A 120
Somersby Gdns. IG4: Ilf....5D 52
Somers Cl. NW1....2H 83
Somers Cres. W2....1C 10 (6C 82)
Somerset Av. DA16: Well....5K 125
Somerset Av. KT9: Chess....4D 162
Somerset Av. SW20....2D 152
Somerset Cl. IG8: Wfd G....1J 51
Somerset Cl. KT3: N Mald....6A 152
Somerset Cl. N17....2D 48
Somerset Cl. SM3: Wor Pk....4E 164
Somerset Ct. IG9: Buck H....2F 37
Somerset Ct. NW1....1C 6 (2H 83)
Somerset Ct. TW11: Tedd....5J 131
Somerset Ct. W7....6K 77
(off Copley Cl.)
Somerset Est. SW11....1B 118
Somerset Gdns. HA0: Wemb....5C 60
Somerset Gdns. N17....7K 33
Somerset Gdns. N6....7E 46
Somerset Gdns. SE13....2D 122
Somerset Gdns. SW16....3K 155
Somerset Gdns. TW11: Tedd....5J 131
Somerset Hall N17....7K 33
Somerset Ho. SW19....3F 135
Somerset House....2G 13 (7K 83)
Somerset Lodge TW8: Bford....6D 96
Somerset Rd. E17....5C 50
Somerset Rd. EN5: New Bar....5E 20
Somerset Rd. HA1: Harr....5G 41
Somerset Rd. KT1: King T....2F 151
Somerset Rd. N17....3F 49
Somerset Rd. N18....5A 34
Somerset Rd. NW4....4E 44
Somerset Rd. SW19....3F 135
Somerset Rd. TW11: Tedd....5J 131
Somerset Rd. TW8: Bford....6C 96
Somerset Rd. UB1: S'hall....5D 76
Somerset Rd. W13....1B 96
Somerset Rd. W4....3K 97
Somerset Sq. W14....2G 99
Somerset Waye TW5: Hest....6C 94
Somersham Rd. DA7: Bex....2E 126
Somers Pl. SW2....7K 119
Somers Rd. E17....4B 50
Somers Rd. SW2....6K 119
Somerston Ho. NW1....1G 83
(off St Pancras Way)
SOMERS TOWN....1C 6 (2H 83)
Somers Town Community Sports Cen....2H 83
Somerton Av. TW9: Rich....3H 115
Somerton Ho. WC1....2D 6 (3H 83)
(off Euston Rd.)
Somerton Rd. NW2....3F 63
Somerton Rd. SE15....4H 121
Somertrees Av. SE12....2K 141
Somervell Rd. HA2: Harr....5D 58
Somerville Av. SW13....6D 98
Somerville Cl. SW9....1K 119
Somerville Point SE16....2B 104
Somerville Rd. RM6: Chad H....6C 54
Somerville Rd. SE20....7K 139
Sonderburg Rd. N7....2K 65
Sondes St. SE17....6D 102
Sonesta Apts. SE15....1H 121
Songhurst Cl. CR0: C'don....6K 155
Sonia Ct. HA1: Harr....6K 41
Sonia Ct. HA8: Edg....7A 28
Sonia Gdns. N12....4F 31
Sonia Gdns. NW10....4B 62
Sonia Gdns. TW5: Hest....7E 94
Sonning Gdns. TW12: Hamp....6D 130
Sonning Ho. E2....2J 9 (3F 85)
(off Swanfield St.)
Sonning Rd. SE25....6G 157
Soper Cl. E4....5G 35
Soper Cl. SE23....1K 139
Soper M. EN3: Enf L....1H 25
Sophia Cl. N7....6K 65
Sophia Ho. W6....5E 98
(off Queen Caroline St.)
Sophia Rd. E10....1D 68
Sophia Rd. E16....6K 87
Sophia Sq. SE16....7A 86
(off Sovereign Cres.)
Sophora Ho. SW11....7F 101
Soprano Ct. E15....1H 87
(off Plaistow Rd.)
Soprano Way KT10: Surb....3B 162
Sopwith NW9....1B 44
Sopwith Av. E17....4K 49
Sopwith Av. KT9: Chess....5E 162
Sopwith Cl. KT2: King T....5F 133
Sopwith Rd. TW5: Hest....7A 94
Sopwith Way KT2: King T....1E 150
Sopwith Way SW11....7F 101
Sorbus Ct. EN2: Enf....2G 23
Sorensen Ct. E10....2D 68
(off Leyton Grange Est.)
Sorrel Cl. SE28....1A 108
Sorrel Gdns. E6....5C 88
Sorrel La. E14....6F 87
Sorrell Cl. SE14....7A 104
Sorrell Cl. SW9....2A 120
Sorrel Mead NW9....7C 44
Sorrento Rd. SM1: Sutt....3K 165
Sotheby Rd. N5....3B 66
Sotheran Cl. E8....1G 85
Sotherby Lodge E2....2J 85
(off Sewardstone Rd.)
Sotheron Pl. SW6....7K 99
Soudan Rd. SW11....1D 118
Souldern Rd. W14....3F 99
Soul St. SE6....1E 140
Sounding All. E3....1C 86
South Access Rd. E17....7A 50
Southacre W2....1C 10 (6C 82)
(off Hyde Pk. Cres.)
Southacre Way HA5: Pinn....1A 40
SOUTH ACTON....2J 97
South Africa Rd. W12....1D 98
SOUTHALL....1D 94
Southall Ct. UB1: S'hall....7D 76
Southall Ent. Cen. UB2: S'hall....2E 94
SOUTHALL GREEN....3C 94
Southall La. TW5: Cran....6K 93
Southall La. UB2: S'hall....4A 94
Southall Pl. SE1....7E 14 (2D 102)
Southall Sports Cen....1C 94
Southall Waterside UB1: S'hall....2B 94
Southam Ho. W10....4G 81
(off Southam St.)
Southampton Bldgs. WC2....6J 7 (5A 84)
Southampton Gdns. CR4: Mitc....5J 155
Southampton M. E16....1K 105
Southampton Pl. WC1....6F 7 (5J 83)
Southampton Rd. NW5....5D 64
Southampton Rd. E. TW6: H'row A....6B 110
Southampton Rd. W. TW6: H'row A....6A 110
Southampton Row WC1....5F 7 (5J 83)
Southampton St. WC2....2F 13 (7J 83)
Southampton Way SE15....7E 102
Southampton Way SE5....7D 102
Southam St. W10....4G 81
South Audley St. W1....3H 11 (7E 82)
South Av. E4....7J 25
South Av. SM5: Cars....7E 166
South Av. TW9: Kew....2G 115
South Av. UB1: S'hall....7D 76
South Av. Gdns. UB1: S'hall....7D 76
Southbank KT7: T Ditt....7B 150
South Bank KT6: Surb....6E 150
South Bank SE1....5G 13 (1K 101)
Southbank Bus. Cen. SW11....1D 118
Southbank Cen....4H 13 (1K 101)
South Bank Ter. KT6: Surb....6E 150
SOUTH BARNET....1K 31
SOUTH BEDDINGTON....6H 167
South Birkbeck Rd. E11....3F 69
South Black Lion La. W6....5C 98
South Block SE1....7G 13 (2K 101)
(off Belvedere Rd.)
South Bolton Gdns. SW5....5K 99
SOUTHBOROUGH....5D 160
SOUTHBOROUGH....1E 162
Southborough Cl. KT6: Surb....1D 162
Southborough Ho. SE17....5E 102
(off Kinglake Est.)
Southborough La. BR2: Broml....5C 160
Southborough Rd. BR1: Broml....3C 160
Southborough Rd. E9....1K 85
Southborough Rd. KT6: Surb....1E 162
Southbourne BR2: Hayes....7J 159
Southbourne Av. NW9....2J 43
Southbourne Cl. HA5: Pinn....7C 40
Southbourne Ct. NW9....2J 43
Southbourne Cres. NW4....4G 45
Southbourne Gdns. HA4: Ruis....1K 57
Southbourne Gdns. IG1: Ilf....5G 71
Southbourne Gdns. SE12....5K 123
Southbridge Pl. CR0: C'don....4C 168
Southbridge Rd. CR0: C'don....4C 168
Southbridge Way UB2: S'hall....2C 94
SOUTH BROMLEY....7E 86
Southbrook M. SE12....6H 123
Southbrook Rd. SE12....6H 123
Southbrook Rd. SW16....1J 155
Southbury NW8....1A 82
(off Loudoun Rd.)
Southbury Av. EN1: Enf....4B 24
Southbury Leisure Cen....3B 24
Southbury Rd. EN1: Enf....3K 23
Southbury Rd. EN3: Pond E....4C 24
South Carriage Dr. SW7....7B 10 (2B 100)
SOUTH CHINGFORD....5G 35
Southchurch Ct. E6....2D 88
(off High St. Sth.)
Southchurch Rd. E6....2D 88
South City Ct. SE15....7E 102
South Cl. DA6: Bex....4D 126
South Cl. EN5: Barn....3C 20
South Cl. HA5: Pinn....7D 40
South Cl. N6....6F 47
South Cl. RM10: Dag....1G 91
South Cl. SM4: Mord....6J 153
South Cl. TW2: Twick....3E 130
South Cl. UB7: W Dray....3B 92
South Colonnade, The E14....1C 104
(not continuous)
Southcombe St. W14....4G 99
South Comn. Rd. UB8: Uxb....6A 56
Southcote Av. KT5: Surb....7H 151
Southcote Av. TW13: Felt....2H 129
Southcote Ri. HA4: Ruis....7F 39
Southcote Rd. E17....5K 49
Southcote Rd. N19....4G 65
Southcote Rd. SE25....5H 157
Southcott Ho. E3....3D 86
(off Devons Rd.)
Southcott Ho. W9....4A 82
(off Clifton Gdns.)
Southcott M. NW8....2C 82
Southcott Rd. TW11: Hamp W....1C 150
South Countess Rd. E17....3B 50
South Cres. E16....4F 87
South Cres. WC1....6C 6 (5H 83)
South Crescent M. WC1....3E 6 (4J 83)
Southcroft Av. BR4: W W'ck....2E 170
Southcroft Av. DA16: Well....3J 125
Southcroft Rd. BR6: Orp....3J 173
Southcroft Rd. SW16....6F 137
Southcroft Rd. SW17....6E 136
South Cross Rd. IG6: Ilf....5G 53
South Croxted Rd. SE21....3D 138
SOUTH CROYDON....5D 168
South Croydon Sports Club....5E 168
Southdean Gdns. SW19....2H 135
South Dene NW7....3E 28
Southdene Ct. N11....3A 32
Southdown Av. W7....3A 96
Southdown Cres. HA2: Harr....1G 59
Southdown Cres. IG2: Ilf....5J 53
Southdown Dr. SW20....7F 135
Southdown Rd. SM5: Cars....7E 166
Southdown Rd. SW20....1F 153
South Dr. BR6: Orp....5J 173
South Dr. HA4: Ruis....1G 57
South Ealing Rd. W5....2D 96
South Eastern Av. N9....3A 34
South Eaton Pl. SW1....3H 17 (4E 100)
South Eden Pk. Rd. BR3: Beck....6D 158
South Edwardes Sq. W8....3H 99
SOUTHEND....4F 141
South End CR0: C'don....4C 168
South End CR2: S Croy....5C 168
South End W8....3K 99
Southend Cl. SE9....6F 125
South End Cl. NW3....4C 64
Southend Cres. SE9....6F 125
South End Grn. NW3....4C 64
Southend La. SE26....4B 140
Southend La. SE6....4B 140
Southend Rd. BR3: Beck....1C 158
Southend Rd. E17....1D 50
Southend Rd. E18....1J 51
Southend Rd. E4....5F 35
Southend Rd. E6....7D 70
Southend Rd. IG8: Wfd G....2A 52
South End Rd. NW3....4C 64
South End Row W8....3K 99
Southern Av. SE25....3F 157
Southern Av. TW14: Felt....1J 129
Southern Cotts. TW19: Stanw M....7B 174
Southerngate Way SE14....7A 104
Southern Gro. E3....3B 86
Southern Perimeter Rd. TW6: H'row A....7C 174
(not continuous)
Southern Perimeter Rd. TW6: Stanw....7C 174
(not continuous)
Southern Pl. HA1: Harr....4K 59
Southern Rd. E13....2K 87
Southern Rd. N2....4D 46
Southern Row W10....4G 81
Southern St. N1....2K 83
Southern Ter. W12....1E 98
Southern Way RM7: Rom....6G 55
Southern Way SE10....4H 105
Southernwood Retail Pk....5F 103
Southerton Rd. W6....4E 98
South Esk Rd. E7....6A 70
Southey Ho. SE17....5C 102
(off Browning St.)
Southey M. E16....1J 105
Southey Rd. N15....5E 48
Southey Rd. SW19....7J 135
Southey Rd. SW9....1A 120
Southey St. SE20....7K 139
Southfield EN5: Barn....6A 20
Southfield Cl. UB8: Hil....4C 74
Southfield Cotts. W7....2K 95
Southfield Ct. E11....3H 69
Southfield Gdns. TW1: Twick....4K 131
Southfield Pk. HA2: Harr....4F 41
Southfield Rd. BR7: Chst....3K 161
Southfield Rd. EN3: Pond E....6C 24
Southfield Rd. W4....2K 97
Southfields KT8: E Mos....6J 149
Southfields NW4....3D 44
SOUTHFIELDS....1H 135
Southfields Av. TW15: Ashf....6D 128
Southfields Ct. SM1: Sutt....2J 165
Southfields M. SW18....6J 117
Southfields Pas. SW18....6J 117
Southfields Rd. SW18....6J 117
Southfleet NW5....6E 64
Southfleet Rd. BR6: Orp....3J 173
South Gdns. HA9: Wemb....2G 61
South Gdns. SE17....4C 102
South Gdns. SW19....7B 136
SOUTHGATE....1C 32
Southgate Av. TW13: Felt....4F 129
SOUTHGATE CIR....1C 32
Southgate Ct. N1....7D 66
(off Downham Rd.)
Southgate Gro. N1....7D 66
Southgate Hockey Cen....3A 22
Southgate Leisure Cen....7C 22
Southgate Rd. N1....1D 84
South Gipsy Rd. DA16: Well....3D 126
South Glade, The DA5: Bexl....1F 145
South Grn. NW9....1A 44
(off Parklea Cl.)
South Gro. E17....5B 50
South Gro. N15....5D 48
South Gro. N6....1E 64
South Gro. Ho. N6....1E 64
SOUTH HACKNEY....1K 85
SOUTH HAMPSTEAD....7A 64
SOUTH HARROW....3G 59
South Harrow Ind. Est. HA2: Harr....2G 59
South Herts Golf Course....1D 30
South Hill BR7: Chst....6D 142
South Hill HA6: Nwood....1G 39
South Hill Av. HA1: Harr....3H 59
South Hill Av. HA2: Harr....3G 59
South Hill Gro. HA1: Harr....4J 59
South Hill Pk. NW3....4C 64
South Hill Pk. Gdns. NW3....3C 64
South Hill Rd. BR2: Broml....3G 159
Southholme Cl. SE19....1E 156
Southill Ct. BR2: Broml....5H 159
Southill La. HA5: Eastc....4K 39
Southill Rd. BR7: Chst....7C 142
Southill St. E14....6D 86
South Island Pl. SW9....7K 101
SOUTH KENSINGTON....4B 16 (4B 100)
South Kensington Sta. Arc. SW7....3B 16 (4B 100)
(off Pelham St.)
SOUTH LAMBETH....7J 101
South Lambeth Pl. SW8....7F 19 (6J 101)
South Lambeth Rd. SW8....7F 19 (6J 101)
Southland Rd. SE18....7K 107
Southlands Av. BR6: Orp....4H 173
Southlands Coll. Roehampton University....5C 116
Southlands Dr. SW19....2F 135
Southlands Gro. BR1: Broml....3C 160
Southlands Rd. BR1: Broml....4C 160
Southlands Rd. BR2: Broml....5A 160
Southland Way TW3: Houn....5H 113
South La. KT1: King T....3D 150
South La. KT3: N Mald....4K 151
South La. W. KT3: N Mald....4K 151
South Lodge E16....1K 105
(off Audley Dr.)
South Lodge NW8....1A 4 (2B 82)
South Lodge SW7....7D 10 (2C 100)
(off Knightsbridge)
South Lodge TW2: Whitt....6G 113
South Lodge Av. CR4: Mitc....4J 155
South Lodge Cres. EN2: Enf....4C 22
(not continuous)
South Lodge Dr. N14....4C 22
South London Crematorium....2G 155
South London Gallery....1E 120
South London Theatre....3B 138
(off Norwood High St.)
South Mall N9....3B 34
(off Plevna Rd.)
South Mall SW18....6K 117
South Mead KT19: Ewe....7B 164
South Mead NW9....1B 44
Southmead Gdns. TW11: Tedd....6A 132
Southmead Rd. SW19....1G 135
Southmere Dr. SE2....2D 108
Southmere Ho. E15....2D 86
(off Highland Street)
South Mill Apts. E2....1F 85
(off Hebden St.)
South Molton La. W1....1J 11 (6F 83)
South Molton Rd. E16....6J 87

South Molton St. – Springwood Cl.

South Molton St. W1.....1J 11 (6F 83)
Southmoor Way E9.....6B 68
South Mt. N20.....2F 31
.....(off High Rd.)
SOUTH NORWOOD.....4F 157
South Norwood Country Pk.....4J 157
South Norwood Country Pk. Vis. Cen......4H 157
South Norwood Hill SE25.....1E 156
South Norwood Leisure Cen......5H 157
South Oak Rd. SW16.....4K 137
Southold Ri. SE9.....3D 142
Southolm St. SW11.....1F 119
Southover BR1: Broml.....5J 141
Southover N12.....3D 30
South Pde. HA8: Edg.....2G 43
South Pde. SM6: W'gton.....6G 167
South Pde. SW3.....5B 16 (5B 100)
South Pde. W4.....4K 97
South Pk. Ct. BR3: Beck.....7C 140
South Pk. Cres. IG1: Ilf.....3H 71
South Pk. Cres. SE6.....1G 141
South Pk. Dr. IG11: Bark.....5J 71
South Pk. Dr. IG3: Ilf.....2J 71
South Pk. Gro. KT3: N Mald.....4J 151
South Pk. Hill Rd. CR2: S Croy.....5D 168
South Pk. M. SW6.....3K 117
South Pk. Rd. IG1: Ilf.....3H 71
South Pk. Rd. SW19.....6J 135
South Pk. Ter. IG1: Ilf.....3J 71
South Pk. Vs. IG3: Ilf.....4J 71
South Pk. Way HA4: Ruis.....6A 58
South Pl. EC2.....5F 9 (5D 84)
South Pl. EN3: Pond E.....5D 24
South Pl. KT5: Surb.....7F 151
South Pl. M. EC2.....6F 9 (5D 84)
Southport Rd. SE18.....4H 107
South Quay Plaza E14.....2D 104
South Quay Sq. E14.....2D 104
Southridge Pl. SW20.....7F 135
South Ri. SM5: Cars.....7C 166
South Ri. W2.....2D 10 (7C 82)
.....(off St George's Flds.)
South Ri. Way SE18.....5H 107
South Rd. RM6: Chad H Dunmow Cl......5C 54
South Rd. RM6: Chad H Mill La......6E 54
South Rd. HA1: Harr.....1A 60
South Rd. HA8: Edg.....1H 43
South Rd. N9.....1B 34
South Rd. SE23.....2K 139
South Rd. SW19.....6A 136
South Rd. TW12: Hamp.....6C 130
South Rd. TW13: Hanw.....5B 130
South Rd. TW2: Twick.....3H 131
South Rd. TW5: Hest.....6B 94
South Rd. UB1: S'hall.....2D 94
South Rd. UB7: W Dray.....3C 92
South Rd. W5.....4D 96
South Row SE3.....2H 123
SOUTH RUISLIP.....4A 58
Southsea Rd. KT1: King T.....4E 150
South Sea St. SE16.....3B 104
Southside N7.....4H 65
South Side N15.....4F 49
South Side W6.....3B 98
Southside Cl. UB10: Uxb.....7A 56
Southside Comn. SW19.....6E 134
Southside Halls SW7.....1B 16 (3B 100)
.....(off Prince's Gdns.)
Southside House.....6E 134
Southside Ind. Est. SW8.....1G 119
.....(off Havelock Ter.)
Southside Shop. Cen......6K 117
Southspring DA15: Sidc.....7H 125
South Sq. NW11.....6K 45
South Sq. WC1.....6J 7 (5A 84)
South Stand N5.....4B 66
South St. BR1: Broml.....2J 159
South St. EN3: Pond E.....5D 24
South St. RM13: Rain.....2J 91
South St. TW7: Isle.....3A 114
South St. W1.....4H 11 (1E 100)
South St. Studios BR1: Broml.....2J 159
.....(off South St.)
South Tenter St. E1.....2K 15 (7F 85)
South Ter. KT6: Surb.....6E 150
South Ter. SW7.....3C 16 (4C 100)
SOUTH TOTTENHAM.....5F 49
South Va. HA1: Harr.....4J 59
South Va. SE19.....6E 138
Southvale Rd. SE3.....2G 123
South Vw. BR1: Broml.....2A 160
South Vw. SW19.....6F 135
Southview Av. NW10.....5B 62
South Vw. Cl. DA5: Bexl.....6F 127
Southview Cl. SW17.....5E 136
South Vw. Ct. SE19.....7C 138
Southview Cres. IG2: Ilf.....6F 53
South Vw. Dr. E18.....3K 51
Southview Gdns. SM6: W'gton.....7G 167
Southview Pde. RM13: Rain.....3K 91
South Vw. Rd. N8.....3H 47
Southview Rd. BR1: Broml.....4F 141
South Vs. NW1.....6H 65
Southville SW8.....1H 119
Southville Cl. KT19: Ewe.....7K 163
Southville Cl. TW14: Bedf.....1G 129
.....(not continuous)
Southville Cl. TW14: Felt.....1G 129
.....(not continuous)
Southville Cres. TW14: Felt.....1G 129
Southville Rd. KT7: T Ditt.....7A 150
Southville Rd. TW14: Felt.....1G 129
South Wlk. BR4: W W'ck.....3G 171
South Wlk. UB3: Hayes.....5F 75
SOUTHWARK.....5B 14 (1B 102)
Southwark Bri. SE1.....3D 14 (7C 84)
Southwark Bri. Bus. Cen. SE1.....5D 14 (1C 102)
.....(off Southwark Bri. Rd.)
Southwark Bri. Rd. SE1.....3B 102
Southwark Cathedral.....4E 14 (1D 102)
Southwark Pk......3H 103
Southwark Pk. Est. SE16.....4H 103
.....(off Southwark Pk. Rd.)
Southwark Pk. Rd. SE16.....4F 103
Southwark Pk. Sports Cen. Track.....4J 103
Southwark Pk. Sports Complex.....4J 103
Southwark Pl. BR1: Broml.....3D 160
Southwark Playhouse.....3C 102
.....(off Newington C'way)
Southwark St George's RC Cathedral.....1K 19 (3A 102)
Southwark St. SE1.....4B 14 (1B 102)
Southwater Cl. BR3: Beck.....7D 140
Southwater Cl. E14.....6B 86
Southway BR2: Hayes.....7J 159
Southway N20.....2D 30
Southway NW11.....6K 45
Southway SM6: W'gton.....4G 167
Southway SW20.....5E 152
South Way CR0: C'don.....3A 170
South Way HA2: Harr.....4E 40
South Way HA9: Wemb.....5G 61
South Way N11.....6B 32
South Way N9.....2D 34
Southway Cl. W12.....2D 98
Southwell Av. UB5: N'olt.....6E 58
Southwell Gdns. SW7.....4A 100
Southwell Gro. Rd. E11.....2G 69
Southwell Ho. SE16.....4H 103
.....(off Anchor St.)
Southwell Rd. CR0: C'don.....6A 156
Southwell Rd. HA3: Kenton.....6D 42
Southwell Rd. SE5.....3C 120
South Western Rd. TW1: Twick.....6A 114
South W. India Dock Entrance E14.....2E 104
South W. Middlesex Crematorium.....1C 130
Southwest Rd. E11.....1F 69
South Wharf Rd. W2.....7A 4 (6B 82)
Southwick M. W2.....7B 4 (6B 82)
Southwick Pl. W2.....1C 10 (6C 82)
Southwick St. W2.....7C 4 (6C 82)
Southwick Yd. W2.....1C 10 (6C 82)
.....(off Titchborne Row)
SOUTH WIMBLEDON.....6K 135
Southwold Dr. IG11: Bark.....5A 72
Southwold Mans. W9.....3J 81
.....(off Widley Rd.)
Southwold Rd. DA5: Bexl.....6H 127
Southwold Rd. E5.....2H 67
Southwood Av. KT2: King T.....1J 151
Southwood Av. N6.....7F 47
Southwood Cl. BR1: Broml.....4D 160
Southwood Cl. KT4: Wor Pk.....1F 165
Southwood Ct. EC1.....2A 8 (3B 84)
.....(off Wynyatt St.)
Southwood Ct. NW11.....5K 45
Southwood Dr. KT5: Surb.....7J 151
SOUTH WOODFORD.....2J 51
South Woodford to Barking Relief Rd. E11.....5B 52
Southwood Gdns. IG2: Ilf.....4F 53
Southwood Gdns. KT10: Hin W.....3A 162
Southwood Hall N6.....6F 47
Southwood Hgts. N6.....7F 47
Southwood Ho. W11.....7G 81
.....(off Avondale Pk. Rd.)
Southwood La. N6.....7E 46
Southwood Lawn Rd. N6.....7E 46
Southwood Mans. N6.....6E 46
.....(off Southwood La.)
Southwood Pk. N6.....7E 46
Southwood Rd. SE28.....1B 108
Southwood Rd. SE9.....2F 143
Southwood Smith Ho. E2.....3H 85
.....(off Florida St.)
Southwood Smith St. N1.....1B 84
South Worple Av. SW14.....3A 116
South Worple Way SW14.....3K 115
Southwyck Ho. SW9.....4B 120
Soval Ct. HA6: Nwood.....1F 39
Sovereign Bus. Cen. EN3: Brim.....3G 25
Sovereign Cl. E1.....7H 85
Sovereign Cl. HA4: Ruis.....1G 57
Sovereign Cl. W5.....5C 78
Sovereign Ct. CR2: S Croy.....5C 168
.....(off Warham Rd.)
Sovereign Ct. HA6: Nwood.....1J 39
Sovereign Ct. HA7: Stan.....7J 27
Sovereign Ct. KT8: W Mole.....4D 148
Sovereign Ct. TW3: Houn.....3E 112
Sovereign Ct. W8.....3K 99
.....(off Wright's La.)
Sovereign Cres. SE16.....7A 86
Sovereign Gro. HA0: Wemb.....3D 60
Sovereign Ho. E1.....4H 85
.....(off Cambridge Heath Rd.)
Sovereign Ho. SE18.....3D 106
.....(off Leda Rd.)
Sovereign Ho. TW15: Ashf.....4A 128
Sovereign M. E2.....2F 85
Sovereign M. EN4: Cockf.....3J 21
Sovereign Pk. NW10.....4H 79
Sovereign Pk. Trad. Est. NW10.....4H 79
Sovereign Pl. HA1: Harr.....5K 41
Sovereign Rd. IG11: Bark.....3C 90
Sowerby Cl. SE9.....5D 124
Spa at Beckenham, The.....1B 158
Spa Bus. Pk. SE16.....3G 103
Space Arts Cen., The.....4C 104
.....(off Westferry Rd.)
Space Bus. Pk. NW10.....3H 79
Spaces Bus. Cen. SW8.....1G 119
Space Waye TW14: Felt.....5J 111
Spa Cl. SE25.....1E 156
Spa Ct. SE16.....3G 103
Spa Ct. SW16.....4K 137
Spafield St. EC1.....3J 7 (4A 84)
Spa Grn. Est. EC1.....1A 8 (3B 84)
Spa Hill SE19.....1D 156
Spalding Cl. HA8: Edg.....7F 29
Spalding Ho. SE4.....4A 122
Spalding Rd. NW4.....7E 44
Spalding Rd. SW17.....5F 137
Spanby Rd. E3.....4C 86
Spaniards Cl. NW11.....1B 64
Spaniards End NW3.....1A 64
Spaniards Rd. NW3.....2A 64
Spanish Pl. W1.....7H 5 (6E 82)
Spanish Rd. SW18.....5A 118
Spanswick Lodge N15.....4B 48
Spare St. SE17.....4C 102
Sparkbridge Rd. HA1: Harr.....4J 41
Sparkes Cl. BR2: Broml.....4K 159
Sparkes Cotts. SW1.....4G 17 (4E 100)
.....(off Graham Ter.)
Sparkford Gdns. N11.....5K 31
Sparkford Ho. SW11.....1B 118
.....(off Battersea Church Rd.)
Sparks Cl. RM8: Dag.....2D 72
Sparks Cl. TW12: Hamp.....6C 130
Sparks Cl. W3.....6K 79
Spa Rd. SE16.....3F 103
Sparrick's Row SE1.....6F 15 (2D 102)
Sparrow Cl. TW12: Hamp.....6C 130
Sparrow Dr. BR5: Farnb.....1G 173
Sparrow Farm Dr. TW14: Felt.....7A 112
Sparrow Farm Rd. KT17: Ewe.....4C 164
Sparrow Grn. RM10: Dag.....3H 73
Sparrow Ho. E1.....4J 85
.....(off Cephas Av.)
Sparrow's Farm - University of Greenwich Avery Hill Campus.....7G 125
Sparrows Herne WD23: Bush.....1A 26
Sparrows La. SE9.....7G 125
Sparrows Way WD23: Bush.....1B 26
Sparsholt Cl. IG11: Bark.....1J 89
.....(off St John's Rd.)
Sparsholt Rd. IG11: Bark.....1J 89
Sparsholt Rd. N19.....1K 65
Spartan Cl. SM6: W'gton.....7J 167
Sparta St. SE10.....1E 122
Speakers' Corner.....2F 11 (7D 82)
Speakers Ct. CR0: C'don.....1D 168
Speakman Ho. SE4.....3A 122
.....(off Arica Rd.)
Spearman Ho. E14.....6C 86
.....(off Upper Nth. St.)
Spearman St. SE18.....6E 106
Spear M. SW5.....4J 99
Spearpoint Gdns. IG2: Ilf.....5K 53
Spears Rd. N19.....1J 65
Speart La. TW5: Hest.....7C 94
Spectacle Works E13.....3A 88
Spectrum Bldg., The N1.....1F 9 (3D 84)
.....(off East Rd.)
Spectrum Pl. SE17.....6D 102
.....(off Lytham St.)
Spectrum Twr. IG1: Ilf.....2G 71
.....(off Hainault St.)
Spectrum Way SW18.....5J 117
Spedan Cl. NW3.....3A 64
Speechly M. E8.....5F 67
Speedbird Way UB7: Harm.....3C 174
Speed Highwalk EC2.....5E 8 (5D 84)
.....(off Silk St.)
Speed Ho. EC2.....5E 8 (5D 84)
.....(off Silk St.)
Speedway Ind. Est. UB3: Hayes.....2F 93
Speedwell Ho. N12.....4E 30
Speedwell St. SE8.....7C 104
Speedy Pl. WC1.....2E 6 (3J 83)
.....(off Cromer St.)
Speer Rd. KT7: T Ditt.....6K 149
Speirs Cl. KT3: N Mald.....6B 152
Speirs Gdns. RM8: Dag.....1E 72
Spekehill SE9.....3D 142
Speke Rd. CR7: Thor H.....2D 156
Speke's Monument.....4A 10 (1B 100)
Speldhurst Cl. BR2: Broml.....5H 159
Speldhurst Rd. E9.....7K 67
Speldhurst Rd. W4.....3K 97
Spellbrook Wlk. N1.....1C 84
Spelman Ho. E1.....6K 9 (5G 85)
.....(off Spelman St.)
Spelman St. E1.....5K 9 (5G 85)
.....(not continuous)
Spelthorne Gro. TW16: Sun.....7H 129
Spelthorne La. TW15: Ashf.....1E 146
Spence Cl. SE16.....2B 104
Spencer Av. N13.....6E 32
Spencer Av. UB4: Hayes.....5J 75
Spencer Cl. BR6: Orp.....2J 173
Spencer Cl. IG8: Wfd G.....5F 37
Spencer Cl. N3.....2J 45
Spencer Cl. NW10.....3F 79
Spencer Ct. BR6: Farnb.....5G 173
Spencer Ct. NW8.....2A 82
.....(off Marlborough Pl.)
Spencer Ct. SW20.....1D 152
Spencer Ctyd. N3.....2H 45
.....(off Regents Pk. Rd.)
Spencer Dr. N2.....6A 46
Spencer Gdns. SE9.....5D 124
Spencer Gdns. SW14.....5J 115
Spencer Hill SW19.....6G 135
Spencer Hill Rd. SW19.....7G 135
Spencer House.....5A 12 (1G 101)
.....(off St James's Pl.)
Spencer Mans. W14.....6G 99
.....(off Queen's Club Gdns.)
Spencer M. SW8.....1K 119
.....(off Lansdowne Way)
Spencer M. W6.....6G 99
Spencer Pk. KT8: E Mos.....5G 149
Spencer Pk. SW18.....5B 118
SPENCER PARK.....5B 118
Spencer Pl. CR0: C'don.....7D 156
Spencer Pl. N1.....7B 66
Spencer Ri. NW5.....4F 65
Spencer Rd. CR4: Mitc Commonside E.....3E 154
Spencer Rd. CR4: Mitc Wood St......7E 154
Spencer Rd. BR1: Broml.....7H 141
Spencer Rd. CR2: S Croy.....5E 168
Spencer Rd. E17.....2E 50
Spencer Rd. E6.....1B 88
Spencer Rd. HA0: Wemb.....2C 60
Spencer Rd. HA3: W'stone.....2J 41
Spencer Rd. IG3: Ilf.....1K 71
Spencer Rd. KT8: E Mos.....4G 149
Spencer Rd. N11.....4A 32
Spencer Rd. N17.....1G 49
Spencer Rd. N8.....5K 47
.....(not continuous)
Spencer Rd. RM13: Rain.....3K 91
Spencer Rd. SW18.....4B 118
Spencer Rd. SW20.....1D 152
Spencer Rd. TW2: Twick.....3J 131
Spencer Rd. TW7: Isle.....1G 113
Spencer Rd. W3.....1J 97
Spencer Rd. W4.....7J 97
Spencer St. EC1.....2A 8 (3B 84)
Spencer St. UB2: S'hall.....2B 94
Spencer Wlk. NW3.....4B 64
Spencer Wlk. SW15.....4F 117
Spencer Way E1.....6H 85
Spencer Yd. SE3.....2H 123
.....(off Tranquil Va.)
Spenlow Ho. SE16.....3G 103
.....(off Jamaica Rd.)
Spenser Gro. N16.....5E 66
Spenser M. SE21.....2D 138
Spenser Rd. SE24.....5B 120
Spenser St. SW1.....1B 18 (3G 101)
Spens Ho. WC1.....4G 7 (4K 83)
.....(off Lamb's Conduit St.)
Spensley Wlk. N16.....3D 66
Speranza St. SE18.....5K 107
Sperling Rd. N17.....2E 48
Spert St. E14.....7A 86
Speyside N14.....6B 22
Spey St. E14.....5E 86
Spey Way RM1: Rom.....1K 55
Spezia Rd. NW10.....2C 80
Sphere, The E16.....6H 87
.....(off Hallsville Rd.)
Sphinx Way EN5: Barn.....5C 20
Spice Ct. E1.....7G 85
Spice Quay Hgts. SE1.....5K 15 (1F 103)
Spicer Cl. EN4: Cockf.....3J 21
Spicer Cl. KT12: Walt T.....6A 148
Spicer Cl. SW9.....2B 120
Spicer Ct. EN1: Enf.....3K 23
Spice's Yd. CR0: C'don.....4C 168
Spiers Gdns. RM8: Dag.....1E 72
.....(off Ager Av.)
Spigurnell Rd. N17.....1D 48
Spikes Bri. Moorings UB4: Yead.....7C 76
Spikes Bri. Rd. UB1: S'hall.....6C 76
Spindle Cl. SE18.....3C 106
Spindle M. BR6: Farnb.....4F 173
Spindlewood Gdns. CR0: C'don.....4E 168
Spindrift Av. E14.....4C 104
Spinel Cl. SE18.....5K 107
Spinnaker Cl. IG11: Bark.....3B 90
Spinnaker Ct. KT1: Hamp W.....1D 150
.....(off Becketts Pl.)
Spinnaker Ho. E14.....2C 104
.....(off Byng St.)
Spinnaker Ho. E16.....2K 105
.....(off Waypoint Way)
Spinnaker Ho. SW18.....4A 118
.....(off Juniper Dr.)
Spinnells Rd. HA2: Harr.....1D 58
Spinner Ho. E8.....1F 85
.....(off Lovelace St.)
Spinney, The DA14: Sidc.....5E 144
Spinney, The EN5: New Bar.....2E 20
Spinney, The HA0: Wemb.....3A 60
Spinney, The HA7: Stan.....4K 27
Spinney, The N21.....7F 23
Spinney, The SM3: Cheam.....4E 164
Spinney, The SW13.....7D 98
Spinney, The SW16.....3G 137
Spinney, The TW16: Sun.....1J 147
Spinney Cl. BR3: Beck.....4D 158
Spinney Cl. KT3: N Mald.....5A 152
Spinney Cl. KT4: Wor Pk.....2B 164
Spinney Cl. UB7: Yiew.....7A 74
Spinney Dr. TW14: Bedf.....7E 110
Spinney Gdns. RM9: Dag.....5E 72
Spinney Gdns. SE19.....5F 139
Spinney Oak BR1: Broml.....2C 160
Spinneys, The BR1: Broml.....2D 160
Spinning Wheel Way SM6: W'gton.....2E 166
Spire Ct. BR3: Beck.....2D 158
.....(off Crescent Rd.)
Spire Ho. W2.....7A 82
.....(off Lancaster Ga.)
Spires Shop. Cen., The.....3B 20
Spirit Quay E1.....1G 103
SPITALFIELDS.....5J 9 (5F 85)
Spitalfields City Farm.....4G 85
Spital Sq. E1.....5H 9 (5E 84)
Spital St. E1.....5K 9 (5G 85)
Spital Yd. E1.....5H 9 (5E 84)
Spitfire Bldg. N1.....1G 7 (2K 83)
.....(off Collier St.)
Spitfire Bus. Pk. CR0: Wadd.....6A 168
Spitfire Est., The TW5: Cran.....5A 94
Spitfire Rd. SM6: W'gton.....7J 167
Spitfire Rd. TW6: H'row A.....6E 110
Spitfire Way TW5: Cran.....5A 94
Splendour Wlk. SE16.....5J 103
.....(off Verney Rd.)
Spode Ho. SE11.....2J 19 (3A 102)
.....(off Lambeth Wlk.)
Spode Wlk. NW6.....5K 63
Spondon Rd. N15.....4G 49
Spoonbill Way UB4: Yead.....5B 76
Spooner Ho. TW5: Hest.....6E 94
Spooners M. W3.....1K 97
Spooner Wlk. SM6: W'gton.....5J 167
Sporle Rd. Ct. SW11.....3B 118
Sports Academy (LSBU).....3B 102
.....(off London Rd.)
Sportsbank St. SE6.....7E 122
Sports Direct Fitness Croydon.....7A 168
Sports Direct Fitness Epsom.....4K 163
SportsDock.....7F 89
Sportsman Pl. E2.....1G 85
Spottiswood Ct. CR0: C'don.....6C 156
.....(off Harry Cl.)
Spottons Gro. N17.....1C 48
Spout Hill CR0: Addtn.....5C 170
Spout La. TW19: Stanw M.....7A 174
Spout La. Nth. TW19: Stanw M.....7C 174
Spratt Hall Rd. E11.....6J 51
Spray La. TW2: Whitt.....6J 113
Spray St. SE18.....4F 107
Spreighton Rd. KT8: W Mole.....4F 149
Spriggs Ho. N1.....7B 66
.....(off Canonbury Rd.)
Sprimont Pl. SW3.....5E 16 (5D 100)
Springall St. SE15.....7H 103
Springalls Wharf SE16.....2G 103
.....(off Bermondsey Wall W.)
Spring Apts. CR0: C'don.....2D 168
.....(off Addiscombe Gro.)
Spring Apts. E14.....2D 104
.....(off Stebondale St.)
Springbank N21.....6E 22
Springbank Rd. SE13.....6F 123
Springbank Wlk. NW1.....7H 65
Springbourne Ct. BR3: Beck.....1E 158
Spring Bri. M. W5.....7D 78
Spring Bri. Rd. W5.....7D 78
Spring Cl. EN5: Barn.....5A 20
Spring Cl. RM8: Dag.....1D 72
Springclose La. SM3: Cheam.....6G 165
Spring Cnr. TW13: Felt.....3J 129
Spring Cotts. KT6: Surb.....5D 150
Spring Ct. KT17: Ewe.....7B 164
Spring Ct. NW6.....6H 63
Spring Ct. W7.....7H 77
Spring Ct. Rd. EN2: Enf.....1F 23
Springcroft Av. N2.....4D 46
Springdale M. N16.....4D 66
Springdale Rd. N16.....4D 66
Spring Dr. HA5: Eastc.....6J 39
Springer Ct. E3.....4E 86
.....(off Navigation Rd.)
Springett Ho. SW2.....5A 120
.....(off St Matthews Rd.)
Springfield E5.....1H 67
Springfield SE25.....3G 157
Springfield WD23: B Hea.....1C 26
Springfield Av. N10.....3G 47
Springfield Av. SW20.....3H 153
Springfield Av. TW12: Hamp.....6F 131
Springfield Cl. HA7: Stan.....3F 27
Springfield Cl. N12.....5E 30
Springfield Ct. IG1: Ilf.....5F 71
Springfield Ct. KT1: King T.....3E 150
.....(off Springfield Rd.)
Springfield Ct. NW3.....7C 64
.....(off Eton Av.)
Springfield Ct. SM6: W'gton.....5F 167
Springfield D. SW17.....2B 136
Springfield Dr. IG2: Ilf.....5G 53
Springfield Gdns. BR1: Broml.....4D 160
Springfield Gdns. BR4: W W'ck.....2D 170
Springfield Gdns. E5.....1H 67
Springfield Gdns. HA4: Ruis.....1K 57
Springfield Gdns. IG8: Wfd G.....7F 37
Springfield Gdns. NW9.....5K 43
Springfield Gro. SE7.....6A 106
Springfield Gro. TW16: Sun.....1H 147
Springfield La. NW6.....1K 81
Springfield Mt. NW9.....5A 44
Springfield Pde. M. N13.....4F 33
Springfield Pk......2B 136
Springfield Pl. KT3: N Mald.....4J 151
Springfield Ri. SE26.....3H 139
Springfield Rd. BR1: Broml.....4D 160
Springfield Rd. CR7: Thor H.....1C 156
Springfield Rd. DA16: Well.....3B 126
Springfield Rd. DA7: Bex.....4H 127
Springfield Rd. E15.....3G 87
Springfield Rd. E17.....6B 50
Springfield Rd. E4.....1B 36
Springfield Rd. E6.....7D 70
Springfield Rd. HA1: Harr.....6J 41
Springfield Rd. KT1: King T.....3E 150
Springfield Rd. N11.....5A 32
Springfield Rd. N15.....4G 49
Springfield Rd. NW8.....1A 82
Springfield Rd. SE26.....5H 139
Springfield Rd. SM6: W'gton.....5F 167
Springfield Rd. SW19.....5H 135
Springfield Rd. TW11: Tedd.....5A 132
Springfield Rd. TW15: Ashf.....5B 128
Springfield Rd. TW2: Whitt.....1E 130
Springfield Rd. UB4: Yead.....1A 94
Springfield Rd. W7.....1J 95
Springfields EN5: New Bar.....5E 20
.....(off Somerset Rd.)
Springfield Wlk. BR6: Orp.....1H 173
.....(off Place Farm Av.)
Springfield Wlk. NW6.....1K 81
Spring Gdns. IG8: Wfd G.....7F 37
Spring Gdns. KT8: W Mole.....5F 149
Spring Gdns. N5.....5C 66
Spring Gdns. RM7: Rom.....5J 55
Spring Gdns. SM6: W'gton.....5G 167
Spring Gdns. SW1.....4D 12 (1H 101)
.....(not continuous)
Spring Gdns. Bus. Pk. RM7: Rom.....6J 55
Spring Gro. CR4: Mitc.....1E 154
Spring Gro. SE19.....7F 139
Spring Gro. TW12: Hamp.....1F 149
Spring Gro. W4.....5G 97
Spring Gro. W7.....7J 77
SPRING GROVE.....1J 113
Spring Gro. Cres. TW3: Houn.....1G 113
Spring Gro. Rd. TW10: Rich.....5F 115
Spring Gro. Rd. TW3: Houn.....1F 113
Spring Gro. Rd. TW3: Isle.....1F 113
Spring Gro. Rd. TW7: Isle.....1H 113
SpringHealth Leisure Club Richmond.....4D 114
.....(within Pools on the Pk.)
Spring Hill E5.....7G 49
Spring Hill SE26.....4J 139
Springhill Cl. SE5.....3D 120
Spring Ho. E17.....2E 50
.....(off Fulbourne Rd.)
Spring Ho. WC1.....2J 7 (3A 84)
.....(off Margery St.)
Springhurst Cl. CR0: C'don.....4B 170
Spring Lake HA7: Stan.....4G 27
Spring La. E5.....7H 49
Spring La. N10.....3E 46
Spring La. SE25.....6H 157
Spring M. KT17: Ewe.....7B 164
Spring M. SE11.....5G 19 (5K 101)
Spring M. TW9: Rich.....4E 114
.....(off Rosedale Rd.)
Spring M. W1.....5F 5 (5D 82)
SPRING PARK.....3C 170
Spring Pk. Av. CR0: C'don.....2K 169
Spring Pk. Dr. N4.....1C 66
Springpark Dr. BR3: Beck.....3E 158
Spring Pk. Rd. CR0: C'don.....2K 169
Spring Pas. SW15.....3F 117
Spring Path NW3.....5B 64
Spring Pl. IG11: Bark.....2G 89
Spring Pl. N3.....3J 45
Spring Pl. NW5.....5F 65
Springpond Rd. RM9: Dag.....5E 72
Spring Prom. UB7: W Dray.....2B 92
Springrice Rd. SE13.....6F 123
Spring Rd. TW13: Felt.....3H 129
Springs Cl. TW19: Stanw.....1A 128
Spring Shaw Rd. BR5: St P.....7A 144
Spring St. KT17: Ewe.....7B 164
Spring St. W2.....1A 10 (6B 82)
Spring Ter. TW9: Rich.....5E 114
Spring Tide Cl. SE15.....1H 121
Spring Va. DA7: Bex.....4H 127
Springvale Av. TW8: Bford.....5D 96
Springvale Ter. W14.....3F 99
Spring Villa Pk. HA8: Edg.....7B 28
Spring Villa Rd. HA8: Edg.....7B 28
Spring Wlk. E1.....5G 85
Springwater WC1.....5G 7 (5K 83)
.....(off New North St.)
Springwater Cl. SE18.....1E 124
Spring Way SE5.....1C 120
Springway HA1: Harr.....7H 41
Springwell Av. NW10.....1B 80
Springwell Cl. SW16.....4K 137
Springwell Rd. SW16.....4A 138
Springwell Rd. TW4: Houn.....2B 112
Springwell Rd. TW5: Hest.....2B 112
Springwood Cl. E3.....2C 86

A–Z London 289

Springwood Ct. – Station Cl.

Springwood Ct. CR2: S Croy 4E **168**
.......................(off Birdhurst Rd.)
Springwood Cres. HA8: Edg...............2C **28**
Sproggit Ind. Est. TW19: Stanw 6B **110**
Sprowston M. E7 ....6J **69**
Sprowston Rd. E7 ....5J **69**
Spruce Ct. W5 ....3E **96**
Sprucedale Gdns. CR0: C'don 4K **169**
Spruce Hills Rd. E17 ....2E **50**
Spruce Ho. SE16 ....2K **103**
........................(off Woodland Cres.)
Spruce Pk. BR2: Broml....................4H **159**
Sprules Rd. SE4 ....2A **122**
Spurfield KT8: W Mole 3F **149**
Spurgeon Av. SE19 ....1D **156**
Spurgeon Rd. SE19 ....1D **156**
Spurgeon St. SE1 ....3D **102**
Spurling Rd. RM9: Dag 6F **73**
Spurling Rd. SE22 ....4F **121**
Spurrell Av. DA5: Bexl 4K **145**
Spur Rd. BR6: Orp 2K **173**
Spur Rd. HA8: Edg 4K **27**
Spur Rd. N15 ....4D **48**
Spur Rd. SE1 ....6J **13** (2A **102**)
Spur Rd. SW1 ....7A **12** (2G **101**)
Spur Rd. TW14: Felt 4K **111**
Spur Rd. TW7: Isle 7B **96**
Spurstowe Rd. E8 ....6H **67**
Spurstowe Ter. E8 ....5G **67**
Spurway Pde. IG2: Ilf 5D **52**
..........................(off Woodford Av.)
Square, The E10 ....3E **68**
Square, The IG1: Ilf 7E **52**
Square, The IG8: Wfd G 5D **36**
Square, The RM8: Dag 1E **72**
Square, The SM5: Cars 5E **166**
Square, The TW9: Rich 5D **114**
Square, The UB11: Stock P 1F **93**
Square, The UB2: S'hall 4A **94**
Square, The UB7: Lford 4C **174**
Square, The W6 ....5E **98**
Square of Fame 4G **61**
................................(off Arena Sq.)
Square Rigger Row SW11 ....3A **118**
Squarey St. SW17 ....3A **136**
Squire Gdns. NW8 ....2A **4** (3B **82**)
..........................(off Grove End Rd.)
Squires, The RM7: Rom 6J **55**
Squire's Bri. Rd. TW17: Shep 4B **146**
Squires Ct. SW19 ....4J **135**
Squires Ct. SW4 ....1J **119**
Squires La. N3 ....2K **45**
Squires Mt. NW3 ....3B **64**
Squire's Rd. TW17: Shep 4C **146**
Squires Wlk. TW15: Ashf 7F **129**
..............................(not continuous)
Squires Way DA2: Wilm 4K **145**
Squires Wood Dr. BR7: Chst 7C **142**
Squirrel Cl. TW4: Houn 3A **112**
Squirrel M. W13 ....7K **77**
Squirrels, The HA5: Pinn 3D **40**
Squirrels, The SE13 ....3F **123**
Squirrels Cl. BR6: Orp 1J **173**
Squirrels Cl. N12 ....4F **31**
Squirrels Cl. UB10: Hil 7C **56**
Squirrels Ct. KT4: Wor Pk 2B **164**
..................................(off The Avenue)
Squirrels Drey BR2: Broml 2G **159**
...............................(off Park Hill Rd.)
Squirrels Grn. KT4: Wor Pk 2B **164**
Squirrel's La. IG9: Buck H 3G **37**
Squirrels Trad. Est. UB3: Hayes 3H **93**
Squirries St. E2 ....3G **85**
SSE Arena Wembley, The 4G **61**
SS Robin 7K **87**
Stable Cl. KT2: King T 6F **133**
Stable Cl. UB5: N'olt 2E **76**
Stable Ct. EC1 ....4B **8** (4B **84**)
..........................(off Clerkenwell Rd.)
Stable Ct. SM6: W'gton 3E **166**
Stable La. DA5: Bexl 2H **145**
Stable M. NW5 ....6F **65**
Stable M. SE27 ....5C **138**
Stable M. SE6 ....1G **141**
Stable M. TW1: Twick 1K **131**
Stable Pl. N4 ....2B **66**
Stables, The IG9: Buck H 1F **37**
Stables End BR6: Farnb 3G **173**
Stables Gallery & Arts Cen. 3C **62**
Stables Lodge E8 ....7H **67**
.....................................(off Mare St.)
Stables Mkt., The NW1 ....7F **65**
Stables Row E11 ....5J **51**
Stable St. N1 ....1J **83**
Stable St. SE18 ....5F **107**
Stables Way SE11 ....5J **19** (5A **102**)
Stables Yd. SW18 ....6J **117**
Stable Vs. BR1: Broml 6B **142**
Stable Wlk. E1 ....6G **85**
...........................(off Boulevard Walkway)
Stable Wlk. N2 ....1B **46**
Stable Way W10 ....6E **80**
Stable Yd. SW1 ....6A **12** (2G **101**)
..................................(off Stable Yd. Rd.)
Stable Yd. SW15 ....3E **116**
Stableyard, The SW9 ....2K **119**
Stableyard M. TW11: Tedd 6K **131**
Stable Yd. Rd. SW1 ....6B **12** (2G **101**)
..................................(not continuous)
Staburn Ct. HA8: Edg 2J **43**
Stacey Av. N18 ....4D **34**
Stacey Cl. E10 ....5F **51**
Stacey St. N7 ....3A **66**
Stacey St. WC2 ....1D **12** (6H **83**)
Stack Ho. SW1 ....4H **17** (4E **100**)
....(off Cundy St.)
Stackhouse St. SW3 ....1E **16** (3D **100**)
....................................(off Rysbrack St.)
Stacy Path SE5 ....7E **102**
Staddon Cl. BR3: Beck 4A **158**
Stadium Bus. Cen. HA9: Wemb 3H **61**
Stadium M. N5 ....3A **66**
Stadium Retail Pk. 3G **61**
Stadium Rd. SE18 ....7C **106**
Stadium Rd. E. NW4 ....7D **44**
Stadium St. SW10 ....7A **100**
Stadium Way HA9: Wemb 4F **61**
Staffa Rd. E10 ....1A **68**
Stafford Cl. E17 ....6B **50**
..................................(not continuous)
Stafford Cl. N14 ....5B **22**
Stafford Cl. NW6 ....3J **81**
Stafford Cl. SM3: Cheam 6G **165**
Stafford Ct. DA5: Bexl 7F **127**
Stafford Ct. SW8 ....7J **101**
Stafford Ct. W7 ....6K **77**
....(off Copley Cl.)
Stafford Ct. W8 ....3J **99**
Stafford Cripps Ho. E2 ....3J **85**
....(off Globe Rd.)
Stafford Cripps Ho. SW6 ....6H **99**
..................................(off Clem Attlee Ct.)
Stafford Cross Bus. Pk. CR0: Wadd
....5K **167**
Stafford Gdns. CR0: Wadd 5K **167**
Stafford Ho. SE1 ....5F **103**
.....................................(off Cooper's Rd.)
Stafford Mans. SW1 ....1A **18** (3G **101**)
.....................................(off Stafford Pl.)
Stafford Mans. SW11 ....7D **100**
.....................................(off Albert Bri. Rd.)
Stafford Mans. SW4 ....4J **119**
Stafford Mans. W14 ....3F **99**
.....................................(off Haarlem Rd.)
Stafford Pl. SW1 ....1A **18** (3G **101**)
Stafford Pl. TW10: Rich 7F **115**
Stafford Rd. CR0: Wadd 4A **168**
Stafford Rd. DA14: Sidc 4J **143**
Stafford Rd. E3 ....2B **86**
Stafford Rd. E7 ....7A **70**
Stafford Rd. HA3: Hrw W 7B **26**
Stafford Rd. HA4: Ruis 4H **57**
Stafford Rd. KT3: N Mald 3J **151**
Stafford Rd. NW6 ....3J **81**
Stafford Rd. SM6: W'gton 6G **167**
Staffordshire St. SE15 ....1G **121**
Stafford St. W1 ....4A **12** (1G **101**)
Stafford Ter. W8 ....3J **99**
Staff St. EC1 ....2F **9** (3D **84**)
Stag Cl. HA8: Edg 2H **43**
Stag Ct. KT2: King T 1G **151**
.....................................(off Coombe Rd.)
Stag La. HA8: Edg 2H **43**
Stag La. IG9: Buck H 2E **36**
Stag La. NW9 ....3J **43**
Stag La. SW15 ....3B **134**
STAG LANE 2B **134**
Stags Way TW7: Isle 6K **95**
Stainbank Rd. CR4: Mitc 3F **155**
Stainby Cl. UB7: W Dray 3A **92**
Stainby Rd. N15 ....4F **49**
Staines Av. SM3: Cheam 2F **165**
Staines Rd. IG1: Ilf 5G **71**
Staines Rd. TW14: Bedf 1C **128**
Staines Rd. TW14: Felt 1C **128**
Staines Rd. TW2: Twick 3E **130**
Staines Rd. TW3: Houn 3F **113**
Staines Rd. TW4: Houn 5B **112**
Staines Rd. E. TW16: Sun 7J **129**
Staines Rd. W. TW15: Ashf 6D **128**
Staines Rd. W. TW16: Sun 7G **129**
Staines Wlk. DA14: Sidc 6C **144**
Stainford Cl. TW15: Ashf 5F **129**
Stainforth Rd. E17 ....4C **50**
Stainforth Rd. IG2: Ilf 7H **53**
Staining La. EC2 ....7D **8** (6C **84**)
Stainmore Cl. BR7: Chst 1H **161**
Stainsbury St. E2 ....2J **85**
Stainsby Rd. E14 ....6C **86**
Stainton Rd. EN3: Enf H 1D **24**
Stainton Rd. SE6 ....6F **123**
Staith Ct. E3 ....3E **86**
.....................................(off Bolinder Way)
Stalbridge Flats W1 ....1H **11** (6E **82**)
.....................................(off Lumley St.)
Stalbridge Ho. NW1 ....1A **6** (2G **83**)
.....................................(off Hampstead Rd.)
Stalbridge St. NW1 ....5D **4** (5C **82**)
Stalham St. SE16 ....3H **103**
Stalham Way IG6: Ilf 1F **53**
Stambourne Way BR4: W W'ck 2E **170**
Stambourne Way SE19 ....7E **138**
Stambourne Woodland Wlk.
SE19 ....7E **138**
Stamford Bridge 7K **99**
Stamford Bri. Studios SW6 ....7K **99**
.....................................(off Wandon Rd.)
Stamford Brook Arches W6 ....4C **98**
Stamford Brook Av. W6 ....3B **98**
Stamford Brook Gdns. W6 ....3B **98**
Stamford Brook Mans. W6 ....4B **98**
.....................................(off Goldhawk Rd.)
Stamford Brook Rd. W6 ....3B **98**
Stamford Bldgs. SW8 ....7J **101**
.....................................(off Meadow Pl.)
Stamford Cl. HA3: Hrw W 7D **26**
Stamford Cl. N15 ....4G **49**
Stamford Cl. NW3 ....3A **64**
.....................................(off Heath St.)
Stamford Cl. UB1: S'hall 7E **76**
Stamford Cotts. SW10 ....7K **99**
.....................................(off Billing St.)
Stamford Ct. W6 ....4C **98**
Stamford Dr. BR2: Broml 4H **159**
Stamford Gdns. RM9: Dag 7C **72**
Stamford Ga. SW6 ....7K **99**
Stamford Ga. Ho. SW6 ....7K **99**
.....................................(off Stamford Ga.)
Stamford Gro. E. N16 ....1G **67**
Stamford Gro. W. N16 ....1G **67**
Stamford Hill N16 ....2F **67**
STAMFORD HILL 1F **67**
Stamford Lodge N16 ....7F **49**
Stamford Rd. E6 ....1C **88**
Stamford Rd. N1 ....7E **66**
Stamford Rd. N15 ....5G **49**
Stamford Rd. RM9: Dag 1B **90**
Stamford Sq. SW15 ....5G **117**
Stamford St. SE1 ....5J **13** (1A **102**)
Stamp Pl. E2 ....1K **9** (2F **85**)
Stanard Cl. N16 ....7E **48**
Stanborough Cl. TW12: Hamp 6D **130**
Stanborough Ho. E3 ....4D **86**
.....................................(off Empson St.)
Stanborough Pas. E8 ....6F **67**
Stanborough Rd. TW3: Houn 3H **113**
Stanbridge Pl. N21 ....2G **33**
Stanbridge Rd. SW15 ....3E **116**
Stanbrook Rd. SE2 ....2B **108**
Stanbury Ct. NW3 ....6D **64**
Stanbury Rd. SE15 ....1H **121**
..............................(not continuous)
Stancroft NW9 ....5A **44**
Standale Gro. HA4: Ruis 5E **38**
Standard Ind. Est. E16 ....2D **106**
Standard Pl. EC2 ....2H **9** (3E **84**)
.....................................(off Rivington St.)
Standard Rd. DA17: Belv 5G **109**
Standard Rd. DA6: Bex 4E **126**
Standard Rd. NW10 ....4J **79**
Standard Rd. TW4: Houn 3C **112**
Standcumbe Ct. BR3: Beck 5B **158**
Standen Rd. SW18 ....7H **117**
Standfield Gdns. RM10: Dag 6G **73**
Standfield Rd. RM10: Dag 5G **73**
Standish Ho. W6 ....4C **98**
.....................................(off St Peter's Gro.)
Standish Rd. W6 ....4C **98**
Standlake Point SE23 ....3K **139**
Stane Cl. SW19 ....7K **135**
Stane Gro. SW9 ....2J **119**
Stanesgate Ho. SE15 ....7G **103**
.....................................(off Friary Est.)
Stane Way SE18 ....7B **106**
Stanfield Ho. NW8 ....3B **4** (4B **82**)
.....................................(off Frampton St.)
Stanfield Ho. UB5: N'olt 2B **76**
.....................................(off Academy Gdns.)
Stanfield Rd. E3 ....2A **86**
Stanford Cl. HA4: Ruis 6E **38**
Stanford Cl. IG8: Wfd G 5H **37**
Stanford Cl. RM7: Rom 6H **55**
Stanford Cl. TW12: Hamp 6D **130**
Stanford Ct. SW6 ....1K **117**
Stanford Ct. W8 ....3K **99**
.....................................(off Cornwall Gdns.)
Stanford M. E8 ....5G **67**
Stanford Pl. SE17 ....4E **102**
Stanford Rd. N11 ....5J **31**
Stanford Rd. SW16 ....2H **155**
Stanford Rd. W8 ....3K **99**
Stanford St. SW1 ....4C **18** (4H **101**)
Stanford Way SW16 ....2H **155**
Stangate SE1 ....1H **19** (3K **101**)
.....................................(off Royal St.)
Stangate Gdns. HA7: Stan 4G **27**
Stangate Lodge N21 ....6E **22**
Stanger Rd. SE25 ....4G **157**
Stanhill Cotts. DA2: Wilm 7K **145**
Stanhope Av. BR2: Hayes 1H **171**
Stanhope Av. HA3: Hrw W 1H **41**
Stanhope Av. N3 ....3H **45**
Stanhope Cl. SE16 ....2K **103**
Stanhope Gdns. IG1: Ilf 1D **70**
Stanhope Gdns. N4 ....6B **48**
Stanhope Gdns. N6 ....6F **47**
Stanhope Gdns. NW7 ....5G **29**
Stanhope Gdns. RM8: Dag 3F **73**
Stanhope Gdns. SW7 ....3A **16** (4A **100**)
Stanhope Ga. W1 ....4H **11** (1E **100**)
Stanhope Gro. BR3: Beck 5B **158**
Stanhope Ho. N11 ....4A **32**
.....................................(off Coppies Gro.)
Stanhope Ho. SE8 ....7B **104**
.....................................(off Adolphus St.)
Stanhope M. E. SW7 ....3A **16** (4A **100**)
Stanhope M. Sth. SW7 ....4A **100**
Stanhope M. W. SW7 ....4A **100**
Stanhope Pde. NW1 ....1A **6** (3G **83**)
Stanhope Pk. Rd. UB6: G'frd 4G **77**
Stanhope Pl. W2 ....2E **10** (7D **82**)
Stanhope Rd. CR0: C'don 3E **168**
Stanhope Rd. DA15: Sidc 4A **144**
Stanhope Rd. DA7: Bex 2E **126**
Stanhope Rd. E17 ....5D **50**
Stanhope Rd. EN5: Barn 6A **20**
Stanhope Rd. N12 ....5F **31**
Stanhope Rd. N6 ....6G **47**
Stanhope Rd. RM8: Dag 2F **73**
Stanhope Rd. SM5: Cars 7E **166**
Stanhope Rd. UB6: G'frd 5G **77**
Stanhope Row W1 ....5J **11** (1F **101**)
Stanhope St. NW1 ....1A **6** (2G **83**)
Stanhope Ter. TW2: Twick 7K **113**
Stanhope Ter. W2 ....2B **10** (7B **82**)
Stanier Cl. W14 ....5H **99**
Stanier Ho. SW6 ....1A **118**
.....................................(off Station Ct.)
Stanlake M. W12 ....1E **98**
Stanlake Rd. W12 ....1E **98**
Stanlake Vs. W12 ....1E **98**
Stanley Av. BR3: Beck 2E **158**
Stanley Av. HA0: Wemb 7E **60**
Stanley Av. IG11: Bark 2K **89**
Stanley Av. KT3: N Mald 5C **152**
Stanley Av. RM8: Dag 1F **73**
Stanley Av. UB6: G'frd 1G **77**
Stanley Bri. Studios SW6 ....7K **99**
.....................................(off King's Rd.)
Stanley Cl. HA0: Wemb 7E **60**
Stanley Cl. SE9 ....1G **143**
Stanley Cl. SW8 ....6K **101**
Stanley Cohen Ho. EC1 ....4D **8** (4C **84**)
.....................................(off Golden La.)
Stanley Ct. SM2: Sutt 7K **165**
Stanley Ct. SM5: Cars 7E **166**
Stanley Ct. W5 ....5C **78**
Stanley Cres. W11 ....7H **81**
Stanleycroft Cl. TW7: Isle 1J **113**
Stanley Gdns. CR4: Mitc 6E **136**
Stanley Gdns. NW2 ....5E **62**
Stanley Gdns. SM6: W'gton 6G **167**
Stanley Gdns. W11 ....7H **81**
Stanley Gdns. W3 ....2A **98**
Stanley Gdns. M. W11 ....7H **81**
.....................................(off Kensington Pk. Rd.)
Stanley Gdns. Rd. TW11: Tedd 5J **131**
Stanley Gro. CR0: C'don 6A **156**
Stanley Gro. SW8 ....2E **118**
Stanley Holloway Ct. E16 ....6J **87**
.....................................(off Coolfin Rd.)
Stanley Ho. E14 ....6C **86**
.....................................(off Saracen St.)
Stanley Ho. SW10 ....7A **100**
.....................................(off Coleridge Gdns.)
Stanley Mans. SW10 ....7A **16** (6A **100**)
.....................................(off Park Wlk.)
Stanley M. SW10 ....7A **100**
.....................................(off Coleridge Gdns.)
Stanley Pk. Dr. HA0: Wemb 1F **79**
Stanley Pk. Rd. SM5: Cars 7C **166**
Stanley Pk. Rd. SM6: W'gton 7E **166**
Stanley Picker Gallery 3E **150**
.....................................(off Springfield Rd.)
Stanley Rd. BR2: Broml 4K **159**
Stanley Rd. BR6: Orp 1K **173**
Stanley Rd. CR0: C'don 7A **156**
Stanley Rd. CR4: Mitc 7E **136**
Stanley Rd. DA14: Sidc 3A **144**
Stanley Rd. E10 ....6D **50**
Stanley Rd. E12 ....5C **70**
Stanley Rd. E18 ....1H **51**
Stanley Rd. E4 ....1A **36**
Stanley Rd. EN1: Enf 3K **23**
Stanley Rd. HA2: Harr 2G **59**
Stanley Rd. HA6: Nwood 1J **39**
Stanley Rd. HA9: Wemb 6F **61**
Stanley Rd. IG1: Ilf 2H **71**
Stanley Rd. N10 ....7A **32**
Stanley Rd. N11 ....6C **32**
Stanley Rd. N15 ....4B **48**
Stanley Rd. N2 ....3B **46**
Stanley Rd. N9 ....1A **34**
Stanley Rd. NW9 ....7C **44**
Stanley Rd. SM2: Sutt 6K **165**
Stanley Rd. SM4: Mord 4J **153**
Stanley Rd. SM5: Cars 7E **166**
Stanley Rd. SW14 ....4H **115**
Stanley Rd. SW19 ....6J **135**
Stanley Rd. TW11: Tedd 4J **131**
Stanley Rd. TW15: Ashf 5A **128**
Stanley Rd. TW2: Twick 3H **131**
Stanley Rd. TW3: Houn 4G **113**
Stanley Rd. UB1: S'hall 7C **76**
Stanley Rd. W3 ....3J **97**
Stanley Sq. SM5: Cars 7D **166**
Stanley St. SE8 ....7B **104**
Stanley Studios SW10 ....6A **100**
.....................................(off Park Wlk.)
Stanley Ter. DA6: Bex 4G **127**
Stanley Ter. N19 ....2J **65**
Stanliff Ho. E14 ....3C **104**
Stanmer St. SW11 ....1C **118**
STANMORE 5G **27**
Stanmore & Edgware Golf Cen. 3J **27**
Stanmore Common Local Nature
Reserve 2E **26**
Stanmore Country Pk. & Local Nature
Reserve 3H **27**
Stanmore Gdns. SM1: Sutt 3A **166**
Stanmore Gdns. TW9: Rich 3F **115**
Stanmore Golf Course 7G **27**
Stanmore Hill HA7: Stan 3F **27**
Stanmore Lodge HA7: Stan 4G **27**
Stanmore Pl. NW1 ....1F **83**
Stanmore Rd. DA17: Belv 4J **109**
Stanmore Rd. E11 ....1H **69**
Stanmore Rd. N15 ....4B **48**
Stanmore Rd. TW9: Rich 3F **115**
Stanmore St. N1 ....1K **83**
Stanmore Ter. BR3: Beck 2C **158**
Stannard Cotts. E1 ....4J **85**
.....................................(off Fox Cl.)
Stannard Ct. SE6 ....1D **140**
Stannard Ho. SW19 ....4A **136**
Stannard M. E8 ....6G **67**
.....................................(off Stannard Rd.)
Stannard Rd. E8 ....6G **67**
Stannary Pl. SE11 ....6K **19** (5A **102**)
Stannary St. SE11 ....7K **19** (6A **102**)
Stannet Way SM6: W'gton 4G **167**
Stansbury Sq. W10 ....3G **81**
Stansfeld Ho. SE1 ....4F **103**
.....................................(off Longfield Est.)
Stansfeld Rd. E16 ....7C **88**
Stansfeld Rd. E6 ....5B **88**
Stansfield Rd. SW9 ....3K **119**
Stansfield Rd. TW4: Cran 2K **111**
Stansgate Rd. RM10: Dag 2G **73**
Stanstead WC1 ....2F **7** (3J **83**)
.....................................(off Tavistock Pl.)
Stanstead Cl. BR2: Broml 5H **159**
Stanstead Gro. SE6 ....1B **140**
Stanstead Ho. E3 ....4E **86**
.....................................(off Devas St.)
Stanstead Mnr. SM1: Sutt 6J **165**
Stanstead Rd. E11 ....5K **51**
Stanstead Rd. SE23 ....1K **139**
Stanstead Rd. SE6 ....1B **140**
Stansted Cres. DA5: Bexl 1D **144**
Stansted Rd. TW6: H'row A 6B **110**
Stanswood Gdns. SE5 ....7E **102**
Stanthorpe Cl. SW16 ....5J **137**
Stanthorpe Rd. SW16 ....5J **137**
Stanton Av. TW11: Tedd 6J **131**
Stanton Cl. KT19: Ewe 5H **163**
Stanton Cl. KT4: Wor Pk 1F **165**
Stanton Ct. CR2: S Croy 5E **168**
.....................................(off Birdhurst Ri.)
Stanton Ho. SE10 ....6E **104**
.....................................(off Thames St.)
Stanton Ho. SE16 ....2B **104**
.....................................(off Rotherhithe St.)
Stanton Rd. CR0: C'don 7C **156**
Stanton Rd. SE26 ....4B **140**
Stanton Rd. SW13 ....2B **116**
Stanton Rd. SW20 ....1F **153**
Stanton Sq. SE26 ....4B **140**
Stanton Way SE26 ....4B **140**
Stanway Ct. N1 ....1H **9** (2E **84**)
.....................................(off Shenfield St.)
Stanway Gdns. HA8: Edg 5D **28**
Stanway Gdns. W3 ....1G **97**
Stanway St. N1 ....2E **84**
STANWELL 6A **110**
Stanwell Cl. TW19: Stanw 6A **110**
STANWELL MOOR 7B **174**
Stanwell Moor Rd. UB7: Lford 5C **174**
Stanwell Rd. TW14: Bedf 7D **110**
Stanwell Rd. TW15: Ashf 2A **128**
Stanwick Rd. W14 ....4H **99**
Stanworth Ct. TW5: Hest 7D **94**
Stanworth St. SE1 ....7J **15** (3F **103**)
Stanyhurst SE23 ....1A **140**
Stapenhill Rd. HA0: Wemb 3B **60**
Staple Cl. DA5: Bexl 3K **145**
Staplefield Cl. SW2 ....1J **137**
Stapleford N17 ....2E **48**
.....................................(off Willan Rd.)
Stapleford Av. IG2: Ilf 5J **53**
Stapleford Cl. E4 ....3K **35**
Stapleford Cl. KT1: King T 2G **151**
Stapleford Cl. SW19 ....7G **117**
Stapleford Rd. HA0: Wemb 7D **60**
Staplehurst Rd. SE13 ....5F **123**
Staplehurst Rd. SM5: Cars 7C **166**
Staple Inn WC1 ....6J **7** (5A **84**)
.....................................(off Staple Inn Bldgs.)
Staple Inn Bldgs. WC1 ....6J **7** (5A **84**)
Staples Cl. SE16 ....1A **104**
STAPLES CORNER 1D **62**
Staples Cnr. Bus. Pk. NW2 ....1D **62**
Staples Cnr. Retail Pk. 1D **62**
Staples Ho. E6 ....6E **88**
.....................................(off Savage Gdns.)
Staple St. SE1 ....7F **15** (2D **102**)
Stapleton Gdns. CR0: Wadd 5A **168**
Stapleton Hall Rd. N4 ....1K **65**
Stapleton Ho. E2 ....3H **85**
.....................................(off Ellsworth St.)
Stapleton Rd. BR6: Orp 4K **173**
Stapleton Rd. DA7: Bex 7F **109**
Stapleton Rd. SW17 ....3E **136**
Stapleton Vs. N16 ....4E **66**
.....................................(off Wordsworth Rd.)
Stapley Rd. DA17: Belv 5G **109**
Stapylton Rd. EN5: Barn 3B **20**
Star All. EC3 ....2H **15** (7E **84**)
.....................................(off Mark La.)
Star & Garter Hill TW10: Rich 1E **132**
Starboard Way E14 ....3C **104**
Starboard Way E16 ....1A **106**
Starbuck Cl. SE9 ....7E **124**
Star Bus. Cen. RM13: Rain 5K **91**
Starch Ho. La. IG6: Ilf 2H **53**
Star Cl. EN3: Pond E 6D **24**
Starcross St. NW1 ....2B **6** (3G **83**)
Starfield Rd. W12 ....2C **98**
Star Hill DA1: Cray 5K **127**
Star La. E16 ....4G **87**
Starley Cl. E17 ....1F **51**
Starlight Way TW6: H'row A 5E **110**
Starling Cl. CR0: C'don 6A **158**
Starling Cl. HA5: Pinn 3A **40**
Starling Cl. IG9: Buck H 1D **36**
Starling Ho. NW8 ....2C **82**
.....................................(off Charlbert St.)
Starling M. KT5: Surb 6F **151**
Starling Wlk. TW12: Hamp 5C **130**
Starmans Cl. RM9: Dag 1E **90**
Star Path UB5: N'olt 2E **76**
.....................................(off Brabazon Rd.)
Star Pl. E1 ....3K **15** (7F **85**)
Star Rd. TW7: Isle 2H **113**
Star Rd. UB10: Hil 4E **74**
Star Rd. W14 ....6H **99**
Star St. W2 ....7C **4** (6C **82**)
Starts Cl. BR6: Farnb 3E **172**
Starts Hill Av. BR6: Farnb 4F **173**
Starts Hill Rd. BR6: Farnb 3E **172**
Starveall Cl. UB7: W Dray 3B **92**
Star Wharf NW1 ....1G **83**
.....................................(off St Pancras Way)
Star Yd. WC2 ....7J **7** (6A **84**)
State Farm Av. BR6: Farnb 4F **173**
Staten Bldg. E3 ....2C **86**
.....................................(off Fairfield Rd.)
Staten Gdns. TW1: Twick 1K **131**
State Pde. IG6: Ilf 2G **53**
Statham Ct. N19 ....3J **65**
.....................................(off Alexander Rd.)
Statham Gro. N16 ....4D **66**
Statham Gro. N18 ....5K **33**
Statham Ho. SW8 ....1G **119**
.....................................(off Wadhurst Rd.)
Station App. DA7: Bex Barnehurst Rd.
....2J **127**
Station App. BR7: Chst Bennetts Copse
....6C **142**
Station App. SE9 Bercta Rd 2G **143**
Station App. SE9 Crossmead 1D **142**
Station App. SW16 Estreham Rd 6H **137**
Station App. SW16 Gleneagle Rd. 5H **137**
Station App. SE26 Lower
....5B **140**
Station App. HA4: Ruis Mahlon Av.
....5K **57**
Station App. HA4: Ruis Pembroke Rd.
....1G **57**
Station App. DA7: Bex Percy Rd 2E **126**
Station App. BR7: Chst Vale Rd 1E **160**
Station App. BR1: Broml 3J **159**
.....................................(off High St.)
Station App. BR2: Hayes 1J **171**
Station App. BR3: Beck 1C **158**
Station App. BR4: W W'ck 7E **158**
Station App. BR6: Orp 2K **173**
Station App. CR2: Sande 7D **168**
Station App. DA16: Well 2A **126**
Station App. DA5: Bexl 1G **145**
Station App. E11 ....5J **51**
Station App. E17 ....5C **50**
Station App. E18 ....2K **51**
Station App. E4 ....6A **36**
Station App. E7 ....4K **69**
Station App. EN5: New Bar 4F **21**
Station App. HA0: Wemb 6B **60**
Station App. HA1: Harr 7J **41**
Station App. HA5: Pinn 3C **40**
Station App. IG8: Wfd G 6E **36**
Station App. IG9: Buck H 4G **37**
Station App. KT1: King T 1G **151**
Station App. KT19: Ewe 5C **164**
Station App. KT4: Wor Pk 1C **164**
Station App. N11 ....5A **32**
Station App. N12 ....4E **30**
Station App. N16 ....2F **67**
.....................................(off Stamford Hill)
Station App. NW1 ....4F **5** (4D **82**)
Station App. NW10 ....3B **80**
Station App. NW11 ....7F **45**
Station App. SE12 ....6J **123**
.....................................(off Burnt Ash Hill)
Station App. SM2: Cheam 7G **165**
Station App. SM5: Cars 4D **166**
Station App. SW14 ....3J **115**
Station App. SW20 ....2D **152**
Station App. SW6 ....3G **117**
Station App. TW12: Hamp 1E **148**
Station App. TW15: Ashf 4B **128**
Station App. TW16: Sun 1J **147**
Station App. TW17: Shep 5E **146**
Station App. TW8: Bford 6C **96**
.....................................(off Sidney Gdns.)
Station App. TW9: Kew 1G **115**
Station App. UB3: Hayes 3H **93**
Station App. UB6: G'frd 7G **59**
Station App. UB7: Yiew 1A **92**
Station App. W7 ....1J **95**
Station App. Nth. DA15: Sidc 2A **144**
Station App. Rd. SE1 ....7J **13** (2A **102**)
Station App. Rd. W4 ....7J **97**
Station App. Sth. DA15: Sidc 2A **144**
.....................................(off Jubilee Way)
Station App. Southside SE9 ....1D **142**
Station Arc. W1 ....4K **5** (4F **83**)
.....................................(off Gt. Portland St.)
Station Av. KT3: N Mald 3A **152**
Station Av. SW9 ....3B **120**
Station Av. TW9: Kew 1G **115**
Station Bldgs. KT1: King T 2E **150**
.....................................(off Fife Rd.)
Station Chambers E6 ....7C **70**
.....................................(off High St. Nth.)
Station Cl. N12 ....4E **30**

Station Cl. – Strand

Station Cl. N3 1J **45**
Station Cl. TW12: Hamp 1F **149**
Station Cotts. BR6: Orp 2K **173**
Station Ct. N15 5F **49**
Station Ct. SW6 1A **118**
Station Cres. HA0: Wemb 6B **60**
Station Cres. N15 4D **48**
Station Cres. SE3 5J **105**
Stationer's Hall Ct. EC4 1B **14** (6B **84**)
Station Est. BR3: Beck 3K **157**
Station Est. E18 2K **51**
Station Est. Rd. TW14: Felt 1K **129**
Station Garage M. SW16 6H **137**
Station Gdns. W4 7J **97**
Station Gro. HA0: Wemb 6E **60**
Station Hill BR2: Hayes 2J **171**
Station Ho. SE8 7C **104**
(off Deptford High St.)
Station Ho. M. N9 4B **34**
Station M. Ter. SE3 5J **105**
Station Pde. UB5: N'olt Accock Gro 4F **59**
Station Pde. UB5: N'olt Court Farm Rd. 7E **58**
Station Pde. BR1: Broml 1J **159**
(off Tweedy Rd.)
Station Pde. DA15: Sidc 2A **144**
Station Pde. E11 5J **51**
Station Pde. E13 1A **88**
(off Green St.)
Station Pde. E5 3H **67**
(off Up. Clapton Rd.)
Station Pde. E6 7C **70**
Station Pde. EN4: Cockf 4K **21**
Station Pde. HA2: Harr 4F **59**
Station Pde. HA3: Kenton 2A **42**
Station Pde. HA4: Ruis 2F **57**
Station Pde. HA8: Edg 7K **27**
Station Pde. IG11: Bark 7G **71**
Station Pde. IG9: Buck H 4G **37**
Station Pde. N14 1C **32**
Station Pde. NW2 6E **62**
Station Pde. RM9: Dag 6G **73**
Station Pde. SM2: Sutt 6A **166**
(off High St.)
Station Pde. SW12 1E **136**
Station Pde. TW14: Felt 1K **129**
Station Pde. TW15: Ashf 4B **128**
Station Pde. TW9: Kew 1G **115**
Station Pde. W3 6G **79**
Station Pde. W4 7J **97**
Station Pde. W5 1F **97**
Station Pas. E18 2K **51**
Station Pas. E20 6E **68**
Station Pas. SE15 1J **121**
Station Path SW6 Putney Bridge 3H **117**
Station Pl. N4 2A **66**
Station Ri. SE27 2B **138**
Station Rd. BR1: Broml 1J **159**
Station Rd. BR2: Broml 2G **159**
Station Rd. BR4: W W'ck 1E **170**
Station Rd. BR6: Orp 2K **173**
Station Rd. CR0: C'don 1C **168**
Station Rd. DA15: Sidc 2A **144**
Station Rd. DA17: Belv 3G **109**
Station Rd. DA7: Bex 3E **126**
Station Rd. E12 4C **70**
Station Rd. E17 6A **50**
Station Rd. E4 1A **36**
Station Rd. E7 4J **69**
Station Rd. EN5: New Bar 5E **20**
Station Rd. HA1: Harr 4K **41**
Station Rd. HA2: Harr 5F **41**
Station Rd. HA8: Edg 6B **28**
Station Rd. IG1: Ilf 3F **71**
Station Rd. IG6: Ilf 3H **53**
Station Rd. KT1: Hamp W 1C **150**
Station Rd. KT2: King T 1G **151**
Station Rd. KT3: N Mald 5D **152**
Station Rd. KT7: T Ditt 7K **149**
Station Rd. KT9: Chess 5E **162**
Station Rd. N11 5A **32**
Station Rd. N17 3G **49**
Station Rd. N19 3G **65**
Station Rd. N21 1G **33**
Station Rd. N22 2J **47**
(not continuous)
Station Rd. N3 1J **45**
Station Rd. NW10 2B **80**
Station Rd. NW4 6C **44**
Station Rd. NW7 6F **29**
Station Rd. RM6: Chad H 7D **54**
Station Rd. RM6: Dag 7D **54**
Station Rd. SE13 3E **122**
Station Rd. SE20 6J **139**
Station Rd. SE25 4F **157**
Station Rd. SM5: Cars 4D **166**
Station Rd. SW13 2B **116**
Station Rd. SW19 1A **154**
Station Rd. TW1: Twick 1K **131**
Station Rd. TW11: Tedd 6A **132**
Station Rd. TW12: Hamp 1E **148**
Station Rd. TW15: Ashf 4B **128**
Station Rd. TW16: Sun 7J **129**
Station Rd. TW17: Shep 5E **146**
Station Rd. TW3: Houn 4F **113**
Station Rd. UB3: Harl 4G **93**
(not continuous)
Station Rd. UB3: Hayes 4G **93**
(not continuous)
Station Rd. UB7: W Dray 2A **92**
Station Rd. W5 6F **79**
Station Rd. W7 1J **95**
Station Rd. Nth. DA17: Belv 3H **109**
Stationside M. IG3: Ilf 1J **71**
Station Sq. BR5: Pet W 5G **161**
Station St. E15 7F **69**
Station St. E16 1F **107**
Station Ter. NW10 2F **81**
Station Ter. SE5 1C **120**
Station Vw. UB6: G'frd 1H **77**
Station Wlk. IG1: Ilf 2F **71**
(within The Exchange)
Station Wlk. W11 7F **81**
(off Bramley Rd.)
Station Way IG9: Buck H 4F **37**
Station Way SE15 2G **121**
Station Way SE18 3F **107**
Station Way SM3: Cheam 6G **165**
Station Yd. HA4: Ruis 2E **56**
Station Yd. TW1: Twick 7A **114**
Staton Ct. E10 7D **50**
(off Kings Cl.)
Staunton Ho. SE17 4E **102**
(off Wansey St.)
Staunton Rd. KT2: King T 6E **132**
Staunton St. SE8 6B **104**
Stave Hill Ecological Pk. 2A **104**
Staveley NW1 1A **6** (3G **83**)
(off Varndell St.)
Staveley Cl. E9 5J **67**
Staveley Cl. N7 4J **65**
Staveley Cl. SE15 1H **121**
Staveley Ct. E11 5J **51**
Staveley Gdns. W4 1K **115**
Staveley Rd. TW15: Ashf 6F **129**
Staveley Rd. W4 6J **97**
Stavers Ho. E3 2B **86**
(off Tredegar Rd.)
Staverton Pl. BR1: Broml 4D **160**
Staverton Rd. NW2 7E **62**
Stave Yd. Rd. SE16 1A **104**
Stavordale Lodge W14 3H **99**
(off Melbury Rd.)
Stavordale Rd. N5 4B **66**
Stavordale Rd. SM5: Cars 7A **154**
Stayner's Rd. E1 4K **85**
Stayton Rd. SM1: Sutt 3J **165**
Stead Cl. BR7: Chst 5E **142**
Steadfast Rd. KT1: King T 1D **150**
Steadman Ct. EC1 3D **8** (4C **84**)
(off Old St.)
Steadman Ho. RM10: Dag 3G **73**
(off Uvedale Rd.)
Stead St. SE17 4D **102**
Steam Farm La. TW14: Felt 4H **111**
Stean St. E8 1F **85**
Stebbing Ho. W11 1F **99**
(off Queensdale Cres.)
Stebbing Way IG11: Bark 2A **90**
Stebondale St. E14 4E **104**
Stedham Pl. WC1 7E **6** (6J **83**)
(off New Oxford St.)
Stedman Cl. DA5: Bexl 3K **145**
Stedman Cl. UB10: Ick 3C **56**
Steedman St. SE17 4C **102**
Steeds Rd. N10 1D **46**
Steele Ct. TW11: Tedd 7C **132**
Steele Ho. E15 2G **87**
(off Eve Rd.)
Steele Rd. E11 4G **69**
Steele Rd. N17 3E **48**
Steele Rd. NW10 2J **79**
Steele Rd. TW7: Isle 4A **114**
Steele Rd. W4 3J **97**
Steele's M. Nth. NW3 6D **64**
Steele's M. Sth. NW3 6D **64**
Steele's Rd. NW3 6D **64**
Steele's Studios NW3 6D **64**
Steele Wlk. DA8: Erith 7H **109**
Steel's La. E1 6J **85**
Steelyard Pas. EC4 3E **14** (7D **84**)
(off Cousin La.)
Steen Way SE22 5E **120**
Steep Cl. BR6: Chels 6K **173**
Steep Hill CR0: C'don 4E **168**
Steep Hill SW16 3H **137**
Steeple Cl. SW19 5G **135**
Steeple Cl. SW6 2G **117**
Steeple Ct. E1 4H **85**
Steeplestone Cl. N18 5H **33**
Steeple Wlk. N1 1C **84**
(off New Nth. Rd.)
Steerforth St. SW18 2A **136**
Steering Cl. N9 1D **34**
Steers Mead CR4: Mitc 1D **154**
Steers Way SE16 2A **104**
Stelfox Ho. WC1 1H **7** (3K **83**)
(off Penton Ri.)
Stella Cl. UB8: Hil 5D **74**
Stellar Ho. N17 6A **34**
Stella Rd. SW17 6D **136**
Stelling Rd. DA8: Erith 7K **109**
Stellman Cl. E5 3G **67**
Stembridge Rd. SE20 2H **157**
Stephan Cl. E8 1G **85**
Stephen Cl. BR6: Orp 3J **173**
Stephendale Rd. SW6 3K **117**
Stephendale Yd. SW6 3K **117**
(off Stephendale Rd.)
Stephen Fox Ho. W4 5A **98**
(off Chiswick La.)
Stephen Jewers Gdns. IG11: Bark 7K **71**
Stephen M. W1 6C **6** (5H **83**)
Stephen Pl. SW4 3G **119**
Stephen Rd. DA7: Bex 3J **127**
Stephens Ct. E16 4H **87**
Stephens Ct. SE4 3A **122**
Stephens Lodge N12 3F **31**
(off Woodside La.)
Stephenson Cl. DA16: Well 2A **126**
Stephenson Cl. E3 3D **86**
Stephenson Ct. SM2: Cheam 7G **165**
(off Station App.)
Stephenson Ho. SE1 3C **102**
Stephenson Rd. E17 5A **50**
Stephenson Rd. TW2: Whitt 7E **112**
Stephenson Rd. W7 6K **77**
Stephenson St. E16 4G **87**
Stephenson St. NW10 3A **80**
Stephenson Way NW1 3B **6** (4G **83**)
Stephen's Rd. E15 1G **87**
Stephen St. W1 6C **6** (5H **83**)
STEPNEY 5K 85
Stepney C'way. E1 6K **85**
Stepney City Apts. E1 5J **85**
Stepney City Farm 5K **85**
Stepney Cl. CR4: Mitc 1E **154**
Stepney Grn. E1 5J **85**
Stepney Grn. Ct. E1 5K **85**
(off Stepney Grn.)
Stepney High St. E1 5K **85**
Stepney Way E1 5H **85**
Sterling Av. HA8: Edg 4A **28**
Sterling Cl. NW10 7C **62**
Sterling Gdns. SE14 6A **104**
Sterling Ind. Est. RM10: Dag 4H **73**
Sterling Pl. W5 4E **96**
Sterling Rd. DA7: Bex 4H **127**
Sterling Rd. EN2: Enf 1J **23**
Sterling St. SW7 1D **16** (3C **100**)
Sterling Way N18 4J **33**
Sterling Way N7 6K **65**
Stern Cl. IG11: Bark 2C **90**
Stern Ct. E3 3E **86**
(off Culvert Dr.)
Sterndale Rd. W14 3F **99**
Sterne St. W12 2F **99**
Sternhall La. SE15 3G **121**
Sternhold Av. SW2 2H **137**
Sterry Cres. RM10: Dag 5G **73**
Sterry Dr. KT19: Ewe 4A **164**
Sterry Dr. KT7: T Ditt 6J **149**
Sterry Gdns. RM10: Dag 6G **73**
Sterry Rd. IG11: Bark 1K **89**
Sterry Rd. RM10: Dag 4G **73**
Sterry St. SE1 7E **14** (2D **102**)
Steucers La. SE23 1A **140**
Stevannie Ct. DA17: Belv 5F **109**
Steve Biko Ct. W10 4F **81**
(off St John's Ter.)
Steve Biko La. SE6 4C **140**
Steve Biko Lodge E13 2J **87**
(off London Rd.)
Steve Biko Rd. N7 3A **66**
Steve Biko Way TW3: Houn 3E **112**
Stevedale Rd. DA16: Well 2C **126**
Stevedore St. E1 1H **103**
Stevenage Rd. E6 6E **70**
Stevenage Rd. SW6 7F **99**
Stevens Av. E9 6J **67**
Stevens Cl. BR3: Beck 6C **140**
Stevens Cl. DA5: Bexl 4K **145**
Stevens Cl. HA5: Eastc 5A **40**
Stevens Cl. TW12: Hamp 6D **130**
Stevens Grn. WD23: B Hea 1B **26**
Stevens La. KT10: Clay 7A **162**
Stevenson Cl. EN5: New Bar 7G **21**
Stevenson Ct. CR4: Mitc 3C **154**
Stevenson Ct. SE6 2H **141**
Stevenson Cres. SE16 5G **103**
Stevenson Ho. NW8 1A **82**
(off Boundary Rd.)
Stevens Rd. RM8: Dag 2C **72**
Stevens St. SE1 7H **15** (3E **102**)
Steventon Rd. W12 7B **80**
Steward Ho. E3 3C **86**
(off Trevithick Way)
Stewards Holte Wlk. N11 4A **32**
Steward St. E1 6H **9** (5E **84**)
Stewart Av. TW17: Shep 4C **146**
Stewart Cl. BR7: Chst 5F **143**
Stewart Cl. NW9 6J **43**
Stewart Cl. TW12: Hamp 6C **130**
Stewart Ho. KT1: King T 3F **151**
Stewart Quay UB3: Hayes 2G **93**
Stewart Rainbird Ho. E12 5E **70**
(off Parkhurst Rd.)
Stewart Rd. E15 4F **69**
Stewartsby Cl. N18 5H **33**
Stewart's Gro. SW3 5B **16** (5B **100**)
Stewart's Pl. SW2 6K **119**
Stewart's Rd. SW8 7G **101**
Stewart St. E14 2E **104**
Stew La. EC4 2C **14** (7C **84**)
Steyne Horn La. W3 1H **97**
Steyne Ho. W3 1J **97**
(off Narrow St.)
Steyne Rd. W3 1H **97**
Steyning Gro. SE9 4D **142**
Steynings Way N12 5D **30**
Steyning Way TW4: Houn 4A **112**
Steynton Av. DA5: Bexl 2D **144**
Stibbington Ho. NW1 2G **83**
(off Cranleigh St.)
Stickland Rd. DA17: Belv 4G **109**
Stickle Ho. SE8 7D **104**
(off Creative Rd.)
Stickleton Cl. UB6: G'frd 3F **77**
Stifford Ho. E1 5J **85**
(off Stepney Way)
Stilecroft Gdns. HA0: Wemb 3B **60**
Stile Hall Gdns. W4 5G **97**
Stile Hall Mans. W4 5G **97**
(off Wellesley Rd.)
Stile Hall Pde. W4 5G **97**
Stileman Ho. E3 5B **86**
(off Ackroyd Dr.)
Stile Path TW16: Sun 3J **147**
Stiles Cl. BR2: Broml 6D **160**
Stiles Cl. DA8: Erith 5H **109**
Stillingfleet Rd. SW13 6C **98**
Stillington St. SW1 3B **18** (4G **101**)
Stillness Rd. SE23 6A **122**
Still Wlk. SE1 5J **15** (1F **103**)
(off Duchess Wlk.)
Stilwell Dr. UB8: Hil 4B **74**
STILWELL RDBT. 7C **74**
Stipularis Dr. UB4: Yead 4B **76**
Stirling Av. HA5: Pinn 1B **58**
Stirling Av. SM6: W'gton 7J **167**
Stirling Av. TW17: Shep 3G **147**
Stirling Cl. DA14: Sidc 4J **143**
Stirling Cl. SW16 1H **155**
Stirling Ct. EC1 3A **8** (4B **84**)
(off St John St.)
Stirling Ct. W13 7B **78**
Stirling Gro. TW3: Houn 2G **113**
Stirling Rd. E13 2K **87**
Stirling Rd. E17 3A **50**
Stirling Rd. HA3: W'stone 3K **41**
Stirling Rd. N17 1G **49**
Stirling Rd. N22 1B **48**
Stirling Rd. SW9 2J **119**
Stirling Rd. TW2: Whitt 7E **112**
Stirling Rd. TW6: H'row A 6B **110**
Stirling Rd. UB3: Hayes 7K **75**
Stirling Rd. W3 3H **97**
Stirling Rd. Path E17 3A **50**
Stirling Wlk. KT5: Surb 6H **151**
Stirling Way CR0: Bedd 7J **155**
Stiven Cres. HA2: Harr 3D **58**
Stockbeck NW1 1B **6** (2G **83**)
(off Ampthill Est.)
Stockbridge Ho. SW18 4A **118**
(off Eltringham St.)
Stockbury Rd. CR0: C'don 6J **157**
Stockdale Rd. RM8: Dag 2F **73**
Stockdove Way UB6: G'frd 3K **77**
Stocker Gdns. RM9: Dag 7C **72**
Stockfield Rd. SW16 3K **137**
Stockford Av. NW7 7A **30**
Stockholm Apts. NW1 7E **64**
(off Chalk Farm Rd.)
Stockholm Ho. E1 7G **85**
(off Swedenborg Gdns.)
Stockholm Rd. SE16 5J **103**
Stockholm Way E1 1G **103**
Stockhurst Cl. SW15 2E **116**
Stockingswater La. EN3: Brim 2G **25**
Stockland Rd. RM7: Rom 6K **55**
Stockleigh Hall NW8 2C **82**
(off Prince Albert Rd.)
Stockley Cl. UB7: W Dray 2D **92**
Stockley Country Pk. 7C **74**
Stockley Farm Rd. UB7: W Dray 3D **92**
STOCKLEY PARK 1D 92
Stockley Pk. Golf Course 7E **74**
Stockley Rd. UB11: Stock P 7D **74**
Stockley Rd. UB7: W Dray 4D **92**
Stockley Rd. UB8: Hil 6C **74**
Stock Orchard Cres. N7 5K **65**
Stock Orchard St. N7 5K **65**
Stockport Rd. SW16 1H **155**
Stocksfield Rd. E17 3E **50**
Stocks Pl. E14 7B **86**
Stocks Pl. UB10: Hil 1C **74**
Stock St. E13 2J **87**
Stockton Cl. EN5: New Bar 4F **21**
Stockton Ct. SW1 2C **18** (3H **101**)
(off Greycoat St.)
Stockton Gdns. N17 7H **33**
Stockton Gdns. NW7 3F **29**
Stockton Ho. E2 3H **85**
(off Ellsworth St.)
Stockton Ho. HA2: Harr 1E **58**
Stockton Rd. N17 7H **33**
Stockton Rd. N18 6B **34**
STOCKWELL 2K 119
Stockwell Av. SW9 3K **119**
Stockwell Cl. BR1: Broml 2K **159**
Stockwell Cl. HA8: Edg 2J **43**
Stockwell Gdns. SW9 1K **119**
Stockwell Gdns. Est. SW9 2J **119**
Stockwell Grn. SW9 2K **119**
Stockwell Grn. Ct. SW9 2K **119**
Stockwell La. SW9 2K **119**
Stockwell M. SW9 2K **119**
Stockwell Pk. Cres. SW9 2K **119**
Stockwell Pk. Est. SW9 2K **119**
Stockwell Pk. Rd. SW9 1K **119**
Stockwell Pk. Wlk. SW9 3A **120**
Stockwell Rd. SW9 2K **119**
Stockwell St. SE10 6E **104**
Stockwell Ter. SW9 1K **119**
Stodart Rd. SE20 1J **157**
Stoddart Ho. SW8 7H **19** (6K **101**)
Stodmarsh Ho. SW9 1A **120**
(off Cowley Rd.)
Stofield Gdns. SE9 3B **142**
Stoford Cl. SW19 7G **117**
Stokenchurch St. SW6 1K **117**
STOKE NEWINGTON 3F 67
Stoke Newington Chu. St. N16 3D **66**
Stoke Newington Comn. N16 3F **67**
Stoke Newington High St. N16 3F **67**
Stoke Newington Rd. N16 5F **67**
Stoke Pl. NW10 3B **80**
Stoke Rd. KT2: King T 7J **133**
Stokesby Rd. KT9: Chess 6F **163**
Stokes Cotts. IG6: Ilf 1G **53**
Stokes Ct. N2 4C **46**
Stokes Field Local Nature Reserve 2B **162**
Stokesley St. W12 6B **80**
Stokes M. TW11: Tedd 5A **132**
Stokes Rd. CR0: C'don 6K **157**
Stokes Rd. E6 4C **88**
Stokley Ct. N8 4J **47**
Stoll Cl. NW2 3E **62**
Stoms Path SE6 5C **140**
(off Maroons Way)
Stonard Rd. N13 3F **33**
Stonard Rd. RM8: Dag 5B **72**
Stondon Pk. SE23 6A **122**
Stondon Wlk. E6 2B **88**
Stonebanks KT12: Walt T 7J **147**
STONEBRIDGE 1K 79
Stonebridge Cen. N15 5F **49**
Stonebridge Gdns. 1F **85**
(off Arbutus St.)
Stonebridge M. SE19 7D **138**
Stonebridge Pk. NW10 7K **61**
Stonebridge Rd. N15 5F **49**
Stonebridge Way HA9: Wemb 6H **61**
Stone Bldgs. WC2 6H **7** (5K **83**)
(off Chancery La.)
Stonechat M. SW15 4C **116**
Stonechat Sq. E6 5C **88**
Stone Cl. RM8: Dag 2F **73**
Stone Cl. SW4 2G **119**
Stone Cl. UB7: Yiew 1B **92**
Stonecot Cl. SM3: Sutt 1G **165**
Stonecot Hill SM3: Sutt 1G **165**
Stone Cres. TW14: Felt 7H **111**
Stonecroft Rd. DA8: Erith 7J **109**
Stonecroft Way CR0: C'don 7J **155**
Stonecrop Cl. NW9 3K **43**
Stonecutter St. EC4 7A **8** (6B **84**)
Stonefield N4 2K **65**
Stonefield Cl. DA7: Bex 3G **127**
Stonefield Cl. HA4: Ruis 5C **58**
Stonefield Mans. N1 1A **84**
(off Cloudesley St.)
Stonefield St. N1 1A **84**
Stonefield Way HA4: Ruis 4C **58**
Stonefield Way SE7 7B **106**
Stonegrove HA8: Edg 4K **27**
STONEGROVE 4A 28
Stone Gro. Ct. HA8: Edg 5A **28**
Stonegrove Gdns. HA8: Edg 5K **27**
Stone Hall W8 3K **99**
(off Stone Hall Gdns.)
Stonehall Av. IG1: Ilf 6C **52**
Stone Hall Gdns. W8 3K **99**
Stone Hall Pl. W8 3K **99**
Stone Hall Rd. N21 7E **22**
Stoneham Rd. N11 5B **32**
Stonehill Cl. SW14 5K **115**
Stonehill Ct. E4 7J **25**
STONEHILL GREEN 7J 145
Stonehill Grn. DA2: Wilm 7J **145**
Stonehill Rd. SW14 5J **115**
Stonehill Rd. W4 5G **97**
Stonehills Ct. SE21 3E **138**
Stonehill Woods Pk. DA14: Sidc 6H **145**
Stonehorse Rd. EN3: Pond E 5D **24**
Stonehouse NW1 1G **83**
(off Plender St.)
Stonehouse Ho. W2 5J **81**
(off Westbourne Pk. Rd.)
Stone Lake Ind. Pk. SE7 4A **106**
Stone Lake Retail Pk. 4A **106**
STONELEIGH 5C 164
Stoneleigh Av. EN1: Enf 1C **24**
Stoneleigh Av. KT4: Wor Pk 4C **164**
Stoneleigh B'way. KT17: Ewe 5C **164**
Stoneleigh Ct. IG5: Ilf 3C **52**
Stoneleigh Cres. KT19: Ewe 5B **164**
Stoneleigh M. E3 2A **86**
Stoneleigh Pk. Av. CR0: C'don 6K **157**
Stoneleigh Pk. Rd. KT19: Ewe 6B **164**
Stoneleigh Pk. Rd. KT4: Wor Pk 4C **164**
Stoneleigh Pl. W11 7F **81**
Stoneleigh Rd. BR1: Broml 3F **161**
Stoneleigh Rd. IG5: Ilf 3C **52**
Stoneleigh Rd. N17 3F **49**
Stoneleigh Rd. SM5: Cars 7C **154**
Stoneleigh St. W11 7F **81**
Stoneleigh Ter. N19 2F **65**
Stonell's Rd. SW11 6D **118**
Stonemason Ct. SE1 7C **14** (2C **102**)
(off Borough Rd.)
Stonemason Ho. SE14 1K **121**
(off Fishers Ct.)
Stonemasons Cl. N15 4D **48**
Stonemasons Yd. SW18 7B **118**
Stonenest St. N4 1K **65**
Stone Pk. Av. BR3: Beck 4C **158**
Stone Pl. KT4: Wor Pk 2C **164**
Stone Rd. BR2: Broml 5H **159**
Stones End St. SE1 7C **14** (2C **102**)
Stonewall E6 5E **88**
Stoneway Wlk. E3 2K **85**
Stone Well Rd. TW19: Stanw 1A **128**
Stonewold Ct. W5 6D **78**
Stoney All. SE18 2E **124**
Stoneyard La. E14 7D **86**
Stoneycroft Cl. SE12 7H **123**
Stoneycroft Rd. IG8: Wfd G 6H **37**
Stoneydeep TW11: Tedd 4A **132**
Stoneydown E17 4A **50**
Stoneydown Av. E17 4A **50**
Stoneydown Ho. E17 4A **50**
(off Stoneydown)
Stoneyfields Gdns. HA8: Edg 4E **28**
Stoneyfields La. HA8: Edg 5D **28**
Stoney La. E1 7J **9** (6F **85**)
Stoney La. SE19 6F **139**
Stoney St. SE1 4E **14** (1D **102**)
Stonhouse St. SW4 4H **119**
Stonor Rd. W14 4H **99**
Stonycroft Cl. EN3: Enf H 2F **25**
Stopes St. SE15 7F **103**
Stopford Rd. E13 1J **87**
Stopford Rd. SE17 5B **102**
Stopher Ho. SE1 7B **14** (2B **102**)
(off Webber St.)
Storehouse M. E14 7C **86**
Storer Dr. DA16: Well 3B **126**
Store Rd. E16 2E **106**
Storers Quay E14 4F **105**
Store St. E15 5F **69**
Store St. WC1 6C **6** (5H **83**)
Storey Cl. UB10: Ick 3E **56**
Storey Ct. NW8 2A **4** (3B **82**)
(off St John's Wood Rd.)
Storey Ho. E14 7D **86**
(off Cottage St.)
Storey Rd. E17 4B **50**
Storey Rd. N6 6D **46**
Storey's Ga. SW1 7D **12** (2H **101**)
Storey St. E16 1E **106**
Stories M. SE5 2E **120**
Stories Rd. SE5 3E **120**
Stork Rd. E7 6H **69**
Storksmead Rd. HA8: Edg 7F **29**
Stork's Rd. SE16 3G **103**
Stormont Lawn Tennis & Squash Club 5D **46**
Stormont Rd. N6 7D **46**
Stormont Rd. SW11 3E **118**
Stormont Way KT9: Chess 5C **162**
Stormount Dr. UB3: Harl 2E **92**
Storrington WC1 2F **7** (3J **83**)
(off Regent Sq.)
Storrington Rd. CR0: C'don 1F **169**
Storth Oaks Mead BR7: Chst 5D **142**
Story St. N1 7K **65**
Stothard Ho. E1 4J **85**
(off Amiel St.)
Stothard Pl. E1 5H **9** (5E **84**)
Stothard St. E1 4J **85**
Stott Cl. SW18 6B **118**
Stoughton Av. SM3: Cheam 5F **165**
Stoughton Cl. SE11 4H **19** (4K **101**)
Stoughton Cl. SW15 1C **134**
Stour Av. UB2: S'hall 3E **94**
Stourcliffe Cl. W1 7E **4** (6D **82**)
Stourcliffe St. W1 1E **10** (6D **82**)
Stour Cl. BR2: Kes 4A **172**
Stourhead Cl. SW19 7F **117**
Stourhead Gdns. SW20 3C **152**
Stourhead Ho. SW1 5C **18** (5H **101**)
(off Tachbrook St.)
Stour Rd. E3 7C **68**
Stour Rd. RM10: Dag 2G **73**
Stourton Av. TW13: Hanw 4D **130**
Stowage SE8 6C **104**
Stow Cres. E17 7F **35**
Stowe Cres. HA4: Ruis 6D **38**
Stowe Gdns. N9 1A **34**
Stowe Ho. NW11 6A **46**
Stowell Ho. N8 4J **47**
(off Pembroke Rd.)
Stowe Pl. N15 3E **48**
Stowe Rd. W12 2D **98**
Stowting Rd. BR6: Orp 4J **173**
Stox Mead HA3: Hrw W 1H **41**
Stracey Rd. E7 4J **69**
Stracey Rd. NW10 1K **79**
Strachan Pl. SW19 6E **134**
Stradbroke Dr. IG7: Chig 6K **37**
Stradbroke Gro. IG5: Ilf 3C **52**
Stradbroke Gro. IG9: Buck H 1G **37**
Stradbroke Pk. IG7: Chig 6K **37**
Stradbroke Rd. N5 4C **66**
Stradbrook Cl. HA2: Harr 3D **58**
Stradella Rd. SE24 6C **120**
Strafford Av. IG5: Ilf 2E **52**
Strafford Ho. SE8 5B **104**
(off Grove St.)
Strafford Rd. EN5: Barn 3B **20**
Strafford Rd. TW1: Twick 7A **114**
Strafford Rd. TW3: Houn 3D **112**
Strafford Rd. W3 2J **97**
Strafford St. E14 2C **104**
Strahan Rd. E3 3A **86**
Straight, The UB1: S'hall 2B **94**
Straightsmouth SE10 7E **104**
Strait Rd. E6 7C **88**
Strakers Rd. SE15 4H **121**
Strale Ho. N1 1E **84**
(off Whitmore Est.)
Strand WC2 3E **12** (7J **83**)

A–Z London 291

Strand Ct. – Sunnyhurst Cl.

Strand Ct. SE18 5K 107
Strand Dr. TW9: Kew 7H 97
Strand E. Twr. E15 2E 86
Strandfield Cl. SE18 5J 107
Strand Ho. BR2: Broml 6B 160
(off Wells Vw. Dr.)
Strand Ho. SE28 1H 107
Strand La. WC2 2H 13 (7K 83)
STRAND ON THE GREEN 6G 97
Strand on the Grn. W4 6G 97
Strand Pl. N18 4K 33
Strand School App. W4 6G 97
Strang Ho. N1 1C 84
Strangways Ter. W14 3H 99
Stranraer Way N1 7J 65
Stranraer Way TW6: H'row A 6A 110
Strasburg Rd. SW11 1E 118
Strata SE1 4C 102
(off Walworth Rd.)
Strata Ct. KT12: Walt T 7H 147
Strata Rd. DA8: Erith 5J 109
Stratfield Pk. Cl. N21 7G 23
STRATFORD 7F 69
Stratford Av. UB10: Hil 2B 74
Stratford Cen., The 7F 69
Stratford Circus (Performing Arts Cen.) 6F 69
Stratford Cl. IG11: Bark 7A 72
Stratford Cl. RM10: Dag 7J 73
Stratford Ct. KT3: N Mald 4K 151
Stratford Eye E15 6F 69
Stratford Gro. SW15 4F 117
Stratford Ho. Av. BR1: Broml 3C 160
STRATFORD NEW TOWN 6F 69
Stratford Office Village, The E15 7G 69
(off Romford Rd.)
Stratford One E20 6D 68
Stratford Picturehouse London 6F 69
Stratford Pl. E20 6E 68
(within Westfield Shop. Cen.)
Stratford Pl. W1 1J 11 (6F 83)
Stratford Rd. CR7: Thor H 4A 156
Stratford Rd. E13 1H 87
(not continuous)
Stratford Rd. NW4 4F 45
Stratford Rd. TW6: H'row A 6D 110
Stratford Rd. UB2: S'hall 4C 94
Stratford Rd. UB4: Yead 4K 75
Stratford Rd. W8 3J 99
Stratford Studios W8 3J 99
Stratford Vs. NW1 7G 65
Stratford Workshops E15 1F 87
(off Burford Rd.)
Strathan Cl. SW18 6G 117
Strathaven Rd. SE12 6K 123
Strathblaine Rd. SW11 5B 118
Strathbrook Rd. SW16 7K 137
Strathcona Rd. HA9: Wemb 2D 60
Strathdale SW16 5K 137
Strathdon Dr. SW17 3B 136
Strathearn Av. TW2: Whitt 1F 131
Strathearn Av. UB3: Harl 7H 93
Strathearn Ho. W2 2C 10 (7C 82)
(off Strathern Pl.)
Strathearn Pl. W2 1C 10 (6C 82)
Strathearn Rd. SM1: Sutt 5J 165
Strathearn Rd. SW19 5J 135
Stratheden Pde. SE3 7J 105
Stratheden Rd. SE3 1J 123
Strathfield Gdns. IG11: Bark 6H 71
Strathleven Rd. SW2 5J 119
Strathmore Ct. NW8 1C 4 (3C 82)
(off Park Rd.)
Strathmore Gdns. HA8: Edg 2H 43
Strathmore Gdns. N3 1K 45
Strathmore Gdns. W8 1J 99
Strathmore Rd. CR0: C'don 7D 156
Strathmore Rd. SW19 3J 135
Strathmore Rd. TW11: Tedd 4J 131
Strathnairn St. SE1 4G 103
(not continuous)
Strathray Gdns. NW3 6C 64
Strath Ter. SW11 4C 118
Strathville Rd. SW18 2J 135
(not continuous)
Strathyre Av. SW16 3A 156
Stratosphere Twr. E15 7F 69
(off Gt. Eastern Rd.)
Stratton Cl. DA7: Bex 3E 126
Stratton Cl. HA8: Edg 6A 28
Stratton Cl. SW19 2J 153
Stratton Cl. TW3: Houn 1E 112
Stratton Ct. HA5: Hat E 1D 40
(off Devonshire Rd.)
Stratton Ct. N1 7E 66
(off Hertford Rd.)
Strattondale St. E14 3E 104
Stratton Dr. IG11: Bark 5J 71
Stratton Gdns. UB1: S'hall 6D 76
Stratton Rd. DA7: Bex 3E 126
Stratton Rd. SW19 2J 153
Stratton Rd. TW16: Sun 2H 147
Stratton St. W1 4K 11 (1F 101)
Strauss Rd. W4 2K 97
Strawberry Flds. BR6: Farnb 5F 173
Strawberry Hill KT9: Chess 6D 162
Strawberry Hill TW1: Twick 3K 131
STRAWBERRY HILL 3K 131
Strawberry Hill 3K 131
Strawberry Hill Cl. TW1: Twick 3K 131
Strawberry Hill Golf Course 3J 131
Strawberry Hill Rd. TW1: Twick 3K 131
Strawberry La. SM5: Cars 3E 166
Strawberry Ter. N10 1D 46
Strawberry Va. N2 1B 46
Strawberry Va. TW1: Twick 3A 132
(not continuous)
Streakes Fld. Rd. NW2 2C 62
Streamdale SE2 6B 108
Streamdale Rd. W3 2H 97
Stream La. HA8: Edg 5C 28
Streamline Ct. SE22 1G 139
(off Streamline M.)
Streamline M. SE22 1G 139
Streamside Cl. BR2: Broml 4J 159
Streamside Cl. N9 1A 34
Streamway DA17: Belv 6G 109
Streatfeild Av. E6 1D 88
Streatfield Rd. HA3: Kenton 3C 42
STREATHAM 3J 137
Streatham Cl. SW16 2J 137
STREATHAM COMMON 6H 137
Streatham Comn. Nth. SW16 5J 137
Streatham Comn. Sth. SW16 6J 137
Streatham Ct. SW16 3J 137
Streatham Green 4H 137
(off Streatham High Road)
Streatham High Rd. SW16 4J 137
Streatham Hill SW2 2J 137
STREATHAM HILL 2J 137
Streatham Ice & Leisure Cen. SW16 5J 137
STREATHAM PARK 5G 137
Streatham Pl. SW2 7J 119
Streatham Rd. CR4: Mitc 1E 154
Streatham Rd. SW16 7F 137
Streatham St. WC1 7E 6 (6J 83)
Streatham Va. SW16 1G 155
STREATHAM VALE 7G 137
Streathbourne Rd. SW17 2E 136
Streatley Pl. NW3 4A 64
Streatley Rd. NW6 7H 63
Street, The E20 6E 68
(within Westfield Shop. Cen.)
St. Abbs Cl. DA16: Well 1A 126
Streeters La. SM6: Bedd 3H 167
Streetfield M. SE3 3J 123
Streimer Rd. E15 2E 86
Strelley Way W3 7A 80
Stretton Mans. SE8 5C 104
Stretton Rd. CR0: C'don 7E 156
Stretton Rd. TW10: Ham 2C 132
Strickland Ct. SE15 3G 121
Strickland Ho. E2 2K 9 (3F 85)
(off Chambord St.)
Strickland Row SW18 7B 118
Strickland St. SE8 2C 122
Strickland Way BR6: Orp 4K 173
Stride Rd. E13 2H 87
Strimon Cl. N9 2D 34
Stringer Ho. N1 1E 84
(off Whitmore Est.)
Strode Cl. N10 7K 31
Strode Rd. E7 4J 69
Strode Rd. N17 2E 48
Strode Rd. NW10 6C 62
Strode Rd. SW6 7G 99
Strome Ho. NW6 2K 81
(off Carlton Vale)
Stromness Wlk. W3 1J 97
Strone Rd. E12 6B 70
Strone Rd. E7 6A 70
Strone Way UB4: Yead 4C 76
Strongbow Cres. SE9 5D 124
Strongbow Rd. SE9 5D 124
Strongbridge Cl. HA2: Harr 1E 58
Stronsa Rd. W12 2B 98
Strood Av. RM7: Rush G 1K 73
Strood Ho. SE1 7F 15 (2D 102)
(off Staple St.)
Stroud Cres. SW15 3C 134
Stroudes Cl. KT4: Wor Pk 7A 152
Stroud Fld. UB5: N'olt 6C 58
Stroud Ga. HA2: Harr 4F 59
STROUD GREEN 7K 47
Stroud Grn. Gdns. CR0: C'don 7J 157
Stroud Grn. Rd. N4 1K 65
Stroud Grn. Way CR0: C'don 7H 157
Stroudley Ho. SW8 1G 119
Stroudley Wlk. E3 3D 86
Stroud Rd. SE25 6G 157
Stroud Rd. SW19 3J 135
Stroud's Cl. RM6: Chad H 5B 54
Stroud Way TW15: Ashf 6D 128
Strouts Pl. E2 1J 9 (3F 85)
Strudwick Ct. SW4 1J 119
(off Binfield Rd.)
Strutton Ct. SW1 2C 18 (3H 101)
(off Gt. Peter St.)
Strutton Ground SW1 1C 18 (3H 101)
Strype St. E1 6J 9 (5F 85)
Stuart Av. BR2: Hayes 1J 171
Stuart Av. HA2: Harr 3D 58
Stuart Av. NW9 7C 44
Stuart Av. W5 2F 97
Stuart Cl. UB10: Hil 6C 56
Stuart Ct. CR0: C'don 3B 168
(off St John's Rd.)
Stuart Cres. CR0: C'don 3B 170
Stuart Cres. N22 1K 47
Stuart Cres. UB3: Hayes 6E 74
Stuart Evans Cl. DA16: Well 3C 126
Stuart Gro. TW11: Tedd 5J 131
Stuart Ho. E16 1K 105
(off Beaulieu Av.)
Stuart Ho. E9 6K 67
(off Queen Anne Rd.)
Stuart Ho. W14 4G 99
(off Windsor Way)
Stuart Mantle Way DA8: Erith 7K 109
(not continuous)
Stuart Mill Ho. N1 1G 7 (2K 83)
(off Killick St.)
Stuart Pl. CR4: Mitc 1D 154
Stuart Rd. CR7: Thor H 4C 156
Stuart Rd. DA16: Well 1B 126
Stuart Rd. EN4: E Barn 7H 21
Stuart Rd. HA3: W'stone 3K 41
Stuart Rd. IG11: Bark 7K 71
Stuart Rd. NW6 3J 81
Stuart Rd. SE15 4J 121
Stuart Rd. SW19 3J 135
Stuart Rd. TW10: Ham 2B 132
Stuart Rd. W3 1J 97
Stuart Twr. W9 3A 82
(off Maida Vale)
Stubbs Cl. NW9 5J 43
Stubbs Ct. W4 5H 97
(off Chaseley Dr.)
Stubbs Dr. SE16 5H 103
Stubbs Ho. E2 3K 85
(off Bonner St.)
Stubbs Ho. SW1 4D 18 (4H 101)
(off Erasmus St.)
Stubbs M. RM8: Dag 4B 72
(off Marlborough Rd.)
Stubbs Point E13 4J 87
Stubbs Way SW19 1B 154
Stucley Pl. NW1 7F 65
Stucley Rd. TW5: Hest 7G 95
Studd St. N1 1B 84
Studholme Ct. NW3 4J 63
Studholme St. SE15 7H 103
Studio Ct. N15 4E 48
Studio La. W5 1D 96
Studio M. NW4 4E 44
Studio Pl. SW1 7F 11 (2D 100)
(off Kinnerton St.)
Studio Plaza 7J 147
Studios, The SW4 4G 119
(off Crescent La.)
Studios, The W8 1J 99
(off Edge St.)
Studios Rd. TW17: Shep 3B 146
Studland SE17 5D 102
(off Portland St.)
Studland Cl. DA15: Sidc 3K 143
Studland Rd. KT2: King T 6E 132
Studland Rd. SE26 5K 139
Studland Rd. W7 6H 77
Studland St. W6 4D 98
Studley Av. E4 7A 36
Studley Cl. E5 5A 68
Studley Ct. DA14: Sidc 5B 144
Studley Ct. E14 7F 87
(off Jamestown Way)
Studley Dr. IG4: Ilf 6B 52
Studley Est. SW4 1J 119
Studley Grange Rd. W7 2J 95
Studley Rd. E7 6K 69
Studley Rd. RM9: Dag 7D 72
Studley Rd. SW4 1J 119
Stukeley Rd. E7 7K 69
Stukeley St. WC2 7F 7 (6J 83)
Stumps Hill La. BR3: Beck 6C 140
Stunell Ho. SE14 6K 103
(off John Williams Cl.)
Sturdee Ho. E2 1K 9 (2G 85)
(off Horatio St.)
Sturdy Ho. E3 2A 86
(off Gernon Rd.)
Sturdy Rd. SE15 2H 121
Sturge Av. E17 2D 50
Sturgeon Rd. SE17 5C 102
Sturges Fld. BR7: Chst 6H 143
Sturgess Av. NW4 7D 44
Sturge St. SE1 6C 14 (2C 102)
Sturmer Way N7 5K 65
Sturminster NW1 7H 65
(off Agar Gro.)
Sturminster Cl. UB4: Yead 6A 76
Sturminster Ho. SW8 7K 101
(off Dorset Rd.)
Sturrock Cl. N15 4D 48
Sturry St. E14 6D 86
Sturts Apts. N1 1D 84
(off Branch Pl.)
Sturt St. N1 1D 8 (2C 84)
Stutfield St. E1 6G 85
Stuttle Ho. E1 4K 9 (4G 85)
(off Buxton St.)
Styles Gdns. SW9 3B 120
Styles Ho. SE1 5A 14 (1B 102)
(off Hatfields)
Styles Way BR3: Beck 4E 158
Stylus Ho. E1 6J 85
Success Ho. SE1 5F 103
(off Cooper's Rd.)
Succession Wlk. E3 7C 68
Sudbourne Rd. SW2 5J 119
Sudbrooke Rd. SW12 6D 118
Sudbrook Gdns. TW10: Ham 3D 132
Sudbrook La. TW10: Ham 1E 132
Sudbury E6 5E 88
SUDBURY 5B 60
Sudbury Av. HA0: Wemb 3C 60
Sudbury Ct. SW8 1H 119
(off Allen Edwards Dr.)
Sudbury Ct. Dr. HA1: Harr 3K 59
Sudbury Ct. Rd. HA1: Harr 3K 59
Sudbury Cres. BR1: Broml 6J 141
Sudbury Cres. HA0: Wemb 5C 60
Sudbury Cft. HA0: Wemb 4K 59
Sudbury Gdns. CR0: C'don 4E 168
Sudbury Golf Course 7C 60
Sudbury Hgts. Av. UB6: G'frd 5K 59
Sudbury Hill HA1: Harr 2J 59
Sudbury Hill Cl. HA0: Wemb 4K 59
Sudbury Ho. SW18 5K 117
Sudbury Rd. IG11: Bark 5K 71
Sudeley Ct. E17 1B 50
(off Broughton Pl.)
Sudeley St. N1 2B 84
Sudlow Rd. SW18 5J 117
Sudrey St. SE1 7C 14 (2C 102)
Suez Av. UB6: G'frd 2K 77
Suez Rd. EN3: Brim 4F 25
SUFFIELD HATCH 4K 35
Suffield Ho. SE17 5B 102
(off Berryfield Rd.)
Suffield Rd. E4 3J 35
Suffield Rd. N15 5F 49
Suffield Rd. SE20 2J 157
Suffolk Ct. E10 7C 50
Suffolk Ct. IG3: Ilf 6J 53
Suffolk Ct. RM6: Chad H 6C 54
Suffolk Ho. CR0: C'don 2D 168
(off George St.)
Suffolk Ho. SE20 1K 157
(off Croydon Rd.)
Suffolk La. EC4 2E 14 (7D 84)
Suffolk Pk. Rd. E17 4A 50
Suffolk Pl. SE2 5C 108
Suffolk Pl. SW1 4D 12 (1H 101)
Suffolk Rd. DA14: Sidc 6C 144
Suffolk Rd. E13 3J 87
Suffolk Rd. EN3: Pond E 5C 24
Suffolk Rd. HA2: Harr 6D 40
Suffolk Rd. IG11: Bark 7H 71
Suffolk Rd. IG3: Ilf 6J 53
Suffolk Rd. KT4: Wor Pk 2B 164
Suffolk Rd. N15 5D 48
Suffolk Rd. NW10 7A 62
Suffolk Rd. RM10: Dag 5J 73
Suffolk Rd. SE25 4F 157
Suffolk Rd. SW13 7B 98
Suffolk St. E7 4J 69
Suffolk St. SW1 3D 12 (7H 83)
Sugar Bakers Ct. EC3 1H 15 (6E 84)
(off Creechurch La.)
Sugar Ho. E1 1K 15 (6G 85)
(off Leman St.)
Sugar Ho. Island Development E15 2E 86
Sugar Ho. La. E15 2E 86
Sugar La. SE16 2G 103
Sugar Loaf Wlk. E2 3J 85
Sugar Quay EC3 3H 15 (7E 84)
(off Sugar Quay Wlk.)
Sugar Quay Wlk. EC3 3H 15 (7E 84)
Sugden Rd. KT7: T Ditt 1B 162
Sugden Rd. SW11 3E 118
Sugden Way IG11: Bark 2K 89
Sulby Ho. SE4 4A 122
(off Turnham Rd.)
Sulgrave Gdns. W6 2E 98
Sulgrave Rd. W6 3E 98
Sulina Rd. SW2 7J 119
Sulivan Ct. SW6 2J 117
Sulivan Ent. Cen. SW6 3K 117
Sulivan Rd. SW6 3J 117
Sulkin Ho. E2 3K 85
(off Knottisford St.)
Sullivan Av. E16 5B 88
Sullivan Cl. KT8: W Mole 3F 149
Sullivan Cl. SW11 3C 118
Sullivan Cl. UB4: Yead 5A 76
Sullivan Ct. E3 4B 86
(off Eric St.)
Sullivan Ct. N16 7F 49
Sullivan Ct. SW5 4J 99
(off Earls Ct. Rd.)
Sullivan Dr. SE9: Sidc 1H 143
Sullivan Ho. SE11 4H 19 (4K 101)
(off Vauxhall St.)
Sullivan Ho. SW1 7K 17 (6F 101)
(off Churchill Gdns.)
Sullivan Rd. SE11 3K 19 (4A 102)
Sullivan Row BR2: Broml 6B 160
Sullivans Reach KT12: Walt T 7H 147
Sultan Ho. SE1 5G 103
(off St James's Rd.)
Sultan Rd. E11 4K 51
Sultan St. BR3: Beck 2K 157
Sultan St. SE5 7C 102
Sultan Ter. N22 2A 48
Sumatra Rd. NW6 5J 63
Sumburgh Rd. SW12 6E 118
Sumeria Ct. SE16 4J 103
(off Rotherhithe New Rd.)
Summer Av. KT8: E Mos 5J 149
Summerbee Ho. SW18 4A 118
(off Eltringham St.)
Summercourt Rd. E1 6J 85
Summer Crossing KT7: T Ditt 5J 149
Summer Dr. UB7: W Dray 2B 92
Summerene Cl. SW16 7G 137
Summerfield BR1: Broml 1K 159
(off Freelands Rd.)
Summerfield Av. NW6 2G 81
Summerfield La. KT6: Surb 2D 162
Summerfield Rd. W5 4B 78
Summerfields Av. N12 6H 31
Summerfield St. SE12 7H 123
Summer Gdns. KT8: E Mos 5J 149
Summer Gdns. UB10: Ick 2E 56
Summer Gro. BR4: W W'ck 2G 171
Summer Hill BR7: Chst 2E 160
Summerhill Cl. BR6: Orp 3J 173
Summerhill Gro. EN1: Enf 6K 23
Summerhill Rd. N15 4D 48
Summerhill Vs. BR7: Chst 1E 160
(off Susan Wood)
Summerhill Way CR4: Mitc 1E 154
Summerhouse Av. TW5: Hest 1C 112
Summerhouse Dr. DA2: Wilm 4K 145
Summerhouse Dr. DA5: Bexl 4K 145
Summerhouse Dr. DA5: Dart 4K 145
Summerhouse La. HA7: Stan 5E 26
Summerhouse La. UB7: Harm 2E 174
Summerhouse Rd. N16 2E 66
Summerland Gdns. N10 3F 47
Summerland Grange N10 3F 47
Summerlands Av. W3 7J 79
Summerlands Lodge BR6: Farnb 4E 172
Summerlee Av. N2 4D 46
Summerlee Gdns. N2 4D 46
Summerley St. SW18 2K 135
Summer Rd. KT7: T Ditt 5K 149
Summer Rd. KT8: E Mos 5H 149
(not continuous)
Summersby Rd. N6 6F 47
Summers Cl. HA9: Wemb 1H 61
Summers Cl. SM2: Sutt 7J 165
Summerskill Cl. SE15 3H 121
Summerskille Cl. N9 3C 34
Summers La. N12 7G 31
Summers Row N12 6H 31
Summers St. EC1 4J 7 (4A 84)
Summerstown SW17 3A 136
SUMMERSTOWN 3A 136
Summerton Ho. E16 2A 106
(off Starboard Way)
Summerton Way SE28 6D 90
Summer Trees TW16: Sun 1K 147
Summerville Gdns. SM1: Sutt 6H 165
Summerwood Rd. TW7: Isle 5K 113
Summit Av. NW9 5K 43
Summit Bus. Pk. TW16: Sun 7J 129
Summit Cl. HA8: Edg 7B 28
Summit Cl. N14 2B 32
Summit Cl. NW9 4K 43
Summit Ct. NW2 5G 63
Summit Dr. IG8: Wfd G 2B 52
Summit Est. N16 7G 49
Summit Ho. BR4: W W'ck 2E 170
Summit Rd. E17 4D 50
Summit Rd. UB5: N'olt 7E 58
Summit Way N14 2A 32
Summit Way SE19 7E 138
Sumner Av. SE15 1F 121
Sumner Bldgs. SE1 4C 14 (1C 102)
(off Sumner St.)
Sumner Cl. BR6: Farnb 4G 173
Sumner Ct. SW8 7J 101
Sumner Est. SE15 7F 103
Sumner Gdns. CR0: C'don 1A 168
Sumner Ho. E3 5D 86
(off Watts Gro.)
Sumner Pl. SW7 4B 16 (4B 100)
Sumner Pl. M. SW7 4B 16 (4B 100)
Sumner Rd. CR0: C'don 1A 168
Sumner Rd. HA1: Harr 7G 41
Sumner Rd. SE15 6F 103
Sumner Rd. Sth. CR0: C'don 1A 168
Sumner St. SE1 4B 14 (1B 102)
Sumpter Cl. NW3 6A 64
Sun All. TW9: Rich 4E 114
Sunbeam Cres. W10 4E 80
Sunbeam Rd. NW10 4J 79
Sunbeam Way NW10 4K 79
Sunbird Wlk. HA2: Harr 2F 59
(off Sandpiper Dr.)
SUNBURY 3A 148
Sunbury Av. NW7 5E 28
Sunbury Av. SW14 4K 115
Sunbury Av. Pas. SW14 4A 116
Sunbury Bus. Cen. TW16: Sun 1H 147
Sunbury Cl. KT12: Walt T 6J 147
SUNBURY COMMON 7H 129
Sunbury Ct. EN5: Barn 4B 20
Sunbury Ct. Island TW16: Sun 3B 148
Sunbury Ct. M. TW16: Sun 2B 148
Sunbury Ct. Rd. TW16: Sun 2A 148
Sunbury Cres. TW13: Felt 4H 129
SUNBURY CROSS 7J 129
Sunbury Cross Cen. TW16: Sun 7H 129
Sunbury Embroidery Gallery, The 3K 147
Sunbury Gdns. NW7 5E 28
Sunbury Golf Course 4F 147
Sunbury Ho. E2 2J 9 (3F 85)
(off Swanfield St.)
Sunbury Ho. SE14 6K 103
(off Myers La.)
Sunbury Ho. TW16: Sun 1G 147
(off Brooklands Cl.)
Sunbury La. KT12: Walt T 6J 147
Sunbury La. SW11 1B 118
(not continuous)
Sunbury Leisure Cen. 1H 147
Sunburylock Ait KT12: Walt T 4K 147
Sunbury Pk. Walled Gdn. 3K 147
Sunbury Rd. SM3: Cheam 3F 165
Sunbury Rd. TW13: Felt 3H 129
Sunbury St. SE18 3D 106
Sunbury Way TW13: Hanw 5A 130
Sunbury Workshops E2 2J 9 (3F 85)
(off Swanfield St.)
Sun Ct. E3 4E 86
(off Navigation Rd.)
Sun Ct. EC3 1F 15 (6D 84)
(off Cornhill)
Suncroft Pl. SE26 3J 139
Sundeala Cl. TW16: Sun 7J 129
(off Hanworth Rd.)
Sunderland Ct. SE22 7G 121
Sunderland Ct. TW19: Stanw 6A 110
(off Whitley Cl.)
Sunderland Ho. W2 5J 81
(off Westbourne Pk. Rd.)
Sunderland Mt. SE23 2K 139
Sunderland Point E16 1G 107
Sunderland Rd. SE23 1K 139
Sunderland Rd. W5 3D 96
Sunderland Ter. W2 6K 81
Sunderland Way E12 2B 70
Sundew Av. W12 7C 80
Sundew Cl. W12 7C 80
Sundew Ct. HA0: Wemb 2E 78
(off Elmore Cl.)
Sundial Av. SE25 3F 157
Sundial Ct. EC1 5D 8 (5C 84)
(off Chiswell St.)
Sundorne Rd. SE7 5A 106
Sundown Rd. TW15: Ashf 5E 128
Sundra Wlk. E1 4K 85
SUNDRIDGE 6K 141
Sundridge Av. BR1: Broml 1B 160
Sundridge Av. BR7: Chst 7C 142
Sundridge Av. DA16: Well 2H 125
Sundridge Ho. E9 7K 67
(off Church Cres.)
Sundridge Pde. BR1: Broml 7K 141
SUNDRIDGE PARK 7K 141
Sundridge Pk. Golf Course 6K 141
Sundridge Park Mans. BR1: Broml 6B 142
Sundridge Pl. CR0: C'don 1G 169
Sundridge Rd. CR0: C'don 7F 157
Sunfields Pl. SE3 7K 105
Sunflower Ct. NW2 2H 63
Sunflower Ct. RM13: Rain 2J 91
Sunflower M. HA7: Stan 5E 26
Sungate Cotts. RM5: Col R 1F 55
Sun Ga. Ho. KT3: N Mald 4B 152
Sunguard Ct. SE1 4A 14 (1B 102)
SUN-IN-THE-SANDS 7K 105
Sunken Rd. CR0: C'don 5J 169
Sunkist Way SM6: W'gton 7J 167
Sunland Av. DA6: Bex 4E 126
Sun La. SE3 7K 105
Sunleigh Rd. HA0: Wemb 1E 78
Sunley Gdns. UB6: G'frd 1A 78
Sun Life Trad. Est. TW14: Felt 3J 111
Sunlight Cl. SW19 6A 136
Sunlight M. SW6 2K 117
Sunlight Sq. E2 3H 85
Sunmead Rd. TW16: Sun 3J 147
Sunna Gdns. TW16: Sun 2K 147
Sunniholme Ct. CR2: S Croy 5C 168
(off Warham Rd.)
Sunningdale N14 5C 32
Sunningdale W13 5B 78
(off Hardwick Grn.)
Sunningdale Av. HA4: Ruis 1A 58
Sunningdale Av. IG11: Bark 1H 89
Sunningdale Av. TW13: Hanw 2C 130
Sunningdale Av. W3 7A 80
Sunningdale Cl. E6 3D 88
Sunningdale Cl. HA7: Stan 6F 27
Sunningdale Cl. KT6: Surb 2E 162
Sunningdale Cl. SE16 5H 103
Sunningdale Cl. SE28 6E 90
Sunningdale Gdns. NW9 5J 43
Sunningdale Gdns. W8 3J 99
(off Stratford Rd.)
Sunningdale Lodge HA8: Edg 5A 28
(off Stonegrove)
Sunningdale Rd. BR1: Broml 4C 160
Sunningdale Rd. SM1: Sutt 3H 165
Sunningfields Cres. NW4 2D 44
Sunningfields Rd. NW4 2D 44
Sunninghill Ct. W3 2J 97
Sunninghill Rd. SE13 2D 122
Sunny Bank SE25 3G 157
Sunny Cres. NW10 7J 61
Sunnycroft Rd. SE25 3G 157
Sunnycroft Rd. TW3: Houn 2F 113
Sunnycroft Rd. UB1: S'hall 5E 76
Sunnydale BR6: Farnb 2E 172
Sunnydale Gdns. NW7 6E 28
Sunnydale Rd. SE12 5K 123
Sunnydene Av. E4 5A 36
Sunnydene Av. HA4: Ruis 1J 57
Sunnydene Gdns. HA0: Wemb 6C 60
Sunnydene St. SE26 4A 140
Sunnyfield NW7 4G 29
Sunnyfield Rd. BR7: Chst 3K 161
Sunny Gdns. Pde. NW4 2D 44
Sunny Gdns. Rd. NW4 2D 44
Sunny Hill NW4 3D 44
Sunnyhill Cl. E5 4A 68
Sunnyhill Rd. SW16 4J 137
Sunnyhurst Cl. SM1: Sutt 3J 165

292 A–Z London

Tabernacle Gdns. – Temple St.

Tabernacle Gdns. E2 2J 9 (3F 85)
(off Hackney Rd.)
Tabernacle St. EC2 4F 9 (4D 84)
Tableer Av. SW4 5G 119
Tabley Rd. N7 4J 65
Tabor Ct. SM3: Cheam 6G 165
Tabor Gdns. SM3: Cheam 6H 165
Tabor Gro. SW19 7H 135
Tabor Rd. W6 3D 98
TA Cen. 6B 64
(off College Cres.)
TA Cen. 3G 117
(off Ranelagh Gdns.)
Tachbrook Est. SW1 6D 18 (5H 101)
Tachbrook M. SW1 3A 18 (4G 101)
Tachbrook Rd. TW14: Felt 7H 111
Tachbrook Rd. UB2: S'hall 4B 94
Tachbrook Rd. UB7: W Dray 1A 92
Tachbrook St. SW1 4B 18 (4G 101)
Tack M. SE4 3C 122
Tadema Ho. NW8 4B 4 (4B 82)
(off Penfold St.)
Tadema Rd. SW10 7A 100
Tadlow KT1: King T 3G 151
(off Washington Rd.)
Tadmor Cl. TW16: Sun 4H 147
Tadmor St. W12 1F 99
Tadworth Av. KT3: N Mald 4B 152
Tadworth Ho. SE1 7A 14 (2B 102)
(off Webber St.)
Tadworth Rd. NW2 2C 62
Taeping St. E14 4D 104
Taffeta Ho. E20 6E 68
(off De Coubertin St.)
Taff Ho. KT2: King T 1D 150
(off Henry Macaulay Av.)
Taffrail Ho. E14 5D 104
(off Burrells Wharf Sq.)
Taffy's How CR4: Mitc 3C 154
Taft Way E3 3D 86
Taggs Ho. KT1: King T 2D 150
(off Market Sq.)
Taggs Island TW12: Hamp 2H 149
Tagore Cl. HA3: W'stone 3K 41
Tagwright Ho. N1 1E 8 (3D 84)
(off Westland Pl.)
Tailor Ho. WC1 4E 6 (4J 83)
(off Colonnade)
Tailworth St. E1 6K 9 (5G 85)
(off Chicksand St.)
Tait Ct. E3 1B 86
(off St Stephen's Rd.)
Tait Ct. SW8 1J 119
(off Lansdowne Grn.)
Tait Ho. SE1 5K 13 (1A 102)
(off Greet St.)
Tait Rd. CR0: C'don 7E 156
Tait Rd. Ind. Est. CR0: C'don 7E 156
(off Tait Rd.)
Tait St. E1 6H 85
Taj Apts. E1 5K 9 (5F 85)
(off Brick La.)
Takeley Cl. RM5: Col R 2K 55
Takhar M. SW11 2C 118
Tala Cl. KT6: Surb 3F 163
Talacre Community Sports Cen. 6E 64
Talacre Rd. NW5 6E 64
Talbot Av. N2 3B 46
Talbot Cl. CR4: Mitc 4G 155
Talbot Cl. N15 4F 49
Talbot Ct. EC3 2F 15 (7D 84)
(off Gracechurch St.)
Talbot Ct. NW9 3K 61
Talbot Cres. NW4 5C 44
Talbot Gdns. IG3: Ilf 2A 72
Talbot Gro. Ho. W11 6G 81
(off Lancaster Rd.)
Talbot Ho. E14 6D 86
(off Girauld St.)
Talbot Ho. N7 3A 66
Talbot Ho. SW11 3B 118
(off York Place)
Talbot Pl. SE3 2G 123
Talbot Rd. CR7: Thor H 4D 156
Talbot Rd. E6 2E 88
Talbot Rd. E7 4J 69
Talbot Rd. HA0: Wemb 6D 60
Talbot Rd. HA3: W'stone 2K 41
Talbot Rd. N15 4F 49
Talbot Rd. N22 2G 47
Talbot Rd. N6 6E 46
Talbot Rd. RM9: Dag 6F 73
Talbot Rd. SE22 4E 120
Talbot Rd. SM5: Cars 5E 166
Talbot Rd. TW15: Ashf 5A 128
Talbot Rd. TW2: Twick 1J 131
Talbot Rd. TW7: Isle 4A 114
Talbot Rd. UB2: S'hall 4C 94
Talbot Rd. W11 6H 81
(not continuous)
Talbot Rd. W13 1A 96
Talbot Rd. W2 6J 81
Talbot Sq. W2 1B 10 (6B 82)
Talbot Wlk. NW10 Church End 6A 62
Talbot Wlk. W11 Notting Hill 6G 81
(off St Mark's Rd.)
Talbot Yd. SE1 5E 14 (1D 102)
Talcott Path SW2 1A 138
Talehangers Cl. DA6: Bex 4D 126
Talfourd Pl. SE15 1F 121
Talfourd Rd. SE15 1F 121
Talgarth Mans. W14 5G 99
(off Talgarth Rd.)
Talgarth Rd. W14 5F 99
Talgarth Rd. W6 5F 99
Talgarth Wlk. NW9 5A 44
Talia Ho. E14 3E 104
(off Manchester Rd.)
Talina Cen. SW6 1A 118
Talisman Cl. IG3: Ilf 1B 72
Talisman Sq. SE26 4G 139
Talisman Way HA9: Wemb 3F 61
Tallack Cl. HA3: Hrw W 7D 26
Tallack Rd. E10 1B 68
Tall Elms Cl. BR2: Broml 5H 159
Talleyrand Ho. SE5 2C 120
(off Lilford Rd.)
Tallis Cl. E16 6K 87
Tallis Gro. SE7 6K 105
Tallis St. EC4 2K 13 (7A 84)
Tallis Vw. NW10 6K 61
Tallow Cl. RM9: Dag 7D 72
Tallow Rd. TW8: Bford 6C 96
Tall Trees SW16 3K 155
Talma Gdns. TW2: Twick 6J 113
Talmage Cl. SE23 7J 121
Talman Gro. HA7: Stan 6J 27
Talma Rd. SW2 4A 120
Talwin St. E3 3D 86
Tamar Cl. E3 1B 86
Tamar Ho. E14 2E 104
(off Plevna St.)
Tamar Ho. SE11 5K 19 (5A 102)
(off Kennington La.)
Tamarind Ct. SE1 6K 15 (2F 103)
(off Gainsford St.)
Tamarind Ct. W8 3K 99
(off Stone Hall Gdns.)
Tamarind Ho. SE15 7G 103
(off Reddins Rd.)
Tamarind Yd. E1 1G 103
(off Kennet St.)
Tamarisk Sq. W12 7B 80
Tamar Sq. IG8: Wfd G 6E 36
Tamar St. SE7 3C 106
Tamar Way N17 3F 49
Tamesis Gdns. KT4: Wor Pk 2A 164
Tamian Ind. Est. TW4: Houn 4A 112
Tamian Way TW4: Houn 4A 112
Tamworth Av. IG8: Wfd G 6B 36
Tamworth La. CR4: Mitc 2F 155
Tamworth Pk. CR4: Mitc 4F 155
Tamworth Pl. CR0: C'don 2C 168
Tamworth Rd. CR0: C'don 2B 168
Tamworth St. SW6 6J 99
Tancred Rd. N4 6B 48
Tandem Cen. 1B 154
Tandem Ho. E17 5B 50
(off Track St.)
Tandem Way SW19 1B 154
Tandridge Dr. BR6: Orp 1H 173
Tandridge Pl. BR6: Orp 1H 173
Tanfield Av. NW2 4B 62
Tanfield Rd. CR0: C'don 4C 168
Tangerine Ho. SE1 7F 15 (2D 102)
(off Long La.)
Tangier Rd. TW10: Rich 4G 115
Tangleberry Cl. BR1: Broml 4D 160
Tangle Tree Cl. N3 2K 45
Tanglewood Cl. CR0: C'don 3J 169
Tanglewood Cl. HA7: Stan 2D 26
Tanglewood Cl. UB10: Hil 4C 74
Tanglewood Way TW13: Felt 3K 129
Tangley Gro. SW15 6B 116
Tangley Pk. Rd. TW12: Hamp 6D 130
Tanglyn Av. TW17: Shep 5D 146
Tangmere N17 2D 48
(off Willan Rd.)
Tangmere WC1 2G 7 (3K 83)
(off Sidmouth St.)
Tangmere Cres. UB10: Uxb 1A 74
Tangmere Gdns. UB5: N'olt 2A 76
Tangmere Gro. KT2: King T 5D 132
Tangmere Way NW9 2A 44
Tan Ho. E9 5A 68
(off Sadler Pl.)
Tanhouse Fld. NW5 5H 65
(off Torriano Av.)
Tanhurst Ho. SW2 7K 119
(off Redlands Way)
Tanhurst Wlk. SE2 3D 108
(off Alsike Rd.)
Tankerton Ho's. WC1 2F 7 (3J 83)
(off Tankerton St.)
Tankerton Rd. KT6: Surb 2F 163
Tankerton St. WC1 2F 7 (3J 83)
Tankerton Ter. CR0: C'don 6K 155
Tankerville Ct. TW3: Houn 3G 113
Tankerville Rd. SW16 7H 137
Tankridge Rd. NW2 2D 62
Tanner Cl. NW9 2A 44
Tanner Ho. E1 5K 85
(off White Horse La.)
Tanner Ho. SE1 7H 15 (2E 102)
(off Tanner St.)
Tanneries, The E1 4J 85
(off Cephas Av.)
Tanner La. W2 7A 4 (6B 82)
Tanner Point E13 1J 87
(off Pelly Rd.)
Tanners Cl. KT12: Walt T 6K 147
Tanners End La. N18 4K 33
Tanner's Hill SE8 1B 122
Tanners La. IG6: Ilf 3G 53
Tanners M. SE8 1B 122
(off Tanner's Hill)
Tanner St. IG11: Bark 6G 71
Tanner St. SE1 7H 15 (2E 102)
Tanners Yd. E2 2H 85
(off Treadway St.)
Tannery, The SE1 Grange Rd. 3E 102
Tannery, The SE1 Whites Grounds 6H 15 (2E 102)
(off Black Swan Yd.)
Tannery Cl. BR3: Beck 5K 157
Tannery Cl. RM10: Dag 3H 73
Tannery Ho. E1 5G 85
(off Deal St.)
Tannery Sq. SE1 3E 102
(off Tannery Way)
Tannery Way SE1 3F 103
Tannington Ter. N5 3B 66
Tannoy Sq. SE27 4D 138
Tannsfeld Rd. SE26 5K 139
Tansley Cl. N7 5H 65
Tanswell St. SE1 7J 13 (2A 102)
Tansy Cl. E6 6E 88
Tantallon Rd. SW12 1E 136
Tant Av. E16 6H 87
Tantony Gro. RM6: Chad H 3D 54
Tanworth Gdns. HA5: Pinn 2K 39
Tanyard Ho. TW8: Bford 7C 96
(off High St.)
Tan Yd. La. DA5: Bexl 7G 127
Tanza Rd. NW3 4D 64
Tapestry Apts. N1 1H 83
Tapestry Bldg. EC2 6H 9 (5E 84)
(off New St.)
Tapestry Cl. SM2: Sutt 7K 165
Tapley Cl. E14 6E 86
Tapley Ho. SE1 7K 15 (2G 103)
(off Wolseley St.)
Taplow NW3 7B 64
Taplow SE17 5D 102
(off Thurlow St.)
Taplow Ct. CR4: Mitc 4C 154
Taplow Ho. E2 2J 9 (3F 85)
(off Palissy St.)
Taplow Rd. N13 4H 33
Taplow St. N1 1D 8 (2C 84)
Tapper Wlk. N1 1J 83
Tappesfield Rd. SE15 3J 121
Tapping Cl. KT2: King T 7G 133
Tapp St. E1 4H 85
Tapster St. EN5: Barn 3C 20
Tara Arts Cen. 1K 135
Tara Ct. BR3: Beck 2D 158
Tara Ho. E14 4C 104
(off Deptford Ferry Rd.)
Tara M. N8 6J 47
Taransay Wlk. N1 6D 66
Tarbert M. N15 5E 48
Tarbert Rd. SE22 5E 120
Tarbert Wlk. E1 7J 85
Tarbuck Ho. SE10 4G 105
(off Manilla Wlk.)
Target Cl. TW14: Felt 6G 111
Target Ho. W13 1B 96
(off Sherwood Cl.)
TARGET RDBT. 1D 76
Tariff Cres. SE8 4B 104
Tariff Rd. N17 6B 34
Tarleton Ct. N22 2A 48
Tarleton Gdns. SE23 2H 139
Tarling Cl. DA14: Sidc 3B 144
Tarling Cl. RM8: Dag 5C 72
Tarling Rd. E16 6H 87
Tarling Rd. N2 2A 46
Tarling St. E1 6H 85
Tarling St. Est. E1 6J 85
Tarmac Way UB7: Harm 3C 174
Tarnbank EN2: Enf 5D 22
Tarnbrook Ct. SW1 4G 17 (4E 100)
(off Holbein Pl.)
Tarns, The NW1 1A 6 (3G 83)
(off Varndell St.)
Tarn St. SE1 3C 102
Tarnwood Pk. SE9 7D 124
Tarplett Ho. SE14 6K 103
(off John Williams Cl.)
Tarquin Ho. SE26 4G 139
(off High Level Dr.)
Tarragon Cl. SE14 7A 104
Tarragon Ct. IG1: Ilf 2J 71
Tarragon Gro. SE26 6K 139
Tarranbrae NW6 7G 63
Tarrant Ho. E2 3J 85
(off Roman Rd.)
Tarrant Ho. W14 3G 99
(off Russell Rd.)
Tarrant Pl. W1 6E 4 (5D 82)
Tarrington Cl. SW16 3H 137
Tartan Ho. E14 6E 86
(off Dee St.)
Tarver Rd. SE17 5B 102
Tarves Way SE10 Lit. Cottage Pl. 7D 104
Tarves Way SE10 Norman Rd. 7D 104
Taryn Gro. BR1: Broml 3D 160
Tash Pl. N11 5A 32
Tasker Cl. UB3: Harl 7E 92
Tasker Ho. E14 5B 86
(off Wallwood St.)
Tasker Ho. IG11: Bark 2H 89
Tasker Lodge W8 2J 99
(off Campden Hill)
Tasker Rd. NW3 5D 64
Tasman Ct. E14 4D 104
(off Westferry Rd.)
Tasman Ct. TW16: Sun 7G 129
Tasman Ho. E1 1H 103
(off Clegg St.)
Tasmania Ter. N18 6H 33
Tasman Rd. SW9 3J 119
Tasman Wlk. E16 6B 88
Tasso Rd. W6 6G 99
Tasso Yd. W6 6G 99
(off Tasso Rd.)
Tatam Rd. NW10 7K 61
Tatchbury Ho. SW15 6B 116
(off Tunworth Cres.)
Tate Apts. E1 6H 85
(off Sly St.)
Tate Britain 4E 18 (4J 101)
Tate Ho. E2 2K 85
(off Mace St.)
Tate Modern 4B 14 (1B 102)
Tate Rd. E16 1D 106
(not continuous)
Tate Rd. SM1: Sutt 5J 165
Tatham Pl. NW8 2B 82
Tatnell Rd. SE23 6A 122
Tatsfield Ho. SE1 7F 15 (3D 102)
(off Pardoner St.)
Tattersall Cl. SE9 5C 124
Tatton Cl. SM5: W'gton 1E 166
Tatton Cres. N16 7F 49
Tatum St. SE17 4D 102
Tauheed Cl. N4 2C 66
Taunton Av. SW20 2D 152
Taunton Av. TW3: Houn 2G 113
Taunton Cl. DA7: Bex 2K 127
Taunton Cl. SM3: Sutt 1J 165
Taunton Dr. EN2: Enf 3F 23
Taunton Dr. N2 2A 46
Taunton Ho. W2 6A 82
(off Hallfield Est.)
Taunton M. NW1 4E 4 (4D 82)
Taunton Pl. NW1 3E 4 (4D 82)
Taunton Rd. SE12 5G 123
Taunton Rd. UB6: G'frd 1F 77
Taunton Way HA7: Stan 2E 42
Tavern Cl. SM5: Cars 7C 154
Tavern Ct. SE1 3C 102
(off New Kent Rd.)
Taverners Cl. W11 1G 99
Taverners Ct. E3 3A 86
(off Grove Rd.)
Taverner Sq. N5 4C 66
Taverners Way E4 1B 36
Tavern La. SW9 2A 120
Tavern Quay SE16 4A 104
Tavistock Av. E17 3K 49
Tavistock Av. NW7 7A 30
Tavistock Av. UB6: G'frd 2A 78
Tavistock Cl. N16 5E 66
Tavistock Cl. TW18: Staines 7A 128
Tavistock Ct. CR0: C'don 1D 168
(off Tavistock Rd.)
Tavistock Ct. WC1 3D 6 (4H 83)
(off Tavistock Sq.)
Tavistock Ct. WC2 2F 13 (7J 83)
(off Tavistock Street)
Tavistock Cres. CR4: Mitc 4J 155
Tavistock Cres. W11 5H 81
(not continuous)
Tavistock Gdns. IG3: Ilf 4J 71
Tavistock Ga. CR0: C'don 1D 168
Tavistock Gro. CR0: C'don 7D 156
Tavistock Ho. IG8: Wfd G 6K 37
Tavistock Ho. WC1 3D 6 (4H 83)
Tavistock M. N19 3J 65
(off Tavistock Ter.)
Tavistock M. W11 6H 81
Tavistock Pl. N14 6A 22
Tavistock Pl. WC1 3E 6 (4J 83)
Tavistock Rd. BR2: Broml 4H 159
Tavistock Rd. CR0: C'don 1D 168
Tavistock Rd. DA16: Well 1C 126
Tavistock Rd. E15 6H 69
Tavistock Rd. E18 3J 51
Tavistock Rd. E7 4H 69
Tavistock Rd. HA8: Edg 1G 43
Tavistock Rd. N4 6D 48
Tavistock Rd. NW10 2B 80
Tavistock Rd. SM5: Cars 1B 166
Tavistock Rd. UB10: Ick 5F 57
Tavistock Rd. W11 6H 81
(not continuous)
Tavistock Sq. WC1 3D 6 (4H 83)
Tavistock St. WC2 2F 13 (7J 83)
Tavistock Ter. N19 3H 65
Tavistock Twr. SE16 3A 104
Tavistock Wlk. SM5: Cars 1B 166
Tavistock Youth Cen. 2B 80
(off Tavistock Rd.)
Taviton St. WC1 3C 6 (4H 83)
Tavy Bridge SE2 2C 108
Tavy Cl. SE11 5K 19 (5A 102)
(off White Hart St.)
Tawney Rd. SE28 7B 90
Tawny Cl. TW13: Felt 3J 129
Tawny Cl. W13 1B 96
Tawny Way SE16 4K 103
Tayben Av. TW2: Twick 6J 113
Tayberry Ho. E20 6D 68
(off Ravens Wlk.)
Taybridge Rd. SW11 3E 118
Tay Bldgs. SE1 7G 15 (3E 102)
(off Decima St.)
Tayburn Cl. E14 6E 86
Tay Ct. E2 3K 85
(off Meath Cres.)
Tay Ct. SE1 7G 15 (3E 102)
(off Decima St.)
Tayfield Cl. UB10: Ick 3F 57
Tay Ho. E3 2B 86
(off St Stephen's Rd.)
Tayler Ct. NW8 1B 82
Taylor Av. TW9: Kew 2H 115
Taylor Cl. BR6: Orp 4K 173
Taylor Cl. N17 7B 34
Taylor Cl. SE8 6B 104
Taylor Cl. TW12: Hamp H 5G 131
Taylor Cl. TW3: Houn 1G 113
Taylor Ct. SE20 2J 157
(off Elmers End Rd.)
Taylor Ho. E14 7C 86
(off Storehouse M.)
Taylor Pl. E3 2D 86
Taylor Rd. CR4: Mitc 7C 136
Taylor Rd. SM6: W'gton 5F 167
Taylors Bldgs. SE18 4F 107
Taylors Cl. DA14: Sidc 3K 143
Taylors Ct. TW13: Felt 2J 129
Taylors Grn. W3 6A 80
Taylor's La. SE26 4H 139
Taylors La. EN5: Barn 1C 20
Taylors La. NW10 6A 62
Taylors Mead NW7 5H 29
Taylors Yd. E1 4K 9 (4F 85)
(off Brick La.)
Taymount Grange SE23 2J 139
Taymount Ri. SE23 2J 139
Tayport Cl. N1 7J 65
Tayside Ct. SE5 4D 120
Tayside Dr. HA8: Edg 3C 28
Taywood Rd. UB5: N'olt 4D 76
Tazzeta Ho. E20 5E 68
(off Victory Pde.)
Teak Cl. SE16 1A 104
Tealby Ct. N7 6K 65
Teal Cl. E16 5B 88
Teal Ct. E1 3K 15 (7G 85)
(off Star Pl.)
Teal Ct. NW10 6K 61
Teal Ct. SE8 6B 104
(off Taylor Cl.)
Teal Ct. SM6: W'gton 5G 167
Teal Dr. HA6: Nwood 1E 38
Teale St. E2 2G 85
Tealing Dr. KT19: Ewe 4K 163
Teal Pl. SM1: Sutt 5H 165
Teal Rd. IG3: Ilf 1A 72
Teal St. SE10 3H 105
TeamSport Indoor Karting Southwark 3H 103
Teamsport Karting Edmonton 4E 34
Teasel Cl. CR0: C'don 1K 169
Teasel Cres. SE28 1J 107
Teasel Way E15 3G 87
Tea Trade Wharf SE1 6K 15 (2F 103)
(off Shad Thames)
Tea Tree Cl. TW15: Ashf 5E 128
Tebworth Rd. N17 7A 34
Technology Pk., The NW9 3A 44
Teck Cl. TW7: Isle 2A 114
Tedder Cl. HA4: Ruis 5J 57
Tedder Cl. KT9: Chess 5C 162
Tedder Cl. UB10: Uxb 7B 56
Tedder Rd. CR2: Sels 7J 169
TEDDINGTON 5A 132
Teddington Bus. Pk. TW11: Tedd 6K 131
(off Station Rd.)
Teddington Lock TW10: Ham 4B 132
TEDDINGTON LOCK 4B 132
Teddington Pk. TW11: Tedd 5K 131
Teddington Pk. Rd. TW11: Tedd 4K 131
Teddington Pool & Fitness Cen. 5A 132
Teddington Riverside TW11: Tedd 5B 132
Teddington Sports Cen. 6D 132
Ted Hennem Ho. RM10: Dag 3H 73
Ted Roberts Ho. E2 2H 85
(off Parmiter St.)
Tedworth Gdns. SW3 6E 16 (5D 100)
Tedworth Sq. SW3 6E 16 (5D 100)
Tee, The W3 6A 80
Tees Av. UB6: G'frd 2J 77
Tees Ct. W7 6H 77
(off Hanway Rd.)
Teesdale Av. TW7: Isle 1A 114
Teesdale Cl. E2 2G 85
Teesdale Gdns. SE25 2E 156
Teesdale Gdns. TW7: Isle 1A 114
Teesdale Rd. E11 6H 51
Teesdale St. E2 2H 85
Teesdale Yd. E2 2H 85
(off Teesdale St.)
Teeswater Ct. DA18: Erith 3D 108
Teevan Cl. CR0: C'don 7G 157
Teevan Rd. CR0: C'don 1G 169
Tegan Cl. SM2: Sutt 7J 165
Teign M. SE9 2C 142
Teignmouth Cl. HA8: Edg 2F 43
Teignmouth Cl. SW4 4H 119
Teignmouth Gdns. UB6: G'frd 2A 78
Teignmouth Pde. UB6: G'frd 2A 78
Teignmouth Rd. DA16: Well 2C 126
Teignmouth Rd. NW2 5F 63
Telcon Way SE10 4G 105
Telcote Way HA4: Ruis 7A 40
Telegraph Av. NW9 3A 44
Telegraph Av. SE10 4G 105
Telegraph Hill NW3 3K 63
Telegraph M. IG3: Ilf 1A 72
Telegraph Pas. SW2 7J 119
(off New Pk. Rd.)
Telegraph Path BR7: Chst 5F 143
Telegraph Pl. E14 4D 104
Telegraph Rd. SW15 7D 116
Telegraph St. EC2 7E 8 (6D 84)
Telephone Pl. SW6 6H 99
Telfer Cl. W3 2J 97
Telfer Ho. EC1 2C 8 (3C 84)
(off Lever St.)
Telferscot Rd. SW12 1H 137
Telford Av. SW2 1H 137
Telford Cl. E17 7A 50
Telford Cl. SE19 6F 139
Telford Dr. KT12: Walt T 7A 148
Telford Ho. SE1 3C 102
(off Tiverton St.)
Telford Rd. N11 5B 32
Telford Rd. SE9 2H 143
Telford Rd. TW2: Whitt 7E 112
Telford Rd. UB1: S'hall 7F 77
Telford Rd. W10 5G 81
Telfords Yd. E1 7G 85
Telford Ter. SW1 7A 18 (6G 101)
Telford Way UB4: Yead 5C 76
Telford Way W3 5A 80
Telham Rd. E6 2E 88
Tell Gro. SE22 4F 121
Tellson Av. SE18 1B 124
Telscombe Cl. BR6: Orp 2J 173
Temair Ho. SE10 7D 104
(off Tarves Way)
Temeraire Pl. TW8: Bford 5F 97
Temeraire St. SE16 2J 103
Tempelhof Av. NW4 7E 44
Temperley Rd. SW12 7E 118
Templar Ct. NW8 2A 4 (3B 82)
(off St John's Wood Rd.)
Templar Ct. RM7: Mawney 4H 55
Templar Dr. SE28 6D 90
Templar Ho. E15 6F 69
(off Leyton Rd.)
Templar Ho. HA2: Harr 2G 59
Templar Ho. NW2 6H 63
Templar Pl. TW12: Hamp 7E 130
Templars Av. NW11 6H 45
Templars Cres. N3 2J 45
Templars Dr. HA3: Hrw W 6C 26
Templars Ho. E16 7F 89
(off University Way)
Templar St. SE5 2B 120
Temple Av. CR0: C'don 2B 170
Temple Av. EC4 2K 13 (7A 84)
Temple Av. N20 7G 21
Temple Av. RM8: Dag 1G 73
Temple Bar 1J 13 (6A 84)
Temple Bar Gate 1B 14 (6B 84)
(off Paternoster Sq.)
Temple Chambers EC4 2K 13 (7A 84)
(off Temple Av.)
Temple Cl. E11 7G 51
Temple Cl. N3 2H 45
Temple Cl. SE28 3G 107
Templecombe Rd. E9 1J 85
Templecombe Way SM4: Mord 5G 153
Temple Ct. E1 5K 85
(off Rectory Sq.)
Temple Ct. SW8 7J 101
(off Thorncroft St.)
Templecroft TW15: Ashf 6F 129
Temple Dwellings E2 2H 85
(off Temple St.)
TEMPLE FORTUNE 5H 45
Temple Fortune Hill NW11 5J 45
Temple Fortune La. NW11 6H 45
Temple Fortune Pde. NW11 5H 45
Temple Gdns. EC4 2J 13 (7A 84)
(off Middle Temple La.)
Temple Gdns. N21 2G 33
Temple Gdns. NW11 6H 45
Temple Gdns. RM8: Dag 3D 72
Temple Gro. EN2: Enf 2G 23
Temple Gro. NW11 6J 45
Temple Hall Ct. E4 2A 36
Temple La. EC4 1K 13 (6A 84)
Templeman Rd. W7 5K 77
Temple Mead Cl. HA7: Stan 6G 27
Templemead Cl. W3 6A 80
Templemead Ho. E9 4A 68
TEMPLE MILLS 4D 68
Temple Mills La. E10 4D 68
Temple Mills La. E15 5E 68
Temple Mills La. E20 4E 68
Temple Pde. EN5: New Bar 7G 21
(off Netherlands Rd.)
Temple Pk. UB8: Hil 3C 74
Temple Pl. WC2 2H 13 (7K 83)
Temple Rd. CR0: C'don 4D 168
Temple Rd. E6 1C 88
Temple Rd. N8 4K 47
Temple Rd. NW2 4E 62
Temple Rd. TW3: Houn 4F 113
Temple Rd. TW9: Rich 2F 115
Temple Rd. W4 3J 97
Temple Rd. W5 3D 96
Temple Sheen SW14 4J 115
Temple Sheen Rd. SW14 4H 115
Temple St. E2 2H 85

Temple Ter. – Thornfield Pde.

Temple Ter. N22 2A **48**
(off Vincent Rd.)
Templeton Av. E4 4H **35**
Templeton Cl. N15 6D **48**
Templeton Cl. N16 5E **66**
Templeton Cl. SE19 1D **156**
Templeton Ct. EN3: Enf W 1D **24**
Templeton Pl. SW5 4J **99**
Templeton Rd. N15 6D **48**
Temple Way SM1: Sutt 3B **166**
Temple W. M. SE11 3B **102**
Templewood W13 5B **78**
Templewood Av. NW3 3K **63**
Templewood Gdns. NW3 3K **63**
Templewood Point NW2 2H **63**
(off Granville Rd.)
Temple Yd. E2 2H **85**
(off Temple St.)
Tempo Ho. UB5: N'olt 3B **76**
Tempsford Cl. EN2: Enf 4H **23**
Tempsford Ct. HA1: Harr 6K **41**
Tempus Apts. EC1 1A **8** (2B **84**)
(off Goswell Rd.)
Tempus Ct. E18 1J **51**
Tempus Wharf SE16 2G **103**
(off Bermondsey Wall W.)
Temsford Cl. HA2: Harr 2G **41**
Tenbury Cl. E7 5B **70**
Tenbury Ct. SW2 1H **137**
Tenby Av. HA3: Kenton 2B **42**
Tenby Cl. N15 4F **49**
Tenby Cl. RM6: Chad H 6E **54**
Tenby Ct. E17 5A **50**
Tenby Gdns. UB5: N'olt 6E **58**
Tenby Ho. UB3: Harl 3E **92**
Tenby Ho. W2 6A **82**
(off Hallfield Est.)
Tenby Mans. W1 5H **5** (5E **82**)
(off Nottingham St.)
Tenby Rd. DA16: Well 1D **126**
Tenby Rd. E17 5A **50**
Tenby Rd. EN3: Pond E 4D **24**
Tenby Rd. HA8: Edg 1F **43**
Tenby Rd. RM6: Chad H 6E **54**
Tench St. E1 1H **103**
Tenda Rd. SE16 4H **103**
Tendring Way RM6: Chad H 5C **54**
Tenham Av. SW2 1H **137**
Tenison Ct. W1 2A **12** (7G **83**)
Tenison Way SE1 5J **13** (1A **102**)
(off York Rd.)
Tenniel Cl. W2 7A **82**
Tennis Ct. La. KT8: E Mos 3K **149**
Tennison Rd. SE25 4F **157**
Tennis St. SE1 6E **14** (2D **102**)
Tenniswood Rd. EN1: Enf 1K **23**
Tennyson CR0: C'don 1C **168**
Tennyson Av. E11 7J **51**
Tennyson Av. E12 7C **70**
Tennyson Av. KT3: N Mald 5D **152**
Tennyson Av. NW9 3J **43**
Tennyson Av. TW1: Twick 1K **131**
Tennyson Cl. DA16: Well 1J **125**
Tennyson Cl. EN3: Pond E 5E **24**
Tennyson Cl. TW14: Felt 6H **111**
Tennyson Ct. NW1 4E **4** (4D **82**)
(off Dorset Sq.)
Tennyson Ho. DA17: Belv 5F **109**
Tennyson Ho. N8 3J **47**
(off Boyton Cl.)
Tennyson Ho. SE17 5C **102**
(off Browning St.)
Tennyson Mans. SW3 7C **16** (6C **100**)
(off Lordship Pl.)
Tennyson Mans. W14 6H **99**
(off Queen's Club Gdns.)
Tennyson Rd. E10 1D **68**
Tennyson Rd. E15 7G **69**
Tennyson Rd. E17 6B **50**
Tennyson Rd. NW6 1H **81**
Tennyson Rd. NW7 5H **29**
Tennyson Rd. SE20 7K **139**
Tennyson Rd. SW19 6A **136**
Tennyson Rd. TW15: Ashf 5A **128**
Tennyson Rd. TW3: Houn 2G **113**
Tennyson Rd. W7 7K **77**
Tennyson St. SW8 2F **119**
Tenpin Acton **4G 79**
Tenpin Bexleyheath **4F 127**
Tenpin Croydon **2K 167**
Tenpin Feltham **2K 129**
Tenpin Kingston upon Thames
2E 150
(within The Rotunda Cen.)
Tensing Rd. UB2: S'hall 3E **94**
Tentelow La. UB2: S'hall 5E **94**
Tenterden Cl. NW4 3F **45**
Tenterden Cl. SE9 4D **142**
Tenterden Dr. NW4 3F **45**
Tenterden Gdns. CR0: C'don 7G **157**
Tenterden Gdns. NW4 3F **45**
Tenterden Gro. NW4 3F **45**
Tenterden Ho. SE17 5E **102**
(off Surrey Gro.)
Tenterden Rd. CR0: C'don 7G **157**
Tenterden Rd. N17 7A **34**
Tenterden Rd. RM8: Dag 2F **73**
Tenterden St. W1 1K **11** (6F **83**)
Tenter Ground E1 6J **9** (5F **85**)
Tent Peg La. BR5: Pet W 5G **161**
Tent St. E1 4H **85**
Tenzing Ct. E14 5D **86**
(off Hillary M.)
Tequila Wharf E14 6A **86**
Tera 40 UB6: G'frd 7G **59**
Terborch Way SE22 5E **120**
Tercelet Ter. NW3 4A **64**
Teredo St. SE16 3K **103**
Terence Ct. DA17: Belv 6F **109**
(off Nuxley Rd.)
Terence McMillan Stadium **4A 88**
Terence Messenger Twr. E10 2D **68**
(off Alpine Rd.)
Teresa M. E17 4C **50**
Teresa Wlk. N10 5F **47**
Terling Cl. E11 3H **69**
Terling Ho. W10 5E **80**
(off Sutton Way)
Terling Rd. RM8: Dag 2G **73**
Terling Wlk. N1 1C **84**
(off Popham St.)
TERMINAL 4 RDBT. **6E 110**
TERMINAL 5 RDBT. **5C 174**
Terminal Ho. HA7: Stan 5J **27**
Terminus Pl. SW1 2K **17** (3F **101**)
Terrace, The E2 3J **85**
(off Old Ford Rd.)
Terrace, The E4 3B **36**
(off Newgate St.)
Terrace, The EC4 1K **13** (6A **84**)
(off King's Bench Wlk.)
Terrace, The IG8: Wfd G 6D **36**
Terrace, The N3 2H **45**
Terrace, The NW6 1J **81**
Terrace, The SE23 7A **122**
Terrace, The SE8 4B **104**
(off Longshore)
Terrace, The SW13 2A **116**
Terrace Apts. N5 5A **66**
Terrace Gdns. SW13 2B **116**
Terrace La. TW10: Rich 6E **114**
Terrace Rd. E13 2J **87**
Terrace Rd. E9 7J **67**
Terrace Rd. KT12: Walt T 7J **147**
Terraces, The E2 2G **85**
(off Garner St.)
Terraces, The NW8 2B **82**
(off Queen's Ter.)
Terrace Wlk. RM9: Dag 5E **72**
Terrace Wlk. SW11 7D **100**
Terrano Ho. TW9: Kew 7H **97**
Terrapin Rd. SW17 3F **137**
Terretts Pl. N1 7B **66**
(off Upper St.)
Terrick Rd. N22 1J **47**
Terrick St. W12 6D **80**
Terrilands HA5: Pinn 3D **40**
Territorial Ho. SE11 4K **19** (4A **102**)
(off Reedworth St.)
Terront Rd. N15 4C **48**
Terry Spinks Pl. E16 5H **87**
(off Barking Rd.)
Tersha St. TW9: Rich 4F **115**
Tesla Ct. W3 2A **98**
Tessa Sanderson Pl. SW8 3F **119**
(off Daley Thompson Way)
Tessa Sanderson Way UB6: G'frd 5H **59**
Testerton Rd. W11 7F **81**
(off Hurstway Wlk.)
Testerton Wlk. W11 7F **81**
Test Rd. TW10: Rich 7B **116**
Testwood Ct. W7 7J **77**
Tetbury Pl. N1 1B **84**
Tetcott Rd. SW10 7A **100**
(not continuous)
Tetherdown N10 3E **46**
Tetty Way BR1: Broml 2J **159**
Tevatree Ho. SE1 5G **103**
(off Old Kent Rd.)
Teversham La. SW8 1J **119**
Teviot Cl. DA16: Well 1B **126**
Teviot Est. E14 5D **86**
Teviot St. E14 5E **86**
Tewkesbury Av. HA5: Pinn 5C **40**
Tewkesbury Av. SE23 1H **139**
Tewkesbury Cl. EN4: E Barn 4G **21**
Tewkesbury Cl. N15 6D **48**
Tewkesbury Gdns. NW9 3H **43**
Tewkesbury Rd. N15 6D **48**
Tewkesbury Rd. SM5: Cars 1B **166**
Tewkesbury Rd. W13 1A **96**
Tewkesbury Ter. N11 6B **32**
Tewson Rd. SE18 5J **107**
Texryte Ho. N1 1D **84**
(off Southgate Rd.)
Textile Ho. E1 5K **85**
(off Duckett St.)
Teynham Av. EN1: Enf 6J **23**
Teynham Ct. BR3: Beck 3D **158**
Teynham Grn. BR2: Broml 5J **159**
Teynton Ter. N17 1C **48**
Thackeray Av. N17 2G **49**
Thackeray Cl. SW19 7F **135**
Thackeray Cl. TW7: Isle 2A **114**
Thackeray Cl. UB8: Hil 6D **74**
Thackeray Ct. NW6 7A **64**
(off Fairfax Rd.)
Thackeray Ct. SW3 5E **16** (5D **100**)
(off Elystan Pl.)
Thackeray Ct. W14 3G **99**
(off Blythe Rd.)
Thackeray Ct. W5 6F **79**
(off Hanger Va. La.)
Thackeray Dr. RM6: Chad H 7A **54**
Thackeray Ho. WC1 3E **6** (4J **83**)
(off Herbrand St.)
Thackeray Lodge TW14: Bedf 6F **111**
Thackeray M. E8 6G **67**
Thackeray Rd. E6 2B **88**
Thackeray Rd. SW8 2F **119**
Thackeray St. W8 3K **99**
Thackery Ct. EC1 5A **8** (5B **84**)
(off Turnmill St.)
Thackrah Cl. N2 2A **46**
(off Simms Gdns.)
Thakeham Cl. SE26 4H **139**
Thalia Cl. SE10 6F **105**
Thalia Ct. E8 7F **67**
(off Albion Dr.)
Thame Rd. SE16 2K **103**
Thames Av. KT4: Wor Pk 1E **164**
Thames Av. RM9: Dag 4H **91**
Thames Av. RM9: Rain 4H **91**
Thames Av. SW10 1A **118**
Thames Av. UB6: G'frd 2K **77**
Thames Bank SW14 2J **115**
Thamesbank Pl. SE28 6C **90**
Thames Barrier **2B 106**
Thames Barrier Ind. Area SE18 3B **106**
(off Faraday Way)
Thames Barrier Info. Cen. **3B 106**
Thames Barrier Pk. **2A 106**
Thamesbrook SW3 6C **16** (5C **100**)
(off Dovehouse St.)
Thames Circ. E14 4C **104**
Thames Cl. TW12: Hamp 2F **149**
Thames Cotts. KT7: T Ditt 6B **150**
Thames Ct. KT8: W Mole 2F **149**
Thames Ct. NW6 2H **81**
(off Albert Rd.)
Thames Ct. SE15 7F **103**
(off Daniel Gdns.)
Thames Ct. W7 6J **77**
(off Hanway Rd.)
Thames Cres. W4 7A **98**
THAMES DITTON 6A 150
Thames Ditton Youth Cen. **7A 150**
Thames Dr. HA4: Ruis 6E **38**
Thames Exchange Bldg. EC4 3D **14** (7C **84**)
(off Queen St. Pl.)
Thames Eyot TW1: Twick 1A **132**
Thamesfield Ct. TW17: Shep 7E **146**
Thamesfield M. TW17: Shep 7E **146**
Thamesgate Cl. TW10: Ham 4B **132**
Thames Gateway RM13: Rain 5K **91**
Thames Gateway RM13: Wenn 5K **91**
Thames Gateway RM9: Dag 2F **91**
Thames Gateway Pk. RM9: Dag 3F **91**
Thames Haven KT6: Surb 5D **150**
Thames Hgts. SE1 6J **15** (2F **103**)
(off Gainsford St.)
Thameshill Av. RM5: Col R 2J **55**
Thames Ho. EC4 3D **14** (7C **84**)
(off Queen St. Pl.)
Thames Ho. KT1: King T 4D **150**
(off Surbiton Rd.)
Thames Ho. SW1 3E **18** (4J **101**)
(off Millbank)
Thameside KT8: W Mole 3F **149**
Thameside TW11: Tedd 7D **132**
Thameside Ind. Est. E16 2B **106**
Thameside Pl. KT1: Hamp W 1D **150**
Thameside Wlk. SE28 6A **90**
Thames Innovation Cen. DA18: Erith
2F **109**
THAMES LOCK **3A 148**
THAMES LOCK **7D 96**
(off Dock Rd.)
Thamesmead KT12: Walt T 6J **147**
THAMESMEAD 1B 108
THAMESMEAD CENTRAL 1A 108
THAMESMEAD EAST 2F 109
THAMESMEAD NORTH 6D 90
Thames Mdw. KT8: W Mole 2E **148**
Thames Mdw. TW17: Shep 7F **147**
THAMESMEAD SOUTH 2D 108
THAMESMEAD SOUTH WEST 2K 107
THAMESMEAD WEST 3G 107
Thamesmere Dr. SE28 7A **90**
Thamesmere Leisure Cen. **7A 90**
Thames Path SE10 3J **105**
Thames Pl. SW15 3F **117**
Thames Point SW6 2A **118**
Thamespoint TW11: Tedd 7D **132**
Thames Police Mus. **1H 103**
Thames Quay E14 2D **104**
Thames Quay SW10 1A **118**
(off Chelsea Harbour)
Thames Reach KT1: Hamp W 1D **150**
Thames Reach SE28 2J **107**
Thames Reach W6 6E **98**
(off Rainville Rd.)
Thames Rd. E16 1B **106**
Thames Rd. IG11: Bark 3K **89**
Thames Rd. W4 6G **97**
Thames Rd. Ind. Est. E16 1B **106**
Thames Side KT1: King T 1D **150**
Thames Side KT7: T Ditt 6B **150**
Thames St. KT1: King T 2D **150**
Thames St. KT12: Walt T 7H **147**
Thames St. SE10 6D **104**
Thames St. TW12: Hamp 1F **149**
Thames St. TW16: Sun 4J **147**
Thames Tunnel Mills SE16 2J **103**
Thamesvale Cl. TW3: Houn 3E **112**
Thames Vw. IG1: Ilf 2G **71**
(off Axon Pl.)
Thamesview Bus. Cen. RM13: Rain
5K **91**
Thamesview Ho's. KT12: Walt T 6J **147**
Thames Vw. Lodge IG11: Bark 3J **89**
Thames Village W4 1J **115**
Thames Wlk. KT12: Walt T 7J **147**
(off Manor Rd.)
Thames Wlk. SW11 7C **100**
Thames Wharf Studios W6 6E **98**
(off Rainville Rd.)
Thanescroft Gdns. CR0: C'don 3E **168**
Thanet Ct. W3 6G **79**
Thanet Dr. BR2: Kes 3B **172**
Thanet Ho. CR0: C'don 4C **168**
(off Coombe Rd.)
Thanet Ho. WC1 2E **6** (3J **83**)
(off Thanet St.)
Thanet Lodge NW2 6G **63**
(off Mapesbury Rd.)
Thanet Pl. CR0: C'don 4C **168**
Thanet Rd. DA5: Bexl 7G **127**
Thanet St. WC1 2E **6** (3J **83**)
Thanet Wharf SE8 6D **104**
(off Copperas St.)
Thane Vs. N7 3K **65**
Thane Works N7 3K **65**
Thanington Ct. SE9 6J **125**
Thant Cl. E10 3D **68**
Tharp Rd. SM6: W'gton 5H **167**
Thatcham Ct. N20 7F **21**
Thatcham Gdns. N20 7F **21**
Thatcher Cl. UB7: W Dray 2A **92**
Thatchers Way TW7: Isle 5H **113**
Thatches Gro. RM6: Chad H 4E **54**
Thavie's Inn EC4 7K **7** (6A **84**)
Thaxted Ct. N1 1F **9** (2D **84**)
(off Murray Gro.)
Thaxted Ho. RM10: Dag 7H **73**
Thaxted Ho. SE16 4J **103**
(off Abbeyfield Est.)
Thaxted Pl. SW20 7F **135**
Thaxted Rd. IG9: Buck H 1H **37**
Thaxted Rd. SE9 3G **143**
Thaxton Pl. E4 1A **36**
Thaxton Rd. W14 6H **99**
Thayers Farm Rd. BR3: Beck 1A **158**
Thayer St. W1 7H **5** (6E **82**)
Theatre Hackney Wick, The **5C 68**
Theatre Bldg. E3 3C **86**
(off Paton Cl.)
Theatre Pl. SE8 7C **104**
(off Speedwell Ct.)
Theatre-Rites **7A 14 (2B 102)**
(off Blackfriars Rd.)
Theatre Royal Drury Lane
1F 13 (6J 83)
(off Catherine St.)
Theatre Royal Haymarket
3D 12 (7H 83)
(off Haymarket)
Theatre Royal Stratford East **7F 69**
Theatre Sq. E15 6F **69**
Theatre St. SW11 3D **118**
Theatre Vw. Apts. SE1 6A **14** (2B **102**)
(off Short St.)
Theatro Technis **1G 83**
(off Crowndale Rd.)
Theatro Twr. SE8 6C **104**
Theberton St. N1 1A **84**
Theed St. SE1 5J **13** (1A **102**)
Thelbridge Ho. E3 3D **86**
(off Bruce Rd.)
Thelma Gdns. SE3 1B **124**
Thelma Gro. TW11: Tedd 6A **132**
Theobald Cres. HA3: Hrw W 1G **41**
Theobald Rd. CR0: C'don 2B **168**
Theobald Rd. E17 7B **50**
Theobalds Av. N12 4F **31**
Theobalds Ct. N4 3C **66**
Theobald's Rd. WC1 5G **7** (5K **83**)
Theobald St. SE1 3D **102**
Theodora Way HA5: Eastc 3H **39**
Theodor Ct. NW9 2K **43**
Theodore Ct. SE13 6F **123**
Theodore Rd. SE13 6F **123**
Therapia La. CR0: Bedd 7H **155**
Therapia La. CR0: C'don 6J **155**
Therapia Rd. SE22 6J **121**
Theresa Rd. W6 4C **98**
Therfield Ct. N4 2C **66**
Thermopylae Ga. E14 4D **104**
Theseus Wlk. N1 1B **8** (2B **84**)
(off City Gdn. Row)
Thesiger Rd. SE20 7K **139**
Thessaly Ho. SW8 7G **101**
(off Thessaly Rd.)
Thessaly Rd. SW8 7G **101**
(not continuous)
Thesus Ho. E14 6E **86**
(off Blair St.)
Thetford Cl. N13 6G **33**
Thetford Gdns. RM9: Dag 7E **72**
Thetford Ho. SE1 7J **15** (3F **103**)
(off St Saviour's Est.)
Thetford Rd. KT3: N Mald 6K **151**
Thetford Rd. RM9: Dag 7D **72**
Thetford Rd. TW15: Ashf 4A **128**
Thetis Ter. TW9: Kew 6G **97**
Theven St. E1 4J **85**
Theydon Gro. IG8: Wfd G 6F **37**
Theydon Rd. E5 2J **67**
Theydon St. E17 7B **50**
Thicket, The UB7: Yiew 6A **74**
Thicket Cres. SM1: Sutt 4A **166**
Thicket Gro. RM9: Dag 6C **72**
Thicket Gro. SE20 7G **139**
Thicket Rd. SE20 7G **139**
Thicket Rd. SM1: Sutt 4A **166**
Thimble Cres. SM6: W'gton 2E **166**
Third Av. E12 4C **70**
Third Av. E13 3J **87**
Third Av. E17 5C **50**
Third Av. EN1: Enf 5A **24**
Third Av. HA9: Wemb 2D **60**
Third Av. RM10: Dag 1H **91**
Third Av. RM6: Chad H 6C **54**
Third Av. UB3: Hayes 1H **93**
Third Av. W10 3G **81**
Third Av. W3 1B **98**
Third Cl. KT8: W Mole 4G **149**
Third Cross Rd. TW2: Twick 2H **131**
Third Way HA9: Wemb 4H **61**
Thirleby Rd. HA8: Edg 1K **43**
Thirleby Rd. NW7 5B **30**
Thirleby Rd. SW1 2B **18** (3G **101**)
Thirlestane Ct. N10 2E **46**
Thirlmere NW1 1K **5** (3F **83**)
(off Cumberland Mkt.)
Thirlmere Av. UB6: G'frd 3C **78**
Thirlmere Gdns. HA9: Wemb 1C **60**
Thirlmere Ho. N16 4D **66**
(off Howard Rd.)
Thirlmere Ho. TW7: Isle 5K **113**
Thirlmere Ri. BR1: Broml 6H **141**
Thirlmere Rd. DA7: Bex 1J **127**
Thirlmere Rd. N10 1F **47**
Thirlmere Rd. SW16 4H **137**
Thirsk Cl. UB5: N'olt 6E **58**
Thirsk Rd. CR4: Mitc 7E **136**
Thirsk Rd. SE25 4D **156**
Thirsk Rd. SW11 3E **118**
Thirty Casson Sq. SE1 5H **13** (1K **101**)
(off Casson Sq.)
Thirza Ho. E1 6J **85**
(off Devonport St.)
Thistlebrook SE2 3C **108**
Thistlebrook Ind. Est. SE2 3C **108**
Thistle Ct. SE12 2J **141**
Thistlecroft Gdns. HA7: Stan 1D **42**
Thistledene KT7: T Ditt 6J **149**
Thistledene Av. HA2: Harr 3C **58**
Thistlefield Cl. DA5: Bexl 1D **144**
Thistle Gro. SW10 5A **100**
Thistle Ho. E14 6E **86**
(off Dee St.)
Thistlemead BR7: Chst 2F **161**
Thistleton Ho. NW9 3B **44**
Thistlewaite Rd. E5 3H **67**
Thistlewood Cl. N7 2K **65**
Thistleworth Cl. TW7: Isle 7H **95**
Thistleworth Marine TW7: Isle 4B **114**
(off Railshead Rd.)
Thistley Cl. N12 6H **31**
Thistley Ct. SE8 6D **104**
Thomas a Beckett Cl. HA0: Wemb 4K **59**
Thomas Baines Rd. SW11 3B **118**
Thomas Barnardo Way IG6: Ilf 3G **53**
Thomas Burt Ho. E2 3H **85**
(off Canrobert St.)
Thomas Coulter Ho. E16 2K **105**
(off Shipwright Street)
Thomas Ct. IG6: Ilf 4G **53**
Thomas Cribb M. E6 6E **88**
Thomas Darby Ct. W11 6G **81**
(off Lancaster Rd.)
Thomas Dean Rd. SE26 4B **140**
Thomas Dinwiddy Rd. SE12 2K **141**
Thomas Doyle St. SE1 7B **14** (3B **102**)
Thomas Dr. UB8: Uxb 6A **56**
Thomas Earle Ho. W14 4H **99**
(off Warwick La.)
Thomas England Ho. RM7: Rom 6K **55**
(off Waterloo Gdns.)
Thomas Frye Ct. E15 2D **86**
(off High St.)
Thomas Fyre Dr. E3 2C **86**
Thomas Hardy Ho. N22 7E **32**
Thomas Hardy M. SW16 5G **137**
Thomas Hewlett Ho. HA1: Harr 4J **59**
Thomas Hollywood Ho. E2 2J **85**
(off Approach Rd.)
Thomas Ho. SM2: Sutt 7K **165**
Thomas Jacomb Pl. E17 4B **50**
Thomas Joseph Ho. SE4 5K **121**
(off St Norbert Rd.)
Thomas La. SE6 7C **122**
Thomas Lodge E17 5D **50**
Thomas More Highwalk
EC2 6C **8** (5C **84**)
(off Aldersgate St.)
Thomas More Ho. EC2 6C **8** (5C **84**)
(off Aldersgate St.)
Thomas More Ho. HA4: Ruis 1G **57**
Thomas More Sq. E1 7G **85**
Thomas More St. E1 3K **15** (7G **85**)
Thomas More Way N2 3A **46**
Thomas Neal's Cen. 1E **12** (6J **83**)
Thomas Pl. W8 3K **99**
Thomas Rd. E14 6B **86**
Thomas Rd. Ind. Est. E14 5C **86**
(not continuous)
Thomas Spencer Hall of Residence
SE18 4E **106**
(off Grand Depot Rd.)
Thomas St. SE18 4F **107**
Thomas Tallis Sports Cen. **3K 123**
Thomas Twr. E8 6F **67**
(off Dalston Sq.)
Thomas Turner Path CR0: C'don 2C **168**
(off George St.)
Thomas Wall Cl. SM1: Sutt 5K **165**
Thomas Watson Cott. Homes
EN5: Barn 4B **20**
(off Leecroft Rd.)
Thompson Av. TW9: Rich 3G **115**
Thompson Cl. IG1: Ilf 2G **71**
Thompson Cl. SM3: Sutt 1J **165**
Thompson Ho. SE14 6K **103**
(off John Williams Cl.)
Thompson Ho. W10 4G **81**
(off Wornington Rd.)
Thompson Rd. RM9: Dag 3F **73**
Thompson Rd. SE22 6F **121**
Thompson Rd. TW3: Houn 4F **113**
Thompson Rd. UB10: Uxb 7A **56**
Thompson's Av. SE5 7C **102**
Thomson Cres. CR0: C'don 1A **168**
Thomson Ho. E14 6C **86**
(off Saracen St.)
Thomson Ho. SE17 4E **102**
(off Tatum St.)
Thomson Ho. SW1 6D **18** (5H **101**)
(off Bessborough Pl.)
Thomson Ho. UB1: S'hall 7C **76**
(off The Broadway)
Thomson Rd. HA3: W'stone 3J **41**
Thonrey Cl. NW9 3B **44**
Thorburn Ho. SW1 7F **11** (2D **100**)
(off Kinnerton St.)
Thorburn Sq. SE1 4G **103**
Thorburn Way SW19 1B **154**
Thoresby St. N1 1D **8** (3C **84**)
Thorkhill Gdns. KT7: T Ditt 1A **162**
Thorkhill Rd. KT7: T Ditt 1A **162**
Thornaby Gdns. N18 6B **34**
Thornaby Ho. E2 3H **85**
(off Canrobert St.)
Thorn Apts. E3 5C **86**
(off St Paul's Way)
Thorn Av. WD23: B Hea 1B **26**
Thornbill Ho. SE15 7G **103**
(off Bird in Bush Rd.)
Thornbury NW4 4D **44**
(off Prince of Wales Cl.)
Thornbury Av. TW7: Isle 7H **95**
Thornbury Cl. N16 5E **66**
Thornbury Cl. NW7 7A **30**
Thornbury Ct. CR2: S Croy 5D **168**
(off Blunt Rd.)
Thornbury Ct. TW7: Isle 7J **95**
Thornbury Ct. W11 7J **81**
(off Chepstow Vs.)
Thornbury Lodge EN2: Enf 3G **23**
Thornbury Rd. SW2 6J **119**
Thornbury Rd. TW7: Isle 7H **95**
Thornbury Sq. N6 1G **65**
Thornbury Way E17 1B **50**
Thornby Rd. E5 3J **67**
Thorncliffe Rd. SW2 6J **119**
Thorncliffe Rd. UB2: S'hall 5D **94**
Thorn Cl. BR2: Broml 6E **160**
Thorn Cl. UB5: N'olt 3D **76**
Thorncombe Rd. SE22 5E **120**
Thorncroft Rd. SM1: Sutt 5K **165**
Thorncroft St. SW8 7J **101**
Thorndean St. SW18 2A **136**
Thorndene Av. N11 1K **31**
Thorndike Av. UB5: N'olt 1B **76**
Thorndike Cl. SW10 7A **100**
Thorndike Ho. SW1 5C **18** (5H **101**)
(off Vauxhall Bri. Rd.)
Thorndike Rd. N1 6D **66**
Thorndike St. SW1 4C **18** (4H **101**)
Thorndon Cl. BR5: St P 2K **161**
Thorndon Gdns. KT19: Ewe 5A **164**
Thorndon Rd. BR5: St P 2K **161**
Thorne Cl. DA8: Erith 6H **109**
Thorne Cl. E11 4F **69**
Thorne Cl. E16 6J **87**
Thorne Cl. KT10: Clay 7A **162**
Thorne Cl. TW15: Ashf 7E **128**
Thorne Ho. E14 3E **104**
(off Launch St.)
Thorne Ho. E2 3J **85**
(off Roman Rd.)
Thorneloe Gdns. CR0: Wadd 5A **168**
Thorne Pas. SW13 2A **116**
Thorne Rd. SW8 7J **101**
Thornes Cl. BR3: Beck 3E **158**
Thornes Ho. SW11 7H **101**
(off Ponton Rd.)
Thorne St. SW13 3A **116**
Thornet Wood Rd. BR1: Broml 3E **160**
Thornewill Ho. E1 7J **85**
(off Cable St.)
Thorney Ct. W8 2A **100**
(off Palace Ga.)
Thorney Cres. SW11 7B **100**
Thorneycroft Cl. KT12: Walt T 6A **148**
Thorneycroft Rd. N20 2G **31**
Thorney Hedge Rd. W4 4H **97**
Thorney St. SW1 3E **18** (4J **101**)
Thornfield Av. NW7 1G **45**
Thornfield Ct. NW7 7B **30**
Thornfield Ho. E14 7C **86**
(off Rosefield Gdns.)
Thornfield Pde. NW7 7B **30**
(off Holders Hill Rd.)

Thornfield Rd. – Torbitt Way

Thornfield Rd. W12 2D 98
(not continuous)
Thornford Rd. SE13 5E 122
Thorngate Rd. W9 4J 81
Thorngrove Rd. E13 1K 87
Thornham Gro. E15 5F 69
Thornham Ind. Est. E15 5F 69
Thornham St. SE10 6D 104
Thornhaugh M. WC1 4D 6 (4H 83)
Thornhaugh St. WC1 4D 6 (4H 83)
Thornhill Av. KT6: Surb 2E 162
Thornhill Av. SE18 7J 107
THORNHILL BRI. 2K 83
(off Caledonian Rd.)
Thornhill Bri. Wharf N1 1K 83
Thornhill Cres. N1 7K 65
Thornhill Gdns. E10 2D 68
Thornhill Gdns. IG11: Bark 7J 71
Thornhill Gro. N1 7K 65
Thornhill Ho. W4 5A 98
(off Wood St.)
Thornhill Ho's. N1 7A 66
(off Thornhill Rd.)
Thornhill M. SW15 4H 117
Thornhill Rd. CR0: C'don 7C 156
Thornhill Rd. E10 2D 68
Thornhill Rd. KT6: Surb 2E 162
Thornhill Rd. N1 7A 66
Thornhill Rd. UB10: Ick 4B 56
Thornhill Sq. N1 7K 65
Thornhill Way TW17: Shep 5C 146
Thornicroft Ho. SW9 2K 119
(off Stockwell Rd.)
Thornlaw Rd. SE27 4A 138
Thornley Cl. N17 7B 34
Thornley Dr. HA2: Harr 2F 59
Thornley Pl. SE10 5G 105
Thornsbeach Rd. SE6 1E 140
Thornsett Pl. SE20 2H 157
Thornsett Rd. SE20 2H 157
Thornsett Rd. SW18 1K 135
Thornsett Ter. SE20 2H 157
(off Croydon Rd.)
Thorn Ter. SE15 3J 121
Thornton Av. CR0: C'don 6K 155
Thornton Av. SW2 1H 137
Thornton Av. UB7: W Dray 3B 92
Thornton Av. W4 4A 98
Thornton Cl. UB7: W Dray 3B 92
Thornton Dene BR3: Beck 2C 158
Thornton Gdns. SW12 1H 137
THORNTON HEATH 4C 156
Thornton Heath Leisure Cen. 4C 156
THORNTON HEATH POND 5A 156
Thornton Hill SW19 7G 135
Thornton Ho. SE17 4E 102
(off Townsend St.)
Thornton Pl. W1 5E 4 (5D 82)
Thornton Rd. BR1: Broml 5J 141
Thornton Rd. CR0: C'don 7K 155
Thornton Rd. CR7: Thor H 6K 155
Thornton Rd. DA17: Belv 4H 109
Thornton Rd. E11 2F 69
Thornton Rd. EN5: Barn 3B 20
Thornton Rd. IG1: Ilf 4F 71
Thornton Rd. N18 3D 34
Thornton Rd. SM5: Cars 1B 166
Thornton Rd. SW12 7H 119
Thornton Rd. SW14 4K 115
Thornton Rd. SW19 6F 135
Thornton Rd. E. SW19 6F 135
Thornton Rd. Ind. Est. CR0: C'don 6K 155
Thornton Row CR7: Thor H 5A 156
Thornton's Farm Av. RM7: Rush G 1J 73
Thornton St. E20 7D 68
Thornton St. SW9 2A 120
Thornton Way NW11 5K 45
Thorntree Ct. W5 5E 78
Thorntree Rd. SE7 5B 106
Thornville Gro. CR4: Mitc 2B 154
Thornville St. SE8 1C 122
Thornwell Ct. W7 2J 95
(off Lwr. Boston Rd.)
Thornwood Cl. E18 2K 51
Thornwood Gdns. W8 2J 99
Thornwood Ho. IG9: Buck H 1H 37
Thornwood Lodge W8 2J 99
(off Thornwood Gdns.)
Thornwood Rd. SE13 5G 123
Thornycroft Ho. W4 5A 98
(off Fraser St.)
Thorogood Gdns. E15 5G 69
Thorogood Way RM13: Rain 1K 91
Thorold Ho. SE1 6C 14 (2C 102)
(off Pepper St.)
Thorold Rd. IG1: Ilf 2F 71
Thorold Rd. N22 7D 32
Thorparch Rd. SW8 1H 119
Thorpebank Rd. W12 1C 98
Thorpe Cl. BR6: Orp 2J 173
Thorpe Cl. SE26 4K 139
Thorpe Cl. W10 6G 81
Thorpe Ct. EN2: Enf 3G 23
Thorpe Cres. E17 2B 50
Thorpedale Gdns. IG2: Ilf 4E 52
Thorpedale Gdns. IG6: Ilf 4F 53
Thorpedale Rd. N4 2J 65
Thorpe Hall Rd. E17 1E 50
Thorpe Ho. N1 1K 83
(off Barnsbury Est.)
Thorpe Rd. E17 2E 50
Thorpe Rd. E6 1D 88
Thorpe Rd. E7 4H 69
Thorpe Rd. IG11: Bark 7H 71
Thorpe Rd. KT2: King T 7E 132
Thorpe Rd. N15 6E 48
Thorpewood Av. SE26 2H 139
Thorpland Av. UB10: Ick 3E 56
Thorsden Way SE19 5E 138
Thorverton Rd. NW2 3G 63
Thoydon Rd. E3 2A 86
Thrale Rd. SW16 4G 137
Thrale St. SE1 5D 14 (1C 102)
Thrasher Cl. E8 1F 85
Thrawl St. E1 6K 9 (5F 85)
Thrayle Ho. SW9 3K 119
(off Benedict Rd.)
Threadgold Ho. N1 6D 66
(off Dovercourt Est.)
Threadneedle St. EC2 1F 15 (6D 84)
Threadneedle Wlk. EC2 1F 15 (6D 84)
(off Throgmorton St.)
Thread St. SM6: W'gton 2E 166
Three Angels Cl. SM6: W'gton 5K 167
Three Bridges Bus. Cen. UB2: S'hall 2G 95
Three Colts La. E2 4H 85
Three Colt St. E14 6B 86
Three Corners DA7: Bex 2H 127
Three Cups Yd. WC1 6H 7 (5K 83)
(off Sandland St.)
Three Kings Yd. W1 2J 11 (7F 83)
Three Meadows M. HA3: Hrw W 1K 41
Three Mill La. E3 3E 86
Three Mills Studios 3E 86
Three Oak La. SE1 6J 15 (2F 103)
Three Oaks Cl. UB10: Ick 3B 56
Three Quays EC3 3H 15 (7E 84)
(off Tower Hill)
Three Quays Wlk. EC3 3H 15 (7E 84)
Threshers Pl. W11 7G 81
Thriffwood SE26 3J 139
Thrigby Rd. KT9: Chess 6F 163
Thring Ho. SW9 2K 119
(off Stockwell Rd.)
Throckmorton Rd. E16 6K 87
Throgmorton Av. EC2 7F 9 (6D 84)
(not continuous)
Throgmorton St. EC2 7F 9 (6D 84)
Throwley Cl. SE2 3C 108
(not continuous)
Throwley Rd. SM1: Sutt 5K 165
Throwley Way SM1: Sutt 4K 165
Thrupp Cl. CR4: Mitc 2F 155
Thrush Grn. HA2: Harr 4E 40
Thrush St. SE17 5C 102
Thunderer St. E13 2A 88
Thunderer Wlk. SE18 3F 107
Thurbarn Rd. SE6 5D 140
Thurland Ho. SE16 4H 103
(off Camilla Rd.)
Thurland Rd. SE16 3G 103
Thurlby Cl. HA1: Harr 6A 42
Thurlby Cl. IG8: Wfd G 5J 37
Thurlby Cft. NW4 3E 44
(off Mulberry Cl.)
Thurlby Rd. HA0: Wemb 6D 60
Thurlby Rd. SE27 4A 138
Thurleigh Av. SW12 6E 118
Thurleigh Ct. SW12 6E 118
Thurleigh Rd. SW12 7D 118
Thurleston Av. SM4: Mord 5G 153
Thurlestone Av. IG3: Bark 4K 71
Thurlestone Av. IG3: Ilf 4K 71
Thurlestone Av. N12 6J 31
Thurlestone Cl. TW17: Shep 6E 146
Thurlestone Ct. UB1: S'hall 6F 77
(off Howard Rd.)
Thurlestone Pde. TW17: Shep 6E 146
(off High St.)
Thurlestone Rd. SE27 3A 138
Thurloe Cl. SW7 3C 16 (4C 100)
Thurloe Ct. SW3 4C 16 (4C 100)
(off Fulham Rd.)
Thurloe Pl. SW7 3B 16 (4B 100)
Thurloe Pl. M. SW7 3B 16 (4B 100)
(off Thurloe Pl.)
Thurloe Sq. SW7 3C 16 (4C 100)
Thurloe St. SW7 3B 16 (4B 100)
Thurlow Cl. E4 6K 35
Thurlow Gdns. HA0: Wemb 5D 60
Thurlow Hill SE21 1C 138
Thurlow Ho. SW16 3J 137
Thurlow Pk. Rd. SE21 2B 138
Thurlow Rd. NW3 5B 64
Thurlow Rd. W7 2A 96
Thurlow St. SE17 5D 102
(not continuous)
Thurlow Ter. NW5 5E 64
Thurlow Wlk. SE17 5E 102
(not continuous)
Thurlstone Rd. HA4: Ruis 3J 57
Thurnby Ct. TW2: Twick 3J 131
Thurnscoe NW1 1G 83
(off Pratt St.)
Thursland Rd. DA14: Sidc 5E 144
Thursley Cres. CR0: New Ad 7E 170
Thursley Gdns. SW19 2F 135
Thursley Ho. SW2 7K 119
(off Holmewood Gdns.)
Thursley Rd. SE9 3D 142
Thurso Ho. NW6 2K 81
Thurso St. SW17 4B 136
Thurstan Dwellings WC2 7F 7 (6J 83)
(off Newton St.)
Thurstan Rd. SW20 7D 134
Thurstan St. SW6 1A 118
Thurston Ho. BR3: Beck 6D 140
Thurston Ho. N1 1K 83
(off Barnsbury Est.)
Thurston Rd. SE13 2D 122
Thurston Rd. UB1: S'hall 6D 76
Thurtle Rd. E2 1F 85
Thwaite Cl. DA8: Erith 6J 109
Thyer Cl. BR6: Farnb 4G 173
Thyme Cl. SE3 3A 124
Thyme Ct. NW7 1G 45
Thyme Wlk. E5 4K 67
Thyra Gro. N12 6E 30
Tibbatt's Rd. E3 4D 86
Tibbenham Pl. SE6 2C 140
Tibbenham Wlk. E13 2H 87
Tibberton Sq. N1 1C 84
Tibbet's Cl. SW19 1F 135
TIBBET'S CORNER 7F 117
Tibbet's Ride SW15 7F 117
Tiber Cl. E3 1C 86
Tiber Gdns. N1 1J 83
Tiber Way BR3: Beck 4D 158
Ticehurst Cl. BR5: St P 7A 144
Ticehurst Rd. SE23 2A 140
Tickford Cl. SE2 2C 108
Tickford Ho. NW8 2C 4 (3C 82)
Tidal Basin Rd. E16 7H 87
(not continuous)
Tidbury Ct. SW8 7G 101
(off Stewart's Rd.)
Tide Cl. CR4: Mitc 1E 154
Tideham Ho. SE28 1H 107
Tidelea Twr. SE28 2G 107
Tidemill Sq. SE10 4G 105
Tidemill Way SE8 7C 104
Tidenham Gdns. CR0: C'don 3E 168
Tideside Ct. SE18 3C 106
Tideslea Path SE28 1H 107
Tideswell Rd. CR0: C'don 3C 170
Tideswell Rd. SW15 4E 116
Tidewaiters Ho. E14 6F 87
(off Blair St.)
Tideway Cl. TW10: Ham 4B 132
Tideway Ct. SE16 1K 103
Tideway Ho. E14 2C 104
(off Strafford St.)
Tideway Ho. E17 4K 49
Tideway Wlk. SW11 7B 18 (6G 101)
Tidey St. E3 5C 86
Tidford Rd. DA16: Well 2K 125
Tidlock Ho. SE28 2H 107
Tidworth Rd. E3 4C 86
Tiepigs La. BR2: Hayes 1H 171
Tiepigs La. BR4: W W'ck 2G 171
Tierney Ct. CR0: C'don 2E 168
Tierney La. W6 6E 98
Tierney Rd. SW2 1J 137
Tiffany Hgts. SW18 7J 117
Tiffin Girls Community Sports Cen. 6E 132
Tiffin Sports Cen. 2F 151
Tiger Cl. IG11: Bark 2B 90
Tiger Ho. WC1 2D 6 (3H 83)
(off Burton St.)
Tiger La. BR2: Broml 4K 159
Tiger Way E5 4H 67
Tiggap Ho. SE10 4G 105
Tigris Cl. N9 2D 34
Tilbrook Rd. SE3 3A 124
Tilbury Cl. HA5: Hat E 1D 40
Tilbury Cl. SE15 7F 103
Tilbury Ho. SE14 6K 103
(off Myers La.)
Tilbury Lodge CR2: S Croy 6E 168
Tilbury Rd. E10 7E 50
Tilbury Rd. E6 2D 88
Tildesley Rd. SW15 6E 116
Tile Farm Rd. BR6: Orp 3H 173
Tile Ho. N1 1J 83
(off Beaconsfield Rd.)
Tilehurst NW1 2K 5 (3F 83)
(off Lit. Albany St.)
Tilehurst Rd. SM3: Cheam 5G 165
Tilehurst Rd. SW18 1B 136
Tile Kiln La. DA5: Bexl Dartford Rd. 2J 145
Tile Kiln La. N13 5H 33
Tile Kiln La. N6 1F 65
Tile Kiln La. UB9: Hare 7D 38
Tile Kiln Studios N6 7G 47
Tilemakers Yd. SW18 2A 136
Tileyard Rd. N7 7J 65
Tilford Av. CR0: New Ad 7E 170
Tilford Gdns. SW19 1F 135
Tilford Ho. SW2 7K 119
(off Holmewood Gdns.)
Tilia Cl. SM1: Sutt 5H 165
Tilia Rd. E5 4H 67
Tilia Wlk. SW9 4B 120
Tiller Ho. N1 1E 84
(off Whitmore Est.)
Tiller Ho. UB2: S'hall 3E 94
(off Lockwood Rd.)
Tiller Leisure Cen. 3C 104
Tiller Rd. E14 3C 104
Tillett Cl. NW10 6J 61
Tillett Sq. SE16 2A 104
Tillett Way E2 3G 85
Tilley Rd. TW13: Felt 1J 129
Tillingbourne Gdns. N3 3H 45
Tillingbourne Grn. BR5: St M Cry 4K 161
Tillingbourne Way N3 4H 45
Tillingham Way N12 4D 30
Tilling Rd. NW2 1E 62
Tillings Cl. SE5 1C 120
Tilling Way HA9: Wemb 2D 60
Tillman St. E1 6H 85
Tilloch St. N1 7K 65
Tillotson Ct. SW8 7H 101
(off Wandsworth Rd.)
Tillotson Rd. HA3: Hrw W 7A 26
Tillotson Rd. IG1: Ilf 7E 52
Tillotson Rd. N9 2A 34
Tilney Ct. EC1 3D 8 (4C 84)
Tilney Ct. IG9: Buck H 2D 36
Tilney Dr. IG9: Buck H 2D 36
Tilney Gdns. N1 6D 66
Tilney Rd. RM9: Dag 6F 73
Tilney Rd. UB2: S'hall 4A 94
Tilney St. W1 4H 11 (1E 100)
Tilson Cl. SE5 7E 102
Tilson Gdns. SW2 7J 119
Tilson Ho. SW2 7J 119
Tilson Rd. N17 1G 49
Tilston Bright Sq. SE2 3C 108
Tilston Cl. E11 3H 69
Tiltman Pl. N7 3K 65
Tilton St. SW6 6G 99
Tiltwood, The W3 7J 79
Tilt Yd. App. SE9 6D 124
Timber Cl. BR7: Chst 2E 160
Timbercroft KT19: Ewe 4A 164
Timbercroft La. SE18 6J 107
Timberdene NW4 2F 45
Timberdene Av. IG6: Ilf 1G 53
Timberland Cl. SE15 7G 103
Timberland Rd. E1 6H 85
Timberley Ct. DA14: Sidc 5K 143
Timber Mill Way SW4 3H 119
Timber Pond Rd. SE16 1K 103
Timbers, The SM3: Cheam 6G 165
Timber St. EC1 4C 8 (4C 84)
Timber Wharf E2 1F 85
Timberwharf Rd. N16 6G 49
Timber Wharves Est. E14 4C 104
(off Copeland Dr.)
Timber Yd., The N1 2H 9 (3E 84)
(off Drysdale St.)
Timberyard M. KT4: Wor Pk 2D 164
Timbrell Pl. SE16 1B 104
Time Sq. E8 5F 67
Times Sq. E1 6G 85
Times Sq. SM1: Sutt 5K 165
Timians Way BR1: Broml 4K 141
Timmins Apts. E2 3K 85
Timms Cl. BR1: Broml 4D 160
Timor Ho. E1 4A 86
(off Duckett St.)
Timothy Cl. DA6: Bex 5E 126
Timothy Cl. SW4 5G 119
Timothy Ho. DA18: Erith 2E 108
(off Kale Rd.)
Timothy Pl. KT8: W Mole 5D 148
Timperley Ct. SW19 1G 135
Timsbury Wlk. SW15 1C 134
Tina Ct. SE6 7B 122
Tindal St. SW9 1B 120
Tinderbox All. SW14 3K 115
Tinderbox Ho. SE8 7C 104
(off Octavius St.)
Tinniswood Cl. N5 5A 66
Tinsley Cl. SE25 3H 157
Tinsley Rd. E1 5J 85
Tintagel Ct. EC1 3A 8 (4B 84)
(off St John St.)
Tintagel Cres. SE22 4F 121
Tintagel Dr. HA7: Stan 4J 27
Tintagel Gdns. SE22 4F 121
Tintern Av. NW9 3H 43
Tintern Cl. SW15 5G 117
Tintern Cl. SW19 6A 136
Tintern Ct. W13 7A 78
Tintern Gdns. N14 7D 22
Tintern Ho. NW1 1K 5 (2F 83)
(off Augustus St.)
Tintern Ho. SW1 4J 17 (4F 101)
(part of Abbots Mnr.)
Tintern Path NW9 6A 44
(off Fryent Gro.)
Tintern Rd. N22 1C 48
Tintern Rd. SM5: Cars 1B 166
Tintern St. SW4 4J 119
Tintern Way HA2: Harr 1F 59
Tinto Rd. E16 4J 87
Tinworth Ct. SE17 6B 102
(off Royal Rd.)
Tinworth St. SE11 5F 19 (5J 101)
Tippett Ct. E6 2D 88
Tippetts Cl. EN2: Enf 1H 23
Tippler Wlk. E15 5F 69
Tipthorpe Rd. SW11 3E 118
Tipton Dr. CR0: C'don 4E 168
Tiptree NW1 7F 65
(off Castlehaven Rd.)
Tiptree Cl. E4 3K 35
Tiptree Cres. IG5: Ilf 3E 52
Tiptree Dr. EN2: Enf 4J 23
Tiptree Rd. HA4: Ruis 4K 57
Tirlemont Rd. CR2: S Croy 7C 168
Tirrell Rd. CR0: C'don 6C 156
Tisbury Ct. W1 2C 12 (7H 83)
(off Wardour St.)
Tisbury Rd. SW16 2J 155
Tisdall Ho. SE17 4D 102
(off Barlow St.)
Tisdall Pl. SE17 4D 102
Tissington Ct. SE16 4J 103
Titan Bus. Est. SE8 7C 104
(off Ffinch St.)
Titan Ct. TW8: Bford 5F 97
Titan Ho. E20 5E 68
(off Napa Cl.)
Titanium Point E2 3K 85
(off Palmer's Rd.)
Titchborne Row W2 1C 10 (6C 82)
Titchfield Rd. NW8 1C 82
Titchfield Rd. SM5: Cars 1B 166
Titchfield Wlk. SM5: Cars 7B 154
Titchwell Rd. SW18 1B 136
Tite St. SW3 6E 16 (5D 100)
Tithe Barn Cl. KT2: King T 1F 151
Tithe Barn Way UB5: N'olt 2K 75
Tithe Cl. KT12: Walt T 6K 147
Tithe Cl. NW7 1C 44
Tithe Cl. UB4: Hayes 5H 75
Tithe Farm Av. HA2: Harr 3E 58
Tithe Farm Cl. HA2: Harr 3E 58
Tithe Farm Social Club 2E 58
Tithe Wlk. NW7 1C 44
Titian Av. WD23: B Hea 1D 26
Titian Hgts. E20 5D 68
(off Scarlet Cl.)
Titley Cl. E4 5H 35
Titmus Cl. UB8: Hil 6E 74
Titmuss Av. SE28 7B 90
Titmuss St. W12 2E 98
Tivendale N8 3J 47
Tiverton Av. IG5: Ilf 3E 52
Tiverton Cl. CR0: C'don 7F 157
Tiverton Dr. SE9 1G 143
Tiverton Ho. EN3: Enf H 3E 24
Tiverton Rd. HA0: Wemb 2E 78
Tiverton Rd. HA4: Ruis 3J 57
Tiverton Rd. HA8: Edg 2F 43
Tiverton Rd. N15 6D 48
Tiverton Rd. N18 5K 33
Tiverton Rd. NW10 1F 81
Tiverton Rd. TW3: Houn 2G 113
Tiverton St. SE1 3C 102
Tiverton Way KT9: Chess 5D 162
Tiverton Way NW7 7A 30
Tivoli Ct. SE16 1B 104
Tivoli M. E14 6J 87
Tivoli Rd. N8 5H 47
Tivoli Rd. SE27 5C 138
Tivoli Rd. TW4: Houn 4C 112
Tivoli Way E14 6B 86
Tizzard Gro. SE3 4K 123
Toad La. TW4: Houn 4D 112
Tobago St. E14 2C 104
Tobin Cl. NW3 7C 64
Toby Ct. N9 7D 24
(off Tramway Av.)
Toby La. E1 4A 86
Toby Way KT5: Surb 2H 163
Todber Ho. W14 3G 99
(off Russell Rd.)
Todd Ho. N2 2B 46
(off The Grange)
Todds Wlk. N7 2K 65
Todhunter Ter. EN5: New Bar 4D 20
Token Ho. CR0: C'don 3C 168
(off Robert St.)
Tokenhouse Yd. EC2 7E 8 (6D 84)
Token Yd. SW15 4G 117
TOKYNGTON 6H 61
Tokyngton Av. HA9: Wemb 6G 61
Toland Sq. SW15 5C 116
Tolcairn Ct. DA17: Belv 5G 109
Tolcarne Dr. HA5: Eastc 2J 39
Tolchurch W11 6H 81
(off Dartmouth Cl.)
Toley Av. HA9: Wemb 7E 42
Tolhurst Dr. W10 3G 81
Tollard Ho. W14 3H 99
(off Kensington High St.)
Toll Bar Ct. SM2: Sutt 7K 165
Tollbridge Cl. W10 4G 81
Tollesbury Gdns. IG6: Ilf 3H 53
Tollet St. E1 4K 85
Tollgate Ct. CR2: S Croy 5D 168
Tollgate Dr. SE21 2E 138
Tollgate Dr. UB4: Yead 7B 76
Tollgate Gdns. NW6 2K 81
(off Oxford Rd.)
Tollgate Ho. NW6 2K 81
(off Tollgate Gdns.)
Tollgate Lodge BR7: Chst 1E 160
(off Caveside Cl.)
Tollgate Rd. E16 5A 88
Tollgate Rd. E6 5B 88
Tollgate Sq. 5D 88
Tollhouse Way N19 2G 65
Tollington Pk. N4 2K 65
Tollington Pl. N4 2K 65
Tollington Rd. N7 4K 65
Tollington Way N7 3J 65
Tolmers Sq. NW1 3B 6 (4G 83)
(not continuous)
Tolpaide Ho. SE11 4J 19 (4A 102)
(off Marylee Way)
Tolpuddle Av. E13 1A 88
Tolpuddle St. N1 2A 84
Tolsford Rd. E5 5H 67
Tolson Rd. TW7: Isle 3A 114
Tolverne Rd. SW20 1E 152
TOLWORTH 2H 163
Tolworth B'way. KT6: Surb 1H 163
Tolworth Cl. KT6: Surb 1H 163
Tolworth Gdns. RM6: Chad H 5D 54
TOLWORTH JUNC. (TOBY JUG) 2H 163
Tolworth Pde. RM6: Chad H 5E 54
Tolworth Pk. Rd. KT6: Surb 2F 163
Tolworth Recreation Cen. 3F 163
Tolworth Ri. Nth. KT5: Surb 1H 163
Tolworth Ri. Sth. KT5: Surb 2H 163
Tolworth Rd. KT6: Surb 2E 162
Tolworth Twr. KT6: Surb 2H 163
Tomahawk Gdns. UB5: N'olt 3B 76
Tomblin M. SW16 2G 155
Tom Coombs Cl. SE9 4C 124
Tom Cribb Rd. SE28 3G 107
Tom Groves Cl. E15 5F 69
Tom Hood Cl. E15 5F 69
Tom Jenkinson Rd. E16 1J 105
Tomkyns Ho. SE11 4J 19 (4A 102)
(off Distin St.)
Tomline Ho. SE1 5C 14 (1C 102)
(off Union St.)
Tomlins All. TW1: Twick 1A 132
Tomlin's Gro. E3 3C 86
Tomlinson Cl. E2 2K 9 (3F 85)
Tomlinson Cl. W4 5H 97
Tomlins Orchard IG11: Bark 1G 89
Tomlins Ter. E14 6A 86
Tomlins Wlk. N7 2K 65
Tom Mann Cl. IG11: Bark 1J 89
Tommy Flowers M. NW7 5A 30
Tom Nolan Cl. E15 2G 87
Tompion Ho. EC1 3B 8 (4B 84)
(off Percival St.)
Tompion St. EC1 2B 8 (3B 84)
(not continuous)
Tom Smith Cl. SE10 6G 105
Tomson Ho. SE1 7J 15 (3F 103)
(off St Saviour's Est.)
Tomswood Ct. IG6: Ilf 1G 53
Tomswood Hill IG6: Ilf 6K 37
Tomswood Rd. IG7: Chig 6K 37
Tom Williams Ho. SW6 6H 99
(off Clem Attlee Ct.)
Tonbridge Cres. HA3: Kenton 4E 42
Tonbridge Ho's. WC1 2F 6 (3J 83)
(off Tonbridge St.)
Tonbridge Rd. KT8: W Mole 4D 148
Tonbridge St. WC1 1E 6 (3J 83)
Toneborough NW8 1K 81
(off Abbey Rd.)
Tonfield Rd. SM3: Sutt 1H 165
Tonge Cl. BR3: Beck 5C 158
Tonsley Hill SW18 5K 117
Tonsley Pl. SW18 5K 117
Tonsley Rd. SW18 5K 117
Tonsley St. SW18 5K 117
Tonstall Rd. CR4: Mitc 2E 154
Tony Cannell M. E3 3B 86
Tony Law Ho. SE20 1H 157
Tony Rawson Way RM10: Dag 3J 73
Tooke Cl. HA5: Pinn 1C 40
Tookey Cl. HA3: Kenton 7F 43
Took's Ct. EC4 7J 7 (6A 84)
Tooley St. SE1 4F 15 (1D 102)
Toorack Rd. HA3: Hrw W 2H 41
Toor Cl. RM6: Chad H 6C 54
TOOTING 5C 136
TOOTING BEC 3D 136
Tooting Bec Gdns. SW16 4H 137
(not continuous)
Tooting Bec Lido 4G 137
Tooting Bec Rd. SW16 4F 137
Tooting Bec Rd. SW17 3E 136
Tooting B'way. SW17 5C 136
TOOTING GRAVENEY 6D 136
Tooting Gro. SW17 5C 136
Tooting High St. SW17 6C 136
Tooting Leisure Cen. 4B 136
Tooting Mkt. SW17 4D 136
Tootswood Rd. BR2: Broml 5G 159
Topaz Ct. E11 1G 69
Topaz Wlk. NW2 7F 45
Topcliffe Dr. BR6: Farnb 4H 173
Topham Ho. SE10 7E 104
(off Prior St.)
Topham Sq. N17 1C 48
Topham St. EC1 3J 7 (4A 84)
Topham Yd. SW19 1K 153
Top Ho. Ri. E4 7K 25
Topiary Sq. TW9: Rich 3F 115
Topley St. SE9 4A 124
Topmast Point E14 2C 104
Top Pk. BR3: Beck 5G 159
Topp Wlk. NW2 2E 62
Topsfield Cl. N8 5H 47
Topsfield Pde. N8 5J 47
(off Tottenham La.)
Topsfield Rd. N8 5J 47
Topsham Rd. SW17 3D 136
Toro Ct. IG9: Buck H 2F 37
Torbay Ct. NW1 7F 65
Torbay Mans. NW6 1H 81
(off Willesden La.)
Torbay Rd. HA2: Harr 2C 58
Torbay Rd. NW6 7H 63
Torbay St. NW1 7F 65
Torbitt Way IG2: Ilf 5K 53

Trinity Cl. – Ullswater Ho.

Trinity Cl. CR2: Sande 7E 168
Trinity Cl. E11 2G 69
Trinity Cl. E8 6F 67
Trinity Cl. NW3 4B 64
Trinity Cl. SE13 4F 123
Trinity Cl. SW4 4G 119
Trinity Cl. TW4: Houn 4C 112
Trinity Cotts. TW9: Rich 3F 115
Trinity Ct. BR1: Broml 1H 159
(off Highland Rd.)
Trinity Ct. CR0: C'don 2C 168
Trinity Ct. EN2: Enf 2H 23
Trinity Ct. N1 1E 84
(off Downham Rd.)
Trinity Ct. N18 6A 34
Trinity Ct. NW2 5E 62
Trinity Ct. SE25 6E 156
Trinity Ct. SE26 3J 139
Trinity Ct. SE7 4B 106
Trinity Ct. SE8 5A 104
(off Evelyn St.)
Trinity Ct. SW9 3K 119
Trinity Ct. W2 6A 82
(off Gloucester Ter.)
Trinity Ct. W9 3H 81
(off Croxley Rd.)
Trinity Ct. WC1 3H 7 (4K 83)
(off Gray's Inn Rd.)
Trinity Cres. SW17 2D 136
Trinity Dr. UB8: Hil 5E 74
Trinity Gdns. E16 5H 87
(not continuous)
Trinity Gdns. SW9 4K 119
Trinity Grn. E1 4J 85
Trinity Gro. SE10 1E 122
Trinity Hospital SE10 5F 105
Trinity Ho. 2J 15 (7F 85)
(off Trinity Sq.)
Trinity Ho. RM8: Dag 5B 72
Trinity Ho. SE1 3C 102
(off Bath Ter.)
Trinity Ho. W14 3H 99
Trinity Laban 6E 104
(within Old Royal Naval College)
Trinity M. E1 5J 85
(off Redman's Rd.)
Trinity M. SE20 1H 157
Trinity M. W10 6F 81
Trinity Pk. E4 6G 35
Trinity Path SE26 3J 139
(not continuous)
Trinity Pl. DA6: Bex 4F 127
Trinity Pl. EC3 2J 15 (7F 85)
Trinity Ri. SW2 1A 138
Trinity Rd. IG6: Ilf 3G 53
Trinity Rd. N2 3B 46
Trinity Rd. N22 7D 32
(not continuous)
Trinity Rd. SW17 1C 136
Trinity Rd. SW18 4A 118
Trinity Rd. SW19 6J 135
Trinity Rd. TW9: Rich 3F 115
Trinity Rd. UB1: S'hall 1C 94
Trinity Sq. E14 6G 87
Trinity Sq. EC3 2H 15 (7E 84)
Trinity St. E16 5H 87
Trinity St. EN2: Enf 2H 23
Trinity St. SE1 7D 14 (2C 102)
(not continuous)
Trinity Ter. IG9: Lough 1E 36
Trinity Twr. E1 7G 85
(off Vaughan Way)
Trinity Twr. E14 3D 104
Trinity Wlk. NW3 6A 64
Trinity Way E4 6G 35
Trinity Way W3 7A 80
Trio Pl. SE1 7D 14 (2C 102)
Triptych Ho. SE8 7C 104
(off Watson's St.)
Triscott Ho. UB3: Hayes 1J 93
Tristan Ct. SE8 6B 104
(off Dorking Cl.)
Tristan Sq. SE3 3G 123
Tristram Cl. E17 3F 51
Tristram Dr. N9 3B 34
Tristram Rd. BR1: Broml 4H 141
Triton Ct. E16 5J 87
(off Robertson Rd.)
Triton Ho. E14 4D 104
(off Cahir St.)
Triton Sq. NW1 3A 6 (4G 83)
Triton St. NW1 3K 5 (4F 83)
Tritton Av. CR0: Bedd 4J 167
Tritton Rd. SE21 3D 138
Triumph Cl. UB3: Harl 1E 110
Triumph Ho. IG11: Bark 3A 90
Triumph Rd. E6 6D 88
Triumph Trad. Est. N17 6B 34
Trocette Mans. SE1 3E 102
(off Bermondsey St.)
Trojan Ct. NW6 7G 63
Trojan Ind. Est. NW10 6B 62
Trojan M. SW19 7J 135
Trojan Way CR0: Wadd 3K 167
Troon Cl. SE16 5H 103
Troon Cl. SE28 6D 90
Troon Ho. E1 6A 86
(off White Horse Rd.)
Troon St. E1 6A 86
Tropical Ct. W10 3F 81
(off Kilburn La.)
Trosley Rd. DA17: Belv 6G 109
Trossachs Rd. SE22 5E 120
Trothy Rd. SE1 4G 103
Trotman Ho. SE14 1J 121
(off Pomeroy St.)
Trott Rd. N10 7J 31
Trott St. SW11 1C 118
Trotwood Ho. SE16 2H 103
(off Wilson Gro.)
Troubridge Sq. E17 3E 50
Troughton Rd. SE7 5K 105
Troutbeck NW1 2K 5 (3F 83)
(off Albany St.)
Troutbeck Rd. SE14 1A 122
Trouville Rd. SW4 6G 119
Trowbridge Est. E9 6B 68
(off Osborne Rd.)
Trowbridge Ho. E9 6B 68
(off Felstead St.)
Trowbridge Rd. E9 6B 68
Trowlock Av. TW11: Tedd 6C 132
Trowlock Island TW11: Tedd 6D 132
Trowlock Way TW11: Tedd 6D 132
Troy Ct. SE18 4F 107
Troy Ct. W8 3J 99
(off Kensington High St.)
Troy Ind. Est. HA1: Harr 5K 41
Troy Rd. SE19 6D 138
Troy Town SE15 3G 121
Trubshaw Rd. UB2: S'hall 3F 95
True Lovers Ct. HA6: Nwood 1F 39
Trueman Cl. HA8: Edg 7C 28
Truesdale Rd. E6 6D 88
Truesdales UB10: Ick 2E 56
truGym Bromley 1J 159
(off East St.)
Trulock Ct. N17 7B 34
Trulock Rd. N17 7B 34
Trumans Rd. N16 5F 67
Truman Wlk. E3 4D 86
Trumpers Way W7 3J 95
Trumpington Rd. E7 4H 69
Trump St. EC2 1D 14 (6C 84)
Trundle Ho. SE1 6C 14 (2C 102)
(off Trundle St.)
Trundlers Way WD23: B Hea 1D 26
Trundle St. SE1 6C 14 (2C 102)
Trundleys Rd. SE8 5K 103
Trundley's Ter. SE8 4K 103
Truro Gdns. IG1: Ilf 7C 52
Truro Ho. HA5: Hat E 1D 40
Truro Ho. W2 5J 81
(off Westbourne Pk. Rd.)
Truro Rd. E17 4B 50
Truro Rd. N22 7D 32
Truro St. NW5 6E 64
Truro Way UB4: Hayes 3G 75
Truslove Rd. SE27 5A 138
Trussley Rd. W6 3E 98
Trust Wlk. SE21 1B 138
Tryfan Cl. IG4: Ilf 5B 52
Tryon Cres. E9 1J 85
Tryon St. SW3 5E 16 (5D 100)
Trystings Cl. KT10: Clay 6A 162
Tuam Rd. SE18 6H 107
Tubbenden Cl. BR6: Orp 3J 173
Tubbenden Dr. BR6: Orp 4H 173
Tubbenden La. BR6: Orp 4H 173
Tubbenden La. Sth. BR6: Farnb 5H 173
Tubbs Rd. NW10 2B 80
Tucana Ct. E1 3K 9 (4F 85)
(off Cygnet St.)
Tucana Hgts. E20 5E 68
(off Cheering La.)
Tucklow Wlk. SW15 7B 116
Tudor Av. KT4: Wor Pk 3D 164
Tudor Av. TW12: Hamp 7E 130
Tudor Cl. BR7: Chst 1D 160
Tudor Cl. HA5: Eastc 5J 39
Tudor Cl. IG7: Chig 4K 37
Tudor Cl. IG8: Wfd G 5E 36
Tudor Cl. KT9: Chess 5E 162
Tudor Cl. N6 7G 47
Tudor Cl. NW3 5C 64
Tudor Cl. NW7 6H 29
Tudor Cl. NW9 2J 61
Tudor Cl. SM3: Cheam 5F 165
Tudor Cl. SM6: W'gton 7G 167
Tudor Cl. SW2 6K 119
Tudor Cl. TW12: Hamp H 5G 131
Tudor Cl. TW15: Ashf 4A 128
Tudor Ct. DA14: Sidc 3A 144
Tudor Ct. E17 7B 50
Tudor Ct. N1 6E 66
Tudor Ct. N22 7D 32
Tudor Ct. SE16 1K 103
(off Princes Riverside Rd.)
Tudor Ct. SE9 4C 124
Tudor Ct. TW11: Tedd 6K 131
Tudor Ct. TW13: Hanw 4A 130
Tudor Ct. TW19: Stanw 6A 110
Tudor Ct. W3 2G 97
Tudor Ct. Nth. HA9: Wemb 5G 61
Tudor Ct. Sth. HA9: Wemb 5G 61
Tudor Cres. EN2: Enf 1H 23
Tudor Dr. KT2: King T 5D 132
Tudor Dr. SM4: Mord 6F 153
Tudor Ent. Pk. HA1: Harr 3K 59
Tudor Ent. Pk. HA3: W'stone 3H 41
Tudor Est. NW10 2H 79
Tudor Gdns. BR4: W W'ck 3E 170
Tudor Gdns. HA3: Hrw W 2H 41
Tudor Gdns. NW9 2J 61
Tudor Gdns. SW13 3A 116
Tudor Gdns. TW1: Twick 1K 131
Tudor Gdns. W3 5G 79
Tudor Gro. E9 7J 67
Tudor Gro. N20 2H 31
Tudor Ho. E16 1K 105
(off Wesley Av.)
Tudor Ho. E9 7J 67
Tudor Ho. HA5: Pinn 2A 40
(off Pinner Hill Rd.)
Tudor Ho. SE1 5J 15 (1F 103)
(off Duchess Wlk.)
Tudor Ho. W14 4F 99
(off Windsor Way)
Tudor M. E17 4B 50
Tudor Pde. RM6: Chad H 7D 54
Tudor Pde. SE9 4C 124
Tudor Pk. Footgolf 3E 20
Tudor Pl. CR4: Mitc 7C 136
Tudor Pl. IG9: Buck H 2H 37
Tudor Pl. SE19 7F 139
Tudor Rd. BR3: Beck 3E 158
Tudor Rd. E4 6J 35
Tudor Rd. E6 1A 88
Tudor Rd. E9 1H 85
Tudor Rd. EN5: New Bar 3D 20
Tudor Rd. HA3: Hrw W 2H 41
Tudor Rd. HA3: W'stone 2H 41
Tudor Rd. HA5: Pinn 2A 40
Tudor Rd. IG11: Bark 1K 89
Tudor Rd. KT2: King T 7G 133
Tudor Rd. N9 7C 24
Tudor Rd. SE19 7F 139
Tudor Rd. SE25 5H 157
Tudor Rd. TW12: Hamp 7E 130
Tudor Rd. TW15: Ashf 6F 129
Tudor Rd. TW3: Houn 4H 113
Tudor Rd. UB1: S'hall 7C 76
Tudor Rd. UB3: Hayes 6F 75
Tudor Sq. UB3: Hayes 5F 75
Tudor Stacks SE24 4C 120
Tudor St. EC4 2K 13 (7A 84)
Tudor Wlk. DA5: Bexl 6E 126
Tudor Way BR5: Pet W 6H 161
Tudor Way N14 1C 32
Tudor Way UB10: Hil 6C 56
Tudor Way W3 2G 97
Tudor Well Cl. HA7: Stan 5G 27
Tudor Works UB4: Yead 1A 94
Tudway Rd. SE3 4A 124
Tufnell Ct. E3 1B 86
(off Old Ford Rd.)
TUFNELL PARK 4G 65
Tufnell Pk. Hall N7 3G 65
Tufnell Pk. Rd. N19 4G 65
Tufnell Pk. Rd. N7 4G 65
Tufton Ct. SW1 2E 18 (3J 101)
(off Tufton St.)
Tufton Gdns. KT8: W Mole 2F 149
Tufton Rd. E4 4H 35
Tufton St. SW1 1E 18 (3J 101)
Tugboat St. SE28 2J 107
Tugela Rd. CR0: C'don 6D 156
Tugela St. SE6 2B 140
Tulett Av. N20 2G 31
Tulip Cl. CR0: C'don 1K 169
Tulip Cl. E6 5D 88
Tulip Cl. TW12: Hamp 6D 130
Tulip Cl. UB2: S'hall 2G 95
Tulip Gdns. E4 3A 36
Tulip Gdns. IG1: Ilf 6F 71
Tullis Ho. E9 7J 67
(off Frampton Pk. Rd.)
Tull St. CR4: Mitc 7D 154
Tulse Cl. BR3: Beck 3E 158
Tulse Hill SW2 6A 120
TULSE HILL 1B 138
Tulse Hill Est. SW2 6A 120
Tulse Ho. SW2 6A 120
Tulsemere Rd. SE27 2C 138
Tumbling Bay KT12: Walt T 6J 147
Tummons Gdns. SE25 2E 156
Tump Ho. SE28 1J 107
Tunbridge Ho. EC1 1A 8 (3B 84)
(off St John St.)
Tuncombe Rd. N18 4K 33
Tunis Rd. W12 1E 98
Tunley Grn. E14 5B 86
Tunley Rd. NW10 1A 80
Tunley Rd. SW17 1E 136
Tunmarsh La. E13 3K 87
Tunnan Leys E6 6E 88
Tunnel App. E14 7A 86
Tunnel App. SE10 2G 105
Tunnel App. SE16 2J 103
Tunnel Av. SE10 2F 105
Tunnel Av. Trad. Est. SE10 2F 105
Tunnel Gdns. N11 7B 32
Tunnel Link Rd. TW6: H'row A 6C 110
Tunnel Rd. SE16 2J 103
Tunnel Rd. E. TW6: H'row A 1D 110
Tunnel Rd. W. TW6: H'row A 1C 110
Tunstall Cl. BR6: Orp 4J 173
Tunstall Rd. CR0: C'don 1E 168
Tunstall Rd. SW9 4K 119
Tunstall Wlk. TW8: Bford 6E 96
Tunstock Way DA17: Belv 3E 108
Tunworth Cl. NW9 6J 43
Tunworth Cres. SW15 6B 116
Tun Yd. SW8 2F 119
(off Peardon St.)
Tupelo Rd. E10 2D 68
Tupman Ho. SE16 2G 103
(off Scott Lidgett Cres.)
Tuppy St. SE28 3G 107
Turenne Cl. SW18 4A 118
Turing St. E20 7E 68
Turin Rd. N9 7D 24
Turin St. E2 2K 9 (3G 85)
Turkey Oak Cl. SE19 1E 156
Turks Boatyard KT1: King T 1D 150
Turks Cl. UB8: Hil 3C 74
Turk's Head Yd. EC1 5A 8 (5B 84)
Turk's Row SW3 5F 17 (5D 100)
Turle Rd. N4 2K 65
Turle Rd. SW16 2J 155
Turlewray Cl. N4 1K 65
Turley Cl. E15 1G 87
Turnagain La. EC4 7A 8 (6B 84)
(off Farringdon St.)
Turnage Rd. RM8: Dag 1E 72
Turnant Rd. N17 1C 48
Turnberry Cl. NW4 2F 45
Turnberry Cl. SE16 5H 103
Turnberry Quay E14 3D 104
Turnberry Way BR6: Orp 1H 173
Turnbull Ho. N1 1B 84
Turnbury Cl. SE28 6D 90
Turnchapel M. SW4 3F 119
Turner Av. CR4: Mitc 1D 154
Turner Av. N15 4E 48
Turner Av. TW2: Twick 3G 131
Turner Cl. HA0: Wemb 6D 60
Turner Cl. NW11 6K 45
Turner Cl. SW9 7B 102
Turner Cl. UB4: Hayes 2E 74
Turner Ct. SE16 2J 103
(off Albion St.)
Turner Cres. CR0: C'don 6C 156
Turner Dr. NW11 6K 45
Turner Ho. E14 2C 104
(off Cassilis Rd.)
Turner Ho. NW6 5A 64
(off Dresden Cl.)
Turner Ho. NW8 2C 82
(off Townshend Est.)
Turner Ho. SW1 4D 18 (4H 101)
(off Herrick St.)
Turner Ho. TW1: Twick 6D 114
(off Clevedon Rd.)
Turner M. SM2: Sutt 7K 165
Turner Pde. N1 7A 66
(off Barnsbury Pk.)
Turner Pl. SW11 5C 118
Turner Rd. E17 3E 50
Turner Rd. HA8: Edg 2E 42
Turner Rd. KT3: N Mald 7K 151
Turners Cl. N20 3J 31
Turners Ct. E15 4E 68
(off Drapers Rd.)
Turners Ct. N15 5D 48
Turners Mdw. Way BR3: Beck 1B 158
Turners Rd. E3 5B 86
Turner St. E1 5H 85
Turner St. E16 6H 87
Turners Way CR0: Wadd 2A 168
Turners Wood NW11 7A 46
Turneville Rd. W14 6H 99
Turney Rd. SE21 7C 120
TURNHAM GREEN 4A 98
Turnham Grn. Ter. W4 4A 98
Turnham Grn. Ter. M. W4 4A 98
Turnham Rd. SE4 5A 122
Turnmill St. EC1 4A 8 (4B 84)
Turnour Ho. E1 6H 85
(off Walburgh St.)
Turnpike Cl. DA16: Well 3A 126
Turnpike Cl. SE8 7B 104
Turnpike Ct. DA6: Bex 4D 126
Turnpike Ho. EC1 2B 8 (3B 84)
Turnpike La. N8 4K 47
Turnpike La. SM1: Sutt 5A 166
Turnpike La. UB10: Uxb 3A 74
Turnpike Link CR0: C'don 2E 168
Turnpike M. N8 3A 48
(off Turnpike La.)
Turnpike Pde. N15 3B 48
(off Green Lanes)
Turnpike Way TW7: Isle 1A 114
Turnpin La. SE10 6E 104
Turnstone Cl. E13 3J 87
Turnstone Cl. NW9 2A 44
Turnstone Cl. UB10: Ick 5D 56
Turnstone Ho. E1 3K 15 (7G 85)
(off Star Pl.)
Turpentine La. SW1 5J 17 (5F 101)
Turpin Cl. E1 7K 85
Turpington Cl. BR2: Broml 7C 160
Turpington La. BR2: Broml 7C 160
Turpin Ho. SW11 1F 119
Turpin Rd. TW14: Felt 6H 111
Turpin's La. IG8: Wfd G 5J 37
Turpins Yd. NW2 5F 63
Turpins Yd. SE10 7E 104
Turpin Way N19 2H 65
Turpin Way SM6: W'gton 7F 167
Turquand St. SE17 4C 102
Turret Gro. SW4 3G 119
Turton Rd. HA0: Wemb 5E 60
Turville Ho. NW8 3C 4 (4C 82)
(off Grendon St.)
Turville St. E2 3J 9 (4F 85)
Tuscan Ho. E2 3J 85
(off Knottisford St.)
Tuscan Rd. SE18 5H 107
Tuscany Corte SE13 3D 122
(off Loampit Va.)
Tuscany Ho. E17 2B 50
Tuscany Ho. IG3: Ilf 6A 54
Tuskar St. SE10 6G 105
Tussah Ho. E2 2J 85
(off Russia La.)
Tustin Est. SE15 6J 103
Tuttlebee La. IG9: Buck H 2D 36
Tuttle Ho. SW1 6C 18 (5H 101)
(off Aylesford St.)
Tweed Ct. W7 6J 77
(off Hanway Rd.)
Tweeddale Gro. UB10: Ick 3E 56
Tweeddale Rd. SM5: Cars 1B 166
Tweed Glen RM1: Rom 1K 55
Tweed Grn. RM1: Rom 1K 55
Tweedmouth Rd. E13 2K 87
Tweed Wlk. E14 4E 86
Tweed Way RM1: Rom 1K 55
Tweedy Cl. EN1: Enf 5A 24
Tweedy Rd. BR1: Broml 1J 159
Tweezer's All. WC2 2J 13 (7A 84)
(off Milford La.)
Tweezers All. WC2 2H 13 (7K 83)
Twelve Acre Ho. E12 3E 70
(off Grantham Rd.)
Twelvetrees Bus. Pk. E3 4F 87
Twelvetrees Cres. E3 4F 86
(not continuous)
Twentyman Cl. IG8: Wfd G 5D 36
TWICKENHAM 1A 132
TWICKENHAM BRI 5C 114
Twickenham Cl. CR0: Bedd 3K 167
Twickenham Gdns. HA3: Hrw W 7D 26
Twickenham Gdns. UB6: G'frd 5A 60
Twickenham Mus. 1A 132
(off The Embankment)
Twickenham Rd. E11 2E 68
Twickenham Rd. TW11: Tedd 4A 132
(not continuous)
Twickenham Rd. TW13: Hanw 3D 130
Twickenham Rd. TW7: Isle 5A 114
Twickenham Rd. TW9: Rich 4C 114
Twickenham Stadium 6J 113
Twickenham Stoop 7J 113
Twickenham Tourist Info. Cen. 1B 132
(off Church St.)
Twickenham Trad. Est. TW1: Twick 6K 113
Twig Folly Cl. E2 2K 85
Twigg Cl. DA8: Erith 7K 109
Twilley St. SW18 7K 117
Twill Way SM6: W'gton 2E 166
Twin Bridges Bus. Pk. CR2: S Croy 6D 168
Twine Cl. IG11: Bark 3B 90
Twine Ct. E1 7J 85
Twineham Grn. N12 4D 30
Twine Ter. E3 4B 86
(off Ropery St.)
Twining Av. TW2: Twick 3G 131
Twin Tumps Way SE28 7A 90
Twisden Rd. NW5 4F 65
Twist Ho. SE1 3E 102
Twitten Gro. BR1: Broml 3D 160
Two Southbank Pl. SE1 6H 13 (2K 101)
(off York Rd.)
Twybridge Way NW10 7J 61
Twycross M. SE10 5G 105
Twyford Abbey Rd. NW10 3F 79
Twyford Av. N2 3D 46
Twyford Av. W3 7G 79
Twyford Ct. HA0: Wemb 2E 78
(off Vicars Bri. Cl.)
Twyford Ct. N10 3E 46
Twyford Cres. W3 1G 97
Twyford Ho. N15 6E 48
(off Chisley Rd.)
Twyford Ho. N5 3B 66
Twyford Pl. WC2 7G 7 (6K 83)
Twyford Rd. HA2: Harr 1F 59
Twyford Rd. IG1: Ilf 5G 71
Twyford Rd. SM5: Cars 1B 166
Twyford Sports Cen. 1H 97
Twyford St. N1 1K 83
Twynholm Mans. SW6 7G 99
(off Lillie Rd.)
Tyas Rd. E16 4H 87
Tybenham Rd. SW19 3J 153
Tyberry Rd. EN3: Enf H 3C 24
Tyburn Ho. NW8 3B 4 (4B 82)
(off Fisherton St.)
Tyburn La. HA1: Harr 7K 41
Tyburn Tree (site of) 2E 10 (7D 82)
(off Marble Arch)
Tyburn Way W1 2F 11 (7D 82)
Tye La. BR6: Farnb 5G 173
Tyers Est. SE1 6G 15 (2E 102)
(off Bermondsey St.)
Tyer's Ga. SE1 7G 15 (2E 102)
Tyers St. SE11 6G 19 (5K 101)
Tyers Ter. SE11 6G 19 (5K 101)
Tyeshurst Cl. SE2 5E 108
Tygan Ho. SM3: Cheam 6G 165
(off The Broadway)
Tylecroft Rd. SW16 2J 155
Tylehurst Gdns. IG1: Ilf 5G 71
Tyler Cl. DA8: Erith 7H 109
Tyler Cl. E2 2F 85
Tyler Ct. SE17 4D 102
(off New Paragon Wlk.)
Tyler Rd. UB2: S'hall 3F 95
Tyler's Ct. W1 1C 12 (6H 83)
(off Wardour St.)
Tylers Ct. E17 4C 50
(off Westbury Rd.)
Tylers Ct. HA0: Wemb 2E 78
Tylers Ga. HA3: Kenton 6E 42
Tylers Path SM5: Cars 4D 166
Tyler St. SE10 5G 105
(not continuous)
Tylney Av. SE19 5F 139
(not continuous)
Tylney Ho. E1 6H 85
(off Nelson St.)
Tylney Rd. BR1: Broml 2B 160
Tylney Rd. E7 4A 70
Tynamara KT1: King T 4D 150
(off Portsmouth Rd.)
Tynan Cl. TW14: Felt 1J 129
Tyndale Ct. E14 5D 104
(off Transom Sq.)
Tyndale Ct. E9 6A 68
(off Brookfield Rd.)
Tyndale Ho. N1 7B 66
(off Tyndale La.)
Tyndale La. N1 7B 66
Tyndale Mans. N1 7B 66
(off Upper St.)
Tyndale Ter. N1 7B 66
Tyndall Gdns. E10 2E 68
Tyndall Rd. DA16: Well 3K 125
Tyndall Rd. E10 2E 68
Tyne Ct. W7 6J 77
(off Hanway Rd.)
Tyneham Cl. SW11 3E 118
Tyneham Rd. SW11 2E 118
Tyne Ho. KT2: King T 1D 150
Tynemouth Cl. E6 6F 89
Tynemouth Dr. EN1: Enf 1B 24
Tynemouth Rd. CR4: Mitc 7E 136
Tynemouth Rd. N15 4F 49
Tynemouth Rd. SE18 5J 107
Tynemouth St. SW6 2A 118
Tyne St. E1 7K 9 (6F 85)
Tynne Ct. E14 4E 86
(off Teviot St.)
Tynsdale Rd. NW10 7A 62
Tynte Ct. E9 5A 68
(off Mabley St.)
Tynwald Ho. SE26 3G 139
Type St. E2 2K 85
Typhoon Way SM6: W'gton 7J 167
Tyrawley Rd. SW6 1K 117
Tyre La. NW9 4A 44
Tyrell Cl. HA1: Harr 4J 59
Tyrell Ct. SM5: Cars 4D 166
Tyrell Gdns. RM10: Dag 7J 73
Tyrell Ho. BR3: Beck 5D 140
(off Beckenham Hill Rd.)
Tyrian Pl. E1 5G 85
Tyrols Rd. SE23 1K 139
Tyrone Rd. E6 2D 88
Tyron Way DA14: Sidc 4J 143
Tyrrell Av. DA16: Well 5A 126
Tyrrell Ho. SW1 7B 18 (6G 101)
(off Churchill Gdns.)
Tyrrell Rd. SE22 4G 121
Tyrrell Sq. CR4: Mitc 1C 154
Tyrwhitt Rd. SE4 3C 122
Tysoe St. EC1 2J 7 (3A 84)
Tyson Gdns. SE23 7J 121
Tyson Rd. SE23 7J 121
Tyssen Pas. E8 6F 67
Tyssen Rd. N16 3F 67
Tyssen St. E8 6F 67
Tyssen St. N1 2E 84
Tytherton E2 2J 85
(off Cyprus St.)
Tytherton Rd. N19 3H 65

U

UAL (London College of Fashion) 6H 7 (5K 83)
(off High Holborn)
Uamvar St. E14 5D 86
Uber E17 4B 50
Uckfield Gro. CR4: Mitc 7E 136
Udall St. SW1 4B 18 (4G 101)
Udimore Ho. W10 5E 80
(off Sutton Way)
Udney Pk. Rd. TW11: Tedd 6A 132
Uffington Rd. NW10 1C 80
Uffington Rd. SE27 4A 138
Ufford Cl. HA3: Hrw W 7A 26
Ufford Rd. HA3: Hrw W 7A 26
Ufford St. SE1 6K 13 (2A 102)
Ufton Ct. UB5: N'olt 3B 76
Ufton Gro. N1 7D 66
Ufton Rd. N1 7D 66
(not continuous)
Uhura Sq. N16 3E 66
Ujima Ct. SW16 4J 137
Ullathorne Rd. SW16 4G 137
Ulleswater Rd. N14 3D 32
Ullin St. E14 5E 86
Ullswater E18 2J 51
Ullswater Cl. BR1: Broml 7G 141
Ullswater Cl. SW15 4K 133
Ullswater Cl. UB4: Hayes 2G 75
Ullswater Ct. HA2: Harr 7E 40
Ullswater Cres. SW15 4K 133
Ullswater Ho. SE15 6J 103
(off Hillbeck Cl.)

298 A–Z London

Ullswater Rd. – Vanbrugh M.

Ullswater Rd. SE27 2B 138
Ullswater Rd. SW13 7C 98
Ulster Gdns. N13 4H 33
Ulster Pl. NW1 4J 5 (4F 83)
Ulster Ter. NW1 3J 5 (4F 83)
Ulundi Rd. SE3 6G 105
Ulva Rd. SW15 5F 117
Ulverscroft Rd. SE22 5F 121
Ulverstone Rd. SE27 2B 138
Ulverston Rd. E17 2F 51
Ulysses Rd. NW6 5H 63
Umberston St. E1 6G 85
Umbria St. SW15 6C 116
Umbriel Pl. E13 2J 87
Umfreville Rd. N4 6B 48
Umpire Vw. HA1: Harr 5G 41
Undercliff Rd. SE13 3C 122
Underhill EN5: Barn 5D 20
UNDERHILL 5D 20
Underhill Ct. EN5: Barn 5D 20
Underhill Gdns. W5 7C 78
Underhill Ho. E14 5C 86 *(off Burgess St.)*
Underhill Pas. NW1 1F 83 *(off Camden High St.)*
Underhill Rd. SE22 5G 121
Underhill St. NW1 1F 83
Underne Av. N14 2A 32
Undershaft EC3 1G 15 (6E 84)
Undershaw Rd. BR1: Broml 3H 141
Underwood, The SE9 2D 142
Underwood CR0: New Ad 5E 170
Underwood Bldg., The EC1 6C 8 (5C 84) *(off Bartholomew Cl.)*
Underwood Ct. E10 1D 68 *(off Leyton Grange Est.)*
Underwood Ho. KT8: W Mole 5E 148 *(off Approach Rd.)*
Underwood Ho. W6 3D 98 *(off Sycamore Gdns.)*
Underwood Rd. E1 4G 85
Underwood Rd. E4 5J 35
Underwood Rd. IG8: Wfd G 7F 37
Underwood Row N1 1D 8 (3C 84)
Underwood St. N1 1D 8 (3C 84)
Undine Rd. E14 4D 104
Undine St. SW17 5D 136
Uneeda Dr. UB6: G'frd 1H 77
Unex Twr. E15 7F 69 *(off Station St.)*
Unicorn Bldg. E1 7K 85 *(off Jardine Rd.)*
Unicorn Theatre London 5H 15 (1E 102)
Unicorn Vw. EN5: Barn 6C 20
Unicorn Works N17 7D 34
Union Cl. E11 4F 69
Union Cotts. E15 7G 69
Union Ct. EC2 7G 9 (6E 84) *(off Old Broad St.)*
Union Ct. SW4 2J 119
Union Ct. TW9: Rich 5E 114
Union Ct. W9 5J 81 *(off Elmfield Way)*
Union Dr. E1 4A 86
Union Gro. SW8 2H 119
Union Ho. CR0: C'don 7C 156
Union La. TW7: Isle 2A 114
Union M. SW4 2J 119
Union Mills Apts. E8 1F 85 *(off Samuel St.)*
Union Pk. SE10 5H 105
Union Rd. BR2: Broml 5B 160
Union Rd. CR0: C'don 7C 156
Union Rd. E17 6B 50
Union Rd. HA0: Wemb 6E 60
Union Rd. N11 6C 32
Union Rd. RM7: Rush G 6K 55
Union Rd. SW4 2H 119
Union Rd. SW8 2H 119
Union Rd. UB5: N'olt 2E 76
Union Sq. N1 1C 84
Union St. EN5: Barn 3B 20
Union St. KT1: King T 2D 150
Union St. SE1 5A 14 (1B 102)
Union Theatre 6B 14 (2B 102)
Union Wlk. E2 1H 9 (3E 84)
Union Wharf N1 Arlington Av. 1C 84
Union Wharf N1 Wenlock Rd. 2C 84 *(off Wenlock Rd.)*
Union Wharf UB7: Yiew 1A 92 *(off Bentinck Rd.)*
Union Yd. W1 1K 11 (6F 83)
Unitair Cen. TW14: Bedf 6E 110
United Dr. TW14: Felt 7H 111
United Ho. SE16 2J 103 *(off Brunel Rd.)*
Unit Workshops E1 6G 85 *(off Adler St.)*
Unity Cl. CR0: New Ad 7D 170
Unity Cl. NW10 6C 62
Unity Cl. SE19 5C 138
Unity Ct. SE1 5F 103 *(off Fortune Pl.)*
Unity M. NW1 2H 83
Unity Pl. E17 3A 50
Unity Ter. HA2: Harr 1F 59
Unity Trad. Est. IG8: Wfd G 2B 52
Unity Way SE18 3B 106
Unity Wharf SE1 6K 15 (2F 103) *(off Mill St.)*
Universal Ho. UB1: S'hall 7C 76
University Cl. NW7 7G 29
University College London Art Mus. 3C 6 (4H 83) *(off Gower St.)*
University College London Bloomsbury Campus 3C 6 (4H 83)
University College London Department of Geological Collections 4C 6 (4H 83) *(off Gower St.)*
University College London Institute of Neurology 4F 7 (4J 83) *(off Queen Sq.)*
University College London Slade School of Fine Art 3C 6 (4H 83) *(off Gower Ct.)*
University College London The Institute of Cancer Research 5A 100
University College London Wolfson Ho. 2B 6 (3G 83) *(off Stephenson Way)*
University College London Medical School Whittington Hospital Campus 2G 65 *(within Whittington Hospital)*
University Gdns. DA5: Bexl 7F 127
University of East London Docklands Campus 7E 88
University of East London Stratford Campus 6G 69
University of Greenwich Avery Hill Campus 6G 125
University of Greenwich Greenwich Campus, King William Wlk. 6F 105
University of Greenwich Maritime Greenwich Campus 6E 104
University of Greenwich Stockwell St. 6E 104
University of London Birkbeck College 5D 6 (5H 83)
University of London Heythrop College 3K 99 *(off Kensington Sq.)*
University of London Institutes of Education & Advanced Legal Studies 4D 6 (4H 83)
University of London School of Hygiene & Tropical Medicine 5D 6 (5H 83) *(off Gower St.)*
University of London School of Oriental & African Studies 4D 6 (4H 83) *(off Torrington Sq.)*
University of London Senate House 5D 6 (5H 83)
University of London Warburg Institute 4D 6 (4H 83)
University of London Observatory 6G 29
University of North London Hornsey Rd. 4A 66
University of North London Ladbrooke House 5C 66
University of North London North London Campus, Spring House 6A 66
University of the Arts London Camberwell College of Arts, Peckham Rd. 1E 120
University of the Arts London Camberwell College of Arts, Wilson Rd. 1E 120
University of the Arts London Chelsea College of Art & Design 5D 18 (5H 101)
University of the Arts London London College of Communication 4B 102
University of the Arts London London College of Fashion, Curtain Rd. 3H 9 (4E 84) *(off Curtain Rd.)*
University of the Arts London London College of Fashion, Golden La. 4C 8 (4C 84) *(off Golden La.)*
University of the Arts London London College of Fashion, Mare St. 7J 67
University of the Arts London Wimbledon College of Art 1G 153
University of West London Brentford Campus 5C 96
University of West London Ealing Campus, Grove House 1D 96
University of West London Ealing Campus, Spesom House 7C 78
University of West London Ealing Campus, St Marys Road 1D 96
University of West London Ealing Campus, Vestry Hall 2D 96
University of West London Ealing Campus, Walpole House 7D 78
University of Westminster Cavendish Campus, Hanson St. 5A 6 (5G 83)
University of Westminster Cavendish Campus, Lit. Titchfield St. 6A 6 (5G 83) *(off Lit. Titchfield St.)*
University of Westminster Harrow Campus 7A 42
University of Westminster Marylebone Campus 5G 5 (5E 82)
University of Westminster Regent Campus, Regent St. 7K 5 (6F 83) *(off Regent St.)*
University of Westminster Regent Campus, Wells St. 6B 6 (5G 83) *(off Wells St.)*
University Pl. DA8: Erith 7J 109
University Rd. SW19 6B 136
University St. WC1 4B 6 (4G 83)
University Way E16 7E 88
Unwin Av. TW14: Felt 5F 111
Unwin Cl. SE15 6G 103
Unwin Ct. N2 4C 46
Unwin Mans. W14 6H 99 *(off Queen's Club Gdns.)*
Unwin Rd. SW7 1B 16 (3B 100)
Unwin Rd. TW7: Isle 3J 113
Unwin Way HA7: Stan 7J 27
Up at The O2 1G 105
Upbrook M. W2 6A 82
Upcerne Rd. SW10 7A 100
Upchurch Cl. SE20 7H 139
Upcott Ho. E3 3D 86 *(off Bruce Rd.)*
Upcott Ho. E9 7J 67 *(off Frampton Pk. Rd.)*
Upcroft Av. HA8: Edg 5D 28
Updale Rd. DA14: Sidc 4K 143
Upfield CR0: C'don 3H 169
Upfield Rd. W7 5K 77
Upgrove Mnr. Way SW2 7A 120
Uphall Rd. IG1: Ilf 5F 71
Upham Pk. Rd. W4 4A 98
Uphill BR2: Broml 4H 159 *(off Westmoreland Rd.)*
Uphill Dr. NW7 5F 29
Uphill Dr. NW9 5J 43
Uphill Gro. NW7 4F 29
Uphill Rd. NW7 4F 29
Upland M. SE22 5G 121
Upland Rd. CR2: S Croy 5D 168
Upland Rd. DA7: Bex 3F 127
Upland Rd. E13 4J 87
Upland Rd. SE22 5G 121 (not continuous)
Upland Rd. SM2: Sutt 7B 166
Uplands, The HA4: Ruis 1J 57
Uplands BR3: Beck 2C 158
Uplands Av. E17 2K 49
Uplands Bus. Pk. E17 3K 49
Uplands Cl. SE18 5F 107
Uplands Cl. SW14 5H 115
Uplands Ct. N21 7F 23 *(off The Green)*
Uplands End IG8: Wfd G 7H 37
Uplands Pk. Rd. EN2: Enf 2F 23
Uplands Rd. EN4: E Barn 1K 31
Uplands Rd. IG8: Wfd G 7H 37
Uplands Rd. N8 5K 47
Uplands Rd. RM6: Chad H 3D 54
Uplands Way N21 5F 23
Upnall Ho. SE15 6J 103
Upney La. IG11: Bark 6J 71
Upnor Way SE17 5E 102
Uppark Dr. IG2: Ilf 6G 53
Upper Abbey Rd. DA17: Belv 4F 109
Upper Addison Gdns. W14 2G 99
Upper Bank St. E14 1D 104 (not continuous)
Upper Bardsey Wlk. N1 6C 66 *(off Douglas Rd. Nth.)*
Upper Belgrave St. SW1 1H 17 (3E 100)
Upper Berenger Wlk. SW10 7B 100 *(off Worlds End Est.)*
Upper Berkeley St. W1 1E 10 (6D 82)
Upper Beulah Hill SE19 1E 156
Upper Blantyre Wlk. SW10 7B 100 *(off Worlds End Est.)*
Upper Brighton Rd. KT6: Surb 6D 150
Upper Brockley Rd. SE4 3B 122 (not continuous)
Upper Brook St. W1 3G 11 (7E 82)
Upper Butts TW8: Bford 6C 96
Upper Caldy Wlk. N1 6C 66 *(off Caldy Wlk.)*
Upper Camelford Wlk. W11 6G 81
Upper Cavendish Av. N3 3J 45
Upper Cheapside Pas. EC2 1C 14 (6C 84) *(off Cheapside)*
Upper Cheyne Row SW3 7C 16 (6C 100)
UPPER CLAPTON 2H 67
Upper Clapton Rd. E5 1H 67
Upper Clarendon Wlk. W11 6G 81 *(off Clarendon Rd.)*
Upper Dartrey Wlk. SW10 7A 100 *(off Worlds End Est.)*
Upper Dengie Wlk. N1 1C 84 *(off Baddow Wlk.)*
Upper Dock Wlk. E16 7G 89 *(off Frobisher Yd.)*
UPPER EDMONTON 5B 34
UPPER ELMERS END 5B 158
Upper Elmers End Rd. BR3: Beck 4A 158
Upper Farm Rd. KT8: W Mole 4D 148
Upper Feilde W1 2G 11 (7E 82) *(off Park St.)*
Upper Fosters NW4 4E 44 *(off New Brent St.)*
Upper Green E. CR4: Mitc 3D 154
Upper Green W. CR4: Mitc 2D 154 (not continuous)
Upper Grosvenor St. W1 3G 11 (7E 82)
Upper Grotto Rd. TW1: Twick 2K 131
Upper Ground SE1 4J 13 (1A 102)
Upper Gro. SE25 4E 156
Upper Grove Rd. DA17: Belv 6F 109
Upper Gulland Wlk. N1 7C 66 *(off Church Rd.)*
UPPER HALLIFORD 4G 147
Upper Halliford By-Pass TW17: Shep 5G 147
Upper Halliford Grn. TW17: Shep 4G 147
Upper Halliford Rd. TW17: Shep 3G 147 (not continuous)
Upper Hampstead Wlk. NW3 4A 64
Upper Ham Rd. KT2: King T 4D 132
Upper Ham Rd. TW10: Ham 4D 132
Upper Handa Wlk. N1 6D 66 *(off Handa Wlk.)*
Upper Hawkwell Wlk. N1 1C 84 *(off Maldon Cl.)*
UPPER HOLLOWAY 2G 65
Upper Holly Hill Rd. DA17: Belv 5H 109
Upper James St. W1 2B 12 (7G 83)
Upper John St. W1 2B 12 (7G 83)
Upper Lismore Wlk. N1 6C 66 *(off Clephane Rd.)*
Upper Lodge W8 1K 99 *(off Palace Grn.)*
Upper Lodge M. TW12: Hamp H 6H 131
Upper Mall W6 5C 98 (not continuous)
Upper Marsh SE1 1H 19 (3K 101)
Upper Montagu St. W1 5E 4 (5D 82)
Upper Mulgrave Rd. SM2: Cheam 7G 165
Upper Nth. St. E14 5C 86
UPPER NORWOOD 1E 156
Upper Pk. Rd. BR1: Broml 1K 159
Upper Pk. Rd. DA17: Belv 4H 109
Upper Pk. Rd. KT2: King T 6G 133
Upper Pk. Rd. N11 5A 32
Upper Pk. Rd. NW3 5D 64
Upper Phillimore Gdns. W8 2J 99
Upper Ramsey Wlk. N1 6D 66 *(off Ramsey Wlk.)*
Upper Rawreth Wlk. N1 1C 84 *(off Basire St.)*
Upper Richmond Rd. SW15 4B 116
Upper Richmond Rd. W. SW14 4H 115
Upper Richmond Rd. W. TW10: Rich 4G 115
Upper Rd. E13 3J 87
Upper Rd. SM6: W'gton 5H 167
UPPER RUXLEY 7G 145
Upper St Martin's La. WC2 2E 12 (7J 83)
Upper Selsdon Rd. CR2: Sande 7F 169
Upper Selsdon Rd. CR2: Sels 7F 169
Upper Sheridan Rd. DA17: Belv 4G 109
UPPER SHIRLEY 4K 169
Upper Shirley Rd. CR0: C'don 2J 169
Upper Sq. TW7: Isle 3A 114
Upper St. N1 2A 84
Upper Sunbury Rd. TW12: Hamp 1C 148
Upper Sutton La. TW5: Hest 7E 94
UPPER SYDENHAM 3H 139
Upper Tachbrook St. SW1 3A 18 (4G 101)
Upper Talbot Wlk. W11 6G 81 *(off Talbot Wlk.)*
Upper Teddington Rd. KT1: Hamp W 7C 132
Upper Ter. NW3 3A 64
Upper Thames St. EC4 2B 14 (7B 84)
Upper Tollington Pk. N4 1A 66 (not continuous)
Upperton Rd. DA14: Sidc 5K 143
Upperton Rd. E. E13 3A 88
Upperton Rd. W. E13 3A 88
UPPER TOOTING 4D 136
Upper Tooting Pk. SW17 2D 136
Upper Tooting Rd. SW17 4D 136
Upper Town Rd. UB6: G'frd 4F 77
Upper Tulse Hill SW2 7K 119
Upper Vernon Rd. SM1: Sutt 5B 166
UPPER WALTHAMSTOW 4F 51
Upper Walthamstow Rd. E17 4E 50
Upper Whistler Wlk. SW10 7A 100 *(off Worlds End Est.)*
Upper Wickham La. DA16: Well 7B 108
Upper Wimpole St. W1 5H 5 (5E 82)
Upper Woburn Pl. WC1 2D 6 (3H 83)
Uppingham Av. HA7: Stan 1B 42
Upsdell Av. N13 6F 33
Upshire Ho. E17 2B 50
Upstairs at the Gatehouse Theatre Highgate 1E 64
Upstall St. SE5 1B 120
UPTON 5D 126
UPTON 7J 69
Upton Av. E7 7J 69
Upton Cl. DA5: Bexl 6F 127
Upton Cl. NW2 3G 63
Upton Ct. SE20 7J 139 *(off Blean Gro.)*
Upton Dene SM2: Sutt 7K 165
Upton Gdns. HA3: Kenton 5B 42
Upton Hgts. E7 7J 69
Upton Ho. E9 5A 68 *(off Ward La.)*
Upton La. E7 7J 69
Upton Lodge E7 6J 69
Upton Lodge Cl. WD23: Bush 1B 26
UPTON PARK 1B 88
Upton Pk. Boleyn Cinema 2B 88
Upton Pk. Rd. E7 7K 69
Upton Rd. CR7: Thor H 2D 156
Upton Rd. DA5: Bexl 6F 127
Upton Rd. DA6: Bex 4E 126
Upton Rd. N18 5B 34
Upton Rd. SE18 6G 107
Upton Rd. TW3: Houn 3E 112
Upton Rd. Sth. DA5: Bexl 6F 127
Upton Vs. DA6: Bex 4E 126
Upway N12 6H 31
Upwey Ho. N1 1E 84
Upwood Rd. SE12 6J 123
Upwood Rd. SW16 1J 155
Urbanest King's Cross N1 1J 83
Urban M. N4 6B 48
Urdang, The 2K 7 (3A 84) *(off Rosebery Av.)*
Urlwin St. SE5 6C 102
Urlwin Wlk. SW9 1A 120
Urmston Dr. SW19 1G 135
Urmston Ho. E14 4E 104 *(off Seyssel St.)*
Urquhart Ct. BR3: Beck 7B 140
Ursa Mans. E20 5E 68 *(off Cheering La.)*
Ursula Gould Way E14 5C 86
Ursula Lodges DA14: Sidc 5B 144
Ursula M. N4 1C 66
Ursula St. SW11 1C 118
Urswick Gdns. RM9: Dag 7E 72
Urswick Rd. E9 5J 67
Urswick Rd. RM9: Dag 7D 72
Usborne M. SW8 7K 101
Usher Hall NW4 4D 44 *(off The Burroughs)*
Usher Rd. E3 1B 86 (not continuous)
Usk Rd. SW11 4A 118
Usk St. E2 3K 85
Utah Bldg. SE13 1D 122 *(off Deal's Gateway)*
Utopia Village NW1 7E 64
Uvedale Rd. EN2: Enf 5J 23
Uvedale Rd. RM10: Dag 3G 73
Uverdale Rd. SW10 7A 100
Uxbridge Ct. KT1: King T 5D 150 *(off Uxbridge Rd.)*
Uxbridge Golf Course 2A 56
Uxbridge Lido 6A 56
Uxbridge Rd. HA3: Hrw W 7B 26
Uxbridge Rd. HA5: Hat E 2A 40
Uxbridge Rd. HA5: Pinn 2A 40
Uxbridge Rd. HA7: Stan 6E 26
Uxbridge Rd. KT1: King T 4D 150
Uxbridge Rd. TW12: Hamp 4E 130
Uxbridge Rd. TW12: Hamp H 4E 130
Uxbridge Rd. TW13: Felt 2A 130
Uxbridge Rd. UB1: S'hall 1E 94
Uxbridge Rd. UB10: Hil 3C 74
Uxbridge Rd. UB4: Hayes 5G 75
Uxbridge Rd. UB4: Yead 5G 75
Uxbridge Rd. W12 1C 98
Uxbridge Rd. W13 1B 96
Uxbridge Rd. W3 1G 97
Uxbridge Rd. W5 7E 78
Uxbridge Rd. W7 1K 95
Uxbridge Rd. Retail Pk. 7A 76
Uxbridge St. W8 1J 99
Uxendon Cres. HA9: Wemb 1E 60
Uxendon Hill HA9: Wemb 1F 61

V

Vaine Ho. E9 6A 68
Vaizeys Wharf SE7 3K 105
Valance Av. E4 1B 36
Valan Leas BR2: Broml 3G 159
Vale, The CR0: C'don 2K 169
Vale, The HA4: Ruis 4A 58
Vale, The IG8: Wfd G 7D 36
Vale, The N10 1E 46
Vale, The N14 7C 22
Vale, The NW11 3F 63
Vale, The SW3 7A 16 (6B 100)
Vale, The TW14: Felt 6K 111
Vale, The TW16: Sun 6J 129
Vale, The TW5: Hest 6C 94
Vale, The W3 1K 97
Vale Cl. BR6: Farnb 4E 172
Vale Cl. N2 3D 46
Vale Cl. TW1: Twick 3A 132
Vale Cl. W9 3A 82
Vale Cotts. SW15 3A 134
Vale Ct. EN5: New Bar 4E 20
Vale Ct. W3 1B 98
Vale Ct. W9 3A 82
Vale Cres. SW15 4A 134
Vale Cft. HA5: Pinn 5C 40
Vale Dr. EN5: Barn 4C 20
Vale End SE22 4F 121
Vale Est., The W3 1A 98
Vale Farm Sports Cen. 4B 60
Vale Gro. N4 7C 48
Vale Gro. W3 2K 97
Vale La. W3 5G 79
Vale Lodge SE23 2J 139
Valence Av. RM8: Dag 1D 72
Valence Cir. RM8: Dag 3D 72
Valence House Mus. 3E 72
Valence Rd. DA8: Erith 7K 109
Valence Wood Rd. RM8: Dag 3D 72
Valencia Cl. E14 6F 87
Valencia Rd. HA7: Stan 4H 27
Valencia Twr. EC1 1C 8 (3C 84) *(off Bollinder Place)*
Valentia Pl. SW9 4A 120
Valentina Av. NW9 2B 44
Valentine Av. DA5: Bexl 2E 144
Valentine Ct. SE23 2K 139 (not continuous)
Valentine Ho. E3 1B 86 *(off Garrison Rd.)*
Valentine Pl. SE1 7A 14 (2B 102)
Valentine Rd. E9 6K 67
Valentine Rd. HA2: Harr 3F 59
Valentine Row SE1 7A 14 (2B 102)
Valentines Mansion & Gdns. 7E 52
Valentines Rd. IG1: Ilf 1F 71
Valentine's Way RM7: Rush G 2K 73
Vale of Health NW3 3B 64
VALE OF HEALTH 3A 64
Vale Pde. SW15 3A 134
Valerian Wlk. N11 2K 31
Valerian Way E15 3G 87
Valerie Ct. SM2: Sutt 7K 165
Valerie Ct. WD23: Bush 1B 26
Valerio M. N1 6D 66
Vale Ri. NW11 1H 63
Vale Rd. BR1: Broml 1E 160
Vale Rd. CR4: Mitc 3H 155
Vale Rd. E7 6K 69
Vale Rd. KT19: Ewe 4B 164
Vale Rd. KT4: Wor Pk 3B 164
Vale Rd. N4 7C 48
Vale Rd. SM1: Sutt 4K 165
Vale Rd. Nth. KT6: Surb 2E 162
Vale Rd. Sth. KT6: Surb 2E 162
Vale Row N5 3B 66
Vale Royal N7 7J 65
Vale Royal Ho. WC2 2D 12 (7H 83) *(off Charing Cross Rd.)*
Valery Pl. TW12: Hamp 7E 130
Valeside Ct. EN5: New Bar 4E 20
Vale St. SE27 3D 138
Valeswood Rd. BR1: Broml 5H 141
Vale Ter. N4 6C 48
Valetta Gro. E13 2J 87
Valetta Ho. SW11 7F 101
Valetta Rd. W3 2A 98
Valette Ct. N10 4F 47 *(off St James's La.)*
Valette Ho. E9 6J 67
Valette St. E9 6J 67
Valiant Cl. RM7: Mawney 2H 55
Valiant Cl. UB5: N'olt 3B 76
Valiant Ho. E14 2E 104 *(off Plevna St.)*
Valiant Ho. SE7 5A 106
Valiant Path NW9 7F 29
Valiant Way E6 5D 88
Vallance Rd. E1 4G 85
Vallance Rd. E2 3G 85
Vallance Rd. N22 2G 47
Vallentin Rd. E17 4E 50
Valley, The 5A 106
Valley Av. N12 4G 31
Valley Cl. HA5: Pinn 2K 39
Valley Dr. NW9 6G 43
Valleyfield Rd. SW16 5K 137
Valley Flds. Cres. EN2: Enf 2F 23
Valley Gdns. HA0: Wemb 7F 61
Valley Gdns. SW19 7B 136
Valley Gro. SE7 5A 106
Valley Leisure Pk. 1J 167
Valleylink Est. EN3: Pond E 6F 25
Valley M. TW1: Twick 2K 131
Valley Point Ind. Est. CR0: Bedd 7J 155
Valley Rd. BR2: Broml 2G 159
Valley Rd. BR5: St P 7B 144
Valley Rd. DA17: Belv 4H 109
Valley Rd. DA8: Erith 4J 109
Valley Rd. SE14 7B 104
Valley Rd. SW16 5K 137
Valley Rd. UB10: Uxb 2A 74
Valley Side E4 2H 35
Valley Side SE7 5B 106
Valley Side Pde. E4 2H 35
Valley Vw. EN5: Barn 6B 20
Valley Wlk. CR0: C'don 2J 169
Valliere Rd. NW10 3C 80
Valliers Wood Rd. DA15: Sidc 1J 143
Vallings Pl. KT6: Surb 7B 150
Vallis Way KT9: Chess 4D 162
Vallis Way W13 5A 78
Val McKenzie Av. N7 3A 66
Valmar Rd. SE5 1C 120
Valmar Trad. Est. SE5 1C 120
Valnay St. SW17 5D 136
Valognes Av. E17 1A 50
Valois Ho. SE1 3F 103 *(off St Saviour's Est.)*
Valonia Gdns. SW18 6H 117
Vambery Rd. SE18 6G 107
Vamey Ct. BR1: Broml 3J 159
V&A Mus. of Childhood 3J 85
Vanbrough Cres. UB5: N'olt 1A 76
Vanbrugh Castle SE10 6G 105 *(off Maze Hill)*
Vanbrugh Cl. E16 5B 88
Vanbrugh Ct. SE11 4K 19 (4A 102) *(off Wincott St.)*
Vanbrugh Dr. KT12: Walt T 7A 148
Vanbrugh Flds. SE3 6H 105
Vanbrugh Hill SE10 5H 105
Vanbrugh Hill SE3 6H 105
Vanbrugh Ho. E9 7J 67 *(off Lodgiges Rd.)*
Vanbrugh M. E15 4G 69

A–Z London 299

Vanbrugh M. – View Cres.

Vanbrugh M. KT12: Walt T ... 7A **148**
Vanbrugh Pk. SE3 ... 7H **105**
Vanbrugh Pk. Rd. SE3 ... 7H **105**
Vanbrugh Pk. Rd. W. SE3 ... 7H **105**
Vanbrugh Rd. W4 ... 3K **97**
Vanbrugh Ter. SE3 ... 1H **123**
Vanburgh Cl. BR6: Orp ... 1J **173**
Vanburgh Ho. E1 ... 5J **9** (5F **85**)
... *(off Folgate St.)*
Vancouver Cl. BR6: Chels ... 4K **173**
Vancouver Ho. E1 ... 1H **103**
... *(off Reardon Path)*
Vancouver Ho. SE16 ... 2K **103**
... *(off Needleman St.)*
Vancouver Mans. HA8: Edg ... 1H **43**
Vancouver Rd. HA8: Edg ... 1H **43**
Vancouver Rd. SE23 ... 2A **140**
Vancouver Rd. TW10: Ham ... 4C **132**
Vancouver Rd. UB4: Yead ... 4K **75**
Vanderbilt Rd. SW18 ... 1K **135**
Vanderbilt Vs. W12 ... 2F **99**
... *(off Sterne St.)*
Vandervell Ct. W3 ... 2A **98**
... *(off Amber Way)*
Vanderville Gdns. N2 ... 2B **46**
Vandome Cl. E16 ... 6K **87**
Vandon Ct. SW1 ... 1B **18** (3G **101**)
... *(off Petty France)*
Vandon Pas. SW1 ... 1B **18** (3G **101**)
Vandon St. SW1 ... 1B **18** (3G **101**)
Van Dyck Av. KT3: N Mald ... 7K **151**
Vandyke Cl. SW15 ... 7F **117**
Vandyke Cross SE9 ... 5C **124**
Vandy St. EC2 ... 4G **9** (4E **84**)
Vane Cl. HA3: Kenton ... 6F **43**
Vane Cl. NW3 ... 5B **64**
Vanessa Cl. DA17: Belv ... 5G **109**
Vanessa Way DA5: Bexl ... 3K **145**
Vane St. SW1 ... 3B **18** (4G **101**)
Vange Ho. W10 ... 5E **80**
... *(off Sutton Way)*
Van Gogh Cl. TW7: Isle ... 3A **114**
Van Gogh Ct. E14 ... 3F **105**
Van Gogh Wlk. SW9 ... 1K **119**
Vanguard NW9 ... 7F **29**
Vanguard Bldg. E14 ... 2B **104**
Vanguard Cl. CR0: C'don ... 1B **168**
Vanguard Cl. E16 ... 5J **87**
Vanguard Cl. RM7: Mawney ... 2G **55**
Vanguard Ct. SE5 ... 1E **120**
Vanguard Ho. E8 ... 7H **67**
Vanguard St. SE8 ... 1C **122**
Vanguard Way E17 ... 4K **49**
Vanguard Way SM6: W'gton ... 7J **167**
Vanguard Way TW6: H'row A ... 2G **111**
Vanilla & Sesame Ct.
SE1 ... 6K **15** (2F **103**)
... *(off Curlew St.)*
Vanneck Sq. SW15 ... 5C **116**
Vanoc Gdns. BR1: Broml ... 4J **141**
Vanquish Cl. TW2: Whitt ... 7E **112**
Vansittart Rd. E7 ... 4H **69**
Vansittart St. SE14 ... 7A **104**
Vanstone Ct. N7 ... 6A **66**
... *(off Blackthorn Av.)*
Vanston Pl. SW6 ... 7J **99**
Vantage Bldg. UB3: Hayes ... 3H **93**
... *(off Station App.)*
Vantage Ct. UB3: Harl ... 7G **93**
Vantage M. E14 ... 1E **104**
... *(off Coldharbour)*
Vantage Pl. TW14: Felt ... 6J **111**
Vantage Pl. W8 ... 3J **99**
Vantage Point BR3: Beck ... 1F **159**
... *(off Albemarle Rd.)*
Vantage Point EN5: Barn ... 4C **20**
... *(off Victors Way)*
Vantage W. TW8: Bford ... 4F **97**
Vantrey Ho. SE11 ... 4J **19** (4A **102**)
... *(off Marylee Way)*
Vant Rd. SW17 ... 5D **136**
Varcoe Gdns. UB3: Hayes ... 6F **75**
Varcoe Rd. SE16 ... 5H **103**
Vardens Rd. SW11 ... 4B **118**
Varden St. E1 ... 6H **85**
Vardon Cl. W3 ... 6K **79**
Varley Dr. TW1: Isle ... 4B **114**
Varley Ho. NW6 ... 1J **81**
Varley Ho. SE1 ... 3C **102**
... *(off County St.)*
Varley Pde. NW9 ... 4A **44**
Varley Rd. E16 ... 6K **87**
Varley Way CR4: Mitc ... 2B **154**
Varna Rd. SW6 ... 7G **99**
Varna Rd. TW12: Hamp ... 1F **149**
Varndell St. NW1 ... 1A **6** (3G **83**)
Varnishers Yd. N1 ... 1F **7** (2J **83**)
... *(off York Way)*
Varsity Dr. TW1: Twick ... 5J **113**
Varsity Row SW14 ... 2J **115**
Vartry Rd. N15 ... 6D **48**
Vascroft Est. NW10 ... 4H **79**
Vassall Ho. E3 ... 3A **86**
... *(off Antill Rd.)*
Vassall Rd. SW9 ... 7A **102**
Vat Ho. SW8 ... 7J **101**
... *(off Rita Rd.)*
Vauban Est. SE16 ... 3F **103**
Vauban St. SE16 ... 3F **103**
Vaudeville Theatre ... 3F 13 (7J 83)
... (off Strand)
Vaughan Almshouses TW15: Ashf
... 5D **128**
... *(off Feltham Hill Rd.)*
Vaughan Av. NW4 ... 5C **44**
Vaughan Av. W6 ... 4B **98**
Vaughan Cl. TW12: Hamp ... 6C **130**
Vaughan Est. E2 ... 1J **9** (3F **85**)
... *(off Diss St.)*
Vaughan Gdns. IG1: Ilf ... 7D **52**
Vaughan Ho. SE1 ... 6A **14** (2B **102**)
... *(off Blackfriars Rd.)*
Vaughan Ho. SW4 ... 7G **119**
Vaughan Rd. DA16: Well ... 2K **125**
Vaughan Rd. E15 ... 6H **69**
Vaughan Rd. HA1: Harr ... 6G **41**
Vaughan Rd. KT7: T Ditt ... 7B **150**
Vaughan Rd. SE5 ... 2C **120**
Vaughan St. SE16 ... 2B **104**
Vaughan Way E1 ... 7G **85**
Vaughan Williams Cl. SE8 ... 7C **104**
Vaughn St. RM8: Dag ... 1E **72**
VAUXHALL ... 6J **101**
Vauxhall Bri. SW1 ... 5E **18** (5J **101**)
Vauxhall Bri. Rd. SW1 ... 2A **18** (3G **101**)
Vauxhall City Farm ... 6G 19 (5K 101)
... (off Tyers St.)
VAUXHALL CROSS ... 6F **19** (5J **101**)
Vauxhall Gdns. CR2: S Croy ... 6C **168**
Vauxhall Gro. SW8 ... 7G **19** (6K **101**)
Vauxhall Leisure Cen. SW8 ... **7F 19 (6J 101)**
Vauxhall St. SE11 ... 5H **19** (5K **101**)
Vauxhall Wlk. SE11 ... 6G **19** (5K **101**)
VauxWall East Climbing Cen.
... 4H 19 (4K 101)
VauxWall West Climbing Cen.
... 7F 19 (6J 101)
... (off Sth. Lambeth Rd.)
Vawdrey Cl. E1 ... 4J **85**
Veals Mead CR4: Mitc ... 1C **154**
Vectis Gdns. SW17 ... 6F **137**
Vectis Rd. SW17 ... 6F **137**
Veda Rd. SE13 ... 4C **122**
Vega Ho. E20 ... 5E **68**
... *(off Prize Wlk.)*
Vega Rd. WD23: Bush ... 1B **26**
Veitch Cl. TW14: Felt ... 7H **111**
Veldene Way HA2: Harr ... 3D **58**
Velde Way SE22 ... 5E **120**
Velletri Ho. E2 ... 2K **85**
... *(off Mace St.)*
Vellum Ct. E17 ... 2A **50**
Vellum Dr. SM5: Cars ... 3E **166**
Velodrome Queen Elizabeth
Olympic Pk. ... 5D 68
Velo Ho. E17 ... 5B **50**
... *(off Track St.)*
Velo Pl. E20 ... 5D **68**
Velvet Ho. E2 ... 2F **85**
... *(off Whiston Rd.)*
Venables Cl. RM10: Dag ... 4H **73**
Venables St. NW8 ... 4B **4** (4B **82**)
Vencourt Pl. W6 ... 4C **98**
Veneer Bldg., The ... 2G **93**
Venerable Ho. E3 ... 4B **86**
... *(off Portia Way)*
Venetian Ho. E20 ... 6D **68**
... *(off Victory Pde.)*
Venetian Rd. SE5 ... 2C **120**
Venetia Rd. N4 ... 6B **48**
Venetia Rd. W5 ... 2D **96**
Venice Corte SE13 ... 3E **122**
... *(off Elmira St.)*
Venice Ct. SE5 ... 7C **102**
... *(off Bowyer St.)*
Venice Ho. HA0: Wemb ... 1E **78**
Venice Wlk. W2 ... 5A **82**
Venner Rd. SE26 ... 6J **139**
... (not continuous)
Venners Cl. DA7: Bex ... 2K **127**
Venn Ho. N1 ... 1K **83**
... *(off Barnsbury Est.)*
Venn St. SW4 ... 4G **119**
Ventnor Av. HA7: Stan ... 1B **42**
Ventnor Dr. N20 ... 3E **30**
Ventnor Gdns. IG11: Bark ... 6J **71**
Ventnor Rd. SE14 ... 7K **103**
Ventnor Rd. SM2: Sutt ... 7K **165**
Venture Cl. DA5: Bexl ... 7E **126**
Venture Ct. SE1 ... 7H **15** (3E **102**)
... *(off Market Yd. M.)*
Venture Ct. SE12 ... 7J **123**
Venture Ho. W10 ... 6F **81**
... *(off Bridge Cl.)*
Venue St. E14 ... 5E **86**
Venus Ho. E14 ... 4C **104**
... *(off Westferry Rd.)*
Venus Ho. E3 ... 1C **86**
... *(off Garrison Rd.)*
Venus M. CR4: Mitc ... 3C **154**
Venus Rd. SE18 ... 3D **106**
Vera Av. N21 ... 5F **23**
Vera Ct. E3 ... 3D **86**
... *(off Grace Pl.)*
Vera Lynn Cl. E7 ... 4J **69**
Vera Rd. SW6 ... 1G **117**
Verbena Cl. E16 ... 4H **87**
Verbena Cl. UB7: W Dray ... 1E **174**
Verbena Gdns. W6 ... 5C **98**
Verdant Ct. SE6 ... 7G **123**
... *(off Verdant La.)*
Verdant La. SE6 ... 7G **123**
Verdayne Av. CR0: C'don ... 2K **169**
Verdi Cres. W10 ... 2G **81**
Verdon Roe Ct. E4 ... 3J **35**
Verdun Rd. SE18 ... 6A **108**
Verdun Rd. SW13 ... 6C **98**
Vere Ct. W2 ... 6K **81**
... *(off Westbourne Gdns.)*
Vereker Dr. TW16: Sun ... 3J **147**
Vereker Rd. W14 ... 5G **99**
Vere St. W1 ... 1J **11** (6F **83**)
Veridion Way DA18: Erith ... 2F **109**
Veritas Ho. DA14: Sidc ... 2A **144**
... *(off Jubilee Way)*
Verity Cl. W11 ... 7G **81**
Verity Ho. E3 ... 3B **86**
... *(off Merchant St.)*
Vermeer Ct. E14 ... 3F **105**
Vermeer Gdns. SE15 ... 4J **121**
Vermilion Apts. E3 ... 1A **86**
... *(off Gunmaker's La.)*
Vermont Cl. EN2: Enf ... 4G **23**
Vermont Ho. E17 ... 2B **50**
Vermont Rd. SE19 ... 6D **138**
Vermont Rd. SM1: Sutt ... 3K **165**
Vermont Rd. SW18 ... 6K **117**
Verna Ho. E20 ... 5E **68**
... *(off Sunrise Cl.)*
Verney Gdns. RM9: Dag ... 4E **72**
Verney Ho. NW8 ... 3C **4** (4C **82**)
... *(off Jerome Cres.)*
Verney Rd. RM9: Dag ... 4E **72**
... (not continuous)
Verney Rd. SE16 ... 6G **103**
Verney St. NW10 ... 3K **61**
Verney Way SE16 ... 5H **103**
Vernham Rd. SE18 ... 6G **107**
Vernon Av. E12 ... 4D **70**
Vernon Av. IG8: Wfd G ... 7E **36**
Vernon Av. SW20 ... 2F **153**
Vernon Cl. KT19: Ewe ... 6J **163**
Vernon Cl. TW19: Stanw ... 1A **128**
Vernon Ct. HA7: Stan ... 1B **42**
Vernon Ct. NW2 ... 3H **63**
Vernon Ct. W5 ... 7C **78**
Vernon Cres. EN4: E Barn ... 6K **21**
Vernon Dr. HA7: Stan ... 1A **42**
Vernon Ho. SE11 ... 6H **19** (5K **101**)
... *(off Vauxhall St.)*
Vernon Ho. WC1 ... 6F **7** (5J **83**)
... *(off Vernon Pl.)*
Vernon Mans. W14 ... 6H **99**
... *(off Queen's Club Gdns.)*
Vernon M. E17 ... 5B **50**
Vernon M. W14 ... 4G **99**
Vernon Pl. WC1 ... 6F **7** (5J **83**)
Vernon Ri. UB6: G'frd ... 5H **59**
Vernon Ri. WC1 ... 1H **7** (3K **83**)
Vernon Rd. E11 ... 1G **69**
Vernon Rd. E15 ... 7G **69**
Vernon Rd. E17 ... 5B **50**
Vernon Rd. E3 ... 2B **86**
Vernon Rd. IG3: Ilf ... 1K **71**
Vernon Rd. N8 ... 3A **48**
Vernon Rd. SM1: Sutt ... 5A **166**
Vernon Rd. SW14 ... 3K **115**
Vernon Rd. TW13: Felt ... 2H **129**
Vernon Sq. WC1 ... 1H **7** (3K **83**)
Vernon St. W14 ... 4G **99**
Vernon Yd. W11 ... 7H **81**
Veroan Rd. DA7: Bex ... 2E **126**
Verona Ct. SE14 ... 6K **103**
... *(off Myers La.)*
Verona Ct. TW15: Ashf ... 4D **128**
Verona Ct. W4 ... 5A **98**
Verona Dr. KT6: Surb ... 2E **162**
Verona Ho. CR4: Mitc ... 3F **155**
... *(off Aventine Av.)*
Verona Rd. E7 ... 7J **69**
Veronica Gdns. SW16 ... 1G **155**
Veronica Ho. E3 ... 3D **86**
... *(off Talwin St.)*
Veronica Ho. SE4 ... 3B **122**
Veronica Rd. SW17 ... 2F **137**
Veronique Gdns. IG6: Ilf ... 5G **53**
Verran Rd. SW12 ... 7F **119**
Versailles Rd. SE20 ... 7G **139**
Verulam Av. E17 ... 6B **50**
Verulam Bldgs. WC1 ... 5H **7** (5K **83**)
... *(off Grays Inn)*
Verulam Ct. NW9 ... 7C **44**
Verulam Ct. UB1: S'hall ... 6G **77**
... *(off Haldane Rd.)*
Verulam Ho. W6 ... 2E **98**
... *(off Hammersmith Gro.)*
Verulam Rd. UB6: G'frd ... 4E **76**
Verulam St. WC1 ... 5J **7** (5A **84**)
Vervian Ho. SE15 ... 7G **103**
... *(off Reddins Rd.)*
Verwood Dr. EN4: Cockf ... 3J **21**
Verwood Ho. SW8 ... 7K **101**
... *(off Cobbett St.)*
Verwood Lodge E14 ... 3F **105**
... *(off Manchester Rd.)*
Verwood Rd. HA2: Harr ... 2G **41**
Veryan Ct. N8 ... 5H **47**
Vesage Ct. EC1 ... 6K **7** (5A **84**)
... *(off Leather La.)*
Vesey Path E14 ... 6D **86**
Vespan Rd. W12 ... 2C **98**
Vespucci Ct. E14 ... 5A **86**
... *(off Oman Way)*
Vesta Ct. SE1 ... 7G **15** (2E **102**)
... *(off City Wlk.)*
Vesta Ho. E20 ... 5E **68**
... *(off Liberty Bri. Rd.)*
Vesta Ho. E3 ... 1C **86**
... *(off Garrison Rd.)*
Vesta Rd. SE4 ... 2A **122**
Vestris Rd. SE23 ... 2K **139**
Voctry Ct. RM7: Rush G ... 6K **55**
Vestry Ct. SW1 ... 2D **18** (3H **101**)
... *(off Monck St.)*
Vestry House Mus. ... 4D 50
Vestry M. SE5 ... 1E **120**
Vestry M. SW18 ... 5B **118**
Vestry Rd. E17 ... 4D **50**
Vestry Rd. SE5 ... 1E **120**
Vestry St. N1 ... 1E **8** (3D **84**)
Vesuvius Apts. E3 ... 2B **86**
... *(off Centurion La.)*
Vevey St. SE6 ... 2B **140**
Veysey Gdns. RM10: Dag ... 3G **73**
Viaduct, The E18 ... 2J **51**
Viaduct, The N10 ... 4F **47**
Viaduct Bldgs. EC1 ... 6K **7** (5A **84**)
Viaduct Gdns. SW11 Ace Way
... 7D **18** (6H **101**)
Viaduct Gdns. SW11 Nine Elms La.
... 7G **101**
Viaduct Pl. E2 ... 3H **85**
Viaduct Rd. N2 ... 2B **46**
Viaduct St. E2 ... 3H **85**
Vian St. SE13 ... 3D **122**
Viant Ho. NW10 ... 7K **61**
... *(off Fawood Av.)*
Vibart Gdns. SW2 ... 7K **119**
Vibart Wlk. N1 ... 1J **83**
... *(off Outram Pl.)*
Vibeca Apts. E1 ... 6K **9** (5F **85**)
... *(off Chicksand St.)*
Vibia Cl. TW19: Stanw ... 7A **110**
Vicarage Av. SE3 ... 7J **105**
Vicarage Cl. DA8: Erith ... 6J **109**
Vicarage Cl. HA4: Ruis ... 7F **39**
Vicarage Cl. KT4: Wor Pk ... 1A **164**
Vicarage Cl. UB5: N'olt ... 7D **58**
Vicarage Ct. BR3: Beck ... 3A **158**
Vicarage Ct. IG1: Ilf ... 5F **71**
Vicarage Ct. TW14: Bedf ... 7E **110**
Vicarage Ct. W8 ... 2K **99**
Vicarage Cres. SW11 ... 1B **118**
Vicarage Dr. BR3: Beck ... 1C **158**
Vicarage Dr. IG11: Bark ... 7G **71**
Vicarage Dr. SW14 ... 5K **115**
Vicarage Farm Ct. TW5: Hest ... 7D **94**
Vicarage Farm Rd. TW3: Houn
... 2C **112**
Vicarage Farm Rd. TW5: Hest ... 1C **112**
Vicarage Flds. KT12: Walt T ... 6A **148**
Vicarage Fld. Shop. Cen. ... 7G **71**
Vicarage Gdns. CR4: Mitc ... 3C **154**
Vicarage Gdns. SW14 ... 5J **115**
Vicarage Gdns. W8 ... 1J **99**
Vicarage Ga. W8 ... 1K **99**
Vicarage Gro. SE5 ... 1D **120**
Vicarage Ho. KT1: King T ... 2F **151**
... *(off Cambridge Rd.)*
Vicarage La. E15 ... 7G **69**
Vicarage La. E6 ... 3D **88**
Vicarage La. IG1: Ilf ... 1H **71**
Vicarage La. KT17: Ewe ... 7C **164**
... (not continuous)
Vicarage M. NW9 ... 2K **61**
Vicarage M. W4 ... 6A **98**
... *(off Bennett St.)*
Vicarage Pde. N15 ... 4C **48**
Vicarage Pk. SE18 ... 5G **107**
Vicarage Path N8 ... 7J **47**
Vicarage Rd. CR0: Wadd ... 3A **168**
Vicarage Rd. DA5: Bexl ... 1H **145**
Vicarage Rd. E10 ... 7C **50**
Vicarage Rd. E15 ... 7H **69**
Vicarage Rd. IG8: Wfd G ... 7H **37**
Vicarage Rd. KT1: Hamp W ... 1C **150**
Vicarage Rd. KT1: King T ... 2D **150**
Vicarage Rd. N17 ... 1G **49**
Vicarage Rd. NW4 ... 6C **44**
Vicarage Rd. RM10: Dag ... 7H **73**
Vicarage Rd. SE18 ... 5G **107**
... (not continuous)
Vicarage Rd. SM1: Sutt ... 3K **165**
Vicarage Rd. SW14 ... 5J **115**
Vicarage Rd. TW11: Tedd ... 5A **132**
Vicarage Rd. TW16: Sun ... 5H **129**
Vicarage Rd. TW2: Twick ... 2J **131**
Vicarage Rd. TW2: Whitt ... 6G **113**
Vicarage Wlk. KT12: Walt T ... 7J **147**
Vicarage Wlk. SW11 ... 1B **118**
Vicarage Way HA2: Harr ... 7E **40**
Vicarage Way NW10 ... 3K **61**
Vicars Bri. Cl. HA0: Wemb ... 2E **78**
Vicar's Cl. E9 ... 1J **85**
Vicars Cl. E15 ... 1J **87**
Vicars Cl. EN1: Enf ... 2K **23**
Vicar's Hill SE13 ... 4D **122**
Vicars Moor La. N21 ... 7F **23**
Vicars Oak Rd. SE19 ... 6E **138**
Vicar's Rd. NW5 ... 5E **64**
Vicars Wlk. RM8: Dag ... 3B **72**
Vicary Ho. EC1 ... 6C **8** (5C **84**)
... *(off Bartholomew Cl.)*
Vicentia Ct. SW11 ... 3A **118**
Viceroy Cl. N2 ... 4C **46**
... *(off East End Rd.)*
Viceroy Ct. CR0: C'don ... 1D **168**
Viceroy Ct. NW8 ... 2C **82**
... *(off Prince Albert Rd.)*
Viceroy Pde. N2 ... 4C **46**
... *(off High Rd.)*
Viceroy Rd. SW8 ... 1J **119**
Vicinity Ho. E14 ... 7C **86**
... *(off Storehouse M.)*
Vic Johnson Ho. E3 ... 1B **86**
... *(off Armagh Rd.)*
Vickers Cl. SM6: W'gton ... 7K **167**
Vickers Ct. N17 ... 3H **49**
Vickers Ct. SE20 ... 7K **139**
Vickers Ct. TW19: Stanw ... 6A **110**
... *(off Whitley Cl.)*
Vickers Rd. DA8: Erith ... 5K **109**
Vickers Way TW4: Houn ... 5C **112**
Vickery Ct. EC1 ... 3D **8** (4C **84**)
... *(off Mitchell St.)*
Vickery's Wharf E14 ... 6C **86**
Victor Cazalet Ho. N1 ... 1B **84**
... *(off Gaskin St.)*
Victor Gro. HA0: Wemb ... 7E **60**
Victor Ho. SE7 ... 6A **106**
Victoria & Albert Mus. ... 2B 16 (3B 100)
Victoria Arc. SW1 ... 2K **17** (3F **101**)
... *(off Victoria St.)*
Victoria Av. E6 ... 1B **88**
Victoria Av. EC2 ... 6H **9** (5E **84**)
Victoria Av. EN4: E Barn ... 4G **21**
Victoria Av. HA9: Wemb ... 6H **61**
Victoria Av. KT6: Surb ... 6D **150**
Victoria Av. KT8: W Mole ... 3F **149**
Victoria Av. N3 ... 1H **45**
Victoria Av. SM6: W'gton ... 3E **166**
Victoria Av. TW3: Houn ... 5E **112**
Victoria Av. UB10: Hil ... 6D **56**
Victoria Bldgs. E8 ... 1H **85**
... *(off Mare St.)*
Victoria Chambers EC2 ... 3G **9** (4E **84**)
... *(off Paul St.)*
Victoria Cl. EN4: E Barn ... 4G **21**
Victoria Cl. HA1: Harr ... 6K **41**
Victoria Cl. KT8: W Mole ... 3E **148**
Victoria Cl. SE22 ... 5G **121**
Victoria Cl. UB3: Hayes ... 6F **75**
Victoria Colonnade WC1 ... 6F **7** (5J **83**)
... *(off Southampton Row)*
Victoria Cotts. E1 ... 5G **85**
... *(off Deal St.)*
Victoria Cotts. N10 ... 2E **46**
Victoria Cotts. TW9: Kew ... 1F **115**
Victoria Ct. E18 ... 3K **51**
Victoria Ct. HA7: Stan ... 7J **27**
... *(off Howard Rd.)*
Victoria Ct. HA9: Wemb ... 6G **61**
Victoria Ct. SE1 ... 4E **102**
... *(off Hendre Rd.)*
Victoria Ct. SE26 ... 6J **139**
Victoria Ct. W3 ... 2G **97**
Victoria Cres. N15 ... 5E **48**
Victoria Cres. SE19 ... 6E **138**
Victoria Cres. SW19 ... 7H **135**
Victoria Dock Rd. E16 ... 7H **87**
Victoria Dr. SW19 ... 7F **117**
Victoria Emb. EC4 ... 2J **13** (7A **84**)
Victoria Emb. SW1 ... 7F **13** (2J **101**)
Victoria Emb. WC2 ... 4F **13** (1J **101**)
Victoria Embankment Gdns.
WC2 ... 4F **13** (1J **101**)
... *(off Victoria Embankment)*
Victoria Gdns. TW5: Hest ... 1C **112**
Victoria Gdns. W11 ... 1J **99**
Victoria Gro. N12 ... 5G **31**
Victoria Gro. W8 ... 3A **100**
Victoria Gro. M. W2 ... 7J **81**
Victoria Hall E16 ... 1J **105**
... *(off Wesley Av.)*
Victoria Ho. SW1 Ebury Bri. Rd.
... 5J **17** (5F **101**)
... *(off Ebury Bri. Rd.)*
Victoria Ho. SW1 Francis St.
... 3B **18** (4G **101**)
... *(off Francis St.)*
Victoria Ho. E6 ... 6E **88**
Victoria Ho. HA8: Edg ... 6C **28**
Victoria Ho. SE16 ... 2J **103**
... *(off Surrey Quays Rd.)*
Victoria Ho. SW8 ... 7J **101**
... *(off Sth. Lambeth Rd.)*
Victoria Ind. Est. W3 ... 5A **80**
Victoria La. EN5: Barn ... 4C **20**
Victoria La. UB3: Harl ... 5F **93**
Victoria Mans. NW10 ... 7D **62**
Victoria Mans. SW8 ... 7J **101**
... *(off Sth. Lambeth Rd.)*
Victoria Mans. W14 ... 6H **99**
... *(off Queen's Club Gdns.)*
Victoria M. E8 ... 6G **67**
Victoria M. NW6 ... 1J **81**
Victoria M. SW18 ... 1A **136**
Victoria M. SW4 ... 4F **119**
Victoria M. W11 ... 1J **99**
Victoria Mills Studios E15 ... 1F **87**
... *(off Burford Rd.)*
Victorian Gro. N16 ... 4E **66**
Victorian Hgts. SW8 ... 2F **119**
... *(off Thackeray Rd.)*
Victorian Rd. N16 ... 3E **66**
Victoria Palace Theatre ... 2A 18 (3G 101)
... (off Victoria St.)
Victoria Pde. SE10 ... 6D **104**
Victoria Pde. TW9: Kew ... 1G **115**
... *(off Sandycombe Rd.)*
Victoria Pk. Hackney ... 1K 85
Victoria Pk. Ct. E9 ... 7J **67**
... *(off Well St.)*
Victoria Pk. Ind. Cen. E9 ... 7C **68**
... *(off Rothbury Rd.)*
Victoria Pk. Rd. E9 ... 1J **85**
Victoria Pk. Sq. E2 ... 3J **85**
Victoria Pk. Studios E9 ... 6J **67**
... *(off Milborne St.)*
Victoria Pas. NW8 ... 3A **4** (4B **82**)
... *(off Fisherton St.)*
Victoria Pl. TW9: Rich ... 5D **114**
Victoria Pl. Shop. Cen. ... 3K **17** (4F **101**)
... *(off Buckingham Pal. Rd.)*
Victoria Point E13 ... 2J **87**
... *(off Victoria Rd.)*
Victoria Retail Pk. South Ruislip ... 5B **58**
Victoria Ri. NW6 ... 7A **64**
... *(off Hilgrove Rd.)*
Victoria Ri. SW4 ... 3F **119**
Victoria Rd. BR2: Broml ... 5B **160**
Victoria Rd. BR7: Chst ... 5E **142**
Victoria Rd. CR4: Mitc ... 7C **136**
Victoria Rd. DA15: Sidc ... 3K **143**
Victoria Rd. DA6: Bex ... 4G **127**
Victoria Rd. DA8: Erith ... 6K **109**
Victoria Rd. E11 ... 4G **69**
Victoria Rd. E13 ... 2J **87**
Victoria Rd. E17 ... 2E **50**
Victoria Rd. E18 ... 2K **51**
Victoria Rd. E4 ... 1B **36**
Victoria Rd. EN4: E Barn ... 4G **21**
Victoria Rd. HA4: Ruis ... 1J **57**
Victoria Rd. IG11: Bark ... 6F **71**
Victoria Rd. IG9: Buck H ... 2G **37**
Victoria Rd. KT1: King T ... 2F **151**
Victoria Rd. KT6: Surb ... 6D **150**
Victoria Rd. N15 ... 4G **49**
Victoria Rd. N18 ... 4A **34**
Victoria Rd. N22 ... 1G **47**
Victoria Rd. N4 ... 7K **47**
Victoria Rd. N9 ... 3A **34**
Victoria Rd. NW10 ... 5K **79**
Victoria Rd. NW4 ... 4E **44**
Victoria Rd. NW6 ... 2H **81**
Victoria Rd. NW7 ... 5G **29**
Victoria Rd. RM10: Dag ... 5H **73**
Victoria Rd. SM1: Sutt ... 5B **166**
Victoria Rd. SW14 ... 3K **115**
Victoria Rd. TW1: Twick ... 7B **114**
Victoria Rd. TW11: Tedd ... 6A **132**
Victoria Rd. TW13: Felt ... 1K **129**
Victoria Rd. UB2: S'hall ... 3D **94**
Victoria Rd. W3 ... 5K **79**
Victoria Rd. W5 ... 5B **78**
Victoria Rd. W8 ... 3A **100**
Victoria Rd. WD23: Bush ... 1A **26**
Victoria Road ... 5H 73
Victoria Sq. SW1 ... 1K **17** (3F **101**)
Victoria St. DA17: Belv ... 5F **109**
Victoria St. E15 ... 7G **69**
Victoria St. SW1 ... 2A **18** (3G **101**)
Victoria Ter. HA1: Harr ... 1J **59**
Victoria Ter. N4 ... 1A **66**
Victoria Ter. NW10 ... 4B **80**
Victoria Ter. W5 ... 1D **96**
Victoria Vs. TW9: Rich ... 3F **115**
Victoria Way HA4: Ruis ... 5B **58**
Victoria Way SE7 ... 5K **105**
Victoria Wharf E14 ... 7A **86**
Victoria Wharf E2 ... 2K **85**
... *(off Palmers Rd.)*
Victoria Wharf SE8 ... 5B **104**
... *(off Dragoon Rd.)*
Victoria Works NW2 ... 2D **62**
Victoria Yd. E1 ... 6G **85**
Victor Rd. HA2: Harr ... 3G **41**
Victor Rd. NW10 ... 3D **80**
Victor Rd. SE20 ... 7K **139**
Victor Rd. TW11: Tedd ... 4J **131**
Victors Dr. TW12: Hamp ... 6C **130**
Victors Way EN5: Barn ... 3C **20**
Victor Vs. N9 ... 3J **33**
Victor Wlk. NW9 ... 2A **44**
Victor Wharf SE1 ... 4E **14** (1D **102**)
... *(off Clink St.)*
Victory Av. SM4: Mord ... 5A **154**
Victory Bus. Cen. TW7: Isle ... 4K **113**
Victory Cl. TW19: Stanw ... 1A **128**
Victory Ct. IG11: Bark ... 4B **90**
Victory Ct. W9 ... 4J **81**
... *(off Hermes Cl.)*
Victory M. UB2: S'hall ... 3C **94**
Victory Pde. E20 ... 6D **68**
Victory Pde. SE18 ... 3F **107**
Victory Pk. HA9: Wemb ... 3D **60**
Victory Pl. E14 ... 7A **86**
Victory Pl. SE17 ... 4D **102**
Victory Pl. SE19 ... 7E **138**
Victory Rd. E11 ... 4J **51**
Victory Rd. SW19 ... 7A **136**
Victory Rd. M. SW19 ... 7A **136**
... *(off Victory Rd.)*
Victory Wlk. SE8 ... 1C **122**
Victory Way RM7: Mawney ... 2H **55**
Victory Way SE16 ... 2A **104**
Victory Way TW5: Cran ... 5A **94**
Vida Ho. SE8 ... 5K **103**
Video Ct. N4 ... 7K **47**
Vidler Cl. KT9: Chess ... 6C **162**
Vienna Cl. IG5: Ilf ... 2B **52**
View, The SE2 ... 5E **108**
View Cl. HA1: Harr ... 4H **41**
View Cl. N6 ... 7D **46**
View Cres. N8 ... 5H **47**

Wallingford Av. – Warwick Way

Wallingford Av. W10 5F 81
WALLINGTON 6F 167
Wallington Cl. HA4: Ruis 6E 38
Wallington Cnr. SM6: W'gton 4F 167
(off Manor Rd. Nth.)
Wallington Ct. SM6: W'gton 6F 167
(off Stanley Pk. Rd.)
WALLINGTON GREEN 4F 167
Wallington Rd. IG3: Ilf 7K 53
Wallington Sq. SM6: W'gton 6F 167
Wallis All. SE1 6D 14 (2C 102)
(off Marshalsea Rd.)
Wallis Cl. SW11 3B 118
Wallis Ho. HA4: Ruis 1F 57
Wallis Ho. SE14 1A 122
Wallis Ho. TW8: Bford 5E 96
Wallis M. N8 3A 48
(off Courcy Rd.)
Wallis Rd. E9 6B 68
Wallis Rd. TW6: H'row A 5C 174
Wallis Rd. UB1: S'hall 6F 77
Wallis's Cotts. SW2 7J 119
Wallman Pl. N22 1K 47
Wallorton Gdns. SW14 4K 115
Wallpaper Apts., The N1 7A 66
(off Offord Rd.)
Wallside EC2 6D 8 (5C 84)
(off Monkwell Sq.)
Wall St. N1 6D 66
Wallwood Rd. E11 7F 51
Wallwood St. E14 5B 86
Walmar Cl. EN4: Had W 1G 21
Walmer Cl. BR6: Farnb 4H 173
Walmer Cl. E4 2J 35
Walmer Cl. RM7: Mawney 2H 55
Walmer Ct. KT5: Surb 5E 150
(off Cranes Pk.)
Walmer Gdns. W13 2A 96
Walmer Ho. W10 6F 81
(off Bramley Rd.)
Walmer Pl. W1 5E 4 (5D 82)
(off Walmer St.)
Walmer Rd. W10 6E 80
Walmer Rd. W11 7G 81
Walmer St. W1 5E 4 (5D 82)
Walmer Ter. SE18 4G 107
Walmgate Rd. UB6: G'frd 1B 78
Walmington Fold N12 6D 30
Walm La. NW2 6E 62
Walney Wlk. N1 6C 66
Walnut Av. UB7: W Dray 3C 92
Walnut Cl. IG6: Ilf 4G 53
Walnut Cl. SE8 6B 104
Walnut Cl. SM5: Cars 5D 166
Walnut Cl. UB3: Hayes 7G 75
Walnut Ct. E17 4E 50
Walnut Ct. W5 2E 96
Walnut Ct. W8 3K 99
(off St Mary's Ga.)
Walnut Flds. KT17: Ewe 7B 164
Walnut Gdns. E15 5G 69
Walnut Gro. EN1: Enf 5J 23
Walnut Ho. E3 1B 86
(off Barge La.)
Walnut M. N22 3A 48
(off High Rd.)
Walnut M. SM2: Sutt 7A 166
Walnut Rd. E10 2C 68
Walnut Tree Av. CR4: Mitc 3C 154
(off De'Arn Gdns.)
Walnut Tree Cl. BR7: Chst 1H 161
Walnut Tree Cl. SW13 1B 116
Walnut Tree Cl. TW17: Shep 3E 146
Walnut Tree Cl. UB10: Ick 4A 56
Walnut Tree Cotts. SW19 5G 135
Walnut Tree Ho. SW10 6K 99
(off Tregunter Rd.)
Walnut Tree Rd. RM8: Dag 2E 72
Walnut Tree Rd. SE10 5G 105
(not continuous)
Walnut Tree Rd. TW17: Shep 2E 146
Walnut Tree Rd. TW5: Hest 6D 94
Walnut Tree Rd. TW8: Bford 6E 96
Walnut Tree Wlk. SE11 3J 19 (4A 102)
Walnut Way HA4: Ruis 6A 58
Walnut Way IG9: Buck H 3G 37
Walpole Av. TW9: Kew 2F 115
Walpole Cl. W13 2C 96
Walpole Ct. NW6 7A 64
(off Fairfax Rd.)
Walpole Ct. TW2: Twick 2J 131
Walpole Ct. W14 3F 99
(off Blythe Rd.)
Walpole Cres. TW11: Tedd 5K 131
Walpole Gdns. TW2: Twick 2J 131
Walpole Gdns. W4 5J 97
Walpole Ho. KT8: W Mole 5E 148
(off Approach Rd.)
Walpole Ho. SE1 7J 13 (2A 102)
(off Westminster Bri. Rd.)
Walpole Ho. SW15 5G 117
(off Plaza Gdns.)
Walpole Lodge W13 1C 96
Walpole M. NW8 1B 82
Walpole M. SW19 6B 136
Walpole Pl. SE18 4F 107
Walpole Pl. TW11: Tedd 5K 131
Walpole Rd. BR2: Broml 5B 160
Walpole Rd. CR0: C'don 2D 168
Walpole Rd. E17 4A 50
Walpole Rd. E18 1H 51
Walpole Rd. E6 7A 70
Walpole Rd. KT6: Surb 7E 150
Walpole Rd. N17 2C 48
(not continuous)
Walpole Rd. SW19 6B 136
Walpole Rd. TW11: Tedd 5K 131
Walpole Rd. TW2: Twick 2J 131
Walpole St. SW3 5E 16 (5D 100)
Walrond Av. HA9: Wemb 5E 60
Walsham Cl. N16 1G 67
Walsham Cl. SE28 7D 90
Walsham Ho. SE14 2K 121
Walsham Ho. SE17 5D 102
(off Blackwood St.)
Walsham How Cl. E17 5F 51
Walsham Rd. SE14 2K 121
Walsham Rd. TW14: Felt 7K 111
Walsingham NW8 1B 82
Walsingham Gdns. KT19: Ewe 4A 164
Walsingham Lodge SW13 1C 116
Walsingham Mans. SW6 7K 99
(off Fulham Rd.)
Walsingham Pk. BR7: Chst 2H 161
Walsingham Pl. SW4 6E 118
Walsingham Rd. CR4: Mitc 5D 154
Walsingham Rd. E5 3G 67
Walsingham Rd. EN2: Enf 4J 23
Walsingham Rd. W13 1A 96
Walsingham Wlk. DA17: Belv 6G 109
Walston Ho. SW1 5C 18 (5H 101)
(off Aylesford St.)
Walter Besant Ho. E1 3K 85
(off Bancroft Rd.)
Walter Ct. W3 6J 79
(off Lynton Ter.)
Walter Grn. Ho. SE15 1J 121
(off Lausanne Rd.)
Walter Ho. SW10 7B 100
(off Riley St.)
Walter Hurford Ho. E12 4E 70
(off Grantham Rd.)
Walter Langley Ct. SE16 2J 103
(off Brunel Rd.)
Walter Rodney Cl. E6 6D 70
Walter Savil Twr. E17 6C 50
(off Colchester Rd.)
Walters Cl. SE17 4D 102
(off Brandon St.)
Walters Cl. UB3: Hayes 2H 93
Walters Ho. N1 1B 84
(off Essex Rd.)
Walters Ho. SE17 6B 102
(off Otto St.)
Walter Sickert Hall N1 1C 8 (2C 84)
(off Graham St.)
Walters Rd. EN3: Pond E 4D 24
Walters Rd. SE25 4E 156
Walter St. E2 3K 85
Walter St. KT2: King T 1E 150
Walters Wlk. HA9: Wemb 4G 61
Walters Way SE23 6K 121
Walters Yd. BR1: Broml 2J 159
Walter Ter. E1 6K 85
Walterton Rd. W9 4H 81
Walter Wlk. HA8: Edg 6D 28
Waltham Av. NW9 6G 43
Waltham Av. UB3: Harl 3E 92
Waltham Dr. HA8: Edg 2G 43
Waltham Forest Feel Good Cen. 2D 50
Waltham Ho. NW8 1A 82
Waltham Pk. Way E17 1C 50
Waltham Rd. IG8: Wfd G 6H 37
Waltham Rd. SM5: Cars 7B 154
Waltham Rd. UB2: S'hall 3C 94
WALTHAMSTOW 3C 50
Walthamstow Av. E4 6G 35
Walthamstow Bus. Cen. E17 2E 50
Walthamstow Leisure Cen. 6B 50
Walthamstow Marsh Nature Reserve 7H 49
Walthamstow Pumphouse Mus. 6A 50
Waltham Way E4 3G 35
Waltheof Av. N17 1D 48
Waltheof Gdns. N17 1D 48
Walton Av. HA2: Harr 5D 58
Walton Av. HA9: Wemb 3H 61
Walton Av. KT3: N Mald 4B 152
Walton Av. SM3: Cheam 3H 165
Walton Bri. KT12: Walt T 7G 147
WALTON BRI. 7G 147
Walton Bri. Rd. TW17: Shep 7G 147
Walton Cl. E4 5H 35
Walton Cl. E5 3K 67
(off Orient Way)
Walton Cl. HA1: Harr 4H 41
Walton Cl. NW2 2D 62
Walton Cl. SW8 7J 101
Walton Ct. CR2: S Croy 5C 168
(off Warham Rd.)
Walton Ct. EN5: New Bar 5F 21
Walton Ct. NW6 7A 64
(off Fairfax Rd.)
Walton Cft. HA1: Harr 4J 59
Walton Dr. HA1: Harr 4H 41
Walton Dr. NW10 6K 61
Walton Gdns. HA9: Wemb 2E 60
Walton Gdns. TW13: Felt 4H 129
Walton Gdns. W3 5H 79
Walton Grn. CR0: New Ad 7D 170
Walton Ho. E17 3D 50
Walton Ho. E2 3K 9 (4F 85)
(off Montclare St.)
Walton Ho. NW1 3K 5 (4F 83)
(off Longford St.)
Walton Ho. SW3 2E 16 (3D 100)
(off Walton St.)
Walton La. TW17: Shep 7F 147
WALTON-ON-THAMES 7J 147
Walton on Thames Camping &
Cvn. Site KT12: Walt T 7E 148
Walton Pl. SW3 1E 16 (3D 100)
Walton Rd. DA14: Sidc 2C 144
Walton Rd. E12 4E 70
(not continuous)
Walton Rd. E13 2A 88
Walton Rd. HA1: Harr 4H 41
Walton Rd. KT12: Walt T 5A 148
Walton Rd. KT8: E Mos 4D 148
Walton Rd. KT8: W Mole 4D 148
Walton Rd. N15 4F 49
Walton Rd. RM5: Col R 1F 55
Walton St. EN2: Enf 1J 23
Walton St. SW3 3D 16 (4C 100)
Walton Vs. N1 7E 66
(off Downham Rd.)
Walton Way CR4: Mitc 4G 155
Walton Way W3 5H 79
Walt Whitman Cl. SE24 4B 120
WALWORTH 5C 102
Walworth Pl. SE17 5C 102
Walworth Rd. SE1 4C 102
Walworth Rd. SE17 4C 102
Walworth Sq. SE17 4C 102
Walwyn Av. BR1: Broml 3B 160
Wanborough Dr. SW15 1D 134
Wanderer Dr. IG11: Bark 3C 90
Wandle Apts. CR2: S Croy 5D 168
Wandle Bank CR0: Bedd 3J 167
Wandle Bank SW19 7B 136
Wandle Ct. CR0: Bedd 3J 167
Wandle Ct. KT19: Ewe 4J 163
Wandle Ct. Gdns. CR0: Bedd 3J 167
Wandle Ho. BR1: Broml 5F 141
Wandle Ho. NW8 5C 4 (5C 82)
(off Penfold St.)
Wandle Industrial Mus. 3D 154
Wandle Meadow Nature Pk. 5A 136
Wandle Pk. 2B 168
Wandle Pk. Trad. Est., The CR0: C'don 2B 168
Wandle Recreation Cen. 6K 117
Wandle Rd. CR0: Bedd 3J 167
Wandle Rd. CR0: C'don 3C 168
Wandle Rd. SM4: Mord 4A 154
Wandle Rd. SM6: W'gton 3F 167
Wandle Rd. SW17 2C 136
Wandle Side CR0: Wadd 3K 167
Wandle Side SM6: W'gton 3F 167
Wandle Trad. Est. CR4: Mitc 7D 154
Wandle Way CR4: Mitc 5D 154
Wandle Way SW18 1K 135
Wandon Rd. SW6 7K 99
WANDSWORTH 5K 117
WANDSWORTH BRI. 3K 117
Wandsworth Bri. Rd. SW6 1K 117
WANDSWORTH COMMON 1D 136
Wandsworth Comn. W. Side
SW18 5A 118
WANDSWORTH GYRATORY 5K 117
Wandsworth High St. SW18 5J 117
Wandsworth Plain SW18 5K 117
Wandsworth Rd. SW8 3F 119
Wangey Rd. RM6: Chad H 7D 54
Wangford Ho. SW9 4B 120
(off Loughborough Pk.)
Wanless Rd. SE24 3C 120
Wanley Rd. SE5 4D 120
Wanlip Rd. E13 4K 87
Wansbeck Ct. EN2: Enf 3G 23
(off Waverley Rd.)
Wansbeck Rd. E9 7B 68
Wansdown Pl. SW6 7K 99
Wansey St. SE17 4C 102
Wansford Rd. IG8: Wfd G 1A 52
WANSTEAD 6K 51
Wanstead Cl. BR1: Broml 2A 160
Wanstead Gdns. IG4: Ilf 6B 52
Wanstead Golf Course 7A 52
Wanstead La. IG1: Ilf 6B 52
Wanstead Leisure Cen. 6A 52
Wanstead Pk. Av. E12 1B 70
Wanstead Pk. Rd. IG1: Ilf 6B 52
Wanstead Pl. E11 6J 51
Wanstead Rd. BR1: Broml 2A 160
Wansunt Rd. DA5: Bexl 1J 145
Wantage Rd. SE12 5H 123
Wantz Rd. RM10: Dag 4H 73
WAPPING 1H 103
Wapping Dock St. E1 1H 103
Wapping High St. E1 1G 103
Wapping La. E1 7H 85
Wapping Wall E1 1J 103
Waratah Dr. BR7: Chst 5D 142
Warbank La. KT2: King T 7B 134
Warbeck Rd. W12 2D 98
Warberry Rd. N22 1K 47
Warboys App. KT2: King T 6H 133
Warboys Cres. E4 5K 35
Warboys Gro. IG11: Bark 4C 90
Warboys Rd. KT2: King T 6H 133
Warburg Ct. NW9 3A 44
(off Mornington Cl.)
Warburton Cl. HA3: Hrw W 6C 26
Warburton Cl. N1 6E 66
(off Culford Rd.)
Warburton Ct. HA4: Ruis 2J 57
Warburton Ho. E8 1H 85
(off Warburton St.)
Warburton Rd. E8 1H 85
Warburton Rd. TW2: Whitt 1F 131
Warburton St. E8 1H 85
Warburton Ter. E17 2D 50
Wardalls Gro. SE14 7J 103
Wardalls Ho. SE8 6B 104
(off Staunton St.)
Ward Cl. CR2: S Croy 6E 168
Ward Cl. DA8: Erith 6K 109
Wardell Cl. NW7 7F 29
Wardell Fld. NW9 1A 44
Wardell Ho. SE10 6E 104
(off Welland St.)
Wardell M. SW4 3F 119
Warden Av. HA2: Harr 1D 58
Warden Rd. NW5 6E 64
Wardens Fld. Cl. BR6: Chels 5K 173
Wardens Gro. SE1 5C 14 (1C 102)
Ward La. E9 5A 68
Wardle St. E9 5K 67
Wardley St. SW18 7K 117
Wardo Av. SW6 1G 117
Wardour M. W1 1B 12 (6G 83)
(off D'Arblay St.)
Wardour St. W1 7B 6 (6G 83)
Ward Point SE11 4J 19 (4A 102)
Ward Rd. E15 1F 87
Ward Rd. N19 3G 65
Ward Rd. SW19 1A 154
Wardrobe, The TW9: Rich 5D 114
(off Old Palace Yd.)
Wardrobe Pl. EC4 1B 14 (6B 84)
(off Carter La.)
Wardrobe Ter. EC4 2B 14 (7B 84)
(off Addle Hill)
Wardroper Ho. SE1 3B 102
(off St George's Rd.)
Wards Rd. IG2: Ilf 7H 53
Wards Wharf App. E16 1B 106
Ware Ct. SM1: Sutt 4H 165
Wareham Cl. TW3: Houn 4F 113
Wareham Ct. N1 7E 66
(off Hertford Rd.)
Wareham Ho. SW8 7K 101
Warehome M. E13 4J 87
(off Jutland Rd.)
Warehouse Ct. SE18 3F 107
Warehouse Way E16 7K 87
Waremead Rd. IG2: Ilf 5F 53
Warepoint Dr. SE28 2H 107
Warfield Rd. NW10 3F 81
Warfield Rd. TW12: Hamp 1F 149
Warfield Rd. TW14: Felt 7G 111
Warfield Yd. NW10 3F 81
(off Warfield Rd.)
Wargrave Av. N15 6F 49
Wargrave Ho. E2 2J 9 (3F 85)
(off Navarre St.)
Wargrave Rd. HA2: Harr 3G 59
Warham Rd. CR2: S Croy 5B 168
Warham Rd. HA3: W'stone 2K 41
Warham Rd. N4 5A 48
Warham St. SE5 7B 102
Waring & Gillow Est. W3 4G 79
Waring Cl. BR6: Chels 6K 173
Waring Dr. BR6: Chels 6K 173
Waring Rd. DA14: Sidc 6C 144
Waring St. SE27 4C 138
Warkworth Gdns. TW7: Isle 7A 96
Warkworth Rd. N17 7J 33
Warland Rd. SE18 7H 107
Warley Av. RM8: Dag 7F 55
Warley Av. UB4: Hayes 6J 75
Warley Cl. E10 1B 68
Warley Rd. IG5: Ilf 1E 52
Warley Rd. IG8: Wfd G 7E 36
Warley Rd. N9 2D 34
Warley Rd. UB4: Hayes 6J 75
Warley St. E2 3K 85
Warlingham Ct. SE13 6E 122
Warlingham Rd. CR7: Thor H 4B 156
Warlock Rd. W9 4H 81
Warlters Cl. N7 4J 65
Warlters Rd. N7 4J 65
Warltersville Mans. N19 7J 47
Warltersville Rd. N19 7J 47
War Memorial Sports Ground 4C 166
Warmington Cl. E5 3K 67
Warmington Rd. SE24 6C 120
Warmington St. E13 4J 87
Warminster Gdns. SE25 2G 157
Warminster Rd. SE25 2F 157
Warminster Sq. SE25 2G 157
Warminster Way CR4: Mitc 1F 155
Warmsworth NW1 1G 83
(off Pratt St.)
Warmwell Av. NW9 1A 44
Warndon St. SE16 4K 103
Warneford Rd. HA3: Kenton 3D 42
Warneford Rd. TW6: H'row A 5C 174
Warneford St. E9 1H 85
Warne Pl. DA15: Sidc 6B 126
Warner Av. SM3: Cheam 2G 165
Warner Cl. E15 5G 69
Warner Cl. TW12: Hamp 5D 130
Warner Cl. UB3: Harl 7F 93
Warner Ho. BR3: Beck 6D 140
Warner Ho. NW8 3A 82
Warner Ho. SE13 2D 122
(off Russett Way)
Warner Pl. E2 2G 85
Warner Rd. BR1: Broml 7H 141
Warner Rd. E17 4A 50
Warner Rd. N8 4H 47
Warner Rd. SE5 1C 120
Warners Cl. IG8: Wfd G 5D 36
Warners La. KT2: King T 4D 132
Warners Path IG8: Wfd G 5D 36
Warner St. EC1 4J 7 (4A 84)
Warner Ter. E14 5D 86
(off Broomfield St.)
Warner Yd. EC1 4J 7 (4A 84)
(off Warner St.)
Warnford Ct. EC2 7F 9 (6D 84)
(off Throgmorton Av.)
Warnford Ho. SW15 6A 116
(off Tunworth Cres.)
Warnford Ind. Est. UB3: Hayes 2G 93
Warnford Rd. BR6: Chels 5K 173
Warnham WC1 2G 7 (3K 83)
(off Sidmouth St.)
Warnham Ct. Rd. SM5: Cars 7D 166
Warnham Ho. SW2 7K 119
(off Up. Tulse Hill)
Warnham Rd. N12 5H 31
Warple M. W3 2A 98
Warple Way W3 2A 98
Warren, The E12 4C 70
Warren, The KT4: Wor Pk 4K 163
Warren, The TW5: Hest 7D 94
Warren, The UB4: Hayes 6J 75
Warren, The 2A 94
Warren Av. BR1: Broml 7G 141
Warren Av. BR6: Chels 5K 173
Warren Av. CR2: Sels 7K 169
Warren Av. E10 3E 68
Warren Av. TW10: Rich 4H 115
Warren Cl. DA6: Bex 5G 127
Warren Cl. HA9: Wemb 2D 60
Warren Cl. N9 7E 24
Warren Cl. SE21 7C 120
Warren Cl. UB4: Yead 5A 76
Warren Ct. BR3: Beck 7C 140
Warren Ct. CR0: C'don 1E 168
Warren Ct. N17 3G 49
(off High Cross Rd.)
Warren Ct. NW1 3A 6 (4G 83)
(off Warren St.)
Warren Ct. SE7 6A 106
Warren Ct. W5 5C 78
Warren Cres. N9 7A 24
Warren Cutting KT2: King T 7K 133
Warrender Rd. N19 3G 65
Warrender Way HA4: Ruis 7J 39
Warren Dr., The E11 7A 52
Warren Dr. HA4: Ruis 7B 40
Warren Dr. UB6: G'frd 4F 77
Warren Dr. Nth. KT5: Surb 1H 163
Warren Dr. Sth. KT5: Surb 1J 163
Warren Farm Cotts. RM6: Chad H 4F 55
Warren Flds. HA7: Stan 4H 27
Warren Footpath TW1: Twick 1C 132
Warren Gdns. BR6: Chels 5K 173
Warren Gdns. E15 5F 69
Warren Ho. E3 3D 86
(off Bromley High St.)
Warren Ho. N17 3G 49
(off High Cross Rd.)
Warren Ho. W14 4H 99
Warren La. HA7: Stan 2F 27
Warren La. SE18 3F 107
Warren M. W1 4A 6 (4G 83)
Warren Pk. KT2: King T 6J 133
Warren Pk. Rd. SM1: Sutt 6B 166
Warren Pl. E1 6K 85
(off Pitsea St.)
Warren Pond Rd. E4 1C 36
Warren Ri. KT3: N Mald 1K 151
Warren Rd. BR2: Hayes 2J 171
Warren Rd. BR6: Chels 5K 173
(not continuous)
Warren Rd. CR0: C'don 1E 168
Warren Rd. DA14: Sidc 3C 144
Warren Rd. DA6: Bex 5G 127
Warren Rd. E10 3E 68
Warren Rd. E11 6A 52
Warren Rd. E4 2K 35
Warren Rd. IG6: Ilf 5H 53
Warren Rd. KT2: King T 6J 133
Warren Rd. NW2 2B 62
Warren Rd. SW19 6C 136
Warren Rd. TW15: Ashf 7G 129
Warren Rd. TW2: Whitt 6G 113
Warren Rd. UB10: Ick 4A 56
Warren Rd. WD23: B Hea 1B 26
Warren Sports Cen. 5F 55
Warrens Shawe La. HA8: Edg 2C 28
Warren St. W1 4A 6 (4G 83)
Warren Ter. RM6: Chad H 4D 54
Warren Wlk. SE7 6A 106
Warren Way HA8: Edg 2H 43
Warren Wood Cl. BR2: Hayes 2H 171
Warriner Dr. N9 3B 34
Warriner Gdns. SW11 1D 118
Warrington Ct. CR0: Wadd 3B 168
(off Warrington Rd.)
Warrington Cres. W9 4A 82
Warrington Gdns. W9 4A 82
(not continuous)
Warrington Rd. CR0: Wadd 3B 168
Warrington Rd. HA1: Harr 5J 41
Warrington Rd. RM8: Dag 2D 72
Warrington Rd. TW10: Rich 5D 114
Warrington Sq. RM8: Dag 2D 72
Warrior Cl. SE28 1H 107
Warrior Ct. SW9 3B 120
(off Coldharbour Rd.)
Warrior Sq. E12 4E 70
Warsaw Cl. HA4: Ruis 6K 57
Warspite Ho. E14 4D 104
(off Cahir St.)
Warspite Rd. SE18 3C 106
Warton Ct. E1 7K 85
(off Cable St.)
Warton Ct. W3 3J 97
(off All Saints Rd.)
Warton Ho. E15 1E 86
(off High St.)
Warton Rd. E15 1E 86
Warwall E6 6F 89
Warwark Ct. KT6: Surb 2E 162
Warwick W14 4H 99
(off Kensington Village)
Warwick Av. HA2: Harr 4D 58
Warwick Av. HA8: Edg 3C 28
Warwick Av. W2 5A 82
Warwick Av. W9 4K 81
Warwick Bldg. SW11 6F 101
Warwick Chambers W8 3J 99
(off Pater St.)
Warwick Cl. DA5: Bexl 7F 127
Warwick Cl. EN4: E Barn 5G 21
Warwick Cl. TW12: Hamp 7G 131
Warwick Cl. W8 3H 99
(off Kensington High St.)
Warwick Cl. WD23: B Hea 1D 26
Warwick Ct. BR2: Broml 2G 159
Warwick Ct. EC4 1B 14 (6B 84)
(off Warwick La.)
Warwick Ct. EN5: New Bar 5E 20
(off Station Rd.)
Warwick Ct. HA1: Harr 3J 41
Warwick Ct. N11 6C 32
Warwick Ct. UB5: N'olt 5E 58
(off Newmarket Av.)
Warwick Ct. W7 6K 77
(off Copley Cl.)
Warwick Ct. WC1 6H 7 (5K 83)
Warwick Cres. UB4: Hayes 4H 75
Warwick Cres. W2 5A 82
Warwick Dene W5 1E 96
Warwick Dr. SW15 3D 116
Warwick Est. W2 5K 81
Warwick Gdns. CR7: Thor H 3A 156
Warwick Gdns. EN5: Barn 1C 20
Warwick Gdns. IG1: Ilf 1F 71
Warwick Gdns. KT7: T Ditt 5K 149
Warwick Gdns. N4 5C 48
Warwick Gdns. W14 3H 99
Warwick Gro. E5 1H 67
Warwick Gro. KT5: Surb 7F 151
Warwick Ho. E16 1J 105
(off Wesley Av.)
Warwick Ho. KT2: King T 1E 150
(off Acre Rd.)
Warwick Ho. SW9 2A 120
Warwick Ho. St. SW1 4D 12 (1H 101)
Warwick La. EC4 7B 8 (6B 84)
Warwick La. W14 4H 99
Warwick Lodge TW2: Twick 3F 131
Warwick Mans. SW5 4J 99
(off Cromwell Cres.)
Warwick Pde. HA3: Kenton 2B 42
Warwick Pas. EC4 7B 8 (6B 84)
(off Old Bailey)
Warwick Pl. KT7: T Ditt 6A 150
Warwick Pl. W5 2D 96
Warwick Pl. W9 5A 82
Warwick Pl. Nth. SW1 4A 18 (4G 101)
Warwick Rd. CR7: Thor H 3A 156
Warwick Rd. DA14: Sidc 5B 144
Warwick Rd. DA16: Well 3C 126
Warwick Rd. E11 5K 51
Warwick Rd. E12 5C 70
Warwick Rd. E15 6H 69
Warwick Rd. E17 1B 50
Warwick Rd. E4 5H 35
Warwick Rd. EN5: New Bar 4E 20
Warwick Rd. KT1: Hamp W 1C 150
Warwick Rd. KT3: N Mald 3J 151
Warwick Rd. KT7: T Ditt 5K 149
Warwick Rd. N11 6C 32
Warwick Rd. N18 4K 33
Warwick Rd. SE20 3H 157
Warwick Rd. SM1: Sutt 4A 166
Warwick Rd. SW5 4J 99
Warwick Rd. TW15: Ashf 5A 128
Warwick Rd. TW2: Twick 1J 131
Warwick Rd. TW4: Houn 3K 111
Warwick Rd. UB2: S'hall 3D 94
Warwick Rd. UB7: W Dray 2A 92
Warwick Rd. W14 4H 99
Warwick Rd. W5 2D 96
Warwick Row SW1 1A 18 (3G 101)
Warwickshire Path SE8 7B 104
Warwickshire Rd. N16 4E 66
Warwick Sq. EC4 7B 8 (6B 84)
Warwick Sq. SW1 5A 18 (5G 101)
(not continuous)
Warwick Sq. M. SW1 4A 18 (4G 101)
Warwick St. W1 2B 12 (7G 83)
Warwick Ter. E17 5F 51
(off Lea Bri. Rd.)
Warwick Ter. SE18 6H 107
Warwick Way SW1 5J 17 (5F 101)

Warwick Yd. – Well Hall Rd.

Warwick Yd. EC1 4D **8** (4C **84**)
Wasdale NW1 1K **5** (3F **83**)
(off Cumberland Mkt.)
Washbourne Ct. N9 2B **34**
(off Acton Cl.)
Washbourne Rd. NW10 1K **79**
Washington Av. E12 4D **70**
Washington Bldg. SE13 1D **122**
(off Deal's Gateway)
Washington Cl. E3 3D **86**
Washington Ho. E17 2B **50**
Washington Ho. SW3 7E **10** (2D **100**)
(off Basil St.)
Washington Rd. E18 2H **51**
Washington Rd. E6 7A **70**
Washington Rd. KT1: King T 2G **151**
Washington Rd. KT4: Wor Pk 2D **164**
Washington Rd. SW13 7C **98**
Washington Rd. TW6: H'row A 6D **174**
Wasp Rd. TW6: H'row A 5C **174**
(off Welland Rd.)
Wastdale Rd. SE23 1K **139**
Watch, The N12 4F **31**
Watchfield Ct. W4 5J **97**
Watcombe Cotts. TW9: Kew 6G **97**
Watcombe Pl. SE25 5H **157**
Watcombe Rd. SE25 5H **157**
Waterbank Ho. SW18 1K **135**
(off Knaresborough Dr.)
Waterbank Rd. SE6 3D **140**
Waterbeach Rd. RM9: Dag 6C **72**
Water Brook La. NW4 5E **44**
Watercress Pl. N1 7E **66**
Waterdale Rd. SE2 6A **108**
Waterden Ct. W11 1G **99**
Waterden Rd. E20 5C **68**
Waterer Ho. SE6 4E **140**
Waterer Ri. SM6: W'gton 6H **167**
Waterfall Cl. N14 3B **32**
Waterfall Cotts. SW19 6B **136**
Waterfall Ho. SW2 5A **120**
(off Brixton Water La.)
Waterfall Rd. N11 4A **32**
Waterfall Rd. N14 3B **32**
Waterfall Rd. SW19 6B **136**
Waterfall Ter. SW17 6C **136**
Waterfall Wlk. N14 1A **32**
Waterfield Cl. DA17: Belv 3G **109**
Waterfield Cl. SE28 1B **108**
Waterfield Gdns. SE25 4D **156**
Waterford Ho. BR1: Broml 1J **159**
(off Newman Rd.)
Waterford Ho. W11 7H **81**
(off Kensington Pk. Rd.)
Waterford Point SW8 7J **101**
Waterford Rd. SW6 7K **99**
Waterford Way NW10 5D **62**
Waterfront W6 6E **98**
Waterfront Dr. SW10 1A **118**
Waterfront Ho. E5 2J **67**
(off Harry Zeital Way)
Waterfront Leisure Cen. Woolwich
3E **106**
Waterfront M. N1 2C **84**
Waterfront Studios Bus. Cen.
E16 1H **105**
(off Dock Rd.)
Water Gdns., The W2 7C **4** (6C **82**)
Watergardens, The KT2: King T
6J **133**
Water Gdns. HA7: Stan 6G **27**
Water Gdns. Sq. SE16 2K **103**
Watergate EC4 2A **14** (7B **84**)
Watergate St. SE8 6C **104**
Watergate Wlk. E14 3D **104**
Watergate Wlk. WC2 4F **13** (1J **101**)
Waterhall Av. E4 4B **36**
Waterhall Cl. E17 1K **49**
Waterhead NW1 1A **6** (3G **83**)
(off Varndell St.)
Waterhouse CR0: C'don 1C **160**
(off Saffron Central Sq.)
Waterhouse Cl. E16 5B **88**
Waterhouse Cl. NW3 5B **64**
Waterhouse Cl. W6 4F **99**
Waterhouse Sq. EC1 6K **7** (5A **84**)
Wateridge Cl. E14 3C **104**
Water La. DA14: Sidc 2F **145**
Water La. E15 6G **69**
Water La. EC3 3H **15** (7E **84**)
Water La. IG3: Ilf 3J **71**
Water La. KT1: King T 1D **150**
Water La. N9 1C **34**
Water La. NW1 7F **65**
Water La. SE14 7J **103**
Water La. TW1: Twick 1A **132**
Water La. TW9: Rich 5D **114**
Water Lily Cl. UB2: S'hall 2G **95**
Waterline Ho. W2 6C **4** (5C **82**)
(off Harbet Rd.)
Waterloo Bri. WC2 3G **13** (7K **83**)
Waterloo Cl. E9 5J **67**
Waterloo Cl. TW14: Felt 1H **129**
Waterloo East Theatre 5K **13** (1A **102**)
(off Brad St.)
Waterloo Gdns. E2 2J **85**
Waterloo Gdns. N1 7B **66**
Waterloo Gdns. RM7: Rom 6K **55**
Waterloo Pas. NW6 7H **63**
Waterloo Pl. SM5: Cars 3D **166**
(off Wrythe Grn.)
Waterloo Pl. SW1 4C **12** (1H **101**)
Waterloo Pl. TW9: Rich 4E **114**
Waterloo Rd. E10 7C **50**
Waterloo Rd. E6 7A **70**
Waterloo Rd. E7 5H **69**
Waterloo Rd. IG6: Ilf 2G **53**
Waterloo Rd. NW2 1C **62**
Waterloo Rd. RM7: Rom 6K **55**
Waterloo Rd. RM7: Rush G 6K **55**
Waterloo Rd. RM7: Rush G 6K **55**
Waterloo Rd. SE1 4H **13** (1K **101**)
Waterloo Rd. SM1: Sutt 5B **166**
Waterloo Ter. N1 7B **66**
Waterlow Bldg., The E3 5B **86**
(off Weatherley Cl.)
Waterlow Ct. NW11 7K **45**
Waterlow Pk. Cen. 1F **65**
Waterlow Rd. N19 1G **65**
Waterman Bldg. E14 2B **104**
Waterman Ho. E15 6F **69**
(off Forrester Way)
Watermans Art Cen., Cinema &
Theatre 6E **96**
Watermans Cl. KT2: King T 7E **132**
Watermans Ct. TW8: Bford 6D **96**
(off High St.)
Watermans Ho. E14 6F **87**
(off New Village Av.)
Watermans M. W5 7E **78**
Waterman's Quay SW6 2A **118**
Waterman St. SW15 3F **117**
Watermans Wlk. SE16 2A **104**
Waterman Way E1 1H **103**
Watermark Ct. RM6: Chad H 6B **54**
(off Quarles Pk. Rd.)
Watermead TW14: Felt 1G **129**
Watermead Ho. E9 5A **68**
Watermead La. SM5: Cars 7D **154**
Watermead Lodge SE16 1K **103**
(off Princes Riverside Rd.)
Watermeadow La. SW6 2A **118**
Watermead Rd. SE6 4E **140**
Watermead Way N17 3H **49**
Watermen's Sq. SE20 7J **139**
Water M. SE15 4J **121**
Watermill Bus. Cen. EN3: Brim 2G **25**
Watermill Cl. TW10: Ham 3C **132**
Water Mill Ho. TW13: Hanw 2E **130**
Watermill La. N18 5K **33**
Watermill Way SW19 1A **154**
Watermill Way TW13: Hanw 2D **130**
Watermint Quay N16 7G **49**
Water Rd. HA0: Wemb 1F **79**
Water's Edge SW6 1E **116**
(off Palemead Cl.)
Watersedge KT19: Ewe 4J **163**
Watersfield Way HA8: Edg 7J **27**
Waters Gdns. RM10: Dag 5G **73**
Waterside BR3: Beck 1B **158**
Waterside E17 6J **49**
Waterside N1 2C **84**
Waterside UB7: Harm 3D **174**
Waterside W2 6A **4** (5B **82**)
(off Nth. Wharf Rd.)
Waterside Apts. N4 1C **66**
(off Goodchild Rd.)
Waterside Av. BR3: Beck 5E **158**
(off Adamson Way)
Waterside Bus. Cen. TW7: Isle 4B **114**
Waterside Cl. E3 1B **86**
Waterside Cl. HA9: Wemb 3J **61**
Waterside Cl. IG11: Bark 4A **72**
Waterside Cl. KT6: Surb 2E **162**
Waterside Cl. SE16 2G **103**
Waterside Cl. SE28 1K **107**
Waterside Cl. TW17: Shep 1E **146**
Waterside Cl. UB5: N'olt 3D **76**
Waterside Ct. SM5: Cars 3E **166**
(off Millpond Pl.)
Waterside Dr. KT12: Walt T 5J **147**
Waterside Hgts. E16 2A **106**
(off Booth Rd.)
Waterside Pl. NW1 1E **82**
Waterside Point SW11 7C **100**
Waterside Rd. UB2: S'hall 3E **94**
Waterside Twr. SW6 2A **118**
(off The Boulevard)
Waterside Trad. Cen. W7 3J **95**
Waterside Way N17 3H **49**
Waterside Way SW17 4A **136**
Watersmeet Pl. N4 1C **66**
Watersmeet Way SE28 6C **90**
Waterson St. E2 1H **9** (3E **84**)
Waters Pl. SW15 2E **116**
Watersplash Cl. KT1: King T 3E **150**
Watersplash La. TW5: Cran 5K **93**
Watersplash La. UB3: Harl 4J **93**
Watersplash Rd. TW17: Shep 5C **146**
Watersreach Apts. N4 1C **66**
(off Kayani Av.)
Waters Rd. KT1: King T 2H **151**
Waters Rd. SE6 3G **141**
Waters Sq. KT1: King T 3H **151**
Water St. E14 1D **104**
Water St. WC2 2J **13** (7A **84**)
(off Maltravers St.)
Water Twr. Cl. UB8: Uxb 5A **56**
Water Twr. Hill CR0: C'don 4D **168**
Water Twr. Pl. N1 1A **84**
Waterview Cl. DA6: Bex 5D **126**
Waterview Dr. SE10 1F **105**
Waterview Ho. E14 5A **86**
(off Carr St.)
Waterway Av. SE13 3D **122**
Waterway Pk. UB3: Hayes 2E **92**
Waterways Bus. Cen. EN3: Enf L 1G **25**
Waterworks Cen. 2A **68**
WATERWORKS CORNER 1G **51**
Waterworks La. E5 2K **67**
Waterworks Nature Reserve 2A **68**
Waterworks Rd. SW2 6K **119**
Waterworks Yd. CR0: C'don 3C **168**
(off Charles St.)
Watery La. DA14: Sidc 6B **144**
Watery La. SW19 1H **153**
Watery La. SW20 2H **153**
Watery La. UB3: Harl 5F **93**
Watery La. UB5: N'olt 2A **76**
Wates Way CR4: Mitc 6D **154**
Wateville Rd. N17 1C **48**
Watford Cl. SW11 1C **118**
Watford Rd. E16 5J **87**
Watford Rd. HA0: Wemb 3B **60**
Watford Rd. HA1: Harr 7A **42**
Watford Way NW4 4C **44**
Watford Way NW7 4F **29**
Watkin Rd. HA9: Wemb 3H **61**
Watkins Cl. HA6: Nwood 1H **39**
Watkins Ho. E14 2E **104**
(off Manchester Rd.)
Watkinson Rd. N7 6K **65**
Watkins Way RM8: Dag 1E **72**
WATLING 7E **28**
Watling Av. HA8: Edg 1J **43**
Watling Ct. EC4 1D **14** (6C **84**)
(off Watling St.)
Watling Farm Cl. HA7: Stan 1H **27**
Watling Gdns. NW2 6G **63**
Watling Ga. NW9 4A **44**
Watling Ho. SE1 4C **102**
(off New Kent Rd.)
Watlings Cl. CR0: C'don 6A **158**
Watling St. DA1: Cray 5K **127**
Watling St. DA6: Bex 4H **127**
Watling St. DA7: Bex 4H **127**
Watling St. EC4 1C **14** (6C **84**)
Watling St. SE15 6E **102**
Watlington Gro. SE26 5A **140**
Watney Cotts. SW14 3J **115**
Watney Mkt. E1 6H **85**
Watney Rd. SW14 3J **115**
Watney's Rd. CR4: Mitc 5H **155**
Watney St. E1 6H **85**
Watson Av. E6 7E **70**
Watson Av. SM3: Cheam 2G **165**
Watson Cl. N16 5D **66**
Watson Cl. SW19 6C **136**
Watson Ct. E3 3C **86**
(off Campbell Rd.)
Watson Ho. SW11 7H **101**
(off Ponton Rd.)
Watson Pl. SE25 5F **157**
Watsons Ho. N1 1E **84**
(off Nuttall St.)
Watson's M. W1 6D **4** (5C **82**)
Watsons Rd. N22 1K **47**
Watsons St. SE8 7C **104**
Watson St. E13 2K **87**
Watt Ct. W3 2A **98**
Watteau Sq. CR0: C'don 1A **168**
Wattisfield Rd. E5 3J **67**
Watts Apts. SW8 7J **101**
(off Cellini St.)
Watts Cl. N15 5E **48**
Wattsdown Cl. E13 1J **87**
Watts Gro. E3 5C **86**
Watts Ho. W10 5G **81**
(off Wornington Rd.)
Watts La. BR7: Chst 1F **161**
Watts La. TW11: Tedd 5A **132**
Watts M. IG6: Ilf 3H **53**
Watts M. SW16 6H **137**
Watts Rd. KT7: T Ditt 7A **150**
Watts St. E1 1H **103**
Watts St. SE15 1F **121**
Wat Tyler Ho. N8 3J **47**
(off Boyton Rd.)
Wat Tyler Rd. SE10 2E **122**
Wat Tyler Rd. SE3 2F **123**
Wauthier Cl. N13 5G **33**
Wave Ct. RM7: Rush G 6K **55**
Wavel Ct. CR0: C'don 5D **168**
(off Hurst Rd.)
Wavel Ct. E1 1J **103**
(off Garnet St.)
Wavelengths Leisure Cen. 7C **104**
Wavell Dr. DA15: Sidc 6J **125**
Wavell Ho. N6 6E **46**
(off Hillcrest)
Wavel M. N8 4H **47**
Wavel M. NW6 7K **63**
Wavel Pl. SE26 4F **139**
Wavendon Av. W4 5K **97**
Waveney Av. SE15 4H **121**
Waveney Cl. E1 1G **103**
Waveney Ho. SE15 4H **121**
Waverley Av. E17 3F **51**
Waverley Av. E4 4G **35**
Waverley Av. HA9: Wemb 5F **61**
Waverley Av. KT5: Surb 6H **151**
Waverley Av. SM1: Sutt 2K **165**
Waverley Av. TW2: Whitt 1D **130**
Waverley Cl. BR2: Broml 5B **160**
Waverley Cl. E18 1A **52**
Waverley Cl. KT8: W Mole 5E **148**
Waverley Cl. UB3: Harl 4F **93**
Waverley Ct. EN2: Enf 3G **23**
Waverley Ct. NW3 6D **64**
Waverley Ct. NW6 7G **63**
Waverley Ct. SE26 5J **139**
Waverley Cres. SE18 5H **107**
Waverley Gdns. E6 5C **88**
Waverley Gdns. HA6: Nwood 1J **39**
Waverley Gdns. IG11: Bark 2J **89**
Waverley Gdns. IG6: Ilf 2G **53**
Waverley Gdns. NW10 2F **79**
Waverley Gro. N3 3F **45**
Waverley Ind. Est. HA1: Harr 3H **41**
Waverley Lodge E15 6G **69**
(off Litchfield Av.)
Waverley Pl. N4 2B **66**
Waverley Pl. NW8 2B **82**
Waverley Rd. E17 3E **50**
Waverley Rd. E18 1A **52**
Waverley Rd. EN2: Enf 3G **23**
Waverley Rd. HA2: Harr 2C **58**
Waverley Rd. KT17: Ewe 5D **164**
Waverley Rd. N17 7C **34**
Waverley Rd. N8 6J **47**
Waverley Rd. SE18 5G **107**
Waverley Rd. SE25 4H **157**
Waverley Rd. UB1: S'hall 7E **76**
Waverley Way SM5: Cars 6C **166**
Waverton Ho. E3 1B **86**
Waverton Rd. SW18 7A **118**
Waverton St. W1 4H **11** (1E **100**)
Wavertree Ct. SW2 1J **137**
Wavertree Rd. E18 2J **51**
Wavertree Rd. SW2 1K **137**
Waxham NW3 5D **64**
Waxlow Cres. UB1: S'hall 6E **76**
Waxlow Ho. UB4: Yead 5B **76**
Waxlow Rd. NW10 2J **79**
Waxlow Way UB5: N'olt 4D **76**
Waxwell Cl. HA5: Pinn 2B **40**
Waxwell Farm Ho. HA5: Pinn 2B **40**
Waxwell La. HA5: Pinn 2B **40**
Wayborne Gro. HA4: Ruis 6E **38**
Waye Av. TW5: Cran 1J **111**
Wayfarer Rd. TW6: H'row A 5C **174**
Wayfarer Rd. UB5: N'olt 3B **76**
Wayfield Link SE9 6H **125**
Wayford St. SW11 2C **118**
Wayland Av. E8 5G **67**
Wayland Ho. SW9 2A **120**
(off Robsart St.)
Waylands UB3: Hayes 5F **75**
Waylands Mead BR3: Beck 1D **158**
Waylett Ho. SE11 6H **19** (5K **101**)
(off Loughborough St.)
Waylett Pl. HA0: Wemb 4D **60**
Waylett Pl. SE27 3B **138**
Wayman Ct. E8 6H **67**
Wayne Cl. BR6: Orp 3K **173**
Wayne Kirkum Way NW6 5H **63**
Waynflete Av. CR0: Wadd 3B **168**
Waynflete Ho. SE1 5C **14** (1C **102**)
(off Union St.)
Waynflete Sq. W10 7F **81**
(not continuous)
Waynflete St. SW18 2A **136**
Waypoint Way E16 2K **105**
Wayside CR0: New Ad 6D **170**
Wayside NW11 1G **63**
Wayside SW14 5J **115**
Wayside Cl. N14 6B **22**
Wayside Commercial Est. IG11: Bark
1K **89**
Wayside Ct. HA9: Wemb 3G **61**
Wayside Ct. TW1: Twick 6C **114**
Wayside Gdns. RM10: Dag 5G **73**
Wayside Gro. SE9 4D **142**
Wayside M. IG2: Ilf 5E **52**
WC1 WC1 4H **7** (4K **83**)
Weald, The BR7: Chst 6D **142**
Weald Cl. BR2: Broml 2C **172**
Weald Cl. SE16 5H **103**
Wealden Ho. E3 3D **86**
(off Talwin St.)
Weald La. HA3: Hrw W 2H **41**
Weald Ri. HA3: Hrw W 7E **26**
Weald Rd. UB10: Hil 2C **74**
Weald Sq. E5 2G **67**
WEALDSTONE 3J **41**
Wealdstone FC 2H **57**
Wealdstone Rd. SM3: Sutt 2H **165**
Weald Village Open Space 1J **41**
Weald Way RM7: Rom 6H **55**
Weald Way UB4: Hayes 3G **75**
Wealdwood Gdns. HA5: Hat E 6A **26**
Weale Rd. E4 3A **36**
Weall Ct. HA5: Pinn 4C **40**
Weardale Gdns. EN2: Enf 1J **23**
Weardale Rd. SE13 4F **123**
Wearmouth Ho. E3 4B **86**
(off Joseph St.)
Wear Pl. E2 3H **85**
(not continuous)
Wearside Rd. SE13 4D **122**
Weatherbury W2 6J **81**
(off Talbot Rd.)
Weatherbury Ho. N19 3H **65**
(off Wedmore St.)
Weatherley Cl. E3 5B **86**
Weaver Cl. CR0: C'don 4F **169**
Weaver Cl. E6 7F **89**
Weaver Ho. E1 4G **85**
(off Pedley St.)
Weavers Almshouses E11 6H **51**
(off Cambridge Rd.)
Weavers Cl. TW7: Isle 4J **113**
Weavers Ho. E11 6J **51**
(off New Wanstead)
Weavers La. SE1 5H **15** (1E **102**)
Weavers Row E20 5D **68**
Weavers Ter. SW6 6J **99**
(off Micklethwaite Rd.)
Weaver St. E1 4G **85**
(not continuous)
Weavers Way NW1 1H **83**
Weaver Wlk. HA9: Wemb 4G **61**
Weaver Wlk. SE27 4B **138**
Webb Cl. W10 4E **80**
Webb Ct. SE28 7B **90**
(off Attlee Rd.)
Webber Ho. IG11: Bark 7G **71**
(off North St.)
Webber Path E14 7E **86**
(off Bullivant St.)
Webber Row SE1 7A **14** (2B **102**)
Webber St. SE1 6K **13** (2A **102**)
Webb Est. E5 7G **49**
Webb Gdns. E13 4J **87**
Webb Ho. E3 3C **86**
(off Trevithick Way)
Webb Ho. RM10: Dag 3G **73**
(off Kershaw Rd.)
Webb Ho. SW8 7H **101**
Webb Ho. TW13: Hanw 3C **130**
Webb Pl. NW10 3B **80**
Webb Rd. SE3 6H **105**
Webbscroft Rd. RM10: Dag 4H **73**
Webb's Rd. SW11 4D **118**
Webbs Rd. UB4: Yead 3K **75**
Webb St. SE1 3E **102**
Webheath NW6 7H **63**
(not continuous)
Webster Gdns. W5 1D **96**
Webster Rd. E11 3E **68**
Webster Rd. SE16 3G **103**
Weddell Ho. E1 4K **85**
(off Duckett St.)
Wedderburn Ho. SW1 5G **17** (5E **100**)
(off Lwr. Sloane St.)
Wedderburn Rd. IG11: Bark 1J **89**
Wedderburn Rd. NW3 5B **64**
Wedgewood Apts. SW8 7J **101**
Wedgewood Ct. BR2: Broml 3H **159**
(off Cumberland Rd.)
Wedgewood Ct. DA5: Bexl 7G **127**
Wedgewood Ho. SW1 6K **17** (5F **101**)
(off Churchill Gdns.)
Wedgewood M. SW6 2G **117**
Wedgewood M. W1 1D **12** (6H **83**)
Wedgwood Ct. N7 4K **65**
Wedgwood Ho. E2 3K **85**
(off Warley St.)
Wedgwood Ho. SE11 2J **19** (3A **102**)
(off Lambeth Wlk.)
Wedgwood Wlk. NW6 5K **63**
(off Dresden Cl.)
Wedgwood Way SE19 7C **138**
Wedlake St. W10 4G **81**
Wedmore Av. IG5: Ilf 1E **52**
Wedmore Gdns. N19 2H **65**
Wedmore M. N19 3H **65**
Wedmore Rd. UB6: G'frd 3H **77**
Wedmore St. N19 3H **65**
Weech Rd. NW6 4J **63**
Weedington Rd. NW5 5E **64**
Weedon Ho. W12 6C **80**
Weekley Sq. SW11 3B **118**
Weigall Rd. SE12 5J **123**
Weighhouse St. W1 1H **11** (6E **82**)
Weightman Ho. SE16 3G **103**
Weighton Rd. HA3: Hrw W 1H **41**
Weighton Rd. SE20 2H **157**
Weihurst Ct. SM1: Sutt 5C **166**
Weihurst Gdns. SM1: Sutt 5B **166**
Weimar St. SW15 3G **117**
Weirdale Av. N20 2J **31**
Weir Hall Av. N18 6J **33**
Weir Hall Gdns. N18 5J **33**
Weir Hall Rd. N17 6J **33**
Weir Hall Rd. N18 5J **33**
Weir Rd. DA5: Bexl 7H **127**
Weir Rd. KT12: Walt T 6J **147**
Weir Rd. SW12 7G **119**
Weir Rd. SW19 3K **135**
Weir's Pas. NW1 1D **6** (3H **83**)
Weiss Rd. SW15 3F **117**
Welbeck Av. BR1: Broml 4J **141**
Welbeck Av. DA15: Sidc 1A **144**
Welbeck Av. UB4: Yead 4K **75**
Welbeck Cl. KT17: Ewe 7C **164**
Welbeck Cl. KT3: N Mald 5B **152**
Welbeck Cl. N12 5G **31**
Welbeck Ct. UB4: Yead 4K **75**
Welbeck Ct. W14 4H **99**
(off Addison Bri. Pl.)
Welbeck Ho. W1 7J **5** (6F **83**)
(off Welbeck St.)
Welbeck Rd. E6 3B **88**
Welbeck Rd. EN4: E Barn 6H **21**
Welbeck Rd. HA2: Harr 1F **59**
Welbeck Rd. SM1: Sutt 2B **166**
Welbeck Rd. SM5: Cars 2B **166**
Welbeck St. W1 6H **5** (5E **82**)
Welbeck Vs. N21 2H **33**
Welbeck Wlk. SM5: Cars 1B **166**
Welbeck Way W1 7J **5** (6F **83**)
Welbury Ct. E8 7E **66**
(off Kingsland Rd.)
Welby Ho. N19 7H **47**
Welby St. SE5 1B **120**
Welch Pl. HA5: Pinn 1A **40**
Welcome Ct. E17 7C **50**
(off Saxon Cl.)
Weldin M. SW18 5J **117**
(off Lebanon Rd.)
Weldon Cl. HA4: Ruis 6K **57**
Weldon Ct. N21 5E **22**
Weldon Dr. KT8: W Mole 4D **148**
Weld Pl. N11 5A **32**
(not continuous)
Weld Works M. SW2 6K **119**
Welfare Rd. E15 7G **69**
Welford Cl. E5 3K **67**
Welford Ct. HA8: Edg 4K **27**
(off Lacey Dr.)
Welford Ct. NW1 7F **65**
(off Castlehaven Rd.)
Welford Ct. SW8 2G **119**
Welford Ct. W9 5J **81**
(off Elmfield Way)
Welford Ho. UB5: N'olt 4D **76**
(off Waxlow Way)
Welford Pl. SW19 4G **135**
Welham Rd. SW16 6F **137**
Welham Rd. SW17 5E **136**
Welhouse Rd. SM5: Cars 1C **166**
Wellacre Rd. HA3: Kenton 6B **42**
Wellan Cl. DA15: Sidc 5B **126**
Welland Ct. SE6 2B **140**
(off Oakham Cl.)
Welland Gdns. UB6: G'frd 2K **77**
Welland Ho. SE15 4J **121**
Welland M. E1 1G **103**
Welland Rd. TW6: H'row A 5C **174**
Wellands Cl. BR1: Broml 2D **160**
Welland St. SE10 6E **104**
Well App. EN5: Barn 5A **20**
Wellbrook Rd. BR6: Farnb 4E **172**
Wellby Cl. N9 1B **34**
Wellby Ct. E13 1A **88**
Well Cl. HA4: Ruis 3C **58**
Well Cl. SW16 4K **137**
Wellclose Sq. E1 7G **85**
(not continuous)
Wellclose St. E1 7G **85**
Wellcome Collection 3C **6** (4H **83**)
(off Euston Rd.)
Wellcome Mus., The 7H **7** (6K **83**)
(within Royal College of Surgeons)
Well Cott. Cl. E11 6A **52**
Well Ct. EC4 1D **14** (6C **84**)
(not continuous)
Wellday Ho. E9 6A **68**
(off Hedger's Gro.)
Welldon Ct. HA1: Harr 5J **41**
Welldon Cres. HA1: Harr 5J **41**
Weller Ct. W11 1H **99**
(off Ladbroke Rd.)
Weller Ho. SE16 2G **103**
(off George Row)
Weller M. BR2: Broml 4K **159**
Weller M. EN2: Enf 1F **23**
Weller St. SE1 6C **14** (2C **102**)
Welles Ct. E14 7C **86**
(off Premiere Pl.)
Wellesley Av. W6 3D **98**
Wellesley Cl. SE7 5A **106**
Wellesley Ct. NW2 2C **62**
Wellesley Ct. SE1 3C **102**
(off Rockingham St.)
Wellesley Ct. SM3: Sutt 1G **165**
Wellesley Ct. W9 3A **82**
Wellesley Ct. Rd. CR0: C'don 2D **168**
Wellesley Cres. TW2: Twick 2J **131**
Wellesley Gro. CR0: C'don 2D **168**
Wellesley Ho. NW1 2C **6** (3H **83**)
(off Wellesley Pl.)
Wellesley Ho. SW1 5J **17** (5F **101**)
(off Ebury Bri. Rd.)
Wellesley Mans. W14 5H **99**
(off Edith Vs.)
Wellesley Pde. TW2: Twick 3J **131**
Wellesley Pk. M. EN2: Enf 2G **23**
Wellesley Pas. CR0: C'don 2C **168**
Wellesley Pl. NW1 2C **6** (3H **83**)
Wellesley Pl. NW5 5E **64**
Wellesley Rd. CR0: C'don 1C **168**
Wellesley Rd. E11 5J **51**
Wellesley Rd. E17 6C **50**
Wellesley Rd. HA1: Harr 5J **41**
Wellesley Rd. IG1: Ilf 2F **71**
Wellesley Rd. N22 2A **48**
Wellesley Rd. NW5 5E **64**
Wellesley Rd. SE18 7E **106**
Wellesley Rd. SM2: Sutt 6A **166**
(not continuous)
Wellesley Rd. TW2: Twick 3H **131**
Wellesley Rd. W4 5G **97**
Wellesley St. E1 5K **85**
Wellesley Ter. N1 1D **8** (3C **84**)
Wellfield Av. N10 3F **47**
Wellfield Rd. SW16 4J **137**
Wellfield Wlk. SW16 4K **137**
Wellfit St. SE24 3B **120**
Wellgarth UB6: G'frd 6B **60**
Wellgarth Rd. NW11 1K **63**
Well Gro. N20 1F **31**
Well Hall Pde. SE9 4D **124**
Well Hall Rd. SE9 3C **124**

WELL HALL RDBT. – Westfield Shop. Cen.

WELL HALL RDBT. 4C 124
Wellhouse La. EN5: Barn 4A 20
Wellhouse Rd. BR3: Beck 4C 158
Wellhurst Cl. BR6: Chels 7K 173
WELLING 3B 126
Welling High St. DA16: Well 3B 126
Wellings Ho. UB3: Hayes 1K 93
Wellington N8 4J 47
(not continuous)
Wellington Arch 6H 11 (2E 100)
Wellington Av. DA15: Sidc 6A 126
Wellington Av. E4 2H 35
Wellington Av. HA5: Hat E 1D 40
Wellington Av. KT4: Wor Pk 3E 164
Wellington Av. N15 6F 49
Wellington Av. N9 3C 34
Wellington Av. TW3: Houn 5E 112
Wellington Bldgs. E3 3C 86
(off Wellington Way)
Wellington Bldgs. SW1 6H 17 (5E 100)
Wellington Cl. KT12: Walt T 7H 147
Wellington Cl. RM10: Dag 7J 73
Wellington Cl. SE14 1K 121
Wellington Cl. W11 6J 81
Wellington Ct. NW8 2B 82
(off Wellington Rd.)
Wellington Ct. SW1 7E 10 (2D 100)
(off Knightsbridge)
Wellington Ct. SW6 1K 117
(off Maltings Pl.)
Wellington Ct. TW12: Hamp H 5H 131
Wellington Ct. TW15: Ashf 5A 128
Wellington Ct. TW19: Stanw 7A 110
Wellington Cres. KT3: N Mald 3J 151
Wellington Dr. RM10: Dag 7J 73
Wellington Gdns. SE7 6A 106
Wellington Gdns. TW2: Twick 4H 131
Wellington Gro. SE10 7F 105
Wellington Ho. E16 1J 105
(off Pepys Cres.)
Wellington Ho. NW3 6D 64
(off Eton Rd.)
Wellington Ho. SE17 6C 102
(off Arnside St.)
Wellington Ho. UB5: N'olt 7E 58
(off The Farmlands)
Wellington Ho. W5 3E 78
Wellington Lodge SE1 7K 13 (2A 102)
(off Waterloo Rd.)
Wellington Mans. E10 1C 68
Wellington Mans. SE7 5A 106
(off Wellington Gdns.)
Wellington Mans. W14 6H 99
(off Queen's Club Gdns.)
Wellington M. N7 6K 65
(off Roman Way)
Wellington M. SE22 4G 121
Wellington M. SE7 6A 106
Wellington M. SW16 3H 137
Wellington Monument London
6H 11 (2E 100)
Wellington Mus. London
6H 11 (2E 100)
Wellington Pde. DA15: Sidc 5A 126
Wellington Pk. Est. NW2 2C 62
Wellington Pas. E11 5J 51
Wellington Pl. N2 5C 46
Wellington Pl. NW8 1B 4 (3B 82)
Wellington Rd. BR2: Broml 4A 160
Wellington Rd. CR0: C'don 7B 156
Wellington Rd. DA17: Belv 5F 109
Wellington Rd. DA5: Bexl 5D 126
Wellington Rd. E10 1A 68
Wellington Rd. E11 5J 51
Wellington Rd. E17 4A 50
Wellington Rd. E6 1D 88
Wellington Rd. E7 4H 69
Wellington Rd. EN1: Enf 5K 23
Wellington Rd. HA3: W'stone 3J 41
Wellington Rd. HA5: Hat E 1D 40
Wellington Rd. NW10 3F 81
Wellington Rd. NW8 1B 4 (2B 82)
Wellington Rd. SW19 2J 135
Wellington Rd. TW12: Hamp H 5H 131
Wellington Rd. TW14: Felt 5G 111
Wellington Rd. TW15: Ashf 5A 128
Wellington Rd. TW2: Twick 4H 131
Wellington Rd. TW6: H'row A 6D 174
(off Whittle Rd.)
Wellington Rd. W5 3C 96
Wellington Rd. Nth. TW4: Houn 3D 112
Wellington Rd. Sth. TW4: Houn 4D 112
Wellington Row E2 1K 9 (3F 85)
Wellington Sq. N1 1J 83
Wellington Sq. SW3 5E 16 (5D 100)
Wellington St. SE18 4E 106
Wellington St. WC2 2G 13 (7K 83)
Wellington Ter. E1 1H 103
Wellington Ter. HA1: Harr 1H 59
Wellington Ter. N8 3A 48
(off Turnpike La.)
Wellington Ter. W2 7J 81
Wellington Way E3 3C 86
Welling United FC 3C 126
Welling Way DA16: Well 3H 125
Welling Way SE9 3G 125
Well La. SW14 5J 115
Wellmeadow Rd. SE13 6G 123
(not continuous)
Wellmeadow Rd. SE6 7G 123
Wellmeadow Rd. W7 4A 96
Wellow Wlk. SM5: Cars 1B 166
Well Pl. NW3 3B 64
Well Rd. NW3 3B 64
Wells, The N14 7C 22
Wellsborough M. SW20 2G 153
Wells Cl. CR2: S Croy 5E 168
Wells Cl. UB5: N'olt 3A 76
Wells Ct. BR2: Broml 2F 159
Wells Ct. NW6 2J 81
(off Cambridge Av.)
Wells Dr. NW9 1K 61
Wells Gdns. IG1: Ilf 7C 52
Wells Gdns. RM10: Dag 5H 73
Wells Ga. Cl. IG8: Wfd G 4D 36
Wells Ho. BR1: Broml 5K 141
(off Pike Cl.)
Wells Ho. EC1 1K 7 (3A 84)
(off Spa Grn. Est.)
Wells Ho. IG11: Bark 7A 72
(off Margaret Bondfield Av.)
Wells Ho. SE16 3J 103
(off Howland Est.)
Wells Ho. W10 4G 81
(off Wornington Rd.)
Wells Ho. W5 7D 78
(off Grove Rd.)
Wells Ho. Rd. NW10 5A 80
Wellside Cl. EN5: Barn 4A 20
Wellside Gdns. SW14 4J 115
Wells La. TW3: Houn 3F 113
Wells M. N11 5C 32
Wells M. W1 6B 6 (5G 83)
Wellsmoor Gdns. BR1: Broml 3E 160
Wells Pk. Rd. SE26 3G 139
Wells Path UB4: Hayes 3G 75
Wells Pl. SW18 7A 118
Wellspring Cl. E14 5E 86
Wellspring Cres. HA9: Wemb 3H 61
Wellspring M. SE26 3H 139
Wells Ri. NW8 1D 82
Wells Rd. BR1: Broml 2D 160
Wells Rd. W12 2E 98
Wells Sq. WC1 2G 7 (3K 83)
Wells St. W1 6A 6 (5G 83)
Wellstead Av. N9 7E 24
Wellstead Rd. E6 2E 88
Wells Ter. N4 2A 66
Wellston Cres. N14 6B 22
Well St. E15 6G 69
Well St. E9 7J 67
Wells Vw. Dr. BR2: Broml 6C 160
Wells Way SE5 6D 102
Wells Way SW7 1A 16 (3B 100)
Wells Yd. N7 5A 66
Well Wlk. NW3 4B 64
Wellwood Rd. IG3: Ilf 1A 72
Welmar M. SW4 5H 119
(off Clapham Pk. Rd.)
Welsby Ct. W5 5C 78
Welsford St. SE1 4G 103
(not continuous)
Welsh Cl. E13 3J 87
Welsh Harp Reservoir 1B 62
Welsh Ho. E1 1H 103
(off Wapping La.)
Welshpool Ho. E8 1G 85
(off Welshpool St.)
Welshpool St. E8 1G 85
(not continuous)
Welshside NW9 6A 44
(off Ruthin Cl.)
Welshside Wlk. NW9 6A 44
Welstead Ho. E1 6H 85
(off Cannon St. Rd.)
Welstead Way W4 4B 98
Weltje Rd. W6 4C 98
Welton Ct. SE5 1E 120
Welton Ho. E1 5K 85
(off Stepney Way)
Welton Rd. SE18 7J 107
Welwyn Av. TW14: Felt 6H 111
Welwyn St. E2 3J 85
Welwyn Way UB4: Hayes 4G 75
WEMBLEY 5E 60
Wembley & Sudbury Tennis & Squash Club 5D 60
Wembley Commercial Cen. HA9: Wemb 2D 60
Wembley Hill Rd. HA9: Wemb East La. 3F 61
Wembley Hill Rd. HA9: Wemb South Way 5F 61
Wembley Leisure Cen. 4G 61
WEMBLEY PARK 3G 61
Wembley Pk. Blvd. HA9: Wemb 5G 61
Wembley Pk. Bus. Cen. HA9: Wemb 4H 61
Wembley Pk. Dr. HA9: Wemb 4F 61
Wembley Pk. Ga. HA9: Wemb 4G 61
Wembley Rd. TW12: Hamp 1E 148
Wembley Sailing Club 2K 61
Wembley Stadium 4G 61
Wembley Stadium Ind. Est. HA9: Wemb 4H 61
Wembley Way HA9: Wemb 6H 61
Wemborough Rd. HA7: Stan 2B 42
Wembury M. N6 7G 47
Wembury Rd. N6 7F 47
Wemyss Rd. SE3 2H 123
Wendela Ct. HA1: Harr 2J 59
Wendell M. W12 2B 98
Wendell Rd. W12 3B 98
Wenderholme CR2: S Croy 5D 168
(off South Pk. Hill Rd.)
Wendle Sq. SW11 1C 118
Wendling NW5 5D 64
Wendling Rd. SM1: Sutt 1B 166
Wendon St. E3 1B 86
Wendover SE17 5E 102
(not continuous)
Wendover Cl. UB4: Yead 4C 76
Wendover Ct. BR2: Broml 3K 159
(off Wendover Rd.)
Wendover Ct. NW10 4H 79
Wendover Ct. NW2 3J 63
Wendover Ct. W1 6G 5 (5E 82)
(off Chiltern St.)
Wendover Dr. KT3: N Mald 6B 152
Wendover Ho. W1 6G 5 (5E 82)
(off Chiltern St.)
Wendover Rd. BR2: Broml 4K 159
Wendover Rd. NW10 2B 80
Wendover Rd. SE9 3B 124
Wendover Way DA16: Well 5A 126
Wendy Cl. EN1: Enf 6A 24
Wendy Way HA0: Wemb 1E 78
Wenham Ho. SW8 7G 101
Wenlake Ho. EC1 3C 8 (4C 84)
(off Old St.)
Wenlock Barn Est. N1 2D 84
(off Wenlock St.)
Wenlock Ct. N1 2D 84
Wenlock Gdns. NW4 4D 44
Wenlock M. E10 7C 50
Wenlock Rd. HA8: Edg 7C 28
Wenlock Rd. N1 2C 84
Wenlock St. N1 1D 8 (2C 84)
Wennington Rd. E3 2K 85
Wensdale Ho. E5 2G 67
Wensley Av. IG8: Wfd G 7C 36
Wensley Cl. N11 6K 31
Wensley Cl. SE9 6D 124
Wensleydale Av. IG5: Ilf 2C 52
Wensleydale Gdns. TW12: Hamp 7F 131
Wensleydale Pas. TW12: Hamp 1E 148
Wensleydale Rd. TW12: Hamp 6E 130
Wensley Rd. N18 6C 34
Wensum Pl. BR2: Hayes 7J 159
Wentland Cl. SE6 2F 141
Wentland Rd. SE6 2F 141
Wentway Ct. W13 4K 77
(off Ruislip Rd. E.)
Wentworth Av. N3 7D 30
Wentworth Cl. BR2: Hayes 2J 171
Wentworth Cl. BR6: Farnb 5J 173
Wentworth Cl. KT6: Surb 2D 162
Wentworth Cl. N3 7E 30
Wentworth Cl. SE28 6D 90
Wentworth Cl. SM4: Mord 7J 153
Wentworth Cl. TW15: Ashf 4D 128
Wentworth Ct. SW1 6J 17 (5F 101)
Wentworth Ct. SW18 6K 117
(off Garratt La.)
Wentworth Ct. TW2: Twick 3J 131
Wentworth Ct. W6 6G 99
(off Paynes Wlk.)
Wentworth Cres. SE15 7G 103
Wentworth Cres. UB3: Harl 3F 93
Wentworth Dr. HA5: Eastc 5J 39
Wentworth Dr. TW6: H'row A 5C 174
Wentworth Dwellings E1 7J 9 (6F 85)
(off Wentworth St.)
Wentworth Flds. UB4: Hayes 2F 75
Wentworth Gdns. N13 3G 33
Wentworth Hill HA9: Wemb 1F 61
Wentworth Ho. IG8: Wfd G 7K 37
(off Victoria Pk. Sq.)
Wentworth M. E3 4A 86
Wentworth M. W3 6A 80
Wentworth Pk. N3 7D 30
Wentworth Pl. HA7: Stan 6G 27
Wentworth Rd. CR0: C'don 7A 156
Wentworth Rd. E12 4B 70
Wentworth Rd. EN5: Barn 3A 20
Wentworth Rd. NW11 6H 45
Wentworth Rd. UB2: S'hall 4A 94
Wentworth St. E1 7J 9 (6F 85)
Wentworth Way HA5: Pinn 4C 40
Wenvoe Av. DA7: Bex 2H 127
Wepham Cl. UB4: Yead 5B 76
Wernbrook St. SE18 6G 107
Werndee Rd. SE25 4G 157
Werneth Hall Rd. IG5: Ilf 3E 52
Werrington St. NW1 2G 83
Werter Rd. SW15 4G 117
Wesleyan Pl. NW5 4F 65
Wesley Apts. SW8 1H 119
Wesley Av. E16 1J 105
Wesley Av. NW10 3K 79
Wesley Av. TW3: Houn 2C 112
Wesley Cl. HA2: Harr 2G 59
Wesley Cl. KT19: Ewe 5J 163
Wesley Cl. N7 2K 65
Wesley Cl. SE17 4B 102
Wesley Ct. SE16 3H 103
Wesley Rd. E10 7E 50
Wesley Rd. NW10 1J 79
Wesley Rd. UB3: Hayes 7J 75
Wesley's House & Mus. of Methodism 3F 9 (4D 84)
Wesley Sq. W11 6G 81
Wesley St. W1 6H 5 (5E 82)
Wessex Av. SW19 3J 153
Wessex Cl. IG3: Ilf 6J 53
Wessex Cl. KT1: King T 1H 151
Wessex Ct. BR1: Broml 2C 160
Wessex Ct. BR3: Beck 1A 158
Wessex Ct. EN5: Barn 4A 20
Wessex Ct. HA9: Wemb 2F 61
Wessex Ct. TW19: Stanw 6A 110
Wessex Dr. HA5: Hat E 1C 40
Wessex Gdns. NW11 1G 63
Wessex Ho. SE1 5F 103
(off Royal Carriage M.)
Wessex La. UB6: G'frd 3H 77
Wessex St. E2 3J 85
Wessex Ter. CR4: Mitc 5C 154
Wessex Wlk. DA2: Wilm 2K 145
Wessex Way NW11 1G 63
Wesson Mead SE5 7C 102
(off Camberwell Rd.)
West 12 Shop. Cen. 2F 99
Westacott UB4: Hayes 5G 75
Westacott Cl. N19 1H 65
West Acre HA2: Harr 2J 59
WEST ACTON 6G 79
West App. BR5: Pet W 5G 161
West Arbour St. E1 6K 85
West Av. E17 4D 50
West Av. HA5: Pinn 6D 40
West Av. N3 6D 30
West Av. NW4 5F 45
West Av. SM6: W'gton 5J 167
West Av. UB1: S'hall 7D 76
West Av. UB3: Hayes 7H 75
West Av. Rd. E17 4C 50
West Bank EN2: Enf 2H 23
West Bank IG11: Bark 1F 89
West Bank N16 7E 48
Westbank Rd. TW12: Hamp H 6G 131
WEST BARNES 5D 152
West Barnes La. KT3: N Mald 3D 152
West Barnes La. SW20 3D 152
WEST BECKTON 6B 88
WEST BEDFONT 6B 110
Westbeech Rd. N22 3A 48
Westbere Dr. HA7: Stan 5J 27
Westbere Rd. NW2 4G 63
West Block SE1 7H 13 (2K 101)
(off York Rd.)
Westbourne Apts. SW6 3K 117
Westbourne Av. SM3: Cheam 2G 165
Westbourne Av. W3 6K 79
Westbourne Bri. W2 5A 82
Westbourne Cl. UB4: Yead 4A 76
Westbourne Ct. W2 5A 82
Westbourne Cres. W2 2A 10 (7B 82)
Westbourne Cres. M. W2 2A 10 (7B 82)
(off Westbourne Cres.)
Westbourne Dr. SE23 2K 139
Westbourne Gdns. W2 6K 81
WESTBOURNE GREEN 5J 81
Westbourne Gro. W11 7H 81
Westbourne Gro. W2 6J 81
Westbourne Gro. M. W11 6J 81
Westbourne Gro. Ter. W2 6K 81
Westbourne Ho. SW1 5J 17 (5F 101)
(off Ebury Bri. Rd.)
Westbourne Ho. TW5: Hest 6E 94
Westbourne Pde. UB10: Hil 4D 74
Westbourne Pk. Pas. W2 5J 81
(off Harrow Rd.)
Westbourne Pk. Rd. W11 6G 81
Westbourne Pk. Rd. W2 5J 81
Westbourne Pk. Vs. W2 5J 81
Westbourne Pl. N9 3C 34
Westbourne Rd. CR0: C'don 6F 157
Westbourne Rd. DA7: Bex 7D 108
Westbourne Rd. N7 6K 65
Westbourne Rd. SE26 6K 139
Westbourne Rd. TW13: Felt 3H 129
Westbourne Rd. UB8: Hil 4D 74
Westbourne St. W2 2A 10 (7B 82)
Westbourne Ter. SE23 2K 139
(off Westbourne Dr.)
Westbourne Ter. W2 6A 82
Westbourne Ter. M. W2 6A 82
Westbourne Ter. Rd. W2 5K 81
WESTBOURNE TER. RD. BRI. 5A 82
(off Westbourne Ter. Rd.)
Westbridge Cl. W12 2C 98
Westbridge Ho. SW11 1C 118
(off Westbridge Rd.)
Westbridge Rd. SW11 1B 118
WEST BROMPTON 6A 100
Westbrook Av. TW12: Hamp 7D 130
Westbrook Cl. EN4: Cockf 3G 21
Westbrook Cres. EN4: Cockf 3G 21
Westbrooke Cres. DA16: Well 3C 126
Westbrooke Rd. DA15: Sidc 2H 143
Westbrooke Rd. DA16: Well 3B 126
Westbrook Ho. E2 3J 85
(off Victoria Pk. Sq.)
Westbrook Rd. CR7: Thor H 1D 156
Westbrook Rd. SE3 1K 123
Westbrook Rd. TW5: Hest 7D 94
Westbrook Sq. EN4: Cockf 3G 21
Westbury Av. HA0: Wemb 7E 60
Westbury Av. N22 3B 48
Westbury Av. UB1: S'hall 4E 76
Westbury Cl. HA4: Ruis 7J 39
Westbury Cl. TW17: Shep 6D 146
Westbury Ct. IG11: Bark 1H 89
(off Ripple Rd.)
Westbury Gro. N12 6D 30
Westbury Ho. E17 4B 50
Westbury Ho. W11 5J 81
(off Aldridge Rd. Vs.)
Westbury La. IG9: Buck H 2E 36
Westbury Lodge Cl. HA5: Pinn 3B 40
Westbury Pde. SW12 6F 119
(off Balham Hill)
Westbury Pl. TW8: Bford 6D 96
Westbury Rd. BR1: Broml 1B 160
Westbury Rd. BR3: Beck 3A 158
Westbury Rd. CR0: C'don 6D 156
Westbury Rd. E17 4B 50
Westbury Rd. E7 6K 69
Westbury Rd. HA0: Wemb 7E 60
Westbury Rd. IG1: Ilf 2E 70
Westbury Rd. IG11: Bark 1H 89
Westbury Rd. IG9: Buck H 2F 37
Westbury Rd. KT3: N Mald 4K 151
Westbury Rd. N11 6D 32
Westbury Rd. N12 6D 30
Westbury Rd. SE20 1K 157
Westbury Rd. TW13: Felt 1B 130
Westbury Rd. W5 6E 78
Westbury Ter. E7 6K 69
Westbush Ct. W12 2D 98
(off Goldhawk M.)
West Cadet Apts. SE18 7E 106
(off Langhorne St.)
West Carriage Dr. W2 Nth. Ride 3C 10 (7C 82)
West Carriage Dr. W2 Rotten Row 6B 10 (2B 100)
West Carriage Ho. SE18 3F 107
(off Royal Carriage M.)
West Central St. WC1 7E 6 (6J 83)
West Chantry HA3: Hrw W 1F 41
Westchester Dr. NW4 3F 45
Westcliffe Apts. W2 6B 4 (5B 82)
West Cl. EN4: Cockf 4K 21
West Cl. HA9: Wemb 1F 61
West Cl. N9 3A 34
West Cl. TW12: Hamp 6C 130
West Cl. TW15: Ashf 4A 128
West Cl. UB6: G'frd 2G 77
Westcombe Av. CR0: C'don 7J 155
Westcombe Ct. SE3 7H 105
Westcombe Dr. EN5: Barn 5D 20
Westcombe Hill SE10 5J 105
Westcombe Hill SE3 7J 105
Westcombe Lodge Dr. UB4: Hayes 5G 75
Westcombe Pk. Rd. SE3 6G 105
West Comn. Rd. BR2: Hayes 1J 171
West Comn. Rd. BR2: Kes 1J 171
West Comn. Rd. UB8: Uxb 5A 56
Westcoombe Av. SW20 1B 152
Westcote Ri. HA4: Ruis 7E 38
Westcote Rd. SW16 5G 137
West Cotts. NW6 5J 63
Westcott Cl. BR1: Broml 5D 160
Westcott Cl. CR0: New Ad 7D 170
Westcott Cl. N15 6F 49
Westcott Cres. W7 6J 77
Westcott Ho. E14 7C 86
Westcott Rd. SE17 6B 102
West Ct. E17 4C 50
West Ct. HA0: Wemb 2C 60
West Ct. TW5: Isle 7G 95
Westcroft Cl. EN3: Enf W 1D 24
Westcroft Cl. NW2 4G 63
Westcroft Est. NW2 4G 63
Westcroft Gdns. SM4: Mord 3H 153
Westcroft Leisure Cen. 4E 166
Westcroft Rd. SM5: Cars 4E 166
Westcroft Rd. SM6: W'gton 4E 166
Westcroft Sq. W6 4C 98
Westcroft Way NW2 4G 63
West Cromwell Rd. SW5 4J 99
West Cromwell Rd. W14 5H 99
West Cross Cen. TW8: Bford 6A 96
West Cross Route W10 7F 81
West Cross Way TW8: Bford 6B 96
Westdale Pas. SE18 6F 107
Westdale Rd. SE18 6F 107
Westdean Av. SE12 1K 141
Westdean Cl. SW18 6K 117
West Dene SM3: Cheam 6G 165
Westdene CR0: C'don 4D 168
(off Chatsworth Rd.)
Westdown Rd. E15 4E 68
Westdown Rd. SE6 7C 122
WEST DRAYTON 2A 92
West Drayton Pk. Av. UB7: W Dray 3A 92
West Drayton Rd. UB8: Hil 6D 74
West Dr. HA3: Hrw W 6C 26
West Dr. SM2: Cheam 7F 165
West Dr. SW16 4G 137
West Dr. Gdns. HA3: Hrw W 6C 26
WEST DULWICH 2D 138
WEST EALING 1B 96
West Ealing Bus. Cen. W13 7A 78
West Eaton Pl. SW1 3G 17 (4E 100)
West Eaton Pl. M. SW1 3G 17 (4E 100)
(off W. Eaton Pl.)
West Ella Rd. NW10 7A 62
West Elms Studios SW8 1G 119
WEST END 2B 76
West End Av. E10 5F 51
West End Av. HA5: Pinn 4B 40
West End Cl. NW10 7J 61
West End Ct. HA5: Pinn 4B 40
West End Ct. NW6 7K 63
West End Gdns. UB5: N'olt 2A 76
West End Grn. 5J 63
(off West End Lane)
West End La. EN5: Barn 4A 20
West End La. HA5: Pinn 3B 40
West End La. NW6 5J 63
(not continuous)
West End La. UB3: Harl 7E 92
West End Quay W2 6B 4 (5B 82)
(off Harbet Rd.)
West End Rd. HA4: Ruis 2G 57
West End Rd. UB1: S'hall 1C 94
West End Rd. UB5: N'olt 7A 58
Westerdale Ct. N5 4B 66
(off Hamilton Pk. W.)
Westerdale Rd. SE10 5J 105
Westerfield Rd. N15 5F 49
Westergate W5 5E 78
Westergate Ho. KT1: King T 4D 150
(off Portsmouth Rd.)
Westergate Rd. SE2 6E 108
Westerham NW1 1G 83
(off Bayham St.)
Westerham Av. N9 3J 33
Westerham Dr. DA15: Sidc 6B 126
Westerham Ho. SE1 3D 102
(off Law St.)
Westerham Lodge BR3: Beck 7C 140
(off Park Rd.)
Westerham Rd. BR2: Kes 6B 172
Westerham Rd. E10 7D 50
Westerley Cres. SE26 5B 140
Westerley Ware TW9: Kew 6G 97
(off Kew Grn.)
Western Av. HA4: Ruis 6E 56
Western Av. NW11 6F 45
Western Av. RM10: Dag 6J 73
Western Av. UB10: Hil 5C 56
Western Av. UB10: Uxb 5C 56
Western Av. UB5: N'olt 7B 58
Western Av. UB6: G'frd 2H 77
Western Av. W3 4G 79
Western Av. W5 4F 79
Western Av. Bus. Pk. W3 4H 79
Western Beach Apts. E16 1J 105
Western Ct. N3 6D 30
Western Ct. NW6 2H 81
Western Ct. W3 6K 79
Western Ctyd. EC2 6H 9 (5E 84)
(off Cutlers Gdns.)
Western Dr. TW17: Shep 6F 147
Western Gdns. W5 7G 79
Western Gateway E16 7J 87
Western Intl. Mkt. UB2: S'hall 4K 93
Western La. SW12 7E 118
Western Mans. EN5: New Bar 5E 20
(off Great Nth. Rd.)
Western M. W9 4H 81
Western Pde. EN5: New Bar 5D 20
Western Perimeter Rd. TW6: H'row A 5C 174
Western Perimeter Rd. TW6: Lford 5C 174
Western Pl. SE16 2J 103
Western Rd. CR4: Mitc 1B 154
Western Rd. E13 2A 88
Western Rd. E17 5E 50
Western Rd. N2 4D 46
Western Rd. N22 2K 47
Western Rd. NW10 4J 79
Western Rd. SM1: Sutt 5J 165
Western Rd. SW19 1B 154
Western Rd. SW9 3A 120
Western Rd. UB2: S'hall 4A 94
Western Rd. W5 7D 78
Western Ter. W6 5C 98
Western Transit Shed N1 1J 83
Western Vw. UB3: Hayes 2H 93
Westernville Gdns. IG2: Ilf 7G 53
Western Wlk. KT1: King T 2E 150
(off Eden Walk Shop. Cen.)
Western Way EN5: Barn 6D 20
Western Way SE28 3H 107
WEST EWELL 7K 163
Westferry Cir. E14 1B 104
Westferry Rd. E14 7B 86
Westfield Av. E20 6D 68
Westfield Cl. EN3: Enf H 3F 25
Westfield Cl. NW9 3J 43
Westfield Cl. SM1: Sutt 4H 165
Westfield Cl. SW10 7A 100
Westfield Ct. KT6: Surb 5D 150
(off Portsmouth Rd.)
Westfield Ct. NW10 3F 81
(off Chamberlayne Rd.)
Westfield Dr. HA3: Kenton 4D 42
Westfield Gdns. HA3: Kenton 4D 42
Westfield Gdns. RM6: Chad H 6C 54
Westfield Ho. SE16 4K 103
(off Rotherhithe New Rd.)
Westfield Ho. SW10 7B 100
(off Worlds End Est.)
Westfield La. HA3: Kenton 5D 42
Westfield Pk. HA5: Hat E 1D 40
Westfield Pk. Dr. IG8: Wfd G 6H 37
Westfield Rd. BR3: Beck 2B 158
Westfield Rd. CR0: C'don 2B 168
Westfield Rd. CR4: Mitc 2C 154
Westfield Rd. DA7: Bex 3J 127
Westfield Rd. KT12: Walt T 7C 148
Westfield Rd. KT6: Surb 5D 150
Westfield Rd. NW7 3E 28
Westfield Rd. RM9: Dag 4E 72
Westfield Rd. SM1: Sutt 4H 165
Westfield Rd. W13 1A 96
Westfields SW13 3B 116
Westfields Av. SW13 3A 116
Westfield Shop. Cen. London 1E 98

304 A–Z London

Westfield Shop. Cen. – Whitby Rd.

Westfield Shop. Cen. Stratford City 6E **68**
Westfields Rd. W3 ....5H **79**
Westfield St. SE18 ....3B **106**
Westfield Way E1 ....3A **86**
Westfield Way HA4: Ruis 3G **57**
West Gdn. Pl. W2 ....1D **10** (6C **82**)
West Gdns. E1 ....7H **85**
West Gdns. SW17 ....6C **136**
Westgate W5 ....3E **78**
Westgate Apts. E16 ....7J **87**
(off Western Gateway)
Westgate Ct. SE12 ....1J **141**
(off Burnt Ash Hill)
Westgate Ct. SW9 ....3A **120**
(off Canterbury Cres.)
Westgate Est. TW14: Bedf 1D **128**
Westgate Ho. TW7: Isle 2H **113**
Westgate Ho. TW8: Bford 5D **96**
(off Ealing Rd.)
Westgate M. W10 ....4G **81**
(off West Row)
Westgate Rd. BR3: Beck 1E **158**
Westgate Rd. SE25 ....4H **157**
Westgate St. E8 ....1H **85**
Westgate Ter. SW10 ....6K **99**
Westglade Ct. HA3: Kenton 5D **42**
WEST GREEN 4B 48
West Grn. Pl. UB6: G'frd 1H **77**
West Grn. Rd. N15 ....4B **48**
West Gro. IG8: Wfd G 6F **37**
West Gro. SE10 ....1E **122**
West Gro. SE17 ....4C **102**
Westgrove La. SE10 ....1E **122**
West Gro. Sq. SE17 ....4C **102**
West Halkin St. SW1 ....1G **17** (3E **100**)
West Hallowes SE9 ....1B **142**
West Hall Rd. TW9: Kew 1H **115**
WEST HAM 1H 87
West Ham La. E15 ....7F **69**
West Ham Pk. E7 ....7J **69**
WEST HAMPSTEAD 6K 63
West Hampstead M. NW6 ....6K **63**
West Ham Utd FC 1D **86**
West Handyside Canopy N1 ....1J **83**
West Harding St. EC4 ....7K **7** (6A **84**)
WEST HARROW 7G 41
West Hatch Mnr. HA4: Ruis 1H **57**
Westhay Gdns. SW14 ....5H **115**
WEST HEATH 6D 108
West Heath Av. NW11 ....1J **63**
West Heath Cl. NW3 ....3J **63**
West Heath Ct. NW11 ....1J **63**
West Heath Dr. NW11 ....1J **63**
West Heath Gdns. NW3 ....2J **63**
West Heath Rd. NW3 ....2J **63**
West Heath Rd. SE2 ....6C **108**
WEST HENDON 7C 44
West Hendon B'way. NW9 ....6B **44**
West Hill HA2: Harr 2J **59**
West Hill HA9: Wemb 1F **61**
West Hill SW15 ....7F **117**
West Hill SW18 ....5H **117**
WEST HILL 6H 117
West Hill Ct. N6 ....3E **64**
Westhill Ct. W11 ....7H **81**
(off Denbigh Rd.)
West Hill Pk. N6 ....2D **64**
(not continuous)
West Hill Rd. SW18 ....6H **117**
West Hill Way N20 ....1E **30**
Westholm NW11 ....4K **45**
West Holme DA8: Erith 1J **127**
Westholme BR6: Orp 7J **161**
Westholme Gdns. HA4: Ruis 1J **57**
Westhope Ho. E2 ....4G **85**
(off Derbyshire St.)
Westhorne Av. SE12 ....7J **123**
Westhorne Av. SE9 ....5B **124**
Westhorpe Gdns. NW4 ....3E **44**
Westhorpe Rd. SW15 ....3E **116**
West Ho. IG11: Bark 6F **71**
West Ho. Cl. SW19 ....1G **135**
West Ho. Cotts. HA5: Pinn 4B **40**
Westhurst Dr. BR7: Chst 5F **143**
West India Av. E14 ....1C **104**
West India Dock Rd. E14 ....7B **86**
West India Ho. E14 ....7C **86**
(off W. India Dock Rd.)
WEST KENSINGTON 4G 99
West Kensington Ct. W14 ....5H **99**
(off Edith Vs.)
West Kensington Mans. W14 ....5H **99**
(off Beaumont Cres.)
WEST KILBURN 3H 81
Westking Pl. WC1 ....2G **7** (3K **83**)
Westlake SE16 ....4J **103**
(off Rotherhithe New Rd.)
Westlake Cl. N13 ....3F **33**
Westlake Cl. UB4: Yead 4C **76**
Westlake Rd. HA9: Wemb 2D **60**
Westland Cl. TW19: Stanw 6A **110**
Westland Ct. UB5: N'olt 3B **76**
(off Seasprite Cl.)
Westland Dr. BR2: Hayes 2H **171**
Westland Ho. E16 ....1E **106**
(off Rymill St.)
Westland Pl. N1 ....1E **8** (3D **84**)
Westlands Cl. UB3: Harl 4J **93**
Westlands Ct. KT8: E Mos 4H **149**
Westlands Est. UB3: Harl 3G **93**
Westlands Ter. SW12 ....6G **119**
West La. SE16 ....2H **103**
Westlea Rd. W7 ....3A **96**
Westleigh Av. SW15 ....5D **116**
Westleigh Ct. CR2: S Croy 4E **168**
(off Birdhurst Rd.)
Westleigh Ct. E11 ....5J **51**
(off Nightingale La.)
Westleigh Dr. BR1: Broml 1C **160**
Westleigh Gdns. HA8: Edg 1G **43**
West Links HA0: Wemb 3D **78**
Westlinton Cl. NW7 ....6B **30**
West Lodge E16 ....1J **105**
(off Britannia Ga.)
West Lodge Av. W3 ....1G **97**
West Lodge Ct. W3 ....1G **97**
West London Crematorium 4D **80**
West London Golf Course 1A **76**
West London Studios SW6 ....7K **99**
(off Fulham Rd.)
Westmacott Dr. TW14: Felt 1H **129**
Westmacott Ho. NW8 ....4B **4** (4B **82**)
(off Hatton St.)
West Mall N9 ....3B **34**
West Mall W8 ....1J **99**
(off Kensington Mall)
Westmark Point SW15 ....1D **134**
(off Norley Va.)
West Mead HA4: Ruis 4A **58**
West Mead KT19: Ewe 6A **164**
Westmead SW15 ....6D **116**
Westmead Cnr. SM5: Cars 4C **166**
Westmead Ct. SE6 ....6C **122**
Westmead Ho. SM1: Sutt 4B **166**
Westmead Rd. SM1: Sutt 4B **166**
Westmere Dr. NW7 ....3E **28**
West Mersea Cl. E16 ....1K **105**
West M. N17 ....7C **34**
West M. SW1 ....4K **17** (4F **101**)
(off W. Warwick Pl.)
West Middlesex Golf Course 7G **77**
WESTMINSTER 7E 12 (2J 101)
Westminster Abbey Chapter House 1E **18** (3J **101**)
(within Abbey)
Westminster Abbey Mus. 1E **18** (3J **101**)
Westminster Abbey Pyx Chamber 1E **18** (3J **101**)
(within Westminster Abbey)
Westminster Av. CR7: Thor H 2B **156**
Westminster Boating Base & Pier 7C **18** (6H **101**)
Westminster Bri. SW1 ....7F **13** (2J **101**)
Westminster Bri. Ho. SE1 ....1K **19** (3B **102**)
(off Lambeth Rd.)
Westminster Bri. Rd. SE1 ....7G **13** (2K **101**)
Westminster Bus. Sq. SE11 ....7G **19** (6K **101**)
(off Durham St.)
Westminster Cl. IG6: Ilf 2H **53**
Westminster Cl. TW11: Tedd 5A **132**
Westminster Cl. TW14: Felt 1J **129**
Westminster Ct. E11 ....6K **51**
(off Cambridge Pk.)
Westminster Ct. NW8 ....4A **4** (4B **82**)
(off Aberdeen Pl.)
Westminster Ct. SE16 ....1K **103**
(off King & Queen Wharf)
Westminster Dr. N13 ....5D **32**
Westminster Gdns. E4 ....1B **36**
Westminster Gdns. IG11: Bark 2J **89**
Westminster Gdns. IG6: Ilf 2G **53**
Westminster Gdns. SW1 ....3E **18** (4J **101**)
(off Vincent St.)
Westminster Hall 7E **12** (2J **101**)
(off St Margaret St.)
Westminster Ind. Est. SE18 ....3B **106**
Westminster Mans. SW1 ....2D **18** (3H **101**)
(off Gt. Smith St.)
Westminster Pal. Gdns. SW1 ....2C **18** (3H **101**)
(off Artillery Row)
Westminster RC Cathedral 2A **18** (3G **101**)
Westminster Rd. N9 ....1C **34**
Westminster Rd. SM1: Sutt 2B **166**
Westminster Rd. W7 ....1J **95**
Westmoat Cl. BR3: Beck 7E **140**
WEST MOLESEY 4E 148
Westmoor Gdns. EN3: Enf H 2E **24**
Westmoor Rd. EN3: Enf H 2E **24**
Westmoor St. SE7 ....3A **106**
Westmore Ct. SW15 ....5G **117**
Westmoreland Av. DA16: Well 3J **125**
Westmoreland Dr. SM2: Sutt 7K **165**
Westmoreland Ho. E16 ....1J **105**
(off Gatcombe Rd.)
Westmoreland Ho. NW10 ....3C **80**
Westmoreland Pl. BR1: Broml 3J **159**
Westmoreland Pl. SW1 ....6K **17** (5F **101**)
Westmoreland Pl. W5 ....5D **78**
Westmoreland Rd. BR1: Broml 3J **159**
Westmoreland Rd. BR2: Broml 5G **159**
Westmoreland Rd. NW9 ....3F **43**
Westmoreland Rd. SE17 ....6D **102**
(not continuous)
Westmoreland Rd. SW13 ....1B **116**
Westmoreland St. W1 ....6H **5** (5E **82**)
Westmoreland Ter. SE20 ....7H **139**
Westmoreland Ter. SW1 ....5K **17** (5F **101**)
Westmoreland Wlk. SE17 ....6D **102**
(not continuous)
Westmorland Cl. E12 ....2B **70**
Westmorland Cl. TW1: Twick 6B **114**
Westmorland Ct. KT6: Surb 7D **150**
Westmorland Rd. E17 ....6C **50**
Westmorland Rd. HA1: Harr 5F **41**
Westmorland Way CR4: Mitc 4H **155**
Westmount Cen. UB4: Yead 7B **76**
Westmount Cl. KT4: Wor Pk 1E **164**
Westmount Ct. W5 ....6F **79**
Westmount Rd. SE9 ....2D **124**
WEST NORWOOD 4C 138
West Norwood Crematorium 3C **138**
West Oak BR3: Beck 1F **159**
Westoe Rd. N9 ....2C **34**
West Officers Apts. SE18 ....7E **106**
Weston Av. KT7: T Ditt 7J **149**
Weston Av. KT8: W Mole 3C **148**
Westonbirt Ct. SE15 ....6F **103**
(off Ebley Cl.)
Weston Ct. KT1: King T 3E **150**
(off Grove Cres.)
Weston Ct. N20 ....7F **21**
(off Farnham Cl.)
Weston Ct. N4 ....3C **66**
Weston Dr. HA7: Stan 1B **42**
West One Ho. W1 ....6A **6** (5G **83**)
(off Wells St.)
Westone Mans. IG11: Bark 7K **71**
(off Upney La.)
West One Shop. Cen. 1H **11** (6E **82**)
(off Gilbert St.)
Weston Gdns. TW7: Isle 1J **113**
WESTON GREEN 7J 149
Weston Grn. KT7: T Ditt Weston Grn. Rd. 7J **149**
Weston Grn. RM9: Dag 4F **73**
Weston Grn. Rd. KT7: T Ditt 7J **149**
Weston Gro. BR1: Broml 1H **159**
Weston Ho. E9 ....1J **85**
(off King Edward's Rd.)
Weston Ho. NW6 ....7G **63**
Weston Pk. KT1: King T 2E **150**
Weston Pk. KT7: T Ditt 7J **149**
Weston Pk. N8 ....6J **47**
Weston Ri. WC1 ....1H **7** (3K **83**)
Weston Rd. BR1: Broml 7H **141**
Weston Rd. EN2: Enf 2J **23**
Weston Rd. RM9: Dag 4E **72**
Weston Rd. W4 ....3J **97**
Weston St. SE1 ....7G **15** (2E **102**)
(not continuous)
Weston Wlk. E8 ....7H **67**
Westover Hill NW3 ....2J **63**
Westover Rd. SW18 ....7A **118**
Westow Hill SE19 ....6E **138**
Westow St. SE19 ....6E **138**
West Pk. SE9 ....2C **142**
Westpark W5 ....6D **78**
West Pk. Av. TW9: Kew 1G **115**
West Park Cl. RM6: Chad H 5D **54**
West Park Cl. TW5: Hest 6D **94**
West Pk. Rd. TW9: Kew 1G **115**
West Pk. Rd. UB2: S'hall 1G **95**
West Parkside SE10 ....2G **105**
West Pk. Wlk. E20 ....6E **68**
West Pl. SW19 ....5E **134**
West Plaza TW15: Ashf 2A **128**
West Point E14 ....7B **86**
(off Grenade St.)
West Point SE1 ....5G **103**
Westpoint Apts. N8 ....3K **47**
West Point Cl. TW4: Houn 3D **112**
(off Grosvenor Rd.)
Westpoint Trad. Est. W3 ....5H **79**
Westpole Av. EN4: Cockf 4K **21**
Westport Ct. UB4: Yead 4A **76**
Westport Rd. E13 ....4K **87**
Westport St. E1 ....6K **85**
West Poultry Av. EC1 ....6A **8** (5B **84**)
West Quarters W12 ....6C **80**
West Quay SW10 ....1A **118**
West Quay Dr. UB4: Yead 5C **76**
West Quay Wlk. E14 ....3D **104**
West Ramp TW6: H'row A 1C **110**
West Reservoir Cen. 1C **66**
West Ridge Gdns. UB6: G'frd 2G **77**
West Ri. W2 ....2D **10** (7C **82**)
(off St George's Flds.)
West Rd. E15 ....1H **87**
West Rd. EN4: E Barn 1K **31**
West Rd. KT2: King T 1J **151**
West Rd. N17 ....6C **34**
West Rd. RM6: Chad H 6D **54**
West Rd. RM7: Rush G 7K **55**
West Rd. SE1 ....6H **13** (2K **101**)
West Rd. SW3 ....6F **17** (5D **100**)
West Rd. SW4 ....5H **119**
West Rd. TW14: Bedf 6F **111**
West Rd. UB7: W Dray 3B **92**
West Rd. W5 ....5E **78**
Westrovia Ct. SW1 ....5C **18** (5H **101**)
(off Moreton St.)
West Row W10 ....4G **81**
Westrow SW15 ....6E **116**
Westrow Dr. IG11: Bark 5A **72**
Westrow Gdns. IG3: Ilf 2K **71**
WEST RUISLIP 2E 56
West Ruislip Ct. HA4: Ruis 2F **57**
(off Ickenham Rd.)
West Sheen Va. TW9: Rich 4F **115**
Westside N2 ....3D **46**
Westside NW4 ....2D **44**
Westside Apts. IG1: Ilf 3E **70**
(off Roden St.)
West Side Comn. SW19 ....5E **134**
West Side Ct. TW16: Sun 7G **129**
(off Scotts Av.)
Westside Ct. W9 ....4J **81**
(off Elgin Av.)
West Smithfield EC1 ....6A **8** (5B **84**)
West Sq. SE11 ....2K **19** (3B **102**)
West Stand N5 ....4B **66**
West St. BR1: Broml 1J **159**
West St. CR0: C'don 4C **168**
West St. DA7: Bex 3F **127**
West St. DA8: Erith 4K **109**
West St. E11 ....3G **69**
West St. E17 ....5D **50**
West St. E2 ....2H **85**
West St. HA1: Harr 1H **59**
West St. SM1: Sutt 5K **165**
West St. SM5: Cars 3D **166**
West St. WC2 ....1D **12** (6H **83**)
West St. La. SM5: Cars 4D **166**
West St. Pl. CR0: C'don 4C **168**
(off West St.)
West Temple Sheen SW14 ....5H **115**
West Tenter St. E1 ....1K **15** (6F **85**)
West Ter. DA15: Sidc 1J **143**
West Thamesmead Bus. Pk. SE28 ....3J **107**
(not continuous)
West Twr. E14 ....2D **104**
(off Pan Peninsula Sq.)
West Twr. SW10 ....1B **118**
West Towers HA5: Pinn 5B **40**
Westvale M. W3 ....2A **98**
West Vw. NW4 ....4E **44**
West Vw. TW14: Bedf 7E **110**
West View Apts. N7 ....7J **65**
(off York Way)
Westview Cl. NW10 ....5B **62**
Westview Cl. W10 ....6E **80**
Westview Cl. W7 ....6J **77**
Westview Ct. N20 ....1F **31**
Westview Cres. N9 ....7K **23**
Westview Dr. IG8: Wfd G 2B **52**
Westville Rd. KT7: T Ditt 1A **162**
Westville Rd. W12 ....2C **98**
West Wlk. EN4: E Barn 7K **21**
West Wlk. UB3: Hayes 1J **93**
West Wlk. W5 ....5E **78**
Westward Pde. E14 ....3D **104**
(off Pepper St.)
Westward Rd. E4 ....5G **35**
(not continuous)
Westward Way HA3: Kenton 6E **42**
West Warwick Pl. SW1 ....4A **18** (4G **101**)
West Way BR4: W W'ck 6F **159**
West Way BR5: Pet W 5H **161**
West Way CR0: C'don 2A **170**
West Way HA4: Ruis 1H **57**
West Way HA5: Pinn 4B **40**
West Way HA8: Edg 6C **28**
West Way N18 ....4J **33**
West Way NW10 ....3K **61**
West Way TW17: Shep 6F **147**
West Way TW5: Hest 1D **112**
Westway SW20 ....3D **152**
Westway W10 ....5H **81**
Westway W12 ....7B **80**
Westway Cl. SW20 ....3D **152**
Westway Ct. UB5: N'olt 1E **76**
Westway Cross Shop. Pk. 1J **77**
Westway Est. W3 ....5A **80**
West Way Gdns. CR0: C'don 2K **169**
Westway Lodge W9 ....5J **81**
(off Amberley Rd.)
West Ways HA6: Nwood 2J **39**
Westways KT19: Ewe 4B **164**
Westway Sports Cen. 6F **81**
Westway Travellers Site W12 ....7F **81**
(off Stable Way)
Westwell M. SW16 ....6J **137**
Westwell Rd. SW16 ....6J **137**
Westwell Rd. App. SW16 ....6J **137**
Westwick KT1: King T 2G **151**
(off Chesterton Ter.)
Westwick Gdns. TW4: Cran 2K **111**
Westwick Gdns. W14 ....2F **99**
WEST WICKHAM 1E 170
West Wickham Leisure Cen. 1E **170**
Westwood Av. HA2: Harr 4F **59**
Westwood Av. SE19 ....1C **156**
Westwood Bus. Cen. NW10 ....4A **80**
Westwood Cl. BR1: Broml 2B **160**
Westwood Cl. HA4: Ruis 6D **38**
Westwood Ct. EN1: Enf 6K **23**
(off Village Rd.)
Westwood Ct. HA0: Wemb 4B **60**
Westwood Ct. UB6: G'frd 5H **59**
Westwood Gdns. SW13 ....3B **116**
Westwood Hill SE26 ....5G **139**
Westwood Ho. W12 ....1E **98**
(off Wood La.)
Westwood La. DA15: Sidc 5A **126**
Westwood La. DA16: Well 3K **125**
Westwood M. E3 ....3C **86**
(off Addington Rd.)
Westwood Pk. SE23 ....7H **121**
Westwood Pk. Trad. Est. W3 ....5H **79**
Westwood Pl. SE26 ....4G **139**
Westwood Rd. E16 ....1K **105**
Westwood Rd. IG3: Ilf 1K **71**
Westwood Rd. SW13 ....3B **116**
West Woodside DA5: Bexl 7E **126**
Wetheral Dr. HA7: Stan 1B **42**
Wetherby Cl. UB5: N'olt 6F **59**
Wetherby Gdns. SW5 ....4A **100**
Wetherby Mans. SW5 ....5K **99**
(off Earls Ct. Sq.)
Wetherby M. SW5 ....5K **99**
Wetherby Pl. SW7 ....4A **100**
Wetherby Rd. EN2: Enf 1H **23**
Wetherby Way KT9: Chess 7E **162**
Wetherden St. E17 ....7B **50**
Wetherell Rd. E9 ....1K **85**
Wetherill Rd. N10 ....1E **46**
Wevco Wharf SE15 ....6H **103**
Wexford Ho. E1 ....5J **85**
(off Sidney St.)
Wexford Rd. SW12 ....7D **118**
Wexner Bldg. E1 ....6J **9** (5F **85**)
(off Strype St.)
Weybourne St. SW18 ....2A **136**
Weybridge Ct. SE16 ....5H **103**
Weybridge Point SW11 ....2D **118**
Weybridge Rd. CR7: Thor H 4A **156**
Wey Ct. KT19: Ewe 4J **163**
Weydown Cl. SW19 ....1G **135**
Weyhill Rd. E1 ....6G **85**
Wey Ho. NW8 ....4B **4** (4B **82**)
(off Church St. Est.)
Wey Ho. UB5: N'olt 4D **76**
(off Taywood Rd.)
Weylands Cl. KT12: Walt T 7D **148**
Weylond Rd. RM8: Dag 3F **73**
Weyman Rd. SE3 ....1A **124**
Weymarks, The N17 ....6J **33**
Weymouth Av. NW7 ....5F **29**
Weymouth Av. W5 ....3C **96**
Weymouth Cl. E6 ....6F **89**
Weymouth Ct. E2 ....2F **85**
Weymouth Ct. SM2: Sutt 7J **165**
Weymouth Ho. BR2: Broml 2H **159**
(off Hill Ho. M.)
Weymouth Ho. SW8 ....7K **101**
(off Bolney St.)
Weymouth M. W1 ....5J **5** (5F **83**)
Weymouth Pl. SE2 ....3A **108**
Weymouth Rd. UB4: Hayes 3G **75**
Weymouth St. W1 ....6H **5** (5E **82**)
Weymouth Ter. E2 ....2F **85**
Weymouth Vs. N4 ....2K **65**
(off Moray Rd.)
Weymouth Wlk. HA7: Stan 6F **27**
Whadcoat St. N4 ....2A **66**
Whaddon Ho. SE22 ....3E **120**
Whalebone Av. RM6: Chad H 6F **55**
Whalebone Ct. EC2 ....7E **8** (6D **84**)
(off Telegraph St.)
Whalebone Gro. RM6: Chad H 6F **55**
Whalebone La. E15 ....7G **69**
Whalebone La. Nth. RM6: Chad H 1E **54**
Whalebone La. Nth. RM6: Col R 1E **54**
Whalebone La. Sth. RM6: Chad H 7F **55**
Whalebone La. Sth. RM6: Dag 7F **55**
Whalebone La. Sth. RM8: Dag 7F **55**
Whales Yd. E15 ....7G **69**
(off West Ham La.)
Wharf, The EC3 ....4J **15** (1F **103**)
Wharfdale Cl. N11 ....6K **31**
Wharfdale Rd. N1 ....2J **83**
Wharfedale Ct. E5 ....4K **67**
Wharfedale Gdns. CR7: Thor H 4K **155**
Wharfedale Ho. NW6 ....1K **81**
(off Kilburn Vale)
Wharfedale St. SW10 ....5K **99**
Wharfedale Yd. N1 ....2J **83**
(off Wharfedale Rd.)
Wharf La. E14 ....6B **86**
Wharf La. TW1: Twick 1A **132**
Wharf Mill Apts. E2 ....1F **85**
(off Laburnum St.)
Wharf Pl. E2 ....1H **85**
Wharf Rd. N1 City Rd. 2C **84**
Wharf Rd. N1 York Way 1J **83**
Wharf Rd. E16 ....1A **106**
Wharf Rd. EN3: Pond E 6F **25**
Wharf Rd. Ind. Est. EN3: Pond E 6F **25**
Wharfside Point Nth. E14 ....7E **86**
(off Poplar High St.)
Wharfside Point Sth. E14 ....7E **86**
Wharfside Rd. E16 ....5G **87**
Wharf St. E16 ....5G **87**
Wharf St. SE8 ....5C **104**
Wharf Vw. Ct. E14 ....6E **86**
(off Blair St.)
Wharncliffe Dr. UB1: S'hall 1H **95**
Wharncliffe Gdns. SE25 ....2E **156**
Wharncliffe M. SW4 ....6H **119**
Wharncliffe Rd. SE25 ....2E **156**
Wharton Cl. NW10 ....6A **62**
Wharton Cotts. WC1 ....2J **7** (3A **84**)
Wharton Ho. E2 ....3K **85**
Wharton Ho. SE1 ....7J **15** (3F **103**)
(off St Saviour's Est.)
Wharton Rd. BR1: Broml 1K **159**
Wharton St. WC1 ....2H **7** (3K **83**)
Whatcott's Yd. N16 ....4E **66**
Whateley Rd. SE20 ....7K **139**
Whateley Rd. SE22 ....5F **121**
Whatley Av. SW20 ....3F **153**
Whatman Ho. E14 ....6B **86**
(off Wallwood St.)
Whatman Rd. SE23 ....7K **121**
Wheatcroft Ct. SM1: Sutt 1K **165**
(off Cleeve Way)
Wheatfield Ho. NW6 ....3J **81**
(off Kilburn Pk. Rd.)
Wheatfields E6 ....6F **89**
Wheatfields EN3: Enf H 1F **25**
Wheatfield Way KT1: King T 2E **150**
Wheathill Ho. SE20 ....2H **157**
(off Penge Rd.)
Wheathill Rd. SE20 ....3H **157**
Wheatland Ho. SE22 ....3E **120**
Wheatlands TW5: Hest 6E **94**
Wheatlands Rd. SW17 ....3E **136**
Wheatley Cl. NW4 ....2C **44**
Wheatley Ct. E3 ....3D **86**
(off Bruce Rd.)
Wheatley Cres. UB3: Hayes 7J **75**
Wheatley Gdns. N9 ....2K **33**
Wheatley Ho. SW15 ....7C **116**
(off Ellisfield Dr)
Wheatley Mans. IG11: Bark 7A **72**
(off Lansbury Av.)
Wheatley M. KT8: E Mos 4H **149**
Wheatley Rd. TW7: Isle 3K **113**
Wheatley's Eyot TW16: Sun 5J **147**
Wheatley St. W1 ....6H **5** (5E **82**)
Wheat Sheaf Cl. E14 ....4D **104**
Wheatsheaf Cl. UB5: N'olt 5C **58**
Wheatsheaf La. SW6 ....7E **98**
Wheatsheaf La. SW8 ....7J **101**
Wheatsheaf Ter. SW6 ....7H **99**
Wheatstone Cl. CR4: Mitc 1C **154**
Wheatstone Ho. SE1 ....3C **102**
(off County St.)
Wheatstone Rd. DA8: Erith 5K **109**
Wheeler Cl. IG8: Wfd G 6J **37**
Wheeler Gdns. N1 ....1J **83**
(off Outram Pl.)
Wheeler Pl. BR2: Broml 4K **159**
Wheelers Cross IG11: Bark 2H **89**
Wheelers Dr. HA4: Ruis 6E **38**
Wheel Farm Dr. RM10: Dag 3J **73**
Wheel Ho. E14 ....5D **104**
(off Burrells Wharf Sq.)
Wheel Ho. E17 ....3K **49**
Wheelock Cl. DA8: Erith 7H **109**
Wheelwright St. N7 ....7K **65**
Whelan Rd. W3 ....3H **97**
Whelan Way SM6: Bedd 3H **167**
Wheler Ho. E1 ....4J **9** (4F **85**)
(off Quaker St.)
Wheler St. E1 ....4J **9** (4F **85**)
Whellock Rd. W4 ....3A **98**
Whenman Av. DA5: Bexl 2J **145**
Whernside Cl. SE28 ....7C **90**
WHETSTONE 2F 31
Whetstone Cl. N20 ....2G **31**
Whetstone Pk. WC2 ....7G **7** (6K **83**)
Whetstone Rd. SE3 ....2A **124**
Whewell Rd. N19 ....2J **65**
Whidborne Bldgs. WC1 ....2F **7** (3J **83**)
(off Whidborne St.)
Whidborne Cl. SE8 ....2C **122**
Whidborne St. WC1 ....2F **7** (3J **83**)
(not continuous)
Whidbourne M. SW8 ....1H **119**
Whimbrel Cl. SE28 ....7C **90**
Whimbrel Way UB4: Yead 6B **76**
Whinchat Rd. SE28 ....3H **107**
Whinfell Cl. SW16 ....5H **137**
Whinyates Rd. SE9 ....3C **124**
Whippendell Way BR5: St P 7B **144**
Whippingham Ho. E3 ....3B **86**
(off Merchant St.)
Whipple La. HA2: Harr 3G **41**
Whipps Cross E17 ....5F **51**
Whipps Cross Ho. E17 ....5F **51**
(off Wood St.)
Whipps Cross Rd. E11 ....5F **51**
(not continuous)
Whiskin St. EC1 ....2A **8** (3B **84**)
Whisperwood Cl. HA3: Hrw W 1J **41**
Whistler Gdns. HA8: Edg 2F **43**
Whistler M. RM8: Dag 5B **72**
(off Fitzstephen Rd.)
Whistler M. SE15 ....7F **103**
Whistlers Av. SW11 ....7B **100**
Whistlers Gro. DA15: Sidc 7J **125**
Whistler St. N5 ....5B **66**
Whistler Twr. SW10 ....7A **100**
(off Worlds End Est.)
Whistler Wlk. SW10 ....7B **100**
Whiston Ho. N1 ....7B **66**
(off Richmond Gro.)
Whiston Rd. E2 ....2F **85**
Whitacre M. SE11 ....6K **19** (5A **102**)
Whitakers Lodge EN2: Enf 1J **23**
Whitbread Cl. N17 ....1G **49**
Whitbread Ho. SW11 ....7H **101**
(off Charles Clowes Wlk.)
Whitbread Rd. SE4 ....4A **122**
Whitburn Rd. SE13 ....4D **122**
Whitby Av. NW10 ....3H **79**
Whitby Ct. N7 ....4J **65**
Whitby Gdns. NW9 ....3G **43**
Whitby Gdns. SM1: Sutt 2B **166**
Whitby Ho. NW8 ....1A **82**
(off Boundary Rd.)
Whitby Pde. HA4: Ruis 2A **58**
Whitby Rd. HA2: Harr 3G **59**
Whitby Rd. HA4: Ruis 3K **57**
Whitby Rd. SE18 ....4D **106**

A–Z London 305

Whitby Rd. SM1: Sutt 2B 166
Whitby St. E1 .... 3J 9 (4F 85)
(not continuous)
Whitcher Cl. SE14 .... 6A 104
Whitcher Pl. NW1 .... 6G 65
Whitchurch Av. HA8: Edg 7A 28
Whitchurch Cl. HA8: Edg 6A 28
Whitchurch Gdns. HA8: Edg 6A 28
Whitchurch Ho. W10 .... 6F 81
(off Kingsdown Cl.)
Whitchurch La. HA8: Edg 7J 27
Whitchurch Pde. HA8: Edg 7B 28
Whitchurch Rd. W11 .... 7F 81
Whitcomb Ct. WC2 .... 3D 12 (7H 83)
(off Whitcomb St.)
Whitcombe M. TW9: Kew 1H 115
Whitcomb St. WC2 .... 3D 12 (7H 83)
Whitcome M. TW9: Kew 1H 115
Whiteadder Way E14 .... 4D 104
Whitear Wlk. E15 .... 6F 69
Whitebarn La. RM10: Dag 1G 91
Whitebeam Av. BR2: Broml 7E 160
Whitebeam Cl. SW9 .... 7K 101
Whitebeam Ho. E15 .... 3G 87
(off Teasel Way)
White Bear Pl. NW3 .... 4B 64
White Bear Yd. EC1 .... 4J 7 (4A 84)
(off Clerkenwell Rd.)
White Bri. Av. CR4: Mitc 3B 154
Whitebridge Cl. TW14: Felt 6H 111
White Butts Rd. HA4: Ruis 3B 58
WHITECHAPEL 5G 85
Whitechapel Art Gallery 7K 9 (6F 85)
Whitechapel High St. E1 .... 7K 9 (6F 85)
Whitechapel Rd. E1 .... 5G 85
Whitechapel Sports Cen. 5H 85
White Church La. E1 .... 7K 9 (6G 85)
White Church Pas. E1 .... 7K 9 (6G 85)
(off White Church La.)
WHITE CITY 6E 80
WHITE CITY 7D 80
White City Cl. W12 .... 7E 80
White City Est. W12 .... 7D 80
White City Rd. W12 .... 7E 80
White Collar Factory EC1 .... 3E 8 (4D 84)
(off City Rd.)
White Conduit St. N1 .... 2A 84
Whitecote Rd. UB1: S'hall 6G 76
Whitecroft Cl. BR3: Beck 4F 159
Whitecroft Way BR3: Beck 5E 158
Whitecross Pl. EC2 .... 5F 9 (5D 84)
Whitecross St. EC1 .... 3D 8 (4C 84)
White Cube Gallery SE1 .... 7G 15 (2E 102)
Whitefield Av. NW2 .... 1E 62
Whitefield Cl. SW15 .... 6G 117
Whitefoot La. BR1: Broml 4E 140
Whitefoot La. SE6 .... 4E 140
Whitefoot Ter. BR1: Broml 3H 141
Whitefriars Av. HA3: W'stone 2J 41
Whitefriars Ct. N12 .... 5G 31
Whitefriars Dr. HA3: Hrw W 2H 41
Whitefriars St. EC4 .... 1K 13 (6A 84)
Whitefriars Trad. Est. HA3: W'stone 3H 41
White Gables Ct. CR2: S Croy 5E 168
White Gdns. RM10: Dag 6G 73
Whitegate Gdns. HA3: Hrw W 7E 26
White Gates KT7: T Ditt 7A 150
Whitehall 6G 165
Whitehall SW1 .... 5E 12 (1J 101)
Whitehall Ct. SW1 .... 5E 12 (1J 101)
(not continuous)
Whitehall Cres. KT9: Chess 5D 162
Whitehall Gdns. E4 .... 1B 36
Whitehall Gdns. SW1 .... 5E 12 (1J 101)
(off Horseguards Av.)
Whitehall Gdns. W3 .... 1G 97
Whitehall Gdns. W4 .... 6H 97
Whitehall La. IG9: Buck H 2D 36
Whitehall Lodge N10 .... 2E 46
Whitehall Pk. N19 .... 1G 65
Whitehall Pk. Rd. W4 .... 6H 97
Whitehall Pl. E7 .... 5J 69
Whitehall Pl. SM6: W'gton 4F 167
Whitehall Pl. SW1 .... 5E 12 (1J 101)
Whitehall Rd. BR2: Broml 5B 160
Whitehall Rd. CR7: Thor H 5A 156
Whitehall Rd. E4 .... 2B 36
Whitehall Rd. HA1: Harr 7J 41
Whitehall Rd. IG8: Wfd G 2C 36
Whitehall Rd. W7 .... 2A 96
Whitehall St. N17 .... 7A 34
White Hart Av. SE18 .... 4K 107
White Hart Av. SE28 .... 3K 107
White Hart Cl. UB3: Harl 6F 93
White Hart Ct. EC2 .... 6G 9 (5E 84)
(off Liverpool St.)
White Hart La. N17 .... 7H 33
White Hart La. N22 .... 1K 47
White Hart La. NW10 .... 6B 62
White Hart La. RM7: Col R 1G 55
White Hart La. RM7: Mawney 1G 55
White Hart La. SW13 .... 2A 116
White Hart Rd. SE18 .... 4J 107
WHITE HART RDBT. Greenford 2B 76
White Hart Slip BR1: Broml 2J 159
White Hart St. EC4 .... 7B 8 (6B 84)
White Hart St. SE11 .... 5K 19 (5A 102)
White Hart Triangle SE28 .... 2K 107
White Hart Triangle Bus. Pk. SE28 .... 2A 108
White Hart Yd. SE1 .... 5E 14 (1D 102)
Whitehaven Cl. BR2: Broml 4J 159
Whitehaven St. NW8 .... 4C 4 (4C 82)
Whitehead Cl. N18 .... 5J 33
Whitehead Cl. SW18 .... 7A 118
Whiteheads Gro. SW3 .... 4D 16 (4C 100)
White Heart Av. UB8: Hil 5E 74
Whiteheath Av. HA4: Ruis 7E 38
White Heather Ho. WC1 .... 2F 7 (3J 83)
(off Cromer St.)
White Heron M. TW11: Tedd 6K 131
White Horse All. EC1 .... 5A 8 (5B 84)
(off Cowcross St.)
White Horse Apts. N1 .... 1A 84
(off Liverpool Rd.)
White Horse Hill BR7: Chst 4E 142
White Horse La. E1 .... 5K 85
Whitehorse La. SE25 .... 4D 156
White Horse M. EN3: Enf H 2E 24
Whitehorse M. SE1 .... 1K 19 (3A 102)
White Horse Rd. E1 .... 6A 86
(not continuous)
White Horse Rd. E6 .... 3D 88
Whitehorse Rd. CR0: C'don 7C 156
Whitehorse Rd. CR7: Thor H 5D 156
White Horse St. W1 .... 5K 11 (1F 101)
White Horse Yd. EC2 .... 7E 8 (6D 84)
White Ho., The NW1 .... 3K 5 (4F 83)
(off Albany St.)
White Ho. CR0: C'don 4D 168
(off Coombe Rd.)
White Ho. SW11 .... 1B 118
White Ho. SW4 .... 7H 119
(off Clapham Pk. Est.)
Whitehouse E10 .... 6E 50
(off Leyton Grn. Rd.)
Whitehouse Apts. SE1 .... 5H 13 (1K 101)
White Ho. Ct. N14 .... 1D 32
White Ho. Dr. HA7: Stan 4H 27
White Ho. Dr. IG8: Wfd G 6C 36
White Ho. La. EN2: Enf 1H 23
White Ho. M. E10 .... 6E 50
Whitehouse Way N14 .... 2A 32
White Kennett St. E1 .... 7J 9 (6F 85)
Whitelands Cres. SW18 .... 7G 117
Whitelands Ho. SW3 .... 5E 16 (5D 100)
(off Cheltenham Ter.)
Whiteledges W13 .... 6C 78
Whitelegg Rd. E13 .... 2H 87
Whiteley Rd. SE19 .... 5D 138
Whiteleys Cen. 6K 81
Whiteleys Pde. UB10: Hil 4D 74
Whiteley's Way TW13: Hanw 3E 130
White Lion Cen. 2A 84
(off White Lion St.)
White Lion Ct. EC3 .... 1G 15 (6E 84)
(off Cornhill)
White Lion Ct. SE15 .... 6J 103
White Lion Ct. TW7: Isle 3B 114
White Lion Hill EC4 .... 2B 14 (7B 84)
White Lion St. N1 .... 2A 84
White Lodge SE19 .... 7B 138
White Lodge W5 .... 5C 78
White Lodge Cl. N2 .... 6B 46
White Lodge Cl. SM2: Sutt 7A 166
White Lodge Cl. TW7: Isle 2A 114
White Lodge Ct. TW16: Sun 1A 148
White Lyon Ct. EC2 .... 4C 8 (4C 84)
(off Fann St.)
Whiteoak Ct. BR7: Chst 6E 142
White Oak Dr. BR3: Beck 2E 158
White Oak Gdns. DA15: Sidc 7K 125
Whiteoaks La. UB6: G'frd 3H 77
White Orchards HA7: Stan 5F 27
White Orchards N20 .... 1C 30
White Post La. E9 .... 7B 68
White Post St. SE15 .... 7J 103
White Rd. E15 .... 7G 69
White Rose Ct. E1 .... 6H 9 (5E 84)
(off Widegate St.)
Whiterose Trad. Est. EN4: E Barn 5G 21
(off Margaret Rd.)
Whites Av. IG2: Ilf 6J 53
Whites Grounds SE1 .... 7H 15 (2E 102)
White's Grounds Est. SE1 .... 6H 15 (2E 102)
(off White's Grounds)
White's Mdw. BR1: Broml 4E 160
White's Row E1 .... 6J 9 (5F 85)
Whites Sq. SW4 .... 4H 119
Whitestile Rd. TW8: Bford 5C 96
Whitestone Cl. EN4: Had W 1H 21
Whitestone La. NW3 .... 3A 64
Whitestone Wlk. NW3 .... 3A 64
Whitestone Way CR0: Wadd 2A 168
White Swan M. W4 .... 5A 98
White Tower, The 3J 15 (7F 85)
White Twr. Way E1 .... 5A 86
Whitewebbs Way BR5: St P 1K 161
Whitfield Ct. IG1: Ilf 7D 52
Whitfield Ct. SW20 .... 2F 153
Whitfield Ho. NW8 .... 4C 4 (4C 82)
(off Salisbury St.)
Whitfield Pl. W1 .... 4A 6 (4G 83)
(off Whitfield St.)
Whitfield Rd. DA7: Bex 7F 109
Whitfield Rd. E6 .... 7A 70
Whitfield St. W1 .... 4B 6 (4G 83)
Whitford Gdns. CR4: Mitc 3D 154
Whitgift Av. CR2: S Croy 5B 168
Whitgift Cen. 2C 168
Whitgift Ct. CR2: S Croy 5C 168
(off Nottingham Rd.)
Whitgift Ho. SE11 .... 3G 19 (4K 101)
Whitgift Ho. SW11 .... 1C 118
Whitgift Sq. CR0: C'don 2C 168
Whitgift St. CR0: C'don 3C 168
Whitgift St. SE11 .... 3G 19 (4K 101)
Whiting Av. IG11: Bark 7F 71
Whiting Cl. DA16: Well 1K 125
Whitings IG2: Ilf 5J 53
Whitings Rd. EN5: Barn 5A 20
Whitings Way E6 .... 5E 88
Whiting Way SE16 .... 4A 104
Whitland Rd. SM5: Cars 1B 166
Whitley Cl. TW19: Stanw 6A 110
Whitley Ho. SW1 .... 7B 18 (6G 101)
(off Churchill Gdns.)
Whitley Rd. N17 .... 2E 48
Whitlock Dr. SW19 .... 7G 117
Whitman Ho. E2 .... 3J 85
(off Cornwall Av.)
Whitman Rd. E3 .... 4A 86
Whitmead Cl. CR2: S Croy 6E 168
Whitmore Bldg. SE16 .... 3F 103
(off Arts La.)
Whitmore Cl. N11 .... 5A 32
Whitmore Est. N1 .... 1E 84
Whitmore Gdns. NW10 .... 2E 80
Whitmore Ho. N1 .... 2E 84
(off Whitmore Est.)
Whitmore Rd. BR3: Beck 3B 158
Whitmore Rd. HA1: Harr 7G 41
Whitmore Rd. N1 .... 1E 84
Whitnell Way SW15 .... 5E 116
(not continuous)
Whitney Av. IG4: Ilf 4B 52
Whitney Rd. E10 .... 7D 50
Whitney Wlk. DA14: Sidc 6E 144
Whitstable Cl. BR3: Beck 1B 158
Whitstable Cl. HA4: Ruis 2G 57
Whitstable Ho. W10 .... 6F 81
(off Silchester Rd.)
Whitstable Pl. CR0: C'don 4C 168
Whitstone Av. W7 .... 6K 77
Whitstone La. BR3: Beck 5D 158
Whittaker Av. TW9: Rich 5D 114
Whittaker Pl. TW9: Rich 5D 114
(off Whittaker Av.)
Whittaker Rd. E6 .... 7A 70
Whittaker Rd. SM3: Sutt 3H 165
Whittaker St. SW1 .... 4G 17 (4E 100)
Whittaker Way SE1 .... 4G 103
Whitta Rd. E12 .... 4B 70
Whittell Gdns. SE26 .... 3J 139
Whittingham N17 .... 7C 34
Whittingham Ct. W4 .... 7A 98
Whittingstall Rd. SW6 .... 1H 117
Whittington Apts. E1 .... 6K 85
(off E. Arbour St.)
Whittington Av. EC3 .... 1G 15 (6E 84)
Whittington Av. UB4: Hayes 5H 75
Whittington Ct. N2 .... 5D 46
Whittington Ho. N19 .... 2H 65
(off Holloway Rd.)
Whittington M. N12 .... 4F 31
Whittington Rd. N22 .... 7D 32
Whittington Way HA5: Pinn 5C 40
Whittlebury Cl. SM5: Cars 7D 166
Whittlebury M. E. NW1 .... 7E 64
Whittlebury M. W. NW1 .... 7E 64
Whittle Cl. E17 .... 6A 50
Whittle Cl. UB1: S'hall 6F 77
Whittle Rd. SE3 .... 4K 123
Whittle Rd. TW5: Hest 7A 94
Whittle Rd. UB2: H'row A 6C 174
Whittle Rd. UB2: S'hall 2F 95
Whittlesea Cl. HA3: Hrw W 7B 26
Whittlesea Path HA3: Hrw W 1G 41
Whittlesea Rd. HA3: Hrw W 7B 26
Whittlesey St. SE1 .... 5J 13 (1A 102)
Whitton NW3 .... 7D 64
WHITTON 7G 113
Whitton Av. E. UB6: G'frd 5J 59
Whitton Av. W. UB5: N'olt 5F 59
Whitton Av. W. UB6: G'frd 5H 59
Whitton Cl. UB6: G'frd 6B 60
Whitton Dene TW3: Houn 5G 113
Whitton Dene TW3: Isle 5G 113
Whitton Dene TW7: Isle 6H 113
Whitton Dr. UB6: G'frd 6A 60
Whitton Mnr. Rd. TW7: Isle 6G 113
Whitton Rd. TW1: Twick 6K 113
Whitton Rd. TW2: Twick 6J 113
Whitton Rd. TW3: Houn 4F 113
WHITTON ROAD RDBT. 6K 113
Whitton Sports & Fitness Cen. 2F 131
Whitton Wlk. E3 .... 3C 86
(not continuous)
Whitton Waye TW3: Houn 6E 112
Whitwell Rd. E13 .... 3J 87
Whitworth Ho. SE1 .... 3C 102
Whitworth Pl. TW4: Houn 7C 112
Whitworth Rd. SE18 .... 7E 106
Whitworth Rd. SE25 .... 3E 156
Whitworth St. SE10 .... 5G 105
Whorlton Rd. SE15 .... 3H 121
Whychcote Point NW2 .... 1E 62
(off Whitefield Av.)
Whymark Av. N22 .... 3A 48
Whytecroft TW5: Hest 7B 94
Whyte M. SM3: Cheam 7G 165
Whyteville Rd. E7 .... 6K 69
Whytlaw Ho. E3 .... 5B 86
(off Baythorne St.)
Wiblin M. NW5 .... 4F 65
Wickersley Rd. SW11 .... 2E 118
Wickers Oake SE19 .... 4F 139
Wicker St. E1 .... 6H 85
Wicket, The CR0: Addtn 5C 170
Wicket Rd. UB6: G'frd 3A 78
Wickets, The TW15: Ashf 4A 128
Wickfield Apts. E15 .... 6F 69
(off Grove Cres. Rd.)
Wickfield Ho. SE16 .... 2H 103
(off Wilson Gro.)
Wickford Ho. E1 .... 4J 85
(off Wickford St.)
Wickford St. E1 .... 4J 85
Wickford Way E17 .... 4K 49
Wickham Av. CR0: C'don 2A 170
Wickham Av. SM3: Cheam 5E 164
Wickham Chase BR4: W W'ck 1F 171
Wickham Cl. E1 .... 5J 85
Wickham Cl. EN3: Enf H 3C 24
Wickham Cl. KT3: N Mald 6B 152
Wickham Ct. KT5: Surb 5F 151
(off Cranes Pk.)
Wickham Ct. Rd. BR4: W W'ck 2E 170
Wickham Cres. BR4: W W'ck 2E 170
Wickham Gdns. SE4 .... 3B 122
Wickham Ho. N1 .... 1E 84
(off Halcomb St.)
Wickham La. DA16: Well 7B 108
Wickham La. SE2 .... 5A 108
Wickham M. SE4 .... 2B 122
Wickham Noakes Ct. BR3: Beck 1D 158
Wickham Rd. BR3: Beck 2D 158
Wickham Rd. CR0: C'don 2K 169
Wickham Rd. E4 .... 7K 35
Wickham Rd. HA3: Hrw W 2H 41
Wickham Rd. SE4 .... 4B 122
Wickham St. DA16: Well 2J 125
Wickham St. SE11 .... 5G 19 (5K 101)
Wickham Theatre Cen. 2F 171
Wickham Way BR3: Beck 4E 158
Wick Ho. KT1: Hamp W 1D 150
(off Station Rd.)
Wick La. E3 .... 1C 86
Wickliffe Av. N3 .... 2G 45
Wickliffe Gdns. HA9: Wemb 2H 61
Wicklow Ho. N16 .... 1F 67
Wicklow St. WC1 .... 1G 7 (3K 83)
Wick Rd. E9 .... 6K 67
Wick Rd. TW11: Tedd 7B 132
Wicks Cl. SE9 .... 4B 142
Wicksteed Cl. DA5: Bexl 3K 145
Wicksteed Ho. SE1 .... 3C 102
Wicksteed Ho. TW8: Bford 5F 97
Wicks Way SE19 .... 6D 138
Wickway Ct. SE15 .... 6F 103
(off Cator St.)
Wickwood St. SE5 .... 2B 120
Widdenham Rd. N7 .... 4K 65
Widdicombe Av. HA2: Harr 2C 58
Widdin St. E15 .... 7G 69
Widecombe Gdns. IG4: Ilf 4C 52
Widecombe Rd. SE9 .... 3C 142
Widecombe Way N2 .... 5B 46
Wideford Dr. RM7: Rush G 6K 55
Widegate St. E1 .... 6H 9 (5E 84)
Widenham Cl. HA5: Eastc 5A 40
Wide Way CR4: Mitc 3H 155
Widewing Cl. TW11: Tedd 7B 132
Widford NW1 .... 6F 65
(off Lewis St.)
Widford Ho. N1 .... 2B 84
(off Colebrooke Rd.)
Widgeon Cl. E16 .... 6K 87
Widgeon Rd. TW6: H'row A 5C 174
Widley Rd. W9 .... 3J 81
Widmer Ct. TW3: Houn 2C 112
WIDMORE 3A 160
WIDMORE GREEN 2B 160
Widmore Lodge Rd. BR1: Broml 2B 160
Widmore Rd. BR1: Broml 2J 159
Widmore Rd. UB8: Hil 4D 74
Wigan Ho. E5 .... 1H 67
Wigeon Path SE28 .... 3H 107
Wigeon Way UB4: Yead 6B 76
Wiggins La. TW10: Ham 2C 132
Wiggins Mead NW9 .... 7G 29
Wigginton Av. HA9: Wemb 6H 61
Wight Ho. KT1: King T 3D 150
(off Portsmouth Rd.)
Wightman Rd. N4 .... 5A 48
Wightman Rd. N8 .... 4A 48
Wighton M. TW7: Isle 2J 113
Wigley Rd. TW13: Felt 2B 130
Wigmore Hall 7J 5 (6F 83)
(off Wigmore St.)
Wigmore Pl. E17 .... 3A 50
Wigmore Pl. W1 .... 7J 5 (6F 83)
Wigmore Rd. SM5: Cars 2B 166
Wigmore St. W1 .... 1G 11 (6E 82)
Wigmore Wlk. SM5: Cars 2B 166
Wigram Ho. E14 .... 7D 86
(off Wade's Pl.)
Wigram Rd. E11 .... 6A 52
Wigram Sq. E17 .... 3E 50
Wigston Cl. N18 .... 5K 33
Wigston Rd. E13 .... 4K 87
Wigton Gdns. HA7: Stan 1E 42
Wigton Pl. SE11 .... 6K 19 (5A 102)
Wigton Rd. E17 .... 1B 50
Wilberforce Ct. BR2: Kes 7B 172
Wilberforce M. SW4 .... 4H 119
Wilberforce Rd. N4 .... 2B 66
Wilberforce Rd. NW9 .... 6C 44
Wilberforce Wlk. E15 .... 5G 69
Wilberforce Way SE25 .... 4F 157
Wilberforce Way SW19 .... 6F 135
Wilbraham Ho. SW8 .... 7J 101
(off Wandsworth Rd.)
Wilbraham Mans. SW1 .... 3G 17 (4E 100)
(off Wilbraham Pl.)
Wilbraham Pl. SW1 .... 3F 17 (4D 100)
Wilbrahams Almshouses EN5: Barn 2C 20
Wilbrooke Pl. SE3 .... 1K 123
Wilbury Way N18 .... 5J 33
Wilby M. W11 .... 1H 99
Wilcox Cl. SW8 .... 7J 101
(not continuous)
Wilcox Gdns. TW17: Shep 3A 146
Wilcox Ho. E3 .... 5B 86
(off Ackroyd Dr.)
Wilcox Pl. SW1 .... 2B 18 (3G 101)
Wilcox Rd. SM1: Sutt 4K 165
Wilcox Rd. SW8 .... 7J 101
Wilcox Rd. TW11: Tedd 4H 131
Wildberry Cl. W7 .... 4A 96
Wildbore Ho. N1 .... 7A 66
(off Liverpool Rd.)
Wildcat Rd. TW6: H'row A 6C 174
(off Wayfarer Rd.)
Wild Ct. WC2 .... 1G 13 (6K 83)
Wildcroft Gdns. HA8: Edg 6J 27
Wildcroft Mnr. SW15 .... 7E 116
Wildcroft Rd. SW15 .... 7E 116
Wilde Cl. E8 .... 1G 85
Wilde Ho. W2 .... 2A 10 (7B 82)
(off Gloucester Ter.)
Wilde Pl. N13 .... 6G 33
Wilde Pl. SW18 .... 7B 118
Wilder Cl. HA4: Ruis 1K 57
Wilderness, The KT8: E Mos 5G 149
Wilderness, The KT8: W Mole 5G 149
Wilderness, The TW12: Hamp H 4F 131
Wildernesse Cl. HA8: Edg 4D 28
Wilderness Island Local Nature Reserve 2E 166
Wilderness Local Nature Reserve, The 7F 101
(off Queenstown Rd.)
Wilderness M. SW4 .... 4F 119
Wilderness Rd. BR7: Chst 7F 143
Wilde Rd. DA8: Erith 7H 109
Wilderton Rd. N16 .... 7E 48
Wilder Wlk. W1 .... 3B 12 (7G 83)
(off Glasshouse St.)
Wildfell Rd. SE6 .... 7D 122
Wild Goose Dr. SE14 .... 1J 121
Wild Hatch NW11 .... 6J 45
Wild's Rents SE1 .... 3E 102
Wild St. WC2 .... 1F 13 (6J 83)
Wildwood Cl. SE12 .... 7H 123
Wildwood Gro. NW3 .... 1A 64
Wildwood Ri. NW11 .... 1A 64
Wildwood Rd. NW11 .... 6K 45
Wildwood Ter. NW3 .... 1A 64
Wilford Cl. EN2: Enf 3J 23
Wilford Rd. CR0: C'don 6C 156
Wilfred Ct. N15 .... 5D 48
(off South Gro.)
Wilfred Owen Cl. SW19 .... 6A 136
Wilfred St. SW1 .... 1A 18 (3G 101)
Wilfred Wood Ct. W6 .... 4E 98
(off Samuel's Cl.)
Wilfrid Gdns. W3 .... 5J 79
Wilkes Cl. NW7 .... 6A 30
Wilkes Rd. TW8: Bford 6E 96
Wilkes St. E1 .... 5K 9 (5F 85)
Wilkie Ho. SW1 .... 5D 18 (5H 101)
(off Cureton St.)
Wilkins Cl. CR4: Mitc 1C 154
Wilkins Cl. UB3: Harl 5H 93
Wilkins Ho. SW1 .... 7K 17 (6F 101)
(off Churchill Gdns.)
Wilkinson Cl. NW2 .... 2E 62
Wilkinson Cl. UB10: Hil 1D 74
Wilkinson Ct. SW17 .... 4B 136
Wilkinson Gdns. SE25 .... 1E 156
Wilkinson Ho. N1 .... 2D 84
(off Cranston Est.)
Wilkinson Rd. E16 .... 6A 88
Wilkinson St. SW8 .... 7K 101
Wilkinson Way W4 .... 2K 97
Wilkin St. NW5 .... 6E 64
Wilkin St. M. NW5 .... 6F 65
Wilks Gdns. CR0: C'don 1A 170
Wilks Pl. N1 .... 2E 84
Willan Rd. N17 .... 2D 48
Willard St. SW8 .... 3F 119
Willcocks Cl. KT9: Chess 3E 162
Willcott Rd. W3 .... 1H 97
Will Crooks Gdns. SE9 .... 4A 124
Willen Fld. Rd. NW10 .... 2J 79
Willenhall Av. EN5: New Bar 6F 21
Willenhall Ct. EN5: New Bar 6F 21
Willenhall Dr. UB3: Hayes 7G 75
Willenhall Rd. SE18 .... 5F 107
Willersley Av. BR6: Orp 3H 173
Willersley Av. DA15: Sidc 1K 143
Willersley Cl. DA15: Sidc 1K 143
WILLESDEN 6C 62
WILLESDEN GREEN 6E 62
Willesden La. NW2 .... 6E 62
Willesden La. NW6 .... 6F 63
Willesden Section Ho. NW6 .... 7F 63
(off Willesden La.)
Willesden Sports Cen. 1D 80
Willesden Sports Stadium 1D 80
Willes Rd. NW5 .... 6F 65
Willett Cl. BR5: Pet W 6J 161
Willett Cl. UB5: N'olt 3A 76
Willett Ho. E13 .... 2K 87
(off Queens Rd. W.)
Willett Pl. CR7: Thor H 5A 156
Willett Rd. CR7: Thor H 5A 156
Willett Way BR5: Pet W 5H 161
William IV St. WC2 .... 3E 12 (7J 83)
William Allen Ho. HA8: Edg 7A 28
William Ash Cl. RM9: Dag 6B 72
William Banfield Ho. SW6 .... 2H 117
(off Munster Rd.)
William Barefoot Dr. SE9 .... 4E 142
William Blake Ho. SW11 .... 1C 118
William Bonney Est. SW4 .... 4H 119
William Booth Ho. E14 .... 6C 86
(off Hind Gro.)
William Booth Rd. SE20 .... 1G 157
William Carey Way HA1: Harr 6J 41
William Caslon Ho. E2 .... 2H 85
(off Patriot Sq.)
William Channing Ho. E2 .... 3H 85
(off Canrobert St.)
William Cl. N2 .... 2B 46
William Cl. RM5: Col R 1J 55
William Cl. SE13 .... 3E 122
William Cl. SE7 .... 5B 106
William Cl. UB2: S'hall 2G 95
William Cobbett Ho. W8 .... 3K 99
(off Scarsdale Pl.)
William Congreve M. N1 .... 1C 84
William Cotton Ct. E14 .... 5C 86
(off Selsey St.)
William Ct. NW8 .... 1A 4 (3A 82)
William Ct. SE10 .... 1D 122
(off Greenwich High Rd.)
William Ct. SE25 .... 3F 157
(off Chalfont Rd.)
William Ct. SW16 .... 7K 137
(off Streatham High Rd.)
William Ct. W5 .... 5C 78
William Covell Cl. EN2: Enf 1E 22
William Dr. HA7: Stan 6F 27
William Dromey Ct. NW6 .... 7H 63
William Dunbar Ho. NW6 .... 2H 81
(off Albert Rd.)
William Dyce M. SW16 .... 4H 137
William Ellis Way SE16 .... 3G 103
(off St James's Rd.)
William Evans Ho. SE8 .... 4K 103
(off Haddonfield)
William Farm La. SW15 .... 3D 116
William Fenn Ho. E2 .... 1K 9 (3G 85)
(off Shipton Rd.)
William Foster La. DA16: Well 2A 126
William Fry Ho. E1 .... 6K 85
(off W. Arbour St.)
William Gdns. SW15 .... 5D 116
William Gibbs Ct. SW1 .... 2C 18 (3H 101)
(off Old Pye St.)
William Gunn Ho. NW3 .... 5C 64
William Guy Gdns. E3 .... 3D 86
William Harvey Ho. SW19 .... 1G 135
(off Whitlock Dr.)
William Henry Wlk. SW11 .... 7C 18 (6H 101)
William Hope Cl. IG11: Bark 2J 89
William Ho. BR1: Broml 3J 159
William Hunt Mans. SW13 .... 6E 98
William Margrie Cl. SE15 .... 2G 121
William Marshall Cl. E17 .... 6A 50
William M. N1 .... 7E 66
William M. SW1 .... 7F 11 (2D 100)
William Morley Cl. E6 .... 1B 88
William Morris Cl. E17 .... 3B 50
William Morris Gallery 3C 50
William Morris Ho. W6 .... 6F 99
William Morris Way SW6 .... 3A 118
William Murdoch Rd. E14 .... 5F 87
William Owston Ct. E16 .... 1C 106
(off Connaught Rd.)
William Parry Ho. E16 .... 2K 105
(off Shipwright Street)
William Perkin Ct. UB6: G'frd 6J 59
William Pike Ho. RM7: Rom 6K 55
(off Waterloo Gdns.)
William Pl. E3 .... 2B 86
William Rathbone Ho. E2 .... 3H 85
(off Florida St.)
William Rd. NW1 .... 2A 6 (3G 83)
William Rd. SM1: Sutt 5A 166
William Rd. SW19 .... 7G 135
William Rushbrooke Ho. SE16 .... 4G 103
(off Rouel Rd.)
Williams Av. E17 .... 1B 50
William Saville Ho. NW6 .... 2H 81
(off Denmark Rd.)
William's Bldgs. E2 .... 4J 85
Williamsburg Plaza E14 .... 7E 86
Williams Cl. N8 .... 6H 47
Williams Cl. SW6 .... 7G 99

Williams Dr. – Windsor Ho.

Williams Dr. TW3: Houn 4E 112
Williams Gro. KT6: Surb 6C 150
Williams Gro. N22 1A 48
Williams Ho. E3 3C 86
(off Alfred St.)
Williams Ho. E9 1H 85
(off King Edward's Rd.)
Williams Ho. NW2 3E 62
(off Stoll Cl.)
Williams Ho. SW1 4D 18 (4H 101)
(off Montaigne Cl.)
William's La. SW14 3J 115
Williams La. SM4: Mord 5A 154
Williams M. SE4 6B 122
William Smith Ho. DA17: Belv 3G 109
(off Ambrooke Rd.)
William Smith Ho. E3 3C 86
(off Ireton St.)
Williamson Cl. SE10 5H 105
Williamson Ct. SE17 5C 102
Williamson Rd. N4 6B 48
Williamson St. N7 4J 65
William Sq. SE16 7A 86
(off Sovereign Cres.)
Williams Rd. UB2: S'hall 4C 94
Williams Rd. W13 1A 96
William Stanley Ho. SE25 4G 157
Williams Ter. CR0: Wadd 6A 168
William St. E10 6D 50
William St. IG11: Bark 7G 71
William St. N17 7A 34
William St. SM5: Cars 3C 166
William St. SW1 7F 11 (2D 100)
Williams Way DA2: Wilm 2K 145
Williams Way HA0: Wemb 5B 60
William Whiffin Sq. E3 4B 86
William Wood Ho. SE26 3J 139
(off Shrublands Cl.)
Willifield Way NW11 4H 45
Willingale Cl. IG8: Wfd G 6F 37
Willingdon Rd. N22 2B 48
Willingham Cl. NW5 5G 65
Willingham Ter. NW5 5G 65
Willingham Way KT1: King T 3G 151
Willington Ct. E5 3A 68
Willington Rd. SW9 3J 119
Willis Av. SM2: Sutt 6C 166
Willis Ct. BR4: W W'ck 2F 171
Willis Ct. CR7: Thor H 6A 156
Willis Ho. E14 7D 86
(off Hale St.)
Willis Rd. CR0: C'don 7C 156
Willis Rd. DA8: Erith 4J 109
Willis Rd. E15 2H 87
Willis St. E14 6D 86
Willis Yd. N14 7C 22
Will Miles Ct. SW19 7A 136
Willmore End SW19 1K 153
Willoughby Av. CR0: Bedd 4K 167
Willoughby Av. UB10: Uxb 2A 74
Willoughby Dr. RM13: Rain 7K 73
Willoughby Gro. N17 7C 34
Willoughby Highwalk EC2 6E 8 (5D 84)
(off Moor La.)
Willoughby Ho. E1 1H 103
(off Reardon Path)
Willoughby Ho. EC2 6E 8 (5D 84)
(off Moor La.)
Willoughby La. BR1: Broml 7K 141
Willoughby La. N17 6C 34
Willoughby M. N17 7C 34
Willoughby M. SW4 4F 119
(off Cedars M.)
Willoughby Pk. Rd. N17 7C 34
Willoughby Pas. E14 1C 104
(off W. India Av.)
Willoughby Rd. KT2: King T 1F 151
Willoughby Rd. N8 3A 48
Willoughby Rd. NW3 4B 64
Willoughby Rd. TW1: Twick 5C 114
(not continuous)
Willoughbys, The SW14 3A 116
Willoughby St. WC1 6E 6 (5J 83)
(off Gt. Russell St.)
Willoughby Way SE7 4K 105
Willow Av. DA15: Sidc 6A 126
Willow Av. SW13 2B 116
Willow Av. UB7: Yiew 7B 74
Willow Bank SW6 3G 117
Willow Bank TW10: Ham 3B 132
Willowbank KT7: T Ditt 1A 162
Willowbay Cl. EN5: Barn 6A 20
Willow Bri. Rd. N1 6C 66
(not continuous)
Willowbrook TW12: Hamp H 5F 131
Willowbrook Est. SE15 7G 103
Willow Brook Rd. SE15 7F 103
Willowbrook Rd. TW19: Stanw 2A 128
Willowbrook Rd. UB2: S'hall 3E 94
Willow Bus. Pk. SE26 3J 139
Willow Cl. BR2: Broml 5D 160
Willow Cl. DA5: Bexl 6F 127
Willow Cl. IG9: Buck H 3G 37
Willow Cl. SE6 1H 141
Willow Cl. TW8: Bford 6C 96
Willow Cotts. TW13: Hanw 3C 130
Willow Cotts. TW9: Kew 6G 97
Willow Ct. E11 2G 69
(off Trinity Cl.)
Willow Ct. EC2 3G 9 (4E 84)
Willow Ct. HA3: Hrw W 1K 41
Willow Ct. HA8: Edg 4K 27
Willow Ct. N12 4E 30
Willow Ct. NW6 7G 63
Willow Ct. SM6: W'gton 7F 167
(off Willow Rd.)
Willow Ct. TW16: Sun 7G 129
(off Staines Rd. W.)
Willow Ct. W4 7A 98
(off Corney Reach Way)
Willow Ct. W9 5J 81
(off Admiral Wlk.)
Willowcourt Av. HA3: Kenton 5B 42
Willow Dene HA5: Pinn 2B 40
Willow Dene WD23: B Hea 1D 26
Willowdene N6 7D 46
Willowdene SE15 7H 103
Willowdene Cl. TW2: Whitt 7G 113
Willowdene Ct. N20 7F 21
(off High Rd. Whetstone)
Willow Dr. EN5: Barn 4B 20
Willow End KT6: Surb 1E 162
Willow End N20 2D 30
Willowfields Cl. SE18 5J 107
Willow Gdns. HA4: Ruis 2H 57
Willow Gdns. TW3: Houn 1E 112
Willow Grange DA14: Sidc 3B 144
Willow Grn. NW9 1A 44
Willow Gro. BR7: Chst 6E 142
Willow Gro. E13 2J 87
Willow Gro. HA4: Ruis 2H 57
Willowhayne Ct. KT12: Walt T 7K 147
(off Willowhayne Dr.)
Willowhayne Dr. KT12: Walt T 7K 147
Willowhayne Gdns. KT4: Wor Pk 3E 164
Willow Ho. BR2: Broml 2G 159
Willow Ho. SE1 4F 103
(off Curtis St.)
Willow Ho. SE4 3A 122
(off Dragonfly Pl.)
Willow Ho. W10 4F 81
(off Maple Wlk.)
Willow La. CR4: Mitc 5D 154
Willow La. SE18 4D 106
Willow La. Bus. Pk. CR4: Mitc 6D 154
Willow La. Ind. Est. CR4: Mitc 6D 154
Willow Lodge RM7: Rom 5K 55
Willow Lodge SW6 1F 117
Willow Lodge TW16: Sun 7H 129
(off Grangewood Dr.)
Willowmead Cl. W5 4D 78
Willow Mt. CR0: C'don 3E 168
Willow Pl. SW1 3B 18 (4G 101)
Willow Rd. EN1: Enf 3K 23
Willow Rd. KT3: N Mald 4J 151
Willow Rd. NW3 4B 64
Willow Rd. RM6: Chad H 6E 54
Willow Rd. SL3: Poyle 5A 174
Willow Rd. SM6: W'gton 7F 167
Willow Rd. W5 2E 96
Willows, The BR3: Beck 1C 158
Willows, The E6 7D 70
Willows, The SE1 4E 102
Willows Av. SM4: Mord 5K 153
Willows Cl. HA5: Pinn 2A 40
Willowside Ct. EN2: Enf 3G 23
Willows Ter. NW10 2B 80
(off Rucklidge Av.)
Willow St. E4 1A 36
Willow St. EC2 3G 9 (4E 84)
Willow St. RM7: Rom 4J 55
Willow Tree Cen. UB9: Hare 5D 38
Willow Tree Cl. E3 1B 86
Willow Tree Cl. SW18 1K 135
Willow Tree Cl. UB4: Yead 4A 76
Willow Tree Cl. UB5: N'olt 6D 58
Willowtree Cl. UB10: Ick 3E 56
Willow Tree Ct. DA14: Sidc 5A 144
Willow Tree Ct. HA0: Wemb 5D 60
Willow Tree La. UB4: Yead 4A 76
WILLOW TREE RDBT. 5B 76
Willow Tree Wlk. BR1: Broml 1K 159
Willowtree Way CR7: Thor H 1A 156
Willow Va. BR7: Chst 6F 143
Willow Va. W12 1C 98
Willow Vw. SW19 1B 154
Willow Wlk. BR6: Farnb 3F 173
Willow Wlk. E17 5B 50
Willow Wlk. IG1: Ilf 2F 71
Willow Wlk. N1 2B 84
Willow Wlk. N15 4B 48
Willow Wlk. N2 2B 46
Willow Wlk. N21 6E 22
Willow Wlk. SE1 3E 102
Willow Wlk. SM3: Sutt 3H 165
Willow Way HA0: Wemb 3A 60
Willow Way KT19: Ewe 6K 163
Willow Way N3 7E 30
Willow Way SE26 3J 139
Willow Way TW16: Sun 4J 147
Willow Way TW2: Twick 2F 131
Willow Way W11 7F 81
Willow Wood Cres. SE25 6E 156
Willow Wren Wharf UB2: S'hall 4K 93
Willrose Cres. SE2 5B 108
Willsbridge Ct. SE15 6F 103
Wills Cres. TW3: Houn 6F 113
Wills Gro. NW7 5H 29
Will Wyatt Ct. N1 2E 84
(off Pitfield St.)
Wilman Gro. E8 7G 67
Wilmar Cl. UB4: Hayes 4F 75
Wilmar Gdns. BR4: W W'ck 1D 170
Wilmcote Ho. W2 5K 81
(off Woodchester Sq.)
Wilment Ct. NW2 3E 62
Wilmer Cl. KT2: King T 5F 133
Wilmer Cres. KT2: King T 5F 133
Wilmer Gdns. N1 1E 84
(not continuous)
Wilmer Ho. E3 2A 86
(off Daling Way)
Wilmer Lea Cl. E15 7F 69
Wilmer Pl. N16 2F 67
Wilmer Way N14 5C 32
Wilmington Av. W4 7K 97
Wilmington Ct. SW16 7J 137
Wilmington Gdns. IG11: Bark 6H 71
Wilmington Sq. WC1 2J 7 (3A 84)
(not continuous)
Wilmington St. WC1 2J 7 (3A 84)
Wilmington Ter. SE16 4H 103
(off Camilla Rd.)
Wilmot Cl. N2 2A 46
Wilmot Cl. SE15 7G 103
Wilmot Ho. SE11 4B 102
(off George Mathers Rd.)
Wilmot Pl. NW1 7G 65
(not continuous)
Wilmot Pl. W7 1J 95
Wilmot Rd. E10 2D 68
Wilmot Rd. N17 3D 48
Wilmot Rd. SM5: Cars 5D 166
Wilmot St. E2 4H 85
Wilmount St. SE18 4F 107
Wilna Rd. SW18 7A 118
Wilsham St. W11 1F 99
Wilshaw Cl. NW4 3C 44
Wilshaw Ho. SE8 7C 104
Wilshaw St. SE14 1C 122
Wilsmere Dr. HA3: Hrw W 7D 26
Wilsmere Dr. UB5: N'olt 6C 58
Wilson Av. CR4: Mitc 7C 136
Wilson Cl. CR2: S Croy 5D 168
Wilson Cl. HA9: Wemb 7F 43
Wilson Ct. NW9 2K 43
Wilson Ct. RM7: Rush G 6K 55
(off Union Rd.)
Wilson Ct. SE28 3G 107
Wilson Dr. HA9: Wemb 7F 43
Wilson Gdns. HA1: Harr 7G 41
Wilson Gro. SE16 2H 103
Wilson Ho. NW6 7A 64
(off Goldhurst Ter.)
Wilson Rd. E6 3B 88
Wilson Rd. IG1: Ilf 7D 52
Wilson Rd. KT9: Chess 6F 163
Wilson Rd. SE5 1E 120
Wilson's Av. N17 2F 49
Wilson's Rd. W6 5F 99
Wilson St. E17 5E 50
Wilson St. EC2 5F 9 (5D 84)
Wilson St. N21 7F 23
Wilson Wlk. W4 4B 98
(off Prebend Gdns.)
Wilstone Cl. UB4: Yead 4C 76
Wiltern Ct. NW2 6G 63
Wilthorne Gdns. RM10: Dag 7H 73
Wilton Av. W4 5A 98
Wilton Cl. UB7: Harm 2E 174
Wilton Ct. E1 6H 85
(off Cavell St.)
Wilton Cres. SW1 7G 11 (2E 100)
Wilton Cres. SW19 1H 153
Wilton Dr. RM5: Col R 1J 55
Wilton Est. E8 6G 67
Wilton Gdns. KT8: W Mole 3E 148
Wilton Gro. KT3: N Mald 6B 152
Wilton Gro. SW19 1H 153
Wilton Ho. CR2: S Croy 5C 168
(off Nottingham Rd.)
Wilton M. E8 6H 67
Wilton M. SW1 1H 17 (3E 100)
Wilton Pde. TW13: Felt 2J 129
Wilton Pl. E4 6A 36
Wilton Pl. HA1: Harr 6K 41
Wilton Pl. SW1 7G 11 (2E 100)
Wilton Plaza SW1 3A 18 (4G 101)
(off Wilton Rd.)
Wilton Rd. EN4: Cockf 4J 21
Wilton Rd. N10 2E 46
Wilton Rd. SE2 4C 108
Wilton Rd. SW1 2K 17 (3F 101)
Wilton Rd. SW19 7C 136
Wilton Rd. TW4: Houn 3B 112
Wilton Row SW1 7G 11 (2E 100)
Wilton's Music Hall 7G 85
(off Graces All.)
Wilton Sq. N1 1D 84
Wilton St. SW1 1J 17 (3F 101)
Wilton Ter. SW1 1G 17 (3E 100)
Wilton Vs. N1 1D 84
(off Wilton Sq.)
Wilton Way E8 6G 67
Wiltshire Cl. NW7 5G 29
Wiltshire Cl. SW3 3E 16 (4D 100)
Wiltshire Ct. CR2: S Croy 5C 168
Wiltshire Ct. IG1: Ilf 6G 71
Wiltshire Ct. N4 1K 65
(off Marquis Rd.)
Wiltshire Gdns. N4 6C 48
Wiltshire Gdns. TW2: Twick 1G 131
Wiltshire La. HA5: Eastc 3H 39
Wiltshire Rd. BR6: Orp 7K 161
Wiltshire Rd. CR7: Thor H 3A 156
Wiltshire Rd. SW9 3A 120
Wiltshire Row N1 1D 84
Wilverley Cres. KT3: N Mald 6A 152
Wimbart Rd. SW2 7K 119
WIMBLEDON 6G 135
Wimbledon All England Lawn Tennis & Croquet Club 4G 135
Wimbledon Bri. SW19 6H 135
Wimbledon Cl. SW20 7F 135
Wimbledon Common 4C 134
Wimbledon Common Golf Course 5D 134
Wimbledon Hill Rd. SW19 6G 135
Wimbledon Lawn Tennis Mus. 3G 135
Wimbledon Leisure Cen. 6K 135
WIMBLEDON PARK 3J 135
Wimbledon Pk. Athletics Track 2H 135
Wimbledon Pk. Ct. SW19 1H 135
Wimbledon Pk. Golf Course 3H 135
Wimbledon Pk. Rd. SW18 1H 135
Wimbledon Pk. Rd. SW19 2G 135
Wimbledon Pk. Side SW19 3F 135
Wimbledon Pk. Watersports Cen. 2H 135
Wimbledon Rd. SW17 4A 136
Wimbledon Stadium Bus. Cen. SW17 3K 135
Wimbledon Theatre 7J 135
Wimbledon Windmill Mus. 3D 134
Wimbolt St. E2 3G 85
Wimborne Av. BR5: St P 4K 161
Wimborne Av. BR7: Chst 3K 161
Wimborne Av. UB2: S'hall 4E 94
Wimborne Av. UB4: Yead 6K 75
Wimborne Cl. IG9: Buck H 2E 36
Wimborne Cl. KT4: Wor Pk 1E 164
Wimborne Cl. SE12 5H 123
Wimborne Ct. SW12 3G 137
Wimborne Ct. UB5: N'olt 6E 58
Wimborne Dr. HA5: Pinn 7B 40
Wimborne Dr. NW9 3G 43
Wimborne Gdns. W13 5B 78
Wimborne Ho. E16 7H 87
(off Victoria Dock Rd.)
Wimborne Ho. NW1 4D 4 (4C 82)
(off Harewood Av.)
Wimborne Ho. SW12 3G 137
Wimborne Ho. SW8 7K 101
(off Dorset Rd.)
Wimborne Rd. N17 2E 48
Wimborne Rd. N9 2B 34
Wimborne Way BR3: Beck 3K 157
Wimbourne Ct. N1 2D 84
(off Wimbourne St.)
Wimbourne St. N1 2D 84
Wimpole Cl. BR2: Broml 4A 160
Wimpole Cl. KT1: King T 2F 151
Wimpole M. W1 5J 5 (5F 83)
Wimpole Rd. UB7: Yiew 1A 92
Wimpole St. W1 6J 5 (5F 83)
Wimshurst Cl. CR0: Wadd 1J 167
Winans Wlk. SW9 2A 120
Winant Ho. E14 7D 86
(off Simpson's Rd.)
Wincanton Ct. N11 6K 31
(off Martock Gdns.)
Wincanton Cres. UB5: N'olt 5E 58
Wincanton Gdns. IG6: Ilf 3F 53
Wincanton Rd. SW18 7H 117
Winchcombe Rd. SM5: Cars 7B 154
Winchcomb Gdns. SE9 3B 124
Winchelsea Av. DA7: Bex 7F 109
Winchelsea Cl. SW15 5F 117
Winchelsea Ho. SE16 2J 103
(off Swan Rd.)
Winchelsea Rd. E7 3J 69
Winchelsea Rd. N17 3E 48
Winchelsea Rd. NW10 1K 79
Winchelsey Ri. CR2: S Croy 6F 169
Winchendon Rd. SW6 1H 117
Winchendon Rd. TW11: Tedd 4H 131
Winchester Av. NW6 1G 81
Winchester Av. NW9 3G 43
Winchester Av. TW5: Hest 6D 94
Winchester Bldgs. SE1 6C 14 (2C 102)
(off Copperfield St.)
Winchester Cl. BR2: Broml 3H 159
Winchester Cl. E6 6D 88
Winchester Cl. EN1: Enf 5K 23
Winchester Cl. KT2: King T 7H 133
Winchester Cl. SE17 4B 102
Winchester Cl. SL3: Poyle 4A 174
Winchester Ct. W8 2J 99
(off Vicarage Ga.)
Winchester Dr. HA5: Pinn 5B 40
Winchester Ho. E14 6C 86
(off New Festival Av.)
Winchester Ho. E3 3B 86
(off Hamlets Way)
Winchester Ho. IG11: Bark 7A 72
(off Margaret Bondfield Av.)
Winchester Ho. SE18 7B 106
(off Portway Gdns.)
Winchester Ho. SW3 7B 16 (6B 100)
(off Beaufort St.)
Winchester Ho. SW9 7A 102
Winchester Ho. W2 6A 82
(off Hallfield Est.)
Winchester M. KT4: Wor Pk 2F 165
Winchester M. NW3 7B 64
(off Winchester Rd.)
Winchester Palace 4E 14 (1D 102)
(off Stoney St.)
Winchester Pk. BR2: Broml 3H 159
Winchester Pl. E8 5F 67
Winchester Pl. N6 1F 65
Winchester Rd. BR2: Broml 3H 159
Winchester Rd. DA7: Bex 2D 126
Winchester Rd. E4 7K 35
Winchester Rd. HA3: Kenton 4E 42
Winchester Rd. HA6: Nwood 2H 39
Winchester Rd. IG1: Ilf 3H 71
Winchester Rd. KT12: Walt T 7J 147
Winchester Rd. N6 7F 47
Winchester Rd. N9 1A 34
Winchester Rd. NW3 7B 64
Winchester Rd. TW1: Twick 6B 114
Winchester Rd. TW13: Hanw 3D 130
Winchester Rd. UB3: Harl 7G 93
Winchester Sq. SE1 4E 14 (1D 102)
(off Winchester Wlk.)
Winchester Sq. SE8 4B 104
Winchester St. SW1 5K 17 (5F 101)
Winchester St. W3 1J 97
Winchester Wlk. SE1 4E 14 (1D 102)
Winchester Wlk. SW15 5H 117
(off Up. Richmond Rd.)
Winchester Wharf SE1 4E 14 (1D 102)
(off Clink St.)
Winchet Wlk. CR0: C'don 6J 157
Winchfield Cl. HA3: Kenton 6C 42
Winchfield Ho. SW15 6B 116
Winchfield Rd. SE26 5A 140
Winch Ho. E14 3D 104
(off Tiller Rd.)
Winch Ho. SW10 7A 100
(off King's Rd.)
Winchilsea Cres. KT8: W Mole 2G 149
Winchilsea Ho. NW8 2A 4 (3B 82)
(off St John's Wood Rd.)
WINCHMORE HILL 7F 23
Winchmore Hill Rd. N14 1C 32
Winchmore Hill Rd. N21 7D 22
Winchmore School Sports Cen. 2H 33
Winchmore Vs. N21 7E 22
(off Winchmore Hill Rd.)
Winchstone Cl. TW17: Shep 4B 146
Winckley Cl. HA3: Kenton 5F 43
Winckworth Ct. N1 2F 9 (3D 84)
(off Charles Sq. Est.)
Wincott Pde. SE11 3K 19 (4A 102)
(off Wincott St.)
Wincott St. SE11 4K 19 (4A 102)
Wincrofts Dr. SE9 4H 125
Windall Cl. SE19 1G 157
Windborough Rd. SM5: Cars 7E 166
Windermere NW1 2K 5 (3F 83)
(off Albany St.)
Windermere Av. HA4: Ruis 7A 40
Windermere Av. HA3: Kenton 7C 42
Windermere Av. HA9: Wemb 7C 42
Windermere Av. N3 3J 45
Windermere Av. NW6 1G 81
Windermere Av. SW19 3K 153
Windermere Cl. BR6: Farnb 3F 173
Windermere Cl. TW14: Felt 1H 129
Windermere Cl. TW19: Stanw 1A 128
Windermere Ct. HA9: Wemb 7C 42
Windermere Ct. SM5: Cars 3E 166
Windermere Ct. SW13 6B 98
Windermere Gdns. IG4: Ilf 5C 52
Windermere Gro. HA9: Wemb 1C 60
Windermere Hall HA8: Edg 5A 28
Windermere Ho. E3 4B 86
Windermere Ho. EN5: New Bar 4E 20
Windermere Ho. TW7: Isle 5K 113
Windermere Point SE15 7J 103
(off Old Kent Rd.)
Windermere Rd. BR4: W W'ck 2G 171
Windermere Rd. CR0: C'don 1F 169
Windermere Rd. DA7: Bex 2J 127
Windermere Rd. N10 1F 47
Windermere Rd. N19 2G 65
Windermere Rd. SW15 4A 134
Windermere Rd. SW16 1G 155
Windermere Rd. UB1: S'hall 5D 76
Windermere Rd. W5 3C 96
Windermere Way UB7: Yiew 1A 92
Winders Cl. BR3: Beck 3K 157
Winders Rd. SW11 2C 118
(not continuous)
Windfield Cl. SE26 4K 139
Windham Rd. TW9: Rich 3F 115
Winding Way RM8: Dag 3C 72
Windlass Ho. E16 2K 105
(off Schooner Rd.)
Windlass Pl. SE8 4A 104
Windlesham Gro. SW19 1F 135
Windlesham Ho. SE1 5J 15 (1F 103)
(off Duchess Wlk.)
Windlesham M. TW12: Hamp H 6G 131
Windley Cl. SE23 2J 139
Windmill WC1 5G 7 (5K 83)
(off New North St.)
Windmill Av. UB2: S'hall 1G 95
Windmill Bri. Ho. CR0: C'don 1E 168
(off Freemasons Rd.)
Windmill Bus. Village TW16: Sun 1G 147
Windmill Cl. KT6: Surb 1C 162
Windmill Cl. SE1 4G 103
(off Beatrice Rd.)
Windmill Cl. SE13 2E 122
Windmill Cl. TW16: Sun 7G 129
Windmill Ct. E4 2B 36
Windmill Ct. HA4: Ruis 1J 57
Windmill Ct. NW2 6G 63
Windmill Ct. W5 4C 96
(off Windmill Rd.)
Windmill Dr. BR2: Kes 4A 172
Windmill Dr. NW2 3G 63
Windmill Dr. SW4 5F 119
Windmill Gdns. EN2: Enf 3F 23
Windmill Grn. TW17: Shep 7G 147
Windmill Gro. CR0: C'don 6C 156
Windmill Hill EN2: Enf 3G 23
Windmill Hill HA4: Ruis 7H 39
Windmill Hill NW3 3A 64
Windmill Ho. E14 4C 104
Windmill Ho. SE1 6K 13 (2A 102)
(off Windmill Wlk.)
Windmill La. E15 6F 69
Windmill La. KT6: Surb 6B 150
Windmill La. TW7: Isle 4J 95
Windmill La. UB2: S'hall 1G 95
Windmill La. UB6: G'frd 6G 77
Windmill La. WD23: B Hea 1D 26
Windmill M. W4 4A 98
Windmill Pas. W4 4A 98
Windmill Pl. UB2: S'hall 1G 95
Windmill Ri. KT2: King T 7H 133
Windmill Rd. CR0: C'don 7C 156
Windmill Rd. CR4: Mitc 5G 155
Windmill Rd. N18 4J 33
Windmill Rd. SW18 6B 118
Windmill Rd. SW19 2D 134
Windmill Rd. TW12: Hamp H 5F 131
Windmill Rd. TW16: Sun 1G 147
Windmill Rd. TW8: Bford 5C 96
Windmill Rd. W4 4A 98
Windmill Rd. W5 4C 96
Windmill Rd. W. TW16: Sun 2G 147
Windmill Row SE11 6J 19 (5A 102)
Windmill St. W1 6C 6 (5H 83)
(not continuous)
Windmill St. WD23: B Hea 1D 26
Windmill Ter. TW17: Shep 7G 147
Windmill Wlk. SE1 5K 13 (1A 102)
Windmill Way HA4: Ruis 1H 57
Windmore Cl. HA0: Wemb 5A 60
Windrose Cl. SE16 2K 103
Windrush KT3: N Mald 4H 151
Windrush SE28 1B 108
Windrush Cl. E8 7G 67
Windrush Cl. N17 1E 48
Windrush Cl. SW11 4B 118
Windrush Cl. UB10: Ick 4B 56
Windrush Cl. W4 1J 115
Windrush Ho. NW8 4B 4 (4B 82)
(off Church St. Est.)
Windrush La. SE23 3K 139
Windrush Rd. NW10 1K 79
Windrush Sq. SW2 4A 120
Windsock Cl. SE16 4B 104
Windsock Way TW6: H'row A 5C 174
Windsor Av. E17 2A 50
Windsor Av. HA8: Edg 4C 28
Windsor Av. KT3: N Mald 5J 151
Windsor Av. KT8: W Mole 3E 148
Windsor Av. SM3: Cheam 3G 165
Windsor Av. SW19 1A 154
Windsor Av. UB10: Hil 1D 74
Windsor Cen., The N1 1B 84
(off Windsor St.)
Windsor Cl. BR7: Chst 5F 143
Windsor Cl. HA2: Harr 3E 58
Windsor Cl. HA6: Nwood 2J 39
Windsor Cl. N3 2G 45
Windsor Cl. SE27 4C 138
Windsor Cl. TW6: H'row A 6D 174
(off Whittle Rd.)
Windsor Cl. TW8: Bford 6B 96
Windsor Cotts. SE14 7B 104
(off Amersham Gro.)
Windsor Ct. E3 2C 86
(off Mostyn Gro.)
Windsor Ct. HA5: Pinn 3B 40
Windsor Ct. KT1: King T 4D 150
(off Palace Rd.)
Windsor Ct. N11 5J 31
Windsor Ct. N14 7B 22
Windsor Ct. NW11 6G 45
(off Golders Grn. Rd.)
Windsor Ct. NW3 4J 63
Windsor Ct. SE16 7K 85
(off King & Queen Wharf)
Windsor Ct. SW11 2B 118
Windsor Ct. SW3 5D 16 (5C 100)
(off Jubilee Pl.)
Windsor Ct. TW16: Sun 7J 129
Windsor Ct. W10 6F 81
(off Bramley Rd.)
Windsor Ct. W2 7K 81
(off Moscow Rd.)
Windsor Ct. WD23: Bush 1B 26
(off Catsey La.)
Windsor Cres. HA2: Harr 3E 58
Windsor Cres. HA9: Wemb 3H 61
Windsor Dr. BR6: Chels 6K 173
Windsor Dr. EN4: E Barn 6J 21
Windsor Gdns. CR0: Bedd 3J 167
Windsor Gdns. UB3: Harl 3F 93
Windsor Gdns. W9 5J 81
Windsor Gro. SE27 4C 138
Windsor Hall E16 1K 105
(off Wesley Av.)
Windsor Ho. E2 3K 85
(off Knottisford St.)
Windsor Ho. E20 5D 68
(off Peloton Av.)

Windsor Ho. – Woodlands Av.

Windsor Ho. N1 2C 84
Windsor Ho. NW1 1K 5 (3F 83)
(off Cumberland Mkt.)
Windsor Ho. NW2 6G 63
(off Chatsworth Rd.)
Windsor Ho. SW16 2K 155
Windsor Ho. UB5: N'olt 6E 58
(off The Farmlands)
Windsor M. SE23 1A 140
Windsor M. SE6 1E 140
Windsor Pk. Rd. UB3: Harl 7H 93
Windsor Pl. SW1 2B 18 (3G 101)
Windsor Rd. CR7: Thor H 2B 156
Windsor Rd. DA6: Bex 4E 126
Windsor Rd. E10 2D 68
Windsor Rd. E11 1J 69
Windsor Rd. E4 4J 35
Windsor Rd. E7 5K 69
Windsor Rd. EN5: Barn 6A 20
Windsor Rd. HA3: Hrw W 1G 41
Windsor Rd. IG1: Ilf 4F 71
Windsor Rd. KT2: King T 7E 132
Windsor Rd. KT4: Wor Pk 2C 164
Windsor Rd. N13 3F 33
Windsor Rd. N17 2G 49
Windsor Rd. N3 2G 45
Windsor Rd. N7 3J 65
Windsor Rd. NW2 6D 62
Windsor Rd. RM8: Dag 3E 72
Windsor Rd. TW11: Tedd 5H 131
Windsor Rd. TW16: Sun 6J 129
Windsor Rd. TW4: Cran 2K 111
Windsor Rd. TW9: Kew 2F 115
Windsor Rd. UB2: S'hall 3D 94
Windsor Rd. W5 7E 78
(not continuous)
Windsors, The IG9: Buck H 2H 37
Windsor St. N1 1B 84
Windsor Ter. N1 1D 8 (3C 84)
Windsor Wlk. SE5 2D 120
Windsor Way W14 4F 99
Windsor Wharf E9 5B 68
Windspoint Dr. SE15 6H 103
Windus M. N16 1F 67
Windus Rd. N16 1F 67
Windus Wlk. N16 1F 67
Windward Ct. E16 7F 89
(off Gallions Rd.)
Windy Ridge BR1: Broml 1C 160
Windy Ridge Cl. SW19 5F 135
Wine Cl. E1 1J 103
(not continuous)
Wine Office Ct. EC4 Peterborough Ct.
1K 13 (6A 84)
Winery La. KT1: King T 3F 151
Winey Cl. KT9: Chess 7C 162
Winford Ct. SE15 1H 121
Winford Ho. E3 7B 68
Winford Pde. UB1: S'hall 6F 77
(off Marconi Way)
Winforton St. SE10 1E 122
Winfrith Rd. SW18 7A 118
Wingate & Finchley FC 7G 31
Wingate Cres. CR0: C'don 6J 155
Wingate Ho. E3 3D 86
(off Bruce Rd.)
Wingate Rd. DA14: Sidc 6C 144
Wingate Rd. IG1: Ilf 5F 71
Wingate Rd. W6 3D 98
Wingate Sq. SW4 3G 119
Wingfield Ct. DA15: Sidc 2K 143
Wingfield Ct. E14 7F 87
(off Newport Av.)
Wingfield Ho. E2 2J 9 (3F 85)
(off Virginia Rd.)
Wingfield M. SE15 3G 121
Wingfield Rd. E15 4G 69
Wingfield Rd. E17 5D 50
Wingfield Rd. KT2: King T 6F 133
Wingfield St. SE15 3G 121
Wingfield Way HA4: Ruis 5K 57
Wingford Rd. SW2 6J 119
Wingmore Rd. SE24 3C 120
Wingrad Ho. E1 5J 85
(off Jubilee St.)
Wingrave Rd. W6 6E 98
Wingreen NW8 1K 81
(off Abbey Rd.)
Wingrove E4 7H 25
Wingrove Ct. RM7: Rom 5J 55
Wingrove Rd. SE6 2G 141
Wings Cl. SM1: Sutt 4J 165
Wings Rd. TW6: H'row A 6C 174
(off Whittle Rd.)
Wing Yip Bus. Cen. NW2 2D 62
Winicotte Ho. W2 5B 4 (5B 82)
(off Paddington Grn.)
Winifred Pl. N12 5F 31
Winifred Rd. DA8: Erith 5K 109
Winifred Rd. RM8: Dag 2E 72
Winifred Rd. SW19 1J 153
Winifred Rd. TW12: Hamp H 4E 130
Winifred St. E16 1D 106
Winifred Ter. EN1: Enf 7A 24
Winkfield Rd. E13 2K 87
Winkfield Rd. N22 1A 48
Winkley Ct. HA2: Harr 3E 58
Winkley Ct. N10 4F 47
(off St James's La.)
Winkley St. E2 2H 85
Winkworth Cotts. E1 4J 85
(off Cephas St.)
Winlaton Rd. BR1: Broml 4F 141
Winmill Rd. RM8: Dag 3F 73
Winn Comn. Rd. SE18 6J 107
Winnepeg Ho. SE16 2J 103
(off Province Dr.)
Winnett St. W1 2C 12 (7H 83)
Winningales Ct. IG5: Ilf 2C 52
Winnings Wlk. UB5: N'olt 6C 58
Winnington Cl. N2 6B 46
Winnington Ho. SE5 7C 102
(off Wyndham Est.)
Winnington Ho. W10 4G 81
(off Southern Row)
Winnington Rd. N2 6B 46
Winnipeg Dr. BR6: Chels 6K 173
Winnock Rd. UB7: Yiew 1A 92
Winn Rd. SE12 1J 141
Winns Av. E17 3B 50
Winns M. N15 4E 48
Winns Ter. E17 3C 50
Winsbeach E17 2F 51
Winscombe Cres. W5 4D 78
Winscombe St. N19 2F 65
Winscombe Way HA7: Stan 5F 27
Winsford Rd. SE6 3B 140
Winsford Ter. N18 5J 33
Winsham Gro. SW11 5E 118
Winsham Ho. NW1 1D 6 (3H 83)
(off Churchway)
Winslade Rd. SW2 5J 119
Winslade Way SE6 7D 122
Winsland M. W2 7A 4 (6B 82)
Winsland St. W2 7A 4 (6B 82)
Winsley St. W1 7A 6 (6G 83)
Winslow SE17 5E 102
Winslow Cl. HA5: Eastc 6K 39
Winslow Cl. NW10 3A 62
Winslow Gro. E4 2B 36
Winslow Rd. W6 6E 98
Winslow Way TW13: Hanw 3B 130
Winsmoor Ct. EN2: Enf 3G 23
WINSOR PARK 5F 89
Winsor Ter. E6 5E 88
Winstanley Est. SW11 3B 118
Winstanley Rd. SW11 3B 118
(not continuous)
Winstead Gdns. RM10: Dag 5J 73
Winston Av. NW9 7A 44
Winston Cl. HA3: Hrw W 6E 26
Winston Cl. KT8: E Mos 6H 149
Winston Cl. RM7: Mawney 4H 55
Winston Ct. BR1: Broml 1K 159
(off Widmore Rd.)
Winston Ct. HA3: Hrw W 7A 26
Winston Ho. W13 2A 96
(off Balfour Rd.)
Winston Ho. WC1 3D 6 (4H 83)
(off Endsleigh St.)
Winston Rd. N16 4D 66
Winston Wlk. W4 3K 97
Winston Way IG1: Ilf 3F 71
Winter Av. E6 1C 88
Winterborne Av. BR6: Orp 3H 173
Winterbourne Ho. W11 7G 81
(off Portland Rd.)
Winterbourne Rd. CR7: Thor H 4A 156
Winterbourne Rd. RM8: Dag 2C 72
Winterbourne Rd. SE6 1B 140
Winter Box Wlk. TW10: Rich 5F 115
Winterbrook Rd. SE24 6C 120
Winterburn Cl. N11 6K 31
Winterfold Cl. SW19 2G 135
Winter Gdns. TW11: Tedd 4K 132
Wintergreen Blvd. UB7: W Dray 2B 92
Wintergreen Cl. E6 5C 88
Winterleys NW6 2H 81
(off Denmark Rd.)
Winter Lodge SE16 5G 103
(off Fern Wlk.)
Winter's Ct. E4 3J 35
Winterslow Ho. SE5 2C 120
(off Flaxman Rd.)
Winterslow Rd. SW9 1B 120
Winters Rd. KT7: T Ditt 7B 150
Winterstoke Gdns. NW7 5H 29
Winterstoke Rd. SE6 1B 140
Winterton Ct. KT1: Hamp W 1D 150
(off Lwr. Teddington Rd.)
Winterton Ct. SE20 2G 157
Winterton Ho. E1 6J 85
(off Deancross St.)
Winterton Pl. SW10 7A 16 (6A 100)
Winterwell Rd. SW2 5J 119
Winthorpe Rd. SW15 4G 117
Winthrop Ho. W12 7D 80
(off White City Est.)
Winthrop St. E1 5H 85
Winthrop Wlk. HA9: Wemb 3E 60
(off Everard Way)
Winton Av. N11 7B 32
Winton Cl. N9 7E 24
Winton Ct. N1 2K 83
(off Calshot St.)
Winton Gdns. HA8: Edg 7A 28
Winton Rd. BR6: Farnb 4F 173
Winton Way SW16 5A 138
Wireworks Ct. SE1 7C 14 (2C 102)
(off Gt. Suffolk St.)
Wirrall Ho. SE26 3G 139
Wirral Wood Cl. BR7: Chst 6E 142
Wirra Rd. TW6: H'row A 5C 174
(off Wayfarer Rd.)
Wisbeach Rd. CR0: C'don 5D 156
Wisbech N4 1K 65
(off Lorne Rd.)
Wisborough Rd. CR2: Sande 7F 169
Wisden Ho. SW8 7H 19 (6K 101)
Wisdom Ct. TW7: Isle 3A 114
(off South St.)
Wisdons Cl. RM10: Dag 1H 73
Wise La. NW7 5H 29
Wiseman Rd. E10 2C 68
Wise Rd. E15 1F 87
Wiseton Rd. SW17 1C 136
Wishart Rd. SE3 2B 124
Wishaw Wlk. N13 6D 32
Wisley Ho. SW1 5C 18 (5H 101)
(off Rampayne St.)
Wisley Rd. BR5: St P 7A 144
Wisley Rd. SW11 5E 118
Wistaria Cl. BR6: Farnb 2F 173
Wisteria Apts. E9 6J 67
(off Chatham Pl.)
Wisteria Cl. IG1: Ilf 5F 71
Wisteria Cl. NW7 6G 29
Wisteria La. N21 1F 33
Wisteria Rd. SE13 4F 123
Wistow Ho. E2 1G 85
(off Whiston Rd.)
Witanhurst La. N6 1E 64
Witan St. E2 3H 85
Witchwood Ho. SW9 3A 120
(off Gresham Rd.)
Witham Ct. E10 3D 68
Witham Ct. SW17 3D 136
Witham Rd. RM10: Dag 5G 73
Witham Rd. SE20 3J 157
Witham Rd. TW7: Isle 1H 113
Witham Rd. W13 1A 96
Witherby Cl. CR0: C'don 5E 168
Witherington Rd. N5 5A 66
Withers Cl. KT9: Chess 6C 162
Withers Mead NW9 1B 44
Withers Pl. EC1 3D 8 (4C 84)
Witherston Way SE9 2E 142
Withycombe Rd. SW19 7F 117
Withy Ho. E1 4K 85
(off Globe Rd.)
Withy La. HA4: Ruis 5E 38
Withy Mead E4 3B 36
Witley Ct. WC1 3E 6 (4J 83)
(off Coram St.)
Witley Cres. CR0: New Ad 6E 170
Witley Gdns. UB2: S'hall 4D 94
Witley Ho. SW2 7J 119
Witley Ind. Est. UB2: S'hall 4D 94
Witley Point SW15 1D 134
(off Wanborough Dr.)
Witley Rd. N19 2G 65
Witney Cl. UB10: Ick 4B 56
Witney Path SE23 3K 139
Wittenham Way E4 3A 36
Wittering Cl. KT2: King T 5D 132
Wittersham Rd. BR1: Broml 5H 141
Witts Ho. KT1: King T 3F 151
(off Winery La.)
Wivenhoe Cl. SE15 3H 121
Wivenhoe Ct. TW3: Houn 4D 112
Wivenhoe Rd. IG11: Bark 2A 90
Wiverton Rd. SE26 6J 139
Wiverton Twr. E1 7K 9 (6F 85)
(off Aldgate Pl.)
Wix Rd. RM9: Dag 1D 90
Wix's La. SW4 3F 119
WLA Community Sports Cen. 1C 76
Woburn W13 5B 78
(off Clivedon Ct.)
Woburn Cl. SE28 6D 90
Woburn Cl. SW19 6A 136
Woburn Ct. CR0: C'don 1C 168
Woburn Ct. E18 2J 51
Woburn Ct. SE16 5H 103
(off Masters Dr.)
Woburn Ct. WC1 4E 6 (4J 83)
(off Bernard St.)
Woburn Mans. WC1 5C 6 (5H 83)
(off Torrington Pl.)
Woburn M. WC1 4D 6 (4H 83)
Woburn Pl. WC1 4E 6 (4J 83)
Woburn Rd. CR0: C'don 1C 168
Woburn Rd. SM5: Cars 1C 166
Woburn Sq. WC1 4D 6 (4H 83)
(not continuous)
Woburn Twr. UB5: N'olt 3B 76
(off Broomcroft Av.)
Woburn Wlk. WC1 2D 6 (3H 83)
Wodeham Gdns. E1 5G 85
Wodehouse Av. SE5 1F 121
Woffington Cl. KT1: Hamp W 1C 150
Wogan Ho. W1 6K 5 (5F 83)
(off Portland Pl.)
Woking Cl. SW15 4B 116
Wolcot Ho. NW1 1B 6 (2G 83)
(off Aldenham St.)
Woldham Pl. BR2: Broml 4A 160
Woldham Rd. BR2: Broml 4A 160
Wolds Dr. BR6: Farnb 4E 172
Wolfe Cl. BR2: Hayes 6J 159
Wolfe Cl. UB4: Yead 3K 75
Wolfe Cres. SE16 2K 103
Wolfe Cres. SE7 5B 106
Wolfe Ho. W12 7D 80
(off White City Est.)
Wolfe Ho. W14 4H 99
Wolferton Rd. E12 4D 70
Wolffe Gdns. E15 6H 69
Wolfington Rd. SE27 4B 138
Wolfram Cl. SE13 5G 123
Wolftencroft Cl. SW11 3C 118
Wollaston Cl. SE1 4C 102
Wollaton Ho. N1 2A 84
(off Batchelor St.)
Wollett Ct. NW1 7G 65
(off St Pancras Way)
Wollstonecraft St. N1 1H 83
Wolmer Cl. HA8: Edg 4B 28
Wolmer Gdns. HA8: Edg 3B 28
Wolseley Av. SW19 2J 135
Wolseley Gdns. W4 6H 97
Wolseley Rd. CR4: Mitc 7E 154
Wolseley Rd. E7 7K 69
Wolseley Rd. HA3: W'stone 3J 41
Wolseley Rd. N22 1K 47
Wolseley Rd. N8 6H 47
Wolseley Rd. RM7: Rush G 7K 55
Wolseley Rd. W4 4J 97
Wolseley St. SE1 7K 15 (2G 103)
Wolsey Av. E17 3B 50
Wolsey Av. E6 3E 88
Wolsey Av. KT7: T Ditt 5K 149
Wolsey Cl. KT2: King T 1H 151
Wolsey Cl. KT4: Wor Pk 4C 164
Wolsey Cl. SE2 2C 108
Wolsey Cl. SW20 7D 134
Wolsey Cl. TW3: Houn 4G 113
Wolsey Cl. UB2: S'hall 3G 95
Wolsey Ct. NW6 7A 64
Wolsey Ct. SE9 6D 124
(off Court Rd.)
Wolsey Ct. SW11 1C 118
(off Westbridge Rd.)
Wolsey Cres. CR0: New Ad 7E 170
Wolsey Cres. SM4: Mord 7G 153
Wolsey Dr. KT12: Walt T 7B 148
Wolsey Dr. KT2: King T 5E 132
Wolsey Gro. HA8: Edg 7E 28
Wolsey M. BR6: Chels 5K 173
Wolsey M. NW5 6G 65
Wolsey Rd. EN1: Enf 2C 24
Wolsey Rd. KT8: E Mos 4H 149
Wolsey Rd. N1 5D 66
Wolsey Rd. TW12: Hamp H 6F 131
Wolsey Rd. TW15: Ashf 4A 128
Wolsey Rd. TW16: Sun 7H 129
Wolsey St. E1 5J 85
Wolsey Way KT9: Chess 5G 163
Wolsley Cl. DA1: Cray 5K 127
Wolstenholme HA7: Stan 5G 27
Wolstonbury N12 5D 30
Wolvercote Rd. SE2 2D 108
Wolverley St. E2 3H 85
Wolverton SE17 5E 102
(not continuous)
Wolverton Av. KT2: King T 1G 151
Wolverton Gdns. W5 7F 79
Wolverton Gdns. W6 4F 99
Wolverton Rd. HA7: Stan 6G 27
Wolverton Way N14 5B 22
Wolves La. N13 6F 33
Wolves La. N22 7F 33
Womersley Rd. N8 6K 47
Wonersh Way SM2: Cheam 7F 165
Wonford Cl. KT2: King T 1A 152
Wontner Cl. N1 7C 66
Wontner Rd. SW17 2D 136
Wooburn Cl. UB8: Hil 4D 74
Woodall Av. EN3: Pond E 6E 24
Woodall Cl. E14 7D 86
Woodall Cl. KT9: Chess 7C 162
Woodall Rd. EN3: Pond E 6E 24
Woodbank Rd. BR1: Broml 3H 141
Woodbastwick Rd. SE26 5K 139
Woodberry Av. HA2: Harr 4F 41
Woodberry Av. N21 2F 33
Woodberry Cl. NW7 7A 30
Woodberry Cl. TW16: Sun 6J 129
Woodberry Cres. N10 3F 47
Woodberry Down N4 7C 48
Woodberry Down Est. N4 7C 48
(not continuous)
Woodberry Gdns. N12 6F 31
Woodberry Gro. DA5: Bexl 3K 145
Woodberry Gro. N12 6F 31
Woodberry Gro. N4 7C 48
Woodberry Way E4 7K 25
Woodberry Way N12 6F 31
Woodbine Cl. TW2: Twick 2H 131
Woodbine Gro. EN2: Enf 1J 23
Woodbine Gro. SE20 7H 139
Woodbine La. KT4: Wor Pk 3D 164
Woodbine Pl. E11 6J 51
Woodbine Rd. DA15: Sidc 1J 143
Woodbines Av. KT1: King T 3D 150
Woodbine Ter. E9 6J 67
Woodborough Rd. SW15 4D 116
Woodbourne Av. SW16 3H 137
Woodbourne Cl. SW16 3J 137
Woodbourne Gdns. SM6: W'gton
7F 167
Woodbridge Cl. N7 2K 65
Woodbridge Cl. NW2 3C 62
Woodbridge Ct. IG8: Wfd G 7H 37
Woodbridge Ho. E11 1H 69
Woodbridge Rd. IG11: Bark 5K 71
Woodbridge St. EC1 3A 8 (4B 84)
(not continuous)
Woodbridge Ter. RM6: Chad H 6B 54
Woodbrook Rd. SE2 6A 108
Woodburn Cl. NW4 5F 45
Woodbury Cl. CR0: C'don 2F 169
Woodbury Cl. E11 4K 51
Woodbury Cres. IG5: Ilf 1D 52
Woodbury Gdns. SE12 3K 141
Woodbury Ho. SE26 3G 139
Woodbury Pk. Rd. W13 4B 78
Woodbury Rd. E17 4D 50
Woodbury St. SW17 5C 136
Woodchester Ho. E14 3D 104
(off Selsdon Way)
Woodchester Sq. W2 5K 81
Woodchurch Cl. DA14: Sidc 3H 143
Woodchurch Dr. BR1: Broml 7B 142
Woodchurch Rd. NW6 7J 63
Wood Cl. E2 4G 85
Wood Cl. HA1: Harr 7H 41
Wood Cl. NW9 7K 43
Woodclyffe Dr. BR7: Chst 2E 160
Woodcock Cl. TW6: H'row A 7C 174
Woodcock Ct. HA3: Kenton 7E 42
Woodcock Dell Av. HA3: Kenton 7D 42
Woodcock Hill HA3: Kenton 5C 42
Woodcock Ho. E14 5C 86
(off Burgess St.)
Woodcocks E16 5A 88
Woodcombe Cres. SE23 1J 139
Woodcote Av. CR7: Thor H 4B 156
Woodcote Av. NW7 6K 29
Woodcote Av. SM6: W'gton 7F 167
Woodcote Cl. EN3: Pond E 6D 24
Woodcote Cl. KT2: King T 5F 133
Woodcote Dr. BR6: Orp 1H 173
Woodcote Ho. SE8 6B 104
(off Prince St.)
Woodcote M. SM6: W'gton 6F 167
Woodcote Pl. SE27 5B 138
Woodcote Rd. E11 7J 51
Woodcote Rd. SM6: W'gton 6F 167
Woodcote Vs. SE27 5C 138
(off Woodcote Pl.)
Wood Cres. W12 7E 80
Wood Crest SM2: Sutt 7A 166
(off Christchurch Pk.)
Woodcroft N21 1F 33
Woodcroft SE9 3D 142
Woodcroft UB6: G'frd 6A 60
Woodcroft Av. HA7: Stan 1A 42
Woodcroft Av. NW7 6F 29
Woodcroft Cl. SE9 6E 124
Woodcroft Cres. UB10: Hil 1D 74
Woodcroft M. SE8 4A 104
Woodcroft Rd. CR7: Thor H 5B 156
Wood Dr. BR7: Chst 6C 142
Woodedge Cl. E4 1C 36
Wood End UB3: Hayes 6G 75
WOOD END 5H 75
WOOD END 5G 59
Woodend SE19 6C 138
Woodend SM1: Sutt 2A 166
Wood End Av. HA2: Harr 4F 59
Wood End Av. UB5: N'olt 4G 59
Wood End Cl. UB5: N'olt 5H 59
Wood End Gdns. UB5: N'olt 5G 59
Woodend Gdns. EN2: Enf 4D 22
WOOD END GREEN 5F 75
Wood End Grn. Rd. UB3: Hayes 5F 75
Wood End La. UB5: N'olt 6F 59
Wood End Rd. HA1: Harr 4H 59
Woodend Rd. E17 2E 50
Wood End Way UB5: N'olt 5G 59
Wooder Gdns. E7 4J 69
Wooderson Cl. SE25 4E 156
Woodfall Av. EN5: Barn 5C 20
Woodfall Rd. N4 2A 66
Woodfall St. SW3 6E 16 (5D 100)
Wood Farm Cl. HA7: Stan 2G 27
Woodfarrs SE5 4D 120
Wood Fld. NW3 5D 64
Woodfield Av. HA0: Wemb 3C 60
Woodfield Av. NW9 4A 44
Woodfield Av. SM5: Cars 6E 166
Woodfield Av. SW16 3H 137
Woodfield Av. W5 4C 78
Woodfield Cl. EN1: Enf 4K 23
Woodfield Cl. SE19 7C 138
Woodfield Cres. W5 4C 78
Woodfield Dr. EN4: E Barn 1K 31
Woodfield Gdns. KT3: N Mald 5B 152
Woodfield Gro. SW16 3H 137
Woodfield Ho. SE23 3K 139
(off Dacres Rd.)
Woodfield La. SW16 3H 137
Woodfield Pl. W9 4H 81
Woodfield Ri. WD23: Bush 1C 26
Woodfield Rd. TW4: Cran 2K 111
Woodfield Rd. W5 4C 78
Woodfield Rd. W9 5H 81
Woodfield Way N11 7C 32
WOODFORD 6F 37
Woodford Av. IG2: Ilf 5D 52
Woodford Av. IG4: Ilf 3B 52
Woodford Av. IG4: Wfd G 3B 52
WOODFORD BRIDGE 6H 37
Woodford Bri. Rd. IG4: Ilf 3B 52
Woodford Ct. W12 2F 99
(off Shepherd's Bush Grn.)
Woodford Cres. HA5: Pinn 2K 39
Woodforde Ct. UB3: Harl 5F 93
Woodford Golf Course 5D 36
WOODFORD GREEN 6D 36
Woodford Green Athletics Club 6H 37
Woodford Hall Path E18 1H 51
Woodford Ho. E18 4J 51
Woodford New Rd. E17 4G 51
Woodford New Rd. E18 1G 51
Woodford New Rd. IG8: Wfd G 7C 36
Woodford Pl. HA9: Wemb 1E 60
Woodford Rd. E18 4J 51
Woodford Rd. E7 3K 69
WOODFORD SIDE 5C 36
Woodford Trad. Est. IG8: Wfd G 2B 52
WOODFORD WELLS 3E 36
Woodgate Av. KT9: Chess 5D 162
Woodgate Dr. SW16 7H 137
Woodger Rd. W12 2E 98
Woodget Cl. E6 6C 88
Woodgrange Av. EN1: Enf 6B 24
Woodgrange Av. HA3: Kenton 5C 42
Woodgrange Av. N12 6G 31
Woodgrange Av. W5 1G 97
Woodgrange Cl. HA3: Kenton 5D 42
Woodgrange Gdns. EN1: Enf 6B 24
Woodgrange Ho. W5 1F 97
(off Woodgrange Av.)
Woodgrange Mans. HA3: Kenton 5D 42
Woodgrange Rd. E7 5K 69
Woodgrange Ter. EN1: Enf 6B 24
WOOD GREEN 2K 47
Wood Grn. Animal Shelter 1B 48
(off Lordship La.)
Wood Grn. Hall N22 2K 47
(off Station Rd.)
Wood Grn. Shop. City 2A 48
Woodhall NW1 2A 6 (3G 83)
(off Robert St.)
Woodhall Av. HA5: Pinn 1C 40
Woodhall Av. SE21 3F 139
Woodhall Cl. UB8: Uxb 5A 56
Woodhall Dr. HA5: Pinn 1B 40
Woodhall Dr. SE21 3F 139
Woodhall Ho. SW18 6B 118
Woodham Ct. E18 4H 51
Woodham Rd. SE6 3E 140
Woodhatch Cl. E6 5C 88
Woodhaven Gdns. IG6: Ilf 4G 53
Woodhayes Rd. SW19 7E 134
Woodhead Dr. BR6: Orp 3J 173
Woodheyes Rd. NW10 5K 61
Woodhill SE18 4C 106
Woodhill Cres. HA3: Kenton 6D 42
Wood Ho. NW6 2H 81
(off Albert Rd.)
Woodhouse Av. UB6: G'frd 2K 77
Woodhouse Cl. SE22 4G 121
Woodhouse Cl. UB3: Harl 3G 93
Woodhouse Cl. UB6: G'frd 1K 77
Woodhouse Gro. E12 6C 70
Woodhouse Rd. E11 3H 69
Woodhouse Rd. N12 6G 31
Woodhurst Av. BR5: Pet W 6G 161
Woodhurst Rd. SE2 5A 108
Woodhurst Rd. W3 7J 79
Woodies La. KT3: N Mald 6K 151
Woodington Cl. SE9 6E 124
Woodknoll Dr. BR7: Chst 1D 160
Woodland App. UB6: G'frd 6A 60
Woodland Cl. IG8: Wfd G 3E 36
Woodland Cl. KT19: Ewe 6A 164
Woodland Cl. NW9 6J 43
Woodland Cl. SE19 6E 138
Woodland Cl. UB10: Ick 2D 56
Woodland Ct. E11 6J 51
(off New Wanstead)
Woodland Ct. N7 6J 65
Woodland Cres. SE10 6G 105
Woodland Cres. SE16 2K 103
Woodland Gdns. N10 5F 47
Woodland Gdns. TW7: Isle 3J 113
Woodland Gro. SE10 5G 105
Woodland Hill SE19 6E 138
Woodland M. SE13 3D 122
(off Loampit Hill)
Woodland M. SW16 3J 137
Woodland Ri. N10 4F 47
Woodland Ri. UB6: G'frd 6A 60
Woodland Rd. CR7: Thor H 4A 156
Woodland Rd. E4 1K 35
Woodland Rd. N11 5A 32
Woodland Rd. SE19 5E 138
Woodlands, The HA1: Harr 2J 59
Woodlands, The HA7: Stan 5G 27
Woodlands, The N12 6F 31
Woodlands, The N14 1A 32
Woodlands, The N5 4C 66
Woodlands, The SE13 7F 123
Woodlands, The SE19 7C 138
Woodlands, The SM6: W'gton 7F 167
Woodlands, The SW9 7B 102
(off Langton Rd.)
Woodlands, The TW7: Isle 2K 113
Woodlands BR2: Broml 4H 159
Woodlands DA6: Bex 5H 127
Woodlands HA2: Harr 4E 40
Woodlands NW11 5G 45
Woodlands SW20 4E 152
WOODLANDS 3J 113
Woodlands Av. DA15: Sidc 1J 143
Woodlands Av. E11 1K 69
Woodlands Av. HA4: Ruis 7A 40
Woodlands Av. KT3: N Mald 1J 151
Woodlands Av. KT4: Wor Pk 2B 164
Woodlands Av. N3 7F 31
Woodlands Av. RM6: Chad H 7E 54
Woodlands Av. W3 1H 97

WOODLANDS BRIDGE – Wyleu St.

WOODLANDS BRIDGE 5H 117
(off Woodlands Way)
Woodlands Cl. BR1: Broml 2D 160
Woodlands Cl. KT10: Clay 7A 162
Woodlands Cl. NW11 5G 45
Woodlands Ct. BR1: Broml 1H 159
Woodlands Ct. HA1: Harr 5K 41
Woodlands Ct. KT12: Walt T 7K 147
Woodlands Ct. NW10 1F 81
(off Wrentham Av.)
Woodlands Ct. SE23 7H 121
Woodlands Dr. HA7: Stan 6E 26
Woodlands Dr. TW16: Sun 2A 148
Woodlands Gdns. E17 4G 51
Woodlands Ga. SW15 5H 117
(off Woodlands Way)
Woodlands Gro. TW7: Isle 2J 113
Woodlands Hgts. SE3 6H 105
(off Vanburgh Hill)
Woodlands Pde. TW15: Ashf 6E 128
Woodlands Pk. DA5: Bexl 4K 145
Woodlands Pk. Rd. N15 5B 48
Woodlands Pk. Rd. SE10 6G 105
(not continuous)
Woodlands Rd. BR1: Broml 2C 160
Woodlands Rd. BR6: Chels 6K 173
Woodlands Rd. DA7: Bex 3E 126
Woodlands Rd. E11 2G 69
Woodlands Rd. E17 3E 50
Woodlands Rd. EN2: Enf 1J 23
Woodlands Rd. HA1: Harr 5K 41
Woodlands Rd. IG1: Ilf 3G 71
Woodlands Rd. KT6: Surb 7D 150
Woodlands Rd. N9 1D 34
Woodlands Rd. SW13 3B 116
Woodlands Rd. TW7: Isle 3H 113
Woodlands Rd. UB1: S'hall 1B 94
Woodlands St. SE13 7F 123
Woodland St. E8 6F 67
Woodlands Way SW15 5H 117
Woodland Ter. SE7 4C 106
Woodland Wlk. SE10 Maze Hill 5G 105
Woodland Wlk. BR1: Broml Southend
4F 141
(not continuous)
Woodland Wlk. KT19: Ewe 6G 163
Woodland Wlk. NW3 5C 64
Woodland Way BR4: W W'ck 4D 170
Woodland Way BR5: Pet W 4G 161
Woodland Way CR0: C'don 1A 170
Woodland Way CR4: Mitc 7E 136
Woodland Way IG8: Wfd G 3E 36
Woodland Way KT5: Surb 2H 163
Woodland Way N21 2F 33
Woodland Way NW7 6G 29
Woodland Way SE2 4D 108
Woodland Way SM4: Mord 4H 153
Wood La. HA4: Ruis 1F 57
Wood La. HA7: Stan 3F 27
Wood La. IG8: Wfd G 4C 36
Wood La. N6 6F 47
Wood La. NW9 7K 43
Wood La. RM10: Dag 2G 73
Wood La. RM8: Dag 4D 72
Wood La. RM9: Dag 4D 72
Wood La. TW7: Isle 6J 95
Wood La. W12 6E 80
Wood La. Studios W12 6E 80
Woodlark Ct. KT10: Clay 6A 162
Woodlawn Cl. SW15 5H 117
Woodlawn Cres. TW2: Whitt 2F 131
Woodlawn Dr. TW13: Felt 2B 130
Woodlawn Rd. SW6 7F 99
Woodlawns KT19: Ewe 7K 163
Woodlea Dr. BR2: Broml 5G 159
Woodlea Rd. N16 3E 66
Woodleigh E18 1J 51
Woodleigh Av. N12 6H 31
Woodleigh Gdns. SW16 3J 137
Woodley Cl. SW17 7D 136
Woodley La. SM5: Cars 3C 166
Wood Lodge Gdns. BR1: Broml 7C 142
Wood Lodge La. BR4: W W'ck 3E 170
Woodman M. TW9: Kew 1H 115
Woodman Pde. E16 1E 106
(off Woodman St.)
Woodmans Gro. NW10 5B 62
Woodman's M. W12 5D 80
Woodmansterne Rd. SW16 7G 137
Woodman St. E16 1E 106
Wood Martyn Ct. BR6: Orp 2K 173
(off Orchard Gro.)
Wood Mead N17 6B 34
Woodmere SE9 1D 142
Woodmere Av. CR0: C'don 7J 157
Woodmere Cl. CR0: C'don 7K 157
Woodmere Cl. SW11 3E 118
Woodmere Ct. N14 7A 22
Woodmere Gdns. CR0: C'don 7K 157
Woodmere Way BR3: Beck 5F 159
Woodmill Cl. SW15 6C 116
Woodmill Rd. E5 2J 67
Woodmill St. SE16 3F 103
Woodnook Rd. SW16 5F 137
Woodpecker Cl. HA3: Hrw W 1K 41
Woodpecker Cl. N9 6C 24
Woodpecker Cl. WD23: Bush 1B 26
Woodpecker M. SE13 4F 123
(off Freshfield Cl.)
Woodpecker Mt. CR0: Sels 7A 170
Woodpecker Rd. SE14 6A 104
Woodpecker Rd. SE28 7C 90
Woodquest Av. SE24 5C 120
Wood Retreat SE18 7H 107
Wood Ride BR5: Pet W 4H 161
Wood Ride EN4: Had W 1G 21
Woodridge Cl. EN2: Enf 1F 23
Woodridings Av. HA5: Hat E 1D 40
Woodridings Cl. HA5: Hat E 1C 40
Woodridings Ct. N22 1H 47
Woodriffe Rd. E11 7F 51
Wood Ri. HA5: Eastc 5J 39
Wood Rd. NW10 7J 61
Wood Rd. TW17: Shep 4C 146
Woodrow SE18 4D 106
Woodrow Av. UB4: Hayes 5H 75
Woodrow Cl. UB6: G'frd 7B 60
Woodrow Ct. N17 7C 34
Woodrow Ct. SE5 1C 120
(off Camberwell Sta. Rd.)
Woodrush Cl. SE14 7A 104
Woodrush Way RM6: Chad H 4D 54
Woods, The UB10: Ick 4D 56
Wood's Bldgs. E1 5H 85
(off Winthrop St.)
Woods Cl. TW3: Houn 3F 113
(off High St.)
Woodseer St. E1 5K 9 (5F 85)
Woodsford SE17 5D 102
(off Portland St.)
Woodsford Sq. W14 2G 99
Woodshire Rd. RM10: Dag 3H 73
Woods Ho. SW1 6J 17 (5F 101)
Woods Ho. SW8 1G 119
(off Wadhurst Rd.)
Woodside IG9: Buck H 2F 37
Woodside N10 3E 46
Woodside NW11 5J 45
WOODSIDE 6G 157
Woodside SW19 6H 135
Woodside Av. BR7: Chst 5G 143
Woodside Av. HA0: Wemb 1E 78
Woodside Av. KT10: Esh 7J 149
Woodside Av. N10 4E 46
Woodside Av. N12 4E 30
Woodside Av. N6 5D 46
Woodside Av. SE25 6H 157
Woodside Cl. DA7: Bex 4K 127
Woodside Cl. HA0: Wemb 1E 78
Woodside Cl. HA4: Ruis 6F 39
Woodside Cl. HA7: Stan 5G 27
Woodside Cl. KT5: Surb 7J 151
Woodside Ct. E12 1A 70
Woodside Ct. N12 4E 30
Woodside Ct. RM7: Mawney 4G 55
Woodside Ct. W5 1E 96
Woodside Ct. Rd. CR0: C'don 7G 157
Woodside Cres. DA15: Sidc 3J 143
Woodside Dr. DA2: Wilm 4K 145
Woodside End HA0: Wemb 1E 78
Woodside Gdns. E4 6J 35
Woodside Gdns. N17 2E 48
Woodside Grange Rd. N12 4E 30
Woodside Grn. SE25 6G 157
Woodside Gro. N12 3F 31
Woodside Ho. SW19 6H 135
Woodside La. DA5: Bexl 6D 126
Woodside La. N12 3F 31
Woodside M. SE22 5F 121
Woodside Pde. DA15: Sidc 3J 143
WOODSIDE PARK 4D 30
Woodside Pk. SE25 6H 157
Woodside Pk. Av. E17 4F 51
Woodside Pk. Rd. N12 4E 30
Woodside Pl. HA0: Wemb 1E 78
Woodside Rd. BR1: Broml 5C 160
Woodside Rd. DA15: Sidc 3J 143
Woodside Rd. DA7: Bex 4K 127
Woodside Rd. E13 4A 88
Woodside Rd. IG8: Wfd G 4D 36
Woodside Rd. KT2: King T 7E 132
Woodside Rd. KT3: N Mald 2K 151
Woodside Rd. N22 7E 32
Woodside Rd. SE25 6H 157
Woodside Rd. SM1: Sutt 3A 166
Woodside Way CR0: C'don 6J 157
Woodside Way CR4: Mitc 1F 155
Woods M. W1 2G 11 (7E 82)
Woodsome Rd. NW5 3E 64
Woods Pl. SE1 3E 102
Woodspring Rd. SW19 2G 135
Woods Rd. SE15 1H 121
Woodstar Ho. SE15 7G 103
(off Reddins Rd.)
Woodstead Gro. HA8: Edg 6K 27
THE WOODSTOCK 7H 153
Woodstock Av. NW11 7G 45
Woodstock Av. SM3: Sutt 7H 153
Woodstock Av. TW7: Isle 5A 114
Woodstock Av. UB1: S'hall 3D 76
Woodstock Av. W13 3A 96
Woodstock Cl. DA5: Bexl 7F 127
Woodstock Cl. HA7: Stan 2E 42
Woodstock Ct. SE11 5H 19 (5K 101)
Woodstock Ct. SE12 6J 123
Woodstock Cres. N9 6C 24
Woodstock Dr. UB10: Ick 4A 56
Woodstock Gdns. BR3: Beck 1D 158
Woodstock Gdns. IG3: Ilf 2A 72
Woodstock Gdns. UB4: Hayes 5H 75
Woodstock Grange W5 1E 96
Woodstock Gro. W12 2F 99
Woodstock La. KT9: Chess 4B 162
Woodstock La. Nth. KT6: Surb 2C 162
Woodstock La. Sth. KT10: Clay 5B 162
Woodstock La. Sth. KT9: Chess
4C 162
Woodstock M. W1 6H 5 (5E 82)
(off Westmoreland St.)
Woodstock Ri. SM3: Sutt 7H 153
Woodstock Rd. CR0: C'don 3D 168
Woodstock Rd. E17 2F 51
Woodstock Rd. E7 7A 70
Woodstock Rd. HA0: Wemb 1F 79
Woodstock Rd. N4 1A 66
Woodstock Rd. NW11 7H 45
Woodstock Rd. SM5: Cars 5E 166
Woodstock Rd. W4 4A 98
Woodstock St. W1 1J 11 (6F 83)
Woodstock Studios W12 2F 99
(off Woodstock Gro.)
Woodstock Ter. E14 7D 86
Woodstock Way CR4: Mitc 2F 155
Woodstone Av. KT17: Ewe 5C 164
Wood St. CR4: Mitc 7E 154
Wood St. E17 3E 50
Wood St. EC2 1D 14 (6C 84)
(not continuous)
Wood St. EN5: Barn 4A 20
Wood St. KT1: King T 2D 150
Wood St. W4 5A 98
WOOD STREET 3E 50
Woodsyre SE26 4F 139
Wood Ter. NW2 3D 62
Woodthorpe Rd. SW15 4D 116
Woodtree Cl. NW4 2F 45
Wood Va. N10 5G 47
Wood Va. SE23 1H 139
Woodvale Av. SE25 3F 157
Woodvale Ct. BR1: Broml 1K 159
(off Widmore Rd.)
Wood Va. Est. SE23 7J 121
Woodvale Wlk. SE27 5C 138
Woodvale Way NW11 3F 63
Woodview Av. E4 4K 35
Woodview Cl. BR6: Farnb 2G 173
Woodview Cl. N4 7B 48
Woodview Cl. SW15 4K 133
Wood Vw. M. RM1: Rom 1K 55
Woodview M. SE19 1E 156
Woodville, The W5 6D 78
(off Woodville Rd.)
Woodville Cl. SE12 5J 123
Woodville Cl. SE3 1K 123
Woodville Cl. TW11: Tedd 4A 132
Woodville Ct. N14 5B 22
Woodville Ct. SE10 1E 122
(off Blissett St.)
Woodville Ct. SE19 1F 157
Woodville Gdns. HA4: Ruis 7E 38
Woodville Gdns. IG6: Ilf 3F 53
Woodville Gdns. KT6: Surb 7D 150
Woodville Gdns. NW11 7F 45
Woodville Gdns. W5 6E 78
Woodville Gro. DA16: Well 3A 126
Woodville Ho. SE1 3F 103
(off St Saviour's Est.)
Woodville Rd. CR7: Thor H 4C 156
Woodville Rd. E11 1H 69
Woodville Rd. E17 4B 50
Woodville Rd. E18 2K 51
Woodville Rd. EN5: New Bar 3E 20
Woodville Rd. N16 5E 66
Woodville Rd. NW11 7F 45
Woodville Rd. NW6 2H 81
Woodville Rd. SM4: Mord 4J 153
Woodville Rd. TW10: Ham 3B 132
Woodville Rd. W5 6D 78
Woodville St. SE18 4C 106
Woodward Av. NW4 5C 44
Woodwarde Rd. SE22 6E 120
Woodward Gdns. HA7: Stan 7E 26
Woodward Gdns. RM9: Dag 7C 72
Woodward Rd. RM9: Dag 7B 72
Woodward's Footpath TW2: Whitt
6G 113
Wood Way BR6: Farnb 2E 172
Woodway Cres. HA1: Harr 6A 42
Woodwell St. SW18 5A 118
Wood Wharf SE10 6D 104
Woodyard Cl. NW5 5E 64
Woodyard La. SE21 7E 120
Woodyates Rd. SE12 6J 123
Woolacombe Rd. SE3 1A 124
Woolacombe Way UB3: Harl 4G 93
Woolbrook Rd. DA1: Cray 6K 127
Woolcombes Ct. SE16 1K 103
(off Princes Riverside Rd.)
Wooldridge Cl. TW14: Bedf 1E 128
Wooler St. SE17 5D 102
Woolf Cl. SE28 1B 108
Woolf M. WC1 3D 6 (4H 83)
(off Burton Pl.)
Woolford Ct. SE5 2C 120
(off Coldharbour La.)
Woolgar M. N16 5E 66
(off Gillett St.)
Woollaston Rd. N4 6B 48
Woolley Ho. SW9 3B 120
(off Loughborough Rd.)
Woollon Ho. E1 6J 85
(off Clark St.)
Woolmead Av. NW9 7C 44
Woolmer Gdns. N18 6B 34
Woolmer Rd. N18 5B 34
Woolmore St. E14 7E 86
Woolneigh St. SW6 3K 117
Woolridge Way E9 7J 67
Wool Rd. SW20 6D 134
Woolstaplers Way SE16 3G 103
Woolston Cl. E17 2K 49
Woolstone Ho. E2 1G 85
(off Whiston Rd.)
Woolstone Rd. SE23 2A 140
WOOLWICH 3D 106
Woolwich Cen., The 4E 106
(off Wellington St.)
Woolwich Chu. St. SE18 3C 106
Woolwich Comn. SE18 6E 106
Woolwich Comn. Youth Club 6E 106
Woolwich Dockyard Ind. Est.
SE18 3C 106
Woolwich High St. SE18 3E 106
Woolwich Ho. UB3: Harl 3E 92
(off Nine Acres Cl.)
Woolwich Mnr. Way E16 2F 107
Woolwich Mnr. Way E6 4D 88
Woolwich New Rd. SE18 5E 106
Woolwich Rd. DA17: Belv 5F 109
Woolwich Rd. DA6: Bex 4G 127
Woolwich Rd. DA7: Bex 3G 127
Woolwich Rd. SE10 5H 105
Woolwich Rd. SE2 6D 108
Woolwich Rd. SE7 5J 105
Woolwich Trade Pk. SE28 3H 107
Wooster Gdns. E14 6F 87
Wooster M. HA2: Harr 3G 41
Wooster Pl. SE1 4D 102
(off Searles Rd.)
Wootton Gro. N3 1J 45
Wootton St. SE1 5K 13 (1A 102)
Worbeck Rd. SE20 2H 157
Worcester Av. N17 7B 34
Worcester Cl. CR0: C'don 2C 170
Worcester Cl. CR4: Mitc 2E 154
Worcester Cl. NW2 3D 62
Worcester Cl. SE20 1G 157
Worcester Ct. HA1: Harr 3J 41
Worcester Ct. KT4: Wor Pk 3A 164
Worcester Ct. N12 5E 30
Worcester Ct. W7 6K 77
(off Copley Cl.)
Worcester Ct. W9 5J 81
(off Elmfield Way)
Worcester Cres. IG8: Wfd G 4E 36
Worcester Cres. NW7 3F 29
Worcester Dr. TW15: Ashf 5D 128
Worcester Dr. W4 2A 98
Worcester Gdns. IG1: Ilf 7C 52
Worcester Gdns. KT4: Wor Pk 3A 164
Worcester Gdns. SW11 5D 118
(off Grandison Rd.)
Worcester Gdns. UB6: G'frd 6H 59
Worcester Ho. SE11 2J 19 (3A 102)
(off Kennington Rd.)
Worcester Ho. SW9 7A 102
(off Cranmer Rd.)
Worcester Ho. W2 6A 82
(off Hallfield Est.)
Worcester M. NW6 6K 63
WORCESTER PARK 1C 164
Worcester Pk. Rd. KT4: Wor Pk 3A 164
Worcester Point EC1 2C 8 (3C 84)
Worcester Rd. E12 4D 70
Worcester Rd. E17 2K 49
Worcester Rd. SM2: Sutt 7J 165
Worcester Rd. SW19 5H 135
Worcesters Av. EN1: Enf 1B 24
Wordsworth Av. E12 7C 70
Wordsworth Av. E18 3H 51
Wordsworth Av. UB6: G'frd 3H 77
Wordsworth Ct. HA1: Harr 7J 41
Wordsworth Dr. SM3: Cheam 4E 164
Wordsworth Ho. NW6 3J 81
(off Stafford Rd.)
Wordsworth Ho. SE18 6E 106
(off Woolwich Comn.)
Wordsworth Mans. W14 6H 99
(off Queens Club Gdns.)
Wordsworth Pde. N8 4B 48
Wordsworth Pl. NW5 5D 64
Wordsworth Rd. DA16: Well 1J 125
Wordsworth Rd. N16 4E 66
Wordsworth Rd. SE1 4F 103
Wordsworth Rd. SE20 7K 139
Wordsworth Rd. SM6: W'gton 6G 167
Wordsworth Rd. TW12: Hamp 4D 130
Wordsworth Wlk. NW11 4J 45
Wordsworth Way UB7: W Dray 4A 92
Worfield St. SW11 7C 100
Worgan St. SE11 5G 19 (5K 101)
Worgan St. SE16 4K 103
Worland Rd. E15 7G 69
World Bus. Cen. TW6: H'row A 1E 110
World of Golf Cen. Croydon 5J 157
World of Golf Cen. New Malden 3C 152
World Rugby Mus. 6J 113
WORLD'S END 3E 22
Worlds End Est. SW10 7B 100
World's End La. EN2: Enf 4E 22
World's End La. N21 5E 22
Worlds End La. BR6: Chels 6K 173
World's End Pas. SW10 7B 100
(off Worlds End Est.)
World's End Pl. SW10 7B 100
(off Worlds End Est.)
Worleys Dr. BR6: Orp 4H 173
Worlidge St. W6 5E 98
Worlingham Rd. SE22 4F 121
Wormholt Rd. W12 7C 80
Wormwood Scrubs Pk. 5B 80
Wormwood St. EC2 7G 9 (6E 84)
Wornington Rd. W10 4G 81
(not continuous)
Woronzow Rd. NW8 1B 82
Worple Av. SW19 7F 135
Worple Av. TW7: Isle 5A 114
Worple Cl. HA2: Harr 1D 58
Worple Rd. SW19 7F 135
Worple Rd. SW20 2E 152
Worple Rd. TW7: Isle 4A 114
Worple Rd. M. SW19 6H 135
Worple St. SW14 3K 115
Worple Way HA2: Harr 1D 58
Worple Way TW10: Rich 5E 114
Worrall La. UB8: Uxb 7A 56
Worship St. EC2 4F 9 (4D 84)
(not continuous)
Worslade Rd. SW17 4B 136
Worsley Bri. Rd. BR3: Beck 7C 140
Worsley Bri. Rd. SE26 4B 140
Worsley Grange BR7: Chst 6G 143
Worsley Gro. E5 4G 67
Worsley Ho. SE23 2J 139
Worsley Rd. E11 4G 69
Worsopp Dr. SW4 5G 119
Worth Cl. BR6: Orp 4J 173
Worthfield Cl. KT19: Ewe 7K 163
Worth Gro. SE17 5D 102
Worthing Cl. E15 1G 87
Worthing Rd. TW5: Hest 6D 94
Worthington Cl. CR4: Mitc 4F 155
Worthington Ho. EC1 1K 7 (3A 84)
(off Myddelton Pas.)
Worthington Rd. KT6: Surb 1F 163
Wortley Rd. CR0: C'don 7A 156
Wortley Rd. E6 7B 70
Worton Ct. TW7: Isle 4J 113
Worton Gdns. TW7: Isle 2H 113
Worton Hall Ind. Est. TW7: Isle 4J 113
Worton Rd. TW7: Isle 4H 113
Worton Way TW3: Houn 2H 113
Worton Way TW7: Houn 2H 113
Worton Way TW7: Isle 2H 113
Wotton Ct. E14 7F 87
(off Jamestown Way)
Wotton Rd. NW2 3E 62
Wotton Rd. SE8 6B 104
Wouldham Rd. E16 6H 87
Wragby Rd. E11 3G 69
Wrampling Pl. N9 1B 34
Wrangthorn Wlk. CR0: Wadd 4A 168
Wraxall Rd. E3 4B 86
(off Hamlets Way)
Wray Av. IG5: Ilf 3E 52
Wrayburn Ho. SE16 2G 103
(off Llewellyn St.)
Wray Cres. N4 2J 65
Wrayfield Rd. SM3: Cheam 3F 165
Wray Rd. SM2: Cheam 7H 165
Wraysbury Cl. TW4: Houn 5C 112
Wrays Way UB4: Hayes 4G 75
Wrekin Rd. SE18 7G 107
Wren Av. NW2 4E 62
Wren Av. UB10: Uxb 1B 74
Wren Av. UB2: S'hall 4D 94
Wren Cl. E16 6H 87
Wren Cl. N9 1E 34
Wren Cl. TW6: H'row A 6C 174
Wren Ct. CR0: C'don 4D 168
(off Coombe Rd.)
Wren Cres. WD23: Bush 1B 26
Wren Gdns. RM9: Dag 5D 72
Wren Ho. E3 2A 86
(off Gernon Rd.)
Wren Ho. KT1: Hamp W 2D 150
(off High St.)
Wren Ho. SW1 6C 18 (5H 101)
(off Aylesford St.)
Wren Landing E14 1C 104
Wren La. HA4: Ruis 6K 39
Wren M. SE11 4H 19 (4K 101)
Wren M. SE13 4G 123
Wrenn Ho. SW13 6E 98
Wren Path SE28 3H 107
Wren Rd. DA14: Sidc 4C 144
Wren Rd. RM9: Dag 5D 72
Wren Rd. SE5 1D 120
Wren's Av. TW15: Ashf 4E 128
Wren's Pk. Ho. E5 2H 67
Wren St. WC1 3H 7 (4K 83)
Wrentham Av. NW10 2F 81
Wrenthorpe Rd. BR1: Broml 4G 141
Wren Vw. N6 7G 47
Wrenwood Way HA5: Eastc 4K 39
Wrexham Rd. E3 2C 86
Wricklemarsh Rd. SE3 2K 123
(not continuous)
Wrigglesworth St. SE14 7K 103
Wright Cl. SE13 4F 123
Wright Gdns. TW17: Shep 5C 146
Wright Rd. TW5: Hest 7A 94
Wrights All. SW19 6E 134
Wrights Cl. RM10: Dag 4H 73
Wrights Grn. SW4 4H 119
Wright's La. W8 3K 99
Wrights Pl. NW10 6J 61
Wright's Rd. E3 2B 86
(not continuous)
Wrights Rd. SE25 3E 156
Wrights Row SM6: W'gton 4F 167
Wrights Wlk. SW14 3K 115
Wright Way TW6: H'row A 5C 174
Wrigley Cl. E4 5A 36
Writtle Ho. NW9 2B 44
Wrotham Ho. BR3: Beck 7B 140
(off Sellindge Cl.)
Wrotham Ho. SE1 3D 102
(off Law St.)
Wrotham Rd. DA16: Well 1C 126
Wrotham Rd. EN5: Barn 2B 20
Wrotham Rd. NW1 7G 65
Wrotham Rd. W13 1C 96
Wrottesley Rd. NW10 2C 80
Wrottesley Rd. SE18 6G 107
Wroughton Rd. SW11 5D 118
Wroughton Ter. NW4 4D 44
Wroxall Rd. RM9: Dag 6C 72
Wroxham Gdns. N11 7C 32
Wroxham Rd. SE28 7D 90
Wroxham Way IG6: Ilf 1F 53
Wroxton Rd. SE15 2J 121
THE WRYTHE 3D 166
Wrythe Grn. SM5: Cars 3D 166
Wrythe Grn. Rd. SM5: Cars 3D 166
Wrythe La. SM5: Cars 1A 166
Wulfstan St. W12 5B 80
Wyatt Cl. SE16 2B 104
Wyatt Cl. TW13: Felt 1B 130
Wyatt Cl. UB4: Hayes 5J 75
Wyatt Cl. WD23: Bush 1C 26
Wyatt Ct. HA0: Wemb 7E 60
Wyatt Ct. W3 3J 97
(off All Saints Rd.)
Wyatt Dr. SW13 6D 98
Wyatt Ho. NW8 4A 4 (4B 82)
(off Frampton St.)
Wyatt Ho. SE3 2H 123
Wyatt Ho. TW1: Twick 6D 114
Wyatt Pk. Rd. SW2 2J 137
Wyatt Point SE28 2G 107
Wyatt Rd. E7 6J 69
Wyatt Rd. N5 3C 66
Wyatts La. E17 3E 50
Wybert St. NW1 3A 6 (4G 83)
Wyborne Ho. NW10 7J 61
Wyborne Way NW10 7J 61
Wyburn Av. EN5: Barn 3C 20
Wychcombe Studios NW3 6D 64
Wyche Gro. CR2: S Croy 7D 168
Wych Elm Cl. KT2: King T 7F 133
Wych Elm Lodge BR1: Broml 7H 141
Wych Elm Pas. KT2: King T 7F 133
Wycherley Cl. SE3 7H 105
Wycherley Cres. EN5: New Bar 6E 20
Wychwood Av. CR7: Thor H 3C 156
Wychwood Av. HA8: Edg 6J 27
Wychwood Cl. HA8: Edg 6J 27
Wychwood Cl. TW16: Sun 6J 129
Wychwood End N6 7G 47
Wychwood Gdns. IG5: Ilf 4D 52
Wychwood Way SE19 6D 138
Wyclif Ct. EC1 2A 8 (3B 84)
(off Wyclif St.)
Wycliffe Cl. DA16: Well 1K 125
Wycliffe Rd. SW11 2E 118
Wycliffe Rd. SW19 6K 135
Wyclif St. EC1 2A 8 (3B 84)
Wycombe Gdns. NW11 2J 63
Wycombe Ho. NW8 3C 4 (4C 82)
(off Grendon St.)
Wycombe Pl. SW18 6A 118
Wycombe Rd. HA0: Wemb 1G 79
Wycombe Rd. IG2: Ilf 5D 52
Wycombe Rd. N17 1G 49
Wycombe Sq. W8 1H 99
Wycombe St. SE14 7B 104
Wydehurst Rd. CR0: C'don 7G 157
Wydell Cl. SM4: Mord 6F 153
Wydeville Mnr. Rd. SE12 4K 141
Wye Cl. BR6: Orp 7K 161
Wye Cl. HA4: Ruis 6E 38
Wye Cl. TW15: Ashf 4D 128
Wye Ct. W13 5B 78
(off Malvern Way)
Wyemead Cres. E4 2B 36
Wye St. SW11 2B 118
Wyevale Cl. HA5: Eastc 3J 39
Wyfields IG5: Ilf 1F 53
Wyfold Ho. SE2 2D 108
(off Wolvercote Rd.)
Wyfold Rd. SW6 7G 99
Wyhill Wlk. RM10: Dag 6J 73
Wyke Cl. TW7: Isle 6K 95
Wyke Gdns. W7 3A 96
Wyke Green Golf Course 6K 95
Wykeham Av. RM9: Dag 6C 72
Wykeham Cl. HA3: W'stone 1K 41
Wykeham Cl. UB7: Sip 6C 92
Wykeham Ct. NW4 5E 44
(off Wykeham Rd.)
Wykeham Grn. RM9: Dag 6C 72
Wykeham Hill HA9: Wemb 1F 61
Wykeham Ho. SE1 5C 14 (1C 102)
(off Union St.)
Wykeham Ri. N20 1B 30
Wykeham Rd. HA3: Kenton 4B 42
Wykeham Rd. NW4 4E 44
Wyke Rd. E3 7C 68
Wyke Rd. SW20 2E 152
Wylchin Cl. HA5: Eastc 3H 39
Wyldes Cl. NW11 1A 64
Wyldfield Gdns. N9 2A 34
Wyld Way HA9: Wemb 6H 61
Wyleu St. SE23 7A 122

Wyllen Cl. – Zulu M.

Wyllen Cl. E1 4J **85**
Wymering Mans. W9 3J **81**
(off Wymering Rd.)
Wymering Rd. W9 3J **81**
Wymondham Ct. NW8 1B **82**
(off Queensmead)
Wymond St. SW15 3E **116**
Wynan Rd. E14 5D **104**
Wynash Gdns. SM5: Cars 5C **166**
Wynaud Ct. N22 6E **32**
Wyncham Av. DA15: Sidc 1J **143**
Wyncham Ho. DA15: Sidc 2A **144**
(off Longlands Rd.)
Wynchgate HA3: Hrw W 7D **26**
Wynchgate N14 1C **32**
Wynchgate N21 7D **22**
Wynchgate UB5: N'olt 5C **58**
Wyncroft Cl. BR1: Broml 3D **160**
Wyndale Av. NW9 6G **43**
Wyndcliff Rd. SE7 6K **105**
Wyndcroft Cl. EN2: Enf 3G **23**
Wyndham Apts. SE10 5G **105**
Wyndham Cl. BR6: Farnb 1G **173**
Wyndham Cl. SM2: Sutt 7J **165**
Wyndham Ct. W7 4A **96**
Wyndham Cres. N19 3G **65**
Wyndham Cres. TW4: Houn 6E **112**
Wyndham Deedes Ho. E2 2G **85**
(off Hackney Rd.)
Wyndham Est. SE5 7C **102**
Wyndham Ho. E14 2D **104**
(off Marsh Wall)
Wyndham Ho. SW1 4G **17** (4E **100**)
(off Sloane Sq.)
Wyndham M. W1 6E **4** (5D **82**)
Wyndham Pl. W1 6E **4** (5D **82**)
Wyndham Rd. E6 7B **70**
Wyndham Rd. EN4: E Barn 1J **31**
Wyndham Rd. KT2: King T 7F **133**
Wyndham Rd. SE5 7C **102**
Wyndham Rd. W13 3B **96**
Wyndhams Ct. E8 7F **67**
(off Celandine Dr.)
Wyndham's Theatre 2E 12 (7J 83)
(off Charing Cross Rd.)
Wyndham St. W1 5E **4** (5D **82**)
Wyndham Yd. W1 6E **4** (5D **82**)
Wyndhurst Cl. CR2: S Croy 7B **168**
Wyneham Rd. SE24 5D **120**
Wynell Rd. SE23 3K **139**
Wynford Pl. DA17: Belv 6G **109**
Wynford Rd. N1 2K **83**
Wynford Way SE9 3D **142**
Wynlie Gdns. HA5: Pinn 2K **39**
Wynn Bri. Cl. IG8: Wfd G 1B **52**
Wynndale Rd. E18 1K **51**
Wynne Rd. SW9 2A **120**
Wynn's Av. DA15: Sidc 5K **125**
Wynnstay Gdns. W8 3J **99**
Wynter St. SW11 4A **118**
Wynton Gdns. SE25 5F **157**
Wynton Pl. W3 6H **79**
Wynyard Ho. SE11 5H **19** (5K **101**)
(off Newburn St.)
Wynyard Ter. SE11 5H **19** (5K **101**)
Wynyatt St. EC1 2A **8** (3B **84**)
Wyre Gro. HA8: Edg 3C **28**
Wyre Gro. UB3: Harl 4J **93**
Wyresdale Cres. UB6: G'frd 3K **77**
Wyteleaf Cl. HA4: Ruis 6E **38**
Wytham Ho. NW8 4B **4** (4B **82**)
(off Church St. Est.)
Wythburn Ct. W1 7E **4** (6D **82**)
(off Wythburn Pl.)
Wythburn Pl. W1 1E **10** (6D **82**)
Wythenshawe Rd. RM10: Dag
3G **73**
Wythens Wlk. SE9 6F **125**
Wythes Cl. BR1: Broml 2D **160**
Wythes Rd. E16 1C **106**
Wythfield Rd. SE9 6D **124**
Wyvell Cl. CR0: C'don 7K **157**
Wyvenhoe Rd. HA2: Harr 4G **59**
Wyvern Est. KT3: N Mald 4C **152**
Wyvil Rd. SW8 7J **101**
Wyvis St. E14 5D **86**

X

Xylon Ho. KT4: Wor Pk 2D **164**

Y

Yabsley St. E14 1E **104**
Yaldham Ho. SE1 4E **102**
(off Old Kent Rd.)
Yalding Rd. SE16 3G **103**
Yale Cl. TW4: Houn 5D **112**
Yale Ct. NW6 5K **63**
Yarborough Rd. SW19 1B **154**
Yard, The N1 1F **7** (2J **83**)
(off Caledonia Rd.)
Yardley Cl. E4 5J **25**
Yardley Ct. SM3: Cheam 4E **164**
Yardley La. E4 5J **25**
Yardley St. WC1 2J **7** (3A **84**)
(not continuous)
Yardmaster Ho. CR0: C'don 1D **168**
Yarlington Ct. N11 5K **31**
(off Sparkford Gdns.)
Yarmouth Cres. N17 5H **49**
Yarmouth Pl. W1 5J **11** (1F **101**)
Yarnfield Sq. SE15 1G **121**
Yarnton Way DA18: Belv 3F **109**
Yarnton Way DA18: Erith 3F **109**
Yarnton Way SE2 2C **108**
Yarrell Mans. W14 6H **99**
(off Queen's Club Gdns.)
Yarrow Cres. E6 5C **88**
Yarrow Ho. E14 3E **104**
(off Stewart St.)
Yarrow Ho. W10 5E **80**
(off Sutton Way)
Yateley St. SE18 3B **106**
Yatesbury Ct. E5 5A **68**
(off Studley Cl.)
Yates Ct. NW2 6F **63**
(off Willesden La.)
Yates Ct. SE1 7K **15** (2F **103**)
(off Abbey St.)
Yates Ho. E2 3G **85**
(off Roberta St.)
Yatton Ho. W10 5E **80**
(off Sutton Way)
YEADING 4A **76**
Yeading Av. HA2: Harr 2C **58**
Yeading Brook Meadows Nature Reserve 4J **75**
Yeading Ct. UB4: Yead 4A **76**
Yeading Fork UB4: Yead 5A **76**
Yeading Gdns. UB4: Yead 5K **75**
Yeading Ho. UB4: Yead 5B **76**
Yeading La. UB4: Yead 6K **75**
Yeading La. UB5: N'olt 3A **76**
Yeading Wlk. HA2: Harr 5D **40**
Yeadon Ho. W10 5E **80**
(off Sutton Way)
Yeames Cl. W13 6A **78**
Yearby Ho. W10 4E **80**
(off Sutton Way)
Yeate St. N1 7D **66**
Yeatman Rd. N6 6D **46**
Yeats Cl. NW10 5A **62**
Yeats Cl. SE13 2F **123**
Yeats Cl. W7 7K **77**
Yeend Cl. KT8: W Mole 4E **148**
Yeldham Ho. W6 5F **99**
(off Yeldham Rd.)
Yeldham Rd. W6 5F **99**
Yeldham Vs. W6 5F **99**
(off Yeldham Rd.)
Yellowhammer Ct. NW9 2A **44**
(off Eagle Dr.)
Yelverton Lodge
TW1: Twick 7C **114**
(off Richmond Rd.)
Yelverton Rd. SW11 2B **118**
Ye Mkt. CR2: S Croy 5D **168**
(off Selsdon Rd.)
Yenston Cl. SM4: Mord 6J **153**
Yeoman Cl. E6 7F **89**
Yeoman Cl. SE27 3B **138**
Yeoman Ct. E14 4E **86**
(off Tweed Wlk.)
Yeoman Ct. TW5: Hest 7D **94**
Yeoman Dr. TW19: Stanw 1A **128**
Yeoman Rd. UB5: N'olt 7C **58**
Yeomans Acre HA4: Ruis 6J **39**
Yeomans M. TW7: Isle 6H **113**
Yeoman's Row SW3 2D **16** (3C **100**)
Yeoman St. SE8 4A **104**
Yeomans Way EN3: Enf H 2D **24**
Yeoman's Yd. E1 2K **15** (7F **85**)
(off Chamber St.)
Yeo St. E3 5D **86**
Yeovil Cl. BR6: Orp 2J **173**
Yeovil Ho. W10 4E **80**
(off Sutton Way)
Yeovilton Pl. KT2: King T 5C **132**
Yerbury Rd. N19 3H **65**
(not continuous)
Yester Dr. BR7: Chst 7C **142**
Yester Pk. BR7: Chst 7D **142**
Yester Rd. BR7: Chst 7C **142**
Yetev Lev Ct. E5 1G **67**
Yew Av. UB7: Yiew 7A **74**
Yew Cl. IG9: Buck H 2G **37**
Yewdale Cl. BR1: Broml 6G **141**
Yewfield Rd. NW10 6B **62**
Yew Gro. NW2 4F **63**
Yew Ho. SE16 2K **103**
(off Woodland Cres.)
Yews, The TW15: Ashf 4D **128**
Yewtree Av. RM10: Dag 5J **73**
Yew Tree Cl. DA16: Well 1A **126**
Yew Tree Cl. KT4: Wor Pk 1A **164**
Yew Tree Cl. N21 7F **23**
Yew Tree Cl. SE13 3E **122**
Yewtree Cl. HA2: Harr 4F **41**
Yewtree Cl. N22 1G **47**
Yew Tree Ct. NW11 5H **45**
(off Bridge La.)
Yew Tree Ct. SM2: Sutt 7A **166**
(off Walnut M.)
Yew Tree Gdns. RM6: Chad H 5E **54**
Yew Tree Gdns. RM7: Rom 5K **55**
Yew Tree Lodge HA4: Ruis 6J **39**
Yew Tree Lodge RM7: Rom 5K **55**
(off Yew Tree Gdns.)
Yew Tree Lodge SW16 4G **137**
Yew Tree Rd. BR3: Beck 3B **158**
Yew Tree Rd. UB10: Uxb 1B **74**
Yew Tree Rd. W12 7B **80**
Yew Trees TW17: Shep 4B **146**
Yew Tree Wlk. TW4: Houn 5D **112**
Yew Wlk. HA1: Harr 1J **59**
YIEWSLEY 1A **92**
Yiewsley Ct. UB7: Yiew 1A **92**
YMCA E16 George Williams College 5K **87**
YMCA W2 German 2A **10** (7A **82**)
(off Craven Ter.)
YMCA KT2: King T Hawker 5D **132**
YMCA UB8: Uxb W. London, Uxbridge
1A **74**
Yoakley Rd. N16 2E **66**
Yoga Way KT4: Wor Pk 2C **164**
Yoke Cl. N7 6J **65**
Yolande Gdns. SE9 5C **124**
Yonge Pk. N4 3A **66**
York Av. DA15: Sidc 2J **143**
York Av. HA7: Stan 1B **42**
York Av. SW14 5J **115**
York Av. UB3: Hayes 5E **74**
York Av. W7 1J **95**
York Bri. NW1 3G **5** (4E **82**)
York Bldgs. WC2 3F **13** (7J **83**)
York Cl. E6 6D **88**
York Cl. SE5 2C **120**
(off Lilford Rd.)
York Cl. SM4: Mord 4K **153**
York Cl. TW18: Staines 6A **128**
York Cl. W7 1J **95**
York Ct. N14 3D **32**
York Ga. N14 7D **22**
York Ga. NW1 4G **5** (4E **82**)
York Gro. SE15 1J **121**
York Hall Leisure Cen. 2H 85
York Hill SE27 3B **138**
York Ho. E16 1J **105**
(off De Quincey M.)
York Ho. EN2: Enf 1J **23**
York Ho. HA9: Wemb 4G **61**
York Ho. KT2: King T 7F **133**
(off Elm Rd.)
York Ho. SE1 2H **19** (3K **101**)
York Ho. SW3 5F **17** (5D **100**)
(off Turks Row)
York Ho. W1 5E **4** (5D **82**)
(off York St.)
York Ho. W8 2K **99**
(off York Ho. Pl.)
York Ho. Pl. W8 2K **99**
Yorkland Av. DA16: Well 3K **125**
York La. CR4: Mitc 2G **155**
Yorkley Ho. W10 4E **80**
(off Sutton Way)
York Mans. SE17 5C **102**
(off Browning St.)
York Mans. SW11 1E **118**
(off Prince of Wales Dr.)
York Mans. SW5 5K **99**
(off Earls Ct. Rd.)
York Mans. W1 5G **5** (5E **82**)
(off Chiltern St.)
York M. IG1: Ilf 3E **70**
York M. NW5 5F **65**
York Pde. NW9 6C **44**
(off W. Hendon B'way.)
York Pde. TW8: Bford 5D **96**
York Pl. IG1: Ilf 2E **70**
York Pl. RM10: Dag 6J **73**
York Pl. SW11 3B **118**
York Pl. WC2 3F **13** (7J **83**)
(off Villiers St.)
York Pl. Mans. W1 5F **5** (5D **82**)
(off Baker St.)
York Ri. BR6: Orp 2J **173**
York Ri. NW5 3F **65**
York Rd. CR0: C'don 7A **156**
York Rd. E10 3E **68**
York Rd. E17 5K **49**
York Rd. E4 4H **35**
York Rd. E7 6J **69**
York Rd. EN5: New Bar 5F **21**
York Rd. HA6: Nwood 2J **39**
York Rd. IG1: Ilf 3E **70**
York Rd. KT2: King T 7F **133**
York Rd. N11 6C **32**
York Rd. N18 6C **34**
York Rd. N21 7J **23**
York Rd. RM13: Rain 7K **73**
York Rd. SE1 6H **13** (2K **101**)
York Rd. SM1: Sutt 6J **165**
York Rd. SM2: Sutt 6J **165**
York Rd. SW11 4A **118**
York Rd. SW18 4A **118**
York Rd. SW19 6A **136**
York Rd. TW10: Rich 5F **115**
York Rd. TW11: Tedd 4J **131**
York Rd. TW3: Houn 3F **113**
York Rd. TW8: Bford 5D **96**
York Rd. W3 6J **79**
York Rd. W5 3C **96**
York Rd. Bus. Cen. SW11 2B **118**
Yorkshire Cl. N16 3E **66**
Yorkshire Gdns. N18 5C **34**
YORKSHIRE GREY 5B **124**
Yorkshire Grey Pl. NW3 4A **64**
Yorkshire Grey Yd. WC1 6G **7** (5K **83**)
(off Eagle St.)
Yorkshire Rd. CR4: Mitc 5J **155**
Yorkshire Rd. E14 6A **86**
York Sq. E14 6A **86**
York St. CR4: Mitc 7E **154**
York St. TW1: Twick 1A **132**
York St. W1 6E **4** (5D **82**)
York St. Chambers W1 5E **4** (5D **82**)
(off York St.)
York Ter. DA8: Erith 1J **127**
York Ter. EN2: Enf 1H **23**
York Ter. SE7 4A **106**
(off Gallon Cl.)
York Ter. E. NW1 4H **5** (4E **82**)
York Ter. W. NW1 4G **5** (4E **82**)
Yorkton St. E2 2G **85**
York Way KT9: Chess 7E **162**
York Way N1 1F **7** (2J **83**)
York Way N20 3J **31**
York Way N7 6H **65**
York Way TW13: Hanw 3D **130**
(not continuous)
York Way Ct. N1 1J **83**
(not continuous)
York Way Est. N7 6J **65**
Young Ct. NW6 7G **63**
Youngmans Cl. EN2: Enf 1H **23**
Young Rd. E16 6A **88**
Youngs Bldgs. EC1 3D **8** (4C **84**)
(off Old St.)
Youngs Ct. SW11 1E **118**
Youngs Rd. IG2: Ilf 5H **53**
Young St. W8 2K **99**
Young Vic Theatre, The 6K 13 (2A 102)
(off The Cut)
Yoxall Ho. W10 4E **80**
(off Sutton Way)
Yoxford Ct. RM6: Chad H 5B **54**
Yoxley App. IG2: Ilf 6G **53**
Yoxley Dr. IG2: Ilf 6G **53**
Ypres Pl. RM9: Dag 1B **90**
Yukon Rd. SW12 7F **119**
Yunus Khan Cl. E17 5C **50**
Yvon Ho. SW11 1E **118**
(off Alexandra Av.)

Z

Zachary Ct. SW1 4D **18** (4H **101**)
(off Montaigne Cl.)
Zachary Ho. SW9 1K **119**
(off Lett Rd.)
Zachary M. E3 3B **86**
(off Tredegar Sq.)
Zahra Ho. NW10 3E **80**
(off Harrow Rd.)
Zambezie Dr. N9 3D **34**
Zampa Rd. SE16 5J **103**
Zanara Ct. SE26 5J **139**
Zander Ct. E2 3G **85**
Zangwill Ho. NW6 2H **81**
(off Carlton Va.)
Zangwill Rd. SE3 1B **124**
Zapotec Ho. SE8 4K **103**
(off Chilton Gro.)
Zealand Av. UB7: Harm 3E **174**
Zealand Ho. SE18 4C **106**
Zealand Ho. SE5 2C **120**
(off Denmark Rd.)
Zealand Rd. E3 2A **86**
Zeller Ho. E20 5D **68**
(off Scarlet Cl.)
Zenith Cl. NW9 3K **43**
Zenith Lodge N3 7E **30**
Zennor Rd. SW12 1G **137**
Zennor Rd. Ind. Est. SW12 1G **137**
Zenobia Mans. W14 6H **99**
(off Queen's Club Gdns.)
Zenoria St. SE22 4F **121**
Zermatt Rd. CR7: Thor H 4C **156**
Zetland Ho. W8 3K **99**
(off Marloes Rd.)
Zetland St. E14 5D **86**
Zeus Ct. UB7: Yiew 1A **92**
Zinc Bldg., The SE13 4G **123**
Zinnia Mans. E20 6D **68**
(off Olympic Pk. Av.)
Zion Ho. E1 6J **85**
(off Jubilee St.)
Zion Pl. CR7: Thor H 4D **156**
Zion Rd. CR7: Thor H 4D **156**
Zoar St. SE1 4C **14** (1C **102**)
Zodiac Cl. HA8: Edg 7B **28**
Zodiac Ct. CR0: C'don 1B **168**
Zodiac Ho. E3 4C **86**
(off Wellington Way)
Zoffany St. N19 2H **65**
Zona Ct. SE1 3F **103**
(off Grange Wlk.)
Zulu M. SW11 2C **118**

310 A–Z London

HOSPITALS, HOSPICES and selected HEALTHCARE FACILITIES
covered by this atlas.

N.B. Where it is not possible to name these facilities on the map, the reference given is for the road in which they are situated.

ASHFORD HOSPITAL 2A **128**
London Road
ASHFORD
TW15 3AA
Tel: 01784 884488

BARKING HOSPITAL 7K **71**
Upney Lane
BARKING
IG11 9LX
Tel: 020 3644 2301

BARNES HOSPITAL 3A **116**
South Worple Way
LONDON
SW14 8SU
Tel: 020 3513 3663

BARNET HOSPITAL 4A **20**
Wellhouse Lane
BARNET
EN5 3DJ
Tel: 020 8216 4600

BECKENHAM BEACON 2B **158**
379 Croydon Road
BECKENHAM
BR3 3QL
Tel: 01689 863000

BETHLEM ROYAL HOSPITAL 7C **158**
Monks Orchard Road
BECKENHAM
BR3 3BX
Tel: 020 3228 6000

THE BLACKHEATH BMI HOSPITAL 3H **123**
40-42 Lee Terrace
LONDON
SE3 9UD
Tel: 020 8318 7722

**THE BLACKHEATH BMI HOSPITAL
OUTPATIENT DEPARTMENT)** 3H **123**
Independents Road
LONDON
SE3 9LF
Tel: 020 8297 4500

BMI CAVELL HOSPITAL 2F **23**
Cavell Drive
ENFIELD
EN2 7PR
Tel: 020 8366 2122

BMI CITY MEDICAL 7G **9** (6E **84**)
17 St Helen's Place
LONDON
EC3A 6DG
Tel: 0845 123 5380

BMI URGENT CARE CEN. 3K **59**
The Clementine Hospital
Sudbury Hill
HARROW
HA1 3RX
Tel: 020 8872 3999

BRENT OLDER PEOPLE DAY HOSPITAL 1C **80**
341 Harlesden Road
LONDON
NW10 3RX
Tel: 020 8459 3562

BRIDGEWAYS DAY HOSPITAL 6C **160**
Turpington Lane
BROMLEY
BR2 8JA
Tel: 020 8629 4900

CAMDEN MEWS DAY HOSPITAL 7G **65**
1-5 Camden Mews
LONDON
NW1 9DB
Tel: 020 3317 4740

CASSEL HOSPITAL 4D **132**
1 Ham Common
RICHMOND
TW10 7JF
Tel: 020 8483 2900

CENTRAL MIDDLESEX HOSPITAL 3J **79**
Acton Lane
LONDON
NW10 7NS
Tel: 020 8965 5733

CHARING CROSS HOSPITAL 6F **99**
Fulham Palace Road
LONDON
W6 8RF
Tel: 020 3311 1234

CHASE FARM HOSPITAL 1F **23**
127 The Ridgeway
ENFIELD
EN2 8JL
Tel: 020 8375 2999

CHELSEA & WESTMINSTER HOSPITAL 6A **100**
369 Fulham Road
LONDON
SW10 9NH
Tel: 020 3315 8000

THE CHILDREN'S HOSPITAL (LEWISHAM) 5D **122**
Lewisham University Hospital
Lewisham High Street
LONDON
SE13 6LH
Tel: 020 8333 3000

CHURCHILL CAMBIAN HOSPITAL 1K **19** (3A **102**)
Barkham Terrace
Lambeth Road
LONDON
SE1 7PW
Tel: 0800 138 1418

**CITY & HACKNEY CENTRE FOR MENTAL
HEALTH** 5K **67**
Homerton Row
LONDON
E9 6SR
Tel: 020 8510 8117

CLAYPONDS HOSPITAL 4E **96**
Sterling Place
LONDON
W5 4RN
Tel: 020 8560 4011

CLEMENTINE CHURCHILL BMI HOSPITAL 2K **59**
Sudbury Hill
HARROW
HA1 3RX
Tel: 020 8872 3872

**THE COBORN CENTRE FOR ADOLESCENT MENTAL
HEALTH** 4B **88**
Glen Road
LONDON
E13 8SP
Tel: 020 7540 6789

CROMWELL BUPA HOSPITAL 4K **99**
162-178 Cromwell Road
LONDON
SW5 0TU
Tel: 020 7460 2000

CROYDON UNIVERSITY HOSPITAL 6B **156**
530 London Road
THORNTON HEATH
CR7 7YE
Tel: 020 8401 3000

CYGNET HOSPITAL, BECKTON 6E **88**
23 Tunnan Leys
LONDON
E6 6ZB
Tel: 020 7511 2299

CYGNET HOSPITAL, BLACKHEATH 1E **122**
80 Blackheath Hill
LONDON
SE10 8AD
Tel: 020 8694 2111

CYGNET LODGE 6E **122**
44 Lewisham Park
LONDON
SE13 6QZ
Tel: 020 8314 5123

DEMELZA HOSPICE CARE FOR CHILDREN 6D **124**
5 Wensley Close
LONDON
SE9 5AB
Tel: 020 8859 9800

DULWICH COMMUNITY HOSPITAL 4E **120**
East Dulwich Grove
LONDON
SE22 8PT
Tel: 020 3049 8800

EALING CYGNET HOSPITAL 5E **78**
22 Corfton Road
LONDON
W5 2HT
Tel: 020 8991 6699

EALING HOSPITAL 1H **95**
Uxbridge Road
SOUTHALL
UB1 3HW
Tel: 020 8967 5000

EAST HAM CARE CENTRE & DAY HOSPITAL 7B **70**
Shrewsbury Road
LONDON
E7 8QP
Tel: 020 8475 2001

EASTMAN DENTAL HOSPITAL 4C **6** (4H **83**)
47-49 Huntley Street
LONDON
WC1E 6DG
Tel: 020 3456 7899

EASTMAN DENTAL INSTITUTE 4C **6** (4H **83**)
Rockefeller Building
21 University Street
LONDON
WC1E 6DE

EDGWARE COMMUNITY HOSPITAL 7C **28**
Burnt Oak Broadway
EDGWARE
HA8 0AD
Tel: 020 8952 2381

EDRIDGE ROAD COMMUNITY HEALTH CEN. 3C **168**
Impact House
2 Edridge Road
CROYDON
CR0 1FE
Tel: 020 3040 0800

ELTHAM COMMUNITY HOSPITAL 6D **124**
Passey Place
LONDON
SE9 5DQ
Tel: 020 3049 0400

ERITH & DISTRICT HOSPITAL 6K **109**
Park Crescent
ERITH
DA8 3EE
Tel: 020 8308 3131

EVELINA CHILDREN'S HOSPITAL 1G **19** (3K **101**)
St Thomas' Hospital
Westminster Bridge Road
LONDON
SE1 7EH
Tel: 020 7188 7188

FINCHLEY MEMORIAL HOSPITAL 7F **31**
Granville Road
LONDON
N12 0JE
Tel: 020 8349 7500

FITZROY SQUARE HOSPITAL 4A **6** (4G **83**)
1 Fitzroy Square
LONDON
W1T 5HF
Tel: 0333 920 9135

GOODMAYES HOSPITAL 5A **54**
Barley Lane
ILFORD
IG3 8XJ
Tel: 0300 555 1200

GORDON HOSPITAL 4C **18** (4H **101**)
Bloomburg Street
LONDON
SW1V 2RH
Tel: 020 3315 8733

**GREAT ORMOND STREET HOSPITAL FOR
CHILDREN** 4F **7** (4J **83**)
Great Ormond Street
LONDON
WC1N 3JH
Tel: 020 7405 9200

**GREENWICH & BEXLEY COMMUNITY
HOSPICE** 5C **108**
185 Bostall Hill
LONDON
SE2 0GB
Tel: 020 8312 2244

GUY'S HOSPITAL 6E **14** (2D **102**)
Great Maze Pond
LONDON
SE1 9RT
Tel: 020 7188 7188

GUY'S NUFFIELD HOUSE 6E **14** (2D **102**)
Guy's Hospital
LONDON
SE1 1YR
Tel: 020 7188 5292

HAMMERSMITH HOSPITAL 6C **80**
Du Cane Road
LONDON
W12 0HS
Tel: 020 3313 1000

THE HARLEY STREET CLINIC 5J **5** (5F **83**)
35 Weymouth Street
LONDON
W1G 8BJ
Tel: 020 3553 6106

HARLINGTON HOSPICE 5F **93**
St Peters Way
HAYES
UB3 5AB
Tel: 020 8759 0453

HARROW CYGNET HOSPITAL 2J **59**
London Road
HARROW
HA1 3JL
Tel: 020 8966 7000

HAVEN HOUSE CHILDREN'S HOSPICE 6C **36**
High Road
WOODFORD GREEN
IG8 9LB
Tel: 020 8505 9944

HAYES GROVE PRIORY HOSPITAL 2J **171**
Prestons Road
Hayes
BROMLEY
BR2 7AS
Tel: 020 8462 7722

HENDON HOSPITAL 3E **44**
46-50 Sunny Gardens Road
LONDON
NW4 1RP
Tel: 020 8457 4500

HIGHGATE HOSPITAL 6D **46**
17- 19 View Road
LONDON
N6 4DJ
Tel: 020 8003 4518

HIGHGATE MENTAL HEALTH CEN. 2F **65**
Dartmouth Park Hill
LONDON
N19 5NX
Tel: 020 7561 4000

HILLINGDON HOSPITAL 5B **74**
Pield Heath Road
UXBRIDGE
UB8 3NN
Tel: 01895 238282

THE HOLLY PRIVATE HOSPITAL 2E **36**
High Road
BUCKHURST HILL
IG9 5HX
Tel: 020 8505 3311

HOMERTON UNIVERSITY HOSPITAL 5K **67**
Homerton Row
LONDON
E9 6SR
Tel: 020 8510 5555

HOSPITAL FOR TROPICAL DISEASES 4B **6** (4G **83**)
Mortimer Market
LONDON
WC1E 6JD
Tel: 020 3447 5959

HOSPITAL OF ST JOHN & ST ELIZABETH 2B **82**
60 Grove End Road
LONDON
NW8 9NH
Tel: 020 7806 4000

HUNTERCOMBE HOSPITAL ROEHAMPTON 7C **116**
Holybourne Avenue
LONDON
SW15 4JD
Tel: 020 8780 6155

JOHN HOWARD CEN. 5A **68**
12 Kenworthy Road
LONDON
E9 5TD
Tel: 020 8510 2003

**KING EDWARD VII'S HOSPITAL SISTER
AGNES** 5H **5** (5E **82**)
5-10 Beaumont Street
LONDON
W1G 6AA
Tel: 020 7486 4411

KING GEORGE HOSPITAL 4A **54**
Barley Lane
ILFORD
IG3 8YB
Tel: 0330 400 4333

KING'S COLLEGE HOSPITAL 2D **120**
Denmark Hill
LONDON
SE5 9RS
Tel: 020 3299 9000

KING'S OAK BMI HOSPITAL 1F **23**
The Ridgeway
ENFIELD
EN2 8SD
Tel: 020 8370 9500

KINGSTON HOSPITAL 1H **151**
Galsworthy Road
KINGSTON UPON THAMES
KT2 7QB
Tel: 020 8546 7711

LAMBETH HOSPITAL 3K **119**
108 Landor Road
LONDON
SW9 9NU
Tel: 020 3228 6000

THE LISTER HOSPITAL 6J **17** (5F **101**)
Chelsea Bridge Road
LONDON
SW1W 8RH
Tel: 020 7730 4345

LONDON BRIDGE HOSPITAL..............4F **15** (1D **102**)
27 Tooley Street
LONDON
SE1 2PR
Tel: 020 7407 3100

LONDON CLINIC.....................................4H **5** (4E **82**)
20 Devonshire Place
LONDON
W1G 6BW
Tel: 020 7935 4444

LONDON EYE HOSPITAL.........................7J **5** (6F **83**)
4 Harley Street
LONDON
W1G 9PB
Tel: 020 7060 2602

LONDON INDEPENDENT BMI HOSPITAL 5K **85**
1 Beaumont Square
LONDON
E1 4NL
Tel: 020 7780 2400

LONDON WELBECK HOSPITAL 6H **5** (5E **82**)
27 Welbeck Street
LONDON
W1G 8EN
Tel: 020 7224 2242

MARGARET CENTRE (HOSPICE).......................6G **51**
Whipps Cross University Hospital
Whipps Cross Road
LONDON
E11 1NR
Tel: 020 8539 5522

MARIE CURIE HOSPICE 5B **64**
11 Lyndhurst Gardens
LONDON
NW3 5NS
Tel: 020 7853 3400

THE MAUDSLEY HOSPITAL 2D **120**
Denmark Hill
LONDON
SE5 8AZ
Tel: 020 3228 6000

MEADOW HOUSE HOSPICE...............................2H **95**
Uxbridge Road
SOUTHALL
UB1 3HW
Tel: 020 8967 5179

MEMORIAL HOSPITAL...2E **124**
Shooters Hill
LONDON
SE18 3RG
Tel: 020 8836 8500

MILDMAY HOSPITAL 2J **9** (3F **85**)
Austin Street
LONDON
E2 7NB
Tel: 0207 613 6300

MILE END HOSPITAL 4K **85**
Bancroft Road
LONDON
E1 4DG
Tel: 020 3416 5000

MINOR INJURIES UNIT (GUY'S HOSPITAL)
....6F **15** (2D **102**)
Great Maze Pond
LONDON
SE1 9RT
Tel: 020 7188 3879

MINOR INJURIES UNIT (ROEHAMPTON) 6C **116**
Roehampton Lane
LONDON
SW15 5PN
Tel: 020 8487 6499

MINOR INJURIES UNIT
(ST BARTHOLOMEW'S HOSPITAL)......6B **8** (5B **84**)
West Smithfield
LONDON
EC1A 7BE
Tel: 020 3465 8843

MOLESEY HOSPITAL 5E **148**
High Street
WEST MOLESEY
KT8 2LU
Tel: 020 8941 4481

MOORFIELDS EYE HOSPITAL 2E **8** (3D **84**)
162 City Road
LONDON
EC1V 2PD
Tel: 020 7253 3411

NATIONAL HOSPITAL FOR NEUROLOGY
& NEUROSURGERY..............................4F **7** (4J **83**)
Queen Square
LONDON
WC1N 3BG
Tel: 020 3456 7890

NEWHAM CENTRE FOR MENTAL HEALTH.........4B **88**
Cherry Tree Way
Glen Road
LONDON
E13 8SP
Tel: 020 7540 4380

NEWHAM UNIVERSITY HOSPITAL.....................4A **88**
Glen Road
LONDON
E13 8SL
Tel: 020 7476 4000

NEW VICTORIA HOSPITAL..................................1A **152**
184 Coombe Lane West
KINGSTON UPON THAMES
KT2 7EG
Tel: 020 8949 9000

NHS WALK-IN CENTRE (ASHFORD) 2A **128**
Ashford Hospital
London Road
ASHFORD
TW15 3AA
Tel: 01784 884000

NHS WALK-IN CENTRE (BARKING HOSPITAL) ...7K **71**
Upney Lane
BARKING
IG11 9LX
Tel: 020 8924 6262

NHS WALK-IN CENTRE
(BELMONT HEALTH CENTRE)........................2A **42**
516 Kenton Lane
HARROW
HA3 7LT
Tel: 020 8866 4100

NHS WALK-IN CENTRE (CLAPHAM JUNCTION)....3C **118**
The Junction Health Centre
Arches 5-8, Clapham Junction Station
Grant Road
LONDON
SW11 2NU
Tel: 0333 200 1718

NHS WALK-IN CENTRE
(CRICKLEWOOD HEALTH CENTRE) 4F **63**
Britannia Business Centre
Cricklewood Lane
LONDON
NW2 1DZ
Tel: 03000 334335

NHS WALK-IN CENTRE (EARL'S COURT) 4K **99**
Earl's Court Health & Wellbeing Centre
2b Hogarth Road
LONDON
SW5 0PT
Tel: 020 7341 0300

NHS WALK-IN CENTRE (EDGWARE)..................7C **28**
Edgware Community Hospital
Burnt Oak Broadway
EDGWARE
HA8 0AD
Tel: 020 8732 6459

NHS WALK-IN CENTRE (FINCHLEY) 7F **31**
Finchley Memorial Hospital
Granville Road
LONDON
N12 0JE
Tel: 020 8349 7470

NHS WALK-IN CENTRE (ISLE OF DOGS) 2C **104**
Barkantine Practice
121 Westferry Road
LONDON
E14 8JH
Tel: 020 7510 4000

NHS WALK-IN CENTRE (PARSONS GREEN) 1J **117**
5-7 Parsons Green
LONDON
SW6 4UL
Tel: 020 8102 4300

NHS WALK-IN CENTRE (PINNER)....................3C **40**
Pinn Medical Centre, The
37 Love Lane
PINNER
HA5 3EE
Tel: 020 8866 5766

NHS WALK-IN CENTRE (SOHO) 1C **12** (6H **83**)
1 Frith Street
LONDON
W1D 3HZ
Tel: 020 7534 6575

NHS WALK-IN CENTRE (TEDDINGTON)...........6J **131**
Teddington Memorial Hospital
Hampton Road
TEDDINGTON
TW11 0JL
Tel: 020 8714 4004

NHS WALK-IN CENTRE (THAMESMEAD) 2J **107**
Thamesmead Health Centre
4-5 Thames Reach
LONDON
SE28 0NY
Tel: 020 8319 5880

NHS WALK-IN CENTRE (WEMBLEY) 6D **60**
116 Chaplin Road
WEMBLEY
HA0 4UZ
Tel: 020 8795 6112

NIGHTINGALE HOSPITAL........................5D **4** (5C **82**)
11-19 Lisson Grove
LONDON
NW1 6SH
Tel: 020 7535 7705

NOAH'S ARK CHILDREN'S HOSPICE 3A **20**
The Ark
Byng Road
BARNET
EN5 4NP
Tel: 02084498877

NORTH LONDON CLINIC 2B **34**
15 Church Street
LONDON
N9 9DY
Tel: 020 8956 1234

NORTH LONDON HOSPICE (FINCHLEY) 3F **31**
47 Woodside Avenue
LONDON
N12 8TT
Tel: 020 8343 8841

NORTH LONDON HOSPICE
(WINCHMORE HILL) 3H **33**
110 Barrowell Green
LONDON
N21 3AY
Tel: 020 8343 8841

NORTH LONDON PRIORY HOSPITAL 1D **32**
The Bourne
LONDON
N14 6RA
Tel: 020 8882 8191

NORTH MIDDLESEX UNIVERSITY HOSPITAL....5K **33**
Sterling Way
LONDON
N18 1QX
Tel: 020 8887 2000

NORTHWICK PARK HOSPITAL...........................7A **42**
Watford Road
HARROW
HA1 3UJ
Tel: 020 8864 3232

OLD BROAD STREET PRIVATE MEDICAL CEN.
....7G **9** (6E **84**)
31 Old Broad Street
LONDON
EC2N 1HT
Tel: 020 7496 3522

ORPINGTON HOSPITAL.....................................4K **173**
Sevenoaks Road
ORPINGTON
BR6 9JU
Tel: 01689 863000

PARK ROYAL CENTRE
(FOR MENTAL HEALTH) 2J **79**
Central Way
LONDON
NW10 7NS
Tel: 020 8955 4400

PARKSIDE HOSPITAL 3F **135**
53 Parkside
LONDON
SW19 5NX
Tel: 020 8971 8000

PEMBRIDGE PALLIATIVE CARE CEN..................5F **81**
St Charles Hospital
Exmoor Street
LONDON
W10 6DZ
Tel: 020 8102 5000

PORTLAND HOSPITAL FOR WOMEN &
CHILDREN 4K **5** (4F **83**)
205-209 Great Portland Street
LONDON
W1W 5AH
Tel: 020 3131 5755

PRINCESS GRACE HOSPITAL 4H **5** (4E **82**)
42-52 Nottingham Place
LONDON
W1U 5NY
Tel: 020 3130 6833

PRINCESS ROYAL UNIVERSITY HOSPITAL......3E **172**
Farnborough Common
ORPINGTON
BR6 8ND
Tel: 01689 863000

PRIORY HOSPITAL ROEHAMPTON 4B **116**
Priory Lane
LONDON
SW15 5JJ
Tel: 020 8876 8261

QUEEN CHARLOTTE'S & CHELSEA
HOSPITAL..6C **80**
Du Cane Road
LONDON
W12 0HS
Tel: 020 3313 1111

QUEEN ELIZABETH HOSPITAL 7C **106**
Stadium Road
LONDON
SE18 4QH
Tel: 020 8836 6000

QUEEN MARY'S HOSPITAL FOR CHILDREN ... 1A **166**
Wrythe Lane
CARSHALTON
SM5 1AA
Tel: 020 8296 2000

QUEEN MARY'S HOSPITAL, ROEHAMPTON ... 6C **116**
Roehampton Lane
LONDON
SW15 5PN
Tel: 020 8487 6000

QUEEN MARY'S HOSPITAL, SIDCUP 6A **144**
Frognal Avenue
SIDCUP
DA14 6LT
Tel: 020 8302 2678

QUEEN'S HOSPITAL..7K **55**
Rom Valley Way
ROMFORD
RM7 0AG
Tel: 01708 435000

RICHARD DESMOND CHILDREN'S EYE CEN
....2E **8** (3D **84**)
Moorfields Eye Hospital
3 Peerless Street
LONDON
EC1V 9EZ
Tel: 020 7253 3411

RICHARD HOUSE CHILDREN'S HOSPICE..........7B **88**
Richard House Drive
LONDON
E16 3RG
Tel: 020 7511 0222

RICHMOND ROYAL HOSPITAL.........................3E **114**
Kew Foot Road
RICHMOND
TW9 2TE
Tel: 020 3513 3200

RODING SPIRE HOSPITAL 3B **52**
Roding Lane South
ILFORD
IG4 5PZ
Tel: 020 3131 4324

ROYAL BROMPTON HOSPITAL...........5C **16** (5C **100**)
Sydney Street
LONDON
SW3 6NP
Tel: 020 7352 8121

ROYAL BROMPTON HOSPITAL
(OUTPATIENTS) 5B **16** (5B **100**)
Fulham Road
LONDON
SW3 6HP
Tel: 020 7352 8121

ROYAL FREE HOSPITAL.....................................5C **64**
Pond Street
LONDON
NW3 2QG
Tel: 020 7794 0500

ROYAL HOSPITAL FOR NEURO-DISABILITY... 6G **117**
West Hill
LONDON
SW15 3SW
Tel: 020 8780 4500

THE ROYAL LONDON HOSPITAL.......................5H **85**
Whitechapel Road
LONDON
E1 1FR
Tel: 020 3416 5000

ROYAL LONDON HOSPITAL FOR
INTEGRATED MEDICINE.......................4F **7** (4J **83**)
Great Ormond Street
LONDON
WC1N 3HR
Tel: 020 3456 7890

THE ROYAL MARSDEN HOSPITAL......5B **16** (5B **100**)
Fulham Road
LONDON
SW3 6JJ
Tel: 020 7352 8171

ROYAL NAT. ORTHOPAEDIC HOSPITAL....4K **5** (4F **83**)
45-51 Bolsover Street
LONDON
W1W 5AQ
Tel: 020 3947 0100

ROYAL NAT. ORTHOPAEDIC HOSPITAL............2H **27**
Brockley Hill
STANMORE
HA7 4LP
Tel: 020 8954 2300

ROYAL NATIONAL THROAT, NOSE &
EAR HOSPITAL 4C **6** (4H **83**)
47-49 Huntley Street
LONDON
WC1E 6DG
Tel: 020 3456 2300

ST ANN'S HOSPITAL 5C **48**
St Ann's Road
LONDON
N15 3TH
Tel: 020 8702 3000

ST ANTHONY'S HOSPITAL..................1F **165**
801 London Road
SUTTON
SM3 9DW
Tel: 020 8337 6691

ST BARTHOLOMEW'S HOSPITAL 6B **8** (5B **84**)
West Smithfield
LONDON
EC1A 7BE
Tel: 020 3416 5000

ST BERNARD'S HOSPITAL 2H **95**
Uxbridge Road
SOUTHALL
UB1 3EU
Tel: 020 8354 8354

ST CHARLES HOSPITAL 5F **81**
Exmoor Street
LONDON
W10 6DZ
Tel: 020 8206 7343

ST CHRISTOPHER'S HOSPICE (SYDNEHAM)...5J **139**
51-59 Lawrie Park Road
LONDON
SE26 6DZ
Tel: 020 8768 4500

ST CHRISTOPHER'S HOSPISCARE (ORPINGTON) ...4K **173**
Tregony Road
ORPINGTON
BR6 9XA
Tel: 01689 825755

ST EBBA'S..7J **163**
Hook Road
EPSOM
KT19 8QJ
Tel: 0300 555 5222

ST GEORGE'S HOSPITAL (TOOTING) 5B **136**
Blackshaw Road
LONDON
SW17 0QT
Tel: 020 8672 1255

ST HELIER HOSPITAL 1A **166**
Wrythe Lane
CARSHALTON
SM5 1AA
Tel: 020 8296 2000

ST JOHN'S HOSPICE..................1A **4** (2B **82**)
60 Grove End Road
LONDON
NW8 9NH
Tel: 020 7806 4040

ST JOSEPH'S HOSPICE.....................................1H **85**
Mare Street
LONDON
E8 4SA
Tel: 020 8525 6000

ST LUKE'S HEALTHCARE FOR THE CLERGY
....4A **6** (4G **83**)
Room 201, Church House
Great Smith Street
LONDON
SW1P 3AZ
Tel: 020 4546 7000

ST LUKE'S HOSPICE 5D **42**
Kenton Road
HARROW
HA3 0YG
Tel: 020 8382 8000

ST MARK'S HOSPITAL (HARROW) 7B **42**
Watford Road
HARROW
HA1 3UJ
Tel: 020 8864 3232

ST MARY'S HOSPITAL.....................7B **4** (6B **82**)
Praed Street
LONDON
W2 1NY
Tel: 020 7886 6666

ST MICHAEL'S HOSPITAL...............................1J **23**
Gater Drive
ENFIELD
EN2 0JB
Tel: 020 8375 2894

ST PANCRAS HOSPITAL...................................1H **83**
4 St Pancras Way
LONDON
NW1 0PE
Tel: 020 3317 3500

ST RAPHAEL'S HOSPICE 2F **165**
London Road
SUTTON
SM3 9DX
Tel: 020 8099 7777

ST THOMAS' HOSPITAL 1G **19** (3K **101**)
Westminster Bridge Road
LONDON
SE1 7EH
Tel: 020 7188 7188

SHIRLEY OAKS BMI HOSPITAL 7J **157**
Poppy Lane
CROYDON
CR9 8AB
Tel: 020 8655 5500

SHOOTING STAR HOUSE, CHILDREN'S
HOSPICE..6D **130**
The Avenue
HAMPTON
TW12 3RA
Tel: 020 8783 2000

THE SLOANE BMI HOSPITAL........................1F **159**
125 Albemarle Road
BECKENHAM
BR3 5HS
Tel: 020 8466 4000

SPIRE BUSHEY HOSPITAL...............................1E **26**
Heathbourne Road
Bushey Heath
BUSHEY
WD23 1RD
Tel: 020 3733 5424

SPRINGFIELD UNIVERSITY HOSPITAL............2C **136**
61 Glenburnie Road
LONDON
SW17 7DJ
Tel: 020 3513 5000

TEDDINGTON MEMORIAL HOSPITAL 6J **131**
Hampton Road
TEDDINGTON
TW11 0JL
Tel: 020 8714 4000

THORPE COOMBE HOSPITAL 3E **50**
714 Forest Road
LONDON
E17 3HP
Tel: 0300 555 1247

TOLWORTH HOSPITAL...................................2G **163**
Red Lion Road
SURBITON
KT6 7QU
Tel: 020 3513 5000

TOWER HAMLETS CENTRE FOR
MENTAL HEALTH 4K **85**
Bancroft Road
LONDON
E1 4DG
Tel: 020 8121 5001

TRINITY HOSPICE..4F **119**
30 Clapham Common North Side
LONDON
SW4 0RN
Tel: 020 7787 1000

UCH MACMILLAN CANCER CEN.............4B **6** (4G **83**)
Huntley Street
LONDON
WC1E 6DH
Tel: 020 3456 7016

UNIVERSITY COLLEGE HOSPITAL...........3B **6** (4G **83**)
235 Euston Road
LONDON
NW1 2BU
Tel: 020 3456 7890

UNIVERSITY COLLEGE HOSPITAL...........4B **6** (4G **83**)
25 Grafton Way
LONDON
WC1E 6DB
Tel: 020 3447 9400

UNIVERSITY COLLEGE HOSPITAL...........6H **5** (5E **82**)
16-18 Westmoreland Street
LONDON
W1G 8PH
Tel: 020 3456 7890

UNIVERSITY HOSPITAL, LEWISHAM 5D **122**
Lewisham High Street
LONDON
SE13 6LH
Tel: 020 8333 3000

URGENT CARE CENTRE (ANGEL MEDICAL
PRACTICE)..2A **84**
34 Ritchie Street
LONDON
N1 0DG
Tel: 020 7837 1663

URGENT CARE CENTRE (BARNET) 4A **20**
Barnet Hospital
Wellhouse Lane
BARNET
EN5 3DJ
Tel: 020 8216 4600

URGENT CARE CENTRE
(BECKENHAM BEACON) 2B **158**
379 Croydon Road
BECKENHAM
BR3 3QL
Tel: 01689 866037

URGENT CARE CENTRE (CARSHALTON) 1A **166**
St Helier Hospital
Wrythe Lane
CARSHALTON
SM5 1AA
Tel: 020 8296 2000

URGENT CARE CENTRE
(CENTRAL MIDDLESEX HOSPITAL)................3J **79**
Acton Lane
LONDON
NW10 7NS
Tel: 0333 999 2575

URGENT CARE CENTRE
(CHASE FARM HOSPITAL)............................1F **23**
The Ridgeway
ENFIELD
EN2 8JL
Tel: 020 8375 1010

URGENT CARE CENTRE (CHELSEA &
WESTMINSTER HOSPITAL) 6A **100**
369 Fulham Road
LONDON
SW10 9NH
Tel: 020 3315 8000

URGENT CARE CENTRE (EALING) 2H **95**
Ealing Hospital
Uxbridge Road
SOUTHALL
UB1 3HW
Tel: 0333 999 2577

URGENT CARE CENTRE (ERITH & DISTRICT
HOSPITAL)...6K **109**
Park Crescent
ERITH
DA8 3EE
Tel: 01322 356116

URGENT CARE CENTRE (FULHAM)....................5F **99**
Charing Cross Hospital
Fulham Palace Road
LONDON
W6 8RF
Tel: 020 8846 1005

URGENT CARE CENTRE
(HAMMERSMITH HOSPITAL).......................6C **80**
Du Cane Road
LONDON
W12 0HS
Tel: 020 3383 4103

URGENT CARE CENTRE (HAMPSTEAD)............5C **64**
Royal Free Hospital
Pond Street
LONDON
NW3 2QG
Tel: 020 7794 0500

URGENT CARE CENTRE
(HILLINGDON HOSPITAL) 5B **74**
Hillingdon Hospital
Pield Heath Road
UXBRIDGE
UB8 3NN
Tel: 01895 238282

URGENT CARE CENTRE
(HOMERTON UNIVERSITY HOSPITAL)..........5K **67**
Homerton Row
LONDON
E9 6SR
Tel: 020 8510 5555

URGENT CARE CENTRE
(KING GEORGE HOSPITAL) 4A **54**
Barley Lane
ILFORD
IG3 8YB
Tel: 020 8983 8000

URGENT CARE CENTRE (NEWHAM) 4A **88**
Newham University Hospital
Glen Road
LONDON
E13 8SL
Tel: 020 7476 4000

URGENT CARE CENTRE (NORTH MIDDLESEX
UNIVERSITY HOSPITAL)...............................5K **33**
Bridport Road
LONDON
N18 1QX
Tel: 020 8887 2398

URGENT CARE CENTRE
(NORTHWICK PARK HOSPITAL) 7A **42**
Watford Road
HARROW
HA1 3UJ
Tel: 020 8869 3743

URGENT CARE CENTRE (PRINCESS ROYAL
UNIVERSITY HOSPITAL).............................4E **172**
Farnborough Common
ORPINGTON
BR6 8ND
Tel: 01689 863050

URGENT CARE CENTRE
(QUEEN ELIZABETH HOSPITAL) 6C **106**
Stadium Road
LONDON
SE18 4QH
Tel: 020 8836 6846

URGENT CARE CENTRE
(QUEEN'S HOSPITAL) 7K **55**
Rom Valley Way
ROMFORD
RM7 0AG
Tel: 01708 435000

URGENT CARE CENTRE
(ST CHARLES CENTRE) 5F **81**
Exmoor Street
LONDON
W10 6DZ
Tel: 020 8102 5111

URGENT CARE CENTRE
(ST GEORGE'S HOSPITAL)............................5C **136**
Blackshaw Road
LONDON
SW17 0QT
Tel: 020 8672 1255

URGENT CARE CENTRE
(ST MARY'S HOSPITAL)....................7A **4** (6B **82**)
Praed Street
LONDON
W2 1NY
Tel: 020 3312 5757

URGENT CARE CENTRE (SIDCUP) 6A **144**
Queen Mary's Hospital
Frognal Avenue
SIDCUP
DA14 6LF
Tel: 020 8308 5611

URGENT CARE CENTRE
(THORNTON HEATH)....................................6B **156**
Croydon University Hospital
530 London Road
THORNTON HEATH
CR7 7YE
Tel: 020 8401 3000

URGENT CARE CENTRE
(UNIVERSITY COLLEGE HOSPITAL)......3B **6** (4G **83**)
235 Euston Road
LONDON
NW1 2BU
Tel: 020 3456 7890

URGENT CARE CENTRE
(UNIVERSITY HOSPITAL LEWISHAM)..........5D **122**
Lewisham High Street
LONDON
SE13 6LH
Tel: 020 8333 3000

URGENT CARE CENTRE (WEST MIDDLESEX
UNIVERSITY HOSPITAL)...............................2A **114**
Twickenham Road
ISLEWORTH
TW7 6AF
Tel: 020 8560 2121

URGENT CARE CENTRE (WHIPPS CROSS
UNIVERSITY HOSPITAL)...............................6F **51**
Whipps Cross Road
LONDON
E11 1NR
Tel: 0300 123 0808

URGENT CARE CENTRE
(WHITTINGTON HOSPITAL) 2G **65**
Magdala Avenue
LONDON
N19 5NF
Tel: 020 7272 3070

THE WELLINGTON HOSPITAL 1B **4** (3B **82**)
34 Circus Road
LONDON
NW8 9LE
Tel: 020 3733 6667

WESTERN EYE HOSPITAL.................5E **4** (5D **82**)
153-173 Marylebone Road
LONDON
NW1 5QH
Tel: 020 7886 6666

WEST MIDDLESEX UNIVERSITY HOSPITAL......2A **114**
Twickenham Road
ISLEWORTH
TW7 6AF
Tel: 020 8560 2121

WEYMOUTH STREET HOSPITAL.............5H **5** (5E **82**)
42-46 Weymouth Street
LONDON
W1G 6NP
Tel: 020 7935 1200

WHIPPS CROSS UNIVERSITY HOSPITAL...........5F **51**
Whipps Cross Road
LONDON
E11 1NR
Tel: 020 8539 5522

WHITTINGTON HOSPITAL.................................2G **65**
Magdala Avenue
LONDON
N19 5NF
Tel: 020 7272 3070

WILLESDEN CENTRE FOR HEALTH & CARE.....7C **62**
Robson Avenue
LONDON
NW10 3RY
Tel: 020 8438 7006

THE WILSON HOSPITAL....................................4D **154**
Cranmer Road
MITCHAM
CR4 4LD
Tel: 020 8648 3021

WOODBURY UNIT 6G **51**
178 James Lane
LONDON
E11 1NR
Tel: 0300 555 1260

London's Rail & Tube services

Key to lines and symbols

▬▬▬ Bakerloo	
▬▬▬ Central	
▬▬▬ Circle	
▬▬▬ District	limited service
▬▬▬ Hammersmith & City	
▬▬▬ Jubilee	
▬▬▬ Metropolitan	
▬▬▬ Northern	
▬▬▬ Piccadilly	
▬▬▬ Victoria	
▬▬▬ Waterloo & City	
▬▬▬ DLR	
▬▬▬ Elizabeth line	
▬▬▬ London Overground	
▬▬▬ London Trams	
▬▬▬ London Cable Car	
Special fares apply	
▬▬▬ c2c	limited service
▬▬▬ Chiltern Railways	
▬▬▬ East Midlands Railway	
▬▬▬ Gatwick Express	
▬▬▬ Great Northern	
▬▬▬ Great Western Railway	limited service
	peak hours only
▬▬▬ Greater Anglia	
▬▬▬ Heathrow Express	
▬▬▬ London Northwestern Railway	
▬▬▬ South Western Railway	peak hours only
▬▬▬ Southeastern	peak hours only
▬▬▬ Southeastern high speed	
	peak hours and limited service
▬▬▬ Southern	peak hours only
▬▬▬ Thameslink	

○	Interchange stations
⊶	Internal interchange
○···○	Under a 10 minute walk between stations
✈	Airport
✈	Bus transfer to Airport
⏴	River services interchange
▭	Victoria Coach Station
Stratford	Station in both fare zones
	Outside fare zones, Oyster not valid
	London Cable Car

tfl.gov.uk

nationalrail.co.uk

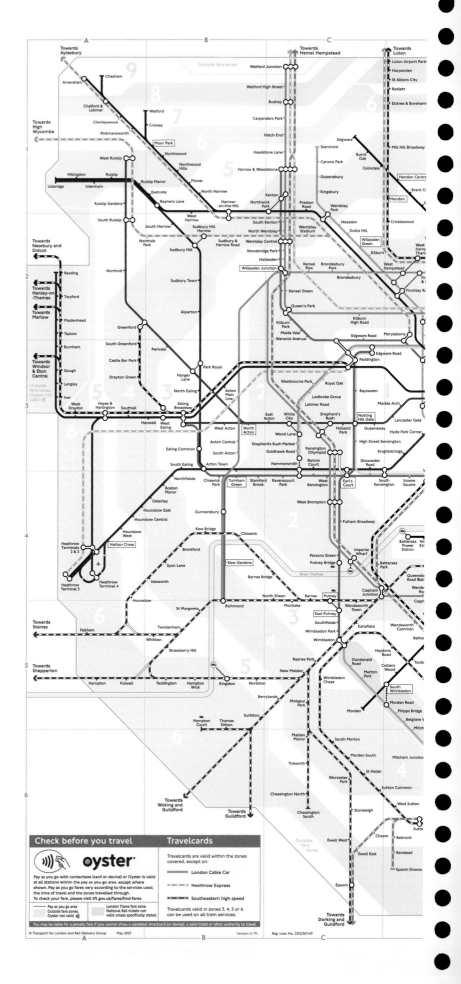

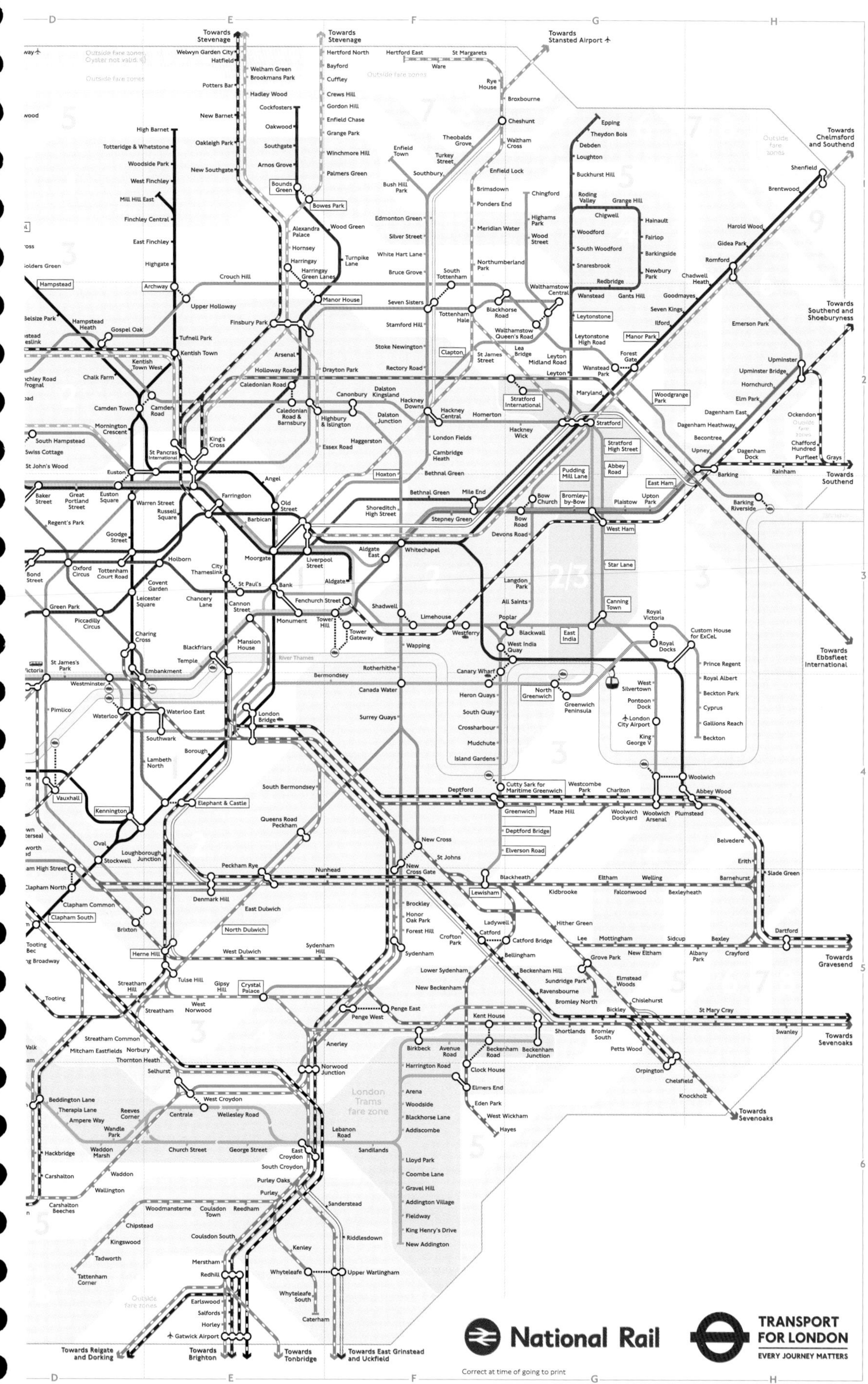
Towards Stevenage
Welwyn Garden City
Hatfield
Welham Green
Brookmans Park
Potters Bar
Hadley Wood
New Barnet
Cockfosters
Oakwood
Southgate
Arnos Grove
Oakleigh Park
New Southgate
High Barnet
Totteridge & Whetstone
Woodside Park
West Finchley
Mill Hill East
Finchley Central
East Finchley
Highgate
Archway
Hampstead
Crouch Hill
Upper Holloway
Hertford North
Bayford
Cuffley
Crews Hill
Gordon Hill
Enfield Chase
Grange Park
Winchmore Hill
Palmers Green
Bounds Green
Bowes Park
Alexandra Palace
Wood Green
Hornsey
Harringay
Turnpike Lane
Harringay Green Lanes
Manor House
Hertford East
St Margarets
Ware
Rye House
Broxbourne
Cheshunt
Theobalds Grove
Waltham Cross
Enfield Town
Turkey Street
Southbury
Bush Hill Park
Enfield Lock
Brimsdown
Ponders End
Edmonton Green
Silver Street
White Hart Lane
Bruce Grove
South Tottenham
Meridian Water
Northumberland Park
Chingford
Highams Park
Wood Street
Towards Stansted Airport
Epping
Theydon Bois
Debden
Loughton
Buckhurst Hill
Roding Valley
Grange Hill
Chigwell
Hainault
Fairlop
Barkingside
Newbury Park
Woodford
South Woodford
Snaresbrook
Redbridge
Wanstead
Gants Hill
Towards Chelmsford and Southend
Shenfield
Brentwood
Harold Wood
Gidea Park
Romford
Chadwell Heath
Goodmayes
Seven Kings
Ilford
Towards Southend and Shoeburyness
Emerson Park
Upminster
Upminster Bridge
Hornchurch
Elm Park
Dagenham East
Dagenham Heathway
Becontree
Upney
Dagenham Dock
Barking
Rainham
Ockendon
Chafford Hundred
Purfleet
Grays
Towards Southend
Barking Riverside
Seven Sisters
Stamford Hill
Stoke Newington
Rectory Road
Tottenham Hale
Blackhorse Road
Walthamstow Central
Walthamstow Queen's Road
Leytonstone
Leytonstone High Road
Manor Park
Clapton
St James Street
Lea Bridge
Leyton Midland Road
Leyton
Wanstead Park
Forest Gate
Maryland
Woodgrange Park
Stratford
Stratford International
Stratford High Street
Abbey Road
Pudding Mill Lane
Hackney Wick
Homerton
Hackney Central
Hackney Downs
Dalston Kingsland
Dalston Junction
Canonbury
Highbury & Islington
Caledonian Road & Barnsbury
Caledonian Road
Holloway Road
Arsenal
Drayton Park
Finsbury Park
Tufnell Park
Kentish Town
Kentish Town West
Gospel Oak
Hampstead Heath
Belsize Park
Chalk Farm
Camden Town
Camden Road
Mornington Crescent
South Hampstead
Swiss Cottage
St John's Wood
Euston
King's Cross
St Pancras International
Haggerston
Essex Road
Hoxton
London Fields
Cambridge Heath
Bethnal Green
Mile End
Bow Church
Bromley-by-Bow
Bow Road
Devons Road
West Ham
East Ham
Plaistow
Upton Park
Star Lane
Canning Town
Royal Victoria
Custom House for ExCeL
Royal Docks
Prince Regent
Royal Albert
Beckton Park
Cyprus
Gallions Reach
Beckton
Towards Ebbsfleet International
Baker Street
Great Portland Street
Euston Square
Warren Street
Russell Square
Regent's Park
Goodge Street
Farringdon
Angel
Old Street
Barbican
Shoreditch High Street
Stepney Green
Whitechapel
Aldgate East
Aldgate
Liverpool Street
Moorgate
Bond Street
Oxford Circus
Tottenham Court Road
Holborn
City Thameslink
St Paul's
Bank
Covent Garden
Leicester Square
Chancery Lane
Cannon Street
Fenchurch Street
Monument
Tower Hill
Tower Gateway
Shadwell
Limehouse
Westferry
Langdon Park
All Saints
Poplar
Blackwall
East India
West India Quay
Green Park
Piccadilly Circus
Charing Cross
Embankment
Temple
Blackfriars
Mansion House
River Thames
Wapping
Rotherhithe
Bermondsey
Canada Water
Surrey Quays
Canary Wharf
Heron Quays
South Quay
Crossharbour
Mudchute
Island Gardens
North Greenwich
Greenwich Peninsula
West Silvertown
Pontoon Dock
London City Airport
King George V
Woolwich
Abbey Wood
St James's Park
Victoria
Westminster
Pimlico
Waterloo
Waterloo East
London Bridge
Southwark
Borough
Lambeth North
Vauxhall
Kennington
Elephant & Castle
South Bermondsey
Queens Road Peckham
Deptford
Cutty Sark for Maritime Greenwich
Greenwich
Westcombe Park
Maze Hill
Charlton
Woolwich Dockyard
Woolwich Arsenal
Plumstead
Deptford Bridge
Elverson Road
Belvedere
Erith
Slade Green
Oval
Stockwell
Loughborough Junction
Peckham Rye
Nunhead
New Cross
St Johns
New Cross Gate
Lewisham
Blackheath
Kidbrooke
Eltham
Falconwood
Welling
Bexleyheath
Barnehurst
Clapham High Street
Clapham North
Clapham Common
Clapham South
Brixton
Denmark Hill
East Dulwich
North Dulwich
Herne Hill
West Dulwich
Sydenham Hill
Brockley
Honor Oak Park
Forest Hill
Sydenham
Crofton Park
Ladywell
Catford
Catford Bridge
Hither Green
Lee
Mottingham
Sidcup
Bexley
Dartford
Towards Gravesend
Crayford
Albany Park
New Eltham
Grove Park
Bellingham
Beckenham Hill
Sundridge Park
Ravensbourne
Bromley North
Elmstead Woods
Chislehurst
Tooting Bec
Tooting
Streatham Hill
Tulse Hill
Gipsy Hill
Crystal Palace
West Norwood
Streatham
Lower Sydenham
New Beckenham
Penge West
Penge East
Kent House
Bickley
St Mary Cray
Swanley
Towards Sevenoaks
Shortlands
Bromley South
Petts Wood
Orpington
Chelsfield
Knockholt
Streatham Common
Mitcham Eastfields
Norbury
Thornton Heath
Selhurst
Anerley
Norwood Junction
Birkbeck
Avenue Road
Beckenham Road
Beckenham Junction
Harrington Road
Clock House
Elmers End
Eden Park
West Wickham
Hayes
Beddington Lane
Therapia Lane
Ampere Way
Reeves Corner
Wandle Park
West Croydon
Centrale
Wellesley Road
London Trams fare zone
Arena
Woodside
Blackhorse Lane
Addiscombe
Hackbridge
Waddon Marsh
Church Street
George Street
East Croydon
Lebanon Road
Sandilands
Lloyd Park
Coombe Lane
Gravel Hill
Addington Village
Fieldway
King Henry's Drive
New Addington
Carshalton
Waddon
Wallington
South Croydon
Purley Oaks
Purley
Sanderstead
Riddlesdown
Carshalton Beeches
Woodmansterne
Coulsdon Town
Reedham
Chipstead
Kingswood
Coulsdon South
Tadworth
Tattenham Corner
Kenley
Merstham
Redhill
Whyteleafe
Upper Warlingham
Whyteleafe South
Caterham
Earlswood
Salfords
Horley
Gatwick Airport
Towards Reigate and Dorking
Towards Brighton
Towards Tonbridge
Towards East Grinstead and Uckfield
Outside fare zones
National Rail
TRANSPORT FOR LONDON
EVERY JOURNEY MATTERS
Correct at time of going to print

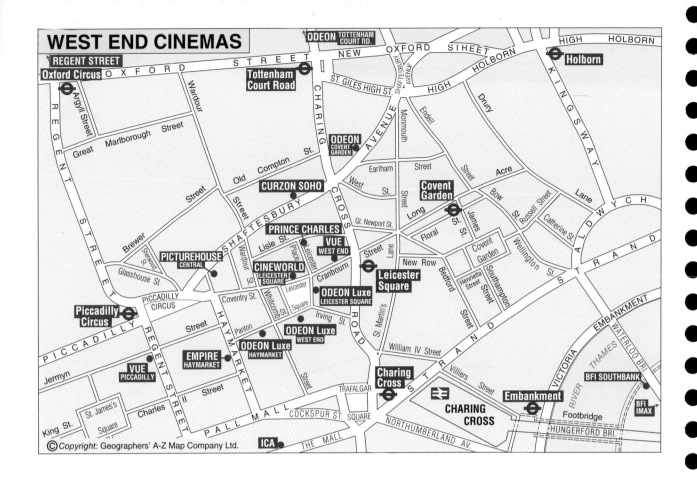

WEST END CINEMAS

REGENT STREET
Oxford Circus

OXFORD STREET

Tottenham Court Road

ODEON TOTTENHAM COURT RD.

NEW OXFORD STREET

HIGH HOLBORN

Holborn

CHARING CROSS ROAD

ST. GILES HIGH ST.

SHAFTESBURY AVENUE

HIGH HOLBORN

KINGSWAY

Marlborough Street
Great
Wardour
Street

Compton St.

ODEON COVENT GARDEN

Earlham Street

Monmouth Street

Endell Street

Drury Lane

Acre

Bow Street

Lane

CURZON SOHO

Old Compton Street

West St.

Covent Garden

DRURY

PRINCE CHARLES

Lisle St.

Gt. Newport St.

Long Acre

James St.

St. Russell Street

Catherine St.

ALDWYCH

STRAND

PICTUREHOUSE CENTRAL

VUE WEST END

Leicester Place

Cranbourn Street

New Row

Floral St.

Covent Garden

Wellington St.

CINEWORLD LEICESTER SQUARE

Leicester Square

Bedford Street

Henrietta Street

Southampton Street

Glasshouse St.

Brewer Sherwood Street

PICCADILLY CIRCUS

Coventry St.

Leicester Square

ODEON Luxe LEICESTER SQUARE

Irving St.

Leicester Square

St. Martin's Lane

EMBANKMENT

WATERLOO BRI.

Piccadilly Circus

Street

Panton

Whitcomb St.

ODEON Luxe WEST END

William IV Street

VICTORIA

RIVER THAMES

PICCADILLY

Regent Street

Haymarket

EMPIRE HAYMARKET

ODEON Luxe HAYMARKET

Charing Cross

BFI SOUTHBANK

Jermyn Street

VUE PICCADILLY

Street

Villiers Street

Embankment

BFI IMAX

King St.

St. James's Square

Charles Street

PALL MALL

COCKSPUR ST.

TRAFALGAR SQUARE

CHARING CROSS

Footbridge

HUNGERFORD BRI.

© Copyright: Geographers' A-Z Map Company Ltd.

ICA

THE MALL

NORTHUMBERLAND AV.

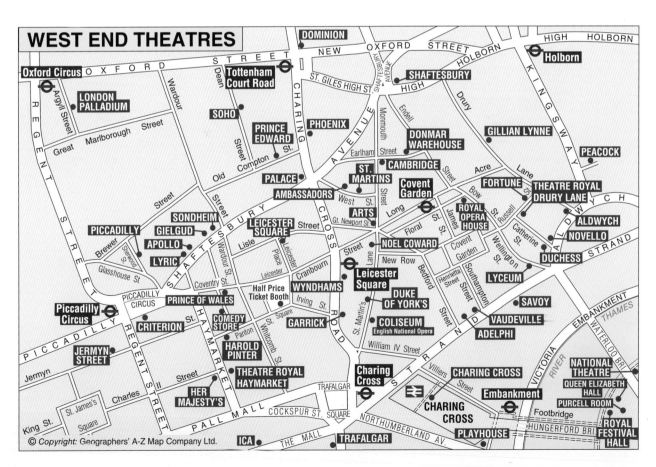

WEST END THEATRES

DOMINION

Oxford Circus

OXFORD STREET

Tottenham Court Road

NEW OXFORD STREET

HIGH HOLBORN

Holborn

LONDON PALLADIUM

Dean Street
Wardour Street

SOHO

CHARING CROSS ROAD

ST. GILES HIGH ST.

SHAFTESBURY

HIGH

KINGSWAY

Marlborough Street
Great

PRINCE EDWARD

PHOENIX

SHAFTESBURY AVENUE

Monmouth Street

Endell Street

Drury Lane

DONMAR WAREHOUSE

GILLIAN LYNNE

Street

Old Compton St.

PALACE

Earlham Street

CAMBRIDGE

Acre

PEACOCK

Street

AMBASSADORS

ST. MARTINS

Covent Garden

Bow Street

FORTUNE

THEATRE ROYAL DRURY LANE

ALDWYCH

SONDHEIM

ARTS

West St.

Gt. Newport St.

Long Acre

James St.

Russell Street

Catherine St.

NOVELLO

STRAND

PICCADILLY

GIELGUD

LEICESTER SQUARE

Lisle St.

NOEL COWARD

Floral St.

ROYAL OPERA HOUSE

Wellington St.

DUCHESS

APOLLO

LYRIC

Leicester Place

Cranbourn Street

New Row

Covent Garden

Henrietta Street

LYCEUM

Glasshouse St.

Brewer Sherwood Street

PICCADILLY CIRCUS

Coventry St.

Half Price Ticket Booth

WYNDHAMS

Leicester Square

Bedford Street

Southampton Street

EMBANKMENT

THAMES

Piccadilly Circus

PRINCE OF WALES

Leicester Square

Irving St.

DUKE OF YORK'S

St. Martin's Lane

SAVOY

WATERLOO BRI.

CRITERION

COMEDY STORE

Panton

GARRICK

COLISEUM English National Opera

VAUDEVILLE

VICTORIA

RIVER

ADELPHI

JERMYN STREET

Whitcomb St.

William IV Street

NATIONAL THEATRE

Jermyn

HAROLD PINTER

Charing Cross

Villiers

CHARING CROSS

Embankment

QUEEN ELIZABETH HALL

THEATRE ROYAL HAYMARKET

Street

Street

PURCELL ROOM

King St.

St. James's Square

HER MAJESTY'S

Charles Street

PALL MALL

COCKSPUR ST.

TRAFALGAR SQUARE

CHARING CROSS

Footbridge

Hungerford BRI.

ROYAL FESTIVAL HALL

© Copyright: Geographers' A-Z Map Company Ltd.

ICA

THE MALL

TRAFALGAR

NORTHUMBERLAND AV.

PLAYHOUSE